Educators
Resource
Directory

2007/08

Seventh Edition

Educators
Resource
Directory

- *No Child Left Behind* Resources
- Associations & Organizations
- Professional Development
- Consultants
- Financial Resources
- Conferences & Trade Shows
- Opportunities Abroad
- Statistics & Rankings

A SEDGWICK PRESS Book

Grey House
Publishing

PUBLISHER:	Leslie Mackenzie
EDITOR:	Richard Gottlieb
EDITORIAL DIRECTOR:	Laura Mars-Proietti
PRODUCTION MANAGER:	Karen Stevens
PRODUCTION ASSISTANTS:	Karynn Ketiinq, Kayla Mathers,
	Ashley Nault, Heather Stuermer
MARKETING DIRECTOR:	Jessica Moody

A Sedgwick Press Book
Grey House Publishing, Inc.
185 Millerton Road
Millerton, NY 12546
518.789.8700
FAX 518.789.0545
www.greyhouse.com
e-mail: books @greyhouse.com

Table of Contents

Introduction

Welcome to the seventh edition of *Educators Resource Directory,* a comprehensive resource designed to provide educators, administrators, and other education professionals with immediate access to a unique combination of over 6,182 educational information resources and 145 charts of education statistics and rankings for both the United States and Canada.

This edition includes 22 carefully organized chapters in categories ranging from **Associations** to **Classroom Supplies.** This revised edition devotes specific chapters on **Teaching Opportunities Abroad, Financial Resources** and **Professional Development,** as well as **Research Centers** and **Testing Resources** – in short, everything you need to make a difference in job and school performance. This one, easy-to-use volume replaces the hours it would take searching through multiple resources to uncover all the information presented here.

The nearly 6,200 entries in *Educators Resource Directory* include not only current name, address, phone numbers, and key contacts, 4,001 fax numbers, 2,462 e-mail addresses and 3,149 web sites. Depending on the chapter, you'll find the specific data you'll need: **Trade Show** listings give the month and size of the show; **Publications** offer frequency and number of pages; **School Supplies** are broken down into seven categories from **Audio Visual Materials** to **Sports & Playground Equipment.**

In addition, this edition includes information on **No Child Left Behind** legislation, with definitions and criteria used by **NCLB** at the federal, state and local levels. This section also includes a separate list of directory entries that relate to **NCLB,** plus definition of **NCLB** terms.

New Canadian Resources and Statistics
New to this edition are more than 100 Canadian educational associations, including the **Association for Canadian Studies in the US, Canadian Association of Independent Schools,** and the **Canadian Council for the Advancement of Education,** as well as 15 tables with statistical data on education in Canada. Topics range from **Educational Attainment** to **Revenues and Expenditures.**

SECTION ONE: Resources
Associations & Organizations disseminate information, host seminars, provide educational literature and promote study councils. The 603 associations in this edition are consolidated in this chapter, and are further organized into 18 distinct categories.

The chapter on **Conferences & Trade Shows** lists everything from large conventions of classroom resource and equipment suppliers to small, specialized conferences that target rural education and specific teaching challenges. The more than 200 listings are arranged in both national and regional categories.

Consultant listings offer information on 192 firms that provide educational consulting services, including curriculum-building guidance, school district organizations, and facility format.

Teaching Opportunities Abroad is arranged in nine geographic categories, from Africa to the West Indies. It includes not only US government schools, but also all American schools overseas. This chapter provides contact information, grade level and enrollment numbers on more than 1,200 schools.

Details on 614 grants, foundations and scholarships can be found in the **Financial Resources** chapter. Here you will find information on how to obtain funds for individual professional advancement, schools, programs, students, and education districts and communities.

Government Agencies lists 381 Federal and State listings, arranged by state with key contact information.

The **Professional Development** chapter offers 500 listings arranged in eight categories, including: Associations; Awards & Honors; Conferences; Career-advancement Programs and Workshops; Handbooks and Periodicals; Software; Internet Resources; and Training Materials.

The chapter on **Publications** includes nearly 1,400 directories, magazines and journals that are subdivided into 17 subject areas from Administration to Technology in Education. Here the education professional will find support for everything from doing research, to getting published, to buying classroom materials.

Publishers include 350 publishers of educational textbooks, testing resources and classroom curriculums.

For those seeking research on general learning and training issues, or data on specific subjects, like Gifted & Talented, Educational Media, or Scientific Learning, *Educators Resource Directory* offers nearly 100 **Research Centers** throughout the country.

The chapter on **School Supplies** focuses on seven categories, including Audio Visual, Electronic and Scientific Equipment, plus Classroom Materials, Furniture and Sports & Playground Equipment.

Software, Hardware & Internet Resources includes 18 subchapters from Administration to Technology in Education for easy access to the exact resources you are looking for. Here you will find educational computer programs, and web sites with information on classroom resources for every level and subject.

Testing Resources includes resources for written materials and web sites in 10 categories.

SECTION TWO: Statistics & Rankings

This section offers 145 tables and charts in nine categories: **Adult Education, College & University Education; Educational Attainment; Elementary & Secondary Education; Federal Programs for Education & Related Activities; International Comparisons of Education; Learning Resources & Technology; Opinions on Education; Outcomes of Education.** Specific topics include degrees, enrollment, completions, dropouts, faculty, revenues, expenditures, and student behavior. Many tables offer state-by-state rankings.

Using the most current data available (December 2005), this section helps to complete the picture for educators making career development decisions, for school administrators interested in comparing fiscal health and educational scores, and for anyone doing educational research. And new for this edition is a separate section of **Canadian Education Statistics**.

SECTION THREE: Indexes

Three indexes offer users access to the information in the *Educators Resource Directory* via several ways:

Entry & Publisher Name Index -- alphabetical list of both entry names and the companies that publish the listed material. Publishers are listed in boldface type.

Geographic Index -- state by state listing of all entries.

Subject Index – alphabetical list of NCLB-relevant listings by certification areas: Arts; Civics & Government; Economics: English; Foreign Language; Geography; History; Math; Reading or Language Arts; and Science. It also includes Special Education, Technology and entries related to *NCLB* Reform.

The 2007/08 edition of *Educators Resource Directory* offers the invaluable combination of educational resources with statistics and rankings, to give users the full educational picture of any given city or state. It is sure to be an indispensable reference for seasoned education professionals, for teachers just beginning their education career, and for all those who service and support the education industry.

11234

1 ➤ **Gifted Children's Association**
2 ➤ 70 International Road
PO Box 594
Anytown, NY 00000

3 ➤ 001-111-1113

4 ➤ 800-000-0000

5 ➤ 001-111-1112

6 ➤ info@GCA.com

7 ➤ www.GCA.com

8 ➤ Provides enrichment and support for gifted children through various national programs.

9 ➤ Director: Gina Thorson
Marketing Manager: Todd Fasco
Production Manager: Sally Felder

10 ➤ **Year Founded:** 1953

User Key

1 ➤ **Entry/Title:** Primary company or product name.

2 ➤ **Address:** Location or permanent mailing address of the company.

3 ➤ **Phone Number:** The listed phone number is usually for the main office, but may also be for sales, marketing, or public relations as provided by the company.

4 ➤ **Toll Free Number:** This is listed when provided by the company.

5 ➤ **Fax Number:** This is listed when provided by the company.

6 ➤ **E-Mail:** Listed when provided by the company, and is usually the main office e-mail

7 ➤ **Web Site:** Listed when provided by the company, and is also referred to as an URL address. To access through the Internet, type http:// before the URL address.

8 ➤ **Title/Entry Description:** This information is provided directly by the company, or abridged from data on their web site or in their literature.

9 ➤ **Key Executives:** Names of key executives in the company.

10 ➤ **Year Founded:** Year company was established.

No Child Left Behind (NCLB)

The *No Child Left Behind Act of 2001 (NCLB)* redefines the federal role in K-12 education and has been called the most sweeping reform of the *Elementary and Secondary Education Act (ESEA)* since it was enacted in 1965. It embodies four basic principles: stronger accountabilty for results; expanded flexibility and local control; expanded options for parents; and an emphasis on teaching methods that have been proven to work. A major focus of *NCLB* is naturally on educators — not only encouraging them to employ proven teaching methods, but also holding those educators accountable for results achieved with those methods. In fact, *NCLB* includes criteria for the "highly qualified" teacher, which we offer below, all in the name of Professional Development.

continued

Who defines "highly qualified" teacher?

Federal
NCLB sets the minimum requirements:
- A bachelor's degree.
- Full state certification, as defined by the state.
- Demonstrated competency, as defined by the state, in each core academic subject the teacher teaches.

NCLB sets a deadline:
- All new teachers of core academic subjects in Title I schools/programs hired beginning with the 2002–03 school year must meet the requirements before entering the classroom.
- All teachers of core academic subjects hired before the 2002–03 school year must meet the requirements by the end of the 2005–06 school year. (Special considerations may apply for multi-subject teachers in eligible small, rural schools.)

The secretary of education is responsible for monitoring state plans and providing assistance to states as they seek to meet these requirements.

State
States define "highly qualified teacher" according to the requirements of NCLB.

States may develop this definition according to their own unique needs. States determine what is meant by "full state certification." They may streamline requirements to make it less burdensome for talented individuals to enter the profession.

States develop a plan with goals for their districts, detailing how they will ensure that all teachers of core academic subjects will be highly qualified by the end of the 2005-06 school year.

States determine ways in which teachers can demonstrate competency in the subjects they teach, according to the requirements in NCLB. (For example, states choose whether or not to adopt their own high, objective, uniform state standard of evaluation [HOUSSE] for current teachers.)

continued

Local
Local Districts ensure that newly hired teachers in Title I schools/programs meet their state's definition of "highly qualified teacher."

Districts work with states to communicate with current teachers regarding the "highly qualified" teacher definition, and provide a way for teachers to determine whether or not they meet the state definition of "highly qualified teacher."

Districts work with states to support teachers who do not meet the "highly qualified" teacher definition in the subjects they teach, providing opportunities or options for them to meet the requirements by the end of the 2005–06 school year.

Who determines what is high-quality professional development?

Federal
In NCLB, the term "high-quality professional development" refers to the definition of professional development in Title IX, Section 9101(34). It includes, but is not limited to, activities that:
- Improve and increase teachers' knowledge of academic subjects.
- Are integral to broad schoolwide and districtwide educational improvement plans.
- Give teachers and principals the knowledge and skills to help students meet challenging state academic standards.
- Improve classroom management skills.
- Are sustained, intensive and classroom-focused and are not one-day or short-term workshops.
- Advance teacher understanding of effective instructional strategies that are supported by scientifically based research.
- Are developed with extensive participation of teachers, principals, parents and administrators.

State
States report to the secretary of education the percentage of teachers involved in high-quality professional development.

States monitor the districts' use of professional development dollars provided by Title II grants, as well as by other federal and state funds.

States must use a minimum of 5 percent of their Title I funds for professional development for teachers and other school-level employees.

Local
To receive federal funds for improving teacher quality (Title II, Part A), districts must perform a needs assessment and use data to make decisions regarding the type of high-quality professional development to be provided for teachers. **Teachers must be involved in this process.**

Districts and schools look at student achievement levels and set professional development goals for teachers.

Who defines and determines adequate yearly progress (AYP)?

Federal

NCLB sets requirements for state definitions of AYP, which is the progress that schools and districts must show in educating all students to grade-level standards, as reflected in student assessments.

NCLB requires subgroup accountability: English language learners, students with disabilities, economically disadvantaged youth, and breakouts by race and ethnicity.

NCLB sets a goal for AYP—100 percent proficiency for all students and each subgroup by the end of the 2013–14 school year.

The secretary of education approves and monitors each state's accountability plan, ensuring that it meets the NCLB minimum requirements.

State

States use assessment data to set benchmarks and determine a trajectory for meeting the goal of 100 percent proficiency by the end of the 2013–14 school year.

States use their own reading and math tests, participation rates in testing and at least one other academic indicator (such as performance on science assessments or graduation rate) when determining AYP.

States must provide assistance to districts in need of improvement and may choose to implement supports for districts, such as professional development, targeting of funds and other assistance.

States oversee districts' actions to help support schools identified as in need of improvement.

Local

Districts provide information to the state about performance on all indicators—math and reading assessments, assessment participation rates, and others.

Districts use this information, as well as determinations of achievement gaps in subgroups of students, to inform decision making at the district and school levels.

At the school level, principals and teachers use assessment data, participation rates and other indicators to help improve student achievement.

Source: U.S. Department of Education, Office of the Deputy Secretary, No Child Left Behind: A Toolkit for Teachers, Washington, D.C., 2004

Definition of Terms

Accountability System
Each state sets academic standards for what every child should know and learn. Student academic achievement is measured for every child, every year. The results of these annual tests are reported to the public.

Achievement Gap
The difference between how well low-income and minority children perform on standardized tests as compared with their peers. For many years, low-income and minority children have been falling behind their white peers in terms of academic achievement.

Adequate Yearly Progress (AYP)
An individual state's measure of yearly progress toward achieving state academic standards. "Adequate Yearly Progress" is the minimum level of improvement that states, school districts and schools must achieve each year.

Alternative Certification
Most teachers are required to have both a college degree in education and a state certification before they can enter the classroom. No Child Left Behind encourages states to offer other methods of qualification that allow talented individuals to teach subjects they know.

Assessment
Another word for "test." Under No Child Left Behind, tests are aligned with academic standards. Beginning in the 2002-03 school year, schools must administer tests in each of three grade spans: grades 3-5, grades 6-9, and grades 10-12 in all schools. Beginning in the 2005-06 school year, tests must be administered every year in grades 3 through 8 in math and reading. Beginning in the 2007-08 school year, science achievement must also be tested.

Charter School
Charter schools are independent public schools designed and operated by educators, parents, community leaders, educational entrepreneurs, and others. They are sponsored by designated local or state educational organizations, who monitor their quality and effectiveness but allow them to operate outside of the traditional system of public schools.

Comprehension
The ability to understand and gain meaning from what has been read.

Corrective Action
When a school or school district does not make yearly progress, the state will place it under a "Corrective Action Plan." The plan will include resources to improve teaching, administration, or curriculum. If a school continues to be identified as in need of improvement, then the state has increased authority to make any necessary, additional changes to ensure improvement.

Disaggregated Data
"Disaggregate" means to separate a whole into its parts. In education, this term means that test results are sorted into groups of students who are economically disadvantaged, from racial and ethnic minority groups, have disabilities, or have limited English fluency. This practice allows parents and teachers to see more than just the average score for their child's school. Instead, parents and teachers can see how each student group is performing.

Distinguished Schools
Awards granted to schools when they make major gains in achievement.

Early Reading First
A nationwide effort to provide funds to school districts and other public or private organizations that serve children from low-income families. The Department of Education will make competitive 6-year grants to local education agencies to support early language, literacy, and pre-reading development of preschool-age children, particularly those from low-income families.

Elementary and Secondary Education Act (ESEA)
ESEA, which was first enacted in 1965, is the principal federal law affecting K-12 education. The No Child Left Behind Act is the most recent reauthorization of the ESEA.

Flexibility
Refers to a new way of funding public education. The No Child Left Behind Act gives states and school districts unprecedented authority in the use of federal education dollars in exchange for strong accountability for results.

Fluency
The capacity to read text accurately and quickly.

Local Education Agency
(LEA) is a public board of education or other public authority within a State which maintains administrative control of public elementary or secondary schools in a city, county, township, school district, or other political subdivision of a state.

National Assessment of Educational Progress
An independent benchmark, NAEP is the only nationally representative and continuing assessment of what American students know and can do in various subject areas. Since 1969, The National Center for Education Statistics has conducted NAEP assessments in reading, mathematics, science, writing, U.S. history, geography, civics, and the arts.

Phonemic Awareness
The ability to hear and identify individual sounds—or phonemes—in spoken words.

Phonics
The relationship between the letters of written language and the sounds of spoken language.

Public School Choice
Students in schools identified as in need of improvement will have the option to transfer to better public schools in their districts. The school districts will be required to provide transportation to the students. Priority will be given to low-income students.

Reading First
A bold new national initiative aimed at helping every child in every state become a successful reader.

State Educational Agency
(SEA) is the agency primarily responsible for the State supervision of public elementary and secondary schools.

Supplemental Services
Students from low-income families who are attending schools that have been identified as in need of improvement for two years will be eligible to receive outside tutoring or academic assistance. Parents can choose the appropriate services for their child from a list of approved providers. The school district will purchase the services.

Teacher Quality
To ensure that every classroom has a highly qualified teacher, states and districts around the country are using innovative programs to address immediate and long-term needs, including alternative recruitment strategies, new approaches to professional development, financial incentive programs, partnerships with local universities, and much more.

Title I
The first section of the ESEA, Title I refers to programs aimed at America's most disadvantaged students. Title I Part A provides assistance to improve the teaching and learning of children in high-poverty schools to enable those children to meet challenging State academic content and performance standards. Title I reaches about 12.5 million students enrolled in both public and private schools.

Transferability
A new ESEA flexibility authority that allows states and local educational agencies (LEAs) to transfer a portion of the funds that they receive under certain Federal programs to other programs that most effectively address their unique needs to certain activities under Title I.

Unsafe School Choice Option
Students who attend persistently dangerous public schools or have been victims of violent crime at school are allowed to transfer to a safer public school.

Vocabulary
The words students must know to read effectively.

Source: U.S. Department of Education, Office of the Deputy Secretary, No Child Left Behind: A Toolkit for Teachers, Washington, D.C., 2004

General

1 ASPIRA Association
1444 Eye Street NW
Suite 800
Washington, DC 20005-6543
202-835-3600
Fax: 202-835-3613
E-mail: info@aspira.org
http://www.aspira.org
Founded in 1961 ASPIRA promotes Latino youth leadership and education. Through its associate ASPIRA organizations and national demonstration projects, it provides a host of leadership development and education programs for Puerto Rican and other Latino youth.

Ronald Blackburn-Moreno, President & CEO
John Villamil-Casanova, Executive Vice President

2 Academy for Educational Development
1825 Connecticut Avenue
Washington, DC 20009-5746
202-884-8000
Fax: 202-884-8400
E-mail: communicationsmail@aed.org
http://www.aed.org
Assists schools, colleges and other educational institutions of developing countries in researching, planning, designing, implementing and evaluating development programs. In the US, manages the Center for Youth Development and Policy Research (disadvantaged youth), Disabilities Studies and Services Center (clearinghouse on special education and children with disabilities), National Institute for Work and Learning (school-to-work transition), and schools and Community Services Department.

Stephen Moseley, Director
Peter B. Johnson, Senior Vice President

3 Advance Program for Young Scholars
Northwestern State University
Po Box 6571
Natchitoches, LA 71497
318-357-4500
Fax: 318-357-4547
E-mail: palmerh@nsula.edu
http://www.advanceprogram.org
From chemistry to history, from foreign languages to ecology, the program offers a broad spectrum of academic opportunities to the qualified 12-17 year old student.

David Wood PhD, Director

4 Alliance for Parental Involvement in Education
PO Box 59
East Chatham, NY 12060-0059
518-392-6900
E-mail: allpie@taconic.net
Seeks to nurture parents' natural teaching abilities and offer tools and resources, public, private and home in becoming active participants in the education of their children.

Katharine Houk, Executive Director

5 American Academy of Pediatrics
141 NW Point Boulevard
Elk Grove Village, IL 60007-1098
847-434-4000
Fax: 847-434-8000
E-mail: kidsdoc@aap.org
http://www.aap.org
Committed to the attainment of optimal physical, mental and social health for all infants, children, adolescents and young adults.

Eileen M Ouellette, MD, President
Errol R Alden, MD, Executive Director

6 American Association for Vocational Instructional Materials (AAVIM)
220 Smithonia Road
Winterville, GA 30683-1418
706-742-5355
800-228-4689
Fax: 706-742-7005
E-mail: sales@aavim.com
http://www.aavim.com/main.html
Develops, publishes and distributes instructional materials for career education instructors, students, and administrators.

Gary Farmer, Director
Vicki J Eaton, Art Director/Production

7 American Council for Drug Education
164 West 74th Street
New York, NY 10023
646-505-2060
800-488-3784
Fax: 212-595-2553
E-mail: acde@phoenixhouse.org
http://www.acde.org/
Distributes packaged information about drugs and the consequences of their use and identifies effective community programs to address the drug problem in the country.

William F Current, Executive Director

8 American Council on Education (ACE)
1 Dupont Circle NW
Suite 800
Washington, DC 20036-1193
202-939-9300
Fax: 202-833-4760
E-mail: comments@ace.nche.edu
http://www.acenet.edu
Represents accredited degree-granting colleges and universities directly and through national and regional higher education associations. Seeks to advance education and serves as an advocate for adult education.

David Ward, President
Sylvia E Robinson, Executive Director

9 American Council on Rural Special Education (ACRES)
Montana Center on Disabilities
MSU-B
1500 University Drive
Billings, MT 59101
435-797-3728
E-mail: inquiries@acres-sped.org
http://www.acres-sped.org/
The organization is comprised of special educators, general educators, related service providers, administrators, teacher trainers, researchers, and parents committed to the enhancement of services to students and individuals living in rural America.

Belva Collins, Chair
David Forbush, Chair Elect

10 American Driver and Traffic Safety Education Association (ADTSEA)
Highway Safety Center
Indiana University of Pennsylvania
R&P Building
Indiana, PA 15705
724-357-4051
800-896-7703
Fax: 724-357-7595
E-mail: arrobin@hsc.iup.edu
http://www.adtsea.org/adtsea/100005.aspx
The purpose of the American Driver and Traffic Safety Education Association is to promote traffic safety and its concomitant benefits by improving and extending driver education/training activities in schools, colleges, universities, the private sector, industry and other institutions.

Allen Robinson Ph.D, CEO
Dana Bowser, Director

11 American Federation of Teachers
555 New Jersey Avenue NW
Washington, DC 20001
202-879-4400
Fax: 202-879-4556
E-mail: online@aft.org
http://www.aft.org
The AFT represents one million teachers, school support staff, higher education faculty and staff, health care professionals, and state and municipal employees. AFT is an affiliated international union of the AFL-CIO.

Edward J McElroy, President

12 American Montessori Society
281 Park Avenue S
New York, NY 10010-6102
212-358-1250
Fax: 212-358-1256
E-mail: info@amshq.org
http://www.amshq.org
Promotes quality Montessori education for all children from birth to 18 years of age.

Michael Dorer, Presidnet
Marilyn Stewart, President-Elect

13 American Public Human Services Association (APHSA)
810 1st Street NE
Suite 500
Washington, DC 20002-4207
202-682-0100
Fax: 202-289-6555
E-mail: jfriedman@aphsa.org
http://www.aphsa.org/Home/home_news.asp
Promotes effective policies and programs to benefit low-income and disabled individuals. Members include all state and many territorial human service agencies, more than 150 local agencies, and several thousand individuals who work in or otherwise have an interest in human service programs.

Jerry W Friedman, Executive Director
Susan Christie, Deputy Executive Director

14 American School Health Association
7263 State Route 43
PO Box 708
Kent, OH 44240-0013
330-678-1601
Fax: 330-678-4526
E-mail: asha@ashaweb.org
http://www.ashaweb.org
A nonprofit organization founded to protect and improve the health and well-being of children and youth by supporting compre-

hensive, preschool-12 school health programs.

David K Lohrmann, President
Phyllis J Lewis, President-Elect

**15 Association for Business
Communication (ABC)**
Baruch College
One Bernard Baruch Way
Box B8-240
New York, NY 10010
646-312-3726
Fax: 646-349-5297
E-mail:
myers@businesscommunication.org
http://www.businesscommunication.org/
Members are varied, with teachers from the
management fields and business communication programs, as well as training directors, public writers and copywriters.
Bestows awards.

Robert J Myers Ph.D, Executive Director
Marsha Bayless, President

**16 Association for Community-Based
Education**
1806 Vernon Street NW
Washington, DC 20009-1217
202-462-6333
Offers technical assistance on planning,
management and program development for
community-based education.

Christofer Zachariadis, Executive
Director

17 Association for Disabled Students
University of Oklahoma
Disability Resource Center
620 Elm Avenue, Suite 166
Norman, OH 73019
405-325-3825
Fax: 405-325-4491
E-mail: publicaffairs@ou.edu
http://drc.ou.edu/content/view/54/
Also known as ADS, this student organization provides a forum for support, regular
meetings, and social and recreational activities. ADS sponsors Disability Awareness
Week each October and Disability Arts
Week the first week of April. ADS also
sponsors a wheelchair basketball team, affiliated with the Intercollegiate Wheelchair Division of the National Wheelchair
Basketball Association. The team competes nationally.

Suzette Dyer, Director

**18 Association for Environmental and
Outdoor Education (AEOE)**
PO Box 187
Angelus Oaks, CA 92305
714-838-8990
714-474-1377
E-mail: tomdrake29@hotmail.com
http://www.aeoe.org
The Association for Environmental and
Outdoor Education supports and inspires
educators in their quest for the knowledge,
skills, and attitudes essential to help all
learners understand, appreciate and care
for their environment.

Tom Drake, President
Helen M De La Maza, Membership Chair

**19 Association for Gender Equity
Leadership in Education**
317 S Division PMB 54
Ann Arbor, MI 48104
734-769-2456
Fax: 734-769-2456
E-mail: agelebusiness@yahoo.com
http://www.agele.org
A national organization for gender equity
specialists and educators. Individuals and
organizations committed to reducing sex
role stereotyping for females and males.
Services include an annual national training conference, a quarterly newsletter and
a membership directory. Members may
join task forces dealing with equity related
topics such as computer/technology issues,
early childhood, male issues, sexual harassment prevention, sexual orientation
and vocational issues.

Marta Larson, Business Manager

20 Association for Integrative Studies
School of Interdisciplinary Studies
Miami University
Oxford, OH 45056
513-529-2659
Fax: 513-529-5849
E-mail: newellwh@muohio.edu
http://www.units.muohio.edu/aisorg/intro
.html
The Association for Integrative Studies is
an interdisciplinary professional organization founded in 1979 to promote the interchange of ideas among scholars and
administrators in all of the arts and sciences on intellectual and organizational issues related to furthering integrative
studies. Incorporated as a non-profit educational association in the State of Ohio, it
has an international membership.

ISSN: 1081-4760
200 attendees

William H Newell, Executive Director
Don Stowe, President

21 Association for Play Therapy
2050 N Winery Avenue
Suite 101
Fresno, CA 93703-2831
559-252-2278
Fax: 559-252-2297
E-mail: info@a4pt.org
http://www.a4pt.org
Founded in 1982 APT is interdisciplinary
and defines play therapy as a distinct group
of interventions which use play as an integral component of the therapeutic process.

Lisa Saldana, President
Bill Burns, Executive Director

**22 Association for Supervision &
Curriculum Development (ASCD)**
1703 N Beauregard Street
Alexandria, VA 22311-1714
703-578-9600
800-933-2723
Fax: 703-575-5400
E-mail: member@ascd.org
http://www.ascd.org
Unique international, nonprofit, nonpartisan association of professional educators
whose jobs cross all grade levels and subject areas.

*600 booths with 11,000 attendees and 450
exhibits*

Nancy Deford, President
Holly Abrams, Executive Program
Marketing

23 Association of Boarding Schools
2141 Wisconsin Avenue NW
Suite H
Washington, DC 20007
202-965-8982
Fax: 202-965-8988
E-mail: tabs@schools.com
http://www.schools.com
A marketing consortium founded in 1975
of 300 boarding schools that seeks to increase the applicant pool of member
schools by increasing public awareness of
benefits and advantages of boarding school
education.

Founded: 1975

Steve Banks, Associate Director
Steven D Ruzicka, Executive Director

**24 Association of Educators in Private
Practice**
104 W Main Street, Suite 101
PO Box 348
Watertown, WI 0348
800-252-3280
Fax: 920-206-1475
E-mail: cyelich@aepp.org
http://www.aepp.org
Represents individuals and small firms
with products and services for elementary
and secondary schools.

**25 Attention Deficit Disorder
Association**
PO Box 543
Pottstown, PA 19464
484-945-2101
Fax: 610-970-7520
E-mail: http://www.add.org
Provides a national network for all ADD
support groups and individuals. The international organization has been in existence
since 1989. The mission of ADDA is to provide information, resources and networking to adults with AD/HD and to the
professionals who work with them. ADDA
generates hope, awareness, empowerment
and connections worldwide in the field of
AD/HD.

David Giwerc, President
Linda Anderson, Vice President

**26 Awards and Recognition
Association**
4700 W Lake Avenue
#500
Glenview, IL 60025
847-375-4800
800-344-2148
Fax: 877-734-9380
E-mail: info@ara.org
http://www.ara.org
The Awards and Recognition Association
is a membership organization devoted to
the awards engraving and recognition industry. Dedicated to advancing the image,
capabilities and business growth of recognition specialists, ARA is committed to delivering educational programs that
enhance technical and business skills.

Ralph Bloch, Director
Jim Weir, Executive Director

27 Better Chance
240 West 35th Street
Floor 9
New York, NY 10001-2506
646-346-1310
800-562-7865
Fax: 646-346-1311
http://www.betterchance.org
Identifies, recruits and places academically talented and motivated minority stu-

dents into leading independent secondary schools and selected public high schools.

Sandra Timmons, President
Colin Lord, Director

28   CHADD: Children & Adults with Attention Deficit/Hyperactivity Disorder
8181 Professional Place
Suite 150
Landover, MD 20785
301-306-7070
800-233-4050
Fax: 301-306-7090
http://www.chadd.org
National nonprofit organization which offers advocacy, information and support for patients and parents of children with attention deficit disorders. Maintains support groups, provides a forum for continuing education about ADHD, and maintains a national resource center for information about ADD.

Russ Shipley, Chief Development Officer
E Clarke Ross, CEO

29   Cable in the Classroom
25 Massachusetts Avenue NW
Suite 100
Washington, DC 20001
202-222-2335
Fax: 202-222-2336
http://www.ciconline.org
Fosters the use of cable content and technology to expand and enhance learning for children and youth nationwide.

Helen Soule PhD, Executive Director
Douglas Levin, Senior Director

30   Center for Civic Education
5145 Douglas Fir Road
Calabasas, CA 91302-1440
818-591-9321
Fax: 818-591-9330
E-mail: cce@civiced.org
http://www.civiced.org
Non-profit, nonpartisan educational corporation dedicated to fostering the development of informed, responsible participation in civic life by citizens committed to values and principles fundamental to American constitutional democracy.

Dick Kean, Director Publication Service

31   Center for Lifelong Learning
American Council on Education
1 Dupont Circle NW
Washington, DC 20036-1110
202-939-9475
E-mail: susan_robinson@ace.nche.edu
http://www.acenet.edu/AM/Template.cfm?
Section=CLLL
Evaluates learning acquired in various non-college settings; monitors educational credit and credentialing policies and provides guidance to postsecondary education institutions for developing policies and procedures for evaluating extra-institutional learning.

Susan Porter Robinson, Vice President
Mary Beth Lakin, Associate Director

32   Center on Education Policy
1001 Connecticut Avenue NW
Suite 522
Washington, DC 20036
202-822-8065
Fax: 202-822-6008
E-mail: cep-dc@cep-dc.org
http://www.cep-dc.org/aboutcep.htm

Promotes, coordinates and conducts research and development activities pertaining to educational policy issues.

John F Jennings, President/CEO
Daine Stark Rentner, Director National Programs

33   Center on Human Policy
805 S Crouse Avenue
Syracuse, NY 13244-2280
315-443-3851
800-894-0826
Fax: 315-443-4338
E-mail: thechp@sued.syr.edu
http://http://thechp.syr.edu
Promotes the integration of individuals with disabilities into the mainstream of society.

Steven J Taylor, Director

34   Civic Practices Network
Florence Heller School for Advanced Studies in Social Welfare, Brandeis Univ
Waltham, MA 02154
617-736-4890
Fax: 617-736-4891
E-mail: cpn@cpn.org
http://www.cpn.org
Collaborative and nonpartisan project bringing together a diverse array of organizations and perspectives within the new citizenship movement.

Carmen Sirianni, Editor-in-Chief
Lewis Friedland, Research Director

35   Constitutional Rights Foundation
601 S Kingsley Drive
Los Angeles, CA 90005
213-487-5590
Fax: 213-386-0459
http://www.crf-usa.org
Seeks to instill in our nation's youth a deeper understanding of citizenship through values expressed in our Constitution and its Bill of Rights, and educate them to become active and responsible participants in our society. Dedicated to assuring our country's future by investing in our youth today.

Todd Clark, Executive Director
JoAnn Burton, Director

36   Council for Advancement & Support of Education
1307 New York Avenue NW
Suite 1000
Washington, DC 20005-4701
202-328-2273
Fax: 202-387-4973
E-mail: MemberServiceCenter@case.org
http://www.case.org
Professional organization for advancement of professionals who work in alumni relations, public relations, publications, government relations, and fund raising at schools, colleges and universities worldwide.

John Lippincott, President

37   Council for Exceptional Children
1110 N Glebe Road
Suite 300
Arlington, VA 22201-5704
703-620-3660
888-232-7733
Fax: 703-264-9494
E-mail: cec@cec.sped.org
The Council for Exceptional Children is the largest international professional organization dedicated to improving educational outcomes for individuals with

exceptionalities, students with disabilities, and/or gifted.

Jacquelyn Alexander, President
Dr Drew Allbritten, Executive Treasurer

38   Council of Graduate Schools
1 Dupont Circle NW
Suite 430
Washington, DC 20036-1173
202-223-3791
Fax: 202-331-7157
E-mail: pmcallister@cgs.nche.edu
http://www.cgsnet.org/
Founded in 1961 members comprise graduate schools in the US and Canada.

Patricia McAllister, VP Government Relations
Stuart Heiser, Manager External Affairs

39   Council on Postsecondary Accreditation
1 Dupont Circle NW
Suite 430
Washington, DC 20036-1173
202-223-3791
Fax: 202-331-7157
http://www.cgsnet.org
Supports, coordinates and improves all voluntary accrediting activities conducted at the postsecondary educational level in the United States.

Debra Syverson, President

40   Disability Rights Education & Defense Fund
2212 6th Street
Berkeley, CA 94710-2219
510-644-2555
Fax: 510-841-8645
E-mail: dredf@dredf.org
http://www.dredf.org
Promotes the full integration of people with disabilities into the mainstream of society. DREDF was founded in 1979.

Beverly Bertaina, President
Kim Connor, Secretary

41   Division for Learning Disabilities
The Council for Exceptional Children
1110 N Glebe Road
Suite 300
Arlington, VA 22201-5704
703-620-3660
Fax: 703-264-9494
http://www.dldcec.org/
The Division for Learning Disabilities founded in 1983 represents professional personnel, students, parents and others interested in promoting the education and general welfare of children and adults with learning disabilities. Offers a journal and newsletter. A full schedule of sessions focusing on learning disabilities at the CEC convention.

Karen Rooney, President
Charles Hughs, Executive Director

42   Drug Information & Strategy Clearinghouse
3109 Lubbock Ave
Fort Worth, TX 76109
800-955-2232
Provides housing officials, residents and community leaders with information and assistance on drug abuse prevention and trafficking control techniques.

Nancy Kay, Director

43 EF Educational Tours
1 Education Street
Cambridge, MA 02141-1803
800-782-2076
Fax: 617-619-1803
http://www.eftours.com
Provides international travel for teachers and students. More than three million people have traveled on an EF tour since 1965.

44 ERIC - Education Resources Information Center
Computer Sciences Corporation
655 15th Street NW, Suite 500
Washington, DC 20005
800-538-3742
http://www.eric.ed.gov/
Coordinates outreach, dissemination and system wide activities; develops new publications and provides reference and referral services. Staffs toll-free information line to 16 subject-specific ERIC Clearinghouses and more than 350 education organizations. Free brochures on themes such as parent involvement available.

Robert Boruch, Chairman
Alvin Walker, Project Development Manager

45 ERIC Clearinghouse on Assessment & Evaluation
University of Maryland
1129 Shriver Lab
College Park, MD 20742-5701
301-405-7449
800-464-3742
Fax: 301-405-8134
E-mail: feedback3@ericae.net
http://www.ericae.net
Disseminates education information on topics pertaining to tests and other measurement devices, research design and methodology.

Dr. Lawrence Rudner, Director
Carol Boston, Associate Director

46 ERIC Clearinghouse on Rural Education & Small Schools
Edvantia
1031 Quarrier Street
Charleston, WV 25301-2337
304-347-0400
800-624-9120
Fax: 304-347-0467
E-mail: ericrc@ael.org
http://www.ael.org/eric
Economic, cultural, social or other factors related to educational programs and practices for rural residents.

Doris Redfield, President
Sara Aikin, Corporate Secretary

47 Easter Seals Communications
Easter Seals
230 W Monroe Street
Suite 1800
Chicago, IL 60606-4703
312-726-6200
800-221-6827
Fax: 312-726-1494
E-mail: info@easter-seals.org
http://www.easterseals.com
One of the nation's largest networks for medical rehabilitation and educational services, offering physical and occupational therapy, speech language services, home health, and specialized therapy and support programs for spinal cord injuries, stroke, post-polio and disabilities that occur as a part of aging. Vocational training and employment provided for young people.

Sara E Brewster, VP
Marketing/Communications
Andrea D Knudsen, Communications Specialist

48 Education Commission of the States
700 Broadway
#1200
Denver, CO 80203-3460
303-299-3600
Fax: 303-296-8332
E-mail: ecs@ecs.org
http://www.ecs.org
Provides a forum for the discussion of major educational issues, and education, research and service function to the member states.

Ted Sanders, President
Mike Huckabee, Chairman

49 Education Development Center
55 Chapel Street
Newton, MA 02458-1060
617-969-7100
Fax: 617-969-5979
http://http://main.edc.org
A nonprofit institution financed by the US government, private educational foundations, foreign governments, and sales of materials for the purpose of comprehensive educational improvement.

Janet Ehitla, President

50 Education Extension
Oklahoma State University-Stillwater
106 Willard
Stillwater, OK 74078-4034
405-744-6254
800-765-8933
Fax: 405-744-7713
E-mail: edext@okstate.edu
http://www.okstate.edu/education/outreach
Provides outreach services to students, teachers and service organizations on a local, state and national basis.

Kenneth A Stern, Director
Adrienne Hyle, Associate Dean

51 Education, Training and Research Associates
4 Carbonero Way
Scotts Valley, CA 95066
831-438-4060
Fax: 831-439-9651
http://www.etr.org
Provides information, resources, training and research to enhance the quality of health and family through education.

Michael Bird, MSW, MPH
John Casken, PhD

52 Educational Equity Concepts
100 5th Avenue
8th Floor
New York, NY 10011
212-243-1110
Fax: 212-627-0407
E-mail: information@edequity.org
http://www.edequity.org
Founded in 1982, promotes bias-free learning through innovative programs and materials.

Merle Froschl, Co-Foundes and Co-Director

53 Educational Register
Vincent-Curtis
29 Simpson Lane
Falmouth, MA 02540
508-457-6473
Fax: 508-457-6499
http://www.educationalregister.com
Hundreds of illustrated announcements describing a variety of private boarding schools and resident summer programs in the United States, Canada and Europe, together with articles by school heads and camp directors of interest to parents of students 10-18.

Stanford B Vincent, Editor

54 Equity Clearinghouse
Mid-Continent Regional Educational Laboratory
2550 S Parker Road
Suite 500
Aurora, CO 80014-1622
303-337-0990
Fax: 303-337-3005
http://www.mcrel.org
Provides information and literature on the topics of desegregation as it relates to education.

Timothy Waters, President
Louis Cicchinelli, Executive Vice President

55 Facing History & Ourselves
16 Hurd Road
Brookline, MA 02445-6919
617-232-1595
Fax: 617-232-0281
http://www.facinghistory.org
Facing History is an international nonprofit that helps teachers and students link the past to moral choices they face today.

Margot Strom, President

56 Family Centered Learning Alternatives (FCLA)
Context Institute
PO Box 946
Langley, WA 98260
360-221-6044
Fax: 360-221-6045
http://www.context.org/ICLIB/IC06/Stewart.htm
Supports parents' right to choose the educational environment best suited for their children's needs and to promote homeschooling as a legal nationwide learning alternative.

Eric Stewart, Founder/Director
Debra Stewart, Founder/Director

57 Foundation for Student Communication
Princeton University
48 University Place
Princeton, NJ 08544
609-258-1111
Fax: 609-258-1222
E-mail: Maggie@businesstoday.org
http://www.businesstoday.org
Student subscribers and conference participants who promote communication among students and business persons.

Michael Short, President
Maggie Orr, Publicity Director

58 Friends Council on Education
1507 Cherry Street
Philadelphia, PA 19102
215-241-7245
E-mail: Info@friendscouncil.org
http://www.friendscouncil.org/

Founded in 1931 the Friends Council on Education acts as a clearinghouse for information on Quaker schools and colleges.

Founded: 1931

Irene McHenry, Executive Director
Sarah Sweeney, Programs & Publications

59 Gifted Child Society
190 Rock Road
Glen Rock, NJ 07452-1736
201-444-6530
Fax: 201-444-9099
E-mail: admin@gifted.org
http://www.gifted.org
Provides educational enrichment and support for gifted children through national advocacy and various programs.

Janet L Chen, Executive Director

60 Girls Incorporated
120 Wall Street
New York, NY 10005-3902
800-374-4475
Fax: 212-509-8708
http://www.girlsinc.org
Represents girls on issues of equality and works to create an environment in which girls can learn and grow to their fullest potential.

Val Ackerman, President

61 HEATH Resource Center
George Washington University
2134 G Street NW
Washington, DC 20052-0001
202-973-0904
800-544-3284
Fax: 202-973-0908
E-mail: askheath@gwu.edu
http://www.HEATH.gwu.edu
The national clearinghouse on post-secondary education for individuals with disabilities. Support from the US Department of Education enables HEATH to serve as an information exchange for support services, policies, procedures and education opportunities.

Donna Martinez, Director
Zavolia Willis, Assistant Director

62 Independent Schools Association of the Southwest (ISAS)
Energy Square
505 N Spring Street
Suite 406
Midland, TX 79701
432-684-9550
Fax: 432-684-9401
E-mail: rdurham@isasw.org
http://www.isasw.org/aboutisas/index.asp
Independent Schools Association of the Southwest (ISAS) is a voluntary membership association of private schools. The membership of ISAS consists of 84 schools located in Arizona, Kansas, Louisiana, Mexico, New Mexico, Oklahoma and Texas enrolling over 38,000 students. A central purpose of ISAS is to encourage, support and develop the highest standard for independent schools of the region and to recognize by formal accreditation those schools in which these standards are maintained.

Rhonda G Durham, Executive Director
Jananne McLaughlin, Accreditation Director

63 Institute for Educational Leadership
1001 Connecticut Avenue NW
Suite 310
Washington, DC 20036-5541
202-822-8405
Fax: 202-872-4050
E-mail: iel@IEL.ORG
http://www.iel.org
The Institute's list of publications on educational trends and policies is available to the public.

Elizabeth Hale, President

64 InterAction - American Council for Voluntary International Action
1400 16th Street, NW
Suite 210
Washington, DC 20036
202-666-7822
Fax: 202-667-8236
E-mail: kgiunta@interaction.org
http://www.interaction.org/
Supports the development of creative, effective and lasting solutions to the challenges of crime, hunger, poverty, illiteracy and homelessness. Action's mission is to stimulate and expand voluntary citizen participation throughthe coordination of efforts with public and private organizations and other government agencies.

Sam Worthington, President/CEO
Ken Giunta, Director

65 International Association of Educators for World Peace
2013 Orba Drive NE
Huntsville, AL 35811-2414
256-534-5501
Fax: 256-536-1018
http://iaewp.net
To contribute to the improvement of man's ability to live at peace, to educate world citizens for peaceful co-existence and cooperation so that all people may have free access to the achievement of science and civilization.

Dr Charles Mercieca, President

66 International Society for Performance Improvement
1400 Spring Street
Suite 260
Silver Spring, MD 20910
301-587-8570
Fax: 301-587-8573
E-mail: info@ispi.org
http://www.ispi.org
Founded in 1962, the International Society for Performance Improvement is dedicated to improving productivity and performance in the workpalce.

Donald Tosti, President

67 Jewish Education Council
Jewish Federation Greater Seattle
2031 Third Avenue
Seattle, WA 98121
206-443-5400
Fax: 206-443-0303
E-mail: info@jewishinseattle.org
http://www.jewishinseattle.org/JF/Education/AboutJEC.asp
Promotes Jewish education and conducts programs to strengthen and improve Jewish life.

Starr Niego, Community Develpment

68 Jewish Education Service of North America
JESNA
111 8th Avenue
Suite 11E
New York, NY 10011-5201
212-284-6950
Fax: 212-284-6951
E-mail: info@jesna.org
http://www.jesna.org
Created in 1981 as the Jewish Federation system's educational coordinating, planning and development agency. JESNA is widely recognized for its leadership in six different areas, including media and technology, reasearch and evaluation, engaging and empowering Jewish youth, educator recruitment and development, day school education, and congregational and communal education.

Jonathan Woocher, President
Amy Amiel, Director/Project Development

69 Jewish Educators Assembly
Broadway and Locust Avenue
Cedarhurst, NY 11516
516-484-9585
Fax: 516-484-9586
E-mail: jewisheducators@aol.com
http://www.jewisheducators.org
Professional educators who are affiliated and functioning within the Conservative movement. A source of trained, experienced and qualified personnel to administer, supervise and instruct on a professionally competent and effective level. Members are professional colleagues dedicated to the perpetuation of Judaism and Jewish life.

Freedman Picker, President

70 John Dewey Society for the Study of Education & Culture
1801 NW 11th Road
Gainesville, FL 32605-5323
352-378-7365
http://www.johndeweysociety.org
Founded in 1935, John Dewey's commitment to the use of critical and reflective intelligence in the search for solutions to crucial problems in education and cuture.

David Hansen, President
Jeanne Connell, Secretary/Treasurer

71 Learning Disabilities Association of America
Learning Disabilities Association of America
4156 Library Road
Pittsburgh, PA 15234-1349
412-341-1515
888-300-6710
Fax: 412-344-0224
E-mail: info@ldaamerica.org
http://www.ldanatl.org
Has 50 state affiliates with more than 300 local chapters. The national office has a resource center of over 500 publications for sale.

Jane Browning, Executive Director

72 Lutheran Education Association
7400 Augusta Street
River Forest, IL 60305-1402
708-209-3343
Fax: 708-209-3458
E-mail: lea@crf.cuis.edu
http://www.lea.org

Seeks to spark ideas, thoughts and practices among Lutherans.

Dr Jonathan Laabs, Executive Director
Kathy Slupik, Executive Assistant

73   MATRIX: A Parent Network and Resource Center
94 Galli Drive
Suite C
Novato, CA 94949
415-884-3535
800-578-2592
Fax: 415-884-3555
E-mail: info@matrixparnets.org
http://www.matirxparents.org
For parents whose child has a special need or disability. Emotional support and information from parents who have been there.

74   Mississippi Library Association
PO Box 13687
Jackson, MS 39236-3687
601-981-4586
Fax: 601-981-4501
http://info@misslib.org
Provides professional leadership for the development, promotion, and the improvement of library and information services and the profession of librarianship in order to enhance learning and ensure access to information for all.

ISBN: M

75   National Academy of Education
School of Education
726 Broadway 5th Floor
New York, NY 10003-9580
212-998-9035
Fax: 212-995-4435
E-mail: nae.info@nyc.edu
http://www.nae.nyu.edu
Offers the Spencer Postdoctoral Fellowship which is designed to promote scholarship in the United States and abroad on matters relevant to the improvement of education in all its forms.

Debbie Leong-Childs, Executive Director

76   National Alliance for Safe Schools
Ice Mountain
PO Box 290
Slanesville, WV 25444-0290
304-496-8100
888-510-6500
Fax: 304-496-8105
E-mail: NASS@raven-villages.net
http://www.safeschools.org
Founded in 1977 NASS a non-profit corporation, ascribes to the belief that schools need to take back control and identify what the local issues are that may be causing fear and anxiety on the part of the students and staff. Once local issues have been identified, school administrators, working with students, teachers, parents and support staff, are able to effect change.

Peter D Blauvelt, CEO/President

77   National Association for Asian and Pacific American Education
Po Box 280346
Northridge, CA 91328-0346
818-677-6853
Fax: 818-366-2714
E-mail: naapae@naapae.net
http://www.naapae.net
Objectives are to enhance awareness of multicultural studies in the United States as well as promoting inclusion of Asian and Pacific American culture and history into the school curricula.

Clara Park, President
Grace Fung-Arto, Vice President

78   National Association for Developmental Education (NADE)
2447 Tiffin Avenue
Suite 207
Findlay, OH 45840
877-233-9455
Fax: 567-202-4385
E-mail: office@nade.net
http://www.nade.net/
Improves the theory and performance at all academic levels.

Hilda Barrow, President
Mickey Hay, Vice President

79   National Association for Legal Support of Alternative Schools (NALSAS)
PO Box 2823
Santa Fe, NM 87504-2823
505-474-0300
E-mail: nalsas@msn.com
http://www.nalsas.org/
Information and legal service center designed to research, coordinate, and support legal actions involving nonpublic educational alternatives.

Ed Nagel, Chairman/Coordinator

80   National Association for Year-Round Education
PO Box 711386
San Diego, CA 92171-1386
619-276-5296
Fax: 858-571-5754
E-mail: info@nayre.org
http://www.NAYRE.org
Founded in 1972 NAYRE fosters and disseminates information about year-round education as a way to improve educational programs.

Marsha Speck, President

81   National Association of Catholic School Teachers
1700 Sansom Street
Suite 903
Philadelphia, PA 19103
215-568-4175
800-996-2278
Fax: 215-568-8270
E-mail: nacst.nacst@verizon.net
http://www.nacst.com/
Unifies, advises and assists Catholic school teachers in matters of collective bargaining.

Rita C Schwartz, President
Michael A Milz, Executive Vice President

82   National Association of Federally Impacted Schools
Hall of the States
444 N Capitol Street NW
Suite 419
Washington, DC 20001-1512
202-624-5455
Fax: 202-624-5468
E-mail: johnfork@nafisdc.org
http://www.sso.org/nafis/
Public school districts receiving federal aid.

John Forkenbrock, Executive Director
Richard Bordeaux, President

83   National Association of State Boards of Education
277 S Washington Street
Suite 100
Alexandria, VA 22314
703-684-4000
Fax: 703-836-2313
E-mail: boards@nasbe.org
http://www.nasbe.org
Aims are to study problems of mutual interest and concern, improve communication among state boards, and exchange and collect information concerning all aspects of education.

52 pages
ISSN: 1540-8000

David Kysilko, Editor
Brenda L Welburn, Executive Director

84   National Association of Student Activity Advisers
1904 Association Drive
Reston, VA 20191-1557
703-860-0200
800-253-7746
Fax: 703-476-5432
E-mail: nhs@nassp.org
http://http://nasccms.principals.org/s_nasc
Promotes leadership training for students involved in the creative process.

85   National Association of Student Councils (NASC)
1904 Association Drive
Reston, VA 20191-1537
703-860-0200
800-253-7746
Fax: 703-620-6534
http://www.nasc.us/s_nasc/index.asp
Supports student councils, relations between teachers and students, as well as directing student-sponsored activities.

Scott D Thompson, Executive Officer

86   National Association of Trade & Industrial Instructors
Canadian Valley Vo Tech
6505 East Highway 66
El Reno, OK 73036-0579
405-262-2629
Fax: 405-422-2354
Founded in 1965 the National Association of Trade and Industrial Instructors seeks to improve communication among members and to support the needs of classroom teachers.

Carol McNish, President

87   National Catholic Educational Association
1077 30th Street NW
Suite 100
Washington, DC 20007-3852
202-337-6232
Fax: 202-333-6706
E-mail: nceaadmin@ncea.org
http://www.ncea.org
Conducts research, works with voluntary groups and government agencies on educational problems, conducts seminars and workshops for educators at all levels.

88 pages Quarterly

Karen M Ristau, Ed.D, President
Donald W Wuerl, Archbishop, Chairman

88 National Catholic Educational Association NCEA
1077 30th Street NW
Suite 100
Washington, DC 20007-3852
202-337-6232
Fax: 202-333-6706
E-mail: nceaadmin@ncea.org
http://www.ncea.org
Provides leadership for groups and individuals who are responsible for policy formation and decision making in Catholic education.

Karen Ristau, President
Claire Helm, VP of Operations

89 National Center for Learning Disabilities
381 Park Avenue S
Room 1401
New York, NY 10016-8806
212-545-7510
888-575-7373
Fax: 212-545-9665
http://www.ncld.org
Provides information, referral, public education and outreach programs on learning disabilities. Provides technical assistance on school to work transition, and referral to state employment services, job training partnership act programs and rehabilitation services.

Frederic Poses, Chairman of the Board

90 National Coalition for Parent Involvement in Education (NCPIE)
1400 Street NW
Suite 300
Washington, DC 20005
202-289-6790
Fax: 703-359-0972
E-mail: ferguson@ncea.com
http://www.ncpie.org/
National Coalition for Parent Involvement in Education (NCPIE) advocates the involvement of parents and families in their children's education, and to foster relationships between home, school, and community to enhance the education of all our nation's young people.

Sue Ferguson, Chair

91 National Coalition of Advocates for Students
100 Boylston Street
Suite 737
Boston, MA 02116
617-357-8507
Fax: 617-357-9549
NCAS is a national education advocacy organization with 21 member groups in 14 states that works to achieve equal access to a quality public education the most vulnerable students those who are poor, children of color, recently immigrated, or children with disabilities. Focusing on kindergarten through grade 12, NCAS informs and mobilizes parents, concerned educators, and communities to help resolve critical education issues. NCAS raises concerns that otherwise might not be addressed.

Judge Nancy Francis, Chairperson

92 National Coalition of Alternative Community Schools
Po Box 6009
Ann Arbor, MI 48106-6009
734-483-7040
888-771-9171
E-mail: ncacs1@earthlink.net
http://www.ncacs.org

A clearinghouse for information regarding alternatives in education for all ages, including home education. Yearly conference, newsletters, mentored Teacher Education Program.

Terri Wheeler, National Office Manager

93 National Coalition of Independent Scholars
PO Box 5743
Berkeley, CA 94705-0743
510-704-0990
http://www.ncis.org
Founded in 1989 the National Coalition of Independent Scholars is comprised of independent teachers and homeschooling professionals.

Founded: 1989

94 National Commission for Cooperative Education
360 Huntington Avenue
Suite 384CP
Boston, MA 02115-5096
617-373-3770
Fax: 617-373-3463
E-mail: ncce@neu.edu
http://www.co-op.edu
Founded in 1962 the national commission for Copperative Education offers brochures and publications describing the structure and benefits of cooperative education. Co-op is an academic program which integrates classroom studies with paid work experience in a field related to a student's goals.

Founded: 1962

Paul Stonely, President

95 National Council for Black Studies
Georgia State University
PO Box 4109
Atlanta, GA 30302-4109
404-463-9483
Fax: 404-651-4883
E-mail: info@ncbsonline.org
http://www.ncbsonline.org
Established in 1975 the NCBS promotes and strengthens academic and community programs in black and/or African-American studies.

Sundiata Cha-Jua, Vice President
Charles E Jones, President

96 National Council for Science and the Environment
1707 H Street NW
Suite 200
Washington, DC 20006
202-530-5810
Fax: 202-628-4311
http://ncseonline.org
NCSE has been working since 1990 to improve the scientific basis of environmental decisionmaking.

Founded: 1990

Shelley Kossak, Director of Development

97 National Council of Higher Education
National Education Association (NEA)
1201 16th Street NW
Washington, DC 20036-3207
202-833-4000
Fax: 202-822-7624
E-mail: nche@nea.org
http://www.nea.org/he/nche
Founded in 1964 the National Council of Higher Education seeks to resolve problems related to quality higher education; pro-

motes collaborations between K-12 and higher education; provides training for members and serves as a vehicle for local input to the National Education Association.

Kathy Sproles, President

98 National Council of Urban Education Associations
National Education Association (NEA)
1201 16th Street NW
Suite 410
Washington, DC 20036-3207
202-822-7364
Fax: 202-822-7624
E-mail: ncuea@nea.org
http://www.nea.org/ncueahome
Founded in 1964 the National Council of Urban Education Association seeks to resolve urban problems related to quality education; promotes improved relations between local and state authorities; provides training for members and serves as a vehicle for local input to the National Education Association.

Susie Jablinske, President
Leon Horne, Vice President

99 National Council on Measurement in Education
1230 17th Street NW
Washington, DC 20036-3078
202-223-9318
Fax: 202-775-1824
E-mail: mwhite@area.net
http://www.ncme.org
Interested in the measurement and use of human abilities, personality characteristics and educational achievement.

Felice Levine, Executive Director
Gerald Sroufe, Administrative Officer

100 National Council on Rehabilitation Education (NCRE)
2012 West Norwood Drive
Carbondale, IL 62901
618-549-3267
Fax: 618-457-3632
E-mail: sbenshoff@ncre-admin.org
http://www.rehabeducators.org/
Promotes the improvement of rehabilitation services available to people with disabilities through quality education and rehabilitation research.

Sharon Benshoff, Administrator
Jorge Garcia, President

101 National Council on Student Development (NCSD)
Univeristy of Illinois
51 Gerty Drive
Room 129
Champaign, IL 61820
217-333-9230
Fax: 217-244-0851
E-mail: ncsd@uiuc.edu
http://www.ncsdonline.org/
Offers information and provides a forum for members and professionals involved in student development.

Debra Bragg, Executive Director
Deborah Garrett, President/Dean

102 National Dissemination Center for Children with Disabilities
PO Box 1492
Washington, DC 20013-1492
202-884-8200
800-695-0285
Fax: 202-884-8441
E-mail: nichcy@aed.org
http://www.nichey.org

Services include personal responses, referrals to other organizations, information packets, publications on current issues, technical assistance to family and professional groups. Provides free information to assist parents, educators, caregivers, advocates and others in helping children and youth with disabilities become participating members of the community.

Lisa Savard, Sales/Marketing Director

103 National Education Association
1201 16th Street NW
Washington, DC 20036-3290
202-833-4000
Fax: 202-822-7974
E-mail: ncuea@nea.org
http://www.nea.org
Advocates for the education profession and the well-being of children; supports campaigns designed to improve the teaching profession and teachers in their efforts to improve teaching; training programs; safe schools; and better working conditions.

Reg Weaver, President
Dennis Van Roekel, Vice President

104 National Education Association Student Program
National Education Association (NEA)
1201 16th Street NW
Washington, DC 20036-3290
202-822-7364
Fax: 202-822-7624
E-mail: ncuea@nea.org
http://www.nea.org
Seeks to improve education and work with and for the student body of America.

105 National Education Association-Retired
National Education Association (NEA)
1201 16th Street NW
Washington, DC 20036-3207
202-822-7125
Fax: 202-822-7624
http://www.nea.org/retired
Serves as a resource in the maintenance of quality public education, promotes improved services and legislation for seniors, provides training for members and serves as a vehicle for local input to the National Education Association.

Jim Sproul, President
Barbara Matteson, Vice President

106 National Education Policy Institute
National Alliance of Black School Educators
310 Pennsylvania Avenue
Washington, DC 20003
202-608-6310
800-221-2654
Fax: 202-608-6319
E-mail: glawson@nabse.org
http://www.nabse.org
Offers a wide array of professional development and information sharing programs for its growing membership of concerned educators. These programs offer hands-on learning opportunities as well as invaluable informational resources for African American educators.

Emma Epps, President
Deborah Hunter-Harvill, President-Elect

107 National Educational Service
304 W Kirkwood Avenue
Suite 2
Bloomington, IN 47404-5132
812-336-7700
800-733-6786
Fax: 812-336-7790
E-mail: info@solution-tree.com
http://www.nesonline.com
Founded in 1989 the National Edcucational Service provides tested and proven resources to help those who work with youth create safe and caring schools, agencies, and communities where all children succeed.
Founded: 1989

Karen Bailey, Representative
Deb McDonald, Representative

108 National Institute for Literacy (NIL)
1775 I Street NW
Suite 730
Washington, DC 20006-2401
202-233-2025
Fax: 202-233-2050
E-mail: ald@nifl.gov
http://www.nifl.gov/
The National Institute for Literacy, a federal agency, provides leadership on literacy issues, including the improvement of reading instruction for children, youth, and adults. In consultation with the U.S. Departments of Education, Labor, and Health and Human Services, the Institute serves as a national resource on current, comprehensive literacy research, practice, and policy.

Sandra Baxter, Director
Elizabeth Hollis, Assistant to Director

109 National Lekotek Center
3204 W Armitage
Chicago, IL 60647
773-276-5164
Fax: 773-276-8644
E-mail: lekotek@lekotek.org
http://www.lekotek.org
Provides play-centered programs for children with disabilities and their families. In 50 US centers children with learning disabilities, Down Syndrome, Cerebral Palsy and developmental delay use play sessions, toy libraries, play groups, computer programs and training. Also provides play experiences through adapted hardware.

Deidre Pate Omahen, Cirector of Programs
Diana Nielander, Executive Director

110 National Middle School Association
4151 Executive Parkway
Suite 300
Westerville, OH 43081
614-895-4730
800-528-6672
Fax: 614-895-4750
E-mail: info@NMSA.org
http://www.nmsa.org
Resource centers, conferences, professional development, and more.

Kathy McAvoy, President

111 National Organization on Disability
910 16th Street NW
Suite 600
Washington, DC 20006-2988
202-293-5960
800-248-ABLE
Fax: 202-293-7999
E-mail: ability@nod.org
http://www.nod.org
Administers a community-based network of more than 2,200 towns, cities, and counties established to improve the participation of people with disabilities in community life.

Alan Reich, President
Michael Deland, Board Chairman

112 National School Boards Association
1680 Duke Street
Alexandria, VA 22314-3455
703-838-6722
Fax: 703-683-7590
E-mail: info@nsba.org
http://www.nsba.org
A nationwide advocacy organization for the public school governance.

Anne Bryant, Executive Director

113 National School Public Relations Association
15948 Denwood Road
Rockville, MD 20855-1109
301-519-0436
Fax: 301-519-0494
E-mail: nspra@nspra.org
http://www.nspra.org
Seeks to further public understanding of its schools.

Jim Dunn, President

114 National Society for Experiential Education
19 Mantua Road
Mt. Royal, NJ 08061
856-423-3427
Fax: 856-423-3420
E-mail: nsee.@talley.com
http://www.nsee.org
The mission of NSEE is to foster the effective use of experience as an integral part of education, in order to empower learners and promote the common good.

Karen Roloff, President
Albert Cabral, President-Elect

115 National Society for the Study of Education (NSSE)
University of Illinois at Chicago
1040 West Harrison Street
Chicago, IL 60607-7133
312-996-4529
773-702-7748
Fax: 773-702-9756
E-mail: nsse@uic.edu
http://www.nsse-chicago.org/
The National Society for the Study of Education (NSSE) is an organization of education scholars, professional educators, and policy makers dedicated to the improvement of education research, policy, and practice. NSSE's mission is to advance the study and practice of education by providing accessible scholarship and promoting informed discourse about the challenges and opportunities of education in a democratic society.

David Hansen, Board of Directors
Deborah Loewenberg Ball, Board of Directors

116 National Student Exchange
4656 W Jefferson Boulevard
Suite 140
Fort Wayne, IN 46804-6839
260-436-2634
Fax: 260-436-5676
E-mail: bworley@fwi.com
http://www.buffalostate.edu/~nse
A cooperative program that allows undergraduate students access to different United States universities.

Bette Worley, President

117 National Student Program
National Education Association (NEA)
1201 16th Street NW
Washington, DC 20036-3207
202-822-7364
Fax: 202-822-7624
E-mail: ncuea@nea.org
http://www.nea.org
Promotes quality pre professional education and training; innovation in teacher training; local and state affiliates and colleges/universities provides training for members and serves as a vehicle for local input to the National Education Association.

Herb Levitt, President
Katrina Thompson, Manager

118 National Telemedia Council
120 E Wilson Street
Madison, WI 53703
608-257-7712
Fax: 608-257-7714
E-mail: ntc@danenet.wicip.org
http://http://danenet.wicip.org/ntc/
A professional, non-profit organization promoting media literacy education through partnership with educators, informed citizens and media producers across the country.

Eric Howland, Director
John Jordan, Community Outreach

119 National Women's Student Coalition (NWSC)
United States Student Association
815 16th Street NW, 4th Floor
Washington, DC 20006
202-637-3924
Fax: 202-637-3931
E-mail: ussa@usstudents.org
http://www.usstudents.org
National Women's Student Coalition (NWSC), an affiliate of the United States Student Association, provides a space for women of different economic backgrounds, races, sexual orientations, religions and abilities to come together and strategize ways to increase campus safety, diversity, fight against bias related violence and build women's leadership.

Jennifer Pae, President
Rebecca Thompson, Legislative Director

120 National Women's Studies Association
University of Maryland
7100 Baltimore Avenue
Suite 502
College Park, MD 20740
301-403-0524
Fax: 301-403-4137
E-mail: nwsaoffice@nwsa.org
http://www.nwsa.org
Founded in 1977 the National Women's Studies Association works to further the social, political and professional development of women's studies programs and projects.

Allison Kimmich, Executive Director
Barbara Howe, President

121 Native American Homeschool Association
474 Brush Creek Road
Fries, VA 24330
540-636-1020
Fax: 540-636-1464
http://www.expage.com/page/nahomeschool2
Association of Native American homeschoolers.

Misty Dawn Thomas Ruff, Tribal Chairwoman

122 North American Association for Environmental Education (NAAEE)
2000 P Street NW
Suite 540
Washington, DC 20036
202-419-0412
Fax: 202-419-0415
E-mail: brian@naaee.org
http://www.naaee.org
The North American Association for Environmental Education is a network of professionals, students, and volunteers working in the field of environmental education throughout North America and in over 55 countries around the world.

Brian A Day, Executive Director
Paul Nowak Jr, Technology Director

123 North American Association of Educational Negotiators
PO Box 1068
Salem, OR 97308
503-588-2800
E-mail: naem@osba.org
http://www.naen.org/
Founded in 1966 the North American Association of Educational Negotiators purpose is to promote and unite those who negotiate on behalf of school boards into a single, strong body and to provide a facility for the effective communication and exchange of information among these individuals.

Mark Pettitt, President

124 North American Students of Cooperation
PO Box 7715
Ann Arbor, MI 48107-7715
734-663-0889
Fax: 734-663-5072
E-mail: info@nasco.coop
http://www.nasco.coop
Founded in 1968 the North American Students of Cooperation supports student cooperatives and offers leadership training in the field.

Holly jo Sparks, Executive Director

125 Northwest Association of Schools & Colleges
1910 University Drive
Boise, ID 83725
208-426-5727
Fax: 208-334-3228
E-mail: sclemens@boisestate.edu
http://www.boisestate.edu/naas
Seeks to advance the concept of education as well as addresses the educational opportunities and services available among schools and colleges. Publishes a 163 page annual paperback, Administrator, Steering Comittee, and Response Team Manual.

Shelli Clemens, Manager

126 Odyssey of the Mind
Creative Competitions, Inc.
1325 Route 130 S
Suite F
Gloucester City, NJ 08030
856-456-7776
Fax: 856-456-7008
E-mail: info@odysseyofthemind.com
http://www.odysseyofthemind.com
Founded in 1979 the Odyssey of the Mind teaches students to learn creative problem-solving methods while having fun in the process; also teaches students how to think divergently by providing open-ended problems that appeal to a wide range of people.

127 PACER Center
8161 Normandale Boulevard
Minneapolis, MN 55437
952-838-9000
888-248-0822
Fax: 952-838-0919
E-mail: pacer@pacer.org
http://www.pacer.org
Founded in 1977 PACER a coalition of organizations founded on the concept of Parents Helping Parents. PACER strives to improve and expand opportunities that enhance the quality of life for children and young adults with disabilities and their families. Helps parents become informed and effective representatives for their children in early childhood, school-age and vocational settings through agencies and appropriate service.
Founded: 1977

Paula Goldberg, Executive Director

128 Parents Rights Organization
Citizens for Educational Freedom
9333 Clayton Road
Saint Louis, MO 63124
314-997-6361
Fax: 314-997-6321
E-mail: citedfree@educational-freedom.org
http://www.educational-freedom.org
Founded in 1959 the Parents Rights Organization secures legal recognition for the right of parents to direct and control the education of their children; secures freedom of choice in education of their children, including an alternative to the government-established school system.
Founded: 1959

Mae Duggan, President/CEF

129 Parents, Let's Unite for Kids
516 N 32nd Street
Billings, MT 59101-6003
406-255-0540
800-222-7585
Fax: 406-255-0523
E-mail: plukinfo@pluk.org
http://www.pluk.org
Formed in 1984 PLUNK informs parents of various resources, workshops, parent training and information in the education field.

130 Peace & Justice Studies Association
5th Floor University Center
2130 Fulton Street
San Francisco, CA 94117-1080
415-422-5238
http://www.peacejusticestudies.org
Dedicated to bringing together academics, K-12 teachers and grassroots activists to explore alternatives to violence and share visions and strategies for peacebuilding, social justice, and social change.
Founded: 2001

131 Public Relations Student Society of America
33 Maiden Lane
11th Floor
New York, NY 10038-5150
212-460-1474
Fax: 212-995-0757
E-mail: prssa@prsa.org
http://www.prssa.org
Cultivates cooperation between students and professional public relations practitioners.

Brent A Hendrix, Manager

132 Religious Education Association (REA)
c/o W Alan Smith, Ph.D
1107 Waterfall Lane
Lakeland, FL 33803
863-430-3893
Fax: 863-644-5477
E-mail: reaapprre@msn.com
http://www.religiouseducation.net/
Religious Education Association was founded in 1903 by William Raney Harper, the first President of the University of Chicago. That year, hundreds of religious and educational leaders from the United States and Canada converged on Chicago for the first convention featuring speakers such as John Dewey and George Albert Coe. Throughout its century-long existence, REA has supported research into moral and religious development in many ways, including conferences, workshops and in-depth studies.

W Alan Smith, Ph.D, REA Executive Secretary
Ronnie Prevost, President/Chairman

133 Renew America
Po Box 77636
Washington, DC 20013-7636
202-721-1545
Fax: 202-467-5780
E-mail: mattcabbott@gmail.com
http://www.renewamerica.us
Works to identify, verify, and recognize successful environmental programs that measurably protect, restore or enhance the environment. Honors successful environmental sustainability projects across the nation through Nation Awards for Environmental Sustainability.

Alan Keys, Chairman

134 Schiller Center
801 Duke Street
Alexandria, VA 22314-3623
703-684-4735
Fax: 703-684-4738
E-mail: schiller@schillercenter.org
http://www.schiller.org
Works extensively with businesses, state, local and national governments and education groups to assist in long-range and strategic planning.

Sherry L Schiller, President

135 Sexuality Information & Education Council of the US
130 W 42nd Street
Suite 350
New York, NY 10036-7802
212-819-9770
Fax: 212-819-9776
E-mail: siecus@siecus.org
http://www.siecus.org
Develops, collects and disseminates information, promotes comprehensive education about sexuality, and advocates the right of individuals to make responsible sexual choices.

Joseph DiNorcia, President/CEO

136 Society for the Advancement of Excellence in Education (SAFE)
225-1889 Springfield Road
Kelowna, British Columbia, Canada
V1Y5V5
250-717-1163
Fax: 250-717-1134
E-mail: info@saee.ca
http://www.saee.ca/
The Society for the Advancement of Excellence in Education (SAEE) provides non-partisan education research and information to policy-makers, education partners and the public. Their mission is to develop new Canadian knowledge on school improvement and foster the understanding of its use. They support public schools and those who work with them to improve outcomes for all students.

Helen Rahem, Research Director
Mame McCrea Silva, General Manager

137 Summit Vision
5640 Lynx Drive
Westerville, OH 43081
614-645-5972
Fax: 614-645-8903
E-mail: tmcbane@wideopenwest.com
http://www.summit-vision.com
Provides specialized programs and activities designed to focus on proficiency objectives, conflict resolution, making smart choices and linking academic concepts to adventure activities.

Trey McBane, Contact
Penn Mallon, Contact

138 Wilderness Education Association
900 East 7th Street
Bloomington, IN 47405
812-855-4095
Fax: 812-855-8697
E-mail: cpelchat@ithaca.edu
http://www.weainfo.org
Promotes environmental, outdoor and wilderness education.

Chris Pelchat, President
Dave Calvin, Vice President

139 Women's Educational & Industrial Union
Crittenton Women's Union
One Washington Mall
2nd Floor
Boston, MA 02108
617-259-2900
Fax: 617-247-8826
E-mail: info@liveworkthrive.org
http://www.weiu.org
Recognizes, supports, maintains and strives to better women's educational opportunities.

Martha Mueller Cook, Chief Operations Officer
Elisabeth D Babcock, President

Administration

140 American Association of Collegiate Registrars & Admissions Officers
1 Dupont Circle NW
Suite 520
Washington, DC 20036-1137
202-293-9161
Fax: 202-872-8857
http://www.aacrao.org
Promotes higher education and furthers the professional development of members working in admissions, enrollment management, financial aid, institutional research, records and registration.

Jerry Sullivan, Executive Director
Martha Henebry, Publications Manager

141 American Association of School Administrators
801 N Quincy Street
Suite 700
Arlington, VA 22203-1730
703-528-0700
Fax: 703-841-1543
E-mail: webmaster@aasa.org
http://www.aasa.org
The mission of the American Association of School Administrators is to support and develop effective school system leaders who are dedicated to the highest quality public education for all children

Paul D Houston, Executive Director

142 American Education Finance Association (AEFA)
8365 Armadillo Trail
Evergreen, CO 80439
303-674-0857
Fax: 303-670-8986
E-mail: eds@aefa.cc
http://www.aefa.cc/
Founded in 1976 the American Education Finance Association fosters communication among groups in educational finance. Interested in public policy, emerging issues and finance concepts and conducting workshops and conventions on these subjects.

Founded: 1976

Christopher Roellken, President
Ed Steinbrecher, Executive Director

143 Association of School Business Officials International
ASBO International Annual Meetings and Exhibits
11401 N Shore Drive
Reston, VA 20190-4200
703-478-0405
Fax: 703-478-0205
E-mail: jmusso@asbointl.org
http://http://asbointl.org
Promotes improvement and advancement of school business management and provides a forum for the exchange of information and ideas among professionals.

John D Musso, Executive Director
Ronald A Skinner, Assistant Executive Director

144 Council of Chief State School Officers
1 Massachusetts Avenue NW
Suite 700
Washington, DC 20001-1431
202-336-7000
Fax: 202-408-8072
http://www.ccsso.org

Organization of public officials who head state departments of education.

David Driscoll, President

145 ERIC Clearinghouse on Educational Management
University of Oregon
5207 University of Oregon
Eugene, OR 97403-5207
541-346-5044
800-438-8841
Fax: 541-346-2334
E-mail: sales@cepm.uoregon.edu
http://www.eric.uoregon.edu
Collects and publishes educational information and materials on topics dealing with all aspects of educational administration and management.

Dr. Philip Piele, Director
Stuart C Smith, Associate Director

146 ERIC Clearinghouse on Languages and Linguistics
4646 40th Street NW
Washington, DC 20016-1859
202-362-0700
800-276-9834
Fax: 202-362-3740
E-mail: info@cal.org
http://www.cal.org
Provides a wide range of services and materials for language educators, most of them free of charge.

Donna Christian, President
Susan Zapata, Executive Assistant

147 Independent Schools Association of the Central States
1165 N Clark Street
Chicago, IL 60610
312-255-1244
Fax: 312-255-1278
E-mail: info@isacs.org
http://www.isacs.org
Founded in 1908 the Independent Schools Association of the Central States provides curricular and research information for private schools on all levels in the midwest. Evaluation/accreditation of independent private schools in a fifteen state region.

1165 pages

Rick Belding, President

148 National Association for Supervision and Curriculum Development (ASCD)
1703 N Beauregard Street
Alexandria, VA 22311-1714
703-578-9600
800-933-2723
Fax: 703-575-5400
E-mail: member@ascd.org
http://www.ascd.org/portal/site/ascd/index.jsp/
Represents administrators of pupil services, promotes the concept of pupil personnel services in school systems to serve the needs of children and youth. Provides communication and professional growth for members.

Gene R Carter Ed.D, Executive Director/CEO
Dick Hanzelka, President

149 National Association of Elementary School Principals
1615 Duke Street
Alexandria, VA 22314-3483
703-684-3345
800-386-2377
Fax: 800-396-2377
E-mail: naesp@naesp.org
http://www.naesp.org
To lead in the advocacy and support for elementary and middle level principals and other education leaders in their commitment to all children.

Al Michelson, President
Raven Padgett, Director of Communications

150 National Association of Principals of Schools for Girls (NAPSG)
23490 Caraway Lakes Drive
Bonita Springs, FL 34135-8441
239-947-6196
Fax: 239-390-3245
E-mail: napsg@mac.com
http://www.napsg.org/
Founded in 1921 the association consists of principals and deans of private and secondary schools for girls.

Bruce W Galbraith, Executive Director
M Burch Tracy Ford, President

151 National Association of Private Schools for Exceptional Children
1522 K Street NW
Suite 1032
Washington, DC 20005-1211
202-408-3338
Fax: 202-408-3340
E-mail: napsec@aol.com
http://www.napsec.com
Strives to ensure access to special education for individuals as a vital component of the continuum of appropriate placements and services in American education.

Sherry L Kolbe, Executive Director/CEO
Sherry DeGroot, Manager

152 National Association of Secondary School Principals
1904 Association Drive
Reston, VA 20191-1537
703-860-0200
Fax: 703-476-5432
http://http://nasspcms.principals.org
To promote excellence in school leadership and to provide members with a wide variety of programs and services to assist them in administration, supervision, curriculum planning, and effective staff development.

Cynthia Rudrud, President

153 National Association of State Directors of Special Education
1800 Diagonal Road
Suite 320
Alexandria, VA 22314
703-519-3800
Fax: 703-519-3808
E-mail: nasdse@nasdse.org
http://www.nasdse.org
A nonprofit corporation that promotes and supports education programs for students with disabilities in the United States and outlying areas.

Mike Armstrong, President
Marcia Harding, Secretary/Treasurer

154 National Association of Student Financial Aid Administrators
1129 20th Street NW
Suite 400
Washington, DC 20036-3453
202-785-0453
Fax: 202-785-1487
E-mail: ask@nasfaa.org
http://www.nasfaa.org
A nonprofit corporation of postsecondary institutions, individuals, agencies and students interested in promoting the effective administration of student financial aid in the United States.

A Dallas Martin Jr, President

155 National Association of Student Personnel Administrators
1875 Connecticut Avenue NW
Suite 418
Washington, DC 20009-5737
202-265-7500
Fax: 202-797-1157
E-mail: office@naspa.org
http://www.naspa.org/
Serves chief student affairs officers of higher education institutions.

Pegke Blake, President
Gwen Dungy, Executive Director

156 National Council of State Directors of Adult Education
444 N Capitol Street
Suite 422
Washington, DC 20001
202-624-5250
Fax: 202-624-1497
E-mail: dc1@naepdc.org
http://www.ncsdae.org
Comprised of state level leaders of adult education from each of the state adult education agencies.

157 National Data Bank for Disabled Student Services
University of Maryland
Room 0126, Shoemaker Building
College Park, MD 20742
301-314-7682
Fax: 301-405-0813
http://www.inform.umd.edu/
Provides assessment of statistics related to services, staff, budget and other components of disabled student services programs across the country.

Dr. Vivian S Boyd, Director
Dr. William Scales, Assistant Director, DSS

158 National Institute for School and Workplace Safety
257 Plaza Drive
Suite B
Oviedo, FL 32765-6457
407-366-4878
Fax: 407-977-1210
http://www.nisws.com
Believes that every school and workplace must implement school and workplace safety standards. Committed to enhance school and workplace safety and to increase awareness of school and workplace safety issues.

Steven Burhoe, CEO

159 National School Safety Center
141 Duesenberg Drive
Suite 11
Westlake Village, CA 91362
805-373-9977
Fax: 805-373-9277
E-mail: info@schoolsafety.us
http://www.schoolsafety.us
Serves as a catalyst and advocate for the prevention of school crime and violence by providing information and resources and identifying strategies and promising programs which support safe schools for school children worldwide.

Dr. Ronald D Stephens, Executive Director
June Lane Arnette, Associate Director

160 Office of Juvenile Justice and Delinquency Prevention
810 7th Street NW
Washington, DC 20531
202-307-5911
Fax: 202-307-2093
E-mail: robert.flores@usdoj.gov
http://www.ojjdp.ncjrs.org/funding/funding.htlm
To provide national leadership, coordination, and resources to prevent and respond to juvenile delinquency and victimization.

J Robert Flores, Administrator
Michele Dekonty, Chief To Staff

161 Psychological Corporation
19500 Bulverde Road
San Antonio, TX 78259
800-211-8378
800-872-1726
Fax: 800-232-1223
http://harcourtassessment.com/
Support to program teachers and administrators.

Micael Hansen, President/CEO
Everett Plante, SVP/Chief Technology Officer

Early Childhood Education

162 Child Care Information Exchange
PO Box 3249
Redmond, WA 98073-3249
800-221-2864
Fax: 425-861-9386
E-mail: infor@ChildCareExchange.com
http://www.ccie.com
Exchange has promoted the exchange of ideas among leaders in early childhood programs worldwide through its magazine, books, training products, trainig seminars, and international conferences for 27 years.

Kay Albrecht, Director
Paul W Axtell, Advertising

163 Dimensions of Early Childhood
Southern Early Childhood Association
PO 55930
Little Rock, AR 72215-5930
501-221-1648
800-305-SECA
Fax: 501-227-5297
E-mail: info@southernearlychildhood.org
http://www.southernearlychildhood.org
Provides opportunities in professional development, leadership and advocacy for early childhood educators, child development specialists and program administrators.

Glenda Bean, Executive Director

164 Division for Early Childhood
The Council for Exceptional Children
27 Fort Missoula Road
Missoula, MT 59804
406-543-0872
Fax: 406-543-0887
Association for individuals who work with or on behalf of children with special needs, birth through age 8, and their families. Includes early childhood intervention professionals as well as parents of children who have disabilities, are gifted, or are at risk.

Sarah Mulligan, Executive Director

165 Education Advisory Group
6239 Woodlawn Avenue North
Seattle, WA 98810
206-323-1838
Fax: 206-267-1325
E-mail: info@eduadvisory.com
http://www.eduadvisory.com
Specializes in matching children with learning environments. Helps families identify concerns and establish priorities about their child's education.

166 National Early Childhood Technical Assistance Center
517 S Greensboro Street
Carrboro, NC 27510
919-962-2001
919-843-3269
Fax: 919-966-7463
E-mail: nectac@unc.edu
http://www.nectas.unc.edu
Assists states and other designated governing jurisdictions as they develop multidisciplinary, coordinated and comprehensive services for children with special needs.

Pascal Trohanis, Director

167 National Educational Systems (NES)
6333 DeZavaia
Suite 106
San Antonio, TX 78249
800-231-4380
Fax: 210-699-4674
E-mail: info@shopnes.com
http://www.shopnes.com/
Offers products and services in parental involvement, bilingual/ESL materials, early childhood development curriculum, multiculturally diverse literature, meeting all new program performance standards and more. Partners with National Head Start Association in serving children, families, communities and our world.

168 National Head Start Association
1651 Prince Street
Alexandria, VA 22314-2818
703-739-0875
Fax: 703-739-0878
http://www.nhsa.org
Dedicated to promoting and protecting the Head Start program. Advocates on the behalf of America's low-income children and families. Publishes many books, periodicals and resource guides. Offers a legislative hotline as well as training programs through the NHSA Academy.

Ron Herndon, President

Elementary Education

169 Center for Play Therapy
University of North Texas
1400 Highland, Suite 114
PO Box 310829
Denton, TX 76203-0829
940-565-3864
Fax: 940-565-4461
E-mail: cpt@unt.edu
http://www.centerforplaytherapy.com
Encourages the unique development and emotional growth of children through the process of play therapy, a dynamic interpersonal relationship between a child and a therapist trained in play therapy procedures. Provides training, research, publications, counseling services and acts as a clearinghouse for literature in the field.

Angela Shelly, Assistant Director
Garry Landreth, Founder

170 Clearinghouse on Early Education and Parenting (CEEP)
University of Illinois at Urbana-Champaign
51 Gerty Drive
Champaign, IL 61820-7469
217-333-1386
877-275-3227
Fax: 212-244-7732
E-mail: ceep@uiuc.edu
http://ceep.crc.uiuc.edu/
The Clearinghouse on Early Education and Parenting (CEEP) is part of the the Early Childhood and Parenting (ECAP) Collaborative at the University of Illinois at Urbana-Champaign. CEEP provides publications and information to the worldwide early childhood and parenting communities on topics relating to the physiological, psychological and cultural development of children from birth through early adolescence.

Lilian G Katz Ph.D, Co-Director
Dianne Rothenberg, Co-Director

171 National Association for the Education of Young Children
1313 L Street, NW
Suite 500
Washington, DC 20005-4101
202-232-8777
800-424-2460
Fax: 202-328-1846
E-mail: naeyc@naeyc.org
http://www.naeyc.org
Supports those interested in serving and acting on behalf of the needs and rights of the education of young children.

Dr. Mark Ginsberg, Executive Director

172 National Association of Elementary School Principals (NACSP)
1615 Duke Street
Alexandria, VA 22314-3483
703-684-3345
800-386-2377
Fax: 703-549-5568
E-mail: naesp@naesp.org
http://www.naesp.org/
To lead in the advocacy and support for elementary and middle level principals and other education leaders in their commitment to all children.

Vincent L Ferrandino Ph.D, Executive Director
Gail Connelly, Chief Operating Officer

173 Tribeca Learning Center-PS 150
334 Greenwich Street
New York, NY 10013
212-732-4392
Fax: 212-766-5895
E-mail: slt@ps150.net
http://www.ps150.net/about.html
Tribeca Learning Center, PS 150 opened in 1987 as a public school that encourages student-centered learning and family involvement fostering the optimal development and learning of every child and reaffirming the pivotal role of the elementary school. The school offers specialized classes in art, music, dance, technology and library as well as daily classroom activities which encourage the integration of a child's academic development, emotional-social growth, and the arts.

Judy Sklover, Co-President
Sandy Van der Zwan Katz, Co-President

174 Voyager Expanded Learning
One Hickory Center
1800 Valley View Suite 400
Dallas, TX 75234-8923
214-932-3213
888-399-1995
Fax: 214-631-0176
E-mail: jnowakowski@voyagerlearning.com
http://www.voyagerlearning.com
Founded in 1997 Voyager Expanded Learning is a national education initiative that provides learning programs to public schools.

Jeri Nowakowski, Executive VP

Employment

175 AAA Teacher's Agency
177 Main Street
Suite 364
Fort Lee, NJ 07024-2540
718-548-3267
Fax: 718-548-3315
A placement agency for teachers, administrators and others in the field of education.

Daniel Shea, Director/Owner

176 Aerospace Industries Association of America
1000 Wilson Boulevard
Suite 1700
Arlington, VA 22209-3901
703-358-1000
E-mail: matt.williams@aia-aerospace.org
http://www.aia-aerospace.org
Offers a series of booklets for students and educators, available by email, regarding employment oppuortunities in the industry.

John W Douglas, AIA President/CEO
Clayton Jones, Vice Chairman

177 Association for Suppliers of Printing & Publishing Technologies
1899 Preston White Drive
Reston, VA 20191-4367
703-264-7200
Fax: 703-620-0994
E-mail: npes@npes.org
http://www.npes.org
Services include career placement.

Regis Delmontagne, President
Kathryn Marx, Vice President

178 Aviation Information Resources
1001 Riverdale Court
Atlanta, GA 30337
800-AIR-APPS
Fax: 404-592-6515
http://www.airapps.com
Services include career placement.

Kit Darby, President

179 BBX Teacher Clearinghouse
Black Business Express
175 Norwood Road
Silver Spring, MD 20905
301-628-9776
Fax: 301-879-8060
E-mail: CEO@BBXOnline.com
http://www.bbxonline.com/bbx-home/TeachersClearingHouse.asp
BBX's Teacher Clearinghouse is a comprehensive resume databank where elementary and secondary school teachers, administrators, and education majors can post their resumes at no charge for review by subscribing school districts. Subscribers are public and private schools with an interest in receiving applications from, and importantly, a commitment to hiring, members of the African American/Black communities.

J R Moore, Administrator

180 English Language Fellow Program
Center for Intercultural Development Center
Georgetown University
PO Box 579400
Washington, DC 20057-9400
202-687-6339
Fax: 202-687-2555
E-mail: elf@georgetown.edu
http://exchanges.state.gov/education/engteaching/fellows.htm
The English Language Fellow Program provides American professional expertise in teaching English as a foreign language by sending American experts on ten-month fellowships to overseas academic institutions to improve foreign teachers' and students' access to diverse perspectives on a broad variety of issues, giving foreign teachers and students information enabling them to better understand and convey concepts about American values, democratic representative government, and free enterprise.

Magdalena Potocka, Project Manager

181 Graphic Arts Education & Research Foundation
1899 Preston White Drive
Reston, VA 20191
703-264-7200
866-381-9839
Fax: 703-620-3165
E-mail: gaerf@npes.org
http://www.npes.org
Services include career placement.

Regis Delmontagne, President

182 Graphic Arts Technical Foundation
200 Deer Run Road
Sewickley, PA 15143
412-741-6860
Fax: 412-741-2311
E-mail: piagatf@piagaft.org
http://www.gain.net.
Services include career placement.

Denna Hower, Marketing Assistant

183 Health Occupations Students of America
6021 Morriss Road
Suite 111
Flower Mound, TX 75028
972-874-0062
800-321-HOSA
Fax: 972-874-0063
http://www.hosa.org
Provides health occupations educators with a student organization used to recruit and develop a competent and motivated work force for the health care field.

Lauren Sheldon, Director

184 International Graphic Arts Education Association
1899 Preston White Drive
Reston, VA 20191-4367
703-758-0595
http://www.igaea.org
Services include career placement.

185 Mountain Pacific Association of Colleges and Employers
16 Santa Ana Place
Walnut Creek, CA 94598
925-934-3877
Fax: 925-906-0922
E-mail: info@mpace.org
http://www.mpace.org
Professional association of approximately 500 college career planning and placement offices and representatives from business, industry and government who recruit, employ and train graduates of colleges and universities in the western states and Canada.

Stan Inman, President
Michael J Mau, VP/President-Elect

186 NASW Job Link: The Social Work Employment Line
750 First Stret NW
Suite 700
Washington, DC 20002-4241
Fax: 800-595-2929
http://www.socialworkers.org
Practical, convenient, and cost effective way to recruit professional social workers.

Gary Bailey, President
Elizabeth Clark, Executive Director

187 National Association of Teachers' Agencies
799 Kings Highway
Fairfield, CT 06432
203-333-0611
Fax: 203-334-7224
E-mail: fairfieldteachers@snet.net
http://www.jobsforteachers.com
Provides placement services for those seeking professional positions at all levels of teaching/administration/support services worldwide.

Mark King, Secretary/Treasurer

188 National Business Education Association
1914 Association Drive
Reston, VA 20191-1596
703-860-8300
Fax: 703-620-4483
E-mail: nbea@nbea.org
http://www.nbea.org
Offers professional service to identify institutions at all educational levels that have positions open, register candidates who are seeking positions, and establish contact be-

tween candidates and representatives of the schools with vacancies.

Peter F Meggison, President
Jim Rucker, President-Elect

189 Printing Industries of America
601 13 Th Street NW
Suite 360N
Washington, DC 20005
202-730-7970
Fax: 202-730-7987
E-mail: llarson@piagatf.org
http://www.gain.net
The world's largest graphic arts trade associations. Promotes the interest of more that 14,000 member companies, including career placement support.

Linda A Larson, Office Manager

190 Windsor Mountain International
One World Way
Windsor, NH 03244
603-478-3166
Fax: 603-478-5260
E-mail: mail@WindsorMountain.org
http://www.windsormountain.org/
Windsor Mountain International was founded in 1961, as Interlocken International Camp, hosting young people from more than 60 countries through international youth travel programs where students learn by doing, thereby enriching their lives with lasting friendships, new skills, self discovery, and increased environmental and cross-cultural awareness.

Richard Herman, Executive Director
Sara Herman, Organizational Director

191 Women's International League for Peace & Freedom
U.S. Section
1213 Race Street
Philadelphia, PA 19107-1691
215-563-7110
Fax: 215-563-5527
http://www.wilpf.org
Agency offering internships in the United States.

Marilyn Clement

Guidance & Counseling

192 American Association of Sex Educators, Counselors & Therapists
PO Box 1960
Ashland, VA 23005
804-752-0026
Fax: 804-752-0056
E-mail: aasect@aasect.org
http://www.aasect.org
The American Association of Sexuality Educators, Counselors and Therapists is a not-for-profit, interdisciplinary professional organization.

Stephen Conley, Executive Director

193 American Counseling Association
5999 Stevenson Avenue
Alexandria, VA 22304-3302
703-823-9800
800-347-6647
Fax: 703-823-0252
http://www.counseling.org
Founded in 1952 the American Counseling Association supports counselors working in higher education settings. Categories in-

clude research studies, professional issues and innovative practice.

Samuel Gladding, President

194 American School Counselor Association
1101 King Street
Suite 625
Alexandria, VA 22314
703-683-2722
800-306-4722
Fax: 703-683-1619
http://www.schoolcounselor,org
Promotes human rights and child welfare, as well as educational rights for children.

Richard Wong, Executive Director

195 Association of Educational Therapists
100 Bush Street
Suite 1500
San Francisco, CA 94104
415-982-2389
800-286-4267
Fax: 415-982-9204
E-mail: aet@aetonline.org
http://www.aetonline.org
Founded in 1979 the Association of Educational Therapists establishes professional standards and defines roles, responsibilities and ethics of educational therapists; studies techniques, technologies, philosophies and research related to educational therapy; represents/defines educational therapy to the community, school and professional group; provides opportunities for continued professional growth.

Deborah Doyle, President
Risa Graff, President-Elect

196 Counseling Association
5999 Stevenson Avenue
Alexandria, VA 22304-3302
703-823-9800
800-347-6647
Fax: 703-823-0252
E-mail: mawakefield@cox.net
http://www.counseling.org
Supports counselors from educational and social service settings across the country.

Marie Wakefield, President
Richard Yep, Executive Office

197 ERIC/CASS Virtual Libraries: Online Resourcesfor Parents, Teachers, and Counselors
Computer Sciences Corporation
655 15th Street SW
Suite 500
Washington, DC 20005
800-538-3742
http://www.eric.ed.gov/sitemap/html_090 0000b80094a7c.html
Collects and disseminates information on counseling, guidance and student services. (ERIC/CASS) serves counseling and student professionals as well as parents who have an interest in personal and social factors that affect learning and development. ERIC/CASS has developed virtual libraries to provide online access to full-text documents on topics within its scope.

Robert Boruch, ERIC Steering Committee
John W Collins III, ERIC Steering Committee

198 International Association of Counseling Services
101 S Whiting Street
Suite 211
Alexandria, VA 22304-3415
703-823-9840
Fax: 703-823-9843
E-mail: iacsinc@earthlink.net
http://www.iacsinc.org
Accreditation association for university, college and private counseling services.

Nancy E Roncketti, Executive Officer

199 National Association of School Psychologists
4340 E West Highway
Suite 402
Bethesda, MD 20814
301-657-0270
Fax: 301-657-0275
E-mail: center@naspweb.org
http://www.masponline.org
Founded in 1977 the National Association of School Psychologists is a professional association representing over 22,000 school psychologists and related professionals.

Leland Huff, President

200 National Association of Social Workers
750 1st Street NE
Suite 700
Washington, DC 20002-4241
202-408-8600
800-638-8799
Fax: 202-336-8313
E-mail: membership@naswdc.org
http://www.naswdc.org
Founded in 1955 the Natioanl Association of Social Workers offers legislative action, professional programs, information through publications, and current developments in their field.

Elvira Craig de Silva, President
Wilie Walker, Vice President

201 National Association of Substance Abuse Trainers & Educators
1521 Hillary Street
New Orleans, LA 70118-4007
504-286-5000
Sustains an information network of substance abuse/chemical dependency training programs in higher education.

Thomas Lief, Director

International

202 Academic Travel Abroad
1920 N Street NW
Suite 200
Washington, DC 20036
202-785-9000
800-556-7896
Fax: 202-342-0317
http://www.academic-travel.com/ata
Seeks to foster intercultural relations and educational cooperation between institutions of higher learning.

David Parry, President

throughout the world, serves many international schools and multinational corporations.

Daniel L Scinto, President
Roger Hove, Executive Vice President

263 International Society for Business Education
US Chapter
1914 Association Drive
Reston, VA 20191-1538
703-860-8300
Fax: 703-620-4483
Focuses on developing and improving the area of business education.

Dr. Janet Treichel, Executive Director

264 International Studies Association (ISA)
University of Arizona
324 Social Sciences
Tucson, AZ 85721
520-621-7715
Fax: 520-621-5780
E-mail: isa@u.arizona.edu
http://www.isanet.org/
A group of scholars and practitioners founded the International Studies Association (ISA) in 1959 to pursue mutual interests in international studies. Representing eighty countries, ISA has over four thousand members worldwide, encouraging research, upgrades teaching and emphasizes a multidisciplinary approach to international dilemmas.

Thomas J Volgy, Executive Director
Dana B Larsen, Director of Administration

265 Mediterranean Association of International Schools
Apartado 80, 28080 Madrid
Spain
34-91-357-2154
Fax: 34-91-357-2678
E-mail: rohale@mais-web.org
http://www.mais-web.org
Professional organization that strives to improve the quality of education in its Member Schools through several venues. It promotes the professional development of faculty, administrators and school board members; effects communication and interchange and creates international understanding.

Reina O'Hale, Executive Director

266 National Council on US-Arab Relations (NCUSAR)
1730 M Street NW
Suite 5030
Washington, DC 20036
202-293-6466
Fax: 202-293-7770
E-mail: info@ncusar.org
http://www.ncusar.org/
The objective of the National Council on U.S.-Arab Relations is to educate Americans about Arab countries, the Middle East, and the Islamic world through leadership development, people-to-people programs, lectures, publications, and grassroots outreach.

John Duke Anthony Ph.D,
President/Founder

267 National Registration Center for Study Abroad
PO Box 1393
Milwaukee, WI 53201-1393
414-278-0631
Fax: 414-271-8884
E-mail: info@nrcsa.com
http://www.nrcsa.com
Founded in 1968 the National Registration Center for Study Abroad provides information about member institutions programs and establishes standards for treatment of visitors from abroad including the appointment of bilingual housing officers and counselors to deal with culture shock.

Mike Wittig, General Manager

268 Near East-South Asia Council of Overseas Schools
The American Colleges of Greece
Gravias 6 St., Aghia Paraskevi 153-42
Athens, Greece
30-210-600-9821
Fax: 30-210-600-9928
E-mail: nesa@ath.forthnet.gr
http://www.nesacenter.org
To serve member school by being the catalyst for their continous improvement and for on-going innovation based in the best practices of American education.

David J Chojnacki, Executive Director

269 Ontario Business Education Partnership
PO Box 91553, 47 Main Street S
Georgetown, ON
L7G-3G2
905-702-0995
888-672-7996
Fax: 905-684-1276
E-mail: info@olpg.on.ca
http://www.olpg.on.ca
Partner with not-for-profit organizations across Ontario committed to advancing business-education co-operation in support of workforce and economic development.

Alice Strachan, Executive Director

270 Ontario Co-operative Education Association
35 Reynar Drive
Quispamsis, NB
E2G-1J9
Fax: 506-849-8375
E-mail: ocea@rogers.com
http://www.ocea.on.ca
A not-for-profit professional organization of Ontario Cooperative Education and Experiential Learning Professionals.

Tammy Belanger-Lamothe, President
Carol Madsen-Tapley,
Membership/Admin. Secretary

271 Operation Crossroads Africa
PO Box 5570
New York, NY 10027
212-289-1949
Fax: 212-289-2526
E-mail: oca@igc.org
http://operationcrossroadsafrica.org/main.php
Agency offering study abroad programs, exchange programs and international internships, financed and unfinanced.

James H Robinson Ph.D,
President/Founder

272 Opportunities Industrialization Centers International (OIC)
240 West Tulpehocken Street
Philadelphia, PA 19144-3295
215-842-0220
Fax: 215-849-7033
E-mail: rhoward@oici.org
http://www.oicinternational.org/
Offers study abroad programs, exchange programs and international internships.

Ronald W Howard, President/CEO
Quy D Nguyen, VP Business Operations

273 Organization of American States (OAS)
17th Street/Constitution Avenue NW
Washington, DC 20006
202-458-3760
Fax: 202-458-6421
E-mail: oasweb@oas.org
http://www.oas.org/
The Organization of American States (OAS) brings together the nations of the Western Hemisphere to strengthen cooperation on democratic values, defend common interests and debate the major issues facing the region and the world. The OAS is a multilateral forum for strengthening democracy, promoting human rights, and confronting shared problems such as poverty, terrorism, illegal drugs and corruption.

Patricia Esquenazi, Director
Communications
Janelle Conaway, Snr Information
Specialist

274 People to People International
501 E Armour Boulevard
Kansas City, MO 64109-2200
816-531-4701
Fax: 816-561-7502
E-mail: ptpi@ptpi.org
http://www.ptpi.org
Various study abroad programs and international internships.

Mary Eisenhower, President/CEO

275 Phi Delta Kappa
408 N Union Street
Po Box 789
Bloomington, IN 47402-0789
812-339-1156
800-766-1156
Fax: 812-339-0018
E-mail: administration@pdkintl.org
http://www.pdkintl.org
Offers various international travel seminars, curriculum materials and international exchange programs.

Sherry Morgan, President

276 Population Institute
107 2nd Street NE
Washington, DC 20002-7303
202-544-3300
Fax: 202-544-0068
Agency offering exchange programs and international internships.

Werner Fornos, President

277 School Milk Foundation of New Foundland and Labrador
27 Sagona Avenue
Mount Pearl NL
A1N-4P8
709-364-2776
Fax: 709-364-8364
E-mail: info@schoolmilkfdn.nf.net
http://www.schoolmilk.nf.ca
Was established in 1991 with a mandate to increase the consumption of milk amongst

school aged children throughout New-foundland and Labrador.

Founded: 1991

278 Service Civil International (SCI)
5505 Walnut Level Road
Crozet, VA 22932-1633
206-350-6585
Fax: 206-350-6585
E-mail: sciinfo@sci-ivs.org
http://www.sciint.org/
Service Civil International (SCI) is a peace organization that coordinates international voluntary projects for people of all ages, cultures, religious and economic back-grounds.

John Westra, International Coordinator
Nico Verzijden, Finance Officer

279 Teach Overseas
International Schools Services
15 Roszel Road
PO Box 5910
Princeton, NJ 08543
609-452-0990
Fax: 609-452-2690
E-mail: iss@iss.edu
http://www.iss.edu/
Placed over 17,000 K-12 teachers and ad-ministrators in overseas schools since 1955. Most candidates attend US-based In-ternational Recruitment Centers where ISS candidates interview with overseas school heads seeking new staff.

Dan Scinto, President
Roger Hove, Executive Vice President

280 Teachers of English to Speakers of Other Languages
700 S Washington Street
Alexandria, VA 22314
703-836-0774
888-547-3369
Fax: 703-836-7864
E-mail: info@tesol.org
http://www.tesol.org
TESOL is an international professional or-ganization whose mission is to ensure ex-cellence in English language to speakers of other languages.

Susan Bayley, Executive Director

281 United Nations Development Program
1 United Nations Plaza
New York, NY 10017-3515
212-906-5364
Fax: 212-906-5307
http://www.undp.org
Agency offering study abroad programs, exchange programs and international in-ternships, financed and unfinanced.

Djibril Diallo, Contact

282 United States Agency for International Development: International Development Intern Program
Ronald Reagan Building
Washington, DC 20523-0001
202-712-4810
Fax: 202-216-3524
http://www.usaid.gov/ OR
www.usaid.gov/policy/ads/400/459.pdf
Agency offering study abroad programs, exchange programs and international in-ternships.

Randall L Tobias, Administrator/Director
Alonzo Fulgham, Chief Operating Officer

283 Visions in Action
2710 Ontario Road NW
Washington, DC 20009-2154
202-625-7402
Fax: 202-588-9344
E-mail: visions@visionsinaction.org
http://www.visionsinaction.org
One year volunteer positions in African and Latin American counties, as well as an additional six month position in South Af-rica. Volunteers select positions within their area of preference. Internships are also available in the fields of international administration, public relations, fundrais-ing and special projects.

Shaun Skelton PhD, Director

284 World Association of Publishers, Manufacturers & Distributors
Worlddidac
Bollwerk 21, PO Box 8866 CH-3001
Berne
Switzerland
41-31-311-7682
Fax: 41-31-312-1744
E-mail: wuethrich@worlddidac.org
http://www.worlddidac.org
Founded in 1996 the World Association of Publishers, Manufacturers and Distribu-tors is a worldwide listing of over 330 pub-lishers, manufacturers and distributors of educational materials. Listings include all contact information, products and school levels/grades.

Beat Jost, Coordinating Education
Lorenz Wuethrich, Project Manager

Language Arts

285 American Association of Teachers of French
Southern Illinois University
Mailcode 4510
Carbondale, IL 62901-4510
618-453-5731
Fax: 618-453-5733
E-mail: abrate@siu.edu
http://www.frenchteachers.org
Founded in 1927, AATF is the largest na-tional association of French teachers in the world.

Dr. Jayne Abrate, Executive Director

286 American Council on Education in Journalism and Mass Communication (ACEJMC)
University of Kansas
Stauffer Flint Hall
1435 Jayhawk Blvd
Lawrence, KS 66045-7575
785-864-3973
Fax: 785-864-5225
E-mail: sshaw@ku.edu
http://www2.ku.edu/~acejmc/
The Accrediting Council on Education in Journalism and Mass Communications, or ACEJMC, is the agency responsible for the evaluation of professional journalism and mass communications programs in col-leges and universities. These programs of-fer education to prepare students for careers in advertising, newspaper or maga-zine journalism, photojournalism, public relations, radio and television broadcast-ing and related fields.

Susanne Shaw, Executive Director
Cheryl Klug, Publications Coordinator

287 American Council on the Teaching of Foreign Languages
700 S Washington Street
Suite 210
Alexandria, VA 22314
703-894-2900
Fax: 703-894-2905
E-mail: headquarters@actfl.org
http://www.actfl.org
National organization dedicated to the im-provement and expansion of the teaching and learning of all languages at all levels of instruction. Individual membership orga-nization of more than 7,000 foreign lan-guage educators and administrators from elementary through graduate education, as well as government industry.

Audrey Heining-Boynton, President
Winnie Merritt, Administrative Assistant

288 American Speech-Language-Hearing Association
10801 Rockville Pike
Rockville, MD 20852-3226
301-897-5700
800-498-2071
Fax: 301-571-0454
E-mail: actioncenter@asha.org
http://www.asha.org
Certifies professionals providing speech, language and hearing services to the pub-lic. It is an accrediting agency for college and university graduate programs in speech-language pathology and audiology.

289 Association of Schools of Journalism and MassCommunication (ASJMC)
234 Outlet Pointe Blvd
Columbia, SC 29210-5667
803-798-0271
Fax: 803-772-3509
E-mail: aejmchq@aol.com
http://www.asjmc.org/
The Association of Schools of Journalism and Mass Communication/ ASJMC seeks to extend collectively on an international level the individual leadership its members practice on their campuses, striving to en-sure that its constituents innovate, manage and lead in a media marketplace undergo-ing fundamental change, ensuring that journalism and mass communication pro-grams broaden, deepen and invigorate the professions they serve.

Jennifer McGill, Executive Director
Judy Van Slyke Turk, Vice President

290 Center for Applied Linguistics
4646 40th Street NW
Washington, DC 20016-1859
202-362-0700
Fax: 202-362-3740
E-mail: info@cal.org
http://www.cal.org
The Center for Applied Linguistics (CAL) is a private, nonprofit organization work-ing to improve communication through better understanding of language and cul-ture. CAL's staff of researchers and educa-tors conduct research, design and develop instructional materials and language tests, provide technical assistance and profes-sional development, conduct needs assess-ments and program evaluations, and disseminate information and resources re-lated to language and culture.

Joy Kreeft Peyton, Language & Culture Director
Grace Burkhart, Language & Literacy Director

291 ERIC Clearinghouse on Languages and Linguistics
4646 40th Street NW
Washington, DC 20016-1859
202-362-0700
800-276-9834
Fax: 202-362-3740
E-mail: info@cal.org
http://www.cal.org/ericcll/
Supports all aspects of second language instruction and learning in all commonly and uncommonly taught languages including English as a second language. Reference and referral service; searches of ERIC database.

Donna Christian, President
Joy Kreeft Peyton, Vice President

292 International Dyslexia Association
8600 LaSalle Road
Chester Building, Suite 382
Baltimore, MD 21286-2044
410-296-0232
800-223-3123
Fax: 410-321-5069
E-mail: info@interdys.org
http://www.interdys.org
Committed to the advancement of the study and treatment of specific language disability, or developmental dyslexia. Sponsors research and encourages successful and appropriate teaching. Offers a strong voice in developing the world-wide understanding of the illness.

Nancy Hennessy, President

293 International Dyslexia Association (IDA)
8600 LaSalle Road
Suite 382
Baltimore, MD 21286-2044
410-296-0232
800-222-3123
Fax: 410-321-5069
E-mail: info@interdys.org
http://www.interdys.org/
The International Dyslexia Association (IDA) is a non-profit organization dedicated to helping individuals with dyslexia, their families and the communities that support them. IDA was founded in 1949 in memory of Dr. Samuel T. Orton, a distinguished neurologist. IDA strives to provide a comprehensive forum for parents, educators, and researchers to share their experiences, methods, and knowledge.

Megan P Cohen MPA/CAE, Executive Director
Robert S Hott, Development Director

294 Journalism Education Association
Kansas State University
103 Kedzie Hall
Manhattan, KS 66506-1505
785-532-5532
Fax: 785-532-5563
E-mail: lindarp@ksu.edu
http://www.jea.org
An organization of about 2,300 journalism teachers and advisers, offers two national teacher-student conventions a year, quarterly newsletter and magazines, bookstore and national certification program. This association serves as a leader in scholastic press freedom and media curriculum.

Ann Visser, President
Jack Kennedy, Vice President

295 National Association for Bilingual Education
National Education Association (NEA)
1030 15th Street NW
Suite 470
Washington, DC 20005
202-898-1829
Fax: 202-789-2866
E-mail: nabe@nabe.org
http://www.nabe.org
Recognizes, promotes and publicizes bilingual education.

Zaida Cintron, President
Marcia Vargas, Vice President

296 National Council of Teachers of English
1111 W Kenyon Road
Urbana, IL 61801-1096
217-328-3870
877-369-6283
Fax: 217-328-9645
E-mail: public_info@ncte.org
http://www.ncte.org
Founded in 1911 the National Council of Teachers of English is devoted to the advancement of English language and literature studies at all levels of education. Publishes 12 periodicals, a member newspaper, and 20-25 books a year, and holds conventions and workshops.

Lori Bianchini, Communications
Jacqui Joseph-Biddle, Convention Director

297 National Federation of Modern Language Teachers Association (NFMLTA)
c/o University of Wisconsin-Madison
Modern Language Journal
1220 Linden Drive/Room 732 Van Hise Hall
Madison, WI 53706-1558
608-262-9741
E-mail: mlj@lss.wisc.edu OR ssmagnan@wisc.edu
http://polyglot.lss.wisc.edu/mlj/nfmlta.htm
The purposes of the National Federation of Modern Language Teachers Associations (NFMLTA) are the expansion, promotion, and improvement of the teaching of languages, literatures, and cultures throughout the United States, by a variety of activities including but not limited to the publication of The Modern Language Journal.

Sally Sieloff Magnan/Professor, Editor/University Wisconsin
Renate Schulz, President Steering Committee

298 National Network for Early Language Learning (NELL)
Wake Forest University
B201 Tribble Hall
Po Box 7266
Winston-Salem, NC 27109
336-758-5341
Fax: 336-758-4591
E-mail: nnell@wfu.edu
http://nnell.org
An organization for educators involved in teaching foreign languages to children. To promote opportunities for all children to develop a high level of competence in at least one language in addition to their own. Provides leadership, suport, and service to those committed to early language learning and coordinates efforts to make language

learning in programs of excellence a reality for all children.

Scott T Wilkolaski, Secretary/Treasurer-Elect
Terry Caccavale, President

299 National Research Center on English Learning and Achievement
School of Education
University of Albany
1400 Washington Avenue
Albany, NY 12222-0100
518-442-5026
Fax: 518-442-5933
E-mail: cela@albany.edu
http://www.cela.albany.edu
Offers information, newsletter, educational materials, download research reports.

Janet I Angelis, Associate Director

300 Sigma Tau Delta
Northern Illinois University
English Department
DeKalb, IL 60115
815-753-1612
http://www.english.org
An honor society for English that offers awards and sponsors competitions.

301 Teachers & Writers Collaborative
5 Union Square W
New York, NY 10003-3306
212-691-6590
888-BOO-KSTW
Fax: 212-675-0171
E-mail: info@twc.org
http://www.twc.org
Brings writers and educators together in collaborations that explore the connections between writing and reading literature and that generate new ideas and materials.

Nancy Shapiro, Director

Library Services

302 American Library Association
50 E Huron Street
Chicago, IL 60611-2795
312-944-6780
800-545-2433
http://www.ala.org
With a membership of over 34,000 across the United States, this Association is the main representative of libraries, school, public and private in the world.

Carol Brey-Casiano, President

303 Asian American Curriculum Project
529 East Third Avenue
San Mateo, CA 94401
650-375-8286
800-874-2242
Fax: 650-375-8797
E-mail: aacpinc@asianamericanbooks.com
http://www.asianamericanbooks.com
Our mission is to educate the public about the greatdiversity of the Asian American experience, through the books that they distrbute; fostering cultural awareness and to educate Asian Americans about their own heritage,instilling a sense of pride. AACP believes that the knowledge which comes from the use of appropriate materials can accomplish these goals.

Florence M Hongo, Preident
Shizue Yoshina, Vice President

304 Association for Library & Information Science Education
65 East Wacker Place
Suite 1900
Chicago, IL 60601
312-795-0996
Fax: 865-481-0390
E-mail: contact@alise.org
http://www.alise.org
Promotes excellence in education for library and information sciences as a means of increasing library services.

Connie Van Fleet, President
Kathleen Combs, Executive Director

305 Council on Library Technical Assistants (COLT)
c/o Lemont Public Library District
50 East Wend Street
Lemont, IL 60439-6439
630-257-6541
Fax: 630-257-7737
E-mail: jlakatos@lemontlibrary.org
http://colt.ucr.edu/
COLT's objectives include that of functioning as a clearinghouse for information relating to library support staff personnel; promoting effective communication between and among library staff at all levels; initiating and promoting research projects and publications for the advancement of knowledge and understanding among library support staff personnel; and studying and developing curricula for the education of library support staff and appropriate standards for that education.

Jackie Latakos, President
Jackie Hite, Vice Presidet

306 International Association of School Librarianship
PMB 292
1903 W 8th Street
Erie, PA 16505
E-mail: pgenco@iu05trc.iu5.org
http://www.ias-slo.org
Provides an international forum for those people interested in promoting effective school library media programmes as viable isntruments in the educational process. Also provides guidance and advice for the development of school library profession.

Peter Genco, President

307 Pacific Northwest Library Association
PO Box 7220
Olympia, WA 98507-7220
425-753-2916
http://www.pnla
Organization of people who work in, with, and for libraries. Provides opportunities in communication, education and leadership that transcend political boundaries.

308 Pro Libra
436 Springfield Avenue
Suite 3
Summit, NJ 07901
908-918-0077
800-262-0070
Fax: 908-918-0977
E-mail: staffing@prolibra.com
http://www.prolibra.com
Library management to academic institutions.

M Bennett Livingston

Mathematics

309 Association for Advancement of Computing in Education
PO Box 1545
Chesapeake, VA 23327-1545
757-366-5606
Fax: 703-997-8760
E-mail: info@aace.org
http://www.aace.org
The Association is an international, educational and not-for profit organization dedicated to the advancement of the knowledge, theory, snd quailty of learning and teaching at all levels with information technology.

Angela Bradley, Conference Contact

310 Eisenhower National Clearinghouse for Mathematics and Science Education
1275 Kinnear Road
Columbus, OH 43212
800-471-1045
Fax: 614-523-0883
E-mail: info@goENC.com
http://www.enc.org
Designed for educators concerned about creating equitable classroom conditions. Provides math and science equity materials to help teachers and administrators acknowledge children's diverse strengths, identify inequities, and improve the ways students with varied needs are served.

Len Simutis, Executive Director

311 Mathematical Association of America
1529 18th Street NW
Washington, DC 20036-1358
202-387-5200
800-741-9415
Fax: 202-265-2384
E-mail: maahq@maa.org
http://www.maa.org
Founded in 1915 the Mathematical Association of America advances the mathematical sciences, especially at the collegiate level.

Carl Cowen, President

312 National Council of Teachers of Mathematics
1906 Association Drive
Reston, VA 20191-1502
703-620-9840
800-235-7566
Fax: 703-476-2970
E-mail: nctm@nctm.org
http://www.nctm.org
Dedicated to the improvement of mathematics education and to meeting the needs of Pre K-12 mathematics teaching. Conferences, journals and a collection of educational materials for teacher development.

Cathy Seeley, President

Music & Art

313 American Art Therapy Association
5999 Stevenson Avenue
Alexandria, VA 22304
703-212-2238
888-290-0878
Fax: 703-823-0252
E-mail: info@arttherapy.org
http://www.arttherapy.org
Seeks to improve the standards of art therapy training and practice and to widen employment opportunities for art therapists.

Amy Crank, Contact

314 American Dance Therapy Association
2000 Century Plaza
Suite 108
Columbia, MD 21044-3273
410-997-4040
Fax: 410-997-4048
E-mail: info@adta.org
http://www.adta.org
Offers free information on educational programs, guidelines for dance therapy training and internship, professional registration requirements and regional professional contacts.

Elissa White, President
Robyn Cruz, Vice President

315 American Musicological Society
201 S 34th Street
Philadelphia, PA 19104-6313
215-898-8698
888-611-4267
Fax: 215-573-3673
E-mail: ams@sas.upenn.edu
http://www.ams-net.org
Founded in 1934 the American Musicological Society advances research and scholarship in music education and its related fields. Bestows awards and publishes journals.

Robert Judd, Executive Director

316 Council on Technology Teacher Education (CTTE) Education
1914 Association Drive
Reston, VA 22091-1539
703-860-2100
703-860-0353
Fax: 480-727-1089
E-mail: iteambrs@iris.org
http://teched.vt.edu/ctte/CTTEMain.html
The Council on Technology Teacher Education (CTTE), formerly known as the American Council of Industrial Arts Teacher Education (ACIATE), stives to support and further the professional ideals of technology education in addition to stimulating research and the dissemination of information of professional interest.

Michael De Miranda Ph.D, President
Marie Hoepfl Ph.D, Vice President

317 Future Music Oregon
School of Music
1225 University of Oregon
Eugene, OR 97403-1225
541-346-3761
Fax: 541-346-0723
http://http://darkwing.uoregon.edu/~fmo
Educational Institute dedicated to the exploration of sound and its creation, and to the innovative use of computers and other recent technologies to create expressive music and media composition.

Jeffrey Stolet, Director
Gary Martin, Associate Dean

318 International Thespian Society
Educational Theatre Association
2343 Auburn Avenue
Cincinnati, OH 45219-2819
513-421-3900
Fax: 513-421-7077
http://www.edta.org
Serves as an honor society for middle school and high school drama students.

319 Kennedy Center Alliance for Arts Education
John F Kennedy Center for the Performing Arts
2700 F Street NW
Washington, DC 20566-0001
202-416-8000
Fax: 202-416-8802
E-mail: kcaaen@kennedy-center.org
http://www.kennedy-center.org/education/kcaaen
Advances education in the arts, collects and disseminates information about arts education, offers technical assistance on arts education to general public and education field.
Nancy Welch w/Andrea Greene, Author
Michael Kaiser, President

320 Music Teachers National Association
441 Vine Street
Suite 505
Cincinnati, OH 45202-2811
513-421-1420
888-512-5278
Fax: 513-421-2503
E-mail: mtnanet@mtna.org
http://www.mtna.org
Founded in 1876, the Music Teachers National Association is a nonprofit association of independent and collegiate music teachers committed to furthering the art of music through teaching, performance, composition and scholarly research.
Gary Ingle, Executive Director

321 National Art Education Association
1916 Association Drive
Reston, VA 20191-1590
703-860-8000
Fax: 703-860-2960
E-mail: sjgabbard@okcps.org
http://www.naea-reston.org
Founded in 1947 the National Art Education Associationh promotes art education through professional development, service, advancement of knowledge and leadership.
Susan J Gabbard, President
Bonnie B Rushlow, President-Elect

322 National Association for Music Education
1806 Robert Fulton Drive
Reston, VA 20191
703-860-4000
800-336-3768
Fax: 703-860-1531
E-mail: dorothyw@menc.org
http://www.menc.org
Offers informative, timely and accurate articles, editorials and features to a national audience of music educators.
72 pages
ISSN: 0027-4321
Dorothy Wagener, Managing Editor

323 National Association of Schools of Music (NASM)
11250 Roger Bacon Drive
Suite 21
Reston, VA 20190-5248
703-437-0700
Fax: 703-437-6312
E-mail: info@arts-accredit.org
http://nasm.arts-accredit.org/
Founded in 1924 the National Association of Schools of Music interested in promoting and funding music schools and conservatories.
Samuel Hope, Executive Director
Karen P Moynahan, Associate Director

324 National Guild of Community Schools of the Arts
520 8th Avenue
Suite 302, 3rd Floor
New York, NY 10018
212-268-3337
Fax: 212-268-3995
E-mail: jonathanherman@nationalguild.org
http://www.nationalguild.org
A nationwide service and educational organization that fosters the growth and development of nonprofit, nondegree-granting community schools offering instruction in the performing and visual arts to students of all ages.
Jonathan Herman, Executive Director
Kenneth Cole, Program Director

325 National Institute of Art and Disabilities
551 23rd Street
Richmond, CA 94804-1626
510-620-0290
Fax: 510-620-0326
E-mail: admin@niadart.org
http://www.niadart.org
An organization which operates a demonstration visual arts program, provides professional training and consultations, helps establish art centers and art programs for children and adults with disabilities, and conducts research. Books, videos, artwork and other items available.
Amanda Cauldwell, Executive Director
Elias Katz, President

Physical Education

326 American Alliance for Health, Physical Educatiion, Recreation and Dance
1900 Association Drive
Reston, VA 20191-1598
703-476-3400
800-213-7193
Fax: 703-476-9527
http://www.aahperd.org
Membership organization in the fields of physical education, recreation, health, safety and dance.
Michael G Davis, CEO

327 American Sports Education Institute
1150 17th Street, NW
Suite 850
Washington, DC 20036
202-775-1762
Fax: 202-296-7462
E-mail: mmay@sgma.com
Boosts amateur sports and physical education at all levels.
Mike May, Executive Director

328 International Council for Health, Physical Education and Recreation
1900 Association Drive
Reston, VA 20191-1598
703-476-3462
Fax: 703-476-9527
E-mail: ichperaahperd.org
http://www.ichpersd.org
Concerned with health and physical education issues related to child development and education.
Dr. Dong Ja Yang, Secretary General

329 National Association for Girls and Women in Sports
1900 Association Drive
Reston, VA 20191-1598
703-476-3400
800-213-7193
Fax: 703-476-4566
E-mail: nagws@aahperd.org
http://www.aahperd.org/nagws
An association of information for girls and women in sports.
Ketra Armstrong, President

330 National Association of Academic Advisors for Athletics
PO Box A-7
College Station, TX 77844-9007
979-862-4310
Fax: 979-862-2461
E-mail: N4A@athletics.tamu.edu
http://www.nfoura.org
Aim is to promote academic achievement and personal development among student athletes.
Steve McDonnell, President

331 National Athletic Trainers' Association
2952 Stemmons Freeway
Dallas, TX 75247-6196
214-637-6282
800-879-6282
Fax: 214-637-2206
E-mail: ebd@nata.org
http://www.nata.org
Offers advertising, corporate membership, exhibiting, list rental and sponsorship opportunities.
Teresa Welch, Assistant Executive Director

332 President's Council on Physical Fitness & Sports
200 Independence Avenue SW
Room 738-H
Washington, DC 20201-0004
202-690-9000
Fax: 202-690-5211
http://www.fitness.gov
Promotes and encourages the development of physical activity fitness and sports programs for all Americans.
Joey Kung, Director Communications
Janice Meer, Public Affairs Specialist

Reading

333 Clearinghouse on Reading, English & Communication
Indiana University School of Education
201 N Rose Avenue
Bloomington, IN 47405-1006
812-856-8500
Fax: 812-856-8440
http://reading.indiana.edu/
Concerned with the acquisition of functional competence in reading, writing, speaking and listening at all educational levels in all social contexts. Catalogue of publications available for free, including ERIC Digests and other publications, Web Resources, and online courses.
Carl B Smith Ph.D, Director
Andy Wisemanane, Systems Administrator

334 International Reading Association
800 Barksdale Road
Newark, DE 19714-8139
302-731-1600
800-336-7323
Fax: 302-731-1057
E-mail: customerservice@reading.org
http://www.reading.org
Proffesional organization dedicated to promoting high levels of literacy for all by improving the quality of reading instruction, disseminating research and information about reading, and encouraging the lifetime reading habit.

Mary Ellen Vogt, President
Richard Allington, President-Elect

335 National Center for ESL Literacy Education
Center for Applied Linguistics
4646 40th Street NW
Washington, DC 20016-1859
202-362-0700
Fax: 202-363-7204
E-mail: miriam@cal.org
http://www.cal.org/
National clearinghouse for adult English as a second language and literacy information.

Miriam Burt, Associate Director
Dora Johnson, Research Associate

336 National Contact Hotline
Contact Center, Inc.
PO Box 81826
Lincoln, NE 68501-1826
800-228-8813
A 25-year-old information and referral agency, to help individuals with literacy problems. Maintains a database of over 7,000 literacy programs across the country and the 7-day hotline.

337 ProLiteracy Worldwide
1320 Jamesville Avenue
Syracuse, NY 13210
315-422-9121
888-528-2224
Fax: 315-422-6369
E-mail: info@proliteracy.org
http://www.proliteracy.org
Now the oldest and largest non-governmental literacy organization in the world and pursues a mission of sponsoring educational programs that help adults and their families acquire the literacy practices and skills they need to function more effectively in their dialy lives.

M Shan Atkins, Chairperson
Walter H Curchack, Secretary

338 Reading Recovery Council of North America
1929 Kenny Road
Suite 100
Columbus, OH 43210-1069
614-292-7111
Fax: 614-292-4404
E-mail: jjohnson@readingrecovery.org
http://www.readingrecovery.org
An early intervention program for children in the primary grades who are having difficulty learning to read and write.

Jady Johnson, Executive Director

Secondary Education

339 American Driver & Traffic Safety Education Association
National Education Association (NEA)
1201 16th Street NW
Washington, DC 20036-3207
202-822-7634
Fax: 202-822-7624
http://http://144.80.48.9/adtsea/default.aspx
Professional association which represents traffic safety educators throughout the United States and abroad. Serves as a national advocate for quality traffic safety education, conducts conferences, workshops and seminars and provides consultative services.

Elizabeth Weaver-Shepard, President
James Gibb, President-Elect

340 Association for Institutional Research
Florida State University
222 Stone Building
Tallahassee, FL 32306
850-644-4470
Fax: 850-644-8824
E-mail: trussell@mailer.fsu.edu
http://www.airweb.org
Membership includes individuals interested in policy research, management, education and statistical information for high schools.

341 Close-Up Foundation
44 Canal Center Plaza
Alexandria, VA 22314-1592
703-706-3300
800-336-5479
Fax: 703-706-0001
http://www.closeup.org
Offers government studies programs for high school students, educators and older Americans.

Barbara Krebs, Director

342 College Board
45 Columbus Avenue
New York, NY 10023-6992
212-713-8000
Fax: 212-713-8282
http://www.collegeboard.org
Champions educational excellence for all students through the ongoing collaboration of nearly 3,000 member schools, colleges, universities, education systems and organizations. Promotes research, programs, policy development,universal access to high standards of learning, equity of opportunity and financial support.

Gaston Caperton, President

343 National Business Education Association
1914 Association Drive
Reston, VA 20191-1596
703-860-8300
Fax: 703-620-4483
E-mail: nbea@nbea.com
http://www.nbea.com
Administers student keyboarding tests and National Business Competency Tests for high school and college students.

Mary Ann Lammers, President
Cynthia Green, President-Elect

344 National Middle School Association
4151 Executive Parkway
Suite 300
Westerville, OH 43081
614-895-4730
800-528-6672
Fax: 614-895-4750
E-mail: info@nmsa.org
http://www.nmsa.org
Promotes the development and growth of middle schools.

Sue Swaim, Executive Director

Science

345 Academy of Applied Science
24 Warren Street
Concord, NH 03301
603-228-4530
Fax: 603-228-4730
E-mail: admin@aas-world.org
http://www.aas-world.org
Founded in 1952 the Academy of Applied Science is dedicated to the advancement of scientific endeavors. Members are active contributors to the applied science field. Sponsors programs and offers research grants.

Robert Rines, President
Joanne Hayes-Rines, Vice-President

346 Air Force Association
1501 Lee Highway
Arlington, VA 22209
703-247-5800
E-mail: aefstaff@aef.org
http://www.aef.org
Dedicated to ensuring America's aerospace excellence through public awareness programs, education and financial assistance.

Danny D Marrs, Executive Vice President
Donald L Peterson, President

347 Association for Advancement of Computing in Education (AACE)
PO Box 1545
Chesapeake, VA 23327-1545
757-366-5606
Fax: 703-997-8760
E-mail: info@aace.org
http://www.aace.org/
Offers support materials and conferences on educational multimedia and hypermedia, mathematics, science education and technology. Conferences are held in March, June and July.

Gary H Marks Ph.D, Executive Director
Angela Bradley, Conference Coordinator

348 Association for Science Education Teachers
Old Dominion University
Curriculum & Instruction
Norfolk, VA 23508
757-683-3283
Fax: 757-683-5862
http://http://theaste.org
Promotes leadership in the professional development of teachers in science, including science teacher educators, staff developers, college-level science instructors, education policy makers, instructional material developers, science supervisors/specialists/coordinators, lead/mentor

Founded in 1924 the Association for Career and Technical Education represents education professionals dedicated to developing programs for advancement and improvement in vocational and business schools.

James Comer, President-Elect
Margaret Hess, Vice-President

377 Association for Educational Communications & Technology

1800 N Stonelake Drive
Suite 2
Bloomington, IN 47404
812-335-7675
877-677-2328
Fax: 812-335-7678
E-mail: aect@aect.org
http://www.aect.org/
Provide leadership in educational communications and technology by linking a wide range of professionals holding a common interest in the use of educational technology and its application learning process.

Ward Cates, President
Phillip Harris, Executive Director

378 Center for Educational Technologies

Wheeling Jesuit University
316 Washington Ave
Wheeling, WV 26003-6243
304-243-2388
Fax: 304-243-2497
E-mail: info@cet.edu
http://www.cet.edu
To enhance lifelong learning and teaching through the effective use of technology. Provides turn-key solutions to schools, school districts, state departments of education, federal agencies, foundations, businesses, and industry—solutions for planning, developing, and implementing advances in educational technologies.

Chuck Wood, Executive Director

379 Computer Using Educators, Inc (CUE)

387 17th Street
Suite 208
Oakland, CA 94612
510-814-6630
Fax: 510-444-4569
E-mail: cueinc@cue.org
http://www.cue.org
Promotes and develops insructional uses of technology in all disciplines and at all educational levels from preschool through college.

Mike Lawrence, Executive Director
Marisol Valles, Conference Manager

380 Consortium for School Networking

1710 Rhode Island Ave, NW
Suite 900
Washington, DC 20036-3007
202-861-2676
866-267-8747
Fax: 202-861-0888
E-mail: membership@cosn.org
http://www.cosn.org
Promotes the use of telecommunications to improve K-12 learning.

Keith Krueger, CEO
Irene Spero, Vice President

381 EDUCAUSE

4772 Walnut Street
Suite 206
Boulder, CO 80301-2538
303-449-4430
Fax: 303-440-0461
E-mail: info@educause.edu
http://www.educause.edu
A nonprofit association whose mission is to advance higher education by promoting the intelligent use of information technology.

Perry Hanson, Chair

382 Educational Technology Center

Harvard Graduate School of Education
Nichols House, Appian Way
Cambridge, MA 02138
617-495-9373
Fax: 617-495-0540
http://http://edetc1.harvard.edu
Investigates and develops methods for using computers and other information technologies to teach K-12 science, mathematics and computing.

383 International Society for Technology in Education

175 West Broadway
Suite 300
Eugene, OR 97401-3003
800-336-5191
Fax: 541-302-3778
E-mail: iste@iste.org
http://www.iste.org
Promotes appropriate uses of information technology to support and improve learning, teaching, and administration in K-12 education and teacher education. Provides information on networking oppportunities and guidance on the challenges of incorporating computers, the Internet, and other new technologies into their schools.

Kurt Steinhaus, President
Trina Davis, President-Elect

384 Learning Independence Through Computers

LINC
1001 Eastern Avenue
#3
Baltimore, MD 21202-4325
410-659-5462
800-772-7372
Fax: 410-659-5472
http://www.linc.org
Offers specially adapted computer technology and quarterly newsletter to children and adults with a variety of disabilities. State-of-the-art systems allow consumers to achieve their potential for productivity and independence at home, school, work and in the community.

Mary Salkever, Executive Director
Susan Pomp, Associate Director

385 MarcoPolo

WorldCom Foundation
14200 Park Meadow Drive
Stamford, CT 06905
215-579-8590
Fax: 215-579-8589
E-mail: oposewa@edumedia.com
http://www.marcopolo-education.org
A non-profit consortium of premier national and international education organizations and the MCI Foundation dedicated to providing high quality internet and professional development to teachers and students throughout the United States.

Oksana Posewa, Project Manager
Della Cronin, Prog Officer
Communications

386 National Association of Media and Technology Centers

PO Box 9844
Cedar Rapids, IA 52409
319-654-0608
Fax: 319-654-0609
http://www.namtc.org
Committed to promoting leadership among its membership through networking, advocacy, and support activities that will enhance the equitable access to media, technology, and information services to educational communities.

Ron Enger, President
Ricki Chowning, President-Elect

387 National Institute on Disability and Rehabilitation Research

U.S. Department of Education
400 Maryland Avenue SW
Washington, DC 20202-2572
202-205-8134
800-872-5327
Fax: 202-401-0689
http://www.ed.gov/about/offices/list/osers/nidrr
Funds 31 state technology assistance projects providing information and technical assistance on technology, related services and devices for individuals with disabilities.

Margaret Spellings, Secretary
Edward R McPherson, Under Secretary

388 Technology & Media Division

The Council for Exceptional Children
1110 N Glede Road
Suite 300
Arlington, VA 22201
703-620-3660
888-232-7733
Fax: 703-264-9494
http://www.tamcec.org
Association promoting availability and effective use of technology and media for individuals with disabilities and/or who are gifted. The membership is comprised of special education teachers, speech and language therapists, rehabilitation therapists, counselors, researchers, teacher educators and others.

John Castellani, President
Joy Zabala, President-Elect

389 Technology Student Association

1914 Association Drive
Reston, VA 20191-1538
703-860-9000
Fax: 703-758-4852
http://www.tsaweb.org
A student organization devoted to the needs of technology education students. TSA is composed of over 100,000 elementary, middle, and high school students in 2,000 schools spanning 45 states; supported by educators, parents, and business leaders who believe in the need for a technologically literate society.

Mike Amrhein, President
Steve Price, President-Elect

390 Technology and Children

International Technology Education Association
1914 Association Drive
Suite 201
Reston, VA 20191-1539
703-860-2100
Fax: 703-860-0353
E-mail: itea@iteaconnect.org
http://iteaconnect.org

The largest professional education association devoted to technology education. Technology educators teach students to use their ingenuity with tools, materials, processes, and resources to create solutions and opportunities that relate to medical, agricultural and related biotechnologies, energy and power, information and communication, transportation, manufacturing, and construction technologies.

Kendall Starkweather, Executive Director
Barry Burke, CATTS Director

391 Telemetrics
6 Leighton Place
Mahwah, NJ 07430-3198
201-848-9818
Fax: 201-848-9819
http://www.telemetrics.com
Telecommunication network for schools, camera remote control systems and robotics.

Anthony Cuomo, President
Jim Wolfe, Sales Manager

392 Twenty First Century Teachers Network: The McGuffey Project
888 17th Street NW
12th Floor
Washington, DC 20006
202-429-0572
Fax: 202-296-2962
E-mail: info@mcguffey.org
http://www.21ct.org/
A nationwide, non-profit initiative of the McGuffey Project, dedicated to assisting K-2 teachers learn, use and effectively integrate technology in the curriculum for improved student learning.

Wade D Sayer, Project Director
Kristina S Ellis, Director Program Development

Alabama

393 Alabama Business Education Association
A&M University
PO Box 429
School of Business
Normal, AL 35762
256-858-4799
Fax: 256-851-5568
E-mail: karzetta@bellsouth.net
http://http://abea2000.tripod.com
Foster business education in the state of Alabama.

Roslyn Moore, President
Annette Haynes, Newsletter Editor

394 Alabama Education Association
422 Dexter Avenue
Montgomery, AL 36104-3743
334-834-9790
800-392-5839
Fax: 334-262-8377
http://www.myaea.org
Serves as an advocate for Alabama teachers and leads in the advancement of equitable and quality public education.

395 Alabama Library Association
400 S Union Street
Suite 395
Montgomery, AL 36104
334-263-1272
877-563-5146
Fax: 334-265-1281
E-mail: allaonline@mindspring.com
http://http://allanet.org/www/council.htm

Non-profit corporation formed to encourage and promote the welfare of libraries and professional interests of librarians in Alabama.

Bettye Forbus, President
Theresa Trawick, President-Elect

Alaska

396 Alaska Association of School Librarians
344 W 3rd Avenue
Suite 125
anchorge, AK 99501
800-776-6566
E-mail: akasl@akla.org
http://www.akla.org/akasl/home.html
advances a high standard for the school librarian profession and the library information program in the schools of Alaska.

Barb Bryson, President
Erika Drain, President-Elect

397 Alaska Library Association
PO Box 81084
Fairbanks, AK 99708
907-459-1020
Fax: 907-459-1024
E-mail: mcgeemb@yahoo.com
http://www.akla.org
Holds a conference in March and publishes a journal.

Mary H McGee, President
Mary Jennings, Executive Officer

Arizona

398 Arizona Library Association
1030 E Baseline Road
Suite 105-1025
Tempe, AZ 85283
480-609-3999
Fax: 480-609-3939
E-mail: admin@azla.org
http://www.azla.org
The mission of the Arizona Library Association shall be to peomote library service and libarianship in libraries of all types in thestate of Arizona.

Debbie Hanson, Executive Director
Kerrall Farmelant, Conference Administrator

399 Arizona School Boards Association
2100 N Central Ave
Suite 200
Phoenix, AZ 85004-1441
602-254-1100
800-238-4701
Fax: 602-254-1177
http://www.azsba.org
Non-profit, non-partisan organization representing more that 225 all-volunteer school district governing boards of Arizona's public school district.

Joan Fleming, President
Rae Waters, President Elect

400 Professional Office Instruction & Training
1325 W 16th Street
Suite 5
Yuma, AZ 85364
928-343-3076
Fax: 520-782-3211
E-mail: rthomp@c2i2.com

Computer software applications training.
Rochelle Thompson, Owner

401 Southeastern Library Association
PO Box 950
Rex, GA 30273
678-466-4325
Fax: 678-466-4349
E-mail: Judith.Gibbons@KY.GOV
http://sela.jsu.edu/
Holds a conference in October and publishes a journal.

Judith Gibbons, President
Faith Line, Vice President

Arkansas

402 Arkansas Business Education Association
Bryant Junior High School
201 Sullivan
Bryant, AR 72022
501-847-5620
Fax: 501-847-5627
E-mail: sherryr@uca.edu
http://www.abea.us
To promote business education, professional growth, quality instruction, and cooperation among state and national organizations related to business education. Also serves as a representative body for business educators.

Sherry J Roberts, President
Rebecca J Timmons, President-Elect

403 Arkansas Education Association
1500 W 4th Street
Little Rock, AR 72201
501-375-4611
Fax: 501-375-4620
E-mail: ttalbot@nea.org
Promotes the cause of public education in Arkansas.

Sid Johnson, President

404 Arkansas Library Association
Po Box 958
Benton, AR 72018-0958
501-860-7585
Fax: 501-776-9709
E-mail: arlib2@sbcglobal.net
http://www.arlib.org
Holds a conference in October and publishes a journal.

Ashley Burris, President
Barbara Martin, Executive Administrator

405 Southeastern Library Association
PO Box 950
Rex, GA 30273
678-466-4325
Fax: 678-466-4349
E-mail: Judith.Gibbons@KY.GOV
http://sela.jsu.edu/
Association of libraries in the Southeast

Judith Gibbons, President
Faith Line, Vice President

California

406 California Business Education Association
Po Box 407
Moraga, CA 94556
925-377-0939
Fax: 925-377-0939
E-mail: CBEAQuestions@cbeaonline.org
http://www.cbeaonline.org
The California Business Education Association is the professional organization for business and computer instructors, administrators and their business/industry partners. CBEA represents and assists programs at middle schools, high schools, regional occupational programs/centers, community colleges, universities and private colleges.

Jane Thompson, Contact

407 California Classical Association-Northern Section
San Francisco State University
Department of Classics
San Francisco, CA 94132
415-253-2267
Fax: 415-338-2514
http://http://userwww.sfsu.edu/~barbaram/cca.htm
Supports programs to enrich and promote Classics.

Michelle Discher, President
Dobbie Nicholls, Vice President

408 California Foundation for Agriculture in the Classroom
2300 River Plaza Drive
Sacramento, CA 95833-3293
916-561-5625
800-700-2482
Fax: 916-561-5697
E-mail: cfaitc@cfaitc.org
http://www.cfaitc.org
Our mission is to increase awarenes and understanding of agriculture among California's educators and students. Our vision is an appreciation of agriculture by all.

Judy Culbertson, Executive Director

409 California Library Association
717 20th Street
Suite 200
Sacramento, CA 95814
916-447-8541
Fax: 916-447-8394
E-mail: info@cla-net.org
http://www.cla-net.org
Provides leadership for the development, promotion, and improvement of library services, librarianship, and the library community. A resource for learning about new ideas and technology.

Susan E Negreen, Executive Director

410 California Reading Association
3186 D-1 Airway
Costa Mesa, CA 92626
714-435-1983
Fax: 714-435-0269
E-mail: kathy@californiareads.org
http://www.californiareads.org
CRA is an independent, self-governing organization dedicated to increasing literacy in California.

Kathy Belanger, Administrative Director

411 California School Library Association
1001 26th Street
Sacramento, CA 95816
916-447-2684
Fax: 916-447-2695
E-mail: csla@pacbell.net
http://www.schoollibrary.org
Organized of library media teachers, classroom teachers, paraprofessionals, district and county coordinators of curriculum, media and technology and others committed to enriching student learning by building a better future for school libraries.

Penny Kastanis, Executive Director
Sue Dalrymple, Office Manager

412 California Teachers Association
1705 Murchison Drive
Burlingame, CA 94010-4583
650-697-1400
Fax: 650-552-5002
E-mail: webmaster@cta.org
http://www.cta.org
Protects and promotes the well-being of California teachers by improving the conditions of teaching and learning and advancing the cause of universal education.

Barbara Kerr, President
David Sanchez, Vice President

413 Northern California Comprehensive Assistance Center
300 Lakeside Drive
18th Floor
Oakland, CA 64612
415-565-3000
877-493-7833
Fax: 415-565-3012
E-mail: plloyd@wested.com
http://www.wested.org/cs/we/view/pj/224
One of 15 comprehensive assistance centers in the country, the Region XI Comprehensive Center is prepared to provide technical assistance to schools, districts, the State Department of Education, community-based organizations, and other entities participating in the implementation of the Improving America's Schools Act of 1994.

Fred Tempes, Director
Rose Owens-West, Assistant Director

414 WestEd
730 Harrison Street
San Francisco, CA 94107-1242
415-615-3144
877-493-7833
Fax: 415-512-2024
E-mail: dtorres@WestEd.org
http://www.WestEd.org
Nonprofit research, development and service agency working with education and other human services communities across the country. As one of the nation's Regional Educational Laboratories, WestEd also has a special relationship serving the states of Arizona, California, Nevada, and Utah. For complete listings of all WestEd developed resources visit us online at www.WestEd.org/catalog.

Danny Torres, Publications Coordinator
Liza Cardinal-Hand, Information/Outreach Manager

Colorado

415 Colorado Association of Libraries
12081 W Alameda Pkwy
Suite 427
Lakewood, CO 80228
303-463-6400
Fax: 303-431-9752
http://www.cal-webs.org
Association of Colorado libraries.

Ellen Greenblatt, President
Judy Barnett, VP

416 Colorado Business Educators
Prairie High School
300 Thomas
Box 82
New Rayemr, CO 80742
970-437-5386
Fax: 970-437-5732
E-mail: Amy@ebusiness4u.biz
http://www.cbeweb.org
Association of Colorado Business Educators.

Cathy Tkacik, President
Myrna Armes, Secretary

417 Colorado Community College & Occupational Education System
9101 E Lowry Blvd
Denver, CO 80230
303-620-4000
Fax: 303-620-4030
E-mail: Barbara.McDonnell@cccs.edu
http://www.cccs.edu
The Colorado Community College System compries the state's largest system of higher education serving more than 117,000 students annually.

Nancy McCallin, President
Terry Hindsman, Assistant To President

418 Colorado Education Association
1500 Grant Street
Denver, CO 80203
303-837-1500
800-332-5939
Fax: 303-837-9006
Advances education in the state of Colorado.

Ron Brady, President
Jane Goff, Vice President

419 Colorado Library Association
12081 W Alameda Parkway
Suite 427
Lakewood, CO 80228
303-463-6400
Fax: 303-431-9752
E-mail: exectivedirector@cal-webs.org
http://www.coloradoea.org
Holds a conference in the fall and publishes one journal and one newsletter.

Beth Wrenn-Estes, President
Kathleen Noland, Executive Director

Connecticut

420 Connecticut Business & Indusry Association (CBIA)
350 Church Street
Hartford, CT 06103-1126
860-244-1900
Fax: 860-278-8562
E-mail: bellj@cbia.com
http://www.cbia.com/home.htm

Fosters business education in the state of Connecticut.

Jim Bell, Business Consulting Director
Nancy Andrews, Media/Public Relations

421 Connecticut Education Association (CEA)
Capitol Place
21 Oak Street
Suite 500
Hartford, CT 06106-8001
860-525-5641
800-842-4316
Fax: 860-725-6323
E-mail: johny@cea.org
http://www.cea.Executive Director
CEA advocates for teachers and public education, lobbying legislators for the resources public schools need and campaigning for high standards for teachers and students.

John Yrchik Ph.D, Executive Director
Alan Currie, Administration/Finance

422 Connecticut Educational Media Association
25 Elmwood Avenue
Trumbull, CT 06611-3594
203-372-2260
E-mail: aweimann@snet.net
http://www.ctcema.org
Professional association of Connecticut school library media specialist.

Janet Roche, President
David Bilmes, Vice President

423 Connecticut School Library Association
New Haven Free Library
133 Elm Street
New Haven, CT 06510-2003
203-946-8130
New Haven Free Public Library provides free and equal access to knowledge and information in an environment conducive to study and resource sharing. Through its collection of media, services and programs, the library promotes literacy, reading, personal development and cultural understanding for the individual and the community at large.

Delaware

424 Delaware Business Education Association
Delcastle High School
140 Brennen Drive
Newark, DE 19713
302-454-2164
E-mail: rhuddj@christina.k12.de.us
Fosters business education in the state of Delaware.

Jennifer Rhudd, President
Lisa Stoner, Membership Director

425 Delaware Library Association
PO Box 816
Dover, DE 19903-0816
302-831-8085
Fax: 302-831-1631
E-mail: dla@dla.lib.de.us
http://www.dla.lib.de.us
This union of public school employees advocates for the rights and interests of its members and outstanding public education for all students.

Barbara Grogg, President
Diane Donohue, Vice President

426 Delaware State Education Association
136 East Water Street
Dover, DE 19901-3630
302-734-5834
866-734-5834
Fax: 302-674-8499
E-mail: pamela.nichols@dsea.org
http://www.dsea.org/
The Delaware State Education Association, a union of public school employees, advocates for the rights and interests of its members and outstanding public education for all students.

Howard Weinberg, Executive Director
Pamela Nichols, Communications Director

District of Columbia

427 American Council on Education Library & Information Service
American Council on Education
1 Dupont Circle NW
Suite 1B-20
Washington, DC 20036-1110
202-939-9300
Fax: 202-833-4730
http://www.acenet.edu
A special collection of books, journals and nonprint materials devoted to the study of higher education. Library services are available to selected education associations in the greater Washington, DC area. Open to the public for on-site use only.

William Kirwan, Chair
M Lee Pelton, Vice Chair

428 Associates for Renewal in Education (ARE)
Brenda Strong Nixon Community Complex
45 P Street NW
Washington, DC 20001-1133
202-483-9424
Fax: 202-667-5299
E-mail: info@areinc.org
http://www.areinc.org/
A multi project agency working to improve the quality of life and education of the young people of the District of Columbia, with an emaphasis on youth-at risk and under served populations.

Thomas W Gore, President/CEO
Evis Saunders Davis, Deputy Finance/HR

429 District of Columbia Library Association
Benjamin Franklin Station
PO Box 14177
Washington, DC 20044
202-872-1112
E-mail: April.King@dc.gov
http://www.dcla.org
Publishes a journal.

Elaine Cline, President
April King, Director

Florida

430 Florida Association for Media in Education
2563 Capital Medical Boulevard
Tallahassee, FL 32308
850-531-8351
Fax: 850-531-8344
E-mail: lbodkin@floridamedia.org
http://www.floridamedia.org

Florida Association for Media in Education is to promote and publicize the library media specialist's role in Florida. FAME participates in the initiative to develop and implement statewide guidelines for teacher library specialists and media specialists. FAME is an efficient, effective, and influential organization that cooperates and collaborates with related professional groups. We care about our libraries, our media centers, and our students. FAME...it's all about the kids

Belinda Vose, President
Sandra Dunnavant, Vice President

431 Florida Business Technology Education Association
c/o Palm Beach County School District
3310 Forest Hill Blvd
C-225
West Palm Beach, FL 33177
561-434-7395
E-mail: sslarsen@bellsouth.net
http://www.fbtea.org/
Fosters business education in the state of Florida.

Linda Robinson, President
Sue Larsen, Treasurer

432 Florida Education Association
213 S Adams Street
Tallahassee, FL 32301-1700
850-201-2800
888-807-8007
Fax: 850-222-1840
http://www.feaweb.org
Represents teachers.

433 Florida Education Association (FEA)
213 S Adams Street
Tallahassee, FL 32301
850-201-4702
Fax: 850-222-1840
E-mail: ANDY.FORD@FLORIDAEA.ORG
http://www.feaweb.org/
Advocates the right to a free, quality public education for all, Empower and support local affiliates. Advance professional growth, development and status of all who serve the students in Florida's public schools. Engage our members and communities to ensure that all students learn and succeed in a diverse world.

Aaron Wallace, Chief of Staff
Andrew Ford, President

434 Florida Library Association (FLA)
3509 Trillium CT
Tallahassee, FL 32312
850-668-6911
850-322-5005
E-mail: flaexecutivedirector@comcast.net
http://www.flalib.org/
Holds a conference in April and publishes a journal.

Ruth O'Donnell, Executive Director
Meghan Wozniak, Conference Manager

Georgia

435 Georgia Association of Educators
100 Crescent Center Parkway
Suite 500
Tucker, GA 30084
678-837-1100
Fax: 678-837-1110

and private educational agencies and institutions with related professional organizations and with business and industry.

Becky Petersen, Executive Director
Jeff Fuller, Board of Directors President

527   North Carolina Department of Public Instruction (DPI)
301 N Wilmington Street
Education Building, Suite 5540
Raleigh, NC 27601
919-807-3300
Fax: 919-807-3445
E-mail: information@dpi.state.nc.us
http://www.ncpublicschools.org/organization/
The North Carolina Department of Public Instruction (DPI) is the agency charged with implementing the State's public school laws and the State Board of Education's policies and procedures governing pre-kindergarten through 12th grade public education. DPI develops the Standard Course of Study which describes the subjects and course content that should be taught in North Carolina public schools and develops the assessments and accountability model used to evaluate school and district success.

Priscilla Maynor, Executive Director
Peter Asmar, Chief Information Officer

528   North Carolina Library Association (NCLA)
1811 Capital Boulevard
Raleigh, NC 27604
919-839-6252
Fax: 919-839-6253
E-mail: nclaonline@ibiblio.org
http://www.nclaonline.org/
An affiliate of the American Library Association and the Southeastern Library Association, the North Carolina Library Association (NCLA) is a statewide organization concerned with the total library community in North Carolina. NCLA's purpose is to promote libraries, library and information services, librarianship, intellectual freedom and literacy. Holds conferences in September and October and publishes a journal.

Robert Burgin Ph.D, President
Phil Barton, Vice President

North Dakota

529   North Dakota Education Association (NDEA)
410 East Thayer Avenue
PO Box 5005
Bismarck, ND 58502-5005
701-223-0450
Fax: 701-224-8535
E-mail: nick.whitman@ndea.org
http://nd.nea.org/
Since 1887, the North Dakota Education Association has been advocating on behalf of North Dakota students and their teachers. NDEA's mission is to improve the political climate and economic conditions for public education and the status of teaching professionals and educational employees, in addition to promoting educational excellence, innovation, and equal opportunity in working toward the elimination of all forms of discrimination.

Nick Whitman, Executive Director
LeAnn Nelson, Professional Development

530   North Dakota Library Association
Po Box 1595
Bismarck, ND 58502-1595
701-777-4640
Fax: 701-777-3319
E-mail: BPostema@cityoffargo.com
http://www.ndla.info
Holds conferences in September and publishes a journal.
ISSN: 0882-4746
150 attendees and 25 exhibits

Cathy Langemo, Executive Secretary
Beth Postema, President

Ohio

531   Ohio Association of School Business Officials
200 East Wilson Bridge
Third Floor
Worthington, OH 43085
614-431-9116
Fax: 614-431-9137
The Ohio Association of School Business Officials is a not-for-profit educational management organization dedicated to learning, utilizing and sharing the best methods and technology of school business administration.

532   Ohio Association of Secondary School Administrators
8050 N High Street
Suite 180
Colcumbus, OH 43235-6484
614-430-8311
Fax: 614-430-8315
The Ohio Association of Secondary School Administrators is dedicated to the adnocacy and welfare of its members. Our mission is to provide high standards of leadership through professional development, political astuteness, legislative influence, positive public relations and collaboration with related organization.

Donald G Wynkoop, President

533   Ohio Library Council
2 Easton Oval
Suite 525
Columbus, OH 43219-7008
614-416-2258
Fax: 614-416-2270
E-mail: olc@olc.org
http://www.olc.org
The Ohio Library Council is the State wide professional associationwhich represents the interests of Ohio's public libraries as well as their trustess, friends and staff. The OLC is governed by a Board of Directors composed of three library employees with an MLIS degree, three library trustees currently serving on library boards, and seven at-1 arge members.

Cindy Lombardo, President
Douglas S. Evans, Executive Director

534   Ohio Technology Education Association (OTEA)
c/o State Supervisor
Ohio Department of Education
25 South Front Street/Room 509
Columbus, OH 43215
614-644-7356
Fax: 614-995-5568
E-mail:
Dick.Dieffenderfer@ode.state.oh.us
http://www.otea.info/
The mission of the Ohio Technology Education Association (OTEA) is to promote

technological literacy for all Ohio students; provide leadership in curriculum and professional development; inform governmental and educational decision makers on technological literacy issues; advocate society wide the understanding of technological literacy and why it is vital; and form and maintain alliances with the business and industrial community.

Richard A Dieffenderfer Ph.D, State Supervisor
Timothy N Tryon, Executive Director

Oklahoma

535   Oklahoma Education Association (OEA)
323 East Madison Avenue
PO 18485
Oklahoma City, OK 73154
402-528-7785
800-439-0393
Fax: 405-524-0350
E-mail: lodom@okea.org
http://www.okea.org
The Oklahoma Education Association (OEA) supports public education as the cornerstone of a democratic society in that education employees, parents, community leaders and elected officials should work together to promote quality education. OEA has 40,000 members, comprised of public school teachers, coaches, counselors, and administrators; nurses, librarians, custodians, cafeteria workers, bus drivers, secretaries; retired teachers; and education majors at Oklahoma colleges and universities.

Roy Bishop, President
Lela Odom, Executive Director

536   Oklahoma Library Association (OLA)
300 Hardy Drive
Edmond, OK 73013
405-348-0506
Fax: 405-348-7027
E-mail: kboies@sbcglobal.net
http://www.oklibs.org/
The Oklahoma Library Association works to strengthen the quality of libraries, library services and librarianship in Oklahoma. Members of OLA work in public, school, academic and special libraries of all sizes. Members include professional, paraprofessional and clerical library staff, library trustees, Friends, students, volunteers, vendors of library products and services and many others. Holds a conference in April and publishes a journal.

Kay Boies, Executive Director
Leslie Langley, Marketing/Communications

Oregon

537   AFT-Oregon (American Federation of Teachers-Oregon)
7035 SW Hampton Street
Tigard, OR 97223-8313
503-595-3880
Fax: 503-595-3887
E-mail: AFTOregon@aft-oregon.org
http://or.aft.org/
Charted in 1952, AFT-Oregon, a state affiliate of the American Federation of Teachers, AFL-CIO, is a non-profit organization representing some 11,000 Oregon workers in K-12, community college and higher educa-

tion in faculty and classified positions; and child care workers, in both public and private sectors. AFT-Oregon, in coalition with other unions and community groups, advocates for quality education and health care for all Oregonians, and gives working people a voice in our state's capitol.

Mark Schwebke, President
Bill Beeson, Vice President

538 Oregon Association of Student Councils (OASC)
707 13th Street SE
Suite 100 Y
Salem, OR 97301-4035
503-581-3141
Fax: 503-581-9840
E-mail: nancy@oasc.org
http://www.oasc.org/
The Oregon Association of Student Councils (OASC) is a non-profit member association, serving middle and high schools throughout the state, that provides leadership development to both students and advisors. OASC's program is sponsored by the Confederation of Oregon School Administrators.

Nancy Moen, Program Director
Val Luukinen, Chair

539 Oregon Education Association (OEA)
6900 SW Atlanta Street
Portland, OR 97223
503-684-3300
800-858-5505
Fax: 503-684-8063
E-mail: larry.wolf@oregoned.org
http://www.oregoned.org/
The mission of the Oregon Education Association (OEA) is to assure quality public education for every student in Oregon by providing a strong, positive voice for school employees. OEA's school funding priority, established in December 2002, seeks to restore stable and adequate funding for Oregon's schools and community colleges so that all Oregon students have access to a quality public education.

Larry Wolf, President
Jerry Caruthers, Executive Director

540 Oregon Educational Media Association
PO Box 277
Terrebonne, OR 97760
503-625-7820
E-mail: j23hayden@aol.com
http://www.oema.net
Conferences, resources for members, newsletters and promotions.

Jim Hayden, Executive Director

541 Oregon Library Association (OLA)
PO Box 2042
Salem, OR 97308
503-370-7019
Fax: 503-587-8063
E-mail: ola@olaweb.org
http://www.olaweb.org/
The mission of the Oregon Library Association is to promote and advance library service through public and professional education and cooperation. Holds a conference in March and publishes two journals.

Aletha Bonebrake, President
Sarah Beasley, Vice President

Pennsylvania

542 Pennsylvania Library Association (PaLA)
220 Cumberland Parkway
Suite 10
Mechanicsburg, PA 17055
717-766-7663
800-622-3308
Fax: 717-766-5440
E-mail: glenn@palibraries.org
http://www.palibraries.org/
Founded in 1901, the Pennsylvania Library Association (PaLA) is a professional library organization serving libraries, library employees, library trustees, and Friends of the Library groups. PaLA represents more than 1,900 personal, institutional, and commercial members affiliated with public, academic, special, and school libraries throughout the Commonwealth. The association provides opportunities for professional growth, leadership development, and continuing education for librarians.

Glenn Miller, Executive Director
Janice Trapp, Board of Directors President

543 Pennsylvania School Librarians Association
9 Saint James Avenue
Somerville, MA 02144
617-628-4451
http://www.plsa.org
Organization of school librarians.

Molly Moyer, Membership Chairman

544 Pennsylvania State Education Association (PSEA)
400 N 3rd Street
Harrisburg, PA 17105-1704
717-255-7000
800-944-7732
Fax: 717-255-7124
E-mail: cdumaresq@psea.org
http://www.psea.org
The mission of the Pennsylvania State Education Association (PSEA), which was formed in 1852, is to advance quality public education for all students while fostering the dignity and worth of members through collective action.

James Weaver, President
Carolyn Dumaresq, Executive Director

Rhode Island

545 National Education Association Rhode Island (NEARI)
99 Bald Hill Road
Cranston, RI 02920
401-463-9630
Fax: 401-463-5337
E-mail: RWalsh@nea.org
http://www.neari.org/matriarch/default.asp
The NEA Rhode Island is both a union and a professional organization. As a union, it provides traditional collective bargaining assistance to its 74 local associations, and representation to its 11,000 members in work-related issues. Members include teachers, education employees, higher education faculty and staff, state and municipal employees, and retirees. As a professional organization, it provides research and training to support these mem-

bers in achieving excellence in their employment.

Robert A Walsh Jr, Executive Director
Vincent P Santaniello Esq, Deputy Executive Director

546 Rhode Island Association of School Business Officials
255 Westminster St
Providence, RI 02903
401-222-2651
http://cynthia.brown@ride.ri.gov
The mission of the Rhode Island School Business Officials, a professional association, is to promote the highest standards of school business management, professional growth and the effective use of educational resources, by providing programs, services and networing opportunities for the benefit of its members.

547 Rhode Island Educational Media Association
PO Box 470
East Greenshich, RI 02818
401-295-9200
Fax: 401-295-8101
http://www.ri.net
Conferences, newsletters and updates on new technologies.

Mike Mello, Membership Chairman

548 Rhode Island Library Association
PO Box 6765
Providence, RI 02940
401-943-9080
Fax: 401-946-5079
E-mail: book_n@yahoo.com
http://www.uri.edu/library/rila/rila/htm
The Rhode Island Library Association is a profesional association of Librarians, Library Staff, Trustees, and library supporters whose purpose is to promote the profession of librarianship and to improve the visibility, accessibility, responsiveness and effectiveness of library and information services throughout Rhode Island.

Cindy Lumghofer, President
Christopher Larouxd, Vice President

South Carolina

549 South Carolina Education Association (SCEA)
421 Zimalcrest Drive
Columbia, SC 29210
803-772-6553
800-422-7232
Fax: 803-772-0922
E-mail: czullinger@thescea.org
http://www.thescea.org
The South Carolina Education Association (The SCEA) is a professional association for educators in South Carolina. Educators from pre-K to 12th grade comprise The SCE, an advocate for educational changge. The SCEA provides instructional development, technology innovation, re-certification assistance, legal services, political action, legislative initiatives, leadership growth and development, and educator benefits to its membership.

Chip Zullinger Ph.D, Executive Director
Carolyn Randolph, Assistant Executive Director

550 South Carolina Library Association
PO Box 1763
Columbia, SC 29202
803-252-1087
Fax: 803-252-0589
E-mail: scla@capconsc.com
http://www.scla.org
Informes members of issues and to provide
training and networking opportunities.

Quincy Pugh, President

South Dakota

**551 Mountain Plains Library
Association (MPLA)**
c/o Interim Executive Secretary
14293 West Center Drive
Lakewood, CO 80228
303-985-7795
E-mail:
mpla_execsecretary@operamail.com
http://www.mpla.us/
The Mountain Plains Library Association
(MPLA) is a twelve state association of librarians, library paraprofessionals and
friends of libraries in Arizona, Colorado,
Kansas, Montana, Nebraska, Nevada, New
Mexico, North Dakota, Oklahoma, South
Dakota, Utah and Wyoming. Its purpose is
to promote the development of librarians
and libraries by providing significant educational and networking opportunities.
Holds conferences in September, October
and November. Also publishes a newsletter.

Judy Zelenski, Interim Executive
Secretary
Dan Chaney, MPLA Webmaster

**552 South Dakota Education
Association (SDEA)**
441 East Capitol Avenue
Pierre, SD 57501
605-224-9263
800-529-0090
Fax: 605-224-5810
E-mail: rhendrickson@nea.org
http://www.sdea.org/
The South Dakota Education Associa-
tion/SDEA advocates new directions for
public education, providing professional
services that benefit students, schools and
the public.

Rachel Hendrickson, Executive Director
Paul McCorkle, CFO/CIO

553 South Dakota Library Association
PO Box 1212
Rapid City, SD 57709
605-343-3750
E-mail: gchapman@rcplib.org
http://www.sdlibraryassociation.org
Holds a conference in October and pub-
lishes a journal.

Greta Chapman, President
Brenda Hemmelman, Secretary/Treasurer

Tennessee

**554 Tennessee Association of Secondary
School Principals (TASSP)**
PO Box 18079
Knoxville, TN 37928
865-687-8965
866-737-2777
Fax: 865-687-8966
E-mail: tommy@tnassp.org
http://www.tnassp.org/

The mission of the Tennessee Association
of Secondary School Principals is: to promote professional standards of practice for
secondary school administrators; provide
high quality professional development experiences for rural, urban, and suburban administrators, statewide, based on their
common and unique professional development needs; and advocate on behalf of secondary administrators in their efforts to
provide high quality education for all students.

Gary Roach, President
Tommy Everette, Executive Director

555 Tennessee Library Association
Po Box 241074
Memphis, TN 38124-1074
615-297-8316
Fax: 615-269-1807
E-mail: Kbwoods1@memphis.edu
http://www.tnla.org
Holds a conference in April and publishes a
journal and a newsletter.

Annelle Huggins, Executive Director
Pat Thompson, President

**556 Tennessee School Boards
Association**
101 French Landing
Nashville, TN 37228
615-741-0666
800-448-6465
Fax: 615-741-2824
http://www.tsba.net
The mission of the Tennessee School
Boards Associationis to assisst school
boards in effectively governing school districts.

Tammy Grissom, Assistant Executive

Texas

**557 Texas Association of Secondary
School Principals (TASSP)**
1833 S IH-35
Austin, TX 78741
512-443-2100
Fax: 512-442-3343
E-mail: archie@tassp.org
http://www.tassp.org/
The Texas Association of Secondary School
Principals is an association formed by and
for over 5000 campus level administrators.
Established in 1922, its purpose is to build
an active network of educators that want to
take responsibility for the quality of school
leadership. TASSP focuses on the need for
collaboration between all stakeholders in
education while using as its foundation a
very effective volunteer force that provides
a statewide knowledge base and informed
leadership.

Archie E McAfee, Executive Director
Tom Leyden, Associate Executive
Director

558 Texas Library Association (TLA)
3355 Bee Cave Road
Suite 401
Austin, TX 78746-6763
512-328-1518
800-580-2852
Fax: 512-328-8852
E-mail: tla@txla.org
http://www.txla.org
The Texas Library Association/TLA is a
professional organization that promotes librarianship and library service in Texas.
Through legislative advocacy, continuing

education events, and networking channels,
TLA offers members opportunities for service to the profession as well as for personal
growth. Holds conferences in March or
April, also publishes a quarterly journal and
a bimonthly newsletter.

Patricia Smith, Executive Director
Gloria Meraz, Communciations Director

Utah

559 Utah Education Association (UEA)
875 East 5180 S
Murray, UT 84107-5299
801-266-4461
800-594-8996
Fax: 801-265-2249
E-mail: mark.mickelsen@utea.org
http://www.utea.org/
The mission of the Utah Education Association (UEA) is to advance the cause of public
education in partnership with others:
strengthen the teaching profession, promote quality schools for Utah's children,
and advocate the well-being of members.

Susan Kuziak, Executive Director
Mark Mickelsen, Director
Communications/PR

560 Utah Library Association (ULA)
PO Box 708155
Sandy, UT 84070-8155
801-422-6763
Fax: 801-422-0466
E-mail: Julie_Williamsen@byu.edu
http://www.ula.org/
The mission of the Utah Library Association is to serve the professional development and educational needs of its members
and to provide leadership and direction in
developing and improving library and information services in the state. The Association also initiates and supports legislation
promoting library development and monitors legislation that might threaten Utah libraries and librarians. Holds a conference
and publishes a journal.

Julie Williamsen, President
Dorothy Horan, Vice President

Vermont

561 Vermont Library Association
PO Box 803
Burlington, VT 05402-0803
802-388-3845
Fax: 802-388-4367
E-mail: vlaorg@sover.net
http://www.vermontlibraries.org
Holds a conference in May and publishes a
quarterly newsletter.

Karen Lane, President
David Clark, Chapter Councilor

**562 Vermont National Education
Association (VTNEA)**
10 Wheelock Street
#567
Montpelier, VT 05602-3737
802-223-6375
Fax: 802-223-1253
E-mail: vtnea@together.net
http://www.vtnea.org/
The Vermont National Education Association is a voluntary organization of 11,000
Vermont teachers and education support
professionals, their purpose being to make
sure that members have a satisfying work
environment where they are acknowledged

for the work they perform and where the work they perform helps students do their best.

Joel DR Cook, Executive Director
Laurie B Huse, Communications Director

563 Volunteers for Peace
1034 Tiffany Road
Belmont, VT 05730
802-259-2759
Fax: 802-259-2922
E-mail: vfp@vfp.org
http://www.vfp.org
Vermont non-profit membership organization promoting over 2,800 international workcamps in 90 countries.

288 pages Paperback/Annually
ISBN: 0-945617-24-0
ISSN: 0896-565X

Peter Coldwell, Director
Jane Skakel, Coordinator

Virginia

564 Action Alliance for Virginia's Children and Youth
701 E Franklin Street
Suite 807
Richmond, VA 23219
804-649-0184
Fax: 804-649-0161
http://www.vakids.org
Nonprofit and non-partisan, Voices for Virginia's Children is a persistent voice of reason in advocating for better lives and futures for children. The Commonwealth's only statewide multi-issue organization advocating for children and youth, Voices promotes sound, far-reaching program and policy solutions, focusing on early care and education, health care, family economic success, and foster care and adoption.

Suzanne Clark Johnson, President

565 Division of Student Leadership Services
PO Box K 170
Richmond, VA 23288-0001
804-285-2829
Fax: 804-285-1379
http://www.vaprincipals.org
Organization that sponsors the Virginia Student Councils Association; the Virginia Association of Honor Societies; and the Virginia Association of Student Activity Advisers.

Dr. Randy Barrack, Executive Director

566 Organization of Virginia Homeschoolers
PO Box 5131
Charlottesville, VA 22905
866-513-6173
Fax: 804-946-2263
http://www.vahomeschoolers.org
The Organization of Virginia Homeschoolers' most effective action is screening legislation for potential impact on homeschoolers. We pay attention to a large list of topics: home instruction statute, tutor provision, religious exemption provision, driver training, truancy, curfews, tax credits, and more.

John Haugherty, President
Kenneth L Payne, Executive Director

567 Southern Association of Colleges & Schools
Virginia Secondary & Middle School Committee
PO Box 7007
Radford, VA 24142-7007
540-831-5399
Fax: 540-831-6309
E-mail: mdalderm@runet.edu
Public and private school accreditation organization. 12,000 member schools in 11 southern state regions. 430 middle and secondary SACS member schools in Virginia.

Dr. Emmett Sufflebarger, President
Lanny Holsinger, President-Elect

568 Virginia Alliance for Arts Education
PO Box 70232
Richmond, VA 23255-0232
804-740-7865
Fax: 804-828-2335
To promote aesthetic and creative art education for the development of the individual at all levels in the commonwealth of Virginia. To assist teachers in improving the quality of art education. To organize and conduct panels, forums, lectures, and tours for art educators and the general public on art and art instruction. To keep the public informed of the arts through whatever means are available.

Margaret Edwards, Division Director

569 Virginia Association for Health, Physical Education, Recreation & Dance
817 W Franklin Street
Box 842037
Richmond, VA 23284-2037
800-918-9899
Fax: 800-918-9899
VAHPERD is a professional association of educators that advocate quality programs in health, physical education, recreation, dance and sport. The association seeks to facilitate the professional growth and educational practices and legislation that will impact the profession.

Judith Clark, President

570 Virginia Association for Supervision and Curriculum Development
1622 Baileys Retreat
Charlottesville, VA 22901
434-296-6804
Fax: 434-296-6971
E-mail: annetchison@earthlink.net
The Virginia affiliate of the Association for Supervision and Curriculum Development (ASCD).

Laurie McCullough, President
Ann Etchison, Executive Director

571 Virginia Association for the Education of the Gifted
PO Box 26212
Richmond, VA 23260-6212
804-355-5945
Fax: 804-355-5137
E-mail: vagifted@comcast.net
http://www.vagifted.org
The Virginia Association for the Gifted supports research in gifted education and advocates specialized preparation for educators of the gifted. The association disseminates information, maintains a statewide network of communication, and cooperates with organizations and agen-

cies to improve the quality of education in the Commonwealth of Virginia.

Liz Nelson, Executive Director

572 Virginia Association of Elementary School Principals
1805 Chantilly Street
Richmond, VA 23230
804-355-6791
Fax: 804-355-1196
E-mail: info@vaesp.org
Nonprofit professional association advocating for public education and equal educational opportunities. Promotes leadership of school administrators, principals as educational leaders, and provides professional development opportunities.

Thomas L Shortt, Executive Director

573 Virginia Association of Independent Specialized Education Facilities
118 N 8th Street
Richmond, VA 23219-2306
804-649-4978
Mary R Simmons, Executive Director
Pam Alteresca, President

574 Virginia Association of Independent Schools
8001 Franklin Farms Drive
Suite 100
Richmond, VA 23229-5108
804-282-3592
Fax: 804-282-3596
E-mail: director@vais.org
http://www.vais.org
The Virginia Association of Independent Schools is a service organization that promotes educational, ethical and professional excellence. Through its school evaluation/accreditation program, attention to professional development and insistence on integrity, the Association safeguards the interests of its member schools.

Andrew A Zvara, Professional Development
Dr. Sally K Boese, Executive Director

575 Virginia Association of School Superintendents
405 Emmet Street
Charlottesville, VA 22903
434-924-0538
Fax: 434-982-2942
The Virginia Association of School Superintendents (VASS) is a professional organization dedicated to the mission of providing leadership and advocacy for public school education throughout the Commonwealth of Virginia.

J Andrew Stamp, Division Director

576 Virginia Association of School Business Officials
Williamsburg-James City County Public Schools
PO Box 8783
Williamsburg, VA 23187-8783
757-253-6748
Fax: 757-253-0173
The mission of the Virginia Association of School Business Officials is to promote the highest standards of school business practices for its membership through professional development, continuing education, networking, and legislative impact.

David C Papenfuse, Division Director

577 Virginia Association of School Personnel Administrators
800 E City Hall Avenue
Norfolk, VA 23510-2723
757-340-1217
Fax: 757-340-1889
E-mail: aaspa@aaspa.org
http://www.aaspa.org
AASPA is the only organization that specifically targets and represents school personnel professionals. If you are a personnel / human resource administrator, personnel support staff, superintendent, principal, or graduate student interested in this field, you will benefit from AASPA membership. The association provides research, reports, professional development activities, and networking opportunities to help you do your job efficiently, legally, and effectively.
Eddid P Antoine II, Division Director

578 Virginia Congress of Parents & Teachers
1027 Wilmer Avenue
Richmond, VA 23227
804-264-1234
Fax: 804-264-4014
E-mail: info@vapta.org
http://www.vapta.org
To promote the welfare of the children and youth in home, school, community, and place of worship. To raise the standards of home life, to secure adequate laws for the care and protection of children and youth, to bring into closer relation the home and the school, that parents and teachers may cooperate intelligently in the education of children and youth.
Sue Glasco, President
Eugene A Goldberg, Executive Director

579 Virginia Consortium of Administrators for Education of the Gifted
RR 5 Box 680
Farmville, VA 23901-9011
804-225-2884
Fax: 814-692-3163
Catherine Cottrell, Division Director

580 Virginia Council for Private Education
1901 Huguenot Road
Suite 301
Richmond, VA 23235
804-423-6435
Fax: 804-423-6436
E-mail: jwebster@vcpe.org
http://www.vcpe.org
VCPE provides a statewide framework for communications and cooperation among private elementary and secondary schools, between such schools and their public school counterparts, and among private schools and state and local governments and other agencies and organizations. In legislative or policy matters, VCPE is available to members of the legislature, to the Board of Education, and to the Department of Education to furnish information about, and to articulate the private school viewpoint.
George McVey, President
Joanne L Webster, Vice President

581 Virginia Council of Administrators of Special Education
Franklin County Public Schools
25 Bernard Road
Rocky Mount, VA 24151
703-493-0280
Fax: 540-483-5806
E-mail: kkirst@k12albemarle.org
http://www.vcase.org
The Virginia Council of Administrators of Special Education is a professional organization that promotes professional leadership through the provision of collegial support and current information on recommended instructional practices as well as local, state and national trends in Special Education for professionals who serve students with disabilities in order to improve the quality and delivery of special education services in Virginia's public Schools
Thomas F Nash, President
Susan Clark, President-Elect

582 Virginia Council of Teachers of Mathematics
1033 Backwoods Road
Virginia Beach, VA 23455-6617
757-671-7316
The purpose of the Virginia Council of Teachers of Mathematics is to stimulate an active interest in mathematics, to provide an interchange of ideas in the teaching of mathematics, to promote the improvement of mathematics education in Virginia, to provide leadership in the professional development of teachers, to provide resources for teachers and to facilitate cooperation among mathematics organizations at the local, state and national levels
Ellen Smith Hook, Division Director

583 Virginia Council on Economic Education
1015 Floyd Avenue, Room 1103
Box 844000
Richmond, VA 23284-4000
804-828-1627
Fax: 804-828-7215
E-mail: shfinley@vcu.edu
http://www.vcee.org
Goal is for students to understand our economy and develop the life-long decision-making skills they need to be effective, informed citizens, consumers, savers, investors, producers and employees.
Yvonne Toms Allmond, Senior Vice President
Sallie Garrett, Contact

584 Virginia Education Association
116 S 3rd Street
Richmond, VA 23219-3744
804-648-5801
Fax: 804-775-8379
Represents teachers.
Jerry Caruthers, Executive Director
Jean Bankos, President

585 Virginia Educational Media Association
PO Box 2743
Fairfax, VA 22031-0743
703-764-0719
Fax: 703-272-3643
E-mail: jremler@pen.k12.va.us
http://www.vema.gan.va.us
Aim is to promote literacy, information access and evaluation, love of literature, effective use of technology, collaboration in the teaching and learning process, intellec-

tual freedom, professional growth, instructional leadership and lifelong learning.
Jean Remler, Executive Director

586 Virginia Educational Research Association
305 Fairway Drive
Radford, VA 24142
540-639-1263
Fax: 540-831-6441
The mission of the Educational Research Service is to improve the education of children and youth by providing educators and the public with timely and reliable research and information.
Dr. Edith Carter, Assistant Professor

587 Virginia High School League
1642 State Farm Boulevard
Charlottesville, VA 22911-8609
804-225-2884
Fax: 804-692-3163
Craig Barbrow, President
Ken Tilley, Executive Director

588 Virginia Library Association
PO Box 8277
Norfolk, VA 23503-0277
757-583-0041
Fax: 757-583-5041
E-mail: lhahne@coastalnet.com
Holds a conference in October and publishes a journal and a newsletter.
Linda Hahne, Executive Director

589 Virginia Middle School Association
11138 Marsh Road
Bealeton, VA 22712-9360
703-439-3207
Fax: 540-439-2051
Mary Barton, Division Director

590 Virginia School Boards Association
2320 Hunters Way
Charlottesville, VA 22911-7931
434-295-8722
800-446-8722
Fax: 434-295-8785
http://www.vsba.org
State school boards association.
Gina Patterson, Assistant Executive Director

591 Virginia Student Councils Association
8001 Franklin Farms Drive
Suite 114
Richmond, VA 23229-5108
804-288-2777
Fax: 804-285-1379
Statewide association of elementary, middle and high school student cuoncils.
Anthony S Morris, Director

592 Virginia Vocational Association
10259 Lakeridge Square Court #G
Ashland, VA 23005-8159
804-365-4556
Jean Holbrook, President
Kathy Williams, Executive Director

Washington

593 Washington Education Association
32032 Weyerhaeuser Way S
PO Box 9100
Federal Way, WA 98063-9100
253-941-6700
Fax: 253-946-4735
Represents teachers.

CT Purdom, President
Leeann Prielipp, VP

594 Washington Library Association
4016 1st Avenue NE
Seattle, WA 98105
206-545-1529
Fax: 206-545-1543
E-mail: washla@wla.org
Holds a conference in April, also publishes
a journal and a newsletter.

ISSN: 8756-4173

Gail Willis, Association Coordinator

West Virginia

595 Edvantia
1031 Quarrier Street
PO Box 1348
Charleston, WV 25325-1348
304-347-0439
800-624-9120
Fax: 304-347-0487
E-mail: carloyn.luzader@edvantia.org
http://www.edvantia.org
Educational research and development organization supported by contracts with the
US Education Department, Office of Educational Research and Improvement. Specialty area: emerging technologies in
education.

Nancy Balow, Author
Patricia Hammer, Director of
Communications
Carolyn S Luzader, Communications
Associate

**596 West Virginia Education
Association**
1558 Quarrier Street
Charleston, WV 25311-2497
304-346-5315
Fax: 304-346-4325
Represents teachers.

Kayetta Meadows, President
Mary Carden, Vice President

597 West Virginia Library Association
PO Box 5221
Charleston, WV 25361
304-558-2045
Fax: 304-558-2044
E-mail: msmith@cabell.lib.wv.us
http://www.wvla.org
Holds conferences in October and November, also publishes a journal.

Ann Farr, President
Olivia L Bravo, First Vice President

Wisconsin

**598 Wisconsin Education Association
Council**
33 Nob Hill Drive
#8003
Madison, WI 53713-2199
608-276-7711
Fax: 608-276-8203
Advocates the ideas of a diverse, democratic society and quality public education.

Mary Lou Zuege, President

**599 Wisconsin Educational Media
Association**
1300 Industrial Drive
Fennimore, WI 53809
http://www.wemaonline.org
Promotes the use of media in education.

600 Wisconsin Library Association
5250 E Terrace Drive
Suite A
Madison, WI 53718-8345
608-245-3640
Fax: 608-245-3646
E-mail: strand@scls.lib.wi.us
Holds conferences in October and November, also publishes a newsletter.

Michael Gelhausen, President
Lisa Strand, Executive Director

Wyoming

601 Wyoming Education Association
115 E 22nd Street
Suite 1
Cheyenne, WY 82001-3795
307-634-7991
800-443-2395
http://www.wyoeg.org
Represents teachers.

Kathyrn Valido, President
Craig Williams, Vice President

602 Wyoming Library Association
PO Box 1387
Cheyenne, WY 82003
307-632-7622
Fax: 307-638-3469
E-mail: grottski@aol.com
http://www.wyla.org
Holds a conference in September and publishes a newsletter.

Ara Anderson, President
Laura Grott, Executive Secretary

**603 Wyoming School Boards
Association**
PO Box 3274
Laramie, WY 82071-3274
307-766-2389
Fax: 307-766-5544
Organization of school boards.

International

604 Association for Childhood Education International Annual Conference

Assn for Childhood Educational International
17904 Georgia Avenue
Suite 215
Olney, MD 20832
301-570-2111
800-423-3563
Fax: 301-570-2212
E-mail: conference@acei.org
http://www.acei.org
Symposium focusing on education for bi-lingual and culturally diverse children. International issues and over 200 workshops.

April
50 booths with 1000 attendees

Lisa Wenger, Director Conferences
Gerald C Odland, Executive Director

605 Association for Experiential Education Annual Conference

3775 Iris Avenue
Suite 4
Boulder, CO 80301-1043
303-440-8844
866-522-8337
Fax: 303-440-9581
E-mail: conferences@aee.org
http://www.aee.org
Annual international and regional conference dedicated to promoting, defining, developing, and applying the theories and practices of experiential education.

November
1,200 attendees

Evan Narotsky, Conference & Events Manager
Amy Green, Membership Coordinator

606 CIEE Annual Conference

Council on International Educational Exchange
7 Custom House Street
3rd Floor
Portland, ME 04101
207-553-7600
800-407-8839
Fax: 207-553-7699
http://www.ciee.org
Open to study-abroad advisors, administrators, faculty and other international education professionals. The conference is an opportunity to share ideas, keep up with developments in the field, and meet with colleagues from around the world.

607 Center for Critical Thinking and Moral Critique Annual International

Po Box 220
Dillon Beach, CA 94929
707-878-9100
Fax: 707-878-9111
E-mail: cct@criticalthinking.org
http://www.criticalthinking.org
Over 1,200 educators participate to discuss critical thinking and educational change.

Dr Linda Elder, President

608 Childhood Education Association International

17904 Georgia Avenue
Suite 215
Olney, MD 20832-2277
301-570-2111
800-423-3563
Fax: 301-570-2212
E-mail: aceihq@aol.com
http://wwwacei.org
To promote and support in the global community the optimal education and development of children, from birth through early adolescence, and to influence the professional growth of educators and the efforts of others who are committed to the needs of children in a changing society.

35 booths

Lisa Wenger, Director of Conference
Jana Pauldin, Public Relations Manager

609 Council for Learning Disabilities International Conference

PO Box 40303
Overland Park, KS 66204-4303
913-492-8755
Fax: 913-492-2546
http://www.cldinternational.org
Intensive interaction with and among professional educators and top LD researchers. Concise, informative and interesting forums on topics from effective instruction to self-reliance are presented by well-known professionals from across the country and around the world.

October
35 booths with 800 attendees

Kirsten McBride, Conference Contact

610 Council of British Independent Schools in the European Communities Annual Conference

14 Fernham Road
Faringdon Oxon SN7—7JY
44-1303-260857
Fax: 44-1303-260857
E-mail: general.secretary@cobisec.org
http://www.cobisec.org
Conference for Heads, Governors and members of Senior Management Teams of schools. Assurance of quality in member schools.

May
75 attendees and 20 exhibits

611 European Council of International Schools

21B Lavant Street
Petersfield, Hampshire GU32 3EL
United Kingdom
44-1730-268-244
Fax: 44-1730-267-914
E-mail: ecis@ecis.org
http://www.ecis.org
Support professional development, curriculum and instruction, leadership and good governance in international schools located in Europe and around the world.

Michelle Daughtry, Events Manager
Peter Price, Executive Officer

612 Hort School: Conference of the Association ofAmerican Schools

International School of Panama
PO Nox 6-7589
El Dorado
Panama
507-266-7037
Fax: 507-266-7808
E-mail: isp@isp.edu.pa
http://www.isp.edu.pa

Founded in 1982 by a group of interested parents from the Panamanian and International community. ISP is a private, independent, non-profit educational institution providing instruction in English for the multinational and Panamanian population residing in Panama City, Panama.

October
600 attendees and 35 exhibits

Dr. Mark G Mend, Director
Laurie Lewter, Business Manager

613 International Association of Teachers of English as a Foreign Language

Darwin College
University of Kent
Canterbury, Kent, UK CT2-7NY
44-1227-276528
Fax: 44-1227-274415
E-mail: generalenquires@iatefl.org
http://www.iatefl.org
Plenary sessions by eminent practitioners, a large number of workshops, talks and round tables given by other speakers, an ELT Resources Exhibition and Pre-Conference Events organised by Special Interest Groups.

April
80 booths with 1500 attendees

Alison Medland, Conference Organizer
Glenda Smart, Executive Officer

614 International Awards Market

Awards and Recognition Association
4700 W Lake Avenue
Glenview, IL 60025
847-375-4800
800-344-2148
Fax: 877-734-9380
E-mail: info@ara.org
http://www.ara.org
Providing outstanding business and educational opportunities for both retailers and suppliers. Retailers can view the latest industry products, take advantage of special show offers and benefit from a full educational program.

Feb, March, Nov
200 booths with 6,000 attendees

Brian Martin, President

615 International Conference

World Associaiton for Symphonic Bands & Ensembles
1037 Mill Street
San Luis Obispo, CA 93401
805-541-8000
Fax: 805-543-9498
E-mail: admin@wasbe2005.com
http://www.wasbe.org/en/conferences/index.html
WASBE is a nonprofit, international association open to individuals, institutions, and industries interested in symphonic bands and wind ensembles. Dedicated to enhancing the quality of the wind band throughout the world and exposing its members to new worlds of repertoire, musical culture, people and places.

Twice a Year

Dennis Johnson, President

616 International Congress for School Effectiveness & Improvement

International Congress Secretariat
PO Box 527-Frankston, VC 3199
Australia
61-037844230
http://www.icsei.net

The purpose of building and using an expanded base for advancing research, practice and policy in the area of school effectiveness and improvement. The Congress offers the opportunity to exchange information and networking for the educational community.

500 attendees

Lejf Moos, President

617 International Dyslexia Association Annual Conference

8600 LaSalle Road
Chester Building, Suite 382
Baltimore, MD 21286-2044
410-296-0232
800-ABC-D123
Fax: 410-321-5069
E-mail: info@interdys.org
http://www.interdys.org
Provide the most comprehensive range of information and services that address the full scope of dyslexia and related difficulties in learning to read and write.

3000 attendees

Margaret Palmer, Conferences Coordinator
Noreen A Frohme, Conference Director

618 International Exhibit

National Institute for Staff & Organizational Dev.
University of Texas
1 University Station
Austin, TX 78712
512-471-7545
Fax: 512-471-9426
E-mail: mpg@mail.utexas.edu
http://www.nisod.org
The largest international conference to focus specifically on the celebration of teaching, learning, and leadership excellence. This conference has enjoyed steady growth since its inception in 1978.

1500 attendees

Margot Perez-Greene, Conference Director

619 International Listening Association Annual Convention

Center for Information & Communication
Ball State University
BC 221
Muncie, IN 47306-0001
765-285-1889
Fax: 765-285-1516
http://www.bsu.edu/cics
Geared toward the teaching of listening in the classroom and various techniques for increasing effectiveness in the classroom setting.

March

Barbara B Nixon, Conference Contact

620 International Reading Association Annual Convention

800 Barksdale Road
PO Box 8139
Newark, DE 19714-8139
302-731-1600
800-336-7323
Fax: 302-731-1057
E-mail: conferences@reading.org
http://www.reading.org
Contains exhibitors involved in various lectures and workshops dealing with illit-

eracy, literature and some library science courses.

May
800 booths with 13M attendees

Maryellen Vogt, President

621 International Symposium

American Association of University Women
1111 16th Street NW
Washington, DC 20036
800-326-2289
Fax: 202-872-1425
E-mail: convention@aauw.org
http://www.aauw.org
The nation's leading voice promoting education and equity for women and girls.

Ashleyr Carr, Media Relations
Christy Jones, Membership Director

622 International Technology Education Association Conference

1914 Association Drive
Suite 201
Reston, VA 20191-1539
703-860-2100
Fax: 703-860-0353
E-mail: itea@iris.org
http://www.iteawww.org
Provides teachers with new and exciting ideas for educating students of all grade levels. The conference gives educators an opportunity for better understanding of the constant changes that take place in technology education.

April
150 booths with 2,200+ attendees

Katie de la Paz, Communications Coordinator

623 International Trombone Festival

International Trombone Association
1 Broomfield Road
Conventry, UK CV5-6JW
903-886-8711
Fax: 903-886-7975
http://www.trombone.net
This annual festival takes place at The Crane School of Music, State University of New York College at Potsdam.

June

Tony Baker, Festival Director
Jon Bohls, ITF Exhibits Coordinator

624 Learner-Centered

Improving Learning and Teaching
8510 49th Avenue
College Park, MD 20740-2412
Fax: 301-474-3473
E-mail: iut2000@aol.com
http://www.iut2000.org
Provides a forum in which participants from across the globe share discoveries, practices and challenges relating to improving the effectiveness of postsecondary teaching and learning. The conference will be held in Johannesburg, South Africa.

July

625 Learning Disabilities Association of America International Conference

4156 Library Road
Pittsburgh, PA 15234-1349
412-341-1515
Fax: 412-344-0224
E-mail: info@ldaamerica.org
http://www.ldaamerica.org
The largest meeting on learning disabilities (LD) in the world. Disabled, parents, various educators and administrators. The con-

ference follows a general theme set by LDAA.

Febuary, March
95 booths with 2600 attendees and 300 exhibits

Andrea Turkheimer, Conference Coordinator

National

626 ACSI Teachers' Convention

Assocation of Christian Schools International
731 Chapel Hills Drive
Colorado City, CO 80920
719-528-6906
800-367-0798
Fax: 562-690-6234
E-mail: exhibitors@acsi.org
http://www.acsi.org
Educational convention for administrators, school board members, and early educators to assist and encourage staff and volunteer development throughout the year.

50000 attendees

Ken Smitherman, President
Janet Stump, Public Relations

627 ASCD Annual Conference & Exhibit Show

Association for Supervision & Curriculum
1703 N Beauregard Street
Alexandria, VA 22311
703-578-9600
800-933-2723
Fax: 703-575-5400
E-mail: member@ascd.org
http://www.ascd.org
Explore the big ideas in education today, or examine new developments in your content area or grade level. Stretch your professional development learning into new areas, or pick an issue you care about most and examine it in depth.

April
12000 attendees

Barbara Gleason, Public Information Director
Christy Guilfoyle, Public Relations Specialist

628 AZLA/MPLA Conference

Arizona Library Association
14449 N 73rd Street
Scottdale, AZ 85260
480-998-1954
Fax: 480-998-7838
E-mail: meetmore@aol.com
http://www.azla.org
Advance the education advantages of the state through libraries, and to promote general interest in library extension (traveling libraries).

October
90+ booths with 2,000 attendees

Christine Bailey, Conference Administrator
Deanna Anderson, Exhibitor & Registration Mgn

629 Advocates for Language Learning Annual Meeting

Kansas City School District
301 E Armour Boulevard #620
Kansas City, MO 64111-1259
301-808-8291
Designed for both language instruction and language learning, the Conference is at-

tended by language teachers, school administrators, directors, principals and parents at the elementary level.

October

Pat Barr-Harrison, Conference Contact

630 American Association School Administrators National Conference on Education
801 N Quincy Street
Suite 700
Arlington, VA 22203
703-528-0700
Fax: 703-841-1543
E-mail: info@aasa.org
http://www.aasa.org
For school superintendents, assistant superintendents, central office staff and those aspiring to the superintendency.

Paul Houston, Executive Director
Marilyn Maury, Conference Assist.
Director

631 American Association for Employment in Education Annual Conference
American Association for Employment in Education
3040 Riverside Drive
Suite 125
Columbus, OH 43221
614-485-1111
Fax: 614-485-9609
E-mail: aaee@osu.edu
http://www.aaee.org
Disseminate information on the educational marketplace, and job search process. Promote ethical standards and practices in the employment process. Promote dialogue and cooperation among institutions which prepare educators and institutions which provide employment opportunities.

November
20 booths with 150-200 attendees

BJ Bryant, Executive Director
Chris Barton, Project Coordinator

632 American Association for Higher Education: Annual Assessment Conference
American Associations for Higher Education
1 Dupont Circle NW
Suite 360
Washington, DC 20036-1137
202-293-6440
Fax: 202-293-0073
E-mail: info@aahe.org
http://www.aahe.org
Bringing together trendsetters - the individuals, institutions, and coalitions in North America and beyond - who demonstrates the courage and imagination to act on the pressing issues of our time.

20 booths with 1700 attendees

Joyce DePass, Conference Director
Robert Mundhenk, Assessment Director

633 American Association for Higher Education: Learning to Change Conference
American Associations for Higher Education
1 Dupont Circle NW
Suite 360
Washington, DC 20036-1137
202-293-6440
Fax: 202-293-0073
E-mail: info@aahe.org
http://www.aahe.org

Widens the circle of faculty and administrators interested in higher education. You will be engaged and excited by a rich mix of learning and networking events.

March
20 booths with 1000 attendees

Joyce DePass, Conference Director
Clara Lovett, President

634 American Association for Higher Education: Summer Academy, Organizing for Learning
American Associations for Higher Education
1 Dupont Circle NW
Suite 360
Washington, DC 20036-1137
202-293-6440
Fax: 202-293-0073
E-mail: info@aahe.org
http://www.aahe.org
Team-based, project-centered experience focused on undergraduate change initiatives that enhance student learning.

July
300 attendees

Joyce DePass, Convention Director

635 American Association of Colleges for TeacherEd Annual Meeting and Exhibits
1307 New York Avenue NW
Suite 300
Washington, DC 20005-4701
202-293-2450
Fax: 202-457-8095
E-mail: aacte@aacte.org
http://www.aacte.org
Identifying and meeting the learning needs of teacher education deans and faculty.

Feb
75 booths with 2400 attendees

Sharon P Robinson, President/CEO
Judy A Beck, VP Professional Development

636 American Association of French Teachers Conference
American Association of French Teachers
Mailcode 4510
Southern Illinois University
Carbondale, IL 62901-4510
618-453-5731
Fax: 618-453-5733
E-mail: aatf@frenchteachers.org
http://www.frenchteachers.org/convention
Takes place in French-speaking areas where our members can benefit from immersion in a French-speaking culture. Representing the French language in North America and to encourage the dissemination, both in the schools and in the general public, of knowledge concerning all aspects of the culture and civilization of France and the French-speaking world.

July
1100 attendees

Dr Jayne Abrate, Executive Director

637 American Association of Physics Teachers National Meeting
One Physics Ellipse
College Park, MD 20740-4129
301-209-3300
Fax: 301-209-0845
E-mail: aapt-meet@aapt.org
http://www.aapt.org
Gives members the opportunity to network, discuss innovations in teaching methods

and share the results of research about teaching and learning.

January & August

Carol Heimpel, Director of Meetings
Maria Elena Khoury, Program Director

638 American Association of School AdministratorsAnnual Convention
American Association of School Administrators
801 N Quincy Street
Suite 700
Arlington, VA 22203-1730
703-528-0700
Fax: 703-841-1543
E-mail: info@aasa.org
http://www.aasa.org
To support and develop effective school system leaders who are dedicated to the highest quality public education for all children.

Marilynn Maury, Conference Assist.
Director
Paul Houston, Executive Director

639 American Association of School Librarians National Conference
American Library Association
50 E Huron Street
Chicago, IL 60611
312-280-4386
800-545-2433
Fax: 312-664-7459
E-mail: aasl@ala.org
http://www.ala.org/aasl
An open conference holding seminars, workshops and tours of local libraries and facilities.

October
3,000 attendees

Laura Hayes, Conference Program Officer
Stephanie Hoerner, Conference Services Manager

640 American Association of Sex Educators, Counselors & Therapists Conference
PO Box 1960
Ashland, VA 23005-1960
804-752-0026
Fax: 804-752-0056
E-mail: aasect@aasect.org
http://www.aasect.org
For professionals and affiliated groups with a focus on continuing education for license renewal.

06/20-06/24
50 booths with 400-500 attendees

Dr Steve Conley, Executive Director
Ashlyn Howell, Confernce Manager

641 American Camping Association National Conference
American Camping Association
5000 State Road 67 N
Martinsville, IN 46151-7902
765-342-8456
Fax: 765-342-2065
E-mail: conference@ACAcamps.org
http://www.acaamps.org
Each year our community comes together to share the work we do and to explore opportunities for the future. With new directions, exciting and creative improvements, and added value for all attendees, the 2005 ACA

National Conference offers you essential opportunities.

Februrary
175 booths with 1500 attendees
Peg Smith, CEO
Kim Bruno, Marketing Manager

642 American Council on Education Annual Meeting
American Council on Education
1 Dupont Circle NW
Washington, DC 20036-1110
202-939-9410
Fax: 202-833-4760
E-mail: annualmeeting@ace.nche.edu
http://www.acenet.edu/meeting/index.cfm
The social compact that has governed and financed U.S. higher education for more than 50 years. A compact among government, citizens, and institutions has made postsecondary education broadly accessible. Join us as we explore the implications behind this highly politicized and provocative topic.

February
74 booths
Stephanie Marshall, Meeting Services Director
Wendy Bresler, Program Planning

643 American Council on the Teaching of Foreign Languages Annual Conference
700 S Washington Street
Suite 210
Alexandria, VA 22314
703-894-2900
Fax: 703-894-2905
E-mail: morehouse@actfl.org
http://www.actfl.org
Annual convention, the largest meeting of second language educators in the US and the only national convention in the continental US for teachers of Chinese, French, Russian, German, Italian, Japanese, Spanish and other languages. It is the professional forum for all languages, and all levels of instruction and the largest exhibition of teaching materials and technology in support of foreign language instruction in the US.

November
250 booths with 5,000+ attendees
Roberta Morehouse, Convention Coordinator
Bret Lovejoy, Executive Director

644 American Counseling Association Annual Convention
American Counseling Association
5999 Stevenson Avenue
Alexandria, VA 22304-3302
703-823-9800
800-347-6647
Fax: 703-823-0252
E-mail: rhayes@counseling.org
http://www.counseling.org
Counseling: A Creative Force in the Fabric of Life. Development of professional counselors, advancing the counseling profession, and using the profession and practice of counseling to promote respect for human dignity and diversity.

March, April
Robin Hayes, Convention & Meeting Contact
Dawn Tullis, Convention & Meeting Contact

645 American Education Finance Association Annual Conference & Workshop
American Education Finance Association
5249 Cape Leyte Drive
Sarasota, FL 34242-1805
941-349-7580
Fax: 941-349-7580
http://www.aefa.cc
Information and discussion relating to critical issues in education finance for administrators, directors and principals.

March
3000 attendees
Marge Plecki, President
Ed Steinbrecher, Executive Director

646 American Educational Research Association Annual Meeting
1230 17th Street NW
Washington, DC 20036-3078
202-223-9485
Fax: 202-775-1824
E-mail: 2005annualmtg@aera.net
http://www.aera.net
Contains exhibiting college and secondary school text publishers, software and hardware manufacturers that emphasize such applications as test development, test scoring and applications.

April
120 booths with 12M attendees
James Mears, Meetings Manager
Robert Smith, Director

647 American Educational Studies Association
Tennessee Technical University
PO Box 5193
Cookeville, TN 38505-0001
931-372-3101
Fax: 931-372-6319
Encourages research and the improvement of teaching in various curriculum areas.

November
Harvey Neufeldt, Conference Contact

648 American Indian Science & Engineering Society Annual Conference
AISES
PO Box 9828
Albuquerque, NM 87106
505-765-1052
Fax: 505-765-5608
E-mail: info@aises.org
http://www.aises.org
Issues of science and technological advances in regard to the various American Indian cultures and possible opportunities in North America. Workshops, seminars, cultural ceremonies, and a job fair with opportunities for employment or receiving scholarships for future academics.

November
3000 attendees
Cristy Davies, Events Coordinator
Pamela Silas, Executive Director

649 American Library Association Annual Conference
American Library Association
50 E Huron Street
Chicago, IL 60611-2795
312-280-3219
800-545-2433
E-mail: ala@ala.org
http://www.ala.org

Bi-Annual conference for librarians.

June/January
Yvonne McLean, Conference Coordinator
Keith Michael Fiels, Executive Director

650 American Mathematical Society
American Mathematical Society
201 Charles Street
Providence, RI 02904
401-455-4000
800-321-4267
Fax: 401-331-3842
E-mail: meet@ams.org
http://www.ams.org
Information on joint mathematics meetings, publications, and professional services of the American Mathematical Society.

January
Diane Saxe, Meetings Director

651 American Montessori Society Conference
281 Park Avenue S
6th Floor
New York, NY 61020
212-358-1250
Fax: 212-358-1256
E-mail: east@amshq.org
http://www.amshq.org
Promotes quality Montessori education for all children from birth to 18 years of age.

May
75 booths with 1000 attendees
Richard A Ungerer, Executive Director
Marcy K Krever, Communication Director

652 American Psychological Association Annual Conference
750 1st Street NE
Washington, DC 20002-4241
202-336-6020
800-374-2721
Fax: 202-336-5919
E-mail: convention@apa.org
http://www.apa.org/convention05
A national conference attended by psychologists from around the world. The conference has workshops, lectures, discussions, roundtables and symposiums.

August

13,000 attendees
Ronald F LeVant, President

653 American Public Health Association Annual Meeting
American Public Health Association
800 I Street NW
Washington, DC 20001
202-777-2742
Fax: 202-777-2534
E-mail: diane.lentini@apha.org
http://www.apha.org/meetings
The premier platform to share successes and failures, discover exceptional best practices and learn from expert colleagues and the latest research in the field.

November
650 booths with 13000 attendees
Diane Lentini, Meeting Information Contact
Karla Pearce, Archives Contact

654 American School Health Association's National School Conference
7263 State Route 43
PO Box 708
Kent, OH 44240-5960
330-678-1601
Fax: 330-678-4526
E-mail: asha@ashaweb.org
http://www.ashaweb.org
Attendees include school nurses, health educators, health counselors, physicians and students. During the five-day conference, presentations are made by ASHA members, government officials and health education professionals.

October
40 booths with 700 attendees

Mary Bamer Ramsier, Meeting Planner
Susan F Wooley, Executive Director

655 American Speech-Language-Hearing Association Annual Convention
ASHA
10801 Rockville Pike
Rockville, MD 20852-3226
301-897-5700
800-638-8255
Fax: 301-571-0457
E-mail: convention@asha.org
http://www.asha.org
A scientific and professional conference of speech-language pathology, audiology and other professionals.

Annual
November
400 booths with 12,000 attendees

Arlene A Pietranton, Executive Director

656 American Technical Education Association Annual Conference
American Technical Education Association
800 6th Street N
Wahpeton,, ND 58076-0002
701-671-2240
Fax: 701-671-2260
E-mail: betty-krump@ndscs.nodak.edu
http://www.ateaonline.org
Over 350 administrators/directors and faculty of various technical institutes, junior colleges, universities and colleges, with 40 exhibitors. Topics cover all aspects of computer assisted instruction, distance education and technical education.

March
35 booths with 700 attendees and 75 exhibits

Betty Krump, Executive Director

657 Annual Academic-Vocational Integrated Curriculum Conference
National School Conference Institute
2525 East Arizona
Biltmore Circle, Suite 240
Phoenix, AZ 85069-7527
602-778-1030
800-242-3419
Fax: 602-778-1032
http://www.nscinet.com
Two pre-conference workshops: Comprehensive Career Guidance K-12, and Curriculum Integration: A New Level of Learning. Conference will also hold over 50 breakout sessions.

March

658 Annual Challenging Learners with Untapped Potential Conference
National School Conference Institute
2525 East Arizona
Biltmore Circle, Suite 240
Phoenix, AZ 85016
602-778-1030
800-242-3419
Fax: 602-778-1032
Two pre-conference workshops: The necessary ingredients for success, and Trends; identification strategies. Conference will also hold over 60 breakout sessions.

February

Carl Boyd, President

659 Annual Conference on Hispanic American Education
National School Conference Institute
2525 East Arizona
Biltmore Circle, Suite 240
Phoenix, AZ 85016
602-778-1030
800-242-3419
Fax: 602-778-1032
Two pre-conference workshops: Hispanic educational success: What schools can do to meet the challenge, and Closing the Hispanic achievement gap: A K-16 strategy using real data and standards-based professional development. Conference will also hold over 60 breakout sessions.

April

660 Annual Effective Schools Conference
National School Conference Institute
2525 East Arizona
Biltmore Circle, Suite 240
Phoenix, AZ 85069-7527
602-778-1030
800-242-3419
Fax: 602-778-1032
Two pre-conference workshops: Making the right changes at the district level to assure successful, sustainable school reform, and The challenges of high standards, accurate assessments, and meaningful accountability. Conference will also hold over 70 breakout sessions.

Bill Daggett

661 Annual Ethics & Technology Conference
Loyola University
820 N Michigan Avenue
School of Business
Chicago, IL 60611-2103
312-915-7394
E-mail: rkizior@luc.edu
http://www.ethicstechconference.org
The primary goal of the conference is to continue the interdisciplinary dialogue about ethical and social challenges triggered by the rapid diffusion of information technology.

June

Dr Ronald Kizior, Conference Chair
Dr Mary Malliaris, Program Chair

662 Annual Microcomputers in Education Conference
Arizona State University
PO Box 870101
Tempe, AZ 85287-0908
480-965-9700
Fax: 480-965-4128
E-mail: info@mec.asu.edu
http://mec.asu.edu
The conference provides a forum to explore emerging educational technology and

draws administrators, teachers, researchers, professionals and technology specialists from Arizona and throughout the country. Conference sessions cover K-12 through university-level applications, and target beginner through experienced users.

March
81 booths with 1,200+ attendees and 80+ exhibits

Dr Gary Bitter, Conference Director
Julie Solomon, Event Coordinator, Sr

663 Annual NCEA Convention & Exposition
National Catholic Educational Association
1077 30th Street NW
Suite 100
Washington, DC 20007-3852
202-337-6232
Fax: 202-333-6706
E-mail: convasst@ncea.org
http://www.ncea.org
For all Catholic educators. 700 special exhibits, 400 engaging sessions and dozens of outstanding speakers.

Annually
April

Sue Arvo, Convention/Exposition Dir.
Stacey Svendgard, Exposition Coordinator

664 Annual Technology & Learning Conference
National School Boards Association
1680 Duke Street
Alexandria, VA 22314
703-838-6722
800-950-6722
Fax: 703-683-7590
E-mail: info@nsba.org
http://www.nsba.org
The latest education technology and the most innovative programming.

October

Anne L Bryant, Executive Director
Sandy Folks, General Conference Contact

665 Association for Advancement of Behavior Therapy Annual Convention
305 7th Avenue
New York, NY 10001-6008
212-647-1890
Fax: 212-647-1865
E-mail: mebrown@aabt.org
http://www.aabt.org
Psychologists, psychology faculty and students, and counselors with information on behavior modification, counseling and guidance and mental health issues.

November
2,000 attendees

Mary Ellen Brown, Convention Manager
Mary Jane Eimer, Executive Director

666 Association for Behavior Analysis Annual Convention
Association for Behavior Analysis
1219 S Park Street
Kalamazoo, MI 49001
269-492-9310
Fax: 269-492-9316
E-mail: convention@abainternational.org
http://www.abainternational.org
Psychologists, psychology faculty and students, counselors and social workers are among the attendees of this conference of-

fering over 25 exhibitors. The conference is research and education oriented.

43 booths

Maria E Malott, PhD, Conference Contact

667 Association for Education in Journalism and Mass Communication Convention

AEJMC
234 Outlet Pointe Boulevard
Columbia, SC 29210-5667
803-798-0271
http://www.aejmc.org/convention
Featuring the latest in technology as well as special sessions on teaching, research and public service in the various components of journalism and mass communication — from advertising and public relations to radio and television journalism to media management and newspapers.

August
1,500 attendees

Fred Williams, Convention Manager
Jennifer McGill, Executive Director

668 Association for Persons with Severe Handicaps Annual Conference

29 W Susquehanna Avenue
Suite 210
Baltimore, MD 21204
410-828-8274
Fax: 410-828-6706
E-mail: info@tash.org
http://www.tash.org
Provides a forum for individuals with disabilities, families, researchers, educators, scholars, and others to create dialogue around creating action for social and systems reform.

December
2,500 attendees

Kelly Nelson, Conference Coordinator
Nancy Weiss, Executive Director

669 Association for Play Therapy Conference

Association for Play Therapy
2050 N Winery Avenue
Suite 101
Fresno, CA 93703-2831
559-252-2278
Fax: 559-252-2297
E-mail: info@a4pt.org
http://www.a4pt.org
Dedicated to the advancement of play therapy. APT is interdisciplinary and defines play therapy as a distinct group of interventions which use play as an integral component of the therapeutic process.

October
1000 attendees

Kathryn Lebby, Events Coordinator
Bill Burns, Executive Director

670 Association for Science Teacher Education Science Annual Meeting

The Association For Science Teacher Education
5040 Haley Center
Auburn, AL 36849
972-690-2496
http://www.aste.chem.pitt.edu
Offers programs in science, mathematics and environmental education with a wide variety of teachers and professors attending.

January

Paul Kuerbis, Conference Chair

671 Association for Supervision & Curriculum Development Annual Conference

ASCD
1703 N Beauregard Street
Alexandria, VA 22311-1717
703-578-9600
800-933-2723
Fax: 703-575-5400
E-mail: member@ascd.org
http://www.ascd.org
Explore the big ideas in education today, or examine new developments in your content area or grade level. Stretch your professional development learning into new areas, or pick an issue you care about most and examine it in depth.

300 booths with 1,100+ attendees

Barbara Gleason, Public Information Director
Christy Guilfoyle, Public Relations

672 Association for the Advancement of International Education

San Diego State University
College of Extended Studies
5250 Campanile Drive
San Diego, CA 92182
619-594-2877
Fax: 619-594-3648
E-mail: ajenkins@mail.sdsu.edu
http://www.aaie.org
Provides the organizational leadership to initiate and promote an understanding of the need for and the support of American/International education.

February
70 booths with 550 attendees

Annie Jenkins, Executive Assistant
Richard Krajcar, Executive Director

673 Association for the Education of Gifted Underachieving Students Conference

PO Box 221
Mountain Lakes, NJ 07046
651-962-5385
http://www.aegus1.org
Attended by teachers, professors, administrators and social workerss, this conference deals with cultural awareness and education of the disabled and gifted students.

April

Lois Baldwin, President
Terry Neu, Vice President

674 Association for the Study of Higher Education Annual Meeting

Michigan State University
424 Erickson Hall
East Lansing, MI 48824
517-432-8805
Fax: 517-432-8806
E-mail: ashemsu@msu.edu
http://www.ashe.ws/index.htm
Promotes collaboration among its members and others engaged in the study of higher education.

November

Gary Rhoades, President

675 Association of American Colleges & Universities Annual Meeting

Association of American Colleges & Universities
1818 R Street NW
Washington, DC 20009-1604
202-387-3760
Fax: 202-265-9532
http://www.aacu-edu.org

Bringing together college educators from across institutional types, disciplines, and departments. Providing participants with innovative ideas and practices, and shaping the direction of their educational reform efforts.

January
1,200 attendees

Carol Geary, President
Ross Miller, Director of Programs

676 Association of Community College TrusteesConference

1233 20th Street NW
Suite 605
Washington, DC 20036-2907
202-775-4667
Fax: 202-223-1297
http://www.acct.org
Exists to develop effective lay governing board leadership to strengthen the capacity of community colleges to achieve their missions on behalf of their communities.

1000 attendees

Ray Taylor, President/CEO
Lila Farmer, Conference Logistics Coord.

677 Association of Science-Technology Centers Incorporated Conference

Association of Science-Technology Centers Incorp.
1025 Vermont Avenue NW
Suite 500
Washington, DC 20005-3516
202-783-7200
Fax: 202-783-7207
E-mail: conference@astc.org
http://www.astc.org
An organization of science centers and museums dedicated to furthering the public understanding of science. ASTC encourages excellence and innovation in informal science learning by serving and linking its members worldwide and advancing the common goals.

October
165 booths with 1600 attendees

Cindy Kong, Meetings/Conference Director
Gareth Rees, Meetings/Conference Coord.

678 CHADD: Children & Adults with Attention Deficit/Hyperactivity Disorder

CHADD
8181 Professional Place
Suite 150
Landover, MD 20785
301-306-7070
800-233-4050
Fax: 301-306-7090
http://www.chadd.org
National non-profit organization which offers advocacy, information and support for patients and parents of children with attention deficit disorders. Maintains support groups, provides a forum for continuing education about ADHD, and maintains a national resource center for information about ADD.

October
60 booths with 1,500 attendees

Alison Harris, Conference Coordinator
Peg Nichols, Communications Director

679 Center for Appalachian Studies & Services Annual Conference
East Tennessee University
PO Box 70556
Johnson City, TN 37614-0918
423-439-7865
Fax: 423-439-7870
E-mail: asa@marshal.edu
http://www.cass.etsu.edu/
Sponsor educational programs and public service activities that enhance the quality of life in Appalachia and that empower people to live more effectively within the region.

March

Elizabeth Fine, Conference Contact

680 Center for Applications of PsychologicalType Biennial Education Conference
2815 NW 13th Street
Suite 401
Gainesville, FL 32609
352-375-0160
800-777-2278
Fax: 352-378-0503
E-mail: fields@capt.org
Promotes the practical application and ethical use of psychological type. Conference sponsored by Center for Applications of Psychological Type (CAPT).

July

Jim Weir, Executive Director

681 Center for Gifted Education and Talent Development Conference
University of Connecticut
2131 Hillside Road
Unit 3007
Storrs Mansfield, CT 06269-3007
860-486-4826
Fax: 860-486-2900
http://www.gifted.uconn.edu
Conducts research on methods and techniques for teaching gifted and talented students.

Annual

Sally M Reis, Professor

682 Center for Rural Education and Small Schools Annual Conference
College of Education
124 Bluemont Hall
1100 Mid-Campus Drive
Manhattan, KS 66506
785-532-5886
Fax: 785-532-7304
E-mail: barbhav@ksu.edu
http://www.coe.ksu.edu/CRESS/conference.html
Annual conference is held which includes over 200 administrators, directors, principals, teachers and university faculty discussing all aspects of education in rural areas.

October
200 attendees and 20 exhibits

Barbara Havlicek, Assistant Director
Robert Newhouse, Director

683 Center on Disabilities Conference
Students with Disabilities Resources
1811 Nordhoff
Northridge, CA 91330-8264
818-677-2684
Fax: 818-677-4932
E-mail: sdr@csun.edu
http://www.csun.edu/cod
This is a comprehensive, international conference, where all technologies across all ages; disabilities; levels of education and training; employment; and independent living is addressed. It is the largest conference of its kind!

March
130 booths with 4,000+ attendees

Marina Sanchez, Participant Coordinator
Sonya Hernandez, Speakers Coordinator

684 Choristers Guild's National Festival & Directors' Conference
Choristers Guild
2834 W Kingsley Road
Garland, TX 75041-2498
972-271-1521
Fax: 972-840-3113
E-mail: conferences@mailcg.org
http://www.choristersguild.org
Enables leaders to nurture the spiritual and musical growth of children and youth.

September

Jim Rindelaub, Director

685 Closing the Gap
526 Main Street
PO Box 68
Henderson, MN 56044-0068
507-248-3294
Fax: 507-248-3810
E-mail: info@closingthegap.com
http://www.closingthegap.com
Provides information on the use of computer technology by and for persons with disabilities and the opportunities available for education and independent learning.

October
150+ booths with 2400 attendees

Maryann Harty, Advertising/Exhibits Manager
Connie Kneip, VP/General Manager

686 Computers on Campus National Conference
University of South Carolina
937 Assembly Street
Suite 108
Columbia, SC 29208
803-777-2260
Fax: 803-777-2663
E-mail: confs@rcce.scarolina.edu
http://www.rcce.sc.edu/coc
This conference provides a national forum for showcasing computer-based instructional models, discussing successful experiences in computer networking, making effective use of computer support in academic assessment, and using computer technology to enhance total student development.

November

Dr Andrew A Sorensen, President
Margaret M Lamb, Media Relations Director

687 Conference for Advancement of Mathematics Teaching
Texas Education Agency
William Travis Building
1701 N Congress Avenue
Austin, TX 78701-1402
512-463-9734
Fax: 512-463-9838
http://www.tea.state.tx.us
Exhibits educational materials useful to mathematics teachers.

July
175 booths with 7.5M-8M attendees

Anita Hopkins, Conference Contact

688 Conference on Information Technology
League for Innovation in the Community College
4505 East Chandler Boulevard
Suite 250
Phoenix, AZ 85048
480-705-8200
Fax: 480-705-8201
E-mail: harris@league.org
http://www.league.org
The premier showcase of the use of information technology to improve teaching and learning, student services, and institutional management. Celebrating 18 years of excellence, CIT features a technologically sophisticated and topically diverse program that enables educators to explore and expand their use of technology.

October
3,000 attendees

Mary K Harris, Conference Manager
Robin Piccilliri, Conference Specialist

689 Council for Advancement and Support of Education
1307 New York Avenue NW
Suite 1000
Washington, DC 20005-4701
202-328-2273
Fax: 202-387-4973
E-mail: conference@case.org
http://www.case.org
Offers numerous opportunities in the United States, Canada, Mexico, mainland Europe, the United Kingdom, and even online, to network with colleagues and learn about Institutional Advancement.

Fall/Winter

Lucinda Lyon-Vaiden, Sr Conference Program Coord.
Richard Salatiello, Sr Conference Program Coord.

690 Council for Exceptional Children Annual Convention
The Council for Exceptional Children
1110 N Glebe Road
Suite 300
Arlington, VA 22201-5704
703-620-3660
800-224-6830
Fax: 703-264-1637
E-mail: victore@cec.sped.org
http://www.cec.sped.org
largest profesional orgenization dedicated to improving educationl results of individuals with disabilities and the gifted. 50,000 members

April
437 booths with 6541 attendees and 299 exhibits

Victor Erickson, Marketing Manager

691 EDUCAUSE
4772 Walnut Street
Suite 206
Boulder, CO 80301-2408
303-449-4430
Fax: 303-440-0461
E-mail: bwilliams@educause.edu
http://www.educause.edu
EDUCAUSE is an international, nonprofit association whose mission is to help shape and enable tranformational change in higher education through the introduction, use, and management of information resources and technologies in teaching, learning, scholarship, research, and institutional management. EDUCAUSE publishes books, magazines, monographs, executive briefings, white papers, and other materials

that provide thoughtful leadership to effect transformational change in higher education.

October
4,000+ attendees and 180 exhibits

Brian L Hawkins, President
Beverly Williams, Conference Director

692 Education Technology Conference

Society for Applied Learning Technology
50 Culpeper Street
Warrenton, VA 20186
540-347-0055
800-457-6812
Fax: 540-349-3169
E-mail: info@lti.org
http://www.salt.org
For over 30 years the Society has sponsored conferences which are educational in nature and cover a wide range of application areas such as distance learning, interactive multimedia in education and training, development of interactive instruction materials, performance support systems applications in education and training, interactive instruction delivery, and information literacy.

August
20 booths with 400 attendees

Raymond G Fox, President

693 Educational Publishing Summit: Creating Managing & Selling Content

Association of Educational Publishers
510 Heron Drive
Suite 201
Logan Township, NJ 08085
856-241-7772
Fax: 856-241-0709
E-mail: mail@edpress.org
http://www.edpress.org
Offers diverse sessions about the latest publishing educational and technology trends and an incomparable opportunity for those in every avenue of the educational publishing community, at every career level, to network with peers.

June

Charlene F Gaynor, Executive Director
Stacey Pusey, Communications Manager

694 Educational Theatre Association Conference

Educational Theatre Association
2343 Auburn Avenue
Cincinnati, OH 45219-2815
513-421-3900
Fax: 513-421-7077
E-mail: mpeitz@edta.org
http://www.edta.org
Promotes and strengthens theatre in education-primarily middle school and high school. Sponsors an honor society, various events, numerous publications, and arts education advocacy activities.

September
2,400 attendees

Michael J Peitz, Executive Director
Kathleen Taylor, Advertising Manager

695 Embracing an Inclusive Society: The Challenge for the New Millennium

National Multicultural Institute
3000 Connecticut Avenue NW
Suite 438
Washington, DC 20008-2556
202-483-0700
Fax: 202-483-5233
E-mail: nmci@nmci.org
http://www.nmci.org
Brings together practitioners from across the country and around the world to explore diversity and multiculturalism in both personal and professional contexts. Leaders from academia, business, and government present the latest thinking and action on diversity issues to conference participants.

June

Maria Morukian, Conference Coordinator
Elizabeth P Salett, President

696 Foundation for Critical Thinking Regional Workshop & Conference

Foundation for Critical Thinking
PO Box 220
Dillon Beach, CA 94929
800-833-3645
Fax: 707-878-9111
E-mail: cct@criticalthinking.org
http://www.criticalthinking.org
Investigates and reports on the value and use of analytical thinking programs and curriculum in the classroom.

July

Dr Linda Elder, President

697 Gifted Child Society Conference

190 Rock Road
Glen Rock, NJ 07452-1736
201-444-6530
Fax: 201-444-9099
E-mail: admin@gifted.org
http://www.gifted.org
Provides educational enrichment and support for gifted children through national advocacy and various programs.

September
250 attendees

Janet L Chen, Executive Director

698 High School Reform Conference

National School Conference Institute
PO Box 37527
Phoenix, AZ 85069-7527
602-371-8655
Fax: 602-371-8790
http://www.nscinet.com
Conference will cover restructuring the high school schedule, designing curriculum and instruction, assessments and student motivation, and information and communication technology. Being held in Las Vegas, Nevada.

April

Robert Lynn Canady
Rick Stiggins

699 Hitting the High Notes of Literacy

Proliteracy Volunteers of America
1320 Jamesville Avenue
Syracuse, NY 13210
315-422-9121
Fax: 315-422-6369
E-mail: lvanat@aol.com
http://www.literacyvolunteers.org
Conference dealing with literacy issues.

November
50 booths with 1,000 attendees

Peggy May, Conference Manager

700 INFOCOMM Tradeshow

8401 Eagle Creek Parkway
Suite 700
Savage, MN 55378
952-894-6280
800-582-6480
Fax: 877-894-6918
E-mail: chief@chiefmfg.com
http://www.chiefmfg.com
Chief Manufacturing is the leader in total mounting solutions for presentation systems. Based in Minnesota, Chief designs, manufactures and distributes worlwide, a full line of mounts, lifts and accessories for LCD/DLP/CRT projectors, large flat panel displays and small flat panel displays.

Cristy Sabatka, Sales Admin.
Coordinator

701 Improving Student Performance

National Study of School Evaluation
1699 E Woodfield Road
Suite 406
Schaumburg, IL 60173-4958
847-995-9080
Fax: 847-995-9088
E-mail: schoolimprovement@nsse.org
http://www.nsse.org
A comprehensive guide for data-driven and research-based school improvement planning.

November

702 Increasing Student Achievement in Reading, Writing, Mathematics, Science

National School Conference Institute
PO Box 37527
Phoenix, AZ 85069-7527
602-371-8655
Fax: 602-371-8790
http://www.nscinet.com

March

Orlando Taylor
George Nelson

703 Independent Education Consultants Association Conference

3251 Old Lee Highway
Suite 510
Fairfax, VA 22030-1504
703-591-4850
800-888-4322
Fax: 703-591-4860
E-mail: requests@IECAonline.com
http://www.IECAonline.com
National professional association of educational counselors working in private practice. Provides counseling in college, secondary schools, learning disabilities and wilderness therapy programs. Publishes a monthly newsletter called 'Insight'.

Spring & Fall
400 booths with 800 attendees

Mark H Sklarow, Executive Director
Susan Millburn, Conference Manager

704 Infusing Brain Research, Multi-Intelligence, Learning Styles and Mind Styles

National School Conference Institute
Crowne Plaza Hotel
Phoenix, AZ 85069-7527
602-371-8655
Fax: 602-371-8790
http://www.nscinet.com
Two pre-conference workshops: Intelligences in the curriculum and classroom, and What do educators need to know

about the human brain? Conference will also hold over 50 breakout sessions.

February
Geoffrey Caine
Renate Caine

705 Instant Access: Critical Findings from the NRC/GT
University of Connecticut
362 Fairfield Road
Storrs, CT 06269
860-486-4826
Fax: 860-486-2900
http://www.gifted.uconn.edu
Conference sponsored by the National Research Center on the Gifted and Talented.

March

706 Integrated/Thematic Curriculum and Performance Assessment
National School Conference Institute
Hyatt Regency Hotel
Phoenix, AZ 85069-7527
602-371-8655
Fax: 602-371-8790
http://www.nscinet.com
Two pre-conference workshops: The door to restructuring, aligning, and integrating the curriculum for the 21st century, and Moving assessment to the top of the charts. Conference will also hold over 50 breakout sessions.

February

Heidi Hayes Jacobs
Roger Taylor

707 International Performance Improvement Conference Expo
International Society for Performance
1400 Spring Street
Suite 260
Silver Spring, MD 20910
301-587-8570
Fax: 301-587-8573
E-mail: info@ispi.org
http://www.ispi.org

April
60 booths with 1500 attendees
Ellen Kaplan, Conference Manager

708 Iteachk
Society for Developmental Education
10 Sharon Road
PO Box 577
Peterborough, NH 03458
800-462-1478
Fax: 800-337-9929
http://www.iteachk.com
National conference for kindergarten teachers.

709 Journalism Education Association
Kansas State University
103 Kedzie Hall
Manhattan, KS 66506-1505
785-532-5532
Fax: 785-532-5563
E-mail: lindarp@ksu.edu
http://www.jea.org/
An organization of about 2,300 journalism teachers and advisers, offers two national teacher-student conventions a year, quarterly newsletter and magazines, bookstore and national certification program. This association serves as a leader in scholastic press freedom and media curriculum.

Linda Puntrey, Executive Director

710 Literacy Volunteers of America National Conference
5795 Widewaters Parkway
Syracuse, NY 13214-1846
315-472-0001
Fax: 315-422-6369
Workshops to promote literacy and reading.

November
30 booths with 1000+ attendees
Peg Price, Conference Contact

711 Lutheran Education Association Convention
Lutheran Education Association
7400 Augusta Street
River Forest, IL 60305-1402
708-209-3343
Fax: 708-209-3458
E-mail: lea@crf.cuis.edu
http://www.lea.org
Equip, and affirms educators in Lutheran ministries, helping them become excellent educators.

Kathy Slupik, Executive Assistant
Jonathan C Laabs, Executive Director

712 Master Woodcraft Inc.
1312 College Street
Oxford, NC 27565
919-693-8811
800-333-2675
Fax: 919-693-1707
Announcement and classroom chalkboards, arts and craft supplies. Cork bulletin boards, dry erase melamine boards, easels, floor, table top, lap boards (white melamine dry erase, chalkboard and magnetic).

2 booths with 6 exhibits
Louis B Moss, Manager

713 Meeting the Tide of Rising Expectations
39 Nathan Ellis Highway
PMB #134
Mashpee, MA 02649-3267
508-539-8844
Fax: 508-539-8868
E-mail: nasdtec@attbi.com
http://www.nasdtec.org
NASDTEC is the National Association of State Directors of Teacher Education and Certification. It is the organization that represents professional standards boards and commissions and state departments of education in all 50 states.

October

Roy Einreinhofer, Executive Director

714 Modern Language Association Annual Conference
10 Astor Place
New York, NY 10003-6935
646-576-5260
Promotes and explains the role of language, specifically second language training, in education.

December

Maribeth Kraus, Conference Contact

715 Music Educators National Conference
1806 Robert Fulton Drive
Reston, VA 20191-4348
703-860-4000
Fax: 703-860-2652
http://www.menc.org

Provides a forum for music educators and other musical development in the school setting.

April

716 Music Teachers Association National Conference
Music Teachers National Association
441 Vine Street
Suite 505
Cincinnati, OH 45202-2811
513-421-1420
888-512-5278
Fax: 513-421-2503
E-mail: mtnanet@mtna.org
http://www.mtna.org
Supports and supplies music teachers with information on development and training.

March
160 booths with 2000 attendees
Rachel Kramer, Assistant Executive Director

717 NAAEE Member Services Office
410 Tarvin Road
Rock Spring, GA 30739
706-764-2926
Fax: 706-764-2094
E-mail: csmith409@aol.com
http://www.naaee.org
Exhibitors seeking to integrate and expand environmental education in school systems and in nonformal settings as well.

September

718 NAFSA: National Association of International Educators
1875 Connecticut Avenue NW
Suite 1000
Washington, DC 20009-5747
202-737-3699
800-836-4994
Fax: 202-737-3657
Annual meeting of professionals in the field of international education, with exhibits of services and products relating to international education.

May
150 booths with 5,500 attendees
Marlene M Johnson, Director/CEO

719 NSTA Educational Workshops
National Science Teachers Association
1840 Wilson Boulevard
Arlington, VA 22201-3000
703-522-5413
888-400-6782
Fax: 703-522-5413
http://www.nsta.org/programs/new
To promote excellence and innovation in science teaching and learning for all.

720 National Academy Foundation Annual Institute for Staff Development
National Academy Foundation
39 Broadway
Sutie 1640
New York, NY 10006
212-635-2400
Fax: 212-635-2409
http://www.naf-education.org
Features several days of intensive peer training, industry presentations, and networking opportunities, with the goal of ensuring that Academy programs are seccessful, focused on the improvement of public education, and dedicated toward helping young people of all backgrounds

continue their education as a step toward building careers.

July

721 National Alliance of Black School Educators Conference
2816 Georgia Avenue NW
Washington, DC 20001-3819
202-483-1549
800-221-2654
Fax: 202-608-6319
E-mail: nabse@nabse.org
http://www.nabse.org
Teachers, principals, specialists, superintendents, school board members and higher education personnel. Workshops, plenary sessions, public forums, networking and fellowship.

November
300 booths with 3,500 attendees

Quentin R Lawson, Conference Manager

722 National Art Education Association Annual Convention
National Art Education Association
1916 Association Drive
Reston, VA 20191-1590
703-860-8000
Fax: 703-860-2960
E-mail: naea@dgs.dgsys.com
http://www.naea-reston.org
Containing booths of art education products and services. New art techniques, skills, and knowledge; renowned speakers and teachers; new ideas for art instruction and curriculum.

March
171 booths with 5,000 attendees

Kathy Duse, Conference Manager

723 National Association for Bilingual Education
1030 15th Street NW
Suite 470
Washington, DC 20005-4018
202-898-1829
Fax: 202-789-2866
E-mail: nabe@nabe.org
http://www.nabe.org
Contains publishers and Fortune 500 companies displaying educational materials and multi-media products.

March
350 booths with 8,000 attendees

Delia Pompa, Executive Director
Josephina Velasco, Conference Manager

724 National Association for College Admission Counseling Conference
Nat'l Association for College Admission Counseling
1631 Prince Street
Alexandria, VA 22314-2818
703-836-2222
Fax: 703-836-8015
http://www.nacac.com
Membership association offering information to counselors and guidance professionals working in the college admissions office.

September
142 booths with 4,000 attendees

Shanda T Ivory, Chief Officer Communications
Amy C Vogt, Assistant Director

725 National Association for Girls and Womenin Sports Yearly Conference
1900 Association Drive
Reston, VA 20191-1599
703-476-3450
800-213-7193
Fax: 703-476-4566
E-mail: nagws@aahperd.org
http://www.aahperd.org/nagws/nagws
An association providing information for girls and women in sports.

March/April
280 booths with 6,000 attendees

Sandra Sumner, Director

726 National Association for Multicultural Education
NAME National Office
1511 K Street NW
Suite 430
Washington, DC 20005
202-628-6263
Fax: 202-628-6264
E-mail: nameorg@erols.com
http://www.inform.umd.edu/name
Keynote speakers and presenters are individuals and educators who value and appreciate diversity and multiculturalism, seek creative approaches to educative practices, and strive to promote social justice through education and training.

727 National Association for Year-Round Education Annual Conference
5404 Napa Street
Suite A
San Diego, CA 92110-7319
619-276-5296
Fax: 858-571-5754
E-mail: info@nayre.org
http://www.NAYRE.org
Fosters the study of year-round education as a way to improve educational programs in terms of providing quality education and adapting the school calendar to community and family living patterns Disseminates information about year-round education.

February
60 booths with 1200 attendees

Marilyn J Stenvall, Executive Director
Don Jeffries, Exhibit Coordinator

728 National Association of Biology Teachers Conference
12030 Sunrise Valley Drive
Sutie 110
Reston, VA 20191
703-264-9696
800-406-0775
Fax: 703-264-7778
E-mail: office@nabt.org
http://www.nabt.org
Contains textbooks, laboratory and classroom supplies and equipment.

November
140 booths with 1,700 attendees

Lisa Walker, Director of Conventions

729 National Association of Elementary School Principals Conference
1615 Duke Street
Alexandria, VA 22314-3406
703-684-3345
Fax: 703-518-6281
E-mail: lburnett@naesp.org
http://www.naesp.org
Products and services in the educational market shopping area. Industry leaders offer practical ways from curriculum resources and instructional aids to fundraising ideas and playground equipment.

April
300 booths

Marguerite Leishman, Director
Lani Burnett, Exhibit Manager

730 National Association of Independent Schools Conference
1620 L Street NW
11th Floor
Washington, DC 20036-5695
202-973-9700
Fax: 202-973-9790
E-mail: bassett@nais.org
http://www.nais.org
Publications, statistics, professional development for independent schools.

February/March
166 booths

Peter D Relic, President

731 National Association of Private Schools for Exceptional Children Conference
1522 K Street NW
Suite 1032
Washington, DC 20005-1211
202-408-3338
Fax: 202-408-3340
E-mail: napsec@aol.com
http://www.napsec.com
This in an annual conference that is held for administrators/directors/principals and private school educators.

January
300 attendees and 8 exhibits

Barb DeGroot, Manager

732 National Association of School Psychologists Annual Convention
4340 EW Highway
Suite 402
Bethesda, MD 20814
301-657-0270
Fax: 301-657-0275
E-mail: center@naspweb.org
http://www.nasponline.org
Gathering of school psychologists and related professionals, offering over 500 workshops, seminars, symposia, papers, presentations and exhibits.

April
100 booths with 4000 attendees

Glenn Reighart, Director
Meeting/Conference

733 National Association of Student Financial Aid Administrators
1129 20th Street NW
Suite 400
Washington, DC 20036-5020
202-785-0453
Fax: 202-785-1487
Exhibits computer hardware and software and banks participating in student loan programs.

July
105 booths

Babara Kay Gordon, Conference Contact

734 National Association of Teachers' Agencies Conference
National Association of Teachers' Agencies
799 Kings Highway
Fairfield, CT 06432
203-333-0611
Fax: 203-334-7224
E-mail: fairfieldteachers@snet.net
http://www.jobsforteachers.com
Mark King, Secretary/Treasurer

735 National Black Child Development Institute Annual Conference
1101 15th Street NW
Suite 900
Washington, DC 20005-2618
202-833-2220
800-556-2234
Fax: 202-833-8222
E-mail: moreinfo@ndcdi.orh
http://www.nbcdi.org
Offers information to counselors and social service workers on African-American Children.

October

Vicki Pinkston, Vice President
Derrell Winder, Program Associate

736 National Catholic Education Association Annual Convention & Exposition
National Catholic Educational Association
1077 30th Street NW
Suite 100
Washington, DC 20007-3852
202-337-6232
Fax: 202-333-6706
http://www.ncea.org
The convention features general sessions with outstanding speakers, special convention liturgies, and a large exposition of many products and services to benefit the educator.

April
675 booths

Leonard DeFiore, President

737 National Center for Montessori Education Conference
PO Box 1543
Roswell, GA 30077-1543
770-434-1128
Focuses on developing and maintaining the Montessori Education system.

March

Kristen Cook, Conference Contact

738 National Coalition for Sex Equity in Education
PO Box 534
Annandale, NJ 08801-0534
908-735-5045
Fax: 908-735-9674
The only national organization for gender equity specialists and educators. Individuals and organizations committed to reducing sex role stereotyping for females and males. Services include an annual national training conference, a quarterly newsletter and a membership directory. Members may join task forces dealing with equity related topics such as computer/technology issues, early childhood, male issues, sexual harassment prevention, sexual orientation and vocational issues.

Theodora Martin, Business Manager

739 National Coalition of Alternative Community Schools
PO Box 15036
Santa Fe, NM 87506-5036
505-474-4312
888-771-9171
A clearinghouse for information regarding alternatives in education for all ages, including home education. Yearly conference, newsletters, mentored Teacher Education Program.

April

Ed Nagel, National Office Manager

740 National Coalition of Title 1-Chapter 1 Parents Conference
Edmonds School Building
9th & D Streets NE
#201
Washington, DC 20002
202-547-9286
Provides lectures and presentations aimed at Chapter 1 parents and professionals.

October

741 National Conference on Student Services
Magna Publications
2718 Dryden Drive
Madison, WI 53704
608-227-8109
800-206-4805
Fax: 608-246-3597
E-mail: carriej@magnapubs.com
http://www.magnapubs.com
Target hard to reach college audiences, and attract campus leaders. Each 4-day conference has potential for the right exhibitor. A second conference will be held in Boston.

October
15 booths with 500 attendees

Carrie Jenson, Conference Manager
David Burns, Associate Publisher

742 National Congress on Aviation and Space Education
Omni Rosen Hotel
Orlando, FL
334-953-5095
E-mail: bspick@cap.af.mil
http://www.cap.af.mil
Provides educators with the tools that make classroom learning fun.

April

743 National Council of Higher Education
National Education Association (NEA)
1201 16th Street NW
Washington, DC 20036-3207
202-822-7162
Fax: 202-822-7624
E-mail: nche@nea.org
http://www.nea.org
Assessing a 20 year journey of the academy.

February, March
400 attendees

Rachel Hendrickson, Coordinator

744 National Council on Alcoholism & Drug Abuse
8790 Manchester Road
Saint Louis, MO 63144
314-962-3456
Fax: 314-968-7394
E-mail: ncada@ncada-stl.org
http://www.ncada-stl.org
A not-for-profit community health agency serving the metropolitian St. Louis area, provides educational materials on substance abuse and addiction, information and referral services, prevention and intervention.

Harriet Kopolow, Director Prevention

745 National Dropout Prevention Center/Network Conference
205 Martin Street
Clemson, SC 29631-1555
864-656-2599
800-443-6392
Fax: 864-656-0136
E-mail: ndpc@clemson.edu
http://www.dropoutprevention.com
Concentrating on programs and services for educators and counselors who deal with at-risk students.

October
100 booths with 1000 attendees

Jay Smink, Executive Director
John Peters, Network Coordinator

746 National Education Association-Retired
National Education Association (NEA)
1201 16th Street NW
Washington, DC 20036-3207
202-822-7125
Fax: 202-822-7624
http://www.nea.org/retired
Serves as a resource in the maintenance of quality public education, promotes improved services and legislation for seniors, provides training for members and serves as a vehicle for local input to the National Education Association.

150 attendees

Deborah C Jackson, Manager
Todd Crenshaw, Coordinator

747 National Guild of Community Schools of theArts Conference
520 8th Avenue
Suite 302, 3rd Floor
New York, NY 10018
212-268-3337
Fax: 212-268-3995
E-mail: info@natguild.org
http://www.nationalguild.org
The National Guild of Community Schools of the Arts fosters and promotes the creation and growth of high-quality arts education in communities across the country. The Guild provides community arts organizations with multiple levels of support, including training, advocacy, information resources, and high-profile leadership in arts education.

November
15 booths with 300 attendees and 15 exhibits

Noah Xifr, Director Membership/Oper.

748 National Head Start Association Annual Conference
1651 Prince Street
Alexandria, VA 22314-2818
703-739-0875
Fax: 703-739-0878
http://www.nhsa.org
Seeks to advance program development, policy and promote training of the Head Start program professionals.

May

A Renee Battle, CMP, Conference Contact
Ruby Lewis-Riar, Conference Assistant

749 National Institute for School and Workplace Safety Conference
160 Internation Parkway
Suite 250
Heathrow, FL 32746
407-804-8310
Fax: 407-804-8306
http://www.nisws.com/
Believes that every school and workplace must implement school and workplace safety standards.
April
80 attendees
Wolfgang Halbig, CEO/Manager

750 National Parent-Teacher Association Annual Convention & Exhibition
1787 Agate Street
Eugene, OR 97403-1923
503-346-4414
Addresses parent-teacher involvement in education. Includes lectures, workshops and seminars for parents and professionals.
June

751 National Reading Styles Institute Conference
179 Lafayette Drive
Syosset, NY 11791-3933
512-224-4555
This conference addresses reading instruction and the problems of illiteracy.
July
Juliet Carbo, Conference Contact

752 National Rural Education Annual Convention
National Rural Education Association
230 Education
Colorado State University
Fort Collins, CO 80523-0001
970-491-1101
Fax: 970-491-1317
Exchanges ideas, practices and better ways to enhance rural educational school systems.
October
30 booths with 400 attendees
Joseph T Newlin, PhD, Conference Contact

753 National Rural Education AssociationAnnual Convention
National Rural Education Association
820 Van Vleet Oval
Room 227
Norman, OK 73019
Fax: 405-325-7959
E-mail: bmooney@ou.edu
http://www.nrea.net
The NREA will be the leading national organization providing services which enhance educational opportunities for rural schools and their communities.
October
35 booths with 400 attendees
Bob Mooneyham, Executive Director

754 National School Boards Annual Conference
1680 Duke Street
Alexandria, VA 22314-3493
703-838-6722
Fax: 703-683-7590
http:// ww.nsba.org/itte
The nation's largest policy and training conference for local education officials on

national and federal issues affecting public schools in the U.S.
March
7,000 attendees and 300 exhibits
Sandra Folks, Conference/Meetings Coord.
Karen Miller, Exhibit Services Manager

755 National School Conference Institute
11202 N 24th Street
Suite 103
Phoenix, AZ 85029
602-371-8655
888-399-8745
Fax: 602-371-8790
http://www.nscinet.com
Our purpose is to increase every student's opportunity for academic success.

756 National School Supply & Equipment Association
NSSEA Essentials
8380 Colesville Road
Silver Spring, MD 20910
301-495-0240
800-395-5550
Fax: 301-495-3330
E-mail: awatts@nssea.org
http://www.nessa.org
Lists 1,500 member dealers and manufacturers representatives for school supplies, equipment and instructional materials.
March
1200 booths with 5,000 attendees and 700 exhibits
Adrienne Dayton, VP of Marketing/Communicatio
DeShuna Spencer, Editor/Communications Manage

757 National Society for Experiential Education Conference
National Society for Experiential Education
3509 Haworth Drive
Suite 207
Raleigh, NC 27609-7235
919-787-3263
Fax: 919-787-3381
E-mail: info@nsee.org
http://www.nsee.org
To foster the effective use of experience as an integral part of education, in order to empower learners and promote the common good.
October
600-700 attendees

758 National Student Assistance Conference
1270 Rakin Drive
Suite F
Troy, MI 48033-2843
800-453-7733
Fax: 800-499-5718
Learn to maintain and improve safe, drug free schools, student assistance programs. Develop skills to implement the Principles of Effectiveness. Choose from workshops and skill building sessions.

759 National Women's History Project Annual Conference
3343 Industrial Drive
Suite #4
Santa Rosa, CA 95403-8518
707-636-2888
Fax: 707-636-2909
E-mail: nwhp@aol.commailto:nwhp@nwhp.org
http://www.nwhp.org
Posters, reference books, curriculum materials and biographies of American women in all subjects for grades K-12.
July
72 attendees
Molly Murphy MacGregor, Conference Manager

760 New Learning Technologies
Society for Applied Learning Technology
50 Culpeper Street
Warrenton, VA 20186
540-347-0055
800-457-6812
Fax: 540-349-3169
E-mail: info@lti.org
http://www.salt.org
To provide a comprehensive overview of the latest in research, design, and development in order to furnish attendees information on systems that are applicable to their organizations.

761 North American Montessori Teachers' Association
13693 Butternnut Road
Burton, OH 44021
440-834-4011
Fax: 440-834-4016
E-mail: staff@montessori-namta.org
http://www.montessori-namta.org/
Professional organization for Montessori teachers and administrators. Services include The NAMTA Journal and other publications, videos and slide shows. Conferences in January and March.
David J Kahn, Executive Director

762 Parents as Teachers National Center Conference
2228 Ball Drive
Saint Louis, MO 63146
314-432-4330
Fax: 314-432-8963
E-mail: patnc@patnc.org
http://www.patnc.org
An international early childhood parent education and family support program designed to enhance child development and school achievement through parent education accessible to all families. Serves families throughout pregnancy and until their child enters kindergarten, usually age 5.
April-May
40 booths with 1400+ attendees
Susan S Stepleton, President/CEO
Cheryl Dyle-Palmer, Director Operations

763 Retention in Education Today for All Indigenous Nations
National Conference Logistics Center
University of Oklahoma
555 E Constitution Street, Suite 208
Norman, OK 73072-7820
405-325-3760
800-203-5494
Fax: 405-325-7075
E-mail: tmonnard@ou.edu
http://www.conferencepros.com

National conference designed to discuss and share retention strategies for indigenous students.

Theresa Monnard, Program Coordinator

764 SERVE Conference
SERVE
PO Box 5367
Greensboro, NC 27435
336-315-7400
800-755-3277
Fax: 336-315-7457
E-mail: jsanders@serve.org
http://www.serve.org
The Regional Educational Laboratories are educational research and development organizations supported by contracts with the US Education Department, National Insititute for Education Sciences. Specialty area: Expanded Learning Opportunities.

October-November

Jack Sanders, Executive Director

765 School Equipment Show
830 Colesville Road
Suite 250
Silver Spring, MD 20910-3297
301-495-0240
Fax: 301-495-3330
Annual show featuring exhibits from manufacturers of school equipment such as bleachers, classroom furniture, lockers, playground and athletic equipment, computer hardware, software, etc.

February

Elizabeth Bradley, Conference Contact

766 Sexual Assault and Harassment on Campus Conference
c/o Sexual Conference
PO Box 1338
Holmes Beach, FL 34218-1338
800-537-4903
http://www.ed.mtu.edu/safe
Topics include gender based hate crime, sexual assault investigators, generational legacy of rape, innovations in the military, sexual harrassment in K-12, updates on date-rape drugs and many more. Hosted by the Hyatt Orlando Hotel in Kissimmee, Florida.

Karen McLaughlin, Conference Co-Chair
Alan McEvoy, Conference Co-Chair

767 Society for Research in Child Development Conference
5720 S Woodlawn Avenue
Chicago, IL 60637-1603
773-702-7700
Fax: 773-702-9756
Working to further research in the area of child development and education.

March/April
40 booths

Barbara Kahn, Conference Contact

768 Teacher Link: An Interactive National Teleconference
Center for the Study of Small/Rural Schools
555 E Constitution Street
Room 138
Norman, OK 73072-7820
405-325-1450
Fax: 405-325-7075
E-mail: jcsimmons@ou.edu
http://cssrs.ou.edu

Prevention Series

Spring
5 booths with 100 attendees
Jan C Simmons, Director

769 Teachers of English to Speakers of Other Languages Convention and Exhibit
700 S Washington Street
Alexandria, VA 22314
703-836-0774
Fax: 703-836-6447
http://www.tesol.org
Leading worldwide professional development opportunity. Simulating program of presentations sponsored by nineteen interest sections, a half-dozen caucus groups and TESOL's advocacy division as well as sessions invited especially for their relevance to our work and our students.

March
245 booths with 8000 attendees
Bart Ecker, Manager

770 Teaching for Intelligence Conference
SkyLight
2626 S Clearbrook Drive
Arlington Heights, IL 60005
847-290-6600
800-348-4474
Fax: 877-260-2530
E-mail: info@irisskylight.com
http://www.iriskylight.com
Focuses on student achievement, brain-based learning and multiple intelligences.

April

771 Technology & Learning Schooltech Exposition & Conference

212-615-6030
http://www.SchoolTechExpo.com
Over 150 targeted sessions specifically designed for all education professionals: technology directors, teachers, principals, superintendents and district administrators.

772 Technology Student Conference
Technology Student Association
1914 Association Drive
Reston, VA 20191-1538
703-860-9000
Fax: 703-758-4852
http://www.tsawww.org
Devoted to the needs of technology education students and supported by educators, parents, and business leaders who believe in the need for a technologically literate society.

June
2,500 attendees
Rosanne White, Conference Manager

773 Technology in 21st Century Schools
National School Conference Institute
PO Box 37527
Phoenix, AZ 85069-7527
602-371-8655
Fax: 602-371-8790
http://www.nscinet.com
Conference will cover managing the Internet, literacy skills, Web Site designs, short and long term planning, creating curriculum, and staff development. Being held at the Boston Park Plaza Hotel in Boston, Massachusetts.

July

Alan November

774 Technology, Reading & Learning Difficulties Conference
International Reading Association
19 Calvert Court
Piedmont, CA 94611
510-594-1249
888-594-1249
Fax: 510-594-1838
http://www.trld.com
Focuses on ways to use technology for reading, learning difficulties, staff development, adult literacy, and more.

January

775 Training of Trainers Seminar
Active Parenting Publishers
810 Franklin Court SE
Suite B
Marietta, GA 30067-8943
770-429-0565
800-825-0060
Fax: 770-429-0334
E-mail: cservice@activeparenting.com
http://www.activeparenting.com
Delivers quality education programs for parents, children and teachers to schools, hospitals, social services organizations, churches and the corporate market.

Dana McKie, Training Coordinator

776 USC Summer Superintendents' Conference
University of Southern California, School of Ed.
Waite Room 901
Los Angeles, CA 90089-0001
213-740-2182
Fax: 213-749-2707
E-mail: lpicus@bcf.usc.edu
A select group of educational leaders nationwide engaged in reform practices offer discussions with nationally renowned speakers; tour innovative schools; and network with colleagues from the United States, Great Britain and Australia.

Lawrence O Picus, Conference Director
Carolyn Bryant, Conference Coordinator

Northeast

777 Clonlara School Annual Conference Home Educators
Clonlara Home Based Education Programs
1289 Jewett Street
Ann Arbor, MI 48104-6201
734-769-4511
Fax: 734-769-9629
E-mail: info@clonlara.org
http://www.clonlara.org
Clonlara School is committed to illuminating educational rights and freedoms through our actions and deep dedication to human rights and dignity.

June
300 attendees
Terri Wheeler, Associate Director

778 Connecticut Library Association
PO Box 85
Williamantic, CT 06226-0085
860-465-5006
Fax: 860-465-5004
E-mail: kmcnulty@avon.lib.ct.us
Holds a conference in April and publishes a journal.

April
1000 attendees and 100 exhibits
Karen McNulty, President
Mary Rupert, Manager

55

779 Hoosier Science Teachers Association Annual Meeting
5007 W 14th Street
Indianapolis, IN 46224-6503
317-244-7238
Fax: 317-486-4838
Papers, workshops, demonstrations and presentations in each area of science.
February
78 booths
Edward Frazer, Conference Contact

780 Illinois Library Association Conference
Illinois Library Association
33 W Grand Avenue
Suite 301
Chicago, IL 60610-4306
312-644-1896
Fax: 312-644-1899
E-mail: ila@ila.org
http://www.ila.org
More than 70 program sessions, exploring nearly every facet of library services, from building projects and professional recruitment to storytelling and the latest revisions of AACR2.
September
2,400+ attendees
Cyndi Robinson, Conference Manager
Bob Doyle, Executive Director

781 Illinois Vocational Association Conference
230 Broadway
Suite 150
Springfield, IL 62701-1138
217-585-9430
Fax: 217-544-0208
E-mail: iva@eosinc.com
Equipment and supplies, publications, teaching aids, computers and food services.
February
75 booths with 600 attendees
Karen Riddle, Conference Contact

782 National Association of Student Financial Aid Administrators
1129 20th Street NW
Suite 400
Washington, DC 20036-3453
202-785-0453
Fax: 202-785-1487
Exists to promote the professional preparation, effectiveness, and mutual support of persons involved in student financial aid administration.
May
40 booths
Suzy Allen, President

783 New Jersey School Boards Association Annual Meeting
413 W State Street
PO Box 909
Trenton, NJ 08605-0909
609-278-5233
Fax: 609-695-0413
School/office supplies, furniture, equipment, counseling services and more.
October
630 booths with 9,000 attendees
Wendy L. Wilson, Conference Contact

784 New York State Council of Student Superintendents Forum
111 Washington Avenue
Suite 104
Albany, NY 12210-2210
518-449-1063
Fax: 518-426-2229
Offers educational products and related services.
February
12 booths
Dr. Claire Brown, Conference Contact

785 Northeast Regional Christian Schools International Association
845 Silver Spring Plaza
Suite B
Lancaster, PA 17601-1183
717-285-3022
Fax: 717-285-2128
40 booths.
November
Alan Graustein, Conference Contact

786 Ohio Library Council Trade Show
35 E Gay Street
Suite 305
Columbus, OH 43215-3138
614-221-9057
Fax: 614-221-6234
Exhibits will offer products and services for library administrators and professionals.
May
Lori Hensley, Exhibits Manager

787 Ohio School Boards Association Capital Conference & Trade Show
700 Brooksedge Boulevard
Westerville, OH 43081-2820
614-891-6466
Provides school officials from Ohio an opportunity to gain information about products, equipment, materials and services.
November
425 booths
Richard Lewis, Conference Contact

788 Satellites and Education Conference
189 Schmucker Science Center
W Chester University
West Chester, PA 19383
610-436-1000
Fax: 610-436-2790
http://www.sated.org/eceos
The Satellite Educators Association was established in 1988 as a professional society to promote the innovative use of satellite technology in education and disseminate information nationally to all members.
March
15 booths with 200 attendees
Nancy McIntyre, Director

789 UNI Overseas Recruiting Fair
University of Northern Iowa
SSC #19
Cedar Falls, IA 50614-0390
319-273-2083
Fax: 319-273-6998
E-mail: overseas.placement@uni.edu
http://www.uni.edu/placement/overseas
About 160 recruiters from 120 schools in 80 countries recruit at this fair for certified K-12 educators.
February
Tracy Roling, Coordinator

790 Wisconsin Vocational Association Conference
44 E Mifflin Street
Suite 104
Madison, WI 53703-2800
608-283-2595
Fax: 608-283-2589
Trade and industry vendor equipment and book publishers.
April
50 booths
Linda Stemper, Conference Contact

Northwest

791 Montana High School Association Conference
1 S Dakota Street
Helena, MT 59601-5111
406-442-6010
School athletic merchandise.
January
15 booths
Dan Freund, Conference Contact

792 Nebraska School Boards Association Annual Conference
140 S 16th Street
Lincoln, NE 68508-1805
402-475-4951
Fax: 402-475-4961
60 booths exhibiting products and services directed at the public school market.
November
Burma Kroger, Conference Contact

793 North Dakota Vocational Educational Planning Conference
State Capitol
15th Floor
Bismarck, ND 58505
701-231-6032
Fax: 701-231-6052
August
30 booths
Ernest Breznay, Conference Contact

794 Pacific Northwest Library Association
Boise Public Library
715 Capitol Boulevard
Boise, ID 83702
208-384-4026
Fax: 208-384-4156
E-mail: sprice@pobox.ci.boise.id.us
Holds a conference in August and publishes a journal.
Susannah Price, President
Colleen Bell, Secretary

795 WA-ACTE Career and Technical Exhibition for Career and Technical Education
Washington Association for Career & Tech Education
PO Box 315
Olympia, WA 98507-0315
360-786-9286
Fax: 360-357-1491
E-mail: kal@wa-acte.org
http://www.wa-acte.org
August
40 booths with 1,000 attendees
Kathleen Lopp, Executive Director

Southeast

796 Association for Continuing Higher Education Conference
Trident Technical College
PO Box 118067
Charleston, SC 29423-8067
843-722-5546
Fax: 843-574-6470
15 tabletops.
October
Dr. Wayne Whelan, Executive VP

797 Center for Play Therapy Summer Institute
University of North Texas
PO Box 311337
Denton, TX 76203
940-565-3864
Fax: 940-565-4461
E-mail: cpt@coefs.coe.unt.edu
http://www.centerforplaytherapy.com
Encourage the unique development and emotional growth of children through the process of play therapy, a dynamic interpersonal relationship between a child and a therapist trained in play therapy procedures. The therapist provides the child with selected play materials and facilitates a safe relationship to express feelings, thoughts, experiences and behaviors through play, the child's natural medium of communication.
July
500 attendees
Garry Landreth PhD, Director

798 Missouri Library Association Conference
1306 Business 63 S
Suite B
Columbia, MO 65201
573-449-4627
Fax: 573-449-4655
E-mail: jmccartn@mail.more.net
http://www.mlnc.com/~mla/
The mission of the Missouri Library Network Corporation (MLNC) is to organize and deliver to its member libraries and other contracting entities OCLC-based information services, related electronic services and content, and training in the management and use of information.
October
75 booths with 400 attendees
Margaret Conroy, President
Jean Ann McCartney, Executive Director

799 National Youth-At-Risk Conference
Georgia Southern University
PO Box 8124
Statesboro, GA 30460
912-681-5557
Fax: 912-681-0306
Stresses education and development for professionals working with at-risk students.
February
Sybil Fickle, Conference Contact

800 Technology and Learning Conference
National School Boards Association
1680 Duke Street
Alexandria, VA 22314
703-838-6722
Fax: 703-683-7590
E-mail: info@nsba.org
http://www.nsba.org
This conference offers programs, equipment, services, and ideas. It will be held at the Dallas Convention Center.

Southwest

801 Children's Literature Festival
Department of Library Science
Sam Houston State University
PO Box 2236
Huntsville, TX 77341-2236
936-294-1614
Fax: 936-294-3780
This annual event is sponsored by the Department of Library Science at Sam Houston State University.

802 Colorado Library Association Conference
12081 W Alameda Parkway
Suite 427
Lakewood, CO 80228
303-463-6400
Fax: 303-431-9752
E-mail: executivedirector@cal-web.org
http://www.cal-webs.org
October
60 booths with 450 attendees
Beth Wrenn, President
Kathleen Noland, Executive Director

803 Phoenix Learning Resources Conference
12 W 31st Street
New York, NY 10001-4415
212-629-3887
800-221-1274
Fax: 212-629-5648
Supplemental and remedial reading and language arts programs for early childhood, K-12, and adult literacy programs.
Alexander Burke, President
John Rothermich, Executive VP

804 Southwest Association College and University Housing Officers
Sam Houston State University
PO Box 2416
Huntsville, TX 77341-2416
936-294-1812
Fax: 936-294-1920
Products and services for college and university housing.
Febuary/March
45 booths
E Thayne King, Conference Contact

805 Texas Classroom Teachers Association Conference
PO Box 1489
Austin, TX 78767-1489
512-477-9415
Fax: 512-469-9527
Educational materials, fundraising and jewelry.
February
150 booths
Jan Lanfear, Conference Contact

806 Texas Library Association Conference
3355 Bee Cave Road
Suite 401
Austin, TX 78746-6763
512-328-1518
800-580-2852
Fax: 512-328-8852
E-mail: pats@txla.org
http://www.txla.org
Established in 1902 to promote and improve library services in Texas.
March
750 booths with 6,000 attendees
Herman L Totten, President
Kathy Pustyovsky, Meetings Manager

807 Texas Vocational Home Economics Teachers Association Conference
3737 Executive Center Drive
Suite 210
Austin, TX 78731-1633
512-794-8370
July/August
Terry Green, Conference Contact

808 Western History Association Annual Meeting
University of New Mexico
Mesa Room 1080
Albuquerque, NM 87131-0001
505-277-5234
Fax: 505-277-6023
Exhibits by book sellers.
October
45 booths
Paul Hutton, Conference Contact

General

809 Accuracy Temporary Services Incorporated
1431 E 12 Mile Road
Madison Hieghts, MI 48071-2653
248-399-0220
Educational consultant for public and private schools.

Howard Weaver, President

810 Add Vantage Learning Incorporated
5430 LB Freeway
Suite 210
Dallas, TX 75240
214-503-6800
Fax: 214-503-6800
Management and educational consultant for the general public.

Jim Pepitone, Chairman

811 Advance Infant Development Program
2232 D Street
Suite 203
LaVerne, CA 91750-5409
909-593-3935
Fax: 909-593-7969
Business and educational consultant for general trade.

812 Aguirre International Incorporated
480 E 4th Avenue
Unit A
San Mateo, CA 94401-3349
650-373-4900
Fax: 650-348-0260
Educational, data, market analysis, statistical and research consultants for US Government Agencies.

Edward Aguirre, President

813 American International Schools
2203 Franklin Road SW
Roanoak, VA 24014-1109
852-233-3812
Fax: 852-233-5276
E-mail: asisadmin@ais.edu.hk
American International School is pledged to preparing students to contribute to an increasingly international and interdependent world. AIS strives to provide an atmosphere conducive to building interpersonal relationships and global awareness. AIS is committed to working closely with students and families to attian academic excellence and to inspire the growth of well-rounded individuals.

Andrew Hurst, President
Lewis C Smith Jr, Executive VP

814 Area Cooperative Educational Services
350 State Street
North Haven, CT 06473
203-498-6881
Fax: 203-498-6899
http://www.aces.k12.ct.us
ACES is the regional educational service center for twenty-five school districts in south central Connecticut.

Robert D Parker, Director/Public Information

815 Aspira of Penna
2726 N 6th Street
Philadelphia, PA 19133-2714
215-229-1226
Educational consultant for educational institutions.

Oscar Cardona, President

816 Association for Refining Cross-Cultured International
Japanese American Cultural Center
244 S San Pedro Street
Suite 505
Los Angeles, CA 90012
213-628-2725
Fax: 213-617-8576
E-mail: wong@jaccc.org
http://www.arcint.com
Educational consultants for international studies.

Chris Aihara, Executive Director
Thomas Lino, Chair

817 Association of Christian Schools International
PO Box 35097
Colorado Springs, CO 80935-3509
719-594-4612
Fax: 719-531-0631
E-mail: david_wilcox@acsi.org
http://www.acsi.org
Educational consultant for Christian Schools.

Ken Smitherman, President

818 Auerbach Central Agency for Jewish Education Incorporated
7607 Old York Road
Elkins Park, PA 19027-3010
215-635-8940
Fax: 215-635-8946
Educational consultants.

Helene Tigay, Executive Director

819 Basics Plus
921 Aris Avenue
Suite C
Metairie, LA 70005-2200
504-832-5111
Fax: 504-832-5110
Educational consultants.

Scott Green, President

820 Beacon Education Management
112 Turnpike Road
Suite 107
Westborough, MA 01581
508-836-4461
800-789-1258
Fax: 508-836-2604
http://www.beaconedu.com
A K-12, education services company that offers contracted management services to public schools and charter school boards. Currently operating 27 charter schools in Massachusetts, Michigan, Missouri and North Carolina.

821 Beverly Celotta
13517 Haddonfield Lane
Gaitherburg, MD 20878
301-330-8803
E-mail: drbev@comcast.net
http://www.celotta.net
Provides psychological and educational services to organizations that serve children and parents.

822 Bluegrass Regional Recycling Corporation
360 Thompson Road
Lexington, KY 40508-2045
859-233-7300
Fax: 859-233-7787
Consultants for educational, training, and services for governments and school systems.

Douglas Castle, Chairman

823 CPM Educational Program
1233 Noonan Drive
Sacramento, CA 95822-2569
916-446-9936
Fax: 916-444-5263
Educational and training consultants for school districts.

Brian Hoey, Executive Director

824 Caldwell Flores Winters
2187 Newcastle Avenue
Suite 201
Cardiff, CA 92007-1848
760-634-4239
800-273-4239
Fax: 760-436-7357
E-mail: cfw@cts.com
Offers educational counsel to school districts.

825 Career Evaluation Systems
1024 N Oakley Boulevard
Chicago, IL 60622-3586
773-645-1363
800-448-7552
Fax: 773-772-5010
Testing instruments for vocational evaluation.

826 Carnegie Foundation for the Advancement of Teaching
51 Vista Lane
Stanford, CA 94305
650-566-5100
Fax: 650-326-0278
Educational consultant for the educational field.

Jacquelyn Tate, Assistant to President

827 Carney Sandoe & Associates
136 Bolyston Street
Boston, MA 02116-4608
617-542-0260
Fax: 617-542-9400
Educational consultant for private schools.

James H Carney, Chairman/President

828 Carter/Tardola Associates
419 Pleasant Street
Suite 307
Beloit, WI 53511
608-365-3163
Fax: 608-365-5961
E-mail: tardola@tucm.net
Evaluates program, administration, staff, resource and time organization, and utilization of resources. Proposal development, language skills development, diversity training.

H Elizabeth Tardola, Educational Consultant

829 Center for Educational Innovation
28 W 44th Street
New York, NY 10036-6600
212-302-8800
Fax: 212-302-0088

Educational consultant for private and commercial accounts.

Steven Kaln, Director

830 Center for Professional Development & Services
408 N Union Street
Po Box 789
Bloomington, IN 47402-0789
812-339-1156
800-766-1156
Fax: 812-339-0018
E-mail: information@pdkintl.org
http://www.pdkintl.org
Examines school district curriculum management system. Determines how effectively a school district designs and delivers its curriculum.

Jo Ann Fujioka, President
John Amato, President-Elect

831 Center for Resource Management
200 International Drive
Suite 201
Portsmouth, NH 03801
603-427-0206
Fax: 603-427-6983
E-mail: info@crminc.com
Employment, human resources, educational, development, training, computer software, organizational and management consultants for Human Service Agencies and Educational Institutions/ Schools.

Mary Ann Lachat, Chairman

832 Child Like Consulting Limited
700 E Rambling Drive
Wellington, FL 33414-5010
Fax: 866-468-4555
Training in literacy, music, classroom and learning center management.

833 Children's Educational Opportunity Foundation
901 McClain Road
Suite 802
Bentonville, AR-9242
479-273-6957
Fax: 479-273-9362
Educational consultant for institutions.

Fritz Steiger, President

834 Childs Consulting Associates
514 Lakeside Drive
Mackinaw City, MI 49701
231-436-4099
Fax: 231-436-4101
E-mail: info@childs.com
http://www.childs.com
Educational, schools and technology consultants for schools, banking and automotive industries.

John W Childs, Chief Executive Officer
Jack Keck, Vice President

835 Classroom
245 5th Avenue
Room 1901
New York, NY 10016-8728
212-545-8400
Fax: 212-481-7178
http://www.classroominc.org
Technology based curriculum and teacher professional development for middle school and high school use.

Shari Bloom, VP

836 Coalition of Essential Schools
1814 Franklin Street
Suite 700
Oakland, CA 94612
510-433-1451
Fax: 510-433-1455
The Coalition of Essential Schools (CES) is a leading comprehensive school reform organization, fundamentally changing the way people think about teaching and learning and transforming American education.

Hudi Podolsky, Executive Director

837 College Bound
17777 Center Court Drive N
Suite 750
Cerritos, CA 90703
562-860-2127
Fax: 562-860-1957
E-mail: info@collegeboundca.org
http://www.collegeboundca.org
Educational consultants.

Johnnie Savoy, President
Cynthia Moore, Executive Assistant

838 College Entrance Examination Board
45 Columbus Avenue
New York, NY 10023-6917
212-713-8000
E-mail: emonts@umich.edu
http://www.collegeboard.com
Educational, research, testing and financial consultant for learning institutions and students.

Gaston Caperton, President
Lester P Monts, Chair

839 Community Connections
PO Box 1064
Athens, GA 30601
706-353-1375
Fax: 706-353-1375
Educational consultant for the general public.

Bess Clark, Director

840 Community Foundation for Jewish Education
618 S Michigan Avenue
10th Floor
Chicago, IL 60605-1901
312-913-1818
Fax: 312-913-1763
Educational consultant for the general public and schools.

Howard Swibel, President

841 Connecting Link
387 Coopers Pond Drive
Siute 1
Lawrenceville, GA 30044-5231
770-979-5804
Fax: 770-931-6831
Business and educational consultants for teachers.

Dr. Bernard F Cleveland, President

842 Conover Company
1789 N Oakwood Road
Oshkosh, WI 54904
920-231-4667
Fax: 920-231-4809
E-mail: sales@conovercompany.com
http://www.conovercompany.com
Training and setting up workplace literacy programs; emotional intelligence assesment and skill enhancement; func-

tional literacy software, career exploration and assessment software

Rebecca Schmitz, Member

843 Consortium on Reading Excellence
5855 Christie Avenue
Suite A
Emeryville, CA 94608-1923
510-595-4803
Educational consultant for public and private schools.

Bill Honing, President

844 Continuous Learning Group Limited Liability Company
500 Cherrington Corprate Center
Site 350
Pittsburgh, PA 15208
412-269-7240
Fax: 412-269-7247
E-mail: clginfo@clg.com
http://www.clg-online.com
Educational consultants.

Brian Caudill, Contact

845 Corporate Design Foundation
20 Park Plaza
Suite 400
Boston, MA 02116-4303
617-566-7676
E-mail: admin@cdf.org
Educational consultant for universities and colleges.

Peter G Lawrence, Chairman

846 Corporate University Enterprise
7600 Leesburg Pike West Building
Suite 202
Falls Church, VA 22043
703-848-0070
866-848-1675
Fax: 703-848-0071
Corporate University Enterprise,Inc. is and educational consulting firm designed to bring a strategic approach to workforce education in both private and public organizations. The company was incorporated in 1998 and has since served clinebts troughout the United States, Europe, and Asia.

John H. Wells, President

847 Council for Aid to Education
342 Madison Avenue
Room 1532
New York, NY 10173-1599
212-661-5800
Fax: 212-661-9766
Non-profit educational consultant for government and commercial concerns.

Roger Benjamin, President

848 Council on Occupational Education
41 Perimeter Center E
North East
Atlanta, GA 30346-1903
770-396-3898
800-917-2081
Fax: 770-396-3790
E-mail: bowmanh@council.org
http://www.council.org
Managerial and educational consultant for post secondary technical education institutions.

Dr. Harry Bowman, President
Cindy Sheldon, Manager

849 Creative Learning Consultants
1610 Brook Lynn Drive
Dayton, OH 45432-1906
937-427-0530
Educational consulting for school districts,
teachers, book stores and parents.
Nancy Johnson, President
Kathy Balsamo, VP

850 Creative Learning Systems
2065 S Escondido Blvd
Suite 108
Escondido, CA 92025
800-458-2880
Fax: 858-592-7055
E-mail:
info@creativelearningsystems.com
http://www.creativelearningsystems.com
Educational consulting firm.
Matt Dickstein, Chief Executive Officer

851 Dawson Education Cooperative
711 Clinton Street
Suite 201
Arkadelphia, AR 71923-5921
870-246-3077
Fax: 870-246-5892
E-mail: rds@dawson.dsc.k12.ar.us
Educational consulting group.

**852 Dawson Education Service
Cooperative**
711 Clinton Street
Suite 201
Arkadelphia, AR 71923-5921
870-246-3077
Fax: 870-246-5892
Educational and organizational consul-
tants for school districts
Patricia Lamb, Contact

853 Designs for Learning
2233 University Ave W
Suite 450
St. Paul, MN 55114-1634
651-645-0200
Fax: 651-645-0240
E-mail: dalley@designlearn.net
http://www,designlearn.net
Educational consultants for primary
schools and the private sector.
David Alley, President
Andrew Adelmann, Project Coordinator

**854 Direct Instructional Support
Systems**
623 High Street
Worthington, OH 43085-4146
614-846-8946
Fax: 614-846-1794
Educational consultant for public and pri-
vate agencies.
Dr Charles L Mand, President

855 Dr. Anthony A Cacossa
4300 N Charles Street
Apartment 9B
Baltimore, MD 21218-1052
410-889-1806
Fax: 410-889-1806
Assists schools in marketing academic pro-
grams that offer internship opportunities.

**856 EPIE InstituteEducational
Products Information Exchange
Institut**
103 West Montauk Highway
PO Box 590
Hampton Bays, NY 11946-4006
631-728-9100
E-mail: kkomoski@epie.org
http://www.epie.org
Curriculum development, training and
evaluation of education products.

857 EPPA Consulting
1116 Comanche Trail
Georgetown, KY 40324-1071
502-867-0157
Fax: 502-867-0157
E-mail: eppa@juno.com
Strategic and operational planning.
Theo R Leverenz, PhD, Contact

**858 East Bay Educational
Collaborative**
317 Market Street
Warren, RI 02885
401-245-4998
Fax: 401-245-9332
Business and educational consultant for
member school districts.
Gerald Kowalczyk, Executive Director

**859 East Central Educational Service
Center**
1601 Indiana Avenue
Connersville, IN 47331
765-825-1247
Fax: 765-825-2532
E-mail: harrison@ecesc.k12.in.us
http://www.ecesc.k12.in.us
Educational services for school districts in
East Central Indiana.
William J Harrison, Executive Director

860 Edge Learning Institute
2217 N 30th Street 200
Tacoma, WA 98403-3320
253-272-3103
Fax: 253-572-2668
Educational consultants for the general
public, commercial concerns, government
agencies and school districts.
Shauni Rock, Contact

861 Edison Schools
521 5th Avenue
15th Floor
New York, NY 10175
212-419-1600
Fax: 212-419-1604
http://www.edisonschools.com
The country's largest private manager of
public schools. Implemented its design in
79 public schools, including 36 charter
schools, which it operates under
mangement contracts with local school districts and charter school boards.

862 Education Concepts
9861 Strausser Street
Canal Fulton, OH 44614
330-497-1055
Fax: 330-966-8000
E-mail: info@ed-concepts.com
http://www.ed-concepts.com
Professional development programs for
early childhood educators.

863 Education Data
1305 E Waterman
Witchata, KS 67211
800-248-4135
Expertise in organizational needs assessments.

864 Education Development Center
55 Chapel Street
Newton, MA 02158
617-969-7100
Fax: 617-244-3436
http://www.edc.org
Developing programs in science, mathematics, reading, writing, health and special
education.

**865 Education Management Consulting
LLC**
Diamond Silver Office Complex
24 Arnett Avenue, Suite 102
Lambertville, NJ 08530
609-397-8989
800-291-0199
Fax: 609-397-1999
E-mail: edragan@edmgt.com
http://www.edmgt.com
Consultation for schools on special education and administration consultation for
lawyers working on education and school
related issues.
Dr. Edward F Dragan, President

866 Educational Consultants of Oxford
10431 Highway 51 S
Courtland, MS 38620
601-563-8954
All areas of educational information services, tutoring, scholarship information,
and non-traditional and overseas training.

867 Educational Credential Evaluators
PO Box 514070
Milwaukee, WI 53202
414-289-3400
Fax: 414-289-3411
E-mail: eval@ece.org
http://www.ece.org
Evaluates foreign educational credentials.
Laura Martinez, Marketing Specialist

868 Educational Data Service
236 Midland Avenue
Saddle Brook, NJ 07663-4604
973-340-8800
Fax: 973-340-0078
Educational and school consulting for
Boards of Education.
Robert F O'Connor, President
Gilbert Wohl, VP

**869 Educational Information &
Resource Center**
606 Delsea Drive
Sewell, NJ 08080
856-582-7000
Fax: 856-582-4206
E-mail: info@eirc.org
http://www.eirc.org
Programs and consulting services for
schools, on many topics from teaching
techniques to technical assistance.

870 Educational Resources
8910 W 62nd Terrace
Shawnee Mission, KS 66202-2814
913-362-4600
Fax: 913-362-4627

Educational consulting for colleges.

Michael Frost, President

Karen Harrison, VP

871 Educational Services Company

5730 W 74th Street
Indianapolis, IN 43278-1754
317-290-4100
Educational and management consulting for primary and secondary schools.

Douglas Cassman, President
William McMaster, Secretary

872 Educational Specialties

9923 S Wood Street
Chicago, IL 60643-1809
773-445-1000
Fax: 773-445-5574
Educational consultant for schools.

Elois W Steward, President

873 Educational Systems for the Future

14650 Viburnum Drive
Dayton, MD 21036
410-531-3737
Fax: 410-531-3939
E-mail: info@esf-protainer.com
http://www.esf-protainer,com
Development of teaching skills, training needs analysis, and training management.

874 Educational Technology Design Consultants

100 Allentown Parkway
Suite 110
Allen, TX 75002
972-727-1234
Fax: 972-727-1491
http://www.etdc.com/html/about_us.html
Developing system design for virtual campus control and support.

875 Educational Testing Service

Rosedale Road
Princeton, NJ 08541-0001
609-921-9000
Educational and professional consulting for schools.

Nancy S Cole, President
Sharon Robison, COO, Senior VP

876 Edusystems Export

820 Wisconsin Street
Walworth, WI 53184-9765
262-275-5761
Fax: 262-275-2009
E-mail: sales@edusystems.com;admin@edusystems.com
Expertise in educational systems.

877 Effective Schools Products

2199 Jolly Road
Suite 160
Okemos, MI 48864-5983
517-349-0941
Fax: 517-349-8852
Publishing consultants for schools, teachers, directors of planning and others in this field.

Ruth Lezotte, PhD, President

878 Effective Training Solutions

39355 California Street
Suite 207
Fremont, CA 94538-1447
510-797-6806
800-949-5035
Fax: 510-797-6805
E-mail: boris@trainingsuccess.com
http://www.trainingsuccess.com
Design and implementation of training strategies. Proficiency training-performance improvement training.

Ingrid Gudenas, CEO

879 Efficacy Institute

182 Felton Street
Waltham, MA 02453-4134
781-547-6060
Fax: 781-547-6077
E-mail: info@efficacy.org
http://www.efficacy.org
Non-profit, educational consultants for educational and community service institutions.

Jeff P Howard, President
Mike Hyter, Treasurer

880 Emerging Technology Consultants

216 Heritage Lane
New Brighton, MN 55112
651-639-3973
Fax: 651-639-3973
Serves as a connection between technology producers and the education and training industries.

Richard Pollak, Chief Executive Officer
Rubyanna Pollak, President

881 Epistemological Engineering

5269 Miles Avenue
Oakland, CA 94618-1044
510-653-3377
Fax: 510-428-1120
E-mail: publications@eeps.com
Educational consultants.

882 Examiner Corporation

600 Marshall Avenue
Suite 100
St. Paul, MN 55102-1723
651-451-7360
800-395-6840
E-mail: examine@xmn.com
http://www.xmn.com
Educational and certification evaluation instruments.

Gary C Brown, President
Michelle Smith, Sales and Marketing

883 Excell Education Centers

3807 Wilshire Boulevard
Los Angeles, CA 90010-3101
213-386-1953
Educational and planning consultants.

Raymond Hahl, Owner

884 FPMI Communications

707 Fiber Street NW
Huntsville, AL 35801-5833
256-539-1850
Fax: 256-539-0911
http://www.fmpi.com
Educational management consulting.

885 First District Resa

110 Zetterower Road
Statesboro, GA 30458-4257
912-842-5000
Fax: 912-842-5161

Educational consultants for the general public and commercial concerns.

Kay Brown, Executive Director

886 Foundation for Educational Innovation

401 M Street SW
2nd Floor, Suite 1
Washington, DC 20024-2610
202-554-7400
Fax: 202-554-7401
Educational consultant for educational/school systems.

Archie Prioleau, President

887 George Dehne & Associates

203 Overlook Drive
Brewster, NY 10509-3836
845-279-6674
Educational and business consultants for commercial concerns and colleges.

George Dehne, President

888 Health Outreach Project

825 Cascade Avenue
Atlanta, GA 30331-8362
404-755-6700
Educational consultants.

Sandra McDonald, President

889 Higher Education Consortium

2233 University Avenue W
Suite 210
St. Paul, MN 55104-1205
651-646-8831
Fax: 651-659-9421
Educational consultants.

Amy Sunderland, Executive Director

890 Highlands Program

PO Box 76168
Atlanta, GA 30358-3915
404-497-0835
Educational consultants for educational institutions, corporations and consumers.

Don Hutcheson, President

891 Howard Greene Associates

60 Post Road W
Westport, CT 06880-4208
203-226-4257
Fax: 203-226-5595
Educational consultants for school systems and individuals.

Howard Greene, President

892 Huntley Pascoe

19125 N Creek Parkway
Bothel, WA 98011-8035
425-485-0900
Fax: 425-487-1825
Educational consultant for architects, utility companies, computer facilities, school districts and hospitals.

Roger Huntley, President

893 Ingraham Dancu Associates

1265 Lakevue Drive
Butler, VA 16002
724-586-8761
Fax: 724-586-6638
E-mail: dedance@msn.com
Development planning for educational and industrial clients.

Dr. Daniel Dancu, Contact

894 Innovative Learning Group
410 Elgin Avenue
Suite F
Forest Park, IL 60130-1780
708-488-1099
Educational consultants for schools and the general public.
Joseph Elliott, President

895 Innovative Programming Systems
9001poplar Bridge Road
Bloomington, MN 55437
612-835-1290
Development of instructional and training programs.

896 Insight
12 S 6th Street
Suite 510
Minneapolis, MN 55402-1510
612-338-5777
Educational consultants for commercial concerns.
Mark Kovatch, President

897 Institute for Academic Excellence
901 Deming Way
Suite 101
Madison, WI 53717-1964
608-664-3880
Fax: 608-664-382
Educational consultants for K-12 schools.
Terrance D Paul, Chairman

898 Institute for Development of Educational Activities
259 Regency Ridge
Dayton, OH 45459
937-434-6969
Fax: 937-434-5203
E-mail: ideadayton@aol.com
http://www.idea.com
Assistance for administrators and teachers of elementary and secondary schools.

899 Institute for Global Ethics
11 Main Street
PO Box 563
Camden, ME 04843-1703
207-236-6658
Fax: 207-236-4014
E-mail: ethics@globalethics.org
http://www.globalethics.org
Educational consultants for the general public, corporations and educators.
Rushworth Kidder, President

900 Interface Network
321 SW 4th Avenue
Suite 502
Portland, OR 97204-2323
503-222-2702
Fax: 503-222-7503
E-mail: www.daggettt.com
http://info@leaderEd.com
Educational consultant for the United States Department of Education, businesses, school districts and other governmental agencies.

901 International Center for Leadership in Education
1587 Route 146
Rexford, NY 12148
518-399-2776
Fax: 518-399-7607
E-mail: info@leadered.com
Educational consultants for educational institutions, governments and commercial concerns.
Willard R Daggett, President

902 International Schools Association
Rue de Carouge 28
CH-1205, Geneva
Switzerland
39-011-645-967
Fax: 39-011-643-298
E-mail: info@isaschools.org
http://www.isaschools.org
Provides advisory and consultative services to its international and internationally minded member schools, as well as to other organizations in the field of education, such as UNESCO. The Association promotes innovations in international education, conducts conferences and workshops and publishes various educational materials.
Lisa Venegas, Executive Administrator

903 J&Kalb Associates
300 Pelham Road
Suite 5K
New Rochelle, NY 10805
914-636-6154
Consulting experience to school districts.

904 JCB/Early Childhood Education Consultant Service
813 Woodchuck Place
Bear, DE 19701
302-836-8505
Program design and cross-cultural staff development through seminars.

905 JJ Jones Consultants
1206 Harrison Avenue
Oxford, MS 38655-3904
662-234-6755
Educational consultant for high school and college students.
JJ Jones, Owner

906 JP Associates Incorporated
131 Foster Avenue
Valley Stream, NY 11580-4726
516-561-7803
Fax: 516-561-4066
Educational consultant for schools.
Jane Dinapoli, President

907 Janet Hart Heinicke
1302 W Boston Avenue
Indianola, IA 50125
515-961-8933
Fax: 515-961-8903
E-mail: heinicke@simpson.edu
Development of new programs and maintenance strategies.

908 Jobs for California Graduates
2525 O Street
Merced, CA 95340-3634
209-385-8466
Educational consultants for high school students.
Obie Obrien, Director

909 John McLaughlin Company
122 S Phillips Avenue
Suite 200
Sioux Falls, SD 57104
605-332-4900
Fax: 605-339-1662
http://www.mclaughlincompany.com
Advises companies regarding private-sector activities in K-12 and higher education.

910 Johnson & Johnson Associates
3970 Chain Bridge Road
Fairfax, VA 2030-3316
703-359-5969
Educational consultants for governmental agencies and commercial concerns.
Dr. Johnson Edosomwan, President/CEO

911 Joseph & Edna Josephson Institute
4640 Admiralty Way
Marina Del Ray, CA 90292-6621
310-306-1868
Fax: 310-827-1864
Educational consultant for organizations, government, businesses and the general public.
Michael Josephson, President

912 Kaludis Consulting Group
1710 Rhode Island Avenue
Suite 400
Washington, DC 20036
202-331-3650
Fax: 202-331-1428
E-mail: info@kaludisconsulting.com
http://www.kaludisconsulting.com
Educational consultants for colleges and universities.
George Kaludis, President/Chairman
Barry M Cohen, Senior Vice President

913 Kentucky Association of School Administrators
152 Consumer Lane
Suite 154
Frankfort, KY 40601-8489
502-875-3411
Fax: 502-875-4634
Educational consultant for school administrators.
V Wayne Young, Director

914 Kleiner & Associates
8441 SE 68th Street
Suite 296
Mercer Island, WA 98040-5235
206-236-0608
Educational consultants for public and private institutions.
Charles Kleiner, Owner

915 Lawrence A Heller Associates
324 Freeport Road
Pittsburgh, PA 15238-3422
412-820-0670
Fax: 412-820-0669
Development and implementation of educational programs.

916 Leona Group
4660 S Hagadorn Road
Suite 500
East Lansing, MI 48823-5353
517-333-9030
Fax: 517-333-4559
http://www.leonagroup.com
Currently manages more than 40 school sites in Michigan, Arizona, Ohio and Indiana

917 Linkage
16 New England Executive Park
Burlington, MA 01803-7305
781-402-5400
Fax: 781-402-5556
E-mail: info@linkage-inc.com
http://www.linkageinc.com

Linkage, Inc. is a global organizational development company that specializes in leadership development.

Philip Harkins, President

918 Logical Systems
411 E 2nd Street
Rome, GA 30161-3109
706-234-9896
Fax: 706-290-0998
Educational consultants for school districts.

Francis Ranwez, President

919 Los Angeles Educational Alliance for Restructuring Now
445 S Figueroa Street
Los Angeles, CA 90071
323-255-3276
Fax: 213-626-5830
E-mail: asant@ccf-la.org
Educational consulting for school systems.

Mary Chambers, Vice President
Michael Roos, President

920 Louisiana Children's Research Center for Development & Learning
208 S Tyler Street
Suite A
Covington, LA 70433-3036
504-893-7777
Fax: 985-893-5443
Educational consultants for the general public.

Alice P Thomas, Executive Director

921 MK & Company
132 Bronte Street
San Francisco, CA 94110
415-826-5923
Program development and project management for educational products, services and organizations.

922 MPR Associates
2150 Shattuck Avenue
Suite 800
Berkeley, CA 94704-1321
510-849-4942
Fax: 510-849-0794
Educational consultants for governmental, educational and commercial concerns including law firms.

E Gareth Hoachlander, President

923 Magi Educational Services Incorporated
7-11 Broadway
Suite 402
White Plains, NY 10601-3546
914-682-1969
Fax: 914-682-1760
http://www.westchesterinst.org
Educational consultant for educational institutions.

Dr. Ronald Szczypkowski, President

924 Management Concepts
8230 Leesburg Pike
Suite 800
Vienna, VA 22182-2639
703-790-9595
Fax: 703-790-1371
E-mail:
csmith@managementconcepts.com
http://www.managementconcepts.com

Educational consultants for commercial and governmental concerns.

Cynthia E Smith, Corporate Director Marketing

925 Management Simulations
540 W Frontage Road
Winnetka, IL 60093-1250
847-441-9041
Fax: 847-441-9044
Educational consultants for comercial concerns and universities.

Daniel Smith, President

926 Marketing Education Resource Center
1375 King Avenue
PO Box 12279
Columbus, OH 43212-2220
800-448-0398
Fax: 614-486-1819
http://www.mark-ed.com
Educational, development and curriculum consulting for high schools and post secondary schools.

927 Maryland Educational Opportunity Center
2700 Gwynns Falls
Baltimore, MD 21216
410-728-3400
800-636-6396
Fax: 410-523-6340
Consultant services for educational institutions.

928 Maryland Elco Incorporated Educational Funding Company
4740 Chevy Chase Drive
Chevy Chase, MD 20815-6461
301-654-8677
Fax: 301-654-7750
Educational, accounting and billing consultants for service and vocational schools and businesses.

Nicholas Peter Cokinos, Chairman

929 Mason Associates
142 N Mountain Avenue
Montclair, NJ 07042
201-744-9143
Educational services for independent secondary schools, colleges and universities.

930 Matrix Media Distribution
28310 Roadside Drive
Suite 237
Agoura, CA 91301-4951
818-865-3470
Educational consultant for the educational market.

Paul Luttrell, President

931 McKenzie Group
1100 17th Street NW
Suite 1100
Washington, DC 20036-4638
202-466-1111
Fax: 202-466-3363
Educational consultant for commercial concerns and government.

Floretta D McKenzie, President

932 Measurement
423 Morris Street
Durham, NC 27701-2128
919-683-2413
Fax: 919-683-1531

Educational, research, testing and printing consultant for schools, state governments and private businesses.

Henry H Scherich, President/CEO

933 Measurement Learning Consultants
80920 Highway 10
Tolovana Park, OR 97145
503-436-1464
Business, educational, testing and development consultants for the general public and commercial concerns such as schools.

Albert G Bennyworth, Partner

934 Merrimack Education Center
101 Mill Road
Chelmsford, MA 01824-4844
978-256-3985
Fax: 978-256-6890
Educational consultant for educational facilities.

John Barranco, Executive Director

935 Michigan Education Council
40440 Palmer Road
Canton, MI 48188-2034
734-729-1000
Educational consultant for individuals.

Dawud Tauhidi, Director

936 Midas Consulting Group
4600 S Syracuse Street
Suite 900
Denver, CO 80237
303-256-6500
Fax: 866-790-9500
E-mail: info@midasconsultinggroup.com
http://www.midasconsultinggroup.com
Educational consultant for schools, universities,training centers and government agencies.

Michael Blimes, Executive Consultant

937 Miller, Cook & Associates
1316 2nd Street SW
Roanoke, VA 24016-4923
540-345-4393
Educational consultants for colleges and universities.

William B Miller, President

938 Model Classroom
4095 173rd Place SW
Bellvue, WA 98008-5929
425-746-0331
Educational consultant for school districts, commercial concerns and the Department of Education.

Cheryl Avena, Owner

939 Modern Educational Systems
15 Limestone Terrace
Ridgefield, CT 06877-2621
203-431-4144
Educational consultant for schools.

Edward T McCormick, President

940 Modern Red Schoolhouse Institute
1901 21st Avenue
South Nashville, TN 37212-1502
888-275-6774
Fax: 615-320-5366
Educational consultant for school districts.

Sally B Kilgore, President

941 Montana School Boards Association
1 S Montana Avenue
Helena, MT 59601-5156
406-442-2180
Fax: 406-442-2194
Training, educational and school districts consultant for school boards.

Karen Richardson, President

942 Montgomery Intermediate Unit 23
1605 W Main Street
Suite B
Norristown, PA 19403-3268
610-539-8550
Fax: 610-539-7411
Educational consultants for professional associations, groups and student organizations.

Len Gircoski

943 Moore Express
865 Pancheri Drive
Idaho Falls, ID 83402
208-523-6276
Educational consultant for public school districts, state and local governments and commercial concerns.

Lawry Wilde, President

944 Mosaica Education
2 Penn Plaza
Suite 1500
New York, NY 10121
212-292-5080
Fax: 212-232-0309
http://www.mosaicaeducation.com
Manages public schools either under contract with local school districts or funded directly by states under charter school laws that permit private management.

945 Multicorp
1912 Avenue K
Suite 210
Plano, TX 75074-5960
972-551-8899
Computer and educational consultant.

Fred Sammet, Chairman

946 National Center on Education & the Economy
700 11th Street NW
Suite 750
Washington, DC 20001-4507
202-783-3668
Fax: 202-783-3672
Educational consultant for schools.

Marc S Tucker, President

947 National Evaluation Systems
30 Gatehouse Road
PO Box 226
Amherst, MA 01004
Fax: 413-256-8221
Educational testing, test development, and assessment for education agencies.

948 National Heritage Academies
3850 Broadmoor Avenue SE
Suite 201
Grand Rapids, MI 49512
877-223-6402
Fax: 616-575-6801
E-mail: info@heritageacademies.com
http://www.heritageacademies.com
Manages 22 charter academies (K-8) in Michigan and North Carolina.

2007, Author

949 National Reading Styles Institute
PO Box 737
Syosset, NY 11791
516-921-5500
800-331-3117
Fax: 516-921-5591
E-mail: readingstyle@nrsi.com
http://www.nrsi.com
Educational consultants for schools and educators.

Marie Carbo, Executive Director

950 National School Safety and Security Services
PO Box 110123
Cleveland, OH 44111
216-251-3067
E-mail: kentrump@aol.com
http://www.schoolsecurity.org
National consulting firm specializing in school security and crisis preparedness training, security assessments, and related safety consulting for K-12 schools, law enforcement, and other youth safety providers.

Kenneth S Trump, President/CEO

951 Noel/Levitz Centers
2101 Act Circle
Iowa City, IA 52245-9581
319-337-4700
Fax: 319-337-5274
Educational consultant for colleges and universities.

Tom Williams, President/CEO

952 Ome Resa
2023 Sunset Boulevard
Steubenville, OH 43952-1349
740-283-2050
Fax: 740-283-2709
Educational consultants for school districts.

Craige Klausser, Executive Director

953 Oosting & Associates
200 Seaboard Lane
Franklin, TN 37067-8237
615-771-7706
Fax: 615-771-7810
Educational consultants for colleges and universities.

Dr. Kenneth Oosting, President

954 Pamela Joy
1049 Whipple Avenue
Suite A
Redwood City, CA 94062-1414
650-368-9968
Fax: 650-368-2794
Educational consultants for schools.

Pamela Joy, Owner

955 Parsifal Systems
155 N Craig Street
Pittsburgh, PA 15213
412-682-8080
Fax: 412-682-6291
Educational consultants for commercial concerns and schools.

Marcia Morton, President

956 Paul H Rosendahl, PHD
204 Waianuenue Avenue
Hilo, HI 96720-2445
808-935-5233
Fax: 808-961-6998
Science, archaeology, historical, resouces and management consultant for develop-

ers, government agencies, educational institutions, groups and individuals.

Paul H Rosendahl, Owner

957 Perfect PC Technologies
15012 Red Hill Avenue
Tustin, CA 92780-6524
714-258-0800
Computer consultants for commercial concerns, schools and institutions.

Neil Lin, President

958 Performa
124 N Broadway
De Pere, WI 54115
920-336-9929
Fax: 920-336-2899
E-mail: jeffk@performaic.com
http://www.performainc.com
Planning and facility consultants for higher education, manufacturing and government agencies.

Jeff Kanzelberger, CEO
Doug Page, Chief Operating Officer

959 Poetry Alive!
70 Woodfin Place
Suite WW4C
Asheville, NC 28801
828-255-7636
800-476-8172
Fax: 828-232-1045
E-mail: poetry@poetryalive.com
http://www.poetryalive.com
Educational consultants for commercial concerns and school systems.

Bob Falls, President

960 Post Secondary Educational Assistance
1210 20th Street S
Suite 200
Birmingham, AL 35205-3814
205-930-4900
Fax: 205-930-4905
Educational consultant for commercial concerns.

John K Jones, President

961 Prevention Service
7614 Morningstar Avenue
Harrisburg, PA 17112-4226
717-651-9510
Educational consultant for corporations, private health clubs, school districts and other organizations.

Mark Everest, President

962 Princeton Review
2315 Broadway
2nd Floor
New York, NY 10024-4332
212-874-8282
Fax: 212-874-0775
Educational consultants for commercial concerns.

John Katzman, President

963 Priority Computer Services
53779 Generations Drive
Suite B
South Bend, IN 46635
574-236-5979
E-mail: priority@pcserv-inc.com
Computer consultant for commercial education.

Ben Hahaj, President

964 Prism Computer Corporation
2 Park Plaza
Suite 1060
Irvine, CA 92614-8520
800-774-7622
Fax: 949-553-6559
Educational consultant for manufacturers, government agencies and colleges.

Micheal A Ellis, President

965 Professional Computer Systems
849 E Greenville Avenue
Winchester, IN 47394-8441
765-584-2288
Fax: 765-584-1283
Computer consultants for businesses, schools and municipalities.

Mark Burkhardt, President

966 Professional Development Institute
280 S County Road
Suite 427
Longwood, FL 32750-5468
407-834-5224
Educational consultants for US Department of Transportation and commercial concerns.

Elsom Eldridge, Jr, President

967 Profiles
507 Highland Avenue
Iowa City, IA 52240-4516
319-354-7600
Fax: 319-354-6813
Educational consultants for school districts and commercial concerns.

Douglas Paul, President

968 Pyramid Educational Consultants
13 Garfield Way
Newark, DE 19713
302-368-2515
Fax: 302-368-2516
E-mail: pyramid@pecs.com
http://www.pecs.com
Educational consultant for general trade, historical commissions and other public bodies.

Andrew Bondy, President
Lori Frost, Vice President

969 Quality Education Development
41 Central Park West
New York, NY 10023
212-724-3335
800-724-2215
Fax: 212-724-4913
E-mail: info@qedconsulting.com
Structures courses that promote knowledge and understanding through interactive learning, and communication programs.

970 Quantum Performance Group
5050 Rushmore Road
Palmyra, NY 14522-9414
315-986-9200
Educational consultant for commercial concerns, including schools.

Dr. Mark Blazey, President

971 Rebus
4111 Jackson Road
Ann Arbor, MI 48103-1827
734-668-4870
Fax: 734-913-4750
Educational consultant for schools and school districts.

Linda Borgsdorf, President

972 Records Consultants
10826 Gulfdale Street
San Antonio, TX 78216-3607
210-366-4127
Fax: 210-366-0776
Educational consultant for school districts and municipalities.

Lang Glotfelty, President

973 Regional Learning Service of Central New York
3049 E Genesee Street
Suite 211
Syracuse, NY 13224-1644
315-446-0500
Fax: 315-446-5869
Educational consultants for commercial concerns.

Rebecca Livengood, Executive Director

974 Reinventing Your School Board
Aspen Group International,Inc
PO Box 260301
Highlands Ranch, CO 80163-0301
303-478-0125
Fax: 208-248-6084

Linda Dawson, Contact
Dr. Randy Quinn, Contact

975 Relearning by Design
447 Forcina Hall
PO Box 7718
Ewing, NJ 08628-0718
609-771-2921
Fax: 609-637-5130
E-mail: info@relearning.org
http://www.relearning.org

Grant Wiggins, Author/Editor
Julia Meneghin, Operations Manager

976 Research Assessment Management
816 Camarillo Springs Road
Camarillo, CA 93012-9441
805-987-5538
Fax: 805-987-2868
Educational consultants for governmental agencies and commercial concerns.

Adrienne McCollum, PhD, President

977 Robert E Nelson Associates
120 Oak Brook Center
Suite 208
Oak Brook, IL 60523
630-954-5585
Fax: 630-954-5606
Consulting for private colleges, universities and secondary schools.

978 Rookey Associates
1740 Little York Xing
Little York, NY 13087
607-749-2325
Educational consultant for school districts, public utility companies and the government.

Ernest J Rookey, President

979 Root Learning
810 W S Boundary Street
Perrysburg, OH 43551-5200
419-874-0077
Fax: 419-874-4801
Business, educational, employment consultant for commercial concerns.

Randall Root, Chairman/CEO

980 School Management Study Group
1649 Lone Peoh Drive
Salt Lake City, UT 84117
801-277-3725
Fax: 801-277-4547
Organization seeking to promote improvement of schools and to involve educators in critical school problems.

Donald Thomas, President
Dale Holden, Associate

981 SchoolMatch by Public Priority Systems
Blendonview Office Park
6167 Deeside Drive
Dublin, OH 43017
614-890-1573
Fax: 614-764-4709
E-mail: bainbridge@schoolmatch.com
http://www.schoolmatch.com
Stategies and information systems for working with public and private schools.

William L Bainbridge, President/CEO
Steve M Sundre, Executive Vice President

982 Sensa of New Jersey
110 Mohawk Trail
Wayne, NJ 07470-5030
973-831-1757
An educational consultant for private and public schools.

John Pinto, President

983 Shirley Handy
19860 Bloss Avenue
Hilmar, CA 95324-8308
209-668-4142
Fax: 209-668-1855
Educational consultants for school districts and teachers.

Shirley Handy, Owner

984 Sidney Kreppel
704 E Benita Boulevard
Vestal, NY 13850-2629
607-754-6870
Educational consultants.

Sidney Kreppel, Owner

985 Solutions Skills
519 1/2 E Tennessee Street
Tallahassee, FL 32308-4981
850-681-6543
Fax: 850-681-6543
Business and educational consultants for state and governments, educational, medical and legal publishing companies.

Randall Vickers, President

986 Special Education Service Agency
2217 E Tudor Road
Suite 1
Anchoage, AK 99507-1068
907-562-7372
Fax: 907-562-0545
http://www.isbe.net
Educational consultant for school districts.

Anthony Sims, State Director Special Edu

987 Sports Management Group
918 Parker Street
Suite A-13
Berkelly, CA 94710
510-849-3090
Fax: 510-849-3094
E-mail: tsmq@sportsmqmt.com
Educational consulting for universities.

Lauren Livingston, President

988 Stewart Howe Alumni Service of New York
3109 N Triphammer Road
Ithaca, NY 14882
607-533-9200
Educational consultants for college organizations.

Peter McChesney, Director

989 Strategies for Educational Change
11 Whitby Court
Mount Holly, NJ 08060
609-261-1702
E-mail: barbd@prodigy.net
Development of programs for youths at risk.

990 Success for All Foundation
200 W Towsontown Boulevard
Baltimore, MD 21204-5200
410-616-2372
800-548-4998
Fax: 410-324-4444
E-mail: sfainfo@successforall.net
http://www.successforall.net
A not-for-profit organization dedicated to the development, evaluation and dissemination of proven reform models for preschool, elementary and middle schools.

Mary Thuman, Contact

991 Teachers Curriculum Institute
E170 E Meadow Drive
Palo Alto, CA 94303-4234
650-856-0565
Fax: 800-343-6828
Educational consultant for schools and teachers.

Bert Bower, President

992 Teachers Service Association
1107 E Lincoln Avenue
Orange, CA 92865-1939
714-282-6342
Educational consultants for schools and teachers.

Richard Ghysels, Secretary Treasurer

993 Tech Ed Services
8255 Firestone Boulevard
Suite 300
Downey, CA 90241
562-869-1913
800-832-4411
Fax: 562-869-5673
E-mail: info@techedservices.com
http://techedservices.com
Computer, planning and training consultant for k-12 educators and adult educators.

Patricia K Sanford, President
Brenna Terrones, Corporate Specialists

994 Technical Education Research Centers
2067 Massachusetts Avenue
Cambridge, MA 02140-1340
617-547-0430
Fax: 617-349-3535
Educational consultant for the National Science Foundation and the Department of Education.

Arthur Nelson, Chairman

995 Tesseract Group
3820 E Ray Raod
Suite 2
Phoenix, AZ 85044
480-706-2500
http://www.tesseractgroup.org

An integrated education management company, serving private and public charter elementary, middle and high schools in six states.

996 Timothy Anderson Dovetail Consulting
936 Nantasket Avenue
Hull, MA 02045-1453
781-925-3078
Fax: 781-925-9830
Educational consultant for businesses.

Eric Anderson, Owner

997 University Research
7200 Wisconsin Avenue
Bethesda, MD 20814-4811
301-654-8338
Fax: 301-941-8427
Educational consultants for the federal government along with other government and private sectors.

Melvin Estrin, CEO

998 University of Georgia-Instructional Technology
G-3 Aderhold Hall
Athens, GA 30602
706-542-6446
Fax: 706-542-0360
E-mail: coeinfo@uga.edu
http://www.coe.uga.edu
Instructional design and development.

Louis A Castenell, Dean
Pedro R Portes, Professor

999 Uplinc
48 Capital Drive
West Springfield, MA 01089
413-693-0700
E-mail: sales@uplinc.com
http://www.uplinc.com
Computer consultants for commercial, general public and educational concerns.

Ron Marino, President

1000 William A Ewing & Company
505 S Main Street
Suite 700
Orange, CA 92868
714-245-1850
Fax: 714-456-1755
E-mail: ewingo@aol.com
http://www.members.aol.com/ewingo
Expertise in compensation and classification.

1001 Wisconsin Technical College System Foundation
1 Foundation Circle
Waunakee, WI 53597-8914
608-849-2424
Fax: 608-849-2468
Educational consultant for educational institutions and businesses.

Loren Brumm, Executive Director

Africa

1002 Alexandra House School
King George V Avenue
Floreal
Mauritius
230-696-4108
Alexandra House is an English language primary school following British/international curriculum catering for Expatriate and Mauritian pupils. Enrollment consists of 100 day students (50 boys; 50 girls), in grades K-6.

M Wrenn-Beejadhur, Principal

1003 American International School-Dhaka
United Nations Road
Dhaka
Bangladesh
880-2-882-2414
Fax: 880-2-883-3175
E-mail: wplotkin@ais-dhaka.net
http://www.ais-dhaka.net
An independent, coeducational day school which offers an educational program from prekindergarten through grade 12 for students of all nationalities.

Walter Plotkin, Superintendent

1004 American International School-Johannesburg
Private Bag X 4
Bryanston 2021
South Africa
27-11-464-1505/6
Fax: 27-11-464-1327
E-mail: lthiessen@aisj-jhb.com
http://www.aisj-jhb.com
Ensure all of our students are inspired life-long learners, motivated global contributors and empowered seekers of personal fulfillment.

Lory Thiessen, Principal

1005 American International School-Lom,
US Embassy Department of State
Washington, DC 20521-2300
E-mail: aisl@cafe.tg
http://www.state.gov/www/about_state/schools/olome.html
Established in 1967 as a private, coeducational day school offering an educational program to students of all nationalities in pre-kindergarten through grade 8.

Geri Branch, Director

1006 American International School-Zambia
2310 Lusaka Place
Washington, DC 20521-2310
260-1-260-50/10
Fax: 260-1-260-538
E-mail: ais@aislusaka.org
http://www.aislusaka.org
Grade levels prekindergarten through twelfth/ enrollment total 220.

Tom Walters, Director

1007 American School of Kinshasa
TASOK/Kinshasa,c/o Panalpina World Transport, Bldg 743,Zone Brucargo, 1931
Zaventem, Brussels, Belguim
243-884-6619
Fax: 243-884-1161
E-mail: bertpbedford@yahoo.com

Grade levels K-12, school year August-June
Bert Bedford, Superintendent
Fiona M Merali, Business Manager

1008 American School-Tangier
Rue Christophe Colomb
Tangier 9000
Morocco
212-39 93 98 27/28
Fax: 212-39 94 75 35
E-mail: ast@tangeroise.net.ma
An independent, coeducational day and boarding school which offers an educational program from prekindergarten through grade 12 for students of all nationalities.

1009 American School-Yaounde
BP 7475
Yaounde
Cameroon
237-223-0421
Fax: 237-223-6011
E-mail: school@asoy.or
Provides highest quality international educational oppurtunities within a nurturing environment that expects students to develop these attributes: excellence in all endeavors, self-discipline, tolerance, creativity, responsibility and a spirit of inquiry and a clear sense of world citizenship.

Nanci Shaw, School Director

1010 Arundel School
PO Box MP 91 Mount Pleasant
Harere
Zimbabwe
263-4-335654/5/6/7
Fax: 335671
E-mail: head@arundel.ac.zw
http://www.arundel.ac.zw/about_our_school
Gives all students the opportunity to reach their full potential, both in and out of the classroom. This is achieved through an active educational program, which encompasses the search for excellence in the fields of academic endeavour, culture, sports and personal development.

G Alcock, Principal

1011 Arusha International School
Po Box 733
Kilimanjaro
Tanzania
255-27-275-5004
Fax: 255-27-275-2877
E-mail: ceo@ismoshi.org
Offers a fully accredited, academically rigorous international education for students of ages three to nineteen years old.

Barry Sutherland, Principal

1012 Asmara International Community School
PO Box 4941
Asmara
Eritrea
291-1-161-705
Fax: 291-1-161-705
E-mail: pjohnston898@yahoo.com
Grade levels pre K-12.

Paul Johnston, Director

1013 Banda School
PO Box 24722
Nairobi
Kenya
254-020-891220
Fax: 254-020-890004
E-mail: bandaschool@swiftkenya.com
Meet the educational needs of children living in and around Nairobi whose parents required a Preparatory School education for their children but who did not wish them to go to boarding school overseas.

Norman Farmer, Principal

1014 Bishop Mackenzie International Schools
PO Box 102
Lilongwe
Malawi
265-1-756-364
Fax: 265-1-751-374
E-mail: info@bmismw.com
International, coeducational day schools which offer an educational program from kindergarten through grade 11 for pupils of all nationalities.

Peter Todd, Director

1015 Braeburn High School
Kisongo Campus
PO Box 45112
Nairobi
Kenya
254-20-3872572
Fax: 254-2-862450
E-mail: ken@bhs.braeburn.ac.uk
Boarding school

Ivor Dougan, Principal

1016 Braeburn School
PO Box 45112
Nairobi
Kenya
254-2-572572
Fax: 254-2-572310
E-mail: primary@braeburn.ac.ke
Provides opprtunities for all children from the early years to the age of 8.

RE Diaper, Principal

1017 British International School Cairo
PO Box 9057
Nasr City, Cairo
Egypt
002-02-758-2881
Fax: 002-02-758-1390
E-mail: info@ncbis.org
Prepares international students for grade level A exams ages 16-18.

Kirsten Rockingham

1018 British School-Lom,
BP 20050
Lome
Togo
228-226-46-06
Fax: 228-226-49-89
E-mail: bsl@cafe.tg
http://www.bsl.tg
This school offers an English based curriculum for 120 day students and 95 boarding students (110 boys; 105 girls), ages 4-18. The school is an independent, co-educational day and boarding school. External exams from the University of London and Cambridge-UK plus International Baccalaureate (IB) is offered. Applications needed to teach include science, pre-school, French, math, social sciences, administration, Spanish, reading, German, English and physical education.

1019 British Yeoward School
Parque Taoro Puerto de la Cruz
Tenerife
Spain
00-34-922-384685
Fax: 00-34-922-37-35-65
E-mail: head@yeowardschool.org
Provides a hogh quality British education for children of all ages in an open multi-cultural environment.

Christopher Black, Head Of Primary

1020 Broadhurst Primary School
Pvt Bag BR 114 Broadhurst
Garborone
Botswana
267-3971-221
Fax: 267-307987
E-mail: headmaster@botsnet.bw
International primary school which children can develop to their full potenial and aquire the knowledge and skills to equip them for living.

Rehana Khan, Principal

1021 Brookhouse Preparatory School
PO Box 24987
Nairobi
Kenya
254-89-46-41-89
E-mail: headmaster@brookschool.com
Provides eduacation in general computer literacy.

Eric Mulind, School Coordinator

1022 Cairo American College
PO Box 39
Digla, Maadi, 11431 Cairo
Egypt
20-2-755-5505
E-mail: support@tc.cac.edu.eg
http://www.cac.edu.eg
Grade levels K-12, school year August-June

1023 Casablanca American School
Amercian Embassy, PSC 74, Box 024
APO AE 09718
Morocco
212-22-214-115
Fax: 212-22-212-488
E-mail: cas@cas.ac.ma
http://www.cas.ac.ma
An independent, university-preparatory, coeducational day school which offers American and International Baccalaureate oriented education from nursery through grade 12.

Allen Hughes, Director

1024 Cavina School
PO Box 43090
Nairobi
Kenya
254-2-577079
Fax: 254-2-566676
E-mail: cavina@iconnect.co.ke
British preparatory school for children aged 3 to thirteen.

RA Massie-Blomfield, Headmaster

1025 Dakar Academy
BP 3189, Rue des Maristes
Dakar
Senegal
221-832-0682
Fax: 221-832-1721
E-mail: daoffice@telecomplus.sn
http://www.dakaracademy.com

Grade levels kindergarten through twelfth, enrollment 160.

Floyd Celi, Director

1026 Greensteds School
Private Bag
Nakuru
Kenya
037-850024
Fax: 037-851248
An international school for boys and girls.

R Albon, Principal

1027 Harare International School
66 Pendennis Road
Harare
Zimbabwe
263-4-883-336
Fax: 263-4-883-371
E-mail: his@his.ac.zw
http://www.his.ac.zw
Grade levels prekindergarten through twelfth, with enrollment of 376.

Paul Poore, Director

1028 Hillcrest Secondary School
PO Box 24819
Nairobi
Kenya
254-20-882-222
Fax: 254-20-882-350
Mixed boarding school.

Christopher Drew, Head Teacher

1029 International Community School-Addis Ababa
PO Box 70282
Addis Adaba
Ethiopia
251-11-371-0722
Fax: 251-11-371-1544
E-mail: info@icsaddis.edu.et
http://www.icsaddisababa.org
An independent, coeducational day school which offers an educational program from prekindergarten through grade 12 for students of all nationalities.

Paul Olson, Director

1030 International School-Kenya
PO Box 14103
Nairobi
Kenya
254-20-418-3622
Fax: 254-20-418-3272
E-mail: isk_admin@isk.ac.ke
http://www.isk.ac.ke
Students from many backgrounds go to this school, which prepares them for successful transitions to other schools and universities around the world, offering both a North American Hogh School Diploma as well as the International Baccalaureate Diploma to its graduates.

Stephen Plisinski, Director

1031 International School-Moshi
PO Box 733
Moshi
Tanzania
255-27-275-5004
Fax: 255-27-275-2877
E-mail: ceo@ismoshi.org
http://www.ecis.org
This international school offers a curriculum in English for 360 day students and 70 boarding students (215 boys and 215 girls), in grades K-12. Teaching applications must be received by January for an August start date. The length of stay is two years and

housing is provided. Applications needed to teach include science, math, social sciences, French, English and physical education. Student/teacher ratio is 10:1.

Geoff Lloyd, Headmaster
Keiron White, Deputy Head

1032 International School-Tanganyika
United Nations Road
PO Box 2651, Dar es Salaam
Tanzania
255-51-151-817-8
Fax: 255-51-152-077
E-mail: ist@raha.com
http://www.istafrica.com
A private, coeducational school which offers PreK-12 and hosts 1,071 students. Offers language courses in French, Kiswahili, Spanish and German.

F Joseph Stucker, Director

1033 John F Kennedy International School
CH-3792 Saanen
Switzerland
033-744-1372
Fax: 033-744-8982
E-mail: lovell@jfk.ch
Boarding day school for boys and girls aged 5-14 years.

William Lovell, Co-Director
Sandra Lovell, Co-Director

1034 Kabira International School
Old Kira Road, PO Box 2020
Kampala
Uganda
256-41-530-472
Fax: 256-41-543-444
E-mail: office@kabiraschool.com
http://www.kabiraschool.com
Grade levels Pre-K through 8, school year - September - July

Harriet Spry, Admissions
Elaine Whelen, Principal

1035 Kestrel Manor School
Ring Road Westlands
PO Box 14489, Nairobi
Kenya
254-2-3740-311
E-mail: info@kestrelmanorschool.com
http://www.kestrelmanorschool.com
Coeducational school for children Kindergarten through secondary schooling.

1036 Khartoum American School
PO Box 699
Khartoum
Sudan
248-183-512042
Fax: 249-183-512044
E-mail: kas@sudanmail.net
An independent, coeducational day school which offers an educational program from prekindergarten through grade 12 for students of all nationalities.

Phil Clinton, Contant

1037 Kigali International School
BP 1375
Kigali
Rwanda
Fax: 250-72128

Jennifer G Sevier, Principal

1038 Kingsgate English Medium Primary School
Box 169
Mafeteng, 900 Lesotho
Africa
Kingsgate is the only non-denominational primary school in the district. The curriculum is English-based offered to a total of 460 day students (240 boys; 220 girls), PreK-7. Overseas teachers are welcome with the length of stay being one year, with housing provided. Applications needed to teach include pre-school and reading.

M Makhothe, Principal

1039 Kisumu International School
PO Box 1276
Kisumu
Kenya
254-35-21678
This school is located on the shores of Lake Victoria and offers a unique education to students of all nationalities and cultural backgrounds. The total enrollment of the school is 35 day students, in grades K-7. The school does participate in the teacher exchange programs, with the length of stay being two years with housing provided by the school. Applications needed to teach include science, preschool, math, social sciences, English and physical education.

Neena Sharma, Principal

1040 Lincoln Community School
American Embassy Accra
Washington
Accra
Ghana
233-21-774-018
Fax: 233-21-774-018
E-mail: lincoln@lincoln.edu.gh
http://www.lincoln.edu.gh
Grade levels preK thru 12.

Don Groves, PhD, Superintendent

1041 Lincoln International School of Uganda
PO Box 4200
Kampala
Uganda
251-41-200374/8/9
Fax: 256-41-200303
E-mail: gmail@lincoln.ac.ug
http://www.lincoln.ac.ug
Grade levels Pre-K through 12, school year August - June

Peter Todd, Director
Mary-Lily Foster, Business Manager

1042 Lincoln International School-Uganda
PO Box 4200
Kampala
Uganda
256-41-200374
Fax: 256-41-200303
E-mail: gmail@lincoln.ac.ug
http://www.lincoln.ac.ug

Peter Todd, Director

1043 Maru A Pula School
Mara a Pula Way
Gaborone
Botswana
267-312953
Fax: 267-373338
http://www.map.ac.bw
independent co-educational secondary school offering international reconized classes.

Neil Smooker, Principal

1044 Mombasa Academy
PO Box 86487
Mombasa
Kenya
254-11-471629
Fax: 254-11-221484
E-mail: msaacademy@swiftmombasa.com
Private school, pupils ranging in the ages of 3-18 years old.

PR Uppal, Principal

1045 Northside Primary School
PO Box 897
Gaborone
Botswana
00-267-395-2440
Fax: 09-267-395-3573
International school that strives to improve the educatin offered to pupils. For boys and girls of all nationalities.

Mandy Watson, Headteacher

1046 Nsansa School
PO Box 70322
Ndola
Zambia
26-2-611753
Fax: 26-2-618465
This school offers an English curriculum to 185 day students (96 boys; 124 girls), in grades K-7. Length of stay for overseas teachers is one year with housing provided. Student/teacher ratio is 20:1.

Nel Mather, Principal

1047 Peterhouse
Private Bag 3741
Marondera
Zimbabwe
263-79-24951
This Anglican school offers an English based curriculum for 19 day students and 790 boarding students (535 boys; 255 girls), in Form I-Form VI. The school is willing to participate in a teacher exchange program with the length of stay being one year, with housing provided. Applications needed to teach include science, math, and physical education.

MW Bawden, Principal

1048 Rabat American School
Po Box 120
Rabat
Morocco
212-37-671-476
Fax: 212-37-670-963
E-mail: info@ras.ma
http://www.ras.ma
An independent, coeducational day school which offers an American educational program from prekindergarten through grade 12 for students of all nationalities.

Paul W Johnson, Director

1049 Rift Valley Academy
PO Box 80
Kijabe, 00220
Kenya
254-20-3246-249
Fax: 254-20-3246-111
E-mail: rva@kijabe.nte
http://www.rva.org
The philosophy is to place the Lord Jesus Christ at the center of the entire program. Emphasis is placed on the positive aspects of Christianity stressing the need for complete obedience to Christ by following His will as revealed in the Holy Scriptures.

Roy E Entwistle, Principal

1050 Rosslyn Academy
PO Box 14146, Westlands
Nairobi, 00800
Kenya
254-020-712-2407
Fax: 254-020-712-1306
E-mail: info@rosslynacademy.com
http://www.rosslynacademy.com
International private Christian coed day school with a North American cirriculum for grades k-12 garde

Dena L Brent, Superintendent

1051 Sandford English Community School
PO Box 30056 MA
Addis Adaba
Ethiopia
251-11-123-38-92
Fax: 251-11-123-3728
E-mail: getu@sandfordschool.org
A co-educational, non-boarding, nursery to pre University institution. Its committed to providing a standard of education that is accepted within Ethiopia and by the international community.

Jon Lane, Head Of Primary School
Kumlachew Aberra, Senior Manager

1052 Schutz American School
PO Box 1000
Alexandria
Egypt 2111
20-3-574-1435
Fax: 20-3-576-0229
E-mail: schutz@schutzschool.org.eg
http://www.schutzschool.org.eg
An independent, coeducational day school which offers an educational program from prekindergarten through grade 12 for students of all nationalities.

Matthew Farwell, Headmaster

1053 Sifundzani School
PO Box A286, Swazi Plaza
Mbabane
Swaziland
268-404-2465
Fax: 268-404-0320
E-mail: sifundzani@realnet.co.sz
A coeducational day school which offers an educational program from grades 1 through 10 for students of all nationalities.

Ella Magongo, Principal

1054 Sir Harry Johnston Primary School
Po Box 52
Zomba
Malawi
265-1525280
Fax: 265-8202374
E-mail: admin@shjzomb.com
http://www.shjzomba.com

Simon McCloskey, Headteacher

1055 St. Barnabas College
PO Box 88188
Newclare 2112
South Africa
011-27-474-2055
Fax: 011-27-474-2249
E-mail: theronn@stbarnabas.co.za
http://www.stbarnabas.co.za
Co-educational secondary school. Grade levels 7-12. The school provides quality secondary education to young people, the main criterion for admission being intellectual potential and the motivation to succeed.

Glynn Blignaut, Headmaster
Faizel Panker, Deputy Headmaster

1056 St. Mary's School
PO Box 40580
Nairobi
Kenya
011-254-57-335007
Grade levels 6-12.

John Awiti, Head of School
Rosemary Abuodha Omogo, Deputy
Principal

1057 St. Paul's College
St. Paul's United Theological College
Po Private Bag
Limuru
Kenya
011-254-154-73157
Fax: 011-254-154-73033
E-mail: principal@stpaulslimuru.ac.ke
http://www.crosslink.org
The school prepares men and women for
ministry in the Christian Chruch and pres-
ent day society.

1058 Tigoni Girls Academy
Box 10
Limuru
Kenya
This Academy is a small, closely knit community of individuals from different cultures in which physical, emotional,
creative and intellectual development is
fortified in all aspects of daily life. Total
enrollment is 40 boarding students, ages
11-16. Applications from overseas include
science, math, social sciences, French,
Spanish and English. Length of stay for
overseas teachers is 2 years with housing
provided. The Academy is affiliated with
the Church of England.

Duncan Kelly, Principal

**1059 Waterford-Kamhlaba United
World College**
Po Box 52
Mbabane
Swaziland
011-268-422-0866
Fax: 011-268-422-0088
E-mail: principal@waterford.sz
http://www.waterford.sz
This school offers a curriculum based in
English for 181 day students and 295
boarding (251 boys; 226 girls), in grades
6-12. Overseas teachers length of stay is
three years with housing provided. Appli-
cations needed to teach include math, Eng-
lish, and physical education.

Laurence Nodder, Principal

1060 Westwood International School
PO Box 2446
Gabarone
Botswana
011-267-390-6736
Fax: 011-267-390-6734
E-mail: westwood@info.bw
http://www.westwood.ac.bw
This International school offers an English
based curriculum to 420 day students (210
boys; 210 girls), in grades K-11. Applications needed to teach include science,
math, English and physical education. The
overall purpose of the school is to provide
an international standard of education for
boys and girls of all ethnic, national and religious backgrounds, enabling them to
re-enter their educational systems of origin.

Brian Turnbull, Principal

1061 Windhoek International School
Private Bag 16007
Windhoek
Namibia
264-61-241-783
Fax: 264-61-243-127
E-mail: kjarman@wis.edu.na
http://www.wis.edu.na
A coeducational day school which offers
educational programs from preschool
through grade 11.

Ken Jarman, Director

Asia, Pacific Rim &
Australia

**1062 Aiyura International Primary
School**
PO Box 407
Ukarumpa Papua
New Guinea

Perry Bradford, Principal

1063 Ake Panya International School
158/1 Moo 3 Hangdong-Samoeng Road
Banpong, Hangdong, Chiang Mai 50230
Thailand
66-53-36-5303
Fax: 66-53-365-304
E-mail: akepanya@cm.ksc.co.th
http://www.akepanya.co.th
Grade levels 1-12, school year August -
June

Barry Sutherland, Headmaster
Holly Shaw, Director of Studies

**1064 Alotau International Primary
School**
PO Box 154
Alotau MBP, Papua
New Guinea

Martha Barss, Principal

**1065 Amelia Earhart Intermediate
School**
Unit 5166
APO Kadena
Okinawa, AP 96368-5166

Rosemarie Arnestad, Principal

**1066 American International
School-Dhaka**
PO Box 6106
Gulshan, Dhaka 1212
Bangladesh
880-2-882-2452
Fax: 880-2-882-3175
E-mail: info@ais-dhaka.net
http://www.ais-dhaka.net
Grade levels Pre-K through 12, school year
August-June

Richard Detwiler, Superintendent

**1067 American International
School-Guangzhou**
3 Yan Yu Street S
Ersha Island, Dongshan District
Guangdong, 510620, China
86-20-8735-3392
Fax: 86-20-8735-3339
E-mail: info@aisgz.edu.cn
http://www.aisgz.edu.cn
Grade levels Pre-K through 12, school year
September-June

David Shawver, PhD, Director

1068 American School-Bombay
SF 2 G Block
Bandra Kurla Complex Road
Mumbai, India 400 051
91-22-652-1837
Fax: 91-22-652-1838
E-mail: asbadmin@bom3.vsnl.net.in
http://www.asbindia.org
Grade levels Pre-K through 13, school year
August - June

James Mains, Superintendent

**1069 American School-Guangzhou
(China)**
N Yan Yu Street S
Ersha Island, Dongshan District
Guangzhou 510105, China
8620-8735-3393
Fax: 8620-8735-3339
E-mail: info@aisgz.edu.cn
http://www.aisgz.edu.cn
An independent, coeducational day school
which offers an educational program from
kindergarten through grade 12.

David Shawver PhD, Director

1070 American School-Japan
1-1 Nomizu 1-chome
Chofu-shi, Tokyo 182-0031
Japan
81-422-34-5300
Fax: 81-422-34-5301
E-mail: info@asij.ac.jp
http://www.asij.ac.jp
The American School in Japan is a private,
coeducational day school which offers an
educational program from nursery through
grade 12 for students of all nationalities,
but it primarily serves the American community living in the Tokyo area. The school
was founded in 1902. The school year comprises 2 semesters extending from September to January and January to June.

Peter R Cooper, Headmaster

1071 Aoba International School
2-10-34 Aobadai
Meguro-Ku, Tokyo 153
Japan
81334611441
Fax: 81334639873
This boys school operates as a US bilingual
(English and Japanese) multicultural. Languages taught-English and Japanese. Special programs include ESL, JSL, PE,
swimming, soroban (abacus). Extra activities include field trips, year book, graduation trips-downtown Tokyo. Total
enrollment is 142 day students in nursery,
kindergarten and preschool with the stu-
dent/teacher ratio is 8:1.

Regina M Doi, Headmistress
Belen Tolentino, VP

1072 Ashgabat International School
Langusova 16
1000 Ljubljana
Slovenia
386-12-007870
Fax: 386-12-007871
E-mail: qsi@qsi.org
http://www.qsi.org
Offers high quality education in the English language for elementary students from
three years through thirteen years of age.

James Gilson, President

1073 Bali International School
PO Box 3259
Denpasar
Bali
62-361-288-770
Fax: 62-361-285-103
E-mail: info@baliis.net
http://www.bdg.centrin.net.id/~bis
A co-educational, private, nonprofit school serving students pre-school to grade 12. All the teachers are fully qualified and experienced in international education.

William D Robertson, Principal

1074 Bandung Alliance International School
Jalan Gunung Agung 14
Bandung, 40142 West Java
Indonesia
62-22-203-1844
Fax: 62-22-203-4202
E-mail: info@baisedu.org
http://www.baisedu.org
Teaches education based on the American philosophy of education from a Christian perspective for students from pre-school through grade 12.

John Havill, Principal

1075 Bandung International School
Kotak Pos 132
Jl Drg Suria Suman, Bandung
Indonesia
62-22-201-4995
Fax: 62-22-201-2688
E-mail: bisadmin@poboxes.com
Teaches students to be educated in knowledgeable, open-mined, well-balanced and reflective thinkers and inquirers who are principled, caring and prepared to take risks.

Oscar Nilsson, Head of School

1076 Bangalore International School
Geddalahalli, Hennur Bagalur Road
Kothanur Post, Bangalore 560077
India
91-802-846-5060
Fax: 91-802-846-5059
E-mail: principal@bisedu.co.in
Provides internationally recognized standards of education with an India ethos and enable students to fulfill their potential in a culturally rich atmosphere.

Anuradha Monga, Principal

1077 Bangkok Patana School
2/38 Soi La Salle, Sukhumbit 105
Bangkok 10260
Thailand
662-398-0200
Fax: 662-399-3179
E-mail: pabe@pantana.ac.th
http://www.patana.com
Language of instruction English. Offers UK National Curriculum, IGCSE and IB examination courses. Accredited by NEASC and ECIS. Currently enrolls 1,950 students and teaches grades N-12.

Andrew Homden, Head Of School

1078 Beacon Hill School
23 Ede Road
Kowloon Tong, Hong Kong
China
852-233-65-221
Fax: 852-233-87-895
E-mail: bhs@bhs.esf.edu.hk
http://www.asioonline.net.hk/beacon

Aim to provide each child with a safe and secure schoool where everyone, irrespective of ability, is an valued individual.

John Brewster, Principal

1079 Beijing BISS International School
#17, Area 4, An Zhen Xi Li
Chaoyang District, Beijing 100029
China
86-10-6443-3151
Fax: 86-10-6443-3156
E-mail: admissions@biss.com.cn
http://www.biss.com.cn
Grade levels K-12, school year August-June

Anne Fowles, Headmaster
Wayne Demnar, Lower School Principal

1080 Bob Hope Primary School
Unit 5166
APO AP 96368-5166
Okinawa
11-81-611-734-0093
Fax: 11-81-98-934-6806
Grade levels K-3.

H. Bud Iles, Principal

1081 Bogor Expatriate School
PO Box 258
Jalan Papandayan 7, Bogor 16151
Indonesia
62-251-324360
Fax: 62-251-328512
Mission is to provide opportunities to foster positive attitdes towards learning.

Chris Rawlins, Head Of School
Lance Kelly, Principal

1082 Bontang International School
15 Roszel Road
Po Box 5910
Princeton, NJ 08543
609-452-0990
62-548551176
Fax: 609-452-2690
E-mail: iss@iss.edu
An international school with an English/Japanese based curriculum for twenty day students (6 boys; 14 girls), grades PreK-8. Student/teacher ration 5:1.

Roger Hove, Executive Vice President

1083 Brent International School-Manila
UL Complex, Meralco Avenue
1603 Pasig City
Philippines
632-631-1265
Fax: 632-633-8420
E-mail: bism@brentmanila.edu.ph
http://www.brentmanila.edu.ph
Grade levels N-12, enrollment 966.

Dick B Robbins, Headmaster

1084 Brent School
PO Box 35
Baguio City 2600
Philippines
63-74-442-2260
Fax: 63-74-442-3638
E-mail:
brentreg@bgo.cyber-space.com.ph
http://www2.mozcom.com/~brent
Coeducational boarding and day college-preparatory school, affiliated with Church of England.

Don Holmes, Headmaster

1085 British International School
PO Box 4120
Jakarta 12041 Indonesia
62-21-745-1670
Fax: 62-21-745-1671
E-mail: bisnet@rad.net.id
Grade level preK through 13.

John Birchill, Principal

1086 British School Manila
PO Box 873
Makati, Metro Manila
Philippines
632-840-1561
Fax: 632-840-1520
School offers education that nurtures the different strengths and talents of the students.

Vanessa Cloutt, BEd, Principal

1087 British School-Muscat
PO Box 1907
Post Code 112
Ruwi Sultanate of Oman
968-600-842
Fax: 968-601-062
E-mail: admin@britishschool.edu.om

Dr. John Scarth, Principal
Ian Forster, Director Finance/Personnel

1088 Calcutta International School Society
18 Lee Road
Calcutta 700 020
India
This school offers an English-based curriculum to 480 day students (230 boys; 250 girls), grades Nursery-12. CIS follows GCE London Curriculum. The cultures represented by the student body include expatriates, NRIs, local children. The student body is mainly Indians. Highly qualified individuals offering excellent results. The school is willing to participate in a teacher exchange program with the length of stay being 1-2 years, with no housing provided.

N Chatterjee, Principal
L Chaturvedi, Faculty Head

1089 Caltex American School
CPI Rumbal
Pekanbaru, Sumatra Riau
Indonesia
62-765-995-501
Fax: 62-765-996-321
Grade level preK through 8.

Daniel Hovde, Superintendent

1090 Camberwell Grammar School
55 Mout Albert Road
Canterbury 3126, Victoria
Australia
03-9836-6266
http://www.asap.unimelb.edu.au/asa/directory/data/342
Independent boys school.

CF Black, Principal

1091 Canadian Academy
4-1 Koyo Cho Naka
Higashinada-Ku, Kobe 658-0032
Japan
81-78-857-0100
Fax: 81-78-857-3250
E-mail: hdmstr@canacad.ac.jp
http://www.canacad.ac.jp/canacad/welcome.html

Grade levels Pre-K through 12, school year August - June

David A Ottaviano EdD, Headmaster
Charles Kite, Assistant Headmaster

1092 Canadian School-India
14/1 Kodigehalli Main Road
Sahakar Nagar, Bangalore 560 092
India
91-80-343-8414
Fax: 91-80-343-6488
E-mail: csib@vsnl.com
http://www.canschoolindia.org
Grade levels K-13, school year August - June

T Alf Mallin, Principal

1093 Canberra Grammar School
Monaro Crescent
Red Hill, Canberra 2603
Australia
02-6260-9700
Fax: 02-6260-9701
E-mail:
canberra.grammar@cgs.act.edu.au
http://www.cgs.act.edu.au
International boys school.

Timothy C Murray, BA, Principal

1094 Carmel School-Hong Kong
10 Borrett Road
Mid Levels, SAR, Hong Kong
China
852-2964-1600
Fax: 852-2813-4121
E-mail: admin@carmel.edu.hk
http://www.carmel.edu.hk
Grade levels N-7, school year September - June

Edwin Epstein, Head of School
Chris Wee, School Manager

1095 Casa Montessori Internationale
17 Palm Avenue Forbes Park Makati
Etro Manila D-3117
Philippines
Pre-nursery, nursery and kindergarten classes.

Carina Lebron, Principal

1096 Cebu International School
Banilad Road
PO Box 735, Cebu City 6401
Philippines
632-32-417-6327
Fax: 632-32-417-6332
E-mail: markb@mozcom.com
http://www2.mozcom.com/~cisram
Grade levels kindergarten through twelfth, enrollment 337.

Mark Bretherton, Superintendent

1097 Central Java Inter-Mission School
PO Box 142
Salatiga 50711, Jaleng
Indonesia
62-298-311673
Fax: 62-298-311780
E-mail: office@mountainviewics.org
http://www.mountainviewics.org
Primary intent of the school is that all students be throughly exposed to Spripture and that they find and sustain a vital relationship to Jesus Christ through Holy Spirit.

Bill Webb, Superintendent
Sid Thornton, Secondary Principal

1098 Central Primary School
Winston Churchill Avenue
Port Vila
Republic of Vanuatu
678-23122
Fax: 678-22526
E-mail: central@vanuatu.com.vu
http://www.vanuatu.com.vu/~central
Co-educational school that conducts lessons in English and encourages students to speak English outside the classroom.

John Path, Chairman

1099 Chiang Mai International School
13 Chetupon Road
Chiang Mai, 50000
Thailand
665-324-2027
Fax: 665-324-2455
E-mail: info@cmis.ac.th
A private, coeducational day school which offers an educational program from pre-school through grade 12 for students of all nationalities. The school year comprises 2 semesters extending from the first week of September to mid-January and from mid-January to the third week of June.

Kamol Boonprohm, Principal

1100 Chinese International School
1 Hau Yuen Path
Braemar Hill, Hong Kong
China
825-251-25918
Fax: 852-251-07378
E-mail: cis_info@cis.edu.hk
http://www.cis.edu.hk
Committed to the achievement of academic excellence and is characterized and enriched by its dual-language program in Chinese and English.

Theodore S Faunce, Headmaster

1101 Chittagong Grammar School
Sarson Valley, 448/B Joynagar,
Chiottagong
Bangladesh
880-31-626-765
E-mail: cgs@gononet.com
Dedicated to the total growth and development of each student. Provides the students a broad, challenging and sound education to enable children to achieve the highest standards of which they are capable.

1102 Colombo International School
28, Gregory's Road
Colombo 7
Sri Lanka
94-11-269-7587
Fax: 94-11-269-9592
E-mail: principal@cis.lk
http://www.cis.lk
An independent, coeducational day school which offers an educational program from preschool through grade 12 for students of all nationalities.

1103 Concordia International School-Shanghai
999 Mingyue Road, Jinqiao, Pudong
Shanghai
201206, China
86-21-5899-0380
Fax: 86-21-5899-1685
E-mail: headofschool@ciss.com.cn
http://www.ciss.com.cn
Preschool through grade 12; school year August-June; WASC accredited pP-12 through June 2008; American cirrculum.

David Rittmann, Head of School

1104 Cummings Elementary School
Unit 5039
APO Misawa
Japan, AP 96319-5039
81-3117-66-2226
Fax: 81-3117-62-5110
Commited to guideing students to become successful learners and responsible citizens.

Dr. Frank Vohovich, Principal

1105 Dalat School
11200 Penang
Tanjung Bunga
Malaysia
60-4-899-2105
Fax: 60-4-890-2141
E-mail: info@dalat.org
Offers North American curriculum and encompasses preschool through grade twelve.

Karl Steinkamp, Interim Director

1106 Dover Court Prep School
Dover Road
Singapore, 139644
Singapore
65-67757664
Fax: 65-67774165
E-mail: admin@dovercourt.edu.sg
To teach goals of the learning process, which is facilitated through encouraging pupils to pose and solve problems, take risks, demonstrare responsible attitudes and behaviour, adopt a critical and self-evaluative approach to their work.

Maureen Roach, Director
Catherine Alliott, Chief Executive Officer

1107 Ela Beach International School
Po Box 1137
Boroko
Papua New Guinea
675-325-2183
Fax: 675-325-7925
E-mail: bmackinlay@temis.iea.ac.pg
This school consists of 262 boys and 222 girl day students in PreK-Grade 6. The length of stay for overseas teachers is three years with housing provided. School enrollment is made up of 260 PNG children, 224 non PNG children, overseas and PNG staff team teaching in mixed age group classrooms.

Bruce E Mackinlay, Principal

1108 Elsternwick Campus-Wesley College
577 St. Kilda Road
Melbourne 3004
Australia
61-3-8102-6000
Fax: 61-3-9510-6284
E-mail: principal@wesleycollege.net
This college is affiliated with the United Church in Australia and offers an English curriculum to 450 day students (250 boys and 220 girls), in pre-preparatory to year ten. The student/teacher ratio currently being 11:1, the school is willing to participate in a teacher exchange program. The length of stay for overseas teachers is one year and the housing provided is exchange housing only.

Jack Moshakis, Executive Director

1109 Faisalabad Grammar School

Kohinoor Nagar
Faisalabad 728593
Pakistan

This Islamic school offers a curriculum taught in both English and Urdu to 2,000 day students (1,000 boys; 1,000 girls), in Junior Nursery up to eighteen years of age. The school runs 50% of classes in Matriculation Streams Local, and 50% in 'O' and 'A' level University of Cambridge UK examinations. Applications needed to teach include science, math, English and computers, with the length of stay for overseas teachers being one year.

RY Saigol Sarfraz, Principal
N Akhtar MSc (Bio), VP

1110 Faith Academy

PO Box 2016 MCPO
0706 Makati City
Philippines
63-2-658-0048
Fax: 63-2-658-0026
E-mail: vanguard@faith.edu.ph
http://www.faith.edu.ph
Grade levels kindergarten through twelfth, enrollment 630 students.

Craig Cook, Superindentent
Martha Macomber, Deputy Superindentent

1111 French International School

165 Blue Pool
Happy Valley, SAR, Hong Kong
China
852-257-76217
Fax: 852-257-79658
E-mail: fis@lfis.edu.hk
Grade levels Pre-K through 13, school year September - June.

Pascal Panthene, Headmaster

1112 Fukuoka International School

3-18-50 Momochi
Sawara-ku, Fukuoka 814-0006
Japan
81-92-841-7601
Fax: 81-92-841-7602
E-mail: adminfis@fka.att.ne.jp
http://www.worldwide.edu/japan/fukuoka
Prekindergarten through grade 12 for English-speaking students of all nationalities. There are English-as-a-Second-Language classes available throughout the grades. The school year comprises 2 semesters extending approximately from September 1 to June 15.

Barry Clough, Headmaster

1113 Garden International School

16 Jalan Kiara 3, Off Jalan Bukit K
50480 Kuala Lumpur
Malaysia
011-60-3-6209-6888
Fax: 011-60-3-6201-2468
E-mail: admissions@gardenschool.edu.my
http://www.gardenschool.edu.my
Grade levels preK through eleventh.

Raymond Davis, Principal

1114 Geelong Grammar School-Glamorgan

14 Douglas Street
Toorak, 3142
Australia
011-61-3-9829-1444
Fax: 011-61-3-9826-2829
E-mail: glamorgan@ggs.vic.edu.au
http://www.ggscorio.vic.edu.au

Boarding day school for girls and boys Nursery to 12.

Fiona Zinn, Coordinator
Stephen Meek, Principal

1115 German Swiss International School

11 Guildford Road, The Peak
Hong Kong
China
011-852-2849-6216
Fax: 011-852-2849-6347
E-mail: gsis@gsis.edu.hk
http://www.mygsis.gsis.edu.hk
Grades levels kindergarten to secondary school. The school follows the German and British School systems.

Sameer Safaya, Alumni Coordinator
Jens-Peter Green, Principal

1116 Glenunga International High School

99 L'Estrange Street
Glenuga 5064
Australia
011-61-8-8379-5629
Fax: 011-61-8-8338-2518
E-mail: glenunga@gihs.sa.edu.au
http://www.gihs.sa.edu.au
Grade levels 8-12.

Robert Knight, Principal
Jeremy Cogan, Deputy Principal

1117 Good Hope School-Kowloon

383 Jat's Incline
Kowloon
Hong Kong
011-852-2327-5294
Fax: 011-852-2329-6403
E-mail: gps-general@hkedcity.net
http://www2.hkedcity.net
Provides equal opportunities to develop their moral, intellectual, physical, social, emotional and artisic aspects of life.

Mary Olga Lam, Supervisor
Lucia Leung Ngan Hei, Principal

1118 Goroka International School

PO Box 845
Goroka EHP
Papua New Guinea
011-675-732-1452
Fax: 011-675-732-2146
E-mail: gorokais@online.net.org
http://www.iea.ac.pg
Grade levels prekindergarten through tenth.

Richard Murke, Principal

1119 Hebron School-Lushington Hall

Lushington Hall, Ootacamund 643-001
Tamil Nadu
India
11-91-42-3244-2372
Fax: 11-91-42-3244-1295
E-mail: admin@hebronooty.org
http://www.hebronooty.org
Independent, international Christain school.

Alastair J Reid, Principal

1120 Hillcrest International School

PO Box 249
Sentani 99352, Papua
Indonesia
011-62-967-591460
Fax: 011-62-967-591673
E-mail: director@hismk.org
http://www.hismk.org
HIS is a Christian international school. Teachers must raise their own support, normally with a mission. Enrollment consists of 97 day students and 24 boarding (53 boys; 68 girls), in grades K-12.

Margaret Hartzler, Director

1121 Hiroshima International School

3-49-1 Kurakake
Asakita-Ku, Hiroshima 739-1743
Japan
011-81-82-843-4111
Fax: 011-81-82-843-6399
E-mail: info@hiroshima-is.ac.jp
http://www.hiroshima-is.ac.jp
The Hiroshima International School is an independent, coeducational day school which offers educational programs from preschool through grade 12. The school year comprises 2 semesters extending from early September to mid-June.

Peter MacKenzie, Principal

1122 Hokkaido International School

1-55, 5-Jo, 19-Chome
Hirahishi, Toyohira-Ku
Sapporo, Hokkaido 062, Japan
011-81-11-816-5000
Fax: 011-81-11-816-2500
E-mail: his@his.ac.jp
http://www.his.ac.jp
A private, coeducational day and boarding school which offers an America-style education from preschool through grade 12.

Wayne Rutherford, Headmaster
Eri Kashiwabara, Business Manager

1123 Hong Kong International School

1 Red Hill Road
Tai Tam, Hong Kong
Republic of China
011-852-3149-7000
Fax: 011-852-2813-8740
E-mail: jwai@hkis.ed.hk
http://www.hkis.edu.hk
The Hong Kong International School is a private, Christian, coeducational day school which offers an educational program from pre-primary through grade 12 for students of all nationalities and religious backgrounds. The school year comprises 2 semesters extending approximately from August 19 to January 16 and from January 19 to June 12.

Richard Mueller, Head of School

1124 Ikego Elementary School

PSC 473 Box 96
APO, Yokosuka
Japan, AP 96349-0005
81-468-72-8320
E-mail: IKEG_ESprincipal@pac.odedodea.edu
Grade levels K-6.

1125 Indianhead School

233-3, Howon-Dong
Uijeongbu City, Gyeonggi-Do
South Korea
011-82-31-870-3475
Fax: 011-82-31-826-3476
E-mail: es@iis.or.kr
http://www.iis.or.kr
Provides a comprehensive and enriched program of education for expatriate children and for those Korean nationals deemed eligible by the Korean Ministry of Education.

Jeong Jin Park, President
Edmund Fitzgerald, Principal

1126 International Christian School
Unit 602A, 6th Floor, Jubilee Court
2-18 Lok King Street, Fotan
N.T. Hong Kong
011-852-2304-6808
Fax: 011-852-2336-6114
E-mail: ics@ics.edu.hk
http://www.ics.edu.hk
Grade levels Pre-K through 12, school year
August - June

Ben Norton, Headmaster

1127 International Community School
1225 The Parkland Road
Bangkok
Thailand
011-66-2-338-0777
Fax: 011-66-2-338-0778
E-mail: info@icsbangkok.com
http://www.icsbangkok.com
Grade levels K-12, school year August -
June

Bill Gerritz, Headmaster
Dalad Karnasut, Secretary

1128 International School Manila
University Parkway
Fort Bonifacio, Taguig 1634
Philippines
011-63-2-840-8400
Fax: 011-63-2-840-8405
E-mail: superintendent@ismanila.com
http://www.ismanila.com
Grades K-12, enrollment 1,868.

Randy Johnson, President
David Toze, Superintendent

**1129 International School of the Sacred
Heart**
4-3-1 Hiroo, Shibuya-ku
Tokyo 150-0012
Japan
011-81-3-3400-3951
Fax: 011-81-3-3400-3496
E-mail: info@issh.ac.jp
http://www.issh.ac.jp
This catholic girls school offers an English
curriculum to 600 day students in grades
K-12.

Masako Egawa, Headmistress

1130 International School-Bangkok
39/7 Soi Nichada Thani,Samakee Road
Nonthaburi 11120
Thailand
011-66-2-963-5800
Fax: 011-66-2-583-5432
E-mail: daladk@isb.ac.th
http://www.isb.ac.th
Grade levels K-1, school year August -
June

Bill Gerritz, Head Of School
Dalad Karnasut, Secretary

1131 International School-Beijing
10 An Hua Street
Shunyi District, Beijing 101300
China
86-10-8046-2345
Fax: 86-10-8046-2001
E-mail: isb-info@isb.bj.edu.cn
http://www.isb.bj.edu.cn
Jointly sponsored by the governments of
Australia, Canada, New Zealand and the
United States, as the successor to the American Educational Association and the former australian, Canadian, and British
schools. ISB is an Eglish language, private,
nonsectarian college preparatory,
coeducational day school offering a pro-

gram ranging from prekindergarten
through grade 12.

Thomas Hawkins, Director

**1132 International School-Eastern
Seaboard**
PO Box 6
Banglamung, Chonburi 20150
Thailand
6638-345-556-9
Fax: 6638-345-156
E-mail: rschultz@ise.ac.th
http://www.ise.ac.th
Grade levels Pre-K through 12 that is a in-
ternational school with an American style
curriculum.

Robert Brewitt, Superintendent

1133 International School-Fiji
PO Box 10828
Laucala Beach Estate, Suva
Fiji
11-679-3393-560
Fax: 11-679-3340-017
E-mail: info@international.school.fj
http://www.international.school.fj
The school provides excellent international education to prepare all students
with the skills necessary to be both positive
members of their communities and responsible global citizens.

Dianne Korare, Principal
Sera Brown, Registrar

**1134 International School-Ho Chi Minh
City**
649A Vo Truong Toan
An Phu, District 2, Ho Ci Minh City
Vietnam
84-8-898-9100
Fax: 84-8-887-4022
E-mail: ishcmc@hcm.vnn.vn
http://www.ishcmc.com
The school provides and teaches the students about intellectual, emotional, social,
creative, linguistic, cultural, moral, aesthetic and physical needs of each students.
The school seeks to involve parents in the
education of their children through regular
communication.

Sean O'Maonaigh, Headmaster
Chris Byrne, Admission And Marketing

**1135 International School-Kuala
Lumpur**
PO Box 12645
50784 Kuala Lumpar
Malaysia
603-4259-5600
Fax: 603-4257-9044
E-mail: Paul_Chmelik@iskl.edu.my
http://www.iskl.edu.my
Offers its students a superior education to
prepare them to be responsible world citizens who think creatively, reason criti-
cally, communicate effectively and learn
enthusiastically throughout life.

Paul Chmelik, Headmaster

1136 International School-Lae
PO Box 2130
Lae 411, Morobe Province
Papua New Guinea
011-675-479-1425
Fax: 011-675-472-3485
E-mail: mmyles@tisol.iea.ac.pg
Offers high quality education, from ages 18
months to grade 8. The curriculum pre-
pares students for national and interna-
tional success.

Mark Myles, Principal

1137 International School-Manila
Univeristy Parkway
Fort Bonifacio, Taguig City 1634
Philippines
632-840-8400
Fax: 632-840-8405
E-mail: superintendent@ismanila.com
http://www.ismanila.com
Multicultural based curriculum to 2200
day students (1100 boys; 1100 girls), in
grades K-12.

Randy Johnson, President

**1138 International
School-Penang-Uplands**
Jalan Sungai Satu, Batu Ferringhi
11100 Penang
Malaysia
011-604-8819-777
Fax: 011-604-8819-778
E-mail: info@uplands.org
http://www.oplands.org
This school provides education to the children of expatriates working in the region.
Students sit for IGCSE and GCE A Level
examinations. Total enrollment of the
school is 415 day students and 55 boarding
(250 boys; 220 girls), grades Nursery
through year thirteen. Student/teacher ratio is currently 12:1, and the applications
needed to teach include Science, French,
Math, Social Sciences, Spanish, German,
English and Physical Education.

Ian Kerr, Principal

**1139 International School-Phnom Penh,
Cambodia**
146 Norodom Boulevard, Po Box 138
Phnom Penh
Cambodia
855-23-213-103
Fax: 855-23-213-104
E-mail: robmockrish@ispp.edu.kh
http://www.ispp.edu.kh
Grades PS-12, enrollment 313.

Rob Mockrish, Director

**1140 International School-Phnom
Penh-Cambodia**
PO Box 138
Phnom Penh
Cambodia
855-23-213-103
Fax: 855-23-361-002
E-mail: ispp@bigpond.com.kh
http://www.ispp.edu.kh
The International School of Phnom Penh is
a private, non-profit, English language,
coeducational day school which offers and
educational program from preschool
through grade 12. The school year consists
of 2 semesters, each of 2 terms.

Terry Hamilton, Director

1141 International School-Pusan
PO Box 77 Nam Pusan Post Office
Sooyoung-Ku, 608-600 Pusan
South Korea
82-51-753-4166
Fax: 82-51-756-4851
E-mail: ispusan@ispusan.co.kr
http://www.ispusan.co.kr
Grade levels prekindergarten through
eighth.

Hugh Younger, Headmaster

1142 International School-Singapore
23 Nam Long Shan Road
Aberdeen
Hong Kong
852-2872-0266
Fax: 852-2872-0431
E-mail: secretary@singapore.edu.hk
ISS offers an integrated curriculum combining an American style high school diploma with the British Examination System. Total enrollment of the school is 650 day students (330 boys; 320 girls), in grades PreK-12.

Mak Lai Ying, Principal

1143 International School-Ulaanbaatar
PO Box 49/564
Ulaanbaatar
Mongolia
976-11-452-839
Fax: 976-11-450-340
E-mail: int.school.ub@gmail.com
http://www.isumongolia.edu.mn
A private, coeducational day school which offers an educational program from preschool through grade 8 for students of all nationalities. The School also offers a grade 9-12 correspondence program.

Deidre Fischer, Director

1144 Island School
20 Borrett Road
Hong Kong, SAR
China
852-2524-7135
Fax: 852-2840-1673
E-mail: school@mail.island.edu.hk
http://www.island.edu.hk
An international, co-educational, comprehensive school, providing secondary education for children of all nations who can benefit from an education through the medium of English.

Pinder Wong, Council Chairman

1145 Ivanhoe Grammar School
PO Box 91
The Ridgeway, Ivanhoe, Victoria 3079
Australia
61-3-9490-3426
Fax: 61-3-9490-3539
E-mail: enrol@igs.vic.edu.au
http://www.igs.vic.edu.au
An international grammar school.

Roderick D Fraser, Principal

1146 JN Darby Elementary School
PSC 485 Box 99
96321 FPO, AP
Japan
81-6160-52-8800
E-mail:
principal_darby_es@pac.odedodea.edu
http://www.darby-es.pac.odedodea.edu
Promote academic excellence so all students will become productive citizens.

1147 Jakarta International School
PO Box 1078/JKS
Jakarta 12010
Indonesia
62-21-769-2555
Fax: 62-21-765-7852
E-mail: admissions@jisedu.or.id
http://www.jisedu.org
Coeducational day school which draws on North American and other curriculum models from preparatory through grade 12.

Niall Nelson, Headmaster

1148 Japan International School
2-10-7 Miyamae
Shibuya-Ku, Tokyo 168-0081
Japan
81-3-3335-6620
Fax: 81-3-3332-6930
Student of all nationalitites, and religions are welcome.

Charles S Barton, Headmaster

1149 John McGlashan College
2 Pilkington Street
Maori Hill, Dunedin
New Zealand
03-467-6620
Fax: 03-467-6622
An all boys college.

K Michael Corkery, Principal

1150 Kansai Christian School
951 Tawaraguchi Cho Ikoma Shi
Nara Ken 630-0243
Japan
0743-73-1754
Fax: 0743-73-1681
E-mail: jm@japanmission.org
http://www3.kcn.ne.jp/~kcsjapan
KCS was established to provide Christian instruction for children of evangelical missionaries. Children from Christian homes are welcome to attend, and children from non-Christian homes may enter on a limited basis. The school's enrollment consists of 15 day students (7 boys; 8 girls), in grades 1-8. Applications needed to teach include math, social sciences, science, reading, and English.

David Verwey, Principal

1151 Kaohsiung American School
35 Sheng Li Road, Tzuo-Ying Dist.
Kaohsiung City 813
Taiwan
886-7-583-0112
Fax: 886-7-582-4536
E-mail: pnanos@kas.kh.edu.tw
http://www.kas.kh.edu.tw
This school offers an English based curriculum for a total of 180 day students (65 boys; 65 girls), in PreK-12. The school is willing to participate in a teacher exchange program with the length of stay being one year. Applications needed to teach include science, math, social sciences, reading and physical education.

Peter Nanos, Director

1152 Kellett School
2 Wah Lok Path
Wah Fu, Pokfulam
Hong Kong
852-2551-8234
Fax: 852-2875-0262
E-mail: kellett@kellettschool.com
Organisation by parents who desire a quality, British style education for their children.

Ann McDonald, Principal

1153 Kilmore International School
40 White Street
Kilmore, Victoria 3764
Australia
61-357-822-211
Fax: 61-357-822-525
E-mail: tkisadmn@kilmore.vic.edu.au
http://www.kilmore.vic.edu.au
This school offers an English curriculum for 29 day students and 121 boarding (100 boys and 50 girls), grades 7-12. The applications needed to teach include science,

math, social sciences, English and physical education. The length of stay for teachers is one year, and housing is only provided if the teacher wishes to be involved in boarding. Student/teacher ratio is 5:1.

John Settle, Principal

1154 Kinabalu International School
PO Box 12080
88822 Kota Kinabalu, Sabah
Malaysia
This school offers an English-based curriculum for 100 day students (50 boys; 50 girls), ages 3-13 years.
1973 pages

Barbara D. Abidin, Principal

1155 King George V School
2 Tin Kwong Road
Homantin, Kowloon
China
852-2711-3029
Fax: 852-2760-7116
E-mail: office@kgv.edu.hk
http://www.kgv.edu.hk
Non selective secondary school which provides a broad.

Ed Wickins, Principal

1156 Kitakyushu International School
Yahata Higashi-ku, Takami 2,
Shinnittetsu, Shijo, Kitakyushu
Japan
81-93-652-0682
This school offers an English based curriculum for 8 day students (2 boys; 6 girls), in kindergarten through elementary. The school is always looking for dedicated and qualified teachers to teach children and adults in school and preschool (especially female teachers). Applications needed include preschool and English.

Ann Ratnayake, Principal

1157 Kodaikanal International School
Seven Roads Junction, Po Box 25
Kodaikanal, 624 101, Tamil Nadu
India
91-4542-247-500
Fax: 91-4542-241-109
E-mail: contact@Kis.in
http://www.kis.in
Grade levels Pre-K through 12, school year July - May

Geoffrey Fisher, Principal
Gregg Faddegon, Vice Principal

1158 Kooralbyn International School
Shop 1, 29 Wellington Bundock Drive
Kooralbyn QLD 4285
Australia
61-7-5544-6111
Fax: 61-7-5544-6702
E-mail: info@kooralbyn.com
http://www.isd.com.au/schools/q7209
Aims to provide students with a broad liberal education.

Geoff Mills, Principal

1159 Kowloon Junior School
20 Perth Street
Ho Man Tin, Hong Kong
China
852-2714-5279
Fax: 852-2394-0684
E-mail: office@kjs.esf.edu.hk
http://www.kjs.edu.hk

Primary students learn English, maths, science, technology, history, geography, art, music and physical education.

Steve Francis, Principal

1160 Kyoto International School

Kitatawara-cho,Nakadachiuri-sagaru,
Yoshiyamachi-Dori, Kamigyo-ku, Kyoto
602-8247, Japan
81-75-451-1022
Fax: 81-75-451-1023
E-mail: kis@kyoto-is.org
http://www.kyoto-is.org
Grade levels Pre-K through 8, school year
September - June

Annette Levy, Contact
Amanda Gillis-Furutaku, Board Chair

1161 Lahore American School

American Consulate General Lahore
LAS
APO, Unit 62216 09812 2216
Pakistan
92-42-576-2406
Fax: 92-42-571-1901
E-mail: las@las.edu.pk
http://www.las.edu.pk
An independent, coeducational day school
which offers an educational program from
nursery through grade 12 for students of all
nationalities.

Ron Dowty, Superintendent
Khurram Karim, Vice President

1162 Lanna International School Thailand

300 Grandview Moo 1
Chiang-Mai to Hang Dong, T. Mae-hea,
Chi
50100, Thailand
66-53-806-231
Fax: 66-53-271-159
E-mail: lannaist@loxinfo.co.th
http://www.lannaist.ac.th
Grade levels Pre-K through 12, school year
August - June

Robert Lewis, Head of School

1163 Lincoln School

Po Box 2673
Rabi Bhawan, Kathmandu
Nepal
977-1-4270482
Fax: 977-1-4272685
E-mail: info@lsnepal.com.np
http://www.lsnepal.com
Grade levels preschool - 12, school year
August - June. The school offers an American curriculum with special programs in
ESL, learning resources, physical education, music, art, French and Nepal Studies.

Allan Bredy, Director
Craig Baker, Principal

1164 Makassar International School

Po Box 1327
Makassar, Sulawesi Selatan 90125
Indonesia
011-62-411-872-591
Fax: 011-62-411-873-035
E-mail: mischool@indosat.net.id
http://www.mischoolsulsel.tripod.com
Grade levels Pre-K through 7, school year
August - June

Chris Sperduto, Principal

1165 Malacca Expatriate School

2443-C Jalan Batang Tiga
76400 Tanjung Kling, Melaka
Malaysia
011-60-6-315-4970
Fax: 011-60-6-315-4970
E-mail: sossb@pd.jaring.my
http://www.meschool.virtualave.net
Mission is provide a high standard of learning. The students benefit from a high level
of individual attention because of their low
student to teacher ratio.

Susheila Samuel, Principal

1166 Marist Brothers International School

1-2-1 Chimori-cho
Suma-ku, Kobe 654-0072
Japan
011-81-787-326266
Fax: 011-81-787-326268
E-mail: info@marist.ac.jp
http://www.marist.ac.jp
Grade levels Pre-K through 12, school year
September - June

James Branni, Principal
Ian Robertson, Headmaster

1167 Matthew C Perry Elementary School

PSC 561 Box 1874
FPO Iwakuni 96310 1874
Japan
011-81-827-79-3447
Fax: 011-81-827-79-6490
Committed to promoting student achievement in a postive safe enviroment. It provides a quality education for every student
based on the needs of each child.

1168 Matthew C Perry Middle & High School

PSC 561 Box 1874
FPO Iwakuni 96310 1874
Japan

Lawrence Wolfe, Principal

1169 Mentone Boys Grammar School

63 Venice Street
Mentone, Victoria 3194
Australia
011-61-3-9584-4211
Fax: 011-61-3-9581-3290
E-mail: admin@mentonegrammar.net
http://www.mentonegrammar.net
Outstanding educational opportunities for
boys from ages 3 years olds to the age of 12.

Mal Cater, Acting Headmaster

1170 Mercedes College

540 Fullarton Road
Springfield 5062
South Australia
011-61-8-8372-3200
Fax: 011-61-8-8379-9540
E-mail:
info@mercedes.adl.catholic.edu.au
http://www.mercedes.adl.catholic.edu.au/
index.cfm
This Catholic school offers a curriculum
based in English for 901 day students (407
boys; 494 girls) in grades Reception-12.
The school is willing to participate in a
teacher exchange program with the length
of stay being one to two years, housing not
provided.

Peter Daw, Principal
Steve Bowley, Business Manager

1171 Methodist Ladies College

207 Barkers Road Kew
Victoria 3101
Australia
011-61-3-9274-6333
Fax: 011-61-3-9819-2345
E-mail: college@mlc.vic.edu.au
http://www.mlc.vic.edu.au
This college prepares its students for the
world of tomorrow by liberating their talents through challenge, enrichment, and
opportunity in a supportive Christian environment. Committed to technology and to
student initiated learning so each girl from
year five onward works with her personal
computer to understand the present and
shape the future. Total enrollment: 2,135
day students; 105 boarding. Grade range
K-12. The school is willing to participate in
a teacher exchange program.

Rosa Swtorelli, Principal

1172 Minsk International School

DOS/Administrative Officer
7010 Minsk Place
Washington, DC 20521-7010
375-172-343-035
Fax: 375-172-343-035
E-mail: mis@open.by
An independent, coeducational day school
which offers an educational program from
kindergarten through grade 8 for students
of all nationalities. Enrollment 11.

Stanley Harrison Orr, Director

1173 Moreguina International Primary School

PO Box 438
Konedobu Papua
New Guinea

Wayne Coleman, Principal

1174 Morrison Christian Academy

136-1 Shui Nan Road
Taichung 40679
Taiwan
11-886-4-2297-3927
Fax: 11-886-4-2292-1174
E-mail: mcgillt@mca.org.tw
http://www.morrison.mknet.org
This academy offers Chinese and Spanish
to 769 students in K-12.

Bruce Moore, Director Of Development
Tim McGill, Superintendent

1175 Mount Hagen International School

PO Box 1050
Mount Hagen
New Guinea

CM White, Principal

1176 Mt Zaagham International School

PT Freeport
Timika Irian Joya 9920
Indonesia
62-9-014-07641
Fax: 62-901-403-170
E-mail: joecuthbertson@efmi.com
Grade levels Pre-K through 98, school year
September - June. Two campuses
Tembagapura and Kula Kencanna

Dr. Joe Cuthbertson, Superintendent
Richard Ledger, Principal

1177 Murray International School
PO Box 1137
Boroko
Papua New Guinea
675-325-2183
Fax: 675-325-7925
E-mail: bmackinlay@temis.iea.ac.pg
Non-profit, private, co-educational day
school that provides quality international
standard education for the expatriate and lo-
cal community in Port Moresby.

Bruce Mackinlay, Principal

1178 Murree Christian School
Jhika Gali
Murree, 47180
Pakistan
92-593-410321
This school offers an English-based curriculum for 20 day students and 140 boarding
students (75 boys; 85 girls), in grades K-12.
Murree Christian School educates the children of missionaries from 14 different countries working in Pakistan and the region.
Living allowances rather than salaries are
awarded. Overseas teacher stay is two years
with housing provided by the school.

Phil Billing, Director
Linda Fisher, HS Faculty Head

1179 Mussoorie International School
Srinagar Estate
248179 Mussoorie, Uttaranchal
India
91-135-2632007
Fax: 91-135-2631160
E-mail: mischool@sacharnet
One of the leading residential educational
institutions for girls and is recognised for its
progressive education with a definite account on India culture and traditions.

HR Rawl, Principal

1180 Nagoya International School
2686 Minamihara, Nakashidami
Moriyama-ku, Nagoya, 463-0002
Japan
81-52-736-2025
Fax: 81-52-736-3883
E-mail: info@nisjapan.net
http://www.nisjapan.net
Grade levels Pre-K through 12, school year
August - June

C Barton, Headmaster

1181 Narrabundah College
Jerrabomberra Avenue
Kingston, ACT 2604
Australia
61-2-6205-6999
Fax: 61-2-6205-6969
E-mail: nick.vonthethoff@ed.act.edu.au
This college offers an English based curriculum for 930 total day students (558 boys;
372 girls), in grades 11 and 12. The school is
willing to participate in a teacher exchange
program with the length of stay being one
year, with no housing provided. This is a
secondary college with teaching special-
ities: International Baccalaureate, foreign
language, performing arts, creative arts,
sciences and ESL.

Steve Kyburz, Head of the School

**1182 New International School of
Thailand**
36 Sukhumvit Soi 15
10110 Bangkok
Thailand
66-2651-2065
Fax: 66-2253-3800

International education to culturally diverse students aged three to eighteen. The
school strives to achieve the academic excellence, attitudes and skills that will allow
success in life-long education.

Simon Leslie, Headmaster

1183 Nile C Kinnick High School
PSC 473 Box 95
FPO Yokosuka 96349-0095
Japan
81-46-816-7392
Fax: 81-46-816-7278

Bruce Derr, Principal

1184 Nishimachi International School
2-14-7 Moto Azabu, Minato-ku
Tokyo 106-0046
Japan
81-3-3451-5520
Fax: 81-3-3456-0197
E-mail: info@nishimachi.org
http://www.nishimachi.ac.jp
Offers a dual-language, multicultural pro-
gram ro 430 student k-9.

Terence Christian, Headmaster

**1185 Okinawa Christian School
International**
1835 Zakimi, Yomitan
Okinawa 904-0391
Japan
81-98-958-3000
Fax: 81-98-958-6279
E-mail: ocschool@ii-okinawa.ne.jp
http://www.ocsi.org
Grade levels K-12, school year August -
June

Rich Barnett, Contact

1186 Osaka International School
4-16 Onohar Nishi 4-Chome
Mino, Osaki, 562-0032
Japan
81-72-727-5050
Fax: 81-72-727-5055
E-mail: addmissions@senri.ed.jp
http://www.senri.ed.jp
OIS is an english-language-based, preK-12
grade coeducational college-preparatory
school.

Karin Caffin, Head of School

**1187 Osaka YMCA International High
School**
1-2-2-800 Benten Minato-ku
Osaka 552-0007
Japan
06-4395-1002
Fax: 06-4395-1004
E-mail: general-inquiry@oyis.org

John Murphy, Principal

1188 Osan American High School
Unit 2037
APO AP 96278-0005
Korea
011-82-31-661-9076
Fax: 011-82-31-661-9121
Provides students with learning experi-
ences that will prepare them to succeed in a
global society.

Marie Cullen, Principal
Georgia Watters, Asstistant Principal

1189 Osan Elementary School
Unit 2037
APO, AP 96278-2037
Korea
011-82-31-661-6912
Fax: 011-82-31-661-5733
E-mail: linda.kidd@pac.dodea.edu
http://www.osan_es.pac.dodea.edu
Provides quality and challenging educa-
tional opportunities for all students to be-
come critical thinkers, life-long learners,
and productive citizens in a global society.

Mia Plourde, Secretary
Linda J Kidd, Principal

1190 Overseas Children's School
PO Box 9, Pelawatte
Battaramulla
Sri Lanka
94-11-2784920-4
Fax: 94-11-2784999
E-mail: lmclellan@osc.lk
http://www.osc.lk
Provides emphasising personal and academic excellence, tolerance and responsibility within frame work of a culturally
diverse and internationally accredited
school.

Laurie McLellan, Head Of School
Ranjith de Silva, Director

1191 Overseas Family School
25 F Paterson Road
238515
Singapore
65-738-0211
Fax: 65-733-8825
E-mail: executive_director@ofs.edu.sg
http://www.ofs.edu.sg
Grade levels prekindergarten through 13,
enrollment 1,660.

David Perry, Chairman

1192 Overseas School of Colombo
Pelawatte
PO Box 9, Battarandulla
Sri Lanka
94-1-864-920
Fax: 94-1-864-999
E-mail: admin@osc.lk
http://www.osc.lk
Grades preSchool-12, enrollment 313.

Peter Gittins, Head of School

**1193 Pacific Harbour International
School**
PO Box 50
Pacific Harbour, Deuba
Fiji Islands

Janet Tuni, Principal

1194 Pasir Ridge International
Unocal-po Box 3-tampines S
Balikpapan 9152
Singapore
62-542-543-474
Fax: 62-542-767-126
http://prschool@bpp.mega.net.id
Grade levels preK through 8.

Kathryn Carter-Golden PhD, Principal

1195 Peak School
20 Plunketts Road
Hong Kong
China

PL Young, Principal

1196 Phuket International Preparatory School
PO Box 432
Phuket 83000
Thailand
Agnes Hebler, Principal

1197 Popondetta International School
PO Box 10
Popondetta, Papua
New Guinea
Michael Whitting, Principal

1198 Prahram Campus-Wesley College
577 St. Kilda Road-Prahran
Victoria 3181 Australia
AB Conabere, Principal

1199 Pusan American School
Do DOS
Pusan 96259
South Korea
82-51-801-7528
Fax: 82-51-803-1729
E-mail: pas@pac.odedodea.edu
http://www.210.107.81.252
Alexia Venglek, Principal

1200 Pusan Elementary & High School
Unit 15625
APO AP 96259-0005, Pusan
Korea
82-52-801-7528
Fax: 82-51-803-1729

1201 QSI International School-Phuket
PO Box 432
Phuket, 83000
Thailand
66-76-354076
Fax: 66-76-354077
E-mail: pkt@qsi.org
http://www.phuketschl.com
Grade levels N-12, school year August-June
Khun Janrita Hnobnorb, Administrative Coordinator

1202 QSI International School-Zhuhai
22 Longxing Street
Zhuhai 519020
China
86-756-815-6134
Fax: 86-756-889-6758
http://www.qsi.org
Grade levels N-8, school year September-June
Bruce Wood, Director

1203 Quarry Bay School
6 Hau Yuen Braemar Hill
North Point, Hong Kong
China
DJ Harrison, Principal

1204 Rabaul International School
PO Box 571
Rabaul Enbp, Papua
New Guinea
Ian Smith, Principal

1205 Richard E Byrd Elementary School
PSC 472 Box 12
FPO Yokohama 96348 0005
Japan
Milton Halloran, Principal

1206 Robert D Edgren High School
Unit 5040
APO Misawa 96319 5040
Japan
Daborah Berry, Principal

1207 Ruamrudee International School
42 Moo 4
Ramkamhaeng 184 Road
Minburi, Bangkok, 10510
66-2-518-0320
Fax: 66-2-518-0334
E-mail: director@rism.ac.th
http://www.rism.ac.th
Grade levels K-12, school year August - June
Fr. Leo Travis, Director
Dave Parsons HS Principal

1208 Saigon South International School
Saigon S Parkway, Tan Phu Ward
Ho Chi Minh City
Vietnam
84-8-873-1375
Fax: 84-8-873-1375
E-mail: ssischool@hcm.vnn.vn
http://www.web.cybercon.com/SSIS
Grade levels Pre-K through 7, school year August - June
Robert Crowther, Headmaster

1209 Sancta Maria International School
41 Karasawa Minami-ku
Yokohama
Japan
Sr Mary Elizabeth Doll, Principal

1210 School at Tembagapura
PO Box 616 Cairns
Queensland 4870
Australia
Bruce Goforth, Principal

1211 Scots PGC College
60 Oxenham Street
Warwick, QLD 4370
Australia
61-7-4666-9922
Fax: 61-7-4666-9999
E-mail: postbox@scotspgc.qld.edu.au
http://www.scotspgc.qld.edu.au
Neil O Bonnell MEd, Principal

1212 Seisen International School
12-15 Yoga 1-chome
Setagaya-Ku, Tokyo 158
Japan
03-3704-2661
Fax: 033701-1033
E-mail: sisinfo@seisen.com
http://www.seisen.com
Grade levels pre-K through twelfth.
Concesa Martin, Headmistress

1213 Semarang International School
Jl Jangli 37, Semarang
Semarang 50254, Central Java
Indonesia
62-24-8311-424
Fax: 62-24-8311-994
E Fitzgerald DipEd, Principal

1214 Seoul Academy
Young Dong
PO Box 85, Seoul
Korea
82-2-562-1690
Fax: 82-2-562-0451
E-mail: unicorn@uriel.net
http://www.uriel.net/~unicorn
Grade levels pre-K through eighth.
Thomas O'Connor, Director

1215 Seoul British School
55 Yonhi Dong Sudaemun Ku
Seoul
Korea
Philip Mayor-Smith, Principal

1216 Seoul Elementary School
Unit 15549
APO, Seoul 96205 0005
Korea
John Blom, Principal

1217 Seoul Foreign School
55 Yonhi-Dong
Seoul 120-113
Korea
82-2-330-3100
Fax: 82-2-335-1857
E-mail: sfsoffice@sfs.or.kr
http://www.sfs-h.ac.kr
Grade levels preK through 12. Offering IB diploma st the HS and both North American and British programs at the Elementary and Middle Schools.
Harlan Lyso PhD, Headmaster
Steven Nurre, Director Human Resources

1218 Seoul High School
Unit 15549
APO, Seouls 96205 0005
South Korea
Dr. Benjamin Briggs, Principal

1219 Shanghai American School
258 Jin Feng Lu
Zhudi Town, Minhang District, Shanghai
201107 China
86-21-6221-1445
Fax: 86-21-6221-1269
E-mail: info@saschina.org
http://www.saschina.org
Grade levels Pre-K through 12, school year August - June
Anthony Horton PhD, Superintendent

1220 Shatin College
3 Lai Wo Lane
Fo Tan, Shatin, Hong Kong
China
This mixed international school provides high quality education through the medium of English, leading to GCSE and A-level examinations. The student body of 900 day students is comprised of 450 boys and 450 girls in grades 7-13. Applications from overseas needed to teach at the school include science, French, math, social sciences, Spanish, German, English and physical education. The student/teacher ratio is 14:1, with a curriculum in English.
David Cottam, MA, MSc, Principal

1221 Shatin Junior College
3A Lai Wo Lane
Sha Tin, Hong Kong
China
BG Lewis, Principal

1222 Shirley Lanham Elementary School
PSC 477 Box 38
FPO Atsugi 96306 0005
Japan

Susan Jackson, Principal

1223 Singapore American School
40 Woodlands Street 41
Singapore 738547
Singapore
65-6360-6309
Fax: 65-6363-3408
E-mail: sasinfo@sas.edu.sg
http://www.sas.edu.sg
Day school which offers an educational program from preschool through grade 12 for students of all nationalities. The school year comprises 2 semesters extending from approximately August 17 to December 18, and from January 11 to June 4.

Bob Gross, Superintendent

1224 Sollars Elementary School
Unit 5041
APO Misawa 96319 5041
Japan

Scarlett Rehrig, Principal

1225 South Island School
50 Nam Fung Road
Hong Kong
China

RE Brookin, Principal

1226 St. Andrews International School-Bangkok
9 Soi Pridi Banomyong 20
Sukhumvit Soi 71, Prakanong, Bangkok
10110, Thailand
2381-2387
Fax: 2390-1780
E-mail: bangkok@at-andrews.ac
http://www.st-andrews.ac
Grade levels N-5, school year September - July

Mary Gibb, Head of School
Janet Gigler, Deputy Head

1227 St. Christopher's School
10 Nunn Road
10350 Penang
Malaysia

JM Wrench, Principal

1228 St. John's International School
1110/1-11 Bipavadee-Rungsit Road
Jatujak, Bangkok 10900
Thailand
662-938-7058-65
Fax: 662-513-8588
E-mail: info@stjohn.ac.th

Chainarong Monthienvic, Principal

1229 St. Joseph International School
85 Yamate-cho Naka-ku
Yokohama 231
Japan
45-641-0065
E-mail: sjislib@gol.com
Coeducational day/boarding school, preschool through grade 12.

James Mueller, Principal

1230 St. Joseph's International Primary School
PO Box 5784
Boroko Papua
New Guinea

Barbara D'Arbon, Principal

1231 St. Mark's College
46 Penntington Tce
North Adelaide
South Australia 5006
08-8334-5600
Fax: 08-8267-4694
E-mail: manager@atmarkscollege.com.au
http://www.stmarkscollege.com.au
Grade levels Pre-K through 12, school year March - December

Gabriela de Martin, Principal
Alejandra Rubio, Vice Head

1232 St. Mary's International School
1-6-19 Seta Setagaya-ku
Tokyo 158
Japan
This international school for boys in grades K-12 offers an America curriculum and international baccalaureate program. The enrollment of the catholic school includes 920 day students with the student/teacher ratio being 20:1. Overseas teachers are welcome for an indefinite time period with the applications needed to teach being science, pre-school, French, math, social sciences, administration, reading, English and physical education.

Michel Jutras, Principal

1233 St. Maur International School
83 Yamate-cho Naka-ku
Yokohama 231-8654
Japan
45-641-5751
This Roman Catholic affiliated school offers an English-based curriculum to 500 day students in grades PreK-12. This is a co-ed K-12 college preparatory catholic international school. Teachers are from US, Canada, UK, Australia and S Africa. Overseas teachers are offered an annual contract that is renewable each year. Housing is provided but deduction from pay is made. Applications needed to teach include science, Montessori preschool, French, math, Spanish and English

Jeanette Thomas, Headmistress
Richard B Rucci, Principal

1234 St. Michael's International School
3-17-2 Nakayamate-Dori
Chuo-ku, Kobe, Hyoyo-Ken 650-0004
Japan
81-78-231-8885
Fax: 81-78-231-8899
E-mail: smis@movenet.or.jp
This Anglican school offers an English curriculum for 95 day students (45 boys; 30 girls), in grades pre-school through 6th.

Aileen Pardon, Principal

1235 St. Stephen's International School
Viphavadi Rangsit Road
Lad Yao, Chatuchak, Bangkok 10900
Thailand
66-2-5130270
Fax: 66-2-9303307
E-mail: info@sis.edu
http://www.sis.edu
Grade levels N-2, enrollment 205

Richard A Ralphs, School Director
Amara Sawasidevi, School Head

1236 St. Xavier's Greenherald School
Asad Ave-Mohammedpur
Dhaka 1207
Bangladesh

Mary Imelda, Principal

1237 Stearley Heights Elementary School
Unit 5166
APO Kadena 96368 5166
Okinawa

Thomas Godbold, Principal

1238 Sullivans Elementary School
PSC 473, Box 96
Yokosuka 96349 0005
Japan

Dr. Carol Cressy, Principal

1239 Surabaya International School
CitraRaya International Village
Tromol Pos 2/SBDK
Surabaya 60225
Indonesia
62-31-741-4300
Fax: 62-31-741-4334
E-mail: Incsupt@rad.net.id
Private, coeducational day school which offers an educational program from preschool through grade 12.

Larry Crouch, Superintendent

1240 TEDA International School-Tianjin
Wei Shan Road, Shuang Gang
Tianjin 300350
China
86-22-2859-2001
Fax: 86-22-2859-2007
E-mail: tist_development@yahoo.com
http://www.tistschool.org
Grade levels N-10, school year August - June

Nick Bowley, Director

1241 Tabubil International School
PO Box 408 Tabubil
W Province, Papua
New Guinea

SE Walker, Principal

1242 Taegu Elementary & High School
Unit 15623
APO Taegu 96218 0005
Korea

Leon Rivers, Principal

1243 Taipei American School
800 Chung Shan N Road
Section 6, Shin Lin 111, Taipei
Taiwan
886-2-287-39900
Fax: 886-2-287-31641
E-mail: mainadmn@tas.edu.tw
http://www.tas.edu.tw
An independent, coeducational school, which offers K-12 for students of all nationalities. Hosts 2,142 students. Offers Mandarin, French, Spanish and Japanese language courses.

Mark Ulfers, Superintendent
Ira B Weislow, Business Manager

1244 Tanglin Trust Schools
Portsdown Road
Songapore 0513
Singapore
65-67780711
Fax: 65-67775862
E-mail: dvmt@tt.edu.sg
http://www.tts.edu.sg

Gade levels prekindergarten through eleventh, enrollment 1550.

Ronald Stones, Head of School

1245 Thai-Chinese International School
Prasertsin Road, Bangplee-Yai
Bangplee, Sumut Prakarm 10540
Thailand
66-2-260-8202
E-mail: tcis@schoolmail.com
Grade levels Pre-K through 12, school year
August - June

1246 Timbertop Campus
Timbertop PB-Mansfield
Victoria 3722
Australia

S Leslie, Principal

1247 Traill Preparatory School
34-36 S01
18 Ramkhamheng Road, Huamark
Bangkok
Thailand

AM Traill, Principal

1248 Ukarumpa High School
PO Box 406
Ukarumpa Via Lae, Papua
New Guinea

Steve Walker, Principal

1249 United Nations International School-Hanoi
2C Van Phuc Diplomatic Compound
Kima Ma Road, Hanoi
Veitnam
84-0-4846-1284
Fax: 84-0-4846-2967
E-mail: postmaster@unishanoi.netnam.vn
http://www.unishanoi.org
A private, nonprofit, English language, coeducational day school which offers an educational program from prekindergarten through grade 12 for the expatriate community of Hanoi.

Frances Rhodes PhD, Director

1250 United World College-SE Asia
Pasir Panjang
PO Box 15, Singapore 9111
Singapore
65-775-5344
Fax: 65-778-5846
E-mail: uwcsea@singnet.com.sg
http://www.uwcsea.edu.sg
Grade levels k-12, enrollment 2,358.

Andrew Bennet, Head of College

1251 University Vacancies in Australia
Australian Vice-Chancellors' Committee
PO Box 1142
Canberra City
Australia
61-02-6285-8200
Fax: 60-02-6285-8211
E-mail: enquiries@avcc.edu.au
http://www.avcc.edu.au

1252 Vientiane International School
PO Box 3180
Vientianne
Laos PDR
856-21-313-606
Fax: 856-21-315-008
E-mail: dragon@laotel.com
http://www.vis.laopdr.com
Grades PS-9, enrollment 159.

John Ritter, Director

1253 Wellesley College
PO Box 41037
Eastbourne, Wellington
New Zealand

G Dreadon, Principal

1254 Wesley International School
Kotak Pos 275
Jalan Simpang Kwoka 1, Malang 65101
Indonesia
62-341-586410
Fax: 62-341-586413
E-mail: wesley@mlg.mega.net.id
http://www.weleyinterschool.org
Grade levels K-12, school year August - May

Paul Richardson, HS Principal

1255 Western Academy of Beijing
PO Box 8547
Chao Yong District, Beijing 100102
China
86-10-8456-4155
Fax: 86-10-6432-2440
E-mail: wabinfo@westernacademy.com
http://www.wab.edu
Grade levels N-8, school year August - June

John McBryde, Director

1256 Wewak International Primary School
PO Box 354
Wewak Esp, Papua
New Guinea

Darian Sullavan, Principal

1257 Woodstock School
Mussoorie 248 179
Uttar Pradesh
India
91-135-632-610
Fax: 91-135-632-885
http://www.woodstock.ac.in
Woodstock is an international Christian boarding school, for grades preK-12.

David Jeffery, Principal

1258 Xiamen International School
Jiu Tian Hu, Xinglin District
Xiamen 361022
China
86-592-625-6581
Fax: 86-592-625-6584
E-mail: JDFISCH47@yahoo.com
http://www.xischina.com
Grade levels Pre-K through 12, school year
August - June

Rob Leveillee PhD, Headmaster

1259 Yew Chung Shanghai International School
11 Shui Cheng Road
20036 Shanghai
China
8621-6242-3243
Fax: 8621-6242-7331
E-mail: inquiry@ycef.com
http://www.ycef.com
Grade levels Pre-K through 12, school year
September - July

Wayne McCullar PhD, Co-Principal
James O'Connor, Co-Principal

1260 Yogyakarta International School
Jl Kaliurang KM5
Pogung Baru Block
Indonesia
62-274-586-067
Fax: 62-274-586-067
E-mail: yisworld@indosat.net.id
Grade levels Pre-K through 6, school year
August - June

Mark Massion, Principal

1261 Yokohama International School
258 Yamate-cho Naka-ku
Yokohama 241
Japan
81-45-622-0084
Fax: 81-45-621-0379
E-mail: yis@yis.ac.jp
http://www.yis.ac.jp
Grade levels N through 12.

Neil Richards, Headmaster

1262 Yokota East Elementary School
DoDDS P J YE Unit 5072
APO, Yokota 96328 5072
Japan
81-3117-55-5503
Fax: 81-3117-55-5502
Yokota East Elementary School is located on Yokota Air Force Base near Tokyo, Japan. There are approximately 900 students grades K-6.

Charles Yahres, Principal

1263 Yokota High School
DoDDS P J YH Unit 5072
APO, Yokota 96328 5072
Japan

Dr. Edward Davies, Principal

1264 Yokota West Elementary School
DoDDS P J YW Unit 5072
APO, Yokota 96328 5072
Japan

James Bowers, Principal

1265 Yonggwang Foreign School
Ceii Site Office
PO Box 9, Yonggwang-Kun 513-880
Korea

Eleanor Jones, Principal

1266 Zama Junior High & High School
USA Garrison, Camp Zama
APO, Honshu 96343 0005
Japan

Samuel Menniti, Principal

1267 Zukeran Elementary School
Unit 35017
FPO 96373 5017
Japan
011-81-611-7452576
Fax: 011-81-611-7457662
E-mail: zessac@hotmail.com
http://www.oki-dso.odedodea/okinawa/schools/zes/zes.html

Sharon Carter, Principal

Central & South America

1268 Academia Cotopaxi American International School
De las Higuerillas y Alondras
Quito, Ecuador, Casilla 1701-199
Ecuador
593-2-246-7373
Fax: 593-2-244-5195
E-mail: director@cotopaxi.k12.ec
http://www.cotopaxi.k12.ec
Grade levels Pre-K through 12, school year August - June

F Joseph Stucker, Director

1269 American Cooperative School
Lawton 20
Paramarobo
Suriname
597-49-9461
Fax: 597-498-853
E-mail: acs_suriname@sil.org
A private, coeducational day school which offers an educational program from prekindergarten through grade 12 for students of all nationalities.

Frank Martens, Administrator

1270 American Elementary & High School
Caixa Postal 7432
01064-970, Sao Paulo
Brazil
55-11-3842-2499
Fax: 55-11-3842-9358
E-mail: graded@eagle.aegsp.br
A private, coeducational day school which offers a full college-preparatory educational program from preschool through grade 12 for students of all nationalities.

Dr. Gunther Brandt, Principal

1271 American International School-Bolivia
PO Box 5309
Cochabamba
Bolivia
591-42-88-577
Fax: 591-42-88-576
E-mail: dsmith@mail.aisb.edu.bo
http://www.aisb.edu.bo

Kathleen Asbun, Director General

1272 American International School-Lincoln Buenos Aires
Andr‚s Ferreyra 4073 La Lucila
1636 La Lucila, Buenos Aires
Argentina
54-11-479-49400
Fax: 54-11-479-02117
E-mail: lincoln@lincoln.edu.ar
http://www.lincoln.edu.ar
Grade levels K-12, school year August-June

Philip Joslin, Superintendent

1273 American School
Final Calle La Mascotta #3
Colonia La Mascota, San Salvador
El Salvador
503-26-38-330
Fax: 503-26-38-385
E-mail: llarsen@ns.amschool.edu.sv
http://www.amschool.edu.sv

Leslie Larsen, General Director

1274 American School Foundation AC
Bondojito #215
Colonia Las Americas, Delegacion Alvaro
Mexico DF, Mexico 01120
52-55-5227-4900
Fax: 52-55-5273-4357
E-mail: asf@www.asf.edu.mx
http://www.asf.edu.mx

Dr. Joyce Lujan Martinez, Head of School

1275 American School Foundation-Guadalajara
Colomos 2100, Col. Providencia
Guadalajara, Jalisco 44640
Mexico
52-3-817-3377
Fax: 52-3-817-3356
E-mail: asfg@warrior.asfg.mx
A private, coeducational day school which offers an educational program from prekindergarten to grade 12.

Charles E Prince, Principal

1276 American School Foundation-Monterrey
Rio Missouri 555 Ote
Coronel del Valle, Garza Garcia
Nuevo Leon 66220, Mexico
52-81-8153-4400
Fax: 52-81-8378-2535
E-mail: jeff.keller@asfm.edu.mx
http://www.asfm.edu.mx
A private, nonprofit, coeducational day school which offers an educational program from nursery through grade 12 for students of all nationalities.

Dr. Jeffrey Keller, Superintendent

1277 American School-Belo Horizonte
Avenida Deputado Cristovan Chiaradia 120
Caixa Postal 1701
Bairro Buritis, Belo Horizonte 30575-440
Brazil
55-31-378-6700
Fax: 55-31-378-6878
E-mail: eabhawk@bhnet.br
A coeducational, private day school which offers an educational program from prekindergarten through grade 12 for students of all nationalities.

Sid Stewart, Principal

1278 American School-Brasilia
Avenicla L-2 Sul
SGAS Q-605-E Brasilia
Brazil
55-61-443-3237
Fax: 55-61-244-4303
E-mail: rwernen@bus.eabdf.br
http://www.eabdf.br
A private, coeducational day school which offers an educational program from prekindergarten through grade 12 for students of all nationalities.

Raymond Lauk PhD, Headmaster

1279 American School-Campinas
Caixa Postal 1183
13100 Campinas Sp, Brazil
55-19-754-1200
Fax: 55-19-754-1212

David Cardenas, Superintendent

1280 American School-Durango
Francisw Sarabia #416 Pte
Durango 34000
Mexico
52-181-33-636
Fax: 52-181-12-839

Dr. Jorge O Nelson, Principal

1281 American School-Guatemala
US Embassy, Unit 3325
APO AA 34024
Guatemala
502-369-8334
Fax: 502-369-8335
E-mail: cagadm@cag.edu.gt
http://www.colegioamericanoguatemula.com
Grade levels K-12, school year January - October

Barbara Barillas, General Director

1282 American School-Guayaquil
PO Box 3304
Guayaquill
Ecuador
593-4-255-503
Fax: 593-4-250-453
E-mail: dir_asg@gye.satnet.net
Grade levels K-12, school year April - January

Francisco Andrade, Interim General Director
Patricia Ayala de Coronel, HS Principal

1283 American School-Laguna Verde
Veracruz, Mexico

Maurice H Blum, Principal

1284 American School-Lima
Apartado 18-0977 Miraflores
Lima 18
Peru
51-14-35-0890
Fax: 51-14-36-0927
E-mail: drandall@amersol.edu.pe
This school offers an English curriculum (with some classes in Spanish) to 741 boys and 565 girls in grades EC2-12. Teacher exchanges are welcome with the length of stay being two years, with an allowance for housing.

David Randall, Principal

1285 American School-Pachuca
Boulevard Valle De San Javier S/N
Pachuca, Hidalgo
Mexico
52-771-39608
Fax: 52-771-85077
E-mail: amerpach@compaq.net.mx
Grade levels prekindergarten through ninth.

Andrew Sherman, General Director

1286 American School-Puebla
Apartado 665
Puebla
Mexico

Dr. Arthur W Chaffee, Principal

1287 American School-Puerto Vallarta
PO Box 275-B
Puerto Vallarta, Jalisco 48300
Mexico
52-3-221-1525
Fax: 52-3-221-1996
E-mail: gsel@pvnet.com.mx
http://www.americanschool-pv.com.mx

Gerald Selitzer, Director

1288 American School-Recife
Rua Sa e Souza, 408
Boa Viagem, Recife
Brazil
55-81-341-4716
Fax: 55-81-341-0142
E-mail: hgueiros@ear.com.br
http://www.ear.com
A private, coeducational day school which offers an instructional program from prekindergarten through grade 12 for students of all nationalities.

Helen Gueiros, Superindendent

1289 American School-Tampico
Hidalgo S/N
Col. Tancol, Tamaulipas
Mexico
52-12-272-081
Fax: 52-12-280-080
E-mail: ast@tamnet.com.mx
http://www.ats.edu.mx
Grade levels N through tenth.

Emma deSalazar, Headmaster

1290 American School-Torreon
Avenue Mayran Y Nogal Col Jardin
27200 Coahula
Mexico
52-8717-135-389
Fax: 52-8717-173-155
E-mail: lsynder@cat.mx
http://www.cat.mx

Larry F Snyder, Director General

1291 Anglo American School
PO Box 3188-1000
San Jose
Costa Rica
506-279-2626
Fax: 506-279-7894
E-mail: angloam@racsa.co.cr
Grade levels Pre-K through 6, school year February - November

Virginia Hine Barrantes, Principal

1292 Anglo Colombian School
Apaptado Aereo 253393
Bogota
Colombia

David Toze, Principal

1293 Anglo-American School
Calle 37
Avenida Central, 1000 San Jose
Costa Rica
E-mail: angloam@sd.racsa.co.cr

Virginia Hine, Principal

1294 Antofagasta International School
Avenida Angamos 587
Antofagasta
Chile
56-55-256-613
Fax: 56-55-256-628
E-mail: ais@ais.cl
http://www.ais.cl
Grade levels Pre-K through 8, school year February - December

Bryan Lewallen, Principal

1295 Asociacion Colegio Granadino
AA 2138
Manizales, Caldas
Colombia
57-68-745-774
Fax: 57-68-746-066
E-mail: granadino@emtelsa.multi.net.co
http://www.granadino.com

Grade levels Pre-K through 12, school year August - June

Gonzalo Arango, General Director

1296 Asociacion Escuelas Lincoln
Andres Ferreyra 4073
1636 La Lucila, Buenos Aires
Argentina
54-11-4794-9400
Fax: 54-11-4790-2117
E-mail: joslin_p@lincoln.edu.ar
http://www.lincoln.edu.ar

Phil Joslin, Superintendent

1297 Balboa Elementary School
Unit 9025
APO Balboa 34002
Panama

Susan Beattie, Principal

1298 Balboa High School
Unit 9025
APO Balboa 34002
Panama

Ernest Holland, Principal

1299 Barker College
Avenida Meeks 337
Lomas de Zamora, Buenos Aires
Argentina

Jimmy Cappanera, Principal

1300 Belgrano Day School
Juramento 3035
1428 Capital Federal, Buenos Aires
Argentina
E-mail: rrpp@bds.esc.edu.ar
This Roman Catholic affiliated school offers an English/Spanish curriculum for 1,002 day students (570 boys and 432 girls) in grades K-12.

Bernard Green, Principal
Carol Halle, Faculty Head

1301 Bilingue School Isaac Newton
Chihuahua, Mexico

Lauya Gonzalez Valenzula, Principal

1302 British American School
AA 4368
Barranquilla
Colombia

Rafael Ortegon Rocha, Principal

1303 British School-Costa Rica
PO Box 8184-1000
San Jose
Costa Rica

David John Lloyd, Principal

1304 British School-Rio de Janeiro
Rua Real Grandeza 87-Cep 22281
Botafogo, Rio de Janeiro
Brazil
55-21-2539-2717
Fax: 55-21-2266-4060
E-mail: wiseman@britishschool.g12.br

David Morley, Principal

1305 British School-Venezuela
Apartado 61.161
Caracas 1060A
Venezuela

JH Sidwell, Principal

1306 Buenos Aires International Christian Academy
Chile 343
1642 San Isidro, Buenos Aires
Argentina
54-114-4732-1914
Fax: 54-114-4732-3329
E-mail: baica@ciudad.com.ar
http://www.baica.com
Grade levels Pre-K through 10, school year August - June

Eric Sticker, Director
Guillermo Larzabal, Principal

1307 Caribbean International School
Box 1594
Cristobal Colon
Panama

Yolanda Anderson, Principal

1308 Centro Cultural Brazil-Elementary School
Rua Jorge Tibirica 5
11100 Santos, Sao Paulo
Brazil

Newton Antonio Martin, Principal

1309 Cochabamba Cooperative School
Casilla 1395
Cochabamba
Bolivia
591-42-987-61
Fax: 591-42-329-06
E-mail: ccs@bo.net

Howard Robertson, Director

1310 Colegio Abraham Lincoln
Calle 170, #50-25
Bos 90339, Bogota
Columbia

Dr. Luis Hernando Ramir, Principal

1311 Colegio Alberto Einstein
PO Box 5018
Quito
Ecuador

Benjamin Tobar, Principal

1312 Colegio Americano De Guayaquil
PO Box 3304
Guayaquil
Ecuador
593-4-255-03
Fax: 593-4-250-453
E-mail: amschool@gye.satnet.net

Stanley Whitman, Principal

1313 Colegio Anglo Colombiano
PO Box 253393
Bogota
Colombia

David Toze, Principal

1314 Colegio Bilingue Juan Enrigue
Pestalozzi AC
Veracruz
Mexico

Michael S Garber, Principal

1315 Colegio Bolivar
Apartado Aereo 26300
Cali
Colombia
57-2-555-2039
Fax: 57-2-555-2041
E-mail:
admisiones@colegiobolivar.edu.co
http://www.colegiobolivar.edu.co

Grade levels Pre-K through 12, school year August-June

Martin Felton, PhD, Director

1316 Colegio Columbo Britanico
Apartado Aereo 5774
Cali
Colombia

Ian Watson, Principal

1317 Colegio Gran Bretana
Carrera 51 #215-20
Bogota
Colombia
57-1-615-0391
Fax: 57-1-676-0426
E-mail: cgbdirector@bigfoot.com
http://www.colgranbret.edu.co
Grade levels N-10, school year August-June

Daryl Barker, Director
David Simpson, Deputy Director

1318 Colegio Granadino
AA 2138 Manizales
Colombia
57-6-874-57-74
Fax: 57-6-874-60-66
E-mail: granadino@emtelsa.multi.net.com

Gonzalo Arango, Principal

1319 Colegio Interamericano de la Montana
Moulevard La Montana
Finca El Socorro, Zona 16
Guatemala City, Guatemala
502-3-641-803
Fax: 502-3-641-779

Dr. Bert Webb, General Director

1320 Colegio Jorge Washington
Apartado Aereo 1899
Cartagena
Colombia
57-5-665-3136
Fax: 57-5-665-6447
E-mail: director@cojowa.edu.co
Grade levels Pre-K through 12, school year August-June

Pete Nonnenkamp, Director

1321 Colegio Karl C Parrish
AA 52962
Barranquilla
Colombia
57-5-359-9484
Fax: 57-5-359-8828
E-mail: drfarr@col13.telecom.com.co
http://www.kcparrish.edu.co
Grade levels N-12, school year August-June

Michael Farr, PhD, Director

1322 Colegio Montelibano
AA 6823 Cerromatoso
Montelibano, Bogota
Colombia

Francisco Cajiao, Principal

1323 Colegio Nueva Granada
AA 51339
Santa Fe de Bogota
Colombia
57-1-235-5350
Fax: 57-1-211-3720
E-mail: sngrana@COL1.telecom.com.co
http://www.cng.edu
A private, coeducational day school which offers an educational program from prekindergarten through grade 12 for students of all nationalities.

Barry McCombs PhD, Director

1324 Colegio Peterson SC
Apartado Postal 10-900
DF 11000
Mexico
52-5-81-30-11-4
Fax: 52-5-81-31-38-5
E-mail: kapm@mail.internet.com.mx

Marvin Peterson, Principal

1325 Colegio San Marcus
Jorges Miles 153
1842 Monte Grande, Buenos Aires
Argentina

Susana Raffo, Principal

1326 Colegio Ward
Hector Coucheiro 599
1706 DF Sarmiento, Ramos Mejia
Buenos Aires, Argentina

Ruben Carlos Urcola, Principal

1327 Costa Rica Academy
Apartado Postal 4941
San Jose 1000
Costa Rica
506-239-03-76
Fax: 506-239-06-25
A private, coeducational school which offers an educational program from prekindergarten through grade 12 for students of all nationalities.

William D Rose, BS, MEd, Principal

1328 Cotopaxi Academy
Casilla 17.01-199
Quito
Ecuador
593-2-246-7411
Fax: 593-2-244-5195
E-mail: director@cotopaxi.kl2.ec
A private, independent, coeducational day school which offers an American program of studies from play group through grade 12 for students of all nationalities.

Arthur Pontes, Principal

1329 Country Day School
Apartado 1139
1250 Escazu, Escazu, Costa Rica
Central America
506-289-8406
Fax: 506-228-2076
E-mail: codasch@sol.racsa.co.cr
http://www.cds.ed.cr
Grade levels through 12, school year August-June.

Timithy Carr, Director

1330 Crandon Institute
Casilla Correo 445
Montevideo
Uruguay
This school offers a curriculum taught in Spanish for 2,000 day students (700 boys; 1,300 girls), in high school through junior college level (home economics, commercial). The school, affiliated with the Methodist church, employs 300 teachers.

Marcos Rocchietti, Principal

1331 Curundu Elementary School
Unit 0925
APO Curundu 34002 0005
Panama

Clifford Drexler, Principal

1332 Curundu Junior High School
Unit 0925
APO Curundu 34002 0005
Panama

Charles Renno, Principal

1333 Edron Academy-Calz Al Desierto
Desierto de los Leones 5578
Mexico City 01740
Mexico
5-585-30-49
Fax: 5-585-28-46

Richard Gilby Travers, Principal

1334 El Abra School
Phelps Dodge Corporation
Calama
Chile
56-55-313-600
Fax: 56-55-315-182
E-mail: elabraschool@hotmail.com
Grade levels K-11, school year August - June

Margaret Maclean, Head Of School

1335 English School
AA 51284
Bogota
Colombia

Leonard Mabe, Principal

1336 Escola Americana do Rio de Janeiro
Estrada Da Gavea 132
Rio de Janeiro 22451-260
Brazil
55-21-512-9830
Fax: 55-21-259-4722
E-mail: americanrio@ax.apc.org
A private coeducational day school which offers an educational program from nursery through grade 12 for students of all nationalities.

Dr. Dennis Klumpp, Principal

1337 Escola Maria Imaculada
Caixa Postal 21293 Brooklin
Sao Paulo 04698
Brazil

Gerald Gates, Principal

1338 Escuela Anaco
Apartado 31
Anaco
Venezuela

Francene Conte, Principal

1339 Escuela Bilingue Santa Barbara
Apartado 342-El Marchito
San Pedro Sila
Honduras
504-659-3053
Fax: 504-659-3059
E-mail: mochitoschool@breakwater.hn
Grade levels preK through 8.

John P Leddy, Principal

1340 Escuela Bilingue Valle De Sula
Apartado 735
San Pedro Sula
Honduras

Carole A Black, Principal

1341 Escuela International Sampedrana
Apartado Postal 565
San Pedro Sula
Honduras
504-566-2722
Fax: 504-566-1458
E-mail: scis@netsys.hn
Gregorg E Werner, Principal

1342 Escuela Las Palmas
Apartdo 6-2637
Panama
Aleida Molina, Principal

1343 Foreign Students School
Avenue Station B
#6617-6615 Esquina 70
Miramar Havana City, Cuba
Gillian P Greenwood, Principal

1344 Fort Clayton Elementary School
Unit 0925
APO, Fort Clayton 34004 0005
Panama
Barbara Seni, Principal

1345 Fort Kobbe Elementary School
Unit 0714
APO, Fort Kobbe 34001 0005
Panama
Dr. Vinita Swenty, Principal

1346 Fundacion Colegio Americano de Quito
Manuel Benigno Cueva N 80-190
Carcelen, Quito
Ecuador
593-2-472-974
Fax: 593-2-472-972
E-mail: dirgeneral@fcaq.k12.ec
http://www.fcaq.k12.ec
Grade levels Pre-K through 12, school year
September - June.
Susan Barbara, Director General

1347 George Washington School
Apartado Aereo 2899
Cartagena
Colombia
57-5-665-3396
Fax: 57-5-665-6447
A private, coeducational day school which
offers and educational program from
prekindergarten through grade 12 for stu-
dents of all nationalities.
Steven Fields, Principal

1348 Grange School
Casilla 218
Correo 12, Santiago
Chile
56-2-396-0101
Fax: 56-2-227-1204
E-mail: admissions@grange.cl
http://www.grange.cl
Grade levels Pre-K through 12, school year
March - December
John Mackenzie, Headmaster
James Cowan, Deputy Headmaster

1349 Greengates School
Circumbalacion Pte 102
Baliones De San Mateo, Naucalpah
Mexico 53200
52-55-5373-0088
Fax: 52-55-5373-0765
E-mail: sarav@greengates.edu.mx

Grade levels prekindergarten through
twelfth.
Susan E Mayer, Principal

1350 Howard Elementary School
Unit 0713
APO, Howard AFB 34001 0005
Panama
Jean Lamb, Principal

1351 Inst Tecnologico De Estudios
Apartado Postal 28B
Chihuahua
Mexico
Hector Chavrez Barron, Principal

1352 International Preparatory School
PO Box 20015-LC
Santiago
Chile
56-2-321-5800
Fax: 56-2-321-5821
E-mail: info@tipschool.com
http://www.tipschool.com
Grade levels Pre-K through 12, school year
March - December
Lesley Easton-Allen, Headmistress
Pamela Thomson, Curriculum
Coordinator

1353 International School Nido de Aguilas
Casilla 27020
Correo 27, Santiago
Chile
56-2-216-6842
Fax: 56-2-216-7603
E-mail: mail@nido.cl
http://www.nido.cl
A private, coeducational day school which
offers a comprehensive educational pro-
gram from prekindergarten through grade
12 for students of all nationalities.
Dr. Clifford Strommen, Headmaster
Joe McDonald, HS Principal

1354 International School-Curitiba
PO Box 7004
80520 Curitiba
Brazil
Ronald James Mccluskey, Principal

1355 International School-La Paz
CC1075870 Villa Dolores
La Paz, Cordoba
Argentina
LH Sullivan, Principal

1356 International School-Panama
PO Box 6-7589
El Dorado
Panama
507-266-7037
Fax: 507-266-7808
E-mail: isp@isp.edu.pa
http://www.isp.edu.pa
A private, coeducational day school which
offers an educational program from
prekindergarten through grade 12 for stu-
dents of all nationalities.
Dr. Mary G Mend, Director
Laurie Lewter, Business Manager

1357 Karl C Parrish School
3598629 AA 52962
Barranquilla
Colombia
57-5-3598590
Fax: 57-5-3598828
E-mail: kcparrish@rnd.net
http://www.kcparrish.edu.co
This school offers a curriculum of Eng-
lish/Spanish to 806 day students (455 boys;
351 girls), in grades 1-12. The length of
stay for overseas teachers is two years,
with housing provided. Applications
needed to teach include science, social sciences, math, reading, English, and physical
education. Other criteria include a BA Degree, two years of successful experience in
grade/subject for which applying. Overseas experience, preferred Spanish language.
Michael Farr, PhD, Director

1358 Liceo Pino Verde
Kilometro 6
Via Cerritos, Pereira Rda
Colombia
963-379368
This school teaches English as a second
language; builds strong human values; develops logical thinking skills and prepares
students for the world of technology and
communication. Enrollment consists of
110 day students (57 boys; 53 girls, in
grades PK-12. Overseas teachers are welcome to apply with the length of stay being
two years, with housing provided. Applications needed to teach include science, math
and English.
Luz Stella Rios Patino, Principal

1359 Limon School
Apartado 565
Limon
Costa Rica
Elexer Arava, Principal

1360 Lincoln International Academy
PO box 20000
Correo 20, Santiago
Chile
56-2-217-1907
Fax: 56-2-215-1080
E-mail: lintac@entelchile.net
http://www.lintac.com
Grade levels Pre-K through 12, school year
March - December
Veronica Caroca, Headmistress
John F Seaquist, Director

1361 Mackay School
Vicuna Mackenna 700 Renaca
Vina del Mar
Chile
Nigel William Blackbur, Principal

1362 Marian Baker School
Apartado 4269
7an Jose
Costa Rica
560-273-3426
Fax: 506-273-4609
E-mail: mbschool@sol.racsa.co.cr
http://www.marianbakerschool.com
Grade level pre-k through 12.
Linda Niehaus, Director

1363 Marymount School
Apartado Aereo #1912
Barranquilla
Colombia

Dr. Kathleen Cunniffe, Principal

1364 Metropolitan School
Tegucigalpa, Honduras

Bertha DeFlores, Principal

1365 Modern American School
Cerro del Hombre #18
Coyoacan CP 04310
Mexico

1366 Northlands Day School
Roma 1210
1636 Olivos, Buenos Aires
Argentina
This bilingual day school for girls offers modern facilities, sports, etc. on a spacious campus. Languages spoken include English and Spanish and total enrollment is 1,100 students, ranging in grade from K1-12. Overseas teachers are accepted, with the length of stay being 2-6 years with housing provided.

Susan Brooke Jackson, MA, Principal

1367 Our Lady of Mercy School
48 Visconde De Caravelas
Botafoga ZC02 Rio de Janeiro
Brazil

Charles Lyndaker, Principal

1368 Pan American Christian Academy
Caixa Postal 12491
04798 Sao Paulo
Brazil
55-11-5929655
Fax: 55-11-59289591
http://www.paca.com.br

Micheal Epp, Superintendent

1369 Pan American School-Bahia
Caixa Postal 231
Salvador Bahia 40901-970
Brazil
55-71-367-9099
Fax: 55-71-367-9090
E-mail: epaba@svn.com.br
A private, coeducational day school which offers a program from preschool through grade 12 for students of all nationalities.

Mary Jo Heatherington, PhD,
Superintendent

1370 Pan American School-Costa Rica
Apartado 118-1150, La Uruca
Monterrey, San Jose
Costa Rica
52-8-342-0778
Fax: 52-8-340-2749
E-mail: dadmission@pas.edu.mx
http://www.pas.edu.mx
Grade levels prekindergarten through eleventh.

Robert Arpee, Director

1371 Pan American School-Monterrey
Hidalgo 656 Pte
Apartado Postal 474, Monterrey 64000
Mexico
52-83-404176
This school offers an English curriculum for 1,393 day students and 100 boarding students (709 boys; 684 girls), grades preschool through nine. The school is willing to participate in a teacher exchange pro-

gram with the length of stay being one year. Applications needed to teach include science, preschool, math, reading, English, and physical education.

Tobert L Arpee, Principal
Lenor Arpee, Faculty Head

1372 Pan American School-Porto Alegre
Rua Joao Paetzel 440
91 330 Porto Alegre
Brazil

Jennifer Sughrue, Principal

1373 Panama Canal College
Unit 0925
APO Balboa 34002 0005
Panama

1374 Prescott Anglo American School
PO Box 1036
Arequipa
Peru
This school offers a Spanish/English curriculum for 1,050 day students (450 boys; 600 girls) in grades K-12. Students are taught English three hours a day, so they can reach an intermediate level in grade 9, and high intermediate in grades 11-12.

Jorge Pachecot, Principal

1375 Redland School
Camino El Alba 11357
Santiago
Chile
This school offers an English/spanish curriculum to 820 day students (420 boys; 400 girls), in grades PreK-12. The student body is mostly Chilean and 90% of the teachers are Chilean. However, overseas teachers are welcome, with the applications being pre-school and English.

Richard Collingwood-Selby, Principal

1376 Reydon School for Girls
5178 Cruz Chica
Sierras de Cordoba, Cordoba
Argentina

NJ Milman, Principal

1377 Saint George's School
Apartado Aereo 51579
Bogota
Colombia

Mary De Acosta, Principal

1378 Santa Cruz Cooperative School
Casilla 753
Santa Cruz
Bolivia
591-3-530-8080
Fax: 591-3-352-6993
E-mail: wmck@hotmial.com
http://www.sccs.edu.bo
A private, coeducational day school which offers an educational program from prekindergarten through grade 12 for students of all nationalities.

William McKelligott, Director General

1379 Santa Margarita School
Avenue Manuel Olguin 961 El Derby
Surco, Lima
Peru

Guillermo Descalzi, Principal

1380 St. Albans College
R Falcon 250
1832 Lomas de Zamora, Buenos Aires
Argentina
This school offers courses to 702 day students (383 boys and 319 girls) in grades K through twelve. The school does participate in teacher exchange programs with the length of stay for teachers being one year. Applications from overseas needed to teach include science, pre-school, math, social sciences, administration, reading, German, English, and physical education.

John R Vibart, Headmaster
Carlos Palermo, Faculty Director

1381 St. Andrew's Scots School
Ruque Sanez Pena
1636 Olivos, Buenos Aires
Argentina
54-114-799-8318
Fax: 54-114-799-8318
E-mail: johntaylor@sanandres.esc.edu.ar
http://www.sanandres.esc.edu.ar
Grades K-12, school year February - December

John Taylor, Headmaster
Ana Repila, Admissions Director

1382 St. Catherine's School
Carbajal 3250
1426 Capital Federal, Buenos Aires
Argentina
54-114-552-4353
Fax: 54-114-554-4113
E-mail: stcath@ciudad.com.ar
http://www.redeseducacion.com.ar
Pre-K through 12, school year March-December

Mabel Manzitti, Principal

1383 St. George's College
Casilla de Correo No 2
1878 Quilmes, Bunos Aires
Argentina
54-11-425-73472
Fax: 54-11-425-30030
E-mail: info@stgeorge.com.ar
http://www.stgeorge.com.ar
Grade levels N-12, school year February - December

James Batten, Headmaster
Peter Ashton, Deputy Headmaster

1384 St. Hilda's College
Cowley Palce
Oxford OX4 1DY
Argentina
44-1865-276884
Fax: 44-1865-276816

Martin Garvie, Principal

1385 St. John School
Casilla 284
Concepcion
Chile
St. John School is a bilingual school that caters to children from PK through grade twelve. The student body includes 1,170 day students (580 boys and 590 girls). The school does participate in teacher exchange programs with the length of stay for teachers being two years. The languages spoken include Spanish and English and the student/teacher ratio is 10:1.

Chris Pugh, Principal

1386 St. Margaret's British School-Girls
Casilla 392-5 Norte
1351 Vina del Mar
Chile
Margery Byrne, Principal

1387 St. Paul's School
Caixa Postal 3472 Cep 01051
Sao Paulo
Brazil
Richardo Pons, Principal

1388 St. Pauls School
5178 Cruz Grande
Cordoba
Argentina
AH Thurn, Principal

1389 St. Peter's School
Pacheco 715
1640 Martinez, Buenos Aires
Argentina
Joy Headland, Principal

1390 Teaching Opportunities in Latin America for US Citizens
Organization of American States
17th & Constitution Avenue NW
Washington, DC 20036
202-458-3000
Fax: 202-458-3967
Supports teaching abroad opportunities.

1391 The American School Foundation of Monterrey
R¡o Missouri, 555 Ote
Garza Garc¡a, Nuevo Leon 66220
Mexico
52-8-158-4409
Fax: 52-8-378-2535
E-mail:
jeff.keller@missouri.asfm.edu.mx
Private international day school founded in 1928 to provide students with a US type of education.
Dr. Jeff Keller, Superintendent

1392 Uruguayan American School
1785 Dublin
Montevideo 11500
Uruguay
598-2-600-7681
Fax: 598-2-606-1935
E-mail: info@uas.edu.uyuy
http://www.uas.edu.uy
Grade level N through twelfth, with enrollment of 207 students.
David Deuel, Director

1393 William T Sampson
Elementary & High School
PSC 1005 Box 49
FPO, Guantanamo Bay 09593 0005
Cuba

Eastern Europe

1394 American Academy Larnaca
PO Box 112-Gregory Afxentious Ave
Larnaca
Cyprus
Maurice Holt, Principal

1395 American College-Sofia
PO Box 873
Sofia 1000
Bulgaria
359-2-975-3695
Fax: 359-2-934-3129
E-mail: acs@acs.bg
http://www.acs.acad.bg
This school offers an English-based curriculum to 530 day students (250 boys; 280 girls), in grades 8-12. This is the oldest American educational institution outside of the United States. The school is very selective regarding the student body and the faculty is 30% American. Student/teacher ratio is 8.5:1. Students are admitted to the best US Universities: Harvard, MIT, Colgate, Cornell, Brown, etc.
Louis J Perske, President

1396 American International School-Bucharest
Sos Pipera-Tunari 196
Com Voluntari-Pipera, Bucharest
Romania
40-1-211-0102/3
Fax: 40-1-211-0104
E-mail: director@aisb.ro
http://www.aisb.ro
Grades preK-12, enrollment 387.
Frederic F Wesson, Director

1397 American International School-Budapest
PO Box 53
Budapest 1525
Hungary
36-1-395-2176
Fax: 36-1-395-2179
http://www.aisb.hu
Grade levels Pre-K through 13, school year August-June
John Johnson, School Director

1398 American International School-Cyprus
PO Box 23847, 11 Kansas Street
1086 Nisocia
Cyprus
357-2-316-345
Fax: 357-2-316-549
E-mail: aisc@aisc.ac.cy
http://www.aisc.ac.cy
Grade levels Pre-K through 12, school year August-June
Joanna Ramos, Director

1399 American International School-Krakow
ul Warnenczyka 14
30-520 Krakow
Poland
48-12-656-3617
Fax: 48-12-656-4952
E-mail: aisk@kompit.com.pl
http://www.aisk.kompit.com.pl
Affiliated with the American School of Warsaw, AISK is an independent, coeducational day school which offers an educational program from preschool through grade 8 for students of all nationalities.
Brain J Marquano, Director

1400 American International School-Vienna
Salmannsdorfer Strasse 47
A-1190 Vienna
Austria
43-1-40-132-0
Fax: 43-1-40-132-5
E-mail: info@ais.at
http://www.ais.at
Grades PK-12, PG Enrollment 750.
Dr. Richard Spradling, Director

1401 American School of Bucharest
Sos Pipera-Tunari 196arest
Com Voluntari-Pipera, Bucharest
Romania
40-21-2044300
Fax: 40-21-2044306
E-mail: fwesson@asb.kappa.ro
An independent, international, coeducational day school which offers an educational program from prekindergarten through grade 12 for students of all nationalities.
F Wesson, Director

1402 Asuncion Christian Academy
American Embassy
APO, Unit #4751 34036 4751
011-595-21-607-378
Fax: 011-595-21-604-855
E-mail: aca@uninet.com.py
A co-educational Christian day school that is interdenominational and international and accredited through both Southern Association of Colleges and Associations of Christian Schools International (ACSI).
Bethany Abreu, Director

1403 Falcon School
PO Box 3640
Nicosia
Cyprus
Nikolas Michael Ieride, Principal

1404 Gimnazija Bezigrad
Periceva 4
61000 Ljublijana Slovenia
Barbara Costisa, Principal

1405 International Elementary School-Estonia
Kannu 67
13418 Tallinn
Estonia
372-660-6072
Fax: 372-660-6128
E-mail: iese@online.ee
http://www.online.ee/~iese
An independent, coeducational day school which offers an educational program for students aged 3 to 14 of all nationalities. Grades PS-10, enrollment 83.
George Lumm, Director

1406 International School-Belgrade
American Embassy Belgrade
Pariska 7, 11001 Belgrade
Yugoslavia
381-11-651-832
Fax: 381-11-652-619
E-mail: isb@eunet.yu
http://www.isb.co.yu
An independent, coeducational day school which offers an edcuational program from kindergarten through grade 8 for students of all nationalities.
Dr. Nikola P Kodzas, Director

1407 International School-Budapest
H-1121
Budapest, Kolkoly-Thege
Hungary
36-1-395-9312
Fax: 36-1-395-9310
E-mail: isb@okk.szamalk.hu
Grade levels N-8, school year August - June

Zsuzsanna Flachner, Headmaster

1408 International School-Estonia
Juhkentali 18 Tallinn
Tallinn 10132
Estonia
372-6-606-072
Fax: 372-6-606-128
E-mail: iese@online.ee
http://www.online.ee/~iese
Grade levels Pre-K through 10, school year
August - June

1409 International School-Latvia
Viestura Iela 6A
Jurmala LV2010
Latvia
371-775-5146
Fax: 371-775-5009
E-mail: isl@latnet.lv
http://www.isl.edu.lv
Grades preSchool-12, enrollment 160.

Sally Hadden, Director

1410 International School-Paphos
PO Box 2018, 22-26 Hellas Avenue
Paphos
Cyprus
061-32236
Fax: 061-34090

Anton Floyd, Principal

1411 International School-Prague
Bohumila Limova
Prague 6 164 00
Czech Republic
420-2-2038-4215
Fax: 420-2-2038-4555
E-mail: ispmail@isp.cz
http://www.isp.cz
Educational program from prekindergarten
through grade 12 for students of all nation-
alities.

Robert Landau, Director

1412 International Teachers Service
47 Papakyriazi Street
Larissa, Greece
41-253856
Fax: 41-251022
A recruitment service for teachers of English in Greece. Must have a BA/BS in education preferably English and/or EFL training
or past experience in EFL and be a native
speaker of English.

Fani Karatzou

1413 Kiev International School
3A Svyatoshinskiy Provilok
Kyiv 03115
Ukraine
380-44-452-2792
Fax: 380-44-452-2998
E-mail: kisukr@sovamua.com
http://www.qsi.org
Grade levels N-12, school year Septem-
ber-June

Michael Tewalthomas, Director
David Pera, Director Instruction

1414 Limassol Grammar-Junior School
Homer St. Ayios Nicolaos
Limassol
Cyprus

EWP Foley, Principal

1415 Logos School of English Education
33-35 Yialousa Street
PO Box 51075 3501 Limassol
Cyprus
357-25336061
Fax: 357-25335578
E-mail: rsee@spidernet.com.cy
http://www.hlogos.ac.cy

Peter Ross, Principal

**1416 Magyar British International
School**
H-1519 Budapest
PO Box 219, Budapest
Hungary

Mary E Pazsit, Principal

1417 Melkonian Educational Institute
PO Box 1907
Nicosia
Cyprus
An Armenian boarding school with high ac-
ademic standards.

S Bedikan, Principal

1418 Private English Junior School
PO Box 2262
Nicosia
Cyprus

Vassos Hajierou, BA, Principal

**1419 QSI International
School-Bratislava**
Karloveska 64
Bratislava
Slovak Republic
421-2-6542-2844
Fax: 421-2-6541-1646
E-mail: phillipsylla@qsi.org
http://www.qsi.org
Grade levels N-12, school year Septem-
ber-June

Philip Sylla, Director
Margaret Davis, Director Instruction

1420 QSI International School-Ljubljana
Puharjehva Ulica 10
100n Ljubljana
Solvenia
386-01-4396300
Fax: 386-01-4396305
E-mail: qsisln@siol.net
http://www.qsi.org
Grade levels N-9, school year Septem-
ber-June

Peter Janda, Director

1421 QSI International School-Tbilisi
10 Topuria Street
Tbilisi
Republic of Georgia
995-32-982909
Fax: 995-32-322607
E-mail: qsi@access.sanet.ge
http://www.qsi.org
Grade levels N-10, school year Septem-
ber-June

Antonio Trujillo, Director

1422 QSI International School-Yerevan
PO Box 82
375010 Yerevan
Republic of Armenia
374-1-391030
Fax: 374-1-284913
Grade levels N-8, school year Septem-
ber-June

Randy Speer, Director

Middle East

1423 ACI & SEV Elementary School
Inonu Cad. #476
Goztepe, Izmir
Turkey
90-232-285-3401
Fax: 90-232-246-1674
E-mail: school@aci.k12.tr
http://www.aci.k12.tr
Grade levels Pre-K through 12, school year
September - June

Kenneth Frank, Superintendent
Kenneth Frank, Turkish First VP

1424 Abdul Hamid Sharaf School
PO Box 6008
Amman
Jordan

Sue Dahdah, Principal

1425 Abquaiq Academy
Box 5150
Abqaiq
Saudi Arabia

Bob Herman, Principal

1426 Al Ain English Speaking School
PO Box 1419 Al Ain
Abu Dhabi
United Arab Emirates
00971-3-7678636
Fax: 00971-3-767-1973

James G Crawford, Principal

1427 Al Bayan Bilingual School
PO Box 24472
Safat 13105
Kuwait
965-531-5125
Fax: 965-533-2836
E-mail: bbsadm@ncc.moc.lcw
http://www2.kems.net/users/bbs
Grade levels N through twelfth.

Lance C Curlin, Sr, PhD, Director

1428 Al Khubairat Community School
PO Box 4001
Abu Dhabi
United Arab Emirates

DJ Holford, Principal

1429 Al Rabeeh School
PO Box 138
Abu Dhabi
United Arab Emirates

HJ Kadri, Principal

1430 Al-Nouri English School
PO Box 46901
Fahaheel
Kuwait

PD Oldfield, Principal

1431 Al-Worood School
PO Box 46673
Abu Ghabi
United Arab Emirates
971-2-444-7655
Fax: 971-2-444-9732
E-mail: alworood@emirates.net.ae
http://www.alworood.sch.ae
Grade levels N-12, school year September
- June

Nazmieh Al-Abed, Principal

1432 American Collegiate Institute
Inonu Caddesi #476 Hatay
Izmir
Turkey
90-232-285-3401
Fax: 90-232-246-4128
E-mail: school@aci.k12.tr
http://www.aci.k12.tr

Fredrick L Thompson, PhD,
Superintendent

1433 American Community School
PO Box 8129
Beirut
Lebanon
961-1-374-370
Fax: 961-1-366-050
E-mail: acs@acs.edu.lb
http://www.acs.edu.lb
Grades N-12, enrollment 997.

Catherine Bashshur, Head of School

1434 American Community School-Abu Dhabi
PO Box 42114
Abu Dhabi
United Arab Emirates
971-2-681-5115
Fax: 971-2-681-6006
E-mail: acs@acs.sch.ae
http://www.acs.sch.ae
An independent, coeducational day school
which offers an educational program from
preschool through grade 12 for English-speaking students of all nationalities.

Dr. David Cramer, Superintendent

1435 American Community School-Beirut
Avenue de Paris JelEl-Bahr
PO Box 11-8129, Riad El Solh, Beirut
Lebanon 11072260
961-1-374-370
Fax: 961-1-366-050
E-mail: acs@acs.edu.lb
http://www.acs.edu.lb
The American Community School at
Beruit is an independent, not-for-profit,
non-sectarian, coeducational preschool
through secondary school serving the international and Lebanese communities.

Catherine Bashshur, Head of School

1436 American International School
PO Box 22090
Doha
Qatar

Dr. Brian J Jones, Principal

1437 American International School-Abu Dhabi
PO Box 5992
Abu Dhabi
United Arab Emirates
971-2-444-4333
Fax: 971-2-444-4005
E-mail: aisa@emirates.net.ae
http://www.aisa.sch.ae

Grade levels kindergarten through twelfth,
with enrollment of 750 students.

Peter J McMurray, Director

1438 American International School-Israel
PO Box 9005
Kfar Shmaryahu
Israel
972-9-961-8100
Fax: 972-9-961-8111
E-mail:
aisrael@american.hasharon.k12.il
An independent, coeducational day school
which offers an educational program from
kindergarten through grade 12 for students
of all nationalities.

Richard Detwiler, Principal

1439 American International School-Kuwait
PO Box 3267
Salmiya 23033
Kuwait
965-564-5083
Fax: 965-564-5089
E-mail: admin@aiskuwait.org
http://www.aiskuwait.org
Grade levels kindergarten through twelfth.

Samera Al Rayes, Owner/Director
Noreen Hawley, Superintendent

1440 American International School-Muscat
PO Box 584
Azaiba, PC 130, Muscat
Sultanate of Oman
968-595-180
Fax: 968-503-815
E-mail: taism@omantel.net.com
http://www.taism.com
Grades preK-12, enrollment 172.

Kevin Schafer, Director

1441 American International School-Riyadh
PO Box 990
Riyadh 11412
Saudi Arabia
966-1-491-4270
Fax: 966-1-491-7101
E-mail: registration@ais-r.edu.sa
http://www.aisr.org
Grades KindergartenI-11, enrollment
1,463.

Dr. Dennis Larkin, Superintendnet

1442 American School-Doha
PO Box 22090
Doha
Qatar
974-442-1377
Fax: 974-442-0885
E-mail: info@asdqatar.org
http://www.asdqatar.org
Grades preK-12, enrollment 470.

Ronald H Schultz, PhD, Director

1443 American School-Kuwait
PO Box 6735
32040 Hawalli
Kuwait
965-266-4341
Fax: 965-265-0438
E-mail: askkewt@kuwait.net
http://www.ask.edu.kw/index1
Founded by a group of American and Kuwaiti citizens for students who wanted to
attend American colleges and universities.
The comprehensive American curriculum

has remained to characteristic to atrract
students to ASK. Provides a solid foundation in essential learning skills preparatory
to higher edudation.

Dr. Peter Nanos, Superintendent

1444 American-British Academy
PO Box 372
Medinat al Sultan Qaboos, 115
Sultanate of Oman
968-603-646
Fax: 968-603-544
An independent, coeducational day school
with an educational program from kindergarten through grade 12 for students of all
nationalities.

Philippa MC Leggate, BA, Principal

1445 Amman Baccalaureate School
PO Box 441
Sweileh Amman 11910
Jordan
962-6-541-1191/7
Fax: 962-6-541-2603
E-mail: abs@go.com.jo
http://www.arabia.com/ABS
School offers Arabic and English language
curriculum for grade levels kindergarten
through twelfth.

Samia Al Farra, Principal

1446 Anglican International School-Jerusalem
82 Prophet Street
Jerusalem 91001
Israel
972-2-567-7200
Fax: 972-2-538-474
E-mail: aisj@netvision.net.il
This Anglican school offers a curriculum
based in English to 320 day students, in
grades K-12. The length of stay for overseas teachers is four years, with some
on-site housing available.

David Jeffery, Principal

1447 Ankara Elementary & High School
PSC 89 Unit 7010
APO, Ankara 09822 7010
Turkey

Robert Marble, Principal

1448 Arab Unity School
PO Box 10563
Rashidiya, Dubai
United Arab Emirates
971-4-886-226
Fax: 971-4-859-885
E-mail: auschool@amirates.net.ae
This school has grown to one of the leading
institutions of learning in the UAE. It has
about 2,700 day students (1,400 boys;
1,300 girls), grades LKG to Senior-6, of
various nationalities drawn from expatriate and local population. The teaching staff
of 120 is also multinational. The school follows IGCSE and AICE and A-Level curriculum of University of Cambridge.

Zainab A Taher

1449 Baghdad International School
PO Box 571
Baghdad
Iraq

Amen A Rihani, Principal

1450 Bahrain Bayan School
PO Box 32411
Isa Town
Bahrain
973-682-227
Fax: 973-780-019
E-mail: bayanschool@bayan.edu.bh
http://www.bayan.edu.bh
Grade levels N-12, school year September-June.

Nabil Sukhun, Director General

1451 Bahrain Elementary & High School
Psc 451
FPO Bahrain
Bahrain 09834-5200
Grade levels K-12.

Dr. Gilbert Fernandes, Principal

1452 Bahrain School
PO Box 934
Juffair
Bahrain
973-727828
Fax: 973-725714

Frithjof R Wannebo, PhD, Principal

1453 Bilkent University Preparatory School-Bilkent International School
E Campus 06533
Bilkent, Ankara 06533
Turkey
90-312-266-4961
Fax: 90-312-266-4963
E-mail: school@bups.bilkent.edu.tr
http://www.bupsbis.bilkent.edu.tr
Grade levels Pre-K through 12, school year September - June.

Roy Lewis, Director

1454 Bishop's School
PO Box 2001
Amman
Jordan
962-6-653668
This Episcopal boy's school, founded in 1936, teaches both the Jordanvian Curricula and the London University General Certification of Education Curriculum. Total enrollment is 855 day students in grades 1-12. Length of stay for teachers is one year with no housing provided. Languages spoken are English and Arabic.

Najib F Elfarr, Principal
Jamil Ismair, Faculty Head

1455 British Aircraft Corp School
PO Box 3843
Riyadh
Saudi Arabia

MR Pound, Principal

1456 British Embassy Study Group
Sehit Ersan Caddesi 46A, 06680
Cankaya Ankara
Turkey
127-43-10

T Gray, Principal

1457 British International School-Istanbul
Dilhayat Sok, #3 Etiler 80600
Istanbul
Turkey
212-265-2558
Fax: 212-257-8842
This international school offers an English based curriculum for 490 day students and 7 boarding (251 boys and 246 girls), ages 2

1/2 to nineteen. Applications needed include science, pre-school, French, math, social sciences, reading, German, English and physical education, with the student/teacher ratio being 14:1.

Graham Pheby, Principal

1458 Cairo American College
PO Box 39
Maadi 11431, Cairo
Egypt
20-2-519-6665
Fax: 20-2-519-6584
E-mail: support@tc.cac.edu.eg
http://www.cac.edu.eg
An independent, coeducational day school which offfers an educational program from kindergarten through grade 12 for students of all nationalities.

Dr. Robert Hetzel, Superintendent

1459 Cambridge High School
PO Box 3004
Dubai
United Arab Emirates

T Jackson, Principal

1460 Continental School (Sais British)
PO Box 6453
Jeddah 21442
Saudi Arabia

Chris Spedding, Principal

1461 Dhahran Academy International School Group
PO Box 31677
Al Khobar 31952
Saudi Arabia
966-3-330-0555
Fax: 966-3-330-2450
E-mail: isg@isgdh.org
Grades preSchool-11, enrollment 994.

Dr. Fred Bowen, Superintendent

1462 Dhahran Central School
Box 73
Dhahran 31311
Saudi Arabia

Jess Arceneaux, Principal

1463 Dhahran Hills School
Box 73
Dhahran 31311
Saudi Arabia

William Parks, Principal

1464 Doha College-English Speaking
PO Box 22090
Doha Qatar
Arabian Gulf
974-806-770
Fax: 974-806-311
E-mail: asdoha@qatar.net.qa
An independent, coeducational day school which offers an educational program from children of all nationalities from kindergarten through grade12.

E Goodwin, Principal

1465 Doha English Speaking School
PO Box 7660
Doha Qatar
Arabian Gulf

GB Savage, Principal

1466 Doha Independent School
PO Box 5404
Doha Qatar
Arabian Gulf

SJ Williams, Principal

1467 Emirates International School
PO Box 6446
Dubai
United Arab Emirates
971-4-348-9804
Fax: 971-4-348-2813
E-mail: eischool@emirates.net.ae
http://www.eischool.com
Grade levels Pre-K through 12, school year September - June

Daryle Russell, EdD, Headmaster
David A Shore, HS Principal

1468 English School-Fahaheel
PO Box 7209
64003 Fahaheel
Kuwait
This school offers English for the British national curriculum, also Arabic language and Islamic studies for 518 day students (298 boys and 220 girls) in grades K-11. The school offers a teacher exchange program with the length of stay being two years (3+ years for heads). The student/teacher ratio is 19:1 and the applications needed include science, pre-school, math, reading, social sciences, English and physical education.

Ibrahim J Shuhaiber, MSc, Chairman
John J MacGregor, Principal

1469 English School-Kuwait
PO Box 379
Safat 13004
Kuwait

William James Strath, Principal

1470 English Speaking School
PO Box 2002, Dubai
United Arab Emirates

Bernadette McCarty, Principal

1471 Enka Okullari-Enka Schools
Sadi Gulcelik Spor Sitesi
Istinye, Istanbul 80860
Turkey
90-212-276-05-4547
Fax: 90-212-286-59-3035
E-mail: mailbox@enkaschools.com
http://www.enkaschools.com
Grade levels N-5, school year September-June.

Andrew Homden, Director

1472 Gulf English School
PO Box 6320
32068 Hawalli
Kuwait
The school, offers an English based curriculum to 1,406 day students (830 boys; 576 girls), in grades KG through university entrance. The school recruits UK trained teachers every February. The length of stay is one year, with housing provided by the school.

Paul Andrews, Principal
Tim Brosnan, Faculty Head

1473 Habara School
PO Box 26516
Bahrain

PM Wrench, Principal

1474 IBN Khuldoon National School
Po Box 20511
Isa Town
Bahrain
973-780-661
Fax: 973-689-028
E-mail: president.office@ikns.edu.bh
This IBN school is a private, fee paying, non-profit, coeducational, accredited middle states school. The curriculum offered to the 1,210 day students (630 boys and 580 girls) in grades K-12, is English/Arabic. The school is willing to participate in a teacher exchange program with the applications needed being science, math, social sciences, pre-school and English.

Samir J Chammaa, President
Ghada R Bou Zeineddine, Principal

1475 Incirlik Elementary School
PSC 94
APO, Incirlik 09827 0005
Turkey

Mary Davis, Principal

1476 Incirlik High School
PSC 94
APO, Incirlik 09824 0005
Turkey

Dr. Donald Torrey, Principal

1477 Infant School-House #45
Khalil Kando Gardens Road, 5651
Manama
Bahrain

Maria Stiles, Principal

1478 International Community School
PO Box 2002
Amman
Jordan

Wendy Bataineh, Principal

1479 International School of Choueifat
PO Box 7212, Abu Dhabi
United Arab Emirates
971-2-446-1444
Fax: 971-2-446-1048
E-mail: iscad@sabis.net
http://www.iscad-sabis.net/
Grade levels Pre-K through 13, school year September - June

Marilyn Abu-Esber, Acting Director

1480 Istanbul International Community School
Karaagac Koyu
Hadimkoy, Istanbul 34866
Turkey
90-212-857-8264
Fax: 90-212-857-8270
E-mail: headmaster@iics.k12.tr
http://www.iics.k12.tr
Grade levels Pre-K through 12, school year August - June

Kenneth Hillmann, Headmaster
Eileen Freely Baker, Primary Principal

1481 Izmir Elementary & High School
PSC 88
APO, Izmir 09821 0005
Turkey

Terry Emerson, Principal

1482 Jeddah Preparatory School
British Consulate, Box 6316
Jeddah 21442 Saudi Arabia

John GF Parsons, Principal

1483 Jubail British Academy
PO Box 10059 Madinat Al Jubail
Al Sinaiyah 31961
Arabia

Norman Edwards, Principal

1484 Jumeirah English Speaking School
PO Box 24942, Dubai
United Arab Emirates
971-4-394-5515
Fax: 971-4-394-3531
E-mail: jumeng@emirates.net.ac

CA Branson, Headmaster

1485 King Faisal School
PO Box 94558, Riyadh 11614
Saudia Arabia
966-1-482-0802
Fax: 966-1-482-1521
E-mail: dgkfs@kff.com
Grade levels preK-12, enrollment 600.

Mohammed Al-Humood, Director General

1486 Koc School
PK 60-Tuzla
Istanbul 34941
Turkey
90-216-304-1003
Fax: 90-216-304-1048
E-mail: info@kocschool.k12.tr
http://www.kocschool.k12.tr
Grade levels K-12, school year September - June

John Chandler, General Director
Jale Onur, Provost

1487 Kuwait English School
PO Box 8640
Salmiya 22057
Kuwait

Rhoda Elizabeth Muhmoo, Principal

1488 Mohammed Ali Othman School
PO Box 5713
Taiz Yeman
Arab Republic

Saleh Zokari, Principal

1489 Nadeen Nursery & Infant School
PO Box 26367
Adliya
Bahrain

Pauline Puri, Principal

1490 New English School
PO Box 6156
32036 Hawalli
Kuwait

Arthur Rodgers, Principal

1491 Pakistan International School-Peshawar
PO Box 3797
Riyadh
Saudi Arabia
92-441-4428
Fax: 92-441-7272
An independent, coeducaional day school which offers an educaional program from prekindergarten through grade 8 and supervised correspondence study for the high school grades for all expatriate nationalities.

Angela Coleridge, Principal

1492 Rahmaniah-Taif-Acad International School
American Consulate General, Dhahran
District Saudi Arabia

Dean May, Principal

1493 Ras Al Khaimah English Speaking School
PO Box 975
Ras Al Khaimah
United Arab Emirates
971-7-362-441
Fax: 971-7-362-445

Deryck M Wilson, Principal

1494 Ras Tanura School
Box 6140
Ras Tanura
Saudi Arabia

Kent Larson, Principal

1495 Sanaa International School
Box 2002
Sanaa
Yemen
967-1-370-191
Fax: 967-1-370-193
E-mail: gordonblackie@qsi.org
http://www.qsi.org
Grade levels N-12, school year September - June

James Gilson, Director

1496 Saudi Arabian International British School
PO Box 85769
Riyadh 11612
Saudi Arabia

Don Martin, Principal

1497 Saudi Arabian International School-Dhahran
SAIS-DD, Box 677
Dhahran International Airport
Dhahran 31932, Saudi Arabia
996-3-330-0555
Fax: 966-3-330-0555
E-mail:
brent_mutsch%sais@macexpress.org

Dr. Leo Ruberto, Principal

1498 Saudi Arabian International School-Riyadh
PO Box 990
Riyadh 11421
Saudi Arabia
966-1-491-4270
Fax: 966-1-491-7101
E-mail: superintendent@saisras.org
An independent, coeducational day school which offers an educational program from kindergarten through grade 9.

Daryle Russell, EdD, Principal

1499 Saudia-Saudi Arabian International School
PO Box 167, CC 100
Jeddah 21231
Saudi Arabia

John Hazelton, Principal

1500 Sharjah English School
PO Box 1600, Sharjah
United Arab Emirates

David Rowlands, Principal

1501 Sharjah Public School
PO Box 6125, Sharjah
United Arab Emirates

Nazim Khan, Principal

1502 St. Mary's Catholic High School
PO Box 1544, Dubai
United Arab Emirates

Fosca Berardi, Principal

1503 Sultan's School
PO Box 9665
Seeb Sultanate of Oman

Alan Henderson, Principal

1504 Sunshine School
PO Box 26922
13130 Safat
Kuwait

David Brinded, Principal

1505 Tarsus American College and SEV Primary
PK 6
33401 Tarsus
Turkey
90-324-613-5402
Fax: 90-324-624-6347
E-mail: school@tac.k12.tr
http://www.tac.k12.tr
This school is a highly competitive international school for Turkish children seeking admission to universities here and abroad. It has a total of 815 day students in grades six through twelve and participates in a teacher exchange program with the length of stay two years, and housing is provided. The applications from overseas that are required to teach at the school are science, French, math, administration, reading, German, and English.

Bernard Mitchell, PhD, Superintendent
Jale Sever, Primary School Principal

1506 Universal American School
PO Box 17035
72451 Khaldiya
Kuwait
965-562-0297/561
Fax: 965-562-5343
E-mail: uas@qualitynet.net
Grade levels N-12.

Nora Al-Ghanim, Administrative Director

1507 Uskudar American Academy
Vakif Sokak Number 1
Baglarbasi, Istanbul 81130
Turkey
90-216-310-6823
Fax: 90-216-333-1818
E-mail: wshepard@uaa.k12.tr
http://www.uaa.k12.tr
Grade levels K-12, school year September - June

Whitman Shepard, Director
Dilek Yakar, Primary Principal

1508 Walworth Barbour American International School in Israel
PO Box 9005
Kfar Shmaryahu
Israel
972-9-961-8100
Fax: 972-9-961-8111
E-mail: aisrael@wbais.org
http://www.american.hasharon.k12.il
Grades K-12, enrollment 619.

Robert A Sills, Superintendent

Western Europe

1509 AC Montessori Kids
Route De Renipont 4
Lasne B-1380
Belgium
32-2-633-6652
Fax: 32-2-633-6652
E-mail: info@acmontessorikids.com
http://www.acmontessorikids.com
Grade levels 1 1/2 years - 9 years, school year September - June

Laurence Randoux, Headmaster
Mark Ciepers, Administrator

1510 AFCENT Elementary & High School
Unit 21606
APO Brunssum 09703 0005
Netherlands

1511 Abbotsholme School
Rocester (Uttoxeter, Staffordshire)
ST14 5BS
England
01889-590217
Fax: 01889-590001
This interdenominational school offers an English-based curriculum for 78 day students and 166 boarding (152 boys; 92 girls), in grades 7-13.

Darrell J Farrant, MA, FRSA, Principal

1512 Academy-English Prep School
Apartado 1300 Palma D Mallorca
07080 Palma de Mallorca
Spain

CA Walker, Principal

1513 Ackworth School, Ackworth
Pontefract, West Yorkshire
WF7 7LT
England
0977-611401
This school offers an English-based curriculum to 264 day students and 111 boarding students (180 boys; 195 girls), ages 11-18 years of age.

Martin J Dickinson, Principal

1514 Alconbury Elementary School
10 CSG CCSH Unit 5570 Box 50
APO, Alconbury 09470 0005
Great Britain
011-44-1480-843620
Fax: 011-44-1480-843172
http://www.alco-hs.odedodea.edu/aes
William Ramos, Principal

1515 Alconbury High School
10 Csg CCSH Unit 5570 Box 60
APO, Alconbury 09470 0005
Great Britain

Darryl Maenpaa, Principal

1516 Alexander M Patch Elementary School
Unit 30401 Box 4003
APO, Vaihingen (Stuttgart) 09131
Germany

Louis Hughes, Principal

1517 Alexander M Patch High School
Unit 30401
APO, Vaihingen 09131 0005
Germany

John Brokaw, Principal

1518 Alfred T Mahan Elementary School
PSC 1003 Box 48
FPO Keflavik 09728
Iceland

Jan Long, Principal

1519 Alfred T Mahan High School
PSC 1003 Box 52
FPO Keflavik 09728 0352
Iceland

M Deatherage, Principal

1520 Amberg Elementary School
CMR 414
APO, Amberg 09173 0005
Germany

Letcher Connell, Principal

1521 Ambrit Rome International School
Via Filippo Tajani, 50
Rome 00149
Italy
39-06-559-5305
Fax: 39-06-559-5309
E-mail: ambrit@email.telpress.it
http://www.ambrit-rome.com
Grade levels Pre-K through 8, school year September - June

Bernard Mullane, Director
Loretta Nannini, Assistant Director

1522 American College-Greece
6 Gravias Street
GR-153 42 Aghia Paraskevi, Athens
Greece
30-1-600-9800
Fax: 30-1-600-9811
E-mail: acgadm@proetheus.hol.gr
http://www.acg.edu
Grae levels 7-12, school year September - June

John Bailey, EdD, President

1523 American Community School-Cobham
Heywood, Portsmouth Road
Cobham, Surrey, KT11 1BL
United Kingdom
44-1932-869-744
Fax: 44-1932-869-789
E-mail: hmulkey@acs-england.co.uk
http://www.acs-england.co.uk
Grade levels N-13, school year August - June

Thomas Lehman, Head of School
Malcolm Kay, Superintendent

1524 American Community School-Egham
Woodlee London Road (A30)
Egham, Surrey, TW20 OHS
United Kingdom
44-1784-430-611
Fax: 44-1784-430-626
E-mail: abarker@acs-england.co.uk
http://www.acs-england.co.uk
Grade levels Pre-K through 11, school year August - June

Malcom Kay, Superintendent
Moyra Hadley, Head of School

1525 American Community School-Hillingdon
108 Vine Lane
Hillingdon, Middlesex, UB10 OBE
United Kingdom
44-189-581-3734
Fax: 44-189-581-0634
E-mail:
hillingdonadmissions@acs-england.co.uk
http://www.acs-england.co.uk
Grade levels Pre-K through 13, school year
August - June

Ginger Apple, Head of School
Rebecca Duesenberg, Dean Addmissions

1526 American Community Schools
108 Vine Court
Hillingdon, Uxbridge, Middlesex
UB100BE
England
44-189-581-3734
Fax: 44-189-581-0634
E-mail: hmulkey@acs-england.co.uk
This school serves the needs of the international business families in Greater London. Programs are nonsectarian, coeducational day schools with lower, middle and high school divisions offering coordinate college preparatory curricula from pre-kindergarten through grade twelve.

Paul Berg, Headmaster

1527 American Community Schools-Athens
129 Aghias Paraskevis Street
152 34 Halandri, Athens
Greece
301-639-3200
Fax: 301-639-0051
E-mail: acs@acs.gr
http://www.acs.gr
Grades preSchool-12, enrollment 718.

Dr. George Besculides, Superintendent

1528 American Embassy School-Reykjavik
American Embassy
PSC 1003 Box 40
Iceland
202-261-8223
Fax: 202-261-8224
E-mail: aes@islandia.is
http://www.state.gov/m/a/os/1438.htm
Grade levels K-6, school year August - May

Barbara Sigurbjornsson, Principal

1529 American International School-Carinthia
Friesacher Strasse 3 Audio ICC
A-9330 Althofen
Austria

Ron Presswood, Principal

1530 American International School-Florence
Via del Carota 23/25
Bagno a Ripoli, Florence 50012
Italy
39-055-646-1007
Fax: 39-055-644-226
E-mail: adminaisf@interbusiness.it
http://www.aisfitaly.org
Grade levels Pre-K through 12, school year
September-June

Laura Mongiat, Head of School
Paul Cook, Deputy Head

1531 American International School-Genoa
Via Quarto 13-C
16148 Genova
Italy
39-010-386-528
Fax: 39-010-398-700
E-mail: aisgdirector@libero.it
http://www.space.tin.it/internet/elrosser
Grade levels Pre-K through 9, school year
September-June

Gary Crippin PhD, Director

1532 American International School-Lisbon
Rua Antonio Dos Reis, 95
Linho, 2710-301 Sintra
Portugal
351-21-923-98-00
Fax: 351-21-923-98-26
E-mail: tesc0893@mail.telepac.pt
http://www.ecis.org/aislisbon/index.html
An independent, coeducational day school which offers an educational program from early childhood through grade 12 for student of all nationalities.

Blannie M Curtis, Director

1533 American International School-Rotterdam
Verhulstlaan 21
3055 WJ Rotterdam
Netherlands
31-10-422-5351
Fax: 31-10-422-4075
E-mail: information@aisr.nl
http://www.aisr.nl
Grades preK-12, enrollment 205.

Alan Conkey, Director

1534 American International School-Salzburg
Moosstrasse 106
Salzburg A-5020
Austria
43-662-824-617
Fax: 43-662-824-555
E-mail: office@ais.salzburg.at
http://www.ais.salzburg.at
Grade levels 7-13, school year September-May

Paul McLean, Headmaster
Harold Morgan, Academic Dean

1535 American International School-Vienna
Salmannsdorfer Strasse 47
Vienna A-1190
Austria
43-1-401-320
Fax: 43-1-401-325
E-mail: info@ais.at
http://www.ais.at
Grade level Pre-K through 12, school year
August-June

Richard Spradling, PhD, Director
Alan Benson, HS Principal

1536 American Overseas School-Rome
Via Cassia, 811
Rome 00189
Italy
39-06-3326-4841
Fax: 39-06-3326-2608
E-mail: aosr@aosr.org
http://www.aosr.org
An independent, coeducational day school for students of all nationalities in prekindergarten through grade 13 and of-fers a boarding program for select students in grades 9-12.

Dr. Larry W Dougherty, Headmaster

1537 American School of the Hague
Rijksstraatweg 200
2241 BX Wassenaar
The Netherlands
31-70-512-1060
Fax: 31-70-511-2400
E-mail: Gerritz@ash.nl
http://www.ash.nl
Grades preK-12, enrollment 1,020.

Paul De Minico, Superintendent

1538 American School-Barcelona
Balmes, 7
Esplugues de Llobregat, Barcelona 08950
Spain
34-93-371-4016
Fax: 34-93-473-4787
E-mail: info@a-s-b.com
http://www.a-s-b.com
Grade levels Pre-K through 12, school year
September - June

Nancy Boyd, Elementary School
Principal
Bill Volckok, Secondary School Principal

1539 American School-Bilbao
Soparda Bidea 10
Berango, Bizkaia 48640
Spain
34-94-668-0860
Fax: 34-94-668-0452
E-mail: asb@asb.saranet.es
http://www.saranet.es/asb
This school offers a curriculum in Spanish and English for 275 day students (137 boys; 138 girls), in grades PreK-10. Length of stay for overseas teachers is two years with no housing provided. Applications needed to teach include math, social sciences and physical education.

Richard Pacheco, Director

1540 American School-Las Palmas
Apartado 15-Tafira Alta
35017 Las Palmas
Spain
34-928-430-023
Fax: 34-928-430-017
E-mail: info@dns.aslp.org
http://www.aslp.org
Grade levels N-12, school year September - June

Carmen Ana Perez, Director
Conchita Neyra, Assistant Director

1541 American School-London
1-8 Loudoun Road
London, NW8 0NP
United Kingdom
44-207-449-1200
Fax: 44-207-449-1350
E-mail: admissions@asl.org
http://www.asl.org
Grade levels Pre-K through 12, school year
September - June

William Mules, EdD, Head of School

1542 American School-Madrid
Apartado 80
Madrid 28080
Spain
34-91-740-1900
Fax: 34-91-357-2678
E-mail: asmadm@amerschmad.org
http://www.amerschmad.org

Grade levels Pre-K through 12, school year September - June

Robert Thompson, Director

1543 American School-Milan

Villaggio Mirasole
Noverasco di Opera, Milan 20090
Italy
39-02-530-001
Fax: 39-02-576-06274
E-mail: director@asmilan.org
http://www.asmilan.org
Grade levels N-13, school year September - June

Shirley Grover, Director

1544 American School-Paris

41, rue Pasteur
Saint Cloud, 92210 Paris
France
33-1-411-28282
Fax: 33-1-460-22390
E-mail: admissions@asparis.org
http://www.asparis.org
Grade levels Pre-K through 13, school year August - June

Pilar Cabeza de Vaca, Headmistress

1545 American School-Valencia

Avenida Sierra Calderona 29
Urb. Los Monasterios, Puzol
Spain
34-96-140-5412
Fax: 34-96-140-5039
E-mail: lalfonso@asvalencia.org
http://www.ecis.org/valencia
Grade levels include N-12 with a total enrollment of 745.

Luis Alfonso, Director

1546 American School-the Hague

Rijkstraatweg 200
2241 BX Wassenaar
Netherlands
31-70-514-0113
Fax: 31-70-511-2400
E-mail: gerritz@ash.nl
An independent, coeducational day school which offers an educational program from prekindergarten through grade 12 for students of all nationalities.

William H Gerritz, PhD, Principal

1547 Anatolia College

PO Box 21021
Pylea, Thessaloniki 55510
Greece
30-31-398-201
Fax: 30-31-327-500
E-mail: jpg@ac.anatolia.edu.gr
http://www.anatolia.edu.gr
Grade levels 7-12, school year September - June

Richard Jackson, President

1548 Anglo-American School-Moscow

American Embassy
Box M, Helsinki 00140
Finland
7-095-231-4488
Fax: 7-095-231-4477
E-mail: director@aas.ru
http://www.aas.ru
An independent, coeducational day school that offers an educational program from First Steps through grade 12.

Ellen Deitsch Stern, Director,   4177650

1549 Anglo-American School-St. Petersburg

US Consulate Box L
00140 Helsinki
Finland
7-812-320-8925
Fax: 7-812-320-8926
E-mail: aassp@glas.apc.prg
Grades K-12, enrollment 104.

Nancy Hope, Principal
Ellen D Stren, Director

1550 Ansbach Elementary School

CMR 454 Box 3616
APO, Ansbach 09250 0005
Germany

Wayne Dozark, Principal

1551 Ansbach High School

Unit 28614
APO, 09250 0005
Germany
49-9802-223
Fax: 49-9802-1496

Dr. Larry E Sessions, Principal

1552 Antwerp International School

Veltwijcklaan 180
B-2180 Ekeren-Antwerpen
Belgium
32-3-543-9300
Fax: 32-3-541-8201
E-mail: ais@ais-antwerp.be
http://www.ais-antwerp.be
Grade levels Pre-K through 12, school year August - June

Robert Schaecher, Headmaster

1553 Argonner Elementary School

Unit 20193 Box 0015
APO, Hanau 09165 0015
Germany

Christine Holsten, Principal

1554 Athens College

PO Box 65005
154 10 Psychico
Greece

Walter McCanny Eggleston, Principal

1555 Aviano Elementary School

PSC 1
APO, Aviano 09601 0005
Italy
011-39-0434-660921
E-mail: joel_hansen@odedodea.edu

Joel K Hansen, Principal

1556 Aviano High School

Unit 6210 Box 180
APO, Aviano 09601 0005
Italy

Robert Bennett, Principal

1557 BEPS 2 Limal International School

13 Rue Leon Deladriere
Limal 1300
Belgium
32-10-417-227
Fax: 32-2-687-2968
E-mail: info@beps.com
http://www.beps.com
Grade levels Pre-K through 6, school year September - June

Charles Gellar, Head
Henny de Waal, Headmistress

1558 Babenhausen Elementary School

CMR 426 Unit 20219
APO, Babenhausen 09089 0005
Germany

Ida Rhodes, Principal

1559 Bad Kissingen Elementary School

CMR 464
APO, Bad Kissingen 09226 0005
Germany

Beatrice McWaters, Principal

1560 Bad Kreuznach Elementary School

CMR 441
APO, Bad Kreuznach 09525 0005
Germany

Peter Grenier, Principal

1561 Bad Kreuznach High School

Unit 24324
APO, Bad Krueznach 09252 0005
Germany

Jennifer Beckwith, Principal

1562 Bad Nauheim Elementary School

Unit 21103
APO, Bad Nauheim 09074 0005
Germany

Raymond Burkard, Principal

1563 Badminton School

Westbury-on-Trym, Bristol
BS9 3BA
England
0272-623141
A non-denominational boarding and day school for girls ages seven to eighteen. Enrollment consists of 163 day students and 195 boarding.

CJT Gould, MA, Principal

1564 Bamberg Elementary School

Unit 27539
APO, Bamberg 09139 0005
Germany

John G Rhyne, Principal

1565 Bamberg High School

Unit 27539
APO, Bamberg 09139 0005
Germany

Lewis Johnson, Principal

1566 Barrow Hills School

Roke Lane
Witley Godalming GU8 5NY
England
01428-683639
Fax: 01428-683639
E-mail: barhills@netcomuk.co.uk
http://www.haslemere.com

Michael Connolly, Headmaster

1567 Baumholder High School

Unit 23816
APO, Baumholder 09034 3816
Germany

William Diesselhorst, Principal

1568 Bavarian International School

Haputstrasse 1
Schloss Haimbausen, Bavaria D-85778
Germany
49-8133-9170
Fax: 49-8133-917-135
E-mail: e.werner@bix-school.com
http://www.bis-school.com

Grade levels Pre-K through 12, school year August - June

Anne Ponisch, Director

1569 Bedales School

Petersfield (Hampshire)
GU32 2DG
England
01730-300100
Fax: 01730-300500
http://www.bedales.org.uk

A Willcocks, MA, Headmaster

1570 Bedford School

De Parys Avenue
Bedford MK40 2TU
England
44-0-1234-362200
Fax: 44-0-1234-362283
E-mail:
registar@bedfordschool.beds.org.uk
http://www.bedfordschool.beds.org.uk/info/contac

This Bedford school provides an English curriculum for 850 day students and 250 boarding students. The all boy school is involved in the teacher exchange program with the length of stay being one year, with housing provided.

Dr. IP Evans, Principal

1571 Bedgebury School

Bedgebury Park, Goudhurst (Kent)
TN17 2SH
England
0580-211954

Boarding school for girls ages eight to eighteen; and day school for girls ages three to eighteen.

ME Anne Kaye, MA, Headmaster

1572 Belgium Antwerp International School

Veltwijcklaan 180
B-2180
Belgium
32-3-543-9300
Fax: 32-3-541-8201
E-mail: ais@ais-antwerp.be
http://www.ais-antwerp.be

Coeducational day school meeting the needs of the international community of Antwerp, with approximately 45 percent of the enrollment from the United States. Grades PS-12, enrollment 588.

Robert F Schaecher, BS, MS, Headmaster

1573 Benjamin Franklin International School

Martorell i Pena 9
08017 Barcelona
Spain
34-93-434-2380
Fax: 34-93-417-3633
E-mail: bfranklin@bfis.org
http://www.bfis.org
Grade levels N-12, school year September - June

Mark Klimesh, Director
Cindy Moyer, Assistant Director

1574 Berlin International School

K"rnerstrasse 11
Berlin 12169
Germany
49-30-790-00370
Fax: 49-30-3790-00370
E-mail:
office@berlin-international-school.de
http://www.berlin-international-school.de

Grade levels N-12, school year August - July

Andreas Wegener, Administrative Director

1575 Berlin Potsdam International School

Am Hochwald 30, Haus 2
14 532 Kleinmachnow
Germany
49-332-086-760
Fax: 49-332-086-7612
E-mail: office@bpis.de
http://www.bpis.de
Grade levels N-12, school year August - June

Stephen Middlebrook, Director

1576 Bitburg Elementary School

52 SPTG CCSE B Unit 3820 Box 45
APO, Bitburg 09126 2045
Germany

Joseph Kane, Principal

1577 Bitburg High School

52 SUG CCSH, Unit 3820 Box 50
APO, Bitburg 09126 2050
Germany

Henry Demps, Principal

1578 Bitburg Middle School

52 SPTG CCSM B, Unit 3820 Box 55
APO, Bitburg 09132
Germany

James Lawther, Principal

1579 Bjorn's International School

Gartnerivej 5
2100 Copenhagen
Denmark

Lea Kroghly, Principal

1580 Black Forest Academy

Postfach 1109
79396 Kandern
Germany
49-7626-91610
Fax: 49-7626-8821
http://www.bfacademy.com

This Academy is a private residential Christian school providing 1-12 education. Admission is conditional upon agreement with the school educational philosophy and preference is given to the children of missionaries. Total enrollment is 115 day students and 100 total boarding (100 boys; 115 girls).

George Durance, Principal
Dave Jones, Faculty Head

1581 Bloxham School

Bloxham (Nr Banbury, Oxfordshire)
OX15 4PE
England
01295-720206
Fax: 01295-721897
E-mail: registar@bloxhamschool.co.uk
http://www.bloxhamschool.com

Boarding and day school for boys ages thirteen to eighteen and girls ages sixteen to eighteen.

MW Vallance, MA, Headmaster

1582 Blue Coat School

Somerset Road, Edgbaston Birmingham
B17 0HR
England
0121-456-3966
E-mail: bcs@argonet.co.uk
http://www.bluecoatschool.org

Brian Bissell, Principal

1583 Boeblingen Elementary School

CMR 445
APO, Boeblingen 09046 0004
Germany

Janette Johnson, Principal

1584 Bonn International School

Martin Luther King Strasse 14
Bonn 53175
Germany
49-228-308-540
Fax: 49-228-308-5420
E-mail: admin@bis.bonn.org
http://www.bis.bonn.org
Grade levels Pre-K through 12, school year August - June

Tom Ulmer, Director

1585 Bordeaux International School

53 Rue De Laseppe
33000 Bordeaux
France
33-557-870-211
Fax: 33-556-790-047
E-mail: bis@easynet.fr
http://http://bordeaux-intl-school.com
Grade levels k-13.

Christine Cussac, Directrice

1586 Brillantmont International School

Avenue Secretan 16
Lausanne, Vaud 1005
Switzerland
41-21-310-0400
Fax: 41-21-320-8417
E-mail: info@brillantmont.ch
http://www.brillantmont.ch
Grade levels include 9-13 with a total enrollment of 130.

Francoise Frei-Huguenin, Headmistress

1587 British Council School-Madrid

Po General Martinez Campos 31
28010 Madrid
Spain
34-91-337-3500
Fax: 34-91-337-3573
E-mail: madris@britishcouncil.com

Jack Cushman, Principal

1588 British Kindergarten

Ctra Del La Coruna Km 17
Las Rozas, 28230 Madrid
Spain

Mary Jane Maybury, Principal

1589 British Primary School

Stationsstraat 3
3080 Brussels
Belgium
32-2-767-3098
Fax: 32-2-767-0351
E-mail: info@britishprimary.com
http://www.britishprimary.com
Grade levels N-4, school year September - July

Dorothy Guy, Headmistress
Bruce Guy, Finacial Manager

1590 British Primary School-Stockholm
Ostra Valhallavagen 17
S182 62 Djursholm
Sweden

Gaye Elliot, Principal

1591 British School-Amsterdam
PO Box 920
1180 AX Amsterdam
Netherlands
31-20-347-1111
Fax: 31-20-347-1222
An independent, coeducational day school which offers an educaitonal program from preschool through grade 13 for students of all nationalities.

MWG Roberts, Principal

1592 British School-Bern
Mattenstrasse 3
3073 Gumligen
Switzerland
41-31-951-2358
Fax: 41-31-951-1710
E-mail: isbern@ibm.net
An independent, coeducational day school which offers and educational program from prekindergarten through grade 12 for students of all nationalities.

Enid Potts, BEd, Principal

1593 British School-Brussels
Leuvensesteenweg 19
B-3080 Tervuren
Belgium
322-767-4700
Fax: 322-767-8070
E-mail: admissions@britishschool.be
http://www.britishschool.be
Coeducational day program, ages three to eighteen.

1594 British School-Netherlands
Tarwekamp 3
2595 XG, Den Haag
Netherlands
071-616958
Fax: 071-617144
E-mail: foundation@britishschool.nl
http://www.britishschool.nl

Michael J Cooper, Principal

1595 British School-Oslo
PO Box 7531, Skillebekk 0205
Oslo 2
Norway

Margaret Stark, Principal

1596 British School-Paris
38 Quai De l'Ecluse, 78290
Croissy-sur-Seine
France
01-34-80-45-94
Fax: 01-39-76-12-69
E-mail: bsprincipal@wanadoo.fr
http://www.ecis.org

Alan Livingston-Smith, Principal

1597 Bromsgrove School
Worcester Road
Bromsgrove Worcestershire B617DU
England
44-0-1527-579679
Fax: 44-0-1527-576177
E-mail:
marketing@bromsgrove-school.co.uk
http://www.bromit.demon.co.uk
This school offers an English curriculum to 840 day students and 350 boarding (700 boys; 490 girls), ages 3 to 18. The curriculum is English based but french, german and Spanish are also taught. Teachers from overseas are welcome with the length of stay being 1-2 years. Applications needed to teach include science, French, math, Spanish, reading, German, English and physical education.

Timothy Malcolm Taylor, Headmaster
John Rogers, Faculty Head

1598 Brooke House College
Leicester Road gh (Leicestershire)
Market Harbourough, Leicestershire
England
44-0-1852-462452
Fax: 44-0-1858-462487
Brooke House is a non-denominational school with an enrollment of twenty day students and seventy boarding students (45 boys and 45 girls), age thirteen to nineteen years.

F Colyer, Headmaster
FJ Colombo, Faculty Head

1599 Brussels American School
PSC 79 Box 003
APO, Brussels 09724 0005
Belgium

Dennis Mcguane, Principal

1600 Brussels English Primary School
13 Rue Leon Deladrire
1300 Limal
Belgium
62-010-41-72-27
Fax: 62-010-40-10-43
E-mail: hdewaal@beps.com
http://www.beps.com
Coeducational day school for ages three to twelve, with the student body representing over 45 countries.

Henny de Waal, Head

1601 Bryanston School
Blandford (Dorset)
DT11 0PX
England
0258-452411
Coeducational boarding school for ages thirteen to eighteen.

Thomas D Wheare, MA, Principal

1602 Buckswood Grange International School
Uckfield (East Sussex)
E Sussex TN22 3PG
United Kingdom
44-182-574-7000
Fax: 44-182-576-5010
E-mail: admissions@buckswood.co.uk
http://www.buckswood.co.uk
A multinational boarding school for British and foreign students which combines the British curriculum with specialist EFL tution and close attention to social skills in an international environment.

Michael Reiser, Principal

1603 Butzbach Elementary School
CMR 452 Box 5500
APO, Butzbach 09045 0005
Germany

Carl Ford, Principal

1604 Byron Elementary School
Via San Zeno 17
Pisa
Italy

Chiara Bernieri, Principal

1605 CIV International School-Sophia Antipolis
BP 97, 190 rue Frederic Mistral
Sophia Antipolis 06902
France
33-4-929-65224
Fax: 33-4-936-52215
E-mail: secretary@civissa.org
http://www.civissa.org
Grade levels 1-12, school year September-June

Andrew Derry, Head of Section

1606 Calpe College International School
Cta. de Cadiz Km 171
29670 Malaga
Spain
95-278-1479
Fax: 95-278-9416
E-mail: calpe@activanet.es

Luis Proetta, Principal

1607 Campion School
PO Box 67484
Pallini GR-15302
Greece
301-813-5901
Fax: 301-813-6492
E-mail: dbaker@hol.gr

Dennis MacKinnon, Principal

1608 Canadian College Italy-The Renaissance School
59 Macamo Courte
Maple, Ontario L6A 1G1
Canada
905-508-7180
800-422-0548
Fax: 905-508-5480
E-mail: cciren@rogers.com
http://www.ccilanciano.com
Grae levels 11-13, school year September - June

1609 Cascais International School
Rua Das Faias, Lt 7 Torre
2750 Cascais
Portugal
An international nursery school, founded in 1996, that caters to children ages 1-6 years on a fulltime or part-time basis. The first language of the school is English and Portuguese is the second. Many other languages are spoken throughout the school. Offers an individual approach, flexible hours and transport. Total enrollment is 75 day students (45 boys; 30 girls).

Evan Lerven Sixma, Principal

1610 Castelli Elementary School
Via Dei Laghi, 8.60
Ligetta Di Marinus, Ag, 00047 Marina
Italy
39-06-9366-1311
Fax: 39-06-9366-1311

Diana Jaworska, Principal

1611 Castelli International School
Via Degli Scozzesi 13
Grottaferrata, Rome 00046
Italy
39-06-943-15779
Fax: 39-06-943-15779
E-mail: maryac@pcg.it
http://www.pcg.it/CIS
Grade levels 1-6, school year September - June

Marianne Palladino, BA, MA, PhD, Director of Studies

1612 Casterton School
Kirkby Lonsdale, Carnforth
LA6 2SG
England
052-42-71202

AF Thomas, MA, Headmaster

1613 Caxton College
Ctra De Barcelona S/N 46530
Puzol Valencia
Spain
34-96-146-4500
Fax: 34-96142-0930
E-mail: oaxton@camerdata.es

Amparo Gil Marques, Principal

1614 Center Academy
92 St. John's Hill Battersea
London SW11 1SH
England
071-821-5760

Robert Detweiler, Principal

1615 Centre International De Valbonne
Civ-bp 097 06902 Sophia
Antipolis Cedex
France
33-4-929-652-24
Fax: 33-4-936-522-15
E-mail: issaciv@riviera.net

Ian Hill, Principal

1616 Charters-Ancaster School
Penland Road, Bexhill on Sea
TN40 2JQ
England
0424-730499
Boarding girls ages eleven to eighteen; day school for boys three to eight and girls three-eighteen.

K Lewis, MA, Headmaster

1617 Children's House
Kornbergvegen 23-4050 Sola
Stavanger
Norway

Christine Grov, Principal

1618 Cite Scolaire International De Lyon
2 Place De Montreal
69007 Lyon
France
33-04-78-69-60-06
Fax: 33-04-78-69-60-36
E-mail: csi-lyon-gerland@ac-lyon.fr
Grade levels 1-12.

Donna Galiana, Director

1619 Cobham Hall
Cobham (Nr Gravesend, Kent)
DA12 3BL
England
0474-82-3371

Rosalind McCarthy, BA, Headmaster

1620 Colegio Ecole
Santa Rosa 12
PO Box 88-Lugone, 33690 Llanera
Spain

Patrick Wilson, Principal

1621 Colegio International-Meres
Apartado 107
33080 Oviedo, Asturias
Spain

Belen Orejas Fernandez, Principal

1622 Colegio International-Vilamoura
Apt 856, 8125 Vilamoura
Loule Algarve
Portugal

Lawrence James, Principal

1623 College Du Leman International School
74 Route De Sauverny
Versoix/Geneva, CH-1290
Switzerland
41-22-775-5555
Fax: 41-22-775-5559
E-mail: info@cdl.ch
http://www.cdl.ch
Grade levels include N-13 with an enrollment of 1700.

Francis Clivaz, General Director

1624 College International-Fontainebleau
48 Rue Guerin 77300
Fontainebleau
France
01-64-22-11-77
Fax: 01-64-23-43-17
E-mail:
glenyskennedy@compuserve.com

Mrs. G. Kennedy, Principal

1625 College Lycee Cevenol International
43400 Le Chambon sur Lignon
France
04-71-59-72-52
Fax: 04-71-65-87-38
E-mail: lecevenol@aol.com

Christiane Minssen, Principal

1626 Copenhagen International School
Hellerupvej 22-26
2900 Hellerup
Denmark
45-39-463-300
Fax: 45-39-612-230
E-mail: cis@cisdk.dk
http://www.cis-edu.dk
Coeducational day school which offers an educational program from prekindergarten through grade 12 for students of all nationalities.

Christopher Bowman, Director

1627 Croughton High School
Unit 5485 Box 15
APO Croughton, 09494 0005
Great Britain

Dr. Charles Recesso, Principal

1628 Danube International School
Josef Gall-Gassee 2
A-1020 Vienna
Austria
00-43-1-720-3110
Fax: 43-1-720-3110-40
http://www.danubeschool.at

Peter Harding, Director

1629 Darmstadt Elementary School
CMR 431
APO, Darmstadt 09175 0005
Germany

Sherry Templeton, Principal

1630 Darmstadt Junior High School
CMR 431
APO, Darmstadt 09175 0005
Germany

Daniel Basarich, Principal

1631 De Blijberg
Postbus 27518-3003 MA
Rotterdam
Netherlands

I Van Der Voordt, Principal

1632 Dean Close School
Shelburne Road, Cheltenham
GL51 6HE
England
0242-522640
E-mail: 9166035.c_57323@clialnet.ls.uk
This school offers an English based curriculum for 157 day students and 279 boarding students (246 boys; 190 girls), ages 13-18 years. The curriculum offered at the coeducational school is an up-to-date balanced curriculum with a wide range of options which aim to outdo the requirements of the national Curriculum. The school is a Church of England foundation and the Evangelical tradition is maintained.

Christopher J. Bacon, MA, Headmaster
Anthony R Barchand, Faculty Head

1633 Dexheim Elementary School
Unit 24027
APO, Dexheim 09110 0005
Germany

Gary Waltner, Principal

1634 Downside School
Stratton-on-the-Fosse, Bath (Avon)
BA3 4RJ
England
0761-232-206
This Roman Catholic boys school offers an English curriculum for 310 boarding students, ages 10-19. Applications needed to teach include science, French, math, social sciences, German, Spanish, English and physical education. many other languages including Mandarin and Arabic are also offered, and the school boasts superb music, drama and sports facilities.

Dom Antony Sutch, MA, Principal

1635 Dresden International School
Goetheallee 18
Dredsen 01309
Germany
49-351-3400428
Fax: 49-351-3400430
E-mail: dis@dredsen-is.de
http://www.dresden-is.de
Grade levels Pre-K through 9, school year August - June

Don Vinge, Director

1636 ECC International School
Jacob Jordaensstraat 85-87
2018 Antwerp
Belgium

Dr. X Nieberding, Principal

1637 Ecole Active Bilingue
70 rue du Theatre
75105 Paris
France
01-44-37-00-80
Fax: 01-45-79-06-66
E-mail: nhourcade@lcnet.fr

Danielle Monod, Principal

1638 Ecole Active Bilingue Jeannine Manuel
70 rue du Theatre
75015 Paris
France
45-44-37-00-80
Fax: 01-45-79-06-66
E-mail: info@eabjm.com
http://www.eabjm.com
Grade levels k-12.

Elizabeth Zeboulon, Directrice

1639 Ecole D'Humanite
CH-6085 Hasliberg-Goldern
Switzerland
41-33-972-9292
Fax: 41-33-972-9211
E-mail: us.office@ecole.ch
150 boys and girls, aged 6 to 20 and faculty live in small family-style groups. International, inter-racial student body. Main language is German, with special classes for beginners.

Kathleen Hennessy, Interim Director

1640 Ecole Des Roches & Fleuris
3961 Bluche
Valais
Switzerland

Marcel Clivez, Principal

1641 Ecole Lemania
Ch. de Preville 3
CP500 1001 Lausanne
Switzerland
41-0-21-320-15-01
Fax: 41-0-21-312-67-00
This international college represents over 65 nationalities offering French and English intensive courses, summer programs, American academic studies at graduate and undergraduate levels, sports and cultural activities, and accommodation in boarding school. Total enrollment: 800 day students; 100 boarding (450 boys; 450 girls), in grades 1-10.

M JP du Pasquier, Principal

1642 Ecole Nouvelle Preparatoire
Route Du Lac 22, Ch-1094
Paudex
Switzerland

Marc Desmet, Principal

1643 Ecole Nouvelle de la Suisse Romande
Ch de Rovereaz 20, CP-161
CH-1000 Lausanne 12
Switzerland
41-21-654-65-00
Fax: 41-21-654-65-05
E-mail: info@ensr.ch

M Lasserre, Administrator

1644 Edinburgh American School
29 Chester Street
Edinburgh EH37EN
Scotland

AW Morris, Principal

1645 Edradour School
Edradour House - Pitlochry
Perthshire PH165JW,
Scotland

JPA Romanes, Principal

1646 El Plantio International School Valencia
Urbanizacion. El Plantio
Calle 233, N36, La Canada, 46182
Paterna
Spain
96-132-14-10
Fax: 96-132-18-41
http://www.plantiointernational.com

Anthony C Nelson, Principal

1647 Ellerslie School
Abbey Road, Malvern
WR14 3HF
England
0684-575701

Elizabeth M Baker, BA, Headmaster

1648 English Junior School
Lilla Danska Vagen 1
412 74 Gothenburg
Sweden
31-401819

Patricia Gabrielsson, Principal

1649 English Kindergarten
Valenjanpolku 2
05880 Hyvinkaa
Finland

Riva Rentto, Principal

1650 English Montessori School
Av. La Salle S/N Aravaca
Madrid 28023
Spain
91-357-26-67
Fax: 91-307-15-43
E-mail: english@acade.es
http://http://www.nabss.org/monte.htm

Eliane Fitzpatrick, Headmistress

1651 English School-Helsinki
Mantytie 14
00270 Helinski
Finland
358-9-477-1123
Fax: 358-9-477-1980
E-mail: english.school@edu.hel.fi
http://www.eschool.edu.hel.fi
An independent, coeducational day school which offers an educational program from kindergarten through grade 12 for students of all nationalities. The school year comprises 2 semesters extending from August to December and from January to June.

Erkki Lehto, Principal
Riitta Pajuniemi, Assistant Principal

1652 English School-Los Olivos
Avda Pino Panera 25, 46110 Godella
Valencia
Spain
96-363-99-38
Fax: 96-364-48-63

Jane Rodriguez, Principal

1653 European Business & Management School
Frederik de Merodestraat, 12-16
2600 Antwerp
Belgium
323-218-8182
Fax: 323-218-5868
E-mail: info@ebms.edu
http://www.ebms.edu
Provides international education in small classes, individual attention and international awareness. Bachelor and Master.

Luc Van Meli

1654 European School Culham
Abingdon Oxfordshire
OX14 3DZ
Great Britain

T Hyem, Principal

1655 European School-Brussels I
Avenue Du Vert Chasseur 46
1180 Brussels
Belgium
02-374-58-44

J Marshall, Principal

1656 European School-Italy
Via Montello 118
21100 Varese
Italy

Jorg Hoffman, Principal

1657 Evangelical Christian Academy
Calle Talia 26
Madrid 28022
Spain
34-91-741-2900
Fax: 34-91-320-8606
E-mail: ECA_Madrid@compuserve.com
http://http://ourworld.compuserve.com/homepages/eca_madrid
This academy offers an English-based curriculum to 75 day students (45 boys; 30 girls), in grades K-12. The length of stay for overseas teachers is one, two or more years with no housing provided. Applications from overseas needed to teach include science, administration, math, English and physical education.

Beth Hornish, Principal
Scot Musser, Business Manager

1658 Feltwell Elementary School
CCSE F Unit 5185 Box 315
APO Feltwell 09461 5315
Grest ritain

Myron Caylor, Principal

1659 Frankfurt International School
An der Waldlust
61440 Frankfurt
Germany
49-6171-2020
Fax: 49-6171-202384
http://www.fis.edu
An independent, coeducational day school which offers an educational program from preprimary through grade 12 for students of all nationalities.

Jutta Kuehne, Director

1660 Frederiksborg Gymnasium
Carlsbergvej 15
3400 Hillerod
Denmark

Peter Kuhlman, Principal

1661 Friends School
Saffron Walden, Essex
CB11 3EB
England
0642-722141
Boarding coed school for ages eleven to eighteen and day coed for ages seven to eighteen.

David G Cook, BEd, Headmaster

1662 Gaeta Elementary & Middle School
PSC Box 811
FPO Gaeta 09609 0005
Italy

Dr. Robert Kirkpatrick, Principal

1663 Garmisch Elementary School
Unit 24511
APO, Garmisch 09053 0005
Germany

Russell Mcclain, Principal

1664 Geilenkirchen Elementary School
Unit 8045
APO, Geilenkirchen 09104 0005
Germany

James Van Dierendonck, Principal

1665 Gelnhausen Elementary School
CMR 465
APO, Gelnhausen 09076 0005
Germany

Jim Harrison, Principal

1666 Geneva English School
36, route de Malagny
1294 Genthod, Geneva
Switzerland
41-22-755-18-55
Fax: 41-22-779-14-29
E-mail: gesadmin.n@iprolink.ch
http://www.geneva-english-school.ch
A private, nonprofit primary school that is owned and managed by an association which is composed of parents whose children attend the school. The main objective of the school is to offer education on British lines for children of primary school age living in or near Geneva, and to prepare them for secondary education in any English-speaking school.

Denis Unsworth, Principal

1667 Giessen Elementary School
414th BSB GSN, Unit 20911
APO, Giessen 09169 0005
Germany

Mary Ann Burkard, Principal

1668 Giessen High School
414th BSB GSB, Unit 20911
APO, Giessen 09169 0005
Germany

Gordon Gartner, Principal

1669 Grafenwoehr Elementary School
Unit 28127
APO, Grafenwoehr 09114 0005
Germany

Richard Sagerman, Principal

1670 Greenwood Garden School
Via Vito Sinisi 5
00189 Rome
Italy
39-06-332-66703
Fax: 39-06-332-66703
E-mail: donnase@tin.it

Donna Seibert Ricci, BA, Principal

1671 Gstaad International School
Ahorn, 3780
Gstaad
Switzerland
41-33-744-2373
Fax: 41-33-744-3578
E-mail: gis@gstaad.ch
http://www.gstaadschool.ch
This school addresses the academic needs of 24 boarding students (15 boys and 9 girls) in grades eight through twelve. Overseas teachers are welcome for a length of three years, with housing provided. Applications from overseas needed to teach are

science, math, social studies, reading, English, economics and business.

Alain Souperbiet, Director

1672 Haagsche School Vereeniging
Nassaulaan 26-2514jt
The Hague
Netherlands

HM Jongeling, Principal

1673 Hainerberg Elementary School
Unit 29647
APO, Wiesbaden 09096 0005
Germany

Maren James, Principal

1674 Halvorsen Tunner Elementary and Middle School
Unit 7565
APO, Rhein Main 09050 0005
Germany

Julie Gaski, Principal

1675 Hanau High School
Unit 20235
APO, Hanau 09165 0005
Germany

Allen Davenport, Principal

1676 Hanau Middle School
Unit 20193
APO, Hanau 09165 0016
Germany

Robert Sennett, Principal

1677 Harrow School
5 High Street
Harrow on the Hill, HA1 3HP
England
01-423-2366
E-mail: hm.harrowschool@cwcom.net

IDS Beer, MA, Headmaster

1678 Hatherop Castle School
Hatherop, Cirencester
GL7 3NB
England
028-575-206

Brian W Forster, BA, MA, Headmaster

1679 Heidelberg High School
Unit 29237
APO, Heidelberg 09102 0005
Germany

Robert Briton, Principal

1680 Heidelberg Middle School
Unit 29237
APO, Heidelberg 09102 0005
Germany

Donald Johnson, Principal

1681 Hellenic College-London
67 Pont Street
London SWIX OBD
England
0171-581-5044
Fax: 0171-589-9055
E-mail: hellenic@rmplc.co.uk
http://www.rmplc.co.uk/eduweb/sites/hellenic

James Wardrobe, Principal

1682 Hellenic-American Education Foundation Athens College-Psychico College
PO Box 65005
Palaio Psychico, 154 10
Greece
30-1-671-2771
Fax: 30-1-674-8156
E-mail: acpresoff@hol.gr
http://www.haef.gr
Grade levels 1-12, school year September - June

Dennis Skiotis, PhD, President

1683 Helsingin Suomalainen
Yhteiskoulu-Isonnevantie 8
00300 Helinski
Finland

Vesa Nikunen, Principal

1684 Het Nederlands Lyceum
Theo Mann-Bouwmeesterlaan 75
2597GV The Hague
Netherlands

Bryan G Morland, Principal

1685 Het Rijnlands Lyceum
Appollolaan 1 2341 BA
Oegstgeest Zh,
Netherlands
31-3771-5155640
Lyceum is a state subsidized school with an international department offering IBMYP and IB. Offers an English/Dutch spoken curriculum to 1,190 day students and 60 boarding (650 boys; 600 girls), in grades 6 through 12. Student/teacher ratio is 15:1, and the school is willing to participate in a teacher exchange program, however, housing will not be provided by the school.

Drs LE Timmerman, Principal

1686 Hillhouse Montessori School
Avenida Alfonso Xiii 30 Y 34
Madrid 2
Spain

Judy Amick, Principal

1687 Hohenfels Elementary School
Unit 28214
APO, Hohenfels 09173 0005
Germany

Susan Somani, Principal

1688 Hohenfels High School
Unit 28214
APO, Hohenfels 09173 0005
Germany

Susan Somani, Principal

1689 Holmwood House
114 Holgate Road, York
(Essex) CO3 5ST
England
44-0-1904-626183
Fax: 44-0-1904-670899
E-mail: holmwood.house@dial.pipex.com
Holmwood House is an independent coeducational day and boarding preparatory school. The total enrollment of the school is 310 day students and 50 boarding students (240 boys and 120 girls), ages 4 1/2 to 13 1/2.

HS Thackrah, Principal

1690 Hvitfeldtska Gymnasiet
Rektorsgatan 2, SE-411 33
Goteborg
Sweden
46-31-367-0623
Fax: 46-31-367-0602
E-mail:
agneta.santesson@educ.goteborg.se
http://www.hvitfeldt.educ.goteborg.se
State school, founded 1647, offers the International Baccalaureate curriculum to a total enrollment of 90 girls and 90 boys, in grades 10-12.

Christen Holmstrom, Principal
Agneta Santesson, Deputy Headmaster

1691 Illesheim Elementary and Middle School
CMR 416 Box J
APO, Hohenfels 09140 0005
Germany
49-9841-8408
Fax: 49-9841-8987

Donald J Ness, Principal

1692 Independent Bonn International School
Tulpenbaumweg 42
Bonn 53177
Germany
49-228-32-31-66
Fax: 49-228-32-39-58
E-mail: ibis@ibis-school.com
http://www.ibis-school.com
Grade levels Pre-K through 7, school year September - July

Graham Fenner, Headmaster

1693 Independent Schools Information Service
Grosveror Gardens House 35-37
Frosvernor Gardens, London SW1W 0BS
England
020-77981575
Fax: 020-77981561
E-mail: national@isis.org.uk
http://www.isis.org.uk
Provides information on 1400 elementary and secondary schools in the United Kingdom and Ireland.

David J Woodhead

1694 Innsbruck International High School
Schonger, Austria A-6141
0-5225-4201
Fax: 0-5225-4202
An accredited coeducational boarding and day school. The school offers an American college preparatory high school curriculum for grades 9-12.

Gunther Wenko, Director
John E Wenrick, Headmaster

1695 Institut Alpin Le Vieux Chalet
1837 Chateau D'oex
Switzerland

Jean Bach, Principal

1696 Institut Auf Dem Rosenberg
Hohenweg 60-9000 St. Gallen
Switzerland

Felicitas Scharli, Principal

1697 Institut Chateau Beau-Cedre
57 Av De Chillion
CH-1820 Territet Montreux
Switzerland
41-21-963-5341
Fax: 41-21-963-4783
E-mail: info@monterosaschool.com
This Institut is an exclusive boarding and finishing international school for girls. American high school with a general culture section for 30 boarding students in grades 9 through twelve. Languages spoken include French and English and the student/teacher ratio is 1:6.

Pierre Gay, Principal

1698 Institut Le Champ Des Pesses
1618 Chatel-st-denis
Montreux
Switzerland

PL Racloz, Principal

1699 Institut Le Rosey
Chateau du Rosey
CH-1180 Rolle
Switzerland
41-21-822-5500
Fax: 41-21-822-5555
E-mail: rosey@rosey.ch
http://www.rosey.ch
Grade levels include 2-13 with a total enrollment of 340.

Philippe Gudin, General Director

1700 Institut Montana Bugerbug-American Schools
Zugerberg
CH 6300 Zug
Switzerland
41-41-711-1722
Fax: 41-41-711-5465
E-mail: kob@montana.zug.ch
http://www.montana.zug.ch
Grade levels include 7-13 with a total enrollment of 111.

Daniel Fredez, Director

1701 Institut Monte Rosa
57, Ave de Chillon,
Montreux/VD CH-1820
Switzerland
021-963-5341
Fax: 021-963-4783

Bernhard Gademann, BS, MS, Principal

1702 Inter-Community School
Strubenacher 3, CH-8126
Zumikon
Switzerland
41-1-919-8300
Fax: 41-1-919-8320
http://www.icsz.ch
This school offers a curriculum in English, Italian, German and French. Grades N-12, enrollment is 659.

John Young, Headmaster
Gary Winning, Principal

1703 International Academy
Via di Grottarossa 295
00189 Rome
Italy
39-340-731-4195

Joan Bafaloukas Bulgarini, Principal

1704 International College Spain
Vereda Norte 3
Lamoraleja, 28109 Aclobendas, Madrid
Spain
34-91-650-2398
Fax: 34-91-650-1035
E-mail: icsmadrid@compuserve.com
http://www.icsmadric.com
An international school with over forty different nationalities among students and fifteen among staff. Programs lead to the International Baccalaureate. Total enrollment is 497 day students; 8 boarding (249 boys; 256 girls), in grades K-12. Applications needed to teach include science, pre-school, French, math, social sciences, administration, Spanish, English, physical education, art and music.

Terry Hedger, Director
Hubert Keulers, Head of Primary School

1705 International Management Institute
Jacob Jordaensstraat 77
2018 Antwerp
Belgium
32-3-21-85-431
Fax: 32-3-21-85-868
E-mail: info@timi.edu
http://www.timi.edu
Bachelor and Master degrees, small classes, individual touch.

Luc Van Mele

1706 International Preparatory School
Rua Do Boror 12 Carcavelos
2775 Parede
Portugal
56-2-321-5800
Fax: 56-2-321-5821
E-mail: info@tipschool.com
http://www.tipschool.com

1707 International School Beverweerd
Beverweerdseweg 60, 3985 RE
Werkhoven
Netherlands
03437-1341
Fax: 03437-2079

Ray Kern, BA, MA, Principal

1708 International School-Aberdeen
296 N Deeside Road
Milltimber, Aberdeen AB13 OAB
England
44-1224-732267
Fax: 44-1224-735648
E-mail: admin@isa.abdn.sch.uk
http://www.isa.abdn.sch.uk

Dan Hovde, Director

1709 International School-Algarve
Apartado 80 Porches 8400
Lagoa Algarve
Portugal

Peter Maddison, Principal

1710 International School-Amsterdam
PO Box 920
1180 AX Amstelveen
The Netherlands
31-20-347-1111
Fax: 31-20-347-1222
E-mail: info@isa.nl
http://www.isa.nl
This school's total enrollment is 573 day students (260 boys; 313 girls), ages toddler through thirteen.

Steve Bannell, Director

1711 International School-Basel
Schulstrasse 5
Bottminger, Ch-4103
Switzerland
41-61-426-96-26
Fax: 41-61-426-96-25

Geoff Tomlinson, Principal

1712 International School-Bergen
Vilhelm Bjerknesvei 15
5081 Landas
Norway
47-55-30-63-30
Fax: 47-55-30-63-31
E-mail: murison@isb.gs.hl.no
http://www.isb.gs.hl.no
Grade levels prekindergarten through tenth.

June Murison, Director

1713 International School-Berne
Mattenstrasse 3
3073 Gumligen
Switzerland
41-31-951-2358
Fax: 41-31-951-1710
E-mail: rosemary.schelker@isberne.ch
http://www.isberne.ch
Grades preK-12, enrollment 290

David Gatley, Director

1714 International School-Brussels
Kattenberg 19
Brussels 1170
Belguim
32-2-661-4211
Fax: 32-2-661-4200
E-mail: admissions@isb.be
http://www.isb.be
Coeducational day school for ages three to eighteen.

Richard P Hall, BA, Director

1715 International School-Cartagena
Manga Club Cp 30385 Cartagena
Los Belones Murcia
Spain
34-68-175000
E-mail: isc@sendanet.es

Robert Risch, Principal

1716 International School-Curacao
PO Box 3090
Koninginnelaan Emmastad, Cuavao
Netherlands Antilles
599-9-737-3633
Fax: 599-90737-3142
E-mail: iscmec@attglobal.net
http://www.isc.an

Margie Elhage, Director

1717 International School-Dusseldorf
Niederrheinstrasse 336
40489 Dusseldorf
Germany
49-211-94066-799
Fax: 49-211-4080-744
E-mail: nmcw@isdedu.de
http://www.isdedu.com
Grade levels preK-13.

Neil McWilliam, Director

1718 International School-Eerde
Kasteellaan 1, 7731 PJ
Ommen
Netherlands
031-0529-451452
Fax: 031-0529-456377
E-mail: ise@landstede.nl

B Schollema, Headmaster

1719 International School-Friuli
Via Delle Grazie 1/A
Pordenone 33170
Italy

Susan Clarke, Principal

1720 International School-Geneva
62 route de Chene
CH-1208 Geneva
Switzerland
41-22-787-2400
Fax: 41-22-787-2410
A coeducational international general academic and college preparatory school.

George Walker, Director General

1721 International School-Hamburg
Holmbrook 20
Hamburg 22605
Germany
49-40-883-1101
Fax: 49-40-1881-1405
E-mail: info@ish.intrasat.org
http://www.ish.intrasat.org
Grade levels Pre-K through 12, school year August - June

Geoffrey Clark, Headmaster

1722 International School-Hannover Region
Bruchmeisterstrasse 16
Hannover, Lower Saxony 30169
Germany
49-511-27041650
Fax: 49-511-557934
E-mail: IntSchoolH@aol.com
http://www.is-hr.de
Grade levels K-11, school year August - June

Derek Malpass, Director

1723 International School-Helsinki
Selk„merenkatu 11
Helsinki 00180
Finland
358-9-686-6160
Fax: 358-9-685-6699
E-mail: mainoffice@ish.edu.hel.fi
http://www.ish.edu.hel.fi
Grade levels K-12, school year August - June

Peter Ostrom, Headmaster

1724 International School-Iita
Carolyn House 26 Dingwall Road
Croydon CR9 3EE
England

Neil Jackson, Principal

1725 International School-Lausanne
73 av CF Ramuz
Pully/Lusanne, VD, 1009
Switzerland
41-21-728-1733
Fax: 41-21-728-7868
E-mail: isl@span.ch
http://www.isl.ch
This International School is Lausanne's only accredited co-educational day school for children ages three to eighteen in grades Nursery through twelfth. ESL, French as

foreign and second language are taught with a wide range of extra activities. The IB Diploma provides a sound college preparatory program for students in Grades 11 and 12. The total enrollment currently 425 students.

Simon G Taylor, Director
John Ivett, Assistant Director

1726 International School-Le Chaperon Rouge
3963 Crans Sur Sierre
Crans/Montana
Switzerland
41-27-4812-500
Fax: 41-27-4812-502

Prosper Bagnoud, Principal

1727 International School-London
139 Gunnersbury Avenue
London W3 8LG
England
44-20-8992-5823
Fax: 44-20-8993-7012
E-mail: islondon@dial.pipex.com
http://www.islondon.com
Grade levels R-13, school year September - June

Ian Hackett, Headmaster
Rita Ward, Deputy Head

1728 International School-Lyon
Ave Tony Garnier
69007 Lyon
France

John Larner, Principal

1729 International School-Naples
Viale della Liberazione, 1
Bagnoli, Napoli 80125
Italy
39-081-721-2037
Fax: 39-081-570-0248
E-mail: isn@na.cybernet.it
http://www.intschoolnaples.it
Grade levels Pre-K through 12, school year September - June

Josephine Sessa, Principal
Patricia Montesano, VP

1730 International School-Nice
15 Avenue Claude Debussy
Nice 02600
France
33-493-210-400
Fax: 33-493-216-911
E-mail: robert.silvetz@cote-azur.cci.fr
Grade levels Pre-K through 12, school year September - June

Robert Silvetz, Director

1731 International School-Paris
6, rue Beethoven
75016 Paris
France
33-1-422-40954
Fax: 33-1-452-71593
E-mail: info@isparis.edu
http://www.isparis.edu
A coeducational elementary and secondary day school founded as a non-profit association. Emphasizing individual attention, the class size is limited to approximately twenty students.

Gareth Jones, Headmaster

1732 International School-Sotogrande
Apartado 15
11310 Sotogrande Pcia de Cadiz
Spain
34-956-79-59-02
Fax: 34-956-79-48-16
E-mail: director@sis.ac
http://www.sis.ac
This school offers various classes to 250 day students and 10 boarding students made up of 138 boys and 122 girls. The grade range covered is K-12 with the student/teacher ratio being 10:1.

Geroge O'Brien, Headmaster

1733 International School-Stavanger
Treskeveien 3
4042 Hafrsfjord
Norway
47-51-559-100
Fax: 47-51-552-962
E-mail: intschol@iss.stavanger.rl.no
http://www.iss.stavager.rl.no
An English language international school providing educaion from preschool up to and including high school graduation.

Linda Duevel, PhD, Director

1734 International School-Stockholm
Johannesgatan 18
Stockholm SE-111 34
Sweden
46-8-412-4000
Fax: 46-8-412-4001
E-mail: admin@intsch.se
http://www.intsch.se
Grade levels include preK-10 with an enrollment of 340.

Claes-Goran Widlund, Principal

1735 International School-Stuttgart
Sigmaringerstr 2578
70 597 Stuttgart-Degerlock
Germany
49-7-11-76-9600-0
Fax: 49-7-11-76-9600-0
E-mail: iss@iss.s.bw.schule.de
http://www.ecis.org/iss

Thomas Schaedler, Director

1736 International School-Trieste
Via Conconello 16 (Opicina)
34016 Trieste
Italy
39-040-211-452
Fax: 39-040-213-122
E-mail: istrieste@interbusiness.it
http://www.geocities.com/athens/oracle/1329
This school offers a curriculum taught in English and Italian to 230 day students (115 boys; 115 girls) in grades PreK-8. Applications needed to teach include science, pre-school, French, math, social sciences, reading, German, English and physical education.

Peter Metzger, Principal

1737 International School-Turin
Vicolo Tiziano 10
10024 Moncalieri
Italy

George Selby, BA, MA, Principal

1738 International School-Venice
The British Center, San Marco
4267A Venice
Italy

John Millerchip, Principal

1739 International School-Zug
Walterswil
Baar 6340
Switzerland
41-41-768-1188
Fax: 41-41-768-1189
E-mail: office@isoz.ch
Grade levels include preK-8 with a total enrollment of 354.

Martin Latter, Head of School

1740 International Schule-Berlin, Potsdam
Seestrasse 45
14467 Potsdam
Germany
49-332-086-760
Fax: 49-332-086-7612
E-mail: office@isbp.p.bb.schule.de
http://www.shuttle.de/p/isbp
This school offers an English curriculum to 157 day students (87 boys and 64 girls) in grades PreK-12. Applications needed to teach include science, pre-school, math, social sciences, reading, English and physical education.

Matthias Truper, Principal

1741 International Secondary School-Eindhoven
Jerusalemlaan 1, 5625 PP Eindhoven
Netherlands
040-413600

JM Westerhout, Principal

1742 Internationale Schule Frankfurt-Rhein-Main
Albert-Blank-Strasse 50
65931 Frankfurt
Germany
49-69-954-3190
Fax: 49-69-954-31920
E-mail: isf@sabis.net
http://www.isf-net.de
Grade levels Pre-K through 13, school year September - June

Richard Long, School Director

1743 Interskolen
Engtoften 22
DK-8260 Viby J
Denmark
45-8611-4560
Fax: 45-8614-9670
http://www.interskolen.com
Coeducational day program for ages five to seventeen.

Tommy Schou Christesen, Principal

1744 John F Kennedy International School
Kirchgasse
CH-3792 Saanen
Switzerland
41-33-744-1372
Fax: 41-33-744-8982
E-mail: lovell@jfk.ch
http://wwwjfk.ch
Grade levels include K-8 with an enrollment of 60.

William M Lovell, Directorl

1745 John F Kennedy School-Berlin
Teltower Damm 87-93
Berlin 14167
Germany
49-30-6321-5711
Fax: 49-30-6321-6377
E-mail: school/ad@jfks.de
http://www.jfks.de

Grade levels K-13, school year August - July

Charles Hanna, Managing Prnicipal

1746 Joppenhof/Jeanne D'arc Clg
PO Box 4050, 6202 Rb Maastricht
Netherlands

L Spronck, Principal

1747 Kaiserslautern Elementary School
86 SPTG CCSE K Unit 3240 Box 425
APO, Kaiserslautern 09094 0005
Germany

Les Haney, Principal

1748 Kaiserslautern High School
86 SPTG CCSH K Unit 3240, Box 440
APO, Kaiserslautern 09094 0005
Germany

William Leclair, Principal

1749 Kaiserslautern Middle School
86 SPTG CCSM K Unit 3240 Box 450
APO, Kaiserslautern 09094 0005
Germany

Richard Nielsen, Principal

1750 Kendale Primary International School
Via Gradoli 86, Via Cassia Km 10300
00189 Rome
Italy
39-06-332-676-08
Fax: 39-06-332-676-08
E-mail: kendale@diesis.com
http://www.diesis.com/kendale

Veronica Said Tani, Principal

1751 Kensington School
Carrer Dels Cavallers 31-33
Pedralbes 08034, Barcelona
Spain

EP Giles, Principal

1752 King Fahad Academy
Bromyard Avenue
London W3 7HD
England
020-7259-3350

Dr. Ibtissam Al-Bassam, Principal

1753 King's College
Paseo de los Andes
Soto De Vinuelas, 28761 Madrid
Spain
91-803-48-00
Fax: 91-803-65-57
E-mail: soto@kingsgroup.com
http://www.kingsgroup.com/idik

CA Clark, Principal

1754 Kitzingen Elementary School
Unit 26124
APO, Kitzingen 09031 0005
Germany

Fred Paesel, Principal

1755 Kleine Brogel Elementary School
58 MUNSS, Unit 21903
kleine Brogel 09713
Belgium

Robert Nance, Principal

1756 La Chataigneraie International School
Geneva La Chataigneraie, 1297
Founex Vaud
Switzerland

Michael Lee, Principal

1757 La Maddalena Elementary School
PSC 816 Box 1755
FPO, La Maddalena, Sardinia 09612
0005
Italy

Janice Barber, Principal

1758 Lajes Elementary School
Unit 7725
APO, Lajes, The Azores 09720 0005
Portugal

David Trukositz, Principal

1759 Lajes High School
Unit 7725
APO, Lajes, The Azores 09720 7725
Portugal

Ira Scheier, Principal

1760 Lakenheath Elementary School
Unit 5185 Box 40
APO, Lakenheath, 09464
Great Britain

Wolfgang Plakinger, Principal

1761 Lakenheath High School
Unit 5185 Box 45
APO, Lakenheath, 09464 8545
Great Britain

Dr. Joan Halloran, Principal

1762 Lakenheath Middle School
Unit 5185 Box 40
APO, Feltwell 09464 8555
Great Britain

Gerorgia Williams, Principal

1763 Lancing College
Lancing (West Sussex)
BN15 ORW
England
0273-452213
Fax: 01273-464720

JS Woodhouse, MA, Headmaster

1764 Landstuhl Elementary and Middle School
CMR 402
APO, Ladstuhl 09180 0005
Germany

James Parker, Principal

1765 Leighton Park School
Shinfield Road
Reading RG2 7DH
England
4-118-987-9600
Fax: 44-118-987-9625
E-mail: info@leightonparkreading.sch.uk
http://www.leightonparkreading.sch.uk
Co-educational day and boarding school
for pupils aged 11-18 years.

John Dunston, Headmaster

1766 Leipzig International School
Konneritzstrasse 47
D-04229 Leipzig
Germany
49-341-421-0574
Fax: 49-341-421-2154
E-mail: admin@intschool-leipzig.com
http://www.intschool-leipzig.com
An independent, coeducational day school
which offers and educational program from
kindergarten through grade 12 for students
of all nationalities. We offer the IGCSE and
IB diploma program.

Michael Webster, Headmaster

1767 Lennen Bilingual School
65 Quai d'Orsay
75007 Paris
France
01-47-05-66-55
Fax: 01-47-05-17-18
This school teaches a curriculum in English and French to 120 day students. The
school is willing to participate in a teacher
exchange program with the length of stay
being one year, with no housing provided
by the school. Bilingual education is offered in the preschool and grade school
(until Grade 3).

Michelle Lennen, Principal

1768 Leys School
Cambridge
CB2 2AD England
44-1223-508-900
Fax: 44-1223-505-333
E-mail: office@theleys.cambs.sch.uk
http://www.theleys.cambs.sch.uk
Boarding and day school for boys ages
eleven to eighteen and girls ages eleven to
eighteen.

Rev Dr John Barrett, Headmaster

1769 Leysin American School
The Savoy, Leysin CH 1864
Switzerland
41-24-493-3777
Fax: 41-24-493-3790
E-mail: admissions@las.ch
http://www.las.ch
The only American boarding school in
Switzerland accredited by the European
Council of International Schools and the
Middle States Association for College and
Secondary Schools.

Steven Oh, Executive Director

1770 Livorno Elementary School
Unit 31301 Box 65
APO, Livorno 09613 0005
Italy

Dr. Robert Kethcart, Principal

1771 Livorno High School
Unit 31301 Box 65
APO, Livorno 09613 0005
Italy, AE 09613-0005

Dr. Frank Calvano, Principal

1772 London Central High School
PSC 821 Box 119
APO, High Wycombe 09421 0005
Great Britain, AE 09421-0005

Dr. Charles Recesso, Principal

1773 Lorentz International School
Groningensingel 1245, 6835HZ
Arnhem
Netherlands
31-26-320-0110
Fax: 31-26-320-0113

Jan M Meens, Principal

1774 Lusitania International College Foundation
Apartado 328
8600 Lagos
Portugal

Krisine Byrne, Principal

1775 Lycee Francais De Belgique
9 Avenue Du Lycee Francais
1180 Brussels
Belgium
02-374-58-78

Jean-Claude Giudicelli, Principal

1776 Lycee International-American Section
Rue du Fer a Cheval
BP 230 Germain En Laye
France
33-34-51-74-85
Fax: 33-30-87-00-49
E-mail: american.lycee.intl@wanadoo.fr
http://www.lycee-intl-american.org

Yves Lemarie, Head of School
Ted Fauance, Head of Section

1777 Lyc,e International-American Section
BP 230, rue du Fer A Cheval
St. Germain-En-Laye, 78104 Cedex
France
33-1-345-17485
Fax: 33-1-308-70049
E-mail: american.lycee@wanadoo.fr
http://http://lycee-intl-american.org
Grade levels Pre-K through 12, school year
September - June

Theodore Faunce, PhD, Director

1778 Malvern College
College Road, Malvern
Worcestershire WR14 3DF
England
01684-581-500
E-mail: inquiry@malcol.org
http://www.malcol.org

Roy de C Chapman, MA, Headmaster

1779 Mannheim Elementary School
Unit 29938
APO, Mannheim 09086
Germany
380-4705
Fax: 0621-723-905
E-mail: mann-es@odedodea.edu
http://www.mann-es.odedodea.edu

Dr. Ardelle Hamilton PhD, Principal
Dr. Ellen Minette, Assisantant Principal

1780 Mannheim High School
Unit 29939
APO, Mannheim 09086 0005
Germany

Barbara Axton, Principal

1781 Margaret Danyers College
N Downs Road, Cheadle Hulme
Cheadle SK8 5HA
England
061-485-4372
Harry Tomlinson, BA, MA, MS, Headmaster

1782 Mark Twain Elementary School
Unit 29237
APO, Heidelberg 09102 0005
Germany
Joseph Newbury, Principal

1783 Marymount International School-Rome
Via di Villa Lauchli 180
00191 Rome
Italy
33-1-462-41051
Fax: 33-1-463-70750
E-mail: school@ecole-marymount.fr
A coeducational, day school for grades prek-12.
Anne Marie Clancy, Headmistress

1784 Marymount International School-United Kingdom
George Road
Kingston upon Thames, Surrey, KT2 7PE
United Kingdom
44-20-8949-0571
Fax: 44-20-8336-2485
E-mail: admissions@marymount.kingston.sch.uk
http://www.marymount.kingston.sch.uk
Grade levels 6-12, school year September - June
Rosaleen Sheridan, Principal

1785 Mattlidens Gymnasium
Mattgardsvagen 20
02230 Esbo
Finland
Hilding Klingenberg, Principal

1786 Mayenne English School
Chateau les Courges 53420
Chailland
France
J Braillard, Principal

1787 Menwith Hill Estates & Middle School
PSC 45 Unit 8435
APO, High Wycombe 09468 0005
Great Britain
Dr. Arnold Watland, Principal

1788 Millfield School
Street, Somerset, BA16 0YD
Glastonbury, Somerset
England
145-844-2291
A coeducational boarding/day school with over 1,250 pupils and 165 members of staff.
CS Martin, Contact

1789 Monkton Combe School
Bath (Avon) BA2 7HG
England
01225-721102
Fax: 01225-721208
E-mail: addmissions@monkton.org.uk
http://www.monktoncombesschool.com
Boarding and day school for girls and boys ages two to nineteen.
Michael J Cuthberton, Head Master
Rus P Neaverson, Registrant

1790 Monti Parioli English School
Via Monti Parioli 50
00197 Rome
Italy
Lynette Surtees, Principal

1791 Mougins School
615 Avenue Drive, Maurice Donat
BP 401, 06251 Mougins Cedex
France
33-4-93-90-15-47
Fax: 33-4-93-75-31-40
E-mail: information@mougins-school.com
http://www.mougins-school.com
International school for Pre-K to Form 13 teaching the British curriculum leading to IGCSE and A Level examinations.
Brian G Hickmore, Headmaster
Sue Dunnachie, Marketing Coordinator

1792 Mountainview School
Bosch 35-6331 Hunenberg
Switzerland
Brenda Moors, Principal

1793 Munich International School
Schloss Buchhof
Starnberg, Munich D82319
Germany
49-8151-366-100
Fax: 49-8151-366-109
E-mail: adminssions@mis-munich.de
http://www.mis-munich.de
Grade levels Pre-K through 12, school year August - June
Ray Taylor, Head of School

1794 Naples Elementary School
PSC 808 Box 39
FPO, Aversa 09618 0039
Italy
Dr. Jacqueline Hulbert, Principal

1795 Naples High School
PSC 808 Box 15
FPO, Aversa 09618 0015
Italy
Carl Albrecht, Principal

1796 Neubruecke Elementary School
Unit 23825
APO, Neubruecke 09034 0005
Germany
Margaret Hoffman-Otto, Principal

1797 Neuchatel Junior College
Cret-Taconnet 4
2002 Neichatel
Switzerland
038-25-27-00
Fax: 038-24-42-59
This school offers an English based curriculum for 80 day students (30 boys; 50 girls) in the pre-university year. The length of stay for overseas teachers is three to five years. Applications needed to teach include science, French, math, social sciences, German, English.
Nancy Edwards, BA, BEd, Principal

1798 New School Rome
Via Della Camilluccia 669
00135 Rome
Italy
39-329-4269
Josette Fusco, Principal

1799 Newton College
Empedrat 4 Elche
Alicante
Spain
David Few, Principal

1800 Norra Reals Gymnasium
Roslagsgatan 1
S-113 55 Stockholm
Sweden
Curt Lagergren, Principal

1801 Numont School
Calle Parma 16
28043 Madrid
Spain
Margaret Ann Swanson, Principal

1802 Oak House School
San Pedro Claver 12-18
08017 Barcelona
Spain
Pauline Ernest, Principal

1803 Oakham School
Chapel Close, Oakham
Rutland, LE15 6DT
England
44-0-1572-758758
Fax: 44-0-1572-758595
E-mail: registrar@oakham.rutland.sch.uk
Graham Smallbone, Headmaster

1804 Oporto British School
Rua Da Cerca 326/338
Oporto 4100
Portugal
Mark Rogers, Principal

1805 Oslo American School
Gml Ringeriksv 53, 1340 Bekkestua
Oslo
Norway
James Mcneil, Principal

1806 Panterra American School
Via Ventre D'oca 41, Fontanella
Pescara 65131
Italy
Virginia Simpson, Principal

1807 Paris American Academy
9, rue Des Ursulines
75005 Paris
France
Enrolls students from sixteen years of age who are interested in studying the French language and culture.
Richard Roy, Headmaster

1808 Patrick Henry Elementary School
Unit 29237
APO, Heidelberg 09102 0005
Germany
Phillip Crooks, Principal

1809 Perse School
Hills Road
Cambridge CB2 2QF
England
0223-248127
GM Stephen, Headmaster

1810 Pinewood Schools of Thessaloniki
PO Box 21001
555 10 Pilea
Greece
30-31-301-221
Fax: 30-31-323-196
E-mail: pinewood@spark.net.gr
Independent, coeducational schools which offer an educational program from prekindergarten through grade 12 and boarding facilities from grade 7 though grade 12 for students of all nationalities. The school year comprises 2 semesters extending from September to January and from January to June.
Peter B Baiter, Director

1811 Pordenone Elementary School
PSC 1
Aviano
Italy
39-0434-28462
Fax: 39-0434-28761
D Jean Waddell, Principal

1812 Priory School
West Bank, Dorking
Surrey RH4 3DG
England
130-688-7337
Fax: 130-688-8715
E-mail: priory.surrey.ss@connect.bt.com
A voluntary aided Church of England School.
A Sohatski, Headteacher

1813 Queen Elizabeth School
Rua Filipe Magalhaes 1
1700 Lisbon
Portugal
Susan Van Den Berg, Principal

1814 Queens College the English School
Juan De Saridakis 64
Palma de Malorca
Spain
809-393-2153
This Methodist affiliated school offers an English-based curriculum to a total of 1,200 female students, grades K1-12. The school does recruit from overseas, offering three year contracts with housing provided for one week at the beginning of the contract, while they find accommodations. Applications needed to teach include science, pre-school, French, math, Spanish, English and physical education.
Philip Cash, Principal

1815 Rainbow Elementary School
Unit 28614 Box 0040
APO, Ansbach 09177 0005
Germany
Thomas Murdock, Principal

1816 Ramstein Elementary School
86 SPTG CCSE R, Unit 3240 Box 430
APO, Unit 3240 Box 430 09094 0005
Germany
Robin Gartner, Principal

1817 Ramstein High School
86 SPTG CCSH R, Unit 3240 Box 445
APO, Ramstein 09094 0005
Germany
Douglas Kelsey, Principal

1818 Ramstein Intermediate School
86 SPTG CCSI R, Unit 3240 Box 600
APO, Ramstein 09094 0005
Germany
Richard Snell, Principal

1819 Ramstein Junior High School
86 SPTG CCSI R, Unit 3240 Box 455
APO, Ramstein 09094 0005
Germany
Richard Snell, Principal

1820 Rathdown School
Glenageary
Dublin
Ireland
01-853133
Stella G Mew, MA, Principal

1821 Regionale Internationale School
Humperdincklaan 4, 5654 PA
Eindhoven
Netherlands
040-2519437
This school teaches a curriculum in Dutch, English, and French for 360 day students (180 boys; 180 girls), 4-12 years of age. The enrollment and teaching staff represent 43 nationalities, and the student/teacher ratio is 14:1.
HA Schol, Principal

1822 Rikkyo School in England
Guildford Road Rudgwick, Sussex
RH12 3BE
Great Britain
M Usuki, Principal

1823 Riverside School
The Salesianum
Arthestrass 55, Zug, 6300
Switzerland
41-41-724-5690
Fax: 41-41-724-5692
E-mail: david.brooks@riverside.ch
http://www.riverside.ch
Grade levels include 7-12 with a total enrollment of 65.
David Brooks, Director

1824 Robinson Barracks Elementary School
CMR 477 Box 2231
APO, Stuttgart 09154 0005
Germany
Clarence Allen, Principal

1825 Rome International School
Via Morgagni 25
00161 Rome
Italy
Gillian Bennett, Principal

1826 Rosall School
Fleetwood
Lancashire FY7 8JW
United Kingdom
Rosall is an anglican school situated on 220 miles N.W. of London in a self-contained campus of 150 acres. The school offers an English based curriculum to 350 day students and 250 boarding students (350 boys; 250 girls), ages 2-19. Teachers are accepted from overseas with housing provided by the school. Applications needed to teach include science, math, and physical education.
RDW Rhodes, Principal
GSH Penelley, Faculty Head

1827 Rosemead
East Street, Littlehampton
BN17 6AL
England
0903-716065
J Bevis, BA, Headmaster

1828 Rota Elementary School
PSC 819 Box 19
FPO Rota 09645 0005
Spain
Charles Callahan, Principal

1829 Rota High School
PSC 819 Box 63
FPO, Rota 09645 0005
Spain
Dr. Robert Jones, Principal

1830 Roudybush Foreign Service School
Place des Arcades, Sauveterre de Rouergue (Averyon)
France
This European school prepares men for the foreign service.
Franklin Roudybush, AB, MA, Headmaster

1831 Rugby School
Lawrence Sheriff Street
Rugby, Warwickshire CV22 5EH
United Kingdom
44-178-854-3465
Fax: 44-178-856-9124
E-mail: postmaster@rugby-school.warwks.sch.uk
http://www.rugby-school.co.uk
MB Mavot, MA, Headmaster

1832 Runnymede College School
Salvia 30
28109 La Moraleja, Madrid
Spain
34-91-650-8302
Fax: 34-91-650-8236
E-mail: mail@runnymede-college.com
http://www.runnymede-college.com
Grade levels include N-13 with a total enrollment of 409.
Frank M Powell, Headmaster

1833 Rygaards International School
Bernstorffsvej 54, DK-2900
Hellerup
Denmark
45-39-62-10-53
Fax: 45-39-62-10-81
E-mail: paulinebrroks@rygaards.com
Coeducational day school for ages five to sixteen.
Mathias Jepsen, Principal

1834 Salzburg International Preparatory School
Moosstrasse 106
A-5020 Salzburg
Austria
662-844485
Fax: 662-847711
A coeducational boarding school offering an American college preparatory high

school curriculum for grades 7 to 12 as well as a post graduate course.

1835 Schiller Academy
51-55 Waterloo Road
London, SE1 8TX
United Kingdom
44-207-928-1372
Fax: 44-207-928-8089
E-mail: office@schiller-academy.org.uk
http://www.schiller-academy.org.uk
Grade levels 9-12, school year August - June

George Selby, Headmaster
Renee Miller, Director Studies

1836 Schools of England, Wales, Scotland & Ireland
J. Burrow & Company
Imperial House, Lypiatt Road
Cheltenham 50201
England

1837 Schweinfurt American Elementary School
CMR 457
APO, Schweinfurt 09033 0005
Germany
09721-81893
Fax: 09721-803905
http://www.schw-es.odedodea.edu
Grades Pre-k to 5th, fully accredited Department of Defense Education Activity school.

Michael Diekmann, Principal

1838 Schweinfurt Middle School
CMR 457
APO, Schweinfurt 09033 0005
Germany

EB Stafford, Principal

1839 Sembach Elementary School
Unit 4240 Box 325
APO, Sembach 09136 0005
Germany

Marlene Knudson, Principal

1840 Sembach Middle School
Unit 4240 Box 320
APO, Sembach 09136 0005
Germany

Shelley Rucker, Principal

1841 Sevenoaks School
Sevenoaks
TN13 IHU
Great Britain

RP Barker, Principal

1842 Sevilla Elementary & Junior High School
496 ABS DODDS Unit 6585
APO Moron AB 09643 0005
Spain

Robert Ludwig, Principal

1843 Shape Elementary School
CMR 451 Box 0005
APO, Shape 09713 0005
Belgium

Judith Mayo, Principal

1844 Shape High School
CMR 451 Box 0005
APO, Shape 09708 0005
Belgium

Dr. Juliana Cardone, Principal

1845 Shape International School
General Services Section
Building 717, 7010 Shape
Belgium
65-44-52-83

Jacques Laurent, Principal

1846 Sherborne School
Abbey Road
Sherborne, Dorset DT9 4AP
England
44-193-581-2249
Fax: 44-193-581-6628
E-mail: enquiries@sherborne.cix.co.uk

Ralph Mowat, Principal

1847 Sidcot School
Winscombe
North Somerset BS25 1PD
England
44-193-484-3102
Fax: 44-193-484-4181
E-mail: addmissions@sidcot.org.uk
http://www.sidcot.org.uk
This friendly school with an international enrollment of 277 day students and 149 boarding students (255 boys; 171 girls), in grades K-12, is set in over one hundred acres of Somerset countryside. The school offers an English-based curriculum and the student/teacher ratio is 10:1.

John Walmsley, Headteacher

1848 Sierra Bernia School
La Caneta s/n
San Rafael 03580
Spain
96-687-51-49
Fax: 96-687-36-33
E-mail: duncan@ctv.es

Duncan M Allan, Principal

1849 Sigonella Elementary & High School
PSC 824 Box 2630
FPO Signoella, Sicily 09627 2630
Italy

Dr. Peter Price, Principal

1850 Sigtunaskolan Humanistiska Laroverket
Manfred Bjorkquists Alle 6-8
Sigtuna S-193 28
Sweden
46-8-592-57100
Fax: 46-8-592-57250
E-mail: info@sshl.se
http://www.sshl.se
Grade levels include 7-12 with an enrollment of 543.

Ingrid Karlsson, Principal

1851 Sir James Henderson School
Via Pisani Dossi 16
Milano 20134
Italy
39-02-264-13310
Fax: 39-02-264-13515
E-mail: sirjames@bbs.infosquare.it
http://www.sirjameshenderson.com
Grade levels N-13, school year September - June

Stephen Anson, Principal

1852 Skagerak Gymnas
PO Box 1545-Veloy
3206 Sandefjord
Norway

Elisabeth Norr, Principal

1853 Smith Elementary School
Unit 23814
APO, Baumholder 09034 0005
Germany

Edward Drozdowski, Principal

1854 Southlands English School
Via Teleclide 20, Casalpalocco
00124 Rome
Italy

Vivien Franceschini, DipEd, Principal

1855 Spangdahlem Elementary School
52 SPTG CCSE S, Unit 3640 Box 50
APO, Spangdahlem 09126 0005
Germany

Lynda Simmons, Principal

1856 Spangdahlem Middle School
52 CSG CCSM, Unit 3640 Box 45
APO, Spangdahlem
Germany 09126-0005

Catherine Ake, Principal

1857 Sportfield Elementary School
Unit 20193 Box 0014
APO, Hanau
Germany, AE 09165-0014

John O'Reilly, Jr, Principal

1858 St. Andrew's College
PO Box 56
Marayong NSW 2148
Ireland
02-9626-1999
E-mail: admin@standrews.nsw.edu.au

Arthur Godsil, Principal

1859 St. Anne's School
Jarama 9
Madrid 2
Spain

Margaret Raines, Principal

1860 St. Anthony's International College
Carretera De Cadiz Km 217
Fuengriola Malaga
Spain

1861 St. Catherine's British School
British Embassy Ploutarchou 1
Athens 106/75
Greece

Michael Toman, Principal

1862 St. Christopher School
Letchworth
Hertfordshire SG6 3JZ
England
0462-679301
Fax: 0462-481578

Colin Reid, MA, Headmaster

1863 St. Clare's Oxford
139 Banbury Road
Oxford OX2 7AL
England
44-186-555-2031
Fax: 44-186-551-3359
E-mail: admissions@stclares.ac.uk

Margaret Skarland, Principal

1864 St. David's School
Justin Hall, Beckenham Road
West Wickham BR4 0QS
England
01784-252494
Fax: 01784-252494
E-mail: office@stdavidsschool.com
Boarding school for girls ages nine to eighteen; day school for girls ages four to eighteen.

Judith G Osborne, BA, Headmaster

1865 St. Dominic's International School
Outeiro de Polima-Arneiro
2775 Sao Domingos da Rana
Lisbon
Portugal
351-21-448-0550
Fax: 351-21-444-3027
E-mail: adm@dominic.mailpac.pt
School offers a curriculum in English to 466 day students (237 boys; 229 girls), in nursery, kindergarten, transitionary, and Grades 1-12.

Maria R Empis, Principal

1866 St. Dominic's Sixth Form College
Mount Park Ave, Harrow on the Hill
Middlesex HA1 3HX
England
020-84228084
Fax: 020-8422-3759
Reformed in 1979, this school offers an English based curriculum to a total of 600 day students (300 boys; 300 girls), in the last two years of high school (pre-university). The school is Roman Catholic affiliated.

John L Lipscomb, Principal

1867 St. Georges English School
Via Cassia Km 16
00123 Rome
Italy
06-3790141
Fax: 06-3792490

Colin Niven, MA, DipEd, Principal

1868 St. Georges School
Vila Goncalve, Quinta Loureiras
2750 Cascais
Portugal

MPB Hoare, Principal

1869 St. Georges School-Switzerland
1815 Clarens-Montreux
Switzerland
21-964-34-11
Fax: 21-964-49-32
A British International School which operates a joint British/U.S. system of secondary boarding school education for girls between the ages of 11-19 years, Grades 7-13.

Alan Locke, MA, Principal

1870 St. Gerard's School
Thornhill Road, Bray Co Wicklow
Republic of Ireland

Michael O'Horan, Principal

1871 St. Helen's School
Eastbury Road
Northwood (Middleeast) HA6 3AS
England
09274-28511
Fax: 0923-835824

YA Burne, Principal

1872 St. John's International School
Dreve Richelle 146
Waterloo 1410
Belguim
32-2-352-0610
Fax: 32-2-352-0630
E-mail: admissions@stjohns.be
http://www.stjohns.be
Grade levels Pre-K through 13, school year August - June

Joseph Doenges, Director
Judith Hoskins, Director Addmissions

1873 St. Mary's School
Ascot (Berkshire)
SL5 9JF
England
0990-23721
Boarding and day school for girls ten to eighteen.

M Mark Orchard, IBVM, BA, Principal

1874 St. Michael's School
St. Michael's Drive
Otford TN14 5SA
England
095-92-2137

Rev. Paul G Cox, BA, Headmaster

1875 St. Stephen's School
Via Aventina 3
00153 Rome
Italy
39-06-575-0605
Fax: 39-06-574-1941
E-mail: ststephens@mclink.it
http://www.ststephens.it
A nonsectarian, coeducational college preparatory school which serves the American and international communities from Rome.

Philip Allen, Headmaster

1876 Stavenger British School
Gauselbakken 107
4032 Gausel
Norway

Zelma Roisli, Principal

1877 Stover School
Newton Abbot (Devon)
TQ12 6QG
England
0626-54505

WE Lunel, BA, Principal

1878 Stowe School
Stowe (Buckingham)
MK18 5EH
England
44-1280-818000
Fax: 44-1280-818181
E-mail: enquiries@stowe.co.uk
Stowe is a leading independent boarding school for boys (13-18) and girls (16-18). It is situated in magnificent country surroundings. Over 90% of its pupils go on to higher education. Around 20% are from expatriate and non-British families. Total enrollment consists of 32 day students and 518 boarding (450 boys; 100 girls), in grades 9-13. The length of stay for overseas teachers is one year, with housing provided by the school.

JGL Nichols, Headmaster
GM Hornby, Faculty Head

1879 Summerfield School SRL
Via Tito Poggi 21 Divino Amore
00134 Rome
Italy

Vivien Franceschini, Principal

1880 Summerhill School
Westward Ho., Leiston (Suffolk)
IP16 4HY
England
0728-830540

Zoe Readhead

1881 Sunny View School
Apartado 175 Cerro De Toril
Torremolinos Malaga
Spain

Jane Barbadillo, Principal

1882 Sutton Park School
St. Fintan's Road, Sutton
Dublin 13
Ireland
353-1-832-2940
Fax: 353-1-832-5929
E-mail: info@suttonpark.ie
http://www.suttonpoark.ie
Grade levels K-12, school year September - June

Laurence J Finnegan, Chief Executive

1883 Sutton Valence School
Sutton Valence, Maidstone (Kent)
ME17 3HL
England
0622-842281

Michael R Haywood, MA, Headmaster

1884 Swans School
Capricho 2, Marbella
29600 Malaga
Spain

TJ Swan, Principal

1885 TASIS Hellenic International School
PO Box 51051
Kifissia Gr-145 10
Greece
30-1-623-3888
Fax: 30-1-623-3160
E-mail: info@tasis.edu.gr
http://www.tasis.com
Grade levels Pre-K through 12, school year September - June

Basile Daskalakis, President

1886 TASIS The American School in England
Coldharbour Lane
Thorpe, Surrey, TW20 8TE
England
44-1932-565-252
Fax: 44-1932-564-644
E-mail: ukadmissions@tasis.com
http://www.tasis.com
Grade levels Pre-K through 12, school year August - June

Barry Breen, Headmaster

1887 Taunus International Montessori School
Altkonigstrasse 1 6370
Oberursel
Germany

Kathleen Hauer, Principal

1888 Teach in Great Britain
5 Netherhall Gardens
London, NW3, England

1889 Thessaloniki International High School & Pinewood Elementary School
PO Box 21001
555 10 Pilea, Thessaloniki
Greece
30-31-301-221
Fax: 30-31-323-196
E-mail: pinewood@spark.net.gr
http://www.users.otenet.gr/~pinewood
Grades preK-12, enrollment 256.

Peter B Baiter, Director

1890 Thomas Jefferson School
13 rue de la Clef
75005 Paris
France

William Wheeler, Principal

1891 United Nations Nursery School
40 Rue Pierre Guerin
75016 Paris
France
33-1-452-72024
Fax: 33-1-428-87146
Pre-K and kindergarten levels.

Brigitte Weill, Directrice

1892 United World College-Adriatic
Via Trieste 29 34013 Duino
Trieste
Italy

DB Sutcliffe, Principal

1893 United World College-Atlantic
St. Donats Castle Llantwit
Major S Glamorgan
United Kingdom

Colin Jenkins, Principal

1894 Vajont Elementary School
PSC 1
Aviano
Italy
427-701553

Nick Suida, Principal

1895 Verdala International School
Fort Pembroke
Pembroke, STJ 14
Malta
356-332-361
Fax: 356-372-387
E-mail: vis@maltanet.net
http://www.verdala.org
An independent, coeducational day and boarding school which offers an educational program from play school through grade 12 for students of all nationalities.

Adam Pleasance, Headmaster

1896 Verona Elementary School
CMR 428
APO, Verona 09628 0005
Italy

Wilma Holt, Principal

1897 Vicenza Elementary School
Unit 31401 Box 11
APO, Vicenza 09630 0005
Italy

Cathy Magni, Principal

1898 Vicenza High School
Unit 31401 Box 11
APO, Vicenza 09630 0005
Italy

Arnold Goldstein, Principal

1899 Vicenza International School
Viale Trento 141
Vicenza 36100
Italy
39-0444-288-475
Fax: 39-0444-963-633
E-mail: vix-ib@vip.it
Grade levels 11-13, school year September - June

Dionigio Tanello, PhD, Director

1900 Vienna Christian School
Wagramerstrasse 175
A-1220 Wien
Austria
43-1-25122-501
E-mail: 100337.1501@compuserve.com
http://www.vienna-christian-sch.org
Grade levels 1-12, school year August - June

Phillip Paden, Directorl
Nancy L Deibert, Principal

1901 Vienna International School
Strasse der Menschenrechte 1
Vienna 1220
Austria
43-1-203-5595
Fax: 43-1-203-0366
E-mail: info@vis.ac.at
http://www.vis.ac.at
Academic curriculum designed to meet the needs of the international community, therefore offering special emphasis to the mastery of languages.

Walther Hetzer, PhD, Director
Malcolm Davis, Head Primary School

1902 Vilseck Elementary School
Unit 28040
APO, Vilseck 09112 0014
Germany

Martin Kinney, Principal

1903 Vilseck High School
Unit 20841
APO, Vilseck 09112 0005
Germany

Andrew Zacharias, Principal

1904 Violen School, International Department
Violenstraat 3, 1214
CJ Hilversum
Netherlands
This school offers an enrollment of 240 day students (125 boys and 115 girls), in grades K through 6. The primary education is in the English language for international mobile families, set up and supported by the Dutch government.

Atse R Spoor, Principal

1905 Vogelweh Elementary School
86 SPTG CCSE V, Unit 3240 Box 435
APO, Kaiserslautern 09094 0005
Germany

Susan Kraebber, Principal

1906 Volkel Elementary School
752 MUNSS Unit 6790
APO, Volkel 09717 5018
Netherlands

Claudia Holtzclaw, Principal

1907 Westwing School
Kyneton House
Thornbury BS122JZ
England
0454-412311

Marjorie Crane, MA, Headmaster

1908 Wetzel Elementary School
Unit 23815
APO, Baumholder 09034 0005
Germany

Robert Richards, Principal

1909 Wiesbaden Middle School
Unit 29647
APO, Wiesbaden 09096 0005
Germany

Patricia Smith, Principal

1910 Wolfert Van Borselen
Bentincklaan 280-3039 KK
Rotterdam
Netherlands

Gilles Schuilenburg, Principal

1911 Worksop College
Worksop (Nottinghamshire)
S80 3AP
England
0909-472391

A Hugh Monro, MA, Headmaster

1912 Worms Elementary School
CMR 455
APO, Worms 09058 0005
Germany

Charles Raglan, Principal

1913 Wuerzburg Elementary School
CMR 475 Box 6
APO, Wuerzburg 09244 6627
Germany

Dee Ann Edwards, Principal

1914 Wuerzburg High School
CMR 475 Box 8
APO, Wuerzburg 09036 0005
Germany

Robert Kubarek, Principal

1915 Wuerzburg Middle School
CMR 475 Box 7
APO, Wuerzburg 09036 0005
Germany

Karen Kroon, Principal

1916 Zurich International School
Steinacherstrasse 140
8820 Wadenswill
Switzerland
41-43-833-2222
Fax: 41-43-833-2223
E-mail: zis@zis.ch
http://www.zis.ch

Day school for grades Pre-School through 12 serving the Zurich international community. Total enrollment is 900 students.

Peter C Mott, BA,MA, Director
Jennifer Saxe, Director Development

West Indies & Caribbean

1917 American School-Santo Domingo
Apartado 20212
Santo Domingo
Dominican Republic
809-565-7946
809-549-5841
E-mail: a.school@codetel.net.do
Grade levels Pre-K through 12, school year August - June

Joseph Dunham, Director

1918 Aquinas College
PO Box N-7540
Nassau
Bahamas

Vincent Ferguson, Principal

1919 Belair School
PO Box 156
Mandeville
Jamaica
1-876-962-2168
Fax: 1-876-962-3396
E-mail: belair.school@cwjamaica.com
Grade levels K-12, school year September - June

Sylvan Shields, Director

1920 Bermuda High School
27 Richmond Road
Pembroke HM 08
Bermuda
1-441-295-6153
Fax: 1-441-295-2754
This girls school offers an English-based curriculum for 620 total day students in grades 1-12.

Eleanor W Kingsbury, Principal

1921 Bermuda Institute-SDA
PO Box SN 114
Southampton SNBX
Bermuda
441-238-1566
A Seventh-day Adventist school that offers an English curriculum for 489 day students (239 boys; 250 girls), in grades K-12.

Sheila Holder, Principal

1922 Bishop Anstey Junior School
Ariapita Road St. Ann's
Port of Spain
Trinidad and Tobago

Joyce Kirton, Principal

1923 Capitol Christian School
C-11 #3 Urb Real Santo Domingo
Dominican Republic

Stacy Lee Blossom, Principal

1924 Ecole Flamboyant
PO Box 1744-A Schweitzer Hosp.
Port-au-Prince
Haiti
509-381-141/2
Fax: 509-381-141
E-mail: has-pap@acn.com

William Dunn, Principal

1925 International School-Aruba
Seroe Colorado
Aruba
Dutch Caribbean
297-845-365
Fax: 297-847-341
E-mail: intschool@satarnet.aw
A nonprofit, coeducational English-speaking day school serving students from prekindergarten to grade 12.

Dennis Klumpp, Headmaster
Violet Marin, Guidance Counselor

1926 International School-Curacao
PO Box 3090
Williamstad
Curacao
5-999-737-3633
Fax: 5-999-737-3142
E-mail: ismec@attglobal.ne
A private, coeducational day school which offers an educational program from kindergarten through grade 12.

Margie Elhage PhD, Director

1927 International School-West Indies
PO Box 278 Leeward
Providenciales
British West Indies

Alison Hodges, Principal

1928 Kingsway Academy
PO Box N4378, Bernard Road
Nassau
Bahamas

Carol Harrison, Principal

1929 Mount Saint Agnes Academy
99 Dundonald Street W
Hamilton HMDX
Bermuda

Judith Marie Rollo, Principal

1930 Queens College
PO Box N7127
Nassau
Bahamas

Rev. Charles Sweeting, Principal

1931 Saltus Cavendish School
Middle Road
Devonshire
Bermuda

Susan Furr, Headteacher

1932 St. Andrew's School
16 Valleton Avenue
Marraval, Port of Spain
Trinidad and Tobago

Peter Harding, Principal

1933 St. Anne's Parish School
PO Box SS6256
Nassau
Bahamas

Rev. Patrick Adderley, Principal

1934 St. John's College
PO Box N4858
Nassau
Bahamas

Arlene Ferguson, Principal

1935 St. Paul's Methodist College
PO Box F897
Freeport
Grand Bahamas

Annette Poitier, Principal

1936 Sunland Lutheran School
PO Box F2469
Freeport
Bahamas

J Pinder, Principal

1937 Tapion School
PO Box 511 Castries
St. Lucia
West Indies
This school offers an English based curriculum to 130 day students (64 boys; 66 girls), in grades 1 to 3. The length of stay for overseas teachers are two years or longer, and the applications needed to teach include French, Spanish and reading.

Wilbert Pickett, Principal

U.S. Branches

1938 Aisha Mohammed International School
Washington, DC 20521-0001

Daryl Barker, Principal

1939 Albania Tirana International School
DOS/Administrative Officer
9510 Tirana Place
Washington, DC 20521-9510
355-42-27734
Fax: 355-42-37734
E-mail: qsialb@albaniaonline.net
An independent, coeducational day school which offers an educational program from kindergarten through grade 10 for students of all nationalities. The school comprises 3 trimesters extending from early September to mid-June. Enrollment 30.

Glenn H Mosher, Director

1940 Alexander Muss High School Israel
12550 Biscayne Boulevard
Suite 604
North Miami, FL 33181
305-891-8868
800-327-5980
Fax: 305-891-8806
E-mail: amhsi1@aol.com
http://www.amhsi.com
8-week intensive academic program for 11th and 12th graders which uses Israel as a living classroom. HS and 6 college credits. Scholarships available.

Joseph E Breman, CEO
Chaim Fischgrund, Headmaster

1941 Almaty International School
DOS/Administrative Officer
7030 Almaty Place
Washington, DC 20521-7030
7-3272-409-412
Fax: 7-3272-409-622
E-mail: director@ais.almaty.kz
http://www.state.gov/www/about_state/schools/oalmaty.html
Grades preK-12, enrollment 169.

Dr. David Pera, Director

1942 American School
DOS/Administrive Officer
3480 Tegucigalpa Place
Washington, DC 20521-3480
504-239-3333
Fax: 504-239-6162
E-mail: info@amschool.org
http://www.amschool.org

Liliana Jenkins, Superintendent

1943 American Cooperative School
DOS/Administrive Officer
3220 La Paz Place
Washington, DC 20521-3220
519-2-792-302
Fax: 591-2-797-218
E-mail: acs@ns.acslp.org
http://www.acslp.org

Dennis Sheehan, Superintendent

1944 American Cooperative School of Tunis
6360 Tunis Place
Washington, DC 20521-6360
216-71-760-905
Fax: 216-71-761-412
E-mail: acst@acst.intl.tn
http://www.acst.net

Dennis Sheehan, Superintendent

1945 American Embassy School
Department of State/AES
9000 New Delhi Place
Washington, DC 20521-9000
91-11-611-7140
Fax: 91-11-687-3320
E-mail: aesindia@aes.ac.in
http://www.serve.com/aesndi
Grade levels Pre-K through 12, school year August - May

Rob Mochrish, PhD, Director

1946 American Embassy School of New Delhi
American Embassy New Delhi
Department of State
Washington, DC 20521-9000
202-234-1494
91-11-611-7140
Fax: 202-234-3159
Fax: 91-11-687-3320
E-mail: aesindia@del2.vsnl.net.in
An independent, coeducational day school which offers an educational program from prekindergarten through grade 12 for all non-Indian students.

Stephen Kapner, Principal

1947 American International School of Nouakchott
DOS/Administrative Officer
2430 Nouakchott Place
Washington, DC 20521-2430
222-2-52967
Fax: 222-2-52967
E-mail: sharon_sperry@opt.mr

Sharon A Sperry, Director

1948 American International School-Abuja
DOS/Administrative Officer
8300 Abuja Place
Washington, DC 20521-8300
234-9-413-4464
Fax: 234-9-413-4464
E-mail: stanjacobsen60@hotmail.com
A coeducational international day school which offers an educational program from preschool to grade 8 for English-speaking students of all nationalities.

Amy Uzoewulu, Superintendent

1949 American International School-Bamako
DOS/Administrative Officer
2050 Bamako Place
Washington, DC 20521
223-222-4738
Fax: 223-222-0853
E-mail: aisb@aisb-ml.org
http://www.aisbmali.org
An independent, coeducational day school which offers an educational program from prekindergarten through grade 10. Supervised study using the University of Nebraska High School correspondence courses for grades 12 may also be arranged.

Irene Epp, Director

1950 American International School-Chennai
DOS/Administrative Officer
6260 Chennai Place
Washington, DC 20521-6260
91-44-499-0881
Fax: 91-44-466-0636
E-mail: officemanager@aisch.org
http://www.aisch.org
Grades preSchool-12, enrollment 160.

Barry Clough, Head of School

1951 American International School-Costa Rica
Interlink 249
PO Box 02-5635
Miami, FL 33102
Fax: 503-239-0625
E-mail: aiscr@cra.ed.cr
http://www.cra.ed.cr

Glenn Grieshaber, Headmaster

1952 American International School-Freetown
2160 Freetown Place
Washington, DC 20521-2160
232-22-232-480
Fax: 232-22-225-471
E-mail: jacquelinejleigh@yahoo.com
A private, coeducational day school which traditionally offers an educational program from preschool through grade 8 to students of all nationalities. Instruction is in English.

1953 American International School-Kingston
DOS/Administrative Officer
3210 Kingston Place
Washington, DC 20521-3210
876-977-3625
Fax: 876-977-3625
E-mail: aiskoff@cwjamaica.com

Eugene Vincent, Principal

1954 American International School-Lesotho
DOS/Administrative Officer
2340 Maseru Place
Washington, DC 20521-2340
266-322-987
Fax: 266-311-963
E-mail: aisl@lesoff.co.za
http://www.aisl.lesoff.co.za
An independent, coeducational day school which offers an American education from preschool through grade 8. The school was founded in 1991 to serve the needs of the American community and other students seeking an English-language education.

Harvey Cohen, Principal

1955 American International School-Libreville
2270 Libreville Place
Washington, DC 20521-2270
241-76-20-03
Fax: 241-74-55-07
E-mail: aisl@internetgabon.com

Paul Sicard, Director

1956 American International School-Lome
DOS/Administrative Officer
2300 Lome Place
Washington, DC 20521-2300
228-221-3000
Fax: 228-221-7952
E-mail: aisl@cafe.tg
http://www.membres.lycos.fr

Geri Branch, Director

1957 American International School-Lusaka
DOS/Administrative Officer
2310 Lusaka Place
Washington, DC 20521-2310
260-1-260-509
Fax: 260-1-260-538
E-mail: aesl@zamnet.zm
http://www.aislusaka.org
An independent, coeducational day school which offers a preschool program for 2-4 year olds and an educational program from prekindergaretn through grade 10.

Walter Plotkin, Director

1958 American International School-Mozambique
DOS/Administrative Officer
2330 Maputo Place
Washington, DC 20521-2330
258-1-49-1994
Fax: 258-1-49-0596
E-mail: aism@aism-moz.com

Don Reeser, Director

1959 American International School-N'Djamena
DOS/Administrative Officer
2410 N'Djamena Place
Washington, DC 20521-2410
235-52-2103
Fax: 235-51-5654
E-mail: aisn@intent.td

Gay Mickle, Director

1960 American International School-Nouakchott
2430 Nouakchott Place
Washington, DC 20521-2430
222-2-52967
Fax: 222-2-52967
E-mail: aisnsahara@yahoo.com
Founded in 1978, a nonprofit, private, coeducational day school which offers an educational program to students from prekindergarten through grade 8 and independent study 9.

1961 American Nicaraguan School
American Embassy Managua
Unit No 2710 Box 7
Washington, DC 20521-3240
505-278-2565
Fax: 505-267-3088
E-mail: director@ans.edu.ni
http://www.ans.edu.ni
A private, nonsectarian coeducaitonal day school which offers an educaional program from prekindergarten through grade 12 for students of all nationalities.

Marvin Happel, Principal

1962 American Samoa Department of Education
Pago Pago
American Samoa 96799
011-684-633-5237
Fax: 011-684-633-5733
For certification information visit www.doe.as or contact (011) 684-633-5237.

Sili K Sataua

1963 American School Honduras
American Embassy Tegucigalpa
Department of State
Washington, DC 20521-3480
504-239-333
Fax: 504-239-6162
A private, coeducational day school which offers an educational program from nursery through grade 12 for students of all nationalities.

James Szoka, Principal

1964 American School-Algiers
American Embassy Algiers
Washington, DC 20520-0001
202-265-2800
Fax: 202-667-2174

Richard Gillogly, Principal

1965 American School-Antananarivo
DOS/Administrative Officer
2040 Antananarivo Place
Dulles, VA 20189-2040
261-20-22-420-39
Fax: 261-20-22-345-39
E-mail: asamad@dts.mg
http://www.asa.blueline.mg

Jay Long, Director

1966 American School-Asuncion
DOS/Administrative Officer
3020 Asuncion Place
Washington, DC 20521-3020
595-21-600-476
Fax: 595-21-603-518
E-mail: asagator@asa.edu.py
http://www.asa.edu.py

Elsa Lamb, Director

1967 American School-Dschang
Washington, DC 20521-0001

Jane French, Principal

1968 American School-Guatemala
DOS/Administrative Officer
3190 Guatemala Place
Washington, DC 20521-3190
502-369-0791
Fax: 502-369-8335
E-mail: bbarilla@shamballa.cag.edu.gt
http://www.cag.edu.gt

Barbara Barillas, General Director

1969 American School-Niamey
DOS/Administrative Officer
2420 Niamey Place
Washington, DC 20521-2420
227-723-942
Fax: 227-723-457
E-mail: asniger@bow.intnet.ne
A coeducational day school offering an educational program from prekindergarten through grade 9, and 10-12 correspondence.

Sharon Sperry, Director

1970 American School-Port Gentil
1100 Louisiana Street
Suite 2500
Houston, TX 77002-5215

Keith Marriott, Principal

1971 American School-Tegucigalpa
American Embassy
Washington, DC 20521-0001

James Shepherd, Principal

1972 American School-Warsaw
DOS/Administrative Officer
5010 Warsaw Place
Washington, DC 20521-5010
48-22-651-9611
Fax: 48-22-642-1506
E-mail: admissions@asw.waw.pl
http://www.asw.waw.pl
An independent, coeducational day school which offers an educational program from prekindergarten through grade 12 for students of all nationalities.

Charles P Barder, Director

1973 American School-Yaounde
BP 7475
Yaounde Place Camaroon
Washington, DC 20521-2520
234-223-0421
Fax: 237-223-6011
E-mail: school@asoy.org
An independent, coeducational day school founded in 1964 which offers an educational program from prekindergarten through grade 12.

Areta Williams, Director

1974 American-Nicaraguan School
DOS/Administrative Officer
3240 Managua Place
Washington, DC 20521-3240
505-2-782-565
Fax: 505-2-673-088
E-mail: msacasa@nicanet.com.ni
http://www.ans.edu.ni

Mary Ellen Normandin, Director

1975 Amoco Galeota School
PO Box 4381
Houston, TX 77210-4381

Barbara Punch, Principal

1976 Andersen Elementary & Middle School
Unit 14057
APO, Mariana Islands 96543 4057
Guam

1977 Anzoategui International School
PO Box 020010, M-42
Jet Cargo International
Miami, FL 33102-0010
58-82-22683
Fax: 58-82-22683
E-mail: aishead@telcel.net.ve
http://www.anaco.net
Grade levels Pre-K through 12, school year August - June

Jorge Nelson EdD, Superintendent

1978 Armenia QSI International School-Yerevan
DOS/Administrative Officer
7020 Yerevan Place
Washington, DC 20521-7020
374-1-391-030
Fax: 374-1-151-438
E-mail: qsiy@arminco.com
An independent, coeducational day school which offers an educational program from preschool (3-4 years) through grade 12 for students of all nationalities. Enrollment 45.

Arthur W Hudson, Director

1979 Atlanta International School
2890 N Fulton Drive
Atlanta, GA 30305
404-841-3840
Fax: 404-816-3060
E-mail: info@aischool.org
http://www.aischool.org
Grade levels prekindergarten through twelfth, with total enrollment of 805 students.

David Hawley,PhD, Headmaster

1980 Awty International School
7455 Awty School Lane
Houston, TX 77055
713-686-4850
Fax: 713-686-4956
E-mail: admin@awty.org
http://www.awty.org
Grade level prekindergarten through twelfth, with total enrollment of 900 students.

David Watson, Headmaster

1981 Azerbaijan Baku International School
DOS/Administrative Officer
Department Of State
Washington, DC 20521-7050
994-12-90-63-52
Fax: 994-12-90-63-51
E-mail: qsi@bis.baku.az
http://www.qsi.org
An independent, coeducational day school which offers an educational program from prekindergarten through grade 10 for students of all nationalities. Enrollment 45.

Beverly McAloon, Director

1982 Baku International School
Administrative Officer
Department of State
Washington, DC 20521-7050
994-12-656352
Fax: 991-12-4105951
E-mail: qsi@bis.baku.az
http://www.qsi.org

Grade levels N-8, school year September - June

Phil Dale, irector

1983 Ball Brothers Foundation
222 S Mulberry Street #1408
Muncie, IN 47305-2802
765-741-5500
Fax: 765-741-5518
Offers support in the areas of higher and other education including health and medical education.

ouglas A Bakken, Executive Director

1984 Banjul American Embassy School
DOS/Administrative Officer
2070 Banjul Place
Washington, DC 20521-2070
220-495-920
Fax: 220-497-181
E-mail: baes@qanet.gm
http://www.baes.gm

Earl Ballard, Headmaster

1985 Bingham Academy Ethiopia
SIM International
PO Box 7900
Charlotte, NC 28241-7900

Harold Jongeward, BAEd, Principal

1986 Bishkek International School
DOS/Administrative Officer
7040 Bishkek Place
Washington, DC 20521-7040
996-312-66-35-03
Fax: 996-312-66-35-03
E-mail: qsibis@elcat.kg
http://www.qsi.org
Grades K-11, enrollment 26.

Gordon Stands, Director

1987 Bosnia-Herzegovina QSI International School-Sarajevo
DOS/Administrative Officer
7130 Sarajevo Place
Washington, DC 20521-7130
387-33-434-756
Fax: 387-33-434-756
E-mail: qsi@bih.net.ba
http://www.qsi.org
An independent, coeducational day school which offers an educational program from preschool (3 and 4 year old class) through grade 8 (13 year old class) for students of all nationalities. Enrollment 53.

Ralph A Reed, Director

1988 Bratislava American International School
American Embassy Bratislava
Department of State
Washington, DC 20521-5850
202-885-1600
421-7-722-844
Fax: 202-885-2494
Fax: 721-7-722-844
E-mail: qsi@ba.sanet.sk
An independent, coeducational day school wich offers an educational program from prekindergarten through grade 12 for students of all nationalities.

Ronald Adams, Principal

1989 Bulgaria Anglo-American School-Sofia
DOS/Administrative Officer
5740 Sophia Place
Washington, DC 20521-5740
359-2-974-4575
Fax: 359-2-974-4483
E-mail: aasregist@infotel.bg
http://www.geocities.com/angloamericanschool
An independent, coeducational day school which offers an educational program from prekindergarten through grade 8 for students of all nationalities. The school year comprises 2 semesters extending from August to December and from January to June. Enrollment 140.

Brian M Garton, Director

1990 Burma International School Yangon
DOS/Administrative Officer
4250 Rangoon Place
Washington, DC 20521-4250
95-1-512-793/795
Fax: 95-1-525-020
E-mail: ISYDIRECTOR@mptmail.net.mm
Grades PK-12, enrollment 331.

Merry Wade, Director

1991 Burns Family Foundation
410 N Michigan Avenue
Room 1600
Chicago, IL 60611-4213
Offers support in secondary school education, higher education and youth services.

1992 Caribbean American School
5 Gates Court
Cranbury, NJ 08512-2926

Ernestine Rochelle, Principal

1993 Caribbean-American School
PO Box 407139
Lynx Air
Ft Lauderdale, FL 33340-7139
509-257-7961
Grade levels Pre-K through 12, school year September - June

Ernestine Roche Robinson, Director

1994 Chinese American International School
150 Oak Street
San Francisco, CA 94102
415-865-6000
Fax: 415-865-6089
E-mail: caishead@aol.com
http://www.cie-cais.org
Grade level preK-8, with total enrollment of 353 students.

David Haack, Principal

1995 Colegio Albania
PO Box 25573
Miami, FL 33102-5573

Eric Spindler, Principal

1996 Colegio Corazon de Maria
Ferrer y Ferrer-Santiago Igles
San Juan 00921
Puerto Rico

M Cyril Stauss, Principal

1997 Colegio De Parvulos
263 Calle San Sebastian
San Juan 00901-1205
Puerto Rico

Maria Dolores Vice, Principal

1998 Colegio Del Buen Pastor
Camino Alejandrino Km 3.4
Rio Piedras 00927
Puerto Rico

Adria M Borges, Principal

1999 Colegio Del Sagrado Corazon
Obispado Final Urb La Alhambra
Ponce 00731
Puerto Rico

Joan G Dedapena, Principal

2000 Colegio Espiritu Santo
PO Box 1715
Hato Rey 00918
Puerto Rico

Carmen Jovet, Principal

2001 Colegio Inmaculada
Carr Militar 2 Km 49.6
Manati 00674
Puerto Rico

Sor Nichlasa Maderea, Principal

2002 Colegio Inmaculada Concepcion
2 Calle Isabela
Guayanilla 00656-1703
Puerto Rico

Sor Alejandrina Torres, Principal

2003 Colegio Internacional-Carabobo
VLN 1010
PO Box 025685
Miami, FL 33102-5685
58-41-421-807
Fax: 58-41-426-510
E-mail: CICadm@telcel.net.ve
http://www.aassa.com
Grade levels Pre-K through 12, school year August-June

Frank Anderson, Superintendent

2004 Colegio Internacional-Caracas
PAKMAIL 6030
PO Box 025323
Miami, FL 33102-5323
58-2-945-0444
Fax: 58-2-945-0533
E-mail: cic@cic-caracas.org
http://www.cic-caracas.org
Grade levels N-12, school year August-June

Winthrop Sargent Jr, Superintendent

2005 Colegio Internacional-Puerto La Cruz
2010 NW 84th Avenue
Suite 8403
Miami, FL 33122
58-281-277-6051
Fax: 58-281-274-1134
E-mail: ciplc@telcel.net.ve
http://www.ciplc.net
Grade levels Pre-K through 12, school year August-June

Dan McClain, Superintendent
Frank Capuccio, Administrative Assistant

2006 Colegio La Inmaculada
1711 Ave Ponce De Leon
San Juan 00909-1905
Puerto Rico
Sor Teresa Del Rio, Principal

2007 Colegio La Milagrosa
107 Calle De Diego
San Juan 00925-3303
Puerto Rico
Maria Flores, Principal

2008 Colegio Lourdes
PO Box 847
Hato Rey 00919
Puerto Rico
Maria Paz Asiain, Principal

2009 Colegio Madre Cabrini
1564 Calle Encarnacion
San Juan 00920-4739
Puerto Rico
Anne Marie Gavin, Principal

2010 Colegio Maria Auxiliadora
PO Box 797
Carolina 00986-0797
Puerto Rico
Leles Rodriguez, Principal

2011 Colegio Marista
Final Santa Ana Alt Torrimar
Guaynabo 00969
Puerto Rico
Hilario Martinez, Principal

2012 Colegio Marista El Salvador
PO Box 462
Manati 00674-0462
Puerto Rico
Hnio Efrain Romo, Principal

2013 Colegio Mater Salvatoris
RR 3 Box 3080
San Juan 00926-9601
Puerto Rico
Maria Luisa Benito, Principal

2014 Colegio Notre Dame Nivel
PO Box 967
Caguas 00726-0967
Puerto Rico
Francisca Suarez, Principal

2015 Colegio Nuestra Senora de La Caridad
PO Box 1164
Caparra Heigh 00920
Puerto Rico
Madre Esperanza Sanchez, Principal

2016 Colegio Nuestra Senora de La Merced
PO Box 4048
San Juan 00936-4048
Puerto Rico
Ivette Lopez, Principal

2017 Colegio Nuestra Senora de Lourdes
1050 Demetrio Odaly-Country Club
Rio Piedras 00924
Puerto Rico
Rita Manzano, Principal

2018 Colegio Nuestra Senora de Valvanera
53 Calle Jose I Quinton # 53
Coamo 00769-3108
Puerto Rico-
Cruz Victor Colon, Principal

2019 Colegio Nuestra Senora del Carmen
RR 2, Box 9KK, Carr Trujillo Alt
Rio Piedras 00721
Puerto Rico
Candida Arrieta, Principal

2020 Colegio Nuestra Senora del Pilar
PO Box 387
Canovanas 00729-0387
Puerto Rico
Sor Leonilda Mallo, Principal

2021 Colegio Nuestra Senora del Rosario
Aa7 Calle 5
Bayamon 00959-3719
Puerto Rico
Theresita Miranda, Principal

2022 Colegio Nuestra Sra del Rosario
PO Box 1334
Ciales 00638-0414
Puerto Rico
787-871-1318
Fax: 787-871-5797
Parrochial School - Prekindergarten to 9th grade.
Angel Mendoza, Principal
Padre Gabriel M Jorres, Director

2023 Colegio Padre Berrios
PO Box 7717
San Juan 00916-7717
Puerto Rico
Sor Enedina Santos, Principal

2024 Colegio Parroquial San Jose
PO Box 1386
Aibonito 00705-1386
Puerto Rico
Maria Maria Malave, Principal

2025 Colegio Ponceno
Coto Laurel, Puerto Rico 00644
809-848-2525
Rev. Jose A Basols, MA, Principal

2026 Colegio Puertorriqueno de Ninas
Urb. Golden Gate
Turquesa Street, Guaynabo 00968
Puerto Rico
787-782-2618
Fax: 787-782-8370
E-mail: cpn@coqui.net
Ivette Nater Prieto, School Director

2027 Colegio Reina de Los Angeles
M19 Frontera Urb Vl Andalucia
San Juan 00926
Puerto Rico
Victorina Ortega, Principal

2028 Colegio Rosa Bell
PO Box 1789
Guaynabo 00970-1789
Puerto Rico
Rose Rodriquez, Principal

2029 Colegio Sacred Heart
Palma Real Urb, Univ. Gardens
San Juan 00927
Puerto Rico
Paul Marie, CSB, Principal

2030 Colegio Sagrada Familia
7 Hostos
Ponce
Puerto Rico 00731
Sor Pilar Becerra, Principal

2031 Colegio Sagrados Corazones
A Esmeralda Urb, Ponce De Leon
Guaynabo 00969
Puerto Rico
Ana Arce de Marrer, Principal

2032 Colegio San Agustin
PO Box 4263
Bayamon 00958-1263
Puerto Rico
Georgina Ortiz, Principal

2033 Colegio San Antonio
PO Box 21350
San Juan 00928-1350
Puerto Rico
809-764-0090
Rev. Paul S Brodie, Principal

2034 Colegio San Antonio Abad
PO Box 729
Humacao 00792-0729
Puerto Rico
Padre Eduardo Torrella, Principal

2035 Colegio San Benito
PO Box 728
Humacao 00792-0728
Puerto Rico
Hermana Carmen Davila, Principal

2036 Colegio San Conrado (K-12)
PO Box 7111
Ponce 00732-7111
Puerto Rico
Fax: 787-841-7303
E-mail: sanconrado@pucpr.edu
Sister Nildred Rodriguez, Principal
Sister Wilma de Echevarria, Assistant Principal

2037 Colegio San Felipe
566 Ave San Luis # 673
Arecibo 00612-3600
Puerto Rico
809-878-3532
Veronica Oravec, Principal

2038 Colegio San Francisco De Asis
PO Box 789
Barranquitas 00794-0789
Puerto Rico
Hermana Maria Carbonell, Principal

2039 Colegio San Gabriel
Gpo Box 347
San Juan 00936
Puerto Rico
Sor Antonia Garatachea, Principal

2040 Colegio San Ignacio de Loyola
Sauco Final Urb Santa Maria
Rio Piedras 00927
Puerto Rico
Rev. Thomas H Feely, Principal

2041 Colegio San Jose
PO Box 21300
San Juan 00928-1300
Puerto Rico
809-751-8177
Rev. Joaquin Suarez SM, Principal

2042 Colegio San Juan Bautista
PO Box E
Orocovis 00720
Puerto Rico
Sor Maria Antonia Miya, Principal

2043 Colegio San Juan Bosco
PO Box 14367
San Juan 00916-4367
Puerto Rico
Rev. P Jose Luis Gomez, Principal

2044 Colegio San Luis Rey
43 Final SE, Urb Reparto Metro
San Juan 00921
Puerto Rico
Rosario Maria, Principal

2045 Colegio San Miguel
GPO Box 1714
San Juan 00936
Puerto Rico
Elvira Gonzalez, Principal

2046 Colegio San Rafael
PO Box 301
Quebradillas 00678-0301
Puerto Rico

2047 Colegio San Vicente Ferrer
PO Box 455
Catano 00963-0455
Puerto Rico
Maria Soledad Colon, Principal

2048 Colegio San Vicente de Paul
PO Box 8699
Santurce 00909
Puerto Rico
Sor Luz Maria Arzuago, Principal

2049 Colegio Santa Clara
Via 14-2JL-456 Villa Fontana
Carolina 00983
Puerto Rico
Elsie Mujica, Principal

2050 Colegio Santa Cruz
PO Box 235
Trujillo Alto 00977-0235
Puerto Rico
Maria Ramon Santiago, Principal

2051 Colegio Santa Gema
PO Box 1705
Carolina 00984-1705
Puerto Rico
Lilia Luna De Anaya, Principal

2052 Colegio Santa Rita
Calle 9, Apartado 1557
Bayamon 00958
Puerto Rico
Elba N Villalba, Principal

2053 Colegio Santa Rosa
Calle Marti, 15 Esquina Maceo
Bayamon 00961
Puerto Rico
Ana Josefa Colon, Principal

2054 Colegio Santa Teresita
342 Victoria
Ponce 00731
Puerto Rico
Mary Terence, Principal

2055 Colegio Santiago Apostol
Calle Celis Aguilera
Fajardo 00738
Puerto Rico
Hilda Velazquez, Principal

2056 Colegio Santisimo Rosario
PO Box 26
Yauco 00698-0026
Puerto Rico
Judith Negron, Principal

2057 Colegio Santo Domingo
192 Calle Comerio
Bayamon 00959-5358
Puerto Rico
Pura Huyke, Principal

2058 Colegio Santo Nino de Praga
PO Box 25
Penuelas 00624-0025
Puerto Rico
Aminta Santos, Principal

2059 Colegio Santos Angeles Custod
3 Sicilia Urb, San Jose
San Juan 00923
Puerto Rico
Roberto Rivera, Principal

2060 Colegio de La Salle
PO Box 518
Bayamon 00960-0518
Puerto Rico
Wilfredo Perez De, Principal

2061 Commandant Gade Special Education School
St. Thomas, Virgin Islands 00801
Miss Jeanne Richards, Principal

2062 Community United Methodist School
PO Box 681
Frederiksted 00841-0681
Virgin Islands
Marva Oneal, Principal

2063 Country Day
RR 1 Box 6199
Kingshill 00850-9803
Virgin Islands
809-778-1974
This school offers an English based curriculum for 440 day students (215 boys; 225 girls) in grades nursery through twelve. The school does participate in teacher exchange

programs. Currently all but the PE position is filled. (Position includes coaching).
James Sadler, Principal
Patricia Bessette, Faculty Head

2064 Croatia American International School-Zagreb
DOS/Administrative Officer
5080 Zagreb Place
Washington, DC 20521-5080
385-1-4680-133
Fax: 385-1-4680-171
E-mail: asz@asz.tel.hr
http://www.asz.tel.hr/asz
Grades K-8, enrollment 112.
Gloria Doll, Director

2065 Dallas International School
6039 Churchill Way
Dallas, TX 75230
972-991-6379
Fax: 972-991-6608
E-mail: rwkdis@metronet.com
http://http://dis.pvt.k12.tx.us
Grade levels prekindergarten through twelfth, with total enrollment of 255 students.
Noelle Delhomme, Headmaster

2066 Dominican Child Development Center
PO Box 5668
Agana
Guam 96910
617-477-7228
Fax: 671-472-4782
Kindergarten and nursery school.
Lednor Flores, Principal

2067 Dorado Academy
PO Box 969
Dorado 00646-0969
Puerto Rico
Liutma Caballero, Principal

2068 Dwight School
291 Central Park W
New York, NY 10024
212-724-2146
Fax: 212-724-2539
E-mail: admissions@dwight.edu
http://www.dwight.edu
Grade levels kindergarten through twelfth, with total enrollment of 425 students.
Susan Hurroit, Director Admissions
Vimmi Snroff, Director Admissions

2069 Educare
3 Storre Gronne Gade
St. Thomas 00802
Virgin Islands
Sara Connell, Principal

2070 Episcopal Cathedral School
PO Box 13305
San Juan 00908-3305
Puerto Rico
787-721-5478
Fax: 787-724-6668
http://www.episcopalcathedralschool.com
Rev. Gary J DeHope, BS, MS, Headmaster

2071 Escole Tout Petit
PO Box 1248
San Juan 00902
Puerto Rico
Vivian Aviles, Principal

2072 Escuela Beata Imelda
PO Box 804
Guanica 00653-0804
Puerto Rico
P Salvador Barber, Principal

2073 Escuela Bella Vista
C-MAR-P 1815
PO Box 02-8537
Miami, FL 33102-8537
58-61-966-696
Fax: 58-61-969-417
E-mail: newtonr@ebv.org.ve
http://www.ebv.org.ve
Grade levels K-12, school year August -
June
Valyn Anderson, Superintendent

2074 Escuela Campo Alegre
8424 NW 56th Street
Suite CCS 00007
Miami, FL 33166
58-2-993-3230
Fax: 58-2-993-0219
E-mail: info@eca.com.ve
http://www.eca.com.ve
Grade levels N-12, school year August -
June.
Bambi Betts, Director

2075 Escuela Campo Alegre-Venezuela
8424 NW 56th Street
Suite CCS00007
Miami, FL 33166
58-2-993-7135
Fax: 58-2-993-0219
E-mail: info@eca.com.ve
A private, coeducational day school offer-
ing a program for students from
prekindergarten through grade 12.
Dr. Forest Broman, Principal

2076 Escuela Caribe Vista School
New Horizon-100 S & 350 E
Marion, IN 46953
765-668-4009
Phil Redwine, Principal

2077 Escuela Las Morochas
Intercomunal, Sector Las Morochas
Zulia, Vanezuela
Miami, FL 33152
58-265-6315-539
Fax: 58-265-6315-539
E-mail: sseb@iamnet.com
Grade levels Pre-K through 12, school year
August - June.
Stephen Sibley, Director

**2078 Escuela Nuestra Senora Del
Carmen**
PO Box 116, Playa De Ponce
Ponce 00731
Puerto Rico 00731
Paquita Alvarado, Principal

2079 Escuela Superior Catolica
PO Box 4245
Bayamon 00958-1245
Puerto Rico
Eledis Diaz, Principal

2080 Evangelical School for the Deaf
PO Box 7111
Luquillo 00773
Puerto Rico 00773
Pamela Eadie, Principal

2081 Fajardo Academy
55 Calle Federico Garcia
PO Box 1146, Fajardo 00648
Puerto Rico
809-863-1001
Miguel A Rivera, BA, MA, MEd,
Principal

2082 Freewill Baptist School
PO Box 6265
Christiansted 00823-6265
Virgin Islands
Joe Postlewaite, Principal

**2083 French-American International
School**
150 Oak Street
San Francisco, CA 94102
415-558-2000
Fax: 415-558-2024
E-mail: fais@fais-ihs.org
http://www.fais-ihs.org
Grade levels preK-12, with total student
enrollment of 813.
Jane Camblin, Head of School

2084 George D Robinson School
5 Nairn Condado
Santurce 00907
Puerto Rico
Daniel W Sheehan, Principal

2085 Georgetown American School
3170 Georgetown Place
Washington, DC 20521-3170
592-225-1595
Fax: 592-226-1459
E-mail: admin@amschoolguyana.net
http://www.geocities.com/Athens/Atlanti
s/6811
Thurston Riehl, Director

**2086 Georgia QSI International
School-Tbilisi**
DOS/Administrative Officer
7060 Tbilisi Place
Washington, DC 20521-7060
995-32-982909
Fax: 995-32-322-607
E-mail: qsi@access.sanet.ge
An independent, coeducational day school
which offers an educational program for
students of all nationalities grades PK-12.
Enrollment 68.
Anthony Trujillo, Director

2087 Glynn Christian School
Club 6, Christian Hill
St. Croix, Kingshill 00851
Virgin Islands
Muriel Francis, Principal

2088 Good Hope School-St. Croix
Estate Good Hope Frederiksted
St. Croix 00840
Virgin Islands
Tanya L Nichols, Principal

2089 Good Shepherd School
PO Box 1069
St. Croix, Kingshill 00851
Virgin Islands 00851
340-772-2280
Fax: 340-772-1021
Mary Ellen Mcencil, Director
Susan P Eversley, Assistant Director

2090 Grace Baptist Academy
PO Box 7490
Christoansted 00823-7490
Virgin Islands
Helen Yasper, Principal

2091 Guam Adventist Academy
1200 Aguilar Road
Taldfofo
Guam 96930
617-789-1515
Fax: 617-789-3547
E-mail: sdagaaguam@netpci.guam
http://www.tagnet.org/gaa
Grade levels K-12.
Murray Cooper, Principal

2092 Guam Department of Education
PO Box DE
Hagatna, Guam 96932
011-671-475-0457
Fax: 011-671-472-5003
For certification information visit
www.guam.net/gov/doe/fpd
Rosie R Tainatongo, Director

2093 Guam High School
PSC 455 Box 192
FPO, Mariana Islands 96540 1192
Guam

**2094 Guam S Elementary & Middle
School**
PSC 455 Box 168
FPO
Mariana Islands, Guam 96540-1054

2095 Guamani School
3 Los Veteranos Km 141.3
Guayama 00787
Puerto Rico 00784
Eduardo Delgado, Principal

2096 Harvest Christian Academy
PO Box 23189
Barrigada
Guam 96921
671-477-6341
Fax: 671-477-7136
http://www.harvestministries.net
Harvest Christian Academy is a K-12th
grade school. It is a ministry of Harvest
Baptist Church.
John McGraw, Principal

2097 Hogar Colegio La Milagrosa
Ave Cotto 987 Barrio Cotto
Arecibo 00612
Puerto Rico 00612
Sor Trinidad Ibizarry, Principal

**2098 India American Embassy
School-New Delhi**
DOS/Administrative Officer
9000 New Delhi Place
Washington, DC 20521-9000
91-11-611-7140
Fax: 91-11-687-3320
E-mail: aesindia@aes.ac.in
http://www.serve.com/aesndi
Grades preK-12, enrollment 944.
Robert M Mockrish Jr, Director

2099 India American International School-Bombay
DOS/Administrative Officer
6240 Mumbai Place
Washington, DC 20521-6240
91-22-652-1837
Fax: 91-22-652-1838
E-mail: asbadmin@vsnl.com
http://www.asbindia.org
Grades N-12, enrollment 291.

James A Mains, Director

2100 Inter-American Academy
Suite 8227
6964 N.W. 50th Street
Miami, FL 33166-5632
593-4-871-790
Fax: 593-4-873-358
E-mail: bgoforth@acig.k12.ec
http://www.acig.k12.ec

Dr. Bruce Goforth, Executive Director

2101 International Community School-Abidjan
DOS/Administrative Officer
2010 Abidjan Place
Washington, DC 20521-2010
225-22-47-11-52
Fax: 225-22-47-19-96
E-mail: rmockrish@icsa.ac.ci
http://www.icsa.ac.ci
American style curriculum from kindergarten through grade 12 for children of all nationalities.

Rob Mockrish, Director

2102 International High School-Yangon
4250 Rangoon Place
Department of State
Washington, DC 20521-4250
95-1-512-793
Fax: 95-1-525-020
E-mail: isydirector@mptmail.net.mm

Merry Wade, Director

2103 International School of Port-of-Spain
POS 1369
1601 NW 97th Avenue
Miami, FL 33166
868-632-4591
Fax: 868-632-4595
E-mail: biatham@isps.edu.ttu.tt
http://www.isps.edu.tt

J Barney Latham, Director

2104 International School-Conakry
DOS/Administrative Officer
2110 Conakry Place
Washington, DC 20521-2110
224-12-661-535
Fax: 224-41-15-22
E-mail: iscgeckos@yahoo.com

Steven Asp-Schussheim, Director

2105 International School-Dakar
DOS/Administrative Officer
2130 Dakar Place
Washington, DC 20521-2130
221-825-0871
Fax: 221-825-5030
E-mail: isd@enda.sn
The only nonsectarian English language school in Kakar. ISD is an independent coeducational day school offering an enriched American educational program to reflect the diverse international background of the student body and the faculty.

Ron Halsey, Director

2106 International School-Grenada
Washington, DC 20521-0001

Mary Delaney Dunn, Principal

2107 International School-Havana
Department of State
Havana Office
Washington, DC 20520-0001

Linda Daly, Principal

2108 International School-Islamabad
DOS/Administrative Officer
8100 Islamabad Place
Washington, DC 20521-8100
92-51-434-950
Fax: 92-51-440-193
E-mail: school@isoi.edu.pkom
http://www.isoi.edu.pk
An independent, coeducational day school which offers an educational program from nursery through grade 12 for students of all nationalities.

Dr. Robert E Ambrogi, Superintendent

2109 International School-Ouagadougou
DOS/Administrative Officer
Ambassade des Etats Unis
Washington, DC 20521-2440
226-36-21-43
Fax: 226-36-22-28
E-mail: isouaga@fasonet.bf
http://http://iso.htmlplanet.com

Patrick M Meyer, Director

2110 International School-Port of Spain
1601 NW 97th Avenue
PO Box 025307h Street
Miami, FL 33102-5307
868-633-4777
Fax: 868-632-4595
E-mail: blatham@isps.edu.tt
http://www.isps.edu.tt
Grade levels Pre-K through 12, school year August - June

Barney Latham, Headmaster

2111 International School-Sfax
Brit Gas 1100 Louisiana
Houston, TX 77002

Sidney Norris, Principal

2112 International School-Yangon
Washington, DC 20521-0001

Dr. David Shawver, Principal

2113 Izmir American Institute
Friends-850 Third Avenue
18th Floor
New York, NY 10022

Richard Curtis, Principal

2114 John F Kennedy School-Queretaro
Cahm 8535 San Gabriel Drive
Laredo, TX 78041
956-580-5401
Fax: 956-580-5415

Dr. Francisco Galicia, Principal

2115 Jordan American Community School
DOS/Administrative Officer
6050 Amman Place
Washington, DC 20521-6050
962-6-581-3944
Fax: 962-6-582-3357
E-mail: school@acsamman.edu.jo
http://www.acsamman.edu.jo

Grades preK-12, enrollment 355.

Dr. Gray Duckett, Superintendent

2116 Karachi American Society School
American Consulate General Karachi
6150 Karachi Place
Washington, DC 20521-6150
92-21-453-909619
Fax: 92-21-453-7305

David Holmer, Principal

2117 Kongeus Grade School
44-46 Gade
St. Thomas 00802
Virgin Islands 00802

Veronica Miller, Principal

2118 Lincoln International School-Kampala
Co of State
Washington, DC 20521-0001

Margaret Bell, Principal

2119 Lincoln School
PO Box 025216
Miami, FL 33102-5216
305-643-4888
Fax: 305-642-8402
E-mail: director@ns.lincoln.ed.cr
A private coeducational day school which offers an educational program from prekindergarten through grade 12 for students of all nationalities.

Dr. Gilbert Brown, Principal

2120 Lincoln-Marti Schools
904 SW 23rd Avenue
Miami, FL 33135
305-643-4200
877-874-1999
Fax: 305-649-2767
E-mail: main@lincoln-marti.com
http://www.lincolnmarti.com
Bilingual private educational institution serving children from birth through 12th grade; offering an exceptional Student Education program as well as accredited childcare programs and K-12 private schooling.

Demitrio Perez, President

2121 Little People's Learning Center
PO Box 12354
St. Thomas 00801-5354
Virgin Islands

Daphne Maynard, Principal

2122 Little School House
47 Kongens Gade
St. Thomas 00802
Virgin Islands

Carol Struiell, Principal

2123 Luanda International School
DOS/Administrative Officer
2550 Luanda Place
Washington, DC 20521-2550
244-2-44-3416
Fax: 244-2-44-3416
E-mail: lis@netangola.com

Ken Hillamn, Director

2124 Lutheran Parish School
#1 Lille Taarne Gade
Charlotte Aml 00802
Puerto Rico 00802

Nancy Gotwalt, Principal

2125 Manor School
236 La Grande Princesse
Christiansted 00820
Virgin Islands 00820

Judith C Gadd, Principal

2126 Maranatha Christian Academy
HC00867, Box 17945, Km 50.3
Fajardo 00738
Puerto Rico 00738

Rev. Gary Sprunger, Principal

2127 Martin De Porress Academy
621 Elmont Road
Elmont, NY 11003
516-616-0580
Fax: 516-616-0582
E-mail: sfagin@mdp.org
http://www.mdp.org/Elmont/Aboutus/abo
utus.html
The Martin De Porress Academy program
provides academic instruction based upon
the NY State Learning Standards as well as
hands on experiences in business enterprises, performing arts, home improvement skills, life skills, culinary arts,
maintenance services and community services.

Thomas Darnowski, Division Director
Sue Fagin, Director Human Resources

2128 Montessori House of Children
PO Box 805
Frederiksted 00841-0805
Virgin Islands

William Myers, Principal

2129 Moravian School
PO Box 1777
Chrisyiansted 00821-1777
Virgin Islands
809-773-8921
This Moravian affiliated school offers a
curriculum based in English for 200 day
students (96 boys; 104 girls), in grades
K-6. The school is willing to participate in
a teacher exchange program, with the
length of stay being one year, with housing
provided. Applications include science,
Spanish and computer skills.

Condon L Joseph, Principal

2130 Morrocoy International
MUN 4051
PO Box 025352
Miami, FL 33102-5352
58-286-9520016
Fax: 58-286-9521861
E-mail: kempenich@telcel.net.ve
http://www.geocities.com/minaspov
Grade levels Pre-K through 10, school year
August - June

Michael Kempenich, Headmaster

2131 Mount Carmel Elementary School
PO Box 7830
Agat 96928 0830
Guam-b830
This Catholic school offers an English (primary) curriculum for 206 day students (100
boys; 106 girls), in Kinder 4 - 8th grade.
Overseas teachers are accepted, with the
length of stay being one year. Applications
needed to teach include reading, English
and counseling/counselor.

Bernadette Quintanilla, Sr, SSND,
Principal
Augustin Gumataotao, Administrator

2132 Nazarene Christian School
#55 Golden Rock
C'sted, St. Croix 00820
Virgin Islands

Pastor Hugh Connor, Principal

2133 Nepal Lincoln School
DOS/Administrative Officer
6190 Kathmandu Place
Washington, DC 20521-6190
977-1-270-482
Fax: 977-1-272-685
E-mail: info@lsnepal.com.np
http://www.lsnepal.com
Grades preschool - 12, enrollment 235.

Dr. Barbara Butterworth, Director

**2134 Northern Mariana Islands
Department of Education**
PO Box 501370 CK
Siapan, MP 96950
011-670-664-3720
Fax: 011-670-664-3798

Rita Hocog Inos, Commissioner

2135 Notre Dame High School
480 S San Miguel Street
Talofofo
Guam 96930-4699
671-789-1676
Notre Dame is a co-educational,
year-round high school run by the School
Sisters of Notre Dame. This Roman Catholic affiliated school offers a curriculum in
English for 191 day students and 9 boarding (32 boys; 168 girls), in grades 9-12.
Student/teacher ratio is 10:1, and the applications needed to teach include science,
math, social sciences, and English.

Regina Paulino, SSND, Principal

2136 Nuestra Senora de La Altagracia
672 Calle Felipe Gutierrez #672
San Juan 00924-2225
Puerto Rico

2137 Nuestra Senora de La Providencia
PO Box 11610
San Juan 00922-1610
Puerto Rico

2138 Okinawa Christian School
PO Box 14250
Gainesville, FL 32604-2250

Paul Gieschen, Principal

2139 Open Classroom
PO Box 4046
St. Thomas 00803
Virgin Islands 00803

Janie Lang, Principal

2140 Osaka International School
International Schools Services
PO Box 5910
Princeton, NJ 08543-5910

James Wiese, Principal

2141 Palache Bilingual School
PO Box 1832
Arecibo 00613-1832
Puerto Rico

Rev. David Valez, Principal

2142 Peace Corp
11 20th Street NW
Washington, DC 20526
202-692-2000
800-424-8580
Fax: 202-692-1897
http://www.peacecorps.gov

2143 Pine Peace School
PO Box 361
Cruz Bay 00830
Virgin Islands

Katharine Hilliard, Principal

2144 Ponce Baptist Academy
72 Calle 1 Belgica
Ponce 00731
Puerto Rico

Vivian Medina, Principal

2145 Prophecy Elementary School
PO Box 10497
APO St. Thomas 00801-3497
Virgin Islands

Verona Rogers, Principal

**2146 Puerto Rico Department of
Education**
Hato Rey 00919
PO Box 190759
San Juan, Puerto Rico 00919
787-763-2171
http://www.de.gobierno.pr

Cesar A Rey-Hernandez, Secretary

2147 QSI International School-Chisinau
DOS/Administrative Officer
7080 Chisinau Place
Washington, DC 20521-7080
373-24-2366
E-mail: qsimdv@qsi.moldline.net
Grades preK-12, enrollment 29.

Mary Kay Smith, Director

2148 QSI International School-Skopje
DOS/Administrative Officer
7120 Skopje Place
Washington, DC 20521-7120
389-91-367-678
Fax: 389-91-362-250
E-mail: qsisk@mt.com.mk
Grades preSchool-8, enrollment 47.

David Dutson, Director

**2149 QSI International
School-Vladivostok**
DOS/Administrative Officer
5880 Vladivostok Place
Washington, DC 20521-5880
7-4232-321-292
Fax: 7-4232-313-684
E-mail: qsiisv@fastmail.vladivostok.ru
Grades preK-9, enrollment 18.

Harold M Strom Jr, Director

2150 Rainbow Development Center
PO Box 7618
Christiansted 00823-7618
Virgin Islands

Gloria Henry, Principal

2151 Rainbow Learning Institute
PO Box 75
Christiansted 00821-0075
Virgin Islands

Alda Lockhart, Principal

2152 Rainbow School
PO Box 422
Charlotte Aml 00801
Virgin Islands
Louise Thomas, Principal

2153 Robinson School
5 Nairn Street
Condado 00907
Puerto Rico
1-787-728-6767
Fax: 1-787-727-7736
E-mail: robinson_school@hotmail.com
http://www.geocities.com
Grade level prekindergarten through twelfth, with enrollment of 445.
Giberto Quintana, Executive Director

2154 Roosevelt Roads Elementary School
PO Box 420132
Roosevelt Roads 00742-0132
Puerto Rico
787-865-3073
Fax: 787-865-4891
http://www.netdial.caribe.net

2155 Roosevelt Roads Middle & High School
PO Box 420131
Roosevelt Roads 00742-0131
Puerto Rico
787-865-4000
Fax: 787-865-4893
E-mail: wjames@caribe.net
http://www.antilles.ododedodea.edu
Waynna James, Principal

2156 Saint Anthony School
529 Chalan San Antonio
Tamuning 96911 3600
Guam
Sor Mary Kathleen Sarmi, Principal

2157 Saint Eheresas Elementary School
Leone
Pago Apgo 96799
American Samoa
Sister Katherine, Principal

2158 Saint Francis Elementary School
520130 Lepua
Pago Pago 96799
American Samoa
Sister Gaynor Ana, Principal

2159 Saint John's School
911 N Marine Drive
Tumon Bay 96911
Guam
671-646-8080
Fax: 617-649-1055
E-mail: info@stjohns.edu.gu
http://www.stjohns.edu.gu
PreK-12th grade college preparatory school.

2160 Saint John's School, Puerto Rico
1466 Ashford Condado
Santurce 00907
Puerto Rico
Louis R Christiansen, Principal

2161 Saints Peter & Paul High School
Box 1706
Charlotte Aml 00801
Virgin Islands
Diana Parker, Principal

2162 Samoa Baptist Academy
Tafuna
Pago Pago 96799
American Samoa
Janice Yerton, Principal

2163 San Carlos & Bishop McManus High School
PO Box Loo 9, Yumet
Aguadilla 00605
Puerto Rico
Nydia U Nieves, Principal

2164 San Vincente Elementary School
San Vincente School Drive
Barrigada 96913
Puerto Rico 96913
671-734-4242
This campus is on five acres of outside Barrigada Village. The average enrollment of 460 students consists of 234 boys and 226 girls in grades PreK-8. SVS holds a Certificate of Accreditation from the Western Association of Schools and Colleges until 1998. Length of stay for overseas teachers is two years, with housing provided. Applications needed to teach include English and physical education.
Adrian Cristobal, Principal
Tarcisia Sablan SSND, Faculty Head

2165 Santa Barbara School
274A W Santa Barbara Avenue
Dededo 96912 1308
Guam

2166 Santiago Christian School
PO Box 5600
Fort Lauderdale, FL 33310-5600
Lloyd Haglund, Principal

2167 School of the Good Shepherd
1069 Kinghill
St. Croix 00851
Virgin Islands 00851
Linda Navarro, Principal

2168 Seventh Day Adventist
PO Box 7909
St. Thomas 00801-0909
Virgin Islands
Josiah Maynard, Principal

2169 Shekou International School
PO Box 4381
Houston, TX 72210-4381
86-755-2669-3669
Fax: 86-755-2667-4099
E-mail: sis@sis.org.cn
http://www.sis.org
Grade levels PK-9, school year August - June
Eleanor Jones, Director
Jennifer Lees, Curriculum Coordinator

2170 Slovak Republic QSI International School of Bratislava
DOS/Administrative Officer
5850 Bratislava Place
Washington, DC 20521-5840
421-2-6541-1636
Fax: 421-2-6541-1646
E-mail: director@qsi.sk
http://www.qsi.sk
Grades preK-12, enrollment 140.
Phil Sylla, Director

2171 Slovenia QSI International School-Ljubljana
DOS/Administrative Officer
7140 Ljubljana Place
Washington, DC 20521-7140
386-1-439-6300
Fax: 386-1-439-6305
E-mail: qsisln@siol.net
http://www.qsi.org
Grades K-8, enrollment 26.
Peter Janda, Director

2172 South Pacific Academy
PO Box 520
Pago Pago 96799 0520
American Samoa
Tina Senrud, Principal

2173 Southern Peru Staff Schools-Peru
180 Maiden Lane
New York, NY 10038-4925
John Dansdill, Principal

2174 St. Croix Christian Academy
PO Box 712
Christiansted 00850
Virgin Islands
Randolph Lockhart, Principal

2175 St. Croix Country Day School
Rt-01, Box 6199
Kingshill 00850
Virgin Islands
1-340-778-1974
Fax: 1-340-779-3331
Grade levels N-12, school year August - June
James Sadler, Headmaster
Susan Gibbons, Business Manager

2176 St. Croix Moravian School
PO Box 117
St. Thomas 00801
Virgin Islands
Condon L Joseph, Principal

2177 St. Croix SDA School
PO Box 930
Kingshill 00851-0930
Virgin Islands
Peter Archer, Principal

2178 St. Joseph High School
PO Box 517
Frederiksted 00841-0517
Virgin Islands
Kevin Marin, Principal

2179 St. Patrick School
PO Box 988
Frderiksted 00841-0988
Virgin Islands
Juliette Clarke, Principal

2180 St. Peter & Paul Elementary School
PO Box 1706
St. Thomas 00803
Virgin Islands
Annamay Komment, Principal

2181 Sunbeam
36 Hospital Ground
St. Thomas 00803
Virgin Islands
Ione Leonard, Principal

2182 Syria Damascus Community School
DOS/Administrative Officer
6110 Damascus Place
Washington, DC 20521-6110
963-11-333-0331
Fax: 963-11-332-1457
E-mail: dcs-dam@net.sy
http://www.syria-guide.com/school/dcs
An independent, coeducational day school which offers an American educational program from preschool through grade 12 for students of all nationalities.
Dr. James L Liebzeit, Director

2183 Tashkent International School
ADM/2 TIS
Dept. of State, 7110 Tashkent Place
Washington, DC 20521-7110
998-71-191-9671
Fax: 998-71-120-6621
E-mail: office@tis.uz
Grade levels K-12, school year August - June
John Thomas, Director

2184 Teaching in Austria
Austrian Institute
11 E 52nd Street
New York, NY 10022-5301
212-579-5165

2185 Temple Christian School
PO Box 3009
Agana 96910
Guam 96910
Rev. Ray Fagan, Principal

2186 Tirana International School-Albania
9510 Tirana Place
Washington, DC 29521-9510
355-4-365-239
Fax: 335-4-227-734
E-mail: qsialb@albaniaonline.net
http://www.qsi.org
Grade levels K-8, school year September - June
Glenn Mosher, Director

2187 Trinity Christian School
PO Box 11343
Yiga 96929 0343
Guam
Craig A Fletcher, Principal

2188 Turkmenistan Ashgabat International School
Box 2002
7070 Ashgabat Place
Washington, DC 20521-7070
967-1-234-437
Fax: 967-1-234-438
E-mail: director@ais.cat.glasnet.ru
Grades K-11, enrollment 75.
Scott Root, Director

2189 Ukraine Kiev International School-An American Institution
EOS/Administrative Officer
5850 Kiev Place
Washington, DC 20521-5850
380-44-452-2792
Fax: 380-44-452-2998
E-mail: kisukr@sovamua.com
An independent, coeducational day school which offers an educational program from

prekindergarten through high school for students of all nationalities.
E Michael Tewalthomas, Director

2190 United Nations International School
24-50 FDR Drive
New York, NY 10010
212-684-7400
Fax: 212-779-2259
E-mail: administration@unis.org
http://www.unis.org
Grade levels kindergarten through twelfth, with total enrollment of 1440 students.
Kenneth Wrye, EdD, Director

2191 University del Sagrado Corazon
PO Box 12383
San Juan 00917-8505
Puerto Rico

2192 Uruguayan American School
1785 Dublin Montevideo
Department of State
Washington, DC 20521-3360
598-2-600-7681
Fax: 598-2-600-1935
E-mail: amschool@chasque.apc.org
A private, nonsectarian, coeducational day school which offers an educational program from nursery through grade 12 for students of all nationalities.
Larry Synder, Principal

2193 Uruguayan American School-Montevideo
DOS/Administrative Officer
3360 Montevideo Place
Washington, DC 20521-3360
598-2-600-7681
Fax: 598-2-606-1935
E-mail: amschool@chasque.apc.org
http://www.uas.edu.uy
David Deuel, Director

2194 Uzbekistan Tashkent International School
DOS/Administrative Officer
7110 Tashkent Place
Washington, DC 20521-7110
998-71-191-9671
Fax: 998-71-120-6621
E-mail: office@tis.uz
Grades K-12, enrollment 138.
John Thomas, Director

2195 Venezuela Colegio Internacional-Carabobo
VLN 1010
PO Box 025685
Miami, FL 33102-5685
58-41-426-551
Fax: 58-41-426-510
E-mail: admin@cic-valencia.org.ve
Grades K-12, enrollment 417.
Frank Anderson, Superintendent

2196 Venezuela Escuela Campo Alegre
8424 NW 56th Street
Suite CCS 00007
Miami, FL 33166
58-2-993-7135
Fax: 58-2-993-0219
E-mail: info@eca.com.ve
http://www.internet.ve/eca
Grades N-12, enrollment 803.
Bambi Betts, Superintendent

2197 Venezuela International School-Caracas
PO Box 025323
CCS 10249
Miami, FL 33102-5323
58-2-945-0422
Fax: 58-2-945-0533
E-mail: wsargent@ciccaracas.com.ve
http://www.cic-caracus.org
Grades PK-12, enrollment 450.
Winthrop Sargent Jr, Headmaster

2198 Virgin Island Montessori School
Vessup Bay Star Route
Charlotte Aml 00801
Virgin Islands 00801
Shournagh Mcweeney, Principal

2199 Virgin Islands Department of Education
44-46 Kongens Gade
Saint Thomas, Virgin Islands 00802
340-774-2810
Fax: 340-774-7153
http://www.networkvi.com/education
Ruby Simmonds, Commissioner

2200 Washington International School
3100 Macomb Street NW
Washington, DC 20008-3324
202-243-1800
Fax: 202-243-1695
E-mail: admissions@wis.edu
http://www.wis.edu
Grade levels preK-12, with total student enrollment of 800.
Anne-Marie Pierce, Head of School

2201 We Care Child Development Center
PO Box 818
Christiansted 00821-0818
Virgin Islands
Pauline Canton, Principal

2202 Wesleyan Academy
PO Box 1489
Guaynabo 00970-1489
Puerto Rico
Jack Mann, Principal

2203 Yakistan International School-Karachi
DOS/Administrative Officer
6150 Karachi Place
Washington, DC 20521-6150
92-21-453-9096
Fax: 92-21-454-7305
E-mail: ameschl@cyber.net.pk
http://www.isk.edu.pk
Grades N-12, enrollment 338.
Glen Shapin, Superintendent

2204 Zion Academy
PO Box 10141
St. Thomas 00801-3141
Virgin Islands
Evelyn Williams, Principal

International

2205 Council for International Exchange of Scholars

3007 Tilden Street NW
Suite 5-L
Washington, DC 20008-3008
202-686-8664
Fax: 202-362-3442
E-mail: scholars@cies.iie.org
http://www.cies.org
Announces each year approximately 1,000 Fulbright awards for Americans to teach or conduct research at universities in about 134 countries.

Patti McGill Peterson, Executive Director
Judy Pehrson, Director External Relations

2206 Defense Language Institute-English Language Branch

US Civil Service Commission, San Antonio Area
8610 Broadway Street
San Antonio, TX 78217-6352
512-229-6622
Employs English language instructors at the school and in numerous overseas locations.

2207 Education Information Services which Employ Americans

Education Information Services
PO Box 620662
Newton, MA 02462-0662
781-433-0125
Fax: 781-237-2842
Devoted to helping Americans who wish to teach in American overseas schools and International Schools in which English is the primary teaching language. Supports those wishing to teach English as a second language. Publish papers covering every country in the world, list of recruiting fairs, internships, volunteers, jobs, summer overseas jobs.

Frederic B Viaux, President

2208 Educational Information Services

PO Box 662
Newtown Lower Falls, MA 02162
617-964-4555
Offers information on employment opportunities including books, periodicals and more for the teaching professional who wishes to teach in American overseas schools, international schools, language (ESL) schools, and Department of Defense Dependencies Schools (DODDS).

Frederick B Viaux, President
Michelle V Curtin, Editor

2209 Educational Placement Sources-US

Education Information Services/Instant Alert
PO Box 620662
Newton, MA 02462-0662
617-433-0125
Lists 100 organizations in the United States that find positions for teachers, educational administrators, counselors and other professionals. Listings are classified by type, listed alphabetically and offer all contact information.

4 pages Annual

FB Viaux, President

2210 Educational Staffing Program

International Schools Services
PO Box 5910
Princeton, NJ 08543
609-452-0990
Fax: 609-452-2690
E-mail: edustaffing@iss.edu
The Educational Staffing Program has placed almost 15,000 K-12 teachers and administrators in overseas schools since 1955. Most candidates obtain their overseas teaching positions by attending our US-based International Recruitment Center where ISS candidates have the potential to interview with overseas school heads seeking new staff. You must be an active ISS candidate to attend an IRC. Applicants must have a bachelor's degree and two years of current relevant experience.

2211 European Council of International Schools

21 Lavant Street
Petersfield, Hampshire GU3 23EL
United Kingdom
44-0-1730-268244
Fax: 44-0-1730-267914
E-mail: ecis@ecis.org
http://www.ecis.org
Provides a variety of services to its 150 member schools in Europe and over 120 associate member schools worldwide: conducts professional conferences, evaluates and accredits international schools, assists schools with staffing, offers placement assistance to teaching candidates and provides comprehensive consultative services.

T Michael Maybury, Executive Secretary

2212 FRS National Teacher Agency

PO Box 298
Seymour, TN 37865-0298
865-577-8143
Offers employment options to educators in the United States and abroad.

2213 Foreign Faculty and Administrative Openings

Education Information Services
PO Box 620662
Newton, MA 02462-0662
617-433-0125
150 specific openings in administration, counseling, library and other professional positions for American teachers in American schools overseas and in international schools in which teaching language is English.

15 pages Every 6 Weeks

FB Viaux, Coordinating Education

2214 Fulbright Teacher Exchange

600 Maryland Avenue SW
Room 235
Washington, DC 20024-2520
800-726-0479
http://www.grad.usda.gov
An organization that offers opportunities for two-year college faculty and secondary school teachers who would like to exchange with teachers in Eastern or Western Europe, Latin America, Australia, Africa, and Canada. To qualify, teachers must be US citizens, have three years full-time teaching experience and be employed in a full-time academic position.

2215 International Educators Cooperative

212 Alcott Road
East Falmouth, MA 02536-6803
508-540-8173
Fax: 508-540-8173
In addition to year round recruitment, International Educators Cooperative hosts Recruitment Centers in the United States each year.

Dr. Lou Fuccillo, Director

2216 National Association of Teachers' Agencies

National Association of Teachers' Agencies
799 Kings Highway
Fairfield, CT 06432
203-333-0611
Fax: 203-334-7224
E-mail: fairfieldteachers@snet.net
http://www.jobsforteachers.com
Provides placement services for those seeking professional positions at all levels of teaching/administration/support services worldwide.

Mark King, Secretary/Treasurer

2217 National Council of Independent Schools' Associations

Curtin ACT 2605
PO Box 324
Australia
06-282-3488
Fax: 06-282-2926
Services include career placement.

Fergus Thomson

2218 Overseas Employment Opportunities for Educators

Department of Defense, Office of Dependent Schools
2461 Eisenhower Avenue
Alexandria, VA 22331-3000
703-325-0867
This publication tells about teaching jobs in 250 schools operated for children of US military and civilian personnel stationed overseas. Applicants usually must qualify in two subject areas.

2219 Recruiting Fairs for Overseas Teaching

Education Information Services/Instant Alert
PO Box 620662
Newton, MA 02462-0662
781-433-0125
Fax: 781-237-2842
Recruiting fairs and sponsors in the US and elsewhere for American educators who wish to teach outside of the United States.

FB Viaux, Coordinating Education

2220 UNI Overseas Recruiting Fair

University of Northern Iowa
SSC #19
Cedar Falls, IA 50614-0390
319-273-2083
Fax: 319-273-6998
E-mail: overseas.placement@uni.edu
http://www.uni.edu/placement/overseas
About 160 recruiters from 120 schools in 80 countries recruit at this fair for certified K-12 educators.

February

Tracy Roling, Coordinator

2221 WorldTeach

Center for International Development
Harvard University
79 John F Kennedy Street
Cambridge, MA 02138-5705
617-495-5527
800-483-2240
Fax: 617-495-1599
E-mail: info@worldteach.org
http://www.worldteach.org
Agency offering volunteers teaching placements in developing countries for English, math, science, and computer education. Summer teaching internships or on a-year programs.

Robin Teater, Executive Director
Harriet Wong, Program Manager

Alabama

2222 Auburn University at Montgomery Library
PO Box 244023
Montgomery, AL 36124-4023
334-244-3649
Fax: 334-244-3720
http://www.aumnicat.aum.edu
Member of The Foundation Center network, maintaining a collection of private foundation tax returns which provide information on the scope of grants dispensed by that particular foundation.

R Best, Dean Administration
T Bailey, ILL/ Reference

2223 Benjamin & Roberta Russell Educational and Charitable Foundation
PO Box 272
Alexander City, AL 35010-0272
256-329-4224
Offers giving in the areas of higher and public education, youth programs and a hospital.

James D Nabors, Executive Director

2224 Birmingham Public Library
Government Documents
2100 Park Place
Birmingham, AL 35203-2794
205-226-3600
Fax: 205-226-3729
http://www.bplonline.org/resources/subjects/gov/deault
Member of The Foundation Center network, maintaining a collection of private foundation tax returns which provide information on the scope of grants dispensed by that particular foundation.

2225 Carolina Lawson Ivey Memorial Foundation
PO Box 340
Smiths, AL 36877-0340
334-826-5760
Scholarships are offered to college juniors and seniors who are pursuing careers of teaching social studies in middle or secondary grades. The grants are also offered to teachers in Alabama and west Georgia for curriculum planning and development, in-service training, the development of instructional materials for use in elementary and secondary schools, and other projects that focus on the cultural approach method of teaching.

2226 Huntsville Public Library
915 Monroe Street SW
Huntsville, AL 35801-5007
256-532-5940
http://www.hpl.lib.al.us/
Member of The Foundation Center network, maintaining a collection of private foundation tax returns which provide information on the scope of grants dispensed by that particular foundation.

Donna B Schremser, Library Director

2227 JL Bedsole Foundation
PO Box 1137
Mobile, AL 36633-1137
251-432-3369
Fax: 251-432-1134
http://www.jlbedsolefoundation.org
The foundation's primary interest is the support of educational institutions within the state of Alabama and civic and eco-nomic development which is limited to the geographical area of Southwest Alabama. The arts, social service and health programs receive limited grants. Organizations or projects outside of the State of Alabama are not considered for funding by the Foundation.

Mabel B Ward, Executive Director
Scott A Morton, Assistant Director

2228 Mildred Weedon Blount Educational and Charitable Foundation
PO Box 607
Tallassee, AL 36078-0007
334-283-4931
Support for Catholic schools, public schools and a scholarship fund for secondary school students.

Arnold B Dopson, Executive Director

2229 Mitchell Foundation
PO Box 1126
Mobile, AL 36633
251-432-1711
Fax: 334-432-1712
Places an emphasis on secondary and higher education, social services programs, youth agencies, and aid for the handicapped.

Augustine Meaher, Executive Director

2230 University of South Alabama
307 University Boulevard
Mobile, AL 36688-0002
251-460-7025
Fax: 251-460-7636
http://http://library.southalabama.edu
Richard Wood, Dean Of Libraries

Alaska

2231 University of Alaska-Anchorage Library
3211 Providence Drive
Anchorage, AK 99508-8000
907-786-1848
Fax: 907-786-6050
http://www.lib.uaa.alaska.edu/
Member of The Foundation Center network, maintaining a collection of private foundation tax returns which provide information on the scope of grants dispensed by that particular foundation.

Stephen J Rollins, Dean Of Library

Arizona

2232 Arizona Department of Education
1535 W Jefferson Street
Phoenix, AZ 85007
602-542-5393
800-352-4558
Fax: 602-542-5440
http://www.ade.state.az.us
Implements procedures that ensure the proper allocation, distribution, and expenditure of all federal and state funds administerd by the department. The following links to our web pages contain information pertaining to educational grants funded from the state or federal programs.

Tom Horne, Superintendent

2233 Arizona Governor's Committee on Employment of People with Disabilities
Samaritan Rehabilitation Institute
1012 E Willetta Street
Phoenix, AZ 85006-3047
602-239-4762
Fax: 602-239-5256

Jim Bruzewski, Executive Director

2234 Education Services
Arizona Department of Education
1535 W Jefferson Street
Phoenix, AZ 85007-3280
602-364-1961
Fax: 602-542-5440
http://www.ade.state.az.us/edservices
Provides quality services and resources to schools, parent groups, government agencies, and community groups to enable them to achieve their goals.

Lillie Sly, Associate Superintendent

2235 Evo-Ora Foundation
2525 E Broadway Boulevard
Suite 111
Tucson, AZ 85716-5398
Giving is primarily aimed at education, especially Catholic high schools and universities.

2236 Flinn Foundation
1802 N Central Avenue
Suite 2300
Phoenix, AZ 85012-2513
602-744-6800
Fax: 602-744-6815
http://www.flinn.org
Supports nonprofit organizations in the state of Arizona for programs in health care, as well as an annual awards competition for Arizona's principal arts institutions and a college scholarship program for Arizona high school graduates. Scholarship provides expenses for four years, two summers of study-related travel abroad and other benefits.

John W Murphy, Executive Director

2237 Phoenix Public Library
Business & Sciences Department
12 E McDowell Road
Phoenix, AZ 85004-1627
602-262-4636
Fax: 602-261-8836
http://www.phxlib.org
Member of The Foundation Center network, maintaining a collection of private foundation tax returns which provide information on the scope of grants dispensed by that particular foundation.

2238 Special Programs
Arizona Department of Education
1535 W Jefferson Street
Phoenix, AZ 85007-3280
602-542-5393
Fax: 602-542-5440

Tom Horne, Superintendent

2239 Support Services
Arizona Department of Education
1535 W Jefferson Street
Phoenix, AZ 85007-3280
602-542-5393
Fax: 602-542-5440

Rachel Arroyo, School Finance

2240 Vocational Technological Education
Arizona Department of Education
1535 W Jefferson Street
Phoenix, AZ 85007-3280
602-542-5393
Fax: 602-542-5440

Tom Horne, Superintendent

Arkansas

2241 Charles A Frueauff Foundation
900 S Shackleford Road
Suite 300
Little Rock, AR 72211-3848
501-219-1410
http://www.frueauffoundation.com
Will review proposals from private four-year colleges and universities.

Zoe Cole Galloway

2242 Roy and Christine Sturgis Charitable and Educational Trust
PO Box 92
Malvern, AR 72104-0092
501-337-5109
Giving is offered to Baptist and Methodist organizations, including schools, churches and higher and secondary education.

Katie Speer, Executive Director

2243 The Jones Center For Families
922 East Emma Avenue
Springdale, AR 72765
479-756-8090
Focuses funds on education, medical resources and religious organizations in Arkansas.

HG Frost Jr, Executive Director
Grace Donoho, Director Of Education

2244 Walton Family Foundation
125 W Central Avenue
Room 217 Po Box 2030
Bentonville, AR 72712-5248
479-464-1570
Fax: 479-464-1580
http://www.wffhome.com
Offers giving for systemic reform of primary education (K-12) and early childhood development.

Stewart T Springfield, Executive Director

2245 Westark Community College
Borham Library
5210 Grand Avenue
Fort Smith, AR 72904-7397
479-788-7200
Fax: 479-788-7209
Member of The Foundation Center network, maintaining a collection of private foundation tax returns which provide information on the scope of grants dispensed by that particular foundation.

2246 William C & Theodosia Murphy Nolan Foundation
200 N Jefferson Avenue
Suite 308
El Dorado, AR 71730-5853
870-863-7118
Fax: 870-863-6528
Supports education and the arts (historic preservation, arts centers) as well as religious welfare and youth organizations in Northern Louisiana and Southern Arkansas.

William C Nolan, Executive Director

2247 Winthrop Rockefeller Foundation
308 E 8th Street
Little Rock, AR 72202-3999
501-376-6854
Fax: 501-374-4797
Dedicated to improving the quality of life and education in Arkansas. Grants go to schools that work to involve teachers and parents in making decisions; to universities and local schools to strengthen both levels of education; and for projects that promote stakeholder participation in the development of educational policy.

Mahlon Martin, President
Jackie Cox-New, Sr Program Officer

California

2248 Ahmanson Foundation
9215 Wilshire Boulevard
Beverly Hills, CA 90210-5538
310-278-0770
Concentrates mainly on education, health and social services in Southern California.

Lee E Walcott, Executive Director

2249 Alice Tweed Tuohy Foundation
205 E Carrillo Street
Suite 219
Santa Barbara, CA 93101-7186
805-962-6430
Priority consideration is given to applications from organizations serving: young people; education; selected areas of interest in health care and medicine; and community affairs.

Harris W Seed, President
Eleanor Van Cott, Executive VP

2250 Arrillaga Foundation
2560 Mission College Boulevard
Suite 101
Santa Clara, CA 95054-1217
408-980-0130
Fax: 408-988-4893
Giving is aimed at secondary schools and higher education in the state of California.

John Arrillaga, Executive Director

2251 Atkinson Foundation
1100 Grundy Lane
Suite 140
San Bruno, CA 94066-3030
650-876-0222
Fax: 650-876-0222
Provides opportunities for people in San Mateo County, California to reach their highest potential and to improve the quality of their lives and to assist educational institutions and supporting organizations with the implementation of effective programs that reach and serve their target populations.

Elizabeth Curtis, Executive Director

2252 BankAmerica Foundation
Bank of America Center
PO Box 37000
San Francisco, CA 94137-0001
415-953-3175
Fax: 415-622-3469
E-mail: bacef@consumer-action.org
Fields of interest include arts/cultural programs, higher education, community development and general federated giving programs.

Elizabeth Nachbaur, Program Director

2253 Bechtel Group Corporate Giving Program
Po Box 193965
San Francisco, CA 94119-3965
415-768-5974
Offers support for higher education and programs related to engineering and construction, math and science in grades K-12 and general charitable programs.

Kathryn M Bandarrae, Executive Director

2254 Bernard Osher Foundation
909 Montgomery
#300
San Francisco, CA 94133
415-861-5587
Fax: 415-677-5868
E-mail: nagle@osherfoundation.org
Funds in the arts, post-secondary education and environmental education on San Francisco and Alameda Counties.

Patricia Nagle, Sr VP

2255 Boys-Viva Supermarkets Foundation
955 Carrillo Drive
Suite 103
Los Angeles, CA 90048-5400
Wide range of support for education of school-aged children, especially the at-risk population, tutoring, and social opportunities.

Fred Snowden, Executive Director

2256 California Community Foundation
445 S Figueroa Street
Suite 3400
Los Angeles, CA 90071-1638
210-413-4130
Fax: 213-622-2979
http://www.calfund.org
Improving human condition through non-profit agencies in Los Angeles County. Integral parts of eligible proposals are, hosting conferences, incurring debt, individuals, sectarian purposes or regranting.

Judy Spiegel, Sr VP of Programs
Antonia Hernandez, President/CEO

2257 Carrie Estelle Doheny Foundation
707 Wilshire Boulevard
Suite 4960
Los Angeles, CA 90017-2659
213-488-1122
Fax: 213-488-1544
http://www.dohenyfoundation.org
This foundation funds a myriad of organizations ranging from the education and medicine field to public health and science areas.

Robert A Smith III, Executive Director

2258 Dan Murphy Foundation
PO Box 711267
Los Angeles, CA 90071-9767
213-623-3120
Fax: 213-623-1421
Funds Roman Catholic institutions, with a primary interest in religious orders and schools.

Daniel J Donohue, Executive Director

2259 David & Lucile Packard Foundation
300 2nd Street
Suite 200
Los Altos Hills, CA 94022-3643
650-948-7658
Fax: 650-941-3151
http://www.packard.org
Concentrates on four categories: education, the arts, conservation and child health. Also allocates funds to companies interested in public improvement and public policy.

Colburn S Wilbur, Executive Director

2260 Evelyn & Walter Haas Jr Fund
One Market Landmark
Suite 400
San Francisco, CA 94105
415-856-1400
Fax: 415-856-1500
Interested in strengthening neighborhoods, communities, and human services. Funds mainly in San Francisco Bay Area.

Ira Hirschfield, President
Clayton Juan, Grants Administrator

2261 Foundation Center-San Francisco
312 Sutter Street
Suite 606
San Francisco, CA 94108-4323
415-397-0902
Fax: 415-397-7670
http://www.fdncenter.org
One of five Foundation Centers nationwide, the Foundation Center - San Francisco is a library which collects information on private foundations, corporate philanthropy, nonprofit management, fundraising and other topics of interest to nonprofit organization representatives.

2262 Foundations Focus
Marin Community Foundation
5 Hamilton Landing
Suite 200
Novato, CA 94949
415-464-2500
Fax: 415-464-2555
http://www.marincf.org
Grants support projects that benefit residents of Marin County, CA.

Don Jen, Program Officer/Education
Thomas Peters, President/CEO

2263 Francis H Clougherty Charitable Trust
500 Newport Center Drive
Suite 720
Newport Beach, CA 92660-7007
Offers grants in the areas of elementary, secondary school and higher education in Southern California.

2264 Freitas Foundation
C/O Fiduciary Resources
1120 Nye Street
Suite 320
San Rafael, CA 94901-2945
Offers giving in the areas of elementary and secondary education, as well as theological education.

Margaret Boyden, Executive Director

2265 Fritz B Burns Foundation
4001 W Alameda Avenue
Suite 201
Burbank, CA 91505-4338
818-840-8802
Fax: 818-840-0468

Grants are primarily focused on education, hospitals and medical research organizations.

Joseph E Rawlinson, Executive Director

2266 George Frederick Jewett Foundation
235 Montgomery Street
Suite 612
San Francisco, CA 94104-2909
415-421-1351
Fax: 415-421-1351
Concerns itself mainly with voluntary, non-profit organizations that promote human welfare.

2267 Grant & Resource Center of Northern California
2280 Benton Drive, Building C
Suite A
Redding, CA 96003
530-244-1219
Fax: 530-244-0905
E-mail: library@grcnc.org
Member of The Foundation Center network, maintaining a collection of private foundation tax returns which provide information on the scope of grants dispensed by that particular foundation.

2268 Greenville Foundation
283 2nd Street E
Suite A
Sonoma, CA 95476-5708
707-938-9377
Fax: 707-939-9311
This foundation focuses its support on education, the environment and human rights. The main focus of the educational grants lie within the areas of elementary, secondary and higher education.

Virginia Hubbell, Executive Director

2269 HN & Frances C Berger Foundation
PO Box 3064
Arcadia, CA 91006
626-447-3351
Provides scholarships and endowments to colleges and universities.

2270 Harry & Grace Steele Foundation
441 Old Newport Boulevard
Suite 301
Newport Beach, CA 92663-4231
949-631-0418
Grants are given in the areas of secondary education, including scholarship funds in the fine arts and youth agencies.

Marie F Kowert, Executive Director

2271 Henry J Kaiser Family Foundation
Quadrus
2400 Sand Hill Road
Menlo Park, CA 94025-6941
650-854-9400
Fax: 650-854-4800
http://www.kff.org
Concentrates on health care, minority groups and South Africa.

Drew Altman, President/CEO

2272 Hon Foundation
25200 La Paz Road
Suite 210
Laguna Hills, CA 92653-5110
949-586-4400
Offers giving in the areas of elementary, secondary and higher education in the states of Hawaii and California.

2273 Hugh & Hazel Darling Foundation
520 S Grand Avenue
7th Floor
Los Angeles, CA 90071-2645
213-683-5200
Fax: 213-627-7795
Supports education in California with special emphasis on legal education; no grants to individuals; grants only to 501(c)(3) organizations.

Richard L Stack, Trustee

2274 Ingraham Memorial Fund
C/O Emrys J. Ross
301 E Colorado Boulevard
Suite 900
Pasadena, CA 91101-1916
Offers giving in the areas of elementary, secondary and higher education, as well as theological education in Claremont and Pasadena, California.

2275 James G Boswell Foundation
101 W Walnut Street
Pasadena, CA 91103-3636
626-583-3000
Fax: 626-583-3090
Funds hospitals, pre-college private schools, public broadcasting and youth organizations.

James G Boswell II, Chairman
Sherman Railsback, EVP/COO

2276 James Irvine Foundation
1 Market, Steuart Tower
Suite 2500
San Francisco, CA 94105-1017
415-777-2244
Fax: 415-777-0869
Giving is primarily aimed at the areas of education, youth and health.

James E Canales, President/CEO
Kristin Nelson, Executive Assistant

2277 James S Copley Foundation
7776 Ivanhoe Avenue #1530
La Jolla, CA 92037-4520
858-454-0411
Fax: 858-729-7629
Support is offered for higher and secondary education, child development, cultural programs and community services.

Anita A Baumgardner, Executive Director

2278 John Jewett & H Chandler Garland Foundation
PO Box 550
Pasadena, CA 91102-0550
Support given primarily for secondary and higher education, social services and cultural and historical programs.

GE Morrow, Executive Director

2279 Joseph Drown Foundation
1999 Avenue of the Stars
Suite 2330
Los Angeles, CA 90067-4611
310-277-4488
Fax: 310-277-4573
http://www.jdrown.org
The Foundation's goal is to assist individuals in becoming successful, self-sustaining, contributing citizens. The foundation is interested in programs that break down any barrier that prevents a person from continuing to grow and learn.

Norman Obrow, Executive Director

2280 Jules & Doris Stein Foundation
PO Box 30
Beverly Hills, CA 90213-0030
213-276-2101
Supports charitable organizations.

2281 Julio R Gallo Foundation
PO Box 1130
Modesto, CA 95353-1130
209-579-3373
Offers grants and support to secondary schools and higher education universities.

Sam Gallo, Chairman

2282 Kenneth T & Eileen L Norris Foundation
11 Golden Shore Street
Suite 450
Long Beach, CA 90802-4214
562-435-8444
Fax: 562-436-0584
E-mail: gerringer@ktn.org
http://www.norrisfoundation.org
Funding categories include medical, education/science, youth, cultural and community.

Ronald Barnes, Executive Director

2283 Koret Foundation
33 New Montgomery Street
Suite 1090
San Francisco, CA 94105-4526
415-882-7740
Fax: 415-882-7775
E-mail: sandyedwards@koretfoundation.org
http://www.koretfoundation.org
Funding includes; public policy and selected programs in K-12 public education, higher education, youth programs, Jewish studies at colleges and universities, and Jewish education. The geographical area for grant-making is the San Francisco Bay area.

Tad Taube, President

2284 Lane Family Charitable Trust
500 Almer Road
Apartment 301
Burlingame, CA 94010-3966
Offers giving in the areas of secondary schools and higher education facilities in California.

Ralph Lane, Trustee
Joan Lane, Trustee

2285 Levi Strauss Foundation
1155 Battery Street
Floor 7
San Francisco, CA 94111-1230
415-501-6000
Fax: 415-501-7112
http://www.levistrauss.com
Grants are made in four areas: AIDS prevention and care; economic empowerment; youth empowerment; and social justice. Grants are limited to communities where Levi Strauss and Company has plants or customer service centers.

Theresa Fay-Buslillos, Executive Director

2286 Louise M Davies Foundation
580 California Street
Suite 1800
San Francisco, CA 94104-1039
Offers giving in the areas of elementary, secondary and higher education, as well as scholarship funding for California students.

Donald Crawford Jr, Executive Director

2287 Lowell Berry Foundation
3685 Mount Diablo Boulevard
Lafayette, CA 94549
925-284-4427
Fax: 925-284-4332
Assists Christian ministry at local church levels.

Debbie Coombe, Office Manager

2288 Luke B Hancock Foundation
360 Bryant Street
Palo Alto, CA 94301-1409
650-321-5536
Fax: 650-321-0697
E-mail: lhancock@lukebhancock.org
http://www.fdcenter.org/grantmaker/hancock
Provides funding for programs which promote the well being of children and youth. Priority is given to programs which address the needs of youth who are at risk of school failure. Additional funding is provided for early childhood development, music education and homeless families.

Ruth M Ramel, Executive Director

2289 Margaret E Oser Foundation
1911 Lyon Court
Santa Rosa, CA 95403-0974
949-553-4202
Offers grants in the areas of elementary and secondary and higher education, which will benefit women.

Carl Mitchell, Executive Director

2290 Marin Community Foundation
17 E Sir Francis Drake Boulevard
Suite 200
Larkspur, CA 94939-1736
415-461-3333
Fax: 415-464-2555
http://www.marincf.org
Established as a nonprofit public benefit corporation to engage in educational and philanthropic activities in Marin County, California.

2291 Mary A Crocker Trust
233 Post Street
Floor 2
San Francisco, CA 94108-5003
415-982-0138
Fax: 415-982-0141
http://www.mactrust.org
Giving is aimed at precollegiate education, as well as conservation and environmental programs.

Barbaree Jernigan, Executive Director

2292 Maurice Amado Foundation
3940 Laurel Canyon Boulevard
Suite 809
Studio City, CA 91604
818-980-9190
Fax: 818-980-9190
E-mail: pkaizer@mauriceamadofdn.org
Concentrates on the Jewish heritage.

Pam Kaizer, Executive Director

2293 McConnell Foundation
PO Box 492050
Redding, CA 96049-2050
530-226-6200
Fax: 530-226-6210
http://www.mcconnellfoundation.org

Interested in cultural, community and health care related projects.

Ana Diaz, Program Assistant

2294 McKesson Foundation
1 Post Street
San Francisco, CA 94104-5203
415-983-8300
http://www.mckesson.com/foundation.html
Giving is primarily to programs for junior high school students and for emergency services such as food and shelter.

Marcia M Argyris, Executive Director

2295 Milken Family Foundation
C/O Foundations of the Milken Families
1250 4th Street
Floor 6
Santa Monica, CA 90401-1350
310-570-4800
http://www.mff.org
Offers support to the educational community to reward educational innovators, stimulate creativity among students, involve parents and other citizens in the school system, and help disadvantaged youth.

Dr. Julius Lesner, Executive Director

2296 Miranda Lux Foundation
57 Post Street
Suite 510
San Francisco, CA 94104-5020
415-981-2966
http://ww.mirandalux.org
Offers support to promising proposals for pre-school through junior college programs in the fields of pre-vocational and vocational education and training.

Kenneth Blum, Executive Director

2297 Northern California Grantmakers
625 Market Street
15th Floor
San Francisco, CA 94105
415-777-4111
Fax: 415-777-1741
E-mail: ncg@ncg.org
Northern California Grantmakers is an association of foundations, corporate contributions programs and other private grantmakers. Its mission is to jpromote the well being of people and their communities in balance with a healthy environment by the thoughtful and creative use of private wealth and resources for the public benefit. To this end, NCG works to enhance the effectiveness of philanthropy, including nonprofit organizations, government, business, media, academia and the public at large.

Colin Lacon, President

2298 Pacific Telesis Group Corporate Giving Program
130 Kearny Street
San Francisco, CA 94108-4818
415-394-3000
Primary areas of interest include K-12 education reform, education of minorities, women and disabled individuals in the math, science, engineering, education and MBA fields; and specific K-12 issues such as dropouts, information technology and parent involvement.

Jere A Jacobs, Executive Director

2299 Peninsula Community Foundation
1700 S El Camino Real
Suite 300
San Mateo, CA 94402-3049
650-358-9369
Fax: 650-358-9817
http://www.pcf.org
Serving a population from Daly City to Mountain View, the foundations focus is on children and youth, adult services, programs serving homeless families and children, prevention of homelessness and civic and public benefit grants.

Sterling K Speirn, Executive Director

2300 Peter Norton Family Foundation
225 Arizona Avenue
Floor 2
Santa Monica, CA 90401-1243
310-576-7700
Fax: 310-576-7701
Offers giving in the areas of early childhood education, elementary school education, higher education, childrens services and AIDS research.

Anne Etheridge, ED, Executive Director

2301 RCM Capital Management Charitable Fund
4 Embarcadero Center
Suite 2900
San Francisco, CA 94111-4189
415-954-5474
Fax: 415-954-8200
Giving is offered in many areas including youth development, early childhood education and elementary education.

Jami Weinman, Executive Director

2302 Ralph M Parsons Foundation
1055 Wilshire Boulevard
Suite 1701
Los Angeles, CA 90017-5600
213-482-3185
Fax: 213-482-8878
http://www.rmpf.org
Giving is focused on higher and pre-collegiate education, with an emphasis on engineering, technology, and science; social impact programs serving families, children and the elderly; health programs targeting underserved populations; civic and cultural programs.

Wendy G Hoppe, Executive Director

2303 Riordan Foundation
300 S Grand Avenue
Suite 29
Los Angeles, CA 90071-3110
213-229-8402
Fax: 213-229-5061
http://www.riordanfoundation.org
Priorities of the foundation include early childhood literacy, youth programs, leadership programs, job training, direct medical services to young children, and cyclical, targeted mini-grants. When determining levels of support, priority is always given to programs which impact young children.

Nike Irvin, President

2304 Royal Barney Hogan Foundation
PO Box 193809
San Francisco, CA 94119-3809
Offers grants specifically for secondary education in the state of California.

2305 SH Cowell Foundation
120 Montgomery Street
Suite 2570
San Francisco, CA 94104-4303
415-397-0285
Fax: 415-986-6786
http://www.shcowell.org
Offers support for educational programs, including pre-school and primary public educational programs.

JD Erickson, Executive Director
Mary S Metz, President

2306 Sacramento Regional Foundation
555 Capitol Mall
Suite 550
Sacramento, CA 95814-4502
916-492-6510
Fax: 916-492-6515
http://www.sacregfoundation.org
Primary interests of this foundation include the arts, humanities and education.

Stephen F Boutin, President
Janice Gow Pettey, CEO

2307 San Diego Foundation
1420 Kettner Boulevard
Suite 500
San Diego, CA 92101-2434
619-235-2300
Fax: 619-239-1710
E-mail: info@sdfoundation.org
http://www.sdfoundation.org
Offers grants in the areas of social services with emphasis on children and families, education and health for San Diego County.

Robert A Kelly, President/CEO
Rebecca Reichmann, VP Programs

2308 San Francisco Foundation
225 Bush Street
Suite 500
San Francisco, CA 94104-4224
415-733-8500
Fax: 415-477-2783
E-mail: rec@sff.org
http://www.sff.org
Addresses community needs in the areas of community health, education, arts and culture, neighborhood revitalization, and environmental justice. Works to support families and communities to help children and youth succeed in school and provide opportunities for them to become confident, caring and contributing adults.

Sandra R Hernandez MD, CEO
Sara Ying Kelley, Director Public Affairs

2309 Santa Barbara Foundation
15 E Carrillo Street
Santa Barbara, CA 93101-2780
805-963-1873
Fax: 805-966-2345
http://www.sbfoundation.org
Offers a student aid program with no interest-1/2 loan and 1/2 scholarship. Funding limited to long-term Santa Barbara County residents.

Claudia Armann, Program Officer
Charles O Slosserm, President/CEO

2310 Sega Youth Education & Health Foundation
255 Shoreline Drive
Suite 200
Redwood City, CA 94065-1428
Offers support only to organizations that address and promote youth education and health issues.

Trizia Carpenter, Executive Director

2311 Sidney Stern Memorial Trust
PO Box 893
Pacific Palisades, CA 90272-0893
310-459-2117
Funding offered includes education, community action groups, the arts and the disabled.

2312 Sol & Clara Kest Family Foundation
5150 Overland Avenue
Culver City, CA 90230-4914
213-204-2050
Offers support for Jewish organizations in the areas of education.

Sol Kest, Executive Director

2313 Szekely Family Foundation
3232 Dove Street
San Diego, CA 92103
619-295-2372
Offers giving in the areas of early childhood education, child development, elementary education, higher education, and adult and continuing education.

Deborah Szekely, Executive Director

2314 Thomas & Dorothy Leavey Foundation
10100 Santa Monica Boulevard
Suite 610
Los Angeles, CA 90067
310-551-9936
Focus is placed on college scholarships, medical research, youth groups and programs, and secondary and higher education purposes.

J Thomas McCarthy, Executive Director

2315 Times Mirror Foundation
202 West First Street
Los Angeles, CA 90012
213-237-3945
Fax: 213-237-2116
http://www.timesmirrorfoundation.org
Giving is largely for higher education purposes including liberal arts and business education.

Cassandra Malry, Executive Director

2316 Timken-Sturgis Foundation
7421 Eads Avenue
La Jolla, CA 92037-5037
619-454-2252
Offers support for education in Southern California and Nevada.

Joannie Barrancotto, Executive Director

2317 Toyota USA Foundation
19001 S Western Avenue
Torrance, CA 90501-1106
310-715-7486
Fax: 310-468-7809
E-mail: b_pauli@toyota
http://www.toyota.com/foundation
Supports K-12 education programs, with strong emphasis on math and science.

William Pauli, National Manager

2318 Turst Funds Incorporated
100 Broadway Street
Floor 3
San Francisco, CA 94111-1404
415-434-3323
Offers grants for Catholic Schools, including elementary and secondary education, in the San Francisco Bay Area.

James T Healy, President

2319 Ventura County Community Foundation

Funding & Information Resource Center
1317 Del Norte Road
Suite 150
Camarillo, CA 93010-8504
805-988-0196
Fax: 805-485-5537
http://www.vccf.org
Member of The Foundation Center network, maintaining a collection of private foundation tax returns which provide information on the scope of grants dispensed by that particular foundation.

Hugh J Ralston, President/CEO
Virginia Weber, Program Officer

2320 WM Keck Foundation

550 S Hope Street
Suite 2500
Los Angeles, CA 90071
213-680-3833
Fax: 213-614-0934
E-mail: info@wmkeck.org
http://www.wmkeck.org
The Foundation also gives some consideration, limited to Southern California, for the support of arts and culture, civic and community services, health care and precollegiate education. The foundation's grant-making is focused primarily on pioneering research efforts in the areas of science, engineering and medical research, and on higher education, including liberal arts.

Maria Pellegrini, Program Director

2321 Walter & Elise Haas Fund

1 Lombard Street
Suite 305
San Francisco, CA 94111-1130
415-398-4474
Fax: 415-986-4779
http://www.haassr.org
Supports education, arts, environment, human services, humanities and public affairs; is especially in projects which have a wide impact within their respective fields through enhancing public education and access to information, serving a central organizing role, addressing public policy, demonstrating creative approaches toward meeting human needs, or supporting the work of a major institution in the field.

Pamela H David, Executive Director
Peter E Hass Jr, President

2322 Walter S Johnson Foundation

525 Middlefield Road
Suite 160
Menlo Park, CA 94025-3447
650-326-0485
Fax: 650-326-4320
http://www.wsjf.org
Giving is centered on education in public schools and social service agencies concerned with the quality of public education in Northern California and Washoe County, Nevada.

Pancho Chang, Executive Director

2323 Wayne & Gladys Valley Foundation

1939 Harrison Street
Suite 510
Oakland, CA 94612-3535
510-466-6060
Fax: 510-466-6067
Supports four areas: education, medical research, community services and special projects.

Michael D Desler, Executive Director

2324 Weingart Foundation

1055 W 7th Street
Suite 3050
Los Angeles, CA 90017-2509
213-688-7799
Fax: 213-688-1515
http://www.weingartfnd.org
Offers support for community services including a student loan program.

William D Schulte, Chairman & CEO
Fred J Ali, President/Chief Adm. Officer

2325 Wells Fargo Foundation

550 California Street
7th Floor MAC A0112-073
San Francisco, CA 94104
415-396-5830
Fax: 415-975-6260
http://www.wellsfargo.com
Offers support for elementary school education, secondary school education and community development.

Tim Hanlon, Executive Director

2326 Wilbur D May Foundation

C/O Brookhill Corporation
2716 Ocean Park Boulevard
Suite 2011
Santa Monica, CA 90405
Gives to youth organizations and hospitals.

2327 William & Flora Hewlett Foundation

2121 Sand Hill Road
Menlo Park, CA 94025-3448
650-234-4500
Fax: 650-234-4501
http://www.hewlett.org
The Hewlett Foundation concentrates its resources on the performing arts, education, population issues, environmental issues, conflict resolution and family and community development. Grants in the education program, specifically the elementary and secondary education part of it, are limited to K-12 areas in California programs, with primary emphasis on public schools in the San Francisco Bay area. The program favors schools, school districts and universities.

Paul Brest, President

2328 William C Bannerman Foundation

9255 Sunset Boulevard
Suite 400
West Hollywood, CA 90069
310-273-9933
Fax: 310-273-9931
Offers grants in the fields of elementary school, secondary schools, education, human services and youth programs K-12 in Los Angeles County, Adult Education and Vocational Training.

Elliot Ponchick, President

2329 Y&H Soda Foundation

2 Theatre Square
Suite 211
Orinda, CA 94563-3346
925-253-2630
Fax: 925-253-1814
E-mail: jNM@silcom.com
Offers support in the areas of early childhood education, child development, elementary education and vocational and higher education.

Judith Murphy, Executive Director

2330 Zellerbach Family Fund

120 Montgomery Street
Suite 1550
San Francisco, CA 94104-4318
415-421-2629
Fax: 415-421-6713
Provides funds to nonprofit organizations in the San Francisco Bay Area.

Cindy Rambo, Executive Director
Linda Avidan, Program Director

Colorado

2331 Adolph Coors Foundation

4100 East Mississippi Avenue
Suite 1850
Denver, CO 80246
303-388-1636
Fax: 303-388-1684
http://www.adolphcoors.org
Giving is primarily offered for programs with an emphasis on education, human services, youth and health.

Sally W Rippey, Executive Director
Jeanne L Bistranin, Program Officers

2332 Boettcher Foundation

600 17th Street
Suite 2210
Denver, CO 80202-5402
303-534-1937
800-323-9640
http://www.boettcherfoundation.org
Offers grants to educational institutions, with an emphasis on scholarships and fellowships.

Timothy W Schultz, President/Executive Director

2333 Denver Foundation

950 S Cherry Street
Suite 200
Denver, CO 80246
303-300-1790
Fax: 303-300-6547
http://www.denverfounation.org
The Foundation serves as the steward and the administrator of the endowment, charged with investing its earned income in programs that meet the community's growing and changing needs. The Foundation has a solid history of supporting a broad array of community efforts. Grants are awarded to nonprofit organizations that touch nearly every meaningful artistic, cultural, civic, educational, human service and health interest of metro Denver's citizens.

David Miller, President/CEO
Betsy Mangone, VP Philanthropic Services

2334 El Pomar Foundation

10 Lake Circle
Colorado Springs, CO 80906-4201
719-633-7733
800-554-7711
Fax: 719-577-5702
http://www.elpomar.org
Founded in 1937, the philosophy of this foundation is simply to help foster a climate for excellence in Colorado's third sector, the nonprofit community, as well as the foundation's own responsibility to improve the quality of life for all residents of Colorado. The foundation gives grants to the arts and humanities, civic and community, education, health, human services, and youth in community service.

William J Hybl, Executive Director

2335 Gates Foundation
3575 Cherry Creek N Drive
Suite 100
Denver, CO 80209-3247
303-722-1881
Fax: 303-698-9031
The purpose of this foundation is to aid, assist, encourage, initiate, or carry on activities that will promote the health, well-being, security and broad education of all people. Because of a deep concern for and confidence in the future of Colorado, the foundation will invest primarily in institutions and programs that will enhance the quality of life for those who live and work in the state.

Thomas C Stokes, Executive Director

2336 Ruth & Vernon Taylor Foundation
518 17th Street
Suite 1670
Denver, CO 80202
303-893-5284
Fax: 303-893-8263
Offers support for education, the arts, human services and conservation.

Friday A Green, Executive Director

2337 US West Foundation
7800 E Orchard Road
Suite 300
Englewood, CO 80111-2526
303-799-3852
Grants are given in the areas of health and human services, including programs for youth, early childhood, elementary, secondary, higher and other.

Janet Rash, Executive Director

Connecticut

2338 Aetna Foundation
151 Farmington Avenue
Hartford, CT 06156-0001
860-273-0123
Fax: 860-273-4764
http://www.aetna.com/foundation/
Aetna gives grants in various areas that improve the community and its citizens. Certain areas include; children's health, education for at-risk students, and community initiatives. Geographic emphasis is placed on organizations and initiatives in Aetna's Greater Hartford headquarters communities; organizations in select communities across the country where Aetna has a significant local presence; and national organizations that can influence state, local or federal policies and programs.

Marilda L Gandara, President
Dave Wilmont, Executive Assistant

2339 Community Foundation of Greater New Haven
70 Audubon Street
New Haven, CT 06510-1248
203-777-2386
Fax: 203-787-6584
http://www.cfgnh.org
Offers a wide variety of giving with an emphasis on social services, youth services, AIDS research and education.

William W Ginsberg, President/CEO
Ronda Maddox, Administrative Assistant

2340 Connecticut Mutual Financial Services
140 Garden Street
Hartford, CT 06154-0200
860-987-6500
Giving is aimed at education, primarily higher education, equal opportunity programs and social services.

Astrida R Olds, Executive Director

2341 Hartford Foundation for Public Giving
85 Gillett Street
Hartford, CT 06105-2693
860-548-1888
Fax: 860-524-8346
E-mail: www.hfpg.org
Offers grants for demonstration programs and capital purposes with emphasis on educational institutions, social services and cultural programs.

Michael R Bangser, Executive Director

2342 Loctite Corporate Contributions Program
Hartford Square North
10 Columbus Boulevard
5th Floor
Hartford, CT 06106-1976
860-571-5100
Fax: 860-571-5430
Offers support in various fields of interest including funding for educational programs for inner city youths in grades K-12.

Kiren Cooley, Corporate Contributions

2343 Louis Calder Foundation
175 Elm Street
New Canaan, CT 06840
203-966-8925
Fax: 203-966-5785
http://www.louiscalderfdn.org
Offers support to organizations who promote education, health and welfare of children and youth in New York City.

Holly Nuechterlein, Program Manager

2344 Sherman Fairchild Foundation
71 Arch Street
Greenwich, CT 06830-6544
203-661-9360
Fax: 203-661-9360
Offers grants in higher education, fine arts and cultural institutions.

Patricia A Lydon, Executive Director

2345 Smart Family Foundation
74 Pin Oak Lane
Wilton, CT 06897-1329
203-834-0400
Fax: 203-834-0412
The foundation is interested in educational projects that focus on primary and secondary school children.

Raymond Smart, Executive Director

2346 Worthington Family Foundation
411 Pequot Avenue
Southport, CT 06490-1386
203-255-9400
Offers grants in the areas of elementary school education and secondary school education in Connecticut.

Worthington Johnson, Executive Director

Delaware

2347 Crystal Trust
Po Box 39
Montchanin, DE 19710-0039
302-651-0533
Grants are awarded for higher and secondary education and social and family services.

Stephen C Doberstein, Executive Director

2348 HW Buckner Charitable Residuary Trust
JP Morgan Services
PO Box 8714
Wilmington, DE 19899-8714
302-633-1900
Focuses giving on educational and cultural organizations in New York, Rhode Island and Massachusetts.

2349 Longwood Foundation
100 W 10th Street
Suite 1109
Wilmington, DE 19801-1694
302-654-2477
Fax: 302-654-2323
Limited grants are offered to educational institutions and cultural programs.

David D Wakefield, Executive Director

District of Columbia

2350 Abe Wouk Foundation
3255 N Street NW
Washington, DC 20007-2845
Offers grants in elementary, secondary education and federated giving programs.

Herman Wouk, Executive Director

2351 Eugene & Agnes E Meyer Foundation
1400 16th Street NW
Suite 360
Washington, DC 20036-2215
202-483-8294
Fax: 202-328-6850
http://www.meyerfoundation.org
Offers grants in the areas of development and housing, education and community services, arts and humanities, law and justice, health and mental health.

Julie L Rogers, President

2352 Foundation Center-District of Columbia
1627 K Street NW
3rd Floor
Washington, DC 20006-1708
202-331-1400
Fax: 202-331-1739
http://www.fdncenter.org/washington/index.jhtml
Member of The Foundation Center network, maintaining a collection of private foundation tax returns which provide information on the scope of grants dispensed to nonprofit organizations by those particular foundations.

2353 Foundation for the National Capitol Region
1201 15th Street NW
Suite 420
Washington, DC 20005
202-955-5890
Fax: 202-955-8084
http://www.cfncr.org
Grants are focused on organization strengthening and regional collaboration. The Foundation wishes to foster collaborations that identify, address, and increase awareness of regional issues, as well as help strengthen the region's existing nonprofit organizations to improve their financial stability. The Foundation welcomes requests from organizations serving the Greater Washington area that are tax-exempt under Section 501(c)(3) of the Internal Revenue Code.

Terry Lee Freeman, President

2354 Gilbert & Jaylee Mead Family Foundation
2700 Virginia Avenue NW #701
Washington, DC 20037-1908
202-338-0208
Offers support for education (K-12), the performing arts and community service programs for Washington, DC, Montgomery County, Maryland, and Geneva, Switzerland.

Linda Smith, Executive Director

2355 Hitachi Foundation
1509 22nd Street NW
Washington, DC 20037-1073
202-457-0588
Fax: 202-296-1098
http://www.hitachi.org
The majority of projects supported by the foundation: promote collaboration across sectors and among institutions, organizations and individuals; reflect multi-or-interdisciplinary perspectives; respect and value diversity of thought, action, and ethnicity. Grants are given in the areas of community development, education, global citizenship and program related investments.

Barbara Dyer, President/CEO

2356 Morris & Gwendolyn Cafritz Foundation
1825 K Street NW
Suite 1400
Washington, DC 20006-1202
202-223-3100
Fax: 202-296-7567
http://www.cafritzfoundation.org
Gives grants to organizations in the metropolitan area, focusing on arts, humanities and scholarships.

Sara Cofrin, Program Assistant

2357 Public Welfare Foundation
1200 U Street NW
Washington, DC 20009-4443
202-965-1800
Fax: 202-265-8851
http://www.publicwelfare.org
Offers grants to grass roots organizations in the US and abroad with emphasis on the environment and education.

Larry Kressley, Executive Director
Teresa Langston, Director Of Programs

2358 Washington Post Company Educational Foundation
1150 15th Street NW
Washington, DC 20071-0002
202-334-6000
Offers support for pre-college and higher education including student scholarships and awards for academic excellence.

Eric Grant, Director Contributions

Florida

2359 Applebaum Foundation
1111 Biscaynees Boulevard
Tower 3, Room 853
North Miami, FL 33181
Offers an emphasis on higher education.

2360 Benedict Foundation for Independent Schools
607 Lantana Lane
Vero Beach, FL 32963-2315
Support is offered primarily for independent secondary schools that have been members of the National Association of Independent Schools for ten consecutive years.

Nancy H Benedict, Executive Director

2361 Chatlos Foundation
PO Box 915048
Longwood, FL 32791-5048
407-862-5077
Fax: 407-862-0708
http://www.chatlos.org
Bible colleges and seminaries, liberal arts colleges, vocation and domestic education, medical education; children, elderly, disabled and learning disabled. The Foundation is non-receptive to primary or secondary education, the arts, medical research, individual churches. No direct scholarship support to individuals.

William J Chatlos, Executive Director

2362 Citibank of Florida Corporate Giving Program
8750 Doral Boulevard
7th Floor
Miami, FL 33718
305-599-5775
Fax: 305-599-5520
Offers support for K-12 education for at-risk children. Funding is also available through the program for housing and community development in the state of Florida.

Susan Yarosz, Executive Director

2363 Dade Community Foundation
200 S Biscayne Boulevard
Suite 505
Miami, FL 33131-2343
305-371-2711
Fax: 305-371-5342
http://www.dadecommunityfoundation.org
Offers support for projects in the fields of education, arts and culture.

Ruth Shack, Executive Director

2364 Innovating Worthy Projects Foundation
Lakeview Corporate Center
6415 Lake Worth Road
Suite 208
Lake Worth, FL 33463-2904
561-439-4445

Offers grants and support for education in the areas of childhood education and elementary education.

Dr. Irving Packer, Executive Director

2365 Jacksonville Public Library
Business, Science & Documents
122 N Ocean Street
Jacksonville, FL 32202-3374
904-630-1994
Fax: 904-630-2431
http://www.neflin.org/members/libraries/jackspub.htm
Member of The Foundation Center network, maintaining a collection of private foundation tax returns which provide information on the scope of grants dispensed by that particular foundation.

Gretchen Mitchell, Business/Science Department

2366 Jessie Ball duPont Fund
One Independent Drive
Suite 1400
Jacksonville, FL 32202-5011
904-353-0890
800-252-3452
Fax: 904-353-3870
E-mail: smagill@dupontfund.org
http://www.dupontfund.org
Grants limited to those institutions to which the donor contributed personally during the five year period ending December 31, 1964. Among the 325 institutions eligible to recieve funds are higher and secondary education intitutions, cultural and historic preservation programs, social services organizations, hospitals, health agencies, churches and church-related organizations and youth agencies.

Dr. Sherry P Magill, President
JoAnn Bennett, Director Administration

2367 Joseph & Rae Gann Charitable Foundation
10185 Collins Avenue
Apartment 317
Bal Harbour, FL 33154-1606
Offers support in the areas of elementary, secondary and theological education.

2368 Orlando Public Library-Orange County Library System
Social Sciences Department
101 E Central Boulivard
Orlando, FL 32801-2471
407-835-7323
Fax: 407-835-7646
E-mail: ajacobe@ocls.lib.fl.us
http://www.ocls.lib.fl.us
Member of The Foundation Center network, maintaining a collection on microfiche of Florida private foundation tax returns which provide information on the scope of grants dispensed by that particular foundation. Other available resources include directories of foundations, guide to funding, and materials on successful grant acquisition. FC Search Foundation Center CD Rom.

Angela C Jacobe, Head Social Science Dpt

2369 Peter D & Eleanore Kleist Foundation
12734 Kenwood Lane
Suite 89
Fort Myers, FL 33907-5638
Support is given to secondary school education and higher education.

Peter D Kleist, Executive Director

2370 Robert G Friedman Foundation
76 Isla Bahia Drive
Fort Lauderdale, FL 33316-2331
Giving is offered to elementary and high
schools, with minor support to indigent individuals and charitable activities.
Robert G Friedman, Executive Director

**2371 Southwest Florida Community
Foundation**
8260 College Parkway
Suite 101
Fort Myers, FL 33919
239-274-5900
Fax: 239-274-5930
E-mail: swflcfo@earthlink.net
http://www.floridacommunity.com
Offers grants and support in the areas of ed-
ucation, higher education, children and
youth services and general charitable giv-
ing to Lee, Charlotte, Hendry, Glades, and
Collier Counties, Florida.
Paul B Flynn, Executive Director
Carol McLaughlin, Program Director

**2372 Student Help and Assistance
Program to Education**
C/O Michael Bienes
141 Bay Colony Drive
Fort Lauderdale, FL 33308-2024
Offers grants and support in the areas of ele-
mentary and secondary education, music
and dance.

**2373 Thomas & Irene Kirbo Charitable
Trust**
1112 W Adams Street
Suite 1111
Jacksonville, FL 32202
904-354-7212
Favors smaller colleges in Florida and
Georgia.
Murray Jenks, Executive Director

2374 Thompson Publishing Group
PO Box 26185
Tampa, FL 33623
800-876-0226
http://www.thompson.com or
www.grantsandfunding.com
Assists education administrators and grant
seekers in successful fundraising in the public and private sectors.
Joel M Drucker, Executive Director

Georgia

2375 Atlanta-Fulton Public Library
Foundation Collection/Ivan Allen
Department
1 Margaret Mitchell Square NW
Atlanta, GA 30303-1089
404-730-1700
Fax: 404-730-1990
http://www.af.public.lib.ga.us
Member of The Foundation Center network, maintaining a collection of private
foundation tax returns which provide information on the scope of grants dispensed by
that particular foundation.

2376 BellSouth Foundation
C/O BellSouth Corporation
1155 Peachtree Street NE
Sutie 7H08
Atlanta, GA 30309-3600
404-249-2396
Fax: 404-249-5696
http://www.bellsouthfoundation.org

The foundation's purpose is to improve education in the South and to address the problem of the inadequate schooling in the
region.
Mary D Boehm, President
Beverly Fleming, Administrative
Assistant

2377 Bradley Foundation
PO Box 1408
Savannah, GA 31402-1408
404-571-6040
Focuses on higher educational facilities, elementary and secondary education, human
services and federated giving programs.

2378 Callaway Foundation
209 W Broome Street
#790
Lagrange, GA 30240-3101
706-884-7348
Fax: 706-884-0201
Offers giving in the areas of elementary,
higher and secondary education, including
libraries and community giving.
JT Gresham, Executive Director

2379 Coca-Cola Foundation
Po Box 1734
Atlanta, GA 30301
404-676-2568
Fax: 404-676-8804
http://www.thecoca-colacompany.com
Committed to serving communities through
education. The foundation supports programs for early childhood education, elementary and secondary schools, public and
private colleges and universities, teacher
training, adult learning and global education programs, among others.
Donald R Greene, Executive Director

2380 J Bulow Campbell Foundation
50 Hurt Plaza
Suite 312
Atlanta, GA 30303
404-658-9066
Fax: 404-659-4802
The purpose of this foundation is to offer
grants and support to privately supported
education, human welfare, youth services
and the arts in the state of Georgia.
John W Stephenson, Executive Director

2381 JK Gholston Trust
C/O NationsBank of Georgia
PO Box 992
Athens, GA 30603-0992
706-357-6271
Support is offered to elementary school and
higher education facilities in the Comer,
Georgia area.
Janey M Cooley, Executive Director

2382 John & Mary Franklin Foundation
C/O Bank South N.A.
PO Box 4956
Atlanta, GA 30302
404-521-7397
Offers grants in secondary school/educa-
tion, higher education and youth services.
Virlyn Moore Sr, Executive Director

**2383 John H & Wilhelmina D Harland
Charitable Foundation**
2 Piedmont Center NE
Suite 106
Atlanta, GA 30305-1502
404-264-9912
Fax: 404-266-8834

Children and higher education.

2384 Joseph B Whitehead Foundation
50 Hurt Plaza SE
Suite 1200
Atlanta, GA 30303-2916
404-522-6755
Fax: 404-522-7026
http://www.jbwhitehead.org
Offers grants in education, cultural pro-
grams, the arts and civic affairs.
Charles H McTier, Executive Director

2385 Lettie Pate Evans Foundation
50 Hurt Plaza SE
Suite 1200
Atlanta, GA 30303-2916
404-522-6755
Fax: 404-522-7026
http://www.lpevans.org
Offers grants in the areas of higher educa-
tion, and support for educational and cul-
tural institutions.
Charles H McTier, Executive Director
Russell Hardin, Vice President/Secretary

2386 McCamish Foundation
1 Buckhead Loop NE #3060
Atlanta, GA 30326-1528
Offers grants for conservation and educational institutions.

**2387 Metropolitan Atlanta Community
Foundation**
50 Hurt Plaza
Suite 449
Atlanta, GA 30303
404-688-5525
Fax: 404-688-3060
http://www.atlcf.org
This foundation was organized for the administration of funds placed in trust for the
purposes of improving education, community development and civic health of the
19-county metropolitan area of Atlanta.
Winsome Hawkins Sr, Executive Director
Alicia Phillip, President

2388 Mill Creek Foundation
PO Box 190
115 North Racetrack Street
Swainsboro, GA 30401-0190
478-237-0101
Fax: 478-237-6187
The foundation's primary interests are edu-
cational programs in all levels of study in
Emanuel County, Georgia.
James H Morgan, Executive Director

**2389 Mills Bee Lane Memorial
Foundation**
Nations Bank of Georgia
PO Box 9626
Savannah, GA 31412-9626
Offers support in various areas of educa-
tion, including higher, secondary, and ele-
mentary.

2390 Peyton Anderson Foundation
577 Mulberry Street
Suite 105
Macon, GA 31201
478-743-5359
Fax: 912-742-5201
Supports organizations and programs that
center on elementary education, higher edu-
cation, adult education, literacy and basic
skills and youth services, in Bibb County,
Georgia only.
Juanita T Jordan, Executive Director

2391 Rich Foundation
11 Piedmont Avenue NE
Atlanta, GA 30303
404-262-2266
Funds are allocated to social services,
health, the arts and education.

Anne Berg, Executive Director

2392 Robert & Polly Dunn Foundation
PO Box 723194
Atlanta, GA 31139-0194
404-816-2883
Fax: 404-237-2150
Offers support in the areas of child devel-
opment, education, higher education, and
children and youth services.

Karen C Wilbanks, Executive Director

2393 Sapelo Foundation
1712 Ellis Street
2nd Floor
Brunswick, GA 31520
912-265-0520
Fax: 912-265-1888
The Sapelo Foundation's scholarship program, The Richard Reynolds Scholarship
Program offers college scholarships only
to students who are legal residents of
McIntosh County, Georgia.

Phyllis Bowen, Administrative Assistant
Alan McGregor, Executive Director

2394 Tull Charitable Foundation
50 Hurt Plaza SE
Suite 1245
Atlanta, GA 30303-2916
404-659-7079
http://www.tullfoundation.org
Offers support to secondary schools, elementary schools and higher education facilities in the state of Georgia.

Barbara Cleveland, Executive Director

**2395 Warren P & Ava F Sewell
Foundation**
PO Box 645
Bremen, GA 30110-0645
Offers support in elementary school, sec-
ondary school education and religion.

Jack Worley, Executive Director

Hawaii

2396 Barbara Cox Anthony Foundation
1132 Bishop Street #120
Honolulu, HI 96813-2807
Offers support to secondary schools,
higher education, and human service organizations in Hawaii.

Barner Anthony, Executive Director

2397 Cooke Foundation
1164 Bishop Street
Suite 800
Honolulu, HI 96813
808-566-5524
888-731-3863
Fax: 808-521-6286
E-mail: foundations@hcf-hawaii.org
http://www.hawaiicommunityfoundation.
org
The environment, the arts, education and
social services are the priority areas for this
foundation.

Lisa Schiff, Private Foundation Service
Samuel Cooke, President & Trustee

2398 Harold KL Castle Foundation
146 Hekili Street
Suite 203A
Kailua, HI 96734-2835
808-262-9413
http://www.castlefoundation.org
Grants are given in the area of education,
community and cultural/community affairs.

Terrence R George, Executive Director
H Mitchell D'Olier, President

**2399 Hawaiian Electric Industries
Charitable Foundation**
PO Box 730
Honolulu, HI 96808-0730
808-532-5862
http://www.hei.com/heicf/heicf.html
Offers support for education, including
higher education, business education, educational associations and secondary
schools.

Scott Shirai, Executive Director
Robert F Clark, President

**2400 James & Abigail Campbell
Foundation**
1001 Kamokila Boulevard
Kapolei, HI 96707-2014
808-674-6674
888-322-2232
Fax: 808-674-3111
Offers support in education for schools and
educational programs related to literacy or
job training in Hawaii.

Theresia McMurdo, Public Relations

2401 Oceanic Cablevision Foundation
200 Akamainui Street
Mililani, HI 96789-3999
808-625-8359
Offers support in a variety of areas with an
emphasis on education, especially early
childhood and cultural programs.

Kit Beuret, Executive Director

**2402 Samuel N & Mary Castle
Foundation**
733 Bishop Street
Suite 1275
Honolulu, HI 96813-2912
808-522-1101
Fax: 808-522-1103
E-mail: acastle@aloha.net
http://www.fdncenter.org
Funding is offered in the areas of educa-
tion, human services and the arts for the
state of Hawaii.

Annually

Al Castle, Executive Director

2403 University of Hawaii
Hamilton Library
2550 The Mall
Honolulu, HI 96822-2233
808-956-7214
Fax: 808-956-5968
http://www.libweb.hawaii.edu/uhmlib
Member of The Foundation Center network, maintaining a collection of private
foundation tax returns which provide information on the scope of grants dispensed by
that particular foundation.

Idaho

2404 Boise Public Library
715 S Capitol Boulevard
Boise, ID 83702-7115
208-384-4076
http://www.boisepubliclibrary.org
Member of The Foundation Center network, maintaining a collection of private
foundation tax returns which provide information on the scope of grants dispensed by
that particular foundation.

**2405 Claude R & Ethel B Whittenberger
Foundation**
PO Box 1073
Caldwell, ID 83606-1073
208-459-0091
E-mail: whittfnd@cableone.net
http://www.whittenberger.org
Offers support for youth and children in
higher and secondary education.

William J Rankin, Executive Director

**2406 Walter & Leona Dufresne
Foundation**
1150 W State Street
Boise, ID 83702-5327
Offers support in the areas of secondary
school education and higher education.

Royce Chigbrow, Executive Director

Illinois

2407 Ameritech Foundation
30 S Wacker Drive
Floor 34
Chicago, IL 60606-7487
312-750-5223
Fax: 312-207-1098
http://www.ntlf.com
A foundation that offers grants to elementary school/education, secondary
school/education and higher education.

Michael E Kuhlin, Executive Director

**2408 Carus Corporate Contributions
Program**
315 5th Street
Peru, IL 61354-2859
815-223-1500
Offers support for higher, secondary, elementary and early childhood education.

Robert J Wilmot, Executive Director

**2409 Chauncey & Marion Deering
McCormick Foundation**
410 N Michigan Avenue
Suite 590
Chicago, IL 60611-4220
312-644-6720
Preschool education, journalism and the
improvement of socio-economic condition
of Metropolitan Chicago are the main areas
of giving for this foundation.

Charles E Schroeder, Executive Director

2410 Chicago Community Trust
11 East Wacker Drive
Suite 1400
Chicago, IL 60601-1088
312-616-8000
Fax: 312-616-7955
E-mail: sandy@cct.org
http://www.cct.org
A community foundation that offers sup-
port for general operating projects and spe-

cific programs and projects in areas including child development, education and higher education.

Sandy Chears, Grants Manager
Terry Mazany, President

2411 Coleman Foundation
575 W Madison Street
Suite 4605-Ii
Chicago, IL 60661-2515
312-902-7120
Fax: 312-902-7124
http://www.colemanfoundation.org
A nonprofit, private foundation established in the state of Illinois in 1951. Major areas of support include health, educational, cultural, scientific and social programs. Grants generally focus on organizations within the Midwest and particularly within the state of Illinois and the Chicago Metropolitan area. No grants are made for programs outside of the United States. Ongoing support is not available, continuing programs must indicate how they will be sustained in the future.

Rosa Janus, Program Manager
Michael W Hennessy, President/CEO

2412 Dellora A & Lester J Norris Foundation
PO Box 4325
Saint Charles, IL 60174-9075
630-377-4111
Education, health and social services are the main concerns of this foundation, with Illinois, Colorado and Florida being their priority.

Eugene W Butler, Executive Director

2413 Dillon Foundation
2804 West Le Fevre Road
Sterling, IL 61081-0537
815-626-9000
Offers support for educational purposes, including higher education and community services.

Peter W Dillon, Executive Director

2414 Dr. Scholl Foundation
1033 Skokie Boulevard
Suite 230
Northbrook, IL 60062
847-559-7430
http://www.drschollfoundation.com
Applications for grants are considered in the following areas: private education at all levels including elementary, secondary schools, colleges and universities and medical and nursing institutions; general charitable organizations and programs, including grants to hospitals and programs for children, developmentally disabled and senior citizens; civic, cultural, social services, health care, economic and religious activities.

Pamela Scholl, Executive Director

2415 Evanston Public Library
1703 Orrington Avenue
Evanston, IL 60201-3886
847-866-0300
Fax: 847-866-0313
http://www.evanston.lib.il.us
Member of The Foundation Center network, maintaining a collection of private foundation tax returns which provide information on the scope of grants dispensed by that particular foundation.

Neal J Ney, Director

2416 Farny R Wurlitzer Foundation
PO Box 418
Sycamore, IL 60178-0418
Offers support in the areas of education, including programs for minorities, early childhood, elementary and secondary institutions, music education and organizations.

William A Rolfing, Executive Director

2417 Grover Hermann Foundation
1000 Hill Grove
Suite 200
Western Springs, IL 60558-6306
708-246-8331
Focus of giving is on higher education and private schooling activities.

Paul K Rhoads, Executive Director

2418 Joyce Foundation
70 W Madison Street
Suite 2750
Chicago, IL 60602
312-782-2464
Fax: 312-782-4160
E-mail: info@joycefdn.org
http://www.joycefdn.org
Based in Chicago with assets of $1 billion, the Joyce foundation supports efforts to strengthen public policies in ways that improve the quality of life in the Great Lakes region. Last year the foundation made nearly $17 million in grants to groups working to inprove public education in Chicago, Cleveland, Detroit and Milwaukee.

Ellen Alberding, President

2419 Lloyd A Fry Foundation
120 S Lasalle Street
Suite 1950
Chicago, IL 60603-4204
312-580-0310
Fax: 312-580-0980
http://www.fryfoundation.org
The foundation primarily supports education, higher education, the performing arts, and social service organizations.

Unmi Song, Executive Director

2420 Northern Trust Company Charitable Trust
Community Affairs Division
50 S Lasalle Street
Chicago, IL 60603-1006
312-630-6000
http://www.ntrs.com
Offers grants in the areas of community development, education and early childhood education.

Marjorie W Lundy, Executive Director

2421 Palmer Foundation
C/O Jay L. Owen
824 N Western Avenue
Lake Forest, IL 60045-1703
Offers grants in elementary and secondary education, as well as youth services and Protestant churches.

2422 Philip H Corboy Foundation
33 N Dearborn Street
Chicago, IL 60602-2502
312-346-3191
http://www.corboydemetrio.com
Offers grants in the areas of elementary, secondary, law school education and health care.

2423 Polk Brothers Foundation
20 W Kinzie Street
Suite 1100
Chicago, IL 60610-4600
312-527-4684
Fax: 312-527-4681
http://www.polkbrosfdn.org
Offers grants for new or ongoing programs to organizations whose work is based in the areas of education, social services and health care.

Nikki W Stein, Executive Director
Shiela A Robinson, Grants Administrator

2424 Prince Charitable Trust
303 West Madison Street
Suite 1900
Chicago, IL 60606-7407
312-419-8700
Fax: 312-419-8558
http://www.fdncenter.org/grantmaker/prin
ce/chicago.html
Offers support for cultural programs, public school programming and social service organizations.

Benna B Wilde, Managing Director
Sharon L Robison, Grants Manager

2425 Regenstein Foundation
8600 W Bryn Mawr Avenue
Suite 705N
Chicago, IL 60631-3579
773-693-6464
Fax: 773-693-2480
Offers grants for educational and general charitable institutions within the metropolitan Chicago area and the state of Illinois.

Joseph Regenstein Jr, Executive Director

2426 Richard H Driehaus Foundation
77 W Wacker Drive
Chicago, IL 60601-1604
312-641-5772
Fax: 312-641-5736
Offers support in elementary, secondary and higher education in the state of Illinois.

Susan M Levy, Executive Director

2427 Robert R McCormick Tribune Foundation
435 N Michigan Avenue
Suite 770
Chicago, IL 60611-4066
312-222-3512
Fax: 312-222-3523
http://www.rrmtf.org
Offers contributions for private higher education and rehabilitation services.

Nicholas Goodban, Senior VP/Philanthropy
Richard A Behrenhausen, President/CEO

2428 Sears-Roebuck Foundation
Sears Tower
Department 903-BSC 51-02
Chicago, IL 60684
312-875-8337
The foundation focuses its giving primarily on projects that address education and volunteerism.

Paula A Banke, Executive Director

2429 Spencer Foundation
875 N Michigan Avenue
Suite 3930
Chicago, IL 60611-1803
312-337-7000
Fax: 312-337-0282
http://www.spencer.org

Supports research aimed at the practice of understanding and expanding knowledge in the area of education.

Michael McPherson, President

2430 Sulzer Family Foundation
1940 W Irving Park Road
Chicago, IL 60613-2437
312-321-4700
Offers giving for education, including higher, secondary, elementary and adult education in the areas of Chicago, Illinois.

John J Hoellen, Executive Director

2431 United Airlines Foundation
PO Box 66919
Chicago, IL 60666-0919
847-952-5714
Offers a wide variety of support programs with an emphasis on education and educational reform.

Eileen Younglove, Executive Director

2432 Valenti Charitable Foundation
Valenti Builders
225 Northfield Road
Northfield, IL 60093-3311
847-446-2200
Fax: 847-446-2610
Offers support in elementary education, secondary school education, higher education and children and youth services.

Valenti Sr Trustee, Executive Director

Indiana

2433 Allen County Public Library
Po Box 2270
Fort Wayne, IN 46802-3699
260-421-1200
Fax: 260-421-1386
http://www.acpl.lib.in.us
Member of The Foundation Center network, maintaining a collection of private foundation tax returns which provide information on the scope of grants dispensed by that particular foundation.

2434 Arvin Foundation
1 Noblitt Plaza #3000
Columbus, IN 47201-6079
812-379-3207
Fax: 812-379-3688
Giving is offered primarily to primary, secondary and higher education and technical training.

E Fred Meyer, Executive Director

2435 Clowes Fund
320 N Meridian Street Suite 316
The Chamber of Commerce Building
Indianapolis, IN 46204-1722
800-943-7209
Fax: 800-943-7286
http://www.clowesfund.org
Offers giving for higher and secondary education; the performing arts; marine biology and social service organizations.

Elizabeth Casselman, Executive Director

2436 Dekko Foundation
PO Box 548
Kendallville, IN 46755-0548
260-347-1278
Fax: 260-347-7103
Offers support for all levels of education and human service organizations.

Linda Speakman, Executive Director

2437 Eli Lilly & Company Corporate Contribution Program
Lilly Corporate Center D.C. 1627
Indianapolis, IN 46285
317-276-2000
Offers support in the areas of secondary school/education, higher education and health care programs.

Thomas King, President

2438 Foellinger Foundation
520 E Berry Street
Fort Wayne, IN 46802-2002
260-422-2900
Fax: 260-422-9436
http://www.foellinger.org
Giving is aimed at higher education and other secondary and elementary projects, community programs and social service organizations.

Harry V Owen, Executive Director

2439 Indianapolis Foundation
615 N Alabama Street
Suite 119
Indianapolis, IN 46204-1498
317-634-2423
Fax: 317-684-0943
http://www.indyfund.org
Offers support in the areas of education and neighborhood services.

Kenneth Gladish, Executive Director

2440 John W Anderson Foundation
402 Wall Street
Valparaiso, IN 46383-2562
219-462-4611
Fax: 219-531-8954
Offers grants in the areas of higher education, youth programs, human services, and arts and humanities. Grants are limited primarily to Northwest Indian organizations.

William Vinovich, Vice Chairman/Trustee

2441 Lilly Endowment
2801 N Meridian Street
Indianapolis, IN 46208-4712
317-924-5471
Fax: 317-926-4431
http://www.lillyendowment.org
Supports the causes of religion, education and community development. Although the Endowment supports efforts of national significance, especially in the field of religion, it is primarily committed to its hometown, Indianapolis, and home state, Indiana.

Sue Ellen Walker, Communications Associate

2442 Moore Foundation
9100 Keystone Xing
Suite 390
Indianapolis, IN 46240-2158
317-848-2013
Fax: 317-571-0744
Offers support in elementary school and secondary school education, higher education, business school education and youth services in Indiana.

Eileen C Ryan, Executive Director

2443 W Brooks Fortune Foundation
7933 Beaumont Green W Drive
Indianapolis, IN 46250-1652
317-842-1303

Support is limited to education-related programs in Indiana.

William Brooks Fortune, Executive Director

Iowa

2444 Cedar Rapids Public Library
Funding Information Center
500 1st Street SE
Cedar Rapids, IA 52401-2095
319-398-5123
Fax: 319-398-0476
http://www.crlibrary.org
Member of The Foundation Center network, maintaining a collection of private foundation tax returns which provide information on the scope of grants dispensed by that particular foundation.

Tamara Glise, Public Services Manager
Eileen C Ryan, Executive Director

2445 RJ McElroy Trust
425 Cedar Street
Suite 312
Waterloo, IA 50701
319-287-9102
312
Fax: 319-287-9105
http://www.mcelroytrust.org
The trust funds grants to educational youth programs in the northeast quarter of Iowa. The trust guidelines do not include grants to individuals.

Linda L Klinger, Executive Director

Kansas

2446 Mary Jo Williams Charitable Trust
PO Box 439
Garden City, KS 67846-0439
Offers support in the areas of early childhood education, higher education, and children and youth services.

Michael E Collins, Executive Director

2447 Sprint Foundation
2330 Shawnee Mission Parkway
Westwood, KS 66205-2090
913-624-3343
Offers grants in a variety of areas with an emphasis on education, including business education, secondary education and higher education.

Don G Forsythe, Executive Director

2448 Wichita Public Library
223 S Main Street
Wichita, KS 67202-3795
316-261-8500
Fax: 316-262-4540
http://www.wichita.lib.ks.us
Member of The Foundation Center network, maintaining a collection of private foundation tax returns which provide information on the scope of grants dispensed by that particular foundation.

Kentucky

2449 Ashland Incorporated Foundation
50 E River Center Boulevard
Covington, KY 41012
859-815-3630
Fax: 859-815-4496
http://www.ashland.com

Offers support to educational organizations, colleges and universities, as well as giving an employee matching gift program to higher education and community funding.

James O'Brien, CEO

2450 Gheens Foundation

One Riverfront Plaza
Suite 705
Louisville, KY 40202
502-584-4650
Fax: 502-584-4652
The foundation's support is aimed at higher and secondary education, ongoing teacher education, and social service agencies.

James N Davis, Executive Director

2451 James Graham Brown Foundation

4350 Brownsboro Road
Suite 200
Louisville, KY 40207
502-896-2440
Fax: 502-896-1774
http://www.jgbf.org
Offers grants in the areas of higher education and social services.

Mason Rummel, Executive Director
Dodie L McKenzie, Program Officer

2452 Louisville Free Public Library

301 York Street
Louisville, KY 40203-2257
502-574-1611
Fax: 502-574-1657
http://www.lfpl.org
Member of The Foundation Center network, maintaining a collection of private foundation tax returns which provide information on the scope of grants dispensed by that particular foundation.

2453 Margaret Hall Foundation

291 S Ashland Avenue
Lexington, KY 40502-1727
859-269-2236
http://www.margarethallfoundation.org
Awards grants and scholarships to private, nonprofit secondary schools for innovative programming.

Helen R Burg, Executive Director

2454 VV Cooke Foundation Corporation

220 Mount Mercy Drive
Pewee Valley, KY 40056
502-241-0303
Offers support in education and youth services with an emphasis on Baptist church and school support.

John B Gray, Executive Director

Louisiana

2455 Baton Rouge Area Foundation

406 N 4th Street
Baton Rouge, LA 70802
225-387-6126
877-387-6126
Fax: 225-387-6153
Offers grants in the area of elementary and secondary education and health.

John G Davies, President

2456 Booth-Bricker Fund

826 Union Street
Suite 300
New Orleans, LA 70112-1421
504-581-2430
Fax: 504-566-4785
Does not have a formal grant procedure or grant application form; nor does it publish an annual report. The Booth-Bricker Fund makes contributions for the purposes of promoting, developing and fostering religious, charitable, scientific, literary or educational programs, primarily in the state of Louisiana. It does not make contributions to individuals.

Gray S Parker, Chairman

2457 East Baton Rouge Parish Library

Centroplex Branch Grants Collection
7711 Goodwood Boulevard
Baton Rouge, LA 70806
225-231-3750
Member of The Foundation Center network, maintaining a collection of private foundation tax returns which provide information on the scope of grants dispensed by that particular foundation.

2458 Fred B & Ruth B Zigler Foundation

PO Box 986
Zigler Building
Jennings, LA 70546-0986
337-824-2413
Fax: 337-824-2414
http://www.ziglerfoundation.org
Offers support to higher, secondary and primary education.

Julie G Berry, President

2459 New Orleans Public Library

Business & Science Division
219 Loyola Avenue
New Orleans, LA 70112-2044
504-529-7323
Fax: 504-596-2609
Member of The Foundation Center network, maintaining a collection of private foundation tax returns which provide information on the scope of grants dispensed by that particular foundation.

2460 Shreve Memorial Library

424 Texas Street
Shreveport, LA 71101-5452
318-226-5897
Fax: 318-226-4780
http://www.shreve-lib.org
Member of The Foundation Center network, maintaining a collection of private Louisiana foundation tax returns which provide information on the scope of grants dispensed by that particular foundation.

Carlos Colon, Reference Supervisor

Maine

2461 Clarence E Mulford Trust

PO Box 290
Fryeburg, ME 04037-0290
207-935-2061
Fax: 207-935-3939
Offers grants to charitable, educational and scientific organizations for the purpose of improving education.

David R Hastings II, Executive Director

2462 Harold Alfond Trust

C/O Dexter Shoe Company
PO Box 353
Dexter, ME 04930-0353
Grants are offered to secondary and higher education in Maine and Maryland.

Keith Burden, Executive Director

Maryland

2463 Abell Foundation

111 S Calvert Street
Suite 2300
Baltimore, MD 21202-6182
410-547-1300
Fax: 410-539-6579
http://www.abell.org
The foundation supports education with an emphasis on public education, including early childhood and elementary, research, and minority education.

Robert C Embry Jr, Executive Director

2464 Aegon USA

1111 N Charles Street
Baltimore, MD 21201-5505
410-576-4571
Fax: 410-347-8685
http://www.aegonins.com
Offers grants in elementary school, secondary school, higher education and medical school education.

Larry G Brown, Executive Director

2465 Clarence Manger & Audrey Cordero Plitt Trust

C/O First National Bank of Maryland
PO Box 1596
Baltimore, MD 21203-1596
410-566-0914
Offers grants to educational institutions for student loans and scholarships.

Mary M Kirgan, Executive Director

2466 Clark-Winchcole Foundation

Air Rights Building
3 Bethesda Metro Center
Suite 550
Bethesda, MD 20814
301-654-3607
Fax: 301-654-3140
Offers grants in the areas of higher education and social service agencies.

Laura E Philips, Executive Director

2467 Commonwealth Foundation

9737 Colesville Road
Suite 800
Silver Spring, MD 20910
301-495-4400
Offers grants in the areas of early childhood education, child development, elementary schools, secondary schools and youth services.

Barbara Bainum, Executive Director

2468 Dresher Foundation

4940 Campbell Boulevard
Suite 110
Baltimore, MD 21236
410-933-0384
http://www.jdgraphicdesign.com/dresher/dresherfoundation/
Offers giving in the areas of elementary school, early childhood education, meals on wheels, and food distribution.

2469 Edward E Ford Foundation
1122 Kenilworth Drive
Suite 105
Towson, MD 21204
410-823-2201
Fax: 410-823-2203
http://www.eeford.org
Offers giving to secondary schools and private education in the US and its protectorates.

Robert Hallett, Executive Director

2470 Enoch Pratt Free Library
Social Science & History Department
400 Cathedral Street
Baltimore, MD 21201-4484
301-396-5430
http://www.pratt.lib.md.us
Member of The Foundation Center network, maintaining a collection of private foundation tax returns which provide information on the scope of grants dispensed by that particular foundation.

2471 France-Merrick Foundation
The Exchange
1122 Kenilworth Drive
Suite 118
Baltimore, MD 21204-2139
410-832-5700
Fax: 410-832-5704
Offers grants in the areas of public education, private and higher education, health, social services and cultural activities.

Frederick W Lafferty, Executive Director

2472 Grayce B Kerr Fund
117 Bay Street
Easton, MD 21601-2769
410-822-6652
Fax: 410-822-4546
E-mail: gbkf@bluecrab.org
The major area of interest to the fund is education, including higher, elementary and early childhood education for the state of Maryland with focus on the Eastern Shore Counties.

Margaret van den Berg, Administrative Assistant

2473 Henry & Ruth Blaustein Rosenberg Foundation
Blaustein Building
10 East Baltimore Street
Suite 1111
Baltimore, MD 21202
410-347-7201
Fax: 410-347-7210
http://www.blaufund.org
Offers grants in the areas of secondary and higher education.

Betsy F Ringel, Executive Director
Henry A Rosenberg Jr, President

2474 James M Johnston Trust for Charitable and Educational Purposes
2 Wisconsin Circle
Suite 600
Chevy Chase, MD 20815-7003
301-907-0135
Grants are given to higher and secondary educational institutions located in Washington, DC and North Carolina.

Julie Sanders, Executive Director

2475 John W Kluge Foundation
6325 Woodside Court
Columbia, MD 21046-1017
Offers grants in higher education and secondary education.

2476 Marion I & Henry J Knott Foundation
3904 Hickory Avenue
Baltimore, MD 21211-1834
410-235-7068
Fax: 410-889-2577
http://www.knottfoundation.org
Grantmaking limited to private nonsectarian schools and Catholic schools geographically located within the Archdiocese of Baltimore, Maryland.

Greg Cantori, Executive Director

2477 Robert G & Anne M Merrick Foundation
The Exchange
1122 Kenilworth Drive
Suite 118
Baltimore, MD 21204-2142
410-832-5700
Fax: 410-832-5704
Offers grants for public education, higher education and social services.

Frederick W Lafferty, Executive Director

Massachusetts

2478 Associated Grantmakers of Massachusetts
55 Court Street
Suite 520
Boston, MA 02108-4304
617-426-2606
Fax: 617-426-2849
http://www.agmconnect.org
Member of The Foundation Center network, maintaining a collection of private foundation tax returns which provide information on the scope of grants dispensed by that particular foundation.

Ron Ancrum, President
Martha Moore, Director Center Philanthropy

2479 Boston Foundation
75 Arlington Street
10th Floor
Boston, MA 02108-4407
617-338-1700
Fax: 617-338-1604
http://www.tbf.org
Supports local educational, social and housing programs and institutions.

Paul Grogan, President

2480 Boston Globe Foundation II
135 Morrissey Boulevard
Boston, MA 02107
617-929-2895
Fax: 617-929-7889
http://www.bostonglobe.com/community/foundation/partner.stm
The foundation's highest priority is community based agencies which understand, represent and are part of the following populations; children and youth with disabilities, children and youth with AIDS, refugees, low-birth weight babies, pregnant and nursing mothers and incarcerated youth.

Suzanne W Maas, Executive Director
Leah P Bailey

2481 Boston Public Library
Social Sciences Reference
700 Boylston Street
Boston, MA 02116-2813
617-536-5400
http://www.bpl.org
Member of The Foundation Center network, maintaining a collection of private foundation tax returns which provide information on the scope of grants dispensed by that particular foundation.

Bernard Margolis, President

2482 Dean Foundation for Little Children
C/O Boston Safe Deposit & Trust Company
1 Boston Pl
Boston, MA 02108-4407
Giving is centered on little children age twelve and under for the care and relief of destitute children. Provides support for preschools, day care, summer camps and other programs.

Nancy Criscitiello, Executive Director

2483 Hyams Foundation
175 Federal Street
Floor 14
Boston, MA 02110-2210
617-426-5600
Fax: 617-426-5696
http://www.hyamsfoundation.org
The foundation seeks to promote understanding and appreciation of diversity, including race, ethnicity, gender, sexual orientation, age, physical ability, class and religion. The foundation's primary objective is to meet the needs of low-income and other underserved populations, striving to address the causes of those needs, whenever possible. Foundation supports low-income communities in their efforts to identify their own problems, solve these problems and improve people's lives.

Elizabeth B Smith, Executive Director

2484 Irene E & George A Davis Foundation
C/O Ann T Keiser
1 Monarch Place
Suite 1450
Springfield, MA 01144-1450
413-734-8336
Fax: 413-734-7845
http://www.davisfdn.org
Education and social service organizations and programs in Western Massachusetts are the primary concern of this foundation.

Mary E Walachy, Executive Director

2485 James G Martin Memorial Trust
122 Pond Street
Jamaica Plain, MA 02130-2714
Giving is centered on elementary education and higher education in Massachusetts.

Ms Martin, Executive Director

2486 Jessie B Cox Charitable Trust
Grants Management Association
60 State Street
Boston, MA 02109-1899
617-227-7940
Fax: 617-227-0781
http://www.hemenwaybarnes.com/selectsrv/jbcox/cox.html
This trust makes grants for projects which will address important social issues in the trust's fields of interest and for which adequate funding from other sources cannot be

obtained. The trust funds projects in New England in the areas of health, education and the environment. The trustees look to support special projects which will assist the applicants to achieve their long-range organizational goals.

Michaelle Larkins, Executive Director
Susan M Fish, Grants Administrator

2487 LG Balfour Foundation

Fleet Bank of Massachusetts
75 State Street
Boston, MA 02109-1775
617-346-4000
Offers support for scholarships and innovative projects designed to eliminate barriers and improve access to education for all potentially qualified students.

Kerry Herliney, Executive Director

2488 Little Family Foundation

33 Broad Street
Suite 10
Boston, MA 02109-4216
617-723-6771
Fax: 617-723-7107
Offers scholarships at various business schools and Junior Achievement programs in secondary schools.

Arthur D Little, Executive Director

2489 Rogers Family Foundation

29 Water Street
Newburyport, MA 01950-4501
978-465-6100
Fax: 978-685-1588
Offers support in the areas of secondary and higher education in the Lawrence, Massachusetts area.

Stephen Rogers, President

2490 State Street Foundation

225 Franklin Street
12th Floor
Boston, MA 02110
617-664-1937
http://www.statestreet.com
Offers grants to organizations that help improve the quality of life in the greater Boston area. Interest includes human services, public and secondary education, vocational education, and arts and culture programs.

Madison Thompson, Executive Director

2491 Sudbury Foundation

278 Old Sudbury Road
Sudbury, MA 01776-1843
978-443-0849
Fax: 978-579-9536
http://www.sudburyfoundation.org
Offers college scholarships to local high school seniors who meet eligibility criteria.

Fredericka Tanner, Executive Director
Marilyn Martino, Program Officer

2492 Trustees of the Ayer Home

PO Box 1865
Lowell, MA 01853-1865
978-452-5914
Fax: 978-452-5914
Funding (greater Lowell, MA only) educational programs (RLF, SMARTS). Primary interests are women and children.

D Donahue, Assistant Treasurer

2493 Weld Foundation

Peter Loring/Janice Palumbo
Loring, Wolcott & Coolidge
30 Congress Street
Boston, MA 02110-2409
617-523-6531
Fax: 617-523-6535
Grants are offered in the areas of elementary, secondary and higher education in Massachusetts.

2494 Western Massachusetts Funding Resource Center

65 Elliot Street
Springfield, MA 01105-1713
413-732-3175
Fax: 413-452-0618
http://www.diospringfield.org/wmfrc.html
Member of The Foundation Center network, maintaining a collection of private foundation tax returns which provide information on the scope of grants dispensed by that particular foundation.

Kathleen Dowd, Director
Jean Los, Administrative Assistant

2495 William E Schrafft & Bertha E Schrafft Charitable Trust

1 Financial Center
Floor 26
Boston, MA 02111-2621
617-457-7327
Giving is primarily allocated to educational programs in the Boston metropolitan area.

2496 Woodstock Corporation

Woodstock Corporation
27 School Street
Suite 200
Boston, MA 02108-2301
617-227-0600
Fax: 617-523-0229
Offers support in the area of secondary school education in the state of Massachusetts.

2497 Worcester Public Library

Grants Resource Center
Salem Square
Worcester, MA 01608
508-799-1655
Fax: 508-799-1652
http://www.worcpublib.org
Member of The Foundation Center network, maintaining a collection of private foundation tax returns which provide information on the scope of grants dispensed by that particular foundation.

J Peck, Director Grants Resource

Michigan

2498 Alex & Marie Manoogian Foundation

21001 Van Born Road
Taylor, MI 48180-1340
313-274-7400
Fax: 313-792-6657
Supports higher and secondary education, cultural programs and human service organizations.

Alex Manoogian, Executive Director

2499 Charles Stewart Mott Foundation

Office of Proposal Entry
503 S Saginaw Street
Suite 1200
Flint, MI 48502-1851
810-238-5651
800-645-1766
Fax: 810-237-4857
E-mail: infocenter@mott.org
http://www.mott.org
Grants are given to nonprofit organizations with an emphasis on programs of volunteerism, at-risk youth, environmental protection, economic development and education.

2500 Chrysler Corporate Giving Program

12000 Chrysler Drive
Detroit, MI 48288-0001
810-576-5741
Offers support for education, especially secondary education and leadership development.

Lynn A Feldhouse, Executive Director

2501 Community Foundation for Southeastern Michigan

333 W Fort Street
Suite 2010
Detroit, MI 48226-3134
313-961-6675
Fax: 313-961-2886
http://www.cfsem.org
Supports projects in the areas of education, culture and social services.

Mariam C Noland, President

2502 Community Foundation of Greater Flint

502 Church Street
Flint, MI 48502-2013
810-767-8270
Fax: 810-767-0496
E-mail: cfgf@cfgf.org
http://www.cfgf.org
A community foundation that makes grants to benefit residents of Genessee County, Michigan. Areas of interest include: arts, education, environment, community services and health and social services.

Kathi Horton, President
Evan M Albert, VP Program

2503 Cronin Foundation

203 E Michigan Avenue
Marshall, MI 49068-1545
616-781-9851
Fax: 616-781-2070
Offers support to expand educational, social and cultural needs of the community within the Marshall, Michigan school district.

Joseph E Schroeder, Executive Director

2504 Detroit Edison Foundation

2000 2nd Avenue
Room 1046
Detroit, MI 48226-1279
313-235-9271
Fax: 313-237-9271
http://www.my.dteenergy.com
Offers support for all levels of education, and local community social services and cultural organizations in Southeast Michigan.

Katharine W Hunt, Executive Director

2505 Ford Motor Company Fund
One American Road
PO Box 1899
Dearborn, MI 48126-2798
888-313-0102
Fax: 313-337-6680
http://www.ford.com
Ford Motor Company Fund continues the legacy of Henry Ford's commitment to innovative education at all levels. We remain dedicated to creating and enriching educational opportunities, especially in the areas of science, engineering, math and business, while promoting diversity in education.

Sandra E Ulsh, President
Jim Graham, Manager Education Programs

2506 Frey Foundation
40 Pearl Street NW
Suite 1100
Grand Rapids, MI 49503-3023
616-451-0303
Fax: 616-451-8481
http://www.freyfdn.org
Awards grants and supports the needs of children in their early years, support for environmental education and protection of our natural resources.

Milton W Rohwer, President
Teresa J Crawford, Grants Manager

2507 General Motors Foundation
13-145 General Motors Building
Detroit, MI 48202
313-556-4260
http://www.gm.com/company/gmability/philanthropy
Offers support for higher education, cultural programs and civic affairs.

Ronald L Theis, Executive Director

2508 Grand Rapids Foundation
209-C Water Building
161 Ottawa Avenue NW
Grand Rapids, MI 49503
616-454-1751
Fax: 616-454-6455
E-mail: mrapp@grfoundation.org
http://www.grfoundation.org
A community foundation established in 1922. The foundation actively serves the people of Kent County by administering funds it receives and by making philanthropic grants to non-profit organizations in response to community needs. Various educational scholarships are offered on the basis of a competitive process which considers academic achievement, extracurricular activities, a statement of one's own personal aspirations and educational goals, and financial need. Kent County Residency required.

Ruth Bishop, Program Associate-Education
Diana Sieger, President

2509 Harry A & Margaret D Towsley Foundation
3055 Plymouth Road
Suite 200
Ann Arbor, MI 48105-3208
312-662-6777
Areas of support include pre-school education, social services, and continuing education.

Margaret Ann Riecker, Executive Director

2510 Henry Ford Centennial Library
Adult Services
16301 Michigan Avenue
Dearborn, MI 48126-2792
313-943-2330
Fax: 313-943-3063
http://www.dearborn.lib.mi.us/aboutus/adult.htm
Member of The Foundation Center network, maintaining a collection of private foundation tax returns which provide information on the scope of grants dispensed by that particular foundation.

2511 Herbert H & Grace A Dow Foundation
1018 W Main Street
Midland, MI 48640
989-631-3699
Fax: 989-631-0675
http://www.hhdowfdn.org
Limited to organizations within Michigan. Has charter goals to improve the educational, religious, economic and cultural lives of Michigan's people.

Margaret Ann Riescker, President
Elysa M Rogers, Assistant VP

2512 Herrick Foundation
150 W Jefferson Avenue
Suite 2500
Detroit, MI 48226-4415
313-496-7585
Offers grants to colleges and universities, health agencies and social service organizations.

Dolores de Galleford, Executive Director

2513 Kresge Foundation
2701 Troy Center Drive
Suite 150
Troy, MI 48084
248-643-9630
Fax: 313-643-0588
http://www.kresge.org
Giving is aimed at areas of interest including arts and humanities, social services and public policy.

John E Marshall III, Executive Director
Sandra McAlister Ambrozy, Senior Program Officer

2514 Malpass Foundation
PO Box 1206
East Jordan, MI 49727-1206
Offers giving in the areas of education and community development.

William J Lorne, Executive Director

2515 McGregor Fund
333 W Fort Street
Suite 2090
Detroit, MI 48226-3134
313-963-3495
Fax: 313-963-3512
http://www.mcgregorfund.org
Social services, health and education grants awarded to organizations located in Ohio, primarily the Detroit area.

C David Campbell, President
Kate Levin Markel, Program Officer

2516 Michigan State University Libraries
Social Sciences/Humanities
Main Library
East Lansing, MI 48824
517-353-8700
Fax: 517-432-3532
http://www.lib.msu.edu

Member of The Foundation Center network, maintaining a collection of private foundation tax returns which provide information on the scope of grants dispensed by that particular foundation.

2517 Richard & Helen DeVos Foundation
190 Muncie NW
Suite 500
Grand Rapids, MI 49503
616-454-4114
Fax: 616-454-4654
Strong geographical preference to Western Michigan. Funding includes Christian education, cultural, community, education (not an individual basis) and government services. Donations are also made on a national level to organizations based in Washington, DC.

Stephanie Roy, Executive Director

2518 Rollin M Gerstacker Foundation
PO Box 1945
Midland, MI 48641-1945
989-631-6097
Fax: 517-832-8842
http://www.tamu.edu/baum/gerstack.html
Primary purpose of this foundation is to carry on, indefinitely, financial aid to charities concentrated in the states of Michigan and Ohio. Grants are given in the areas of community support, schools, education, social services, music and the arts, youth activities, health care and research, churches and other areas.

Carl A Gerstacker, Executive Director

2519 Steelcase Foundation
PO Box 1967, CH-4E
Grand Rapids, MI 49501-1967
616-246-4695
Fax: 616-475-2200
E-mail: sbroman@steelcse.com
http://www.steelcase.com
Offers support for human services and education, to improve the quality of life for children, the elderly and the disabled in the areas where there are manufacturing plants.

Susan Broman, Executive Director

2520 Wayne State University
Purdy-Kresge Library
5265 Cass Avenue
Detroit, MI 48202-3930
313-577-6424
http://www.lib.wayne.edu
Member of The Foundation Center network, maintaining a collection of private foundation tax returns which provide information on the scope of grants dispensed by that particular foundation.

2521 Whirlpool Foundation
2000 N M 63
Benton Harbor, MI 49022-2632
269-923-5580
Fax: 269-925-0154
Giving centers on learning, cultural diversity, adult education, and scholarships for children of corporation employees.

Ddaniel Hopp, President & Chairman
Barbara Hall, Program Officer

Minnesota

2522 Andersen Foundation
Andersen Corporation
100 4th Avenue N
Bayport, MN 55003-1096
651-264-5150
Fax: 651-264-5537
Grants are given in the areas of higher education, health, youth and the arts in Minnesota.

2523 Bush Foundation
E-900 First National Bank Building
332 Minnesota Street
Saint Paul, MN 55101-1314
651-227-0891
Fax: 651-297-6485
http://www.bushfoundation.org
The foundation is predominantly a regional grantmaking foundation, with broad interests in education, human services, health, arts and humanities and in the development of leadership.

Anita M Pampusch, President
John Archabal, Senior Program Officer

2524 Cargill Foundation
PO Box 9300
Minneapolis, MN 55440-9300
952-742-4311
Fax: 612-742-7224
http://www.cargill.com
Offers grants in the areas of education, health, human service organizations, arts and cultural programs and social service agencies.

Audrey Tulberg, Executive Director

2525 Charles & Ellora Alliss Educational Foundation
332 Minnesota Street #64704
Saint Paul, MN 55101-1314
651-244-4581
Fax: 651-244-0860
The foundation is organized exclusively for support of the education of young people, up to and including the period of postgraduate study. As a matter of policy, the foundation generally has limited its program to universities and colleges located in Minnesota. Grants are made to such institutions in support of undergraduate scholarship programs administered by their student aid offices. The foundation makes no direct grants to individuals.

John Bultena, Executive Director

2526 Duluth Public Library
520 W Superior Street
Duluth, MN 55802-1578
218-723-3802
Fax: 218-723-3815
http://www.duluth.lib.mn.us
Member of The Foundation Center network, maintaining a collection of private foundation tax returns which provide information on the scope of grants dispensed by that particular foundation.

Elizabeth Kelly, Library Director

2527 FR Bigelow Foundation
600 Fifth Street
Center 55th Street East
St. Paul, MN 55101-1797
651-224-5463
Fax: 651-224-8123
http://www.frbigelow.org
Offers support in early childhood education, elementary and secondary education, higher and adult education and human services.

Jon A Theobald, Chair
Carleen K Rhodes, Secretary

2528 First Bank System Foundation
PO Box 522
Minneapolis, MN 55480-0522
612-973-2440
Offers support for public elementary and secondary education, arts and cultural programs.

Cheryl L Rantala, Executive Director

2529 Hiawatha Education Foundation
360 Vila Street
Winona, MN 55987-1500
507-453-5550
Giving is centered on Catholic high schools and colleges, as well as awarding scholarships to college-bound high school graduates.

Robert Kierlin, Executive Director

2530 IA O'Shaughnessy Foundation
First Trust
PO Box 64704
Saint Paul, MN 55164-0704
612-291-5164
Giving is centered on cultural programs, secondary and higher education, human services and medical programs.

John Bultena, Executive Director

2531 Marbrook Foundation
730 2nd Avenue
1450 US Trust Building
Minneapolis, MN 55402
612-752-1783
Fax: 612-752-1780
E-mail: marbrook@brooksinc.net
Offers grants in the areas of the environment, the arts, social empowerment, spiritual endeavors, basic human needs and health.
Annual Report

Conley Brooks Jr, Executive Director
Julie S Hara, Program Officer

2532 Medtronic Foundation
7000 Central Avenue NE
Minneapolis, MN 55432-3576
763-514-4000
800-328-2518
Fax: 763-514-8410
http://www.medtronic.com
Offers grants in the areas of education (especially at the pre-college level), community funding and social services.

Penny Hunt, Executive Director

2533 Minneapolis Foundation
800 Ids Center 80 S 8th Street
Minneapolis, MN 55402
612-672-3878
Fax: 612-672-3846
http://www.minneapolisfoundation.org
The foundation strives to strengthen the community for the benefit of all citizens. Grants are awarded for the purposes of achieving this goal in the areas of early childhood education, child development, and education.

Karen Kelley-Ariwoola, VP Community Philanthropy

2534 Minneapolis Public Library
Music, Art, Sociology & Humanities
250 S Marquette
Minneapolis, MN 55401-2188
612-630-6000
Fax: 612-630-6220
http://www.mplib.org
Member of The Foundation Center network, maintaining a collection of private foundation tax returns which provide information on the scope of grants dispensed by that particular foundation.

Katherine G Hadle, Director

2535 Otto Bremer Foundation
445 Minnesota Street
Suite 2250
Saint Paul, MN 55101-2135
651-227-8036
Fax: 651-312-3665
http://www.fdncenter.org/grantmaker/bremer/
Offers support for post-secondary education, human services and community affairs.

John Kostishack, Executive Director
Karen Starr, Senior Program Officer

2536 Saint Paul Foundation
55 Fifth Street East
Suite 600
St. Paul, MN 55101-1797
651-224-5463
Fax: 651-224-8123
http://www.saintpaulfoundation.org
Offers support for educational, charitable and cultural purposes of a public nature.

Carleen K Rhodes, President
Mindy K Molumby, Grants Administrator

2537 TCF Foundation
Code EXO-02-C
200 Lake Street
East Wayzata, MN 55391-1693
952-745-2757
Fax: 612-661-8554
http://www.tcfexpress.com
Giving is primarily for education through grants and employee matching gifts, including secondary schools, higher education and organizations that increase public knowledge.

Neil I Whitehouse, Executive Director

Mississippi

2538 Foundation for the Mid South
1230 Raymond Road
Box 700
Jackson, MS 39204
601-355-8167
Fax: 601-355-6499
http://www.fndmidsouth.org
Makes grants in the area of education, as well as economic development and families and children.

George Penick, Executive Director

2539 Jackson-Hinds Library System
300 N State Street
Jackson, MS 39201-1705
601-968-5803
http://www.jhlibrary.com
Member of The Foundation Center network, maintaining a collection of private foundation tax returns which provide information on the scope of grants dispensed by that particular foundation.

Carolyn McCallum, Executive Director

2540 Mississippi Power Foundation
PO Box 4079
Gulfport, MS 39502-4079
228-864-1211
http://www.southerncompany.com/mspow
er/edufound
The foundation is dedicated to the improvement and enhancement of education in Mississippi from kindergarten to twelfth grade.

Huntley Biggs, Executive Director

2541 Phil Hardin Foundation
Citizens National Bank
1921 24th Avenue
Meridian, MS 39301-5800
601-483-4282
Fax: 601-483-5665
http://www.philhardin.org
Offers giving in Mississippi for schools and educational institutions and programs.

C Thompson Wacaster, Executive Director

Missouri

2542 Ameren Corporation Charitable Trust
Ameren Corporation
PO Box 66149
MC 100
Saint Louis, MO 63166-6149
314-554-2789
877-426-3736
Fax: 314-554-2888
E-mail: sbell@ameren.com
http://www.ameren.com
Offers giving in the areas of education, environment, youth and seniors; giving restricted to nonprofits located in Ameren service area in Missouri and Illinois.

Annually

Susan M Bell, Sr Community Relations
Otis Cowan, Community Relations Manger

2543 Clearinghouse for Midcontinent Foundations
University of Missouri
5110 Cherry Street
Suite 310
Kansas City, MO 64110-2426
816-253-1176
Fax: 816-235-5727
Member of The Foundation Center network, maintaining a collection of private foundation tax returns which provide information on the scope of grants dispensed by that particular foundation.

2544 Danforth Foundation
211 N Broadway
Suite 2390
Saint Louis, MO 63102-2733
314-588-1900
Fax: 314-588-0035
E-mail: banderson@info.csd.org
http://www.orgs.muohio.edu/forumscp/in
dez.html
This foundation is aimed at enhancing human life through activities which emphasize the theme of improvement in teaching and learning. Serves the pre-collegiate education through grantmaking and program activities.

Dr. Bruce J Anderson, President

2545 Enid & Crosby Kemper Foundation
C/O UMB Bank, N.A.
PO Box 419692
Kansas City, MO 64141-6692
816-860-7711
Fax: 816-860-5690
Giving is primarily allocated to organizations and programs focusing on educational and cultural needs.

Stephen J Campbell, Executive Director

2546 Hall Family Foundation
Charitable & Crown Investment - 323
PO Box 419580
Kansas City, MO 64141-8400
816-274-8516
Fax: 816-274-8547
Offers grants in the areas of all levels of education, performing and visual arts, community development, and children, youth and families.

Wendy Burcham, Program Officer
Peggy Collins, Program Officer

2547 James S McDonnell Foundation
1034 S Brentwood Boulevard
Suite 1850
Saint Louis, MO 63117-1284
314-721-1532
Fax: 314-721-7421
http://www.jsmf.org
Foundation Program, Cognitive Studies for Educational Practice, funding available through competition in broadly announced requests for proposals. Program grant guidelines are announced in 3 year cycles.

John T Bruer, President
Cheryl A Washington, Grants Manager

2548 Kansas City Public Library
14 West 10th Street
Kansas City, MO 64105
816-701-3400
Fax: 816-701-3401
http://www.kclibrary.org
Member of The Foundation Center network, maintaining a collection of private foundation tax returns which provide information on the scope of grants dispensed by that particular foundation.

2549 Mary Ranken Jordan & Ettie A Jordan Charitable Foundation
Mercantile Bank
PO Box 387
Saint Louis, MO 63166-0387
314-231-7626
Giving is limited to charitable institutions with an emphasis on secondary education and cultural programs, as well as higher education and social services.

Fred Arnold, Executive Director

2550 McDonnell Douglas Foundation
PO Box 516
MC S100-1510
Saint Louis, MO 63166-0516
314-234-0360
Fax: 314-232-7654
Offers various grants with an emphasis on higher and other education and community funding.

AM Bailey, Executive Director

2551 Monsanto Fund
800 N Lindbergh Boulevard
Saint Louis, MO 63167-0001
314-694-1000
Fax: 314-694-7658
E-mail: monsanto.fund@monsanto.com
http://www.monsanto.com/monsanto/abo
ut_us/monsanto_fund
Giving is offered primarily in the area of education, specifically science and math.

Deborah J Patterson, President

Montana

2552 Eastern Montana College Library
Special Collections-Grants
1500 N 30th Street
Billings, MT 59101-0245
406-657-1662
Fax: 406-657-2037
http://www.msubillings.edu/library
Member of The Foundation Center network, maintaining a collection of private foundation tax returns which provide information on the scope of grants dispensed by that particular foundation.

Joan Bares, Grants Manager

2553 Montana State Library
Library Services
1515 E 6th Avenue
Helena, MT 59601-4542
406-444-3115
Fax: 406-444-5612
http://www.msl.state.mt.us/
Member of The Foundation Center network, maintaining a collection of private foundation tax returns which provide information on the scope of grants dispensed by that particular foundation.

Barbara Duke, Administrative Assistant

Nebraska

2554 Dr. CC & Mabel L Criss Memorial Foundation
US Bank
1700 Farnam Streets
Omaha, NE 68102
800-441-2117
Fax: 402-348-6666
Offers support for educational and scientific purposes, including higher education.

2555 Thomas D Buckley Trust
PO Box 647
Chappell, NE 69129-0647
308-874-2212
Fax: 308-874-3491
Offers giving in the areas of education, health care and youth and religion. Grants awarded in Chappell, NE, community and surrounding area.

Connie Loos, Secretary

2556 W Dale Clark Library
Social Sciences Department
215 S 15th Street
Omaha, NE 68102-1601
402-444-4826
Fax: 402-444-4504
http://www.omahapubliclibrary.org
Member of The Foundation Center network, maintaining a collection of private foundation tax returns which provide information on the scope of grants dispensed by that particular foundation.

Angela Green-Garland, President

Nevada

2557 Conrad N Hilton Foundation
100 W Liberty Street
Suite 840
Reno, NV 89501-1988
775-323-4221
Fax: 775-323-4150
http://www.hiltonfoundation.org
Founded in 1944 as a Trust, this foundation is dedicated to fulfilling and expanding Conrad Hilton's philanthropic vision by carrying out grantmaking activities. The foundation's giving is focused primarily in two areas: the alleviation of human suffering, particularly among disadvantaged children; and the human services works of the Catholic Sisters through a separate entity as described under Major Projects (supportive housing, disabled, education and prevention of domestic violence).

Donald H Hubbs, Executive Director
Steven M Hilton, President

2558 Cord Foundation
E.L. Cord Foundation Center For Learning Literacy
College Of Education/Mail Stop 288
University Of Nevada, Reno
Reno, NV 89557-0215
775-784-4951
Fax: 775-784-4758
http://www.unr.edu/cll
Offers support for secondary and higher education, including youth organizations and cultural programs.

Donald Bear, Director/Professor

2559 Donald W Reynolds Foundation
1701 Village Center Circle
Las Vegas, NV 89134
702-804-6000
Fax: 702-804-6099
E-mail: generalquestions@dwrf.org
http://www.dwreynolds.org
Devotes funds to further the cause of free press and journalism education.

Fred Smith, Chairman

2560 EL Wiegand Foundation
Wiegand Center
165 W Liberty Street
Reno, NV 89501-1915
775-333-0310
Fax: 775-333-0314
Offers grants in of culture and the arts, organizations, health and medical institutions, with an emphasis on Roman Catholic organizations.

Kristen A Avansino, Executive Director

2561 Las Vegas-Clark County
Library District
833 Las Vegas Boulevard N
Las Vegas, NV 89101-2030
702-382-5280
Fax: 702-382-5491
http://www.lvccld.org
Member of The Foundation Center network, maintaining a collection of private foundation tax returns which provide information on the scope of grants dispensed by that particular foundation.

Daniel L Walters, Executive Director

2562 Washoe County Library
301 S Center Street
Reno, NV 89501-2102
775-327-8349
Fax: 775-327-8341
http://www.washoe.lib.nv.us/
Member of The Foundation Center network, maintaining a collection of private foundation tax returns which provide information on the scope of grants dispensed by that particular foundation.

New Hampshire

2563 Lincolnshire
Liberty Lane
Hampton, NH 03842
Giving is primarily for secondary school education, business school education and recreation.

William Coffey, Executive Director

2564 New Hampshire Charitable Foundation
37 Pleasant Street
Concord, NH 03301-4005
603-225-6641
Fax: 603-225-1700
E-mail: scg@nhcf.org
http://www.nhcf.org
Offers grants for charitable and educational purposes including college scholarships, existing charitable organizations, child welfare, community services, health and social services and new programs that emphasize programs rather than capital needs.

Racheal Stuart, VP Program

2565 Plymouth State College
Herbert H. Lamson Library
Highland Street MSC #47
Plymouth, NH 03264
603-535-2258
Fax: 603-535-2445
http://www.plymouth.edu/psc/library
Member of The Foundation Center network, maintaining a collection of private foundation tax returns which provide information on the scope of grants dispensed by that particular foundation.

New Jersey

2566 Community Foundation of New Jersey
Knox Hill Road
PO Box 338
Morristown, NJ 07963-0338
973-267-5533
Fax: 973-267-2903
E-mail: cfnj@bellatlantic.net
http://www.cfnj.org
Offers support for programs that offer a path of solution of community problems in the areas of education, leadership development and human services.

Hans Dekker, President

2567 Fund for New Jersey
Kilmer Square
94 Church Street
Suite 303
New Brunswick, NJ 08901-1242
732-220-8656
Fax: 732-220-8654
http://www.fundfornj.org
Offers grants on projects which provide the basis of action in education, AIDS research, minorities/immigrants, public policy and community development.

Mark M Murphy, Executive Director

2568 Hoechst Celanese Foundation
Route 202-206 N
PO Box 2500
Somerville, NJ 08876
908-522-7500
Fax: 908-598-4424
Provides support for education, particularly in the sciences.

Lewis F Alpaugh, Executive Director

2569 Honeywell Foundation
101 Columbia Road
Morristown, NJ 07960-4658
973-455-2000
Fax: 973-455-4807
http://www.honeywell.com/about/foundation.html
Offers support for education, including fellowship and scholarship aid to colleges.

2570 Hyde & Watson Foundation
437 Southern Boulevard
Chatham, NJ 07928-1454
973-966-6024
Fax: 973-966-6404
http://www.fdncenter.org/grantmaker/hydeandwatson
Support of capital projects of lasting value which tend to increase quality, capacity, or efficiency of a grantee's programs or services, such as purchase or relocation of facilities, capital equipment, instructive materials development, and certain medical research areas. Broad fields include health, education, religion, social services, arts, and humanities. Geographic areas served include the New York City Metropolitan region and primarily Essex, Union, and Morris Counties in New Jersey.

Hunter W Corbin, President

2571 Mary Owen Borden Memorial Foundation
160 Hodge Road
Princeton, NJ 08540-3014
609-924-3637
Fax: 609-252-9472
E-mail: tborden@ibm.net
http://www.fdncenter.org/grantmaker/borden/index.htm
Offers grants in the areas of childhood education, child development, education, conservation and health and human services.

Thomas Borden, Executive Director

2572 Merck Company Foundation
1 Merck Drive #100
Whitehouse Station, NJ 08889-3400
908-423-2042
http://www.merck.com
Offers support of education, primarily medical through community programs, grants and matching gift programs for colleges and secondary education.

John R Taylor, Executive Director

2573 Prudential Foundation
Prudential Plaza
751 Broad Street
Floor 15
Newark, NJ 07102-3714
973-802-4791
http://www.prudential.com
Focus is on children and youth for services that can better their lives. Grants are made in the areas of education, health and human services, community and urban develop-

ment, business and civic affairs, culture and the arts. Emphasis is placed on programs that serve the city of Newark and the surrounding New Jersey urban centers, programs in cities where The Prudential has a substantial presence and national programs that further the company's objectives.

Barbara L Halaburda, Executive Director

2574 Turrell Fund
21 Van Vleck Street
Montclair, NJ 07042-2358
201-783-9358
Fax: 973-783-9283
E-mail: turrell@bellatlantic.net
http://www.fdncenter.org/grantmaker/turrell
Offers grants to organizations and agencies that are dedicated to the care of children and youth under twelve years of age, with an emphasis on education, early childhood education, delinquency prevention and child and youth services.

E Belvin Williams, Executive Director

2575 Victoria Foundation
946 Bloomfield Avenue
Glen Ridge, NJ 07028
973-748-5300
Fax: 973-748-0016
E-mail: cmcfarvic@aol.com
http://www.victoriafoundation.org
Grants are limited to Newark, New Jersey in the following areas: elementary and secondary education, after school enrichment programs, teacher training and academic enrichment.

Catherine M McFarland, Executive Officer
Nancy K Zimmerman, Senior Program Officer

2576 Warner-Lambert Charitable Foundation
201 Tabor Road
Morris Plains, NJ 07950-2614
212-573-2323
Fax: 212-573-7851
Grants are given in the areas of education, health care, culture and the arts. Supports higher institutions of learning which concentrate on pharmacy, medicine, dentistry, the sciences and mathematics. Current support is aimed at the higher levels of education, but the foundation has begun to place more of its attention on the growing needs that impact elementary and secondary training.

Evelyn Self, Community Affairs
Richard Keelty, VP Investor Affair

2577 Wilf Family Foundation
820 Morris Tpke
Short Hills, NJ 07078-2619
973-467-5000
Awards grants in the areas of Jewish higher education and religion.

Joseph Wilf, Executive Director

New Mexico

2578 Dale J Bellamah Foundation
PO Box 36600
Albuquerque, NM 87176-6600
858-756-1154
Fax: 858-756-3856

Offers grants for higher education including military academies, hospitals and social service organizations.

AF Potenziani, Executive Director

2579 New Mexico State Library
Information Services
1209 Camino Carlos Rey
Santa Fe, NM 87507
505-476-9700
Fax: 505-476-9701
http://www.stlib.state.nm.us
Member of The Foundation Center network, maintaining a collection of private foundation tax returns which provide information on the scope of grants dispensed by that particular foundation.

2580 RD & Joan Dale Hubbard Foundation
PO Box 1679
Ruidoso Downs, NM 88346-1679
505-378-4142
Giving is offered in the areas of childhood education, elementary, secondary and higher education as well as other cultural programs.

Jim Stoddard, Executive Director

New York

2581 Achelis Foundation
767 3rd Avenue
4th Floor
New York, NY 10017
212-644-0322
Fax: 212-759-6510
E-mail: achelis@aol.com
http://fdncenter.org/grantmaker/achelis-bodman
Grants include biomedical research at Rockefeller University, rebuilding the Hayden Planetarium at the American Museum of Natural History, support for the arts and culture, the charter school movement, youth organizations, and special efforts to curb father absence and strengthen family life with awards.

Russell P Pennoyer, President
Joseph S Dolan, Executive Director

2582 Adrian & Jessie Archbold Charitable Trust
401 East 60th Street
New York, NY 10022
212-371-1152
Eastern United States educational institutions and health care service organizations are the main recipients of the Trust.

Myra Mahon, Executive Director

2583 Alfred P Sloan Foundation
630 5th Avenue
Suite 2550
New York, NY 10111-0100
212-649-1649
Fax: 212-757-5117
E-mail: www.sloan.org
A nonprofit foundation offering Sloan Research Fellowships which are awarded in chemistry, computer science, economics, mathematics, neuroscience and physics. These are competitive grants given to young faculty members with high research potential on the recommendation of department heads and other senior scientists.

Ralph E Gomory, President

2584 Altman Foundation
521 5th Avenue
35th Floor
New York, NY 10175
212-682-0970
http://www.altmanfoundation.org
In education, the Altman Foundation supports programs that identify, sponsor and tutor talented disadvantaged youngsters and help them to obtain educations in non-public and independent schools. The Foundation awards grants only in New York State with an almost-exclusive focus on the five boroughs of New York City. The Foundation does not award grants or scholarships to individuals.

Karen L Rosa, VP/Executive Director

2585 Ambrose Monell Foundation
C/O Fulton, Duncombe & Rowe
1 Rockefeller Plaza
Room 301
New York, NY 10020-2002
212-586-0700
Fax: 212-245-1863
http://www.monellvetlesen.org
Broad range of allocation including education, social service, cultural organizations and the environment.

Ambrose K Monell, Executive Director

2586 American Express Foundation
American Express Company
World Financial Center
New York, NY 10285
212-640-5661
http://www.home3.americanexpress.com/corp/philanthropy/contacts.asp
The foundation's giving focuses on three areas including community service, education and employment.

Mary Beth Salerno, Executive Director
Angela Woods, Philanthropic Program

2587 Andrew W Mellon Foundation
140 E 62nd Street
New York, NY 10021-8187
212-838-8400
Fax: 212-223-2778
http://www.mellon.org
Offers grants in the areas of higher education, cultural affairs and public affairs.

William G Bowen, President

2588 Arnold Bernhard Foundation
220 E 42nd Street
Floor 6
New York, NY 10017-5806
212-907-1500
Offers funding in the areas of education with the emphasis placed on college and universities as well as college preparatory schools.

Jean B Buttner, Executive Director

2589 Atran Foundation
23-25 East 21st Street
3rd Floor
New York, NY 10010
212-505-9677
Offers grants and funding to nonprofit educational and religious organizations.

2590 Beatrice P Delany Charitable Trust
The Chase Manhattan Bank
1211 Avenue of the Americas
34th Floor
New York, NY 10036
212-935-9935

Giving is offered for education, especially higher education and religion.

John HF Enteman, Executive Director

2591 Bodman Foundation
767 3rd Avenue
4th Floor
New York, NY 10017
212-644-0322
Fax: 212-759-6510
E-mail: bodmanfnd@aol.com
Grants include biomedical research at Rockefeller University, building the Congo Gorilla Forest Education Center at the Bronx Zoo through the Wildlife Conservation Society, rebuilding of the Hayden Planetarium for Science and Technology at the American Museum of Natural History, support for Symphony Space, the charter school movement, youth organizations, and the Rutgers University Foundation.

John N Irwin III, President
Joseph S Dolan, Executive Director

2592 Bristol-Myers Squibb Foundation
345 Park Avenue
Floor 43
New York, NY 10154-0004
212-546-4331
http://www.bms.com
Offers support for elementary and secondary school, math and science education reform, civic affairs and health care.

Cindy Johnson, Executive Director

2593 Buffalo & Erie County Public Library
History Department
Lafayette Square
Buffalo, NY 14203
716-858-8900
Fax: 716-858-6211
http://www.buffalolib.org/libraries/central
Member of The Foundation Center network, maintaining a collection of private foundation tax returns which provide information on the scope of grants dispensed by that particular foundation.

Michael C Mahaney, Director

2594 Caleb C & Julia W Dula Educational & Charitable Foundation
C/O Chemical Bank
270 Park Avenue
Floor 21
New York, NY 10017-2014
212-270-9066
Offers grants to charities with an emphasis on secondary and higher education.

G Price-Fitch, Executive Director

2595 Capital Cities-ABC Corporate Giving Program
77 W 66th St
New York, NY 10023-6201
212-456-7498
Fax: 212-456-7909
Offers support in adult education, literary and basic skills, reading, and AIDS research.

Bernadette Longford Williams, Executive Director

2596 Carl & Lily Pforzheimer Foundation
476 5th Avenue
New York, NY 10018
212-764-0655

Offers support primarily for higher and secondary education, cultural programs, public administration, and health care.

Carl H Pforzheimer III, Executive Director

2597 Carnegie Corporation of New York
437 Madison Avenue
New York, NY 10022-7001
212-374-3200
Fax: 212-754-4073
http://www.carnegie.org
The foundation has several program goals including education and healthy development of children and youth, including early childhood health and education, early adolescence educational achievement, science education and education reform.

Vartan Gregorian, President

2598 Chase Manhattan Corporation Philanthropy Department
1 Chase Manhattan Plaza
Floor 9
New York, NY 10005-1401
212-552-7087
Offers support to various organizations to enhance the well-being of the communities Chase Manahattan serves. Grants are awarded in the areas of education, youth services, community and economic development, homeless, library science, health care and housing development.

Steven Gelston, Executive Director

2599 Christian A Johnson Endeavor Foundation
1060 Park Avenue
New York, NY 10128-1008
212-534-6620
http://www.csuohio.edu/uored/funding/johnson.htm
Offers support to private institutions of higher education at the baccalaureate level and on educational outreach programs.

Wilmot H Kidd, Executive Director

2600 Cleveland H Dodge Foundation
670 W 247th Street
Bronx, NY 10471-3292
212-543-1220
Fax: 718-543-0737
http://www.chdodgefoundation.org
Bestows funding for nonprofit organizations aimed at improving higher education and youth organizations.

William D Rueckert, President

2601 Cowles Charitable Trust
630 5th Avenue
Suite 1612
New York, NY 10111-0100
212-765-6262
Funding for higher education and cultural organizations.

2602 Daisy Marquis Jones Foundation
1600 S Avenue
Suite 250
Rochester, NY 14620
585-461-4950
Fax: 585-461-9752
http://www.dmjf.org
Offers grants for nonprofit organizations focusing on improving the lives of children, youth and the elderly, in Monroe and Yates counties in New York State.

Roger L Gardner, President
Marless A Honan, Administrative Assistant

2603 DeWitt Wallace-Reader's Digest Fund
2 Park Avenue
Floor 23
New York, NY 10016-9301
212-251-9700
Fax: 212-679-6990
E-mail: www.wallacefoundation.org
The mission of this foundation is to invest in programs and projects that enhance the quality of educational and career development opportunities for all school-age youth.

M Christine De Vita, President

2604 Edna McConnell Clark Foundation
415 Madison Avenue
10th Floor
New York, NY 10017
212-551-9100
Fax: 212-421-9325
http://www.emcf.org
Supports select youth, serving organizations working with children 9-24 during the non-school hours.

Michael Bailin, President

2605 Edward John Noble Foundation
32 E 57th Street
Floor 19
New York, NY 10022-2513
212-759-4212
Fax: 212-888-4531
Offers grants to major cultural organizations in New York City, especially for arts educational programs and management training internships.

June Noble Larkin, Chairman

2606 Edward W Hazen Foundation
90 Broad Street
Suite 604
New York, NY 10004
212-889-3034
E-mail: hazen@hazenfoundation.org
http://www.hazenfoundation.org
The foundation focuses giving on public education and youth development in the area of public education.

Lori Bezahler, President

2607 Edwin Gould Foundation for Children
126 East 31st Street
New York, NY 10016
212-251-0907
Fax: 212-982-6886
Supports projects that promote the welfare and education of children. Interests lies in early childhood education, higher education, children and youth services and family services.

Michael W Osheowitz, Executive Director

2608 Elaine E & Frank T Powers Jr Foundation
81 Skunks Misery Road
Locust Valley, NY 11560-1306
Offers support in the areas of secondary and higher education as well as youth services.

2609 Elmer & Mamdouha Bobst Foundation
Elmer Holmes Bobst Library, NYU
70 Washington Square S
New York, NY 10012-1019
212-998-2440
Fax: 212-995-4070
Offers grants and funding in the areas of youth, community development and the arts.

141

2610 Equitable Foundation
787 7th Avenue
Floor 39
New York, NY 10019-6018
212-554-3511
Offers grants in the areas of secondary school education, arts, community services, art and cultural programs, and higher education.

Kathleen A Carlson, Executive Director

2611 Ford Foundation
320 E 43rd Street
New York, NY 10017-4890
212-573-5000
Fax: 212-351-3677
E-mail: offsec@fordfound.rog
http://www.fordfound.org
Offers grants to advance public well-being and educational opportunities. Grants are given in the areas of education, secondary school/education, early childhood education, development services, human services, citizenship, academics and more.

Barron M Tenny, Secretary

2612 Frances & Benjamin Benenson Foundation
708 3rd Avenue
Floor 28
New York, NY 10017-4201
212-867-0990
Offers grants in elementary/secondary education, higher education and human services.

Charles B Benenson, Executive Director

2613 George F Baker Trust
477 Madison Avenue
New York, NY 10022
212-755-1890
Fax: 212-319-6316
Offers giving in the areas of higher and secondary education, social services, civic affairs and international affairs.

Rocio Suarez, Executive Director

2614 George Link Jr Foundation
C/O Emmet, Marvin & Martin
120 Broadway
32nd Floor
New York, NY 10271
212-238-3000
Fax: 212-238-3100
Giving is primarily centered on higher education, secondary school/education and medical research.

Michael J Catanzaro, Executive Director

2615 Gladys & Roland Harriman Foundation
63 Wall Street
Floor 23
New York, NY 10005-3001
212-493-8182
Fax: 212-493-5570
Giving is centered on education and support for youth and social service agencies.

William F Hibberd, Executive Director

2616 Gladys Brooks Foundation
1055 Franklin Avenue
Garden City, NY 11530
212-943-3217
http://www.gladysbrooksfoundation.org
The purpose of this foundation is to provide for the intellectual, moral and physical welfare of the people of this country by establishing and supporting nonprofit libraries, educational institutions, hospitals and clinics. In the area of education, grant applications will be considered generally for (a) educational endowments to fund scholarships based solely on leadership and academic ability of the student; (b) endowments to support salaries of educators.

Harman Hawkins, Chairman
Robert E Hill, Executive Director

2617 Green Fund
14 E 60th Street
Suite 702
New York, NY 10022-1006
212-755-2445
Fax: 212-755-0021
Offers grants in the area of higher and secondary education.

Cynthia Green Colin, Executive Director

2618 Hagedorn Fund
C/O JPMorgan Private Bank
Global Foundations Group
345 Park Avenue 4th Floor
New York, NY 10154
212-473-1587
http://www.fdncenter.org/grantmaker/hagedorn/
Offers support for higher and secondary education, youth agencies and social service agencies.

Monica J Neal, Vice President

2619 Hasbro Children's Foundation
10 Rockefeller Plaza
16th Floor
New York, NY 10020
212-713-7654
Fax: 212-645-4055
http://www.hasbro.org
Offers support to improve the quality of life for children. Areas of interest include education, AIDS research, literacy, special education, and youth services.

Eve Weiss, Executive Director

2620 Henry Luce Foundation
111 W 50th Street
Room 3710
New York, NY 10020-1202
212-489-7700
Fax: 212-581-9541
http://www.hluce.org
Offers grants for specific programs and projects in the areas of higher education and scholarship, social sciences at private colleges and universities, American arts and public affairs.

Michael Gilligan, President

2621 Herman Goldman Foundation
61 Broadway
Floor 18
New York, NY 10006-2701
212-797-9090
Fax: 212-797-9161
This foundation offers grants in the areas of social, legal and organizational approaches to aid for deprived or handicapped people; education for new or improved counseling for effective pre-school, vocational, and paraprofessional training; and the arts.

Richard K Baron, Executive Director

2622 Hess Foundation
1185 Avenue of the Americas
New York, NY 10036-2601
212-997-8500
Fax: 212-536-8390
E-mail: webmaster@hess.com
http://www.hess.com
Offers grants that focus on higher education, performing arts, and welfare organizations.

Leon Hess, Executive Director

2623 Horace W Goldsmith Foundation
375 Park Avenue
Suite 1602
New York, NY 10152-1699
212-319-8700
800-319-2881
Fax: 212-319-2881
Offers giving and support for education, higher education, cultural programs and museums.

James C Slaughter, Executive Director

2624 IBM Corporate Support Program
Old Orchard Road
Armonk, NY 10504
914-765-1900
The mission of this fund is to improve the areas and the communities that IBM operates in. Grants are awarded in various areas including early childhood education, elementary education, secondary education, business school/education, and engineering school/education.

Stanley Litow, Executive Director

2625 JI Foundation
C/O Patterson, Belknap, Webb & Tyler
1133 Avenue of the Americas
New York, NY 10036
212-336-2000
Offers grants in the areas of elementary education, higher education, and general charitable giving.

2626 JP Morgan Charitable Trust
60 Wall Street
Floor 46
New York, NY 10005-2836
212-648-9673
Offers support in the area of education, housing, economic development, advocacy and international affairs.

Roberta Ruocco, Executive Director

2627 Joukowsky Family Foundation
410 Park Avenue
Suite 1610
New York, NY 10022-4407
212-355-3151
Fax: 212-355-3147
http://www.joukowsky.org
Giving is focused on higher and secondary education.

Nina J Koprulu, Director/President
Emily R Kessler, Executive Director

2628 Julia R & Estelle L Foundation
1 HSBC Center
Suite 3650
Buffalo, NY 14203-1217
716-856-9490
Fax: 716-856-9493
http://www.oisheifdt.org
This fund offers grants in the areas of higher and secondary education, medical research, social services and support agencies.

Thomas E Baker, President

2629 Leon Lowenstein Foundation
575 Madison Avenue
New York, NY 10022-3613
212-605-0444
Fax: 212-688-0134

Support is given for New York City public education and medical research.

John F Van Gorder, Executive Director

2630 Levittown Public Library
1 Bluegrass Lane
Levittown, NY 11756-1292
516-731-5728
Fax: 516-735-3168
http://www.nassaulibrary.org/levtown/
Member of The Foundation Center network, maintaining a collection of private foundation tax returns which provide information on the scope of grants dispensed by that particular foundation.

Margaret Santer, President

2631 Louis & Anne Abrons Foundation
C/O First Manhattan Company
437 Madison Avenue
New York, NY 10022-7001
212-756-3376
Fax: 212-832-6698
Offers support in the areas of education, improvement programs, environmental and cultural projects.

Richard Abrons, Executive Director

2632 Margaret L Wendt Foundation
40 Fountain Plaza
Suite 277
Buffalo, NY 14202-2200
716-855-2146
Fax: 716-855-2149
Offers various grants with an emphasis on education, the arts and social services in Buffalo and Western New York.

Robert J Kresse, Executive Director

2633 McGraw-Hill Foundation
1221 Avenue of the Americas
Room 2917
New York, NY 10020
212-512-6113
800-442-9685
Offers support to educational organizations in the areas of company operations or to national organizations.

Susan A Wallman, Executive Director

2634 New York Foundation
350 5th Avenue
Suite 2901
New York, NY 10118-2996
212-594-8009
Fax: 212-594-5918
http://www.nyf.org
Provides support for the implementation of programs that offer support for the quality of life including educational services, health organizations, centers and services, civil rights, public policy, research and more.

Madeline Lee, Executive Director

2635 Palisades Educational Foundation
C/O Gibney, Anthony & Flaherty
665 5th Avenue
Floor 2
New York, NY 10022-5305
Offers support for secondary and higher education in New York, New Jersey and Connecticut.

Ralph F Anthony, Executive Director

2636 Robert Sterling Clark Foundation
135 E 64th Street
New York, NY 10021-7307
212-288-8900
Fax: 212-288-1033
http://www.rsclark.org
For more than 15 years, this foundation has provided support to New York City's cultural community. During this time, the Foundation has tried to structure a grants program so that it is flexible and meets the needs of the institutions and organizations. Grants are given in the areas of cultural institutions, arts advocacy, family planning services and supporting new initiatives in the area of arts and education.

Winthrop R Munyan, President
Margaret C Ayers, Executive Director

2637 Rochester Public Library
Business, Economics & Law
115 S Avenue
Rochester, NY 14604-1896
585-428-8045
Fax: 585-428-8353
http://www.rochester.lib.ny.us/central
Member of The Foundation Center network, maintaining a collection of private foundation tax returns which provide information on the scope of grants dispensed by that particular foundation.

Emeterio M Otero, President

2638 Ronald S Lauder Foundation
767 5th Avenue
42nd Floor
New York, NY 10153-0023
212-572-6966
Offers giving in the areas of elementary/secondary education, human services and religion.

Marjorie S Federbush, Executive Director

2639 SH & Helen R Scheuer Family Foundation
350 5th Avenue
Suite 3410
New York, NY 10118-0110
212-947-9009
Fax: 212-947-9770
Offers support in the areas of higher education, welfare funding and cultural programs.

2640 Samuel & May Rudin Foundation
345 Park Avenue
New York, NY 10154-0004
212-407-2544
Fax: 212-407-2540
Offers support for higher education, social services, religious welfare agencies, hospitals and cultural programs.

Susan H Rapaport, Executive Director

2641 Seth Sprague Educational and Charitable Foundation
C/O U.S. Trust Company of New York
114 W 47th Street
New York, NY 10036-1510
212-852-3683
Fax: 212-852-3377
Offers support in the areas of education, culture, the arts, human services, community development and government/public administration.

Maureen Augusciak, Executive Director

2642 Starr Foundation
70 Pine Street
New York, NY 10270-0002
212-770-6881
Fax: 212-425-6261
http://www.fdncenter.org/grantmaker/starr
Support is given for educational projects with an emphasis on higher education, including scholarships under specific programs.

Ta Chun Hsu, Executive Director

2643 Tiger Foundation
101 Park Avenue
47th Floor
New York, NY 10178-0002
212-984-2565
Fax: 212-949-9778
http://www.tigerfoundation.org
Support is given primarily for early childhood education, youth programs and job training.

Phoebe Boyer, Executive Director

2644 Tisch Foundation
667 Madison Avenue
New York, NY 10021-8029
212-545-2000
Support is given in the area of education, especially higher education, and includes institutions in Israel and research-related programs.

Laurence A Tisch, Executive Director

2645 Travelers Group
388 Greenwich Street
New York, NY 10013-2375
212-816-8000
Fax: 212-816-5944
The main purpose of this foundation is to support public education, offering grants in the communities that the company serves.

Dee Topol, Executive Director

2646 White Plains Public Library
100 Martine Avenue
White Plains, NY 10601-2599
914-422-1400
Fax: 914-422-1462
http://www.whiteplainslibrary.org
Member of The Foundation Center network, maintaining a collection of private foundation tax returns which provide information on the scope of grants dispensed by that particular foundation.

2647 William Randolph Hearst Foundation
888 7th Avenue
Floor 45
New York, NY 10106-0001
212-586-5404
Fax: 212-586-1917
http://www.hearstfdn.org
Offers support to programs that aid priority-level and minority groups, educational programs especially private secondary and higher education, health systems and cultural programs.

Robert M Frehse Jr, Executive Director
Ilene Mack, Senior Program Officer

2648 William T Grant Foundation
570 Lexington Avenue
Floor 18
New York, NY 10022-6837
212-752-0071
Fax: 212-752-1398
E-mail: info@wtgrantfdn.org
http://www.wtgrantfoundation.org

The goal of the foundation is to help create a society that values people and helps them to reach their potential. The Foundation is interested in environmentally friendly approaches

Edward Seidman, Senior VP Programs
Robert Granger, President

North Carolina

2649 AE Finley Foundation
1151 Newton Road
Raleigh, NC 27615
919-782-0565
Fax: 919-782-6978
Private foundation contributing and supporting to charitable, scientific, literary, religious and educational organizations. It endeavors to contribute to soundly managed and operated qualifying organizations which fundamentally give service with a broad scope and impact, aid all kinds of people and contribute materially to the general welfare.

Robert C Brown, Executive Director

2650 Cannon Foundation
PO Box 548
Concord, NC 28026-0548
704-786-8216
Fax: 704-785-2052
http://www.thecannonfoundationinc.org
Offers support for higher and secondary education, cultural programs, and grants to social service and youth agencies.

Frank Davis, Executive Director
William C Cannon Jr, President

2651 Dickson Foundation
301 S Tryon Street
Suite 1800
Charlotte, NC 28202
704-372-5404
Fax: 704-372-6409
Main focus is on areas of education & healthcare. Considers funding programs in the Southeast.

Susan Patterson, Secretary/Treasurer

2652 Duke Endowment
100 N Tryon Street
Suite 3500
Charlotte, NC 28202-4012
704-376-0291
Fax: 704-376-9336
http://www.dukeendowment.org
Support is given to higher education, children and youth services, churches and hospitals.

Eugene W Cochrane Jr, Executive Director

2653 First Union University
Two 1st Union Center
Charlotte, NC 28288
704-374-6868
Fax: 704-374-4147
Offers support for higher education and special programs for public elementary and secondary schools.

Ann D Thomas, Executive Director

2654 Foundation for the Carolinas
PO Box 3479
Charlotte, NC 28234
704-973-4500
800-973-7244
Fax: 704-376-1243
http://www.fftc.org

Offers support for education, the arts and health in North Carolina and South Carolina.

Michael Marsicano, President/CEO

2655 Kathleen Price and Joseph M Bryan Family Foundation
3101 N Elm Street
Greensboro, NC 27408-3184
336-288-5455
Grants are primarily offered in the fields of higher, secondary, and early childhood education.

William Massey, Executive Director

2656 Mary Reynolds Babcock Foundation
2920 Reynolda Road
Winston Salem, NC 27106-4618
336-748-9222
Fax: 336-777-0095
http://www.mrbf.org
This foundation traditionally provides funds to programs in education, social services, the environment, the arts and citizen participation in the development of public policy. The foundation prefers to fund programs of two kinds: those particularly sensitive to the changing and emerging needs of society and those addressing society's oldest needs in new and imaginative ways.

Gayle W Dorman, Executive Director
Sandra H Mikush, Assitant Director

2657 Non-Profit Resource Center/Pack Memorial Library
Learning Resources Center
67 Haywood Street
Asheville, NC 28801-4897
828-254-4960
Fax: 828-251-2258
http://www.buncombecounty.org
Cooperating collection of the Foundation Center. Other resources for non-profit organizations are also available.

Ed Sheary, Library Director

2658 State Library of North Carolina
Government & Business Services
109 E Jones Street
Raleigh, NC 27601-2806
919-807-7450
Fax: 919-733-5679
http://www.statelibrary.dcr.state.nc.us
Member of The Foundation Center network, maintaining a collection of private foundation tax returns which provide information on the scope of grants dispensed by that particular foundation.

2659 William R Kenan Jr Charitable Trust
Kenan Center
PO Box 3858
Chapel Hill, NC 27515-3858
919-962-0343
Fax: 919-962-3331
The focus of this foundation is on education, primarily at private institutions in the US. The emphasis now is on national literacy and the importance of early childhood education. Grants have just established an institute for the arts and an institute for engineering, technology and science. No grants are given to individuals for scholarships, for research or other special projects or for medical, public health or social welfare projects. This Trust does not accept unsolicited requests.

William C Friday, Executive Director

2660 Winston-Salem Foundation
860 W 5th Street
Winston Salem, NC 27101-2506
336-725-2382
Fax: 336-727-0581
http://www.wsfoundation.org
Educational grants and loans to residents of Forsyth County, North Carolina in most areas.

Scott Wierman, President
Donna Rader, VP Grants & Programs

2661 Z Smith Reynolds Foundation
147 S Cherry Street
Suite 200
Winston Salem, NC 27101
336-725-7541
800-443-8319
Fax: 336-725-6069
http://www.zsr.org
Grants are limited to the state of North Carolina. General purpose foundation provides for their current priorities including community economic development, women's issues, minority issues, environment and pre-collegiate education. No grants are given to individuals.

Thomas W Ross, Executive Director

North Dakota

2662 Myra Foundation
PO Box 13536
Grand Forks, ND 58208-3536
701-775-9420
Offers grants in the areas of secondary school, and higher education to residents of Grand Forks County, North Dakota.

Edward C Gillig, Executive Director

2663 Tom & Frances Leach Foundation
PO Box 1136
Bismarck, ND 58502-1136
701-255-0479
Offers grants in the areas of higher and other education in North Dakota.

Clement C Weber, Executive Director

Ohio

2664 Akron Community Foundation
345 W Cedar Street
Akron, OH 44307-2407
330-376-8522
Fax: 330-376-0202
E-mail: acf_fund@ix.netcom.com
http://www.akroncommunityfdn.org
The foundation receives donations to permanent endowment and makes grants to qualified nonprofit organizations within Summit County, Ohio.

Jody Bacon, President

2665 American Foundation Corporation
720 National City Bank Building
Cleveland, OH 44114
216-241-6664
Fax: 216-241-6693
Offers support in the areas of higher and secondary education, the arts and community funds.

Maria G Muth, Executive Director

2666 Burton D Morgan Foundation
PO Box 1500
Akron, OH 44309-1500
330-258-6512
Fax: 330-258-6559
http://www.bdmorganfdn.org
The foundation's present areas of interest include economics, education, mental health and organizations principally located in Northeast Ohio. No grants are made to individuals and few grants are made to social service organizations.

John V Frank, President

2667 Dayton Foundation
2300 Kettering Tower
Dayton, OH 45423-1395
937-222-0410
Fax: 937-222-0636
http://www.daytonfoundation.org
Educational and community service grants.

Michael M Parks, President

2668 Eva L & Joseph M Bruening Foundation
1422 Euclid Avenue
Suite 627
Cleveland, OH 44115-1952
216-621-2632
Fax: 216-621-8198
http://www.fmscleveland.com/bruening
Support is offered in the fields of education, early childhood education, education fund-raising, higher education, youth services and health agencies.

Janet E Narten, Executive Director

2669 GAR Foundation
50 S Main Street #1500
Akron, OH 44308-1828
330-643-0201
800-686-2825
Fax: 330-252-5584
http://www.garfdn.org
Established in 1967 as a charitable trust, the foundation offers grants to organizations located primarily in Akron, Ohio area or, secondarily, in Northeastern Ohio or elsewhere in the United States at the discretion of the Distribution Committee. Grants for research projects of educational or scientific institutions, capital improvement projects, or matching campaigns are the priorities of this foundation.

Richard A Chenoweth, Executive Director
Robert W Briggs, Co-Trustee

2670 George Gund Foundation
1845 Guildhall Building
45 Prospect Avenue
West Cleveland, OH 44115
216-241-3114
Fax: 216-241-6560
E-mail: info@gundfdn.org
http://www.gundfdn.org
The primary interest of this foundation is in educational projects, with an emphasis on inventive movements in teaching and learning, and on increasing educational opportunities for the disadvantaged.

David Abbott, Executive Director
Marcia Egbert, Senior Program Officer

2671 Hoover Foundation
101 E Maple Street
North Canton, OH 44720-2517
330-499-9200
Fax: 330-966-5433

Offers grants for elementary education, secondary and higher education and youth agencies.

LR Hoover, Executive Director

2672 Kettering Fund
40 N Main Street
Suite 1440
Dayton, OH 45423-1001
937-228-1021
Support is offered for social and educational studies and research as well as community development and cultural programs.

Richard F Beach, Executive Director

2673 Kulas Foundation
Tower City Center
50 Public Square
Suite 924
Cleveland, OH 44113-2203
216-623-4770
Fax: 216-623-4773
http://www.fdncenter.org/grantmaker/kulas/
A major general interest foundation, but with an emphasis on music. Giving is limited to Cuyahoga County and its surrounding area. Provides support to musical educational programs at Baldwin Wallace College, Case Western Reserve University and Cleveland Institute of Music. Also provides tickets to cultural programs to students in 16 colleges and universities in the area. The Foundation does not provide grants or loans to individuals. Support is geared to local primary and secondary schools.

Nancy W McCann, President/Treasurer

2674 Louise H & David S Ingalls Foundation
20600 Chagrin Boulevard
Suite 301
Shaker Heights, OH 44122-5334
216-921-6000
Offers support to organizations whose primary interest in the improvement of the educational, physical and mental condition of humanity throughout the world. Grants are given in secondary, elementary, and educational research.

Jane W Watson, Executive Director

2675 Louise Taft Semple Foundation
425 Walnut Street
Suite 1800
Cincinnati, OH 45202-3948
513-381-2838
Fax: 513-381-0205
Support is offered in the areas of secondary school/education, higher education, human services and health care organizations.

Dudley S Taft, Executive Director

2676 Martha Holden Jennings Foundation
Advisory & Distribution Committee Office
1228 Euclid Avenue
Suite 710
Cleveland, OH 44115-1831
216-589-5700
Fax: 216-589-5730
http://mhjf.org
The purpose of this foundation is to foster the development of young people to the maximum possible extent through improving the quality of teaching in secular elementary and secondary schools.

William T Hiller, Executive Director
Kathy L Kooyman, Grants Manager

2677 Mead Corporation Foundation
Courthouse Plz NE
Dayton, OH 45463-0001
937-495-3883
Fax: 937-495-4103
Grants are given to elementary, secondary, higher and minority education.

Ronald F Budzik, Executive Director

2678 Nord Family Foundation
747 Milan Avenue
Amherst, OH 44001
440-984-3939
Fax: 440-984-3934
http://www.nordff.org
Offers support for a variety of programs, including giving for early childhood, secondary, and higher education, social services, cultural affairs and civic activities.

David R Ashenhurst, Executive Director

2679 Ohio Bell Telephone Contribution Program
45 Erieview Plaza
Room 870
Cleveland, OH 44114-1814
216-822-4445
800-257-0902
Offers support of elementary school/education, secondary school/education, higher education, literacy and basic skills.

William W Boag Jr, Executive Director

2680 Ohio State Library Foundation Center
Kent H. Smith Library
1422 Euclid Avenue
Suite 1356
Cleveland, OH 44115-2001
216-861-1933
Fax: 216-861-1936
Member of The Foundation Center network, maintaining a collection of private foundation tax returns which provide information on the scope of grants dispensed by that particular foundation.

2681 Owens-Corning Foundation
PO Box 1688
Toledo, OH 43603-1688
419-248-8000
Fax: 419-325-4273
Offers support for education, including religious schools and science and technology programs.

Emerson J Ross, Executive Director

2682 Procter & Gamble Fund
PO Box 599
Cincinnati, OH 45201-0599
513-983-1100
Fax: 513-983-8250
Always considers the interests of the company's employees helping in the community, the arts, improving of schools and universities and to meet the needs of the less-fortunate neighbors. Some donations into the education program include grants to the United Negro College Fund, The National Hispanic Scholarship Fund, The Leadership Conference on Civil Rights Education Fund and more than 600 colleges and universities.

RL Wehling, President
G Talbot, VP

2683 Public Library of Cincinnati
Grants Resource Center
800 Vine Street #Library
Cincinnati, OH 45202-2009
513-369-6940
Fax: 513-369-6993
http://www.cincinnatilibrary.org
Member of The Foundation Center network, maintaining a collection of private foundation tax returns which provide information on the scope of grants dispensed by that particular foundation.

Kimber L Fender, Director

2684 Thomas J Emery Memorial
Frost & Jacobs
201 E 5th Street
Suite 2500
Cincinnati, OH 45202-4113
513-621-3124
Offers support in secondary school/education, higher education, health care, human services and arts/cultural programs.

Henry W Hobson Jr, Executive Director

2685 Timken Foundation of Canton
200 Market Avenue N
Suite 210
Canton, OH 44702-1622
330-452-1144
Fax: 330-455-1752
Offers support to promote the broad civic betterment including the areas of education, conservation and recreation. Grants restricted to caption projects only.

Don D Dickes, Secretary
Nancy Kuvdsen

2686 Wolfe Associates
34 S 3rd Street
Columbus, OH 43215-4201
614-461-5220
Fax: 614-469-6126
The foundation supports those organizations whose programs educate the individual and cultivate the individual's ability to participate in and contribute to the community or which enhance the quality of life which the community can offer to its citizens. The foundation has six general program areas in which it focuses its support: health and medicine, religion, education, culture, community service and environment.

AK Pierce Jr, Executive Director

Oklahoma

2687 Grace & Franklin Bernsen Foundation
15 W 6th Street
Suite 1308
Tulsa, OK 74119-5407
918-584-4711
Fax: 918-584-4713
E-mail: gfbersen@aol.com
http://www.bernsen.org
The foundation is limited by its policies to support of nonprofit organizations within the metropolitan area of Tulsa. The foundation discourages applications for general support or reduction of debt or for continuing or additional support for the same programs, although a single grant may cover several years. No grant is made to individuals or for the benefit of specific individuals and the applications must be received before the twelfth of each month.

John Strong Jr, Trustee

2688 Mervin Bovaird Foundation
100 W 5th Street
Suite 800
Tulsa, OK 74103-4291
918-583-1777
Fax: 918-592-5809
Awards scholarships to the University of Tulsa. Recipients are selected by Tulsa Area high schools and by Tulsa Junior College. No individual grants are made.

R Casey Cooper, President

2689 Oklahoma City University
Dulaney Brown Library
2501 N Blackwelder Avenue
Oklahoma City, OK 73106-1493
405-521-5000
Fax: 405-521-5291
Member of The Foundation Center network, maintaining a collection of private foundation tax returns which provide information on the scope of grants dispensed by that particular foundation.

Victoria Swinney, Director

2690 Public Service Company of Oklahoma Corporate Giving Program
212 E 6th Street #201
Tulsa, OK 74119-1295
918-586-0420
Offers support in the areas of elementary, secondary and higher education.

Mary Polfer, Executive Director

2691 Samuel Roberts Noble Foundation
PO Box 2180
Ardmore, OK 73402-2180
580-223-5810
Fax: 580-224-6380
http://www.noble.org
Offers support in the areas of higher education, agricultural research, human services and educational grants for health research pertaining to degenerative diseases, cancer and for health delivery systems.

Michael A Cawley, Executive Director

Oregon

2692 Collins Foundation
1618 SW 1st Avenue
Suite 305
Portland, OR 97201-5708
503-227-7171
Fax: 503-295-3794
http://www.collinsfoundation.org
Offers general support with an emphasis on higher education, hospices and health agencies, youth programs and arts and culture.

Jerry E Hudson, Executive Vice President
Cynthia G Adams, Director Of Programs

2693 Ford Family Foundation
1600 NW Stewart Parkway
Roseburg, OR 97470-0252
541-957-5574
Fax: 541-957-5720
E-mail: info@tfff.org
http://www.tfff.org
Giving is centered on education, youth organizations and human service programs in Oregon and Siskiyou County in California.

Bart Howard, Director Scholarship Program
Sarah Reeve, Scholarship Program Officer

2694 Meyer Memorial Trust
425 NW 10th Avenue
Suite 400
Portland, OR 97209
503-228-5512
Fax: 503-228-5840
E-mail: mmt@mmt.org
http://www.mmt.org
The Trust operates three different funding programs, all of which are restricted primarily to Oregon: 1) a broad-based General Purpose program that provides funds for education, arts, and humanities, health, social welfare, community development, and other activities; 2) a Small Grants program that provides up to $12,000 for small projects in the general purpose categories; and 3) the Support for Teacher Initiatives program, which provides grants of up to $7,000- to teachers.

Doug Stamm, Executive Director

2695 Multnomah County Library
Government Documents
801 SW 10th Avenue
Portland, OR 97205-2597
503-988-5123
Fax: 503-988-8014
http://www.multcolib.org
Member of The Foundation Center network, maintaining a collection of private foundation tax returns which provide information on the scope of grants dispensed by that particular foundation.

2696 Oregon Community Foundation
1221 SW Yamhill
Suite 100
Portland, OR 97205
503-227-6846
Fax: 503-274-7771
http://www.ocfl.org
The purpose of this foundation is to improve the cultural, educational and social needs in all levels of society throughout the state of Oregon.

Gregory A Chaille, Executive Director

2697 Tektronix Foundation
PO Box 1000
Wilsonville, OR 97070-1000
503-627-7111
http://www.tek.com
Offers support for education, especially science, math and engineering, and some limited art grants.

Jill Kirk, Executive Director

Pennsylvania

2698 Alcoa Foundation
201 Isabella Street
Pittsburgh, PA 15212-5858
412-553-2348
Fax: 412-553-4498
http://www.alcoa.com
Grants are given for education, arts and cultural programs.

F Worth Hobbs, Executive Director

2699 Annenberg Foundation
St. David's Center
150 N Radnor Chester Road
Suite A200
Saint Davids, PA 19087-5293
610-341-9066
Fax: 610-964-8688
E-mail: info@annenbergfoundation.org
http://www.annenbergfoundation.org

Primary support is given to childhood and K-12 education.

Dr. Gail C Levin Sr, Executive Director

2700 Arcadia Foundation

105 E Logan Street
Norristown, PA 19401-3058
215-275-8460
Gives only in Eastern Pennsylvania, no personal scholarships, accepts proposals only between June 1-August 15. These will be considered for the following calendar year. Proposal has to be no more than 2 pages long and longer submissions will be discarded. Must have a copy of the IRS tax-identified letter with no other enclosures.

Marilyn Lee Steinbright, Executive Director

2701 Audrey Hillman Fisher Foundation

2000 Grant Building
Pittsburgh, PA 15219
412-338-3466
Fax: 412-338-3463
Offers support for secondary school/education, higher education, rehabilitation, science and engineering.

Ronald W Wertz, Executive Director

2702 Bayer Corporation

100 Bayer Court
Pittsburgh, PA 15205
412-777-2000
Fax: 412-777-3468
http://www.bayerus.com/about/community/
Support is given primarily in education, especially science programs, chemistry and the arts.

Rebecca Lucore, Executive Director

2703 Buhl Foundation

650 Smithfield Street
Pittsburgh, PA 15222-1207
412-566-2711
Fax: 412-566-2714
Grants are given to colleges and universities, secondary schools and educational associations, community educational and training programs, and other community programs offering health and education to the community. Grants are not made for building funds, overhead costs, accumulated deficits, ordinary operating budgets, general fund-raising campaigns, loans, scholarships and fellowships, other foundations, nationally funded organized groups or individuals.

Dr. Doreen Boyce, President

2704 Connelly Foundation

One Tower Bridge
Suite 1450
West Conshohocken, PA 19428
610-834-3222
Fax: 610-834-0866
http://www.connellyfdn.org
Offers support for education, health, human service, culture and civic programs to nonprofit organizations located in the city of Philadelphia and the greater Delaware Valley region.

Victoria K Flaville, VP Administration
Josephine C Mandeville, President/CEO

2705 Eden Hall Foundation

Pittsburgh Office And Research Park
600 Grant Street
Suite 3232
Pittsburgh, PA 15219
412-642-6697
Fax: 412-642-6698
http://www.edenhallfdn.org
This foundation offers support for higher education, social welfare and the improvement of conditions of the poor and needy.

Sylvia V Fields, Program Director
George C Greer, Chairman/President

2706 Erie County Library System

160 E Front Street
Erie, PA 16507-1554
814-451-6927
Fax: 814-451-6969
http://www.ecls.lib.pa.us
Member of The Foundation Center network, maintaining a collection of private foundation tax returns which provide information on the scope of grants dispensed by that particular foundation.

2707 Foundation Center-Carnegie Library of Pittsburgh

Foundation Collection
4400 Forbes Avenue
Pittsburgh, PA 15213-4080
412-281-7143
Fax: 412-454-7001
E-mail: foundati@carnegielibrary.org
http://www.clpgh.org/clp/Foundation
Member of the Foundation Center network, of cooperating collections; providing current, factual information about grants and grantmaking organizations, and other aspects of philanthropy to the local nonprofit community.

Jim Lutton, Manager
Herb Elish, Director

2708 HJ Heinz Company Foundation

PO Box 57
Pittsburgh, PA 15230-0057
412-456-5772
Fax: 412-456-7859
E-mail: heinz.foundation@hjheinz.com
http://www.heinz.com/jsp/foundation.jsp
Offers support for higher education, employee matching gifts, social service agencies and cultural programs.

Loretta M Oken, Executive Director

2709 John McShain Charities

540 N 17th Street
Philadelphia, PA 19130-3988
215-564-2322
Offers support for higher and secondary education, Roman Catholic church support and social welfare.

Mary McShain, Executive Director

2710 Mary Hillman Jennings Foundation

625 Stanwix Street
Apt 2203
Pittsburgh, PA 15222-1408
412-434-5606
Fax: 412-434-5907
Offers grants to schools, youth agencies, and hospitals and health associations.

Paul Euwer Jr, Executive Director

2711 McCune Foundation

750 Six PPG Place
Pittsburgh, PA 15222
412-644-8779
Fax: 412-644-8059
http://www.mccune-db.mccune.org

The foundation provides support to independent higher education and human services.

Henry S Beukema, Executive Director

2712 Pew Charitable Trusts

One Commerce Square
2005 Market Street
Suite 1700
Philadelphia, PA 19103-7077
215-575-9050
Fax: 215-575-4939
http://www.pewtrusts.com
Offers support for education (including theology), arts culture, as well as public policy and religion.

Rebecca W Rimel, Executive Director

2713 Richard King Mellon Foundation

One Mellon Bank Center
500 Grant Street
Suite 4106
Pittsburgh, PA 15219-2502
412-392-2800
Fax: 412-392-2837
http://fdncenter.org/grantmaker/rkmellon/
Offers local grant programs with an emphasis on education, social services and the environment.

Seward Prosser Mellon, Trustee/President

2714 Rockwell International Corporation Trust

625 Liberty Avenue
Pittsburgh, PA 15222-3110
414-212-5200
Fax: 414-212-5201
Offers support in the areas of K-12 math and science education, and higher education in the field of engineering and science.

William R Fitz, Executive Director

2715 Samuel S Fels Fund

1616 Walnut Street
Suite 800
Philadelphia, PA 19103-5308
215-731-9455
Fax: 215-731-9457
http://www.samfels.org
Offers grants in continuing support that help prevent, lessen or resolve contemporary social problems including education, arts/cultural programs, and community development.

Helen Cunningham, Executive Director
Nell Williams, Office Administrator

2716 Sarah Scaife Foundation

Three Mellon Bank Center
301 Grant Street
Suite 3900
Pittsburgh, PA 15219-6402
412-392-2900
http://www.scaife.com
Offers grants in the areas of education and community development.

Joanne B Beyer, Executive Director
Michael W Gleba, Executive Vice President

2717 Shore Fund

C/O Melton Bank N.A.
PO Box 185
Pittsburgh, PA 15230-0185
412-234-4695
Fax: 412-234-3551
Although the foundation appreciates funding opportunities within the field of education, most grants given out have been to

schools with which the foundation's trustees have been personally involved.

Helen M Collins, Executive Director

2718 Stackpole-Hall Foundation
44 S Saint Marys Street
Saint Marys, PA 15857-1667
814-834-1845
Fax: 814-834-1869
Offers support for higher education and secondary education, literacy and vocational projects, social services, arts and cultural programs, and community development.

William C Conrad, Executive Director

2719 United States Steel Foundation
600 Grant Street
Suite 639
Pittsburgh, PA 15219-2800
412-433-5237
Fax: 412-433-2792
http://www.psc.uss.com/usxfound
Grants are awarded for capital development, special projects or operating needs. Support is limited to organizations within the United States, with preference to those in the US Steel Corporation's operating areas. US Steel does not award grants for religious purposes. Additionally, grants are not awarded for conferences, seminars or symposia, travel, publication of papers, books or magazines, or production of films, videotapes or other audiovisual materials.

Craig D Mallick, General Manager
Pamela E DiNardo, Program
Administrator

2720 William Penn Foundation
2 Logan Square 11th Floor
100 North 18th Street
Philadelphia, PA 19103-2757
215-988-1830
Fax: 215-988-1823
http://www.williampennfoundation.org
The foundation supports culture, environment, human development, including programs for youth and elderly, education, including early childhood, secondary, elementary and higher.

Kathryn J Engebretson, President

Rhode Island

2721 Champlin Foundations
300 Centerville Road
Suite 300 S
Warick, RI 02868
401-736-0370
Fax: 401-736-7248
E-mail: champlinfons@worldnet.att.net
http://www.fdncenter.org/grantmaker/champlin
Offers giving in the areas of higher, secondary and other education. Exclusively in Rhode Island.

David A King, Executive Director

2722 Providence Public Library
Reference Department
150 Empire Street
Providence, RI 02903-3219
401-455-8005
http://www.provlib.org
Member of The Foundation Center network, maintaining a collection of private foundation tax returns which provide infor-

mation on the scope of grants dispensed by that particular foundation.

Dale Thompson, Director

2723 Rhode Island Foundation
One Union Station
Providence, RI 02903-4630
401-274-4564
Fax: 401-331-8085
http://www.rifoundation.org
Promotes charitable activities which tend to improve the living conditions and well-being of the residents of Rhode Island.

Ronald V Gallo, President

South Carolina

2724 Charleston County Library
68 Calhoun Street
Charleston, SC 29401
843-805-6801
Fax: 843-727-3741
http://www.ccpl.org
Member of The Foundation Center network, maintaining a collection of private foundation tax returns which provide information on the scope of grants dispensed by that particular foundation.

Jan Buvinger, Director

2725 South Carolina State Library
1500 Senate Street
Columbia, SC 29201-3815
803-734-8666
Fax: 803-734-8676
http://www.state.sc.us/scsl/
Member of The Foundation Center network, maintaining a collection of private foundation tax returns which provide information on the scope of grants dispensed by that particular foundation.

James B Johnson Jr, Director

South Dakota

2726 South Dakota Community Foundation
207 E Capitol Avenue
Suite 296
Pierre, SD 57501-3159
605-224-1025
800-888-1842
Fax: 605-224-5364
http://www.sdcommunityfoundation.org
The mission of the foundation is to promote philanthropy, receive and administer charitable gifts and invest in a wide range of programs promoting the social and economic well being of the people of the South Dakota. Grants given in South Dakota only.

Bob Sutton, Executive Director

2727 South Dakota State Library
Reference Department
800 Governors Drive
Pierre, SD 57501-2294
605-773-5070
Fax: 605-773-4950
http://www.sdstatelibrary.com
Member of The Foundation Center network, maintaining a collection of private foundation tax returns which provide information on the scope of grants dispensed by that particular foundation.

Tennesse

2728 Benwood Foundation
736 Market Street
Chattanooga, TN 37402-4803
423-267-4311
Fax: 423-267-9049
The general purpose of this foundation is to support such religious, charitable, scientific, literary and educational activities as will promote the advancement of mankind in any part of the United States of America. It should be recognized by all prospective grantees that while the foundation is not limited to the Chattanooga, Tennessee area, the bulk of the grants are made to organizations in the immediate area.

Jean R McDaniel, Executive Director

2729 Christy-Houston Foundation
1296 Dow Street
Murfreesboro, TN 37130-2413
615-898-1140
Fax: 615-895-9524
Offers grants for education, arts, culture and health care to residents and organizations of Rutherford County, Tennessee.

James R Arnhart, Executive Director

2730 Frist Foundation
3100 West End Avenue
Suite 1200
Nashville, TN 37203
615-292-3868
Fax: 615-292-5843
http://www.fristfoundation.org
Broad general-purposed charitable foundation whose grants are restricted primarily to Nashville.

Peter F Bird Jr, President/CEO

2731 JR Hyde Foundation
First Tennessee Bank
PO Box 84
Memphis, TN 38101-0084
901-523-4883
Fax: 901-523-4266
Offers grants for higher education, including scholarships for the children of Malone and Hyde employees, community funds, secondary education and youth services.

JR Hyde III, Executive Director

2732 Lyndhurst Foundation
517 E 5th Street
Chattanooga, TN 37403
423-756-0767
Fax: 423-756-0770
http://www.lyndhurstfoundation.org
Support local arts and culture and downtown revitalzation efforts in Chattanooga. Support the protection and enhancement of the natural environment of the Southern Appalachian Region. Support the elementary and secondary public schools in Chattanooga.

Jack E Murrah, President

2733 Nashville Public Library
Business Information Division
615 Church Street
Nashville, TN 37219
615-862-5800
http://www.library.nashville.org
Member of The Foundation Center network, maintaining a collection of private foundation tax returns which provide information on the scope of grants dispensed by that particular foundation.

2734 Plough Foundation
6410 Poplar Avenue
Suite 710
Memphis, TN 38119-5736
901-761-9180
Fax: 901-761-6186
Offers grants for community projects, including a community fund, early childhood and elementary education, social service agencies and the arts.

Noris R Haynes Jr, Executive Director

2735 RJ Maclellan Charitable Trust
Provident Building
Suite 501
Chattanooga, TN 37402
423-755-1366
Supports higher and theological education, social services and youth programs.

Hugh O Maclellan Jr, Executive Director

Texas

2736 Albert & Ethel Herzstein Charitable Foundation
6131 Westview Drive
Houston, TX 77055-5421
713-681-7868
Fax: 713-681-3652
http://www.herzsteinfoundation.org
Concentrates support on temples and medical research with grants offered to medical schools.

L Michael Hajtman, President

2737 Burlington Northern Foundation
3800 Continental Plaza
777 Main Street
Fort Worth, TX 76102
817-352-6425
Fax: 817-352-7924
The major channel of philanthropy for Burlington Northern and its subsidiaries. The foundation administers a consistent contribution program in recognition of the company's opportunity to support and improve the general welfare and quality of life in communities it serves.

Beverly Edwards, President
Becky Blankenship, Grant Administrator

2738 Burnett Foundation
801 Cherry Street
Suite 1400
Fort Worth, TX 76102-6814
817-877-3344
Fax: 817-338-0448
Focus is on Fort Worth and Santa Fe, NM, seeking to be a positive force in the community, supporting the energy and creativity that exist in the nonprofit sector, and building capacity in organizations and people in the fields of education, health, community affairs, human services and arts and humanities.

Thomas F Beech, Executive Director

2739 Cooper Industries Foundation
PO Box 4446
Houston, TX 77210-4446
713-209-8607
Fax: 713-209-8982
E-mail: evans@cooperindustries.com
http://www.cooperindustries.com
The policy of this foundation is to carry out the responsibilities of corporate citizenship, by supporting nonprofit organizations in areas where employees are located, which best serve the educational, health,

welfare, civic, cultural and social needs of the foundation's communities. All gifts are consistent with the company's objectives to enhance the quality of life and to honor the principles and freedoms that have enabled the company to prosper and grow. Average Grant: $5,000.

Victoria Guennewig, President
Jennifer L Evans, Secretary

2740 Corpus Christi State University
Library-Reference Department
805 Comanche
Corpus Christi, TX 78401
361-880-7000
Fax: 361-880-7005
http://www.library.ci.corpus-christi.tx.us
Member of The Foundation Center network, maintaining a collection of private foundation tax returns which provide information on the scope of grants dispensed by that particular foundation.

Denise Landry

2741 Cullen Foundation
601 Jefferson Street
Floor 40
Houston, TX 77002-7900
713-651-8837
Fax: 713-651-2374
http://www.cullenfdn.org
Supports educational, medical purposes, community funds and conservation.

Alan M Stewart, Executive Director
Sue A Alexander, Grants Administrator

2742 Dallas Public Library
Urban Information
1515 Young Street
Dallas, TX 75201-5499
214-670-1487
Fax: 214-670-1451
http://www.dallaslibrary.org
Member of The Foundation Center network, maintaining a collection of private foundation tax returns which provide information on the scope of grants dispensed by that particular foundation.

2743 El Paso Community Foundation
Historic Cortez Building
310 North Mesa 10th Floor
El Paso, TX 79901
915-533-4020
Fax: 915-532-0716
http://www.epcf.org
Grants to 501(c)(3) organizations in the El Paso geographic area. Fields of interest are arts and humanities, education, environment, health and disabilities, human services and civic benefits. No grants to individuals are offered.

Janice Windle, President
Virginia Martinez, Executive VP

2744 Ellwood Foundation
PO Box 52482
Houston, TX 77052-2482
713-739-0763
Scholarships for social services and education.

H Wayne Hightower, Executive Director

2745 Eugene McDermott Foundation
3808 Euclid Avenue
Dallas, TX 75205-3102
214-521-2924
Offers support primarily for higher and secondary education, health, cultural programs, and general community interests.

Eugene McDermott, Executive Director

2746 Ewing Halsell Foundation
711 Navarro Street
Suite 535
San Antonio, TX 78205-1786
210-223-2649
Fax: 210-271-9089
Offers grants in the areas of art and cultural programs, education, medical research, human services and youth services.

2747 Exxon Education Foundation
5959 Las Colinas Boulevard
Irving, TX 75039-2298
972-444-1106
Fax: 972-444-1405
http://www.exxon.mobile.com
Grants are given in the areas of environment, education, public information and policy research, united appeals and federated drives, health, civic and community service organizations, minority and women-oriented service organizations, arts, museums and historical associations. In the education area grants are awarded to mathematics education programs, elementary and secondary school improvement programs, undergraduate general education programs, research, training and support programs.

EF Ahnert, Executive Director

2748 Fondren Foundation
7 TCT 37
PO Box 2558
Houston, TX 77252
713-236-4403
Provides support in various areas of interest with an emphasis on higher and secondary education, social services and cultural organizations.

Melanie Scioneaus, Executive Director

2749 George Foundation
310 Morton Street
PMB Suite C
Richmond, TX 77469-3135
281-342-6109
Fax: 281-341-7635
http://www.thegeorgefoundation.org
Offers giving for religious, educational, charitable or scientific purposes.

Roland Adamson, Executive Director

2750 Gordon & Mary Cain Foundation
8 E Greenway Plaza
Suite 702
Houston, TX 77046-0892
713-960-9283
Fax: 713-877-1824
The foundation is not limited to education but does contribute a large amount to that area. For a company to apply for a grant they must offer a statement of purpose or a summary of the project needing funding; budget with balance sheet, fund balance, distribution of funds, audited statement and number of employees; latest copy of IRS tax-exempt status letter 501(c)(3); current projects needing funding with amounts needed for entire project and the amount of the grant being requested.

James D Weaver, Executive Director

2751 Haggar Foundation
6113 Lemmon Avenue
Dallas, TX 75209-5715
214-352-8481
Fax: 214-956-4446
Offers support in various areas with an emphasis on higher and secondary education,

including a program for children of company employees.

Mary Vaughan Rumble, Executive Director

2752 Hobby Foundation
2131 San Felipe Street
Houston, TX 77019-5620
713-521-4694
Fax: 713-521-3950
Offers grants to educational facilities in the state of Texas.

Oveta Culp Hobby, Executive Director

2753 Houston Endowment
600 Travis Street
Suite 6400
Houston, TX 77002-3000
713-238-8100
Fax: 713-238-8101
E-mail: info@houstonendowment.org
http://www.houstonendowment.org
Offers support for charitable, religious or educational organizations.

H Joe Nelson III, Executive Director

2754 Houston Public Library
Bibliographic Information Center
500 McKinney Street
Houston, TX 77002-2534
832-238-9640
Fax: 832-393-1383
http://www.hpl.lib.tx.us/hpl/hplhome
Member of The Foundation Center network, maintaining a collection of private foundation tax returns which provide information on the scope of grants dispensed by that particular foundation.

2755 James R Dougherty Jr Foundation
PO Box 640
Beeville, TX 78104-0640
361-358-3560
Fax: 361-358-9693
Offers support for Roman Catholic church-related industries including education, higher, secondary and other education.

Hugh Grove Jr, Executive Director

2756 Leland Fikes Foundation
3050 Lincoln Plaza
500 N Akard
Dallas, TX 75201
214-754-0144
Fax: 214-855-1245
Giving is focused on education, youth services, family planning, public interest and cultural programs.

Nancy Solana, Executive Director

2757 MD Anderson Foundation
PO Box 2558
Houston, TX 77252-2558
713-658-2316
The purpose of this foundation is to improve lives in the areas of health care, education, human service, youth and research.

John W Lowrie, Executive Director

2758 Meadows Foundation
3003 Swiss Avenue
Wilson Historic Block
Dallas, TX 75204-6049
214-826-9431
800-826-9431
Fax: 214-824-0642
E-mail: besterline@mfi.org
http://www.mfi.org

Support is given in the area of arts and culture, civic and public affairs, education, health, including mental health, and human services.

Bruce Esterline, VP Grants
Carol Stabler, Director Communications

2759 Moody Foundation
2302 Post Office Street
Suite 704
Galveston, TX 77550-1994
409-763-5333
Fax: 409-763-5564
http://www.moodyf.org
Provides major support for two foundation-initiated projects: the Transitional Learning Center, a residential rehabilitation and research facility for the treatment of traumatic brain injury, and Moody Gardens, a world-class education and recreation complex that includes a 1-acre enclosed rainforest, the area's largest aquarium, a space museum, IMAX theater, and the Moody Hospitality Institute.

Peter M Moore, Grants Director

2760 Paul & Mary Haas Foundation
PO Box 2928
Corpus Christi, TX 78403-2928
361-887-6955
Offers scholastic grants to graduating high school seniors from Corpus Christi, Texas. The student must have above average grades and ability to prove financial need. The Foundation asks that the senior contact them in the Fall of his/her senior year in order to begin the in-house application process. The grant is a maximum of $1,500 per semester and is renewable for a total of eight semesters if the student maintains a 3.0 GPA. The student may attend college or university of his choice.

Karen Wesson, Executive Director

2761 Perot Foundation
12377 Merit Drive
Suite 1700
Dallas, TX 75251-2239
972-788-3000
Fax: 972-788-3091
Educational grants, medical research funding and grantmaking for the arts and cultural organizations.

Bette Perot, Executive Director

2762 RW Fair Foundation
PO Box 689
Tyler, TX 75710-0689
903-592-3811
Grants are given for secondary and higher education, church-related programs and legal education.

Wilton H Fair, Executive Director

2763 Sid W Richardson Foundation
309 Main Street
Fort Worth, TX 76102-4006
817-336-0494
Fax: 817-332-2176
E-mail: www.sidrichardson.org
This foundation was established for the purpose of supporting organizations that serve the people of Texas. Grants are given in the areas of education, health, the arts and human services.

Valleau Wilkie Jr, Executive Director

2764 Strake Foundation
712 Main Street
Suite 3300
Houston, TX 77002-3210
713-546-2400
Fax: 713-216-2401
Foundation gives primarily in Texas in the areas of operating budgets, continuing support, annual campaigns, special projects, research, matching funds and general purposes.

George W Strake Jr, Executive Director

2765 Trull Foundation
404 4th Street
Palacios, TX 77465-4812
361-972-5241
Fax: 361-972-1109
E-mail: trullfdn@ncnet.net
http://www.trullfoundation.org
1. A concern for the needs of the Palacios, Matagorda county are, where the foundation has its roots. Local health care, the senior center, and other local projects were considered and supported. 2. A concern for children and families. Grants are given to direct and channel lives away from child abuse, neglect from hunger, and poverty. 3. A concern for those persons and families devastated by the effects of substance abuse.

Gail Purvis, Executive Director
Lucja White, Administrative Assistant

Utah

2766 Marriner S Eccles Foundation
79 S Main Street
Salt Lake City, UT 84111-1901
801-246-5155
General support for Utah's human services, education and the arts programs.

Erma E Hogan, Executive Director

2767 Ruth Eleanor Bamberger and John Ernest Bamberger Memorial Foundation
136 S Main Street
Salt Lake City, UT 84101
801-364-2045
Fax: 801-322-5284
Offers support for secondary education, especially undergraduate scholarships for student nurses and for schools.

William H Olwell, Executive Director

2768 Salt Lake City Public Library
210 East 400 south
Salt Lake City, UT 84111-3280
801-524-8200
Fax: 801-524-8272
http://www.slcpl.lib.ut.us
Member of The Foundation Center network, maintaining a collection of private foundation tax returns which provide information on the scope of grants dispensed by that particular foundation.

Dana Tumtowsky, Comm Relations Coordinator
Nancy Tessman, Director

Vermont

2769 Vermont Community Foundation
PO Box 30
Three Court Street
Middlebury, VT 05753-0030
802-388-3355
Fax: 802-388-3398
http://www.vermontcf.org
Offers support for the arts and education, the environment, preservation of the community, public affairs and more for the betterment of Vermont.

Brian T Byrnes, President/CEO
Mary Conlon, Program Director

2770 Vermont Department of Libraries
Reference Services
109 State Street
Montpelier, VT 05609-0001
802-828-3268
Fax: 802-828-2199
http://www.dol.state.vt.us
Member of The Foundation Center network, maintaining a collection of private foundation tax returns which provide information on the scope of grants dispensed by that particular foundation.

2771 William T & Marie J Henderson Foundation
PO Box 600
Stowe, VT 05672-0600
Offers grants in the areas of elementary and secondary education.

William T Henderson, Executive Director

Virginia

2772 Beazley Foundation
3720 Brighton Street
Portsmouth, VA 23707-3902
757-393-1605
Fax: 757-393-4708
http://www.beazleyfoundation.org
The purpose of this foundation to further the causes of charity, education and religion. Offers support for higher, secondary and medical education, youth agencies, community agencies and development.

Richard Bray, President
Donna Russell, Associate Director

2773 Flagler Foundation
PO Box 644
Richmond, VA 23205
804-648-5033
Offers support for secondary and higher education, cultural programs and restoration.

Lawrence Lewis Jr, Executive Director

2774 Hampton Public Library
4207 Victoria Boulevard
Hampton, VA 23669-4200
757-727-1154
Fax: 757-727-1152
http://www.hampton.va.us
Member of The Foundation Center network, maintaining a collection of private foundation tax returns which provide information on the scope of grants dispensed by that particular foundation.

2775 Jeffress Memorial Trust
Bank Of America Private Bank
Po Box 26688
Richmond, VA 23261-6688
804-788-3698
Fax: 804-788-2700
http://www.wm.edu/grants/opps/jeffress.htm
Funds research in higher education.

Richard B Brandt, Advisor

2776 Kentland Foundation
PO Box 837
Berryville, VA 22611-0837
540-955-1082
Focuses on civic affairs organizations and education.

Helene Walker, Executive Director

2777 Longview Foundation for Education in World Affairs/International Understanding
8639 B Sixteenth Street
Box 211
Silver Spring, MD 20910
301-681-0899
Fax: 301-681-0925
http://www.fdncenter.org/grantmaker/longview/index.html
Offers grants and scholarships with an emphasis on pre-collegiate education, primarily elementary education, and also supports teacher education.

Betsy Devlin-Foltz, Director

2778 Richmond Public Library
Business, Science & Technology Department
101 E Franklin Street
Richmond, VA 23219-2193
804-646-7223
Fax: 804-646-4757
http://www.richmondpubliclibrary.org
Member of The Foundation Center network, maintaining a collection of private foundation tax returns which provide information on the scope of grants dispensed by that particular foundation.

2779 Virginia Foundation for Educational Leadership
2204 Recreation Drive
Virginia Beach, VA 23456-6178
757-430-2412
Fax: 757-430-3247

George E McGovern, Division Director

Washington

2780 Comstock Foundation
S 2607 SE Boulevard #B115
Spokane, WA 99223
509-534-6499
The Foundation contributes only to 501(c)(3) organizations, limited to Spokane County and its environs. In the field of general education, Comstock Foundation favors grants only to private institutions of higher learning, and no grants are made to individuals.

Horton Herman, Trustee
Charles M Leslie, Trustee

2781 Foster Foundation
1201 3rd Avenue
Suite 2101
Seattle, WA 98101-3086
206-624-5200

Offers support in art, culture, higher education, adult education, literacy and basic reading, health care and children and youth services.

Jill Goodsell, Executive Director

2782 MJ Murdock Charitable Trust
703 Broadway Street
Suite 701
Vancouver, WA 98660-3308
360-694-8415
Fax: 360-694-1819
http://www.murdock-trust.org
Offers support primarily for special projects of private organizations in the areas of education, higher education, human services and program development.

John Van Zytveld, Senior Program Director

2783 Seattle Foundation
200 5th Avenue
Suite 1300
Seattle, WA 98101-3151
206-622-2294
Fax: 206-622-7673
http://www.seattlefoundation.org
A community foundation that facilitates charitable giving; administers charitable funds, trusts and bequests; and distributes grants to non-profit organizations that are making a positive difference in our community. Grants are awarded to organizations working in areas that include social service, children and youth, civic, culture, elderly, conservation, education and health/rehabilitation.

Phyllis J Campbell, President/CEO
Molly Stearns, Senior Vice President

2784 Seattle Public Library
Science, Social Science
1000 4th Avenue
Seattle, WA 98104-1193
206-386-4636
Fax: 206-386-4634
http://www.spl.org
Member of The Foundation Center network, maintaining a collection of private foundation tax returns which provide information on the scope of grants dispensed by that particular foundation.

2785 Spokane Public Library
Funding Information Center
906 West Main Street
Spokane, WA 99201-0903
509-444-5300
Fax: 509-444-5364
http://www.spokanelibrary.org
Member of The Foundation Center network, maintaining a collection of private foundation tax returns which provide information on the scope of grants dispensed by that particular foundation.

Jan Sanders, Director

West Virginia

2786 Clay Foundation
1426 Kanawha Boulevard E
Charleston, WV 25301-3084
304-344-8656
Fax: 304-344-3805
Private charitable foundation making grants for health, education and programs for the aging or disadvantaged children.

Charles M Avampao, Executive Director

2787 Kanawha County Public Library
123 Capitol Street
Charleston, WV 25301-2686
304-343-4646
Fax: 304-348-6530
http://www.kanawha.lib.wv.us
Member of The Foundation Center network, maintaining a collection of private foundation tax returns which provide information on the scope of grants dispensed by that particular foundation.

2788 Phyllis A Beneke Scholarship Fund
Security National Bank & Trust Company
PO Box 511
Wheeling, WV 26003-0064
Offers support and scholarships for secondary education.

GP Schramm Sr, Executive Director

Wisconsin

2789 Faye McBeath Foundation
1020 N Broadway
Suite 112
Milwaukee, WI 53202-3157
414-272-2626
Fax: 414-272-6235
http://www.fayemcbeath.org
The purpose of the foundation is to provide Wisconsin people the best in education, child welfare, homes and care for the elderly and research in civics and government.

Scott E Gelzer, Executive Director
Aileen Mayer, Executive Assistant

2790 Lynde & Harry Bradley Foundation
1241 N Franklin Place
Milwaukee, WI 53202-2901
414-291-9915
Fax: 414-291-9991
http://www.bradleyfdn.org
The Foundation encourages projects that focus on cultivating a renewed, healthier and more vigorous sense of citizenship among the American people, and among peoples of all nations, as well. Grants are awarded to organizations and institutions exempt from federal taxation under Section 501(c)(3) and publicly supported under section 509(a), favor projects which are not normally financed by public tax funds, consider requests from religious organizations and institutions as well.

Michael W Grebe, President/CEO
Terri L Famer, Director Of Administration

2791 Marquette University Memorial Library
1415 W Wisconsin Avenue
Milwaukee, WI 53233-2287
414-288-1515
Fax: 414-288-5324
http://www.marquette.edu/library/
Member of The Foundation Center network, maintaining a collection of private foundation tax returns which provide information on the scope of grants dispensed by that particular foundation.

2792 Siebert Lutheran Foundation
2600 N Mayfair Road
Suite 390
Wauwatosa, WI 53226-1392
414-257-2656
Fax: 414-257-1387
E-mail: rdjslf@execpc.com
http://www.siebertfoundation.org
Offers support in elementary and secondary, higher education and early childhood education.

Ronald D Jones, President
Deborah Engel, Administrative Assistant

2793 University of Wisconsin-Madison
Memorial Library
728 State Street
Madison, WI 53706-1418
608-262-3242
Fax: 608-262-8569
E-mail: grantsinfo@library.wisc.edu
http://www.grants.library.wisc.edu
Member of The Foundation Center network, maintaining a collection of private foundation tax returns which provide information on the scope of grants dispensed by that particular foundation.

Wyoming

2794 Natrona County Public Library
307 E 2nd Street
Casper, WY 82601-2598
307-237-4935
Fax: 307-266-3734
http://www.library.natrona.net
Member of The Foundation Center network, maintaining a collection of private foundation tax returns which provide information on the scope of grants dispensed by that particular foundation.

Grants, Federal & Private

2795 American Honda Foundation
PO Box 2205
Torrance, CA 90509-2205
310-781-4090
Fax: 310-781-4270
http://www.hondacorporate.com/community
Offers support for national organizations whose areas of interest include youth and scientific education. Grants reach private elementary, secondary, higher, vocational and scientific education.

Kathryn A Carey, Manager

2796 Awards for University Administrators and Librarians
Association of Commonwealth Universities
John Foster House
36 Gordon Square
London WC1H OPF, England
171 3878572
Fax: 171 3872655
E-mail: pubinfo@acu.ac.uk;
acusales@acu.ac.uk
Lists approximately 40 sources of financial assistance for administrative and library staff for universities worldwide. Includes name, address, phone, fax, tenure place and length, amount of aid, requirements for eligibility and application procedure, and frequency and number of grants available.
40 pages Biennial
ISSN: 0964-2714

Moira Hunter, Editor

2797 Awards for University Teachers and Research Workers
Association of Commonwealth Universities
36 Gordon Square
London
WC1H OPF, England
44-20-7380-6700
Fax: 44-20-7387-2655
E-mail: info@devry.edu
http://www.devry.edu
Lists approximately 740 awards open to university teachers and research workers in one country for research, study visits or teaching at a university in another country. Offers fellowships, visiting professorships and lectureships and travel grants.
364 pages Biennial
ISSN: 0964-2706

2798 Educational Foundation of America
35 Church Lane
Westport, CT 06880-3515
203-226-6498
Fax: 203-227-0424
http://www.efaw.org
Funds projects in arts, education and programs benefiting Native Americans.

Diane M Allison, Executive Director

2799 Foundation Center
79 5th Avenue
Floor 8
New York, NY 10003-3076
212-620-4230
Fax: 212-807-3677
http://www.fdncenter.org
A national service organization which disseminates information on private giving through public service programs, publications, and through a national network of library reference collections for free public use. Over 100 network members have sets of private foundation information returns, and the New York, Washington, DC, Cleveland and San Francisco reference collections operated by the Foundation offer a wide variety of services and collections of information on foundations and grants.

Cheryl Loe, Director Of Communications
Laura Cascio, Fulfillment Management

2800 GTE Foundation
PO Box 152257
Irving, TX 75015-2257
972-507-5434
Fax: 972-615-4310
http://www.gte.com
The emphasis of giving for the foundation is on higher education in math, science and technology. It also sponsors scholarships and supports community funds and social service agencies that emphasize literacy training.

Maureen Gorman, VP

2801 George I Alden Trust
370 Main Street
Worcester, MA 01608-1714
508-798-8621
Fax: 508-791-6454
http://www.aldentrust.org
Gives to higher education organizations and facilities with an emphasis on scholarship endowments.

Francis H Dewey III, Executive Director

2802 Gershowitz Grant and Evaluation Services
505 Merle Hay Tower
Des Moines, IA 50310
515-270-1718
Fax: 515-270-8325
E-mail: gershowitz@netins.net
To give schools an edge in funding their technology programs
Michael V Gershowitz, PhD
Steve Panyan, PhD

2803 Grants and Contracts Service
Department of Education/Regional Office Building
7th & D Streets
Suite 3124
Washington, DC 20202-0001
202-401-2000
Fax: 202-260-7225
To support improvements in teaching and learning and to help meet special needs of schools and students in elementary and secondary education
Gary J Rasmussen, Director

2804 Grantsmanship Center
PO Box 17220
Los Angeles, CA 90017-0220
213-482-9860
Fax: 213-482-9863
E-mail: norton@tgci.com
http://www.tgci.com
The world's oldest and largest training organization for the nonprofit sector. Since it was founded in 1972, the has trained trains more than 75,000 staff members of public and private agencies; training provided includes grantsmanship, program management and fundraising. Center also produces publications on grantsmanship, fundraising, planning, management and personnel issues for nonprofit agencies.
Norton Kiritz, President

2805 John S & James L Knight Foundation
Wachovia Financial Center
Suite 3300
200south Biscayne Boulevard
Miami, FL 33131-2349
305-908-2635
http://www.knightfdn.org
The foundation makes national grants in journalism, education and the field of arts and culture. It also supports organizations in communities where the Knight brothers were involved in publishing newspapers but is wholly separate from and independent of those newspapers.
James D Spaniolo, Executive Director

2806 National Academy of Education
School of Education
Ceras 108
Stanford, CA 94305
212-998-9035
Fax: 212-995-4435
Offers the Spencer Postdoctoral Fellowship which is designed to promote scholarship in the United States and abroad on matters relevant to the improvement of education in all its forms.
Debbie Leong-Childs, Executive Director

2807 National Science Foundation
4201 Wilson Boulevard
Arlington, VA 22230
703-292-5111
Fax: 703-292-9184
http://www.nsf.gov

Offers grants, workshops and curricula for all grade levels.
Arden L Bement Jr, Director

2808 Trust to Reach Education Excellence
1904 Association Drive
Reston, VA 20191-1537
703-860-0200
800-253-7746
Fax: 703-476-5432
E-mail: tree@principals.org
http://http://tree.principals.org
Founded to make grants to educators and students who would ordinarily not have access to outstanding NASSP programs, such as camps, programs and workshops on leadership, technology and school reform.
Dr. Anne Miller, Executive Director

2809 Union Carbide Foundation
39 Old Ridgebury Road
Danbury, CT 06817-0001
203-794-6945
Fax: 203-794-7031
Offers grants in the areas of elementary and secondary education, with an emphasis on systemic reform; higher education with a focus on science and engineering; and environmental protection awareness.
Nancy W Deibler, Executive Director

2810 United States Institute of Peace
1200 17th Street NW
Washington, DC 20036
202-457-1700
Fax: 202-429-6063
http://www.usip.org
Includes grants, fellowships, a National Peace Essay Contest for high school students and teacher training institutes.
Richard H Solomon, President

2811 United States-Japan Foundation
145 E 32nd Street
Floor 12
New York, NY 10016-6055
212-481-8753
Fax: 212-481-8762
E-mail: info@us-jf.org
http://www.us-jf.org
A nonprofit, philanthropic organization with the principal mission of promoting a greater mutual knowledge between United States and Japan and to contribute to a strengthened understanding of important public policy issues of interest to both countries. Currently the focus is on precollegiate education, policy studies, and communications and public opinion.

2812 Westinghouse Foundation
Westinghouse Electric Corporation
Po Box 355
ECE 575C
Pittsburgh, PA 15230-0355
412-374-6824
Fax: 412-642-4874
Http://www.westinghousenuclear.com
Makes charitable contributions to community priorities primarily where Westinghouse has a presence. Areas of emphasis include: education, health and welfare, culture and the arts and civic and social grants. Support for education is central to Westinghouse's contributions program, particularly higher education in the areas of engineering, applied science and business. Also encourages educational programs that

strengthen public schools through enhanced student learning opportunities.
G Reynolds Clark, Executive Director

2813 Xerox Foundation
800 Long Ridge Road #1600
Stamford, CT 06902-1227
203-968-3445
http://www.xerox.com
Offers giving in the areas of higher education to prepare qualified men and women for careers in business, government and education.
Joseph M Cahalan, Executive Director

Fundraising

2814 A&L Fund Raising
95 Leggett Street
East Hartford, CT 06108-1140
860-242-2476
800-286-7247
Offers many successful fundraising programs including Christmas gifts, designer gift wraps from Ashley Taylor and Geoffrey Boehm chocolates. A&L sells only the highest quality items at affordable prices with great service to schools and organizations.
Anita Brown

2815 A+ Enterprises
1426 Route 33
Hamilton Square, NJ 08690-1704
609-587-1765
800-321-1765
A promotional corporation offering a variety of fundraising programs for schools and educational institutions, ranging from Christmas campaigns to chocolates, as well as magnets and gift campaigns.

2816 Aid for Education
CD Publications
8204 Fenton Street
Sliver Spring, MD 20910
301-588-6380
800-666-6380
Fax: 301-588-0519
E-mail: afe@cdpublications.com
http://cdpublications.com
18 pages Newsletter
ISSN: 1058-1324
Frank Kimko, Editor

2817 All Sports
21 Round Hill Road
Wethersfield, CT 06109
860-721-0273
800-829-0273
Fax: 860-257-9609
http://www.graduationshirts.com
Fundraising and school promotion company offering crew sweatshirts, hoods, tees, jackets, caps, gymwear and specialty signature shirts for graduating classes.
Wally Schultz, Owner

2818 Art to Remember
5535 Macy Drive
Indianapolis, IN 46236
317-826-0870
800-895-8777
Fax: 317-823-2822
E-mail: brackney@arttoremember.com
http://www.arttoremember.com
Raises funds for art departments and special school programs.

2819 Childrens Youth Funding Report
CD Publications
8204 Fenton Street
Sliver Spring, MD 20910
301-588-6380
800-666-6380
Fax: 301-588-0519
E-mail: cye@cdpublications.com
http://cdpublications.com
Detailed coverage of federal and private grant opportunities and legislative initiatives effecting childrens programs in such areas as child welfare, education healthcare.
18 pages Monthly
Steve Albright, Editor

2820 Dutch Mill Bulbs
25 Trinidad Avenue
PO Box 407
Hershey, PA 17033-1386
717-534-2900
800-533-8824
Fax: 800-556-0539
E-mail: info@dutchmillbulbs.com
http://www.dutchmillbulbs.com
Fundraising with flower bulbs since 1960. 50% profit-no hidden costs. Guaranteed to bloom. Free shipping. No cash up front.
Jeffrey E Ellenberger, President

2821 E-S Sports Screenprint Specialists
47 Jackson Street
Holyoke, MA 01040-5512
413-534-5634
800-833-3171
Fax: 413-538-8648
Scholastic Spirit Division offers screenprinted T-shirts, sweatshirts, shorts and apparel. This program offers schools and organizations an easy way to increase school spirit with no risk, no minimum orders and prompt delivery.
Aaron Porchelli, Division Director

2822 Fundraising USA
1395 State Route 23
Butler, NJ 07405-1736
973-283-1946
800-428-6178
Fundraiser offering a variety of programs for schools and organizations including Walk-A-Thons. This program is fast becoming the most popular way for schools to raise money. The walks are designed to take place at your own school, and children are not responsible for collecting any money. Fundraising USA collects all donations through the mail.

2823 Gold Medal Products
10700 Medallion Drive
Cincinnati, OH 45241-4807
513-769-7676
800-543-0862
Fax: 513-769-8500
E-mail: info@gmpopcorn.com
http://www.gmpopcorn.copm
Offers a full line of fundraising products popcorn poppers and supplies and programs including candy, clothing and sports programs for schools and colleges.
Chris Petroff
Dan Kroeger, President

2824 Human-i-Tees
400 Columbus Avenue
Valhalla, NY 10595-1335
800-275-2638
Fax: 914-745-1799
http://www.humanitees.com

Environmental T-shirt fundraisers that provide large profits while raising environmental awareness for thousands of school, youth and service organizations across the country.

2825 Hummel Sweets
PO Box 232
Forestville, MD 20747
800-998-8115
Offer fundraising programs with 45% to 50% profit.

2826 M&M Mars Fundraising
800 High Street
Hackettstown, NJ 07840-1552
908-852-1000
Fax: 908-850-2734
Offers America's favorite candies for fundraising programs throughout the year.

2827 QSP
Subsidiary of the Reader's Digest Association
PO Box 2003
Ridgefield, CT 06877-0903
203-756-3022
For twenty-seven years, this fundraiser has helped students raise more than $900,000,000 for extracurricular programs and projects that are essential to a meaningful, well-rounded education. With QSP programs, students earn money to fund worthwhile projects and learn about the business world at the same time. QSP offers various fundraising programs including: Family Reading Programs; The Music Package; Delightful Edibles; and The Parade of Gifts.
Robert L Metivier, Sales Manager

2828 Sally Foster Gift Wrap
PO Box 539
Duncan, SC 29334-0539
800-552-5875
Fax: 800-343-0809
Fundraiser offers gift wrap packages to schools. Offers high quality merchandise, including the heaviest papers and foils available. This proven two-week program is quick, easy and profitable offering your school or organization the opportunity to raise thousands of dollars to buy computers, books, athletic equipment and more. Organizations and schools keep 50% of all the profits, and there are no up-front costs or risks.
Mark Metcalfe, Sr VP

2829 School Identifications
Chas. E. Petrie Comapny
PO Box 12
Long Beach, CA 90801-0012
562-591-0666
800-772-0798
Fax: 562-591-0071
E-mail: info@schoolidents.com
http://www.schoolidents.com
An easy fundraising project for schools, offering school identification cards and tags for students.

2830 School Memories Collection
Fundcraft Publishing
PO Box 340
Collierville, TN 38027
901-853-7070
800-390-2129
Fax: 901-853-6196
E-mail: info@schoolplanners.com
http://www.schoolmemories.com

Memory books with games and activities.
Chris Bradley, Marketing Director

2831 Sports Shoes & Apparel
3 Moulton Drive
Londonderry, NH 03053-4061
603-437-7844
800-537-7844
Fax: 603-437-2300
Offers customized sweatshirts, T-shirts and beach towels at group discount, with several complete fund raising programs being available as well. Beach towels for fundraising.
Bill McMahon, Regional Manager

2832 Steve Wronker's Funny Business
39 Boswell Road
W Hartford, CT 06107-3708
860-233-6716
800-929-swfb
Fax: 860-561-8910
http://www.swfb.net/swfb.htm
Comedy and educational magic shows available for preschool and elementary school aged children. Award winning programs such as The Magic of Books and Magic from Around the World are available for any size audience. For middle schools and high schools, comedy hypnosis is a perfect venue for entertainment as a fundraising program, for high school after-prom parties, graduation parties, or just for an evening's entertainment.
Steve Wronker

2833 T-Shirt People/Wearhouse
10722 Hanna Street
Beltsville, MD 20705-2123
301-937-4843
800-638-7070
Fax: 301-937-2916
Fundraiser offering customized T-shirts to boost school spirit, raise funds, instill school pride and save money.

2834 Troll Book Fairs
100 Corporate Drive
Mahwah, NJ 07430-2041
201-529-4000
Fax: 201-529-8282
A profit-making program designed to introduce children to the wonderful world of books.

2835 Union Pen Company
70 Riverdale Avenue
Greenwich, CT 06831
800-846-6600
Fax: 800-688-4877
E-mail: unionpen@aol.com
http://www.unionpen.com
This company offers advertising gifts including customized pens and key chains that will increase confidence, school spirit and community goodwill in education. Group discounts are available.
Matt Roberts, General Manager
Morton Tenny, President

2836 www.positivepins.com
802 E 6th Streetve
PO Box 52528
Tulsa, OK 74152
918-587-2405
800-282-0085
Fax: 918-382-0906
E-mail: pinrus@aol.com
http://www.thepinman-pins.com
Fundraising organization used by educational organizations. Designer and manu-

facturer of lapel pins used for employee service, appreciation, volunteer recognition, donor incentives and recognition, public relations and spirit.

Bern L Gentry, President
Michelle Anderson, VP

Scholarships & Financial Aid

2837 AFL-CIO Guide to Union Sponsored Scholarships, Awards & Student Aid
AFL-CIO
815 16th Street NW
Suite 407
Washington, DC 20006-4104
202-637-5000
http://www.unionplus.org
Lists international and national unions, local unions, state federations and labor councils offering scholarships, awards or financial aid to students.

100 pages Annual

2838 American-Scandinavian Foundation
58 Park Avenue
New York, NY 10016
212-879-9779
Fax: 212-249-3444
E-mail: info@amscan.org
http://www.amscan.org
The Foundation provides information, scholarships and grants on the study programs in Scandinavia.

Andrey Henkin, Assistant
Fellowship/Grant

2839 Arts Scholarships
Jewish Foundation for Education of Women
135 E 64th Street
New York, NY 10019-1827
212-288-3931
Fax: 212-288-5798
E-mail: fdnscholar@aol.com
http://www.jfew.org
These scholarships are being offered at the Julliard School, Tisch School, of the Arts at New York University, and the Manhattan School of Music to qualified students enrolled in their programs. Faculty members will select recipients.

Marge Goldwater, Executive Director

2840 CUNY Teacher Incentive Program
Jewish Foundation for Education of Women
135 E 64th Street
New York, NY 10019-1827
212-288-3931
Fax: 212-288-5798
E-mail: fdnscholar@aol.com
http://www.jfew.org
Provide stipends to CUNY graduates who are studying for a master's degree in education and interested in a teaching career in the New York City public school system. Contact the office of the Vice Chancellor for Academic Affairs at CUNY for further information.

Marge Goldwater, Executive Director

2841 College Board
45 Columbus Avenue
New York, NY 10023-6992
212-713-8000
Fax: 212-713-8282
http://www.collegeboard.org
The College Board is a national, nonprofit membership association that supports educational transitions through programs and services in assessment, guidance, admission, placement, financial aid, and educational reform.

2842 Dissertation Fellowships in the Humanities
Jewish Foundation for Education of Women
330 W 58th Street
New York, NY 10019-1827
212-883-9315
Fax: 212-288-5798
E-mail: fdnscholar@aol.com
http://www.jfew.org
A small number of fellowships will be awarded through the CUNY Graduate Center to qualified applicants.

Marge Goldwater, Executive Director

2843 George & Mary Kremer Foundation
1100 5th Avenue S
Suite 411
Naples, FL 34102-7415
941-261-2367
Fax: 941-261-1494
Provides scholarship funding for needy children in elementary Catholic schools throughout the Continental United States.

Mary Anderson Goddard, Director
Sister MT Ballrach, Assistant Director

2844 Intel Science Talent Search Scolarship
1719 N Street NW
Washington, DC 20036-2888
202-785-2255
Fax: 202-785-1243
E-mail: sciedu@sciserv.org
http://www.sciserv.org
Offers a variety of services to teachers and students, including Intel Science Talent Search Scholarship competition, science fairs and publications.

2845 Jewish Foundation for Education of Women
330 W 58th Street
New York, NY 10019-1827
212-288-3931
Fax: 212-288-5798
E-mail: fdnscholar@aol.com
http://www.jfew.org
The Jewish Foundation for Education of Women is a private, nonsectarian foundation providing scholarships to women for higher education in the New York City area. A variety of specific programs are available. Most programs are administered collaboratively with area schools and organizations; the Foundation's mission is to help women of all ages attain the education and training needed to make them productive, economically independent members of the community.

Marge Goldwater, Executive Director

2846 Octameron Associates
1900 Mount Vernon Avenue
Alexandria, VA 22301-0748
703-836-5480
Fax: 703-836-5650
E-mail: info@octameron.com
http://www.octameron.com
Octameron is a publishing and consulting firm with over 25 years experience in financial aid and admissions.

2847 Scholarship America
One Scholarship Way
Saint Peter, MN 56082-1556
507-931-1682
800-537-4180
Fax: 507-931-9250
E-mail: dsnatoff@aol.com
http://dollarsforscholars.org
Provides community volunteers with the tools and support to create, develop and sustain legally constituted community-based scholarship foundations. Over 15,000 volunteers are active on 760 Dollars for Scholars chapter boards and committees throughout the United States. In addition, 20,000 high school youth and community residents are active in fund-raising events and academic support programs. Since the late 1950's, over 155,000 students have received Dollars for Scholars scholarships.

David Bach, VP

2848 Scholarships in the Health Professions
Jewish Foundation for Education of Women
135 E 64th Street
New York, NY 10021
212-288-3931
Fax: 212-288-5798
E-mail: fdnscholar@aol.com
http://www.jfew.org
Provides scholarships to emigres from the former Soviet Union who are studying medicine, dentistry, nursing, pharmacy, OT, PT, dental hygiene, and physician assistanceship.

Marge Goldwater, Executive Director

Federal Listings

2849 Accounting & Financial Management Services
Department of Education/1175 Main Building
400 Maryland Avenue SW
Washington, DC 20202-0001
Fax: 202-401-0207

Mitchell L Laine, Chief Officer

2850 Assistance to States Division
Department of Education/3042 Mary E. Switzer Bldg.
330 C Street
Washington, DC 20202
202-401-2000
Fax: 202-260-7225

Tom Irvin, Acting Director

2851 Civil Rights
Department of Education/Mary E. Switzer Building
330 C Street
Suite 50001
Washington, DC 20202
202-205-5413
Fax: 202-260-7225

Norma Y Canto, Assistant Secretary

2852 Compensatory Education Program
US Department of Education
400 Maryland Avenue SW
Washington, DC 20202
202-260-0826
Fax: 202-260-7764

Mary Jean LeTendre, Director

2853 Elementary & Secondary Education
Department of Education/4000 Portals Building
1250 Maryland Avenue SW
Washington, DC 20024-2141
202-401-0113
Fax: 202-205-0303

Thomas W Payzant, Assistant Secretary

2854 Elementary Secondary Bilingual & Research Branch
Department of Education/Regional Office Bldg.
7th & D Streets
Suite 3653
Washington, DC 20202
202-401-0113
Fax: 202-260-7225

Queenola Tyler, Bureau Chief

2855 Elementary, Secondary & Vocational Analysis
Department of Education
400 Maryland Avenue SW
3043 Main Building
Washington, DC 20202-0001
202-401-0318
Fax: 202-260-7225

Thomas Corwin, Division Director

2856 Human Resources and Administration
Department of Education/3181 Main Building
400 Maryland Avenue SW
Washington, DC 20202-0001
202-401-0470
Fax: 202-260-7225

Rodney A McCowan, Assistant Secretary

2857 International Educational Exchange
Teacher Exchange, Off. of International Education
US Department of Education
Washington, DC 20202
202-708-5366
Offers educational information on student and teacher exchanges abroad.

2858 Legislation & Congressional Affairs
Department of Education/3153 Main Building
400 Maryland Avenue SW
Washington, DC 20202-0001
202-401-0020
Fax: 202-260-7225

Kay Casstevens, Assistant Secretary

2859 Library Programs
Department of Education
402 Capitol Place
555 New Jersey
Washington, DC 20202
202-219-2293
Fax: 202-260-7225

Inez Frazier, Administrative Officer

2860 Management Services
Department of Education/3005 Main Building
400 Maryland Avenue SW
Washington, DC 20202-0001
202-401-0500
Fax: 202-260-7225

2861 National Center for Education Statistics
Department of Education
400 Capitol Place
555 New Jersey
Washington, DC 20202
202-401-2000
Fax: 202-260-7225

Emerson J Elliott, Commissioner

2862 National Council on Disability
1331 F Street
Suite 1050
Washington, DC 20004-1107
202-272-2004
Fax: 202-272-2022
E-mail: mquighley@ncd.gov
http://www.ncd.gov/
An independent federal agency comprised of 15 members appointed by the President and confirmed by the Senate.

2863 National Institute of Child Health and Human Development
Office of Research Reporting
Building 31 Room 2A32
MSC 2425
Bethesda, MD 20892-2425
301-496-5133
Fax: 301-496-7101
http://www.nichd.nih.gov
Develops research to solve problems in the physical and mental evolution of develop-

ment. Including some of the most emotionally draining disorders, learning disabilities, behavioral disabilities, birth defects and infant mortality. Acts as a clearinghouse of materials, information and referrals and more.

Duane Alexander, Director
Yvonne Thompson Maddox, Deputy Director

2864 National Trust for Historic Preservation: Office of Education Initiatives
1785 Massachusetts Avenue NW
Washington, DC 20036-2117
202-588-6296
http://www.nationaltrust.org
Teaching with Historic Places, a program offered by the National Park Service's National Register of Historic Places, and the National Trust for Historic Preservation Press.

2865 No Child Left Behind
Department of Education
400 Maryland Avenue, SW
Washington, DC 20202
202-401-2000
800-872-5327
Fax: 202-401-0689
http://www.ed.gov/nclb

Margaret Spelling, Secretary of Education

2866 Office of Bilingual Education and Minority Language Affairs
Department of Education/5082 Mary E. Switzer Bldg.
330 C Street
Washington, DC 20202
202-205-5463
Fax: 202-260-7225

Eugene E Garcia, Division Director

2867 Office of Indian Education
Department of Education/4300 Portals Building
1250 Maryland Avenue SW
Washington, DC 20024-2141
202-260-3774
Fax: 202-260-7225

John Wade, Division Director

2868 Office of Migrant Education
Department of Education/4100 Portals Building
1250 Maryland Avenue SW
Washington, DC 20024-2141
202-260-1164
Fax: 202-260-7225

Francis Corrigan, Division Director

2869 Office of Overseas Schools
US Department of State
US Department of State
Room H 328, SA 1
Washington, DC 20522-0132
202-261-8200
Fax: 202-261-8224
E-mail: OverseasSchools@state.gov
http://www.state.gov
Maintains detailed information on 190 overseas elementary and secondary schools which receive some assistance from the US Department of State. These schools provide an American-type education which prepares students for schools, colleges and universities in the United States.

Dr. Keith D Miller, Director

2870 Office of Public Affairs
Department of Education/4181 Main
Building
400 Maryland Avenue SW
Washington, DC 20202-0001
202-401-3026
Fax: 202-260-7225

Kay Kahler, Division Director

**2871 Office of Special Education
Programs**
Department of Education/3086 Mary E.
Switzer Bldg.
600 Independence Avenue SW
Washington, DC 20202-2570
202-205-5507
Fax: 202-260-7225
E-mail: thomas_hehir@ed.gov
http://www.ed.gov./offices/osers/idea/inde
x.htm

Thomas Hehir, Director

**2872 Office of Student Financial
Assistance Programs**
Department of Education/5102 Regional
Office Bldg.
7th & D Sts
Washington, DC 20202-0001
202-401-2000
Fax: 202-260-7225

Leo Kornfeld, Deputy Assistant

2873 Planning & Evaluation Service
Department of Education
Elementary Secondary Division
3127 Main Building, 400 Maryland
Washington, DC 20202
202-401-1968
Fax: 202-260-7225

Val Ptisko, Division Director

**2874 Policy, Planning & Management
Services**
Department of Education
330 C Street SW
Suite 4022
Washington, DC 20201-0001
202-205-9960
Fax: 202-260-7225

Gen. John P Higgins Jr, Assistant
Inspector

**2875 Programs for the Improvement of
Practice**
Department of Education
500 N Capitol Street NW
Suite 555
Washington, DC 20001-1531
202-219-2164
Fax: 202-260-7225

Ronald W Cartwright, Sr Program
Manager

**2876 Rehabilitation Services
Administration**
Department of Education/3028 Mary E.
Switzer Bldg.
330 C Street
Washington, DC 20202
202-205-5482
Fax: 202-260-7225
E-mail: fredric_schroeder@ed.gov

Fredric K Schroeder, Commissioner

2877 Research to Practice Division
Department of Education/3530 Mary E.
Switzer Bldg.
330 C Street
Washington, DC 20202
202-205-9864
Fax: 202-260-7225
http://www.ed.gov/offices/osers/osef

Louis Danielson, Director

2878 School Assistance Division
Department of Education/4200 Portals
Building
1250 Maryland Avenue SW
Washington, DC 20024-2141
202-260-2270
Fax: 202-260-7225

Catherine Schagh, Division Director

**2879 School Improvement
Programs-Drug Free Schools &
Communities Division**
Department of Education/4500 Portals
Building
1250 Maryland Avenue SW
Washington, DC 20024-2141
202-260-3693
Fax: 202-260-7225

**2880 School Improvement
Programs-Equity and Educational
Excellence Division**
Department of Education/4500 Portals
Building
1250 Maryland Avenue SW
Washington, DC 20024-2141
202-260-3693
Fax: 202-260-7225

Janice Williams-Madison, Division
Director

**2881 School Improvement
Programs-School Effectiveness
Division**
Department of Education/4500 Portals
Building
1250 Maryland Avenue SW
Washington, DC 20024-2141
202-260-3693
Fax: 202-260-7225

Daniel F Bonner, Division Director

2882 Training & Development Programs
Brody Communications Ltd.
815 Green Wood Avenue
Suite 8
Jenkintown, PA 19046
215-886-1688
800-726-7936
Fax: 215-886-1699
E-mail:
brody@brodycommunications.com
http://www.brodycommunications.com
Brody offers tailored training programs, executive coaching and presentations in the
areas of communication skills and professional development.

Maryann Roddy, Manager of Maximum
Exposure

**2883 US Department of Defense
Dependents Schools**
2461 Eisenhower Avenue
Alexandria, VA 22331-3000
571-325-0867

Marilyn Witcher

2884 US Department of Education
400 Maryland Avenue SW
Washington, DC 20202
800-872-5327
Fax: 202-401-0689
E-mail: customerservice@inet.ed.gov
http://www.ed.gov
Ensures equal access to education and promotes educational excellence for all Americans.

Margaret Spellings, Secretary of
Education

2885 Vocational & Adult Education
Department of Education/4090 Mary E.
Switzer Bldg.
330 C Street
Washington, DC 20202
202-205-5451
Fax: 202-260-7225

Augusta Souza Kappner, Assistant
Secretary

**2886 Washington DC Department of
Education**
825 N Capitol Street NE
Suite 900
Washington, DC 20202-4210
202-442-5885
Fax: 202-442-5026

Paul L Varce, Superintendent

Alabama

**2887 Alabama State Department of
Education**
50 N Ripley Street
PO Box 302101
Montgomery, AL 36130-2101
334-242-9700
Fax: 334-242-9708
http://www.alsde.edu
Mission is to provide a state system of education which is committed to academic excellence and which provides education of
the highest quality to all Alabama students,
preparing them for the 21st century. For certification information contact the Alabama
certification office at 334-242-9977.

Edward R Richardson, Superintendent

**2888 Assistant Superintendent &
Financial Services**
Alabama Department of Education
50 N Ripley Street
Montgomery, AL 36130-0624
334-242-9741
Fax: 334-242-9708

William C Berryman, Division Director

2889 Deputy Superintendent
Alabama Department of Education
50 N Ripley Street
Montgomery, AL 36130-0624
334-242-9700
Fax: 334-242-9708

Thomas Ingram, Assistant Superintendent

2890 Disability Determination Division
Alabama Department of Education
50 N Ripley Street
Montgomery, AL 36130-0624
205-989-2100
Fax: 800-524-6489

Tommy Warren, General Counsel

2891 General Administrative Services
Alabama Department of Education
50 N Ripley Street
Montgomery, AL 36130-0624
334-242-9700
Fax: 334-242-9708

William J Rutherford, Assistant
Superintendent

2892 General Counsel
Alabama Department of Education
50 N Ripley Street
Montgomery, AL 36130-0624
334-242-9700
Fax: 334-242-9708

Richard N Meadows, General Counsel

2893 Instructional Services
Alabama Department of Education
50 N Ripley Street
Montgomery, AL 36130-0624
334-242-9700
Fax: 334-242-9708

Charlie G Williams, Assistant
Superintendent

2894 Professional Services
Alabama Department of Education
50 N Ripley Street
Montgomery, AL 36130-0624
334-242-9700
Fax: 334-242-9708

Eddie R Johnson, Assistant
Superintendent

2895 Rehabilitation Services
Alabama Department of Rehabilitation
Services
2129 E S Boulevard
PO Box 11586
Montgomery, AL 36111-0586
334-281-8780
800-441-7607
Fax: 334-281-1973
http://www.rehab.state.al.us
State agency that provides and services and
assistance to Alabama's children and
adults with disabilities and their families.

Steve Shrivers, Commissioner

2896 Special Education Services
Alabama Department of Education
50 N Ripley Street
Montgomery, AL 36130-0624
334-242-8114
Fax: 334-242-9192

Bill East, Division Director

2897 Student Instructional Services
Alabama Department of Education
50 N Ripley Street
Montgomery, AL 36130-0624
334-242-8256
Fax: 334-242-9708

Martha V Beckett, Assistant
Superintendent

2898 Superintendent
Alabama Department of Education
50 N Ripley Street
Montgomery, AL 36130-0624
334-242-9700
Fax: 334-242-9708

Ed Richardson, Superintendent

2899 Vocational Education
Alabama Department of Education
50 N Ripley Street
Montgomery, AL 36130-0624
334-242-9111
Fax: 334-353-8861

Stephen B Franks, Division Director

Alaska

2900 Alaska Commission on Postsecondary Education
Alaska Department of Education & Early
Development
3030 Vintage Boulevard
Juneau, AK 99801-7100
907-465-2962
800-441-2962
Fax: 907-465-5316
E-mail: custsvc@acpe.state.ak.us
http://www.state.ak.us/acpc
This state agency coordinates administration of state-funded education financial assistance for students and their families.
This agency is also responsible for licensing and regulating postsecondary institutions to operate in Alaska.

Diane Barrans, Executive Director
Dennis Watson, SFA Director

2901 Alaska Department of Education Administrative Services
801 W 10th Street
Suite 200
Juneau, AK 99801-1894
907-465-2802
Fax: 907-465-4156
For certification information visit
www.eed.state.ak.us/TeacherCertification
/ or contact 907-465-2831.

Shirley J Halloway, Commissioner

2902 Alaska Department of Education & Early Development
801 W 10th Street
Suite 200
Juneau, AK 99801
907-465-2800
Fax: 907-465-3452
http://www.educ.state.ak.us

Gerald Covey, Commissioner

2903 Education Program Support
Alaska Department of Education
801 W 10th Street
Suite 200
Juneau, AK 99801-1878
907-465-2800
Fax: 907-465-4156

Harry Gamble, Information Officer

2904 Libraries, Archives & Museums
Alaska Department of Education &
Energy Developmnt
PO Box 110571
Juneau, AK 99811
907-465-2910
Fax: 907-465-2151
E-mail: ase@eed.state.ak.us
http://www.energy.state.ak.us

Karen Crane, Division Director

2905 School Finance & Data Management
Alaska Department of Education
801 W 10th Street
Suite 200
Juneau, AK 99801-1878
907-465-2800
Fax: 907-465-3452

Duane Guiley, Division Director

2906 Vocational Rehabilitation
Alaska Department of Labor &
Workforce Development
801 W 10th Street
Suite A
Juneau, AK 99801-1878
907-465-2814
Fax: 907-465-2856
http://www.labor.state.ak.us/dur/home.ht
m

Duane French, Division Director

Arizona

2907 National Council of State Supervisors of Music
Arizona Department of Education
1535 W Jefferson Street
Phoenix, AZ 85007-3209
602-542-5393
800-352-4558
Fax: 602-542-3590
E-mail: mgiffor@mail1.ade.state.az.com
http://http://ade.state.az.us/
Strives to improve the supervision and education of music on the state level and to encourage coordination between states.

Arkansas

2908 Arkansas Department of Education
4 State Capitol Mall
Room 304A
Little Rock, AR 72201-1071
501-682-4475
Fax: 501-682-1079
http://http://arkedu.state.ar.us
Mission is to provide the highest quality
leadership, service, and support to school
districts and schools in order that they may
provide equitable, quality education for all
to ensure that all public schools comply
with the Standards. For certification information visit http://arkedu.state.us/teach-
ers/index.html or contact 501-371-1580.

T.Kenneth James, Education Director

2909 Arkansas Department of Education: Special Education
4 State Capitol Mall
Room 105C
Little Rock, AR 72201-1071
501-682-4221
Fax: 501-682-5159
E-mail: mharding@arkedu.k12.ar.us
http://http://arkedu.state.ar.us

Marcia Harding, Associate Director

2910 Federal Programs
Arkansas Department of Education
4 State Capitol
Room 304A
Little Rock, AR 72201-1011
501-682-4268
Fax: 501-682-5010

Clearence Lovell, Associate Director

2911 Human Resources Office
Arkansas Department of Education
4 State Capitol
Room 304A
Little Rock, AR 72201-1011
501-682-4210
Fax: 501-682-1193

Clemetta Hood, Personnel Manager

California

2912 California Department of Education
721 Capitol Mall
1430 N Street
Sacramento, CA 95814-4702
916-657-4766
Fax: 916-657-4975
http://www.cde.ca.gov
For certification information visit www.ctc.ca.gov or contact 916-445-8778.

Delaine A Easton, Superintendent

2913 California Department of Education Catalog
CDE Books & Videos
PO Box 271
Sacramento, CA 95812-0271
916-323-4583
800-995-4099
Fax: 916-323-0823
Offers new techniques and fresh perspectives in handbooks, guides, videos and more.

2914 California Department of Special Education
721 Capitol Mall
Sacramento, CA 95814-4702
916-445-4613
Fax: 916-327-3516

Alice Parker, Director

2915 Curriculum & Instructional Leadership Branch
California Department of Education
721 Capitol Mall
Sacramento, CA 95814-4702
916-657-3043

Harvey Hunt, Deputy

2916 Department Management Services Branch
California Department of Education
721 Capitol Mall
Sacramento, CA 95814-4785
916-657-5474
Fax: 916-319-0106

Diane Kirkham, Deputy

2917 Executive Office & External Affairs
California Department of Education
721 Capitol Mall
Sacramento, CA 95814-4702
916-657-3027
Fax: 916-657-4975

Susie Lange, Division Director

2918 Field Services Branch
California Department of Education
721 Capitol Mall
Sacramento, CA 95814-4702
916-657-4748
Fax: 916-319-0155

Robert W Agee, Division Director

2919 Governmental Policy Branch
California Department of Education
721 Capitol Mall
Sacramento, CA 95814-4702
916-657-5461

Joe Holsinger, Deputy

2920 Legal & Audits Branch
California Department of Education
1430 N Street
Suite 5319
Sacramento, CA 95814-4702
916-319-0860
Fax: 916-319-0155

Marsha Bedwell, General Counsel

2921 Region 9: Education Department
50 United Nations Plaza
San Francisco, CA 94102-4912
415-556-4920

2922 Specialized Programs Branch
California Department of Education
721 Capitol Mall
Sacramento, CA 95814-4702
916-657-2642
Fax: 916-319-0155

Shirley A Thornton, Chief Counsel

Colorado

2923 Colorado Department of Education
201 E Colfax Avenue
Denver, CO 80203-1799
303-866-6600
Fax: 303-866-6938
http://www.cde.state.co.us
For certification information visit www.cde.state.co.us/index_license.htm or contact 303-866-6628.

William T Moloney, Commissioner

2924 Educational Services
Colorado Department of Education
201 E Colfax Avenue
Denver, CO 80203-1704
303-866-6600
Fax: 303-866-6811

Arthur J Ellis, Commissioner

2925 Federal Program Services
Colorado Department of Education
201 E Colfax Avenue
Denver, CO 80203-1704
303-866-6782
Fax: 303-866-6647

Betty Hinkle, Executive Director

2926 Management, Budget & Planning
Colorado Department of Education
201 E Colfax Avenue
Denver, CO 80203-1704
303-866-6822
Fax: 303-866-6938

Karen Stroup, Division Director

2927 Public School Finance
Colorado Department of Education
201 E Colfax Avenue
Denver, CO 80203-1704
303-866-6845

Dan Stewart, Division Director

2928 Special Services
Colorado Department of Education
201 E Colfax Avenue
Denver, CO 80203-1704
303-866-6782
Fax: 303-866-6785

Brian McNulty, Assistant Commissioner

2929 State Library
Colorado Department of Education
201 E Colfax Avenue
Denver, CO 80203-1704
303-866-6900
Fax: 303-866-6940

Nancy Bolt, Assistant Commissioner

2930 Teacher Certification & Professional Education
Colorado Department of Education
201 E Colfax Avenue
Denver, CO 80203-1704
303-866-6851
Fax: 303-866-6968

Gene Campbell, Assistant Commissioner

2931 US Department of Education: Region VIII
1244 Speer Boulevard
Suite 310
Denver, CO 80204-3582
303-844-3544
Fax: 303-844-2524
http://www.ed.gov

Helen Littlejohn, Public Affairs Officer

Connecticut

2932 Connecticut Department of Education
165 Capitol Avenue
Hartford, CT 06106
860-713-6500
Fax: 860-713-7001
E-mail: thomas.murphy@po.state.ct.us
http://www.state.ct.us/sdel
For certification information visit www.state.ct.us/sde or contact 860-713-6969.

Betty Sternberg, Commissioner

2933 Connecticut Early Childhood Unit
Department of Education
PO Box 2219
Hartford, CT 06145
860-566-5497
Offers programs for children, infants and toddlers with disabilities.

Kay Halverson, Coordinator

2934 Connecticut Governor's Committee on Employment of the Handicapped
Labor Department Building
200 Folly Brook Boulevard
Wethersfield, CT 06109-1153
860-263-6000
Fax: 860-263-6216

2935 Education Programs & Services
Connecticut Department of Education
25 Industrial Park Road
Middletown, CT 06457-1520
860-807-2005
Fax: 860-635-7125

Theodore S Sergi, Division Director

2936 Finance & Administrative Services
Connecticut Department of Education
165 Capitol Avenue Office Building
Hartford, CT 06106-1659
860-566-4879
Fax: 860-713-7011

John G Coroso, Division Director

2937 Human Services
Connecticut Department of Education
165 Capitol Avenue Office Building
Hartford, CT 06106-1659
860-713-6690
Fax: 860-713-7011

Dick Wilber, Division Director

2938 Information Systems
Connecticut Department of Education
165 Capitol Avenue Office Building
Hartford, CT 06106-1659
860-647-5064
Fax: 860-647-5027

Greg Vassar, Division Director

2939 Office of State Coordinator of Vocational Education for Disabled Students
Vocational Prgs. for the Disabled &
Disadvantaged
PO Box 2219
Hartford, CT 06145
860-807-2001
Fax: 860-807-2196

2940 Teaching & Learning Division
Connecticut Department of Education
165 Capitol Ave Ofc Building
Hartford, CT 06106-1659
203-566-8113

Betty J Sternberg, Division Director

2941 Vocational-Technical School Systems
Connecticut Department of Education
25 Industrial Park Road
Middletown, CT 06457-1520
860-822-6832
Fax: 860-807-2196

Delaware

2942 Assessments & Accountability Branch Delaware Department of Education
Federal & Lockerman Streets
#279
Dover, DE 19903
302-739-6700
Fax: 302-739-3092

Marsha DeLain, Associate Supervisor

2943 Delaware Department of Education
401 Federal Street
PO Box 1402
Dover, DE 19903-1402
302-739-4601
Fax: 302-739-4654
E-mail: dedoe@doe.k12.de.us
http://www.doe.state.de.us
Our mission is to promote the highest quality education for every Delaware student by providing visionary leadership and superior service. For certification informa-

tion visit www.doe.state.de.us or contact
302-739-4686.

Joseph A Pika PhD, President State
Board of Ed.
Valerie A Woodruff, Executive Secretary

2944 Delaware Department of Education: Administrative Services
Townsend Building, Suite 2
PO Box 1402
Dover, DE 19903-1402
302-739-4601
Fax: 302-739-4654
E-mail: dedoe@doe.k12.de.us
http://www.doe.state.de.us

Valerie Woodroff, Secretary

2945 Improvement & Assistance Branch Delaware Department of Education
Federal & Lockerman Streets
#279
Dover, DE 19903
302-739-3772
Fax: 302-739-7645

Valerie Woodruff, Associate
Superintendent

District of Columbia

2946 DC Division of Special Education
10th & H Streets NW
Washington, DC 20001
202-724-4800
Fax: 202-442-5517

Doris Woodson, Superintendent

2947 District of Columbia Department of Education
415 APO Street NW
Presidential Building
Washington, DC 20004
204-724-4222
For certification information visit
www.k12.dc.us.

Franklin L Smith, Superintendent

2948 Grants Administration Branch
District of Columbia
415 12th St NW, Presidential Building
Washington, DC 20004
202-274-5597
Fax: 202-274-5264

Barbara Jackson, Division Director

2949 Management Systems & Technology Services Division
District of Columbia
415 12th St NW, Presidential Building
Washington, DC 20004
202-724-4062

Ulysses Keyes, Division Director

2950 State Services Division District of Columbia
415 12th Street NW
Presidential Building
Washington, DC 20004
202-624-5490
Fax: 202-624-8588

Andrew E Jenkins, Division Director

Florida

2951 Florida Department of Education
Turlington Building Suite 1514
325 West Gaines Street
Tallahassee, FL 32399
850-245-0505
Fax: 850-245-9667
E-mail: mccueq@mail.doe.state.fl.us
http://www.firn.edu/doe/
Offers information on community colleges, vocational education, public schools, human resources, financial assistance, adult education and more. For certification information visit www.fldoe.org or contact 850-488-2317.

John Winn, Commissioner

Georgia

2952 Georgia Department of Education
2066 Twin Towers E
Atlanta, GA 30334
404-656-2800
877-729-7867
Fax: 404-651-6867
E-mail: help.desk@doe.k12.ga.us
http://www.gadoe.org
Among many other features, this organization offers agriculture education, federal programs, Leadership Development Academy, school and community nutrition progams, Spanish language and cultural program, technology/career (vocational) education and more. For certification information visit www.gapsc.com or contact 404-657-9000.

Ron Newcomb, Commission Staff
Director
Kathy Cox, Superintendent

Hawaii

2953 Business Services Office
Hawaii Department of Education
1390 Miller Street
Honolulu, HI 96813-2418
808-586-3444
Fax: 808-586-3445

Alfred Suga, Division Director

2954 Hawaii Department of Education
PO Box 2360
1390 Miller Street
Honolulu, HI 96804
808-586-3349
Fax: 808-586-3234
E-mail: boe_hawaii@notes.k12.hi.us
http://www.k12.hi.us
For certification information visit
http://doe.k12.hi.us.

Patricia Hamamoto, Superintendent

2955 Information & Telecommunications Services
Hawaii Department of Education
1390 Miller Street
Honolulu, HI 96813-2418
808-586-3307
Fax: 808-586-3645

Philip Bossert, Division Director

2956 Instructional Services
Hawaii Department of Education
1390 Miller Street
Honolulu, HI 96813-2418
808-586-3446
Fax: 808-586-3429

Mildred Higashi, Division Director

2957 Office of the State Director for Career & Technical Education
University of Hawaii
Lower Campus Road
Lunalilo Freeway Portable 1
Honolulu, HI 96822-2489
808-956-7461
Fax: 808-956-9096
E-mail: kjones@hawaii.edu
http://www.hawaii.edu/cte

Karla Jones, State Director

2958 Personnel Services
Hawaii Department of Education
1390 Miller Street
Honolulu, HI 96813-2418
808-586-3400
Fax: 808-586-3419

Donald Nugent, Division Director

2959 State Public Library System
Hawaii Department of Education
1390 Miller Street
Honolulu, HI 96813-2418
808-586-3704
Fax: 808-586-3715

Batholomew Kane, State Librarian

Idaho

2960 Idaho Department of Education
PO Box 83720-0027
650 West State Street
Boise, ID 83702-0027
208-332-6800
Fax: 208-334-2228
E-mail: mhoward@sde.state.id.us
http://www.sde.state.id.us
For certification information visit www.sde.state.id.us/certification or contact 808-586-2616.

Marilyn Howard, Superintendent

2961 Vocational Education Division
Idaho State Department of Education
605 W State Street
Boise, ID 83702-0096
208-334-3390
Fax: 208-334-5305
http://www.sde.state.id.us
Committed to empower people with disabilities with appropriate resources to make informed choices about their futures.

Dr.Michael Graham, Administrator

Illinois

2962 Executive Deputy Superintendent
Illinois Department of Education
100 N 1st Street
Springfield, IL 62777
217-782-0342
Fax: 217-782-5333

2963 Finance & Support Services
Illinois Department of Education
100 N 1st Street
Springfield, IL 62777
217-782-5596
Fax: 217-782-4550

Karol Richardson, Division Director

2964 Illinois Department of Education
100 N 1st Street
Springfield, IL 62777
217-782-2221
Fax: 217-785-8585
http://www.isbe.state.il.us
For certification information visit www.isbe.state.il.us/teachers/default.htm.

Ernest R Wish, Superintendent

2965 Planning, Research & Evaluation
Illinois Department of Education
100 N 1st Street
Springfield, IL 62702-5199
217-782-3950
Fax: 217-524-7784

Connie Wise, Division Director

2966 Programs & Accountability
Illinois Department of Education
100 N 1st Street
Springfield, IL 62702-5199
217-782-2221
Fax: 217-524-4928

2967 Recognition & Supervision of Schools
Illinois Department of Education
100 N 1st Street
Springfield, IL 62702-5199
217-782-4123
Fax: 217-524-6125

Dick Haney, Division Director

2968 Region 5: Education Department
6130 W Walcott Avenue
Chicago, IL 60636
773-535-9570
Fax: 773-535-9582

2969 School Finance
Illinois Department of Education
100 N 1st Street
Springfield, IL 62702-5199
217-782-5439
Fax: 217-785-7650

Gary Ey, Division Director

2970 School Improvement & Assessment Services
Illinois Department of Education
100 N 1st Street
Springfield, IL 62702-5199
217-782-5439
Fax: 217-785-7650

Tom Kerins, Division Director

2971 Special Education
Illinois State Board of Education
100 N 1st Street
Springfield, IL 62702-5199
217-782-5589
Fax: 217-782-0372
E-mail: asims@isbe.net
http://www.isbe.net

Anthony Sims, Manager Special Education

2972 Specialized Programs
Illinois Department of Education
100 N 1st Street
Springfield, IL 62702-5199
312-814-2223
Fax: 312-814-2282

Brenda Heffner, Division Director

2973 Student Development Services
Illinois Department of Education
100 N 1st Street
Springfield, IL 62702-5199
217-782-0995
Fax: 217-785-7849

Frank Llano, Division Director

2974 Teacher Education & Certification
Illinois Department of Education
100 N 1st Street
Springfield, IL 62702-5199
217-782-3774
Fax: 217-524-1289

Sue Bentz, Division Director

Indiana

2975 Administration & Financial Management Center
Indiana Department of Education
100 N Capitol Avenue, Room 229
Indianapolis, IN 46204-2203
317-232-0808
Fax: 317-233-6326

Patty Bond, Director

2976 Center for School Assessment & Research
Indiana Department of Education
100 N Capitol Avenue, Room 229
Indianapolis, IN 46204-2203
317-232-9050
Fax: 317-233-2196

Wes Bruce, Director

2977 Community Relations & Special Populations
Indiana Department of Education
100 N Capitol Avenue, Room 229
Indianapolis, IN 46204-2203
317-232-0520
Fax: 317-233-6502

Linda Miller, Senior Officer

2978 External Affairs
Indiana Department of Education
100 N Capitol Avenue, Room 229
Indianapolis, IN 46204-2203
317-232-6614
Fax: 317-232-8004

Joe DiLaura, Division Director

2979 Indiana Department of Education
200 W Washington Street
State House, Room 229
Indianapolis, IN 46204-2798
317-232-6665
Fax: 317-232-8004
http://www.doe.state.in.us
For certification information visit www.in.gov/psb or contact 866-542-3672.

Suellen K Reed, Superintedent

2980 Office of the Deputy Superintendent
Indiana Department of Education
100 N Capitol Avenue, Room 229
Indianapolis, IN 46204-2203
317-232-0510
Fax: 317-232-0589

Robert Dalton, Division Director

2981 Policy & Planning
Indiana Department of Education
100 N Capitol Avenue
Room 229
Indianapolis, IN 46204-2203
317-232-6648

Evelyn Sayers, Policy Analyst

2982 School Improvement & Performance Center
Indiana Department of Education
100 N Capitol Avenue, Room 229
Indianapolis, IN 46204-2203
317-232-9100
Fax: 317-232-9121

Phyllis Land Usher, Division Director

2983 State Board Relations & Legal Services
Indiana Department of Education
100 N Capitol Avenue, Room 229
Indianapolis, IN 46204-2203
317-232-6622
Fax: 317-232-8004

Jeffrey Zaring, Administrator

Iowa

2984 Community Colleges Division
Iowa Department of Education
14th E & Grand Streets
Des Moines, IA 50319-0001
515-281-8260

Harriet Custer, Division Director

2985 Division of Library Services
Iowa Department of Education
14th E & Grand Streets
Des Moines, IA 50319-0001
515-281-4105

Sharman B Smith, Administrator

2986 Educational Services for Children & Families
Iowa Department of Education
14th E & Grand Streets
Des Moines, IA 50319-0001
515-281-3575

Susan J Donielson, Administrator

2987 Elementary & Secondary Education
Iowa Department of Education
14th E & Grand Streets
Des Moines, IA 50319-0001
515-281-3333

Ted Stilwill, Administrator

2988 Financial & Information Services
Iowa Department of Education
Grimes State Office Buildings
Des Moines, IA 50319-0001
515-281-5293
Fax: 515-242-5988
E-mail: lee.tack@ed.state.ia.us
http://www.state.ia.us/educate

Leland Tack, Administrator

2989 Iowa Department of Education
Grimes State Office Building
400 E 14th & Grand Streets
Des Moines, IA 50319-0146
515-281-5294
Fax: 515-281-5988
E-mail: webmaster@ed.state.ia.us
http://www.state.ia.us/educate
Serves the students of Iowa by providing leadership and resources for schools, area education agencies and community colleges. For certification information visit www.state.ia.us/boee or contact 515-281-3245.

Ted Stilwill, Director

2990 Iowa Public Television
Iowa Department of Education
14th E & Grand Streets
Des Moines, IA 50319-0001
515-242-3150

David Bolender, Executive Director

2991 Vocational Rehabilitation Services
Iowa Department of Education
14th E & Grand Streets
Des Moines, IA 50319-0001
515-281-6731

Margaret Knudsen, Administrator

Kansas

2992 Assistant Commissioner's Office
Kansas Department of Education
120 SE 10th Avenue
Topeka, KS 66612
785-296-2303
Fax: 785-296-1413
E-mail: sfreden@ksbe.state.ks.us
http://www.ksbe.state.ks.us

Sharon Freden, Assistant Commissioner

2993 Fiscal Services & Quality Control
Kansas Department of Education
120 SE 10th Avenue
Topeka, KS 66612
785-296-3871
Fax: 785-296-0459

Dale M Dennis, Deputy Commissioner

2994 Kansas Department of Education
120 SE Tenth Avenue
Topeka, KS 66612-1182
785-296-3201
Fax: 785-796-7933
http://www.ksbe.state.ks.us
For certification information visit www.ksde.org or contact 785-291-3678.

John A Tompkins, Commissioner

2995 Kansas Division of Special Education
120 E 10th Street
Topeka, KS 66612
785-296-4945
Fax: 785-296-1413

Kentucky

2996 Chief of Staff Bureau
Kentucky Department of Education
500 Mero Street, 19th Floor
Frankfort, KY 40601-1957
502-564-3141
Fax: 502-564-6470

Hunt Helm, Office Communications

2997 Communications Services
Kentucky Department of Education
500 Mero Street
19th Floor
Frankfort, KY 40601-1957
502-564-3421
Fax: 502-564-6470
http://www.kde.state.ky.us

Hunt Helm, Associate Commissioner

2998 Curriculum, Assessment & Accountability Services
Kentucky Department of Education
500 Mero Street, 19th Floor
Frankfort, KY 40601-1957
502-564-4394
Fax: 502-564-7749

Neal Klingston, Division Director

2999 Education Technology Office
Kentucky Department of Education
500 Mero Street, 19th Floor
Frankfort, KY 500 M-1957
502-564-6900
Fax: 502-564-4695

Don Coffman, Division Director

3000 Kentucky Department of Education
500 Mero Street
Capitol Plaza Tower
Frankfort, KY 40601-1957
502-564-3141
Fax: 502-564-5680
http://www.kde.state.ky.us
For certification information visit www.kyepsb.net or contact 502-573-4606.

Gene Wilhoit, Commissioner

3001 Learning Results Services Bureau
Kentucky Department of Education
500 Mero Street, 19th Floor
Frankfort, KY 40601-1957
502-564-2256
Fax: 502-564-7749

Vickie Basham, Division Director

3002 Office of Learning Programs Development
Kentucky Department of Education
500 Mero Street, 19th Floor
Frankfort, KY 40601-1957
502-564-3010
Fax: 502-564-6952

Linda Hargan, Division Director

3003 Regional Services Centers
Kentucky Department of Education
500 Mero Street
19th Floor
Frankfort, KY 40601-1957
502-564-9850
Fax: 502-564-9848
E-mail: svice@kde.state.ky.us
http://www.kde.state.ky.us

Sheila Vice, Principal Assistant

3004 Special Instructional Services
Kentucky Department of Education
500 Mero Street, 19th Floor
Frankfort, KY 40601-1957
502-564-4970
Fax: 502-564-6721

Ken Warlick, Division Director

3005 Support Services Bureau on Learning
Kentucky Department of Education
500 Mero Street, 19th Floor
Frankfort, KY 40601-1957
502-564-3301
Fax: 502-564-6952

Lois Adams-Rodgers, Division Director

3006 Teacher Education & Certification
Kentucky Department of Education
500 Mero Street, 19th Floor
Frankfort, KY 40601-1957
502-564-4606

Roland Goddu, Division Director

Louisiana

3007 Academic Programs Office
Louisiana Department of Education
626 N 4th Street
Baton Rouge, LA 70802-5363
225-342-4411
Fax: 225-342-0193

Moselle Dearborne, Division Director

3008 Educational Support Programs
Louisiana Department of Education
626 N 4th Street
Baton Rouge, LA 70802-5363
225-342-4411
Fax: 225-342-0781

Gayle Neal, Division Director

3009 Louisiana Department of Education
2758-D Brightside Drive
PO Box 94064
Baton Rouge, LA 70804-9064
504-342-3607
Fax: 504-342-7316
http://www.doe.state.la.us
Provides leadership and enacts policies that result in improved academic achievement and responsible citizenship for all students. For certification information visit www.louisianaschools.net or contact 225-342-3490.

Cecil J Picard, Superintendent

3010 Management & Finance Office
Louisiana State Department of Education
PO Box 64064
Baton Rouge, LA 70804-9064
225-342-3617
877-453-2721
Fax: 225-219-7538
E-mail: mlangley@doe.state.la.us
http://www.doe.state.la.us

Marlyn J Langley, Deputy Superintendent

3011 Office of Vocational Education
Louisiana Department of Education
626 N 4th Street
Baton Rouge, LA 70802-5363
225-342-4411
Fax: 225-342-0781

Chris Strother, Division Director

3012 Research & Development Office
Louisiana Department of Education
626 N 4th Street
Baton Rouge, LA 70802-5363
225-342-4411
Fax: 225-342-0781

Mari Ann Fowler, Division Director

3013 Special Education Services
Louisiana Department of Education
626 N 4th Street
Baton Rouge, LA 70802-5363
225-342-4411
Fax: 225-342-0781

Leon L Borne Jr, Division Director

Maine

3014 Applied Technology & Adult Learning
Maine Department of Education
23 State House Station
Augusta, ME 04333-0023
207-287-5854

Chris Lyons, Division Director

3015 Division of Compensatory Education
Maine Department of Education
23 State House Station
Augusta, ME 04333-0023
207-624-6705
Fax: 207-624-6706

Kathryn Manning, Division Director

3016 Maine Department of Education
23 State House Station
Augusta, ME 04333-0023
207-624-6620
Fax: 207-624-6601
http://www.state.me.us/education

Susan Gendron, Commissioner

Maryland

3017 Career Technology & Adult Learning
Maryland Department of Education
200 W Baltimore Street
Baltimore, MD 21201-2502
410-767-0158

Katharine Oliver, Division Director

3018 Certification & Accreditation
Maryland Department of Education
200 W Baltimore Street
Baltimore, MD 21201-2502
410-333-2141

A Skipp Sanders, Division Director

3019 Compensatory Education & Support Services
Maryland Department of Education
200 W Baltimore Street
Baltimore, MD 21201-2502
410-333-2400

Ellen Gonzales, Division Director

3020 Division of Business Services
Maryland Department of Education
200 W Baltimore Street
Baltimore, MD 21201-2502
410-333-2648

Raymond H Brown, Division Director

3021 Instruction Division
Maryland Department of Education
200 W Baltimore Street
Baltimore, MD 21201-2502
410-767-0316

Colleen Seremet, Assistant Superintendent

3022 Library Development & Services
Maryland Department of Education
00 W Baltimore Street
Baltimore, MD 21201-2502
410-333-2113

Irene Padilla, Division Director

3023 Maryland Department of Education
200 W Baltimore Street
Baltimore, MD 21201-2502
410-767-0600
888-246-0016
Fax: 410-333-6033
http://www.msde.state.md.us
Mission of MSDE is to provide leadership, support, and accountability for effective systems of public education, library services and rehabilitation services. For certification information visit www.certification.msde.state.md.us or contact 410-767-0412.

Nancy S Grasmick, Superintendent

3024 Planning, Results & Information Management
Maryland Department of Education
200 W Baltimore Street
Baltimore, MD 21201-2502
410-333-2045

Mark Moody, Division Director

3025 Rehabilitation Services Division
Maryland Department of Education
200 W Baltimore Street
Baltimore, MD 21201-2502
410-554-3276

James S Jeffers, Division Director

3026 Special Education
Maryland Department of Education
200 W Baltimore Street
Baltimore, MD 21201-2502
410-767-0261
800-535-0182
Fax: 410-333-8166

Richard J Steinke, Division Director

Massachusetts

3027 Massachusetts Department of Education
350 Main Street
Malden, MA 02148-5023
781-338-3000
Fax: 781-338-3770
http://www.doe.mass.edu

David P Driscoll, Commissioner

3028 Massachusetts Department of Educational Improvement
350 Main Street
Malden, MA 02148-5089
781-388-3300

Andrea Perrault, Division Director

3029 Region 1: Education Department
J.W. McCormick Post Office & Courthouse
540 McCormick Courthouse
Boston, MA 02109-4557
617-223-9317
Fax: 617-223-9324

Michael Sentance

Michigan

3030 Administrative Services Office
Michigan Department of Education
608 W Allegan Street
Lansing, MI 48933-1524
517-373-3324
Fax: 517-335-4565
http://www.michigan.gov
Calvin C Cupidore, Director

3031 Adult Extended Learning Office
Michigan Department of Education
608 W Allegan Street
Lansing, MI 48933-1524
517-373-3324
Fax: 517-335-4565
http://www.michigan.gov
Ronald Gillum, Director

3032 Career & Technical Education
Michigan Department of Education
608 W Allegan Street
Lansing, MI 48933-1524
517-373-3324
Fax: 517-373-8776
http://www.michigan.gov
William Welsgerber, Director

3033 Higher Education Management Office
Michigan Department of Education
608 W Allegan Street
Lansing, MI 48933-1524
517-373-3324
Fax: 517-373-2759
http://www.michigan.gov
Ronald L Root, Director

3034 Instructional Programs
Michigan Department of Education
608 W Allegan Street
Lansing, MI 48933-1524
517-373-3324
Fax: 517-335-4565
http://www.michigan.gov

3035 Michigan Department of Education
608 W Allegan Street
PO Box 30008
Lansing, MI 48909
517-373-3324
Fax: 517-335-4565
E-mail: MDEweb@michigan.gov
http://www.michigan.gov/mde
Thomas D Watkins, Superintendent

3036 Office of School Management
Michigan Department of Education
608 W Allegan Street
Lansing, MI 48933-1524
517-373-3324
Fax: 517-335-4565
http://www.michigan.gov
Roger Lynas, Director

3037 Office of the Superintendent
Michigan Department of Education
608 W Allegan Street
Lansing, MI 48933-1524
517-373-3324
Fax: 517-335-4565
http://www.michigan.gov

3038 Postsecondary Services
Michigan Department of Education
608 W Allegan Street
Lansing, MI 48909
517-373-3324
Fax: 517-335-4565
http://www.michigan.gov

3039 School Program Quality
Michigan Department of Education
608 W Allegan Street
Lansing, MI 48933-1524
517-373-3324
Fax: 517-373-4565
http://www.michigan.gov
Anne Hansen, Division Director

3040 Special Education
Michigan Department of Education
608 W Allegan Street
Lansing, MI 48933-1524
517-373-3324
Fax: 581-733-5456
Richard Baldwin, Director

3041 Student Financial Assistance
Michigan Department of Education
608 W Allegan Street
Lansing, MI 48933-1524
517-373-3324
Fax: 517-335-4565
Jack Nelson, Director

3042 Teacher & Administrative Preparation
Michigan Department of Education
608 W Allegan Street
Lansing, MI 48933-1524
514-373-3324
Fax: 517-335-4565
http://www.michigan.gov
Carolyn Logan, Director

Minnesota

3043 Data & Technology
Minnesota Department of Education
550 Cedar Street
Saint Paul, MN 55101-2233
612-297-3151
Mark Manning, Division Director

3044 Data Management
Minnesota Department of Education
1500 Highway 39 W
Roseville, MN 55113
651-582-8296
Fax: 651-582-8873
Carol Hokenson, Manager Data Management

3045 Education Funding
Minnesota Department of Education
550 Cedar Street
Saint Paul, MN 55101-2233
651-297-2194
Tom Melcher, Division Director

3046 Financial Conditions & Aids Payment
Minnesota Department of Education
550 Cedar Street
Saint Paul, MN 55101-2233
612-296-4431
Gary Farland, Division Director

3047 Government Relations
Minnesota Department of Education
550 Cedar Street
Saint Paul, MN 55101-2233
612-296-5279
Sliv Carlson, Division Director

3048 Human Resources Office
Minnesota Department of Education
550 Cedar Street
Saint Paul, MN 55101-2233
651-582-8200
William O'Neill, Division Director

3049 Minnesota Department of Children, Families & Learning
1500 Highway 36 W
Roseville, MN 55113-4266
651-582-8204
Fax: 651-582-8724
http://cfl.state.mn.us
Works to help communities to measurably improve the well-being of children through programs that focus on education, community services, prevention, and the preparation of young people for the world of work. All department efforts emphasize the achievement of positive results for children and their families.
Dr.Cheri Pierson, Commissioner

3050 Minnesota Department of Education
1500 Highway 36 W
Roseville, MN 55113-4266
651-582-8204
Fax: 651-582-8724
http://www.education.state.mn.us
Christine Jax, Commissioner

3051 Residential Schools
Minnesota Department of Education
550 Cedar Street
Saint Paul, MN 55101-2233
507-332-3363
Wade Karli, Division Director

Mississippi

3052 Community Outreach Services
Mississippi Department of Education
PO Box 771
Jackson, MS 39205-1113
601-359-3513
Fax: 601-359-3033
Sarah Beard, Division Director

3053 Educational Innovations
Mississippi Department of Education
PO Box 771
Jackson, MS 39205-0771
601-359-3499
Fax: 601-359-2587
David Robinson, Division Director

3054 External Relations
Mississippi Department of Education
PO Box 771
372 Central High Building
Jackson, MS 39201
601-359-3515
Fax: 601-359-3033
Andrew P Mullins, Division Director

3055 Management Information Systems
Mississippi Department of Education
PO Box 771
Jackson, MS 39205
601-359-3487
Fax: 601-359-3033
Rusty Purvis, Division Director

3056 Mississippi Department of Education
359 NW Street
PO Box 771
Jackson, MS 39205-0771
601-359-3512
Fax: 601-359-3242
http://www.mde.k12.ms.us
Dr.Henry Johnson, Superintendent

3057 Mississippi Employment Security Commission
PO Box 1699
Jackson, MS 39215-1699
601-961-7400
Fax: 601-961-7405
http://www.mesc.state.ms

3058 Office of Accountability
Mississippi Department of Education
PO Box 771
Jackson, MS 39205
601-359-2038
Fax: 601-359-1748
Judy Rhodes, Division Director

3059 Vocational Technical Education
Mississippi Department of Education
359 NW Street
PO Box 771
Jackson, MS 39292
601-359-3090
Fax: 601-359-3989
Samuel McGee, Division Director

Missouri

3060 Deputy Commissioner
Missouri Department of Education
205 Jefferson Street
PO Box 480 Floor 6
Jefferson City, MO 65101-2901
573-751-3503
Fax: 573-751-1179
Dr.Bert Schulte, Deputy Commissioner

3061 Division of Instruction
Missouri Department of Education
205 Jefferson Street
Floor 6
Jefferson City, MO 65101-2901
573-751-4234
Fax: 573-751-8613
Otis Baker, Division Director

3062 Missouri Department of Education
205 Jefferson Street, 6th Floor
PO Box 480
Jefferson City, MO 65102-0480
573-751-4212
Fax: 573-751-8613
E-mail: pubinfo@mail.dese.state.mo.us
http://www.dese.state.mo.us
A team of dedicated individuals working for the continuous improvement of education and services for all citizens. We believe that we can make a positive difference in the quality of life for all Missourians by provid-ing exceptional service to students, educators, schools and citizens.
D Kent King, Commissioner

3063 Region 7: Education Department
10220 NW Executive Hills Boulevard
Kansas City, MO 64153-2312
816-891-7972
Fax: 816-891-7972

3064 Special Education Division
Missouri Department of Education
205 Jefferson Street
PO Box 480 Floor 6
Jefferson City, MO 65102-2901
573-751-5739
Fax: 573-526-4404
John F Allan, Division Director

3065 Urban & Teacher Education
Missouri Department of Education
205 Jefferson Street
Floor 6
Jefferson City, MO 65101-2901
573-751-2931
Fax: 573-751-8613
L Celestine Ferguson, Division Director

3066 Vocational & Adult Education
Missouri Department of Education
205 Jefferson Street, 5th Floor
PO Box 480
Jefferson City, MO 65102-0480
573-751-2660
Fax: 573-526-4261
E-mail: nheadrick@mail.dese.state.mo.us
http://www.dese.state.mo.us
Nancy J Headrick, Assistant Commissioner

3067 Vocational Rehabilitation
Missouri Department of Education
3024 Dupont Circle
Jefferson City, MO 65109-0525
573-751-3251
Fax: 573-751-1441
Don L Gann, Division Director

Montana

3068 Accreditation & Curriculum Services Department
Montana Department of Education
106 State Capitol
Helena, MT 59620
406-444-5726
Fax: 406-444-2893
Dr.Linda Vrooman, Administrator

3069 Division of Information-Technology Support
Montana Department of Education
106 State Capitol
Helena, MT 59620
406-444-4326
Fax: 406-444-2893
Scott Buswell, Division Director

3070 Montana Department of Education
1227 11th Avenue
PO Box 202501
Helena, MT 59620-2501
406-444-3095
Fax: 406-444-2893
http://www.opi.state.mt.us
For certification information visit www.opi.state.mt.us or contact 406-444-3150.
Linda McCulloch, Superindtendent

3071 Operations Department
Montana Department of Education
106 State Capitol
Helena, MT 59620
406-444-3095
Fax: 406-444-2893

Nebraska

3072 Administrative Services Office
Nebraska Department of Education
301 Centennial Mall S
Lincoln, NE 68508-2529
402-471-2295
Fax: 402-471-6351
http://www.nde.state.ne.us/ADSS/index.html
To provide quality services and support in the areas of finance human resource management continuous quality improvement, office/building services,and technical assistant.
Mike Stefkovich, Division Director

3073 Division of Education Services
Nebraska Department of Education
301 Centennial Mall S
Lincoln, NE 68508-2529
402-471-2783
Fax: 402-471-0117
Marge Harouff, Division Director

3074 Nebraska Department of Education
301 Centennial Mall S
PO Box 94987
Lincoln, NE 68509-4987
402-471-5020
Fax: 402-471-4433
http://www.nde.state.ne.us
Douglas D Christensen, Commissioner

3075 Rehabilitation Services Division
Nebraska Department of Education
301 Centennial Mall S 6th Floor
PO Box 94987
Lincoln, NE 68509-2529
402-471-3649
877-637-3422
Fax: 402-471-0788
http://www.bocrehab.state.ne.us
Frank C Lloyd, Director

Nevada

3076 Administrative & Financial Services
Nevada Department of Education
400 W King St
Carson City, NV 89703-4204
775-687-9102
888-590-6726
Fax: 702-486-5803
Douglas Thunder

3077 Instructional Services Division
Nevada Department of Education
400 W King St
Carson City, NV 89703-4204
775-687-3104
Mary L Peterson, Division Director

3078 Nevada Department of Education
700 E 5th Street
Carson City, NV 89701-5096
775-687-9200
Fax: 775-687-9101
http://www.nsn.k12.nv.us
Mission is to lead Nevada's citizens in accomplishing lifelong learning and educational excellence.

Jack McLaughlin, Superintendent

New Hampshire

3079 Information Services
New Hampshire Department of Education
101 Pleasent Street
Concord, NH 03301-3852
603-271-2778
Fax: 603-271-1953
http://www.ed.state.nh.us
New Hampshire schools enrollment, financial, assessment information.

Dr.Judith Fillion, Division Director

3080 New Hampshire Department of Education
101 Pleasant Street
State Office Park S
Concord, NH 03301-3860
603-271-3494
800-339-9900
Fax: 603-271-1953
E-mail: llovering@ed.state.nh.us
http://www.state.nh.us/doe
Mission is to provide educational leadership and services which promote equal educational opportunities and quality practices and programs than enable New Hampshire residents to become fully productive members of society.

Nicholas C Donohue, Commissioner

3081 New Hampshire Division of Instructional Services
101 Pleasant Street
Concord, NH 03301-3852
603-271-3880

William B Evert, Division Director

3082 Standards & Certification Division
New Hampshire Dept of Education
101 Pleasant St
Concord, NH 03301-3852
603-271-3453
Fax: 603-271-8709

Judith D Fillion, Divisions Director

New Jersey

3083 New Jersey Department of Education
100 Riverview Plaza
PO Box 500
Trenton, NJ 08625-0500
609-292-4450
Fax: 609-777-4099
http://www.state.nj.us/education
Develops and implements policies that address the major education issues in New Jersey. The State Board will engage in an effort to ensure that all children receive a quality public education that prepares them to succeed as responsible, productive citizens in a global society.

William L Librera, Commissioner

3084 New Jersey Department of Education: Finance
100 Riverview Plaza
PO Box 500
Trenton, NJ 08625-0500
609-292-4421
Fax: 609-292-6794
http://www.state.nj.us/education

Richard Rosenberg, Assistant Commissioner

3085 New Jersey Division of Special Education
100 Riverview Plaza
PO Box 500
Trenton, NJ 08625
609-292-0147
Fax: 609-984-8422

Jeffrey Osowski, Divsion Director

3086 New Jersey State Library
PO Box 520
Trenton, NJ 08625-0520
609-292-6200
Fax: 609-292-2746
E-mail: nblake@njstatelib.org
http://www.njstatelib.org

Norma E Blake, State Librarian

3087 Professional Development & Licensing
New Jersey Department of Education
100 Riverview Plaza, PO Box 500
Trenton, NJ 08625
609-292-2070
Fax: 609-292-3768

Hilda Hidalgo, Division Director

3088 Urban & Field Services
New Jersey Department of Education
100 Riverview Plaza, PO Box 500
Trenton, NJ 08625
609-292-4442
Fax: 609-292-3830

Elena Scambio, Division Director

New Mexico

3089 Agency Support
New Mexico Department of Education
300 Don Gaspar, Education Building
Santa Fe, NM 87501-2786
505-827-6330

Tres Giron, Division Director

3090 Learning Services
New Mexico Department of Education
300 Don Gaspar, Education Building
Santa Fe, NM 87501
505-827-6508
Fax: 505-827-6689

Albert Zamora, Division Director

3091 New Mexico Department of Education
300 Don Gaspar
Education Building
Santa Fe, NM 87501-2786
505-827-6688
Fax: 505-827-6520
http://www.sde.state.nm.us

Michael J Davis, Superintendent

3092 New Mexico Department of School-Transportation & Support Services
300 Don Gaspar, Education Building
Santa Fe, NM 87501
505-827-6683

Susan Brown, Division Director

3093 School Management Accountability
New Mexico Department of Education
300 Don Gaspar, Education Building
Santa Fe, NM 87501
505-827-3876
Fax: 505-827-6689

Michael J Davis, Division Director

3094 Vocational Education
New Mexico Department of Education
300 Don Gaspar, Education Building
Santa Fe, NM 87501
505-827-6511

Tom Trujillo, Division Director

New York

3095 Cultural Education
New York Department of Education
Madison Avenue
Albany, NY 12230
518-474-5976
Fax: 518-474-2718
E-mail: CISINFO@mail.nysed.gov

Carole F Huxley, Division Director

3096 Elementary, Middle & Secondary Education
New York Department of Education
89 Washington Avenue
Room 875 EBA
Albany, NY 12234-0001
518-474-5915
Fax: 518-474-2718
E-mail: emscgen@mail.nysed.gov

James Kadamus, Deputy

3097 Higher & Professional Education
New York Department of Education
111 Education Avenue W Mezzanine
2nd Floor
Albany, NY 12234-0001
518-474-5851
Fax: 518-474-2718

Johanna Duncan-Poitier, Deputy Commissioner

3098 New York Department of Education
89 Washington Avenue
Education Building, Room 111
Albany, NY 12234
518-474-5844
Fax: 518-473-4909
E-mail: rmills@mail.nysed.gov
http://www.nysed.gov

Richard P Mills, President

3099 Professional Responsibility Office
New York Department of Education
89 Wolf Road Suite 204
Albany, NY 12205-2643
518-485-9350
Fax: 518-485-9361

3100 Region 2: Education Department
75 Park Place
New York, NY 10007
212-264-7005
Fax: 212-264-4427

3101 Vocational & Educational Services for Disabled
New York Department of Education
80 Wolf Road Suite 200
Albany, NY 12205
518-473-8097
800-272-5448
Fax: 518-457-4562

David Segalla, Regional Coordinator

North Carolina

3102 Auxiliary Services
North Carolina Department of Education
301 N Wilmington Street
Raleigh, NC 27601-2825
919-733-1110
Fax: 919-733-5279

Charles Weaver, Division Director

3103 Financial & Personnel Services
North Carolina Department of Education
301 N Wilmington Street
Raleigh, NC 27601-2825
919-807-3600

James O Barber, Division Director

3104 North Carolina Department of Education
301 N Wilmington Street
Raleigh, NC 27601-2825
919-715-1299
Fax: 919-807-3279
http://www.ncpublicschools.org

Bob R Etheridge, Division Director

3105 North Carolina Department of Instructional Services
301 N Wilmington Street
Raleigh, NC 27601-2825
919-715-1506
Fax: 919-807-3279

Henry Johnson, Division Director

3106 Staff Development & Technical Assistance
North Carolina Department of Education
301 N Wilmington Street
Raleigh, NC 27601-2825
919-715-1315

Nancy Davis, Division Director

North Dakota

3107 North Dakota Department of Education
600 E Boulevard Avenue
State Capitol Building, Floor 11
Bismarck, ND 58505-0440
701-328-4572
Fax: 701-328-2461
http://www.state.nd.us/espb

Wayne G Sanstead, Superintendent

3108 North Dakota Department of Public Instruction Division
600 E Boulevard Avenue, Dept. 201
Floor 9,10, & 11
Bismarck, ND 58505-0440
701-328-2260
Fax: 701-328-2461
E-mail: wsanstea@mail.dpi.state.nd.us
http://www.dpi.state.nd.us/dpi/index.htm

Dr. Wayne G Sanstead, State Superintendent

3109 North Dakota State Board for Vocational & Technical Education
600 E Boulevard Avenue
Floor 15
Bismarck, ND 58505-0660
701-224-2259
Fax: 701-328-2461

Reuben Guenthner, Division Director

3110 Study & State Film Library
North Dakota Department of Education
600 E Boulevard Avenue
Floor 11
Bismarck, ND 58505-0660
701-237-7282

Robert Stone, Division Director

Ohio

3111 Blind School
Ohio Department of Education
65 S Front Street
Columbus, OH 43215-4131
614-466-3641
Fax: 614-752-1713

Dennis Holmes, Division Director

3112 Curriculum, Instruction & Professional Development
Ohio Department of Education
65 S Front Street
Columbus, OH 43215-4131
614-466-2761
Fax: 704-992-5168

Nancy Eberhart, Division Director

3113 Early Childhood Education
Ohio Department of Education
65 S Front Street
Columbus, OH 43215-4131
614-466-0224
Fax: 614-728-2338

Jane Wiechel, Division Director

3114 Federal Assistance
Ohio Department of Education
65 S Front Street
Columbus, OH 43215-4131
614-466-4161
Fax: 704-992-5168

William Henry, Division Director

3115 Ohio Department of Education
25 S Front Street
7th Floor
Columbus, OH 43215-4183
614-466-7578
877-644-6338
Fax: 614-728-4781
http://www.ode.state.oh.us
Works in partnership with school districts to assure high achievements for all learners, promote a safe and orderly learning environment, provide leadership, support, and build capacity, and provide support to

school districts particularly those who need it most.
Susan T Zelman, Superintendent

3116 Personnel Services
Ohio Department of Education
65 S Front Street
Columbus, OH 43215-4131
614-466-3763
Fax: 704-992-5168

Larry Cathell, Division Director

3117 School Finance
Ohio Department of Education
65 S Front Street
Columbus, OH 43215-4131
614-466-6266
Fax: 704-992-5168
E-mail: sf_tavakolia@ode.ohio.gov
http://www.ode.state.ohio.us/foundation/www_.html

Susan Tavakolian, Division Director

3118 School Food Service
Ohio Department of Education
65 S Front Street
Columbus, OH 43215-4131
614-466-2945
Fax: 704-992-5168

Lorita Myles, Division Director

3119 School for the Deaf
Ohio Department of Education
65 S Front Street
Columbus, OH 43215-4131
614-466-3641
Fax: 704-992-5168

Edward C Corbett Jr, Division Director

3120 Special Education
Ohio Department of Education
933 High Street
Worthington, OH 43085
614-466-2650
Fax: 704-992-5168
E-mail: se_herner@ode.ohio.gov

John Herner, Director Special Education

3121 Student Development
Ohio Department of Education
65 S Front Street
Columbus, OH 43215-4131
614-466-3641
Fax: 704-992-5168

Hazel Flowers, Division Director

3122 Teacher Education & Certification
Ohio Department of Education
65 S Front Street
Columbus, OH 43215-4131
614-466-3430
Fax: 704-992-5168

Darrell Parks, Division Director

3123 Vocational & Career Education
Ohio Department of Education
65 S Front Street
Columbus, OH 43215-4131
614-466-3430
Fax: 704-992-5168

Darrell Parks, Division Director

Oklahoma

3124 Accreditation & Standards Division
Oklahoma Department of Education
2500 N Lincoln Boulevard
Oklahoma City, OK 73105-4503
405-521-3333
Fax: 405-521-6205

Sharon Lease, Division Director

3125 Federal/Special/Collaboration Services
Oklahoma Department of Education
2500 N Lincoln Boulevard
Oklahoma City, OK 73105-4503
405-521-4873
Fax: 405-522-3503

Sid Hudson, Division Director

3126 Oklahoma Department of Career and Technology Education
1500 W 7th Avenue
Stillwater, OK 74074-4398
405-743-5444
Fax: 405-743-5541

Roy Peters Jr, Division Director

3127 Oklahoma Department of Education
2500 N Lincoln Boulevard
Hodge Education Building
Oklahoma City, OK 73105-4599
405-521-4485
Fax: 405-521-6205
http://http://sde.state.ok.us

Sandy Garrett, Superindentdent

3128 Oklahoma Department of Education; Financial Services
Oklahoma Department of Education
2500 N Lincoln Boulevard
Oklahoma City, OK 73105-4503
405-521-3371
Fax: 405-521-6205

Don Shive, Division Director

3129 Professional Services
Oklahoma Department of Education
2500 N Lincoln Boulevard
Oklahoma City, OK 73105-4503
405-521-4311
Fax: 405-521-6205

Paul Simon, Division Director

3130 School Improvement
Oklahoma Department of Education
2500 N Lincoln Boulevard
Oklahoma City, OK 73105-4503
405-521-4869
Fax: 405-521-6205

Hugh McCrabb, Division Director

Oregon

3131 Assessment & Evaluation
Oregon Department of Education
255 Capitol Street NE
Salem, OR 97310-0203
503-378-3600
Fax: 503-378-5156
E-mail: firstname.lastname@state.or.us
http://www.ode.state.or.us

Doug Kosty, Assistant Superintendent

3132 Community College Services
Oregon Department of Education
225 Capitol Street NE
Salem, OR 97310-1341
503-378-3600
Fax: 503-378-5156

Stan Bunn, Superintendent

3133 Compensatory Education Office
Oregon Department of Education
225 Capitol Street NE
Salem, OR 97310-1341
503-378-3569
Fax: 503-378-5156

Jerry Fuller, Division Director

3134 Deputy Superintendent Office
Oregon Department of Education
225 Capitol Street NE
Salem, OR 97310-1341
503-378-3573
Fax: 503-378-5156

Bob Burns, Division Director

3135 Early Childhood Council
Oregon Department of Education
225 Capitol Street NE
Salem, OR 97310-1341
503-378-5585
Fax: 503-378-5156

Judy Miller, Division Director

3136 Government Relations
Oregon Department of Education
225 Capitol Street NE
Salem, OR 97310-1341
503-378-8549
Fax: 503-378-5156

Greg McMurdo, Division Director

3137 Management Services
Oregon Department of Education
225 Capitol Street NE
Salem, OR 97310-1341
503-378-8549
Fax: 503-378-5156

Chris Durham, Division Director

3138 Office of Field, Curriculum & Instruction Services
Oregon Department of Education
225 Capitol Street NE
Salem, OR 97310-1341
503-378-8004
Fax: 503-378-5156

Roberta Hutton, Division Director

3139 Oregon Department of Education
225 Capitol Street NE
Salem, OR 97310-0203
503-378-3569
Fax: 503-378-5156
E-mail: ode.frontdesk@ode.state.or.us
http://www.ode.state.or.us

Susan Castillo, Superintendent

3140 Professional Technical Education
Oregon Department of Education
225 Capitol Street NE
Salem, OR 97310-1341
503-378-3584
Fax: 503-378-5156

JD Hoye, Division Director

3141 Special Education
Oregon Department of Education
225 Capitol Street NE
Salem, OR 97310-1341
503-378-3600
Fax: 503-378-5156
http://www.ode.state.or.us

Steve Johnson, Division Director

3142 Student Services Office
Oregon Department of Education
225 Capitol Street NE
Salem, OR 97310-1341
503-378-5585
Fax: 503-378-5156

Judy Miller, Division Director

3143 Twenty First Century Schools Council
Oregon Department of Education
225 Capitol Street NE
Salem, OR 97310-1341
503-378-3600
Fax: 503-378-5156

Joyce Reinke, Division Director

Pennsylvania

3144 Chief Counsel
Pennsylvania Department of Education
333 Market Street
Harrisburg, PA 17101-2210
717-787-5500
Fax: 717-783-0347

Jeffrey Champagne, Division Director

3145 Chief of Staff Office
Pennsylvania Department of Education
333 Market Street
Harrisburg, PA 17101-2210
717-787-9744
Fax: 717-787-7222

Terry Dellmuth, Chief of Staff

3146 Higher Education/Postsecondary Office
Pennsylvania Department of Education
333 Market Street
Harrisburg, PA 17101-2210
717-787-5041
Fax: 717-783-0583

Charles Fuget, Division Director

3147 Office of Elementary and Secondary Education
Pennsylvania Department of Education
333 Market Street
5th Floor
Harrisburg, PA 17101
717-787-2127
Fax: 717-783-6802
E-mail: dhaines@state.pa.us
http://www.pde.state.pa.us

Debra Haines, Executive Secretary

3148 Office of the Comptroller
Pennsylvania Department of Education
333 Market Street
Harrisburg, PA 17101-2210
717-787-5506
Fax: 717-787-3593

William Hardenstine, Division Director

3149 Pennsylvania Department of Education
333 Market Street
Harrisburg, PA 17126
717-783-6788
Fax: 717-787-7222
http://www.teaching.state.pa.us

Charles B Zogby, Secretary

3150 Region 3: Education Department
3535 Market Street
Philadelphia, PA 19104-3309
215-596-1001

Rhode Island

3151 Career & Technical Education
Rhode Island Department of Education
255 Westminster Street
Providence, RI 02903-3414
401-222-4600
Fax: 401-222-2537
http://www.ridoe.net

Frank M Santoro, Division Director

3152 Equity & Access Office
Rhode Island Department of Education
255 Westminster Street
Providence, RI 02903-3414
401-222-4600
Fax: 401-222-2537
http://www.ridoe.net

Frank R Walker III, Division Director

3153 Human Resource Development
Rhode Island Department of Education
255 Westminster Street
Providence, RI 02903-3414
401-222-4600
Fax: 401-222-2537
http://www.ridoe.net

Paula A Rossi, Division Director

3154 Instruction Office
Rhode Island Department of Education
255 Westminster Street
Providence, RI 02903-3414
401-222-4600
Fax: 401-222-2537
http://www.ridoe.net

Marie C DiBiasio, Division Director

3155 Office of Finance
Rhode Island Department of Education
255 Westminster Street
Providence, RI 02903-3414
401-222-4600
Fax: 401-222-2537
http://www.ridoe.net

Frank A Pontarelli, Division Director

3156 Outcomes & Assessment Office
Rhode Island Department of Education
255 Westminster Street
Providence, RI 02903-3414
401-222-4600
Fax: 401-222-2537
http://www.ridoe.net

Pasquale J DeVito, Division Director

3157 Resource Development
Rhode Island Department of Education
255 Westminster Street
Providence, RI 02903-3414
401-222-4600
Fax: 401-222-6033
http://www.ridoe.net

Edward T Costa, Division Director

3158 Rhode Island Department of Education
255 Westminster Street
Providence, RI 02903
401-222-4600
Fax: 401-222-6178
E-mail: ride0001@ride.ri.net
http://www.ridoe.net
Goal of all our work is to improve student performance and help all students meet or exceed a high level of performance. Standards, instruction, and assessment intertwine to provide a system that ensures a strong education for our students.

Peter McWalters, Commissioner

3159 School Food Services Administration
Rhode Island Department of Education
255 Westminster Street
Providence, RI 02903-3414
401-222-4600
Fax: 401-222-3080
http://www.ridoe.net

Virginia da Mora, Dir Integrated Soc Service

3160 Special Needs Office
Rhode Island Department of Education
255 Westminster Street
Providence, RI 02903-3414
401-456-9331
Fax: 401-456-8699
http://www.ridoe.net

Dr.Frances Gallo, Acting Dirctor

3161 Teacher Education & Certification Office
Rhode Island Department of Education
255 Westminster Street
Providence, RI 02903-3414
401-222-4600
Fax: 401-222-2048
http://www.ridoe.net

Louis E DelPapa, Division Director

South Carolina

3162 Budgets & Planning
South Carolina Department of Education
1201 Main Street
Suite 950
Columbia, SC 29201-3730
803-734-2280
Fax: 803-734-0645

Les Boles, Division Director

3163 Communications Services
South Carolina Department of Education
1429 Senate Street
Columbia, SC 29201-3730
803-734-8500
Fax: 803-734-3389

Jerry Adams, Division Director

3164 General Counsel
South Carolina Department of Education
1429 Senate Street
Columbia, SC 29201-3730
803-734-8500
Fax: 803-734-4384

Shelly Carrigg, Esq, Division Director

3165 Internal Administration
South Carolina Department of Education
1429 Senate Street
Columbia, SC 29201-3730
803-734-8500
Fax: 803-734-6225

Jackie Rosswurm, Division Director

3166 Policy & Planning
South Carolina Department of Education
1429 Senate Street
Columbia, SC 29201-3730
803-734-8500
Fax: 803-734-8624

Valerie Truesdale, Division Director

3167 South Carolina Department of Education
1429 Senate Street
Columbia, SC 29201
803-734-8492
Fax: 803-734-3389
http://www.state.sc.us
Provides leadership and services to ensure a system of public education in which all students become educated, responsible, and contributing citizens. For certification information visit www.myscschools.com or contact 803-734-5280.

Inez M Tenenbaum, Superintendent

3168 Support Services
South Carolina Department of Education
1429 Senate Street
Columbia, SC 29201-3730
803-734-8500
Fax: 803-734-8254

Donald Tudor, Division Director

South Dakota

3169 Finance & Management
South Dakota Department of Education
700 Governors Drive
Pierre, SD 57501-2291
605-773-3248
Fax: 605-773-6139

Stacy Krusemark, Division Director

3170 Services for Education
South Dakota Department of Education
700 Governors Drive
Pierre, SD 57501-2291
605-773-4699
Fax: 605-773-3782

Donlynn Rice, Division Director

3171 South Dakota Department of Education & Cultural Affairs
700 Governors Drive
Pierre, SD 57501-2291
605-773-2291
Fax: 605-773-6139
E-mail: ray.christensen@state.sd.us
http://www.state.sd.us/deca/
Advocates for education, facilitate the delivery of statewide educational and cultural services, and promote efficient, appropri-

ate, and quality educational opportunities for all persons residing in South Dakota.

Ray Christensen, Secretary
Patrick Keating, Division Director

3172 South Dakota State Historical Society
South Dakota Dept of Education & Cultural Affairs
900 Governors Drive
Pierre, SD 57501-2291
605-773-3458
Fax: 605-773-6041
E-mail: jay.vogt@state.sd.us
http://www.state.sd.us/deca/
Program areas: Archaeology, archives, historic preservation, museum, research, and publishing

Jay D Vogt, History Manager

3173 Special Education Office
South Dakota Department of Education
700 Governors Drive
Pierre, SD 57501-2291
605-773-3678
Fax: 605-773-3782

Michelle Powers, Division Director

Tennessee

3174 Special Education
Tennessee Department of Education
710 John Robertson Parkway
6th Floor
Nashville, TN 37243
615-741-2851
Fax: 615-532-9412

Joe Fisher, Division Director

3175 Teaching and Learning
Tennessee Department of Education
710 James Robertson Parkway
5th Floor
Nashville, TN 37243
615-532-6195
Fax: 615-741-1837
E-mail: wprotoe@mail.state.tn.us
http://www.state.tn.us/education

Wilma Protoe, Assitant Commissioner

3176 Tennessee Department of Education
710 James Robertson Parkway
6th Floor
Nashville, TN 37243-0375
615-741-2731
Fax: 615-741-6236
E-mail: jwalters@mail.state.tn.us
http://www.state.tn.us/education

Lana Seivers, Commissioner

3177 Vocational Education
Tennessee Department of Education
710 John Robertson Parkway
4th Floor
Nashville, TN 37243-0383
615-532-2800
Fax: 615-532-8226

Ralph Barnett, Assistant Commissioner

Texas

3178 Accountability Reporting and Research
Texas Education Agency
1701 Congress Avenue
WBT Building Room 3-111
Austin, TX 78701-1494
512-475-3523
Fax: 512-475-0028
E-mail: ccloudt@tmail.tea.state.tx.us
http://www.tea.state.tx.us

Criss Cloudt, Associate Commissioner

3179 Chief Counsel
Texas Department of Education
1701 Congress Avenue
Austin, TX 78701-1402
512-463-9720
Fax: 512-463-9838

Kewin O'Hanlon, Division Director

3180 Continuing Education
Texas Education Agency
1701 Congress Avenue
Austin, TX 78701-1402
512-463-9322
Fax: 512-463-6782
E-mail: wtillian@tea.state.tx.us

Walter Tillian, Manager

3181 Curriculum Development & Textbooks
Texas Department of Education
1701 Congress Avenue
Austin, TX 78701-1402
512-463-9581
Fax: 512-463-8057

Ann Smisko, Division Director

3182 Curriculum, Assessment & Professional Development
Texas Department of Education
1701 Congress Avenue
Austin, TX 78701-1402
512-463-9328
Fax: 512-475-3640

Linda Cimusz, Division Director

3183 Curriculum, Assessment and Technology
Texas Department of Education
1701 Congress Avenue
Austin, TX 78701-1402
512-463-9087
Fax: 512-475-3667
E-mail: asmisko@tea.tetn.net

Ann Smisko, Associate Commissioner

3184 Education of Special Populations & Adults
Texas Department of Education
1701 Congress Avenue
Austin, TX 78701-1402
512-463-8992
Fax: 512-463-9176

Jay Cummings, Division Director

3185 Field Services
Texas Department of Education
1701 Congress Avenue
Austin, TX 78701-1402
512-463-9354
Fax: 512-463-9227

3186 Internal Operations
Texas Department of Education
1701 Congress Avenue
Austin, TX 78701-1402
512-463-9437
Fax: 512-475-4293

3187 Operations & School Support
Texas Department of Education
1701 Congress Avenue
Austin, TX 78701-1494
512-463-8994
Fax: 512-463-9227

Roberto Zamora, Division Director

3188 Permanent School Fund
Texas Department of Education
1701 Congress Avenue
Room 5-120
Austin, TX 78701-1402
512-463-9169
Fax: 512-463-9432

Carlos Resendez, Division Director

3189 Region 6: Education Department
1200 Main Tower
Dallas, TX 75202-4325
214-767-3626

3190 Texas Department of Education
1701 N Congress Avenue
William B Travis Building
Austin, TX 78701-1494
512-463-8985
Fax: 512-463-9008
http://www.sbec.state.tx.us

Dr.Shirley Neeley, Commissioner

Utah

3191 Applied Technology Education Services
Utah Department of Education
250 E 500 S
Salt Lake City, UT 84111-4200
801-538-7840
Fax: 801-538-7868
E-mail: rbrems@usoe.kiz.ut.us
http://www.usoe.k12.ut.us
State agency for career and technical education.

Rod Brems, Associate Superintendent
Leslee Andelean, Administrative Assistant

3192 Instructional Services Division
Utah Department of Education
250 E 500 S
Salt Lake City, UT 84111-3204
801-538-7515
Fax: 801-538-7768

Jerry P Peterson, Division Director

3193 Schools for the Deaf & Blind
Utah Department of Education
250 E 500 S
Salt Lake City, UT 84111-3204
801-629-4700
Fax: 801-629-4896

Wayne Glaus, Division Director

3194 Utah Office of Education
250 E 500 South
PO Box 144200
Salt Lake City, UT 84111
801-538-7510
Fax: 801-538-7768
http://www.usoe.k12.ut.us
Steven O Laing, Superintendent

3195 Utah Office of Education; Agency Services Division
250 E 500 S
PO Box 144200
Salt Lake City, UT 84114-4200
801-538-7500
Fax: 801-538-7768
http://www.usoe.k12.ut.us
Patrick Ogden, Associate Superintendent

Vermont

3196 Career & Lifelong Learning
Vermont Department of Education
120 State Street
Montpelier, VT 05620-0001
802-828-3101
Fax: 802-828-3146
Charles Stander, Division Director

3197 Core Services
Vermont Department of Education
120 State Street
Montpelier, VT 05620-0001
802-828-3135
Fax: 802-828-3140
Eleanor Perry, Division Director

3198 Family & School Support
Vermont Department of Education
120 State Street
Montpelier, VT 05620-0001
802-828-2447
Fax: 802-828-3140
Jo Busha, Division Director

3199 Financial Management Team
Vermont Department of Education
120 State Street
Montpelier, VT 05620-0001
802-828-3155
Fax: 802-828-3140
Mark O'Day, Division Director

3200 School Development & Information
Vermont Department of Education
120 State Street
Montpelier, VT 05620-0001
802-828-2756
Fax: 802-828-3140
Douglas Chiappetta, Division Director

3201 Teaching & Learning
Vermont Department of Education
120 State Street
Montpelier, VT 05620-0001
802-828-3111
Fax: 802-828-3140
Marguerite Meyer, Division Director

3202 Vermont Department of Education
120 State Street
Montpelier, VT 05620-2501
802-828-3135
Fax: 802-828-3140
http://Vermont.gov

For certification information visit www.pen.k12.va.us or contact 804-225-2022.
Richard Cate, Commissioner

3203 Vermont Special Education
120 State Street
Montpelier, VT 05602-2703
802-828-3141
Theodore Riggen, Division Director

Virginia

3204 Administrative Services
Virginia Department of Education
14th & Franklin Streets
PO Box 2120
Richmond, VA 23216
804-225-3252
Fax: 804-786-5828
Edward W Carr, Division Director

3205 Policy, Assessment, Research & Information Systems
Virginia Department of Education
101 N 4th Street
PO Box 2120
Richmond, VA 23218-2120
804-225-2102
800-292-3820
Fax: 804-371-8978
E-mail: charris@pen.k12.va.us
http://www.pen.k12.va.us
Anne Wescott, Assistant Superintendent

3206 Student Services
Virginia Department of Education
14th & Franklin Streets
PO Box 2120
Richmond, VA 23216
804-225-2757
Fax: 804-786-5828
Dr.Cynthia Cave, Division Director

3207 Virginia Centers for Community Education
Virginia Department of Education
PO Box 2120
Richmond, VA 23218-2120
804-225-2293
Fax: 804-786-5828
Dr. Lenox L McLendon, Division Director

3208 Virginia Department of Education
James Monroe Building
101 N 14th Street
Richmond, VA 23219
804-225-2023
800-292-3820
Fax: 804-371-2099
E-mail: rlayman@pen.k12.va.us
http://www.pen.k12.va.us
Jo Lynne DeMary, Superintendent

Washington

3209 Region 10: Education Department
915 2nd Avenue
Room 3362
Seattle, WA 98174-1001
206-220-7800
Fax: 202-220-7806
http://www.ed.gov

3210 Washington Department of Education
PO Box 47200
Olympia, WA 98504-7200
360-725-6000
Fax: 360-753-6712
http://www.k12.wa.us
Theresa Bergeson, Superintendent

3211 Washington Department of Education; Instruction Program
PO Box 47200
Olympia, WA 98504-7200
206-753-1545
Fax: 360-586-0247
John Pearson, Division Director

3212 Washington Department of Education; Commission on Student Learning Administration
PO Box 47200
Olympia, WA 98504-7200
360-664-3155
Fax: 360-664-3028
Terry Bergeson, Division Director

3213 Washington Department of Education; Executive Services
PO Box 47200
Olympia, WA 98504-7200
360-586-9056
Fax: 360-753-6754
Ken Kanikeberg, Division Director

3214 Washington Department of Education; School Business & Administrative Services
PO Box 47200
Olympia, WA 98504-7200
206-753-6742
David Moberly, Division Director

West Virginia

3215 Division of Administrative Services
West Virginia Department of Education
1900 Kanawha Boulevard E
Building 6
Charleston, WV 25305-0009
304-558-2441
Fax: 304-558-8867
Carolyn Arrington, Division Director

3216 Research, Accountability & Professional
West Virginia Department of Education
1900 Kanawha Boulevard E
Building 6
Charleston, WV 25305-0009
304-558-3762
Fax: 304-558-8867
William J Luff Jr, Division Director

3217 Student Services & Instructional Services
West Virginia Department of Education
1900 Kanawha Boulevard E
Building 6
Charleston, WV 25305-0009
304-558-2691
Fax: 304-558-8867
Keith Smith, Division Director

3218 Technical & Adult Education Services
West Virginia Department of Education
1900 Kanawha Boulevard E
Building 6
Charleston, WV 25305-0009
304-558-2346
Fax: 304-558-8867

Adam Sponaugle, Division Director

3219 West Virginia Department of Education
1900 Kanawha Boulevard E
Building 6, Room B-358
Charleston, WV 25305-0330
304-558-2681
Fax: 304-558-0048
http://www.wvde.state.wv.us
The constitutional mission is to provide supervision of the K-12 education system.

David Stewart, Superintendent
Audrey Horne, President

Wisconsin

3220 Division for Learning Support: Equity & Advocacy
Wisconsin Department of Education
125 S Webster Street
PO Box 7841
Madison, WI 53707-7841
608-266-1649
Fax: 608-267-3746
http://www.dpi.state.wi.us

Carolyn Stanford-Taylor, Division Director

3221 Instructional Services Division
Wisconsin Department of Education
125 S Webster Street
PO Box 7841
Madison, WI 53707-7841
608-266-3361
Fax: 608-267-3746
http://www.dpi.state.wi.us

Pauline Nikolay, Division Director

3222 Library Services Division
Wisconsin Department of Education
125 S Webster Street
PO Box 7841
Madison, WI 53707-7841
608-266-2205
Fax: 608-267-3746
http://www.dpi.state.wi.us

William Wilson, Division Director

3223 School Financial Resources & Management
Wisconsin Department of Education
125 S Webster Street
PO Box 7841
Madison, WI 53707-7841
608-266-3851
Fax: 608-267-3746
http://www.dpi.state.wi.us

Bambi Statz, Division Director

3224 Wisconsin College System Technical
310 Price Place
PO Box 7874
Madison, WI 53707-7874
608-266-1770
Fax: 608-266-1285
E-mail: wtcsb@board.tec.wi.us
http://www.board.tec.wi.us

Richard Carpenter, President

3225 Wisconsin Department of Public Instruction
125 S Webster Street
PO Box 7841
Madison, WI 53707-7841
608-266-1771
800-441-4563
Fax: 608-266-5188
http://www.dpi.state.wi.us

Elizabeth Burmaster, Superintendent

Wyoming

3226 Accounting, Personnel & School Finance Unit
Wyoming Department of Education
2300 Capitol Avenue
Floor 2
Cheyenne, WY 82001-3644
307-777-6392
Fax: 307-777-6234

Barry Nimmo, Division Director

3227 Applied Data & Technology Unit
Wyoming Department of Education
2300 Capitol Avenue
Floor 2
Cheyenne, WY 82001-3644
307-777-6213
Fax: 307-777-6234

Steven King, Division Director

3228 Services for Individuals with Hearing Loss
Wyoming Department of Education
2300 Capitol Avenue
Floor 2
Cheyenne, WY 82001-3644
307-777-4686
Fax: 307-777-6234

Tim Sanger, Division Director

3229 Support Programs & Quality Results Division
Wyoming Department of Education
2300 Capitol Avenue
Floor 2
Cheyenne, WY 82001-3644
307-777-6213
Fax: 307-777-6234

Dr. Alan Sheinker, Division Director

3230 Wyoming Department of Education
2300 Capitol Avenue
Hathaway Building, 2nd Floor
Cheyenne, WY 82002-0050
307-777-7675
Fax: 307-777-6234
http://www.k12.wy.us

Dr.Trent Blankenship, Superintendent

Associations

3231 Academic Alliances
American Association of Higher Education
1 Dupont Circle NW
Suite 360
Washington, DC 20036-1143
202-293-6440
Fax: 202-293-0073
E-mail: info@aahe.net
http://www.aahe.org
Encourages quality education and the professional development of all teachers and educators.

J.Michael Ortiz, Chair Elect

3232 Agency for Instructional Technology
1800 N StoneLake Drive
Box A
Bloomington, IN 47402-0120
812-339-2203
800-457-4509
Fax: 812-333-4218
E-mail: info@ait.net
http://www.ait.net
Professional development, school-to-career, employability skills of problem solving, self management and teamwork.

George Turner, Chair
Sandra McBrayer, Vice Chair

3233 American Association of Colleges for Teacher Education
1307 New York Avenue NW
Suite 300
Washington, DC 20005-4701
202-293-2450
Fax: 202-457-8095
E-mail: aacte@aacte.org
http://www.aacte.org
Colleges and universities concerned with the preparation and development of professionals in education.

Sharon Robinson, President/CEO

3234 American Educational Research Association
1230 17th Street NW
Washington, DC 20036-3078
202-223-9485
Fax: 202-775-1824
E-mail: aera@gmu.edu
http://www.aera.net
Supports improvement of the educational process through the encouragement of scholarly inquiry related to education, the dissemination of research results, and their practical application. Holds a conference and publishes books, videos, and magazines.

Marilyn Cochran-Smith, President

3235 American Educational Studies Association
302 Buchtel Mall
Akron, OH 44325
330-972-7111
http://www.uakron.edu/aesa
Encourages research and the improvement of teaching in various curriculum areas.

Kathleen Bennett deMarrais, President

3236 American Foundation for Negro Affairs
117 S 17th Street
Suite 1200
Philadelphia, PA 19103-5011
215-854-1470
Fax: 215-854-1487
Offers a model for educational programs preparing minority students for professional careers.

Samuel L Evans, President

3237 American Society for Training and Development Information Center
1640 Duke Street
Alexandria, VA 22314-3407
703-683-8100
Fax: 703-683-8103
Serves as the educational society for persons engaged in training and development of business, industry, education and government personnel.

Edith Allen, Director

3238 American Speech-Language-Hearing Association
10801 Rockville Pike
Rockville, MD 20852-3226
301-897-5700
800-638-8255
Fax: 301-571-0457
E-mail: actioncenter@asha.org
http://www.asha.org
Certifies professionals providing speech, language and hearing services to the public. It is an accrediting agency for college and university graduate programs in speech-language pathology and audiology.

3239 Association of Teacher Educators
1900 Association Drive
Sute Ate
Reston, VA 20191-1502
703-620-3110
Fax: 703-620-9530
E-mail: ATE@aol.com
http://www.ate1.org/pubs/home.cfm
Found in 1920 ATE, promotes quality teacher education programs.

Ed Pultorak, President

3240 Center for Rural Studies
University of Vermont, College of Agriculture
108 Morrill Hall
146 University Place
Burlington, VT 05405-0106
802-656-3021
Fax: 802-656-0290
http://crs.uvm.edu
Disseminates information on social, economic, organizational and natural resource aspects of rural life and conducts training and workshops for the professional.

Jane Kolodinsky, Co-Director
Fred Schmidt, Co-Director

3241 Committee on Continuing Education for School Personnel
Kean College of New Jersey
Academic Services
Union, NJ 07083
908-737-5326
Fax: 908-737-5845
Develops activities for professional and personal growth among teachers and educators.

George Sisko, Director

3242 Council for Learning Disabilities
PO Box 4014
Leesburg, VA 20177
571-258-1010
Fax: 571-258-1011
http://www.cldinternational.org
Provides services to professionals who work with individuals with learning disabilities including conferences and publications.

Kirsten McBride, Executive Director

3243 Council of Administrators of Special Education
The Council for Exceptional Children
Fort Valley State University
1005 State University Drive
Fort Valley, GA 31030
478-825-7667
888-232-7733
Fax: 478-825-7811
E-mail: lpurcell@bellsouth.net
http://www.casecec.org
Promotes professional leadership and opportunities for personal and professional advancement. CASE's 5,400 members include administrators, directors and supervisors of special education programs and services.

Steve Milliken, President

3244 Distance Education & Training Council
1601 18th Street NW
Washington, DC 20009-2529
202-234-5100
Fax: 202-332-1386
E-mail: detc@detc.org
http://www.detc.org
A voluntary association of accredited distance education institutions.

Henry Spille, Chair

3245 ERIC Clearinghouse on Teaching and Teacher Education
American Association of Colleges for Teacher Ed.
1307 New York Avenue NW
Suite 300
Washington, DC 20055-4701
202-293-2450
Fax: 202-457-8095
E-mail: aacte@aacte.org
http://www.aacte.org
Teacher recruitment, selection, licensing, certification, training, preservice and inservice preparation, evaluation, retention and retirement. Includes theory, philosophy and teaching practice.

Dr. Mary Dilworth, Director
Deborah Newby, Associate Director

3246 Educational Leadership Institute
4455 Connecticut Avenue NW
Suite 310
Washington, DC 20008
202-822-8405
Fax: 202-872-4050
E-mail: iel@iel.org
http://www.iel.org
Seeks to improve the quality of educational leadership at all levels through field-level research and training programs.

Elizabeth Hale, President

3247 International Council on Education for Teaching
1000 Capitol Drive
Wheeling, IL 60090
847-465-0191
Fax: 847-465-5617
E-mail: icet@nl.edu
http://www.nl.edu
International association dedicated to the improvement of teacher education and all forms of education and training related to national development.

Darrell Bloom, Executive Director
Barbara Spence, Administrative Assistant

3248 National Association of State Directors of Teacher Education & Certification
22 Bates Road
PMB #134
Mashpee, MA 02649-3267
508-539-8844
Fax: 508-539-8868
E-mail: nasdtec@attbi.com
http://www.nasdtec.org
Provides leadership in matters related to the preparation and certification of professional school personnel.

Roy Einreinhofer, Executive Director

3249 National Center for Community Education
1017 Avon Street
Flint, MI 48503-2797
810-238-0463
800-811-1105
Fax: 810-238-9211
E-mail: nccenet@earthlink.net
http://www.nccenet.org
Provides short term training workshops for persons entering and/or working in the field of community education.

Duane R Brown, Director

3250 National Council for the Accreditation of Teacher Education
2010 Massachusetts Avenue NW
Washington, DC 20036-1023
202-466-7496
Fax: 202-296-6620
E-mail: ncate@ncate.org
http://www.ncate.org
Professional accrediting organization for schools, colleges, and departments of education in the United States.

Arthur E Wise, President
Donna M Gollnick, Sr VP

3251 National Education Association
1201 16th Street NW
Washington, DC 20036-3290
202-833-4000
Fax: 202-822-7974
E-mail: ncuea@nea.org
http://www.nea.org
Advocates for the education profession and the well-being of children; supports campaigns designed to improve the teaching profession, teachers in their efforts to improve teaching; training programs, safe schools and better working conditions.

Reg Weaver, President
Dennis Van Roekel, Vice President

3252 National Middle School Association
4151 Executive Parkway
Suite 300
Westerville, OH 43081
614-895-4730
800-528-6672
Fax: 614-895-4750
E-mail: info@NMSA.org
http://www.nmsa.org
Resource centers, conferences, professional development, and more.

Kathy McAvoy, President

3253 National Staff Development Council
5995 Fairfield Road
Suite 4
Oxford, OH 45056
513-523-6029
Fax: 513-523-0638
http://www.nsdc.org
Researches and organizes staff development theories and practices for various school districts.

Dennis Sparks, Executive Director

3254 National Women's Studies Association
7100 Baltimore Boulevard
University of Maryland
College Park, MD 20740
301-403-0524
Fax: 301-403-4137
E-mail: nwsa@umail.umd.edu
http://www.nwsa.org
Works to further the social, political and professional development of women's studies programs and projects.

Jacquelyn Zita, President

3255 Recruiting New Teachers
385 Concord Avenue
Suite 103
Belmont, MA 02478-3037
617-489-6000
800-45 -EACH
Fax: 617-489-6005
E-mail: rnt@rnt.org
http://www.rnt.org/channels/clearinghouse
Conducts public service advertising campaign encouraging people to consider teaching careers.

Mildred Hudson, CEO/RNT

3256 Search Associates
PO Box 636
Dallas, PA 18612-0636
570-696-5400
Fax: 570-696-9500
Sponsors recruiting fairs across the country.

Dr. John Magagna

3257 Teacher Education Division
The Council for Exceptional Children
1920 Association Drive
Reston, VA 20191-1545
703-620-3660
888-232-773
Fax: 703-264-9494
Association promoting preparation and continuing development of effective professionals in special education and related fields such as general education, allied health, speech and language pathology, rehabilitation, legal services and more.

3258 Apple Education Grants
Apple Computer
2420 Ridge Point Drive
Austin, TX 78754
800-800-2775
Fax: 512-919-2992
http://www.apple.com
Awarded each year to teams of K-12 educators working on educational technology plans. Potential awardees find innovative uses of technology in the classroom and come from schools that would otherwise have limited access to technology.

3259 Bayer/NSF Award for Community Innovation
105 Terry Drive
Suite 120
Newtown, PA 18940
215-579-8590
800-291-6020
Fax: 215-579-8589
E-mail: success@edumedia.com
http://www.bayernsfaward.com
A community-based science and technology competition to give all sixth, seventh and eighth-graders a hands-on experience with real-world problems using the scientific method.

Stephanie Hallman, Program Manager
Stacey Gall, Competition Coordinator

3260 Excellence in Teaching Cabinet Grant
Curriculm Associates
PO Box 2001
North Billericka, MA 01862
800-225-0248
Fax: 800-366-1158
http://www.curriculumassociates.com
Awarded to educators who wish to implement unique educational projects. Potential awardees propose projects using a variety of teaching tools, including technology and print.

3261 Magna Awards
American School Board Journal
1680 Duke Street
Alexandria, VA 22314
703-549-6719
Fax: 703-549-6719
Recognizes local school boards that are putting student achievement and community engagement at the center of their work. October 31st deadline.
Annual

3262 NSTA Award for Principals
National Science Teachers Association
1840 Wilson Boulevard
Arlington, VA 22201
703-243-7100
888-400-NSTA
Fax: 703-243-7177
E-mail: mbulter@nsta.org
http://www.nsta.org
The 1999 Exemplary Middle Level and High School Principal Awards recognizes one middle level and one high school principal who have demonstrated leadership in developing, implementing, and maintaining an outstanding science progam; supported staff development; promoted positive relationships, and served as an advocate and leader.

Michelle Butler, Manager
Linda Froschauer, President

3263 NSTA Awards
National Science Teachers Association
1840 Wilson Boulevard
Arlington, VA 22201-3000
703-243-7100
Fax: 703-243-7177
Awards for excellence in dozens of fields
and programs.

3264 National Teachers Hall of Fame
1320 C of E Drive
Emporia, KS 66801
620-341-9131
800-968-3224
Fax: 620-341-5912
E-mail: hallfame@emporia.edu
http://www.nthf.org
Founded for the purpose of recognizing the
exceptional qualities possessed by our nation's teachers. Candidates eligible for in-
duction must have at least 20 years of
full-time classroom teaching in grades
pre-kindergarten through high school. Candidates may be active or retired.

David John, President
Cora Hedstrom, Coordinator/Teacher

**3265 Presidential Awards for Excellence
in Mathematics and Science
Teaching**
National Science Foundation
4201 Wilson Boulevard
Arlington, VA 22230
703-292-8620
Fax: 703-292-9044
E-mail: msaul@nsf.gov
http://www.ehr.nsf.gov
This award is the nation's highest commen-
dation for K-12 math and science teachers.
Approximately 108 teachers are recognized
annually with this prestigious award.

Mark Saul, Director

3266 Senior Researcher Award
Music Education Research Council
Deptartment of Music
138 Fine Arts Center
Columbia, MO 65211
573-884-1604
Fax: 573-884-7444
For recognition of a significant scholarly
achievement maintained over a period of
years.

**3267 Toyota Tapestry Grants for
Teachers**
National Science Teachers Association
1840 Wilson Boulevard
Arlington, VA 22201-3000
800-807-9852
Fax: 703-522-6193
E-mail: tapestry@nsta.org
http://www.nsta.org/programs/tapestry
Sponsored by Toyota Motor Sales USA, this
offers a minimum of 70 grants totaling
$550,000 each year to K-12 teachers of sci-
ence who wish to implement an innovative,
community based science project. 50 large
grants of up to $10,000 each will be avail-
able as well as a minimum of 20 mini-grants
of up to $2,500 each. Categories include
Physical Science, Environmental Science
and Literacy and Science.

Eric Crossley, Industry/Education
Programs

Conferences

3268 ACE Fellows Program
American Council on Education
1 Dupont Circle NW
Washington, DC 20036-1193
202-939-9420
Fax: 808-785-8056
E-mail: fellows@ace.nche.edu
http://www.acenet.edu
Provides comprehensive leadership development for senior faculty and administrators of universities and colleges. Offers
mentor-intern relationships programs. Special institutional grants available for candidates from community colleges, tribal
colleges and private historical black universities and colleges.

**3269 ASQ Annual Koalaty Kid
Conference**
ASQ
611 E Wisconsin Avenue
Milwaukee, WI 53201
414-272-8717
Fax: 414-272-1247
http://www.asq.org
A professional association headquartered in
Milwaukee, Wisconsin, creates better
workplaces and communities worldwide by
advancing learning, quality improvement,
and knowledge exchange.

April

Andrew Hohensee

**3270 Alaska Department of Education
Bilingual & Bicultural Education
Conference**
University of Alaska, Conference &
Special Events
117 Eielson Building
Fairbanks, AK 99775
907-474-7396
Stresses the importance of literacy and
multicultural education for Alaskan educa-
tors.

February

**3271 American Association of Collegiate
Registrars & Admissions Officers**
1 Dupont Circle NW
Suite 520
Washington, DC 20036-1137
202-293-9161
Fax: 202-872-8857
http://www.aacrao.org
Promotes higher education and furthers the
professional developmentof members
working in admissions, enrollment management, financial aid, institutional research,
records and registration.

April
125 booths with 2500 attendees

Jerry Sullivan, Executive Director
Martha Henebry, Publications Manager

**3272 American Federation of Teachers
Biennial Convention & Exhibition**
AFL-CIO
555 New Jersey Avenue NW
Washington, DC 20001-2029
202-879-4400
Fax: 202-879-4558
E-mail: online@aft.org
http://www.aft.org
represent the economic, social and professional interests of classroom teachers

Edward McElroy, President

**3273 American Society for
Training-Development
International Conference**
1640 King Street
Po Box 1443
Alexandria, VA 22313-2043
703-683-8100
800-628-2783
Fax: 703-683-1523
http://www.astd.org/astd/conferences/abou
t_conferences
Explore the newest training theories and
models. ASTD conferences ensure that
you're up-to-date with the latest thinking
and trends affecting workplace learning and
performance. Attended by international
teachers and professors, counselors and human relations personnel.

May

Tony Bingham, President/CEO
Christopher Palazio, Advertising
Coordinator

**3274 Annual Building Championship
Schools Conference**
Center for Peak Performing Schools
2021 Clubhouse Drive
Greeley, CO 80634
970-339-9277
Interested in curriculum development and
instructional assessment. Members include
administrators at all levels of education.

February

3275 Annual Convention
New York School Board Association
24 Century Hill Drive
Suite 200
Latham, NY 12210-2125
518-783-0200
Fax: 518-783-0211
E-mail: info@nyssba.org
http://www.nyssba.org
Contains exhibitors representing various
educational industries including: buses,
athletic and recreational services, school
furnishings and public utilities.

October
240 booths with 3,000 attendees

Cheryl Brenn, Marketing Manager

**3276 Annual New England Kindergarten
Conference**
Lesley University
29 Everett Street
Cambridge, MA 02138
617-349-8922
800-999-1959
Fax: 617-349-8125
E-mail: kindconf@mail.lesley.edu
http://www.lesley.edu
November
1000 attendees

Mary Mindess, Conference Coordinator
Kari Nygaard, Conference Manager

**3277 Annual State Convention of
Association of Texas Professional
Educators**
305 E Huntland Drive
Suite 300
Austin, TX 78752
512-467-0071
800-777-2873
Fax: 512-467-2203
E-mail: atpe@atpe.org
http://www.atpe.org

Professional association for Texas public school educators.

March
100 booths with 1,300 attendees

Doug Rogers, Executive Director
Kara Lacke, Conference Manager

3278 Association for Educational Communications & Technology Annual Convention

AECT
1800 N Stonelake Drive
Suite 2
Bloomington, IN 47404
812-335-7675
Fax: 812-335-7678
E-mail: aect@aect.org
http://www.aect.org/Events/default.htm
Offers training tracks focusing on a variety of special interest areas. Special sessions examine such topics as hypermedia, TQM, school reform, and advanced telecommunications. Half-day workshops offer in-depth training on the latest technology applications for education.

Dr Phillip Harris, Executive Director
Ned Shaw, Mktg & Communications Dir.

3279 Association for Library & Information Science Education Annual Conference

ALISE
1009 Commerce Park Drive
Suite 150
Oak Ridge, TN 37830
865-425-0155
Fax: 865-481-0390
E-mail: contact@alise.org
http://www.alise.org
An annual conference attended by over 250 university/college faculty librarians with over 10 co-sponsors. Although a special interest conference, it has open registration and includes a job placement service.

January

Deborah York, Executive Director
Lance Vowell, Information Management

3280 Association of Teacher Educators

Po Box 793
Manassas, VA 20113
703-331-0911
Fax: 703-331-3666
E-mail: dritchey@ate1.org
http://www.ate1.org
Exhibits publications, teaching materials, model programs, and other related merchandise.

February
25 booths

David Ritchey, Conference Contact

3281 California Council for Adult Education

1006 4th Street
Suite 260
Sacramento, CA 95814-3314
916-444-3323
Fax: 916-557-1152
A state conference of adult educators representing school districts, community colleges and related products and services to the education field.

April
40 booths

Richard Whiteman, Conference Contact

3282 California Kindergarten Association Annual Conference

California Kindergarten Association
3009 Douglas Blvd
Suite 120
Roseville, CA 95661
916-780-5331
Fax: 916-780-5330
E-mail: cka@ckanet.org
http://www.ckanet.org
A conference catering to early childhood education professionals.

January
120 booths with 2,000 attendees and 100 exhibits

Armando Argandona, President

3283 California School Boards Association Conference

PO Box 1660
West Sacramento, CA 95691-6660
916-371-4691
Fax: 916-371-3407
E-mail: colcese@csba.org
http://www.csba.org
Products and services targeted to the California public schools.

December
200 booths

Chris Olcese, Conference Contact

3284 Careers Conference

Center on Education and Work
964 Educational Sciences Building
1025 W. Johnson Street
Madison, WI 53706-1706
608-263-4779
800-446-0399
Fax: 608-262-3063
E-mail: cewconf@education.wisc.edu
http://www.cew.wisc.edu
Designed to serve all practitioners concerned with career development and education for work. This annual conference presents learning opportunities at all levels, from a basic introduction to keeping current with the very latest in advanced practices.

Jan - Feb
40 booths with 1500 attendees

Carol Edds, Conference Director

3285 Center for Play Therapy Fall Conference

University of North Texas
PO Box 311337
Denton, TX 76203
940-565-3864
Fax: 940-565-4461
E-mail: cpt@coefs.coe.unt.edu
http://www.centerforplaytherapy.com

October
4 booths with 350 attendees

Garry Landreth PhD, Director

3286 Central States Conference on the Teaching of Foreign Languages

University of Nebraska at Omaha
Omaha, NE 68182
402-554-2403
Offers various information, updates and programs to advance the teaching of foreign languages and foreign language educators.

3287 Chicago Principals Association Education Conference

221 N Lasalle Street
Suite 3316
Chicago, IL 60601-1505
312-263-7767
Fax: 312-263-2012
Educational or fund raising products including copy machines, computers, book companies, etc.

February

Beverly Tunney, Conference Contact

3288 Classroom Connect

8000 Marina Boulevard
Suite 400
Brisbane, CA 94005
650-351-5100
800-638-1639
Fax: 650-351-5300
E-mail: conect@classroom.com
http://www.classroom.com
A leading provider of professional development programs and online instructional content for K-12 education.

October

3289 Colorado Association of School Executives Conference

4101 S Bannock Street
Englewood, CO 80110-4605
303-762-8762
Fax: 303-762-8697
47 booths exhibiting school administration and education/construction related products.

August

Janice Hartmangruber, Conference Contact

3290 Education Conference

International Honor and Professional Association
PO Box 6626
Bloomington, IN 47407-6626
812-339-3411
800-487-3411
Fax: 812-339-3462
E-mail: office@pilambda.org
http://www.pilambda.org
Honor outstanding educators and inspire them to be effective leaders who address critical issues in education.

400 attendees

Juli Knutson, Conference Manager

3291 Florida Elementary School Principals Association Conference

206 S Monroe Street
Suite B
Tallahassee, FL 32301-1801
800-593-3626
Fax: 850-224-3892
Exhibitors from fundraisers to computer companies.

November
50 booths

Lisa Begue, Conference Contact

3292 Florida School Administrators Association Summer Conference

206 S Monroe Street
Suite B
Tallahassee, FL 32301-1801
850-224-3626
800-593-3626
Fax: 850-224-3892
E-mail: sgray@fasa.net
Exhibits include computer software, textbooks and school supplies, fundraising

companies, schoolyear book and ring companies, video and audio companies, furniture suppliers and other school related products.

Jan./June/Nov.
700/300 attendees and 100/85 exhibits

Sharon Gray, Conference Coordinator
Kim Beaty, Director Communications

3293 Florida Vocational Association Conference

1420 N Paul Russell Road
Tallahassee, FL 32301-4835
850-878-6860
Fax: 850-878-5476
Curriculum materials, industrial equipment and supplies, computer hardware and software, medical equipment and other materials utilized by vocational educators.

July
150 booths

Donna Harper, Conference Contact

3294 Illinois Assistant Principals Conference

2990 Baker Drive
Springfield, IL 62703-2800
217-525-1383
Fax: 217-525-7264
http://http://ipa.vsat.net
Professional member association dedicated to the improvement of elementary and secondary education.

February
120 booths with 200 attendees

David Turner, Executive Director
Pam Burdine, Exhibit Contact

3295 Illinois Principals Professional Conference

2990 Baker Drive
Springfield, IL 62703-2800
217-525-1383
Fax: 217-525-7264
http://http:ipa.vsat.net
Professional member association dedicated to the improvement of elementary and secondary education.

October
120 booths with 800 attendees

Julie Weichert, Associate Director
David Turner, Executive Director

3296 Illinois Resource Center Conference of Teachers of Linguistically Diverse Students

Illinois Resource Center
1855 S Mount Prospect Road
Des Plaines, IL 60018-1805
847-803-3112
Fax: 847-803-2828
A conference that caters to those educators involved with teaching multi-licensed pupils.

March

3297 Illinois School Boards Association

430 E Vine Street
Springfield, IL 62703-2236
217-528-9688
Fax: 217-528-2831
School equipment, supplies, building maintenance, insurance and bond sales programs, supplies and equipment.

November
235 booths

Sandra Boston, Conference Contact

3298 Indiana School Boards Association Annual Conference

1 N Capitol Avenue
Suite 1215
Indianapolis, IN 46204-2095
317-639-0330
Educational products and services.

September/October
158 booths

Mary A. Chapman, Conference Contact

3299 International Association for Social Science Information Service & Technology

Institute for Social Science
Research/UCLA Archive
405 Hilgard Avenue
Attn: Wendy Treadwell
Los Angeles, CA 90095-9000
612-624-4389
Fax: 612-626-9353
http://www.iassistdata.org/conferences
Conference for association members offering the latest information on research and technology in the social sciences fields.

May
May

Ann Green, President

3300 Iowa Council Teachers of Math Conference

1712 55th Street
Des Moines, IA 50310-1548
515-242-7846
Math teachers conference.

February
48 booths

Michael Link, Conference Contact

3301 Iowa Reading Association Conference

512 Lynn Avenue
Ames, IA 50014-7320
515-292-0126
100 tabletops.

April

Evelyn Beavers, Conference Contact

3302 Iowa School Administrators Association Annual Convention

4500 Westown Parkway
Suite 140
West Des Moines, IA 50266-6717
515-267-1115
Fax: 515-267-1066
150 booths.

August

Gaylord Tryon, Conference Contact

3303 Iowa School Boards Association

700 2nd Avenue
Suite 100
Des Moines, IA 50309-1713
515-288-1991

November
135 booths

Wayne R Beal, Conference Contact

3304 Kansas School Boards Association Conference

1420 SW Arrowhead Road
Topeka, KS 66604-4001
785-273-3600
Fax: 785-273-7580

Wide variety of school district vendors and contacts for products and services.

December
70 booths

3305 Kansas United School Administrators Conference

515 S Kansas Avenue
Suite 201
Topeka, KS 66032-3415
785-232-6566
Fax: 785-232-9776
E-mail: usaoffice@usa-ks.org
http://www.usa-ks.org
Exhibits of the latest educational goods and services.

January
180 booths

Dennis Stones, President
Rob Balsters, President-Elect

3306 Kentucky School Boards Association Conference

260 Democrat Drive
Frankfort, KY 40601-9214
502-695-4630
Fax: 502-695-5451

February
45 booths

Ann Booten, Conference Contact

3307 Kentucky School Superintendents Association Meeting

154 Consumer Lane
Frankfort, KY 40601-8489
502-875-3411
Fax: 502-875-4634
A variety of education services and sales, and products from architecture to computers.

June
36 booths

Dr. Roland Haun, Conference Contact

3308 Lilly Conference on College Teaching

Miami University
102 Roudebush Hau
Oxford, OH 45056
513-529-6648
Fax: 513-529-3762
E-mail: lillyconference@muohio.edu
http://www.muohio.edu/lillyconference/
Celebrating 23 years of presenting the Scholarship of Teaching. The Lilly Conference specializes in training and teaching methodology for higher education professionals through approximately 160 sessions by over 150 presenters. Many of the presenters are nationally or internationally known experts in Scholarship of Teaching.

November
660 attendees

Melody Barton, Conference Manager
Milton Cox, Conference Director

3309 Lilly Conferences on College and University Teaching

International Alliance of Teacher Scholars
Box 1000
Claremnont, CA 91711
800-718-4287
Fax: 909-621-8270
E-mail: alliance@iats.com
http://www.iats.com
Lilly Conferences are retreats that combine workshops, discussion sessions and major addresses, with opportunities for informal discussion about excellence in college and university teaching and learning. Interna-

tionally known scholars join new and experienced faculty members and administrators from all over the world.

November

Laurie Richlin, Director

3310 Louisiana School Boards Association Conference
7912 Summa Avenue
Baton Rouge, LA 70809-3416
504-769-3191
60 booths of school and classroom related products and/or services.

February

James V Soileau, Conference Contact

3311 Maine Principals Association Conference
PO Box 2468
Augusta, ME 04338-2468
207-622-0217
50 booths.

April

Barbara Proko, Conference Contact

3312 Massachusetts Elementary School Principals Association Conference
28 Lord Road
Suite 125
Marlborough, MA 01752-4548
508-624-0500
Fax: 508-485-9965
Educational products, texts and fundraising products.

May
100 booths

Nadya Aswad Higgins, Conference Contact

3313 Massachusetts School Boards Association Meeting
90 Topsfield Road
Ipswich, MA 01938-1650
978-356-5453

May
100 booths

Capt. Edward Bryant, NCCC, Conference Contact

3314 Michigan Association of Elementary and Middle School Principals Conference
1405 S Harrison Road
Suite 210
East Lansing, MI 48823-5245
517-353-8770
Fax: 517-432-1063
Exhibits offer books, fundraisers, camps, insurance groups and non-profit organizations.

October
100 booths

William Hays, Jr, Conference Contact

3315 Michigan School Boards Association Fall Leadership Conference and Exhibit Show
1001 Centennial Way
Lansing, MI 48917
517-327-5900
Fax: 517-327-0776
E-mail: mkreh@masb.org
http://www.masb.org
Educational conference for school board members, plus exhibit show, companies such as construction, facilities technology,

student achievement, food service and transportation.

110 booths with 500 attendees and 110 exhibits

Deborah L Keys, Director

3316 Michigan Science Teachers Association Annual Conference
Western Michigan University
Office of Conferences
Kalamazoo, MI 49008
616-387-4174
Fax: 616-387-4189
A conference that aims to supply science teachers with information and research.

February

3317 Mid-South Educational Research Association Annual Meeting
Louisiana State University, School of Dentistry
1100 Florida Avenue
#223
New Orleans, LA 70119-2714
504-619-8700
Fax: 504-619-8740
Focuses on assessment and involvement in education by releasing research and statistics.

November

Diana Gardiner PhD, Conference Contact

3318 Middle States Council for the Social Studies Annual Regional Conference
Rider College
2083 Lawrenceville Road
Lawrenceville, NJ 08648-3001
717-865-2117
Seeks to develop and implement new curriculum into the social studies area.

April

Dan Sidelnick, Conference Contact

3319 Minnesota Leadership Annual Conference
Minnesota School Boards Association
1900 W Jefferson Avenue
St. Peter, MN 56082-3014
507-934-2450
800-324-4459
Fax: 507-931-1515
http://www.mnmsba.org
A prime networking opportunity combined with sessions discussing the latest information and ideas in school governance and operations.

January
200+ booths with 2,000+ attendees

Mike Torkelson, Deputy Executive Director
Tiffany Rodning, Coordinator Finance

3320 Minnesota School Administrators Association
1884 Como Avenue
Saint Paul, MN 55108-2715
651-645-7231
Fax: 651-645-7518
E-mail: members@mnasa.org
http://wwwmnasa.org
Educational materials and school building products.

October
70 booths

Charles Kyle, Executive Director
Mia Vrick, Conference Contact

3321 Minnesota School Boards Association Annual Meeting
1900 W Jefferson Street
Saint Peter, MN 56082-3014
507-931-2450
Fax: 507-931-1515
School supplies and services as diverse as buses and architectural services.

January
190 booths

Mike Torkelson, Conference Contact

3322 Missouri National Education Association Conference
1810 E Elm Street
Jefferson City, MO 65101-4174
573-634-3202
Fax: 573-634-5646
http://www.mo.nea.org

November annual
95 booths with 1,500 attendees

Carol Schmoock, Conference Manager
Ann Claypool, Conference Manager

3323 Missouri School Boards Association Annual Meeting
2100170 Drive SW
Columbia, MO 65203
573-445-9920
Fax: 573-445-9981
Education-related products and services.

October
125 booths

Evelyn Graham, Conference Contact

3324 Missouri State Teachers Association Conference
PO Box 458
Columbia, MO 65205-0458
573-442-3127
Fax: 573-443-5079
Educational materials.

November
280 booths

Kent King, Conference Contact

3325 Montana Association of Elementary School Principals Conference
1134 Butte Avenue
Helena, MT 59601-5178
406-442-2510
Fax: 406-442-2518

January/Febuary
20 booths

Loran Frazier, Conference Contact

3326 National Association of Secondary School Principals Annual Convention and Exposition
1904 Association Drive
Reston, VA 22019
703-860-0200
800-253-7746
Fax: 703-620-6534
http://www.nasspconvention.org
Offers workshops for principals on leadership training, student personnel services, and how to deal with at-risk students. Convention highlights include more than 200 educational sessions, special interest forums and luncheons and spotlights on the latest education products and services.

Phoenix
March
290 booths

Gayle Mercer, Conference Contact

3327 National Association of State Boards of Education Conference
277 S Washington Street
Suite 100
Alexandria, VA 22314
703-684-4000
Fax: 703-836-2313
E-mail: boards@nasbe.org
http://www.nasbe.org
October
24 booths with 150 attendees

Doris Cruel, Conference Contact

3328 National Career Development Association Conference
4700 Reed Road
Suite M
Columbus, OH 43220-3074
703-823-9800
Fax: 703-823-0252
Supplies information and guidance for vocational-technical and career development professionals.
January

3329 National Conference on Education
American Association of School
Administrators
801 N Quincy Street
Suite 700
Arlington, VA 22203-1730
703-528-0700
Fax: 703-841-1543
E-mail: info@aasa.org
http://www.aasa.org
Ensures the highest quality education systems for all learners through the support and development of leadership on the building, district and state levels. Containing 5,000 attendees.
March
3/1-3/4

Andrea Saris, Manager

3330 National Conference on Standards and Assessment
National School Conference Institute
Riviera Hotel
Las Vegas, NV 89101
602-371-8655
Fax: 602-371-8790
http://www.nscinet.com
Two pre-conference workshops: The five most important things that educators need to know when using information for continuous program improvement, and The key to sustained leadership effectiveness. Conference will also hold over 60 breakout sessions.
April

Bill Daggett
Bob Marzano

3331 National Council for Geographic Education Annual Meeting
700 Pelham Road N
Jacksonville, AL 36265
256-782-5293
Fax: 256-782-5336
E-mail: ncge@jsucc.jsu.edu
http://www.nege.org
Stresses the essential value of geographic education and knowledge in schools.
October
45 booths with 800 attendees

Michael LeVasseur, Executive Director
Angelia Mance, Associate Director

3332 National Council for History Education Conference
National Council for History Education
26915 Westwood Road
Suite B-2
Westlake, OH 44145-4657
440-835-1776
Fax: 440-835-1295
E-mail: nche@nche.net
http://www.history.org/nche
Discovering history, places, documents and artifacts.
October
750 attendees and 75 exhibits

Elaine W Reed, Manager

3333 National Council for Social Studies Annual Conference
National Council for the Social Studies
8555 Sixteenth Street
Suite 500
Silver Spring, MD 20910
301-588-1800
800-683-0812
Fax: 301-588-2049
E-mail: sgriffin@ncss.org
http://www.socialstudies.org
Focuses on social studies educators.
November-December
11/30-12/2
150 booths

Peter Stavros, Conference Contact

3334 National Council of English Teachers Conference
National Council of Teachers of English
1111 W Kenyon Road
Urbana, IL 61801-1010
217-328-3870
800-369-6283
Fax: 217-328-9645
http://www.ncte.org

Jacqui Joseph-Biddle, Conference Manager

3335 National Council of Teachers of Mathematics Annual Meeting
1906 Association Drive
Reston, VA 20191-1593
703-620-9840
Fax: 703-476-2970
E-mail: annimtg@nctm.org
http://www.nctm.org
Elementary school teachers at a school that is an NCTM member are entitled to a special individual member registration fee at our conferences. Consult your school administration about the Title II Dwight D. Eisenhower funds earmarked for teacher training. Ask us about group discounts.
April
620 booths with 18M attendees

Patty Markusson, Conference Manager

3336 National Council of Teachers of English Annual Convention
1111 W Kenyon Road
Urbana, IL 61801-1010
217-328-3870
800-369-6283
Fax: 217-278-3763
E-mail: public_info@ncte.org
http://www.ncte.org
Provides a forum for English educators of all grade levels.
November
290+ booths with 6500 attendees

Jacqui Joseph-Biddle, Conference Contact

3337 National Council of Teachers of Mathematics Conference
1906 Association Drive
Reston, VA 20191-9988
703-620-9840
800-235-7566
Fax: 703-476-2970
E-mail: nctm@nctm.org
http://www.nctm.org
Dedicated to the improvement of mathematics education and to meeting the needs of Pre K-12 mathematics teaching. Conferences, journals and a collection of educational materials for teacher development.
January

Cynthia Rosse, Directorf Marketing Services
Barbara Thode, Conference Manager

3338 National Education Association Annual Meeting
National Education Association (NEA)
1201 16th Street NW
Washington, DC 20036-3290
202-822-7364
Fax: 202-822-7624
E-mail: ncuea@nea.org
http://www.nea.org
A general conference that addresses all facets and concerns of the educator.
July

Gloria Durgin, Conference Contact

3339 National Educational Computing Conference
Washington State Convention & Trade Center
800 Convention Place
Seattle, WA 98101-2350
206-694-5000
Fax: 206-694-5399
E-mail: info@wsctc.com
http://www.neccsite.com
Strengthen the role of technology in education by sharpening your skills, learning new ones, sharing with colleagues, and becoming involved.
June
417 booths with 12,500 attendees

Dr Heidi Rogers, First Executive Director

3340 National Middle School Association's Annual Conference and Exhibition
National Middle School Association
4151 Executive Parkway
Suite 300
Westerville, OH 43081
800-528-6672
E-mail: info@nmsa.org
http://www.nmsa.org
Provides professional development, journals, books, research and other valuable information to assist educators on an ongoing basis.
October

3341 National Occupational Information Coordinating Committee Conference
2100 M Street NW
Suite 156
Washington, DC 20037-1207
202-653-7680
Focuses on policy, social issues and social services addressing career development and occupational information.
August

Mary Susan Vickers, Conference Contact

179

3342 National School Boards Association Annual Conference & Exposition
1680 Duke Street
Alexandria, VA 22314-3455
703-838-6788
Fax: 703-549-6719
Distributes information on issues confronting school administration today.
Februrary
550 booths

Teresaa Dumochelle, Conference Contact

3343 National Science Teachers Association Area Convention
1840 Wilson Boulevard
Arlington, VA 22201-3000
703-243-7100
800-782-6782
Fax: 703-243-7177
Three area conventions are held in Portland, Minneapolis and Las Vegas.
March/April

Sallie Snyder, Conference Contact

3344 New England Kindergarten Conference
Lesley University
29 Everett Street
Cambridge, MA 02138-2702
617-868-9600
Fax: 617-349-8544
E-mail: srice@lesley.edu
http://www.lesley.edu/kc
100 booths consisting of materials and products that help educators work more effectively with children.
November
100 booths with 2000 attendees

Margaret A McKenna, President
Sandra J Doran, Chief To Staff

3345 New England League of Middle Schools
New England League of Middle Schools
460 Boston Street
Suite 4
Topsfield, MA 01983-1223
978-887-6263
Fax: 978-887-6504
E-mail: nelms@nelms.org
http://www.nelms.org
Offers vendors the opportunity to showcase educationally supportive ideas and meet one-on-one with professionals who are resources for advice on new products appropriate to the middle level.
March
160+ booths with 3800+ attendees

Jeannette Southall, Exhibit Manager
Adrian Aleckna, Conference Planner

3346 New Mexico School Boards Association Conference Annual Meeting
300 Galisteo Street
Suite 204
Santa Fe, NM 87501-2606
505-983-5041
Fax: 505-983-2450
December
20 booths

Wesley H Lane, Conference Contact

3347 New York School Superintendents Association Annual Meeting
111 Washington Avenue
Suite 404
Albany, NY 12210-2210
518-449-1063
Fax: 518-426-2229
Provides leadership and membership services through a professional organization of school superintendents.
October
50 booths

Dr. Claire Brown, Conference Contact

3348 New York Science Teachers Association Annual Meeting
2449 Union Boulevard
Apartment 20B
Islip, NY 11751-3117
516-783-5432
Fax: 516-783-5432
Education related publications, equipment, supplies and services.
November
110 booths

Harold Miller, Conference Contact

3349 New York State United Teachers Conference
159 Wolf Road
Albany, NY 12205-1106
518-213-6000
Fax: 518-213-6415
February
40 booths

Anthony Bifaro, Conference Contact

3350 New York Teachers Math Association Conference
92 Governor Drive
Scotia, NY 12302-4802
518-399-0149
October-November
50 booths

Phil Reynolds, Conference Contact

3351 North American Association for Environmental Education
1825 Connecticut Avenue NW
Suite 800
Washington, DC 20009-5708
202-884-8942
Fax: 202-884-8455
E-mail: email@naaee.org
http://www.naaee.org
A network of professionals and students working in the field of environmental education throughout North America and 45 other countries. The Association promotes environmental education and supports the work of environmental educators for over 25 years.
October

Elaine Andrews, President

3352 North Carolina Association for Career and Technical Education Conference
PO Box 25159
Raleigh, NC 27611-5159
919-782-0708
Fax: 919-782-8096
http://www.ncacte.org

Educational books, supplies, materials, interactive video, computers, lasers, robotics, child care equipment and hand tools.
July
110 booths with 3000 + attendees

Dr. Clifton Belcher, Conference Contact

3353 North Carolina School Administrators Conference
PO Box 1629
Raleigh, NC 27602-1629
919-828-1426
Fax: 919-828-6099
March
40 booths

Joyce Myers, Conference Contact

3354 North Central Association Annual Meeting
North Central Association Commission on Accred.
Arizona State University
PO Box 874705
Tempe, AZ 85287-4705
303-722-6019
Fax: 303-593-2849
http://www.ncacasi.org
Sponsored by the North Central Association Commission on Accreditation and School Improvement.
April
30 booths with 1,800 attendees

Teri Schwindt, Conference Contact
Ron Stastney, Conference Manager

3355 North Central Conference on Summer Schools
Summer School
University of Wisconsin
410 S 3rd Street
River Falls, WI 54022
715-425-3851
Fax: 715-425-3785
E-mail: roger.a.swanson@uwrf.edu
http://www.conted.ufuc.edu
The NCCSS is an organization of colleges and universities offering undergraduate and/or graduate programs in the summer months. The organization's boundries roughly coincide with those of North Central Association of Colleges and Schools. The NCCSS is able to address concerns unique to this area and is dedicated to maintaining high standards in summer programs.
March

Dr. Roger Swanson, Manager

3356 Northeast Conference on the Teaching of Foreign Languages
Northeast Conference at Dickinson College
PO Box 1773
Carlisle, PA 17013-2896
717-245-1977
Fax: 717-245-1976
E-mail: nectfl@dickinson.edu
http://www.dickinson.edu/nectfl
Annual conference on the teaching of foreign languages; juried periodical, advocacy, information clearinghouse.
April
160 booths with 2500 attendees

Rebecca Kline, Executive Director

3357 Northeast Teachers Foreign Language Conference
St. Michael's College
29 Ethan Allen Avenue
Dupont Building
Colchester, VT 05446
802-654-2000
Fax: 802-654-2595
Foreign language textbooks, supplementary materials, audio equipment, computer software, travel abroad program materials and other related teaching aids and publications.

April
130 booths

Elizabeth L Holekamp, Conference Contact

3358 Northwest Association of Schools & Colleges Annual Meeting
1910 University Drive
Boise, ID 83725-1060
208-426-5727
Fax: 208-334-3228
http://www2.idbsu.edu/nasc
Serves the educational administration community by addressing topics that concern colleges, schools and other educational institutions.

December
120 attendees

Shelli D Clemens, Manager

3359 Northwest Regional Educational Laboratory Conference
101 SW Main Street
Suite 500
Portland, OR 97204-3297
800-547-6339
Concentrates on career education and educational change for professionals in vocational education, counseling and social work.

October/November

Francie Lindner, Conference Contact

3360 Ohio Business Teachers Association
Wright State University, Lake Campus
7600 State Route 703
Celina, OH 45822-2921
419-586-0337
Fax: 419-586-0368

October
40 booths

Roger Fulk, Conference Contact

3361 Ohio Public School Employees Association Convention
6805 Oak Creek Drive
Columbus, OH 43229
614-890-4770
Fax: 614-890-3540

May
15 booths

Joe Rugola, Conference Contact

3362 Ohio Secondary School Administrators Association Fall Conference
750 Brooksedge Boulevard
Westerville, OH 43081-2881
614-430-8311
Fax: 614-430-8315
Ring companies, furniture, computer software and fundraising companies.

October
42 booths

Jo Anne Rubsam, Conference Contact

3363 Oklahoma School Boards Association & School Administrators Conference
2801 N Lincoln Boulevard
Oklahoma City, OK 73105-4223
405-528-3571
Fax: 405-528-5695
School-related products and/or services.

August
195 booths

Joann Yandell, Conference Contact

3364 Oregon School Boards Association Annual Convention
PO Box 1068
Salem, OR 97308-1068
503-588-2800
Fax: 503-588-2813
This convention addresses various issues emerging in the Oregon school system.

November

Pat Fitzwater, Conference Contact

3365 Pacific Northwest Council on Languages Annual Conference
PO Box 4649
Portland, OR 97208-4649
503-287-8539
E-mail: pncfl@uoregon.edu
http://www.babel.uoregon.edu
Focuses on learning, instruction and training practices in second language development.

April

Robert Davis, President
Greg Hopper-Moore, Executive Director

3366 Pennsylvania Council for the Social Studies Conference
Pennsylvania Council for the Social Studies
1212 Smallman Street
Senator John Heinz Regional Histiry Cnt.
Pittsburgh, PA 15222-4200
717-238-8768
E-mail: JKEARNEY@CBSD.ORG
http://www.pcssonline.org
Committed to the promotion of the teaching and learning of the Social Studies in the Commonwealth of Pennsylvania.

October
50 booths with 500 attendees

David Trevaskis, President Elect
Ken Kubistek, Executive Secretary

3367 Pennsylvania School Boards Association Annual Meeting
774 Limekiln Road
New Cumberland, PA 17070-2315
717-774-2331
Fax: 717-774-0718
School\office products, services and information for public education systems.

October
140 booths

Wayne W Updegraff, Conference Contact

3368 Pennsylvania Science Teachers Association
Center for Science & Technology Education
PO Box 330
Shippenville, PA 16254-0330
814-782-6301

December
70 booths

Dr. Ken Mechling, Conference Contact

3369 Principals' Center Spring Institute Conference
Harvard Graduate School of Education
6 Appian Way
#336
Cambridge, MA 02138-3704
617-495-1825
Fax: 617-495-5900
Administrative professionals get together to discuss issues, policy and procedures.

April

Nindy Leroy, Conference Contact

3370 Restructuring Curriculum Conference
National School Conference Institute
PO Box 35099
Phoenix, AZ 85069-5099
602-674-8990
Presents research, studies, and new information relevant to curriculum development.

January

3371 SchoolTech Forum
Miller Freeman
600 Harrison Street
San Francisco, CA 94109
415-947-6657
Fax: 415-947-6015
National forum for educational technology professional development and exhibits, devoted to intensive instruction by today's leading practitioners, eye-opening special events, unparalleled networking opportunities, and exposure to products and services.

3372 Sonoma State University Annual Conference
1801 E Colati Avenue
Sonoma State University, Carson Hall 65
Rohnert Park, CA 94928-3613
707-664-2940
800-833-3645
Fax: 707-878-9111
E-mail: cct@criticalthinking.org
http://www.criticalthinking.org
Participants to discuss promoting critical thinking and educational change.

July-August
1200 attendees

Paul Binker, Author

3373 South Carolina Library Association Conference
PO Box 1763
Columbia, SC 29202
803-252-1087
Fax: 803-252-0589
E-mail: scla@capconsc.com
http://www.scla.org

October
125 booths with 350 attendees

Tom Gilson, President

3374 Southern Association Colleges & Schools
1866 Southern Lane
Decatur, GA 30033-4033
404-679-4500
Fax: 404-679-4556
http://www.saes.org
Exhibits publications, data and word processing equipment, school photography, charter bus services and more.

December
50 booths with 3700 attendees

Dr. James Rogers, Chhief Academic Officer

181

3375 Southern Early Childhood Annual Convention
Southern Early Childhood Association
PO Box 55930
Little Rock, AR 72215-5930
800-305-7322
Fax: 501-227-5297
E-mail:
info@SouthernEarlyChildhood.org
http://www.southernearlychildhood.org
April
2,500 attendees
Sherry Hamilton, Dir Administrative Services

3376 Summer Leadership Institute
American Association of School Administrators
801 N Quincy Street
Suite 700
Arlington, VA 22203-1730
703-528-0700
Fax: 703-841-1543
E-mail: info@aasa.org
http://www.aasa.org
Speakers will include prominent superintendents, cutting-edge reformers and others concerned about increasing achievement in high-achieving districts.
July 19 - July 22

3377 Superintendents Work Conference
Teachers College, Columbia University
525 W 120th Street
PO Box 7
New York, NY 10027-6696
212-678-3783
Fax: 212-678-3682
E-mail: TCSuper@columbia.edu
http://www.conference.tc.columbia.edu
Offers practicing school superintendents a unique opportunity for professional growth in stimulating surroundings.
July
60 attendees
Thomas Sobol, Conference Chair
Gibran Matdalany, Associate Chair

3378 Teachers Association in Instruction Conference
150 W Market Street
Indianapolis, IN 46204-2806
317-634-1515
Exhibits a wide variety of teaching materials and information from Grades K-12.
October
150 booths
Barbara Stainbrook, Conference Contact

3379 Tennessee School Boards Association Conference
1130 Nelson Merry Street
Nashville, TN 37203-2884
615-741-0666
800-448-6465
Fax: 615-741-2824
http://www.tsba.net
Contains exhibiting equipment, materials and services used by schools and selected by boards of education.
November
60 booths with 1,000 attendees
Tammy Grissom, Conference Manager

3380 Texas Middle School Association Conference
PO Box 18896
Austin, TX 78760-8896
512-462-1105

25 booths.
February
Cecil Floyd, Conference Contact

3381 Texas School Boards Association Conference
7620 Guadalupe Street
Austin, TX 78752-1348
512-467-0222
Fax: 512-483-7100
275 booths exhibiting sports equipment, computers, and more.
September
Susan Bell, Conference Contact

3382 Texas State Teachers Association
318 W 12th Street
Austin, TX 78701-1815
512-476-5355
Fax: 512-476-9555
April
120 booths
Carla Bond, Conference Contact

3383 Training & Presentations
Chief Manufacturing, Inc.
14310 Ewing Avenue S
Burnsville, MN 55306-4839
612-894-6280
800-582-6480
Fax: 877-894-6918
E-mail: chief@chiefmfg.com
http://www.chiefmfg.com
Chicago, Illinois
February
Liz Sorensen, Marketing Assistant
Sharon McCubbin, Marketing Manager

3384 University Continuing Education Association Annual Conference
Leadership for Lifelong Learning
1 Dupont Circle NW
Suite 615
Washington, DC 20036-1134
202-659-3130
Fax: 202-785-0374
Focuses on life-long training and postgraduate work.
70 booths with 1,000 attendees
Frances Glover, Conference Manager

3385 Virginia Association of Elementary School Principals Conference
2116 Dabney Road
Suite A-4
Richmond, VA 23230
804-355-6791
Fax: 804-355-1196
E-mail: vaesp@earthlink.net
http://www.vaesp.org
Nonprofit professional association advocating for public education and equal educational opportunities. Promotes leadership of school administrators, principal as educational leaders, and provides professional development opportunities.
October
50 booths with 300 attendees
Thomas L Shortt, Executive Director
Judy Grady, Financial Director

3386 Virginia Association of Independent Schools-Conference
8001 Franklin Farms Drive
Suite 100
Richmond, VA 23229-5108
804-282-3592
Fax: 804-282-3596
E-mail: director@vais.org
http://www.vais.org
November
1,500 attendees
Andrew A Zvara, Manager

3387 Virginia Educators Annual Conference
Virginia ASCD
106 Yorkview Road
Yorktown, VA 23692
757-898-4434
Fax: 757-898-4344
E-mail: jbyrne@visi.net
December
30 booths with 600 attendees
Joan S Byrne, Executive Director

3388 Virginia School Boards Association Conference
2320 Hunters Way
Charlottesville, VA 22911-7931
434-295-8722
800-446-8722
Fax: 434-295-8785
http://www.vsba.org
State school boards association.
Barbara Coyle, Conference Manager

3389 Wisconsin Association of School Boards Annual Conference
Wisconsin Association of School Boards
122 W Washington Avenue
#400
Madison, WI 53703-2718
608-257-2622
Fax: 608-257-8386
E-mail: info@wasb.org
http://www.wasb.org
Contains sports equipment, textbooks, computers, office equipment and management, architects, contractors, food service and more.
January
370 booths with 3,000 attendees
Dianne Calgaro, Conference Contact
Carrie Tobin, Exhibit Show Manager

3390 Wisconsin Association of School District Administrators Conference
4797 Hayes Road
Madison, WI 53704-3288
608-242-1090
Fax: 608-242-1290
Annual convention featuring exhibits of school equipment, supplies and services.
April/May
70 booths
Miles Turner, Conference Contact

3391 Wisconsin School Administrators Association Conference
4797 Hayes Road Stop 1
Madison, WI 53704-3288
608-241-0300
Fax: 608-249-4973
School equipment, supplies and services including books, fundraising and computers.
October
60 booths
Charles R Hilston, Conference Contact

Directories & Handbooks

3392 American Association of Colleges for Teacher Education-Directory
American Association of Colleges for Teacher Ed.
1307 New York Avenue NW
Suite 300
Washington, DC 20005-4701
202-293-2450
Fax: 202-457-8095
E-mail: aacte@aacte.org
http://www.aacte.org
Offers listings of over 750 member schools, colleges and departments of education offering programs in teacher education, including more than 6,300 academic administrators and faculty. Publishes a paperback book annually.

144 pages Annual
ISSN: 0516-9313

Kristin McCabe, Publications Manager/Editor
Brinda Albert, Conference Manager

3393 American Society for Training/Development-Training Video
American Society for Training & Development
1640 King Street
Alexandria, VA 22314-2746
703-683-8100
Fax: 703-683-1523
Two volumes listing producers and distributors of about 22,000 training videos covering management, career development and technical skills.

3394 Appropriate Inclusion and Paraprofessionals
National Education Association (NEA)
1201 16th Street NW
Washington, DC 20036-3207
202-822-7364
Fax: 202-822-7624
E-mail: ncuea@nea.org
http://www.nea.org
A book offering information on mainstreaming disabled students and the work of paraprofessionals in the education process.

10 pages

3395 Assessing Student Performance: Exploring thePurpose and Limits of Testing
Jossey-Bass/Pfeiffer
989 Market Street
San Francisco, CA 94103-1741
415-433-1740
Fax: 415-433-0499
http://www.josseybass.com
A powerful and well-written work, which begins by raising a fundamental question: What is assessment and how does testing differ from it?

336 pages Softcover
ISBN: 0-7879-5047-5

3396 Association for Continuing Higher Education Directory
Trident Technical College, CE-M
PO Box 118067
Charleston, SC 29423-8067
843-574-6658
800-807-ACHE
Fax: 843-574-6470
E-mail: zpbarrineau@al.trident.tec.sc.us
http://charleston.net/org/ache/

Directory includes information on 500 individual education professionals and approximately 300 member institutions. Includes name, address, titles and phone numbers of institutions and name, title, address and phone numbers of individuals.

102 pages Annual/March
10 booths with 250 attendees

Wayne L Whelan, Executive VP

3397 Before the School Bell Rings
Phi Delta Kappa Educational Foundation
408 N Union Street
PO Box 789
Bloomington, IN 47402-0789
812-339-1156
800-766-1156
Fax: 812-339-0018
http://www.pdkintl.org
Early childhood teachers and administrators, childcare providers and parents will enjoy and learn from this practical, insightful book.

84 pages Paperback
ISBN: 0-87367-476-6

Carol B Hillman, Author
George Kersey, Executive Director
Donovan R Walling, Editor, Special Publications

3398 Beyond Tracking: Finding Success in Inclusive Schools
Phi Delta Kappa Educational Foundation
PO Box 789
Bloomington, IN 47402-0789
812-339-1156
800-766-1156
Fax: 812-339-0018
http://www.pdkintl.org
Research data, practical ideas and reports from educators involved in untracking schools make this an authoritative and useful collection of important articles.

293 pages Hardcover
ISBN: 0-87367-470-7

Harbison Pool and Jane A Page, Author
George Kersey, Executive Director
Donovan R Walling, Dir Publications/Research

3399 Book of Metaphors, Volume II
AEE and Kendall/Hunt Publishing Company
4050 Westmark Drive
Dubuque, IA 52004-1840
563-589-1000
800-228-0810
Fax: 800-772-9165
http://www.kendallhunt.com
A compilation of presentations designed to enhance learning for those participating in adventure-based programs. Practitioners share how they prepare experiences for presentations.

256 pages Paperback
ISBN: 0-7872-0306-8

AEE, Author
Karen Berger, Customer Service Assistant

3400 Brief Legal Guide for the Independent Teacher
441 Vine Street
Suite 505
Cincinnati, OH 45202-2811
Offering insights into the most common legal issues faced by independent music teachers.

28 pages

3401 Building Life Options: School-Community Collaborations
Academy for Educational Development
1255 23rd Street NW
Washington, DC 20037-1125
202-884-8800
Fax: 202-884-8400
A handbook for family life educators on how to prevent pregnancy in the middle grades.

3402 Closing the Achievement Gap
Master Teacher
Leadership Lane
PO Box 1207
Manhattan, KS 66505-1207
785-539-0555
800-669-9633
Fax: 800-669-1132
http://www.masterteacher.com
A complete step-by-step approach to building a system that narrows the gap between student potenial and student performance—between success and failure.

162 pages
ISBN: 0-914607-73-1

Kristy Meeks, Author

3403 Coming Up Short? Practices of Teacher Educators Committed to Character
Character Education Partnership
1025 Connecticut Avenue NW
Suite 1011
Washington, DC 20036
202-296-7743
800-988-8081
Fax: 202-296-7779
http://www.character.org

Henry Huffman, Author
Andrea Grenadier, Director Communications
Esther Schaeffer, CEO/Executive Director

3404 Competency-Based Framework for Professional Development of Certified Health Specialists
Nat'l Health Education Credentialing
Columbia University
Department of Health Education
New York, NY 10027
212-854-1754
Fax: 212-678-4048
Aims to help the health education profession provide the leadership necessary for improving health in a rapidly changing, culturally pluralistic and technologically complex society. Provides universities, professional organizations, and accreditation a common basis of skills for the development, assessment, and improvement of professional preparation for health educators.

3405 Contracting Out: Strategies for Fighting Back
National Education Association (NEA)
1201 16th Street NW
Washington, DC 20036-3207
202-822-7364
Fax: 202-822-7624
E-mail: ncuea@nea.org
http://www.nea.org
Offers information for teachers and administration on how to stop contracting out, subcontracting, and other forms of privatization of public services that are a threat to school employees and the communities they serve.

3406 Directory of Curriculum Materials Centers
Association of College & Research Libraries
50 E Huron Street
Chicago, IL 60611-5295
312-280-2517
Fax: 312-280-2520
Listing of over 275 centers that have collections of curriculum materials to aid in elementary and secondary teaching preparation.
200 pages

3407 Distance Learning Directory
Virginia A Ostendorf
PO Box 2896
Littleton, CO 80161-2896
303-797-3131
Fax: 303-797-3524
E-mail: ostendorf@vaostendorf.com
Comprehensive list of distance learning practitioners and vendors. Each listing includes names, addresses, e-mail, fax and phones, credits awarded, program content, peripherals and technologies used, class configurations and more. Includes a lists of vendors offering descriptions of distance learning products, services and programming.
308 pages Annual
Virginia A Ostendorf, President
Ronald Ostendorf, VP

3408 Ethical Issues in Experiential Education
AEE and Kendall/Hunt Publishing Company
4050 Westmark Drive
Dubuque, IA 52002-2624
319-589-1000
800-228-0810
Fax: 800-772-9165
http://www.kendallhunt.com
An examination of ethical issues in the field of adventure programming and experiential education. Topics include ethical theory, informed consent, sexual issues, student rights, environmental concerns and programming practices.
144 pages
ISBN: 0-7872-93083
Karen Berger, Customer Service Assistant

3409 Finishing Strong: Your Personal Mentoring & Planning Guide for the Last 60 Days of Teaching
Master Teacher
Leadership Lane
PO Box 1207
Manhattan, KS 66505-1207
785-539-0555
800-669-9633
Fax: 800-669-1132
http://www.masterteacher.com
In this book we've selected from the 32 years of The Master Teacher, the writings we know you would most like your teachers to have to support that last 60 days of the school year.
132 pages
ISBN: 1-58992-095-3
Robert L De Bruyn, Author

3410 How to Plan and Develop a Career Center
Center on Education and Work
964 Educational Sciences Building
1025 W Johnson Street
Madison, WI 53706-1796
800-446-0399
Fax: 608-262-9197
E-mail: cewmail@soemadison.wisc.edu
http://www.cew.wisc.edu
High school, postsecondary, adult, and virtual career centers-a comprehensive blueprint that covers all the bases.

3411 How to Raise Test Scores
Skylight Professional Development
1900 E Lake Avenue
Glenview, IL 60025
847-657-7450
800-348-4474
Fax: 847-486-3183
E-mail: info@skylightedu.com
http://www.skylightedu.com
Addresses the teaching and learning process at its most basic and important level-the classroom.
30 pages Softcover
ISBN: 1575171635
Robin Fogarty, Author

3412 Inclusion: The Next StepDVD
Master Teacher
Leadership Lane
PO Box 1207
Manhattan, KS 66505-1207
785-539-0555
800-669-9633
Fax: 800-669-1132
http://www.masterteacher.com
Offers practical help for regular classroom teachers and special education teachers in meeting the challenges of inclusion.
225 pages
ISBN: 0-914607-69-3
Wendy Dover, Author

3413 Law of Teacher Evaluation: A Self-Assestment Handbook
Phi Delta Kappa Educational Foundation
PO Box 789
Bloomington, IN 47402-0789
812-339-1156
800-766-156
Fax: 812-339-0018
http://www.pdkintl.org
This handy guidebook provides a concise, authoritative overview of US state statutes, regulations and guidelines regarding the performance evaluation of educators.
51 pages Paperback
ISBN: 0-87367-488-X
Perry A. Zirkel, Author
DR Walling, Dir Publications/Research

3414 Learning for Life
1325 W Walnut Hill Lane
PO Box 152079
Irving, TX 75015-2079
972-580-2433
Fax: 972-580-2137
http://www.learning-for-life.org
Emphasizes respect, responsibility, honesty, and kindness from the very start.

3415 Lesson Plans for the Substitue Teacher: Elementary Edition
Master Teacher
Po Box 1207
Manhattan, KS 66505-1207
785-539-0555
800-669-9633
Fax: 800-669-1132
http://www.masterteacher.com
Gives you more than 100 lessons developed and tested by teachers across the curriculum and at all grade levels.
145 pages
ISBN: 1-58992-107-0
Robert L DeBruyn, Author

3416 Libraries Unlimited
88 Post Road West
Westport, CT 06881
203-226-3571
800-225-5800
Fax: 203-222-1502
E-mail: lu-books@lu.com
http://www.lu.com
Publisher of resource books written by educators for educators. The books offer innovative ideas, practical lessons, and classroom-tested activities in the areas of math, science, social studies, whole language literature and library connections.

3417 Life Skills Training
711 Westchester Avenue
White Plains, NY 10604
914-421-2525
800-293-4969
Fax: 914-683-6998
E-mail: lstinfo@nhpanet.com
http://www.LifeSkillsTraining.com
A powerful prevention program with a proven record of effectiveness.

3418 List of Regional, Professional & Specialized Accrediting Association
Educational Information Services
PO Box 662
Newton Lower Falls, MA 02162
617-964-4555
A list of those associations involved in accreditation for the education fields.

3419 MacMillan Guide to Correspondence Study
MacMillan Publishing Company
1633 Broadway
New York, NY 10019
212-512-2000
Fax: 800-835-3202
Listing of 175 colleges, accredited trade, technical and vocational schools that offer home study courses.
500 pages

3420 Middle Grades Education in an Era of Reform
Academy for Educational Development
1255 23rd Street NW
Washington, DC 20037-1125
202-884-8800
Fax: 202-884-8400
Reviews middle-grades educational reform policies and practices.

3421 Middle School Teachers Guide to FREE Curriculum Materials
Educators Progress Service
214 Center Street
Randolph, WI 53956-1408
920-326-3126
888-951-4469
Fax: 920-326-3127
E-mail: epsinc@centurytel.net
http://www.freeteachingaids.com
Lists and describes free supplementary teaching aids for the middle school and junior high level.
290 pages Annual
ISBN: 87708-401-7
Kathy Nehmer, President

3422 NASDTEC Knowledge Base
22 Bates Road
PMB #134
Mashpee, MA 02649-3267
508-539-8844
Fax: 508-539-8868
E-mail: nasdtec@comcast.com
http://www.nasdtec.org
Annually
ISBN: 0-9708628-3-0
June
10 booths with 275 attendees and 10 exhibits
Roy Einreinhofer, Executive Director

3423 Orators & Philosophers: A History of the Idea of Liberal Education
College Board Publications
45 Columbus Avenue
New York, NY 10023-6917
212-713-8165
800-323-7155
Fax: 800-525-5562
http://www.collegeboard.org
A cogent study of the historical evolution of the idea of liberal education. Clearly and forcefully argued, the book portrays this evolution as a struggle between two contending points of view, one oratorical and the other philosophical.
308 pages
Bruce A Kimball, Author

3424 Parent Training Resources
PACER Center
8161 Normandale Boulevard
Minneapolis, MN 55437
952-838-9000
800-537-2237
Fax: 952-838-0199
E-mail: pacer@pacer.org
http://www.pacer.org
Booklets, information handouts, videotapes, newsletters and training materials for parents of children and adults with disabilities, individuals with disabilities, educators and other professionals.
130 pages
Paula Goldberg, Executive Director

3425 Personal Planner and Training Guide for the Paraprofessional
Master Teacher
Po Box 1207
Manhattan, KS 66505-1207
785-539-0555
800-669-9633
Fax: 800-669-1132
http://www.masterteacher.com
Includes numerous forms which allow each para to keep track of vital information he or

she will need in working with specific teachers and their special students.
128 pages
ISBN: 0-914607-39-1
Wendy Dover, Author

3426 Practical Handbook for Assessing Learning Outcomes in Continuing Education
International Association for Continuing Education
Departmant #3087
Washington, DC 20042-0001
202-463-2905
Fax: 202-463-8498
Innovative guide offers readers a series of steps to help select an assessment plan which will work for any organization.

3427 Principles of Good Practice in Continuing Education
International Association for Continuing Education
Department #3087
Washington, DC 20042-0001
202-463-2905
Fax: 202-463-8498
Principles from many sources for the field of continuing education, placing a pervasive emphasis on learning outcomes for the individual learner.

3428 Professional Learning Communities at Work
National Educational Service
304 W Kirkwood Avenue
Suite 2
Bloomington, IN 47404-5132
812-336-7700
800-733-6786
Fax: 812-336-7790
E-mail: nes@nesonline.com
http://www.nesonline.com
This publication provides specific, practical, how-to information on the best practices in use in schools through the US and Canada for curriculum development, teacher preparation, school leadership, professional development programs, school-parent partnerships, assessment practices and much more.

3429 Programs for Preparing Individuals for Careers in Special Education
The Council for Exceptional Children
1920 Association Drive
Reston, VA 20191-1545
703-620-3660
800-232-7323
Fax: 703-264-1637
This directory offers over 600 colleges and universities with programs in special education. Information includes institution name, address, contact person, telephone, fax, Internet, accreditation status, size of faculty, level of program, and areas of specialty.
256 pages

3430 Quality School Teacher
National Professional Resources
25 S Regent Street
Port Chester, NY 10573-8295
914-937-8897
800-453-7461
Fax: 914-937-9327
E-mail: info@nprinc.com
http://www.nprinc.com
Provides the specifics that classroom teachers are asking for as they begin the move to quality schools. It is written for educators

who are trying to give up the old system of boss-managing, and to create classrooms that produce quality work.
144 pages
ISBN: 0060-952857
William Glasser, Author
Robert Hanson, President
Helene Hanson, VP

3431 Requirements for Certification of Teachers & Counselors
University of Chicago Press
5801 S Ellis Avenue
Floor 4
Chicago, IL 60637-5418
312-702-7700
800-621-2736
Fax: 800-621-8476
A list of state and local departments of education for requirements including teachers, counselors, librarians, and administrators for elementary and secondary schools.
256 pages Annual
ISBN: 0-226-42850-8
Elizabeth Kaye, Author
John Tryneski, Coordinating Education

3432 Research for Better Schools Publications
112 N Broad Street
Philadelphia, PA 19102
215-568-6150
Fax: 215-568-7260
E-mail: maguire@rbs.org
http://www.rbs.org
Offers a variety of books on thinking skills, classroom materials, school and student assessment, at-risk students, school restructuring and improvement. As well as professional development resources for students.
Louis M Maguire, Executive Co-Director

3433 Resources for Teaching Middle School Science
National Academy Press
Arts & Industries Bldg Room 1201
900 Jefferson Drive SW
Washington, DC 20560-0403
202-287-2063
Fax: 202-287-2070
E-mail: outreach@nas.edu
http://www.si.edu/nsrc
Second in a series of resource guides for elementary, middle school, and high school science teachers, this book is an annotated guide to hands-on, inquiry-centered curriculum materials and sources of help in teaching science in grades six through eight. Produced by the National Science Resources Center.
496 pages
National Science Resources Center, Author
Douglas Lapp, Executive Director

3434 Restructuring in the Classroom: Teaching,Learning, and School Organization
Jossey-Bass/Pfeiffer
989 Market Street
San Francisco, CA 94103-1741
415-433-1740
Fax: 415-433-0499
http://www.josseybass.com
Teaching, learning and school organization.
288 pages Hardcover
ISBN: 0-7879-0239-X
Riched Elmore, Penelope Peterson & Sara McCarthey, Author

3435 Revolution Revisited: Effective Schools and Systemic Reform
Phi Delta Kappa Educational Foundation
PO Box 789
Bloomington, IN 47402-0789
812-339-1156
800-766-1156
Fax: 812-339-0018
http://www.pdkintl.org
The authors examine the Effective Schools movement of the past quarter century as a school reform philosophy and renewal process for today and for the coming years.

132 pages Paperback
ISBN: 0-873674-83-9

BO Taylor and P Bullard, Author
Donovan R Walling, Dir
Publications/Research

3436 Seminar Information Service
17752 Sky Park Circle
Suite 210
Irvine, CA 92614-4469
949-261-9104
877-SEM-INFO
Fax: 949-261-1963
E-mail: info@seminarinformation.com
http://www.seminarinformation.com
Offers information on over 700 sponsors of more than 100,000 business and technical seminars.

1,000 pages Annual

Mona Pointkowski, VP

3437 Service-Learning and Character Education: One Plus One is More Than Two
Character Education Partnership
1025 Connecticut Avenue NW
Suite 1011
Washington, DC 20036
202-296-7743
800-988-8081
Fax: 202-296-7779
http://www.character.org

Andrea Grenadier, Director
Communications
Esther Schaeffer, CEO/Executive
Director

3438 Teacher Created Resources
Teacher Created Resources
6421 Industry Way
Westminster, CA 92683-3652
714-891-7895
800-662-4321
Fax: 714-892-0283
E-mail: custserv@teachercreated.com
http://www.teachercreated.com
Publishes supplementary materials for Pre-K to grade 8 educators and parents in the areas of language arts, social studies, science, math, and classroom management. Submissions should include tentative table of contents or outline, introduction and 8-12 sample pages.

Ina Levin, Managing Editor
Karen Goldfluss, Managing Editor

3439 Teachers as Educators of Character: Are the Nations Schools of Education Coming Up Short?
Character Education Partnership
1025 Connecticut Avenue NW
Suite 1011
Washington, DC 20036
202-296-7743
800-988-8081
Fax: 202-296-7779
http://www.character.org
Henry Huffman, Author
Andrea Grenadier, Director
Communications
Esther Schaeffer, CEO/Executive
Director

3440 Teachers as Leaders
Phi Delta Kappa Educational Foundation
PO Box 789
Bloomington, IN 47402-0789
812-339-1156
800-766-1156
Fax: 812-339-0018
http://www.pdkintl.org
Examines teacher recruitment, retention, professional development and leadership. The central theme of these twenty essays is excellence in education and how to achieve it.

320 pages Hardcover
ISBN: 0-873674-68-5

Donovan R Walling, Author
Donovan R Walling, Dir
Publications/Research

3441 Teachers in Publishing
Pike Publishing Company
221 Town Center W
Suite 112
Santa Maria, CA 93458-5083
Editorial, research, sales, consulting, in-office positions or travel to learn teachers' needs and instruct new texts.

3442 Teaching About Islam & Muslims in the Public School Classroom
9300 Gardenia Avenue
#B3
Fountain Valley, CA 92708-2253
714-839-2929
Fax: 714-839-2714

117 pages
ISBN: 1-930109-008

Susan Douglas, Author
Shabbir Mansuri, Founding Director

3443 Teaching as the Learning Profession: Handbook of Policy and Practice
Jossey-Bass/Pfeiffer
989 Market Street
San Francisco, CA 94103-1741
415-433-1740
Fax: 415-433-0499
Provides the best essays about the status of teaching, and the contributing writers are among the best thinkers in education today.

426 pages Hardcover

Linda Darling-Hammond, Editor
Gary Sykes, Editor

3444 Teaching for Results
Master Teacher
Leadership Lane
PO Box 1207
Manhattan, KS 66505-1207
800-669-9633
Fax: 800-669-1132
http://www.masterteacher.com

An easy-to-implement powerful method for helping to ensure sucess in the classroom.

45 pages
ISBN: 1-58992-120-8

3445 Their Best Selves: Building Character Education and Service Learning Together
Character Education Partnership
1025 Connecticut Avenue NW
Suite 1011
Washington, DC 20036
202-296-7743
800-988-8081
Fax: 202-296-7779
http://www.character.org

Andrea Grenadier, Director
Communications
Esther Schaeffer, CEO/Executive
Director

3446 Theory of Experiential Education
AEE and Kendall/Hunt Publishing
Company
4050 Westmark Drive
Dubuque, IA 52002-2624
319-589-1000
800-228-0810
Fax: 800-772-9165
http://www.kendallhunt.com
This groundbreaking resource looks at the theoretical foundations of experiential education from philosophical, historical, psychological, social and ethical perspectives.

496 pages
ISBN: 0-7872-0262-2

AEE, Author
Karen Berger, Customer Service
Assistant

3447 Time to Teach, Time to Learn: Changing the Pace of School
Northeast Foundation for Children
39 Montague City Road
Greenfield, MA 01301
413-772-2066
800-360-6332
Fax: 413-774-1129
E-mail: info@responsiveclassroom.org
Giving students the chance to learn and their teachers the chance to teach.

322 pages Softcover

Chip Wood, Author

3448 Top Quality School Process (TQSP)
National School Services
390 Holbrook Drive
Wheeling, IL 60090-5812
847-541-2768
800-262-4511
Fax: 847-541-2553
A customized School Improvement Program that incorporates input from all stakeholders in the educational process to establish baseline data, implement a continuous process of school improvement, and select quality programs for professional development.

3449 US Department of Education: Office of Educational Research & Improvement
National Library of Education
555 New Jersey Avenue NW
Washington, DC 20001-2029
877-433-7827
800-424-1616
Fax: 202-401-0457

Offers a variety of publications for professional development. The list of sources includes statistical reports, topical reports and effective programs, schools and practices.

John Blake, Reference/Information
Nancy Cavanaugh, Collection Development

3450 Understanding and Relating To Parents Professionally

Master Teacher
Leadership Lane
PO Box 1207
Manhattan, KS 66505-1207
800-669-9633
Fax: 800-669-1132
http://www.masterteacher.com
Gives teachers both the perspective and the techniques to relate to parents professionally to secure the maximum benefit for students.

70 pages
ISBN: 0-914607-65-0
Robert L DeBruyn, Author

3451 Welcome to Teaching and our Schools

Master Teacher
Leadership Lane
PO Box 1207
Manhattan, KS 66505-1207
800-669-9633
Fax: 800-669-1132
http://www.masterteacher.com
Sets the stage for teachers so that they can have an enthusiastic and successful year in the classroom.

50 pages
ISBN: 0-914607-49-9
Robert L DeBryon, Author

3452 World Exchange Program Directory

Center for U.N. Studies, GPO Box 2786
Ramna
Dacca 1000, Bangladesh
Offers listings, by geographical location, of exchange programs available to United States and abroad students. Listings include all contact information, schedules, fields and levels of study and bilingual information.

Biennial

3453 You Can Handle Them All

Master Teacher
Leadership Lane
PO Box 1207
Manhattan, KS 66505-1207
800-669-9633
Fax: 800-669-1132
http://www.masterteacher.com
Encyclopedia of student misbehaviors offering answers that work. one hundred seventeen student misbehaviors are covered.

320 pages
ISBN: 0-914607-04-9
Robert L DeBruyn, Author

3454 Your Personal Mentoring & Planning Guide for the First 60 Days of Teaching

Master Teacher
Leadership Lane
PO Box 1207
Manhattan, KS 66505-1207
800-669-9633
Fax: 800-669-1132
http://www.masterteacher.com

In this book we've selected from 32 years of The Master Teacher, the writings we know you would most like your teachers to have to support the first 60 days of the school year.

116 pages
ISBN: 1-58992-056-2

Periodicals

3455 AACTE Briefs

American Association of Colleges for Teacher Ed.
1307 New York Avenue NW
Suite 300
Washington, DC 20005-4701
202-293-2450
Fax: 202-457-8095
E-mail: aacte@aacte.org
http://www.aacte.org
Covers current events in teacher education including public policy, research and programs. Publishes a newsletter and there is a conference.

4-12 pages Monthly
ISSN: 0731-602x
Kristin McCabe, Publications Manager/Editor
Brinda Albert, Conference Manager

3456 ATEA Journal

American Technical Education Association
800 N 6th Street N
Wahpeton, ND 58076-0002
701-671-2240
Fax: 701-671-2260
E-mail: bett.krump@ndscs.edu
http://www.ateaonline.org
Dedicated to excellence in the quality of postsecondary technical education, with an emphasis on professional development.

32 pages Quarterly
ISSN: 0889-6488
Betty M Krump, Executive Director
Edward Mann, Editor

3457 Action in Teacher Education

University of Georgia, College of Education
427 Aderhold Hall
Athens, GA 30602
706-542-4238
Fax: 706-542-4277
The official publication of the Association of Teacher Educators, serving as a forum for the exchange of information and ideas related to the improvement of teacher education at all levels.

Quarterly
Brenda H Manning, Editor
H James McLaughlin, Editor

3458 American Educational Research Journal

Columbia University Teachers College
PO Box 51
New York, NY 10027-0051
212-678-3498
Fax: 212-678-4048
Focuses on teaching development and human resource training.

Quarterly
Lyn Corno, Co-Editor
Gary Natriello, Co-Editor

3459 American Educator

American Federation of Teachers
555 New Jersey Avenue NW
Washington, DC 20001-2029
202-879-4420
Contains articles on education, politics, media and social commentary.

Quarterly
Elizabeth McPike, Editor
Mary Kearney, Advertising/Sales

3460 Arts Management in Community Institutions: Summer Training

National Guild of Community Schools of the Arts
520 8th Avenue
Suite 302, 3rd Floor
New York, NY 10018
212-268-3337
Fax: 212-268-3995
E-mail: info@natguild.org
http://www.nationalguild.org

June
Noah Xifr, Director Membership/Oper.

3461 Balance Sheet

ITP South-Western Publishing
5101 Madison Road
Cincinnati, OH 45227-1427
513-271-8811
800-824-5179
Fax: 800-487-8488
Informational publication for high school accounting educators. Articles contain information about innovations in teaching accounting, producing an extensive line of educational texts and software for K-postsecondary markets.

2x Year
Larry Qualls, Editor
Carol Bross-McMahon, Coordinating Editor

3462 Better Teaching

The Parent Institute
PO Box 7474
Fairfax Station, VA 22039-7474
703-323-9170
Fax: 703-323-9173
http://www.parent-institute.com
Newsletter for teachers (grades 1-12) that offers tips and techniques to improve student learning.

Monthly
ISSN: 1061-1495
John Wherry, Publisher

3463 C/S Newsletter

Center for Instructional Services
Purdue University
W. Lafayette, IN 47907
317-494-9454
Contains descriptions of CIS services and articles about instructional techniques.

4 pages 7x Year
Vickie Lojek

3464 Curriculum Brief

International Technology Education Association
1914 Association Drive
Reston, VA 20191-1538
703-860-2100
Fax: 703-860-0353
Seeks to advance technological literacy through professional development activities and publications.

4x Year
Kendall Starkweather, Executive Director

3465 Education & Treatment of Children
Pressley Ridge School
530 Marshall Avenue
Pittsburgh, PA 15214-3016
412-321-6995
Fax: 412-321-5313
A journal devoted to the dissemination of information concerning the development and improvement of services for children and youth. Its primary criterion for publication is that the material be of direct value to educators and other child care professionals in improving their teaching/training effectiveness. Various types of material are appropriate for publication including originial experimental research, experimental replications, adaptations of previously reported research and reviews.

Quarterly

Bernie Fabry, Managing Editor

3466 Educational Placement Sources-US
Education Information Services/Instant Alert
PO Box 620662
Newton, MA 02462-0662
617-433-0125
Lists 100 organizations in the United States that find positions for teachers, educational administrators, counselors and other professionals. Listings are classified by type, listed alphabetically and offers all contact information.

4 pages Annual

FB Viaux, President

3467 Exceptional Child Education Resources
The Council for Exceptional Children
1920 Association Drive
Reston, VA 20191-1545
703-620-3660
800-328-0272
Fax: 703-264-1637
E-mail: askeric@ericir.syr.edu
A quarterly abstract journal that helps teachers stay abreast of the book, nonprint media, and journal literature in special and gifted education.

Quarterly
ISSN: 0160-4309

3468 Extensions - Newsletter of the High/Scope Curriculum
High/Scope Educational Research Foundation
600 N River Street
Ypsilanti, MI 48198-2821
734-485-2000
800-40P-RESS
Fax: 734-485-0704
E-mail: info@highscope.org
http://www.highscope.org
Teacher guide for users of the High/Scope curriculum. Articles on classroom strategies, training techniques, problem-solving ideas, and news from the field. Also includes updated training data.

8 pages BiMonthly
ISSN: 0892-5135

Sharon Adams-Taylor, Associate Executive Director
Clay Shouse, Vice President

3469 Guild Notes Bi-Monthly Newsletter
National Guild of Community Schools of the Arts
520 8th Avenue
Suite 302, 3rd Floor
New York, NY 10018
212-268-3337
Fax: 212-268-3995
E-mail: info@natguild.org
http://www.nationalguild.org

Bi-Monthly

Noah Xifr, Director Membership/Oper.

3470 Infocus: A Newsletter of the University Continuing Education Association
University Continuing Education Association
1 Dupont Circle NW
Suite 615
Washington, DC 20036-1134
202-659-3130
Fax: 202-785-0374
E-mail: kjkohl@ucea.edu
http://www.ucea.edu
Reports on higher education activities, federal legislation and government agencies, innovative programming at institutions across the country; member institutions; trends in continuing and part-time education; resources; professional development opportunities within the field; and changes in member personnel.

12-20 pages Monthly

Roger Whitaker, President
Kay J Kohl, Executive Director/CEO

3471 Innovator
University of Michigan Association
4001 School of Education Building
Ann Arbor, MI 48104
734-764-0394
Fax: 734-763-6934
For professional educators and alumni of University of Michigan's School of Education.

20 pages Quarterly

Eric Warden, Contact

3472 International Journal of Instructional Media
Westwood Press
149 Goose Lane
Tolland, CT 06084-3822
860-875-5484
A professional journal directly responsive to the need for precise information on the application of media to your instructional and training needs.

Quarterly

Dr. Phillip J. Sleeman, Editor

3473 Intervention in School and Clinic
Pro-Ed., Inc.
8700 Shoal Creek Boulevard
Austin, TX 78757-6816
512-451-3246
800-897-3202
Fax: 512-302-9129
http://www.proedinc.com
The hands-on how-to resource for teachers and clinicians working with students (especially LD and BD) for whom minor curiculum and environmental medications are ineffective.

64 pages 5x Year Magazine
ISSN: 1053-4512

Judith K Voress, Periodicals Director
Brenda Smith Myles, Editor

3474 Journal of Classroom Interaction
University of Houston-University Park
Farish Hall
Room 240
Houston, TX 77004
713-743-5919
Fax: 713-743-8664
E-mail: jci@bayou.uh.edu
http://www.coe.uh.edu
Reports on student and teacher rapport as well as classroom activities that promote interaction.

Bi-Annually

Dr. Jerome Freiberg, Editor

3475 Journal of Economic Education
Heldref Publications
1319 18th Street NW
Washington, DC 20036-1802
202-296-6267
800-365-9753
Fax: 202-296-5149
http://www.heldref.org
The Journal of Economic Education offers original articles on innovations and evaluations of teaching techniques, materials, and programs in economics. Articles, tailored to the needs of instructors of introductory through graduate-level economics, cover content and pedagogy in a variety of mediums.

Quarterly

William E Becker, Editor

3476 Journal of Experiential Education
Association for Experiental Education
2305 Canyon Boulevard
Suite 100
Boulder, CO 80302-5651
303-440-8844
Fax: 303-440-9581
E-mail: ED@aee.org
http://www.aee.org
A professional journal that publishes a diverse range of articles in such subject areas as outdoor adventure programming, service learning, experiential school based programming, environmental education, cultural journalism, internships, therapeutic applications, research and theory, the creative arts, etc.

64 pages 3x Year
ISSN: 1053-8259

Alan Ewert, Coordinating Editor
Sue Beggs, Executive Director

3477 Journal on Excellence in College Teaching
Miami University
Langstroth Cottage
Oxford, OH 45056
513-529-9265
Fax: 531-529-9264
E-mail: wentzegw@muohio.edu
http://http://celt.muohio.edu/ject
A peer-reviewed journal published by and for faculty at colleges and universities to increase student learning through effective teaching, interest in and enthusiasm for the profession of teaching, and communication among faculty about their classroom experiences. The Journal provides a scholarly forum for faculty to share proven, innovative pedagogies and thoughtful, inspirational insights about teaching.

Journal 3x/Yr
ISSN: 1052-4800

Gregg Wentzell, Author
Gregg Wentzell, Managing Editor
Milton Cox, Editor-in-Chief

3478 Journalism Education Association
Kansas State University
103 Kedzie Hall
Manhattan, KS 66506-1505
785-532-5532
Fax: 785-532-5563
E-mail: lindarp@ksu.edu
http://www.jea.org/
An organization of about 2,300 journalism
teachers and advisers, offers two national
teacher-student conventions a year, quarterly newsletter and magazines, bookstore
and national certification program. This association serves as a leader in scholastic
press freedom and media curriculum.
April & November
25-30 booths with 4700 attendees
Linda Puntrey, Executive Director

3479 NCRTL Special Report
National Center for Research on Teacher
Education
Michigan State University
East Lansing, MI 48824
517-355-9302
E-mail: floden@msu.edu
http://www.ncrtb.msu.edu
Membership news and updates.

3480 NCSIE Inservice
National Council of States on Inservice
Education
Syracuse University
402 Huntington Hall
Syracuse, NY 13244
315-443-1870
Fax: 315-443-9082
Professional development, staff develop-
ment and inservice education.
20 pages Quarterly
James Collins

**3481 On The Go! for the Educational
OfficeProfessional**
Master Teacher
Leadership Lane
PO Box 1207
Manhattan, KS 66505-1207
800-669-9633
Fax: 800-669-1132
http://www.masterteacher.com
Positive, practical, and successful insights
and techniques to help you manage and
work with your support staff.
1 pages Monthly Newsletter
Tracey H DeBruyn, Executive Editor

**3482 On-The-Go For Educational Office
Professionals**
Master Teacher
Leadership Lane
PO Box 1207
Manhattan, KS 66505-1207
785-539-0555
800-669-9633
Fax: 800-669-1132
http://www.masterteacher.com
The publication that provides you with
great articles to complete your in-house
newsletters and newsletters to parents,
without fear of copyright violations.
1 pages Monthly Newsletter
Erica Parkinson, Executive Editor

**3483 Paraeducator's Guide to
Instructional & Curricular
Modifications**
Master Teacher
Leadership Lane
PO Box 1207
Manhattan, KS 66505-1207
800-669-9633
Fax: 800-669-1132
http://www.masterteacher.com
An indispensible tool your paras can use to
understand, plan for and carry out appropri-
ate modification for students with all types
of special needs.
100 pages
ISBN: 0-914607-88-X
Wendy Dover, Author

3484 Pennsylvania Education
Pennsylvania Department of Education
333 Market Street
Harrisburg, PA 17101-2210
717-783-9802
Fax: 717-783-8230
A newsletter to keep educators informed on
activities of the state education department,
schools and other educational institutions.
Also contains information on conferences
and workshops on relevant educational topics.
8-10 pages 8x Year
Gary Tuma, Press Secretary
Beth Boyer, Information Specialist

3485 Performance Improvement Journal
International Society for Performance
1400 Spring Street
Suite 260
Silver Spring, MD 20910
301-587-8570
Fax: 301-587-8573
E-mail: info@ispi.org
http://www.ispi.org
48 pages Monthly
ISSN: 1090-8811
April Davis, Publications Director

3486 Preventing School Failure
Heldref Publications
1319 18th Street NW
Washington, DC 20036-1826
202-296-6267
800-365-9753
Fax: 202-296-5149
E-mail: psf@heldref.org
http://www.heldref.org
The journal for educators and parents seeking strategies to promote the success of students who have learning and behavior
problems. It includes practical examples of
programs and practices that help children
and youth in schools, clinics, correctional
institutions, and other settings. Articles are
written by educators and concern teaching
children with various kinds of special
needs.
48 pages Quarterly
ISSN: 1045-988X
Mary O'Donnell, Managing Editor

3487 Prevention Researcher
Integrated Research
66 Club Road
Suite 370
Eugene, OR 97401
541-683-9278
800-929-2955
Fax: 541-683-2621
E-mail: orders@TPRonline.org
http://www.TPRonline.org

Quarterly newsletter for professionals who
work with youth. Each issue addresses a
single topic, such as gun violence, dating violence, eating disorders, and drug abuse.
Annual resource issue included
24 pages Magazine/Quarterly
ISSN: 1086-4385
Steven Ungerleider PhD, Editor

3488 Progressive Teacher
Progressive Publishing Company
2678 Henry Street
Augusta, GA 30904-4656
770-868-1691
Offers new information and updates for the
improvement and development of higher
education.
Quarterly
ISSN: 0033-0825
MS Adcock

3489 Retaining Great Teachers
Master Teacher
Leadership Lane
PO Box 1207
Manhattan, KS 66505-1207
800-669-9633
Fax: 800-669-1132
http://www.masterteacher.com
This book will help you and your staff
reconize the common dilemmas new teach-
ers face and will empower you, lead teach-
ers, and mentors with practical solutions to
help new teachers over the hurdles.
85 pages
ISBN: 1-58992-097-X
Michael J Lovett PhD, Author

**3490 Rural Educator-Journal for Rural
and Small Schools**
National Rural Education Association
246 E Ed Building
Colorado State University
Ft. Collins, CO 80523-1588
970-491-7022
Fax: 970-491-1317
E-mail: jnewlin@lamar.colostate.edu
http://www.colostate.edu
Official journal of the NREA. A nationally
recognized publication that features timely
and informative articles written by leading
rural educators from all levels of education.
All NREA members are encouraged to submit research articles and items of general information for publication.
40 pages Quarterly Magazine
ISSN: 0273-446X
Joseph T Newlin, Editor

3491 TED Newsletter
The Council for Exceptional Children
1920 Association Drive
Reston, VA 20191-1545
703-620-3660
888-232-7733
Fax: 703-264-9494
Newsletter of the Teacher Education Division offering information about TED activities, upcoming events, current trends and
practices, state and national legislation, recently published materials and practical information of interest to persons involved in
the preparation and continuing professional
development of effective professionals in
special education and related service fields.
3x Year
Diana Hammitte, Co-Editor
Laurence O'Shea, Editor

3492 TESOL Journal: A Journal of Teaching and Classroom Research
Teachers of English to Speakers of Other Languages
1600 Cameron Street
Suite 300
Alexandria, VA 22314-2705
703-836-0774
Fax: 703-836-7864
E-mail: tescol@tesol.edu
http://www.tesol.edu
TESOL's mission is to develop the expertise of its members and others involved in teaching English to speakers of other languages to help them foster communication in diverse settings. The association advances standards for professional preparation and employment, continuing education, and student programs, produces programs, services, and products, and promotes advocacy to further the profession. TESOL has 91 affiliates worldwide.

50 pages Quarterly
Christian J Faltis, Editor
Marilyn Kupetz, Managing Editor

3493 Teacher Education Reports
Feistritzer Publishing
4401-A Connecticut Avenue NW
#212
Washington, DC 20008-2302
202-362-3444
Fax: 202-362-3493
Covers the field of teacher education for elementary and secondary schools, including pre-service preparation, in-service training and professional development, related federal programs, legislation and funding.

8 pages BiWeekly
David T Chester, Editor

3494 Teacher Education and Special Education
The Council for Exceptional Children
1920 Association Drive
Reston, VA 20191-1545
703-620-3660
Fax: 352-392-7159
Contains information on current research, exemplary practices, timely issues, legislation, book reviews, and new programs and materials relative to the preparation and continuing professional development of effective professionals in special education and related service fields.

Quarterly
Vivian Correa, Editor

3495 Teacher Magazine
6935 Arlington Road
Suite 100
Bethesda, MD 20814
301-280-3100
800-346-1834
Fax: 301-280-3250
E-mail: ads@epe.org
http://www.edweek.org
Articles for educators.

3496 Teacher's Guide to Classroom Management
Economics Press
12 Daniel Road
Fairfield, NJ 07004-2507
973-227-1224
Bulletins showing teachers how to solve problems and avoid problematic situations.

BiWeekly
Robert Guder

3497 Teachers in Touch
ISM Independent School Management
1316 N Union Street
Wilmington, DE 19806-2534
302-656-4944
800-955-4944
Fax: 302-656-0647
Faculty professional development publication with strategies for career satisfaction, good teaching practices and stress-reducing techniques. The forum for professional sharing for private-independent school educators.

4 pages 5x Year
Rozanne S Elliott, Publisher
Kelly Rawlings, Editor

3498 Teaching Education
University of South Carolina, College of Education
Wardlaw College
Room 231
Columbia, SC 29208-0001
803-777-6301
Fax: 803-777-3068
Focuses on the actual profession of teaching and new methodology by which to learn.

2x Year
James T. Sears, PhD, Editor

3499 Teaching Exceptional Children
The Council for Exceptional Children
1920 Association Drive
Reston, VA 20191-1545
703-620-3660
800-232-7323
Fax: 703-264-1637
A practical classroom-oriented magazine that explores instructional methods, materials and techniques for working with children who have disabilities or who are gifted.

BiMonthly
ISSN: 0040-0599
H William Heller, Editor
Fred Spooner, Editor

3500 Techniques-Connecting Education and Careers
Association for Career and Technical Education
1410 King Street
Alexandria, VA 22314-2749
703-683-3111
800-826-9972
Fax: 703-683-7424
E-mail: sackley@acteonline.org
http://www.acteonline.org
Each issue is packed with information on subjects of successful partnerships, new education models, career exploration, balancing work and family responsibilities, adapting to new workplace practices and technologies, positioning in the global market, teaching approaches and safety issues.

Newsletter/Magazine
Steve Ackley, Asst Exec Dir Communications

3501 Technology Integration for Teachers
Master Teacher
Po Box 1207
Manhattan, KS 66505-1207
785-539-0555
800-669-9633
Fax: 800-669-1132
http://www.masterteacher.com
The publication that provides teachers with innovative strategies for integratinjg technology into the classroom.

Monthly Newsletter
Brad Roberts, Executive Editor

3502 The Board
Master Teacher
Po Box 1207
Manhattan, KS 66505-1207
785-539-0555
800-669-9633
Fax: 800-669-1132
http://www.masterteacher.com
A complete program of in-service training for school board members.

2 pages
Robert DeBruyn, Executive Editor

3503 The Professor In The Classroom
Master Teacher
Po Box 1207
Manhattan, KS 66505-1207
785-539-0555
800-669-9633
Fax: 800-669-1132
http://www.masterteacher.com
a complete program of unservice training for college faculty members and graduate teaching assistants.

1 pages Semi-Monthly
Robert DeBruyn, Author

3504 Today's Catholic Teacher
2621 Dryden Road
Suite 300
Dayton, OH 45439
937-293-1415
Fax: 937-293-1310
E-mail: mnoschang@peterli.com
http://www.catholicteacher.com
The voice of Catholic education for over a quarter of a century. Lists teaching suggestions, curriculum strategies and ready-to-use classroom ideas. Editorial and special columns are also included in each issue.

72 pages Bimonthly
ISSN: 0040-8441
Mary C Noschang, Editor

3505 Training Research Journal: The Science and Practice of Training
Educational Technology Publications
700 Paliside Avenue
Englewood Cliffs, NJ 07632
Fax: 201-871-4009
Peer-reviewed publication, published once yearly by Educational Technology Publications, is now in its fourth volume. Provides a high-quality, peer-reviewed forum for theoretical and empirical work relevant to training.

Annually

Software, Hardware & Internet Resources

3506 Analog & Digital Peripherals
251 S Mulberry Street
Troy, OH 45373-3585
937-339-2241
800-758-1041
Fax: 937-339-0070
Rewritable optical desk systems with storage from 128 meg. to 1.3 Gig for all operating systems. Backup systems for all

operating systems, one system backs up all PC's.

Lyle Ellicott

3507 E-Z Grader Software

E-Z Grader Company
PO Box 23608
Chagrin Falls, OH 44023
800-432-4018
http://www.ezgrader.com
Electronic guidebook designed by teachers for teachers.

3508 Education Index

H.W. Wilson Company
950 University Avenue
Bronx, NY 10452-4224
718-588-8400
800-367-6770
Fax: 718-590-1617
E-mail: rsky@hwwilson.com
http://www.hwwilson.com
Contains more than 456,000 citations to articles, interviews, editorials and letters, reviews of books, educational films, and software for approximately 427 English-language periodicals, monographs and yearbooks in the field of education. Available electronically on the Web with index, abstracts and full text versions.

Monthly

Roseward Sky, Assistant Manager/Marketing
Harold Regan, President

3509 Educational Administration Resource Centre Database

University of Alberta
Department of Chemistry
Edmonton, AB, Canada, T6 G 2G2
780-492-3254
Fax: 780-492-8231
Over 3,650 bibliographic descriptions of the Centre's collection of educational administration print and audiovisual materials.

3510 KidsCare Childcare Management Software

770 Cochituate Road
Framingham, MA 01701-4672
508-875-3451
Sells software programs to education professionals involved in childcare to aid their development and understanding.

3511 Mental Edge

Learning ShortCuts
PO Box 382367
Germantown, TN 38183-2367
901-755-4732
Fax: 309-406-5358
E-mail: learning@learningshortcuts.com
http://www.learningshortcuts.com
A teacher information network.

3512 http://www.gsn.org

Global Schoolhouse

http://www.gsn.org
Collaborative projects, communication tools and professional development.

3513 http://www.usajobs.opm.gov/b1c.htm

Institute of Int'l Education Overseas Employment
Info-Teachers United States Office of Personnel Management

3514 www.K12jobs.com

E-mail: info@k12jobs.com
Concentrates in posting job opportunities available at elementary, junior high, high schools and vocational schools.

3515 www.aasa.org

American Association of School Administrators
801 N Quincy Street
Suite 700
Arlington, VA 22203-1730
703-528-0700
Fax: 703-841-1543
E-mail: info@aasa.org
http://www.aasa.org
Leadership news online.

3516 www.cftl.org

Center for the Future of Teaching & Learning

A not-for-profit organization with roots in California's education reform movement. Our primary focus is strengthening California's teacher workforce.

3517 www.classbuilder.com

Free teachers toolbox! Grade book, Create tests, Reports, Lessons, Distance Learning Courseware, and more.

3518 www.ed.gov/free

Federal Resources for Educational Excellence

Provides hundreds of searchable teaching and learning resources from across 35 federal government agencies. Links to 30 offerings on physics, language, arts, history, current events and other areas. Publishes input from teachers, students and parents.

3519 www.eduverse.com

eduverse.com

Leading Internet e-Knowledge software developer building core technologies for powering international distance education.

3520 www.freeteachingaids.com

Free Teaching Aids.com

Guides for finding free resources for teachers.

3521 www.imagescape.com/helpweb/www/oneweb.html

An Overview of the World Wide Web
A New Surfer's Guide
Let this Web site, ease you gently into World Wide Web vocabulary and history. Click Index to find A Guide to Getting Started on the Internet.

3522 www.learningpage.com

http://www.sitesforteachers.com
A wealth of resource links to teacher organizations, sites to recommend to parents, administrators, and students.

3523 www.mmhschool.com

McGraw Hill School Division

A collection of some Web links that offer basic information to guide you. From simple definitions, to a brief description of the history of the Wide Web, to a list of ways to use Web technology with students.

3524 www.nprinc.com

National Professional Resources

Major distributor of professional development materials to support our nation's teachers in the field of education.

3525 www.onlinelearning.net

OnlineLearning.net

Leading online supplier of instructor-led continuing/adult education.

3526 www.pagestarworld.com

Pagestar

Software products that are specifically designed for teachers. Over 600 electronic forms that are commonly used by teachers for planning, administering, delivering and assessing student learning.

3527 www.pbs.org

PBS TeacherSource

Quick access to a collection of resources for teachers including more than 1,400 lesson plans, teacher's guides and online student activities.

3528 www.pbs.org/uti/quicktips.html

QuickTips

On understanding and using the Internet, you'll find tips on navigating the Web.

3529 www.rhlschool.com

RHL School

Free worksheets for english basics, math computation, math problem solving, reading comprehension and research skills.

3530 www.sanjuan.edu/select/structures.html

San Juan Select - Structures

A Web site that examines various ways to structure and facilitate student projects using Internet capabilities. Each suggestion is accompanied by a specific example of how that structure can be or is being used on the Internet.

3531 www.schoolrenaissance.com

School Renaissance Model

The School Renaissance Model combines the #1 software in education with professional development and consulting services to help you dramatically improve student performance.

3532 www.teachingjobs.com

The Teachers Employment Network

http://
Leading resource for education employment.

3533 www.usajobs.opm.gov/b1c.htm
Overseas Employment Info- Teachers
US Office of Personnel Management
Covers eligibility, position categories and
special requirements, application procedures, program information and entitle-
ment, housing, living/working conditions,
shipment of household goods, and complete application forms and guidance.

3534 www.webworkshops.com
Web Work Shops

A series of on-line courses, designed to
prepare teachers to integrate both the
Internet and classroom computer applications into daily lessons.

Training Materials

**3535 At-Risk Students: Identification
and Assistance Strategies**
Center for the Study of Small/Rural
Schools
555 E Constitution Street
Room 138
Norman, OK 73072-7820
405-325-1450
Fax: 405-325-7075
E-mail: jcsimmons@ou.edu
http://cssrs.ou.edu
Series II
Video

Jan C Simmons, Director

**3536 Character Education: Making a
Difference**
Character Education Partnership
1025 Connecticut Avenue NW
Suite 1011
Washington, DC 20036
202-296-7743
800-988-8081
Fax: 202-296-7779
http://www.character.org

Andrea Grenadier, Director
Communications
Esther Schaeffer, CEO/Executive
Director

**3537 Character Education: Restoring
Respect & Responsibility in our
Schools**
Master Teacher
Po Box 1207
Manhattan, KS 66505-1207
785-539-0555
800-669-9633
Fax: 800-669-1132
http://www.masterteacher.com
Provides a comprehensive model for character education in our nations schools. Specific classroom stategies as well as school
wide approaches are outlines in a clear and
compelling fashion.

Thomas Lickona PhD, Author

3538 Cisco Educational Archives
University of North Carolina at Chapel
Hill
CB# 3456, Manning Hall
Chapel Hill, NC 27599-3455
http://www.sunsite.unc.edu/cisco/cisco-h
ome
Resource for education programs, dis-
counts and special offers.

**3539 Classroom Teacher's Guide for
Working withParaeducators Video
Set**
Master Teacher
Po Box 1207
Manhattan, KS 66505-1207
785-539-0555
800-669-9633
Fax: 800-669-1132
http://www.masterteacher.com
Covers a range of nuts-and-bolts topics including why the job duties of paras have
changed so much over the years, what a
classroom teacher needs to know to get
started working effectively with a para.
Useful tips for managing another adult, and
how para factor into the planning process.

Wendy Dover, Author

**3540 Clinical Play Therapy Videos:
Child-Centered Developmental &
Relationship Play Therapy**
University of North Texas
PO Box 311337
Denton, TX 76203
940-565-3864
Fax: 940-565-4461
E-mail: cpt@coefs.coe.unt.edu
http://www.centerforplaytherapy.com

Garry Landreth PhD, Director

**3541 Conferencing with Students &
Parents Video Series**
Master Teacher
Po Box 1207
Manhattan, KS 66505-1207
785-539-0555
800-669-9633
Fax: 800-669-1132
http://www.masterteacher.com
Will help teachers turn both formal and in-
formal conferences with students and par-
ents into opportunities for student success.

**3542 Conflict Resolution Strategies in
Schools**
Center for the Study of Small/Rural
Schools
555 E Constitution Street
Room 138
Norman, OK 73072-7820
405-325-1450
Fax: 405-325-7075
E-mail: jcsimmons@ou.edu
http://cssrs.ou.edu
Series IV
Video

Jan C Simmons, Director

3543 Conover Company
2926 Hidden Road
Oshkosh, WI 54902
920-231-4667
Fax: 920-231-4809
E-mail: conover@execpc.com
http://www.conovercompany.com
Emotional intelligence related to learning,
leadership, teamwork and change, anger
management, violence prevention; functional literary, career exploration and assessment.

3544 Cooperative Learning Strategies
Center for the Study of Small/Rural
Schools
555 E Constitution Street
Room 138
Norman, OK 73072-7820
405-325-1450
Fax: 405-325-7075
E-mail: jcsimmons@ou.edu
http://cssrs.ou.edu
Series I
Video

Jan C Simmons, Director

**3545 Creating Schools of Character
Video Series**
Master Teacher
Po Box 1207
Manhattan, KS 66505-1207
785-539-0555
800-669-9633
Fax: 800-669-1132
http://www.masterteacher.com
Visit a Blue Ribbon School of excellence
and hear staff and others discuss how to
create or improve a whole school charecter
education program.
ISBN: 0-914607-90-1

3546 Crisis Management in Schools
Center for the Study of Small/Rural
Schools
555 E Constitution Street
Room 138
Norman, OK 73072-7820
405-325-1450
Fax: 405-325-7075
E-mail: jcsimmons@ou.edu
http://cssrs.ou.edu
Series IV
Video

Jan C Simmons, Director

3547 Critical Thinking Video Set
Master Teacher
Po Box 1207
Manhattan, KS 66505-1207
785-539-0555
800-669-9633
Fax: 800-669-1132
http://www.masterteacher.com
Will help teachers challange students to
think in a new way. Research shows that
when we engage students in critical and
creative though, retention increases tre-
mendously.
ISBN: 1-58992-079-1

**3548 Curriculum Alignment: Improving
Student Learning**
Center for the Study of Small/Rural
Schools
555 E Constitution Street
Room 138
Norman, OK 73072-7820
405-325-1450
Fax: 405-325-7075
E-mail: jcsimmons@ou.edu
http://cssrs.ou.edu
Series I
Video

Jan C Simmons, Director

3549 Datacad
20 Tower Lane
Avon, CT 06001
860-677-4004
800-394-2231
Fax: 860-677-2610
E-mail: info@datacad.com
http://www.datacad.com
Software for AKC professionals.

Mark F Madura, President/CEO

3550 Discipline Techniques you can Master in a Minute Video Series
Master Teacher
Leadership Lane
PO Box 1207
Manhattan, KS 66505-1207
800-669-9633
Fax: 800-669-1132
http://www.masterteacher.com
Key attitudes and strategies for maximizing your options, handle chronic and habitual discipline problems, approaches and actions to get the responses you want, critical mistakes that cause or perpetuate misbehavior.

ISBN: 1-58992-040-6

3551 Educational Productions Inc
6433 SW Laber Road
Portland, OR 97221
503-297-6393
800-950-4949
Fax: 503-297-6395
E-mail: custserv@edpro.com
http://www.edpro.com
Video-rich training for all adults working with children birth to eight years of age.

Linda Freedman, President

3552 Eleven Principals of Effective Character Education
Master Teacher
Leadership Lane
PO Box 1207
Manhattan, KS 66505-1207
800-669-9633
Fax: 800-669-1132
http://www.masterteacher.com
Takes you to schools in Maryland, New York, and Missouri, where quality character education programs are being implemented by skilled and resourceful staff.

ISBN: 1-887943-13-7

Thomas Lickona PhD, Author

3553 Eleven Principles of Effective Character Educaion
Character Education Partnership
1025 Connecticut Avenue NW
Suite 1011
Washington, DC 20036
202-296-7743
800-988-8081
Fax: 202-296-7779
http://www.character.org

Andrea Grenadier, Director
Communications
Esther Schaeffer, CEO/Executive Director

3554 Eye on Education
6 Depot Way W
Larchmont, NY 10538
914-833-0551
Fax: 914-833-0761
http://www.eyeoneducation.com
Books on performance-based learning and assessment.

3555 Great Classroom Management SeriesDVD
Master Teacher
Leadership Lane
PO Box 1207
Manhattan, KS 66505-1207
800-669-9633
Fax: 800-669-1132
http://www.masterteacher.com
Effestive classroom management is getting more difficult everday. teachers face increasing demands and expectations in ebery aspect of their jobs.

ISBN: 0-914607-90-1

3556 Great Classroom Management Video SeriesVHS
Master Teacher
Leadership Lane
PO Box 1207
Manhattan, KS 66505-1207
800-669-9633
Fax: 800-669-1132
http://www.masterteacher.com
Effective classroom management is getting more difficult everyday. teachers face increasing demands and expectations in everyday. Teachers face increasing demands and expectations in every aspect of their jobs.

ISBN: 1-58992-121-6

3557 Handling Chronically Disruptive Students at Risk Video Series
Master Teacher
Leadership Lane
PO Box 1207
Manhattan, KS 66505-1207
800-669-9633
Fax: 800-669-1132
http://www.masterteacher.com
Implement and utlize a CARE couscil, develop and individual Action plan, strategies for enhancing individual action plan.

ISBN: 1-58992-031-7

3558 Hearlihy & Company
Po Box 1747
Pittaburg, KS 66762
866-622-1003
Fax: 800-443-2260
E-mail: kbolte@hearlihy.com
http://www.hearlihy.com
Training and installation for schools purchasing modular labratories.

Kevin Bolte, Contact

3559 Improving Parent/Educator Relationships
Center for the Study of Small/Rural Schools
555 E Constitution Street
Room 138
Norman, OK 73072-7820
405-325-1450
Fax: 405-325-7075
E-mail: jcsimmons@ou.edu
http://cssrs.ou.edu
Series I

Video

Jan C Simmons, Director

3560 Improving Student Thinking in the Content Area
Center for the Study of Small/Rural Schools
555 E Constitution Street
Room 138
Norman, OK 73072-7820
405-325-1450
Fax: 405-325-7075
E-mail: jcsimmons@ou.edu
http://cssrs.ou.edu
Series II

Video

Jan C Simmons, Director

3561 Inclusion: The Next Step the Video Series
Master Teacher
Leadership Lane
PO Box 1207
Manhattan, KS 66505-1207
800-669-9633
Fax: 800-669-1132
http://www.masterteacher.com
Will help you propel your inclusion efforts to a new level of success giving you the necessary insights and stategies for building consensus; weighing your program, curriculum, and instructional options.

ISBN: 1-58992-012-0

Wendy Dover, Author

3562 Integrating Technology into the CurriculumVideo Series
Master Teacher
Leadership Lane
PO Box 1207
Manhattan, KS 66505-1207
800-669-9633
Fax: 800-669-1132
http://www.masterteacher.com
Gives teachers the tools and strategies they need to make information technology work for then and for students while empowering then to teach the skills necessary for students to be productive in a technology driven world.

ISBN: 1-58992-007-Y

3563 International Clearinghouse for the Advancement of Science Teaching
University of Maryland
Benjamin Building
Room 226
College Park, MD 20742-1100
301-405-3161
Fax: 301-314-9055
Provides curriculum information about science and mathematics teaching.

Dr. David Lockard, Director

3564 Lesson Plans and Modifications for Inclusion and Collaborative Classrooms
Master Teacher
Leadership Lane
PO Box 1207
Manhattan, KS 66505-1207
800-669-9633
Fax: 800-669-1132
http://www.masterteacher.com
Discover specific strategies lesson plans and activity modifications to enhance learning for all students in the inclusive classroom.

ISBN: 1-58992-022-8

Professional Development/Training Materials

3565 Managing Students Without Coercion
Center for the Study of Small/Rural Schools
555 E Constitution Street
Room 138
Norman, OK 73072-7820
405-325-1450
Fax: 405-325-7075
E-mail: jcsimmons@ou.edu
http://cssrs.ou.edu
Series II
Video
Jan C Simmons, Director

3566 Mentoring Teachers to Mastery Video Series
Master Teacher
Leadership Lane
PO Box 1207
Manhattan, KS 66505-1207
800-669-9633
Fax: 800-669-1132
http://www.masterteacher.com
This 5 tape set will provide your staff with the focus, ideas, and stategies necessary for developing the skills of a Master Teacher.
ISBN: 1-58992-001-5

3567 Motivating Students in the Classroom Video Series
Master Teacher
Leadership Lane
PO Box 1207
Manhattan, KS 66505-1207
800-669-9633
Fax: 800-669-1132
http://www.masterteacher.com
Will help teachers with the tough job of motivating students to want to learn.
ISBN: 1-58992-074-0

3568 Multicultural Education: Teaching to Diversity
Center for the Study of Small/Rural Schools
555 E Constitution Street
Room 138
Norman, OK 73072-7820
405-325-1450
Fax: 405-325-7075
E-mail: jcsimmons@ou.edu
http://cssrs.ou.edu
Series II
Video
Jan C Simmons, Director

3569 Outcome-Based Education: Making it Work
Center for the Study of Small/Rural Schools
555 E Constitution Street
Room 138
Norman, OK 73072-7820
405-325-1450
Fax: 405-325-7075
E-mail: jcsimmons@ou.edu
http://cssrs.ou.edu
Series III
Video
Jan C Simmons, Director

3570 Overview of Prevention: A Social Change Model
Center for the Study of Small/Rural Schools
555 E Constitution Street
Room 138
Norman, OK 73072-7820
405-325-1450
Fax: 405-325-7075
E-mail: jcsimmons@ou.edu
http://cssrs.ou.edu
Prevention Series
Video
Jan C Simmons, Director

3571 Quality School
Center for the Study of Small/Rural Schools
555 E Constitution Street
Room 138
Norman, OK 73072-7820
405-325-1450
Fax: 405-325-7075
E-mail: jcsimmons@ou.edu
http://cssrs.ou.edu
Series II
Video
Jan C Simmons, Director

3572 SAP Today
Performance Resource Press
1270 Rankin Drive
Suite F
Troy, MI 48083-2843
800-453-7733
Fax: 800-499-5718
Overview offers the basics of student assistance.

3573 School-Wide Stratigies for Retaining Great Teachers Video Series
Master Teacher
Leadership Lane
PO Box 1207
Manhattan, KS 66505-1207
800-669-9633
Fax: 800-669-1132
http://www.masterteacher.com
You will hear proven strategies for supporting new teachers through all those typical expirences that cansabatage their efforts and cause them to leave your district or even abandon teaching all together.
ISBN: 1-58992-098-8

3574 Site-Based Management
Center for the Study of Small/Rural Schools
555 E Constitution Street
Room 138
Norman, OK 73072-7820
405-325-1450
Fax: 405-325-7075
E-mail: jcsimmons@ou.edu
http://cssrs.ou.edu
Series III
Video
Jan C Simmons, Director

3575 Strategic Planning for Outcome-Based Education
Center for the Study of Small/Rural Schools
555 E Constitution Street
Room 138
Norman, OK 73072-7820
405-325-1450
Fax: 405-325-7075
E-mail: jcsimmons@ou.edu
http://cssrs.ou.edu
Series II
Video
Jan C Simmons, Director

3576 Strengthening the Family: An Overview of a Holistic Family Wellness Model
Center for the Study of Small/Rural Schools
555 E Constitution Street
Room 138
Norman, OK 73072-7820
405-325-1450
Fax: 405-325-7075
E-mail: jcsimmons@ou.edu
http://cssrs.ou.edu
Prevention Series
Video
Jan C Simmons, Director

3577 Students-at-Risk Video Series
Master Teacher
Leadership Lane
PO Box 1207
Manhattan, KS 66505-1207
800-669-9633
Fax: 800-669-1132
http://www.masterteacher.com
Gives you specific stategies for reaching those students who are giving up.
ISBN: 1-58992-060-0
Mildred Odom Bradley, Author

3578 Superintendent/School Board Relationships
Center for the Study of Small/Rural Schools
555 E Constitution Street
Room 138
Norman, OK 73072-7820
405-325-1450
Fax: 405-325-7075
E-mail: jcsimmons@ou.edu
http://cssrs.ou.edu
Series I
Video
Jan C Simmons, Director

3579 TQM: Implementing Quality Management in Your School
Center for the Study of Small/Rural Schools
555 E Constitution Street
Room 138
Norman, OK 73072-7820
405-325-1450
Fax: 405-325-7075
E-mail: jcsimmons@ou.edu
http://cssrs.ou.edu
Series III
Video
Jan C Simmons, Director

3580 Teachers as Heros
Center for the Study of Small/Rural
Schools
555 E Constitution Street
Room 138
Norman, OK 73072-7820
405-325-1450
Fax: 405-325-7075
E-mail: jcsimmons@ou.edu
http://cssrs.ou.edu
Series IV
Video
Jan C Simmons, Director

3581 Teaching for Intelligent Behavior
Center for the Study of Small/Rural
Schools
555 E Constitution Street
Room 138
Norman, OK 73072-7820
405-325-1450
Fax: 405-325-7075
E-mail: jcsimmons@ou.edu
http://cssrs.ou.edu
Series IV
Video
Jan C Simmons, Director

3582 The Master Teacher
Master Teacher
Leadership Lane
PO Box 1207
Manhattan, KS 66505-1207
800-669-9633
Fax: 800-669-1132
http://www.masterteacher.com
Program of staff development and leadership. It provides a continuous inspiration
each week to correspond to the mood and
activities present in schools.
2 pages Weekly

**3583 Training Video Series for the
Substitute Teacher**
Master Teacher
Leadership Lane
PO Box 1207
Manhattan, KS 66505-1207
800-669-9633
Fax: 800-669-1132
http://www.masterteacher.com
Will help you provide the consistent direc-
tion and training for substitute teachers.
ISBN: 0-914607-95-2

**3584 Voices in the Hall: High School
Principals at Work**
Phi Delta Kappa Educational Foundation
PO Box 789
Bloomington, IN 47402-0789
812-339-1156
800-766-1156
Fax: 812-339-0018
http://www.pdkintl.org
William E Webster's visits to more than 150
schools for this three-year study yield in-
sights into the new roles of the high school
principal in American education.
William E Webster, Author
Donovan R Walling, Dir
Publications/Research

3585 Wavelength
4753 N Broadway
Suite 808
Chicago, IL 60640
Fax: 773-784-1079
E-mail: winwave@aol.com
http://www.wavelengthinc.com

Humorous programs and videos cover a variety of topics including team building, motivation, diversity, mentoring, brain
research and character education.

**3586 You Can Handle Them All
Discipline Video Series**
Master Teacher
Leadership Lane
PO Box 1207
Manhattan, KS 66505-1207
800-669-9633
Fax: 800-669-1132
http://www.masterteacher.com
Based upon the best selling books You Can
Handle Them All and BEfore you can Disci-
pline by Robert L Debruyn. It contains the
vital professional foundations that must un-
derpin and solid philosophy of discipline.
ISBN: 1-58992-035-X
Robert L DeBruyn, Author

Workshops & Programs

3587 ACE Fellows Program
American Council on Education
1 Dupont Circle NW
Washington, DC 20036-1193
202-939-9300
Fax: 202-785-8056
E-mail: fellows@ace.nche.edu
http://www.acenet.edu/programs/fellows
Providing senior faculty and administrators
with the knowledge, skills, and experience
to manage change.
William Kirwan, Chair
M Lee Pelton, Vice Chair

**3588 ART New England Summer
Workshops**
Art New England Workshops
425 Washington Street
Brighton, MA 02135
617-879-7175
E-mail: nmccarthy@massart.edu
http://www.massart.edu/at_massart/acade
mic_prgms/continuing/
Offers painting, drawing, photography,
jewelry making, sculpting, computer imaging and ceramics.
Nancy McCarthy, Administrator

**3589 Annual Conductor's Institute of
South Carolina**
University of South Carolina
School of Music
Columbia, SC 29208
803-777-7500
Fax: 803-777-9774
E-mail: CI@mozart.sc.edu
http://www.conductorsinstitute.com
Since its inception, more than 600 conduc-
tors have traveled to Columbia to study with
guest conductors and composers. Academic
credit is available.
Donald Portnoy, Director

**3590 Annual Summer Institute for
Secondary Teachers**
Rock and Roll Hall of Fame

E-mail: soehler@rockhall.org
http://www.rockhall.com/programs/institu
te.asp
The institute provides teachers with the
knowledge and tools needed to bring popular music into the curriculum. The program

includes a rock and roll history survey;
guest speakers; discussions and workshops.
June
Susan Oehler, Education Programs
Manager

3591 Ball State University
Department of Industry & Technology
Applied Technology Building 131
Muncie, IN 47306-0255
765-285-5641
Fax: 765-285-2162
http://www.bsu.edu/cast/itech
Summer programs in manufacturing, print-
ing, graphic arts, technology education, in-
dustrial vocational/technical education.

3592 Bryant and Stratton College
200 Bryant and Stratton Way
Williamsville, NY 14231-0142
716-821-9331
Fax: 716-821-9343
http://www.bryantstratton.edu
Summer programs in information technology, data communications and networking,
logic and program design.

**3593 Center for Educational Leadership
Trinity University**
Trinity University
715 Stadium Drive
San Antonio, TX 78212-7200
210-999-7501
Fax: 210-999-7696
E-mail: paul.kelleher@trinity.edu
http://http://carme.cs.trinity.edu/education
/index.asp
Offers three Masters degree programs for
Arts, Teaching, Psychology and School Administration. The school also offers summer
institutes and training programs for educators and administrators. Also see information regarding the Master of Education:
School Administration at
http://carme.cs.trinity.edu/education/grad-
uate/medschoolleadership.htm

3594 Center for Global Education
Augsbury College
2211 Riverside Avenue
Minneapolis, MN 55454-1350
612-330-1159
800-299-8889
Fax: 612-330-1695
E-mail: globaled@augsburg.edu
http://www.augsburg.edu/global
Offers travel seminars for educators, 7-21
day programs to Mexico, Central America,
Southern Africa and Cuba. Explores social
change, human rights, development and US
policy. Educators reflect upon teaching
goals, methods and curricula and discover
new models of teaching.

**3595 Center for Image Processing in
Education**
PO Box 13750
Tucson, AZ 85732-3750
520-322-0118
800-322-9884
Fax: 520-327-0175
E-mail: kRISR@evisual.org
http://www.evisual.org
Disseminates curriculum materials and
in-service workshops for using digital image processing in classroom applications.
The materials are designed for hands-on,
open-ended exploration and discovery, using professional scientific software. Workshops provide the needed background and

training for teachers to effectively implement image processing.

Steve Moore, Executive Director
Kristine Rees, Business Operations Director

3596 Center for Learning Connections

Highline Community College 25-55A
PO Box 98000
Des Moines, IA 98198-9800
206-870-3783
Fax: 206-870-3787
http://www.learningconnections.org
Workshops, seminars, conferences, focus groups and retreats; education reform, school-to-career, project design and management.

3597 Center for Occupational Research & Development

601 Lake Air Drive
Waco, TX 76710
800-231-3015
Fax: 254-776-3906
E-mail: twarner@cord.org
http://www.cord.org
Workshops, onsite workshops and video conferencing courses in education technology applications.

Teemus Warner, Training Coordinator

3598 Center for Play Therapy

University of North Texas
PO Box 311337
Denton, TX 76203
940-565-3864
Fax: 940-565-4461
E-mail: cpt@unt.edu
http://www.centerforplaytherapy.com
Encourages the unique development and emotional growth of children through the process of play therapy, a dynamic interpersonal relationship between a child and a therapist trained in play therapy procedures. Provides training, research, publications, counseling services and acts as a clearinghouse for literature in the field.

Sue Bratton, Director

3599 Classroom Connect

8000 Marina Boulevard
Suite 400
Brisbane, CA 94005
650-351-5100
800-638-1639
Fax: 650-351-5300
E-mail: conect@classroom.com
http://www.classroom.com
A leading provider of professional development programs and online instructional content for K-12 education.

Jim Bowler, President
Melinda Cook, Vice President Sales

3600 College of the Ozarks

PO Box 17
Point Lookout, MO 65726
417-334-6411
Fax: 417-335-2618
E-mail: admiss4@cofo.edu
http://www.cofo.edu

3601 Connect

Synergy Learning
116 Birge Street
PO Box 60
Brattleboro, VT 05302-0060
802-257-2629
800-769-6199
Fax: 802-254-5233
E-mail: casey@synergylearning.org
http://www.synergylearning.org
Sponsors literature teacher institutes and on-site workshops in math, science and design technology. Publishes Connect magazine for teachers of grades K-8 focusing on Math, Science and technology.

28 pages
ISSN: 1041-682X

Casey Murrow, Director
Susan Hathaway, Circulation Manager

3602 Critical Issues in Urban Special Education: The Implications of Whole-School Change

Harvard Graduate School of Education
Programs in Professional Education
339 Gutman Library
Cambridge, MA 02138
617-495-3572
800-545-1849
Fax: 617-496-8051
E-mail: ppe@harvard.edu
http://www.gse.harvard.edu/~ppe
A one-week summer seminar that examines the implications of whole-school change on students with disabilities, policy, procedure, and practice. The program will clarify competing agendas, illuminate various models, and identify unified approaches to ensuring measurable benefits to all children.

Genet Jeanjean, Program Coordinator

3603 Critical and Creative Thinking in the Classroom

National Center for Teaching Thinking
815 Washington Street
Suite 8
Newtonville, MA 02460
617-965-4604
Fax: 617-965-4674
A unique summer program of courses for K-12 teachers, curriculum developers, staff-development specialists, school/district administrators, teacher educators and college faculty.

3604 Curriculum Center - Office of Educational Services

3430 Constitution Drive
Suite 114
Springfield, IL 62707-9402
217-786-3010
Fax: 217-786-3020
E-mail: oesiscc@siu.edu
http://www.oes.siu.edu
Programs in vocational areas, career awareness, career development, integration, technology, tech preparation.

3605 Darryl L Sink & Associates

60 Garden Court
Suite 101
Monterey, CA 93940
831-649-8384
800-650-7465
Fax: 831-649-3914
E-mail: info@dsink.com
http://www.dsink.com
Three-day workshop based on proven instructional design principles adapted for web-based training.

3606 DeVry University

1 Tower Lane
Oakbrook Terrace, IL 60181
630-571-7700
800-295-8694
Fax: 630-574-1973
http://www.devry.edu
Subjects include communications, computer technology, electronics, graphic communications, and training and development.

3607 Delmar Thomson Learning

3 Columbia Circle
Albany, NY 12212
518-464-3500
Fax: 518-464-7000
E-mail: info@delmar.com
http://www.delmar.com
Subjects include welding, HVAC-R, electrical, electronics, automotive, CADD and drafting, construction, blueprint reading, and fire science.

3608 Depco

3305 Airport Drive
PO Box 178
Pittsburg, KS 66762
620-231-0019
800-767-1062
Fax: 620-231-0024
E-mail: sales@depcoinc.com
http://www.depcoinc.com
Subjects include technology service, linear and non-linear video production, and autodesk product training.

3609 Eastern Illinois University School of Technology

600 Lincoln Avenue
Charleston, IL 61920
217-581-3226
Fax: 217-581-6607
http://www.eiu-edu/~tech1
Subjects include manufacturing, construction, electronics, graphic communications, training and development.

3610 Edison Welding Institute

EWI
1250 Arthur E Adams Drive
Columbus, OH 42321
614-688-5000
Fax: 614-688-5001
E-mail: ewi@ewi.org
http://www.ewi.org
Welding courses taught by world experts in materials joining.

3611 Educational Summit

The Principals' Center
20 Nassau Street
Suite 211
Princeton, NJ 08542-4509
609-497-1907
Fax: 609-497-1927
An educational summit held in August for school principals to explore, debate and design new models for schooling in America with implications for choice, charters and the community.

3612 Effective Strategies for School Reform

Harvard Graduate School of Education
Programs in Professional Education
339 Gutman Library
Cambridge, MA 02138
617-495-3572
800-545-1849
Fax: 617-496-8051
E-mail: ppe@harvard.edu
http://www.gse.harvard.edu/~ppe
A two-week residential program on the Harvard campus for leadership teams from school districts that are involved in the process of school reform or restructuring. Participants will gain practical skills for leading change in their districts, and will forge effective action plans for school reform to take back to their districts.

Genet Jeanjean, Program Coordinator

3613 Electronics Industries Alliance/CEA

2500 Wilson Boulevard
Arlington, VA 22201-3834
703-907-7670
Fax: 703-907-7968
http://www.CEMAweb.org
Electronics workshops.

3614 Elementary Education Professional DevelopmentSchool

Pennsylvania State University
148 Chambers Building
Pennsylvania State University
University Park, PA 16802
814-865-2243
E-mail: n78@psu.edu
http://www.ed.psu/pds
Through courses and training seminars teachers can engage in research and rethinking of pracice, thus creating an opportunity for the profession to expand its knowledge base.

James Nolan, Professor of Education

3615 Emco Maier Corporation

2841 Charter Street
Columbus, OH 43228
614-771-5991
Fax: 614-771-5990
E-mail: info@emcomaier-usa.com
http://www.emcomaier-usa.com
Subjects include CNC training - turning and milling.

Josh Dack, Sales Manager
Karen Fahy, Sales/Marketing Coordinator

3616 Energy Concepts

404 Washington Boulevard
Mundelein, IL 60060
847-837-8191
800-621-1247
Fax: 847-837-8171
http://www.energy-concepts-inc.com
Subjects include material science technology, principles of technology year I&II.

3617 Fastech

1750 Westfield Drive
Findlay, OH 45840
419-425-2233
Fax: 419-425-9431
E-mail: info@fastechinc.net
http://www.fastechinc.net
Subjects include mastercam training, and FMMT CD's.

3618 Festo Corporation

395 Moreland Road
Hauppauge, NY 11788
631-435-0800
Fax: 631-435-0576
E-mail: HR.department@us.festo.com
http://www.festo-usa.com
Subjects include fluid power, PLC, industrial automation.

Fred Zieram, Sales Manager
Petra Milks, Product Coordinator

3619 Foundation for Critical Thinking

PO Box 7087
Dillon Beach, CA 94929
707-878-9100
E-mail: cct@criticalthinking.org
http://www.criticalthinking.org
Nonprofit organization which distributes books, videotapes, audiotapes and micropublications on critical thinking. Also hosts regional workshops which are geared toward educators.

3620 Four State Regional Technology Conference

Pittsburg State University
College of Technology
1701 S Broadway
Pittsburg, KS 66762
620-235-4365
800-854-7488
Fax: 620-235-4343
E-mail: tbaldwin@pittstate.edu
http://www.pittstate.edu
Subjects include educational technology and technology management.

November
30 booths with 250 attendees

Tom Baldwin, Dean College of Technology

3621 Graduate Programs for Professional Educators

North Central Association of Colleges & Schools
Walden University
155 5th Avenue S
Minneaoplis, MN 55401
800-444-6795
Fax: 941-498-4266
E-mail: request@waldenu.edu
Both the MS and PhD in Education allow study from home or work. The Master of Science in Education serves classroom teachers and the PhD in education serves the advanced learning needs of educators from a wide range that serves practice fields and levels.

3622 Grand Canyon University College of Education

30 N LaSalle Street
Chicago, IL 60602
312-263-0456
800-621-7440
Fax: 312-263-7462
http://www.ncahigherlearningcommission.org
A program created specifically to answer the needs of teachers with practical application of teaching strategies based on theory and research; work at your own pace within term deadlines.

3623 Harvard Institute for School Leadership

Harvard Graduate School of Education
14 Story Street
4th Floor
Cambridge, MA 02138
617-495-3572
800-545-1849
Fax: 617-496-8051
E-mail: ppe@harvard.edu
http://www.gse.harvard.edu/~ppe
An intensive residential program for leadership teams from school districts. Participants will gain new perspectives on the processes and goals of school reform and practical skills for leading change in their districts.

July

3624 Harvard Seminar for Superintendents

Harvard Graduate School of Education
Programs in Professional Education
339 Gutman Library
Cambridge, MA 02138
617-495-3572
800-545-1849
Fax: 617-496-8051
E-mail: ppe@harvard.edu
http://www.gse.harvard.edu/~ppe
Veteran superintendents from around the country participate in a week of intellectually stimulating conversations with Harvard faculty and networking with colleagues. Topics discussed include the arts, science, social science, and current events.

July

Valencia Miner, Program Assistant

3625 Hobart Institute of Welding Technology

400 Trade Square East
Troy, OH 45373
800-332-9448
Fax: 937-332-5200
http://www.welding.org
Preparation course for CWI/CWE exams. Instructor course devoted to welding theory and hand-son practice.

Elmer Swank, Contact

3626 Indiana University-Purdue University of Indianapolis, IUPUI

Department of Construction Technology
799 W Michigan Street
ET 309
Indianapolis, IN 46202-5160
317-274-2413
Fax: 317-278-3669
E-mail: dilpatto@iupui.edu
http://www.engr.iupui.edu/cnt
Subjects include architectural technology, civil engineering technology, construction technology, interior design.

E Sener, Chairman
Diane Patton, Adminstative Assistant

3627 Industrial Training Institute

3385 Wheeling Road
Lancaster, OH 43130
740-687-5262
800-638-4180
Fax: 740-687-5262
E-mail: drbillstevens1@msn.com
http://www.trainingrus.com
Subjects include basic electricity, motors, controls, PLC's, NEC and process control; custom designed training and consulting.

3628 Institute of Higher Education
General Board of Higher Education &
Ministry/UMC
1001 Nineteenth Avenue
PO Box 340007
Nashville, TN 37203-0007
615-340-7406
Fax: 615-340-7379
E-mail: scu@gbhem.org
http://www.gbhem.org/highed.html
An annual seminar for administrators and
faculty of United Methodist-related educa-
tional institutions addressing current
themes related to the college's mission.

June
125 attendees

Dr. James A Noseworthy, Assistant
General Secretary

**3629 International Curriculum
Management Audit Center**
Phi Delta Kappa International
Professional Development & Services
PO Box 789
Bloomington, IN 47402-0789
812-339-1156
800-776-1156
Fax: 812-339-0018
E-mail: cpds@pdkintl.org
http://www.pdkintl.org
Training in the curriculum audit process
empowers you to look objectively at the en-
tire curriculum management system.

3630 International Graduate School
Berne University
35 Center Street
Suite 18
Wolfeboro Falls, NH 03896-1080
603-569-8648
866-755-5557
Fax: 603-569-4052
E-mail: berne@berne.edu
http://www.berne.edu
Doctoral Degrees in one to two years, Specialist Diplomas in six to twelve months in:
business, education (all specialties), government, health services, international relations, psychology, religion, social work
and human services.

3631 International Workshops
187 Aqua View Drive
Cedarburg, WI 53012
262-377-7062
Fax: 262-377-7096
E-mail: thintz@execpc.com
http://www.internationalworkshops.org
Music education, accompanying, chamber
music, improvisation, jazz, technique, pedagogy, storing and piano repertoire and
chorus.

400 attendees

Tori Hintz, Manager

**3632 Island Drafting & Technical
Institute**
128 Broadway
Amityville, NY 11701
631-691-8733
Fax: 631-691-8738
E-mail: info@islanddrafting.com
http://www.islanddrafting.com
Subjects include CAD, drafting, computer
repair, electronics technology, novel CNE,
microsoft MSCE, and networking. Degree
and non-degree programs.

John G Diliberto, VP

3633 Janice Borla Vocal Jazz Camp
N Central College, Music Department
30 N Brainard
Naperville, IL 60566
630-416-3911
Fax: 630-416-6249
E-mail: jborla@aol.com
http://www.janiceborlavocaljazzcamp.org
Solo vocal jazz workshops, music education, vocal jazz history, improvisation, repertoire, technique and theory.

Janice Borla, Director

3634 Jefferson State Community College
2601 Carson Road
Birmingham, AL 35215
205-856-8517
Fax: 205-856-8572
E-mail: alfie@jscc.cc.al.us
http://www.jeffstateonline.com
Certificate and degree programs in automated manufacturing, electromechanical
systems, industrial maintenance, and
CAD.

3635 July in Rensselaer
St. Joseph's College, Graduate Dept
PO Box 984
Rensselaer, IN 47978
219-866-6352
Fax: 219-866-6102
E-mail: jamesc@saintjoe.edu
Solo, ensemble, liturgy, accompanying,
history, improvisation, private lessons,
technique, repertoire, sight reading, work-
shops, theory and sacred choral music.

Rev. James Challancin, Director

3636 K'nex Education Division
2990 Bergey Road
PO Box 700
Hatfield, PA 19440
888-ABC-KNEX
Fax: 215-996-4222
E-mail: abcknex@knex.com
http://www.knexeducation.com
Introductory, set specific, regional and design your own professional development
programs offered for any/all K-12 technology, math and science sets.

3637 Kaleidoscope
Consulting Psychologists Press
3803 E Bayshore Road
Palo Alto, CA 94303-4300
800-624-1765
Fax: 650-969-8608
An institute for educators that develops insights into teaching styles and learning
styles; administers and interprets the
Myers-Briggs Type Indicator (personality
inventory); learn new techniques to help
children understand and value their unique
qualities; create and deliver lessons that
enlighten all students and more.

July

3638 Kent State University
School of Technology
117 Van Deusen Hall
Kent, OH 44242-0001
330-672-2892
Fax: 330-672-2894
http://www.tech.kent.edu
Subjects include aeronautics, electronics,
manufacturing engineering, computer
technology, and automotive engineering
technology.

3639 Kentucky State University
Department of Industrial Technology
East Main Street, Shauntee Hall
Frankfort, KY 40601
502-597-6897
Fax: 502-227-6236
http://www.kysu.edu
Associates in applied science in drafting
and design technology and applied science
in electronics technology.

**3640 Kodaly Teaching Certification
Program**
DePaul University, School of Music
804 West Belden Avenue
Chicago, IL 60614
773-325-4355
Fax: 773-325-7263
Music education, pedagogy and work-
shops.

Robert Krueger, Director Operations

3641 Lab Volt Systems
1710 Highway 34 N
Wall, NJ 07727
732-938-2000
800-522-2658
Fax: 732-774-8573
E-mail: us@labvolt.com
http://www.labvolt.com
Hands-on training in the concepts, skills
and procedures that work best in modular,
multimedia technology education programs.

Eric Maynard, Contact

**3642 Leadership and the New
Technologies**
Harvard Graduate School of Education
Programs in Professional Education
339 Gutman Library
Cambridge, MA 02138
617-495-3572
800-545-1849
Fax: 617-496-8051
E-mail: ppe@harvard.edu
http://www.gse.harvard.edu/~ppe
Programs designed to help teams of school
leaders anticipate the far-reaching impacts
that new technologies can have on students, teachers, curriculum, and communication. Participants make long-term plans
for the use of technology in their schools
and districts and learn how to take advantage of federal and state technology initiatives.

July

Ann Doyle, Program Coordinator

3643 Learning & The Enneagram
National Enneagram Institute at Milton
Academy
230 Atherton Street
Milton, MA 02186-2424
617-898-1798
Fax: 617-898-1712
An educational enterprise dedicated to
guiding individuals and organizations in
the most responsible and effective format
for their needs. Programs include exploration of what every educator needs to know;
why we learn in the way we do; and how we
teach.

July

Regina Pyle, Coordinator

3644 Learning Materials Workshop
274 N Winooski Avenue
Burlington, VT 05401-3621
802-802-8399
800-693-7164
Fax: 802-862-0794
E-mail: mail@learningmaterialswork.com
http://www.learningmaterialswork.com
Learning Materials Workshop Blocks are learning tools in the hands of young children. They are open-ended, yet carefully designed in a variety of colors, sizes, shapes, and textures that stimulate and develop perpetual, motor, and language skills. Learning Materials Workshops are designed for early childhood/primary grade teachers, paraprofessionals, curriculum coordinators, special education teachers, ESL teachers, and teachers of the gifted and talented to help develop the learning process.

Karen Hewitt, President

3645 Light Machines

http://www.Imcorp.com/_vti_bin/shtml.exe/search/index.html
Subjects include demonstrations and comprehensive training on CNC routers, turning machines and milling machines, and CAD/CAM software.

3646 MPulse Maintenance Software
PO Box 22906
Eugene, OR 97402
800-944-1796
Fax: 541-302-6680
E-mail: info@mpulsesoftware.com
http://www.mpulsesoftware.com
Subjects include maintenance and facility management software.

3647 Marcraft International Corporation
100 N Morain Street
Suite 302
Kennwick, WA 99336
509-374-1951
800-441-6006
Fax: 509-374-9250
E-mail: info@mic-inc.com
http://www.moc-inc.com
Subjects include A+ certification, network+ certification, i-net+ certification and copper and optical cabling certifications.

Robert Krug, National Sales Manager

3648 Maryland Center for Career and Technology Education
1415 Key Highway
Baltimore, MD 21230
410-685-1648
Fax: 410-685-0032
Subjects include technology education and occupational education certification.

3649 Media and American Democracy
Harvard Graduate School of Education
Programs in Professional Education
339 Gutman Library
Cambridge, MA 02138
617-495-3572
800-545-1849
Fax: 617-496-8051
E-mail: ppe@harvard.edu
http://www.gse.harvard.edu/~ppe
Participants learn about the interaction between the media and American democratic process, develop curriculum units, and examine ways to help students become thoughtful consumers of media messages about politics. Designed for secondary school teachers of history, social studies, English, journalism, and humanities.

August

Tracy Ryder, Program Assistant

3650 Miller Electric Manufacturing Company
1635 W Spencer Street
Appleton, WI 54914
800-426-4553
Fax: 877-327-8132
http://www.millerwelds.com
Subjects include welding.

3651 Millersville University
Department of Industry & Technology
PO Box 1002, Osborn Hall
Millersvile, PA 54914
800-426-4553
Fax: 877-327-8132
http://www.millersv.edu
Subjects include continuing education in technology education, computers, internet for educators, aerospace/aviation, and websites for classroom use.

3652 Morehead State University
Dept. of Industrial Ed. & Tech
210 Loyd Cassity Building, MSU
Morehead, KY 40651
606-783-2418
Fax: 606-783-5030
E-mail: r.hayes@morehead-st.edu
http://www.morehead-st.edu/colleges/science/iet
AAS and BS in Industrial Technology, BS in Industrial Education, MS in Vocational Education and Technology.

3653 Musikgarten
507 Arlington Street
Greensboro, NC 27406
336-272-5303
800-216-6864
Fax: 336-272-0581
E-mail: musgarten@aol.com
http://www.musikgarten.org
Early childhood music education workshops teaching music and understanding children.

Lorna Heyge, Speaker

3654 NASA Educational Workshop
NSTA
1840 Wilson Boulevard
Arlington, VA 22201-3000
888-400-6782
Fax: 703-522-5413
http://www.nsta.org/programs/new.htm
Two week workshop at a NASA Center, professional development opportunity for K-12 teachers in mathematics, science, and technology, teachers and curriculum specialists at the K-12 levels; media specialists, resource teachers, elementary curriculum developers, counselors, and others with special interest in mathematics, science, technology, and geography.

3655 NCSS Summer Workshops
National Council for the Social Studies
8555 Sixteenth Street
Suite 500
Siver Spring, MD 20910
301-588-1800
800-683-0812
Fax: 301-588-2049
E-mail: sgriffin@ncss.org
http://www.socialstudies.org
Offers independent workshops and conferences concentrating on the social studies classroom.

July

Susan Griffin

3656 National Center for Construction Education & Research
PO Box 141104
Gainsville, FL 32614-1104
352-334-0911
Fax: 352-334-0932
E-mail: info@nccer.org
http://www.nccer.org
Subjects include industry-developed standardized craft training program covering more than 25 craft trades. Accredited, competency-based, task driven, and modular in format.

3657 National Computer Systems
4401 L Street NW
Suite 550
Edina, MN 55435
612-995-8997
800-328-6172
Fax: 952-830-8564
http://www.ncs.com
Programs offer skills to teach technology in the classroom.

3658 National Head Start Association
1651 Prince Street
Alexandria, VA 22314-2818
703-739-0875
Fax: 703-739-0878
http://www.nhsa.org
Dedicated to promoting and protecting the Head Start program. Advocates on the behalf of America's low-income children and families. Publishes many books, periodicals and resource guides. Offers a legislative hotline as well as training programs through the NHSA Academy.

Ron Herndon, President
Blanche Russ-Glover, VP

3659 Northern Arizona University
AZTEC Lab
Box 6025
Flagstaff, AZ 86011-6025
520-523-2560
Fax: 520-523-6395
E-mail: tlc2@dana.ucc.nau.edu
http://www.nau.edu/~ifwfd/aztec
Offers computer and technology workshops on site or off. Lab available for rental for training.

Nicole Snow, Director
Tracy Cooper, Lab Assistant

3660 Orff-Schulwerk Teacher Certification Program
DePaul University, School of Music
804 West Belden Avenue
Chicago, IL 60614
773-325-7260
Fax: 773-325-7264
E-mail: ahutchen@wppost.depaul.edu.
Music education, pedagogy and workshops.

Judy Bundra, Associate Dean

3661 Owens Community College
PO Box 10000
Toledo, OH 43699-1947
567-661-7000
800-466-9367
Fax: 419-661-7664
http://www.owens.cc.oh.us

199

Subjects include welding, machining, electronics, automotive, diesel, environmental, quality, and mechanical and digital media.

Ronald A McMaster, Chair
John Moore, Vice Chair

3662 Paideia Group
PO Box 3423
Chapel Hill, NC 27515-3423
919-929-0600
Fax: 919-932-3905
E-mail: paideiapgi@aol.com
http://http://hometown.aol.com/paideiapgi/webpage.html
Programs are designed with options for beginner and advanced levels. Activities include seminars and sessions that focus on socratic teaching, coaching, evaluation and curriculum design.

March
150 attendees

Patricia Weiss, PhD, President

3663 Pamela Sims & Associates
54 Mozart Crescent
Brampton, Ontario
Canada L6Y 2W7
905-455-7331
888-610-7467
Fax: 905-455-0207
E-mail: loveofkids@aol.com
http://www.pamelasims.com
Seminars and workshops for educators and parents.

Pamela Sims, President
Kelly Smith, Marketing Director

3664 Pennsylvania State University-Workforce Education & Development Program
301 Keller Building
University Park, PA 16802-1303
814-863-2584
Fax: 814-863-7532
http://www.ed.psu.edu/wfed
Subjects include educational, business, and industrial for vocational instructors, counselors, administrators, and students.

3665 Performance Learning Systems
72 Lone Oak Drive
Cadiz, KY 42211
270-522-2000
866-757-2527
Fax: 270-522-2010
E-mail: info@plsweb.com
http://www.plswed.com
Training programs with a specialization in teacher education, professional development and online classes.

Jackie Futrell, Resource Manager

3666 Piano Workshop
Goshen College, Music Department
1700 S Main Street
Goshen, IN 46526
574-535-7364
Fax: 574-535-7949
E-mail: beverlykl@goshen.edu
Solo, ensemble, music education, technique, pedagogy, repertoire, workshops and master classes.

Beverly Lapp

3667 Pittsburg State University
College of Technology
1701 S Broadway
Pittsburg, KS 66762
620-235-4365
800-854-7488
Fax: 620-235-4343
E-mail: tbaldwin@pittstate.edu
http://www.pittstate.edu
Subjects include educational technology and technology management. Hosts a regional conference in November.

Tom Baldwin, Dean College of Technology

3668 Polaroid Education Program
565 Technology Square
#3B
Cambridge, MA 02139-3539
781-386-2000
Fax: 781-386-3925
This program offers workshops for professional educators, preK-12; the Visual Learning Workshop and an Instant Image Portfolio Workshop.

3669 Professional Development Institutes
Center for Professional Development & Services
Phi Delta Kappa International
PO Box 789
Bloomington, IN 47402-0789
812-339-1156
800-766-1156
Fax: 812-339-0018
E-mail: cpds@pdkintl.org
http://www.pdkintl.org
Offers programs such as active learning strategies for extended blocks of time; block scheduling; efficacy in action/working to get smart.

3670 Professional Development Workshops
Rebus
4111 Jackson Road
Ann Arbor, MI 48103
734-668-4870
800-435-3085
Fax: 734-668-4728
http://www.rebusinc.com
Workshops that promote success by assessing children in the context of active learning.

June/July

Sam Meisels, CEO
Linda Borgsdorf, President

3671 Project Zero Classroom
Harvard Graduate School of Education
Programs in Professional Education
339 Gutman Library
Cambridge, MA 02138
617-495-3572
800-545-1849
Fax: 617-496-8051
E-mail: ppe@harvard.edu
http://www.gse.harvard.edu/~ppe
Renowned educators Howard Gardner and David Perkins and their Project Zero colleagues work with K-12 educators to help them reshape their classroom practices to promote student understanding. The week focuses on five concepts: teaching for understanding, multiple intelligences, the thinking classroom, authentic assessment, and learning with and through the arts.

July

Deana Tassi, Program Assistant

3672 Robert McNeel & Associates
3670 Woodland Park Avenue N
Seattle, WA 98103
206-545-7000
Fax: 206-545-7321
E-mail: bob@mcneelcom
http://www.rhino3d.com
3D modeling workshop for design, drafting, graphics, and technology educators.

3673 Rockford Systems
4620 Hydraulic Road
Rockford, IL 61109-2695
815-874-7891
800-922-7533
Fax: 815-874-6144
E-mail: sales@rockfordsystems.com
http://www.rockfordsystems.com
Machine safegaurding seminar for technology educators.

3674 SUNY College at Oswego
7060 Route 104
Oswego, NY 13126-3599
315-312-2500
Fax: 315-312-2863
E-mail: stanley@oswego.edu
http://www.oswego.edu
Subjects include technical and computer drafting, CADD, design, energy technology, materials processing, and manufacturing systems.

October
26 booths with 350-400 attendees

Deborah F Stanley, President
Howard Gordon, Executive Assistant to Presi

3675 School of Music
Georgia State University
PO Box 4097
Atlanta, GA 30302-4097
404-651-1720
Offers high school piano camp, music education leadership, summer opera workshops, and much more.

3676 Southern Polytechnic State University
1100 S Marietta Parkway
Marietta, GA 30060
770-528-7240
Fax: 770-528-7490
E-mail: coned@spsu.edu
http://www.spsu.edu/oce
Information technology continuing education.

3677 Southwestern Oklahoma State University
Industrial and Engineering Technology Department
100 Campus Drive
Weatherford, OK 73096
580-774-3162
Fax: 580-774-7028
E-mail: tech@swosu.edu
http://www.swosu.edu
Subjects include technology education, engineering technology and industrial technology.

Gary Bell, Chair
Jeff Short, Program Coordinator

3678 Specialized Solutions
24703 US Highway 19-N
Suite 200
Clearwater, FL 33763
727-669-1415
888-840-2378
Fax: 888-200-5959
E-mail: sales@quickcert.com
http://www.specializedsolutions.com
Technology based training and certification self study programs.

Sheri Nash, Contact

3679 Staff Development Workshops & Training Sessions
National School Conference Institute
PO Box 37527
Phoenix, AZ 85069-7527
602-371-8655
Fax: 602-371-8790
Offers twenty relevant and leading edge programs including curriculum instruction assessment, restructuring your school, improving student performance and gifted at-risk students. Ten monthly sessions of each program are available, with monthly feedback to follow-up. Accelerates restructuring efforts and also offers graduate credit.

3680 Standards and Accountability: Their Impact on Teaching and Assessment
Harvard Graduate School of Education
Programs in Professional Education
339 Gutman Library
Cambridge, MA 02138
617-495-3572
800-545-1849
Fax: 617-496-8051
E-mail: ppe@harvard.edu
http://www.gse.harvard.edu/~ppe
Examines educational and policy issues by new approaches to standards, assessment, and accountability. Focuses on issues of excellence and equity, aligning assessments with standards, strengthening professional development, impacts of challenges on school communities, and political and legal issues surrounding standards and forms of accountability. Designed for public school leaders whose responsibilities include evaluation and testing.

July

Tracy Ryder, Program Assistant

3681 Storytelling for Educational Enrichment The Magic of Storytelling
2709 Oak Haven Drive
San Marcos, TX 78666-5065
512-392-0669
800-322-3199
Fax: 512-392-9660
E-mail: krieger@corridor.net
Teacher in-service and training in storytelling and puppetry for teachers of Pre-K through third grades. The Magic of Storytelling is for all ages and levels, specializing in original stories of enlightenment and environmental education. Over ten years experiences with many national and regional conferences and training.

Cherie Krieger, President

3682 Summer Institute in Siena
University of Siena-S/American
Universities
Music Director
595 Prospect Road
Waterbury, CT 06706
203-754-5741
Fax: 203-753-8105
http://www.sienamusic.org
Programs offered in cooperation with the University of Siena-S and American Universities and Colleges. The program in Siena Italy is open to qualified graduates, undergraduates, professionals, teachers, 19 years of age or above. Special diploma; credit or non-credit; in-service credit; auditions; trips to Rome, Florence, Assisi, Venice, Pisa, three days in Switzerland; a Puccini Opera.

3683 Summer Programs for School Teams
National Association of Elementary
School Principa
1615 Duke Street
Alexandria, VA 22314-3406
703-684-3345
800-386-2377
Fax: 703-518-6281
http://www.naesp.org
Events focused on the key to exceptional instruction. Effective teaching and learning for school teams, must include the principal.

Ann R Walker, Assistant Executive Director
Herrie Hahn, Director Programs

3684 Supplemental Instruction, Supervisor Workshops
University of Missouri-Kansas City
5100 Rockhill Road
SASS 210
Kansas City, MO 64110-2499
816-235-1174
Fax: 816-235-5156
E-mail: cad@umkc.edu
http://www.umkc.edu/cad/si
Training dates in February, April, June, July, September and November.

Kim Wilcox, Coordinator of Training

3685 THE Institute & Knowvation
800-840-0003
http://www.thejournal.com/institute
Online courses helping educators become comfortable with technology tools, integrating technology into their classroom and delivering high quality content for their professional growth.

3686 TUV Product Service
5 Cherry Hill Drive
Danvers, MA 01923
800-TUV-0123
Fax: 978-762-7637
E-mail: info@tuvps.com
http://www.tuvglobal.com
Subjects include ISO 9000:2000, ISO 14001, SEMI, and CE Marking.

3687 Teacher Education Institute
1079 W Morse Boulivard
Winter Park, FL 32789-3751
800-331-2208
Fax: 800-370-2600
E-mail: tei@teachereducation.com
http://www.teachereducation.com
Programs and courses needed by educators and administrators.

Ken Miller, President

3688 Teachers College: Columbia University
Center for Technology & School Change
Teachers College
Box 8, 525 W 120th Street
New York, NY 10002
212-678-3773
Fax: 212-678-4048
E-mail: hb50@columbia.edu
http://www.tc.columbia.edu/~academic/ctsc
Earn an MA degree in Computing and Education or Instructional Technology in 2 or 3 July sessions in New York, plus independent study. Concentrate in: multimedia design, technology leadership and teaching and learning with technology.

Howard Budin, Contact

3689 Technology Training for Educators
Astronauts Memorial Foundation
321-452-2887
800-792-3494
Fax: 321-452-6244
http://www.amfcse.org
Microsoft NT Administration; Technology Specialist; Management of Technology; Advanced Technology Specialist.

3690 Tooling University
15700 S Waterloo Road
Cleveland, OH 44110
866-706-8665
Fax: 216-706-6601
E-mail: info@toolingu.com
http://www.toolingu.com
Offers online training for manufacturing via the website.

Gene Jones, Director Marketing

3691 Total Quality Schools Workshop
Pennsylvania State University
302F Rackley Building
University Park, PA 16802
814-843-3765
E-mail: hli@psu.edu
http://www.ed.psu.edu/ctqs/index.html
Designed for public school educators at the state, national, and international level, this training program provides information in the philosophy, tools, and techniques of total quality management in education. The three day-six week program focuses on leadership, reform models, and education decision making.

William Hartman, Director

3692 University of Arkansas at Little Rock
2801 S University Avenue
Little Rock, AR 72204
501-569-8222
Fax: 501-569-8206
E-mail: mdstewart@ualr.edu
http://www.ualr.edu/~autocad
Computer aided design training classes on autodesk products; autoCAD 2000, mechanical desktop R4, and inventor R2.

Mike Stewart, Contact

3693 University of Central Florida
12424 Research Parkway
Suite 264
Orlando, FL 32826-3271
407-823-4908
Fax: 407-270-4911
http://www.distrib.ucf.edu
Web-based vocational teacher education courses.

3694 University of Michigan-Dearborn Center for Corporate & Professional Development

4901 Evergreen Road
CCPD-2000
Dearborn, MI 48128
313-593-5000
Fax: 313-593-5111
E-mail: info@umich.edu
http://www.umd.umich.edu
Over 230 professional development seminars, workshops, and conferences targeted for line-managers to mid- and senior-level management.

Daniel Little, Chancellor
Ray Metz, Chief to Staff

3695 Wavelength

4753 N Broadway
Suite 808
Chicago, IL 60640
Fax: 773-784-1079
E-mail: winwave@aol.com
http://www.wavelengthinc.com
Humorous programs and videos cover a variety of topics including team building, motivation, diversity, mentoring, brain research and character education.

3696 Wids Learning Design System

One Foundation Circle
Waunakee, WI 53597
800-821-6313
Fax: 608-849-2468
E-mail: info@wids.org
http://www.wids.org
Subjects include instructional design, developing outcomes, designing assessments and assessing standards.

Lisa Laabs, Office Manager
Judy Neill, Director

3697 Workforce Education and Development

Southern Illinois University Carbondale
Pulliem Hall
Carbondale, IL 62901-4603
618-453-3321
Fax: 618-453-1934
E-mail: wed@siu.edu
http://www.siu.edu/~wed01/OCDP/OCDP Frame.htm
Students majoring in workforce education and development are prepared as instructors and instructional support personnel in education, business, industry, labor, and government training organizations.

Directories & Handbooks: General

3698 106 Ways Parents Can Help Students Achieve
American Association of School Administrators
801 N Quincy Street
Suite 700
Arlington, VA 22203-1730
703-528-0700
Fax: 703-841-1543
http://www.aasa.org
Provides parents with useful information about the importance of parental involvement, concrete ways to work with children and schools to promote success, and a list of resources for further reading.
Set of 10
ISBN: 0-8108-4220-3

3699 A Personal Planner & Training Guide for the Substitute Teacher
Master Teacher
Leadership Lane
PO Box 1207
Manhattan, KS 66505-1207
800-669-9633
Fax: 800-669-1132
http://www.masterteacher.com
Helps substitute teachers set the tone for a positive experience.
90 pages
ISBN: 0-914607-89-8
John Eller, Author

3700 Academic Year & Summer Programs Abroad
American Institute for Foreign Study
102 Greenwich Avenue
Greenwich, CT 06830-5504
203-869-9090
800-727-2437
Fax: 203-399-5590
E-mail: college.info@aifs.com
http://www.aifs.com
Offers school names, addresses, courses offered, tuition and fee information.
224 pages Annual

3701 Accredited Institutions of Postsecondary Education
MacMillan Publishing Company
1633 Broadway
New York, NY 10019
212-654-8500
Fax: 800-835-3202
Lists over 5,000 accredited institutions and programs for postsecondary education in the United States.
600 pages Annual

3702 Activities and Strategies for Connecting Kids with Kids: Elementary Edition
Master Teacher
Leadership Lane
PO Box 1207
Manhattan, KS 66505-1207
800-669-9633
Fax: 800-669-1132
http://www.masterteacher.com
Activities, lesson plans, and strategies that celebrate each student's individual differences while developing cooperation, tolerance, understanding, sharing and caring.
159 pages
ISBN: 0-914607-74-X

3703 Activities and Strategies for Connecting Kids with Kids: Secondary Edition
Master Teacher
Leadership Lane
PO Box 1207
Manhattan, KS 66505-1207
800-669-9633
Fax: 800-669-1132
http://www.masterteacher.com
Activities, lesson plans, and strategies that celebrate each student's individual differences while developing cooperation, tolerance, understanding, sharing and caring.
136 pages
ISBN: 0-914607-75-8

3704 American School Directory
PO Box 20002
Murfreesboro, TN 37129
866-273-2797
Fax: 800-929-3408
E-mail: asdwebmaster@asd.com
http://www.asd.com
More than 104,000 school sites are loaded with pictures, art, calendars, menus, local links and notes from students, parents and alumni. Choose the school by name, state list, or by ASD number.

3705 Amusing and Unorthodox Definitions
Careers/Consultants Consultants in Education
3050 Palm Aire Drive N
#310
Pompano Beach, FL 33069
954-974-5477
Fax: 954-974-5477
E-mail: carconed@aol.com
Collection of amusing and unorthodox definitions. The meanings, purposes and implications assigned to the words appearing here will delight audiences, enliven conversations and keep you chuckling.
ISBN: 0-7392-0089-5
ISSN: 99-94623
Dr. Robert M Bookbinder, President/Author

3706 Associated Schools Project in Education for International Co-operation
UNESCO Associated Schools Project Network
7 Place de Fontenoy
F-75700 Paris
France
1-45681000
Lists 1,970 secondary and primary schools, teacher training institutions and nursery schools in 95 countries that participate in the UNESCO Associated School Project.
200 pages Annual

3707 Association for Community-Based Education Directory of Members
Association for Community Based Education
1805 Florida Avenue NW
Washington, DC 20009-1708
202-462-6333
Offers information on 100 private community organizations concerned with alternative education including colleges that award degrees without residency requirements and more.
115 pages Annual

3708 Awakening Brilliance: How to Inspire Children to Become Successful Learners
Pamela Sims & Associates
54 Mozart Crescent
Canada L6Y 2W7
905-455-7331
888-610-7467
Fax: 905-455-0207
E-mail: loveofkids@aol.com
http://www.pamelasims.com
Seminars and workshops for educators and parents. Upcoming workshops include themes of awakening students' potential and team leadership skills.
248 pages Paperback
ISBN: 0-9651126-0-8
Pamela Sims, Author/Editor
Kelly Smith, Marketing Director

3709 Beyond the Bake Sale
Master Teacher
Leadership Lane
PO Box 1207
Manhattan, KS 66505-1207
800-669-9633
Fax: 800-669-1132
http://www.masterteacher.com
A notebook containing 101 detailed plans that not only provide you with fundraising ideas, but get you started, keep you on track, and lead your team through the finishing touches.
101 pages
ISBN: 1-58992-119-4

3710 Biographical Membership Directory
American Educational Research Association
1230 17th Street NW
Washington, DC 20036-3078
202-223-9485
Fax: 202-775-1824
Membership directory of more than 23,000 persons involved in education research and development, including the names, addresses, phone numbers, highest degree held and year received, occupational specialization areas, e-mail addresses and more.
420 pages Bi-Annual
Thomas J Campbell, Director Publications

3711 CASE Directory of Advancement Professionals in Education
Council for Advancement & Support of Education
1307 New York Avenue NW
Suite 1000
Washington, DC 20005-4701
202-328-2273
Fax: 202-387-4973
E-mail: info@case.org
http://www.case.org
Membership directory of 16,000 professionals in alumni relations, communications and fund raising at educational institutions worldwide.
Publication Date: 1995 200 pages Annual
ISBN: 0-899643-10-8
Cedric Calhoun, Membership Director

3712 Cabells Directory of Publishing Opportunities in Educational Curriculum & Methods
Cabell Publishing Company
Box 5428
Tobe Hahn Station
Beaumont, TX 77726
409-898-0575
Fax: 409-866-9554
E-mail: publish@cabells.com
http://www.cabells.com
Provides information on editor's contact information, manuscript guidelines, acceptance rate, review information and circulation data for over 350 academic journals.
799 pages Annual
ISBN: 0-911753-27-3
David WE Cabell, Editor
Deborah L English, Editor

3713 Cadet Gray: Your Guide to Military Schools-Military Colleges & Cadet Programs
Reference Desk Books
PO Box 22925
Santa Barbara, CA 93121
805-772-8806
This is a comprehensive reference book which describes 55 American military schools, grade schools, high schools, junior colleges, senior colleges, and the federal service academies. Descriptions include school histories, academic requirements, military environment, extracurricular activities and costs.
Publication Date: 1990 212 pages
ISBN: 0-962574-90-2

3714 Character Education Evaluation Tool Kit
Character Education Partnership
1025 Connecticut Avenue NW
Suite 1011
Washington, DC 20036
202-296-7743
800-988-8081
Fax: 202-296-7779
http://www.character.org
Julea Posey, Matthew Davison, Meg Korpi, Author
Andrea Grenadier, Director Communications
Esther Schaeffer, CEO/Executive Director

3715 Character Education Kit: 36 Weeks of Success: Elementary Edition
Master Teacher
Leadership Lane
PO Box 1207
Manhattan, KS 66505-1207
800-669-9633
Fax: 800-669-1132
http://www.masterteacher.com
Takes the guesswork out of delivering your character education message by providing you with all the pieces of a well-rounded program including important components for 36 character traits.
428 pages
ISBN: 1-58992-096-1

3716 Choosing Your Independent School in the United Kingdom & Ireland
Independent Schools Information Service
56 Buckingham Gate
London SW1E 6AG
England
71-63087934

1,400 independent schools in the United Kingdom and Ireland with contact information, entry requirements, fees, scholarships available, subjects and exam boards.
293 pages Annual/September

3717 Classroom Teacher's Guide for Working with Paraeducators
Master Teacher
Leadership Lane
PO Box 1207
Manhattan, KS 66505-1207
800-669-9633
Fax: 800-669-1132
http://www.masterteacher.com
This workbook includes numerous forms that allow teachers to communicate more effectively to paras the vital information they will need in working with special students.
60 pages
ISBN: 1-58992-127-5
Wendy Dover, Author

3718 Commonwealth Universities Yearbook
Association of Commonwealth Universities
36 Gordon Square
London WC1H 0PF
England
44-20-7380-6700
Fax: 44-20-738-2655
E-mail: info@acu.ac.uk
http://www.acu.ac.uk
Offers information on over 700 university institutions of recognized academic standing in 36 Commonwealth countries or regions, including Africa, Asia, Australia, Britain, Canada and the Pacific.
2,600 pages Annual
ISBN: 0-85143-188-7
ISSN: 0069-7745

3719 Complete Learning Disabilities Directory
Grey House Publishing
185 Millerton Road
Millerton, NY 12546
518-789-8700
800-562-2139
Fax: 518-789-0545
E-mail: books@greyhouse.com
http://www.greyhouse.com
A one-stop sourcebook for people of all ages with learning disabilities and those who work with them. This comprehensive database in print includes information about associations and organizations, schools, government agencies, testing materials, camps, books, newsletters and more.
800 pages Annual/Softcover
ISBN: 1-59237-049-7
Leslie Mackenzie, Publisher
Richard Gottlieb, Editor

3720 Computer and Web Resources for People with Disabilities
Alliance for Technology Access/Hunter House
1304 Southpoint Boulevard
Suite 240
Petaluma, CA 94954
707-778-3011
800-914-3017
Fax: 707-765-2080
E-mail: atainfo@ataccess.org
http://www.ataccess.org
This directory shows how America's forty-five million people with disabilities

can potentially benefit from using computer technology to achieve goals and change their lives. Written by experts in the field, this important work provides a comprehensive, step-by-step guide to approaching computer innovations. It explains how to identify the appropriate technology, how to seek funding, how to set it up and what to consider.
Publication Date: 1996 400 pages Paperback/CD ROM
ISBN: 0-89793-433-4
Libbie Butler, Information/Referral Assista

3721 Contemporary World Issues: Public Schooling in America
ABC-CLIO
130 Cremona Drive
#1911
Santa Barbara, CA 93117-5599
805-963-4221
800-368-6868
Fax: 805-685-9685
Offers information on organizations and agencies involved with public education systems.

3722 Cornocopia of Concise Quotations
Careers/Consultants Consultants in Education
3050 Palm Aire Drive N
#310
Pompano Beach, FL 33069
954-974-5477
Fax: 954-974-5477
E-mail: carconed@aol.com
Wealth of practical reminders of the enduring ideas. The book furthers humane understandings by gathering and preserving the wisdom of the wise and experienced.
ISBN: 0-7392-0275-8
ISSN: 99-95201
Dr. Robert M Bookbinder, President

3723 Council for Educational Development and Research Directory
National Education Association (NEA)
1201 16th Street NW
Washington, DC 20036-3290
202-833-4000
Fax: 202-822-7974
E-mail: ncuea@nea.org
http://www.nea.org
Offers 15 member educational research and development institutions.
50 pages Annual

3724 Digest of Supreme Court Decisions
Phi Delta Kappa Educational Foundation
PO Box 789
408 N Union Street
Bloomington, IN 47402-0789
812-339-1156
800-786-1156
Fax: 812-339-0018
http://www.pdkintl.org
Designed as a ready reference, this edition of a popular digest provides a concise set of individual summaries of cases decided by the Supreme Court. Fully indexed.
256 pages Paperback
ISBN: 0-87367-835-4
Perry A Zirkel, Author
George Kersey, Executive Director
Donovan R Walling, Dir Publications/Research

3725 Directory for Exceptional Children
Porter Sargent Publishers, Inc.
11 Beacon Street
Suite 1400
Boston, MA 02108-3028
617-523-1670
800-342-7470
Fax: 617-523-1021
E-mail: info@portersargent.com
http://www.portersargent.com
A comprehensive survey of 2,500 schools, facilities and organizations across the country serving children and young adults with developmental, physical and medical disabilities. With 15 distinct chapters covering a range of disabilities, this work is an invaluable aid to parents and professionals seeking the optimal environment for special-needs children. Hardcover.
Publication Date: 1994 1152 pages BiAnnual
ISSN: 0070-5012

Dan McKeever, Senior Editor

3726 Directory of Catholic Special Educational Programs & Facilities
National Catholic Educational Association
1077 30th Street NW
Suite 100
Washington, DC 20007-3829
202-337-6232
Fax: 202-333-6706
Lists approximately 950 Catholic schools and day and residential school programs for children and adolescents with special education needs.
Publication Date: 1989 100 pages

3727 Directory of Central Agencies for Jewish Education
Jewish Education Service of North America
111 8th Avenue
New York, NY 10011
212-284-6882
Fax: 212-284-6951
E-mail: info@jesna.org
http://www.jesna.org
Offers educational resources for professionals in Jewish education, including general education information, materials and services.

Rika Levin, Director
Marketing/Communica

3728 Directory of College Cooperative Education Programs
National Commission for Cooperative Education
360 Huntington Avenue
#384CP
Boston, MA 02115-5096
617-373-3770
Fax: 617-373-3463
E-mail: ncce@neu.edu
http://www.co-op.edu
A publication providing detailed information on cooperative education programs at 460 colleges throughout the United States.
Publication Date: 1962 219 pages
ISBN: 0-89774-998-4

Polly Hutcheson, VP
Paul Stonely, President

3729 Directory of ERIC Information Service Providers
Educational Resources Information Ctr./Access ERIC
1600 Research Boulevard
Rockville, MD 20850-3172
301-656-9723

Offers information on more than 1,000 government agencies, nonprofit and profit organizations, individuals and foreign organizations that provide access to ERIC microfiche collections, search services and abstract journal collections.
100 pages Biennial

3730 Directory of Graduate Programs
Graduate Record Examinations Program/ETS
PO Box 6014
Princeton, NJ 08541-6014
609-951-1542
Accredited institutions that offer graduate degrees.
1,400 pages 4 Volumes

3731 Directory of Indigenous Education
Floyd Beller - Wested
730 Harrison Street
San Francisco, CA 94107
415-565-3000
877-4we-sted
Fax: 415-565-3012
E-mail: fbeller@WestEd.org
http://www.wested.org
This revised and expanded edition incorporates a wider scope of information, including a list of Head Start, Child Care and Title IX programs and JOM contractors, which enhances our principal goal of improving educational services to native students and communities.
Publication Date: 1998 94 pages

Floyd Beller, Research Associate

3732 Directory of International Internships: A World of Opportunities
International Studies & Programs
209 International Center
Michigan State University
East Lansing, MI 48824-1035
517-353-5589
Fax: 517-353-7254
E-mail: gliozzo@msu.edu
http://www.isp.msu.edu
A directory containing information about a wide range of overseas internship oppotunities. Over 500 entries of international internships sponsored by educational institutions, government agencies, and private organizations. There are indexes of topics in geographical areas listed by countries and geographical areas listed by topic.

Charles Gliozzo

3733 Directory of Member Institutions and Institutional Representatives
Council of Graduate Schools
1 Dupont Circle NW
Suite 430
Washington, DC 20036-1136
202-223-3791
Fax: 202-331-7157
Offers listings of over 400 member graduate schools in the US and Canada.
85 pages Annually

Nancy A Goffney, Administrator/Editor
Kathy Baker, Assistant

3734 Directory of Overseas Educational Advising Centers
College Board Publications
45 Columbus Avenue
New York, NY 10023-6917
212-713-8165
800-323-7155
Fax: 800-525-5562
http://www.collegeboard.org
This directory has been developed as a means through which institutions of higher education can communicate directly with overseas education advisers and through which advisers can communicate more directly with each other.
Publication Date: 1995 165 pages

3735 Directory of Postsecondary Institutions
National Center for Education Statistics
K Street NW
Washington, DC 20006
202-502-7300
877-4ED-PUBS
Fax: 301-470-1244
E-mail: edpubs@inet.ed.gov
http://www.ed.pubs/
Postsecondary institutions in the US, Puerto Rico, Virgin Islands and territories in the Pacific United States. Two volumes: Volume I Degree-Granting Institutions, Volume II Non-Degree-Granting Institutions.
Publication Date: 1990 500 pages Biennial

3736 Directory of Public School Systems in the United States
American Association for Employment in Education
3040 Riverside Drive
Suite 125
Columbus, OH 43221
614-485-1111
Fax: 614-485-9609
E-mail: aaee@osu.edu
http://www.aaee.org
Lists 15,000 public school systems in the United States, their administrative personnel and size/type of district.
212 pages Bi-Annually

BJ Bryant, Executive Director

3737 Directory of Youth Exchange Programs
UN Educational, Scientific & Cultural Association
Youth Division, 1 Rue Miollis
Paris F-75015
France
1-4563842
Offers about 370 nonprofit organizations and governmental agencies in 95 countries that organize youth and student exchanges, study tours and correspondence exchanges.
Publication Date: 1992 225 pages

3738 Diversity, Accessibility and Quality
College Board Publications
45 Columbus Avenue
New York, NY 10023-6917
212-713-8165
800-323-7155
Fax: 800-525-5562
http://www.collegeboard.org
Primarily for non-Americans, this overview is designed to examine aspects of US education that have particular importance in programs of student exchange.
Publication Date: 1995 47 pages
ISBN: 0-874474-24-8

Clifford F Sjogren, Author

3739 Education Sourcebook: Basic Information about National Education Expectations and Goals
Omnigraphics
615 Griswold Street
Detroit, MI 48226
313-961-1340
800-234-1340
Fax: 313-961-1383
E-mail: info@omnigraphics.com
http://www.omnigraphics.com
A collection of education-related documents and articles for parents and students.

1123 pages
ISBN: 0-7808-0179-2

Jeanne Gough, Author
Paul Rogers, Publicity Associate

3740 Educational Placement Sources-Abroad
Education Information Services/Instant Alert
PO Box 620662
Newton, MA 02462-0662
617-433-0125
Lists 150 organizations, arranged by type, in the United States and abroad that place English-speaking teachers and education administrators in positions abroad.

19 pages Annual

FB Viaux, President

3741 Educational Rankings Annual
Gale Group
27500 Drake Road
Farmington Hills, MI 48331-3535
248-699-GALE
800-414-5043
Fax: 248-699-8069
E-mail: galeord@galegroup.com
http://www.galegroup.com
Top 10 lists from popular and scholarly periodicals, government publications, and others. The lists cover all facets of education.

890 pages Annual Hardcover
ISBN: 0-7876-7419-2

Lynn C Hattendorf Westney, Author
Kathleen Maki Petts, Coordinating Editor

3742 Educational Resources Catalog
CDE Press
PO Box 271
Sacramento, CA 95812-0271
916-445-1260
800-995-4099
Fax: 916-323-0823
http://www.cde.ca.gov/cdepress
Resource catalog from the California Department of Education.

3743 Educator's Desk Reference: A Sourcebook of Educational Information & Research
MacMillan Publishing Company
1633 Broadway
New York, NY 10019
212-654-8500
Fax: 800-835-3202
Directory includes national and regional education organizations.

Publication Date: 1989

3744 Educator's Scrapbook
Careers/Consultants Consultants in Education
3050 Palm Aire Drive N
#310
Pompano Beach, FL 33069
954-974-5477
Fax: 954-974-5477
E-mail: carconed@aol.com
Collection of education morsels offered to those who who would seek to redefine and clarify the aims and purposes of today's education. The book attempts to help its readers refocus upon the real purposes of education and their relationships to current education practices.

ISBN: 0-9703623-0-7
ISSN: 00-93185

Dr. Robert M Bookbinder, President

3745 Educators Guide to FREE Computer Materials and Internet Resources
Educators Progress Service
214 Center Street
Randolph, WI 53956-1408
920-326-3126
888-951-4469
Fax: 920-326-3127
E-mail: epsinc@centurytel.net
http://www.freeteachingaids.com
Lists and describes almost 2000 web sites of educational value. Available in two grade specific editions.

317 pages Annual
ISBN: 87708-362-2

Kathy Nehmer, President

3746 Educators Guide to FREE Films, Filmstrips and Slides
Educators Progress Service
214 Center Street
Randolph, WI 53956-1408
920-326-3126
888-951-4469
Fax: 920-326-3127
E-mail: epsinc@centurytel.net
http://www.freeteachingaids.com
Lists and describes free and free-loan films, filmstrips, slides, and audiotapes for all age levels.

135 pages Annual
ISBN: 87708-400-9

Kathy Nehmer, President

3747 Educators Guide to FREE Multicultural Material
Educators Progress Service
214 Center Street
Randolph, WI 53956-1408
920-326-3126
888-951-4469
Fax: 920-326-3127
E-mail: epsinc@centurytel.net
http://www.freeteachingaids.com
Lists and describes FREE films, videotapes, filmstrips, slides, web sites, and hundreds of free printed materials in the field of multicultural and diversity education for all age levels.

198 pages Annual
ISBN: 87708-412-2

Kathy Nehmer, President

3748 El-Hi Textbooks and Serials in Print
RR Bowker Reed Reference
121 Chanlon Road
New Providence, NJ 07974-1541
908-464-6800
Fax: 908-665-6688
Listing of about 995 publishers of elementary and secondary level textbooks and related teaching materials.

Annual

3749 Exceptional Children Education Resources
The Council for Exceptional Children
110 N Glebe Road
Suite 300
Arlington, VA 22201-5704
703-620-3660
800-232-7323
Fax: 703-264-9494
E-mail: cec@cec.sped.org
http://www.cec.sped.org/bk/catalog/journals.htm
A proprietary database that includes bibliographic data and abstract information on journal articles, and audiovisual materials in special education, and gifted education.

ISSN: 0160-4309

3750 Family Services Report
CD Publictions
8204 Fenton Street
Sliver Spring, MD 20910
301-588-6380
301-666-6380
Fax: 301-588-0519
E-mail: fsr@cdpublications.com
http://cdpublications.com
Private grants for family service programs

18 pages
ISSN: 1524-9484

Ray Sweeney, Editor

3751 Fifty State Educational Directories
Career Guidance Foundation
8090 Engineer Road
San Diego, CA 92111-1906
619-560-8051
A collection on microfiche consisting of reproductions of the state educational directories published by each individual state department of education.

3752 Funny School Excuses
Careers/Consultants Consultants in Education
3050 Palm Aire Drive N
#310
Pompano Beach, FL 33069
954-974-5477
Fax: 954-974-5477
E-mail: carconed@aol.com
Collection of illustrations, cartoons and excuses gathered from authentic notes written by parents and sometimes their children. The book is wonderfully entertaining and recommended for its unusual humor, variety, and revelations of human nature.

ISBN: 0-7392-0309-6
ISSN: 99-95349

Dr. Robert M Bookbinder, President

3753 Ganley's Catholic Schools in America
Fisher Publishing Company
PO Box 15070
Scottsdale, AZ 85267-5070
800-759-7615
Fax: 480-657-9422
E-mail: publisher@ganleyscatholicschools.com
http://www.ganleyscatholicschool.com
Comprehensive listings on all Catholic Schools in America. Listings include phone numbers, addresses, names of administrators, number of students, complete diocesan, state, regional and national statistics. Includes an extensive analysis of demographic trends within Catholic elementary and secondary education, prepared by the National Catholic Education Association.

450+ pages Annual/June
ISBN: 1-558331-59-0

Millard T Fischer, Publisher

3754 Graduate & Undergraduate Programs & Courses in Middle East Studies in the US, Canada
Middle East Studies Association of North America
University of Arizona
1643 E Helen Street
Tucson, AZ 85721
520-621-5850
Fax: 520-626-9095
E-mail: mesana@u.arizona.edu
http://www.acls.org

3755 Guide to International Exchange, Community Service & Travel for Persons with Disabilities
Mobility International USA
45 W Broadway Suite 202
PO Box 10767
Eugene, OR 97401
541-343-1284
Fax: 541-343-6812
E-mail: info@miusa.org
http://www.miusa.org
This directory lists an impressive array of information regarding international study, living, travel, funding and contact organizations for people with disabilities.

Publication Date: 1997
ISBN: 1-880034-24-7

Christa Bucks, Editor

3756 Guide to Schools and Departments of Religion and Seminaries
MacMillan Publishing Company
1633 Broadway
New York, NY 10019
800-858-7674
Fax: 201-767-5029
Over 700 accredited programs and institutions granting degrees in theology, divinity and religion.

3757 Guide to Summer Camps & Schools
Porter Sargent Publishers
11 Beacon Street
Suite 1400
Boston, MA 02108-3028
617-523-1670
800-342-7470
Fax: 617-523-1021
E-mail: info@portersargent.com
http://www.portersargent.com
Covers the broad spectrum of recreational and educational summer opportunities. Current facts from 1,500 camps and schools, as well as programs for those with special needs or learning disabilities, makes the guide a comprehensive and convenient resource.

816 pages Biannual
ISBN: 0-875581-33-1

HJ Lane Coordinating Editor, Author
J Yonce, General Manager
Daniel McKeever, Sr Editor

3758 Guidelines for Effective Character Education Through Sports
Character Education Partnership
1025 Connecticut Avenue NW
Suite 1011
Washington, DC 20036
202-296-7743
800-988-8081
Fax: 202-296-7779
http://www.character.org
Guidelines for turning sports and physical education programs into the powerful, positive forces they should be.

Andrea Grenadier, Director Communications
Esther Schaeffer, CEO/Executive Director

3759 Handbook of Private Schools
Porter Sargent Publishers
11 Beacon Street
Suite 1400
Boston, MA 02108-3028
617-523-1670
800-342-7470
Fax: 617-523-1021
E-mail: info@portersargent.com
http://www.portersargent.com
Continuing a tradition that began in 1915, this handbook provides optimal guidance in the choice of educational environments and opportunities for students. Totally revised and updated, this 83rd edition presents current facts on 1,700 elementary and secondary boarding and day schools across the United States. Complete statistical data on enrollments, tuition, graduates, administrators and faculty have been compiled and objectively reported. Hardcover.

1472 pages Annual
ISBN: 0-875581-44-7

J Yonce, General Manager
Daniel McKeever, Sr Editor

3760 Handbook of United Methodist-Related Schools, Colleges, Universities & Theological Schools
General Board of Higher Education & Ministry/UMC
1001 19th Avenue
PO Box 340007
Nashville, TN 37203-0007
615-340-7406
Fax: 615-340-7379
E-mail: scu@gbhem.org
http://www.gbhem.org/highed.html
Includes two pages of information about each of United Methodist's 123 institutions, a chart indicating major areas of study, information about United Methodist loan and scholarship programs, as well as information about how to select a college. Published every four years.

344 pages Paperback

Dr. James A Noseworthy, Assistant General Secretary

3761 Hidden America
Place in the Woods
3900 Glenwood Avenue
Golden Valley, MN 55422-5302
763-374-2120
Fax: 952-593-5593
E-mail: placewoods@aol.com
Set of five reference-essay books on American minorities (African America; Hispanic America, the People (Native Americans); American women; My Own Book! classroom reference for elementary through secondary).

36+ pages Paperback Book

Roger Hammer, Publisher

3762 Higher Education Directory
Higher Education Publications
6400 Arlington Boulevard
Suite 648
Falls Church, VA 22042-2342
703-532-2300
888-349-7915
Fax: 703-532-2305
E-mail: info@hepinc.com
http://www.hepinc.com
Lists over 4,364 degree granting colleges and universities accredited by approved agencies, recognized by the US Secretary of Education successor to the Department of Education's: Education Directory, Colleges and Universities and Council for Higher Education Accreditation (CHEA).

Publication Date: 1994 1,040 pages Annual/Paperback
ISBN: 0-914927-44-2
ISSN: 0736-0197

Jeanne Burke, Editor
Fred Hafner JR, Vice President Operations

3763 Higher Education Opportunities for Women & Minorities: Annotated Selections
U.S. Office of Postsecondary Education
400 Maryland Avenue SW
Room 3915
Washington, DC 20202-0001
202-708-9180
Programs of public and private organizations and state and federal government agencies that offer loans, scholarships and fellowship opportunities for women and minorities.

143 pages Biennial

3764 Home from Home (Educational Exchange Programs)
Central Bureau for Educational Visits & Exchanges
10 Spring Gardens
London, SW1A 2BN, England
171-389-4004
Fax: 171-389-4426
150 organizations and agencies worldwide that arrange stays with families for paying guests or on an exchange basis. Organizations are geographically listed including a description of program, costs, insurance information, overseas representation and language instruction.

216 pages

3765 Homeschooler's Guide to FREE Teaching Aids
Educators Progress Service
214 Center Street
Randolph, WI 53956-1408
920-326-3126
888-951-4469
Fax: 920-326-3127
E-mail: epsinc@centurytel.net
http://www.freeteachingaids.com
Lists and describes free print materials specifically available to homeschoolers with students of all age levels.

277 pages
ISBN: 87708-375-4

Kathy Nehmer, President

3766 Homeschooler's Guide to FREE Videotapes
Educators Progress Service
214 Center Street
Randolph, WI 53956-1408
920-326-3126
888-951-4469
Fax: 920-326-3127
E-mail: epsinc@centurytel.net
http://www.freeteachingaids.com
Lists and describes free and free-loan videotapes specifically available to homeschoolers with students of all age levels.

248 pages Annual
ISBN: 87708-411-4

Kathy Nehmer, President

3767 IIEPassport: Academic Year Abroad 2007
Institute of International Education
809 United Nations Plaza
New York, NY 10017-3580
412-741-0930
Fax: 212-984-5496
E-mail: iiebooks@abdintl.com
http://www.iiebooks.org
Over 3,100 undergraduate and graduate study-abroad programs conducted worldwide during the academic year by United States and foreign colleges, universities, and private organizations.

Publication Date: 2007 Annual
ISBN: 87206-279-1

Marie O'Sullivan, Author
Daniel Obst, Sr Editor

3768 ISS Directory of Overseas Schools
International Schools Services
15 Roszel Road
PO Box 5910
Princeton, NJ 08540-6729
609-452-0990
Fax: 609-452-2690
E-mail: jlarsson@iss.edu
http://www.iss.edu
The only comprehensive guide to American and international schools around the world. The Directory is carefully researched and compiled to include current and complete information on over 600 international schools.

590 pages Paperback
ISBN: 0-913663-13-1

Jane Larsson, Director Of Education

3769 Inclusion Guide for Handling Chronically Disruptive Behavior
Master Teacher
Leadership Lane
PO Box 1207
Manhattan, KS 66505-1207
800-669-9633
Fax: 800-669-1132
http://www.masterteacher.com
A comprehensive process for ensuring that no disruptive behavior is tolerated, no student is turned away, and all students are served.

150 pages
ISBN: 0-914607-40-5

Teresa VanDover, Author

3770 Incorporating Multiple Intelligences into the Curriculum and into the Classroom: Elementary
Master Teacher
Leadership Lane
PO Box 1207
Manhattan, KS 66505-1207
800-669-9633
Fax: 800-669-1132
http://www.masterteacher.com
Contains lesson plans and teaching methods that address the needs of students and help them identify their strengths according to the domains of multiple intelligences.

181 pages
ISBN: 0-914607-63-4

3771 Incorporating Multiple Intelligences into the Curriculum and into the Classroom: Secondary
Master Teacher
Leadership Lane
PO Box 1207
Manhattan, KS 66505-1207
800-669-9633
Fax: 800-669-1132
http://www.masterteacher.com
Contains lesson plans and teaching methods that address the needs of students and help them identify their strengths according to the domains of multiple intelligences.

147 pages
ISBN: 0-914607-64-2

3772 Independent Schools Association of the Southwest-Membership List
Independent Schools Association of the Southwest
PO Box 52297
Tulsa, OK 74152-0297
817-569-9200
Fax: 817-569-9103
A geographical index of 65 independent elementary and secondary schools accredited by the association.

5 pages Annual/August

Richard W Ekdahl, Coordinating Education

3773 Independent Study Catalog
Peterson's Guides
PO Box 2123
Princeton, NJ 08543-2123
800-338-3282
Fax: 609-896-4531
A comprehensive listing of over 10,000 correspondence course offerings at 100 accredited colleges and universities nation-

wide, for those seeking the flexibility and convenience of at-home study.

293 pages
ISBN: 1-560794-60-7

3774 Industry Reference Handbooks
Gale Group
27500 Drake Road
Farmington Hills, MI 48331
248-699-4253
Fax: 248-699-8064
http://www.galegroup.com
Brings together and supplements Gale and D&B data on specific industries for reference use in public and academic libraries.

Hardcover
ISBN: 0787639567

Alen W Paschal, President

3775 International Federation of Organizations for School Correspondence/Exchange
FIOCES
29, rue d'ulm, F-75230 Paris
F-75230 Paris
France
Governmental agencies and other organizations concerned with scholastic correspondence and student exchange programs.

Publication Date: 1991 3 pages

3776 International Schools Directory
European Council of International Schools
21B Lavant Street, Petersfield,
Hampshire GU3 23EL
United Kingdom
1730-268244
Fax: 1730-267914
E-mail: 100412.242@compuserve.com
Over 420 ECIS schools in more than 90 countries; 300 affiliated colleges and universities worldwide; educational publishers and equipment suppliers.

550 pages Annual

JS Henleu, Coordinating Education

3777 International Study Telecom Directory
WorldWide Classroom
PO Box 1166
Milwaukee, WI 53201-1166
414-224-3476
Fax: 414-224-3466
E-mail: info@worldwide.edu
http://www.worldwide.edu
Comprehensive directory for locating educational resources both internationally and throughout the US Provides contact information on educational institutions including address, phone, fax, e-mail and URL. New icon system offers additional information on the type of programs offered. Resource guide at beginning includes useful web sites, airline and car rental contact numbers, currency converters, international organizations and international publications.

Mike Witley, President
Stacy Hargarten, Classroom Publications

3778 International Voluntary Service Directory
Volunteers for Peace
1034 Tiffany Road
Belmont, VT 05730
802-259-2759
Fax: 802-259-2922
E-mail: vfp@vfp.org
http://www.vfp.org
Comprehensive listing of over 3,400 workcamps in 100 countries around the world. Organized by country.
289 pages Annual
ISBN: 0-945617-20-B

Peter Coldwell, Director

3779 International Who's Who in Education
International Biographical Centre/Melrose Press
3 Regal Lane, Soham, Ely
Cambridgeshire CB7 5BA
United Kingdom
353-721091
Lists about 5,000 persons at all levels of teaching and educational administration.
1,000 pages

3780 International Yearbook of Education: Education in the World
UN Educational, Scientific & Cultural Assn.
7, place de Fontenoy
F-75700 Paris
France
1-45681000
Describes and offers information on educational systems worldwide.
Publication Date: 1989 200 pages

3781 Legal Basics: A Handbook for Educators
Phi Delta Kappa International
408 N Union Street
PO Box 789
Bloomington, IL 47402-0789
812-339-1156
800-766-1156
Fax: 812-339-0018
http://www.pdkintl.org
Superintendents, principals, counselors, teachers, and paraprofessionals need to pay close attention to their actions in schools and classrooms because, from a legal standpoint, those settings may contain hazardous conditions. Legal Basics points out the pitfalls and how to avoid them.
Publication Date: 1998 120 pages Paperback
ISBN: 0-8736-806-0

Evelyn B Kelly, Author
DR Walling, Dir Publications/Research

3782 Lesson Plans and Modifications for Inclusion and Collaborative Classrooms
Master Teacher
Leadership Lane
PO Box 1207
Manhattan, KS 66505-1207
800-669-9633
Fax: 800-669-1132
http://www.masterteacher.com
Each modification is a complete lesson plan that gives the teacher a description of the activity and objetive the materials need and a step-by-step guide of how to carry out the learning process.
242 pages
ISBN: 0-914607-37-5

3783 Lesson Plans for Character Education: Elementary Edition
Master Teacher
Leadership Lane
PO Box 1207
Manhattan, KS 66505-1207
800-669-9633
Fax: 800-669-1132
http://www.masterteacher.com
Gives you more than 140 practical lessons developed and tested by teachers across the curriculum and in all grade levels.
207 pages
ISBN: 0-914607-53-7

3784 List of Over 70 Higher Education Association
Educational Information Services
PO Box 662
Newton Lower Falls, MA 02162
617-964-4555
Provides descriptions and contact information on associations for individuals in higher education.

3785 List of State Boards of Higher Education
Educational Information Services
PO Box 662
Newton Lower Falls, MA 02162
617-964-4555
A compilation of the boards of education for all the states in the union.

3786 List of State Community & Junior College Board Offices
Educational Information Services
PO Box 662
Newton Lower Falls, MA 02162
617-964-4555
A list of the board officers and state officers within community, junior and university institutions.

3787 MDR School Directory
Market Data Retrieval
1 Forest Parkway
Shelton, CT 06484-6216
203-926-4800
800-333-8802
Fax: 203-929-5253
E-mail: msubrizi@dnb.com
MDR's school directories provide comprehensive data on every public school district and school, Catholic and other independent schools, regional and county centers in all fifty states and the District of Columbia. Updated each year, each state directory contains current names and job titles of key decision makers, school and district addresses, phone numbers, current enrollments and much more. Also available on CD-ROM and diskette.
51 Volume Set

Mike Subrizi, Director Marketing

3788 Minority Student Guide to American Colleges
Paoli Publishing
1708 E Lancaster Avenue
Suite 287
Paoli, PA 19301-1553
215-640-9889
Covers colleges, military schools, and financial aid information for minority students.
89 pages

3789 NAFSA's Guide to Education Abroad for Advisers & Administrators
NAFSA: Association of International Educators
1307 New York Avenue NW
8th Floor
Washington, DC 20005-4701
202-737-3699
800-836-4994
Fax: 202-737-3657
E-mail: inbox@nafsa.org
http://www.nafsa.org

Marlene M Johnson, Director/CEO

3790 NEA Almanac of Higher Education
National Education Association (NEA)
1201 16th Street NW
Washington, DC 20036-3207
202-833-4000
Fax: 202-822-7624
E-mail: nche@nea.org
http://www.nea.org
Annually
ISSN: 0743-670X

Con Lehane, Author

3791 National Directory of Children, Youth & Families Services
Contexo Media
2755 E Cottonwood Parkway
Suite 400
Salt Lake City, UT 84120
800-343-6681
Fax: 801-365-0710
E-mail: customersupport@contexomedia.com
http://www.contexomedia.com
Organized by state and county, this directory lists over 30,000 organizations and 46,000 contacts that focus on helping anyone who is committed to providing the best possible service to our nation's at-risk children, youth and families.
1456 pages Annually

Treavor Peterson, President
Kim Luna, Product Manager

3792 National Guide to Educational Credit for Training Programs
American Council on Education
1 Dupont Circle NW
Suite 535
Washington, DC 20036-1110
202-939-9430
Fax: 202-833-4762
More than 4,500 courses offered by over 280 government agencies, business firms and nonprofit groups.
1,018 pages Annual

3793 National Reference Directory of Year-Round Education Programs
National Association for Year-Round Education
PO Box 711386
San Diego, CA 92171-1386
619-276-5296
Fax: 858-571-5754
E-mail: info@nayre.org
http://www.nayre.org
Six hundred fifty school districts in the US with year-round programs are covered in this directory, listed by geographical location, including all contact information and descriptions.
178 pages Annual Paperback

Shirley Jennings, Directory Editor
Samuel Pepper, Executive Director

3794 National Schools of Character: Best Practices and New Perspectives
Character Education Partnership
1025 Connecticut Avenue NW
Suite 1011
Washington, DC 20036
202-296-7743
800-988-8081
Fax: 202-296-7779
http://www.character.org
Andrea Grenadier, Director Communications
Esther Schaeffer, CEO/Executive Director

3795 National Schools of Character: Practices to Adopt & Adapt
Character Education Partnership
1025 Connecticut Avenue NW
Suite 1011
Washington, DC 20036
202-296-7743
800-988-8081
Fax: 202-296-7779
http://www.character.org
Andrea Grenadier, Director Communications
Esther Schaeffer, CEO/Executive Director

3796 National Society for Experiential Education
515 King Street
Suite 420
Alexandria, VA 22314
703-706-9552
Fax: 703-684-6048
E-mail: info@nsee.org
http://www.nsee.org
28 pages Quarterly
Linda Goff, Author

3797 New England Association of Schools and Colleges
New England Association of Schools and Colleges
209 Burlington Road
Bedford, MA 01730-1433
781-271-0022
Fax: 781-271-0950
Listing of over 1,575 institutions of higher education, public and independent schools and vocational-technical schools in New England.
65 pages Annual

3798 Overseas American-Sponsored Elementary and Secondary Schools
US Department of State, Office Overseas Schools
Room 245, SA-29
Washington, DC 20522
202-647-4000
Fax: 202-261-8224
Lists nearly 180 independent schools overseas and 10 regional associations of schools.
30 pages Annual

3799 Paradigm Lost: Leading America Beyond It'sFear of Educational Change
American Association of School Administrators
801 N Quincy Street
Suite 700
Arlington, VA 22203-1730
703-528-0700
Fax: 703-841-1543
E-mail: info@aasa.org
http://www.aasa.org
Explores the beliefs and assumptions upon which schools operate, provides powerful and practical insights and improvement strategies.
Publication Date: 1998 158 pages Softcover
ISBN: 0-87652-232-0
William G Spady, Editor

3800 Patterson's American Education
Educational Directories Inc
Po Box 68097
Schaumburg, IL 60168
847-459-0605
800-357-6183
Fax: 847-891-0945
E-mail: info@ediusa.com
http://www.ediusa.com
Lists more than 11,000 public school districts; 300 parochial superintendents; 400 territorial schools; 400 state department of education personnel; and 400 educational associations in one easy to use consistent format. Arranged alphabetically by state then by city. City listings include the city name, telephone area code, city population, county name, public school district name, enrollment, grade range, superintendent's name, address and phone number. Index of secondary schools included.
Publication Date: 1994 974 pages Annual
ISBN: 0-9771602-3-8
ISSN: 0079-0230
Linda Moody, Office Manager

3801 Patterson's Schools Classified
Educational Directories Inc.
1025 W Wise Road
PO Box 68097
Schaumburg, IL 60168
847-891-1250
800-357-6183
Fax: 847-891-0945
E-mail: info@ediusa.org
http://www.ediusa.org
Contains 7,000 accredited postsecondary schools, the broadest assortment available in a single directory. Universities, colleges, community colleges, junior colleges, career schools and teaching hospitals are co-mingled under 50 academic disciplines but retain their school type identification. School professional accreditation is shown in 32 classifications. The basic entry includes school name, mailing address and contact person, with additional descriptive material supplied by the school.
Publication Date: 2006 302 pages Annual
ISBN: 0-9771602-2-X
Wayne Moody, Coordinating Education

3802 Persons as Resources
World Council for Curriculum & Instruction
School of Education
Indiana University
Bloomington, IN 47405
812-336-4702
Fax: 812-856-8088

Listing of about 600 member individuals and institutions concerned with curriculum and instruction in schools, colleges, universities and non-school agencies.
75 pages Triennial

3803 Peterson's Competitive Colleges
Peterson's, A Nelnet Company
Princeton Pike Corporate Center
2000 Lenox Drive PO Box 67005
Lawrenceville, NJ 08648
609-896-1800
800-338-3282
Fax: 609-896-4531
E-mail: custsvc@petersons.com
http://www.petersons.com
The most trusted source of advice for excellent students searching for high-quality schools. Provides objective criteria to compare more than 440 leading colleges and universities.
524 pages
ISBN: 1-560795-98-0

3804 Peterson's Guide to Four-Year Colleges
Peterson's, A Nelnet Company
Princeton Pike Corporate Center
2000 Lenox Drive PO Box 67005
Lawrenceville, NJ 08648
609-896-1800
800-338-3282
Fax: 609-896-1811
E-mail: custsvc@petersons.com
http://www.petersons.com
Includes descriptions of over 2,000 colleges, providing guidance on selecting the right school, getting in and financial aid.
2,922 pages

3805 Peterson's Guide to Two-Year Colleges
Peterson's, A Nelnet Company
Princeton Pike Corporate Center
2000 Lenox Drive PO Box 67005
Lawrenceville, NJ 08648
609-896-1800
800-338-3282
Fax: 609-896-4531
E-mail: custsvc@petersons.com
http://www.petersons.com
The only two-year college guide available, this new and expanded directory is the most complete source of information on institutions that grant an associate as their highest degree.
Publication Date: 2006 712 pages
ISBN: 1-560796-05-7

3806 Peterson's Regional College Guide Set
Peterson's, A Nelnet Company
Princeton Pike Corporate Center
2000 Lenox Drive PO Box 67005
Lawrenceville, NJ 08648
609-896-1800
800-338-3282
Fax: 609-896-4531
E-mail: custsvc@petersons.com
http://www.petersons.com
Six individual regional guides that help students compare colleges in a specific geographic area.

3807 Power of Public Engagement Book Set
Master Teacher
Leadership Lane
PO Box 1207
Manhattan, KS 66505-1207
800-669-9633
Fax: 800-669-1132
http://www.masterteacher.com
Learn how to engage your community to make the changes needed to ensure the best education for its children.
ISBN: 1-58992-128-3

William G O'Callaghan Jr, Author

3808 Private Independent Schools
Bunting & Lyon
238 N Main Street
Wallingford, CT 06492-3728
203-269-3333
Fax: 203-269-5697
E-mail: BuntingandLyon@aol.com
http://www.buntingandlyon.com
Provides information on more than 1,100 elementary and secondary private schools and summer programs in the United States and abroad. This annual guide, now in its 56th edition, is the most concise, current resource available on private school programs.
Publication Date: 1996 644 pages Annual Hardcover
ISBN: 0-913094-56-0
ISSN: 0079-5399

Peter G Bunting, Publisher

3809 Private School Law in America
Progressive Business Publications
370 Technology Drive
Malvern, PA 19355
800-220-5000
Fax: 610-647-8089
E-mail: customer_service@pbp.com
http://www.pbp.com
An up-to-date compilation of summarized federal and state appellate court decisions which affect private education. The full legal citation is supplied for each case. A brief introductory note on the American judicial system is provided along with updated appendices of recent US Supreme Court cases and recently published law review articles. Also included are portions of the US Constitution which are most frequently cited in private education cases.
500 pages Annually
ISBN: 0-939675-80-3

3810 Public Schools USA: A Comparative Guide to School Districts
Peterson's, A Nelnet Company
Princeton Pike Corporate Center
2000 Lenox Drive PO Box 67005
Lawrenceville, NJ 08648
609-896-1800
800-338-3282
Fax: 609-896-4531
E-mail: custsvc@petersons.com
http://www.petersons.com
Lists over 400 school districts in 52 metropolitan areas throughout the United States.
490 pages Annual

Charles Hampton Harrison, Author

3811 School Foodservice Who's Who
Information Central
PO Box 3900
Prescott, AZ 86302-3900
520-778-1513

Listing of over 2,500 food service programs in public and Catholic school systems.
110 pages Triennial

3812 School Guide
School Guide Publications
210 N Avenue
New Rochelle, NY 10801-6402
914-632-7771
800-433-7771
Fax: 914-632-3412
E-mail: info@schoolguides.com
http://schoolguides.com
Listing of over 3,000 colleges, vocational schools and nursing schools in the US.
280 pages Annual/Paperback
ISBN: 1-893275-30-2

Janette Aiello, Editor

3813 Schools Abroad of Interest to Americans
Porter Sargent Publishers
11 Beacon Street
Suite 1400
Boston, MA 02108-3028
617-523-1670
800-342-7470
Fax: 617-523-1021
E-mail: info@portersargent.com
http://www.portersargent.com
Lists and authoritatively describes 800 elementary and secondary schools in 130 countries. Written for the educator, personnel advisor, student and parent as well as diplomatic and corporate officials, this unique guide is an indispensable reference for American students seeking preparatory schooling overseas. Hardcover.
Publication Date: 1991 544 pages BiAnnual

J Yonce, General Manager
Daniel McKeever, Sr Editor

3814 Schools-Business & Vocational Directory
American Business Directories
5711 S 86th Circle
Omaha, NE 68127-4146
402-593-4600
888-999-1307
Fax: 402-331-5481
A complete listing of business and vocational schools nationwide. Includes phone numbers, contact names, employee sizes and more.
Annual

Jerry Venner, Coordinating Education

3815 Treasury of Noteworthy Proverbs
Careers/Consultants Consultants in Education
3050 Palm Aire Drive N
#310
Pompano Beach, FL 33069
954-974-5477
Fax: 954-974-5477
E-mail: carconed@aol.com
Tapestry of maxims, aphorisims, and pithy sayings. A revealing picture of the wisdom, philosophy, and humor of the people of this and many other nations throughout the world.
ISBN: 0-7392-0208-1
ISSN: 99-943-75

Dr. Robert M Bookbinder, President

3816 US Supreme Court Education Cases
Progressive Business Publications
370 Technology Drive
Malvern, PA 19355
800-220-5000
Fax: 610-647-8089
E-mail: customer_service@pbp.com
http://www.pbp.com
A compilation of summarized US Supreme Court decisions since 1954 which affect education. The full legal citation is supplied for each case. Also included are portions of the US Constitution which are most frequently cited in education cases.
Annually

3817 Vincent-Curtis Educational Register
Vincent-Curtis
29 Simpson Lane
Falmouth, MA 02540-2230
508-457-6473
Fax: 508-457-6499
http://www.vincentcurtis.com
Hundreds of illustrated announcements describing a variety of private boarding schools and resident summer programs in the United States, Canada and Europe, together with articles by school heads and camp directors of interest to parents of students 10-18.
Publication Date: 1994 236 pages Annual/June

Stanford B Vincent, Coordinating Education

3818 Western Association of Schools and Colleges
Western Association of Schools and Colleges
3060 Valencia Avenue
#70
Aptos, CA 95003-4126
831-688-7575
Listing of schools and colleges in California, Hawaii, Guam, American Samoa and East Asia.
130 pages Annual

3819 Whole Nonprofit Catalog
Grantmanship Center
PO Box 17720
Los Angeles, CA 90017
Offers information on training programs offered by the Center, publications and other services available to the nonprofit sector.

3820 Working Together: A Guide to Community-Based Educational Resources
Research, Advocacy & Legislation/Council of LaRaza
810 1st Street NE
Suite 300
Washington, DC 20002-4227
202-289-1380
Listing of about 30 community-based organizations nationwide providing educational services to Hispanic Americans.
35 pages

3821 World of Learning
Gale Group
27500 Drake Road
Farmington Hills, MI 48331
248-699-4253
800-877-4253
Fax: 248-699-8064
E-mail: galeord@galegroup.com
http://www.galegroup.com

Contains information for over 26,000 universities, colleges, schools of art and music, libraries, archives, learned societies, research institutes, museums and art galleries in more than 180 countries.

ISBN: 0-7876-5004-8

Allen W Paschal, President

Directories & Handbooks: Administration

3822 American Association of Collegiate Registrars & Admissions Officers
American Association of Collegiate Registrars
1 Dupont Circle NW
Suite 330
Washington, DC 20036-1137
202-293-9161
Fax: 202-872-8857
Offers more than 2,300 member institutions and 8,400 college and university registrars, financial aid information and admissions officers.

Publication Date: 1995 224 pages Annual

3823 American School & University - Who's Who Directory & Buyer's Guide
Prism Business Media
9800 Metcalf Avenue
Overland Park, KS 66212-2286
913-967-1960
Fax: 913-967-1905
E-mail: jagron@asumag.com
http://www.asumag.com
Comprehensive directory of suppliers and products for facility needs; listings of architects by region; listing of associations affiliated with the education industry; article index for quick and easy reference; in-depth calendar of events.

Annual

Joe Agron, Editor-In-Chief
Susan Lustig, Executive Editor

3824 Bricker's International Directory
Peterson's, A Nelnet Company
Princeton Pike Corporate Center
2000 Lenox Drive PO Box 67005
Lawrenceville, NJ 08648
609-896-1800
800-338-3282
Fax: 609-896-4531
E-mail: custsvc@petersons.com
http://www.petersons.com
Offers over 400 residential management development programs at academic institutions in the United States and abroad.

Annual

3825 Cabells Directory of Publishing Opportunities in Educational Psychology and Administration
Cabell Publishing Company
Box 5428
Tobe Hahn Station
Beaumont, TX 77726
409-898-0575
Fax: 409-866-9554
E-mail: publish@cabells.com
http://www.cabells.com
Provides information on editor contact information, manuscript guidelines, acceptance rate, review information and

circulation data for over 225 academic journals.

799 pages Annual
ISBN: 0-911753-28-1

David WE Cabell, Editor
Deborah L English, Associate Editor

3826 Character Education Questions & Answers
Character Education Partnership
1025 Connecticut Avenue NW
Suite 1011
Washington, DC 20036
202-296-7743
800-988-8081
Fax: 202-296-7779
http://www.character.org

Andrea Grenadier, Director Communications
Esther Schaeffer, CEO/Executive Director

3827 Character Education Resource Guide
Character Education Partnership
1025 Connecticut Avenue NW
Suite 1011
Washington, DC 20036
202-296-7743
800-988-8081
Fax: 202-296-7779
http://www.character.org

Andrea Grenadier, Director Communications
Esther Schaeffer, CEO/Executive Director

3828 Character Education: The Foundation for Teacher Education
Character Education Partnership
1025 Connecticut Avenue NW
Suite 1011
Washington, DC 20036
202-296-7743
800-988-8081
Fax: 202-296-7779
http://www.character.org

Andrea Grenadier, Director Communications
Esther Schaeffer, CEO/Executive Director

3829 Continuing Education Guide
International Association for Continuing Education
Department #3087
Washington, DC 20042-0001
202-463-2905
Fax: 202-463-8498
Explores how to interpret and use the Continuing Education Unit or other criteria used for continuing education programs. This guide, written by continuing education and training consultant, Louis Phillips, is a reference source complete with sample forms, charts, checklists and everything you need to plan, develop and evaluate your school's continuing education program.

3830 Creating Quality Reform: Programs, Communities and Governance
Pearson Education Communications
1 Lake Street
Upper Saddle River, NJ 07458
201-236-7000
Fax: 877-260-2530
E-mail: communications@pearsoned.com
http://www.pearsoned.com

Publication Date: 2002

J Thomas Owens, Editor
Jan C Simmons, Editor

3831 Designing & Implementing a Leadership Academy in Character Education
Character Education Partnership
1025 Connecticut Avenue NW
Suite 1011
Washington, DC 20036
202-296-7743
800-988-8081
Fax: 202-296-7779
http://www.character.org

Andrea Grenadier, Director Communications
Esther Schaeffer, CEO/Executive Director

3832 Deskbook Encyclopedia of American School Law
Progressive Business Publications
370 Technology Drive
Malvern, PA 19355
800-220-5000
Fax: 610-647-8089
E-mail: customer_service@pbp.com
http://www.pbp.com
An up-to-date compilation of summarized federal and state appellate court decisions which affect education. The full legal citation is supplied for each case with a brief introductory note on the American judicial system is provided along with updated appendices of recent US Supreme Court cases and recently published law review articles.

Annually

3833 Developing a Character Education Program
Character Education Partnership
1025 Connecticut Avenue NW
Suite 1011
Washington, DC 20036
202-296-7743
800-988-8081
Fax: 202-296-7779
http://www.character.org

Henry Huffman, Author
Andrea Grenadier, Director Communications
Esther Schaeffer, CEO/Executive Director

3834 Development Education: A Directory of Non-Governmental Practitioners
U.N. Non-Governmental Liaison Service
Palais des Nations, CH 1211
Geneva 10
Switzerland
Lists about 800 national non-governmental organizations in industrialized countries and international non-governmental networks concerned with developmental education.

Publication Date: 1992 400 pages

3835 Directory of Chief Executive Officers of United Methodist Schools, Colleges & Universities
General Board of Higher Education & Ministry/UMC
1001 19th Avenue
PO Box 340007
Nashville, TN 37203-0007
615-340-7406
Fax: 615-340-7379
E-mail: scu@gbhem.org
http://www.gbhem.org/highed.html
123 United Methodist educational institutions including theology schools, professional schools, two year colleges and colleges and universities with all contact information arranged by institution type. Paperback.
32 pages Annual
Dr. James A Noseworthy, Assistant General Secretary

3836 Directory of Organizations in Educational Management
ERIC Clearinghouse on Educational Management
1787 Agate Street
Eugene, OR 97403-1923
541-346-5043
800-438-8841
Fax: 541-346-2334
E-mail: sales@oregon.uoregon.edu
http://www.eric.uoregon.edu
Offers listings of 163 organizations in the field of educational management at the elementary and secondary school levels.
Dr. Philip Piele, Director
Stuart C Smith, Associate Director

3837 Directory of State Education Agencies
Council of Chief State School Officers
1 Massachusette Avenue NW
Suite 700
Washington, DC 20001-1431
202-336-7000
Fax: 202-408-8072
http://www.ccsso.org
A reference to state and national education agency contracts. Arranged state-by-state, it includes state education agency personnel titles, addresses, phone numbers, and fax numbers when applicable. National information includes key contacts and information for 33 national education associations and 5 pages of names, titles, addresses, and numbers for the US Department of Education.
103 pages
ISBN: 1-884037-66-6
Kathleen Neary, Editor

3838 Educating for Character
Master Teacher
Leadership Lane
PO Box 1207
Manhattan, KS 66505-1207
800-669-9633
Fax: 800-669-1132
http://www.masterteacher.com
Dr. Licona has developed a 12 point program that offers practical strategies designed to create a working coalition of parents, teachers and communities.
428 pages
ISBN: 0-553-37052-9
Thomas Lickona PhD, Author

3839 Educating for Character: How Our Schools Can Teach Respect and Responsibility
Character Education Partnership
1025 Connecticut Avenue NW
Suite 1011
Washington, DC 20036
202-296-7743
800-988-8081
Fax: 202-296-7779
http://www.character.org
Tom Likona, Author
Andrea Grenadier, Director Communications
Esther Schaeffer, CEO/Executive Director

3840 Education Budget Alert
Committee for Education Funding
122 C Street NW
Suite 280
Washington, DC 20001-2109
202-383-0083
Fax: 202-383-0097
E-mail: jchang@cef.org
http://www.cef.org
Federal programs currently help over 63 million Americans to engage in formal learning. This guidebook explains what these programs do, what types of activities are supported, the reasons the federal government initiated these programs, and their level at funding.
150 pages Annually
Jennifer Chang, Administrative Assistant
Michael Pons, Editor

3841 Educational Consultants Directory
American Business Directories, Inc.
5711 S 86th Circle
PO Box 27347
Omaha, NE 68127
402-593-4600
800-555-6124
Fax: 402-331-5481
E-mail: directory@abi.com
A list of more than 5,000 entries, including name, address, phone, size of advertisement, name of owner or manager and number of employees.

3842 Educational Dealer-Buyers' Guide Issue
Fahy-Williams Publishing
171 Reed Street
Geneva, NY 14456-2137
315-789-0458
Fax: 315-789-4263
List of approximately 2,000 suppliers of educational materials and equipment.
Annual

3843 Executive Summary Set
Master Teacher
Leadership Lane
PO Box 1207
Manhattan, KS 66502
800-669-9633
Fax: 800-669-1132
http://www.masterteacher.com
An easy, effective and practical way to orient new board members before they attend their first meeting. Executive Summary Sets cover the vital information board members must have in eight areas: tenets of education; powers and responsibilities; decision making; communication for maximum results; resource management; assessment of programs; assessment of personnel and conflict resolution.
Robert DeBruyn, Editor

3844 Grants and Contracts Handbook
Association of School Business Officials Int'l
11401 N Shore Drive
Reston, VA 20190-4232
703-478-0405
Fax: 703-478-0205
This is a basic reference for grant applicants, executors, project managers, administrators and staff. The ideas are school-tested and based on information gathered from institutions and agencies over the past two decades.
32 pages
ISBN: 0-910170-52-5
Peg D Kirkpatrick, Editor/Publisher
Robert Gluck, Managing Editor

3845 Hispanic Yearbook-Anuario Hispano
TIYM Publishing
6718 Whittier Avenue
Suite 130
McLean, VA 22101
703-734-1632
Fax: 703-356-0787
E-mail: TIYM@aol.com
http://www.tiym.com
This guide lists Hispanic organizations, publications, radio and TV stations, through not specifically for grant-giving purposes.
Annually
John O Zavala, COO
Ramon Palencia, Director PR

3846 Leading to Change: The Challenge of the NewSuperintendency
Jossey-Bass/Pfeiffer
989 Market Street
San Francisco, CA 94103-1741
415-433-1740
Fax: 415-433-0499
http://www.josseybass.com
The challenge of the new superintendency.
352 pages
ISBN: 0-7879-0214-4
Susan Moore Johnson, Author

3847 Legal Basics: A Handbook for Educators
Phi Delta Kappa International
PO Box 789
Bloomington, IL 47402-0789
812-339-1156
Fax: 812-339-0018
http://www.pdkintl.org
Superintendents, principals, counselors, teachers, and paraprofessionals need to pay close attention to their actions in schools and classrooms because, from a legal standpoint, those settings may contain hazardous conditions. Legal Basics points out the pitfalls and how to avoid them.
120 pages Paperback
ISBN: 8-87367-806-0
Evelyn B Kelly, Author
DR Walling, Dir Publications/Research

3848 Legal Issues and Education Technology
National School Board Association
PO Box 161
Annapolis Junction, MD 20701
800-706-6722
Fax: 703-683-7590
Helps administrators craft an acceptable-use policy.
Publication Date: 1999
ISSN: 0314510

3849 Lifeworld of Leadership: Creating Culture,Community, and Personal Meaning in Our Schools
Jossey-Bass Publishers
989 Market Street
San Francisco, CA 94103-1741
415-433-1740
Fax: 415-433-0499
http://www.josseybass.com
Explores the crucial link between school improvement and school character.
Publication Date: 2004   240 pages   Paperback
ISBN: 0-7879-7277-6

Thomas J Sergiovanni

3850 Looking at Schools: Instruments & Processes for School Analysis
Research for Better Schools
112 N Broad Street
Philadelphia, PA 19102
215-568-6150
Fax: 215-568-7260
http://www.rbs.org
Thirty-five institutions that offer instruments and processes to assess the performance of students, teachers and administrators, school climate effectiveness and school-community relations.
Publication Date: 1991   140 pages

Carol Crociante, Executive Secretary
Keith M Kershner, Executive Co-Director

3851 Market Data Retrieval-National School Market Index
Market Data Retrieval
1 Forest Parkway
Shelton, CT 06484-0947
203-926-4800
800-333-8802
Fax: 203-929-5253
E-mail: msubrizi@dnb.com
An annual report on school spending patterns for instructional materials in the United States. The Index now in its twenty-fifth year of publication, lists the expenditures for instructional materials for all 15,000 US senior districts.
Publication Date: 1996
ISBN: 0-897708-25-3

Mike Subrizi, Marketing Director

3852 National Association of Principals of Schools for Girls Directory
National Association of Principals/Girls Schools
4050 Little River Road
Hendersonville, NC 28739-8317
828-693-8248
Fax: 828-693-1490
List of 575 principals and deans of private and secondary schools for girls and coeducational schools, colleges and admissions officers.
Annual

3853 National School Public Relations Association Directory
National School Public Relations Association
1501 Lee Highway
Arlington, VA 22209-1109
703-528-6713
Lists over 2,800 school system public relations directors and school administration officers.
100 pages   Annual

3854 National School Supply & Equipment Association Membership/Buyers' Guide Directory
National School Supply & Equipment Association
830 Colesville Road
Suite 250
Silver Spring, MD 20910
301-495-0240
800-395-5550
Fax: 301-495-3330
E-mail: awatts@nssea.org
http://www.nssea.org
Lists 1,500 member dealers, manufacturers and manufacturers' representatives for school supplies, equipment and instructional materials.
200 pages   Annual

Adrienne Watts, Author
Adrienne Watts, VP Marketing
Kathy Jentz, Director Communications

3855 National Schools of Character
Character Education Partnership
1025 Connecticut Avenue NW
Suite 1011
Washington, DC 20036
202-296-7743
800-988-8081
Fax: 202-296-7779
http://www.character.org
Andrea Grenadier, Director Communications
Esther Schaeffer, CEO/Executive Director

3856 Proactive Leadership in the 21st Century
Master Teacher
Leadership Lane
PO Box 1207
Manhattan, KS 66505-1207
800-669-9633
Fax: 800-669-1132
http://www.masterteacher.com
Contain the laws and principals of leadership and people management as they had never been defined and described before giving school administrators a set of guidelines that if followed would guarantee success.
ISBN: 0-914607-44-8

Robert L DeBruyn, Author

3857 QED's State School Guides
Quality Education Data
1625 Broadway Street
Suite 250
Denver, CO 80203
303-860-1832
800-525-5811
Fax: 303-209-9444
E-mail: info@qeddata.com
http://www.qeddata.com
Complete directories of every US school district and public, Catholic and private school. Directories are available for individual states, geographic regions and the entire United States. Each directory includes names of district administrators, school principals and school librarians, as well as addresses, phone numbers and enrollment information. QED's State school guide also includes key demographic and instructional technology data for each district and school.
Publication Date: 1993   Yearly
ISBN: 0-887476-49-0

Liz Stephens, Marketing

3858 School Promotion, Publicity & Public Relations: Nothing but Benefits
Master Teacher
Leadership Lane
PO Box 1207
Manhattan, KS 66505-1207
785-539-0555
800-669-9633
Fax: 785-539-7739
http://www.masterteacher.com
Contains the vital foundations an administrator must have to understand and implement a program of publicity, promotion and public relations, in a school or school district.
327 pages
ISBN: 0-914607-25-1

Tracey H DeBruyn, Author

3859 Schoolwide Discipline Strategies that Make a Difference in Teaching & Learning
Master Teacher
Leadership Lane
PO Box 1207
Manhattan, KS 66505-1207
800-669-9633
Fax: 800-669-1132
http://www.masterteacher.com
This approach to discipline will help your school or district eliminate the dependecy on one individual, provide guidance for present and new teachers, allow disipline to become a K-12 program, an bring about consistancy in the handling of all student misbehaviors.
150 pages
ISBN: 1-58992-000-7

Larry Dixon, Author

3860 The Teaching Professor
Magna Publications
2718 Dryden Drive
Madison, WI 53704
608-246-3590
Fax: 608-246-3597
E-mail: billh@magnapubs.com
http://www.magnapubs.com
This newsletter has been a leading source of information and inspiration for educators committed to creating a better learning environment.
Publication Date: 1995   530 pages   Paperback
November
1000 attendees and 10+ exhibits

William Haight, President
Jody Glynn Patrick, Vice President

Directories & Handbooks: Elementary Education

3861 Educational Impressions
PO Box 77
Hawthorne, NJ 07507-0077
973-423-4666
800-451-7450
Fax: 973-423-5569
E-mail: awpeller@worldnet.att.net
Educational workbooks, activity books, literature guides, and audiovisuals. Grades K-8, with emphasis on intermediate and middle grades.
Paperback/Video/Audi

Neil Peller, Marketing Director
Lori Brown, Sales/Marketing

3862 Educators Guide to FREE Videotapes-Elementary/ Middle School Edition
Educators Progress Service
214 Center Street
Randolph, WI 53956-1408
920-326-3126
888-951-4469
Fax: 920-326-3127
E-mail: epsinc@centurytel.net
http://www.freeteachingaids.com
Lists and describes free and free-loan videotapes for the elementary and middle school level.
Annual
ISBN: 0-877082-67-7
Kathy Nehmer, President

3863 Educators Guide to FREE Videotapes-Secondary Edition
Educators Progress Service
214 Center Street
Randolph, WI 53956-1408
920-326-3126
888-951-4469
Fax: 920-326-3127
E-mail: epsinc@centurytel.net
http://www.freeteachingaids.com
Lists and describes free and free-loan videotapes for the elementary and middle school level.
Annual
ISBN: 0-877082-67-7
Kathy Nehmer, President

3864 Elementary Teachers Guide to FREE Curriculum Materials
Educators Progress Service
214 Center Street
Randolph, WI 53956-1408
920-326-3126
888-951-4469
Fax: 920-326-3127
E-mail: epsinc@centurytel.net
http://www.freeteachingaids.com
Lists and describes free supplementary teaching aids for the elementary level.
Annual
ISBN: 0-877082-64-2
Kathy Nehmer, President

3865 KIDSNET Media Guide and News
KIDSNET
6856 Eastern Avenue NW
Suite 208
Washington, DC 20012
202-291-1400
Fax: 202-882-7315
E-mail: kidsnet@kidsnet.org
http://www.kidsnet.org
Contains children's television, radio and video listings. Also lists related teaching materials and copyright guidelines.
150 pages Monthly

3866 Lesson Plans, Integrating Technology into the Classroom: Elementary Edition
Master Teacher
Leadership Lane
PO Box 1207
Manhattan, KS 66505-1207
800-669-9633
Fax: 800-669-1132
http://www.masterteacher.com
Gives teachers practical lessons developed and tested by teachers across the curricu-

lum, with students of all levels of ability in using technology.
130 pages
ISBN: 0-914607-59-6

3867 Nursery Schools & Kindergartens Directory
American Business Directories
5711 S 86th Circle
Omaha, NE 68127-4146
402-593-4600
888-999-1307
Fax: 402-331-5481
A geographical listing of 34,900 nursery schools and kindergartens including all contact information, first year in Yellow Pages and descriptions. Also available are regional editions and electronic formats.
Annual
Jerry Venner, Coordinating Education

3868 Parent Involvement Facilitator: Elementary Edition
Master Teacher
Leadership Lane
PO Box 1207
Manhattan, KS 66505-1207
800-669-9633
Fax: 800-669-1132
http://www.masterteacher.com
Packed with ideas for you and your teachers to implement along with the exact steps for you to follow.
169 pages
ISBN: 0-914607-45-6

3869 Patterson's Elementary Education
Educational Directories Inc.
1025 W Wise Road
PO Box 68097
Schaumberg, IL 60168
847-891-1250
800-357-6183
Fax: 847-891-0945
E-mail: info@ediusa.org
http://www.ediusa.org
A directory to more than 13,000 public school districts; 71,000 public, private and Catholic elementary and middle schools; 1,600 territorial schools; and 400 state department of education personnel in one easy to use consistent format. Arranged alphabetically by state then city. City listings include city name, telephone area code, city population, county name, public school district name, enrollment, grade range, superintendent's name, address and phone number.
Publication Date: 1994 870 pages Annual
ISBN: 0-910536-59-7
Douglas Moody, Coordinating Education

3870 Teaching Our Youngest-A Guide for PreschoolTeachers and Child Care and Family Providers
PO Box 1398
Jessup, MD 20794-1398
877-4ED-PUBS
Fax: 301-470-1244
E-mail: edpubs@inet.ed.gov
http://www.edpubs.org
This booklet draws from scientifically based research about what can be done to help children develop their language abilities, increase their knowledge, become familiar with books and other printed materials,learn letters and sounds, recognize numbers and learn to count.

Directories & Handbooks: Employment

3871 AAEE Job Search Handbook for Educators
American Association for Employment in Education
3040 Riverside Drive
Suite 125
Columbus, OH 43221
614-485-1111
Fax: 614-485-9609
E-mail: aaee@osu.edu
http://www.aaee.org
Information for those pursuing work as educators.
72 pages Annually
BJ Bryant, Executive Director

3872 Cabell's Directory of Publishing Opportunities in Education
Cabell Publishing
Box 5428
Tobe Hahn Station
Beaumont, TX 77726-5428
409-898-0575
Fax: 409-866-9554
E-mail: publish@cabells.com
http://www.cabells.com
Includes list of more than 430 education journals that consider manuscripts for publication. Includes contact names and addresses for submitting manuscripts, topics considered, publication guidelines, fees, and circulation information.
1,200 pages
David WE Cabell, Editor
Deborah L English, Associate Editor

3873 Cabell's Directory of Publishing Opportunities in Accounting
Cabell Publishing Company
Box 5428
Tobe Hahn Station
Beaumont, TX 77726
409-898-0575
Fax: 409-866-9554
E-mail: publish@cabells.com
http://www.cabells.com
Contains information on 130 journal. Entries include manuscript guidelines for authors: editor's address, phone, fax and e-mail. Review process and the time required, acceptance rates, readership circulation and subscription rates. The Index classifies journals by 15 topics areas and provides information on type of review, acceptance rate and review time.
425 pages Annual
ISBN: 0-911753-13-3
David WE Cabell, Editor
Deborah L English, Editor

3874 Cabell's Directory of Publishing Opportunities in Economics & Finance
Cabell Publishing Company
Box 5428
Tobe Hahn Station
Beaumont, TX 77726-5428
409-898-0575
Fax: 409-866-9554
E-mail: publish@cabells.com
http://www.cabells.com
Contains information on 350 journals. Each journal entry includes manuscript guidelines for authors: editor's address, phone, fax and e-mail, review process and time required, acceptance rates, readership, circu-

lation and subscription prices. The Index classifies journals by 15 topic areas and provides information on type of review, acceptance rate and review time.

Publication Date: 1995 1100 pages Annual
ISBN: 0-911753-14-1

David WE Cabell, Editor
Deborah L English, Associate Editor

3875 Cabells Directory of Publishing Opportunities in Management
Cabell Publishing Company
Box 5428
Tobe Hahn Station
Beaumont, TX 77726
409-898-0575
Fax: 409-866-9554
E-mail: publish@cabells.com
http://www.cabells.com
Provides editor contact information, acceptance rates, review information, manuscript guidelines and circulation data for over 540 academic journals.

Publication Date: 1973 648 pages
ISBN: 0-911753-15-X

David WE Cabell, Editor
Deborah L English, Associate Editor

3876 Career Book
VGM Career Books
4255 W Touhy Avenue
Lincolnwood, IL 60712
732-329-6991
Fax: 732-329-6994
Offers information on educational employment opportunities in America and abroad.

BiAnnual Hard/Paper

Joyce Lain Kennedy & Darryl Laramore, Author

3877 Career Development Activities for Every Classroom
University of Wisconsin-Madison
1025 W Johnson Street
Madison, WI 53706-1796
608-263-3696
800-446-0399
Fax: 608-262-9197
E-mail: cewmail@soemadison.wisc.edu
http://www.cew.wisc.edu
Four volumes containing hundreds of career development activities, and separate activity masters to duplicate. All lessons are keyed to National Career Development Guidelines Competencies and subject matter areas. Each volume is available individually.

3878 Career Information Center; 13 Volumes
MacMillan Publishing Company
1633 Broadway
New York, NY 10019
212-512-2000
Fax: 800-835-3202
13 volumes covering 3,000 careers, 633 job summaries with 800 photos. Up-to-date information on salaries and occupational outlooks for nearly 3,000 careers.

2.6M pages Triennial
ISBN: 0-028974-52-2

3879 Careers Information Officers in Local Authorities
Careers Research & Advisory
Centre/Hobsons Pub.
Bateman Street
Cambridge CB2 1LZ England
223-354551

1,100 United Kingdom institutions offering collections of career information and audio-visual materials covering career opportunities and current job markets. Arranged alphabetically listing address, phone, contact name and titles, type of materials held and a description of the facilities.

165 pages 12.95 pounds

3880 Certification and Accreditation Programs Directory
Gale Research
27500 Drake Road
Farmington Hills, MI 48331-3535
248-699-4253
800-877-4253
Fax: 248-699-8064
E-mail: galeord@gale.com
http://www.galegroup.com
Directory of private organizations that offer more than 1,700 voluntary certification programs and approximately 300 accreditation programs. Also on CD-ROM.

Publication Date: 1995 620 pages
ISSN: 1084-2128

Allen W Paschal, President

3881 Council of British Independent Schools in the European Communities-Members Directory
Lucy's Hill
Hythe, Kent CT21 5ES
England
44-1303-260857
Fax: 44-1303-260857
E-mail: secretariat@cobisec.org
http://www.cobisec.org

Annual

Roger Fry CBE, Chairman
Sybil Melchers MBE, Honorary Secretary

3882 Directory of English Language Schools in Japan Hiring English Teachers
Information Career Opportunities
Research Center
Box 1100, Station F
Toronto M4Y 2T7
Canada
416-925-8878
English-language schools in Japan.

15 pages Annual

3883 Directory of International Internships Michigan State University
MSU: Dean's Office of Int'l Studies and Programs
209 International Center
East Lansing, MI 48824
517-355-2350
Fax: 517-353-7254
E-mail: gliozzo@pilot.msu.edu
http://www.isp.msu.edu
International internships sponsored by academic institutions, private corporations and the federal government.

Publication Date: 1994 168 pages Paperback

Charles A Gliozzo, Coordinating Editor

3884 Directory of Schools, Colleges, and Universities Overseas
Overseas Employment Services
EBSCO Industries
PO Box 1943
Birmingham, AL 35201
205-991-1330
Fax: 205-995-1582
Directory of 300 educational institutions worldwide that hire teachers to teach different subjects in English.

21 pages Annual

Leonard Simcoe, Editor

3885 Directory of Work and Study in Developing Countries
Vacation-Work Publishers
9 Park End Street
Oxford OX1 1HJ
England
865-241978
Offers information on about 420 organizations worldwide offering employment and study opportunities in over 100 developing countries.

215 pages

3886 Earn & Learn: Cooperative Education Opportunities
Octameron Associates
1900 Mount Vernon Avenue
PO Box 2748
Alexandria, VA 22301-0748
703-836-5480
Fax: 703-836-5650
E-mail: info@octameron.com
http://www.octameron.com
Explains how students may participate in cooperative work-study education programs with federal government agencies.

Publication Date: 1997 48 pages BiAnnual
ISBN: 1-57509-023-6

3887 English in Asia: Teaching Tactics for New English Teachers
Global Press
697 College Parkway
Rockville, MD 20850-1135
303-393-7645
Directory covering 1,000 private English-language schools in Asia, to which applications can be sent to teach.

Publication Date: 1992 180 pages

3888 European Council of International Schools Directory
European Council of International
Schools
21 Lavant Street, Petersfield
Hampshire GU3 23EL
United Kingdom
44-1730-26-8244
Fax: 44-1730-267914
E-mail: 100412.242@compuserve.com
More than 420 member elementary and secondary international schools in Europe and worldwide.

480 pages Annual

JS Henley, President

3889 Faculty Exchange Center Directory and House Exchange Supplement
Faculty Exchange Center
962 Virginia Avenue
Lancaster, PA 17603-3116
717-393-1130
Offers information for college and faculty members wishing to exchange positions

and/or homes temporarily with faculty members at other institutions.

35 pages Annual

3890 Foreign Faculty and Administrative Openings

Education Information Services
PO Box 620662
Newton, MA 02462-0662
617-433-0125
150 specific openings in administration, counseling, library and other professional positions for American teachers in American schools overseas and in international schools in which teaching language is English.

15 pages Every 6 Weeks

FB Viaux, Coordinating Education

3891 Guide to Educational Opportunities in Japan

Embassy of Japan
2520 Massachusetts Avenue NW
Washington, DC 20008
202-238-6700
Fax: 202-328-2187
http://www.embjapan.org
This guide describes opportunities for study in Japan and outlines different forms of financial assistance.

3892 How to Create a Picture of Your Ideal Job or Next Career

Ten Speed Press
PO Box 7123
Berkeley, CA 94707-0123
415-845-8414
800-841-BOOK
Fax: 510-524-4588
Offers handy tips on how to choose the right career, and then go out and get it.

Publication Date: 1989

Richard Nelson Bolles, Author

3893 How to Plan and Develop a Career Center

Center on Education and Work
964 Educational Sciences Building
1025 W Johnson Street
Madison, WI 53706-1796
800-446-0399
Fax: 608-262-9197
E-mail: cewmail@soemadison.wisc.edu
http://www.cew.wisc.edu
High school, postsecondary, adult, and virtual career centers-a comprehensive blueprint that covers all the bases.

3894 Jobs in Russia & the Newly Independent States

Impact Publications
9104 Manassas Drive
Sutie N
Manassas Park, VA 20111-5211
703-361-7300
Fax: 703-335-9486
E-mail: info@impactpublications.com
http://www.impactpublications.com
This guide provides background information on the Russian Federation, the Baltics, the Eastern Slavic Republics, the Transcaucasian Republics and the Asiatic Republics.

3895 Leading Educational Placement Sources in the US

Educational Information Services
PO Box 662
Newton Lower Falls, MA 02162
617-964-4555

An index of the host placement agencies in America for education professionals.

3896 List of Over 200 Executive Search Consulting Firms in the US

Educational Information Services
PO Box 662
Newton Lower Falls, MA 02162
617-964-4555
Covers companies with active search committees in America.

3897 List of Over 600 Personnel & Employment Agencies

Educational Information Services
PO Box 662
Newton Lower Falls, MA 02162
617-964-4555
Contains information on personnel and employment agencies.

3898 Living in China: A Guide to Studying, Teaching & Working in the PRC & Taiwan

China Books & Periodicals
360 Swift Avenue
Suite 48
South San Francisco, CA 94080
650-872-7076
800-818-2017
Fax: 650-872-7808
E-mail: info@chinabooks.com
http://www.chinabooks.com
America's #1 source of publications about China since 1960.

284 pages Paperback
ISBN: 0835125823
November

Chellis Ying, Marketing Director
Jane Lau, Customer Support Specialist

3899 National Directory of Internships

National Society for Experiential Education
3509 Haworth Drive
Suite 207
Raleigh, NC 27609-7235
631-728-9100
Fax: 631-728-9228
E-mail: info@nsee.org
http://www.nsee.org
Directory contains internship descriptions for hundreds of organizations in 85 fields in nonprofit organizations, government and corporations. Lists work and service experiences for high school, college and graduate students, people entering the job market, mid-career professionals and retired persons. Includes indexes by field of interest, location and host organization.

Publication Date: 1995 703 pages
ISBN: 0-536-01123-0

3900 Opening List in US Colleges, Public & Private Schools

Education Information Services/Instant Alert
PO Box 620662
Newton, MA 02462-0662
617-433-0125
Offers about 150 current professional openings in US colleges and public and private schools.

10 pages Every 6 weeks

FB Viaux, Coordinating Education

3901 Opening List of Professional Openings in American Overseas Schools

Education Information Services/Instant Alert
PO Box 620662
Newton, MA 02462-0662
617-433-0125
About 150 current professional openings for teachers, administrators, counselors, librarians and educational specialists in American overseas schools and international schools at which the teaching language is primarily English.

FB Viaux, Coordinating Education

3902 Overseas Employment Opportunities for Educators

Department of Defense, Office of Dependent Schools
2461 Eisenhower Avenue
Alexandria, VA 22331-3000
703-325-0867
This publication tells about teaching jobs in 250 schools operated for children of US military and civilian personnel stationed overseas. Applicants usually must qualify in two subject areas.

3903 Private School, Community & Junior College Four Year Colleges & Universities

Educational Information Services
PO Box 662
Newton Lower Falls, MA 02162
617-964-4555
Names, addresses and phones for any state or region in the United States offering employment opportunities.

3904 Research, Study, Travel, & Work Abroad

US Government Printing Office
732 N Capitol Street NW
Washington, DC 20401
202-512-1999
Fax: 202-512-1293
E-mail: admin@access.gpo.gov
http://www.access.gpo.gov

3905 Teaching Overseas

KSJ Publishing Company
PO Box 2311
Sebastopol, CA 95473-2311
A directory of information on how to find jobs teaching overseas.

Publication Date: 1992 89 pages 2nd Edition
ISBN: 0-962044-55-5

3906 Thirty-Four Activities to Promote Careers in Special Education

The Council for Exceptional Children
1920 Association Drive
Reston, VA 20191-1545
703-620-3660
800-232-7323
Fax: 703-264-1637
This guide introduces individuals to the opportunities, rewards and delights of working with children with exceptionalities. It provides directions on how to plan, develop, and implement activities in the school and community that will increase people's awareness of careers in special education and related services.

Publication Date: 1996 120 pages
ISBN: 0-865862-77-0

3907 VGM's Careers Encyclopedia
VGM Career Books/National Textbook
Company
4255 W Touhy Avenue
Lincolnwood, IL 60646-1933
708-679-5500
A list of over 200 professional associations
that provide career guidance information.

**3908 Work Abroad: The Complete
Guide to Finding a Job Overseas**
Transitions Abroad
PO Box 745
Bennington, VT 05201
802-442-4827
Fax: 802-442-4827
E-mail: editor@transitionsabroad.com
http://www.transitionsabroad.com
Resource for finding both short- and
long-term jobs abroad. Organized by re-
gion and country, includes websites and
phone numbers.

**3909 Workforce Preparation: An
International Perspective**
PO Box 8623
Ann Arbor, MI 48107-8623
800-530-9673
Fax: 734-975-2787
Excellent collection of material by 20
prominent educators describes efforts in
developed and developing countries
worldwide to prepare youth and adults for
work.

3910 World of Learning
Europa Publications
18 Bedford Square
London WC1B 3JN
England
171-580-8236
Fax: 171-636-1664
Details over 26,000 educational, cultural
and scientific institutions throughout the
world, together with an exhaustive directory of over 150,000 people active within
them.
2,072 pages Annual
ISBN: 0-946653-92-5

Directories & Handbooks:
Financial Aid

**3911 Catalog of Federal Domestic
Assistance**
Office of Management & Budget
Washington, DC 20402
Offers information from all federal agencies that have assistance programs (loans,
scholarships and technical assistance as
well as grants) and compiles these into the
CFDA. The individual entries are grouped
by Department of Agency and includes an
excellent set of instructions and several indices. Indices allow the user to search for
grants by subject matter, agency, deadline
date or eligibility criteria.

3912 Chronicle Financial Aid Guide
Chronicle Guidance Publications
66 Aurora Street
Moravia, NY 13118-3576
315-497-0330
800-622-7284
Fax: 315-497-3359
E-mail:
customerservice@chronicleguidance.com
http://www.chronicleguidance.com
Financial aid programs offered primarily
by noncollegiate organizations, independ-

ent and AFL-CIO affiliated labor unions
and federal and state governments for high
school seniors and undergraduate and graduate students.
460 pages Annual
ISBN: 1-5563-310-1

Janet Seemann, Author
Janet Seemann, Author/Editor

**3913 College Costs and Financial Aid
Handbook**
College Board Publications
PO Box 869010
Plano, TX 75074-6917
800-323-7155
Fax: 888-321-7183
http://www.collegeboard.org
A step-by-step guide providing the most
up-to-date facts on costs plus financial aid
and scholarship availability at 3,200 two-
and four-year institutions.
Publication Date: 2003
ISBN: 0-874476-83-6

3914 College Financial Aid Annual
Arco/Macmillan
1633 Broadway
Floor 7
New York, NY 10019-6708
212-654-8933
Lists of private businesses, academic institutions and other organizations that provide awards and scholarships for financial
aid; guide to federal and state financial aid.

**3915 Directory of Educational Contests
for Students K-12**
ABC-CLIO
130 Cremona Drive
#1911
Santa Barbara, CA 93117-5599
805-968-1911
800-368-6868
Fax: 805-685-9685
Offers about 200 competitive scholarship
programs and other educational contests
for elementary and secondary school students.
Publication Date: 1991 253 pages

**3916 Directory of Financial Aid for
Women**
Reference Service Press
5000 Windplay Drive
Suite 4
El Dorado Hills, CA 95762
916-939-9620
Fax: 916-939-9626
E-mail: rspinfo@aol.com
http://www.rspfunding.com
Offers information on more than 1,500
scholarships, fellowships, loan sources,
grants, awards and internships.
490 pages

**3917 Directory of Institutional Projects
Funded by Office of Educational
Research**
U.S. Office of Educational Research &
Improvement
555 New Jersey Avenue NW
Washington, DC 20001-2029
202-219-2050
Publication Date: 1990 60 pages

**3918 Directory of International Grants
& Fellowships in the Health
Sciences**
National Institutes of Health
31 Center Drive MSC 2220
Building 31, Room B2C29
Bethesda, MD 20892-2220
301-496-2075
Fax: 301-594-1211
E-mail: ficinfo@nih.gov
http://www.nih.gov/fic
Fellowships and grants listed separately in
this guide. Each listing includes a complete
program description with contact informa-
tion.

**3919 Don't Miss Out: The Ambitous
Students Guide to Financial Aid**
Octameron Associates
1900 Mt Vernon Avenue
Alexandria, VA 22301-0748
703-836-5480
Fax: 703-836-5650
E-mail: info2octameron.com
http://www.octameron.com
192 pages Anually

**3920 Fellowships in International
Affairs-A Guide to Opportunities
in the US & Abroad**
Lynne Rienner Publishing
1800 30th Street
Suite 314
Boulder, CO 80301
303-444-6684
Fax: 303-444-0824
E-mail: questions@rienner.com
http://www.rienner.com
This guide lists fellowships meant to en-
courage women to pursue careers in inter-
national security.

**3921 Fellowships, Scholarships and
Related Opportunities**
Center for International Ed./University of
TN
201 Aconda Court
Knoxville, TN 37996
865-974-1000
Fax: 865-974-2985
140 grants, scholarships and fellowships
available to citizens of the United States
for study or research abroad.
50 pages Biennial

**3922 Financial Aid for Research &
Creative Activities Abroad**
Reference Service Press
5000 Windplay Drive
Suite 4
El Dorado Hills, CA 95762
916-939-9620
Fax: 916-939-9626
E-mail: webagent@rspfunding.com
http://www.rspfunding.com
This book lists opportunities fir high
school students and undergraduates, grad-
uates, postdoctoral students, professionals
and others.
432 pages
ISBN: 1588410625

Gail Schlachter, Author
R.David Weber, Author

3923 Financial Aid for Study Abroad: a Manual for Advisers & Administrators
NAFSA: Association of International Educators
1307 New York Avenue NW
8th Floor
Washington, DC 20005-4701
202-737-3699
800-836-4994
Fax: 202-737-3657
E-mail: inbox@nafsa.org
http://www.nafsa.org
Publication Date: 1989 105 pages
Marlene M Johnson, Director/CEO

3924 Financial Resources for International Study
Institute of International Education
809 United Nations Plaza
New York, NY 10017-3580
412-741-0930
Fax: 212-984-5452
E-mail: iiebooks@abdintl.com
http://www.iiebooks.org
Directory of more than 600 awards that can be used for international study.
Publication Date: 1996 320 pages
ISBN: 087206-220-1

3925 Foundation Grants to Individuals
Foundation Center
79 Fifth Avenue
New York, NY 10003-3076
212-260-4230
Fax: 212-807-3677
Features current information for grant seekers.

3926 Free Money for College: Fifth Edition
Facts On File
132 West 31st Street
17th Floor
New York, NY 10001
800-678-3633
E-mail: llikoff@factsonfile.com
http://www.factsonfile.com
1,000 grants and scholarships.
Publication Date: 1999 240 pages Annual
Hardcover
ISBN: 081603947X
Laurie Blum, Author
Laurie Likoff, Editorial Director

3927 Free Money for Foreign Study: A Guide to 1,000 Grants for Study Abroad
Facts On File
132 West 31st Street
17th Floor
New York, NY 10001
800-678-3633
E-mail: llikoff@factsonfile.com
http://www.factsonfile.com
Lists organizations and institutions worldwide offering scholarships and grants for study outside the United States.
262 pages
Laurie Likoff, Editorial Director

3928 Fulbright and Other Grants for USIA Graduate Study Abroad
U.S. Student Programs Division
809 United Nations Plaza
New York, NY 10017-3503
212-984-5330
Fax: 212-984-5325
http://www.iie.org

Mutual educational exchange grants for pre-doctoral students offered by foreign governments.
90 pages Annual

3929 Fund Your Way Through College: Uncovering 1,100 Opportunities in Aid
Visible Ink Press/Gale Research
830 Penobscot Building
Detroit, MI 48226
313-961-2242
1,100 scholarships, grants, loans, awards and prizes for undergraduate students.
470 pages

3930 German-American Scholarship Guide-Exchange Opportunities for Historians and Social Scientist
German Historical Institute
1607 New Hampshire Avenue NW
Washington, DC 20009-2562
202-387-3355
Fax: 202-483-3430
http://www.ghi-dc.org
This guide is divided into two sections: scholarships for study and research in the US and scholarships for study and research in Germany.

3931 Getting Funded: The Complete Guide to WritingGrant Proposals
Continuing Education Press
PO Box 1394
Portland, OR 97207-1394
503-725-4891
866-647-7377
Fax: 503-725-4715
E-mail: press@pdx.edu
http://www.cep.pdx.edu
A step-by-step guide to writing successful grants and proposals. An indispensible reference for experienced and first-time grant writers alike.
180 pages Paperback
ISBN: 0-87678-071-0
Mary Hall, Author
Mary Hall, Author

3932 Graduate Scholarship Book
Pearson Education
1 Lake Street
Upper Saddle River, NJ 07458
201-909-6200
Fax: 201-767-5029
A complete guide to scholarships, grants and loans for graduate and professional study.
441 pages Biennial

3933 Grant Opportunities for US Scholars & Host Opportunities for US Universities
International Research & Exchange Board
2121 K Street NW
Suite 700
Washington, DC 20037
202-628-8188
Fax: 202-628-8189
E-mail: irex@irex.org
http://www.irex.org
This pamphlet lists programs in advanced research, language and development, short-term travel, special projects and institutional opportunities.

3934 Grant Writing Beyond The Basics: Proven Strategies Professionals Use To Make Proposals Work
Continuing Education Press
PO Box 1394
Portland, OR 97207-1394
503-725-4891
866-647-7377
Fax: 503-725-4840
E-mail: press@pdx.edu
http://www.cep.pdx.edu
Designed to inspire those with grant writing experience who want to take their development strategies to the next level.
128 pages Paperback
ISBN: 0-87678-117-2
Michael K Wells, Author
Alba Scholz, Manager
Martha Ketchum, Customer Service

3935 Grants & Awards Available to American Writers
PEN American Center
588 Broadway
Suite 303
New York, NY 10012
212-334-1660
Fax: 212-334-2181
E-mail: ftw@pen.org
http://www.pen.org
Includes a full program description and is then broken down by type of writing. Awards for work in a particular country are listed alphabetically by country.
340 pages Paperback
ISBN: 0-934638-20-9

3936 Grants Register
St. Martin's Press
175 5th Avenue
New York, NY 10010
212-674-5151
888-330-8477
Fax: 800-672-2054
E-mail: firstname.lastname@stmartins.com
http://www.vhpsva.com
This directory offers a comprehensive list of programs organized alphabetically with special attention to eligibility requirements. Index by subject.

3937 Grants, Fellowships, & Prizes of Interest to Historians
American Historical Association
400 A Street SE
Washington, DC 20003-3889
202-544-2422
Fax: 202-544-8307
E-mail: aha@theaha.org
http://www.theaha.org
This guide offers information on awards for historians from undergraduate to postgraduate grants, fellowships, prizes, internships and awards.

3938 Guide to Department of Education Programs
US Department of Education
400 Maryland Avenue SW
Washington, DC 20202-0001
202-401-0765
Programs of financial aid offered by the Department of Education.
35 pages Annual

3939 Harvard College Guide to Grants
Office of Career Services
Harvard University
54 Dunster Street
Cambridge, MA 02138
617-495-2595
Fax: 617-496-6880
http://www.ocs.fas.harvard.edu
This guide describes national and regional grants and fellowships for study in the US, study abroad and work and practical experience.

234 pages Paperback

3940 How to Find Out About Financial Aid & Funding
Reference Service Press
5000 Windplay Drive
Suite 4
El Dorado Hills, CA 95762
916-939-9620
Fax: 916-939-9626
E-mail: rspinfo@aol.com
http://www.rspfunding.com
Over 700 financial aid directories and Internet sites described and evaluated.

432 pages Hardcover
ISBN: 1588410935

Gail A Schlachter, Author

3941 International Foundation Directory
Europa Publications
11 New Fetter Lane
London
England EC4P 4EE
44-0-20-7842-2110
Fax: 44-0-20-7842-2249
http://www.europapublications.co.uk
A world directory of international foundations, trusts and similar non-profit institutions. Provides detailed information on over 1,200 institutions in some 70 countries throughout the world.

Publication Date: 1994 736 pages
ISBN: 1-857430-01-8

Paul Kelly, Editorial Director

3942 International Scholarship Book: The Complete Guide to Financial Aid
Pearson Education
1 Lake Street
Upper Saddle River, NJ 07458
201-909-6200
Fax: 201-767-5029
Offers information on private organizations providing financial aid for university students interested in studying in foreign countries.

335 pages Cloth

3943 Journal of Student Financial Aid
University of Notre Dame
Office of Financial Aid
Notre Dame, IN 46556
574-631-6436
Offers a listing of private and federal sources of financial aid for college bound students.

3x Year

Joseph A Russo, Editor

3944 Loans and Grants from Uncle Sam
Octameron Associates
1900 Mount Vernon Avenue
PO Box 2748
Alexandria, VA 22301-0748
703-836-5480
Fax: 703-836-5650
E-mail: info@octameron.com
http://www.octameron.com
Offers information on federal student loan and grant programs and state loan guarantee agencies.

72 pages Annual
ISBN: 1-57509-097-X

Anna Leider, Author

3945 Money for Film & Video Artists
American for the Art
1000 Vermont Avenue NW
6th Floor
Washington, DC 20005
202-371-2830
Fax: 202-371-0424
http://www.artsusa.org
The listings are organized by sponsoring organization and entries include basic application and program information.

3946 Money for International Exchange in the Arts
American for the Art
1000 Vermont Avenue NW
12th Floor
Washington, DC 20005
202-371-2830
Fax: 202-371-0424
http://www.artsusa.org
A guide to the various resources available to support artists and arts organizations in international work.

3947 Money for Visual Artists
America for the Art
1000 Vermont Avenue NW
6th Floor
Washington, DC 20005
202-371-2830
Fax: 202-371-0424
http://www.artsusa.org
Programs are listed alphabetically by sponsor with detailed program description.

3948 National Association of State Scholarship and Grant Program Survey Report
National Association of State Scholarship Programs
660 Boas Street
Harrisburg, PA 17102-1324
717-257-2794
Listing of over 50 member state agencies administering scholarship and grant programs for student financial aid.

150 pages

3949 National Association of Student Financial Aid Administrators Directory
1129 20th Street NW
Suite 400
Washington, DC 20036-5001
202-785-0453
Fax: 202-785-1487
Offers information on over 3,000 institutions of postsecondary education and their financial aid administrators.

230 pages Annual

3950 Need A Lift?
The American Legion
700 N Pennsylvania Street
PO Box 1055
Indianapolis, IN 46206-1050
317-630-1200
888-453-4466
Fax: 317-630-1223
http://www.EMBLEM.legion.org
Sources of career, scholarship and loan information or assistance.

144 pages Annual/Paperback

Robert Caudell, Author

3951 Peterson's Grants for Graduate and Postdoctoral Study
Peterson's, A Nelnet Company
Princeton Pike Corporate Center
2000 Lenox Drive PO Box 67005
Lawrenceville, NJ 08648
609-698-1800
800-338-3282
Fax: 609-896-4531
E-mail: custsvc@petersons.com
http://www.petersons.com
Only comprehensive source of current information on grants and fellowships exclusively for graduate and postdoctoral students.

Publication Date: 1998 5th Edition
ISBN: 1-560794-01-1

3952 Peterson's Sports Scholarships and College Athletic Programs
Peterson's, A Nelnet Company
Princeton Pike Corporate Center
2000 Lenox Drive
Lawrenceville, NJ 08648
609-896-1800
800-338-3282
Fax: 609-896-4531
E-mail: custsvc@petersons.com
http://www.petersons.com
A college-by-college look at scholarships designated exclusively for student athletes in 32 men's and women's sports.

Publication Date: 2004 624 pages 5th Edition
ISBN: 0768915244

3953 Scholarship Handbook
The College Board
45 Columbus Avenue
New York, NY 10023
800-323-7155
http://www.collegeboard.org
Useful text for college-bound students, their families and guidance counselors. Offers more than 2,000 descriptions of national and state level award programs, public and private education loan programs, intership opportunities and more.

3954 Scholarships for Emigres Training for Careers in Jewish Education
Jewish Foundation for Education of Women
135 E 64th Street
New York, NY 10021
212-288-3931
Fax: 212-288-5798
E-mail: fdnscholar@aol.com
http://www.jfew.org
Open to emigres from the former Soviet Union who are pursuing careers in Jewish education. Candidates in Jewish education, rabbinical and cantorial studies, and Jewish studies are invited to write the Foundation.

Marge Goldwater, Executive Director

3955 Scholarships, Fellowships and Loans
Gale Research
PO Box 33477
Detroit, MI 48232-5477
800-877-GALE
Fax: 800-414-5043
http://www.galegroup.com
Written especially for professionals, students, counselors, parents and others interested in education. This resource provides more than 3,700 sources of education-related financial aid and awards at all levels of study.
Publication Date: 1995 1,290 pages Annual
ISBN: 0-810391-14-7

3956 Student Guide
Federal Student Aid Information Center
PO Box 84
Washington, DC 20044-0084
800-433-3243
800-433-3243
Describes the federal student aid programs, and general information about the eligibility criteria, application procedures and award levels, and lists important deadlines and phone numbers.
54 pages
John J McCarthy, Director

3957 Study Abroad
U.N. Educational, Scientific & Cultural Assn.
7, place de Fontenoy
F-75700 Paris
France
1-45681123
Listing of over 200,000 scholarships, fellowships and educational exchange opportunities offered for study in 124 countries.
1,300 pages Biennial

3958 Write Now: A Complete Self-Teaching Program Foor Better Handwriting
Continuing Education Press
PO Box 1394
Portland, OR 97207-1394
503-725-4891
866-647-7377
Fax: 503-725-4840
E-mail: press@pdx.edu
http://www.cep.pdx.edu
A step-by-step guide to improving one's handwriting. Develop clean and legible italic handwriting with regular practice.
128 pages Paperback
ISBN: 0-87678-089-3
Barbara Getty & Inga Dubay, Author
Alba Scholz, Manager
Martha Ketchum, Customer Service

Directories & Handbooks: Guidance & Counseling

3959 Accredited Institutions of Postsecondary Education
MacMillan Publishing Company
1633 Broadway
New York, NY 10019
212-512-2000
Fax: 800-835-3202
Lists over 5,000 accredited institutions and programs for postsecondary education in the United States.
600 pages Annual

3960 Adolescent Pregnancy Prevention Clearinghouse
Children's Defense Fund Education & Youth Develop.
122 C Street NW
#400
Washington, DC 20001-2109
202-628-8787
Fax: 202-662-3560
Provides information and clarification on the connection between pregnancy and broader life questions for youth.
Marian Wright Edelman, Coordinating Education

3961 COLLEGESOURCE
Career Guidance Foundation
8090 Engineer Road
San Diego, CA 92111-1906
800-854-2670
Fax: 858-278-8960
http://www.collegesource.org
CD-ROM and Web College Catalog Collection. Contains colleges and universitie's catalogs from throughout the US, over 2,600. Also a college search program that can be searched by major, tuition costs, and more. Foreign catalogs available.
Annette Crone, Account Coordinator
David Hunt, Account Coordinator

3962 Cabells Directory of Publishing Opportunities in Educational Psychology and Administration
Cabell Publishing Company
Box 5428
Tobe Hahn Station
Beaumont, TX 77726
409-898-0575
Fax: 409-866-9554
E-mail: publish@cabells.com
http://www.cabells.com
Provides information on editor contact information, manuscript guidelines, acceptance rate, review information and circulation data for over 225 academic journals.
799 pages Annual
ISBN: 0-911753-19-2
David WE Cabell, Editor
Deborah L English, Associate Editor

3963 Career & Vocational Counseling Directory
American Business Directories
5711 S 86th Circle
Omaha, NE 68127-4146
402-593-4600
888-999-1307
Fax: 402-331-5481
Nationwide listing of 3,300 companies/consultants available in print, computer magnetic tape and diskette, mailing labels, and index cards listing the name, address, phone, size of advertisement, contact person and number of employees.
Annual
Jerry Venner, Coordinating Education

3964 College Handbook
College Board Publications
45 Columbus Avenue
New York, NY 10023-6992
212-713-8000
Fax: 800-525-5562
E-mail: puborderinfo@collegeboard.org
http://www.collegeboard.org

Descriptions of 3,200 colleges and universities.
Publication Date: 1994 1728 pages Annually
Kea Waithe, Director Customer Service

3965 College Handbook Foreign Student Supplement
College Board Publications
45 Columbus Avenue
New York, NY 10023-6917
212-713-8000
Fax: 800-525-5562
Lists about 2,800 colleges and universities that are open to foreign students.
Publication Date: 1994 288 pages Annual
ISBN: 0-877474-83-3

3966 College Transfer Guide
School Guide Publications
210 N Avenue
New Rochelle, NY 10801-6402
914-632-7771
800-433-7771
Fax: 914-632-3412
Five hundred four-year colleges in the Northeast and Midwest that accept transfer students listing transfer requirements, deadlines, fees, enrollment, costs and contact information. Circulation, 60,000.
125 pages Annual/January

3967 Community College Exemplary Instructional Programs
Massachusetts Bay Community College Press
50 Oakland Street
Wellsley Hills, MA 02181
781-237-1100
Fax: 781-237-1061
Community college programs identified as outstanding by the National Council of Instructional Administrators.

3968 Comparative Guide to American Colleges for Students, Parents & Counselors
HarperCollins
10 E 53rd Street
New York, NY 10022-5244
212-207-7000
Fax: 212-207-7145
Accredited four-year colleges in the United States.
800 pages Cloth

3969 Directory of Play Therapy Training
University of North Texas
PO Box 310829
Denton, TX 76203
940-565-3864
Fax: 940-565-4461
E-mail: cpt@coefs.coe.unt.edu
http://www.centerforplaytherapy.com
Provides training, research publications and serves as a clearinghouse for literature in the field.
Paperback
Rinda Thomas, Office Manager
Sue C Bratton, Center Director

3970 Educators Guide to FREE Guidance Materials
Educators Progress Service
214 Center Street
Randolph, WI 53956-1408
920-326-3126
888-951-4469
Fax: 920-326-3127
E-mail: epsinc@centurytel.net
http://www.freeteachingaids.com
Lists and describes free films, videotapes, filmstrips, slides, web sites, and hundreds of free printed materials in the field of career education and guidance for all age levels.
190 pages Annual
ISBN: 87708-406-8

Kathy Nehmer, President

3971 Index of Majors and Graduate Degrees
College Board Publications
45 Columbus Avenue
New York, NY 10023-6992
212-713-8000
Fax: 800-525-5562
http://www.collegeboard.org
Includes descriptions of over 600 majors and identifies the 3,200 colleges, universities, and graduate schools that offer them.
Annual
ISBN: 0-87447-592-9

3972 Tests: a Comprehensive Reference for Psychology, Education & Business
PRO-ED
8700 Shoal Creek Boulevard
Austin, TX 78757-6897
512-451-3246
800-897-3202
Fax: 800-397-7633
E-mail: info@proedinc.com
http://www.proedinc.com
This fifth edition groups updated information on approximately 2,000 assessment instruments into three primary classifications-psychology, education, and business-and 89 subcategories, enabling users to readily identify the tests that meet their assessment needs. Each entry contains a statement of the instrument's purpose, a concise description of the instrument, scoring procedures, cost, and publisher information.
Publication Date: 1991 809 pages Paperback/Hardcover
ISBN: 0-89079-709-9

Taddy Maddox, General Editor

3973 Vocational Biographies
PO Box 31
Sauk Centre, MN 56378-0031
320-352-6516
800-255-0752
Fax: 320-352-5546
E-mail: careers@vocbio.com
http://www.vocbio.com
Real life career success stories of persons in every walk of life that allow students to see a career through the eyes of a real person. New for 2005: Internet Access to 1001 Career Success Stories.

Toby Behnen, President
Roxann Behnen, Customer Service/Sales

3974 What Works and Doesn't With at Risk Students
BKS Publishing
3109 150th Place SE
Mill Creek, WA 98012-4864
425-745-3029
Fax: 425-337-4837
E-mail: DocBlokk@aol.com
http://www.literacyfirst.com
Publication Date: 1919 162 pages Paperback
ISBN: 0-9656713-0-5

Jan Glaes, Author
Bill Blokker, Owner

3975 World of Play Therapy Literature
Center for Play Therapy
PO Box 311337
Denton, TX 76203
940-565-3864
Fax: 940-565-4461
E-mail: cpt@coefs.coe.unt.edu
http://www.centerforplaytherapy.com
Author and topical listings of over 6,000 books, dissertations, documents, and journal articles on play therapy, updated every two years.
Publication Date: 1995 306 pages

Landreth, Homeyer, Bratton, Kale, Hipl, Schumann, Author

Directories & Handbooks: Language Arts

3976 Classroom Strategies for the English Language Learner
Master Teacher
Leadership Lane
PO Box 1207
Manhattan, KS 66505-1207
800-669-9633
Fax: 800-669-1132
http://www.masterteacher.com
A practical model for accelerating both oral language and literacy development, based on the latest research for effective instruction of both Native English speakers and English language learners.
266 pages
ISBN: 1-58992-068-6

Socrro Herrera EdD, Author

3977 Italic Handwriting Series-Book A
Continuing Education Press
PO Box 1394
Portland, OR 97207-1394
503-725-4891
866-647-7377
Fax: 503-725-4840
E-mail: press@pdx.edu
http://www.cep.pdx.edu
Book A is the first workbook of a seven-part series. Designed for the beginning reader and writer, it introduces the alphabet one letter at a time. Illustrated.
64 pages Paperback
ISBN: 0-87678-092-3

Barbara Getty & Inga Dubay, Author
Alba Scholz, Manager

3978 Italic Handwriting Series-Book B
Continuing Education Press
PO Box 1394
Portland, OR 97207-1394
503-725-4891
866-647-7377
Fax: 503-725-4840
E-mail: press@pdx.edu
http://www.cep.pdx.edu
Book B is the second workbook of a seven-part series. Designed for the beginning reader and writer. Introduces words and sentences, lowercase and capitol print script, one letter per page. Illustrated.
59 pages Paperback
ISBN: 0-87678-093-1

Barbara Getty & Inga Dubay, Author
Alba Scholz, Manager

3979 Italic Handwriting Series-Book C
Continuing Education Press
PO Box 1394
Portland, OR 97207-1394
503-725-4891
866-647-7377
Fax: 503-725-4840
E-mail: press@pdx.edu
http://www.cep.pdx.edu
Book C is the third workbook of a seven-part series. Covers basic italic and introduces the cursive. Words and sentences include days of week, months of year, modes of transportation, and tongue twisters. Illustrated.
60 pages Paperback
ISBN: 0-87678-094-X

Barbara Getty & Inga Dubay, Author
Alba Scholz, Manager

3980 Italic Handwriting Series-Book D
Continuing Education Press
PO Box 1394
Portland, OR 97207-1394
503-725-4891
866-647-7377
Fax: 503-725-4840
E-mail: press@pdx.edu
http://www.cep.pdx.edu
Book D is the fourth workbook of a seven-part series. Reviews basic italic and covers the total cursive program. Includes prefixes, suffixes, capitalization, and playful poems. Explores history of the alphabet. Illustrated.
80 pages Paperback
ISBN: 0-87678-095-8

Barbara Getty & Inga Dubay, Author
Alba Scholz, Manager

3981 Italic Handwriting Series-Book E
Continuing Education Press
PO Box 1394
Portland, OR 97207-1394
503-725-4891
866-647-7377
Fax: 503-725-4840
E-mail: press@pdx.edu
http://www.cep.pdx.edu
Book E is the fifth workbook of a seven-part series. Reviews basic italic and covers the total cursive program. Writing practice covers natural history— plants, volcanoes, cities. Explores history of the alphabet. Illustrated.
56 pages Paperback
ISBN: 0-87678-096-6

Barbara Getty & Inga Dubay, Author
Alba Scholz, Manager

3982 Italic Handwriting Series-Book F
Continuing Education Press
PO Box 1394
Portland, OR 97207-1394
503-725-4891
866-647-7377
Fax: 503-725-4840
E-mail: press@pdx.edu
http://www;.cep.pdx.edu
Book F is the sixth workbook of a seven-part series. Reviews basic italic and covers the total cursive program. Writing practice emphasizes figures of speech (e.g. homophones, puns, metaphors, acronyms). Explores history of the alphabet. Illustrated.

56 pages Paperback
ISBN: 0-87678-097-4

Barbara Getty & Inga Dubay, Author
Alba Scholz, Manager

3983 Italic Handwriting Series-Book G
Continuing Education Press
PO Box 1394
Portland, OR 97207-1394
503-725-4891
866-647-7377
Fax: 503-725-4840
E-mail: press@pdx.edu
http://www.cep.pdx.edu
Book G is the seventh workbook of a seven-part series. A comprehensive self-instruction program in basic and cursive italic. Writing content follows a central theme-the history of our alphabet. Suitable for older students. Illustrated.

56 pages Paperback
ISBN: 0-87678-098-2

Barbara Getty & Inga Dubay, Author
Alba Scholz, Manager

3984 Language Schools Directory
American Business Directories
5711 S 86th Circle
Omaha, NE 68127-4146
402-593-4600
888-999-1307
Fax: 402-331-5481
A listing of language schools, arranged by geographic location, offering contact information which is updated on a continual basis, and printed on request. Directory is also available in electronic formats.

Jerry Venner, Coordinating Education

3985 Picture Book LearningVolume-1
Picture Book Learning Inc.
PO Box 270075
Louisville, CO 80027
303-548-2809
E-mail: todd@picturebooklearning.com
http://www.picturebooklearning.com
Teachers can use this fun method of teaching elementary children basic language arts skills through the use of picture books.

60 pages
ISBN: 0-9760725-0-5

Todd Osborne, Co-President
Corinne Osborne, Editor

3986 Process of Elimination - a Method of Teaching Basic Grammar - Teacher Ed
Scott & McCleary Publishing Company
2482 11th Street SW
Akron, OH 44314-1712
702-566-8756
800-765-3564
Fax: 702-568-1378
E-mail: jscott7576@aol.com
http://www.scottmccleary.com

Series of 7 steps designed to teach basic grammar skills to students in middle grades through college. Available in a teacher edition and a student workbook.

50 pages
ISBN: 0-9636225-2-8
ISSN: 0-9636225-

Milton Metheny, Author
Janet Scott, Publisher
Sheila McCleary, Publisher

3987 Process of Elimination: A Method of Teaching Basic Grammar - Student Ed
Scott & McCleary Publishing Company
2482 11th Street SW
Akron, OH 44314-1712
702-566-8756
800-765-3564
Fax: 702-568-1378
E-mail: jscott7576@aol.com
http://www.scottmccleary.com
Series of 7 steps designed to teach basic grammar skills to students in middle grades through college. Available in a teacher edition and a student workbook.

Milton Metheny, Author
Janet Scott, Publisher
Sheila McCleary, Publisher

3988 Put Reading First: The Research BuildingBlocks For Teaching Children To Read
PO Box 1398
Jessup, MD 20794-1398
877-4ED-PUBS
Fax: 301-470-1244
E-mail: edpubs@inet.ed.gov
http://www.edpubs.org
Provides analysis and discussion in five areas of reading instruction: phonemic awareness, phonics, fluency, vocabulary and text comprehension.

3989 Write Now: A Complete Self Teaching Program for Better Handwriting
Continuing Education Press
PO Box 1394
Portland, OR 97207-1394
503-725-4891
866-647-7377
Fax: 503-725-4840
E-mail: press@pdx.edu
http://www.cep.pdx.edu
Finally, a handwriting improvement book for adults. Teach yourself to write legibly and retain it over time using this step-by-step guide to modern italic handwriting with complete instructions as well as practice exercises and tips. The secret to legible handwriting is the absence of loops in letterform, making it easier to write and easier to read.

96 pages Paperback
ISBN: 0-87678-089-3

Barbara Getty & Inga Dubay, Author
Alba Scholz, Manager
Wendi Johnson, Customer Service

Directories & Handbooks: Library Services

3990 Directory of Manufacturers & Suppliers
Special Libraries Association
331 S Patrick Street
Alexandria, VA 22314-3501
703-647-4900
Fax: 703-647-4901
E-mail: sla@sla.org
http://www.sla.org
The SLA network consists of nearly 15,000 librarians and information professionals who specialize in the arts, communication, business, social science, biomedical sciences, geosciences and environmental studies, and industry, business, research, educational and technical institutions, government, special departments of public and university libraries, newspapers, museums, and public or private organizations that provide or require specialized information.

3991 Directory of Members of the Association for Library and Information Science Education
1009 Commerce Park Drive Suite 150
PO Box 4219
Oak Ridge, TN 37830
865-425-0155
Fax: 865-481-0390
E-mail: contact@alise.org
http://www.alise.org
The Directory is designed to serve as a handbook for the association, including a list of officers, committees, and interest groups and strategic planning information for the association. Also listed are graduate schools of library and information science and their faculty.

Annual Paperback

Rand Price, Executive Director
Maureen Thompson, Administrator

3992 Libraries Unlimited Academic Catalog
88 Post Road W
Westport, CT 06881
203-226-3571
Fax: 203-222-1502
E-mail: lu-books@lu.com
http://www.lu.com
Catalog includes reference, collection development, library management, cataloging, and technology.

3993 Managing Info Tech in School Library Media Center
Libraries Unlimited
88 Post Road West
Westport, CT 06881
203-226-3571
800-225-5800
Fax: 203-222-1502
E-mail: lu-books@lu.com
http://www.lu.com

Publication Date: 2000 290 pages Hardcover
ISBN: 1-56308-724-3

L Anne Clyde

3994 Managing Media Services Theory and Practice
Libraries Unlimited
88 Post Road West
Westport, CT 06881
203-226-3571
800-225-5800
Fax: 203-222-1502
E-mail: lu-books@lu.com
http://www.lu.com
Publication Date: 2002 418 pages Cloth
ISBN: 1-56308-530-5
L Anne Clyde

Directories & Handbooks: Music & Art

3995 College Guide for Visual Arts Majors
Peterson's, A Nelnet Company
Princeton Pike Corporate Center
2000 Lenox Drive PO Box 67005
Lawrenceville, NJ 08648
609-896-1800
800-338-3282
Fax: 609-896-4531
E-mail: custsvc@petersons.com
http://www.petersons.com
Offers descriptions of over 700 accredited US colleges and universities, music conservatories, and art/design schools that grant undergraduate degrees in the areas of studio art.
Publication Date: 2006 404 pages
ISBN: 1-560795-36-0

3996 Community Outreach and Education for the Arts Handbook
Music Teachers National Association
441 Vine Street
Cincinnati, OH 45202
513-421-1420
888-512-5278
Fax: 513-421-2503
E-mail: mtnanet@mtaa.org
http://www.mtaa.org
Resource booklet for independent music teachers.
Paperback
March
150 booths with 2500 attendees
Chad Schwatbach, Pr/Marketing Associate

3997 Italic Letters
Continuing Education Press
PO Box 1394
Portland, OR 97207-1394
503-725-4891
866-647-7377
Fax: 503-725-4840
E-mail: press@pdx.edu
http://www.cep.pdx.edu
Italic Letters is for professional and amateur calligraphers, art teachers, and enthusiasts of the book arts. Numerous tips on letter shapes, spacing, slant, pen edge angle, and other secrets to handsome writing.
128 pages Paperback
ISBN: 0-87678-091-5
Barbara Getty & Inga Dubay, Author
Alba Scholz, Manager

3998 Money for Film & Video Artists
American for the Art
1000 Vermont Avenue NW
6th Floor
Washington, DC 20005
202-371-2830
Fax: 202-371-0424
http://www.artsusa.org
The listings are organized by sponsoring organization and entries include basic application and program information.

3999 Money for Visual Artists
America for the Art
1000 Vermont Avenue NW
12th Floor
Washington, DC 20005
202-371-2830
Fax: 202-371-0424
http://www.artsusa.org
Programs are listed alphabetically by sponsor with detailed program description.

4000 Music Teachers Guide to Music Instructional Software
Music Teachers National Association
441 Vine Street
Suite 505
Cincinnati, OH 45202-2811
888-512-5278
Fax: 513-421-2503
E-mail: mtnanet@mtna.org
http://www.mtna.org
Evaluations of music software for the macintosh and PC, including CD-ROMs, music skills and keyboard technique drill software, sequencers and soundequipment controllers.

4001 Resource Booklet for Independent Music Teachers
Music Teachers National Association
441 Vine Street
Suite 505
Cincinnati, OH 45202-2811
888-512-5278
Fax: 513-421-2503
E-mail: mtnanet@mtna.org
http://www.mtna.org
A booklet for organizing information about community resources.

4002 School Arts
50 Portland Street
Worcester, MA 01608
800-533-2847
Fax: 508-753-3834
Companies offering products, materials, and art education resources or programs that focus on the history of art, multicultural resources such as Fine Art, reproductions, CD-Roms, museum education, programs, slides, books, videos, exhibits, architecture, timelines, and resource kits.

Directories & Handbooks: Physical Education

4003 Educators Guide to FREE HPER Materials
Educators Progress Service
214 Center Street
Randolph, WI 53956-1408
920-326-3126
888-951-4469
Fax: 920-326-3127
E-mail: epsinc@centurytel.net
http://www.freeteachingaids.com
Lists and describes free films, videotapes, filmstrips, slides, web sites, and hundreds of free printed materials in the field of health, physical education, and recreation for all age levels.
184 pages Annual
ISBN: 87708-407-6
Kathy Nehmer, President

4004 Schools & Colleges Directory
Association for Experiential Education
3775 Iris Avenue
Suite 4
Boulder, CO 80301-2043
303-440-8844
Fax: 303-440-9581
E-mail: publications@aee.org
http://www.aee.org
Provides information about many schools, colleges and universities that have programs or offer degrees related to the field of outdoor/experiential education. Listings include programs in high schools and independent organizations as well as institutions of higher learning. Paperback.
Publication Date: 1995 Paperback
Natalie Kurylke, Publications Manager

Directories & Handbooks: Reading

4005 Diagnostic Reading Inventory for Bilingual Students in Grades 1-8
Scott & McCleary Publishing Company
2482 11th Street SW
Akron, OH 44314-1712
702-566-8756
800-765-3564
Fax: 702-568-1378
E-mail: jscott7576@aol.com
http://www.scottmccleary.com
Series of 13 tests designed to access reading performance. IRI, spelling, phonics, visual and auditory discrimination and listening comprehension are just some of the tests included.
155 pages
ISBN: 0-9636225-1-X
Janet M Scott, Co-Author
Sheila C McCleary, Co-Author

4006 Diagnostic Reading Inventory for Primary and Intermediate Grades K-8
Scott & McCleary Publishing Company
2482 11th Street SW
Akron, OH 44314-1712
702-566-8756
800-765-3564
Fax: 702-568-1378
E-mail: jscott7576@aol.com
http://www.scottmccleary.com
Designed to assess reading performance in grades K-8. Tests include: word recognition, oral reading inventory, comprehension, listening comprehension, auditory and visual discrimination, auditory and visual memory, learning modalities inventory, phonics mastery tests, structural analysis, word association and a diagnostic spelling test.
260 pages
ISBN: 0-9636225-4-4
Janet M Scott, Co-Author
Sheila C McCleary, Co-Author

4007 Educational Leadership
Assn. for Supervision & Curriculum Dev. (ASCD)
1703 N Beauregard Street
Alexandria, VA 22311-1714
703-578-9600
800-933-2723
Fax: 703-575-5400
E-mail: el@ascd.org
http://www.ascd.org
For educators by educators. With a circulation of 175,000, Educational Leadership is acknowledged throughout the world as an authoritative source of information about teaching and learning, new ideas and practices relevant to practicing educators, and the latest trends and issues affecting prekindergarten through higher education.

Marge Scherer, Executive Editor

4008 Laubach Literacy Action Directory
Laubach Literacy Action
1320 Jamesville Avenue
Syracuse, NY 13210
315-422-9121
888-528-2224
Fax: 315-422-6369
E-mail: info@laubach.org
http://www.laubach.org
Listing of over 1,100 local literacy councils and associates who teach the Laubach Method.

90 pages Annual

4009 Ready to Read, Ready to Learn
PO Box 1398
Jessup, MD 20794-1398
877-4ED-PUBS
Fax: 301-470-1244
E-mail: edpubs@inet.ed.gov
http://www.edpubs.org

4010 Tips for Reading Tutors
PO Box 1398
Jessup, MD 20794-1398
877-4ED-PUBS
Fax: 301-470-1244
E-mail: edpubs@inet.ed.gov
http://www.edpubs.org
Basic tips for reading tutors

Directories & Handbooks: Secondary Education

4011 College Board Guide to High Schools
College Board Publications
45 Columbus Avenue
New York, NY 10023-6917
212-713-8165
800-323-7155
Fax: 800-525-5562
http://www.collegeboard.org
Offers listings and information on over 25,000 public and private high schools nationwide.

Publication Date: 1994 2,024 pages
ISBN: 0-874474-66-3

4012 Compendium of Tertiary & Sixth Forum Colleges
SCOTVIC: S McDonald, Principal
Ridge College
Manchester
England
61-4277733
Offers listings of over 200 Sixth Form and Tertiary Colleges in the United Kingdom of-

fering courses preparing secondary students for university study.
Publication Date: 1990 200 pages Biennial

4013 Directory of Public Elementary and Secondary Education Agencies
US National Center for Education Statistics
555 New Jersey Avenue NW
Washington, DC 20208-5651
202-219-1916
800-424-1616
Fax: 202-502-7466
Directory of approximately 17,000 local education agencies that operate their own schools or pay tuition to other local education agencies.

400 pages Annual

John Sietsema, Statistician
Lena McDowell, Contact

4014 Educators Guide to FREE Family and Consumer Education Materials
Educators Progress Service
214 Center Street
Randolph, WI 53956-1408
920-326-3126
888-951-4469
Fax: 920-326-3127
E-mail: epsinc@centurytel.net
http://www.freeteachingaids.com
Lists and describes free films, videotapes, filmstrips, slides, web sites, and hundreds of free printed materials in the field of home econominics and consumer education for all age levels.

161 pages Annual
ISBN: 87708-408-4

Kathy Nehmer, President

4015 Focus on School
ABC-CLIO
130 Cremona Drive
#1911
Santa Barbara, CA 93117-5599
805-968-1911
800-368-6868
Fax: 805-685-9685
Hotlines, print and nonprint resources on education for young adults.
Publication Date: 1990

4016 Great Source Catalog
Great Source Education Group
PO Box 7050
Wilmington, MA 01887
800-289-4490
Fax: 800-289-3994
http://www.greatsource.com
Alternative, affordable, student-friendly K-12 materials to make teaching and learning fun for educators and students.

4017 Helping Your Child Succeed In School: Elementary and Secondary Editions
Master Teacher
Po Box 1207
Manhattan, KS 66505-1207
785-539-0555
800-669-9633
Fax: 800-669-1132
http://www.masterteacher.com
Provides a way for school administrators to help parents help their children succeed in school. Published in English and Spanish.

Erica Paronson, Executive Editor

4018 Lesson Plans for Integrating Technology into the Classroom: Secondary Edition
Master Teacher
Leadership Lane
PO Box 1207
Manhattan, KS 66505-1207
800-669-9633
Fax: 800-669-1132
http://www.masterteacher.com
Gives teachers practical lessons developed and tested by teachers across the curriculum, with students of all levels of ability in using technology.

104 pages
ISBN: 1-58992-152-6

4019 Lesson Plans for Problem-Based Learning: Secondary Edition
Master Teacher
Leadership Lane
PO Box 1207
Manhattan, KS 66505-1207
800-669-9633
Fax: 800-669-1132
http://www.masterteacher.com
An instructional technique which organizes the curriculum around a major problem that students work to solve over the weeks or months.

117 pages
ISBN: 0-914607-87-1

4020 Lesson Plans for the Substitute Teacher: Secondary Edition
Master Teacher
Leadership Lane
PO Box 1207
Manhattan, KS 66505-1207
800-669-9633
Fax: 800-669-1132
http://www.masterteacher.com
Gives you more than 100 lessons developed and tested by teachers across the curriculum and at all grade levels.

177 pages
ISBN: 1-58992-108-9

4021 Peterson's Private Secondary Schools
Peterson's, A Nelnet Company
Princeton Pike Corporate Center
2000 Lenox Drive PO Box 67005
Lawrenceville, NJ 08648-2123
609-896-1800
800-338-3282
Fax: 609-896-4531
E-mail: custsvc@petersons.com
http://www.petersons.com
Listing of over 1,400 accredited and state-approved private secondary schools in the US and abroad.

1,300 pages Annual

4022 Secondary Teachers Guide to FREE Curriculum Materials
Educators Progress Service
214 Center Street
Randolph, WI 53956-1408
920-326-3126
888-951-4469
Fax: 920-326-3127
E-mail: epsinc@centurytel.net
http://www.freeteachingaids.com
Lists and describes free supplementary teaching aids for the high school and college level.

296 pages Annual
ISBN: 87708-399-1

Kathy Nehmer, President

Directories & Handbooks: Science

4023 Earth Education: A New Beginning
Institute for Earth Education
Cedar Cove
PO Box 115
Greenville, WV 24945
304-832-6404
Fax: 304-832-6077
E-mail: iee1@aol.com
http://www.eartheducation.org
This book proposes another direction-an alternative that many environmental leaders and teachers around the world have already taken. It is called The Earth Education Path, and anyone can follow it in developing a genuine program made up of magical learning adventures.

334 pages Paperback
ISBN: 0917011023

Steve Van Matre, Chairman

4024 Earthkeepers
Institute for Earth Education
Cedar Cove
PO Box 115
Greenville, WV 24945
304-832-6404
Fax: 304-832-6077
E-mail: iee1@aol.com
http://www.eartheducation.org
This book will give you the best picture of what a complete earth education program involves. Even if you can't set up the complete Earthkeepers program, there are many activities you can use to build an earth education program in your own settting and situation.

108 pages Paperback
ISBN: 0917011015

Bruce Johnson, Chairman

4025 Educators Guide to FREE Science Materials
Educators Progress Service
214 Center Street
Randolph, WI 53956-1408
920-326-3126
888-951-4469
Fax: 920-326-3127
E-mail: epsinc@centurytel.net
http://www.freeteachingaids.com
Lists and describes free films, videotapes, filmstrips, slides, web sites, and hundreds of free printed materials in the field of science for all age levels.

Annual

Kathy Nehmer, President

4026 K-6 Science and Math Catalog
Carolina Biological Supply Co.
2700 York Road
Burlington, NC 27215-3398
336-584-0381
800-334-5551
Fax: 800-222-7112
http://www.carolina.com
Service teaching materials for grades Pre K through 8, including charts, computers, software, books, living animals and plants, microscopes, microscope slides, models, teaching kits and more.

4027 Science for All Children; A Guide to Improving Science Education
National Academy Press
Arts & Industries Bldg Room 1201
900 Jefferson Drive SW
Washington, DC 20560-0403
202-287-2063
Fax: 202-287-2070
E-mail: outreach@nas.edu
http://www.si.edu/nsrc
Provides concise and practical guidelines for implementing science education reform at local level, including the elements of an effective, inquiry-based, hands-on science program. Produced by the National Science Resources Center. Published by National Academy Press.

240 pages
ISBN: 0-309-05297-1

National Science Resources Center, Author
Douglas Lapp, Executive Director

4028 Sunship Earth
Institute for Earth Education
Cedar Cove
PO Box 115
Greenville, WV 24945
304-832-6404
Fax: 304-832-6077
E-mail: iee1@aol.com
http://www.eartheducation.org
Contains clear descriptions of key ecological concepts and concise reviews of important learning principals, plus over 200 additional pages of ideas, activities and guidelines for setting up a complete Sunship Earth Study Station.

265 pages Paperback
ISBN: 0876030460

Bruce Johnson, Chairman

4029 Sunship III
Institute for Earth Education
Cedar Cove
PO Box 115
Greenville, WV 24945
304-832-6404
Fax: 304-832-6077
E-mail: iee1@aol.com
http://www.eartheducation.org
Examines perception and choice in our daily habits and routines. It is about exploration and discovery in the larger context of where and how we live, and examining alteratives and making sacrifices on behalf of a healthier home planet.

133 pages Paperback
ISBN: 0917011031

Bruce Johnson, Chairman

4030 UNESCO Sourcebook for Out-of-School Science & Technology Education
U.N. Educational, Scientific & Cultural Assn.
7, place de Fontenoy
F-75700 Paris
France
Offers information on science clubs, societies and congresses, science fairs and museums.

145 pages

Directories & Handbooks: Social Studies

4031 Directory of Central America Classroom Resources
Central American Resource Center
317 17th Avenue SE
Minneapolis, MN 55414-2012
612-627-9445
Offers information on suppliers of education resource materials about Central America, including curricula, materials, directories and organizations providing related services.

Publication Date: 1990   200 pages

4032 Educators Guide to FREE Social Studies Materials
Educators Progress Service
214 Center Street
Randolph, WI 53956-1408
920-326-3126
888-951-4469
Fax: 920-326-3127
E-mail: epsinc@centurytel.net
http://www.freeteachingaids.com
Lists and describes free films, videotapes, filmstrips, slides, web sites, and hundreds of free printed materials in the field of social studies for all age levels.

287 pages Annual
ISBN: 87708-405-X

Kathy Nehmer, President

4033 Geography: A Resource Guide for Secondary Schools
ABC-CLIO
130 Cremona Drive
#1911
Santa Barbara, CA 93117-5599
805-968-1911
800-368-6868
Fax: 805-685-9685
List of organizations and associations to use as resources for secondary education geography studies.

Directories & Handbooks: Technology in Education

4034 American Trade Schools Directory
Croner Publications
10951 Sorrento Valley Road
Suite 1D
San Diego, CA 92121
858-546-1954
800-441-4033
Fax: 858-546-1955
E-mail: paul@croner.com
http://www.croner.com
Loose leaf binder directory listing trade and technical schools throughout the United States, in alphabetical order, by state, then city, then school name.

411 pages
ISBN: 0-875140-02-5

Rosa Padilla, Office Manager

4035 Association for Educational Communications & Technology: Membership Directory
Association for Educational Communications & Tech.
1025 Vermont Avenue NW
Suite 820
Washington, DC 20005-3516
202-965-2059

Five thousand audiovisual and instructional materials specialists and school media specialists, with audio-visual and TV production personnel. Also listed are committees, task force divisions, auxiliary affiliates, state organizations and directory of corporate members.

200 pages Annual/Spring

4036 Chronicle Vocational School Manual
Chronicle Guidance Publications
66 Aurora Street
Moravia, NY 13118-3569
315-497-0330
800-899-0454
Fax: 315-497-3359
E-mail: customerservice@chronicleguidance.com
http://www.chronicleguidance.com
A geographical index of more than 3,500 vocational schools including all contact information, programs, admissions requirements, costs, financial aid programs and student services.
Publication Date: 1996 300 pages Annual
ISBN: 1-556312-50-4
Patricia F Hammon, Research Associate
Stephen Thompson, Managing Editor

4037 Directory of Public Vocational-Technical Schools & Institutes in the US
Media Marketing Group
PO Box 611
DeKalb, IL 60115-0611
360-576-5864
Offers information on over 1,400 post secondary vocational and technical education programs in public education; private trade and technical schools are not included.
Publication Date: 1994 400 pages Biennial
ISBN: 0-933474-51-2

4038 Directory of Vocational-Technical Schools
Media Marketing Group
PO Box 611
DeKalb, IL 60115-0611
360-576-5864
Offers information on public, postsecondary schools offering degree and non-degree occupational education.
Publication Date: 1996 450 pages Biennial
ISBN: 0-933474-52-0

4039 Educational Film & Video Locator
RR Bowker Reed Reference
121 Chanlon Road
New Providence, NJ 07974-1541
908-464-6800
Fax: 908-665-6688
Producers and distributors of educational films.
Publication Date: 1990

4040 Guide to Vocational and Technical Schools East & West
Peterson's, A Nelnet Company
Princeton Pike Corporare Center
2000 Lenox Drive PO Box 67005
Lawrenceville, NJ 08648
609-896-1800
800-338-3282
Fax: 690-896-4531
E-mail: custsvc@petersons.com
http://www.petersons.com
These two directories cover the full range of training programs in over 240 career fields divided into the categories of Business,

Technology, Trade, Personal Services, and Health Care. East edition covers East of Mississippi; West edition covers West of the Mississippi.
Publication Date: 2006 579 pages Per Volume

4041 Industrial Teacher Education Directory
National Assn. of Industrial Teacher Educators
University of Northern Iowa
Cedar Falls, IA 50614-0001
319-273-2561
Fax: 319-273-5818
http://www.uni.edu/indtech
Listing of about 2,800 industrial education faculty members at 250 universities and four-year colleges in the United States, Canada, Australia, Japan and Taiwan.
108 pages Annual
M Fahmy, Professor/Head of Department
Charles Johnson, Coordinator of Tech Ed. Prog

4042 Information Literacy: Essential Skills for the Information Age
Syracuse University
4-194 Center for Science & Tech.
Syracuse, NY 13244-0001
315-443-3640
800-464-9107
Fax: 315-443-5448
E-mail: eric@ericir.sye.edu
Traces history, development, and economic necessity of information literacy. Reports on related subject matter standards. Includes reports on the National Educational Goals (1991), the Secretary's Commission on Achieving Necessary Skills Report (1991), and the latest updates from ALA's Information Power (1998).
377 pages
ISBN: 0-937597-44-9
Kathleen L Spitzer, Editor

4043 Internet Resource Directory for Classroom Teachers
Regulus Communications
140 N 8th Street
Suite 201
Lincoln, NE 68508-1358
402-432-2680
Directory offering information on all resources available on-line for classroom teachers, including e-mail addresses, Home Page URL's, phone and fax numbers, surface-mail addresses, classroom contacts and teaching resources. Available in paper and electronic formats.
Publication Date: 1996 272 pages Paper Format
Jane A Austin, Coordinating Education

4044 K-12 District Technology Coordinators
Quality Education Data
1625 Broadway
Suite 250
Denver, CO 80202-4715
303-860-1832
800-525-5811
Fax: 303-209-9444
E-mail: info@qeddata.com
http://www.qeddata.com
The first in QED's National Educator Directories, this comprehensive directory of technology coordinators combines QED's exclusive database of technology and demographic data with names of technology coordinators in the 7,000 largest US school

districts. The directory includes district phone number, number of students in the district, number of computers, student/computer ratio and predominant computer brand.
Publication Date: 1994 400 pages
Laurie Christensen, Coordinating Education

4045 NetLingo Internet Dictionary
805-794-8687
E-mail: info@netlingo.com
http://www.netlingo.com
A smart looking easy-to-understand dictionary of 3000 internet terms, 1200 chat acronyms, and much more. Modem reference book for international students, educators, industry professionals and online businesses and organizations.
Erin Jansen, Author

4046 Quick-Source
AM Educational Publishing
3745 Suffolk Drive
Suite D
Tallahassee, FL 32308-3048
850-668-4148
Educational technology directory with over 1,100 names, addresses, phones/faxes, and brief descriptions of the products/services of companies/organizations; supports major works/word processors (MS-DOS/MAC); conferences and other educational technology listings.
Annual/September

4047 Schools Industrial, Technical & Trade Directory
American Business Directories
5711 S 86th Circle
Omaha, NE 68127-4146
402-593-4600
888-999-1307
Fax: 402-331-5481
A geographical listing of over 3,750 schools with all contact information, size of advertisement and first year in Yellow Pages. Also available in electronic formats.
Annual
Jerry Venner, Coordinating Education

4048 TESS: The Educational Software Selector
EPIE Institute
103 W Montauk Highway
PO Box 590
Hampton Bays, NY 11946-4003
631-728-9100
Fax: 631-728-9228
E-mail: kkomoski@epie.org
http://www.epie.org
A list of over 1,200 suppliers of educational software and over 18,000 educational software products (on CD-ROM) for pre-school through college information. Includes description of program, grade level data, price, platform and review citations.
Nancy Boland, Coordinating Education

4049 Tech Directions-Directory of Federal & Federal and State Officials Issue
Prakken Publications
416 Longshore Drive
Ann Arbor, MI 48105-1624
313-577-4042
Fax: 313-577-1672

Listing of federal and state officials concerned with vocational, technical, industrial trade and technology education in the United States and Canada.

Annual

4050 Technology in Public Schools
Quality Education Data
1624 Broadway
Suite 250
Denver, CO 80202-4715
303-860-1832
800-525-5811
Fax: 303-209-9444
E-mail: info@qeddata.com
http://www.qeddata.com
Annual survey of instructional technology represents more than 67% of all US K-12 students. Includes computer brand and processor type market share, CD-ROM, networks, LAN, modem, cable and in-depth internet access installed base information.

Publication Date: 1994   160 pages   Yearly
ISBN: 0-88947-925-1

Liz Stephens, Marketing Coordinator

Periodicals: General

4051 AACS Newsletter
American Association of Christian Schools
4500 S Selsa Road
Blue Springs, MO 64015-2221
816-252-9900
Fax: 703-252-6700
Association news offering the most up-to-date information relating to Christian education.

4 pages   Monthly
Dr. Carl Herbster, Contact

4052 AAHE Bulletin
American Association for Higher Education
1 Dupont Circle
Suite 360
Washington, DC 20036
202-293-6440
Fax: 202-293-0073
http://www.aahebulletin.com
Electronic newsletter

16 pages   Monthly
Vicky Hendly Dobin, Manager

4053 ACJS Today
Academy of Criminal Justice Services
7339 Hanover Parkway
Suite A
Greenbelta, MD 20770
301-446-6300
800-757-2257
Fax: 301-446-2819
http://www.acjs.org
Provides upcoming events, news releases, ACJS activities, ads, book reviews and miscellaneous information.

24-32 pages   Quarterly
Laura Myers, Editor
Laura Monaco, Association Manager

4054 ASCD Update
Assn. for Supervision & Curriculum Development
1703 N Beauregard Street
Alexandria, VA 22311
703-578-9600
Fax: 703-575-5400

News on contemporary education issues and information on ASCD programs.
Ronald Brandt, Publisher
John O'Neil, Editor

4055 ASSC Newsletter
Arkansas School Study Council
255 Graduate Education Building
Fayetteville, AR 72701
479-442-8464
Fax: 479-442-2038
Monthly up-date on education, finance, new legislation, mandates for Arkansas public schools.

3-10 pages
Martin Schoppmeyer, Editor

4056 AV Guide Newsletter
Educational Screen
380 E NW Highway
Des Plaines, IL 60016-2201
847-298-6622
Fax: 847-390-0408
Provides concise and practical information on audiovisually oriented products with an emphasis on new ideas and methods of using learning media, including educational computer software.

Monthly
ISSN: 0091-360X

HS Gillette, Publisher
Natalie Ferguson, Editor

4057 Academe
American Association of University Professors
1012 14th Street NW
Suite 500
Washington, DC 20005-3406
202-737-5900
Fax: 202-737-5526
E-mail: academe@aaup.org
http://www.aaup.org
A thoughtful and provocative review of developments affecting higher education faculty. With timely features and informative departments, Academe delivers the latest on the state of the profession, legal and legislative trends, and issues in academia.

BiMonthly
Lawrence Hanley, Editor, Author
Gwendolyn Bradley, Managing Co-Director
Wendi Maloney, Managing Editor

4058 Aero Gramme
Alternative Education Resource Organizations
417 Roslyn Road
Roslyn Heights, NY 11577-2620
516-621-2195
800-769-4171
Fax: 516-625-3257
Networks all forms of educational alternatives, from public and private alternative schools to homeschooling.

Quarterly
Jerry Mintz, Editor

4059 Agenda: Jewish Education
Jewish Education Service of North America
111 Eighth Avenue
Suite 11E
New York, NY 10011
212-284-6950
Fax: 212-284-6951
E-mail: info@jesna.org
http://www.jesna.org

Seeks to create a community of discourse on issues of Jewish public policy dealing with Jewish education and the indications of policy options for the practice of Jewish education.

Quarterly
ISSN: 1072-1150

Amy Skin, Dir
Marketing/Communication

4060 American Council on Education: GED Testing Service
American Council on Education
1 Dupont Circle NW
Suite 800
Washington, DC 20036-1193
202-939-9300
Fax: 202-833-4760
Information relating to GED items and testing.

8 pages   5x Year
Colleen Allen, Contact

4061 American Journal of Education
University of Chicago
5835 S Kimbark Avenue
Chicago, IL 60637
773-702-1555
Fax: 773-702-6207
E-mail: aje@uchicago.edu

Quarterly
Robert Dreeben and Zalman Usiskin, Author
John E Craig, Editor
Susan S Stodolsky, Editor

4062 American Scholar
1785 Massachusetts Avenue NW
4th Floor
Washington, DC 20036-2117
202-265-3808
A general interest magazine that includes articles on science, literature, and book reviews.

Quarterly
Anne Fadiman, Editor

4063 American Students & Teachers Abroad
US Government Printing Office
732 N Capitol Street NW
Washington, DC 20401
202-512-0000
Fax: 202-512-1293
E-mail: admin@access.gpo.gov
http://www.access.gpo.gov

4064 Annual Report
Jessie Ball duPont Fund
One Dependent Drive
Suite 1400
Jacksonville, FL 32202-5011
904-353-0890
800-252-3452
Fax: 904-353-3870
E-mail: contactus@dupontfund.org
http://www.dupontfund.org
Focused on a variety of good work aimed at growing the capacity of the nonprofit sector.

Annually

4065 Association of Orthodox Jewish Teachers of the New York Public Schools
Association of Orthodox Jewish Teachers of the NY
1577 Coney Island Avenue
Brooklyn, NY 11230
718-258-3585
Fax: 718-258-3586
E-mail: aojt@juno.com
Newsletter representing observant Jewish teachers in the New York City Public Schools.

8-12 pages Quarterly Newsletter

Max Zakon, Executive Director

4066 Between Classes-Elderhostel Catalog
Elderhostel
75 Federal Street
Boston, MA 02110-1913
617-426-7788
Fax: 617-426-8351
http://www.elderhostel.org
Seasonal listings of elderhostel educational programs offered by educational cultural institutions in the US and 60 countries overseas.

120 pages Quarterly

Heather Baynes, Contact

4067 Blumenfeld Education Newsletter
PO Box 45161
Boise, ID 83711-5161
Providing knowledge to parents and educators who want to save children of America from destructive forces that endanger them. Children in public schools are at grave risk in 4 ways: academically, spiritually, morally, physically, and only a well-informed public will be able to reduce these risks.

8 pages

Peter F Watt, Publisher
Samuel L Blumenfeld, Editor

4068 Brighton Times
Brighton Academy/Foundation of Human Understanding
1121 NE 7th Street
Grants Pass, OR 97526-1421
541-474-6865
Fax: 541-474-6866
Home schooling information.

Monthly

Cynthia Coumoyer, Contact

4069 Brochure of American-Sponsored Overseas Schools
Office of Overseas Schools, Department of State
Room 245
SA-29
Washington, DC 20522
202-261-8200
Fax: 202-261-8224

4070 Business-Education Insider
Heritage Foundation
214 Massachusetts Avenue NE
Washington, DC 20002-4958
202-546-4400
Fax: 202-546-8328
Deals with issues relating to the corporate/business world, and the effects it has on education.

Monthly

Jeanne Allen, Contact

4071 CBE Report
Association for Community Based Education
1806 Vernon Street NW
Washington, DC 20009-1217
202-462-6333
Educational institutions covering news, workshops and resources.

Monthly

4072 CEDS Communique
The Council for Exceptional Children
1920 Association Drive
Reston, VA 20191-1545
703-620-3660
888-232-7733
Fax: 703-264-9494
Reports on the activities of the Council for Educational Diagnostic Services and information about special programs, upcoming events, current trends and practices, and other topical matters.

Quarterly

Lamoine Miller, Contact

4073 Center Focus
Center of Concern
1225 Otis Street NE
Washington, DC 20017-2516
202-635-2757
Fax: 202-832-9494
E-mail: coc@coc.org
http://www.coc.org
Newsletters addressing the everchanging needs and concerns in the education field.

6 pages BiMonthly

Jane Deren, Publisher/Editor

4074 Center for Continuing Education of Women Newsletter
University of Michigan
Ann Arbor, MI 48109
734-763-1400
Fax: 734-936-1641
Association news focusing on the concerns of women in education.

4 pages

4075 Center for Parent Education Newsletter
81 Wyman Street
Wapham, MA 02160
617-964-2442
Offers information and tips to address parent involvement in the education of their children.

BiMonthly

4076 Change
Heldref Publications
1319 18th Street NW
Washington, DC 20036-1802
202-296-6267
800-365-9753
Fax: 202-296-5149
http://www.heldref.org
Perspectives on the critical issues shaping the world of higher education. It is not only issue-oriented and reflective, but challenges the status quo in higher education.

BiMonthly

Margaret A Miller, President
Theodore J Marchese, VP/Editor

4077 Clearing House: A Journal of Educational Research
Heldref Publications
1319 18th Street NW
Washington, DC 20036-1826
202-296-6267
800-365-9753
Fax: 202-296-5149
E-mail: tch@heldfred.org
Each issue offers a variety of articles for teachers and administrators of middle schools and junior and senior high schools. It includes experiments, trends and accomplishments in courses, teaching methods, administrative procedures and school programs.

4 pages BiMonthly
ISSN: 0009-8655

Deborah N Cohen, Promotions Manager
Judy Cusick, Managing Editor

4078 Commuter Perspectives
National Clearinghouse for Commuter Programs
1195 Stamp Union
College Park, MD 30314-9634
301-405-0986
Fax: 301-314-9874
E-mail: nccp@accmail.umd.edu
http://www.umd.edu/NCCP
A quarterly newsletter published by the National Clearinghouse for Commuter Programs for professionals who work for, with, and on behalf of commuter students.

8 pages Quarterly

Barbara Jacoby, Contact

4079 Congressional Digest
Congressional Digest Corp.
4416 East West Highway
Suite 400
Bethesda, MD 20814-4568
301-634-3113
800-637-9915
Fax: 301-634-3189
E-mail: griff.thomas@pro-and-con.org
http://www.pro-and-con.org
An independent publication featuring controversies in Congress, pro-and-con.

ISSN: 0010-5899

Delores Baisden, Assistant

4080 Contemporary Education
Indiana State University, School of Education
SE 1005th
Terre Haute, IN 47809-0001
877-856-8005
Fax: 812-856-8088
A readable and currently informative journal of topics in the mainstream of educational thought.

Quarterly
ISSN: 0010-7476

Todd Whitaker, Editor
Beth Whitaker, Editor

4081 Creative Child & Adult Quarterly
Nat'l Assn. for Creative Children & Adults
8080 Springvalley Drive
Cincinnati, OH 45236-1352
513-631-1777

Quarterly

Anne Fabe Isaacs, Editor

4082 Creativity Research Journal
Lawrence Erlbaum Associates
10 Industrial Avenue
Mahwah, NJ 07430-2262
201-258-2200
800-926-6579
Fax: 201-236-0072
E-mail: journals@erlbaum.com
http://www.erlbaum.com
A peer-reviewed journal covering a full range of approaches including behavioral, cognitive, clinical developmental, educational, social and organizational. Online access is available by visiting LEAonline.com
Quarterly
ISSN: 1040-0419

Mark A Runco, PhD., Editor

4083 Currents
Council for Advancement & Support of Education
1307 New York Avenue NW
Suite 1000
Washington, DC 20005-4726
703-379-4611
A how-to magazine covering educational fund raising and public relations publications.
Monthly

Sue Partyke, Editor

4084 DCDT Network
The Council for Exceptional Children
1920 Association Drive
Reston, VA 20191-1545
703-620-3660
888-232-7733
Fax: 703-264-9494
Newsletter of the Division on Career Development and Transition. Provides the latest information on legislation, projects, resource materials and implementation strategies in the field of career development and transition for persons with disabilities and/or who are gifted. Carries information about Division activities, upcoming events, announcements and reports of particular interest to DCDT members.
3x Year

Sherrilyn Fisher, Contact

4085 DECA Dimensions
1908 Association Drive
Reston, VA 20191-1503
703-860-5000
Fax: 703-860-4013
http://www.deca.org
An educational nonprofit association news management for marketing education students across the country, Canada, Guam and Puerto Rico. Offers information on DECA activities, leadership, business and career skills, which help develop future leaders in business, marketing and management.
36 pages Quarterly
ISSN: 1060-6106

Carol Lund, Author

Carol Lund, Editor

4086 DLD Times
The Council for Exceptional Children
1920 Association Drive
Reston, VA 20191-1589
703-620-3660
800-CEC-SPED
Fax: 703-264-1637
Information concerning education and welfare of children and youth with learning disabilities.
8 pages TriQuarterly

Katherine Garnett

4087 Decision Line
Decision Sciences Institute
University Plaza
Atlanta, GA 30303
404-651-4000
Fax: 404-651-2896
Contains articles on education, business and decision sciences as well as available positions and textbook advertising.
32 pages 5x Year

K Roscoe Davis

4088 Desktop Presentations & Publishing
Doron & Associates
1213 Ridgecrest Circle
Denton, TX 76205-5421
940-320-0068
Fax: 940-591-9586
Computer generated presentations and visual aids for education and business.
16 pages BiMonthly

Tom Doron, Contact

4089 Development and Alumni Relations Report
LRP Publications
1901 N Moore Street
Suite 700
Arlington, VA 22209
703-516-7002
800-341-7874
Fax: 703-516-9313
E-mail: custserve@lrp.com
http://www.lrp.com
Provides colleges and universities with innovative ideas for improving: alumni relations; the involvement of alumni in clubs and chapters; annual giving; endowment and capital campaigns; and planned giving. Plus, you can recieve free e-mail updates on crucial news affecting your job with your paid subscription.
Monthly Newsletter

4090 Different Books
Place in the Woods
3900 Glenwood Avenue
Golden Valley, MN 55422-5302
763-374-2120
Fax: 952-593-5593
E-mail: differentbooks@aol.com
Special imprint of books by, for and about persons on a different path. Features main characters with disabilities as heroes and heroines in storyline. For hi-lo reading in early elementary grades (3-7).
Paperback

Roger Hammer, Publisher

4091 Directions
AFS Intercultural Programs USA
198 Madison Avenue
Floor 8
New York, NY 10016
212-299-9000
Fax: 212-299-9090
News of AFS US volunteers.
6 pages Monthly

Pedro Valez, Contact

4092 Disability Compliance for Higher Education
LRP Publications
1901 N Moore Street
Suite 700
Arlington, VA 22209
703-516-9313
800-341-7874
Fax: 703-516-9313
E-mail: custserve@lrp.com
http://www.lrp.com
Newsletter helps colleges determine if they're complying with the Americans with Disabilities Act (ADA) and Section 504 of the Rehabilitation Act- so they can avoid costly litigation. Gives tips on how to provide reasonable accommodations in test-taking, grading, admissions, and accessibility to programs and facilities.
Monthly
ISSN: 1086-1335

Edward Filo, Author

4093 Diversity 2000
Holocaust Resource Center
Kean College
1000 Morris Avenue
Union, NJ 07083
Offers ideas and issues on multicultural school education programs.
BiMonthly

J Preill, Contact

4094 ERIC/CRESS Bulletin
AEL, Inc.
PO Box 1348
Charleston, WV 25325-1348
304-347-0437
800-624-9120
Fax: 304-347-0467
E-mail: ericrc@ael.org
Announces new developments in the ERIC system nationally, and publications and events relevant to American Indians, Alaska Natives, Mexican Americans, migrants, outdoor education and rural, small schools.
3x Year Newsletter

Patricia Hammer Cahape, Associate Director

4095 Eagle Forum
Eagle Education Fund
8383 E 123rd Avenue
Brighton, CO 80601-8110
News on the Eagle Education Fund.
Quarterly

Jayne Schindler, Editor

4096 EdPress News
Association of Educational Publishers
510 Heron Drive
Suite 201
Logan Township, NJ 08085
856-241-7772
Fax: 856-241-0709
E-mail: mail@edpress.org
http://www.edpress.org
The Association supports the growth of educational publishing and it's positive effects on learning and teaching. EdPress provides information and analysis of markets and trends, education and legislative policy, learning and teaching research, and intellectual property. The Association also provides training and staff development programs, promotes supplemental learning resources as essential curriculum materi-

als, and advocates on issues relevant to its constituents.

Charlene F Gaynor, Executive Director
Stacey Pusey, Communications Director

4097 Education
Project Innovation
1362 Santa Cruz Court
Chula Vista, CA 91910-7114
760-630-9938
E-mail: rcassel5@aol.com
http://www.rcassel.com
Original investigations and theoretical articles dealing with education. Preference given to innovations, real or magical, which promise to improve learning.

160 pages Quarterly
ISSN: 0013-1172

Dr. Russell Cassel, Editor
Lan Mieu Cassel, Managing Editor

4098 Education Digest
Prakken Publications
PO Box 8623
3970 Varsity Drive
Ann Arbor, MI 48107-8623
734-975-2800
800-530-9673
Fax: 734-975-2787
E-mail: publisher@techdirectories.com
http://www.eddigest.com
Offers outstanding articles condensed for quick review from over 200 magazines, monthlies, books, newsletters and journals, timely and important for professional educators and others interested in the field.

80 pages Monthly
ISSN: 0013-127X

George F Kennedy, Publisher
Kenneth Schroeder, Managing Editor

4099 Education Hotline
6935 Arlington Road
Suite 100
Bethesda, MD 20814
301-280-3100
800-346-1834
Fax: 301-280-3250
E-mail: ads@epe.org
http://www.edweek.org
Education newsletter.

4100 Education Newsletter LibraryCounterpoint
LRP Publications
1901 N Moore Street
Suite 700
Alington, VA 22209
703-516-7002
800-341-7874
Fax: 703-516-9313
E-mail: custserve@lrp.com
http://www.lrp.com
Offers its readers concise, informative and timely articles covering innovative practices in special education. Covers: special education news from the states; updates on curriculum; developments in special education technology; classified ads; descriptions of new products and publications; and more.

On-Line

4101 Education Newsline
National Association of Christian Educators
PO Box 3200
Costa Mesa, CA 92628-3200
949-251-9333
Articles pertinent to public education for teachers and parents, current trends and so-

lutions and the work of Citizens for Excellence in Education.

8 pages BiMonthly

Robert Simonds, Publisher
Kathi Hudson, Editor

4102 Education Now and in the Future
Northwest Regional Educational Laboratory
101 SW Main Street
Suite 500
Portland, OR 97204-3213
503-275-9500
800-597-6339
Fax: 503-275-0458
E-mail: info@nwrel.org
http://www.nwrel.org
Contains articles about products, events, research and publications produced or sponsored by the NW Regional Educational Laboratory, a private nonprofit educational institution whose mission is to help schools improve outcomes for all students.

Carol F Thomas, CEO

4103 Education Quarterly
New Jersey State Department of Education
100 Riverview Plaza
PO Box 500
Trenton, NJ 08625
609-292-4040
New Jersey education information and updates.

6 pages Quarterly

Richard Vespucci, Contact

4104 Education USA
LRP Publications
1901 N Moore Street
Suite 1106
Arlington, VA 22209
703-516-7002
800-341-7874
Fax: 703-516-9313
E-mail: custserve@lrp.com
http://www.lrp.com
Offers information on court decisions, federal funding, the national debate over standards, education research, school finance, and more. Subscribers receive biweekly reports on Education Department policies on Title I, special education, bilingual education, drug-free schools and other issues affecting schools nationwide.

8-10 pages BiWeekly

4105 Education Update
Heritage Foundation
214 Massachusetts Avenue NE
Washington, DC 20002-4958
202-546-4400
Fax: 202-544-7330
http://www.heritage.org
Contains analyses of policy issues and trends in US education.

4106 Education Week
6935 Arlington Road
Suite 100
Bethesda, MD 20814
301-280-3100
800-346-1834
Fax: 301-280-3250
E-mail: ads@epe.org
http://www.edweek.org
For principals, superintendents, director, managers and other administrators.

4107 Education in Focus
Books for All Times
PO Box 2
Alexandria, VA 22313-0002
703-548-0457
E-mail: jdavid@bfat.com
Examines failures and successes of public and private education by looking beneath the surface for answers and explanations.

6 pages BiAnnually
ISSN: 1049-7250

Joe David, Editor

4108 Educational Forum
University of Colorado-Denver, School of Education
PO Box 173364
Campus Box 106
Denver, CO 80217-3364
303-556-3402
Fax: 303-556-4479
E-mail: education@cudenver.edu
http://www.cudenver.edu/sehd
The university is recognized as one of the leading public universities in the nation and offers a broad range of academic opportunities to students.

Quarterly

Hank Brown, President
Michel Dahlin, Interim Vice President

4109 Educational Freedom Spotlight On Homeschooling
Clonlara Home Based Education Programs
1289 Jewett Street
Ann Arbor, MI 48104-6201
734-769-4511
Fax: 734-769-9629
E-mail: clonlara@wash.k12.mi.us
http://www.clonlara.org
Clonlara School is committed to illuminating educational rights and freedoms through our actions and deep dedication to human rights and dignity.

12 pages Monthly

Susan Andrews, Editor
Carmen Amabile, Coordinator

4110 Educational Horizons
P. Lambda Theta, Int'l Honor & Professional Assn.
PO Box 6626
Bloomington, IN 47407-6626
812-339-3411
Fax: 812-339-3462
E-mail: root@pilambda.org
http://www.pilambda.org
Founded in the spirit of academic excellence in order to provide leadership in addressing educational, social and cultural issues of national and international significance and to enhance the status of educators by providing a recognized forum for sharing new perspectives, research findings and scholarly essays.

48 pages Quarterly
ISSN: 0013-175X

Juli Knutson, Editor

4111 Educational Research Forum
American Educational Research Association
1230 17th Street NW
Washington, DC 20036-3078
202-223-9485
Fax: 202-775-1824
E-mail: aera@gmu.edu
Contains news and information on educational research, teaching, counseling and school administration.

4112 Educational Researcher
American Educational Research
Association
1230 17th Street NW
Washington, DC 20036-3078
202-223-9485
Fax: 202-775-1824
E-mail: aera@gmu.edu
Publishes research news and commentary
on events in the field of educational re-
search and articles of a wide interest to any-
one involved in education.

9x Year

Robert Donmoyer, Editor
Leannah Harding, Managing Editor

4113 Educational Theory
University of Illinois at Urbana
1310 S 6th Street
Champaign, IL 61820-6925
217-333-3003
Fax: 217-244-3711
E-mail: edtheory@uiuc.edu
http://www.ed.uiuc.edu/educational-theor
y
The purpose of this journal is to foster the
continuing development of educational
theory and encourage wide and effective
discussion of theoretical problems with the
educational profession. Publishes articles
and studies in the foundations of education
and in related disciplines outside the field
of education which contribute to the advancement of education theory.

570 pages Quarterly
ISSN: 0013-2004

Nicholas C Burbules, Editor
Diane E Beckett, Business Manager

4114 Exceptional Children
The Council for Exceptional Children
1920 Association Drive
Reston, VA 20191-1545
703-620-3660
800-232-7323
Fax: 703-264-1637
Informs readers through research studies,
articles by authorities in the field of special
education, and discussions of current issues and problems.

Quarterly
ISSN: 0014-4029

Bob Algozzine, Editor
Martha Thurlow, Editor

4115 Focus on Autism
Pro-Ed., Inc.
8700 Shoal Creek Boulevard
Austin, TX 78757-6816
512-451-3246
800-897-3202
Fax: 512-302-9129
http://www.proedinc.com
Hands-on tips, techniques, methods and
ideas from top authorities for improving
the quality of assessment, instruction and
management.

Brenda Smith Myles, PhD, Editor

4116 Focus on Research
The Council for Exceptional Children
1920 Association Drive
Reston, VA 20191-1545
703-620-3660
888-232-7733
Fax: 703-264-9494
Contains member opinion articles, debates
on research issues, descriptions and dates
of specific projects, notices of funded program priorities in special education, the
availability of research dollars, and the dis-

cussion of emerging issues that may affect
research in special education.

3x Year

Mavis Donahue, Co-Editor
Eileen Ball, Co-Editor

4117 Foreign Student Service Council
2263 12th Place NW
Washington, DC 20009-4405
202-232-4979
Non-profit organization dedicated to promoting understanding between international students and Americans.

Quarterly

4118 Fortune Education Program
105 Terry Drive
Suite 120
Newtown, PA 18940-1872
800-448-3399
Fax: 215-579-8589
Professional program that offers 75% off
the cover price of Fortune magazine, a free
educator's desk reference, a free 2-page
teaching guide, fast delivery, choice of billing options. Plus quality customer service.

Pat Sproehnle, Editor

4119 Forum
Educators for Social Responsibility
23 Garden Street
Cambridge, MA 02138-3623
617-492-1764
Fax: 617-864-5164
E-mail: educators@esrnational.org
http://www.esrnational.org
Edited for educators concerned with teach-
ing in the nuclear age.

12 pages Quarterly

Susan Pittman, Contact

**4120 Foundation for Exceptional
Children: Focus**
The Council for Exceptional Children
1920 Association Drive
Reston, VA 20191-1545
703-620-3660
888-232-7733
Fax: 703-264-9494
Membership and association news.

6 pages TriQuarterly

Ken Collins, Contact

4121 Fulbright News
Metro International Program Services of
New York
285 W Broadway
Room 450
New York, NY 10013-2269
212-431-1195
Fax: 212-941-6291
A four page newsletter distributed 5 times a
year to visiting Fulbright scholars in the
New York area. Contains a scholar profile,
information about activities, tips for living
in the United States, events in the New
York area, and relevant announcements.

4 pages

Kristen Pendleton, Publisher

4122 GED Items
Center for Adult Learning & Education
Credentials
1 Dupont Circle NW
Washington, DC 20036-1110
202-939-9490
Newsletter of the GED Testing Service
with articles focusing on adult education
programs, teaching tips, GED graduate

success stories and administration of GED
testing.

12 pages BiMonthly

4123 Gifted Child Society Newsletter
190 Rock Road
Glen Rock, NJ 07452-1736
201-444-6530
Fax: 201-444-9099
E-mail: admin@gifted.org
http://www.gifted.org
Provides educational enrichment and support for gifted children through national
advocacy and various programs.

Bi-Annual

Janet L Chen, Executive Director

4124 Harvard Education Letter
8 Story Street
5th Floor
Cambridge, MA 02138
617-495-3432
800-513-0763
Fax: 617-496-3584
E-mail: editor@edletter.org
http://www.edletter.org
Published by the Harvard Graduate School
of Education and reports on current research and innovative practice in PreK-12.

8 pages Bi-Monthly
ISSN: 8755-3716

Douglas Clayton, Publisher
David T Gordon, Editor

4125 Health in Action
American School Health Association
PO Box 708
Kent, OH 44240-0013
330-678-1601
800-445-2742
Fax: 330-678-4526
E-mail: asha@ashaweb.org
http://www.ashaweb.org

24 pages Quarterly
ISSN: 1540-2479

Tom Reed, Assistant Executive Director

**4126 Help! I'm in Middle School... How
Will I Survive?**
NRS Publications
1482 51st Road
Douglass, KS 67039
620-986-5472
E-mail: info@englishthrough.com
http://www.nsrpublications.com
The goal of NRS Publibcations is "the success of every child." We provide a varity of
books, educational games, posters, educational dice, overhead tiles, science kits, the
SHAPES parts of speech learning system
and creative play toys to help meet that
goal.

Merry L Gumm, President
Tanya L Hein, Vice President

**4127 Higher Education & National
Affairs**
American Council on Education
1 Dupont Circle NW
Suite 800
Washington, DC 20036-1132
202-939-9365
National newsletter with Capitol Hill and
Administration updates on issues that affect colleges and universities. Includes stories on the federal budget, student financial
aid, tax laws, Education Department regulations and research, legal issues and minorities in higher education.

Janetta Hammock, Contact

4128 History of Education Quarterly
Indian University
School of Education
Bloomington, IN 47405
812-855-9334
Fax: 812-855-3631
Discusses current and historical movements in education.

Quarterly

Amy Schutt, Editor

4129 Homeschooling Marketplace Newsletter
13106 Patrici Circle
Omaha, NE 68164
Offers information, strategies and tips for homeschooling.

Clarice Routh, Contact

4130 IDRA Newsletter
Intercultural Development Research Association
5835 Callaghan Road
Suite 350
San Antonio, TX 78228-1125
210-444-1710
Fax: 210-444-1714
E-mail: idra@txdirect.net
http://www.idra.org
Mini-journal covering topics in the education of minority, poor and language-minority students in public institutions. It provides research-based solutions and editorial materials for education.

Monthly

Maria Robledo Montecel, Executive Director

4131 IEA Reporter
Idaho Education Association
620 N 6th Street
Boise, ID 83702-5542
208-344-1341
Fax: 208-336-6967
http://www.idahoea.org

Quarterly

Diana Mikesell, VP
Kathy Phelan, President

4132 Inclusive Education Programs
LRP Publications
1901 N Moore Street
Suite 700
Arlington, VA 22209
703-516-7002
800-341-7874
Fax: 703-516-9313
E-mail: custserve@lrp.com
http://www.lrp.com
Newsletter covers the legal and practical issues of educating children with disabilities in regular education environments. It provides practical, how-to-advice, real life examples, and concise case summaries of the most recent judicial case laws.

Monthly
ISSN: 1076-8548

4133 Independent Scholar
National Coalition of Independent Scholars
PO Box 5743
Berkeley, CA 94705-0743
510-704-0990
A newsletter for independent scholars and their organizations.

Quarterly

Murray Wax, Contact

4134 Innovative Higher Education
Kluwer Academic/Human Sciences Press
233 Spring Street
New York, NY 10013
212-620-8000
800-221-9369
Fax: 212-463-0742
http://www.wkpa.nl
Provides educators and scholars with the latest creative strategies, programs and innovations designed to meet contemporary challenges in higher education. Professionals throughout the world contribute high-quality papers on the changing rules of vocational and liberal arts education, the needs of adults reentering the education process, and the reconciliation of faculty desires to economic realities, among other topics.

Quarterly
ISSN: 0742-5627

Carol Bischoff, Publisher
Ronald Simpson, Editor

4135 Insight
Independent Education Consultants Association
3251 Old Lee Highway
Suite 510
Fairfax, VA 22030-1504
703-591-4850
800-888-4322
Fax: 703-591-4860
E-mail: requests@IECAonline.com
http://www.IECAonline.com
Publication of national professional association of educational counselors working in private practice. Association provides counseling in college, secondary schools, learning disabilities and wilderness therapy programs.

Rebecca Peek, Author
Mark H Sklarow, Executive Director

4136 International Debates
Congressional Digest Corp.
4416 East West Highway
Suite 400
Bethesda, MD 20814-4568
301-634-3113
800-637-9915
Fax: 301-634-3189
E-mail: griff.thomas@pro-and-con.org
http://www.pro-and-con.org
An independent publication featuring global controversies in the United Nations and other international forums, pro and cons.

ISSN: 1542-0345

Delores Baisden, Assistant

4137 International Education
University of Tennessee
College of Education
Health & Human Services
Knoxville, TN 37996-3400
865-974-5252
Fax: 865-974-8718
E-mail: scarey@utk.edu
Publishes articles related to various international topics.

Publication Date: 1997 BiAnnual/Paperback
ISSN: 0160-5429

Sue Carey, Managing Editor

4138 International Journal of Qualitive Studies in Education
Sanchez 310
University of Texas at Austin
Austin, TX 78712
512-232-1552
Fax: 512-471-5975
E-mail: 8se@uts.cc.utexas.edu
http://www.tandF.co.uk/journals
Aims to enhance the theory of qualitative research in education.

6 Issues Per Year

Jim Scheurich, Editor
Angela Valenzuela, Editor

4139 International Volunteer
Volunteers for Peace
1034 Tiffany Road
Belmont, VT 05730-9988
802-259-2759
Fax: 802-259-2922
E-mail: vfp@vfp.org
http://www.vfp.org
Newsletter of Volunteers for Peace, which provides intercultural education and community services.

8 pages Annual

Peter Coldwell, Author

4140 It Starts in the Classroom
National School Public Relations Association
1501 Lee Highway
Suite 201
Arlington, VA 22209-1109
703-528-5840
Devoted to classroom and teacher public relations techniques and ideas.

8 pages Monthly

Joseph Scherer, Publisher
Judi Cowan, Editor

4141 Journal of Behavioral Education
Kluwer Academic/Human Sciences Press
233 Spring Street
New York, NY 10013
212-620-8000
800-221-9369
Fax: 212-463-0742
http://www.wkpa.nl
Provides the first single-source forum for the publication of research on the application of behavioral principles and technology to education. Publishes original empirical research and brief reports covering behavioral education in regular, special and adult education settings. Subject populations include handicapped, at-risk, and non-handicapped students of all ages.

Quarterly
ISSN: 1053-0819

Carol Bischoff, Publisher
Christopher Skinner, Co-Editor

4142 Journal of Creative Behavior
Creative Education Foundation
289 Bay Road
Hadley, MA 01035
413-559-6614
800-447-2774
Fax: 413-559-6615
E-mail: contact@creativeeducationfoundation.org
http://www.cef-cpsi.org
Devoted to the serious general reader with vocational/avocational interests in the fields of creativity and problem solving. Its articles are authored not only by established writers in the field, but by up-and coming contributors as well. The criteria for select-

ing articles include reference, clarity, interest and overall quality.

Quarterly

Grace A Guzzetta, Managing Editor
Mary Pokojowczyk, Circulation Manager

4143 Journal of Curriculum Theorizing

Colgate University
Department of Education
Hamilton, NY 13346
315-228-1000
Fax: 315-228-7998
Analyzes and provides insights to curriculum movements and evolution.

Quarterly

JoAnne Pagano, Editor

4144 Journal of Disability Policy Studies

Pro-Ed., Inc.
8700 Shoal Creek Boulevard
Austin, TX 78757-6816
512-451-3246
800-897-3202
Fax: 512-302-9129
E-mail: proed1@aol.com
http://www.proedinc.com
Devoted exclusively to disability policy topics and issues.

Quarterly Magazine
ISSN: 1044-2073

Craig R Fiedler, JD, PhD, Editor
Billie Jo Rylance, PhD, Editor

4145 Journal of Educational Research

Heldref Publications
1319 18th Street NW
Washington, DC 20036-1826
202-296-6267
800-365-9753
Fax: 202-296-5149
http://www.heldref.org
Since 1920, this journal has contributed to the advancement of educational practice in elementary and secondary schools. Authors experiment with new procedures, evaluate traditional practices, replicate previous research for validation and perform other work central to understanding and improving the education of today's students and teachers. This Journal is a valuable resource for teachers, counselors, supervisors, administrators, planners and educational researchers.

64 pages BiMonthly
ISSN: 0022-0671

Deborah Cohen, Promotions Editor

4146 Journal of Experimental Education

Heldref Publications
1319 18th Street NW
Washington, DC 20036-1826
202-296-6267
800-365-9753
Fax: 202-296-5149
E-mail: jxe@heldref.org
http://www.heldref.org
Aims to improve educational practice by publishing basic and applied research studies using the range of quantitative and qualitative methodologies found in the behavioral, cognitive and social sciences. Published studies address all levels of schooling, from preschool through graduate and professional education, and various educational context, including public and private education in the United States and abroad.

96 pages Quarterly

Paige Jackson, Managing Editor

4147 Journal of Law and Education

University of South Carolina Law School
Columbia, SC 29208
803-777-4155
Fax: 803-777-9405
A periodical offering information on the newest laws and legislation affecting education.

Quarterly

Eldon D Wedlock Jr, Editor

4148 Journal of Learning Disabilities

Pro-Ed., Inc.
8700 Shoal Creek Boulevard
Austin, TX 78757-6816
512-451-3246
800-897-3202
Fax: 512-302-9129
E-mail: proed1@aol.com
http://www.proedinc.com
Special series, feature articles and research articles.

Bi-Monthly Magazine
ISSN: 0022-2194

Wayne P Hresko, PhD, Editor-in-Chief

4149 Journal of Negro Education

Howard University
PO Box 311
Washington, DC 20059-0001
202-806-8120
Fax: 202-806-8434
E-mail: jne@howard.edu
A Howard University quarterly review of issues incident to the education of Black people; tracing educational developments and presenting research on issues confronting Black students in the US and around the world.

120+ pages Quarterly
ISSN: 0022-2984

D. Kamili Anderson, Associate Editor
Dr. Sylvia T. Johnson, Editor-in-Chief

4150 Journal of Positive Behavior Interventions

Pro-Ed., Inc.
8700 Shoal Creek Boulevard
Austin, TX 78757-6816
512-451-3246
800-897-3202
Fax: 512-302-9129
http://www.proedinc.com
Sound, research-based principles of positive behavior support for use in home, school and community settings for people with challenges in behavioral adaptation.

Glen Dunlap, PhD, Editor
Robert L Koegel, PhD, Editor

4151 Journal of Research and Development in Education

University of Georgia, College of Education
427 Tucker Hall
Athens, GA 30602
404-542-1154
A magazine offering insight and experimental and theoretical studies in education.

Quarterly

4152 Journal of Research in Character Education

Character Education Partnership
1025 Connecticut Avenue NW
Suite 1011
Washington, DC 20036
202-296-7743
800-988-8081
Fax: 202-296-7779
http://www.character.org

Andrea Grenadier, Director
Communications
Esther Schaeffer, CEO/Executive Director

4153 Journal of Research in Rural Education

University of Maine, College of Education
5766 Shibles Hall
Orono, ME 04469-5766
207-581-2493
Fax: 207-581-2423
http://www.umaine.edu
Publishes the results of educational research relevant to rural settings.

3x Year Journal

Theodore Coladarci, Editor
Sara Sheppard, Managing Editor

4154 Journal of School Health

American School Health Association
PO Box 708
Kent, OH 44240-0013
330-678-1601
800-445-2742
Fax: 330-678-4526
E-mail: asha@ashaweb.org
http://www.ashaweb.org
Contains material related to health promotion in school settings. A non-profit organization founded in 1927, ASHA's mission is to protect and improve the health and well-being of children and youth by supporting comprehensive, preschool-12 school health programs. ASHA and its 4,000 members (school nurses, health educators, and physicians) work to improve school health services and school health environments.

40 pages Monthly
ISSN: 0022-4391

Tom Reed, Assistant Executive Director

4155 Journal of Special Education

Pro-Ed., Inc.
8700 Shoal Creek Boulevard
Austin, TX 78757-6816
512-451-3246
800-897-3202
Fax: 512-302-9129
http://www.proedinc.com
Timely, sound special education research.

Lynn S Fuchs, PhD, Editor
Douglas Fuchs, PhD, Editor

4156 Journal of Urban & Cultural Studies

University of Massachusetts at Boston
Department of English
Harbor Campus
Boston, MA 02125
617-287-5760
Fax: 617-287-6511
Explores various issues in education that deal with urban and cultural affairs.

Donaldo Macedo, Editor

4157 Kaleidoscope
Evansville-Vanderburgh School
Corporation
1 SE 9th Street
Evansville, IN 47708-1821
812-435-8453
A staff publication for and about employees
of the Evansville-Vanderburgh School Corporation.

8 pages Monthly

Patti S Coleman, Contact

4158 LD Forum
Council for Learning Disabilities
PO Box 40303
Overland Park, KS 68204
913-492-8755
Fax: 913-492-2546
Provides updated information and research
on the activities of the Council for Learning
Disabilities.

60 pages Quarterly
ISSN: 0731-9487

4159 Learning Disability Quarterly
Council for Learning Disabilities
PO Box 40303
Overland Park, KS 66204-4303
913-492-8755
Fax: 913-492-2546
Aimed at learning disabled students, their
parents and educators. Accepts advertising.

Quarterly

**4160 Learning Point
MagazineLaboratory**
North Central Regional Educational
Laboratory
1900 Spring Road
Suite 300
Oak Brook, IL 60523-1447
630-649-6500
Fax: 630-649-6700
E-mail: info@ncrel.org
http://www.ncrel.org
Applies research and technology to learn-
ing.

16 pages Quarterly

Jeri Nowakowski, Director

**4161 Learning Unlimited Network of
Oregon**
31960 SE Chin Street
Boring, OR 97009-9708
503-663-5153
Cuts through all barriers to communication
and learning; institutional, personal, physical, psychological, spiritual. It focuses on
basic communication/language skills but
sets no limits on means or tools, subjects or
participants in seeking maximum balance
and productivity for all.

10 pages 9x Year

Gene Lehman, Contact

**4162 Let It Grow. Let It Grow. Let It
Grow. Hands-on Activities to
Explore the Planet Kingdom**
NSR Publications
1482 51st Road
Douglass, KS 67039
620-986-5472
E-mail: info@englishthrough.com
http://www.nsrpublications.com
The goal of NSR Publication is "the success
of every child." We provide a variety of
books, educational games, posters, educational dice, overhead tiles, science kits, the

SHAPES parts of speech learning system
and creative play toys to help meet that goal.

58 pages

Merry L Gumm, President
Tanya L Hein, Vice President

4163 Liaison Bulletin
National Assn. of State Directors of
Special Ed.
1800 Diagonal Road
Suite 320
Alexandria, VA 22314-2840
703-519-3800
Fax: 703-519-3808
Membership news for persons affiliated
with the National Association of State Di-
rectors of Special Education.

BiWeekly

Dr. William Schipper

4164 Liberal Education
Association of American Colleges &
Universities
1818 R Street NW
Washington, DC 20009-1604
202-387-3760
Fax: 202-265-9532
http://www.aacu-edu.org
Concentrates on issues currently affecting
American higher education. Promotes and
strengthens undergraduate curriculum,
classroom teaching and learning, collaborative leadership, faculty leadership, diversity. Other publications on higher education
include books, monographs, peer review,
and on campus with women.

64 pages Quarterly
ISSN: 0024-1822

Bridget Puzon, Editor
Debra Humphreys, Comm/Public Affairs
VP

4165 Link
AEL, Inc.
PO Box 1348
Charleston, WV 25325-1348
304-347-0400
800-624-9120
Fax: 304-347-0487
E-mail: aelinfo@ael.org
http://www.ael.org
A newsletter for educators providing re-
search summaries, education news, and
news of AEL products, services and events.

12 pages Quarterly Newsletter

Carolyn Luzader, Communications
Associate

4166 Lisle-Interaction
433 W Sterns Street
Temperance, MI 48182-9568
734-847-7126
800-477-1538
Fax: 512-259-0392
Reports on domestic and international programs, annual meetings and board meetings
of the Lisle Fellowship which seeks to
broaden global awareness and appreciation
of different cultures. Occasional special articles on topics such as racism, book reviews. News of members are also included.

16 pages Quarterly

Mark Kinney, Executive Director
Dianne Brause, VP

4167 MEA Today
Montana Education Association
1232 E 6th Avenue
Helena, MT 59601-3927
406-442-4250
Fax: 406-443-5081
National and state association news, legis-
lative policies, and classroom features.

8 pages Monthly

Nancy Robbins

**4168 Massachusetts Home Learning
Association Newsletter**
23 Mountain Street
Sharon, MA 02067-2234
781-784-8006
A source for information gleaned from all
the major national magazines and many
state newsletters. Calendar of events for
Massachusetts homeschooling and several
feature articles on legal, educational or fa-
milial issues.

24 pages Quarterly

Sharon Terry, Editor
Patrick Terry, Editor

4169 Mel Gabler's Newsletter
Educational Research Analysts
PO Box 7518
Longview, TX 75607-7518
972-753-5993
Educational information pertaining to cur-
ricula used in schools.

8 pages SemiAnnually

Mel Gabler, Publisher
Chad Rosenberger, Editor

4170 Minnesota Education Update
Office of Library Development & Services
440 Capital Square
550 Cedar Street
St. Paul, MN 55101
651-296-2821
Policies and activities in elementary and
secondary education in the state of Minnesota.

8 pages Monthly

James Lee

4171 Missouri Schools
Missouri Department of Education
PO Box 480
Jefferson City, MO 65102-0480
573-751-3469
Fax: 573-751-8613
State education policy.

28 pages BiMonthly

James L Morris

4172 Momentum
National Catholic Educational Association
1077 30th Street NW
Suite 100
Washington, DC 20007-3852
202-337-6232
Fax: 202-333-6706
http://www.ncea.org
The association offers a quarterly publication, conducts research, works with voluntary groups and government agencies on
educational problems, conducts seminars
and workshops for all levels of educators.

Quarterly

Catherine T McNamee, CSJ, President

4173 Montana Schools
Montana Office of Public Instruction
State Capitol
Helena, MT 59620
406-444-3095
Fax: 406-444-2893
Information about people and programs in
the Montana education system.

12 pages 5x Year
Ellen Meloy

4174 Montessori Observer
International Montessori Society
9525 Georgia Avenue
Suite 200
Silver Spring, MD 20910-4570
301-589-1127
800-301-3131
Fax: 301-589-0733
E-mail: havis@erols.com
http://http://imsmontessori.org
Provides news and information about Montessori education and the work of the International Montessori Society.

ISSN: 0889-5643
Lee Havis, Editor

4175 NAEIR Advantage
Nat'l Assn. for Exchange of Industrial
Resources
560 McClure Street
Galesburg, IL 61401-4286
309-343-0704
800-562-0955
Fax: 309-343-3519
E-mail: member.naeir@misslink.net
http://www.freegoods.com
News of the National Association for the
Exchange of Industrial Resources, which
collects donations of new excess inventory
from corporations and redistributes them
to American schools and nonprofits.

8 pages BiMonthly
Gary C Smith, President/CEO
Jack Zavada, Communications Director

4176 NAEN Bulletin
Nort American Association of Education
Negotiators
NAEN
PO Box 1068
Salem, OR 97308
503-588-2800
Fax: 503-588-2813
E-mail: naen@osba.org
http://www.naen.org
Association news and notes.

Members Only

4177 NAFSA Newsletter
NAFSA: Association of International
Educators
1875 Connecticut Avenue NW
8th Floor
Washington, DC 20009-5728
202-737-3699
800-836-4994
Fax: 202-737-3657
E-mail: inbox@nafsa.org
http://www.nafsa.org
Publishes news and information related to
international education and exchange.

40 pages Weekly & Quarterly
Marlene M Johnson, Director/CEO

4178 NAPSEC News
Assn. of Private Schools for Exceptional
Children
1522 K Street NW
Suite 1032
Washington, DC 20005-1202
202-408-3338
Fax: 202-408-3340
Association news and events.

8-12 pages Quarterly
Sherry L Kolbe, Executive Director/CEO
Barb DeGroot, Manager

4179 NEA Higher Education Advocate
National Education Association (NEA)
1201 16th Street NW
Washington, DC 20036-3207
202-822-7364
Fax: 202-822-7624
E-mail: ncuea@nea.org
http://www.nea.org
Reports on NEA and general higher educa-
tion news.

4 pages Monthly
Alicia Sandoual, Publisher
Rebecca Robbins, Editor

4180 NEA Today
National Education Association (NEA)
1201 16th Street NW
Washington, DC 20036-3290
202-822-7364
Fax: 202-822-7624
E-mail: ncuea@nea.org
http://www.nea.org
Contains news and features of interest to
classroom teachers and other employees of
schools.

8x Year
Bill Fischer, Editor
Suzanne Wade, Advertising Coordinator

4181 NEWSLINKS
International Schools Services
15 Roszel Road
Princeton, NJ 08540-6248
609-452-0990
Fax: 609-452-2690
E-mail: newslinks@iss.edu
http://www.iss.edu
Regularly published newspaper of International Schools Services that is distributed
free of charge to overseas teachers, school
administrators and libraries, US universities, educational organizations, multinational corporations, school supply
companies and educational publishers.

32-40 pages Quarterly
Judy Seltz, Director Communications

4182 NJEA Review
New Jersey Education Association
180 W State Street
PO Box 1211
Trenton, NJ 08607
609-599-4561
Fax: 609-392-6321
Monthly educational journal of the New
Jersey Education Association which focuses on educational news and issues related to New Jersey public schools. Its
readers are active and retired teaching staff
members and support staff, administrators,
board members, teacher education students, and others in New Jersey public
schools and colleges.

80 pages Monthly
ISSN: 0027-6758
Martha O DeBlieu, Editor
Rosemary Kaub, Conference Manager

4183 NREA News
National Rural Education Association
Education Room 246
Fort Collins, CO 80523-0001
Fax: 970-491-1317
E-mail: jnewlin@lamar.colostate.edu
http://www.colostate.edu
Keeps all members up-to-date on Associa-
tion activities, events, rural education con-
ferences and meetings, and research
projects in progress.

8 pages Quarterly Newsletter
ISSN: 0273-4460
Joseph T Newlin, Editor

**4184 National Accrediting Commission
of Cosmetology, Arts and Sciences**
National Accrediting Commission of
Cosmetology
901 N Stuart Street
Suite 900
Arlington, VA 22203-1816
703-527-7600
Fax: 703-379-2200
E-mail: naccas@naccas.org
http://www.naccas.org
Information on accreditation, cosmetology
schools and any federal regulations affecting accreditation and postsecondary education.

20 pages 6x Year
Clifford A Culbreath, Editor

**4185 National Alliance of Black School
Educators (NABSE)**
2816 Georgia Avenue NW
Washington, DC 20001-3819
202-483-1549
800-221-2654
Fax: 202-608-6319
E-mail: nabse@nabse.org
http://www.nabse.org
For teachers, principals, specialists, superintendents, school board members and
higher education personnel.

15-25 pages 3x Year

**4186 National Homeschool Association
Newsletter**
National Homeschool Association
PO Box 290
Hartland, MI 48353-0290
425-432-1544
Information on what's happening in the
homeschooling community.

28 pages Quarterly

4187 National Monitor of Education
CA Monitor of Education
1331 Fairmount Avenue
Suite 61
El Cerrito, CA 94530
510-527-4430
Fax: 510-528-9833
E-mail: jsod@aol.com
http://www.e-files.org
Supports traditional moral and academic
values in education. Reports on litigation
and reviews various education publications. Issues reported on include parents'
rights and movement to restore basic academics.

8 pages Bi-Monthly/Paperback
Susan O'Donnell, Publisher
Susan Sweet, Newsletter Design

4188 New Hampshire Educator
National Education Association, New Hampshire
103 N State Street
Concord, NH 03301-4334
603-224-7751
Fax: 603-224-2648
Reports on the advancements in education in the state and nation and promotes the welfare of educators.
10 pages Monthly
Carol Carstarphen

4189 New Images
METCO
55 Dimock Street
Boston, MA 02119-1029
617-427-1545
Mailed to METCO parents and educational institutions local and national.
4 pages Quarterly
JM Mitchell

4190 New York Teacher
New York State United Teachers
PO Box 15008
Albany, NY 12212-5008
518-213-6000
800-342-9810
Fax: 518-213-6415
Edited primarily for teaching personnel in elementary, intermediate and high schools and colleges. News and features cover organizations' development, progress of legislation affecting education at local state and national levels and news of the labor movement.
BiWeekly
Nicki Rhue, Advertising Director
Bob Fitzpatrick, Production Manager

4191 News N' Notes
NTID at Rochester Institute of Technology
LBJ 2264
Box 9687
Rochester, NY 14623
716-475-6201
Convention news, membership information, education legislation advocacy and personal contributions to the scholarly society.
12 pages Quarterly
Judy Egleston

4192 Non-Credit Learning News
Learning for All Seasons
6 Saddle Club Road
#579X
Lexington, MA 02420-2115
781-861-0379
Marketing information for directors and marketers of non-credit programs.
8 pages 10x Year
Susan Capon

4193 Notes from the Field
Jessie Ball duPont Fund
One Dependent Drive
Suite 1400
Jacksonville, FL 32202-5011
904-353-0890
800-252-3452
Fax: 904-353-3870
E-mail: contactus@dupontfund.org
http://www.dupontfund.org
Provides information on the various organizations and institutes the Jessie Ball duPont Fund reaches out to every year.
3x

4194 Occupational Programs in California Community Colleges
Leo A Myer Associates/LAMA Books
2381 Sleepy Hollow Avenue
Hayward, CA 94545
510-785-1091
888-452-6244
Fax: 510-785-1099
E-mail: lama@lmabooks.com
http://www.lamabooks.com
Writers and publishers of HVAC books.
186 pages Bi-Annually
ISBN: 0-88069
Steve Meyer, President

4195 Our Children: The National PTA Magazine
330 N Wabash Avenue
Suite 2100
Chicago, IL 60611-3603
312-670-6782
Fax: 312-670-6783
http://www.pta.org
Written by, for and about the National PTA. A nonprofit organization of parents, educators, students, and other citizens active in their schools and communities.
5x Year
Douglas Seibold, Editor
Laura Martinelli, Graphic Designer

4196 PTA National Bulletin
National Association of Hebrew Day School PTA'S
160 Broadway
New York, NY 10038-4201
212-227-1000
Fax: 212-406-6934
Educational events in day school relating to PTA movement. News of national and regional groups.
Quarterly

4197 PTA in Pennsylvania
Pennsylvania PTA
4804 Derry Street
Harrisburg, PA 17111-3440
717-564-8985
Fax: 717-564-9046
E-mail: info@papta.org
http://www.papta.org
Topical articles about issues affecting education and children, such as safety and health, AIDS, parents involvement and guidance, environmental concerns and special education.
24 pages Quarterly
ISSN: 1072-3242
250 attendees and 40-50 exhibits
Peg Fallon, Executive Director
Mary Hess, Membership Coordinator

4198 Parents as Teachers National Center
2228 Ball Drive
Saint Louis, MO 63146
314-432-4330
Fax: 314-432-8963
E-mail: patnc@patnc.org
http://www.patnc.org
Provides information, training and technical assistance for those interested in adopting the home-school-community partnership program. Offers parents the information and support needed to give their children the best possible start in life.
Quarterly
Julie Robbens, Editor, Author
Susan S Stepleton, President/CEO
Cheryl Dyle-Palmer, Director Operations

4199 Passing Marks
San Bernadino City Unified School District
777 N F Street
San Bernardino, CA 92410-3017
909-381-1250
Fax: 909-388-1451
Educational resume of school activities, covering instruction, personnel, administration, board of education, etc.
12 pages Monthly
Jan Bell

4200 Pennsylvania Home Schoolers Newsletter
RR 2 Box 117
Kittanning, PA 16201-9311
724-783-6512
Fax: 724-783-6512
A support newsletter directed to homeschooling families in Pennsylvania. Articles, reviews of curriculum, advice, calendar, support group listing, children's writing section.
32 pages Quarterly
Howard Richman, Publisher
Susan Richman, Editor

4201 Pennsylvania State Education Association
400 N 3rd Street
Harrisburg, PA 17101-1346
717-255-7000
Fax: 717-255-7124
http://www.psea.org
16 pages 9x Year
ISSN: 0896-6605
William H Johnson, Editor

4202 Phi Delta Kappa Educational Foundation
PO Box 789
Bloomington, IN 47402-0789
812-339-1156
800-766-1156
Fax: 812-339-0018
E-mail: information@pdkintl.org
http://www.pdkintl.org
Articles concerned with educational research, service, and leadership; issues, trends and policy are emphazied.
350 pages 10x Year
ISBN: 0-87367-835-4
November
600 attendees and 30 exhibits
Perry A. Zirkel, Author
William Bushaw, Executive Director
Donovan Walling, Director Publications

4203 Planning for Higher Education
Society for College and University Planning (SCUP)
399 East Liberty Street
Suite 300
Ann Arbor, MI 48104
734-998-7832
Fax: 734-998-6532
E-mail: info@scup.org
http://www.scup.org/phe
A quarterly, peer-reviewed journal devoted to the advancement and application of the best planning practices for colleges and universities.
70+ pages Quarterly Journal
ISSN: 0736-0983
July
150 booths with 1,200 attendees and 150 exhibits
Tom Longin, Executive Editor
Chantelle Neumann, Managing Editor

4204 Policy & Practice
American Public Human Services
Association
810 1st Street NE
Suite 500
Washington, DC 20002-4207
202-682-0100
Fax: 202-289-6555
http://www.aphsa.org
This quarterly magazine presents a comprehensive look at issues important to public human services administrators. It also features a wide spectrum of views by the best thinkers in social policy.

52 pages Quarterly
ISSN: 1520-801X
Sybil Walker Barnes, Editor

4205 Population Educator
Population Connection
1400 16th Street NW
Suite 320
Washington, DC 20036-2215
202-332-2200
800-767-1956
Fax: 202-332-2302
E-mail:
poped@populationconnection.org
http://www.populationeducation.org
Offers population education news, classroom activities and workshop schedules for grades K-12.

4 pages Quarterly
Pamela Wasseman

4206 Public Education Alert
Public Education Association
39 W 32nd Street
New York, NY 10001-3803
212-868-1640
Fax: 212-302-0088
E-mail: info@peaonline.org
http://www.pea-online.org
Provides information and consumer-oriented analysis of law policy issues and current developments in New York City public education. PEA Alert back issues; e-guide to New York City's public high school offering comparative data.

Ray Domanico, Publisher
Jessica Wolfe, Editor

4207 QEG
Friends Council on Education
1507 Cherry Street
Philadelphia, PA 19102-1403
215-241-7245
Informal news sheet for Quaker schools.

4 pages BiMonthly
Irene McHenry

**4208 QUIN: Quarterly University
International News**
University of Minnesota, Office in
Education
149 Nicholson Hall
Minneapolis, MN 55455
612-625-1915
Fax: 612-624-6839
International campus update for students, faculty, staff and the community.

TriQuarterly
Gayla Marty

4209 Reclaiming Children and Youth
Pro-Ed., Inc.
8700 Shoal Creek Boulevard
Austin, TX 78757-6816
512-451-3246
800-897-3202
Fax: 512-302-9129
E-mail: proed1@aol.com
http://www.proedinc.com
Provides positive, creative solutions to professionals serving youth in conflict.

Quarterly Magazine
Nicholas J Long, PhD, Editor
Larry K Brendtro, PhD, Editor

4210 Recognition Review
Awards and Recognition Association
4700 W Lake Avenue
Glenview, IL 60025
847-375-4800
Fax: 877-734-9380
E-mail: rbloch@accessgroup.com
http://www.ara.org
Published monthly by the Awards and Recognition Association. Recognition Review is the leading voice of the awards, engraving and recognition industry.

Monthly
Stacy McTaggert, Editor

4211 Regional Spotlight
Southern Regional Education Board
592 10th Street NW
Atlanta, GA 30318-5776
404-875-9211
News of educational interest directed to 15 SREB-member states.

9 pages
Margaret Sullivan

4212 Remedial and Special Education
Pro-Ed., Inc.
8700 Shoal Creek Boulevard
Austin, TX 78757-6816
512-451-3246
800-897-3202
Fax: 512-302-9129
E-mail: proed1@aol.com
http://www.proedinc.com
Highest-quality interdisciplinary scholarship that bridges the gap between theory and practice involving the education of individuals for whom typical instruction is not effective.

Bi-Monthly Magazine
ISSN: 0741-9325
Edward A Polloway, EdD,
Editor-in-Chief

4213 Renaissance Educator
Renaissance Educational Associates
4817 N County Road 29
Loveland, CO 80538-9515
970-679-4300
Quarterly publication highlighting educators around the world who are revealing the effectiveness of integrity in education.

8 pages Quarterly
Kristy Clark

4214 Research in Higher Education
Kluwer Academic/Human Sciences Press
233 Spring Street
New York, NY 10013
212-620-8000
800-221-9369
Fax: 212-463-0742
http://www.wkpa.nl
Essential source of new information for all concerned with the functioning of postsecondary educational institutions. Publishes original, quantitative research articles which contribute to an increased understanding of an institution, aid faculty in making more informed decisions about current or future operations, and improve the efficiency of an institution.

Bimonthly
ISSN: 0361-0365
Carol Bischoff, Publisher
John C Smart, Editor

4215 Research in the Schools
Mid-South Educational Research
Association
University of Alabama
Tuscaloosa, AL 35487-0001
Fax: 205-348-6873
A nationally refereed journal sponsored by the Mid-South Educational Research Association and the University of Alabama. RITS publishes original contributions in the following areas: 1) Research in practice; 2) Topical Articles; 3) Methods and Techniques; 4) Assessment and 5) Other topics of interest dealing with school-based research. Contributions should follow the guidelines in the latest edition of the Publications Manual of the American Psychological Association.

James E McLean, Co-Editor
Alan S Kaufman, Co-Editor

**4216 Roeper Review: A Journal on
Gifted Education**
Roeper Institute
PO Box 329
Bloomfield Hills, MI 48303-0329
248-203-7321
Fax: 248-203-7310
E-mail: tcross@bsu.edu
http://www.roeperreview.org
A journal that focuses on gifted and talented education, the Roeper Review applies the highest standards of peer review journalism to cover a broad range of issues. For professionals who work with teachers and for professionals who work directly with gifted and talented children and their families, the journal provides readable coverage of policy issues. Each issue covers one or more subjects. Regular departments include research reports and book reviews.

60-80 pages Quarterly
ISSN: 0278-3193
Tracy L Cross PhD, Editor
Vicki Rossbach, Subsciption

**4217 Rural Educator: Journal for Rural
and Small Schools**
National Rural Education Association
246 E Ed Building
Colorado State University
Fort Collins, CO 80523-1588
970-491-7022
Fax: 970-491-1317
E-mail: jnewlin@lamar.colostate.edu
http://www.colostate.edu
Official journal of the NREA. A nationally recognized publication that features timely and informative articles written by leading rural educators from all levels of education. All NREA members are encouraged to submit research articles and items of general information for publication.

40 pages TriAnnual
Joseph T Newlin, Editor

4218 SKOLE: A Journal of Alternative Education
Down-To-Earth Books
72 Philip Street
Albany, NY 12202-1729
518-432-1578
Publishes articles, poems, and research by people engaged in alternative education.
200 pages SemiAnnually
Mary Leue

4219 SNEA Impact: The Student Voice of the Teaching Profession
National Education Association (NEA)
1201 16th Street NW
Washington, DC 20036-3207
202-822-7131
Fax: 202-822-7624
Offers articles and views on current events and the educational system through students' eyes for education professionals.
7x Year

4220 Safety Forum
Safety Society
1900 Association Drive
Reston, VA 20191-1502
703-476-3440
Offers articles and up-to-date information on school safety.
4 pages TriQuarterly
Linda Moore

4221 School Bus Fleet
Bobit Business Media
3520 Challenger Street
Torrance, CA 90503
310-533-2400
Fax: 310-533-2512
E-mail: sbf@bobit.com
http://www.schoolbusfleet.com
Coverage of federal vehicle and education regulations that affect pupil transportation, policy and management issues and, of course, how to improve the safety of children riding yellow buses. Special sections include how to transport students with disabilities, a state report on regulations and legislation, and various other departments. School officials that manage finance operations at school districts, private contractors, school bus manufacturers are the audience.
Frank Di Giacomo, Publisher
Steve Hirano, Editor/Associate Publisher

4222 School Foodservice & Nutrition
1600 Duke Street
Floor 7
Alexandria, VA 22314-3421
703-739-3900
800-877-8822
Fax: 703-739-3915
For foodservice professionals presenting current articles on industry issues, management events, legislative issues, public relations programs and professional development news.
11x Year
Adrienne Gall Tufts, Editor

4223 School Law Bulletin
Quinlan Publishing
23 Drydock Avenue
Boston, MA 02210-2336
617-542-0048
Covers cases and laws pertaining to schools.
8 pages Monthly

4224 School Safety
National School Safety Center
141 Duesenberg Drive
Suite 11
Westlake Village, CA 91362-3815
805-373-9977
800-453-7461
Fax: 805-373-9277
E-mail: rstephens@nssc1.org
http://www.nssc1.org
For educators, law enforcers, judges and legislators on the prevention of drugs, gangs, weapons, bullying, discipline problems and vandalism; also on-site security and character development as they relate to students and schools.
Monthly
Dr. Ronald D Stephens, Executive Director
June Lane Arnette, Editor

4225 School Transportation News
STN Media Company Inc.
700 Torrance Boulevard
Suite C
Redondo Beach, CA 90277
310-792-2226
Fax: 310-792-2231
E-mail: bpaul@stnonline.com
http://www.stnonline.com
Covers school district and contractor fleets, special needs and prekindergarten transportation, Head Start, and more on a monthly basis. Reports developments affecting public school transportation supervisors and directors, state directors of school transportation, school bus contractors, special needs transportation, Head Start transportation, private school transportation, school business officials responsible for transportation and industry suppliers.
Magazine/Monthly
100 booths
Bill Paul, Author
Colette Paul, VP
Bill Paul, Publisher/Editor

4226 School Zone
West Aurora Public Schools, District 129
80 S River Street
#14
Aurora, IL 60506-5178
630-844-4400
Informs the community of what is happening in their schools, with their students, and with their tax dollars.
4 pages 5x Year
Laurel Chivari

4227 Shaping the Future
Lutheran Education Association
7400 Augusta Street
River Forest, IL 60305-1402
708-209-3343
Fax: 708-209-3458
E-mail: lea@lea.org
http://www.lea.org
Newsletter for LEA members to focus on the unique spiritual and professional needs of church workers and to celebrate life in the ministry. Resource information for the organization, upcoming events, encouragement for pre-planning.
Dr. Johnathan Laabs, Contact

4228 Sharing Space
Creative Urethanes, Children's Creative Response
PO Box 271
Nyack, NY 10960-0271
845-358-4601

Trains all those working with children to communicate positivity and cooperation.
12 pages TriAnnually

4229 Southwest Educational Development Laboratory Letter
211 E 7th Street
Austin, TX 78701-3218
512-476-6861
800-476-6861
Fax: 512-476-2286
E-mail: whoover@sedl.org
http://www.sedl.org
32 pages Tri-Annually
Lesile A Blair, Editor, Author

4230 Special Education Leadership
LifeWay Church Resources
One LifeWay Plaza
Nashville, TN 37234
615-251-2000
Fax: 615-251-5933
Covers special education issues relating to religious education.
52 pages Quarterly
Ben Garner, Editor-in-Chief
Ellen Beene, Editor

4231 Special Educator
LRP Publications
1901 N Moore Street
Suite 700
Arlington, VA 22209
703-516-7002
800-341-7874
Fax: 703-516-9313
E-mail: custserve@lrp.com
http://www.lrp.com
Covers important issues in the field of special education, including such topics as law and administrative policy.
22 pages 22 Issues Per Year
ISSN: 1047-1618

4232 Star News
Jefferson Center for Character Education
PO Box 1283
Monrovia, CA 91017-1283
949-770-7602
Fax: 949-450-1100
Mission is to produce and promote programs to teach children the concepts, skills and behavior of good character, common core values, personal and civic responsibility, workforce readiness and citizenship.
Quarterly
Robert Jamieson, CEO
Sharon McClenahan, Administrative Assistant

4233 Statewise: Statistical & Research Newsletter
State Board of Education, Planning & Research
PO Box 1402
Dover, DE 19903-1402
302-736-4601
Fax: 302-739-4654
Statistical data relating to Delaware public schools.
2 pages

4234 Street Scenes
(APO Street College of Education
610 W 112th Street
New York, NY 10025-1898
212-222-6700
Fax: 212-222-6700

New ideas in education.

8 pages SemiAnnually

Renee Creange

4235 Supreme Court Debates
Congressional Digest Corp.
4416 East West Highway
Suite 400
Bethesda, MD 20814-4568
301-634-3113
800-637-9915
Fax: 301-634-3189
E-mail: griff.thomas@pro-and-con.org
http://www.pro-and-con.org
An independent publication featuring controversies before the U.S. Supreme Court, pro-and-con.

ISSN: 1099-5390

Delores Baisden, Assistant

4236 Teacher$ Talk
Teachers Insurance and Annuity
Association
730 3rd Avenue
New York, NY 10017-3206
212-490-9000
Fax: 800-914-8922
Offers timely information and helpful hints about savings, investments, finance and insurance for teachers and educators.

Quarterly

Robert D Williams, Editor

4237 Telluride Newsletter
217 W Avenue
Ithaca, NY 14850-3980
607-273-5011
Fax: 607-272-2667
News of interest to alumni of Telluride Association sponsored programs.

8 pages TriQuarterly

Eric Lemer

4238 Tennessee Education
University of Tennessee
College of Education
Knoxville, TN 37996-0001
865-974-5252
Fax: 865-974-8718
E-mail: scarey@utk.edu
Publishes articles on topics related to K through higher education.

BiAnnually
ISSN: 0739-0408

Sue Carey, Editor

4239 Tennessee School Board Bulletin
Tennessee School Boards Association
500 13th Avenue N
Nashville, TN 37203-2884
Articles of interest to boards of education.

6 pages

Daniel Tollett, Publisher
Holly Hewitt, Editor

4240 The Sounds and Spelling Patterns of English: PHonics for Teachers and Parents
Oxton House Publishers, LLC
Po Box 209
Farmington, ME 04938
207-779-1923
800-539-7323
Fax: 207-779-0623
E-mail: info@oxtonhouse.com
http://www.oxtonhouse.com
A clear, concise, practical, jargon-free overview of the sounds that make up the

English language and the symbols that we use to represent them in writing. It includes a broad range of strategies for helping beginning readers develop fluent decoding skills.

62 pages

William Berlinghoff, Managing Editor
Bobby Brown, Marketing Director

4241 Theory Into Practice
Ohio State University, College of
Education
122 Ramseyer Hall
29 W Woodruff Avenue
Columbus, OH 43210
614-292-3407
Fax: 614-292-7900
E-mail: tip@osu.edu
http://www.coe.ohio-state.edu
Nationally recognized for excellence in educational journalism; thematic format, providing comprehensive discussion of single topic with many diverse points of view.

Quarterly
ISSN: 0040-5841

Anita Woolfolk Hey, Author
Anita Woolfolk Hey, Editor

4242 This Active Life
National Education Association (NEA)
1201 16th Street NW
Washington, DC 20036-3207
202-822-7125
Fax: 202-822-7624
http://www.nea.org/retired
Serves as a resource in the maintenance of quality public education.

20 pages Bi-Monthly
ISSN: 1526-9342

John O'Neil, Editor

4243 Three R'S for Teachers: Research, Reports & Reviews
Master Teacher
Po Box 1207
Manhattan, KS 66502
785-539-0555
800-669-9633
Fax: 800-669-1132
http://www.masterteacher.com
The publication that synthesizes the most recent educational research, data and trends on specific topics for teachers.

Quarterly

Alice King, Executive Editor

4244 Tidbits
Assn. for Legal Support of Alternative
Schools
PO Box 2823
Santa Fe, NM 87504-2823
505-471-6928
Information and legal advice to those involved in non-public educational facilities.

12 pages Quarterly

Ed Nagel

4245 Transitions Abroad: The Guide to Learning, Living, & Working Abroad
Transitions Abroad
PO Box 745
Bennington, VT 05201
802-442-4827
Fax: 802-442-4827
E-mail: editor@transitionsabroad.com
http://www.transitionsabroad.com

This magazine contains articles and bibliographies on travel, study, teaching, internships and work abroad.

Bi-Monthly

4246 Unschoolers Network
2 Smith Street
Farmingdale, NJ 07727-1006
732-938-2473
Information and support for families teaching their children at home.

14 pages Monthly

Nancy Plent

4247 VSBA Newsletter
Vermont School Boards Association
2 Prospect Street
Montpelier, VT 05602-3555
802-223-3580
General information.

16 pages Monthly

Donald Jamieson

4248 WCER Highlights
Wisconsin Center for Education Research
1025 W Johnson Street
Suite 785
Madison, WI 53706-1706
608-263-8814
Fax: 608-263-6448
News about research conducted at the Wisconsin Center for Education Research.

8 pages Quarterly
ISSN: 1073-1882

Paul Baker, Editor

4249 WestEd: Focus
WestEd
730 Harrison Street
San Francisco, CA 94107-1242
415-615-3144
877-493-7833
Fax: 415-512-2024
E-mail: info@WestEd .org
http://www.WestEd.org
Improving education through research, development and service.

Mark Kerr, Manager of Organizational
Danny Torres, Publications Manager

4250 Western Journal of Black Studies
Washington State University
Heritage House
Pullman, WA 99164-0001
509-335-8681
Fax: 509-335-8338
A journal which canvasses topical issues affecting Black studies and education.

Quarterly

Talmadge Anderson, Editor

4251 World Gifted
World Council for Gifted & Talented
Children
Purdue University
1446 S Campus
West Lafayette, IN 47907
Offers information and articles on gifted education for the professional.

4252 Young Audiences Newsletter
115 E 92nd Street
New York, NY 10128-1688
212-831-8110
Fax: 212-289-1202

Organization news of performing arts education programs in schools and communities.

Annual

Jane Bak

Periodicals: Administration

4253 AACRAO Data Dispenser

American Association of Collegiate Registrars
1 Dupont Circle NW
Suite 330
Washington, DC 20036-1137
202-293-9161
Fax: 202-872-8857
Association newsletter for US and foreign postsecondary education institution professionals involved in admissions, records and registration.

12 pages 10x Year

Eileen Kennedy

4254 AASA Bulletin

American Association of School Administrators
801 N Quincy Street
Suite 700
Arlington, VA 22203-1730
703-528-0700
Fax: 703-841-1543
E-mail: info@aasa.org
http://www.aasa.org
The AASA Bulletin is a supplement to The School Administrator. It contains the Job Bulletin and information for school leaders about the many products, services and events available to them from AASA.

Ginger O'Neil, Editor
Kari Arfstrom, Project Director

4255 ACCT Advisor

Association of Community College Trustees
1233 20th Street NW
Suite 605
Washington, DC 20036-2907
202-775-4667
Fax: 202-223-1297
http://www.acct.org
Provides news of association events, federal regulations, activities, state activities, legal issues and other news of interest to community college governing board members.

Ray Taylor, ACCT President
Alvin Major II, Director Mktg/Communications

4256 AVA Update

Association for Volunteer Administration
PO Box 4584
Boulder, CO 80306-4584
303-447-0558
Information of value to administrators of volunteer services.

4 pages BiMonthly

Martha Martin

4257 Accreditation Fact Sheet

NAPNSC Accrediting Commission for Higher Education
182 Thompson Road
Grand Junction, CO 81503-2246
970-243-5441
Fax: 970-242-4392
E-mail: director@napnsc.org
http://www.napnsc.org
Newsletter reporting on the origin, history, developments, procedures and changes of educational institution accreditation.

Annually

H. Earl Heusser, Author
H Earl Heusser, Executive Director

4258 Administrative Information Report

Nat'l Association of Secondary School Principles
1904 Association Drive
Reston, VA 20191-1502
703-860-0200
800-253-7746
Fax: 703-620-6534
Offers school statistics and administrative updates for secondary school principals and management officers.

4 pages Monthly

Thomas Koerner

4259 American School & University Magazine

Intertec Publishing
PO Box 12960
Overland Park, KS 66282-2960
913-967-1960
Fax: 913-967-1905
Directed at business and facilities administrators in the nation's public and private schools.

Monthly

Joe Agron, Editor

4260 American School Board Journal

National School Boards Association
1680 Duke Street
Alexandria, VA 22314-3455
703-838-6722
Fax: 703-549-6719
E-mail: editor@asbj.com
Published primarily for school board members and school system superintendents serving public elementary and secondary schools in the United States and Canada.

Monthly

Anne L Bryant, Executive Publisher
Harold P Seamon, Deputy Executive Publisher

4261 Board

Master Teacher
Leadership Lane
PO Box 1207
Manhattan, KS 66502
800-669-9633
Fax: 800-669-1132
http://www.masterteacher.com
Designed to be a continuous form of communication to help board members know and understand the duties, responsibilities, and commitments of the office; view the superintendent of schools as the educational leader; improve administrator-board working relationships; better understand the purpose of education; and work at their responsibilities in a prudent, calm, and rational manner.

Monthly

Robert DeBruyn, Editor

4262 Building Leadership Bulletin

2990 Baker Drive
Springfield, IL 62703-2800
217-525-1383
Fax: 217-525-7264
http://www.ipa.vsta.net
Topical, timely issues.

8 pages 11x Year

Julie Weichert, Associate Director

4263 Business Education Forum

National Business Education Association
1914 Association Drive
Reston, VA 20191-1538
703-860-8300
Fax: 703-620-4483
A journal of distinctive articles dealing with current issues and trends, future directions and exemplary programs in business education at all instructional levels. Articles focus on international business, life-long learning, cultural diversity, critical thinking, economics, state-of-the-art technology and the latest research in the field.

200 pages Quarterly

Janet M Treichel, Executive Director
Regina McDowell, Editor

4264 CASE Currents

1307 New York Avenue NW
Suite 1000
Washington, DC 20036-1226
202-328-2273
Fax: 202-387-4973
Covers the world of fund raising, alumni administration, public relations, periodicals, publications and student recruitment in higher education.

10x Year

Karla Taylor, Editor

4265 CASE Newsletter

The Council for Exceptional Children
1920 Association Drive
Reston, VA 20191-1545
703-620-3660
888-232-7733
Fax: 703-264-9494
News about CASE activities, upcoming events, current trends and practices, state and national legislation, and other practical information relevant to the administration of special education programs.

5x Year

Jo Thomason

4266 CASE in Point

The Council for Exceptional Children
1920 Association Drive
Reston, VA 20191-1545
703-620-3660
888-232-7733
Fax: 703-264-9494
A journal reporting on emerging promising practices, current research, contact points for expanded information, and field-based commentary relevant to the administration of special education programs.

BiAnnual

Donnie Evans, Editor

4267 California Schools Magazine

California School Boards Association
3100 Beacon Boulevard
West Sacramento, CA 95691
916-371-4691
Fax: 916-372-3369
For school board members, superintendents and school business managers, responsible for the operation of California's public

schools. Articles of interest to parents, teachers, community members and anyone else concerned with public education.

20 pages Quarterly
ISSN: 1081-8936

Mina G Fasulo, Executive Editor

4268 Clearing House: A Journal of Educational Research

Heldref Publications
1319 18th Street NW
Washington, DC 20036-1826
202-296-6267
800-365-9753
Fax: 202-296-5149
E-mail: tch@heldfred.org
Each issue offers a variety of articles for teachers and administrators of middle schools and junior and senior high schools. It includes experiments, trends and accomplishments in courses, teaching methods, administrative procedures and school programs.

4 pages BiMonthly
ISSN: 0009-8655

Deborah N Cohen, Promotions Manager
Judy Cusick, Managing Editor

4269 Connection

National Association of State Boards of Education
277 S Washington Street
Suite 100
Alexandria, VA 22314
703-684-4000
Fax: 703-836-2313
Quarterly magazine for state board of education members.

10 pages

David Kysilko, Editor

4270 Developer

National Staff Development Council
PO Box 240
Oxford, OH 45056-0240
513-523-6029
Fax: 513-523-0638
Devoted to staff development for educational personnel.

8 pages 10x Year

Dennis Sparks

4271 ERS Spectrum

Educational Research Service
2000 Clarendon Boulevard
Arlington, VA 22201-2908
703-243-2100
800-791-9308
Fax: 703-243-1985
E-mail: editor@ers.org
http://www.ers.org
A quarterly journal of school research and information. Publishes practical research and information for school decisions. Authors include practicing administrators and other educators in local school districts.

48 pages Quarterly
ISSN: 0740-7874

Deborah Perkins-Gough, Editor-in-Chief, Editor

4272 Education Daily

LRP Publications
1901 N Moore Street
Suite 1106
Arlington, VA 22209
703-516-7002
800-341-7874
Fax: 703-516-9313
E-mail: custserve@lrp.com
http://www.lrp.com
News on national education policy. Offers daily reports of Education Department policies, initiatives and priorities— how they are developed and how they affect school programs.

6-8 pages Daily

4273 Educational Administration Quarterly

University of Wisconsin, Milwaukee
PO Box 413
Milwaukee, WI 53201-0413
414-229-4740
Fax: 414-229-5300
Deals with administrative issues and policy.

Quarterly

Dr. James Cibulka, Editor

4274 Electronic Learning

Scholastic
555 Broadway
New York, NY 10012-3919
212-343-6100
800-724-6527
Fax: 212-343-4801
Published for the administrative level, education professionals who are directly responsible for the implementing of electronic technology at the district, state and university levels.

8x Year

Lynn Diamond, Advertising Director
Therese Mageau, Editor

4275 Enrollment Management Report

LRP Publications
1901 N Moore Street
Suite 700
Arlington, VA 22209
703-516-7002
800-341-7874
Fax: 703-516-9313
E-mail: custserve@lrp.com
http://www.lrp.com
Provides colleges and universities with solutions and strategies for recruitment, admissions, retention and financial aid. Reviews the latest trends, research studies and their findings and gives a profile on how other institutions are handling their enrollment management issues.

Monthly
ISSN: 1094-3757

4276 Galileo For Superintendents And District LevelAdministrators

Master Teacher
Po Box 1207
Manhattan, KS 66505-1207
785-539-0555
800-669-9633
Fax: 800-669-1132
http://www.masterteacher.com
The monthly web and print service provides direction & strategies for superintendents and district level administrators.

Monthly Newsletter

Rick Stultz, Executive Editor

4277 HR on Campus

LRP Publications
1901 N Moore Street
Suite 700
Arlington, VA 22209
703-516-7002
800-341-7874
Fax: 703-516-9313
E-mail: custserve@lrp.com
http://www.lrp.com
This monthly newsletter provides coverage of the latest and most inovative programs higher education institutions use to handle their human resource challenges. Plus, you can recieve free e-mail updates on crucial news affecting your job with your paid subscription.

Monthly
ISSN: 1098-9293

4278 IPA Newsletter

2990 Baker Drive
Springfield, IL 62703-2800
217-525-1383
Fax: 217-525-7264
http://www.ipa.vsta.net
Provides current information on Illinois principals and the profession.

8 pages 11x Year

David Turner, Author
Julie Weichert, Associate Director

4279 Journal of Curriculum & Supervision

Association for Supervision & Curriculum Develop.
1703 N Beauregard Street
Alexandria, VA 22311-1714
512-471-4611
Fax: 512-471-8460
E-mail: oldavisjr@mail.uteyas.edu
http://www.ascd.org/framejcs.html
Offers professional updates and news as well as membership/association information.

Quarterly Paperback

OL Davis Jr, Editor

4280 Journal of Education for Business

Heldref Publications
1319 18th Street NW
Washington, DC 20036-1802
202-296-6267
800-365-9753
Fax: 202-296-5149
http://www.heldref.org
Offers information to instructors, supervisors, and administrators at the secondary, postsecondary and collegiate levels. The journal features basic and applied research-based articles in accounting, communications, economics, finance, information systems, management, marketing and other business disciplines.

BiMonthly

4281 Keystone Schoolmaster Newsletter

Pennsylvania Assn. of Secondary School Principals
PO Box 953
Easton, PA 18044-0953
215-253-8516
Reports achievements, honors, problems and innovations by officers and established authorities.

4 pages Monthly

Joseph Mamana, Contact

4282 LSBA Quarter Notes
Louisiana School Boards Association
7912 Summa Avenue
Baton Rouge, LA 70809-3416
News articles relative to the association, feature stories on research.

6 pages BiMonthly

Victor Hodgkins

4283 Legal Notes for Education
Progressive Business Publications
370 Technology Drive
Malvern, PA 19355
800-220-5000
Fax: 610-647-8089
E-mail: customer_service@pbp.com
http://www.pbp.com
Reports the latest school law cases and late-breaking legislation along with the most recent law review articles affecting education. Federal and state appellate court decisions are summarized and the full legal citation is supplied for each case.

Monthly

4284 Maintaining Safe Schools
LRP Publications
1901 N Moore Street
Suite 700
Arlington, VA 22209
703-516-7002
800-341-7874
Fax: 703-516-9313
E-mail: custserve@lrp.com
http://www.lrp.com
Focuses on the legal and practical issues involved in preventing and responding to violent acts by students in schools, and highlights successful violence prevention programs in school districts across the country. Offers strategies for mediation, discipline and crisis managment.

Monthly
ISSN: 1082-4774

4285 Managing School Business
LRP Publications
1901 N Moore Street
Suite 700
Arlington, VA 22209
703-516-7002
800-341-7874
Fax: 703-516-9313
E-mail: custserve@lrp.com
http://www.lrp.com
Newsletter provides school business managers with tips on how to solve the problems they face in managing finance, operations, personnel, and their own career.

Biweekly
ISSN: 1092-2229

Angela Childers, Author

4286 Memo to the President
American Assn. of State Colleges & Universities
1307 New York Avenue
Washington, DC 20005
202-293-7070
Fax: 202-296-5819
http://www.aascu.org
Monitors public policies at national, state and campus level on higher education issues. Reports on activities of the Association and member institutions.

20 pages Monthly
November

Susan Chilcott, Director Communications

4287 NASPA Forum
National Assn. of Student Personnel Administrators
1875 Connecticut Avenue NW
Suite 418
Washington, DC 20009-5737
202-265-7500
Fax: 202-797-1157
Offers information for personnel administrators and strategies, updates and tips on the education system.

Monthly

Sybil Walker

4288 National Faculty Forum
National Faculty of Humanities, Arts & Sciences
1676 Clifton Road NE
Atlanta, GA 30329-4050
404-727-5788
Offers administrative news and updates for persons in higher education.

TriQuarterly

4289 Network
National School Public Relations Association
1501 Lee Highway
Suite 201
Arlington, VA 22209-1109
301-519-0496
Fax: 301-519-0494
E-mail: nspra@nspra.org
http://www.nspra.org
Monthly newsletter for and about our members. Some articles about school public relations, issues that affect school public relations people.

Andy Grunig, Editorial Coordinator
Tommy Jones, Advertising/Sales

4290 OASCD Journal
Oklahoma Curriculum Development
3705 S. 98th East Avenue
Tulsa, OK 74146
918-627-4403
Fax: 918-627-4433
A refereed journal which prints contributions on curriculum theory and practices, leadership in education, staff development and supervision. The Editorial Board welcomes photographs, letters to the editor, program descriptions, interviews, research reports, theoretical pieces, reviews of books and non-print media, poetry, humor, cartoons, satire and children's art and writing, as well as expository articles.

Annual

Blaine Smith, Executive Secretary

4291 On Board
New York State School Boards Association
24 Century Hill Drive
Suite 200
Latham, NY 12110-2125
518-783-0200
800-342-3360
Fax: 518-783-0211
E-mail: info@nyssba.org
http://www.nyssba.org
Contains general educational news, state and federal legislative activity, legal and employee relations issues, commentary, issues in education, and successful education programs around the state.

21x Year

4292 Perspectives for Policymakers
New Jersey School Boards Association
413 W State Street
#909
Trenton, NJ 08618-5617
609-695-7600
Each issue focuses on a specific topic in education providing background, activities and resources.

8 pages SemiAnnually

Missy Martin

4293 Planning & Changing
Illinois State University
Dept. of Ed. Admin. & Foundations
Normal, IL 61790-5900
309-438-2399
Fax: 309-438-8683
http://http://coe.ilstu.edu/eafdept/pandc.htm
An educational leadership and policy journal. This journal attempts to disseminate timely and useful reports of practice and theory with particular emphasis on change, and planning in K-12 educational settings and higher education settings. Paperback.

64 pages Quarterly
ISSN: 0032-0684

Judith Mogilka, Editor
Lilly J Meiner, Publications Manager

4294 Principal
Nat'l Association of Elementary School Principals
1615 Duke Street
Alexandria, VA 22314-3406
703-684-3345
Fax: 800-396-2377
A professional magazine edited for elementary and middle school principals and others interested in education.

5x Year

Leon E Greene, Editor
Louanne M Wheeler, Production Manager

4295 Principal Communicator
National School Public Relations Association
15948 Derwood Road
Rockville, MD 20855
301-519-0496
Fax: 301-519-0494
E-mail: nspra@nspra.org
http://www.napra.org
Tips for building public relations people.

6 pages Monthly

Andy Grunig, Manager of Communications

4296 Private Education Law Report
Progressive Business Publications
370 Technology Drive
Malvern, PA 19355
800-220-5000
Fax: 610-647-8089
E-mail: customer_service@pbp.com
http://www.pbp.com
Reports the latest school law cases and late-breaking legislation along with the most recent law review articles affecting private education. Federal and state appellate court decisions are summarized and the full legal citation is supplied for each case.

Monthly

4297 Public Personnel Management
International Personnel Management
Association
1617 Duke Street
Alexandria, VA 22314-3406
703-549-7100
Fax: 703-684-0948
Caters to those professionals in human resource management.

Quarterly
Sarah AI Shiffert, Editor

4298 Rural Educator-Journal for Rural and Small Schools
National Rural Education Association
246 E Ed Building
Colorado State University
Ft. Collins, CO 80523-1588
970-491-7022
Fax: 970-491-1317
E-mail: jnewlin@lamar.colostate.edu
http://www.colostate.edu
Official journal of the NREA. A nationally recognized publication that features timely and informative articles written by leading rural educators from all levels of education. All NREA members are encouraged to submit research articles and items of general information for publication.

40 pages Quarterly Magazine
ISSN: 0273-446X

Joseph T Newlin, Editor

4299 School Administrator
American Association of School
Administrators
801 N Quincy Street
Suite 700
Arlington, VA 22203-1730
703-528-0700
Fax: 703-841-1543
E-mail: info@aasa.org
http://www.aasa.org
Ensures the highest quality education systems for all learners through the support and development of leadership on the building, district and state levels.

52 pages Monthly
Paul D Houston, Executive Director

4300 School Business Affairs
Association of School Business Officials
Int'l
11401 N Shore Drive
Reston, VA 20190-4232
703-478-0405
Fax: 703-478-0205
For school business administrators responsible for the administration and purchase of products and services for the schools.

Monthly
Peg D Kirkpatrick, Editor/Publisher
Robert Gluck, Managing Editor

4301 School Law Briefings
LRP Publications
1901 N Moore Street
Suite 700
Arlington, VA 22209
703-516-7002
800-341-7874
Fax: 703-516-9313
E-mail: custserve@lrp.com
http://www.lrp.com
Gives you summaries of general education, special education, and early childhood court cases, as well as administrative hearings.

Monthly
ISSN: 1094-3749

4302 School Law News
LPR Publications
1901 N Moore Street
Suite1106
Arlington, VA 22209
703-516-7002
800-341-7874
Fax: 703-516-9313
E-mail: custserve@lrp.com
http://www.lrp.com
Advises administrators to avoid legal pitfalls by monitoring education-related court action across the nation. With School Law News, administrators receive the latest information on issues like sexual harassment liability, special education, religion in the schools, affirmative action, youth violence, student-faculty rights, school finance, desegregation and much more.

8-10 pages Monthly

4303 School Planning & Management
Peter Li Education Group
330 Progress Road
Dayton, OH 45449-2322
937-293-1415
800-523-4625
Fax: 415-626-0554
For the business needs of school administrators featuring issues, ideas and technology at work in public, private and independent schools.

Monthly
ISSN: 1086-4628

Peter J Li, Publisher
Deborah Moore, Editor

4304 Section 504 Compliance Advisor
LRP Publications
1901 N Moore Street
Suite 700
Arlington, VA 22209
703-516-7002
800-341-7874
Fax: 703-516-9313
E-mail: custserve@lrp.com
http://www.lrp.com
Newsletter examines the requirements of Section 504 of the Rehabilitation Act and analyzes their impact on disciplining students. Provides educators and administrators with detailed tips and advice to help them solve the discipline problems they face everyday and keep their policies and programs in compliance.

Monthly
ISSN: 1094-3730

4305 Special Education Law Monthly
LRP Publications
1901 N Moore Street
Suite 700
Arlington, VA 22209
703-516-7002
800-341-7874
Fax: 703-516-9313
E-mail: custserve@lrp.com
http://www.lrp.com
Covers court decisions and administrative rulings affecting the education of students with disabilities.

Monthly
ISSN: 1094-3773

4306 Special Education Law Report
Progressive Business Publications
370 Technology Drive
Malvern, PA 19355
800-220-5000
Fax: 610-647-8089
E-mail: customer_service@pbp.com
http://www.pbp.com

Reports the latest school law cases and late-breaking legislation along with the most recent law review articles affecting special education. Federal and state appellate court decisions are summarized and the full legal citation is supplied for each case.

Monthly

4307 Special Education Report
LPR Publications
1901 N Moore Street
Suite 1106
Arlington, VA 22209
703-516-7002
800-341-7874
Fax: 703-516-9313
E-mail: custserve@lrp.com
The special education administrator's direct pipeline to federal legislation, regulation and funding of programs for children and youths with disabilities.

6-8 pages Monthly

4308 Student Affairs Today
LRP Publications
1901 N Moore Street
Suite 700
Arlington, VA 22209
703-516-7002
800-341-7874
Fax: 703-516-9313
E-mail: custserve@lrp.com
http://www.lrp.com
Newsletter provides strategies and tips for handling higher education institutions' student affairs challenges and problems involving: sexual harassment, binge drinking, fraternity and sorority activities, student housing and more. Gives profiles of other colleges programs.

Monthly
ISSN: 1098-5166

4309 Superintendents Only Notebook
Master Teacher
Leadership Lane
PO Box 1207
Manhattan, KS 66502
800-669-9633
Fax: 800-669-1132
http://www.masterteacher.com
Offers superintendents hundreds of solid ideas to help their jobs run more smoothly. Written by practicing superintendents and business executives, this publication saves hundreds of hours of anguish over the course of the year.

Monthly

4310 THE JournalTechnology Horizons in Education
T.H.E Journal
16261 Laguna Canyon Road
Suite 130
Irvine, CA 92618
949-265-1520
Fax: 949-265-1528
E-mail: wladuke@1105media.com
http://www.thejournal.com
A forum for administrators and managers in school districts to share their experiences in the use of technology-based educational aids.

Wendy LaDuke, Publisher/CEO
Matthew Miller, Editor

4311 Thrust for Educational Leadership
Association of California School
Administrators
1517 L Street
Sacramento, CA 95814-4004
916-444-3216
Fax: 916-444-3245
Designed for school administrators who
must stay abreast of educational developments, management and personnel practices, social attitudes and issues that impact
schools.

7x Year

Tom DeLapp, Communications Director
Susan Davis, Editor

4312 Title I Handbook
Thompson Publishing Group, Inc.
Customer Service Center
PO Box 26185
Tampa, FL 33623-6185
800-677-3789
Fax: 800-759-7179
http://www.titleionline.com
Two-volume looseleaf provides complete,
up-to-date coverage of Title I, the largest
federal program of aid for elementary and
secondary education. The book contains all
the laws, regulations and guidance needed
to sucessfully operate the grant program,
and insightful articles on key Title I topics,
ongoing budget coverage, and special reports on issues like Title I testing,
schoolwide programs, and audits. Also included is a compilation of official Title I
policy letters, found nowhere else.

1,500 pages Quarterly

Cheryl L. Sattler, Author

4313 Title I Monitor
Thompson Publishing Group, Inc.
Customer Service Center
PO Box 26185
Tampa, FL 33623-6185
202-872-4000
800-876-0226
Fax: 202-739-9578
http://www.titleionline.com
This newsletter provides continuing coverage of Title I, the largest federal program of
aid for elementary and secondary education. Title I is at the heart of the debate over
education reform, and the Monitor ensures
that educators have the most up-to-date information about developments in this
ever-changing program. Breaking news
about the Title I budget, new legislation and
regulations, court cases and other issues.

Monthly
ISSN: 1086-2455

Cheryl L Sattler, Author

4314 Training Magazine
Lakewood Publications
50 S 9th Street
Minneapolis, MN 55402-3118
612-333-0471
800-328-4329
Fax: 612-333-6526
Focuses on corporate training and employee
development, as well as management and
human performance issues.

Monthly

Jack Gordon, Editor

4315 Updating School Board Policies
National School Boards Association
1680 Duke Street
Alexandria, VA 22314-3455
703-838-6722
Fax: 703-683-7590

Offers information and statistics for school
boards and administrative offices across the
country.

16 pages BiMonthly
ISSN: 1081-8286

Michael Wessely

Periodicals: Early Childhood Education

4316 Child Development
Arizona State University
Department of Psychology
Tempe, AZ 85287
480-965-3326
Fax: 480-965-8544
http://www.asu.edu
Offers professionals working with children
news on childhood education, books, reviews, questions and answers and professional articles of interest.

BiMonthly

Susan C Somerville

4317 Child Study Journal
Buffalo State College
1300 Elmwood Avenue
#306
Buffalo, NY 14222-1004
716-878-5302
Articles of interest related to childhood education.

Quarterly

Donald E Carter

4318 Children Today
ACF Office of Public Affairs
370 Lenfant Plaza SW
Floor 7
Washington, DC 20560-0002
202-401-9218
Fax: 202-205-9688
An interdisciplinary magazine published by
the Administration for Children and Families (ACF). The content is a mix of theory
and practice, research and features, news
and opinions for its audience.

Quarterly

4319 Children and Families
National Head Start Association
1651 Prince Street
Alexandria, VA 22314-2818
703-739-0875
Fax: 703-739-0878
http://www.nhsa.org
Designed to support the Head Start programs, directors, staff, parents and volunteers.

Quarterly
ISSN: 1091-7578

Julie Konieczny, Editor

**4320 Division for Children with
Communication Disorders
Newsletter**
The Council for Exceptional Children
1920 Association Drive
Reston, VA 20191-1545
703-620-3660
800-232-7323
Fax: 703-264-1637
Information concerning education and wel-
fare of children with communication disor-
ders.

12 pages SemiAnnually

Christine DeSouza, Editor

4321 Early Childhood Education Journal
Kluwer Academic/Human Sciences Press
233 Spring Street
New York, NY 10013
212-620-8000
Fax: 212-463-0742
http://www.wkpa.nl
Provides professional guidance on instructional methods and materials, child development trends, funding and administrative
issues and the politics of day care.

Quarterly
ISSN: 1082-3301

Carol Bischoff, Publisher
Mary Renck Jalongo, Editor

4322 Early Childhood Report
LRP Publications
1901 N Moore Street
Suite 700
Arlington, VA 22209
703-516-7002
800-341-7874
Fax: 703-516-9313
E-mail: custserve@lrp.com
http://www.lrp.com
Educational newsletter for parents and professionals involved at the local state and
federal levels responsible for the design and
implementation of early childhood programs.

Monthly
ISSN: 1058-6482

**4323 Early Childhood Research
Quarterly**
Department of Individuals & Family
Syudies
111 Alison Annex
University of Delaware
Newark, DE 19716
302-831-8552
Fax: 302-831-8776
Addresses various topics in the develop-
ment and education of young children.

Quarterly

Dr. Marion Hyson, Editor

4324 Early Childhood Today
Scholastic
555 Broadway
New York, NY 10012
212-343-6100
800-724-6527
Fax: 212-343-4801
E-mail: ect@scholastic.com
http://www.scholastic.com
The magazine for all early childhood professionals working with infants to
six-year-olds. Each issue provides child development information resources, staff development information and parent
communication information.

8x Year
ISSN: 1070-1214

Ellen Christian, Publisher
Jill Strauss, Managing Editor

4325 Highlights for Children
PO Box 269
Columbus, OH 43216
800-255-9517
Magazine featuring Fun with a Purpose, to
all children preschool to preteen. Features
stories, hidden pictures, reading and thinking exercises, crafts, puzzles, and more.

4326 Journal of Early Intervention
The Council for Exceptional Children
1920 Association Drive
Reston, VA 20191-1545
703-620-3660
800-232-7323
Fax: 703-264-1637

Quarterly
ISSN: 0885-3460

4327 Journal of Research in Childhood Education
Association for Childhood Education International
17904 Georgia Avenue
Suite 215
Olney, MD 20832
301-570-2111
800-423-3563
Fax: 301-570-2212
Current research in education and related fields. It is intended to advance knowledge and theory of the education of children, from infancy through early adolescence. The journal seeks to stimulate the exchange of research ideas through publication of: reports of empirical research; theroretical articles; ethnographic and case studies; cross-cultural studies and studies addressing international concerns; participant observation studies and, studies, deriving data collected.

142 pages BiAnnual
ISSN: 0256-8543

4328 NHSA Journal
National Head Start Association
1651 Prince Street
Alexandria, VA 22314-2818
703-739-0875
Fax: 703-739-0878
Edited for Head Start communities serving children 3 to 5 years of age throughout the country. The journal is an invaluable resource containing current research, innovative programming ideas, details on the Head Start conferences and training events.

Quarterly

Ethan Salwen, Editor

4329 National Guild of Community Schools of the Arts
National Guild of Community Schools of the Arts
520 8th Avenue
Suite 302, 3rd Floor
New York, NY 10018
212-268-3337
Fax: 212-268-3995
E-mail: info@natguild.org
http://www.nationalguild.org
National association of community based arts education institutions employment opportunities, guildnotes newsletter, publications catalog. See www.nationalguild.org.

Monthly

Noah Xifr, Director Membership/Oper.

4330 Parents Make the Difference!: School Readiness Edition
The Parent Institute
PO Box 7474
Fairfax Station, VA 22039-7474
703-323-9170
Fax: 703-323-9173
http://www.parent-institute.com

Newsletter focusing on parent involvement in education. Focuses on parents of children ages infant to five.

Monthly
ISSN: 1089-3075

John Wherry, Publisher

4331 Pre-K Today
Scholastic
555 Broadway
New York, NY 10012-3919
212-343-6100
800-724-6527
Fax: 212-343-4801
Edited to serve the needs of early childhood professionals, owners, directors, teachers and administrators in preschools and kindergarten.

8x Year

Ellen Christian, Editor

4332 Report on Preschool Programs
Business Publishers
8737 Colesville Road
Suite 1100
Silver Spring, MD 20910-3928
301-587-6300
800-274-6737
Fax: 301-585-9075
E-mail: bpinews@bpinews.com
http://www.bpinews.com
Reports on information about Head Start regulations, federal funding policies, state trends in Pre-K and research news. Also covers information on grant and contract opportunities.

8 pages BiWeekly

Eric Easton, Publisher
Chuck Devarics, Editor

4333 Topics in Early Childhood Special Education
Pro-Ed
8700 Shoal Creek Boulevard
Austin, TX 78757-6816
512-451-3246
800-897-3202
Fax: 512-302-9129
http://www.proedinc.com
Provides program developers, advocates, researchers, higher education faculty and other leaders with the most current, relevant research on all aspects of early childhood education for children with special needs.

Judith J Carta, PhD, Editor

4334 Totline Newsletter
Frank Schaffer Publications
23740 Hawthorne Boulevard
Torrance, CA 90505
310-378-1137
800-421-5533
Fax: 800-837-7260
E-mail: fspcustsrv@aol.com
http://www.frankschaffer.com
Creative activities for working with toddlers and preschool children.

32 pages BiMonthly

4335 Vision
SERVE
PO Box 5367
Greensboro, NC 27435
336-315-7400
800-755-3277
Fax: 336-315-7457
E-mail: cahearn@serve.org
http://www.serve.org

Publication of the Regional Educational Laboratories, an educational research and development organization supported by contracts with the US Education Department, National Institute for Education Sciences. Specialty area: Extended Learning Opportunity including Before and After School programs and Early Childhood.

Quarterly

Charles Ahearn, Author
Jack Sanders, Executive Director

Periodicals: Elementary Education

4336 Children's Literature in Education
Kluwer Academic/Human Sciences Press
233 Spring Street
New York, NY 10013
212-620-8000
Fax: 212-463-0742
http://www.wkpa.nl
Source for stimulating articles and interviews on noted children's authors, incisive critiques of classic and contemporary writing for young readers, and original articles describing successful classroom reading projects. Offers timely reviews on a variety of reading-related topics for teachers and teachers-in-training, librarians, writers and interested parents.

Quarterly
ISSN: 0045-6713

Margaret Mackey & Geoff Fox, Editors, Author
Carol Bischoff, Publisher

4337 Creative Classroom
Creative Classroom Publishing
149 5th Avenue
12th Floor
New York, NY 10010
212-353-3639
Fax: 212-353-8030
http://www.creativeclassroom.com
A magazine for teachers of K-8, containing innovative ideas, activities, classroom management tips and information on contemporary social problems facing teachers and students.

BiMonthly

Susan Eveno, Editorial Director
Laura Axler, Associate Editor

4338 Dragonfly
National Science Teachers Association
1840 Wilson Boulevard
Arlington, VA 22201-3000
703-243-7100
800-782-6782
Fax: 703-243-7177
http://www.nsta.org
A fun-filled interdisciplinary magazine for children grades 3-6. A teacher's companion is also available. The teacher's companion is designed to help you integrate Dragonfly into your curriculum.

Dr. Gerald Wheeler, Executive Director
Shelley Johnson Carey, Managing Editor

4339 Educate@Eight
US Department of Education, Region VIII
1244 Speer Boulevard
Suite 310
Denver, CO 80204-3582
303-844-3544
Fax: 303-844-2524
http://www.ed.gov
8 pages
Helen Littlejohn, Author

4340 Elementary School Journal
University of Missouri
1507 E Broadway
Hillcrest Hall
Columbia, MO 65211
573-882-7889
Academic journal publishing primarily
original studies but also reviews of research
and conceptual analyses for researchers and
practitioners interested in elementary
schooling. Emphasizes papers dealing with
educational theory and research and their
implications.
5x Year
Thomas L Good, Editor
Gail M Hinkel, Managing Editor

4341 Elementary Teacher's Ideas and Materials Workshop
Princeton Educational Publishers
117 Cuttermill Road
Great Neck, NY 11021-3101
516-466-9300
Articles on teaching for elementary
schools.
16 pages 10x Year
Barry Pavelec

4342 Helping Your Child Succeed in Elementary School
Rowman & Littlfield Education
4501 Forbes Boulevard
Suite 200
Lanham, MD 20706
301-459-3366
Fax: 301-429-5748
http://www.rowmaneducation.com
Provides parents with useful information
about the importance of parental involvement, concrete ways to work with children
and schools to promote success, and a list of
resources for further reading.

4343 Highlights for Children
PO Box 269
Columbus, OH 43216-0269
800-255-9517
Fax: 614-876-8564
Magazine featuring Fun with a Purpose, to
all children preschool to preteen. Features
stories, hidden pictures, reading and thinking exercises, crafts, puzzles, and more.

4344 Independent School
National Association of Independent
Schools
75 Federal Street
Boston, MA 02110-1913
617-451-2444
Contains information and opinion about
secondary and elementary education in gen-
eral and independent education in particu-
lar.
TriAnnually
Thomas W Leonhardt, Editor
Kurt R Murphy, Advertising/Editor

4345 Instructor
Scholastic
555 Broadway
New York, NY 10012-3919
212-343-6100
800-724-6527
Fax: 212-343-4801
http://www.scholastic.com/instructor
Edited for teachers, curriculum coordina-
tors, principals and supervisors of primary
grades through junior high school.
Monthly
Claudia Cohl, Publisher
Lynn Diamond, Advertising Director

4346 Journal of Research in Childhood Education
Association for Childhood Education
International
17904 Georgia Avenue
Suite 215
Olney, MD 20832
301-570-2111
800-423-3563
Fax: 301-570-2212
Current research in education and related
fields. It is intended to advance knowledge
and theory of the education of children,
from infancy through early adolescence.
The journal seeks to stimulate the exchange
of research ideas through publication of: reports of empirical research; theroretical articles; ethnographic and case studies;
cross-cultural studies and studies addressing international concerns; participant observation studies and, studies, deriving data
collected.
142 pages BiAnnual
ISSN: 0256-8543

4347 Montessori LIFE
American Montessori Society
281 Park Avenue S
6th Floor
New York, NY 10010
212-358-1250
Fax: 212-358-1256
E-mail: kate@amshq.org
http://www.amshq.org
Magazine for parents and educators.
Quarterly
ISSN: 1054-0040
Joy Turner, Author
Eileen Roper, Executive Assistant

4348 Parents Make the Difference!
The Parent Institute
PO Box 7474
Fairfax Station, VA 22039-7474
703-323-9170
Fax: 703-323-9173
http://www.parent-institute.com
Newsletter focusing on parent involvement
in children's education. Focuses on parents
of preschool-aged children.
9x Year
John Wherry, Publisher

4349 Teaching K-8 Magazine
Early Years
40 Richards Avenue
Norwalk, CT 06854-2319
203-855-2650
800-249-9363
Fax: 203-855-2656
E-mail: patricia@teachingk-8.com
http://www.teachingk-8.com

Written for teachers in the elementary
grades, kindergarten through eighth, offer-
ing classroom tested ideas and methods.
Monthly Magazine
ISSN: 0891-4508
November-December
Allen A Raymond, Publisher
Patricia Broderick, Editorial Director

Periodicals: Employment

4350 AACE Careers Update
American Association for Career
Education
2900 Amby Place
Hermosa Beach, CA 90254
310-376-7378
Fax: 310-376-2926
Connects careers, education and work
through career education for all ages. Career awareness, exploration, decision making, and preparation. Employability,
transitions, continuing education, paid and
nonpaid work, occupations, career tips, resources, partnerships, conferences and
workshops. Awards and recognition, trends
and futures. A newsletter is published.
8+ pages Quarterly/Newsletter
ISBN: 1074-9551
Dr.Pat Nellor Wickwire, Author
Dr. Pat Nellor Wickwire, Editor

4351 Career Development for Exceptional Individuals
The Council for Exceptional Children
1920 Association Drive
Reston, VA 20191-1545
703-620-3660
888-232-7733
Fax: 703-264-9494
Contains articles dealing with the latest research activities, model programs, and issues in career development and transition
planning for individuals with disabilities
and/or who are gifted.
2x Year
Gary Greene, Executive Editor

4352 Career Education News
Diversified Learning
72300 Vallat Road
Rancho Mirage, CA 92270-3906
619-346-3336
Reports on programs, materials and training
for career educators.
4 pages BiWeekly
Webster Wilson Jr, Publisher
Webster Wilson, Editor

4353 Careers Bridge Newsletter
St. Louis Public Schools
901 Locust Street
Saint Louis, MO 63101-1401
314-231-3720
Available to educators and business/com-
munity persons on collaborative activities
and promotion of career and self-awareness
education in preschool to grade 12.
BiMonthly
Susan Katzman, Contact

4354 Chronicle of Higher Education
Subscription Department
PO Box 1955
Marion, OH 43305-1955
800-347-6969

Newspaper published weekly advertising many teaching opportunities overseas.

Weekly

4355 Current Openings in Education in the USA

Education Information Services
PO Box 620662
Newton, MA 02462-0662
617-433-0125
This publication is a booklet listing about 140 institutions or school systems, each with one to a dozen or more openings for teachers, librarians, counselors and other personnel.

15 pages Every 6 Weeks

F Viaux, Coordinating Education

4356 Education Jobs

National Education Service Center
PO Box 1279
Riverton, WY 82501-1279
307-856-0170
Offers information on employment in the education field.

Weekly

Lucretia Ficht, Contact

4357 Employment Opportunities

National Guild of Community Schools of the Arts
520 8th Avenue
Suite 302, 3rd Floor
New York, NY 10018
212-268-3337
Fax: 212-268-3995
E-mail: info@natguild.org
http://www.nationalguild.org

Monthly

Noah Xifr, Director Membership/Oper.

4358 Faculty, Staff & Administrative Openings in US Schools & Colleges

Educational Information Services
PO Box 662
Newton Lower Falls, MA 02162
617-964-4555
A listing of available positions in the educational system in the United States.

Monthly

4359 International Educator

PO Box 513
Cummaquid, MA 02637-0513
508-580-1880
A newspaper listing over 100 teaching positions overseas.

Quarterly

4360 Jobs Clearinghouse

Association for Experiential Education
2305 Canyon Boulevard
Suite 100
Boulder, CO 80302-5651
303-440-8844
Fax: 303-440-9581
E-mail: jch@aee.org
http://www.aee.org
A newsletter that is one of the most comprehensive and widely-used monthly listings of full-time, part-time, and seasonal employment and internship opportunities in the experiential/adventure education field for both employers and job seekers.

Monthly

Kristen Cherry

4361 Journal of Cooperative Education

University of Waterloo
200 University Avenue
Waterloo, ON N2L 3G1 Canada
519-888-4567
519-885-1211
Fax: 519-746-8631
Dedicated to the publication of thoughtful and timely articles concerning work-integrated education. It invites manuscripts which are essays that analyze issues, reports of research, descriptions of innovative practices.

3x Year

Patricia M Rowe, Editor

4362 Journal of Vocational Education Research

Colorado State University
202 Education
Fort Collins, CO 80523-0001
970-491-6835
Fax: 970-491-1317
Publishes refereed articles dealing with research and research-related topics in vocational education. Manuscripts based on original investigations, comprehensive reviews of literature, research methodology and theoretical constructs in vocational education are encouraged.

Quarterly

Brian Cobb, Editor

4363 New Jersey Education Law Report

Whitaker Newsletters
313 S Avenue
#340
Fanwood, NJ 07023-1364
908-889-6336
800-359-6049
Fax: 908-889-6339
Court decisions and rulings on employment in New Jersey schools.

8 pages
ISSN: 0279-8557

Joel Whitaker, Publisher
Fred Rossu, Editor

4364 SkillsUSA Champions

Vocational Industrial Clubs of America
PO Box 3000
Leesburg, VA 20177-0300
703-777-8810
Fax: 703-777-8999
E-mail: anyinfo@skillsusa.org
http://www.skillsusa.org
To individuals interested in cultivating leaderships skills, SkillsUSA is a dynamic resource that inspires and connencts all members creating a virtual community through its revalent and useful content.

28 pages Quarterly
ISSN: 1040-4538

E Thomas Hah, Director Office Publications
Timothy W Lawrence, Executive Director

4365 VEWAA Newsletter

Vocational Evaluation & Work Adjustment Assn.
1234 Haley Circle
Auburn University
Auburn, AL 36849
334-844-3800

News and information about the practice of vocational evaluation and work adjustment.

8 pages Quarterly

Ronald Fru, Publisher
Clarence D Brown, Editor

4366 Views & Visions

Wisconsin Vocational Association
44 E Mifflin Street
Suite 104
Madison, WI 53703-2800
608-283-2595
Fax: 608-283-2589
For teachers of vocational and adult education.

8 pages BiMonthly

Linda Stemper

4367 Vocational Training News

Aston Publications
701 King Street
Suite 444
Alexandria, VA 22314-2944
703-683-4100
800-453-9397
Fax: 703-739-6517
Contains timely, useful reports on the federal Job Training Partnership Act and the Carl D Perkins Vocational Education Act. Other areas include literacy, private industry councils and training initiatives.

10 pages Weekly

Cynthia Carter, Publisher
Matthew Dembicki, Editor

Periodicals: Financial Aid

4368 American-Scandinavian Foundation Magazine

American-Scandinavian Foundation
58 Park Avenue
New York, NY 10016-5025
212-879-9779
Fax: 212-686-1157
E-mail: info@amscan.org
http://www.amscan.org
Covers politics, culture and lifestyles of Denmark, Finland, Iceland, Norway and Sweden.

100 pages Quarterly Magazine

Richard J Litell, Editor

4369 Education Grants Alert

LPR Publications
1901n Moore Street
Suite 700
Arlington, VA 22209-2944
703-516-7002
800-341-7874
Fax: 703-516-9313
E-mail: custserve@lrp.com
http://www.lrp.com
Dedicated to helping schools increase funding for K-12 programs. This newsletter will uncover new and recurring grant competitions from federal agencies that fund school projects, plus scores of corporate and foundation sources.

Weekly

4370 Federal Research Report
Business Publishers
8737 Colesville Road
Suite 1100
Silver Spring, MD 20910-3928
301-587-6300
800-274-6737
Fax: 301-585-9075
E-mail: bpinews@bpinews.com
http://www.bpinews.com
Identifies critical funding sources supplying administrator's with contact names, addresses, telephone numbers, RFP numbers and other vital details.
8 pages Weekly
Eric Easton, Publisher
Leonard Eiserer, Editor

4371 Foundation & Corporate Grants Alert
LRP Publishing
1901 N Moore Street
Suite 1106
Arlington, VA 22209
703-516-7002
800-341-7874
Fax: 703-516-9313
E-mail: custserve@lrp.com
http://www.lrp.com
Offers information on funding trends, new foundations and hard-to-find regional funders. You'll also get to foundation and corporate funders from the inside, with foundation profiles and interviews with program officers.
Monthly

4372 Grants for School Districts Monthly
Quinlan Publishing
23 Drydock Avenue
Boston, MA 02210-2336
617-542-0048
Listing of grants available for schools across the country.
Monthly

4373 Informativo
LASPAU (Latin America Scholarship Program)
25 Mount Auburn Street
Cambridge, MA 02138-6028
617-495-5255
Administers scholarships for staff members nominated by Latin American and Caribbean education and development organizations and other public and private sector entities.
8 pages SemiAnnually
Carole Biederman, Contact

4374 NASFAA Newsletter
National Assn. of Student Financial Aid Admin.
1920 L Street NW
Suite 200
Washington, DC 20036-5010
202-785-0453
Fax: 202-785-1487
News covering student financial aid legislation and regulations.
24 pages SemiMonthly
Madeleine McLean

4375 United Student Aid Funds Newsletter
PO Box 6180
Indianapolis, IN 46206-6180
317-578-6094

USA Funds Education Loan products and services information.
8 pages BiMonthly
Nelson Scharadin, Publisher
Dena Weisbard, Editor

Periodicals: Guidance & Counseling

4376 ASCA Counselor
American Counseling Association
5999 Stevenson Avenue
Alexandria, VA 22304-3302
703-823-9800
Fax: 703-823-0252
Aimed at the guidance counselor.
16 pages BiMonthly
Dolores Ehrlich

4377 Adolescence
Libra Publishers
3089C Clairemont Drive
San Diego, CA 92117-6802
858-571-1414
Fax: 858-571-1414
E-mail: librapublishers@juno.com
Articles contributed by professionals spanning issues relating to teenage education, counseling and guidance. Paperback.
256 pages Quarterly
ISSN: 0001-8449
Jon Kroll, Editor
William Kroll, Author

4378 Association for Play Therapy Newsletter
2050 N Winery Avenue
Suite 101
Fresno, CA 93703-2831
559-252-2278
Fax: 559-252-2297
E-mail: info@a4pt.org
http://www.a4pt.org
Dedicated to the advancement of play therapy. APT is interdisciplinary and defines play therapy as a distinct group of interventions which use play as an integral component of the therapeutic process.
Quarterly
William S Burns CAE, Executive Director
Kathryn Lebby MS, General Manager

4379 Attention
CHADD
8181 Professional Place
Suite 150
Landover, MD 20785
301-306-7070
800-233-4050
Fax: 301-306-7090
E-mail: attention@chadd.org
http://www.chadd.org
Magazine for children and adults with Attention Deficit/Hyperactivity Disorder, and their families.
48 pages Bi-Monthly
ISSN: 1551-0980
70+ booths with 1,400 attendees and 70+ exhibits
Marsha Bokman, Manager

4380 Before You Can Discipline
Master Teacher
Leadership Lane
PO Box 1207
Manhattan, KS 66505-1207
800-669-9633
Fax: 800-669-1132
http://www.masterteacher.com
Understand exactly how student's primary and secondary needs can and do influence acceptable and unacceptable behavior. Develop professional attitudes toward discipline problems and learn the laws and principals of managing people.
170 pages
ISBN: 0-914607-03-0
Robert L DeBruyn, Author

4381 Child Psychiatry & Human Development
Kluwer Academic/Human Sciences Press
233 Spring Street
New York, NY 10013
212-620-8000
800-221-9369
Fax: 212-463-0742
http://www.wkpa.nl
Interdisciplinary international journal serving the groups represented by child and adolescent psychiatry, clinical child/pediatric/family psychology, pediatrics, social science, and human development. Publishes research on diagnosis, assessment, treatment, epidemiology, development, advocacy, training, cultural factors, ethics, policy, and professional issues as related to clinical disorders in children, adolescents and families.
Quarterly
ISSN: 0009-398X
Carol Bischoff, Publisher
Kenneth J Tarnowski, Editor

4382 Child Welfare
Child Welfare League of America
440 1st Street NW
Suite 310
Washington, DC 20001-2085
202-638-2952
Fax: 202-638-4004
BiMonthly
Eve Klein, Editor

4383 Child and Adolescent Social Work Journal
Kluwer Academic/Human Sciences Press
233 Spring Street
New York, NY 10013
212-620-8000
800-221-9369
Fax: 212-463-0742
http://www.wkpa.nl
Features original articles that focus on clinical social work practice with children, adolescents and their families. The journal addresses current issues in the field of social work drawn from theory, direct practice, research, and social policy, as well as focuses on problems affecting specific populations in special settings.
Bimonthly
ISSN: 0738-0151
Carol Bischoff, Publisher
Thomas Kenemore, Editor

4384 College Board News
College Board Publications
45 Columbus Avenue
New York, NY 10023-6992
212-713-8165
800-323-7155
Fax: 800-525-5562
http://www.collegeboard.org
Sent free to schools and colleges several times a year, the News reports on the activities of the College Board. Its articles inform readers about the Board's services in such areas as high school, guidance, college admission, curriculum and placement, testing, financial aid, adult education and research.

4385 College Board Review
College Board Publications
45 Columbus Avenue
New York, NY 10023-6992
212-713-8165
800-323-7155
Fax: 800-525-5562
http://www.collegeboard.org
Each issue of the Review probes key problems and trends facing education professionals concerned with student transition from high school to college.

4386 College Times
College Board Publications
45 Columbus Avenue
New York, NY 10023-6917
212-713-8165
800-323-7155
Fax: 800-525-5562
http://www.collegeboard.org
This annual magazine is a one-stop source to college admission. It provides valuable advice to help students through the complex college selection, application and admission process.
Publication Date: 1995 32 pages Package of 50

4387 Communique
National Association of School Psychologists
4340 EW Highway
Suite 402
Bethesda, MD 20814
301-657-0270
Fax: 301-657-0275
E-mail: center@naspweb.org
http://www.nasponline.org
50 pages 8x Year
ISSN: 0164-775X

4388 Counseling & Values
American Counseling Association
5999 Stevenson Avenue
Alexandria, VA 22304-3302
703-823-9800
Fax: 703-823-0252
Editorial content focuses on the roles of values and religion in counseling and psychology.
3x Year
Stephen Brooks, Advertising Director
Susan Lausch, Advertising/Sales

4389 Counseling Today
American Counseling Association
5999 Stevenson Avenue
Alexandria, VA 22304-3302
703-823-9800
Fax: 703-823-0252
Covers national and international counseling issues and reports legislative and governmental activities affecting counselors.
Monthly
Kathy Maguire, Advertising Director
Mary Morrissey, Editor-in-Chief

4390 Counselor Education & Supervision
American Counseling Association
5999 Stevenson Avenue
Alexandria, VA 22304-3302
703-823-9800
Fax: 703-823-0252
Covers counseling theories, techniques and skills, teaching and training.
Quarterly
Stephven Brooks, Advertising Director
Susan Lausch, Advertising/Sales

4391 ERIC Clearinghouse on Counseling & Student Services
201 Ferguson Building UNCG
Greensboro, NC 27402-6171
336-334-4114
800-414-9769
Fax: 336-334-4116
E-mail: ericcass@uncg.edu.edu
http://ericcass.uncg.edu
Covers news about ERIC and the counseling clearinghouse and developments in the fields of education and counseling.
4 pages Quarterly
Garry R Walz, Co-Director
Jeanne C Bleuer, Co-Director

4392 Educational & Psychological Measurement
Sage Publications
2455 Telle Road
Thousand Oaks, CA 91320
805-499-9774
Fax: 805-375-1700
E-mail: order@sagepub.com
http://www.sagepub.com
Quarterly

4393 Elementary School Guidance & Counseling
American Counseling Association
5999 Stevenson Avenue
Alexandria, VA 22304-3300
703-823-9800
Fax: 703-823-0252
http://www.counseling.org
Journal concerned with enhancing the role of the elementary, middle school and junior high school counselor.
Quarterly
ISSN: 0013-5976
Michael Comlish, Editor

4394 Family Relations
Miami University
Family & Child Studies Center
Oxford, OH 45056
513-529-4909
Fax: 513-529-7270
Quarterly
Timothy H Brubaker, Editor

4395 Family Therapy: The Journal of the California Graduate School of Family Psychology
Libra Publishers
3089C Clairemont Drive
PNB 383
San Diego, CA 92117-6802
858-571-1414
Fax: 858-571-1414
Articles contributed by professionals spanning issues relating to teenage education, counseling and guidance. Paperback.
96 pages Quarterly
ISSN: 0091-6544
William Kroll, Editor

4396 Health & Social Work
National Association of Social Workers
750 First Street NE
Suite 700
Washington, DC 20002-4241
202-408-8600
800-638-8799
Fax: 202-336-8311
http://www.socialworkers.org
Covers practice, innovation, research, legislation, policy , planning, and all the professional issues relevant to social work services in all levels of education.
Mal Milburn, Marketing/Sales Associate
Lyn Carter, Advertising Specialist

4397 ICA Quarterly
Western Illinois University
Counseling Center
Memorial Hall
Macomb, IL 61455
309-298-2453
Fax: 309-298-3253
Official publication of the Illinois Counseling Association. Focus is on material of interest and value to professional counselors.
Quarterly
Michael Illovsky, Editor

4398 International Journal of Play Therapy
2050 N Winery Avenue
Suite 101
Fresno, CA 93703-2831
559-252-2278
Fax: 559-252-2297
E-mail: info@a4pt.org
http://www.a4pt.org
Dedicated to the advancement of play therapy. APT is interdisciplinary and defines play therapy as a distinct group of interventions which use play as an integral component of the therapeutic process.
Publication Date: 1982 BiAnnual
William S Burns CAE, Executive Director
Kathryn Lebby MS, General Manager

4399 Journal for Specialists in Group Work
American Counseling Association
5999 Stevenson Avenue
Alexandria, VA 22304-3302
703-823-9800
Fax: 703-823-0252
Contains theory, legal issues and current literature reviews.
Quarterly
Stephven Brooks, Editor

4400 Journal of At-Risk Issues
Clemson University
209 Martin Street
Clemson, SC 29631-1555
864-656-2599
800-443-6392
Fax: 864-656-0136
E-mail: NDPC@clemson.edu
http://www.dropoutprevention.org
36 pages
ISBN: 1098-1608
Dr. Judy Johnson, Author
Dr. Judy Johnson, Author
Dr. Alice Fisher, Editor

4401 Journal of Child and Adolescent Group Therapy
Kluwer Academic/Human Sciences Press
233 Spring Street
New York, NY 10013
212-620-8000
800-221-9369
Fax: 212-463-0742
http://www.wkpa.nl
Addresses the whole spectrum of professional issues relating to juvenile and parent group treatment. Promotes the exchange of new ideas from a wide variety of disciplines concerned with enhancing treatments for this special population. The multidisciplinary contributions include clinical reports, illustrations of new technical methods, and studies that contribute to the advancement of therapeutic results, as well as articles on theoretical issues, applications, and the group process.
Quarterly
ISSN: 1053-0800
Carol Bischoff, Publisher
Edward S Soo, Editor

4402 Journal of College Admission
Nat'l Association for College Admission Counseling
1631 Prince Street
Alexandria, VA 22314-2818
703-836-2222
Fax: 703-836-8015
http://www.nacac.com
Membership association offering information to counselors and guidance professionals working in the college admissions office.
32 pages Quarterly
ISSN: 0734-6670
Elaina Loveland, Author
Shanda T Ivory, Chief Officer
Communications
Amy C Vogt, Assistant Director

4403 Journal of Counseling and Development
American Counseling Association
5999 Stevenson Avenue
Alexandria, VA 22304-3302
703-823-9800
Fax: 703-823-0252
Edited for counseling and human development specialists in schools, colleges and universities.
Monthly
Stephven Brooks, Editor

4404 Journal of Drug Education
California State University
Department of Health Science
Northridge, CA 91330-8285
818-677-3101
Fax: 818-677-2045
Offers information to counselors and guidance professionals dealing with areas of

drug and substance abuse education in the school system.
Quarterly
Robert Huff, Contact

4405 Journal of Emotional and Behavioral Disorders
Pro-Ed
8700 Shoal Creek Boulevard
Austin, TX 78757-6816
512-451-3246
800-897-3202
Fax: 512-302-9129
http://www.proedinc.com
Presents high-quality interdisciplinary scholarship in the area of emotional and behavioral disabilities. Explores issues including youth violence, emotional problems among minority children, long-term foster care placement, mental health services, social development and educational strategies.
Michael H Epstein, EdD, Editor
Douglas Cullinan, EdD, Editor

4406 Journal of Employment Counseling
American Counseling Association
5999 Stevenson Avenue
Alexandria, VA 22304-3302
703-823-9800
Fax: 703-823-0252
Editorial content includes developing trends in case studies and newest personnel practices.
Quarterly
Stephven Brooks, Editor

4407 Journal of Humanistic Education and Development
Ohio University
201 McCracken Hall
Athens, OH 45701
740-593-4000
Fax: 740-593-0569
Focuses on the humanities and promotes their place in the educational system.
Quarterly

4408 Journal of Multicultural Counseling & Development
American Counseling Association
5999 Stevenson Avenue
Alexandria, VA 22304-3302
703-823-9800
Fax: 703-823-0252
Contains articles with focus on research, theory and program application related to multicultural counseling.
Quarterly
Stephven Brooks, Editor

4409 Journal of Sex Education & Therapy
American Association of Sex Educators
PO Box 5488
Richmond, VA 23220-0488
804-644-3288
Fax: 804-644-3290
E-mail: aasect@worldnet.att.net
http://www.aasect.org
Provides education and training in all areas of sexual health.
110 pages Quarterly
ISSN: 0161-4576
Michael Plant, Author

4410 Measurement & Evaluation in Counseling and Development
American Counseling Association
5999 Stevenson Avenue
Alexandria, VA 22304-3302
703-823-9800
Fax: 703-823-0252
Editorial focuses on research and applications in counseling and guidance.
Quarterly
Stephven Brooks, Advertising Director
Susan Lausch, Advertising/Sales

4411 NACAC Bulletin
Nat'l Association for College Admission Counseling
1631 Prince Street
Alexandria, VA 22314-2818
703-836-2222
Fax: 703-836-8015
http://www.nacac.com
Membership association offering information to counselors and guidance professionals working in the college admissions office.
Monthly
Shanda T Ivory, Chief Officer
Communications
Amy C Vogt, Assistant Director

4412 NASW News
National Association of Social Workers
PO Box 431
Annapolis Junction, MD 20701-0431
301-317-8688
800-638-8799
Fax: 301-206-7989
Features in-depth coverage of developments in social work practice, news of national social policy developments, political and legislative news in social services, noteworthy achievements of social workers and association news.
Monthly
Scott Moss

4413 National Coalition for Sex Equity in Education
PO Box 534
Annandale, NJ 08801
908-735-5045
Fax: 908-735-9674
E-mail: info@ncsee.org
http://www.ncsee.org
The only national organization for gender equity specialists and educators. Individuals and organizations committed to reducing sex role stereotyping for females and males. Services include an annual national training conference, a quarterly newsletter and a membership directory. Members may join task forces dealing with equity related topics such as computer/technology issues, early childhood, male issues, sexual harassment prevention, sexual orientation and vocational issues.
Quarterly Newsletter
Theodora Martin, Business Manager

4414 New Horizons
National Registration Center for Study Abroad
PO Box 1393
Milwaukee, WI 53201-1393
414-278-0631
Fax: 414-271-8884
E-mail: info@nrcsa.com
http://www.nrcsa.com
Provides information about member institution's programs and establishes standards for treatment of visitors from abroad includ-

ing the appointment of bilingual housing officers and counselors to deal with culture shock.

16 pages Quarterly
ISBN: 1-977864-43-3

Anne Wittig, Author
Mike Wittig, General Manager

4415 Rehabilitation Counseling Bulletin
Pro-Ed
8700 Shoal Creek Boulevard
Austin, TX 78757-6816
512-451-3246
800-897-3202
Fax: 512-302-9129
E-mail: proed1@aol.com
http://www.proedinc.com
International journal providing original empirical research, essays of a theoretical nature, methodological treatises and comprehensive reviews of the literature, intensive case studies and research critiques.

Quarterly Magazine
ISSN: 0034-3552

Douglas Strohmer, PhD, Editor

4416 School Counselor
American Counseling Association
5999 Stevenson Avenue
Alexandria, VA 22304-3302
703-823-9800
Fax: 703-823-0252
Includes current issues and information affecting teens and how counselors can deal with them.

5x Year

Stephven Brooks, Advertising Director
Susan Lausch, Advertising/Sales

4417 School Psychology Review
National Association of School Psychologists
4340 EW Highway
Suite 402
Bethesda, MD 20814
301-657-0270
Fax: 301-657-0275
E-mail: center@naspweb.org
http://www.nasponline.org

170 pages Quarterly
ISSN: 0279-6015

4418 Social Work Research Journal
National Association of Social Workers
750 1st Street NE
Suite 700
Washington, DC 20002-4241
202-408-8600
800-638-8799
Fax: 202-336-8311
http://www.socialworkers.org
Contains orginal research papers that contribute to knowledge about social work issues and problems. Topics include new technology, strategies and methods, and resarch results.

Quarterly
ISSN: 1070-5309

Stuart A Kirk, Editor

4419 Social Work in Education
National Association of Social Workers
750 1st Street NE
Suite 700
Washington, DC 20002-4241
202-408-8600
Fax: 202-336-8310
http://www.socialworkers.org
Covers practice, innovation, research, legislation, policy, planning, and all the pro-

fessional issues relevant to social work services in all levels of education.

Mal Milburn, Marketing/Sales Associate
Lyn Carter, Advertising Specialist

4420 SocialWork
National Association of Social Workers
750 1st Street NE
Suite 700
Washington, DC 20002-4241
202-408-8600
800-638-8799
Fax: 202-336-8311
http://www.socialworkers.org
Covers important research findings, critical analyses, practice issues, and information on current social issues such as AIDS, homelessness, and federal regulation of social programs. Case management, third-party reimbursement, credentialing, and other professional issues are addressed.

Mal Milburn, Marketing/Sales Associate
Lyn Carter, Advertising Specialist

4421 Today's School Psychologist
LRP Publications
1901 N Moore Street
Suite 700
Arlington, VA 22209
703-516-7002
800-341-7874
Fax: 703-516-9313
E-mail: custserve@lrp.com
http://www.lrp.com/ed
An in-depth guide to a school psychologist's job, offering practical strategies and tips for handling day-to-day responsibilites, encouraging change, and improving professional standing and performance.

Monthly
ISSN: 1098-9277

4422 Washington Counseletter
Chronicle Guidance Publications
66 Aurora Street
Moravia, NY 13118-1190
315-497-0330
800-622-7284
Fax: 315-497-3359
E-mail: customerservice@chronicleguidance.com
http://www.chronicleguidance.com
Monthly report highlighting federal, state, and local developments affecting the counseling and education professions. Items list events, programs, activities and publications of interest to counselors and educators.

8 pages 8x Year

Gary Fickeisen, President
Priscilla Lorah, Coordinator

Periodicals: Language Arts

4423 AATF National Bulletin
American Association of Teachers of French
Mailcode 4510
Southern Illinois University
Carbondale, IL 62901
618-453-5731
Fax: 618-453-5733
E-mail: abrate@siu.edu
http://www.frenchteachers.org

Announcements and short articles relating to the association on French language and cultural activities.

30-50 pages 5x Year

Jayne Abrate, Executive Director
Marie-Christine Koop, President

4424 ACTFL Newsletters
American Council on the Teaching of Foreign Lang.
6 Executive Plaza
Yonkers, NY 10701-6832
914-963-8830
Fax: 914-963-1275
A quarterly newsletter containing topical and timely information on matters of interest to foreign language educators. Regular columns include Languages in the News and Washington Watch.

20 pages Quarterly

C Edward Scebold, C-Editor
Jamie Draper, Co-Editor

4425 ADE Bulletin
Association of Departments of English
26 Broadway
Third Floor
New York, NY 10004-1789
646-576-5133
Fax: 646-458-0033
http://www.ade.org
This bulletin concentrates on developments in scholarship, curriculum and teachers in English.

64 pages
ISSN: 0001-0888

4426 Beyond Words
1534 Wells Drive NE
Albuquerque, NM 87112-6383
505-275-2558
Offers information on literature, language arts and English for the teaching professional.

10x Year

4427 Bilingual Research Journal
National Association for Bilingual Education
1030 15th Street NW
Suite 470
Washington, DC 20005-4018
202-898-1829
Fax: 202-789-2866
E-mail: nabe@nabe.org
http://www.nabe.org
Journal published by National Association for Bilingual Education.

Quarterly
8,000 attendees

Delia Pompa, Executive Director
Alicia Sosa, Membership Director

4428 Bilingual Review Press
Arizona State University
Hispanic Research Center
Tempe, AZ 85287
480-965-3990
Fax: 480-965-0315
Offers information and reviews on books, materials and the latest technology available to bilingual educators.

3x Year

Gary D Keller, Editor

4429 CEA Forum
College English Association
English Department
Youngstown State University
Youngstown, OH 44555-0001
330-941-3415
Fax: 330-941-2304
E-mail: Daniel.Robinson@widener.edu
http://www.as.ysu.edu/~english/cea/forum
1.htm
Publishes articles on professional issues
and pedagogy related to the teaching of
English. Subscription includes CEA Critic,
a scholarly journal that appears 3x annually.

Newsletter
ISSN: 0007-8034

Daniel Robinson, Editor

4430 Classroom Notes Plus
National Council of Teachers of English
1111 W Kenyon Road
Urbana, IL 61801-1010
217-328-3870
800-369-6283
Fax: 217-278-3761
E-mail: notesplus@ncte.org
http://www.ncte.org
Secondary periodical for English/Language
Arts featuring usable teaching ideas for
teachers by teachers.

16 pages Quarterly

Felice Kaufmann, Communications
Director

**4431 Communication Disorders
Quarterly**
Pro-Ed., Inc.
8700 Shoal Creek Boulevard
Austin, TX 78757-6816
512-451-3246
800-897-3202
Fax: 512-302-9129
E-mail: proed1@aol.com
http://www.proedinc.com
Research, intervention and practice in
speech, language and hearing.

Quarterly Magazine
ISSN: 1525-7401

Alejandro Brice, Editor

**4432 Communication: Journalism
Education Today**
Truman High School
3301 S Noland Road
Independence, MO 64055-1318
816-521-2710
Fax: 816-521-2913
A quarterly journal for the Journalism Education Association, based at Kansas State
University, Manhattan, KS. Most articles
are designed to relate to a theme. The magazine focuses on secondary and collegiate
journalism educators.

Quarterly

Molly J Clemons, Editor

**4433 Composition Studies Freshman
English News**
De Paul University
802 W Belden Avenue
Chicago, IL 60614
312-362-8000
Fax: 773-325-7328
Theoretical and practical articles on rhetori-
cal theory.

44 pages SemiAnnually

Peter Vandenberg, English Department

4434 Council-Grams
National Council of Teachers of English
1111 W Kenyon Road
Urbana, IL 61801-1010
217-328-3870
800-369-6283
Fax: 217-328-9645
http://www.ncte.org
Offers information and updates in the areas
of English, language arts and reading.

16 pages 5x Year

Michael Spooner

4435 Counterforce
Society for the Advancement of Good
English
4501 Riverside Avenue
#30
Anderson, CA 96007-2759
530-365-8026
Offers updates and information for English
teachers and professors.

Quarterly

4436 English Education
New York University
635 E Building
New York, NY 10003
212-998-8857
Fax: 212-995-4376
Offers updates and information for reading
and English teachers, and professors.

Quarterly

Gordon M Pradl, Editor

4437 English Journal
National Council of Teachers of English
1111 W Kenyon Road
Urbana, IL 61801-1010
217-328-3870
800-369-6283
Fax: 217-328-9645
http://www.ncte.org
An ideal magazine for middle school, junior
and senior high school English teachers.

Biannual
ISSN: 0013-8274

Carrie Stewart, Editor

4438 English Leadership Quarterly
National Council of Teachers of English
1111 W Kenyon Road
Urbana, IL 61801-1010
217-328-3870
800-369-6283
Fax: 217-328-9645
http://www.ncte.org
Teaching of English for secondary school
English Department chairpersons.

12 pages Quarterly

James Strickland

4439 English for Specific Purposes
University of Michigan
Ann Arbor, MI 48109
619-594-6331
Fax: 619-594-6530
Concerned with English education and its
importance to the developing student.

3x Year

John Swales, Editor

4440 Foreign Language Annals
American Council on the Teaching of
Foreign Lang.
6 Executive Plaza
Yonkers, NY 10701-6832
914-963-8830
Fax: 914-963-1275

Dedicated to advancing all areas of the profession of foreign language teaching. It
seeks primarily to serve the interests of
teachers, administrators and researchers,
regardless of educational level of the language with which they are concerned. Preference is given in this scholarly journal to
articles that describe innovative and successful teaching methods, that report educational research or experimentation, or that
are relevant to the concerns and problems of
the profession.

128 pages Quarterly

C Edward Scebold, Executive Director

4441 Journal of Basic Writing
City University of NY, Instructional
Resource Ctr.
535 E 80th Street
New York, NY 10021-0767
212-794-5445
Fax: 212-794-5706
Publishes articles of theory, research and
teaching practices related to basic writing.
Articles are referred by members of the Edi-
torial Board and the editors.

Spring & Fall

Karen Greenberg, Editor
Trudy Smoke, Editor

**4442 Journal of Children's
Communication Development**
The Council for Exceptional Children
1920 Association Drive
Reston, VA 20191-1545
703-620-3660
800-232-7323
Fax: 703-264-1637
Provides in-depth research and practical application articles in communication assessment and intervention. The journal
frequently contains a practitioner's section
that addresses professional questions, reviews tests and therapy materials, and describes innovative programs and service
delivery models.

2x Year
ISSN: 0735-3170

Richard Nowell, Editor

4443 Journal of Teaching Writing
Indiana Teachers of Writing
IUPUI Department of English CA502L
425 University Boulevard
Indianapolis, IN 46202-5148
317-278-2054
Fax: 317-278-1287
E-mail: sfox@iupui.edu
http://www.iupui.edu/~jtw
A refereed journal for classroom teachers
and researchers at all academic levels
whose interest or emphasis is the teaching
of writing. Appearing semiannually, JTW
publishes articles on the theory, practice,
and teaching of writing throughout the curriculum. Each issue covers a range of topics, from composition theory and discourse
analysis to curriculum development and innovative teaching techniques. Contributors
are reminded to tailor their writing for a diverse readership.

12-20 pages Semiannually

4444 Journalism Quarterly
George Washington University
School of Journalism
Washington, DC 20052-0001
202-994-6227
Fax: 202-994-5806

Information on all facets of writing and journalism for the student and educator.

Quarterly

Jean Folkerts, Editor

4445 Language & Speech
Kingston Press Services, Ltd.
43 Derwent Road, Whitton
Twickenham, Middlesex TW2 7HQ
United Kingdom
0-20-8893-3015
Fax: 208-893-3015
E-mail: sales@kingstonepress.com
http://www.kingstonepress.com
Psychological research articles, speech perception, speech production, psycholinguistics and reading.

Quarterly

4446 Language Arts
National Council of Teachers of English
1111 W Kenyon Road
Urbana, IL 61801-1010
217-328-3870
800-369-6283
Fax: 217-328-9645
http://www.ncte.org
Edited for instructors in language arts at the elementary level.

Monthly

Kent Williamson, Editor

4447 Language, Speech & Hearing Services in School
Ohio State University
110 Pressey Hall
1070 Carmack Road
Columbus, OH 43210
614-292-8207
Fax: 614-292-7504
Interested in innovative technology and growth in language development in schools.

Wayne A Secord, PhD, Editor

4448 Merlyn's Pen: Fiction, Essays and Poems by America's Teens
PO Box 910
East Greenwich, RI 02818-0964
401-885-5175
800-247-2027
Fax: 401-885-5199
E-mail: merlynspen@aol.com
http://www.merlynspen.com
Merlyns' Pen magazine is a selective publisher of model writing by America's students in grades 6-12. Products include Merlyn's Pen magazine (a reproducible annual magazine) and the American Teen Writer Series, collections of anthologized short fiction and nonfiction by brilliant teen writers. Used for models, inspiration, and instruction in literature and writing.

100 pages Annually
ISSN: 0882-2050

Jim Stahl, Editor

4449 Modern Language Journal
Case Western Reserve University
Department of Modern Languages
Cleveland, OH 44106
216-368-2000
Fax: 216-368-2216

Quarterly

David P Benseler, Editor

4450 NABE News
National Association for Bilingual Education
1030 15th Street NW
Suite 470
Washington, DC 20005-4018
202-898-1829
Fax: 202-789-2866
E-mail: nabe@nabe.org
http://www.nabe.org
Magazine published by the National Association for Bilingual Education.

Bi-Monthly

Delia Pompa, Executive Director
Alicia Sosa, Membership Director

4451 NASILP Journal
National Assn. of Self-Instructional Language
Temple University
Philadelphia, PA 19122
215-204-7000
Articles, news and book reviews on language instructional methodology.

12 pages SemiAnnually

Dr. John Means

4452 National Clearinghouse for Bilingual Education Newsletter
George Washington University
2121 K Street NW
Suite 260
Washington, DC 20037-1214
202-467-0867
800-321-6223
E-mail: askncbe@ncbe.gwu.edu
http://www.ncbe.gwu.edu
Provides information to practitioners on the education of language minority students.

Weekly

Dr. Minerva Gorena, Director

4453 PCTE Bulletin
Pennsylvania Council of Teachers of English
Williamsport Area Community College
Williamsport, PA 17701
Focuses on Pennsylvania literacy issues.

SemiAnnually

Robert Ulrich

4454 Quarterly Journal of Speech
National Communication Association
1765 N Street NW
Washington, DC 20036
202-464-4622
Fax: 202-464-4600
http://www.natcom.org
Main academic journal in the speech/communication field of education.

Quarterly

James Gaudino, Executive Director

4455 Quarterly Review of Doublespeak
National Council of Teachers of English
1111 W Kenyon Road
Urbana, IL 61801-1010
217-328-3870
800-369-6283
Fax: 217-328-9645
http://www.ncte.org
Provides information on the misuses and abuse of language.

8 pages Quarterly

Harry Brent

4456 Quarterly of the NWP
National Writing Project
2105 Bancroft Way
Suite 1042
Berkeley, CA 94720-1042
510-642-0963
Fax: 510-642-4545
E-mail: writingproject.org
http://www.writingproject.org
Journal on the research in and practice of teaching writing at all grade levels.

40 pages Quarterly Magazine
ISSN: 0896-3592

Art Peterson, Amy Bauman; Editors, Author
Art Peterson, Senior Editor
Amy Bauman, Managing Editor

4457 Quill and Scroll
University of Iowa School of Journalism
100 Adler Journalism Builing
Room E346
Iowa City, IA 52242
319-335-3457
Fax: 319-335-3989
E-mail: quill-scroll@uiowa.edu
http://www.uiowa.edu/~quill-sc
Founded and distributed for the purpose of encouraging and rewarding individual achievements in journalism and allied fields. This magazine is published bi-monthly during the school year and has a variety of pamphlets and lists of publications available as resources.

BiMonthly

Richard P Johns, Executive Director

4458 Research in the Teaching of English
Harvard Graduate School of Education
Larsen Hall
Appian Way
Cambridge, MA 02138
617-495-3521
Fax: 617-495-0540
A research journal devoted to original research on the relationships between teaching and learning for language development in reading, writing and speaking at all age levels.

Quarterly

Sandra Stotsky, Editor

4459 Rhetoric Review
University of Arizona
Department of English
Tucson, AZ 85721-0001
520-621-3371
Fax: 520-621-7397
http://http://members.aol.com/sborrowman/rr/html
A journal of rhetoric and composition publishing scholarly and historical studies, theoretical and practical articles, views of the profession, review essays of professional books, personal essays about writing and poems.

200+ pages Quarterly
ISSN: 0735-0198

Theresa Enos, Editor

4460 Slate Newsletter
National Council of Teachers of English
1111 W Kenyon Road
Urbana, IL 61801-1010
217-328-3870
800-369-6283
Fax: 217-328-9645
http://www.ncte.org
Short articles on topics such as censorship, trends and issues and testing.

4461 Studies in Second Language Acquisition
Cambridge University Press
1105 Atwater
Bloomington, IN 47401-5020
812-855-6874
Fax: 812-855-2386
E-mail: ssla@indiana.edu
http://www.indiana.edu/~ssla
Referred journal devoted to problems and issues in second and foreign language acquisition of any language.
140 pages Quarterly Paperback
ISSN: 0272-2631
Albert Valdman, Editor

4462 TESOL Journal: A Journal of Teaching and Classroom Research
Teachers of English to Speakers of Other Languages
1600 Cameron Street
Suite 300
Alexandria, VA 22314-2705
703-836-0774
Fax: 703-836-7864
E-mail: tescol@tesol.edu
http://www.tesol.edu
TESOL's mission is to develop the expertise of its members and others involved in teaching English to speakers of other languages to help them foster communication in diverse settings. The association advances standards for professional preparation and employment, continuing education, and student programs, produces programs, services, and products, and promotes advocacy to further the profession. TESOL has 91 affiliates worldwide.
50 pages Quarterly
Christian J Faltis, Editor
Marilyn Kupetz, Managing Editor

4463 TESOL Quarterly
Teachers of English to Speakers of Other Languages
1600 Cameron Street
Suite 300
Alexandria, VA 22314-2705
703-836-0774
Fax: 703-836-7864
E-mail: tesol@tesol.edu
http://www.tesol.com
TESOL Quarterly is our scholarly journal containing articles on academic research, theory, reports, reviews. Articles about linguistics, ethnographies, and more describe the theoretic basis for ESL/EFL teaching practices. Readership is approximately 23,400.
830 pages Quarterly
Carol Chapelle, Editor

4464 Writing Lab Newsletter
Purdue University, Department of English
500 Oval Drive
W. Lafayette, IN 47907-2038
765-494-7268
Fax: 765-494-3780
E-mail: wln@purdue.edudue.edu
http://www.owl.english.purdue.edu/lab/newsletter/index.html
Monthly newsletter for readers involved in writing centers and/or one-to-one instruction in writing skills.
16 pages Monthly/Newsletter
ISSN: 1040-3779
Muriel Harris, Editor
Shawna McCaw, Managing Editor

Periodicals: Library Services

4465 ALA Editions Catalog
Membership Services American Library Association
50 E Huron Street
Chicago, IL 60611
800-545-2433
Fax: 312-836-9958
http://www.ala.org
Contains over 1,000 job listings, news and reports on the latest technologies in 11 issues annually. Also scholarships, grants and awards are possibilities.
Annually

4466 American Libraries
American Library Association
50 E Huron Street
Chicago, IL 60611-2795
312-944-6780
Fax: 312-440-9374
A news magazine covering library development today. Includes news on trends, recent developments and subjects of interest to modern library professionals.
Monthly
Tom Gaughan, Editor

4467 Booklist
American Library Association
50 E Huron Street
Chicago, IL 60611-5295
312-944-6780
Fax: 312-440-9374
http://www.ala.org/booklist
A guide to current print and audiovisual materials worthy of consideration for purchase by small and medium-sized public libraries and school library media centers.
Semimonthly
Bill Ott, Editor

4468 Catholic Library World
Catholic Library Association
461 W Lancaster Avenue
Haverford, PA 19041-1412
734-722-7185
A periodical geared toward the professional librarian in order to keep them abreast of new publications, library development, association news and technology.
Quarterly
Allen Gruenke, Executive Director

4469 Choice
Current Reviews for Academic Libraries
100 Riverview Center
Middletown, CT 06457-3445
860-347-6933
Fax: 860-346-8586
E-mail: adsales@ala-choice.org
http://www.ala.org/acrl/choice
A magazine distributed to librarians and other organizations that analyzes various materials, offers book reviews and information on the latest technology available for the library acquisitions departments.
11x Year
Steven Conforti, Subscriptions Manager
Stuart Foster, Advertising Manager

4470 Emergency Librarian
Ken Haycock and Associates
101-1001 W Braodway
Vancouver
British Columbia
604-925-0266
604-925-056
Professional journal targeted to the specific needs and concerns of teachers and teacher-librarians.
5x Year
Dr. Ken Haycock

4471 ILA Reporter
33 W Grand Avenue
Suite 301
Chicago, IL 60610-4306
312-644-1896
Fax: 312-644-1899
E-mail: ila@ila.org
http://www.ila.org
30 pages
ISSN: 0018-9979
Robert P Doyle, Arthor

4472 Information Technology & Libraries
University of the Pacific
William Knox Holt Library
Stockton, CA 95211-0001
209-946-2434
Fax: 209-946-2805
Offers information on the latest technology, systems and electronics offered to the library market.
Quarterly
Thomas W Leonhardt, Editor
Karen Hope

4473 Journal of Education for Library and Information Sciences
Kent State University
School of Library Science
Kent, OH 44242-0001
330-672-2782
Fax: 330-672-7965
The latest information on books, publications, electronics and technology for the librarian.
Quarterly

4474 Libraries & Culture
University of Texas at Austin/Univ. of Texas Press
PO Box 7819
Austin, TX 78713-7819
512-232-7618
Fax: 512-232-7178
E-mail: dgdavis@gslis.utexas.edu
An interdisciplinary journal that explores the significance of collections of recorded knowledge. Scholarly articles and book reviews cover international topics dealing with libraries, books, reviews, archives, personnel, and their history; for scholars, librarians, historians, readers interested in the history of books and libraries.
100 pages Quarterly
ISSN: 0894-8631
Dr. Donald G Davis Jr, Editor
Colleen Daly, Assistant Editor

4475 Library Collections, Acquisitions & Technical Services
Pergamon Press, Elsevier Science
The Boulevard, Lanngford Lane
Kidlington, Oxford
United Kingdom
614-292-4738
Fax: 614-292-7859
E-mail: deidrichs.1@osu.edu
http://www.elsvier.com
Offers information on policy, practice, and research on the collection management and technical service areas of libraries.
500 pages Quarterly
ISSN: 1464-9055
Carol Pitts Diedrichs, Editor

4476 Library Issues: Briefings for Faculty and Administrators
Mountainside Publishing Company
PO Box 8330
Ann Arbor, MI 48107-8330
734-662-3925
Fax: 734-662-4450
E-mail: apdougherty@compuserve.com
http://www.libraryissues.com
Offers overviews of the trends and problems affecting campus libraries. Explained in layman's terms as they relate to faculty, administrators and the parent institution.
4-6 pages Bi-Monthly
ISSN: 0734-3035
Dr. Richard M Dougherty, Editor
Ann Dougherty, Managing Editor

4477 Library Quarterly
Indiana University, School of Library Science
Lib 013
Bloomington, IN 47405
812-855-5113
Fax: 812-855-6166
Updates, information, statistics, book reviews and publications for librarians.
Quarterly
Stephen P Harter, Editor

4478 Library Resources & Technical Services
Columbia University, School of Library Sciences
516 Butler Library
New York, NY 10027
212-854-3329
Fax: 212-854-8951
Quarterly
Richard P Smirgalia, Editor

4479 Library Trends
Grad. School Library & Info. Science
501 E Daniel Street
Champaign, IL 61820
217-333-1359
Fax: 217-244-7329
E-mail: puboff@alexia.lis.uiuc.edu
http://www.edfu.lis.uiuc.edu/puboff
A scholarly quarterly devoted to invited papers in library and information science. Each issue is devoted to a single theme.
208 pages Quarterly
FW Lancaster, Editor
James Dowling, Managing Editor

4480 Media & Methods Magazine
American Society of Educators
1429 Walnut Street
Philadelphia, PA 19102-3218
215-563-6005
Fax: 215-587-9706
E-mail: claudette@media-methods.com
http://www.media-methods.com
Leading pragmatic magazine for K-12 educators and administrators. The focus is on how to integrate today's technologies and presentation tools into the curriculum. Very up-to-date and well respected national source publication. Loyal readers are media specialists, school librarians, technology coordinators, administrators and classroom teachers.
5x Year
Michele Sokoloff, Publisher
Christine Weiser, Editor

4481 Read, America!
Place in the Woods
3900 Glenwood Avenue
Golden Valley, MN 55422-5302
763-374-2120
Fax: 952-593-5593
E-mail: readamerica10732@aol.com
News, book reviews, ideas for librarians and reading program leaders; short stories and poetry pages for adults and children; and an annual Read America! collection with selections of new books solicited from 350 publishers.
12 pages Quarterly Newsletter
ISSN: 0891-4214
Roger Hammer, Editor/Publisher

4482 School Library Journal
360 Park Avenue
New York, NY 10010
646-746-6759
Fax: 646-746-6689
E-mail: slj@reedbusiness.com
http://www.schoollibraryjournal.com
For children, young adults and school librarians.
Francine Fialkoff, Editorial Director
Brian Kenney, Editor-in-Chief

4483 School Library Media Activities Monthly
LMS Associates
17 E Henrietta Street
Baltimore, MD 21230-3910
301-685-8621
Monthly
Paula Montgomery, Editor

4484 School Library Media Quarterly
American Library Association
50 E Huron Street
Chicago, IL 60611-5295
312-944-6780
Fax: 312-280-3255
For elementary and secondary building level library media specialists, district supervisors and others concerned with the selection and purchase of print and nonprint media.
Quarterly
Judy Pitts, Editor
Barbara Stripling, Editor

4485 Special Libraries
Special Libraries Association
1700 18th Street NW
Washington, DC 20009-2514
202-234-4700
Fax: 202-265-9317
Includes information and manuscripts on the administration, organization and operation of special libraries.
Quarterly
Maria Barry, Editor

4486 Specialist
Special Libraries Association
1700 18th Street NW
Washington, DC 20009-2514
202-234-4700
Fax: 202-265-9317
Contains news and information about the special library/information field.
Monthly
Alisa Nesmith Cooper, Editor

Periodicals: Mathematics

4487 Focus on Learning Problems in Math
Center for Teaching/Learning Math
PO Box 3149
Framingham, MA 01701-3149
508-877-7895
Fax: 508-788-3600
E-mail: msharma@rea.com
An interdisciplinary journal. Edited jointly by the Research Council for Diagnostic and Prescription Mathematics and the Center for Teaching/Learning of Mathematics. The objective of focus is to make available the current research, methods of identification, diagnosis, and remediation of learning problems in mathematics. Contribution from the fields of education psychology and mathematics having the potential to import on classroom or clinical practice are valued.
64-96 pages Quarterly
Mahesh Sharma, Editor

4488 Journal for Research in Mathematics Education
National Council of Teachers of Mathematics
1906 Association Drive
Reston, VA 20191-1502
703-620-9840
Fax: 703-476-2970
E-mail: nctm@nctm.org
http://www.nctm.org
A forum for disciplined inquiry into the teaching and learning of math at all levels— from preschool through adult. Available in print or online version.
5x Year
ISSN: 0021-8251
Harry B Tunis, Publications Director
Rowena G Martelino, Promotions Manager

4489 Journal of Computers in Math & Science
PO Box 2966
Charlottesville, VA 22902-2966
804-973-3087
Fax: 703-997-8760
Quarterly

4490 Journal of Recreational Mathematics
4761 Bigger Road
Kettering, OH 45440-1829
631-691-1470
Fax: 631-691-1770

Promotes the creative practice of mathematics for educational learning.

Quarterly

Joseph S Madachy, Editor

4491 Math Notebook
Center for Teacher/Learning Math
PO Box 3149
Framingham, MA 01705-3149
508-877-7895
Fax: 508-788-3600
A publication for teachers and parents to improve mathematics instruction.

4x/5x Year

Mahesh Sharma, Editor

4492 Mathematics & Computer Education
MAYTC Journal
PO Box 158
Old Bethpage, NY 11804-0158
516-822-5475
Contains a variety of articles pertaining to the field of mathematics.

TriAnnually

George Miller, Editor

4493 Mathematics Teacher
National Council of Teachers of Mathematics
1906 Association Drive
Reston, VA 20191-1502
703-620-9840
Fax: 703-295-0973
E-mail: nctm@nctm.org
http://www.nctm.org
Devoted to the improvement of mathematics instruction in grades 9 and higher.

Monthly
ISSN: 0025-5769

Harry B Tunis, Publications Director
Rowena G Martellino, Promotions Manager

4494 Mathematics Teaching in the Middle School
National Council of Teachers of Mathematics
1906 Association Drive
Reston, VA 20191-1593
703-620-9840
Fax: 703-476-2970
E-mail: nctm@nctm.org
http://www.nctm.org
Addresses the learning needs of students in grades 5-9.

Monthly
ISSN: 1072-0839

Harry B Tunis, Publications Director
Rowena G Martelino, Promotions Manager

4495 NCTM News Bulletin
National Council of Teachers of Mathematics
1906 Association Drive
Reston, VA 20191-9988
703-620-9840
Fax: 703-476-2970
E-mail: nctm@nctm.org
http://www.nctm.org
Publication that reaches all of NCTM's individual and institutional members of more than 107,000 math teachers and school personnel.

Harry B Tunis, Director Publications
Krista Hopkins, Director Marketing Services

4496 Notices of the American Mathematical Society
American Mathematical Society
PO Box 6248
Providence, RI 02940-6248
401-455-4000
Fax: 401-331-3842
Announces programs, meetings, conferences and symposia of the AMS and other mathematical groups.

10x Year

Dr. John S Bradley, Managing Editor
Anne Newcomb, Avertising Coordinator

4497 SSMart Newsletter
School Science & Mathematics Association
Curriculum & Foundations
Bloomsburg, PA 17815
570-389-3894
Fax: 570-389-3894
Membership news offering information, updates, reviews, articles and association news for professionals in the science and mathematics fields of education.

8 pages Quarterly

Darrel Fyffe, Publisher
Norbert Kuenzi, Editor

4498 Teaching Children Mathematics
National Council of Teachers of Mathematics
1906 Association Drive
Reston, VA 20191-1502
703-620-9840
Fax: 703-476-2970
E-mail: nctm@nctm.org
http://www.nctm.org
Concerned primarily with the teaching of mathematics from Pre-K through grade 6.

Monthly
ISSN: 1073-5836

Harry B Tunis, Publications Director
Rowena G Martelino, Promotions Manager

Periodicals: Music & Art

4499 American Academy of Arts & Sciences Bulletin
Norton Woods, 136 Irving Street
Cambridge, MA 02138
617-576-5000
Fax: 617-576-5050
Covers current news of the Academy as well as developments in the arts and sciences.

Alexandra Oleson

4500 Art Education
National Art Education Association
1916 Association Drive
Reston, VA 20191-1590
703-860-8000
Fax: 703-860-2960
A professional journal in the field of art education devoted to articles on all education levels.

6x Year

Thomas A Hatfield, Editor
Beverly Jeanne Davis, Managing Editor

4501 Arts & Activities
Arts & Activities Magazine
12345 World Trade Drive
San Diego, CA 92128
858-605-0242
E-mail: subs@artsandactivities.com
http://www.artsandactivities.com

For classroom teachers, art teachers and other school personnel teaching visual art from kindergarten through college levels.

Monthly
ISSN: 0004-3931

4502 Arts Education Policy Review
Heldref Publications
1319 18th Street NW
Washington, DC 20036-1826
202-296-6267
800-365-9753
Fax: 202-296-5149
http://www.heldref.org
Discusses major policy issues concerning K-12 education in the various arts. The journal presents a variety of views rather than taking sides and emphasizes analytical exploration. Its goal is to produce the most insightful, comprehensive and rigorous exchange of ideas ever available on arts education. The candid discussions are a valuable resource for all those involved in the arts and concerned about their role in education.

40 pages BiWeekly
ISSN: 1063-2913

Leila Saad, Managing Editor

4503 CCAS Newsletter
Council of Colleges of Arts & Sciences
186 University Hall
Columbus, OH 43210
614-292-1882
Fax: 614-292-8666
Membership newsletter to inform deans about arts and sciences issues in education.

4-10 pages BiMonthly

Richard J Hopkins, Contact

4504 Choral Journal
American Choral Directors Association
PO Box 6310
Lawton, OK 73506-0310
903-935-7963
Fax: 903-934-8114
E-mail: jmoore@etbu.edu
Publishes scholarly, practical articles and regular columns of importance to professionals in the fields of choral music and music education. Articles explore conducting teachnique, rehearsal strategies, historical performance practice, choral music history and teaching materials.

Monthly

James A Moore, President

4505 Clavier
200 Northfield Road
Northfield, IL 60093
847-446-5000
Fax: 847-446-6263
Published 10 times each year for piano and organ teachers, with issues in all months except June and August.

Monthly

4506 Dramatics
Educational Theatre Association
2343 Auburn Avenue
Cincinnati, OH 45219-2815
513-421-3900
Fax: 513-421-7055
E-mail: info@etassoc.org
http://www.etassoc.org

Magazine published by Educational Theatre Association, a professional association for theatre educators/artists.

Monthly

David LaFleche, Dir
Membership/Leadership

4507 Flute Talk
200 Northfield Road
Northfield, IL 60093
847-446-5000
Fax: 847-446-6263
Published 10 times each year for flute teachers and intermediate or advanced students, with issues every month except June and August.

Monthly

4508 Instrumentalist
200 Northfield Road
Northfield, IL 60093
847-446-5000
Fax: 847-446-6263
Published 12 times each year for band and orchestra directors and teachers of instruments in these groups.

Monthly

4509 Journal of Experiential Education
Association of Experiential Education
2305 Canyon Boulevard
Suite 100
Boulder, CO 80302
303-440-8844
Fax: 303-440-9581
E-mail: aewert@indiana.edu
http://www.aee.org
A professional journal that publishes articles in outdoor adventure programming, service learning, environmental education, therapeutic applications, research and theory, the creative arts, and much more. An invaluable reference tool for anyone in the field of experiential education.

3x Year
ISSN: 1053-8259

Alan Ewert, Editor

4510 Music Educators Journal
National Association for Music Education
1806 Robert Fulton Drive
Reston, VA 20191-4348
703-860-4000
Fax: 703-860-1531
http://www.menc.org
Offers informative, timely and accurate articles, editorials, and features to a national audience of music educators.

BiMonthly
ISSN: 0027-4321

Frances Ponick, Editor, Author

4511 Music Educators Journal and Teaching Music
National Association for Music Education
1806 Robert Fulton Drive
Reston, VA 20191-4348
703-860-4000
Fax: 703-860-4826
http://www.menc.org
Informative, timely and accurate articles, editorials, and features to a national audience of music educators.

BiMonthly
ISSN: 1069-7446

Jeanne Spaeth, Editor

4512 NAEA News
National Art Education Association
1916 Association Drive
Reston, VA 20191-1502
703-860-8000
Fax: 703-860-2960
E-mail: naea@dgs.dgsys.com
http://www.naea-reston.org
National, state and local news affecting visual arts education.

24 pages BiMonthly

Dr. Thomas Hatfield, Executive Director

4513 National Guild of Community Schools of the Arts
National Guild of Community Schools of the Arts
520 8th Avenue
Suite 302, 3rd Floor
New York, NY 10018
212-268-3337
Fax: 212-268-3995
E-mail: info@natguild.org
http://www.nationalguild.org
National association of community based arts education institutions employment opportunities, guildnotes newsletter, publications catalog. See www.nationalguild.org.

Monthly

Noah Xifr, Director Membership/Oper.

4514 Oranatics Journal
Educational Theatre Association
2343 Auburn Avenue
Cincinnati, OH 45219-2815
513-451-3900
Fax: 513-421-7077
http://www.etassoc.org
Promotes and strengthens theatre in education - primarily middle school and high school. Sponsors an honor society, various events, numerous publications, and arts education advocacy activities.

9x Year

David LaFleche, Director Membership

4515 SchoolArtsDavis Publications
50 Portland Street
Worcester, MA 01682
800-533-2847
Fax: 508-791-0779
http://www.davis-art.com/
Davis has promoted and advocated for art education at both the local and national levels, providing good ideas for teachers and celebrating cultural diversity and the contributions of world cultures through a wide range of art forms.

Wyatt Wade, Publisher
Claire Mowbray Golding, Managing Editor

4516 SchoolArts Magazine
Davis Publications
50 Portland Street
Worcester, MA 01608-2013
508-754-7201
800-533-2847
Fax: 508-791-0779
Aimed at art educators in public and private schools, elementary through high school. Articles offer ideas and information involving art media for the teaching profession and for use in classroom activities.

Monthly
ISSN: 0036-3463

Wyatt Wade, Publisher
Eldon Katter, Editor

4517 Studies in Art Education
Louisiana State University, Dept. of Curriculum
Baton Rouge, LA 70803-0001
225-578-3202
Fax: 225-578-9135
Reports on developments in art education.

Quarterly

Karen A Hamblen, Editor

4518 Teaching Journal
Educational Theatre Association
2343 Auburn Avenue
Cincinnati, OH 45219-2815
513-421-3900
Fax: 513-421-7055
E-mail: info@etassoc.org
http://www.etassoc.org
Journal published by Educational Theatre Association, a professional association for theatre educators/artists.

Quarterly

David LaFleche, Dir
Membership/Leadership

4519 Teaching Music
National Association for Music Education
1806 Robert Fulton Drive
Reston, VA 20191-4348
703-860-4000
Fax: 703-860-4826
http://www.menc.org
Offers informative, timely and accurate articles, editorials, and features to a national audience of music educators.

BiMonthly
ISSN: 1069-7446

Christine Stinson, Editor

4520 Ultimate Early Childhood Music Resource
Miss Jackie Music Company
10001 El Monte Street
Shawnee Mission, KS 66207-3631
913-381-3672
Designed to assist parents and teachers engaged in early childhood.

16 pages Quarterly

Jackie Weissman, Publisher
Emily Smith, Editor

Periodicals: Physical Education

4521 Athletic Director
National Association for Sport & Physical Ed.
1900 Association Drive
Reston, VA 20191-1502
703-476-3410
Fax: 703-476-8316
Of interest to athletic directors and coaches.

4 pages SemiAnnually

4522 Athletic Management
College Athletic Administrator
2488 N Triphammer Road
Ithaca, NY 14850-1014
607-272-0265
Fax: 607-273-0701
Offers information on how athletic managers can improve their operations, focusing

on high school and college athletic departments.

BiMonthly

Mark Goldberg, Publisher
Eleanor Frankel, Editor

4523 Athletic Training
National Athletic Trainers' Association
2952 N Stemmons Freeway
Dallas, TX 75247-6103
214-637-6282
800-879-6282
Fax: 214-637-2206
http://www.nata.org
Edited for athletic trainers.

100 pages Quarterly Magazine

4524 Athletics Administration
NACDA
PO Box 16428
Cleveland, OH 44116
440-892-4000
Fax: 440-892-4007
E-mail: jwork@nacda.com
http://www.nacda.com
The official publication of the National Association of Collegiate Directors of Athletics (NACDA), Athletics Administration focuses on athletics facilities, new ideas in marketing, promotions, development, legal ramifications and other current issues in collegiate athletics administrations.

44-48 pages BiMonthly
ISSN: 0044-9873

Julie Work, Editor

4525 Journal of Environmental Education
Heldref Publications
1319 18th Street NW
Washington, DC 20036-1826
202-296-6267
800-365-9753
Fax: 202-296-5149
E-mail: jee@heldref.org
http://www.heldref.org
An excellent resource for department chairpersons and directors of programs in environmental, resources, and outdoor education.

48 pages Quarterly
ISSN: 0095-8964

B Alison Panko, Managing Editor

4526 Journal of Experiential Education
Association for Experiential Education
2305 Canyon Boulevard
Suite 100
Boulder, CO 80302
303-440-8844
800-787-7979
Fax: 303-440-9581
E-mail: simps_sv@mail.uwlax.edu
http://www.aee.org
A professional journal that publishes articles in outdoor adventure programming, service learning, environmental education, therapeutic applications, research and theory, the creative arts, and much more. An invaluable reference tool for anyone in the field of experiential education.

3x Year

Steve Simpson, Editor

4527 Journal of Physical Education, Recreation and Dance
American Alliance for Health, Phys. Ed. & Dance
1900 Association Drive
Reston, VA 20191-1502
703-476-3495
Fax: 703-476-9527
Presents new books, teaching aids, facilities, equipment, supplies, news of the profession and related groups.

9x Year

Fran Rowan, Editor

4528 Journal of Teaching in Physical Education
Human Kinetics Incorporation
1607 N Market Street
Champaign, IL 61820
217-351-5076
800-747-4457
Fax: 217-351-2674
http://www.humankinetics.com/jtpe
Journal for in-service and pre-service teachers, teacher educators, and administrators, that presents research articles based on classroom and laboratory studies, descriptive and survey studies, summary and review articles, as well as discussions of current topics.

132 pages Quarterly
ISSN: 0273-5024

M Solmon, Author/Editor
R McBride, Author/Editor

4529 Marketing Recreation Classes
Learning Resources Network
1550 Hayes Drive
Manhattan, KS 66502-5068
785-539-5376
800-678-5376
Successful new class ideas and promotion techniques for recreation instructors.

8 pages Monthly

William Draves, Publisher
Julie Coates, Production Manager

4530 National Association for Sport & Physical Education News
National Association for Sport & Physical Ed.
1900 Association Drive
Reston, VA 20191-1502
703-476-3410
800-321-0789
Fax: 703-476-8316
News of conventions, new publications, workshops, and more, all tailored for people in the field of sports, physical education, coaching, etc. Legislative issues are covered as well as news about the over 20 structures in NASPE.

12 pages Monthly

Paula Kun

4531 National Standards for Dance Education News
National Dance Association
1900 Association Drive
Reston, VA 20191-1502
703-476-3400
Fax: 703-476-9527
E-mail: nda@aahperd.org
http://www.aahperd.org/nda
News of the National Dance Association activities, national events in dance education and topics of interest to recreation and athletic directors.

12 pages Quarterly

Barbara Hernandez, Executive Director

4532 Physical Education Digest
11 Cerilli Crescent
Sudbury
Ontario, Canada P3E5R5
705-523-3331
800-455-8782
Fax: 705-523-3331
E-mail: coach@pedigest.com
http://www.pedigest.com
Edited for physical educators and scholastic coaches. Condenses practical ideas from periodicals and books.

36 pages Quarterly
ISSN: 0843-2635

Dick Moss, Editor

4533 Physical Educator
Arizona State University
Editorial Office
Department of ESPE
Tempe, AZ 85287
480-965-3875
Fax: 480-965-2569
Offers articles for the physical educator.

Quarterly

Robert Pangrazi, Editor

4534 Quest
Louisiana State University/Dept. of Kinesiology
Huey Room 112
Baton Rouge, LA 70803-0001
225-388-2036
Fax: 225-388-3680
Publishes articles concerning issues critical to physical education in higher education. Its purpose is to stimulate professional development within the field.

Quarterly

4535 Teaching Elementary Physical Education
Human Kinetics Publishers
1607 N Market Street
Champaign, IL 61820-2220
217-351-5076
800-747-4457
Fax: 217-351-2674
A resource for elementary physical educators, by physical educators. Each 32-page issue includes informative articles on current trends, teaching hints, activity ideas, current resources and events, and more.

32 pages BiMonthly Magazine
ISSN: 1045-4853

G Jake Jaquet, Director Journal Division
Margery Robinson, Managing Editor

Periodicals: Reading

4536 Beyond Words
1534 Wells Drive NE
Albuquerque, NM 87112-6383
505-275-2558
Offers information on literature, language arts and English for the teaching professional.

10x Year

4537 Christian Literacy Outreach
Christian Literacy Association
541 Perry Highway
Pittsburgh, PA 15229-1851
412-364-3777
Association news offering membership information, convention news, books and arti-

cles for the Christian education professional.

4 pages Quarterly

Joseph Mosca

4538 Exercise Exchange
Appalachian State University
222 Duncan Hall
Boone, NC 28608-0001
828-262-2234
Fax: 828-262-2128
Bi-annual journal which features classroom-tested approaches to the teaching of English language arts from middle school through college; articles are written by classroom practitioners.

BiAnnual
ISSN: 0531-531X

Charles R Duke, Editor

4539 Forum for Reading
Fitchburg State College, Education
Department
160 Pearl Street
Fitchburg, MA 01420-2631
978-343-2151
Offers articles, reviews, question and answer columns and more for educators and students.

2x Year

Rona F Flippo, Editor

4540 Journal of Adolescent & Adult Literacy
International Reading Association
800 Barksdale Road
#8139
Newark, DE 19714
302-731-1600
800-336-7323
Fax: 302-731-1057
E-mail: journals@reading.org
http://www.reading.org
Carries articles and departments for those who teach reading in adolescent and adult programs. Applied research, instructional techniques, program descriptions, training of teachers and professional issues.

80-96 pages 8x Year
ISSN: 1081-3004

John Elleins, Editor

4541 Laubach LitScape
Laubach Literacy Action
1320 Jamesville Avenue
Syracuse, NY 13210
315-422-9121
888-528-2224
Fax: 315-422-6369
E-mail: info@laubach.org
http://www.laubach.org
Includes articles about national literacy activities as well as support and information on tutoring, resources, training, new readers, program management, and recruitment and retention of students and volunteers.

12 pages Quarterly

Linda Church, Managing Editor

4542 Literacy Advocate
Laubach Literacy Action
1320 Jamesville Avenue
Syracuse, NY 13210
315-422-9121
888-528-2224
Fax: 315-422-6369
E-mail: info@laubach.org
http://www.laubach.org

Covers United States and international programs and membership activities.

8 pages Quarterly

Beth Kogut, Editor

4543 News for You
Laubach Literacy Action
1320 Jamesville Avenue
Syracuse, NY 13210
315-422-9121
888-528-2224
Fax: 315-422-6369
E-mail: info@laubach.org
http://www.laubach.org
A newspaper for older teens and adults with special reading needs. Includes US and world news written at a 4th to 6th grade reading level.

4 pages Weekly
ISSN: 0884-3910

Heidi Stephens, Editor

4544 Phonics Institute
PO Box 98785
Tacoma, WA 98498-0785
253-588-3436
E-mail: mah@readingstore.com
http://www.readingstore.com
Restoration of intensive phonics to beginning reading instruction.

8 pages 5x Year

4545 RIF Newsletter
Smithsonian Institution
900 Jefferson Drive SW
Washington, DC 20560-0004
202-357-2888
Fax: 202-786-2564
Describes RIF's nationwide reading motivation program.

TriQuarterly

4546 Read, America!
Place in the Woods
3900 Glenwood Avenue
Golden Valley, MN 55422-5302
763-374-2120
Fax: 952-593-5593
E-mail: readamerica10732@aol.com
News, book reviews, ideas for librarians and reading program leaders; short stories and poetry pages for adults and children; and an annual Read America! collection with selections of new books solicited from 350 publishers.

12 pages Quarterly Newsletter
ISSN: 0891-4214

Roger Hammer, Editor/Publisher

4547 Reading Improvement
Project Innovation of Mobile
PO Box 8508
Mobile, AL 36689-0508
334-633-7802
A journal dedicated to improving reading and literacy in America.

Quarterly

Dr. Phil Feldman, Editor

4548 Reading Psychology
Texas A&M University, College of Education
Department of Education
College Station, TX 77843-0001
979-845-7093
Fax: 979-845-9663

Quarterly

Dr. William H. Rupley, Editor

4549 Reading Research Quarterly
Ohio State University
1945 N High Street
Columbus, OH 43210-1120
614-292-8054
Fax: 614-292-1816
Delves into reading ratings and special concerns in the field of literacy.

Quarterly

Dr. Robert Tierney, Editor

4550 Reading Research and Instruction
Appalachian State University, College of Education
Dept. of Curriculum & Instruction
Boone, NC 28608-0001
828-262-6055

Quarterly

William E Blanton, Editor

4551 Reading Teacher
International Reading Association
800 Barksdale Road
#8139
Newark, DE 19711-3204
302-731-1600
800-336-READ
Fax: 301-731-1057
Carries articles and departments for those who teach reading in preschool and elementary schools. Applied research, instructional techniques, program descriptions, the training of teachers, professional issues and special feature reviews of children's books and ideas for classroom practice.

8x Year

Dr. James Baumann, Journal Editor
Linda Hunter, Advertising Manager

4552 Reading Today
International Reading Association
800 Barksdale Road
#8139
Newark, DE 19711-3204
302-731-1600
800-336-READ
Fax: 302-731-1057
Edited for IRA individual and institutional members offering information for teachers, news of the education profession and information for and relating to parents, councils and international issues.

36-44 pages BiMonthly

Linda Hunter, Advertising Manager
John Mickles, Editor

4553 Recording for the Blind & Dyslexic
69 Mapleton Road
Princeton, NJ 08540
609-750-1830
Fax: 609-750-9653
E-mail: scampbell@rfbd.org
http://www.rfbd.org
Textbooks on tape for students who cannot read standard print.

Stephanie Campbell, Executive Director

4554 Report on Literacy Programs
Business Publishers
8737 Colesville Road
Suite 1100
Silver Spring, MD 20910-3928
301-587-6300
800-274-6737
Fax: 301-585-9075
E-mail: bpinews@bpinews.com
http://www.bpinews.com
Reports on the efforts of business and government to provide literacy training to

adults— focusing on the effects of literacy on the workforce.

8-10 pages BiWeekly

Eric Easton, Publisher
Dave Speights, Editor

4555 Visual Literacy Review & Newsletter
International Visual Literacy Association
Virginia Tech
Old Security Building
Blacksburg, VA 24061
540-231-8992
Forum for sharing research and practice within an educational context in the area of visual communication.

8 pages BiMonthly

Richard Couch

4556 WSRA Journal
University of Wisconsin - Oshkosh
1863 Doty Street
Oshkosh, WI 54901-6978
920-424-7231
Fax: 920-326-6280
E-mail: wsra@centurytel.net
A quarterly publication of the Wisconsin State Reading Association that publishes articles about literacy for academicians, teachers, libraries and literary workers.

Quarterly

Dr. Margaret Humadi Genisio, Editor

4557 What's Working in Parent Involvement
The Parent Institute
PO Box 7474
Fairfax Station, VA 22039-7474
703-323-9170
Fax: 703-323-9173
http://www.parent-institute.com
Focuses on parent involvement in children's reading education.

10x Year

John Wherry, Publisher

Periodicals: Secondary Education

4558 ACTIVITY
American College Testing
2201 Dodge
Iowa City, IA 52243-0001
319-337-1410
Fax: 319-337-1014
Distributed free of charge to more than 100,000 persons concerned with secondary and postsecondary education. ACT, an independent nonprofit organization provides a broad range of educational programs and services throughout this country and abroad.

Quarterly

Dan Lechay, Editor

4559 Adolescence
Libra Publishers
3089C Clairemont Drive
PNB 383
San Diego, CA 92117-6802
858-571-1414
Fax: 858-571-1414

Articles contributed by professionals spanning issues relating to teenage education, counseling and guidance. Paperback.

256 pages Quarterly
ISSN: 0001-8449

William Kroll, Editor

4560 American Secondary Education
Bowling Green State University
Education Room 531
Bowling Green, OH 43403-0001
419-372-7379
Fax: 419-372-8265
Serves those involved in secondary education— administrators, teachers, university personnel and others. Examines and reports on current issues in secondary education and provides readers with information on a wide range of topics that impact secondary education professionals. Professionals are provided with the most up-to-date theories and practices in their field.

Quarterly

Gregg Brownell, Editor
Madu Ireh, Graduate Editor

4561 Child and Youth Care Forum
Kluwer Academic/Human Sciences Press
233 Spring Street
New York, NY 10013
212-620-8000
800-221-9369
Fax: 212-463-0742
http://www.wkpa.nl
Independent, professional publication committed to the improvement of child and youth care practice in a variety of day and residential settings and to the advancement of this field. Designed to serve child and youth care practitioners, their supervisors, and other personnel in child and youth care settings, the journal provides a channel of communication and debate including material on practice, selection and training, theory and research, and professional issues.

Bimonthly
ISSN: 1053-1890

Carol Bischoff, Publisher
Doug Magnuson, Co-Editor

4562 Family Therapy: The Journal of the California Graduate School of Family Psychology
Libra Publishers
3089C Clairemont Drive
PNB 383
San Diego, CA 92117-6802
858-571-1414
Fax: 858-571-1414
Articles contributed by professionals spanning issues relating to teenage education, counseling and guidance. Paperback.

96 pages Quarterly
ISSN: 0091-6544

William Kroll, Editor

4563 High School Journal
University of North Carolina
212-D #3500
Chapel Hill, NC 27599-0001
919-962-1395
Fax: 919-962-1533
The Journal publishes articles dealing with adolescent growth, development, interests, beliefs, values, learning, etc., as they effect school practice. In addition, it reports on research dealing with teacher, administrator and student interaction within the school setting. The audience is primarily second-

ary school teachers and administrators, as well as college level educators.

60 pages Quarterly
ISSN: 0018-1498

Dr. George Noblit, Editor

4564 Independent School
National Association of Independent Schools
75 Federal Street
Boston, MA 02110-1913
617-451-2444
Contains information and opinion about secondary and elementary education in general and independent education in particular.

TriAnnually

Thomas W Leonhardt, Editor
Kurt R Murphy, Advertising/Editor

4565 Journal of At-Risk Issues
Clemson University
209 Martin Street
Clemson, SC 29631-1555
864-656-2599
800-443-6392
Fax: 864-656-0136
E-mail: NDPC@clemson.edu
http://www.dropoutprevention.org

36 pages
ISBN: 1098-1608

Dr. Judy Johnson, Author
Dr. Judy Johnson, Author
Dr. Alice Fisher, Editor

4566 NASSP Bulletin
National Assn. of Secondary School Principals
1904 Association Drive
Reston, VA 20191-1537
703-860-0200
800-253-7746
Fax: 703-620-6534
E-mail: nassp@nassp.org
For administrators at the secondary school level dealing with subjects that range from the philosophical to the practical.

TriAnnual

Eugenia Cooper Potter, Editor

4567 Parents Still Make the Difference!
The Parent Institute
PO Box 7474
Fairfax Station, VA 22039-7474
703-323-9170
Fax: 703-323-9173
http://www.parent-institute.com
Newsletter focusing on parent involvement in children's education. Focuses on parents of children in grades 7-12.

Monthly
ISSN: 1523-2395

Betsie Millar, Author
John Wherry, Publisher

4568 Parents Still Make the Difference!: Middle School Edition
The Parent Institute
PO Box 7474
Fairfax Station, VA 22039-7474
703-323-9170
Fax: 703-323-9173
http://www.parent-institute.com
Newsletter focusing on parent involvement in children's education. Focuses on parents of children in grades 7-12.

Monthly
ISSN: 1071-5118

John Wherry, Publisher

Periodicals: Science

4569 American Biology Teacher
National Association of Biology Teachers
12030 Sunrise Valley Drive
Reston, VA 20191
703-264-9696
800-406-0775
Fax: 703-264-7778
E-mail: office@nabt.org
http://www.nabt.org
Edited for elementary, secondary school, junior college, four-year college and university teachers of biology.

80 pages 9 times a year

Cheryl Merrill, Managing Editor
Kay Acevedo, Publications Specialist

4570 AnthroNotes
Smithsonian Institution Anthropology
Outreach Offi
PO Box 37012
Washington, DC 20013-7012
202-633-1917
Fax: 202-357-2208
E-mail: anthroutreach@si.edu
http://www.nmnsi.edu/anthro
Offers archeological, anthropological research in an engaging style.

20 pages

Ann Krupp, Editor

4571 Appraisal: Science Books for Young People
Children's Science Book Review
Committee
Boston University
School of Education
Boston, MA 02215
617-353-4150
This is a journal dedicated to the review of science books for children and young adults. Now in its 27th year of publication, Appraisal reviews nearly all of the science books published yearly for pre-school through high-school age young people. Each book is examined by a children's librarian and by a specialist in its particular discipline.

Quarterly

Diane Holzheimer, Editor

4572 Association of Science-Technology Centers Dimensions
1025 Vermont Avenue NW
Suite 500
Washington, DC 20005-3516
202-783-7200
Fax: 202-783-7207
E-mail: info@astc.org
http://www.astc.org
20 pages
ISSN: 1528-820X

Carolyn Sutterfield, Author
Bonnie VanDorn, Executive Director
Wendy Pollock, Dir
Communication/Research

4573 CCAS Newsletter
Council of Colleges of Arts & Sciences
186 University Hall
Columbus, OH 43210
614-292-1882
Fax: 614-292-8666
Membership newsletter to inform deans about arts and sciences issues in education.

4-10 pages BiMonthly

Richard J Hopkins, Contact

4574 Journal of College Science Teaching
National Science Teachers Association
1840 Wilson Boulevard
Arlington, VA 22201-3000
703-243-7100
800-782-6782
Fax: 703-243-7177
http://www.nsta.org
Professional journal for college and university teachers of introductory and advanced science with special emphasis on interdisciplinary teaching of nonscience majors. Contains feature articles and departments including a science column, editorials, lab demonstrations, problem solving techniques and book reviews.

6x Year

Dr. Gerald Wheeler, Executive Director
Michael Byrnes, Managing Editor

4575 Journal of Environmental Education
Heldref Publications
1319 18th Street NW
Washington, DC 20036-1826
202-296-6267
800-365-9753
Fax: 202-296-5149
A vital research journal for everyone teaching about the environment. Each issue features case studies of relevant projects, evaluation of new research, and discussion of public policy and philosophy in the area of environmental education. The Journal is an excellent resource for department chairpersons and directors of programs in outdoor education.

Quarterly

Kerri P Kilbane, Editor

4576 Journal of Research in Science Teaching
Wiley InterScience
Wiley Corporate Headquarters
111 River Street
Hoboken, NJ 07030-5774
201-748-6000
Fax: 201-748-6088
http://www.interscience.wiley.com

10x Year

4577 NSTA Reports!
National Science Teachers Association
1840 Wilson Boulevard
Arlington, VA 22201-3000
703-243-7100
800-782-6782
Fax: 703-243-7177
http://www.nsta.org
The association's timely source of news on issues of interest to science teachers of all levels. Includes national news, information on teaching materials, announcements of programs for teachers and students, and advance notice about all NSTA programs, conventions and publications.

52 pages BiMonthly

Dr. Gerald Wheeler, Executive Director
Jodi Peterson, Editor

4578 Odyssey
Cobblestone Publishing
30 Grove Street
Suite C
Peterborough, NH 03458-1453
603-924-7209
800-821-0115
Fax: 603-924-7380
E-mail: custsvc@cobblestonepub.org
http://www.odysseymagazine.com

Secrets of science are probed with each theme issues's articles, interviews, activities and math puzzles. Astronomical concepts are experienced with Jack Horkheimer's Star Gazer cartoon and Night-Sky Navigation.

48 pages Monthly
ISSN: 0163-0946

Elizabeth E Lindstrom, Editor

4579 Physics Teacher
American Association of Physics
Teachers
One Physics Ellipse
College Park, MD 20740-3845
301-209-3300
Fax: 301-209-0845
E-mail: aapt-web@aapt.org
http://www.aapt.org
Published by the American Association of Physics Teachers and dedicated to the improvement of the teaching of introductory physics at all levels.

9x Year

Karl C Mamola, Editor
Pamela R Brown, Senior Editorial
Associate

4580 Quantum
National Science Teachers Association
1840 Wilson Boulevard
Arlington, VA 22201-3000
703-243-7100
800-782-6782
Fax: 703-243-7177
http://www.nsta.org
Illustrated magazine containing material translated from Russian magazine Kvant as well as original material specifically targeted to American students. In addition to feature articles and department pieces, Quantum offers olympiad-style problems and brainteasers. Each issue also contains an answer section.

BiMonthly

Dr. Gerald Wheeler, Executive Director
Mike Donaldson, Managing Editor

4581 Reports of the National Center for Science Education
National Center for Science Education
925 Kearney Street
El Cerrito, CA 94530-2810
510-601-7203
800-290-6006
Fax: 510-601-7204
E-mail: ncse@ncseweb.org
http://www.ncseweb.org
An examination of issues and current events in science education with a focus on evolutionary science, and the evolution/creation controversy.

36-44 pages BiMonthly Newsletter
ISSN: 1064-2358

Eugenie C Scott, PhD, Publisher
Andrew J Petto PhD, Editor

4582 Science Activities
Heldref Publications
1319 18th Street NW
Washington, DC 20036-1826
202-296-6267
800-365-9753
Fax: 202-296-5149
E-mail: sa@heldref.org
http://www.heldref.org
A storehouse of up-to-date creative science projects and curriculum ideas for the K-12 classroom teacher. A one-step source of experiments, projects and curriculum innovations in the biological, physical and

behavioral sciences, the journal's ideas have been teacher tested, providing the best of actual classroom experiences. Regular departments feature news notes, computer news, book reviews and new products and resources for the classroom.

48 pages Quarterly
ISSN: 0036-8121

Betty Bernard, Managing Editor

4583 Science News Magazine
1719 N Street NW
Washington, DC 20036-2888
202-785-2255
Fax: 202-659-0365
Information and programs in all areas of science.

Weekly

4584 Science Scope
National Science Teachers Association
1840 Wilson Boulevard
Arlington, VA 22201-3000
703-243-7100
800-782-6782
Fax: 703-243-7177
http://www.nsta.org
Specifically for middle-school and junior-high science teachers. Science Scope addresses the needs of both new and veteran teachers. The publication includes classroom activities, posters and teaching tips, along with educational theory on the way adolescents learn.

8x Year

Dr. Gerald Wheeler, Executive Director
Ken Roberts, Managing Editor

4585 Science Teacher
National Science Teachers Association
1840 Wilson Boulevard
Arlington, VA 22201-3000
703-243-7100
800-782-6782
Fax: 703-243-7177
http://www.nsta.org
Professional journal for junior and senior high school science teachers. Offers articles on a wide range of scientific topics, innovative teaching ideas and experiments, and current research news. Also offers reviews, posters, information on free or inexpensive materials, and more.

9x Year

Dr. Gerald Wheeler, Executive Director
Shelley Johnson Carey, Managing Editor

4586 Science and Children
National Association of Science Teachers
1840 Wilson Boulevard
Arlington, VA 22201-3000
703-243-7100
800-782-6782
Fax: 703-243-7177
http://www.nsta.org
Dedicated to preschool through middle school science teaching provides lively how-to articles, helpful hints, software and book reviews, colorful posters and inserts, think pieces and on-the-scene reports from classroom teachers.

8x Year

Dr. Gerald Wheeler, Executive Director
Linda L Roswog, Managing Editor

4587 Sea Frontiers
International Oceanographic Foundation
4600 Rickenbacker Causeway
Key Biscayne, FL 33149-1031
305-361-4888

A general interest magazine about science education including underwater studies.

BiMonthly

Bonnie Gordon, Editor

4588 Universe in the Classroom
Astronomical Society of the Pacific
390 Ashton Avenue
San Francisco, CA 94112-1722
415-337-1100
Fax: 415-337-5205
E-mail: astroed@astrosociety.org
http://www.astrosociety.org/uitc
On teaching astronomy in grades 3-12, including astronomical news, plain-English explanations, teaching resources and classroom activities.

8 pages Quarterly

Noel Encaracian, Customer Service

Periodicals: Social Studies

4589 Alumni Newsletter
Jewish Labor Committee
25 E 21st Street
Floor 2
New York, NY 10010-6207
212-477-0707
Fax: 212-477-1918
Newsletter of American public secondary school teachers who teach about the Holocaust and Jewish Resistance to the Nazis during World War II.

8 pages SemiAnnually

Arieh Lebowitz

4590 American Sociological Review
Pennsylvania State University
206 Oswald Tower, Sociology Dept
University Park, PA 16802
814-865-5021
Fax: 814-865-0705
Addresses most aspects of sociology in a general range of categories for academic and professional sociologists.

Bimonthly

Glenn Firebaugh, Editor

4591 AnthroNotes
Anthropology Outreach Office
PO Box 37012
Washington, DC 20013-7012
202-357-1592
Fax: 202-357-2208
Offers archeological, anthropological research in an engaging style.

4592 AppleSeeds
Cobblestone Publishing
30 Grove Street
Suite C
Peterborough, NH 03458-1453
603-924-7209
800-821-0115
Fax: 603-924-7380
E-mail: custsvc@cobblestonepub.com
http://www.cobblestonepub.com
A delightful way to develop love of non-fiction reading in grades 2-4. Full color articles, photographs, maps, activities that grab student and teacher interest. Children's doings and thinking around the world in Mail Bag.

32 pages Monthly
ISSN: 1099-7725

Susan Buckey, Barb Burt, Editors, Author
Lou Waryncia, Managing Editor

4593 Boletin
Center for the Teaching of the Americas
Immaculata College
Immaculata, PA 19345
610-647-4400
School teaching of the Americas.

Quarterly

Sr. Mary Consuela

4594 California Weekly Explorer
California Weekly Reporter
285 E Main Street
Suite 3
Tustin, CA 92780-4429
714-730-5991
Fax: 714-730-3548
Resources, events, awards and reviews relating to California history.

16 pages Weekly

Don Oliver

4595 Calliope
Cobblestone Publishing
30 Grove Street
Suite C
Peterborough, NH 03458-1453
603-924-7209
800-821-0115
Fax: 603-924-7380
E-mail: custsvc@cobblestonepub.com
http://www.cobblestonepub.com
Invests in world history with reality not only through articles, stories and maps but also current events and resource lists. Calliope's themes are geared to topics studied in world history classrooms.

48 pages Monthly
ISSN: 1058-7086

Lou Waryncia, Managing Editor
Charles F Baker, Editors

4596 Capitalism for Kids
National Schools Commitee for Economic Education
330 East 70th Street
Suite 5J
New York, NY 10021-8641
212-535-9534
Fax: 212-535-4167
E-mail: info@nscee.org
http://www.nscee.org
Teaches young people about capitalism and the free enterprise system in a clear and entertaining styl. Discusses the practical aspects of starting a small business.

247 pages

John E Donnelly, Executive Director

4597 Cobblestone
Cobblestone Publishing
30 Grove Street
Suite C
Peterborough, NH 03458-1445
603-924-7209
800-821-0115
Fax: 603-924-7380
E-mail: custsvc@cobblestonepub.com
http://www.cobblestonepub.com
Blends sound information with excellent writing, a combination that parents and teachers appreciate. Cobblestone offers imaginative approaches to introduce young readers to the world of American history.

48 pages Monthly
ISSN: 0199-5197

Lou Waryncia, Managing Editor
Meg Chorlian, Editor

4598 Colloquoy on Teaching World Affairs
World Affairs Council of North California
312 Sutter Street
Suite 200
San Francisco, CA 94108-4311
415-982-3263
Fax: 415-982-5028
Offers information, articles and updates for the history teacher.
3x Year
Cassie Todd

4599 Faces
Cobblestone Publishing
30 Grove Street
Suite C
Peterborough, NH 03458-1453
603-924-7209
800-821-0115
Fax: 603-924-7380
E-mail: custsvc@cobblestonepub.com
http://www.cobblestonepub.com
The world is brought to the classroom through the faces of its people. World culture encourages young readers' perspectives through history, folk tales, news and activities.
48 pages Monthly
ISSN: 0749-1387
Lou Waryncia, Managing Editor
Elizabeth Crooker Carpentiere, Editor

4600 Focus
Freedoms Foundation at Valley Forge
PO Box 706
Valley Forge, PA 19482-0706
215-933-8825
800-896-5488
Fax: 610-935-0522
E-mail: tsueta@ffvf.org
http://www.ffvf.org
Strives to teach America and promote responsible citizenship through educational programs and awards designed to recognize outstanding Americans.
6 pages Quarterly
Thomas M Sueat, Editor

4601 Footsteps
Cobblestone Publishing
30 Grove Street
Suite C
Peterborough, NH 03458-1453
603-924-7209
800-821-0115
Fax: 603-924-7380
E-mail: custsvc@cobblestonepub.com
http://www.cobblestonepub.com
Celebrates heritage of African Americans and explores their contributions to culture from colonial times to present. Courage, perserverance mark struggle for freedom and equality in articles, maps, photos, etc.
48 pages 9x Year
ISSN: 1521-5865
Lou Waryncia, Managing Editor
Charles Baker, Editor

4602 History Matters Newsletter
National Council for History Education
26915 Westwood Road
Suite B-2
Westlake, OH 44145-4657
440-835-1776
Fax: 440-835-1295
E-mail: nche@nche.nett
http://www.history.org/nche

Serves as a resource to help members improve the quality and quantity of history learning.
8 pages Monthly
ISSN: 1090-1450
Elaine W Reed, Executive Director

4603 Inquiry in Social Studies: Curriculum, Research & Instruction
University of North Carolina-Charlotte
Dept of Curriculum & Instruction
Charlotte, NC 28223
704-547-4500
Fax: 704-547-4705
An annual journal of North Carolina Council for the Social Studies with a readership of 1,400.
Annual
John A Gretes, Editor
Jeff Passe, Editor

4604 Journal of American History
Organization of American Historians
121 N Bryan Street
Bloomington, IN 47408-4136
812-855-7311
800-446-8923
Fax: 812-855-0696
Contains articles and essays concerning the study and investigation of American history.
Quarterly
Tamzen Meyer, Editor

4605 Journal of Economic Education
Heldref Publications
1319 18th Street NW
Washington, DC 20036-1826
202-296-6267
800-365-9753
Fax: 202-296-5149
Offers original articles on innovations in and evaluations of teaching techniques, materials and programs in economics.
Quarterly
ISSN: 0022-4085

4606 Journal of Geography
National Council for Geographic Education
700 Pelham Road N
Jacksonville, AL 36265
256-782-5293
Fax: 256-782-5336
E-mail: ncge@jsu.edu
http://www.ncge.org
Stresses the essential value of geographic education and knowledge in schools.
Quarterly
ISSN: 0022-1341
Michal LeVasseur, Executive Director
Allison Newton, Associate Director

4607 Magazine of History
Organizations of American History
112 N Bryan Avenue
Bloomington, IN 47408-4199
812-855-7311
800-446-8923
Fax: 812-855-0696
E-mail: oah@oah.org
http://www.oah.org
Includes informative articles, lesson plans, current historiography and reproducible classroom materials on a particular theme. In addition to topical articles, such columns as Dialogue, Studentspeak and His-

tory Headlines allow for the exchange of ideas from all levels of the profession.
70-90 pages Quarterly Magazine
ISSN: 0882-228X
Michael Regoli, Managing Editor

4608 New England Journal of History
Bentley College
Dept of History
Waltham, MA 02254
781-891-2509
Fax: 781-891-2896
Covers all aspects of American history for the professional and student.
3x Year
Joseph Harrington, Editor

4609 News & Views
Pennsylvania Council for the Social Studies
11533 Clematis Boulevard
Pittsburgh, PA 15235-3105
717-238-8768
E-mail: lguru1@aol.com
http://www.pcss.org
Offers news, notes, and reviews of interest to social studies educators.
20 pages 5x Year
ISSN: 0894-8712
Jack Suskind, Executive Secretary
Leo R West, Editor

4610 Perspective
Association of Teachers of Latin American Studies
PO Box 620754
Flushing, NY 11362-0754
718-428-1237
Fax: 718-428-1237
Promotes the teaching of Latin America in US schools and colleges.
10 pages BiMonthly
Daniel Mugan

4611 Social Education
National Council for the Social Studies
8555 Sixteenth Street
Suite 500
Silver Spring, MD 20910
301-588-1800
800-683-0812
Fax: 301-588-2049
E-mail: sgriffin@ncss.org
http://www.socialstudies.org
Journal for the social studies profession serves middle school, high school and college and university teachers. Social Education features research on significant topics relating to social studies, lesson plans that can be applied to various disciplines, techniques for using teaching materials in the classroom and information on the latest instructional technology.
7x Year
ISSN: 0337-7724
Michael Simpson, Editor
Robin Hayes, Manager

4612 Social Studies
Heldref Publications
1319 18th Street NW
Washington, DC 20036-1826
202-296-6267
800-365-9753
Fax: 202-296-5149
Offers K-12 classroom teachers, teacher educators and curriculum administrators an independent forum for publishing their ideas about the teaching of social studies at all levels. The journal presents teachers'

methods and classroom-tested suggestions for teaching social studies, history, geography and the social sciences.

48 pages BiMonthly

Helen Kress, Managing Editor

4613 Social Studies Journal

Pennsylvania Council for the Social Studies
11533 Clematis Boulevard
Pittsburgh, PA 15235-3105
717-238-8768
E-mail: lguru1@aol.com
http://www.pcss.org
Delves into matters of social studies, history, research and statistics for the education professional and science community.

80 pages Annual

Leo R West, Editor
Dr. Saundra McKee, Editor

4614 Social Studies Professional

National Council for the Social Studies
8555 Sixteenth Street
Suite 500
Silver Spring, MD 20910
301-588-1800
800-683-0812
Fax: 301-588-2049
E-mail: sgriffin@ncss.org
http://www.socialstudies.org
Newsletter focusing on strategies, tips and techniques for the social studies educator. New product announcements, professional development opportunities, association news, state and regional meetings.

6 Times

Terri Ackermann, Editor

4615 Social Studies and the Young Learner

National Council for the Social Studies
8555 Sixteenth Street
Suite 500
Silver Spring, MD 20910
301-588-1800
800-683-0812
Fax: 301-588-2049
E-mail: sgriffin@ncss.org
http://www.socialstudies.org
This publication furthers creative teaching in grades K-6, meeting teachers' needs for new information and effective teaching activities.

Quarterly

Martharose Laffey, Editor

4616 Society For History Education/History Teacher

California State University - Long Beach
CSULB, 1250 Bellflower Blvd.
Long Beach, CA 90840-1601
562-985-2573
Fax: 562-985-5431
E-mail: historytacherjournal@gmail.com
http://www.thehistoryteacher.org
The most widely recognized journal in the United States suppoting all areas of history education, pre-collegiate through university level, with practical and insightful professional analyses of both traditional and innovative teaching techniques.

150 pages Quarterly
ISSN: 0018-2745

Jane Dabel, Editor
Elisa Herrera, Executive Director

4617 Teaching Georgia Government Newsletter

Carl Vinson Institute of Government
201 N Milledge Avenue
Athens, GA 30602-5027
706-542-2736
Fax: 706-542-6239
Substantive and supplementary material for social studies teachers in Georgia. Topics of government, history, archaeology, geography, citizenship, etc. are covered. Publications available and upcoming social studies meetings in the state are also announced.

8 pages TriAnnually

Inge Whittle, Editor
Ed Jackson, Editor

4618 Theory and Research in Social Education

National Council for the Social Studies
8555 Sixteenth Street
Suite 500
Silver Spring, MD 20910
301-588-1800
800-683-0812
Fax: 301-588-2049
E-mail: sgriffin@ncss.org
http://www.socialstudies.org
Features articles covering a variety of topics: teacher training, learning theory, and child development research; instructional strategies; the relationship of the social sciences, philosophy, history and the arts to social education; models and theories used in developing social studies curriculum; and schemes for student participation and social action.

Quarterly

4619 Wall Street Journal - Classroom Edition

PO Box 7019
Chicopee, MA 01021
800-544-0522
Fax: 413-598-2332
E-mail: classroom.edition@wsj.com
http://www.wsjclassroom.com
Monthly student newspaper, with stories drawn from the daily journal that show international, business, economic, and social issues affect students' lives and futures. The newspaper is supported by posters, monthly teacher guides, and videos. Regular features on careers, enterprise, marketing, personal finance and technology. Helps teachers prepare students for the world of work by combining timely articles with colorful graphics, etc.

Monthly

Krishnan Anantharamanz, Editor

4620 Women's History Project News

National Women's History Project
3343 Industrial Drive
Suite #4
Santa Rosa, CA 95403
707-636-2888
Fax: 707-636-2909
E-mail: nwhp@aol.com
http://www.nwhp.org
Monthly E-mail newsletter about US women's history, for educators, researchers, program planners, and general women's history enthusiasts.

Monthly

Molly Murphy MacGregor, Exec. Dir./Co-Founder

Periodicals: Technology in Education

4621 Cable in the Classroom

CCI/Crosby Publishing
214 Lincoln Street
Suite 112
Boston, MA 02134
617-254-9481
Fax: 617-254-9776
http://www.ciconline.org
Most comprehensive guide to integrating educational video with the Internet and other curriculum resources for K-12 educators.

54 pages Monthly
ISSN: 1054-5409

Stephen P Crosby, Publisher
Al Race, Executive Editor

4622 EDUCAUSE Quarterly

EDUCAUSE
4772 Walnut Street
Suite 206
Boulder, CO 80301-2538
303-544-5665
Fax: 303-440-0461
E-mail: pdeblois@educause.edu
http://www.educause.edu
Strategic policy advocacy; teaching and learning initiatives; applied research; special interest collaboration communities; awards for leadership and exemplary practices; and extensive online information services.

Quarterly Magazine
ISSN: 1528-5324

Nancy Hays, Author
Peter DeBlois, Director Communications

4623 EDUCAUSE Review

EDUCAUSE
4772 Walnut Street
Suite 206
Boulder, CO 80301-2408
303-544-5665
Fax: 303-440-0461
E-mail: pdeblois@educause.edu
http://www.educause.edu
Strategic policy advocacy; teaching and learning initiatives applied research; special interest collaboration communities; awards for leadership and exemplary practices; and extensive online information services.

Monthly
ISSN: 1527-6619

Nancy Hays, Author
Peter DeBlois, Director Communications

4624 Education Technology News

Business Publishers
8737 Colesville Road
Suite 1100
Silver Spring, MD 20910-3928
301-587-6300
800-274-6737
Fax: 301-585-9075
E-mail: bpinews@bpinews.com
http://www.bpinews.com
Offers information on computer hardware, multimedia products, software applications, public and private funding and integration of technology into K-12 classrooms.

8 pages BiWeekly

Eric Easton, Publisher
Brian Love, Editorial Coordinato

4625 Educational Technology
700 E Palisade Avenue
Englewood Cliffs, NJ 07632-3040
201-871-4007
800-952-BOOK
Fax: 201-871-4009
Published since 1961, periodical covering
the entire field of educational technology.
Issues feature essays by leading authorities
plus a Research Section. With many special
issues covering aspects of the field in
depth. Readers are found in some 120 countries.
9x Year

Lawrence Lipsitz, Editor

4626 Electronic Learning
Scholastic
555 Broadway
New York, NY 10012-3919
212-343-6100
800-724-6527
Fax: 212-343-4801
Published for the administrative level, education professionals who are directly responsible for the implementing of
electronic technology at the district, state
and university levels.

8x Year

Lynn Diamond, Advertising Director
Therese Mageau, Editor

4627 Electronic School
1680 Duke Street
Alexandria, VA 22314
703-838-6722
Fax: 703-683-7590
E-mail: cwilliams@nsba.org
http://www.electronic-school.com
The school technology authority.

Cheryl S Williams, Director
Ann Lee Flynn, Director Ed/Technology
Part

4628 Information Searcher
Datasearch Group
14 Hadden Road
Scarsdale, NY 10583-3328
914-723-1995
Fax: 914-723-1995
http://www.infosearcher.com
Quarterly newsletter for the Internet and
curriculum-technology integration in
school.

32 pages

Pam Berger, President
Bill Berger, Treasurer

4629 Journal of Computing in Childhood Education
AACE
PO Box 2966
Charlottesville, VA 22902-2966
757-623-7588
Fax: 703-997-8760
Discusses the realm of software and tech-
nology now merging with primary educa-
tion.
Quarterly

4630 Journal of Educational Technology Systems
58 New Mill Road
Smithtown, NY 11787-3342
516-632-8767
A compendium of articles submitted by
professionals regarding the newest technology in the educational field.
Quarterly

Dr. Thomas Liao, Editor

4631 Journal of Information Systems Education
Bryant University
1150 Douglas Pike
Smithfield, RI 02917-1291
401-232-6393
Fax: 401-232-6319
Publishes original articles on current topics of special interest to Information Systems Educators and Trainers. Focus is
applications-oriented articles describing
curriculum, professional development or
facilities issues. Topics include course pro-
jects/cases, lecture materials, curriculum
design and/or implementation, workshops,
faculty/student intern/extern programs,
hardware/software selection and industry
relations.
Quarterly

Richard Glass, Contact

4632 Journal of Research on Computing in Education
International Society for Technology in
Education
480 Charnelton Street
Eugene, OR 97401-2626
541-302-3777
800-336-5191
Fax: 541-302-3778
E-mail: cust_serv@ccmail.uoregon.edu
http://www.iste.org
A quarterly journal of original research and
detailed system and project evaluations. It
also defines the state of the art and future
horizons of educational computing.
Quarterly

Diane McGrath, Editor

4633 Journal of Special Education Technology
The Council for Exceptional Children
1920 Association Drive
Reston, VA 20191-1545
703-620-3660
888-232-7733
Fax: 703-264-9494
Provides professionals in the field with information on new technologies, current research, exemplary practices, relevant
issues, legislative events and more concerning the availability and effective use of
technology and media for individuals with
disabilities and/or who are gifted.
Quarterly

Herbert Rieth, Editor

4634 Matrix Newsletter
Department of CCTE, Teachers
College/Communication
PO Box 8
New York, NY 10027-0008
212-678-3344
Fax: 212-678-8227
Newsletter describing activities and inter-
ests of Department of Communication,
Computing and Technology.
14 pages SemiAnnually

Marie Sayer

4635 MultiMedia Schools
Information Today
143 Old Marlton Pike
Medford, NJ 08055-8750
609-654-6266
800-300-9868
Fax: 609-654-4309
E-mail: custserv@infotoday.com
http://www.infotoday.com

A practical journal of multimedia,
CD-Rom, online and Internet in K-12.

Thomas H Hogan, Publisher
Ferdi Serim, Editor

4636 National Forum of Instructional Technology Journal
McNeese State University
324 Prewitt Street
Lake Charles, LA 70601-5915
337-475-5000
Fax: 318-475-5467

Dr. J Mark Hunter, Editor

4637 Society for Applied Learning Technology
50 Culpeper Street
Warrenton, VA 20186
540-347-0055
800-457-6812
Fax: 540-349-3169
E-mail: info@lti.org
http://www.salt.org
Quarterly

4638 TAM Connector
The Council for Exceptional Children
1920 Association Drive
Reston, VA 20191-1545
703-620-3660
888-232-7733
Fax: 703-264-9494
Contains information about upcoming
events, current trends and practices, state
and national legislation, recently published materials and practical information
relative to the availability and effective use
of technology and media for individuals
who are gifted or are disabled.
Quarterly

Cynthia Warger

4639 TECHNOS Quarterly for Education & Technolgy
Agency for Instructional Technology
PO Box A
Bloomington, IN 47402-0120
812-339-2203
Fax: 812-333-4218
E-mail: info@technos.net
http://www.technos.net
TECHNOS Quarterly is a forum for the dis-
cussion of ideas about the use of technol-
ogy in education, with a focus on reform.

36 pages Quarterly
ISSN: 1060-5649

Michael F Sullivan, Executive Director
Carole Novak, Manager TECHNOS Press

4640 Tech Directions
Prakken Publications
275 Meity Drive
Suite 1
Ann Arbor, MI 48107
734-975-2800
Fax: 734-975-2787
E-mail: publisher@techdirections.com
http://www.eddigest.com
Issues programs, projects for educators in
career-technical and technology education
and monthly features on technology, com-
puters, tech careers.
Monthly
ISSN: 1062-9351

Tom Bowden, Managing Editor

4641 Technology & Learning
CMP Media
600 Harrison Street
San Francisco, CA 94107
516-562-5000
800-607-4410
Fax: 516-562-7013
http://www.techlearning.com
Product reviews; hard-hitting, straightforward editorial features; ideas on challenging classroom activities; and more. Tailor made to the special needs of a professional and an educator.

60-80 pages Monthly Magazine
ISSN: 1053-6728
March & October

Susan McLester, Author
Judy Salpeter, Editor-in-Chief
Jo-Ann McDevitt, Publisher

4642 Technology Integration for Teachers
Master Teacher
Leadership Lane
PO Box 1207
Manhattan, KS 66505-1207
800-669-9633
Fax: 800-669-1132
http://www.masterteacher.com

4 pages Monthly

4643 Technology Teacher
International Technology Education Association
1914 Association Drive
Suite 201
Reston, VA 20191-1538
703-860-2100
Fax: 703-860-0353
E-mail: itea@iris.org
http://www.iteawww.org
Seeks to advance technological literacy through professional development activities and publications.

40 pages 8x Year

Kendall Starkweather, Executive Director
Kathleen de la Paz, Editor

4644 Technology in Education Newsletter
111 E 14th Street
#140
New York, NY 10003-4103
800-443-7432
This newsletter for K-12 educators and administrators, covers national trends of technology in education.

4645 Web Feet Guides
Thomson Gale
Thomson Gale World Headquarters
27500 Drake Road
Farmington Hills, MI 48331-3535
248-699-4253
http://www.webfeetguides.com
The premier subject guides to the Internet, rigorously reviewed by librarians and educators, fully annotated, expanded and updated monthly. Appropriate for middle school through adult. Available in print, online, or MARC records. For more information, free trials and free samples.

Monthly

4646 eSchool News
7920 Norfolk Avenue
Suite 900
Bethesda, MD 20814
301-913-0115
800-394-0115
Fax: 301-913-0119
http://www.eschoolnews.com

Monthly newspaper dedicated to providing news and information to help educators use technology to improve education.
Monthly
Gregs Downey, Publisher

General

4647 ABC Feelings Adage Publications
Po Box 7280
Ketchum, ID 83340
208-788-5399
Fax: 208-788-4195
E-mail: info@theattitudedoc.com
http://www.abcfeelings.com
Interactive line of children's products that relate feelings to each letter of the alphabet. Encourages dialogue, understanding, communication, enhances self-esteem. Books, audiotape, poster, placemats, charts, activity cards, t-shirts and multicultural activity guides, floor puzzles, feelings dictionary, carpets.
Ages 3-10
Dr. Alexandra Delis-Abrams, President

4648 ABDO Publishing Company
4940 Viking Drive
Suite 622
Edina, MN 55435-5300
452-831-2120
800-800-1312
Fax: 952-831-1632
E-mail: info@abdopub.com
http://www.abdopub.com
K-8 nonfiction books, including Abdo and Daughters imprint, high/low books for reluctant readers and Checkerboard Library with K-3 science, geography, and biographics for beginning readers. Sand Castle for pre-K to second grade, graduated reading program.
Jill Abdo Hansen, President
James Abdo, Publisher

4649 AGS
4201 Woodland Road
Circle Pines, MN 55014-1796
763-786-4343
800-328-2560
Fax: 800-471-8457
Major test publisher and distributor of tests for literature, reading, English, mathematics, sciences, aptitude, and various other areas of education. Includes information on timing, scoring, teacher's guides and student's worksheets.

4650 AIMS Education Foundation
1595 S Chestnut Avenue
Fresno, CA 93702-4706
559-255-4094
888-733-2467
Fax: 559-255-6396
E-mail: aimsed@fresno.edu
http://www.aimsedu.org
A nonprofit educational foundation that focuses on preparing materials for science and mathematics areas of education.

4651 Ablex Publishing Corporation
PO Box 811
Stamford, CT 06904-0811
201-767-8450
Fax: 201-767-8450
Publishes academic books and journals dealing with many different subject areas. Some of these include: education, linguistics, psychology, library science, computer and cognitive science, writing research and sociology.
Kristin K Butter, President

4652 Acorn Naturalists
155 El Camino Real
Tustin, CA 92780
714-838-4888
800-422-8886
Fax: 714-838-5309
http://www.acornnaturalists.com
Publishes and distributes science and environmental education materials for teachers, naturalists and outdoor educators. A complete catalog is available.
World Wildlife Fund, Author
Jennifer Rigby, Director
Mika Stonehawk, Operations Manager

4653 Active Child
PO Box 2346
Salem, OR 97308-2346
503-371-0865
Publishes creative curriculum for young children.

4654 Active Learning
10744 Hole Avenue
Riverside, CA 92505-2867
909-689-7022
Fax: 909-689-7142
Interactive learning center publishing materials for childhood education.

4655 Active Parenting Publishers
1955 Vaughn Road NW
Suite 108
Kennesaw, GA 30144-7808
770-429-0565
800-825-0060
Fax: 770-429-0334
E-mail: cservice@activeparenting.com
http://www.activeparenting.com
Produces and sells books and innovative video-based programs for use in parent education, self-esteem education and loss education groups/classes.

4656 Addison-Wesley Publishing Company
2725 Sand Hill Road
Menlo Park, CA 94025-7019
650-854-0300
Publisher and distributor of a wide range of fiction, nonfiction and textbooks for grades K-12 in the areas of mathematics, reading, language arts, science, social studies and counseling.

4657 Advance Family Support & Education Program
301 S Frio Street
Suite 103
San Antonio, TX 78207-4422
210-270-4630
Fax: 210-270-4612
Offers books and publications on counseling and support for the family, student and educator.

4658 Alarion Press
PO Box 1882
Boulder, CO 80306-1882
303-443-9039
800-523-9177
Fax: 303-443-9098
E-mail: info@alarion.com
http://www.alarion.com
Video programs, posters, activities, manuals and workbooks dealing with History Through Art and Architecture for grades K-12.

4659 Albert Whitman & Company
6340 Oakton Street
Morton Grove, IL 60053-2723
847-581-0033
Children's books.

4660 Allyn & Bacon
160 Gould Street
Needham Heights, MA 02194
781-455-1250
Fax: 781-455-1220
Publisher of college textbooks and professional reference books.

4661 Alpha Publishing Company
1910 Hidden Point Road
Annapolis, MD 21401-6002
410-757-5404
Educational materials for K-12 curricula.

4662 American Association for State & Local History
1717 Church Street
Nashville, TN 37203-2921
615-320-3203
Fax: 615-327-9013
How-to books for anyone teaching history or social studies.

4663 American Association of School Administrators
1801 N Moore Street
Arlington, VA 22209-1813
703-528-0700
Fax: 703-528-2146
http://www.aasa.org
Paul Houston, Executive Director

4664 American Guidance Service
4201 Woodland Road
Circle Pines, MN 55014-1796
612-786-4343
800-328-2560
Fax: 763-783-4658
Largest distributor of educational materials focusing on guidance counselors and educators in the field of counseling. Materials include books, pamphlets, workshops and information on substance abuse, childhood education, alcoholism, inner-city subjects and more.
Matt Keller, Marketing Director

4665 American Institute of Physics
2 Huntington Quadrangle
Suite 1NO1
Melville, NY 11747
516-576-2200
Fax: 516-349-9704
Physics books.
Marc Brodsky, Executive Director

4666 American Nuclear Society
Outreach Department
555 N Kensington Avenue
La Grange Park, IL 60526-5592
708-352-6611
800-323-3044
Fax: 708-352-0499
E-mail: outreach@ans.org
http://www.aboutnuclear.com
Nuclear science and technology, supplemental educational materials for grades K-12. ReActions newsletters.

4667 American Physiological Society
9050 Rockville Pike
Bethesda, MD 20814
301-530-7132
Fax: 301-634-7098

Videotapes, tracking materials and free teacher resource packets.

4668 American Technical Publishers
1155 W 175th Street
Homewood, IL 60430-4600
708-957-1100
800-323-3471
Fax: 708-957-1101
E-mail: service@americantech.net
http://www.go2atp.com
Offers instructional materials for a variety of vocational and technical training areas.

4669 American Water Works Association
6666 W Quincy Avenue
Denver, CO 80235-3098
303-794-7711
Fax: 303-795-1989
Activity books, teacher guides and more on science education.

4670 Ampersand Press
750 Lake Street
Port Townsend, WA 98368
360-379-5187
800-624-4263
Fax: 360-379-0324
E-mail: info@ampersandpress.com
http://www.ampersandpress.com
Nature and science educational games.

Lou Haller, Owner

4671 Amsco School Publications
315 Hudson Street
New York, NY 10013-1009
212-675-7000
Fax: 212-675-7010
Basal textbooks, workbooks and supplementary materials for grades 7-12.

4672 Anderson's Bookshops
PO Box 3832
Naperville, IL 60567-3832
630-355-2665
The very latest and best trade books to use in the classroom.

4673 Annenberg/CPB Project
901 E Street NW
Washington, DC 20004-2037
202-393-7100
Fax: 202-879-6707
Offers teaching resources in chemistry, geology, physics and environmental science.

4674 Art Image Publications
PO Box 568
Champlain, NY 12919-0568
800-361-2598
Fax: 800-559-2598
Offers various products including art appreciation kits, art image mini-kits and visual arts programs for grades K-12.

Rachel Ross, President

4675 Art Visuals
PO Box 925
Orem, UT 84059-0925
801-226-6115
Fax: 801-226-6115
E-mail: artvisuals@sisna.com
http://www.members.tripod.com
Social studies and art history products including an Art History Timeline, 20 feet long that represents over 50 different styles, ranging from prehistoric to contemporary art; Modern Art Styles, set of 30 posters depicting 20th century styles; Multicultural Posters, Africa, India, China, Japan and the World of Islam, with 18 posters in each cul-

ture. Sets on women artists and African American Artists. Each set is printed on hard cardstock, laminated and ultraviolet protected.

Diane Asay, Owner

4676 Asian American Curriculum Project
83-37th Avenue
San Mateo, CA 94403
650-357-1088
800-874-2242
Fax: 650-357-6908
E-mail: aacpinc@best.com
http://www.asianamericanbooks.com
Develops, promotes and disseminates Asian-American books to schools, libraries and Asian-Americans. Over 1,500 titles.

Florence M Hongo, General Manager

4677 Association for Science Teacher Education
University of Florida
11000 University Parkway
Pensacola, FL 32514-5732
850-474-2000
Fax: 850-474-3205
Yearbooks, journals, newsletters and information on AETS.

4678 Association for Supervision & Curriculum Development
ASCD
1703 N Beauregard Street
Alexandria, VA 22311-1717
703-578-9600
800-933-2723
Fax: 703-575-5400
E-mail: member@ascd.org
http://www.ascd.org
Publishers of educational leadership books, audios and videos focusing on teaching and learning in all subjects and grade levels.

4679 Association of American Publishers
71 5th Avenue
Floor 12
New York, NY 10003
212-255-0200
Fax: 212-255-7007
Association for the book publishing industry.

4680 Atheneum Books for Children
MacMillan Publishing Company
1633 Broadway
New York, NY 10019
212-512-2000
Fax: 800-835-3202
Hardcover trade books for children and young adults.

4681 Australian Press-Down Under Books
15235 Brand Boulevard
Suite A107
Mission Hills, CA 91345-1423
818-837-3755
Big Books, models for writing, small books and teacher's ideas books from Australia.

4682 Avon Books
1350 Avenue of the Americas
New York, NY 10019-4702
212-481-5600
Fax: 212-532-2172
Focuses on middle grade paperbacks for the classroom and features authors such as Cleary, Avi, Borks, Hous, Reeder, Hobbs, Hahn, Taylor and Prish.

4683 Ballantine/Del Rey/Fawcett/Ivy
201 E 50th Street
New York, NY 10022-7703
212-782-9000
800-638-6460
Fax: 212-782-8438
Offer paperback books for middle school and junior and senior high.

4684 Barron's Educational Series
250 Wireless Boulevard
Hauppauge, NY 11788-3924
631-434-3311
800-645-3476
Fax: 631-434-3217
E-mail: barrons@barronseduc.com
http://www.barronseduc.com
Educational books, including a full line of juvenile fiction and non-fiction, and titles for test prep and guidance, ESL, foreign language, art history and techniques, business, and reference.

Frederick Glasser, Director
School/Library Sale

4685 Baylor College of Medicine
One Baylor Plaza
Houston, TX 77030
713-798-4951
Fax: 713-798-6521
http://www.bcm.edu
Offers materials and programs in the scientific area from Texas Scope, Sequence and Coordination projects.

Peter G Traber, President
Robert H Allen, Chairman

4686 Beech Tree Books
1350 Avenue of the Americas
New York, NY 10019-4702
212-261-6500
Fax: 212-261-6518
Curriculum offering reading materials, fiction and nonfiction titles.

4687 Black Butterfly Children's Books
625 Broadway
Floor 10
New York, NY 10012-2611
212-982-3158
A wide variety of books focusing on children, hardcover and paperback.

4688 Blake Books
2222 Beebee Street
San Luis Obispo, CA 93401-5505
805-543-7314
800-727-8550
Fax: 805-543-1150
Photo books on nature, endangered species, habitats, etc. for ages 10 and up.

Paige Torres, President

4689 Bluestocking Press Catalog
Bluestocking Press
PO Box 1014
Placerville, CA 95997-1014
530-622-8586
800-959-8586
Fax: 530-642-9222
E-mail: Jane@bluestockingpress.com
http://www.bluestockingpress.com
Approximately 800 items with a concentration in American History, economics and law. That includes fiction, nonfiction, primary source material, historical documents, facsimile newspapers, historical music, hands-on-kits, audio history, coloring books and more.

Jane A Williams, Coordinating Editor

4690 Boyds Mill Press
815 Church Street
Honesdale, PA 18431-1889
570-253-1164
Fax: 570-253-0179
Publishes books for children from pre-school to young adult.

4691 BridgeWater Books
100 Corporate Drive
Mahwah, NJ 07430-2041
Distinctive children's hardcover books featuring award-winning authors and illustrators, including Laurence Yep, Babette Cole, Joseph Bruchac and others. An imprint of Troll Associates.

4692 Bright Ideas Charter School
2507 Central Freeway East
Wichita Falls, TX 76302-5802
940-767-1561
Fax: 940-767-1904
E-mail: lydiaplmr@aol.com
K-12 curriculum framework for educators struggling to move toward a global tomorrow.

Lynda Plummer, President

4693 Brown & Benchmark Publishers
25 Kessel Court
Madison, WI 63711
608-273-0040
College textbooks in language arts and reading.

**4694 Bureau for At-Risk Youth
Guidance Channel**
Guidance Channel
135 Dupont Street
PO Box 760
Plainview, NY 11803-0760
516-349-5520
800-999-6884
Fax: 800-262-1886
E-mail: info@at-risk.com
http://www.at-risk.com
Publisher and distributor of educational curriculums, videos, publications and products for at-risk youth and the counselors and others who work with them. Bureau products focus on areas such as violence and drug prevention, character education, parenting skills and more.

Sally Germain, Editor-in-Chief

4695 Business Publishers
PO Box 17592
Baltimore, MD 21297
301-587-6300
800-274-6737
Fax: 301-585-9075
E-mail: bpinews@bpinews.com
http://www.bpinews.com
Publishes education related materials.

4696 CLEARVUE/eav
6465 N Avondale Avenue
Chicago, IL 60631
773-775-9433
800-253-2788
Fax: 773-775-9855
E-mail: slucas@clearvue.com
http://www.clearvue.com
CLEARVUE/eav offers educators the largest line of curriculum-oriented media in the industry. CLEARVUE/eav programs have, and will continue to enhance students' interest, learning, motivation and skills.

Sarah M Lucas, Communications Coordinator
Kelli Campbell, VP

4697 Calculators
7409 Fremont Avenue S
Minneapolis, MN 55423-3971
800-533-9921
Fax: 612-866-9030
Calculators and calculator books for K thru college level instruction. Calculator products by Texas Instruments, Casio, Sharp and Hewlett-Packard.

Richard Nelson, President

4698 Cambridge University Press
Edinburgh Building
Shaftesbury Road
Cambridge, England CB22RU
http://www.cup.cam.ac.uk
Curriculum materials and textbooks for science education for grades K-12.

4699 Candlewick Press
2067 Massachusetts Avenue
Cambridge, MA 02140-1340
617-661-3330
Fax: 617-661-0565
High quality trade hardcover and paperback books for children and young adults.

4700 Capstone Press
151 Good Counsel Drive
Mankato, MN 56001-3143
952-224-0529
888-262-6135
Fax: 888-262-0705
E-mail: timadsen@capstone-press.com
http://www.capstonepress.com
PreK-12 Nonfiction publisher

Tim Mandsen, Director Marketing

**4701 Careers/Consultants in Education
Press**
3050 Palm Aire Drive N
#310
Pompano Beach, FL 33069
954-974-3511
Fax: 954-974-5477
E-mail: carconed@aol.com
Current education job lists for teacher and administrator positions in schools and colleges. Plus nine differently titled desk/reference paperback books.

Dr. Robert M Bookbinder, President

4702 Carolrhoda Books
A Division of Lerner Publishing Group
241 1st Avenue N
Minneapolis, MN 55401-1607
612-332-3344
800-328-4929
Fax: 612-332-7615
http://www.lernerbooks.com
Fiction and nonfiction for readers K through grade 6. List includes picture books, biographies, nature and science titles, multicultural and introductory geography books, and fiction for beginning readers.

Rebecca Poole, Submissions Editor

**4703 Carson-Dellosa Publishing
Company**
PO Box 35665
Greensboro, NC 27425-5665
336-632-0084
800-321-0943
Fax: 336-632-087
Textbooks, manuals, workbooks and materials aimed at increasing students reading skills.

4704 Center for Play Therapy
University of North Texas
PO Box 311337
Denton, TX 76203
940-565-3864
Fax: 940-565-4461
E-mail: cpt@coefs.coe.unt.edu
http://www.centerforplaytherapy.com
Encourages the unique development and emotional growth of children through the process of play therapy, a dynamic interpersonal relationship between a child and a therapist trained in play therapy procedures. Provides training, research, publications, counseling services and acts as a clearinghouse for literature in the field.

Garry Landreth PhD, Director

**4705 Central Regional Educational
Laboratory**
2550 S Parker Road
Suite 500
Aurora, CO 80014
303-337-0990
Fax: 303-337-3005
E-mail: twaters@mcrel.org
The Regional Educational Laboratories are educational research and development organizations supported by contracts with the US Education Department, Office of Educational Research and Improvement. Specialty area: curriculum, learning and instruction.

Dr. J Timothy Waters, Executive Director

4706 Charles Scribner & Sons
MacMillan Publishing Company
1633 Broadway
New York, NY 10019
212-632-4944
Fax: 800-835-3202
Hardcover trade books for children and young adults.

4707 Chicago Board of Trade
141 W Jackson Boulevard
Chicago, IL 60604-2992
312-435-3500
Educational materials including a new economics program entitled Commodity Challenge.

4708 Children's Book Council
12 West 37th Street
2nd Floor
New York, NY 10018-7480
212-966-1990
800-999-2160
Fax: 212-966-2073
E-mail: staff@cbcbooks.org
http://www.cbcbooks.org
The Children's Book Council, Inc is the nonprofit trade association of publishers and packagers of trade books and related materials for children and young adults.

JoAnn Sabatino-Falkenstein, VP Marketing

4709 Children's Press
Grolier Publishing
90 Sherman Turnpike
Danbury, CT 06816
800-621-1115
Fax: 800-374-4329
http://publishing.grolier.com
Leading supplier of reference and children's nonfiction and fiction books.

4710 Children's Press/Franklin Watts
PO Box 1330
Danbury, CT 06813-1330
203-797-3500
Fax: 203-797-3197
K-12 curriculum materials.

4711 Children's Television Workshop
1 Lincoln Plaza
New York, NY 10023-7129
212-875-6809
Fax: 212-875-7388
Hands-on books for elementary school use
in the area of science education.

Brenda Pilson, Review Coordinator
Elaine Israel, Editor-in-Chief

4712 Chime Time
2440-C Pleasantdale Road
Atlanta, GA 30340-1562
770-662-5664
Early childhood products and publications.

4713 Choices Education Project
Watson Institute for International Studies
Brown University
PO Box 1948
Providence, RI 02912-1948
401-863-3155
Fax: 401-863-1247
E-mail: choices@brown.edu
http://www.choices.edu
Develops interactive, supplementary cur-
riculum resources on current and historical
international issues. Makes complex cur-
rent and historic international issues acces-
sible for secondary school students.
Materials are low-cost, reproducible, up-
dated annually.

Annually

4714 Close Up Publishing
44 Canal Center Plaza
Alexandria, VA 22314-1592
800-765-3131
Fax: 703-706-3564
Offers textbooks, workbooks and other publications focusing on self-esteem, learning
and counseling.

4715 Cognitive Concepts
PO Box 1363
Evanston, IL 60204-1363
888-328-8199
Fax: 847-328-5881
http://www.cogcon.com
Leading provider of language and literacy
software, books, internet services and staff
development. Specialize in integrating
technology with scientific principles and
proven instructional methods to offer effective and affordable learning solutions for
educators, specialists and families.

4716 College Board
45 Columbus Avenue
New York, NY 10023-6992
212-713-8000
Fax: 212-713-8282
http://www.collegeboard.org
Publishers of books of interest to educational researchers, policymakers, students,
counselors, teachers; products to prepare
students for college and test prep materials.

4717 Coloring Concepts
1732 Jefferson Street
Suite 7
Napa, CA 94559-1737
707-257-1516
800-257-1516
Fax: 707-253-2019
E-mail: chris@coloringconcepts.com
http://www.coloringconcepts.com
Colorable active learning books for middle
school through college that combine scientifically correct text with colorable illustrations to provide an enjoyable and
educational experience that helps the user
retain more information than during normal
reading. Subjects include Anatomy, Marine
Biology, Zoology, Botany, Human Evolution, Human Brain, Microbiology and biology.

Christopher Elson, Operations

**4718 Comprehensive Health Education
Foundation**
22419 Pacific Hwy S
Seattle, WA 98198-5106
206-824-2907
800-833-6388
E-mail: info@chef.org
http://www.chef.org
Primarily Health gives K-3 kids a dynamic,
hands-on health program while teaching academic skills.

Larry Clark, President
Marvin Hamanishi, Vice President

4719 Computer Learning Foundation
PO Box 60007
Palo Alto, CA 94306-0007
408-720-8898
Fax: 408-730-1191
E-mail: clf@computerlearning.org
http://www.computerlearning.org
Publishes books and videos on using tech-
nology.

4720 Computer Literacy Press
Computer Literacy Press
PO Box 562
Earlysville, VA 22936
513-600-3455
513-530-0110
Fax: 800-833-5413
E-mail: info@complitpress.com
http://www.complitpress.com
Instructional materials using hands-on,
step-by-step format, appropriate for
courses in adult and continuing education,
business education, computer literacy and
applications, curriculum integration,
Internet instruction, and training and staff
development. Products are available for
ranging from middle school through high
school as well as post secondary, teacher
training and adult/senior courses.

Robert First

4721 Concepts to Go
PO Box 10043
Berkeley, CA 94709-5043
510-848-3233
Fax: 510-486-1248
Develops and distributes manipulative ac-
tivities for language arts and visual commu-
nications for ages 3-8.

4722 Congressional Quarterly
1414 22nd Street NW
Washington, DC 20037-1003
202-887-8500
Fax: 202-293-1487
Comprehensive publications and reference
and paperback books pertaining to Con-

gress, US Government and politics, the
presidency, the Supreme Court, national affairs and current issues.

4723 Continental Press
520 E Bainbridge Street
Elizabethtown, PA 17022-2299
717-367-1836
800-233-0759
Fax: 717-367-5660
E-mail:
cpeducation@continentalpress.com
http://www.continentalpress.com
Publisher of print for PreK-12 (plus adult
education). Programs relate to skill areas in
reading, math, comprehension, phonics,
etc. Producers of Testlynx Software.

4724 Cottonwood Press
107 Cameron Drive
Suite 398
Fort Collins, CO 80525
970-204-0715
800-864-4297
Fax: 970-204-0761
E-mail:
cottonwood@cottonwwodpress.com
http://www.cottonwoodpress.com
Publishes books focusing on teaching language arts and writing, grades 5-12.

Cheryl Thurston

4725 Council for Exceptional Children
The Council for Exceptional Children
1920 Association Drive
Reston, VA 20191-1589
703-620-3660
800-232-7323
Fax: 703-264-9494
E-mail: cec@cec.sped.org
http://www.cec.sped.org
The Council for Exceptional Children is a
major publisher of special education literature and produces a catalog semiannually.

4726 Creative Teaching Press
Po Box 2723
Huntington Beach, CA 92647-0723
800-287-8879
Fax: 800-229-9929
E-mail:
customerservice@creativeteaching.com
http://www.creativeteaching.com
Offers language and literature-based books
including Teaching Basic Skills through
Literature, Literature-Based Homework
Activities, I Can Read! I Can Write!, Multi-
cultural Art Activities, Responding to Liter-
ature, and Linking Math and Literature.

Jim Connelly, President
Luella Connelly, Co-Founder

4727 Cricket Magazine Group
315 5th Street
Peru, IL 61354-2859
815-223-1500
Magazines of high quality children's literature.

4728 Curriculum Associates
PO Box 2001
North Billerica, MA 01862-0901
978-667-8000
800-225-0248
Fax: 800-366-1158
E-mail: cainfo@curriculumassociates.com
http://www.curriculumassociates.com
Supplementary educational materials;
cross-curriculum, language arts, reading,
study skills, test preparation, diagnostic assessments, emergent readers, videos, and
software.

4729 DC Heath & Company
125 Spring Street
Lexington, MA 02421-7801
781-862-6650
Publishes resources for all academic levels ranging from textbooks, fiction and nonfiction titles to business and college guides.

4730 DLM Teaching Resources
PO Box 4000
Allen, TX 75013-1302
972-248-6300
800-527-4747
Offers a variety of teacher's resources and guides for testing in all areas of education.

4731 Dawn Publications
14618 Tyler Foote Road
Nevada City, CA 95959-9316
530-478-7540
800-545-7475
Fax: 530-478-0112
Specializes in nature, children and health and healing books, tapes and videos and dedicated to helping people experience unity and harmony.

Bob Rinzler, Publisher
Glenn Hoveman, Editor

4732 Delta Education
PO Box 950
Hudson, NH 03051-0950
800-442-5444
Fax: 800-282-9560
Science programs, materials and curriculum kits.

4733 Dial Books for Young Readers
345 Hudson Street
New York, NY 10014-3658
212-366-2800
Fax: 212-366-2938
http://www.penguinputnam.com
General hardcover, children's books, from toddler through young adult, fiction and nonfiction.

4734 Didax Educational Resources
PO Box 507
Rowley, MA 01969-0907
978-948-2340
800-458-0024
Fax: 978-948-2813
E-mail: info@didaxinc.com
http://www.didaxinc.com
High quality educational materials featuring Unifix and hundreds of math and reading supplements.

Brian Scarlett, President
Martin Kennedy, VP

4735 Dinah-Might Activities
PO Box 39657
San Antonio, TX 78218-6657
210-698-0123
Fax: 210-698-0095
Learn how to integrate language arts, math, map and globe skills and more into a science curriculum. Books include The Big Book of Books and Activities, Organizing the Integrated Classroom, Write Your Own Thematic Units and Reading and Writing All Day Long.

4736 Dinocardz Company
146 5th Avenue
San Francisco, CA 94118-1310
415-751-5809
Dinosaur curriculums for grades 1-3 and 4-6.

4737 Disney Press
Disney Juvenile Publishing
114 5th Avenue
New York, NY 10011-5604
212-633-4400
Fax: 212-633-5929
Hardcover trade and library editions and paperback books for children, grades K-12.

Liisa-Ann Fink, President

4738 Dominic Press
1949 Kellogg Avenue
Carlsbad, CA 92008-6582
619-481-3838
Offers a range of materials for the Reading Recovery Program and Chapter 1 programs.

4739 Dorling Kindorley Company
95 Madison Avenue
New York, NY 10016
212-213-4800
Fax: 212-689-5254
Science books for all grade levels.

4740 Dover Publications
31 E 2nd Street
Mineola, NY 11501
516-294-7000
Fax: 516-742-6953
Fun and educational storybooks, coloring, activity, cut-and-assemble toy books, science for children.

Clarence Strowbridge, President

4741 Dutton Children's Books
375 Hudson Street
New York, NY 10014-3658
212-366-2000
Fax: 212-366-2948
General hardcover children's books from toddler through young adult, fiction and nonfiction.

4742 DynEd International
1350 Bayshore Highway
Suite 850
Burlingame, CA 94010
800-765-4375
Fax: 650-375-7017
http://www.dyned.com
Pre-K-adult listening and speaking skill development English language acquisition software.

Steven Kearney, Sales
Sue Young, Operations

4743 ETA - Math Catalog
620 Lakeview Parkway
Vernon Hills, IL 60061-1828
847-816-5050
800-445-5985
Fax: 847-816-5066
E-mail: info@etauniverse.com
http://www.etauniverse.com
Offers a full line of mathematics products, materials, books, textbooks and workbooks for grades K-12.

Mary Cooney, Product Development Manager
Monica Butler, Director Marketing

4744 ETR Associates
4 Carbonero Way
Scotts Valley, CA 95066
831-438-4060
800-321-4407
Fax: 800-435-8433
http://www.etr.org
ETR Associate's mission is to enhance the well-being of individuals, families and communities by providing leadership, educational resources, training and research in health promotion with an emphasis on sexuality and health education.

Robert Keet, President
Arnold W. Kriegel, Vice President

4745 EVAN-Motor Corporation
18 Lower Ragsdale Drive
Monterey, CA 93940-5728
831-649-5901
Fax: 800-777-4332
Resource materials for K-6 science educational programs.

4746 Early Start-Fun Learning
PO Box 350187
Jacksonville, FL 32235-0187
904-641-6138
Preschool materials for the educator.

4747 Earth Foundation
5151 Mitchelldale
B11
Houston, TX 77092-7200
713-686-9453
Fax: 713-686-6561
Join the largest active network of educators working to save endangered ecosystems and their species! Multi-disciplinary, hands-on curriculum and videos for the classroom.

Cynthia Everage, President

4748 Editorial Projects in Education
6935 Arlington Road
Suite 100
Bethesda, MD 20814-5233
301-280-3100
800-346-1834
Fax: 301-280-3250
E-mail: customercare@epe.org
http://www2.edweek.org
Publishes various newsletters and publications in the fields of history and education.

Christopher B Swanson, Director
Carole Vinograd Bausell, Assistant Director

4749 Edmark
Riverdeep Inc.
100 Pine Street
Suite 1900
San Francisco, CA 94111
415-659-2000
888-242-6747
Fax: 415-659-2020
E-mail: info@riverdeep.net
http://www.edmark.com
Develops innovative and effective educational materials for children.

Barry O'Callaghan, Chairman
Tony Mulderry, Executive Vice President

4750 Education Center
3515 W Market Street
Greensboro, NC 27403-1309
336-273-9409
Publishers of the Mailbox, teacher's helper magazines, learning centers clubs, classroom beautiful bulletin board clubs, the storybook club and more.

4751 Educational Marketer
SIMBA Information
11 Riverbend Drive
PO Box 4234
Stamford, CT 06907-0234
800-307-2529
Fax: 203-358-5824

Contains a range of print and electronic tools, including software and multimedia materials for educational institutions.

4752 Educational Press Association of America
Glassboro State College
Glassboro, NJ 08028
609-445-7349
Offers various publications and bibliographic data focusing on all aspects of education.

4753 Educational Productions
9000 SW Gemini Drive
Beaverton, OR 97008
503-644-7000
800-950-4949
Fax: 503-350-7000
E-mail: custserv@edpro.com
http://www.edpro.com
Video training programs that help increase parenting skills and help every teacher meet performance standards. Offers training on preventing discipline problems, increasing parenting skills, supporting literacy efforts and more.

4754 Educational Teaching Aids
620 Lakeview Pkwy
Vernon Hills, IL 60061-1838
847-816-5050
800-445-5985
Fax: 847-816-5066
E-mail: info@etauniverse.com
http://www.etauniverse.com
Manipulatives to enhance understanding of basic concepts and to help bridge the gap between the concrete and the abstract.

4755 Educators Progress Service
214 Center Street
Randolph, WI 53956
920-326-3127
888-951-4469
Fax: 920-326-3126
http://www.freeteachingaids.com
A complete spectrum of curriculum and mixed media resources for allgrade levels.

4756 Educators Publishing Service
31 Smith Place
Cambridge, MA 02138-1089
617-547-6706
800-225-5750
Fax: 617-547-0412
http://www.epsbooks.com
Supplementary workbooks and teaching materials in reading, spelling, vocabulary, comprehension, and elementary math, as well as materials for assessment and learning differences.

4757 Edumate-Educational Materials
2231 Morena Boulevard
San Diego, CA 92110-4134
619-275-7117
Multicultural and multilingual materials in the form of toys, puzzles, books, videos, music, visuals, games, dolls and teacher resources. Special emphasis on Spanish and other languages. Literature offered from North and South America.

Gustavo Blankenburg, President

4758 Ellis
406 W 10600 S
Suite 610
Salt Lake City, UT 84003
801-374-3424
888-756-1570
Fax: 801-374-3495
http://www.ellis.com
Publish software that teaches English.

4759 Encyclopaedia Britannica
333 N La Salle Street
Chicago, IL 60610
312-347-7159
800-323-1229
Fax: 312-294-2104
http://www.britannica.com
Books and related educational materials.

4760 Energy Learning Center
USCEA
1776 I Street NW
Suite 400
Washington, DC 20006-3700
703-741-5000
Fax: 703-741-6000
Energy learning materials.

4761 Essential Learning Products
PO Box 2590
Columbus, OH 43216-2590
800-357-3570
Fax: 614-487-2272
Publishers of phonics workbooks.

4762 Ethnic Arts & Facts
PO Box 20550
Oakland, CA 94620-0550
510-465-0451
888-278-5652
Fax: 510-465-7488
E-mail: eaf@ethnicartsnfacts.com
http://www.ethnicartsnfacts.com
Kit titles include: Traditional Africa, Urban Africa, China, Guatemala, Peru, Huichol Indians of Mexico, Chinese Shadow Puppet Kit. African-American Music History Mini-Kit. Artifact kits/resource booklets designed to enhance appreciation of cultural diversity, improve geographic literacy and sharpen critical thinking and writing skills.

Susan Drexler, Curriculum Specialist

4763 Evan-Moor Corporation
18 Lower Ragsdale Drive
Monterey, CA 93940-5728
How to Make Books with Children and other fine teacher resources and reproducible materials for all curriculum areas grades PreK-6.

4764 Everyday Learning Corporation
PO Box 812960
Chicago, IL 60681-2960
800-382-7670
Fax: 312-233-7860
University of Chicago school mathematics project. Everyday Mathematics enriched curriculum for grades K-6.

4765 Exploratorium
3601 Lyon Street
San Francisco, CA 94123-1099
415-563-7337
Fax: 415-561-0307
http://www.exploratorium.edu
Exploratorium is dedicated to the formal and informal teaching of science using innovative interactive methods of inquiry. It publishes materials for educators and pro-

vides professional development opportunities both in print and online.
Quarterly/Monthly

4766 Extra Editions K-6 Math Supplements
PO Box 38
Urbana, IL 61803-0038
Fax: 614-794-0107
Special needs math supplements offering 70 single-topic units from K-6 that reach students your basic math program misses. Extra Editions newspaper-like format uses animation with a hands-on approach to show real life necessity for computational skills, time, money, problem solving, critical thinking, etc. Ideal for Chapter One, Peer-Tutoring, Parental Involvement, Home Use, and more.

Craig Rucker, General Manager
Earl Ockenga, Author/Owner

4767 F(G) Scholar
Future Graph
538 Street Road
Suite 200
Southhampton, PA 18966-3780
215-396-0721
Fax: 215-396-0724
A revolutionary program for teaching, learning and using math. This single program allows students and teachers easy answers to Algebra, Trigonometry, Pre-Calculus, Calculus, Statistics, Probability and more. It combines all of the power of a graphing calculator, spreadsheet, drawing tools, mathematics and programming/scripting language and much more, and makes it simple and fun to use.

4768 Facts on File
11 Penn Plaza
New York, NY 10001
212-967-8800
800-322-8755
Fax: 212-967-9196
E-mail: llikoff@factsonfile.com
http://www.factsonfile.com
Reference books for teacher education, software, hardware and educational computer systems.
9 Hardcover Books

Laurie Likoff, Editorial Director

4769 Farrar, Straus & Giroux
19 Union Square W
New York, NY 10003-3304
212-741-6900
Fax: 212-633-9385
Children's, young adult and adult trade books in hardcover and paperback, including Sunburst Books, Aerial Miraso/libros juveniles and Hill and Wang.

4770 First Years
1 Kiddie Drive
Avon, MA 02322-1171
508-588-1220
Early childhood books, hardcover and paperback.

4771 Forbes Custom Publishing
60 5th Avenue
New York, NY 10011-8802
513-229-1000
800-355-9983
Fax: 800-451-3661
E-mail: fcpinfo@forbes.com
http://www.forbescp.com
Offers educators and teachers the opportunity to select unique teaching material to

create a book designed specifically for their courses.

4772 Formac Distributing
5502 Atlantic Street
Halifax, NS E3HIG-4
902-421-7022
800-565-1905
Fax: 902-425-0166
Contemporary and historical fiction for ages 6-15. Multicultural themes featuring Degrassi Y/A series; first novel chapter books.

4773 Frank Schaffer Publications
3195 Wilson Drive NW
Grand Rapids, MI 49534
800-417-3261
Fax: 888-203-9361
E-mail:
cpg_custserve@schoolspecialty.com
http://www.frankschaffer.com
Best-selling supplemental materials including charts, literature notes, resource materials and more.

4774 Franklin Watts
Grolier Publishing
Sherman Turnpike
Danbury, CT 06816
800-621-1115
800-843-3749
Fax: 800-374-4329
Publisher of library bound books, paperback and Big Books for literature based, multicultural classrooms and school libraries.

4775 Free Spirit Publishing
217 Fifth Avenue N
Suite 200
Minneapolis, MN 55401-1299
612-338-2068
Fax: 612-337-5050
Free Spirit is the leading publisher of learning tools that support young people's social and emotional health.

4776 Frog Publications
PO Box 280996
Tampa, FL 33682
813-935-5845
Fax: 813-935-3764
http://www.frog.com
An organized system of cooperative games for K-5 reading, language arts, thinking skills, math, social studies, Spanish and multicultural studies. Parental Involvement Program, Learning Centers, Test Preperation, Afterschool Program Materials. Drops in the Bucket daily practice books.

4777 Gareth Stevens
330 W Olive Street
Suite 100
Milwaukee, WI 53212
414-332-3520
800-542-2595
Fax: 414-336-0156
E-mail: info@gsinc.com
http://garethstevens.com
Complete display of supplemental children's reading material for grades K-6, including our New World Almanac Library imprint grades 6-12.

Bi-Annually
ISSN: 0-8368

Mark Sachner, Author
Juanita Jones, Marketing Manager
Jonathan Strickland, National Sales Manager

4778 Glencoe/Div. of Macmillan/McGraw Hill
936 Eastwind Drive
Westerville, OH 43081-3329
708-615-3360
800-442-9685
Fax: 972-228-1982
Secondary science programs.

4779 Goethe House New York
1014 5th Avenue
New York, NY 10028-0104
Teaching materials on Germany for the social studies classroom in elementary, middle and high schools.

4780 Goodheart-Willcox Publisher
18604 W Creek Drive
Tinley Park, IL 60477-6243
800-323-0440
Fax: 888-409-3900
E-mail: custerv@goodheartwillcox.com
http://www.goodheartwillcox.com
Comprehensive text designed to help young students learn about themselves, others, and the environment. Readers will develop skills in clothing, food, decision making, and life management. Case studies throughout allow students to apply learning to real-life situations.

4781 Greenhaven Press
PO Box 289009
San Diego, CA 92198-9009
800-231-5163
800-231-5163
Fax: 248-699-8035
E-mail: info@greenhaven.com
Publishers of the Opposing Viewpoints Series, presenting viewpoints in an objective, pro/con format on some of today's controversial subjects.

4782 Greenwillow Books
1350 Avenue of the Americas
New York, NY 10019-4702
212-261-6500
Fax: 212-261-6518
Offers publications for all reading levels.

4783 Grey House Publishing
185 Millerton Road
PO Box 860
Millerton, NY 12546
518-789-8700
800-562-2139
Fax: 518-789-0545
E-mail: books@greyhouse.com
http://www.greyhouse.com
Publisher of educational reference directories.

Richard Gottlieb, President
Leslie Mackenzie, Publisher

4784 Grolier Publishing
90 Sherman Turnpike
Danbury, CT 06816
203-797-3500
800-621-1115
Fax: 203-797-3197
http://www.publishing.grolier.com
Publisher of library bound and paperback books in the areas of social studies, science, reference, history, and biographies for schools and libraries for grades K-12.

4785 Gryphon House
Gryphon House
PO Box 275
Mount Rainier, MD 20712-0275
301-779-6200
Fax: 301-595-0051
E-mail: info@ghbooks.com
http://www.ghbooks.com
Resource and activity books for early childhood teachers and directors.

Cathy Callootte, Marketing Director

4786 Hands-On Prints
PO Box 5899-268
Berkeley, CA 94705
510-601-6279
Fax: 510-601-6278
Specializes in cultural and language materials for children with an emphasis on internationalism and multiculturalism.

Christina Cheung, President

4787 Hardcourt Religion Publishers
6277 Sea Harbor Drive
Orlando, FL 32887
563-557-3700
800-922-7696
Fax: 563-557-3719
E-mail: hardcourtreligion.com
Publishers of religion education materials for schools and parishes.

4788 Hazelden Educational Materials
PO Box 176
Center City, MN 55012-0176
651-257-4010
Fax: 651-213-4590
Educational publisher of materials supporting both students and faculty in areas of substance abuse and related topics.

4789 Heinemann
361 Hanover Street
Portsmouth, NH 03801-3959
603-431-7894
Fax: 203-750-9790
Holistic/student-centered publications, videotapes and workshops for parents, teachers and administrators.

4790 Henry Holt & Company
175 Fifth Avenue
New York, NY 10010
646-307-5095
800-628-9658
Fax: 212-633-0748
Books and materials for classroom teachers, grades 6-adult, including programs on science literacy.

4791 Henry Holt Books for Young Readers
115 W 18th Street
New York, NY 10011-4113
800-628-9658
Fax: 212-647-0490
Hardcover and paperback trade books for preschool through young adult, fiction and nonfiction. Also, big books and promotional materials are available.

4792 High Touch Learning
PO Box 754
Houston, MN 55943-0754
507-896-3500
800-255-0645
Fax: 507-896-3243
Classroom interactive learning maps promoting the hands-on approach to the teaching of social studies.

4793 High/Scope Educational Research Foundation
600 N River Street
Ypsilanti, MI 48198-2821
734-485-2000
800-40 -RESS
Fax: 734-485-4467
Early childhood, elementary, movement and music, and adolescent materials. Over 300 titles of books, videos, cassettes and CDs from which to choose. Research and training materials as well as curriculum and development materials are based on the acclaimed High/Scope active learning approach.

Emily Koepp, President

4794 Holiday House
425 Madison Avenue
New York, NY 10017-1110
212-688-0085
Fax: 212-688-0395
Hardcover and paperback children's books. General fiction and nonfiction, preschool through high school.

4795 Hoover's
5800 Airport
Dallas, TX 78752-3812
512-374-4500
Fax: 512-374-4501
Everything educational, for the early childhood and K-12 market. As a partner for over 100 years, the company is eager to extend their commitment to produce quality, timely shipping and customer service to the public. Offer over 10,000 products for infants, toddlers, pre-school and school age educational needs.

4796 Horn Book Guide
Horn Book
56 Roland Street
Suite 200
Boston, MA 02129
617-628-0225
800-325-1170
Fax: 617-628-0882
E-mail: info@hbook.com
http://http://www.hbook.com
The most comprehensive review source of children's and young adult books available. Published each spring and fall, the Guide contains concise, critical reviews of almost every hardcover trade children's and young adult book published in the United States - nearly 2,000 books each issue.

BiAnnually
ISSN: 1044-405X

Anne Quirk, Marketing Manager
Roger Sutton, Editor

4797 Houghton Mifflin Books for Children
222 Berkeley Street
Boston, MA 02116-3748
617-351-5000
800-225-3362
Fax: 617-351-1111
http://www.hmco.com
Wide variety of children's and young adult books, fiction and nonfiction.

4798 Houghton Mifflin Company: School Division
222 Berkeley Street
Boston, MA 02116-3748
617-351-5000
Fax: 617-651-1106
Children's literature; K-12 reading and language arts print and software programs; and testing and evaluation for K-12.

4799 Hyperion Books for Children
114 5th Avenue
New York, NY 10011-5604
212-633-4400
Fax: 212-633-5929
Children's books in paperback and hardcover editions.

4800 ITP South-Western Publishing Company
5101 Madison Road
Cincinnati, OH 45227-1427
800-824-5179
Fax: 800-487-8488
Innovative instructional materials for teaching integrated science.

4801 Idea Factory
10710 Dixon Drive
Riverview, FL 33569-7406
813-677-6727
Teacher resource books, science project ideas, materials and more for elementary and middle school teachers.

4802 Institute for Chemical Education
University of Wisconsin
1101 University Avenue
Madison, WI 53706-1322
608-262-3033
800-991-5534
Fax: 608-265-8094
E-mail: ice@chem.wisc.edu
http://ice.chem.wisc.edu
Hands-on activities, publications, kits and videos.

4803 Institute for Educational Leadership
1001 Connecticut Avenue NW
Suite 310
Washington, DC 20036-5541
202-822-8405
Fax: 202-872-4050
The Institute's list of publications on educational trends and policies is available to the public.

Michael C Usdan, President

4804 IntelliTools
1720 Corporate Circle
Petaluma, CA 94954
707-773-2000
800-899-6687
Fax: 707-773-2001
http://www.intellitools.com
Provider of hardware and software giving students with special needs comprehensive access to learning.

4805 Intellimation
130 Cremona Drive
Santa Barbara, CA 93117-5599
805-968-2291
800-346-8355
Fax: 805-968-8899
Educational materials in all areas of curriculum for early learning through college level. Over 400 titles are available in video, and software and multimedia exclusively for the Macintosh. Free catalogs avaiable.

Karin Fisher, Marketing Associate
Marlene Carlyle, Marketing Supervisor

4806 Intercultural Press
100 City Hall Plaza
Suite 501
Boston, MA 02108
617-523-3801
888-273-2539
Fax: 617-523-3708
E-mail: books@interculturalpress.com
http://www.interculturalpress.com
Publishes over 100 titles.

Judy Carl-Hendrick, Managing Editor

4807 J Weston Walch, Publisher
PO Box 658
Portland, ME 04104-0658
207-772-2846
800-558-2846
Fax: 207-772-3105
http://www.walch.com
Walch Publishing is an independent, family-owned publisher of educational supplemental materials for grades 3 through 12 and adult makets.

4808 Jacaranda Designs
3000 Jefferson Street
Boulder, CO 80304-2638
707-374-2543
Fax: 707-374-2543
Authentic African children's books from Kenya, including modern concept stories for K-3 in bilingual editions, folktales, and traditional cultural stories for older readers. All books are written and illustrated by African Kenyans.

Carrie Jenkins Williams, President

4809 Jarrett Publishing Company
PO Box 1460
Ronkonkoma, NY 11779
631-981-4248
Fax: 631-588-4722
Offers a wide range of books for today's educational needs.

4810 JayJo Books
Guidance Channel
135 Dupont Street
PO Box 760
Plainview, NY 11803
516-349-5520
800-999-6884
Fax: 516-349-5521
E-mail:
jayjobooks@guidancechannel.com
http://www.jayjo.com
Publisher of books to help teachers, parents and children cope with chronic illnesses, special needs and health education in classroom, family and social settings.

Sally Germain, Editor-in-Chief

4811 John Wiley & Sons
111 River Street
Hoboken, NJ 07030-5774
201-748-6000
Fax: 201-748-6088
Publish science and nature books for children and adults.

4812 Jossey-Bass: An Imprint of Wiley
Jossey-Bass/Pfeiffer
989 Market Street
San Francisco, CA 94103-1741
415-433-1740
Fax: 415-433-0499
http://www.josseybass.com
Creating educational incentives that work.

Adrianne Biggs, Publicity/Manager
Jennifer A O'Day, Editor

4813 Junior Achievement
1 Education Way
Colorado Springs, CO 80906-4477
719-540-8000
Fax: 719-540-6127
Provides business and economics-related materials and programs to students in grades K-12. All programs feature volunteers from the local business community. Materials are free, but available only from local Junior Achievement offices.

4814 Kaeden Corporation
PO Box 16190
19915 Lake Road
Rocky River, OH 44116
440-356-0030
800-890-7323
Fax: 440-356-5081
E-mail: lcowan@kaedeen.com
http://www.kaeden.com
Books for emergent readers at the K, 1 and 2 levels, ideal for Title 1 and Reading Recovery and other at-risk reading programs.

Laura Cowan, Sales Manager
Joan Hoyer, Office Manager

4815 Kane/Miller Book Publishers
PO Boxn 8515
La Jolla, CA 92038-0529
858-456-0540
Fax: 858-456-9641
E-mail: info@kanemiller.com
http://www.kanemiller.com
English translation of foreign children's picture books. Distributors of Spanish language children's books.

Byron Parnell, Sales Manager
Kira Lynn, President

4816 Keep America Beautiful
1010 Washington Boulevard
Stamford, CT 06901
203-323-8987
Fax: 203-325-9199
E-mail: info@kab.org
http://www.kab.org
K-12 curriculum specializing in litter prevention and environmental education. Education posters with lesson plans printed right on the back of each poster and school recycling guides.

4817 Kendall-Hunt Publishing Company
4050 Westmark Drive
Dubuque, IA 52002-2624
319-589-1000
800-228-0810
Fax: 800-772-9165
E-mail: webmaster@kendallhunt.com
http://www.kendallhunt.com
A leading custom publisher in the United States with over 6,000 titles in print. Kendall/Hunt publishes educational materials for kindergarten through college to continuing education creditation and distance learning courses.

Karen Berger, Customer Service Assistant

4818 Knowledge Adventure
2377 Crenshaw Blvd
Suite 302
Torrance, CA 90501
310-533-3400
Fax: 310-533-3700
E-mail: editorial@education.com
http://www.knowledgeadventure.com
Develops, publishes, and distributes best-selling multimedia educational software for use in both homes and schools.

4819 Knowledge Unlimited
PO Box 52
Madison, WI 53701-0052
800-356-2303
Fax: 608-831-1570
http://www.newscurrents.com
NewsCurrents, the most effective current events programs for grades 3-12. Now available on DVD or Online.

4820 Kraus International Publications
358 Saw Mill River Road
Millwood, NY 10546-1035
914-762-2200
800-223-8323
Fax: 914-762-1195
Offers teacher resource notebooks with complete resource information for teachers and administrators at all levels. Great for program planning, quick reference, inservice training. Also offers books on early childhood education, English/language arts, mathematics, science, health education and visual arts.

Barry Katzen, President

4821 Lake Education
AGS/Lake Publishing Company
500 Harbor Boulevard
Belmont, CA 94002-4075
650-592-1606
800-328-2560
Fax: 800-471-8457
Alternative learning materials for underachieving students grades 6-12, RSL and adult basic education. High interest, low readability fiction, adapted classic literature, lifeskills and curriculum materials to supplement and support many basal programs.

Phil Schlenter
Carol Hegarty, VP Editorial

4822 Landmark Editions
PO Box 270169
Kansas City, MO 64127-0169
816-241-4919
Books written and illustrated by children.

4823 Langenseheidt Publishing
515 Valley Street
Maplewood, NJ 07040-1337
800-526-4953
Fax: 908-206-1104
E-mail: edusales@hammond.com
http://www.hammondmap.com
World maps, atlases, general reference guides and CD-Roms.

4824 Lawrence Hall of Science
University of California
Berkeley, CA 94720
510-642-5132
Fax: 510-642-1055
E-mail: lhsinfo@uclink.berkeley.edu
http://www.lawrencehallofscience.org
Offers programs and materials in the field of science and math education for teachers, families and interested citizens. Exhibits include Equals, Family Math, CePUP and FOSS.

Linda Schneider, Marketing Manager
Mike Salter, Marketing/PR Associate

4825 Leap Frog Learning Materials
6401
Suite 100
Emeryville, CA 94608-1071
510-596-3333
800-701-5327
Learning materials, books, posters, games and toys for children.

4826 Learning Connection
19 Devane Street
Frostproof, FL 33843-2017
863-635-5610
800-338-2282
Fax: 863-635-4676
Thematic, literature-based units with award-winning books, media and hands-on for PK-12 including parent involvement, early childhood, bilingual, literacy, math, writing, science and multicultural.

4827 Learning Disabilities Association of America
Learning Disabilities Association of America
4156 Library Road
Pittsburgh, PA 15234-1349
412-341-1515
888-300-6710
Fax: 412-344-0224
E-mail: info@ldaamerica.org
http://www.ldaamerica.org
Has 50 state affiliates with more than 300 local chapters. The national office has a resource center of over 500 publications for sale.

4828 Learning Links
2300 Marcus Avenue
New Hyde Park, NY 11042-1083
516-437-9075
800-724-2616
Fax: 516-437-5392
E-mail: learningLx@aol.com
http://www.learinglinks.com
All you need for literature based instruction; Noveltie, study guides, thematic units books and more.

4829 Lee & Low Books
95 Madison Avenue
Suite 606
New York, NY 10016-3303
212-779-4400
Fax: 212-683-1894
E-mail: info@leeandlow.com
http://www.leeandlow.com
A multicultural children's book publisher. Our primary focus is on picture books, especially stories set in contemporary America. Spanish language titles are available.

Craig Low, VP Publisher
Louise May, Executive Editor

4830 Leo A Myer Associates/LAMA Books
20956 Corsair Boulevard
Hayward, CA 94545-1002
510-785-1091
Fax: 510-785-1099
E-mail: lama@lmabooks.com
Writers and publishers of HVAC books.

Barbara Ragura, Marketing Assistant

4831 Lerner Publishing Group
A Division Lerner Publications Group
241 1st Avenue N
Minneapolis, MN 55401-1607
612-332-3344
800-328-4929
Fax: 612-332-7615
http://www.lernerbooks.com
Primarily nonfiction for readers of all grade levels. List includes titles encompassing nature, geography, natural and physical science, current events, ancient and modern history, world art, special interests, sports, world cultures, and numer-

ous biography series. Some young adult and middle grade fiction.

Jennifer Martin, Submissions Editor

4832 Linden Tree Children's Records & Books
170 State Street
Los Altos Hills, CA 94022-2863
650-949-3390
Fax: 650-949-0346
Offers a wide variety of books, audio cassettes and records for children.

4833 Listening Library
One Park Avenue
Old Greenwich, CT 06870-1727
203-637-3616
800-243-4504
Fax: 800-454-0606
E-mail: moreinfo@listeninglib.com
http://www.listeninglib.com
A producer of quality unabridged audiobooks for listeners of all ages. Specializing in children's literature and adult classics.

BiAnnually

Annette Imperati, Director
Sales/Marketing

4834 Little, Brown & Company
3 Center Plaza
Boston, MA 02108-2084
617-227-0730
Fax: 617-263-2854
Trade books for children and young adults, hardcover and paper, including Sierra Club Books for Children.

4835 Lodestar Books
375 Hudson Street
New York, NY 10014-3658
212-366-2000
General hardcover children's books from toddler through young adult, fiction and nonfiction.

4836 Lothrop, Lee & Shepard Books
1350 Avenue of the Americas
New York, NY 10019-4702
212-261-6500
Fax: 212-261-6518
Children's books.

4837 Lynne Rienner Publishing
1800 30th Street
Suite 314
Boulder, CO 80301
303-333-3003
800-803-8488
Fax: 303-333-4037
E-mail: karen-hemmes@mindspring.com
http://www.fireflybooks.com
Publishes academic-level books with a focus on international and domestic social sciences.

Karen Hemmes, Publicist
Mary Kay Opicka, Publicist

4838 MHS
PO Box 950
North Tonawanda, NY 14120-0950
416-492-2627
800-456-3003
Fax: 416-492-3343
E-mail: customer_service@mhs.com
http://www.mhs.com
Publishers and distributors of professional assessment materials.

Steven J Stein, PhD, President

4839 MacMillan Children's Books
1633 Broadway
New York, NY 10019
212-512-2000
Fax: 800-835-3202
Hardcover trade books for children and young adults.

4840 MacMillan Reference
1633 Broadway
New York, NY 10019
212-512-2000
Fax: 800-835-3202
A wide variety of titles for students and teachers of all grade levels.

4841 Macmillan/McGraw-Hill School Division
1633 Broadwaty
New York, NY 10019
212-654-8500
800-442-9685
Fax: 800-835-3202
Quality literature for the student and excellent support for the teacher. Programs and educational materials for all grade levels.

4842 Macro Press
18242 Peters Court
Fountain Valley, CA 92708-5873
310-823-9556
Fax: 310-306-2296
Includes resources to conduct thematic hands-on science lessons and integrated curriculum; and, student materials offering a Scientist's Notebook and reading materials to integrate hands-on (grade specific) scientific thinking, problem solving and documenting skills to benefit all students. Nine award-winning K-6 teachers (200+ years combined experience) joined together to address the real needs of today's high student load.

Leigh Hoven Swenson, President

4843 Magna Publications
2718 Dryden Drive
Madison, WI 53704
608-227-8109
800-206-4805
Fax: 608-246-3597
E-mail: carriej@magnapubs.com
http://www.magnapubs.com
Produces eight subscriptions newsletters in the field of higher education.

Carrie Jenson, Conference Manager
David Burns, Associate Publisher

4844 Major Educational Resources Corporation
10153 York Road
Suite 107
Hunt Valley, MD 21030-3340
800-989-5353
Multimedia curriculum tools for educators.

4845 Margaret K McElderry Books
1633 Broadway
New York, NY 10019
212-512-2000
Fax: 800-835-3202
Hardcover trade books for children and young adults.

4846 Mari
3215 Pico Boulevard
Santa Monica, CA 90405-4603
310-829-2212
800-955-9494
Fax: 310-829-2317
http://www.mariinc.com

The best literature learning materials for K-12. Offers Mini-Units for writing and critical thinking skills, Literature Extenders that extend literature across the curriculum and Basic Skills Through Literature that combine literature and skill work.

4847 MasterTeacher
Leadership Lane
PO Box 1207
Manhattan, KS 66505-1207
800-669-9633
Fax: 800-669-1132
http://www.masterteacher.com
A publisher of videotapes for the professional. Offers programs on inclusion, tests and testing, student motivation, discipline and more.

4848 MathSoft
101 Main Street
Cambridge, MA 02142
617-577-1017
800-628-4223
Fax: 617-577-8829
http://www.mathsoft.com
Provider of math, science and engineering software for business, academia, research and government.

4849 McCracken Educational Services
PO Box 3588
Blaine, WA 98231
360-332-1881
800-447-1462
Fax: 360-332-7332
E-mail: mes@mccrackened.com
http://www.mccrackened.com
Materials for beginning reading, writing and spelling. Big Books, manipulative materials, teacher resource books, spelling through phonics, posters and both audio and video tapes.

Robert & Marlene McCracken, Author

4850 McGraw Hill Children's Publishing
PO Box 1650
Grand Rapids, MI 49501-1650
616-363-1290
Fax: 800-543-2690
New self-esteem literature based reading and multicultural literature based reading.

4851 Mel Bay Publications
4 Industrial Drive
PO Box 66
Pacific, MO 63069-0066
637-257-3970
800-863-5229
Fax: 636-257-5062
E-mail: email@melbay.com
http://www.melbay.com
Music supply distributors.

Sheri Stephens, Customer Service Supervisor

4852 Merriam-Webster
47 Federal Street
#281
Springfield, MA 01105-3805
413-734-3134
Fax: 413-734-0257
A wide variety of titles for students and teachers of all grade levels.

4853 Millbrook Press
1251 Washington Avenue N
Minneapolis, MN 55401
203-740-2220
800-328-4929
Fax: 800-332-1132
http://www.millbrookpress.com
Exceptional nonfiction juvenile and young adult books for schools and public libraries.

4854 Milton Roy Company
820 Linden Avenue
Rochester, NY 14625-2710
716-248-4000
Teacher support materials, scientific kits and manuals.

4855 Mimosa Publications
90 New Montgomery Street
San Francisco, CA 94105-4501
415-982-5350
A language based K-3 math program featuring big books, language and activity based math topics and multicultural math activities.

4856 Model Technologies
2420 Van Layden Way
Modesto, CA 95356-2454
209-575-3445
Curriculum guides and scientific instruction kits.

4857 Mondo Publishing
980 Avenue Of The Americas
New York, NY 10018
Fax: 888-532-4492
E-mail: mondopub@aol.com
http://www.mondopub.com
Offers multicultural big books and music cassettes: Folk Tales from Around the World series; Exploring Habitats series; and, Let's Write and Sing a Song, whole language activities through music.

4858 Morning Glory Press
6595 San Haroldo Way
Buena Park, CA 90620-3748
714-828-1998
888-612-8254
Fax: 714-828-2049
E-mail: info@morningglorypress.com
http://www.morningglorypress.com
Publishes books and materials for teenage parents.
Quarterly
Jeanne Lindsay, President
Carole Blum, Promotion Director

4859 Music for Little People
PO Box 1460
Redway, CA 95560-1460
707-923-3991
Fax: 707-923-3241
Science and environmental education materials set to music for younger students.

4860 N&N Publishing Company
18 Montgomery Street
Middletown, NY 10940-5116
Low-cost texts and workbooks.

4861 NASP Publications
National Association of School Psychologists
4340 EW Highway
Suite 402
Bethesda, MD 20814
301-657-0270
Fax: 301-657-0275
E-mail: center@naspweb.org
http://www.naspionline.org
Over 100 hard-to-find books and videos centering on counseling, psychology and guidance for students.
Betty Somerville, President

4862 NCTM Educational Materials
National Council of Teachers of Mathematics
1906 Association Drive
Reston, VA 20191-1502
703-620-9840
Fax: 703-476-2970
E-mail: nctm@nctm.org
http://www.nctm.org
Publications, videotapes, software, posters and information to improve the teaching and learning of mathematics.
Harry B Tunis, Publications Director
Cynthia C Rosso, Director Marketing Services

4863 NYSTROM
3333 N Elston Avenue
Chicago, IL 60618-5898
773-463-1144
800-621-8086
Fax: 773-463-0515
Maps, globes, hands-on geography and history materials.

4864 Narrative Press
PO Box 145
Crabtree, OR 97335
800-315-9005
Fax: 541-259-2154
E-mail: service@narrativepress.com
http://www.narrativepress.com
Publisher of first person narratives of adventure and exploration.
Vickie Zimmer, Editor

4865 National Aeronautics & Space Administration
NASA Headquarters
300 E Street SW
Washington, DC 20546
202-358-0000
Fax: 202-358-3251
Over 10 different divisions offering a wide variety of classroom and educational materials in the areas of science, physics, aeronautics and more.

4866 National Center for Science Teaching & Learning/Eisenhower Clearinghouse
1929 Kenny Road
Columbus, OH 43210-1015
Collects and creates the most up-to-date listing of science and mathematics curriculum materials in the nation.

4867 National Council for the Social Studies
8555 Sixteenth Street
Suite 500
Silver Spring, MD 20910
301-588-1800
800-683-0812
Fax: 301-588-2049
E-mail: sgriffin@ncss.org
http://www.ncss.org
Publishes books, videotapes and journals in the area of social education and social studies.

4868 National Council of Teachers of English
1111 W Kenyon Road
Urbana, IL 61801-1096
217-328-3870
800-369-6283
Fax: 217-328-9645
E-mail: public_info@ncte.org
http://www.ncte.org
Devoted to the advancement of English language and literature studies at all levels of education. Publishes 12 periodicals, a member newspaper, and 20-25 books a year, and holds conventions and workshops.
Lori Bianchini, Public Affairs

4869 National Council on Economic Education
1140 Avenue of the Americas
New York, NY 10036-5803
212-730-7007
Offers various programs including their latest, US History: Eyes on the Economy, a council program for secondary education teachers.

4870 National Geographic School Publishing
1145 17th Street NW
Washington, DC 20036
800-368-2728
Fax: 515-362-3366
Books, magazines, videos, and software in the areas of science, geography and social studies.

4871 National Geographic Society
PO Box 10041
Des Moines, IA 50340-0597
800-548-9797
Fax: 301-921-1575
http://www.nationalgeographic.com
Science materials, videos, CD-ROM's and telecommunications program.

4872 National Head Start Association
1651 Prince Street
Alexandria, VA 22314-2818
703-739-0875
Fax: 703-739-0878
http://www.nhsa.org
Dedicated to promoting and protecting the Head Start program. Advocates on the behalf of America's low-income children and families. Publishes many books, periodicals and resource guides. Offers a legislative hotline as well as training programs through the NHSA Academy.
Ron Herndon, President
Blanche Russ-Glover, VP

4873 National Textbook Company
4255 W Touhy Avenue
Lincolnwood, IL 60646-1975
847-679-5500
800-323-4900
Fax: 847-679-2494
Offers various textbooks for students grades K-college level.

4874 National Women's History Project
3343 Industrial Drive
Suite #4
Santa Rosa, CA 95403
707-636-2888
Fax: 707-636-2909
E-mail: nwhp@aol.com
http://www.nwhp.org
Non-profit organization, the clearinghouse for information about multicultural US women's history. Initiated March as National Women's History Month; issues a catalog of women's history materials. Provides teacher-training nationwide; coordinates the Women's History Network; produces videos, posters, curriculum units and other curriculum materials.

Molly Murphy MacGregor, Exec. Dir./Co-Founder

4875 National Writing Project
University of California, Berkeley
2105 Bancroft Way
#1042
Berkeley, CA 94720-1042
510-642-6096
Fax: 510-642-4545
http://www.writingproject.org
Technical reports and occasional paper series: a series of research reports and essays on the research in and practice of teaching writing at all grade levels.

4876 New Canaan Publishing Company
PO Box 752
New Canaan, CT 06840
203-966-3408
800-705-5698
Fax: 203-966-3408
http://www.newcanaanpublishing.com
Children's publications.

4877 New Press
38 Greene Street
4th Floor
New York, NY 10013
212-629-8802
Fax: 212-629-8617
Multicultural teaching materials, focusing on the social studies.

4878 NewsBank
5020 Tamiami Trail N
Suite 110
Naples, FL 34103-2837
941-263-6004
Electronic information services that support the science curriculum.

4879 North South Books
11 E 26th Street
17 Floor
New York, NY 10010-2007
212-706-4545
Fax: 212-706-4544
Publisher of quality children's books by authors and illustrators from around the world.

4880 Nystrom, Herff Jones
3333 N Elston Avenue
Chicago, IL 60618-5811
913-432-8100
Fax: 913-432-3958
Charts for earth, life and physical science for upper elementary and high school grades.

4881 Options Publishing
PO Box 1749
Merrimack, NH 03054
603-429-2698
800-782-7300
Fax: 603-424-4056
E-mail: serviceoptionspublishing.com m
http://www.optionspublishing.com
Publishers of supplemental materials in reading, math and language arts.

Marty Furlong, VP

4882 Organization of American Historians
112 N Bryan Avenue
Bloomington, IN 47408-4136
812-855-7311
800-446-8923
Fax: 812-855-0696
E-mail: oah@oah.org
http://www.oah.org
Offers various products and literature dealing with American history, as well as job registries, Magazine of History, Journal of American History, OAH Newsletter, and more.

Damon Freeman, Marketing Manager
Michael Regoli, Publications Director

4883 Oxton House Publishers, LLC
Po Box 209
Farmington, ME 04938
207-779-1923
800-539-7323
Fax: 207-779-0623
E-mail: info@oxtonhouse.com
http://www.oxtonhouse.com
Publishes high quality, innovative, affordable materials for teaching, reading and mathematics and for dealing with learning disabilities.

William Berlinghoff, Managing Editor
Bobby Brown, Marketing Director

4884 PF Collier
1315 W 22nd Street
Suite 250
Oak Brook, IL 60523-2061
A leading educational publisher for more than 110 years, creating the home learning center. Products include: Collier's Encyclopedia, Quickstart and Early Learning Fun.

4885 PRO-ED
8700 Shoal Creek Boulevard
Austin, TX 78757-6897
512-451-3246
800-897-3202
Fax: 800-397-7633
E-mail: info@proedinc.com
http://www.proedinc.com
A leading publisher of assessments, therapy materials and resource/reference books in the areas of speech, language, and hearing; psychology; special education; and occupational therapy.

4886 Parenting Press
PO Box 75267
11065 5th Avenue NE
Seattle, WA 98125-0267
206-364-2900
800-992-6657
Fax: 206-364-0702
E-mail: office@ParentingPress.com
http://www.ParentingPress.com
Publishes books for parents, children, and professionals who work with them. Nonfiction books include topics on parenting, problem solving, dealing with feelings, safety, and special issues.

Carolyn J Threadgill, Publisher

4887 Penguin USA
375 Hudson Street
New York, NY 10014-3658
212-366-2000
Fax: 212-366-2934
http://www.penguinputnam.com
Children's and adult hardcover and paperback general trade books, including classics and multiethnic literature.

4888 Perfection Learning Corporation
Perfection Learning
10520 New York Avenue
Des Moines, IA 50322
303-333-3003
800-803-8488
Fax: 303-333-4037
E-mail: karen-hemmes@mindspring.com
http://www.fireflybooks.com
Perfection Learning publishes high interest-low reading level fiction and non-fiction books for young adults.

Karen Hemmes, Publicist
Mary Kay Opicka, Publicist

4889 Perma Bound Books
E Vandalia Road
Jacksonville, IL 62650
217-243-5451
800-637-6581
Fax: 800-551-1169
Thematically arranged for K-12 classroom use with 480,000 titles available in durable Perma-Bound bindings; related library services also available.

Ben Mangum, President

4890 Personalizing the Past
1534 Addison Street
Berkeley, CA 94703-1454
415-388-9351
Museum quality artifact history kits complete with integrated lesson plan teachers guide. Copy-ready student worksheets, literature section, videos and audio tapes. United States and ancient world history.

4891 Perspectives on History Series
Discovery Enterprises, Ltd.
31 Laurelwood Drive
Carlisle, MA 01741
978-287-5401
800-729-1720
Fax: 978-287-5402
E-mail: ushistorydocs@aol.com
http://www.ushistorydocs.com
Primary and secondary source materials for middle school to college levels; bibliographies; plays for grades 5-9 on American history topics. Educators curriculum guides for using primary source documents. 75-volumes of primary source documents on American history may be purchased individually or in sets. New Researching American History Series presents documents with summaries and vocabulary on each

page (20 volumes) sold individually or in sets.

JoAnne Deitch, President

4892 Peytral Publications Inc
PO Box 1162
Minnetonka, MN 55345
952-949-8707
877-739-8725
Fax: 952-906-9777
E-mail: inquiry@peytral.com
http://www.peytral.com
Books and videos for educators.

Peggy Hammeken, Owner

4893 Phelps Publishing
PO Box 22401
Cleveland, OH 44122
216-752-4938
Fax: 216-752-4941
E-mail: earl@phelpspublishing.com
http://www.phelpspublishing.com
Publisher of art instruction books for ages 8 to 108.

Earl Phelps, President

4894 Phoenix Learning Resources
12 W 31st Street
New York, NY 10001-4415
212-629-3887
800-221-1274
Fax: 212-629-5648
Phoenix Learning Resources provides all students with the skills to be successful, lifelong learners.

Alexander Burke, President
John Rothermich, Executive VP

4895 Pleasant Company Publications
8400 Fairway Pl
Middleton Branch, WI 53562-2554
608-836-4848
800-233-0264
Fax: 800-257-3865
The American Girls Collection historical fiction series.

4896 Pocket Books/Paramount Publishing
1230 Avenue of the Americas
New York, NY 10020-1513
212-698-7000
Books for children and young adults in hardcover and paperback originals and reprints of bestselling titles.

4897 Population Connection
1400 16th Street NW
Suite 320
Washington, DC 20036-2290
800-767-1956
Fax: 202-332-2302
E-mail: poped@populationconnection.org
http://www.populationconnection.org
Curriculum materials for grades K-12 to teach students about population dynamics and their social, political and environmental effects in the United States and the world.

Pamela Wasserman, Director Education

4898 Prentice Hall School Division
340 Rancheros Drive
Suite 160
San Marcos, CA 92069
760-510-0222
Fax: 760-510-0230
Superb language arts textbooks and ancillaries for students grades 6-12.

4899 Prentice Hall School Division - Science
1 Lake Street
Upper Saddle River, NJ 07458
201-236-7000
Fax: 201-236-3381
Science textbooks and ancillaries for grades 6-12 and advanced placement students.

4900 Prentice Hall/Center for Applied Research in Education
1 Lake Street
Upper Saddle River, NJ 07458
201-236-7000
Fax: 201-236-3381
Publisher of practical, time and work saving teaching/learning resources for PreK-12 teachers and specialists in all content areas.

4901 Project Learning Tree
American Forest Foundation
1111 19th Street NW
Suite 780
Washington, DC 20036-3603
202-463-2462
Fax: 202-463-2461
Pre-K through grade 12 curriculum materials containing hundreds of hands-on science activities. PLT uses the forest as a window into the natural world to increase students' understanding of our complex environment. Stimulates critical and creative thinking; develops the ability to make informed decisions on environmental issues; and instills the confidence and commitment to take action on them.

Kathy McGlauflin, President

4902 Prufrock Press
PO Box 8813
Waco, TX 76714
800-998-2208
Fax: 800-240-0333
http://www.prufrock.com
Exciting classroom products for gifted and talented education.

4903 Puffin Books
375 Hudson Street
New York, NY 10014-3658
212-366-2819
Fax: 212-366-2040
Offers the Puffin Teacher Club set.

Lisa Crosby, President

4904 RR Bowker
Reed Reference Publishing Company
121 Chanlon Road
New Providence, NJ 07974-1541
908-464-6800
Fax: 908-665-6688
A leading information provider to schools and libraries for over one hundred years, RR Bowker provides quality resources to help teachers and librarians make informed reading selections for children and young adults.

4905 Raintree/Steck-Vaughn
Harcourt Achieve
6277 Sea Harbor Drive
Orlando, FL 32887
800-531-5015
Fax: 800-699-9459
http://www.steck-vaughn.com
Reference materials for K-8 students and texts for underachieving students K-12.

Tim McEwen, President
Martijn Tel, Chief Financial Officer

4906 Rand McNally
8255 Central Park Avenue
Skokie, IL 60076-2970
847-674-2151
Cross-curricular products featuring reading/language arts in the social studies.

4907 Random House
201 E 50th Street
New York, NY 10022-7703
212-751-2600
Fax: 212-572-8700
Offers a line of science trade books for grades K-8.

4908 Random House/Bullseye/Alfred A Knopf/Crown Books for Young Readers
201 E 50th Street
New York, NY 10022-7703
212-751-2600
Fax: 212-572-8700
Publisher of hardcover books, paperbacks, books and cassettes and videos for children.

4909 Recorded Books
270 Skipjack Road
Prince Frederick, MD 20678-3410
800-638-1304
Professionally narrated, unabridged books on standard-play audio cassettes, classroom ideas and combinations of print book, cassettes and teacher's guides.

Linda Hirshman, President

4910 Redleaf Press
10 Yorkton Court
Saint Paul, MN 55117-1065
800-428-8309
Fax: 800-641-0115
E-mail: jward@redleafpress.org
http://www.redleafpress.org
Publisher of curriculum, activity, and childrens books for early childhood professionals.

Sid Farrer, Editor In Chief
JoAnne Voltz, Marketing Manager

4911 Reference Desk Books
430 Quintana Road
Suite 146
Morro Bay, CA 93442-1948
805-772-8806
Offers a variety of books for the education professional.

4912 Rhythms Productions
PO Box 34485
Los Angeles, CA 90034-0485
310-836-4678
800-544-7244
Fax: 310-837-1534
Producer and publisher of songs and games for learning through music. Cassettes, CDs, books for birth through elementary featuring rhythms, puppet play, art activities, and more. Titles include Lullabies, Singing Games, Watch Me Grow series, Mr. Windbag concept stories, phonics, First Reader's Kit, Hear-See-Say-Do Musical Math series, Themes, and more. Also publishes a line of folk dances from elementary through adult.

Audio

Ruth White, President

4913 Richard C Owen Publishers
PO Box 585
Katonah, NY 10536
914-232-3903
800-336-5588
Fax: 914-232-3977
E-mail: mfrund@rcowen.com
http://www.rcowen.com
Focus child-centered learning, Books for Young Learners, professional books, the Learning Network and Meet the Author series.

Mary Frundt, Marketing

4914 Riverside Publishing Company
425 Spring Lake Drive
Ithaca, IL 60143
630-467-7000
800-323-9540
Fax: 630-467-7192
http://www.riverpub.com
Offers a full line of reading materials, including fiction and nonfiction titles for all grade levels.

4915 Roots & Wings Educational Catalog-Australia for Kids
PO Box 19678
Boulder, CO 80308-2678
303-776-4796
800-833-1787
Fax: 303-776-6090
E-mail: roos@boulder.net
http://www.rootsandwingscatalog.com/
www.australiaforkids.com
Catalog company providing materials for the education of the young child, specializing in the following topics: Australia, multiculturalism, parenting and families, teaching, special needs, environment and peace.

Susan Ely, President/Sales
Anne Wilson, VP/Marketing

4916 Rosen Publishing Group
29 E 21st Street
New York, NY 10010-6209
212-777-3017
800-237-9932
Fax: 888-436-4643
Nonfiction books on self-help and guidance for young adults. Books also available for reluctant readers on self-esteem, values and drug abuse prevention.

4917 Routledge/Europa Library Reference
Taylor & Francis Books
29 W 35 Street
New York, NY 10001-2299
212-216-7800
800-634-7064
Fax: 212-564-7854
E-mail: reference@routledge-ny.com
http://www.reference.routlege-ny.com
Publisher of a wide range of print and online library reference titles, including the renowned Europa World Yearbook and the award-winning Routledge Encyclopedia of Philosophy (both available in online and print formats), Garland Encyclopedia of World Music, Routledge Religion and Society Encyclopedias, Chronological History of US Foreign Relations, and many other acclaimed resources.

Koren Thomas, Sr Marketing/Library Ref
Elizabeth Sheehan, Marketing/Library Reference

4918 Runestone Press
A Divisions of Lerner Publishing Group
241 1st Avenue N
Minneapolis, MN 55401-1607
612-332-3344
800-328-4929
Fax: 612-332-7615
http://www.lernerbooks.com
Nonfiction for readers in Grades 5 and up. Newly revised editions of previously out-of-print books. List includes Buried Worlds archaeology series and titles of Jewish and Native American interest. Complete catalog is available.

Harry J Lerner, President
Mary M Rodgers, Editorial Director

4919 Saddleback Educational
Three Watson
Irvine, CA 92618-2767
949-860-2500
800-637-8715
Fax: 888-734-4010
Supplementary curriculum materials for K-12 and adult students.

4920 SafeSpace Concepts
1424 N Post Oak Road
Houston, TX 77055-5401
713-956-0820
800-622-4289
Fax: 713-956-6416
E-mail: safespacec@aol.com
http://www.safespaceconcepts.com
Manufactures young children's play equipment and furnishings.

Barbara Carlson, PhD, President
Jerry Johnson, Marketing Director

4921 Sage Publications
Sage Publications
2455 Teller Road
Thousand Oaks, CA 91320
303-333-3003
800-803-8488
Fax: 303-333-4037
E-mail: karen-hemmes@mindspring.com
http://www.fireflybooks.com
Sage Publications publishes handbooks and guides with a focus on research and science.

Karen Hemmes, Publicist
Mary Kay Opicka, Publicist

4922 Santillana Publishing
901 W Walnut Street
Compton, CA 90220-5109
310-763-0455
800-245-8584
Fax: 305-591-9145
Publishers of K-12 and adult titles in Spanish.Imprints include: Altea, Alfagunea, Taurus and Aguilar.

Marla Norman, Publisher/Trade Book
Antonio de Marco, President

4923 Scholastic
555 Broadway
New York, NY 10012
212-343-6100
800-724-6527
Fax: 212-343-4801
http://www.scholastic.com
Publisher and distributor of children's books. Provides professional and classroom resources for K-12.

4924 School Book Fairs
PO Box 835105
Richardson, TX 75083
972-231-9838

A children's book publisher that provides distribution of leisure reading materials to elementary and middle schools through book fair fund-raising events via a North American network with 97 locations.

4925 Science Inquiry Enterprises
14358 Village View Lane
Chino Hills, CA 91709-1706
530-295-3338
Fax: 530-295-3334
Selected science teaching materials.

4926 Scott & McCleary Publishing Company
2482 11th Street SW
Akron, OH 44314-1712
702-566-8756
800-765-3564
Fax: 702-568-1378
E-mail: jscott7576@aol.com
http://www.scottmccleary.com
Diagnostic reading and testing material.

Janet M Scott, Publisher
Sheila C McCleary, Publisher

4927 Scott Foresman Company
1900 E Lake Avenue
Glenview, IL 60025-2086
800-554-4411
Fax: 800-841-8939
Science tests and reading/language arts materials for teachers and students. Celebrate Reading! is the K-8 literature-based reading/integrated language arts program designed to meet the needs of all children. Book Festival is a literature learning center that offers teachers a collection of trade books for independent reading.

Bert Crossland, Reading Product Manager
Jim Fitzmaurice, VP Editor Group

4928 Sharpe Reference
M.E. Sharpe, Inc.
80 Business Park Drive
Armonk, NY 10504
914-273-1800
800-541-6563
Fax: 914-273-2106
E-mail: custserv@mesharpe.com
http://www.mesharpe.com
Historical, political, geographical and art reference books.

Diana McDermott, Director Marketing

4929 Signet Classics
375 Hudson Street
New York, NY 10014-3658
212-366-2000
Fax: 212-366-2888
Publishes books on literature, poetry and reading.

4930 Silver Moon Press
160 5th Avenue
Suite 622
New York, NY 10010-7003
212-242-6499
800-874-3320
Fax: 212-242-6799
Informational and entertaining books for young readers. Subjects include history, multiculturalism and science.

4931 Simon & Schuster Children's Publishing
1230 Avenue of the Americas
New York, NY 10020
212-698-7000
Fax: 212-698-7007
http://www.simonsayskids.com

Fiction and nonfiction, in hardcover and paperback editions, for preschool through young adult.

4932 Social Issues Resources Series
1100 Holland Drive
Boca Raton, FL 33487-2701
561-994-0079
Fax: 561-994-2014
Provides information systems in print format and CD-ROM format.

4933 Social Science Education Consortium
Box 21270
Boulder, CO 80308-4270
303-492-8154
Fax: 303-449-3925
E-mail: singletl@stripe.colorado.edu
http://www.ssecinc.org
Produces curriculum guides, instructional units and collections of lesson plans on US history, law-related education, global studies, public issues and geography. Develops projects for social studies teachers and evaluates social studies programs.

James Cooks, Executive Director
Laurel Singleton, Associate Director

4934 Social Studies School Service
10200 Jefferson Boulevard
Culver City, CA 90232-3598
310-839-2436
800-421-4246
Fax: 310-839-2249
E-mail: access@socialstudies.com
http://www.socialstudies.com
Supplemental materials in all areas of social studies, language arts.

4935 Special Education & Rehabilitation Services
330 C Street
Washington, DC 20202
202-205-5465
Fax: 202-260-7225

Judith E Heuman, Assistant Secretary

4936 Speech Bin
1965 25th Avenue
Vero Beach, FL 32960-3000
561-770-0007
800-477-3324
Fax: 561-770-0006
Publisher and distributor of books and materials for professionals in rehabilitation, speech-language pathology, occupational and physical therapy, special education, and related fields. Major product lines include professional and children's books, computer software, diagnostic tests.

Jan J Binney, VP

4937 Stack the Deck Writing Program
PO Box 5352
Chicago, IL 60680-0429
312-675-1000
Fax: 312-765-0453
E-mail: stockthedeck@sbcglobal.net
http://www.stackthedeck.com
Composition textbooks, grades 1-12, plus computer software.

4938 Stenhouse Publishers
477 Congress Street
Suite 4B
Portland, ME 04101-3417
888-363-0566
Fax: 800-833-9164
http://www.stenhouse.com

Professional materials for teachers by teachers.

4939 Story Teller
PO Box 921
Salem, UT 84653-0921
801-423-2560
Fax: 801-423-2568
E-mail: patti@thestoryteler.com
http://www.thestoryteller.com
Felt board stories books and educational sets.

Patti Gardner, VP Sales

4940 Summit Learning
7755 Rockwell Avenue
PO Box 755
Fort Atkinson, WI 53538-0755
800-777-8817
800-777-8817
Fax: 800-317-2194
E-mail: info@summitlearning.com
http://www.summitlearning.com
Summit learning is a distributor of manipulative-based math and science materials, provides you with a carefully selected group of the most popular high-quality products at low prices.

Gary Otto, Marketing Manager

4941 Sunburst Technology
1550 Executive Drive
Elgin, IL 60123
914-747-3310
800-338-3457
Fax: 914-747-4109
http://www.sunburst.com
K-12 educational software, guidance and health materials, and online teacher resources.

4942 Sundance Publishing
234 Taylor Street
PO Box 1326
Littleton, MA 01460
978-486-9201
800-343-8204
Fax: 978-486-8759
E-mail: kjasmine@sundancepub.com
http://www.sindancepub.com
A supplementary educational publisher of instructional materials for shared, guided, and independent reading, phonics, and comprehension skills for grades K-9. Some of its programs include AlphKids, SunLit Fluency, Popcorns and Little Readers. Its Second Chance Reading Program for below-level readers features high-interest titles, written for upper elementary/middle school students. It also distributes paperback editions of some of the most widely taught literature titles for grades K-1

Katherine Jasmine, VP Marketing

4943 Synergistic Systems
2297 Hunters Run Drive
Reston, VA 20191-2834
703-758-9213
Science education curriculum materials.

4944 TASA
PO Box 382
Brewster, NY 10509-0382
845-277-8100
800-800-2598
Fax: 845-277-3548
Degrees of Literacy Power Program; English Language Profiles, primary, standard and advanced DRP tests, Degrees of World Meaning Tests.

4945 TL Clark Incorporated
5111 SW Avenue
St. Louis, MO 63110
314-865-2525
800-859-3815
Fax: 314-865-2240
E-mail: general@tlclarkinc.com
http://www.tlclarkinc.com
Educational products for grades Pre-K-3. Rest time products including cots and mats, sand and water play tubs, active play items including tunnels, tricycles and foam play items.

Jim Fleminla, President

4946 TMC/Soundprints
353 Main Avenue
Norwalk, CT 06851-1508
203-846-2274
800-228-7839
Fax: 203-846-1776
E-mail: sndprnts@ixinctcom.com
http://www.soundprints.com
Children's story books for children ages 4 through 8 under the license of the Smithsonian Institute and the National Wildlife Federation. Each 32 page four color book highlights a unique aspect of the animal featured in the book so as to provide education while still being entertaining. Each book can be bought with an audiocassette read-a-long and plush toy. Over 80 books in print.

Ashley Anderson, Associate Publisher
Chelsea Shriver

4947 Tambourine Books
1350 Avenue of the Americas
New York, NY 10019-4702
212-261-6500
Fax: 212-261-6518
A wide variety of books to increase creativity and reading skills in students.

4948 Taylor & Francis Publishers
7625 Empire Drive
Florence, KY 41042
800-624-7064
Fax: 800-248-4724
Publisher of professional texts and references in several fields including the behavioral sciences; arts, humanities, social sciences, science technology and medicine.

Chris Smith, Customer Service Manager

4949 Teacher's Friend Publications
3240 Trade Center Drive
Riverside, CA 92507
909-682-4748
800-343-9680
Fax: 909-682-4680
Complete line of the original monthly and seasonal Creative Idea Books. Plus, two new cooperative-learning language series and much more.

Karen Sevaly, Author
Richard Sevaly, President/CEO
Kim Marsh, National Sales Manager

4950 Teaching Comprehension: Strategies for Stories
Oxton House Publishers, LLC
Po Box 209
Farmington, ME 04938
207-779-1923
800-539-7323
Fax: 207-779-0623
E-mail: info@oxtonhouse.com
http://www.oxtonhouse.com
A detailed roadmap for providing students with effective strategies for comprehend-

ing and remembering stories. It includes story-line masters for helping students to organize their thinking and to accurately depict character and sequence events.

62 pages

William Berlinghoff, Managing Editor
Bobby Brown, Marketing Director

4951 Theme Connections

Perfection Learning
PO Box 500
Logan, IA 51546-0500
800-831-4190
Fax: 712-644-2392
Features 135 best-selling literature titles and related theme libraries for students to develop lifelong learning strategies.

4952 Ther-A-Play Products

PO Box 2030
Lodi, CA 95241-2030
209-368-6787
800-308-6749
Fax: 209-365-2157
E-mail: madgic@attbi.com
Children's books, play therapy books, sandplay and sandtray manipulatives, puppets, games, doll houses and furniture. Playmobile and educational toys, specializing in counselors' tools. Books on abuses, illness, death, behavior and parenting.

Madge Geiszler, Owner

4953 Thomson Learning

115 5th Avenue
New York, NY 10003-1004
212-979-2210
800-880-4253
Fax: 248-699-8061
Book publisher of library and classroom-oriented educational resources for children and young adults. Over 200 books are available in 30 different subjects.

4954 Time-Life Books

2000 Duke Street
Alexandria, VA 22314-3414
703-838-7000
Fax: 703-838-7166
A wide-ranging selection of quality reference and supplemental books for students from elementary to high school.

4955 Tiny Thought Press

1427 S Jackson Street
Louisville, KY 40208-2720
502-637-6916
Fax: 502-634-1693
Children's books that build character and self-esteem.

4956 Tom Snyder Productions

80 Coolidge Hill Road
Watertown, MA 02472
800-342-0236
Fax: 800-304-1254
E-mail: ask@tomsynder.com
http://www.tomsynder.com
Developer and publisher of educational software.

John McAndrews, Contact

4957 Tor Books/Forge/SMP

175 5th Avenue
New York, NY 10010-7703
212-388-0100
Fax: 212-388-0191
Science-fiction and fantasy children's books, mysteries, Westerns, general fiction and classics publications.

4958 Tricycle Press

PO Box 7123
Berkeley, CA 94707-0123
510-559-1600
800-841-2665
Fax: 510-559-1637
Publisher of books and posters for children ages 2-12 and their grown-ups. Catalog available.

Christine Longmuir, Publicity/Marketing

4959 Troll Associates

100 Corporate Drive
Mahwah, NJ 07430-2322
201-529-4000
Fax: 201-529-8282
Publisher of children's books and products, including paperbacks and hardcovers, special theme units, read-alongs, videos, software and big books.

4960 Trumpet Club

1540 Broadway
New York, NY 10036-4039
212-492-9595
School book club featuring hardcover and paperback books, in class text sets and author video visits.

4961 Turn-the-Page Press

203 Baldwin Avenue
Roseville, CA 95678-5104
916-786-8756
800-959-5549
Fax: 916-786-9261
E-mail: mleeman@ibm.net
http://www.turnthepage.com
Books, cassettes and videos focusing on early childhood education.

Michael Leeman, President

4962 USA Today

1000 Wilson Boulevard
Arlington, VA 22209-3901
703-276-3400
Fax: 703-854-2103
Educational programs focusing on social studies.

4963 Upstart Books

PO Box 800
Fort Atkinson, WI 53538-0800
920-563-9571
800-558-2110
Fax: 920-563-7395
http://www.hpress.highsmith.com
Publishes teacher activity resources, reading activities, library and information seeking skills, Internet.

Matt Mulder, Director
Virginia Harrison, Editor

4964 Useful Learning

711 Meadow Lane Court
Apartment 12
Mount Vernon, IA 52314-1549
319-895-6155
800-962-3855
The Useful Spelling Textbook series for Grades 2-8, represents a curriculum based upon the scientific knowledge of research studies conducted during the past 80 years at The University of Iowa, Iowa City, IA. Incorporates the New Iowa Spelling Scale and is composed of qualitative curriculum, qualitative learning practices and qualitative instructional procedures.

Larry D. Zenor, PhD, President
Bradley M Loomer, PhD, Board Chairman

4965 VIDYA Books

PO Box 7788
Berkeley, CA 94707-0788
510-527-9932
Fax: 510-527-2936
Supplemental materials about India and the surrounding region for K-12 lesson plans.

4966 Viking Children's Books

375 Hudson Street
New York, NY 10014-3658
212-941-8780
General hardcover children's books, from toddler through young adult, fiction and nonfiction.

4967 Vision 23

Twenty-Third Publications
185 Willow Street
Mystic, CT 06355-2636
860-536-2611
Fax: 800-572-0788
A wide variety of children's products including books, games, clothing and toys.

4968 WH Freeman & Company

41 Madison Avenue
New York, NY 10010-2202
212-576-9400
Fax: 212-481-1891
Books relating to the world of mathematics.

4969 Wadsworth Publishing School Group

10 Davis Drive
Belmont, CA 94002-3002
650-595-2350
Fax: 800-522-4923
College and advanced placement/honors high school materials in biology, chemistry and environmental science.

4970 Walker & Company

104 Fifth Avenue
New York, NY 10011
212-727-8300
800-289-2553
Fax: 212-727-0984
http://www.walkerbooks.com
Hardcover and paperback trade titles for Pre-K-12th grade, including picture books, photo essays, fiction and nonfiction titles appropriate for every curriculum need.

4971 Warren Publishing House

11625-G Airport Road
Everett, WA 98204-3790
425-353-3100
New Totline Teaching Tales with related activities plus quality whole language teacher activity books including Alphabet Theme-A-Saurus and Piggyback Songs.

4972 Waterfront Books

85 Crescent Road
Burlington, VT 05401-4126
802-658-7477
800-639-6063
Fax: 802-860-1368
E-mail: helpkids@waterfrontbooks.com
http://www.waterfrontbooks.com
Publishes and distributes books on special issues for children: barriers to learning, coping skills, mental health, prevention strategies, family/parenting, etc. for grades K-12. Titles include: The Divorce Workbook; Josh, a Boy with Dyslexia; What's a Virus, Anyway? The Kids' Book About AIDS and more.

Sherrill N Musty, Publisher
Michelle Russell, Order Fulfillment

4973 Web Feet Guides
Rock Hill Communications
14 Rock Hill Road
Bala Cynwyd, PA 19004
610-667-2040
888-762-5445
Fax: 610-667-2291
E-mail:
info@rockhillcommunications.com
http://www.webfeetguides.com
The premier subject guides to the Internet, rigorously reviewed by librarians and educators, fully annotated, expanded and updated monthly. Appropriate for middle school through adult. Available in print, online, or marc records. For more information, free trials and Web casts, and free interactive Web Quests for your K-8 students, visit our Web site.

Linda Smith, Marketing Coordinator

4974 West Educational Publishing
620 Opperman Drive
#645779
Saint Paul, MN 55123-1340
A leader in quality social studies textbooks and ancillaries for grades K-12.

4975 Western Psychological Services
12031 Wilshire Boulevard
Los Angeles, CA 90025-1251
310-478-2061
800-648-8857
Fax: 310-478-7838
http://www.wpspublish.com
Assessment tools for professionals in education, psychology and allied fields. Offer a variety of tests, books, software and therapeutic games.

4976 Wildlife Conservation Society
Bronx Zoo
Education Department
2300 Southern Boulevard
Bronx, NY 10460
718-220-5131
800-937-5131
Fax: 718-733-4460
E-mail: sscheio@wes.org
http://www.wcs.com
Environmental science and conservation biology curriculum materials and information regarding teacher training programming for Grades K-12, on site or off site, nationally and locally. Science programming for grades pre-K-12 available on site.

Sydell Schein, Manager/Program Services
Ann Robinson, Director National Programs

4977 William Morrow & Company
1350 Avenue of the Americas
New York, NY 10019-4702
212-261-6500
Fax: 212-261-6518
High quality hardcover and paperback books for children.

4978 Winston Derek Publishers
101 French Landing Drive
Nashville, TN 37228-1511
615-321-0535
A cross section of African American books and educational materials, including preschool and primary grade books.

4979 Wolfram Research
100 Trade Centre Drive
Champaign, IL 61820-7237
800-441-MATH
Fax: 217-398-1108

Offers mathematics publications, statistics and information to educators of grades K-12.

4980 Workman Publishing
708 Broadway
New York, NY 10003-9508
212-254-5900
Fax: 212-254-8098
Children's curriculum, books, textbooks, workbooks, fiction and nonfiction titles.

4981 World & I
News World Communications
2800 New York Avenue NE
Washington, DC 20002-1945
202-636-3365
800-822-2822
Fax: 202-832-5780
E-mail: ckim@worldandimag.com
http://www.worldandi.com
With over 40 articles each month, The World & I presents an enlightening look at our changing world through the eyes of noted scholars and experts covering current issues, the arts, science, book reviews, lifestyles, cultural perspectives, philosophical trends, and the millennium. For educators, students and libraries. Free teacher's guides year round. Also, online archives available at www.worldandi.com.

Charles Kim, Business Director

4982 World Association of Publishers, Manufacturers & Distributors
Worlddidac
Bollwerk 21, PO Box 8866 CH-3001
Berne
Switzerland
41-31-3121744
Fax: 41-31-3121744
E-mail: info@worlddidac.org
A worldwide listing of over 330 publishers, manufacturers and distributors of educational materials. Listings include all contact information, products and school levels/grades.

160 pages Annual

Beat Jost, Coordinating Education

4983 World Bank
1818 H Street NW
Room T-8061
Washington, DC 20433-0002
202-477-1234
Fax: 202-477-6391
Maps, poster kits, case studies and videocassettes that teach about life in developing countries.

4984 World Book Educational Products
525 W Monroe Street
20th Floor
Chicago, IL 60661
312-729-5800
Fax: 312-729-5600
Reference books and the World Book Encyclopedia on CD-Rom.

4985 World Eagle
111 King Street
Littleton, MA 01460-1527
978-486-9180
800-854-8273
Fax: 978-486-9652
E-mail: info@ibaradio.org
http://www.worldeagle.com
Publishes an online, social studies educational resource magazine: comparative data, graphs, maps and charts on world is-

sues. Publishes world regional atlases, and supplies maps and curriculum materials.

Valentina Bardawil Powers, Author
Martine Crandall-Hollick, President

4986 World Resources Institute
10 G Street, NE
Suite 800
Washington, DC 20002
202-729-7600
Fax: 202-729-7610
The world Resources Institute is an environmental think tank that goes beyond research to create practical ways to protect the Earth and improve people's lives. our mission is to move human society to live in ways that protect Earth's environment for surrent and future generations.

Jonathan Lash, President

4987 World Scientific Publishing Company
27 Warren Street
Suite 401-402
Hackensack, NJ 07601
201-487-9655
Fax: 201-487-9695
E-mail: wspc@wspc.com
http://www.wspc.com
This is one of the world's leading academic publishers. It now publishes more than 400 books and 100 journals a year in diverse fields of science technology, medicine, business and management.

Ruth Zhou, Marketing Executive

4988 World of Difference Institute
Anti-Defamation League
823 United Nations Plaza
New York, NY 10017-3518
212-490-2525
Fax: 212-867-0779
E-mail: webmaster@adl.org
http://www.adl.org
Materials and training, as well as Pre K-12 curriculum resources, Anti-bias and diversity.

Lindsay J Friedman, Director

4989 Worth Publishers
33 Irving Plaza
New York, NY 10003-2332
212-475-6000
Fax: 212-689-2383
A balanced and comprehensive account of the U.S. past is accompanied by an extensive set of supplements.

4990 Wright Group
19201 120th Avenue NE
Bothell, WA 98011-9507
800-523-2371
Fax: 425-486-7704
http://www.wrightgroup.com
Supplementary program materials for reading education.

4991 Write Source Educational Publishing House
PO Box 460
Burlington, WI 53105-0460
262-763-8258
Fax: 262-763-2651
Publishes Writers Express, a writing, thinking and learning handbook series for grades 4 and 5. Also offer the latest editions of Write Source 2000 and Writers INC for grades 6-8 and 9-12.

4992 Zaner-Bloser K-8 Catalog
2200 W 5th Avenue
Columbus, OH 43215
614-486-0221
800-421-3018
Fax: 614-487-2699
http://www.zaner-bloser.com
Publisher of handwriting materials and
reading, writing, spelling and study skills
programs.

Robert Page, President

4993 Zephyr Press
PO Box 66006
Tucson, AZ 85728-6006
520-322-5090
800-232-2187
Fax: 520-323-9402
E-mail: neways2learn@zephyrpress.com
http://www.zephyrpress.com
Zephyr Press publishes effective,
state-of-the-art-teaching materials for
classroom use.

Joey Tanner MEd, President

4994 ZooBooks
ZooBooks/Wildlife Education. Ltd.
12233 Thatcher Court
Poway, CA 92064-6880
619-513-7600
800-477-5034
Fax: 858-513-7660
E-mail: animals@zoobooks.com
http://www.zoobooks.com
Reference books offering fascinating insights into the world of wildlife. Created in
collaboration with leading scientists and
educators, these multi-volume Zoobooks
make important facts and concepts about
nature, habitat and wildlife understandable
to children. From alligators to zebras,
aquatic to exotic, each Zoobook is colorful,
scientifically accurate and easy to read.

General

4995 AVKO Educational Research Foundation
3084 W Willard Road
Clio, MI 48420-7801
810-686-9283
866-285-6612
Fax: 810-686-1101
E-mail: avkoemail@aol.com
http://www.avko.org
Comprised of teachers and individuals interested in helping others learn to read and spell. Develops reading training materials for individuals with dyslexia or other learning disabilities using a method involving audio, visual, kinesthetic and oral diagnosis and remediation. Conducts research into the causes of reading, spelling and writing disabilities.

Donald J McCabe, Executive Director

4996 Assistive Technology Clinics
Children's Hospital
1056 E 19th Avenue
#030
Denver, CO 80218-1007
303-861-6250
Fax: 303-764-8214
A diagnostic clinic providing evaluation, information and support to families with children with disabilities in the areas of seating and mobility. Offers augmentative communication and assistive technology access.

Tracey Kovach, Coordinator

4997 Center for Equity and Excellence in Education
George Washington University
1555 Wilson Blvd
Suite 515
Arlington, VA 22209-2004
703-528-3588
800-925-3223
Fax: 703-528-5973
E-mail: crivera@ceee.gwu.edu
http://www.ceee.gwu.edu
Mission is to advance education reform so that all students achieve high standards. Operates under the umbrella of the Institute for Education Policy Studies within the Graduate School of Education and Human Development. Designs and conducts program evaluation for states, districts and schools and conducts program evalutaion, policy and applied research effecting equitable educational opportunities for all students.

Charlene Rivera, Executive Director
Kristina Anstrom, Assistant Director

4998 Center for Learning
The Center for Learning
Po Box 910
Villa Maria, PA 16155
724-964-8083
800-767-9090
Fax: 724-964-8992
E-mail: customerservice@centerforlearning.org
http://www.centerforlearning.org
Sopplementary curriculum units for all grade levels in English, Language Arts, Novel-Dramas, and Social Studies.

4999 Center for Research on the Context of Teaching
Stanford University
School of Education, CERAS Building
Stanford, CA 94305
650-723-4972
Fax: 650-723-7578
Conducts research on ways in which secondary school teaching and learning are affected by their contexts.

5000 Center for Research on the Education of Students Placed at Risk
Johns Hopkins University
3003 N Charles Street
Baltimore, MD 21218-2404
410-516-8800
Fax: 410-516-8890
http://www.csos.jhu.edu
Conducts research, development, evaluation and dissemination to transform schooling for students placed at risk, especially by supporting a talent development model of school organization and instruction.

James McPortland, Director
Marc Cutright, Communication Director

5001 Center for Social Organization of Schools
Johns Hopkins University
3003 N Charles Street
Suite 200
Baltimore, MD 21218-3888
410-516-8800
Fax: 410-516-8890
E-mail: jmcpartland@csos.jhu.edu
http://www.csos.jhu.edu
Conducts research, development, evaluation and dissemination to transform low performing schools especially by supporting a talent development modelof school organization and instruction. Programs for early childhood, middle grades, high schools and parents involvement.

James McPartland, Director
Mary Maushard, Communication Director

5002 Center for Technology in Education
Bank Street College of Education
610 W 112th Street
New York, NY 10025-1898
212-875-4467
Fax: 212-875-4753
Studies and demonstrates the role technology can play in improving student learning and achievement in schools.

Jan Hawkins, Director

5003 Center for the Study of Reading
University of Illinois
175 Children's Research Center
Champaign, IL 61820
217-333-2552
Fax: 217-244-4501
Conducts basic and applied research on the better understanding of reading.

Richard C Anderson, Director

5004 Center for the Study of Small/Rural Schools
University of Oklahoma
555 E Constitution Street
Room 138
Norman, OK 73072-7820
405-325-3760
Fax: 405-325-7075
E-mail: jcsimmons@ou.edu
http://cssrs.ou.edu
Provides services to small and/or rural schools while conducting research projects that generate knowledge to improve the quality of education.

Jan C Simmons, Director

5005 Center on Families, Schools, Communities & Children's Learning
Northeastern University
50 Nightingale Hall
Boston, MA 02215
617-373-2595
Fax: 617-373-8924
Examines how families, communities and schools can work in partnership to promote children's motivation, learning and development, including disseminating information.

Nancy Ames, Vice President

5006 Center on Organization & Restructuring of Schools
1025 W Johnson Street
Madison, WI 53706-1706
608-263-7575
Fax: 608-263-6448
Focuses on restructuring K-12 schools in various areas of student development and progress.

Fred M Newman, Director

5007 Cirriculum Research and Development Group
1776 University Avenue
Honolulu, HI 96822-2463
808-956-4949
800-799-8111
Fax: 808-956-6730
E-mail: crdg@hawaii.edu
http://www.hawaii.edu/crdg
Develops new curricular and instructional materials for K-12. Professional development for teachers and ongoing assistance to schools that adopt our programs is also offered.

Lani Abrigana, Marketing Manager
Glen Schmitt, Marketing Specialist

5008 Council for Educational Development and Research
National Education Association (NEA)
1201 16th Street NW
Washington, DC 20036-3207
202-822-7364
Fax: 202-822-7624
E-mail: ncuea@nea.org
http://www.nea.org
Advances research and development in education.

E Joseph Schneider, Executive Director

5009 Division for Research
The Council for Exceptional Children
DOR Admin Offices 2000
Broadway Oakland 94612
510-891-3400
Association devoted to the advancement of research in the education of individuals with disabilities and/or who are gifted. Members include university personnel,

teachers, researchers, administrators and others.

5010 Educational Information & Resource Center
Research Department
606 Delsea Drive
Sewell, NJ 08080-9399
856-582-7000
Fax: 856-582-4206
Provides information on education-related services and programs to parents, schools and communities.

Art Rainear, Director

5011 Educational Research Service
1001 N Fairfax Street
Suite 500
Alexandria, VA 22314
703-243-2100
800-759-9308
Fax: 703-243-1985
E-mail: ers@ers.org
http://www.ers.org
ERS is an independent, nonprofit research organization founded in 1973 by seven national education assocations of school management. Offers objective research and information to school district administrators. Publishes reports and periodicals dealing with issues in school management, instruction, curriculum and compensation.

Dr. John Forsyth, President
Katherin A Behrens, Chief
Marketing/Business Off

5012 Educational Testing Service
Rosedale Road
MS 26-C
Princeton, NJ 08541
609-921-9000
Fax: 609-734-5410
Private educational measurement institution and a leader in educational research.

Susan Keipper, Program Director

5013 Florida Atlantic University-Multifunctional Resource Center
1515 W Commercial Boulevard
Suite 303
Boco Raton, FL 33309-3095
561-297-3000
800-328-6721
Fax: 561-297-2141
Provides training and technical assistance to Title VII-funded classroom instructional projects and other programs serving limited-English proficient students.

Dr. Ann C Willig, Director
Elaine Sherr, Research Assistant

5014 Higher Education Center
National Education Association (NEA)
1201 16th Street NW
Washington, DC 20036-3207
202-822-7162
Fax: 202-822-7624
E-mail: ncuea@nea.org
http://www.nea.org
The center provides data and other research products to NEA higher education affiliates. The Research Advisory Group, composed of higher education leaders and staff, meets twice a year to review products from the NEA Research Center for Higher Education and make recommendations about additional research needs. The center currently provides salary reports, Higher Education Contract Analysis System, and budget analysis.

5015 Information Center on Education
Eba Room 385
Albany, NY 12234-0001
518-474-8716
Fax: 518-473-7737
Coordinates data collection procedures within the New York State Education Department.

Leonard Powell, Director

5016 Information Exchange
Maine State Library
64 State House Station
Augusta, ME 04333-0064
207-287-5620
800-322-8899
Fax: 207-287-5624
Provides access to the latest education research and information for teachers.

Edna M Comstock, Director

5017 Institute for Research in Learning Disabilities
The University of Kansas
3060 Robert
Lawrence, KS 66045-0001
785-864-4780
Fax: 785-864-5728
Although the focus of the Institute's research is children, they have a sizeable publication list with some of their research having relevance for adults.

5018 Instructional Materials Laboratory
University of Missouri-Columbia
8 London Hall
Columbia, MO 65211-2230
314-882-2884
Prepares and disseminates instructional materials for the vocational education community.

Dr. Harley Schlichting, Director

5019 Learning Research and Development Center
University of Pittsburgh
3939 O'Hara Street
Pittsburgh, PA 15260
412-624-7020
Fax: 412-624-9149
E-mail: asklrdc@vms.cis.pitt.edu
http://www.lrdc.pitt.edu
Interdisciplinary center conducting fundamental and applied research in learning in schools, workplaces, and other institutions, investigates cognitive processes involved in learning and instruction; engages in analysis and design of teaching and training programs; and disseminates findings to other researchers, practitioners, and policy makers.

Lauren Resnick, Director
Alan Lesgold, Executive Associate

5020 Life Lab Science Program
1156 High Street
Santa Cruz, CA 95064
831-459-2001
Fax: 831-459-3483
E-mail: lifelab@zzyx.ucsc.edu
http://www.lifelab.org
Develops and provides garden-centered educational programs connecting science to all other areas of learning.

Gail Harlamoff, Executive Director
Erika Perloff, Education Director

5021 Merrimack Education Center
101 Mill Road
Chelmsford, MA 01824-4899
978-256-3985
Fax: 978-256-6890
Offers programs and services to teachers and students with a special focus on technology.

Richard Lavin, Director

5022 Mid-Atlantic Regional Educational Laboratory
1301 Cecil B. Moore Avenue
Philadelphia, PA 19122
215-204-3000
Fax: 215-204-5130
E-mail: robert.sullivan@temple.edu
http://www.temple.edu/lss
The Regional Educational Laboratories are educational research and development organizations supported by contracts with the US Education Department. Specialty area: Education Leadership.

William Evans, Director

5023 Mid-Continent Regional Educational Laboratory
2550 S Parker Road
Suite 500
Aurora, CO 80014-1678
303-337-0990
Fax: 303-337-3005
Focuses on improvement of education practices in Colorado, Kansas, Missouri, Nebraska, Wyoming, North Dakota and South Dakota.

C. Lawrence Hutchins, Director

5024 Midwestern Regional Educational Laboratory
1900 Spring Road
Suite 300
Oak Brook, IL 60521
630-649-6500
Fax: 630-649-6700
E-mail: nowakows@ncrel.org
The Regional Educational Laboratories are educational research and development organizations supported by contracts with the US Education Department, Office of Educational Research and Improvement. Specialty area: Technology.

Dr. Jeri Nowakowski, Executive Director

5025 Missouri LINC
401 E Stewart Road
Columbia, MO 65211
573-882-2733
800-392-0533
Fax: 573-882-5071
Serves students with special needs through a resource and technical assistance center.

Linda Bradley, Director

5026 Music Teachers National Association
441 Vine Street
Suite 505
Cincinnatti, OH 45202
513-421-1420
Research reports dealing with any aspects of music, music teaching, music learning and related subjects.

Rachel Kramer, Executive Director
Programs

5027 NEA Foundatrion for the Improvement of Education
1201 16th Street NW
Washington, DC 20036-3207
202-822-7840
Fax: 202-822-7779
E-mail:
info@neafoundation@list.nea.org
http://www.neafoundation.org
Works through grants, publications and reports to give educators the resources they need to create better learning environments for students.

Ian Blyth, Communications Associate
Nedra J Helenburg, Administrative Assistant

5028 National Black Child Development Institute
1313 L Street, NW
Suite 110
Washington, DC 20005-4110
202-833-2220
800-556-2234
Fax: 202-833-8222
E-mail: moreinfo@nbcdi.org
http://www.nbcdi.org
Offers information and training to advocates, educators, and childcare professionals on African American children.

Carol Brunson Day, President
Gillian Shurland, Contact

5029 National Center for Improving Science Education
2000 L Street NW
Suite 616
Washington, DC 20036-4917
202-467-0652
Fax: 202-467-0659
Promotes change in state and local policies and practices in science curricula, teaching, and assessment.

Senta A Raizen, Director

5030 National Center for Research in Mathematical Sciences Education
University of Wisconsin-Madison
1025 W Johnson Street
#557
Madison, WI 53706-1706
608-263-4285
Fax: 608-263-3406
Provides a research base for the reform of school mathematics.

Thomas A Romberg, Director

5031 National Center for Research in Vocational Education
University of California, Berkeley
2030 Addison Street
Suite 500
Berkeley, CA 94720-1674
510-642-0323
800-762-4093
E-mail: NCRVE@berkeley.edu
http://http://vocserve.berkeley.edu
Enables educators, employers, researchers and policymakers to stay up-to-date on work-related education reform. Offers hands-on guides for educators interested in developing or redesigning a career development system.

5032 National Center for Research on Teacher Learning
Michigan State University, College of Education
116 Erickson Hall
East Lansing, MI 48824-1034
517-355-9302
Fax: 517-432-2795
Researches the development of elementary and secondary teacher expertise in teaching the subjects of the curriculum.

Bob Fludon, Director

5033 National Center for Science Teaching & Learning
Ohio State University
1314 Kinnear Road
Columbus, OH 43212-1156
614-292-3339
Fax: 614-292-0263
Seeks to understand how non-curricular factors affect how science is taught in grades K-12.

Arthur L White, Director

5034 National Center for the Study of Privatization in Education
525 West 120th Street
Box 181
New York, NY 10027
212-678-3259
Fax: 212-678-3474
E-mail: ncspe@columbia.edu
An independent research center.

5035 National Center on Education & the Economy
39 State Street
Suite 500
Rochester, NY 14614-1312
888-361-6233
Fax: 585-482-1284
http://www.ncee.org
Develops proposals for building a world-class education and training system.

Marc S Tucker, Director

5036 National Center on Education in the Inner Cities
Temple University
13th Street & Cecil B Moore Avenue
Philadelphia, PA 19122
215-893-8400
Fax: 215-735-9718
Conducts systematic studies of innovative initiatives for improving the quality and outcomes of schooling and broad-based efforts to strengthen and improve education.

Margaret C Wang, Director

5037 National Child Labor Committee
1501 Broadway
Suite 1111
New York, NY 10036-5592
212-840-1801
Fax: 212-768-0963
Produces and disseminates information on youth employment and child labor laws with the aim of advocating the rights and dignity of youth.

Jeffrey Newman, Director

5038 National Clearinghouse for Alcohol & Drug Information
PO Box 2345
Rockville, MD 20847-2345
301-468-2600
800-729-6686
Fax: 301-468-6433
http://health.org

Serves to collect, disseminate and exchange alcohol and drug information.

John Noble, Director

5039 National Clearinghouse for Bilingual Education
George Washington University
2121 K Street NW
Suite 260
Washington, DC 20037-1214
202-467-0867
800-321-6223
Fax: 202-467-4283
E-mail: askncela@ncela.gwu.edu
http://www.ncela.gwu.edu
Provides information to practitioners on the education of language minority students. Operates a web site, sponsors discussion groups and an electronic newsletter.

Nancy Zelasko, Director
Minerva Gorena, Senior Advisor

5040 National Clearinghouse for Information on Business Involvement in Education
National Association for Industry-Education Co-op
235 Hendricks Boulevard
Buffalo, NY 14226-3304
716-834-7047
Fax: 718-834-7047
E-mail: www2.pecom/naiec
http://www2.pecom.net/naiec
Seeks to foster industry-education cooperation in the US and Canada in the areas of school improvement, career education and human resource/economic development.

Dr. Donald Clark, Director

5041 National Dropout Prevention Center
Clemson University
209 Martin Street
Clemson, SC 29631-1555
864-656-2599
Fax: 864-656-0136
E-mail: NDPC@clemson.edu
http://www.dropoutprevention.org
Seeks to reduce America's dropout rate significantly by fostering public-private partnerships in local school districts and communities throughout the nation.

Dr. Jay Smink, Director
Marty Duckenfield, Information Coordinator

5042 National Early Childhood Technical Assistance System
137 E Franklin Street
Room 500
Chapel Hill, NC 27514
919-962-2001
Fax: 919-966-7463
http://www.nectas.unc.edu
Provides technical assistance to state agencies and model projects sponsored by the US Dept of Education in the development of services for children with special needs and their families.

Pascal Trohanis, Director

5043 National Information Center for Educational Media
PO Box 8640
Albuquerque, NM 87198-8640
505-265-3591
800-926-8328
Fax: 505-256-1080
E-mail: mhlava@accessinn.com
http://www.nicem.com/index.html

Maintains the world's largest database of information about educational media and materials and makes the information available on CD-rom and the Internet.

Marjorie Hlava, President
Jay Van Eman, Chief Executive Officer

5044 National Research Center on the Gifted & Talented
University of Connecticut
362 Fairfield Road
Unit U-7
Storrs Mansfield, CT 06269-2007
860-486-4826
Fax: 860-486-2900
Conducts research on methods and techniques for teaching gifted and talented students.

Joseph S Renzulli, Director
Phillip E Austin, President

5045 National Resource Center on Self-Care & School-Age Child Care
American Home Economics Association
1555 King Street
Alexandria, VA 22314-2738
703-706-4620
800-252-SAFE
Fax: 703-706-4663
Provides materials to parents, educators, child care professionals and others concerned about the number of latchkey children and about quality school-age child care.

Dr. Margaret Plantz, Director

5046 National School Boards Association Library
1680 Duke Street
Alexandria, VA 22314-3455
703-838-6731
Fax: 703-683-7590
Maintains up-to-date collection of resources concerning education issues, with an emphasis on school board policy issues.

Adria Thomas, Director

5047 National School Safety Center
14 Duesenberg Drive
Suite 11
Westlake Village, CA 91362-3815
805-373-9977
Fax: 805-373-9277
Provides training, technical assistance and resources on school safety and school crime prevention.

Dr. Ronald Stephens, Executive Director
June Arnette, Editor

5048 National Science Resources Center
901 D Street SW
Suite 704B
Washington, DC 20024
202-633-2792
Fax: 202-287-2070
E-mail: nsrcinfo@si.edu
http://www.nsrconline.org
Works to improve teaching of science in the nation's schools. Through national outreach to build consensus, dissemination of information on resources for teaching science, and development of curriculum materials. NSRC offers strategic planning institutes for school district teams every summer. Operated by the Smithsonian Institution and the National Academies.

Sally Shuler, Executive Director
Barbara Thomas, Director

5049 North Central Regional Educational Laboratory
1120 E Diehl Drive
Suite 200
Naperville, IL 60563
630-649-6500
Fax: 630-649-6700
E-mail: info@ncrel.org
http://www.ncrel.org
Applies research and technology to learning. Makes connections between researchers and educators on a wide variety of topics.

Gina Burkhard, Executive Director

5050 Northeast Regional Center for Drug-Free Schools & Communities
12 Overton Avenue
Sayville, NY 11782-2437
718-340-7000
Fax: 516-589-7894
Works to support the prevention of alcohol and other drug use in the northeast region of the United States.

Dr. Gerald Edwards, Director

5051 Northeast and Islands Regional Educational Laboratory
222 Richmond Street
Suite 300
Providnce, RI 02903
401-274-9548
800-521-9550
Fax: 401-421-7650
E-mail: info@lab.brown.edu
http://www.lab.brown.edu
The LAB at Brown University is one of ten federally funded labs performing applied research and development to improve teaching and learning and promote effective school reform. We focus on education issues in New England, New York, Puerto Rico and the Virgin Islands. Our national leadership area is teaching diverse learners. We examine ways that learning standards, portfolio assessment systems and math and science instructional practices can be revised to more effectively challenge students.

Lisa DiMartino, Administrative Assistant
Eileen Harrington, Public Information Associate

5052 Northwest Regional Educational Laboratory
101 SW Main Street
Suite 500
Portland, OR 97204-3297
503-275-9500
800-547-6339
Fax: 503-275-0458
E-mail: info@nwrel.org
http://www.nwrel.org
The Regional Educational Laboratories are educational research and development organizations supported by contracts with the US Education Department, Office of Educational Research and Improvement. Specialty area: school change processes.

Carol F Thomas, CEO

5053 Pacific Regional Educational Laboratory
1099 Alakea Street
Suite 2500
Honolulu, HI 96813
808-969-3482
Fax: 808-969-3483
E-mail: kofelj@prel.hawaii.edu
The Regional Educational Laboratories are educational research and development organizations supported by contracts with the

U.S. Education Department, Office of Educational Research and Improvement. Specialty area: Language and Cultural Diversity.

Dr. John Kofel, Executive Director

5054 Parent Educational Advocacy Training Center
2405 Jefferson Avenue
Richmond, VA 23223
804-819-1999
E-mail: partners@peatc.org
http://www.peatc.org
The Parent Educational Advocacy Training Center assists the families of children with disabilities through education, information and training. PEATC builds parent-professional partnerships to promote success in school and community life.

Felicia Kessel-Crawley, Director

5055 Parents as Teachers National Center
2228 Ball Drive
Saint Louis, MO 63146
314-432-4330
Fax: 314-432-8963
E-mail: patnc@patnc.org
http://www.patnc.org
Provides information about PAT, plus training and technical assistance for those interested in adopting the program. PAT is a home-school-community partnership designed to provide all parents from birth, (or prenatally) to kindergarten entry the information and support needed to give their children the best possible start in life. Independent evaluations show strong positive outcomes for children and parents. Publishes a quarterly newsletter.

Susan S Stepleton, President/CEO
Cheryl Dyle-Palmer, Director Operations

5056 Public Education Fund Network
601 13th Street NW
Suite 209
Washington, DC 20005-3807
202-628-7460
Fax: 202-628-1893
Dedicated to improving public education, especially for disadvantaged children.

Wendy D Puriefoy, Director

5057 Quality Education Data
1700 Lincoln Street
Suite 3600
Denver, CO 80203
303-209-9328
800-525-5811
Fax: 303-209-9444
E-mail: qedinfo@qeddata.com
http://www.qeddata.com
Gathers information about K-12 schools, colleges and other educational institutions, offers an on-line database on education, directories of public and nonpublic schools and research reports.

Jeanne Hayes, President

5058 Regional Laboratory for Educational Improvement of the Northeast
300 Brickstone Square
Suite 900
Andover, MA 01810-1435
800-347-4200
Fax: 781-481-1120
Seeks to improve education in Connecticut, Maine, Massachusetts, New Hampshire,

New York, Rhode Island, Vermont, Puerto Rico and the Virgin Islands.

David P Crandall, Director

5059 Research for Better Schools
1818 N Street NW
Suite 350
Washington, DC 20036-2471
215-574-9300
Fax: 215-574-0133
Seeks to improve schools and classroom instruction in Delaware, the District of Columbia, Maryland, New Jersey and Pennsylvania.

Peter J Donahoe, Director

5060 SERVE
PO Box 5367
Greensboro, NC 27435
336-315-7400
Fax: 336-315-7457
E-mail: info@serve.org
http://www.serve.org
Regional Educational Laboratories is an educational research and development organization supported by contracts with the US Education Department, National Institute for Education Sciences. Specialty area: Extended Learning Opporunity including Before and After School programs and Early Childhood.

Ludy van Broekhuizen, Executive Director

5061 SIGI PLUS
Educational Testing Service
105 Terry Drive
Suite 120
Newtown, PA 18940-1872
800-257-7444
Fax: 215-579-8589
A computerized career guidance program developed by Educational Testing Service. Covers all the major aspects of career decision making and planning through a carefully constructed system of nine separate but interrelated sections, including a Tech Prep module and Internet Hydrolink Connectivity.

Annie Schofer, Sales Manager

5062 Satellite Educational Resources Consortium
939 S Stadium Road
Columbia, SC 29201-4724
803-252-2782
Fax: 803-252-5320
Seeks to expand educational opportunities by employing the latest telecommunication technologies to make quality education in math, science, and foreign languages available equally and cost-effectively to students regardless of their geographic location.

John Chambers, Director Education Services

5063 Scientific Learning
300 Frank H. Ogawa Plaza
Suite 600
Oakland, CA 94612-2040
888-665-9707
888-665-9707
Fax: 510-444-3580
E-mail: customerservice@scilearn.com
http://www.scientificlearning.com
Scientific Learning bases their products and services on neuroscience research and scientifically validated efficacy and deliver them using the most efficient technologies. We also provide beneficial products

and services to our customers that are easy to use and access.

Cynthia Myers, VP Public Affairs

5064 Smithsonian Institution/Office of Elementary & Secondary Education
PO Box 3701263
Washington, DC 20560-0001
202-357-2700
Fax: 202-357-2116
E-mail: info@si.edu
Helps K-12 teachers incorporate museums and other community resources into their curricula.

Ann Bay, Director

5065 Society for Research in Child Development
University of Chicago Press
5720 S Woodlawn Avenue
Chicago, IL 60637-1603
773-702-7700
Fax: 773-702-9756
Works to further research in the area of child development.

Barbara Kahn, Business Manager

5066 Southeast Regional Center for Drug-Free Schools & Communities
Spencerian Office Plaza
Louisville, KY 40292-0001
502-588-0052
800-621-7372
Fax: 502-588-1782
Works to support the prevention of alcohol and drug use among youth in the Southeast region.

Nancy J Cunningham, Director

5067 Southern Regional Education Board
592 10th Street NW
Atlanta, GA 30318-5790
404-875-9211
Fax: 404-872-1477
Identifies and directs attention to key education issues.

Mark D Musick, Director

5068 Southwest Comprehensive Regional Assistance Center-Region IX
New Mexico Highlands University
121 Tijeras Avenue NE, Suite 2100
Albuquerque, NM 87102-3461
800-247-4269
Fax: 505-243-4456
National network of 15 technical assistance centers, funded through the US Department of Education, designed to support federally funded educational programs. Specifically, these centers will provide comprehensive training and technical assistance under the Improving America's Schools Act (IASA) to States, Tribes, community based organizations, local education agencies, schools and other recipients of funds under the Act.

Paul E Martinez EdD, Director

5069 Southwestern Educational Development Laboratory
211 E 7th Street
Austin, TX 78701
512-476-6861
800-476-6861
Fax: 512-476-2286
E-mail: whoover@sedl.org
http://www.sedl.org

SEDL is a private not-for-profit corporation that conducts education research, development, technical assistance, and professional development. SEDL holds contracts with the US Education Department for the Regional Educational Laboratory, the Eisenhower Math & Science Consortium, and the Regional Technology on Education Consortium serving Arkansas, Louisiana, New Mexico, Oklahoma and Texas.

Dr. Wesley A Hoover, Executive Director
Dr. Joyce S Pollard, Director Institutional Comm.

5070 Special Interest Group for Computer Science Education
Computer Science Department
University of Texas at Austin
Austin, TX 78712
512-471-9539
Fax: 512-471-8885
Provides a forum for solving problems common in developing, implementing and evaluating computer science education programs and courses.

Nell B Dale, Director

5071 TACS/WRRC
University of Oregon
1268 University of Oregon
Eugene, OR 97403
541-346-5641
Fax: 541-346-0322
E-mail: wrrc@oregon.uoregon.edu
http://http://interact.uoregon.edu/wrrc/wrrc.html
Supports state education agencies in their task of ensuring quality programs and services for children with disabilities and their families.

Richard Zeller, Co-Director
Caroline Moore, Co-Director

5072 TERC
2067 Massachusetts Avenue
Cambridge, MA 02140-1340
617-547-0430
Fax: 617-349-3535
E-mail: communications@terc.edu
http://www.terc.edu
Researches, develops, and disseminates innovative programs in science, mathematics and technology for educators, schools and other learning environments.

24 pages
ISSN: 0743-0221

Kenneth Mayer, Author
Peggy Kapisovsky, Communications Director

5073 UCLA Statistical Consulting
University of California, Los Angeles
8130 MSB, UCLA
PO Box 951554
Los Angeles, CA 90095-1554
310-825-8299
Fax: 310-206-5658
Provides statistical consulting services to UCLA and off-campus students. The staff is faculty members, graduate students and the Department of Statistics. Specializes in the quantitative analysis of research problems in a wide variety of fields.

Debbie Barrera, Administrator
Richard Berk, Director

Audio Visual Materials

5074 AGC/United Learning
Discovery Education
1560 Sherman Avenue
Suite 100
Evanston, IL 60201
847-328-6700
800-323-9084
Fax: 847-328-6706
http://www.discoveryed.com
A publisher/producer of educational videos and digital content K-College curriculum based.

Coni Rechner, Director Marketing
Ronald Reed, Sr. Vice President

5075 Active Parenting Publishing
810 Franklin Court
Suite B
Marietta, GA 30067
800-825-0060
Fax: 770-429-0334
E-mail: cservice@activeparenting.com
http://www.activeparenting.com
Videos and books on parenting, character education, substance abuse prevention, divorce and step-parenting, ADHD and more.

5076 Agency for Instructional Technology/AIT
PO Box A
Bloomington, IN 47402-0120
800-457-4509
Videodiscs, videocassettes, films and electronics.

5077 Allied Video Corporation
PO Box 702618
Tulsa, OK 74170-2618
918-587-6477
800-926-5892
Fax: 918-587-1550
E-mail: allied@farpointer.net
http://www.alliedvd.com
Produces the educational video series, The Assistant Professor. Animations and three-dimensional graphics clearly illustrate concepts in mathematics, science and music. Companion supplementary materials are also available.

Video

Charles Brown, President

5078 Altschul Group Corporation
1560 Sherman Avenue
Suite 100
Evanston, IL 60201-4817
800-323-9084
Video and film educational programs.

5079 Ambrose Video Publishing Inc
145 West 45th Street
New York, NY 10036
212-768-7373
800-526-4663
Fax: 212-768-9282
http://www.ambrosevideo.com
A leading distributor of broadcast quality documentation/educational videos to individuals (in the home) and schools, libraries and other institutions. The company also sells through catalog, sales staff and television advertising.

5080 Anchor Audio
3415 Lomita Boulevard
Torrance, CA 90505-5010
310-784-2300
800-262-4671
Fax: 310-784-0533
http://www.anchoraudio.com
Various audio visual products for the school and library.

5081 Association for Educational Communications & Technology
1025 Vermont Avenue NW
Suite 820
Washington, DC 20005-3516
202-347-7834
Offers a full line of videotapes and films for the various educational fields including language arts, science and social studies.

5082 BUILD Sucess Through the Values of Excellence
Center for the Study of Small/Rural Schools
555 E Constitution Street
Room 138
Norman, OK 73072-7820
405-325-1450
Fax: 405-325-7075
E-mail: jcsimmons@ou.edu
http://cssrs.ou.edu
Series IV

Video

Jan C Simmons, Director

5083 Bergwall Productions
540 Baltimore Pike
Chadds Ford, PA 19317-9304
800-645-3565
Educational videotapes and films.

5084 Cedrus
1420 Buena Vista Avenue
McLean, VA 22101-3510
703-883-0986
Videodiscs, videocassettes and filmstrips for educational purposes.

5085 Character Education
Center for the Study of Small/Rural Schools
555 E Constitution Street
Room 138
Norman, OK 73072-7820
405-325-1450
Fax: 405-325-7075
E-mail: jcsimmons@ou.edu
http://cssrs.ou.edu
Series IV

Video

Jan C Simmons, Director

5086 Chip Taylor Communications
2 E View Drive
Derry, NH 03038-5728
603-434-9262
800-876-2447
Fax: 603-432-2723
E-mail: sales@chiptaylor.com
http://www.chiptaylor.com
Quality educational videotapes and DVDs and multimedia in all areas of interest.

Video

Chip Taylor, President

5087 Churchill Media
6677 N NW Highway
Chicago, IL 60631-1304
310-207-6600
800-334-7830
Fax: 800-624-1678
Videos, videodiscs and curriculum packages for schools and libraries.

5088 College Board Publications
College Board Publications
45 Columbus Avenue
New York, NY 10023-6992
212-713-8165
800-323-7155
Fax: 800-525-5562
http://www.collegeboard.org
Offers a variety of educational videotapes and publications focusing on college issues.

5089 Computer Prompting & Captioning Company
1010 Rockville Pike
Suite 306
Rockville, MD 20852-3035
301-738-8487
800-977-6678
Fax: 301-738-8488
E-mail: info@cpcweb.com
http://www.cpcweb.com
Closed captioning systems and service.

Sid Hoffman, Project Manager

5090 Concept Media
2493 Du Bridge Avenue
Irvine, CA 92606-5022
949-660-0727
800-233-7078
Fax: 949-660-0206
E-mail: info@conceptmedia.com
http://www.conceptmedia.com
Videos for students and professionals focused on child development, early childhood education, and the challenges facing many young children. Effective educational media for development specialists, regular and special education staff in elementary school, preschool teachers, childcare providers, health care workers and parents.

Dennis Timmerman, Sr Account Executive

5091 Crystal Productions
PO Box 2159
Glenview, IL 60025-6159
847-657-8144
800-255-8629
Fax: 800-657-8149
E-mail: custserv@crystalproductions.com
http://www.crystalproductions.com
Producer and distributor of educational resource material in art and sciences. Resources include videotapes, posters, books, videodiscs, CD-Rom, reproductions, games.

132 pages

Amy Woodworth, President

5092 Dukane Corporation
Audio Visual Products Division
2900 Dukane Drive
St Charles, IL 60174-3395
630-584-2300
Fax: 630-584-5156
Full line of audio visual products, LCD display panels, computer data projectors, overhead projectors, microfilm readers and silent and sound filmstrip projectors.

Stew deLacey

5093 Early Advantage
270 Monroe Turnpike
PO Box 4063
Monroe, CT 06468-4063
888-999-4670
Fax: 800-301-9268
E-mail:
customerservice@early-advantage.com
http://www.earlyadvantage.com
Features the Muzzy video collection for
teaching children beginning second language skills.

5094 Educational Video Group
291 S Wind Way
Greenwood, IN 46142-9190
317-888-6581
Fax: 317-888-5857
E-mail: evg@insightbb.com
http://www.evgonline.com
Award-winning video programs and textbooks in education, presenting new offerings in speech, government and historic
documentaries.

Roger Cook, President

**5095 English as a Second Language
Video Series**
Master Teacher
Leadership Lane
PO Box 1207
Manhattan, KS 66505-1207
800-669-9633
Fax: 800-669-1132
http://www.masterteacher.com
Assessing the needs of culturally diverse
learners, you will learn what must be done
to evaluate the learning needs and progress
of ESL students.

ISBN: 1-58992-045-7

5096 Fase Productions
4801 Wilshire Boulevard
Suite 215
Los Angeles, CA 90010-3813
213-965-8794
Educational videotapes and films.

5097 Films for Humanities & Sciences
PO Box 2053
Princeton, NJ 08543-2053
609-419-8000
800-257-5126
Fax: 609-419-8071
A leading publisher/distributor of over
four thousand educational programs, including NOVA and TV Ontario, for school
and college markets. Also a leader in the
production and distribution of videotapes
and videodiscs to the educational, institutional and government markets.

5098 First Steps/Concepts in Motivation
18105 Town Center Drive
Olney, MD 20832-1479
301-774-9429
800-947-8377
Educational videotapes and accessories
promoting physical fitness for preschool-
ers and young children. Using choreo-
graphed dance movement, familiar and fun
children's music, colorful mats, bean bags
and rhythm sticks, First Steps teaches balance, gross and fine motor skills, rhythm,
coordination, and primary learning skills.

Dale Rimmey, Marketing Director
Larry Rose, President/Owner

5099 Future of Rural Education
Center for the Study of Small/Rural
Schools
555 E Constitution Street
Room 138
Norman, OK 73072-7820
405-325-1450
Fax: 405-325-7075
E-mail: jcsimmons@ou.edu
http://cssrs.ou.edu
Series I
Video

Jan C Simmons, Director

5100 GPN Year 2005 Literacy Catalog
GPN Educational Media
PO Box 80669
Lincoln, NE 68501-0669
402-472-2007
800-228-4630
Fax: 402-472-4076
E-mail: gpn@unl.edu
http://www.gpn.unl.edu
DVD, VHS, CD-ROM and slides for K-12
libraries and higher education. Free previews and satisfaction guaranteed. The
sole source of Reading Rainbow and many
other quality programs seen on PBS.

Annually/Video

Stephen C Lenzen, Executive Director
John Vondracek, Director Marketing

**5101 Gangs in Our Schools:
Identification, Response, and
Prevention Strategies**
Center for the Study of Small/Rural
Schools
555 E Constitution Street
Room 138
Norman, OK 73072-7820
405-325-1450
Fax: 405-325-7075
E-mail: jcsimmons@ou.edu
http://cssrs.ou.edu
Series III
Video

Jan C Simmons, Director

5102 Guidance Associates
PO Box 1000
Mount Kisco, NY 10549-7000
800-431-1242
Fax: 914-666-5319
E-mail: sales@guidanceassociates.com
http://www.guidanceassociates.com
Curriculum based videos in health/guid-
ance, social studies, math, science, Eng-
lish, the humanities and career education.

Will Goodman, President

5103 Health Connection
55 W Oak Ridge Drive
Hagerstown, MD 21740
800-548-8700
Fax: 888-294-8405
E-mail: sales@healthconnection.org
http://www.healthconnection.org
Tools for freedom from tobacco and other
drugs.

5104 Human Relations Media
175 Tompkins Avenue
Pleasantville, NY 10570-3144
800-431-2050
Fax: 914-244-0485
Offers a wide variety of videotapes and
videodiscs in the areas of guidance, social
services, human relations, self-esteem and
student services.

**5105 IIEPassport: Short Term Study
Abroad**
Institute of International Education
809 United Nations Plaza
New York, NY 10017-3580
412-741-0930
Fax: 212-984-5496
E-mail: iiebooks@abdintl.com
http://www.iiebooks.org
Over 2,900 short-term study abroad pro-
grams offered by universities, schools, as-
sociations and other organizations.

Annual
ISBN: 087206-296-1

Daniel Obst, Sr Editor

5106 INSIGHTS Visual Productions
374-A N Highway 101
Encinitas, CA 92024-2527
760-942-0528
Fax: 760-944-7793
Science video for K-12 and teacher training.

**5107 INTELECOM Intelligent
Telecommunications**
150 E Colorado Boulevard
Suite 300
Pasadena, CA 91105-3710
626-796-7300
Fax: 626-577-4282
Videos and educational films.

Bob Miller, VP Marketing/Sale

5108 In Search of Character
Performance Resource Press
1270 Rankin Drive
Suite F
Troy, MI 48083-2843
800-453-7733
Fax: 800-499-5718
http://www.pronline.net
Character education videos.

**5109 Instructional Resources
Corporation**
1819 Bay Ridge Avenue
Annapolis, MD 21403-2835
American History Videodisc.

5110 Intermedia
1165 Eastlake Ave East
Suite 400
Seattle, WA 98109-3571
206-284-2995
800-553-8336
Fax: 206-283-0778
http://www.intermedia-inc.com
Distributes a wide range of high-quality,
social interest videos on topics such as teen
pregnancy prevention, substance abuse
prevention, domestic violence, sexual harassment, dating violence, date rape, gang
education, cultural diversity, AIDS prevention and teen patenting. Offer free 30
day previews of the programs which are developed to address the needs of educators
who must deal with the pressing social
problems of today.

Paperback/Video

Susan Hoffman, President
Ted Fitch, General Manager

5111 International Historic Films
3533 S Archer Avenue
Chicago, IL 60609-1135
773-927-2900
Fax: 773-927-9211
E-mail: info@ihffilm.com
http://www.ihffilm.com

Military, political and social history of the 20th century.

Video/Audio

5112 January Productions

PO Box 66
Hawthorne, NJ 07507-0066
973-423-4666
800-451-7450
Fax: 973-423-5569
E-mail: anpeller@worldnet.att.net
Educational videotapes, read-a-long books, and CD-Rom.

Paperback/Video/Audi

Lori Brown, Sales/Marketing

5113 Karol Media

350 N Pennsylvania Avenue
Wilkes Barre, PA 18702-4415
570-822-8899
Fax: 570-822-8226
Science videos.

5114 Kimbo Educational

PO Box 477
Long Branch, NJ 07740-0477
800-631-2187
Manufacturer of children's audio-musical learning fun. Also offers videos and music by other famous children's artists such as Raffi, Sharon, Lois and Bram.

5115 Leadership: Rethinking the Future

Center for the Study of Small/Rural Schools
555 E Constitution Street
Room 138
Norman, OK 73072-7820
405-325-1450
Fax: 405-325-7075
E-mail: jcsimmons@ou.edu
http://cssrs.ou.edu
Series IV

Video

Jan C Simmons, Director

5116 MPC Multimedia Products Corp

1010 Sherman Avenue
Hamden, CT 06514
203-407-4623
800-243-2108
Fax: 203-407-4636
E-mail: sales@800-pickmpc.com
http://www.800-pickmpc.com
Over 5,000 most frequently requested high quality audio, visual and video products and materials offered at deep discount prices. Manufacturer of high quality tape records, CD's record players, PA systems, headphones

148 pages BiAnnual

T. Guercia, Author
T Guercia, VP
A Melillo, Sales Manager

5117 Main Street Foundations: Building Community Teams

Center for the Study of Small/Rural Schools
555 E Constitution Street
Room 138
Norman, OK 73072-7820
405-325-1450
Fax: 405-325-7075
E-mail: jcsimmons@ou.edu
http://cssrs.ou.edu
Prevention Series

Video

Jan C Simmons, Director

5118 Marshmedia

Marsh Media
8025 Ward Parkway Plaza
Kansas City, MO 64114
816-523-1059
800-821-3303
Fax: 816-333-7421
E-mail: order@marshmedia.com
http://www.marshmedia.com
Children's educational videotapes, books and teaching guides.

32 pages Bi-Annual
ISBN: 1-55942-xxx

Joan K Marsh, President

5119 Media Projects

5215 Homer Street
Dallas, TX 75206-6623
214-826-3863
Fax: 214-826-3919
E-mail: mediaprojects@noval.net
http://www.mediaprojects.org
Educational videotapes in all areas of interest, including drug education, violence prevention, women's studies, history, youth issues and special education.

5120 Middle School: Why and How

Center for the Study of Small/Rural Schools
555 E Constitution Street
Room 138
Norman, OK 73072-7820
405-325-1450
Fax: 405-325-7075
E-mail: jcsimmons@ou.edu
http://cssrs.ou.edu
Series III

Video

Jan C Simmons, Director

5121 Multicultural Educations: Valuing Diversity

Center for the Study of Small/Rural Schools
555 E Constitution Street
Room 138
Norman, OK 73072-7820
405-325-1450
Fax: 405-325-7075
E-mail: jcsimmons@ou.edu
http://cssrs.ou.edu
Series I

Video

Jan C Simmons, Director

5122 NUVO, Ltd.

PO Box 1729
Chula Vista, CA 91912
619-426-8440
Fax: 619-691-1525
E-mail: nuvoltd@aol.com
Produces and distributes how-to videotapes for teens and adults on beginning reading and decorative napkin folding useful in classroom instruction and individual practice. Also distributes two bilingual (Spanish/English) books by psychologist Dr. Jorge Espinoza.

5123 National Film Board

1251 Avenue of the Americas
New York, NY 10020-1104
800-542-2164
Fax: 845-774-2945
Educational films and videos ranging from documentaries on nature and science to social issues such as teen pregnancy.

5124 National Geographic School Publishing

PO Box 10579
Washington, DC 20090-8019
800-368-2728
Fax: 515-362-3366
Offers a wide variety of videodiscs, videotapes and educational materials in the area of social studies, geography, science and social sciences.

5125 PBS Video

1320 Braddock Pl
Alexandria, VA 22314-1649
703-739-5380
800-424-7963
Fax: 703-739-5269
Award-winning programs from PBS, public television's largest video distributors. Video and multimedia programming including interactive videodiscs for schools, colleges and libraries. The PBS Video Resource Catalog is organized into detailed subject categories.

5126 PICS Authentic Foreign Video

University of Iowa
270 International Center
Iowa City, IA 52242-1802
319-335-2335
800-373-PICS
Fax: 319-335-0280
Provides educators with authentic foreign language videos in French, German and Spanish on videotapes and videodisc. Also offers software to accompany the videodiscs as well as written materials in the form of transcripts and videoguides with pedagogical hints and tips.

Becky Bohde, German Coll Editor
Anny Ewing, French Coll Editor

5127 Penton Overseas

2470 Impala Drive
Carlsbad, CA 92008-7226
800-748-5804
Fax: 760-431-8110
Educational videotapes and videodiscs in a wide variety of interests for classroom use.

5128 Phoenix Films/BFA Educ Media/Coronet/MII

Phoenix Learning Group
2349 Chaffee Drive
St. Louis, MO 63146
314-569-0211
800-777-8100
Fax: 314-569-2834
E-mail: phoenixdealer@aol.com
http://www.phoenixlearninggroup.com
Educational multi-media - VHS, CD-Rom, DVD, streaming & broadcast.

Video

Kathy Longsworth, Vice President, Market Dev

5129 Presidential Classroom

119 Oronoco Street
Alexandria, VA 22314-2015
703-683-5400
800-441-6533
Fax: 703-548-5728
E-mail: eriedel@presidentialclassroom.org
http://www.presidentialclassroom.org
Video of civic education programs in Washington, DC for high school juniors and seniors. Each one week program provides students with an inside view of the federal

government in action and their role as responsible citizens and future leaders.

Annual
400 attendees

Jack Buechner, President/CEO
Emily Davisriedel, Director Marketing

5130 Rainbow Educational Media Charles Clark Company
4540 Preslyn Drive
Raleigh, NC 27616
919-954-7550
800-331-4047
Fax: 919-954-7554
E-mail: karencf@rainbowedumedia.com
http://www.rainbowedumedia.com
Educational videocassettes and CD-Roms.

Karen C Francis, Business Analyst

5131 Rainbow Educational Video
170 Keyland Court
Bohemia, NY 11716-2638
800-331-4047
Producer and distributor of educational videos.

Wesley Clark, Marketing Director

5132 Reading & O'Reilly: The Wilton Programs
PO Box 302
Wilton, CT 06897-0302
800-458-4274
Producers and distributors of award-winning audiovisual educational programs in art appreciation, history, multicultural education, social studies and music. Titles include: African-American Art and the Take-a-Bow, musical production series. Free catalog is available of full product line.

Lee Reading, President
Gretchen O'Reilly, VP

5133 SAP Today
Performance Resource Press
1270 Rankin Drive
Suite F
Troy, MI 48083-2843
800-453-7733
Fax: 800-499-5718
Overview offers the basics of student assistance.

5134 SVE: Society for Visual Education
55 E Monroe Street
Suite 3400
Chicago, IL 60603-5710
312-849-9100
800-829-1900
Fax: 800-624-1678
Producer and distributor of curriculum based instructional materials including videodisc, microcomputer software, video cassettes and filmstrips for grade levels PreK-12.

5135 Slow Learning Child Video Series
Master Teacher
Leadership Lane
PO Box 1207
Manhattan, KS 66505-1207
800-669-9633
Fax: 800-669-1132
http://www.masterteacher.com
Provides a full understangding of the slow learning child and allows all educators to share in the excitment of teaching this

invidual in ways that develop his or her emerging potenial to the fullest.

ISBN: 1-58992-157-0

Mildred Odom Bradley, Author

5136 Spoken Arts
PO Box 100
New Rochelle, NY 10802-0100
727-578-7600
Literature-based audio and visual products for library and K-12 classrooms.

5137 Teacher's Video Company
8150 S Krene Road
Tempe, AZ 85284
800-262-8837
Fax: 800-434-5638
http://www.teachersvideo.com
Video for teachers.

5138 Teen Court: An Alternative Approach to Juvenile Justice
Center for the Study of Small/Rural Schools
555 E Constitution Street
Room 138
Norman, OK 73072-7820
405-325-1450
Fax: 405-325-7075
E-mail: jcsimmons@ou.edu
http://cssrs.ou.edu
Prevention Series

Video

Jan C Simmons, Director

5139 Tools to Help Youth
529 S 7 Street
Suite 570
Minneapolis, MN 55415
800-328-0417
Fax: 612-342-2388
http://www.communityintervention.com
Books and videos on counseling, character education, anger management, life skills, and achohol, tobacco and other drug uses.

5140 Training Video Series for the Professional School Bus Driver
Master Teacher
Leadership Lane
PO Box 1207
Manhattan, KS 66505-1207
800-669-9633
Fax: 800-669-1132
http://www.masterteacher.com
Will help you provide bus drivers with consistent direction and training for the many situations thay will encounter beyond driving safety.

ISBN: 1-58992-082-1

5141 True Colors
Center for the Study of Small/Rural Schools
555 E Constitution Street
Room 138
Norman, OK 73072-7820
405-325-1450
Fax: 405-325-7075
E-mail: jcsimmons@ou.edu
http://cssrs.ou.edu
Series III

Video

Jan C Simmons, Director

5142 United Transparencies
435 Main Street
Johnson City, NY 13790-1935
607-729-6368
800-477-6512
Fax: 607-729-4820
A full line of overhead transparencies for Junior-Senior high school and colleges and technical programs.

D Hetherington

5143 Video Project
200 Estates Drive
Ben Lomond, CA 95005
800-475-2638
Fax: 905-278-2801
E-mail: videoproject@igc.org
http://www.videoproject.org
Distributor of environmental videos with a collection of over 500 programs for all grade levels, including Oscar and Emmy award winners. Many videotapes come with teacher's guides. Free catalogs available.

Terry Thiermann, Administrative Director
Ian Thiermann, Executive Director

5144 Weston Woods Studios
265 Post Road West
Westport, CT 06880
203-845-0197
800-243-5020
Fax: 203-845-0498
E-mail: wstnwoods@aol.com
Audiovisual adaptations of classic children's literature.

Video

Cindy Cardozo, Marketing Coordinator

Classroom Materials

5145 ABC School Supply
3312 N Berkeley Lake Road NW
Duluth, GA 30096-3024
Instructional materials and supplies.

5146 ADP Lemco
5970 W Dannon Way
West Jordan, UT 84088
801-280-4000
800-575-3626
Fax: 801-280-4040
E-mail: sales@adplemco.com
http://www.adplemco.com
Announcement boards, schedule boards, chalkboards, tackboard, marker boards, trophy cases, athletic equipment, gym divider curtains and basketball backstops.

David L Hall, Sr VP

5147 APCO
388 Grant Street SE
Atlanta, GA 30312-2227
404-688-9000
Fax: 404-577-3847
Classroom supplies including announcement and chalkboards.

Anne M Gallup

5148 AbleNet
2808 Fairview Avenue N
Roseville, MN 55113-1308
651-294-2200
800-322-0956
Fax: 651-294-2259
http://www.ablenetinc.com
Adaptive devices for students with disabilities from Pre-K through adult, as well as

activities and games for students of all abilities.

5149 Accounter Systems USA
1107 S Mannheim Road
Suite 305
Westchester, IL 60154-2560
800-229-8765
Sports timers and clocks and classroom supplies.

5150 Accu-Cut Systems
1035 E Dodge Street
Fremont, NE 68025
402-721-4134
800-288-1670
Fax: 402-721-5778
E-mail: info@accucut.com
http://www.accucut.com
Manufacturer of die cutting machines dies.

5151 Airomat Corporation
2916 Engle Road
Fort Wayne, IN 46809-1198
260-747-7408
800-348-4905
Fax: 260-747-7409
E-mail: airomat@airomat.com
http://www.airomat.com
Mats and matting.

Jody Feasel, VP
Janie Feasel, President/CEO

5152 Airspace USA
89 Patton Avenue
Asheville, NC 28801
828-258-1319
800-872-1319
Fax: 828-258-1390
E-mail: sales@airspace-usa.com
http://www.airspacesolutions.com
Airspace Soft Center Play and Learn Systems provide a comprehensive range of play, learning and physical development opportunities using commercial grade and foam filled play equipment. Play manual provided.

Daniel Brenman, VP Sales/Marketing
Tracy Syxes, Administrator

5153 All Art Supplies
Art Supplies Wholesale
4 Enon Street
North Beverly, MA 01915
800-462-2420
Fax: 800-462-2420
E-mail: info@allartsupplies.com
http://www.allartsupplies.com
Art supplies at wholesale prices.

5154 American Foam
HC 37 Box 317 H
Lewisburg, WV 24901
304-497-3000
800-344-8997
Fax: 304-497-3001
http://www.bfoam.com
Carving blocks of foam.

5155 American Plastics Council
1300 Wilson Boulevard
Arlington, VA 22209
800-243-5790
http://www.plastics.org
Offers classroom materials on recycling and environmental education.

5156 Anatomical Chart Company
8221 Kimball Avenue
Skokie, IL 60076-2956
847-679-4700
http://www.anatomical.com
Maps and charts for educational purposes.

5157 Angels School Supply
600 E Colorado Boulevard
Pasadena, CA 91101-2006
626-584-0855
Fax: 626-584-0888
http://www.angelschoolsupply.com
School and classroom supplies.

Jennifer , Sales Representitive

5158 Aol@School
22070 Broderick Drive
Dulles, VA 20166
888-468-3768
E-mail: aol at school@aol.com
http://www.school.aol.com
Age-appropriate, high-quality educational content tailored for K-12 students and educators. Aol@School focuses and filters the Web for us, providing appropriate, developmental access to the vast educational resources on the internet.

5159 Armada Art Materials
Armada Art Inc.
142 Berkeley Street
Boston, MA 02116
617-859-3800
800-435-0601
Fax: 617-859-3808
E-mail: info@armadaart.com
http://www.armadaart.com

5160 Art Materials Catalog
United Art and Education
PO Box 9219
Fort Wayne, IN 46899
800-322-3247
Fax: 800-858-3247
http://www.unitednow.com
Art materials.

5161 Art Supplies Wholesale
4 R Enon Street
N Beverly, MA 01915
800-462-2420
Fax: 978-922-1495
E-mail: info@allartsupplies.com
http://www.allartsupplies.com
Wholesale art supplies.

5162 Art to Remember
10625 Deme Drive
Unit E
Indianapolis, IN 46236
317-826-0870
800-895-8777
Fax: 317-823-2822
http://www.arttoremember.com
A unique program that encourages your students' artisic creativity while providing an opportunity to raise funds for schools.

5163 Artix
PO Box 25008
Kelowna, BC V1W3Y
250-861-5345
800-665-5345
http://www.artix.bc.ca
Papermaking kits.

5164 Assessories by Velma
PO Box 2580
Shasta, CA 96087-2580
Multicultural education-related products.

5165 At-Risk Resources
135 Dupont Street
PO Box 760
Plainview, NY 11803-0706
800-999-6884
Fax: 800-262-1886
Dealing with drug violence prevention, character education, self-esteem, teen sexuality, dropout prevention, safe schoolks, career development, parenting crisis and trauma, and professional development.

5166 Atlas Track & Tennis
19495 SW Teton Avenue
Tualatin, OR 97062-8846
800-423-5875
Fax: 503-692-0491
Specialty sport surfaces; synthetic running tracks, tennis courts, and athletic flooring for schools.

5167 Audio Forum
69 Broad Street
Guildford, CT 06437
203-453-9794
Fax: 203-453-9774
E-mail: info@audioforum.com
http://www.audioforum.com
Cassettes, CD's and books for language study.

5168 Badge-A-Minit
PO Box 800
La Salle, IL 61301-0800
815-883-8822
800-223-4103
Fax: 815-883-9696
E-mail: questions@badgeaminit.com
http://www.badgeaminit.com
Awards, trophies, emblems and badges for educational purposes.

5169 Bag Lady School Supplies
9212 Marina Pacifica Drive N
Long Beach, CA 90803-3886
Classroom supplies.

5170 Bale Company
PO Box 6400
Providence, RI 02940-6400
800-822-5350
Fax: 401-831-5500
http://www.bale.com
Awards, medals, pins, plaques and trophies.

5171 Bangor Cork Company
William & D Streets
Pen Argyl, PA 18072
610-863-9041
Fax: 610-863-6275
Announcement boards.

Janice Cory, Customer Services Rep

5172 Baumgarten's
144 Ottley Drive
Atlanta, GA 30324-4016
404-874-7675
800-247-5547
Fax: 800-255-5547
E-mail: mlynch@baumgartens.com
http://www.baumgartens.com
Products available include pencil sharpeners, pencil grips, pocket binders, disposable aprons, American flags, practical colorful clips, fastening devices in a variety of shapes and sizes, identification security items, lamination, magnifiers and key chains.

Michael Lynch, National Sales Manager

5173 Best Manufacturing Sign Systems
PO Box 577
Montrose, CO 81402-0577
970-249-2378
800-235-2378
Fax: 970-249-0223
E-mail: sales@bestsigns.com
http://www.bestsigns.com
Architectural and ADA signs, announcement boards.

Mary Phillips, Sales Manager

5174 Best-Rite
201 N Crockett Avenue
#713
Cameron, TX 76520-3376
254-778-4727
800-749-2258
Fax: 866-888-7483
E-mail: boards@bestrite.com
http://www.bestrite.com
Quality visual display products which include a complete line of chalk, marker, tack, bulletin, fabric and projection boards. Display and trophy cases, beginner boards, reversible boards, mobile easels, desk-top and floor carrels and early childhood products are also manufactured.

Bob Wilson, VP
Greg Moore, Executive VP

5175 Binney & Smith
1100 Church Lane
Easton, PA 18044
610-253-6271
800-CRA-YOLA
Fax: 610-250-5768
http://www.crayola.com
Crayons.

5176 Black History Month
Guidance Channel
135 Dupont Street
PO Box 760
Plainview, NY 44803-0706
800-999-6884
Fax: 800-262-1886
Products to celebrate Black history, multicultutral resources.

5177 Blackboard Resurfacing Company
50 N 7th Street
Bangor, PA 18013-1731
610-588-0965
Fax: 610-863-1997
Chalk and announcement boards.

Karin Karpinski, Administrative Assistant

5178 Bob's Big Pencils
1848 E 27th Street
Hays, KS 67601-2108
Large novelty pencils, plaques, bookends and many pencil related items.

5179 Book It!/Pizza Hut
9111 E Douglas Avenue
Wichita, KS 67207-1205
316-687-8401
National reading incentive program with materials, books and incentive display items to get students interested in reading.

5180 Borden
Home & Professional Products Group
180 E Broad Street
Columbus, OH 43215-3799
614-225-7479
Fax: 614-225-7167
Arts and crafts supplies, maintenance and repair supplies.

5181 Bulman Products
1650 McReynolds NW
Grand Rapids, MI 49504
616-363-4416
Fax: 616-363-0380
E-mail: bulman@macatawa.com
Art craft paper.

5182 Bydee Art
8603 Yellow Oak Street
Austin, TX 78729-3739
512-474-4343
Fax: 512-474-5749
Prints, books, T-shirts with the Bydee People focusing on education.

5183 C-Thru Ruler Company
6 Britton Drive
Bloomfield, CT 06002-3632
860-243-0303
Fax: 860-243-1856
http://www.CThruRuler.com
Arts, crafts and classroom supplies.

Ross Zachs, Manager

5184 CHEM/Lawrence Hall of Science
University of California
Berkeley, CA 94720
510-642-6000
Fax: 510-642-1055
E-mail: lhsinfo@uclink.berkley.edu
http://www.lawrencehallofscience.org
Activities for grades 5-6 and helps students understand the use of chemicals in our daily lives.

Linda Schnieder, Marketing Manager
Mike Slater, Marketing/PR Associate

5185 CORD Communications
324 Kelly Street
Waco, TX 76710-5709
254-776-1822
Fax: 254-776-3906
Instructional materials for secondary and postsecondary applications in science education.

5186 Califone International
21300 Superior Street
Chatsworth, CA 91311-4328
818-407-2400
800-722-0500
Fax: 818-407-2491
http://www.califone.com
Multisensory, supplemental curricula on magnetic cards for use with all Card Reader/Language master equipment.

Nelly Spievak, Sales Coordinator

5187 Cardinal Industries
PO Box 1430
Grundy, VA 24614-1430
276-935-4545
800-336-0551
Fax: 276-935-4970
Awards, emblems, trophies and badges.

5188 Carousel Productions
1100 Wilcrest Drive
Suite 100
Houston, TX 77042-1642
281-568-9300
Fax: 281-568-9498
Moments in History T-shirts, as well as other various educational gifts and products.

5189 Cascade School Supplies
1 Brown Street
PO Box 780
North Adams, MA 01247
800-628-5078
Fax: 413-663-3719
Offers a variety of school supplies and more.

5190 Celebrate Diversity
Guidance Channel
135 Dupont Street
PO Box 760
Plainview, NY 44803-0706
800-999-6884
Fax: 800-262-1886
Educational resources that celebrate diversity.

5191 Celebrate Earth Day
Guidance Channel
135 Dupont Street
PO Box 760
Plainview, NY 44803-0706
800-999-6884
Fax: 800-262-1886
Educational resources for celebrating earth day.

5192 Center Enterprises
PO Box 33161
West Hartford, CT 06110
860-953-4423
Fax: 800-373-2923
Clifford individual curriculum and storybook stamp sets, individual, grading, curriculum based and Sweet Arts rubber stamp line, stamp pads, embossing inks and powders.

5193 Center for Learning
21590 Center Ridge Road
Rocky River, OH 44116-3963
440-331-1404
800-767-9090
Fax: 888-767-8080
E-mail: cfl@stratos.net
http://www.centerforlearning.org
Supplementary curriculum units for all grade levels in biography, language arts, novel/drama and social studies.

5194 Center for Teaching International Relations
University of Denver
Denver, CO 80208
303-871-3106
Reproducible teaching activities and software promoting multicultural understanding and international relations in the classroom for grades K-adult.

5195 Childcraft Education Corporation
20 Kilmer Avenue
Edison, NJ 08817
732-572-6100
Distributes children's toys, products, materials and publications to schools.

5196 Childswork/Childsplay
The Guidence Channel
135 Dupont Street
PO Box 760
Plainview, NY 11803-0760
800-962-1141
Fax: 800-262-1886
http://www.childswork.com

Contains over 450 resources to address the social and emotional needs of children and adolescents.

Lawrence C Shapiro, PhD, President
Constance H Logan, Development Coordinator

5197 Chroma
205 Bucky Drive
Lititz, PA 17543
717-626-8866
800-257-8278
Fax: 717-626-9292
http://www.chromaonline.com
Tempera and acrylic paints.

5198 Chroma-Vision Sign & Art System
PO Box 434
Greensboro, NC 27402-0434
336-275-0602
Refillable and renewable felt tip markers used with non-toxic, water soluable, fast drying colors for making signs, posters, and general art work with no messy cleanup.

S Gray, President

5199 Citizenship Through Sports and Fine Arts Curriculum
National Federation of State High School Assoc.
PO Box 20626
Kansas City, MO 64195-0626
816-464-5400
800-776-3462
Fax: 816-891-2414
http://www.nfhs.org
High school activities curriculum package that includes an introductory video, Rekindling the Spirit, along with the Overview booklet, plus two insightful books covering eight targets of the curriculum.

5200 Claridge Products & Equipment
Claridge Products & Equipment
601 Highway 62-65 S
PO Box 910
Harrison, AR 72601-0910
870-743-2200
Fax: 870-743-1908
E-mail: claridge@claridgeproducts.com
http://www.claridgeproducts.com
Claridge manufactures chalkboards, markerboards, bulletin boards, display and trophy cases, bulletin and directory board cabinets, easels, lecterns, speakers' stands, wood lecture units with matching credenzas and much more.

Terry McCutchen, Sales Manager

5201 Collins & Aikman Floorcoverings
311 Smith Industrial Boulevard
Dalton, GA 30722
800-248-2878
Fax: 706-259-2666
E-mail: tellis@powerbond.com
http://www.powerbond.com
An alternative to conventional carpet to improve indoor air quality and reduce maintenance cost. Powerboard floor covering.

T Ellis, General Manager/Edu Markets

5202 Columbia Cascade Company
1975 SW 5th Avenue
Portland, OR 97201-5293
503-223-1157
Fax: 503-223-4530
E-mail: hq@timberform.com
http://www.timberform.com
Playground equipment and site furniture.

Dale Gordon, Sales Manager

5203 Creative Artworks Factory
19031 McGuire Road
Perris, CA 92570-8305
909-780-5950
Screenprinted T-shirts, posters and gifts for educational purposes.

5204 Creative Educational Surplus
9801 James Avenue S
#C
Bloomington, MN 55431-2919
Art and classroom materials.

5205 Crizmac Art & Cultural Education Materials Inc
PO Box 65928
Tucson, AZ 85728
520-323-8555
800-913-8555
Fax: 520-323-6194
E-mail: customerservice@crizmac.com
http://www.crizmac.com
Publisher of art and cultural education materials includes curriculum, books, music,and folk art.

Stevie Mack, President

5206 Crown Mats & Matting
2100 Commerce Drive
Fremont, OH 43420-1048
419-332-5531
800-628-5463
Fax: 800-544-2806
E-mail: sales@crown-mats.com
http://www.crown-mats.com
Mats, matting and flooring for schools.

5207 Dahle USA
375 Jaffrey Road
Peterborough, NH 03458
603-924-0003
800-243-8145
Fax: 603-924-1616
E-mail: info@dahleusa.com
http://www.dahleusa.com
Arts and crafts supplies, school and office products, office shreddars and more.

5208 Designer Artwear I
8475 C-1 Highway 6 N
Houston, TX 77095
281-446-6641
Specialty clothing, accessories, etc. all educationally designed.

5209 Dexter Educational Toys
Dexter Educational Toys, Inc.
PO Box 630861
Aventura, FL 33163-0861
305-931-7426
Fax: 305-931-0552
Manufacturer and distributor of education material. Dress-ups for children 2-7 years. Multicultural hand puppets, finger puppets, head masks puppet theaters, rag dolls, dress-ups for teddy bears and dolls, cloth books, export manufacturing under special designs and orders.

Genny Silverstein, VP Secretary

5210 Dick Blick Art Materials
PO Box 1267
Galesburg, IL 61402
800-828-4584
Fax: 800-621-8293
E-mail: info@dickblick.com
http://www.dickblick.com
Classroom art supplies.

5211 Dinorock Productions
407 Granville Drive
Silver Spring, MD 20901-3238
301-588-9300
Musical, Broadway puppet shows for early childhood fun and education.

5212 Discovery Toys
12443 Pine Creek Road
Cerritos, CA 90703-2044
562-809-0331
Fax: 562-809-0331
http://www.discoverytoyslink.com/elizabeth
Emphasizes child physical, social and educational development through creative play. Educational toys, games and books are available for all ages. Services include home demonstrations, fund raisers, phone and catalog orders. New Book of Knowledge Encyclopedia and patenting video tapes are also available.

5213 Disney Educational Productions
500 S Buena Vista Street
Burbank, CA 91521-0001
800-777-8100
Creates and manufactures classroom aids for the educational field.

5214 Dixie Art Supplies
2612 Jefferson Highway
New Orleans, LA 70121
800-783-2612
Fax: 504-831-5738
http://www.dixieart.com
Fine art supplier.

5215 Dr. Playwell's Game Catalog
Guidance Channel
135 Dupont Street
PO Box 760
Plainview, NY 44803-0706
800-999-6884
Fax: 800-262-1886
Games that develop character and life skills.

5216 Draper
125 S Pearl Street
Spiceland, IN 47385
765-987-7999
800-238-7999
Fax: 765-987-7142
E-mail: draper@draper.com
http://www.draperinc.com
Projection screens, video projector mounts and lifts, plasma display mounts, presentation easels, window shades and gymnasium equipment.

Chris Broome, Contract Market Manager
Bob Mathes, AV/Video Market Manager

5217 Draw Books
Peel Productions
PO Box 546
Columbus, NC 28722-0546
828-859-3879
800-345-6665
Fax: 801-365-9898
http://www.drawbooks.com
How-to-draw books for elementary and middle school.

Paperback
ISBN: 0-939217

5218 Dupont Company
Corlan Products
CRP-702
Wilmington, DE 19880
302-774-1000
800-436-7426
Fax: 800-417-1266
Arts and crafts supplies.

5219 Durable Corporation
75 N Pleasant Street
Norwalk, OH 44857-1218
419-668-8138
800-537-1603
Fax: 419-668-8068
Furniture, classroom supplies, arts and crafts and educational products.

5220 EZ Grader
PO Box 23608
Chagrin Falls, OH 44023
800-732-4018
Fax: 800-689-2772
Electronic gradebook designed by teachers for teachers. It is an incredible time saver and computes percentage scores accurately, quickly and easily.

5221 Early Ed
3110 Sunrise Drive
Crown Point, IN 46307-8905
Teacher sweatshirts, cardigans, T-shirts, tote bags and jewelry.

5222 Education Department
Wildlife Conservation Society
2300 Southern Boulevard
Bronx, NY 10460
718-220-5131
800-937-5131
Fax: 718-733-4460
http://www.wcs.com
Year round programs for school and general audience. Teacher training, grades K-12.

Sydell Schein, Manager/Program Services
Ann Robinson, Director/National Programs

5223 Educational Equipment Corporation of Ohio
845 Overholt Road
Kent, OH 44240-7529
330-673-4881
Fax: 330-673-4915
E-mail: mkaufman@mkco.com
Chalkboards, tackboards, trophy cases, announcement boards.

Michael Kaufman, General Manager
Eric Baughman, Sales Manager

5224 Electronic Book Catalog
Franklin Learning Resources
1 Franklin Plaza
Burlington, NJ 08016-4908
800-BOO-MAN
Fax: 609-387-1787
Electronic translation machines, calculators and supplies.

5225 Ellison Educational Equipment
25862 Commercentre Drive
Lake Forest, CA 92630-8804
800-253-2238
Fax: 888-270-1200
E-mail: info@ellison.com
http://www.ellison.com
Serves the educational and craft community with time-saving equipment, supplies and ideas.

5226 Endura Rubber Flooring
2 University Office Park
Waltham, MA 02453-3421
781-647-5375
Fax: 781-647-4543
Floorcoverings, mats and matting for schools.

5227 Fairgate Rule Company
22 Adams Avenue
Cold Spring, NY 10516-1501
845-265-3677
Fax: 845-265-4128
Arts and crafts supplies.

5228 Family Reading Night Kit
Renaissance Learning
PO Box 8036
Wisconsin Rapids, WI 54495-8036
715-424-3636
800-338-4204
Fax: 715-424-4242
E-mail: answers@renlearn.com
http://www.renlearn.com
Kit to start a family reading night where parents and children spent quality time together sharing enthusiasm over books.

5229 Fascinating Folds
PO Box 10070
Glendale, AZ 85318
602-375-9979
Fax: 602-375-9978
http://www.fascinating-folds.com
World's large supplier of origami and paper arts products.

5230 Fiskars Corporation
636 Science Drive
Madison, WI 53711
608-233-1649
Fax: 608-294-4790
http://www.fiskars.com
School scissors.

5231 Fox Laminating Company
84 Custer Street
W Hartford, CT 06110-1955
860-953-4884
800-433-2468
Fax: 860-953-1277
E-mail: sales@foxlam.com
http://www.foxlam.com
Easy, simple, and inexpensive do-it-yourself laminators. A piece of paper can be laminated for just pennies. Badges, ID's and luggage tags can also be made. Also laminated plaques for awards, diplomas, and mission statements.

Joe Fox, President
John Mills, Marketing Manager

5232 George F Cram Company
PO Box 426
Indianapolis, IN 46206-0426
317-635-5564
Fax: 317-687-2845
Classroom geography maps, state maps, social studies skills and globes.

5233 Gift-in-Kind Clearinghouse
PO Box 850
Davidson, NC 28036-0850
704-892-7228
Fax: 704-892-3825
Educational and classroom supplies, computers and gifts for teachers.

5234 Gold's Artworks
2100 N Pine
Lumberton, NC 28358
910-739-9605
800-356-2306
Fax: 910-739-9605
http://www.goldsartworks.20m.com
Papermaking supplies.

5235 Golden Artist Colors
188 Bell Road
New Berlin, NY 13411-9527
800-959-6543
E-mail: goldenart@goldenpaints.com
http://www.goldenpaints.com
Acrylic paints.

5236 Graphix
19499 Miles Road
Cleveland, OH 44128-4109
216-581-9050
Fax: 216-581-9041
E-mail: sales@grafixarts.com
http://www.grafixarts.com
Art and crafts supplies and a source for creative plastic films.

Tanya Lutz, National Sales Manager

5237 Grolier Multimedial Encyclopedia
Grolier Publishing
PO Box 1716
Danbury, CT 06816
203-797-3703
800-371-3908
Fax: 203-797-3899
Encyclopedia software.

5238 Hands-On Equations
Borenson & Associates
PO Box 3328
Allentown, PA 18106
800-993-6284
Fax: 610-398-7863
http://www.borenson.com
System to teach algebraic concepts to elementary and middle school students.

5239 Harrisville Designs
Center Village
PO Box 806
Harrisville, NH 03450
603-827-3333
800-938-9415
Fax: 603-827-3335
http://www.harrisville.com
Award-winning weaving products for children.

5240 Hayes School Publishing
321 Penwood Avenue
Pittsburgh, PA 15221
800-245-6234
Fax: 800-543-8771
E-mail: info@hayespub.com
http://www.hayespub.com
Suppliers of certificates and awards.

5241 Henry S Wolkins Company
605 Myles Standish Boulevard
Taunton, MA 02780
800-233-1844
Fax: 877-965-5467
http://www.wolkins.com
Art and craft materials, teaching aids, early learning products, furniture, general school equipment.

5242 Hooked on Phonics Classroom Edition
665 3rd Street
Suite 225
San Francisco, CA 94107
714-437-3450
800-222-3334
E-mail: customerservice@hop.com
http://www.hop.com
Program that teaches students to learn letters and sounds to decoding words, and then reading books.

5243 Hydrus Galleries
PO Box 4944
San Diego, CA 92164-4944
800-493-7299
Fax: 619-283-7466
E-mail: info@hydra9.com
http://www.hydra9.com
Curriculum-based classroom activities including papyrus outlines for students to paint.

5244 Insect Lore
PO Box 1535
Shafter, CA 93263
800-548-3284
Fax: 661-746-0334
E-mail: livebug@insectlore.com
http://www.insectlore.com
Science materials for elementary and preschool students.

5245 J&A Handy-Crafts
165 S Pennsylvania Avenue
Lindenhurst, NY 11757-5058
631-226-2400
888-252-1130
Fax: 631-226-2564
E-mail: info@jacrafts.com
http://www.jacrafts.com
Arts, crafts and educational supplies.

Paul Siegelman, Marketing

5246 Jiffy Printers Products
35070 Maria Road
Cathedral City, CA 92234
760-321-7335
Fax: 760-770-1955
E-mail: jiffyprod@aol.com
Adhesive wax sticks.

Ivan Zwelling, Owner

5247 Key-Bak
Division of West Coast Chain
Manufacturing Co.
4245 Pacific Privado
Ontario, CA 91761
909-923-7800
800-685-2403
Fax: 800-565-6202
E-mail: sales@keybak.com
http://www.keybak.com
Badges, awards and emblems for educational purposes.

5248 Keyboard Instructor
Advanced Keyboard Technology, Inc.
PO Box 2418
Paso Robles, CA 93447-2418
805-237-2055
Fax: 805-239-8973
http://www.keyboardinstructor.com
Mobile keyboarding lab with individualized instruction.

5249 Kids Percussion Buyer's Guide
Percussion Marketing Council

818-753-1310
E-mail: DLevine360@aol.com
http://www.playdrums.com
This guide is divided into two sections- recreational instruments and those for beginning traditional drummers.

5250 Kids at Heart & School Art Materials
PO Box 94082
Seattle, WA 98124-9482
Classroom and art materials.

5251 Kidstamps
PO Box 18699
Cleveland Heights, OH 44118-0699
216-291-6884
Fax: 216-291-6887
E-mail: kidstamps@apk.net
http://www.kidstamps.com
Rubber stamps, T-shirts, bookplates and mugs designed by leading children's illustrators.

5252 Knex Education Catalog
Knex Education
2990 Bergey Road
PO Box 700
Hatfield, PA 19440-0700
888-ABC-KNEX
E-mail: abcknex@knex.com
http://www.knexeducation.com
Hands-on, award-winning curriculum supported K-12 math, science and technology sets.

5253 Lauri
PO Box 0263
Smethport, PA 16749
800-451-0520
Fax: 207-639-3555
Lacing puppets craft kits, crepe rubber picture puzzles, phonics kits and math manipulatives for pre-K and up. Catalog offers 200 manipulatives for early childhood.

5254 Learning Materials Workshop
274 N Winooski Avenue
Burlington, VT 05401-3621
802-802-8399
800-693-7164
Fax: 802-862-0794
E-mail: mail@learningmaterialswork.com
http://www.learningmaterialswork.com
Designs and produces open-ended blocks and construction sets for early childhood classrooms. An education guide and video, as well as training workshops are offered.

Karen Hewitt, President

5255 Learning Needs Catalog
Riverdeep Interactive Learning
PO Box 97021
Redmond, WA 98073-9721
800-362-2890
http://www.learningneeds.com
Hardware, software and print products designed for specialized student needs for Pre-K to grade 12.

5256 Learning Power and the Learning Power Workbook
Great Source Education Group
181 Ballardvale
Willmington, MA 01887
800-289-4490

Student materials for 8th and 9th grade critical thinking, study skills, life management, and other student success course.

218 pages
ISBN: 0-963813-33-1

5257 Learning Well
111 Kane Street
Baltimore, MD 21224-1728
800-645-6564
Fax: 800-413-7442
E-mail: learningwell@wclm.com
Drawing compass/ruler.

5258 Linray Enterprises
167 Corporation Road
Hyannis, MA 02601-2204
800-537-9752
Mats and matting for gym classes.

5259 Loew-Coenell
563 Chestnut Avenue
Teaneck, NJ 07666-2491
201-836-8110
Fax: 201-836-7070
E-mail: sales@loew-cornell.com
http://www.loew-cornell.com
Leader in art and craft brushes, painting accessories and artists' tools.

5260 Longstreth
PO Box 475
Parker Ford, PA 19457-0475
610-495-7022
Fax: 610-495-7023
Awards, emblems, badges and trophies, sports timers and clocks.

5261 Love to Teach
693 Glacier Pass
Westerville, OH 43081-1295
614-899-2118
800-326-8361
Fax: 614-899-2070
http://www.lovetoteach.com
Gifts for teachers.

Linda Vollmer, Contact

5262 Lyra
78 Browne Street
Suite 3
Brookline, MA 02146
888-PEN-LYRA
E-mail: mshoham@aol.com
Drawing supplies.

5263 MPI School & Instructional Supplies
PO Box 24155
Lansing, MI 48909-4155
517-393-0440
Fax: 517-393-8884
School and classroom supplies, arts and crafts.

5264 Magnetic Aids
133 N 10th Street
Paterson, NJ 07522-1220
973-790-1400
800-426-9624
Fax: 973-790-1425
E-mail: magneticaids@worldnet.att.com
http://www.magneticaids.com
Announcement and chalkboards, office supplies and equipment. Magnetic book supports.

Paul Pecka, VP Sales

5265 Mailer's Software
970 Calle Negocio
San Clemente, CA 92673-6201
949-492-7000
Fax: 949-589-5211
Charts, maps, globes and software for the classroom.

5266 Marsh Industries
Div. of Marsh Lumber Company
PO Box 509
Dover, OH 44622-1935
330-343-8825
800-426-4244
Fax: 330-343-9515
E-mail: wdsinghaus@marsh-ind.com
http://www.marsh-ind.com
Marker boards chalkboards, and tacknoards for new rennovative construction projects. Glass enclosed bulletin and directory boards. Map rail and accessories.

William Singhaus, Sales Manager

5267 Master Woodcraft
1312 College Street
Oxford, NC 27565
919-693-8811
800-333-2675
Fax: 919-693-1707
Announcement and classroom chalkboards, arts and craft supplies. Cork bulletin boards, dry erase melamine boards, easels, floor and table top.

J Moss, VP

5268 Material Science Technology
Energy Concepts
595 Bond Street
Lincolnshire, IL 60069
800-621-1247
http://www.energy-concepts-inc.com
Provides practical knowledge of the use and development of materials in todays world. Each unit combines theory with hands-on experience.

5269 Midwest Publishers Supply
4640 N Olcott Avenue
Harwood Heights, IL 60706
800-621-1507
Fax: 800-832-3189
E-mail: info@mps-co.com
http://www.mps-co.com
Arts and crafts supplies.

Bonnie Cready, Sales Manager

5270 Miller Multiplex
1555 Larkin Williams Road
Fenton, MO 63026-3008
636-343-5700
800-325-3350
Fax: 636-326-1716
E-mail: info@millermultiplex.com
Announcement boards, classroom displays, charts and photography, books towers, posters, frames, kiosk displays, presentation displays.

12 pages Annually

Kathy Webster, Director Marketing

5271 Monsanto Company
800 N Lindbergh Boulevard
Saint Louis, MO 63167-0001
314-694-3902
Fax: 314-694-7625
Arts and crafts supplies.

5272 Morrison School Supplies
304 Industrial Road
San Carlos, CA 94070-6285
650-592-3000
Fax: 650-592-1679
School supplies, classroom equipment, furniture and toys.

5273 Names Unlimited
2300 Spikes Lane
Lansing, MI 48906-3996
Chalkboard and markerboard slates and tablets.

5274 Nasco Arts & Crafts Catalog
Nasco
901 Janesville Avenue
PO Box 901
Fort Atkinson, WI 53538-0901
920-563-2446
800-558-9595
Fax: 920-563-8296
http://www.eNASCO.com
Complete line of arts and craft materials for the art educator and individual artist.

Kris Bakke, Arts & Crafts Director

5275 Nasco Early Learning & Afterschool Essential Catalogs
Nasco
901 Janesville Avenue
PO Box 901
Fort Atkinson, WI 53538-0901
920-563-2446
800-558-9595
Fax: 920-563-8296
E-mail: info@enasco.com
http://www.eNasco.com
Features low prices on classroom supplies, materials, furniture and equipment for early childhood and afterschool programs.

Scott J Beyer, Director, Sales & Marketing

5276 Nasco Math Catalog
Nasco
901 Janesville
PO Box 901
Fort Atkinson, WI 53538-0901
920-563-2446
800-558-9595
Fax: 920-563-8296
http://www.nascofa.com
Features hands-on manipulatives and real-life problem-solving projects.

5277 National Teaching Aids
PO Box 2121
Fort Collins, CO 80522
970-484-7445
800-289-9299
Fax: 970-484-1198
E-mail: bevans@amep.com
http://www.hubbardscientific.com
Learning math, alphabet, and geography skills is easy with our Clever Catch Balls. These colorful 24" inflatable vinyl balls provide an excellent way for children to practice math, alphabet and geography skills. Excellent learning tool in organized classroom activities, on the playground, or at home.

Barbara Evans, Customer Service Manager
Candy Coffman, National Sales Manger

5278 New Hermes
2200 Northmont Parkway
Duluth, GA 30096
770-623-0331
800-843-7637
Fax: 800-533-7637
E-mail: sales@newhermes.com
http://www.newhermes.com
Announcement boards, trophies, badges, emblems.

5279 Newbridge Discovery Station
PO Box 5267
Clifton, NH 07015
Monthly quick tips and activities for teachers.

5280 Newbridge Jumbo Seasonal Patterns
PO Box 5267
Clifton, NJ 07015
Art projects, games, bulletin boards, flannel boards, story starters, learning center displays, costumes, masks and more for grades Pre K-3.

5281 NewsCurrents
Knowledge Unlimited
PO Box 52
Madison, WI 53701
800-356-2303
Fax: 608-831-1570
E-mail: sales@newscurrents.com
http://www.newscurrents.com
Current issues discussion programs for grades 3 and up.

5282 Partners in Learning Programs
1065 Bay Boulevard
Suite H
Chula Vista, CA 91911-1626
619-407-4744
Fax: 619-407-4755
Manufacturers and produces books, manuals, materials, supplies and gifts, such as banners for classroom purposes.

5283 Pearson Education Technologies
827 W Grove Avenue
Mesa, AZ 85210
520-615-7600
800-222-4543
Fax: 520-615-7601
http://www.pearsonedtech.com
SuccessMaker is a multimedia K-Adult learning system which includes math, reading, language arts and science courseware.

5284 Pentel of America
2805 Columbia Street
Torrance, CA 90509-3800
310-320-3831
800-421-1419
Fax: 310-533-0697
http://www.pentel.com
Office supplies and equipment.

5285 Pin Man
Together Inc.
802 E 6th Street
PO Box 52528
Tulsa, OK 74105-3264
918-587-2405
800-282-0085
Fax: 918-382-0906
http://www.thepinmanok.com
Manufacturer of custom designed lapel pins, totes for Chapter 1, reading, scholastic achievement, honor roll, parent involvement, staff awards and incentives

with over 25,000 items available for imprint.

Bern Gentry, CEO

5286 PlayConcepts
2275 Huntington Drive
#305
San Marino, CA 91108-2640
800-261-2584
Fax: 626-795-1177
Creative, 3-D scenery that stimulates dramatic play. The scenes complement integrated curriculum. They are age and developmentally appropriate, non-biased, and effective for groups or individuals.

5287 Polyform Products Company
1901 Estes Avenue
Elk Grove Village, IL 60007
847-427-0020
Fax: 847-427-0020
E-mail: polyform@sculpey.com
http://www.sculpey.com
Manufacturer of sculpey modeling clay.

5288 Presidential Classroom
119 Oronoco Street
Alexandria, VA 22314-2015
703-683-5400
800-441-6533
Fax: 703-548-5728
E-mail:
eriedel@presidentialclassroom.org
http://www.presidentialclassroom.org
Civic education programs in Washington, DC for high school juniors and seniors. Each one week program provides students with an inside view of the federal government in action and their role as responsible citizens and future leaders.

Jan-March, June+July
400 attendees

Jack Buechner, President/CEO
Ginger King, Dean

5289 Professor Weissman's Software
Professor Weissman's Software
246 Crafton Avenue
Staten Island, NY 10314-4227
718-698-5219
Fax: 718-698-5219
E-mail: mathprof@hotmail.com
http://www.math911.com
Algebra comic books, learn by example algebra flash cards, step-by-step software tutorials for algebra, trigonometry, precalculus, statistics, network versions for all software.

Martin Weissman, Owner
Keith Morse, VP

5290 Pumpkin Masters
PO Box 61456
Denver, CO 80206-8456
303-860-8006
Fax: 303-860-9826
Classroom pumpkin carving kits featuring whole language curriculum with safer and easier carving tools and patterns.

5291 Puppets on the Pier
Pier 39
Box H4
San Francisco, CA 94133
415-781-4435
800-443-4463
Fax: 415-379-9544
E-mail: onepuppet@earthlink.net
http://www.puppetdream.com

Puppets, arts, crafts and other creative educational products for children.

Arthur Partner

5292 Qwik-File Storage Systems
1000 Allview Drive
Crozet, VA 22932-3144
804-823-4351
Schedule boards and classroom supplies.

5293 RC Musson Rubber Company
1320 E Archwood Avenue
Akron, OH 44306-2825
330-773-7651
800-321-3281
Fax: 330-773-3254
E-mail: info@mussonrubber.com
http://www.mussonrubber.com
Rubber floorcoverings, mats and athletic matting.

Mark Reese, Customer Service Manager
Robert Segers, VP

5294 RCA Rubber Company
1833 E Market Street
Akron, OH 44305-4214
330-784-1291
Fax: 330-784-2899
Floorcoverings, athletic mats and more for the physical education class.

5295 Reading is Fundamental
600 Maryland Avenue SW
Suite 600
Washington, DC 20024-2520
202-673-1641
Fax: 202-673-1633
Distributor of posters, bookmarks, and parent guide brochures.

5296 Reconnecting Youth
National Educational Service
304 W Kirkwood Avenue
Suite 2
Bloomington, IN 47404-5132
812-336-7700
800-733-6786
Fax: 812-336-7790
E-mail: nes@nesonline.com
http://www.nesonline.com
Curriculum to help discouraged learners achieve in school, manage their anger, and decrease drug use, depression, and suicide risk. The program was piloted for five years with over 600 urban Northwestern public high school students with funding from the National Institute on Drug Abuse and the National Institute of Mental Health, and has since been successful in many educational settings.

3 Ring Binder Circul
ISBN: 1-879639-42-4

Jane St. John, Sales Marketing Director

5297 Red Ribbon Resources
135 Dupont Street
PO Box 760
Plainview, NY 11803
800-646-7999
Fax: 800-262-1886
http://ww.redribbonresources.com
Over 250 low cost giveaways to promote your safe and drug-free school and community.

5298 Renaissance Graphic Arts
69 Steamwhistle Drive
Ivyland, PA 18974
888-833-3398
Fax: 215-357-5258
E-mail: pat@printmaking-materials.com
http://www.printmaking-materials.com
Tools, papers, plates, inks and assorted products necessary for printmaking.

5299 Rock Paint Distributing Corporation
PO Box 482
Milton, WI 53563
608-868-6873
Fax: 800-715-7625
E-mail: handyart@handyart.com
http://www.handyart.com
Tempera paint, India ink, acrylic paint, block inc, washable paint, fabric paint.

5300 S&S Worldwide
S&S Arts & Crafts
75 Mill Street
Department 2030
Colchester, CT 06415-1263
800-243-9232
Fax: 800-566-6678
Arts and crafts, classroom games and group paks.

5301 Safe & Drug Free Catalog
Performance Resource Press
1270 Rankin Drive
Suite F
Troy, MI 48083-2843
800-453-7733
Fax: 800-499-5718
http://www.pronline.net
Books, videos, CD-Roms, phamlets and posters toassist students with social skills, counseling, drug and violence prevention.

5302 Sakura of America
30780 San Clemente Street
Hayward, CA 94544-7131
510-475-8880
800-776-6257
Fax: 510-475-0973
E-mail: express@sakuraofamerica.com
http://www.gellyroll.com
Gelly Roll pens, Cray pas oil pastels, Fantasia watercolors, Pigma micron pens, Pentouch and Aqua Wipe markers and other art supplies for the classroom.

John Crook
Donna Wilson, Marketing Director

5303 Sanford Corporation
A Lifetime of Color
2711 Washington Boulevard
Bellwood, IL 60104-1970
708-547-6650
800-323-0749
Fax: 708-547-6719
E-mail:
consumer.service@sanfordcorp.com
http://www.sanfordcorp.com
Writing instruments, art supplies.

Angela Nigl, Author
Sharon Meyers, PR Manager

5304 Sax Visual Art Resources
Sax Arts and Crafts
2725 S Moorland Road
bept. SA
New Berlin, WI 53151
800-558-6696
Fax: 800-328-4729
E-mail: catalog@saxfcs.com
http://www.saxfcs.com

Variety of resources for slides, books, videos, fine art posters and CD-Roms.

5305 School Mate
PO Box 2225
Jackson, TN 38302
731-935-2000
Fax: 800-668-7610
E-mail: school@schoolmateinc.com
Pre-school and elementary art products.

5306 SchoolMatters
Current
The Current Building
Colorado Springs, CO 80941-0001
800-525-7170
Fax: 800-993-3232
Offers a variety of creative classroom ideas including stickers, mugs, posters, signs and more for everyday and holidays and everyday of the year.

5307 Scott Sign Systems
PO Box 1047
Tallevast, FL 34270-1047
941-355-5171
800-237-9447
Fax: 941-351-1787
E-mail: mail@scottsigns.com
http://www.scottsigns.com
Educational supplies including announcement, letters, signs, graphics and chalkboards.

5308 Scratch-Art Company
PO Box 303
Avon, MA 02322
508-583-8085
800-377-9003
Fax: 508-583-8091
E-mail: info@scratchart.com
http://www.scratchart.com
Offers materials for drawing, sketching and rubbings.

5309 Sea Bay Game Company
PO Box 162
Middletown, NJ 07748-0162
732-583-7902
Fax: 732-583-7284
Manufacturer and distributor of products, games and creative play to nursery schools and preschools.

5310 Seton Identification Products
20 Thompson Road
PO Box 819
Branford, CT 06405
203-488-8059
800-243-6624
Fax: 203-488-4114
http://www.seton.com
Manufacturer of all types of identification products including signs, tags, labels, traffic control, OSHA, ADA and much more.

5311 Shapes, Etc.
PO Box 400
Dansville, NY 14437-0400
585-335-6619
Fax: 585-335-6070
Notepads and craft materials for creative writing projects. Coordinates with literature themes. Perfect for storystarters, bulletin boards, awards and motivators.

5312 Sign Product Catalog
Scott Sign Systems, Inc.
PO Box 1047
Tallevast, FL 34270-1047
845-355-5171
800-237-9447
Fax: 941-351-1787
E-mail: scottsigns@mindspring.com
http://www.scottsigns.com
Educational supplies including announcement, letters, signs, graphics and chalkboards.

Robert Lew, Account Executive

5313 Small Fry Originals
2700 S Westmoreland Road
Dallas, TX 75233-1312
214-330-8671
800-248-9443
Children's original artwork preserved in plastic plates and mugs.

5314 Southwest Plastic Binding Corporation
109 Millwell Drive
Maryland Heights, MO 63043-2509
800-986-2001
Fax: 800-942-2010
Overhead transparencies, maps, charts and classroom supplies.

5315 Spectrum Corporation
10048 Easthaven Boulevard
Houston, TX 77075-3298
800-392-5050
Fax: 713-944-1290
Announcement boards, scoreboards and sports equipment, sports timers and clocks.

5316 Speedball Art Products Company
2226 Speedball Road
PO Box 5157
Statesville, NC 28687
704-838-1475
800-898-7224
Fax: 704-838-1472
E-mail: tonyahill@speedballart.com
http://www.speedballart.com
Art products for stamping, calligraphy, printmaking, drawing and painting.

Rita Madsen, Manager
Tonya Hill, Director of Sales

5317 Sponge Stamp Magic
525 S Anaheim Hills Road
Apartment C314
Anaheim, CA 92807-4726
Rubber stamps and games for classroom use.

5318 Staedtler
PO Box 2196
Chatsworth, CA 91313-2196
818-882-6000
800-776-5544
Fax: 818-882-3767
E-mail: rhoye@staedtler-usa.com
http://www.staedtler-usa.com
Arts and crafts supplies, office supplies and equipment.

Dick Hoye, National Sales Manager

5319 Sylvan Learning Systems
1000 Lancaster Street
Baltimore, MD 21202
410-843-6828
888-779-5826
Fax: 410-783-3832
http://www1.sylvan.net
Provides public school academic programs that are traditional sylvan programs modified to fit the needs of individual school districts and performance guarantees.

Jody Madron, Contact

5320 Tandy Leather Company
PO Box 791
Fort Worth, TX 76101-0791
817-451-1480
Fax: 817-451-5254
Arts and crafts supplies, computer peripherals and systems.

5321 Teacher Appreciation
Guidance Channel
135 Dupont Street
PO Box 760
Plainview, NY 44803-0706
800-999-6884
Fax: 800-262-1886
Products for celebrating teacher appreciation week.

5322 Teachers Store
PO Box 24155
Lansing, MI 48909-4155
517-393-0440
Fax: 517-393-8884
School and classroom supplies, arts and crafts.

5323 Texas Instruments
12500 TI Boulevard
Dallas, TX 75243-4136
800-336-5236
Fax: 972-995-4360
http://www.ti.com
Manufacturer of calculators.

5324 Triarco Arts & Crafts
14650 28th Avenue N
Plymouth, MN 55447
763-559-5590
800-328-3360
Fax: 736-559-2215
E-mail: info@triarcoarts.com
Art supplies.

5325 Vanguard Crafts
1081 E 48th Street
Brooklyn, NY 11234
718-377-5188
800-662-7238
Fax: 888-692-0056
Arts and crafts supplier.

5326 Wagner Zip-Change
3100 W Hirsch Avenue
Melrose Park, IL 60160-1741
800-323-0744
Fax: 708-681-4165
Non-lighted changeable letter message activity signs, changeable letters in all sizes and colors.

CJ Krasula, Marketing VP
Jim Leone, Sales Manager

5327 Walker Display
6520 Grand Avenue
Duluth, MN 55807-2242
218-624-8990
Fax: 888-695-4647
Arts, crafts, classroom supplies and displays.

5328 Wellness Reproductions
Guidance Channel
135 Dupont Street
PO Box 760
Plainview, NY 44803-0706
800-999-6884
Fax: 800-262-1886
Mental and life skills educational materials.

5329 Wikki Stix One-of-a-Kind Creatables
Omnicor
2432 W Peoria Avenue #1188
Suite 1188
Phoenix, AZ 85029-4735
602-870-9937
800-869-4554
Fax: 602-870-9877
E-mail: info@wikkistix.com
http://www.wikkistix.com
Unique, one-of-a-kind twistable, stickable, creatable, hands-on teaching tools. Ideal for Pre-K through 8 for science, language arts, math, arts and crafts, positive behavior rewards, rainy day recess, classroom display, diagrams and 3-D work. Self-stick; no glue needed.

Kem Clark, President

5330 Wilson Language Training
175 W Main Strete
Millbury, MA 01527-1441
508-865-5699
Fax: 508-865-9644
Multisensory language program.

5331 Wilton Art Appreciation Programs
Reading & O'Reilley
PO Box 646
Botsford, CT 06404
203-270-6336
800-458-4274
Fax: 203-270-5569
E-mail: ror@wiltonart.com
http://www.wiltonart.com
Materials for art appreciation including CD-ROMS, videos, fine art prints, slides, workbooks, teacher' guides, lessons, puzzles and games.

Diana O'Neill, President

5332 Young Explorers
1810 E Eisenhower Boulevrd
Loveland, CO 80539
800-239-7577
Fax: 888-876-8847
http://www.youngexplorers.com
Educational material for children.

Electronic Equipment

5334 AIMS Multimedia
9710 De Soto Avenue
Chatsworth, CA 91311-4409
818-773-4300
800-367-2467
Fax: 818-341-6700
E-mail: info@aimsmultimedia.com
http://www.aimsmultimedia.com
Film, video, laserdisc producer and distributor, offering a free catalog available materials. Also provides internet video streaming.

David Sherman, President
Biff Sherman, President

5335 Advance Products Company
1101 E Central Avenue
Wichita, KS 67214-3922
316-263-4231
Fax: 316-263-4245
Manufacturer of steel mobile projection and television tables, video cabinets, easels, computer furniture, wall and ceiling TV mounts, and study tables and carrels.

Paul Keck

5336 All American Scoreboards
Everbrite
401 S Main Street
Pardeeville, WI 53954
608-429-2121
800-356-8146
Fax: 608-429-9216
E-mail: score@everbrite.com
http://www.allamericanscoreboards.com
Scoreboards.

Doug Winkelmann, Product Manager

5337 American Time & Signal Company
140 3rd Avenue S
Dassel, MN 55325
800-328-8996
Fax: 800-789-1882
Sports timers and clocks.

5338 Arts & Entertainment Network
235 E 45th Street
Floor 9
New York, NY 10017-3354
212-210-1400
Fax: 212-210-9755
Cable network offering free educational programming to schools.

5339 Barr Media/Films
12801 Schabarum Avenue
Irwindale, CA 91706-6808
626-338-7878
K-12 film, video and interactive Level I and III laserdisc programs.

5340 Buhl Optical Company
1009 Beech Avenue
Pittsburgh, PA 15233-2013
412-321-0076
Fax: 412-322-2640
Overhead projectors and transparencies.

5341 C-SPAN Classroom
4000 N Capitol Street NW
Washington, DC 20001
800-523-7586
Fax: 202-737-6226
C-SPAN School Bus travels through more than 80 communities during each school year. This bus is a mobile television production studio and learning center designed to give hands-on experience with C-SPAN's programming.

5342 CASIO
570 Mount Pleasant Avenue
Dover, NJ 07801-1631
973-361-5400
Fax: 570-868-6898
Cameras, overhead projectors and electronics.

5343 CASPR
100 Park Center Plaza
Suite 550
San Jose, CA 95113-2204
800-852-2777
http://www.caspr.com
Leader in the field of library automation for schools. Integrated library automa-

tion-cross platforms: Macintosh, Windows, Apple IIe/IIGS. Multimedia source.

Norman Kline, President

5344 Cable in the Classroom
1800 N Beauregard Street
Suite 100
Alexandria, VA 22311-1710
703-845-1400
Fax: 703-845-1409
http://www.ciconline.org
Represents the cable tele-communications industry's commitment to improving teaching and learning for children in schools, at home and in their communities.

5345 Canon USA
1 Canon Plaza
New Hyde Park, NY 11042-1198
516-488-1400
Fax: 516-328-5069
School equipment and supplies including a full line of electronics, cameras, calculators and other technology.

5346 Caulastics
5955 Mission Street
Daly City, CA 94014-1397
415-585-9600
Overhead projectors, transparencies and electronics.

5347 Cheshire Corporation
Cheshire Corporation
PO Box 61109
Denver, CO 80206-8109
303-333-3003
Fax: 303-333-4037
E-mail: karen-hemmes@mindspring.com
Cheshire corporation is a publicist for book, video, CD-ROM and internet publishers in the school and library market.

Karen Hemmes, Publicist
Mary Kay Opicka, Publicist

5348 Chief Manufacturing
14310 Ewing Avenue S
Burnsville, MN 55306-4839
612-894-6280
800-582-6480
Fax: 877-894-6918
E-mail: chief@chiefmfg.com
http://www.chiefmfg.com
Manufacturer of Communications Support Systems for audio visual and video equipment. Chief's product includes a full-line of mounts, electric lifts, carts, and accessories for LCD/DLP projectors, plasma displays and TV/monitors.

Liz Sorensen, Marketing Assistant
Sharon McCubbin, Marketing Manager

Manufacturer of Communications Support Systems for audio visual and video equipment. Chief's product includes a full-line of mounts, electric lifts, carts, and accessories for LCD/DLP projectors, plasma displays and TV/monitors.

Liz Sorensen, Marketing Assistant
Sharon McCubbin, Marketing Manager

5349 Chisholm

7019 Realm Drive
San Jose, CA 95119-1321
800-888-4210
Computer peripherals, overhead projectors and overhead transparencies.

5350 Daktronics

331 32nd Avenue
Brookings, SD 57006-4704
605-697-4300
888-325-8766
Fax: 605-697-4300
E-mail: sales@daktronics.com
http://www.daktronics.com
Scoreboards, electronic message displays statistics software.

Gary Gramm, HSPR Market Manager

5351 Depco- Millennium 3000

3305 Airport Drive
PO Box 178
Pittsburg, KS 66762
316-231-0019
800-767-1062
Fax: 316-231-0024
E-mail: sales@depcoinc.com
http://www.depcoinc.com
Program tracks and schedules for you, the test taker delivers tests electronically, as well as, automatic final exams. There are workstation security features to help keep students focused on their activities.

5352 Discovery Networks

7700 Wisconsin Avenue
Bethesda, MD 20814-3578
301-986-0444
Manages and operates The Discovery Channel, offering the finest in nonfiction documentary programming, as well as The Learning Channel, representing a world of ideas to learners of all ages.

5353 Echolab

175 Bedford Street
Burlington, MA 01803-2794
781-273-1512
Fax: 978-250-3335
Cameras, equipment, projectors and electronics.

5354 Eiki International

Audio Visual/Video Products
26794 Vista Terrace Drive
Lake Forest, CA 92630
949-457-0200
Fax: 949-457-7878
Video projectors, overhead projectors and transparencies.

5355 Elmo Manufacturing Corporation

1478 Old Country Road
Plainview, NY 11803-5034
516-501-1400
800-654-7628
Fax: 516-501-0429
Overhead projectors and transparencies.

5356 Fair-Play Scoreboards

1700 Delaware Avenue
Des Moines, IA 50317-2999
800-247-0265
Fax: 515-265-3364
E-mail: sales@fair-play.com
http://www.fair-play.com
Scoreboards and sports equipment.

5357 Festo Corporation

395 Moreland Road
PO Box 18023
Hauppauge, NY 11788
631-435-0800
Fax: 631-435-3847
http://www.festo-usa.com

5358 General Audio-Visual

333 W Merrick Road
Valley Stream, NY 11580-5219
516-825-8500
Fax: 516-568-2057
Offers a full line of audio-visual equipment and supplies, cameras, projectors and various other electronics for the classroom.

5359 Hamilton Electronics

2003 W Fulton Street
Chicago, IL 60612-2365
312-421-5442
Fax: 312-421-0818
Electronics, equipment and supplies.

5360 JR Holcomb Company

3205 Harvard Avenue
Cleveland, OH 44101
216-341-3000
800-362-9907
Fax: 216-341-5151
A full line of electronics including calculators, overhead projectors and overhead transparencies.

5361 JVC Professional Products Company

41 Slater Drive
Elmwood Park, NJ 07407-1311
201-794-3900
Electronics line including cameras, projectors, transparencies and other technology for the classroom.

5362 Labelon Corporation

10 Chapin Street
Canandaigua, NY 14424-1589
585-394-6220
800-428-5566
Fax: 585-394-3154
Electronics, supplies and equipment for schools.

5363 Learning Channel

7700 Wisconsin Avenue
Bethesda, MD 20814
800-346-0032
Offers educational programming for schools.

5364 Learning Station/Hug-a-Chug Records

3950 Bristol Court
Melbourne, FL 32904-8712
321-728-8773
800-789-9990
Fax: 321-722-9121
http://www.learningstationmusic.com
Early childhood products including OMH, cassettes, CD's and videos. Also, the Learning Station performs children and family concerts and are internationally acclaimed for their concert/keynote presentations for early childhood conferences and other educational organizations.

Don Monopoli, President
Laurie Monopoli, VP

5365 Learning Well

2200 Marcus Avenue
#3759
New Hyde Park, NY 11042-1042
800-645-6564
Fax: 800-638-6499
Instructional material including computer and board games, videos, cassettes, audio tapes, theme units, manipulatives for grades PreK-8.

Mona Russo, President

5366 Leightronix

2330 Jarco Drive
Holt, MI 48842-1210
517-694-5589
Fax: 517-694-1600
Educational cable programming for schools and institutions.

5367 MCM Electronics

650 Congress Park Drive
Centerville, OH 45459
800-543-4330
Fax: 800-765-6960
http://www.mcmelectronics.com
Offers a full line of electronics products and components for use in the classroom or at home. Over 40,000 parts.

5368 Magna Plan Corporation

1320 Route 9
Champlain, NY 12919-5007
518-298-8404
800-361-1192
Fax: 518-298-2368
E-mail: info@visualplanning.com
http://www.visualplanning.com
Overhead projectors.

Joseph P Josephson, Managing Director
Joel Boloten, Manager Consultation Service

5369 Mitsubishi Professional Electronics

200 Cottontail Lane
Somerset, NJ 08873-1231
732-563-9889
Video projectors and electronics.

5370 Multi-Video

PO Box 35444
Charlotte, NC 28235-5444
704-563-4279
800-289-0111
Fax: 704-568-0219
Cameras, projectors and equipment.

5371 Naden Scoreboards

505 Fair Avenue
PO Box 636
Webster City, IA 50595-0636
515-832-4290
800-467-4290
Fax: 515-832-4293
E-mail: naden@ncn.net
http://www.naden.com
Electronic scoreboards for sports.

Russ Naden, President

5372 Neumade Products Corporation
30 Pecks Lane
Newtown, CT 06470-2361
203-270-1100
Fax: 203-270-7778
E-mail: neumadeGJ@aol.com
http://www.neumade.com
Overhead projectors, overhead transparencies, video projectors and electronics.

Gregory Jones, VP Sales

5373 Nevco Scoreboard Company
301 E Harris Avenue
Greenville, IL 62246-2151
618-664-0360
800-851-4040
Fax: 618-664-0398
E-mail: info@nevco.com
http://www.nevco.com
Nevco is a premier manufacturer and distributor of scoreboards, message centers and video displays.

Phil Robertson, Sales Manager

5374 Panasonic Communications & System Company
1 Panasonic Way
Secaucus, NJ 07094-2917
201-392-4818
800-524-1064
Fax: 201-392-4044
Cameras, projectors, equipment, players, CD-ROM equipment and school supplies.

5375 Quickset International
3650 Woodhead Drive
Northbrook, IL 60062-1895
800-247-6563
Fax: 847-498-1258
Telecommunication equipment, cameras, projectors and electronics.

5376 RMF Products
PO Box 520
Batavia, IL 60510-0520
630-879-0020
Fax: 630-879-6749
E-mail: mail@rmfproducts.com
http://www.rmfproducts.com
Complete line of slide-related products including two and three-projector dissolve controls, programmers, multi-track tape recorders, audio-visual cables, remote controls and slide mounts.

Richard Frieders, President

5377 RTI-Research Technology International
4700 W Chase Avenue
Lincolnwood, IL 60646-1608
800-323-7520
Fax: 800-784-6733
TapeChek Videotape Cleaner/Inspector/Rewinders make videotapes last longer and perform better. Find damage before tape is circulated. Also available is videotape/laser disc storage, shipping and care products.

Bill Wolavka, Marketing Director

5378 Recreation Equipment Unlimited
PO Box 4700
Pittsburgh, PA 15206-0700
412-731-3000
Fax: 412-731-3052
Scoreboards and sports/recreation equipment.

5379 Reliance Plastics & Packaging
25 Prospect Street
Newark, NJ 07105-3300
973-473-7200
Fax: 973-589-6440
Vinyl albums for audio or video cassettes, video discs, slides, floppy disks, CDs Protect, store and circulate valuable media properly.

5380 Resolution Technology
26000 Avenida Aeropuerto Spc 22
San Juan Capistrano, CA 92675-4736
949-661-6162
Fax: 949-661-0114
Video systems and videomicroscopy equipment.

5381 RobotiKits Direct
17141 Kingsview Avenue
Suite B
Carson, CA 90746
310-515-6800
877-515-6652
Fax: 310-515-0927
E-mail: info@owirobot.com
http://www.robotikitsdirect.com
New science and robotic kits for the millenium.

Craig Morioka, President
Armer Amante, General Manger

5382 S'Portable Scoreboards
3058 Alta Vista Drive
Fallbrook, CA 92028-8738
800-323-7745
Fax: 270-759-0066
Portable scoreboards, manual and electronic, sports timers and clocks.

5383 SONY Broadcast Systems Product Division
1 Sony Drive
Park Ridge, NJ 07656
800-472-SONY
Interactive videodisc players for multimedia applications, VTRs, monitors, projection systems, video cameras, editing systems, printers and scanners, video presentation stands, audio cassette duplicators and video library systems.

5384 Scott Resources/ Hubbard Scientific
National Training Aids
PO Box 2121
Fort Collins, CO 80522-2121
970-484-7445
800-289-9299
Fax: 970-484-1198
E-mail: sgranger@amep.com
http://www.hubbardscientific.com
Microslide system is a comprehensive, classroom-ready to help students learn. The microslide system combines superb photo-materials with detailed curriculum material and reproducible student activity sheets at an affrdable price.

Shelley Granger, OEM/Retail Sales Manager
Candy Coffman, National Sales Manager

5385 Shure Brothers
222 Hartrey Avenue
Evanston, IL 60202-3696
847-866-2200
Fax: 847-866-2551
Electronics, hardware and classroom supplies.

5386 Swift Instruments
1190 N 4th Street
San Jose, CA 95112
408-293-2380
800-523-4544
Fax: 408-292-7967
http://www.swiftmicroscope.com
Capture live or still microscopic images through your compound or stereo microscope and background sound images through your VCR or computer.

5387 Tech World
Lab-Volt
PO Box 686
Farmingdale, NJ 07727
732-938-2000
800-522-8658
Fax: 732-774-8573
E-mail: us@labvolt.com
http://www.labvolt.com
Tech World provides superior hands-on instruction using state-of-the-art technology and equipment. Lab-Volt also offers a full line of attractive, durable, and flexible modular classroom furniture.

5388 Technical Education Systems
814 Chestnut Street
PO Box 1203
Rockford, IL 61102
815-966-2525
800-451-2169
Fax: 815-965-4836
http://www.tii-tech.com
Hands-on application-oriented training systems integrating today's real world technologies in a flexible and easy-to-understand curriculum format.

5389 Telex Communications
12000 Portland Avenue S
Burnsville, MN 55337
952-884-4051
800-828-6107
Fax: 952-884-0043
http://www.telex.com
Telex manufactures a variety of products for the educational market, including multimedia headphones, headsets and microphones; LCD computer and multimedia projection panels, group listening centers, video projectors, slide projectors, portable sound systems, wired and wireless intercoms, and wired and wireless microphones.

Dawn Wiome, Marketing Coordinator

5390 Three M Visual Systems
3M Austin Center
6801 River Place Boulevard
Austin, TX 78726-4530
800-328-1371
Fax: 512-984-6529
Overhead projectors, audiovisual carts and tables, and overhead transparencies.

5391 Tom Snyder Productions
80 Coolidge Hill Road
Watertown, MA 02472-7013
617-926-6000
800-342-0236
Fax: 800-304-1254
E-mail: ask@tpmsnyder.com
http://www.tomsnyder.com
Educational videotapes, videodiscs and computer programs.

5392 Varitronics Systems
PO Box 234
Minneapolis, MN 55440
800-637-5461
Fax: 800-543-8966

Computer electronics, hardware, software and systems.

5393 Wholesale Educational Supplies
PO Box 120123
East Haven, CT 06512-0123
800-243-2518
Fax: 800-452-5956
E-mail: wes4@snet.net
http://www.discountav.com
Over 5,000 audio visual and video equipment and supplies offered at deep discount prices. Free 148 page catalog.

J Fields, President

Furniture & Equipment

5394 ASRS of America
225 W 34th Street
Suite 1708
New York, NY 10122-0049
212-760-1607
Fax: 212-714-2084
E-mail: elecompack@erols.com
http://www.elecompack.com
Offers Elecompack, high density compact shelving which offers double storage capacity, automatic passive safety systems and custom front panels.

Walter M Kaufman

5395 Adden Furniture
26 Jackson Street
Lowell, MA 01852-2199
978-454-7848
800-625-3876
Fax: 978-453-1449
E-mail: fsafran@addenfurniture.com
http://www.addenfurniture.com
Manufacturer of dormitory furniture, bookcases and shelving products.

Frank Safran, Education/Sales Director

5396 Air Technologies Corporation
27130 Paseo Espada
Suite 1405-A
San Juan Capistrano, CA 92675
949-661-5060
800-759-5060
Fax: 949-661-2454
E-mail: sales@airtech.net
http://www.airtech.net
Develop and manufacture professional ergonomic computer products.

5397 Alma Industries
1300 Prospect Street
High Point, NC 27260-8329
336-578-5700
Fax: 336-578-0105
Bookcases and shelving for educational purposes.

5398 Angeles Group
Dailey Industrial Park
9 Capper Drive
Pacific, MO 63069
636-257-0533
Fax: 636-257-5473
http://www.angeles-group.com
Housekeeping furniture and children play kitchen's made of durable and sturdy molded polyethylene. Baseline Furniture: tables, chairs, lockers, cubbies, bookcases, bookracks, silver rider trikes, spaceline cots, basic trikes, and bye bye buggies.

Dianna Pritcjett, Customer Service Manager
Tami Warren, Customer Service Manager

5399 Anthro Corporation Technology Furniture
10450 SW Manhasset
Tualatin, OR 97062
503-691-2556
800-325-3841
Fax: 800-325-0045
http://www.anthro.com
Durable computer workstations and accessories; educational discounts; and dozens of shapes and sizes.

Mila Graham, Educational Sales

5400 Architectural Precast
10210 Winstead Lane
Cincinnati, OH 45231
513-772-4670
Fax: 513-772-4672
Furniture, tables, playground equipment, desks.

5401 Blanton & Moore Company
PO Box 70
Barium Springs, NC 28010-0070
704-528-4506
Fax: 704-528-6519
http://www.blantonandmoore.com
Standard and custom library furniture crafted from fine hardwoods.

Billy Galliher, Manager Sales Administration

5402 Borroughs Corporation
3002 N Burdick Street
Kalamazoo, MI 49004-3483
616-342-0161
800-627-6767
Bookcases and shelving products for educational purposes.

5403 Brady Office Machine Security
11056 S Bell Avenue
Chicago, IL 60643-3935
773-779-8349
800-326-8349
Fax: 773-779-9712
E-mail: b.brady1060@aol.com
The Brady Office Machine Security physically protects all office machines, computer components, faxes, printers, VCRs, have wall and ceiling mounts for TVs.

Bernadette Brady, President
Don Brady, VP

5404 Bretford Manufacturing
9715 Soreng Avenue
Schiller Park, IL 60176-2186
540-678-2545
Manufacturer of a full line of AV and computer projection screens, television mounts, wood office furniture and a full line of combination wood shelving and steel library shelving.

5405 Brixey
30414 Ganado Drive
Suite A
Palos Verdes Estates, CA 90275-6221
310-544-6098
Furniture for the classroom.

5406 Brodart Company, Automation Division
500 Arch Street
Williamsport, PA 17701
570-326-2461
800-233-8467
Fax: 570-327-9237
E-mail: salesmkt@brodart.com
http://www.brodart.com

Brodart's Automation Division has been providing library systems, software, and services for over 25 years. Products include: library management systems, media management systems, Internet solutions, cataloged web sites, cataloging resource tools, union catalog solutions, public access catalogs, and bibliographic services.

Kasey Dibble, Marketing Coordinator
Sally Wilmoth, Director Marketing/Sales

5407 Buckstaff Company
Buckstaff Company
1127 S Main Street
PO Box 2506
Oshkosh, WI 54902
920-235-5890
800-755-5890
Fax: 920-235-2018
E-mail: tmugerauer@buckstaff.com
http://www.buckstaff.com
The premier manufacturer of library furniture in the United States. Quality and durability has been the Buckstaff trademark for 150 years.

Tom Mugerauer, Sales Manager, National

5408 Carpets for Kids Etc...
115 SE 9th Avenue
Portland, OR 97214-1301
503-232-1203
Fax: 503-232-1394
http://www.carpetforkids.com
Carpets, flooring and floorcoverings for educational purposes.

5409 Children's Factory
505 N Kirkwood Road
Saint Louis, MO 63122-3913
314-821-1441
Fax: 877-726-1714
Manufactures children's indoor play furniture.

5410 Children's Furniture Company
Gressco Ltd.
328 Moravian Valley Road
Waunakee, WI 53597
800-697-3408
Fax: 608-849-6300
E-mail: caroline@gresscoltd.com
http://www.gressco.com
Commercial quality furniture for children of all ages.

Robert Childers, President
Caroline Ashmore, Marketing/Sales

5411 Community Playthings
PO Box 901
Rifton, NY 12471-0901
800-777-4244
Fax: 800-336-5948
E-mail: sales@bruderhof.com
Unstructured maple toys and furniture including innovative products, especially for infants and toddlers.

5412 Continental Film
PO Box 5126
Chattanooga, TN 37406-0126
423-622-1193
888-909-3456
Fax: 423-629-0853
E-mail: cfpc@chattanooga.net
http://www.continentalfilm.com
LCD projectors, distance learning systems, interactive white boards, document cameras.

Jim Webster, President
Courtney Sisk, VP

5413 Counterpoint
17237 Van Wagoner Road
Spring Lake, MI 49456-9702
800-628-1945
Fax: 616-847-3109
Audiovisual carts and tables.

5414 CyberStretch By Jazzercise
2460 Impala Drive
Carlsbad, CA 92008
760-476-1750
Fax: 760-602-7180
E-mail: cyberstretch@cyberstretch.com
http://www.jazzercize.com
To foster and promote wellness through the production of free interactive software programs for business, government, educational and personal use.

Kathy Missett, Contact

5415 Da-Lite Screen Company
3100 N Detroit Street
Warsaw, IN 46582
574-267-8101
800-622-3737
Fax: 574-267-7804
E-mail: info@dalite.com
http://www.da-lite.com
Projection screens, monitor mounts, audiovisual carts and tables, overhead projectors and transparencies.

5416 DeFoe Furniture 4 Kids
910 S Grove Avenue
Ontario, CA 91761-8011
909-947-4459
Fax: 909-947-3377
Furniture, floorcoverings, toys, constructive playthings and more for children grades PreK-5.

5417 Decar Corporation
7615 University Avenue
Middleton Branch, WI 53562-3142
606-836-1911
Library shelving, storage facilities and furniture.

5418 DecoGard Products
Construction Specialties
Route 405
PO Box 400
Muncy, PA 17756
570-546-5941
Fax: 570-546-5169
Physical fitness and athletic floorcoverings and mats.

5419 Engineering Steel Equipment Company
1307 Boissevain Avenue
Norfolk, VA 23507-1307
757-627-0762
Fax: 757-625-5754
Audiovisual carts and tables, bookcases and library shelving.

5420 Environments
PO Box 1348
Beaufort, SC 29901-1348
843-846-8155
800-348-4453
Fax: 843-846-2999
Publishes a catalog featuring equipment and materials for child care and early education. Offers durable and easy-to-maintain products with values that promote successful preschool, kindergarden, special needs and multi-age programs.

5421 Flagship Carpets
PO Box 1189
Chatsworth, GA 30705-1189
Carpets, flooring and floorcoverings.

5422 Fleetwood Group
PO Box 1259
Holland, MI 49422-1259
616-396-1142
800-257-6390
Fax: 616-820-8300
E-mail: www.fleetwoodfurniture.com
Offers library and school furniture including shelving, check out desks and multimedia units.

5423 Fordham Equipment Company
3308 Edson Avenue
New York, NY 10469
718-379-7300
800-249-5922
Fax: 718-379-7312
E-mail: alrobbi@attglobal.net
http://www.fordhamequip.com
Distributor and manufacturer of complete line of library supplies. Specialize in professional library shelving and furniture (wood and metal), mobile shelving and displayers. Catalog on request.

Al Robbins, President

5424 Good Sports
6031 Broad Street Mall
Pittsburgh, PA 15206-3009
412-661-9500
Mats, matting, floorcoverings and athletic training mats.

5425 Grafco
ERD
PO Box 71
Catasauqua, PA 18032-0071
800-367-6169
Fax: 610-782-0813
E-mail: info@grafco.com
http://www.grafco.com
GRAFCO manufacturers sturdy and durable computer furniture and tables designed for the educational environment.

Art Grafenberg, President

5426 Grammer
6989 N 55th Street
Suite A
Oakdale, MN 55128
651-770-6515
800-367-7328
http://www.grammerusa.com
Leading manufacturer and designer of ergonomically sound seating. Offers a chair designed especially for children.

5427 Greeting Tree
2709 Oak Haven Drive
San Marcos, TX 78666
512-392-0669
800-322-3199
Fax: 512-392-9660
E-mail: krieger@corridor.net
http://www.greetingtree.com
Solid wood furniture for Reading Recovery, Reading Library, Primary and Early Childhood. Specializes in quality and customized furniture for today's classroom. Kitchen learning centers, storage units of all sizes and sorts, easels with over fourteen different display front possibilities.

BiAnnually

Cherie Krieger, Owner

5428 Gressco Ltd.
Gressco
328 Moravian Valley Road
PO Box 339
Waunakee, WI 53597
608-849-6300
800-345-3480
Fax: 608-849-6304
E-mail: custserv@gresscoltd.com
http://www.gressco.com
Gressco is a supplier of a complete line of commercial children's HABA furniture and library displays for all types of medias. Kwik-case for the security protection of CDs, videos, and audiocassettes. Catalog available.

Caroline Ashmore, Marketing/Sales

5429 H Wilson Company
555 W Taft Drive
South Holland, IL 60473-2071
708-339-5111
800-245-7224
Fax: 800-245-8224
E-mail: sales@wilson.com
http://www.hwilson.com
Manufacturer of furniture for audio, video, and computers. Complete line of TV wall and ceiling mounts. Makers of the famous Tuffy color carts.

Matthew Glowiak, Director
Sales/Marketing

5430 HON Company
200 Oak Street
#769
Muscatine, IA 52761-4341
563-264-7100
Fax: 563-264-7505
Bookcases and shelving units.

5431 Haworth
One Haworth Center
Holland, MI 49423-9570
616-393-3000
800-344-2600
Fax: 616-393-1570
http://www.haworth.com
Steel and wood desks, systems furniture, seating, files, bookcases, shelving units, and tables.

5432 Joy Carpets
104 W Forrest Road
Fort Oglethorpe, GA 30742-3675
706-866-3335
800-645-2787
Fax: 706-866-7928
E-mail: joycarpets@joycarpets.com
http://www.joycarpets.com
Manufacturer of recreational and educational carpet for the classroom, home, or business. With a 10 year wear warranty, Class #1 Flammability rating, anti-stain and anti-bacterial treatment.

Joy Dobosh, Director Marketing

5433 KI
PO Box 8100
Green Bay, WI 54308-8100
920-468-8100
Fax: 920-468-2232
Library shelving, furniture, bookcases and more.

5434 Kensington Technology Group
2855 Campus Drive
San Mateo, CA 94403
650-572-2700
Fax: 650-572-9675
http://www.kensington.com

Offers several ergonomic mice.

5435 Kimball Office Furniture Company

1600 Royal Street
Jasper, IN 47549-1022
812-482-1600
Fax: 812-482-8300
Bookcases, office equipment and shelving units for educational institutions.

5436 Lee Metal Products

PO Box 6
Littlestown, PA 17340-0006
717-359-4111
Fax: 717-359-4414
http://www.leemetal.com
Carts, tables, bookcases and storage cabinets.

Richard Kemper, President

5437 Library Bureau

172 Industrial Road
Fitchburg, MA 01420
978-345-7942
800-221-6638
Fax: 978-345-0188
E-mail: melvil@librarybureau.com
http://www.librarybureau.com
Library shelving, bookcases, cabinets, circulation desks, carrels, computer workstations, upholstered seating.

Dennis Ruddy, Sr Project Manager

5438 Library Store

Library Store
112 E S Street
PO Box 964
Tremont, IL 61568
309-925-5571
800-548-7204
Fax: 800-320-7706
E-mail: libstore@thelibrarystore.com
http://www.thelibrarystore.com
The Library Store offers through its full-line catalog, supplies and furniture items for librarians, schools, and churches. Free catalog available containing special product discounts.

Janice Smith, Marketing Director

5439 Little Tikes Company

2180 Barlow Road
Hudson, OH 44236-4199
330-656-3906
800-321-4424
Fax: 330-650-3221
Offers a wide variety of furniture, educational games and toys and safety products for young children.

5440 Lucasey Manufacturing Company

2744 E 11th Street
Oakland, CA 94601-1429
510-534-1435
800-582-2739
Fax: 510-534-6828
E-mail: janrence@lucasey.com
Audiovisual carts, tables, and TV mounts

Jan RenceTurnbull, National Accountant

5441 Lundia

600 Capitol Way
Jacksonville, IL 62650-1096
800-726-9663
Fax: 800-869-9663
Bookcases and shelving products, as well as furniture for educational institutions.

5442 Lyon Metal Products

PO Box 671
Aurora, IL 60507-0671
630-892-8941
Fax: 630-892-8966
Bookcases and library shelving.

5443 Mateflex-Mele Corporation

1712 Erie Street
Utica, NY 13502-3337
315-733-4600
800-926-3539
Fax: 315-733-3183
http://www.mateflex.com
Manufacturers of Mateflex gymnasium flooring for basketball/gym courts. Mateflex II tennis court surfaces and Mateflex/Versaflex gridded safety floor tiles.

Gabe Martini, Sales Manager

5444 Microsoft Corporation

One Microsoft Way
Redmond, WA 98502-6399
425-882-8080
Fax: 206-703-2641
http://www.microsoft.com
Strives to produce innovative products and services that meet our costomers' evolving needs.

5445 Miller Multiplex

1555 Larkin Williams Road
Fenton, MO 63026-3008
636-343-5700
800-325-3350
Fax: 636-326-1716
E-mail: info@millermultiplex.com
Announcement boards, classroom displays, charts and pghtography, books towers, posters, frames, kiosk displays, presentation displays.

12 pages

Kathy Webster, Director Marketing

5446 ModuForm

ModuForm, Inc.
172 Industry Road
Fitchburg,, MA 01420
978-345-7942
800-221-6638
Fax: 978-345-0188
E-mail: guestlog@moduform.com
http://www.moduform.com
Residence hall furniture, loung seating, tables, stacking chairs, fully upholstered seating.

Robert Kushnir, Nationals Sales Manager
Darlene Bailey, VP Sales/Marketing

5447 Morgan Buildings, Pools, Spas, RV's

PO Box 660280
Dallas, TX 75266-0280
972-864-7300
800-935-0321
Fax: 972-864-7382
E-mail: rmoran@morganusa.com
http://www.morganusa.com
Classrooms, campus and other buildings custom designed to meet your projects needs. Permanent and relocatable modular classrooms or complete custom facilities. Rent, lease or purchase options available.

5448 Norco Products

Division of USA McDonald Corporation
PO Box 4227
Missoula, MT 59806
406-251-3800
800-662-2300
Fax: 406-251-3824
E-mail: john@norcoproducts.com
http://www.norcoproducts.com
Mobile cabinets, YRE funiture, tables, science labs, home economics displays, bookcases and shelving units, laboratory equipment, casework, cabinets, computer labs, podiums, award display cabinets, flags and flag poles.

Jim McDonald, President
John Schrom, Office Manger

5449 Nova

421 W Industrial Avenue
PO Box 725
Effingham, IL 62401
800-730-6682
Fax: 800-940-6682
E-mail: novadesk@effingham.net
http://www.novadesk.com
Patented furniture solution for computer mounting incorporates the downward gaze, our visual system's natural way of viewing close objects. Scientific evidence indicates that viewing a computer monitor at a downward gaze angle is a better solution than with traditional monitor placement.

5450 Oscoda Plastics

5585 N Huron Avenue
PO Box 189
Oscoda, MI 48750
989-739-6900
800-544-9538
Fax: 800-548-7678
E-mail: sales@oscodaplastics.com
http://www.oscodaplastics.com
Oscoda Plastics manufactures Protect-All Specialty Flooring from 100% recycled post-industrial vinyls. Protect-All is perfect for use in locker rooms, kitchen/walk-in cooler floors, fitness areas, weight rooms, gym floors, or as a temporary gym floor cover.

Joe Brinn, National Sales Manager
Rick Maybury, Sales Coordinator

5451 Palmer Snyder

201 High Street
Conneautville, PA 16406
814-587-6313
800-762-0415
Fax: 814-587-2375
Tables are built with the highest quality materials for long life and low maintenance. A complete range of rugged options.

5452 Paragon Furniture

2224 E Randol Mill Road
Arlington, TX 76011
817-633-3242
800-451-8546
Fax: 817-633-2733
E-mail: customerservice@paragoninc.com
http://www.paragoninc.com
Offers a line of furniture for classroom, labs, science, and libraries.

Carl Brockway, VP Sales
Mark Hubbard, President

5453 Pawling Corporation
Borden Lane
Wassaic, NY 12592
845-373-9300
800-431-3456
Fax: 800-451-2200
E-mail: sales@pawling.com
Pawling is an approved manufacturer by E&I cooperative buying for athletic flooring, traffic safety products, wall and corner protection and entrance mat systems.

Richard Meyer, Sales Manager

5454 Peerless Sales Company
1980 N Hawthorne Avenue
Melrose Park, IL 60160-1167
708-865-8870
Fax: 708-865-2941
Auidovisual carts and tables.

5455 RISO
300 Rosewood Drive
Suite 210
Danvers, MA 01923-4527
978-777-7377
800-876-7476
Fax: 978-777-2517
The Risograph digital printer offers high speed copy/duplicating at up to 130 pages per minute. A 50-sheet document feeder lets people print multi-page documents quickly and inexpensively. Specifically designed to handle medium run length jobs that are too strenuous for copiers. Offers various other products and office equipment available to the education community.

5456 Research Technology International
4700 Chase Avenue
Lincolnwood, IL 60646-1689
847-677-3000
800-323-7520
Fax: 847-677-1311
E-mail: sales@rtico.com
http://www.ritco.com
Tape check, Video tape cleaner, disk chack optical, disc rejestor.

5457 Russ Bassett Company
8189 Byron Road
Whittier, CA 90606-2615
800-350-2445
Fax: 562-689-8972
Shelving units, furniture and bookcases for educational institutions.

5458 SNAP-DRAPE
2045 Westgate
Suite 100
Carrollton, TX 75006-5116
972-466-1030
800-527-5147
Fax: 800-230-1330
E-mail: mecton@snapdrape.com
http://www.snapdrape.com
Table and stage skirting

Melissa Acton, Marketing/Sales Assistant

5459 Screen Works
2201 W Fulton Street
Chicago, IL 60612
312-243-8265
800-294-8111
Fax: 312-243-8290
E-mail: daveh@thescreenworks.com
http://www.thescreenworks.com
Manufacturers the E-Z Fold brand of portable projection screens and offers a full line of portable presentation accessories and services, including: an extensive screen rental inventory; audio-visula roll carts; lecterns and PaperStand flip charts. Custom

screen sizes, screen surface cleaning and frame repair service also available.

David Hull, National Sales Manager

5460 Spacemaster Systems
155 W Central Avenue
Zeeland, MI 49464-1601
616-772-2406
Fax: 616-772-2100
Standard and Custom Shelving Systems and USEFUL AISLE Storage Systems.

5461 Spacesaver Corporation
1450 Janesville Avenue
Fort Atkinson, WI 53538-2798
920-563-6362
800-492-3434
Fax: 920-563-2702
E-mail: ssc@spacesaver.com
http://www.spacesaver.com
Flexible Spacesaver custom designs high-density mobile storage systems. Will double your storage and filing capacity while increasing usable floor space. Store files, supplies, manuals, books, drawings, multi-media, etc.

5462 Synsor Corporation
1920 Merrill Creek Pkwy
Everett, WA 98203-5859
800-426-0193
Fax: 425-551-1313
Offers a full line of educational furniture.

5463 Tab Products Company
1400 Page Mill Road
Palo Alto, CA 94304-1124
800-672-3109
Fax: 920-387-1802
Bookcases and shelving products for library/media centers.

5464 Tepromark International
206 Mosher Avenue
Woodmere, NY 11598-1662
516-569-4533
800-645-2622
Fax: 516-295-5991
Trolley Rail wall guards, corner guards, wall guards with hand rails, door plates, chair rolls, kick plates, vinyl floor mats and carpet mats. All mats promote safety from slipping in wet areas.

Robert Rymers

5465 Tesco Industries
1038 E Hacienda Street
Bellville, TX 77418-2828
979-865-3176
Fax: 979-865-9026
Bookcases and shelving units.

5466 Texwood Furniture
1353 N 2nd Street
Taylor, TX 76574
512-352-3000
888-878-0000
Fax: 512-352-3084
E-mail: ajohnson@texwood.com
http://www.texwood.com
Wood library furniture, shelving, computer tables and circulation desks and early childhood furniture.

Andrea Johnson, Director Marketing
Dave Gaskers, VP Sales/Marketing

5467 Tot-Mate by Stevens Industries
704 W Main Street
Teutopolis, IL 62467-1212
217-857-6411
800-397-8687
Fax: 217-857-3638
E-mail: timw@stevens.com
Early learning furniture manufactured by Stevens Industries. Features include 16 color choices, plastic laminate surfacing, rounded corners, beveled edges, safe and strong designs. Items offered include change tables, storage shelving, book displays, teacher cabinets, housekeeping sets and locker cubbies.

Randy Ruholl, Sales Representative
Paul Jones, Customer Service

5468 University Products
University Products
517 Main Street
PO Box 101
Holyoke, MA 01041-0101
413-532-3372
800-628-1912
Fax: 413-532-9281
E-mail: info@universityproducts.com
http://www.universityproducts.com
University Products specializes in top-quality archival materials for conservation and preservation as well as library and media centers supplies, equipment, and furnishings.

John A Dunphy

5469 W. C. Heller & Company
Heller
201 W Wabash Avenue
Montpelier, OH 43543
419-485-3176
Fax: 419-485-8694
E-mail: wcheller@hotmail.com
Complete line of wood library furniture in oak and birch, custom cabinetry and special modifications. Over 110 years in business.

Robert L Heller II, VP Sales

5470 Wheelit
PO Box 352800
Toledo, OH 43635-2800
419-531-4900
800-523-7508
Fax: 419-531-6415
Carts and storage containers.

5471 White Office Systems
50 Boright Avenue
Kenilworth, NJ 07033-1015
908-272-8888
Fax: 908-931-0840
Shelving, bookcases, furniture and products for libraries, media centers, schools and offices.

5472 Whitney Brothers Company
PO Box 644
Keene, NH 03431-0644
603-352-2610
Fax: 603-357-1559
Manufactures children's furniture products for preschools and day care centers.

5473 Winsted Corporation
10901 Hampshire Avenue S
Minneapolis, MN 55438-2385
952-944-9050
800-447-2257
Fax: 800-421-3839
E-mail: racks@winsted.com
http://www.winsted.com

Video furniture, accessories, tape storage systems and lan rack systems.

Randy Smith, President

5474 Wood Designs
PO Box 1308
Monroe, NC 28111-1308
704-283-7508
800-247-8465
Fax: 704-289-1899
E-mail: p.schneider@tip-me-not.com
Manufactures wooden educational equipment and teaching toys for early learning environments. Sold through school supply dealers and stores.

Dennis Gosney, President
Paul Schneider, VP Sales/Marketing

5475 Worden Company
199 E 17th Street
Holland, MI 49423-4298
800-748-0561
Fax: 616-392-2542
Furniture for office, business, school or library.

Maintenance

5476 American Locker Security Systems
608 Allen Street
Jamestown, NY 14701-3966
716-664-9600
800-828-9118
Fax: 716-664-2949
E-mail: 103303.1432@compuserve.com
http://www.americanlocker.com
Lockers featuring coin operated lockers.

David L Henderson, VP/General Manager

5477 Atlantic Fitness Products
PO Box 300
Linthicum Hts, MD 21090-0300
800-445-1855
School lockers and fitness/physical education products and equipment.

5478 Barco Products
11 N Batavia Avenue
Batavia, IL 60510-1961
800-338-2697
Maintenance and safety products made from recycled materials.

Kitt Pittman, Office Manager
Judy Leonard, Marketing Manager

5479 Blaine Window Hardware
17319 Blaine Drive
Hagerstown, MD 21740-2394
800-678-1919
Fax: 301-797-2510
E-mail: user533955@aol.com
http://www.blainewindow.com
Window and door parts including window repair hardware, custom screens locker hardware, chair glides, panic exit hardware, balance systems, door closers and motorized operators.

William Pasquerette, VP
Robert Slick, Purchasing Agent

5480 Bleacherman, M.A.R.S.
105 Mill Street
Corinth, NY 12822-1021
518-654-9084
School lockers.

5481 Burkel Equipment Company
14670 Hanks Drive
Red Bluff, CA 96080-9475
800-332-3993
School lockers, hardware and security equipment, maintenance and repair supplies.

5482 Chemtrol
Santa Barbara Control Systems
5375 Overpass Road
Santa Barbara, CA 93111-5879
800-621-2279
Fax: 805-683-1893
E-mail: chemtrol@slocontrol.com
http://www.chemtrolcontrol.com
Maintenance supplies for educational institutions.

Kevin R Smith, Sales Manager

5483 Contact East
335 Willow Street S
N Andover, MA 01845-5995
978-682-2000
800-225-5370
Fax: 978-688-7829
E-mail: sales@contacteast.com
http://www.contacteast.com
Maintenance supplies and equipment.

5484 DeBourgh Manufacturing Company
27505 Otero Avenue
La Junta, CO 81050-9403
719-384-8161
Fax: 719-384-7713
Security equipment, hardware, storage and school lockers.

5485 Dow Corning Corporation
PO Box 0994
Midland, MI 48686-0001
989-496-4000
Fax: 989-496-4572
Maintenance supplies and equipment.

5486 Dri-Dek Corporation
2706 Horseshoe Drive S
Naples, FL 34104-6142
941-643-0578
800-348-2378
Fax: 800-828-4248
E-mail: dri-dek@kictr.com
http://www.dri-dek.com
Oxy-BI vinyl compound in the Dri-Dek flooring systems helps halt the spread of infectious fungus and bacteria in areas with barefooted traffic. This compound makes Dri-Dek's anti-skid, self-draining surface ideal for use in the wettest conditions.

5487 Esmet
Tufloc Group
1406 5th Street SW
Canton, OH 44702-2062
330-452-9132
Fax: 330-452-2557
Lockers for the educational institution.

5488 Ex-Cell Metal Products
11240 Melrose Avenue
Franklin, IL 60131
847-451-0451
Fax: 847-451-0458
Maintenance supplies and repair equipment.

5489 Facilities Network
PO Box 868
Mahopac, NY 10541-0868
845-621-1664

School lockers and security system units.

5490 Fibersin Industries
37031 E Wisconsin Avenue
Oconomowoc, WI 53066
262-567-4427
Fax: 262-567-4814
School lockers and maintenance supplies. Desks, cradenzas, bookcases for school adm. Tables for cafeteria and adm.

5491 Flagpole Components
4150A Kellway Circle
Addison, TX 75001-4205
972-250-0893
800-634-4926
Fax: 972-380-5143
Maintenance and repair supplies and equipment.

5492 Flexi-Wall Systems
PO Box 89
Liberty, SC 29657-0089
Maintenance and repair supplies for educational institutions.

5493 Flo-Pac Corporation
700 Washington Avenue N
Suite 400
Minneapolis, MN 55401-1130
612-332-6240
Fax: 612-344-1663
Maintenance and repair supplies.

5494 Four Rivers Software Systems
2400 Ardmore Boulevard
7th Floor
Pittsburgh, PA 15221-1451
412-273-6400
Fax: 412-273-6420
Maintenance and repair supplies, business and administrative software and supplies.

5495 Friendly Systems
3878 Oak Lawn Avenue
#1008-300
Dallas, TX 75219-4460
972-857-0399
Maintenance and repair supplies.

5496 GE Capitol Modular Space
40 Liberty Boulevard
Malvern, PA 19355
610-225-2836
800-523-7918
Fax: 610-225-2762
School lockers, shelving and storage facilities.

5497 Glen Products
13765 Alton Parkway
Suite A
Irvine, CA 92618-1627
800-486-4455
Storage facilities, lockers and security systems.

5498 Global Occupational Safety
22 Harbor Park Drive
Port Washington, NY 11050-4650
516-625-4466
Safety storage facilities, shelving, lockers and hardware.

5499 Graffiti Gobbler Products
6428 Blarney Stone Court
Springfield, VA 22152-2106
800-486-2512
Educational maintenance and repair supplies and equipment.

5500 H&H Enterprises
PO Box 585
Grand Haven, MI 49417-9430
616-846-8972
800-878-7777
Fax: 616-846-1004
E-mail: hhenterprises@novagate.com
Maintenance and repair supplies.

5501 HAZ-STOR
2454 Dempster Street
Des Plaines, IL 60016
217-345-4422
800-727-2067
Fax: 217-345-4475
E-mail: info@hazstor.com
http://www.hazstor.com
Manufacturer of pre-fabricated steel structures including hazardous material storage buildings and outdoor flammables lockers as well as waste compactors and drum crushers, secondary containment products and process shelters.

Roger Quinlan, National Sales Manager
Antoinette Balthazor, Marketing Coordinator

5502 HOST/Racine Industries
1405 16th Street
Racine, WI 53403-2249
800-558-9439
Fax: 262-637-1624
Maintenance and repair supplies.

5503 Hako Minuteman
111 S Rohlwing Road
Addison, IL 60101-4244
630-627-6900
Fax: 630-627-1130
Maintenance and repair supplies for educational institutions.

5504 Haws Corporation
PO Box 2070
Sparks, NV 89432-2070
775-359-4712
Fax: 775-359-7424
E-mail: haws@hawsco.com
http://www.hawsco.com
Manufacturer of drinking fountains, electric water coolers, emergency drench showers and eyewashes.

Jim Bowers, Marketing Manager

5505 Honeywell
Home & Building Control
PO Box 524
Minneapolis, MN 55440-0524
973-455-2001
Fax: 973-455-4807
Maintenance and cleaning products for educational purposes.

5506 Insta-Foam Products
2050 N Broadway Street
Joliet, IL 60435-2571
800-800-FOAM
Fax: 800-326-1054
Maintenance supplies, cleaning products and repair hardware.

5507 Interstate Coatings
1005 Highway 301 S
Wilson, NC 27895
800-533-7663
Hardware, repair, maintenance and cleaning supplies.

5508 J.A. Sexauer
PO Box 1000
White Plains, NY 10602-1000
800-431-1872
Fax: 856-439-1333
Cleaning and maintenance supplies for educational institutions.

5509 Karnak Corporation
330 Central Avenue
Clark, NJ 07066-1199
732-388-0300
800-526-4236
Fax: 732-388-9422
Maintenance and cleaning supplies.

5510 Kool Seal
Unifex Professional Maintenance Products
1499 Enterprise Pkwy
Twinsburg, OH 44087-2241
800-321-0572
Fax: 330-425-9778
Maintenance, repair and cleaning supplies.

5511 LDSystems
9535 Monroe Road
Suite 140
Charlotte, NC 28270
704-847-1338
Fax: 704-847-1354
E-mail: ds@starkpr.com
http://www.bottompump.com
Environmentally-safe bottom pump air powered spray containers to dispense cleaning supplies such as window sprays, for cooling during workouts and general storage containers.

Dick Stark

5512 List Industries
401 NW 12th Avenue
Deerfield Beach, FL 33442-1707
954-429-9155
Fax: 954-428-3843
School lockers and storage facilities.

5513 Maintenance
1051 W Liberty Street
Wooster, OH 44691-3307
330-264-6262
800-892-6701
Fax: 800-264-2578
Provides pavement maintenance products for parking lots, driveways, tennis courts, etc.

Robert E Huebner

5514 Master Bond
PO Box 522
Teaneck, NJ 07666
201-343-8983
Fax: 201-343-2132
E-mail: main@masterbond.com
http://www.masterbond.com
Repair hardware, maintenance and cleaning products for schools.

5515 Master Builders
Admixture Division
23700 Chagrin Boulevard
Cleveland, OH 44122-5554
216-831-5500
Fax: 216-839-8815
School hardware, maintenance and repair supplies and equipment.

5516 Medart
Division of Carriage Industries
PO Box 435
Garrettsville, OH 44231-0435
662-453-2506

School lockers.

5517 Modular Hardware
8190 N Brookshire Court
Tucson, AZ 85741-4037
520-744-4424
800-533-0042
Fax: 800-533-7942
School hardware, for repair and maintenance purposes.

5518 Penco Products
99 Brower Avenue
PO Box 378
Oaks, PA 19456-0378
610-666-0500
800-562-1000
Fax: 610-666-7561
E-mail: general@pencoproducts.com
http://www.pencoproducts.com
School lockers.

5519 Permagile Industries
910 Manor Lane
Bay Shore, NY 11706-7512
516-349-1100
Maintenance and cleaning products and supplies.

5520 Powr-Flite Commercial Floor Care Equipment
3301 Wichita Court
Fort Worth, TX 76140
817-551-0700
800-880-2913
Fax: 817-551-0719
http://www.powrflite.com
School maintenance supplies focusing on floor care equipment products, accessories and parts.

Curtis Walton, Contact

5521 ProCoat Products
260 Centre Street
Suite D
Holbrook, MA 02343-1074
781-767-2270
Fax: 781-767-2271
E-mail: info@procoat.com
http://www.procoat.com
Designed to restore aged and discolored acoustical ceiling tiles. Acoustical and fire retarding qualities are maintained. Ceiling restoration is cost effective, time efficient and avoids solid waste disposal. Products available also for preventative maintenance programs.

Kenneth Woolf, President

5522 Rack III High Security Bicycle Rack Company
675 Hartz Avenue
Suite 306
Danville, CA 94526-3859
800-733-1971
Lockers, bicycle racks, storage facilities and hardware.

5523 Republic Storage Systems Company
1038 Belden Avenue NE
Canton, OH 44705-1454
330-438-5800
Fax: 330-452-5071
Storage facilities, containers, maintenance products, shelving and lockers.

5524 Safety Storage
2301 Bert Drive
Hollister, CA 95023-2547
800-344-6539
Fax: 831-637-7405
Equipment, supplies and storage containers for maintenance and educational purposes.

5525 Salsbury Industries
1010 E 62nd Street
Los Angeles, CA 90001-1598
800-624-5269
Fax: 800-624-5299
E-mail: salsbury@mailboxes.com
http://www.mailboxes.com
School lockers, maintenance products and storage facilities.

5526 Servicemaster
Education Management Services
One Servicemaster Way
Downers Grove, IL 60515
800-926-9700
http://www.servicemaster.com
A provider of facility management support services to education.

5527 Sheffield Plastics
DSM Engineered Plastics Company
119 Salisbury Road
Sheffield, MA 01257-9706
413-229-8711
Maintenance and cleaning products for schools.

5528 Southern Sport Surfaces
PO Box 1817
Cumming, GA 30028-1817
770-887-3508
800-346-1632
Maintenance and cleaning products for schools.

5529 System Works
3301 Windy Ridge Parkway
Marietta, GA 30067
770-952-8444
800-868-0497
Fax: 770-955-2977
Addresses the capacity, quality and safety requirements of maintenance operations. Comprehensive and interactive it maximizes maintenance resources, people, tools and replacement parts, for increased productivity and equipment reliability, reduced inventories and accurate cost accounting.

Karen Kharlead

5530 TENTEL Corporation
4475 Golden Foothill Parkway
El Dorado Hills, CA 95762-9638
800-538-6894
Fax: 916-939-4114
Cleaning, repair and maintenance products for educational institutions.

5531 Tiffin Systems
450 Wall Street
Tiffin, OH 44883-1366
419-447-8414
800-537-0983
Fax: 419-447-8512
E-mail: tiffin@bpsom.com
http://www.tiffinmetal.com
Lockers, storage containers and shelving.

5532 Topog-E Gasket Company
1224 N Utica Avenue
Tulsa, OK 74110-4682
918-587-6649
Fax: 918-587-6961
Maintenance supplies and products.

5533 Tru-Flex Recreational Coatings
Touraine Paints
1760 Revere Beach Pkwy
Everett, MA 02149-5906
800-325-0017
Maintenance, floor care, coatings and repair supplies for upkeep of schools and institutions.

5534 Wagner Spray Tech Corporation
1770 Fernbrook Lane N
Plymouth, MN 55447-4663
763-553-7000
Fax: 763-553-7288
Maintenance supplies, floor care, cleaning and repair products and equipment.

5535 Wilmar
303 Harper Drive
Moorestown, NJ 08057
609-439-1222
800-523-7120
Fax: 800-220-3291
Maintenance and repair products, hardware and supplies.

5536 Witt Company
4454 Steel Place
Cincinnati, OH 45209-1184
513-979-3127
800-543-7417
Fax: 513-979-3134
Lockers, maintenance supplies and storage containers for educational purposes.

5537 Zep Manufacturing
1310 Seaboard Industrial Blvd NW
Atlanta, GA 30318-2807
404-352-1680
Maintenance and cleaning supplies.

Scientific Equipment

5538 Adventures Company
435 Main Street
Johnson City, NY 13790-1935
607-729-6512
800-477-6512
Fax: 607-729-4820
A full line of supplies and equipment for science and technology education.

D Hetherington

5539 Alfa Aesar
30 Bond Street
Ward Hill, MA 01835-8042
800-343-0660
Laboratory equipment and supplies.

5540 American Chemical Society
1155 16th Street NW
Washington, DC 20036-4800
202-872-4600
800-ACS-5558
Fax: 202-833-7732
Exhibits hands-on activities and programs for K-12 and college science curriculum.

5541 Arbor Scientific
PO Box 2750
Ann Arbor, MI 48106-2750
800-367-6695
Fax: 734-477-9570
E-mail: mail@arborsci.com
http://www.arborsci.com
Innovative products for Science Education.

56 pages Bi-Annual Catalog

Dave Barnes, Marketing Director

5542 Astronomy to Go
1115 Melrose Avenue
Melrose Park, PA 19027-3017
215-782-8970
Fax: 215-831-0486
E-mail: astro2go@aol.com
http://www.astronomytogo.com
Programs include Starlab Planetarium presentations, hands-on demonstrations, slides and lecture shows and energy observing sessions with our many telescopses. We are funded through our traveling museum shop which carries a large assortment of t-shirts, jewelry, gifts, books, and teaching supplies as well as an extensive selection of meteorites.

Bob Summerfield, Director

5543 CEM Corporation
3100 Smith Farm Road
Matthews, NC 28104-5044
704-821-7015
Fax: 704-821-7894
Laboratory and scientific supplies, furniture, casework and equipment.

5544 Carolina Biological Supply Company
2700 York Road
Burlington, NC 27215-3398
336-584-0381
800-334-5551
Fax: 800-222-7112
E-mail: carolina@carolina.com
http://www.carolina.com
Educational products for teachers and students of biology, molecular biology, biotechnology, chemistry, earth science, space science, physics, and mathematics. Carolina serves elementary schools through universities with living and preserved animals and plants, prepared microscope slides, microscopes, audiovisuals, books, charts, models, computer software, games, apparatus, and much more.

5545 Challenger Center for Space Science Education
1250 N Pitt Street
Alexandria, VA 22314
703-683-9740
Fax: 703-683-7546
E-mail: mail@challenger.org
http://www.challenger.org
Is a global not-for-profit education organization created in 1986 by familes of the astronauts tragically lost during the last flight of the Challenger Space Shuttle. Dedicated to the educaltional spirit of that mission, Challenger center develops Learning Centers and othe educational programs worldwide to continue the mission to engage students in science and math education

Glenn Ono, Marketing/Communications
Tracy Martin, Marketing Assistant

5546 ChronTrol Corporation
9975 Businesspark Avenue
San Diego, CA 92131-1644
619-282-8686
Fax: 619-563-6563
Scientific equipment, laboratory supplies
and furniture.

5547 Classic Modular Systems
1911 Columbus Street
Two Rivers, WI 54241-2898
920-793-2269
800-558-7625
Fax: 920-793-2896
E-mail: cms@dataplusnet.com
http://www.dct.com/cms
Laboratory equipment, shelving, cabinets
and markerboards.

Cathy Albers, Advertising Manager

5548 Columbia University's Biosphere 2 Center
Highway 77 & Biosphere Road
Oracle, AZ 85623
520-896-6200
Fax: 520-896-6471
Educational programs and products.

5549 Connecticut Valley Biological Supply Company
82 Valley Road
PO Box 326
Southampton, MA 01073-9536
413-527-4030
800-628-7748
Fax: 800-355-6813
E-mail: connval@ctvalleybio.com
Cultures and specimens, instruments,
equipment, hands-on kits, books, software,
audiovisuals, models and charts for teaching botany, zoology, life science, anatomy,
physiology, genetics, astronomy, entomol-
ogy, microscopy, AP Biology, microbiology, horticulture, biotechnology, earth
science, natural history and environmental
science.

5550 Crow Canyon Archaeological Center
23390 County Road K
Cortez, CO 81321-9408
970-565-8975
800-422-8975
Fax: 970-565-4859
E-mail: jsimpson@crowcanyon.org
http://www.crowcanyon.org
Experiential education programs in archaeology and Native American history. Programs offered for school groups, teachers
and other adults.

ISBN: 0-7872-6748-1

M Elaine Davis and Marjorie R Connelly,
Author
Joyce Simpson, Director Marketing
Elaine Davis, Director Education

5551 Cuisenaire Company of America
10 Bank Street
#5026
White Plains, NY 10606-1933
914-997-2600
Fax: 914-684-6137
Science materials and equipment.

5552 DISCOVER Science Program
105 Terry Drive
Suite 120
Newtown, PA 18940-1872
800-448-3399
Fax: 215-579-8589

Features the newest developments in a wide
range of science topics and provides an easy
way for teachers to stay current and
up-to-date in the world of science. The DIS-
COVER Program offers the DISCOVER
magazine at the lowest possible price.

5553 Delta Biologicals
PO Box 26666
Tucson, AZ 85726-6666
520-790-7737
800-821-2502
Fax: 520-745-7888
E-mail: sales@deltabio.com
http://www.deltabio.com
Products and supplies for science and biology educators for over 30 years. Preserves
specimens, laboratory furniture, microscopes, anatomy models, balances and
scales, dissection supplies, lab safety supplies, multimedia, plant presses.

Lynn Hugins, Marketing
Darlene Harris, Customer Service
Manager

5554 Delta Biologicals Catalog
PO Box 26666
Tucson, AZ 85726-6666
520-790-7737
800-821-2502
Fax: 520-745-7888
E-mail: sales@deltabio.com
http://www.deltabio.com

96 pages

Lynn Hugins, Marketing
Darlene Harris, Customer Service
Manager

5555 Detecto Scale Corporation
203 E Daugherty Street
Webb City, MO 64870-1929
417-673-4631
800-641-2008
Fax: 417-673-5001
E-mail: detecto@cardet.com
http://www.detectoscale.com
Scientific equipment and supplies for educational laboratories.

5556 Dickson Company
930 S Westwood Avenue
Addison, IL 60101-4997
630-543-3747
Laboratory instruments, electronics, furniture and equipment.

5557 Donald K. Olson & Associates
PO Box 858
Bonsall, CA 92003-0858
Mineral and fossil samples for educational
purposes.

5558 Dranetz Technologies
1000 Durham Road
Edison, NJ 08818
732-287-3680
Fax: 732-287-9014
Laboratory instruments, equipment and
supplies.

5559 Edmund Scientific - Scientifics Catalog
E726 Edscorp Building
Department 16A1
Barrington, NJ 08007
856-547-3488
Fax: 856-573-6295
Over 5,000 products including a wide selec-
tion of microscopes, telescopes, astronomy
aids, fiber optic kits, demonstration optics,

magnets and science discover products used
in science fair projects.

Nancy McGonigle, President

5560 Educational Products
1342 N I35 E
Carrollton, TX 75006
972-245-9512
Fax: 972-245-5468
Science display boards, workshop materials
and science fair accessories.

5561 Edwin H. Benz Company
73 Maplehurst Avenue
Providence, RI 02908-5324
401-331-5650
Fax: 401-331-5685
E-mail: sales@benztesters.com
http://www.benztesters.com
Laboratory equipment.

5562 Electro-Steam Generator Corporation
1000 Bernard Street
Alexandria, VA 22314-1299
703-549-0664
800-634-8177
Fax: 703-836-2581
E-mail: jharlineclectrostream.com
http://www.electrosteam.com
Laboratory equipment and supplies. Manufacture steam generators for sterilizers, au-
toclaves, clean rooms, pure steam
humidification, laboratories, steam rooms,
and cleaning of all kinds.

Jack Harlin, Sales/Marketing Associate

5563 Estes-Cox Corporation
1295 H Street
Penrose, CO 81240-9676
719-372-6565
800-820-0202
Fax: 719-372-3217
E-mail: info@esteseducator.com
http://www.esteseducator.com
Supplier of model rockets, engines and supporting videos, curriculums and educational publications for K-12.

Ann Grimm, Director Education

5564 FOTODYNE
950 Walnut Ridge Drive
Hartland, WI 53029-9388
262-369-7000
800-362-3642
Fax: 262-369-7017
Biotechnology curriculum equipment.

5565 First Step Systems
PO Box 2304
Jackson, TN 38302-2304
800-831-0877
Fax: 216-361-0829
Developed an effective, safe and less expen-
sive approach to blood exposure safety for
schools and classrooms that both help comply with OSHA requirements and is easy to
purchase and resupply.

Susan Staples, Account Manager
Renee Carr, Bid Support

5566 Fisher Scientific Company
1410 Wayne Avenue
Indiana, PA 15701-3940
724-357-1000
Fax: 724-357-1019
A full line of laboratory and scientific supplies and equipment for educational institutions.

5567 Fisher Scientific/EMD
3970 John Creek Court
Suite 500
Suwanee, GA 30024
770-871-4500
800-766-7000
Fax: 800-926-1166
Supplier of chemistry, biology and physics
laboratory supplies and equipment.

5568 Fisons Instruments
8 Forge Parkway
Franklin, MA 02038-3157
978-524-1000
Laboratory equipment and instruments for
the scientific classroom.

5569 Flinn Scientific
PO Box 219
Batavia, IL 60510-0219
630-879-6900
800-452-1261
Fax: 630-879-6962
Laboratory safety supplies.

5570 Forestry Supplies
PO Box 8397
Jackson, MS 39284-8397
601-354-3565
800-647-5368
Fax: 800-543-4203
E-mail: fsi@forestry-suppliers.com
http://www.forestry-suppliers.com
Field and lab equipment for earth, life and
environmental sciences.

Ken Peacock, VP Marketing
Debbie Raddin, Education Specialist

5571 Frank Schaffer Publications
23740 Hawthorne Boulevard
Torrance, CA 90505-5927
310-378-1133
800-421-5565
Fax: 800-837-7260
Charts, animal posters, floor puzzles, resource books and more.

5572 Frey Scientific
905 Hickory Lane
Mansfield, OH 44905-2862
800-225-FREY
Fax: 419-589-1522
Name brand scientific products including
Energy Physics, Earth Science, Chemistry
and Applied Science. Over 12,000 products and kits for grades 5-14 are available.

5573 Great Adventure Tours
1717 Old Topanga Canyon Road
Topanga, CA 90290-3934
800-642-3933
Educational science field trips and adventures.

5574 Guided Discoveries
PO Box 1360
Claremont, CA 91711-1360
Outdoor educational science programs.

5575 HACH Company
PO Box 389
Loveland, CO 80539-0389
970-669-3050
Fax: 970-669-2932
Water and soil test kits for field and labora-
tory work.

5576 Heathkit Educational Systems
455 Riverview Drive
Benton Harbor, MI 49022-5015
616-925-6000
800-253-0570
Fax: 616-925-3895
Electronics educational products from basic electricity to high-tech lasers and microscopes and beyond. Comprehensive
line of different media to fit varied applications. Including Computer-Aided Instruction and Computer-Aided Troubleshooting
services and Heathkit's PC Servicing,
Troubleshooting and Networking courses.

Carolyn Feltner, Sales Coordinator
Patrick Beckett, Marketing Manager

5577 Holometrix
25 Wiggins Avenue
Bedford, MA 01730-2314
781-275-3300
Fax: 781-275-3705
Laboratory instruments.

5578 Howell Playground Equipment
1714 E Fairchild Street
Danville, IL 61832-3616
217-442-0482
800-637-5075
Fax: 217-442-8944
E-mail: howellequipment@aol.com
http://www.primestripe.com
Playground equipment and bicycle racks.

Nina Payne, President

5579 Hubbard Scientific
PO Box 2121
Fort Collins, CO 80522-2121
Earth science and life science models, kits,
globes and curriculum materials.

5580 Innova Corporation
115 George Lamb Road
Bernardston, MA 01337-9742
Science kits and globes.

5581 Insect Lore
PO Box 1535
Shafter, CA 93263-1535
661-746-6047
800-548-3284
Fax: 661-746-0334
E-mail: orders@insectlore.com
http://www.insectlore.com
Science and nature materials for preschool
through grade 6. Raises butterflies, frogs,
ladybugs and more. Features books, curriculum units, videos, puppet, posters, and
other nature oriented products.

5582 Insights Visual Productions
PO Box 230644
Encinitas, CA 92023-0644
800-942-0528
Laboratory instruments, manuals, and sup-
plies.

5583 Instron Corporation
100 Royall Street
Canton, MA 02021-1089
781-828-2500
Fax: 781-575-5776
Laboratory and scientific equipment, supplies and furniture.

5584 Johnsonite
16910 Munn Road
Chagrin Falls, OH 44023-5493
800-899-8916
Fax: 440-632-5643

Physical education mats, matting and
floors.

5585 Justrite Manufacturing Company
2454 E Dempster Street
Des Plaines, IL 60016-5315
847-298-9250
Fax: 847-298-3429
E-mail: justrite@justritemfg.com
http://www.justritemfg.com
Supplies and equipment aimed at the scientific classroom or laboratory.

5586 KLM Bioscientific
8888 Clairemont Mesa Boulevard
Suite D
San Diego, CA 92123
858-571-5562
Fax: 858-571-5587
A mail order company that provides high
quality, reasonably priced, on time living
and preserved biological specimens. The
Biology Store also carries a wide range of
instructional materials including books,
charts, models and videos. Also available
is a wide range of general labware.

Loli Victorio, President

**5587 Ken-a-Vision Manufacturing
Company**
5615 Raytown Road
Kansas City, MO 64133-3388
816-353-4787
Fax: 816-358-5072
E-mail: info@ken-a-vision.com
http://www.ken-a-vision.com
Video Flex, Vison Viewer, Pupil CAM, Mi-
croscopes and Microrojectors

Steve Dunn, Domestic/International Op.
Ben Hoke, Sales Manger

5588 Kepro Circuit Systems
3640 Scarlet Oak Boulevard
Kirkwood, MO 63122-6606
800-325-3878
Fax: 636-861-9109
Laboratory equipment.

5589 Kewaunee Scientific Corporation
2700 W Front Street
Statesville, NC 28677-2894
704-873-7202
Fax: 704-873-1275
E-mail: humanresources@kewaunee.com
http://www.kewaunee.com
Science and laboratory supplies.

Bob Neals, Human Resources

5590 Knex Education Catalog
Knex Education
2990 Bergey Road
PO Box 700
Hatfield, PA 19440-0700
888-ABC-KNEX
E-mail: abcknex@knex.com
http://www.knexeducation.com
Hands-on, award-winning curriculum supported K-12 math, science and technology
sets.

5591 Koffler Sales Company
100A Oakwood Road e
Lake Zurich, IL 60047-1524
847-438-1152
800-323-0951
Fax: 847-438-1514
http://www.kofflersales.com
Floor mats, Matting and stair treads.

5592 Komodo Dragon
PO Box 822
The Dalles, OR 97058-0822
541-773-5808
Museum-quality fossils and minerals.

5593 Kreonite
715 E 10th Street N
Wichita, KS 67214-2918
316-263-1111
Fax: 316-263-6829
Laboratory equipment, furniture and hardware.

5594 Kruger & Eckels
1406 E Wilshire Avenue
Santa Ana, CA 92705-4423
714-547-5165
Fax: 714-547-2009
Laboratory and scientific instruments for institutional or educational use.

5595 LEGO Data
PO Box 1600
Enfield, CT 06083-1600
860-749-2291
Fax: 860-763-7477
Curriculum programs and materials for science education.

5596 LINX System
Science Source
PO Box 727
Waldoboro, ME 04572-0727
207-832-6344
800-299-5469
Fax: 207-832-7281
E-mail: info@thesciencesource.com
http://www.thesciencesource.com
A building system that integrates science, mathematics and technology at the K-9 level.

5597 Lab Safety Supply
PO Box 1368
Janesville, WI 53547-1368
608-754-2345
Fax: 800-543-9910
Extensive variety of school products, including lab and safety apparel and floorcoverings.

5598 Lab Volt Systems
PO Box 686
Farmingdale, NJ 07727-0686
Educational materials and equipment for the science educator.

5599 Lab-Aids
17 Colt Center
Ronkonkoma, NY 11779-6949
631-737-1133
800-381-8003
Fax: 631-737-1286
E-mail: mkt@lab-aids.com
http://www.lab-aids.com
Science kits, published curriculum materials.

John Weatherby, Sales/Marketing Director
David M Frank, President

5600 Labconco Corporation
8811 Prospect Avenue
Kansas City, MO 64132-2696
816-333-8811
Fax: 816-363-0130
Laboratory equipment and supplies.

5601 Lakeside Manufacturing
1977 S Allis Street
Milwaukee, WI 53207-1295
414-481-3900
Fax: 414-481-9313
Laboratory and scientific instruments, equipment, furniture and supplies.

5602 Lane Science Equipment Company
225 W 34th Street
Suite 1412
New York, NY 10122-1496
212-563-0663
Fax: 212-465-9440
Scientific equipment, technology and supplies.

5603 Lasy USA
1309 Webster Avenue
Fort Collins, CO 80524-2756
800-444-2126
Fax: 970-221-4352
Building sets that encourage children to encounter technology through problem solving activities, planning, co-operation and perseverance. Allows students to build and learn programming skills in areas of communication, construction, manufacturing and transportation.

Dave Nayak

5604 Learning Technologies
40 Cameron Avenue
Somerville, MA 02144-2404
617-628-1459
800-537-8703
Fax: 617-628-8606
E-mail: starlab@starlab.com
http://www.starlab.com
STARLAB portable planetarium systems and the Project STAR hands-on science materials.

Jane Sadler, President

5605 Leica Microsystems EAD
PO Box 123
Buffalo, NY 14240-0123
716-686-3000
Fax: 716-686-3085
Educational microscopes for elementary through university applications.

5606 Life Technologies
7335 Executive Way
Suite A
Frederick, MD 21704-8354
716-774-6700
800-952-9166
Fax: 716-774-6727
Supplier of biology and cell culture products.

5607 Lyon Electric Company
1690 Brandywine Avenue
Chula Vista, CA 91911-6021
619-216-3400
Fax: 619-216-3434
Electrical tabletop incubators for science classrooms and tabletop animal intensive care units, hatchers and brooders.

Caroline Vazquez, Sales Manager
Jose Madrigal, Marketing Manager

5608 Magnet Source
607 S Gilbert Street
Castle Rock, CO 80104-2221
303-688-3966
888-293-9190
Fax: 303-688-5303
E-mail: magnet@magnetsource.com
http://www.magnetsource.com
Educational magnetic products and magnetic toys designed to stimulate creativity and encourage exploration of science with fun magnets. Kits include experiments, fun games, activities and powerful magnets. Moo Magnets, rare earth magnets, horseshoes, and bulk magnets.

Jim Madsen, Sales Manager

5609 Meiji Techno America
Meiji Techno America
2186 Bering Drive
San Jose, CA 95131-2041
408-428-9654
800-832-0060
Fax: 408-428-0472
http://www.meijitechno.com
A full line of elementary, secondary, grade school and college-level microscopes and accessories.

James J Dutkiewicz, General Manager

5610 Metrologic Instruments
Coles Road at Route 42
Blackwood, NJ 08012
800-436-3876
Fax: 856-228-0653
Manufactures low-power lasers and laser accessories for the classroom, a range of helium-neon lasers, a modulated VLD laser, optics lab, sandbox holography kit, speed of light lab, optics bench system and digital laser power meter, as well as a selection of pin carriers, mounting pins, lenses and mirrors. Sponsors the Physics Bowl, a yearly national physics competition for high school students by the American Association of Physics Teachers.

Betty Williams

5611 Modern School Supplies
PO Box 958
Hartford, CT 06143-0958
860-243-9565
Fax: 800-934-7206
Products for hands-on science education.

5612 Mohon International
1600 Porter Court
Paris, TN 38242
731-642-4251
Fax: 731-642-4262
Classroom equipment and supplies, directed at the scientific classroom and laboratory.

5613 Museum Products Company
84 Route 27
Mystic, CT 06355-1226
860-536-6433
800-395-5400
Fax: 860-572-9589
E-mail: museumprod@aol.com
http://www.museumproducts.net
Field guides, rock collections, environmental puzzles, posters, charts, books, magnets, magnifiers, microscopes and other lab equipment. Also weather simulators, physics demonstration, games, toys in space, animal track replicas and fossils. Free catalog.

John Bannister, President

5614 Nalge Company
PO Box 20365
Rochester, NY 14602-0365
585-586-8800
800-625-4327
Fax: 585-586-8987
Plastic labware and safety products for the scientific classroom.

5615 National Instruments
6504 Bridge Point Parkway
Austin, TX 78730-5039
512-794-0100
Fax: 512-683-5794
Laboratory/scientific instruments.

5616 National Optical & Scientific Instruments
11113 Landmark 35 Drive
San Antonio, TX 78233-5786
210-590-7010
800-275-3716
Fax: 210-590-1104
E-mail: natlopt@sbcglobal.net
http://www.nationaloptical.com
Wholesale distributor of national comppound, stero and digital miocroscopes for K-12 and college.

Michael Hart, Director Sales/Marketing

5617 Ohaus Corporation
19 A Chapin Road
Pine Brook, NJ 07058-1408
973-377-9000
800-672-7722
Fax: 973-593-0359
Scientific supplies and equipment for the classroom or laboratory.

5618 PASCO Scientific
10101 Foothills Boulevard
Roseville, CA 95747-7100
916-786-3800
800-772-8700
Fax: 916-786-7565
E-mail: jbrown@pasco.com
http://ww.pasco.com
US manufacturers of physics apparatus and probe warer that enable teachers to improve science literacy and meet the standards

Justine Brown, Copy Writer

5619 Quest Aerospace Education
350 E 18th Street
Yuma, AZ 85364
602-595-9506
Fax: 520-783-9534
A complete line of model rockets and related teaching materials.

5620 Resources for Teaching Elementary School Science
National Academy Press
Arts & Industries Bldg Room 1201
900 Jefferson Drive SW
Washington, DC 20560-0403
202-287-2063
Fax: 202-287-2070
E-mail: outreach@nas.edu
http://www.si.edu
Resource guides for elementary, middle school, and high school science teachers. Annotated guides to hands-on, inquiry-centered curriculum materials and sources of help in teaching science from kindergarten through sixth grades. Produced by the National Science Resources Center.

National Science Resources Center, Author
Douglas Lapp, Executive Director

5621 Rheometrics
1 Possumtown Road
Piscataway, NJ 08854-2100
732-560-8550
Laboratory/science supplies and equipment.

5622 SARUT
107 Horatio Street
New York, NY 10014-1569
212-691-9453
Science and nature-related educational tools.

5623 Safe-T-Rack Systems
4325 Dominguez Road
Suite A
Rocklin, CA 95677-2146
916-632-1121
Fax: 916-632-1173
Laboratory furniture, safety storage containers and equipment.

5624 Sargent-Welch Scientific Company
911 Commerce Court
Buffalo Grove, IL 60089-2375
847-459-6625
Models, books and instruments for the scientific classroom.

5625 Science Instruments Company
6122 Reisterstown Road
Baltimore, MD 21215-3423
410-358-7810
Develops, manufactures and markets unique hands-on programs in biotechnology, biomedical instrumentation, telecommunications, electronics and industrial controls.

5626 Science Source
PO Box 727
Waldoboro, ME 04572-0727
207-832-6344
800-299-5469
Fax: 207-832-7281
E-mail: info@thesciencesource.com
http://www.thesciencesource.com
Design technology books, teacher resource and student books on design and technology, design technology materials, equipment and supplies used in the construction of design challenges.

Michelle Winter, Sales/Marketing Support
Rudolf Graf, President

5627 Science for Today & Tomorrow
1840 E 12th Street
Mishawaka, IN 46544
574-258-5397
Fax: 574-258-5594
Hands-on science activities packaged for K-3 students.

5628 Scientific Laser Connection, Incorporated
5021 N 55th Avenue
Suite 10
Glendale, AZ 85301-7535
623-939-6711
877-668-7844
Fax: 623-939-3369
E-mail: sales@slclaser.com
http://www.slclasers.com
Laser education modules.

Don Morris, President
Travis Gatrin, Service

5629 Shain/Shop-Bilt
509 Hemlock Street
Philipsburg, PA 16866-2937
814-342-2820
Fax: 814-342-6180
Laboratory casework and cabinets.

5630 Sheldon Lab Systems
PO Box 836
Crystal Springs, MS 39059-0836
601-892-2731
Fax: 601-892-4364
Laboratory casework and technical equipment for K-12, college and university level.

5631 Skilcraft
CRAFT House Corporation
328 N Westwood Avenue
Toledo, OH 43607-3317
419-537-9090
Fax: 419-537-9160
Microchemistry sets.

5632 Skullduggery Kits
624 S B Street
Tustin, CA 92780-4318
800-336-7745
Fax: 714-832-1215
Social studies kits offers hands-on learning, art projects, complete lesson plans, authentic replicas, and challenging products designed for small groups of students with increasing levels of difficulty.

5633 Skulls Unlimited International
10313 S Sunnylane Road
Oklahoma City, OK 73160
405-794-9300
800-659-SKUL
Fax: 405-794-6985
E-mail: sales@skullsunlimited.com
http://www.skullsunlimited.com
Leading supplier of specimen supplies to the educational community.

5634 Society of Automotive Engineers
400 Commonwealth Drive
Warrendale, PA 15086-7511
724-776-4841
877-606-7323
Fax: 724-776-5760
E-mail: info@sae.org
http://www.sae.org
Award-winning science unit for grades 4-6.

Steve Yaeger, Corporate PR Manager
Kathleen O'Conner, K-12 Education Program Mgr

5635 Southern Precision Instruments Company
3419 E Commerce Street
San Antonio, TX 78220-1322
210-212-5055
800-417-5055
Fax: 210-212-5062
E-mail: spico@flash.net
http://www.flash.net/spico
Microscopes and microprojectors for grades K-1-K-12 and college levels. Stereo and compound microscopes, along with CCTV color systems.

Victor Spiroff, VP/General Manager

5636 Southland Instruments
17741 Metzler Lane
Unit A
Huntington Beach, CA 92647-6246
714-847-5007
Fax: 714-893-3613
Microscopes.

5637 Spectronics Corporation
956 Brush Hollow Road
Westbury, NY 11590-1714
516-333-4840
800-274-8888
Fax: 800-491-6868
E-mail: vvvv@aol.com
http://www.spectroline.com
Laboratory and scientific classroom equipment, hardware and shelving.

Gloria Blusk, Manager Customer Service
Vincent McKenna, Publicist

5638 Spitz
Transnational Industries
PO Box 198
Chadds Ford, PA 19317-0198
215-459-5200
Offers scientific and laboratory instruments and accessories.

5639 Swift Instruments
1190 N 4th Street
San Jose, CA 95112-4946
408-293-2380
Educational microscopes and other laboratory instruments.

5640 TEDCO
498 S Washington Street
Hagerstown, IN 47346-1596
765-489-4527
800-654-6357
Fax: 765-489-5752
E-mail: sales@tedcotoys.com
http://www.tedcotoys.com
Bill Nye Extreme Gyro, Prisms, Educational Toys Solar Science Kit.

Jane Shadle

5641 Telaire Systems
6489 Calle Real
Goleta, CA 93117-1538
805-964-1699
Fax: 805-964-2129
Laboratory instruments and hardware.

5642 Tooltron Industries
103 Parkway
Boerne, TX 78006-9224
830-249-8277
800-293-8134
Fax: 830-755-8134
E-mail: easyleut@gvtc.comt
http://www.tooltron.com
Scientific hardware and laboratory equipment, including instruments and accessories. School scissors and craft supplies.

Thomas Love, Owner/VP Marketing

5643 Triops
PO Box 10852
Pensacola, FL 32524-0852
850-479-4415
800-200-DINO
Fax: 850-479-3315
E-mail: triopsinc@aol.com
http://www.triops.com
Classroom activities and kits in environmental, ecological and biological sciences.

Dr. Eugene Hull, President
Peter Bender, Office Manager

5644 Trippense Planetarium Company
Science First
95 Botsford Place
Buffalo, NY 14216
716-874-0133
800-875-3214
Fax: 716-874-9853
E-mail: info@sciencefirst.com
http://www.sciencefirst.com
Astronomy and earth science models and materials, including the Trippense planetarium, Elementary planetarium, Copernican and Ptolemic solar systems, Milky Way model, Explore Celestial Globes and the patented top quality educational astronomy models since 1905.

Kris Spors, Customer Service Manager
Nancy Bell, President

5645 Unilab
967 Mabury Road
San Jose, CA 95133
800-288-9850
Fax: 408-975-1035
E-mail: unilab@richnet.net
http://www.unilabinc.com
Designs and manufactures products for teaching science and technology.

Gerald A Beer, VP

5646 Vibrac Corporation
16 Columbia Drive
Amherst, NH 03031-2304
603-882-6777
Fax: 603-271-3454
Scientific instruments and hardware.

5647 Wild Goose Company
5181 S 300 W
Murray, UT 84107-4709
801-466-1172
Hands-on science kits for elementary-aged students 3 and up and resource books for all levels of general science.

5648 Wildlife Supply Company
95 Botsford Place
Buffalo, NY 14216-d
716-877-9518
800-799-8301
Fax: 716-874-9853
E-mail: goto@wildco.com
http://www.wildco.com
Aquatic sampling equipment including Fieldmaster Field Kits, Water Bottle Kits, Secchi Disks, line and messengers and a NEW Mini Ponar bottom grab. Also, a variety of professional Wildco bottom grabs, water bottles, plankton nets, hand corers and other materials.

Aaron Bell, Product Manager
Bruce Izard, Customer Service Manager

5649 WoodKrafter Kits
PO Box 808
Yarmouth, ME 04096-0808
207-846-3722
Fax: 207-846-1019
Science kits, hands-on curriculum-based science kits for ages 4 and up, classroom packs, supplies and science materials also available.

Sports & Playground Equipment

5650 American Playground Corporation
6406 Production Drive
Anderson, IN 46013-9408
765-642-0288
800-541-1602
Fax: 765-649-7162
E-mail: sales@american-playgroud.com
http://www.american-playground.com
Playground equipment and supplies.

Julie Morson, Inside Sales Manager
Marty Bloyd, General Manager

5651 American Swing Products
2533 N Carson Street
Suite 1062
Carson City, NV 89706-0147
800-433-2573
800-433-2573
Fax: 775-883-4874
E-mail: play@americanswing.com
http://www.americanswing.com
Replacement playground parts, including commercial and residential swing sets, swing hangers for pipes and wood beams, spring animals, S-hooks, spring connectors, and more.

Susan Watson, President

5652 BCI Burke Company
660 Van Dyne Road
Fond Du Lac, WI 54937-1447
920-921-9220
Fax: 920-921-9566
Playground equipment.

5653 Belson Manufacturing
111 N River Road
North Aurora, IL 60542-1396
800-323-5664
Playground equipment.

5654 Colorado Time Systems
1551 E 11th Street
Loveland, CO 80537-5056
970-667-1000
800-279-0111
Fax: 970-667-5876
E-mail: sales@colooradotimes.com
http://www.coloradotime.com
Been the system of choice for sports timing and scoring. Has a timing system for almost every sport including swimming, basketball, football, baseball, track, soccer and most others. Has a wide variety of displays ranging from fixed digit scoreboards to animation LED boards to fullcolor video displays and ribbon boards.

Randy Flint, Sr Sales Representative
Rick Connell, CDS Sales Manager

5655 Constructive Playthings
1227 E 119th Street
Grandview, MO 64030-1178
Playground, recreational and indoor fun equipment for children grades PreK-3.

5656 Creative Outdoor Designs
142 Pond Drive
Lexington, SC 29073-8009
803-957-9259
Fax: 803-957-7152
Playground equipment.

5657 Curtis Marketing Corporation
2550 Rigel Road
Venice, FL 34293-3200
941-493-8085
Playground equipment.

5658 GameTime
PO Box 680121
Fort Payne, AL 35968-0099
256-845-5610
800-235-2440
Fax: 256-845-9361
E-mail: info@gametime.com
http://www.gametime.com
Playground equipment.

Doris Dellinger, Marketing Service
Manager

5659 Gared Sports
707 N 2nd Street
Suite 220
Saint Louis, MO 63102
800-325-2682
Fax: 314-421-6014
E-mail: laura@garedsports.com
http://www.garedsports.com
Basketball, Volleyball, Soccer, Equipment
and training aids for indoor and outdoor facilities.

Laura St George, Sales/Marketing
Manager

5660 Gerstung/Gym-Thing
6308 Blair Hill Lane
Baltimore, MD 21209-2102
800-922-3575
Physical education mats, matting and
floorcoverings.

5661 Grounds for Play
1401 E Dallas Road
Mansfield, TX 76063
817-477-5482
800-552-7529
Fax: 817-477-1140
E-mail:
jimdempsey@groundsforplay.com
http://www.groundsforplay.com
Playground equipment, flooring,
floorcoverings, play eviroment design,
lanscape architecure, installation, and
safety insepection.

Jim Dempsey, Senior VP
Emily Smith, Office Manager

5662 Iron Mountain Forge
One Iron Mountain Drive
Farmington, MO 63640
800-325-8828
Fax: 573-760-7441
Playground equipment.

5663 JCH International
978 E Hermitage Road NE
Rome, GA 30161-9641
800-328-9203
Coverings, mats and physical education
matting.

5664 Jaypro
Jaypro Sports
976 Hartford Tpke
Waterford, CT 06385-4002
860-447-3001
800-243-0533
Fax: 860-444-1779
E-mail: info@jaypro.com
http://www.jaypro.com
Sports equipment.

Linda Andels, Marketing Manager
Bill Wild, VP Sales/Marketing

5665 Kidstuff Playsystems
5400 Miller Avenue
Gary, IN 46403-2844
800-255-0153
Fax: 219-938-3340
E-mail:
rhagelberg@kidstuffplaysystems.com
http://www.fun-zone.com
Preschool and grade school playground
equipment, Health Trek Fitness Course,
park site furnishings.

Dick Hagelberg, CEO

5666 Kompan
7717 New Market Street
Olympia, WA 98501
360-943-6374
800-426-9788
Fax: 360-943-5575
http://www.kompan.com
Unique playgrond equipment.

Tom Grover, Marketing Director

5667 LA Steelcraft Products
1975 Lincoln Avenue
Pasadena, CA 91103-1395
626-798-7401
800-371-2438
Fax: 626-798-1482
E-mail: info@lasteelcraft.com
http://www.lasteelcraft.com
Manufacturer of quality athletic, park and
playground equipment for schools, parks
and industry. Features indoor/outdoor fi-
berglass furniture, court and field equipment, site furnishings, bike racks,
flagpoles, baseball and basketball backstops.

James D Holt, President
John C Gaudesi, COO

5668 Landscape Structures
PO Box 198
Delano, MN 55328-0198
612-972-3391
Playground equipment.

5669 MMI-Federal Marketing Service
PO Box 241367
Montgomery, AL 36124-1367
334-286-0700
Fax: 334-286-0711
Playground equipment, sports timers,
clocks and school supplies.

5670 Matworks
Division of Janitex Rug Service
Corporation
11900 Old Baltimore Pike
Beltsville, MD 20705-1265
800-523-5179
Fax: 301-595-0740
Mats, matting and floorcoverings for en-
trances, gymnasiums, and all other facilities where the potential for slip and fall
exists.

**5671 Miracle Recreation Equipment
Company**
PO Box 420
Monett, MO 65708-0420
417-235-6917
Fax: 417-235-6816
Playground and recreation equipment.

5672 National Teaching Aids
PO Box 2121
Fort Collins, CO 80522
970-484-7445
800-289-9299
Fax: 970-484-1198
E-mail: bevans@amep.com
http://www.hubbardscientific.com
Learning math, alphabet, and geography
skills is easy with our Clever Catch Balls.
These colorful 24" inflatable vinyl balls
provide an excellent way for children to
practice math, alphabet and geography
skills. Excellent learning tool in organized
classroom activities, on the playground, or
at home.

Barbara Evans, Customer Service
Manager
Candy Coffman, National Sales Manger

**5673 New Braunfels General Store
International**
3150 Interstate H 35 S
New Braunfels, TX 78130-7927
830-620-4000
Fax: 830-620-0598
Playground equipment, supplies and class-
room supplies.

5674 Outback Play Centers
1280 W Main Street
Sun Prairie, WI 53590-0010
608-825-2140
800-338-0522
Fax: 608-825-2114
http://www.outbackplaycenters.com
Playground equipment.

Jack Garczynskl, President

5675 PlayDesigns
1000 Buffalo Road
Lewisburg, PA 17837-9795
800-327-7571
Fax: 570-522-3030
E-mail: webmaster@playdesigns.com
http://www.playdesigns.com
Playground and recreational equipment,
flooring and matting.

5676 Playground Environments
22 Old Country Road
PO Box 578
Quogue, NY 11959
631-231-1300
800-662-0922
Fax: 631-231-1329
E-mail: peplay@mindspring.com
Designs and manufactures integrated play
and recreational areas for children, providing them with new experiences in a safe, accessible, educationally supportive and fun
environment.

5677 Playnix
3530 S Logan Street
Englewood, CO 80110-3731
303-761-5630
Fax: 303-781-6749
Wood products and playground equipment.

5678 Playworld Systems
1000 Buffalo Road
Lewisburg, PA 17837-9795
570-522-9800
800-233-8404
Fax: 570-522-3030
E-mail:
webmaster@playworldsystems.com
http://www.playworldsystems.com
Playground and recreational equipment.

5679 Porter Athletic Equipment Company
Porter Athletic Equipment Company
2500 S 25th Avenue
Broadview, IL 60155-3870
708-338-2000
800-947-6783
Fax: 708-338-2060
E-mail: porter@porter-ath.com
http://www.porter-ath.com
Athletic equipment, floorcoverings, mats and supplies.

Dan Morgan, VP Sales/Marketing

5680 Quality Industries
PO Box 765
Hillsdale, MI 49242-0765
800-766-9458
Fax: 517-439-1878
Recycled plastic park and playground equipment.

5681 Real ACT Prep Guide
Peterson's, A Nelnet Company
Princeton Pike Corporate Center
2000 Lenox Drive PO Box 67005
Lawrenceville, NJ 08648
609-896-1800
800-338-3282
Fax: 609-896-4531
Familiarizes students with the test's format, reviews skills, and provides the all-important practice that helps build confidence.

621 pages
ISBN: 0-768919-75-4

Elaine Bender, Mark Weinfeld, et al., Author

5682 Recreation Creations
PO Box 955
Hillsdale, MI 49242-0955
517-439-0300
800-888-0977
Fax: 517-439-0303
Heavy duty park and playground equipment for school and public use. Equipment is both colorful and safe.

DC Shaneour

5683 Roppe Corporation
1602 N Union Street
Fostoria, OH 44830-1958
419-435-8546
Fax: 419-435-1056
Floorcoverings, mats and matting.

5684 Safety Play
10460 Roosevelt Boulevard
#295
St Petersburgh, FL 33716-3818
727-522-0061
888-878-0244
Fax: 727-522-0061
http://www.mindspring.com
Playground and recreational accident consultants. Experienced in insepctions, design, expert witness. Creators of Playground Safety Signs as required to be on the playground.

Scott Burmon, Contact

5685 Sport Court
939 S 700 W
Salt Lake City, UT 84104-1504
801-972-0260
800-421-8112
Fax: 801-975-7752
E-mail: info@sportcourt.com
http://www.sportcourt.com

Sport flooring, portable flooring, outdoor-indoor educational institutions.
Finnika Lundmark, Director Marketing

5686 Sport Floors
PO Box 1478
Cartersville, GA 30120-1478
800-322-3567
Fax: 574-293-2381
Sport floors, flooring, floorcoverings, mats and matting.

5687 Sportmaster
6031 Broad Street Mall
Pittsburgh, PA 15206-3009
412-243-5100
Fax: 412-731-3052
Playground equipment, sports timers and clocks.

5688 Stackhouse Athletic Equipment Company
1505 Front Street NE
Salem, OR 97303-6949
503-363-1840
Fax: 503-363-0511
E-mail: bob@stackhouseathletic.com
http://www.stackhouseathletic.com
Volleyball, soccer, football and baseball hardgoods.

Greg Henshaw, VP Marketing

5689 Swedes Systems - HAGS Play USA
2180 Stratingham Drive
Dublin, OH 43016-8907
Fax: 614-889-9026
Playground safety consultants.

5690 Ultra Play Systems
Parek Stuff
425 Sycamore Street
Anderson, IN 46016-1000
800-45 -LTRA
Playground and recreational equipment.

5691 Wausau Tile
PO Box 1520
Wausau, WI 54402-1520
715-359-3121
800-388-8728
Fax: 715-355-4627
E-mail: wtile@wausautile.com
http://www.wausautile.com
Playground and recreation equipment.

Rob Geurink, Furnishings Division Manager

5692 Wear Proof Mat Company
2156 W Fulton Street
Chicago, IL 60612-2392
312-733-4570
Fax: 800-322-7105
http://www.notracks.com
Mats, matting and floorcoverings for the physical education class.

5693 Wolverine Sports
745 State Circle
Ann Arbor, MI 48108-1647
734-761-5690
Fax: 800-654-4321
Playground, sports and physical fitness furniture and equipment.

General

5694 A-V Online
National Information Center for
Educational Media
PO Box 8640
Albuquerque, NM 87198
505-265-3591
800-926-8328
Fax: 505-256-1080
E-mail: nicem@nicem.com
http://www.nicem.com
A CD-ROM that contains over 400,000 citations with abstracts, to non-print educational materials for all educational levels. It is available on an annual subscription basis and comes with semiannual updates.

Lisa Savard, Marketing and Sales

5695 AASA Daily News
American Association of School
Administrators
801 N Quincy Street
Suite 700
Arlington, VA 22203-1730
703-528-0700
Fax: 703-841-1543
E-mail: info@aasa.org
http://www.aasa.org

Jay Goldman, Editor

5696 ACT
2201 N Dodge Street
PO Box 168
Iowa City, IA 52243-0168
319-337-1000
Fax: 319-339-3021
http://www.act.org
Help individuals and organizations make informed decisions about education and work.

5697 AMX Corporation
11995 Forestgate Drive
Dallas, TX 75243-5481
972-644-3048
Fax: 972-624-7153
Multiple products, equipment and supplies.

5698 ASC Electronics
2 Kees Pl
Merrick, NY 11566-3625
516-623-3206
Fax: 516-378-2672
High tech multimedia system. Completely software driven, featuring interactive video, audio and data student drills. Novell network. System includes CD-ROM, laserdisc and digital voice card technology.

5699 Accelerated Math
Renaissance Learning
PO Box 8036
Wisconsin Rapids, WI 54495-8036
715-424-3636
800-338-4204
Fax: 715-424-4242
E-mail: answers@renlearn.com
http://www.renlearn.com
Math management software that helps teachers increase student math achievement in grades 1 through calculus.

5700 Accelerated Reader
Renaissance Learning
PO Box 8036
Wisconsin Rapids, WI 54495-8036
715-424-3636
800-338-4204
Fax: 715-424-4242
E-mail: answers@renlearn.com
http://www.renlearn.com
Software program that helps teachers manage literature-based reading.

5701 Actrix Systems
6315 San Ignacio Avenue
San Jose, CA 95119-1202
800-422-8749
Fax: 509-744-2851
Computer networks.

5702 Allen Communications
5 Triac Center
5th Floor
Salt Lake Cty, UT 84180
801-537-7800
Fax: 801-537-7805
Software.

5703 Alltech Electronics Company
602 Garrison Street
Oceanside, CA 92054-4865
760-721-0093
Fax: 760-732-1460
Computer hardware.

5704 Anchor Pad Products
Anchor Pad Products
11105 Dana Circle
Cypress, CA 90630-5133
714-799-4071
800-626-2467
Fax: 714-799-4094
E-mail: kris@anchor.com
http://www.anchorpad.com
Cost effective physical security systems for computers, computer peripherals and office equipment.

Kris Jones, Marketing Associate
Melanie Rustle, Marketing Associate

5705 Apple Computer
1 Infinite Loop
Cupertino, CA 95014-2084
408-996-1010
Fax: 408-974-2786
Offers a wide selection of software systems and programs for the student, educator, professional and classroom use. Program areas include reading, science, social studies, history, language arts, mathematics and more.

5706 Ascom Timeplex
400 Chestnut Ridge Road
Woodcliff Lake, NJ 07675-7604
201-646-1571
Fax: 201-646-0485
Computer networks.

5707 BGS Systems
128 Technology Drive
Waltham, MA 02453-8909
617-891-0000
Facility planning and evaluation software.

5708 BLS Tutorsystems
5153 W Woodmill Drive
Wilmington, DE 19808-4067
800-545-7766
Computer software.

5709 Broderbund Software
500 Redwood Boulevard
Novato, CA 94947-6921
319-395-9626
800-223-8941
Fax: 319-395-7449
Educational software.

5710 Bulletin Boards for Busy Teachers

http://www.geocities.com/VisionTeacher
wv/
Bulletin board tips and education links.

5711 CASL Software
6818 86th Street E
Puyallup, WA 98371-6450
206-845-7738
Educational software for schools and institutions in all areas of interest.

5712 CCU Software
PO Box 6724
Charleston, WV 25362-0724
800-843-5576
Fax: 800-321-4297
Educational software.

5713 CCV Software
5602 36th Street S
Fargo, ND 58104-6768
800-541-6078
Fax: 800-457-6953
All varieties of software and hardware for the educational fields of interest including language arts, math, social studies, science, history and more.

**5714 Cambridge Development
Laboratory**
86 West Street
Waltham, MA 02451-1110
800-637-0047
Fax: 781-890-2894
E-mail: customerservice@edumatch.com
http://www.edumatch.com
Meets all educational software needs in language arts, mathematics, science, social studies early learning and special education.

5715 Chariot Software Group
123 Camino De La Reina W Building
San Diego, CA 92108-3002
619-298-0202
800-242-7468
Fax: 619-491-0021
E-mail: info@chariot.com
http://www.chariot.com
Academic software.

5716 Child's Play Software
5785 Emporium Square
Columbus, OH 43231-2802
614-833-1836
Fax: 614-833-1837
Markets learning games and creative software to schools.

5717 Claris Corporation
5201 Patrick Henry Drive
Santa Clara, CA 95054-1171
800-747-7483
Educational software.

5718 Classroom Direct
20200 E 9 Mile Road
Saint Clair Shores, MI 48080-1791
800-777-3642
Fax: 800-628-6250

Full line of hardware and software for Mac, IBM and Apple II at discount prices.

5719 College Board/SAT
45 Columbus Avenue
New York, NY 10023-6992
217-713-8000
http://http://sat.org/

5720 Computer City Direct
2000 Two Tandy Center
Fort Worth, TX 76102
800-538-0586
Hardware.

5721 Computer Friends
10200 SW Eastridge Street
Portland, OR 97225
800-547-3303
Fax: 503-643-5379
E-mail: cfi@cfriends.com
http://www.cfriends.com
Computer hardware, software and networks, printer support products.

Jimmy Moglia, Marketing Director

5722 Data Command
PO Box 548
Kankakee, IL 60901-0548
800-528-7390
Educational software.

5723 Davidson & Associates
19840 Pioneer Avenue
Torrance, CA 90503-1690
800-545-7677
Educational software and systems.

5724 Dell Computer Corporation
9595 Arboretum Boulevard
Austin, TX 78759-6337
512-338-4400
800-388-1450
Hardware.

5725 Digital Divide Network

http://www.digitaldividenetwork.org
Knowledge to help everyone succeed in the digital age.

5726 Digital Equipment Corporation
Educational Computer Systems Group
2 Iron Way
Marlboro, MA 01752
Computer hardware and networks.

5727 Don Johnston Developmental Equipment
1000 N Rand Road
Suite 115
Wauconda, IL 60084-1190
847-526-2682
800-999-4660
Develops educational software for special needs. Products include the Ukandu Series for emergent literacy, LD, ESL, students Co-Writer and Write: OutLoud.

5728 Edmark Corporation
6727 185th Avenue NE
PO Box 97021
Redmond, WA 98052-5037
425-556-8400
800-691-2986
Fax: 425-556-8430
Markets educational software.

5729 EduQuest, An IBM Company
PO Box 2150
Atlanta, GA 30301-2150
Offers exciting educational software in various fields of interest including history, social studies, reading, math and language arts, as well as computers.

5730 Educational Activities
1937 Grand Avenue
Baldwin, NY 11510-2889
516-223-4666
800-645-3739
Fax: 516-623-9282
http://www.edact.com
Supplemental materials.

Roni Hofbauer, Office Manager
Carol Stern, VP

5731 Educational Resources
1550 Executive Drive
Elgin, IL 60123-9330
630-213-8681
Fax: 630-213-8681
The largest distributor of educational software and technology in the education market. Features Mac, APL, ligs and IBM school versions, lab packs, site licenses, networking and academic versions. Hardware, accessories and multimedia is also available.

5732 Electronic Specialists Inc.
PO Box 389
Natick, MA 01760-0004
508-655-1532
810-225-4876
Fax: 508-653-0268
E-mail: esp@elect-spec.com
http://www.elect-spec.com
Computer and electronics, including networks and computer systems plus transformers and power converters.

F Stifter, President

5733 Environmental Systems Research Institute
380 New York Street
Redlands, CA 92373-8118
Demonstrates a full range of geographic information system software products.

5734 Eversan Inc.
34 Main Street
Whitesboro, NY 13492
800-383-6060
Fax: 315-736-4058
E-mail: sales&eversan.com
http://www.eversan.com
Announcement boards, scoreboards and classroom supplies, sports timers and clocks.

Michelle Moran, Sales Representative
Elsa Kucherna, Sales Representative

5735 GAMCO Educational Materials
PO Box 1911
Big Spring, TX 79721-1911
800-351-1404
Publishes software in math, language arts, reading, social studies, early childhood education and teacher tools for Macintosh, Apple, IBM and MS-DOS compatible.

5736 Games2Learn
1936 East Deere Avenue
Suite 120
Santa Ana, CA 92705
714-751-4263
888-713-4263
Fax: 714-442-0869
E-mail: CustomerService@Games2Learn.com
http://www.games2learn.com
Develops, markets and provides children and adults with quality, fun, interactive educational products designed to increase their skills in language, math and general knowledge. Creator of The Phonics Game.

5737 Gateway Learning Corporation
665 3rd Street
Suite 225
San Francisco, CA 94107
800-544-7323
http://www.hop.com
Develop and sell innovative educational products for home learning.

5738 Greene & Associates
1834 E Manhatton Drive
Tempe, AZ 85282-5857
480-491-1151
Educational software.

5739 Grolier
PO Box 1716
Danbury, CT 06816
800-371-3908
Fax: 800-456-4402
Multimedia software for education.

5740 Hubbell
Kellems Division
14 Lords Hill Road
Stonington, CT 06378-2604
860-535-5350
Fax: 860-535-1719
Computer hardware, software, systems, and networks.

5741 Indiana Cash Drawer
1315 S Miller Street
Shelbyville, IN 46176-2424
317-398-6643
Fax: 317-392-0958
Computer peripherals.

5742 Ingenuity Works
1123 Fir Avenue
Blaine, WA 98230-9702
604-412-1555
800-665-0667
Fax: 604-431-7996
E-mail: info@ingenuityworks.com
http://www.ingenuityworks.com
Publishes K-12 educational software for classroom use. Key curriculum areas include geography, keyboarding, and math (K-9). Network and district licenses are available.

Brigetta , Director Marketing

5743 Instructional Design
WIDS-Worldwide Instructional Design System
1 Foundation Circle
Waunakee, WI 53597-8914
608-849-2411
800-677-9437
Fax: 608-849-2468
E-mail: info@wids.org
http://www.wids.org
Performance-based curriculum design software and professional devlopment tools. Use software to write curriculum, imple-

ment standards, create assessments, and build in learning styles. Excellent upfront online design tool.

Robin Nickel, Associate Director

5744 Instructor
Scholastic
555 Broadway
New York, NY 10012-3919
212-343-6100
800-724-6527
Fax: 212-343-4801
http://www.scholastic.com/instructor
Edited for teachers, curriculum coordinators, principals and supervisors of primary grades through junior high school.

Monthly

Claudia Cohl, Publisher
Lynn Diamond, Advertising Director

5745 Jostens Learning Corporation
4920 Pacific Heights Boulevard
Suite 500
San Diego, CA 92121
858-587-0087
800-521-8538
Fax: 858-587-1629
Educational software and CD-ROM's.

5746 Journey Education
1325 Capital Parkway
Suite 130
Carrollton, TX 75006
800-874-9001
Fax: 972-245-3585
E-mail: sales@journeyed.com
http://www.journeyed.com
Software for students.

5747 Ken Cook Education Systems
9929 W Silver Spring Drive
PO Box 25267
Milwaukee, WI 53225-1024
800-362-2665
Fax: 414-466-0840
Classroom curricular software.

5748 Kensington Microwave
2855 Campus Drive
San Mateo, CA 94403-2510
650-572-2700
800-535-4242
Fax: 650-572-9675
http://www.kensington.com
Computer systems and peripherals.

5749 Lapis Technologies
1100 Marina Village Parkway
Alameda, CA 94501-1043
510-748-1600
Computer peripherals.

5750 Laser Learning Technologies
120 Lakeside Avenue
#3240
Seattle, WA 98122-6533
800-722-3505
Educational CD-ROM's and interactive videos.

5751 Lawrence Productions
1800 S 35th Street
Galesburg, MI 49053-9687
800-421-4157
Fax: 616-665-7060
More than 60 proven software titles for PreK to adult, covering problem solving, early learning hand leadership skills.

5752 Learning Company
500 Redwood Boulevard
Novato, CA 94947
800-825-4420
Fax: 877-864-2275
http://www.learningcompanyschool.com
School educational software.

5753 Library Corporation, Sales & Marketing
1501 Regency Way
Woodstock, GA 30189-5487
Computer networks.

5754 LinkNet
Introlink
1400 E Touhy Avenue
Suite 260
Des Plaines, IL 60018-3339
847-390-8700
Fax: 847-390-9435
Computer networks.

5755 MECC
6160 Summit Drive N
Minneapolis, MN 55430-2100
800-685-MECC
Educational software, hardware and overhead projectors.

5756 Mamopalire of Vermont
PO Box 24
Warren, VT 05674
802-496-4095
888-496-4094
Fax: 802-496-4096
E-mail: bethumpd@wcvt.com
http://www.bethumpd.com
Provides quality educational books and board games for the whole family.

Rebecca Cahilly, President
Glenn Cahilly, CEO

5757 McGraw-Hill Educational Resources
11 W 19th Street
New York, NY 10011-4209
800-442-9685
Fax: 972-228-1982
Educational software for all areas of interest including social studies, science, mathematics and reading.

5758 Microsoft Corporation
1 Microsoft Way
Redmond, WA 98052-8300
425-882-8080
Fax: 425-936-7329
One of the largest publishers and distributors of educational software, hardware, equipment and supplies.

5759 Misty City Software
11866 Slater Avenue NE
Kirkland, WA 98034-4103
206-820-2219
800-795-0049
Fax: 425-820-4298
Publisher of Grade Machine, gradebook software for Macintosh, MS-DOS, and Apple II. Grade Machine used by thousands of teachers in hundreds of schools worldwide. Grade Machine has full-screen editing, flexible reports, large class capacity, excellent documentation and reasonable cost.

Roberta Spiro, Business Manager
Russell Cruickshanks, Sales Manager

5760 NCR Corporation
1700 S Patterson Boulevard
Dayton, OH 45479-0002
937-445-5000
Computer networks, systems (large, mini, micro, medium and personal).

5761 NetLingo The Internet Dictionary
PO Box 627
Ojai, CA 93024
805-640-3754
Fax: 805-640-3654
E-mail: info@netlingo.com
http://www.NetLingo.com
A smart-looking and easy to understand dictionary of 3000 internet terms, 1200 chat acronyms, and much more. NetLingo is a modern reference book fo international students, educators, industry professionals, and online businesses and organizations.

528 pages Paperback
ISBN: 0-9706396-7-8

Erin Jansen, Author
Erin Jansen, Author/Publisher

5762 NetZero
2555 Townsgate Road
Westlake Village, CA 91361-2650
805-418-2020
Fax: 805-418-2075
http://www.netzero.com
Free Internet access.

5763 New Century Education Corporation
220 Old New Brunswick Road
Piscataway, NJ 08854
732-981-0820
800-833-6232
Fax: 732-981-0552
E-mail: jharrison@ncecorp.com
http://www.ncecorp.com
ILS systems.

Janice Harrison, Marketing Representative

5764 OnLine Educator

http://faldo.atmos.uiuc.edu/CLA
A comprehensive archive of educational sites with useful search capabilities and descriptions of the sites.

5765 Online Computer Systems
1 Progress Drive
Horsham, PA 19044-3502
CD-ROM networking, CD-ROM titles and CD-ROM tower units.

5766 PBS TeacherSource

http://www.pbs.org/teachersource
Includes an on-line inventory of more than 1,000 free lesson plans, teacher guides and other activities designed to complement PBS television programs.

5767 Parent Link
Parlant Technology
290 N University Avenue
Provo, UT 84601
801-373-9669
800-735-2930
Fax: 801-373-9697
E-mail: info@parlant.com
http://www.parlant.com
School to home communication systems allow scholls to create messages — emails, telephone calls, web content, printed letters, about student information, grades, at-

tendance, homework, and activities. Also provides inbound access via internet and telephone.

George Joeckel, Marketing

5768 Peopleware
1621 114th Avenue SE
Suite 120
Bellevue, WA 98004-6905
425-454-6444
Fax: 425-454-7634
Classroom curricular software.

5769 Phillips Broadband Networks
100 Fairgrounds Drive
Manlius, NY 13104-2437
315-682-9105
Fax: 315-682-1022
Computer networks.

5770 Pioneer New Media Technologies
2265 E 220th Street
Long Beach, CA 90810-1639
800-LAS-R ON
DRM-604X CD-ROM mini-changer, world's fastest CD-ROM drive for multimedia. Also offers special packages including The Mystery Reading Bundle, CLD-V2400RB which includes the CLD-V2400 LaserDisc player, educator's remote control, UC-V109BC barcode reader and membership in the Pioneers in Learning Club and The Case of the Missing Mystery Writer videodisc from Houghton Mifflin.

5771 Polaroid Corporation
575 Tech Square
Cambridge, MA 02139
781-386-2000
Fax: 781-386-3925
Computer repair, hardware and peripherals, equipment and various size systems.

5772 Power Industries
37 Walnut Street
Wellsley Hills, MA 02181
800-395-5009
Educational software.

5773 Quetzal Computers
1708 E 4th Street
Brooklyn, NY 11223-1925
718-375-1186
Computer systems and networks, peripherals and hardware.

5774 RLS Groupware
Realtime Learning Systems
2700 Connecticut Avenue NW
Washington, DC 20008-5330
202-483-1510
Classroom curricular software.

5775 Radio Shack
100 Throckmorton Street
Suite 1800
Ft. Worth, TX 76102
817-415-3700
Fax: 817-415-2335
Computer networks and peripherals.

Laura Moore, Sr VP Public Relations

5776 Rose Electronics
10850 Wilcrest Drive
Suite 900
Houston, TX 77099-3599
281-933-7673
Fax: 281-933-0044
Computer peripherals and hardware.

5777 STAR Reading & STAR Math
Renaissance Learning
PO Box 8036
Wisconsin Rapids, WI 54495-8036
715-424-3636
800-338-4204
Fax: 715-424-4242
E-mail: answers@renlearn.com
http://www.renlearn.com
Computer-adaptive tests provide instructional levels, grade equivalents and percentile ranks.

5778 SVE & Churchill Media
6677 N NW Highway
Chicago, IL 60631
773-775-9550
800-829-1900
Fax: 773-775-5091
E-mail: slucas@svemedia.com
http://www.svemedia.com
Has brought innovative media technology into america's pre-K through high school classrooms. By producing programs to satisfy state curriculum standards, SVE consistently provides educators with high-quality and award-winning videos, CD-ROMs, eLMods, and DVDs in science, social studies, english and health/guidance.

Sarah M Lucas, Communications Coordinator
Kelli Campbell, VP Marketing/Development

5779 School Cruiser
Time Cruiser Computing Corporation
9 Law Drive
3rd Floor, Ottawa, Ontario
Canada K1N 7G1
613-562-9847
877-450-9482
Fax: 613-562-4768
http://www.epals.com
School Cruiser provides online tools and resources to promote academic and community interaction. It lets you access and share school calenders, lesson plans, homework assignments, announcements and other school related information.

5780 SchoolHouse

http://www.encarta.msn.com/schoolhouse/maincontent.asp
The Encarta Lesson Collection and other educational resources.

5781 Seaman Nuclear Corporation
7315 S 1st Street
Oak Creek, WI 53154-2095
414-762-5100
Fax: 414-762-5106
Facility planning and evaluation software.

5782 Skills Bank Corporation
7104 Ambassador Road
Suite 1
Baltimore, MD 21244-2732
800-451-5726
Educational manufacturing company offering computer and electronic resources, software, programs and systems focusing on home education and tutoring.

5783 Sleek Software Corporation
2404 Rutland Drive
Suite 600
Austin, TX 78758
800-337-5335
Fax: 888-353-2900
http://www.sleek.com

Specializes in Algorithm-Based tutorial and test-generating software.

5784 Smartstuff Software
PO Box 82284
Portland, OR 97282-0284
415-763-4799
800-671-3999
Fax: 877-278-7456
E-mail: info@smartstuff.com
http://www.smartstuff.com
Foolproof Security is a dual platform desktop security product that prevents unwanted changes to the desktop and a product line for the internet that protects browser settings, filters content, and allows guided activities.

5785 Society for Visual Education
1345 W Diversey Parkway
Chicago, IL 60614-1249
773-775-9550
Fax: 800-624-1678
Educational software dealing specifically with special education.

5786 SofterWare
540 Pennsylvania Avenue
Suite 200
Fort Washington, PA 19034-3388
215-628-0400
800-220-4111
Fax: 215-628-0585
E-mail: info@softerware.com
http://www.softerware.com
Offers software, support and administrative solutions to four markets: childcare centers, public and private schools, nonprofit organizations and institutions, and camps.

5787 SpecialNet
GTE Educational Network Services
5525 N Macarthur Boulevard
Suite 320
Irving, TX 75038-2600
214-518-8500
800-927-3000
Fax: 757-852-8277
Contains news and information on trends and developments in educational services and programs. Databases, bulletin boards, school packages, student/teacher packages, online magazines, distance learning, vocational education, school health, educational laws, and more.

5788 Student Software Guide

800-874-9001
E-mail: journey.com
Discounts on a variety of software materials.

5789 Sun Microsystems
2550 Garcia Avenue
#6-13
Mountain View, CA 94043-1100
714-643-2688
800-555-9786
Fax: 650-934-9776
Computer networks and peripherals.

5790 Sunburst/Wings for Learning
101 Castleton Street
Pleasantville, NY 10570-3405
914-747-3310
800-338-3457
Fax: 914-747-4109
Educational materials, including software, print materials, videotapes, videodisc and interdisciplinary packages.

5791 Support Systems International Corporation
136 S 2nd Street
Richmond, CA 94804-2110
510-234-9090
800-777-6269
Fax: 510-233-8888
E-mail: info@support-systems-intl.com
http://www.fiberopticcableshop.com
Fiber optic patch cables, converters, and switches.

Ben Parsons, General Manager

5792 Surfside Software
PO Box 1112
East Orleans, MA 02643-1112
800-942-9008
Educational software.

5793 Target Vision
1160 Pittsford Victor Road
Suite K
Pittsford, NY 14534-3825
800-724-4044
Fax: 585-248-2354
TVI DeskTop expands your show directly to desktop PC utilizing existing LANS. View information by topics or as a screen saver. Features: graphic importing, VCR interface, advanced scheduling and more.

5794 Teacher Universe
5900 Hollis Street
Suite A
Emeryville, CA 94608
877-248-3224
Fax: 415-763-4917
E-mail: info@teacheruniverse.com
http://www.teacheruniverse.com
Creates technology-rich solutions for improving the quality of life and work for teachers worldwide.

5795 Technolink Corporation
24 Depot Square
Tuckahoe, NY 10707-4004
914-961-1900
Computer systems and electronics.

5796 Tom Snyder Productions
80 Coolidge Hill Road
Watertown, MA 02472
800-342-0236
Fax: 800-304-1254
E-mail: ask@tomsnyder.com
http://www.tomsnyder.com
Educational CD-ROM products and Internet services for schools.

5797 Tripp Lite
500 N Orleans Street
Chicago, IL 60610-4117
312-329-1601
Peripherals, hardware and computer systems.

5798 True Basic
12 Commerce Avenue
West Lebanon, NH 03784-1669
800-436-2111
Fax: 603-298-7015
E-mail: john@truebasic.com
http://www.truebasic.com
Educational software.

5799 U.S. Public School Universe Database
U.S. National Center for Education Statistics
555 New Jersey Avenue NW
Washington, DC 20001-2029
202-219-1335
85,000 public schools of elementary and secondary levels, public special education, vocational/technical education and alternative education schools.

5800 USA CityLink Project
USA CityLink Project
Floppies for Kiddies
4060 Highway 59
Mandeville, LA 70471
985-898-2158
Fax: 985-892-8535
Collects used and promotional disketts from the masses for redistribution to school groups and nonprofits throughout the county.

Carol Blake, Contact

5801 Unisys
PO Box 500
Blue Bell, PA 19424-0001
215-986-3501
Fax: 215-986-3279
A full line of computers (sizes ranging from mini/micro to medium/large and personal).

5802 Ventura Educational Systems
910 Ramona Avenue
Suite E
Grover Beach, CA 93433-2154
805-473-7383
800-336-1022
Fax: 805-473-7382
E-mail: sales@venturaes.com
http://www.venturaes.com
Publishers of curriculum based educational software for all grade levels, specializing in interactive math and science software. Programs include teacher's guide with student worksheets.

5803 Viziflex Seels
16 E Lafayette Street
Hackensack, NJ 07601-6895
201-487-8080
Peripherals, hardware and electronics, floorcoverings, mats and matting.

5804 Waterford Institute
1590 E 9400 S
Sandy, UT 84093-3009
800-767-9976
Fax: 801-572-1667
Produces children's educational software for math and reading.

5805 Web Connection
Education Week

301-280-3100
E-mail: ads@epe.org
http://www.edweek.org
Information about education suppliers.

5806 Wiremold Company
60 Woodlawn Street
W Hartford, CT 06110-2383
800-243-8421
Computer networks and peripherals.

5807 Wisconsin Technical College System Foundation
1 Foundation Cir
Waunakee, WI 53597-8914
800-821-6313
Fax: 608-849-2468
E-mail: foundation@wtcsf.tec.wi.us
Interactive videodiscs, self-paced instruction or with barcodes. Students learn faster, become more motivated and retain more information. Math, algebra and electronics courseware are also available.

5808 Word Associates
3226 Robincrest Drive
Northbrook, IL 60062-5125
847-291-1101
Fax: 847-291-0931
E-mail: microlrn@aol.com
http://www.wordassociates.com
Software tutorials featuring lessons in question format, with tutorial and test mode. 15 titles include Math SAT, 2 English SAT; US Constitution Tutor; Phraze Maze; Geometry: Planely Simple, Concepts and Proofs, Right Triangles; Life Skills Math; Algebra; Reading: Myths and More Myths, Magic and Monsters; Economics; American History. Windows, Macintosh, CD's or disks.

Software

Myrna Helfand, President
Sherry Azaria, Marketing

5809 Ztek Company
PO Box 11768
Lexington, KY 40577-1768
859-281-1611
800-247-1603
Fax: 859-281-1521
E-mail: cs@ztek.com
http://www.ztek.com
Offers physics multimedia lessons on CD-ROM, DVD, videodisc and videotape. Also, carries Pioneer New Media DVD and videodisc players as well as Bretford Manufacturing's line of audio-visual furniture.

5810 ePALS.com
Classroom Exchange

http://www.epals.com
World's largest online classroom community, connecting over 3 million students and teachers through 41,044 profiles.

5811 http://ericir.syr.edu
AskERIC

Ask a question about education and receive a personalized e-mail response in two business days.

5812 http://gsn.bilkent.edu.tr
Ballad of an EMail Terrorist
Global SchoolNet Foundation
One pitfall of the internet is danger of vulgarity and/or obscenity to a child via e-mail.

5813 http://suzyred.home.texas.net
The Little Red School House

Offers sections on music, writing, quotes, web quests, jokes, poetry, games, activities and more.

5814 www.FundRaising.Com
FundRaising.Com

800-443-5353

Internet fundraising company.

5815 www.abcteach.com

E-mail: sandkems@abcteach.com
Offers ideas and activities for kids, parents, students and teachers. Features section on many topics in education, including writing, poetry, word searches, crosswords, games, maps, mazes and more.

5816 www.abctooncenter.com
ABC Toon Center

This family orientated site offers games, cartoons, storybook, theater, information stations and more. This site is open to children of differnt languages. Can be translated into Italian, French, Spanish, German and Russian.

5817 www.americatakingaction.com
America Taking Action

Provides every school with a free, 20 page website with resources for teachers, parents, students and the community. Created entirely by involved parents, teachers and community leaders as a public service.

5818 www.awesomelibrary.org
Awesome Library

Organizes the Web with 15,000 carefully reviewed resources, including the top 5 percent in education. Offers sections of mathematics, science, social studies, english, health, physical education, technology, languages, special education, the arts and more. Features a section involved with today's current issues facing our world, like pollution, gun control, tobacco, and other changing 'hot' topics. Site can be browsed in English, German, Spanish, French or Portuguese.

5819 www.bigchalk.com
Big Chalk-The Education Network

Educational web site tailored to fit teachers' and students' needs.

5820 www.brunchbunch.org
Brunch Bunch

The foundation names all of the grants it makes after teachers who have demonstrated excellence. The foundation regularly makes significant grants to aid teachers' efforts.

5821 www.busycooks.com
BusyCooks.com

A hit with home economics teachers, enjoying free recipes and online cooking shows. Tapping into the experience of thousands to nuture your culinary creativity.

5822 www.chandra.harvard.edu
Chandra X-ray Observatory Center

Find teacher-developed, classroom-ready materials based on results from the Chandra mission. Classroom-ready activities, interactive games, activities, quizzes, and printable activities which will keep students absorbed with interest.

5823 www.cherrydale.com
Cherrydale Farms

Website offers company information, fund raising products and information, online mega mall, card shop, career opportunities and much more. Produces fine chocolates and confections. Many opportunities for schools to raise funds with various Cherrydale programs.

5824 www.cleverapple.com
Education Station

Offers links to many sites involved with education.

5825 www.edhelper.com
edhelper.com

Keeps you up to date with the latest educational news.

5826 www.education-world.com
Education World

Features and education-specific search engine with links to over 115,000 sites. Offers monthly reviews of other educational web sites, and other original content on a weekly basis.

5827 www.eduverse.com

Software developer building core technologies for powering international distance education. Features an online distance education engine, product information, news releases and more.

5828 www.efundraising.com
efundraising.com

Provides non-profit groups with quality products, low prices and superior service. Helping thousands of schools, youth sports teams and community groups reach their fundraising goals each year.

5829 www.embracingthechild.com
Embracing the Child

Educational resource for teachers and parents that provides a structural resource for home and classroom use, lesson planning, as well as a child-safe site, for children's research, classroom use and homework fulfillment.

5830 www.enc.org
Eisenhower National Clearinghouse

For math and science teachers-anywhere in the K-12 spectrum. This organization contains a wealth of information, activities, resources, and demonstrations for the sciences and math.

5831 www.englishhlp.com
English Help

E-mail: englishhlpr@hotmail.com
This page is a walk through of Microsoft Power Point. The goal is to show in a few simple steps how to make your own website. Created by Rebecca Holland.

5832 www.expage.com/Just4teachers
Just 4 Teachers

The ultimate website for educators! Teaching tips, resources, themeunits, search engines, classroom management and sites for kids.

5833 www.fraboom.com
Fraboom

This site's tools let you specify areas within your state's standards and search for a list of 'Flying Rhinoceros' lessons that meet your criteria. Offers other information sources for teachers and students.

5834 www.globalschoolnet.org
Global Schoolhouse

Connects teachers, administrators, and parents with options and possibilities the Internet has to offer the schools of the world.

5835 www.gradebook.org/
The Classroom

Dedicated to the students and teachers of the world.

5836 www.homeworkspot.com
HomeworkSpot

A free online homework resource center developed by educators, students, parents and journalists for K-12 students. It simplifies the search for homework help, features a top-notch reference cetner, current events, virtual field trips and expeditions, extracurricular activities and study breaks, parent and teacher resources and much more.

5837 www.iearn.org
iEARN USA

Utilizes projects for students ages 6 through 19. Projects are concerned with the environment as well as arts, politics, and the health and welfare of all the Earth's citizens.

5838 www.jasonproject.org
Jason Project

Founded in 1989 as a tool for live, interactive programs for students in the fourth through eighth grades. Annual projects are funded through a variety of public corporations and governmental organizations.

5839 www.junebox.com
JuneBox.com

A classroom superstore that features the leading suppliers of educational products and services. A gateway to project ideas and educational links.

5840 www.k12planet.com
Chancery Software

Chancery Software is announcing a new school to home extension that will provide student information systems to give parents, students, and educators access to accurate information about students in one, easy-to-use website.

5841 www.kiddsmart.com
Institute for Child Development

E-mail: dcornell@kiddsmart.com
The ICD develops educational materials and resources designed to facilitate children's social and emotional development. Offers the previous materials as well as research summaries, lesson plans, training, workshops, games, multi-cultural materials and other resources to teachers, educational centers, parents, counselors, corporations, non-profits and others involved in the child-care professions.

5842 www.lessonplansearch.com
Lesson Plan Search

220 lesson plans from cooking to writing.

5843 www.lessonplanspage.com
lessonplanspage.com

A collection of over 1,000 free lesson plans for teachers to use in their classrooms. Lesson plans are organized by subject and grade level.

5844 www.library.thinkquest.org
Think Quest Library of Entries

The Arti FAQS 2100 Project is designed to predict how art will influence our lives in the next hundred years. Students can use available data to make reasonable predictions for the future.

5845 www.ncspearson.com
NCS Pearson

E-mail: info@ncs.com
NCS Pearson is at the forefront of the education space with curriculum, contant, tools, assessment, and interface to enterprise systems

5846 www.negaresa.org
LearningGate

For teachers, electronic web-based grade book aplication eGRader 2000. Many educational resource links as well has discussion groups, a news and events section, and even links to online shopping.

5847 www.netrover.com/~kingskid/108.html
Room 108
An educational activity center for kids. Offers lots of fun for children with educational focus; like songs, art, math, kids games, children's stories and much more. Sections with pen pal information, puzzles, crosswords, teachers store, spelling, kids sites, email, music, games and more.

5848 www.pcg.cyberbee.com
Postcard Geography

Offered to classes all over the world via the internet. Your class commits to exchanging picture postcards with all other participants. Appropriate for all ages, for public and private schools, for youth groups and for home- schools.

5849 www.pitt.edu
EdIndex

E-mail: poole@pitt.edu

A web resource for teachers and students, offers course information, MS Office tutorials, personal and professional pages, and more.

5850 www.riverdeep.net
Riverdeep Interactive Learning

Riverdeep's interactive science, language and math arts programs deliver high quality educational experiences.

5851 www.safedayeducation.com
Safe Day Education

The leader in bully prevention and street proofing education for kids; safe dating preparation programs for teens; and re-empowerment and assault prevention training for women.

5852 www.safekids.com/child_safety.htm
SafeKids.Com

Cyberspace is a fabulous tool for learning, but some of it can be exploitative and even criminal.

5853 www.sdcoe.k12.ca.us

Researches a coral reef and creates a diorama for The Cay by Theodore Taylor.

5854 www.shop2gether.com
Collective Publishing Service

We are committed to helping all schools buy better by shopping together. Building upon a scalable, dynamic procurement platform and group buying technology, we also provide a unique ecommerce system, delivering next generation procurement services over the Internet.

5855 www.spaceday.com
Space Day

Program engineered to build problem-solving and teamwork skills.

5856 www.specialednews.com
Special Education News

E-mail: info@specialednews.com
Consists of breaking news stories from Washington and around the country. These stories are complied together in the Special Education News letter is sent via e-mail once a week.

5857 www.straightscoop.org
Straight Scoop News Bureau

SSNB increases the frequency of anti-drug themes and messages in junior high and high school student media.

5858 www.tcta.org
Texas Classroom Teachers Association

Compromised of Texas educators, provides interest for teachers everywhere. Education laws and codes are presented here.

5859 www.teacherszone.com
TeachersZone.Com

Lesson plans, free stuff for teachers, contests, sites for kids, conferences and work-

shops, schools and organizations, job listings, products for school.

5860 www.teacherweb.com
TeacherWeb

TeacherWeb, your free personal website that's as easy to use as the bulletin board in your classroom. This site offers a secure, password-protected service.

5861 www.teachingheart.com
Teaching is A Work of Heart

Chock-full of ideas, projects, motivational thoughts, behavior ideas.

5862 www.thelearningworkshop.com
Learning Workshop.com

Services for teachers, students, and parents. For teachers online gradebooks and grade tracking, students can check their grades online, parents enjoy articles written expressly for them and a tutor search by zip code.

5863 www.tutorlist.com
TutorList.com

Offers information on tips on how to find and choose a tutor, what a tutor does, educational news and more.

5864 www.worksafeusa.org
WorkSafeUSA

Addresses the alarming injury and death rates experienced by America's adolescent workers. This non-profit site publishes and distributes A Teen Guide to Workplace Safety, available in English and Spanish.

5865 www1.hp.com
Compaq Computer Corporation

Compaq is one of the leading corporations in educational technology, working on developing solutions that will connect students, teachers and the community.

Administration

5866 ASQC
611 E Wisconsin Avenue
Milwaukee, WI 53202-4695
800-248-1946
Fax: 414-272-1734
Business and administrative software.

5867 Anchor Pad
Anchor Pad Products
11105 Dana Cir
Cypress, CA 90630-5133
714-799-4071
800-626-2467
Fax: 714-799-4094
E-mail: anchor@anchor.com
http://www.anchorpad.com
Computer and office security

Caroline Jones, COO
Melanie Ruste, Sales/Marketing Associate

5868 Applied Business Technologies
4631 W Chester Pike
Newtown Square, PA 19073-2225
610-359-0700
800-220-2281
Fax: 610-359-9420
Computer networks and administrative
software.

5869 AskSam Systems
121 S Jefferson Street
Perry, FL 32347-3232
850-584-6590
800-800-1997
Fax: 850-584-7481
E-mail: info@asksam.com
http://www.asksam.com
Business and administrative free form database software.

Dottie Sheffield, Sales Manager

5870 Autodesk Retail Products
1725 220th Street
Suite C101
Bothell, WA 98021-8809
425-487-2233
Fax: 425-486-1636
Administrative and business software.

5871 Avcom Systems
250 Cox Lane
PO Box 977
Cutchogue, NY 11935-1303
631-734-5080
800-645-1134
Fax: 631-734-7204
Supplies for making and mounting transparencies. Products includes economy and self-adhesive mounts; transparent rolls and sheets; markers, pens and cleaners; thermo, computer graphics and plain-paper copier transparency films and laminating supplies.

Joseph K Lukas

5872 Bobbing Software
67 Country Oaks Drive
Buda, TX 78610-9338
800-688-6812
Administrative software and systems.

5873 Bull HN Information Systems
Technology Park
Billerica, MA 01821
978-294-6000
Fax: 978-294-7999
Computer networks, computers (large, medium, micro and mini), and supplies.

5874 Bureau of Electronic Publishing
745 Alexander Road
#728
Princeton, NJ 08540-6343
973-808-2700
Administrative software, hardware and systems.

5875 CRS
17440 Dallas Parkway
Suite 120
Dallas, TX 75287-7307
800-433-9239
Administrative software and systems.

5876 Campus America
900 E Hill Avenue
Suite 205
Knoxville, TN 37915-2580
865-523-4477
877-536-0222
Fax: 617-492-9081
http://www.campus.com

Computer supplies, equipment, systems and networks.

5877 Century Consultants
150 Airport Road
Suite 1500
Lakewood, NJ 08701-3309
732-363-9300
Fax: 732-363-9374
E-mail: marketing@centuryltd.com
http://www.centuryltd.com
Develops, markets, and services Oracle based web-enabled Management software, STAR_BASE, for school districts K-12.

5878 Computer Resources
PO Box 60
Barrington, NH 03825-0060
603-664-5811
Fax: 603-664-5864
The Modular Management System for Schools is a school administrative software system designed to handle all student record keeping and course scheduling needs. A totally integrated modular system built around a central Student Master File. Additional modules handle student scheduling, grades, attendance and discipline reporting.

Raymond J Perreault, VP Marketing
Robert W Cook, National Sales Manager

5879 Cyborg Systems
2 N Riverside Plaza
Chicago, IL 60606-2600
312-454-1865
Administrative and business software programs.

5880 Diskovery Educational Systems
1860 Old Okeechobee Road
Suite 105
West Palm Beach, FL 33409-5281
561-683-8410
800-331-5489
Fax: 561-683-8416
http://www.diskovery.com
Computer supplies, equipment, and various size systems.

5881 Doron Precision Systems
Doron Precision Systems
174 Court Street
PO Box 400
Binghamton, NY 13902-0400
607-772-1610
Fax: 607-772-6760
http://www.doronprecision.com
Business and classroom curriculum software. Driving Simulation Systems and Entertainment Simulation Systems.

5882 Educational Data Center
180 De La Salle Drive
Romeoville, IL 60446-1895
800-451-7673
Fax: 815-838-9412
Administration software.

5883 EnrollForecast: K-12 Enrollment Forecasting Program
Association of School Business Officials Int'l
11401 N Shore Drive
Reston, VA 20190-4232
703-478-0405
Fax: 703-478-0205
A powerful planning tool that helps project student enrollment.

Peg D Kirkpatrick, Editor/Publisher
Robert Gluck, Managing Editor

5884 Epson America
20770 Madrona Avenue
Torrance, CA 90503-3778
800-289-3776
Computer repair and peripherals.

5885 FMJ/PAD.LOCK Computer Security Systems
741 E 223rd Street
Carson, CA 90745-4111
310-549-3221
800-322-3365
Fax: 310-549-2921
E-mail: info@fmjpadlock.com
Computer peripherals, supplies and equipment.

Tom Separa

5886 Geist
Geist Manufacturing
1821 Yolande Avenue
Lincoln, NE 68521-1835
402-474-3400
Fax: 402-474-4369
E-mail: products@geistmfg.com
http://www.geistmfg.com
Power distribution for racks, cabinets and data centers.

Terri Rockeman, Customer Service Supervisor

5887 Global Computer Supplies
11 Harbor Park Drive
Port Washington, NY 11050-4622
516-625-6200
Fax: 516-484-8533
Computer supplies, equipment, hardware, software and systems.

5888 Harrington Software
658 Ridgewood Road
Maplewood, NJ 07040-2536
201-761-5914
Administrative and business software.

5889 Information Design
7009 S Potomac Street
Suite 110
Englewood, CO 80112
303-792-2990
800-776-2469
Fax: 303-792-2378
E-mail: sales@idesgninc.com
http://www.idesigninc.com
Administrative and business software including systems focusing on payroll, personnel, financial accounting, purchasing, budgeting, fixed asset accounting and salary administration.

5890 International Rotex
7171 Telegraph Road
Los Angeles, CA 90040-3227
800-648-1871
Computer supplies.

5891 Jay Klein Productions Grade Busters
1695 Summit Point Court
Colorado Springs, CO 80919-3444
719-599-8786
Fax: 719-599-8312
A line of teacher productivity tools, the most highly recognized integrated gradebooks, attendance records, seating charts and scantron packages in K-12 education today (Mac, DOS, Windows, Apple II).

Jay A Klein, President
Angela C Wormley, Office Manager

5892 Jostens Learning Corporation
5521 Norman Center Drive
Minneapolis, MN 55437-1040
800-635-1429
The leading provider of comprehensive multimedia instruction, including hardware, software and service.

5893 MISCO Computer Supplies
1 Misco Plaza
Holmdel, NJ 07733-1033
800-876-4726
Computer supplies, networks, equipment and accessories.

5894 Mathematica
Wolfram Research
100 Trade Centre Drive
Champaign, IL 61820-7237
217-398-0700
800-441-6284
Fax: 217-398-0747
E-mail: info@wolfram.com
http://www.wolfram.com
Classroom curricular software and business/administrative software.

5895 Media Management & Magnetics
N94W14376 Garwin Mace Drive
Menomonee Falls, WI 53051-1629
262-251-5511
800-242-2090
Fax: 262-251-4737
E-mail: medmgt@execpc.com
http://www.computersupplypeople.com
Computer supplies, equipment and systems, Koss headphones.

John Schimberg, Education Sales

5896 MicroAnalytics
Student Transportation Systems
2300 Clarendon Boulevard
Suite 404
Arlington, VA 22201-3331
703-841-0414
Fax: 703-527-1693
Automates bus routing and scheduling for school districts with fleets of 5 to 500 buses. BUSTOPS is flexible, affordable and easy to use. Offers color maps and graphics, efficient routing, report writing, planning and more to improve your pupil transportation system.

Mary Buchanan, Sales Manager

5897 MicroLearn Tutorial Series
Word Associates
3226 Robincrest Drive
Northbrook, IL 60062-5125
847-291-1101
Fax: 847-291-0931
E-mail: microlrn@aol.com
http://www.wordassociates.com
Software tutorials featuring lessons in question format, with tutorial and test mode. 15 titles include Math SAT, 2 English SAT; US Constitution Tutor; Phraze Maze; Geometry: Planely Simple, Concepts and Proofs, Right Triangles; Life Skills Math; Algebra; Reading: Myths and More Myths, Magic and Monsters; Economics; American History. Windows, Macintosh, CD's or disks.

Software

Myrna Helfand, President

5898 NCS Marketing
11000 Prairie Lakes Drive
Eden Prairie, MN 55344-3885
800-447-3269
Fax: 612-830-7788
http://www.ncspearson.com
OpScan optical mark reading scanners from NCS process data at speeds of up to 10,000 sheets per hour for improved accuracy and faster turnaround. Also provides software and scanning applications and services that manage student, financial, human resources, instructional and assessment information.

Sheryl Kyweriga

5899 National Computer Systems
11000 Prairie Lakes Drive
Minneapolis, MN 55440
800-447-3269
Fax: 952-830-8564
Administrative software and systems.

5900 Parlant Technologies
290 N University Avenue
Provo, UT 84601-2821
800-735-2930
Fax: 801-373-9697
Administrative software and systems.

5901 Quill Corporation
100 Schelter Road
Lincolnshire, IL 60069-3621
847-634-4800
Fax: 847-634-5708
Computer and office supplies and equipment.

5902 Rauland Borg
3450 Oakton Street
Skokie, IL 60076-2958
847-679-0900
Fax: 800-217-0977
Administrative software and systems.

5903 Rediker Administration Software
2 Wileraham Road
Hampden, MA 01036-9685
800-882-2994
Fax: 413-566-2274
E-mail: sales@rediker.com
School administrative software for the teaching professional.

5904 Scantron Corporation
PO Box 2411
Tustin, CA 92781-2411
714-259-8887
Computer peripherals, administrative software and services.

5905 SourceView Software International
PO Box 578
Concord, CA 94522-0578
925-825-1248
Classroom curricular, business and administrative software.

5906 Systems & Computer Technology Services
4 Country View Road
Malvern, PA 19355-1408
610-647-5930
Fax: 610-578-7778
Administrative and business software programs and services.

5907 Trapeze Software
23215 Commerce Park Drive
Suite 200
Beachwood, OH 44122
216-595-3100
Fax: 216-595-3113
E-mail: clint@mail.trapezesoftware.com
http://www.trapezesoftware.com
Computerized bus routing, boundary planning and redistricting software and services, and AVL (automatic vehicle locator software).

Clint Rooley, Director of Sales

5908 University Research Company
4724 W 2100 N
Cedar City, UT 84720-7846
800-526-4972
Supplies Quiz-A-Matic electronics for quiz competitions.

5909 Velan
4153 24th Street
Suite 1
San Francisco, CA 94114-3667
415-949-9150
Administrative software and systems.

5910 WESTLAW
West Group
610 Opperman Drive
Eagan, MN 55123-1340
612-687-7000
800-757-9378
Fax: 651-687-5827
http://www.westlaw.com
Online service concerning the complete text of U.S. federal court decisions, state court decisions from all 50 states, regulations, specialized files, and texts dealing with education.

5911 http://teacherfiles.homestead.com/index~ns4

Offers sections on clip art, quotes, slogans, lesson plans, organizations, web quests, political involvement, grants, publications, special education, professional development, humor and more.

5912 www.abcteach.com
Abcteach

E-mail: sandkems@abcteach.com
Free printable materials for kids, parents, student teachers and teachers. Theme units, spelling word searches, research help, writing skills and much more.

5913 www.apple.com
PowerSchool

PowerSchool's web-based architecture makes it easy to learn and easy to use.

5914 www.atozteacherstuff.com
A to Z Teacher Stuff

E-mail: webmaster@atozteacherstuff.com
Features quick indexes to online lesson plans and teacher resources, educational sites for teachers, articles, teacher store and more.

5915 www.awesomelibrary.org
Awesome Library

Organizes the Web with 15,000 carefully reviewed resources, including the top 5 percent in education. Offers sections of mathematics, science, social studies, english, health, physical education, technology, languages, special education, the arts and more. Features a section involved with today's current issues facing our world, like pollution, gun control, tobacco, and other changing 'hot' topics. Site can be browsed in English, German, Spanish, French or Portuguese.

5916 www.easylobby.com
EasyLobby

The complete electronic visitor management system.

5917 www.fraboom.com
Stan D. Bird's WhizBang Thang

This site's tools let's you specify areas within your state's standards and search for a list of 'Flying Rhinoceros' lessons that meet your criteria. Offers other information sources for teachers and students.

5918 www.fundraising.com

800-443-5353
http://www.fundraising.com
Internet fundraising company.

5919 www.hoagiesgifted.org
Hoagies Gifted Education Page

Features the latest research on parenting and educating gifted children. Offers ideas, solutions and other things to try for parents of gifted children. Sections with world issues facing children and other important social topics.

5920 www.kiddsmart.com
Institute for Child Development

E-mail: dcornell@kiddsmart.com
The ICD develops educational materials and resources designed to facilitate children's social and emotional development. Offers the previous materials as well as research summaries, lesson plans, training, workshops, games, multi-cultural materials and other resources to teachers, educational centers, parents, counselors, corporations, non-profits and others involved in the child-care professions.

5921 www.nycteachers.com
NYCTeachers.com

Designed for NYC teachers that work within public school systems. Speaks out on controversial issues facing the broadening, funding, development, staffing and other concerns about public schools. Welcomes your suggestions and comments about the site and the issues involved.

5922 www.songs4teachers.com
O'Flynn Consulting

E-mail: oflynn4@home.com
Offers many resources for teachers including songs made especially for your classroom. Sections with songs and activities for holidays, seasons and more. Features books and audios with 101 theme songs for use in the classroom or anywhere children gather to sing.

5923 www.thecanadianteacher.com
Free Stuff for Canadian Teachers

Site where educators can find the latest links to free resources, materials, lesson plans, software, samples and computers. Some links are for Canadians only.

5924 www.welligent.Com
Welligent

A web-based software program that improves student health management and your school's finances at the same time.

Early Childhood Education

5925 Jump Start Math for Kindergartners
Knowledge Adventure
Torrance, CA
800-545-7677
http://www.knowledgeadventure.com
The program covers important and essential kindergarten math skills such as, writing numbers, sorting, and problem solving/following directions.

5926 Mindplay
160 W Fort Lowell Road
Tucson, AZ 85705
520-888-1800
800-221-7911
Fax: 520-888-7904
E-mail: mail@mindplay.com
http://www.mindplay.com
Educational software focusing on early childhood education and adult literacy.

Stacie Johnson, Communication Coordinator

5927 Nordic Software
PO Box 5403
Lincoln, NE 68505
402-489-1557
800-306-6502
Fax: 402-489-1560
E-mail: info@nordicsoftware.com
http://www.nordicsoftware.com
Specializes in developing and publishing educational software titles. Well-known for its software titles that make it easy for children to learn while playing on the computer. Develops and publishes elementary software products for the Macintosh and Windows platforms. Products include Turbo Math Facts, Clock Shop, Coin Critters, Language Explorer and Preschool Parade, and more.

Tammy Hurlbut, Finance/Operations

5928 Personalized Software
PO Box 359
Phoenix, OR 97535
541-535-8085
Fax: 541-535-8889
Offers a full line of childcare management and development software programs.

5929 Science for Kids
9950 Concord Church Road
Lewisville, NC 27023-9720
336-945-9000
800-572-4362
Fax: 336-945-2500
E-mail: sci4kids@aol.com
http://www.scienceforkids.com
Developers and publishers of CD-ROM science and early learning programs for children ages 5-14; for Macintosh and Windows

computers; school and home programs available.

Charles Moyer, Executive VP

5930 http://daycare.about.com/parenting /daycare
About Parenting/Family Daycare

5931 www.booksofwonder.com

New and vintage childrens books.

5932 www.lil-fingers.com
Lil' Fingers

A computer storybook site for toddlers. Parents and children are encouraged to enjoy the colorful drawings and animations. Offers games, storybooks, coloring pages, the Lil' Store and more.

Elementary Education

5933 Educational Institutions Partnership Program
Defense Information Systems Agency
Automation Resources Information
701 S Courthouse Road
Arlington, VA 22204-2199
703-607-6900
Fax: 703-607-4371
Makes available used computer equipment for donation of transfer to eligible schools, including K-12 schools recognized by the US Department of Education, Universities, colleges, Minority Institutions and nonporfit groups.

5934 Houghton Mifflin Company
222 Berkeley Street
Boston, MA 02116-3748
617-351-5000
Fax: 617-351-1106
Offers literature-based technology products for grades K-8 including CD's Story Time, a Macintosh based CD-ROM programs for grades 1 and 2 and Channel R.E.A.D., a videodisc series for grades 3-8.

5935 Kid Keys 2.0
Knowledge Adventure

800-545-7677
Keyboarding for grades K-2.

5936 Kinder Magic
1680 Meadowglen Lane
Encinitas, CA 92024-5652
760-632-6693
Fax: 760-632-9995
Educational software for ages 4-11.

Dr. Ilse Ortabasi, President

5937 Micrograms Publishing
9934 N Alpine Road
Suite 108
Machesney Park, IL 61115-8240
800-338-4726
Fax: 815-877-1482
http://www.micrograms.com
Micrograms develops educational software for schools and homes.

5938 Tudor Publishing Company
17218 Preston Road
Suite 400
Dallas, TX 75252-4018
Grade level evaluation (GLE) is a computer-adaptive assessment program for elementary and secondary students.

5939 Wordware Publishing
2320 Los Rios Boulevard
#200
Plano, TX 75074-8157
214-423-0090
Fax: 972-881-9147
Publisher of computer reference tutorials, regional Texas and Christian books. Educational division produces a diagnostic and remediation software for grade levels 3-8. Content covers over 3,000 objectives in reading, writing and math. Contact publisher for dealer information.

Eileen Schnett, Product Manager

5940 World Classroom
Global Learning Corporation
PO Box 201361
Arlington, TX 76006-1361
214-641-3356
800-866-4452
An educational telecommunications network that prepares students, K-12 to use real-life data to make real-life decisions about themselves and their environment. Participating countries have included Argentina, Australia, Belgium, Canada, Denmark, France, Germany, Hungary, Iceland, Indonesia, Kenya, Russia, Lithuania, Mexico, Singapore, Taiwan, the Netherlands, the United States and Zimbabwe.

5941 http://k-6educators....education/k-6 educators
About Education Elementary Educators

5942 http://www.etacuisenaire.com/index.htm
ETA Cuisenaire

Over 5,000 manipulative-based education and supplemental materials for grades K-12.

5943 http://www.wnet.org/wnetschool
wNet School

212-560-2713
Helps K-12 teachers by providing free standards based lesson plans, classroom activities, multimedia primers, online mentors, links to model technology schools, and more. Online workshops are also included in the WNET TV site.

5944 www.cherrydale.com/
Cherrydale Farms

Website offers company information, fund raising products and information, online mega mall, card shop, career opportunities and much more. Produces fine chocolates and confections. Many opportunities for schools to raise funds with various Cherrydale programs.

5945 www.efundraising.com
eFundraising

Provides non-profit groups with quality products, low prices and superior service. Helping thousands of schools, youth sports teams and community groups reach their fundraising goals each year.

5946 www.hoagiesgifted.org
Hoagies' Gifted Education Page

Features the latest research on parenting and educating gifted children. Offers ideas, solutions and other things to try for parents of gifted children. Sections with world issues facing children and other important social topics.

5947 www.netrover.com/~kingskid/108.html
Room 108

An educational activity center for kids. Offers lots of fun for children with educational focus; like songs, art, math, kids games, children's stories and much more. Sections with pen pal information, puzzles, crosswords, teachers store, spelling, kids sites, email, music, games and more.

5948 www.netrox.net
Dr. Labush's Links to Learning

General links for teachers with internet help, coloring pages, and enrichment programs.

5949 www.primarygames.com
PrimaryGames.com

Contains educational games for elementary students.

5950 www.usajobs.opm.gov/b1c.htm
Overseas Employment Info-Teachers

Employment

5951 Educational Placement Service
90 S Cascade
Suite 1110
Colorado Springs, CO 80903
http://www.teacherjobs.com
Largest teacher placement service in the U.S.

5952 Job Bulletin
American Association of School Administrators
801 N Quincy Street
Arlington, VA 22203-1730
703-528-0700
Fax: 703-841-1543
E-mail: info@aasa.org
http://www.aasa.org
The Job Bulletin was made to help employers and job candidates save time finding one another.

Jay Goldman, Editor

5953 Teachers@Work
PO Box 430
Vail, CO 81658
970-476-5008
Fax: 970-476-1496
http://www.teachersatwork.com
Electronic employment service designed to match the professional staffing needs of schools with teacher applicants.

5954 www.SchoolJobs.com
SchoolJobs.com

Provides principals, superintendents and other administrators the ability to market their job openings to a national pool of candidates, also gives educational professionals the chance to search for opportunities matching their skills.

5955 www.aasa.org
American Association of School Administrators
801 N Quincy Street
Suite 700
Arlington, VA 22203-1730
703-528-0700
Fax: 703-841-1543
E-mail: info@aasa.org
http://www.aasa.org
Leadership news online.

Guidance & Counseling

5956 Alcohol & Drug Prevention for Teachers, Law Enforcement & Parent Groups
PO Box 4656
Reading, PA 19606
610-582-2090
Fax: 610-404-0406
E-mail: nodrugs@earthlink.net
http://www.nodrugs.com
Local organizations and international groups against drugs.

5957 Live Wire Media
3450 Sacramento Street
619
San Francisco, CA 94118
800-359-5437
Fax: 415-665-8006
E-mail: info@livewiremedia.com
http://www.livewiremedia.com/
Videos for youth guidance and character development, and teacher training.

Christine Hollander, Director Marketing

5958 Phillip Roy Multimedia Materials
PO Box 130
Indian Rocks Beach, FL 34635
727-593-2700
800-255-9085
Fax: 727-595-2685
E-mail: info@philliproy.com
http://www.philliproy.com
Multimedia materials for use with alternative education, Chapter 1, dropout prevention, Even Start, Head Start, JTPA/PIC, special education students, at-risk students, transition to work programs. Focuses on basic skills, conflict resolution, remediation, vocational education, critical thinking skills, communication skills, reasoning and decision making skills. Materials can be duplicated networked at no cost.

Phil Padol, Consultant
Regina Jacques, Customer Support

5959 www.goodcharacter.com
Character Education

Teaching guides for k-12 character education, packed with discussion questions, assignments, and activities that you can use as your own lesson plans.

International

5960 www.aed.org
Academy for Educational Development

The site provides information on international exchange, fellowshipand training.

5961 www.asce.org
American Society of Civil Engineers

This site lists scholarships and fellowships available only to ASCE members.

5962 www.cie.uci.edu
International Opportunities Program

Valuable links for exploring opportunities for study and research abroad.

5963 www.ciee.org
Council on International Educational Exchange

Study abroad programs by region, work abroad opportunities, international volunteer projects and Council-administered financial aid and grant information .

5964 www.cies.org
Council for International Exchange of Scholars

Information on the Fulbright Senior Scholar Program which is made available to Fulbright alumni,grantees, prospective applicants and public at large.

5965 www.daad.org
German Academic Exchange Service (DADD)

Promotes international academic relations and contains links to research grants, summer language grants,annual grants, grants in German studies andspecial programs.

5966 www.ed.gov
US Department of Education
Office of Higher Education Programs
This site describes programs and fellowships offered by the International Education and Graduate Programs office of the US Department of Education.

5967 www.finaid.org
FinAid

A free, comprehensive, independent and ojective guide to student financial aid.

5968 www.iie.org
Institute of International Education
809 United Nations Plaza
New York, NY 10017-3580
412-741-0930
Fax: 212-984-5452
E-mail: iiebooks@abdintl.com
http://www.iiebooks.org
The largest not-for-profit international educational organization in the United States. This site provides information regarding IIE's programs, services and resources, including the Filbright Fellowship.

5969 www.iiepasspport.org
Institute of International Education
IIE Passport: Study Abroad
1350 Edgmont Avenue Suite 1100
Chester, PA 19013
877-404-0338
Fax: 610-499-9205
E-mail: info@iiepassport.org
http://www.iiepassport.org
A student guide on the web to 5,000 learning oppurtunities worldwide.

5970 www.irex.org
International Research and Exchange Board

Academic exchanges between the United States and Russia. Lists a variety of programs as well as grant and fellowship oppurtunities.

5971 www.isp.msu.edu/ncsa
Michigan State University
National Consortium for Study in Africa
Provides a comprehensive lists of sponsors for African exchange.

5972 www.istc.umn.edu/
University of Minnesota
International Study and Travel Center
Comprehensive and searchable links to study, work and travel abroad opportunities.

5973 www.languagetravel.com
Language Travel Magazine

Resource for finding study abroad language immersion courses.

5974 www.nsf.gov/
National Science Foundation
Encourages exchange in science and engineering. The site has inter-national component, providing links with valuable information on fellowships   grants and awards, summer institutes, workshops,research and education projects and international programs.

5975 www.si.edu/
Smithsonian Institution

Fellowships link to Smithsonian Oppurtunities for research and study.

5976 www.studiesinaustralia.com/study
Studies in Australia

Listing of study abroad oppurtunities in Australia, providing details of academic and training institutions and the programs they offer to prospective international students and education professionals.

5977 www.studyabroad.com/
Educational Directories Unlimited, Inc.

Study abroad information resource listing study abroad programs worldwide.

5978 www.studyabroad.com/.
StudyAbroad.com

A commercial site with thousands of study abroad programs in over 100 countries with links to study abroad program home pages.

5979 www.ucis.pitt.edu/crees
University of Pittsburgh
Center for Russian/European Studies
Index of electronic resources for the student interested in Russian and European language and culture study.

5980 www.upenn.edu/oip/scholarships.html
University of Pennsylvania
Scholarships/Graduate Study Abroad
Provides links for graduate study abroad and scholarship opportunities.

5981 www.usc.edu
University of Southern California
Resources for Colleges and
Universities in International Exchange
Links for browsing all aspects of international exchange, including study, research, work and teaching abroad, financial aid, grants and scholarships.

5982 www.usinfo.state/gov
US Department of State International Information Programs
Comprehensive desriptions of all IIP programs, sections on policy issues, global and regional issues and IIP publications.

5983 www.wes.org
World Education Services

Features information on WES' foreign credentials evaluation services, world education workshops, and the journals World Education and News Reviews.

5984 www.world-arts-resources.com/
World Wide Arts Resources

Focuses solely on the arts, this site provides links for funding sources, university programs and arts organizations all over the world.

5985 www.yfu.org/
Youth for Understanding (YFU)

Oppurtunities for young people around the world to spend a summer, semester or year with a host family in another country.

5986 wwww.sas.upenn.edu
African Studies Center, University of Pennsylvania
African Studies WWW
Links to Africa-related internet sources, African Studies Association and UPenn African Studies Center.

Language Arts

5987 Advantage Learning Systems
Renaissance Learning
PO Box 8036
Wisconsin Rapids, WI 54495-8036
715-424-3636
800-338-4204
Fax: 715-424-4242
E-mail: answers@renlearn.com
http://www.renlearn.com
Accelerated Reader software and manuals that motivate K-12 students to read more and better books. The program boosts reading scores and library circulation. Lets educators quickly and accurately assess student reading while motivating students to read more and better books.

5988 Bytes of Learning Incorporated
150 Consumers Road
Suite 2021
Willowdale, ON, Canada, M2 J 1P9
800-465-6428
Single and site licensed software for Macintosh, Apple II, DOS and Windows-network compatible too. Keyboarding, language arts, career exploration and more on diskette and CD-ROM.

5989 Humanities Software
408 Columbia Street
#950
Hood River, OR 97031-2044
503-386-6737
800-245-6737
Fax: 541-386-1410
Over 150 whole language, literature-based language arts software titles for grades K-12.

Karen Withrow, Marketing Assistant
Charlotte Arnold, Marketing Director

5990 Teacher Support Software
3542 NW 97th Boulevard
Gainesville, FL 32606-7322
352-332-6404
800-228-2871
Fax: 352-332-6779
E-mail: tss@tssoftware.com
http://www.tssoftware.com
Language arts, Title 1, special ed, at-risk and ESL, curriculum-based networkable software for grades K-12. Vocabulary software that develops sight word recognition, provides basal correlated databases, tests reading comprehension, tracks student's progress and provides powerful teacher tools.

5991 Weaver Instructional Systems
6161 28th Street SE
Grand Rapids, MI 49546-6931
616-942-2891
Fax: 616-942-1796
Reading and language arts computer software programs for K-college.

5992 www.caslt.org
Canadian Association of Second Language Teachers

Promotes the advancement of second language education throughout Canada.

5993 www.riverdeep.net
Riverdeep Interactive Learning

Riverdeep's interactive science, language and math arts programs deliver high quality educational experiences.

5994 www.signit2.com
Aylmer Press

Website hosted by Aylmer Press which produces video's to teach kids sign language as well as music.

5995 www.usajobs.opm.gov/b1c.html
Overseas Employment Info- Teachers
US Office of Personnel Management

Library Services

5996 American Econo-Clad Services
2101 N Topeka
Topeka, KS 66601
800-255-3502
Fax: 785-233-3129
A full service supplier of educational materials for the library, curriculum and software resource needs including MatchMaker, CD-ROM and ABLE (Analytically Budgeted Library Expenditures) computer systems.

5997 Anchor Audio
3415 Lomita Boulevard
Torrance, CA 90505-5010
310-784-2300
800-262-4671
Fax: 310-784-0533
http://www.anchoraudio.com
Various audio visual products for the school and library.

5998 Baker & Taylor
8140 Lehigh Avenue
Morton Grove, IL 60053-2627
847-965-8060
Nation's leading wholesale supplier of audio, computer software, books, videocassettes and other accessories to schools and libraries.

5999 Brodart Company, Automation Division
500 Arch Street
Williamsport, PA 17701
570-326-2461
800-233-8467
Fax: 570-327-9237
E-mail: salesmkt@brodart.com
http://www.brodart.com
Brodart's Automation Division has been providing library systems, software, and services for over 25 years. Products include: library management systems, media management systems, Internet solutions, cataloged web sites, cataloging resource tools, union catalog solutions, public access catalogs, and bibliographic services.

Kasey Dibble, Marketing Coordinator
Sally Wilmoth, Director Marketing/Sales

6000 Catalog Card Company
12219 Nicollet Avenue
Burnsville, MN 55337-1650
612-882-8558
800-442-7332
Fax: 785-290-1223
MARC records compatible with all software for retrospective conversions and new book orders. Catalog Card's conversion services include barcode labels to complement circulation software. MARC records generated from Dewey/Sears and Library of Congress databases are in standard USMARC or MicroLIF format.

6001 Chancery Student Management Solutions
3001 Wayburne Drive
Burnbay
Canada V5G 4W3
604-294-1233
800-999-9931
Fax: 604-294-2225
http://www.chancery.com
Online catalog searches and checking materials in and out.

6002 Data Trek
5838 Edison Place
Carlsbad, CA 92008-6519
800-876-5484
Turn-key library automation systems and computer networks.

6003 Demco
PO Box 7488
Madison, WI 53707-7488
800-356-1200
Fax: 608-241-1799
A leader in educational and library supplies for more than 80 years, Demco offers library audio and visual supplies and equipment plus display furniture.

6004 Dewey Decimal Classification
OCLC Forest Press
6565 Frantz Road
Dublin, OH 43017-3395
800-848-5878
Fax: 888-339-3921
E-mail: orders@oclc.org
http://www.oclc.org/fp
OCLC Forest Press publishes the Dewey Decimal Classification (DDC) system and many related print and CD-ROM products that teach librarians and library users about the DDC.

Libble Clawford, Marketing Manager

6005 Ebsco Subscription Services
International Headquarters
PO Box 1943
Birmingham, AL 35201-1943
205-991-1480
Fax: 205-980-6700
Periodical subscription and ordering and customer service equipment, computer and CD-ROM supplies, products and hardware for libraries.

Shannon Hayslip

6006 Electronic Bookshelf
5276 S Country Road, 700 W
Frankfort, IN 46041
765-324-2182
Fax: 765-324-2183
Reading motivation, testing management system and various computer systems and networks for educational purposes.

Rosalie Carter

6007 Filette Keez Corporation/Colorworks Diskette Organizing System
3204 Channing Lane
Bedford, TX 76021-6506
817-283-5428
Produces ten filing inventions for classroom library, lab and district technology resources management. SelecTsideS folders store multimedia in Press-an-Inch Technology Slings and keep instruction, printouts, pamphlets and blackliners altogether. The diskette/CD portfolio color coordinates with the student/magazine Spbinder, plastic LaceLox fastener and all

systems paper supplies: CD envelopes, storage box dividers, sheeted cards, perforated tractor labels and keys, available in 7 tech colors.

Roxanne Kay Harbert, Founder/President
Ray L Harbert, VP

6008 Follett Software Company

1391 Corporate Drive
McHenry, IL 60050
815-344-8700
800-323-3397
Fax: 815-344-8774
E-mail: marketing@fsc.follett.com
http://www.fsc.follett.com
Helping K-12 schools and districts create a vital library-to-classroom link to improve student achievement. FSC combines award-winning library automation with practical applications of the Internet. From OPAC data enhancement and easy-to-implement Internet technology to innovative information literacy solutions, FSC helps simplify resource management, increase access to resources inside and outside your collection and provide tools to integrate technology into the curriculum.

Patricia Yonushonis, Marketing Manager
Ann Reist, Conference Manager

6009 Foundation for Library Research

1200 Bigley Avenue
Charleston, WV 25302-3752
304-343-6480
Fax: 304-343-6489
The Automated Library Systems integrated library automation software.

Robert Evans

6010 Gaylord Brothers

PO Box 4901
Syracuse, NY 13221-4901
800-448-6160
Fax: 315-457-8387
Library, AV supplies and equipment; security systems; and library furniture.

Tim Krein

6011 Highsmith Company

W5527 Highway 106
Fort Atkinson, WI 53538
414-563-9571
Catalog of microcomputer and multimedia curriculum products and software.

Barbara R Endl

6012 Information Access Company

362 Lakeside Drive
Foster City, CA 94404-1171
800-227-8431
Offers automation products and electronics for library/media centers.

6013 LePAC NET

Brodart Automation
500 Arch Street
Williamsport, PA 17705
570-326-2461
800-233-8467
Fax: 570-327-9237
E-mail: salesmkt@brodart.com
http://www.brodart.com
Software for searching thousands of library databases with a single search. Schools can use to take multiple individual library databases and consolidate them, while deleting duplicate listings, into a union database.

Shawn Knight, Assistant Marketing Manager
Denise Macafee, Marketing Manager

6014 Library Corporation

Library Corporation
Research Park
Inwood, WV 25428-9733
800-325-7759
http://www.tlcdelivers.com
Web-based library management systems allows patrons to have easy and immediate access to books and other library resources.

6015 Lingo Fun

International Software
PO Box 486
Westerville, OH 43086-0486
800-745-8258
Providers of microcomputer software including CD-ROM's for Macintosh and MPC, on-line dictionaries, translation assistants; teaching programs for elementary presentation, review and reinforcement, test preparation, and literary exploration.

6016 MARCIVE

PO Box 47508
San Antonio, TX 78265-7508
210-646-6161
800-531-7678
Fax: 210-646-0167
E-mail: info@marcive.com
http://www.marcive.com
Economical, fast 100% conversion. Full MARC records with SEARS or LC headings. Free authorities processing smart barcode labels, reclassification, MARC Record enrichment

6017 Medianet/Dymaxion Research Limited

5515 Cogswell Street
Halifax, Nova Scotia, B3 J 1R2
902-422-1973
Fax: 902-421-1267
E-mail: info@medianet.ns.ca
http://www.medianet.ns.ca
Medianet is the scheduling system for equipment and media that has consistently been rated as best in its class. Features include book library system integration, time-of-day booking, catalog production, WWW and touch tone phone booking by patrons.

Peter Mason, President

6018 Mitinet/Marc Software

6409 Odana Road
Madison, WI 53719-1125
800-824-6272
Fax: 608-270-1107
Import/export USMARC, MICROLIF to USMARC conversions.

6019 Orange Cherry Software

69 Westchester Avenue
PO Box 390
Pound Ridge, NY 10576-1702
914-764-4104
800-672-6002
Fax: 914-764-0104
http://www.orangecherry.com
Educational software products for libraries and media centers.

Biannual

Nicholas Vazzana, President

6020 Right on Programs

778 New York Avenue
Huntington, NY 11743-4240
631-424-7777
Fax: 631-424-7207
E-mail: friends@rightonprograms.com
http://www.rightonprograms.com

Computer software for Windows and networks for library management including circulation, cataloging, periodicals, catalog cardmaking, inventory and thirty more. Used in more than 24,000 schools and libraries of all sizes.

D Farren, VP

6021 SOLINET, Southeastern Library Network

1438 W Peachtree Street NW
Suite 200
Atlanta, GA 30309-2955
404-892-0943
800-999-8558
Fax: 404-892-7879
E-mail: information@solinet.net
http://www.solinet.net
SOLINET provides access, training and support for OCLC products and services; offers discounted library products and services, including licensed databases; provides electronic information solutions; workflow consulting, training and customized workshops; and supports a regional preservation of materials program.

Cathie Gharing, Marketing Coordinator
Liz Hornsby, Editor

6022 Sirsi Corporation

101 Washington Street SE
Huntsville, AL 35801-4827
256-704-7000
800-917-4774
Fax: 256-704-7007
E-mail: sales@sirsi.com
http://www.sirsi.com
Unicorn Collection Management Systems are fully integrated UNIX-based library systems, automating all of a library's operation. Modules include: cataloging, authority control, public access, materials booking, circulation, academic reserves, acquisitions, serials control, reference database manager and electronic mail. Modules can be configured for all types and sizes of libraries.

Vicki Smith, Communication Specialist

6023 Social Issues Resources Series

PO Box 2348
Boca Raton, FL 33427
561-994-0079
800-232-SIRS
Fax: 561-994-4704
Publisher of CD-ROM reference systems for PC and Macintosh computers. Databases of full-text articles carefully selected from 1,000 domestic and international sources. Also provides PC-compatible and stand-alone and network packages.

Paula Jackson, Marketing Director
Suzanne Panek, Customer Service

6024 TekData Systems Company

1111 W Park Avenue
Libertyville, IL 60048-2952
847-367-8800
Fax: 847-367-0235
E-mail: tekdata@tekdata.com
http://www.tekdata.com
Scheduling and booking systems for intranets and internets.

Randy Kick, Sales Manager

6025 Three M Library Systems

Three M Center
Building 225-4N-14
St. Paul, MN 55144
800-328-0067
Fax: 800-223-5563

Materials Flow Management system is the first comprehensive system for optimizing the handling, processing and security of your library materials - from processing to checkout to check-in. The SelfCheck System and Staff Workstation automate the processing of virtually all of your library materials, while the Tattle-Tape Security Strips and Detection Systems help ensure the security of those materials.

6026 UMI
300 N Zeeb Road
Ann Arbor, MI 48103-1553
800-521-0600
Fax: 800-864-0019
Information products in microform, CD-ROM, online and magnetic tape.

6027 University Products
517 Main Street
#101
Holyoke, MA 01040-5514
413-532-3372
800-628-1912
Fax: 413-452-0618
Complete selection of library and media center supplies and equipment.

Juhn Dunpay

6028 WLN
PO Box 3888
Lacey, WA 98509-3888
360-923-4000
800-342-5956
Fax: 360-923-4009
School and media librarians experience 95% hit rates with WLN's LaserCat, CD-ROM database, a cataloging product and MARC record service.

6029 Winnebago Software Company
457 E S Street
Caledonia, MN 55921-1356
800-533-5430
Fax: 507-725-2301
E-mail: sales@winnebago.com
http://www.winnebago.com
Comprehensive, user-friendly circulation and catalog software for Windows, Mac OS, and MS-DOS systems-plus Internet technology, online periodical databases, outstanding customer support, and retrospective conversion services-all developed within the quality guidelines of Winnebago's ISO 9001 certification with TickIT accreditation.

6030 www.awesomelibrary.org
Awesome Library

Organizes the Web with 15,000 carefully reviewed resources, including the top 5 percent in education. Offers sections of mathematics, science, social studies, english, health, physical education, technology, languages, special education, the arts and more. Features a section involved with today's current issues facing our world, like pollution, gun control, tobacco, and other changing 'hot' topics. Site can be browsed in English, German, Spanish, French or Portuguese.

6031 www.techlearning.com
Technology & Learning

Open 24 hours, every day of the week, with an extensive and up-to-date catalog of over 53,000 software and hardware products. Powerful search engine will help you find the right education-specific products.

Mathematics

6032 Accelerated Math
Renaissance Learning
PO Box 8036
Wisconsin Rapids, WI 54495-8036
715-424-3636
800-338-4204
Fax: 715-424-4242
E-mail: answers@renlearn.com
http://www.renlearn.com
Accelerated Math provides 17 different reports, providing individualized, constructive feedback to students, parents, and teachers.

6033 Applied Mathematics Program
Prime Technology Corporation
PO Box 2407
Minneola, FL 34755-2407
352-394-7558
Fax: 352-394-3778
http://www.primetechnology.net
Provides students with comprehensive instruction in 11 math areas. In working with this program, students develop employment and life skills. The program will also lead the student to greater success on the mathematics sections of any standardized test.

Paul Scime, President

6034 CAE Software
3608 Shepherd Street
Chevy Chase, MD 20815-4132
301-907-9845
800-354-3462
Provides educational software for mathematics, grades 3-12. Simulations, tutorials, games, and problem solving. Titles include Mathematics Life Skills Services, Reading and Making Graphs Series, MathLab Series, Meaning of Fractions, Using Fractions and Using Decimals, ALG Football, GEO Pool and GEO Billiards, Paper Route, Mathematics Achievement Project, and others.

Alan R Chap, President

6035 EME Corporation
PO Box 1949
Stuart, FL 34995-1949
800-848-2050
Fax: 561-219-2209
E-mail: emecorp@aol.com
http://www.emescience.com
Publishers of award-winning science and math software, elementary through high school levels.

6036 Logal Software
125 Cambridgepark Drive
Cambridge, MA 02140-2329
617-491-4440
Fax: 617-491-5855
Math and science products for high school through college.

Martha Cheng, President

6037 MathType
Design Science
4028 E Broadway
Long Beach, CA 90803-1502
562-433-0685
800-827-0685
Fax: 562-433-6969
http://www.mathtype.com
Designed to make the creation of complex equations on a computer simple and fast. It works in conjunction with the software ap-

plications you already own, such as word processing programs, graphics programs, presentation programs, and web-authoring applications. Create research papers, tests, slides, books or web pages quickly and easily. MathType is the powerful, professional version of the Equation Editor in Microscoft Word, and Wordperfect.

Bruce Virga, VP Sales/Marketing
Nicole Jessey, Sale/Marketing Coordinator

6038 Mathematica
Wolfram Research

877-239-7149
http://www.wolfram.com
Mathematica is an indispensable tool for finding and communicating solutions quickly and easily.

6039 MindTwister Math
Edmark Corporation
PO Box 97021
Redmond, WA 98073-9721
425-556-8400
800-691-2986
Fax: 425-556-8430
E-mail: edmarkteam@edmark.com
http://www.edmark.com
Software to help students in grade 3 and 4 build math fact fluency, practice mental math and improve estimating skills as they compete in a series of math challenges.

6040 Multimedia - The Human Body
Sunburst Technology
101 Castleton Street
Pleasantville, NY 10570
914-747-3310
800-321-7511
Fax: 914-747-4109
http://www.sunburst.com
Multimedia production of the intricate workings of the human body.

6041 Texas Instruments
Consumer Relations
PO Box 53
Lubbock, TX 79408-0053
800-842-2737
Fax: 972-917-0874
Instructional calculators offer features matched to math concepts taught at each of conceptional development. Classroom accessories and teacher support programs that support the Texas Instruments products enhance instruction and learning. TI also offers a complete range of powerful notebook computers and laser printers for every need.

6042 William K. Bradford Publishing Company
35 Forest Ridge Road
Concord, MA 01742-5414
800-421-2009
Fax: 978-318-9500
http://www.wkbradford.com
Educational software for grades K-12. Especially math and grade book.

Hal Wexler, VP

6043 www.mathgoodies.com
Mrs. Glosser's Math Goodies

Free educational site featuring interactive math lessons. Use a problem-solving approach and actively engage students in the learning process.

6044 www.mathstories.com
MathStories.com

The goal of this site is to help grade school children improve their math problem-solving and critical thinking skills. Offers over 4000 math word problems for children.

6045 www.riverdeep.net
Riverdeep Interactive Learning

Riverdeep's interactive science, language and math arts programs deliver high quality educational experiences.

6046 www.themathemagician.8m.com
The Mathemagician

Offers the help of a real live person to help students correct and understand math and other home work problems.

Music & Art

6047 Harmonic Vision
68 E Wacker Place
Chicago, IL 60610
312-332-9200
800-474-0903
http://www.harmonicvision.com
Leading musical education software to teach effectiveness of music in the home, school and studio.

6048 Midnight Play
Simon & Schuster Interactive

800-793-9972
http://www.simonandschuster.com
Electronic picture book with an unusual look at creativity.

6049 Music Teacher Find
33 W 17th Street
10th Floor
New York, NY 10011
212-242-2464
http://www.MusicTeacherFind.com
Comprehensive Music Teacher Database designed to help music students find quality teachers in their neighborhood.

6050 Music and Guitar

http://www.nl-guitar.com
Original music programs for schools, courses and encounters with music.

6051 Pure Gold Teaching Tools
PO Box 16622
Tuscon, AZ 85732
520-747-5600
866-692-6500
Fax: 520-571-9077
E-mail: info@puregoldteachingtools.com
http://www.puregoldteachingtools.com
Exciting teaching methods and fabulous gifts for teachers, parents, students, pre-schoolers, homeschoolers and music therapists.

Heidi Goldman, President

6052 http://library.thinkquest.org
Think Quest

The Arti FAQS 2100 Project is designed to predict how art will influence our lives in the next hundred years. Students can use available data to make reasonable predictions for the future.

6053 http://members.truepath.com/head oftheclass
Head of The Class

Offers three galleries with clip art for teachers and children, several lesson plans, teaching tips, songs for teachers, lounge laughs, teacher tales and more.

6054 www.billharley.com
BillHarley.com

Humerous, yet meaningful songs which chronicle the lives of children at school and at home. His recordings of songs and stories can be used most effectively in the classroom as inspirational tools for the motivation of learning.

6055 www.sanford-artedventures.com
Sanford- A Lifetime of Color

800-323-0749
Teaches students about art and color theory while they play a game. Lessons plans, newsletter and product information.

6056 www.songs4teachers.com
O'Flynn Consulting

E-mail: oflynn4@home.com
Offers many resources for teachers including songs made especially for your classroom. Sections with songs and activities for holidays, seasons and more. Features books and audios with 101 theme songs for use in the classroom or anywhere children gather to sing.

6057 www.ushistory.com
History Happens

Teaches integrating art, music, literature, science, math, library skills, and American history. The Primary source is stories from American history presented in musci video style.

Physical Education

6058 InfoUse
2560 9th Street
Suite 216
Berkeley, CA 94710-2557
510-549-6520
Fax: 510-549-6512
An award-winning, multimedia development and products firm, features CD-ROM, websites on health, education and disability. For training, education or presentations, our services include: research, instructional design, interface design, graphics, animation, content acquisition, videoing, analog and digital editing and evaluation. Products include SafeNet, (HIV prevention for fifth and sixth grade children), Place Math and Math Pad (math tools and lessons for students with disabilities).

Lewis E Kraus, VP
Susan Stoddard, President

6059 www.sports-media.org
Sports Media

A tool for p.e. teachers, coaches, students and everyone who is interested in p.e./fitness and sports. Interactive p.e. lesson plans, sports pen-apls for the kids, European p.e. mailing list, and developing teaching skills in physical education.

Reading

6060 Accelerated Reader
Renaissance Learning
PO Box 8036
Wisconsin Rapids, WI 54495-8036
715-424-3636
800-338-4204
Fax: 715-424-4242
E-mail: answers@renlearn.com
http://www.renlearn.com
Helps teachers increase literature-based reading practice for all k-12 students

Secondary Education

6061 New York Times
New York, NY
646-698-8000
Fax: 646-698-8344
http://www.nytimes.com/learning
A resource for educators, parents and students in grades six through 12. Provides a daily lesson plan and comprehensive interactive resources based on newspaper content.

Rob Larson, Education Editor
Diane Morgan, Director Marketing

6062 Wm. C. Brown Communications
2460 Kerper Boulevard
Dubuque, IA 52001-2224
College textbooks, software, CD-ROM and more for grades 10-12.

6063 http://adulted.about.com/education/ adulted
Adult/Continuing Education

6064 http://englishhlp.www5.50megs.com
English Help

E-mail: englishhlpr@hotmail.com
This page is a walk through of Microsoft Power Point. The goal is to show in a few simple steps how to make your own website. Created by Rebecca Holland.

6065 www.number2.com
Number2.com

Currently offer SAT and GRE prep along with a vocabulary builder. Practice questions and word drill are adapted to the ability level of the user.

Science

6066 Academic Software Development Group
University of Maryland
University of Maryland
Computer Science Center
College Park, MD 20742-0001
301-405-5100
Fax: 301-405-0726
Offers BioQuest Library which is a set of peer-reviewed resources for science education.

6067 Accu-Weather
385 Science Park Road
State College, PA 16803-2215
814-237-0309
Fax: 814-238-1339
Offers a telecommunications weather and oceanography database.

6068 AccuLab Products Group
614 Senic Drive
Suite 104
Modesto, CA 95350
209-522-8874
Fax: 209-522-8875
Science laboratory software.

6069 Learning Team
10 Long Pond Road
Armonk, NY 10504-2625
914-273-2226
800-793-TEAM
Fax: 914-273-2227
Offers CD-ROM, including MathFinder, Science Helper and Small Blue Planet and Redshift, the Learning Team edition.

Thomas Laster

6070 Problem Solving Concepts
611 N Capitol Avenue
Indianapolis, IN 46204-1205
317-267-9827
800-755-2150
Fax: 317-262-5044
Pro Solv provides students with a new approach to learning introductory physics problem solving techniques. Multi-experiential exercises with supporting text introduce students to relevant variables and their interrelations, principles, graphing and the development of problem solving skills through the quiz/tutorial mode.

Thomas D Feigenbaum, President
Gean R Shelor, Administrative Assistant

6071 Quantum Technology
PO Box 8252
Searcy, AR 72145-8252
A microcomputer database collection system that allows users to perform experiments in chemistry, biology and applied physics.

6072 SCI Technologies
SCI Technologies
105 Terry Drive
Suite 120
Newtown, PA 18940
215-579-8590
800-421-9881
Fax: 215-579-8589
E-mail: cgreenblatt@scitechnologies.com
http://www.scitechnologies.com
A computer-based interface with an integrated hardware and software package that allows the focus of a science lab to shift from data collection to data analysis and experiment design.

Colleen Greenblatt, Sales Manager
Michelle Trexler, Event Coordinator

6073 Videodiscovery
1700 Westlake Avenue N
Suite 600
Seattle, WA 98109-3040
206-285-5400
800-548-3472
Fax: 206-285-9245
Publishers of award winning science videodiscs and multimedia software for kindergarten through post-secondary classes.

6074 www.kidsastronomy.com
KidsAstronomy.com

Offers information on astronomy, deep space, the solar system, space exploration, a teachers corner and more.

6075 www.riverdeep.net
Riverdeep Interactive Learning

Riverdeep's interactive science, language and math arts programs deliver high quality educational experiences.

Social Studies

6076 AccuNet/AP Multimedia Archive
AccuWeather, Inc.
385 Science Park Road
State College, PA 16803
814-235-8600
800-566-6606
Fax: 814-231-0453
E-mail: salesmail@accuwx.com
http://www.ap.accuweather.com
The Photo Archive is an on-line database containing almost a half-million of Associated Press's current and historic images for the last 150 years.

Michael Warfield, Southeastern Sales Manager
Richard Towne, Northeastern Sales Manager

6077 Gale Research
PO Box 33477
Detroit, MI 48232-5477
800-877-GALE
Fax: 800-414-5043
Offers CD-Rom information that offer students contextual understanding of the most commonly-studies persons, events and social movements in U.S. history; concepts, theories, discoveries and people involved in the study of science; current geopolitical data with cultural information on 200 nations of the world as well as all U.S. states and dependencies; poetry and literary information; and more in various databases for education.

6078 World Geography Web Site
ABC-CLIO Schools
130 Cremona Drive
#1911
Santa Barbara, CA 93117-5599
805-968-1911
800-368-6868
Fax: 805-685-9685
Provides convenient internet access to curriculum-based reference and research materials for media specialist, educators and students.

CD-ROM

Judy Fay, Managing Editor
Valerie Mercado, Customer Service

6079 WorldView Software
76 N Broadway
Suite 4009
Hicksville, NY 11801-4241
516-681-1773
800-347-8839
Fax: 516-681-1775
E-mail: history@worldviewsoftware.com
WorldView Software's interactive social studies programs for middle school and high school are comprehensive, curriculum-based tools that may be used along with or in place of textbooks. Each dy-

namic program contains Socratic learning sessions, writing activities and exams with instant feedback. Resource materials in every program include sketches and artwork. Used nationllly in classrooms, computer labs and learning centers.

Grades 7-12

Jerrold Kleinstein, President

6080 http://faculty.acu.edu
M.I. Smart Program

Site designed for teacher and students. Offers electronic resources for historical and cultural geography. Features games, quizzes, trivia and virtual tours for students and thier teachers.

Technology in Education

6081 BLINKS.Net
PO Box 79321
Atlanta, GA 30357
404-243-5202
Fax: 404-241-4992
E-mail: info@blinks.net
http://www.blinks.net
Fastest growing free Internet service provider and community portal for information and resources for the African American, Caribbean, Latino, and African markets.

6082 Boyce Enterprises
360 Sharry Lane
Santa Maria, CA 93455
805-937-4353
Fax: 805-934-1765
Development of computer-based vocational curriculums.

6083 Center for Educational Outreach and Innovation
Teachers College-Columbia University
525 W 120th Street
Box 132
New York, NY 10027
212-678-3987
800-209-1245
Fax: 212-678-8417
E-mail: ceoi-mail@tc.columbia.edu
http://www.tc.columbia.edu
Lifelong learning programs, including distance learning courses, certificates and workshoops in education related topics.

6084 Depco
3305 Airport Drive
PO Box 178
Pittsburg, KS 66762
316-231-0019
800-767-1062
Fax: 316-231-0024
E-mail: sales@depcoinc.com
http://www.depcoinc.com
Program tracks and schedules for you, the test taker delivers tests electronically, as well as, automatic final exams. There are workstation security features to help keep students focused on their activities.

6085 Dialog Information Services
Worldwide Headquaters
3460 Hillview Avenue
#10010
Palo Alto, CA 94304-1338
415-858-3785
800-334-2564
Fax: 650-858-7069

The world's most comprehensive online information source offering over 450 databases containing over 330 million articles, abstracts and citations - covering an unequaled variety of topics, with particular emphasis on news, business, science and technology. Dialog has offices throughout the United States and around the world.

6086 Distance Education Database
International Centre for Distance Learning
Open University, Walton Hall
Milton Keynes
England
441-085-3537
Fax: 441-086-4173
Contains information on distance education, including more than 22,000 distance-taught programs and courses in the Commonwealth of Learning, an organization created by the Commonwealth Heads of Government. On-line and CD-Rom versions of the database contain detailed information on over 30,000 distance-taught courses, 900 distance teaching instructions, and nearly 9,000 books, journals, reports and papers.

Keith Harry, Director

6087 EDUCAUSE
1112 16th Street NW
Suite 600
Washington, DC 20036-4822
202-872-4200
Fax: 202-872-4318
http://www.educause.edu
Aims to link practitioners in primary and secondary education through computer-mediated communications networks.

John Clement, Director

6088 Educational Structures
NCS Pearson
827 W Grove Avenue
Mesa, AZ 85210
800-736-4357
http://www.ncspearson.com
Features complete lesson plans and resources in social studies, mathematics, science, and language arts.

6089 Gibson Tech Ed
1216 S 1580 West
Building C
Orem, UT 84058
800-422-1100
Fax: 800-470-1606
E-mail: gary@gibsonteched.com
http://www.gibsonteched.com
Educational materials to teach electronics, from middle, junior, high school and college.

Gary Gibson, Manager
Tim Gibson, President

6090 Grolier Interactive
Grolier Publishing
90 Sherman Turnpike
Danbury, CT 06816
800-371-3908
Fax: 800-456-4402
http://http://publishing.grolier.com
Instructional software including reference, science, mathematics, music, social studies, early learning, art and art history, language arts/literature.

6091 Heifner Communications
4451 Interstate 70 Drive NW
Columbia, MO 65202-3271
573-445-6163
800-445-6164
Fax: 512-527-2395
Offers educational-merit, cable-programming available via satellite. HCI Distance Learning systems are designed for dependable services and ease of operation and competitive prices.

Vicky Roberts

6092 In Focus
27700 B SW Parkway Avenue
Wilsonville, OR 97070-9215
503-685-8887
800-294-6400
Fax: 503-685-8887
LCD panels, video projectors and systems.

6093 JonesKnowledge.com
9697 E Mineral Avenue
Englewood, CO 80112
800-701-6463
For administrators, that means and integrated solution-with no minimum commitment, or upfront investment. For instructors, it means getting your course online your way, without being a web expert, and for students it means, an accessible and convenient online experience.

6094 Mastercam
CNC Software
5717 Wollochet Drive NW
Suite 2A
Gig Harbor, WA
800-275-6226
Fax: 253-858-6737
E-mail: mcinfo@mastercam.com
http://www.mastercamedu.com

6095 Merit Audio Visual
Merit Software
132 W 21st Street
New York, NY 10011-3203
212-675-8567
800-753-6488
Fax: 212-675-8607
E-mail: sales@meritsoftware.com
http://www.merutsoftware.com
Easy to use, interactive basic skills software for Windows 9x/ME/NT/2000/XP computers. Lessons for reading, writing, grammar and math with appropriate graphics for teens and adults.

Ben Weintraub, Marketing Manager

6096 National Information Center for Educational Media
PO Box 8640
Albuquerque, NM 87198
505-265-3591
800-926-8328
Fax: 505-256-1080
E-mail: nicem@nicem.com
http://www.nicem.com
NICEM maintains a comprehensive database describing educational media materials for all ages and subjects. It is available on CD-ROM and online.

Lisa Savard, Sales/Marketing Director

6097 NoRad Corporation
4455 Torrance Boulevard
#2806513
Torrance, CA 90503-4398
310-605-0808
Fax: 323-934-2101

Mini, personal, medium and large computer systems for educational institutions.

6098 Proxima Corporation
9440 Carroll Park Drive
San Diego, CA 92121
858-457-5500
800-294-6400
Fax: 503-685-7239
http://www.proxima.com
Proxima Corporation is a global leader in the multimedia projection market, providing world class presentation solutions to corporate enterprises, workgroups, mobile professionals, trainers, and professional public speakers.

Kim Gallagher, Public Relations Manager
Kathy Bankerd, Director Marketing Programs

6099 RB5X: Education's Personal Computer Robot
General Robotics Corporation
760 S Youngfield Court
Suite 8
Lakewood, CO 80228-2813
303-988-5636
800-422-4265
Fax: 303-988-5303
E-mail: cbrown@generalrobotics.com
http://www.edurobot.com
RB5X: Education's Personal Computer Robot. All grade levels. Self learn, self teach, hands on modular system. Problem solving, basic learning skills, increases self-esteem. Expanable open-ended, motivation at its best.

Constant Brown, President

6100 SEAL
550 Spring Street
Naugatuck, CT 06770-1906
203-729-5201
Complete line of systems and electronics for schools.

6101 Sharp Electronics Corporation
LCD Products Group
Sharp Plaza
Mall Stop One
Mahwah, NJ 07430
201-529-8731
Fax: 201-529-9636
E-mail: prolcd@sharpsec.com
http://www.sharplcd.com
Offers a full line of LCD-based video and computer multimedia projectors and projection panels for use in a wide range of educational applications. Sharp's product line also includes industrial VHS format VCRs, color TV monitors.

J Ganguzza, Director/Marketing

6102 Valiant
PO Box 3171
S Hackensack, NJ 07606-1171
800-631-0867
Fax: 201-814-0418
Distributors of LCD projection panels, P/A systems, overhead/slide and filmstrip projectors, cassette recorders, classroom record players, laser pointers, laminating equipment, lecturns, listening centers and headphones.

Sheldon Goldstein

6103 Vernier Software
8565 SW Beaverton Hillsdale Hwy
Portland, OR 97225-2429
Laboratory interacting software for the Macintosh, IBM and Apple II.

6104 Websense
10240 Sorrento Valley Road
San Diego, CA 92121
858-320-8000
800-723-1166
Fax: 858-458-2950
http://www.websense.com
Internet filtering.

6105 http://di...elearn/cs/eductechnology/index.htm
About Education Distance Learning

6106 http://futurekids.com
FUTUREKIDS School Technology
Solutions

http://www.futurekids.com
Helping schools use technology to transform education.

6107 http://online.uophx.edu
University of Phoenix Online

Offers you the convenience and flexibility of attending classes from your personal computer. Students are discussing issues, sharing ideas, testing theories, essentially enjoying all of the advantages of an on-campus degree programs. Interaction is included like e-mail, so you practice at your convenience.

6108 http://www.crossteccorp.com
NetOp

800-675-0729
Fax: 561-391-5820
http://www.crossteccorp.com
A powerful combination of seven essential tools for networked classrooms. Based on the award winning technology of NetOp Remote Control and is easy-to-use software only solution.

6109 http://www.growsmartbrains.com
GrowSmartBrains.com

Website for parents and educators who want research based information and practical stradegies for raising children in a media age.

6110 http://www.zdnet.com
ZDNet

Full-service destination for people looking to buy, use and learn more about technology.

6111 www.21ct.org
Twenty First Century Teachers Network

A nationwide, non-profit initiative of the McGuffey Project, dedicated to assisting k-12 teachers learn, use and effectively integrate technology in the curriculum for improved student learning.

6112 www.aboutonehandtyping.com/
One Hand Typing and Keyboarding
Resources

This site dishes up a blend of messages and stories, resources for one-hand typists, links to alternative keyboards, teaching links, and more.

6113 www.digitaldividenetwork.org
Digital Divide Network

E-mail: ddivide@benton.org
The goal of bridging the divide is to use communications technology to help improve the quality of life of all communities and their citizens; provide them with the tools, skills and information they need to help them realize their socioeconomic, educational and cultural potential.

6114 www.getquizzed.com
GetQuizzed

Designed as a free service that provides a database that allows users to create, store and edit Multiple Choice or Question and Answer quizzes, under password protected conditions.

6115 www.guidetogeekdom.com
Guide to Geekdom

E-mail: info@guidetogeekdom.com
Designed especially for Homeschoolers, step-by-step lessons teach students how to use the computer and troubleshoot computer problems. Offers workbooks, sample lesson and more.

6116 www.happyteachers.com
HappyTeachers.com

Information about technical and vocational education programs, products and curriculum.

6117 www.integratingit.com
Integrating Information Technology for the
Classroom, School, & District
Dedicated to providing the education community a place to find real world strategies, solutions, and resources for integrating technology. Organized by the perspective of the classroom teacher, the school administrator, and the district.

6118 www.livetext.com
LiveText Curriculum Manager

Provides tools for engaged learning classroom projects and provides online professional development for teachers.

6119 www.ncrel.org
North Central Regional Educational
Laboratory

Offers research results regarding the effective use of technology.

6120 www.ncrtec.org
N Central Regional Technology
in Education Consortiums
Provides a variety of tools and information to improve technology-related professional development programs.

Elementary Education

6121 Curriculum Associates
153 Rangeway Road
No. Billerica, MA 01862
800-225-0248
Fax: 800-366-1158
http://www.curriculumassociates.com
Test preparation material with a guarantee
of success; skill instruction and assessment.

6122 Diagnostic Reading Inventory for Primaryand Intermediate Grades K-8
Scott and McCleary Publishing Co.
2482 11th Street SW
Akron, OH 44314-1712
702-566-8756
800-765-3564
Fax: 702-568-1378
E-mail: jscott7576@aol.com
http://www.scottmccleary.com
A series of 13 tests at each grade level, 10
can be given in a group setting. 3 Forms of
the IRI teacher friendly. Easy to administer.

Spiral Paperback
ISBN: 0-9636225-4-4

Janet M. Scott and Sheila C. McCeary,
Author
Janet Scott, Co-Author
Sheila McCleary, Co-Author

6123 Lexia Learning Systems
PO Box 466
Lincoln, MA 01773-0466
781-259-8752
Fax: 781-259-1349
E-mail: info@lexialearning.com
http://www.lexialearning.com
Reading software and assessment programs
for children and adults, professional development programs for teachers, principals
and administrators.

6124 LinguiSystems
3100 4th Avenue
East Moline, IL 61244-9700
800-776-4332
Fax: 800-577-4555
E-mail: service@linguisystems.com
http://www.linguisystems.com
Offers tests and print materials for speech
language pathologists, teachers of the learning disabled, middle school language arts
and reading teachers.

6125 National Study of School Evaluation
1699 E Woodfield Road
Suite 406
Schaumburg, IL 60173-4958
847-995-9080
800-843-6773
Fax: 847-995-9088
E-mail: schoolimprovement@nsse.org
http://www.nsse.org
Provides educational leaders with
state-of-the-art assessment and evaluation
materials to enhance and promote student
growth and school improvement.

Dr. Kathleen A. Fitzpatrick, Executive
Director

6126 Testing Miss Malarky
Walker And Company
435 Hudson Street
New York, NY 10014
212-727-8300
800-289-2553
Fax: 212-727-0984
http://www.walkerbooks.com
Author and artist exploit the mania that ac-
companies the classes first standardized
test.

32 pages
ISBN: 0-8027-8737-1

Judy Finchler, Contact

Language Arts

6127 CTB/McGraw-Hill
20 Ryan Ranch Road
Monterey, CA 93940-5703
831-393-0700
800-538-9547
Fax: 800-282-0266
http://www.ctb.com
K-12 achievement tests, early literacy assessment, language proficiency evaluation,
adult basic skills tests, and test management
and instructional planning software.

6128 SLEP Program Office
PO Box 6155
Princeton, NJ 08541-6155
Offers information on the Secondary Level
English Proficiency Test.

Mathematics

6129 Psychological Assessment Resources
PO Box 998
Odessa, FL 33556
800-331-TEST
Fax: 800-727-9329
http://www.parinc.com
Catalog of professional testing resources.

6130 Summing It Up: College Board Mathematics Assessment Programs
College Board Publications
45 Columbus Avenue
New York, NY 10023-6917
212-713-8165
800-323-7155
Fax: 800-525-5562
http://www.collegeboard.org
An overview of SAT I: Reasoning Tests and
PSAT/NMSQT, SAT II: Subject Tests, De-
scriptive Tests of Mathematical Skills
(DTMS), CPTs in Mathematics, CLEP
Mathematics Examinations, AP Exams in
Mathematics, AP Exams in Computer Sci-
ences, and Pacesetter Mathematics.

30 pages

Music & Art

6131 A&F Video's Art Catalog
PO Box 264
Geneseo, NY 14454
http://www.aandfvideo.com
New listing of titles for Art Teachers and
Art Lovers.

6132 All Art Supplies
Art Supplies Wholesale
4 Enon Street
North Beverly, MA 01915
800-462-2420
http://www.allartsupplies.com
Art supplies at wholesale prices.

6133 American Art Clay Company
6060 Guion Road
Indianapolis, IN 46254
317-244-6871
800-374-1600
Fax: 317-248-9300
E-mail: catalog@amaco.com
http://www.amaco.com
Provides ceramic materials and equipment.

6134 Arnold Grummer
PO Box 13245
Milwaukee, WI 53213
800-453-1485
Fax: 414-453-1495
E-mail: webmaster@arnoldgrummer.com
http://www.arnoldgrummer.com
Products and information to meet most any
papermaking need.

6135 Arrowmont School of Arts & Crafts
556 Parkway
Gainsburg, TN 37738
865-438-5860
Fax: 865-438-4101
http://www.arrowmont.org
The art school of tomorrow.

6136 Art & Creative Materials Institute
PO Box 479
Hanson, MA 02341
781-293-4100
Fax: 781-294-0808
E-mail: debbieg@acminec.org
http://www.acminec.org
A non-profit trade association whose
memebers are manufacturers of art and creative materials. Sponsors a certification
program to ensure that art materials are
non-toxic or affixed with health warning labels where appropriate. Publishes a booklet
on the safe use of art materials and a listing
of products that are approved under its certification program. Both of these publications are free of charge.

Deborah Fanning, Executive Vice
President
Deborah Gustafson, Associate Director

6137 Art Instruction Schools
3309 Broadway Street NW
Minneapolis, MN 55413
http://www.artists-ais.com

6138 Art to Remember
10625 Deme Drive
Unit E
Indianapolis, IN 46236
317-826-0870
800-895-8777
Fax: 317-823-2822
http://www.arttoremember.com
A unique program that encourages your students' artisic creativity while providing an
oppurtunity to raise funds for schools.

6139 ArtSketchbook.com
487 Hulsetown Road
Campbell Hall, NY 10916
845-496-4709
http://www.artsketchbook.com
Provides instructions and work examples by
an elementary student, secondary student
and a professional artist.

6140 Arts Institutes International
Education Management Corporation
300 6th Avenue
Suite 800
Pittsburgh, PA 15222
800-275-2440
Post-secondary career education. Offers associate's, bachelor's and non-degree programs in design, media arts, technology, culinary arts and fashion.

6141 Museum Stamps
PO Box 356
New Canaan, CT 06840
800-659-2787
Fax: 203-966-2729
http://www.museumstamps.com
Rubber stamps of famous works of art, stamp accessories, classroom projects.

6142 Music Ace 2
Harmonic Vision
68 E Wacker Place
8th Floor
Chicago, IL 60610
312-332-9200
800-474-0903
Fax: 312-726-1946
http://www.harmonicvision.com
Introduces concepts such as standard notation, rhythm, melody, time signatures, harmony, intervals and more.

6143 http://www.ilford.com
Ilford

Partners in imaging.

6144 www.schoolrenaissance.com
School Renaissance Model

The School Renaissance Model combines the #1 software in education with professional development and consulting services to help you dramatically improve student performance.

6145 www.speedballart.com

Speedball lesson plans and teaching aids for calligraphy, stamping, printmaking, drawing, painting and more.

Reading

6146 Advantage Learning Systems
2911 Peach Street
PO Box 8036
Wisconsin Rapids, WI 54495-8036
800-338-4204
Fax: 715-424-4242
http://www.advlearn.com
New computer-adaptive tests that assess student reading and math levels in just 15 minutes or less.

6147 Educational Testing Service/Library
Test Collection
Rosedale Road
Princeton, NJ 08541
609-734-5686
Fax: 609-734-5410
Provides information on tests and related materials to those in research and advisory services and educational activities.

Janet Williams, President

6148 National Foundation for Dyslexia
4801 Hermitage Road
Richmond, VA 23227-3332
804-262-0586
800-SOS-READ
Provides screenings for schools or individuals and assists individuals with IEP's. Provides information about support groups and organizations and teacher training workshops.

Jo Powell, Executive Director

6149 Psychological Assessment Resources
PO Box 998
Odessa, FL 33556
800-331-TEST
Fax: 800-727-9329
http://www.parinc.com
Catalog of professional testing resources.

6150 www.schoolrenaissance.com
Renaissance Learning and School Renaissance Inst.

The School Renaissance Model combines the #1 software in education with professional development and consulting services to help you dramatically improve student performance.

6151 www.voyagerlearning.com
Voyager Expanded Learning

Improves students performance in reading for those at different grade levels.

Secondary Education

6152 ACT
PO Box 4060
Iowa City, IA 52243-0001
319-337-1000
800-498-6065
Offers a full-service catalog of tests for intermediate and secondary schools organized by assessment, career and educational planning, study skills, surveys and research services.

Catalog

6153 Admission Officer's Handbook for the New SAT Program
College Board Publications
45 Columbus Avenue
New York, NY 10023-6917
212-713-8165
800-323-7155
Fax: 800-525-5562
http://www.collegeboard.org
Designed to help college admission staff quickly find information on the new SAT program, the Handbook has detailed descriptions of score reports and special services for colleges.

56 pages

6154 American College Testing
ACT
2201 Dodge
#168
Iowa City, IA 52243-0001
319-337-1028
Fax: 319-337-1014
E-mail: gullettk@act.org
http://www.act.org
Provides educational assessment services to students and their parents, high schools, colleges and professional associations.

Also workforce development services, including a network of ACT Centers and the Workkeys program.

Ken Gullette, Director, Media Relations

6155 College-Bound Seniors
College Board Publications
45 Columbus Avenue
New York, NY 10023-6917
212-713-8165
800-323-7155
Fax: 800-525-5562
http://www.collegeboard.org
Profile of SAT and achievement test takers, national report.

13 pages

6156 CollegeChoice, StudentChoice
College Board Publications
45 Columbus Avenue
New York, NY 10023-6917
212-713-8165
800-323-7155
Fax: 800-525-5562
http://www.collegeboard.org
This video provides a reassuring perspective on the SAT's importance and how the college admission process really works. It shows how SAT scores are only one of many elements in the admission picture and emphasizes academic preparation for college and discusses the SAT within the context of the entire admission process.

15 Minutes

6157 Counselor's Handbook for the SAT Program
College Board Publications
45 Columbus Avenue
New York, NY 10023-6917
212-713-8165
800-323-7155
Fax: 800-525-5562
http://www.collegeboard.org
Easy-to-use reference provides details on the new SAT program tests and services.

64 pages

6158 Destination College: Planning with the PSAT/NMSQT
College Board Publications
45 Columbus Avenue
New York, NY 10023-6917
212-713-8165
800-323-7155
Fax: 800-525-5562
http://www.collegeboard.org
This new video offers schools an ideal format for explaining the features and benefits of the PSAT/NMSQT Score Report to groups of students.

18 Minutes

6159 Educational Testing Service
Rosedale Road
MS 26-C
Princeton, NJ 08541
609-921-9000
Fax: 609-734-5410
Private educational measurement institution and a leader in educational research.

Susan Keipper, Program Director

6160 Focus on the SAT: What's on it, How to Prepare & What Colleges Look For
College Board Publications
45 Columbus Avenue
New York, NY 10023-6917
212-713-8165
800-323-7155
Fax: 800-525-5562
http://www.collegeboard.org
The authoritative video for students on how to prepare for the SAT and PSAT/NMSQT. It provides test-taking tips, sample test questions, and an explanation of how SAT is developed.

20 Minutes

6161 GED Testing Service
American Council on Education
1 Dupont Cir NW
Washington, DC 20036-1110
202-939-9490
Fax: 202-775-8578
The largest testing service in the United States. Maintains a full line of tests and testing resources for all areas of education and all grade levels K-college level testing.

6162 Guide to the College Board Validity Study Service
College Board Publications
45 Columbus Avenue
New York, NY 10023-6917
212-713-8165
800-323-7155
Fax: 800-525-5562
http://www.collegeboard.org
The purpose of this manual is to assist Validity Study Service users in designing and interpreting validity studies. It provides design suggestions, sample admission and placement studies, advice on interpreting studies, and a discussion of basic statistical concepts.

60 pages

6163 Look Inside the SAT I: Test Prep from the Test Makers Video
College Board Publications
45 Columbus Avenue
New York, NY 10023-6917
212-713-8165
800-323-7155
Fax: 800-525-5562
http://www.collegeboard.org
Brings the College Board's test-taking tips to life through interviews with people from different backgrounds who recount their SAT experiences.

30 Minutes
ISBN: 0-874475-29-5

6164 Master The GMAT
Peterson's, A Nelnet Company
Princeton Pike Corporate Center
2000 Lenox Drive PO Box 67005
Lawrenceville, NJ 08648
609-896-1800
800-338-3282
Fax: 690-896-4531
E-mail: custsvc@petersons.com
http://www.petersons.com
Helps test takers get ready, develop test-preparation strategies and manage test anxiety constructively, whether they have seven weeks to prepare or just one day.

672 pages Book & Disk
Martinson, Author

6165 Master The SAT
Peterson's, A Nelnet Company
Princeton Pike Corporate Center
2000 Lenox Drive PO Box 67005
Lawrenceville, NJ 08648
609-896-1800
800-338-3282
Fax: 609-896-4531
E-mail: custsvc@petersons.com
http://www.petersons.com
Features easily accessible Red Alert sections offering essential tips for test-taking success. Provides students with the critical skills they need to tackle the SAT.

821 pages Book & Disk
ISBN: 1-560796-06-5
John Davenport Carris with Michael R. Crystal, Author

6166 National Center for Fair & Open Testing
342 Broadway
Cambridge, MA 02139-1843
617-864-4810
Fax: 617-497-2224
Dedicated to ensuring that America's students and workers are assessed using fair, accurate, relevant and open tests.

Cinthia Schuman, President

6167 National Study of School Evaluation
1699 E Woodfield Road
Suite 406
Schaumburg, IL 60173-4958
847-995-9080
800-843-6773
Fax: 847-995-9088
E-mail: schoolimprovement@nsse.org
http://www.nsse.org
Provides educational leaders with state-of-the-art assessment and evaluation materials to enhance and promote student growth and school improvement.

Dr. Kathleen A. Fitzpatrick, Executive Director

6168 Official Guide to the SAT II: Subject Tests
College Board Publications
45 Columbus Avenue
New York, NY 10023-6917
212-713-8165
800-323-7155
Fax: 800-525-5562
http://www.collegeboard.org
The authoritative preparation guide for students taking the SAT II: Subject Tests. The guide includes full-length practice Subject Tests, along with answer sheets, answer keys, and scoring instructions for Writing, Literature, American History, World History, Math I, Math IIC, Biology, Chemistry and Physics. It also includes minitests in French (reading only), German (reading only), Italian, Latin, Modern Hebrew, and Spanish.

380 pages
ISBN: 0-874474-88-4

6169 One-On-One with the SAT
College Board Publications
45 Columbus Avenue
New York, NY 10023-6917
212-713-8165
800-323-7155
Fax: 800-525-5562
http://www.collegeboard.org
Gives students easy access to proven advice and test-taking strategies directly from the test makers, as well as a unique chance to take a real SAT on computer. This program

also includes password protection for each student record and toll-free technical support.

Home License

6170 Panic Plan for the SAT
Peterson's, A Nelnet Company
Princeton Pike Corporate Center
2000 Lenox Drive PO Box 67005
Lawrenceville, NJ 08648
609-896-1800
800-338-3282
Fax: 609-896-4531
E-mail: custsvc@petersons.com
http://www.petersons.com
An excellent, two-week review, featuring actual questions from the SAT. Helps students make the most out of the limited time they have left to study.

368 pages
ISBN: 1-560794-32-1
Michael R Crystal, Author

6171 Preventing School Failure
Heldref Publications
1319 Eighteenth Street NW
Washington, DC 20036-1802
202-296-6267
800-365-9753
Fax: 202-296-5149
http://www.heldref.org
The articles cover a broad array of specific topics, from important technical aspects and adaptions of functional behavioral assessment to descriptions of projects in which functional behavioral assessment is being used to provide technical assistance to preschools, schools, and families who must deal eith children and adolescents who present serious challenging behaviors.

Quarterly
ISSN: 1045-988X
Sheldon Braaten, Executive Editor

6172 Psychological Corporation
555 Academic Court
San Antonio, TX 78204-2498
210-921-8701
Assessment materials for teachers in all areas of curricula.

6173 Psychometric Affiliates
PO Box 807
Murfreeboro, TN 37133
615-890-6296
Testing instruments for use by educational institutions.

Jeannette Heritage

6174 Real SAT's
College Board Publications
45 Columbus Avenue
New York, NY 10023-6917
212-713-8165
800-323-7155
Fax: 800-525-5562
http://www.collegeboard.org
The only preparation guide that contains actual scorable tests. It has been developed to help the millions of students taking the tests each year to do their best on the PSAT/NMSQT and SAT and to improve their scores.

396 pages
ISBN: 0-874475-11-2

6175 Registration Bulletin
College Board Publications
45 Columbus Avenue
New York, NY 10023-6917
212-713-8165
800-323-7155
Fax: 800-525-5562
http://www.collegeboard.org
Available in five regional and a New York
State edition, the Bulletin provides information
on how to register for the SAT I and
SAT II, and on how to use the related services.

24 pages

**6176 SAT Services for Students with
Disabilities**
College Board Publications
45 Columbus Avenue
New York, NY 10023-6917
212-713-8165
800-323-7155
Fax: 800-525-5562
http://www.collegeboard.org
Describes arrangements for students with
physical, hearing, visual and learning disabilities
who wish to take the SAT I and/or
SAT II.

6 pages

6177 Scholastic Testing Service
480 Meyer Road
Bensenville, IL 60106-1617
630-766-7150
800-642-6STS
Fax: 630-766-8054
E-mail: stslh25@aol.com
http://www.ststesting.com
Publisher of assessment materials from
birth into adulthood, ability and achievement
tests for kindergarten through grade
twelve. Tests are also constructed on contract
for educational agencies and school
districts. Publish the Torrance Tests of Creative
Thinking, Thinking Creatively in Action
and Movement, the STS High School
Placement Test and Educational Development
Series.

OF Anderhalter, President
John D Kauffman, VP Marketing

6178 TOEFL Test and Score Manual
College Board Publications
45 Columbus Avenue
New York, NY 10023-6917
212-713-8165
800-323-7155
Fax: 800-525-5562
http://www.collegeboard.org
Focuses on information that college admissions
officers, foreign student advisers and
other users of TOEFL score reports need to
know about the operation of the TOEFL
program, the test itself, and the interpretation
of scores.

48 pages

6179 Taking the SAT I: Reasoning Test
College Board Publications
45 Columbus Avenue
New York, NY 10023-6917
212-713-8165
800-323-7155
Fax: 800-525-5562
http://www.collegeboard.org
A complete guide for students who plan to
take the SAT I: Reasoning Test.

80 pages

**6180 Taking the SAT II: The Official
Guide to the SAT II: Subject Tests**
College Board Publications
45 Columbus Avenue
New York, NY 10023-6917
212-713-8165
800-323-7155
Fax: 800-525-5562
http://www.collegeboard.org
Provides information about the content and
format of each of the SAT II: Subject Tests,
as well as test-taking advice and sample
questions.

95 pages

6181 TestSkills
College Board Publications
45 Columbus Avenue
New York, NY 10023-6917
212-713-8165
800-323-7155
Fax: 800-525-5562
http://www.collegeboard.org
A preparation program for the
PSAT/NMSQT that helps students, particularly
those from minority and disadvantaged
groups, sharpen skills and increase
confidence needed to succeed on the tests.

Spiral-Bound

**6182 Think Before You Punch: Using
Calculators on the New SAT I and
PSAT/NMSQT**
College Board Publications
45 Columbus Avenue
New York, NY 10023-6917
212-713-8165
800-323-7155
Fax: 800-525-5562
http://www.collegeboard.org
This video looks at the pros and cons of calculators
usage on a test. In it, students talk
about using them, and College Board and
ETS staff explain the new calculator policy.
It works through math questions that
may or may not best be answered with the
help of a calculator.

12 Minutes

Participation of employed persons, 17 years old and over, in career-related adult education during the previous 12 months, by selected characteristics of participants: 1995, 1999, and 2003

Characteristic of employed persons	1995 Percent of adults participating in career or job-related courses	1995 Number of career or job-related courses taken, per employee	1999 In career or job-related courses	1999 In apprentice programs	1999 Number of career or job-related courses taken, per employee	2003 Employed persons, in thousands	2003 In career or job-related courses[1]	2003 In apprentice programs	2003 In less formal work-related learning activities	2003 Number of career or job-related courses taken, in thousands	2003 Number of career or job-related courses taken, per employee[1]
1	2	3	4	5	6	7	8	9	10	11	12
Total	31.1	0.8	30.5 (1.14)	2.2 (0.41)	0.7 (0.03)	130,025	46.0 (0.70)	1.1 (0.14)	76.5 (0.70)	119,948	0.9 (0.02)
Sex											
Males	29.0	0.7	28.3 (1.15)	3.0 (0.45)	0.6 (0.03)	67,453	42.7 (1.15)	1.6 (0.26)	76.1 (0.94)	54,870	0.8 (0.03)
Females	33.4	0.9	32.9 (1.14)	1.4 (0.32)	0.8 (0.03)	62,572	49.4 (0.99)	0.6 (0.11)	76.9 (1.05)	65,078	1.0 (0.03)
Age											
17 to 24 years	18.6	0.4	19.1 (1.91)	4.4 (1.41)	0.4 (0.06)	16,113	33.9 (2.31)	2.6 (0.72)	83.2 (1.51)	8,777	0.5 (0.06)
25 to 29 years	31.2	0.8	34.3 (2.44)	3.7 (0.93)	0.8 (0.08)	14,393	49.7 (2.62)	2.4 (0.74)	82.2 (2.44)	13,059	0.9 (0.05)
30 to 34 years	31.6	0.8	34.4 (2.50)	2.9 (0.82)	0.8 (0.08)	13,691	48.4 (2.50)	1.6 (0.47)	76.6 (2.20)	12,823	0.9 (0.06)
35 to 39 years	35.1	0.9	29.2 (2.15)	1.6 (0.52)	0.7 (0.07)	16,281	48.8 (2.32)	0.5 (0.23)	74.9 (1.98)	15,841	1.0 (0.06)
40 to 44 years	36.6	0.9	36.4 (2.44)	1.5 (0.60)	0.8 (0.07)	19,794	46.1 (2.23)	0.9 (0.32)	77.3 (1.97)	18,055	0.9 (0.06)
45 to 49 years	39.6	1.0	30.4 (2.42)	1.8 (0.75)	0.7 (0.06)	17,030	50.8 (2.15)	0.3 (0.11)	74.9 (2.58)	18,360	1.1 (0.06)
50 to 54 years	34.4	0.9	34.7 (2.57)	1.3 (0.54)	0.8 (0.07)	13,296	52.5 (2.21)	0.6 (0.23)	77.6 (2.04)	16,305	1.2 (0.08)
55 to 59 years	26.7	0.7	30.3 (2.83)	0.8 (0.56)	0.6 (0.08)	9,884	46.3 (2.49)	0.4 (0.19)	72.0 (2.42)	9,990	1.0 (0.06)
60 to 64 years	21.1	0.5	27.2 (3.80)	0.8 (0.82)	0.7 (0.15)	5,318	37.8 (2.63)	0.1 (0.09)	64.1 (3.07)	4,198	0.8 (0.08)
65 and over	13.7	0.4	20.3 (4.21)	0.2 (0.25)	0.4 (0.08)	4,226	— (†)	— (†)	— (†)	2,541	— (†)
65 to 69 years	—	—	— (†)	— (†)	— (†)	2,379	33.5 (3.42)	0.6 (0.57)	66.3 (3.73)	1,679	0.7 (0.08)
70 years and over	—	—	— (†)	— (†)	— (†)	1,847	22.3 (3.35)	# (†)	55.8 (5.53)	862	0.5 (0.09)
Racial/ethnic group											
White, non-Hispanic	33.2	0.8	32.8 (0.98)	1.7 (0.25)	0.6 (0.03)	94,603	48.5 (0.85)	1.1 (0.18)	78.5 (0.77)	92,576	1.0 (0.02)
Black, non-Hispanic	26.2	0.7	28.1 (2.34)	4.1 (1.27)	1.0 (0.07)	13,513	43.4 (2.19)	0.8 (0.31)	75.2 (1.98)	12,385	0.9 (0.06)
Hispanic	18.1	0.4	16.4 (1.83)	4.3 (1.45)	0.5 (0.05)	15,694	31.8 (2.32)	1.1 (0.31)	66.3 (2.69)	9,356	0.6 (0.06)
Asian/Pacific Islander	25.5	0.6	32.8 (4.84)	# (†)	0.4 (0.15)	4,056	50.4 (4.77)	0.6 (0.51)	78.1 (4.89)	3,393	0.8 (0.09)
American Indian/Alaska Native	34.0	0.9	29.5 (11.52)	6.8 (5.57)	0.7 (0.52)	760	40.0 (15.14)	3.1 (3.28)	55.0 (17.49)	498	0.7 (0.25)
Highest level of education completed											
Less than high school completion	8.8	0.1	7.9 (2.29)	2.5 (1.66)	0.4 (0.05)	15,070	— (†)	— (†)	— (†)	3,000	— (†)
Eighth grade or less	—	—	— (†)	— (†)	— (†)	4,753	9.9 (3.11)	0.2 (0.19)	49.4 (5.57)	668	0.1 (0.05)
9th to 12th grade, no completion	—	—	— (†)	— (†)	— (†)	10,318	16.3 (2.32)	1.7 (1.00)	56.2 (3.97)	2,332	0.2 (0.04)
High school completion	20.9	0.4	21.4 (1.45)	2.4 (0.59)	0.8 (0.03)	34,412	33.2 (1.39)	1.0 (0.23)	68.7 (1.79)	19,407	0.6 (0.03)
Some vocational/technical	32.3	0.8	28.7 (5.76)	5.1 (3.23)	0.9 (0.17)	4,372	41.7 (3.26)	3.9 (1.40)	83.2 (2.39)	4,299	1.0 (0.11)
Some college	29.9	0.7	29.0 (1.78)	3.0 (0.71)	0.7 (0.06)	26,448	45.6 (1.83)	1.7 (0.45)	78.4 (1.42)	23,294	0.9 (0.05)
Associate's degree	39.2	1.0	39.7 (3.07)	2.6 (0.90)	0.9 (0.09)	8,851	54.5 (2.74)	1.1 (0.41)	82.3 (2.09)	9,966	1.1 (0.07)
Bachelor's degree	44.6	1.2	43.8 (2.01)	1.0 (0.31)	1.0 (0.06)	24,024	64.2 (1.42)	0.4 (0.13)	86.6 (1.35)	31,875	1.3 (0.05)
Some graduate work (or study)	50.2	1.4	46.8 (4.17)	1.4 (1.02)	1.2 (0.14)	16,849	71.5 (1.87)	0.5 (0.20)	90.2 (1.08)	28,107	1.7 (0.07)
No degree	44.3	1.2	54.2 (4.94)	0.9 (0.65)	1.2 (0.14)	2,466	68.3 (4.90)	0.1 (0.12)	86.7 (2.76)	3,984	1.6 (0.15)
Master's	50.5	1.4	45.3 (2.97)	0.9 (0.45)	1.1 (0.11)	9,834	73.4 (2.44)	0.7 (0.34)	92.7 (1.05)	17,108	1.7 (0.09)
Doctor's	40.4	1.0	34.4 (4.79)	3.2 (1.45)	0.7 (0.12)	1,727	58.9 (6.15)	# (†)	84.3 (5.91)	2,457	1.4 (0.25)
Professional	67.6	2.0	67.6 (6.98)	1.4 (1.42)	1.9 (0.31)	2,822	75.3 (4.63)	0.5 (0.34)	88.2 (4.01)	4,558	1.6 (0.16)
Urbanicity											
Urban	32.4	0.8	31.5 (1.67)	2.3 (0.49)	0.7 (0.05)	103,185	48.0 (0.75)	1.1 (0.15)	78.1 (0.72)	99,576	1.0 (0.02)
Urban, inside urbanized area	33.3	0.8	31.2 (0.99)	2.4 (0.35)	0.7 (0.03)	88,626	47.7 (0.88)	1.2 (0.17)	78.3 (0.78)	85,210	1.0 (0.02)
Urban, outside urbanized area	27.9	0.7	32.9 (2.48)	1.8 (0.64)	0.8 (0.08)	14,559	49.5 (2.19)	0.6 (0.24)	77.0 (2.21)	14,366	1.0 (0.06)
Rural	26.9	0.7	27.1 (1.74)	2.0 (0.65)	0.6 (0.05)	26,841	38.2 (2.08)	1.2 (0.42)	70.1 (2.03)	20,373	0.8 (0.05)

See notes at end of table.

Participation of employed persons, 17 years old and over, in career-related adult education during the previous 12 months, by selected characteristics of participants: 1995, 1999, and 2003—Continued

Characteristic of employed persons	1995 Percent of adults participating in career or job-related courses	1995 Number of career or job-related courses taken, per employee	1999 Percent participating: In career or job-related courses	1999 Percent participating: In apprentice programs	1999 Number of career or job-related courses taken, per employee	2003 Employed persons, in thousands	2003 Percent: In career or job-related courses[1]	2003 Percent: In apprentice programs	2003 Percent: In less formal work-related learning activities	2003 Number of career or job-related courses taken, in thousands	2003 Number of career or job-related courses taken, per employee[1]
1	2	3	4	5	6	7	8	9	10	11	12
Occupation											
Executive, administrative, or managerial	42.9	1.2	40.6 (2.06)	1.2 (0.41)	1.0 (0.07)	15,613	61.7 (2.13)	0.6 (0.31)	85.9 (1.83)	20,867	1.3 (0.06)
Engineers, surveyors, and architects	44.2	1.1	52.1 (6.96)	6.0 (4.34)	1.0 (0.16)	2,376	66.8 (4.60)	1.4 (1.01)	92.0 (2.49)	3,046	1.3 (0.13)
Natural scientists and mathematicians	59.7	1.7	46.0 (6.61)	1.4 (0.90)	0.8 (0.14)	2,405	60.7 (5.89)	# (†)	93.4 (2.05)	2,894	1.2 (0.13)
Social scientists and workers, lawyers	59.5	1.8	56.9 (5.66)	0.7 (0.65)	1.7 (0.24)	2,875	77.7 (3.90)	0.8 (0.81)	87.5 (3.02)	5,518	1.9 (0.15)
Teachers, elementary/secondary	53.9	1.5	52.1 (3.53)	0.4 (0.24)	1.2 (0.11)	7,102	76.5 (2.43)	0.2 (0.10)	88.7 (1.53)	12,734	1.5 (0.19)
Teachers, postsecondary	41.6	1.0	35.6 (5.85)	2.1 (1.30)	0.7 (0.14)	1,731	65.7 (5.63)	0.6 (0.48)	94.4 (2.28)	2,543	1.8 (0.09)
Physicians, dentists, veterinarians	68.6	2.0	65.2 (11.99)	4.5 (4.50)	1.5 (0.50)	1,049	88.5 (4.11)	# (†)	96.1 (2.15)	2,093	2.0 (0.24)
Registered nurses, pharmacists	72.8	2.2	72.2 (5.04)	0.2 (0.17)	1.8 (0.21)	3,309	84.9 (2.80)	0.3 (0.33)	90.2 (3.12)	6,229	1.9 (0.11)
Writers, artists, entertainers, and athletes	23.4	0.5	30.6 (6.21)	2.5 (1.34)	0.6 (0.18)	2,820	35.1 (4.84)	0.4 (0.30)	69.4 (5.20)	1,729	0.6 (0.11)
Health technologists and technicians	50.0	1.4	41.8 (6.00)	5.2 (3.48)	1.0 (0.19)	2,581	59.4 (6.12)	1.7 (1.06)	84.6 (4.18)	3,728	1.4 (0.21)
Technologists, except health	43.8	1.1	37.6 (4.87)	4.0 (2.84)	1.0 (0.15)	5,371	51.9 (3.47)	1.8 (0.72)	84.4 (2.84)	6,251	1.2 (0.14)
Marketing and sales occupations	25.2	0.6	21.1 (2.27)	1.7 (0.73)	0.4 (0.06)	15,258	38.7 (2.36)	0.2 (0.10)	79.0 (2.39)	9,759	0.6 (0.05)
Administrative support, including clerical	30.8	0.7	27.4 (2.02)	0.9 (0.32)	0.6 (0.05)	19,535	45.1 (2.20)	0.4 (0.19)	74.2 (2.29)	15,201	0.8 (0.04)
Service occupations	22.6	0.6	21.0 (2.15)	2.3 (0.71)	0.5 (0.07)	17,838	37.2 (2.04)	1.0 (0.25)	66.8 (1.98)	13,773	0.8 (0.06)
Agriculture, forestry, and fishing	12.4	0.3	12.2 (4.09)	6.9 (6.56)	0.2 (0.07)	2,232	33.9 (6.19)	1.6 (1.40)	62.0 (6.22)	1,172	0.5 (0.09)
Mechanics and repairers	29.1	0.7	15.0 (3.40)	6.1 (2.26)	0.3 (0.09)	4,212	32.1 (3.84)	3.6 (1.32)	81.0 (3.19)	2,819	0.7 (0.11)
Construction and extractive occupations	18.6	0.3	13.2 (3.16)	6.0 (2.41)	0.2 (0.06)	6,470	22.1 (2.87)	4.7 (1.72)	65.9 (4.43)	2,287	0.4 (0.06)
Precision production	25.6	0.6	18.3 (6.52)	11.9 (5.25)	0.4 (0.12)	1,702	22.5 (6.15)	6.6 (5.84)	70.5 (9.38)	760	0.5 (0.13)
Production workers	14.8	0.3	23.0 (3.17)	2.4 (1.18)	0.5 (0.08)	8,044	27.6 (3.04)	1.9 (0.66)	63.6 (3.27)	3,843	0.5 (0.07)
Transportation, material moving	15.8	0.3	18.4 (3.62)	1.6 (0.95)	0.3 (0.06)	4,657	25.8 (3.39)	0.5 (0.28)	59.5 (4.27)	1,721	0.4 (0.05)
Handler, equipment, cleaners, helpers, and laborers	11.7	0.2	6.8 (3.45)	1.7 (1.35)	0.2 (0.12)	2,711	15.9 (4.27)	1.4 (1.06)	63.5 (7.07)	784	0.3 (0.11)
Miscellaneous occupations	38.8	1.0	14.2 (4.62)	3.7 (2.33)	0.3 (0.08)	133	63.0 (21.53)	# (†)	96.9 (3.35)	198	1.5 (0.61)
Annual household income											
$10,000 or less	12.6	0.2	9.5 (3.09)	1.9 (1.54)	0.2 (0.05)	4,812	— (†)	— (†)	— (†)	1,408	— (†)
$5,000 or less	—	—	— (†)	— (†)	— (†)	1,829	19.4 (4.50)	1.8 (1.26)	70.9 (5.79)	570	0.3 (0.09)
$5,001 to $10,000	—	—	— (†)	— (†)	— (†)	2,983	17.5 (2.85)	0.4 (0.28)	61.6 (5.77)	838	0.3 (0.04)
$10,001 to $15,000	15.1	0.4	8.3 (1.88)	2.5 (1.69)	0.1 (0.03)	5,718	20.1 (3.00)	0.2 (0.18)	70.4 (3.46)	1,679	0.3 (0.05)
$15,001 to $20,000	20.1	0.4	16.3 (2.75)	1.9 (0.94)	0.3 (0.05)	5,160	22.7 (3.44)	1.1 (0.39)	61.7 (6.96)	1,937	0.4 (0.07)
$20,001 to $25,000	20.4	0.5	18.8 (2.79)	4.4 (2.12)	0.4 (0.08)	6,373	29.4 (2.73)	0.9 (0.53)	64.1 (3.38)	3,402	0.5 (0.07)
$25,001 to $30,000	24.7	0.5	22.2 (2.73)	2.7 (1.24)	0.5 (0.07)	7,165	27.7 (2.60)	0.7 (0.29)	70.5 (3.18)	3,721	0.5 (0.07)
$30,001 to $40,000	30.2	0.8	26.6 (2.82)	2.3 (0.95)	0.6 (0.07)	15,835	40.4 (2.43)	1.2 (0.37)	71.9 (2.34)	12,740	0.8 (0.06)
$40,001 to $50,000	34.7	0.8	32.3 (2.34)	2.6 (0.76)	0.7 (0.07)	12,653	47.9 (2.50)	1.4 (0.42)	76.9 (2.00)	11,985	1.0 (0.07)
$50,001 to $75,000	40.0	1.0	36.6 (1.86)	2.5 (0.59)	0.9 (0.06)	31,465	49.3 (1.57)	1.7 (0.38)	75.9 (1.39)	31,471	1.0 (0.04)
More than $75,000	45.2	1.3	42.5 (1.79)	1.2 (0.33)	1.0 (0.06)	40,844	60.5 (1.36)	0.8 (0.28)	85.5 (1.05)	51,604	1.3 (0.04)

—Not available.
†Not applicable.
#Rounds to zero.
[1]Estimates are not directly comparable to 1995 and 1999 due to wording in questions.

NOTE: Data do not include persons enrolled in high school or below. Detail may not sum to totals because of rounding. Race/ethnicity categories may not sum to totals because they do not include an "other" race/ethnicity category. Standard errors appear in parentheses.
SOURCE: U.S. Department of Education, National Center for Education Statistics, Adult Education Survey (AE-NHES:1995 and AE-NHES:1999) and Adult Education for Work-Related Reasons Survey (AEWR-NHES:2003) of the National Household Education Surveys Program. (This table was prepared April 2005.)

Participation of persons, 17 years old and over, in adult education during the previous 12 months, by selected characteristics of participants: Selected years, 1991 through 2003

Characteristic of participants	Percent participating in any program, 1991[1]	Percent participating in any program, 1995	Percent participating in any program, 1999	2001 — Percent participating							2003 — Percent participating	
				In any program	In basic education[2]	In English as a second language	In part-time postsecondary education	In career or job-related courses	In apprentice programs	In personal development courses	In career or job-related courses	In less formal work-related learning activities
1	2	3	4	5	6	7	8	9	10	11	12	13
Total	33.0	40.2	44.5 (0.77)	46.4 (0.55)	0.9 (0.12)	1.2 (0.17)	4.4 (0.20)	29.7 (0.47)	1.3 (0.14)	21.3 (0.54)	33.2 (0.51)	58.3 (0.54)
Sex												
Males	32.6	38.2	41.7 (1.15)	43.1 (0.83)	0.9 (0.19)	1.5 (0.32)	3.9 (0.28)	29.0 (0.73)	1.7 (0.22)	16.3 (0.72)	32.9 (0.90)	62.2 (0.82)
Females	33.2	42.1	47.1 (1.02)	49.5 (0.78)	1.0 (0.15)	0.9 (0.11)	4.9 (0.31)	30.4 (0.67)	1.0 (0.16)	25.9 (0.71)	33.5 (0.65)	54.8 (0.82)
Age												
17 to 24 years	37.8	47.0	49.9 (2.34)	52.8 (2.04)	4.6 (0.81)	3.8 (0.94)	11.6 (1.30)	22.4 (1.66)	2.9 (0.77)	27.6 (1.58)	30.9 (1.92)	73.4 (1.66)
25 to 29 years	40.0	49.6	56.5 (2.53)	52.9 (2.60)	0.4 (0.18)	1.8 (0.42)	9.6 (1.13)	35.3 (2.09)	3.1 (0.97)	19.8 (1.72)	42.4 (2.20)	75.4 (2.06)
30 to 34 years	37.6	47.3	56.2 (2.57)	53.7 (2.18)	1.0 (0.27)	2.6 (1.01)	6.2 (0.72)	35.0 (1.95)	2.3 (0.57)	21.5 (1.64)	40.7 (2.09)	68.4 (2.22)
35 to 39 years	42.1	47.7	50.1 (2.43)	54.0 (1.71)	0.9 (0.31)	1.2 (0.38)	4.3 (0.66)	40.7 (1.68)	1.3 (0.31)	19.8 (1.35)	41.6 (2.08)	67.5 (1.93)
40 to 44 years	49.2	50.9	50.5 (2.43)	53.5 (1.88)	0.5 (0.18)	0.6 (0.19)	3.5 (0.60)	41.1 (1.63)	1.3 (0.39)	19.8 (0.58)	40.7 (1.88)	70.4 (1.95)
45 to 49 years	40.0	48.7	49.8 (2.69)	55.4 (2.02)	0.2 (0.13)	0.3 (0.16)	3.5 (0.48)	42.8 (1.95)	1.0 (0.31)	23.0 (1.92)	42.2 (1.85)	65.3 (2.37)
50 to 54 years	26.8	42.5	47.2 (2.51)	51.1 (2.22)	0.7 (0.57)	0.3 (0.18)	2.3 (0.44)	39.8 (2.05)	0.5 (0.21)	21.9 (1.57)	43.6 (1.89)	65.7 (1.99)
55 to 59 years	29.0	32.2	38.0 (2.60)	44.1 (1.98)	0.3 (0.18)	0.2 (0.09)	1.4 (0.42)	30.1 (1.75)	‡	22.5 (1.87)	34.9 (1.69)	56.3 (2.09)
60 to 64 years	17.4	23.7	31.4 (2.83)	30.8 (2.18)	‡	‡	0.4 (0.19)	15.7 (1.81)	‡	18.3 (1.76)	21.7 (1.44)	39.4 (2.13)
65 to 69 years	14.2	18.1	25.4 (2.54)	20.5 (1.74)	‡	‡	0.2 (0.13)	7.0 (0.93)	‡	16.2 (1.65)	11.9 (0.93)	27.0 (1.82)
70 years and over	8.6	13.8	15.0 (1.38)	21.7 (1.37)	‡	‡	0.1 (0.08)	3.0 (0.41)	‡	19.6 (1.36)	4.7 (0.47)	12.9 (0.94)
Racial/ethnic group												
White, non-Hispanic	34.1	41.5	44.4 (0.89)	47.4 (0.59)	0.6 (0.13)	0.1 (0.05)	4.4 (0.25)	31.7 (0.54)	1.3 (0.17)	21.6 (0.59)	34.6 (0.63)	58.7 (0.57)
Black, non-Hispanic	25.9	37.0	46.3 (2.30)	43.3 (1.50)	1.7 (0.42)	0.4 (0.17)	4.9 (0.67)	23.4 (1.45)	1.1 (0.33)	25.7 (1.50)	31.3 (1.57)	56.1 (1.82)
Hispanic	31.4	33.7	41.3 (2.51)	41.7 (2.28)	2.2 (0.51)	8.3 (1.41)	3.6 (0.52)	21.6 (1.22)	1.6 (0.50)	16.3 (1.58)	25.4 (1.74)	56.6 (2.00)
Asian/Pacific Islander	35.9	39.7	51.1 (4.63)	49.5 (3.81)	1.7 (0.75)	3.2 (0.88)	7.7 (2.30)	34.3 (3.73)	0.9 (0.48)	18.2 (2.70)	38.1 (3.17)	67.2 (3.61)
American Indian/Alaska Native	29.3	38.8	36.3 (9.16)	50.2 (8.28)	1.0 (0.58)	‡	3.2 (2.06)	38.4 (7.66)	2.9 (2.21)	10.4 (4.01)	33.0 (9.26)	53.0 (10.44)
Highest level of education completed												
Eighth grade or less	7.7	10.0	14.7 (2.92)	19.7 (2.84)	1.6 (0.45)	6.1 (1.87)	‡	3.8 (1.05)	0.3 (0.17)	10.6 (2.37)	4.1 (1.18)	26.8 (2.85)
9th to 12th grade, no completion	15.8	20.2	25.6 (2.55)	25.5 (1.53)	4.1 (0.74)	1.5 (0.45)	0.5 (0.23)	10.2 (1.02)	0.7 (0.24)	10.3 (1.19)	13.8 (1.41)	35.9 (2.09)
High school completion	24.1	30.7	34.8 (1.37)	33.9 (1.07)	0.3 (0.11)	0.6 (0.16)	2.2 (0.28)	19.7 (0.93)	1.5 (0.25)	16.1 (0.88)	23.7 (0.91)	50.8 (1.19)
Some vocational/technical	34.2	41.9	41.1 (3.97)	50.7 (3.51)	1.6 (0.72)	3.9 (1.27)	2.1 (0.85)	30.8 (2.81)	2.6 (0.90)	22.0 (3.14)	28.4 (2.25)	57.4 (2.95)
Some college	41.4	49.3	51.1 (1.76)	57.4 (1.29)	1.0 (0.39)	0.5 (0.17)	9.3 (0.82)	34.6 (1.31)	2.4 (0.60)	27.6 (1.28)	35.6 (1.53)	64.2 (1.23)
Associate's degree	49.2	56.1	56.6 (2.93)	62.5 (2.15)	0.2 (0.13)	0.6 (0.35)	7.0 (1.03)	46.1 (2.24)	1.4 (0.44)	24.6 (2.02)	44.3 (2.19)	72.2 (1.84)
Bachelor's degree	51.1	56.9	60.3 (1.84)	64.5 (1.39)	†	0.4 (0.14)	5.4 (0.56)	48.6 (1.27)	1.1 (0.28)	27.9 (1.31)	52.3 (1.28)	75.3 (1.36)
Some graduate work (or study)	55.1	59.9	63.6 (1.96)	68.9 (1.64)	†	0.8 (0.44)	0.8 (0.92)	53.4 (1.51)	0.3 (0.11)	33.8 (1.41)	58.2 (1.58)	77.8 (1.23)
No degree	—	62.2	64.7 (4.39)	64.2 (3.54)	‡	‡	12.0 (2.34)	49.2 (3.50)	‡	31.7 (3.24)	57.6 (4.24)	81.1 (2.91)
Master's	—	59.1	65.7 (2.64)	70.7 (2.10)	‡	0.5 (0.29)	7.6 (1.25)	55.7 (2.07)	0.3 (0.16)	34.3 (2.02)	58.5 (2.09)	78.6 (1.67)
Doctor's	—	54.0	53.1 (4.73)	63.7 (3.98)	‡	3.2 (2.92)	7.1 (2.34)	41.1 (4.27)	‡	33.4 (4.30)	48.7 (4.58)	69.4 (4.55)
Professional	—	65.9	72.5 (5.75)	72.8 (3.79)	‡	‡	4.5 (1.68)	61.9 (4.36)	‡	34.8 (3.76)	64.0 (4.21)	77.5 (3.81)
Urbanicity												
Urban	34.5	41.8	46.0 (0.88)	48.0 (0.70)	1.1 (0.15)	1.5 (0.22)	4.7 (0.22)	30.5 (0.55)	1.3 (0.18)	22.4 (0.61)	34.8 (0.58)	60.2 (0.57)
Urban, inside urbanized area	—	42.3	46.5 (0.95)	49.3 (0.78)	1.1 (0.15)	1.7 (0.25)	4.9 (0.27)	31.3 (0.63)	1.4 (0.20)	23.1 (0.66)	34.9 (0.66)	60.6 (0.63)
Urban, outside urbanized area	—	39.5	43.4 (2.23)	41.6 (1.70)	1.3 (0.56)	0.7 (0.34)	3.9 (0.53)	26.3 (1.36)	0.7 (0.29)	19.1 (1.37)	34.3 (1.62)	57.7 (1.61)
Rural	28.3	35.4	39.9 (1.58)	41.6 (1.17)	0.5 (0.14)	0.1 (0.04)	3.4 (0.41)	27.5 (1.03)	1.5 (0.24)	18.0 (0.96)	27.0 (1.32)	51.4 (1.56)
Labor force status												
In labor force	40.7	49.8	52.1 (0.94)	— (†)	— (†)	— (†)	— (†)	— (†)	— (†)	—	44.2 (0.68)	74.6 (0.72)
Employed	42.0	50.7	52.5 (0.96)	— (†)	— (†)	— (†)	— (†)	— (†)	— (†)	—	46.0 (0.70)	76.5 (0.70)
Unemployed	26.0	36.6	44.9 (4.60)	— (†)	— (†)	— (†)	— (†)	— (†)	— (†)	—	25.1 (2.31)	54.6 (2.99)
Not in labor force	15.7	21.3	24.9 (1.17)	— (†)	— (†)	— (†)	— (†)	— (†)	— (†)	—	8.8 (0.62)	22.3 (0.85)

See notes at end of table.

Participation of persons, 17 years old and over, in adult education during the previous 12 months, by selected characteristics of participants: Selected years, 1991 through 2003—Continued

Characteristic of participants	Percent participating in any program, 1991[1]	Percent participating in any program, 1995	Percent participating in any program, 1999	2001 — In any program	2001 — In basic education[2]	2001 — In English as a second language	2001 — In part-time postsecondary education	2001 — In career or job-related courses	2001 — In apprentice programs	2001 — In personal development courses	2003 — In career or job-related courses	2003 — In less formal work-related learning activities
1	2	3	4	5	6	7	8	9	10	11	12	13
Occupation												
Executive, administrative, or managerial	49.3	55.8	57.0 (2.11)	66.2 (1.61)	‡ (†)	‡ (†)	7.6 (0.88)	54.3 (1.73)	0.4 (0.14)	28.0 (1.69)	60.4 (2.08)	85.2 (1.76)
Engineers, surveyors, and architects	62.6	65.5	79.8 (6.01)	68.1 (4.46)	‡ (†)	‡ (†)	8.9 (3.68)	53.5 (4.89)	‡ (†)	25.5 (4.83)	61.4 (4.72)	90.5 (2.62)
Natural scientists and mathematicians	48.2	72.3	60.5 (6.74)	74.0 (4.46)	‡ (†)	‡ (†)	5.4 (1.78)	60.6 (5.29)	‡ (†)	33.4 (4.38)	58.5 (5.69)	92.7 (2.11)
Social scientists and workers, lawyers	55.6	76.6	79.3 (4.35)	83.5 (3.05)	‡ (†)	‡ (†)	8.1 (2.92)	76.6 (3.80)	‡ (†)	26.2 (4.49)	76.4 (3.57)	87.6 (2.87)
Teachers, elementary/secondary	55.0	54.8	66.5 (5.61)	79.9 (2.95)	‡ (†)	‡ (†)	11.4 (1.65)	70.4 (3.15)	‡ (†)	30.4 (2.50)	73.8 (2.40)	87.5 (1.53)
Teachers, postsecondary	45.5	76.7	78.4 (3.11)	69.4 (4.60)	‡ (†)	‡ (†)	11.6 (3.29)	53.0 (5.92)	0.2 (0.22)	31.5 (5.12)	64.6 (5.55)	90.5 (2.77)
Physicians, dentists, veterinarians	67.1	71.1	79.8 (9.02)	78.5 (6.38)	‡ (†)	‡ (†)	11.0 (4.55)	69.5 (7.42)	‡ (†)	32.4 (5.43)	86.5 (4.02)	93.8 (2.69)
Registered nurses, pharmacists	59.6	86.7	85.4 (4.10)	82.7 (3.83)	‡ (†)	‡ (†)	7.0 (2.05)	78.7 (3.84)	‡ (†)	32.5 (4.18)	84.8 (2.73)	90.0 (3.00)
Writers, artists, entertainers, and athletes	42.9	49.9	50.0 (6.93)	46.8 (6.03)	‡ (†)	‡ (†)	4.5 (1.63)	22.0 (3.89)	‡ (†)	31.3 (5.85)	34.7 (4.52)	68.0 (4.84)
Health technologists and technicians	68.6	74.8	66.9 (6.16)	85.6 (3.25)	‡ (†)	‡ (†)	10.8 (3.08)	76.1 (4.37)	3.1 (1.32)	27.5 (4.80)	59.1 (5.89)	84.3 (4.00)
Technologists, except health	55.4	64.3	59.6 (5.07)	70.2 (3.32)	‡ (†)	‡ (†)	11.9 (2.51)	56.7 (3.54)	2.1 (1.21)	25.5 (2.98)	50.1 (3.20)	83.2 (2.69)
Marketing and sales occupations	34.4	44.2	44.4 (2.73)	51.1 (2.10)	1.4 (0.59)	0.7 (0.29)	4.0 (0.83)	34.0 (1.77)	1.0 (0.45)	23.8 (1.90)	36.4 (2.18)	76.9 (2.29)
Administrative support, including clerical	29.9	51.7	50.1 (2.29)	58.7 (1.72)	0.9 (0.46)	0.4 (0.15)	7.3 (0.90)	39.8 (1.67)	1.0 (0.25)	25.6 (1.66)	43.8 (2.04)	73.0 (2.08)
Service occupations	25.2	46.5	50.9 (2.74)	49.3 (2.24)	2.7 (0.72)	3.0 (1.15)	4.5 (0.66)	27.0 (1.59)	1.1 (0.37)	19.4 (1.53)	36.6 (1.78)	66.1 (1.89)
Agriculture, forestry, and fishing	14.3	26.4	34.3 (7.16)	46.4 (6.80)	‡ (†)	9.5 (6.11)	6.0 (3.78)	23.7 (6.19)	‡ (†)	21.0 (6.28)	31.7 (5.94)	65.1 (5.44)
Mechanics and repairers	32.1	47.6	42.2 (5.44)	35.1 (3.40)	‡ (†)	0.9 (0.53)	1.5 (0.76)	26.6 (2.99)	3.4 (1.24)	6.9 (1.42)	31.1 (3.57)	79.0 (3.51)
Construction and extractive occupations	21.9	38.0	34.5 (4.78)	32.3 (3.19)	0.3 (0.22)	1.9 (1.24)	2.1 (0.88)	16.7 (2.29)	5.5 (1.43)	10.7 (2.48)	21.5 (2.72)	66.1 (4.01)
Precision production	31.2	43.0	38.3 (8.48)	35.1 (6.19)	‡ (†)	‡ (†)	‡ (†)	22.6 (6.23)	11.1 (5.90)	16.4 (4.31)	30.2 (8.97)	71.9 (8.61)
Production workers	21.1	30.7	38.0 (3.47)	39.4 (2.82)	1.3 (0.55)	2.5 (0.70)	2.0 (0.64)	25.3 (2.42)	4.5 (1.33)	12.9 (2.12)	27.2 (2.94)	62.7 (3.23)
Transportation, material moving	20.7	28.4	33.3 (4.25)	30.4 (3.29)	‡ (†)	‡ (†)	1.2 (0.75)	19.8 (2.78)	‡ (†)	13.3 (2.49)	23.6 (3.19)	59.5 (3.70)
Handler, equipment, cleaners, helpers, and laborers	20.8	25.1	19.6 (4.56)	18.2 (3.20)	1.6 (0.83)	1.0 (0.54)	1.4 (0.78)	10.6 (2.72)	‡ (†)	5.6 (1.91)	16.8 (4.06)	64.1 (5.92)
Miscellaneous occupations	—	56.6	43.0 (7.98)	64.9 (7.07)	‡ (†)	‡ (†)	4.8 (3.05)	52.0 (8.78)	‡ (†)	26.8 (7.83)	58.5 (19.72)	90.1 (8.16)
Annual household income												
$5,000 or less	13.6	21.3	21.0 (3.22)	25.1 (2.92)	3.9 (1.51)	2.2 (0.89)	1.1 (0.50)	8.3 (1.88)	0.5 (0.26)	14.6 (2.55)	11.3 (2.03)	36.5 (3.56)
$5,001 to $10,000	17.5	23.9	24.5 (3.39)	28.0 (2.74)	1.7 (0.47)	2.2 (0.61)	1.3 (0.81)	12.4 (1.86)	1.7 (1.22)	14.0 (1.85)	11.4 (1.88)	36.0 (3.11)
$10,001 to $15,000	22.8	26.7	22.8 (2.45)	28.6 (2.30)	0.9 (0.61)	2.4 (0.65)	2.2 (0.99)	10.5 (1.52)	2.2 (1.04)	17.3 (2.17)	13.2 (1.62)	42.4 (2.47)
$15,001 to $20,000	21.9	31.8	31.4 (2.75)	30.2 (2.48)	1.5 (0.55)	2.5 (1.21)	4.5 (0.90)	13.3 (1.50)	0.4 (0.19)	13.2 (1.64)	14.3 (2.39)	41.3 (4.26)
$20,001 to $25,000	26.7	31.4	35.8 (2.81)	35.2 (2.27)	2.3 (0.90)	2.9 (1.19)	3.3 (0.72)	17.8 (1.72)	1.5 (0.55)	16.6 (1.61)	17.2 (1.45)	40.7 (2.33)
$25,001 to $30,000	32.1	37.9	36.7 (2.61)	38.3 (2.43)	1.0 (0.58)	2.3 (0.80)	2.8 (0.56)	19.0 (1.74)	1.0 (0.39)	19.9 (2.08)	20.6 (1.71)	52.3 (2.63)
$30,001 to $40,000	35.6	42.7	45.2 (2.05)	44.6 (1.54)	0.4 (0.17)	0.5 (0.19)	5.1 (0.66)	27.6 (1.37)	1.2 (0.30)	20.4 (1.43)	31.6 (1.63)	58.3 (1.86)
$40,001 to $50,000	44.8	46.8	47.9 (2.31)	49.1 (1.93)	1.2 (0.32)	1.1 (0.37)	4.3 (0.73)	30.8 (1.70)	2.2 (0.58)	22.5 (1.51)	36.3 (1.65)	59.9 (1.64)
$50,001 to $75,000	46.6	52.0	55.1 (1.80)	55.7 (1.48)	0.4 (0.13)	0.4 (0.17)	5.6 (0.58)	39.3 (1.28)	1.4 (0.31)	24.3 (1.29)	40.2 (1.29)	64.0 (1.32)
More than $75,000	48.7	58.0	56.9 (1.66)	59.5 (1.29)	0.5 (0.23)	0.3 (0.15)	5.5 (0.52)	44.6 (1.19)	1.0 (0.20)	26.2 (0.93)	49.0 (1.09)	72.8 (0.99)

—Not available.
†Not applicable.
‡Reporting standards not met.
[1]Adult education is defined as all education activities, except full-time enrollment in higher education credential programs. Examples of adult education activities include part-time college attendance, classes or seminars given by employers, and classes taken for adult literacy purposes, or for recreation and enjoyment.
[2]The estimates of participation in basic education include only those participating in courses to improve "reading, writing, and math skills," and do not count participation in GED or other high-school equivalency courses.

NOTE: Data are based on a sample survey of the civilian noninstitutional population. Data do not include persons enrolled in high school or below. Data revised from previously published figures. Detail may not sum to totals because of rounding. Race/ethnicity categories may not sum to totals because they do not include "other" races/ethnicities. Occupation categories may not sum to totals because they exclude those not in the labor force. Standard errors appear in parentheses.
SOURCE: U.S. Department of Education, National Center for Education Statistics, Adult Education Survey (AE-NHES:1991, AE-NHES:1995, and AE-NHES:1999); Adult Education and Lifelong Learning Survey (AELL-NHES:2001); and Adult Education for Work-Related Reasons Survey (AEWR-NHES:2003) of the National Household Education Surveys Program. (This table was prepared November 2005.)

Degrees conferred by degree-granting institutions, by level of degree and sex of student: Selected years, 1869–70 through 2013–14

Year	Associate's degrees			Bachelor's degrees			Master's degrees			First-professional degrees			Doctor's degrees[1]		
	Total	Males	Females	Total	Males	Females	Total	Males	Females	Total	Males	Females	Total	Males	Females
1	2	3	4	5	6	7	8	9	10	11	12	13	14	15	16
1869–70	—	—	—	[2] 9,371	[2] 7,993	[2] 1,378	0	0	0	(3)	(3)	(3)	1	1	0
1879–80	—	—	—	[2] 12,896	[2] 10,411	[2] 2,485	879	868	11	(3)	(3)	(3)	54	51	3
1889–90	—	—	—	[2] 15,539	[2] 12,857	[2] 2,682	1,015	821	194	(3)	(3)	(3)	149	147	2
1899–1900	—	—	—	[2] 27,410	[2] 22,173	[2] 5,237	1,583	1,280	303	(3)	(3)	(3)	382	359	23
1909–10	—	—	—	[2] 37,199	[2] 28,762	[2] 8,437	2,113	1,555	558	(3)	(3)	(3)	443	399	44
1919–20	—	—	—	[2] 48,622	[2] 31,980	[2] 16,642	4,279	2,985	1,294	(3)	(3)	(3)	615	522	93
1929–30	—	—	—	[2] 122,484	[2] 73,615	[2] 48,869	14,969	8,925	6,044	(3)	(3)	(3)	2,299	1,946	353
1939–40	—	—	—	[2] 186,500	[2] 109,546	[2] 76,954	26,731	16,508	10,223	(3)	(3)	(3)	3,290	2,861	429
1949–50	—	—	—	[2] 432,058	[2] 328,841	[2] 103,217	58,183	41,220	16,963	(3)	(3)	(3)	6,420	5,804	616
1959–60	—	—	—	[2] 392,440	[2] 254,063	[2] 138,377	74,435	50,898	23,537	(3)	(3)	(3)	9,829	8,801	1,028
1960–61	—	—	—	365,174	224,538	140,636	84,609	57,830	26,779	25,253	24,577	676	10,575	9,463	1,112
1961–62	—	—	—	383,961	230,456	153,505	91,418	62,603	28,815	25,607	24,836	771	11,622	10,377	1,245
1962–63	—	—	—	411,420	241,309	170,111	98,684	67,302	31,382	26,590	25,753	837	12,822	11,448	1,374
1963–64	—	—	—	461,266	265,349	195,917	109,183	73,850	35,333	27,209	26,357	852	14,490	12,955	1,535
1964–65	—	—	—	493,757	282,173	211,584	121,167	81,319	39,848	28,290	27,283	1,007	16,467	14,692	1,775
1965–66	111,607	63,779	47,828	520,115	299,287	220,828	140,602	93,081	47,521	30,124	28,982	1,142	18,237	16,121	2,116
1966–67	139,183	78,356	60,827	558,534	322,711	235,823	157,726	103,109	54,617	31,695	30,401	1,294	20,617	18,163	2,454
1967–68	159,441	90,317	69,124	632,289	357,682	274,607	176,749	113,552	63,197	33,939	32,402	1,537	23,089	20,183	2,906
1968–69	183,279	105,661	77,618	728,845	410,595	318,250	193,756	121,531	72,225	35,114	33,595	1,519	26,158	22,722	3,436
1969–70	206,023	117,432	88,591	792,316	451,097	341,219	208,291	125,624	82,667	34,918	33,077	1,841	29,866	25,890	3,976
1970–71	252,311	144,144	108,167	839,730	475,594	364,136	230,509	138,146	92,363	37,946	35,544	2,402	32,107	27,530	4,577
1971–72	292,014	166,227	125,787	887,273	500,590	386,683	251,633	149,550	102,083	43,411	40,723	2,688	33,363	28,090	5,273
1972–73	316,174	175,413	140,761	922,362	518,191	404,171	263,371	154,468	108,903	50,018	46,489	3,529	34,777	28,571	6,206
1973–74	343,924	188,591	155,333	945,776	527,313	418,463	277,033	157,842	119,191	53,816	48,530	5,286	33,816	27,365	6,451
1974–75	360,171	191,017	169,154	922,933	504,841	418,092	292,450	161,570	130,880	55,916	48,956	6,960	34,083	26,817	7,266
1975–76	391,454	209,996	181,458	925,746	504,925	420,821	311,771	167,248	144,523	62,649	52,892	9,757	34,064	26,267	7,797
1976–77	406,377	210,842	195,535	919,549	495,545	424,004	317,164	167,783	149,381	64,359	52,374	11,985	33,232	25,142	8,090
1977–78	412,246	204,718	207,528	921,204	487,347	433,857	311,620	161,212	150,408	66,581	52,270	14,311	32,131	23,658	8,473
1978–79	402,702	192,091	210,611	921,390	477,344	444,046	301,079	153,370	147,709	68,848	52,652	16,196	32,730	23,541	9,189
1979–80	400,910	183,737	217,173	929,417	473,611	455,806	298,081	150,749	147,332	70,131	52,716	17,415	32,615	22,943	9,672
1980–81	416,377	188,638	227,739	935,140	469,883	465,257	295,739	147,043	148,696	71,956	52,792	19,164	32,958	22,711	10,247
1981–82	434,526	196,944	237,582	952,998	473,364	479,634	295,546	145,532	150,014	72,032	52,223	19,809	32,707	22,224	10,483
1982–83	449,620	203,991	245,629	969,510	479,140	490,370	289,921	144,697	145,224	73,054	51,250	21,804	32,775	21,902	10,873
1983–84	452,240	202,704	249,536	974,309	482,319	491,990	284,263	143,595	140,668	74,468	51,378	23,090	33,209	22,064	11,145
1984–85	454,712	202,932	251,780	979,477	482,528	496,949	286,251	143,390	142,861	75,063	50,455	24,608	32,943	21,700	11,243
1985–86	446,047	196,166	249,881	987,823	485,923	501,900	288,567	143,508	145,059	73,910	49,261	24,649	33,653	21,819	11,834
1986–87	436,304	190,839	245,465	991,264	480,782	510,482	289,349	141,269	148,080	71,617	46,523	25,094	34,041	22,061	11,980
1987–88	435,085	190,047	245,038	994,829	477,203	517,626	299,317	145,163	154,154	70,735	45,484	25,251	34,870	22,615	12,255
1988–89	436,764	186,316	250,448	1,018,755	483,346	535,409	310,621	149,354	161,267	70,856	45,046	25,810	35,720	22,648	13,072
1989–90	455,102	191,195	263,907	1,051,344	491,696	559,648	324,301	153,653	170,648	70,988	43,961	27,027	38,371	24,401	13,970
1990–91	481,720	198,634	283,086	1,094,538	504,045	590,493	337,168	156,482	180,686	71,948	43,846	28,102	39,294	24,756	14,538
1991–92	504,231	207,481	296,750	1,136,553	520,811	615,742	352,838	161,842	190,996	74,146	45,071	29,075	40,659	25,557	15,102
1992–93	514,756	211,964	302,792	1,165,178	532,881	632,297	369,585	169,258	200,327	75,387	45,153	30,234	42,132	26,073	16,059
1993–94	530,632	215,261	315,371	1,169,275	532,422	636,853	387,070	176,085	210,985	75,418	44,707	30,711	43,185	26,552	16,633
1994–95	539,691	218,352	321,339	1,160,134	526,131	634,003	397,629	178,598	219,031	75,800	44,853	30,947	44,446	26,916	17,530
1995–96	555,216	219,514	335,702	1,164,792	522,454	642,338	406,301	179,081	227,220	76,734	44,748	31,986	44,652	26,841	17,811
1996–97	571,226	223,948	347,278	1,172,879	520,515	652,364	419,401	180,947	238,454	78,730	45,564	33,166	45,876	27,146	18,730
1997–98	558,555	217,613	340,942	1,184,406	519,956	664,450	430,164	184,375	245,789	78,598	44,911	33,687	46,010	26,664	19,346
1998–99[4]	559,954	218,417	341,537	1,200,303	518,746	681,557	439,986	186,148	253,838	78,439	44,339	34,100	44,077	25,146	18,931
1999–2000	564,933	224,721	340,212	1,237,875	530,367	707,508	457,056	191,792	265,264	80,057	44,239	35,818	44,808	25,028	19,780
2000–01	578,865	231,645	347,220	1,244,171	531,840	712,331	468,476	194,351	274,125	79,707	42,862	36,845	44,904	24,728	20,176
2001–02	595,133	238,109	357,024	1,291,900	549,816	742,084	482,118	199,120	282,998	80,698	42,507	38,191	44,160	23,708	20,452
2002–03	632,912	253,060	379,852	1,348,503	573,079	775,424	512,645	211,381	301,264	80,810	41,834	38,976	46,024	24,341	21,683
2003–04	665,301	260,033	405,268	1,399,542	595,425	804,117	558,940	229,545	329,395	83,041	42,169	40,872	48,378	25,323	23,055
2004–05[5]	668,000	257,000	411,000	1,416,000	584,000	832,000	562,000	224,000	338,000	85,000	42,000	43,000	47,200	24,600	22,600

See notes at end of table.

Degrees conferred by degree-granting institutions, by level of degree and sex of student: Selected years, 1869–70 through 2013–14—Continued

Year	Associate's degrees			Bachelor's degrees			Master's degrees			First-professional degrees			Doctor's degrees[1]		
	Total	Males	Females	Total	Males	Females	Total	Males	Females	Total	Males	Females	Total	Males	Females
1	2	3	4	5	6	7	8	9	10	11	12	13	14	15	16
2005–06[5]...............	668,000	256,000	412,000	1,431,000	586,000	845,000	580,000	229,000	350,000	87,600	42,700	44,900	48,500	25,100	23,300
2006–07[5]...............	676,000	258,000	418,000	1,449,000	590,000	859,000	596,000	236,000	361,000	89,600	43,300	46,400	49,500	25,600	24,000
2007–08[5]...............	689,000	262,000	427,000	1,475,000	598,000	877,000	615,000	243,000	373,000	91,600	43,800	47,800	50,200	25,700	24,400
2008–09[5]...............	705,000	266,000	438,000	1,507,000	608,000	898,000	634,000	249,000	384,000	93,700	44,500	49,200	50,600	25,800	24,800
2009–10[5]...............	719,000	271,000	448,000	1,538,000	618,000	920,000	650,000	255,000	395,000	95,700	45,200	50,500	51,100	25,900	25,200
2010–11[5]...............	728,000	273,000	454,000	1,558,000	625,000	933,000	661,000	260,000	402,000	97,200	45,700	51,500	51,800	26,100	25,700
2011–12[5]...............	731,000	274,000	457,000	1,570,000	629,000	941,000	671,000	264,000	407,000	98,500	46,200	52,300	52,700	26,400	26,200
2012–13[5]...............	733,000	275,000	458,000	1,578,000	632,000	946,000	680,000	269,000	411,000	99,600	46,700	52,900	53,800	26,900	26,900
2013–14[5]...............	735,000	275,000	460,000	1,582,000	633,000	949,000	693,000	275,000	418,000	99,000	47,300	53,700	54,900	27,300	27,600

—Not available.

[1]Includes Ph.D., Ed.D., and comparable degrees at the doctoral level. Excludes first-professional, such as M.D., D.D.S., and law degrees.

[2]Includes first-professional degrees.

[3]First-professional degrees are included with bachelor's degrees.

[4]Data for 1998–99 were imputed using alternative procedures. (See Guide to Sources for details.)

[5]Projected.

NOTE: Data for 1869–70 to 1994–95 are for institutions of higher education. Institutions of higher education were accredited by an agency or association that was recognized by the U.S. Department of Education, or recognized directly by the Secretary of Education. The new degree-granting classification is very similar to the earlier higher education classification, except that it includes some additional institutions, primarily 2-year colleges, and excludes a few higher education institutions that did not award associate's or higher degrees. Some data have been revised from previously published figures. Detail may not sum to totals because of rounding.

SOURCE: U.S. Department of Education, National Center for Education Statistics, *Earned Degrees Conferred*, 1869–70 through 1964–65; *Projections of Education Statistics to 2014*; Higher Education General Information Survey (HEGIS), "Degrees and Other Formal Awards Conferred" surveys, 1965–66 through 1985–86; and 1986–87 through 2003–04 Integrated Postsecondary Education Data System, "Completions Survey" (IPEDS-C:87–99), and Fall 2000 through Fall 2004. (This table was prepared July 2005.)

Degrees conferred by degree-granting institutions, by control, level of degree, and state or jurisdiction: 2003–04

State or jurisdiction	Public					Private				
	Associate's degrees	Bachelor's degrees	Master's degrees	First-professional degrees[1]	Doctor's degrees (Ph.D., Ed.D., etc.)	Associate's degrees	Bachelor's degrees	Master's degrees	First-professional degrees[1]	Doctor's degrees (Ph.D., Ed.D., etc.)
1	2	3	4	5	6	7	8	9	10	11
United States	524,875	905,718	285,138	34,499	29,706	140,426	493,824	273,802	48,542	18,672
Alabama	7,735	17,643	8,535	637	479	1,179	3,743	524	379	42
Alaska	922	1,288	501	0	20	64	117	84	0	0
Arizona	9,662	17,350	6,423	473	828	4,356	8,875	11,041	297	103
Arkansas	4,689	8,537	2,326	465	219	198	2,247	271	0	0
California	74,564	104,322	25,233	2,333	2,995	14,970	38,096	28,060	6,370	2,918
Colorado	5,827	19,135	5,476	518	658	4,000	4,972	4,551	429	122
Connecticut	3,556	8,149	2,972	356	257	1,181	8,494	5,409	593	423
Delaware	912	3,811	754	0	177	247	1,290	1,186	243	24
District of Columbia	138	302	67	25	0	678	9,133	8,401	2,630	576
Florida	43,440	42,797	12,815	1,370	1,458	14,486	21,014	10,360	2,099	1,450
Georgia	9,678	23,638	8,735	858	877	3,249	12,524	5,707	1,260	257
Hawaii	2,296	3,314	1,053	143	116	1,358	2,185	844	2	11
Idaho	1,723	4,378	993	161	105	1,550	1,664	123	0	0
Illinois	23,718	31,678	11,827	1,136	1,065	5,020	27,859	20,905	3,286	1,433
Indiana	9,148	24,522	7,121	1,093	956	4,105	11,866	3,715	571	168
Iowa	9,457	11,122	2,621	547	538	1,619	9,052	1,346	979	68
Kansas	7,069	12,624	4,324	727	433	663	3,398	1,665	14	0
Kentucky	6,451	13,123	5,100	804	339	2,209	4,120	1,090	236	85
Louisiana	4,609	17,450	4,710	824	444	1,232	3,886	1,704	886	127
Maine	1,778	3,600	851	82	40	474	2,459	691	120	3
Maryland	8,518	18,295	6,733	980	687	505	5,704	6,266	160	376
Massachusetts	8,473	13,299	4,657	98	438	2,900	32,284	23,111	4,130	2,046
Michigan	17,873	38,615	16,832	1,677	1,493	3,963	12,551	7,372	1,039	66
Minnesota	10,990	17,330	4,126	715	592	3,199	9,994	7,307	944	440
Mississippi	7,923	9,774	2,940	395	357	301	1,889	728	133	0
Missouri	8,514	17,647	5,078	756	417	3,882	16,359	11,207	1,801	816
Montana	1,637	4,772	1,037	134	80	174	597	50	0	0
Nebraska	3,621	7,145	2,601	346	274	674	4,294	1,029	467	108
Nevada	2,296	4,714	1,347	169	121	576	422	449	0	0
New Hampshire	1,713	4,125	969	0	46	1,576	3,783	1,870	158	81
New Jersey	12,712	22,185	6,713	1,128	699	1,494	8,379	5,322	534	483
New Mexico	4,019	5,948	2,402	243	283	252	1,269	581	0	0
New York	39,492	43,882	18,040	1,254	1,199	16,142	63,113	45,230	7,119	2,791
North Carolina	16,399	26,441	8,233	836	950	1,118	12,333	3,145	1,052	298
North Dakota	1,891	4,226	788	181	90	281	807	266	0	0
Ohio	16,919	35,860	11,948	2,013	1,373	5,391	20,396	7,298	1,199	477
Oklahoma	8,002	13,767	4,361	745	366	699	3,657	1,246	353	36
Oregon	6,889	12,114	4,134	409	413	1,412	4,550	1,743	661	91
Pennsylvania	12,966	37,569	9,734	1,693	1,370	11,610	37,774	16,554	2,855	1,429
Rhode Island	1,177	3,137	825	78	85	2,363	6,114	1,346	243	164
South Carolina	6,829	12,972	3,831	619	414	1,210	4,919	934	201	18
South Dakota	1,790	3,349	881	185	89	718	1,403	235	19	2
Tennessee	6,362	15,756	5,059	724	503	2,371	9,227	3,245	707	343
Texas	33,691	66,182	23,574	3,061	2,345	5,611	19,357	6,975	2,021	407
Utah	8,225	12,008	2,595	260	280	1,176	7,901	1,572	156	82
Vermont	795	2,328	513	90	53	595	2,320	961	157	2
Virginia	10,659	27,027	9,321	1,341	1,101	3,375	8,633	2,627	1,066	148
Washington	22,362	20,456	4,685	648	670	1,314	6,784	3,796	522	59
West Virginia	2,344	7,442	2,479	453	169	979	1,659	350	0	0
Wisconsin	10,458	23,401	5,845	585	703	882	8,358	3,310	451	99
Wyoming	1,964	1,670	420	131	42	845	0	0	0	0
U.S. Service Schools[2]	0	3,499	0	0	0	†	†	†	†	†
Other jurisdictions	2,070	8,526	875	357	68	2,964	9,353	3,047	517	114
American Samoa	149	0	0	0	0	0	0	0	0	0
Federated States of Micronesia	171	0	0	0	0	0	0	0	0	0
Guam	87	280	100	0	0	3	7	0	0	0
Marshall Islands	80	0	0	0	0	0	0	0	0	0
Northern Marianas	98	32	0	0	0	0	0	0	0	0
Palau	69	0	0	0	0	0	0	0	0	0
Puerto Rico	1,339	8,024	703	357	68	2,961	9,346	3,047	517	114
Virgin Islands	77	190	72	0	0	0	0	0	0	0

†Not applicable.
[1]Includes degrees that require at least 6 years of college work for completion (including at least 2 years of preprofessional training). See Definitions for details.
[2]Excludes Uniformed Services University of the Health Sciences, National Defense University, Air Force Institute of Technology, Community College of the Air Force, Naval Postgraduate School, Joint Military Intelligence College, and the U.S. Army Command and General Staff College.

SOURCE: U.S. Department of Education, National Center for Education Statistics, 2003–04 Integrated Postsecondary Education Data System (IPEDS), Fall 2004. (This table was prepared July 2005.)

Degrees conferred by degree-granting institutions, by control of institution, level of degree, and discipline division: 2003–04

Discipline division	Public institutions				Private institutions			
	Associate's degrees	Bachelor's degrees	Master's degrees	Doctor's degrees[1]	Associate's degrees	Bachelor's degrees	Master's degrees	Doctor's degrees[1]
1	2	3	4	5	6	7	8	9
All fields, total	524,875	905,718	285,138	29,706	140,426	493,824	273,802	18,672
Agriculture and natural resources..........................	5,989	19,655	4,095	1,110	294	3,180	688	75
Architecture and related services	446	6,696	3,404	109	46	2,142	2,020	64
Area, ethnic, cultural, and gender studies	100	4,349	1,000	126	5	2,832	683	83
Biological and biomedical sciences.........................	1,402	41,295	4,924	3,556	54	20,214	2,733	1,686
Business.......................................	67,583	177,962	52,399	695	38,721	129,187	86,948	786
Communications, journalism, and related programs	1,808	49,275	3,337	331	636	21,693	3,198	87
Communications technologies............................	2,505	1,057	86	0	896	977	279	8
Computer and information sciences	22,220	30,202	9,935	549	19,625	29,286	10,208	360
Construction trades	2,849	109	0	0	711	10	0	0
Education....................................	11,070	75,152	83,978	4,639	1,395	31,126	78,367	2,449
Engineering	1,869	48,593	23,350	4,294	868	14,965	9,348	1,629
Engineering technologies[2]........................	21,689	10,338	1,445	12	15,226	4,053	1,054	46
English language and literature/letters	817	37,143	5,585	898	11	16,841	2,371	309
Family and consumer sciences	8,883	16,278	1,371	228	595	2,894	423	101
Foreign languages, literatures, and linguistics..................	999	11,966	2,273	672	48	5,788	851	359
Health professions and related clinical sciences	81,665	48,560	23,997	2,266	24,543	25,374	20,942	2,095
Legal professions and studies	4,994	1,717	1,027	24	4,472	1,124	3,216	95
Liberal arts and sciences, general studies, and humanities	218,520	29,581	1,812	22	9,130	12,525	1,885	73
Library science	113	72	4,863	42	1	0	1,152	5
Mathematics and statistics	790	8,651	3,246	689	11	4,676	945	371
Mechanics and repair technologies	8,727	123	0	0	3,826	36	0	0
Military technologies..............................	293	10	0	0	0	0	0	0
Multi/interdisciplinary studies........................	14,587	21,228	2,535	462	207	7,934	1,512	414
Parks, recreation, leisure and fitness studies	782	17,157	2,564	205	141	5,007	635	17
Philosophy and religious studies	104	4,682	528	249	300	6,470	1,050	346
Physical sciences and science technologies.............	2,635	11,939	4,129	2,697	41	6,044	1,441	1,118
Precision production	1,834	22	0	0	134	39	13	0
Psychology	1,778	54,469	7,319	2,079	109	27,629	10,579	2,748
Public administration and social service professions.........	3,441	13,335	17,749	371	287	7,217	10,501	278
Security and protective services.......................	17,679	20,495	1,795	51	2,894	7,680	1,922	3
Social sciences and history	6,046	99,282	9,857	2,423	199	51,075	6,253	1,388
Social sciences.....................	5,688	80,043	7,924	1,860	187	40,506	5,664	1,096
History............................	358	19,239	1,933	563	12	10,569	589	292
Theology and religious vocations	2	4	0	0	490	8,122	5,486	1,304
Transportation and materials moving..................	825	2,094	88	0	392	2,730	640	0
Visual and performing arts	9,831	42,227	6,447	907	14,118	34,954	6,459	375

[1]Includes Ph.D., Ed.D., and comparable degrees at the doctoral level. Excludes first-professional degrees, such as M.D., D.D.S., and law degrees.
[2]Excludes "Construction trades" and "Mechanics and repair technologies," which are listed separately.
NOTE: To facilitate trend comparisons, certain aggregations have been made of the degree fields as reported in the IPEDS Fall survey: "Agriculture and natural resources" includes Agriculture, agriculture operations, and related sciences and Natural resources and conservation; and "Business" includes Business management, marketing, and related support services and Personal and culinary services.
SOURCE: U.S. Department of Education, National Center for Education Statistics, 2003–04 Integrated Postsecondary Education Data System (IPEDS), Fall 2004. (This table was prepared July 2005.)

First-professional degrees conferred by degree-granting institutions in dentistry, medicine, and law, by sex of student, and number of institutions conferring degrees: Selected years, 1949–50 through 2003–04

| Year | Dentistry (D.D.S. or D.M.D.) | | | | Medicine (M.D.) | | | | Law (LL.B. or J.D.) | | | |
| | Number of institutions conferring degrees | Degrees conferred | | | Number of institutions conferring degrees | Degrees conferred | | | Number of institutions conferring degrees | Degrees conferred | | |
		Total	Males	Females		Total	Males	Females		Total	Males	Females
1	2	3	4	5	6	7	8	9	10	11	12	13
1949–50	40	2,579	2,561	18	72	5,612	5,028	584	—	—	—	—
1951–52	41	2,918	2,895	23	72	6,201	5,871	330	—	—	—	—
1953–54	42	3,102	3,063	39	73	6,712	6,377	335	—	—	—	—
1955–56	42	3,009	2,975	34	73	6,810	6,464	346	131	8,262	7,974	288
1957–58	43	3,065	3,031	34	75	6,816	6,469	347	131	9,394	9,122	272
1959–60	45	3,247	3,221	26	79	7,032	6,645	387	134	9,240	9,010	230
1961–62	46	3,183	3,166	17	81	7,138	6,749	389	134	9,364	9,091	273
1963–64	46	3,180	3,168	12	82	7,303	6,878	425	133	10,679	10,372	307
1964–65	46	3,108	3,086	22	81	7,304	6,832	472	137	11,583	11,216	367
1965–66	47	3,178	3,146	32	84	7,673	7,170	503	136	13,246	12,776	470
1967–68	48	3,422	3,375	47	85	7,944	7,318	626	138	16,454	15,805	649
1968–69	—	3,408	3,376	32	—	8,025	7,415	610	—	17,053	16,373	680
1969–70	48	3,718	3,684	34	86	8,314	7,615	699	145	14,916	14,115	801
1970–71	48	3,745	3,703	42	89	8,919	8,110	809	147	17,421	16,181	1,240
1971–72	48	3,862	3,819	43	92	9,253	8,423	830	147	21,764	20,266	1,498
1972–73	51	4,047	3,992	55	97	10,307	9,388	919	152	27,205	25,037	2,168
1973–74	52	4,440	4,355	85	99	11,356	10,093	1,263	151	29,326	25,986	3,340
1974–75	52	4,773	4,627	146	104	12,447	10,818	1,629	154	29,296	24,881	4,415
1975–76	56	5,425	5,187	238	107	13,426	11,252	2,174	166	32,293	26,085	6,208
1976–77	57	5,138	4,764	374	109	13,461	10,891	2,570	169	34,104	26,447	7,657
1977–78	57	5,189	4,623	566	109	14,279	11,210	3,069	169	34,402	25,457	8,945
1978–79	58	5,434	4,794	640	109	14,786	11,381	3,405	175	35,206	25,180	10,026
1979–80	58	5,258	4,558	700	112	14,902	11,416	3,486	179	35,647	24,893	10,754
1980–81	58	5,460	4,672	788	116	15,505	11,672	3,833	176	36,331	24,563	11,768
1981–82	59	5,282	4,467	815	119	15,814	11,867	3,947	180	35,991	23,965	12,026
1982–83	59	5,585	4,631	954	118	15,484	11,350	4,134	177	36,853	23,550	13,303
1983–84	60	5,353	4,302	1,051	119	15,813	11,359	4,454	179	37,012	23,382	13,630
1984–85	59	5,339	4,233	1,106	120	16,041	11,167	4,874	181	37,491	23,070	14,421
1985–86	59	5,046	3,907	1,139	120	15,938	11,022	4,916	181	35,844	21,874	13,970
1986–87	58	4,741	3,603	1,138	121	15,428	10,431	4,997	179	36,056	21,561	14,495
1987–88	57	4,477	3,300	1,177	122	15,358	10,278	5,080	180	35,397	21,067	14,330
1988–89	58	4,265	3,124	1,141	124	15,460	10,310	5,150	182	35,634	21,069	14,565
1989–90	57	4,100	2,834	1,266	124	15,075	9,923	5,152	182	36,485	21,079	15,406
1990–91	55	3,699	2,510	1,189	121	15,043	9,629	5,414	179	37,945	21,643	16,302
1991–92	52	3,593	2,431	1,162	120	15,243	9,796	5,447	177	38,848	22,260	16,588
1992–93	55	3,605	2,383	1,222	122	15,531	9,679	5,852	184	40,302	23,182	17,120
1993–94	53	3,787	2,330	1,457	121	15,368	9,544	5,824	185	40,044	22,826	17,218
1994–95	53	3,897	2,480	1,417	119	15,537	9,507	6,030	183	39,349	22,592	16,757
1995–96	53	3,697	2,374	1,323	119	15,341	9,061	6,280	183	39,828	22,508	17,320
1996–97	52	3,784	2,387	1,397	118	15,571	9,121	6,450	184	40,079	22,548	17,531
1997–98	53	4,032	2,490	1,542	117	15,424	9,006	6,418	185	39,331	21,876	17,455
1998–99	53	4,144	2,674	1,470	118	15,562	8,954	6,608	188	39,167	21,628	17,539
1999–2000	54	4,250	2,547	1,703	118	15,286	8,761	6,525	190	38,152	20,638	17,514
2000–01	54	4,391	2,696	1,695	118	15,403	8,728	6,675	192	37,904	19,981	17,923
2001–02	53	4,239	2,608	1,631	118	15,237	8,469	6,768	192	38,981	20,254	18,727
2002–03	53	4,344	2,653	1,691	118	15,034	8,221	6,813	194	39,067	19,916	19,151
2003–04	53	4,335	2,532	1,803	118	15,442	8,273	7,169	195	40,209	20,332	19,877

—Not available.

NOTE: Data for 1998–99 were imputed using alternative procedures. (See Guide to Sources for details.)

SOURCE: U.S. Department of Education, National Center for Education Statistics, Earned Degrees Conferred, 1949–50 through 1964–65; Higher Education General Information Survey (HEGIS), "Degrees and Other Formal Awards Conferred" surveys, 1965–66 through 1985–86; and 1986–87 through 2003–04 Integrated Postsecondary Education Data System (IPEDS), "Completions Survey" (IPEDS-C:87–99), and Fall 2000 through Fall 2004. (This table was prepared July 2005.)

Statistical profile of persons receiving doctor's degrees in education: Selected years, 1979–80 through 2002–03

Selected characteristic	1979–80	1989–90	1990–91	1991–92	1992–93	1993–94	1994–95	1995–96	1996–97	1997–98	1998–99	1999–2000	2000–01	2001–02	2002–03
1	2	3	4	5	6	7	8	9	10	11	12	13	14	15	16
Number of degrees	7,576	6,510	6,454	6,677	6,689	6,708	6,649	6,772	6,497	6,559	6,557	6,420	6,324	6,488	6,627
Sex (percent)															
Male	55.5	42.4	41.9	40.5	41.3	39.1	38.4	38.3	36.7	37.0	35.8	35.1	35.4	33.8	33.9
Female	44.5	57.6	58.1	59.5	58.7	60.9	61.6	61.7	63.3	63.0	64.2	64.9	64.6	66.2	66.1
Racial/ethnic group (percent)[1]															
White, non-Hispanic..................	86.3	86.0	85.6	84.8	83.7	83.9	81.6	82.2	81.1	79.1	79.3	78.3	78.8	77.2	76.3
Black, non-Hispanic	9.1	8.2	7.9	8.4	9.4	8.6	10.4	10.1	10.2	11.6	11.7	12.6	12.6	13.0	14.0
Hispanic	2.4	3.3	3.3	3.5	3.7	4.0	4.4	3.6	4.6	5.1	4.8	5.1	5.1	6.2	6.2
Asian[2]	1.3	1.8	2.2	2.4	2.4	2.9	3.0	3.1	3.2	3.2	3.1	3.1	2.7	2.6	2.8
American Indian/Alaska Native..	0.8	0.6	1.0	0.8	0.8	0.6	0.7	1.0	0.9	0.9	1.1	0.9	0.8	0.9	0.7
Citizenship (percent)															
United States	88.7	84.4	84.8	86.8	86.4	87.4	86.8	86.6	82.6	84.3	82.8	86.2	84.0	81.2	83.0
Foreign.............................	8.2	9.7	10.2	10.7	10.8	11.0	11.0	9.9	8.2	9.1	10.6	10.3	9.7	9.0	10.8
Unknown.............................	3.1	5.8	5.0	2.4	2.7	1.6	2.3	3.4	9.3	6.6	6.5	3.5	6.2	9.8	6.2
Median age at doctorate (years)....	37.0	41.6	42.1	42.7	43.0	43.6	43.8	44.3	44.0	44.3	44.3	44.4	43.8	44.2	43.5
Percent with bachelor's degree in same field as doctorate	39.0	37.5	39.3	38.7	37.4	36.9	37.0	36.1	34.1	35.0	34.8	33.7	33.2	30.6	31.0
Median time lapse from bachelor's to doctorate (years)															
Total time..........................	13.1	17.9	18.4	18.9	19.2	19.7	19.9	20.2	20.0	20.0	19.9	19.4	19.0	19.0	18.2
Registered time......................	6.9	8.1	8.1	8.2	8.2	8.1	8.2	8.2	8.4	8.4	8.2	8.1	8.3	8.5	8.3

[1]Distribution by race/ethnicity based on U.S. citizens and those with permanent visas only.
[2]Does not include Native Hawaiians or other Pacific Islanders.
NOTE: Longitudinal comparisons by race/ethnicity should be done with extreme care, due to periodic changes in the survey. In particular, large numbers of Asians converted from temporary visas to permanent visas in the mid-1990s. The classification of degrees by field used in this survey differs somewhat from that in most publications of the National Center for Educa-

tion Statistics (NCES). The total number of degrees also differs slightly from that reported in the NCES "Completions" survey. Detail may not sum to totals because of rounding.
SOURCE: *Doctorate Recipients From United States Universities, 2003*, Survey of Earned Doctorates, National Science Foundation, National Institutes of Health, U.S. Department of Education, National Endowment for the Humanities, U.S. Department of Agriculture, and the National Aeronautics and Space Administration. (This table was prepared April 2005.)

Total fall enrollment in degree-granting institutions, by attendance status, age, and sex:
Selected years, 1970 through 2014
[In thousands]

Sex, age, and attendance status	1970[1]	1980[1]	1990[1]	1995[1]	2000[2]	2001[2]	2002[2]	2003[2]	2004[2]	Projected[2] 2005	Projected[2] 2010	2014
1	2	3	4	5	6	7	8	9	10	11	12	13
Males and females	**8,581**	**12,097**	**13,819**	**14,262**	**15,312**	**15,928**	**16,612**	**16,900**	**17,272**	**17,350**	**18,816**	**19,470**
14 to 17 years old	259	247	177	148	145	133	202	193	198	201	216	215
18 and 19 years old	2,600	2,901	2,950	2,894	3,531	3,595	3,571	3,578	3,671	3,705	4,067	3,951
20 and 21 years old	1,880	2,424	2,761	2,705	3,045	3,408	3,366	3,420	3,508	3,456	3,848	3,845
22 to 24 years old	1,457	1,989	2,144	2,411	2,617	2,760	2,932	3,069	3,138	3,143	3,384	3,686
25 to 29 years old	1,074	1,871	1,982	2,120	1,960	2,014	2,102	2,235	2,280	2,374	2,724	2,913
30 to 34 years old	487	1,243	1,322	1,236	1,265	1,290	1,300	1,296	1,319	1,290	1,399	1,573
35 years old and over	823	1,421	2,484	2,747	2,749	2,727	3,139	3,109	3,157	3,181	3,178	3,287
Males	5,044	5,874	6,284	6,343	6,722	6,961	7,202	7,256	7,387	7,356	7,872	8,084
14 to 17 years old	130	99	87	61	63	54	82	80	82	83	87	84
18 and 19 years old	1,349	1,375	1,421	1,338	1,583	1,629	1,616	1,595	1,628	1,622	1,760	1,701
20 and 21 years old	1,095	1,259	1,368	1,282	1,382	1,591	1,562	1,604	1,637	1,586	1,739	1,726
22 to 24 years old	964	1,064	1,107	1,153	1,293	1,312	1,342	1,408	1,435	1,417	1,498	1,617
25 to 29 years old	783	993	940	962	862	905	890	903	918	949	1,071	1,133
30 to 34 years old	308	576	537	561	527	510	547	536	543	533	569	636
35 years old and over	415	507	824	986	1,012	961	1,164	1,131	1,145	1,166	1,148	1,186
Females	3,537	6,223	7,535	7,919	8,591	8,967	9,410	9,645	9,885	9,995	10,945	11,386
14 to 17 years old	129	148	90	87	82	79	121	113	116	118	129	130
18 and 19 years old	1,250	1,526	1,529	1,557	1,948	1,966	1,955	1,984	2,043	2,084	2,308	2,250
20 and 21 years old	786	1,165	1,392	1,424	1,663	1,817	1,804	1,816	1,871	1,870	2,108	2,119
22 to 24 years old	493	925	1,037	1,258	1,324	1,448	1,590	1,661	1,704	1,726	1,886	2,069
25 to 29 years old	291	878	1,043	1,159	1,099	1,110	1,212	1,332	1,362	1,425	1,653	1,780
30 to 34 years old	179	667	784	675	738	780	753	761	776	757	831	937
35 years old and over	409	914	1,659	1,760	1,736	1,767	1,976	1,978	2,012	2,015	2,030	2,102
Full-time	**5,816**	**7,098**	**7,821**	**8,129**	**9,010**	**9,448**	**9,946**	**10,312**	**10,610**	**10,483**	**11,563**	**11,902**
14 to 17 years old	242	223	144	123	125	122	161	156	161	162	174	174
18 and 19 years old	2,406	2,669	2,548	2,387	2,932	2,929	2,942	2,955	3,040	3,043	3,352	3,266
20 and 21 years old	1,647	2,075	2,151	2,109	2,401	2,662	2,759	2,827	2,908	2,840	3,173	3,178
22 to 24 years old	881	1,121	1,350	1,517	1,653	1,757	1,922	2,041	2,099	2,062	2,235	2,443
25 to 29 years old	407	577	770	908	878	883	1,013	1,154	1,188	1,208	1,400	1,509
30 to 34 years old	100	251	387	430	422	494	465	478	493	467	514	584
35 years old and over	134	182	471	653	599	602	684	700	721	701	714	748
Males	3,505	3,689	3,808	3,807	4,111	4,300	4,501	4,632	4,739	4,584	4,955	5,034
14 to 17 years old	124	87	71	54	51	43	65	63	65	64	67	65
18 and 19 years old	1,265	1,270	1,230	1,091	1,250	1,329	1,327	1,310	1,340	1,315	1,427	1,379
20 and 21 years old	990	1,109	1,055	999	1,106	1,249	1,275	1,325	1,356	1,294	1,419	1,408
22 to 24 years old	650	665	742	789	839	854	936	1,002	1,025	986	1,043	1,122
25 to 29 years old	327	360	401	454	415	397	467	491	502	500	564	596
30 to 34 years old	72	124	156	183	195	216	183	188	193	179	191	213
35 years old and over	75	74	152	238	256	212	247	253	259	247	244	251
Females	2,311	3,409	4,013	4,321	4,899	5,148	5,445	5,680	5,871	5,899	6,608	6,868
14 to 17 years old	117	136	73	69	74	78	96	93	96	98	107	109
18 and 19 years old	1,140	1,399	1,318	1,296	1,682	1,600	1,615	1,645	1,700	1,729	1,926	1,887
20 and 21 years old	657	966	1,096	1,111	1,296	1,413	1,484	1,502	1,552	1,546	1,754	1,770
22 to 24 years old	231	456	608	729	814	903	985	1,039	1,074	1,076	1,193	1,321
25 to 29 years old	80	217	369	455	463	486	546	663	686	708	836	913
30 to 34 years old	28	127	231	247	227	277	282	290	300	288	323	371
35 years old and over	59	108	319	415	343	390	437	447	462	454	470	498
Part-time	**2,765**	**4,999**	**5,998**	**6,133**	**6,303**	**6,480**	**6,665**	**6,589**	**6,662**	**6,867**	**7,253**	**7,568**
14 to 17 years old	17	38	32	25	20	11	41	37	37	39	42	41
18 and 19 years old	194	418	402	507	599	666	628	624	630	662	715	686
20 and 21 years old	233	441	610	596	644	746	607	593	600	616	675	667
22 to 24 years old	576	844	794	894	964	1,003	1,010	1,028	1,039	1,081	1,149	1,243
25 to 29 years old	668	1,209	1,213	1,212	1,083	1,132	1,088	1,080	1,092	1,166	1,324	1,404
30 to 34 years old	388	905	935	805	843	796	835	818	827	823	885	989
35 years old and over	689	1,145	2,012	2,093	2,150	2,126	2,456	2,409	2,436	2,480	2,464	2,539

See notes at end of table.

Total fall enrollment in degree-granting institutions, by attendance status, age, and sex:
Selected years, 1970 through 2014—Continued
[In thousands]

Sex, age, and attendance status	1970[1]	1980[1]	1990[1]	1995[1]	2000[2]	2001[2]	2002[2]	2003[2]	2004[2]	Projected[2] 2005	Projected[2] 2010	Projected[2] 2014
1	2	3	4	5	6	7	8	9	10	11	12	13
Males	1,540	2,185	2,476	2,535	2,611	2,661	2,701	2,624	2,648	2,772	2,917	3,050
14 to 17 years old......................	5	17	16	7	11	11	17	17	17	18	19	19
18 and 19 years old....................	84	202	191	246	333	300	288	285	288	307	333	323
20 and 21 years old....................	105	201	313	283	276	342	287	278	281	292	320	318
22 to 24 years old......................	314	392	365	365	454	458	405	406	410	432	455	495
25 to 29 years old......................	456	594	539	508	447	508	423	412	416	450	507	538
30 to 34 years old......................	236	397	381	378	332	294	364	347	351	354	378	423
35 years old and over..................	340	382	672	748	757	749	917	878	886	919	905	935
Females	1,225	2,814	3,521	3,598	3,692	3,820	3,964	3,965	4,014	4,096	4,336	4,518
14 to 17 years old......................	12	20	17	18	9	1	24	20	20	21	22	22
18 and 19 years old....................	110	215	211	261	266	366	340	339	343	355	382	363
20 and 21 years old....................	128	240	297	313	368	404	320	315	319	324	355	349
22 to 24 years old......................	262	452	429	529	510	545	605	622	630	649	693	748
25 to 29 years old......................	212	616	674	704	636	624	666	668	677	716	817	866
30 to 34 years old......................	151	507	554	427	511	502	471	470	476	469	507	566
35 years old and over..................	349	762	1,340	1,345	1,393	1,377	1,539	1,531	1,550	1,561	1,560	1,604

[1]Data are for institutions that were accredited by an agency or association that was recognized by the U.S. Department of Education, or recognized directly by the Secretary of Education.
[2]Data are for 4-year and 2-year degree-granting institutions that were participating in Title IV federal financial aid programs.
NOTE: Distributions by age are estimates based on samples of the civilian noninstitutional population. Some data have been revised from previously published figures. Detail may not sum to totals because of rounding.

SOURCE: U.S. Department of Education, National Center for Education Statistics, Higher Education General Information Survey (HEGIS), "Fall Enrollment in Colleges and Universities" surveys, 1970 and 1980; 1990 through 2004 Integrated Postsecondary Education Data System, "Fall Enrollment Survey" (IPEDS-EF:90–99), and Spring 2001 through Spring 2005; and *Projections of Education Statistics to 2014*. (This table was prepared September 2005.)

Total fall enrollment in degree-granting institutions, by attendance status, sex of student, and control of institution: Selected years, 1947 through 2004

Year	Total enrollment	Full-time	Part-time	Percent part-time	Male	Female	Percent female	Public	Total	Not-for-profit	For-profit
		Attendance status			Sex of student			Control of institution		Private	
1	2	3	4	5	6	7	8	9	10	11	12
Institutions of higher education											
1947[1]	2,338,226	—	—	—	1,659,249	678,977	29.0	1,152,377	1,185,849	—	—
1948[1]	2,403,396	—	—	—	1,709,367	694,029	28.9	1,185,588	1,217,808	—	—
1949[1]	2,444,900	—	—	—	1,721,572	723,328	29.6	1,207,151	1,237,749	—	—
1950[1]	2,281,298	—	—	—	1,560,392	720,906	31.6	1,139,699	1,141,599	—	—
1951[1]	2,101,962	—	—	—	1,390,740	711,222	33.8	1,037,938	1,064,024	—	—
1952[1]	2,134,242	—	—	—	1,380,357	753,885	35.3	1,101,240	1,033,002	—	—
1953[1]	2,231,054	—	—	—	1,422,598	808,456	36.2	1,185,876	1,045,178	—	—
1954[1]	2,446,693	—	—	—	1,563,382	883,311	36.1	1,353,531	1,093,162	—	—
1955[1]	2,653,034	—	—	—	1,733,184	919,850	34.7	1,476,282	1,176,752	—	—
1956[1]	2,918,212	—	—	—	1,911,458	1,006,754	34.5	1,656,402	1,261,810	—	—
1957	3,323,783	—	—	—	2,170,765	1,153,018	34.7	1,972,673	1,351,110	—	—
1959	3,639,847	2,421,016	[2] 1,218,831	33.5	2,332,617	1,307,230	35.9	2,180,982	1,458,865	—	—
1961	4,145,065	2,785,133	[2] 1,359,932	32.8	2,585,821	1,559,244	37.6	2,561,447	1,583,618	—	—
1963	4,779,609	3,183,833	[2] 1,595,776	33.4	2,961,540	1,818,069	38.0	3,081,279	1,698,330	—	—
1964	5,280,020	3,573,238	[2] 1,706,782	32.3	3,248,713	2,031,307	38.5	3,467,708	1,812,312	—	—
1965	5,920,864	4,095,728	[2] 1,825,136	30.8	3,630,020	2,290,844	38.7	3,969,596	1,951,268	—	—
1966	6,389,872	4,438,606	[2] 1,951,266	30.5	3,856,216	2,533,656	39.7	4,348,917	2,040,955	—	—
1967	6,911,748	4,793,128	[2] 2,118,620	30.7	4,132,800	2,778,948	40.2	4,816,028	2,095,720	—	—
1968	7,513,091	5,210,155	2,302,936	30.7	4,477,649	3,035,442	40.4	5,430,652	2,082,439	—	—
1969	8,004,660	5,498,883	2,505,777	31.3	4,746,201	3,258,459	40.7	5,896,868	2,107,792	—	—
1970	8,580,887	5,816,290	2,764,597	32.2	5,043,642	3,537,245	41.2	6,428,134	2,152,753	—	—
1971	8,948,644	6,077,232	2,871,412	32.1	5,207,004	3,741,640	41.8	6,804,309	2,144,335	—	—
1972	9,214,820	6,072,350	3,142,470	34.1	5,238,718	3,976,102	43.1	7,070,635	2,144,185	—	—
1973	9,602,123	6,189,493	3,412,630	35.5	5,371,052	4,231,071	44.1	7,419,516	2,182,607	—	—
1974	10,223,729	6,370,273	3,853,456	37.7	5,622,429	4,601,300	45.0	7,988,500	2,235,229	—	—
1975	11,184,859	6,841,334	4,343,525	38.8	6,148,997	5,035,862	45.0	8,834,508	2,350,351	—	—
1976	11,012,137	6,717,058	4,295,079	39.0	5,810,828	5,201,309	47.2	8,653,477	2,358,660	2,314,298	44,362
1977	11,285,787	6,792,925	4,492,862	39.8	5,789,016	5,496,771	48.7	8,846,993	2,438,794	2,386,652	52,142
1978	11,260,092	6,667,657	4,592,435	40.8	5,640,998	5,619,094	49.9	8,785,893	2,474,199	2,408,331	65,868
1979	11,569,899	6,794,039	4,775,860	41.3	5,682,877	5,887,022	50.9	9,036,822	2,533,077	2,461,773	71,304
1980	12,096,895	7,097,958	4,998,937	41.3	5,874,374	6,222,521	51.4	9,457,394	2,639,501	2,527,787	[3] 111,714
1981	12,371,672	7,181,250	5,190,422	42.0	5,975,056	6,396,616	51.7	9,647,032	2,724,640	2,572,405	[3] 152,235
1982	12,425,780	7,220,618	5,205,162	41.9	6,031,384	6,394,396	51.5	9,696,087	2,729,693	2,552,739	[3] 176,954
1983	12,464,661	7,261,050	5,203,611	41.7	6,023,725	6,440,936	51.7	9,682,734	2,781,927	2,589,187	192,740
1984	12,241,940	7,098,388	5,143,552	42.0	5,863,574	6,378,366	52.1	9,477,370	2,764,570	2,574,419	190,151
1985	12,247,055	7,075,221	5,171,834	42.2	5,818,450	6,428,605	52.5	9,479,273	2,767,782	2,571,791	195,991
1986	12,503,511	7,119,550	5,383,961	43.1	5,884,515	6,618,996	52.9	9,713,893	2,789,618	2,572,479	[4] 217,139
1987	12,766,642	7,231,085	5,535,557	43.4	5,932,056	6,834,586	53.5	9,973,254	2,793,388	2,602,350	[4] 191,038
1988	13,055,337	7,436,768	5,618,569	43.0	6,001,896	7,053,441	54.0	10,161,388	2,893,949	2,673,567	220,382
1989	13,538,560	7,660,950	5,877,610	43.4	6,190,015	7,348,545	54.3	10,577,963	2,960,597	2,731,174	229,423
1990	13,818,637	7,820,985	5,997,652	43.4	6,283,909	7,534,728	54.5	10,844,717	2,973,920	2,760,227	213,693
1991	14,358,953	8,115,329	6,243,624	43.5	6,501,844	7,857,109	54.7	11,309,563	3,049,390	2,819,041	230,349
1992	14,487,359	8,162,118	6,325,241	43.7	6,523,989	7,963,370	55.0	11,384,567	3,102,792	2,872,523	230,269
1993	14,304,803	8,127,618	6,177,185	43.2	6,427,450	7,877,353	55.1	11,189,088	3,115,715	2,888,897	226,818
1994	14,278,790	8,137,776	6,141,014	43.0	6,371,898	7,906,892	55.4	11,133,680	3,145,110	2,910,107	235,003
1995	14,261,781	8,128,802	6,132,979	43.0	6,342,539	7,919,242	55.5	11,092,374	3,169,407	2,929,044	240,363
1996	14,300,255	8,213,490	6,086,765	42.6	6,343,992	7,956,263	55.6	11,090,171	3,210,084	2,940,557	269,527

See notes at end of table.

Total fall enrollment in degree-granting institutions, by attendance status, sex of student, and control of institution: Selected years, 1947 through 2004—Continued

Year	Total enrollment	Attendance status			Sex of student			Control of institution			
		Full-time	Part-time	Percent part-time	Male	Female	Percent female	Public	Private		
									Total	Not-for-profit	For-profit
1	2	3	4	5	6	7	8	9	10	11	12
Degree-granting institutions											
1996................................	14,367,520	8,302,953	6,064,567	42.2	6,352,825	8,014,695	55.8	11,120,499	3,247,021	2,942,556	304,465
1997................................	14,502,334	8,438,062	6,064,272	41.8	6,396,028	8,106,306	55.9	11,196,119	3,306,215	2,977,614	328,601
1998................................	14,506,967	8,563,338	5,943,629	41.0	6,369,265	8,137,702	56.1	11,137,769	3,369,198	3,004,925	364,273
1999[5]............................	14,791,224	8,786,494	6,004,730	40.6	6,490,646	8,300,578	56.1	11,309,399	3,481,825	3,051,626	430,199
2000................................	15,312,289	9,009,600	6,302,689	41.2	6,721,769	8,590,520	56.1	11,752,786	3,559,503	3,109,419	450,084
2001................................	15,927,987	9,447,502	6,480,485	40.7	6,960,815	8,967,172	56.3	12,233,156	3,694,831	3,167,330	527,501
2002................................	16,611,711	9,946,359	6,665,352	40.1	7,202,116	9,409,595	56.6	12,751,993	3,859,718	3,265,476	594,242
2003................................	16,900,471	10,311,814	6,588,657	39.0	7,255,551	9,644,920	57.1	12,857,059	4,043,412	3,340,718	702,694
2004................................	17,272,044	10,610,177	6,661,867	38.6	7,387,262	9,884,782	57.2	12,980,112	4,291,932	3,411,685	880,247

—Not available.
[1]Degree-credit enrollment only.
[2]Includes part-time resident students and all extension students.
[3]Large increases are due to the addition of schools accredited by the Accrediting Commission of Career Schools and Colleges of Technology.
[4]Because of imputation techniques, data are not consistent with figures for other years.
[5]Data were imputed using alternative procedures. (See Guide to Sources for details.)
NOTE: Institutions of higher education were accredited by an agency or association that was recognized by the U.S. Department of Education, or recognized directly by the Secretary of Education. The new degree-granting classification is very similar to the earlier higher education classification, except that it includes some additional institutions, primarily

2-year colleges, and excludes a few higher education institutions that did not award associate's or higher degrees. These degree-granting institutions participated in Title IV federal financial aid programs. (See Guide to Sources for details.)
SOURCE: U.S. Department of Education, National Center for Education Statistics, *Biennial Survey of Education in the United States; Opening Fall Enrollment in Higher Education,* 1963 through 1965; Higher Education General Information Survey (HEGIS), "Fall Enrollment in Colleges and Universities" surveys, 1966 through 1985; and 1986 through 2004 Integrated Postsecondary Education Data System, "Fall Enrollment Survey" (IPEDS-EF:86–99), and Spring 2001 through Spring 2005. (This table was prepared September 2005.)

College enrollment and enrollment rates of recent high school completers, by sex: 1960 through 2004

[Numbers in thousands]

Year	Number of high school completers[1]						Enrolled in college[2]											
	Total		Males		Females		Total				Males				Females			
							Number		Percent		Number		Percent		Number		Percent	
1	2		3		4		5		6		7		8		9		10	
1960	1,679	(43.8)	756	(31.8)	923	(29.6)	758	(40.9)	45.1	(2.13)	408	(29.5)	54.0	(3.18)	350	(28.2)	37.9	(2.80)
1961	1,763	(46.0)	790	(33.2)	973	(31.3)	847	(42.9)	48.0	(2.09)	445	(30.8)	56.3	(3.10)	402	(29.9)	41.3	(2.77)
1962	1,838	(43.6)	872	(31.5)	966	(30.0)	900	(43.2)	49.0	(2.05)	480	(31.1)	55.0	(2.96)	420	(30.0)	43.5	(2.80)
1963	1,741	(44.2)	794	(32.1)	947	(30.0)	784	(41.5)	45.0	(2.09)	415	(29.8)	52.3	(3.11)	369	(28.8)	39.0	(2.78)
1964	2,145	(43.0)	997	(31.9)	1,148	(28.5)	1,037	(45.6)	48.3	(1.89)	570	(32.9)	57.2	(2.75)	467	(31.4)	40.7	(2.54)
1965	2,659	(47.7)	1,254	(35.1)	1,405	(32.0)	1,354	(51.4)	50.9	(1.70)	718	(36.7)	57.3	(2.45)	636	(35.8)	45.3	(2.33)
1966	2,612	(45.0)	1,207	(33.8)	1,405	(29.0)	1,309	(50.2)	50.1	(1.72)	709	(36.0)	58.7	(2.49)	600	(34.8)	42.7	(2.32)
1967	2,525	(37.9)	1,142	(28.4)	1,383	(24.3)	1,311	(40.9)	51.9	(1.42)	658	(28.9)	57.6	(2.09)	653	(28.9)	47.2	(1.92)
1968	2,606	(37.3)	1,184	(28.2)	1,422	(23.8)	1,444	(41.7)	55.4	(1.39)	748	(29.6)	63.2	(2.00)	696	(29.3)	48.9	(1.89)
1969	2,842	(36.0)	1,352	(26.8)	1,490	(23.7)	1,516	(42.5)	53.3	(1.34)	812	(30.3)	60.1	(1.90)	704	(29.7)	47.2	(1.85)
1970	2,758	(37.4)	1,343	(26.1)	1,415	(26.8)	1,427	(42.2)	51.7	(1.36)	741	(29.7)	55.2	(1.94)	686	(29.8)	48.5	(1.90)
1971	2,875	(38.0)	1,371	(26.6)	1,504	(27.1)	1,538	(43.2)	53.5	(1.33)	790	(30.3)	57.6	(1.90)	749	(30.8)	49.8	(1.84)
1972	2,964	(37.8)	1,423	(27.0)	1,542	(26.4)	1,459	(43.1)	49.2	(1.31)	750	(30.4)	52.7	(1.89)	709	(30.5)	46.0	(1.81)
1973	3,058	(37.1)	1,460	(27.6)	1,599	(24.6)	1,424	(43.0)	46.6	(1.29)	730	(30.6)	50.0	(1.87)	694	(30.2)	43.4	(1.77)
1974	3,101	(38.6)	1,491	(27.8)	1,611	(26.8)	1,475	(43.7)	47.6	(1.28)	736	(30.8)	49.4	(1.85)	740	(31.1)	45.9	(1.77)
1975	3,185	(38.6)	1,513	(27.3)	1,672	(27.2)	1,615	(44.8)	50.7	(1.26)	796	(31.2)	52.6	(1.83)	818	(32.1)	49.0	(1.75)
1976	2,986	(39.8)	1,451	(28.9)	1,535	(27.3)	1,458	(43.6)	48.8	(1.31)	685	(30.4)	47.2	(1.87)	773	(31.2)	50.3	(1.82)
1977	3,141	(40.7)	1,483	(29.7)	1,659	(27.7)	1,590	(45.4)	50.6	(1.29)	773	(31.8)	52.1	(1.87)	817	(32.4)	49.3	(1.77)
1978	3,163	(39.7)	1,485	(29.3)	1,677	(26.7)	1,585	(45.2)	50.1	(1.28)	759	(31.6)	51.1	(1.87)	827	(32.4)	49.3	(1.76)
1979	3,160	(40.0)	1,475	(29.2)	1,685	(27.2)	1,559	(45.1)	49.3	(1.28)	744	(31.4)	50.4	(1.88)	815	(32.4)	48.4	(1.76)
1980	3,088	(39.4)	1,498	(28.4)	1,589	(27.3)	1,523	(44.6)	49.3	(1.30)	700	(30.9)	46.7	(1.86)	823	(32.0)	51.8	(1.81)
1981	3,056	(42.2)	1,491	(30.4)	1,565	(29.1)	1,648	(45.8)	53.9	(1.30)	817	(32.4)	54.8	(1.86)	831	(32.4)	53.1	(1.82)
1982	3,100	(40.4)	1,509	(29.0)	1,592	(28.2)	1,569	(46.9)	50.6	(1.36)	741	(32.7)	49.1	(1.95)	828	(33.6)	52.0	(1.90)
1983	2,963	(41.6)	1,389	(30.4)	1,573	(28.2)	1,562	(46.7)	52.7	(1.39)	721	(32.3)	51.9	(2.03)	841	(33.6)	53.4	(1.91)
1984	3,012	(36.5)	1,429	(28.7)	1,584	(21.9)	1,663	(46.0)	55.2	(1.37)	801	(32.7)	56.0	(1.99)	862	(32.3)	54.5	(1.90)
1985	2,668	(40.1)	1,287	(28.7)	1,381	(27.9)	1,540	(45.1)	57.7	(1.45)	755	(31.6)	58.6	(2.08)	785	(32.1)	56.8	(2.02)
1986	2,786	(38.6)	1,332	(28.5)	1,454	(26.0)	1,498	(45.0)	53.8	(1.43)	743	(31.7)	55.8	(2.06)	755	(31.9)	51.9	(1.99)
1987	2,647	(40.9)	1,278	(29.8)	1,369	(28.0)	1,503	(45.1)	56.8	(1.46)	746	(31.9)	58.3	(2.09)	757	(31.9)	55.3	(2.04)
1988	2,673	(47.0)	1,334	(34.1)	1,339	(32.3)	1,575	(50.3)	58.9	(1.57)	761	(35.6)	57.1	(2.24)	814	(35.4)	60.7	(2.20)
1989	2,450	(46.5)	1,204	(32.9)	1,246	(32.8)	1,460	(48.7)	59.6	(1.64)	693	(34.0)	57.6	(2.35)	767	(34.8)	61.6	(2.27)
1990	2,362	(43.0)	1,173	(30.6)	1,189	(30.2)	1,420	(45.9)	60.1	(1.60)	680	(32.2)	58.0	(2.29)	740	(32.6)	62.2	(2.24)
1991	2,276	(41.0)	1,140	(29.0)	1,136	(29.0)	1,423	(44.8)	62.5	(1.62)	660	(31.4)	57.9	(2.33)	763	(31.9)	67.1	(2.22)
1992	2,397	(40.4)	1,216	(29.1)	1,180	(28.1)	1,483	(45.4)	61.9	(1.58)	729	(32.3)	60.0	(2.24)	754	(31.8)	63.8	(2.23)
1993	2,342	(41.4)	1,120	(30.6)	1,223	(27.7)	1,467	(45.4)	62.6	(1.59)	670	(31.9)	59.9	(2.33)	797	(32.1)	65.2	(2.17)
1994	2,517	(38.1)	1,244	(27.9)	1,273	(25.9)	1,559	(43.0)	61.9	(1.43)	754	(30.6)	60.6	(2.05)	805	(30.2)	63.2	(1.99)
1995	2,599	(40.9)	1,238	(29.9)	1,361	(27.7)	1,610	(44.5)	61.9	(1.41)	775	(31.3)	62.6	(2.03)	835	(31.5)	61.3	(1.95)
1996	2,660	(40.5)	1,297	(29.5)	1,363	(27.7)	1,729	(46.1)	65.0	(1.42)	779	(32.4)	60.1	(2.09)	950	(32.5)	69.7	(1.92)
1997	2,769	(41.8)	1,354	(31.0)	1,415	(27.9)	1,856	(47.3)	67.0	(1.38)	860	(33.6)	63.6	(2.01)	995	(32.9)	70.3	(1.87)
1998	2,810	(43.9)	1,452	(31.0)	1,358	(31.0)	1,844	(48.3)	65.6	(1.38)	906	(34.4)	62.4	(1.96)	938	(33.9)	69.1	(1.93)
1999	2,897	(41.5)	1,474	(29.9)	1,423	(28.8)	1,822	(47.8)	62.9	(1.38)	905	(34.1)	61.4	(1.95)	917	(33.4)	64.4	(1.95)
2000	2,756	(45.3)	1,251	(33.6)	1,505	(29.7)	1,745	(48.4)	63.3	(1.41)	749	(33.4)	59.9	(2.13)	996	(34.4)	66.2	(1.88)
2001	2,549	(46.5)	1,277	(33.7)	1,273	(32.0)	1,574	(47.5)	61.8	(1.48)	767	(33.7)	60.1	(2.11)	808	(33.3)	63.5	(2.08)
2002	2,796	(42.7)	1,412	(31.3)	1,384	(29.0)	1,824	(46.1)	65.2	(1.31)	877	(33.0)	62.1	(1.88)	947	(32.1)	68.4	(1.82)
2003	2,677	(42.2)	1,306	(29.9)	1,372	(29.7)	1,711	(45.2)	63.9	(1.35)	799	(31.5)	61.2	(1.97)	913	(32.3)	66.5	(1.86)
2004	2,752	(40.0)	1,327	(29.1)	1,425	(27.3)	1,835	(44.9)	66.7	(1.31)	815	(31.5)	61.4	(1.95)	1,020	(31.6)	71.5	(1.74)

[1]Individuals ages 16 to 24 who graduated from high school or completed a GED during the preceding 12 months.
[2]Enrollment in college as of October of each year for individuals ages 16 to 24 who completed high school during the preceding 12 months.
NOTE: Data are based on sample surveys of the civilian population. High school completion data in this table differ from figures appearing in other tables because of varying survey procedures and coverage. High school completers include GED recipients. Some data have been revised from previously published figures. Standard errors appear in parentheses. Detail may not sum to totals because of rounding.
SOURCE: American College Testing Program, unpublished tabulations, derived from statistics collected by the Census Bureau, 1960 through 1969. U.S. Department of Commerce, Census Bureau, Current Population Survey (CPS), October 1970 through October 2004, unpublished tabulations. (This table was prepared September 2005.)

Total undergraduate fall enrollment in degree-granting institutions, by attendance status, sex of student, and control of institution: 1969 through 2004
[In thousands]

Year	Total	Full-time	Part-time	Males	Females	Males Full-time	Males Part-time	Females Full-time	Females Part-time	Males Public	Males Private	Females Public	Females Private
1	2	3	4	5	6	7	8	9	10	11	12	13	14
Institutions of higher education													
1969	6,884	4,991	1,893	4,008	2,876	2,952	1,056	2,039	837	2,997	1,011	2,162	714
1970	7,376	5,280	2,096	4,254	3,122	3,097	1,157	2,183	939	3,241	1,013	2,387	735
1971	7,743	5,512	2,231	4,418	3,325	3,201	1,217	2,311	1,014	3,427	991	2,580	745
1972	7,941	5,488	2,453	4,429	3,512	3,121	1,308	2,367	1,145	3,467	962	2,756	756
1973	8,261	5,580	2,681	4,538	3,723	3,135	1,403	2,445	1,278	3,579	959	2,943	780
1974	8,798	5,726	3,072	4,765	4,033	3,191	1,574	2,535	1,498	3,799	966	3,232	801
1975	9,679	6,169	3,510	5,257	4,422	3,459	1,798	2,710	1,712	4,245	1,012	3,581	841
1976	9,429	6,030	3,399	4,902	4,527	3,242	1,660	2,788	1,739	3,949	953	3,668	859
1977	9,717	6,094	3,623	4,897	4,820	3,188	1,709	2,906	1,914	3,937	960	3,906	914
1978	9,691	5,967	3,724	4,766	4,925	3,072	1,694	2,895	2,030	3,812	954	3,974	951
1979	9,998	6,080	3,919	4,821	5,178	3,087	1,734	2,993	2,185	3,865	956	4,181	995
1980	10,475	6,362	4,113	5,000	5,475	3,227	1,773	3,135	2,340	4,014	985	4,427	1,048
1981	10,755	6,449	4,306	5,109	5,646	3,261	1,848	3,188	2,458	4,090	1,018	4,558	1,088
1982	10,825	6,484	4,341	5,170	5,655	3,299	1,871	3,184	2,470	4,140	1,031	4,573	1,081
1983	10,846	6,514	4,332	5,158	5,688	3,304	1,854	3,210	2,478	4,117	1,042	4,580	1,107
1984	10,618	6,348	4,270	5,007	5,611	3,195	1,812	3,153	2,459	3,990	1,017	4,504	1,107
1985	10,597	6,320	4,277	4,962	5,635	3,156	1,806	3,163	2,471	3,953	1,010	4,525	1,110
1986	10,798	6,352	4,446	5,018	5,780	3,146	1,871	3,206	2,575	4,002	1,015	4,658	1,122
1987	11,046	6,463	4,584	5,068	5,978	3,164	1,905	3,299	2,679	4,076	992	4,842	1,136
1988	11,317	6,642	4,674	5,138	6,179	3,206	1,931	3,436	2,743	4,113	1,024	4,990	1,189
1989	11,743	6,841	4,902	5,311	6,432	3,279	2,032	3,562	2,869	4,272	1,039	5,216	1,216
1990	11,959	6,976	4,983	5,380	6,579	3,337	2,043	3,639	2,940	4,353	1,027	5,357	1,223
1991	12,439	7,221	5,218	5,571	6,868	3,436	2,135	3,786	3,082	4,531	1,040	5,617	1,251
1992	12,538	7,244	5,293	5,583	6,955	3,425	2,158	3,820	3,135	4,537	1,046	5,679	1,275
1993	12,324	7,179	5,144	5,484	6,840	3,382	2,102	3,797	3,043	4,447	1,036	5,565	1,276
1994	12,263	7,169	5,094	5,422	6,840	3,342	2,081	3,827	3,013	4,394	1,028	5,551	1,290
1995	12,232	7,145	5,086	5,401	6,831	3,297	2,105	3,849	2,982	4,380	1,021	5,524	1,307
1996	12,259	7,211	5,049	5,411	6,848	3,304	2,107	3,907	2,942	4,368	1,043	5,537	1,311
1997	12,298	7,306	4,992	5,405	6,893	3,330	2,075	3,976	2,917	4,385	1,021	5,574	1,319
Degree-granting institutions													
1996	12,327	7,299	5,028	5,421	6,906	3,339	2,082	3,960	2,947	4,383	1,038	5,553	1,354
1997	12,451	7,419	5,032	5,469	6,982	3,380	2,089	4,039	2,943	4,408	1,060	5,599	1,383
1998	12,437	7,539	4,898	5,446	6,991	3,428	2,018	4,111	2,880	4,361	1,085	5,589	1,402
1999[1]	12,681	7,735	4,946	5,559	7,122	3,516	2,044	4,219	2,903	4,431	1,128	5,679	1,443
2000	13,155	7,923	5,232	5,778	7,377	3,588	2,190	4,335	3,042	4,622	1,156	5,917	1,460
2001	13,716	8,328	5,388	6,004	7,711	3,769	2,236	4,559	3,152	4,804	1,200	6,182	1,529
2002	14,257	8,734	5,523	6,192	8,065	3,934	2,258	4,800	3,265	4,960	1,232	6,473	1,592
2003	14,474	9,035	5,439	6,224	8,250	4,044	2,180	4,991	3,259	4,956	1,269	6,566	1,684
2004	14,781	9,284	5,496	6,340	8,441	4,141	2,199	5,144	3,297	5,009	1,331	6,641	1,799

[1]Data for 1999 were imputed using alternative procedures. (See Guide to Sources for details.)
NOTE: Data include unclassified undergraduate students. Institutions of higher education were accredited by an agency or association that was recognized by the U.S. Department of Education, or recognized directly by the Secretary of Education. The new degree-granting classification is very similar to the earlier higher education classification, except that it includes some additional institutions, primarily 2-year colleges, and excludes a few higher education institutions that did not award associate's or higher degrees. (See Guide to Sources for details.) Detail may not sum to totals because of rounding.
SOURCE: U.S. Department of Education, National Center for Education Statistics, Higher Education General Information Survey (HEGIS), "Fall Enrollment in Colleges and Universities" surveys, 1969 through 1985; and 1986 through 2004 Integrated Postsecondary Education Data System, "Fall Enrollment Survey" (IPEDS-EF:86–99), and Spring 2001 through Spring 2005. (This table was prepared September 2005.)

Total graduate fall enrollment in degree-granting institutions, by attendance status, sex of student, and control of institution: 1969 through 2004
[In thousands]

Year	Total	Full-time	Part-time	Male	Female	Male Full-time	Male Part-time	Female Full-time	Female Part-time	Male Public	Male Private	Female Public	Female Private
1	2	3	4	5	6	7	8	9	10	11	12	13	14
Institutions of higher education													
1969...............	955	363	593	590	366	252	338	111	255	393	197	273	93
1970...............	1,031	379	651	630	400	264	366	115	285	423	207	301	99
1971...............	1,012	388	621	615	394	269	346	119	275	415	200	296	100
1972...............	1,066	394	671	626	439	268	358	126	313	427	199	330	109
1973...............	1,123	410	715	648	477	273	375	137	340	442	206	358	119
1974...............	1,190	427	762	663	526	276	387	151	375	454	209	398	128
1975...............	1,263	453	810	700	563	290	410	163	400	481	219	425	138
1976...............	1,333	463	870	714	619	287	427	176	443	477	237	454	165
1977...............	1,319	473	845	700	617	289	411	184	434	458	243	443	174
1978...............	1,312	468	844	682	630	280	402	188	442	441	241	453	177
1979...............	1,309	476	833	669	640	280	389	196	444	427	242	457	182
1980...............	1,343	485	860	675	670	281	394	204	466	426	247	474	195
1981...............	1,343	484	859	674	669	277	397	207	462	419	255	468	201
1982...............	1,322	485	838	670	653	280	390	205	447	417	253	453	200
1983...............	1,340	497	843	677	663	286	391	211	452	418	259	454	209
1984...............	1,345	501	844	672	673	286	386	215	459	411	261	459	215
1985...............	1,376	509	867	677	700	289	388	220	479	414	263	477	223
1986...............	1,435	522	913	693	742	294	399	228	514	433	260	508	234
1987...............	1,452	527	925	693	759	294	400	233	525	429	264	516	243
1988...............	1,472	553	919	697	774	304	393	249	526	429	268	520	254
1989...............	1,522	572	949	710	811	309	401	263	548	437	273	541	271
1990...............	1,586	599	987	737	849	321	416	278	571	456	281	567	282
1991...............	1,639	642	997	761	878	341	419	300	578	471	290	580	299
1992...............	1,669	666	1,003	772	896	351	421	314	582	474	298	584	313
1993...............	1,688	688	1,000	771	917	355	416	334	584	473	298	590	327
1994...............	1,721	706	1,016	776	946	359	417	347	598	472	304	603	343
1995...............	1,732	717	1,015	768	965	356	412	361	604	464	304	610	355
1996...............	1,743	736	1,007	760	983	358	403	378	604	456	305	613	370
1997...............	1,751	750	1,000	756	994	359	398	392	603	452	304	618	377
Degree-granting institutions													
1996...............	1,742	737	1,005	759	983	358	401	379	604	456	303	613	370
1997...............	1,753	752	1,001	758	996	360	398	393	603	452	306	618	377
1998...............	1,768	754	1,014	754	1,013	355	399	398	615	444	310	623	390
1999[1]...............	1,807	781	1,026	766	1,041	363	403	418	623	446	320	630	411
2000...............	1,850	813	1,037	780	1,071	377	402	436	635	447	332	642	428
2001...............	1,904	843	1,061	796	1,108	388	408	455	653	460	336	659	449
2002...............	2,036	926	1,109	847	1,189	421	425	505	684	487	360	700	489
2003...............	2,098	981	1,117	865	1,233	439	426	542	691	491	374	710	523
2004...............	2,157	1,024	1,133	879	1,278	448	431	576	702	486	393	708	570

[1]Data for 1999 were imputed using alternative procedures. (See Guide to Sources for details.)
NOTE: Data include unclassified graduate students. Institutions of higher education were accredited by an agency or association that was recognized by the U.S. Department of Education, or recognized directly by the Secretary of Education. The new degree-granting classification is very similar to the earlier higher education classification, except that it includes some additional institutions, primarily 2-year colleges, and excludes a few higher education institutions that did not award associate's or higher degrees. Detail may not sum to totals because of rounding.
SOURCE: U.S. Department of Education, National Center for Education Statistics, Higher Education General Information Survey (HEGIS), "Fall Enrollment in Colleges and Universities" surveys, 1969 through 1985; and 1986 through 2004 Intergrated Postsecondary Education Data System, "Fall Enrollment Survey" (IPEDS-EF:86–99), and Spring 2001 through Spring 2005. (This table was prepared September 2005.)

Total fall enrollment in degree-granting institutions, by state or jurisdiction: Selected years, 1970 through 2004

State or jurisdiction	Institutions of higher education			Degree-granting institutions							Percent change, 1999 to 2004
	Fall 1970	Fall 1980	Fall 1990	Fall 1998	Fall 1999[1]	Fall 2000	Fall 2001	Fall 2002	Fall 2003	Fall 2004	
1	2	3	4	5	6	7	8	9	10	11	12
United States	8,580,887	12,096,895	13,818,637	14,506,967	14,791,224	15,312,289	15,927,987	16,611,711	16,900,471	17,272,044	16.8
Alabama	103,936	164,306	218,589	216,241	223,144	233,962	236,146	246,414	253,846	255,826	14.6
Alaska	9,471	21,296	29,833	27,652	26,948	27,953	27,756	29,546	31,035	30,869	14.6
Arizona	109,619	202,716	264,148	302,123	326,159	342,490	366,485	401,605	430,661	490,925	50.5
Arkansas	52,039	77,607	90,425	113,751	115,092	115,172	122,282	127,372	133,950	138,399	20.3
California	1,257,245	1,790,993	1,808,740	1,949,508	2,017,483	2,256,708	2,380,090	2,474,024	2,338,846	2,374,045	17.7
Colorado	123,395	162,916	227,131	257,247	261,744	263,872	269,292	282,343	289,243	300,914	15.0
Connecticut	124,700	159,632	168,604	153,336	156,907	161,243	165,027	170,606	170,976	172,775	10.1
Delaware	25,260	32,939	42,004	46,260	46,613	43,897	47,104	49,228	49,595	49,804	6.8
District of Columbia	77,158	86,675	79,551	72,388	72,118	72,689	87,252	91,014	95,297	99,988	38.6
Florida	235,525	411,891	588,086	661,187	684,745	707,684	753,554	792,079	839,735	866,665	26.6
Georgia	126,511	184,159	251,786	303,685	311,812	346,204	376,098	397,604	411,061	434,283	39.3
Hawaii	36,562	47,181	56,436	61,615	62,578	60,182	62,079	65,368	67,390	67,225	7.4
Idaho	34,567	43,018	51,881	63,085	64,661	65,594	69,674	72,072	75,370	76,311	18.0
Illinois	452,146	644,245	729,246	729,084	733,182	743,918	748,444	776,622	796,774	801,401	9.3
Indiana	192,668	247,253	284,832	299,176	304,725	314,334	338,715	342,064	350,091	356,801	17.1
Iowa	108,902	140,449	170,515	181,944	186,780	188,974	194,822	202,546	213,958	217,646	16.5
Kansas	102,485	136,605	163,733	177,561	176,737	179,968	184,943	188,049	190,291	191,590	8.4
Kentucky	98,591	143,066	177,852	180,550	181,626	188,341	214,839	225,489	235,743	240,097	32.2
Louisiana	120,728	160,058	186,840	221,110	221,348	223,800	228,871	232,140	244,455	246,301	11.3
Maine	34,134	43,264	57,186	56,986	57,822	58,473	61,127	63,308	64,222	65,415	13.1
Maryland	149,607	225,526	259,700	265,173	268,820	273,745	288,224	300,269	307,543	312,493	16.2
Massachusetts	303,809	418,415	417,833	415,501	419,695	421,142	425,071	431,224	436,068	439,245	4.7
Michigan	392,726	520,131	569,803	557,011	558,998	567,631	585,998	605,835	615,765	620,980	11.1
Minnesota	160,788	206,691	253,789	271,612	282,756	293,445	308,233	323,791	337,780	349,021	23.4
Mississippi	73,967	102,364	122,883	132,438	133,170	137,389	137,882	147,077	148,584	152,115	14.2
Missouri	183,930	234,421	289,899	310,507	317,480	321,348	331,580	348,146	359,680	365,204	15.0
Montana	30,062	35,177	35,876	44,150	43,114	42,240	44,932	45,111	47,240	47,173	9.4
Nebraska	66,915	89,488	112,831	111,123	110,806	112,117	113,817	116,737	119,511	121,053	9.2
Nevada	13,669	40,455	61,728	83,120	89,711	87,893	93,368	95,671	100,995	105,961	18.1
New Hampshire	29,400	46,794	59,510	60,784	63,366	61,718	65,031	68,523	69,608	70,163	10.7
New Jersey	216,121	321,610	324,286	325,885	330,537	335,945	346,507	361,733	372,632	380,374	15.1
New Mexico	44,461	58,283	85,500	108,810	111,896	110,739	112,861	120,997	126,852	131,577	17.6
New York	806,479	992,237	1,048,286	1,014,220	1,020,991	1,043,395	1,057,794	1,107,270	1,126,087	1,141,525	11.8
North Carolina	171,925	287,537	352,138	387,407	395,907	404,652	427,784	447,335	464,430	472,709	19.4
North Dakota	31,495	34,069	37,878	39,441	40,348	40,248	42,843	45,800	48,402	49,533	22.8
Ohio	376,267	489,145	557,690	542,077	548,545	549,553	569,223	587,996	603,378	614,234	12.0
Oklahoma	110,155	160,295	173,221	178,507	179,055	178,016	189,785	198,423	207,781	207,625	16.0
Oregon	122,177	157,458	165,741	171,056	175,635	183,065	191,378	204,565	198,701	199,985	13.9
Pennsylvania	411,044	507,716	604,060	595,749	605,283	609,521	630,299	654,826	675,574	688,780	13.8
Rhode Island	45,898	66,869	78,273	73,970	74,821	75,450	77,235	77,417	79,085	80,377	7.4
South Carolina	69,518	132,476	159,302	181,353	183,626	185,931	191,590	202,007	207,601	208,910	13.8
South Dakota	30,639	32,761	34,208	41,545	42,147	43,221	45,534	47,751	48,967	48,708	15.6
Tennessee	135,103	204,581	226,238	251,319	252,915	263,910	258,534	261,899	267,969	278,055	9.9
Texas	442,225	701,391	901,437	978,550	990,587	1,033,973	1,076,678	1,152,369	1,188,727	1,229,197	24.1
Utah	81,687	93,987	121,303	151,232	161,591	163,776	177,045	178,932	185,772	194,324	20.3
Vermont	22,209	30,628	36,398	37,054	36,728	35,489	36,351	36,537	37,831	38,639	5.2
Virginia	151,915	280,504	353,442	370,142	377,970	381,893	389,853	404,966	414,881	425,181	12.5
Washington	183,544	303,603	263,384	298,974	306,723	320,840	325,132	338,820	345,469	343,524	12.0
West Virginia	63,153	81,973	84,790	88,107	88,657	87,888	91,319	93,723	97,005	97,884	10.4
Wisconsin	202,058	269,086	299,774	301,963	304,776	307,179	315,850	329,443	329,691	331,506	8.8
Wyoming	15,220	21,147	31,326	29,707	29,002	30,004	31,095	32,605	33,695	33,955	17.1
U.S. Service Schools[2]	17,079	49,808	48,692	13,991	13,344	13,475	14,561	14,420	14,628	14,754	10.6

See notes at end of table.

Total fall enrollment in degree-granting institutions, by state or jurisdiction: Selected years, 1970 through 2004—Continued

State or jurisdiction	Institutions of higher education			Degree-granting institutions							
	Fall 1970	Fall 1980	Fall 1990	Fall 1998	Fall 1999[1]	Fall 2000	Fall 2001	Fall 2002	Fall 2003	Fall 2004	Percent change, 1999 to 2004
1	2	3	4	5	6	7	8	9	10	11	12
Other jurisdictions	67,237	137,749	164,618	181,244	185,244	194,633	201,642	211,204	217,655	220,920	19.3
American Samoa	0	976	1,219	909	1,172	297	1,178	1,367	1,537	1,550	32.3
Federated States of Micronesia...............	0	224	975	772	1,506	1,576	2,243	2,173	2,558	2,608	73.2
Guam	2,719	3,217	4,741	5,758	5,727	5,215	4,869	5,157	4,710	4,642	-18.9
Marshall Islands...................................	0	0	0	513	616	328	220	224	601	623	1.1
Northern Marianas	0	0	661	1,239	1,080	1,078	982	1,299	1,237	1,101	1.9
Palau..	0	0	491	424	569	581	579	668	727	651	14.4
Puerto Rico...	63,073	131,184	154,065	168,983	171,832	183,290	188,430	197,781	203,745	207,180	20.6
Virgin Islands.......................................	1,445	2,148	2,466	2,646	2,742	2,268	3,141	2,535	2,540	2,565	-6.5

[1]Data were imputed using alternative procedures. (See Guide to Sources for details.)
[2]Data for 1998 and later years reflect substantial changes in survey coverage.
NOTE: Institutions of higher education were accredited by an agency or association that was recognized by the U.S. Department of Education, or recognized directly by the Secretary of Education. The new degree-granting classification is very similar to the earlier higher education classification, except that it includes some additional institutions, primarily 2-year colleges, and excludes a few higher education institutions that did not award associate's or higher degrees. These degree-granting institutions participated in Title IV federal financial aid programs. (See Guide to Sources for details.)

SOURCE: U.S. Department of Education, National Center for Education Statistics, Higher Education General Information Survey (HEGIS), "Fall Enrollment in Colleges and Universities" surveys, 1970 and 1980; and 1990 through 2004 Integrated Postsecondary Education Data System, "Fall Enrollment Survey" (IPEDS-EF:90–99), and Spring 2001 through Spring 2005. (This table was prepared September 2005.)

Total fall enrollment in public degree-granting institutions, by state or jurisdiction: Selected years, 1970 through 2004

State or jurisdiction	Institutions of higher education			Degree-granting institutions							Percent change, 1999 to 2004
	Fall 1970	Fall 1980	Fall 1990	Fall 1998	Fall 1999[1]	Fall 2000	Fall 2001	Fall 2002	Fall 2003	Fall 2004	
1	2	3	4	5	6	7	8	9	10	11	12
United States	6,428,134	9,457,394	10,844,717	11,137,769	11,309,399	11,752,786	12,233,156	12,751,993	12,857,059	12,980,112	14.8
Alabama	87,884	143,674	195,939	190,685	197,173	207,435	208,385	217,883	225,347	226,989	15.1
Alaska........................	8,563	20,561	27,792	26,296	25,687	26,559	26,550	28,314	29,821	29,515	14.9
Arizona	107,315	194,034	248,213	268,102	276,268	284,522	294,174	307,496	310,679	317,974	15.1
Arkansas	43,599	66,068	78,645	102,264	103,326	101,775	108,950	113,509	119,920	123,973	20.0
California	1,123,529	1,599,838	1,594,710	1,646,329	1,692,607	1,927,771	2,043,182	2,121,106	1,978,831	1,987,283	17.4
Colorado	108,562	145,598	200,653	216,351	219,436	217,897	222,815	233,740	236,883	239,308	9.1
Connecticut..................	73,391	97,788	109,556	94,299	96,834	101,027	104,066	108,522	108,815	110,354	14.0
Delaware	21,151	28,325	34,252	37,362	36,895	34,194	36,510	37,344	37,621	38,243	3.7
District of Columbia	12,194	13,900	11,990	5,410	5,349	5,499	5,589	5,603	5,424	5,388	0.7
Florida........................	189,450	334,349	489,081	531,921	540,967	556,912	588,921	617,754	643,784	649,857	20.1
Georgia	101,900	140,158	196,413	229,928	237,411	271,755	298,215	317,180	330,052	335,979	41.5
Hawaii........................	32,963	43,269	45,728	45,270	46,479	44,579	45,994	48,163	50,316	50,569	8.8
Idaho.........................	27,072	34,491	41,315	51,330	52,615	53,751	56,673	57,996	60,481	60,695	15.4
Illinois.......................	315,634	491,274	551,333	533,294	533,522	534,155	534,280	554,093	566,137	563,593	5.6
Indiana.......................	136,739	189,224	223,953	228,450	230,810	240,023	259,258	258,627	262,957	266,916	15.6
Iowa..........................	68,390	97,454	117,834	129,302	133,753	135,008	140,227	145,798	149,195	149,776	12.0
Kansas	88,215	121,987	149,117	158,594	157,088	159,976	164,173	167,741	169,384	170,149	8.3
Kentucky	77,240	114,884	147,095	146,344	146,558	151,973	178,349	188,518	196,474	197,991	35.1
Louisiana	101,127	136,703	158,290	189,896	188,573	189,213	194,790	197,547	207,923	208,218	10.4
Maine.........................	25,405	31,878	41,500	38,636	40,349	40,662	42,425	44,850	46,714	47,284	17.2
Maryland......................	118,988	195,051	220,783	219,055	220,809	223,797	236,795	246,792	252,026	256,582	16.2
Massachusetts................	116,127	183,765	186,035	178,376	181,514	183,248	186,891	187,874	189,334	187,873	3.5
Michigan......................	339,625	454,147	487,359	462,580	461,825	467,861	482,154	495,676	501,821	500,873	8.5
Minnesota	130,567	162,379	199,211	200,422	207,474	218,617	225,941	235,513	240,714	241,245	16.3
Mississippi	64,968	90,661	109,038	120,831	121,369	125,355	125,656	134,130	134,318	137,543	13.3
Missouri	132,540	165,179	200,093	194,462	199,324	201,509	206,721	214,022	216,777	214,561	7.6
Montana.......................	27,287	31,178	31,865	38,768	38,336	37,387	39,368	40,615	42,444	42,289	10.3
Nebraska	51,454	73,509	94,614	89,040	88,386	88,531	89,639	92,111	93,432	93,195	5.4
Nevada	13,576	40,280	61,242	79,147	85,270	83,120	86,790	89,547	94,205	96,773	13.5
New Hampshire	15,979	24,119	32,163	32,187	34,927	35,870	37,224	40,958	41,324	40,642	16.4
New Jersey	145,373	247,028	261,601	260,092	263,752	266,921	275,655	289,275	298,906	305,034	15.7
New Mexico	40,795	55,077	83,403	101,150	103,125	101,450	103,758	111,667	117,245	121,339	17.7
New York......................	449,437	563,251	616,884	567,202	566,306	583,417	584,607	610,756	613,895	623,192	10.0
North Carolina	123,761	228,154	285,405	314,110	321,311	329,422	350,684	367,861	383,720	389,143	21.1
North Dakota	30,192	31,709	34,690	35,264	35,940	36,014	38,560	41,134	43,383	43,275	20.4
Ohio..........................	281,099	381,765	427,613	408,487	411,541	411,161	425,265	441,738	450,369	454,377	10.4
Oklahoma	91,438	137,188	151,073	155,796	155,361	153,699	163,336	171,369	178,612	179,281	15.4
Oregon	108,483	140,102	144,427	144,326	148,177	154,756	162,645	173,698	166,129	165,375	11.6
Pennsylvania.................	232,982	292,499	343,478	338,047	336,930	339,229	353,950	370,386	381,254	384,525	14.1
Rhode Island	25,527	35,052	42,350	38,368	38,650	38,458	39,149	38,867	39,937	39,920	3.3
South Carolina...............	47,101	107,683	131,134	152,542	153,496	155,519	158,661	167,563	171,893	172,386	12.3
South Dakota.................	23,936	24,328	26,596	34,088	34,197	34,857	37,310	37,760	38,179	37,598	9.9
Tennessee	98,897	156,835	175,049	193,393	193,646	202,530	194,696	194,202	196,088	199,904	3.2
Texas	365,522	613,552	802,314	849,075	862,271	896,534	935,826	1,006,549	1,036,008	1,071,926	24.3
Utah..........................	49,588	59,598	86,108	111,315	120,558	123,046	133,790	135,778	140,282	145,182	20.4
Vermont	12,536	17,984	20,910	20,549	20,580	20,021	20,480	21,238	22,607	22,980	11.7
Virginia	123,279	246,500	291,286	305,455	311,536	313,780	326,758	337,286	341,948	343,391	10.2
Washington	162,718	276,028	227,632	257,047	263,415	273,928	277,023	293,007	298,079	293,145	11.3
West Virginia.................	51,363	71,228	74,108	76,322	76,777	76,136	78,304	79,741	82,273	83,274	8.5
Wisconsin	170,374	235,179	253,529	247,462	249,608	249,737	257,888	268,010	266,805	266,884	6.9
Wyoming	15,220	21,121	30,623	28,757	27,944	28,715	29,545	30,666	31,666	31,597	13.1
U.S. Service Schools[2]	17,079	49,808	48,692	13,991	13,344	13,475	14,561	14,420	14,628	14,754	10.6

See notes at end of table.

Total fall enrollment in public degree-granting institutions, by state or jurisdiction: Selected years, 1970 through 2004—Continued

State or jurisdiction	Institutions of higher education			Degree-granting institutions							
	Fall 1970	Fall 1980	Fall 1990	Fall 1998	Fall 1999[1]	Fall 2000	Fall 2001	Fall 2002	Fall 2003	Fall 2004	Percent change, 1999 to 2004
1	2	3	4	5	6	7	8	9	10	11	12
Other jurisdictions	**46,680**	**60,692**	**66,244**	**82,537**	**83,919**	**84,464**	**85,535**	**86,484**	**85,468**	**83,831**	**-0.1**
American Samoa...............................	0	976	1,219	909	1,172	297	1,178	1,367	1,537	1,550	32.3
Federated States of Micronesia...............	0	224	975	772	1,506	1,576	2,243	2,173	2,558	2,608	73.2
Guam..	2,719	3,217	4,741	5,758	5,727	5,215	4,869	5,038	4,546	4,470	-21.9
Marshall Islands...............................	0	0	0	513	616	328	220	224	601	623	1.1
Northern Marianas	0	0	661	1,239	1,080	1,078	982	1,299	1,237	1,101	1.9
Palau..	0	0	491	424	569	581	579	668	727	651	14.4
Puerto Rico....................................	42,516	54,127	55,691	70,276	70,507	73,121	73,173	73,180	71,722	70,263	-0.3
Virgin Islands..................................	1,445	2,148	2,466	2,646	2,742	2,268	2,291	2,535	2,540	2,565	-6.5

[1]Data were imputed using alternative procedures. (See Guide to Sources for details.)
[2]Data for 1998 and later years reflect substantial changes in survey coverage.
NOTE: Institutions of higher education were accredited by an agency or association that was recognized by the U.S. Department of Education, or recognized directly by the Secretary of Education. The new degree-granting classification is very similar to the earlier higher education classification, except that it includes some additional institutions, primarily 2-year colleges, and excludes a few higher education institutions that did not award associate's or higher degrees. These degree-granting institutions participated in Title IV federal financial aid programs. (See Guide to Sources for details.)
SOURCE: U.S. Department of Education, National Center for Education Statistics, Higher Education General Information Survey (HEGIS), "Fall Enrollment in Colleges and Universities" surveys, 1970 and 1980; and 1990 through 2004 Integrated Postsecondary Education Data System, "Fall Enrollment Survey" (IPEDS-EF:90–99), and Spring 2001 through Spring 2005. (This table was prepared September 2005.)

Total fall enrollment in all degree-granting institutions, by attendance status, sex, and state or jurisdiction: 2003 and 2004

		Fall 2003					Fall 2004			
		Full-time		Part-time			Full-time		Part-time	
State or jurisdiction	Total	Males	Females	Males	Females	Total	Males	Females	Males	Females
1	2	3	4	5	6	7	8	9	10	11
United States	**16,900,471**	**4,631,735**	**5,680,079**	**2,623,816**	**3,964,841**	**17,272,044**	**4,739,355**	**5,870,822**	**2,647,907**	**4,013,960**
Alabama	253,846	73,357	97,046	32,248	51,195	255,826	74,392	98,345	32,392	50,697
Alaska	31,035	5,533	7,132	6,725	11,645	30,869	5,746	7,384	6,393	11,346
Arizona	430,661	112,560	134,879	74,507	108,715	490,925	133,969	169,730	76,537	110,689
Arkansas	133,950	37,599	51,870	16,618	27,863	138,399	38,407	53,404	17,085	29,503
California	2,338,846	527,748	662,349	499,657	649,092	2,374,045	534,469	669,926	508,808	660,842
Colorado	289,243	77,863	88,564	49,411	73,405	300,914	82,202	93,690	50,320	74,702
Connecticut	170,976	47,161	58,199	24,428	41,188	172,775	48,488	60,198	23,456	40,633
Delaware	49,595	13,204	18,079	6,526	11,786	49,804	13,520	18,416	6,188	11,680
District of Columbia	95,297	24,667	34,415	14,651	21,564	99,988	25,616	35,493	15,322	23,557
Florida	839,735	199,866	258,664	149,501	231,704	866,665	209,498	274,647	150,186	232,334
Georgia	411,061	116,080	153,414	52,635	88,932	434,283	124,187	167,539	51,488	91,069
Hawaii	67,390	16,962	23,231	11,149	16,048	67,225	16,716	23,607	10,738	16,164
Idaho	75,370	24,520	27,416	9,428	14,006	76,311	24,838	27,925	9,578	13,970
Illinois	796,774	202,407	241,400	138,998	213,969	801,401	204,219	245,392	139,236	212,554
Indiana	350,091	112,345	129,092	44,214	64,440	356,801	114,572	131,827	45,406	64,996
Iowa	213,958	68,279	77,456	26,490	41,733	217,646	67,279	78,144	27,716	44,507
Kansas	190,291	53,127	58,584	31,228	47,352	191,590	53,593	59,703	31,054	47,240
Kentucky	235,743	63,889	85,809	37,088	48,957	240,097	65,056	87,840	36,995	50,206
Louisiana	244,455	73,418	103,019	24,209	43,809	246,301	74,073	105,109	23,625	43,494
Maine	64,222	17,401	21,412	7,946	17,463	65,415	18,041	22,030	8,130	17,214
Maryland	307,543	71,316	91,148	53,971	91,108	312,493	72,210	93,404	54,938	91,941
Massachusetts	436,068	132,621	161,895	52,937	88,615	439,245	134,644	164,786	51,649	88,166
Michigan	615,765	158,005	193,918	104,426	159,416	620,980	161,695	197,831	102,243	159,211
Minnesota	337,780	97,140	118,758	49,375	72,507	349,021	99,282	125,724	49,794	74,221
Mississippi	148,584	46,042	67,912	11,621	23,009	152,115	46,663	69,760	11,997	23,695
Missouri	359,680	96,012	118,181	57,420	88,067	365,204	97,658	122,578	57,498	87,470
Montana	47,240	17,081	18,737	4,397	7,025	47,173	16,954	19,002	4,288	6,929
Nebraska	119,511	36,093	41,956	17,092	24,370	121,053	36,743	42,829	17,038	24,443
Nevada	100,995	19,126	25,202	24,331	32,336	105,961	21,577	28,652	24,080	31,652
New Hampshire	69,608	20,583	25,179	8,536	15,310	70,163	21,157	25,682	8,187	15,137
New Jersey	372,632	100,887	119,759	58,109	93,877	380,374	103,233	122,613	59,205	95,323
New Mexico	126,852	28,904	38,183	23,277	36,488	131,577	29,655	39,117	23,983	38,822
New York	1,126,087	348,476	437,432	124,678	215,501	1,141,525	352,558	446,836	125,270	216,861
North Carolina	464,430	126,472	170,259	61,231	106,468	472,709	126,963	172,686	62,503	110,557
North Dakota	48,402	18,843	18,251	4,735	6,573	49,533	19,107	18,771	4,802	6,853
Ohio	603,378	182,728	220,775	78,003	121,872	614,234	184,876	226,639	79,000	123,719
Oklahoma	207,781	62,557	72,306	28,729	44,189	207,625	62,690	73,461	28,415	43,059
Oregon	198,701	55,467	64,283	33,834	45,117	199,985	55,996	66,195	33,087	44,707
Pennsylvania	675,574	225,229	257,495	71,319	121,531	688,780	229,746	264,945	70,172	123,917
Rhode Island	79,085	25,494	30,096	8,487	15,008	80,377	26,415	31,016	8,123	14,823
South Carolina	207,601	58,800	79,309	22,732	46,760	208,910	59,459	81,173	22,118	46,160
South Dakota	48,967	15,448	17,267	5,818	10,434	48,708	15,441	17,479	5,518	10,270
Tennessee	267,969	83,248	107,920	28,749	48,052	278,055	87,349	113,876	28,681	48,149
Texas	1,188,727	305,337	361,883	213,492	308,015	1,229,197	310,783	375,882	222,925	319,607
Utah	185,772	61,350	55,748	33,327	35,347	194,324	61,725	56,982	37,499	38,118
Vermont	37,831	12,778	14,023	3,655	7,375	38,639	13,391	14,412	3,531	7,305
Virginia	414,881	110,727	137,458	66,426	100,270	425,181	114,236	142,856	66,439	101,650
Washington	345,469	98,094	117,101	53,610	76,664	343,524	97,336	116,923	52,967	76,298
West Virginia	97,005	32,858	39,110	9,241	15,796	97,884	33,388	39,681	9,118	15,697
Wisconsin	329,691	94,218	114,733	47,451	73,289	331,506	95,172	116,782	47,249	72,303
Wyoming	33,695	9,655	9,304	5,150	9,586	33,955	10,163	9,355	4,937	9,500
U.S. Service Schools	14,628	12,160	2,468	0	0	14,754	12,209	2,545	0	0

See notes at end of table.

Total fall enrollment in all degree-granting institutions, by attendance status, sex, and state or jurisdiction: 2003 and 2004—Continued

State or jurisdiction	Fall 2003					Fall 2004				
	Total	Full-time		Part-time		Total	Full-time		Part-time	
		Males	Females	Males	Females		Males	Females	Males	Females
1	2	3	4	5	6	7	8	9	10	11
Other jurisdictions	**217,655**	**63,796**	**100,148**	**20,611**	**33,100**	**220,920**	**65,959**	**102,561**	**20,024**	**32,376**
American Samoa................................	1,537	362	445	271	459	1,550	303	446	270	531
Federated States of Micronesia...............	2,558	962	1,027	291	278	2,608	956	992	339	321
Guam..	4,710	900	1,581	911	1,318	4,642	978	1,503	886	1,275
Marshall Islands................................	601	237	205	104	55	623	284	214	69	56
Northern Marianas	1,237	274	564	169	230	1,101	307	509	99	186
Palau..	727	225	245	85	172	651	205	224	72	150
Puerto Rico......................................	203,745	60,536	95,152	18,495	29,562	207,180	62,611	97,730	18,009	28,830
Virgin Islands...................................	2,540	300	929	285	1,026	2,565	315	943	280	1,027

NOTE: Data are for 4-year and 2-year degree-granting institutions that participated in Title IV federal financial aid programs.

SOURCE: U.S. Department of Education, National Center for Education Statistics, 2003 and 2004 Integrated Postsecondary Education Data System (IPEDS), Spring 2004 and Spring 2005. (This table was prepared September 2005.)

365

Total fall enrollment in private degree-granting institutions, by state or jurisdiction: Selected years, 1970 through 2004

State or jurisdiction	Institutions of higher education			Degree-granting institutions							
	Fall 1970	Fall 1980	Fall 1990	Fall 1998	Fall 1999[1]	Fall 2000	Fall 2001	Fall 2002	Fall 2003	Fall 2004	Percent change, 1999 to 2004
1	2	3	4	5	6	7	8	9	10	11	12
United States	**2,152,753**	**2,639,501**	**2,973,920**	**3,369,198**	**3,481,825**	**3,559,503**	**3,694,831**	**3,859,718**	**4,043,412**	**4,291,932**	**23.3**
Alabama	16,052	20,632	22,650	25,556	25,971	26,527	27,761	28,531	28,499	28,837	11.0
Alaska	908	735	2,041	1,356	1,261	1,394	1,206	1,232	1,214	1,354	7.4
Arizona	2,304	8,682	15,935	34,021	49,891	57,968	72,311	94,109	119,982	172,951	246.7
Arkansas	8,440	11,539	11,780	11,487	11,766	13,397	13,332	13,863	14,030	14,426	22.6
California	133,716	191,155	214,030	303,179	324,876	328,937	336,908	352,918	360,015	386,762	19.0
Colorado	14,833	17,318	26,478	40,896	42,308	45,975	46,477	48,603	52,360	61,606	45.6
Connecticut	51,309	61,844	59,048	59,037	60,073	60,216	60,961	62,084	62,161	62,421	3.9
Delaware	4,109	4,614	7,752	8,898	9,718	9,703	10,594	11,884	11,974	11,561	19.0
District of Columbia	64,964	72,775	67,561	66,978	66,769	67,190	81,663	85,411	89,873	94,600	41.7
Florida	46,075	77,542	99,005	129,266	143,778	150,772	164,633	174,325	195,951	216,808	50.8
Georgia	24,611	44,001	55,373	73,757	74,401	74,449	77,883	80,424	81,009	98,304	32.1
Hawaii	3,599	3,912	10,708	16,345	16,099	15,603	16,085	17,205	17,074	16,656	3.5
Idaho	7,495	8,527	10,566	11,755	12,046	11,843	13,001	14,076	14,889	15,616	29.6
Illinois	136,512	152,971	177,913	195,790	199,660	209,763	214,164	222,529	230,637	237,808	19.1
Indiana	55,929	58,029	60,879	70,726	73,915	74,311	79,457	83,437	87,134	89,885	21.6
Iowa	40,512	42,995	52,681	52,642	53,027	53,966	54,595	56,748	64,763	67,870	28.0
Kansas	14,270	14,618	14,616	18,967	19,649	19,992	20,770	20,308	20,907	21,441	9.1
Kentucky	21,351	28,182	30,757	34,206	35,068	36,368	36,490	36,971	39,269	42,106	20.1
Louisiana	19,601	23,355	28,550	31,214	32,775	34,587	34,081	34,593	36,532	38,083	16.2
Maine	8,729	11,386	15,686	18,350	17,473	17,811	18,702	18,458	17,508	18,131	3.8
Maryland	30,619	30,475	38,917	46,118	48,011	49,948	51,429	53,477	55,517	55,911	16.5
Massachusetts	187,682	234,650	231,798	237,125	238,181	237,894	238,180	243,350	246,734	251,372	5.5
Michigan	53,101	65,984	82,444	94,431	97,173	99,770	103,844	110,159	113,944	120,107	23.6
Minnesota	30,221	44,312	54,578	71,190	75,282	74,828	82,292	88,278	97,066	107,776	43.2
Mississippi	8,999	11,703	13,845	11,607	11,801	12,034	12,226	12,947	14,266	14,572	23.5
Missouri	51,390	69,242	89,806	116,045	118,156	119,839	124,859	134,124	142,903	150,643	27.5
Montana	2,775	3,999	4,011	5,382	4,778	4,853	5,564	4,496	4,796	4,884	2.2
Nebraska	15,461	15,979	18,217	22,083	22,420	23,586	24,178	24,626	26,079	27,858	24.3
Nevada	93	175	486	3,973	4,441	4,773	6,578	6,124	6,790	9,188	106.9
New Hampshire	13,421	22,675	27,347	28,597	28,439	25,848	27,807	27,565	28,284	29,521	3.8
New Jersey	70,748	74,582	62,685	65,793	66,785	69,024	70,852	72,458	73,726	75,340	12.8
New Mexico	3,666	3,206	2,097	7,660	8,771	9,289	9,103	9,330	9,607	10,238	16.7
New York	357,042	428,986	431,402	447,018	454,685	459,978	473,187	496,514	512,192	518,333	14.0
North Carolina	48,164	59,383	66,733	73,297	74,596	75,230	77,100	79,474	80,710	83,566	12.0
North Dakota	1,303	2,360	3,188	4,177	4,408	4,234	4,283	4,666	5,019	6,258	42.0
Ohio	95,168	107,380	130,077	133,590	137,004	138,392	143,958	146,258	153,009	159,857	16.7
Oklahoma	18,717	23,107	22,148	22,711	23,694	24,317	26,449	27,054	29,169	28,344	19.6
Oregon	13,694	17,356	21,314	26,730	27,458	28,309	28,733	30,867	32,572	34,610	26.0
Pennsylvania	178,062	215,217	260,582	257,702	268,353	270,292	276,349	284,440	294,320	304,255	13.4
Rhode Island	20,371	31,817	35,923	35,602	36,171	36,992	38,086	38,550	39,148	40,457	11.8
South Carolina	22,417	24,793	28,168	28,811	30,130	30,412	32,929	34,444	35,708	36,524	21.2
South Dakota	6,703	8,433	7,612	7,457	7,950	8,364	8,224	9,991	10,788	11,110	39.7
Tennessee	36,206	47,746	51,189	57,926	59,269	61,380	63,838	67,697	71,881	78,151	31.9
Texas	76,703	87,839	99,123	129,475	128,316	137,439	140,852	145,820	152,719	157,271	22.6
Utah	32,099	34,389	35,195	39,917	41,033	40,730	43,255	43,154	45,490	49,142	19.8
Vermont	9,673	12,644	15,488	16,505	16,148	15,468	15,871	15,299	15,224	15,659	-3.0
Virginia	28,636	34,004	62,156	64,687	66,434	68,113	63,095	67,680	72,933	81,790	23.1
Washington	20,826	27,575	35,752	41,927	43,308	46,912	48,109	45,813	47,390	50,379	16.3
West Virginia	11,790	10,745	10,682	11,785	11,880	11,752	13,015	13,982	14,732	14,610	23.0
Wisconsin	31,684	33,907	46,245	54,501	55,168	57,442	57,962	61,433	62,886	64,622	17.1
Wyoming	0	26	703	950	1,058	1,289	1,550	1,939	2,029	2,358	122.9

See notes at end of table.

Total fall enrollment in private degree-granting institutions, by state or jurisdiction: Selected years, 1970 through 2004—Continued

State or jurisdiction	Institutions of higher education			Degree-granting institutions							Percent change, 1999 to 2004
	Fall 1970	Fall 1980	Fall 1990	Fall 1998	Fall 1999[1]	Fall 2000	Fall 2001	Fall 2002	Fall 2003	Fall 2004	
1	2	3	4	5	6	7	8	9	10	11	12
Other jurisdictions	**20,557**	**77,057**	**98,374**	**98,707**	**101,325**	**110,169**	**116,107**	**124,720**	**132,187**	**137,089**	**35.3**
American Samoa	0	0	0	0	0	0	0	0	0	0	†
Federated States of Micronesia	0	0	0	0	0	0	0	0	0	0	†
Guam	0	0	0	0	0	0	0	119	164	172	†
Marshall Islands	0	0	0	0	0	0	0	0	0	0	†
Northern Marianas	0	0	0	0	0	0	0	0	0	0	†
Palau	0	0	0	0	0	0	0	0	0	0	†
Puerto Rico	20,557	77,057	98,374	98,707	101,325	110,169	115,257	124,601	132,023	136,917	35.1
Virgin Islands	0	0	0	0	0	0	850	0	0	0	†

†Not applicable.
[1]Data were imputed using alternative procedures. (See Guide to Sources for details.)
NOTE: Institutions of higher education were accredited by an agency or association that was recognized by the U.S. Department of Education, or recognized directly by the Secretary of Education. The new degree-granting classification is very similar to the earlier higher education classification, except that it includes some additional institutions, primarily 2-year colleges, and excludes a few higher education institutions that did not award associ-

ate's or higher degrees. These degree-granting institutions participated in Title IV federal financial aid programs. (See Guide to Sources for details.)
SOURCE: U.S. Department of Education, National Center for Education Statistics, Higher Education General Information Survey (HEGIS), "Fall Enrollment in Colleges and Universities" surveys, 1970 and 1980; and 1990 through 2004 Integrated Postsecondary Education Data System, "Fall Enrollment Survey" (IPEDS-EF:90–99), and Spring 2001 through Spring 2005. (This table was prepared September 2005.)

**Total fall enrollment in public degree-granting institutions, by attendance status, sex,
and state or jurisdiction: 2003 and 2004**

State or jurisdiction	Total	Fall 2003				Total	Fall 2004			
		Full-time		Part-time			Full-time		Part-time	
		Males	Females	Males	Females		Males	Females	Males	Females
1	2	3	4	5	6	7	8	9	10	11
United States	12,857,059	3,282,703	3,982,346	2,228,865	3,363,145	12,980,112	3,325,073	4,044,359	2,234,403	3,376,277
Alabama	225,347	63,482	83,818	30,353	47,694	226,989	64,224	84,879	30,405	47,481
Alaska	29,821	5,276	6,750	6,485	11,310	29,515	5,469	6,927	6,155	10,964
Arizona	310,679	62,223	73,091	71,376	103,989	317,974	64,896	76,680	72,177	104,221
Arkansas	119,920	32,223	45,238	15,912	26,547	123,973	32,729	46,801	16,388	28,055
California	1,978,831	401,258	505,269	465,124	607,180	1,987,283	403,771	505,546	467,917	610,049
Colorado	236,883	60,998	68,840	42,318	64,727	239,308	61,997	69,780	42,441	65,090
Connecticut	108,815	26,004	31,832	18,675	32,304	110,354	27,351	33,552	18,083	31,368
Delaware	37,621	10,797	14,711	4,319	7,794	38,243	11,120	14,909	4,289	7,925
District of Columbia	5,424	887	1,264	1,112	2,161	5,388	919	1,302	1,024	2,143
Florida	643,784	137,683	182,703	122,865	200,533	649,857	141,662	188,098	122,270	197,827
Georgia	330,052	87,845	114,039	47,361	80,807	335,979	89,679	117,610	46,159	82,531
Hawaii	50,316	12,398	15,982	8,565	13,371	50,569	12,436	16,253	8,495	13,385
Idaho	60,481	18,374	19,912	8,896	13,299	60,695	18,301	20,316	8,912	13,166
Illinois	566,137	130,361	151,520	112,738	171,518	563,593	131,649	151,928	111,569	168,447
Indiana	262,957	80,552	89,495	38,571	54,339	266,916	81,620	90,713	39,649	54,934
Iowa	149,195	48,491	51,103	20,547	29,054	149,776	47,051	50,581	21,580	30,564
Kansas	169,384	46,378	50,565	28,908	43,533	170,149	46,788	51,533	28,668	43,160
Kentucky	196,474	51,756	68,097	33,616	43,005	197,991	51,993	68,767	33,572	43,659
Louisiana	207,923	62,066	84,657	21,891	39,309	208,218	62,560	85,827	21,067	38,764
Maine	46,714	12,188	14,358	6,506	13,662	47,284	12,515	14,749	6,594	13,426
Maryland	252,026	56,845	71,989	45,363	77,829	256,582	57,801	73,268	46,468	79,045
Massachusetts	189,334	47,393	57,307	30,306	54,328	187,873	47,591	56,791	29,739	53,752
Michigan	501,821	129,095	152,342	88,347	132,037	500,873	131,888	154,965	85,102	128,918
Minnesota	240,714	70,269	77,868	38,559	54,018	241,245	70,043	78,842	37,755	54,605
Mississippi	134,318	41,926	60,313	10,884	21,195	137,543	42,502	61,807	11,277	21,957
Missouri	216,777	57,948	71,303	32,512	55,014	214,561	58,369	71,978	31,196	53,018
Montana	42,444	15,617	16,506	4,031	6,290	42,289	15,371	16,674	3,922	6,322
Nebraska	93,432	27,170	29,637	15,402	21,223	93,195	27,407	29,661	15,139	20,988
Nevada	94,205	16,475	21,348	24,196	32,186	96,773	18,099	23,428	23,789	31,457
New Hampshire	41,324	10,843	13,348	6,232	10,901	40,642	11,257	13,663	5,747	9,975
New Jersey	298,906	75,832	94,394	48,677	80,003	305,034	77,858	96,465	49,587	81,124
New Mexico	117,245	25,706	33,563	22,592	35,384	121,339	26,215	34,150	23,275	37,699
New York	613,895	174,915	217,010	81,575	140,395	623,192	179,130	221,469	81,916	140,677
North Carolina	383,720	97,074	131,680	56,403	98,563	389,143	96,711	132,623	57,746	102,063
North Dakota	43,383	17,093	15,620	4,524	6,146	43,275	17,088	15,630	4,505	6,052
Ohio	450,369	131,048	156,300	64,452	98,569	454,377	131,826	158,484	64,946	99,121
Oklahoma	178,612	50,239	60,468	26,414	41,491	179,281	51,090	61,398	26,301	40,492
Oregon	166,129	43,984	49,529	31,142	41,474	165,375	43,938	50,041	30,386	41,010
Pennsylvania	381,254	122,813	137,316	44,338	76,787	384,525	125,111	139,991	42,974	76,449
Rhode Island	39,937	9,066	12,905	5,832	12,134	39,920	9,290	13,091	5,612	11,927
South Carolina	171,893	46,610	61,793	20,892	42,598	172,386	47,422	63,474	19,889	41,601
South Dakota	38,179	13,045	13,145	4,087	7,902	37,598	12,916	13,057	3,956	7,669
Tennessee	196,088	56,419	74,082	24,522	41,065	199,904	57,983	76,414	24,282	41,225
Texas	1,036,008	253,646	302,720	194,203	285,439	1,071,926	257,727	311,866	204,248	298,085
Utah	140,282	42,091	36,408	30,082	31,701	145,182	42,231	36,788	32,645	33,518
Vermont	22,607	6,431	7,821	2,640	5,715	22,980	6,662	8,043	2,572	5,703
Virginia	341,948	85,421	104,377	60,670	91,480	343,391	86,649	105,164	59,870	91,708
Washington	298,079	82,209	95,560	49,350	70,960	293,145	80,662	94,273	48,131	70,079
West Virginia	82,273	28,260	31,369	8,471	14,173	83,274	28,673	32,150	8,377	14,074
Wisconsin	266,805	76,155	89,348	40,879	60,423	266,884	76,787	90,092	40,700	59,305
Wyoming	31,666	7,665	9,265	5,150	9,586	31,597	7,837	9,323	4,937	9,500
U.S. Service Schools	14,628	12,160	2,468	0	0	14,754	12,209	2,545	0	0

See notes at end of table.

Total fall enrollment in public degree-granting institutions, by attendance status, sex, and state or jurisdiction: 2003 and 2004—Continued

State or jurisdiction	Fall 2003					Fall 2004				
	Total	Full-time		Part-time		Total	Full-time		Part-time	
		Males	Females	Males	Females		Males	Females	Males	Females
1	2	3	4	5	6	7	8	9	10	11
Other jurisdictions	**85,468**	**25,115**	**40,476**	**7,284**	**12,593**	**83,831**	**25,681**	**40,549**	**6,423**	**11,178**
American Samoa...	1,537	362	445	271	459	1,550	303	446	270	531
Federated States of Micronesia...............	2,558	962	1,027	291	278	2,608	956	992	339	321
Guam..	4,546	867	1,537	859	1,283	4,470	936	1,442	851	1,241
Marshall Islands..	601	237	205	104	55	623	284	214	69	56
Northern Marianas	1,237	274	564	169	230	1,101	307	509	99	186
Palau..	727	225	245	85	172	651	205	224	72	150
Puerto Rico..	71,722	21,888	35,524	5,220	9,090	70,263	22,375	35,779	4,443	7,666
Virgin Islands..	2,540	300	929	285	1,026	2,565	315	943	280	1,027

NOTE: Data are for 4-year and 2-year degree-granting institutions that participated in Title IV federal financial aid programs.

SOURCE: U.S. Department of Education, National Center for Education Statistics, 2003 and 2004 Integrated Postsecondary Education Data System (IPEDS), Spring 2004 and Spring 2005. (This table was prepared September 2005.)

Total fall enrollment in private degree-granting institutions, by attendance status, sex, and state or jurisdiction: 2003 and 2004

State or jurisdiction	Total	Fall 2003 Full-time Males	Full-time Females	Part-time Males	Part-time Females	Total	Fall 2004 Full-time Males	Full-time Females	Part-time Males	Part-time Females
1	2	3	4	5	6	7	8	9	10	11
United States	4,043,412	1,349,032	1,697,733	394,951	601,696	4,291,932	1,414,282	1,826,463	413,504	637,683
Alabama	28,499	9,875	13,228	1,895	3,501	28,837	10,168	13,466	1,987	3,216
Alaska	1,214	257	382	240	335	1,354	277	457	238	382
Arizona	119,982	50,337	61,788	3,131	4,726	172,951	69,073	93,050	4,360	6,468
Arkansas	14,030	5,376	6,632	706	1,316	14,426	5,678	6,603	697	1,448
California	360,015	126,490	157,080	34,533	41,912	386,762	130,698	164,380	40,891	50,793
Colorado	52,360	16,865	19,724	7,093	8,678	61,606	20,205	23,910	7,879	9,612
Connecticut	62,161	21,157	26,367	5,753	8,884	62,421	21,137	26,646	5,373	9,265
Delaware	11,974	2,407	3,368	2,207	3,992	11,561	2,400	3,507	1,899	3,755
District of Columbia	89,873	23,780	33,151	13,539	19,403	94,600	24,697	34,191	14,298	21,414
Florida	195,951	62,183	75,961	26,636	31,171	216,808	67,836	86,549	27,916	34,507
Georgia	81,009	28,235	39,375	5,274	8,125	98,304	34,508	49,929	5,329	8,538
Hawaii	17,074	4,564	7,249	2,584	2,677	16,656	4,280	7,354	2,243	2,779
Idaho	14,889	6,146	7,504	532	707	15,616	6,537	7,609	666	804
Illinois	230,637	72,046	89,880	26,260	42,451	237,808	72,570	93,464	27,667	44,107
Indiana	87,134	31,793	39,597	5,643	10,101	89,885	32,952	41,114	5,757	10,062
Iowa	64,763	19,788	26,353	5,943	12,679	67,870	20,228	27,563	6,136	13,943
Kansas	20,907	6,749	8,019	2,320	3,819	21,441	6,805	8,170	2,386	4,080
Kentucky	39,269	12,133	17,712	3,472	5,952	42,106	13,063	19,073	3,423	6,547
Louisiana	36,532	11,352	18,362	2,318	4,500	38,083	11,513	19,282	2,558	4,730
Maine	17,508	5,213	7,054	1,440	3,801	18,131	5,526	7,281	1,536	3,788
Maryland	55,517	14,471	19,159	8,608	13,279	55,911	14,409	20,136	8,470	12,896
Massachusetts	246,734	85,228	104,588	22,631	34,287	251,372	87,053	107,995	21,910	34,414
Michigan	113,944	28,910	41,576	16,079	27,379	120,107	29,807	42,866	17,141	30,293
Minnesota	97,066	26,871	40,890	10,816	18,489	107,776	29,239	46,882	12,039	19,616
Mississippi	14,266	4,116	7,599	737	1,814	14,572	4,161	7,953	720	1,738
Missouri	142,903	38,064	46,878	24,908	33,053	150,643	39,289	50,600	26,302	34,452
Montana	4,796	1,464	2,231	366	735	4,884	1,583	2,328	366	607
Nebraska	26,079	8,923	12,319	1,690	3,147	27,858	9,336	13,168	1,899	3,455
Nevada	6,790	2,651	3,854	135	150	9,188	3,478	5,224	291	195
New Hampshire	28,284	9,740	11,831	2,304	4,409	29,521	9,900	12,019	2,440	5,162
New Jersey	73,726	25,055	25,365	9,432	13,874	75,340	25,375	26,148	9,618	14,199
New Mexico	9,607	3,198	4,620	685	1,104	10,238	3,440	4,967	708	1,123
New York	512,192	173,561	220,422	43,103	75,106	518,333	173,428	225,367	43,354	76,184
North Carolina	80,710	29,398	38,579	4,828	7,905	83,566	30,252	40,063	4,757	8,494
North Dakota	5,019	1,750	2,631	211	427	6,258	2,019	3,141	297	801
Ohio	153,009	51,680	64,475	13,551	23,303	159,857	53,050	68,155	14,054	24,598
Oklahoma	29,169	12,318	11,838	2,315	2,698	28,344	11,600	12,063	2,114	2,567
Oregon	32,572	11,483	14,754	2,692	3,643	34,610	12,058	16,154	2,701	3,697
Pennsylvania	294,320	102,416	120,179	26,981	44,744	304,255	104,635	124,954	27,198	47,468
Rhode Island	39,148	16,428	17,191	2,655	2,874	40,457	17,125	17,925	2,511	2,896
South Carolina	35,708	12,190	17,516	1,840	4,162	36,524	12,037	17,699	2,229	4,559
South Dakota	10,788	2,403	4,122	1,731	2,532	11,110	2,525	4,422	1,562	2,601
Tennessee	71,881	26,829	33,838	4,227	6,987	78,151	29,366	37,462	4,399	6,924
Texas	152,719	51,691	59,163	19,289	22,576	157,271	53,056	64,016	18,677	21,522
Utah	45,490	19,259	19,340	3,245	3,646	49,142	19,494	20,194	4,854	4,600
Vermont	15,224	6,347	6,202	1,015	1,660	15,659	6,729	6,369	959	1,602
Virginia	72,933	25,306	33,081	5,756	8,790	81,790	27,587	37,692	6,569	9,942
Washington	47,390	15,885	21,541	4,260	5,704	50,379	16,674	22,650	4,836	6,219
West Virginia	14,732	4,598	7,741	770	1,623	14,610	4,715	7,531	741	1,623
Wisconsin	62,886	18,063	25,385	6,572	12,866	64,622	18,385	26,690	6,549	12,998
Wyoming	2,029	1,990	39	0	0	2,358	2,326	32	0	0

See notes at end of table.

Total fall enrollment in private degree-granting institutions, by attendance status, sex, and state or jurisdiction: 2003 and 2004—Continued

State or jurisdiction	Fall 2003					Fall 2004				
		Full-time		Part-time			Full-time		Part-time	
	Total	Males	Females	Males	Females	Total	Males	Females	Males	Females
1	2	3	4	5	6	7	8	9	10	11
Other jurisdictions	**132,187**	**38,681**	**59,672**	**13,327**	**20,507**	**137,089**	**40,278**	**62,012**	**13,601**	**21,198**
American Samoa......................	0	0	0	0	0	0	0	0	0	0
Federated States of Micronesia...............	0	0	0	0	0	0	0	0	0	0
Guam..	164	33	44	52	35	172	42	61	35	34
Marshall Islands......................	0	0	0	0	0	0	0	0	0	0
Northern Marianas	0	0	0	0	0	0	0	0	0	0
Palau..	0	0	0	0	0	0	0	0	0	0
Puerto Rico..............................	132,023	38,648	59,628	13,275	20,472	136,917	40,236	61,951	13,566	21,164
Virgin Islands.............................	0	0	0	0	0	0	0	0	0	0

NOTE: Data are for 4-year and 2-year degree-granting institutions that participated in Title IV federal financial aid programs.

SOURCE: U.S. Department of Education, National Center for Education Statistics, 2003 and 2004 Integrated Postsecondary Education Data System (IPEDS), Spring 2004 and Spring 2005. (This table was prepared September 2005.)

Fall enrollment in degree-granting institutions, by race/ethnicity of student and by state or jurisdiction: 2004

State or jurisdiction	Total	White, non-Hispanic	Minority, by race/ethnicity					Non-resident alien	Percentage distribution of students							
			Total	Black, non-Hispanic	Hispanic	Asian/Pacific Islander	American Indian/Alaska Native		Total	White, non-Hispanic	Minority, by race/ethnicity					Non-resident alien
											Total	Black, non-Hispanic	Hispanic	Asian/Pacific Islander	American Indian/Alaska Native	
1	2	3	4	5	6	7	8	9	10	11	12	13	14	15	16	17
United States	**17,272,044**	**11,422,770**	**5,259,107**	**2,164,683**	**1,809,593**	**1,108,693**	**176,138**	**590,167**	**100.0**	**66.1**	**30.4**	**12.5**	**10.5**	**6.4**	**1.0**	**3.4**
Alabama	255,826	166,656	83,180	74,412	3,568	3,342	1,858	5,990	100.0	65.1	32.5	29.1	1.4	1.3	0.7	2.3
Alaska	30,869	22,316	7,637	1,094	1,044	1,344	4,155	916	100.0	72.3	24.7	3.5	3.4	4.4	13.5	3.0
Arizona	490,925	315,925	148,215	34,908	78,300	17,588	17,419	26,785	100.0	64.4	30.2	7.1	15.9	3.6	3.5	5.5
Arkansas	138,399	104,737	31,174	25,271	2,375	1,996	1,532	2,488	100.0	75.7	22.5	18.3	1.7	1.4	1.1	1.8
California	2,374,045	1,040,123	1,259,027	182,775	609,600	444,352	22,300	74,895	100.0	43.8	53.0	7.7	25.7	18.7	0.9	3.2
Colorado	300,914	231,068	63,150	14,002	33,308	11,490	4,350	6,696	100.0	76.8	21.0	4.7	11.1	3.8	1.4	2.2
Connecticut	172,775	126,513	39,738	17,903	13,673	7,440	722	6,524	100.0	73.2	23.0	10.4	7.9	4.3	0.4	3.8
Delaware	49,804	35,935	12,485	9,255	1,679	1,371	180	1,384	100.0	72.2	25.1	18.6	3.4	2.8	0.4	2.8
District of Columbia	99,988	48,634	44,654	33,207	4,444	6,627	376	6,700	100.0	48.6	44.7	33.2	4.4	6.6	0.4	6.7
Florida	866,665	492,832	343,545	156,587	154,246	29,044	3,668	30,288	100.0	56.9	39.6	18.1	17.8	3.4	0.4	3.5
Georgia	434,283	262,308	159,462	131,236	11,168	15,616	1,442	12,513	100.0	60.4	36.7	30.2	2.6	3.6	0.3	2.9
Hawaii	67,225	17,952	44,218	1,523	1,954	40,412	329	5,055	100.0	26.7	65.8	2.3	2.9	60.1	0.5	7.5
Idaho	76,311	67,429	6,263	596	3,202	1,397	1,068	2,619	100.0	88.4	8.2	0.8	4.2	1.8	1.4	3.4
Illinois	801,401	524,866	252,406	110,995	91,517	47,237	2,657	24,129	100.0	65.5	31.5	13.9	11.4	5.9	0.3	3.0
Indiana	356,801	295,973	47,495	29,117	9,947	7,115	1,316	13,333	100.0	83.0	13.3	8.2	2.8	2.0	0.4	3.7
Iowa	217,646	189,641	20,621	9,598	5,442	4,466	1,115	7,384	100.0	87.1	9.5	4.4	2.5	2.1	0.5	3.4
Kansas	191,590	156,552	29,079	11,177	8,082	6,737	3,083	5,959	100.0	81.7	15.2	5.8	4.2	3.5	1.6	3.1
Kentucky	240,097	208,553	27,200	21,041	2,661	2,799	699	4,344	100.0	86.9	11.3	8.8	1.1	1.2	0.3	1.8
Louisiana	246,301	150,456	88,085	75,586	5,919	5,037	1,543	7,760	100.0	61.1	35.8	30.7	2.4	2.0	0.6	3.2
Maine	65,415	60,277	3,753	1,106	772	1,013	862	1,385	100.0	92.1	5.7	1.7	1.2	1.5	1.3	2.1
Maryland	312,493	182,062	117,357	84,638	11,594	19,868	1,257	13,074	100.0	58.3	37.6	27.1	3.7	6.4	0.4	4.2
Massachusetts	439,245	319,010	93,579	33,961	26,054	31,650	1,914	26,656	100.0	72.6	21.3	7.7	5.9	7.2	0.4	6.1
Michigan	620,980	475,409	122,438	80,171	16,644	20,515	5,108	23,133	100.0	76.6	19.7	12.9	2.7	3.3	0.8	3.7
Minnesota	349,021	292,323	47,417	21,732	6,687	14,877	4,121	9,281	100.0	83.8	13.6	6.2	1.9	4.3	1.2	2.7
Mississippi	152,115	88,612	61,481	58,345	1,128	1,254	754	2,022	100.0	58.3	40.4	38.4	0.7	0.8	0.5	1.3
Missouri	365,204	290,291	65,107	43,938	9,939	8,993	2,237	9,806	100.0	79.5	17.8	12.0	2.7	2.5	0.6	2.7
Montana	47,173	40,219	6,109	287	717	503	4,602	845	100.0	85.3	13.0	0.6	1.5	1.1	9.8	1.8
Nebraska	121,053	104,754	12,814	5,076	3,949	2,790	999	3,485	100.0	86.5	10.6	4.2	3.3	2.3	0.8	2.9
Nevada	105,961	69,004	34,307	8,044	13,963	10,777	1,523	2,650	100.0	65.1	32.4	7.6	13.2	10.2	1.4	2.5
New Hampshire	70,163	63,040	5,450	1,552	1,734	1,784	380	1,673	100.0	89.8	7.8	2.2	2.5	2.5	0.5	2.4
New Jersey	380,374	228,670	136,474	53,986	49,132	32,232	1,124	15,230	100.0	60.1	35.9	14.2	12.9	8.5	0.3	4.0
New Mexico	131,577	57,086	71,423	3,721	53,672	2,527	11,503	3,068	100.0	43.4	54.3	2.8	40.8	1.9	8.7	2.3
New York	1,141,525	698,133	380,889	160,941	127,658	88,274	4,016	62,503	100.0	61.2	33.4	14.1	11.2	7.7	0.4	5.5
North Carolina	472,709	320,135	140,844	112,820	10,878	11,252	5,894	11,730	100.0	67.7	29.8	23.9	2.3	2.4	1.2	2.5
North Dakota	49,533	42,560	5,236	743	611	488	3,394	1,737	100.0	85.9	10.6	1.5	1.2	1.0	6.9	3.5

See notes at end of table.

Fall enrollment in degree-granting institutions, by race/ethnicity of student and by state or jurisdiction: 2004—Continued

State or jurisdiction	Total	Minority, by race/ethnicity						Non-resident alien	Percentage distribution of students							
		White, non-Hispanic	Total	Black, non-Hispanic	Hispanic	Asian/Pacific Islander	American Indian/Alaska Native		Total	White, non-Hispanic	Minority, by race/ethnicity					Non-resident alien
											Total	Black, non-Hispanic	Hispanic	Asian/Pacific Islander	American Indian/Alaska Native	
1	2	3	4	5	6	7	8	9	10	11	12	13	14	15	16	17
Ohio	614,234	497,895	98,273	71,307	11,649	12,994	2,323	18,066	100.0	81.1	16.0	11.6	1.9	2.1	0.4	2.9
Oklahoma	207,625	146,224	51,294	18,771	6,834	4,674	21,015	10,107	100.0	70.4	24.7	9.0	3.3	2.3	10.1	4.9
Oregon	199,985	163,889	30,616	4,509	10,230	12,606	3,271	5,480	100.0	82.0	15.3	2.3	5.1	6.3	1.6	2.7
Pennsylvania	688,780	546,202	119,657	69,837	19,496	28,457	1,867	22,921	100.0	79.3	17.4	10.1	2.8	4.1	0.3	3.3
Rhode Island	80,377	64,546	13,219	4,596	4,866	3,420	337	2,612	100.0	80.3	16.4	5.7	6.1	4.3	0.4	3.2
South Carolina	208,910	140,288	65,134	58,099	3,115	3,088	832	3,488	100.0	67.2	31.2	27.8	1.5	1.5	0.4	1.7
South Dakota	48,708	42,049	5,509	672	515	396	3,926	1,150	100.0	86.3	11.3	1.4	1.1	0.8	8.1	2.4
Tennessee	278,055	207,872	64,758	53,992	4,652	5,143	971	5,425	100.0	74.8	23.3	19.4	1.7	1.8	0.3	2.0
Texas	1,229,197	645,856	533,491	150,899	315,988	60,221	6,383	49,850	100.0	52.5	43.4	12.3	25.7	4.9	0.5	4.1
Utah	194,324	170,333	18,408	1,865	8,590	5,643	2,310	5,583	100.0	87.7	9.5	1.0	4.4	2.9	1.2	2.9
Vermont	38,639	35,301	2,550	706	772	828	244	788	100.0	91.4	6.6	1.8	2.0	2.1	0.6	2.0
Virginia	425,181	293,131	121,185	80,684	14,946	23,322	2,233	10,865	100.0	68.9	28.5	19.0	3.5	5.5	0.5	2.6
Washington	343,524	262,771	71,161	14,507	18,084	32,297	6,273	9,592	100.0	76.5	20.7	4.2	5.3	9.4	1.8	2.8
West Virginia	97,884	88,168	7,379	5,006	946	1,072	355	2,337	100.0	90.1	7.5	5.1	1.0	1.1	0.4	2.4
Wisconsin	331,506	285,736	38,577	16,759	9,126	9,191	3,501	7,193	100.0	86.2	11.6	5.1	2.8	2.8	1.1	2.2
Wyoming	33,955	30,700	2,753	329	1,509	298	617	502	100.0	90.4	8.1	1.0	4.4	0.9	1.8	1.5
U.S. Service Schools	14,754	11,755	2,831	801	1,014	836	180	168	100.0	79.7	19.2	5.4	6.9	5.7	1.2	1.1
Other jurisdictions	**220,920**	**529**	**219,674**	**2,145**	**207,064**	**10,448**	**17**	**717**	**100.0**	**0.2**	**99.4**	**1.0**	**93.7**	**4.7**	**#**	**0.3**
American Samoa	1,550	7	1,370	0	2	1,368	0	173	100.0	0.5	88.4	0.0	0.1	88.3	0.0	11.2
Federated States of Micronesia	2,608	4	2,604	0	0	2,604	0	0	100.0	0.2	99.8	0.0	0.0	99.8	0.0	0.0
Guam	4,642	222	4,356	40	35	4,274	7	64	100.0	4.8	93.8	0.9	0.8	92.1	0.2	1.4
Marshall Islands	623	0	623	0	0	623	0	0	100.0	0.0	100.0	0.0	0.0	100.0	0.0	0.0
Northern Marianas	1,101	48	890	2	2	884	2	163	100.0	4.4	80.8	0.2	0.2	80.3	0.2	14.8
Palau	651	0	645	0	0	645	0	6	100.0	0.0	99.1	0.0	0.0	99.1	0.0	0.9
Puerto Rico	207,180	113	206,930	34	206,864	28	4	137	100.0	0.1	99.9	#	99.8	#	#	0.1
Virgin Islands	2,565	135	2,256	2,069	161	22	4	174	100.0	5.3	88.0	80.7	6.3	0.9	0.2	6.8

#Rounds to zero.
NOTE: Data are for 2-year and 4-year degree-granting institutions that participated in Title IV federal financial aid programs. Detail may not sum to totals because of rounding.

SOURCE: U.S. Department of Education, National Center for Education Statistics, 2004 Integrated Postsecondary Education Data System (IPEDS), Spring 2005. (This table was prepared September 2005.)

Average salary of full-time instructional faculty on 9-month contracts in degree-granting institutions, by academic rank, sex, and control and type of institution: Selected years, 1980–81 through 2004–05

[In current dollars]

Academic year, control and type of institution	All faculty	Academic rank						Sex	
		Professor	Associate professor	Assistant professor	Instructor	Lecturer	No academic rank	Males	Females
1	2	3	4	5	6	7	8	9	10
1980–81									
All institutions	$23,302	$30,753	$23,214	$18,901	$15,178	$17,301	$22,334	$24,499	$19,996
4-year	23,693	31,016	23,265	18,867	15,056	17,375	17,380	24,909	19,809
University	25,949	33,622	24,392	19,684	15,530	17,327	17,856	27,206	20,736
Other 4-year	22,230	28,798	22,558	18,398	14,887	17,425	17,334	23,271	19,372
2-year	21,898	26,528	22,750	19,166	15,621	16,222	22,615	22,736	20,434
Public institutions	23,745	31,077	23,772	19,431	15,613	17,620	22,820	24,873	20,673
4-year	24,373	31,442	23,898	19,442	15,486	17,712	19,240	25,509	20,608
University	25,571	32,945	24,268	19,637	15,305	17,426	17,358	26,788	20,564
Other 4-year	23,500	30,097	23,639	19,315	15,567	17,997	19,798	24,499	20,633
2-year	22,177	26,880	22,947	19,370	15,928	16,458	22,875	22,965	20,778
Private institutions	22,093	29,994	21,833	17,767	14,192	15,899	15,946	23,493	18,073
4-year	22,325	30,089	21,887	17,816	14,316	15,971	16,706	23,669	18,326
University	26,897	35,227	24,730	19,792	16,197	16,956	18,933	28,251	21,176
Other 4-year	19,996	26,173	20,502	16,939	13,905	14,741	16,617	21,040	17,342
2-year	15,065	18,645	17,685	14,663	12,155	12,441	14,993	16,075	13,892
1990–91									
All institutions	42,165	55,540	41,414	34,434	26,332	30,097	36,395	45,065	35,881
4-year	43,693	56,485	41,811	34,657	25,772	30,209	31,494	46,519	36,574
University	49,430	63,437	44,877	37,838	27,105	31,748	31,533	52,426	39,788
Other 4-year	40,313	51,467	39,994	33,020	25,370	29,009	31,488	42,660	35,135
2-year	36,642	44,916	37,650	32,253	27,933	28,048	36,752	38,465	34,224
Public institutions	42,317	55,371	42,101	35,137	26,907	29,881	36,990	45,084	36,459
4-year	44,510	56,668	42,742	35,520	26,134	29,956	32,349	47,168	37,573
University	47,499	60,536	43,851	36,889	25,647	30,429	30,412	50,405	38,363
Other 4-year	42,499	53,704	41,969	34,680	26,316	29,664	33,507	44,804	37,147
2-year	37,055	45,411	38,051	32,673	28,389	28,780	37,096	38,787	34,720
Private institutions	41,788	55,911	39,983	33,116	24,928	30,864	28,523	45,019	34,359
4-year	42,224	56,127	40,122	33,235	25,159	31,053	31,122	45,319	34,898
University	53,875	69,732	47,405	40,013	31,239	34,444	36,211	56,989	43,273
Other 4-year	36,888	47,405	36,965	30,688	23,973	25,416	30,915	39,162	32,251
2-year	24,088	29,520	26,353	24,587	20,911	—	23,187	25,937	22,585
1999–2000									
All institutions	55,888	74,410	54,524	44,978	34,918	38,194	47,389	60,084	48,997
4-year	58,087	76,419	55,198	45,312	33,950	38,124	40,452	62,348	50,124
University	67,507	88,079	59,996	50,678	35,465	40,306	44,591	72,363	56,060
Other 4-year	52,716	67,985	52,404	42,902	33,479	36,295	39,851	55,908	47,454
2-year	48,012	57,677	47,844	41,730	37,433	39,928	48,012	49,819	46,096
Public institutions	55,011	72,475	54,641	45,285	35,007	37,403	47,990	58,984	48,714
4-year	57,950	75,204	55,681	45,822	33,528	37,261	40,579	62,030	50,168
University	63,595	82,344	57,984	48,671	33,230	38,576	41,147	68,135	53,216
Other 4-year	54,255	69,641	54,062	44,293	33,641	36,351	40,430	57,618	48,527
2-year	48,240	57,806	48,056	41,984	37,634	40,061	48,233	50,033	46,340
Private institutions	58,013	78,490	54,295	44,410	34,641	40,652	39,630	62,631	49,737
4-year	58,323	78,582	54,384	44,494	34,809	40,674	40,381	62,905	50,052
University	76,132	99,634	64,782	55,232	43,456	43,822	49,454	81,418	62,787
Other 4-year	50,415	65,277	50,087	40,971	33,197	36,056	39,572	53,271	45,926
2-year	35,925	39,454	36,349	31,499	27,178	25,965	37,532	38,636	32,951
2003–04									
All institutions	62,615	85,352	61,744	51,808	49,076	43,689	47,746	67,509	55,425
4-year	65,355	87,930	62,677	52,418	38,291	43,815	47,340	70,391	56,965
University	76,595	102,722	68,937	59,097	38,569	45,476	51,944	82,774	63,870
Other 4-year	58,963	77,106	59,102	49,358	38,201	42,486	46,340	62,458	53,778
2-year	52,890	62,775	52,485	46,107	55,129	41,059	47,836	54,436	51,410
Public institutions	60,912	82,329	61,196	51,701	50,604	42,539	47,563	65,508	54,445
4-year	64,398	85,843	62,545	52,626	37,611	42,627	43,899	69,290	56,183
University	71,511	94,813	65,883	56,386	36,861	43,041	45,222	77,161	60,207
Other 4-year	59,788	78,584	60,230	50,581	37,906	42,373	43,640	63,629	54,004
2-year	53,080	62,943	52,736	46,297	55,359	41,120	47,937	54,630	51,592
Private institutions	66,693	91,272	62,778	52,005	39,214	47,578	49,291	72,026	57,989
4-year	66,953	91,400	62,894	52,087	39,529	47,600	50,221	72,248	58,255
University	87,340	118,142	76,044	65,069	43,622	50,048	56,790	94,290	72,103
Other 4-year	57,749	74,909	57,570	47,674	38,667	43,121	48,674	60,708	53,452
2-year	36,429	43,982	39,158	36,349	33,174	33,028	36,442	35,734	36,980

See notes at end of table.

Average salary of full-time instructional faculty on 9-month contracts in degree-granting institutions, by academic rank, sex, and control and type of institution: Selected years, 1980–81 through 2004–05—Continued

[In current dollars]

Academic year, control and type of institution	All faculty	Academic rank						Sex	
		Professor	Associate professor	Assistant professor	Instructor	Lecturer	No academic rank	Males	Females
1	2	3	4	5	6	7	8	9	10
2004–05									
All institutions...............	64,234	88,158	63,558	53,308	49,730	44,514	48,942	69,337	56,926
4-year.................	67,153	90,789	64,585	54,018	39,436	44,395	48,194	72,407	58,631
University	79,124	106,608	71,482	61,192	40,199	46,292	51,214	85,502	66,252
Other 4-year	60,367	79,181	60,706	50,715	39,198	42,902	47,401	63,997	55,137
2-year.................	53,762	64,386	53,333	46,914	55,621	47,086	49,123	55,201	52,423
Public institutions	62,346	84,921	62,950	53,209	51,131	43,362	48,803	67,130	55,780
4-year.................	66,053	88,511	64,457	54,296	38,767	43,132	45,006	71,145	57,714
University	73,913	98,398	68,315	58,522	38,363	44,063	46,540	79,769	62,389
Other 4-year	60,986	80,463	61,817	51,983	38,914	42,557	44,633	64,936	55,215
2-year.................	53,932	64,571	53,513	47,095	55,819	47,257	49,222	55,398	52,566
Private institutions	68,755	94,392	64,702	53,493	40,420	48,453	50,021	74,318	59,919
4-year.................	68,995	94,527	64,794	53,574	40,714	48,493	50,814	74,540	60,143
University	90,108	122,461	78,841	67,156	45,388	50,665	54,656	97,280	74,838
Other 4-year	59,451	77,305	59,205	48,953	39,681	44,780	49,742	62,588	55,025
2-year.................	37,329	44,704	41,706	35,187	34,058	40,319	37,098	34,970	39,291

—Not available.
NOTE: Data for 1980–81 and 1990–91 are for institutions of higher education. Institutions of higher education were accredited by an agency or association that was recognized by the U.S. Department of Education, or recognized directly by the Secretary of Education. The new degree-granting classification is very similar to the earlier higher education classification, except that it includes some additional institutions, primarily 2-year colleges, and excludes a few higher education institutions that did not award associate's or higher degrees. (See Guide to Sources for details.)

SOURCE: U.S. Department of Education, National Center for Education Statistics, Higher Education General Information Survey (HEGIS), "Faculty Salaries, Tenure, and Fringe Benefits," 1980–81; and 1990–91 through 2004–05 Integrated Postsecondary Education Data System, "Salaries, Tenure, and Fringe Benefits of Full-Time Instructional Faculty Survey" (IPEDS-SA:90–99), Winter 2003–04, and Winter 2004–05. (This table was prepared September 2005.)

Average salary of full-time instructional faculty on 9-month contracts in degree-granting institutions, by control and type of institution and state or jurisdiction: 2004–05

State or jurisdiction	All institutions	Public institutions					Private institutions				
		Total	4-year institutions			2-year	Total	4-year institutions			2-year
			Total	University	Other 4-year			Total	University	Other 4-year	
1	2	3	4	5	6	7	8	9	10	11	12
United States	**$64,234**	**$62,346**	**$66,053**	**$73,913**	**$60,986**	**$53,932**	**$68,755**	**$68,995**	**$90,108**	**$59,451**	**$37,329**
Alabama	54,269	55,321	59,999	69,203	54,054	44,135	48,803	49,112	†	49,112	30,422
Alaska	57,492	58,130	58,114	59,828	56,915	60,494	46,346	46,346	†	46,346	†
Arizona	67,271	68,058	72,085	76,925	59,209	61,231	51,948	51,948	†	51,948	†
Arkansas	48,668	48,872	52,907	65,221	49,523	38,833	47,553	47,697	†	47,697	24,245
California	76,119	74,856	78,488	100,865	74,161	70,751	81,182	81,416	100,014	71,606	47,356
Colorado	60,256	59,600	63,379	73,524	55,337	43,045	64,411	64,411	71,357	57,736	†
Connecticut	77,311	71,940	75,871	85,960	66,452	60,045	82,631	82,631	108,512	70,419	†
Delaware	75,312	76,093	79,664	82,578	59,327	57,895	68,249	69,153	†	69,153	41,476
District of Columbia	78,303	69,396	69,396	†	69,396	†	78,596	78,596	80,820	62,094	†
Florida	59,786	59,548	64,409	74,797	60,516	48,790	60,577	60,577	75,447	56,144	†
Georgia	59,453	58,481	61,155	73,734	58,514	42,801	62,165	62,363	102,165	52,035	48,126
Hawaii	63,045	63,468	68,550	71,066	55,937	54,216	61,287	61,287	†	61,287	†
Idaho	49,954	50,347	51,858	57,719	49,815	42,705	45,673	45,673	†	45,673	†
Illinois	66,464	62,899	65,220	71,268	60,168	58,665	72,193	72,386	94,865	57,368	30,056
Indiana	62,033	61,525	64,863	69,798	55,407	43,218	63,169	63,312	94,675	53,797	37,939
Iowa	58,186	62,279	71,291	74,329	60,982	43,675	51,519	51,531	63,740	50,147	49,052
Kansas	54,735	56,814	62,255	66,622	53,065	44,077	40,651	41,214	†	41,214	32,035
Kentucky	53,382	54,782	58,692	68,972	52,968	44,974	47,632	47,632	†	47,632	†
Louisiana	53,652	52,929	54,830	67,108	51,366	40,666	56,799	56,799	61,126	49,451	†
Maine	58,899	55,175	57,673	61,920	55,451	46,391	64,945	65,073	†	65,073	52,153
Maryland	65,231	63,829	67,555	82,996	60,853	57,320	69,748	69,748	89,761	58,680	†
Massachusetts	79,186	66,330	71,826	82,956	67,364	52,896	85,068	85,256	98,788	70,971	41,559
Michigan	68,342	70,449	70,959	83,701	61,048	68,296	56,535	56,610	61,606	56,073	33,965
Minnesota	62,114	64,001	69,382	87,064	60,051	55,657	57,741	57,826	†	57,826	39,508
Mississippi	48,500	48,900	53,922	58,803	50,236	42,591	44,974	44,974	†	44,974	†
Missouri	57,825	55,934	58,185	67,905	55,938	48,554	61,567	61,974	81,846	47,697	39,323
Montana	49,359	50,574	52,524	54,917	46,962	38,046	41,474	42,610	†	42,610	31,395
Nebraska	56,427	59,026	63,498	74,463	55,577	42,720	50,029	50,153	60,269	45,880	34,143
Nevada	67,796	67,845	68,860	75,649	66,190	60,057	61,618	61,618	†	61,618	†
New Hampshire	65,435	64,317	70,443	76,147	61,139	42,993	66,867	67,124	†	67,124	30,571
New Jersey	76,266	74,678	79,394	87,591	76,505	63,218	80,142	80,180	102,517	64,780	45,000
New Mexico	54,906	54,852	59,914	64,649	48,965	42,555	55,916	55,916	†	55,916	†
New York	71,944	66,120	69,007	79,358	67,494	60,413	77,328	77,625	91,586	67,038	38,592
North Carolina	56,214	53,601	65,391	79,568	59,815	39,359	64,420	64,640	90,770	49,368	35,329
North Dakota	46,340	47,912	50,889	55,681	42,073	37,779	38,557	41,378		41,378	30,971
Ohio	62,549	64,088	68,111	70,160	61,197	51,439	59,155	59,304	88,371	55,993	37,254
Oklahoma	52,848	52,881	55,993	63,501	48,751	41,759	52,712	52,712	69,544	45,672	†
Oregon	56,289	55,358	57,425	61,269	53,114	52,699	59,473	59,473	†	59,473	†
Pennsylvania	69,148	67,944	70,236	80,708	63,883	54,977	70,508	70,902	96,829	62,448	38,348
Rhode Island	72,047	62,343	65,374	69,548	57,461	52,581	78,467	78,467	†	78,467	†
South Carolina	54,342	55,426	62,207	71,350	53,330	41,960	49,337	49,606	†	49,606	37,275
South Dakota	48,941	50,070	51,977	53,201	50,455	40,284	43,880	43,880	†	43,880	†
Tennessee	56,613	55,729	59,705	68,505	56,726	43,481	58,507	58,748	91,091	47,186	26,882
Texas	60,105	59,189	65,185	73,598	57,873	47,627	64,350	64,552	76,063	55,053	31,853
Utah	61,184	55,319	58,179	64,400	50,378	41,467	76,549	76,844	78,973	56,803	47,893
Vermont	59,565	57,032	57,032	62,965	45,030	†	61,951	64,642	†	64,642	33,141
Virginia	61,854	63,604	68,569	76,049	64,323	46,309	56,523	56,523	†	56,523	†
Washington	57,646	57,370	64,982	71,556	55,155	47,880	58,679	58,679	†	58,679	†
West Virginia	50,034	51,469	53,009	61,338	48,968	41,269	42,574	42,574	†	42,574	†
Wisconsin	61,632	63,234	63,247	84,113	56,150	63,214	55,040	55,152	68,313	50,826	39,508
Wyoming	55,290	55,290	64,981	64,981	†	44,840	†	†	†	†	†
U.S. Service Schools	79,058	79,058	79,058	†	79,058	†	†	†	†	†	†
Other jurisdictions	**48,612**	**48,866**	**52,163**	**†**	**52,163**	**29,526**	**27,437**	**27,437**	**†**	**27,437**	**†**
American Samoa	27,388	27,388	†	†	†	27,388	†	†	†	†	†
Federated States of Micronesia	21,348	21,348	†	†	†	21,348	†	†	†	†	†
Guam	51,880	51,880	56,439	†	56,439	44,671	†	†	†	†	†
Marshall Islands	28,077	28,077	†	†	†	28,077	†	†	†	†	†
Northern Marianas	41,276	41,276	41,276	†	41,276	†	†	†	†	†	†
Palau	17,733	17,733	†	†	†	17,733	†	†	†	†	†
Puerto Rico	51,848	52,263	52,263	†	52,263	†	27,437	27,437	†	27,437	†
Virgin Islands	51,580	51,580	51,580	†	51,580	†	†	†	†	†	†

†Not applicable.
NOTE: Data include imputations for nonrespondent institutions.

SOURCE: U.S. Department of Education, National Center for Education Statistics, 2004–05 Integrated Postsecondary Education Data System (IPEDS), Winter 2004–05. (This table was prepared September 2005.)

Average salary of full-time instructional faculty on 9-month contracts in 4-year degree-granting institutions, by type and control of institution, rank of faculty, and state or jurisdiction: 2004–05

State or jurisdiction	Public university			Public other 4-year			Private university			Private other 4-year		
	Professor	Associate professor	Assistant professor	Professor	Associate professor	Assistant professor	Professor	Associate professor	Assistant professor	Professor	Associate professor	Assistant professor
1	2	3	4	5	6	7	8	9	10	11	12	13
United States	**$98,398**	**$68,315**	**$58,522**	**$80,463**	**$61,817**	**$51,983**	**$122,461**	**$78,841**	**$67,156**	**$77,305**	**$59,205**	**$48,953**
Alabama	91,411	65,146	54,498	70,680	57,289	48,367	†	†	†	63,745	50,161	41,895
Alaska	79,171	60,321	52,252	74,091	58,202	50,918	†	†	†	64,254	52,806	41,892
Arizona	99,179	68,468	60,970	76,459	60,588	49,917	†	†	†	52,900	67,054	49,102
Arkansas	86,126	64,892	55,208	64,501	55,443	46,597	†	†	†	57,620	48,946	41,492
California	122,458	78,596	69,678	92,316	68,148	57,709	130,792	85,512	74,829	90,818	68,236	56,740
Colorado	94,809	69,526	59,796	72,941	56,547	48,506	93,233	69,570	57,998	79,676	53,711	49,144
Connecticut	110,922	78,961	63,824	81,645	63,298	52,598	146,414	83,138	69,874	91,967	68,506	55,329
Delaware	111,112	76,580	62,807	68,339	62,640	55,189	†	†	†	96,271	69,420	52,795
District of Columbia	†	†	†	81,706	64,579	52,056	108,466	75,968	60,895	89,802	67,449	52,169
Florida	94,567	65,638	58,970	81,629	62,212	53,735	108,960	72,918	63,485	74,843	56,438	48,353
Georgia	95,755	64,635	57,970	83,294	60,447	50,802	132,809	83,007	76,589	61,811	52,739	44,219
Hawaii	89,394	67,574	58,756	68,807	57,924	50,371	†	†	†	80,331	67,700	55,725
Idaho	70,922	58,182	48,921	63,567	53,279	45,451	†	†	†	52,127	45,045	38,910
Illinois	100,705	68,026	58,590	81,128	62,700	52,428	131,671	81,685	67,853	71,397	58,446	47,713
Indiana	94,510	66,852	56,398	77,213	59,729	49,981	118,670	78,750	67,677	66,893	53,053	46,169
Iowa	97,061	68,969	60,262	77,770	61,522	52,920	84,564	59,511	48,836	61,919	50,689	43,351
Kansas	86,441	63,468	53,910	70,842	55,104	47,071	†	†	†	46,811	42,830	37,718
Kentucky	89,538	63,747	54,445	72,109	56,371	49,462	†	†	†	58,781	47,535	41,209
Louisiana	93,662	67,574	59,359	69,257	54,727	46,866	87,874	64,634	53,323	62,323	53,364	45,272
Maine	74,166	63,102	49,034	67,419	55,335	45,069	†	†	†	89,933	62,659	50,302
Maryland	108,149	73,990	73,781	84,820	64,715	54,219	115,074	76,178	66,840	76,049	60,286	50,557
Massachusetts	103,371	82,128	62,544	81,258	66,184	54,187	131,702	81,463	71,817	92,741	68,337	56,262
Michigan	110,538	77,056	64,668	78,703	61,859	51,493	80,632	61,357	50,404	67,425	56,215	46,869
Minnesota	107,484	71,900	62,475	74,475	59,820	50,036	†	†	†	73,266	57,958	48,425
Mississippi	81,811	63,368	54,035	65,850	54,210	47,391	†	†	†	58,723	47,834	41,735
Missouri	93,644	66,159	53,335	73,697	56,654	48,495	114,105	72,874	62,663	57,496	49,857	43,076
Montana	69,251	54,303	47,621	57,801	47,760	43,296	†	†	†	52,063	43,126	36,955
Nebraska	96,673	69,110	58,579	68,563	57,753	49,127	87,563	59,241	46,740	56,815	47,862	40,890
Nevada	101,691	75,685	57,230	76,727	73,317	60,361	†	†	†	75,231	52,305	53,020
New Hampshire	95,319	70,396	59,611	73,710	60,474	49,863	†	†	†	91,121	64,258	49,061
New Jersey	113,068	77,074	62,426	99,863	76,273	59,610	141,826	77,413	67,243	85,046	67,727	50,535
New Mexico	82,819	61,061	53,424	57,252	51,565	44,291	†	†	†	62,298	49,570	44,392
New York	103,736	72,964	60,392	87,633	66,517	54,962	122,313	81,803	69,486	90,442	67,112	54,354
North Carolina	105,772	72,618	64,817	79,631	62,090	54,730	125,022	83,107	65,525	61,667	51,016	43,279
North Dakota	72,270	58,452	51,751	53,254	46,346	41,684	†	†	†	50,352	43,381	39,241
Ohio	94,658	66,400	54,780	81,672	62,495	50,461	109,619	85,440	78,053	70,916	55,866	47,000
Oklahoma	84,691	61,480	52,809	61,590	53,059	45,537	92,758	64,763	55,150	58,582	46,323	40,362
Oregon	81,514	60,573	55,001	67,290	53,228	44,989	†	†	†	76,529	56,988	47,571
Pennsylvania	110,206	75,276	64,600	86,006	68,050	55,264	127,650	83,829	71,830	82,905	63,008	51,900
Rhode Island	85,757	62,451	56,070	65,061	54,925	48,143	†	†	†	104,125	70,601	60,285
South Carolina	92,215	66,392	59,783	66,006	56,636	46,735	†	†	†	64,795	49,556	42,909
South Dakota	69,087	56,660	48,362	69,208	50,021	46,097	†	†	†	54,517	48,409	39,912
Tennessee	91,365	68,309	57,192	71,926	57,134	48,353	124,263	79,040	64,990	58,201	48,939	41,540
Texas	99,797	66,899	59,352	78,519	61,740	53,449	104,504	72,236	65,410	70,966	53,776	45,105
Utah	84,366	60,775	55,044	60,779	51,519	46,550	100,373	74,673	65,390	66,842	58,699	50,544
Vermont	86,359	64,657	54,908	52,587	42,945	34,586	†	†	†	87,653	61,543	51,336
Virginia	102,757	72,166	59,696	85,322	64,357	52,577	†	†	†	73,707	55,937	46,120
Washington	90,744	65,438	60,997	68,125	56,209	49,086	†	†	†	73,145	58,933	49,481
West Virginia	76,966	59,619	48,818	59,989	49,994	42,042	†	†	†	52,014	45,415	36,938
Wisconsin	99,017	73,990	62,753	70,212	57,638	49,657	92,973	68,752	56,862	62,261	51,688	44,282
Wyoming	83,955	63,230	59,081	†	†	†	†	†	†	†	†	†
U.S. Service Schools	†	†	†	103,698	82,767	67,789	†	†	†	†	†	†
Other jurisdictions	†	†	†	**62,807**	**53,013**	**43,832**	†	†	†	†	**27,600**	**31,110**
American Samoa	†	†	†	†	†	†	†	†	†	†	†	†
Federated States of Micronesia	†	†	†	†	†	†	†	†	†	†	†	†
Guam	†	†	†	56,439	74,550	55,998	†	†	†	†	†	†
Marshall Islands	†	†	†	†	†	†	†	†	†	†	†	†
Northern Marianas	†	†	†	†	†	†	†	†	†	†	†	†
Palau	†	†	†	†	†	†	†	†	†	†	†	†
Puerto Rico	†	†	†	62,078	52,469	43,776	†	†	†	†	27,600	31,110
Virgin Islands	†	†	†	65,318	53,379	44,008	†	†	†	†	†	†

†Not applicable.
NOTE: Data include imputations for nonrespondent institutions.

SOURCE: U.S. Department of Education, National Center for Education Statistics, 2004–05 Integrated Postsecondary Education Data System (IPEDS), Winter 2004–05. (This table was prepared September 2005.)

Full-time instructional staff with tenure for degree-granting institutions with a tenure system, by academic rank, sex, and control and type of institution: Selected years, 1993–94 through 2003–04

Academic year, control and type of institution	Percent with tenure														No academic rank
	All ranks			Professor			Associate professor			Assistant professor			Instructor	Lecturer	
	Total	Male	Female	Total	Male	Female	Total	Male	Female	Total	Male	Female			
1	2	3	4	5	6	7	8	9	10	11	12	13	14	15	16
1993–94															
All institutions	56.2	62.6	42.7	91.9	92.8	87.7	76.8	77.5	75.1	14.4	13.6	15.5	38.3	10.8	26.0
4-year	54.0	61.0	38.0	93.0	93.5	90.6	76.2	77.0	74.3	12.1	11.5	12.9	4.8	9.6	9.4
University	54.3	61.0	35.8	94.1	94.5	91.3	78.0	78.6	76.4	6.6	6.2	7.3	5.7	10.5	9.9
Other	53.8	61.1	39.4	92.1	92.5	90.2	74.9	75.7	73.1	15.7	15.4	16.0	4.4	8.3	8.7
2-year	69.3	74.7	62.4	80.8	83.7	75.7	83.8	86.1	81.1	46.6	50.5	43.2	67.9	41.2	65.6
Public institutions	58.9	65.4	45.6	92.6	93.6	87.5	80.8	81.6	78.9	17.1	16.1	18.5	45.5	7.2	28.6
4-year	56.3	63.5	39.3	94.3	94.7	92.0	80.4	81.2	78.4	13.8	13.0	14.8	4.4	5.4	6.1
University	57.0	64.2	37.2	95.6	96.0	92.5	83.9	84.4	82.6	7.6	7.0	8.6	3.1	1.0	7.0
Other	55.7	62.9	40.8	93.2	93.5	91.7	77.5	78.3	75.5	18.1	17.6	18.7	5.1	9.8	4.9
2-year	69.9	75.4	63.0	80.7	83.7	75.5	84.2	86.4	81.5	47.7	51.1	44.6	68.9	39.9	65.7
Private institutions	49.5	56.0	35.4	90.3	90.8	88.1	67.6	68.1	66.5	9.0	8.7	9.4	6.8	21.9	18.8
4-year	49.5	56.0	35.4	90.3	90.8	88.0	67.6	68.1	66.5	9.0	8.7	9.4	5.5	21.6	15.7
University	48.4	54.1	32.9	90.8	91.1	89.1	63.2	64.1	60.6	4.7	4.8	4.7	10.4	30.0	15.4
Other	50.3	57.5	36.8	89.9	90.5	87.4	70.2	70.7	69.1	11.6	11.5	11.7	3.1	1.4	16.3
2-year	45.4	51.9	36.8	89.8	86.8	95.0	62.9	64.1	61.8	12.0	11.8	12.0	25.8	—	64.8
1999–2000															
All institutions	53.6	59.6	43.1	92.8	93.2	91.2	76.8	76.8	76.7	11.7	10.9	12.8	34.1	3.4	18.4
4-year	51.5	58.3	38.5	92.9	93.2	91.5	76.3	76.5	76.0	9.1	8.6	9.7	3.6	2.5	4.9
University	50.1	57.1	34.5	92.5	92.9	90.3	77.1	77.4	76.6	4.1	3.9	4.5	1.7	0.9	1.3
Other	52.6	59.4	41.1	93.2	93.5	92.2	75.7	75.8	75.7	12.4	12.1	12.8	4.7	4.4	11.6
2-year	67.7	70.6	64.6	91.3	92.3	89.9	83.2	83.3	83.1	53.5	55.9	51.6	60.9	21.1	64.5
Public institutions	55.9	61.9	45.5	93.9	94.4	91.9	81.0	81.2	80.7	14.0	13.0	15.2	39.9	4.1	21.2
4-year	53.1	60.3	39.3	94.2	94.6	92.5	80.8	81.0	80.3	10.0	9.6	10.6	3.9	3.0	4.0
University	53.0	60.4	36.7	94.2	94.7	91.4	83.0	83.2	82.7	4.6	4.3	5.1	2.3	0.7	1.7
Other	53.2	60.2	41.2	94.1	94.4	93.1	78.9	79.0	78.5	13.8	13.5	14.1	4.8	5.2	7.5
2-year	67.8	70.7	64.6	91.3	92.3	89.8	83.4	83.5	83.4	53.7	56.0	51.8	61.0	21.2	64.4
Private institutions	48.3	54.3	37.0	90.3	90.5	89.7	68.1	67.9	68.5	7.5	6.9	8.2	4.1	1.2	8.6
4-year	48.2	54.3	36.8	90.3	90.5	89.7	68.1	67.9	68.5	7.4	6.8	8.2	3.1	1.2	7.2
University	44.1	50.3	29.8	88.9	89.1	87.9	64.1	64.6	62.8	3.2	3.1	3.3	0.4	1.3	0.4
Other	51.4	57.7	41.1	91.4	91.7	90.6	70.6	70.2	71.3	10.1	9.6	10.6	4.6	1.0	28.3
2-year	59.9	60.3	59.6	95.9	92.0	100.0	60.0	66.7	55.8	33.8	40.0	30.0	50.5	—	68.8
2001–02															
All institutions	50.8	56.5	41.5	92.0	92.3	90.7	75.6	75.4	75.9	10.0	9.1	11.1	30.0	3.2	18.9
4-year	48.7	55.2	36.9	92.0	92.3	90.7	75.0	74.9	75.1	7.5	6.8	8.2	3.1	2.0	3.4
University	47.8	54.5	33.5	91.9	92.3	89.6	76.0	76.2	75.8	3.4	3.1	3.7	1.4	0.5	1.1
Other	49.4	55.8	39.2	92.1	92.4	91.3	74.1	73.9	74.6	10.2	9.6	10.9	4.0	3.8	7.4
2-year	64.2	66.6	61.8	91.8	92.2	91.2	84.0	83.9	84.0	49.6	51.5	48.0	53.0	31.5	67.8
Public institutions	52.6	58.2	43.5	93.2	93.6	91.8	79.4	79.3	79.5	11.9	10.8	13.3	34.4	3.9	22.1
4-year	49.8	56.6	37.4	93.4	93.7	92.0	78.9	78.9	78.8	8.1	7.5	9.0	2.5	2.4	2.4
University	50.2	57.3	35.5	93.7	94.2	91.4	81.3	81.6	80.6	3.6	3.2	4.1	1.8	0.6	0.8
Other	49.4	56.0	38.7	93.0	93.2	92.3	76.9	76.6	77.4	11.3	10.7	12.0	2.8	4.2	4.8
2-year	64.3	66.6	61.8	91.8	92.3	91.2	84.0	83.9	84.1	49.9	51.9	48.2	53.0	30.6	67.9
Private institutions	46.5	52.4	36.2	89.3	89.6	88.2	67.7	67.3	68.4	6.3	5.7	7.0	6.6	1.1	6.8
4-year	46.5	52.3	36.0	89.3	89.6	88.2	67.7	67.3	68.4	6.3	5.7	7.0	4.4	0.9	6.0
University	42.7	48.9	29.1	88.0	88.4	85.8	64.4	64.5	64.2	3.0	3.0	3.0	0.6	0.4	1.7
Other	49.4	55.2	40.3	90.4	90.7	89.6	69.7	69.2	70.4	8.4	7.7	9.0	6.3	2.1	18.6
2-year	61.0	63.0	58.1	88.7	86.5	91.1	80.4	81.0	80.0	24.2	17.1	30.0	57.8	—	65.6
2003–04															
All institutions	50.4	56.0	41.5	91.8	92.0	91.1	74.6	74.2	75.3	9.0	8.2	9.9	30.7	2.1	22.5
4-year	48.2	54.6	37.2	91.9	92.1	91.3	74.2	73.8	74.8	6.6	6.1	7.3	3.2	1.5	3.9
University	47.4	54.0	34.0	91.7	91.9	90.5	75.0	74.8	75.4	3.1	3.0	3.2	1.1	0.4	1.7
Other	48.8	55.1	39.4	92.1	92.2	91.8	73.6	73.0	74.5	9.0	8.3	9.7	4.3	2.6	9.6
2-year	65.2	68.2	62.2	90.6	91.3	89.7	81.2	82.0	80.5	45.6	48.4	43.2	57.2	22.1	69.8
Public institutions	53.0	58.6	44.2	93.6	93.8	92.9	78.9	78.7	79.4	11.1	10.2	12.1	35.7	2.6	28.6
4-year	50.2	56.9	38.5	93.9	94.0	93.7	78.7	78.4	79.2	7.5	7.0	8.2	2.4	1.7	4.4
University	51.1	58.0	37.2	93.8	94.0	92.9	81.2	81.2	81.3	3.7	3.6	3.9	1.5	0.4	2.6
Other	49.4	56.0	39.4	94.0	94.0	94.2	76.6	76.0	77.6	10.1	9.4	10.8	2.8	2.7	8.3
2-year	65.2	68.3	62.2	90.5	91.3	89.6	81.3	82.1	80.6	45.9	48.8	43.5	57.2	22.0	69.8
Private institutions	44.7	50.3	35.0	88.2	88.4	87.2	66.2	65.5	67.3	5.2	4.6	5.9	6.7	0.7	3.7
4-year	44.6	50.3	34.9	88.2	88.4	87.1	66.2	65.5	67.3	5.2	4.6	5.9	4.9	0.7	2.8
University	40.5	46.6	27.9	87.5	87.8	85.6	62.1	61.9	62.6	2.0	2.0	2.0	0.4	0.2	0.3
Other	47.9	53.6	39.3	88.7	89.0	88.0	68.7	68.1	69.7	7.2	6.5	8.0	7.2	1.8	14.0
2-year	61.5	60.2	62.7	94.9	91.7	97.7	65.4	61.9	67.7	15.6	14.3	16.7	63.0	37.5	68.1

—Not available.

NOTE: The coverage of this tabulation differs from similar tables published in editions of the *Digest* prior to 2003. Previous tenure tabulations included only instructional staff classified as full-time faculty; this table includes all staff with full-time instructional duties, including faculty and other instructional staff. Data for 1993–94 are for institutions of higher education that were accredited by an agency or association that was recognized by the U.S. Department of Education, or recognized directly by the Secretary of Education. The new degree-granting classification is very similar to the earlier higher education classification, except that it includes some additional institutions, primarily 2-year colleges, and excludes a few higher education institutions that did not award associate's or higher degrees. (See Guide to Sources for details.)

SOURCE: U.S. Department of Education, National Center for Education Statistics, 1993–94 through 2003–04 Integrated Postsecondary Education Data System, "Fall Staff Survey" (IPEDS-S:93–99), Winter 2001–02, and Winter 2003–04. (This table was prepared March 2005.)

Degree-granting institutions, by control and type of institution: Selected years, 1949–50 through 2004–05

Year	All institutions			Public			Private		
	Total	4-year	2-year	Total	4-year	2-year	Total	4-year	2-year
1	2	3	4	5	6	7	8	9	10
Institutions of higher education,[1] excluding branch campuses									
1949–50..........	1,851	1,327	524	641	344	297	1,210	983	227
1959–60..........	2,004	1,422	582	695	367	328	1,309	1,055	254
1960–61..........	2,021	1,431	590	700	368	332	1,321	1,063	258
1961–62..........	2,033	1,443	590	718	374	344	1,315	1,069	246
1962–63..........	2,093	1,468	625	740	376	364	1,353	1,092	261
1963–64..........	2,132	1,499	633	760	386	374	1,372	1,113	259
1964–65..........	2,175	1,521	654	799	393	406	1,376	1,128	248
1965–66..........	2,230	1,551	679	821	401	420	1,409	1,150	259
1966–67..........	2,329	1,577	752	880	403	477	1,449	1,174	275
1967–68..........	2,374	1,588	786	934	414	520	1,440	1,174	266
1968–69..........	2,483	1,619	864	1,011	417	594	1,472	1,202	270
1969–70..........	2,525	1,639	886	1,060	426	634	1,465	1,213	252
1970–71..........	2,556	1,665	891	1,089	435	654	1,467	1,230	237
1971–72..........	2,606	1,675	931	1,137	440	697	1,469	1,235	234
1972–73..........	2,665	1,701	964	1,182	449	733	1,483	1,252	231
1973–74..........	2,720	1,717	1,003	1,200	440	760	1,520	1,277	243
1974–75..........	2,747	1,744	1,003	1,214	447	767	1,533	1,297	236
1975–76..........	2,765	1,767	998	1,219	447	772	1,546	1,320	226
1976–77..........	2,785	1,783	1,002	1,231	452	779	1,554	1,331	223
1977–78..........	2,826	1,808	1,018	1,241	454	787	1,585	1,354	231
1978–79..........	2,954	1,843	1,111	1,308	463	845	1,646	1,380	266
1979–80..........	2,975	1,863	1,112	1,310	464	846	1,665	1,399	266
1980–81..........	3,056	1,861	1,195	1,334	465	869	1,722	1,396	[2] 326
1981–82..........	3,083	1,883	1,200	1,340	471	869	1,743	1,412	[2] 331
1982–83..........	3,111	1,887	1,224	1,336	472	864	1,775	1,415	[2] 360
1983–84..........	3,117	1,914	1,203	1,325	474	851	1,792	1,440	352
1984–85..........	3,146	1,911	1,235	1,329	461	868	1,817	1,450	367
1985–86..........	3,155	1,915	1,240	1,326	461	865	1,829	1,454	375
Institutions of higher education,[1] including branch campuses									
1974–75..........	3,004	1,866	1,138	1,433	537	896	1,571	1,329	242
1975–76..........	3,026	1,898	1,128	1,442	545	897	1,584	1,353	231
1976–77..........	3,046	1,913	1,133	1,455	550	905	1,591	1,363	228
1977–78..........	3,095	1,938	1,157	1,473	552	921	1,622	1,386	236
1978–79..........	3,134	1,941	1,193	1,474	550	924	1,660	1,391	269
1979–80..........	3,152	1,957	1,195	1,475	549	926	1,677	1,408	269
1980–81..........	3,231	1,957	1,274	1,497	552	945	1,734	1,405	[2] 329
1981–82..........	3,253	1,979	1,274	1,498	558	940	1,755	1,421	[2] 334
1982–83..........	3,280	1,984	1,296	1,493	560	933	1,787	1,424	[2] 363
1983–84..........	3,284	2,013	1,271	1,481	565	916	1,803	1,448	355
1984–85..........	3,331	2,025	1,306	1,501	566	935	1,830	1,459	371
1985–86..........	3,340	2,029	1,311	1,498	566	932	1,842	1,463	379
1986–87[3]..........	3,406	2,070	1,336	1,533	573	960	1,873	1,497	376
1987–88[3]..........	3,587	2,135	1,452	1,591	599	992	1,996	1,536	460
1988–89[3]..........	3,565	2,129	1,436	1,582	598	984	1,983	1,531	452
1989–90[3]..........	3,535	2,127	1,408	1,563	595	968	1,972	1,532	440
1990–91[3]..........	3,559	2,141	1,418	1,567	595	972	1,992	1,546	446
1991–92[3]..........	3,601	2,157	1,444	1,598	599	999	2,003	1,558	445
1992–93[3]..........	3,638	2,169	1,469	1,624	600	1,024	2,014	1,569	445
1993–94[3]..........	3,632	2,190	1,442	1,625	604	1,021	2,007	1,586	421
1994–95[3]..........	3,688	2,215	1,473	1,641	605	1,036	2,047	1,610	437
1995–96[3]..........	3,706	2,244	1,462	1,655	608	1,047	2,051	1,636	415

See notes at end of table.

379

Degree-granting institutions, by control and type of institution: Selected years, 1949–50 through 2004–05—Continued

Year	All institutions			Public			Private		
	Total	4-year	2-year	Total	4-year	2-year	Total	4-year	2-year
1	2	3	4	5	6	7	8	9	10
Title IV eligible institutions, including branch campuses									
1996–97............................	4,009	2,267	1,742	1,702	614	1,088	2,307	1,653	654
1997–98............................	4,064	2,309	1,755	1,707	615	1,092	2,357	1,694	663
1998–99............................	4,048	2,335	1,713	1,681	612	1,069	2,367	1,723	644
1999–2000........................	4,084	2,363	1,721	1,682	614	1,068	2,402	1,749	653
2000–01............................	4,182	2,450	1,732	1,698	622	1,076	2,484	1,828	656
2001–02............................	4,197	2,487	1,710	1,713	628	1,085	2,484	1,859	625
2002–03............................	4,168	2,466	1,702	1,712	631	1,081	2,456	1,835	621
2003–04............................	4,236	2,530	1,706	1,720	634	1,086	2,516	1,896	620
2004–05............................	4,216	2,533	1,683	1,700	639	1,061	2,516	1,894	622

[1]Institutions that were accredited by an agency or association that was recognized by the U.S. Department of Education, or recognized directly by the Secretary of Education.
[2]Large increases are due to the addition of schools accredited by the Accrediting Commission of Career Schools and Colleges of Technology.
[3]Because of revised survey procedures, data are not entirely comparable with figures for earlier years. The number of branch campuses reporting separately has increased since 1986–87.
NOTE: Title IV eligible institutions are postsecondary institutions that meet the criteria for participating in the federal student financial aid program. See Guide to Sources and appendix B for more details. (Approximately 96 percent of all postsecondary institutions are Title IV eligible.)
SOURCE: U.S. Department of Education, National Center for Education Statistics, *Education Directory, Colleges and Universities*, 1949–50 through 1965–66; Higher Education General Information Survey (HEGIS), "Institutional Characteristics of Colleges and Universities" surveys, 1966–67 through 1985–86; and 1986–87 through 2004–05 Integrated Postsecondary Education Data System, "Institutional Characteristics Survey" (IPEDS-IC:86–99), and Fall 2000 through Fall 2004. (This table was prepared August 2005.)

Degree-granting institutions and branches, by type and control of institution and state or jurisdiction: 2004–05

State or jurisdiction	Total	All public institutions	Public 4-year institutions						Public 2-year	All private institutions	Private 4-year institutions						Private 2-year
			Total	Doctoral, extensive[1]	Doctoral, intensive[2]	Master's[3]	Bacca-laureate[4]	Other 4-year[5]			Total	Doctoral, extensive[1]	Doctoral, intensive[2]	Master's[3]	Bacca-laureate[4]	Other 4-year[5]	
1	2	3	4	5	6	7	8	9	10	11	12	13	14	15	16	17	18
United States	4,216	1,700	639	102	63	280	103	91	1,061	2,516	1,894	49	45	362	532	906	622
Alabama	69	42	16	3	3	9	1	0	26	27	23	0	0	4	9	10	4
Alaska	8	5	3	0	1	2	0	0	2	3	3	0	0	1	1	1	0
Arizona	77	25	5	2	1	1	0	1	20	52	31	0	1	6	1	23	21
Arkansas	47	33	11	1	1	5	2	2	22	14	12	0	0	1	8	3	2
California	399	144	34	8	2	20	2	2	110	255	192	4	7	30	25	126	63
Colorado	77	28	13	2	2	3	4	2	15	49	32	1	0	6	3	22	17
Connecticut	45	22	10	1	0	7	1	1	12	23	20	1	3	5	4	7	3
Delaware	10	5	2	1	0	1	0	0	3	5	4	0	1	0	1	2	1
District of Columbia	15	2	2	0	0	1	0	1	0	13	13	5	0	4	1	3	0
Florida	163	40	16	4	2	4	1	5	24	123	91	1	3	20	24	43	32
Georgia	128	74	21	3	0	13	1	4	53	54	44	1	1	4	15	23	10
Hawaii	20	10	3	1	0	0	2	0	7	10	8	0	0	3	1	4	2
Idaho	14	7	4	1	1	1	1	0	3	7	6	0	0	1	1	4	1
Illinois	172	60	12	4	1	7	0	0	48	112	100	3	3	15	20	59	12
Indiana	99	29	14	2	3	6	3	0	15	70	47	1	0	8	20	18	23
Iowa	64	19	3	2	0	1	0	0	16	45	42	0	0	4	22	16	3
Kansas	63	36	9	2	1	4	0	2	27	27	23	0	0	8	10	5	4
Kentucky	76	31	8	2	0	6	0	0	23	45	30	0	0	4	16	10	15
Louisiana	90	59	17	1	3	9	0	4	42	31	13	1	0	3	5	4	18
Maine	30	15	8	1	0	1	5	1	7	15	12	0	0	3	5	4	3
Maryland	57	30	13	2	1	9	1	0	17	27	23	1	0	5	6	11	4
Massachusetts	122	31	15	1	2	7	1	4	16	91	82	7	2	15	21	37	9
Michigan	105	45	15	4	3	8	0	0	30	60	55	0	1	9	17	28	5
Minnesota	105	42	12	1	0	7	3	1	30	63	52	0	3	6	13	30	11
Mississippi	40	25	9	3	1	3	1	1	16	15	11	0	0	2	5	4	4
Missouri	125	33	13	1	3	6	2	1	20	92	70	2	0	12	14	42	22
Montana	23	18	6	0	2	2	1	1	12	5	4	0	0	1	2	1	1
Nebraska	39	15	7	1	0	5	0	1	8	24	20	0	0	4	8	8	4
Nevada	20	7	5	1	1	0	1	2	2	13	6	0	0	1	2	3	7
New Hampshire	26	9	5	1	0	2	2	0	4	17	15	0	2	2	5	6	2
New Jersey	59	33	14	1	2	8	2	1	19	26	24	1	2	6	6	9	2
New Mexico	43	28	8	2	1	3	0	2	20	15	13	0	0	3	4	6	2
New York	307	78	43	5	1	20	7	10	35	229	177	9	7	32	34	95	52
North Carolina	127	75	16	2	2	8	3	1	59	52	46	1	1	7	25	12	6
North Dakota	21	14	7	0	2	1	3	1	7	7	5	0	0	1	1	3	2
Ohio	194	61	27	5	5	1	6	10	34	133	77	1	2	15	25	34	56
Oklahoma	54	29	16	2	0	7	3	4	13	25	19	0	1	5	7	6	6
Oregon	59	26	9	2	1	3	1	2	17	33	30	0	0	6	9	15	3
Pennsylvania	260	65	44	3	1	17	20	3	21	195	105	3	3	28	34	37	90
Rhode Island	14	3	2	1	0	1	0	0	1	11	10	1	0	4	1	4	1
South Carolina	63	33	13	2	1	5	3	2	20	30	25	0	0	3	15	7	5
South Dakota	26	14	9	0	2	2	2	3	5	12	11	0	0	2	5	4	1
Tennessee	97	22	9	2	3	4	0	0	13	75	55	1	0	11	16	27	20
Texas	208	109	42	6	6	20	2	8	67	99	62	2	2	14	20	24	37
Utah	27	13	7	2	0	2	2	1	6	14	9	1	0	2	1	5	5
Vermont	25	6	5	1	0	2	1	1	1	19	17	0	0	6	7	4	2
Virginia	99	39	15	4	2	6	3	0	24	60	49	0	0	8	18	23	11
Washington	81	46	11	2	0	8	1	0	35	35	32	0	0	11	4	17	3
West Virginia	43	21	12	1	0	1	9	1	9	22	10	0	0	2	7	1	12
Wisconsin	67	31	13	2	0	11	0	0	18	36	34	1	0	8	10	15	2
Wyoming	9	8	1	1	0	0	0	0	7	1	1	0	0	0	0	0	1
U.S. Service Schools	5	5	5	0	0	0	0	5	0	†	†	†	†	†	†	†	†
Other jurisdictions	90	29	18	0	1	4	7	6	11	61	44	0	0	7	19	18	17
American Samoa	1	1	0	0	0	0	0	0	1	0	0	0	0	0	0	0	0
Federated States of Micronesia	4	4	0	0	0	0	0	0	4	0	0	0	0	0	0	0	0
Guam	3	2	1	0	0	1	0	0	1	1	1	0	0	0	0	1	0
Marshall Islands	1	1	0	0	0	0	0	0	1	0	0	0	0	0	0	0	0
Northern Marianas	1	1	1	0	0	0	0	1	0	0	0	0	0	0	0	0	0
Palau	1	1	0	0	0	0	0	0	1	0	0	0	0	0	0	0	0
Puerto Rico	77	17	14	0	1	1	7	5	3	60	43	0	0	7	19	17	17
Virgin Islands	2	2	2	0	0	2	0	0	0	0	0	0	0	0	0	0	0

†Not applicable.
[1]Doctoral, extensive institutions are committed to graduate education through the doctorate, and award 50 or more doctor's degrees per year across at least 15 disciplines.
[2]Doctoral, intensive institutions are committed to education through the doctorate and award at least 10 doctor's degrees per year across 3 or more disciplines or at least 20 doctor's degrees overall.
[3]Master's institutions offer a full range of baccalaureate programs and are committed to education through the master's degree. They award at least 20 master's degrees per year.
[4]Baccalaureate institutions primarily emphasize undergraduate education.

[5]Other specialized 4-year institutions award degrees primarily in single fields of study, such as medicine, business, fine arts, theology, and engineering. Includes some institutions that have 4-year programs, but have not reported sufficient data to identify program category. Also, includes institutions classified as 4-year under the IPEDS system, which had been classified as 2-year in the Carnegie classification system because they primarily award associate's degrees.
NOTE: New institutions that do not have sufficient data to report by detailed level are included under "other 4-year" or 2-year, depending on the level reported by the institution.
SOURCE: U.S. Department of Education, National Center for Education Statistics, 2004–05 Integrated Postsecondary Education Data System (IPEDS), Fall 2004. (This table was prepared August 2005.)

Scores on Graduate Record Examination (GRE) and subject matter tests: 1965 through 2004

Academic year ending	Number of GRE takers	GRE takers as a percent of bachelor's degrees[1]	Verbal	Quantitative	Analytical reasoning	Analytical writing	Biochemistry, cell and molecular biology	Biology	Chemistry	Computer science	Education	Engineering	Literature	Mathematics	Physics	Psychology
1	2	3	4	5	6	7	8	9	10	11	12	13	14	15	16	17
1965	93,792	18.7	530 (124)	533 (137)	† (†)	† (†)	†	617 (117)	628 (114)	†	481 (86)	618 (108)	591 (95)	— (†)	— (†)	556 (91)
1966	123,960	23.8	520 (124)	528 (133)	† (†)	† (†)	†	610 (115)	618 (110)	†	474 (87)	609 (106)	588 (94)	— (†)	— (†)	552 (91)
1967	151,134	27.0	519 (125)	528 (134)	† (†)	† (†)	†	613 (114)	615 (104)	†	476 (90)	603 (104)	582 (91)	— (†)	— (†)	553 (93)
1968	182,432	28.8	520 (124)	527 (135)	† (†)	† (†)	†	614 (114)	617 (104)	†	478 (87)	601 (105)	572 (91)	— (†)	— (†)	547 (93)
1969	206,113	28.3	515 (124)	524 (132)	† (†)	† (†)	†	613 (112)	613 (104)	†	477 (88)	591 (103)	569 (89)	— (†)	— (†)	543 (89)
1970	265,359	33.5	503 (123)	516 (132)	† (†)	† (†)	†	603 (111)	613 (113)	†	462 (92)	586 (110)	556 (90)	— (†)	— (†)	532 (91)
1971	293,600	35.0	497 (125)	512 (134)	† (†)	† (†)	†	603 (114)	618 (117)	†	457 (95)	587 (115)	546 (91)	— (†)	— (†)	530 (92)
1972	293,506	33.1	494 (126)	508 (136)	† (†)	† (†)	†	606 (115)	624 (124)	†	446 (93)	594 (119)	544 (96)	— (†)	— (†)	528 (92)
1973	290,104	31.5	497 (125)	512 (135)	† (†)	† (†)	†	619 (110)	630 (114)	†	459 (96)	593 (114)	545 (96)	— (†)	— (†)	529 (92)
1974	301,070	31.8	492 (126)	509 (137)	† (†)	† (†)	†	624 (110)	634 (115)	†	452 (93)	591 (121)	547 (99)	— (†)	— (†)	530 (95)
1975	298,335	32.3	493 (125)	508 (137)	† (†)	† (†)	†	— (†)	— (†)	—	— (†)	— (†)	— (†)	— (†)	— (†)	— (†)
1976	299,292	32.3	492 (127)	510 (138)	† (†)	† (†)	†	627 (112)	627 (107)	—	454 (93)	594 (119)	539 (101)	— (†)	— (†)	531 (93)
1977	287,715	31.3	490 (129)	514 (139)	498 (126)	† (†)	†	625 (113)	630 (109)	—	453 (93)	592 (115)	532 (101)	— (†)	— (†)	532 (95)
1978	286,383	31.1	484 (128)	518 (135)	504 (128)	† (†)	†	622 (113)	624 (108)	—	452 (91)	594 (114)	530 (102)	— (†)	— (†)	529 (97)
1979	282,482	30.7	476 (130)	517 (135)	512 (129)	† (†)	†	621 (117)	623 (104)	—	451 (89)	592 (115)	525 (102)	— (†)	— (†)	530 (97)
1980	272,281	29.3	474 (131)	522 (136)	516 (129)	† (†)	†	619 (115)	618 (105)	—	449 (90)	590 (116)	521 (105)	— (†)	— (†)	534 (98)
1981	262,855	28.1	473 (128)	523 (136)	520 (129)	† (†)	†	617 (115)	615 (103)	—	453 (90)	590 (116)	520 (99)	— (†)	— (†)	532 (97)
1982	256,381	26.9	469 (130)	533 (137)	521 (128)	† (†)	†	616 (114)	616 (105)	—	456 (89)	593 (115)	521 (100)	— (†)	— (†)	532 (97)
1983	263,674	27.2	473 (131)	541 (138)	528 (128)	† (†)	†	623 (115)	620 (105)	—	459 (90)	599 (114)	527 (98)	— (†)	— (†)	542 (95)
1984	265,221	27.2	475 (130)	541 (139)	530 (129)	† (†)	†	622 (115)	619 (102)	—	461 (90)	604 (114)	530 (97)	— (†)	— (†)	543 (96)
1985	271,972	27.8	474 (126)	545 (140)	534 (128)	† (†)	†	619 (114)	621 (101)	—	459 (89)	615 (120)	531 (95)	— (†)	— (†)	541 (95)
1986	279,428	28.3	475 (126)	552 (140)	536 (129)	† (†)	†	612 (114)	628 (106)	—	464 (87)	616 (119)	527 (96)	— (†)	— (†)	542 (97)
1987	293,560	29.6	477 (126)	550 (140)	537 (129)	† (†)	†	616 (116)	629 (104)	—	465 (86)	619 (119)	526 (95)	— (†)	— (†)	536 (95)
1988	303,703	30.5	483 (123)	557 (140)	541 (129)	† (†)	†	615 (114)	631 (108)	—	467 (85)	622 (120)	525 (94)	— (†)	— (†)	537 (94)
1989	326,096	32.0	484 (125)	560 (142)	541 (129)	† (†)	†	612 (114)	642 (117)	—	465 (87)	626 (116)	528 (91)	— (†)	— (†)	538 (95)
1990	344,572	32.8	486 (123)	562 (143)	544 (131)	† (†)	†	612 (114)	662 (123)	—	461 (84)	617 (111)	523 (92)	— (†)	— (†)	537 (95)
1991	379,882	34.7	485 (122)	562 (141)	549 (131)	† (†)	†	609 (113)	660 (123)	—	457 (85)	611 (111)	523 (93)	— (†)	— (†)	535 (95)
1992	411,528	36.2	483 (120)	561 (140)	548 (129)	† (†)	†	605 (113)	654 (128)	—	462 (82)	610 (117)	525 (92)	— (†)	— (†)	536 (95)
1993	400,246	34.4	481 (117)	557 (140)	543 (133)	† (†)	†	606 (114)	662 (133)	—	462 (80)	602 (115)	516 (94)	— (†)	— (†)	536 (97)
1994	399,395[2]	34.2	479 (116)	553 (139)	542 (133)	† (†)	†	620 (116)	627 (113)	—	493 (104)[3]	601 (115)	517 (95)	— (†)	— (†)	538 (96)
1995	389,539[2]	33.6	477 (115)	553 (140)	† (†)	† (†)	—	622 (116)	675 (138)	—	488 (102)[3]	596 (113)	513 (96)	— (†)	— (†)	544 (98)
1996	376,013[2]	32.3	473 (114)	558 (139)	† (†)	† (†)	—	614 (114)	678 (135)	—	489 (104)[3]	604 (119)	512 (97)	— (†)	— (†)	547 (99)
1997	376,062[2]	32.1	472 (113)	562 (139)	† (†)	† (†)	—	620 (115)	684 (143)	—	487 (103)[3]	602 (114)	525 (100)	— (†)	— (†)	554 (99)
1998	364,554[2]	30.8	471 (113)	569 (141)	† (†)	† (†)	—	628 (113)	686 (137)	—	477 (100)[3]	609 (118)	530 (100)	— (†)	— (†)	563 (100)
1999[4]	396,330	33.0	468 (114)	565 (143)	† (†)	† (†)	—	626 (114)	684 (137)	—	†[3] (†)	604 (115)	527 (100)	— (†)	— (†)	559 (99)

See notes at end of table.

Scores on Graduate Record Examination (GRE) and subject matter tests: 1965 through 2004—Continued

Academic year ending	Number of GRE takers	GRE takers as a percent of bachelor's degrees[1]	Verbal	Quantitative	Analytical reasoning	Analytical writing	Subject matter tests Biochemistry, cell and molecular biology	Biology	Chemistry	Computer science	Education	Engineering	Literature	Mathematics	Physics	Psychology
1	2	3	4	5	6	7	8	9	10	11	12	13	14	15	16	17
2000[4]	340,785	27.5	465 (116)	578 (147)	562 (141)	†	— (†)	629 (114)	686 (133)	— (†)	† (†)	—	530 (99)	— (†)	— (†)	563 (98)
2001	384,205	—	— (†)	— (†)	— (†)	†	— (†)	— (†)	— (†)	— (†)	† (†)	†	— (†)	— (†)	— (†)	— (†)
2002	507,216	39.3	473 (123)	597 (151)	571 (139)	†	— (†)	— (†)	— (†)	— (†)	† (†)	†	— (†)	— (†)	— (†)	— (†)
2003[5]	563,787	41.8	470 (120)	593 (147)	†	4.2 (0.96)	517 (100)	635 (114)	682 (125)	712 (97)	† (†)	†	538 (98)	620 (131)	669 (151)	580 (101)
2004[5]	491,066	35.1	— (†)	— (†)	†	—	517 (101)	643 (115)	675 (120)	715 (93)	† (†)	†	537 (97)	621 (130)	665 (148)	586 (101)

—Not available.

†Not applicable.

[1]GRE takers include examinees from inside and outside of the United States, while the bachelor's degree recipients include U.S. institutions only.

[2]Total includes examinees who received no score on one or more general test measures.

[3]Data reported for 1994 through 1998 are from the revised education test.

[4]Subject test score data reflect the three-year average for all examinees who tested between October 1 three years prior to the reported test year and September 30 of the reported test year. These data are not directly comparable with data for most other years.

[5]Subject test score data reflect the three-year average for all examinees who tested between July 1 three years prior to the reported test year and June 30 of the reported test year. These data are not directly comparable with previous years, except for 1999 and 2000.

NOTE: GRE data include test takers from both within and outside of the United States. GRE scores for the verbal, quantitative, and analytical reasoning sections range from 200 to 800. Scores for the analytical writing section range from 0 to 6, in half-point increments. The range of scores is different for the various subject tests, from as low as 200 to as high as 990. The analytical reasoning section of the GRE, a multiple-choice test, was discontinued in September 2002, and replaced by the analytical writing section, an essay-based test. The education subject test was administered for the final time in April 1998. The engineering subject test was administered for the final time in April 2001. Some data have been revised from previously published figures. Standard deviations appear in parentheses.

SOURCE: Graduate Record Examination Board, Examinee and Score Trends for the GRE General Test, 1964–65 through 1985–86; A Summary of Data Collected From Graduate Record Examinations Test-Takers During 1986–87; Guide to the Use of Scores, 1987–88 through 2001–02; Sex, Race, Ethnicity, and Performance on the GRE General Test, 2000–01 through 2001–02; Factors That Can Influence Performance on the GRE General Test, 2003; GRE Volumes by Country 2000–04, 2005; and unpublished tabulations. U.S. Department of Education, National Center for Education Statistics, Higher Education General Information Survey (HEGIS), "Degrees and Other Formal Awards Conferred" surveys, 1964–65 through 1985–86, and 1986–87 through 2003–04; Integrated Postsecondary Education Data System (IPEDS), "Completions Survey" (IPEDS-C:87–99), and Fall 2000 through Fall 2004. (This table was prepared August 2005.)

Percentage of degree-granting institutions with first-year undergraduates using various selection criteria for admission, by type and control of institution: Selected years, 2000–01 through 2004–05

	All institutions			Public institutions			Private institutions								
										Not-for-profit			For-profit		
Selection criteria	Total	4-year	2-year	Total	4-year	2-year	Total	4-year	2-year	Total	4-year	2-year	Total	4-year	2-year
1	2	3	4	5	6	7	8	9	10	11	12	13	14	15	16
	Number of institutions with first-year undergraduates														
2000–01	3,717	2,034	1,683	1,647	580	1,067	2,070	1,454	616	1,383	1,247	136	687	207	480
2002–03	3,796	2,105	1,691	1,655	577	1,078	2,141	1,528	613	1,392	1,268	124	749	260	489
2003–04	3,861	2,158	1,703	1,665	580	1,085	2,196	1,578	618	1,383	1,265	118	813	313	500
2004–05	3,835	2,158	1,677	1,644	584	1,060	2,191	1,574	617	1,355	1,245	110	836	329	507
	Percent of institutions														
Open admissions															
2000–01	40.2	12.9	73.2	63.8	12.1	91.9	21.4	13.3	40.7	14.0	11.7	34.6	36.5	22.7	42.5
2002–03	43.3	16.2	76.9	66.5	12.5	95.4	25.3	17.7	44.4	14.6	12.5	36.3	45.3	43.1	46.4
2003–04	43.6	16.9	77.3	66.5	12.9	95.2	26.1	18.4	46.0	14.5	12.6	33.9	46.0	41.5	48.8
2004–05	44.0	17.1	78.1	65.2	13.3	93.0	27.9	18.4	51.9	14.7	12.6	37.3	50.3	42.2	55.4
Some admission requirements[1]															
2000–01	58.4	85.8	25.1	35.4	87.4	7.1	76.6	85.2	56.3	84.5	86.8	63.2	60.7	75.4	54.4
2002–03	55.4	82.5	21.6	33.2	87.0	4.5	72.5	80.8	51.9	84.0	86.1	62.1	51.1	54.6	49.3
2003–04	55.2	82.1	21.1	33.1	86.6	4.5	72.0	80.5	50.3	84.5	86.4	64.4	50.7	56.5	47.0
2004–05	54.2	82.3	18.7	33.3	87.2	4.5	70.1	80.5	43.5	82.8	85.5	54.2	48.5	60.4	41.0
Secondary grades															
2000–01	34.6	58.7	5.5	23.9	63.4	2.4	43.0	56.7	10.7	60.1	64.1	23.5	8.7	12.6	7.1
2002–03	34.3	58.1	4.8	24.2	65.5	2.1	42.1	55.2	9.5	61.4	64.6	28.2	6.4	9.6	4.7
2003–04	33.9	57.0	4.5	24.6	66.6	2.1	40.9	53.5	8.6	61.5	64.7	27.1	5.9	8.6	4.2
2004–05	34.2	57.7	4.3	25.1	68.3	2.0	41.0	53.9	8.3	61.0	64.5	23.7	7.0	10.9	4.6
Secondary class rank															
2000–01	13.7	24.3	1.0	10.9	30.3	0.3	16.0	21.9	2.3	23.2	25.1	5.9	1.6	2.4	1.3
2002–03	12.5	21.9	0.7	10.5	29.8	0.2	14.0	18.9	1.6	21.0	22.6	5.6	0.8	1.2	0.6
2003–04	11.8	20.5	0.7	10.3	29.3	0.2	12.8	17.2	1.6	19.8	21.1	5.9	1.0	1.6	0.6
2004–05	11.6	20.2	0.7	10.5	29.8	0.2	12.4	16.7	1.6	19.2	20.4	5.9	1.0	1.6	0.6
Secondary school record															
2000–01	45.8	70.3	16.2	29.4	72.9	5.8	58.7	69.2	34.1	73.2	75.5	52.2	29.5	30.9	29.0
2002–03	48.3	73.1	17.4	29.2	75.7	4.4	63.0	72.1	40.3	76.4	78.3	57.3	38.1	41.9	36.0
2003–04	48.6	73.4	17.3	29.5	77.1	4.1	63.1	72.1	40.3	77.2	78.9	59.3	39.1	44.4	35.8
2004–05	48.3	74.3	15.3	30.0	78.3	4.2	62.1	72.8	34.6	76.4	78.8	50.8	37.6	48.6	30.8
College preparatory program															
2000–01	15.5	27.3	1.2	16.2	44.0	1.1	14.9	20.7	1.3	22.1	24.1	4.4	0.4	0.5	0.4
2002–03	15.7	27.6	0.8	17.3	47.8	1.0	14.4	20.0	0.5	22.1	24.1	2.4	0.1	0.4	0.0
2003–04	15.5	27.2	0.8	17.5	48.4	0.9	14.0	19.3	0.5	22.2	24.0	2.5	0.1	0.3	0.0
2004–05	15.6	27.4	0.6	17.3	48.1	0.8	14.3	19.8	0.3	22.6	24.6	1.7	0.2	0.6	0.0
Recommendations															
2000–01	20.4	34.4	3.5	2.7	7.4	0.2	34.4	45.1	9.3	46.6	49.2	22.8	10.0	20.8	5.4
2002–03	20.0	33.8	2.9	3.1	8.5	0.3	33.1	43.4	7.5	48.4	51.1	21.0	4.7	5.8	4.1
2003–04	19.7	33.0	2.8	2.8	7.6	0.3	32.5	42.4	7.1	49.2	51.8	22.0	3.9	4.5	3.6
2004–05	19.2	32.5	2.3	2.9	7.9	0.2	31.6	41.6	6.1	47.9	50.7	18.6	3.8	4.8	3.2
Demonstration of competencies[2]															
2000–01	8.0	12.1	3.0	2.2	5.0	0.7	12.7	15.0	7.1	12.1	12.7	7.4	13.7	29.0	7.1
2002–03	7.0	9.5	3.8	2.5	6.8	0.3	10.4	10.5	10.1	9.8	10.2	5.6	11.6	12.3	11.2
2003–04	7.1	9.5	4.1	2.2	5.7	0.3	10.9	11.0	10.7	10.1	10.3	8.5	12.2	13.7	11.2
2004–05	6.9	9.5	3.5	2.2	5.9	0.3	10.4	10.9	9.1	9.7	9.9	7.6	11.6	15.0	9.4
Test scores[3]															
2000–01	47.2	72.5	16.7	33.2	83.4	5.8	58.5	68.2	35.6	70.3	73.4	41.9	34.6	36.7	33.8
2002–03	43.3	69.1	11.2	31.5	83.5	3.7	52.5	63.7	24.5	67.2	71.3	25.0	25.1	26.5	24.3
2003–04	43.3	68.5	11.4	31.3	83.1	3.6	52.4	63.1	25.1	68.4	71.5	34.7	25.2	29.1	22.8
2004–05	39.7	65.0	7.7	31.4	83.4	3.6	46.0	58.2	14.9	66.5	70.3	26.3	11.2	9.6	12.2
TOEFL[4]															
2000–01	43.4	71.2	9.9	30.2	77.4	4.6	54.0	68.7	19.2	66.2	70.1	30.9	29.3	60.4	15.8
2002–03	42.4	69.2	8.9	30.0	79.0	3.7	51.9	65.5	18.1	66.8	70.3	31.5	24.3	42.3	14.7
2003–04	42.5	69.3	8.5	30.2	79.5	3.9	51.8	65.6	16.7	67.3	70.8	29.7	25.5	44.4	13.6
2004–05	42.0	69.3	7.4	30.5	80.0	4.0	50.8	65.4	13.4	66.4	70.2	26.3	24.1	46.0	10.4
No admission requirements, only recommendations															
2000–01	1.4	1.2	1.7	0.8	0.5	0.9	1.9	1.5	2.9	1.5	1.4	2.2	2.8	1.9	3.1
2002–03	1.4	1.3	1.5	0.3	0.5	0.2	2.2	1.6	3.8	1.4	1.4	1.6	3.6	2.3	4.3
2003–04	1.2	1.0	1.5	0.4	0.5	0.3	1.9	1.1	3.7	1.0	0.9	1.7	3.3	1.9	4.2
2004–05	1.1	0.6	1.7	0.2	0.2	0.2	1.8	0.8	4.4	0.5	0.4	1.7	4.1	2.6	5.0

[1]Many institutions have more than one admission requirement.
[2]Formal demonstration of competencies (e.g. portfolios, certificates of mastery, assessment instruments).
[3]Includes SAT, ACT, or other admission tests.
[4]Test of English as a Foreign Language.

NOTE: Detail may not sum to totals because of rounding.
SOURCE: U.S. Department of Education, National Center for Education Statistics, 2000–01 through 2004–05 Integrated Postsecondary Education Data System, Fall 2000 through Fall 2004. (This table was prepared August 2005.)

Total expenditures of private not-for-profit degree-granting institutions, by purpose and type of institution: 1996–97 through 2002–03

Year and type of institution	Total expenditures	Instruction	Research	Public service	Academic support	Student services	Institutional support	Auxiliary enterprises[1]	Net grant aid to students[2]	Hospitals	Independent operations	Other
1	2	3	4	5	6	7	8	9	10	11	12	13
	In thousands of current dollars											
All institutions												
1996–97	$67,399,563	$21,126,357	$6,702,520	$1,621,583	$4,942,411	$4,430,241	$8,226,648	$7,079,116	$1,529,456	—	—	$11,741,232
1997–98	69,300,699	23,404,428	7,267,877	1,672,991	5,738,254	4,903,988	9,138,895	7,698,614	1,297,749	$6,395,808	$1,782,095	—
1998–99[3]	75,516,696	25,181,848	7,779,001	1,521,440	6,349,076	5,295,059	9,901,658	8,027,492	1,222,565	7,258,939	2,979,619	—
1999–2000	80,613,037	26,012,599	8,381,926	1,446,958	6,510,951	5,688,499	10,585,850	8,300,021	1,180,882	7,355,110	2,753,679	2,396,563
2000–01	85,625,016	27,607,324	9,025,739	1,473,292	7,368,263	6,117,195	11,434,074	9,010,853	1,176,160	7,255,376	3,134,609	2,022,132
2001–02	92,192,297	29,689,041	10,035,480	1,665,884	7,802,637	6,573,185	12,068,120	9,515,829	1,188,690	7,633,043	3,397,979	2,622,409
2002–03	99,757,733	32,062,218	11,079,532	1,878,380	8,156,688	7,096,223	13,158,794	9,938,658	1,187,285	7,586,208	3,879,736	3,734,011
4-year												
1996–97	66,668,808	20,922,069	6,701,053	1,616,019	4,902,188	4,294,812	8,095,791	7,011,791	1,502,866	—	—	11,622,219
1997–98	68,677,274	23,164,693	7,267,228	1,669,650	5,704,216	4,817,585	8,988,203	7,621,887	1,276,848	6,395,610	1,771,355	—
1998–99[3]	74,805,484	24,823,398	7,778,900	1,513,641	6,308,251	5,224,455	9,766,020	7,957,265	1,198,516	7,257,021	2,978,017	—
1999–2000	79,699,659	25,744,199	8,376,568	1,438,544	6,476,338	5,590,978	10,398,914	8,228,409	1,162,570	7,355,110	2,752,019	2,176,011
2000–01	85,048,123	27,413,897	9,019,966	1,467,325	7,333,851	6,036,478	11,292,310	8,957,973	1,160,660	7,253,479	3,133,099	1,979,086
2001–02	91,612,337	29,492,583	10,035,394	1,658,781	7,768,870	6,497,127	11,914,149	9,470,557	1,173,725	7,632,942	3,396,831	2,571,376
2002–03	99,146,893	31,866,310	11,079,332	1,871,274	8,122,181	7,014,149	12,997,886	9,879,117	1,174,881	7,586,208	3,854,471	3,701,085
2-year												
1996–97	730,755	204,288	1,467	5,564	40,223	135,429	130,857	67,324	26,590	—	—	119,013
1997–98	623,424	239,735	649	3,341	34,038	86,403	150,692	76,726	20,901	198	10,740	—
1998–99[3]	711,212	358,450	101	7,799	40,826	70,603	135,638	70,226	24,049	1,917	1,602	—
1999–2000	913,378	268,400	5,358	8,415	34,612	97,521	186,936	71,612	18,311	0	1,660	220,553
2000–01	576,893	193,428	5,772	5,967	34,412	80,717	141,764	52,880	15,500	1,896	1,510	43,046
2001–02	579,960	196,459	86	7,102	33,767	76,058	153,971	45,271	14,965	100	1,147	51,033
2002–03	610,840	195,909	200	7,106	34,506	82,074	160,908	59,541	12,404	0	25,265	32,926
	Percentage distribution											
All institutions												
1996–97	100.00	31.34	9.94	2.41	7.33	6.57	12.21	10.50	2.27	—	—	17.42
1997–98	100.00	33.77	10.49	2.41	8.28	7.08	13.19	11.11	1.87	9.23	2.57	—
1998–99[3]	100.00	33.35	10.30	2.01	8.41	7.01	13.11	10.63	1.62	9.61	3.95	—
1999–2000	100.00	32.27	10.40	1.79	8.08	7.06	13.13	10.30	1.46	9.12	3.42	2.97
2000–01	100.00	32.24	10.54	1.72	8.61	7.14	13.35	10.52	1.37	8.47	3.66	2.36
2001–02	100.00	32.20	10.89	1.81	8.46	7.13	13.09	10.32	1.29	8.28	3.69	2.84
2002–03	100.00	32.14	11.11	1.88	8.18	7.11	13.19	9.96	1.19	7.60	3.89	3.74
4-year												
1996–97	100.00	31.38	10.05	2.42	7.35	6.44	12.14	10.52	2.25	—	—	17.43
1997–98	100.00	33.73	10.58	2.43	8.31	7.01	13.09	11.10	1.86	9.31	2.58	—
1998–99[3]	100.00	33.18	10.40	2.02	8.43	6.98	13.06	10.64	1.60	9.70	3.98	—
1999–2000	100.00	32.30	10.51	1.80	8.13	7.02	13.05	10.32	1.46	9.23	3.45	2.73
2000–01	100.00	32.23	10.61	1.73	8.62	7.10	13.28	10.53	1.36	8.53	3.68	2.33
2001–02	100.00	32.19	10.95	1.81	8.48	7.09	13.00	10.34	1.28	8.33	3.71	2.81
2002–03	100.00	32.14	11.17	1.89	8.19	7.07	13.11	9.96	1.18	7.65	3.89	3.73
2-year												
1996–97	100.00	27.96	0.20	0.76	5.50	18.53	17.91	9.21	3.64	—	—	16.29
1997–98	100.00	38.45	0.10	0.54	5.46	13.86	24.17	12.31	3.35	0.03	1.72	—
1998–99[3]	100.00	50.40	0.01	1.10	5.74	9.93	19.07	9.87	3.38	0.27	0.23	—
1999–2000	100.00	29.39	0.59	0.92	3.79	10.68	20.47	7.84	2.00	0.00	0.18	24.15
2000–01	100.00	33.53	1.00	1.03	5.96	13.99	24.57	9.17	2.69	0.33	0.26	7.46
2001–02	100.00	33.87	0.01	1.22	5.82	13.11	26.55	7.81	2.58	0.02	0.20	8.80
2002–03	100.00	32.07	0.03	1.16	5.65	13.44	26.34	9.75	2.03	0.00	4.14	5.39
	Expenditure per full-time-equivalent student in current dollars											
All institutions												
1996–97	$27,880	$8,739	$2,772	$671	$2,044	$1,833	$3,403	$2,928	$633	—	—	$4,857
1997–98	28,270	9,547	2,965	682	2,341	2,000	3,728	3,141	529	$2,609	$727	—
1998–99[3]	30,291	10,101	3,120	610	2,547	2,124	3,972	3,220	490	2,912	1,195	—
1999–2000	31,751	10,246	3,301	570	2,564	2,241	4,169	3,269	465	2,897	1,085	944
2000–01	33,069	10,662	3,486	569	2,846	2,363	4,416	3,480	454	2,802	1,211	781
2001–02	34,841	11,220	3,793	630	2,949	2,484	4,561	3,596	449	2,885	1,284	991
2002–03	36,482	11,725	4,052	687	2,983	2,595	4,812	3,635	434	2,774	1,419	1,366

See notes at end of table.

Total expenditures of private not-for-profit degree-granting institutions, by purpose and type of institution: 1996–97 through 2002–03—Continued

Year and type of institution	Total expenditures	Instruction	Research	Public service	Academic support	Student services	Institutional support	Auxiliary enterprises[1]	Net grant aid to students[2]	Hospitals	Independent operations	Other
1	2	3	4	5	6	7	8	9	10	11	12	13
4-year												
1996–97	28,327	8,890	2,847	687	2,083	1,825	3,440	2,979	639	—	—	4,938
1997–98	28,740	9,694	3,041	699	2,387	2,016	3,761	3,190	534	2,676	741	—
1998–99[3]	30,706	10,189	3,193	621	2,589	2,145	4,009	3,266	492	2,979	1,222	—
1999–2000	32,064	10,357	3,370	579	2,605	2,249	4,184	3,310	468	2,959	1,107	875
2000–01	33,359	10,753	3,538	576	2,877	2,368	4,429	3,514	455	2,845	1,229	776
2001–02	35,139	11,312	3,849	636	2,980	2,492	4,570	3,633	450	2,928	1,303	986
2002–03	36,746	11,810	4,106	694	3,010	2,600	4,817	3,661	435	2,812	1,429	1,372
2-year												
1996–97	11,426	3,194	23	87	629	2,118	2,046	1,053	416	—	—	1,861
1997–98	10,094	3,882	11	54	551	1,399	2,440	1,242	338	3	174	—
1998–99[3]	12,514	6,307	2	137	718	1,242	2,387	1,236	423	34	28	—
1999–2000	17,148	5,039	101	158	650	1,831	3,510	1,345	344	0	31	4,141
2000–01	14,494	4,860	145	150	865	2,028	3,562	1,329	389	48	38	1,081
2001–02	14,890	5,044	2	182	867	1,953	3,953	1,162	384	3	29	1,310
2002–03	16,846	5,403	6	196	952	2,263	4,438	1,642	342	0	697	908
Expenditure per full-time-equivalent student in constant 2004–05 dollars[4]												
All institutions												
1996–97	$33,631	$10,542	$3,344	$809	$2,466	$2,211	$4,105	$3,532	$763	—	—	$5,859
1997–98	33,505	11,315	3,514	809	2,774	2,371	4,418	3,722	627	$3,092	$862	—
1998–99[3]	35,289	11,768	3,635	711	2,967	2,474	4,627	3,751	571	3,392	1,392	—
1999–2000	35,952	11,601	3,738	645	2,904	2,537	4,721	3,702	527	3,280	1,228	1,069
2000–01	36,205	11,673	3,816	623	3,116	2,587	4,835	3,810	497	3,068	1,325	855
2001–02	37,481	12,070	4,080	677	3,172	2,672	4,906	3,869	483	3,103	1,381	1,066
2002–03	38,402	12,342	4,265	723	3,140	2,732	5,066	3,826	457	2,920	1,494	1,437
4-year												
1996–97	34,171	10,724	3,435	828	2,513	2,201	4,149	3,594	770	—	—	5,957
1997–98	34,062	11,489	3,604	828	2,829	2,389	4,458	3,780	633	3,172	879	—
1998–99[3]	35,773	11,871	3,720	724	3,017	2,498	4,670	3,805	573	3,470	1,424	—
1999–2000	36,306	11,728	3,816	655	2,950	2,547	4,737	3,748	530	3,351	1,254	991
2000–01	36,522	11,772	3,873	630	3,149	2,592	4,849	3,847	498	3,115	1,345	850
2001–02	37,801	12,169	4,141	684	3,206	2,681	4,916	3,908	484	3,150	1,402	1,061
2002–03	38,680	12,432	4,322	730	3,169	2,736	5,071	3,854	458	2,960	1,504	1,444
2-year												
1996–97	13,784	3,853	28	105	759	2,554	2,468	1,270	502	—	—	2,245
1997–98	11,963	4,600	12	64	653	1,658	2,892	1,472	401	4	206	—
1998–99[3]	14,579	7,348	2	160	837	1,447	2,780	1,440	493	39	33	—
1999–2000	19,417	5,706	114	179	736	2,073	3,974	1,522	389	0	35	4,689
2000–01	15,868	5,320	159	164	947	2,220	3,899	1,454	426	52	42	1,184
2001–02	16,018	5,426	2	196	933	2,101	4,253	1,250	413	3	32	1,409
2002–03	17,732	5,687	6	206	1,002	2,383	4,671	1,728	360	0	733	956

—Not available.

[1]Essentially self-supporting operations of institutions that furnish a service to students, faculty, or staff, such as residence halls and food services.

[2]Excludes tuition and fee allowances and agency transactions, such as student awards made from contributed funds or grant funds.

[3]Data were imputed using alternative procedures. (See Guide to Sources for details.)

[4]Constant dollars based on the Consumer Price Index, prepared by the Bureau of Labor Statistics, U.S. Department of Labor, adjusted to a school-year basis.

NOTE: Detail may not sum to totals because of rounding.

SOURCE: U.S. Department of Education, National Center for Education Statistics, 1996–97 through 2002–03 Integrated Postsecondary Education Data System, "Fall Enrollment Survey" (IPEDS-EF:96–99) and "Finance Survey" (IPEDS-F:FY97–99), and Spring 2001 through Spring 2004. (This table was prepared February 2006.)

Total expenditures of private not-for-profit degree-granting institutions, by purpose and type of institution: 2002–03

Type of institution	Total expenditures	Instruction	Research	Public service	Academic support	Student services	Institutional support	Auxiliary enterprises[1]	Net grant aid to students[2]	Hospitals	Independent operations	Other
1	2	3	4	5	6	7	8	9	10	11	12	13
In thousands of current dollars												
Total	$99,757,733	$32,062,218	$11,079,532	$1,878,380	$8,156,688	$7,096,223	$13,158,794	$9,938,658	$1,187,285	$7,586,208	$3,879,736	$3,734,011
4-year	99,146,893	31,866,310	11,079,332	1,871,274	8,122,181	7,014,149	12,997,886	9,879,117	1,174,881	7,586,208	3,854,471	3,701,085
Doctoral, extensive[3]	48,662,324	14,686,125	9,063,188	677,344	3,556,282	1,735,140	4,293,260	3,884,887	340,383	6,407,547	3,523,156	495,011
Doctoral, intensive[4]	7,417,914	2,839,130	592,943	234,376	1,017,141	577,163	1,124,708	807,653	78,993	0	47,540	98,268
Master's[5]	15,870,186	6,183,203	214,747	202,987	1,560,350	2,000,170	2,933,818	2,166,393	221,746	97,567	130,161	159,044
Baccalaureate[6]	14,492,163	5,051,232	128,140	145,887	1,277,136	2,053,186	2,773,685	2,422,846	319,812	0	73,924	246,316
Specialized institutions[7]	12,704,306	3,106,620	1,080,314	610,680	711,272	648,490	1,872,415	597,338	213,948	1,081,094	79,690	2,702,446
Art, music, or design	1,287,191	483,044	592	19,718	107,286	105,322	233,890	116,009	75,225	0	21,797	124,307
Business and management	712,037	225,057	4,003	10,301	97,903	110,086	159,176	73,408	16,817	0	8,426	6,860
Engineering or technology	437,132	146,058	46,725	2,593	28,871	33,771	100,130	34,794	7,089	0	2,782	34,319
Medical or other health	6,978,732	1,286,851	1,017,907	524,647	207,622	117,030	698,495	116,862	27,886	1,080,526	32,058	1,868,848
Theological	1,435,288	441,191	3,862	27,531	129,454	121,159	383,525	165,682	61,822	305	13,028	87,729
Tribal[8]	30,823	10,562	0	4,203	1,588	1,804	5,389	1,422	4,064	0	0	1,792
Other specialized	1,823,103	513,856	7,226	21,686	138,549	159,318	291,810	89,160	21,045	262	1,599	578,591
2-year	610,840	195,909	200	7,106	34,506	82,074	160,908	59,541	12,404	0	25,265	32,926
Associate's of arts	557,573	185,084	92	3,937	29,624	75,167	145,839	57,329	10,250	0	25,265	24,986
Tribal[8]	53,267	10,824	108	3,170	4,882	6,907	15,070	2,212	2,154	0	0	7,940
Percentage distribution												
Total	100.00	32.14	11.11	1.88	8.18	7.11	13.19	9.96	1.19	7.60	3.89	3.74
4-year	100.00	32.14	11.17	1.89	8.19	7.07	13.11	9.96	1.18	7.65	3.89	3.73
Doctoral, extensive[3]	100.00	30.18	18.62	1.39	7.31	3.57	8.82	7.98	0.70	13.17	7.24	1.02
Doctoral, intensive[4]	100.00	38.27	7.99	3.16	13.71	7.78	15.16	10.89	1.06	0.00	0.64	1.32
Master's[5]	100.00	38.96	1.35	1.28	9.83	12.60	18.49	13.65	1.40	0.61	0.82	1.00
Baccalaureate[6]	100.00	34.85	0.88	1.01	8.81	14.17	19.14	16.72	2.21	0.00	0.51	1.70
Specialized institutions[7]	100.00	24.45	8.50	4.81	5.60	5.10	14.74	4.70	1.68	8.51	0.63	21.27
Art, music, or design	100.00	37.53	0.05	1.53	8.33	8.18	18.17	9.01	5.84	0.00	1.69	9.66
Business and management	100.00	31.61	0.56	1.45	13.75	15.46	22.36	10.31	2.36	0.00	1.18	0.96
Engineering or technology	100.00	33.41	10.69	0.59	6.60	7.73	22.91	7.96	1.62	0.00	0.64	7.85
Medical or other health	100.00	18.44	14.59	7.52	2.98	1.68	10.01	1.67	0.40	15.48	0.46	26.78
Theological	100.00	30.74	0.27	1.92	9.02	8.44	26.72	11.54	4.31	0.02	0.91	6.11
Tribal[8]	100.00	34.27	0.00	13.64	5.15	5.85	17.48	4.61	13.18	0.00	0.00	5.81
Other specialized	100.00	28.19	0.40	1.19	7.60	8.74	16.01	4.89	1.15	0.01	0.09	31.74
2-year	100.00	32.07	0.03	1.16	5.65	13.44	26.34	9.75	2.03	0.00	4.14	5.39
Associate's of arts	100.00	33.19	0.02	0.71	5.31	13.48	26.16	10.28	1.84	0.00	4.53	4.48
Tribal[8]	100.00	20.32	0.20	5.95	9.17	12.97	28.29	4.15	4.04	0.00	0.00	14.91
Expenditure per full-time-equivalent student												
Total	$36,482	$11,725	$4,052	$687	$2,983	$2,595	$4,812	$3,635	$434	$2,774	$1,419	$1,366
4-year	36,746	11,810	4,106	694	3,010	2,600	4,817	3,661	435	2,812	1,429	1,372
Doctoral, extensive[3]	82,571	24,920	15,379	1,149	6,034	2,944	7,285	6,592	578	10,872	5,978	840
Doctoral, intensive[4]	28,356	10,853	2,267	896	3,888	2,206	4,299	3,087	302	0	182	376
Master's[5]	17,817	6,942	241	228	1,752	2,246	3,294	2,432	249	110	146	179
Baccalaureate[6]	22,652	7,895	200	228	1,996	3,209	4,335	3,787	500	0	116	385
Specialized institutions[7]	40,115	9,810	3,411	1,928	2,246	2,048	5,912	1,886	676	3,414	252	8,533
Art, music, or design	28,456	10,679	13	436	2,372	2,328	5,171	2,565	1,663	0	482	2,748
Business and management	15,074	4,765	85	218	2,073	2,331	3,370	1,554	356	0	178	145
Engineering or technology	26,879	8,981	2,873	159	1,775	2,077	6,157	2,139	436	0	171	2,110
Medical or other health	121,135	22,337	17,669	9,107	3,604	2,031	12,124	2,028	484	18,756	556	32,439
Theological	19,966	6,137	54	383	1,801	1,685	5,335	2,305	860	4	181	1,220
Tribal[8]	20,869	7,151	0	2,846	1,075	1,221	3,648	963	2,751	0	0	1,213
Other specialized	23,681	6,675	94	282	1,800	2,069	3,790	1,158	273	3	21	7,516
2-year	16,846	5,403	6	196	952	2,263	4,438	1,642	342	0	697	908
Associate's of arts	16,087	5,340	3	114	855	2,169	4,208	1,654	296	0	729	721
Tribal[8]	33,250	6,757	67	1,979	3,047	4,311	9,407	1,381	1,345	0	0	4,956

[1]Essentially self-supporting operations of institutions that furnish a service to students, faculty, or staff, such as residence halls and food services.

[2]Excludes tuition and fee allowances and agency transactions, such as student awards made from contributed funds or grant funds.

[3]Doctoral, extensive institutions are committed to graduate education through the doctorate, and award 50 or more doctor's degrees per year across at least 15 disciplines.

[4]Doctoral, intensive institutions are committed to education through the doctorate, and award at least 10 doctor's degrees per year across 3 or more disciplines or at least 20 doctor's degrees overall.

[5]Master's institutions offer a full range of baccalaureate programs and are committed to education through the master's degree. They award at least 20 master's degrees per year.

[6]Baccalaureate institutions primarily emphasize undergraduate education.

[7]Specialized 4-year institutions award degrees primarily in single fields of study, such as medicine, business, fine arts, theology, and engineering. Includes some institutions that have 4-year programs, but have not reported sufficient data to identify program category. Also includes institutions classified as 4-year under the IPEDS system, which had been classified as 2-year in the Carnegie system because they primarily award associate's degrees.

[8]Tribally controlled colleges are located on reservations and are members of the American Indian Higher Education Consortium.

NOTE: Detail may not sum to totals because of rounding.

SOURCE: U.S. Department of Education, National Center for Education Statistics, 2002–03 Integrated Postsecondary Education Data System (IPEDS), Spring 2003 and Spring 2004. (This table was prepared August 2005.)

Total expenditures of private not-for-profit and for-profit degree-granting institutions, by level and state or jurisdiction: 1996–97 through 2002–03
[In thousands of current dollars]

State or jurisdiction	Not-for-profit institutions									For-profit institutions	
	1996–97	1997–98	1998–99	1999–2000	2000–01	2001–02	2002–03 Total	4-year	2-year	2001–02	2002–03
1	2	3	4	5	6	7	8	9	10	11	12
United States	**$67,399,563**	**$69,300,699**	**$75,516,696**	**$80,613,037**	**$85,625,016**	**$92,192,297**	**$99,757,733**	**$99,146,893**	**$610,840**	**$5,087,292**	**$6,112,791**
Alabama	303,786	351,948	366,326	393,465	400,987	419,872	435,190	428,948	6,242	35,639	40,885
Alaska	15,033	10,202	16,663	19,042	19,106	19,823	20,561	20,561	†	4,109	3,975
Arizona	73,447	117,603	129,980	143,698	160,787	162,471	182,548	179,106	3,441	462,998	606,684
Arkansas	151,209	160,182	164,307	230,860	197,313	213,645	216,809	215,496	1,313	8,418	8,815
California	6,952,432	5,740,704	7,417,634	7,871,651	8,682,192	9,588,524	10,268,563	10,137,881	130,682	836,835	970,021
Colorado	293,573	303,769	335,298	376,887	399,613	430,242	450,245	447,119	3,126	180,798	202,309
Connecticut	1,688,760	1,792,100	1,894,898	2,094,981	2,193,752	2,343,067	2,517,664	2,513,285	4,379	22,009	24,930
Delaware	36,143	37,647	43,320	52,533	56,670	62,625	70,783	68,300	2,484	†	†
District of Columbia	2,542,826	2,492,285	2,641,207	2,267,409	2,230,368	2,387,245	2,530,695	2,530,695	†	78,861	96,971
Florida	1,683,998	1,776,443	1,905,829	2,031,623	2,247,374	2,472,362	2,695,985	2,681,075	14,909	399,232	555,859
Georgia	1,857,238	2,289,149	2,508,080	2,635,438	2,795,105	2,946,777	3,188,042	3,165,206	22,836	168,316	270,926
Hawaii	112,706	111,103	122,340	209,135	138,660	146,050	152,348	152,348	†	13,647	16,924
Idaho	101,342	104,558	110,393	118,150	130,256	139,029	147,022	147,022	†	7,417	8,369
Illinois	4,520,613	4,720,747	5,130,189	5,668,566	5,910,538	6,188,489	6,304,076	6,293,535	10,541	247,570	322,046
Indiana	1,105,549	1,125,545	1,246,522	1,343,315	1,425,665	1,525,312	1,612,609	1,599,669	12,940	129,166	136,851
Iowa	669,201	673,346	689,698	740,760	767,891	800,428	847,857	837,020	10,836	32,563	30,287
Kansas	184,317	187,707	196,897	208,729	222,036	232,720	237,781	224,966	12,814	4,973	7,356
Kentucky	338,377	347,011	375,598	400,513	406,358	437,092	458,584	452,900	5,684	68,198	78,431
Louisiana	614,566	673,645	692,914	746,629	773,107	828,300	876,419	876,419	†	40,429	52,983
Maine	255,458	271,228	290,439	316,114	341,350	373,835	384,085	383,247	839	7,089	5,171
Maryland	1,897,904	1,994,345	2,113,725	2,205,880	2,410,284	2,725,616	3,019,626	3,018,157	1,469	21,577	25,306
Massachusetts	6,378,048	6,845,932	7,218,867	7,591,344	8,187,834	8,831,619	9,506,793	9,487,775	19,018	27,453	44,673
Michigan	924,441	901,576	936,454	995,384	1,065,100	1,134,361	1,206,723	1,204,114	2,609	35,959	37,532
Minnesota	807,941	874,507	930,959	1,004,427	1,093,937	1,164,763	1,157,173	1,137,542	19,631	180,115	216,771
Mississippi	129,996	130,497	136,859	150,123	156,292	158,464	167,822	167,822	†	4,156	5,363
Missouri	1,923,345	1,988,750	2,019,795	2,144,299	2,380,876	2,561,036	3,355,385	3,309,810	45,576	134,260	126,696
Montana	57,356	57,049	64,772	69,426	74,446	72,297	78,561	70,931	7,629	†	†
Nebraska	326,591	338,473	355,512	387,569	422,879	445,634	840,326	837,290	3,036	14,214	14,444
Nevada	6,828	7,440	7,679	7,006	9,130	10,919	9,657	9,657	†	34,788	43,598
New Hampshire	497,014	523,575	572,609	589,823	654,213	719,549	786,283	786,283	†	36,832	37,787
New Jersey	1,133,757	1,160,843	1,252,181	1,362,090	1,479,492	1,588,295	1,641,561	1,639,941	1,620	73,205	74,683
New Mexico	36,130	51,204	47,256	54,280	63,824	60,571	59,119	51,461	7,659	35,067	32,449
New York	10,577,464	10,525,903	11,511,493	12,519,671	13,099,910	14,177,942	15,801,483	15,749,209	52,274	462,997	540,167
North Carolina	2,617,089	2,761,327	3,292,928	3,530,337	3,845,125	3,978,481	4,224,812	4,214,447	10,365	18,562	24,574
North Dakota	42,576	45,200	51,613	56,000	59,677	63,207	68,513	46,843	21,671	1,785	2,012
Ohio	1,791,534	1,912,254	2,017,835	2,211,035	2,368,824	2,530,980	2,637,737	2,627,753	9,984	151,129	167,023
Oklahoma	310,567	323,212	319,214	338,276	360,772	363,611	370,604	370,604	†	42,195	49,721
Oregon	362,663	398,742	424,420	456,683	447,516	473,270	487,996	487,996	†	44,821	57,669
Pennsylvania	6,417,195	6,952,322	7,219,858	7,590,629	7,841,530	8,397,080	8,894,900	8,791,678	103,222	361,163	401,065
Rhode Island	669,548	696,398	737,297	828,715	897,056	978,710	1,062,719	1,062,719	†	†	†
South Carolina	332,525	366,727	392,369	408,127	432,035	483,551	507,157	496,530	10,627	11,163	13,949
South Dakota	55,944	59,837	64,155	69,555	75,488	90,290	94,117	91,623	2,493	15,592	17,721
Tennessee	1,599,099	1,804,783	1,842,893	1,971,564	2,131,732	2,367,380	2,609,840	2,603,013	6,828	82,624	91,545
Texas	1,936,660	2,080,235	2,249,979	2,490,597	2,662,275	2,921,130	3,142,104	3,128,579	13,524	206,915	247,302
Utah	523,384	553,754	610,830	648,035	694,025	741,519	785,441	779,649	5,792	45,113	49,031
Vermont	299,844	306,150	333,738	347,293	369,832	382,794	400,154	383,096	17,058	26,474	24,224
Virginia	786,696	833,774	891,622	944,905	1,000,236	1,057,465	1,109,551	1,109,551	†	122,616	158,870
Washington	484,063	492,504	544,781	600,315	594,393	639,129	674,622	674,622	†	74,081	84,366
West Virginia	160,524	160,681	162,994	170,653	185,101	194,652	201,085	201,085	†	17,841	19,713
Wisconsin	812,263	865,782	913,475	999,502	1,062,053	1,160,074	1,258,006	1,252,317	5,689	24,364	28,456
Wyoming	†	†	†	†	†	†	†	†	†	31,965	36,289
Other jurisdictions	**347,011**	**372,019**	**413,323**	**431,216**	**456,532**	**494,476**	**680,257**	**671,583**	**8,673**	**46,898**	**58,180**
Guam	†	†	†	†	†	1,160	1,161	1,161	†	†	†
Puerto Rico	347,011	372,019	413,323	431,216	456,532	493,316	679,096	670,422	8,673	46,898	58,180

†Not applicable.
NOTE: Detail may not sum to totals because of rounding.
SOURCE: U.S. Department of Education, National Center for Education Statistics, 1996–97 through 2002–03 Integrated Postsecondary Education Data System, "Finance Survey" (IPEDS-F:FY97–99), and Spring 2001 through Spring 2004. (This table was prepared August 2005.)

Average undergraduate tuition and fees and room and board rates charged for full-time students in degree-granting institutions, by type and control of institution: 1964–65 through 2004–05

Year and control of institution	Total tuition, room, and board					Tuition and required fees (in-state)					Dormitory rooms					Board (7-day basis)[1]				
	All institutions	All 4-year	Universities	Other 4-year	2-year	All institutions	All 4-year	Universities	Other 4-year	2-year	All institutions	All 4-year	Universities	Other 4-year	2-year	All institutions	All 4-year	Universities	Other 4-year	2-year
1	2	3	4	5	6	7	8	9	10	11	12	13	14	15	16	17	18	19	20	21
All institutions																				
1976–77	$2,275	$2,577	$2,647	$2,527	$1,598	$924	$1,218	$1,210	$1,223	$346	$603	$611	$649	$584	$503	$748	$748	$788	$719	$750
1977–78	2,411	2,725	2,777	2,685	1,703	984	1,291	1,269	1,305	378	645	654	691	628	525	781	780	818	752	801
1978–79	2,587	2,917	2,967	2,879	1,828	1,073	1,397	1,370	1,413	411	688	696	737	667	575	826	825	860	800	842
1979–80	2,809	3,167	3,223	3,124	1,979	1,163	1,513	1,484	1,530	451	751	759	803	729	628	895	895	936	865	900
1980–81	3,101	3,499	3,535	3,469	2,230	1,289	1,679	1,634	1,705	526	836	846	881	821	705	976	975	1,020	943	1,000
1981–82	3,489	3,951	4,005	3,908	2,476	1,457	1,907	1,860	1,935	590	950	961	1,023	919	793	1,083	1,082	1,121	1,055	1,094
1982–83	3,877	4,406	4,466	4,356	2,713	1,626	2,139	2,081	2,173	675	1,064	1,078	1,150	1,028	873	1,187	1,189	1,235	1,155	1,165
1983–84	4,167	4,747	4,793	4,712	2,854	1,783	2,344	2,300	2,368	730	1,145	1,162	1,211	1,130	916	1,239	1,242	1,282	1,214	1,208
1984–85	4,563	5,160	5,236	5,107	3,179	1,985	2,567	2,539	2,583	821	1,267	1,282	1,343	1,242	1,058	1,310	1,311	1,353	1,282	1,301
1985–86[2]	4,885	5,504	5,597	5,441	3,367	2,181	2,784	2,770	2,793	888	1,338	1,355	1,424	1,309	1,107	1,365	1,365	1,403	1,339	1,372
1986–87	5,206	5,964	6,124	5,857	3,295	2,312	3,042	3,042	3,042	897	1,405	1,427	1,501	1,376	1,034	1,489	1,495	1,581	1,439	1,364
1987–88	5,494	6,272	6,339	6,226	3,263	2,458	3,201	3,168	3,220	809	1,488	1,516	1,576	1,478	1,017	1,549	1,555	1,596	1,529	1,437
1988–89	5,869	6,725	6,801	6,673	3,573	2,658	3,472	3,422	3,499	979	1,575	1,609	1,665	1,573	1,085	1,636	1,644	1,715	1,601	1,509
1989–90	6,207	7,212	7,347	7,120	3,705	2,839	3,800	3,765	3,819	978	1,638	1,675	1,732	1,638	1,105	1,730	1,737	1,850	1,663	1,622
1990–91	6,562	7,602	7,709	7,528	3,930	3,016	4,009	3,958	4,036	1,087	1,743	1,782	1,848	1,740	1,182	1,802	1,811	1,903	1,751	1,660
1991–92	7,077	8,238	8,390	8,142	4,092	3,286	4,385	4,368	4,394	1,189	1,874	1,921	1,996	1,875	1,210	1,918	1,931	2,026	1,872	1,692
1992–93	7,452	8,758	8,934	8,648	4,207	3,517	4,752	4,665	4,795	1,276	1,939	1,991	2,104	1,926	1,240	1,996	2,015	2,165	1,927	1,692
1993–94	7,931	9,296	9,495	9,186	4,449	3,827	5,119	5,104	5,127	1,399	2,057	2,111	2,190	2,068	1,332	2,047	2,067	2,201	1,992	1,718
1994–95	8,306	9,728	9,863	9,646	4,633	4,044	5,391	5,287	5,441	1,488	2,145	2,200	2,281	2,155	1,396	2,116	2,138	2,295	2,049	1,750
1995–96	8,800	10,330	10,560	10,195	4,725	4,338	5,786	5,733	5,812	1,522	2,264	2,318	2,423	2,260	1,473	2,199	2,226	2,404	2,123	1,730
1996–97	9,206	10,841	11,033	10,726	4,895	4,564	6,118	6,055	6,150	1,543	2,365	2,422	2,518	2,368	1,522	2,276	2,301	2,460	2,208	1,830
1997–98	9,588	11,277	11,382	11,205	5,192	4,755	6,351	6,232	6,408	1,695	2,444	2,507	2,575	2,469	1,598	2,389	2,419	2,576	2,327	1,900
1998–99[3]	10,076	11,888	12,123	11,752	5,291	5,013	6,723	6,713	6,728	1,725	2,557	2,626	2,710	2,578	1,616	2,506	2,540	2,700	2,446	1,950
1999–2000	10,444	12,352	12,613	12,198	5,408	5,238	7,044	7,026	7,052	1,721	2,682	2,749	2,845	2,695	1,733	2,524	2,559	2,741	2,451	1,954
2000–01	10,818	12,922	13,177	12,775	5,460	5,377	7,372	7,360	7,377	1,698	2,819	2,893	2,999	2,833	1,744	2,622	2,658	2,818	2,565	2,017
2001–02	11,380	13,639	13,942	13,468	5,718	5,646	7,786	7,788	7,785	1,800	2,981	3,060	3,184	2,992	1,848	2,753	2,793	2,970	2,692	2,070
2002–03	12,014	14,439	14,827	14,233	6,252	6,002	8,309	8,406	8,264	1,903	3,179	3,263	3,377	3,201	2,077	2,832	2,867	3,044	2,767	2,272
2003–04	12,955	15,504	16,096	15,203	6,716	6,608	9,027	9,267	8,922	2,175	3,360	3,448	3,599	3,368	2,206	2,987	3,028	3,230	2,914	2,335
2004–05[4]	13,743	16,465	17,206	16,100	7,020	7,074	9,662	10,037	9,497	2,323	3,567	3,658	3,811	3,577	2,310	3,102	3,145	3,358	3,026	2,387
Public institutions																				
1964–65	950	—	1,051	867	638	243	—	298	224	99	271	—	291	241	178	436	—	462	402	361
1965–66	983	—	1,105	904	670	257	—	327	241	109	281	—	304	255	194	445	—	474	408	367
1966–67	1,026	—	1,171	947	710	275	—	360	259	121	294	—	321	271	213	457	—	490	417	376
1967–68	1,064	—	1,199	997	789	283	—	366	268	144	313	—	337	292	243	468	—	496	437	402
1968–69	1,117	—	1,245	1,063	883	295	—	377	281	170	337	—	359	318	278	485	—	509	464	435
1969–70	1,203	—	1,362	1,135	951	323	—	427	306	178	369	—	395	346	308	511	—	540	483	465
1970–71	1,287	—	1,477	1,206	998	351	—	478	332	187	401	—	431	375	338	535	—	568	499	473
1971–72	1,357	—	1,579	1,263	1,073	376	—	526	354	192	430	—	463	400	366	551	—	590	509	515
1972–73	1,458	—	1,668	1,460	1,197	407	—	566	455	233	476	—	500	455	398	575	—	602	550	566
1973–74	1,517	—	1,707	1,506	1,274	438	—	581	463	274	480	—	505	464	409	599	—	621	579	591

See notes at end of table.

Average undergraduate tuition and fees and room and board rates charged for full-time students in degree-granting institutions, by type and control of institution: 1964–65 through 2004–05—Continued

Year and control of institution	Total tuition, room, and board					Tuition and required fees (in-state)					Dormitory rooms					Board (7-day basis)[1]				
	All insti-tutions	4-year institutions			2-year	All insti-tutions	4-year institutions			2-year	All insti-tutions	4-year institutions			2-year	All insti-tutions	4-year institutions			2-year
		All 4-year	Univer-sities	Other 4-year			All 4-year	Univer-sities	Other 4-year			All 4-year	Univer-sities	Other 4-year			All 4-year	Univer-sities	Other 4-year	
1	2	3	4	5	6	7	8	9	10	11	12	13	14	15	16	17	18	19	20	21
1974–75	1,563	—	1,760	1,558	1,339	432	—	599	448	277	506	—	527	497	424	625	—	634	613	638
1975–76	1,666	—	1,935	1,657	1,386	433	—	642	469	245	544	—	573	533	442	689	—	720	655	699
1976–77	1,789	1,935	2,067	1,827	1,491	479	617	689	564	283	582	592	614	572	465	728	727	763	692	742
1977–78	1,888	2,038	2,170	1,931	1,590	512	655	736	596	306	621	631	649	616	486	755	752	785	720	797
1978–79	1,994	2,145	2,289	2,027	1,691	543	688	777	622	327	655	664	689	641	527	796	793	823	764	837
1979–80	2,165	2,327	2,487	2,198	1,822	583	738	840	662	355	715	725	750	703	574	867	865	898	833	893
1980–81	2,373	2,550	2,712	2,421	2,027	635	804	915	722	391	799	811	827	796	642	940	936	969	904	994
1981–82	2,663	2,871	3,079	2,705	2,224	714	909	1,042	813	434	909	925	970	885	703	1,039	1,036	1,067	1,006	1,086
1982–83	2,945	3,196	3,403	3,032	2,390	798	1,031	1,164	936	473	1,010	1,030	1,072	993	755	1,136	1,134	1,167	1,103	1,162
1983–84	3,156	3,433	3,628	3,285	2,534	891	1,148	1,284	1,052	528	1,087	1,110	1,131	1,092	801	1,178	1,175	1,213	1,141	1,205
1984–85	3,408	3,682	3,899	3,518	2,807	971	1,228	1,386	1,117	584	1,196	1,217	1,237	1,200	921	1,241	1,237	1,276	1,201	1,302
1985–86[2]	3,571	3,859	4,146	3,637	2,981	1,045	1,318	1,536	1,157	641	1,242	1,263	1,290	1,240	960	1,285	1,278	1,320	1,240	1,380
1986–87	3,805	4,138	4,469	3,891	2,989	1,106	1,414	1,651	1,248	660	1,301	1,323	1,355	1,295	979	1,398	1,401	1,464	1,348	1,349
1987–88	4,050	4,403	4,619	4,250	3,066	1,218	1,537	1,726	1,407	706	1,378	1,410	1,410	1,409	943	1,454	1,456	1,482	1,434	1,417
1988–89	4,274	4,678	4,905	4,526	3,183	1,285	1,646	1,846	1,515	730	1,457	1,496	1,483	1,506	965	1,533	1,536	1,576	1,504	1,488
1989–90	4,504	4,975	5,324	4,723	3,299	1,356	1,780	2,035	1,608	756	1,513	1,557	1,561	1,554	962	1,635	1,638	1,728	1,561	1,581
1990–91	4,757	5,243	5,585	5,004	3,467	1,454	1,888	2,159	1,707	824	1,612	1,657	1,658	1,655	1,050	1,691	1,698	1,767	1,641	1,594
1991–92	5,138	5,693	6,050	5,458	3,623	1,628	2,117	2,409	1,931	936	1,731	1,785	1,789	1,787	1,074	1,780	1,792	1,852	1,745	1,612
1992–93	5,379	6,020	6,442	5,740	3,799	1,782	2,349	2,604	2,192	1,025	1,756	1,816	1,856	1,787	1,106	1,841	1,854	1,982	1,761	1,668
1993–94	5,694	6,365	6,710	6,146	3,996	1,942	2,537	2,820	2,360	1,125	1,873	1,934	1,897	1,958	1,190	1,880	1,895	1,993	1,828	1,681
1994–95	5,965	6,670	7,077	6,409	4,137	2,057	2,681	2,977	2,499	1,192	1,959	2,023	1,992	2,044	1,232	1,949	1,967	2,108	1,866	1,712
1995–96	6,256	7,014	7,448	6,730	4,217	2,179	2,848	3,151	2,660	1,239	2,057	2,121	2,104	2,133	1,297	2,020	2,045	2,192	1,937	1,681
1996–97	6,530	7,334	7,792	7,035	4,404	2,271	2,987	3,323	2,778	1,276	2,148	2,214	2,187	2,232	1,339	2,111	2,133	2,282	2,025	1,789
1997–98	6,813	7,673	8,210	7,318	4,509	2,360	3,110	3,486	2,877	1,314	2,225	2,301	2,285	2,312	1,401	2,228	2,263	2,438	2,130	1,795
1998–99[3]	7,107	8,027	8,625	7,631	4,604	2,430	3,229	3,640	2,974	1,327	2,330	2,409	2,408	2,410	1,450	2,347	2,389	2,576	2,247	1,828
1999–2000	7,310	8,275	8,912	7,852	4,720	2,506	3,349	3,768	3,091	1,338	2,440	2,519	2,516	2,521	1,549	2,364	2,406	2,628	2,239	1,834
2000–01	7,586	8,653	9,321	8,218	4,839	2,562	3,501	3,979	3,208	1,333	2,569	2,654	2,657	2,652	1,600	2,455	2,499	2,686	2,358	1,906
2001–02	8,022	9,196	9,948	8,715	5,137	2,700	3,735	4,273	3,409	1,380	2,723	2,816	2,838	2,801	1,722	2,598	2,645	2,837	2,504	2,036
2002–03	8,502	9,787	10,604	9,280	5,601	2,903	4,046	4,686	3,668	1,483	2,930	3,029	3,023	3,032	1,954	2,669	2,712	2,895	2,580	2,164
2003–04	9,249	10,674	11,679	10,063	6,020	3,319	4,587	5,363	4,141	1,702	3,107	3,212	3,232	3,198	2,086	2,823	2,875	3,084	2,724	2,233
2004–05[4]	9,877	11,441	12,604	10,741	6,334	3,638	5,038	5,948	4,520	1,847	3,304	3,418	3,431	3,409	2,154	2,935	2,985	3,226	2,813	2,333
Private institutions																				
1964–65	1,907	—	2,202	1,810	1,455	1,088	—	1,297	1,023	702	331	—	390	308	289	488	—	515	479	464
1965–66	2,005	—	2,316	1,899	1,557	1,154	—	1,369	1,086	768	356	—	418	330	316	495	—	529	483	473
1966–67	2,124	—	2,456	2,007	1,679	1,233	—	1,456	1,162	845	385	—	452	355	347	506	—	548	490	487
1967–68	2,205	—	2,545	2,104	1,762	1,297	—	1,534	1,237	892	392	—	455	366	366	516	—	556	501	504
1968–69	2,321	—	2,673	2,237	1,876	1,383	—	1,638	1,335	956	404	—	463	382	391	534	—	572	520	529
1969–70	2,530	—	2,920	2,420	1,993	1,533	—	1,809	1,468	1,034	436	—	503	409	413	561	—	608	543	546
1970–71	2,738	—	3,163	2,599	2,103	1,684	—	1,980	1,603	1,109	468	—	542	434	434	586	—	641	562	560
1971–72	2,917	—	3,375	2,748	2,186	1,820	—	2,133	1,721	1,172	494	—	576	454	449	603	—	666	573	565
1972–73	3,038	—	3,512	2,934	2,273	1,898	—	2,226	1,846	1,221	524	—	622	490	457	616	—	664	598	595
1973–74	3,164	—	3,717	3,040	2,410	1,989	—	2,375	1,925	1,303	533	—	622	502	483	642	—	720	613	624

See notes at end of table.

Average undergraduate tuition and fees and room and board rates charged for full-time students in degree-granting institutions, by type and control of institution: 1964–65 through 2004–05—Continued

Year and control of institution	Total tuition, room, and board					Tuition and required fees (in-state)					Dormitory rooms					Board (7-day basis)[1]				
	All insti-tutions	4-year institutions			2-year	All insti-tutions	4-year institutions			2-year	All insti-tutions	4-year institutions			2-year	All insti-tutions	4-year institutions			2-year
		All 4-year	Univer-sities	Other 4-year			All 4-year	Univer-sities	Other 4-year			All 4-year	Univer-sities	Other 4-year			All 4-year	Univer-sities	Other 4-year	
1	2	3	4	5	6	7	8	9	10	11	12	13	14	15	16	17	18	19	20	21
1974–75	3,403	—	4,076	3,156	2,591	2,117	—	2,614	1,954	1,367	586	—	691	536	564	700	—	771	666	660
1975–76	3,663	—	4,467	3,385	2,711	2,272	—	2,881	2,084	1,427	636	—	753	583	572	755	—	833	718	712
1976–77	3,906	3,977	4,715	3,714	2,971	2,467	2,534	3,051	2,351	1,592	649	651	783	604	607	790	791	882	759	772
1977–78	4,158	4,240	5,033	3,967	3,148	2,624	2,700	3,240	2,520	1,706	698	702	850	648	631	836	838	943	800	811
1978–79	4,514	4,609	5,403	4,327	3,389	2,867	2,958	3,487	2,771	1,831	758	761	916	704	700	889	890	1,000	851	858
1979–80	4,912	5,013	5,891	4,700	3,751	3,130	3,225	3,811	3,020	2,062	827	831	1,001	768	766	955	957	1,078	912	923
1980–81	5,470	5,594	6,569	5,249	4,303	3,498	3,617	4,275	3,390	2,413	918	921	1,086	859	871	1,054	1,056	1,209	1,000	1,019
1981–82	6,166	6,330	7,443	5,947	4,746	3,953	4,113	4,887	3,853	2,605	1,038	1,039	1,229	970	1,022	1,175	1,178	1,327	1,124	1,119
1982–83	6,920	7,126	8,536	6,646	5,364	4,439	4,639	5,583	4,329	3,008	1,181	1,181	1,453	1,083	1,177	1,300	1,306	1,501	1,234	1,179
1983–84	7,508	7,759	9,308	7,244	5,571	4,851	5,093	6,217	4,726	3,099	1,278	1,279	1,531	1,191	1,253	1,380	1,387	1,559	1,327	1,219
1984–85	8,202	8,451	10,243	7,849	6,203	5,315	5,556	6,843	5,135	3,485	1,426	1,426	1,753	1,309	1,424	1,462	1,469	1,647	1,405	1,294
1985–86[2]	8,885	9,228	11,034	8,551	6,512	5,789	6,121	7,374	5,641	3,672	1,553	1,557	1,940	1,420	1,500	1,542	1,551	1,720	1,490	1,340
1986–87	9,676	10,039	12,278	9,276	6,384	6,316	6,658	8,118	6,171	3,684	1,658	1,673	2,097	1,518	1,266	1,702	1,708	2,063	1,587	1,434
1987–88	10,512	10,659	13,075	9,854	7,078	6,988	7,116	8,771	6,574	4,161	1,748	1,760	2,244	1,593	1,380	1,775	1,783	2,060	1,687	1,537
1988–89	11,189	11,474	14,073	10,620	7,967	7,461	7,722	9,451	7,172	4,817	1,849	1,863	2,353	1,686	1,540	1,880	1,889	2,269	1,762	1,609
1989–90	12,018	12,284	15,098	11,374	8,670	8,147	8,396	10,348	7,778	5,196	1,923	1,935	2,411	1,774	1,663	1,948	1,953	2,339	1,823	1,811
1990–91	12,910	13,237	16,503	12,220	9,302	8,772	9,083	11,379	8,389	5,570	2,063	2,077	2,654	1,889	1,744	2,074	2,077	2,470	1,943	1,989
1991–92	13,892	14,258	17,572	13,201	9,632	9,419	9,759	12,037	9,060	5,754	2,221	2,241	2,825	2,042	1,788	2,252	2,257	2,709	2,098	2,090
1992–93	14,634	15,009	18,898	13,882	9,903	9,942	10,294	13,055	9,533	6,059	2,348	2,362	3,018	2,151	1,970	2,344	2,354	2,825	2,197	1,875
1993–94	15,496	15,904	20,097	14,640	10,406	10,572	10,952	13,874	10,100	6,370	2,490	2,506	3,277	2,261	2,067	2,434	2,445	2,946	2,278	1,970
1994–95	16,207	16,602	21,041	15,363	11,170	11,111	11,481	14,537	10,653	6,914	2,587	2,601	3,469	2,347	2,233	2,509	2,520	3,035	2,362	2,023
1995–96	17,208	17,612	22,502	16,198	11,563	11,864	12,243	15,605	11,297	7,094	2,738	2,751	3,680	2,473	2,371	2,606	2,617	3,218	2,429	2,098
1996–97	18,039	18,442	23,520	16,994	11,954	12,498	12,881	16,552	11,871	7,236	2,878	2,889	3,826	2,602	2,537	2,663	2,672	3,142	2,520	2,181
1997–98	18,516	19,070	24,116	17,717	12,921	12,801	13,344	17,229	12,338	7,464	2,954	2,964	3,756	2,731	2,672	2,762	2,761	3,132	2,648	2,785
1998–99[3]	19,368	19,929	25,443	18,430	13,319	13,428	13,973	18,340	12,815	7,854	3,075	3,091	3,914	2,850	2,581	2,865	2,865	3,188	2,765	2,884
1999–2000	20,186	20,706	26,534	19,127	13,965	14,081	14,588	19,307	13,361	8,235	3,224	3,237	4,070	2,976	2,808	2,882	2,881	3,157	2,790	2,922
2000–01	21,368	21,856	27,676	20,247	14,788	15,000	15,470	20,106	14,233	9,067	3,374	3,392	4,270	3,121	2,722	2,993	2,993	3,300	2,893	3,000
2001–02	22,413	22,896	29,115	21,220	15,825	15,742	16,211	21,176	14,923	10,076	3,567	3,576	4,478	3,301	3,116	3,104	3,109	3,462	2,996	2,633
2002–03	23,340	23,787	31,043	21,965	17,753	16,383	16,826	22,716	15,416	10,651	3,752	3,764	4,724	3,478	3,232	3,206	3,197	3,602	3,071	3,870
2003–04	24,636	25,083	32,886	23,166	19,559	17,327	17,777	24,128	16,298	11,546	3,945	3,952	4,979	3,647	3,581	3,364	3,354	3,778	3,222	4,432
2004–05[4]	26,025	26,489	34,698	24,481	19,899	18,374	18,838	25,600	17,261	12,182	4,165	4,166	5,244	3,849	4,162	3,486	3,485	3,854	3,371	3,556

—Not available.

[1] Data for 1986–87 and later years reflect a basis of 20 meals per week. Because of this revision in data collection and tabulation procedures, data are not entirely comparable with figures for previous years. In particular, data on board rates are somewhat higher than earlier years because they reflect the basis of 20 meals per week rather than meals served 7 days per week. Since many institutions serve fewer than 3 meals each day, the 1986–87 and later data reflect a more accurate accounting of total board costs.

[2] Room and board data are estimated.

[3] Data were imputed using alternative procedures. (See Guide to Sources for details.)

[4] Preliminary data based on fall 2003 enrollment weights.

NOTE: Data are for the entire academic year and are average total charges for full-time attendance. Tuition and fees were weighted by the number of full-time-equivalent undergraduates, but were not adjusted to reflect student residency. Room and board were based on full-time students. The data have not been adjusted for changes in the purchasing power of the dollar over time. Data for 1976–77 to 1996–97 are for institutions of higher education. Data for 1986–87 and later years are for institutions of higher education. Institutions of higher education were accredited by an agency or association that was recognized by the U.S. Department of Education, or recognized directly by the Secretary of Education. The new degree-granting classification is very similar to the earlier higher education classification, except that it includes some additional institutions, primarily 2-year colleges, and excludes a few higher education institutions that did not award associate's or higher degrees. Because of their low response rate, data for private 2-year colleges must be interpreted with caution. Some data have been revised from previously published figures. Detail may not sum to totals because of rounding.

SOURCE: U.S. Department of Education, National Center for Education Statistics, Higher Education General Information Survey (HEGIS), "Institutional Characteristics of Colleges and Universities" surveys, 1965–66 through 1985–86; "Fall Enrollment in Institutions of Higher Education" surveys, 1965 through 1985; and 1986–87 through 2004–05 Integrated Postsecondary Education Data System (IPEDS), "Fall Enrollment Survey" (IPEDS-EF:86–99), "Institutional Characteristics Survey" (IPEDS-C:86–99), Spring 2001 through Spring 2004, and Fall 2000 through Fall 2004. (This table was prepared August 2005.)

Average undergraduate tuition, fees, room, and board charged for full-time students in degree-granting institutions, by type and control of institution and state or jurisdiction: 2003–04 and 2004–05

State or jurisdiction	Public 4-year, 2003–04		Public 4-year, 2004–05[1]				Private 4-year, 2003–04		Private 4-year, 2004–05[1]				Public 2-year, tuition only (in-state)	
	Total	Tuition and required fees (in-state)	Total	Tuition and required fees (in-state)	Room	Board	Total	Tuition and required fees	Total	Tuition and required fees	Room	Board	2003–04	2004–05[1]
1	2	3	4	5	6	7	8	9	10	11	12	13	14	15
United States	$10,674	$4,587	$11,441	$5,038	$3,418	$2,985	$25,083	$17,777	$26,489	$18,838	$4,166	$3,485	$1,702	$1,847
Alabama	8,962	3,970	9,819	4,377	2,574	2,868	16,557	11,056	17,520	11,671	2,906	2,943	2,479	2,735
Alaska	10,132	3,430	9,936	3,782	3,332	2,822	17,958	11,877	21,423	14,093	3,002	4,328	1,790	1,945
Arizona	10,149	3,587	10,863	4,076	3,854	2,934	19,147	12,466	19,448	13,197	2,922	3,329	1,141	1,226
Arkansas.................................	8,337	4,006	8,734	4,297	2,321	2,116	15,956	11,041	17,040	11,811	2,537	2,692	1,659	1,700
California	12,288	3,800	13,356	4,323	4,578	4,456	28,337	19,749	30,186	21,046	5,082	4,058	486	721
Colorado	9,763	3,451	10,243	3,518	3,184	3,541	26,030	17,472	27,361	18,583	4,670	4,108	1,796	1,850
Connecticut.............................	12,790	5,777	13,824	6,385	3,948	3,491	32,326	23,434	33,965	24,664	5,132	4,169	2,307	2,404
Delaware.................................	12,502	6,183	13,353	6,671	3,765	2,917	16,294	9,680	17,368	10,458	3,499	3,411	1,992	2,088
District of Columbia	†	2,070	†	2,070	†	†	29,236	20,312	31,594	22,240	6,020	3,334	†	†
Florida	8,956	2,534	9,335	2,633	3,775	2,927	22,800	15,845	23,793	16,599	3,814	3,380	1,639	1,745
Georgia	9,052	3,192	9,439	3,392	3,629	2,418	23,241	16,090	24,734	17,146	4,313	3,275	1,421	1,470
Hawaii	8,747	3,235	9,131	3,347	3,130	2,653	17,922	9,196	17,866	9,585	3,813	4,468	1,118	1,175
Idaho.......................................	8,082	3,321	9,066	3,589	2,459	3,018	10,905	5,155	11,388	5,502	2,315	3,571	1,657	1,817
Illinois.....................................	11,795	5,642	12,803	6,497	3,152	3,154	25,543	18,049	26,966	18,996	4,743	3,226	1,782	1,952
Indiana	11,619	5,370	12,240	5,666	3,085	3,489	25,116	18,871	26,490	20,112	3,274	3,104	2,468	2,599
Iowa	10,876	4,991	11,541	5,407	3,017	3,118	21,774	16,394	23,012	17,339	2,658	3,015	2,688	2,876
Kansas	8,587	3,674	9,397	4,181	2,536	2,680	18,632	13,438	19,736	14,260	2,496	2,979	1,792	1,882
Kentucky	8,515	3,859	9,400	4,502	2,703	2,195	18,197	12,684	19,262	13,577	2,790	2,895	2,266	2,562
Louisiana	7,460	3,185	7,973	3,526	2,355	2,093	25,543	18,262	26,583	19,312	4,144	3,126	1,228	1,429
Maine	10,994	5,001	11,826	5,565	3,186	3,075	26,813	19,627	28,371	20,711	3,779	3,881	2,781	2,802
Maryland..................................	13,407	6,224	14,108	6,632	4,180	3,296	28,784	21,006	30,515	22,284	4,831	3,400	2,595	2,837
Massachusetts.........................	12,245	6,069	13,687	7,010	3,868	2,809	33,652	24,524	35,470	25,935	5,404	4,131	2,723	2,844
Michigan	12,187	5,994	12,658	6,189	3,268	3,202	18,147	12,434	19,286	13,253	3,066	2,967	1,865	1,936
Minnesota................................	10,826	5,728	11,958	6,478	3,054	2,426	24,498	18,559	25,946	19,510	3,433	3,003	3,416	3,839
Mississippi	8,535	3,750	9,019	3,986	2,458	2,575	15,811	10,993	16,460	11,442	2,574	2,444	1,390	1,510
Missouri	10,355	5,396	11,356	5,833	3,196	2,327	20,462	14,322	21,431	15,045	3,281	3,105	1,940	2,128
Montana..................................	9,347	4,155	9,867	4,511	2,437	2,920	16,740	11,458	17,918	12,172	2,688	3,058	2,569	2,558
Nebraska	9,611	4,238	10,704	4,679	2,889	3,137	19,090	13,750	19,725	14,412	2,778	2,535	1,672	1,772
Nevada	10,310	2,720	10,464	2,477	4,622	3,365	18,840	11,428	20,594	11,928	4,977	3,689	1,509	1,496
New Hampshire	13,843	7,615	14,651	8,086	3,998	2,567	28,320	20,499	29,728	21,452	4,796	3,480	4,821	5,338
New Jersey	15,088	7,255	16,349	7,989	5,286	3,073	28,210	19,710	29,751	20,910	4,750	4,092	2,443	2,569
New Mexico	8,255	3,164	8,675	3,395	2,539	2,741	18,237	12,138	19,304	13,034	3,161	3,109	1,002	1,072
New York	12,004	4,884	12,441	4,922	4,280	3,238	29,375	20,522	30,907	21,632	5,373	3,902	2,951	3,074
North Carolina	8,780	3,239	9,450	3,563	3,190	2,697	23,186	16,982	24,600	18,139	3,248	3,214	1,166	1,248
North Dakota	8,035	3,837	9,011	4,549	1,803	2,659	13,511	9,501	12,525	8,571	1,647	2,306	2,421	2,850
Ohio...	13,346	6,589	15,256	8,041	4,092	3,123	24,279	17,901	25,594	18,941	3,368	3,285	2,823	2,999
Oklahoma................................	7,907	3,201	8,451	3,507	2,455	2,489	17,379	11,848	19,168	13,446	2,742	2,980	1,648	1,719
Oregon	11,632	4,667	12,177	5,151	3,469	3,556	26,059	19,531	27,493	20,593	3,493	3,407	2,427	2,558
Pennsylvania............................	13,734	7,615	14,771	8,347	3,601	2,823	28,930	21,098	30,637	22,306	4,418	3,913	2,512	2,751
Rhode Island	12,767	5,391	13,541	5,866	4,112	3,563	29,295	21,110	30,907	22,394	4,663	3,850	2,120	2,310
South Carolina.........................	12,668	7,442	12,165	6,749	3,156	2,261	20,133	14,569	21,237	15,426	2,915	2,896	2,632	2,816
South Dakota...........................	8,406	4,453	8,944	4,720	1,872	2,352	17,097	12,440	18,076	13,161	2,344	2,571	2,798	2,840
Tennessee	8,934	4,039	9,445	4,258	2,606	2,581	21,025	15,074	22,035	15,873	3,314	2,848	2,076	2,209
Texas	9,180	3,559	10,233	4,423	3,164	2,647	20,855	14,798	22,218	15,929	3,308	2,981	1,166	1,228
Utah	7,878	2,896	8,348	3,177	2,134	3,036	10,069	4,537	10,521	4,767	2,864	2,889	1,954	2,089
Vermont...................................	14,769	8,263	15,658	8,771	4,393	2,495	25,517	18,166	27,261	19,838	3,947	3,476	3,604	3,796
Virginia....................................	10,903	5,068	11,616	5,556	3,243	2,817	22,248	16,162	23,277	17,010	3,165	3,101	1,802	1,929
Washington..............................	11,335	4,626	11,902	4,926	3,334	3,642	24,671	17,983	26,021	19,031	3,746	3,245	2,228	2,390
West Virginia............................	8,764	3,170	9,450	3,572	3,003	2,876	18,373	12,685	19,067	13,284	2,823	2,960	2,920	3,105
Wisconsin	9,061	4,676	9,872	5,290	2,688	1,894	23,318	17,386	24,574	18,380	3,148	3,046	2,589	2,796
Wyoming..................................	8,485	3,090	8,514	2,721	2,590	3,203	†	†	†	†	†	†	1,614	1,680

†Not applicable.
[1]Preliminary data based on fall 2003 enrollments.
NOTE: Data are for the entire academic year and are average charges. Tuition and fees were weighted by the number of full-time-equivalent undergraduates in 2003, but are not adjusted to reflect student residency. Room and board are based on full-time students.

(See Guide to Sources for details.) Some data have been revised from previously published figures. Detail may not sum to totals because of rounding.
SOURCE: U.S. Department of Education, National Center for Education Statistics, 2003–04 and 2004–05 Integrated Postsecondary Education Data System (IPEDS), Fall 2003, Fall 2004, and Spring 2004. (This table was prepared August 2005.)

Average graduate and first-professional tuition and required fees in degree-granting institutions, by first-professional discipline and control of institution: 1987–88 through 2004–05

Year and control	Average full-time graduate tuition	Average full-time first-professional tuition									
		Chiropractic	Dentistry	Medicine	Optometry	Osteopathic medicine	Pharmacy	Podiatry	Veterinary medicine	Law	Theology
1	2	3	4	5	6	7	8	9	10	11	12
All institutions											
1987–88	$3,599	$6,996	$9,399	$9,034	$7,926	$10,674	$5,201	$12,736	$4,503	$6,636	$3,572
1988–89	3,728	7,972	9,324	9,439	8,503	11,462	4,952	13,232	4,856	7,099	3,911
1989–90	4,135	8,315	10,515	10,597	9,469	11,888	5,890	14,611	5,470	8,059	4,079
1990–91	4,488	9,108	10,270	10,571	9,512	12,830	5,889	15,143	5,396	8,708	4,569
1991–92	5,116	10,226	12,049	11,646	9,610	13,004	6,731	16,257	6,367	9,469	4,876
1992–93	5,475	11,117	12,710	12,265	10,858	14,297	6,635	17,426	6,771	10,463	5,331
1993–94	5,973	11,503	14,403	13,074	10,385	15,038	7,960	17,621	7,159	11,552	5,253
1994–95	6,247	12,324	15,164	13,834	11,053	15,913	8,315	18,138	7,741	12,374	5,648
1995–96	6,741	12,507	15,647	14,860	11,544	16,785	8,602	18,434	8,208	13,278	5,991
1996–97	7,111	12,721	16,585	15,481	12,250	17,888	9,207	19,056	8,668	14,081	6,558
1997–98	7,246	13,131	17,393	16,075	12,685	18,654	9,544	19,355	9,013	14,877	6,761
1998–99	7,685	13,582	18,800	17,110	14,066	19,718	9,636	19,547	9,392	15,590	7,147
1999–2000	8,071	14,256	19,314	17,775	14,389	20,817	10,601	20,102	9,865	16,399	7,425
2000–01	8,429	15,092	21,696	18,935	15,360	21,685	11,175	20,313	10,365	17,659	10,100
2001–02	8,857	15,605	22,643	19,973	16,066	22,753	12,008	21,115	10,940	18,577	8,543
2002–03	9,226	—	—	—	—	—	—	—	—	—	—
2003–04	10,308	—	—	—	—	—	—	—	—	—	—
2004–05[1]	10,888	—	—	—	—	—	—	—	—	—	—
Public[2]											
1987–88	1,827	†	4,614	5,245	2,789	5,125	2,462	†	3,523	2,810	†
1988–89	1,913	†	5,286	5,669	3,455	6,269	2,218	†	3,889	2,766	†
1989–90	1,999	†	5,728	6,259	3,569	6,521	2,816	†	4,505	3,196	†
1990–91	2,206	†	5,927	6,437	3,821	7,188	2,697	†	4,840	3,430	†
1991–92	2,524	†	6,595	7,106	4,161	7,699	2,871	†	5,231	3,933	†
1992–93	2,791	†	7,006	7,867	5,106	8,404	2,987	†	5,553	4,261	†
1993–94	3,050	†	7,525	8,329	5,325	8,640	3,567	†	6,107	4,835	†
1994–95	3,250	†	8,125	8,812	5,643	8,954	3,793	†	6,571	5,307	†
1995–96	3,449	†	8,806	9,585	6,130	9,448	4,100	†	6,907	5,821	†
1996–97	3,607	†	9,434	10,057	6,561	9,932	4,884	†	7,343	6,565	†
1997–98	3,744	†	9,657	10,501	7,366	10,358	5,065	19,541	7,742	7,004	†
1998–99	3,897	†	10,277	11,141	7,890	10,802	5,482	19,818	7,975	7,425	†
1999–2000	4,043	†	10,615	11,569	8,021	11,211	5,897	19,578	8,601	7,740	†
2000–01	4,243	†	11,574	12,074	8,302	11,516	6,245	20,228	8,964	8,326	†
2001–02	4,496	†	12,446	13,264	9,060	12,587	7,020	21,254	9,524	9,043	†
2002–03	4,842	†	—	—	—	—	—	—	—	—	†
2003–04	5,544	†	—	—	—	—	—	—	—	—	†
2004–05[1]	6,080	†	—	—	—	—	—	—	—	—	†
Private											
1987–88	6,769	6,996	16,201	14,945	11,635	13,311	8,834	12,736	12,544	9,048	3,572
1988–89	6,945	7,972	16,127	15,610	12,050	13,536	9,692	13,232	13,285	9,892	3,911
1989–90	7,881	8,315	16,800	16,826	13,640	14,117	10,656	14,611	14,184	10,901	4,079
1990–91	8,507	9,108	18,270	17,899	13,767	15,009	11,546	15,143	14,159	12,247	4,569
1991–92	9,592	10,226	20,318	19,225	14,366	16,098	12,937	16,257	15,816	12,946	4,876
1992–93	10,008	11,117	21,309	19,585	14,459	17,098	13,373	17,426	17,103	13,975	5,331
1993–94	10,790	11,503	23,824	20,769	14,156	17,720	14,838	17,621	17,433	15,193	5,253
1994–95	11,338	12,324	24,641	21,819	14,497	18,422	14,894	18,138	17,940	16,201	5,648
1995–96	12,083	12,507	25,678	23,001	15,235	19,619	15,618	18,434	19,380	17,251	5,991
1996–97	12,537	12,721	26,618	24,242	15,949	20,714	15,934	19,056	19,526	18,276	6,558
1997–98	12,774	13,151	29,923	25,189	16,415	21,710	16,307	19,316	20,299	19,171	6,761
1998–99	13,299	13,582	31,659	26,502	17,848	22,796	16,905	19,492	21,286	20,154	7,147
1999–2000	13,782	14,256	32,268	27,694	18,087	23,838	18,091	20,193	21,772	21,081	7,425
2000–01	14,420	15,092	35,234	29,863	19,592	24,712	19,031	20,329	22,600	22,775	10,100
2001–02	15,165	15,605	36,207	30,485	20,463	25,779	20,459	21,089	23,303	23,911	8,543
2002–03	14,983	—	—	—	—	—	—	—	—	—	—
2003–04[1]	16,241	—	—	—	—	—	—	—	—	—	—
2004–05[1]	16,998	—	—	—	—	—	—	—	—	—	—

—Not available.

†Not applicable.

[1]Preliminary data based on fall 2003 enrollment.

[2]Data are based on in-state tuition only.

NOTE: Average graduate student tuition weighted by fall full-time-equivalent graduate enrollment. Average first-professional tuition weighted by number of degrees conferred during the academic year. Some year-to-year fluctuations in tuition data may reflect nonreporting by individual institutions. Excludes institutions not reporting degrees conferred and institutions not reporting tuition. Data for 1987–88 to 1997–98 are for institutions of higher education. Institutions of higher education were accredited by an agency or association that was recognized by the U.S. Department of Education, or recognized directly by the Secretary of Education. The new degree-granting classification is very similar to the earlier higher education classification, except that it includes some additional institutions, primarily 2-year colleges, and excludes a few higher education institutions that did not award associate's or higher degrees. Some data have been revised from previously published figures. Detail may not sum to totals because of rounding.

SOURCE: U.S. Department of Education, National Center for Education Statistics, 1987–88 through 2004–05 Integrated Postsecondary Education Data System, "Fall Enrollment Survey" (IPEDS-EF:87–99); "Completions Survey," (IPEDS-C:88–99); "Institutional Characteristics Survey" (IPEDS-IC:87–99); Fall 2000 through Fall 2004; and Spring 2001 through Spring 2004. (This table was prepared August 2005.)

Percentage of undergraduates receiving aid, by type and source of aid and selected student characteristics: 2003–04

Selected student characteristic	Enrollment of undergraduates,[1] in thousands	Any aid			Grants			Loans			Work study	Other		
		Total[2]	Federal	Nonfederal	Total	Federal	Nonfederal	Total	Federal[3]	Nonfederal	Total[4]	Total	Federal	Nonfederal
1	2	3	4	5	6	7	8	9	10	11	12	13	14	15
All undergraduates	19,054 (0.0)	63.2 (0.36)	48.0 (0.28)	40.9 (0.48)	50.7 (0.41)	27.6 (0.17)	36.8 (0.46)	35.2 (0.23)	34.0 (0.22)	5.9 (0.19)	7.5 (0.22)	3.6 (0.16)	2.9 (0.13)	0.8 (0.09)
Sex														
Male	8,073 (73.8)	60.6 (0.54)	44.8 (0.50)	40.1 (0.58)	46.5 (0.55)	22.8 (0.36)	35.6 (0.57)	33.7 (0.45)	32.3 (0.43)	6.3 (0.29)	7.4 (0.24)	5.3 (0.22)	4.7 (0.21)	0.7 (0.09)
Female	10,980 (73.8)	65.2 (0.41)	50.4 (0.36)	41.4 (0.54)	53.7 (0.47)	31.1 (0.28)	37.7 (0.51)	36.4 (0.34)	35.2 (0.34)	5.6 (0.17)	7.6 (0.25)	2.3 (0.17)	1.5 (0.11)	0.8 (0.11)
Race/ethnicity[5]														
White, non-Hispanic	12,025 (144.6)	61.5 (0.56)	44.4 (0.53)	41.7 (0.54)	47.8 (0.58)	21.3 (0.39)	37.7 (0.54)	35.5 (0.48)	34.2 (0.48)	6.2 (0.22)	7.3 (0.27)	3.5 (0.18)	2.6 (0.14)	0.9 (0.13)
Black, non-Hispanic	2,666 (117.6)	75.8 (0.88)	64.6 (1.11)	41.6 (1.07)	64.3 (0.98)	47.7 (1.03)	37.2 (1.01)	43.2 (1.63)	42.0 (1.65)	5.1 (0.46)	8.5 (0.45)	5.1 (0.38)	4.4 (0.34)	0.8 (0.15)
Hispanic	2,426 (81.3)	63.2 (0.82)	51.9 (0.87)	37.4 (1.02)	53.4 (0.84)	37.7 (0.80)	33.3 (1.04)	29.9 (0.96)	28.7 (0.95)	5.4 (0.42)	6.8 (0.52)	3.1 (0.19)	2.5 (0.17)	0.5 (0.09)
Asian Pacific Islander	1,127 (41.7)	51.5 (1.51)	38.1 (1.18)	37.0 (1.35)	41.2 (1.38)	22.7 (0.87)	33.7 (1.26)	25.3 (0.97)	23.6 (0.87)	5.3 (0.57)	9.1 (0.55)	2.1 (0.32)	1.8 (0.32)	0.3 (0.07)
American Indian/Alaska Native	176 (20.5)	67.4 (3.84)	50.4 (3.94)	46.1 (3.35)	59.1 (3.69)	35.8 (3.44)	41.8 (3.41)	32.5 (2.99)	31.4 (2.98)	5.0 (1.08)	5.1 (1.27)	3.3 (0.98)	2.4 (0.77)	1.0 (0.41)
Age														
Younger than 24	10,820 (98.6)	64.2 (0.49)	49.4 (0.42)	44.7 (0.54)	51.4 (0.47)	25.7 (0.24)	40.5 (0.51)	37.9 (0.42)	36.3 (0.42)	7.5 (0.24)	10.6 (0.31)	2.0 (0.10)	1.6 (0.08)	0.4 (0.05)
24 to 29 years old	3,299 (53.0)	66.8 (0.74)	55.0 (0.76)	35.2 (0.72)	52.7 (0.72)	36.9 (0.55)	30.7 (0.64)	39.5 (0.66)	38.3 (0.68)	5.0 (0.34)	4.1 (0.23)	5.7 (0.42)	5.1 (0.41)	0.6 (0.07)
30 years old or over	4,935 (79.6)	58.8 (0.78)	40.3 (0.72)	36.2 (0.75)	47.6 (0.75)	25.4 (0.49)	32.7 (0.79)	26.7 (0.60)	25.8 (0.60)	3.0 (0.19)	3.0 (0.18)	5.7 (0.35)	4.0 (0.28)	1.7 (0.24)
Marital status[6]														
Not married	14,613 (78.1)	64.4 (0.44)	50.2 (0.32)	42.5 (0.51)	52.0 (0.47)	28.6 (0.19)	38.3 (0.50)	37.6 (0.30)	36.3 (0.30)	6.7 (0.21)	8.9 (0.26)	2.8 (0.13)	2.2 (0.11)	0.6 (0.06)
Married	4,056 (76.4)	57.5 (0.78)	38.1 (0.84)	35.2 (0.76)	44.2 (0.90)	21.1 (0.66)	31.6 (0.70)	26.0 (0.64)	25.1 (0.65)	3.1 (0.22)	2.9 (0.18)	6.3 (0.41)	5.1 (0.35)	1.3 (0.22)
Separated	385 (14.3)	78.5 (1.96)	67.7 (2.43)	37.9 (1.98)	69.8 (2.10)	58.1 (2.22)	33.1 (1.94)	41.8 (2.32)	40.4 (2.39)	4.5 (0.75)	4.0 (0.52)	5.4 (0.73)	4.2 (0.66)	1.2 (0.35)
Attendance status														
Full-time, full-year	7,824 (93.5)	76.1 (0.40)	61.7 (0.42)	54.3 (0.52)	62.2 (0.48)	33.2 (0.32)	49.3 (0.51)	49.9 (0.44)	48.5 (0.43)	9.0 (0.31)	13.5 (0.41)	3.2 (0.17)	2.4 (0.12)	0.8 (0.09)
Part-time or part-year	11,230 (93.5)	54.3 (0.56)	38.5 (0.44)	31.5 (0.59)	42.7 (0.57)	23.6 (0.35)	28.1 (0.57)	25.0 (0.30)	23.8 (0.30)	3.7 (0.16)	3.4 (0.14)	3.9 (0.20)	3.2 (0.19)	0.8 (0.10)
Dependency status and family income														
Dependent	9,476 (106.4)	63.8 (0.53)	48.5 (0.44)	45.9 (0.58)	50.4 (0.51)	22.8 (0.25)	41.7 (0.56)	38.6 (0.46)	37.0 (0.46)	7.9 (0.26)	11.2 (0.32)	1.6 (0.10)	1.3 (0.08)	0.3 (0.04)
Less than $20,000	1,241 (29.1)	62.7 (0.49)	47.5 (0.49)	35.9 (0.57)	51.0 (0.50)	32.3 (0.33)	31.9 (0.56)	32.0 (0.43)	31.0 (0.43)	3.9 (0.19)	4.0 (0.15)	5.6 (0.27)	4.4 (0.24)	1.2 (0.15)
$20,000–$39,999	1,827 (27.3)	77.8 (0.87)	67.2 (0.95)	50.9 (1.13)	63.7 (0.96)	43.6 (0.96)	48.0 (1.12)	36.2 (1.01)	34.9 (1.07)	5.6 (0.46)	14.2 (0.77)	1.6 (0.25)	1.3 (0.25)	0.3 (0.06)
$40,000–$59,999	1,710 (27.5)	76.2 (0.78)	65.2 (0.73)	54.0 (0.92)	69.6 (0.83)	53.6 (0.81)	49.9 (0.86)	43.1 (0.70)	41.8 (0.73)	7.7 (0.45)	15.0 (0.61)	1.7 (0.18)	1.4 (0.17)	0.4 (0.06)
$60,000–$79,999	1,596 (32.7)	63.2 (0.83)	48.0 (0.79)	46.8 (0.83)	48.4 (0.77)	18.0 (0.51)	42.6 (0.81)	41.4 (0.82)	39.9 (0.79)	8.8 (0.36)	12.1 (0.54)	1.8 (0.23)	1.4 (0.20)	0.4 (0.11)
$80,000–$99,999	1,124 (27.5)	58.7 (1.09)	40.9 (1.00)	44.3 (0.94)	40.6 (0.90)	3.3 (0.25)	39.7 (0.91)	39.6 (0.98)	37.7 (0.97)	8.9 (0.42)	10.2 (0.47)	1.6 (0.13)	1.1 (0.13)	0.5 (0.10)
$100,000 or more	1,978 (43.6)	60.5 (1.30)	41.6 (1.05)	44.3 (1.24)	39.9 (1.24)	0.9 (0.15)	39.6 (1.25)	41.1 (1.08)	39.0 (1.03)	9.9 (0.48)	9.6 (0.64)	1.5 (0.32)	1.3 (0.31)	0.1 (0.05)
Independent	9,578 (106.4)	62.7 (0.49)	47.5 (0.49)	35.9 (0.57)	51.0 (0.76)	32.3 (0.33)	31.9 (0.56)	32.0 (0.43)	31.0 (0.43)	3.9 (0.19)	4.0 (0.15)	5.6 (0.27)	4.4 (0.24)	1.2 (0.15)
Less than $9,999	2,157 (36.5)	70.5 (0.79)	61.6 (0.85)	38.5 (0.86)	65.7 (0.76)	56.2 (0.77)	34.0 (0.84)	37.8 (0.85)	36.6 (0.86)	4.7 (0.39)	8.0 (0.46)	4.2 (0.36)	3.0 (0.31)	1.2 (0.17)
$10,000–$19,999	1,745 (35.6)	73.3 (0.86)	62.7 (0.84)	38.6 (0.92)	63.4 (1.05)	49.3 (0.84)	33.9 (0.89)	40.7 (0.97)	39.5 (0.99)	4.9 (0.34)	5.2 (0.34)	5.9 (0.39)	4.6 (0.37)	1.3 (0.21)
$20,000–$29,999	1,512 (35.6)	68.4 (1.05)	55.9 (1.18)	35.0 (0.94)	53.8 (0.96)	37.2 (0.89)	30.5 (0.91)	38.1 (1.09)	37.2 (1.09)	3.8 (0.35)	3.2 (0.28)	6.1 (0.47)	4.4 (0.33)	1.7 (0.30)
$30,000–$49,999	1,809 (44.1)	60.6 (0.89)	42.3 (0.95)	36.1 (0.83)	46.3 (0.77)	23.2 (0.82)	32.4 (0.82)	29.6 (0.84)	28.7 (0.83)	3.8 (0.31)	2.6 (0.27)	6.4 (0.47)	5.5 (0.42)	1.0 (0.17)
$50,000 or more	2,356 (50.8)	45.6 (0.97)	22.0 (0.74)	31.9 (0.92)	30.1 (0.97)	1.8 (0.18)	29.2 (0.95)	18.1 (0.64)	17.2 (0.61)	2.5 (0.22)	0.9 (0.14)	5.7 (0.50)	4.9 (0.49)	0.9 (0.16)
Housing status														
School-owned	2,632 (69.3)	79.2 (0.60)	62.3 (0.78)	64.9 (0.77)	66.3 (0.70)	25.7 (0.59)	60.3 (0.79)	57.2 (0.82)	55.5 (0.83)	12.9 (0.66)	22.6 (0.72)	1.8 (0.16)	1.3 (0.14)	0.4 (0.09)
Off-campus, not with parents	10,524 (89.4)	62.9 (0.50)	47.4 (0.47)	37.9 (0.58)	49.9 (0.56)	28.8 (0.36)	33.7 (0.55)	33.7 (0.40)	32.5 (0.39)	4.8 (0.20)	5.1 (0.19)	4.6 (0.22)	3.7 (0.19)	1.0 (0.13)
With parents	5,899 (77.7)	56.7 (0.69)	42.7 (0.54)	35.5 (0.66)	45.1 (0.65)	26.2 (0.41)	31.8 (0.63)	28.2 (0.55)	26.9 (0.53)	4.7 (0.19)	5.2 (0.23)	2.6 (0.16)	2.1 (0.14)	0.5 (0.07)

[1] Numbers of undergraduates may not equal figures reported in other tables, since these data are based on a sample survey of students who enrolled at any time during the school year. Includes all postsecondary institutions.
[2] Includes students who reported they were awarded aid, but did not specify the source or type of aid.
[3] Includes Parent Loans for Undergraduate Students (PLUS).
[4] Details on federal and nonfederal work study participants are not available.
[5] Excludes persons not reported by race/ethnicity.
[6] Includes students who were single, divorced, or widowed.

NOTE: Rows may not sum to totals because of rounding and/or the fact that some students receive aid from multiple sources. Data include undergraduates in degree-granting and non-degree-granting institutions. Estimates for loans include PLUS loans and may differ from previously published figures. Standard errors appear in parentheses. Data include Puerto Rico.
SOURCE: U.S. Department of Education, National Center for Education Statistics, 2003–04 National Postsecondary Student Aid Study (NPSAS:04). (This table was prepared September 2005.)

Percentage of persons age 25 and over and 25 to 29, by race/ethnicity, years of school completed, and sex: Selected years, 1910 through 2005

Age and year	Total			White, non-Hispanic[1]			Black, non-Hispanic[1]			Hispanic		
	Less than 5 years of elementary school	High school completion or higher[2]	Bachelor's or higher degree[3]	Less than 5 years of elementary school	High school completion or higher[2]	Bachelor's or higher degree[3]	Less than 5 years of elementary school	High school completion or higher[2]	Bachelor's or higher degree[3]	Less than 5 years of elementary school	High school completion or higher[2]	Bachelor's or higher degree[3]
1	2	3	4	5	6	7	8	9	10	11	12	13
Males and females, 25 and over												
1910 [4]	23.8 (—)	13.5 (—)	2.7 (—)	— (†)	— (†)	— (†)	— (†)	— (†)	— (†)	— (†)	— (†)	— (†)
1920 [4]	22.0 (—)	16.4 (—)	3.3 (—)	— (†)	— (†)	— (†)	— (†)	— (†)	— (†)	— (†)	— (†)	— (†)
1930 [4]	17.5 (—)	19.1 (—)	3.9 (—)	— (†)	— (†)	— (†)	— (†)	— (†)	— (†)	— (†)	— (†)	— (†)
April 1940	13.7 (—)	24.5 (—)	4.6 (—)	10.9 (—)	26.1 (—)	4.9 (—)	41.8 (—)	7.7 (—)	1.3 (—)	— (†)	— (†)	— (†)
April 1950	11.1 (—)	34.3 (—)	6.2 (—)	8.9 (—)	36.4 (—)	6.6 (—)	32.6 (—)	13.7 (—)	2.2 (—)	— (†)	— (†)	— (†)
April 1960	8.3 (—)	41.1 (—)	7.7 (—)	6.7 (—)	43.2 (—)	8.1 (—)	23.5 (—)	21.7 (—)	3.5 (—)	— (†)	— (†)	— (†)
March 1970	5.3 (—)	55.2 (—)	11.0 (—)	4.2 (—)	57.4 (—)	11.6 (—)	14.7 (—)	36.1 (—)	6.1 (—)	— (†)	— (†)	— (†)
March 1975	4.2 (—)	62.5 (—)	13.9 (—)	2.6 (—)	65.8 (—)	14.9 (—)	12.3 (—)	42.6 (—)	6.4 (—)	18.2 (—)	38.5 (—)	6.6 (—)
March 1980	3.4 (0.08)	68.6 (0.20)	17.0 (0.16)	1.9 (0.07)	71.9 (0.21)	18.4 (0.18)	9.1 (0.40)	51.4 (0.69)	7.9 (0.38)	15.8 (0.74)	44.5 (1.01)	7.6 (0.54)
March 1985	2.7 (0.07)	73.9 (0.18)	19.4 (0.16)	1.4 (0.05)	77.5 (0.19)	20.8 (0.19)	6.1 (0.31)	59.9 (0.64)	11.1 (0.41)	13.5 (0.58)	47.9 (0.85)	8.5 (0.48)
March 1986	2.7 (0.07)	74.7 (0.18)	19.4 (0.16)	1.4 (0.05)	78.2 (0.19)	20.9 (0.19)	5.3 (0.29)	62.5 (0.62)	10.9 (0.40)	12.9 (0.55)	48.5 (0.83)	8.4 (0.46)
March 1987	2.4 (0.06)	75.6 (0.17)	19.9 (0.16)	1.3 (0.05)	79.0 (0.18)	21.4 (0.19)	4.9 (0.27)	63.6 (0.61)	10.8 (0.39)	11.9 (0.52)	50.9 (0.81)	8.6 (0.45)
March 1988	2.4 (0.06)	76.2 (0.17)	20.3 (0.16)	1.2 (0.05)	79.8 (0.18)	21.8 (0.19)	4.8 (0.27)	63.5 (0.60)	11.2 (0.40)	12.2 (0.52)	51.0 (0.79)	10.0 (0.47)
March 1989	2.5 (0.06)	76.9 (0.17)	21.1 (0.16)	1.2 (0.05)	80.7 (0.18)	22.8 (0.19)	5.2 (0.27)	64.7 (0.59)	11.7 (0.40)	12.2 (0.50)	50.9 (0.77)	9.9 (0.46)
March 1990	2.4 (0.06)	77.6 (0.17)	21.3 (0.16)	1.1 (0.05)	81.4 (0.17)	23.1 (0.19)	5.1 (0.27)	66.2 (0.58)	11.3 (0.39)	12.3 (0.50)	50.8 (0.75)	9.2 (0.44)
March 1991	2.4 (0.06)	78.4 (0.16)	21.4 (0.16)	1.1 (0.05)	82.4 (0.17)	23.3 (0.19)	4.7 (0.26)	66.8 (0.57)	11.5 (0.39)	12.5 (0.49)	51.3 (0.74)	9.7 (0.44)
March 1992	2.1 (0.06)	79.4 (0.16)	21.4 (0.16)	0.9 (0.04)	83.4 (0.16)	23.2 (0.19)	3.9 (0.23)	67.7 (0.56)	11.9 (0.39)	11.8 (0.47)	52.6 (0.73)	9.3 (0.42)
March 1993	2.1 (0.06)	80.2 (0.16)	21.9 (0.16)	0.8 (0.04)	84.1 (0.16)	23.8 (0.19)	3.7 (0.22)	70.5 (0.54)	12.2 (0.39)	11.8 (0.46)	53.1 (0.71)	9.0 (0.41)
March 1994	1.9 (0.05)	80.9 (0.15)	22.2 (0.16)	0.8 (0.04)	84.9 (0.16)	24.3 (0.19)	2.7 (0.19)	73.0 (0.52)	12.9 (0.39)	10.8 (0.42)	53.3 (0.67)	9.1 (0.39)
March 1995	1.8 (0.05)	81.7 (0.15)	23.0 (0.16)	0.7 (0.04)	85.9 (0.16)	25.4 (0.19)	2.5 (0.18)	73.8 (0.52)	13.3 (0.40)	10.6 (0.41)	53.4 (0.67)	9.3 (0.39)
March 1996	1.8 (0.05)	81.7 (0.16)	23.6 (0.17)	0.6 (0.04)	86.0 (0.16)	25.9 (0.20)	2.2 (0.18)	74.6 (0.53)	13.8 (0.42)	10.3 (0.42)	53.1 (0.69)	9.3 (0.40)
March 1997	1.7 (0.05)	82.1 (0.14)	23.9 (0.16)	0.6 (0.03)	86.3 (0.15)	26.2 (0.19)	2.0 (0.16)	75.3 (0.49)	13.3 (0.38)	9.4 (0.36)	54.7 (0.62)	10.3 (0.38)
March 1998	1.6 (0.05)	82.8 (0.14)	24.4 (0.16)	0.6 (0.03)	87.1 (0.14)	26.6 (0.19)	1.7 (0.14)	76.4 (0.47)	14.8 (0.40)	9.3 (0.35)	55.5 (0.60)	11.0 (0.38)
March 1999	1.6 (0.05)	83.4 (0.14)	25.2 (0.16)	0.6 (0.03)	87.7 (0.14)	27.7 (0.19)	1.7 (0.15)	77.4 (0.46)	15.5 (0.40)	9.0 (0.34)	56.1 (0.60)	10.9 (0.37)
March 2000	1.6 (0.05)	84.1 (0.13)	25.6 (0.16)	0.5 (0.03)	88.4 (0.14)	28.1 (0.19)	1.6 (0.14)	78.9 (0.45)	16.6 (0.41)	8.7 (0.33)	57.0 (0.58)	10.6 (0.36)
March 2001	1.6 (0.05)	84.3 (0.13)	26.1 (0.16)	0.5 (0.03)	88.7 (0.13)	28.6 (0.19)	1.3 (0.12)	79.5 (0.44)	16.1 (0.40)	9.3 (0.34)	56.5 (0.57)	11.2 (0.37)
March 2002	1.6 (0.03)	84.1 (0.09)	26.7 (0.11)	0.5 (0.02)	88.7 (0.10)	29.4 (0.14)	1.6 (0.10)	79.2 (0.32)	17.2 (0.30)	8.7 (0.22)	57.0 (0.39)	11.1 (0.25)
March 2003	1.6 (0.03)	84.6 (0.09)	27.2 (0.11)	0.5 (0.02)	89.4 (0.09)	30.0 (0.14)	1.5 (0.10)	80.3 (0.33)	17.4 (0.31)	8.2 (0.18)	57.0 (0.33)	11.4 (0.21)
March 2004	1.5 (0.03)	85.2 (0.09)	27.7 (0.11)	0.4 (0.02)	90.0 (0.09)	30.6 (0.14)	1.3 (0.09)	81.1 (0.32)	17.7 (0.31)	8.1 (0.18)	58.4 (0.32)	12.1 (0.21)
March 2005	1.6 (0.03)	85.2 (0.09)	27.6 (0.11)	0.5 (0.02)	90.1 (0.09)	30.5 (0.14)	1.5 (0.10)	81.5 (0.32)	17.7 (0.31)	7.9 (0.17)	58.5 (0.32)	12.0 (0.21)
Males and females, 25 to 29												
1920 [4]	— (†)	— (†)	— (†)	12.9 (—)	22.0 (—)	4.5 (—)	44.6 (—)	6.3 (—)	1.2 (—)	— (†)	— (†)	— (†)
April 1940	5.9 (—)	38.1 (—)	5.9 (—)	3.4 (—)	41.2 (—)	6.4 (—)	27.0 (—)	12.3 (—)	1.6 (—)	— (†)	— (†)	— (†)
April 1950	4.6 (—)	52.8 (—)	7.7 (—)	3.3 (—)	56.3 (—)	8.2 (—)	16.1 (—)	23.6 (—)	2.8 (—)	— (†)	— (†)	— (†)
April 1960	2.8 (—)	60.7 (—)	11.0 (—)	2.2 (—)	63.7 (—)	11.8 (—)	7.2 (—)	38.6 (—)	5.4 (—)	— (†)	— (†)	— (†)
March 1970	1.1 (—)	75.4 (—)	16.4 (—)	0.9 (—)	77.8 (—)	17.3 (—)	2.2 (—)	58.4 (—)	10.0 (—)	— (†)	— (†)	— (†)
March 1975	1.0 (—)	83.1 (—)	21.9 (—)	0.6 (—)	86.6 (—)	23.8 (—)	0.5 (—)	71.1 (—)	10.5 (—)	8.0 (—)	53.1 (—)	8.8 (—)
March 1980	0.8 (0.10)	85.4 (0.40)	22.5 (0.47)	0.3 (0.07)	89.2 (0.40)	25.0 (0.55)	0.6 (0.27)	76.7 (1.41)	11.6 (1.07)	6.7 (1.12)	58.0 (2.22)	7.7 (1.20)
March 1985	0.7 (0.09)	86.1 (0.37)	22.2 (0.45)	0.2 (0.06)	89.5 (0.38)	24.4 (0.53)	0.4 (0.20)	80.5 (1.22)	11.6 (0.99)	6.0 (0.91)	60.9 (1.86)	11.1 (1.20)
March 1986	0.9 (0.10)	86.1 (0.37)	22.4 (0.45)	0.4 (0.07)	89.6 (0.37)	25.2 (0.53)	0.5 (0.22)	83.5 (1.13)	11.8 (0.99)	5.6 (0.83)	59.1 (1.78)	9.0 (1.04)
March 1987	0.9 (0.10)	86.0 (0.37)	22.0 (0.44)	0.4 (0.08)	89.4 (0.38)	24.6 (0.53)	0.4 (0.20)	83.4 (1.13)	11.5 (0.97)	4.8 (0.76)	59.8 (1.75)	8.7 (1.01)
March 1988	1.0 (0.11)	85.9 (0.37)	22.7 (0.45)	0.3 (0.07)	89.7 (0.38)	25.1 (0.54)	0.3 (0.18)	80.9 (1.20)	12.0 (0.99)	6.0 (0.82)	62.3 (1.68)	11.3 (1.10)
March 1989	1.0 (0.11)	85.5 (0.38)	23.4 (0.45)	0.3 (0.07)	89.3 (0.38)	26.3 (0.55)	0.5 (0.22)	82.3 (1.16)	12.6 (1.01)	5.4 (0.76)	61.0 (1.65)	10.1 (1.02)
March 1990	1.2 (0.12)	85.7 (0.38)	23.2 (0.46)	0.3 (0.07)	90.1 (0.37)	26.4 (0.55)	1.0 (0.31)	81.7 (1.17)	13.4 (1.03)	7.3 (0.88)	58.2 (1.66)	8.1 (0.92)
March 1991	1.0 (0.11)	85.4 (0.39)	23.2 (0.46)	0.4 (0.08)	89.8 (0.39)	26.7 (0.56)	0.5 (0.22)	81.8 (1.17)	11.0 (0.95)	5.8 (0.80)	56.7 (1.69)	9.2 (0.99)
March 1992	0.9 (0.10)	86.3 (0.38)	23.6 (0.47)	0.3 (0.07)	90.7 (0.38)	27.2 (0.58)	0.8 (0.28)	80.9 (1.21)	11.0 (0.97)	5.2 (0.75)	60.9 (1.66)	9.5 (1.00)
March 1993	0.7 (0.09)	86.7 (0.38)	23.7 (0.48)	0.3 (0.07)	91.2 (0.37)	27.2 (0.59)	0.2 (0.15)	82.6 (1.17)	13.3 (1.05)	4.0 (0.65)	60.9 (1.64)	8.3 (0.93)
March 1994	0.8 (0.10)	86.1 (0.39)	23.3 (0.47)	0.2 (0.07)	91.1 (0.38)	27.1 (0.60)	0.6 (0.24)	84.1 (1.13)	13.6 (1.06)	3.6 (0.57)	60.3 (1.51)	8.0 (0.84)
March 1995	0.9 (0.11)	86.8 (0.39)	24.7 (0.49)	0.3 (0.08)	92.5 (0.36)	28.8 (0.62)	0.2 (0.14)	86.7 (1.06)	15.4 (1.13)	4.9 (0.67)	57.1 (1.55)	8.9 (0.89)
March 1996	0.8 (0.11)	87.3 (0.40)	27.1 (0.53)	0.2 (0.07)	92.6 (0.38)	31.6 (0.67)	0.4 (0.20)	86.0 (1.14)	14.6 (1.16)	4.3 (0.66)	61.1 (1.58)	10.0 (0.98)
March 1997	0.8 (0.10)	87.4 (0.37)	27.8 (0.50)	0.1 (0.05)	92.9 (0.35)	32.6 (0.63)	0.6 (0.23)	86.9 (1.03)	14.2 (1.07)	4.2 (0.59)	61.8 (1.42)	11.0 (0.91)

See notes at end of table.

Percentage of persons age 25 and over and 25 to 29, by race/ethnicity, years of school completed, and sex: Selected years, 1910 through 2005—Continued

Age and year	Total			White, non-Hispanic[1]			Black, non-Hispanic[1]			Hispanic		
	Less than 5 years of elementary school	High school completion or higher[2]	Bachelor's or higher degree[3]	Less than 5 years of elementary school	High school completion or higher[2]	Bachelor's or higher degree[3]	Less than 5 years of elementary school	High school completion or higher[2]	Bachelor's or higher degree[3]	Less than 5 years of elementary school	High school completion or higher[2]	Bachelor's or higher degree[3]
1	2	3	4	5	6	7	8	9	10	11	12	13
March 1998	0.7 (0.09)	88.1 (0.36)	27.3 (0.50)	0.1 (0.05)	93.6 (0.34)	32.3 (0.64)	0.4 (0.19)	88.2 (0.98)	15.8 (1.11)	3.7 (0.55)	62.8 (1.41)	10.4 (0.89)
March 1999	0.6 (0.09)	87.8 (0.37)	28.2 (0.51)	0.1 (0.05)	93.0 (0.35)	33.6 (0.66)	0.2 (0.15)	88.7 (0.97)	15.0 (1.09)	3.2 (0.52)	61.6 (1.44)	8.9 (0.84)
March 2000	0.7 (0.09)	88.1 (0.37)	29.1 (0.52)	0.1 (0.04)	94.0 (0.33)	34.0 (0.67)	# (†)	86.8 (1.06)	17.8 (1.20)	3.8 (0.55)	62.8 (1.40)	9.7 (0.85)
March 2001	0.8 (0.11)	87.7 (0.38)	28.6 (0.52)	0.2 (0.06)	93.3 (0.36)	33.0 (0.68)	0.1 (0.09)	87.0 (1.05)	17.8 (1.19)	4.7 (0.62)	63.2 (1.41)	11.1 (0.92)
March 2002	1.1 (0.08)	86.4 (0.28)	29.3 (0.37)	0.1 (0.04)	93.0 (0.26)	35.9 (0.50)	0.6 (0.18)	87.6 (0.76)	18.0 (0.88)	4.7 (0.39)	62.4 (0.89)	8.9 (0.53)
March 2003	1.0 (0.08)	86.5 (0.27)	28.4 (0.36)	0.2 (0.04)	93.7 (0.25)	34.2 (0.49)	0.6 (0.19)	88.5 (0.78)	17.5 (0.93)	4.0 (0.30)	61.7 (0.75)	10.0 (0.47)
March 2004	1.1 (0.08)	86.6 (0.27)	28.7 (0.36)	0.3 (0.05)	93.3 (0.26)	34.5 (0.49)	0.3 (0.13)	88.7 (0.76)	17.1 (0.90)	4.1 (0.31)	62.4 (0.75)	10.9 (0.48)
March 2005	1.0 (0.08)	86.1 (0.27)	28.6 (0.36)	0.3 (0.05)	92.8 (0.26)	34.1 (0.48)	0.4 (0.15)	86.9 (0.79)	17.5 (0.89)	3.6 (0.28)	63.3 (0.74)	11.2 (0.48)
Males, 25 and over												
April 1940	15.1 (—)	22.7 (—)	5.5 (—)	12.0 (—)	24.2 (—)	5.9 (—)	46.2 (—)	6.9 (—)	1.4 (—)	— (†)	— (†)	— (†)
April 1950	12.2 (—)	32.6 (—)	7.3 (—)	9.8 (—)	34.6 (—)	7.9 (—)	36.9 (—)	12.6 (—)	2.1 (—)	— (†)	— (†)	— (†)
April 1960	9.4 (—)	39.5 (—)	9.7 (—)	7.4 (—)	41.6 (—)	10.3 (—)	27.7 (—)	20.0 (—)	3.5 (—)	— (†)	— (†)	— (†)
March 1970	5.9 (—)	55.0 (—)	14.1 (—)	4.5 (—)	57.2 (—)	15.0 (—)	17.9 (—)	35.4 (—)	6.8 (—)	— (†)	— (†)	— (†)
March 1980	3.6 (0.12)	69.2 (0.30)	20.9 (0.26)	2.0 (0.10)	72.4 (0.31)	22.8 (0.29)	11.3 (0.67)	51.2 (1.06)	7.7 (0.56)	16.5 (1.11)	44.9 (1.49)	9.2 (0.87)
March 1990	2.7 (0.09)	77.7 (0.24)	24.4 (0.25)	1.3 (0.07)	81.6 (0.25)	26.7 (0.29)	6.4 (0.45)	65.8 (0.88)	11.9 (0.60)	12.9 (0.73)	50.3 (1.09)	9.8 (0.65)
March 1995	2.0 (0.08)	81.7 (0.22)	26.0 (0.25)	0.8 (0.06)	86.0 (0.22)	28.9 (0.29)	3.4 (0.32)	73.5 (0.78)	13.7 (0.61)	10.8 (0.59)	52.9 (0.95)	10.1 (0.57)
March 1996	1.9 (0.08)	81.9 (0.23)	26.0 (0.26)	0.7 (0.06)	86.1 (0.23)	28.8 (0.30)	2.9 (0.31)	74.6 (0.80)	12.5 (0.61)	10.1 (0.59)	53.0 (0.97)	10.3 (0.59)
March 1997	1.8 (0.07)	82.0 (0.21)	26.2 (0.24)	0.6 (0.05)	86.3 (0.21)	29.0 (0.28)	2.9 (0.28)	73.8 (0.75)	12.5 (0.56)	9.2 (0.50)	54.9 (0.87)	10.6 (0.54)
March 1998	1.7 (0.07)	82.8 (0.20)	26.5 (0.24)	0.7 (0.05)	87.1 (0.21)	29.3 (0.28)	2.3 (0.25)	75.4 (0.72)	14.0 (0.58)	9.3 (0.50)	55.7 (0.85)	11.1 (0.54)
March 1999	1.6 (0.07)	83.4 (0.20)	27.5 (0.24)	0.6 (0.05)	87.7 (0.20)	30.6 (0.28)	2.0 (0.24)	77.2 (0.70)	14.3 (0.58)	9.0 (0.49)	56.0 (0.85)	10.7 (0.53)
March 2000	1.6 (0.07)	84.2 (0.19)	27.8 (0.24)	0.6 (0.05)	88.5 (0.20)	30.8 (0.28)	2.1 (0.24)	79.1 (0.67)	16.4 (0.61)	8.2 (0.46)	56.6 (0.83)	10.7 (0.52)
March 2001	1.6 (0.07)	84.4 (0.19)	28.0 (0.24)	0.6 (0.05)	88.6 (0.19)	30.9 (0.28)	1.7 (0.21)	80.6 (0.65)	15.9 (0.60)	9.4 (0.48)	55.6 (0.82)	11.1 (0.52)
March 2002	1.7 (0.05)	83.8 (0.14)	28.5 (0.17)	0.5 (0.03)	88.5 (0.14)	31.7 (0.20)	1.9 (0.16)	79.0 (0.48)	16.5 (0.44)	9.0 (0.32)	56.1 (0.55)	11.0 (0.34)
March 2003	1.7 (0.05)	84.1 (0.13)	28.9 (0.17)	0.5 (0.03)	89.0 (0.14)	32.3 (0.20)	1.9 (0.17)	79.9 (0.50)	16.8 (0.47)	8.3 (0.26)	56.3 (0.46)	11.2 (0.29)
March 2004	1.7 (0.05)	84.8 (0.13)	29.4 (0.17)	0.5 (0.03)	89.9 (0.13)	32.9 (0.20)	1.5 (0.15)	80.8 (0.49)	16.6 (0.46)	8.4 (0.25)	57.3 (0.45)	11.8 (0.30)
March 2005	1.7 (0.05)	84.9 (0.13)	28.9 (0.17)	0.5 (0.03)	89.9 (0.13)	32.3 (0.20)	1.7 (0.16)	81.4 (0.48)	16.1 (0.45)	8.0 (0.24)	58.0 (0.44)	11.8 (0.29)
Females, 25 and over												
April 1940	12.4 (—)	26.3 (—)	3.8 (—)	9.8 (—)	28.1 (—)	4.0 (—)	37.5 (—)	8.4 (—)	1.2 (—)	— (†)	— (†)	— (†)
April 1950	10.0 (—)	36.0 (—)	5.2 (—)	8.1 (—)	38.2 (—)	5.4 (—)	28.6 (—)	14.7 (—)	2.4 (—)	— (†)	— (†)	— (†)
April 1960	7.4 (—)	42.5 (—)	5.8 (—)	6.0 (—)	44.7 (—)	6.0 (—)	19.7 (—)	23.1 (—)	3.6 (—)	— (†)	— (†)	— (†)
March 1970	4.7 (—)	55.4 (—)	8.2 (—)	3.9 (—)	57.7 (—)	8.6 (—)	11.9 (—)	36.6 (—)	5.6 (—)	— (†)	— (†)	— (†)
March 1980	3.2 (0.11)	68.1 (0.28)	13.6 (0.21)	1.8 (0.09)	71.5 (0.30)	14.4 (0.23)	7.4 (0.49)	51.5 (0.94)	8.1 (0.52)	15.3 (1.03)	44.2 (1.42)	6.2 (0.69)
March 1990	2.2 (0.08)	77.5 (0.23)	18.4 (0.22)	1.0 (0.06)	81.3 (0.24)	19.8 (0.25)	4.0 (0.33)	66.5 (0.79)	10.8 (0.52)	11.7 (0.69)	51.3 (1.07)	8.7 (0.61)
March 1995	1.7 (0.07)	81.6 (0.21)	20.2 (0.22)	0.6 (0.05)	85.8 (0.22)	22.1 (0.26)	1.7 (0.21)	74.1 (0.69)	13.0 (0.53)	10.4 (0.58)	53.8 (0.94)	8.4 (0.52)
March 1996	1.7 (0.07)	81.6 (0.22)	21.4 (0.23)	0.5 (0.05)	85.9 (0.22)	23.2 (0.27)	1.6 (0.21)	74.6 (0.72)	14.8 (0.58)	10.5 (0.60)	53.3 (0.97)	8.3 (0.54)
March 1997	1.6 (0.06)	82.2 (0.20)	21.7 (0.21)	0.5 (0.04)	86.3 (0.20)	23.7 (0.25)	1.3 (0.17)	76.5 (0.64)	14.0 (0.52)	9.5 (0.51)	54.6 (0.87)	10.1 (0.53)
March 1998	1.6 (0.06)	82.9 (0.19)	22.4 (0.21)	0.6 (0.04)	87.1 (0.20)	24.1 (0.25)	1.2 (0.16)	77.1 (0.63)	15.4 (0.54)	9.2 (0.50)	55.3 (0.86)	10.9 (0.54)
March 1999	1.5 (0.06)	83.3 (0.19)	23.1 (0.22)	0.5 (0.04)	87.6 (0.19)	25.0 (0.26)	1.5 (0.18)	77.5 (0.62)	16.5 (0.55)	9.0 (0.48)	56.3 (0.83)	11.0 (0.53)
March 2000	1.5 (0.06)	84.0 (0.19)	23.6 (0.22)	0.4 (0.04)	88.4 (0.19)	25.5 (0.26)	1.1 (0.16)	78.7 (0.60)	16.8 (0.55)	9.3 (0.48)	57.5 (0.81)	10.6 (0.50)
March 2001	1.5 (0.06)	84.2 (0.18)	24.3 (0.22)	0.4 (0.04)	88.8 (0.19)	26.5 (0.26)	1.0 (0.15)	78.6 (0.60)	16.3 (0.54)	9.1 (0.47)	57.4 (0.80)	11.3 (0.51)
March 2002	1.5 (0.04)	84.4 (0.13)	25.1 (0.15)	0.5 (0.03)	88.9 (0.13)	27.3 (0.19)	1.4 (0.12)	79.4 (0.42)	17.7 (0.40)	8.3 (0.31)	57.9 (0.55)	11.2 (0.35)
March 2003	1.5 (0.04)	85.0 (0.13)	25.7 (0.15)	0.4 (0.03)	89.7 (0.13)	27.9 (0.19)	1.2 (0.12)	80.7 (0.44)	18.0 (0.43)	8.1 (0.26)	57.8 (0.46)	11.6 (0.30)
March 2004	1.4 (0.04)	85.4 (0.12)	26.1 (0.15)	0.4 (0.02)	90.1 (0.12)	28.4 (0.19)	1.1 (0.12)	81.2 (0.43)	18.5 (0.43)	7.8 (0.25)	59.5 (0.46)	12.3 (0.31)
March 2005	1.5 (0.04)	85.4 (0.12)	26.5 (0.15)	0.4 (0.03)	90.3 (0.12)	28.9 (0.19)	1.3 (0.12)	81.5 (0.42)	18.9 (0.43)	7.8 (0.25)	58.9 (0.45)	12.1 (0.30)

—Not available.
†Not applicable.
#Rounds to zero.
[1]Includes persons of Hispanic origin for years prior to 1980.
[2]Data for years prior to 1993 are for persons with 4 or more years of high school.
[3]Data for years prior to 1993 are for persons with 4 or more years of college.
[4]Estimates based on Census Bureau retrojection of 1940 census data on education by age.

NOTE: Total includes other racial/ethnic groups not separately shown. Standard errors appear in parentheses.
SOURCE: U.S. Department of Commerce, Census Bureau, U.S. Census of Population, 1960, Volume 1, part 1; Current Population Reports, Series P-20; Current Population Survey, March 1970 through March 2005; and 1960 Census Monograph, Education of the American Population, by John K. Folger and Charles B. Nam. (This table was prepared September 2005.)

Persons age 18 and over who hold at least a bachelor's degree in specific fields of study, by sex, race/ethnicity, and age: 2001

Numbers in thousands

Field of study	Total	Sex — Males	Sex — Females	White, non-Hispanic	Black, non-Hispanic	Hispanic	Asian/Pacific Islander	American Indian/Alaska Native	Age — 18 to 29 years old	30 to 49 years old	50 years old and over
	2	3	4	5	6	7	8	9	10	11	12
Total population, 18 and over	208,762 (680.6)	99,811 (484.3)	108,951 (477.6)	151,898 (779.3)	23,314 (234.3)	23,580 (273.6)	8,097 (252.9)	1,873 (135.5)	44,447 (572.0)	85,830 (721.6)	78,485 (703.0)
Number of persons with bachelor's or higher degree	49,144 (595.5)	24,977 (422.6)	24,166 (419.3)	40,138 (548.5)	3,192 (142.5)	2,189 (145.7)	3,389 (177.9)	235 (49.2)	7,016 (245)	24,666 (444)	17,461 (378.5)
Percent of population	23.5 (0.57)	25.0 (0.81)	22.2 (0.79)	26.4 (0.65)	13.7 (1.61)	9.3 (2.00)	41.9 (2.73)	12.6 (6.96)	15.8 (1.29)	28.7 (0.85)	22.2 (0.93)
Agriculture/forestry	540 (68.7)	421 (60.6)	‡ (†)	473 (64.3)	‡ (†)	‡ (†)	‡ (†)	‡ (†)	‡ (†)	254 (47.1)	239 (45.7)
Art/architecture	1,450 (112.4)	649 (75.2)	801 (83.5)	1,156 (100.4)	‡ (†)	‡ (†)	‡ (†)	‡ (†)	259 (47.6)	748 (80.8)	443 (62.2)
Business/management	8,976 (275.8)	5,679 (218.3)	3,297 (167.9)	7,254 (248.7)	623 (65.4)	426 (66.1)	633 (80.2)	‡ (†)	1,202 (102.4)	5,102 (209.4)	2,672 (152.2)
Communications	1,164 (100.7)	577 (70.9)	586 (71.5)	945 (90.8)	‡ (†)	‡ (†)	166 (41.4)	‡ (†)	301 (51.3)	706 (78.5)	157 (37.1)
Computer and information sciences	1,249 (104.3)	871 (87.0)	378 (57.4)	895 (88.4)	‡ (†)	‡ (†)	181 (43.2)	‡ (†)	268 (48.4)	828 (85.0)	152 (36.5)
Education	7,102 (246.1)	1,750 (123.0)	5,351 (212.3)	6,160 (229.6)	490 (58.1)	234 (49.1)	559 (75.5)	‡ (†)	663 (76.1)	2,891 (158.2)	3,548 (175.1)
Engineering	3,959 (184.8)	3,558 (174.2)	401 (59.2)	3,085 (163.4)	‡ (†)	173 (42.3)	‡ (†)	‡ (†)	459 (63.3)	2,057 (133.7)	1,443 (112.1)
English/literature	1,527 (115.3)	597 (72.1)	930 (89.9)	1,316 (107.1)	‡ (†)	‡ (†)	‡ (†)	‡ (†)	241 (45.9)	633 (74.3)	654 (75.6)
Foreign languages	448 (62.6)	135 (34.4)	313 (52.3)	344 (54.9)	‡ (†)	‡ (†)	‡ (†)	‡ (†)	‡ (†)	219 (43.7)	189 (40.6)
Health sciences	2,298 (141.3)	482 (64.8)	1,817 (125.3)	1,811 (125.5)	173 (34.8)	‡ (†)	213 (46.9)	‡ (†)	382 (57.8)	1,247 (104.2)	670 (76.5)
Liberal arts/humanities	2,846 (157.0)	1,150 (99.9)	1,695 (121.1)	2,444 (145.6)	146 (31.9)	‡ (†)	142 (38.3)	‡ (†)	400 (59.1)	1,308 (106.7)	1,137 (99.6)
Mathematics/statistics	869 (87.1)	507 (66.5)	362 (56.2)	567 (70.4)	‡ (†)	‡ (†)	149 (39.2)	‡ (†)	‡ (†)	386 (58.1)	363 (56.3)
Natural sciences (biological and physical)	2,910 (158.8)	1,756 (123.2)	1,153 (100.1)	2,260 (140.1)	190 (36.4)	‡ (†)	345 (59.5)	‡ (†)	413 (60.1)	1,426 (111.4)	1,071 (96.6)
Philosophy/religion/theology	628 (74.1)	437 (61.8)	191 (40.9)	533 (68.3)	‡ (†)	‡ (†)	‡ (†)	‡ (†)	‡ (†)	268 (48.4)	255 (47.2)
Pre-professional	596 (72.1)	397 (58.9)	199 (41.7)	448 (62.6)	‡ (†)	‡ (†)	‡ (†)	‡ (†)	‡ (†)	306 (51.7)	216 (43.4)
Psychology	1,903 (128.6)	606 (72.7)	1,297 (106.1)	1,561 (116.6)	157 (33.0)	‡ (†)	‡ (†)	‡ (†)	428 (61.2)	940 (90.6)	535 (68.3)
Social sciences/history	2,436 (145.4)	1,026 (94.4)	1,410 (110.5)	1,981 (131.2)	260 (42.5)	‡ (†)	‡ (†)	‡ (†)	359 (56.0)	1,092 (97.6)	985 (92.7)
Other fields	8,243 (264.6)	4,377 (192.6)	3,866 (181.5)	6,907 (242.8)	417 (53.7)	337 (58.8)	559 (75.5)	‡ (†)	1,253 (104.5)	4,256 (191.5)	2,734 (153.9)

Percentage distribution of degree holders, by field

Field of study	Total	Sex — Males	Sex — Females	White, non-Hispanic	Black, non-Hispanic	Hispanic	Asian/Pacific Islander	American Indian/Alaska Native	Age — 18 to 29 years old	30 to 49 years old	50 years old and over
Total	100.0 (†)	100.0 (†)	100.0 (†)	100.0 (†)	100.0 (†)	100.0 (†)	100.0 (†)	100.0 (†)	100.0 (†)	100.0 (†)	100.0 (†)
Agriculture/forestry	1.1 (0.14)	1.7 (0.24)	0.5 (0.13)	1.2 (0.16)	0.7 (0.38)	1.1 (0.73)	0.5 (0.40)	4.4 (4.32)	0.7 (0.29)	1.0 (0.19)	1.4 (0.26)
Art/architecture	3.0 (0.23)	2.6 (0.30)	3.3 (0.34)	2.9 (0.25)	3.3 (0.83)	4.8 (1.47)	2.2 (0.81)	‡ (†)	3.7 (0.67)	3.0 (0.32)	2.5 (0.35)
Business/management	18.3 (0.52)	22.7 (0.78)	13.6 (0.65)	18.1 (0.57)	19.5 (1.86)	19.5 (2.72)	18.7 (2.16)	17.5 (7.98)	17.1 (1.33)	20.7 (0.76)	15.3 (0.81)
Communications	2.4 (0.20)	2.3 (0.28)	2.4 (0.29)	2.4 (0.22)	3.2 (0.82)	3.3 (1.23)	1.2 (0.60)	‡ (†)	4.3 (0.72)	2.9 (0.31)	0.9 (0.21)
Computer and information sciences	2.5 (0.21)	3.5 (0.34)	1.6 (0.24)	2.2 (0.22)	3.9 (0.91)	2.6 (1.10)	4.9 (1.19)	‡ (†)	3.8 (0.68)	3.4 (0.34)	0.9 (0.21)
Education	14.5 (0.47)	7.0 (0.48)	22.1 (0.79)	15.3 (0.53)	15.3 (1.69)	10.7 (2.13)	5.3 (1.24)	16.0 (7.69)	9.5 (1.03)	11.7 (0.61)	20.3 (0.90)
Engineering	8.1 (0.36)	14.2 (0.65)	1.7 (0.24)	7.7 (0.39)	3.6 (0.87)	7.9 (1.86)	16.5 (2.05)	11.4 (6.67)	6.5 (0.87)	8.3 (0.52)	8.3 (0.62)
English/literature	3.1 (0.23)	2.4 (0.29)	3.8 (0.37)	3.3 (0.26)	2.6 (0.75)	3.1 (1.19)	1.7 (0.71)	‡ (†)	3.4 (0.64)	2.6 (0.30)	3.7 (0.43)
Foreign languages	0.9 (0.13)	0.5 (0.14)	1.3 (0.22)	0.9 (0.14)	0.8 (0.42)	1.7 (0.90)	1.0 (0.56)	‡ (†)	0.6 (0.27)	0.9 (0.18)	1.1 (0.23)
Health sciences	4.7 (0.28)	1.9 (0.26)	7.5 (0.50)	4.5 (0.31)	5.4 (1.06)	4.4 (1.41)	6.3 (1.34)	2.1 (2.99)	5.4 (0.80)	5.1 (0.41)	3.8 (0.43)
Liberal arts/humanities	5.8 (0.31)	4.6 (0.39)	7.0 (0.49)	6.1 (0.35)	4.6 (0.98)	4.7 (1.45)	4.2 (1.11)	4.5 (4.37)	5.7 (0.82)	5.3 (0.42)	6.5 (0.55)
Mathematics/statistics	1.8 (0.18)	2.0 (0.26)	1.5 (0.23)	1.4 (0.17)	2.4 (0.72)	2.4 (1.05)	4.4 (1.13)	10.4 (6.41)	1.6 (0.46)	1.6 (0.23)	2.1 (0.32)
Natural sciences (biological and physical)	5.9 (0.31)	7.0 (0.48)	4.8 (0.41)	5.6 (0.34)	6.0 (1.11)	4.9 (1.49)	10.2 (1.67)	2.7 (3.41)	5.9 (0.83)	5.8 (0.44)	6.1 (0.54)
Philosophy/religion/theology	1.3 (0.15)	1.8 (0.25)	0.8 (0.17)	1.3 (0.17)	0.9 (0.45)	1.8 (0.90)	0.8 (0.49)	‡ (†)	1.5 (0.43)	1.1 (0.20)	1.5 (0.27)
Pre-professional	1.2 (0.15)	1.6 (0.23)	0.8 (0.17)	1.1 (0.16)	1.6 (0.59)	2.0 (0.97)	1.5 (0.67)	‡ (†)	1.1 (0.36)	1.2 (0.21)	1.2 (0.25)
Psychology	3.9 (0.26)	2.4 (0.29)	5.4 (0.43)	3.9 (0.29)	4.9 (1.01)	5.0 (1.50)	1.7 (0.72)	7.9 (5.65)	6.1 (0.85)	3.8 (0.36)	3.1 (0.39)
Social sciences/history	5.0 (0.29)	4.1 (0.37)	5.8 (0.45)	4.9 (0.32)	8.1 (1.28)	4.7 (1.45)	2.4 (0.85)	4.7 (4.45)	5.1 (0.78)	4.4 (0.39)	5.6 (0.52)
Other fields	16.8 (0.50)	17.5 (0.71)	16.0 (0.70)	17.2 (0.56)	13.1 (1.58)	15.4 (2.48)	16.5 (2.05)	9.9 (6.26)	17.9 (1.35)	17.3 (0.71)	15.7 (0.81)

†Not applicable.
‡Reporting standards not met.
NOTE: Data are based on a sample survey of the civilian noninstitutional population. Detail may not sum to totals because of rounding. Standard errors appear in parentheses.

SOURCE: U.S. Department of Commerce, Census Bureau, Survey of Income and Program Participation, 2001, unpublished tabulations. (This table was prepared September 2005.)

Number of persons age 18 and over, by highest level of education attained, age, sex, and race/ethnicity: 2005

[In thousands]

Age, sex, and race/ethnicity	Total	Elementary — Less than 7 years	Elementary — 7 or 8 years	High school — 1 to 3 years	High school — 4 years	High school — Completion		College — Some college	College — Associate's degree	College — Bachelor's degree		College — Master's degree		College — Professional degree	College — Doctor's
1	2	3	4	5	6	7		8	9	10		11		12	13
Total															
18 and over	217,334	7,105	5,619	18,206	3,220	69,308	(244.1)	41,647	17,587	36,456	(193.2)	12,902	(121.4)	2,936	2,347
18 and 19 years old	7,570	74	99	2,626	431	2,151	(50.7)	2,131	42	14	(4.1)	#	(†)	2	#
20 to 24 years old	20,402	334	280	1,877	389	6,240	(85.6)	7,717	1,241	2,223	(51.5)	86	(10.2)	10	5
25 years old and over	189,362	6,697	5,240	13,703	2,400	60,917	(234.3)	31,798	16,303	34,219	(188.2)	12,816	(121.0)	2,925	2,343
25 to 29 years old	19,499	553	322	1,476	355	5,734	(82.2)	3,814	1,665	4,372	(72.0)	907	(33.0)	222	79
30 to 34 years old	19,808	604	307	1,322	277	5,568	(81.0)	3,550	1,859	4,423	(72.4)	1,441	(41.6)	280	178
35 to 39 years old	20,651	636	307	1,242	271	6,374	(86.5)	3,452	1,964	4,297	(71.3)	1,461	(41.8)	378	270
40 to 49 years old	44,933	1,207	656	2,657	505	14,633	(128.8)	7,760	4,602	8,599	(100.0)	3,028	(60.1)	754	530
50 to 59 years old	36,489	1,071	730	2,021	355	11,363	(114.3)	6,406	3,451	6,531	(87.5)	3,307	(62.7)	627	627
60 to 64 years old	12,769	431	391	997	165	4,443	(72.5)	2,016	960	1,962	(48.4)	982	(34.3)	173	250
65 years old and over	35,213	2,194	2,527	3,989	474	12,801	(120.9)	4,800	1,802	4,036	(69.2)	1,691	(45.0)	491	409
Males															
18 and over	104,945	3,671	2,735	9,012	1,665	33,779	(187.2)	19,433	7,484	17,534	(140.0)	6,145	(85.0)	1,899	1,589
18 and 19 years old	3,760	56	68	1,423	230	1,054	(35.6)	906	18	3	(2.0)	#	(†)	2	#
20 to 24 years old	10,288	205	165	995	240	3,551	(65.0)	3,659	541	903	(32.9)	22	(5.1)	3	5
25 years old and over	90,896	3,410	2,502	6,594	1,195	29,173	(175.9)	14,869	6,925	16,628	(136.6)	6,123	(84.8)	1,894	1,584
25 to 29 years old	9,825	328	180	753	218	3,223	(61.9)	1,853	781	1,983	(48.7)	353	(20.6)	122	30
30 to 34 years old	9,851	324	173	700	162	3,013	(59.9)	1,731	839	2,048	(49.5)	608	(27.0)	152	100
35 to 39 years old	10,264	353	175	690	144	3,397	(63.6)	1,624	838	2,031	(49.3)	654	(28.1)	213	146
40 to 49 years old	22,139	658	359	1,423	270	7,622	(94.3)	3,597	1,911	4,005	(68.9)	1,491	(42.3)	467	337
50 to 59 years old	17,624	556	372	930	167	5,245	(78.7)	3,028	1,493	3,377	(63.4)	1,585	(43.6)	432	438
60 to 64 years old	6,044	254	178	462	70	1,876	(47.4)	910	400	1,049	(35.5)	528	(25.2)	131	187
65 years old and over	15,151	938	1,065	1,638	165	4,797	(75.3)	2,125	663	2,134	(50.5)	904	(32.9)	376	345
Females															
18 and over	112,389	3,434	2,884	9,194	1,555	35,530	(191.1)	22,213	10,103	18,922	(145.0)	6,757	(89.0)	1,037	759
18 and 19 years old	3,810	18	31	1,202	201	1,097	(36.3)	1,225	24	11	(3.6)	#	(†)	#	#
20 to 24 years old	10,114	129	115	882	149	2,690	(56.6)	4,059	700	1,320	(39.8)	64	(8.8)	7	#
25 years old and over	98,465	3,287	2,739	7,110	1,205	31,743	(182.3)	16,929	9,379	17,591	(140.2)	6,693	(88.6)	1,031	759
25 to 29 years old	9,674	225	142	723	136	2,510	(54.7)	1,961	885	2,389	(53.4)	554	(25.8)	100	49
30 to 34 years old	9,957	280	134	622	114	2,556	(55.2)	1,819	1,019	2,374	(53.2)	833	(31.6)	127	78
35 to 39 years old	10,387	284	132	552	127	2,977	(59.5)	1,827	1,126	2,266	(52.0)	806	(31.1)	165	124
40 to 49 years old	22,794	550	298	1,235	235	7,011	(90.6)	4,162	2,692	4,594	(73.7)	1,537	(42.9)	288	192
50 to 59 years old	18,865	515	358	1,091	189	6,119	(84.8)	3,379	1,958	3,153	(61.3)	1,721	(45.4)	195	188
60 to 64 years old	6,724	177	212	535	95	2,567	(55.3)	1,106	559	913	(33.1)	454	(23.4)	42	63
65 years old and over	20,063	1,256	1,461	2,351	308	8,004	(96.6)	2,675	1,139	1,902	(47.7)	788	(30.8)	114	64
White, non-Hispanic															
18 and over	152,059	1,392	3,180	10,159	1,550	49,388	(217.6)	30,035	13,402	28,334	(173.7)	10,395	(109.5)	2,351	1,875
18 and 19 years old	4,723	10	41	1,584	233	1,360	(40.4)	1,461	24	9	(3.2)	#	(†)	2	#
20 to 24 years old	12,621	18	105	787	151	3,683	(66.1)	5,189	888	1,735	(45.6)	53	(8.0)	8	5
25 years old and over	134,715	1,363	3,034	7,788	1,166	44,346	(208.9)	23,386	12,490	26,590	(168.9)	10,342	(109.3)	2,341	1,870
25 to 29 years old	11,616	48	86	593	112	3,309	(62.7)	2,404	1,097	3,110	(60.8)	648	(27.9)	145	62
30 to 34 years old	12,053	44	84	481	85	3,351	(63.1)	2,227	1,284	3,151	(61.2)	1,025	(35.1)	200	122
35 to 39 years old	13,333	43	82	555	109	4,143	(70.1)	2,291	1,436	3,126	(61.0)	1,061	(35.7)	297	189
40 to 49 years old	31,593	136	277	1,364	219	10,306	(109.1)	5,557	3,591	6,705	(88.7)	2,427	(53.8)	601	410
50 to 59 years old	27,539	191	374	1,165	197	8,542	(99.7)	5,047	2,793	5,331	(79.3)	2,853	(58.3)	530	518
60 to 64 years old	9,945	111	234	639	103	3,561	(65.0)	1,659	760	1,656	(44.5)	856	(32.1)	153	212
65 years old and over	28,636	790	1,897	2,992	340	11,133	(113.2)	4,200	1,529	3,511	(64.6)	1,472	(42.0)	415	357
Black, non-Hispanic															
18 and over	24,389	598	542	3,075	585	8,962	(99.5)	5,034	1,778	2,742	(59.4)	836	(33.5)	138	98
18 and 19 years old	1,082	0	14	428	62	328	(21.1)	240	6	4	(2.4)	#	(†)	#	#
20 to 24 years old	2,732	11	24	369	84	957	(35.8)	988	123	167	(15.1)	7	(3.2)	#	#
25 years old and over	20,575	586	505	2,278	440	7,676	(93.6)	3,806	1,649	2,571	(57.6)	828	(33.3)	138	98
25 to 29 years old	2,480	19	14	227	63	940	(35.5)	558	224	369	(22.4)	57	(8.8)	9	#
30 to 34 years old	2,418	13	14	157	42	859	(33.9)	596	223	382	(22.7)	104	(11.9)	20	7
35 to 39 years old	2,485	24	12	190	55	1,016	(36.8)	460	212	380	(22.7)	105	(12.0)	18	13
40 to 49 years old	5,296	46	39	492	103	2,128	(52.6)	1,054	436	731	(31.3)	202	(16.6)	35	30
50 to 59 years old	3,795	92	82	398	75	1,436	(43.6)	674	339	431	(24.1)	210	(16.9)	28	30
60 to 64 years old	1,208	41	48	193	33	477	(25.4)	172	88	93	(11.3)	50	(8.2)	2	10
65 years old and over	2,893	350	295	620	70	820	(33.2)	292	128	184	(15.8)	100	(11.7)	26	7

See notes at end of table.

Number of persons age 18 and over, by highest level of education attained, age, sex, and race/ethnicity: 2005—Continued
[In thousands]

Age, sex, and race/ethnicity	Total	Elementary		High school				College						
		Less than 7 years	7 or 8 years	1 to 3 years	4 years	Completion		Some college	Associate's degree	Bachelor's degree		Master's degree		Professional degree	Doctor's
1	2	3	4	5	6	7		8	9	10		11		12	13
Hispanic															
18 and over.............................	27,509	4,590	1,618	4,175	852	7,849	(73.8)	4,175	1,407	2,045	(42.0)	553	(22.4)	150	95
18 and 19 years old	1,283	61	44	464	93	358	(18.1)	253	10	1	(1.1)	#	(†)	#	#
20 to 24 years old	3,675	302	141	634	129	1,264	(33.4)	915	145	139	(11.3)	7	(2.5)	#	#
25 years old and over..........	22,551	4,227	1,433	3,077	630	6,228	(67.9)	3,006	1,252	1,904	(40.6)	546	(22.3)	150	95
25 to 29 years old.............	3,948	476	206	607	161	1,205	(32.7)	608	244	360	(18.1)	52	(6.9)	19	10
30 to 34 years old.............	3,688	535	194	620	127	1,064	(30.8)	507	223	317	(17.0)	77	(8.4)	19	6
35 to 39 years old.............	3,298	542	198	452	100	924	(28.8)	471	179	323	(17.2)	81	(8.6)	17	12
40 to 49 years old.............	5,314	958	292	658	148	1,473	(36.0)	735	335	491	(21.1)	155	(11.9)	49	20
50 to 59 years old.............	3,135	692	210	359	52	849	(27.6)	415	138	265	(15.6)	108	(10.0)	19	28
60 to 64 years old.............	973	234	88	121	16	251	(15.2)	121	60	46	(6.5)	26	(4.9)	7	3
65 years old and over.......	2,194	791	245	260	27	461	(20.5)	149	74	103	(9.7)	47	(6.6)	21	15

†Not applicable.
#Rounds to zero.
NOTE: Total includes other racial/ethnic groups not shown separately. Although cells with fewer than 75,000 weighted persons are subject to relatively wide sampling variation, they are included in the table to permit various types of aggregations. Detail may not sum to totals because of rounding. Standard errors appear in parentheses.
SOURCE: U.S. Department of Commerce, Census Bureau, Current Population Survey (CPS), March 2005, unpublished tabulations. (This table was prepared September 2005.)

Educational Attainment

Educational attainment of persons 18 years old and over, by state: Selected years, 1994 through 2004

State	Percent of population, 25 years old and over, by education level, 2000					Percent of population, 25 years old and over, by education level, 2004		Percent of 18- to 24-year-olds who were high school completers[1]	
	Percent with less than high school completion	Percent with high school completion or higher	Percent with bachelor's or higher degree			Percent with high school completion or higher	Percent with bachelor's or higher degree	1994 through 1996	1999 through 2001
			Total	Bachelor's degree	Graduate or professional degree				
1	2	3	4	5	6	7	8	9	10
United States	19.6	80.4	24.4	15.5	8.9	85.2 (0.09)	27.7 (0.11)	85.8 (0.19)	86.3 (0.19)
Alabama	24.7	75.3	19.0	12.1	6.9	82.4 (0.73)	22.3 (0.79)	87.2 (1.37)	82.0 (1.70)
Alaska	11.7	88.3	24.7	16.1	8.6	90.2 (0.67)	25.5 (0.91)	87.4 (4.11)	90.9 (3.64)
Arizona	19.0	81.0	23.5	15.1	8.4	84.4 (0.79)	28.0 (0.97)	84.0 (1.56)	77.6 (1.64)
Arkansas	24.7	75.3	16.7	11.0	5.7	79.2 (0.79)	18.8 (0.79)	88.6 (1.70)	86.7 (1.94)
California	23.2	76.8	26.6	17.1	9.5	81.3 (0.36)	31.7 (0.43)	78.6 (0.64)	85.1 (0.55)
Colorado	13.1	86.9	32.7	21.6	11.1	88.3 (0.55)	35.5 (0.79)	87.9 (1.42)	82.4 (1.73)
Connecticut	16.0	84.0	31.4	18.1	13.3	88.8 (0.55)	34.5 (0.79)	96.1 (1.01)	93.6 (1.45)
Delaware	17.4	82.6	25.0	15.6	9.4	86.5 (0.73)	26.9 (0.97)	90.3 (3.09)	90.8 (3.16)
District of Columbia	22.2	77.8	39.1	18.1	21.0	86.4 (0.73)	45.7 (1.09)	86.2 (3.85)	88.2 (3.82)
Florida	20.1	79.9	22.3	14.2	8.1	85.9 (0.43)	26.0 (0.49)	80.1 (0.97)	83.8 (0.91)
Georgia	21.4	78.6	24.3	16.0	8.3	85.2 (0.67)	27.6 (0.85)	81.3 (1.26)	84.7 (1.17)
Hawaii	15.4	84.6	26.2	17.8	8.4	88.0 (0.67)	26.6 (0.91)	92.6 (2.05)	91.3 (2.51)
Idaho	15.3	84.7	21.7	14.9	6.8	87.9 (0.67)	23.8 (0.85)	84.9 (2.73)	88.3 (2.50)
Illinois	18.6	81.4	26.1	16.6	9.5	86.8 (0.43)	27.4 (0.55)	87.9 (0.83)	88.4 (0.86)
Indiana	17.9	82.1	19.4	12.2	7.2	87.2 (0.55)	21.1 (0.67)	89.7 (1.12)	89.4 (1.26)
Iowa	13.9	86.1	21.2	14.7	6.5	89.8 (0.55)	24.3 (0.79)	91.9 (1.35)	92.4 (1.45)
Kansas	14.0	86.0	25.8	17.1	8.7	89.6 (0.55)	30.0 (0.79)	91.6 (1.53)	88.2 (1.79)
Kentucky	25.9	74.1	17.1	10.2	6.9	81.8 (0.73)	21.0 (0.79)	82.2 (1.79)	87.4 (1.57)
Louisiana	25.2	74.8	18.7	12.2	6.5	78.7 (0.91)	22.4 (0.91)	82.2 (1.63)	82.6 (1.63)
Maine	14.6	85.4	22.9	15.0	7.9	87.1 (0.55)	24.2 (0.73)	91.4 (2.36)	93.6 (2.19)
Maryland	16.2	83.8	31.4	18.0	13.4	87.4 (0.61)	35.2 (0.91)	93.4 (1.07)	84.9 (1.60)
Massachusetts	15.2	84.8	33.2	19.5	13.7	86.9 (0.55)	36.7 (0.79)	92.4 (1.01)	91.4 (1.08)
Michigan	16.6	83.4	21.8	13.7	8.1	87.9 (0.43)	24.4 (0.61)	89.1 (0.89)	88.1 (0.92)
Minnesota	12.1	87.9	27.4	19.1	8.3	92.3 (0.43)	32.5 (0.79)	95.3 (0.91)	93.1 (1.06)
Mississippi	27.1	72.9	16.9	11.1	5.8	83.0 (0.79)	20.1 (0.85)	82.0 (2.07)	84.3 (2.00)
Missouri	18.7	81.3	21.6	14.0	7.6	87.9 (0.61)	28.1 (0.79)	89.9 (1.19)	90.4 (1.18)
Montana	12.8	87.2	24.4	17.2	7.2	91.9 (0.55)	25.5 (0.91)	89.8 (3.08)	92.4 (2.67)
Nebraska	13.4	86.6	23.7	16.4	7.3	91.3 (0.55)	24.8 (0.85)	93.0 (1.76)	90.8 (1.94)
Nevada	19.3	80.7	18.2	12.1	6.1	86.3 (0.67)	24.5 (0.79)	81.5 (3.09)	79.6 (2.84)
New Hampshire	12.6	87.4	28.7	18.7	10.0	90.8 (0.55)	35.4 (0.85)	87.4 (3.03)	86.6 (3.30)
New Jersey	17.9	82.1	29.8	18.8	11.0	87.6 (0.49)	34.6 (0.67)	93.0 (0.86)	89.3 (1.07)
New Mexico	21.1	78.9	23.5	13.7	9.8	82.9 (0.85)	25.1 (0.97)	78.8 (2.86)	85.0 (2.59)
New York	20.9	79.1	27.4	15.6	11.8	85.4 (0.36)	30.6 (0.49)	86.4 (0.72)	86.8 (0.76)
North Carolina	21.9	78.1	22.5	15.3	7.2	80.9 (0.67)	23.4 (0.73)	85.3 (1.16)	84.7 (1.23)
North Dakota	16.1	83.9	22.0	16.5	5.5	89.5 (0.55)	25.2 (0.79)	97.9 (1.56)	96.8 (2.01)
Ohio	17.0	83.0	21.1	13.7	7.4	88.1 (0.43)	24.6 (0.55)	87.7 (0.88)	87.0 (0.91)
Oklahoma	19.4	80.6	20.3	13.5	6.8	85.2 (0.67)	22.9 (0.79)	89.5 (1.55)	86.0 (1.74)
Oregon	14.9	85.1	25.1	16.4	8.7	87.4 (0.61)	25.9 (0.79)	81.1 (2.02)	86.3 (1.70)
Pennsylvania	18.1	81.9	22.4	14.0	8.4	86.5 (0.43)	25.3 (0.55)	89.6 (0.82)	89.8 (0.83)
Rhode Island	22.0	78.0	25.6	15.9	9.7	81.1 (0.67)	27.2 (0.73)	87.5 (3.33)	85.5 (3.46)
South Carolina	23.7	76.3	20.4	13.5	6.9	83.6 (0.73)	24.9 (0.91)	88.4 (1.48)	84.5 (1.71)
South Dakota	15.4	84.6	21.5	15.5	6.0	87.5 (0.61)	25.5 (0.79)	89.6 (3.24)	91.6 (2.90)
Tennessee	24.1	75.9	19.6	12.8	6.8	82.9 (0.73)	24.3 (0.85)	83.3 (1.46)	86.6 (1.36)
Texas	24.3	75.7	23.2	15.6	7.6	78.3 (0.49)	24.5 (0.49)	79.3 (0.78)	79.9 (0.79)
Utah	12.3	87.7	26.1	17.8	8.3	91.0 (0.61)	30.8 (1.03)	91.3 (1.56)	88.9 (1.67)
Vermont	13.6	86.4	29.4	18.3	11.1	90.8 (0.61)	34.2 (0.97)	87.2 (3.99)	86.6 (4.47)
Virginia	18.5	81.5	29.5	17.9	11.6	88.4 (0.61)	33.1 (0.85)	86.3 (1.23)	88.2 (1.20)
Washington	12.9	87.1	27.7	18.4	9.3	89.7 (0.61)	29.9 (0.91)	86.8 (1.30)	88.3 (1.25)
West Virginia	24.8	75.2	14.8	8.9	5.9	80.9 (0.67)	15.3 (0.61)	87.7 (2.25)	88.5 (2.26)
Wisconsin	14.9	85.1	22.4	15.2	7.2	88.8 (0.55)	25.6 (0.73)	94.2 (0.91)	90.3 (1.19)
Wyoming	12.1	87.9	21.9	14.9	7.0	91.9 (0.55)	22.5 (0.79)	89.4 (3.93)	87.3 (4.51)

[1]High school completers include diploma recipients and those completing through alternative credentials, such as a GED. Data reflect 3-year averages.

NOTE: Standard errors appear in parentheses. Detail may not sum to totals because of rounding. Some data have been revised from previously published figures.

SOURCE: U.S. Department of Commerce, Census Bureau, *Census 2000 Brief,* "Educational Attainment: 2000" and "Educational Attainment in the United States: 2004," retrieved on March 23, 2005, from http://www.census.gov/population/www/socdemo/education/cps2004.html; and Census 2000 Summary File 3, retrieved on March 23, 2005, from http://www.census.gov/Press-Release/www/2002/sumfile3.html. U.S. Department of Education, National Center for Education Statistics, *Dropout Rates in the United States, 2001.* (This table was prepared March 2005.)

Percentage of 12- to 17-year-olds reporting drug use during the past 30 days and past year, by drug used: Selected years, 1982 through 2003

Year	Percent reporting drug use during past 30 days					Percent reporting drug use during past year				
	Illicit drug use			Alcohol	Cigarettes	Illicit drug use			Alcohol	Cigarettes
	Any[1]	Marijuana	Cocaine			Any[1]	Marijuana	Cocaine		
1	2	3	4	5	6	7	8	9	10	11
1982	— (†)	9.9 —	1.9 —	34.9 —	— (†)	— (†)	17.7 —	3.7 —	46.1 —	— (†)
1985	13.2 —	10.2 —	1.5 —	41.2 —	29.4 —	20.7 —	16.7 —	3.4 —	52.7 —	29.9 —
1988	8.1 —	5.4 —	1.2 —	33.4 —	22.7 —	14.9 —	10.7 —	2.5 —	45.5 —	26.8 —
1990	7.1 —	4.4 —	0.6 —	32.5 —	22.4 —	14.1 —	9.6 —	1.9 —	41.8 —	26.2 —
1993	5.7 —	4.0 —	0.4 —	23.9 —	18.5 —	11.9 —	8.5 —	0.7 —	35.9 —	22.5 —
1994	8.2 —	6.0 —	0.3 —	21.6 —	18.9 —	15.5 —	11.4 —	1.1 —	36.2 —	24.5 —
1995	10.9 —	8.2 —	0.8 —	21.1 —	20.2 —	18.0 —	14.2 —	1.7 —	35.1 —	26.6 —
1996	9.0 —	7.1 —	0.6 —	18.8 —	18.3 —	16.7 —	13.0 —	1.4 —	32.7 —	24.2 —
1997	11.4 —	9.4 —	1.0 —	20.5 —	19.9 —	18.8 —	15.8 —	2.2 —	34.0 —	26.4 —
1998	9.9 —	8.3 —	0.8 —	19.1 —	18.2 —	16.4 —	14.1 —	1.7 —	31.8 —	23.8 —
1999	9.8 (0.23)	7.2 (0.20)	0.5 (0.06)	16.5 (0.30)	14.9 (0.31)	19.8 (0.32)	14.2 (0.29)	1.6 (0.10)	34.1 (0.41)	23.4 (0.37)
2000	9.7 (0.24)	7.2 (0.21)	0.6 (0.07)	16.4 (0.29)	13.4 (0.28)	18.6 (0.31)	13.4 (0.27)	1.7 (0.12)	33.0 (0.39)	20.8 (0.34)
2001	10.8 (0.26)	8.0 (0.24)	0.4 (0.06)	17.3 (0.33)	13.0 (0.28)	20.8 (0.36)	15.2 (0.32)	1.5 (0.10)	33.9 (0.39)	20.0 (0.35)
2002	11.6 (0.29)	8.2 (0.24)	0.6 (0.07)	17.6 (0.32)	13.0 (0.30)	22.2 (0.38)	15.8 (0.32)	2.1 (0.13)	34.6 (0.42)	20.3 (0.35)
2003	11.2 (0.27)	7.9 (0.24)	0.6 (0.06)	17.7 (0.33)	12.2 (0.29)	21.8 (0.36)	15.0 (0.31)	1.8 (0.11)	34.3 (0.42)	19.0 (0.36)

—Not available.

†Not applicable.

[1]Includes other illegal drug use not shown separately.

NOTE: Marijuana includes hashish usage for 1996 and later years. Due to changes in the survey instrument and administration and to improve comparability with new data, estimates for 1982 through 1993 have been adjusted and may differ from those reported in previous years. Data for 1999 have been revised from previously published figures. Data for 1999 and later years were gathered using Computer Assisted Interviewing (CAI) and may not be directly comparable to previous years. Standard errors appear in parentheses.

SOURCE: U.S. Department of Health and Human Services, Substance Abuse and Mental Health Services Administration, National Survey on Drug Use and Health (formerly called National Household Survey on Drug Abuse), 1982 through 2003. (This table was prepared August 2005.)

Percentage of high school seniors reporting drug use, by type of drug and frequency of use:
Selected years, 1975 through 2004

Type of drug	Class of 1975		Class of 1980		Class of 1985		Class of 1989		Class of 1990		Class of 1991		Class of 1992		Class of 1993		Class of 1994		Class of 1995	
1	2		3		4		5		6		7		8		9		10		11	
Percent reporting having ever used drugs																					
Alcohol[1]	90.4	(0.69)	93.2	(0.46)	92.2	(0.48)	90.7	(0.51)	89.5	(0.57)	88.0	(0.61)	87.5	(0.60)	80.0	(0.71)	80.4	(0.73)	80.7	(0.73)
Any illicit drug	55.2	(1.68)	65.4	(1.23)	60.6	(1.26)	50.9	(1.27)	47.9	(1.33)	44.1	(1.33)	40.7	(1.28)	42.9	(1.27)	45.6	(1.31)	48.4	(1.32)
Marijuana only	19.0	(1.32)	26.7	(1.15)	20.9	(1.05)	19.5	(1.00)	18.5	(1.03)	17.2	(1.01)	15.6	(0.94)	16.2	(0.94)	18.0	(1.01)	20.3	(1.06)
Any illicit drug other than marijuana[2]	36.2	(1.33)	38.7	(1.04)	39.7	(1.04)	31.4	(0.96)	29.4	(0.99)	26.9	(0.97)	25.1	(0.93)	26.7	(0.93)	27.6	(0.97)	28.1	(0.97)
Use of selected drugs																					
Cocaine.........................	9.0	(0.73)	15.7	(0.72)	17.3	(0.74)	10.3	(0.59)	9.4	(0.59)	7.8	(0.55)	6.1	(0.47)	6.1	(0.47)	5.9	(0.47)	6.0	(0.48)
Heroin	2.2	(0.21)	1.1	(0.12)	1.2	(0.12)	1.3	(0.12)	1.3	(0.13)	0.9	(0.11)	1.2	(0.12)	1.1	(0.12)	1.2	(0.12)	1.6	(0.14)
LSD................................	11.3	(0.81)	9.3	(0.57)	7.5	(0.52)	8.3	(0.53)	8.7	(0.57)	8.8	(0.58)	8.6	(0.56)	10.3	(0.59)	10.5	(0.62)	11.7	(0.64)
Marijuana/hashish...........	47.3	(1.68)	60.3	(1.27)	54.2	(1.29)	43.7	(1.26)	40.7	(1.30)	36.7	(1.29)	32.6	(1.22)	35.3	(1.22)	38.2	(1.28)	41.7	(1.30)
PCP	—	(†)	9.6	(0.33)	4.9	(0.24)	3.9	(0.21)	2.8	(0.19)	2.9	(0.19)	2.4	(0.17)	2.9	(0.19)	2.8	(0.19)	2.7	(0.18)
Percent reporting use of drugs in the past 12 months																					
Alcohol[1]	84.8	(0.84)	87.9	(0.59)	85.6	(0.63)	82.7	(0.67)	80.6	(0.73)	77.7	(0.78)	76.8	(0.77)	72.7	(0.80)	73.0	(0.82)	73.7	(0.81)
Any illicit drug	45.0	(1.64)	53.1	(1.26)	46.3	(1.26)	35.4	(1.18)	32.5	(1.21)	29.4	(1.19)	27.1	(1.13)	31.0	(1.16)	35.8	(1.23)	39.0	(1.26)
Marijuana only	18.8	(1.29)	22.7	(1.06)	18.9	(0.99)	15.4	(0.89)	14.6	(0.91)	13.2	(0.88)	12.2	(0.83)	13.9	(0.87)	17.8	(0.98)	19.6	(1.02)
Any illicit drug other than marijuana[2]	26.2	(1.15)	30.4	(0.92)	27.4	(0.89)	20.0	(0.78)	17.9	(0.79)	16.2	(0.76)	14.9	(0.72)	17.1	(0.75)	18.0	(0.78)	19.4	(0.81)
Use of selected drugs																					
Cocaine.........................	5.6	(0.52)	12.3	(0.58)	13.1	(0.59)	6.5	(0.42)	5.3	(0.40)	3.5	(0.33)	3.1	(0.31)	3.3	(0.31)	3.6	(0.33)	4.0	(0.35)
Heroin	1.0	(0.13)	0.5	(0.07)	0.6	(0.07)	0.6	(0.07)	0.5	(0.07)	0.4	(0.06)	0.6	(0.08)	0.5	(0.07)	0.6	(0.08)	1.1	(0.10)
LSD................................	7.2	(0.59)	6.5	(0.43)	4.4	(0.36)	4.9	(0.37)	5.4	(0.41)	5.2	(0.40)	5.6	(0.40)	6.8	(0.44)	6.9	(0.45)	8.4	(0.49)
Marijuana/hashish...........	40.0	(1.61)	48.8	(1.27)	40.6	(1.24)	29.6	(1.13)	27.0	(1.15)	23.9	(1.11)	21.9	(1.05)	26.0	(1.10)	30.7	(1.19)	34.7	(1.23)
PCP	—	(†)	4.4	(0.20)	2.9	(0.16)	2.4	(0.15)	1.2	(0.11)	1.4	(0.12)	1.4	(0.11)	1.4	(0.11)	1.6	(0.12)	1.8	(0.13)
Percent reporting use of drugs in the past 30 days																					
Alcohol[1]	68.2	(1.10)	72.0	(0.81)	65.9	(0.85)	60.0	(0.86)	57.1	(0.92)	54.0	(0.93)	51.3	(0.91)	48.6	(0.89)	50.1	(0.92)	51.3	(0.92)
Any illicit drug	30.7	(1.35)	37.2	(1.09)	29.7	(1.03)	19.7	(0.88)	17.2	(0.87)	16.4	(0.86)	14.4	(0.79)	18.3	(0.86)	21.9	(0.95)	23.8	(0.98)
Marijuana only	15.3	(1.06)	18.8	(0.88)	14.8	(0.80)	10.6	(0.68)	9.2	(0.67)	9.3	(0.67)	8.1	(0.62)	10.4	(0.68)	13.1	(0.77)	13.8	(0.79)
Any illicit drug other than marijuana[2]	15.4	(0.80)	18.4	(0.66)	14.9	(0.60)	9.1	(0.48)	8.0	(0.47)	7.1	(0.45)	6.3	(0.41)	7.9	(0.45)	8.8	(0.49)	10.0	(0.52)
Use of selected drugs																					
Cocaine.........................	1.9	(0.25)	5.2	(0.31)	6.7	(0.35)	2.8	(0.23)	1.9	(0.20)	1.4	(0.17)	1.3	(0.16)	1.3	(0.16)	1.5	(0.18)	1.8	(0.19)
Heroin	0.4	(0.08)	0.2	(0.04)	0.3	(0.05)	0.3	(0.05)	0.2	(0.04)	0.2	(0.04)	0.3	(0.05)	0.2	(0.04)	0.3	(0.05)	0.6	(0.08)
LSD................................	2.3	(0.28)	2.3	(0.21)	1.6	(0.18)	1.8	(0.18)	1.9	(0.20)	1.9	(0.20)	2.0	(0.20)	2.4	(0.21)	2.6	(0.23)	4.0	(0.28)
Marijuana/hashish...........	27.1	(1.30)	33.7	(1.07)	25.7	(0.98)	16.7	(0.82)	14.0	(0.80)	13.8	(0.80)	11.9	(0.73)	15.5	(0.81)	19.0	(0.90)	21.2	(0.94)
PCP	—	(†)	1.4	(0.11)	1.6	(0.12)	1.4	(0.11)	0.4	(0.06)	0.5	(0.07)	0.6	(0.08)	1.0	(0.10)	0.7	(0.08)	0.6	(0.08)

See notes at end of table.

Percentage of high school seniors reporting drug use, by type of drug and frequency of use: Selected years, 1975 through 2004—Continued

Type of drug	Class of 1996		Class of 1997		Class of 1998		Class of 1999		Class of 2000		Class of 2001		Class of 2002		Class of 2003		Class of 2004	
1	12		13		14		15		16		17		18		19		20	
Percent reporting having ever used drugs																		
Alcohol[1]	79.2	(0.77)	81.7	(0.71)	81.4	(0.72)	80.0	(0.78)	80.3	(0.80)	79.7	(0.81)	78.4	(0.83)	76.6	(0.80)	76.8	(0.80)
Any illicit drug	50.8	(1.37)	54.3	(1.31)	54.1	(1.32)	54.7	(1.40)	54.0	(1.44)	53.9	(1.44)	53.0	(1.44)	51.1	(1.35)	51.1	(1.35)
Marijuana only	22.3	(1.14)	24.3	(1.13)	24.7	(1.14)	25.3	(1.22)	25.0	(1.25)	23.2	(1.22)	23.5	(1.22)	23.4	(1.15)	22.4	(1.13)
Any illicit drug other than marijuana[2]	28.5	(1.01)	30.0	(0.99)	29.4	(0.99)	29.4	(1.05)	29.0	(1.08)	30.7	(1.09)	29.5	(1.08)	27.7	(0.99)	28.7	(1.00)
Use of selected drugs																		
Cocaine	7.1	(0.53)	8.7	(0.57)	9.3	(0.59)	9.8	(0.63)	8.6	(0.62)	8.2	(0.60)	7.8	(0.59)	7.7	(0.55)	8.1	(0.56)
Heroin	1.8	(0.16)	2.1	(0.16)	2.0	(0.16)	2.0	(0.17)	2.4	(0.19)	1.8	(0.17)	1.7	(0.16)	1.5	(0.14)	1.5	(0.14)
LSD	12.6	(0.69)	13.6	(0.69)	12.6	(0.67)	12.2	(0.70)	11.1	(0.69)	10.9	(0.69)	8.4	(0.61)	5.9	(0.49)	4.6	(0.43)
Marijuana/hashish	44.9	(1.36)	49.6	(1.32)	49.1	(1.33)	49.7	(1.40)	48.8	(1.45)	49.0	(1.45)	47.8	(1.44)	46.1	(1.35)	45.7	(1.35)
PCP	4.0	(0.23)	3.9	(0.22)	3.9	(0.22)	3.4	(0.22)	3.4	(0.23)	3.5	(0.23)	3.1	(0.22)	2.5	(0.18)	1.6	(0.15)
Percent reporting use of drugs in the past 12 months																		
Alcohol[1]	72.5	(0.85)	74.8	(0.80)	74.3	(0.81)	73.8	(0.86)	73.2	(0.89)	73.3	(0.89)	71.5	(0.91)	70.1	(0.86)	70.6	(0.86)
Any illicit drug	40.2	(1.31)	42.4	(1.27)	41.4	(1.28)	42.1	(1.35)	40.9	(1.39)	41.4	(1.39)	41.0	(1.38)	39.3	(1.29)	38.8	(1.29)
Marijuana only	20.4	(1.08)	21.7	(1.06)	21.2	(1.06)	21.4	(1.12)	20.5	(1.14)	19.8	(1.12)	20.1	(1.13)	19.5	(1.05)	18.3	(1.02)
Any illicit drug other than marijuana[2]	19.8	(0.84)	20.7	(0.83)	20.2	(0.82)	20.7	(0.88)	20.4	(0.90)	21.6	(0.92)	20.9	(0.91)	19.8	(0.83)	20.5	(0.85)
Use of selected drugs																		
Cocaine	4.9	(0.40)	5.5	(0.41)	5.7	(0.42)	6.2	(0.46)	5.0	(0.43)	4.8	(0.42)	5.0	(0.42)	4.8	(0.39)	5.3	(0.41)
Heroin	1.0	(0.10)	1.2	(0.11)	1.0	(0.10)	1.1	(0.11)	1.5	(0.13)	0.9	(0.10)	1.0	(0.11)	0.8	(0.09)	0.9	(0.10)
LSD	8.8	(0.52)	8.4	(0.49)	7.6	(0.48)	8.1	(0.52)	6.6	(0.49)	6.6	(0.49)	3.5	(0.36)	1.9	(0.25)	2.2	(0.27)
Marijuana/hashish	35.8	(1.28)	38.5	(1.25)	37.5	(1.25)	37.8	(1.33)	36.5	(1.36)	37.0	(1.36)	36.2	(1.35)	34.9	(1.26)	34.3	(1.25)
PCP	2.6	(0.16)	2.3	(0.15)	2.1	(0.14)	1.8	(0.14)	2.3	(0.16)	1.8	(0.14)	1.1	(0.11)	1.3	(0.11)	0.7	(0.08)
Percent reporting use of drugs in the past 30 days																		
Alcohol[1]	50.8	(0.95)	52.7	(0.92)	52.0	(0.92)	51.0	(0.98)	50.0	(1.01)	49.8	(1.01)	48.6	(1.00)	47.5	(0.94)	48.0	(0.94)
Any illicit drug	24.6	(1.03)	26.2	(1.01)	25.6	(1.01)	25.9	(1.07)	24.9	(1.09)	25.7	(1.10)	25.4	(1.09)	24.1	(1.01)	23.4	(1.00)
Marijuana only	15.1	(0.85)	15.5	(0.83)	14.9	(0.82)	15.5	(0.88)	14.5	(0.89)	14.7	(0.89)	14.1	(0.87)	19.5	(0.93)	18.3	(0.91)
Any illicit drug other than marijuana[2]	9.5	(0.53)	10.7	(0.53)	10.7	(0.54)	10.4	(0.56)	10.4	(0.58)	11.0	(0.59)	11.3	(0.60)	10.4	(0.54)	10.8	(0.55)
Use of selected drugs																		
Cocaine	2.0	(0.21)	2.3	(0.22)	2.4	(0.22)	2.6	(0.24)	2.1	(0.23)	2.1	(0.23)	2.3	(0.24)	2.1	(0.21)	2.3	(0.22)
Heroin	0.5	(0.07)	0.5	(0.07)	0.5	(0.07)	0.5	(0.07)	0.7	(0.09)	0.4	(0.07)	0.5	(0.08)	0.4	(0.06)	0.5	(0.07)
LSD	2.5	(0.23)	3.1	(0.25)	3.2	(0.26)	2.7	(0.25)	1.6	(0.20)	2.3	(0.24)	0.7	(0.13)	0.6	(0.11)	0.7	(0.12)
Marijuana/hashish	21.9	(0.98)	23.7	(0.98)	22.8	(0.97)	23.1	(1.03)	21.6	(1.04)	22.4	(1.05)	21.5	(1.03)	21.2	(0.96)	19.9	(0.94)
PCP	1.3	(0.12)	0.7	(0.08)	1.0	(0.10)	0.8	(0.09)	0.9	(0.10)	0.5	(0.08)	0.4	(0.07)	0.6	(0.08)	0.4	(0.06)

—Not available.

†Not applicable.

[1]Survey question changed in 1993; data are not comparable to figures for earlier years.

[2]Other illicit drugs include any use of LSD or other hallucinogens, crack or other cocaine, or heroin, or any use of other narcotics, amphetamines, barbiturates, or tranquilizers not under a doctor's orders.

NOTE: Standard errors appear in parentheses. Standard errors were calculated from formulas to perform trend anaysis over an interval greater than one year (for example, a comparison between 1975 and 1990). A revised questionnaire was used in 1982 and later years to reduce the inappropriate reporting of nonprescription stimulants. This slightly reduced the positive responses for some types of drug abuse.

SOURCE: University of Michigan, Institute for Social Research, Monitoring the Future, various years. (This table was prepared March 2005.)

Percentage of students in grades 9 through 12 who reported experience with drugs and violence on school property, by race/ethnicity, grade, and sex: Selected years, 1997 through 2003

Type of violence or drug-related behavior	1997 total	1999 total	2001 total	2003 Total	White, non-Hispanic	Black, non-Hispanic	Hispanic	Grade 9	10	11	12
1	2	3	4	5	6	7	8	9	10	11	12
Felt too unsafe to go to school[1]											
Total	4.0 (0.6)	5.2 (1.3)	6.6 (0.51)	5.4 (0.41)	3.1 (0.31)	8.4 (0.61)	9.4 (0.77)	6.9 (0.61)	5.2 (0.56)	4.5 (0.51)	3.8 (0.56)
Male	4.1 (0.8)	4.8 (1.6)	5.8 (0.56)	5.5 (0.51)	3.3 (0.36)	7.9 (1.12)	8.9 (1.07)	7.1 (0.87)	5.3 (0.56)	4.3 (0.61)	3.8 (0.77)
Female	3.9 (0.7)	5.7 (1.5)	7.4 (0.66)	5.3 (0.51)	2.9 (0.41)	9.0 (0.66)	10.0 (1.22)	6.6 (0.71)	5.1 (0.87)	4.6 (0.71)	3.9 (0.66)
Carried a weapon on school property[1,2]											
Total	8.5 (1.5)	6.9 (1.2)	6.4 (0.51)	6.1 (0.56)	5.5 (0.56)	6.9 (0.97)	6.0 (0.56)	5.3 (1.12)	6.0 (0.51)	6.6 (0.82)	6.4 (0.66)
Male	12.5 (2.9)	11.0 (2.1)	10.2 (0.87)	8.9 (0.77)	8.5 (0.82)	8.4 (1.28)	7.7 (1.02)	6.6 (0.82)	8.9 (0.87)	10.3 (1.48)	10.2 (1.02)
Female	3.7 (0.7)	2.8 (0.7)	2.9 (0.26)	3.1 (0.51)	2.2 (0.66)	5.5 (1.12)	4.2 (0.71)	3.8 (1.53)	3.0 (0.51)	2.7 (0.61)	2.5 (0.51)
Threatened or injured with a weapon on school property[3]											
Total	7.4 (0.9)	7.7 (0.8)	8.9 (0.56)	9.2 (0.77)	7.8 (0.77)	10.9 (0.82)	9.4 (1.22)	12.1 (1.28)	9.2 (1.02)	7.3 (0.71)	6.3 (0.92)
Male	10.2 (1.4)	9.5 (1.6)	11.5 (0.66)	11.6 (0.97)	9.6 (1.07)	14.3 (1.33)	11.9 (1.53)	15.4 (2.04)	11.3 (1.28)	9.2 (0.97)	8.5 (1.43)
Female	4.0 (0.6)	5.8 (1.2)	6.5 (0.51)	6.5 (0.61)	5.8 (0.56)	7.5 (0.77)	6.9 (1.43)	8.3 (0.87)	7.0 (0.97)	5.4 (1.12)	3.9 (0.77)
Engaged in a physical fight on school property[3]											
Total	14.8 (1.3)	14.2 (1.3)	12.5 (0.51)	12.8 (0.77)	10.0 (0.71)	17.1 (1.28)	16.7 (1.12)	18.0 (1.22)	12.8 (0.92)	10.4 (0.92)	7.3 (0.71)
Male	20.0 (2.0)	18.5 (1.4)	18.0 (0.77)	17.1 (0.92)	14.3 (0.82)	21.5 (1.68)	19.3 (1.48)	23.3 (1.58)	18.1 (1.33)	14.2 (1.38)	9.6 (1.07)
Female	8.6 (1.5)	9.8 (1.9)	7.2 (0.46)	8.0 (0.71)	5.3 (0.92)	12.6 (1.43)	13.8 (1.63)	12.2 (1.17)	7.3 (0.77)	6.4 (0.87)	4.7 (0.82)
Property stolen or deliberately damaged on school property[3]											
Total	32.9 (2.6)	— (†)	— (†)	29.8 (0.71)	28.2 (0.71)	30.4 (1.48)	32.3 (1.17)	34.8 (1.53)	30.5 (1.12)	27.2 (1.07)	24.2 (1.07)
Male	36.1 (2.6)	— (†)	— (†)	33.1 (0.87)	30.6 (1.02)	33.9 (1.73)	37.0 (1.63)	37.4 (1.84)	34.3 (1.22)	30.5 (1.38)	27.9 (1.58)
Female	29.0 (3.7)	— (†)	— (†)	26.2 (0.82)	25.6 (0.87)	27.0 (2.09)	27.6 (1.33)	31.9 (1.63)	26.6 (1.53)	23.9 (1.38)	20.2 (1.58)
Cigarette use on school property[1]											
Total	14.6 (1.5)	14.0 (1.9)	9.9 (0.61)	8.0 (0.71)	8.9 (0.87)	5.9 (0.71)	6.0 (0.61)	7.5 (0.97)	7.7 (0.92)	8.2 (0.92)	8.3 (0.87)
Male	15.9 (1.7)	14.8 (2.0)	11.3 (0.66)	8.2 (0.66)	8.2 (0.77)	8.4 (0.97)	6.2 (0.87)	7.3 (0.97)	7.5 (0.87)	8.1 (1.07)	10.5 (1.22)
Female	13.0 (2.2)	13.2 (2.0)	8.5 (0.71)	7.6 (0.92)	9.6 (1.28)	3.5 (0.66)	5.8 (0.77)	7.7 (1.22)	8.0 (1.22)	8.4 (1.48)	5.9 (0.97)
Smokeless tobacco use on school property[4]											
Total	5.1 (1.4)	4.2 (1.8)	5.0 (0.61)	5.9 (1.53)	6.7 (2.14)	2.5 (0.51)	3.6 (1.38)	5.2 (1.48)	5.2 (1.63)	7.1 (3.62)	6.3 (3.21)
Male	9.0 (2.5)	8.1 (3.5)	9.4 (1.17)	8.5 (1.48)	9.9 (2.09)	3.2 (0.82)	4.6 (1.89)	6.0 (1.33)	7.7 (1.68)	10.8 (5.51)	10.1 (5.15)
Female	0.4 (0.2)	0.3 (0.2)	0.7 (0.15)	3.3 (1.68)	3.3 (2.35)	1.8 (0.51)	2.6 (0.97)	4.4 (1.73)	2.6 (0.36)	3.2 (1.63)	2.3 (1.17)
Alcohol use on school property[1]											
Total	5.6 (0.7)	4.9 (0.7)	4.9 (0.26)	5.2 (0.46)	3.9 (0.46)	5.8 (0.82)	7.6 (1.07)	5.1 (0.66)	5.6 (0.61)	5.0 (0.56)	4.5 (0.66)
Male	7.2 (1.3)	6.1 (1.1)	6.1 (0.41)	6.0 (0.61)	4.5 (0.56)	7.9 (1.22)	7.4 (1.17)	5.1 (0.77)	6.1 (0.71)	6.4 (0.87)	6.5 (1.12)
Female	3.6 (0.7)	3.6 (0.7)	3.8 (0.41)	4.2 (0.41)	3.2 (0.51)	3.8 (0.87)	7.9 (1.28)	5.2 (0.92)	5.0 (0.61)	3.5 (0.51)	2.6 (0.56)
Marijuana use on school property[1]											
Total	7.0 (1.0)	7.2 (1.4)	5.4 (0.36)	5.8 (0.66)	4.5 (0.66)	6.6 (0.87)	8.2 (0.71)	6.6 (1.02)	5.2 (0.71)	5.6 (0.71)	5.0 (0.77)
Male	9.0 (1.3)	10.1 (2.6)	8.0 (0.56)	7.6 (0.87)	5.8 (0.82)	9.7 (1.12)	10.4 (1.07)	8.1 (1.12)	7.2 (1.12)	7.9 (1.12)	7.1 (1.02)
Female	4.6 (1.1)	4.4 (0.8)	2.9 (0.31)	3.7 (0.46)	3.1 (0.56)	3.6 (0.92)	6.0 (0.71)	5.1 (1.02)	3.0 (0.56)	3.3 (0.56)	2.6 (0.66)
Offered, sold, or given an illegal drug on school property[3]											
Total	31.7 (1.8)	30.2 (2.4)	28.5 (1.02)	28.7 (1.94)	27.5 (2.70)	23.1 (1.43)	36.5 (1.94)	29.5 (2.40)	29.2 (2.04)	29.9 (2.35)	24.9 (2.24)
Male	37.4 (2.3)	34.7 (3.3)	34.6 (1.22)	31.9 (2.09)	30.2 (2.81)	27.7 (1.28)	40.6 (2.45)	32.1 (2.35)	31.9 (2.30)	33.5 (2.35)	29.7 (2.65)
Female	24.7 (2.4)	25.7 (2.4)	22.7 (1.02)	25.0 (1.94)	24.5 (2.70)	18.3 (1.94)	32.5 (1.94)	26.7 (1.63)	26.5 (2.40)	26.1 (2.70)	19.6 (2.30)

—Not available.

†Not applicable.

[1]One or more times during the 30 days preceding the survey.

[2]Such as a gun, knife, or club.

[3]One or more times during the 12 months preceding the survey.

[4]Used chewing tobacco or snuff one or more times during the 30 days preceding the survey.

NOTE: Totals include other racial/ethnic groups not shown separately. Standard errors appear in parentheses.

SOURCE: U.S. Department of Health and Human Services, Centers for Disease Control and Prevention, *CDC Surveillance Summaries*, MMWR 47(SS-03), 51(SS-04), and 53(SS-02). (This table was prepared July 2005.)

Average scale score in mathematics, by age and selected student and school characteristics: Selected years, 1973 through 2004

Selected student and school characteristic	1973		1978		1982		1986		1990		1992		1994		1996		1999		2004	
1	2		3		4		5		6		7		8		9		10		11	
9-year-olds																				
All students	219	(0.8)	219	(0.8)	219	(1.1)	222	(1.0)	230	(0.8)	230	(0.8)	231	(0.8)	231	(0.8)	232	(0.8)	241	(0.9)
Sex																				
Male	218	(0.7)	217	(0.7)	217	(1.2)	222	(1.1)	229	(0.9)	231	(1.0)	232	(1.0)	233	(1.2)	233	(1.0)	243	(1.1)
Female	220	(1.1)	220	(1.0)	221	(1.2)	222	(1.2)	230	(1.1)	228	(1.0)	230	(0.9)	229	(0.7)	231	(0.9)	240	(1.1)
Race/ethnicity																				
White, non-Hispanic	225	(1.0)	224	(0.9)	224	(1.1)	227	(1.1)	235	(0.8)	235	(0.8)	237	(1.0)	237	(1.0)	239	(0.9)	247	(0.9)
Black, non-Hispanic	190	(1.8)	192	(1.1)	195	(1.6)	202	(1.6)	208	(2.2)	208	(2.0)	212	(1.6)	212	(1.4)	211	(1.6)	224	(2.1)
Hispanic	202	(2.4)	203	(2.2)	204	(1.3)	205	(2.1)	214	(2.1)	212	(2.3)	210	(2.3)	215	(1.7)	213	(1.9)	230	(2.0)
Region																				
Northeast	227	(1.9)	227	(1.9)	226	(1.8)	226	(2.7)	236	(2.1)	235	(1.9)	238	(2.2)	236	(2.0)	242	(1.7)	245	(2.0)
Southeast	208	(1.3)	209	(1.2)	210	(2.5)	218	(2.5)	224	(2.4)	221	(1.7)	229	(1.4)	227	(2.0)	226	(2.6)	240	(2.2)
Central	224	(1.5)	224	(1.5)	221	(2.7)	226	(2.3)	231	(1.3)	234	(1.6)	233	(1.8)	233	(2.3)	233	(1.4)	240	(1.5)
West	216	(2.2)	213	(1.3)	219	(1.8)	217	(2.4)	228	(1.8)	229	(2.3)	226	(1.6)	229	(1.3)	228	(1.7)	241	(1.8)
13-year-olds																				
All students	266	(1.1)	264	(1.1)	269	(1.1)	269	(1.2)	270	(0.9)	273	(0.9)	274	(1.0)	274	(0.8)	276	(0.8)	281	(1.0)
Sex																				
Male	265	(1.3)	264	(1.3)	269	(1.4)	270	(1.1)	271	(1.2)	274	(1.1)	276	(1.3)	276	(0.9)	277	(0.9)	283	(1.2)
Female	267	(1.1)	265	(1.1)	268	(1.1)	268	(1.5)	270	(0.9)	272	(0.9)	273	(1.0)	272	(1.0)	274	(1.1)	279	(1.0)
Race/ethnicity																				
White, non-Hispanic	274	(0.9)	272	(0.8)	274	(1.0)	274	(1.3)	276	(1.1)	279	(0.9)	281	(0.9)	281	(0.9)	283	(0.8)	288	(0.9)
Black, non-Hispanic	228	(1.9)	230	(1.9)	240	(1.6)	249	(2.3)	249	(2.3)	250	(1.9)	252	(3.5)	252	(1.3)	251	(2.6)	262	(1.6)
Hispanic	239	(2.2)	238	(2.0)	252	(1.7)	254	(2.9)	255	(1.8)	259	(1.8)	256	(1.9)	256	(1.6)	259	(1.7)	265	(2.0)
Parents' highest level of education																				
Not high school graduate	—	(†)	245	(1.2)	251	(1.4)	252	(2.3)	253	(1.8)	256	(1.0)	255	(2.1)	254	(2.4)	256	(2.8)	262	(2.2)
Graduated high school	—	(†)	263	(1.0)	263	(0.8)	263	(1.2)	263	(1.2)	263	(1.2)	266	(1.1)	267	(1.1)	264	(1.1)	271	(1.7)
Some education after high school	—	(†)	273	(1.2)	275	(0.9)	274	(0.8)	277	(1.0)	278	(1.0)	277	(1.6)	277	(1.4)	279	(0.9)	283	(1.0)
Graduated college	—	(†)	284	(1.2)	282	(1.5)	280	(1.4)	280	(1.0)	283	(1.0)	285	(1.2)	283	(1.2)	286	(1.0)	292	(0.9)
Region																				
Northeast	275	(2.4)	273	(2.4)	277	(2.0)	277	(2.2)	275	(2.3)	274	(2.2)	284	(1.5)	275	(2.1)	279	(2.7)	284	(2.1)
Southeast	255	(3.2)	253	(3.3)	258	(2.2)	263	(1.4)	266	(1.9)	271	(2.5)	269	(2.0)	270	(1.8)	270	(2.3)	278	(2.1)
Central	271	(1.8)	269	(1.8)	273	(2.1)	266	(4.5)	272	(2.4)	275	(1.5)	275	(3.4)	280	(1.3)	278	(1.8)	283	(2.2)
West	262	(1.9)	260	(1.9)	266	(2.4)	270	(2.1)	269	(1.6)	272	(1.4)	272	(1.7)	273	(1.9)	276	(1.4)	280	(1.4)
17-year-olds																				
All students	304	(1.1)	300	(1.0)	298	(0.9)	302	(0.9)	305	(0.9)	307	(0.9)	306	(1.0)	307	(1.2)	308	(1.0)	307	(0.8)
Sex																				
Male	309	(1.2)	304	(1.0)	301	(1.0)	305	(1.2)	306	(1.1)	309	(1.1)	309	(1.4)	310	(1.3)	310	(1.4)	308	(1.0)
Female	301	(1.1)	297	(1.0)	296	(1.0)	299	(1.0)	303	(1.1)	305	(1.1)	304	(1.1)	305	(1.4)	307	(1.0)	305	(0.9)
Race/ethnicity																				
White, non-Hispanic	310	(1.1)	306	(0.9)	304	(0.9)	308	(1.0)	309	(1.0)	312	(0.8)	312	(1.1)	313	(1.4)	315	(1.1)	313	(0.7)
Black, non-Hispanic	270	(1.3)	268	(1.3)	272	(1.2)	279	(2.1)	289	(2.8)	286	(2.2)	286	(1.8)	286	(1.7)	283	(1.5)	285	(1.6)
Hispanic	277	(2.2)	276	(2.3)	277	(1.8)	283	(2.9)	284	(2.9)	292	(2.6)	291	(3.7)	292	(2.1)	293	(2.5)	289	(1.8)
Parents' highest level of education																				
Not high school graduate	—	(†)	280	(1.2)	279	(1.0)	279	(2.3)	285	(2.2)	285	(2.3)	284	(2.4)	281	(2.4)	289	(1.8)	287	(2.4)
Graduated high school	—	(†)	294	(0.8)	293	(0.8)	293	(1.0)	294	(0.9)	298	(1.7)	295	(1.1)	297	(2.4)	299	(1.6)	295	(1.1)
Some education after high school	—	(†)	305	(0.9)	304	(0.9)	305	(1.2)	308	(1.0)	308	(1.1)	305	(1.3)	307	(1.5)	308	(1.6)	306	(1.1)
Graduated college	—	(†)	317	(1.0)	312	(1.0)	314	(1.4)	316	(1.3)	316	(1.0)	318	(1.4)	317	(1.3)	317	(1.2)	317	(0.9)
Region																				
Northeast	312	(1.8)	307	(1.8)	304	(2.0)	307	(1.9)	304	(2.1)	311	(2.0)	313	(2.9)	309	(3.0)	313	(2.4)	310	(1.4)
Southeast	296	(1.8)	292	(1.7)	292	(2.1)	297	(1.4)	301	(2.3)	301	(1.9)	301	(1.6)	303	(2.1)	300	(1.4)	302	(1.3)
Central	306	(1.8)	305	(1.9)	302	(1.4)	304	(1.9)	311	(2.1)	312	(2.0)	307	(2.2)	314	(2.0)	310	(2.0)	313	(1.0)
West	303	(2.0)	295	(1.8)	294	(1.9)	299	(2.7)	302	(1.5)	303	(2.3)	305	(2.4)	304	(2.3)	310	(2.0)	303	(1.9)

—Not available.

†Not applicable.

NOTE: Excludes persons not enrolled in school and those who were unable to be tested due to limited proficiency in English or due to a disability. Includes public and private schools. A score of 150 implies the knowledge of some basic addition and subtraction facts, and most students at this level can add two-digit numbers without regrouping. They recognize simple situations in which addition and subtraction apply. A score of 200 implies considerable understanding of two-digit numbers and knowledge of some basic multiplication and division facts. A score of 250 implies an initial understanding of the four basic operations. Students at this level can also compare information from graphs and charts and are developing an ability to analyze simple logical relations. A score of 300 implies an ability to compute decimals, simple fractions, and percents. Students at this level can identify geometric figures, measure lengths and angles, and calculate areas of rectangles. They are developing the skills to operate with signed numbers, exponents, and square roots. A score of 350 implies an ability to apply a range of reasoning skills to solve multistep problems. Students at this level can solve routine problems involving fractions and percents, recognize properties of basic geometric figures, and work with exponents and square roots. Scale ranges from 0 to 500. Totals include other racial/ethnic groups not shown separately. Some data have been revised from previously published figures. Standard errors appear in parentheses.

SOURCE: U.S. Department of Education, National Center for Education Statistics, National Assessment of Educational Progress (NAEP), *NAEP 2004 Trends in Academic Progress*; and unpublished tabulations, NAEP Data Explorer (http://nces.ed.gov/nationsreportcard/nde/), retrieved July 2005. (This table was prepared July 2005.)

Average scale score in mathematics, percentage attaining mathematics achievement levels, and selected statistics on mathematics education of 4th-graders in public schools, by state or jurisdiction: Selected years, 1992 through 2005

State or jurisdiction	Average scale score				Percent attaining mathematics achievement levels, 2005[1]				Percent of students with 5 or more hours of math instruction each week, 2005	Percent of students, 2003	
	1992	2000	2003	2005	Below basic	Basic or above[2]	Proficient or above[3]	Advanced[4]		Spending 30 minutes or more on math homework each day[5]	Watching 6 hours or more of television each day
1	2	3	4	5	6	7	8	9	10	11	12
United States	219 (0.8)	224 (1.0)	234 (0.2)	237 (0.2)	21 (0.2)	80 (0.2)	35 (0.2)	5 (0.1)	83 (0.4)	49	21 (0.2)
Alabama	208 (1.6)	217 (1.2)	223 (1.2)	225 (0.9)	34 (1.3)	66 (1.3)	21 (1.1)	2 (0.4)	92 (1.6)	47	22 (1.1)
Alaska	— (†)	— (†)	233 (0.8)	236 (1.0)	23 (1.1)	77 (1.1)	34 (1.7)	5 (0.6)	78 (2.9)	—	— (†)
Arizona	215 (1.1)	219 (1.3)	229 (1.1)	230 (1.1)	30 (1.3)	70 (1.3)	28 (1.6)	3 (0.7)	80 (3.2)	52	19 (1.0)
Arkansas	210 (0.9)	216 (1.1)	229 (0.9)	236 (0.9)	22 (1.2)	78 (1.2)	34 (1.4)	4 (0.5)	91 (1.8)	51	24 (1.0)
California[6]	208 (1.6)	213 (1.6)	227 (0.9)	230 (0.6)	29 (0.7)	71 (0.7)	28 (0.8)	4 (0.4)	87 (1.3)	56	20 (0.7)
Colorado	221 (1.0)	— (†)	235 (1.0)	239 (1.1)	20 (1.4)	81 (1.4)	39 (1.6)	6 (0.8)	88 (1.9)	50	15 (0.8)
Connecticut	227 (1.1)	234 (1.1)	241 (0.8)	242 (0.8)	16 (1.0)	84 (1.0)	43 (1.4)	7 (0.6)	86 (2.2)	42	21 (0.8)
Delaware	218 (0.8)	— (†)	236 (0.5)	240 (0.5)	16 (0.8)	84 (0.8)	36 (1.2)	4 (0.5)	85 (0.4)	49	25 (0.7)
District of Columbia	193 (0.5)	192 (1.1)	205 (0.7)	211 (0.8)	55 (1.2)	45 (1.2)	10 (0.8)	1 (0.3)	86 (0.5)	52	32 (1.0)
Florida	214 (1.5)	— (†)	234 (1.1)	239 (0.7)	18 (0.6)	82 (0.6)	37 (1.1)	5 (0.7)	86 (1.4)	50	26 (1.0)
Georgia	216 (1.2)	219 (1.1)	230 (1.0)	234 (1.0)	24 (1.3)	76 (1.3)	30 (1.5)	4 (0.5)	90 (2.1)	48	23 (1.1)
Hawaii	214 (1.3)	216 (1.0)	227 (1.0)	230 (0.8)	27 (1.1)	73 (1.1)	27 (1.3)	3 (0.4)	78 (3.0)	58	23 (1.1)
Idaho[6]	222 (1.0)	224 (1.4)	235 (0.7)	242 (0.7)	14 (0.8)	86 (0.8)	40 (1.6)	5 (0.6)	77 (2.5)	49	14 (0.6)
Illinois[6]	— (†)	223 (1.9)	233 (1.1)	233 (1.0)	26 (1.2)	74 (1.2)	32 (1.5)	5 (0.8)	69 (2.9)	50	21 (0.9)
Indiana[6]	221 (1.0)	233 (1.1)	238 (0.9)	240 (0.9)	16 (0.9)	84 (0.9)	38 (1.7)	5 (0.6)	78 (2.8)	50	23 (0.9)
Iowa[6]	230 (1.0)	231 (1.2)	238 (0.7)	240 (0.7)	15 (1.0)	85 (1.0)	37 (1.3)	4 (0.4)	72 (3.2)	46	17 (1.0)
Kansas[6]	— (†)	232 (1.6)	242 (1.0)	246 (1.0)	12 (0.7)	88 (0.7)	47 (1.6)	8 (0.8)	92 (1.5)	48	19 (1.1)
Kentucky	215 (1.0)	219 (1.4)	229 (1.1)	232 (0.9)	25 (1.2)	75 (1.2)	26 (1.4)	3 (0.5)	68 (3.3)	49	24 (0.8)
Louisiana	204 (1.5)	218 (1.4)	226 (1.0)	230 (0.9)	26 (1.3)	74 (1.3)	24 (1.3)	2 (0.4)	92 (2.0)	43	24 (1.2)
Maine[6]	232 (1.0)	230 (1.0)	238 (0.7)	241 (0.8)	16 (0.9)	84 (0.9)	39 (1.4)	5 (0.6)	77 (2.8)	46	15 (0.9)
Maryland	217 (1.3)	222 (1.2)	233 (1.3)	238 (1.0)	21 (1.3)	79 (1.3)	38 (1.5)	7 (1.0)	95 (1.2)	42	25 (1.1)
Massachusetts	227 (1.2)	233 (1.2)	242 (0.8)	247 (0.8)	9 (0.7)	91 (0.7)	49 (1.5)	8 (0.7)	89 (1.9)	47	19 (0.7)
Michigan[6]	220 (1.7)	229 (1.6)	236 (0.9)	238 (1.2)	21 (1.5)	79 (1.5)	38 (1.7)	5 (0.7)	73 (3.0)	46	22 (0.9)
Minnesota[6]	228 (0.9)	234 (1.3)	242 (0.9)	246 (1.0)	12 (0.9)	88 (0.9)	47 (1.7)	8 (0.8)	81 (2.7)	48	15 (0.8)
Mississippi	202 (1.1)	211 (1.1)	223 (1.0)	227 (0.9)	31 (1.4)	69 (1.4)	19 (1.2)	1 (0.3)	91 (1.5)	51	24 (1.0)
Missouri	222 (1.2)	228 (1.2)	235 (0.9)	235 (0.9)	21 (1.3)	79 (1.3)	31 (1.3)	3 (0.5)	83 (2.5)	49	21 (1.0)
Montana[6]	— (†)	228 (1.7)	236 (0.8)	241 (0.8)	15 (1.1)	85 (1.1)	38 (1.4)	4 (0.5)	73 (2.0)	49	13 (0.7)
Nebraska	225 (1.2)	225 (1.8)	236 (0.8)	238 (0.9)	20 (1.0)	80 (1.0)	36 (1.3)	5 (0.6)	75 (2.5)	51	19 (1.1)
Nevada	— (†)	220 (1.0)	228 (0.8)	230 (0.8)	28 (1.0)	72 (1.0)	26 (1.2)	3 (0.4)	92 (1.3)	47	19 (0.8)
New Hampshire	230 (1.2)	— (†)	243 (0.9)	246 (0.9)	11 (0.9)	89 (0.9)	47 (1.5)	6 (0.6)	69 (2.9)	45	15 (0.8)
New Jersey	227 (1.5)	— (†)	239 (1.1)	244 (1.1)	14 (1.1)	86 (1.1)	45 (1.7)	8 (0.9)	78 (3.6)	45	20 (1.1)
New Mexico	213 (1.4)	213 (1.5)	223 (1.1)	224 (0.8)	35 (1.5)	65 (1.5)	19 (1.1)	2 (0.4)	76 (2.0)	55	18 (0.8)
New York[6]	218 (1.2)	225 (1.4)	236 (0.9)	238 (0.9)	19 (1.0)	81 (1.0)	36 (1.3)	5 (0.5)	77 (2.2)	47	23 (1.0)
North Carolina	213 (1.1)	230 (1.1)	242 (0.8)	241 (0.9)	17 (1.1)	83 (1.1)	40 (1.4)	7 (0.8)	86 (2.4)	50	20 (0.8)
North Dakota	229 (0.8)	230 (1.2)	238 (0.7)	243 (0.5)	11 (0.8)	89 (0.8)	40 (1.5)	4 (0.6)	63 (0.6)	48	14 (0.7)
Ohio[6]	219 (1.2)	230 (1.5)	238 (1.0)	242 (1.0)	16 (1.2)	84 (1.2)	43 (1.5)	7 (0.7)	79 (2.6)	45	21 (1.0)
Oklahoma	220 (1.0)	224 (1.0)	229 (1.0)	234 (1.0)	21 (1.2)	79 (1.2)	29 (1.5)	2 (0.4)	75 (2.4)	48	21 (1.0)
Oregon[6]	— (†)	224 (1.8)	236 (0.9)	238 (0.8)	20 (0.9)	80 (0.9)	37 (1.3)	6 (0.6)	77 (2.8)	49	16 (0.8)
Pennsylvania	224 (1.3)	— (†)	236 (1.1)	241 (1.2)	18 (1.2)	82 (1.2)	42 (1.6)	6 (0.8)	85 (2.5)	41	23 (1.0)
Rhode Island	215 (1.5)	224 (1.1)	230 (1.0)	233 (0.9)	24 (1.3)	76 (1.3)	31 1.2	4 (0.5)	87 (1.8)	44	19 (1.0)
South Carolina	212 (1.1)	220 (1.4)	236 (0.9)	238 (0.9)	19 (1.1)	82 (1.1)	36 (1.5)	5 (0.6)	86 (2.3)	47	25 (0.9)
South Dakota	— (†)	— (†)	237 (0.7)	242 (0.5)	14 (0.8)	86 (0.8)	41 (1.3)	4 (0.5)	71 (0.6)	55	14 (0.8)
Tennessee	211 (1.4)	220 (1.4)	228 (1.0)	232 (1.2)	26 (1.5)	74 (1.5)	28 (1.7)	3 (0.5)	82 (2.3)	50	23 (0.9)
Texas	218 (1.2)	231 (1.1)	237 (0.9)	242 (0.6)	13 (0.6)	87 (0.6)	40 (0.9)	5 (0.5)	92 (1.1)	53	19 (0.9)
Utah	224 (1.0)	227 (1.3)	235 (0.8)	239 (0.8)	17 (1.0)	83 (1.0)	37 (1.5)	4 (0.6)	72 (2.5)	46	15 (0.8)
Vermont[6]	— (†)	232 (1.6)	242 (0.8)	244 (0.5)	13 (0.8)	87 (0.8)	44 (1.1)	6 (0.6)	86 (0.6)	47	14 (0.9)
Virginia	221 (1.3)	230 (1.0)	239 (1.1)	241 (0.9)	17 (1.1)	83 (1.1)	39 (1.5)	6 (0.8)	77 (2.6)	46	23 (1.0)
Washington	— (†)	— (†)	238 (1.0)	242 (0.9)	16 (1.1)	84 (1.1)	42 (1.5)	6 (0.7)	86 (2.1)	51	17 (0.9)
West Virginia	215 (1.1)	223 (1.3)	231 (0.8)	231 (0.7)	25 (1.1)	75 (1.1)	25 (1.3)	2 (0.3)	82 (2.5)	47	22 (0.9)
Wisconsin[6]	229 (1.1)	— (†)	237 (0.9)	241 (0.9)	16 (1.2)	84 (1.2)	40 (1.4)	5 (0.6)	77 (2.7)	49	17 (0.7)
Wyoming	225 (0.9)	229 (1.1)	241 (0.6)	243 (0.6)	13 (0.9)	87 (0.9)	43 (1.4)	5 (0.7)	88 (0.4)	56	15 (0.7)

See notes at end of table.

Average scale score in mathematics, percentage attaining achievement levels, and selected statistics on mathematics education of 4th-graders in public schools, by state or jurisdiction: Selected years, 1992 through 2005—Continued

State or jurisdiction	Average scale score				Percent attaining mathematics achievement levels, 2005[1]				Percent of students with 5 or more hours of math instruction each week, 2005	Percent of students, 2003	
	1992	2000	2003	2005	Below basic	Basic or above[2]	Proficient or above[3]	Advanced[4]		Spending 30 minutes or more on math homework each day[5]	Watching 6 hours or more of television each day
1	2	3	4	5	6	7	8	9	10	11	12
Department of Defense dependents schools[7] .	— (†)	— (†)	— (†)	239 (0.5)	15 (1.0)	85 (1.0)	35 (1.2)	3 (0.4)	74 (0.5)	—	— (†)
Domestic schools.........	— (†)	228 (1.4)	237 (0.7)	— (†)	— (†)	— (†)	— (†)	— (†)	— (†)	51	21 (1.2)
Overseas schools	— (†)	226 (0.9)	237 (0.5)	— (†)	— (†)	— (†)	— (†)	— (†)	— (†)	52	18 (0.6)
Other jurisdictions											
American Samoa	— (†)	152 (2.5)	— (†)	— (†)	— (†)	— (†)	— (†)	— (†)	— (†)	—	— (†)
Guam	193 (0.8)	184 (1.7)	— (†)	— (†)	— (†)	— (†)	— (†)	— (†)	— (†)	—	— (†)
Virgin Islands	— (†)	181 (1.8)	— (†)	— (†)	— (†)	— (†)	— (†)	— (†)	— (†)	—	— (†)

—Not available.

†Not applicable.

[1]Achievement levels are in trial status.

[2]The basic level denotes partial mastery of prerequisite knowledge and skills that are fundamental for proficient work at the 4th-grade level.

[3]This level represents solid academic mastery for 4th-graders. Students reaching this level have demonstrated competency over challenging subject matter, including subject-matter knowledge, application of such knowledge to real-world situations, and analytical skills appropriate to the subject matter.

[4]This level signifies superior performance.

[5]Percentage of students who report spending 30 minutes, 45 minutes, 1 hour, and over 1 hour on mathematics homework each day.

[6]Did not meet one or more of the guidelines for school sample participation rates in 2000. Data are subject to appreciable nonresponse bias.

[7]The definition of the national sample changed in 2005; it now includes all of the Department of Defense schools.

NOTE: Excludes students unable to be tested due to limited proficiency in English or due to a disability. Forty-three jurisdictions (states, the District of Columbia, and Department of Defense schools) participated in the 2000 State Assessment of 4th-graders and met student and school participation criteria for reporting results. Fifty-three jurisdictions participated in the 2003 and 2005 state assessment and met student and school participation criteria for reporting results. Data for 2000, 2003, and 2005 are for situations where student accommodations for the testing were permitted. Scale ranges from 0 to 500. Detail may not sum to totals because of rounding. Standard errors appear in parentheses.

SOURCE: U.S. Department of Education, National Center for Education Statistics, National Assessment of Educational Progress (NAEP), *The Nation's Report Card: Mathematics, 2000* and *The Nation's Report Card: Mathematics Highlights*, 2003 and 2005; and unpublished tabulations, NAEP Data Explorer (http://nces.ed.gov/nationsreportcard/nde/), retrieved October 2005. (This table was prepared October 2005.)

Average scale score in mathematics and percentage attaining mathematics achievement levels of 8th-graders in public schools, by level of parental education and state or jurisdiction: Selected years, 1990 through 2005

State or jurisdiction	Average scale score						Percent attaining mathematics achievement levels, 2005[1]				Average scale score, by highest level of education attained by parents, 2005[2]			
	1990	1992	1996	2000	2003	2005	Below basic	Basic or above[3]	Proficient or above[4]	Advanced[5]	Did not finish high school	Graduated high school	Some education after high school	Graduated college
1	2	3	4	5	6	7	8	9	10	11	12	13	14	15
United States	262 (1.4)	267 (1.0)	271 (1.2)	272 (0.9)	276 (0.3)	278 (0.2)	32 (0.2)	68 (0.2)	29 (0.2)	6 (0.1)	259 (0.5)	267 (0.3)	280 (0.3)	289 (0.3)
Alabama	253 (1.1)	252 (1.7)	257 (2.1)	264 (1.8)	262 (1.5)	262 (1.5)	47 (1.9)	53 (1.9)	15 (1.4)	2 (0.7)	245 (2.8)	254 (1.6)	267 (1.8)	272 (2.1)
Alaska[6]	— (†)	— (†)	278 (1.8)	— (†)	279 (0.9)	279 (0.8)	31 (1.5)	69 (1.5)	29 (1.3)	6 (0.6)	‡ (†)	‡ (†)	‡ (†)	‡ (†)
Arizona[6]	260 (1.3)	265 (1.3)	268 (1.6)	269 (1.8)	271 (1.2)	274 (1.1)	36 (1.5)	64 (1.5)	26 (1.2)	5 (0.4)	255 (1.7)	266 (1.6)	278 (1.9)	290 (1.5)
Arkansas	256 (0.9)	256 (1.2)	262 (1.5)	257 (1.5)	266 (1.2)	272 (1.2)	36 (1.6)	64 (1.6)	22 (1.1)	3 (0.4)	263 (2.5)	264 (1.8)	279 (1.5)	279 (1.7)
California[6]	256 (1.3)	261 (1.7)	263 (1.9)	260 (2.1)	267 (1.2)	269 (0.7)	43 (0.8)	57 (0.8)	22 (0.6)	5 (0.4)	253 (1.2)	258 (1.3)	274 (1.2)	284 (1.0)
Colorado	267 (0.9)	272 (1.0)	276 (1.1)	— (†)	283 (1.1)	281 (1.2)	30 (1.6)	71 (1.6)	32 (1.4)	6 (0.8)	257 (1.9)	266 (2.0)	282 (1.9)	294 (1.1)
Connecticut	270 (1.0)	274 (1.1)	280 (1.1)	281 (1.3)	284 (1.2)	281 (1.4)	30 (1.7)	70 (1.7)	35 (1.4)	8 (0.7)	252 (3.6)	264 (1.8)	280 (1.7)	294 (1.5)
Delaware	261 (0.9)	263 (1.0)	267 (0.9)	— (†)	277 (0.7)	281 (0.6)	28 (1.0)	72 (1.0)	30 (1.0)	5 (0.5)	267 (2.7)	271 (1.7)	284 (1.2)	289 (1.0)
District of Columbia	231 (0.9)	235 (0.9)	233 (1.3)	235 (1.1)	243 (0.8)	245 (0.9)	69 (1.3)	31 (1.3)	7 (0.6)	2 (0.3)	243 (3.6)	238 (1.3)	252 (1.8)	253 (1.3)
Florida	255 (1.2)	260 (1.5)	264 (1.8)	— (†)	271 (1.5)	274 (1.1)	35 (1.3)	65 (1.3)	26 (1.2)	5 (0.7)	260 (2.1)	267 (1.8)	279 (1.6)	282 (1.5)
Georgia	259 (1.3)	259 (1.2)	262 (1.6)	265 (1.2)	270 (1.2)	272 (1.1)	38 (1.3)	62 (1.3)	23 (1.2)	4 (0.5)	252 (2.6)	261 (2.0)	275 (1.9)	284 (1.5)
Hawaii	251 (0.8)	257 (0.9)	262 (1.0)	262 (1.4)	266 (0.8)	266 (0.7)	44 (1.0)	56 (1.0)	18 (0.8)	3 (0.4)	250 (4.4)	255 (1.7)	271 (1.4)	274 (1.3)
Idaho[6]	271 (0.8)	275 (0.7)	— (†)	277 (1.0)	280 (0.9)	281 (0.9)	27 (1.0)	73 (1.0)	30 (1.0)	5 (0.6)	255 (2.3)	270 (1.9)	283 (2.2)	290 (1.0)
Illinois[6]	261 (1.7)	— (†)	— (†)	275 (1.7)	277 (1.2)	278 (1.1)	32 (1.2)	68 (1.2)	29 (1.3)	5 (0.6)	255 (2.0)	266 (1.4)	279 (1.4)	289 (1.4)
Indiana[6]	267 (1.2)	270 (1.1)	276 (1.4)	281 (1.4)	281 (1.1)	282 (1.0)	26 (1.2)	74 (1.2)	30 (1.3)	5 (0.7)	264 (2.5)	267 (1.8)	286 (1.7)	291 (1.5)
Iowa[6]	278 (1.1)	283 (1.0)	284 (1.3)	— (†)	284 (0.8)	284 (0.9)	25 (1.1)	76 (1.1)	34 (1.2)	6 (0.6)	264 (2.6)	272 (1.7)	285 (1.3)	293 (1.0)
Kansas[6]	— (†)	— (†)	— (†)	283 (1.7)	284 (1.3)	284 (1.0)	23 (1.3)	77 (1.3)	34 (1.4)	5 (0.6)	261 (2.7)	273 (1.8)	286 (1.3)	294 (1.6)
Kentucky	257 (1.2)	262 (1.1)	267 (1.1)	270 (1.3)	274 (1.2)	274 (1.2)	36 (1.6)	64 (1.6)	23 (1.4)	3 (0.6)	256 (1.9)	264 (1.4)	277 (1.8)	285 (1.6)
Louisiana	246 (1.2)	250 (1.7)	252 (1.6)	259 (1.5)	266 (1.5)	268 (1.4)	41 (2.1)	59 (2.1)	16 (1.4)	2 (0.4)	260 (2.6)	260 (2.3)	274 (1.6)	275 (1.7)
Maine[6]	— (†)	279 (1.0)	284 (1.3)	281 (1.1)	282 (0.9)	281 (0.8)	26 (1.0)	74 (1.0)	30 (1.1)	5 (0.5)	264 (3.1)	271 (1.7)	284 (1.7)	290 (1.1)
Maryland	261 (1.4)	265 (1.3)	270 (2.1)	272 (1.7)	278 (1.0)	278 (1.1)	34 (1.5)	66 (1.5)	30 (1.3)	7 (0.7)	255 (4.2)	268 (2.2)	277 (1.9)	288 (1.5)
Massachusetts	— (†)	273 (1.0)	278 (1.7)	279 (1.5)	287 (0.9)	292 (0.9)	20 (1.1)	80 (1.1)	43 (1.4)	11 (0.8)	271 (3.2)	278 (1.7)	286 (1.6)	302 (0.9)
Michigan[6]	264 (1.2)	267 (1.4)	277 (1.8)	278 (1.9)	276 (2.0)	277 (1.5)	32 (1.6)	68 (1.6)	29 (1.8)	6 (0.8)	254 (4.0)	265 (2.4)	281 (1.7)	286 (1.9)
Minnesota	275 (0.9)	282 (1.0)	284 (1.3)	287 (1.4)	291 (1.1)	290 (1.2)	21 (1.3)	79 (1.3)	43 (1.6)	11 (0.9)	263 (4.4)	275 (2.5)	291 (1.9)	300 (1.2)
Mississippi	— (†)	246 (1.2)	250 (1.2)	254 (1.1)	261 (1.1)	263 (1.2)	48 (1.7)	52 (1.7)	14 (0.9)	1 (0.3)	254 (2.0)	253 (1.6)	269 (1.8)	269 (1.5)
Missouri	— (†)	271 (1.2)	273 (1.4)	271 (1.5)	279 (1.1)	276 (1.1)	32 (1.8)	68 (1.8)	26 (1.4)	4 (0.6)	263 (3.0)	272 (1.9)	277 (1.9)	285 (1.8)
Montana[6]	280 (0.9)	280 (0.9)	283 (1.3)	285 (1.4)	286 (0.9)	286 (0.7)	21 (1.0)	80 (1.0)	36 (1.1)	6 (0.6)	262 (3.2)	254 (1.3)	288 (1.3)	293 (0.9)
Nebraska	276 (1.0)	278 (1.1)	283 (1.0)	280 (1.2)	282 (0.9)	284 (1.0)	25 (1.2)	75 (1.2)	35 (1.6)	6 (0.6)	263 (3.0)	271 (2.4)	285 (2.0)	293 (1.1)
Nevada	— (†)	— (†)	— (†)	265 (0.8)	268 (0.8)	270 (0.8)	40 (1.1)	60 (1.1)	21 (0.9)	3 (0.5)	257 (2.2)	261 (2.5)	281 (1.9)	281 (1.1)
New Hampshire	273 (0.9)	278 (1.0)	— (†)	— (†)	286 (0.8)	285 (0.8)	23 (0.9)	77 (0.9)	35 (1.6)	7 (0.7)	269 (2.8)	275 (1.6)	283 (2.0)	294 (1.0)
New Jersey	270 (1.1)	272 (1.6)	— (†)	— (†)	281 (1.1)	284 (1.4)	26 (1.4)	74 (1.4)	36 (1.5)	9 (1.0)	266 (3.2)	272 (1.9)	283 (1.8)	294 (1.7)
New Mexico	256 (0.7)	260 (0.9)	262 (1.2)	259 (1.3)	263 (1.0)	263 (0.9)	47 (1.5)	53 (1.5)	14 (1.1)	1 (0.3)	249 (1.8)	254 (1.3)	270 (1.7)	276 (1.4)
New York[6]	261 (1.4)	266 (2.1)	270 (1.7)	271 (2.2)	280 (1.1)	280 (0.9)	30 (1.1)	70 (1.1)	31 (1.3)	6 (0.5)	263 (1.9)	271 (1.4)	280 (1.4)	289 (1.3)
North Carolina	250 (1.1)	258 (1.2)	268 (1.4)	276 (1.3)	281 (1.0)	282 (0.9)	28 (1.2)	72 (1.2)	32 (1.1)	7 (0.8)	265 (3.1)	270 (1.4)	283 (1.5)	294 (1.5)
North Dakota	281 (1.2)	283 (1.1)	284 (0.9)	282 (1.1)	287 (0.8)	287 (0.6)	19 (1.1)	81 (1.1)	35 (1.2)	5 (0.5)	271 (3.7)	274 (1.8)	286 (1.5)	292 (0.8)

See notes at end of table.

Average scale score in mathematics and percentage attaining mathematics achievement levels of 8th-graders in public schools, by level of parental education and state or jurisdiction: Selected years, 1990 through 2005—Continued

State or jurisdiction	Average scale score						Percent attaining mathematics achievement levels, 2005[1]				Average scale score, by highest level of education attained by parents, 2005[2]			
	1990	1992	1996	2000	2003	2005	Below basic	Basic or above[3]	Proficient or above[4]	Advanced[5]	Did not finish high school	Graduated high school	Some education after high school	Graduated college
1	2	3	4	5	6	7	8	9	10	11	12	13	14	15
Ohio	264 (1.0)	268 (1.5)	— (†)	281 (1.6)	282 (1.3)	283 (1.1)	26 (1.4)	74 (1.4)	33 (1.4)	7 (0.6)	266 (3.8)	272 (1.6)	283 (1.9)	294 (1.3)
Oklahoma	263 (1.3)	268 (1.1)	— (†)	270 (1.3)	272 (1.1)	271 (1.0)	37 (1.2)	64 (1.2)	21 (1.3)	2 (0.4)	252 (2.1)	262 (2.0)	275 (1.5)	281 (1.3)
Oregon[6]	271 (1.0)	—	276 (1.5)	280 (1.5)	281 (1.3)	282 (1.0)	28 (1.1)	72 (1.1)	34 (1.3)	7 (0.8)	262 (3.2)	270 (1.8)	283 (2.0)	295 (1.3)
Pennsylvania	266 (1.6)	271 (1.5)	— (†)	— (†)	279 (1.1)	281 (1.5)	28 (1.6)	72 (1.6)	31 (1.6)	6 (0.8)	263 (2.9)	269 (1.9)	283 (2.0)	292 (1.5)
Rhode Island	260 (0.6)	266 (0.7)	269 (0.9)	269 (1.3)	272 (0.7)	272 (0.8)	37 (1.1)	64 (1.1)	24 (0.9)	3 (0.5)	255 (2.7)	263 (1.9)	276 (1.6)	284 (1.0)
South Carolina	—	261 (1.0)	261 (1.5)	265 (1.5)	277 (1.3)	281 (0.9)	29 (1.4)	71 (1.4)	30 (0.9)	7 (0.7)	270 (2.8)	273 (1.8)	285 (2.0)	289 (1.2)
South Dakota	— (†)	— (†)	— (†)	— (†)	285 (0.8)	287 (0.6)	20 (0.8)	80 (0.8)	37 (1.0)	7 (0.7)	267 (2.2)	276 (1.7)	287 (1.3)	295 (0.9)
Tennessee	— (†)	259 (1.4)	263 (1.4)	262 (1.5)	268 (1.8)	271 (1.1)	39 (1.6)	61 (1.6)	21 (1.3)	3 (0.4)	259 (2.1)	263 (1.6)	275 (1.9)	279 (1.7)
Texas	258 (1.4)	265 (1.3)	270 (1.4)	273 (1.6)	277 (1.1)	281 (0.6)	28 (0.7)	72 (0.7)	31 (0.8)	6 (0.4)	268 (1.3)	272 (1.2)	286 (1.2)	293 (1.0)
Utah	—	274 (0.7)	277 (1.0)	274 (1.2)	281 (1.0)	279 (0.7)	29 (1.0)	71 (1.0)	30 (1.1)	5 (0.6)	259 (2.8)	262 (1.5)	280 (1.5)	289 (0.9)
Vermont[6]	— (†)	—	279 (1.0)	281 (1.5)	286 (0.8)	287 (0.8)	23 (1.0)	78 (1.0)	38 (1.1)	9 (0.7)	265 (3.8)	275 (1.4)	285 (1.8)	298 (1.1)
Virginia	264 (1.5)	268 (1.2)	270 (1.6)	275 (1.3)	282 (1.3)	284 (1.1)	25 (1.2)	75 (1.2)	33 (1.5)	8 (0.9)	266 (2.2)	271 (1.9)	282 (2.6)	295 (1.3)
Washington	— (†)	—	276 (1.3)	— (†)	281 (0.9)	285 (1.0)	25 (1.2)	75 (1.2)	36 (1.4)	9 (0.8)	264 (3.0)	277 (1.7)	287 (1.5)	295 (1.3)
West Virginia	256 (1.0)	259 (1.0)	265 (1.0)	266 (1.2)	271 (1.2)	269 (1.0)	40 (1.5)	60 (1.5)	18 (1.0)	1 (0.3)	251 (2.4)	263 (1.4)	273 (1.3)	279 (1.4)
Wisconsin	274 (1.3)	278 (1.5)	283 (1.5)	— (†)	284 (1.3)	285 (1.2)	24 (1.4)	76 (1.4)	36 (1.4)	7 (0.7)	264 (3.8)	276 (1.7)	288 (2.0)	293 (1.3)
Wyoming	272 (0.7)	275 (0.9)	275 (0.9)	276 (1.0)	284 (0.7)	282 (0.8)	24 (1.1)	76 (1.1)	29 (1.4)	4 (0.4)	262 (3.6)	274 (1.5)	283 (1.5)	290 (1.1)
Department of Defense dependents schools[7]	— (†)	— (†)	— (†)	— (†)	— (†)	284 (0.7)	24 (0.9)	76 (0.9)	33 (1.6)	5 (0.6)	‡ (‡)	273 (2.3)	284 (1.7)	288 (1.0)
Domestic schools	—	—	269 (2.3)	274 (1.8)	282 (1.5)	—	—	—	—	—	— (†)	— (†)	— (†)	— (†)
Overseas schools	—	—	275 (0.9)	278 (1.1)	286 (0.7)	—	—	—	—	—	— (†)	— (†)	— (†)	— (†)
Other jurisdictions														
American Samoa	—	235 (1.0)	239 (1.7)	192 (5.5)	— (†)	— (†)	—	—	—	—	— (†)	— (†)	— (†)	— (†)
Guam	232 (0.7)	235 (1.0)	—	234 (2.6)	282 (1.5)	— (†)	—	—	—	—	— (†)	— (†)	— (†)	— (†)
Virgin Islands	219 (0.9)	223 (1.1)	— (†)	—	286 (0.7)	— (†)	—	—	—	—	— (†)	— (†)	— (†)	— (†)

—Not available.
†Not applicable.
‡Reporting standards not met.
[1]Achievement levels are in trial status.
[2]Excludes students who responded "I don't know" to the question about educational level of parents.
[3]The basic level denotes partial mastery of prerequisite knowledge and skills that are fundamental for proficient work at the 8th-grade level.
[4]This level represents solid academic performance for 8th-graders. Students reaching this level have demonstrated competency over challenging subject matter, including subject-matter knowledge, application of such knowledge to real-world situations, and analytical skills appropriate to the subject matter.
[5]This level signifies superior performance.

[6]Did not meet one or more of the guidelines for school participation in 2000. Data are subject to appreciable nonresponse bias.
[7]The definition of the national sample changed in 2005; it now includes all of the international Department of Defense schools.
NOTE: Excludes persons not enrolled in school and those who were unable to be tested due to limited proficiency in English or due to a disability. Fifty states, the District of Columbia, and Department of Defense school systems participated in the 2005 State Assessment of 8th-graders and met student and school participation criteria for reporting results. Scale ranges from 0 to 500. Data for 2000, 2003, and 2005 are for situations where student accommodations for the testing were permitted. Detail may not sum to totals because of rounding. Standard errors appear in parentheses.
SOURCE: U.S. Department of Education, National Center for Education Statistics, National Assessment of Educational Progress (NAEP), *The Nation's Report Card: Mathematics,* 2003 and 2005; and unpublished tabulations, NAEP Data Explorer (http://nces.ed.gov/nationsreportcard/nde/), retrieved October 2005. (This table was prepared October 2005.)

Average mathematics scale scores and percentage of students within each achievement level, grade 4 public schools: By state, 2005

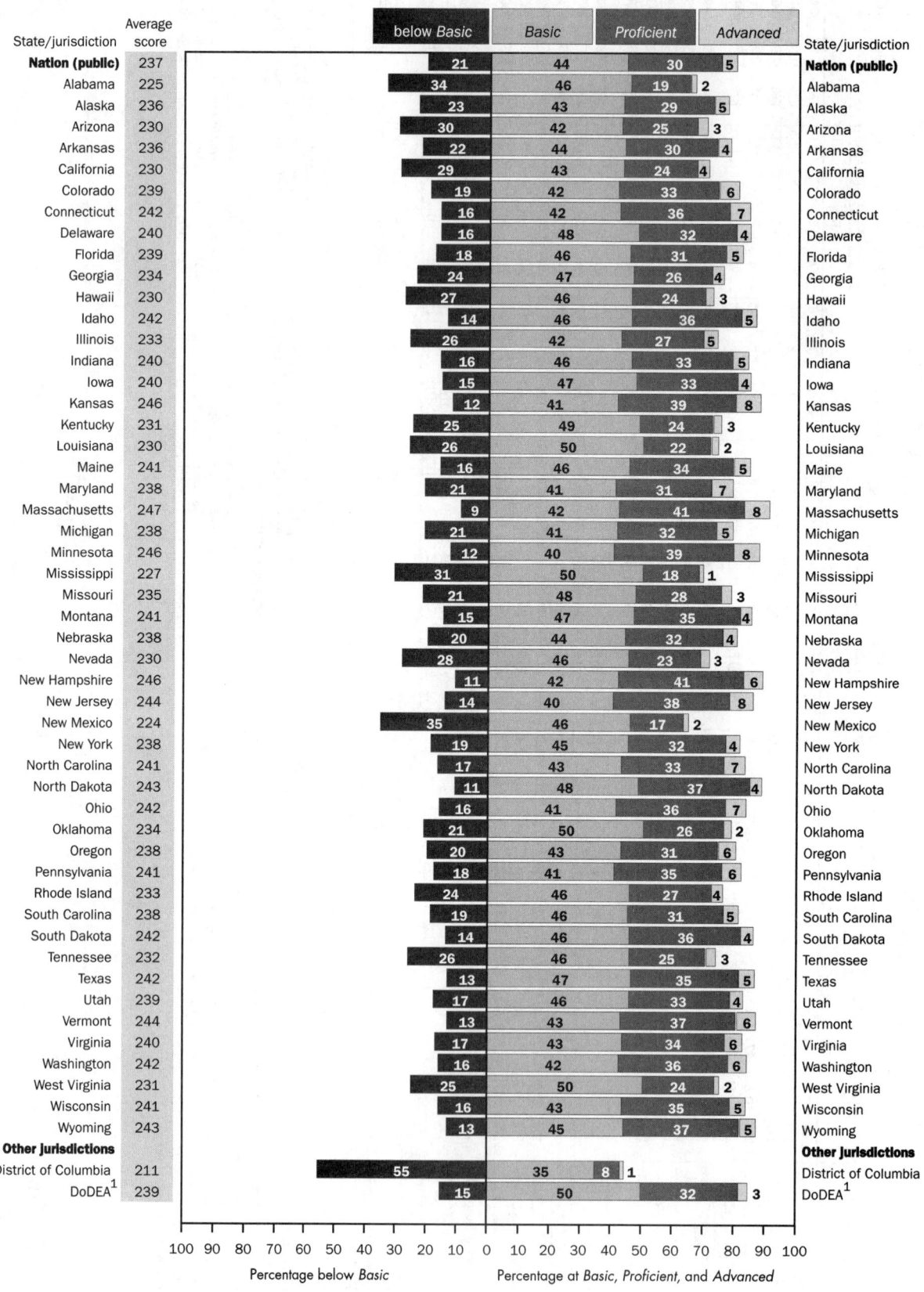

State/jurisdiction	Average score	below Basic	Basic	Proficient	Advanced	State/jurisdiction
Nation (public)	237	21	44	30	5	**Nation (public)**
Alabama	225	34	46	19	2	Alabama
Alaska	236	23	43	29	5	Alaska
Arizona	230	30	42	25	3	Arizona
Arkansas	236	22	44	30	4	Arkansas
California	230	29	43	24	4	California
Colorado	239	19	42	33	6	Colorado
Connecticut	242	16	42	36	7	Connecticut
Delaware	240	16	48	32	4	Delaware
Florida	239	18	46	31	5	Florida
Georgia	234	24	47	26	4	Georgia
Hawaii	230	27	46	24	3	Hawaii
Idaho	242	14	46	36	5	Idaho
Illinois	233	26	42	27	5	Illinois
Indiana	240	16	46	33	5	Indiana
Iowa	240	15	47	33	4	Iowa
Kansas	246	12	41	39	8	Kansas
Kentucky	231	25	49	24	3	Kentucky
Louisiana	230	26	50	22	2	Louisiana
Maine	241	16	46	34	5	Maine
Maryland	238	21	41	31	7	Maryland
Massachusetts	247	9	42	41	8	Massachusetts
Michigan	238	21	41	32	5	Michigan
Minnesota	246	12	40	39	8	Minnesota
Mississippi	227	31	50	18	1	Mississippi
Missouri	235	21	48	28	3	Missouri
Montana	241	15	47	35	4	Montana
Nebraska	238	20	44	32	4	Nebraska
Nevada	230	28	46	23	3	Nevada
New Hampshire	246	11	42	41	6	New Hampshire
New Jersey	244	14	40	38	8	New Jersey
New Mexico	224	35	46	17	2	New Mexico
New York	238	19	45	32	4	New York
North Carolina	241	17	43	33	7	North Carolina
North Dakota	243	11	48	37	4	North Dakota
Ohio	242	16	41	36	7	Ohio
Oklahoma	234	21	50	26	2	Oklahoma
Oregon	238	20	43	31	6	Oregon
Pennsylvania	241	18	41	35	6	Pennsylvania
Rhode Island	233	24	46	27	4	Rhode Island
South Carolina	238	19	46	31	5	South Carolina
South Dakota	242	14	46	36	4	South Dakota
Tennessee	232	26	46	25	3	Tennessee
Texas	242	13	47	35	5	Texas
Utah	239	17	46	33	4	Utah
Vermont	244	13	43	37	6	Vermont
Virginia	240	17	43	34	6	Virginia
Washington	242	16	42	36	6	Washington
West Virginia	231	25	50	24	2	West Virginia
Wisconsin	241	16	43	35	5	Wisconsin
Wyoming	243	13	45	37	5	Wyoming
Other jurisdictions						**Other jurisdictions**
District of Columbia	211	55	35	8	1	District of Columbia
DoDEA[1]	239	15	50	32	3	DoDEA[1]

Percentage below *Basic* — Percentage at *Basic, Proficient,* and *Advanced*

[1] Department of Defense Education Activity.
NOTE: The NAEP mathematics scale sranges from 0 to 500. Detail may not sum to totals because of rounding. The shaded bars are graphed using unrounded numbers.
SOURCE: U.S. Department of Education, Institute of Education Sciences, National Center for Education Statistics, National Assessment of Educational Progress (NAEP), 2005 Mathematics Assessment.

Average mathematics scale scores and achievement-level results, by race/ethnicity, grade 4 public schools: By state, 2005

State/jurisdiction	White					Black					Hispanic				
			Percentage of students					Percentage of students					Percentage of students		
	Percentage of all students	Average scale score	Below Basic	At or above Basic	At or above Proficient	Percentage of all students	Average scale score	Below Basic	At or above Basic	At or above Proficient	Percentage of all students	Average scale score	Below Basic	At or above Basic	At or above Proficient
Nation (public)	57	246	11	89	47	17	220	40	60	13	20	225	33	67	19
Alabama	57	235	20	80	30	38	211	53	47	7	2	‡	‡	‡	‡
Alaska	56	244	13	87	44	4	226	33	67	20	4	227	35	65	23
Arizona	45	243	14	86	43	5	217	46	54	13	41	218	43	57	14
Arkansas	71	242	14	86	42	22	214	50	50	10	5	229	28	72	25
California	31	245	12	88	46	7	215	47	53	12	49	219	41	59	14
Colorado	64	247	10	90	49	5	222	39	61	18	27	223	37	63	18
Connecticut	69	250	7	93	53	14	219	42	58	11	13	223	35	65	15
Delaware	54	249	7	93	50	33	226	29	71	15	9	229	26	74	18
Florida	48	247	9	91	49	23	224	33	67	16	24	233	22	78	28
Georgia	48	243	13	87	43	39	221	39	61	12	8	229	27	73	22
Hawaii	17	241	14	86	42	3	221	39	61	16	3	219	37	63	21
Idaho	82	245	10	90	44	1	‡	‡	‡	‡	13	226	32	68	17
Illinois	54	245	11	89	44	19	212	54	46	9	22	219	41	59	14
Indiana	73	245	11	89	45	16	221	38	62	13	6	230	25	75	21
Iowa	85	242	13	87	40	5	224	32	68	15	6	222	37	63	17
Kansas	74	249	8	92	52	9	228	30	70	24	11	234	21	79	30
Kentucky	84	234	22	78	29	12	217	44	56	9	2	‡	‡	‡	‡
Louisiana	48	241	12	88	38	49	219	40	60	9	1	‡	‡	‡	‡
Maine	97	241	15	85	39	1	‡	‡	‡	‡	#	‡	‡	‡	‡
Maryland	51	250	9	91	53	35	220	40	60	14	8	232	28	72	26
Massachusetts	75	252	5	95	57	9	228	27	73	18	11	225	27	73	14
Michigan	72	245	11	89	46	20	211	55	45	8	4	‡	‡	‡	‡
Minnesota	79	251	7	93	54	9	219	43	57	15	6	223	37	63	15
Mississippi	47	238	14	86	32	51	216	46	54	7	1	‡	‡	‡	‡
Missouri	76	240	15	85	37	17	215	47	53	9	4	221	37	63	10
Montana	85	243	11	89	41	1	‡	‡	‡	‡	2	234	20	80	30
Nebraska	75	244	12	88	44	8	211	55	45	7	13	219	41	59	10
Nevada	46	240	15	85	38	12	214	48	52	10	33	219	42	58	13
New Hampshire	94	246	10	90	48	2	‡	‡	‡	‡	2	226	36	64	17
New Jersey	57	251	7	93	55	18	224	33	67	17	15	230	26	74	25
New Mexico	30	238	17	83	34	2	213	55	45	6	56	218	43	57	13
New York	53	247	9	91	49	21	222	36	64	13	19	226	30	70	17
North Carolina	59	250	8	92	52	27	225	34	66	17	8	234	20	80	26
North Dakota	88	245	9	91	43	1	‡	‡	‡	‡	1	‡	‡	‡	‡
Ohio	72	248	9	91	51	21	221	41	59	16	2	231	24	76	21
Oklahoma	59	240	15	85	36	11	217	46	54	11	9	226	28	72	16
Oregon	71	243	13	87	42	3	222	34	66	12	17	218	45	55	14
Pennsylvania	74	247	11	89	50	17	219	40	60	13	7	220	40	60	16
Rhode Island	73	241	14	86	37	8	211	54	46	9	16	211	52	48	9
South Carolina	55	250	8	92	53	41	223	34	66	13	3	236	17	83	30
South Dakota	84	245	10	90	45	2	‡	‡	‡	‡	2	‡	‡	‡	‡
Tennessee	69	238	17	83	35	26	214	50	50	9	3	229	31	69	26
Texas	38	254	4	96	60	13	228	25	75	18	46	235	18	82	28
Utah	81	242	13	87	41	1	‡	‡	‡	‡	13	220	40	60	13
Vermont	96	244	13	87	44	1	‡	‡	‡	‡	1	‡	‡	‡	‡
Virginia	61	247	11	89	50	24	224	34	66	14	8	230	25	75	22
Washington	69	246	11	89	48	6	231	26	74	26	15	224	34	66	17
West Virginia	95	231	24	76	25	4	226	31	69	17	1	‡	‡	‡	‡
Wisconsin	77	247	9	91	48	11	210	54	46	7	7	224	34	66	16
Wyoming	85	245	11	89	45	1	‡	‡	‡	‡	9	234	22	78	31
Other jurisdictions															
District of Columbia	4	266	1	99	78	86	207	59	41	5	8	215	49	51	11
DoDEA[1]	47	245	9	91	46	20	227	27	73	15	14	235	18	82	28

See notes at end of table.

Average mathematics scale scores and achievement-level results, by race/ethnicity, grade 4 public schools: By state, 2005—Continued

State/jurisdiction	Asian/Pacific Islander					American Indian/Alaska Native				
	Percentage of all students	Average scale score	Percentage of students			Percentage of all students	Average scale score	Percentage of students		
			Below Basic	At or above Basic	At or above Proficient			Below Basic	At or above Basic	At or above Proficient
Nation (public)	4	251	11	89	54	1	227	31	69	22
Alabama	1	‡	‡	‡	‡	1	‡	‡	‡	‡
Alaska	8	238	20	80	36	26	220	43	57	15
Arizona	3	241	15	85	43	6	‡	‡	‡	‡
Arkansas	1	‡	‡	‡	‡	1	‡	‡	‡	‡
California	10	249	11	89	51	1	228	31	69	27
Colorado	3	242	19	81	42	1	‡	‡	‡	‡
Connecticut	3	253	7	93	57	#	‡	‡	‡	‡
Delaware	3	260	6	94	70	#	‡	‡	‡	‡
Florida	2	259	4	96	66	#	‡	‡	‡	‡
Georgia	3	255	5	95	57	#	‡	‡	‡	‡
Hawaii	66	229	29	71	25	1	‡	‡	‡	‡
Idaho	2	‡	‡	‡	‡	2	‡	‡	‡	‡
Illinois	4	258	8	92	66	#	‡	‡	‡	‡
Indiana	1	‡	‡	‡	‡	#	‡	‡	‡	‡
Iowa	2	‡	‡	‡	‡	1	‡	‡	‡	‡
Kansas	3	262	8	92	71	2	‡	‡	‡	‡
Kentucky	1	‡	‡	‡	‡	#	‡	‡	‡	‡
Louisiana	1	‡	‡	‡	‡	#	‡	‡	‡	‡
Maine	1	‡	‡	‡	‡	#	‡	‡	‡	‡
Maryland	6	256	5	95	59	#	‡	‡	‡	‡
Massachusetts	5	258	5	95	64	#	‡	‡	‡	‡
Michigan	3	‡	‡	‡	‡	#	‡	‡	‡	‡
Minnesota	5	242	18	82	40	2	‡	‡	‡	‡
Mississippi	1	‡	‡	‡	‡	#	‡	‡	‡	‡
Missouri	2	‡	‡	‡	‡	#	‡	‡	‡	‡
Montana	1	‡	‡	‡	‡	11	223	38	62	17
Nebraska	2	‡	‡	‡	‡	2	‡	‡	‡	‡
Nevada	8	243	12	88	42	1	‡	‡	‡	‡
New Hampshire	2	‡	‡	‡	‡	#	‡	‡	‡	‡
New Jersey	9	264	3	97	74	#	‡	‡	‡	‡
New Mexico	1	‡	‡	‡	‡	10	217	44	56	9
New York	7	254	7	93	61	1	‡	‡	‡	‡
North Carolina	2	256	6	94	63	2	‡	‡	‡	‡
North Dakota	1	‡	‡	‡	‡	8	223	34	66	13
Ohio	1	‡	‡	‡	‡	#	‡	‡	‡	‡
Oklahoma	1	‡	‡	‡	‡	19	229	24	76	21
Oregon	5	248	16	84	54	2	‡	‡	‡	‡
Pennsylvania	2	‡	‡	‡	‡	#	‡	‡	‡	‡
Rhode Island	2	240	17	83	39	1	‡	‡	‡	‡
South Carolina	1	‡	‡	‡	‡	#	‡	‡	‡	‡
South Dakota	1	‡	‡	‡	‡	11	221	38	62	13
Tennessee	1	‡	‡	‡	‡	#	‡	‡	‡	‡
Texas	3	264	4	96	72	#	‡	‡	‡	‡
Utah	3	235	24	76	33	1	‡	‡	‡	‡
Vermont	1	‡	‡	‡	‡	#	‡	‡	‡	‡
Virginia	5	256	5	95	64	#	‡	‡	‡	‡
Washington	8	245	16	84	46	2	‡	‡	‡	‡
West Virginia	1	‡	‡	‡	‡	#	‡	‡	‡	‡
Wisconsin	3	236	20	80	29	1	‡	‡	‡	‡
Wyoming	1	‡	‡	‡	‡	3	‡	‡	‡	‡
Other jurisdictions										
District of Columbia	1	‡	‡	‡	‡	#	‡	‡	‡	‡
DoDEA[1]	7	239	15	85	32	1	‡	‡	‡	‡

\# The estimate rounds to zero.

‡ Reporting standards not met. Sample size is insufficient to permit a reliable estimate.

[1] Department of Defense Education Activity.

NOTE: Results are not shown for students whose race/ethnicity was "unclassified." Detail may not sum to totals because of rounding.

SOURCE: U.S. Department of Education, Institute of Education Sciences, National Center for Education Statistics, National Assessment of Educational Progress (NAEP), 2005 Mathematics Assessment.

Average mathematics scale scores and achievement-level results, by gender, grade 4 public schools: By state, 2005

State/jurisdiction	Male					Female				
	Percentage of all students	Average scale score	Percentage of students			Percentage of all students	Average scale score	Percentage of students		
			Below Basic	At or above Basic	At or above Proficient			Below Basic	At or above Basic	At or above Proficient
Nation (public)	51	238	20	80	37	49	236	21	79	33
Alabama	51	225	34	66	22	49	225	33	67	20
Alaska	50	236	24	76	35	50	235	22	78	32
Arizona	52	233	26	74	32	48	227	33	67	24
Arkansas	53	236	22	78	36	47	235	22	78	32
California	51	231	28	72	30	49	229	30	70	26
Colorado	52	241	18	82	41	48	238	21	79	36
Connecticut	51	244	14	86	45	49	241	17	83	40
Delaware	51	241	15	85	38	49	238	16	84	34
Florida	50	240	17	83	38	50	238	19	81	35
Georgia	51	234	24	76	30	49	233	24	76	29
Hawaii	51	229	29	71	26	49	231	26	74	28
Idaho	51	242	14	86	42	49	241	14	86	39
Illinois	51	234	25	75	33	49	232	28	72	30
Indiana	50	240	16	84	38	50	240	16	84	38
Iowa	53	242	14	86	40	47	238	17	83	34
Kansas	52	247	11	89	48	48	245	12	88	45
Kentucky	51	233	24	76	29	49	230	26	74	24
Louisiana	52	231	25	75	26	48	229	27	73	21
Maine	51	243	14	86	41	49	239	17	83	36
Maryland	51	240	21	79	40	49	237	22	78	36
Massachusetts	49	248	9	91	50	51	247	10	90	48
Michigan	51	240	19	81	41	49	236	23	77	34
Minnesota	50	247	12	88	50	50	245	13	87	45
Mississippi	51	227	30	70	20	49	226	32	68	18
Missouri	51	237	21	79	34	49	233	22	78	28
Montana	50	243	13	87	42	50	239	16	84	34
Nebraska	50	239	19	81	39	50	236	21	79	33
Nevada	51	231	28	72	28	49	229	29	71	24
New Hampshire	51	247	10	90	50	49	244	12	88	44
New Jersey	52	246	13	87	47	48	242	16	84	43
New Mexico	51	225	35	65	21	49	223	36	64	17
New York	50	240	18	82	39	50	237	19	81	33
North Carolina	51	242	17	83	41	49	241	16	84	38
North Dakota	50	244	10	90	43	50	241	12	88	38
Ohio	51	243	16	84	45	49	241	16	84	40
Oklahoma	51	235	20	80	31	49	233	22	78	26
Oregon	51	239	20	80	37	49	238	19	81	37
Pennsylvania	51	241	18	82	44	49	240	18	82	39
Rhode Island	51	234	24	76	32	49	233	23	77	29
South Carolina	50	238	20	80	37	50	238	18	82	35
South Dakota	51	243	13	87	43	49	240	14	86	38
Tennessee	50	233	26	74	30	50	231	26	74	25
Texas	50	244	12	88	43	50	240	15	85	37
Utah	51	240	16	84	39	49	237	18	82	34
Vermont	53	246	11	89	47	47	241	15	85	39
Virginia	51	242	17	83	42	49	239	18	82	37
Washington	50	242	15	85	43	50	241	17	83	41
West Virginia	52	232	23	77	28	48	229	27	73	22
Wisconsin	51	242	15	85	42	49	239	18	82	39
Wyoming	51	244	12	88	45	49	242	13	87	40
Other jurisdictions										
District of Columbia	49	212	56	44	11	51	211	55	45	9
DoDEA[1]	49	241	14	86	38	51	237	17	83	31

[1] Department of Defense Education Activity.
NOTE: Detail may not sum to totals because of rounding.
SOURCE: U.S. Department of Education, Institute of Education Sciences, National Center for Education Statistics, National Assessment of Educational Progress (NAEP), 2005 Mathematics Assessment.

Average mathematics scale scores and percentage of students within each achievement level, grade 8 public schools: By state, 2005

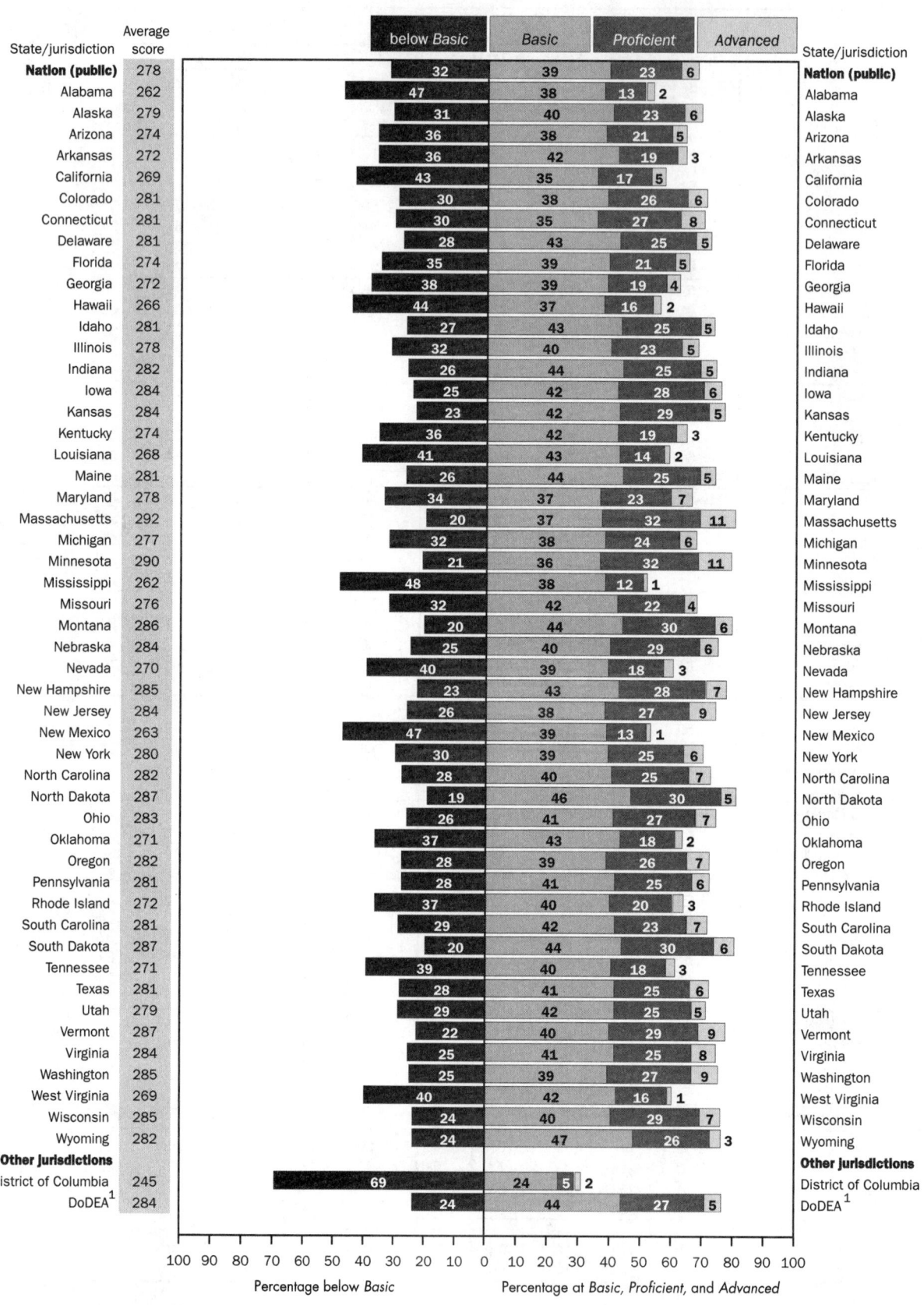

State/jurisdiction	Average score	below Basic	Basic	Proficient	Advanced
Nation (public)	278	32	39	23	6
Alabama	262	47	38	13	2
Alaska	279	31	40	23	6
Arizona	274	36	38	21	5
Arkansas	272	36	42	19	3
California	269	43	35	17	5
Colorado	281	30	38	26	6
Connecticut	281	30	35	27	8
Delaware	281	28	43	25	5
Florida	274	35	39	21	5
Georgia	272	38	39	19	4
Hawaii	266	44	37	16	2
Idaho	281	27	43	25	5
Illinois	278	32	40	23	5
Indiana	282	26	44	25	5
Iowa	284	25	42	28	6
Kansas	284	23	42	29	5
Kentucky	274	36	42	19	3
Louisiana	268	41	43	14	2
Maine	281	26	44	25	5
Maryland	278	34	37	23	7
Massachusetts	292	20	37	32	11
Michigan	277	32	38	24	6
Minnesota	290	21	36	32	11
Mississippi	262	48	38	12	1
Missouri	276	32	42	22	4
Montana	286	20	44	30	6
Nebraska	284	25	40	29	6
Nevada	270	40	39	18	3
New Hampshire	285	23	43	28	7
New Jersey	284	26	38	27	9
New Mexico	263	47	39	13	1
New York	280	30	39	25	6
North Carolina	282	28	40	25	7
North Dakota	287	19	46	30	5
Ohio	283	26	41	27	7
Oklahoma	271	37	43	18	2
Oregon	282	28	39	26	7
Pennsylvania	281	28	41	25	6
Rhode Island	272	37	40	20	3
South Carolina	281	29	42	23	7
South Dakota	287	20	44	30	6
Tennessee	271	39	40	18	3
Texas	281	28	41	25	6
Utah	279	29	42	25	5
Vermont	287	22	40	29	9
Virginia	284	25	41	25	8
Washington	285	25	39	27	9
West Virginia	269	40	42	16	1
Wisconsin	285	24	40	29	7
Wyoming	282	24	47	26	3
Other jurisdictions					
District of Columbia	245	69	24	5	2
DoDEA[1]	284	24	44	27	5

100 90 80 70 60 50 40 30 20 10 0 10 20 30 40 50 60 70 80 90 100

Percentage below *Basic*   Percentage at *Basic, Proficient,* and *Advanced*

[1] Department of Defense Education Activity.

NOTE: The NAEP mathematics scale ranges from 0 to 500. Detail may not sum to totals because of rounding. The shaded bars are graphed using unrounded numbers.

SOURCE: U.S. Department of Education, Institute of Education Sciences, National Center for Education Statistics, National Assessment of Educational Progress (NAEP), 2005 Mathematics Assessment.

Average mathematics scale scores and achievement-level results, by race/ethnicity, grade 8 public schools: By state, 2005

State/jurisdiction	White					Black					Hispanic				
	Percentage of all students	Average scale score	Percentage of students			Percentage of all students	Average scale score	Percentage of students			Percentage of all students	Average scale score	Percentage of students		
			Below Basic	At or above Basic	At or above Proficient			Below Basic	At or above Basic	At or above Proficient			Below Basic	At or above Basic	At or above Proficient
Nation (public)	60	288	21	79	37	17	254	59	41	8	17	261	50	50	13
Alabama	59	276	32	68	22	37	240	73	27	3	2	‡	‡	‡	‡
Alaska	57	288	21	79	38	5	266	48	52	19	4	272	36	64	21
Arizona	50	288	21	79	38	5	261	50	50	15	38	260	52	48	13
Arkansas	71	281	25	75	28	23	243	70	30	4	4	266	44	56	15
California	33	284	26	74	34	8	248	65	35	7	45	254	58	42	9
Colorado	64	292	18	82	43	7	256	56	44	11	25	260	52	48	10
Connecticut	66	293	17	83	46	15	249	63	37	6	14	254	59	41	10
Delaware	56	291	15	85	40	33	264	47	53	13	7	268	43	57	16
Florida	52	286	22	78	36	22	251	61	39	8	22	265	44	56	16
Georgia	51	284	24	76	34	37	255	57	43	8	6	258	52	48	12
Hawaii	15	277	31	69	25	2	‡	‡	‡	‡	3	257	53	47	9
Idaho	85	284	23	77	33	1	‡	‡	‡	‡	12	261	52	48	11
Illinois	61	289	18	82	39	21	249	66	34	6	14	265	45	55	13
Indiana	81	286	20	80	34	12	257	56	44	9	4	261	51	49	14
Iowa	88	286	22	78	36	4	256	59	41	8	5	264	46	54	9
Kansas	77	289	17	83	39	8	256	56	44	12	9	266	44	56	14
Kentucky	86	276	33	67	24	10	255	57	43	9	1	‡	‡	‡	‡
Louisiana	53	281	23	77	25	44	252	63	37	5	2	‡	‡	‡	‡
Maine	96	281	26	74	30	2	‡	‡	‡	‡	1	‡	‡	‡	‡
Maryland	50	292	18	82	43	40	258	54	46	11	4	262	53	47	19
Massachusetts	76	297	14	86	49	8	263	50	50	15	10	265	45	55	15
Michigan	73	285	23	77	36	20	247	66	34	6	4	265	48	52	16
Minnesota	81	296	15	85	49	8	251	63	37	9	4	263	47	53	10
Mississippi	46	279	26	74	24	51	247	69	31	4	1	‡	‡	‡	‡
Missouri	77	284	23	77	32	19	247	68	32	4	2	‡	‡	‡	‡
Montana	86	290	16	84	39	#	‡	‡	‡	‡	2	‡	‡	‡	‡
Nebraska	83	289	19	81	40	5	243	75	25	2	9	261	52	48	10
Nevada	55	280	27	73	29	10	247	66	34	7	29	256	56	44	10
New Hampshire	94	286	22	78	35	1	‡	‡	‡	‡	2	‡	‡	‡	‡
New Jersey	57	295	15	85	47	20	260	50	50	11	15	264	42	58	15
New Mexico	34	279	28	72	26	2	257	56	44	13	51	255	57	43	8
New York	55	290	17	83	41	19	259	54	46	11	18	262	49	51	14
North Carolina	60	292	18	82	42	29	263	47	53	12	6	265	41	59	16
North Dakota	88	290	16	84	37	1	‡	‡	‡	‡	1	‡	‡	‡	‡
Ohio	80	289	19	81	38	15	255	58	42	7	1	259	47	53	11
Oklahoma	62	278	29	71	26	11	249	65	35	4	7	257	55	45	11
Oregon	76	287	23	77	38	3	258	50	50	9	13	257	56	44	10
Pennsylvania	78	287	20	80	36	15	250	65	35	7	5	267	40	60	13
Rhode Island	73	281	27	73	30	8	249	66	34	5	15	244	71	29	4
South Carolina	57	294	14	86	44	39	263	49	51	10	3	269	42	58	19
South Dakota	86	291	15	85	40	1	‡	‡	‡	‡	2	‡	‡	‡	‡
Tennessee	75	278	30	70	26	22	246	70	30	3	2	‡	‡	‡	‡
Texas	43	295	14	86	46	15	264	47	53	13	39	271	37	63	19
Utah	84	283	25	75	33	1	‡	‡	‡	‡	10	255	55	45	9
Vermont	96	288	21	79	39	2	‡	‡	‡	‡	1	‡	‡	‡	‡
Virginia	61	293	16	84	43	26	263	48	52	9	6	270	37	63	20
Washington	74	289	20	80	39	4	265	44	56	15	10	262	50	50	15
West Virginia	95	270	39	61	18	4	251	64	36	6	1	‡	‡	‡	‡
Wisconsin	79	291	16	84	42	11	246	70	30	5	6	265	44	56	16
Wyoming	87	284	21	79	32	1	‡	‡	‡	‡	7	265	43	57	11
Other jurisdictions															
District of Columbia	4	317	6	94	69	88	241	73	27	4	7	252	61	39	9
DoDEA[1]	45	292	15	85	41	20	267	42	58	16	13	280	28	72	28

See notes at end of table.

Average mathematics scale scores and achievement-level results, by race/ethnicity, grade 8 public schools: By state, 2005—Continued

State/jurisdiction	Asian/Pacific Islander					American Indian/Alaska Native				
	Percentage of all students	Average scale score	Percentage of students			Percentage of all students	Average scale score	Percentage of students		
			Below Basic	At or above Basic	At or above Proficient			Below Basic	At or above Basic	At or above Proficient
Nation (public)	5	294	19	81	46	1	266	45	55	14
Alabama	1	‡	‡	‡	‡	1	‡	‡	‡	‡
Alaska	7	270	40	60	19	26	264	47	53	15
Arizona	2	‡	‡	‡	‡	5	259	53	47	10
Arkansas	1	‡	‡	‡	‡	1	‡	‡	‡	‡
California	12	293	20	80	45	1	‡	‡	‡	‡
Colorado	2	‡	‡	‡	‡	1	‡	‡	‡	‡
Connecticut	4	292	22	78	46	#	‡	‡	‡	‡
Delaware	3	306	9	91	59	#	‡	‡	‡	‡
Florida	2	299	13	87	51	#	‡	‡	‡	‡
Georgia	3	301	16	84	52	#	‡	‡	‡	‡
Hawaii	68	264	47	53	17	#	‡	‡	‡	‡
Idaho	1	‡	‡	‡	‡	1	‡	‡	‡	‡
Illinois	4	300	10	90	50	#	‡	‡	‡	‡
Indiana	1	‡	‡	‡	‡	#	‡	‡	‡	‡
Iowa	2	‡	‡	‡	‡	1	‡	‡	‡	‡
Kansas	2	‡	‡	‡	‡	2	‡	‡	‡	‡
Kentucky	1	‡	‡	‡	‡	#	‡	‡	‡	‡
Louisiana	1	‡	‡	‡	‡	1	‡	‡	‡	‡
Maine	1	‡	‡	‡	‡	#	‡	‡	‡	‡
Maryland	5	304	13	87	55	1	‡	‡	‡	‡
Massachusetts	5	314	9	91	68	#	‡	‡	‡	‡
Michigan	2	‡	‡	‡	‡	#	‡	‡	‡	‡
Minnesota	5	285	28	72	34	2	‡	‡	‡	‡
Mississippi	1	‡	‡	‡	‡	#	‡	‡	‡	‡
Missouri	1	‡	‡	‡	‡	#	‡	‡	‡	‡
Montana	1	‡	‡	‡	‡	10	259	52	48	11
Nebraska	1	‡	‡	‡	‡	1	‡	‡	‡	‡
Nevada	6	281	27	73	30	1	‡	‡	‡	‡
New Hampshire	2	‡	‡	‡	‡	#	‡	‡	‡	‡
New Jersey	7	309	8	92	63	#	‡	‡	‡	‡
New Mexico	1	‡	‡	‡	‡	12	253	61	39	4
New York	7	298	17	83	50	#	‡	‡	‡	‡
North Carolina	2	303	13	87	53	1	‡	‡	‡	‡
North Dakota	1	‡	‡	‡	‡	9	261	51	49	9
Ohio	2	‡	‡	‡	‡	#	‡	‡	‡	‡
Oklahoma	2	‡	‡	‡	‡	18	267	40	60	15
Oregon	4	299	18	82	50	2	274	37	63	23
Pennsylvania	2	297	18	82	49	#	‡	‡	‡	‡
Rhode Island	3	278	26	74	26	#	‡	‡	‡	‡
South Carolina	1	‡	‡	‡	‡	#	‡	‡	‡	‡
South Dakota	1	‡	‡	‡	‡	10	260	52	48	11
Tennessee	1	‡	‡	‡	‡	#	‡	‡	‡	‡
Texas	3	308	10	90	61	#	‡	‡	‡	‡
Utah	3	273	37	63	26	2	‡	‡	‡	‡
Vermont	1	‡	‡	‡	‡	#	‡	‡	‡	‡
Virginia	6	300	14	86	53	#	‡	‡	‡	‡
Washington	8	294	19	81	45	2	273	36	64	26
West Virginia	#	‡	‡	‡	‡	#	‡	‡	‡	‡
Wisconsin	3	286	30	70	32	1	‡	‡	‡	‡
Wyoming	1	‡	‡	‡	‡	3	262	46	54	8
Other jurisdictions										
District of Columbia	1	‡	‡	‡	‡	#	‡	‡	‡	‡
DoDEA[1]	8	290	20	80	41	1	‡	‡	‡	‡

The estimate rounds to zero.
‡ Reporting standards not met. Sample size is insufficient to permit a reliable estimate.
[1] Department of Defense Education Activity.
NOTE: Results are not shown for students whose race/ethnicity was "unclassified." Detail may not sum to totals because of rounding.
SOURCE: U.S. Department of Education, Institute of Education Sciences, National Center for Education Statistics, National Assessment of Educational Progress (NAEP), 2005 Mathematics Assessment.

Average mathematics scale scores and achievement-level results, by gender, grade 8 public schools: By state, 2005

State/jurisdiction	Male					Female				
	Percentage of all students	Average scale score	Percentage of students			Percentage of all students	Average scale score	Percentage of students		
			Below Basic	At or above Basic	At or above Proficient			Below Basic	At or above Basic	At or above Proficient
Nation (public)	51	278	32	68	30	49	277	33	67	27
Alabama	49	261	48	52	15	51	264	46	54	15
Alaska	53	280	30	70	30	47	278	32	68	27
Arizona	52	274	36	64	26	48	274	36	64	25
Arkansas	51	270	38	62	22	49	273	34	66	22
California	51	269	42	58	23	49	268	44	56	20
Colorado	49	281	30	70	33	51	281	29	71	31
Connecticut	50	281	31	69	35	50	281	30	70	34
Delaware	50	283	26	74	32	50	279	29	71	27
Florida	52	276	33	67	28	48	272	37	63	23
Georgia	51	273	38	62	24	49	272	38	62	23
Hawaii	54	265	45	55	19	46	266	44	56	18
Idaho	50	280	28	72	30	50	282	25	75	30
Illinois	51	279	30	70	30	49	276	34	66	27
Indiana	51	283	25	75	32	49	280	27	73	28
Iowa	50	283	25	75	34	50	284	24	76	33
Kansas	51	285	23	77	35	49	283	23	77	33
Kentucky	51	275	34	66	24	49	273	37	63	21
Louisiana	51	267	42	58	16	49	268	40	60	16
Maine	49	282	26	74	31	51	280	26	74	29
Maryland	48	278	35	65	31	52	278	33	67	28
Massachusetts	49	291	21	79	43	51	292	19	81	43
Michigan	50	279	30	70	31	50	275	34	66	27
Minnesota	50	291	22	78	45	50	289	20	80	41
Mississippi	49	263	48	52	15	51	262	49	51	12
Missouri	52	278	31	69	28	48	275	33	67	24
Montana	52	286	22	78	36	48	287	19	81	36
Nebraska	50	285	24	76	37	50	283	26	74	33
Nevada	51	270	39	61	23	49	269	40	60	20
New Hampshire	50	286	23	77	36	50	285	22	78	33
New Jersey	51	286	25	75	39	49	282	27	73	33
New Mexico	50	264	47	53	15	50	262	48	52	13
New York	50	280	30	70	31	50	280	30	70	30
North Carolina	51	281	29	71	32	49	282	26	74	32
North Dakota	51	287	20	80	36	49	287	19	81	33
Ohio	50	284	25	75	34	50	282	26	74	32
Oklahoma	50	272	37	63	22	50	271	37	63	19
Oregon	52	284	27	73	35	48	281	28	72	32
Pennsylvania	52	283	26	74	33	48	279	30	70	29
Rhode Island	51	272	37	63	24	49	273	36	64	23
South Carolina	50	282	29	71	31	50	281	28	72	29
South Dakota	51	287	20	80	36	49	287	20	80	37
Tennessee	49	270	39	61	21	51	271	39	61	20
Texas	50	283	26	74	33	50	279	29	71	28
Utah	52	280	29	71	32	48	278	29	71	27
Vermont	50	287	23	77	38	50	287	22	78	38
Virginia	50	285	25	75	35	50	283	26	74	32
Washington	51	285	26	74	37	49	285	24	76	35
West Virginia	51	268	40	60	18	49	270	40	60	18
Wisconsin	49	285	24	76	36	51	284	24	76	36
Wyoming	52	283	24	76	31	48	281	23	77	27
Other jurisdictions										
District of Columbia	47	246	68	32	7	53	245	71	29	6
DoDEA[1]	52	285	23	77	34	48	283	25	75	31

[1] Department of Defense Education Activity.
NOTE: Detail may not sum to totals because of rounding.
SOURCE: U.S. Department of Education, Institute of Education Sciences, National Center for Education Statistics, National Assessment of Educational Progress (NAEP), 2005 Mathematics Assessment.

Average reading scale score, by age and selected student and school characteristics: Selected years, 1971 through 2004

Selected student and school characteristic	1971	1975	1980	1984	1988	1990	1992	1994	1996	1999	2004
1	2	3	4	5	6	7	8	9	10	11	12
9-year-olds											
All students	208 (1.0)	210 (0.7)	215 (1.0)	211 (0.8)	212 (1.1)	209 (1.2)	211 (0.9)	211 (1.2)	212 (1.0)	212 (1.3)	219 (1.1)
Sex											
Male	201 (1.1)	204 (0.8)	210 (1.1)	207 (1.0)	207 (1.4)	204 (1.7)	206 (1.3)	207 (1.3)	207 (1.4)	209 (1.6)	216 (1.4)
Female	214 (1.0)	216 (0.8)	220 (1.1)	214 (0.9)	216 (1.3)	215 (1.2)	215 (0.9)	215 (1.4)	218 (1.1)	215 (1.5)	221 (1.0)
Race/ethnicity											
White, non-Hispanic	214 (0.9)	217 (0.7)	221 (0.8)	218 (0.9)	218 (1.4)	217 (1.3)	218 (1.0)	218 (1.3)	220 (1.2)	221 (1.6)	226 (1.1)
Black, non-Hispanic	170 (1.7)	181 (1.2)	189 (1.8)	186 (1.3)	189 (2.4)	182 (2.9)	185 (2.2)	185 (2.3)	191 (2.6)	186 (2.3)	200 (2.2)
Hispanic	1 (†)	183 (2.2)	190 (2.3)	187 (3.0)	194 (3.5)	189 (2.3)	192 (3.1)	186 (3.9)	195 (3.4)	193 (2.7)	205 (1.7)
Region											
Northeast	213 (1.7)	215 (1.3)	221 (2.1)	216 (2.2)	215 (2.6)	217 (2.2)	218 (2.6)	217 (2.9)	220 (1.8)	222 (3.5)	223 (2.5)
Southeast	194 (2.9)	201 (1.2)	210 (2.3)	204 (2.0)	207 (2.1)	197 (3.2)	199 (2.0)	208 (3.0)	206 (2.8)	205 (2.3)	218 (1.8)
Central	215 (1.2)	215 (1.2)	217 (1.4)	215 (1.9)	218 (2.2)	213 (2.0)	216 (1.6)	214 (2.3)	215 (2.6)	215 (3.9)	221 (2.3)
West	205 (2.0)	207 (2.0)	213 (1.8)	209 (2.0)	208 (2.6)	210 (2.8)	209 (2.3)	205 (2.8)	210 (1.9)	206 (1.8)	215 (1.5)
13-year-olds											
All students	255 (0.9)	256 (0.8)	258 (0.9)	257 (0.6)	257 (1.0)	257 (0.8)	260 (1.2)	258 (0.9)	258 (1.0)	259 (1.0)	259 (1.0)
Sex											
Male	250 (1.0)	250 (0.8)	254 (1.1)	253 (0.7)	252 (1.3)	251 (1.1)	254 (1.7)	251 (1.2)	251 (1.2)	254 (1.3)	254 (1.2)
Female	261 (0.9)	262 (0.9)	263 (0.9)	262 (0.7)	263 (1.0)	263 (1.1)	265 (1.2)	266 (1.2)	264 (1.2)	265 (1.2)	264 (1.3)
Race/ethnicity											
White, non-Hispanic	261 (0.7)	262 (0.7)	264 (0.7)	263 (0.6)	261 (1.1)	262 (0.9)	266 (1.2)	265 (1.1)	266 (1.0)	267 (1.2)	266 (1.0)
Black, non-Hispanic	222 (1.2)	226 (1.2)	233 (1.5)	236 (1.2)	243 (2.4)	241 (2.2)	238 (2.3)	234 (2.4)	234 (2.6)	238 (2.4)	244 (2.0)
Hispanic	1 (†)	232 (3.0)	237 (2.0)	240 (2.0)	240 (3.5)	238 (2.3)	239 (3.5)	235 (1.9)	238 (2.9)	244 (2.9)	242 (1.6)
Parents' highest level of education											
Not high school graduate	— (†)	— (†)	239 (1.1)	240 (1.2)	246 (2.1)	241 (1.8)	239 (2.6)	237 (2.4)	239 (2.8)	238 (3.4)	240 (2.7)
Graduated high school	— (†)	— (†)	253 (0.9)	253 (0.8)	253 (1.2)	251 (0.9)	252 (1.7)	251 (1.4)	251 (1.5)	251 (1.8)	251 (1.6)
Some education after high school	— (†)	— (†)	268 (1.0)	266 (1.1)	265 (1.7)	267 (1.7)	265 (2.7)	266 (1.9)	268 (2.3)	269 (2.4)	264 (2.0)
Graduated college	— (†)	— (†)	273 (0.9)	268 (0.9)	265 (1.6)	267 (1.1)	271 (1.5)	269 (1.2)	269 (1.4)	270 (1.2)	270 (1.0)
Region											
Northeast	261 (2.0)	259 (1.8)	260 (1.8)	261 (0.8)	259 (2.4)	259 (1.8)	265 (3.2)	269 (2.0)	259 (2.6)	263 (2.9)	265 (1.9)
Southeast	245 (1.7)	249 (1.5)	253 (1.6)	256 (1.9)	258 (2.2)	256 (2.2)	254 (2.5)	253 (2.5)	251 (3.3)	254 (2.4)	257 (2.3)
Central	260 (1.8)	261 (1.4)	265 (1.4)	258 (1.3)	256 (2.0)	257 (1.5)	263 (3.0)	259 (3.3)	267 (1.8)	261 (1.9)	260 (2.1)
West	254 (1.3)	253 (1.7)	256 (2.0)	254 (1.1)	258 (2.1)	256 (1.6)	258 (1.6)	253 (2.1)	257 (1.7)	259 (2.2)	255 (1.6)

See notes at end of table.

Average reading scale score, by age and selected student and school characteristics: Selected years, 1971 through 2004—Continued

Selected student and school characteristic	1971		1975		1980		1984		1988		1990		1992		1994		1996		1999		2004	
1	2		3		4		5		6		7		8		9		10		11		12	
17-year-olds																						
All students	285	(1.2)	286	(0.8)	285	(1.2)	289	(0.8)	290	(1.0)	290	(1.1)	290	(1.1)	288	(1.3)	288	(1.1)	288	(1.3)	285	(1.2)
Sex																						
Male	279	(1.2)	280	(1.0)	282	(1.3)	284	(0.8)	286	(1.5)	284	(1.6)	284	(1.6)	282	(2.2)	281	(1.3)	281	(1.6)	278	(1.5)
Female	291	(1.3)	291	(1.0)	289	(1.2)	294	(0.9)	294	(1.5)	296	(1.2)	296	(1.1)	295	(1.5)	295	(1.2)	295	(1.4)	292	(1.3)
Race/ethnicity																						
White, non-Hispanic	291	(1.0)	293	(0.6)	293	(0.9)	295	(0.9)	295	(1.2)	297	(1.2)	297	(1.4)	296	(1.5)	295	(1.2)	295	(1.4)	293	(1.1)
Black, non-Hispanic	239	(1.7)	241	(2.0)	243	(1.8)	264	(1.2)	274	(2.4)	267	(2.3)	261	(2.1)	266	(3.9)	266	(2.7)	264	(1.7)	264	(2.7)
Hispanic	‡	(†)	252	(3.6)	261	(2.7)	268	(2.9)	271	(4.3)	275	(3.6)	271	(3.7)	263	(4.9)	265	(4.1)	271	(3.9)	264	(2.9)
Parents' highest level of education																						
Not high school graduate	—	(†)	—	(†)	262	(1.5)	269	(1.4)	267	(2.0)	270	(2.8)	271	(3.9)	268	(2.7)	267	(3.2)	265	(3.6)	259	(3.4)
Graduated high school	—	(†)	—	(†)	277	(1.0)	281	(0.8)	282	(1.3)	283	(1.4)	280	(1.6)	276	(1.9)	273	(1.7)	274	(2.1)	274	(1.6)
Some education after high school	—	(†)	—	(†)	295	(1.2)	298	(0.9)	299	(2.2)	295	(1.9)	293	(1.9)	294	(1.6)	295	(2.2)	295	(1.8)	286	(1.9)
Graduated college	—	(†)	—	(†)	301	(1.0)	302	(0.9)	300	(1.4)	302	(1.5)	301	(1.7)	300	(1.7)	299	(1.5)	298	(1.3)	298	(1.3)
Region																						
Northeast	291	(2.8)	289	(1.7)	286	(2.4)	291	(2.5)	295	(2.9)	296	(1.8)	297	(3.2)	297	(4.2)	292	(2.8)	295	(4.0)	290	(2.5)
Southeast	271	(2.4)	277	(1.4)	280	(2.2)	284	(2.1)	286	(2.1)	285	(2.5)	278	(2.9)	283	(2.8)	279	(2.6)	279	(2.4)	281	(2.1)
Central	291	(2.1)	292	(1.4)	287	(2.2)	290	(1.8)	291	(1.9)	294	(2.4)	294	(2.1)	286	(3.7)	293	(2.1)	292	(1.5)	291	(2.2)
West	284	(1.8)	282	(1.9)	287	(2.1)	289	(1.6)	289	(1.8)	287	(2.6)	290	(2.3)	288	(2.8)	287	(2.4)	286	(3.0)	280	(2.5)

—Not available.
†Not applicable.
‡Test scores of Hispanics were not tabulated separately.
NOTE: The NAEP scores have been evaluated at certain performance levels. Scale ranges from 0 to 500. Students at reading score level 150 are able to follow brief written directions and carry out simple, discrete reading tasks. Students at reading score level 200 are able to understand, combine ideas, and make inferences based on short uncomplicated passages about specific or sequentially related information. Students at reading score level 250 are able to search for specific information, interrelate ideas, and make generalizations about literature, science, and social studies materials. Students at reading score level 300 are able to find, understand, summarize, and explain relatively complicated literary and informational material. Includes public and private schools. Excludes persons not enrolled in school and those who were unable to be tested due to limited proficiency in English or due to a disability. Some data have been revised from previously published figures. Standard errors appear in parentheses.
SOURCE: U.S. Department of Education, National Center for Education Statistics, National Assessment of Educational Progress (NAEP), NAEP 2004 Trends in Academic Progress; and unpublished tabulations, NAEP Data Explorer (http://nces.ed.gov/nationsreportcard/nde/), retrieved January 2006. (This table was prepared February 2006.)

Average scale score in reading and percentage of 4th-graders in public schools attaining reading achievement levels, by race/ethnicity and state or jurisdiction: Selected years, 1994 through 2005

State or jurisdiction	1994 average	1998 average	2002 average	2003 average	2005 Average	2005 Race/ethnicity[1] White, non-Hispanic	Black, non-Hispanic	Hispanic	Asian/ Pacific Islander	American Indian/ Alaska Native	Percent attaining reading achievement levels,[2] 2005 Below basic	Basic or above[3]	Proficient or above[4]	Advanced[5]
1	2	3	4	5	6	7	8	9	10	11	12	13	14	15
United States[6]	212 (1.1)	213 (1.2)	217 (0.5)	216 (0.3)	217 (0.2)	228 (0.2)	199 (0.3)	201 (0.5)	227 (0.9)	205 (1.3)	38 (0.3)	63 (0.3)	30 (0.2)	7 (0.1)
Alabama	208 (1.5)	211 (1.9)	207 (1.4)	207 (1.7)	208 (1.2)	220 (1.3)	188 (1.8)	‡ (†)	‡ (†)	‡ (†)	47 (1.3)	53 (1.3)	22 (1.3)	5 (0.6)
Alaska	— (†)	— (†)	— (†)	212 (1.6)	211 (1.4)	225 (1.3)	212 (3.9)	209 (3.6)	206 (4.0)	183 (3.0)	42 (1.5)	58 (1.5)	27 (1.3)	5 (0.5)
Arizona	206 (1.9)	206 (1.4)	205 (1.5)	209 (1.2)	207 (1.6)	224 (1.9)	193 (3.4)	192 (1.7)	224 (5.3)	‡ (†)	48 (1.7)	52 (1.7)	24 (1.7)	6 (0.6)
Arkansas	209 (1.7)	209 (1.6)	213 (1.4)	214 (1.4)	217 (1.1)	225 (1.0)	194 (1.9)	212 (4.2)	‡ (†)	‡ (†)	37 (1.4)	63 (1.4)	30 (1.1)	6 (0.6)
California[7,8]	197 (1.8)	202 (2.5)	206 (2.5)	206 (1.2)	207 (0.7)	225 (1.2)	195 (1.4)	193 (0.8)	223 (1.8)	213 (3.9)	50 (0.9)	50 (0.9)	21 (0.7)	5 (0.4)
Colorado	213 (1.3)	220 (1.4)	— (†)	224 (1.2)	224 (1.1)	232 (1.2)	207 (3.0)	206 (1.6)	231 (3.9)	‡ (†)	31 (1.3)	70 (1.3)	37 (1.6)	8 (0.9)
Connecticut	222 (1.6)	230 (1.6)	229 (1.1)	228 (1.1)	226 (1.0)	234 (1.1)	201 (1.9)	203 (2.2)	236 (4.2)	‡ (†)	29 (1.2)	71 (1.2)	38 (1.2)	12 (1.0)
Delaware	206 (1.1)	207 (1.7)	224 (0.6)	224 (0.7)	226 (0.8)	235 (0.9)	212 (1.1)	216 (2.2)	239 (4.5)	‡ (†)	27 (1.4)	73 (1.4)	34 (1.2)	7 (0.8)
District of Columbia	— (†)	179 (1.2)	191 (0.9)	188 (0.9)	191 (1.0)	252 (3.9)	187 (1.0)	193 (3.4)	‡ (†)	‡ (†)	67 (1.0)	33 (1.0)	11 (0.8)	2 (0.4)
Florida	205 (1.7)	206 (1.4)	214 (1.4)	218 (1.1)	220 (0.9)	228 (1.4)	203 (1.6)	215 (1.6)	230 (4.0)	‡ (†)	35 (1.0)	65 (1.0)	30 (1.2)	7 (0.7)
Georgia	207 (2.4)	209 (1.4)	215 (1.0)	214 (1.3)	214 (1.2)	226 (1.2)	199 (1.5)	203 (4.2)	243 (5.1)	‡ (†)	42 (1.5)	58 (1.5)	26 (1.5)	6 (0.7)
Hawaii	201 (1.7)	200 (1.5)	208 (0.9)	208 (1.4)	210 (1.0)	224 (1.7)	206 (4.8)	211 (4.8)	206 (1.1)	‡ (†)	47 (1.2)	53 (1.2)	23 (1.4)	5 (0.6)
Idaho	— (†)	— (†)	220 (1.1)	218 (1.0)	218 (0.9)	226 (0.8)	‡ (†)	199 (2.8)	‡ (†)	‡ (†)	31 (1.1)	69 (1.1)	33 (1.4)	7 (0.6)
Illinois	— (†)	— (†)	— (†)	216 (1.6)	217 (1.2)	230 (1.1)	194 (2.1)	199 (2.5)	230 (4.8)	‡ (†)	38 (1.3)	62 (1.3)	29 (1.3)	7 (0.7)
Indiana	220 (1.3)	— (†)	222 (1.4)	220 (1.0)	218 (1.1)	223 (1.2)	197 (2.4)	208 (2.9)	‡ (†)	‡ (†)	36 (1.3)	64 (1.3)	30 (1.4)	7 (0.7)
Iowa[7,8]	223 (1.3)	220 (1.6)	223 (1.1)	223 (1.1)	221 (0.9)	224 (0.9)	201 (3.6)	200 (2.9)	224 (5.9)	‡ (†)	33 (1.3)	68 (1.3)	33 (1.2)	7 (0.5)
Kansas[7,8]	— (†)	221 (1.4)	222 (1.4)	220 (1.2)	221 (1.3)	225 (1.3)	196 (2.5)	203 (2.8)	238 (4.9)	‡ (†)	34 (1.5)	66 (1.5)	33 (1.3)	8 (1.0)
Kentucky	212 (1.6)	218 (1.5)	219 (1.1)	219 (1.3)	220 (1.1)	222 (1.1)	203 (2.3)	‡ (†)	‡ (†)	‡ (†)	35 (1.5)	65 (1.5)	31 (1.2)	8 (0.8)
Louisiana	197 (1.3)	200 (1.8)	207 (1.7)	205 (1.4)	209 (1.3)	223 (1.1)	195 (1.7)	204 (3.6)	216 (4.6)	‡ (†)	47 (1.8)	53 (1.8)	20 (1.4)	4 (0.6)
Maine	228 (1.3)	225 (1.3)	225 (1.1)	224 (1.0)	225 (0.9)	225 (1.0)	197 (2.4)	208 (2.9)	‡ (†)	‡ (†)	29 (1.2)	71 (1.2)	35 (1.3)	9 (0.8)
Maryland	210 (1.5)	212 (1.6)	217 (1.5)	219 (1.4)	220 (1.1)	233 (1.5)	201 (1.5)	210 (2.7)	239 (3.6)	‡ (†)	35 (1.4)	65 (1.4)	32 (1.5)	8 (0.7)
Massachusetts[7]	223 (1.3)	223 (1.4)	234 (1.1)	228 (1.2)	231 (0.9)	237 (0.9)	211 (1.9)	203 (2.4)	234 (4.1)	‡ (†)	22 (1.2)	78 (1.2)	44 (1.4)	12 (0.9)
Michigan	220 (1.5)	216 (1.5)	219 (1.1)	219 (1.3)	218 (1.5)	226 (1.4)	190 (2.7)	202 (2.5)	‡ (†)	‡ (†)	37 (1.7)	63 (1.7)	32 (1.4)	7 (0.9)
Minnesota[7,8]	218 (1.4)	219 (1.7)	225 (1.7)	223 (1.1)	225 (1.3)	231 (1.3)	192 (3.8)	204 (3.6)	216 (4.6)	210 (2.0)	29 (1.6)	71 (1.6)	38 (1.7)	11 (0.9)
Mississippi	202 (1.6)	203 (1.3)	203 (1.3)	205 (1.3)	204 (1.4)	220 (1.0)	190 (1.6)	‡ (†)	‡ (†)	‡ (†)	52 (1.7)	48 (1.7)	18 (1.4)	3 (0.5)
Missouri	217 (1.5)	216 (1.3)	220 (1.3)	222 (1.2)	221 (0.9)	226 (0.9)	200 (2.6)	210 (4.8)	‡ (†)	‡ (†)	33 (1.2)	67 (1.2)	33 (1.3)	7 (0.8)
Montana[7,8]	222 (1.4)	225 (1.5)	224 (1.8)	223 (1.5)	225 (1.1)	228 (1.1)	‡ (†)	226 (4.5)	‡ (†)	210 (2.0)	29 (1.2)	71 (1.2)	36 (1.4)	8 (0.9)
Nebraska[9]	220 (1.5)	— (†)	222 (1.5)	221 (1.0)	221 (1.2)	228 (1.2)	194 (2.5)	202 (2.5)	‡ (†)	‡ (†)	32 (1.4)	68 (1.4)	34 (1.4)	7 (0.8)
Nevada	— (—)	206 (1.8)	209 (1.2)	207 (1.2)	207 (1.2)	219 (1.5)	192 (2.6)	195 (1.7)	212 (3.4)	‡ (†)	48 (1.5)	52 (1.5)	21 (1.3)	4 (0.6)
New Hampshire[7]	223 (1.5)	226 (1.7)	— (†)	228 (0.9)	227 (0.9)	228 (0.9)	‡ (†)	‡ (†)	‡ (†)	‡ (†)	26 (1.1)	74 (1.1)	39 (1.4)	9 (0.8)
New Jersey	219 (1.2)	— (†)	— (†)	225 (1.2)	223 (1.3)	233 (1.1)	199 (2.4)	206 (2.3)	241 (2.6)	‡ (†)	32 (1.6)	68 (1.6)	37 (1.5)	10 (0.8)
New Mexico	205 (1.7)	205 (1.4)	208 (1.6)	203 (1.5)	207 (1.3)	225 (1.5)	206 (5.3)	199 (1.6)	‡ (†)	190 (2.6)	49 (1.5)	51 (1.5)	21 (1.4)	4 (0.5)
New York[7,8]	212 (1.4)	215 (1.6)	222 (1.5)	222 (1.1)	223 (1.1)	232 (0.9)	207 (1.8)	208 (1.9)	237 (2.9)	‡ (†)	31 (1.5)	69 (1.5)	33 (1.2)	8 (0.6)
North Carolina	214 (1.5)	213 (1.6)	222 (1.0)	221 (1.0)	217 (1.0)	227 (1.2)	201 (1.5)	204 (2.4)	221 (6.2)	‡ (†)	39 (1.5)	62 (1.5)	29 (1.4)	7 (0.6)
North Dakota[8]	225 (1.2)	— (†)	224 (1.0)	222 (0.9)	225 (0.7)	228 (0.7)	‡ (†)	‡ (†)	‡ (†)	199 (2.9)	28 (1.1)	72 (1.1)	36 (1.1)	7 (0.6)

See notes at end of table.

Average scale score in reading and percentage of 4th-graders in public schools attaining reading achievement levels, by race/ethnicity and state or jurisdiction: Selected years, 1994 through 2005—Continued

State or jurisdiction	1994 average	1998 average	2002 average	2003 average	2005 Average	White, non-Hispanic	Black, non-Hispanic	Hispanic	Asian/ Pacific Islander	American Indian/ Alaska Native	Below basic[3]	Basic or above[3]	Proficient or above[4]	Advanced[5]
1	2	3	4	5	6	7	8	9	10	11	12	13	14	15
Ohio	— (†)	— (†)	222 (1.3)	222 (1.2)	223 (1.4)	230 (1.3)	197 (1.9)	211 (5.6)	‡ (†)	‡ (†)	31 (1.6)	69 (1.6)	34 (1.6)	8 (0.9)
Oklahoma	— (†)	219 (1.2)	213 (1.2)	214 (1.2)	214 (1.1)	219 (1.3)	197 (2.9)	204 (3.2)	‡ (†)	211 (1.8)	40 (1.6)	60 (1.6)	25 (1.5)	5 (0.7)
Oregon	— (†)	212 (1.8)	220 (1.4)	218 (1.3)	217 (1.4)	223 (1.2)	200 (4.8)	194 (2.2)	221 (4.2)	‡ (†)	38 (1.7)	62 (1.7)	29 (1.5)	7 (0.7)
Pennsylvania[9]	215 (1.6)	— (†)	221 (1.2)	219 (1.3)	223 (1.3)	229 (1.3)	200 (2.5)	203 (4.3)	234 (5.4)	‡ (†)	31 (1.6)	69 (1.6)	36 (1.5)	9 (0.8)
Rhode Island[9]	220 (1.3)	218 (1.4)	220 (1.2)	216 (1.3)	216 (1.2)	224 (1.1)	197 (3.2)	192 (2.5)	219 (6.1)	‡ (†)	38 (1.5)	62 (1.5)	30 (1.3)	7 (0.8)
South Carolina	203 (1.4)	209 (1.4)	214 (1.3)	215 (1.3)	213 (1.3)	225 (1.7)	197 (1.4)	215 (4.4)	‡ (†)	‡ (†)	43 (1.7)	57 (1.7)	26 (1.3)	6 (0.7)
South Dakota	— (†)	— (†)	— (†)	222 (1.2)	222 (0.5)	222 (0.6)	‡ (†)	‡ (†)	‡ (†)	201 (2.3)	30 (1.1)	70 (1.1)	33 (1.3)	6 (0.7)
Tennessee[8,9]	213 (1.7)	212 (1.4)	214 (1.2)	212 (1.6)	214 (1.4)	222 (1.5)	195 (2.5)	199 (4.9)	‡ (†)	‡ (†)	41 (1.7)	59 (1.7)	27 (1.8)	6 (0.8)
Texas	212 (1.9)	214 (1.9)	217 (1.7)	215 (1.0)	219 (0.8)	232 (1.0)	206 (1.7)	210 (1.2)	234 (3.6)	‡ (†)	36 (1.1)	64 (1.1)	29 (0.9)	6 (0.5)
Utah	217 (1.3)	216 (1.2)	222 (1.0)	219 (1.0)	221 (1.1)	226 (1.0)	‡ (†)	199 (2.4)	218 (4.2)	‡ (†)	32 (1.3)	68 (1.3)	34 (1.3)	8 (0.8)
Vermont	— (†)	— (†)	227 (1.1)	226 (0.9)	227 (0.9)	227 (0.9)	‡ (†)	‡ (†)	‡ (†)	‡ (†)	28 (1.3)	72 (1.3)	39 (1.2)	10 (1.0)
Virginia	213 (1.5)	217 (1.2)	225 (1.3)	223 (1.5)	226 (0.8)	233 (1.0)	207 (1.2)	218 (2.2)	239 (2.7)	‡ (†)	28 (1.5)	72 (1.5)	37 (1.4)	8 (0.8)
Washington[8]	213 (1.5)	218 (1.4)	224 (1.2)	221 (1.1)	224 (1.1)	228 (1.1)	212 (2.8)	202 (2.5)	230 (2.6)	‡ (†)	30 (1.4)	70 (1.4)	36 (1.4)	8 (0.9)
West Virginia	213 (1.1)	216 (1.7)	219 (1.2)	219 (1.0)	215 (0.8)	215 (0.8)	202 (3.2)	‡ (†)	‡ (†)	‡ (†)	40 (1.1)	61 (1.1)	26 (1.0)	5 (0.7)
Wisconsin[7,8,9]	224 (1.1)	222 (1.1)	— (†)	221 (1.0)	221 (1.0)	227 (1.0)	194 (2.5)	208 (3.5)	226 (4.5)	‡ (†)	33 (1.3)	67 (1.3)	33 (1.4)	7 (0.7)
Wyoming	221 (1.2)	218 (1.5)	221 (1.0)	222 (0.8)	223 (0.7)	227 (0.8)	199 (†)	204 (3.3)	‡ (†)	‡ (†)	29 (1.2)	71 (1.2)	35 (1.4)	7 (0.6)
Department of Defense dependents schools[10]	— (†)	— (†)	— (†)	— (†)	226 (0.6)	232 (0.9)	218 (2.0)	219 (1.7)	223 (3.0)	‡ (†)	25 (1.0)	75 (1.0)	36 (1.4)	7 (0.8)
Domestic schools	— (†)	219 (1.6)	225 (0.7)	223 (1.2)	— (†)	— (†)	— (†)	— (†)	— (†)	— (†)	— (†)	— (†)	— (†)	— (†)
Overseas schools	218 (0.9)	221 (1.0)	224 (0.5)	225 (0.6)	— (†)	— (†)	— (†)	— (†)	— (†)	— (†)	— (†)	— (†)	— (†)	— (†)
Other jurisdictions														
Guam	181 (1.2)	— (†)	185 (1.3)	—	— (†)	— (†)	— (†)	— (†)	— (†)	— (†)	— (†)	— (†)	— (†)	— (†)
Virgin Islands	— (†)	174 (2.2)	179 (1.9)	—	— (†)	— (†)	— (†)	— (†)	— (†)	— (†)	— (†)	— (†)	— (†)	— (†)

—Not available.
†Not applicable.
‡Reporting standards not met.
[1]Based on school records.
[2]Achievement levels are in trial status.
[3]The basic level denotes partial mastery of the knowledge and skills that are fundamental for proficient work at the 4th-grade level.
[4]This level represents solid academic performance for 4th-graders. Students reaching this level have demonstrated competency over challenging subject matter.
[5]This level signifies superior performance.
[6]Based on nationally representative sample. Forty-one states and Guam participated in the test in 1994; 44 jurisdictions (state, territory, and Department of Defense schools) participated in 1998; 50 participated in 2002; and 53 participated in 2003 and 2005.

[7]Did not satisfy one or more of the guidelines for school sample participation rates in 1998. Data are subject to appreciable nonresponse bias.
[8]Did not satisfy one or more of the guidelines for school sample participation rates in 2002. Data are subject to appreciable nonresponse bias.
[9]Did not satisfy one or more of the guidelines for school sample participation rates in 1994. Data are subject to appreciable nonresponse bias.
[10]The definition of the national sample changed in 2005; it now includes all of the Department of Defense schools.
NOTE: The reading data include students for whom accommodations were permitted. Scale ranges from 0 to 500. Standard errors appear in parentheses.
SOURCE: U.S. Department of Education, National Center for Education Statistics, National Assessment of Educational Progress (NAEP), *Reading Report Card for the Nation and the States*, 1994, 1998, 2002, 2003, and 2005; and unpublished tabulations, NAEP Data Explorer (http://nces.ed.gov/nationsreportcard/nde/), retrieved October 2005. (This table was prepared October 2005.)

Average scale score in reading and percentage of 8th-graders in public schools attaining reading achievement levels, by locale and state or jurisdiction: Selected years, 1998 through 2005

State or jurisdiction	1998 average		2002 average		2003 average		Percent attaining reading achievement levels, 2005[1] Below basic		Basic or above[2]		Proficient or above[3]		Advanced[4]		2005 Average		Locale Central city		Urban fringe/large town		Rural/small town	
1	2		3		4		5		6		7		8		9		10		11		12	
United States[5]	261	(0.8)	263	(0.5)	261	(0.2)	29	(0.2)	71	(0.2)	29	(0.2)	3	(0.1)	260	(0.2)	254	(0.4)	264	(0.3)	262	(0.4)
Alabama	255	(1.4)	253	(1.3)	253	(1.5)	37	(1.4)	63	(1.4)	22	(1.4)	2	(0.6)	252	(1.4)	246	(2.8)	260	(3.1)	250	(1.6)
Alaska	—	(†)	—	(†)	256	(1.1)	30	(1.3)	70	(1.3)	26	(1.4)	2	(0.3)	259	(0.9)	‡	(†)	‡	(†)	‡	(†)
Arizona	260	(1.1)	257	(1.3)	255	(1.4)	35	(1.3)	65	(1.3)	23	(1.1)	2	(0.3)	255	(1.0)	253	(1.5)	258	(2.2)	253	(4.5)
Arkansas	256	(1.3)	260	(1.1)	258	(1.3)	31	(1.4)	69	(1.4)	26	(1.3)	2	(0.4)	258	(1.1)	257	(2.8)	261	(2.0)	257	(1.3)
California[6,7,8]	252	(1.6)	250	(1.8)	251	(1.3)	40	(0.7)	60	(0.7)	21	(0.6)	2	(0.2)	250	(0.6)	249	(0.9)	251	(0.9)	257	(3.6)
Colorado	264	(1.0)	—	(†)	268	(1.2)	25	(1.3)	75	(1.3)	32	(1.4)	4	(0.5)	265	(1.1)	260	(2.1)	268	(1.5)	266	(2.0)
Connecticut	270	(1.0)	267	(1.2)	267	(1.1)	26	(1.2)	75	(1.2)	34	(1.6)	4	(0.8)	264	(1.3)	245	(3.0)	270	(1.5)	269	(1.8)
Delaware	254	(1.3)	267	(0.5)	265	(0.7)	20	(1.1)	80	(1.1)	30	(0.9)	2	(0.4)	266	(0.6)	266	(2.4)	265	(0.7)	269	(1.4)
District of Columbia	236	(2.1)	240	(0.9)	239	(0.8)	55	(1.2)	45	(1.2)	12	(0.9)	1	(0.3)	238	(0.9)	238	(0.9)	‡	(†)	‡	(†)
Florida	255	(1.4)	261	(1.6)	257	(1.3)	34	(1.4)	66	(1.4)	25	(1.1)	2	(0.3)	256	(1.2)	252	(2.4)	257	(1.5)	257	(2.6)
Georgia	257	(1.4)	258	(1.0)	258	(1.1)	33	(1.5)	67	(1.5)	25	(1.6)	3	(0.5)	257	(1.3)	245	(2.8)	261	(2.1)	257	(2.1)
Hawaii	249	(1.0)	252	(0.9)	251	(0.9)	42	(1.0)	58	(1.0)	18	(1.0)	1	(0.2)	249	(0.9)	255	(1.6)	249	(1.4)	243	(1.5)
Idaho	—	(†)	266	(1.1)	264	(0.9)	24	(1.4)	76	(1.4)	32	(1.2)	2	(0.6)	264	(1.1)	266	(1.3)	264	(1.4)	263	(2.0)
Illinois	—	(†)	—	(†)	266	(1.0)	25	(1.2)	75	(1.2)	31	(1.3)	3	(0.6)	264	(1.0)	256	(1.9)	268	(1.5)	266	(2.1)
Indiana	—	(†)	265	(1.3)	265	(1.0)	27	(1.3)	73	(1.3)	28	(1.5)	2	(0.4)	261	(1.1)	254	(2.1)	265	(2.0)	263	(1.6)
Iowa	—	(†)	—	(†)	268	(0.8)	21	(1.0)	79	(1.0)	34	(1.5)	3	(0.4)	267	(0.9)	262	(1.5)	272	(2.3)	268	(1.4)
Kansas[6,7,8]	268	(1.4)	269	(1.3)	266	(1.5)	22	(1.3)	78	(1.3)	35	(1.4)	3	(0.4)	267	(1.0)	262	(2.6)	270	(1.7)	267	(1.1)
Kentucky	262	(1.4)	265	(1.0)	266	(1.3)	25	(1.5)	75	(1.5)	31	(1.4)	3	(0.5)	264	(1.1)	271	(2.3)	262	(2.1)	263	(1.6)
Louisiana	252	(1.4)	256	(1.5)	253	(1.6)	36	(2.2)	64	(2.2)	20	(1.5)	1	(0.4)	253	(1.6)	247	(2.8)	255	(2.8)	255	(1.9)
Maine	271	(1.2)	270	(0.9)	268	(1.0)	19	(1.0)	81	(1.0)	38	(1.4)	4	(0.6)	270	(1.0)	269	(2.6)	277	(2.1)	269	(1.1)
Maryland[6,7]	261	(1.8)	263	(1.7)	262	(1.4)	31	(1.7)	69	(1.7)	30	(1.4)	4	(0.5)	261	(1.2)	251	(3.6)	262	(1.5)	266	(2.7)
Massachusetts	269	(1.4)	271	(1.3)	273	(1.0)	17	(1.0)	83	(1.0)	44	(1.6)	5	(0.7)	274	(1.0)	258	(1.4)	280	(1.3)	282	(3.1)
Michigan	—	(†)	265	(1.6)	264	(1.8)	27	(1.4)	73	(1.4)	29	(1.6)	2	(0.5)	261	(1.2)	251	(2.9)	265	(1.4)	266	(2.2)
Minnesota[6,7]	265	(1.4)	—	(†)	268	(1.1)	20	(1.2)	80	(1.2)	37	(1.6)	3	(0.5)	268	(1.2)	264	(3.2)	272	(1.6)	267	(1.6)
Mississippi	251	(1.2)	255	(0.9)	255	(1.4)	40	(1.7)	60	(1.7)	19	(1.4)	1	(0.3)	251	(1.3)	246	(2.9)	254	(2.2)	250	(1.8)
Missouri	262	(1.3)	268	(1.0)	267	(1.0)	24	(1.3)	76	(1.3)	31	(1.4)	3	(0.4)	265	(1.0)	258	(3.0)	267	(1.3)	266	(1.6)
Montana[6,7]	271	(1.3)	270	(1.0)	270	(1.0)	19	(1.0)	82	(1.0)	37	(1.2)	3	(0.6)	269	(0.7)	270	(1.6)	271	(1.8)	268	(0.9)
Nebraska	—	(†)	270	(0.9)	266	(0.9)	20	(1.0)	80	(1.0)	35	(1.5)	3	(0.5)	268	(0.9)	266	(1.6)	268	(1.6)	268	(1.4)
Nevada	258	(1.0)	251	(0.8)	252	(0.8)	37	(1.3)	63	(1.3)	22	(0.9)	1	(0.5)	253	(1.0)	253	(1.4)	251	(1.4)	256	(1.5)
New Hampshire	—	(†)	—	(†)	271	(0.9)	20	(1.1)	80	(1.1)	38	(1.6)	4	(0.5)	270	(1.2)	264	(2.1)	270	(2.0)	272	(1.9)
New Jersey	—	(†)	—	(†)	268	(1.2)	20	(1.5)	80	(1.5)	38	(1.7)	4	(0.6)	269	(1.2)	‡	(†)	270	(1.2)	278	(3.0)
New Mexico	258	(1.2)	254	(1.0)	252	(0.9)	38	(1.5)	62	(1.5)	19	(1.1)	1	(0.2)	251	(1.0)	256	(1.9)	249	(1.9)	248	(1.7)
New York[6,7]	265	(1.5)	264	(1.5)	265	(1.3)	25	(0.9)	75	(0.9)	34	(1.3)	3	(0.5)	265	(1.0)	252	(1.5)	275	(1.4)	272	(1.4)
North Carolina	262	(1.1)	265	(1.1)	262	(1.0)	31	(1.3)	69	(1.3)	27	(1.2)	2	(0.4)	258	(0.9)	257	(1.6)	261	(1.9)	258	(1.5)
North Dakota[7]	—	(†)	268	(0.8)	270	(0.8)	17	(1.1)	83	(1.1)	37	(1.3)	3	(0.6)	270	(0.6)	271	(1.5)	270	(1.8)	270	(0.8)
Ohio	—	(†)	268	(1.6)	267	(1.3)	23	(1.4)	78	(1.4)	36	(1.4)	4	(0.7)	267	(1.3)	248	(3.1)	272	(1.6)	272	(2.2)
Oklahoma	265	(1.2)	262	(0.8)	262	(0.9)	28	(1.6)	72	(1.6)	25	(1.4)	1	(0.4)	260	(1.1)	252	(4.0)	264	(1.3)	259	(1.4)
Oregon[3]	266	(1.5)	268	(1.3)	264	(1.2)	26	(1.3)	74	(1.3)	33	(1.5)	3	(0.5)	263	(1.1)	264	(2.2)	264	(1.7)	261	(1.9)
Pennsylvania	—	(†)	265	(1.0)	264	(1.2)	23	(1.6)	77	(1.6)	36	(1.6)	3	(0.6)	267	(1.3)	247	(3.9)	273	(1.9)	268	(1.4)
Rhode Island	264	(0.9)	262	(0.8)	261	(0.7)	29	(1.1)	71	(1.1)	29	(1.0)	2	(0.4)	261	(0.7)	245	(1.4)	267	(1.0)	275	(1.8)
South Carolina	255	(1.1)	258	(1.1)	258	(1.3)	33	(1.3)	67	(1.3)	25	(1.2)	2	(0.4)	257	(1.1)	259	(2.5)	262	(1.6)	253	(1.5)
South Dakota	—	(†)	—	(†)	270	(0.8)	18	(0.8)	82	(0.8)	35	(1.1)	2	(0.3)	269	(0.6)	267	(1.1)	271	(2.4)	269	(0.7)
Tennessee[7]	258	(1.2)	260	(1.4)	258	(1.2)	29	(1.2)	71	(1.2)	26	(1.4)	1	(0.5)	259	(0.9)	252	(1.7)	264	(2.3)	260	(1.6)
Texas	261	(1.4)	262	(1.4)	259	(1.1)	31	(0.8)	69	(0.8)	26	(0.8)	2	(0.3)	258	(0.6)	256	(1.1)	261	(1.1)	259	(1.6)
Utah	263	(1.0)	263	(1.1)	264	(0.8)	27	(0.9)	73	(0.9)	29	(1.2)	2	(0.4)	262	(0.8)	261	(1.4)	262	(1.0)	264	(3.0)
Vermont	—	(†)	272	(0.9)	271	(0.8)	21	(1.0)	79	(1.0)	37	(1.2)	4	(0.4)	269	(0.8)	‡	(†)	‡	(†)	‡	(†)
Virginia	266	(1.1)	269	(1.0)	268	(1.1)	22	(1.2)	78	(1.2)	36	(1.4)	3	(0.5)	268	(1.0)	260	(1.7)	273	(1.6)	266	(2.1)
Washington[7]	264	(1.2)	268	(1.2)	264	(0.9)	25	(1.3)	75	(1.3)	34	(1.5)	3	(0.4)	265	(1.3)	264	(2.4)	265	(1.5)	265	(2.3)
West Virginia	262	(1.0)	264	(1.0)	260	(1.0)	33	(1.5)	67	(1.5)	22	(1.3)	1	(0.3)	255	(1.2)	261	(2.0)	259	(2.7)	252	(1.3)
Wisconsin[6,7]	265	(1.8)	—	(†)	266	(1.3)	23	(1.3)	77	(1.3)	35	(1.4)	3	(0.5)	266	(1.1)	255	(2.6)	276	(1.6)	266	(1.6)
Wyoming	263	(1.3)	265	(0.7)	267	(0.5)	19	(1.0)	81	(1.0)	36	(1.4)	2	(0.4)	268	(0.7)	267	(1.6)	270	(3.7)	269	(0.8)

See notes at end of table.

Average scale score in reading and percentage of 8th-graders in public schools attaining reading achievement levels, by locale and state or jurisdiction: Selected years, 1998 through 2005—Continued

State or jurisdiction	1998 average		2002 average		2003 average		Percent attaining reading achievement levels, 2005[1]						2005						
							Below basic		Basic or above[2]		Proficient or above[3]		Advanced[4]		Average		Locale					
																	Central city		Urban fringe/ large town		Rural/ small town	
1	2		3		4		5		6		7		8		9		10		11		12	
Department of Defense dependents schools[9]							16	(1.2)	84	(1.2)	37	(1.4)	2	(0.5)	271	(0.7)	‡	(†)	‡	(†)	‡	(†)
Domestic schools.........	268	(4.5)	272	(1.0)	269	(1.4)	—	(†)	—	(†)	—	(†)	—	(†)	—	(†)	‡	(†)	‡	(†)	‡	(†)
Overseas schools	269	1.0	273	(0.6)	273	(0.7)	—	(†)	—	(†)	—	(†)	—	(†)	—	(†)	‡	(†)	‡	(†)	‡	(†)
Other jurisdictions																						
American Samoa	—	(†)	198	(1.7)	—	(†)	—	(†)	—	(†)	—	(†)	—	(†)	—	(†)	—	(†)	—	(†)	—	(†)
Guam	—	(†)	240	(1.2)	—	(†)	—	(†)	—	(†)	—	(†)	—	(†)	—	(†)	—	(†)	—	(†)	—	(†)
Virgin Islands	231	(2.1)	241	(1.3)	—	(†)	—	(†)	—	(†)	—	(†)	—	(†)	—	(†)	—	(†)	—	(†)	—	(†)

—Not available.
†Not applicable.
‡Reporting standards not met.
[1]Achievement levels are in trial status.
[2]The basic level denotes partial mastery of the knowledge and skills that are fundamental for proficient work at the 8th-grade level.
[3]This level represents solid academic performance for 8th-graders. Students reaching this level have demonstrated competency over challenging subject matter.
[4]This level signifies superior performance.
[5]Based on nationally representative sample. Forty-four jurisdictions (state, District of Columbia, territory, and Department of Defense overseas schools) participated in 1998; 50 participated in 2002; and 53 participated in 2003 and 2005.
[6]Did not satisfy one or more of the guidelines for school sample participation rates in 1998. Data are subject to appreciable nonresponse bias.

[7]Did not satisfy one or more of the guidelines for school sample participation rates in 2002. Data are subject to appreciable nonresponse bias.
[8]Did not satisfy one or more of the guidelines for school sample participation rates in 2003. Data are subject to appreciable nonresponse bias.
[9]The definition of the national sample changed in 2005; it now includes all of the Department of Defense schools.
NOTE: The reading data include students for whom accommodations were permitted. Scale ranges from 0 to 500. Standard errors appear in parentheses.
SOURCE: U.S. Department of Education, National Center for Education Statistics, National Assessment of Educational Progress (NAEP), *Reading Report Card for the Nation and the States*, 2002, 2003, and 2005; unpublished tabulations, NAEP Data Explorer (http://nces.ed.gov/nationsreportcard/nde/), retrieved October 2005. (This table was prepared October 2005.)

Average reading scale scores and percentage of students within each achievement level, grade 4 public schools: By state, 2005

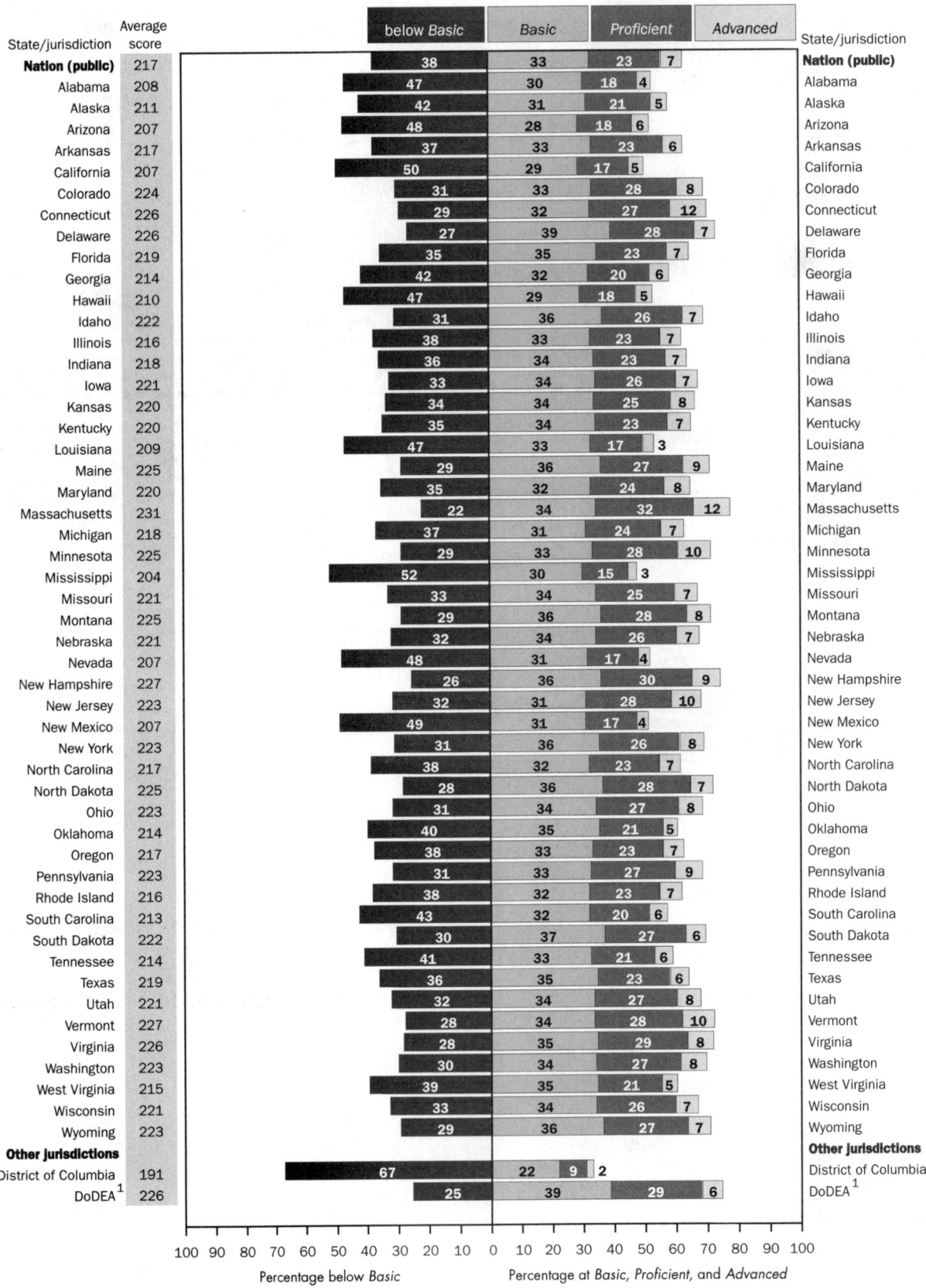

State/jurisdiction	Average score	below Basic	Basic	Proficient	Advanced	State/jurisdiction
Nation (public)	217	38	33	23	7	**Nation (public)**
Alabama	208	47	30	18	4	Alabama
Alaska	211	42	31	21	5	Alaska
Arizona	207	48	28	18	6	Arizona
Arkansas	217	37	33	23	6	Arkansas
California	207	50	29	17	5	California
Colorado	224	31	33	28	8	Colorado
Connecticut	226	29	32	27	12	Connecticut
Delaware	226	27	39	28	7	Delaware
Florida	219	35	35	23	7	Florida
Georgia	214	42	32	20	6	Georgia
Hawaii	210	47	29	18	5	Hawaii
Idaho	222	31	36	26	7	Idaho
Illinois	216	38	33	23	7	Illinois
Indiana	218	36	34	23	7	Indiana
Iowa	221	33	34	26	7	Iowa
Kansas	220	34	34	25	8	Kansas
Kentucky	220	35	34	23	7	Kentucky
Louisiana	209	47	33	17	3	Louisiana
Maine	225	29	36	27	9	Maine
Maryland	220	35	32	24	8	Maryland
Massachusetts	231	22	34	32	12	Massachusetts
Michigan	218	37	31	24	7	Michigan
Minnesota	225	29	33	28	10	Minnesota
Mississippi	204	52	30	15	3	Mississippi
Missouri	221	33	34	25	7	Missouri
Montana	225	29	36	28	8	Montana
Nebraska	221	32	34	26	7	Nebraska
Nevada	207	48	31	17	4	Nevada
New Hampshire	227	26	36	30	9	New Hampshire
New Jersey	223	32	31	28	10	New Jersey
New Mexico	207	49	31	17	4	New Mexico
New York	223	31	36	26	8	New York
North Carolina	217	38	32	23	7	North Carolina
North Dakota	225	28	36	28	7	North Dakota
Ohio	223	31	34	27	8	Ohio
Oklahoma	214	40	35	21	5	Oklahoma
Oregon	217	38	33	23	7	Oregon
Pennsylvania	223	31	33	27	9	Pennsylvania
Rhode Island	216	38	32	23	7	Rhode Island
South Carolina	213	43	32	20	6	South Carolina
South Dakota	222	30	37	27	6	South Dakota
Tennessee	214	41	33	21	6	Tennessee
Texas	219	36	35	23	6	Texas
Utah	221	32	34	27	8	Utah
Vermont	227	28	34	28	10	Vermont
Virginia	226	28	35	29	8	Virginia
Washington	223	30	34	27	8	Washington
West Virginia	215	39	35	21	5	West Virginia
Wisconsin	221	33	34	26	7	Wisconsin
Wyoming	223	29	36	27	7	Wyoming
Other jurisdictions						**Other jurisdictions**
District of Columbia	191	67	22	9	2	District of Columbia
DoDEA[1]	226	25	39	29	6	DoDEA[1]

100 90 80 70 60 50 40 30 20 10 0 10 20 30 40 50 60 70 80 90 100

Percentage below *Basic*   Percentage at *Basic, Proficient,* and *Advanced*

[1] Department of Defense Education Activity.

NOTE: The NAEP reading scale ranges from 0 to 500. Detail may not sum to totals because of rounding. The shaded bars are graphed using unrounded numbers.

SOURCE: U.S. Department of Education, Institute of Education Sciences, National Center for Education Statistics, National Assessment of Educational Progress (NAEP), 2005 Reading Assessment.

Average reading scale scores and achievement-level results, by race/ethnicity, grade 4 public schools: By state, 2005

State/jurisdiction	White					Black					Hispanic				
	Percentage of all students	Average scale score	Percentage of students			Percentage of all students	Average scale score	Percentage of students			Percentage of all students	Average scale score	Percentage of students		
			Below Basic	At or above Basic	At or above Proficient			Below Basic	At or above Basic	At or above Proficient			Below Basic	At or above Basic	At or above Proficient
Nation (public)	57	228	25	75	39	17	199	59	41	12	19	201	56	44	15
Alabama	58	220	33	67	32	38	188	69	31	8	2	‡	‡	‡	‡
Alaska	55	225	27	73	36	4	212	42	58	24	5	209	45	55	19
Arizona	46	224	30	70	37	5	193	67	33	12	40	192	63	37	11
Arkansas	69	225	27	73	37	24	194	66	34	10	5	212	45	55	21
California	31	225	29	71	37	8	195	62	38	11	49	193	66	34	10
Colorado	64	232	21	79	46	5	207	48	52	18	27	206	51	49	17
Connecticut	69	234	19	81	47	13	201	58	42	12	13	203	55	45	15
Delaware	56	235	15	85	46	32	212	46	54	15	9	216	36	64	22
Florida	49	228	25	75	39	23	203	55	45	13	23	215	39	61	25
Georgia	49	226	27	73	37	39	199	60	40	12	7	203	54	46	14
Hawaii	17	224	31	69	37	3	205	51	49	21	3	211	47	53	27
Idaho	83	226	26	74	37	1	‡	‡	‡	‡	13	199	58	42	11
Illinois	55	230	22	78	42	20	194	65	35	9	21	199	56	44	14
Indiana	76	223	30	70	35	15	197	59	41	12	4	208	48	52	11
Iowa	85	224	29	71	36	5	201	58	42	12	6	200	55	45	15
Kansas	74	225	28	72	37	8	196	60	40	10	11	203	54	46	14
Kentucky	85	222	33	67	33	11	203	55	45	15	2	‡	‡	‡	‡
Louisiana	49	223	30	70	32	48	195	65	35	9	2	‡	‡	‡	‡
Maine	97	225	29	71	35	1	‡	‡	‡	‡	1	‡	‡	‡	‡
Maryland	52	232	21	79	45	35	201	58	42	12	8	210	46	54	21
Massachusetts	76	237	15	85	51	9	211	43	57	20	10	203	55	45	11
Michigan	71	226	28	72	38	19	190	69	31	10	5	‡	‡	‡	‡
Minnesota	81	231	23	77	43	8	192	64	36	10	5	204	51	49	18
Mississippi	47	220	34	66	31	51	190	70	30	7	1	‡	‡	‡	‡
Missouri	76	226	27	73	38	18	200	57	43	14	4	210	46	54	21
Montana	85	228	25	75	39	1	‡	‡	‡	‡	2	226	25	75	36
Nebraska	77	228	25	75	40	8	194	65	35	10	12	202	55	45	12
Nevada	47	219	35	65	28	12	192	65	35	10	32	194	63	37	12
New Hampshire	94	228	25	75	39	1	‡	‡	‡	‡	2	‡	‡	‡	‡
New Jersey	58	232	21	79	46	17	199	58	42	15	16	206	51	49	19
New Mexico	31	225	28	72	36	3	206	50	50	24	54	199	57	43	14
New York	53	232	20	80	43	20	207	50	50	17	18	208	48	52	17
North Carolina	58	227	26	74	39	27	200	59	41	13	8	204	54	46	17
North Dakota	88	228	25	75	38	1	‡	‡	‡	‡	1	‡	‡	‡	‡
Ohio	74	230	23	77	41	20	197	62	38	10	2	211	43	57	24
Oklahoma	61	219	33	67	30	10	197	60	40	10	8	204	55	45	17
Oregon	71	223	31	69	34	4	200	55	45	15	16	194	64	36	10
Pennsylvania	75	229	24	76	42	17	200	57	43	15	6	203	56	44	19
Rhode Island	72	224	30	70	36	8	197	60	40	15	16	192	65	35	11
South Carolina	54	225	30	70	36	41	197	60	40	11	3	215	43	57	29
South Dakota	84	226	25	75	37	2	‡	‡	‡	‡	2	‡	‡	‡	‡
Tennessee	70	222	32	68	33	25	195	63	37	11	3	199	64	36	13
Texas	40	232	21	79	44	14	206	51	49	15	43	210	46	54	19
Utah	82	226	27	73	38	1	‡	‡	‡	‡	12	199	59	41	14
Vermont	96	227	28	72	38	1	‡	‡	‡	‡	1	‡	‡	‡	‡
Virginia	61	233	20	80	45	25	207	51	49	15	6	218	35	65	26
Washington	71	228	25	75	40	5	212	43	57	20	13	202	55	45	14
West Virginia	93	215	39	61	26	6	202	54	46	15	1	‡	‡	‡	‡
Wisconsin	77	227	26	74	38	13	194	66	34	10	6	208	51	49	20
Wyoming	84	227	25	75	38	1	‡	‡	‡	‡	11	204	52	48	16
Other jurisdictions															
District of Columbia	4	252	8	92	70	85	187	71	29	8	9	193	63	37	12
DoDEA[1]	48	232	18	82	44	19	218	35	65	24	14	219	34	66	26

See notes at end of table.

Average reading scale scores and achievement-level results, by race/ethnicity, grade 4 public schools: By state, 2005—Continued

State/jurisdiction	Asian/Pacific Islander					American Indian/Alaska Native				
	Percentage of all students	Average scale score	Percentage of students			Percentage of all students	Average scale score	Percentage of students		
			Below *Basic*	At or above *Basic*	At or above *Proficient*			Below *Basic*	At or above *Basic*	At or above *Proficient*
Nation (public)	4	227	28	72	40	1	205	51	49	19
Alabama	1	‡	‡	‡	‡	1	‡	‡	‡	‡
Alaska	7	206	50	50	19	26	183	71	29	9
Arizona	2	224	30	70	36	6	‡	‡	‡	‡
Arkansas	1	‡	‡	‡	‡	1	‡	‡	‡	‡
California	10	222	32	68	35	1	213	46	54	23
Colorado	3	231	20	80	42	1	‡	‡	‡	‡
Connecticut	4	236	20	80	49	1	‡	‡	‡	‡
Delaware	3	239	20	80	55	#	‡	‡	‡	‡
Florida	2	230	24	76	43	#	‡	‡	‡	‡
Georgia	3	243	16	84	57	#	‡	‡	‡	‡
Hawaii	65	205	52	48	19	#	‡	‡	‡	‡
Idaho	1	‡	‡	‡	‡	2	‡	‡	‡	‡
Illinois	3	230	25	75	44	#	‡	‡	‡	‡
Indiana	1	‡	‡	‡	‡	#	‡	‡	‡	‡
Iowa	2	224	32	68	40	1	‡	‡	‡	‡
Kansas	2	238	22	78	55	2	‡	‡	‡	‡
Kentucky	1	‡	‡	‡	‡	#	‡	‡	‡	‡
Louisiana	1	‡	‡	‡	‡	#	‡	‡	‡	‡
Maine	1	‡	‡	‡	‡	#	‡	‡	‡	‡
Maryland	5	239	17	83	55	#	‡	‡	‡	‡
Massachusetts	5	234	20	80	47	#	‡	‡	‡	‡
Michigan	3	‡	‡	‡	‡	#	‡	‡	‡	‡
Minnesota	5	216	38	62	28	2	‡	‡	‡	‡
Mississippi	1	‡	‡	‡	‡	#	‡	‡	‡	‡
Missouri	2	‡	‡	‡	‡	#	‡	‡	‡	‡
Montana	1	‡	‡	‡	‡	10	201	55	45	13
Nebraska	2	‡	‡	‡	‡	2	‡	‡	‡	‡
Nevada	8	212	44	56	24	1	‡	‡	‡	‡
New Hampshire	2	‡	‡	‡	‡	#	‡	‡	‡	‡
New Jersey	8	241	16	84	57	#	‡	‡	‡	‡
New Mexico	1	‡	‡	‡	‡	11	190	67	33	8
New York	7	237	19	81	50	1	‡	‡	‡	‡
North Carolina	3	221	37	63	31	2	‡	‡	‡	‡
North Dakota	1	‡	‡	‡	‡	9	198	60	40	9
Ohio	1	‡	‡	‡	‡	#	‡	‡	‡	‡
Oklahoma	1	‡	‡	‡	‡	21	211	43	57	22
Oregon	5	220	34	66	35	3	‡	‡	‡	‡
Pennsylvania	3	233	22	78	47	#	‡	‡	‡	‡
Rhode Island	3	219	36	64	29	1	‡	‡	‡	‡
South Carolina	1	‡	‡	‡	‡	#	‡	‡	‡	‡
South Dakota	1	‡	‡	‡	‡	11	201	56	44	14
Tennessee	1	‡	‡	‡	‡	#	‡	‡	‡	‡
Texas	3	234	24	76	47	#	‡	‡	‡	‡
Utah	3	218	38	62	30	1	‡	‡	‡	‡
Vermont	2	‡	‡	‡	‡	1	‡	‡	‡	‡
Virginia	6	239	16	84	53	#	‡	‡	‡	‡
Washington	8	230	22	78	40	2	‡	‡	‡	‡
West Virginia	#	‡	‡	‡	‡	#	‡	‡	‡	‡
Wisconsin	3	226	29	71	34	1	‡	‡	‡	‡
Wyoming	1	‡	‡	‡	‡	3	‡	‡	‡	‡
Other jurisdictions										
District of Columbia	2	‡	‡	‡	‡	#	‡	‡	‡	‡
DoDEA[1]	7	223	30	70	33	1	‡	‡	‡	‡

\# The estimate rounds to zero.

‡ Reporting standards not met. Sample size is insufficient to permit a reliable estimate.

[1] Department of Defense Education Activity.

NOTE: Results are not shown for students whose race/ethnicity was "unclassified." Detail may not sum to totals because of rounding.

SOURCE: U.S. Department of Education, Institute of Education Sciences, National Center for Education Statistics, National Assessment of Educational Progress (NAEP), 2005 Reading Assessment.

Average reading scale scores and achievement-level results, by gender, grade 4 public schools:
By state, 2005

State/jurisdiction	Male					Female				
			Percentage of students					Percentage of students		
	Percentage of all students	Average scale score	Below *Basic*	At or above *Basic*	At or above *Proficient*	Percentage of all students	Average scale score	Below *Basic*	At or above *Basic*	At or above *Proficient*
Nation (public)	50	214	41	59	27	50	220	34	66	33
Alabama	52	205	49	51	22	48	211	45	55	23
Alaska	51	207	45	55	24	49	215	38	62	29
Arizona	51	203	51	49	21	49	211	44	56	26
Arkansas	49	213	42	58	26	51	221	33	67	34
California	50	203	53	47	19	50	210	47	53	24
Colorado	52	221	33	67	33	48	227	27	73	41
Connecticut	52	222	33	67	34	48	230	25	75	43
Delaware	49	223	30	70	30	51	229	24	76	38
Florida	50	217	38	62	28	50	222	33	67	33
Georgia	50	210	47	53	22	50	219	37	63	30
Hawaii	50	205	51	49	20	50	214	43	57	27
Idaho	49	218	34	66	29	51	225	28	72	37
Illinois	52	215	38	62	28	48	218	37	63	30
Indiana	50	214	39	61	27	50	222	33	67	34
Iowa	50	218	35	65	29	50	224	30	70	37
Kansas	50	218	36	64	30	50	223	32	68	35
Kentucky	52	218	38	62	29	48	222	32	68	33
Louisiana	51	208	48	52	19	49	211	46	54	22
Maine	49	221	31	69	31	51	228	27	73	39
Maryland	48	217	38	62	30	52	223	33	67	35
Massachusetts	51	230	24	76	42	49	233	21	79	45
Michigan	50	216	39	61	29	50	221	35	65	34
Minnesota	49	221	32	68	34	51	229	25	75	42
Mississippi	48	200	56	44	16	52	208	48	52	21
Missouri	50	218	35	65	30	50	224	31	69	36
Montana	50	222	31	69	33	50	227	26	74	38
Nebraska	51	219	35	65	31	49	224	30	70	36
Nevada	50	203	53	47	17	50	212	43	57	24
New Hampshire	52	224	28	72	35	48	231	23	77	43
New Jersey	53	221	34	66	34	47	226	29	71	40
New Mexico	51	203	53	47	17	49	211	44	56	24
New York	50	220	33	67	30	50	225	29	71	36
North Carolina	51	213	42	58	26	49	221	34	66	33
North Dakota	50	222	30	70	33	50	227	26	74	38
Ohio	50	219	35	65	31	50	226	28	72	37
Oklahoma	50	211	43	57	23	50	217	37	63	27
Oregon	49	213	42	58	26	51	220	34	66	33
Pennsylvania	50	219	35	65	32	50	227	28	72	40
Rhode Island	50	212	42	58	26	50	221	34	66	34
South Carolina	51	210	46	54	23	49	217	39	61	28
South Dakota	53	219	35	65	29	47	227	25	75	38
Tennessee	49	210	44	56	23	51	218	38	62	30
Texas	50	216	40	60	26	50	222	32	68	32
Utah	50	216	37	63	29	50	226	27	73	40
Vermont	48	223	31	69	35	52	230	25	75	42
Virginia	48	223	31	69	34	52	228	26	74	39
Washington	50	219	34	66	30	50	228	26	74	41
West Virginia	50	211	43	57	23	50	218	36	64	28
Wisconsin	51	219	36	64	31	49	224	30	70	35
Wyoming	51	221	32	68	33	49	226	27	73	36
Other jurisdictions										
District of Columbia	46	186	72	28	9	54	195	63	37	13
DoDEA[1]	50	222	29	71	31	50	230	21	79	40

[1] Department of Defense Education Activity.
NOTE: Detail may not sum to totals because of rounding.
SOURCE: U.S. Department of Education, Institute of Education Sciences, National Center for Education Statistics, National Assessment of Educational Progress (NAEP), 2005 Reading Assessment.

Average reading scale scores and percentage of students within each achievement level, grade 8 public schools: By state, 2005

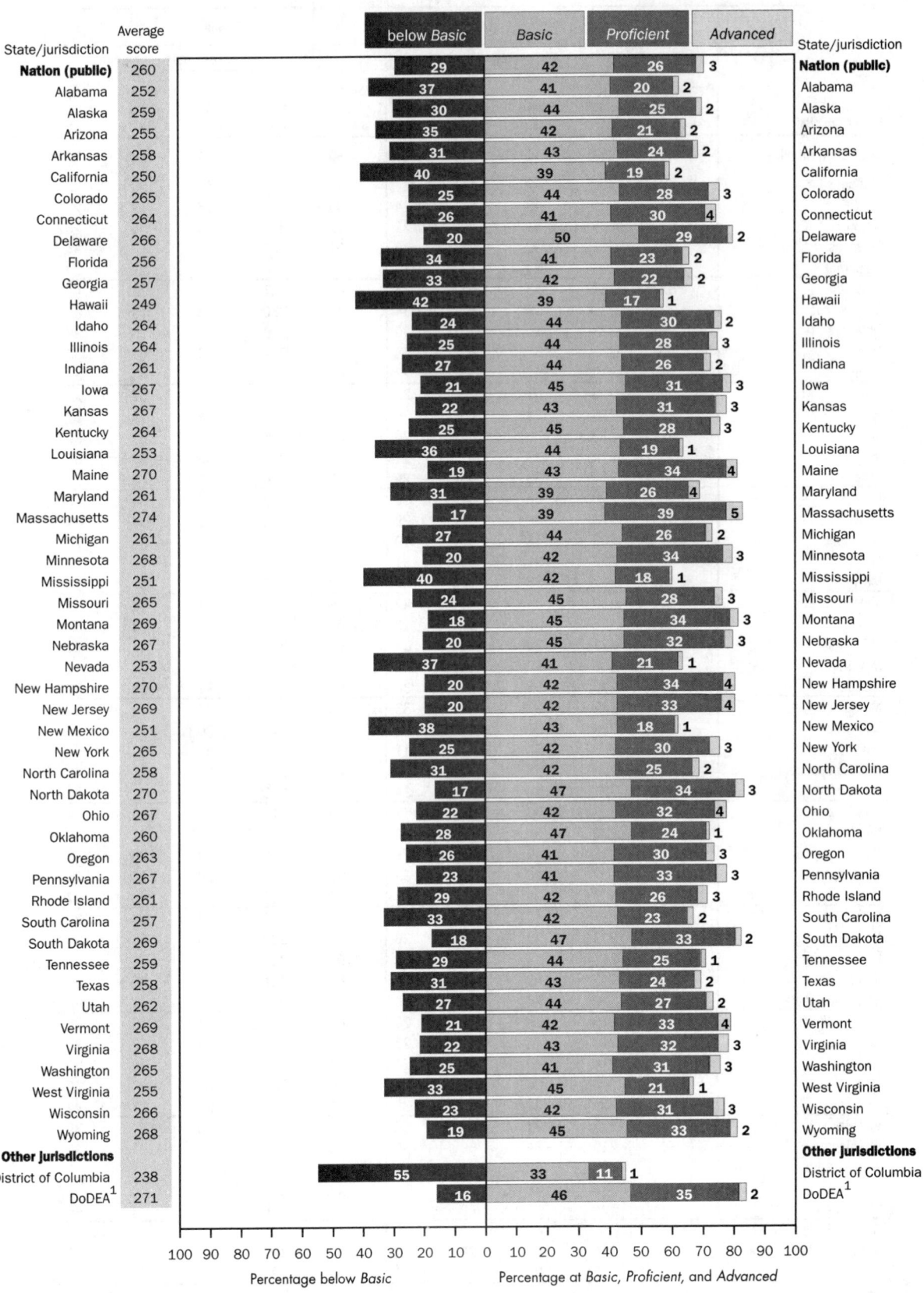

State/jurisdiction	Average score	below Basic	Basic	Proficient	Advanced	State/jurisdiction
Nation (public)	260	29	42	26	3	**Nation (public)**
Alabama	252	37	41	20	2	Alabama
Alaska	259	30	44	25	2	Alaska
Arizona	255	35	42	21	2	Arizona
Arkansas	258	31	43	24	2	Arkansas
California	250	40	39	19	2	California
Colorado	265	25	44	28	3	Colorado
Connecticut	264	26	41	30	4	Connecticut
Delaware	266	20	50	29	2	Delaware
Florida	256	34	41	23	2	Florida
Georgia	257	33	42	22	2	Georgia
Hawaii	249	42	39	17	1	Hawaii
Idaho	264	24	44	30	2	Idaho
Illinois	264	25	44	28	3	Illinois
Indiana	261	27	44	26	2	Indiana
Iowa	267	21	45	31	3	Iowa
Kansas	267	22	43	31	3	Kansas
Kentucky	264	25	45	28	3	Kentucky
Louisiana	253	36	44	19	1	Louisiana
Maine	270	19	43	34	4	Maine
Maryland	261	31	39	26	4	Maryland
Massachusetts	274	17	39	39	5	Massachusetts
Michigan	261	27	44	26	2	Michigan
Minnesota	268	20	42	34	3	Minnesota
Mississippi	251	40	42	18	1	Mississippi
Missouri	265	24	45	28	3	Missouri
Montana	269	18	45	34	3	Montana
Nebraska	267	20	45	32	3	Nebraska
Nevada	253	37	41	21	1	Nevada
New Hampshire	270	20	42	34	4	New Hampshire
New Jersey	269	20	42	33	4	New Jersey
New Mexico	251	38	43	18	1	New Mexico
New York	265	25	42	30	3	New York
North Carolina	258	31	42	25	2	North Carolina
North Dakota	270	17	47	34	3	North Dakota
Ohio	267	22	42	32	4	Ohio
Oklahoma	260	28	47	24	1	Oklahoma
Oregon	263	26	41	30	3	Oregon
Pennsylvania	267	23	41	33	3	Pennsylvania
Rhode Island	261	29	42	26	3	Rhode Island
South Carolina	257	33	42	23	2	South Carolina
South Dakota	269	18	47	33	2	South Dakota
Tennessee	259	29	44	25	1	Tennessee
Texas	258	31	43	24	2	Texas
Utah	262	27	44	27	2	Utah
Vermont	269	21	42	33	4	Vermont
Virginia	268	22	43	32	3	Virginia
Washington	265	25	41	31	3	Washington
West Virginia	255	33	45	21	1	West Virginia
Wisconsin	266	23	42	31	3	Wisconsin
Wyoming	268	19	45	33	2	Wyoming
Other jurisdictions						**Other jurisdictions**
District of Columbia	238	55	33	11	1	District of Columbia
DoDEA[1]	271	16	46	35	2	DoDEA[1]

Percentage below *Basic* | Percentage at *Basic*, *Proficient*, and *Advanced*

[1] Department of Defense Education Activity.

NOTE: The NAEP reading scale ranges from 0 to 500. Detail may not sum to totals because of rounding. The shaded bars are graphed using unrounded numbers.

SOURCE: U.S. Department of Education, Institute of Education Sciences, National Center for Education Statistics, National Assessment of Educational Progress (NAEP), 2005 Reading Assessment.

Average reading scale scores and achievement-level results, by race/ethnicity, grade 8 public schools: By state, 2005

State/jurisdiction	White					Black					Hispanic				
			Percentage of students					Percentage of students					Percentage of students		
	Percentage of all students	Average scale score	Below Basic	At or above Basic	At or above Proficient	Percentage of all students	Average scale score	Below Basic	At or above Basic	At or above Proficient	Percentage of all students	Average scale score	Below Basic	At or above Basic	At or above Proficient
Nation (public)	60	269	19	81	37	17	242	49	51	11	17	245	45	55	14
Alabama	58	263	25	75	31	38	235	56	44	9	2	‡	‡	‡	‡
Alaska	57	268	20	80	35	5	249	41	59	18	4	254	32	68	20
Arizona	49	267	21	79	34	6	242	47	53	12	37	242	51	49	11
Arkansas	69	266	22	78	33	25	236	54	46	9	4	250	39	61	13
California	33	264	25	75	32	8	240	53	47	11	45	239	53	47	10
Colorado	65	273	16	84	40	7	254	35	65	18	24	247	44	56	15
Connecticut	69	272	17	83	42	16	240	50	50	11	13	245	46	54	13
Delaware	58	274	11	89	41	32	252	35	65	13	7	253	34	66	16
Florida	51	265	25	75	33	23	238	53	47	11	21	252	38	62	21
Georgia	52	268	21	79	35	37	241	51	49	10	6	247	41	59	14
Hawaii	14	261	28	72	29	2	‡	‡	‡	‡	3	242	51	49	15
Idaho	87	267	22	78	34	1	‡	‡	‡	‡	10	246	43	57	14
Illinois	61	272	16	84	39	21	244	47	53	12	14	253	35	65	19
Indiana	81	265	23	77	32	13	241	51	49	10	3	247	44	56	17
Iowa	89	269	19	81	36	4	246	44	56	15	4	256	33	67	20
Kansas	77	271	18	82	39	8	247	44	56	15	9	249	40	60	14
Kentucky	88	266	23	77	32	9	248	42	58	15	1	‡	‡	‡	‡
Louisiana	52	264	23	77	30	44	240	52	48	9	2	‡	‡	‡	‡
Maine	96	270	18	82	39	2	‡	‡	‡	‡	1	‡	‡	‡	‡
Maryland	51	272	19	81	42	40	244	47	53	12	4	256	33	67	23
Massachusetts	77	279	12	88	50	8	253	35	65	18	10	246	44	56	15
Michigan	73	268	20	80	34	21	239	52	48	10	3	250	39	61	16
Minnesota	81	273	15	85	42	8	239	52	48	11	4	244	45	55	14
Mississippi	48	264	23	77	30	50	237	56	44	7	1	‡	‡	‡	‡
Missouri	78	270	18	82	36	18	242	49	51	9	3	258	33	67	23
Montana	87	272	15	85	40	1	‡	‡	‡	‡	2	‡	‡	‡	‡
Nebraska	84	271	16	84	38	6	243	52	48	13	8	245	46	54	12
Nevada	53	261	27	73	29	10	240	51	49	12	28	241	50	50	11
New Hampshire	95	270	19	81	38	2	‡	‡	‡	‡	2	‡	‡	‡	‡
New Jersey	59	278	12	88	48	20	251	38	62	14	14	251	35	65	14
New Mexico	33	264	24	76	33	2	‡	‡	‡	‡	53	245	45	55	12
New York	57	276	13	87	45	18	242	49	51	11	18	250	39	61	16
North Carolina	61	267	21	79	35	29	240	51	49	10	5	248	43	57	17
North Dakota	89	272	15	85	38	1	‡	‡	‡	‡	1	‡	‡	‡	‡
Ohio	78	272	17	83	41	17	243	46	54	10	2	245	47	53	14
Oklahoma	62	265	20	80	30	11	243	49	51	13	7	247	44	56	13
Oregon	77	267	22	78	36	3	245	47	53	18	11	245	47	53	15
Pennsylvania	78	273	16	84	41	15	239	52	48	12	5	246	45	55	17
Rhode Island	74	268	22	78	36	8	243	47	53	11	14	237	52	48	9
South Carolina	58	267	22	78	34	38	242	50	50	11	2	‡	‡	‡	‡
South Dakota	86	272	14	86	38	1	‡	‡	‡	‡	2	‡	‡	‡	‡
Tennessee	75	265	23	77	31	22	240	52	48	9	2	‡	‡	‡	‡
Texas	42	270	18	82	39	15	246	44	56	14	39	248	41	59	15
Utah	84	265	24	76	32	1	‡	‡	‡	‡	10	243	48	52	12
Vermont	96	269	21	79	38	1	‡	‡	‡	‡	1	‡	‡	‡	‡
Virginia	61	275	15	85	45	27	251	37	63	16	7	259	30	70	23
Washington	75	268	22	78	38	6	255	33	67	27	10	245	45	55	15
West Virginia	94	256	32	68	22	4	236	56	44	10	1	‡	‡	‡	‡
Wisconsin	80	271	18	82	40	10	236	56	44	9	6	247	43	57	18
Wyoming	87	270	17	83	38	1	‡	‡	‡	‡	7	256	32	68	21
Other jurisdictions															
District of Columbia	3	301	6	94	74	89	235	58	42	9	6	247	41	59	18
DoDEA[1]	43	276	12	88	47	22	258	27	73	20	13	268	17	83	30

See notes at end of table.

Average reading scale scores and achievement-level results, by race/ethnicity, grade 8 public schools: By state, 2005—Continued

State/jurisdiction	Asian/Pacific Islander					American Indian/Alaska Native				
	Percentage of all students	Average scale score	Percentage of students			Percentage of all students	Average scale score	Percentage of students		
			Below Basic	At or above Basic	At or above Proficient			Below Basic	At or above Basic	At or above Proficient
Nation (public)	4	270	21	79	39	1	251	39	61	18
Alabama	1	‡	‡	‡	‡	1	‡	‡	‡	‡
Alaska	7	260	29	71	24	25	240	51	49	10
Arizona	2	‡	‡	‡	‡	6	240	54	46	12
Arkansas	1	‡	‡	‡	‡	1	‡	‡	‡	‡
California	12	264	25	75	33	1	‡	‡	‡	‡
Colorado	3	269	24	76	42	2	‡	‡	‡	‡
Connecticut	3	279	12	88	50	#	‡	‡	‡	‡
Delaware	3	276	10	90	42	#	‡	‡	‡	‡
Florida	2	273	18	82	47	#	‡	‡	‡	‡
Georgia	3	275	21	79	47	#	‡	‡	‡	‡
Hawaii	68	246	45	55	16	#	‡	‡	‡	‡
Idaho	1	‡	‡	‡	‡	1	‡	‡	‡	‡
Illinois	3	281	8	92	49	#	‡	‡	‡	‡
Indiana	1	‡	‡	‡	‡	#	‡	‡	‡	‡
Iowa	2	‡	‡	‡	‡	1	‡	‡	‡	‡
Kansas	2	‡	‡	‡	‡	2	‡	‡	‡	‡
Kentucky	1	‡	‡	‡	‡	#	‡	‡	‡	‡
Louisiana	1	‡	‡	‡	‡	1	‡	‡	‡	‡
Maine	1	‡	‡	‡	‡	#	‡	‡	‡	‡
Maryland	4	283	14	86	58	#	‡	‡	‡	‡
Massachusetts	5	282	14	86	52	#	‡	‡	‡	‡
Michigan	2	‡	‡	‡	‡	1	‡	‡	‡	‡
Minnesota	6	262	28	72	29	1	‡	‡	‡	‡
Mississippi	1	‡	‡	‡	‡	#	‡	‡	‡	‡
Missouri	1	‡	‡	‡	‡	#	‡	‡	‡	‡
Montana	1	‡	‡	‡	‡	10	248	43	57	16
Nebraska	1	‡	‡	‡	‡	1	‡	‡	‡	‡
Nevada	6	263	28	72	32	2	‡	‡	‡	‡
New Hampshire	1	‡	‡	‡	‡	#	‡	‡	‡	‡
New Jersey	6	291	5	95	66	#	‡	‡	‡	‡
New Mexico	1	‡	‡	‡	‡	11	240	51	49	7
New York	6	274	18	82	45	#	‡	‡	‡	‡
North Carolina	2	275	16	84	46	2	‡	‡	‡	‡
North Dakota	1	‡	‡	‡	‡	8	250	38	62	15
Ohio	1	‡	‡	‡	‡	#	‡	‡	‡	‡
Oklahoma	2	‡	‡	‡	‡	19	254	34	66	19
Oregon	5	267	24	76	35	2	‡	‡	‡	‡
Pennsylvania	2	275	18	82	47	#	‡	‡	‡	‡
Rhode Island	3	257	33	67	26	1	‡	‡	‡	‡
South Carolina	1	‡	‡	‡	‡	#	‡	‡	‡	‡
South Dakota	1	‡	‡	‡	‡	10	245	45	55	13
Tennessee	1	‡	‡	‡	‡	#	‡	‡	‡	‡
Texas	3	280	13	87	50	#	‡	‡	‡	‡
Utah	3	266	23	77	31	2	‡	‡	‡	‡
Vermont	1	‡	‡	‡	‡	1	‡	‡	‡	‡
Virginia	4	282	9	91	52	#	‡	‡	‡	‡
Washington	7	270	18	82	36	3	255	33	67	24
West Virginia	1	‡	‡	‡	‡	#	‡	‡	‡	‡
Wisconsin	3	262	27	73	28	1	‡	‡	‡	‡
Wyoming	#	‡	‡	‡	‡	4	251	35	65	15
Other jurisdictions										
District of Columbia	1	‡	‡	‡	‡	#	‡	‡	‡	‡
DoDEA[1]	10	274	11	89	41	1	‡	‡	‡	‡

The estimate rounds to zero.

‡ Reporting standards not met. Sample size is insufficient to permit a reliable estimate.

[1] Department of Defense Education Activity.

NOTE: Results are not shown for students whose race/ethnicity was "unclassified." Detail may not sum to totals because of rounding.

SOURCE: U.S. Department of Education, Institute of Education Sciences, National Center for Education Statistics, National Assessment of Educational Progress (NAEP), 2005 Reading Assessment.

Average reading scale scores and achievement-level results, by gender, grade 8 public schools: By state, 2005

State/jurisdiction	Male					Female				
			Percentage of students					Percentage of students		
	Percentage of all students	Average scale score	Below Basic	At or above Basic	At or above Proficient	Percentage of all students	Average scale score	Below Basic	At or above Basic	At or above Proficient
Nation (public)	50	255	34	66	24	50	266	24	76	34
Alabama	50	245	45	55	17	50	260	30	70	27
Alaska	50	253	36	64	21	50	265	24	76	32
Arizona	51	249	41	59	19	49	260	30	70	27
Arkansas	50	252	37	63	20	50	263	25	75	31
California	50	246	45	55	17	50	255	35	65	24
Colorado	52	261	28	72	28	48	268	21	79	36
Connecticut	52	258	30	70	28	48	270	21	79	40
Delaware	48	261	25	75	25	52	271	15	85	35
Florida	49	249	41	59	20	51	262	27	73	30
Georgia	49	251	39	61	20	51	263	27	73	30
Hawaii	53	242	50	50	14	47	256	34	66	23
Idaho	51	258	30	70	25	49	271	17	83	39
Illinois	51	258	30	70	25	49	269	21	79	37
Indiana	51	256	33	67	23	49	267	21	79	34
Iowa	51	261	26	74	27	49	273	15	85	41
Kansas	51	262	27	73	30	49	271	18	82	40
Kentucky	50	258	30	70	25	50	270	19	81	36
Louisiana	49	247	43	57	16	51	259	30	70	24
Maine	51	264	24	76	31	49	276	13	87	46
Maryland	51	256	36	64	25	49	266	26	74	35
Massachusetts	49	269	21	79	38	51	278	13	87	50
Michigan	50	256	32	68	24	50	266	23	77	33
Minnesota	51	263	26	74	31	49	274	15	85	44
Mississippi	48	246	45	55	14	52	255	35	65	22
Missouri	49	260	29	71	25	51	270	19	81	36
Montana	51	265	22	78	30	49	274	15	85	43
Nebraska	51	261	26	74	27	49	274	15	85	43
Nevada	50	247	42	58	18	50	258	31	69	27
New Hampshire	51	264	25	75	32	49	275	15	85	44
New Jersey	50	266	23	77	33	50	273	17	83	42
New Mexico	51	247	43	57	17	49	255	33	67	22
New York	50	260	30	70	28	50	270	20	80	38
North Carolina	52	251	38	62	21	48	266	24	76	33
North Dakota	50	267	20	80	32	50	274	14	86	41
Ohio	49	261	27	73	30	51	272	18	82	41
Oklahoma	50	254	33	67	19	50	265	23	77	31
Oregon	50	258	31	69	28	50	268	21	79	37
Pennsylvania	50	262	27	73	31	50	271	19	81	41
Rhode Island	50	256	33	67	26	50	266	24	76	33
South Carolina	48	252	39	61	20	52	262	28	72	29
South Dakota	50	264	21	79	29	50	273	14	86	41
Tennessee	52	255	34	66	22	48	264	25	75	31
Texas	51	254	35	65	22	49	263	26	74	30
Utah	49	255	33	67	22	51	269	21	79	36
Vermont	51	262	26	74	30	49	276	15	85	45
Virginia	50	263	26	74	30	50	273	17	83	41
Washington	50	260	29	71	29	50	269	20	80	39
West Virginia	52	250	39	61	17	48	261	27	73	27
Wisconsin	53	261	29	71	29	47	273	17	83	42
Wyoming	50	264	22	78	30	50	272	16	84	41
Other jurisdictions										
District of Columbia	47	230	64	36	7	53	245	47	53	15
DoDEA[1]	51	266	20	80	31	49	276	12	88	44

[1] Department of Defense Education Activity.
NOTE: Detail may not sum to totals because of rounding.
SOURCE: U.S. Department of Education, Institute of Education Sciences, National Center for Education Statistics, National Assessment of Educational Progress (NAEP), 2005 Reading Assessment.

Average fourth-grade NAEP science scores and percentage of students in each achievement level in 2005, by state

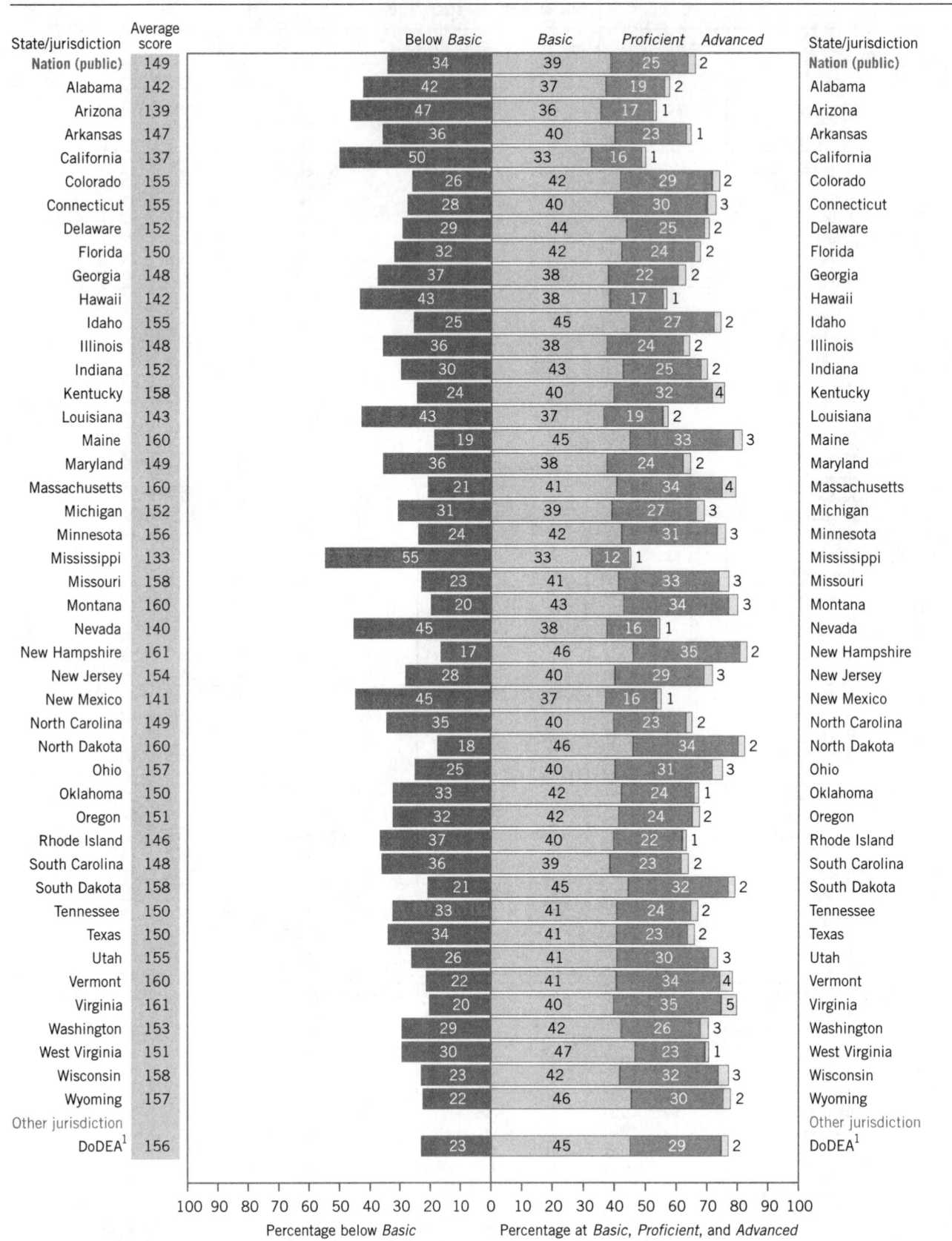

State/jurisdiction	Average score	Below Basic	Basic	Proficient	Advanced
Nation (public)	149	34	39	25	2
Alabama	142	42	37	19	2
Arizona	139	47	36	17	1
Arkansas	147	36	40	23	1
California	137	50	33	16	1
Colorado	155	26	42	29	2
Connecticut	155	28	40	30	3
Delaware	152	29	44	25	2
Florida	150	32	42	24	2
Georgia	148	37	38	22	2
Hawaii	142	43	38	17	1
Idaho	155	25	45	27	2
Illinois	148	36	38	24	2
Indiana	152	30	43	25	2
Kentucky	158	24	40	32	4
Louisiana	143	43	37	19	2
Maine	160	19	45	33	3
Maryland	149	36	38	24	2
Massachusetts	160	21	41	34	4
Michigan	152	31	39	27	3
Minnesota	156	24	42	31	3
Mississippi	133	55	33	12	1
Missouri	158	23	41	33	3
Montana	160	20	43	34	3
Nevada	140	45	38	16	1
New Hampshire	161	17	46	35	2
New Jersey	154	28	40	29	3
New Mexico	141	45	37	16	1
North Carolina	149	35	40	23	2
North Dakota	160	18	46	34	2
Ohio	157	25	40	31	3
Oklahoma	150	33	42	24	1
Oregon	151	32	42	24	2
Rhode Island	146	37	40	22	1
South Carolina	148	36	39	23	2
South Dakota	158	21	45	32	2
Tennessee	150	33	41	24	2
Texas	150	34	41	23	2
Utah	155	26	41	30	3
Vermont	160	22	41	34	4
Virginia	161	20	40	35	5
Washington	153	29	42	26	3
West Virginia	151	30	47	23	1
Wisconsin	158	23	42	32	3
Wyoming	157	22	46	30	2
Other jurisdiction					
DoDEA[1]	156	23	45	29	2

100 90 80 70 60 50 40 30 20 10 0 10 20 30 40 50 60 70 80 90 100

Percentage below *Basic*   Percentage at *Basic*, *Proficient*, and *Advanced*

[1] Department of Defense Education Activity.
NOTE: The shaded bars are graphed using unrounded numbers. Percentages may not add to 100 due to rounding.
SOURCE: U.S. Department of Education, Institute of Education Sciences, National Center for Education Statistics, National Assessment of Educational Progress (NAEP), 2005 Science Assessment.

Average fourth-grade NAEP science scores and achievement-level performance, by state

| State/jurisdiction | Average scale score | | Percentage of students | | | | | |
| | | | At or above *Basic* | | At or above *Proficient* | | At *Advanced* | |
	2000	2005	2000	2005	2000	2005	2000	2005
Nation (public)	145*	149	61*	66	26	27	3	2
Alabama	143	142	58	58	22	21	2	2
Alaska	—	—	—	—	—	—	—	—
Arizona	140	139	55	53	22	18	2	1
Arkansas	145	147	62	64	23	24	2	1
California	129*	137	45	50	13*	17	1	1
Colorado	—	155	—	74	—	32	—	2
Connecticut	156	155	75	72	35	33	3	3
Delaware	—	152	—	71	—	27	—	2
Florida	—	150	—	68	—	26	—	2
Georgia	142*	148	57*	63	23	25	3	2
Hawaii	136*	142	51*	57	16	19	1	1
Idaho	152	155	74	75	29	29	2	2
Illinois	150	148	68	64	31	27	3	2
Indiana	154	152	74	70	32	27	3	2
Iowa	159	—	79	—	36	—	3	—
Kansas	—	—	—	—	—	—	—	—
Kentucky	152*	158	69*	76	28*	36	2*	4
Louisiana	139	143	54	57	18	20	2	2
Maine	161	160	82	81	37	36	4	3
Maryland	145*	149	61	64	24	27	3	2
Massachusetts	161	160	81	79	42	38	5	4
Michigan	152	152	70	69	32	30	3	3
Minnesota	157	156	78	76	34	33	3	3
Mississippi	133	133	46	45	13	12	1	1
Missouri	157	158	76	77	34	36	3	3
Montana	160	160	80	80	36	37	3	3
Nebraska	150	—	68	—	26	—	2	—
Nevada	142	140	58	55	19	17	1	1
New Hampshire	—	161	—	83	—	37	—	2
New Jersey	—	154	—	72	—	32	—	3
New Mexico	140	141	54	55	17	18	1	1
New York	148	—	66	—	24	—	2	—
North Carolina	147	149	63	65	23	25	2	2
North Dakota	160	160	81	82	36	36	3	2
Ohio	155	157	73	75	31	35	3	3
Oklahoma	151	150	70	67	26	25	2	1
Oregon	148	151	66	68	27	26	3	2
Pennsylvania	—	—	—	—	—	—	—	—
Rhode Island	148	146	65	63	25	23	2*	1
South Carolina	140*	148	54*	64	20*	25	2	2
South Dakota	—	158	—	79	—	35	—	2
Tennessee	145*	150	61*	67	24	26	2	2
Texas	145*	150	62	66	23	25	2	2
Utah	154	155	73	74	31	33	3	3
Vermont	160	160	79	78	38	38	4	4
Virginia	155*	161	72*	80	32*	40	3	5
Washington	—	153	—	71	—	28	—	3
West Virginia	149	151	68	70	24	24	2	1
Wisconsin	‡	158	‡	77	‡	35	‡	3
Wyoming	156	157	77	78	31	32	2	2
Other jurisdictions								
District of Columbia	—	—	—	—	—	—	—	—
DoDEA[1]	156	156	76	77	30	32	3	2

— Not available. The jurisdiction did not participate.

‡ Reporting standards not met.

* Significantly different from 2005 when only one jurisdiction or the nation is being examined.

[1] Department of Defense Education Activity. Before 2005, DoDEA overseas and domestic schools were separate jurisdictions in NAEP. For this table, 2000 data were recalculated for comparability.

SOURCE: U.S. Department of Education, Institute of Education Sciences, National Center for Education Statistics, National Assessment of Educational Progress (NAEP), 2000 and 2005 Science Assessments.

Average eighth-grade NAEP science scores and percentage of students in each achievement level in 2005, by state

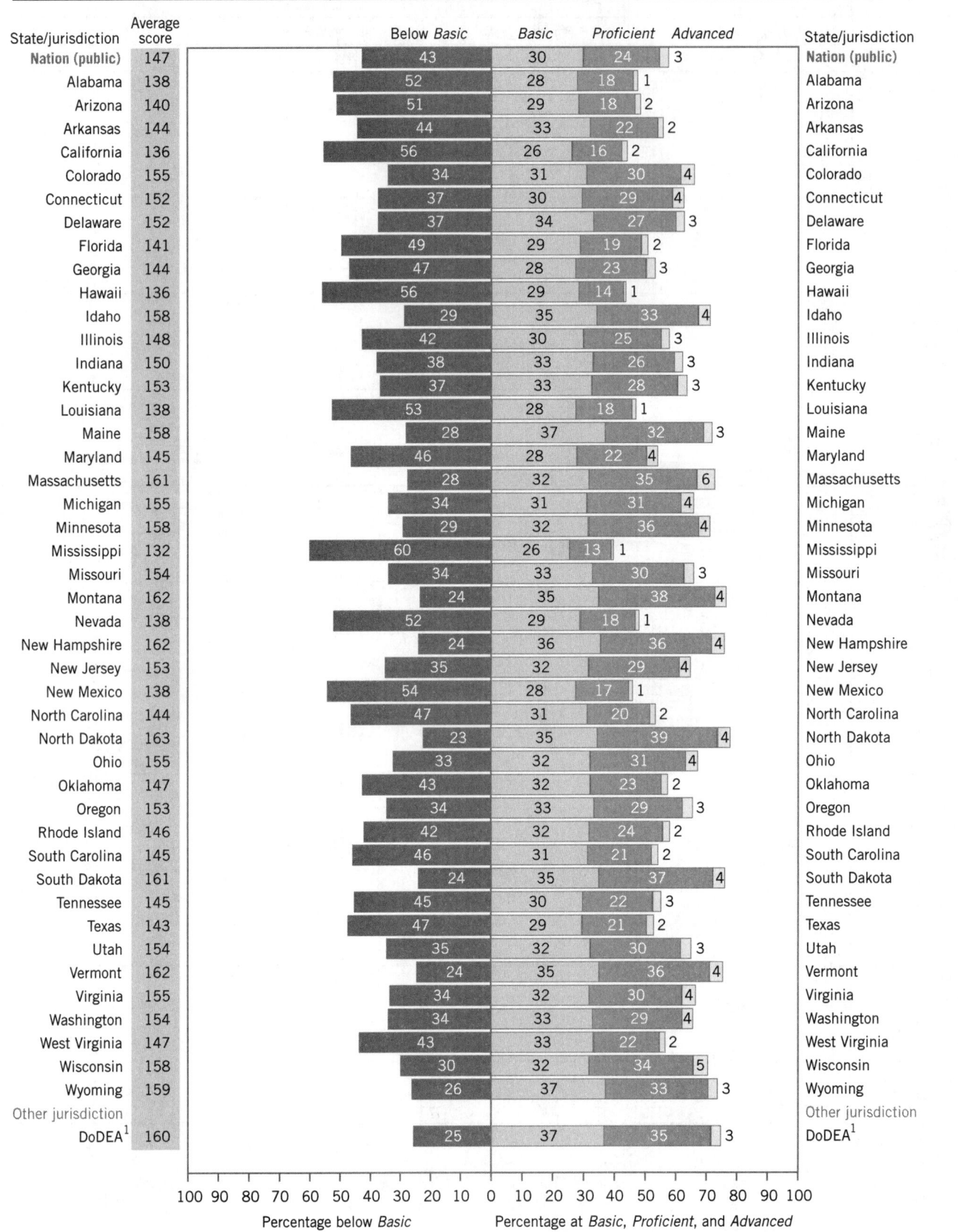

State/jurisdiction	Average score	Below Basic	Basic	Proficient	Advanced
Nation (public)	147	43	30	24	3
Alabama	138	52	28	18	1
Arizona	140	51	29	18	2
Arkansas	144	44	33	22	2
California	136	56	26	16	2
Colorado	155	34	31	30	4
Connecticut	152	37	30	29	4
Delaware	152	37	34	27	3
Florida	141	49	29	19	2
Georgia	144	47	28	23	3
Hawaii	136	56	29	14	1
Idaho	158	29	35	33	4
Illinois	148	42	30	25	3
Indiana	150	38	33	26	3
Kentucky	153	37	33	28	3
Louisiana	138	53	28	18	1
Maine	158	28	37	32	3
Maryland	145	46	28	22	4
Massachusetts	161	28	32	35	6
Michigan	155	34	31	31	4
Minnesota	158	29	32	36	4
Mississippi	132	60	26	13	1
Missouri	154	34	33	30	3
Montana	162	24	35	38	4
Nevada	138	52	29	18	1
New Hampshire	162	24	36	36	4
New Jersey	153	35	32	29	4
New Mexico	138	54	28	17	1
North Carolina	144	47	31	20	2
North Dakota	163	23	35	39	4
Ohio	155	33	32	31	4
Oklahoma	147	43	32	23	2
Oregon	153	34	33	29	3
Rhode Island	146	42	32	24	2
South Carolina	145	46	31	21	2
South Dakota	161	24	35	37	4
Tennessee	145	45	30	22	3
Texas	143	47	29	21	2
Utah	154	35	32	30	3
Vermont	162	24	35	36	4
Virginia	155	34	32	30	4
Washington	154	34	33	29	4
West Virginia	147	43	33	22	2
Wisconsin	158	30	32	34	5
Wyoming	159	26	37	33	3
Other jurisdiction					
DoDEA[1]	160	25	37	35	3

Percentage below *Basic*

Percentage at *Basic*, *Proficient*, and *Advanced*

[1] Department of Defense Education Activity.

NOTE: The shaded bars are graphed using unrounded numbers. Percentages may not add to 100 due to rounding.

SOURCE: U.S. Department of Education, Institute of Education Sciences, National Center for Education Statistics, National Assessment of Educational Progress (NAEP), 2005 Science Assessment.

Average eighth-grade NAEP science scores and achievement-level performance, by state

State/jurisdiction	Average scale score			Percentage of students								
				At or above *Basic*			At or above *Proficient*			At *Advanced*		
	1996[1]	2000	2005	1996[1]	2000	2005	1996[1]	2000	2005	1996[1]	2000	2005
Nation (public)	148	148	147	60	57	57	27	29	27	3	4*	3
Alabama	139	143*	138	47	53	48	18	23	19	1	2	1
Alaska	153	—	—	65	—	—	31	—	—	3	—	—
Arizona	145*	145*	140	55*	55*	49	23	23	20	2	2	2
Arkansas	144	142	144	55	53	56	22	22	23	1	1	2
California	138	129*	136	47	38*	44	20	14*	18	1	1	2
Colorado	155	—	155	68	—	66	32	—	35	2*	—	4
Connecticut	155	153	152	68*	64	63	36	35	33	3	4	4
Delaware	142*	—	152	51*	—	63	21*	—	29	1*	—	3
Florida	142	—	141	51	—	51	21	—	21	1	—	2
Georgia	142	142	144	49	52	53	21*	23	25	1*	2	3
Hawaii	135	130*	136	42	40	44	15	14	15	1	1	1
Idaho	—	158	158	—	71	71	—	37	36	—	4	4
Illinois	—	148	148	—	59	58	—	29	27	—	3	3
Indiana	153	154*	150	65	66	62	30	33	29	2	3	3
Iowa	158	—	—	71	—	—	36	—	—	3	—	—
Kansas	—	—	—	—	—	—	—	—	—	—	—	—
Kentucky	147*	150*	153	58*	60	63	23*	28	31	2	3	3
Louisiana	132*	134*	138	40*	44	47	13*	18	19	1*	1	1
Maine	163*	158	158	78*	72	72	41*	35	34	4	3	3
Maryland	145	146	145	55	57	54	25	27	26	2*	3	4
Massachusetts	157*	158*	161	69	70	72	37	39	41	4*	5	6
Michigan	153	155	155	65	68	66	32	35	35	3	4	4
Minnesota	159	159	158	72	72	71	37	41	39	3	4	4
Mississippi	133	134	132	39	41	40	12	15	14	1	1	1
Missouri	151	154	154	64	66	66	28*	33	33	2	3	3
Montana	162	164	162	77	79	76	41	44	42	3	5	4
Nebraska	157	158	—	71	71	—	35	38	—	3	4	—
Nevada	‡	141*	138	‡	52	48	‡	22	19	‡	2	1
New Hampshire	‡	—	162	‡	—	76	‡	—	41	‡	—	4
New Jersey	‡	—	153	‡	—	65	‡	—	33	‡	—	4
New Mexico	141*	139	138	49	48	46	19	20	18	1	1	1
New York	146	145	—	57	58	—	27	28	—	2	2	—
North Carolina	147	145	144	56	54	53	24	25	22	2	3	2
North Dakota	162	159*	163	78	72*	77	41	38*	43	3	4	4
Ohio	—	159	155	—	72	67	—	39	35	—	5	4
Oklahoma	—	149	147	—	60	57	—	25	25	—	2	2
Oregon	155	154	153	68	68	66	32	34	32	3	3	3
Pennsylvania	—	—	—	—	—	—	—	—	—	—	—	—
Rhode Island	149*	148	146	59	58	58	26	27	26	2	2	2
South Carolina	139*	140*	145	45*	48*	54	17*	20	23	1	2	2
South Dakota	—	—	161	—	—	76	—	—	41	—	—	4
Tennessee	143	145	145	53	55	55	22	24	25	2	2	3
Texas	145	143	143	55	52	53	23	23	23	1	2	2
Utah	156*	154	154	70*	67	65	32	34	33	2*	3	3
Vermont	157*	159*	162	70*	71*	76	34*	39	41	3*	4	4
Virginia	149*	151*	155	59*	61*	66	27*	29*	35	2*	3	4
Washington	150*	—	154	61*	—	66	27*	—	33	2*	—	4
West Virginia	147	146	147	56	57	57	21	24	23	1*	2	2
Wisconsin	160	‡	158	73	‡	70	39	‡	39	4	‡	5
Wyoming	158	156*	159	71	69*	74	34	34*	37	2	3	3
Other jurisdictions												
District of Columbia	113	—	—	19	—	—	5	—	—	#	—	—
DoDEA[2]	155*	158*	160	67*	71*	75	30*	36	38	2	4	3

— Not available. The jurisdiction did not participate.

The estimate rounds to zero.

‡ Reporting standards not met.

* Significantly different from 2005 when only one jurisdiction or the nation is being examined.

[1] Accommodations were not permitted for this assessment.

[2] Department of Defense Education Activity. Before 2005, DoDEA overseas and domestic schools were separate jurisdictions in NAEP. For this table, 1996 and 2000 data were recalculated for comparability.

SOURCE: U.S. Department of Education, Institute of Education Sciences, National Center for Education Statistics, National Assessment of Educational Progress (NAEP), 1996, 2000, and 2005 Science Assessments.

Percentage of students at or above selected writing proficiency levels, by grade level and selected student characteristics: 2002

Selected student characteristic	Percentage of 4th-graders				Percentage of 8th-graders				Percentage of 12th-graders			
	Below basic	At or above basic	At or above proficient	At advanced	Below basic	At or above basic	At or above proficient	At advanced	Below basic	At or above basic	At or above proficient	At advanced
1	2	3	4	5	6	7	8	9	10	11	12	13
All students	**14** (0.4)	**86** (0.4)	**28** (0.4)	**2** (0.1)	**15** (0.4)	**85** (0.4)	**31** (0.6)	**2** (0.1)	**26** (0.7)	**74** (0.7)	**24** (0.8)	**2** (0.2)
Sex												
Male	19 (0.5)	81 (0.5)	20 (0.5)	1 (0.1)	21 (0.6)	79 (0.6)	21 (0.6)	1 (0.1)	37 (1.0)	63 (1.0)	14 (0.8)	1 (0.1)
Female	9 (0.3)	91 (0.3)	36 (0.6)	3 (0.2)	9 (0.3)	91 (0.3)	42 (0.8)	3 (0.2)	15 (0.7)	85 (0.7)	33 (1.0)	3 (0.3)
Race/ethnicity												
White, non-Hispanic	9 (0.2)	91 (0.2)	35 (0.4)	3 (0.2)	9 (0.4)	91 (0.4)	39 (0.6)	3 (0.2)	20 (0.7)	80 (0.7)	28 (0.9)	2 (0.3)
Black, non-Hispanic	21 (0.6)	79 (0.6)	15 (0.7)	1 (0.2)	25 (1.0)	75 (1.0)	13 (0.6)	# (0.1)	41 (1.8)	59 (1.8)	9 (1.0)	# (†)
Hispanic	22 (1.1)	78 (1.1)	18 (0.7)	1 (0.2)	27 (0.8)	73 (0.8)	17 (0.9)	1 (0.2)	38 (1.5)	62 (1.5)	13 (1.2)	# (0.2)
Asian/Pacific Islander	7 (0.8)	93 (0.8)	42 (2.0)	4 (0.7)	10 (1.0)	90 (1.0)	42 (2.3)	3 (0.6)	24 (2.5)	76 (2.5)	26 (3.2)	3 (1.0)
American Indian/Alaska Native	20 (1.2)	80 (1.2)	16 (1.0)	1 (0.3)	23 (2.5)	77 (2.5)	18 (2.9)	1 (#)	—	—	—	—
Parents' highest level of education												
Not high school graduate	— (†)	— (†)	— (†)	— (†)	26 (1.3)	74 (1.3)	14 (1.0)	# (†)	43 (2.1)	57 (2.1)	8 (1.4)	# (†)
Graduated high school	— (†)	— (†)	— (†)	— (†)	19 (0.7)	81 (0.7)	20 (0.6)	1 (0.2)	32 (1.2)	68 (1.2)	14 (1.1)	1 (0.2)
Some college	— (†)	— (†)	— (†)	— (†)	11 (0.6)	89 (0.6)	31 (0.8)	1 (0.2)	23 (1.0)	77 (1.0)	22 (1.3)	1 (0.2)
Graduated college	— (†)	— (†)	— (†)	— (†)	9 (0.4)	91 (0.4)	43 (0.8)	4 (0.2)	18 (0.9)	82 (0.9)	32 (1.0)	3 (0.4)
Free/reduced-price lunch eligibility												
Eligible	22 (0.8)	78 (0.8)	15 (0.5)	1 (0.1)	26 (0.6)	74 (0.6)	16 (0.6)	1 (0.1)	40 (1.5)	60 (1.5)	11 (1.0)	1 (0.2)
Not eligible	8 (0.3)	92 (0.3)	36 (0.6)	3 (0.2)	9 (0.4)	91 (0.4)	39 (0.8)	3 (0.2)	23 (0.8)	77 (0.8)	26 (1.0)	2 (0.3)
Information not available	10 (1.1)	90 (1.1)	34 (1.6)	3 (0.3)	11 (0.7)	89 (0.7)	39 (1.7)	4 (0.6)	19 (1.3)	81 (1.3)	29 (1.6)	2 (0.4)

—Not available.

†Not applicable.

#Rounds to zero.

NOTE: Includes public and private schools. Excludes persons unable to be tested due to limited proficiency in English or due to a disability (and the accommodations provided were not sufficient to enable the test to properly reflect the students' writing proficiency). Beginning in 2002, the NAEP national sample was obtained by aggregating the samples from each state, rather than by obtaining an independently selected national sample. As a consequence, the size of the national sample increased, and smaller differences between years or between types of students were found to be statistically significant than would have been detected in previous assessments. Detail may not sum to totals because of rounding. Standard errors appear in parentheses.

SOURCE: U.S. Department of Education, National Center for Education Statistics, National Assessment of Educational Progress (NAEP), 2002 Writing Assessment; and unpublished tabulations, NAEP Data Explorer (http://nces.ed.gov/nationsreportcard/nde/), retrieved August 2003. (This table was prepared August 2003.)

Percentage of students at or above selected U.S. history proficiency levels, by grade level and selected student characteristics: 2001

Selected student characteristic	Percentage of 4th-graders				Percentage of 8th-graders				Percentage of 12th-graders			
	Below basic	At or above basic	At or above proficient	At advanced	Below basic	At or above basic	At or above proficient	At advanced	Below basic	At or above basic	At or above proficient	At advanced
1	2	3	4	5	6	7	8	9	10	11	12	13
All students	**33** (1.1)	**67** (1.1)	**18** (1.0)	**2** (0.5)	**36** (0.9)	**64** (0.9)	**17** (0.8)	**2** (0.3)	**57** (1.2)	**43** (1.2)	**11** (0.9)	**1** (0.4)
Sex												
Male	34 (1.3)	66 (1.3)	19 (1.2)	2 (0.7)	35 (1.1)	65 (1.1)	18 (1.0)	2 (0.3)	55 (1.6)	45 (1.6)	12 (1.1)	1 (0.5)
Female	32 (1.4)	68 (1.4)	17 (1.1)	2 (0.4)	37 (1.2)	63 (1.2)	15 (0.8)	1 (0.4)	59 (1.3)	41 (1.3)	10 (0.9)	1 (0.3)
Race/ethnicity												
White, non-Hispanic	21 (1.3)	79 (1.3)	24 (1.4)	3 (0.7)	25 (1.0)	75 (1.0)	21 (1.1)	2 (0.4)	51 (1.4)	49 (1.4)	13 (1.0)	1 (0.4)
Black, non-Hispanic	56 (2.1)	44 (2.1)	6 (1.0)	# (0.3)	62 (2.4)	38 (2.4)	4 (0.8)	# (†)	80 (1.5)	20 (1.5)	3 (0.6)	# (†)
Hispanic	58 (3.0)	42 (3.0)	7 (1.1)	1 (0.3)	60 (1.7)	40 (1.7)	5 (0.7)	# (0.2)	74 (2.4)	26 (2.4)	5 (1.1)	# (†)
Asian/Pacific Islander	29 (3.8)	71 (3.8)	19 (3.2)	3 (1.9)	32 (3.8)	68 (3.8)	20 (3.6)	2 (0.8)	47 (5.1)	53 (5.1)	21 (6.0)	5 (2.3)
American Indian/Alaska Native	47 (6.4)	53 (6.4)	12 (4.6)	4 (†)	50 (7.1)	50 (7.1)	8 (3.5)	1 (†)	66 (7.2)	34 (†)	1 (†)	# (†)
Parents' highest level of education												
Not high school graduate	— (†)	— (†)	— (†)	— (†)	59 (3.3)	41 (3.3)	3 (1.8)	# (†)	80 (2.1)	20 (2.1)	2 (0.7)	# (†)
Graduated high school	— (†)	— (†)	— (†)	— (†)	48 (1.7)	52 (1.7)	7 (1.0)	# (†)	74 (1.3)	26 (1.3)	4 (0.8)	# (0.1)
Some college	— (†)	— (†)	— (†)	— (†)	30 (1.3)	70 (1.3)	14 (1.3)	1 (0.3)	61 (1.3)	39 (1.3)	8 (0.7)	1 (0.2)
Graduated college	— (†)	— (†)	— (†)	— (†)	22 (1.0)	78 (1.0)	27 (1.1)	3 (0.5)	42 (1.5)	58 (1.5)	18 (1.5)	2 (0.8)
Free/reduced-price lunch eligibility												
Eligible	53 (1.7)	47 (1.7)	6 (0.8)	1 (0.2)	59 (1.4)	41 (1.4)	6 (0.7)	# (0.2)	77 (1.8)	23 (1.8)	3 (0.7)	# (†)
Not eligible	21 (1.7)	79 (1.7)	25 (1.6)	3 (0.8)	27 (1.2)	73 (1.2)	20 (1.2)	2 (0.3)	55 (1.5)	45 (1.5)	11 (1.1)	1 (0.6)
Not available	25 (2.8)	75 (2.8)	24 (2.9)	3 (1.1)	30 (2.4)	70 (2.4)	22 (2.1)	3 (0.6)	47 (2.9)	53 (2.9)	17 (2.3)	2 (0.6)
Region												
Northeast	27 (3.1)	73 (3.1)	23 (2.9)	3 (1.1)	28 (2.2)	72 (2.2)	22 (2.1)	2 (0.8)	55 (3.8)	45 (3.8)	13 (3.2)	2 (†)
Southeast	34 (2.7)	66 (2.7)	16 (2.2)	2 (1.2)	38 (2.3)	62 (2.3)	16 (1.3)	2 (0.4)	61 (2.3)	39 (2.3)	10 (1.3)	1 (0.3)
Central	25 (2.3)	75 (2.3)	24 (2.4)	3 (1.1)	29 (2.2)	71 (2.2)	19 (1.5)	2 (0.5)	54 (2.2)	46 (2.2)	11 (1.3)	1 (0.4)
West	41 (2.5)	59 (2.5)	13 (1.2)	1 (0.4)	45 (1.7)	55 (1.7)	12 (1.3)	1 (0.2)	58 (2.2)	42 (2.2)	11 (1.5)	1 (0.4)

—Not available
†Not applicable.
#Rounds to zero.

NOTE: Includes public and private schools. Excludes persons unable to be tested due to limited proficiency in English or due to a disability (and the accommodations provided were not sufficient to enable the test to properly reflect the students' history proficiency). Detail may not sum to totals because of rounding. Standard errors appear in parentheses.
SOURCE: U.S. Department of Education, National Center for Education Statistics, National Assessment of Educational Progress (NAEP), *The Nation's Report Card: U.S. History 2001.* (This table was prepared May 2002.)

Percentage of students at or above selected geography proficiency levels, by grade level and selected student characteristics: 2001

Selected student characteristic	Percentage of 4th-graders				Percentage of 8th-graders				Percentage of 12th-graders			
	Below basic	At or above basic	At or above proficient	At advanced	Below basic	At or above basic	At or above proficient	At advanced	Below basic	At or above basic	At or above proficient	At advanced
1	2	3	4	5	6	7	8	9	10	11	12	13
All students	**26** (1.2)	**74** (1.2)	**21** (1.0)	**2** (0.3)	**26** (0.9)	**74** (0.9)	**30** (1.2)	**4** (0.6)	**29** (0.9)	**71** (0.9)	**25** (1.1)	**1** (0.3)
Sex												
Male	25 (1.3)	75 (1.3)	24 (1.4)	3 (0.5)	25 (1.0)	75 (1.0)	33 (1.5)	5 (0.7)	27 (1.1)	73 (1.1)	28 (1.5)	2 (0.4)
Female	28 (1.6)	72 (1.6)	18 (1.1)	1 (0.4)	27 (1.2)	73 (1.2)	26 (1.4)	3 (0.6)	30 (1.0)	70 (1.0)	21 (1.0)	1 (0.3)
Race/ethnicity												
White, non-Hispanic	13 (1.3)	87 (1.3)	29 (1.5)	3 (0.5)	14 (0.9)	86 (0.9)	39 (1.7)	5 (0.8)	19 (0.9)	81 (0.9)	31 (1.4)	2 (0.4)
Black, non-Hispanic	56 (2.1)	44 (2.1)	5 (0.9)	# (†)	60 (2.3)	40 (2.3)	6 (0.8)	# (†)	65 (2.3)	35 (2.3)	4 (0.7)	# (†)
Hispanic	51 (3.0)	49 (3.0)	6 (1.0)	# (†)	52 (1.9)	48 (1.9)	10 (1.0)	1 (0.2)	48 (2.6)	52 (2.6)	10 (1.4)	# (0.1)
Asian/Pacific Islander	23 (3.4)	77 (3.4)	25 (3.0)	1 (0.9)	21 (3.4)	79 (3.4)	32 (3.2)	4 (1.8)	28 (4.3)	72 (4.3)	26 (4.7)	1 (0.7)
Free/reduced-price lunch eligibility												
Eligible	49 (2.2)	51 (2.2)	6 (0.9)	# (†)	50 (1.8)	50 (1.8)	11 (1.2)	1 (0.3)	49 (2.3)	51 (2.3)	11 (1.6)	# (†)
Not eligible	14 (1.1)	86 (1.1)	29 (1.5)	3 (0.6)	17 (0.9)	83 (0.9)	37 (1.7)	5 (0.8)	25 (1.2)	75 (1.2)	26 (1.6)	1 (0.4)
Not available	16 (2.5)	84 (2.5)	27 (3.2)	3 (0.8)	21 (2.1)	79 (2.1)	33 (2.5)	4 (0.9)	24 (2.0)	76 (2.0)	31 (2.1)	2 (0.4)
Region												
Northeast	22 (3.7)	78 (3.7)	24 (2.2)	3 (0.9)	22 (2.5)	78 (2.5)	34 (3.3)	4 (1.3)	29 (2.3)	71 (2.3)	26 (4.1)	2 (1.1)
Southeast	28 (2.5)	72 (2.5)	18 (1.9)	1 (0.6)	27 (2.4)	73 (2.4)	26 (1.6)	3 (0.6)	33 (1.6)	67 (1.6)	21 (1.3)	1 (0.3)
Central	18 (1.7)	82 (1.7)	30 (2.5)	3 (0.7)	18 (2.3)	82 (2.3)	38 (3.7)	6 (1.3)	24 (1.8)	76 (1.8)	28 (1.9)	1 (0.5)
West	34 (2.7)	66 (2.7)	14 (1.7)	1 (0.3)	34 (1.7)	66 (1.7)	23 (1.7)	2 (0.6)	30 (1.9)	70 (1.9)	23 (1.8)	1 (0.4)

†Not applicable.
#Rounds to zero.
NOTE: Includes public and private schools. Excludes students unable to be tested due to limited proficiency in English or due to a disability (and the accommodations provided were not sufficient to enable the test to properly reflect the students' proficiency in geography). Totals include other racial/ethnic groups not shown separately. Detail may not sum to totals because of rounding. Standard errors appear in parentheses.

SOURCE: U.S. Department of Education, National Center for Education Statistics, National Assessment of Educational Progress (NAEP), *The Nation's Report Card: Geography 2001*. (This table was prepared July 2002.)

SAT score averages of college-bound seniors, by race/ethnicity: Selected years, 1986–87 through 2004–05

Race/ethnicity	1986–87	1990–91	1995–96	1996–97	1999–2000	2000–01	2001–02	2002–03	2003–04	2004–05	Score change 1986–87 to 1996–97	Score change 1990–91 to 2000–01	Score change 1999–2000 to 2000–01	Score change 2000–01 to 2001–02	Score change 2001–02 to 2002–03	Score change 2002–03 to 2003–04	Score change 2003–04 to 2004–05
1	2	3	4	5	6	7	8	9	10	11	12	13	14	15	16	17	18
SAT-Verbal																	
All students	507	499	505	505	505	506	504	507	508	508	-2	7	1	-2	3	1	0
White	524	518	526	526	528	529	527	529	528	532	2	11	1	-2	2	-1	4
Black	428	427	434	434	434	433	430	431	430	433	6	6	-1	-3	1	-1	3
Hispanic or Latino	464	458	465	466	461	460	458	457	461	463	2	2	-1	-2	-1	4	2
Mexican American	457	454	455	451	453	451	446	448	451	453	-6	-3	-2	-5	2	3	2
Puerto Rican	436	436	452	454	456	457	455	456	457	460	18	21	1	-2	1	1	3
Asian American	479	485	496	496	499	501	501	508	507	511	17	16	2	0	7	-1	4
American Indian	471	470	483	475	482	481	479	480	483	489	4	11	-1	-2	1	3	6
Other	480	486	511	512	508	503	502	501	494	495	32	17	-5	-1	-1	-7	1
SAT-Mathematics																	
All students	501	500	508	511	514	514	516	519	518	520	10	14	0	2	3	-1	2
White	514	513	523	526	530	531	533	534	531	536	12	18	1	2	1	-3	5
Black	411	419	422	423	426	426	427	426	427	431	12	7	0	1	-1	1	4
Hispanic or Latino	462	462	466	468	467	465	464	464	465	469	6	3	-2	-1	0	1	4
Mexican American	455	459	459	458	460	458	457	457	458	463	3	-1	-2	-1	0	1	5
Puerto Rican	432	439	445	447	451	451	451	453	452	457	15	12	0	0	2	-1	5
Asian American	541	548	558	560	565	566	569	575	577	580	19	18	1	3	6	2	3
American Indian	463	468	477	475	481	479	483	482	488	493	12	11	-2	4	-1	6	5
Other	482	492	512	514	515	512	514	513	508	513	32	20	-3	2	-1	-5	5

NOTE: Data are for seniors who took the SAT any time during their high school years through March of their senior year. If a student took a test more than once, the most recent score was used. The SAT was formerly known as the Scholastic Assessment Test and the Scholastic Aptitude Test. Possible scores on each part of the SAT range from 200 to 800.

SOURCE: College Entrance Examination Board, *National Report on College-Bound Seniors*, selected years 1986–87 through 2004–05. (This table was prepared August 2005.)

SAT score averages of college-bound seniors, by sex: 1966–67 through 2004–05

School year	SAT[1]						Scholastic Aptitude Test (old scale)					
	Verbal score			Mathematics score			Verbal score			Mathematics score		
	Total	Male	Female	Total	Male	Female	Total	Male	Female	Total	Male	Female
1	2	3	4	5	6	7	8	9	10	11	12	13
1966–67	543	540	545	516	535	495	466	463	468	492	514	467
1967–68	543	541	543	516	533	497	466	464	466	492	512	470
1968–69	540	536	543	517	534	498	463	459	466	493	513	470
1969–70	537	536	538	512	531	493	460	459	461	488	509	465
1970–71	532	531	534	513	529	494	455	454	457	488	507	466
1971–72	530	531	529	509	527	489	453	454	452	484	505	461
1972–73	523	523	521	506	525	489	445	446	443	481	502	460
1973–74	521	524	520	505	524	488	444	447	442	480	501	459
1974–75	512	515	509	498	518	479	434	437	431	472	495	449
1975–76	509	511	508	497	520	475	431	433	430	472	497	446
1976–77	507	509	505	496	520	474	429	431	427	470	497	445
1977–78	507	511	503	494	517	474	429	433	425	468	494	444
1978–79	505	509	501	493	516	473	427	431	423	467	493	443
1979–80	502	506	498	492	515	473	424	428	420	466	491	443
1980–81	502	508	496	492	516	473	424	430	418	466	492	443
1981–82	504	509	499	493	516	473	426	431	421	467	493	443
1982–83	503	508	498	494	516	474	425	430	420	468	493	445
1983–84	504	511	498	497	518	478	426	433	420	471	495	449
1984–85	509	514	503	500	522	480	431	437	425	475	499	452
1985–86	509	515	504	500	523	479	431	437	426	475	501	451
1986–87	507	512	502	501	523	481	430	435	425	476	500	453
1987–88	505	512	499	501	521	483	428	435	422	476	498	455
1988–89	504	510	498	502	523	482	427	434	421	476	500	454
1989–90	500	505	496	501	521	483	424	429	419	476	499	455
1990–91	499	503	495	500	520	482	422	426	418	474	497	453
1991–92	500	504	496	501	521	484	423	428	419	476	499	456
1992–93	500	504	497	503	524	484	424	428	420	478	502	457
1993–94	499	501	497	504	523	487	423	425	421	479	501	460
1994–95	504	505	502	506	525	490	428	429	426	482	503	463
1995–96	505	507	503	508	527	492	—	—	—	—	—	—
1996–97	505	507	503	511	530	494	—	—	—	—	—	—
1997–98	505	509	502	512	531	496	—	—	—	—	—	—
1998–99	505	509	502	511	531	495	—	—	—	—	—	—
1999–2000	505	507	504	514	533	498	—	—	—	—	—	—
2000–01	506	509	502	514	533	498	—	—	—	—	—	—
2001–02	504	507	502	516	534	500	—	—	—	—	—	—
2002–03	507	512	503	519	537	503	—	—	—	—	—	—
2003–04	508	512	504	518	537	501	—	—	—	—	—	—
2004–05	508	513	505	520	538	504	—	—	—	—	—	—

—Not available.

[1] Formerly known as the Scholastic Assessment Test. Data for 1967 to 1986 were converted to the recentered scale by using a formula applied to the original mean and standard deviation. For 1987 to 1995, individual student scores were converted to the recentered scale and recomputed. For 1996 to 2003, most students received scores on the recentered scale score. Any score on the original scale was converted to the recentered scale prior to recomputing the mean.

NOTE: Data for the years 1966–67 through 1970–71 are estimates derived from the test scores of all participants. Data for 1971–72 and later are for seniors who took the SAT test any time during their high school years through March of their senior year. If a student took a test more than once, the most recent score was used. The SAT was formerly known as the Scholastic Assessment Test and the Scholastic Aptitude Test. Possible scores on each part of the SAT range from 200 to 800.
SOURCE: College Entrance Examination Board, *National Report on College-Bound Seniors*, selected years, 1966–67 through 2004–05. (This table was prepared August 2005.)

SAT score averages of college-bound seniors, by selected student characteristics: Selected years, 1995-96 through 2004-05

Selected student characteristic	1995-96			1997-98[1]		1999-2000			2002-03[1]		2003-04			2004-05[1]	
	Verbal score	Mathematics score	Percentage distribution	Verbal score	Mathematics score	Verbal score	Mathematics score	Percentage distribution	Verbal score	Mathematics score	Verbal score	Mathematics score	Percentage distribution	Verbal score	Mathematics score
1	2	3	4	5	6	7	8	9	10	11	12	13	14	15	16
All students	505	508	100	505	512	505	514	100	507	519	508	518	100	508	520
High school rank															
Top decile	591	606	22	590	607	589	608	‡	585	607	584	602	29	585	606
Second decile	530	539	22	530	543	528	543	‡	522	539	522	537	24	523	540
Second quintile	494	496	28	494	500	493	500	‡	486	494	486	494	22	488	499
Third quintile	455	448	24	454	453	455	453	‡	449	449	449	451	20	452	455
Fourth quintile	429	418	4	427	421	425	419	‡	420	417	422	421	4	425	424
Fifth quintile	411	401	1	408	403	408	401	‡	410	410	415	418	1	426	430
High school grade point average															
A+ (97-100)	617	632	6	613	629	610	628	7	607	625	606	620	6	607	625
A (93-96)	573	583	14	569	582	567	582	16	566	583	567	580	18	570	585
A- (90-92)	545	554	15	542	554	540	553	17	538	552	537	549	17	541	555
B (80-89)	486	485	49	483	487	482	486	47	480	485	480	486	47	484	491
C (70-79)	432	426	15	430	428	428	426	12	425	424	429	431	11	430	432
D, E, or F (below 70)	414	408	#	408	411	405	406	#	416	430	421	446	#	415	439
Intended college major															
Agriculture/natural resources	491	484	2	491	487	490	486	1	484	482	484	483	1	487	486
Architecture/environmental design	492	519	3	494	524	494	524	2	483	511	479	510	2	495	527
Arts: visual/performing	520	497	6	520	502	518	502	8	514	500	517	501	8	521	506
Biological sciences	546	545	6	545	546	544	548	5	543	553	544	552	6	547	558
Business and commerce	483	500	13	484	505	487	510	14	489	512	486	509	13	491	515
Communications	527	497	4	523	501	526	505	4	524	506	525	505	4	527	509
Computer or information sciences	497	522	3	500	529	499	533	6	503	535	504	532	5	508	535
Education	487	477	8	483	480	483	481	9	482	483	483	482	8	486	488
Engineering	525	569	8	525	571	523	573	8	525	574	525	573	9	529	579
Foreign/classical languages	556	534	#	552	538	558	539	1	564	545	570	545	1	575	551
General/interdisciplinary	576	553	#	568	549	562	545	#	547	539	547	545	1	546	535
Health and allied services	500	505	19	497	505	497	505	16	489	498	487	495	17	490	501
Home economics	458	452	#	458	459	462	462	#	462	462	460	461	#	463	466
Language and literature	605	545	1	605	549	608	552	1	603	550	603	547	2	606	552
Library and archival sciences	554	512	#	547	525	556	511	#	572	512	567	515	#	577	511
Mathematics	552	628	1	552	629	551	630	1	545	626	541	621	1	545	626
Military sciences	503	505	#	504	507	505	512	#	513	516	516	520	1	522	526
Philosophy/religion/theology	560	536	1	558	538	560	539	1	562	544	560	539	1	561	542
Physical sciences	575	595	1	571	592	569	592	1	563	588	564	587	2	565	591
Public affairs and services	458	448	3	459	453	459	454	3	462	458	464	459	3	465	463
Social sciences and history	532	509	11	531	512	532	513	11	531	514	534	515	10	540	522
Technical and vocational	435	441	1	440	448	442	452	1	441	450	443	453	1	445	456
Undecided	500	507	7	510	520	512	521	7	516	528	514	526	6	517	530
Degree-level goal															
Certificate program	434	439	1	436	447	439	453	1	441	456	441	456	1	445	463
Associate's degree	422	415	2	421	419	420	419	2	417	416	417	417	1	420	421
Bachelor's degree	476	476	23	475	480	478	483	25	475	481	474	479	24	481	487
Master's degree	514	518	29	513	523	515	526	31	513	524	511	520	29	516	526
Doctor's or related degree	548	552	24	548	554	547	554	22	542	552	540	547	21	542	552
Other	430	438	1	435	446	442	454	1	441	453	439	457	1	442	464
Undecided	502	503	20	505	510	508	514	19	514	523	513	521	23	517	527

See notes at end of table.

SAT score averages of college-bound seniors, by selected student characteristics: Selected years, 1995–96 through 2004–05—Continued

Selected student characteristic	1995–96			1997–98[1]		1999–2000			2002–03[1]		2003–04			2004–05[1]	
	Verbal score	Mathematics score	Percentage distribution	Verbal score	Mathematics score	Verbal score	Mathematics score	Percentage distribution	Verbal score	Mathematics score	Verbal score	Mathematics score	Percentage distribution	Verbal score	Mathematics score
1	2	3	4	5	6	7	8	9	10	11	12	13	14	15	16
Family income															
Less than $10,000	429	444	4	427	446	425	447	‡	420	444	422	450	5	426	458
$10,000, but less than $20,000	456	464	8	451	463	447	460	‡	437	452	440	457	8	443	463
$20,000, but less than $30,000	482	482	10	477	482	471	478	‡	460	467	459	467	10	463	474
$30,000, but less than $40,000	497	495	12	495	497	490	493	‡	480	484	478	482	11	480	487
$40,000, but less than $50,000	509	507	10	506	509	503	505	‡	495	498	493	496	9	496	500
$50,000, but less than $60,000	517	517	9	514	518	511	515	‡	504	508	501	504	9	505	509
$60,000, but less than $70,000	524	525	7	521	525	517	522	‡	511	514	507	510	8	511	515
$70,000, but less than $80,000	531	533	6	527	532	524	530	‡	518	523	515	518	8	517	522
$80,000 to $100,000	541	544	7	539	546	536	543	‡	529	536	527	530	12	529	534
More than $100,000	560	569	9	559	572	558	571	‡	555	568	553	562	20	554	565
Highest level of parental education															
No high school diploma	414	439	4	411	441	413	442	4	413	443	415	445	5	419	452
High school diploma	475	474	31	473	477	472	477	33	470	475	469	474	33	471	479
Associate's degree	489	487	7	489	491	488	491	9	487	491	486	490	9	489	494
Bachelor's degree	525	529	25	525	532	525	533	29	525	534	523	531	28	527	536
Graduate degree	556	558	23	556	563	558	566	25	559	569	558	564	25	561	570

#Rounds to zero.
‡Reporting standards not met.
[1]Percentage distribution not reported since this year had less than 80 percent combined unit and item response rate.
NOTE: Data are for seniors who took the SAT test any time during their high school years through March of their senior year. If a student took a test more than once, the most recent score was used. The SAT was formerly known as the Scholastic

Assessment Test and the Scholastic Aptitude Test. Possible scores on each part of the SAT range from 200 to 800. Detail may not sum to totals because of rounding and survey item nonresponse.
SOURCE: College Entrance Examination Board, *National Report on College-Bound Seniors*, selected years 1995–96 through 2004–05. (This table was prepared August 2005.)

SAT score averages of college-bound seniors, by state or jurisdiction: Selected years, 1987–88 through 2004–05

State or jurisdiction	1987–88 Verbal	1987–88 Mathematics	1995–96 Verbal	1995–96 Mathematics	2000–01 Verbal	2000–01 Mathematics	2001–02 Verbal	2001–02 Mathematics	2002–03 Verbal	2002–03 Mathematics	2003–04 Verbal	2003–04 Mathematics	2004–05 Verbal	2004–05 Mathematics	Percent of graduates taking SAT, 2003–04	Percent of graduates taking SAT, 2004–05
1	2	3	4	5	6	7	8	9	10	11	12	13	14	15	16	17
United States	**505**	**501**	**505**	**508**	**506**	**514**	**504**	**516**	**507**	**519**	**508**	**518**	**508**	**520**	**48**	**49**
Alabama	554	540	565	558	559	554	560	559	559	552	560	553	567	559	10	10
Alaska	518	501	521	513	514	510	516	519	518	518	518	514	523	519	53	52
Arizona	531	523	525	521	523	525	520	523	524	525	523	524	526	530	32	33
Arkansas	554	536	566	550	562	550	560	556	564	554	569	555	563	552	6	6
California	500	508	495	511	498	517	496	517	499	519	501	519	504	522	49	50
Colorado	537	532	536	538	539	542	543	548	551	553	554	553	560	560	27	26
Connecticut	513	498	507	504	509	510	509	509	512	514	515	515	517	517	85	86
Delaware	510	493	508	495	501	499	502	500	501	501	500	499	503	502	73	74
District of Columbia	479	461	489	473	482	474	480	473	484	474	489	476	490	478	77	79
Florida	499	495	498	496	498	499	496	499	498	498	499	499	498	498	67	65
Georgia	480	473	484	477	491	489	489	491	493	491	494	493	497	496	73	75
Hawaii	484	505	485	510	486	515	488	520	486	516	487	514	490	516	60	61
Idaho	543	523	543	536	543	542	539	541	540	540	540	539	544	542	20	21
Illinois	540	540	564	575	576	589	578	596	583	596	585	597	594	606	10	10
Indiana	490	486	494	494	499	501	498	503	500	504	501	506	504	508	64	66
Iowa	587	588	590	600	593	603	591	602	586	597	593	602	596	608	5	5
Kansas	568	557	579	571	577	580	578	580	578	582	584	585	585	588	9	9
Kentucky	551	535	549	544	550	550	550	552	554	552	559	557	561	559	12	12
Louisiana	551	533	559	550	564	562	561	559	563	559	564	561	565	562	8	8
Maine	508	493	504	498	506	500	503	502	503	501	505	501	509	505	76	75
Maryland	509	501	507	504	508	510	507	513	509	515	511	515	511	515	68	71
Massachusetts	508	499	507	504	511	515	512	516	516	522	518	523	520	527	85	86
Michigan	532	533	557	565	561	572	558	572	564	576	563	573	568	579	11	10
Minnesota	546	549	582	593	580	589	581	591	582	591	587	593	592	597	10	11
Mississippi	557	539	569	557	566	551	559	547	565	551	562	547	564	554	5	4
Missouri	547	539	570	569	577	577	574	580	582	583	587	585	588	588	8	7
Montana	547	547	546	547	539	539	541	547	538	543	537	539	540	540	29	31
Nebraska	562	561	567	568	562	568	561	570	573	578	569	576	574	579	8	8
Nevada	517	510	508	507	509	515	509	518	510	517	507	514	508	513	40	39
New Hampshire	523	511	520	514	520	516	519	519	522	521	522	521	525	525	80	81
New Jersey	500	495	498	505	499	513	498	513	501	515	501	514	503	517	83	86
New Mexico	553	543	554	548	551	542	551	543	548	540	554	543	558	547	14	13
New York	497	495	497	499	495	505	494	506	496	510	497	510	497	511	87	92
North Carolina	478	470	490	486	493	499	493	505	495	506	499	507	499	511	70	74
North Dakota	572	569	596	599	592	599	597	610	602	613	582	601	590	605	5	4
Ohio	529	521	536	535	534	539	533	540	536	541	538	542	539	543	28	29
Oklahoma	558	542	566	557	567	561	565	562	569	562	569	566	570	563	7	7
Oregon	517	507	523	521	526	526	524	528	526	527	527	528	526	528	56	59
Pennsylvania	502	489	498	492	500	499	498	500	500	502	501	502	501	503	74	75
Rhode Island	508	496	501	491	501	499	504	503	502	504	503	502	503	505	72	72
South Carolina	477	468	480	474	486	488	488	493	493	496	491	495	494	499	62	64
South Dakota	585	573	574	566	577	582	576	586	588	588	594	597	589	589	5	5
Tennessee	560	543	563	552	562	553	562	555	568	560	567	557	572	563	16	16
Texas	494	490	495	500	493	499	491	500	493	500	493	499	493	502	52	54
Utah	572	553	583	575	575	570	563	559	566	559	565	556	566	557	7	7
Vermont	514	499	506	500	511	506	512	510	515	512	516	512	521	517	66	67
Virginia	507	498	507	496	510	501	510	506	514	510	515	509	516	514	71	73
Washington	525	517	519	519	527	527	525	529	530	532	528	531	532	534	52	55
West Virginia	528	519	526	506	527	512	525	515	522	510	524	514	523	511	19	20
Wisconsin	549	551	577	586	584	596	583	599	585	594	587	596	592	599	7	6
Wyoming	550	545	544	544	547	545	531	537	548	549	551	546	544	543	12	12

NOTE: Data are for seniors who took the SAT test any time during their high school years through March of their senior year. If a student took a test more than once, the most recent score was used. The SAT was formerly known as the Scholastic Assessment Test and the Scholastic Aptitude Test. Possible scores on each part of the SAT range from 200 to 800.

SOURCE: College Entrance Examination Board, *College-Bound Seniors: 2005 Profile of SAT Program Test Takers*. (This table was prepared August 2005.)

ACT score averages and standard deviations, by selected characteristics, sex, and race/ethnicity: Selected years, 1995 through 2004

Selected characteristic	Number									Standard deviation							
	1995	1997	1998	1999	2000	2001	2002	2003	2004	1997	1998	1999	2000	2001	2002	2003	2004
1	2	3	4	5	6	7	8	9	10	11	12	13	14	15	16	17	18
Total test takers (in thousands)	**945**	**959**	**995**	**1,019**	**1,065**	**1,070**	**1,116**	**1,175**	**1,171**	†	†	†	†	†	†	†	†
Average test score[1]																	
Composite, total	20.8	21.0	21.0	21.0	21.0	21.0	20.8	20.8	20.9	4.7	4.7	4.7	4.7	4.7	4.8	4.8	4.8
Male	21.0	21.1	21.2	21.1	21.2	21.1	20.9	21.0	21.0	4.9	4.9	4.9	4.9	4.9	5.0	5.0	5.0
Female	20.7	20.8	20.9	20.9	20.9	20.9	20.7	20.8	20.9	4.6	4.6	4.6	4.6	4.6	4.7	4.7	4.7
Race/ethnicity																	
White, non-Hispanic	—	22.8	22.7	22.7	22.7	21.8	22.6	21.7	21.8	—	—	—	—	—	—	—	—
Black, non-Hispanic	—	17.9	17.9	17.9	17.8	16.9	17.6	16.9	17.1	—	—	—	—	—	—	—	—
Mexican American/ Chicano	—	19.9	19.6	19.6	19.5	18.5	19.0	18.3	18.4	—	—	—	—	—	—	—	—
Puerto Rican/Hispanic	—	20.1	20.7	20.7	20.5	19.4	20.0	19.0	18.8	—	—	—	—	—	—	—	—
Asian American or Pacific Islander	—	22.5	22.6	22.3	22.4	21.7	22.3	21.8	21.9	—	—	—	—	—	—	—	—
American Indian/Alaska Native	—	20.4	20.4	20.4	20.4	18.8	20.1	18.7	18.8	—	—	—	—	—	—	—	—
English, total	20.2	20.3	20.4	20.5	20.5	20.5	20.2	20.3	20.4	5.4	5.4	5.5	5.5	5.6	5.8	5.8	5.9
Male	19.8	19.9	19.9	20.0	20.0	20.0	19.7	19.8	19.9	5.4	5.4	5.5	5.6	5.6	5.8	5.8	5.9
Female	20.6	20.7	20.8	20.9	20.9	20.8	20.6	20.7	20.8	5.4	5.4	5.5	5.5	5.6	5.7	5.8	5.8
Mathematics, total	20.2	20.6	20.8	20.7	20.7	20.7	20.6	20.6	20.7	5.0	5.1	5.0	5.0	5.0	5.0	5.1	5.0
Male	20.9	21.3	21.5	21.4	21.4	21.4	21.2	21.2	21.3	5.2	5.3	5.2	5.2	5.2	5.3	4.8	5.3
Female	19.7	20.1	20.2	20.2	20.2	20.2	20.1	20.1	20.2	4.7	4.8	4.7	4.8	4.7	4.8	5.3	4.8
Reading, total	21.3	21.3	21.4	21.4	21.4	21.3	21.1	21.2	21.3	6.1	6.0	6.0	6.1	6.0	6.1	6.1	6.0
Male	21.1	21.2	21.1	21.1	21.2	21.1	20.9	21.0	21.1	6.1	6.2	6.1	6.1	6.1	6.3	5.3	6.1
Female	21.4	21.5	21.6	21.6	21.5	21.5	21.3	21.4	21.5	6.0	5.9	5.9	6.0	6.0	6.1	4.8	5.9
Science reasoning, total	21.0	21.1	21.1	21.0	21.0	21.0	20.8	20.8	20.9	4.7	4.6	4.5	4.5	4.6	4.6	4.6	4.6
Male	21.6	21.7	21.8	21.5	21.6	21.6	21.3	21.3	21.3	4.9	4.9	4.8	4.8	4.9	4.9	4.9	4.9
Female	20.5	20.6	20.6	20.6	20.6	20.6	20.4	20.4	20.5	4.4	4.3	4.2	4.3	4.3	4.3	4.3	4.3
Percent																	
Obtaining composite scores of—																	
28 or above	—	10	10	10	10	10	10	10	10	†	†	†	†	†	†	†	†
17 or below	—	26	25	25	25	25	27	27	26	†	†	†	†	†	†	†	†
Planned major field of study																	
Business[2]	13	12	12	12	11	11	10	10	9	†	†	†	†	†	†	†	†
Engineering[3]	8	8	8	8	8	7	7	7	6	†	†	†	†	†	†	†	†
Social science[4]	9	9	9	9	9	9	8	8	7	†	†	†	†	†	†	†	†
Education[5]	8	9	9	9	9	8	8	7	7	†	†	†	†	†	†	†	†

—Not available.

†Not applicable.

[1]Minimum score, 1; maximum score, 36.

[2]Includes business and management, business and office, and marketing and distribution.

[3]Includes engineering and engineering-related technologies.

[4]Includes social science and philosophy, religion, and theology.

[5]Includes education and teacher education.

SOURCE: The American College Testing program, *High School Profile Report*, selected years 1995 through 2004. (This table was prepared April 2005.)

Enrollment in public elementary and secondary schools, by state or jurisdiction: Selected years, 1990 through 2005

State or jurisdiction	Total										Fall 2001			Fall 2002			Fall 2003			Projected 2004 enrollment	Projected 2005 enrollment
	Fall 1990	Fall 1992	Fall 1993	Fall 1994	Fall 1995	Fall 1996	Fall 1997	Fall 1998	Fall 1999	Fall 2000	Total	Prekindergarten to grade 8[1]	Grades 9 to 12[2]	Total	Prekindergarten to grade 8[1]	Grades 9 to 12[2]	Total	Prekindergarten to grade 8[1]	Grades 9 to 12[2]		
1	2	3	4	5	6	7	8	9	10	11	12	13	14	15	16	17	18	19	20	21	22
United States	41,216,683	42,823,312	43,464,916	44,111,482	44,840,481	45,611,046	46,126,897	46,538,585	46,857,149	47,203,539	47,671,877	33,937,653	13,734,224	48,183,086	34,115,888	14,067,198	48,540,725	34,202,239	14,338,486	48,270,100	48,375,400
Alabama	721,806	731,634	734,288	736,531	746,149	747,932	749,207	747,980	740,732	739,992	737,190	535,580	201,610	739,366	533,207	206,159	731,220	525,313	205,907	729,100	725,000
Alaska	113,903	122,487	125,948	127,057	127,618	129,919	132,123	135,373	134,391	133,356	134,358	94,897	39,461	134,364	94,380	39,984	133,933	93,695	40,238	133,300	133,200
Arizona	639,853	673,477	709,453	737,424	743,566	799,250	814,113	848,262	852,612	877,696	922,180	671,658	250,522	937,755	660,363	277,392	1,012,068	704,327	307,741	957,300	967,300
Arkansas	436,286	441,490	444,271	447,565	453,257	457,349	456,497	452,256	451,034	449,959	449,805	317,925	131,880	450,985	318,828	132,157	454,523	321,509	133,014	448,000	447,500
California	4,950,474	5,254,844	5,327,231	5,407,475	5,536,406	5,686,198	5,803,887	5,926,037	6,038,590	6,140,814	6,247,726	4,479,063	1,768,663	6,353,667	4,526,030	1,827,637	6,413,862	4,540,362	1,873,500	6,456,300	6,518,000
Colorado	574,213	612,635	625,062	640,521	656,279	673,438	687,167	699,135	708,109	724,508	742,145	529,156	212,989	751,862	534,465	217,397	757,693	536,325	221,368	761,700	768,600
Connecticut	469,123	488,476	496,298	506,824	517,935	527,129	535,164	544,698	553,993	562,179	570,228	410,017	160,211	570,023	405,998	164,025	577,203	407,794	169,409	568,900	567,300
Delaware	99,658	104,321	105,547	106,813	108,461	110,549	111,960	113,262	112,836	114,676	115,560	81,303	34,257	116,342	82,221	34,121	117,668	82,898	34,770	116,200	116,400
District of Columbia	80,694	80,937	80,678	80,450	79,802	78,648	77,111	71,889	77,194	68,925	75,392	57,951	17,441	76,166	58,794	17,372	78,057	59,482	18,575	74,300	73,900
Florida	1,861,592	1,981,407	2,040,763	2,111,188	2,176,222	2,242,212	2,294,077	2,337,633	2,381,396	2,434,821	2,500,478	1,797,414	703,064	2,539,929	1,809,279	730,650	2,587,628	1,832,376	755,252	2,587,400	2,609,100
Georgia	1,151,687	1,207,186	1,235,304	1,270,948	1,311,126	1,346,761	1,375,980	1,401,291	1,422,762	1,444,937	1,470,634	1,075,195	395,439	1,496,012	1,088,561	407,451	1,522,611	1,103,181	419,430	1,519,500	1,530,700
Hawaii	171,708	177,448	180,410	183,795	187,180	187,653	189,887	188,069	185,860	184,360	184,546	131,881	52,665	183,829	130,862	52,967	183,609	130,054	53,555	182,200	181,700
Idaho	220,840	231,668	236,774	240,448	243,097	245,252	244,403	244,722	245,136	245,117	246,521	171,423	75,098	248,604	173,249	75,355	252,120	175,424	76,696	251,800	254,200
Illinois	1,821,407	1,873,567	1,893,078	1,916,172	1,943,623	1,973,040	1,998,289	2,011,530	2,027,600	2,048,792	2,071,391	1,484,207	587,184	2,084,187	1,487,654	596,533	2,100,961	1,492,730	608,231	2,086,700	2,091,000
Indiana	954,525	960,630	965,633	969,022	977,263	982,876	986,836	989,001	988,702	989,267	996,133	711,471	284,662	1,003,875	714,013	289,862	1,011,130	716,825	294,305	1,011,900	1,015,900
Iowa	483,652	494,839	498,519	500,440	502,343	502,941	501,054	498,214	497,301	495,080	485,932	329,670	156,262	482,210	325,879	156,331	481,226	326,846	154,380	470,500	466,700
Kansas	437,034	451,536	457,614	460,838	463,008	466,293	468,687	472,353	472,188	470,610	470,205	322,426	147,779	470,957	321,886	149,071	470,490	322,575	147,915	461,600	459,400
Kentucky	636,401	655,041	655,265	657,642	659,821	656,089	669,322	655,687	648,180	665,850	654,363	473,499	180,864	660,782	476,758	184,024	663,885	478,258	185,627	645,700	642,500
Louisiana	784,757	797,985	800,560	797,933	797,366	793,296	776,813	768,734	756,579	743,089	731,328	536,951	194,377	730,464	536,881	193,583	727,709	536,390	191,319	713,600	709,100
Maine	215,149	216,453	216,995	212,601	213,569	213,593	212,579	211,051	209,253	207,037	205,586	143,864	61,722	204,337	141,785	62,552	202,084	139,420	62,664	195,800	192,500
Maryland	715,176	751,850	772,638	790,938	805,544	818,583	830,744	841,671	846,582	852,920	860,640	610,907	249,733	866,743	610,384	256,359	869,113	605,905	263,208	864,900	862,600
Massachusetts	834,314	859,948	877,726	893,727	915,007	933,898	949,006	962,317	971,425	975,150	973,139	699,495	273,644	982,989	701,050	281,939	980,459	692,130	288,329	972,200	966,400
Michigan	1,584,431	1,603,610	1,599,377	1,614,784	1,641,456	1,685,714	1,702,717	1,720,287	1,725,639	1,720,626	1,730,669	1,222,763	507,906	1,785,160	1,253,811	531,349	1,757,604	1,229,121	528,483	1,788,800	1,789,700
Minnesota	756,374	793,724	810,233	821,693	835,166	847,204	853,621	856,455	854,034	854,340	851,384	573,028	278,356	846,891	567,701	279,190	842,854	564,049	278,805	827,600	822,600
Mississippi	502,417	506,668	505,907	505,962	506,272	503,967	504,792	502,379	500,716	497,871	493,507	361,648	131,859	492,645	360,287	132,358	493,540	360,913	132,627	486,200	484,000
Missouri	816,558	859,357	866,378	878,541	889,881	900,517	910,613	913,494	914,110	912,744	909,792	642,513	267,279	906,499	634,675	271,824	905,941	632,230	273,711	913,400	911,800
Montana	152,974	160,011	163,009	164,341	165,547	164,627	162,335	159,988	157,556	154,875	151,947	102,721	49,226	149,995	101,177	48,818	148,356	100,160	48,196	144,800	142,900
Nebraska	274,081	282,414	285,097	287,100	289,744	291,967	292,681	291,140	288,261	286,199	285,095	194,653	90,442	285,402	195,113	90,289	285,542	195,417	90,125	280,600	279,800
Nevada	201,316	222,974	235,800	250,747	265,041	282,131	296,621	311,061	325,610	340,706	356,814	262,473	94,341	369,498	270,941	98,557	385,401	280,735	104,666	399,200	410,600
New Hampshire	172,785	181,247	185,360	189,319	194,171	198,308	201,629	204,713	206,783	208,461	206,847	144,489	62,358	207,671	143,618	64,053	207,417	142,033	65,384	203,300	201,100
New Jersey	1,089,646	1,130,560	1,151,307	1,174,206	1,197,381	1,227,832	1,250,276	1,268,996	1,289,256	1,313,405	1,341,656	971,934	369,722	1,367,438	978,762	388,676	1,380,753	978,589	402,164	1,394,000	1,399,800
New Mexico	301,881	315,668	322,292	327,248	329,640	332,632	331,673	328,753	324,495	320,306	320,260	225,036	95,224	320,234	224,497	95,737	323,066	226,032	97,034	317,000	316,400
New York	2,598,337	2,689,686	2,733,813	2,766,208	2,813,230	2,843,131	2,861,823	2,877,143	2,887,776	2,882,188	2,872,132	2,017,342	854,790	2,888,233	2,016,810	871,423	2,864,775	1,978,673	886,102	2,858,500	2,842,800
North Carolina	1,086,871	1,114,083	1,133,231	1,156,767	1,183,090	1,210,108	1,236,083	1,254,821	1,275,925	1,293,638	1,315,363	955,965	359,398	1,335,954	963,967	371,987	1,360,209	974,019	386,190	1,349,200	1,354,500
North Dakota	117,825	118,734	119,127	119,288	119,100	120,123	118,572	114,927	112,751	109,201	106,047	70,454	35,593	104,225	69,089	35,136	102,233	67,870	34,363	99,300	97,600

See notes at end of table.

Enrollment in public elementary and secondary schools, by state or jurisdiction: Selected years, 1990 through 2005—Continued

State or jurisdiction	Fall 1990	Fall 1992	Fall 1993	Fall 1994	Fall 1995	Fall 1996	Fall 1997	Fall 1998	Fall 1999	Fall 2000	Fall 2001 Total	Fall 2001 Prekindergarten to grade 8[1]	Fall 2001 Grades 9 to 12[2]	Fall 2002 Total	Fall 2002 Prekindergarten to grade 8[1]	Fall 2002 Grades 9 to 12[2]	Fall 2003 Total	Fall 2003 Prekindergarten to grade 8[1]	Fall 2003 Grades 9 to 12[2]	Projected 2004 enrollment	Projected 2005 enrollment
1	2	3	4	5	6	7	8	9	10	11	12	13	14	15	16	17	18	19	20	21	22
Ohio	1,771,089	1,795,199	1,807,319	1,814,290	1,836,015	1,844,698	1,847,114	1,842,163	1,836,554	1,835,049	1,830,985	1,286,632	544,353	1,838,285	1,283,795	554,490	1,845,428	1,278,202	567,226	1,812,900	1,804,300
Oklahoma	579,087	597,096	604,076	609,718	616,393	620,695	623,681	628,492	627,032	623,110	622,139	445,997	176,142	624,548	449,039	175,509	626,160	450,319	175,841	610,600	608,500
Oregon	472,394	510,122	516,611	521,945	527,914	537,854	541,346	542,809	545,033	546,231	551,480	381,695	169,785	554,071	382,005	172,066	551,273	378,072	173,201	554,200	555,700
Pennsylvania	1,667,834	1,717,613	1,744,082	1,764,946	1,787,533	1,804,256	1,815,151	1,816,414	1,816,716	1,814,311	1,821,627	1,254,692	566,935	1,816,747	1,241,636	575,111	1,821,146	1,235,624	585,522	1,798,600	1,785,000
Rhode Island	138,813	143,798	145,676	147,487	149,799	151,324	153,321	154,785	156,454	157,347	158,046	112,783	45,263	159,205	112,544	46,661	159,375	111,209	48,166	160,100	159,600
South Carolina	622,112	640,464	643,696	648,725	645,586	652,816	659,273	664,600	666,780	677,411	676,198	486,723	189,475	694,389	500,427	193,962	699,198	500,743	198,455	688,000	688,800
South Dakota	129,164	134,573	142,825	143,482	144,685	143,331	142,443	132,495	131,037	128,603	127,542	86,982	40,560	130,048	89,450	40,598	125,537	86,015	39,522	123,900	122,700
Tennessee	824,595	855,231	866,557	881,425	893,770	904,818	893,044	905,454	916,202	909,161	924,899	674,507	250,392	927,608	673,337	254,271	936,681	675,276	261,405	923,500	923,900
Texas	3,382,887	3,541,769	3,608,262	3,677,171	3,748,167	3,828,975	3,891,877	3,945,367	3,991,783	4,059,619	4,163,447	3,016,214	1,147,233	4,259,823	3,079,665	1,180,158	4,331,751	3,132,584	1,199,167	4,317,600	4,365,200
Utah	446,652	463,870	471,365	474,675	477,121	481,812	482,957	481,176	480,255	481,485	484,677	338,016	146,661	489,262	342,655	146,607	495,981	348,890	147,091	492,700	498,200
Vermont	95,762	98,558	102,755	104,533	105,565	106,341	105,984	105,120	104,559	102,049	101,179	69,299	31,880	99,978	68,034	31,944	99,103	66,732	32,371	95,600	93,700
Virginia	998,601	1,031,925	1,045,471	1,060,809	1,079,854	1,096,093	1,110,815	1,124,022	1,133,994	1,144,915	1,163,091	826,184	336,907	1,177,229	831,504	345,725	1,192,092	837,258	354,834	1,189,900	1,193,200
Washington	839,709	896,475	915,952	938,314	956,572	974,504	991,235	998,053	1,003,714	1,004,770	1,009,200	696,257	312,943	1,014,798	697,191	317,607	1,021,349	699,248	322,101	1,008,200	1,008,500
West Virginia	322,389	318,296	314,383	310,511	307,112	304,052	301,419	297,530	291,811	286,367	282,885	199,803	83,082	282,455	200,002	82,453	281,215	198,836	82,379	275,700	273,500
Wisconsin	797,621	829,415	844,001	860,581	870,175	879,259	881,780	879,542	877,753	879,476	879,361	591,804	287,557	881,231	591,703	289,528	880,031	589,812	290,219	863,600	858,700
Wyoming	98,226	100,313	100,899	100,314	99,859	99,058	97,115	95,241	92,105	89,940	88,128	59,093	29,035	88,116	59,926	28,190	87,462	59,759	27,703	84,200	83,400
Bureau of Indian Affairs	—	—	—	—	—	—	—	50,125	49,076	46,938	46,476	35,021	11,455	46,126	34,392	11,734	45,828	33,671	12,157	—	—
Department of Defense dependents schools																					
Overseas schools	—	—	—	—	—	80,715	78,254	78,170	3 108,035	73,581	73,212	58,750	14,462	72,889	58,214	14,675	71,053	56,226	14,827	—	—
Domestic schools	—	—	—	—	—	—	—	—	—	34,058	32,847	29,389	3,458	32,115	28,759	3,356	30,603	27,500	3,103	—	—
Other jurisdictions																					
American Samoa	12,463	13,994	14,484	14,445	14,576	14,766	15,214	15,372	15,477	15,702	15,897	11,911	3,986	15,984	11,838	4,146	15,893	11,772	4,121	—	—
Guam	26,391	30,077	30,920	32,185	32,960	33,393	32,444	32,222	32,951	32,473	31,992	23,133	8,859	15,984	11,838	—	31,572	22,551	9,021	—	—
Northern Marianas	6,449	8,086	8,188	8,429	8,809	9,041	9,246	9,498	9,732	10,004	10,479	8,015	2,464	11,251	8,379	2,872	11,244	8,192	3,052	—	—
Puerto Rico	644,734	637,034	631,460	621,121	627,620	618,861	617,157	613,862	613,019	612,725	604,177	438,053	166,124	596,502	429,351	167,151	584,916	418,588	166,328	—	—
Virgin Islands	21,750	22,887	22,752	23,126	22,737	22,385	22,136	20,976	20,866	19,459	18,780	13,421	5,359	18,333	12,933	5,400	17,716	12,738	4,978	—	—

—Not available.
[1]Includes elementary unclassified.
[2]Includes secondary unclassified.
[3]Includes both overseas and domestic schools.

NOTE: Some data have been revised from previously published figures.
SOURCE: U.S. Department of Education, National Center for Education Statistics, Common Core of Data (CCD), "State Nonfiscal Survey of Public Elementary/Secondary Education," 1990–91 through 2003–04, and *Projections of Education Statistics to 2014.* (This table was prepared August 2005.)

Percentage distribution of enrollment in public elementary and secondary schools, by race/ethnicity and state or jurisdiction: Fall 1993 and fall 2003

State or jurisdiction	Percentage distribution, fall 1993						Percentage distribution, fall 2003					
	Total	White, non-Hispanic	Black, non-Hispanic	Hispanic	Asian or Pacific Islander	American Indian/ Alaska Native	Total	White, non-Hispanic	Black, non-Hispanic	Hispanic	Asian or Pacific Islander	American Indian/ Alaska Native
1	2	3	4	5	6	7	8	9	10	11	12	13
United States[1]	100.0	66.1	16.6	12.7	3.6	1.1	100.0	58.7	17.2	18.5	4.4	1.2
Alabama	100.0	62.4	35.8	0.4	0.6	0.8	100.0	59.9	36.4	2.1	0.9	0.8
Alaska	100.0	65.2	4.9	2.4	4.1	23.4	100.0	58.9	4.7	3.9	6.5	26.0
Arizona	100.0	59.6	4.2	27.6	1.6	6.9	100.0	49.2	4.8	37.2	2.2	6.6
Arkansas	100.0	74.4	23.8	0.9	0.7	0.3	100.0	69.9	23.1	5.3	1.1	0.6
California	100.0	42.3	8.7	37.1	11.2	0.8	100.0	32.9	8.2	46.7	11.3	0.8
Colorado	100.0	74.1	5.4	17.1	2.4	1.0	100.0	64.5	5.8	25.3	3.1	1.2
Connecticut	100.0	73.3	13.0	11.1	2.4	0.2	100.0	68.3	13.6	14.6	3.2	0.3
Delaware	100.0	66.2	28.5	3.4	1.7	0.2	100.0	57.3	31.9	7.9	2.6	0.3
District of Columbia[2]	100.0	4.0	88.5	6.1	1.3	#	100.0	4.3	83.7	10.4	1.6	0.1
Florida	100.0	59.6	24.7	13.8	1.7	0.2	100.0	51.3	24.3	22.1	2.0	0.3
Georgia	100.0	59.9	37.0	1.5	1.4	0.2	100.0	52.1	38.3	6.9	2.5	0.2
Hawaii	100.0	23.7	2.6	5.0	68.4	0.3	100.0	20.2	2.4	4.5	72.4	0.5
Idaho	100.0	89.6	0.5	7.5	1.1	1.3	100.0	84.1	0.9	12.0	1.5	1.6
Illinois	100.0	64.7	21.1	11.2	2.9	0.1	100.0	57.4	21.1	17.7	3.6	0.2
Indiana	100.0	85.9	11.1	2.1	0.8	0.2	100.0	81.5	12.4	4.8	1.1	0.2
Iowa	100.0	93.3	3.1	1.6	1.5	0.4	100.0	88.2	4.5	4.9	1.8	0.6
Kansas	100.0	83.6	8.3	5.3	1.8	1.0	100.0	76.4	8.9	11.0	2.3	1.4
Kentucky	100.0	89.3	9.8	0.3	0.5	0.1	100.0	87.0	10.4	1.5	0.8	0.2
Louisiana	100.0	51.7	45.4	1.1	1.3	0.5	100.0	48.5	47.7	1.8	1.3	0.7
Maine[3]	100.0	97.6	0.7	0.4	0.8	0.5	100.0	95.8	1.7	0.8	1.2	0.5
Maryland	100.0	58.9	34.2	2.9	3.7	0.3	100.0	50.4	37.9	6.4	4.9	0.4
Massachusetts	100.0	79.3	8.1	8.8	3.7	0.2	100.0	74.6	8.8	11.5	4.7	0.3
Michigan	100.0	78.0	17.3	2.4	1.4	1.0	100.0	72.7	20.1	4.1	2.2	1.0
Minnesota	100.0	88.8	4.2	1.7	3.5	1.9	100.0	80.2	7.8	4.6	5.4	2.1
Mississippi	100.0	47.9	50.9	0.3	0.5	0.4	100.0	47.3	50.7	1.1	0.7	0.2
Missouri	100.0	82.3	15.7	0.9	0.9	0.2	100.0	77.7	18.0	2.6	1.4	0.4
Montana	100.0	87.8	0.5	1.4	0.8	9.6	100.0	85.1	0.7	2.1	1.0	11.0
Nebraska	100.0	88.3	5.7	3.6	1.2	1.3	100.0	79.5	7.1	10.1	1.7	1.6
Nevada	100.0	70.5	9.2	14.3	4.0	2.0	100.0	50.8	10.7	30.2	6.7	1.7
New Hampshire	100.0	96.9	0.8	1.0	1.0	0.2	100.0	94.2	1.4	2.4	1.7	0.3
New Jersey	100.0	63.4	18.6	12.8	5.1	0.1	100.0	57.9	17.7	17.2	7.0	0.2
New Mexico	100.0	40.5	2.3	46.0	0.9	10.2	100.0	32.8	2.4	52.5	1.2	11.2
New York	100.0	58.2	20.1	16.5	4.8	0.4	100.0	53.9	19.7	19.4	6.6	0.5
North Carolina	100.0	65.7	30.3	1.3	1.1	1.6	100.0	58.3	31.6	6.7	2.0	1.5
North Dakota	100.0	91.5	0.8	0.8	0.7	6.3	100.0	88.0	1.2	1.4	0.8	8.5
Ohio	100.0	82.8	14.8	1.3	1.0	0.1	100.0	79.4	17.0	2.1	1.3	0.1
Oklahoma	100.0	71.6	10.3	3.3	1.2	13.7	100.0	61.5	10.9	7.6	1.5	18.5
Oregon	100.0	86.7	2.4	5.9	3.1	1.9	100.0	76.6	3.1	13.6	4.4	2.3
Pennsylvania	100.0	81.1	13.8	3.3	1.7	0.1	100.0	76.3	15.8	5.5	2.3	0.1
Rhode Island	100.0	81.1	6.8	8.6	3.1	0.4	100.0	71.2	8.5	16.4	3.2	0.6
South Carolina	100.0	57.0	41.6	0.5	0.7	0.2	100.0	54.2	41.3	3.2	1.1	0.3
South Dakota	100.0	84.9	0.7	0.6	0.7	13.0	100.0	84.9	1.5	1.8	1.0	10.7
Tennessee	100.0	75.8	22.9	0.4	0.7	0.1	100.0	70.7	25.0	2.8	1.3	0.2
Texas	100.0	47.7	14.3	35.5	2.2	0.2	100.0	38.7	14.3	43.8	2.9	0.3
Utah	100.0	91.5	0.6	4.5	2.0	1.4	100.0	83.4	1.1	11.0	2.9	1.5
Vermont	100.0	97.5	0.7	0.3	0.9	0.6	100.0	95.9	1.2	0.8	1.5	0.6
Virginia	100.0	67.9	25.8	2.8	3.3	0.2	100.0	61.3	26.8	6.6	4.7	0.5
Washington	100.0	79.9	4.4	6.9	6.2	2.6	100.0	71.5	5.7	12.3	7.9	2.7
West Virginia	100.0	95.4	4.0	0.2	0.4	0.1	100.0	94.1	4.6	0.5	0.6	0.1
Wisconsin	100.0	84.3	9.1	2.9	2.4	1.3	100.0	78.8	10.5	5.8	3.4	1.4
Wyoming	100.0	89.4	1.0	6.2	0.7	2.7	100.0	86.0	1.4	8.2	1.0	3.5

See notes at end of table.

Percentage distribution of enrollment in public elementary and secondary schools, by race/ethnicity and state or jurisdiction: Fall 1993 and fall 2003—Continued

State or jurisdiction	Percentage distribution, fall 1993						Percentage distribution, fall 2003					
	Total	White, non-Hispanic	Black, non-Hispanic	Hispanic	Asian or Pacific Islander	American Indian/ Alaska Native	Total	White, non-Hispanic	Black, non-Hispanic	Hispanic	Asian or Pacific Islander	American Indian/ Alaska Native
1	2	3	4	5	6	7	8	9	10	11	12	13
Bureau of Indian Affairs	—	—	—	—	—	—	100.0	0.0	0.0	0.0	0.0	100.0
Department of Defense dependents schools												
Overseas schools	—	—	—	—	—	—	100.0	55.2	20.0	13.5	10.5	0.9
Domestic schools............	—	—	—	—	—	—	100.0	48.6	23.6	22.7	4.2	1.0
Other jurisdictions												
American Samoa	100.0	0.0	0.0	0.0	100.0	0.0	100.0	0.0	0.0	0.0	100.0	0.0
Guam	100.0	9.1	1.9	0.6	88.4	0.1	100.0	1.3	0.3	0.2	98.1	0.1
Northern Marianas.........	100.0	1.3	0.0	0.0	98.7	0.0	100.0	0.4	#	0.0	99.6	0.0
Puerto Rico....................	100.0	0.0	0.0	100.0	0.0	0.0	100.0	0.0	0.0	100.0	0.0	0.0
Virgin Islands	100.0	0.9	85.3	13.3	0.4	0.1	100.0	0.8	84.3	14.5	0.2	0.2

—Not available.
#Rounds to zero.
[1]Fall 1993 figures include estimates for Maine based on fall 1994 report; fall 2003 figures include estimates for District of Columbia based on fall 2002 report.
[2]Estimate for fall 2003 based on fall 2002 report.
[3]Estimate for fall 1993 based on fall 1994 report.

NOTE: Percentage distribution based on students for whom race/ethnicity was reported, which may be less than the total number of students in the state. Detail may not sum to totals because of rounding.
SOURCE: U.S. Department of Education, National Center for Education Statistics, Common Core of Data (CCD), "State Nonfiscal Survey of Public Elementary/Secondary Education," 1993–94 and 2003–04. (This table was prepared August 2005.)

Enrollment of 3-, 4-, and 5-year-old children in preprimary programs, by level of program, control of program, and attendance status: Selected years, 1965 through 2004

[In thousands]

Year and age	Total population, 3 to 5 years old	Total	Percent enrolled	Nursery school Public	Nursery school Private	Kindergarten Public	Kindergarten Private	Full-day	Part-day	Percent full-day
1	2	3	4	5	6	7	8	9	10	11
Total, 3 to 5 years old										
1965	12,549 (144.5)	3,407 (87.1)	27.1 (0.69)	127 (19.6)	393 (34.1)	2,291 (75.6)	596 (41.6)	— (†)	— (†)	— (†)
1970	10,949 (109.4)	4,104 (71.5)	37.5 (0.65)	332 (25.3)	762 (37.6)	2,498 (62.0)	511 (31.1)	698 (36.1)	3,405 (34.0)	17.0 (0.83)
1975	10,185 (105.8)	4,955 (71.2)	48.7 (0.70)	570 (32.7)	1,174 (45.5)	2,682 (62.7)	528 (31.6)	1,295 (47.4)	3,659 (43.6)	26.1 (0.88)
1980	9,284 (102.6)	4,878 (68.8)	52.5 (0.74)	628 (34.6)	1,353 (48.6)	2,438 (60.6)	459 (29.9)	1,551 (51.4)	3,327 (46.5)	31.8 (0.95)
1985	10,733 (115.6)	5,865 (77.6)	54.6 (0.72)	846 (42.0)	1,631 (56.0)	2,847 (68.8)	541 (34.1)	2,144 (62.3)	3,722 (55.5)	36.6 (0.95)
1989	11,039 (129.9)	6,026 (87.2)	54.6 (0.79)	930 (48.7)	1,894 (66.1)	2,704 (75.4)	497 (36.3)	2,238 (70.4)	3,789 (62.5)	37.1 (1.04)
1990	11,207 (124.2)	6,659 (82.3)	59.4 (0.73)	1,199 (51.8)	2,180 (66.4)	2,772 (72.3)	509 (34.9)	2,577 (70.6)	4,082 (63.0)	38.7 (0.95)
1991	11,370 (125.1)	6,334 (83.9)	55.7 (0.74)	996 (47.8)	1,828 (62.0)	2,967 (74.2)	543 (36.0)	2,408 (69.0)	3,926 (61.2)	38.0 (0.97)
1992	11,545 (126.0)	6,402 (84.6)	55.5 (0.73)	1,073 (49.4)	1,783 (61.5)	2,995 (74.6)	550 (36.3)	2,410 (69.2)	3,992 (61.4)	37.6 (0.96)
1993	11,954 (128.0)	6,581 (86.1)	55.1 (0.72)	1,205 (52.1)	1,779 (61.6)	3,020 (75.3)	577 (37.1)	2,642 (71.9)	3,939 (63.0)	40.1 (0.96)
1994[1]	12,328 (130.6)	7,514 (86.3)	61.0 (0.70)	1,848 (63.1)	2,314 (69.0)	2,819 (74.3)	534 (36.0)	3,468 (79.5)	4,046 (68.8)	46.2 (0.92)
1995[1]	12,518 (131.5)	7,739 (86.6)	61.8 (0.69)	1,950 (64.6)	2,381 (69.9)	2,800 (74.2)	608 (38.3)	3,689 (81.2)	4,051 (70.0)	47.7 (0.90)
1996[1]	12,378 (135.7)	7,580 (89.5)	61.2 (0.72)	1,830 (65.2)	2,317 (71.7)	2,853 (77.4)	580 (38.8)	3,562 (83.2)	4,019 (71.8)	47.0 (0.95)
1997[1]	12,121 (134.3)	7,860 (86.8)	64.9 (0.72)	2,207 (70.2)	2,231 (70.5)	2,847 (77.1)	575 (38.7)	3,922 (85.1)	3,939 (73.2)	49.9 (0.93)
1998[1]	12,078 (134.1)	7,788 (86.9)	64.5 (0.72)	2,213 (70.2)	2,299 (71.2)	2,674 (75.4)	602 (39.5)	3,959 (85.2)	3,829 (72.9)	50.8 (0.94)
1999[1]	11,920 (133.3)	7,844 (85.5)	65.8 (0.72)	2,209 (70.0)	2,298 (71.1)	2,777 (76.2)	560 (38.2)	4,154 (85.9)	3,690 (73.0)	53.0 (0.93)
2000[1]	11,858 (133.0)	7,592 (86.3)	64.0 (0.73)	2,146 (69.2)	2,180 (69.7)	2,701 (75.4)	565 (38.3)	4,008 (85.1)	3,584 (71.8)	52.8 (0.95)
2001[1]	11,899 (133.2)	7,602 (86.5)	63.9 (0.73)	2,164 (69.5)	2,201 (69.9)	2,724 (75.7)	512 (36.6)	3,940 (84.8)	3,662 (71.9)	51.8 (0.95)
2002[1]	11,524 (131.2)	7,697 (79.2)	66.8 (0.69)	2,376 (68.0)	2,179 (65.8)	2,621 (70.5)	521 (34.9)	4,191 (80.9)	3,507 (68.4)	54.4 (0.89)
2003[1]	12,204 (134.8)	7,921 (82.6)	64.9 (0.68)	2,512 (70.0)	2,347 (68.2)	2,539 (70.2)	523 (35.0)	4,429 (83.2)	3,492 (69.2)	55.9 (0.87)
2004[1]	12,362 (145.9)	7,969 (83.3)	64.5 (0.67)	2,428 (69.2)	2,243 (67.1)	2,812 (73.0)	484 (33.8)	4,507 (83.8)	3,461 (69.3)	56.6 (0.87)
3 years old										
1965	4,149 (84.9)	203 (24.3)	4.9 (0.59)	41 (11.1)	153 (21.2)	5 (3.9)	4 (3.5)	— (†)	— (†)	— (†)
1970	3,516 (63.2)	454 (28.1)	12.9 (0.80)	110 (14.6)	322 (24.1)	12 (4.9)	10 (4.5)	142 (16.5)	312 (13.9)	31.3 (3.07)
1975	3,177 (60.2)	683 (32.7)	21.5 (1.03)	179 (18.3)	474 (28.3)	11 (4.7)	18 (6.0)	259 (21.8)	423 (17.9)	37.9 (2.62)
1980	3,143 (60.7)	857 (35.7)	27.3 (1.14)	221 (20.5)	604 (31.6)	16 (5.7)	17 (5.9)	321 (24.3)	536 (20.3)	37.5 (2.36)
1985	3,594 (68.2)	1,035 (40.8)	28.8 (1.14)	278 (24.1)	679 (35.3)	52 (10.8)	26 (7.6)	350 (26.7)	685 (22.9)	33.8 (2.21)
1989	3,713 (76.8)	1,005 (45.2)	27.1 (1.22)	277 (26.7)	707 (39.9)	3 (3.1)	18 (7.1)	390 (31.2)	615 (25.8)	38.8 (2.56)
1990	3,692 (72.7)	1,205 (45.1)	32.6 (1.22)	347 (28.1)	840 (40.3)	11 (5.4)	7 (4.2)	447 (31.4)	758 (26.6)	37.1 (2.20)
1991	3,811 (73.8)	1,074 (44.0)	28.2 (1.15)	313 (26.8)	702 (37.9)	38 (9.7)	22 (7.3)	388 (29.6)	687 (24.9)	36.1 (2.32)
1992	3,905 (74.7)	1,081 (44.3)	27.7 (1.13)	336 (27.8)	685 (37.6)	26 (8.0)	34 (9.3)	371 (29.0)	711 (24.7)	34.3 (2.29)
1993	4,053 (76.1)	1,097 (44.8)	27.1 (1.11)	369 (29.0)	687 (37.8)	20 (7.1)	20 (7.1)	426 (30.9)	670 (25.6)	38.9 (2.33)
1994[1]	4,081 (76.8)	1,385 (48.2)	33.9 (1.18)	469 (32.5)	887 (42.0)	19 (7.0)	9 (4.9)	670 (37.7)	715 (29.6)	48.4 (2.14)
1995[1]	4,148 (77.4)	1,489 (49.2)	35.9 (1.19)	511 (33.7)	947 (43.0)	15 (6.1)	17 (6.5)	754 (39.6)	736 (30.7)	50.6 (2.06)
1996[1]	4,045 (79.3)	1,506 (50.8)	37.2 (1.26)	511 (34.9)	947 (44.5)	22 (7.7)	26 (8.4)	657 (38.8)	848 (31.8)	43.7 (2.11)
1997[1]	3,947 (78.3)	1,528 (50.5)	38.7 (1.28)	643 (38.3)	843 (42.5)	25 (8.2)	18 (7.0)	754 (40.8)	774 (32.3)	49.4 (2.11)
1998[1]	3,989 (78.7)	1,498 (50.5)	37.6 (1.27)	587 (37.0)	869 (43.1)	27 (8.6)	14 (6.2)	735 (40.4)	763 (32.0)	49.1 (2.13)
1999[1]	3,862 (77.5)	1,505 (50.0)	39.0 (1.30)	621 (37.7)	859 (42.7)	13 (6.0)	12 (5.7)	773 (41.1)	732 (32.0)	51.3 (2.13)
2000[1]	3,929 (78.2)	1,541 (50.5)	39.2 (1.29)	644 (38.3)	854 (42.7)	27 (8.5)	16 (6.7)	761 (40.9)	779 (32.4)	49.4 (2.10)
2001[1]	3,985 (78.7)	1,538 (50.7)	38.6 (1.27)	599 (37.3)	901 (43.6)	14 (6.2)	23 (7.9)	715 (40.0)	823 (32.3)	46.5 (2.10)
2002[1]	3,831 (77.2)	1,711 (48.2)	44.7 (1.26)	779 (39.0)	864 (40.5)	45 (10.5)	24 (7.6)	937 (41.7)	775 (32.3)	54.7 (1.88)
2003[1]	4,260 (81.3)	1,806 (50.5)	42.4 (1.19)	783 (39.6)	915 (42.0)	83 (14.1)	24 (7.7)	979 (43.0)	826 (33.2)	54.2 (1.84)
2004[1]	4,089 (85.7)	1,583 (48.8)	38.7 (1.19)	674 (37.2)	849 (40.6)	40 (9.9)	20 (7.0)	808 (39.9)	775 (31.2)	51.0 (1.97)
4 years old										
1965	4,238 (85.8)	683 (41.8)	16.1 (0.99)	68 (14.3)	213 (24.9)	284 (28.4)	118 (18.7)	— (†)	— (†)	— (†)
1970	3,620 (64.1)	1,007 (38.0)	27.8 (1.05)	176 (18.3)	395 (26.5)	318 (24.0)	117 (15.0)	230 (20.7)	776 (18.8)	22.8 (1.87)
1975	3,499 (63.1)	1,418 (41.0)	40.5 (1.17)	332 (24.5)	644 (32.3)	313 (23.8)	129 (15.7)	411 (26.9)	1,008 (24.1)	29.0 (1.70)
1980	3,072 (60.0)	1,423 (39.5)	46.3 (1.29)	363 (25.6)	701 (33.3)	239 (21.2)	120 (15.4)	467 (28.5)	956 (25.3)	32.8 (1.78)
1985	3,598 (68.2)	1,766 (45.1)	49.1 (1.25)	496 (31.1)	859 (38.5)	276 (24.0)	135 (17.1)	643 (34.6)	1,123 (30.4)	36.4 (1.72)
1989	3,692 (76.6)	1,882 (50.7)	51.0 (1.37)	524 (35.4)	1,055 (45.8)	202 (23.1)	100 (16.5)	592 (37.2)	1,290 (33.6)	31.4 (1.79)
1990	3,723 (73.0)	2,087 (48.0)	56.1 (1.29)	695 (37.7)	1,144 (44.6)	157 (19.4)	91 (14.9)	716 (38.1)	1,371 (34.4)	34.3 (1.65)
1991	3,763 (73.4)	1,994 (48.5)	53.0 (1.29)	584 (35.2)	982 (42.7)	287 (25.8)	140 (18.4)	667 (37.1)	1,326 (33.4)	33.5 (1.67)
1992	3,807 (73.8)	1,982 (48.8)	52.1 (1.28)	602 (35.7)	971 (42.6)	282 (25.6)	126 (17.5)	632 (36.4)	1,350 (32.9)	31.9 (1.66)
1993	4,044 (76.0)	2,178 (50.2)	53.9 (1.24)	719 (38.5)	957 (42.8)	349 (28.3)	154 (19.3)	765 (39.5)	1,413 (35.3)	35.1 (1.62)

See notes at end of table.

Enrollment of 3-, 4-, and 5-year-old children in preprimary programs, by level of program, control of program, and attendance status: Selected years, 1965 through 2004—Continued

[In thousands]

Year and age	Total population, 3 to 5 years old		Enrollment by level and control										Enrollment by attendance					
			Total		Percent enrolled		Nursery school				Kindergarten				Full-day		Part-day		Percent full-day
							Public		Private		Public		Private						
1	2		3		4		5		6		7		8		9		10		11
1994[1]	4,202	(77.9)	2,532	(50.5)	60.3	(1.20)	1,020	(44.3)	1,232	(47.0)	198	(21.9)	82	(14.3)	1,095	(45.3)	1,438	(39.7)	43.2	(1.57)
1995[1]	4,145	(77.4)	2,553	(49.9)	61.6	(1.20)	1,054	(44.6)	1,208	(46.6)	207	(22.3)	84	(14.5)	1,104	(45.3)	1,449	(39.9)	43.3	(1.56)
1996[1]	4,148	(80.3)	2,454	(52.3)	59.2	(1.26)	1,029	(45.9)	1,168	(47.8)	180	(21.7)	77	(14.3)	1,034	(46.0)	1,420	(40.4)	42.1	(1.65)
1997[1]	4,033	(79.2)	2,665	(49.6)	66.1	(1.23)	1,197	(47.9)	1,169	(47.6)	207	(23.1)	92	(15.7)	1,161	(47.5)	1,505	(42.3)	43.5	(1.59)
1998[1]	4,002	(78.9)	2,666	(49.3)	66.6	(1.23)	1,183	(47.7)	1,219	(48.1)	210	(23.3)	53	(11.9)	1,179	(47.6)	1,487	(42.3)	44.2	(1.59)
1999[1]	4,021	(79.0)	2,769	(48.5)	68.9	(1.21)	1,212	(48.1)	1,227	(48.2)	207	(23.1)	122	(18.0)	1,355	(49.5)	1,414	(43.4)	48.9	(1.57)
2000[1]	3,940	(78.3)	2,556	(49.5)	64.9	(1.26)	1,144	(47.0)	1,121	(46.8)	227	(24.2)	65	(13.2)	1,182	(47.5)	1,374	(41.6)	46.2	(1.63)
2001[1]	3,927	(78.1)	2,608	(48.9)	66.4	(1.24)	1,202	(47.7)	1,121	(46.7)	236	(24.6)	49	(11.5)	1,255	(48.3)	1,354	(42.1)	48.1	(1.62)
2002[1]	3,851	(77.4)	2,615	(45.4)	67.9	(1.18)	1,198	(45.0)	1,163	(44.6)	174	(20.2)	80	(13.9)	1,259	(45.6)	1,355	(40.0)	48.2	(1.53)
2003[1]	4,076	(79.6)	2,785	(46.5)	68.3	(1.14)	1,324	(46.8)	1,176	(45.3)	184	(20.7)	101	(15.5)	1,400	(47.5)	1,384	(41.3)	50.3	(1.48)
2004[1]	4,339	(88.2)	2,969	(48.0)	68.4	(1.11)	1,462	(48.8)	1,213	(46.3)	208	(22.1)	85	(14.3)	1,484	(48.9)	1,485	(42.7)	50.0	(1.44)
5 years old[2]																			
1965	4,162	(85.1)	2,521	(55.1)	60.6	(1.32)	18	(7.4)	27	(9.1)	2,002	(56.3)	474	(35.8)	—	(†)	—	(†)	—	(†)
1970	3,814	(65.8)	2,643	(40.2)	69.3	(1.05)	45	(9.4)	45	(9.4)	2,168	(43.2)	384	(26.2)	326	(24.4)	2,317	(23.9)	12.3	(0.90)
1975	3,509	(63.2)	2,854	(32.6)	81.3	(0.93)	59	(10.7)	57	(10.6)	2,358	(39.2)	381	(26.0)	625	(32.0)	2,228	(31.2)	21.9	(1.09)
1980	3,069	(60.0)	2,598	(28.6)	84.7	(0.93)	44	(9.4)	48	(9.8)	2,183	(35.9)	322	(24.3)	763	(34.2)	1,835	(33.2)	29.4	(1.28)
1985	3,542	(67.7)	3,065	(30.6)	86.5	(0.86)	73	(12.7)	94	(14.4)	2,519	(40.6)	379	(27.7)	1,151	(41.9)	1,914	(40.3)	37.6	(1.32)
1989	3,633	(76.0)	3,139	(34.5)	86.4	(0.95)	129	(18.6)	132	(18.8)	2,499	(46.6)	378	(30.7)	1,255	(47.8)	1,883	(45.8)	40.0	(1.46)
1990	3,792	(73.7)	3,367	(30.8)	88.8	(0.81)	157	(19.4)	196	(21.6)	2,604	(45.2)	411	(30.3)	1,414	(47.2)	1,953	(45.4)	42.0	(1.35)
1991	3,796	(73.7)	3,267	(33.8)	86.0	(0.89)	100	(15.6)	143	(18.6)	2,642	(44.9)	382	(29.4)	1,354	(46.7)	1,913	(44.6)	41.4	(1.37)
1992	3,832	(74.1)	3,339	(32.8)	87.1	(0.86)	135	(18.1)	127	(17.5)	2,688	(44.9)	390	(29.6)	1,408	(47.3)	1,931	(45.2)	42.2	(1.35)
1993	3,857	(74.3)	3,306	(34.4)	85.7	(0.89)	116	(16.8)	136	(18.1)	2,651	(45.6)	403	(30.1)	1,451	(47.7)	1,856	(45.2)	43.9	(1.37)
1994[1]	4,044	(76.4)	3,597	(31.8)	88.9	(0.79)	359	(28.8)	194	(21.6)	2,601	(48.5)	442	(31.6)	1,704	(50.0)	1,893	(47.7)	47.4	(1.33)
1995[1]	4,224	(78.1)	3,697	(34.2)	87.5	(0.81)	385	(29.8)	226	(23.3)	2,578	(50.5)	507	(33.7)	1,830	(51.3)	1,867	(48.4)	49.5	(1.31)
1996[1]	4,185	(80.6)	3,621	(36.5)	86.5	(0.87)	290	(27.1)	202	(22.9)	2,652	(51.5)	477	(34.0)	1,870	(53.1)	1,750	(49.7)	51.7	(1.37)
1997[1]	4,141	(80.2)	3,667	(33.8)	88.5	(0.82)	368	(30.2)	219	(23.8)	2,616	(51.3)	465	(33.5)	2,007	(53.1)	1,660	(49.8)	54.7	(1.36)
1998[1]	4,087	(79.7)	3,624	(33.5)	88.7	(0.82)	442	(32.8)	211	(23.3)	2,437	(51.8)	535	(35.6)	2,044	(52.8)	1,579	(49.3)	56.4	(1.36)
1999[1]	4,037	(79.2)	3,571	(33.5)	88.4	(0.83)	376	(30.5)	212	(23.4)	2,557	(50.6)	426	(32.2)	2,027	(52.5)	1,544	(48.9)	56.8	(1.37)
2000[1]	3,989	(78.7)	3,495	(34.3)	87.6	(0.86)	359	(29.8)	206	(23.1)	2,447	(50.8)	484	(34.1)	2,065	(52.1)	1,431	(48.0)	59.1	(1.37)
2001[1]	3,987	(78.7)	3,456	(35.4)	86.7	(0.89)	363	(30.0)	179	(21.6)	2,474	(50.6)	440	(32.7)	1,970	(52.1)	1,485	(48.1)	57.0	(1.39)
2002[1]	3,841	(77.3)	3,371	(31.8)	87.8	(0.83)	399	(29.6)	153	(19.0)	2,403	(47.0)	417	(30.2)	1,994	(48.5)	1,377	(44.7)	59.2	(1.33)
2003[1]	3,867	(77.5)	3,331	(33.7)	86.1	(0.87)	404	(29.8)	256	(24.2)	2,272	(47.9)	398	(29.6)	2,050	(48.6)	1,281	(44.0)	61.5	(1.32)
2004[1]	3,934	(84.1)	3,417	(33.2)	86.9	(0.84)	293	(25.8)	181	(20.6)	2,564	(46.8)	380	(29.0)	2,215	(48.7)	1,201	(43.7)	64.8	(1.28)

—Not available.
†Not applicable.
[1]Data collected using new procedures. May not be comparable with figures prior to 1994.
[2]Enrollment data include only those students in preprimary programs.
NOTE: Data are based on sample surveys of the civilian noninstitutional population. Although cells with fewer than 75,000 children are subject to wide sampling variation, they are included in the table to permit various types of aggregations. Some data have been revised from previously published figures. Detail may not sum to totals because of rounding. Standard errors appear in parentheses.
SOURCE: U.S. Department of Education, National Center for Education Statistics, *Preprimary Enrollment*, 1965, 1970, and 1975. U.S. Department of Commerce, Census Bureau, Current Population Survey (CPS), October 1980 through October 2004, unpublished tabulations. (This table was prepared November 2005.)

Children 3 to 21 years old served in federally supported programs for the disabled, by type of disability:
Selected years, 1976–77 through 2003–04

Type of disability	1976–77	1980–81	1990–91	1992–93	1993–94	1994–95	1995–96	1996–97	1997–98	1998–99	1999–2000	2000–01	2001–02	2002–03	2003–04
1	2	3	4	5	6	7	8	9	10	11	12	13	14	15	16
Number served (in thousands)															
All disabilities	3,694	4,144	4,710	5,036	5,216	5,378	5,573	5,730	5,903	6,055	6,190	6,296	6,407	6,523	6,634
Specific learning disabilities	796	1,462	2,129	2,351	2,408	2,489	2,579	2,649	2,725	2,789	2,830	2,843	2,846	2,848	2,831
Speech or language impairments	1,302	1,168	985	994	1,014	1,015	1,022	1,043	1,056	1,068	1,078	1,084	1,084	1,412	1,441
Mental retardation	961	830	534	518	536	555	570	579	589	597	600	599	592	602	593
Emotional disturbance	283	347	389	400	414	427	438	445	453	462	468	473	476	485	489
Hearing impairments	88	79	58	60	64	64	67	68	69	70	70	70	70	78	79
Orthopedic impairments	87	58	49	52	56	60	63	66	67	69	71	72	73	83	77
Other health impairments	141	98	55	65	82	106	133	160	190	221	254	292	337	403	464
Visual impairments	38	31	23	23	24	24	25	25	25	26	26	25	25	29	28
Multiple disabilities	—	68	96	102	108	88	93	98	106	106	111	121	127	138	140
Deaf-blindness	—	3	1	1	1	1	1	1	1	2	2	1	2	2	2
Autism and traumatic brain injury	—	—	—	19	24	29	39	44	54	67	80	94	118	159	186
Developmental delay	—	—	—	—	—	—	—	—	4	12	19	28	45	283	305
Preschool disabled[1]	—	—	390	450	486	519	544	552	564	568	582	592	612	†	†
Percentage distribution of children served															
All disabilities	100.0	100.0	100.0	100.0	100.0	100.0	100.0	100.0	100.0	100.0	100.0	100.0	100.0	100.0	100.0
Specific learning disabilities	21.5	35.3	45.2	46.7	46.2	46.3	46.3	46.2	46.2	46.1	45.7	45.2	44.4	43.7	42.7
Speech or language impairments	35.2	28.2	20.9	19.7	19.4	18.9	18.3	18.2	17.9	17.6	17.4	17.2	16.9	21.6	21.7
Mental retardation	26.0	20.0	11.3	10.3	10.3	10.3	10.2	10.1	10.0	9.9	9.7	9.5	9.2	9.2	8.9
Emotional disturbance	7.7	8.4	8.3	7.9	7.9	7.9	7.9	7.8	7.7	7.6	7.6	7.5	7.4	7.4	7.4
Hearing impairments	2.4	1.9	1.2	1.2	1.2	1.2	1.2	1.2	1.2	1.2	1.1	1.1	1.1	1.2	1.2
Orthopedic impairments	2.4	1.4	1.0	1.0	1.1	1.1	1.1	1.2	1.1	1.1	1.1	1.1	1.1	1.3	1.2
Other health impairments	3.8	2.4	1.2	1.3	1.6	2.0	2.4	2.8	3.2	3.6	4.1	4.6	5.3	6.2	7.0
Visual impairments	1.0	0.7	0.5	0.5	0.5	0.4	0.4	0.4	0.4	0.4	0.4	0.4	0.4	0.4	0.4
Multiple disabilities	—	1.6	2.0	2.0	2.1	1.6	1.7	1.7	1.8	1.8	1.8	1.9	2.0	2.1	2.1
Deaf-blindness	—	0.1	#	#	#	#	#	#	#	#	#	#	#	#	#
Autism and traumatic brain injury	—	—	—	0.4	0.5	0.5	0.7	0.8	0.9	1.1	1.3	1.5	1.8	2.4	2.8
Developmental delay	—	—	—	—	—	—	—	—	0.1	0.2	0.3	0.4	0.7	4.3	4.6
Preschool disabled[1]	—	—	8.3	8.9	9.3	9.7	9.8	9.6	9.6	9.4	9.4	9.4	9.6	†	†
Number served as a percent of total enrollment[2]															
All disabilities	8.3	10.1	11.4	11.8	12.0	12.2	12.4	12.6	12.8	13.0	13.2	13.3	13.4	13.5	13.7
Specific learning disabilities	1.8	3.6	5.2	5.5	5.5	5.6	5.8	5.8	5.9	6.0	6.0	6.0	6.0	5.9	5.8
Speech or language impairments	2.9	2.9	2.4	2.3	2.3	2.3	2.3	2.3	2.3	2.3	2.3	2.3	2.3	2.9	3.0
Mental retardation	2.2	2.0	1.3	1.2	1.2	1.3	1.3	1.3	1.3	1.3	1.3	1.3	1.2	1.2	1.2
Emotional disturbance	0.6	0.8	0.9	0.9	1.0	1.0	1.0	1.0	1.0	1.0	1.0	1.0	1.0	1.0	1.0
Hearing impairments	0.2	0.2	0.1	0.1	0.1	0.1	0.1	0.1	0.1	0.2	0.1	0.1	0.1	0.2	0.2
Orthopedic impairments	0.2	0.1	0.1	0.1	0.1	0.1	0.1	0.1	0.1	0.1	0.2	0.2	0.2	0.2	0.2
Other health impairments	0.3	0.2	0.1	0.2	0.2	0.2	0.3	0.4	0.4	0.5	0.5	0.6	0.7	0.8	1.0
Visual impairments	0.1	0.1	0.1	0.1	0.1	0.1	0.1	0.1	0.1	0.1	0.1	0.1	0.1	0.1	0.1
Multiple disabilities	—	0.2	0.2	0.2	0.2	0.2	0.2	0.2	0.2	0.2	0.2	0.3	0.3	0.3	0.3
Deaf-blindness	—	#	#	#	#	#	#	#	#	#	#	#	#	#	#
Autism and traumatic brain injury	—	—	—	#	0.1	0.1	0.1	0.1	0.1	0.1	0.2	0.2	0.2	0.3	0.4
Developmental delay	—	—	—	—	—	—	—	#	#	#	0.1	0.1	0.6	0.6	
Preschool disabled[1]	—	—	0.9	1.1	1.1	1.2	1.2	1.2	1.2	1.2	1.2	1.3	1.3	†	†

—Not available.
†Not applicable.
#Rounds to zero.
[1]Includes preschool children ages 3–5 served under Chapter 1 and IDEA, Part B. Prior to 1987–88, these students were included in the counts by disability condition. Beginning in 1987–88, states were no longer required to report preschool children (ages 0–5) by disability condition. Beginning in 2002–03, preschool children were again identified by disability condition.
[2]Based on the total enrollment in public schools, prekindergarten through 12th grade.
NOTE: Includes students served under Chapter 1 and Individuals with Disabilities Education Act (IDEA), formerly the Education of the Handicapped Act. Prior to October 1994, children and youth with disabilities were served under the Individuals with Disabilities Education Act, Part B, and Chapter 1 of the Elementary and Secondary Education Act. In October 1994, Congress passed the Improving America's Schools Act, in which funding for children and youth with disabilities was consolidated under IDEA, Part B. Data reported in this table for years prior to 1993–94 include children ages 0–21 served under Chapter 1. Counts are based on reports from the 50 states and the District of Columbia only (i.e., figures from other jurisdictions are not included). Increases since 1987–88 are due in part to new legislation enacted in fall 1986, which mandates public school special education services for all disabled children ages 3 through 5, in addition to age groups previously mandated. Some data have been revised from previously published figures. Detail may not sum to totals because of rounding.
SOURCE: U.S. Department of Education, Office of Special Education and Rehabilitative Services, Annual Report to Congress on the Implementation of The Individuals with Disabilities Education Act, various years, and unpublished tabulations; and Individuals with Disabilities Education Act (IDEA) database. Retrieved on April 18, 2005, from http://www.ideadata.org/tables26th/ar_aa7.htm. National Center for Education Statistics, Statistics of Public Elementary and Secondary Day Schools, various years; and Common Core of Data (CCD), "State Nonfiscal Survey of Public Elementary/Secondary Education," 1990–91 through 2003–04. (This table was prepared April 2005.)

Percentage distribution of disabled students 6 to 21 years old receiving education services for the disabled, by educational environment and type of disability: Fall 1989 through fall 2004

Type of disability	All environments	Regular school, outside regular class			Separate public school facility	Separate private school facility	Public residential facility	Private residential facility	Homebound/ hospital placement
		Less than 21 percent	21–60 percent	More than 60 percent					
1	2	3	4	5	6	7	8	9	10
All disabled students									
1989...........................	100.0	31.7	37.5	24.9	3.2	1.3	0.7	0.3	0.6
1990...........................	100.0	33.1	36.4	25.0	2.9	1.3	0.6	0.3	0.5
1991...........................	100.0	35.1	36.2	23.4	2.5	1.4	0.6	0.3	0.5
1992...........................	100.0	40.0	31.5	23.4	2.4	1.2	0.6	0.3	0.5
1993...........................	100.0	43.7	29.3	22.6	2.2	1.0	0.5	0.3	0.5
1994...........................	100.0	44.8	28.5	22.4	2.0	1.0	0.5	0.3	0.6
1995...........................	100.0	45.7	28.5	21.5	2.1	1.0	0.4	0.3	0.5
1996...........................	100.0	46.1	28.3	21.4	2.0	1.0	0.4	0.3	0.5
1997...........................	100.0	46.8	28.8	20.4	1.8	1.0	0.4	0.3	0.5
1998...........................	100.0	46.0	29.9	20.0	1.8	1.1	0.4	0.3	0.5
1999...........................	100.0	45.9	29.8	20.3	1.9	1.0	0.4	0.3	0.5
2000...........................	100.0	46.5	29.8	19.5	1.9	1.1	0.4	0.3	0.5
2001...........................	100.0	48.2	28.5	19.2	1.7	1.2	0.4	0.4	0.4
2002									
All disabled students..........	**100.0**	**48.2**	**28.7**	**19.0**	**1.7**	**1.2**	**0.3**	**0.4**	**0.5**
Specific learning disabilities...............	100.0	46.9	38.6	13.5	0.3	0.4	0.1	0.1	0.2
Speech or language impairments...............	100.0	87.0	7.5	4.7	0.1	0.6	#	#	0.1
Mental retardation.........................	100.0	10.9	30.5	52.6	4.0	0.9	0.2	0.3	0.5
Emotional disturbance.....................	100.0	28.8	23.0	30.7	7.2	5.2	1.3	2.5	1.4
Multiple disabilities.......................	100.0	11.5	17.2	47.0	12.5	7.4	1.0	1.4	2.1
Hearing impairments	100.0	43.0	19.3	23.7	4.1	2.5	6.8	0.4	0.2
Orthopedic impairments..................	100.0	45.8	22.2	27.5	2.1	0.6	0.1	0.1	1.6
Other health impairments	100.0	49.5	31.4	15.3	0.9	0.8	0.1	0.3	1.8
Visual impairments	100.0	52.6	17.3	16.5	4.0	1.8	6.3	0.9	0.6
Autism.......................................	100.0	24.7	17.8	45.5	5.8	4.6	0.1	1.0	0.4
Deaf-blindness.............................	100.0	17.3	20.3	32.2	10.5	6.1	8.5	4.0	1.2
Traumatic brain injury....................	100.0	28.4	34.8	27.9	2.9	3.5	0.2	0.7	1.7
Developmental delay	100.0	46.3	32.4	19.7	0.5	0.9	0.1	#	0.2
2003									
All disabled students..........	**100.0**	**49.9**	**27.7**	**18.5**	**1.7**	**1.1**	**0.3**	**0.4**	**0.5**
Specific learning disabilities...............	100.0	48.8	37.3	13.0	0.3	0.3	0.1	0.1	0.2
Speech or language impairments...............	100.0	88.2	6.8	4.6	0.1	0.2	#	#	0.1
Mental retardation.........................	100.0	11.7	30.3	51.8	4.4	1.0	0.2	0.3	0.5
Emotional disturbance.....................	100.0	30.3	22.6	30.2	6.6	5.4	1.1	2.6	1.2
Multiple disabilities.......................	100.0	12.1	17.2	45.8	12.7	7.6	1.0	1.5	2.2
Hearing impairments	100.0	45.0	19.1	22.2	4.4	2.5	6.2	0.4	0.2
Orthopedic impairments..................	100.0	46.8	20.9	26.2	3.6	0.7	0.1	0.1	1.6
Other health impairments	100.0	51.1	30.5	15.0	0.8	0.7	0.1	0.2	1.6
Visual impairments	100.0	54.6	16.9	15.6	3.9	2.0	5.4	0.9	0.6
Autism.......................................	100.0	26.8	17.7	43.9	5.6	4.6	0.1	0.9	0.3
Deaf-blindness.............................	100.0	22.0	14.0	33.6	8.5	8.0	8.3	4.2	1.4
Traumatic brain injury....................	100.0	34.6	30.0	27.1	2.7	3.3	0.3	0.7	1.5
Developmental delay	100.0	51.2	28.2	18.6	0.6	1.1	0.1	#	0.2
2004									
All disabled students..........	**100.0**	**51.9**	**26.5**	**17.6**	**1.8**	**1.2**	**0.3**	**0.3**	**0.4**
Specific learning disabilities...............	100.0	51.2	35.8	12.0	0.3	0.4	0.1	0.1	0.2
Speech or language impairments...............	100.0	88.3	6.5	4.7	0.1	0.2	#	#	0.1
Mental retardation.........................	100.0	13.1	29.7	50.8	4.4	1.0	0.3	0.3	0.4
Emotional disturbance.....................	100.0	32.3	22.0	28.4	7.2	5.8	1.2	2.0	1.2
Multiple disabilities.......................	100.0	12.8	16.9	45.2	12.7	8.1	0.9	1.3	2.2
Hearing impairments	100.0	46.9	18.8	20.9	4.3	2.6	5.9	0.4	0.2
Orthopedic impairments..................	100.0	48.2	19.5	25.8	4.0	0.8	0.1	0.1	1.5
Other health impairments	100.0	53.7	29.3	13.6	0.8	0.8	0.1	0.2	1.4
Visual impairments	100.0	56.1	16.1	15.0	3.7	2.1	5.7	0.8	0.5
Autism.......................................	100.0	29.1	17.8	41.8	5.5	4.7	0.1	0.7	0.3
Deaf-blindness.............................	100.0	19.4	15.6	35.1	8.5	6.9	7.6	2.9	3.9
Traumatic brain injury....................	100.0	37.5	28.4	25.9	2.7	3.1	0.2	0.6	1.5
Developmental delay	100.0	56.8	25.2	16.7	0.7	0.2	0.1	#	0.2

#Rounds to zero.
NOTE: Data are for the 50 United States, the District of Columbia, and the Bureau of Indian Affairs schools taken on the Child Count date of the last Friday in October or December 1. Data by disability status are only reported for 6- to 21-year-old students. Detail may not sum to totals because of rounding.

SOURCE: U.S. Department of Education, Office of Special Education Programs, Individuals with Disabilities Education Act (IDEA) database. Retrieved January 20, 2006, from http://www.ideadata.org/docs/PartBTrendData/B4A.xls. (This table was prepared January 2006.)

Number and percentage of children served under Individuals with Disabilities Education Act, Part B, by age group and state or jurisdiction: Selected years, 1990–91 through 2003–04

State or jurisdiction	Ages 3 to 21						Disabled students as a percent of public school enrollment, 2003–04[1]	Percent change, ages 3 to 21, 1990–91 to 2003–04	Ages 3 to 5					
	1990–91	1999–2000	2000–01	2001–02	2002–03	2003–04	2003–04		1990–91	1999–2000	2000–01	2001–02	2002–03	2003–04
1	2	3	4	5	6	7	8	9	10	11	12	13	14	15
United States	**4,710,089**	**6,190,235**	**6,295,816**	**6,407,418**	**6,523,428**	**6,633,902**	**13.7**	**38.5**	**389,751**	**581,997**	**592,087**	**612,084**	**638,394**	**670,406**
Alabama	94,601	99,733	99,828	96,477	95,194	93,056	12.7	-1.6	7,154	7,316	7,554	7,526	7,854	7,843
Alaska	14,390	17,495	17,691	18,017	18,116	17,959	13.4	24.8	1,458	1,633	1,637	1,678	1,774	1,968
Arizona	56,629	93,333	96,442	100,886	103,488	112,125	11.1	98.0	4,330	9,076	9,144	9,906	10,606	11,952
Arkansas	47,187	60,864	62,222	63,969	65,610	66,793	14.7	41.5	4,626	9,031	9,376	9,504	10,007	10,670
California	468,420	640,815	645,287	657,671	669,447	675,763	10.5	44.3	39,627	58,491	57,651	58,456	60,265	61,950
Colorado	56,336	76,858	78,715	80,083	81,327	82,447	10.9	46.3	4,128	8,059	8,202	8,581	9,200	9,673
Connecticut	63,886	74,722	73,886	74,016	74,126	73,952	12.8	15.8	5,466	7,275	7,172	7,390	7,722	8,135
Delaware	14,208	16,287	16,760	17,295	17,817	18,417	15.7	29.6	1,493	1,641	1,652	1,875	1,836	2,031
District of Columbia	6,290	9,348	10,559	12,456	12,065	13,242	17.0	110.5	411	560	374	436	400	301
Florida	234,509	356,198	367,335	379,609	390,883	397,758	15.4	69.6	14,883	29,363	30,660	32,590	34,387	35,258
Georgia	101,762	164,374	171,292	178,239	184,142	190,948	12.5	87.6	7,098	15,922	16,560	17,709	18,689	20,260
Hawaii	12,705	22,964	23,951	23,526	23,509	23,266	12.7	83.1	809	1,860	1,919	1,930	2,112	2,284
Idaho	21,703	29,112	29,174	29,100	29,062	29,092	11.5	34.0	2,815	3,626	3,591	3,650	3,684	3,807
Illinois	236,060	287,475	297,316	306,355	311,436	318,111	15.1	34.8	22,997	27,689	28,787	29,664	31,140	32,718
Indiana	112,949	151,599	156,320	161,519	167,584	171,896	17.0	52.2	7,243	14,499	15,101	16,347	17,448	18,439
Iowa	59,787	71,970	72,461	73,084	73,563	73,717	15.3	23.3	5,421	5,599	5,580	5,487	5,773	5,985
Kansas	44,785	60,036	61,267	61,873	63,905	65,139	13.8	45.4	3,881	7,334	7,728	8,135	8,685	9,190
Kentucky	78,853	91,521	94,572	98,146	100,298	103,783	15.6	31.6	10,440	15,897	16,372	17,747	18,637	20,219
Louisiana	72,825	96,632	97,938	99,325	100,942	101,933	14.0	40.0	6,703	9,671	9,957	10,061	10,769	11,386
Maine	27,987	35,139	35,633	36,580	37,139	37,784	18.7	35.0	2,895	3,954	3,978	4,230	4,482	4,647
Maryland	88,017	111,711	112,077	112,426	113,128	113,865	13.1	29.4	7,163	9,750	10,003	10,614	11,510	12,105
Massachusetts	149,743	165,013	162,216	150,003	155,561	159,042	16.2	6.2	12,141	14,568	14,328	13,070	13,955	14,822
Michigan	166,511	213,585	221,456	226,061	231,799	238,292	13.6	43.1	14,547	19,236	19,937	20,887	22,325	23,465
Minnesota	79,013	107,860	109,880	110,964	112,626	114,193	13.5	44.5	8,646	11,366	11,522	11,804	12,370	12,987
Mississippi	60,872	62,359	62,281	62,196	63,807	66,848	13.5	9.8	5,642	6,812	6,944	6,902	7,268	7,994
Missouri	101,166	134,950	137,381	141,524	144,165	143,593	15.9	41.9	4,100	10,683	11,307	12,222	13,966	15,140
Montana	16,955	19,039	19,313	19,262	19,274	19,435	13.1	14.6	1,751	1,614	1,635	1,687	1,728	1,798
Nebraska	32,312	42,577	42,793	43,864	43,891	44,561	15.6	37.9	2,512	3,707	3,724	3,896	4,290	4,445
Nevada	18,099	35,703	38,160	40,227	42,532	45,201	11.7	149.7	1,401	3,664	3,676	3,976	4,401	4,933
New Hampshire	19,049	28,597	30,077	30,270	30,981	31,311	15.1	64.4	1,468	2,193	2,387	2,452	2,570	2,586
New Jersey	178,870	214,875	221,715	228,844	235,515	241,272	17.5	34.9	14,741	16,058	16,361	16,716	17,433	18,545
New Mexico	36,000	52,346	52,256	52,225	51,904	51,814	16.0	43.9	2,210	5,115	4,970	5,145	5,207	5,656
New York	307,366	434,347	441,333	440,232	440,515	442,665	15.5	44.0	26,266	50,140	51,665	53,313	54,328	55,588
North Carolina	122,942	173,067	173,067	186,972	190,806	193,956	14.3	57.8	10,516	17,361	17,361	19,010	19,921	21,018
North Dakota	12,294	13,612	13,652	13,627	13,901	14,044	13.7	14.2	1,164	1,283	1,247	1,294	1,394	1,501

See notes at end of table.

Number and percentage of children served under Individuals with Disabilities Education Act, Part B, by age group and state or jurisdiction: Selected years, 1990–91 through 2003–04—Continued

State or jurisdiction	Ages 3 to 21						Disabled students as a percent of public school enrollment, 2003–04[1]	Percent change, ages 3 to 21, 1990–91 to 2003–04	Ages 3 to 5					
	1990–91	1999–2000	2000–01	2001–02	2002–03	2003–04			1990–91	1999–2000	2000–01	2001–02	2002–03	2003–04
1	2	3	4	5	6	7	8	9	10	11	12	13	14	15
Ohio	205,440	236,200	237,643	238,547	248,127	253,878	13.8	23.6	12,487	19,341	18,664	19,075	19,182	19,659
Oklahoma	65,457	83,149	85,577	87,801	91,226	93,045	14.9	42.1	5,163	6,077	6,393	6,714	7,414	7,769
Oregon	54,422	73,531	75,204	76,129	77,100	76,083	13.8	39.8	2,854	6,387	6,926	7,227	7,370	7,453
Pennsylvania	214,254	233,273	242,655	249,731	262,325	273,259	15.0	27.5	17,982	21,161	21,477	21,885	23,265	24,459
Rhode Island	20,646	29,895	30,727	31,816	32,718	32,223	20.2	56.1	1,682	2,651	2,614	2,692	2,830	2,930
South Carolina	77,367	103,153	105,922	110,037	110,195	111,077	15.9	43.6	7,948	11,352	11,775	11,967	11,927	11,818
South Dakota	14,726	16,246	16,825	16,931	17,441	17,760	14.1	20.6	2,105	2,267	2,286	2,244	2,362	2,540
Tennessee	104,853	126,732	125,863	126,245	125,389	122,627	13.1	17.0	7,487	10,690	10,699	11,132	10,449	11,121
Texas	344,529	493,850	491,642	492,857	496,234	506,771	11.7	47.1	24,848	36,079	36,442	37,244	37,396	40,607
Utah	46,606	54,957	53,921	54,570	56,085	57,745	11.6	23.9	3,424	5,899	5,785	5,922	6,381	6,733
Vermont	12,160	14,073	13,623	13,886	13,722	13,670	13.8	12.4	1,097	1,391	1,237	1,293	1,307	1,378
Virginia	112,072	157,995	162,212	170,518	169,558	172,788	14.5	54.2	9,892	14,023	14,444	15,145	15,691	16,422
Washington	83,545	116,235	118,851	120,970	122,484	123,673	12.1	48.0	9,558	11,623	11,760	11,881	12,445	13,010
West Virginia	42,428	50,314	50,333	50,136	50,443	50,772	18.1	19.7	2,923	5,409	5,445	5,332	5,400	5,604
Wisconsin	85,651	121,209	125,358	127,035	127,031	127,828	14.5	49.2	10,934	13,934	14,383	14,574	14,802	15,393
Wyoming	10,852	13,307	13,154	13,286	13,292	13,430	15.4	23.8	1,221	1,667	1,695	1,867	2,037	2,211
Bureau of Indian Affairs	6,997	12,913	8,448	8,571	8,310	8,343	18.2	19.2	1,092	386	338	266	306	344
Other jurisdictions	38,986	63,981	70,670	71,440	74,964	83,948	12.7	115.3	3,892	6,750	8,168	7,845	8,720	9,392
American Samoa	363	703	697	813	969	1,135	7.1	212.7	48	55	48	64	102	138
Guam	1,750	2,230	2,267	2,368	2,406	2,460	7.8	40.6	198	195	205	218	230	200
Northern Marianas	411	568	569	590	588	669	5.9	62.8	211	48	53	52	52	69
Palau	—	123	131	169	—	—	—	—	—	11	10	13	—	—
Puerto Rico	35,129	58,740	65,504	65,874	69,327	77,932	13.3	121.8	3,345	6,274	7,746	7,378	8,159	8,806
Virgin Islands	1,333	1,617	1,502	1,626	1,674	1,752	9.9	31.4	90	167	106	120	177	179

—Not available.

[1] Percent of students that are disabled is based on the enrollment in public schools, prekindergarten through 12th grade.
NOTE: Prior to 1994, children and youth with disabilities were served under the Individuals with Disabilities Education Act (IDEA), Part B, and Chapter 1 of the Elementary and Secondary Education Act. In October 1994, Congress passed the Improving America's Schools Act, in which funding for children and youth with disabilities was consolidated under IDEA, Part B. Data reported in this table for years prior to 1994 include children served under Chapter 1. Some data have been revised from previously published figures.

SOURCE: U.S. Department of Education, Office of Special Education and Rehabilitative Services, *Annual Report to Congress on the Implementation of The Individuals with Disabilities Education Act*, various years. Individuals with Disabilities Education Act (IDEA) database. Retrieved on April 18, 2005, from http://www.ideadata.org/tables26th/ar_aa1.htm and http://www.ideadata.org/tables27th/ar_aa1.htm. National Center for Education Statistics, Common Core of Data (CCD), "State Nonfiscal Survey of Public Elementary/Secondary Education," 2003–04. (This table was prepared April 2005.)

High school graduates, by sex and control of school: Selected years, 1869–70 through 2004–05

[Numbers in thousands]

| | High school graduates | | | | |
| | | Sex | | Control | |
School year	Total[1]	Males	Females	Public[2]	Private[3]
1	2	3	4	5	6
1869–70	16	7	9	—	—
1879–80	24	11	13	—	—
1889–90	44	19	25	22	22
1899–1900	95	38	57	62	33
1909–10	156	64	93	111	45
1919–20	311	124	188	231	80
1929–30	667	300	367	592	75
1939–40	1,221	579	643	1,143	78
1949–50	1,200	571	629	1,063	136
1959–60	1,858	895	963	1,627	231
1960–61	1,964	955	1,009	1,725	239
1961–62	1,918	938	980	1,678	240
1962–63	1,943	956	987	1,710	233
1963–64	2,283	1,120	1,163	2,008	275
1964–65	2,658	1,311	1,347	2,360	298
1965–66	2,665	1,323	1,342	2,367	298
1966–67	2,672	1,328	1,344	2,374	298
1967–68	2,695	1,338	1,357	2,395	300
1968–69	2,822	1,399	1,423	2,522	300
1969–70	2,889	1,430	1,459	2,589	300
1970–71	2,938	1,454	1,484	2,638	300
1971–72	3,002	1,487	1,515	2,700	302
1972–73	3,035	1,500	1,535	2,729	306
1973–74	3,073	1,512	1,561	2,763	310
1974–75	3,133	1,542	1,591	2,823	310
1975–76	3,148	1,552	1,596	2,837	311
1976–77	3,152	1,548	1,604	2,837	315
1977–78	3,127	1,531	1,596	2,825	302
1978–79	3,101	1,517	1,584	2,801	300
1979–80	3,043	1,491	1,552	2,748	295
1980–81	3,020	1,483	1,537	2,725	295
1981–82	2,995	1,471	1,524	2,705	290
1982–83	2,888	1,437	1,451	2,598	290
1983–84	2,767	—	—	2,495	272
1984–85	2,677	—	—	2,414	263
1985–86	2,643	—	—	2,383	260
1986–87	2,694	—	—	2,429	265
1987–88	2,773	—	—	2,500	273
1988–89	2,744	—	—	2,459	285
1989–90	2,589	—	—	2,320	269
1990–91	2,493	—	—	2,235	258
1991–92	2,478	—	—	2,226	252
1992–93	2,480	—	—	2,233	247
1993–94	2,464	—	—	2,221	243
1994–95	2,520	—	—	2,274	246
1995–96	2,518	—	—	2,273	245
1996–97	2,612	—	—	2,358	254
1997–98	2,704	—	—	2,439	265
1998–99	2,759	—	—	2,486	273
1999–2000	2,833	—	—	2,554	279
2000–01	2,848	—	—	2,569	279
2001–02	2,908	—	—	2,622	286
2002–03	3,021	—	—	2,720	301
2003–04[4]	3,063	—	—	2,758	305
2004–05[4]	3,089	—	—	2,780	309

—Not available.

[1]Includes graduates of public and private schools.

[2]Data for 1929–30 and preceding years are from *Statistics of Public High Schools* and exclude graduates from high schools that failed to report to the Office of Education.

[3]For most years, private school data have been estimated based on periodic private school surveys.

[4]Projected.

NOTE: Includes graduates of regular day school programs. Excludes graduates of other programs, when separately reported, and recipients of high school equivalency certificates. Some data have been revised from previously published figures. Detail may not sum to totals because of rounding.

SOURCE: U.S. Department of Education, National Center for Education Statistics, *Annual Report of the Commissioner of Education*, 1870 through 1910; *Biennial Survey of Education in the United States*, 1919–20 through 1949–50; *Statistics of State School Systems*, 1951–52 through 1957–58; *Statistics of Public Elementary and Secondary School Systems*, 1958–59 through 1980–81; *Statistics of Nonpublic Elementary and Secondary Schools*, 1959 through 1980; Common Core of Data (CCD), "State Nonfiscal Survey of Public Elementary/Secondary Education," 1981–82 through 2003–04; Private School Universe Survey (PSS), 1989 through 2001; and *Projections of Education Statistics to 2014.* (This table was prepared January 2006.)

Public high school graduates, by state or jurisdiction: Selected years, 1969–70 through 2003–04

State or jurisdiction	1969–70	1980–81	1985–86	1990–91	1995–96	1999–2000	2000–01	2001–02[1]	2002–03	Projected 2003–04, graduates	Percent change, 1990–91 to 2003–04
1	2	3	4	5	6	7	8	9	10	11	12
United States	2,588,639	2,725,285	2,382,616	2,234,893	2,273,109	2,553,844	2,568,956	2,621,534	2,719,947	2,757,540	23.4
Alabama	45,286	44,894	39,620	39,042	35,043	37,819	37,082	35,887	36,741	37,610	-3.7
Alaska	3,297	5,343	5,464	5,458	5,945	6,615	6,812	6,945	7,297	7,100	30.1
Arizona	22,040	28,416	27,533	31,282	30,008	38,304	46,773	47,175	49,986	57,010	82.2
Arkansas	26,068	29,577	26,227	25,668	25,094	27,335	27,100	26,984	27,555	26,890	4.8
California	260,908	242,172	229,026	234,164	259,071	309,866	315,189	325,895	341,097	342,580	46.3
Colorado	30,312	35,897	32,621	31,293	32,608	38,924	39,241	40,760	42,379	42,920	37.2
Connecticut	34,755	38,369	33,571	27,290	26,319	31,562	30,388	32,327	33,667	34,380	26.0
Delaware	6,985	7,349	5,791	5,223	5,609	6,108	6,614	6,482	6,817	6,840	31.0
District of Columbia[2]	4,980	4,848	3,875	3,369	2,696	2,695	2,808	3,090	2,725	3,150	-6.5
Florida	70,478	88,755	83,029	87,419	89,242	106,708	111,112	119,537	127,484	129,020	47.6
Georgia	56,859	62,963	59,082	60,088	56,271	62,563	62,499	65,983	66,890	69,720	16.0
Hawaii	10,407	11,472	9,958	8,974	9,387	10,437	10,102	10,452	10,013	10,300	14.8
Idaho	12,296	12,679	12,059	11,961	14,667	16,170	15,941	15,874	15,858	15,460	29.3
Illinois	126,864	136,795	114,319	103,329	104,626	111,835	110,624	116,657	117,507	121,270	17.4
Indiana	69,984	73,381	59,817	57,892	56,330	57,012	56,172	56,722	57,897	57,610	-0.5
Iowa	44,063	42,635	34,279	28,593	31,689	33,926	33,774	33,789	34,860	33,820	18.3
Kansas	33,394	29,397	25,587	24,414	25,786	29,102	29,360	29,541	29,963	30,040	23.0
Kentucky	37,473	41,714	37,288	35,835	36,641	36,830	36,957	36,337	37,654	36,170	0.9
Louisiana	43,641	46,199	39,965	33,489	36,467	38,430	38,314	37,905	37,610	36,220	8.2
Maine	14,003	15,554	13,006	13,151	11,795	12,211	12,654	12,593	12,947	13,380	1.7
Maryland	46,462	54,050	46,700	39,014	41,785	47,849	49,222	50,881	51,864	53,030	35.9
Massachusetts	63,865	74,831	60,360	50,216	47,993	52,950	54,393	55,272	55,987	57,930	15.4
Michigan	121,000	124,372	101,042	88,234	85,530	97,679	96,515	95,001	100,301	106,320	20.5
Minnesota	60,480	64,166	51,988	46,474	50,481	57,372	56,581	57,440	59,432	59,780	28.6
Mississippi	29,653	28,083	25,134	23,665	23,032	24,232	23,748	23,740	23,810	23,610	-0.2
Missouri	55,315	60,359	49,204	46,928	49,011	52,848	54,138	54,487	56,925	56,980	21.4
Montana	11,520	11,634	9,761	9,013	10,139	10,903	10,628	10,554	10,657	10,520	16.7
Nebraska	21,280	21,411	17,845	16,500	18,014	20,149	19,658	19,910	20,161	20,020	21.3
Nevada	5,449	9,069	8,784	9,370	10,374	14,551	15,127	16,270	16,378	16,220	73.1
New Hampshire	8,516	11,552	10,648	10,059	10,094	11,829	12,294	12,452	13,210	13,250	31.7
New Jersey	86,498	93,168	78,781	67,003	67,704	74,420	76,130	77,664	81,391	88,330	31.8
New Mexico	16,060	17,915	15,468	15,157	15,402	18,031	18,199	18,094	16,923	18,050	19.1
New York	190,000	198,465	162,165	133,562	134,401	141,731	141,884	140,139	143,818	150,880	13.0
North Carolina	68,886	69,395	65,865	62,792	57,014	62,140	63,288	65,955	69,696	71,380	13.7
North Dakota	11,150	9,924	7,610	7,573	8,027	8,606	8,445	8,114	8,169	7,790	2.9
Ohio	142,248	143,503	119,561	107,484	102,098	111,668	111,281	110,608	115,762	116,270	8.2
Oklahoma	36,293	38,875	34,452	33,007	33,060	37,646	37,458	36,852	36,694	36,670	11.1
Oregon	32,236	28,729	26,286	24,597	26,570	30,151	29,939	31,153	32,587	32,530	32.3
Pennsylvania	151,014	144,645	122,871	104,770	105,981	113,959	114,436	114,943	119,933	121,550	16.0
Rhode Island	10,146	10,719	8,908	7,744	7,689	8,477	8,603	9,006	9,318	9,280	19.8
South Carolina	34,940	38,347	34,500	32,999	30,182	31,617	29,742	31,302	32,482	32,110	-2.7
South Dakota	11,757	10,385	7,870	7,127	8,532	9,278	8,881	8,796	8,999	9,090	27.5
Tennessee	49,000	50,648	43,263	44,847	43,792	41,568	40,642	40,894	44,113	43,620	-2.7
Texas	139,046	171,665	161,150	174,306	171,844	212,925	215,316	225,167	238,111	236,670	35.8
Utah	18,395	19,886	19,774	22,219	26,293	32,501	31,036	30,183	29,527	29,920	34.7
Vermont	6,095	6,424	5,794	5,212	5,867	6,675	6,856	7,083	6,970	7,030	34.9
Virginia	58,562	67,126	63,113	58,441	58,166	65,596	66,067	66,519	72,943	71,740	22.8
Washington	50,425	50,046	45,805	42,514	49,862	57,597	55,081	58,311	60,435	60,410	42.1
West Virginia	26,139	23,580	21,870	21,064	20,335	19,437	18,440	17,128	17,287	17,070	-19.0
Wisconsin	66,753	67,743	58,340	49,340	52,651	58,545	59,341	60,575	63,272	62,270	26.2
Wyoming	5,363	6,161	5,587	5,728	5,892	6,462	6,071	6,106	5,845	5,730	#

See notes at end of table.

Public high school graduates, by state or jurisdiction: Selected years, 1969–70 through 2003–04—Continued

State or jurisdiction	1969–70	1980–81	1985–86	1990–91	1995–96	1999–2000	2000–01	2001–02[1]	2002–03	Projected 2003–04, graduates	Percent change, 1990–91 to 2003–04
1	2	3	4	5	6	7	8	9	10	11	12
Bureau of Indian Affairs	—	—	—	—	—	—	—	—	—	—	—
Department of Defense dependents schools											
Overseas schools	—	—	—	—	2,674	2,642	2,621	2,554	3,231	—	—
Domestic schools.....................	—	—	—	—	—	560	568	565	—	—	—
Other jurisdictions											
American Samoa	[3] 367	—	608	597	719	698	722	823	832	—	—
Guam.....................................	972	—	840	1,014	987	1,406	1,371	—	1,502	—	—
Northern Marianas...................	—	—	—	273	325	360	361	416	422	—	—
Puerto Rico.............................	24,917	—	31,597	29,329	29,499	30,856	30,154	30,278	31,408	—	—
Virgin Islands	[3] 432	—	1,044	981	937	1,060	966	883	886	—	—

—Not available.

#Rounds to zero.

[1]Revised from previously published figures.

[2]Beginning in 1985–86, graduates from adult programs are excluded.

[3]Data are for 1970–71.

NOTE: Data include graduates of regular day school programs, but exclude graduates of other programs and persons receiving high school equivalency certificates. Detail may not sum to totals because of rounding. Some data have been revised from previously published figures.

SOURCE: U.S. Department of Education, National Center for Education Statistics, *Statistics of Public Elementary and Secondary Day Schools, 1969–70*; Common Core of Data (CCD), "State Nonfiscal Survey of Public Elementary/Secondary Education," 1981–82 through 2003–04; and *Projections of Education Statistics to 2014*. (This table was prepared January 2006.)

Public high school graduates and dropouts, by race/ethnicity and state or jurisdiction: 2001–02

State or other jurisdiction	High school graduates, by race/ethnicity, 2001–02						Percent of 9th- to 12th-graders who dropped out during 2001–02, by race/ethnicity[1]					
	Total	White, non-Hispanic	Black, non-Hispanic	Hispanic	Asian/Pacific Islander	American Indian/Alaska Native	Total	White, non-Hispanic	Black, non-Hispanic	Hispanic	Asian/Pacific Islander	American Indian/Alaska Native
1	2	3	4	5	6	7	8	9	10	11	12	13
United States[2,3]	2,618,941	1,800,190	345,497	314,093	132,040	27,121	—	—	—	—	—	—
Alabama	35,887	23,462	11,374	245	347	459	3.7	3.6	3.9	4.5	1.6	2.1
Alaska	6,945	4,734	252	197	422	1,340	8.1	6.2	11.4	8.9	6.7	13.4
Arizona	47,175	28,640	2,008	12,479	1,286	2,762	10.5	6.8	13.4	15.2	3.9	19.0
Arkansas	26,984	20,138	5,779	626	323	118	5.3	4.6	7.0	7.7	4.3	6.9
California	324,152	140,421	23,451	109,038	48,206	3,036	—	—	—	—	—	—
Colorado	40,760	31,506	1,798	5,700	1,442	314	—	—	—	—	—	—
Connecticut	32,327	24,721	3,617	2,886	1,029	74	2.6	1.9	4.0	5.3	2.4	4.9
Delaware[2]	6,482	4,358	1,683	241	185	15	6.2	4.6	9.0	11.6	3.5	5.1
District of Columbia	3,090	128	2,684	209	66	3	—	—	—	—	—	—
Florida	119,537	70,862	24,960	20,067	3,345	303	3.7	3.0	4.9	4.5	1.9	3.6
Georgia	65,983	40,801	21,357	1,593	2,151	81	6.5	5.8	7.6	9.8	3.6	7.5
Hawaii	10,452	2,013	167	467	7,771	34	5.1	5.5	5.5	6.4	4.9	6.6
Idaho	15,874	14,296	76	1,063	248	191	3.9	—	—	—	—	—
Illinois	116,657	82,454	16,294	12,242	5,234	433	6.4	3.7	13.6	10.4	2.6	5.7
Indiana	56,722	49,846	4,650	1,428	657	141	2.3	2.1	3.1	4.0	1.1	2.8
Iowa	33,789	31,608	756	660	657	108	2.4	2.1	6.8	7.1	2.7	6.6
Kansas	29,541	25,219	1,856	1,498	685	283	3.1	2.6	5.3	5.9	2.4	5.4
Kentucky	36,337	32,556	3,151	249	350	31	3.9	3.8	5.3	4.0	1.7	0.0
Louisiana	37,905	21,252	15,322	484	622	225	7.0	5.0	9.5	6.9	5.1	7.3
Maine	12,593	12,201	110	61	144	77	2.8	2.8	4.4	3.7	2.7	5.0
Maryland	50,881	29,363	16,745	1,890	2,725	158	3.9	3.0	5.5	3.7	1.4	4.1
Massachusetts	55,272	44,973	3,944	3,526	2,693	136	—	—	—	—	—	—
Michigan	95,001	77,947	11,619	2,284	2,250	901	—	—	—	—	—	—
Minnesota	57,440	51,052	2,122	1,032	2,573	661	3.8	2.7	9.9	14.5	4.4	14.2
Mississippi	23,740	12,174	11,195	120	219	32	3.9	3.1	4.7	4.1	2.2	2.2
Missouri	54,487	45,627	7,195	696	821	148	3.6	3.2	5.8	5.8	1.6	4.8
Montana	10,554	9,537	34	158	112	713	3.9	3.2	6.7	5.2	2.0	10.3
Nebraska	19,910	17,851	796	756	357	150	4.2	3.1	11.3	11.7	3.3	11.9
Nevada	16,270	10,879	1,285	2,728	1,123	255	6.4	5.0	8.9	9.3	5.2	5.6
New Hampshire	12,452	—	—	—	—	—	4.0	3.9	6.5	7.8	3.2	7.5
New Jersey	77,664	50,347	11,909	9,657	5,619	132	2.5	1.5	4.9	4.7	0.9	2.2
New Mexico	18,094	—	—	—	—	—	5.2	3.5	2.6	6.4	3.4	5.8
New York	140,139	94,528	19,686	15,524	9,946	455	7.1	3.3	12.9	14.2	5.9	9.4
North Carolina	65,955	44,888	17,385	1,559	1,410	713	5.7	4.9	7.0	9.4	3.7	9.9
North Dakota	8,114	7,564	58	68	62	362	2.0	1.5	2.7	3.4	1.9	8.0
Ohio[2]	110,090	95,036	11,945	1,441	1,568	100	3.1	2.4	7.2	6.6	2.0	7.1
Oklahoma	36,852	25,385	3,299	1,562	650	5,956	4.4	3.8	6.7	9.4	3.2	3.8
Oregon[2]	30,821	26,464	594	1,990	1,283	490	4.6	4.0	9.9	10.5	3.6	0.0
Pennsylvania	114,943	97,397	11,655	3,093	2,696	102	3.3	2.4	7.0	8.9	2.9	3.3
Rhode Island	9,006	7,132	657	857	317	43	4.3	3.3	6.9	8.2	4.6	5.9
South Carolina	31,302	—	—	—	—	—	3.3	3.1	3.7	3.9	1.7	3.1
South Dakota	8,796	8,232	49	62	99	354	2.8	2.0	7.3	6.1	1.9	13.0
Tennessee	40,894	—	—	—	—	—	3.8	—	—	—	—	—
Texas	225,167	112,386	30,030	74,466	7,707	578	3.8	2.2	4.9	5.5	1.6	4.1
Utah	30,183	27,307	172	1,574	817	313	3.7	3.1	8.8	8.2	5.2	8.1
Vermont	7,083	—	—	—	—	—	4.0	3.9	7.3	9.0	2.2	5.9
Virginia	66,519	45,485	15,084	2,454	3,353	143	2.9	2.3	4.0	5.8	2.0	4.1
Washington	58,311	45,918	2,306	3,937	5,030	1,120	7.1	5.6	16.8	12.3	6.6	15.2
West Virginia	17,128	16,281	600	70	148	29	3.7	3.7	3.9	1.8	1.8	8.9
Wisconsin	60,575	53,255	3,148	1,792	1,757	623	1.9	1.2	8.3	5.6	1.8	4.1
Wyoming	6,106	5,569	60	324	51	102	5.8	5.2	9.9	12.3	2.7	13.0

See notes at end of table.

Public high school graduates and dropouts, by race/ethnicity and state or jurisdiction: 2001–02—Continued

State or other jurisdiction	High school graduates, by race/ethnicity, 2001–02						Percent of 9th- to 12th-graders who dropped out during 2001–02, by race/ethnicity[1]					
	Total	White, non-Hispanic	Black, non-Hispanic	Hispanic	Asian/ Pacific Islander	American Indian/ Alaska Native	Total	White, non-Hispanic	Black, non-Hispanic	Hispanic	Asian/ Pacific Islander	American Indian/ Alaska Native
1	2	3	4	5	6	7	8	9	10	11	12	13
Bureau of Indian Affairs schools	—	—	—	—	—	—	—	—	—	—	—	—
Department of Defense dependents schools												
Overseas schools	2,052	1,130	417	163	342	0	—	—	—	—	—	—
Domestic schools...........	498	193	101	187	17	0	—	—	—	—	—	—
Other jurisdictions												
American Samoa	823	0	0	0	823	0	1.1	—	—	—	1.1	—
Guam.............................	—	—	—	—	—	—	—	—	—	—	—	—
Northern Marianas........	416	1	0	0	415	0	7.1	0.0	16.7	—	7.2	—
Puerto Rico...................	30,278	0	0	30,278	0	0	1.2	—	—	1.2	—	—
Virgin Islands	883	3	811	68	0	1	—	—	—	—	—	—

—Not available.

[1]Alabama, Alaska, Arizona, Florida, Illinois, Maryland, New Jersey, New York, Tennessee, Vermont, and Puerto Rico reported data on an alternative July through June cycle, rather than the specified October through September cycle for dropout data.

[2]Includes estimates for nonreporting states, based on 2001 12th-grade enrollment racial/ethnic distribution reported by state.

[3]Data differ slightly from figures reported in other tables due to varying reporting practices for racial/ethnic survey data.

SOURCE: U.S. Department of Education, National Center for Education Statistics, Common Core of Data (CCD), "State Nonfiscal Survey of Public Elementary/Secondary Education," 2002–03, and "Local Education Agency Universe Survey Dropout and Completion Data File," 2001–02; and unpublished tabulations. (This table was prepared January 2006.)

Percentage of high school dropouts (status dropouts) among persons 16 to 24 years old, by sex and race/ethnicity: 1960 through 2004

Year	Total				Male				Female			
	All races[1]	White, non-Hispanic	Black, non-Hispanic	Hispanic origin	All races[1]	White, non-Hispanic	Black, non-Hispanic	Hispanic origin	All races[1]	White, non-Hispanic	Black, non-Hispanic	Hispanic origin
1	2	3	4	5	6	7	8	9	10	11	12	13
1960[2]	27.2 (—)	— (†)	— (†)	— (†)	27.8 (—)	— (†)	— (†)	— (†)	26.7 (—)	— (†)	— (†)	— (†)
1967[3]	17.0 (—)	15.4 (—)	28.6 (—)	— (†)	16.5 (—)	14.7 (—)	30.6 (—)	— (†)	17.3 (—)	16.1 (—)	26.9 (—)	— (†)
1968[3]	16.2 (—)	14.7 (—)	27.4 (—)	— (†)	15.8 (—)	14.4 (—)	27.1 (—)	— (†)	16.5 (—)	15.0 (—)	27.6 (—)	— (†)
1969[3]	15.2 (—)	13.6 (—)	26.7 (—)	— (†)	14.3 (—)	12.6 (—)	26.9 (—)	— (†)	16.0 (—)	14.6 (—)	26.7 (—)	— (†)
1970[3]	15.0 (0.29)	13.2 (0.30)	27.9 (1.22)	— (†)	14.2 (0.42)	12.2 (0.42)	29.4 (1.82)	— (†)	15.7 (0.41)	14.1 (0.42)	26.6 (1.65)	— (†)
1971[3]	14.7 (0.28)	13.4 (0.29)	24.0 (1.14)	— (†)	14.2 (0.41)	12.6 (0.41)	25.5 (1.70)	— (†)	15.2 (0.40)	14.2 (0.42)	22.6 (1.54)	— (†)
1972	14.6 (0.28)	12.3 (0.29)	21.3 (1.07)	34.3 (2.22)	14.1 (0.40)	11.6 (0.40)	22.3 (1.59)	33.7 (3.23)	15.1 (0.39)	12.8 (0.41)	20.5 (1.44)	34.8 (3.05)
1973	14.1 (0.27)	11.6 (0.28)	22.2 (1.06)	33.5 (2.24)	13.7 (0.38)	11.5 (0.39)	21.5 (1.53)	30.4 (3.16)	14.5 (0.38)	11.8 (0.39)	22.8 (1.47)	36.4 (3.16)
1974	14.3 (0.27)	11.9 (0.28)	21.2 (1.05)	33.0 (2.08)	14.2 (0.39)	12.0 (0.40)	20.1 (1.51)	33.8 (2.99)	14.3 (0.38)	11.8 (0.39)	22.1 (1.45)	32.2 (2.90)
1975	13.9 (0.27)	11.4 (0.27)	22.9 (1.06)	29.2 (2.02)	13.3 (0.37)	11.0 (0.38)	23.0 (1.56)	26.7 (2.84)	14.5 (0.38)	11.8 (0.39)	22.9 (1.44)	31.6 (2.86)
1976	14.1 (0.27)	12.0 (0.28)	20.5 (1.00)	31.4 (2.01)	14.1 (0.38)	12.1 (0.39)	21.2 (1.49)	30.3 (2.94)	14.2 (0.37)	11.8 (0.39)	19.9 (1.35)	32.3 (2.76)
1977	14.1 (0.27)	11.9 (0.28)	19.8 (0.99)	33.0 (2.02)	14.5 (0.38)	12.6 (0.40)	19.5 (1.45)	31.6 (2.89)	13.8 (0.37)	11.2 (0.38)	20.0 (1.36)	34.3 (2.83)
1978	14.2 (0.27)	11.9 (0.28)	20.2 (1.00)	33.3 (2.00)	14.6 (0.38)	12.2 (0.40)	22.5 (1.52)	33.6 (2.88)	13.9 (0.37)	11.6 (0.39)	18.3 (1.31)	33.1 (2.78)
1979	14.6 (0.27)	12.0 (0.28)	21.1 (1.01)	33.8 (1.98)	15.0 (0.39)	12.6 (0.40)	22.4 (1.52)	33.0 (2.83)	14.2 (0.37)	11.5 (0.38)	20.0 (1.35)	34.5 (2.77)
1980	14.1 (0.26)	11.4 (0.27)	19.1 (0.97)	35.2 (1.89)	15.1 (0.39)	12.3 (0.40)	20.8 (1.47)	37.2 (2.72)	13.1 (0.36)	10.5 (0.37)	17.7 (1.28)	33.2 (2.61)
1981	13.9 (0.26)	11.3 (0.27)	18.4 (0.93)	33.2 (1.80)	15.1 (0.38)	12.5 (0.40)	19.9 (1.40)	36.0 (2.61)	12.8 (0.35)	10.2 (0.36)	17.1 (1.24)	30.4 (2.48)
1982	13.9 (0.27)	11.4 (0.29)	18.4 (0.97)	31.7 (1.93)	14.5 (0.40)	12.0 (0.42)	21.2 (1.50)	30.5 (2.73)	13.3 (0.38)	10.8 (0.40)	15.9 (1.26)	32.8 (2.71)
1983	13.7 (0.27)	11.1 (0.29)	18.0 (0.97)	31.6 (1.93)	14.9 (0.41)	12.2 (0.43)	19.9 (1.46)	34.3 (2.84)	12.5 (0.37)	10.1 (0.39)	16.2 (1.28)	29.1 (2.61)
1984	13.1 (0.27)	11.0 (0.29)	15.5 (0.91)	29.8 (1.91)	14.0 (0.40)	11.9 (0.43)	16.8 (1.37)	30.6 (2.78)	12.3 (0.37)	10.1 (0.39)	14.3 (1.22)	29.0 (2.63)
1985	12.6 (0.27)	10.4 (0.29)	15.2 (0.92)	27.6 (1.93)	13.4 (0.40)	11.1 (0.42)	16.1 (1.37)	29.9 (2.76)	11.8 (0.37)	9.8 (0.39)	14.3 (1.23)	25.2 (2.68)
1986	12.2 (0.27)	9.7 (0.28)	14.2 (0.90)	30.1 (1.88)	13.1 (0.40)	10.3 (0.42)	15.0 (1.33)	32.8 (2.66)	11.4 (0.37)	9.1 (0.39)	13.5 (1.21)	27.2 (2.63)
1987	12.6 (0.28)	10.4 (0.30)	14.1 (0.90)	28.6 (1.84)	13.2 (0.40)	10.8 (0.43)	15.0 (1.35)	29.1 (2.57)	12.1 (0.38)	10.0 (0.41)	13.3 (1.21)	28.1 (2.64)
1988	12.9 (0.30)	9.6 (0.31)	14.5 (1.00)	35.8 (2.30)	13.5 (0.44)	10.3 (0.46)	15.0 (1.48)	36.0 (3.19)	12.2 (0.42)	8.9 (0.43)	14.0 (1.36)	35.4 (3.31)
1989	12.6 (0.31)	9.4 (0.32)	13.9 (0.98)	33.0 (2.19)	13.6 (0.45)	10.3 (0.47)	14.9 (1.46)	34.4 (3.08)	11.7 (0.42)	8.5 (0.43)	13.0 (1.32)	31.6 (3.11)
1990	12.1 (0.29)	9.0 (0.30)	13.2 (0.94)	32.4 (1.91)	12.3 (0.42)	9.3 (0.44)	11.9 (1.30)	34.3 (2.71)	11.8 (0.41)	8.7 (0.42)	14.4 (1.34)	30.3 (2.70)
1991	12.5 (0.30)	8.9 (0.31)	13.6 (0.95)	35.3 (1.93)	13.0 (0.43)	8.9 (0.44)	13.5 (1.37)	39.2 (2.74)	11.9 (0.41)	8.9 (0.43)	13.7 (1.31)	31.1 (2.70)
1992[4]	11.0 (0.28)	7.7 (0.29)	13.7 (0.95)	29.4 (1.86)	11.3 (0.41)	8.0 (0.42)	12.5 (1.32)	32.1 (2.67)	10.7 (0.39)	7.4 (0.40)	14.8 (1.36)	26.6 (2.56)
1993[4]	11.0 (0.28)	7.9 (0.29)	13.6 (0.94)	27.5 (1.79)	11.2 (0.40)	8.2 (0.42)	12.6 (1.32)	28.1 (2.54)	10.9 (0.40)	7.6 (0.41)	14.4 (1.34)	26.9 (2.52)
1994[4]	11.4 (0.26)	7.7 (0.27)	12.6 (0.75)	30.0 (1.16)	12.3 (0.38)	8.0 (0.38)	14.1 (1.14)	31.6 (1.60)	10.6 (0.36)	7.5 (0.37)	11.3 (0.99)	28.1 (1.66)
1995[4]	12.0 (0.27)	8.6 (0.28)	12.1 (0.74)	30.0 (1.15)	12.2 (0.38)	9.0 (0.40)	11.1 (1.05)	30.0 (1.59)	11.7 (0.37)	8.2 (0.39)	12.9 (1.05)	30.0 (1.66)

See notes at end of table.

Percentage of high school dropouts (status dropouts) among persons 16 to 24 years old, by sex and race/ethnicity: 1960 through 2004—Continued

	Total				Male				Female			
Year	All races[1]	White, non-Hispanic	Black, non-Hispanic	Hispanic origin	All races[1]	White, non-Hispanic	Black, non-Hispanic	Hispanic origin	All races[1]	White, non-Hispanic	Black, non-Hispanic	Hispanic origin
1	2	3	4	5	6	7	8	9	10	11	12	13
1996[4]	11.1 (0.27)	7.3 (0.27)	13.0 (0.80)	29.4 (1.19)	11.4 (0.38)	7.3 (0.38)	13.5 (1.18)	30.3 (1.67)	10.9 (0.38)	7.3 (0.39)	12.5 (1.08)	28.3 (1.69)
1997[4]	11.0 (0.27)	7.6 (0.28)	13.4 (0.80)	25.3 (1.11)	11.9 (0.39)	8.5 (0.41)	13.3 (1.16)	27.0 (1.55)	10.1 (0.36)	6.7 (0.37)	13.5 (1.11)	23.4 (1.59)
1998[4]	11.8 (0.27)	7.7 (0.28)	13.8 (0.81)	29.5 (1.12)	13.3 (0.40)	8.6 (0.41)	15.5 (1.24)	33.5 (1.59)	10.3 (0.36)	6.9 (0.37)	12.2 (1.05)	25.0 (1.56)
1999[4]	11.2 (0.26)	7.3 (0.27)	12.6 (0.77)	28.6 (1.11)	11.9 (0.38)	7.7 (0.39)	12.1 (1.10)	31.0 (1.58)	10.5 (0.36)	6.9 (0.37)	13.0 (1.08)	26.0 (1.54)
2000[4]	10.9 (0.26)	6.9 (0.26)	13.1 (0.78)	27.8 (1.08)	12.0 (0.38)	7.0 (0.37)	15.3 (1.20)	31.8 (1.56)	9.9 (0.35)	6.9 (0.37)	11.1 (1.00)	23.5 (1.48)
2001[4]	10.7 (0.25)	7.3 (0.26)	10.9 (0.71)	27.0 (1.06)	12.2 (0.38)	7.9 (0.39)	13.0 (1.12)	31.6 (1.55)	9.3 (0.34)	6.7 (0.36)	9.0 (0.90)	22.1 (1.42)
2002[4]	10.5 (0.24)	6.5 (0.24)	11.3 (0.70)	25.7 (0.93)	11.8 (0.35)	6.7 (0.35)	12.8 (1.07)	29.6 (1.32)	9.2 (0.32)	6.3 (0.34)	9.9 (0.91)	21.2 (1.27)
2003[4,5]	9.9 (0.23)	6.3 (0.24)	10.9 (0.69)	23.5 (0.90)	11.3 (0.34)	7.1 (0.35)	12.5 (1.05)	26.7 (1.29)	8.4 (0.30)	5.6 (0.32)	9.5 (0.89)	20.1 (1.23)
2004[4,5]	10.3 (0.23)	6.8 (0.24)	11.8 (0.70)	23.8 (0.89)	11.6 (0.34)	7.1 (0.35)	13.5 (1.08)	28.5 (1.30)	9.0 (0.31)	6.4 (0.34)	10.2 (0.92)	18.5 (1.18)

—Not available.
†Not applicable.
[1]Includes other racial/ethnic categories not separately shown.
[2]Based on the April 1960 decennial census.
[3]White and Black include persons of Hispanic origin.
[4]Because of changes in data collection procedures, data may not be comparable with figures for years prior to 1992.
[5]White, non-Hispanic and Black, non-Hispanic categories exclude persons identifying themselves as more than one race.

NOTE: "Status" dropouts are 16- to 24-year-olds who are not enrolled in school and who have not completed a high school program regardless of when they left school. People who have received GED credentials are counted as high school completers. All data except for 1960 are based on October counts. Data are based on sample surveys of the civilian noninstitutionalized population. Standard errors appear in parentheses.
SOURCE: U.S. Department of Commerce, Census Bureau, Current Population Survey (CPS), October 1967 through October 2004, unpublished tabulations. (This table was prepared September 2005.)

461

Number of students with disabilities exiting special education, by basis of exit, age, and type of disability: United States and other jurisdictions, 2001–02 and 2002–03

Age and type of disability	Total exiting special education	Graduated with diploma	Received a certificate of attendance	Reached maximum age[1]	No longer receives special education	Died	Moved, known to continue	Moved, not known to continue	Dropped out[2]
1	2	3	4	5	6	7	8	9	10
					2001–02				
Total, 14 and over	596,233	190,951	35,610	4,790	65,744	1,841	157,082	60,471	79,744
Age									
14..	67,990	—	131	—	17,880	292	36,565	10,427	2,695
15..	70,454	—	123	—	14,941	316	37,056	12,074	5,944
16..	79,519	1,506	370	—	13,410	356	34,578	13,106	16,193
17..	131,428	52,906	6,109	—	10,836	323	26,921	11,861	22,472
18..	151,207	87,936	14,376	—	6,169	285	14,654	7,590	20,197
19..	62,557	36,059	8,225	—	1,742	117	4,482	3,174	8,758
20..	17,523	7,579	3,050	559	481	76	1,783	1,433	2,562
21 and over	15,555	4,965	3,226	4,231	285	76	1,043	806	923
Type of disability									
Specific learning disabilities............	350,422	128,776	15,745	1,140	39,786	588	84,333	34,124	45,930
Mental retardation.........................	66,013	17,702	12,147	1,979	2,340	374	16,885	5,268	9,318
Emotional disturbance	95,457	16,539	2,837	388	7,105	200	36,833	14,272	17,283
Speech or language impairments....	20,495	4,346	584	59	8,846	18	3,852	1,499	1,291
Multiple disabilities........................	10,789	3,347	1,229	652	424	260	2,954	808	1,115
Other health impairments	31,435	10,881	1,161	112	5,431	212	7,617	2,926	3,095
Hearing impairments	6,610	3,080	485	55	486	15	1,521	485	483
Orthopedic impairments	6,300	2,433	614	116	782	101	1,204	487	563
Visual impairments	2,543	1,322	163	28	192	21	485	157	175
Autism...	3,198	1,142	480	193	149	24	816	230	164
Deaf-blindness	231	81	18	19	17	2	49	18	27
Traumatic brain injury.....................	2,740	1,302	147	49	186	26	533	197	300
					2002–03				
Total, 14 and over	615,894	195,090	47,649	5,035	67,807	1,867	172,135	44,576	81,735
Age									
14..	69,321	—	60	—	18,426	268	39,829	8,012	2,726
15..	71,404	—	66	—	15,673	301	40,289	8,780	6,295
16..	81,182	1,572	429	—	14,142	379	38,599	9,327	16,734
17..	144,799	60,211	10,709	—	11,103	354	30,569	8,521	23,332
18..	156,966	89,373	19,882	—	6,049	253	15,580	5,535	20,294
19..	58,691	32,442	8,953	—	1,671	131	4,610	2,359	8,525
20..	18,206	7,342	3,832	820	469	104	1,677	1,248	2,714
21 and over	15,325	4,150	3,718	4,215	274	77	982	794	1,115
Type of disability									
Specific learning disabilities............	359,616	129,984	23,362	1,053	40,258	613	92,797	24,903	46,646
Mental retardation.........................	68,673	17,846	14,149	2,185	2,314	370	17,943	4,743	9,123
Emotional disturbance	95,658	17,331	3,611	417	7,179	206	39,532	9,584	17,798
Speech or language impairments....	21,777	4,859	694	58	9,561	36	4,008	1,093	1,468
Multiple disabilities........................	11,102	3,414	1,398	674	448	234	3,112	745	1,077
Other health impairments	36,613	12,251	2,039	122	6,163	221	9,703	2,289	3,825
Hearing impairments	6,541	2,974	589	48	566	11	1,503	360	490
Orthopedic impairments	6,318	2,390	660	130	654	109	1,437	318	620
Visual impairments	2,396	1,194	227	39	196	14	458	109	159
Autism...	4,066	1,431	696	236	242	32	989	233	207
Deaf-blindness	182	71	14	8	13	4	37	14	21
Traumatic brain injury.....................	2,952	1,345	210	65	213	17	616	185	301

—Not available.

[1]The upper age mandate for providing special education and related services as defined by state law, practice, or court order.

[2]"Dropped out" is defined as the total who were enrolled at some point in the reporting year, were not enrolled at the end of the reporting year, and did not exit through any of the other bases described. This category includes dropouts, runaways, GED recipients, expulsions, status unknown, and other exiters.

SOURCE: U.S. Department of Education, Office of Special Education Programs, Individuals with Disabilities Education Act (IDEA) database. Retrieved April 18, 2005, from http://www.ideadata.org/tables26th/ar_ad2.htm and http://www.ideadata.org/tables27th/ar_ad2.htm. (This table was prepared April 2005.)

Private elementary and secondary enrollment, teachers, and schools, by orientation of private schools and selected school characteristics: Fall 2001

Selected school characteristic	Kindergarten to grade 12 enrollment				Teachers[1]				Schools			
	Total	Catholic	Other religious	Non-sectarian	Total	Catholic	Other religious	Non-sectarian	Total	Catholic	Other religious	Non-sectarian
1	2	3	4	5	6	7	8	9	10	11	12	13
	Number											
Total..........................	5,341,513	2,515,524	1,924,874	901,114	425,406	155,514	166,005	103,887	29,273	8,207	14,388	6,678
Level of school												
Elementary..................	2,883,010	1,793,593	783,676	305,741	202,071	103,897	64,549	33,625	17,427	6,763	7,367	3,297
Secondary...................	835,328	615,711	123,843	95,773	67,318	42,671	12,096	12,551	2,704	1,110	747	847
Combined	1,623,175	106,220	1,017,355	499,600	156,017	8,946	89,361	57,711	9,142	335	6,275	2,533
School enrollment												
Less than 50	232,342	7,026	150,807	74,509	32,476	977	19,856	11,643	8,955	210	5,938	2,808
50 to 149...................	765,056	163,222	407,906	193,927	80,269	14,247	40,744	25,279	8,336	1,562	4,529	2,245
150 to 299.................	1,408,132	748,451	479,634	180,047	104,858	46,542	38,544	19,772	6,554	3,398	2,302	854
300 to 499.................	1,223,135	699,302	361,396	162,436	87,317	41,890	28,303	17,124	3,199	1,813	958	427
500 to 749.................	829,642	480,667	240,301	108,674	57,324	27,160	18,315	11,849	1,392	810	400	182
750 or more	883,205	416,856	284,829	181,520	63,161	24,698	20,243	18,221	836	415	261	161
Percent minority students												
None	303,880	49,725	236,288	17,867	27,013	3,502	21,425	2,085	3,961	368	3,131	462
1 to 9 percent..............	2,232,596	1,181,229	795,358	256,008	169,073	72,785	67,820	28,468	9,592	3,658	4,510	1,423
10 to 29 percent...........	1,458,232	598,849	470,477	388,907	125,852	38,782	40,492	46,578	7,163	1,784	3,007	2,372
30 to 49 percent............	433,749	208,004	136,020	89,726	34,833	12,566	11,389	10,878	2,560	644	1,034	882
50 percent or more	913,056	477,718	286,732	148,606	68,636	27,880	24,879	15,877	5,997	1,753	2,706	1,539
Community type												
Central city	2,276,808	1,142,738	745,261	388,809	176,559	70,187	62,523	43,849	10,117	3,415	4,136	2,566
Urban fringe/large town ..	2,276,823	1,140,523	783,038	353,262	176,173	68,597	66,066	41,511	10,948	3,420	4,779	2,749
Rural/small town	787,882	232,263	396,575	159,044	72,674	16,730	37,417	18,527	8,209	1,372	5,473	1,363
	Standard errors											
Total..........................	(26,746.8)	(11,607.2)	(12,812.8)	(15,869.1)	(3,022.3)	(822.3)	(1,857.3)	(1,849.7)	(336.4)	(48.6)	(227.7)	(193.0)
Level of school												
Elementary..................	(14,519.5)	(9,608.4)	(5,813.3)	(8,303.5)	(1,137.6)	(603.0)	(452.1)	(701.5)	(184.6)	(38.0)	(124.2)	(121.7)
Secondary...................	(3,438.2)	(2,292.7)	(2,004.7)	(2,001.1)	(362.7)	(262.5)	(101.5)	(199.7)	(62.7)	(6.3)	(20.2)	(47.6)
Combined	(15,716.5)	(1,758.9)	(11,080.2)	(11,019.0)	(2,333.4)	(179.4)	(1,779.3)	(1,550.2)	(232.5)	(21.2)	(199.7)	(96.5)
School enrollment												
Less than 50	(5,591.1)	(277.8)	(4,112.5)	(4,136.5)	(726.8)	(23.2)	(552.6)	(497.4)	(235.6)	(11.0)	(187.6)	(154.7)
50 to 149...................	(10,884.8)	(2,086.5)	(9,146.9)	(4,094.4)	(1,648.4)	(207.7)	(1,517.5)	(506.5)	(140.5)	(26.1)	(115.8)	(59.1)
150 to 299.................	(8,751.8)	(4,036.9)	(4,831.0)	(5,509.4)	(564.4)	(297.2)	(332.0)	(288.6)	(44.2)	(19.5)	(28.5)	(25.6)
300 to 499.................	(6,561.4)	(4,750.7)	(1,510.7)	(4,074.1)	(478.7)	(343.5)	(160.8)	(251.0)	(17.6)	(11.9)	(4.0)	(12.1)
500 to 749.................	(5,053.4)	(0.0)	(5,053.4)	(0.0)	(408.3)	(0.0)	(408.3)	(0.0)	(8.4)	(0.0)	(8.4)	(0.0)
750 or more	(11,013.5)	(5,418.6)	(2,415.1)	(8,108.7)	(1,468.1)	(313.5)	(112.1)	(1,383.6)	(10.0)	(5.1)	(2.2)	(7.6)
Percent minority students												
None	(6,606.9)	(2,302.9)	(6,051.9)	(1,655.6)	(437.2)	(149.3)	(410.4)	(129.4)	(139.1)	(8.5)	(115.8)	(65.9)
1 to 9 percent..............	(12,911.9)	(4,829.2)	(9,178.1)	(5,600.6)	(1,684.9)	(286.7)	(1,544.5)	(480.3)	(143.0)	(25.5)	(105.6)	(69.7)
10 to 29 percent...........	(9,345.5)	(7,103.4)	(3,192.6)	(6,535.2)	(726.9)	(413.6)	(342.8)	(525.0)	(126.6)	(17.8)	(89.4)	(88.0)
30 to 49 percent............	(4,739.3)	(258.5)	(2,184.6)	(3,606.8)	(349.0)	(47.3)	(108.8)	(305.2)	(50.7)	(3.7)	(20.2)	(42.5)
50 percent or more	(15,930.5)	(3,918.4)	(4,164.5)	(11,139.0)	(2,050.8)	(410.7)	(385.7)	(1,610.1)	(123.3)	(25.6)	(89.2)	(53.8)
Community type												
Central city	(23,936.4)	(10,430.4)	(6,096.5)	(14,174.0)	(2,487.2)	(742.6)	(1,807.1)	(460.9)	(202.7)	(36.5)	(82.7)	(133.0)
Urban fringe/large town ..	(11,361.1)	(4,477.7)	(6,384.6)	(7,314.4)	(868.5)	(320.9)	(497.1)	(575.7)	(126.8)	(28.0)	(60.7)	(87.0)
Rural/small town	(10,437.7)	(0.0)	(9,971.6)	(2,237.8)	(1,743.5)	(0.0)	(233.1)	(1,720.0)	(222.1)	(0.0)	(206.8)	(81.2)

[1]The teacher estimates are for full-time-equivalent (FTE) teachers.
NOTE: Includes special education, vocational/technical education, and alternative schools. Includes only schools that offer first or higher grade. Excludes prekindergarten students. Detail may not sum to totals because of rounding. Standard errors appear in parentheses.

SOURCE: U.S. Department of Education, National Center for Education Statistics, Private School Universe Survey (PSS), 2001–2002. (This table was prepared September 2004.)

Private elementary and secondary schools, enrollment, teachers, and high school graduates, by state: Selected years, 1991 through 2001

State	Schools 2001		Enrollment[1] Fall 1991		Fall 1997		Fall 1999		Fall 2001		Teachers Fall 2001		High school graduates 2000–01	
1	2		3		4		5		6		7		8	
United States[2]	29,273	(336.4)	4,889,545	(26,471)	5,076,118	(15,549)	5,162,684	(25,410.2)	5,341,513	(26,746.8)	425,406	(3,022.3)	278,773	(4,385.4)
Alabama	442	(23.4)	69,441	(8,390)	72,486	(682)	73,352	(2,527.0)	76,634	(1,283.1)	6,368	(192.1)	4,234	(111.5)
Alaska	86	(7.9)	5,520	(543)	6,253	(220)	6,172	(63.3)	6,747	(266.5)	657	(29.8)	247	(4.9)
Arizona	299	(24.6)	39,460	(3)	44,991	(652)	44,060	(428.2)	44,360	(1,457.5)	3,458	(133.6)	2,079	(28.6)
Arkansas	202	(11.4)	22,792	(3)	26,645	(290)	26,424	(1,233.1)	29,290	(439.1)	2,382	(74.9)	1,236	(25.8)
California	3,508	(107.1)	613,067	(16,643)	609,506	(3,730)	619,067	(1,532.5)	655,502	(8,815.2)	47,033	(753.4)	30,285	(389.3)
Colorado	376	(27.0)	57,352	(11,374)	52,563	(1,109)	52,142	(397.0)	54,450	(1,571.8)	4,751	(136.7)	2,418	(43.2)
Connecticut	341	(18.5)	67,374	(3)	69,293	(494)	70,058	(224.2)	71,147	(1,694.2)	7,298	(253.4)	5,126	(124.7)
Delaware	121	(5.8)	22,803	(3)	24,193	(911)	22,779	(303.1)	26,365	(260.8)	2,144	(37.9)	1,534	(19.7)
District of Columbia	90	(9.2)	17,776	(322)	16,671	(155)	16,690	(700.5)	20,043	(1,931.5)	2,386	(277.5)	1,555	(142.0)
Florida	1,779	(94.0)	205,600	(2,988)	273,628	(2,359)	290,872	(8,152.0)	303,093	(3,799.5)	25,427	(679.7)	14,038	(227.2)
Georgia	660	(34.3)	96,683	(4,078)	107,065	(1,477)	116,407	(4,156.8)	117,229	(1,622.4)	10,889	(260.1)	6,622	(120.0)
Hawaii	137	(6.5)	36,306	(3)	33,300	(350)	32,193	(168.5)	40,199	(603.9)	3,269	(47.9)	3,388	(20.9)
Idaho	108	(7.8)	6,644	(3)	9,635	(203)	10,209	(96.0)	10,291	(362.4)	813	(28.0)	461	(9.2)
Illinois	1,375	(17.2)	301,374	(1,158)	298,620	(1,101)	299,871	(1,364.5)	293,290	(1,700.7)	19,910	(133.1)	15,621	(73.6)
Indiana	750	(24.0)	99,450	(7,004)	105,358	(1,836)	105,533	(1,460.5)	111,257	(1,865.9)	7,809	(140.0)	4,593	(63.5)
Iowa	284	(5.0)	51,431	(3)	50,138	(520)	49,565	(445.5)	47,647	(469.0)	3,652	(49.0)	2,667	(42.9)
Kansas	226	(6.9)	35,077	(3)	40,573	(363)	43,113	(1,731.0)	41,027	(1,081.4)	2,985	(104.1)	1,903	(41.4)
Kentucky	398	(18.6)	65,990	(3)	70,731	(413)	75,084	(1,926.5)	72,819	(752.0)	5,615	(129.7)	3,654	(94.3)
Louisiana	444	(13.6)	139,248	(3)	141,633	(696)	138,135	(1,982.1)	137,266	(2,521.7)	9,526	(207.2)	8,398	(243.0)
Maine	145	(9.9)	14,854	(3)	17,187	(292)	18,287	(133.1)	18,779	(554.8)	1,896	(80.3)	2,045	(44.7)
Maryland	785	(38.1)	113,774	(3)	129,898	(937)	144,131	(4,700.1)	153,861	(1,858.8)	13,745	(321.4)	7,666	(97.8)
Massachusetts	691	(24.3)	125,006	(3,419)	127,165	(1,163)	132,154	(506.1)	140,810	(2,323.1)	13,688	(312.0)	9,686	(130.3)
Michigan	1,060	(23.2)	187,095	(710)	187,740	(1,538)	179,579	(1,553.7)	177,026	(1,963.5)	12,555	(162.8)	9,226	(70.0)
Minnesota	590	(13.5)	93,404	(2,401)	90,400	(918)	92,795	(1,046.7)	101,180	(1,141.5)	7,238	(98.9)	4,563	(36.0)
Mississippi	249	(10.8)	58,757	(1,377)	54,529	(457)	51,369	(1,357.0)	52,565	(820.4)	4,268	(109.2)	3,452	(86.8)
Missouri	659	(15.3)	116,440	(1,884)	119,534	(964)	122,387	(1,076.3)	124,326	(1,404.0)	9,444	(133.2)	6,883	(73.0)
Montana	109	(7.6)	9,644	(3)	8,341	(220)	8,711	(88.2)	9,941	(273.2)	842	(25.9)	543	(12.0)
Nebraska	251	(6.4)	39,673	(3)	40,943	(320)	42,141	(415.0)	43,137	(513.2)	2,976	(41.7)	2,375	(38.7)
Nevada	118	(9.9)	8,482	(3)	12,847	(241)	13,926	(81.4)	16,623	(496.7)	1,211	(36.9)	605	(13.1)
New Hampshire	162	(16.8)	18,712	(1,330)	21,143	(297)	23,383	(192.9)	24,750	(950.5)	2,427	(128.6)	2,189	(63.1)
New Jersey	989	(39.5)	209,913	(8,195)	205,126	(1,535)	198,631	(784.5)	218,187	(2,832.4)	18,121	(392.6)	12,345	(222.2)
New Mexico	219	(19.2)	23,236	(3)	19,251	(534)	23,055	(195.0)	23,637	(852.1)	2,258	(77.2)	1,362	(23.6)
New York	2,009	(86.6)	498,668	(7,158)	467,520	(1,821)	475,942	(1,226.9)	492,518	(5,494.7)	39,414	(786.5)	26,601	(239.0)
North Carolina	706	(46.6)	63,255	(5,224)	88,127	(1,260)	96,262	(3,775.3)	103,219	(1,694.2)	9,681	(300.4)	4,299	(107.6)
North Dakota	56	(1.2)	7,518	(3)	7,332	(72)	7,148	(97.0)	6,782	(87.5)	532	(10.6)	374	(5.8)
Ohio	1,042	(18.3)	269,064	(13,362)	251,543	(1,528)	254,494	(1,694.3)	256,427	(2,187.7)	17,044	(166.2)	13,869	(152.2)
Oklahoma	192	(11.3)	34,025	(9,317)	27,675	(345)	31,276	(1,049.0)	30,579	(651.2)	2,879	(83.8)	1,581	(24.9)
Oregon	374	(27.5)	30,918	(1,003)	44,290	(1,364)	45,352	(1,286.7)	45,448	(1,288.7)	3,643	(106.2)	2,517	(42.1)
Pennsylvania	1,971	(216.3)	359,440	(6,920)	343,191	(4,401)	339,484	(2,953.6)	331,471	(9,061.7)	24,543	(908.5)	18,092	(449.9)
Rhode Island	119	(5.5)	21,242	(3)	25,597	(195)	24,738	(126.6)	26,125	(475.7)	2,211	(75.3)	1,616	(29.9)
South Carolina	366	(20.6)	46,086	(2,013)	56,169	(700)	55,612	(2,506.1)	58,937	(1,063.1)	5,282	(162.3)	2,923	(79.5)
South Dakota	97	(2.3)	10,539	(3)	9,794	(143)	9,364	(231.9)	10,950	(178.9)	934	(19.4)	510	(11.7)
Tennessee	567	(32.0)	82,969	(2,953)	84,651	(746)	93,680	(3,519.1)	92,099	(1,116.1)	8,167	(197.9)	5,462	(82.3)
Texas	1,362	(47.5)	170,670	(472)	223,294	(1,703)	227,645	(7,260.1)	241,674	(2,349.1)	21,832	(437.2)	10,500	(140.9)
Utah	111	(8.8)	9,836	(3)	12,653	(201)	12,614	(114.0)	16,814	(466.0)	1,359	(39.5)	820	(16.6)
Vermont	129	(14.3)	8,351	(3)	10,823	(196)	12,170	(198.6)	13,058	(541.5)	1,539	(93.6)	1,342	(31.1)
Virginia	631	(33.8)	80,887	(1,872)	98,307	(1,071)	100,171	(4,170.8)	109,993	(1,813.4)	10,617	(297.3)	5,470	(98.7)
Washington	606	(44.8)	66,556	(2,798)	76,956	(1,462)	76,885	(519.4)	82,189	(2,102.9)	6,580	(171.7)	3,526	(36.5)
West Virginia	176	(12.1)	12,908	(3)	14,640	(225)	15,895	(974.4)	15,737	(305.1)	1,434	(59.7)	827	(40.3)
Wisconsin	1,066	(28.8)	142,399	(220)	143,577	(1,748)	139,455	(1,828.4)	141,812	(3,173.3)	10,424	(215.3)	5,387	(57.0)
Wyoming	41	(3.6)	1,840	(3)	2,593	(110)	2,221	(45.1)	2,209	(113.4)	252	(12.5)	54	(2.5)

[1]Excludes prekindergarten enrollment.
[2]NCES employed an area frame sample to account for noninclusion of schools at the national level. However, caution should be exercised in interpreting state-by-state characteristics since the samples were not designed to produce such numbers.
[3]Insufficient data to compute a standard error.
NOTE: Includes special education, vocational/technical education, and alternative schools. Standard errors for states are root mean squared errors to correct for bias in model-based estimates for all years except for 1991–92. Tabulation includes only schools that offer first or higher grade. Some data have been revised from previously published figures. Detail may not sum to totals because of rounding.
SOURCE: U.S. Department of Education, National Center for Education Statistics, Private School Universe Survey (PSS), 1999–2000 and 2001–2002; and *Indirect State-Level Estimation for the Private School Survey, 1999.* (This table was prepared April 2005.)

Revenues for public elementary and secondary schools, by source and state or jurisdiction: 2002–03

State or jurisdiction	Total (in thousands)	Federal Amount (in thousands)	Federal Per student	Federal Percent of total	State Amount (in thousands)	State Percent of total	Local and intermediate Amount (in thousands)	Local Percent of total	Private[1] Amount (in thousands)	Private Percent of total
1	2	3	4	5	6	7	8	9	10	11
United States	$440,157,299	$37,515,909	$779	8.5	$214,277,407	48.7	$178,091,027	40.5	$10,272,956	2.3
Alabama	5,153,795	595,456	805	11.6	2,966,979	57.6	1,326,004	25.7	265,356	5.1
Alaska........................	1,468,276	260,064	1,936	17.7	834,259	56.8	341,859	23.3	32,093	2.2
Arizona......................	7,351,310	839,278	895	11.4	3,555,570	48.4	2,724,540	37.1	231,923	3.2
Arkansas....................	3,266,318	382,871	849	11.7	1,804,362	55.2	940,009	28.8	139,076	4.3
California	57,021,363	5,629,649	886	9.9	33,561,358	58.9	17,264,265	30.3	566,092	1.0
Colorado	6,299,536	409,359	544	6.5	2,715,206	43.1	2,921,298	46.4	253,673	4.0
Connecticut................	7,087,302	369,444	648	5.2	2,652,212	37.4	3,955,348	55.8	110,298	1.6
Delaware....................	1,197,512	102,929	885	8.6	759,290	63.4	320,385	26.8	14,907	1.2
District of Columbia	1,114,021	153,246	2,012	13.8	†	†	952,265	85.5	8,511	0.8
Florida.......................	18,984,106	1,999,264	787	10.5	8,285,654	43.6	7,958,615	41.9	740,573	3.9
Georgia......................	13,448,966	1,083,873	725	8.1	6,489,049	48.2	5,649,478	42.0	226,566	1.7
Hawaii........................	2,078,876	170,377	927	8.2	1,873,316	90.1	15,681	0.8	19,502	0.9
Idaho.........................	1,698,503	166,626	670	9.8	1,003,508	59.1	500,910	29.5	27,460	1.6
Illinois.......................	19,154,705	1,618,737	777	8.5	6,327,132	33.0	10,807,708	56.4	401,128	2.1
Indiana.......................	7,926,062	605,523	603	7.6	4,663,625	58.8	2,387,990	30.1	268,924	3.4
Iowa	4,241,508	315,454	654	7.4	1,974,707	46.6	1,734,159	40.9	217,187	5.1
Kansas.......................	4,071,712	370,506	787	9.1	2,326,819	57.1	1,269,069	31.2	105,317	2.6
Kentucky....................	4,764,253	504,713	764	10.6	2,799,254	58.8	1,358,009	28.5	102,277	2.1
Louisiana	5,549,582	732,835	1,003	13.2	2,723,938	49.1	2,031,773	36.6	61,037	1.1
Maine	2,161,238	193,403	946	8.9	927,774	42.9	999,641	46.3	40,420	1.9
Maryland....................	8,668,097	582,440	672	6.7	3,317,559	38.3	4,508,430	52.0	259,667	3.0
Massachusetts..................	11,801,318	705,875	718	6.0	4,827,630	40.9	6,091,947	51.6	175,867	1.5
Michigan	17,954,395	1,407,777	789	7.8	11,358,303	63.3	4,782,850	26.6	405,464	2.3
Minnesota	8,349,227	494,757	584	5.9	6,165,549	73.8	1,426,647	17.1	262,274	3.1
Mississippi	3,263,897	502,816	1,021	15.4	1,754,445	53.8	908,159	27.8	98,476	3.0
Missouri	7,662,199	616,043	680	8.0	2,743,289	35.8	4,005,033	52.3	297,833	3.9
Montana.....................	1,204,497	174,685	1,165	14.5	558,114	46.3	422,865	35.1	48,833	4.1
Nebraska	2,550,525	225,769	791	8.9	877,657	34.4	1,319,520	51.7	127,579	5.0
Nevada	2,784,681	196,258	531	7.0	840,435	30.2	1,646,777	59.1	101,210	3.6
New Hampshire	1,957,267	101,904	491	5.2	957,850	48.9	853,865	43.6	43,649	2.2
New Jersey	18,905,028	805,498	589	4.3	8,230,289	43.5	9,464,543	50.1	404,698	2.1
New Mexico	2,685,725	402,471	1,257	15.0	1,936,713	72.1	297,040	11.1	49,501	1.8
New York....................	37,894,517	2,645,471	916	7.0	17,267,655	45.6	17,663,906	46.6	317,484	0.8
North Carolina	9,379,577	899,045	673	9.6	5,975,983	63.7	2,268,536	24.2	236,014	2.5
North Dakota	825,135	126,029	1,209	15.3	303,925	36.8	353,481	42.8	41,700	5.1
Ohio...........................	18,143,062	1,166,816	635	6.4	8,132,703	44.8	8,212,728	45.3	630,815	3.5
Oklahoma...................	4,161,621	528,646	846	12.7	2,277,241	54.7	1,149,332	27.6	206,402	5.0
Oregon.......................	4,599,717	416,281	751	9.1	2,342,430	50.9	1,711,109	37.2	129,897	2.8
Pennsylvania..............	18,751,160	1,453,198	800	7.7	6,867,531	36.6	10,076,486	53.7	353,945	1.9
Rhode Island	1,744,838	113,611	714	6.5	733,211	42.0	875,428	50.2	22,588	1.3
South Carolina..................	5,732,697	563,752	812	9.8	2,757,948	48.1	2,200,380	38.4	210,617	3.7
South Dakota	963,997	151,235	1,163	15.7	325,091	33.7	457,932	47.5	29,738	3.1
Tennessee	6,114,870	613,615	662	10.0	2,680,969	43.8	2,419,001	39.6	401,284	6.6
Texas	34,605,869	3,417,588	802	9.9	14,146,697	40.9	16,269,993	47.0	771,591	2.2
Utah..........................	2,912,991	269,728	551	9.3	1,643,684	56.4	940,094	32.3	59,486	2.0
Vermont	1,149,920	80,022	800	7.0	779,215	67.8	272,841	23.7	17,842	1.6
Virginia......................	10,283,182	678,459	576	6.6	4,072,761	39.6	5,330,297	51.8	201,665	2.0
Washington................	8,696,472	779,564	768	9.0	5,373,852	61.8	2,262,619	26.0	280,437	3.2
West Virginia..............	2,552,446	271,770	962	10.6	1,568,125	61.4	685,820	26.9	26,731	1.0
Wisconsin	8,858,181	536,643	609	6.1	4,727,338	53.4	3,380,439	38.2	213,762	2.4
Wyoming	961,248	84,536	959	8.8	489,201	50.9	373,920	38.9	13,590	1.4
Other jurisdictions										
American Samoa	68,812	53,676	3,358	78.0	12,591	18.3	2,447	3.6	98	0.1
Guam	—	—	—	—	—	—	—	—	—	—
Northern Marianas.........	60,712	23,183	2,060	38.2	37,230	61.3	282	0.5	17	0.0
Puerto Rico	2,619,532	802,703	1,346	30.6	1,816,733	69.4	13	#	82	#
Virgin Islands	177,087	37,119	2,025	21.0	0	0.0	139,757	78.9	212	0.1

—Not available.
†Not applicable.
#Rounds to zero.
[1]Includes revenues from gifts, and tuition and fees from patrons.

NOTE: Excludes revenues for state education agencies. Detail may not sum to totals because of rounding.
SOURCE: U.S. Department of Education, National Center for Education Statistics, Common Core of Data (CCD), "National Public Education Financial Survey," 2002–03. (This table was prepared July 2005.)

465

Current expenditures for public elementary and secondary education, by state or jurisdiction: Selected years, 1969–70 through 2002–03

[In thousands of dollars]

State or jurisdiction	1969–70	1979–80	1980–81	1989–90	1990–91	1992–93	1993–94	1994–95	1995–96	1996–97	1997–98	1998–99	1999–2000	2000–01	2001–02[1]	2002–03
1	2	3	4	5	6	7	8	9	10	11	12	13	14	15	16	17
United States	$34,217,773	$86,984,142	$94,321,093	$188,229,359	$202,037,752	$220,948,052	$231,542,764	$243,877,582	$255,106,683	$270,174,298	$285,485,370	$302,876,294	$323,888,508	$348,360,841	$368,378,006	$387,592,494
Alabama	422,730	1,146,713	1,393,137	2,275,233	2,475,216	2,610,514	2,809,713	3,026,287	3,240,364	3,436,406	3,633,159	3,880,188	4,176,082	4,354,794	4,444,390	4,657,643
Alaska	81,374	377,947	476,368	828,051	854,499	967,765	1,002,515	1,020,675	1,045,022	1,069,379	1,092,750	1,137,610	1,183,499	1,229,036	1,284,854	1,326,226
Arizona	281,941	949,753	1,075,362	2,258,660	2,469,543	2,753,504	2,911,304	3,144,540	3,327,969	3,527,473	3,740,889	3,963,455	4,288,739	4,846,105	5,395,814	5,891,105
Arkansas	235,083	666,949	709,394	1,404,545	1,510,092	1,703,621	1,782,645	1,873,595	1,994,748	2,074,113	2,149,237	2,241,244	2,380,331	2,505,179	2,822,877	2,923,401
California	3,831,595	9,172,158	9,936,642	21,485,782	22,748,218	24,219,792	25,140,639	25,949,033	27,334,639	29,909,168	32,759,492	34,379,878	38,129,479	42,908,787	46,265,544	47,983,402
Colorado	369,218	1,243,049	1,369,883	2,451,833	2,642,850	2,919,916	2,954,793	3,232,976	3,360,529	3,577,211	3,886,872	4,140,699	4,401,010	4,758,173	5,151,003	5,551,506
Connecticut	588,710	1,227,892	1,440,881	3,444,520	3,540,411	3,739,497	3,943,891	4,247,328	4,366,123	4,522,718	4,763,653	5,075,580	5,402,836	5,693,207	6,031,062	6,302,988
Delaware	108,747	269,108	270,439	520,953	543,933	600,161	643,915	694,473	726,241	788,715	830,731	872,786	937,630	1,027,224	1,072,875	1,127,745
District of Columbia	141,138	298,448	295,155	639,983	647,901	670,677	713,427	666,938	679,106	632,952	647,202	693,712	780,192	830,299	912,432	902,318
Florida	961,273	2,766,468	3,336,657	8,228,531	9,045,710	9,661,012	10,331,896	11,019,735	11,480,359	12,018,676	12,737,325	13,534,374	13,885,988	15,023,514	15,535,864	16,355,123
Georgia	599,371	1,608,028	1,688,714	4,505,962	4,804,225	5,273,143	5,643,843	6,136,689	6,629,646	7,230,405	7,770,241	8,537,177	9,158,624	10,011,343	10,853,496	11,630,576
Hawaii	141,324	351,889	395,038	700,012	827,579	946,074	998,143	1,028,729	1,040,682	1,057,069	1,112,351	1,143,713	1,213,695	1,215,968	1,348,381	1,489,092
Idaho	103,107	313,927	352,912	627,794	708,045	804,231	859,088	951,350	1,019,594	1,090,597	1,153,778	1,239,755	1,302,817	1,403,190	1,481,803	1,511,862
Illinois	1,896,067	4,579,355	4,773,179	8,125,493	8,932,538	9,942,737	10,076,889	10,640,279	10,727,091	11,720,249	12,473,064	13,602,965	14,462,773	15,634,490	16,480,787	17,271,301
Indiana	809,105	1,851,292	1,898,194	4,074,578	4,379,142	4,797,946	5,064,685	5,243,761	5,493,653	6,055,055	6,234,563	6,697,468	7,110,930	7,548,487	7,704,547	8,088,684
Iowa	527,086	1,186,659	1,337,504	2,004,742	2,136,561	2,459,141	2,527,434	2,622,510	2,753,425	2,885,943	3,005,421	3,110,585	3,264,336	3,430,885	3,565,796	3,652,022
Kansas	362,593	830,133	958,281	1,848,302	1,938,012	2,224,080	2,325,247	2,406,580	2,488,077	2,568,525	2,684,244	2,841,147	2,971,814	3,264,698	3,450,923	3,510,675
Kentucky	353,265	1,054,459	1,096,472	2,134,011	2,480,363	2,823,134	2,952,119	2,988,892	3,171,495	3,382,062	3,489,205	3,696,331	3,837,794	4,047,392	4,268,608	4,401,627
Louisiana	503,217	1,303,902	1,767,692	2,838,283	3,023,690	3,199,919	3,309,018	3,475,926	3,545,832	3,747,508	4,029,139	4,264,981	4,391,189	4,485,878	4,802,565	5,056,583
Maine	155,907	385,492	401,355	1,048,195	1,070,965	1,217,418	1,208,411	1,281,706	1,313,759	1,372,571	1,433,175	1,510,024	1,604,438	1,704,422	1,812,798	1,909,268
Maryland	721,794	1,783,056	1,937,159	3,894,644	4,240,862	4,556,266	4,783,023	5,083,380	5,311,207	5,529,309	5,843,685	6,165,934	6,545,135	7,044,881	7,480,723	7,933,957
Massachusetts	907,341	2,638,734	2,794,762	4,760,390	4,906,828	5,281,067	5,637,337	6,062,303	6,435,458	6,846,610	7,381,784	7,948,502	8,564,039	9,272,387	9,957,292	10,281,820
Michigan	1,799,945	4,642,847	5,196,249	8,025,621	8,545,805	9,532,994	9,816,830	10,440,206	11,137,877	11,686,124	12,003,818	12,785,460	13,994,294	14,243,597	14,975,150	15,674,698
Minnesota	781,243	1,786,768	1,900,322	3,474,398	3,740,820	4,135,284	4,328,093	4,622,930	4,844,879	5,087,353	5,452,571	5,836,186	6,140,442	6,531,198	6,586,559	6,867,403
Mississippi	262,760	756,018	716,878	1,472,710	1,510,552	1,600,752	1,725,386	1,921,480	2,000,321	2,035,675	2,164,592	2,293,188	2,510,376	2,576,457	2,642,116	2,853,531
Missouri	642,030	1,504,988	1,643,258	3,288,738	3,487,786	3,710,426	3,981,614	4,275,217	4,531,192	4,775,931	5,067,720	5,348,366	5,655,531	6,076,169	6,491,885	6,793,957
Montana	127,176	358,118	380,092	641,345	719,963	785,159	822,015	844,257	868,892	902,252	929,197	955,695	994,770	1,041,760	1,073,005	1,124,291
Nebraska	231,612	581,615	629,017	1,233,431	1,297,643	1,430,039	1,513,971	1,594,928	1,648,104	1,707,455	1,743,775	1,821,310	1,926,500	2,067,290	2,206,946	2,304,223
Nevada	87,273	281,901	287,752	712,898	864,379	1,035,623	1,099,685	1,186,132	1,296,629	1,434,395	1,570,576	1,738,009	1,875,467	1,978,480	2,169,000	2,251,044
New Hampshire	101,370	295,400	340,518	821,671	890,116	972,963	1,007,129	1,053,966	1,114,540	1,173,958	1,241,255	1,316,946	1,418,503	1,518,792	1,641,378	1,781,594
New Jersey	1,343,564	3,638,533	3,648,914	8,119,336	8,897,612	9,915,482	10,448,096	10,776,982	11,208,558	11,771,941	12,056,560	12,874,579	13,327,645	14,773,650	15,822,609	17,185,966
New Mexico	183,736	515,451	560,213	1,020,148	1,134,156	1,240,310	1,323,459	1,441,078	1,517,517	1,557,376	1,659,891	1,788,382	1,890,274	2,022,093	2,204,165	2,281,608
New York	4,111,839	8,760,500	9,259,948	18,090,978	19,514,583	20,898,267	22,059,949	22,989,629	23,522,461	24,237,291	25,332,735	26,885,444	28,433,240	30,884,292	32,218,975	34,546,965
North Carolina	676,193	1,880,862	2,112,417	4,342,826	4,605,384	4,930,823	5,145,416	5,440,426	5,582,994	5,964,939	6,497,648	7,097,882	7,713,293	8,201,901	8,543,290	8,766,968
North Dakota	97,895	228,483	254,197	459,391	460,581	511,095	522,377	534,632	557,043	577,498	599,443	625,428	638,946	668,814	711,437	716,007
Ohio	1,639,805	3,836,576	4,149,858	7,994,379	8,407,428	9,173,393	9,612,678	10,030,956	10,408,022	10,948,074	11,448,722	12,138,937	12,974,575	13,893,495	14,774,065	15,868,494
Oklahoma	339,105	1,055,844	1,193,373	1,905,332	2,107,513	2,442,320	2,680,153	2,763,721	2,804,088	2,990,044	3,138,690	3,332,697	3,382,581	3,750,542	3,875,547	3,804,570
Oregon	403,844	1,126,812	1,292,624	2,297,944	2,453,934	2,849,009	2,852,723	2,948,539	3,056,801	3,184,100	3,474,714	3,706,044	3,896,287	4,112,069	4,214,512	4,150,747
Pennsylvania	1,912,644	4,584,320	4,955,115	9,496,788	10,087,322	10,944,392	11,236,417	11,587,027	12,374,073	12,820,704	13,084,859	13,532,211	14,120,112	14,895,316	15,550,975	16,344,439
Rhode Island	145,443	362,046	395,389	801,908	823,655	934,815	990,094	1,050,969	1,094,185	1,151,888	1,215,595	1,283,859	1,393,143	1,465,703	1,533,455	1,647,587
South Carolina	367,689	997,984	1,006,088	2,322,618	2,494,254	2,690,009	2,790,878	2,920,230	3,085,495	3,296,661	3,507,017	3,759,042	4,087,355	4,492,161	4,744,809	4,888,250

See notes at end of table.

Current expenditures for public elementary and secondary education, by state or jurisdiction: Selected years, 1969–70 through 2002–03—Continued

[In thousands of dollars]

State or jurisdiction	1969–70	1979–80	1980–81	1989–90	1990–91	1992–93	1993–94	1994–95	1995–96	1996–97	1997–98	1998–99	1999–2000	2000–01	2001–02[1]	2002–03
1	2	3	4	5	6	7	8	9	10	11	12	13	14	15	16	17
South Dakota......	109,375	238,332	242,215	447,074	481,304	553,005	584,894	612,825	610,640	628,753	665,082	696,785	737,998	796,133	819,296	851,429
Tennessee......	473,226	1,319,303	1,429,938	2,790,808	2,903,209	3,139,223	3,305,579	3,540,682	3,728,486	4,145,380	4,409,338	4,638,924	4,931,734	5,170,379	5,501,029	5,674,773
Texas......	1,518,181	4,997,689	5,310,181	12,763,954	13,695,327	15,121,655	16,193,722	17,572,269	18,801,462	20,167,238	21,188,676	22,430,153	25,098,703	26,546,557	28,191,128	30,399,603
Utah......	179,981	518,251	587,648	1,130,135	1,235,916	1,376,319	1,511,205	1,618,047	1,719,782	1,822,725	1,916,688	2,025,714	2,102,655	2,250,339	2,374,702	2,366,897
Vermont......	78,921	189,811	224,901	546,901	599,018	616,212	643,828	665,559	684,864	718,092	749,786	792,664	870,198	934,031	992,149	1,045,213
Virginia......	704,677	1,881,519	2,045,412	4,621,071	4,958,213	5,228,326	5,441,384	5,750,318	5,969,608	6,343,768	6,736,863	7,137,419	7,757,598	8,335,805	8,718,554	9,208,329
Washington......	699,984	1,825,782	1,791,477	3,550,819	3,906,471	4,679,698	4,892,690	5,138,928	5,394,507	5,587,803	5,987,060	6,098,008	6,399,885	6,782,136	7,103,817	7,359,566
West Virginia......	249,404	678,386	754,889	1,316,637	1,473,640	1,626,005	1,663,868	1,758,557	1,806,004	1,847,560	1,905,940	1,986,562	2,086,937	2,157,568	2,219,013	2,349,833
Wisconsin......	777,288	1,908,523	2,035,879	3,929,920	4,292,434	4,954,900	5,170,343	5,422,264	5,670,826	5,975,122	6,280,696	6,620,653	6,852,178	7,249,081	7,592,176	7,934,755
Wyoming......	69,584	226,067	271,153	509,084	521,549	547,938	558,353	577,144	581,817	591,488	603,901	651,622	683,918	704,695	761,830	791,732
Other jurisdictions																
American Samoa......	16,652	—	—	21,838	24,946	23,636	25,161	28,643	30,382	33,780	33,088	35,092	42,395	40,642	46,192	47,566
Guam......	—	—	—	101,130	116,406	161,477	160,797	161,434	158,303	156,561	168,716	—	—	—	—	—
Northern Marianas......	—	—	—	20,476	26,822	38,784	32,824	45,008	44,037	53,140	56,514	50,450	49,832	49,151	46,508	50,843
Puerto Rico......	—	—	713,000	1,045,407	1,142,863	1,295,452	1,360,762	1,501,485	1,667,640	1,740,074	1,981,603	2,024,499	2,086,414	2,257,837	2,152,724	2,541,385
Virgin Islands......	—	—	—	128,065	119,950	120,510	120,556	122,094	122,286	122,188	131,315	146,474	135,174	125,252	107,343	125,405

—Not available.

[1]Data have been revised from previously published figures.

NOTE: Beginning in 1980–81, expenditures for state administration are excluded. Detail may not sum to totals because of rounding.

SOURCE: U.S. Department of Education, National Center for Education Statistics, *Statistics of State School Systems, 1969–70; Revenues and Expenditures for Public Elementary and Secondary Education, 1979–80* and *1980–81;* and Common Core of Data (CCD), "National Public Education Financial Survey," 1989–90 through 2002–03. (This table was prepared July 2005.)

Total and current expenditure per pupil in public elementary and secondary schools: Selected years, 1919–20 through 2002–03

| | Expenditure per pupil in average daily attendance | | | | Expenditure per pupil in fall enrollment[1] | | | | |
| | Unadjusted dollars | | Constant 2004–05 dollars[2] | | Unadjusted dollars | | Constant 2004–05 dollars[2] | | |
School year	Total expenditure[3]	Current expenditure	Total expenditure[3]	Current expenditure	Total expenditure[3]	Current expenditure	Total expenditure[3]	Current expenditure	Annual percent change in current expenditure
1	2	3	4	5	6	7	8	9	10
1919–20	$64	$53	$643	$536	$48	$40	$481	$401	—
1929–30	108	87	1,215	971	90	72	1,006	804	—
1931–32	97	81	1,288	1,078	82	69	1,090	913	—
1933–34	76	67	1,103	977	65	57	937	830	—
1935–36	88	74	1,227	1,036	74	63	1,038	877	—
1937–38	100	84	1,334	1,122	86	72	1,145	963	—
1939–40	106	88	1,450	1,208	92	76	1,257	1,047	—
1941–42	110	98	1,353	1,209	94	84	1,158	1,035	—
1943–44	125	117	1,372	1,287	105	99	1,156	1,084	—
1945–46	146	136	1,533	1,433	124	116	1,306	1,221	—
1947–48	205	181	1,685	1,493	179	158	1,472	1,304	—
1949–50	260	210	2,107	1,703	231	187	1,870	1,511	—
1951–52	314	246	2,294	1,794	275	215	2,008	1,571	—
1953–54	351	265	2,502	1,888	312	236	2,225	1,679	—
1955–56	387	294	2,760	2,098	354	269	2,523	1,918	—
1957–58	447	341	3,003	2,290	408	311	2,739	2,088	—
1959–60	471	375	3,073	2,447	440	350	2,871	2,286	—
1961–62	517	419	3,298	2,672	485	393	3,095	2,507	—
1963–64	559	460	3,472	2,861	520	428	3,232	2,663	—
1965–66	654	538	3,928	3,230	607	499	3,647	2,999	—
1967–68	786	658	4,433	3,711	732	612	4,124	3,452	—
1969–70	955	816	4,846	4,141	879	751	4,462	3,812	—
1970–71	1,049	911	5,064	4,397	970	842	4,682	4,065	6.6
1971–72	1,128	990	5,254	4,610	1,034	908	4,818	4,228	4.0
1972–73	1,211	1,077	5,421	4,822	1,117	993	5,000	4,448	5.2
1973–74	1,364	1,207	5,607	4,963	1,244	1,101	5,113	4,526	1.7
1974–75	1,545	1,365	5,717	5,050	1,423	1,257	5,267	4,653	2.8
1975–76	1,697	1,504	5,867	5,197	1,563	1,385	5,402	4,786	2.9
1976–77	1,816	1,638	5,932	5,348	1,674	1,509	5,466	4,928	3.0
1977–78	2,002	1,823	6,128	5,579	1,842	1,677	5,637	5,131	4.1
1978–79	2,210	2,020	6,184	5,654	2,029	1,855	5,679	5,192	1.2
1979–80	2,491	2,272	6,150	5,610	2,290	2,088	5,654	5,157	-0.7
1980–81	[4] 2,742	2,502	[4] 6,068	5,536	[4] 2,529	2,307	[4] 5,597	5,106	-1.0
1981–82	[4] 2,973	2,726	[4] 6,057	5,552	[4] 2,754	2,525	[4] 5,610	5,143	0.7
1982–83	[4] 3,203	2,955	[4] 6,256	5,772	[4] 2,966	2,736	[4] 5,793	5,344	3.9
1983–84	[4] 3,471	3,173	[4] 6,538	5,976	[4] 3,216	2,940	[4] 6,056	5,537	3.6
1984–85	[4] 3,722	3,470	[4] 6,746	6,290	[4] 3,456	3,222	[4] 6,263	5,840	5.5
1985–86	[4] 4,020	3,756	[4] 7,081	6,616	[4] 3,724	3,479	[4] 6,561	6,129	5.0
1986–87	[4] 4,308	3,970	[4] 7,424	6,842	[4] 3,995	3,682	[4] 6,884	6,345	3.5
1987–88	[4] 4,654	4,240	[4] 7,701	7,016	[4] 4,310	3,927	[4] 7,132	6,498	2.4
1988–89	5,109	4,645	8,081	7,347	4,738	4,307	7,494	6,813	4.8
1989–90	5,550	4,980	8,379	7,518	5,174	4,643	7,812	7,009	2.9
1990–91	5,885	5,258	8,424	7,526	5,486	4,902	7,853	7,017	0.1
1991–92	6,074	5,421	8,425	7,519	5,629	5,023	7,807	6,967	-0.7
1992–93	6,281	5,584	8,448	7,510	5,804	5,160	7,807	6,939	-0.4
1993–94	6,492	5,767	8,511	7,561	5,996	5,327	7,861	6,984	0.6
1994–95	6,725	5,989	8,571	7,633	6,208	5,529	7,912	7,046	0.9
1995–96	6,962	6,147	8,638	7,627	6,443	5,689	7,994	7,059	0.2
1996–97	7,300	6,393	8,806	7,712	6,764	5,923	8,159	7,145	1.2
1997–98	7,703	6,676	9,130	7,912	7,142	6,189	8,464	7,335	2.7
1998–99	8,118	7,013	9,458	8,170	7,533	6,508	8,776	7,582	3.4
1999–2000	8,592	7,394	9,729	8,372	8,033	6,912	9,095	7,827	3.2
2000–01	9,183	7,904	10,054	8,653	8,575	7,380	9,387	8,080	3.2
2001–02	9,614	8,259	10,342	8,884	8,996	7,727	9,677	8,313	2.9
2002–03	9,941	8,600	10,464	9,053	9,299	8,044	9,788	8,468	1.9

—Not available.

[1]Data for 1919–20 to 1953–54 are based on school-year enrollment.

[2]Constant dollars based on the Consumer Price Index, prepared by the Bureau of Labor Statistics, U.S. Department of Labor, adjusted to a school-year basis.

[3]Excludes "Other current expenditures," such as community services, private school programs, adult education, and other programs not allocable to expenditures per student at public schools.

[4]Estimated.

NOTE: Beginning in 1980–81, state administration expenditures are excluded from both "total" and "current" expenditures. Current expenditures include instruction, student support services, food services, and enterprise operations. Total expenditures include current expenditures, capital outlay, and interest on debt. Beginning in 1988–89, extensive changes were made in the data collection procedures. Some data have been revised from previously published figures.

SOURCE: U.S. Department of Education, National Center for Education Statistics, *Biennial Survey of Education in the United States*, 1919–20 through 1955–56; *Statistics of State School Systems*, 1957–58 through 1969–70; *Revenues and Expenditures for Public Elementary and Secondary Education*, 1970–71 through 1986–87; Common Core of Data (CCD), "National Public Education Financial Survey," 1987–88 through 2002–03. (This table was prepared February 2006.)

Total and current expenditures per pupil in fall enrollment in public elementary and secondary education, by function and state or jurisdiction: 2002–03

Current expenditures, capital expenditures, and interest on school debt

State or jurisdiction	Total[1]	Current expenditures		Student services										Capital outlay[2]	Interest on school debt
		Total	Instruction	Total	Students[4]	Instructional staff[5]	General administration	School administration	Operation and maintenance	Student transportation	Other support services	Food services	Enterprise operations[3]		
	2	3	4	5	6	7	8	9	10	11	12	13	14	15	16
1															
United States	$9,299	$8,044	$4,934	$2,782	$415	$385	$165	$452	$764	$325	$275	$310	$19	$1,016	$239
Alabama	7,031	6,300	3,812	2,058	301	257	172	387	551	270	121	430	0	588	144
Alaska	11,896	9,870	5,740	3,798	486	627	157	564	1,262	389	313	285	47	1,843	183
Arizona	7,474	6,282	3,765	2,221	328	159	103	313	693	213	410	296	0	908	283
Arkansas	7,275	6,482	3,961	2,196	289	334	210	365	601	230	166	325	0	638	155
California	8,740	7,552	4,591	2,678	339	493	68	515	720	181	362	272	11	1,100	88
Colorado	8,846	7,384	4,230	2,900	324	358	106	502	684	220	706	228	26	1,098	365
Connecticut	12,653	11,057	7,052	3,612	612	382	229	609	996	519	264	297	97	1,348	248
Delaware	11,382	9,693	5,965	3,276	461	130	109	540	913	540	584	452	0	1,538	151
District of Columbia	14,419	11,847	6,216	5,331	1,087	1,202	320	473	1,320	626	303	300	0	2,573	0
Florida	7,773	6,439	3,786	2,338	327	395	73	388	687	269	200	315	0	1,149	185
Georgia	9,041	7,774	4,925	2,459	352	417	104	477	570	292	247	383	7	1,145	122
Hawaii	8,745	8,100	4,833	2,839	882	480	51	524	579	138	186	428	0	349	296
Idaho	6,978	6,081	3,721	2,098	344	283	140	349	579	279	124	262	0	752	144
Illinois	9,851	8,287	4,952	3,068	512	333	292	442	832	402	254	268	0	1,309	255
Indiana	9,587	8,057	4,932	2,797	356	263	146	456	871	447	257	329	0	838	692
Iowa	8,659	7,574	4,508	2,511	482	341	212	408	635	233	200	335	219	952	133
Kansas	8,268	7,454	4,413	2,697	420	339	265	449	741	295	187	345	0	531	283
Kentucky	7,012	6,661	4,066	2,233	269	329	192	382	561	323	177	362	0	202	148
Louisiana	7,638	6,922	4,203	2,291	293	321	164	374	635	355	148	428	0	563	153
Maine	10,288	9,344	6,269	2,774	315	294	213	500	886	402	163	300	0	728	216
Maryland	10,051	9,153	5,693	3,042	356	531	82	599	788	451	234	270	149	793	106
Massachusetts	11,045	10,460	6,656	3,486	626	500	192	457	957	438	316	318	0	277	307
Michigan	10,593	8,781	5,002	3,509	599	436	198	588	920	361	408	269	0	1,437	375
Minnesota	9,907	8,109	5,201	2,536	272	442	211	309	615	440	246	339	32	1,376	422
Mississippi	6,356	5,792	3,466	1,966	252	261	192	325	579	249	109	359	1	427	137
Missouri	8,600	7,495	4,570	2,602	368	336	230	443	731	355	138	324	0	847	258
Montana	8,100	7,496	4,606	2,583	359	289	236	414	757	327	201	296	11	525	79
Nebraska	9,371	8,074	5,151	2,360	338	269	284	415	682	214	158	316	247	1,106	191
Nevada	8,110	6,092	3,812	2,080	226	255	111	419	608	226	235	200	0	1,562	456
New Hampshire	9,802	8,579	5,569	2,746	567	260	293	482	705	375	63	264	0	1,035	188
New Jersey	13,884	12,568	7,424	4,757	1,137	427	349	652	1,242	695	254	292	95	1,105	211
New Mexico	8,469	7,125	3,953	2,842	722	330	221	438	689	320	122	325	4	1,230	115
New York	13,316	11,961	8,213	3,459	385	325	252	495	1,029	588	384	290	0	1,100	255
North Carolina	7,529	6,562	4,173	2,023	336	230	127	416	513	237	164	366	0	756	210
North Dakota	7,721	6,870	4,102	2,230	275	210	332	342	610	315	146	327	211	767	85

See notes at end of table.

469

Total and current expenditures per pupil in fall enrollment in public elementary and secondary education, by function and state or jurisdiction: 2002–03—Continued

State or jurisdiction	Total[1]	Current expenditures — Total	Instruction	Student services — Total	Students[4]	Instructional staff[5]	General administration	School administration	Operation and maintenance	Student transportation	Other support services	Food services	Enterprise operations[3]	Capital outlay[2]	Interest on school debt
1	2	3	4	5	6	7	8	9	10	11	12	13	14	15	16
Ohio	10,096	8,632	4,956	3,390	514	544	243	525	803	384	378	285	1	1,274	190
Oklahoma	6,611	6,092	3,528	2,160	395	197	170	328	676	196	199	334	69	436	84
Oregon	8,921	7,491	4,438	2,798	500	292	110	482	618	329	468	253	2	1,093	336
Pennsylvania	10,445	8,997	5,557	3,088	436	335	271	398	920	444	283	315	36	1,039	410
Rhode Island	10,731	10,349	6,685	3,396	826	432	141	532	811	408	246	267	0	199	184
South Carolina	8,577	7,040	4,199	2,464	476	452	89	414	628	219	186	351	25	1,262	276
South Dakota	7,656	6,547	3,836	2,361	363	332	231	338	635	213	249	332	17	942	167
Tennessee	6,962	6,118	3,933	1,885	216	333	124	325	582	213	92	300	0	691	153
Texas	8,598	7,136	4,307	2,469	347	404	116	392	757	193	259	360	0	1,118	343
Utah	5,969	4,838	3,103	1,461	180	229	54	295	446	151	106	258	16	950	181
Vermont	11,075	10,454	6,713	3,458	742	380	268	719	809	330	209	275	8	466	154
Virginia	8,854	7,822	4,809	2,705	376	489	118	463	771	369	119	306	2	908	124
Washington	8,755	7,252	4,317	2,582	506	328	166	345	719	280	238	237	116	1,184	319
West Virginia	8,936	8,319	5,115	2,742	287	230	226	467	857	557	118	463	0	580	37
Wisconsin	10,347	9,004	5,566	3,149	410	468	244	466	802	350	409	289	0	775	568
Wyoming	10,313	8,985	5,381	3,317	526	447	203	511	935	382	314	286	1	1,252	76
Other jurisdictions															
American Samoa	3,225	2,976	1,543	893	127	184	39	140	283	40	79	540	0	249	0
Guam	—	—	—	—	—	—	—	—	—	—	—	—	—	—	—
Northern Marianas	4,555	4,519	3,871	437	58	14	307	0	0	9	48	211	0	36	0
Puerto Rico	4,324	4,260	3,145	606	87	76	25	0	220	95	103	509	0	32	31
Virgin Islands	7,163	6,840	4,459	2,168	385	215	332	388	486	239	123	171	42	323	0

—Not available.

[1]Excludes "Other current expenditures," such as community services, private school programs, adult education, and other programs not allocable to expenditures per pupil in public schools.

[2]Includes expenditures for property and for buildings and alterations completed by school district staff or contractors.

[3]Includes expenditures for operations funded by sales of products or services (e.g., school bookstore or computer time).

[4]Includes expenditures for health, attendance, and speech pathology services.

[5]Includes expenditures for curriculum development, staff training, libraries, and media and computer centers.

NOTE: Excludes expenditures for state education agencies. "0" indicates none or less than $0.50. Some data have been revised from previously published figures. Detail may not sum to totals because of rounding.

SOURCE: U.S. Department of Education, National Center for Education Statistics, Common Core of Data (CCD), "National Public Education Financial Survey," 2002–03. (This table was prepared July 2005.)

Selected statistics on enrollment, teachers, dropouts, and graduates in public school districts enrolling more than 15,000 students, by state: 1990, 2000, 2001–02, and 2003

Name of district	State	Enrollment, fall 1990	Enrollment, fall 2000	Enrollment, fall 2003	White, non-Hispanic	Minority Total	Black, non-Hispanic	Hispanic	Asian/Pacific Islander	American Indian/Alaska Native	Number of classroom teachers, fall 2003	Pupil/teacher ratio, fall 2003	Total number of staff, fall 2003	Student/staff ratio, fall 2003	Dropouts Total	Grade 9	Grade 10	Grade 11	Grade 12	Number of high school graduates, 2001–02[2]	Number of schools, fall 2003
1	2	3	4	5	6	7	8	9	10	11	12	13	14	15	16	17	18	19	20	21	22
Districts with more than 15,000 students	†	16,807,641	20,106,176	20,844,627	40.8	59.2	24.9	27.2	6.4	0.7	1,229,398	17.0	2,229,666	8.9	—	—	—	—	—	1,014,087	29,886
Baldwin County	AL	17,479	22,656	24,037	80.8	19.2	16.3	2.0	0.5	0.5	1,717	14.0	3,145	7.6	3.1	2.1	3.2	5.2	2.3	1,093	45
Birmingham City	AL	41,536	37,843	34,099	1.2	98.8	97.3	1.3	0.2	#	2,211	15.4	4,047	8.4	2.1	1.9	2.6	2.2	1.8	1,706	80
Huntsville City	AL	23,945	22,832	22,590	51.0	49.0	43.2	2.7	2.5	0.5	1,600	14.1	2,903	7.8	3.1	4.6	2.5	1.7	3.0	1,146	49
Jefferson County	AL	40,664	40,726	38,659	69.3	30.7	28.3	1.7	0.5	0.1	2,468	15.7	4,466	8.7	4.1	2.7	4.7	4.7	4.6	2,278	58
Madison County	AL	13,861	15,675	17,023	77.8	22.2	15.1	1.3	0.9	5.0	1,032	16.5	1,904	8.9	4.9	5.7	5.1	4.5	3.9	813	25
Mobile County	AL	67,203	64,976	64,774	46.2	53.8	50.3	0.7	2.0	0.8	4,237	15.3	8,073	8.0	4.0	4.2	4.1	4.6	3.0	2,854	104
Montgomery County	AL	35,956	33,267	32,553	21.4	78.6	76.0	1.0	1.4	0.2	2,172	15.0	4,160	7.8	4.4	2.0	3.8	7.4	5.1	1,607	62
Shelby County	AL	16,089	20,129	22,541	83.2	16.8	11.6	3.7	1.4	0.2	1,590	14.2	2,940	7.7	2.6	1.3	2.2	3.2	4.1	1,040	35
Tuscaloosa County	AL	14,426	15,666	16,073	74.1	25.9	24.5	0.9	0.4	0.1	1,033	15.6	1,952	8.2	3.7	3.6	3.6	4.0	3.5	753	31
Anchorage	AK	42,300	49,526	49,722	59.2	40.8	8.7	6.4	11.4	14.2	2,832	17.6	5,561	8.9	8.6	5.4	8.5	9.8	11.3	2,505	94
Amphitheater Unified District	AZ	13,835	16,857	16,868	59.7	40.3	3.7	31.7	2.9	2.0	926	18.2	1,885	8.9	3.4	1.8	2.7	3.6	6.3	947	22
Cartwright Elementary	AZ	14,369	17,746	19,864	9.9	90.1	5.5	83.0	0.6	1.1	961	20.7	2,244	8.9	†	†	†	†	†	†	24
Chandler Unified	AZ	11,038	21,703	26,915	57.8	42.2	5.9	30.4	4.4	1.5	1,221	22.0	2,447	11.0	4.1	4.7	3.7	3.2	4.5	1,021	28
Deer Valley Unified	AZ	15,898	27,158	31,691	80.4	19.6	3.1	12.2	3.3	0.9	1,585	20.0	3,029	10.5	6.3	5.5	5.2	6.9	8.0	1,320	34
Gilbert Unified	AZ	10,863	29,188	35,218	77.1	22.9	3.8	14.4	3.8	0.9	1,909	18.4	3,687	9.6	2.5	0.8	2.6	2.7	4.3	1,817	38
Kyrene Elementary	AZ	10,487	19,446	18,579	69.7	30.3	6.4	13.8	7.8	2.4	1,017	18.3	1,803	10.3	†	†	†	†	†	†	26
Mesa Unified	AZ	62,470	73,587	75,401	60.7	39.3	3.7	29.5	2.3	3.8	3,704	20.4	7,644	9.9	3.8	3.4	4.9	3.6	2.8	4,014	91
Paradise Valley Unified	AZ	26,698	34,882	34,884	75.5	24.5	3.1	17.5	2.8	1.1	1,788	19.5	3,177	11.0	5.9	4.9	4.4	6.4	8.0	2,136	50
Peoria Unified	AZ	20,846	32,608	36,719	70.1	29.9	4.9	20.8	3.1	1.2	1,938	18.9	3,543	10.4	2.4	1.3	3.0	3.2	2.5	1,990	37
Phoenix Union High	AZ	18,182	22,192	23,989	12.3	87.7	10.1	72.8	1.5	3.3	1,295	18.5	2,660	9.0	11.2	7.4	11.6	12.9	14.6	3,534	14
Scottsdale Unified	AZ	19,741	26,958	26,559	80.6	19.4	2.2	12.5	3.4	1.4	1,395	19.0	2,460	10.8	1.4	1.2	1.4	1.8	1.3	1,708	34
Sunnyside Unified	AZ	13,058	14,518	15,861	6.5	93.5	2.0	86.8	0.6	4.2	874	18.1	1,843	8.6	12.3	13.1	12.1	10.5	12.3	580	23
Tucson Unified	AZ	56,177	61,869	61,448	36.1	63.9	6.6	50.6	2.6	4.1	3,356	18.3	6,672	9.2	4.7	4.0	5.1	5.7	3.8	3,309	126
Washington Elementary	AZ	22,446	24,723	24,438	48.8	51.2	6.5	38.2	2.9	3.5	1,284	19.0	2,560	9.5	†	†	†	†	†	†	32
Little Rock	AR	25,813	25,502	25,346	25.1	74.9	68.6	4.2	1.8	0.3	1,726	14.7	3,692	6.9	12.1	12.2	11.7	11.5	13.3	1,334	52
Pulaski County Special	AR	21,495	18,735	18,522	57.2	42.8	39.6	2.1	0.8	0.3	1,202	15.4	2,922	6.3	7.5	7.9	6.4	7.5	8.3	816	36
ABC Unified	CA	20,972	22,303	22,226	10.9	89.1	9.8	38.6	40.4	0.3	988	22.5	1,888	11.8	—	—	—	—	—	1,636	30
Alvord Unified	CA	14,853	17,664	19,441	23.4	76.6	5.7	65.0	5.4	0.4	854	22.8	1,460	13.3	†	†	†	†	†	837	19
Anaheim Elementary	CA	14,972	22,275	21,963	8.0	92.0	1.9	83.7	6.2	0.3	1,027	21.4	1,809	12.1	—	—	—	—	—	—	23
Anaheim Union High	CA	23,086	29,363	32,468	24.7	75.3	3.4	55.2	16.2	0.5	1,278	25.4	2,357	13.8	†	†	†	†	†	3,688	21
Antelope Valley Union High	CA	10,937	19,056	22,148	37.8	62.2	21.2	36.3	4.1	0.7	839	26.4	1,611	13.7	†	†	†	†	†	2,992	13
Antioch Unified	CA	13,045	20,018	21,628	40.1	59.9	18.2	29.1	11.4	1.3	1,003	21.6	1,514	14.3	†	†	†	†	†	1,254	23
Bakersfield City Elementary	CA	24,911	27,674	28,315	16.3	83.7	12.9	68.0	1.7	1.2	1,357	20.9	2,656	10.7	—	—	—	—	—	†	42
Baldwin Park Unified	CA	15,878	17,473	19,287	6.0	94.0	2.1	85.9	5.7	0.3	779	24.8	1,580	12.2	†	†	†	†	†	713	22
Bellflower Unified	CA	9,917	14,935	15,522	23.2	76.8	16.4	48.9	11.1	0.5	690	22.5	1,207	12.9	†	†	†	†	†	780	15
Burbank Unified	CA	12,057	16,170	17,066	50.3	49.7	3.0	37.1	9.2	0.4	779	21.9	1,402	12.2	†	†	†	†	†	1,094	20
Cajon Valley Union Elementary	CA	17,328	19,059	18,070	60.4	39.6	7.2	28.3	3.1	1.0	818	22.1	1,476	12.2	—	—	—	—	—	—	28
Capistrano Unified	CA	26,852	45,074	49,746	72.2	27.8	1.4	19.0	7.0	0.3	2,159	23.0	3,782	13.2	†	†	†	†	†	2,644	56
Chaffey Joint Union High	CA	13,505	19,851	23,341	30.4	69.6	11.6	51.5	6.0	0.5	940	24.8	1,705	13.7	†	†	†	†	†	3,873	11
Chino Valley Unified	CA	23,257	31,763	33,340	36.0	64.0	4.7	46.2	13.0	0.2	1,383	24.1	2,419	13.8	—	—	—	—	—	1,865	35

See notes at end of table.

Selected statistics on enrollment, teachers, dropouts, and graduates in public school districts enrolling more than 15,000 students, by state: 1990, 2000, 2001–02, and 2003—Continued

Name of district	State	Enrollment, fall 1990	Enrollment, fall 2000	Enrollment, fall 2003	Percentage distribution of enrollment, by race, fall 2003						Number of classroom teachers, fall 2003	Pupil/ teacher ratio, fall 2003	Total number of staff, fall 2003	Student/ staff ratio, fall 2003	Percent dropouts from grades 9–12, 2001–02[1]					Number of high school graduates, 2001–02[2]	Number of schools, fall 2003
					White, non-Hispanic	Minority															
						Total	Black, non-Hispanic	Hispanic	Asian/ Pacific Islander	American Indian/ Alaska Native					Total	Grade 9	Grade 10	Grade 11	Grade 12		
1	2	3	4	5	6	7	8	9	10	11	12	13	14	15	16	17	18	19	20	21	22
Chula Vista Elementary	CA	17,604	23,132	25,292	17.1	82.9	4.9	64.5	13.1	0.4	1,292	19.6	2,441	10.4	†	†	—	—	—	—	†	40
Clovis Unified	CA	23,224	32,717	34,663	59.1	40.9	3.6	21.7	14.2	1.3	1,604	21.6	2,868	12.1	†	†	—	—	—	—	2,052	39
Colton Joint Unified	CA	16,415	22,118	24,936	15.0	85.0	9.4	71.1	3.9	0.6	1,099	22.7	1,830	13.6	—	—	—	—	—	—	789	28
Compton Unified	CA	27,585	31,037	32,486	0.2	99.8	29.4	69.3	1.0	#	1,374	23.6	2,852	11.4	—	—	—	—	—	—	902	40
Conejo Valley Unified	CA	17,209	20,999	22,243	72.3	27.7	1.6	17.3	8.1	0.7	992	22.4	1,782	12.5	†	†	—	—	—	—	1,413	29
Corona-Norco Unified	CA	23,036	37,487	43,998	41.4	58.6	6.2	45.3	6.8	0.4	2,086	21.1	3,455	12.7	—	—	—	—	—	—	2,170	42
Covina-Valley Unified	CA	11,666	14,422	15,035	22.2	77.8	5.7	61.8	9.9	0.4	662	22.7	1,299	11.6	—	—	—	—	—	—	979	20
Cupertino Union Elementary	CA	12,227	15,670	16,048	33.2	66.8	1.3	4.5	60.8	0.2	743	21.6	1,222	13.1	†	†	—	—	—	—	†	24
Desert Sands Unified	CA	16,058	23,500	26,122	31.0	69.0	2.1	64.6	1.8	0.4	1,190	22.0	2,217	11.8	†	†	—	—	—	—	1,394	28
Downey Unified	CA	15,418	21,474	22,523	14.2	85.8	4.0	75.6	5.7	0.4	971	23.2	1,717	13.1	—	—	—	—	—	—	1,292	22
East Side Union High	CA	21,973	24,282	25,176	14.0	86.0	4.4	44.4	36.7	0.4	1,147	21.9	2,063	12.2	—	—	—	—	—	—	4,467	21
Elk Grove Unified	CA	27,246	47,736	55,613	33.8	66.2	18.9	19.8	26.3	1.1	2,660	20.9	4,574	12.2	—	—	—	—	—	—	2,728	55
Escondido Union Elementary	CA	14,663	19,312	20,164	31.2	68.8	3.3	59.6	5.3	0.6	995	20.3	1,771	11.4	†	†	—	—	—	—	†	22
Fairfield-Suisun Unified	CA	20,227	22,263	23,241	33.7	66.3	22.5	26.8	16.0	0.9	1,114	20.9	1,829	12.7	†	†	—	—	—	—	1,106	27
Folsom-Cordova Unified	CA	12,656	16,277	18,041	66.5	33.5	9.2	13.0	10.4	0.9	835	21.6	1,503	12.0	—	—	—	—	—	—	898	31
Fontana Unified	CA	27,043	37,244	41,343	9.8	90.2	8.6	78.9	2.1	0.6	1,771	23.3	3,248	12.7	—	—	—	—	—	—	1,793	38
Fremont Unified	CA	27,172	31,078	31,844	30.7	69.3	5.5	14.7	48.3	0.7	1,469	21.7	2,294	13.9	†	†	—	—	—	—	1,972	41
Fresno Unified	CA	71,500	79,007	81,408	17.5	82.5	11.5	53.7	16.6	0.7	3,927	20.7	7,390	11.0	—	—	—	—	—	—	3,721	100
Fullerton Joint Union High	CA	12,729	15,165	16,398	28.3	71.7	2.2	49.8	19.3	0.3	566	29.0	1,077	15.2	—	—	—	—	—	—	2,670	8
Garden Grove Unified	CA	37,969	48,742	50,172	16.8	83.2	1.1	51.9	29.9	0.3	2,138	23.5	4,126	12.2	—	—	—	—	—	—	2,738	67
Glendale Unified	CA	25,459	30,329	29,433	57.5	42.5	1.0	22.6	18.7	0.2	1,346	21.9	2,423	12.1	—	—	—	—	—	—	2,002	32
Grossmont Union High	CA	18,647	23,639	24,456	62.2	37.8	8.2	21.3	6.1	2.2	1,186	20.6	2,154	11.4	—	—	—	—	—	—	4,387	19
Hacienda La Puente Unified	CA	23,267	24,646	25,499	7.4	92.6	2.8	72.7	16.7	0.4	1,172	21.8	2,151	11.9	—	—	—	—	—	—	1,345	39
Hayward Unified	CA	19,122	24,205	24,014	13.5	86.5	16.0	48.9	21.0	0.6	1,198	20.0	1,961	12.2	†	†	—	—	—	—	1,264	33
Hemet Unified	CA	12,811	17,451	19,693	54.6	45.4	6.1	34.8	3.4	1.1	899	21.9	1,564	12.6	—	—	—	—	—	—	995	22
Hesperia Unified	CA	13,113	15,360	17,051	50.9	49.1	5.3	41.2	2.1	0.5	710	24.0	1,355	12.6	—	—	—	—	—	—	857	22
Inglewood Unified	CA	16,355	17,295	17,969	0.6	99.4	41.8	56.7	0.8	#	857	21.0	1,477	12.2	—	—	—	—	—	—	666	20
Irvine Unified	CA	20,735	23,961	24,930	50.1	49.9	2.5	7.6	39.2	0.6	1,076	23.2	1,847	13.5	†	†	—	—	—	—	1,838	33
Jurupa Unified	CA	15,419	19,839	20,924	26.1	73.9	4.4	66.9	2.2	0.4	885	23.6	1,477	14.2	—	—	—	—	—	—	797	24
Kern Union High	CA	20,183	29,333	32,357	39.6	60.4	8.1	47.6	4.0	0.8	1,411	22.9	2,829	11.4	—	—	—	—	—	—	5,741	23
Lake Elsinore Unified	CA	11,000	17,178	19,711	51.2	48.8	4.8	39.6	3.6	0.9	877	22.5	1,611	12.2	—	—	—	—	—	—	900	22
Lancaster Elementary	CA	11,248	14,433	15,799	30.2	69.8	29.1	36.9	3.2	0.7	728	21.7	1,331	11.9	†	†	—	—	†	—	†	18
Lodi Unified	CA	23,954	27,339	29,178	36.9	63.1	7.8	32.3	22.3	0.7	1,443	20.2	1,931	15.1	†	†	—	—	—	—	1,456	47
Long Beach Unified	CA	71,342	93,694	97,560	16.9	83.1	18.6	49.0	15.2	0.3	4,439	22.0	9,436	10.3	—	—	—	—	—	—	4,664	91
Los Angeles Unified	CA	625,086	721,346	747,009	9.1	90.9	11.8	72.5	6.3	0.3	35,493	21.0	74,103	10.1	†	†	—	—	—	—	27,720	693
Lynwood Unified	CA	15,469	18,237	19,658	0.3	99.7	8.9	90.5	0.4	#	733	26.8	1,312	15.0	—	—	—	—	—	—	824	14
Madera Unified	CA	13,728	15,957	17,247	17.4	82.6	3.4	77.7	1.4	0.2	828	20.8	1,451	11.9	—	—	—	—	—	—	796	20
Manteca Unified	CA	13,356	19,746	22,627	39.8	60.2	8.6	38.7	11.5	1.4	1,017	22.2	1,684	13.4	—	—	—	—	—	—	1,061	24
Modesto City Elementary	CA	17,405	18,740	18,803	28.7	71.3	5.1	58.0	7.2	1.0	925	20.3	1,620	11.6	†	†	—	—	†	—	†	27
Modesto City High	CA	10,697	14,547	15,581	45.8	54.2	5.1	37.5	10.5	1.1	632	24.7	1,201	13.0	—	—	—	—	—	—	2,815	6
Montebello Unified	CA	32,938	34,794	35,952	2.6	97.4	0.4	93.0	4.0	0.1	1,507	23.9	2,811	12.8	—	—	—	—	—	—	1,543	29
Moreno Valley Unified	CA	29,064	32,730	34,792	20.9	79.1	22.3	50.8	5.5	0.4	1,539	22.6	2,654	13.1	—	—	—	—	—	—	2,161	33
Mt. Diablo Unified	CA	32,840	36,648	36,821	56.9	43.1	5.2	25.1	12.4	0.5	1,845	20.0	3,074	12.0	—	—	—	—	—	—	1,694	55
Murrieta Valley Unified	CA	3,990	12,065	17,480	64.5	35.5	6.2	25.1	7.7	0.5	774	22.6	1,373	12.7	—	—	—	—	—	—	690	16
Napa Valley Unified	CA	13,705	16,392	17,023	52.0	48.0	1.9	39.3	5.1	1.7	834	20.4	1,475	11.5	—	—	—	—	—	—	998	37

See notes at end of table.

Selected statistics on enrollment, teachers, dropouts, and graduates in public school districts enrolling more than 15,000 students, by state: 1990, 2000, 2001–02, and 2003—Continued

Name of district	State	Enrollment, fall 1990	Enrollment, fall 2000	Enrollment, fall 2003	White, non-Hispanic	Minority Total	Black, non-Hispanic	Hispanic	Asian/Pacific Islander	American Indian/Alaska Native	Number of classroom teachers, fall 2003	Pupil/teacher ratio, fall 2003	Total number of staff, fall 2003	Student/staff ratio, fall 2003	Dropouts Total	Grade 9	Grade 10	Grade 11	Grade 12	Number of high school graduates, 2001–02[1]	Number of schools, fall 2003
1	2	3	4	5	6	7	8	9	10	11	12	13	14	15	16	17	18	19	20	21	22
Newport-Mesa Unified	CA	16,434	21,658	22,383	53.2	46.8	1.2	39.2	6.1	0.3	1,036	21.6	2,025	11.1	—	—	—	—	—	1,118	31
Norwalk-La Mirada Unified	CA	19,179	23,610	24,101	16.5	83.5	4.3	70.7	8.1	0.4	1,066	22.6	2,109	11.4	—	—	—	—	—	1,192	29
Oakland Unified	CA	52,095	54,863	50,437	5.8	94.2	42.7	34.0	17.1	0.5	2,544	19.8	4,924	10.2	—	—	—	—	—	1,617	118
Oceanside Unified	CA	17,034	22,354	22,484	30.5	69.5	10.2	50.3	8.2	0.7	1,069	21.0	1,767	12.7	—	—	—	—	—	957	28
Ontario-Montclair Elementary	CA	21,033	26,407	27,010	9.2	90.8	4.5	83.0	3.0	0.3	1,194	22.6	2,098	12.9	†	†	†	†	†		34
Orange Unified	CA	25,224	31,097	32,032	42.4	57.6	1.7	42.5	12.6	0.7	1,521	21.1	2,923	11.0	—	—	—	—	—	2,065	42
Oxnard Elementary	CA	12,212	16,249	16,851	8.8	91.2	2.6	84.6	3.5	0.5	785	21.5	1,322	12.7	†	†	†	†	†		21
Oxnard Union High	CA	11,512	14,552	15,746	23.1	76.9	3.5	64.6	7.6	1.1	603	26.1	1,150	13.7	—	—	—	—	—	2,529	9
Pajaro Valley Joint Unified	CA	16,355	19,964	19,522	20.7	79.3	0.6	76.4	2.0	0.2	995	19.6	2,013	9.7	—	—	—	—	—	1,009	29
Palm Springs Unified	CA	14,427	20,847	22,499	26.0	74.0	5.0	64.5	3.7	0.9	1,069	21.0	1,829	12.3	—	—	—	—	—	950	23
Palmdale Elementary	CA	13,199	20,853	22,736	20.6	79.4	20.8	55.0	2.8	0.7	927	24.5	1,624	14.0	†	†	†	†	†		26
Paramount Unified	CA	12,855	16,862	17,013	3.1	96.9	11.0	82.5	3.2	0.2	786	21.6	1,333	12.8	—	—	—	—	—	593	18
Pasadena Unified	CA	21,802	23,559	22,669	15.8	84.2	26.2	54.4	3.5	0.4	1,076	21.1	1,940	11.7	—	—	—	—	—	970	32
Placentia-Yorba Linda Unified	CA	21,438	26,046	26,774	57.8	42.2	1.9	30.4	9.5	0.1	1,180	22.7	2,163	12.4	—	—	—	—	—	1,656	30
Pomona Unified	CA	26,918	34,479	35,412	7.3	92.7	8.0	77.8	6.8	0.5	1,544	22.9	2,805	12.6	—	—	—	—	—	1,410	40
Poway Unified	CA	24,662	32,532	33,051	65.5	34.5	3.4	9.7	20.8	0.8	1,479	22.3	2,760	12.0	—	—	—	—	—	2,230	31
Redlands Unified	CA	16,002	19,411	20,643	45.9	54.1	8.3	34.4	10.7	0.2	916	22.5	1,516	13.6	—	—	—	—	—	1,313	20
Rialto Unified	CA	19,794	28,060	30,431	9.1	90.9	23.2	64.9	2.5	0.2	1,325	23.0	2,334	13.0	—	—	—	—	—	1,392	27
Riverside Unified	CA	31,326	38,124	42,012	37.5	62.5	10.0	47.2	4.8	0.5	1,808	23.2	3,174	13.2	—	—	—	—	—	2,251	46
Rowland Unified	CA	19,143	18,972	18,384	6.0	94.0	3.9	60.7	29.3	0.1	827	22.2	1,606	11.4	—	—	—	—	—	1,072	22
Sacramento City Unified	CA	49,557	52,734	52,103	22.7	77.3	22.6	29.6	23.5	1.5	2,659	19.6	4,539	11.5	—	—	—	—	—	2,237	88
Saddleback Valley Unified	CA	25,130	35,199	35,349	66.8	33.2	2.2	20.3	10.4	0.4	1,459	24.2	2,445	14.5	—	—	—	—	—	2,157	37
San Bernardino City Unified	CA	40,589	52,031	57,818	16.0	84.0	19.9	60.2	2.9	1.0	2,691	21.5	4,943	11.7	—	—	—	—	—	1,933	65
San Diego City Unified	CA	121,152	141,804	137,960	25.9	74.1	14.5	41.9	17.2	0.5	7,421	18.6	13,911	9.9	—	—	—	—	—	6,504	185
San Francisco Unified	CA	61,688	59,979	57,805	9.9	90.1	14.9	22.0	52.7	0.6	3,139	18.4	4,951	11.7	—	—	—	—	—	3,399	118
San Jose Unified	CA	29,630	33,015	32,314	28.9	71.1	3.5	50.7	15.2	1.7	1,627	19.9	2,526	12.8	—	—	—	—	—	1,740	57
San Juan Unified	CA	47,690	50,266	50,906	70.8	29.2	7.6	13.1	6.4	2.1	2,418	21.4	4,784	10.6	—	—	—	—	—	3,556	83
San Ramon Valley Unified	CA	16,119	20,742	21,988	76.6	23.4	1.8	4.4	16.4	0.7	1,026	21.4	1,824	12.1	—	—	—	—	—	1,491	28
Santa Ana Unified	CA	45,964	60,643	62,874	3.3	96.7	0.7	92.0	3.9	0.1	2,833	22.2	5,125	12.3	—	—	—	—	—	2,484	56
Simi Valley Unified	CA	18,262	21,181	21,727	69.9	30.1	1.5	20.1	7.5	0.9	961	22.6	1,988	10.9	—	—	—	—	—	1,148	29
Stockton City Unified	CA	32,687	37,573	39,483	11.6	88.4	13.4	52.0	19.6	3.4	2,004	19.7	3,698	10.7	—	—	—	—	—	1,309	50
Sweetwater Union High	CA	27,894	35,330	39,228	13.9	86.1	4.8	68.9	11.9	0.6	1,773	22.1	3,477	11.3	—	—	—	—	—	4,768	28
Temecula Valley Unified	CA	7,596	18,980	23,496	65.3	34.7	5.0	19.9	8.5	1.3	1,094	21.5	1,791	13.1	—	—	—	—	—	1,049	24
Torrance Unified	CA	19,645	24,118	25,229	41.7	58.3	3.9	18.1	35.5	0.7	1,139	22.2	2,067	12.2	—	—	—	—	—	1,813	30
Tracy Joint Unified	CA	—	13,816	16,063	41.1	58.9	7.7	34.6	15.4	1.2	752	21.4	1,277	12.6	—	—	—	—	—	927	21
Tustin Unified	CA	10,831	16,963	18,950	37.8	62.2	2.8	44.5	14.6	0.3	808	23.5	1,400	13.5	—	—	—	—	—	944	26
Vallejo City Unified	CA	19,049	20,270	19,462	15.3	84.7	35.0	23.7	25.3	0.6	916	21.2	1,643	11.8	—	—	—	—	—	1,099	29
Ventura Unified	CA	15,383	17,527	17,794	53.9	46.1	2.4	39.2	3.3	1.2	787	22.6	1,592	11.2	—	—	—	—	—	1,024	29
Visalia Unified	CA	21,309	23,989	25,258	38.2	61.8	2.5	51.7	6.5	1.1	1,145	22.1	2,138	11.8	—	—	—	—	—	1,310	32
Vista Unified	CA	18,489	27,651	26,989	41.6	58.4	5.4	46.5	5.8	0.7	1,193	22.6	2,200	12.3	—	—	—	—	—	1,996	28
Walnut Valley Unified	CA	12,613	14,849	15,458	18.7	81.3	4.2	18.5	58.5	0.1	686	22.5	1,162	13.3	—	—	—	—	—	1,288	15
West Contra Costa Unified	CA	31,292	34,499	33,672	14.5	85.5	29.5	38.9	16.9	0.2	1,698	19.8	2,965	11.4	—	—	—	—	—	1,770	64
William S. Hart Union High	CA	10,278	17,001	21,122	62.2	37.8	4.1	24.9	8.3	0.5	839	25.2	1,487	14.2	—	—	—	—	—	2,393	13

See notes at end of table.

Selected statistics on enrollment, teachers, dropouts, and graduates in public school districts enrolling more than 15,000 students, by state: 1990, 2000, 2001–02, and 2003—Continued

Name of district	State	Enrollment, fall 1990	Enrollment, fall 2000	Enrollment, fall 2003	White, non-Hispanic	Minority Total	Black, non-Hispanic	Hispanic	Asian/ Pacific Islander	American Indian/ Alaska Native	Number of classroom teachers, fall 2003	Pupil/ teacher ratio, fall 2003	Total number of staff, fall 2003	Student/ staff ratio, fall 2003	Dropouts Total	Grade 9	Grade 10	Grade 11	Grade 12	Number of high school graduates, 2001–02[1]	Number of high schools, fall 2003
1	2	3	4	5	6	7	8	9	10	11	12	13	14	15	16	17	18	19	20	21	22
Academy 20	CO	10,986	17,628	19,083	84.7	15.3	3.7	6.3	4.4	0.9	1,165	16.4	2,280	8.4	—	—	—	—	—	1,205	22
Adams 12 Five Star Schools	CO	20,838	30,079	34,869	64.9	35.1	2.5	26.6	5.0	1.1	1,767	19.7	3,585	9.7	—	—	—	—	—	1,566	26
Adams-Arapahoe	CO	25,897	30,453	32,530	31.8	68.2	22.0	41.4	4.0	0.8	1,739	18.7	3,707	8.8	—	—	—	—	—	1,120	47
Boulder Valley	CO	21,502	27,508	27,804	78.9	21.1	1.6	13.0	5.8	0.7	1,629	17.1	3,487	8.0	—	—	—	—	—	1,810	47
Cherry Creek	CO	29,210	42,320	46,594	70.8	29.2	11.9	9.9	6.9	0.5	2,738	17.0	5,413	8.6	—	—	—	—	—	2,922	53
Colorado Springs	CO	30,009	32,699	31,840	66.6	33.4	10.2	19.0	2.7	1.5	1,918	16.6	3,773	8.4	—	—	—	—	—	1,816	50
Denver County	CO	59,013	70,847	72,100	19.7	80.3	18.8	57.1	3.1	1.2	4,218	17.1	8,352	8.6	—	—	—	—	—	2,612	65
Douglas County	CO	13,125	34,918	41,924	87.7	12.3	1.8	6.3	3.6	0.6	2,351	17.8	4,627	9.1	—	—	—	—	—	1,898	145
Greeley	CO	11,657	15,998	17,598	48.9	51.1	1.2	48.3	0.9	0.7	1,055	16.7	1,946	9.0	—	—	—	—	—	870	63
Jefferson County	CO	76,275	87,703	87,172	78.3	21.7	1.8	15.2	3.5	1.1	4,765	18.3	9,847	8.9	—	—	—	—	—	5,334	167
Littleton	CO	15,524	16,516	16,458	85.3	14.7	2.1	9.0	3.0	0.7	945	17.4	1,822	9.0	—	—	—	—	—	1,223	31
Mesa County Valley	CO	17,024	19,688	20,167	80.8	19.2	1.1	15.9	0.9	1.3	1,155	17.5	2,269	8.9	—	—	—	—	—	1,179	25
Poudre	CO	18,589	24,052	24,891	79.8	20.2	1.9	13.9	3.3	1.1	1,434	17.4	2,863	8.7	—	—	—	—	—	1,503	38
Pueblo City	CO	18,364	17,636	17,693	38.3	61.7	2.4	57.0	0.6	1.7	1,104	16.0	2,163	8.2	—	—	—	—	—	907	50
St. Vrain Valley	CO	15,070	19,620	21,596	69.9	30.1	1.1	25.1	3.1	0.9	1,218	17.7	2,228	9.7	—	—	—	—	—	1,134	38
Bridgeport	CT	19,687	22,432	22,828	10.3	89.7	43.3	43.2	3.1	0.1	1,486	15.4	2,803	8.1	10.0	7.3	10.8	14.0	9.2	834	35
Hartford	CT	25,418	22,543	22,578	4.6	95.4	40.3	54.3	0.8	0.1	1,717	13.1	3,336	6.8	6.3	8.7	5.8	5.1	2.2	785	40
New Haven	CT	17,881	19,549	20,457	11.1	88.9	55.5	32.2	1.2	#	1,411	14.5	3,292	6.2	5.2	4.7	6.1	5.9	4.0	788	50
Stamford	CT	11,574	14,791	15,307	43.7	56.3	24.5	26.3	5.5	#	1,210	12.7	2,036	7.5	2.7	3.9	1.8	2.7	2.7	795	22
Waterbury	CT	13,323	16,282	17,714	31.0	69.0	26.7	39.8	2.1	0.4	1,308	13.5	2,490	7.1	3.0	3.4	2.8	3.1	2.0	578	29
Christina	DE	17,872	19,882	19,407	47.0	53.0	38.9	9.9	4.0	0.1	1,316	14.7	2,638	7.4	10.5	13.6	10.5	7.8	8.0	857	28
Red Clay Consolidated	DE	14,551	15,827	15,556	50.7	49.3	28.8	16.6	3.8	0.1	965	16.1	1,802	8.6	7.9	10.3	7.0	7.6	5.4	758	28
District of Columbia	DC	80,694	68,925	65,099	4.9	95.1	83.6	9.7	1.7	0.1	4,898	13.3	9,583	6.8	—	—	—	—	—	2,894	169
Alachua County	FL	26,305	29,712	29,448	53.2	46.8	38.6	4.7	3.3	0.2	1,667	17.7	4,073	7.2	6.1	5.4	6.3	5.3	7.9	1,651	64
Bay County	FL	21,827	25,755	26,708	79.5	20.5	16.2	2.0	1.9	0.4	1,564	17.1	3,297	8.1	1.8	1.7	1.6	2.2	1.7	1,230	41
Brevard County	FL	56,503	70,597	73,901	78.3	21.7	14.0	5.7	1.7	0.3	4,303	17.2	8,506	8.7	0.9	1.2	0.8	1.1	0.4	3,578	107
Broward County	FL	161,101	251,129	272,835	36.3	63.7	36.8	23.5	3.0	0.3	14,264	19.1	26,909	10.1	1.6	2.0	1.2	1.4	1.7	11654	259
Charlotte County	FL	13,030	17,170	18,298	84.5	15.5	8.4	5.4	1.4	0.3	970	18.9	2,313	7.9	4.2	2.0	2.7	3.8	8.7	1,076	22
Citrus County	FL	11,697	15,199	15,517	90.6	9.4	4.3	3.5	1.3	0.4	949	16.4	2,084	7.4	4.8	4.9	4.6	4.3	5.2	830	23
Clay County	FL	21,925	28,115	31,370	82.3	17.7	10.6	4.7	2.2	0.4	1,797	17.5	3,599	8.7	2.8	4.1	2.5	2.1	1.7	1,627	33
Collier County	FL	20,850	34,203	40,157	50.7	49.3	11.2	36.9	0.9	0.4	2,332	17.2	5,125	7.8	4.4	4.4	5.3	4.2	3.2	1,711	56
Dade County	FL	292,023	368,625	371,785	10.4	89.6	28.9	59.4	1.1	0.1	18,887	19.7	36,585	10.2	4.8	4.4	3.9	4.0	7.5	16,638	362
Duval County	FL	111,142	125,846	129,557	47.8	52.2	44.1	4.8	3.1	0.1	6,976	18.6	12,125	10.7	6.7	7.8	5.9	5.5	6.6	5,260	177
Escambia County	FL	42,950	45,012	43,998	57.6	42.4	37.0	1.9	2.7	0.7	2,511	17.5	5,312	8.3	2.8	3.1	3.1	2.7	2.2	2,320	76
Hernando County	FL	12,831	17,215	19,596	83.4	16.6	6.9	8.5	0.9	0.3	1,090	18.0	2,500	7.8	2.3	3.1	2.6	1.7	0.9	923	20
Hillsborough County	FL	124,337	164,311	181,900	48.7	51.3	23.6	25.0	2.4	0.3	11,020	16.5	21,377	8.5	2.8	4.2	2.0	2.2	1.6	7,968	232
Indian River County	FL	11,683	14,979	16,637	70.1	29.9	15.8	12.6	1.2	0.3	932	17.9	1,921	8.7	1.8	1.7	1.1	2.3	2.1	821	26
Lake County	FL	21,065	29,293	33,992	71.2	28.8	15.6	11.5	1.3	0.4	1,758	19.3	2,950	11.5	5.5	4.1	5.6	6.4	6.5	1,531	51
Lee County	FL	43,240	58,401	66,466	62.2	37.8	15.0	21.1	1.3	0.4	3,624	18.3	7,532	8.8	9.0	9.4	8.5	7.2	11.0	2,846	81
Leon County	FL	27,241	32,050	32,194	54.1	45.9	41.1	2.5	2.2	0.1	1,817	17.7	4,159	7.7	3.7	4.7	3.4	3.4	2.7	1,788	53
Manatee County	FL	26,207	36,569	40,269	64.2	35.8	16.4	18.2	1.0	0.1	2,279	17.7	4,870	8.3	3.7	2.7	4.0	3.4	6.1	1,709	70
Marion County	FL	29,577	38,562	40,382	67.7	32.3	20.8	10.2	1.0	0.4	2,299	17.6	5,417	7.5	3.5	3.1	3.3	3.6	4.5	1,960	62

See notes at end of table.

Selected statistics on enrollment, teachers, dropouts, and graduates in public school districts enrolling more than 15,000 students, by state: 1990, 2000, 2001–02, and 2003—Continued

Name of district	State	Enrollment, fall 1990	Enrollment, fall 2000	Enrollment, fall 2003	Percentage distribution of enrollment, by race, fall 2003						Number of classroom teachers, fall 2003	Pupil/ teacher ratio, fall 2003	Total number of staff, fall 2003	Student/ staff ratio, fall 2003	Percent dropouts from grades 9–12, 2001–02[1]					Number of high school graduates, 2001–02[2]	Number of schools, fall 2003
					White, non-Hispanic	Minority Total	Black, non-Hispanic	Hispanic	Asian/ Pacific Islander	American Indian/ Alaska Native					Total	Grade 9	Grade 10	Grade 11	Grade 12		
1	2	3	4	5	6	7	8	9	10	11	12	13	14	15	16	17	18	19	20	21	22
Martin County	FL	11,692	16,308	17,783	72.7	27.3	10.0	16.0	1.0	0.2	974	18.3	1,987	8.9	0.6	0.6	0.4	0.5	0.9	842	27
Okaloosa County	FL	26,140	30,344	31,489	80.4	19.6	12.5	3.8	2.8	0.5	1,695	18.6	3,472	9.1	3.6	3.0	2.5	3.5	5.8	1,978	54
Orange County	FL	102,672	150,681	165,992	40.3	59.7	28.5	26.9	3.8	0.4	9,495	17.5	20,125	8.2	3.4	3.5	2.7	2.4	4.9	7,361	187
Osceola County	FL	19,514	34,566	43,911	42.4	57.6	9.7	45.5	2.3	0.2	2,219	19.8	5,284	8.3	5.6	5.6	5.8	5.4	5.7	1,853	57
Palm Beach County	FL	105,712	153,871	170,260	46.3	53.7	29.7	21.1	2.3	0.2	9,359	18.2	18,315	9.3	3.1	3.4	3.9	1.9	2.4	7,687	208
Pasco County	FL	33,891	49,704	57,510	84.6	15.4	4.1	9.7	1.4	0.3	3,196	18.0	7,044	8.2	4.2	3.8	4.4	3.8	5.2	2,453	71
Pinellas County	FL	92,976	113,027	114,510	70.2	29.8	19.5	6.7	3.3	0.3	6,632	17.3	14,092	8.1	6.3	7.4	6.4	5.0	5.0	5,413	163
Polk County	FL	64,579	79,477	84,135	60.7	39.3	22.4	15.6	1.1	0.2	5,284	15.9	11,032	7.6	3.6	3.5	3.3	3.3	4.1	3,815	147
Saint Johns County	FL	12,080	20,090	23,191	86.8	13.2	9.1	2.6	1.1	0.1	1,319	17.6	2,691	8.6	2.5	2.3	1.5	3.1	3.4	1,097	33
Saint Lucie County	FL	22,224	29,540	32,799	55.1	44.9	29.1	14.2	1.4	0.3	1,645	19.9	3,677	8.9	1.6	1.7	1.7	2.7	1.8	1,258	42
Santa Rosa County	FL	15,708	22,633	24,429	90.5	9.5	5.3	2.1	1.6	0.6	1,329	18.4	2,329	10.5	2.1	1.3	1.3	1.5	3.7	1,333	36
Sarasota County	FL	26,881	35,533	39,534	79.4	20.6	9.5	9.3	1.6	0.2	2,389	16.5	5,049	7.8	3.6	3.6	3.9	3.3	3.5	1,895	48
Seminole County	FL	48,831	60,869	64,904	67.2	32.8	13.8	15.6	3.1	0.2	3,788	17.1	7,083	9.2	1.5	1.5	1.7	1.5	1.3	3,420	72
Volusia County	FL	48,342	61,517	64,089	71.7	28.3	15.2	11.6	1.2	0.2	3,807	16.8	8,257	7.8	1.9	1.7	2.0	1.9	2.2	3,386	87
Atlanta City	GA	60,714	58,230	52,103	7.6	92.4	88.2	3.6	0.6	#	3,692	14.1	7,310	7.1	8.9	7.7	7.7	10.5	10.8	2,270	105
Bibb County	GA	24,378	24,739	25,276	25.9	74.1	71.4	1.2	1.3	0.3	1,487	17.0	3,184	7.9	10.3	11.7	10.1	9.5	8.3	831	45
Chatham County	GA	34,044	35,344	34,514	29.5	70.5	66.1	2.5	1.7	0.2	2,337	14.8	4,425	7.8	16.8	20.8	15.3	12.1	16.3	1,197	55
Cherokee County	GA	16,086	26,043	29,711	86.2	13.8	4.6	7.8	1.2	0.3	1,898	15.7	3,555	8.4	4.5	2.5	4.1	6.7	5.2	1,271	34
Clayton County	GA	34,754	46,930	50,555	13.1	86.9	72.8	9.6	4.4	0.1	2,954	17.1	6,590	7.7	8.2	8.4	8.0	7.2	9.3	1,791	57
Cobb County	GA	69,441	95,781	102,034	57.9	42.1	27.7	10.3	3.8	0.2	6,867	14.9	12,616	8.1	3.6	2.1	3.4	4.3	4.8	5,231	106
Columbia County	GA	14,096	18,756	20,063	79.9	20.1	14.3	2.4	3.3	0.1	1,185	16.9	2,517	8.0	4.8	3.6	5.0	5.6	5.2	1,051	28
Coweta County	GA	10,430	16,766	19,035	73.4	26.6	22.2	3.6	0.7	0.1	1,172	16.2	2,505	7.6	5.5	4.3	6.4	6.4	5.3	788	28
DeKalb County	GA	74,108	95,958	99,550	11.7	88.3	77.8	7.0	3.4	0.1	6,409	15.5	12,942	7.7	6.8	7.5	6.6	6.1	6.5	4,191	141
Dougherty County	GA	18,482	16,799	16,844	15.0	85.0	83.8	0.7	0.4	0.1	1,029	16.4	2,412	7.0	8.0	9.7	7.9	8.1	4.5	711	29
Douglas County	GA	14,002	17,489	19,697	60.3	39.7	33.4	4.8	1.4	0.1	1,122	17.6	2,358	8.4	5.7	3.7	7.5	6.7	4.7	899	31
Fayette County	GA	13,105	19,590	21,224	75.6	24.4	17.9	3.2	3.2	0.1	1,394	15.2	2,665	8.0	2.0	2.1	1.6	2.4	1.8	1,380	30
Forsyth County	GA	7,742	17,131	22,067	90.9	9.1	0.8	7.0	1.3	0.1	1,361	16.2	2,693	8.2	2.7	1.5	2.0	3.5	4.6	765	24
Fulton County	GA	41,195	68,583	73,319	45.2	54.8	39.3	8.8	6.6	0.1	4,891	15.0	9,641	7.6	2.5	1.6	2.4	2.6	4.1	3,360	87
Gwinnett County	GA	63,930	110,075	129,014	52.7	47.3	21.4	16.0	9.7	0.1	8,221	15.7	15,425	8.4	3.2	2.8	2.8	3.3	4.0	6,116	98
Hall County	GA	13,738	20,330	22,535	66.9	33.1	5.5	26.2	1.0	0.4	1,395	16.2	2,635	8.6	6.2	1.3	8.2	6.1	12.7	869	33
Henry County	GA	10,929	23,601	29,843	66.1	33.9	28.0	3.6	2.1	0.2	1,844	16.2	3,499	8.5	4.0	1.1	4.0	5.1	7.7	1,157	32
Houston County	GA	16,249	21,529	23,395	61.8	38.2	33.1	3.0	1.8	0.2	1,528	15.3	3,073	7.6	5.8	5.6	7.0	6.0	4.3	1,208	37
Muscogee County	GA	30,038	32,916	33,055	34.8	65.2	60.5	3.2	1.4	0.2	2,187	15.1	4,945	6.7	6.8	6.4	6.9	7.1	6.8	1,502	62
Paulding County	GA	7,604	16,587	20,459	83.0	17.0	13.9	2.4	0.3	0.4	1,257	16.3	2,456	8.3	7.7	3.0	8.6	9.7	13.7	652	26
Richmond County	GA	33,660	35,424	34,400	25.6	74.4	71.2	2.0	1.0	0.1	2,209	15.6	4,681	7.3	5.0	5.4	4.1	4.7	6.0	1,576	58
Hawaii Dept. of Education	HI	171,309	184,360	183,609	20.2	79.8	2.4	4.5	72.4	0.5	11,129	16.5	21,112	8.7	5.1	2.8	5.4	5.8	7.6	10,452	284
Boise City Independent	ID	23,394	26,598	26,211	87.4	12.6	1.9	7.0	3.1	0.6	1,466	17.9	2,671	9.8	4.0	2.3	3.8	6.2	3.9	1,737	54
Meridian Junction	ID	14,802	23,854	26,987	92.0	8.0	1.4	3.4	2.5	0.8	1,361	19.8	2,415	11.2	3.5	3.4	2.9	3.9	3.8	1,498	40
City of Chicago	IL	408,714	435,261	434,419	9.1	90.9	50.3	37.3	3.2	0.2	22,951	18.9	27,583	15.7	17.6	22.9	18.2	15.3	8.0	15,653	633
Community Unit 300	IL	11,196	16,711	18,175	67.2	32.8	4.5	24.3	3.5	0.5	864	21.0	1,032	17.6	3.0	3.2	2.4	2.8	3.7	1,037	24
Indian Prairie	IL	7,670	23,173	26,779	73.6	26.4	8.5	5.9	11.8	0.2	1,639	16.3	1,950	13.7	0.9	0.1	0.7	1.2	1.9	1,282	31
Naperville	IL	16,212	18,762	18,933	79.8	20.2	3.3	3.4	13.4	0.1	1,050	18.0	1,282	14.8	0.5	0.0	0.1	0.5	1.4	1,348	21

See notes at end of table.

Selected statistics on enrollment, teachers, dropouts, and graduates in public school districts enrolling more than 15,000 students, by state: 1990, 2000, 2001–02, and 2003—Continued

Name of district	State	Enrollment, fall 1990	Enrollment, fall 2000	Enrollment, fall 2003	White, non-Hispanic	Minority Total	Black, non-Hispanic	Hispanic	Asian/ Pacific Islander	American Indian/ Alaska Native	Number of classroom teachers, fall 2003	Pupil/ teacher ratio, fall 2003	Total number of staff, fall 2003	Student/ staff ratio, fall 2003	Total	Grade 9	Grade 10	Grade 11	Grade 12	Number of high school graduates, 2001–02	Number of schools, fall 2003
1	2	3	4	5	6	7	8	9	10	11	12	13	14	15	16	17	18	19	20	21	22
Peoria	IL	17,378	15,724	15,863	34.9	65.1	59.0	3.8	2.2	0.1	1,066	14.9	1,240	12.8	12.1	11.8	11.9	12.0	12.9	775	45
Plainfield	IL	3,324	11,986	18,964	75.8	24.2	7.5	13.3	3.3	0.2	1,061	17.9	1,223	15.5	3.0	0.8	1.3	2.9	8.7	748	20
Rockford	IL	27,255	27,399	28,612	46.1	53.9	32.2	18.3	3.2	0.2	1,681	17.0	1,998	14.3	6.4	8.4	7.2	4.5	3.3	1,187	53
School District 46	IL	27,726	36,767	38,821	49.2	50.8	7.4	36.2	7.1	0.2	1,878	20.7	2,206	17.6	4.7	2.8	6.7	5.6	3.9	1,914	53
Springfield	IL	15,813	15,387	15,212	58.8	41.2	37.8	1.2	2.0	0.2	945	16.1	1,121	13.6	3.6	0.9	4.0	6.6	3.4	803	36
Valley View	IL	11,781	13,558	15,949	45.9	54.1	25.8	23.0	5.3	#	786	20.3	921	17.3	3.8	1.3	2.3	5.2	7.2	753	17
Waukegan	IL	12,116	15,510	16,260	9.7	90.3	20.7	67.4	2.2	0.1	860	18.9	1,036	15.7	11.2	13.6	10.3	10.4	8.2	648	24
Evansville-Vanderburgh SC	IN	22,918	22,875	22,408	82.1	17.9	15.7	1.2	0.8	0.3	1,400	16.0	2,730	8.2	1.0	0.1	1.3	1.3	1.2	1,344	42
Fort Wayne Community	IN	31,611	31,843	31,815	62.2	37.8	26.4	8.6	2.2	0.5	1,763	18.0	3,519	9.0	2.9	1.7	3.5	2.6	4.3	1,596	54
Gary Community SC	IN	26,620	19,206	17,381	0.6	99.4	97.9	1.2	0.2	0.1	1,002	17.3	2,869	6.1	0.5	0.6	0.5	0.2	0.5	706	35
Indianapolis	IN	48,140	41,008	39,989	30.6	69.4	59.7	9.1	0.4	0.2	2,770	14.4	5,516	7.2	2.2	3.1	1.8	1.6	1.2	1,203	92
M.S.D. Lawrence Township	IN	11,066	15,692	16,201	59.2	40.8	33.3	5.5	1.9	0.2	922	17.6	2,142	7.6	1.4	1.6	1.1	2.2	0.7	871	19
South Bend Community SC	IN	21,425	21,536	21,871	48.4	51.6	37.6	12.4	1.2	0.5	1,343	16.3	3,151	6.9	1.5	1.2	1.7	1.6	1.7	1,206	38
Vigo County SC	IN	16,982	16,545	16,377	91.6	8.4	6.6	0.6	1.1	0.1	1,017	16.1	1,992	8.2	3.8	2.3	3.4	5.1	4.7	997	29
Cedar Rapids	IA	16,988	17,780	17,324	83.0	17.0	12.1	2.4	2.1	0.4	1,126	15.4	2,258	7.7	2.6	0.1	2.4	3.7	4.4	1,013	34
Davenport	IA	17,841	16,874	16,366	70.9	29.1	18.0	7.3	2.6	1.1	1,112	14.7	1,914	8.6	4.2	2.3	4.6	6.5	3.8	956	32
Des Moines Independent	IA	30,514	32,435	31,086	66.7	33.3	15.9	12.2	4.6	0.7	2,329	13.3	4,222	7.4	4.6	5.0	4.0	5.3	3.5	1,659	61
Blue Valley	KS	9,432	17,111	19,055	88.5	11.5	3.3	1.8	6.2	0.3	1,250	15.2	2,283	8.3	0.7	0.1	0.4	1.2	1.3	1,190	29
Kansas City	KS	21,948	21,173	20,868	20.3	79.7	48.2	27.7	3.3	0.5	1,476	14.1	2,799	7.5	4.8	3.3	5.2	6.0	5.2	938	42
Olathe	KS	14,868	20,703	22,917	83.9	16.1	5.9	6.1	3.6	0.4	1,537	14.9	2,874	8.0	1.8	0.1	1.1	3.0	3.0	1,319	39
Shawnee Mission	KS	30,563	30,765	29,389	82.9	17.1	6.7	6.8	3.1	0.5	1,815	16.2	3,392	8.7	2.0	0.5	2.0	2.5	3.2	2,226	50
Wichita	KS	46,847	48,228	48,894	48.7	51.3	23.6	19.7	5.4	2.7	3,069	15.9	5,606	8.7	8.7	4.9	8.3	7.9	14.6	2,147	90
Boone County	KY	9,911	13,445	15,406	93.9	6.1	2.2	2.2	1.5	0.1	895	17.2	1,902	8.1	2.1	1.7	2.2	2.3	2.2	722	18
Fayette County	KY	32,083	33,130	34,259	68.5	31.5	23.3	5.1	2.9	0.2	2,534	13.5	5,010	6.8	5.0	5.1	5.8	4.1	4.9	1,643	60
Jefferson County	KY	91,450	96,860	95,582	59.9	40.1	35.0	2.7	1.9	0.4	5,656	16.9	13,624	7.0	5.9	4.6	6.1	7.2	6.4	4,932	173
Ascension Parish School Board	LA	13,001	15,038	15,810	67.7	32.3	28.6	2.9	0.6	0.3	1,105	14.3	2,178	7.3	4.7	3.8	5.3	5.1	4.8	772	23
Bossier Parish SB	LA	17,804	18,797	18,771	64.9	35.1	30.5	2.9	1.4	0.3	1,170	16.0	2,378	7.9	4.6	3.8	4.7	3.8	6.1	983	35
Caddo Parish SB	LA	51,375	45,119	44,473	35.4	64.6	62.8	0.9	0.8	0.2	2,928	15.2	6,485	6.9	10.0	7.7	8.5	8.3	17.2	2,223	75
Calcasieu Parish SB	LA	32,917	32,261	32,149	64.5	35.5	33.8	0.7	0.7	0.2	2,185	14.7	4,441	7.2	4.8	3.9	4.8	4.9	5.6	1,747	59
East Baton Rouge Parish SB	LA	61,669	54,246	46,644	20.5	79.5	75.8	1.3	2.3	0.1	3,137	14.9	6,573	7.1	8.5	8.3	9.0	8.2	8.5	2,815	98
Jefferson Parish SB	LA	58,177	50,891	51,453	35.3	64.7	51.1	8.7	4.2	0.7	3,372	15.3	6,937	7.4	9.7	9.8	11.3	9.3	7.6	2,261	84
Lafayette Parish SB	LA	29,403	28,931	29,813	56.9	43.1	40.2	1.4	1.3	0.3	2,118	14.1	3,955	7.5	7.8	7.2	9.1	8.9	5.8	1,624	45
Livingston Parish SB	LA	16,310	19,723	20,743	93.7	6.3	5.2	0.7	0.2	0.2	1,354	15.3	2,572	8.1	1.2	1.3	1.2	1.4	1.0	1,056	37
Orleans Parish SB	LA	82,925	77,610	67,922	3.4	96.6	93.6	1.1	1.9	0.1	4,657	14.6	8,945	7.6	9.1	7.1	9.7	7.5	12.5	3,471	128
Ouachita Parish SB	LA	17,667	17,479	18,324	70.7	29.3	27.8	0.8	0.6	0.1	1,283	14.3	2,747	6.7	7.1	7.7	5.4	7.2	8.2	923	35
Rapides Parish SB	LA	24,765	23,467	22,646	53.9	46.1	42.9	1.1	1.2	0.9	1,573	14.4	3,213	7.0	8.7	7.4	9.4	8.4	10.1	1,294	53
Saint Landry Parish SB	LA	17,213	15,457	15,231	43.5	56.5	55.7	0.4	0.3	0.1	1,046	14.6	2,142	7.1	5.0	4.4	5.4	5.0	5.6	805	38
Saint Tammany Parish SB	LA	27,522	32,392	34,750	79.5	20.5	17.1	1.3	1.1	0.4	2,492	13.9	4,952	7.0	4.0	3.7	3.8	4.9	3.7	1,834	51
Tangipahoa Parish SB	LA	16,724	18,197	18,465	52.8	47.2	45.4	1.3	0.5	0.1	1,058	17.5	2,252	8.2	7.0	6.7	9.3	7.0	4.4	1,030	37
Terrebonne Parish SB	LA	21,116	19,774	19,256	61.1	38.9	27.8	1.3	1.3	8.4	1,386	13.9	2,649	7.3	8.3	7.9	9.6	6.4	9.8	1,007	41

See notes at end of table.

Selected statistics on enrollment, teachers, dropouts, and graduates in public school districts enrolling more than 15,000 students, by state: 1990, 2000, 2001–02, and 2003—Continued

Name of district	State	Enrollment, fall 1990	Enrollment, fall 2000	Enrollment, fall 2003	Percentage distribution of enrollment, by race, fall 2003						Number of classroom teachers, fall 2003	Pupil/ teacher ratio, fall 2003	Total number of staff, fall 2003	Student/ staff ratio, fall 2003	Percent dropouts from grades 9–12, 2001–02[1]					Number of high school graduates, 2001–02[2]	Number of schools, fall 2003
					White, non-Hispanic	Minority															
						Total	Black, non-Hispanic	Hispanic	Asian/ Pacific Islander	American Indian/ Alaska Native					Total	Grade 9	Grade 10	Grade 11	Grade 12		
1	2	3	4	5	6	7	8	9	10	11	12	13	14	15	16	17	18	19	20	21	22
Anne Arundel County	MD	65,011	74,491	74,508	72.2	27.8	20.9	3.4	3.1	0.3	4,501	16.6	8,050	9.3	4.4	4.8	4.5	4.7	3.2	4,466	119
Baltimore City	MD	108,663	99,859	94,049	9.1	90.9	88.6	1.4	0.6	0.3	6,268	15.0	11,223	8.4	11.5	10.3	12.7	13.0	10.1	4,524	189
Baltimore County	MD	86,737	106,898	108,523	56.0	44.0	36.7	2.5	4.3	0.5	7,292	14.9	13,297	8.2	3.0	2.5	3.2	3.8	2.5	6,859	167
Calvert County	MD	10,398	16,170	17,423	81.7	18.3	15.7	1.2	1.2	0.2	1,042	16.7	2,025	8.6	3.3	3.1	3.4	3.2	3.7	1,043	25
Carroll County	MD	21,835	27,528	28,832	94.4	5.6	2.8	1.3	1.3	0.3	1,709	16.9	3,009	9.6	2.0	1.3	2.2	2.7	1.9	1,910	42
Cecil County	MD	12,868	15,905	16,475	89.0	11.0	7.5	2.3	0.8	0.3	1,044	15.8	1,817	9.1	3.0	2.5	2.6	3.8	3.5	878	31
Charles County	MD	18,708	23,468	25,610	52.6	47.4	41.1	2.7	2.8	0.9	1,447	17.7	2,568	10.0	3.3	3.2	3.4	3.6	3.0	1,481	34
Frederick County	MD	26,848	36,885	38,950	82.8	17.2	9.9	4.1	2.9	0.3	2,408	16.2	4,426	8.8	1.8	1.3	2.4	1.5	2.2	2,465	59
Harford County	MD	31,500	39,520	40,200	78.1	21.9	16.3	2.7	2.3	0.5	2,297	17.5	4,465	9.0	3.4	2.1	3.4	4.3	4.1	2,425	51
Howard County	MD	29,949	44,946	47,833	65.9	34.1	18.4	3.6	11.8	0.2	3,324	14.4	6,299	7.6	2.0	1.7	2.4	1.8	2.0	2,990	71
Montgomery County	MD	103,757	134,180	139,201	44.6	55.4	22.1	18.7	14.3	0.3	9,007	15.5	17,870	7.8	1.9	1.9	1.8	1.9	2.0	8,282	194
Prince George's County	MD	108,868	133,723	137,285	8.0	92.0	77.6	10.8	3.1	0.6	8,119	16.9	15,130	9.1	3.1	3.7	3.5	2.5	2.5	7,552	203
Saint Mary's County	MD	12,549	15,151	16,261	76.5	23.5	18.6	2.1	2.1	0.6	1,004	16.2	1,745	9.3	3.1	2.2	3.9	2.8	3.8	845	27
Washington County	MD	17,778	19,782	20,338	87.1	12.9	9.5	2.0	1.1	0.2	1,292	15.7	2,294	8.9	3.1	2.1	3.3	4.2	3.1	1,234	46
Boston	MA	60,543	63,024	60,150	14.0	86.0	46.4	30.4	8.8	0.4	3,926	15.3	7,918	7.6	—	—	—	—	—	2,816	136
Brockton	MA	14,529	16,791	16,454	37.8	62.2	45.9	12.4	2.9	0.9	1,148	14.3	2,257	7.3	—	—	—	—	—	689	25
Lowell	MA	13,488	15,989	15,105	43.5	56.5	5.7	21.2	29.4	0.2	1,111	13.6	1,997	7.6	—	—	—	—	—	732	25
Springfield	MA	24,194	26,526	26,132	20.7	79.3	28.3	48.5	2.4	0.2	2,302	11.4	4,595	5.7	—	—	—	—	—	839	48
Worcester	MA	21,066	25,828	25,028	48.2	51.8	12.2	30.8	8.2	0.6	1,892	13.2	3,543	7.1	—	—	—	—	—	1,087	47
Ann Arbor	MI	14,199	16,539	16,701	68.1	31.9	15.4	3.6	12.5	0.5	1,055	15.8	2,130	7.8	—	—	—	—	—	1,141	33
Dearborn City	MI	13,380	17,129	18,083	93.5	6.5	3.0	2.1	0.8	0.6	1,072	16.9	2,079	8.7	—	—	—	—	—	1,014	32
Detroit City	MI	168,116	162,194	153,034	3.0	97.0	90.8	5.1	0.8	0.3	6,719	22.8	19,620	7.8	—	—	—	—	—	5,540	261
Flint City	MI	27,601	22,532	20,465	18.7	81.3	77.9	2.7	0.3	0.4	1,209	16.9	2,628	7.8	—	—	—	—	—	714	39
Grand Rapids City	MI	26,250	25,625	24,166	27.8	72.2	44.0	25.4	1.4	1.5	1,633	14.8	3,464	7.0	—	—	—	—	—	708	88
Lansing	MI	21,350	17,610	16,979	37.6	62.4	41.1	15.2	5.0	1.2	304	55.9	322	52.7	—	—	—	—	—	778	42
Livonia	MI	16,373	18,347	18,379	91.8	8.2	3.7	1.5	2.7	0.3	1,035	17.8	2,103	8.7	—	—	—	—	—	1,315	34
Plymouth-Canton Community Schools	MI	14,955	16,518	18,121	81.8	18.2	5.1	1.8	10.8	0.5	890	20.4	1,678	10.8	—	—	—	—	—	1,008	25
Utica Community	MI	23,960	27,786	28,935	92.6	7.4	1.8	2.3	3.1	0.1	1,546	18.7	3,177	9.1	—	—	—	—	—	1,867	43
Walled Lake Consolidated	MI	9,059	14,438	15,205	89.2	10.8	3.4	1.7	5.2	0.5	888	17.1	1,767	8.6	—	—	—	—	—	811	24
Warren Consolidated	MI	14,336	14,602	15,421	88.8	11.2	5.3	0.8	4.5	0.7	802	19.2	1,490	10.3	—	—	—	—	—	970	26
Anoka-Hennepin	MN	34,524	41,314	41,254	87.0	13.0	4.8	2.1	4.6	1.4	2,256	18.3	4,373	9.4	3.9	0.5	1.5	4.0	9.5	2,372	60
Minneapolis	MN	36,763	48,834	43,397	27.1	72.9	42.1	13.5	13.1	4.2	3,025	14.3	6,067	7.2	12.5	6.9	12.3	13.9	17.6	2,180	142
Osseo	MN	19,483	22,017	21,698	67.1	32.9	16.9	3.4	11.8	0.8	998	21.7	2,285	9.5	2.3	0.2	1.7	2.9	4.4	1,342	31
Rochester	MN	13,897	15,929	16,470	76.7	23.3	9.9	4.7	8.5	0.4	938	17.6	1,879	8.8	2.9	1.6	2.2	3.6	4.4	1,068	40
Rosemount-Apple Valley-Eagan	MN	17,029	28,330	28,561	85.0	15.0	5.8	3.0	5.7	0.6	1,750	16.3	3,301	8.7	1.9	0.0	0.6	2.3	4.8	1,865	37
St. Paul	MN	32,366	45,115	42,510	29.4	70.6	28.1	11.8	28.9	1.8	2,754	15.4	5,427	7.8	6.6	1.0	3.4	5.7	15.2	2,127	123
South Washington County	MN	11,260	14,953	15,629	84.7	15.3	5.1	3.4	6.2	0.6	864	18.1	1,653	9.5	2.5	0.0	1.0	2.4	6.6	1,031	24
Desoto County	MS	13,470	19,812	23,672	75.1	24.9	20.5	3.2	1.0	0.2	1,266	18.7	2,564	9.2	0.9	1.1	0.8	0.9	0.8	862	26
Jackson	MS	33,546	31,351	31,640	3.2	96.8	96.2	0.3	0.2	#	1,901	16.6	4,546	7.0	7.0	9.5	5.8	6.3	5.1	1,239	61
Rankin County	MS	12,824	15,013	16,014	76.7	23.3	21.5	0.9	0.8	0.1	1,047	15.3	2,007	8.0	1.6	1.3	1.8	1.8	1.8	795	23

See notes at end of table.

Selected statistics on enrollment, teachers, dropouts, and graduates in public school districts enrolling more than 15,000 students, by state: 1990, 2000, 2001–02, and 2003—Continued

Name of district	State	Enrollment, fall 1990	Enrollment, fall 2000	Enrollment, fall 2003	White, non-Hispanic	Minority Total	Black, non-Hispanic	Hispanic	Asian/Pacific Islander	American Indian/Alaska Native	Number of classroom teachers, fall 2003	Pupil/teacher ratio, fall 2003	Total number of staff, fall 2003	Student/staff ratio, fall 2003	Dropouts Total	Grade 9	Grade 10	Grade 11	Grade 12	Number of high school graduates, 2001–02	Number of schools, fall 2003
1	2	3	4	5	6	7	8	9	10	11	12	13	14	15	16	17	18	19	20	21	22
Columbia	MO	12,786	16,178	16,498	71.4	28.6	21.1	2.6	4.6	0.4	1,234	13.4	2,463	6.7	4.5	0.7	3.5	5.7	8.3	1,039	22
Ft. Zumwalt R-II	MO	10,110	16,521	18,138	93.2	6.8	4.1	1.5	1.1	0.2	1,065	17.0	2,346	7.7	2.7	1.5	3.3	2.3	4.2	1,073	31
Francis Howell R-III	MO	13,391	19,497	18,360	92.6	7.4	4.4	1.3	1.5	0.3	1,188	15.5	2,022	9.1	2.8	1.5	2.7	3.8	3.5	1,232	23
Hazelwood	MO	16,985	18,855	19,311	40.8	59.2	57.1	1.1	0.9	#	1,133	17.0	2,362	8.2	4.6	2.3	6.0	6.4	3.8	1,247	25
Kansas City	MO	34,486	37,298	38,285	13.3	86.7	69.8	14.5	2.1	0.2	2,601	14.7	4,869	7.9	7.6	8.0	10.0	6.8	3.7	1,409	89
Lee's Summit R-VII	MO	7,132	14,340	15,862	87.7	12.3	7.6	2.7	1.8	0.2	957	16.6	2,094	7.6	2.2	0.8	1.8	3.5	2.8	956	22
North Kansas City	MO	15,732	17,258	17,004	81.0	19.0	7.9	7.0	3.2	0.9	1,214	14.0	2,463	6.9	2.9	0.6	2.2	4.4	4.5	1,137	30
Parkway C-2	MO	21,542	20,433	19,578	71.9	28.1	17.3	1.7	9.0	0.1	1,200	16.3	2,469	7.9	1.1	0.4	0.7	1.2	2.1	1,438	28
Rockwood R-VI	MO	15,608	21,203	22,658	83.9	16.1	11.7	1.2	3.0	0.2	1,343	16.9	2,910	7.8	1.9	0.8	2.1	3.3	1.3	1,474	30
St. Louis City	MO	43,284	44,412	40,827	15.5	84.5	81.4	1.5	1.5	0.1	3,227	12.7	6,730	6.1	8.2	8.4	8.2	8.0	7.8	1,424	108
Springfield R-XII	MO	23,631	24,630	24,285	88.6	11.4	6.1	2.4	2.2	0.6	1,456	16.7	2,882	8.4	4.9	1.8	5.2	6.0	6.9	1,464	55
Lincoln	NE	27,986	31,354	32,120	82.1	17.9	7.4	5.3	3.8	1.4	2,342	13.7	4,533	7.1	6.2	0.6	3.9	8.8	11.3	1,896	66
Millard	NE	16,764	19,160	19,904	92.4	7.6	2.2	2.3	2.8	0.3	1,275	15.6	2,313	8.6	1.3	0.3	1.0	1.3	2.7	1,513	34
Omaha	NE	41,699	45,197	46,035	47.6	52.4	31.1	18.1	1.7	1.5	3,101	14.8	6,227	7.4	10.9	12.9	10.6	10.8	8.0	2,168	84
Clark County	NV	121,959	231,655	270,529	44.0	56.0	14.1	33.2	7.8	0.9	13,483	20.1	21,049	12.9	8.1	6.1	5.3	3.2	19.6	10,215	298
Washoe County	NV	38,466	56,268	62,103	60.6	39.4	3.6	27.1	6.0	2.8	3,614	17.2	6,775	9.2	3.4	3.1	2.6	1.7	6.2	2,851	102
Manchester	NH	14,604	17,407	17,655	83.4	16.6	4.6	9.2	2.3	0.5	1,160	15.2	1,918	9.2	6.8	4.0	7.0	7.5	10.0	1,180	22
Camden City	NJ	19,497	17,517	18,997	1.1	98.9	54.1	42.9	1.7	0.1	1,547	12.3	2,482	7.7	14.1	18.4	14.4	13.4	6.2	505	31
Elizabeth City	NJ	15,266	19,674	21,998	10.7	89.3	23.9	63.3	2.1	#	2,008	11.0	4,032	5.5	5.9	5.7	6.5	5.4	5.8	877	26
Jersey City	NJ	28,585	31,347	35,161	9.5	90.5	35.6	39.3	14.3	1.3	2,702	13.0	5,440	6.5	8.6	12.1	9.2	7.2	3.6	1,293	40
Newark City	NJ	48,433	42,150	46,825	8.3	91.7	59.4	31.3	0.8	0.1	3,687	12.7	7,470	6.3	4.2	4.5	4.5	3.8	3.6	1,699	77
Paterson City	NJ	22,109	24,629	27,734	6.0	94.0	37.6	53.8	2.5	0.1	2,420	11.5	4,154	6.7	9.3	12.0	11.0	4.8	4.3	754	36
Tom's River Regional	NJ	16,002	17,621	19,190	88.9	11.1	3.6	4.9	2.5	0.1	1,177	16.3	2,227	8.6	2.4	0.5	2.1	3.7	3.5	1,188	17
Albuquerque	NM	88,295	85,276	90,537	36.4	63.6	3.9	52.6	2.3	4.8	6,191	14.6	12,170	7.4	7.1	9.0	6.8	6.9	4.6	4,708	148
Las Cruces	NM	19,216	22,185	23,101	27.5	72.5	2.3	68.3	1.0	0.9	1,545	15.0	3,178	7.3	5.5	6.9	5.9	5.5	2.9	1,417	37
Brentwood Unified	NY	11,749	15,565	16,607	15.0	85.0	20.7	62.5	1.7	0.1	1,073	15.5	2,230	7.4	3.7	0.1	4.7	5.7	4.9	641	18
Buffalo City	NY	47,235	45,721	41,089	25.9	74.1	58.5	12.8	1.3	1.5	3,023	13.6	5,420	7.6	7.6	5.4	6.0	7.2	13.4	1,638	68
New York City	NY	944,113	1,066,516	1,023,674	14.8	85.2	33.7	38.4	12.7	0.4	70,171	14.6	107,532	9.5	14.2	5.4	23.9	16.9	12.4	37,915	1,225
Rochester City	NY	32,705	36,294	34,598	13.7	86.3	64.4	19.8	1.8	0.4	2,833	12.2	5,780	6.0	13.0	12.4	15.0	12.2	11.7	1,021	62
Sachem CSD	NY	15,187	14,948	15,378	90.3	9.7	1.0	5.0	3.5	0.2	1,162	13.2	2,014	7.6	1.2	0.2	0.3	0.9	3.9	910	15
Syracuse City	NY	22,432	23,015	22,405	36.2	63.8	51.4	8.6	2.6	1.2	1,804	12.4	3,849	5.8	3.8	2.5	3.9	5.3	4.6	627	35
Yonkers City	NY	18,621	26,237	26,201	18.5	81.5	29.2	46.2	5.9	0.2	1,883	13.9	3,854	6.8	7.7	9.6	7.8	5.7	5.9	724	39
Alamance-Burlington	NC	10,322	20,729	21,788	59.9	40.1	26.8	11.6	1.4	0.3	1,457	15.0	2,617	8.3	5.5	5.5	5.9	4.1	6.8	1,081	33
Buncombe County	NC	22,026	24,708	24,828	85.5	14.5	8.5	4.6	0.9	0.5	1,626	15.3	3,192	7.8	6.4	7.7	5.8	6.6	4.8	1,370	41
Cabarrus County	NC	12,853	19,115	21,860	73.8	26.2	17.1	7.4	1.3	0.4	1,423	15.4	2,368	9.2	5.1	5.3	6.0	4.8	4.0	1,097	28
Catawba County Schools	NC	12,770	16,250	16,635	77.5	22.5	8.7	6.1	7.5	0.2	1,063	15.6	2,009	8.3	4.7	3.5	5.2	6.0	4.3	827	25
Charlotte-Mecklenburg	NC	77,069	103,336	114,071	41.6	58.4	44.5	9.0	4.3	0.6	7,350	15.5	14,651	7.8	5.5	6.8	5.7	3.9	4.4	5,087	137
Cumberland County	NC	44,612	50,850	53,159	40.4	59.6	50.4	5.9	1.6	1.7	3,255	16.3	6,360	8.4	4.3	5.4	5.2	4.0	1.8	2,809	85
Davidson County	NC	16,426	19,136	19,549	93.7	6.3	3.1	2.1	0.8	0.3	1,178	16.6	2,139	9.1	5.9	6.1	6.2	6.1	5.2	1,046	29
Durham	NC	18,517	29,728	30,889	27.8	72.2	59.7	10.0	2.2	0.3	2,094	14.8	3,991	7.7	6.5	7.7	6.3	6.3	4.6	1,435	43

See notes at end of table.

Selected statistics on enrollment, teachers, dropouts, and graduates in public school districts enrolling more than 15,000 students, by state: 1990, 2000, 2001–02, and 2003—Continued

Name of district	State	Enrollment, fall 1990	Enrollment, fall 2000	Enrollment, fall 2003	White, non-Hispanic	Total	Black, non-Hispanic	Hispanic	Asian/Pacific Islander	American Indian/Alaska Native	Number of classroom teachers, fall 2003	Pupil/teacher ratio, fall 2003	Total number of staff, fall 2003	Student/staff ratio, fall 2003	Total	Grade 9	Grade 10	Grade 11	Grade 12	Number of high school graduates, 2001–02[2]	Number of schools, fall 2003
1	2	3	4	5	6	7	8	9	10	11	12	13	14	15	16	17	18	19	20	21	22
Forsyth County	NC	37,625	44,769	47,788	49.8	50.2	37.6	11.1	1.3	0.2	3,251	14.7	5,504	8.7	6.3	5.3	5.7	7.7	6.7	2,271	69
Gaston County	NC	29,631	30,603	31,288	73.0	27.0	20.8	4.7	1.4	0.2	1,932	16.2	3,423	9.1	6.4	6.0	5.8	7.6	6.7	1,466	52
Guilford County	NC	24,575	63,417	66,971	45.7	54.3	43.9	5.4	4.4	0.7	4,390	15.3	8,007	8.4	3.9	4.8	3.8	3.7	2.7	3,304	105
Harnett County	NC	11,890	16,338	16,914	56.8	43.2	32.9	8.9	0.4	0.9	1,064	15.9	2,046	8.3	7.9	7.0	8.0	10.1	6.7	759	25
Iredell-Statesville	NC	10,610	17,235	19,098	72.9	27.1	18.1	6.2	2.6	0.2	1,204	15.9	2,198	8.7	6.1	6.1	7.5	5.8	4.6	821	32
Johnston County	NC	14,647	21,334	24,946	66.0	34.0	22.4	10.8	0.4	0.4	1,785	14.0	3,386	7.4	6.5	7.0	6.9	4.9	6.6	942	34
Nash-Rocky Mount	NC	11,653	18,342	18,526	38.5	61.5	54.5	5.3	1.3	0.4	1,226	15.1	2,341	7.9	6.2	3.8	7.5	8.3	5.2	918	29
New Hanover County	NC	19,090	21,605	22,268	65.7	34.3	30.1	2.7	1.1	0.4	1,470	15.1	3,063	7.3	5.5	4.1	6.3	6.2	6.0	1,272	34
Onslow County	NC	18,605	20,984	21,745	63.5	36.5	29.3	4.8	1.1	1.0	1,344	16.2	2,694	8.1	6.0	4.9	6.3	6.9	6.3	1,161	33
Pitt County	NC	17,629	20,040	21,412	42.4	57.6	52.0	4.2	1.3	0.2	1,440	14.9	2,811	7.6	6.7	6.5	7.7	6.9	5.6	994	28
Randolph County	NC	13,572	17,271	18,211	84.9	15.1	6.6	7.3	0.7	0.4	1,140	16.0	2,232	8.2	6.5	7.4	6.6	6.8	4.4	825	41
Robeson County	NC	23,251	23,911	24,352	20.4	79.6	30.9	5.2	0.4	43.1	1,470	16.6	3,167	7.7	9.1	8.5	10.4	9.9	7.1	963	30
Rowan-Salisbury	NC	16,403	20,472	20,907	69.4	30.6	23.2	5.8	1.3	0.3	1,323	15.8	2,573	8.1	5.6	5.0	6.4	5.7	5.2	1,093	34
Union County	NC	16,864	22,862	26,993	73.5	26.5	17.2	8.1	0.9	0.3	1,684	16.0	3,080	8.8	4.7	4.6	3.8	6.2	4.4	1,085	26
Wake County	NC	64,266	98,950	109,424	58.3	41.7	29.9	7.3	4.3	0.3	7,302	15.0	13,457	8.1	3.7	4.1	3.6	3.4	3.3	5,411	126
Wayne County	NC	13,653	19,279	19,424	47.5	52.5	43.7	7.2	1.3	0.1	1,283	15.1	2,495	7.8	4.8	3.9	5.7	5.2	4.6	996	31
Akron City	OH	33,213	31,464	28,816	47.1	52.9	50.0	1.0	1.8	0.1	3,134	9.2	6,444	4.5	5.0	5.1	4.0	6.3	4.7	1,526	63
Cincinnati City	OH	50,394	46,562	40,374	25.4	74.6	72.7	0.9	0.9	0.1	3,133	12.9	6,173	6.5	8.2	9.1	8.6	7.8	5.5	1,305	84
Cleveland Municipal	OH	68,924	75,684	69,655	18.0	82.0	71.4	9.6	0.7	0.3	5,109	13.6	11,591	6.0	15.1	17.1	13.3	14.9	13.2	2,443	122
Columbus City	OH	63,956	64,511	63,098	32.0	68.0	62.1	3.4	2.2	0.2	3,838	16.4	8,594	7.3	8.7	8.6	9.6	10.0	6.2	2,600	151
Dayton City	OH	28,000	23,522	18,491	27.3	72.7	70.8	1.6	0.3	#	1,418	13.0	2,906	6.4	8.4	9.8	6.4	7.5	8.8	858	39
Lakota Local SD	OH	9,356	14,659	16,358	87.0	13.0	6.4	2.2	4.4	0.1	965	17.0	1,905	8.6	0.9	0.2	1.1	1.8	0.3	963	19
South-Western City	OH	16,605	19,216	21,230	80.7	19.3	11.9	5.4	1.7	0.3	1,327	16.0	2,541	8.4	5.9	6.2	5.2	6.0	6.4	1,003	35
Toledo City	OH	40,126	37,738	34,486	44.4	55.6	47.3	7.5	0.6	0.1	2,539	13.6	4,633	7.4	6.7	6.8	7.5	7.0	5.0	1,478	66
Edmond	OK	13,041	17,084	18,158	81.6	18.4	8.1	3.4	3.2	3.7	1,031	17.6	1,824	10.0	2.5	2.6	3.1	2.2	2.2	1,267	21
Lawton	OK	17,727	17,338	17,069	50.2	49.8	31.9	9.2	2.2	6.5	1,025	16.7	2,057	8.3	4.8	2.2	7.5	4.8	4.2	894	35
Moore	OK	16,630	18,101	18,946	66.7	33.3	5.6	5.7	4.3	17.6	1,069	17.7	1,805	10.5	3.9	1.2	4.9	5.6	4.4	1,137	27
Oklahoma City	OK	36,038	39,750	40,599	27.3	72.7	34.8	29.6	2.6	5.6	2,345	17.3	4,435	9.2	12.1	14.6	13.9	10.0	6.0	1,441	89
Putnam City	OK	18,071	19,506	19,365	61.3	38.7	21.6	8.9	4.3	3.9	1,145	16.9	1,864	10.4	5.9	9.1	6.3	4.1	2.3	1,185	26
Tulsa	OK	40,732	42,812	42,280	39.7	60.3	35.9	14.3	1.2	8.8	2,567	16.5	5,535	7.6	7.7	7.3	7.3	8.1	8.6	1,758	86
Beaverton	OR	24,874	33,600	35,333	68.7	31.3	3.3	13.9	13.3	0.9	1,699	20.8	3,227	10.9	4.1	2.2	2.6	4.9	7.0	1,957	49
Eugene	OR	17,904	18,432	18,476	78.9	21.1	3.1	7.0	5.7	5.3	814	22.7	1,707	10.8	3.1	1.7	2.3	3.5	5.3	1,378	48
Hillsboro	OR	—	18,315	18,951	66.0	34.0	2.0	24.6	6.8	0.6	793	23.9	1,783	10.6	3.1	1.8	2.7	3.2	5.4	888	31
North Clackamas	OR	12,403	14,876	16,170	81.9	18.1	2.0	9.1	6.0	0.9	788	20.5	1,635	9.9	4.0	2.6	2.6	5.4	5.8	789	27
Portland	OR	53,042	53,141	48,344	60.9	39.1	15.8	11.0	10.2	2.1	2,685	18.0	4,862	9.9	10.8	9.8	9.6	11.7	12.5	2,592	97
Salem/Keizer	OR	27,756	35,108	37,785	68.4	31.6	1.6	24.7	3.6	1.8	1,773	21.3	3,733	10.1	7.4	3.0	5.4	6.9	16.0	1,810	67
Allentown City	PA	13,519	16,424	16,964	29.8	70.2	16.1	52.0	1.9	0.1	883	19.2	1,723	9.8	9.3	7.4	9.3	11.4	10.2	686	23
Central Bucks	PA	10,286	17,305	19,089	94.4	5.6	1.6	1.2	2.7	#	984	19.4	2,002	9.5	1.2	0.0	0.5	1.4	3.3	1,082	21
Philadelphia City	PA	190,978	201,190	189,779	14.6	85.4	65.2	14.7	5.3	0.2	10,194	18.6	22,554	8.4	9.8	7.4	10.5	11.9	12.3	8,559	263
Pittsburgh	PA	39,896	38,560	34,658	38.6	61.4	59.0	0.7	1.6	0.1	2,687	12.9	5,214	6.6	5.4	3.7	6.0	5.8	7.2	1,899	92
Reading	PA	11,965	15,487	16,515	19.3	80.7	14.8	64.7	1.1	0.1	931	17.7	1,778	9.3	8.7	2.5	9.6	12.2	13.4	570	19

See notes at end of table.

Selected statistics on enrollment, teachers, dropouts, and graduates in public school districts enrolling more than 15,000 students, by state: 1990, 2000, 2001–02, and 2003—Continued

Name of district	State	Enrollment, fall 1990	Enrollment, fall 2000	Enrollment, fall 2003	White, non-Hispanic	Total	Black, non-Hispanic	Hispanic	Asian/Pacific Islander	American Indian/Alaska Native	Number of classroom teachers, fall 2003	Pupil/teacher ratio, fall 2003	Total number of staff, fall 2003	Student/staff ratio, fall 2003	Total	Grade 9	Grade 10	Grade 11	Grade 12	Number of high school graduates, 2001–02 [2]	Number of schools, fall 2003
1	2	3	4	5	6	7	8	9	10	11	12	13	14	15	16	17	18	19	20	21	22
Providence	RI	20,908	26,937	27,900	14.2	85.8	22.1	55.4	7.6	0.7	1,779	15.7	1,779	15.7	8.2	8.0	10.5	7.3	6.1	1,122	54
Aiken County	SC	23,964	25,147	25,333	60.0	40.0	35.7	3.3	0.7	0.3	1,544	16.4	1,798	14.1	3.2	3.6	3.4	3.2	2.1	1,218	39
Beaufort County	SC	12,525	16,721	18,328	46.0	54.0	40.7	12.1	1.1	0.2	1,295	14.2	1,503	12.2	1.7	1.4	2.2	2.1	1.2	759	26
Berkeley County	SC	27,392	26,635	27,899	58.6	41.4	35.8	3.4	1.9	0.3	1,624	17.2	2,037	13.7	4.3	4.0	5.7	3.5	3.8	1,302	36
Charleston County	SC	43,667	44,767	44,109	39.9	60.1	55.5	3.1	1.3	0.2	3,160	14.0	3,746	11.8	3.2	4.4	3.0	2.6	2.0	1,666	80
Dorchester County	SC	13,737	16,678	18,137	66.9	33.1	28.7	2.2	1.7	0.6	1,120	16.2	1,329	13.6	3.6	2.4	4.6	4.9	3.0	883	17
Greenville County	SC	51,471	59,875	64,245	63.9	36.1	28.3	6.0	1.7	0.1	3,835	16.8	4,799	13.4	2.6	2.6	2.8	2.7	2.3	2,934	93
Horry County	SC	24,085	29,894	31,648	69.0	31.0	25.8	3.7	1.2	0.3	2,102	15.1	2,679	11.8	2.1	2.0	2.4	2.6	1.5	1,335	46
Lexington County #01	SC	11,204	17,285	19,099	87.6	12.4	8.0	2.5	1.5	0.5	1,277	15.0	1,513	12.6	2.4	1.8	2.1	2.6	3.6	906	20
Lexington County #05	SC	11,688	15,064	15,865	69.6	30.4	26.5	1.5	2.3	0.1	1,083	14.6	1,276	12.4	1.8	1.5	1.9	1.9	1.7	1,002	18
Pickens County	SC	14,298	15,938	16,262	88.0	12.0	8.9	2.1	0.9	0.1	1,022	15.9	1,176	13.8	6.3	7.2	6.9	5.1	5.3	755	25
Richland #01	SC	27,071	27,061	26,990	18.6	81.4	78.7	1.9	0.7	0.1	1,987	13.6	2,435	11.1	3.2	2.8	3.6	3.9	2.5	1,178	50
Richland #02	SC	12,792	17,409	19,865	37.9	62.1	55.7	3.5	2.7	0.2	1,333	14.9	1,602	12.4	2.6	1.3	2.4	3.9	3.4	958	23
York #03	SC	12,690	14,925	16,307	57.7	42.3	35.5	3.5	1.6	1.6	997	16.4	1,185	13.8	1.7	1.1	2.4	2.1	1.2	755	23
Sioux Falls	SD	16,120	19,097	20,053	84.1	15.9	5.1	4.6	2.3	3.9	1,241	16.2	2,307	8.7	4.2	1.6	2.7	5.6	7.8	1,131	43
Hamilton County	TN	22,874	39,915	40,100	—	—	—	—	—	—	2,739	14.6	6,476	6.2	5.8	5.6	5.2	7.2	5.6	1,715	81
Knox County	TN	50,429	51,944	52,659	—	—	—	—	—	—	3,609	14.6	6,664	7.9	3.0	0.1	0.6	3.6	8.6	2,553	88
Memphis City	TN	106,223	113,730	116,224	—	—	—	—	—	—	7,275	16.0	12,943	9.0	8.6	6.9	8.4	9.0	11.5	3,933	185
Montgomery County	TN	17,532	23,339	24,924	—	—	—	—	—	—	1,558	16.0	2,984	8.4	3.3	1.9	2.1	2.7	7.5	1,063	30
Nashville-Davidson	TN	67,452	67,669	68,651	—	—	—	—	—	—	4,858	14.1	9,292	7.4	7.6	7.9	6.7	8.5	7.0	2,609	126
Rutherford County	TN	18,228	25,356	29,529	—	—	—	—	—	—	1,792	16.5	2,734	10.8	2.2	0.7	1.2	2.3	5.4	1,506	38
Shelby County	TN	37,605	46,972	46,808	—	—	—	—	—	—	2,649	17.7	5,059	9.3	2.1	0.8	1.6	2.8	3.6	2,550	49
Sumner County	TN	19,650	22,347	24,002	—	—	—	—	—	—	1,576	15.2	3,006	8.0	1.4	0.4	1.6	1.3	2.9	1,477	42
Williamson County	TN	11,502	19,545	21,956	—	—	—	—	—	—	1,361	16.1	2,512	8.7	1.7	0.1	0.5	1.3	5.5	745	33
Abilene ISD	TX	18,217	18,118	17,036	54.1	45.9	12.7	31.5	1.2	0.5	1,295	13.2	2,659	6.4	4.9	3.6	4.7	5.5	6.4	1,032	38
Aldine ISD	TX	41,372	52,520	56,292	6.5	93.5	33.1	58.0	2.4	0.1	3,616	15.6	7,799	7.2	5.8	4.3	7.1	6.3	6.0	2,149	66
Alief ISD	TX	29,774	42,151	45,344	6.7	93.3	36.8	43.1	13.3	0.1	2,977	15.2	5,968	7.6	3.3	1.8	5.1	2.8	3.9	1,960	40
Amarillo ISD	TX	27,374	28,908	29,527	48.7	51.3	10.6	37.9	2.5	0.3	2,026	14.6	3,829	7.7	3.1	1.8	3.1	3.6	4.6	1,544	52
Arlington ISD	TX	44,958	58,866	62,454	39.5	60.5	22.7	30.5	6.9	0.5	3,991	15.6	8,089	7.7	2.7	3.7	2.4	2.1	2.0	2,875	77
Austin ISD	TX	65,797	77,816	79,007	30.2	69.8	13.6	53.2	2.7	0.2	5,354	14.8	10,432	7.6	6.0	4.8	6.3	6.4	7.0	3,705	111
Beaumont ISD	TX	18,684	20,696	20,732	22.1	77.9	63.9	11.0	2.8	0.2	1,456	14.2	2,855	7.3	4.4	3.8	5.2	3.8	5.0	1,153	36
Birdville ISD	TX	18,466	21,246	22,507	65.4	34.6	6.1	22.3	5.6	0.5	1,355	16.6	2,621	8.6	1.9	1.8	1.8	2.0	1.8	1,164	32
Brownsville ISD	TX	34,906	40,898	45,923	1.8	98.2	0.1	97.7	0.3	#	3,014	15.2	6,960	6.6	4.1	4.0	5.6	2.8	3.7	1,854	51
Carrollton-Farmers Branch	TX	16,234	24,134	25,638	33.3	66.7	13.1	41.1	12.0	0.5	1,742	14.7	3,242	7.9	2.1	1.3	2.1	2.5	3.1	1,277	39
Clear Creek ISD	TX	22,372	29,875	32,810	67.2	32.8	7.4	15.6	9.4	0.5	1,996	16.4	3,767	8.7	1.8	1.2	1.3	1.9	3.2	1,844	38
Conroe ISD	TX	23,288	34,928	39,246	70.7	29.3	5.4	20.9	2.4	0.5	2,496	15.7	5,116	7.7	1.8	1.9	2.0	1.5	1.6	2,202	46
Corpus Christi ISD	TX	41,881	39,138	39,310	20.2	79.8	5.5	72.5	1.5	0.3	2,409	16.3	5,172	7.6	4.8	4.5	3.9	4.6	6.4	2,119	62
Cypress-Fairbanks ISD	TX	41,196	63,497	74,877	51.9	48.1	11.1	28.7	8.2	0.2	4,884	15.3	9,821	7.6	1.1	0.8	0.9	1.1	1.9	3,938	60
Dallas ISD	TX	135,320	161,548	160,584	6.3	93.7	31.3	61.0	1.1	0.3	10,323	15.6	20,115	8.0	5.1	4.1	6.4	4.5	6.2	6,532	227
Denton ISD	TX	10,690	13,645	15,951	58.5	41.5	11.5	27.4	2.1	0.5	1,170	13.6	2,266	7.0	4.7	3.4	5.3	5.4	5.1	720	25
Ector County ISD	TX	26,993	26,831	26,090	35.4	64.6	5.4	57.8	0.7	0.7	1,671	15.6	3,281	8.0	9.0	5.8	10.5	9.3	11.1	1,478	42
Edinburg ISD	TX	13,685	22,005	25,373	2.6	97.4	0.2	96.8	0.4	#	1,632	15.5	3,652	6.9	3.5	3.5	4.3	3.1	3.0	1,038	37

See notes at end of table.

Selected statistics on enrollment, teachers, dropouts, and graduates in public school districts enrolling more than 15,000 students, by state: 1990, 2000, 2001–02, and 2003—Continued

Name of district	State	Enrollment, fall 1990	Enrollment, fall 2000	Enrollment, fall 2003	Percentage distribution of enrollment, by race, fall 2003 — White, non-Hispanic	Minority Total	Minority Black, non-Hispanic	Minority Hispanic	Minority Asian/ Pacific Islander	Minority American Indian/ Alaska Native	Number of classroom teachers, fall 2003	Pupil/ teacher ratio, fall 2003	Total number of staff, fall 2003	Student/ staff ratio, fall 2003	Percent dropouts from grades 9–12, 2001–02[1] — Total	Grade 9	Grade 10	Grade 11	Grade 12	Number of high school graduates, 2001–02[2]	Number of schools, fall 2003
1	2	3	4	5	6	7	8	9	10	11	12	13	14	15	16	17	18	19	20	21	22
El Paso ISD	TX	64,092	62,325	63,200	13.3	86.7	4.4	80.6	1.3	0.3	4,505	14.0	9,081	7.0	4.1	2.8	3.8	4.4	6.5	3,353	92
Fort Bend ISD	TX	36,270	53,999	61,248	31.7	68.3	29.8	20.2	18.2	0.2	3,720	16.5	7,561	8.1	2.2	1.4	1.8	1.3	4.9	3,630	59
Fort Worth ISD	TX	69,163	79,661	80,335	17.8	82.2	28.1	52.1	1.8	0.2	4,793	16.8	10,399	7.7	6.5	5.0	7.5	5.8	9.0	3,222	145
Galena Park ISD	TX	15,593	18,885	20,454	11.2	88.8	21.3	65.9	1.5	0.1	1,461	14.0	2,846	7.2	3.0	1.3	3.6	3.6	4.3	1,077	23
Garland ISD	TX	37,978	50,312	55,114	39.5	60.5	18.2	34.9	7.0	0.5	3,509	15.7	6,522	8.5	1.7	1.2	1.5	1.8	2.8	2,689	69
Goose Creek ISD	TX	17,654	18,003	19,247	35.5	64.5	17.6	45.6	1.2	0.2	1,217	15.8	2,419	8.0	5.1	2.8	6.8	4.6	7.3	899	26
Grand Prairie ISD	TX	16,482	20,257	22,132	25.3	74.7	15.0	54.9	4.0	0.8	1,478	15.0	2,798	7.9	3.7	2.8	4.5	4.1	3.9	1,035	33
Harlingen Consolidated ISD	TX	13,805	15,857	17,051	10.8	89.2	0.7	87.8	0.6	#	1,049	16.3	2,401	7.1	4.8	4.0	4.8	5.0	5.9	807	25
Houston ISD	TX	194,435	208,462	211,499	9.1	90.9	29.7	58.1	3.0	0.1	12,277	17.2	25,507	8.3	6.0	4.6	9.0	4.0	8.0	7,945	308
Humble ISD	TX	19,560	24,684	27,009	65.7	34.3	12.3	18.2	3.4	0.4	1,745	15.5	3,534	7.6	1.7	0.2	0.6	3.6	2.6	1,653	30
Hurst-Euless-Bedford ISD	TX	18,733	19,203	19,527	59.5	40.5	11.9	18.3	9.3	0.9	1,272	15.4	2,474	7.9	1.9	1.2	1.8	2.2	2.2	1,227	31
Irving ISD	TX	23,509	29,097	31,249	24.3	75.7	12.7	57.8	4.8	0.5	2,088	15.0	3,893	8.0	3.3	2.5	3.7	4.1	3.3	1,308	39
Judson ISD	TX	13,145	16,603	17,981	29.5	70.5	25.5	42.0	2.6	0.4	1,229	14.6	2,467	7.3	2.9	2.0	2.2	2.9	6.1	842	22
Katy ISD	TX	19,507	34,503	42,116	63.6	36.4	6.7	22.1	7.4	0.2	2,802	15.0	5,320	7.9	1.1	1.1	1.5	0.9	1.1	2,112	42
Keller ISD	TX	8,212	21,803	21,803	77.3	22.7	5.1	11.3	5.9	0.4	1,249	17.5	2,278	9.6	2.2	1.0	2.1	2.6	3.8	1,013	25
Killeen ISD	TX	22,131	29,687	32,583	35.7	64.3	40.4	18.9	4.4	0.7	2,303	14.1	4,970	6.6	3.5	2.5	2.2	2.6	7.5	1,358	48
Klein ISD	TX	26,220	32,376	35,558	54.4	45.6	13.7	23.8	7.9	0.3	2,219	16.0	4,333	8.2	2.5	1.6	2.5	2.4	4.3	2,112	34
La Joya ISD	TX	8,523	17,641	21,765	0.3	99.7	#	99.6	#	#	1,366	15.9	3,148	6.9	7.6	5.4	8.7	7.1	10.8	765	27
Lamar Consolidated ISD	TX	12,335	15,159	17,864	35.6	64.4	14.1	47.5	2.6	0.1	1,155	15.5	2,451	7.3	3.2	2.6	3.1	3.1	4.6	796	28
Laredo ISD	TX	23,304	23,304	24,846	0.5	99.5	0.1	99.2	0.2	#	1,553	16.0	3,660	6.8	4.6	3.6	4.1	4.4	6.6	765	29
Leander ISD	TX	5,419	14,499	18,201	74.0	26.0	5.0	17.2	3.2	0.6	1,216	15.0	2,304	7.9	2.0	0.9	1.8	2.3	3.3	2,267	23
Lewisville ISD	TX	20,776	39,096	44,024	68.6	31.4	8.3	16.0	6.6	0.5	3,063	14.4	5,236	8.4	1.1	0.8	0.8	1.2	1.8	1,737	58
Lubbock ISD	TX	30,786	29,026	29,020	38.1	61.9	14.8	45.3	1.5	0.3	2,074	14.0	3,756	7.7	3.8	1.2	3.7	4.0	6.6	791	57
Mansfield ISD	TX	7,570	14,888	21,060	59.9	40.1	19.4	15.7	4.5	0.5	1,367	15.4	2,529	8.3	2.1	2.0	1.6	2.6	2.7	1,270	22
McAllen ISD	TX	18,432	21,747	23,492	8.2	91.8	0.6	89.3	1.9	#	1,541	15.2	3,545	6.6	4.8	5.0	5.5	4.1	4.5	1,270	32
McKinney ISD	TX	4,703	12,000	16,663	66.8	33.2	9.2	21.2	3.6	0.8	1,102	15.1	1,825	9.1	2.7	2.0	3.0	3.5	2.5	604	25
Mesquite ISD	TX	25,920	32,334	34,414	45.8	54.2	21.3	28.5	3.6	0.5	2,150	16.0	4,309	8.0	2.9	1.8	3.3	3.1	3.6	1,956	44
Midland ISD	TX	21,082	20,522	20,921	42.7	57.3	9.8	46.2	0.9	0.2	1,362	15.4	2,678	7.8	5.5	4.1	5.8	6.3	6.3	1,207	36
North East ISD	TX	39,909	50,875	56,298	45.4	54.6	9.5	41.8	3.0	0.3	3,671	15.3	7,242	7.8	1.8	1.3	1.5	1.8	2.7	3,208	65
Northside ISD	TX	50,229	63,739	71,798	31.3	68.7	7.2	58.7	2.5	0.3	4,594	15.6	10,188	7.0	3.0	2.2	2.9	2.7	4.5	3,928	93
Pasadena ISD	TX	37,643	42,577	46,142	19.4	80.6	6.4	70.8	3.2	0.2	2,681	17.2	5,554	8.3	5.4	4.0	4.9	6.5	7.1	2,028	56
Pflugerville ISD	TX	6,482	14,545	16,592	40.7	59.3	21.0	29.6	8.3	0.4	1,029	16.1	1,794	9.2	1.8	0.9	1.4	2.4	2.8	864	24
Pharr-San Juan-Alamo ISD	TX	16,563	22,537	26,493	1.2	98.8	0.2	98.6	0.1	#	1,580	16.8	3,648	7.3	6.1	5.2	6.5	6.1	7.5	1,045	36
Plano ISD	TX	28,398	47,161	51,869	62.3	37.7	8.8	13.0	15.6	0.3	3,826	13.6	7,034	7.4	1.5	0.6	0.7	1.6	3.1	2,795	69
Richardson ISD	TX	32,555	35,138	34,536	40.1	59.9	25.1	25.7	8.6	0.5	2,419	14.3	4,493	7.7	2.0	0.9	1.8	2.4	3.3	1,891	57
Round Rock ISD	TX	19,636	31,536	35,553	60.4	39.6	9.6	21.0	8.5	0.4	2,344	15.2	4,417	8.0	2.1	1.4	1.9	2.3	3.1	1,977	45
San Angelo ISD	TX	16,488	16,092	15,126	44.2	55.8	6.3	48.2	1.1	0.2	971	15.6	1,883	8.0	4.3	3.0	3.8	4.2	6.8	960	27
San Antonio ISD	TX	60,161	57,273	56,914	3.6	96.4	8.8	87.2	0.3	0.1	3,527	16.1	7,877	7.2	7.1	6.2	6.8	6.7	9.5	2,727	107
Socorro ISD	TX	14,350	26,711	32,241	5.4	94.6	1.3	92.6	0.4	0.3	1,911	16.9	3,942	8.2	1.9	1.4	1.7	1.9	3.3	1,533	34
Spring Branch ISD	TX	23,661	31,659	33,005	34.7	65.3	6.3	52.7	6.2	0.1	2,226	14.8	4,728	7.0	3.2	2.9	3.6	2.7	3.9	1,751	49
Spring ISD	TX	18,537	23,034	26,768	31.0	69.0	31.8	31.2	5.7	0.2	1,787	15.0	3,940	6.8	2.9	1.6	3.3	3.1	4.2	1,334	27
Tyler ISD	TX	16,182	16,626	17,394	32.9	67.1	34.0	31.7	1.2	0.2	1,253	13.9	2,470	7.0	4.4	2.8	3.8	5.0	7.0	901	29
United ISD	TX	12,553	27,556	32,262	2.1	97.9	0.2	97.2	0.4	#	1,953	16.5	4,733	6.8	1.8	1.6	2.1	1.4	2.4	1,360	37
Waco ISD	TX	14,304	15,433	15,669	16.9	83.1	36.9	45.8	0.4	0.1	1,041	15.1	2,189	7.2	8.1	7.2	7.4	9.0	10.2	588	36

See notes at end of table.

Selected statistics on enrollment, teachers, dropouts, and graduates in public school districts enrolling more than 15,000 students, by state: 1990, 2000, 2001–02, and 2003—Continued

Name of district	State	Enroll-ment, fall 1990	Enroll-ment, fall 2000	Enroll-ment, fall 2003	White, non-Hispanic	Minority Total	Black, non-Hispanic	Hispanic	Asian/Pacific Islander	American Indian/Alaska Native	Number of classroom teachers, fall 2003	Pupil/teacher ratio, fall 2003	Total number of staff, fall 2003	Student/staff ratio, fall 2003	Total	Grade 9	Grade 10	Grade 11	Grade 12	Number of high school graduates, 2001–02[2]	Number of schools, fall 2003
1	2	3	4	5	6	7	8	9	10	11	12	13	14	15	16	17	18	19	20	21	22
Wichita Falls ISD	TX	15,011	15,013	15,063	56.8	43.2	17.5	22.3	2.5	0.9	1,113	13.5	2,124	7.1	1.9	1.6	2.3	1.3	2.6	1,071	36
Ysleta ISD	TX	49,974	46,394	46,668	6.8	93.2	2.2	90.1	0.4	0.5	3,000	15.6	6,274	7.4	5.6	2.2	4.9	5.5	10.9	2,842	63
Alpine	UT	38,852	47,117	51,240	90.1	9.9	0.6	6.8	1.9	0.6	2,117	24.2	3,097	16.5	2.1	0.3	0.7	2.5	4.8	2,726	63
Davis	UT	55,558	59,578	60,749	90.1	9.9	1.4	5.9	2.1	0.6	2,627	23.1	5,243	11.6	2.4	0.3	0.9	2.0	6.1	3,765	96
Granite	UT	78,554	71,328	70,771	71.7	28.3	1.6	19.1	6.4	1.2	3,206	22.1	5,663	12.5	6.0	3.0	5.0	6.1	10.2	4,170	109
Jordan	UT	64,991	73,158	74,761	90.4	9.6	0.7	6.0	2.4	0.6	3,054	24.5	5,711	13.1	4.4	2.3	2.9	5.0	7.4	4,916	85
Nebo	UT	16,393	21,094	24,129	91.7	8.3	0.4	6.1	1.0	0.8	1,007	24.0	1,857	13.0	2.0	0.1	0.8	1.4	6.0	1,303	35
Salt Lake City	UT	24,766	25,367	24,443	50.3	49.7	3.9	33.7	10.1	1.9	1,230	19.9	2,867	8.5	11.2	7.7	8.8	12.5	16.3	1,202	44
Washington	UT	13,264	18,374	20,482	88.2	11.8	0.6	7.3	1.6	2.3	892	23.0	1,591	12.9	0.8	0.0	0.1	1.2	2.1	1,214	35
Weber	UT	25,425	27,783	28,196	90.2	9.8	1.2	6.6	1.6	0.5	1,237	22.8	2,153	13.1	2.2	0.0	0.7	2.6	5.7	1,898	48
Arlington County	VA	14,825	18,870	19,158	42.3	57.7	14.5	32.9	10.2	0.1	1,775	10.8	3,531	5.4	3.0	3.4	1.9	3.9	2.6	923	32
Chesapeake City	VA	29,533	37,645	39,412	60.2	39.8	35.3	2.0	2.2	0.3	2,877	13.7	5,021	7.8	2.8	2.5	1.7	2.6	4.6	2,298	46
Chesterfield County	VA	44,480	51,212	55,393	67.3	32.7	25.1	4.3	2.8	0.5	3,846	14.4	5,412	10.2	4.3	5.0	4.5	3.1	4.6	3,292	60
Fairfax County	VA	128,766	156,412	164,235	55.1	44.9	11.2	15.8	17.6	0.4	12,293	13.4	25,260	6.5	2.7	2.0	2.2	2.9	3.7	10,450	204
Hampton City	VA	21,383	23,290	23,009	35.0	65.0	60.5	2.4	1.8	0.3	1,868	12.3	3,283	7.0	3.7	4.5	3.6	2.1	4.4	1,279	36
Hanover County	VA	11,328	16,611	18,139	86.9	13.1	10.3	1.1	1.4	0.3	1,404	12.9	2,372	7.6	0.7	0.2	0.6	0.4	1.8	1,060	21
Henrico County	VA	32,638	41,655	45,354	56.3	43.7	36.0	3.0	4.4	0.3	3,175	14.3	5,641	8.0	2.3	1.4	2.4	2.3	3.6	2,400	66
Loudoun County	VA	14,485	31,804	40,750	72.6	27.4	8.4	9.9	8.8	0.3	3,017	13.5	5,226	7.8	1.1	0.6	1.0	1.2	1.7	1,766	61
Newport News City	VA	28,925	33,008	32,893	34.9	65.1	56.9	4.8	2.5	0.9	2,425	13.6	4,354	7.6	3.0	3.0	3.1	3.1	2.9	1,570	48
Norfolk City	VA	36,541	37,349	36,724	26.4	73.6	68.6	2.8	2.0	0.2	2,586	14.2	4,995	7.4	4.6	6.6	3.3	3.3	2.7	1,348	58
Portsmouth City	VA	18,405	16,473	16,545	26.8	73.2	71.3	1.1	0.8	0.1	1,155	14.3	2,193	7.5	3.3	2.6	6.5	1.6	2.6	736	27
Prince William County	VA	41,888	54,646	63,404	51.8	48.2	23.9	18.2	5.8	0.4	4,125	15.4	8,365	7.6	4.0	3.3	2.9	4.0	6.1	3,196	75
Richmond City	VA	27,021	27,237	25,399	7.0	93.0	89.9	2.4	0.6	0.1	1,892	13.4	2,733	9.3	3.1	6.1	2.9	1.7	0.0	1,058	59
Spotsylvania County	VA	12,227	18,876	22,075	75.4	24.6	18.0	4.2	2.1	0.3	1,663	13.3	3,035	7.3	2.2	2.4	1.5	2.6	2.5	1,119	30
Stafford County	VA	12,555	21,124	24,869	73.0	27.0	19.5	4.6	2.5	0.4	1,736	14.3	3,146	7.9	2.5	2.4	1.8	2.9	2.9	1,359	24
Virginia Beach City	VA	70,266	76,586	76,304	60.5	39.5	28.8	4.6	5.8	0.3	5,555	13.7	10,137	7.5	1.2	2.0	1.4	0.7	0.3	4,455	86
Bellevue	WA	14,748	15,431	16,125	66.0	34.0	2.5	8.2	22.9	0.4	863	18.7	1,749	9.2	2.5	0.6	1.1	2.0	5.7	1,090	32
Bethel	WA	11,669	16,029	17,397	70.6	29.4	10.2	6.2	9.7	3.3	825	21.1	1,712	10.2	7.1	3.2	7.8	8.0	10.1	975	29
Edmonds	WA	18,868	22,067	21,984	72.5	27.5	5.5	7.0	13.5	1.6	1,071	20.5	2,276	9.7	6.9	1.9	3.3	5.6	19.5	1,111	42
Everett	WA	15,343	18,683	18,610	75.5	24.5	4.5	7.2	11.1	1.8	874	21.3	1,744	10.7	11.6	11.8	9.7	7.7	17.6	885	31
Evergreen	WA	14,810	21,650	23,979	81.6	18.4	4.1	5.5	7.7	1.1	1,288	18.6	2,405	10.0	6.3	1.5	3.1	7.5	14.1	1,147	35
Federal Way	WA	16,168	22,623	22,538	57.4	42.6	13.0	11.6	16.7	1.4	1,126	20.0	2,233	10.1	5.9	1.5	7.2	8.7	6.3	1,151	46
Highline	WA	16,208	18,024	17,711	43.7	56.3	13.6	19.8	20.8	2.2	938	18.9	1,973	9.0	10.0	14.0	9.9	7.8	5.7	984	32
Issaquah	WA	8,888	14,259	15,146	80.5	19.5	1.8	3.6	13.4	0.7	730	20.7	1,463	10.4	6.6	10.0	5.0	4.0	6.9	896	23
Kent	WA	21,027	26,535	26,860	64.9	35.1	10.4	8.1	15.4	1.2	1,371	19.6	2,845	9.4	2.7	2.1	3.1	2.8	2.9	1,535	42
Lake Washington	WA	23,050	23,662	24,144	77.9	22.1	2.6	6.2	12.5	0.8	1,187	20.3	2,263	10.7	1.8	0.3	0.6	0.7	5.3	1,651	49
Northshore	WA	17,511	20,255	20,088	80.8	19.2	2.5	5.8	9.8	1.1	1,012	19.8	2,053	9.8	1.3	0.4	0.5	0.6	3.7	1,413	35
Puyallup	WA	15,100	19,757	20,043	81.8	18.2	4.4	5.6	6.3	1.8	1,021	19.6	1,892	10.6	7.4	4.9	5.3	6.3	13.9	1,153	32
Seattle	WA	43,593	47,575	47,588	40.7	59.3	22.8	11.2	23.0	2.4	2,577	18.5	5,183	9.2	24.4	21.4	21.6	25.3	29.2	2,629	129
Spokane	WA	29,186	31,725	31,068	85.3	14.7	5.0	3.1	2.8	3.8	1,753	17.7	3,420	9.1	3.9	4.9	3.0	3.9	3.8	1,793	66
Tacoma	WA	30,169	34,093	33,605	52.8	47.2	22.3	10.0	12.8	2.0	1,765	19.0	3,562	9.4	5.0	5.7	5.0	4.2	4.7	1,462	61
Vancouver	WA	16,423	21,892	22,119	77.7	22.3	5.2	10.0	4.9	2.1	1,140	19.4	2,420	9.1	10.5	5.2	9.2	12.5	15.6	1,170	37

See notes at end of table.

Selected statistics on enrollment, teachers, dropouts, and graduates in public school districts enrolling more than 15,000 students, by state: 1990, 2000, 2001–02, and 2003—Continued

| | | | | | Percentage distribution of enrollment, by race, fall 2003 | | | | | | | | | | Percent dropouts from grades 9–12, 2001–02[1] | | | | | | |
| | | | | | | | Minority | | | | | | | | | | | | | | |
Name of district	State	Enrollment, fall 1990	Enrollment, fall 2000	Enrollment, fall 2003	White, non-Hispanic	Total	Black, non-Hispanic	Hispanic	Asian/Pacific Islander	American Indian/Alaska Native	Number of classroom teachers, fall 2003	Pupil/teacher ratio, fall 2003	Total number of staff, fall 2003	Student/staff ratio, fall 2003	Total	Grade 9	Grade 10	Grade 11	Grade 12	Number of high school graduates, 2001–02[2]	Number of schools, fall 2003
1	2	3	4	5	6	7	8	9	10	11	12	13	14	15	16	17	18	19	20	21	22
Kanawha County	WV	34,284	29,250	28,306	86.6	13.4	11.7	0.5	1.1	0.1	1,934	14.6	3,667	7.7	5.3	5.9	4.7	5.4	5.1	1,630	71
Appleton Area	WI	12,876	14,793	15,275	82.4	17.6	2.4	4.2	10.2	0.9	948	16.1	1,556	9.8	0.8	0.0	0.0	0.4	2.8	1,109	33
Green Bay Area	WI	18,048	20,104	20,297	69.9	30.1	4.5	12.2	8.4	5.0	1,463	13.9	2,460	8.3	1.6	0.0	0.0	0.7	6.0	1,131	36
Kenosha	WI	16,219	20,099	21,426	69.1	30.9	14.4	14.5	1.7	0.4	1,444	14.8	2,419	8.9	3.3	2.3	3.4	4.2	3.5	1,305	41
Madison Metropolitan	WI	23,214	25,087	24,913	59.3	40.7	19.8	10.1	10.1	0.7	1,992	12.5	3,754	6.6	3.0	2.1	2.9	3.6	3.5	1,607	51
Milwaukee	WI	92,784	97,985	97,359	17.3	82.7	59.4	18.0	4.4	0.9	5,930	16.4	11,252	8.7	9.0	10.7	9.5	8.5	4.9	3,912	223
Racine	WI	21,904	21,102	21,457	56.3	43.7	26.3	15.9	1.3	0.3	1,324	16.2	2,485	8.6	5.2	1.5	3.6	6.2	11.5	1,163	35

—Not available.
†Not applicable.
#Rounds to zero.
[1] Alabama, Alaska, Arizona, Florida, Illinois, Maryland, New Jersey, New York, Tennessee, and Vermont reported data on an alternative July through June cycle, rather than the specified October through September cycle.
[2] Includes regular diplomas only.

NOTE: Total enrollment, staff, and teacher data in this table reflect totals reported by school districts and may differ from data derived from summing school-level data to school district aggregates. SB=School board. SC=School corporation. ISD=Independent school district. Detail may not sum to totals because of rounding.
SOURCE: U.S. Department of Education, National Center for Education Statistics, Common Core of Data (CCD), "Public Elementary/Secondary School Universe Survey," 2003–04, and "Local Education Agency Universe Survey," 1990–91, 2000–01, 2002–03, and 2003–04. (This table was prepared August 2005.)

Enrollment, poverty, and federal funds for the 100 largest school districts, by enrollment size: Selected years, 2001–02 through 2005–06

Name of district	State	Rank order	Enrollment, fall 2003	5- to 17-year-old population, 2001–02	5- to 17-year-old population below the poverty level, 2001–02	Poverty rate of 5- to 17-year-olds, 2001–02	Revenues by source of funds (in thousands), 2002–03 — Total	Federal	Federal as a percent of total	Federal revenue per student, 2002–03[1]	Revenue for selected federal programs (in thousands), 2002–03 — Title I, basic and concentration grants	School lunch	Vocational education	Drug-free schools	Eisenhower math and science	Special education	Title I allocations for 2005–06 (in thousands) — Basic grants	Concentration grants	Targeted grants	Education finance incentive grants
1	2	3	4	5	6	7	8	9	10	11	12	13	14	15	16	17	18	19	20	21
New York City	NY	1	1,023,674	1,358,965	392,397	28.9	$13,140,359	$1,437,401	10.9	$1,334	$502,532	$258,513	$4,557	—	—	$202,368	$394,193	$94,005	$201,659	$162,082
Los Angeles Unified	CA	2	747,009	877,488	260,902	29.7	6,978,828	824,683	11.8	1,104	283,927	196,516	12,728	$7,838	$60,331	99,764	192,867	46,135	104,982	105,952
City of Chicago	IL	3	434,419	529,686	147,008	27.8	3,837,867	602,702	15.7	1,382	199,226	146,246	8,769	5,781	50,914	71,267	132,381	31,666	70,421	67,366
Dade County	FL	4	371,785	417,064	95,822	23.0	2,976,518	335,837	11.3	899	97,366	87,109	6,431	3,710	18,466	58,451	62,401	14,927	32,189	27,551
Broward County	FL	5	272,835	306,758	42,793	14.0	2,013,451	174,974	8.7	653	39,366	41,562	3,051	1,415	9,603	36,343	27,911	6,676	12,857	11,005
Clark County	NV	6	270,529	293,016	38,978	13.3	1,893,171	122,989	6.5	479	24,751	28,234	2,468	1,165	188	24,881	26,087	6,240	11,835	9,904
Houston ISD	TX	7	211,499	242,281	62,700	25.9	1,709,699	205,044	12.0	967	66,029	69,174	3,176	2,169	2	15,589	46,022	11,009	22,683	20,949
Philadelphia City	PA	8	189,779	271,660	73,967	27.2	2,005,429	283,834	14.2	1,473	109,115	59,205	5,022	867	—	21,392	71,341	17,065	36,056	46,280
Hawaii Dept. of Education	HI	9	183,609	212,069	27,134	12.8	2,078,877	170,377	8.2	927	27,939	31,487	3,282	3,090	964	29,069	24,351	5,104	9,147	8,941
Hillsborough County	FL	10	181,900	199,791	32,172	16.1	1,398,341	192,811	13.8	1,099	35,651	35,036	2,511	1,704	1,703	29,069	21,471	5,136	9,379	8,027
Palm Beach County	FL	11	170,260	193,685	24,984	12.9	1,392,058	104,384	7.5	633	27,592	25,989	1,332	319	228	21,777	16,337	3,908	6,981	5,975
Orange County	FL	12	165,992	178,371	28,678	16.1	1,204,883	104,053	8.6	656	22,261	23,356	1,991	1,229	7,087	30,609	18,666	4,465	8,068	6,906
Fairfax County	VA	13	164,235	183,747	9,730	5.3	1,666,632	66,801	4.0	411	10,471	12,017	1,650	474	474	21,995	7,892	1,888	2,891	3,393
Dallas ISD	TX	14	160,584	188,312	51,951	27.6	1,359,491	165,779	12.2	1,015	52,853	46,703	1,951	1,237	—	18,976	37,840	9,052	18,097	16,714
Detroit City	MI	15	153,034	215,674	66,759	31.0	1,659,070	236,429	14.3	1,361	112,356	33,926	5,314	1,401	676	19,821	64,043	15,319	31,900	41,560
Montgomery County	MD	16	139,201	166,707	10,523	6.3	1,717,136	68,686	4.0	494	14,605	12,222	1,029	690	597	18,284	9,847	2,355	3,672	3,308
San Diego City Unified	CA	17	137,960	163,074	31,367	19.2	1,516,967	162,374	10.7	1,154	51,108	28,692	1,672	2,382	9,385	22,821	24,516	5,756	10,247	9,108
Prince George's County	MD	18	137,285	160,651	15,351	9.6	1,267,462	87,537	6.9	646	18,124	25,259	1,263	712	428	17,083	14,261	3,411	5,734	5,428
Duval County	FL	19	129,557	156,418	22,220	14.2	909,284	91,828	10.1	717	26,321	22,627	1,234	789	3,938	24,257	14,717	3,520	6,224	5,327
Gwinnett County	GA	20	129,014	131,094	11,030	8.4	1,139,910	42,487	3.7	347	—	13,926	—	—	—	—	8,893	2,127	3,363	3,984
Memphis City	TN	21	116,224	133,320	30,899	23.2	865,001	109,676	12.7	929	27,932	32,945	2,459	—	—	19,191	20,448	4,891	8,901	11,196
Pinellas County	FL	22	114,510	135,911	19,354	14.2	854,304	79,604	9.3	694	20,949	15,981	1,537	1,014	4,788	20,761	12,765	3,053	5,312	4,547
Charlotte-Mecklenburg	NC	23	114,071	136,217	16,770	12.3	1,038,967	66,067	6.4	602	—	19,676	—	—	—	—	11,412	2,730	4,664	5,168
Wake County	NC	24	109,424	126,926	10,618	8.4	851,758	44,803	5.3	427	—	10,651	—	—	—	—	7,134	1,706	2,666	2,954
Baltimore County	MD	25	108,523	133,261	10,564	7.9	1,052,878	61,499	5.8	568	12,688	11,484	1,048	616	574	15,095	10,194	2,438	3,834	3,474
Cobb County	GA	26	102,034	111,161	8,696	7.8	937,155	41,996	4.5	418	—	8,547	—	—	—	—	7,115	1,702	2,532	2,872
DeKalb County	GA	27	99,550	107,622	16,777	15.6	900,104	54,728	6.1	559	—	23,007	—	—	—	—	13,408	3,207	5,471	6,809
Long Beach Unified	CA	28	97,560	106,052	32,654	30.8	757,771	104,562	13.8	1,076	27,713	23,953	1,029	821	5,728	10,970	24,038	5,750	10,501	9,342
Milwaukee	WI	29	97,359	120,503	33,446	27.8	1,099,821	164,362	14.9	1,689	58,795	21,776	2,006	—	—	18,103	31,725	7,589	13,913	17,757
Jefferson County	KY	30	95,582	120,752	18,610	15.4	773,945	45,700	5.9	478	—	—	—	—	—	—	14,031	3,356	5,825	8,147
Baltimore City	MD	31	94,049	112,180	27,631	24.6	1,004,690	143,103	14.2	1,487	51,469	23,048	1,796	1,062	456	18,597	27,442	6,564	11,890	11,758
Albuquerque	NM	32	90,537	104,811	16,982	16.2	638,542	58,432	9.2	663	15,519	14,210	416	462	1,576	9,033	11,654	2,788	4,776	5,512
Jefferson County	CO	33	87,172	96,677	5,465	5.7	715,561	30,195	4.2	343	7,878	4,946	617	271	2,127	10,273	4,217	594	1,377	1,475
Polk County	FL	34	84,135	92,122	16,393	17.8	598,573	69,077	11.5	841	19,904	18,949	923	1,050	344	13,739	10,678	2,554	4,338	3,713
Fresno Unified	CA	35	81,408	86,516	32,357	37.4	753,759	98,909	13.1	1,218	39,028	21,815	1,398	470	5,030	10,699	23,876	5,711	10,424	9,272
Fort Worth ISD	TX	36	80,335	93,957	22,161	23.6	653,873	72,571	11.1	895	22,783	18,778	1,122	672	—	8,249	16,233	3,883	6,856	6,332
Austin ISD	TX	37	79,007	90,756	16,187	17.8	824,586	61,882	7.5	787	17,178	16,147	799	513	—	11,043	11,944	2,857	4,853	4,482
Virginia Beach City	VA	38	76,304	87,400	7,631	8.7	605,100	55,192	9.1	727	9,664	7,424	1,190	279	249	11,676	6,141	1,469	2,077	2,293
Mesa Unified	AZ	39	75,401	93,326	11,043	11.8	538,798	42,099	7.8	559	9,598	10,452	1,363	437	3,281	9,097	7,450	1,782	2,830	2,879
Cypress-Fairbanks ISD	TX	40	74,877	68,939	4,188	6.1	548,169	18,017	3.3	253	1,724	6,014	247	237	—	6,317	3,080	—	952	880

See notes at end of table.

Enrollment, poverty, and federal funds for the 100 largest school districts, by enrollment size: Selected years, 2001–02 through 2005–06—Continued

Name of district	State	Rank order	Enrollment, fall 2003	5- to 17-year-old population, 2001–02	5- to 17-year-old population below the poverty level, 2001–02	Poverty rate of 5- to 17-year-olds, 2001–02	Revenues by source of funds (in thousands), 2002–03				Revenue for selected federal programs (in thousands), 2002–03						Title I allocations for 2005–06 (in thousands)			
							Total	Federal	Federal as a percent of total	Federal revenue per student, 2002–03[1]	Title I, basic and concentration grants	School lunch	Vocational education	Drug-free schools	Eisenhower math and science	Special education	Basic grants	Concentration grants	Targeted grants	Education finance incentive grants
1	2	3	4	5	6	7	8	9	10	11	12	13	14	15	16	17	18	19	20	21
Jordan	UT	41	74,761	81,875	4,153	5.1	425,717	26,698	6.3	362	3,582	6,839	786	—	672	8,258	2,814	—	874	1,034
Anne Arundel County	MD	42	74,508	91,637	5,368	5.9	687,725	36,209	5.3	484	6,913	4,700	666	401	181	11,280	4,979	844	1,607	1,327
Brevard County	FL	43	73,901	83,397	9,629	11.5	501,962	43,045	8.6	593	11,741	7,842	743	360	—	12,411	6,302	1,508	2,294	1,963
Fulton County	GA	44	73,319	80,902	6,211	7.7	773,098	30,813	4.0	432	—	9,965	—	—	—	—	5,156	1,233	1,710	1,854
Denver County	CO	45	72,100	83,155	18,723	22.5	649,333	68,940	10.6	958	22,900	13,701	1,125	1,713	5,343	9,750	13,874	3,319	5,754	7,173
Northside ISD	TX	46	71,798	74,165	9,340	12.6	549,010	40,883	7.4	589	6,448	10,762	529	315	1,951	10,310	6,932	1,658	2,512	2,320
Granite	UT	47	70,771	74,337	7,480	10.1	385,148	41,947	10.9	589	6,751	9,668	758	213	—	8,470	4,946	1,183	1,670	2,022
Cleveland Municipal	OH	48	69,655	94,573	27,636	29.2	784,024	139,462	17.8	1,947	11,436	25,373	436	1,114	—	13,021	24,586	5,772	10,378	14,898
Nashville-Davidson	TN	49	68,651	87,091	14,657	16.8	524,769	43,910	8.4	646	11,436	12,135	1,242	—	—	10,942	9,908	2,370	3,978	4,773
Orleans Parish SB	LA	50	67,922	87,428	30,703	35.1	529,221	94,142	17.8	1,340	34,761	23,820	3,281	131	4,902	12,352	21,701	5,191	9,429	9,514
Guilford County	NC	51	66,971	75,553	11,280	14.9	482,067	41,289	8.6	629	10,372	14,005	966	—	74	9,754	7,607	1,820	2,886	3,199
Lee County	FL	52	66,466	73,298	10,138	13.8	502,261	46,188	9.2	731	10,372	11,157	966	356	—	10,892	6,621	1,584	2,443	2,091
District of Columbia	DC	53	65,099	74,805	21,767	29.1	1,114,061	152,599	13.7	2,260	34,472	17,135	3,678	1,362	1,138	11,476	24,835	5,941	10,625	8,959
Seminole County	FL	54	64,904	72,493	6,800	9.4	454,552	32,739	7.2	516	8,353	6,507	419	306	1,964	14,302	4,416	1,056	1,472	1,260
Mobile County	AL	55	64,774	78,335	18,708	23.9	449,312	65,632	14.6	1,025	21,598	17,428	1,589	586	4,368	10,538	12,240	2,928	5,067	5,858
Greenville County	SC	56	64,245	72,550	10,239	14.1	485,956	34,973	7.2	553	7,481	9,349	1,199	325	1,384	9,451	7,557	1,808	2,811	3,799
Volusia County	FL	57	64,089	71,618	11,105	15.5	491,233	40,371	8.2	641	12,825	9,552	961	478	3,107	5,939	7,371	1,763	2,793	2,390
Prince William County	VA	58	63,404	67,804	4,412	6.5	565,455	20,616	3.6	341	2,782	5,091	597	203	198	6,774	3,546	—	1,107	1,196
El Paso ISD	TX	59	63,200	65,424	23,122	35.3	479,632	67,200	14.0	1,064	25,730	15,860	1,261	569	—	7,942	16,738	4,004	7,092	6,550
Columbus City	OH	60	63,098	76,345	18,469	24.2	674,296	60,154	8.9	937	—	15,309	1,793	470	—	7,942	16,156	3,865	6,691	9,382
Santa Ana Unified	CA	61	62,874	64,994	15,647	24.1	573,085	53,938	9.4	848	14,041	16,005	324	223	2,380	6,966	11,416	2,731	4,605	3,912
Arlington ISD	TX	62	62,454	68,799	8,849	12.9	458,183	28,849	6.3	466	4,981	10,026	449	262	—	7,473	6,467	1,547	2,295	2,119
Washoe County	NV	63	62,103	67,157	6,745	10.0	429,620	31,454	7.3	521	6,723	6,861	563	240	1,742	6,312	4,630	1,108	1,552	1,065
Tucson Unified	AZ	64	61,448	81,081	16,202	20.0	449,579	56,080	12.5	905	15,467	12,411	1,554	559	3,846	8,633	10,922	2,613	4,452	4,738
Fort Bend ISD	TX	65	61,248	64,127	4,098	6.4	435,536	18,914	4.3	318	2,790	4,505	349	260	1,527	6,243	3,111	—	964	890
Davis	UT	66	60,749	60,856	3,563	5.9	331,830	25,868	7.8	429	3,269	6,681	807	176	—	6,649	2,354	—	702	820
Boston	MA	67	60,150	80,657	21,131	26.2	1,016,975	97,365	9.6	1,582	38,686	10,435	1,587	864	7,496	15,501	21,135	5,056	8,897	11,578
San Bernardino City Unified	CA	68	57,818	59,520	21,278	35.7	492,864	56,564	11.5	1,008	20,115	16,960	639	134	4,625	6,946	15,815	3,783	6,659	5,804
San Francisco Unified	CA	69	57,805	73,357	11,689	15.9	539,958	65,637	12.2	1,127	16,243	9,349	603	259	3,320	312	8,949	2,131	3,434	2,833
Pasco County	FL	70	57,510	60,510	9,501	15.7	392,460	36,455	9.3	663	9,776	9,778	532	353	2,244	7,008	6,255	1,496	2,272	1,944
San Antonio ISD	TX	71	56,914	66,506	23,121	34.8	517,535	81,270	15.7	1,423	29,218	23,502	1,271	642	—	7,930	17,139	4,100	7,279	6,723
North East ISD	TX	72	56,298	61,085	6,289	10.3	438,835	26,679	6.1	485	4,037	7,200	463	264	—	8,800	4,645	—	1,537	1,420
Aldine ISD	TX	73	56,292	54,021	12,092	22.4	448,966	47,220	10.5	853	9,019	18,159	575	296	1,742	7,213	8,935	2,137	3,448	3,184
Elk Grove Unified	CA	74	55,613	53,431	6,951	13.0	469,357	28,982	6.2	553	6,295	7,867	355	379	—	6,188	5,415	1,295	1,825	1,365
Chesterfield County	VA	75	55,393	56,906	3,482	6.1	422,464	18,303	4.3	341	3,052	2,849	601	163	1,653	7,287	2,789	—	825	876
Garland ISD	TX	76	55,114	56,322	5,533	9.8	370,969	21,419	5.8	397	3,345	7,615	358	187	121	5,321	4,028	—	1,307	1,207
Cumberland County	NC	77	53,159	56,702	10,417	18.4	351,184	42,558	12.1	817	5,585	12,086	—	—	—	—	7,032	1,682	2,618	2,901
Knox County	TN	78	52,659	62,126	8,650	13.9	353,030	22,172	6.3	415	—	6,635	—	—	—	130	5,906	1,413	2,109	2,335
Sacramento City Unified	CA	79	52,103	65,982	16,202	24.6	499,416	71,837	14.4	1,359	23,480	13,671	905	596	3,929	7,489	13,209	2,950	5,032	4,306
Atlanta City	GA	80	52,103	66,133	21,344	32.3	720,923	69,171	9.6	1,259	—	18,215	—	—	—	—	18,916	4,189	7,388	9,377

See notes at end of table.

Enrollment, poverty, and federal funds for the 100 largest school districts, by enrollment size: Selected years, 2001–02 through 2005–06—Continued

Name of district	State	Rank order	Enrollment, fall 2003	5- to 17-year-old population, 2001–02	5- to 17-year-old population below the poverty level, 2001–02	Poverty rate of 5- to 17-year-olds, 2001–02	Revenues by source of funds (in thousands), 2002–03: Total	Federal	Federal as a percent of total, 2002–03	Federal revenue per student, 2002–03[1]	Revenue for selected federal programs (in thousands), 2002–03: Title I, basic and concentration grants	School lunch	Vocational education	Drug-free schools	Eisenhower math and science	Special education	Title I allocations for 2005–06 (in thousands): Basic grants	Concentration grants	Targeted grants	Education finance incentive grants
1	2	3	4	5	6	7	8	9	10	11	12	13	14	15	16	17	18	19	20	21
Plano ISD	TX	81	51,869	66,353	2,708	4.1	557,312	14,418	2.6	282	1,199	2,828	318	167	—	5,764	2,001	—	—	—
Jefferson Parish SB	LA	82	51,453	80,197	17,170	21.4	392,032	55,362	14.1	1,075	13,546	13,808	903	752	4,001	8,533	12,148	2,906	4,967	5,012
Alpine	UT	83	51,240	51,126	4,285	8.4	256,461	14,385	5.6	293	2,124	5,098	498	128	1,038	5,175	2,826	—	878	1,039
San Juan Unified	CA	84	50,906	60,554	6,607	10.9	416,990	38,352	9.2	735	9,483	5,912	468	391	2,069	6,435	5,170	1,237	1,733	1,295
Clayton County	GA	85	50,555	55,898	9,527	17.0	410,649	33,123	8.1	668	—	12,322	—	—	—	—	7,682	1,838	2,797	3,227
Oakland Unified	CA	86	50,437	71,360	16,924	23.7	535,822	60,308	11.3	1,149	22,172	11,417	789	594	3,423	7,500	13,439	3,056	5,240	4,497
Garden Grove Unified	CA	87	50,172	55,668	10,341	18.6	374,552	33,913	9.1	677	11,522	2,498	337	316	1,549	5,869	8,124	3,417	3,067	2,496
Capistrano Unified	CA	88	49,746	57,668	3,474	6.0	359,936	14,397	4.0	296	1,867	—	154	161	607	5,752	2,535	798	748	539
Anchorage	AK	89	49,722	56,609	4,614	8.2	414,075	49,899	12.1	997	8,974	6,763	905	504	453	8,358	5,811	—	2,686	2,733
Wichita	KS	90	48,894	58,112	9,290	16.0	418,629	49,101	11.7	1,004	14,297	10,385	—	590	—	—	8,012	1,917	2,951	4,857
Portland	OR	91	48,344	61,929	8,906	14.4	480,659	47,612	9.9	922	13,125	9,391	765	2,350	2,350	8,382	7,429	1,777	2,672	3,767
Howard County	MD	92	47,833	53,648	1,970	3.7	516,846	14,447	2.8	306	2,325	1,840	412	165	148	5,830	1,842	—	1,838	—
Forsyth County	NC	93	47,788	55,704	7,976	14.3	349,248	30,294	8.7	647	—	8,292	—	—	—	7,326	5,361	1,282	1,838	2,036
Seattle	WA	94	47,588	60,149	8,082	13.4	513,336	48,581	9.5	1,015	13,325	6,990	609	—	—	8,109	6,366	1,901	2,234	2,842
Newark City	NJ	95	46,825	56,070	16,325	29.1	930,827	65,928	7.1	1,555	31,186	11,724	—	—	—	6,264	17,519	3,992	6,820	9,918
Shelby County	TN	96	46,808	47,040	2,152	4.6	283,109	13,808	4.9	304	1,885	3,179	365	—	—	5,665	1,573	—	410	402
Ysleta ISD	TX	97	46,668	44,775	14,202	31.7	348,062	49,392	14.2	1,057	16,189	12,456	775	358	—	8,463	10,262	2,455	4,067	3,756
East Baton Rouge Parish SB	LA	98	46,644	68,551	14,735	21.5	432,445	55,303	12.8	1,055	12,647	16,053	1,005	436	3,252	5,263	10,402	2,488	4,152	4,189
Cherry Creek	CO	99	46,594	46,037	2,360	5.1	389,053	11,015	2.8	241	1,453	2,256	—	147	719	—	1,781	—	467	467
Pasadena ISD	TX	100	46,142	47,203	7,912	16.8	330,929	26,171	7.9	584	6,274	10,238	430	242	—	4,485	5,800	1,387	1,983	1,832

—Not available

[1] Federal revenue per student is based on fall enrollment collected by the Bureau of the Census.

SOURCE: U.S. Department of Education, National Center for Education Statistics, Common Core of Data (CCD), "National Public Education Financial Survey," 2002–03; "Local Education Agency Universe Survey," 2003–04; and unpublished Department of Education budget data. (This table was prepared August 2005.)

Number of public school districts and public and private elementary and secondary schools: Selected years, 1869–70 through 2003–04

School year	Regular public school districts[1]	Public schools[2] Total, all schools[4]	Total, schools with reported grade spans[5]	Schools with elementary grades Total	Schools with elementary grades One-teacher	Schools with secondary grades	Private schools[2,3] Total[4]	Schools with elementary grades	Schools with secondary grades
1	2	3	4	5	6	7	8	9	10
1869–70	—	116,312	—	—	—	—	—	—	—
1879–80	—	178,122	—	—	—	—	—	—	—
1889–90	—	224,526	—	—	—	—	—	—	—
1899–1900	—	248,279	—	—	—	—	—	—	—
1909–10	—	265,474	—	—	212,448	—	—	—	—
1919–20	—	271,319	—	—	187,948	—	—	—	—
1929–30	—	248,117	—	238,306	148,712	23,930	—	9,275	3,258
1939–40	117,108	226,762	—	—	113,600	—	—	11,306	3,568
1949–50	83,718	—	—	128,225	59,652	24,542	—	10,375	3,331
1951–52	71,094	—	—	123,763	50,742	23,746	—	10,666	3,322
1959–60	40,520	—	—	91,853	20,213	25,784	—	13,574	4,061
1961–62	35,676	—	—	81,910	13,333	25,350	—	14,762	4,129
1963–64	31,705	—	—	77,584	9,895	26,431	—	—	4,451
1965–66	26,983	—	—	73,216	6,491	26,597	17,849	15,340	4,606
1967–68	22,010	—	94,197	70,879	4,146	27,011	—	—	—
1970–71	17,995	—	89,372	65,800	1,815	25,352	—	14,372	3,770
1973–74	16,730	—	88,655	65,070	1,365	25,906	—	—	—
1975–76	16,376	88,597	87,034	63,242	1,166	25,330	—	—	—
1976–77	16,271	—	86,501	62,644	1,111	25,378	19,910	16,385	5,904
1978–79	16,014	—	84,816	61,982	1,056	24,504	19,489	16,097	5,766
1979–80	15,929	87,004	—	—	—	—	—	—	—
1980–81	15,912	85,982	83,688	61,069	921	24,362	20,764	16,792	5,678
1982–83	15,824	84,740	82,039	59,656	798	23,988	—	—	—
1983–84	15,747	84,178	81,418	59,082	838	23,947	[6] 27,694	[6] 20,872	[6] 7,862
1984–85	—	84,007	81,147	58,827	825	23,916	—	—	—
1985–86	—	—	—	—	—	—	[6] 25,616	[6] 20,252	[6] 7,387
1986–87	[7] 15,713	83,455	82,190	60,784	763	23,389	—	—	—
1987–88	[7] 15,577	83,248	81,416	59,754	729	23,841	[6] 26,807	[6] 22,959	[6] 8,418
1988–89	[7] 15,376	83,165	81,579	60,176	583	23,638	—	—	—
1989–90	[7] 15,367	83,425	81,880	60,699	630	23,461	—	—	—
1990–91	[7] 15,358	84,538	82,475	61,340	617	23,460	[6] 24,690	[6] 22,223	[6] 8,989
1991–92	[7] 15,173	84,578	82,506	61,739	569	23,248	[6] 25,998	[6] 23,523	[6] 9,282
1992–93	[7] 15,025	84,497	82,896	62,225	430	23,220	—	—	—
1993–94	[7] 14,881	85,393	83,431	62,726	442	23,379	[6] 26,093	[6] 23,543	[6] 10,555
1994–95	[7] 14,772	86,221	84,476	63,572	458	23,668	—	—	—
1995–96	[7] 14,766	87,125	84,958	63,961	474	23,793	[6] 27,686	[6] 25,153	[6] 10,942
1996–97	[7] 14,841	88,223	86,092	64,785	487	24,287	—	—	—
1997–98	[7] 14,805	89,508	87,541	65,859	476	24,802	[6] 27,402	[6] 24,915	[6] 10,779
1998–99	[7] 14,891	90,874	89,259	67,183	463	25,797	—	—	—
1999–2000	[7] 14,928	92,012	90,538	68,173	423	26,407	[6] 27,223	[6] 24,685	[6] 10,693
2000–01	[7] 14,859	93,273	91,691	69,697	411	27,090	—	—	—
2001–02	[7] 14,559	94,112	92,696	70,516	408	27,468	[6] 29,273	[6] 26,569	[6] 11,846
2002–03	[7] 14,465	95,615	93,869	71,270	366	28,151	—	—	—
2003–04	[7] 14,383	95,726	93,977	71,195	376	28,219	—	—	—

—Not available.

[1]Includes operating and nonoperating districts.

[2]Schools with both elementary and secondary programs are included under elementary schools and also under secondary schools.

[3]Data for most years prior to 1976–77 are partly estimated.

[4]Includes regular schools and special schools not classified by grade span.

[5]Includes elementary, secondary, and combined elementary/secondary schools.

[6]These data cannot be compared directly with the data for earlier years.

[7]Because of expanded survey coverage, data are not directly comparable with figures prior to 1986.

SOURCE: U.S. Department of Education, National Center for Education Statistics, *Annual Report of the Commissioner of Education*, 1870 through 1910; *Biennial Survey of Education in the United States*, 1919–20 through 1949–50; *Statistics of State School Systems*, 1959–60 through 1967–68; *Statistics of Public Elementary and Secondary School Systems*, 1970–71 through 1980–81; *Statistics of Nonpublic Elementary and Secondary Schools*, 1970–71 through 1979–80; *Private Schools in American Education*; Schools and Staffing Survey (SASS), "Private School Questionnaire," 1987–88 and 1990–91; Private School Universe Survey (PSS), 1991–92 through 2001–2002; and Common Core of Data (CCD), "Local Education Agency Universe Survey" and "Public Elementary/Secondary School Universe Survey," 1982–83 through 2003–04. (This table was prepared August 2005.)

Public elementary and secondary schools, by type of school: Selected years, 1970–71 through 2003–04

		Schools with reported grade spans											
			Elementary schools				Secondary schools						
Year	Total, all public schools	Total	Total[2]	Middle schools[3]	One-teacher schools	Other elementary schools	Total[4]	Junior high[5]	3-year or 4-year high schools	5-year or 6-year high schools	Other secondary schools	Combined elementary/ secondary schools[6]	Other schools[1]
1	2	3	4	5	6	7	8	9	10	11	12	13	14
1970–71	—	89,372	64,020	2,080	1,815	60,125	23,572	7,750	11,265	3,887	670	1,780	—
1975–76	88,597	87,034	61,704	3,916	1,166	56,622	23,792	7,521	11,572	4,113	586	1,538	1,563
1976–77	—	86,501	61,123	4,180	1,111	55,832	23,857	7,434	11,658	4,130	635	1,521	—
1978–79	—	84,816	60,312	5,879	1,056	53,377	22,834	6,282	11,410	4,429	713	1,670	—
1980–81	85,982	83,688	59,326	6,003	921	52,402	22,619	5,890	10,758	4,193	1,778	1,743	2,294
1982–83	84,740	82,039	58,051	6,875	798	50,378	22,383	5,948	11,678	4,067	690	1,605	2,701
1983–84	84,178	81,418	57,471	6,885	838	49,748	22,336	5,936	11,670	4,046	684	1,611	2,760
1984–85	84,007	81,147	57,231	6,893	825	49,513	22,320	5,916	11,671	4,021	712	1,596	2,860
1986–87	83,455	82,190	58,801	7,452	763	50,586	21,406	5,142	11,453	4,197	614	1,983	[7] 1,265
1987–88	83,248	81,416	57,575	7,641	729	49,205	21,662	4,900	11,279	4,048	1,435	2,179	[7] 1,832
1988–89	83,165	81,579	57,941	7,957	583	49,401	21,403	4,687	11,350	3,994	1,372	2,235	[7] 1,586
1989–90	83,425	81,880	58,419	8,272	630	49,517	21,181	4,512	11,492	3,812	1,365	2,280	[7] 1,545
1990–91	84,538	82,475	59,015	8,545	617	49,853	21,135	4,561	11,537	3,723	1,314	2,325	2,063
1991–92	84,578	82,506	59,258	8,829	569	49,860	20,767	4,298	11,528	3,699	1,242	2,481	2,072
1992–93	84,497	82,896	59,676	9,152	430	50,094	20,671	4,115	11,651	3,613	1,292	2,549	1,601
1993–94	85,393	83,431	60,052	9,573	442	50,037	20,705	3,970	11,858	3,595	1,282	2,674	1,962
1994–95	86,221	84,476	60,808	9,954	458	50,396	20,904	3,859	12,058	3,628	1,359	2,764	1,745
1995–96	87,125	84,958	61,165	10,205	474	50,486	20,997	3,743	12,168	3,621	1,465	2,796	2,167
1996–97	88,223	86,092	61,805	10,499	487	50,819	21,307	3,707	12,424	3,614	1,562	2,980	2,131
1997–98	89,508	87,541	62,739	10,944	476	51,319	21,682	3,599	12,734	3,611	1,738	3,120	1,967
1998–99	90,874	89,259	63,462	11,202	463	51,797	22,076	3,607	13,457	3,707	1,305	3,721	1,615
1999–2000	92,012	90,538	64,131	11,521	423	52,187	22,365	3,566	13,914	3,686	1,199	4,042	1,474
2000–01	93,273	91,691	64,601	11,696	411	52,494	21,994	3,318	13,793	3,974	909	5,096	1,582
2001–02	94,112	92,696	65,228	11,983	408	52,837	22,180	3,285	14,070	3,917	908	5,288	1,416
2002–03	95,615	93,869	65,718	12,174	366	53,178	22,599	3,263	14,330	4,017	989	5,552	1,746
2003–04	95,726	93,977	65,758	12,341	376	53,041	22,782	3,251	14,595	3,840	1,096	5,437	1,749

—Not available.

[1]Includes special education, alternative, and other schools not classified by grade span.
[2]Includes schools beginning with grade 6 or below and with no grade higher than 8.
[3]Includes schools with grade spans beginning with 4, 5, or 6 and ending with 6, 7, or 8.
[4]Includes schools with no grade lower than 7.
[5]Includes schools with grades 7 and 8 or grades 7 through 9.
[6]Includes schools beginning with grade 6 or lower and ending with grade 9 or above.

[7]Because of revision in data collection procedures, figures not comparable to data for other years.
SOURCE: U.S. Department of Education, National Center for Education Statistics, *Statistics of State School Systems, 1975–76; Statistics of Public Elementary and Secondary Day Schools*, 1970–71, and 1976–77 through 1980–81; and Common Core of Data (CCD), "Public Elementary/Secondary School Universe Survey," 1982–83 through 2003–04. (This table was prepared July 2005.)

Public elementary and secondary schools, by type and state or jurisdiction: 1990–91, 2000–01, and 2003–04

State or jurisdiction	Total, all schools, 1990–91	Total, all schools, 2000–01	Number of schools, 2003–04			Combined elementary/secondary[3]				Other[4]	Alternative[5]	Special education[5]	Charter[5]	One-teacher schools[5]
			Total	Elementary[1]	Secondary[2]	Total	Pre-kindergarten, kindergarten, or 1st grade to grade 12	Other schools ending with grade 12	Other combined schools					
1	2	3	4	5	6	7	8	9	10	11	12	13	14	15
United States	84,538	93,273	95,726	65,758	22,782	5,437	2,822	2,136	479	1,749	5,958	2,328	2,977	376
Alabama	1,297	1,517	1,518	938	403	177	120	48	9	0	74	26	0	0
Alaska	498	515	520	194	85	241	220	14	7	0	23	3	19	21
Arizona	1,049	1,724	2,016	1,261	560	151	74	52	25	44	76	13	505	11
Arkansas	1,098	1,138	1,150	711	424	15	4	5	6	0	5	4	13	1
California	7,913	8,773	9,223	6,579	2,187	456	360	75	21	1	1,187	128	444	54
Colorado	1,344	1,632	1,672	1,196	401	75	37	33	5	0	74	17	96	5
Connecticut	985	1,248	1,247	824	240	180	163	12	5	3	200	27	12	0
Delaware	173	191	204	137	44	23	18	4	1	0	10	16	13	0
District of Columbia	181	198	206	139	43	9	7	1	1	15	7	13	37	0
Florida	2,516	3,316	3,427	2,350	481	596	193	369	34	0	185	117	257	6
Georgia	1,734	1,946	2,458	1,637	356	42	19	20	3	423	174	271	51	0
Hawaii	235	261	284	208	54	22	18	1	3	0	1	3	26	3
Idaho	582	673	685	417	223	45	25	15	5	0	67	10	17	7
Illinois	4,239	4,342	4,416	3,189	1,005	126	45	62	19	96	169	256	28	0
Indiana	1,915	1,976	1,986	1,420	448	92	40	46	6	26	47	51	17	0
Iowa	1,588	1,534	1,493	1,023	424	37	2	35	0	9	43	10	0	6
Kansas	1,477	1,430	1,413	977	423	2	1	1	0	11	5	4	17	0
Kentucky	1,400	1,526	1,436	1,007	337	91	22	67	2	1	158	11	0	0
Louisiana	1,533	1,530	1,544	1,037	312	195	142	48	5	0	112	39	16	0
Maine	747	714	694	518	156	20	12	7	1	0	0	4	0	5
Maryland	1,220	1,383	1,408	1,085	269	36	19	11	6	18	72	50	1	0
Massachusetts	1,842	1,905	1,867	1,464	334	65	35	22	8	4	27	5	51	1
Michigan	3,313	3,998	4,000	2,698	843	187	81	70	36	272	244	179	212	11
Minnesota	1,590	2,362	2,545	1,256	836	106	29	48	29	347	638	275	105	1
Mississippi	972	1,030	1,051	599	327	116	70	45	1	9	61	0	1	0
Missouri	2,199	2,368	2,372	1,560	650	162	77	82	3	0	84	23	26	0
Montana	900	879	859	497	362	0	0	0	0	0	4	2	0	71
Nebraska	1,506	1,326	1,248	885	333	30	30	0	0	0	0	46	0	79
Nevada	354	511	558	406	127	23	7	14	2	2	40	13	15	12
New Hampshire	439	526	473	375	97	1	0	0	1	0	0	0	0	0
New Jersey	2,272	2,410	2,467	1,911	462	14	1	8	5	80	18	83	51	0
New Mexico	681	765	814	575	205	34	14	16	4	0	56	16	34	2
New York	4,010	4,336	4,531	3,187	995	179	84	62	33	170	195	73	50	—
North Carolina	1,955	2,207	2,268	1,770	390	85	24	49	12	23	71	19	93	0
North Dakota	663	579	556	322	200	2	0	2	0	32	0	30	0	5

See notes at end of table.

Public elementary and secondary schools, by type and state or jurisdiction: 1990–91, 2000–01, and 2003–04—Continued

State or jurisdiction	Total, all schools, 1990–91	Total, all schools, 2000–01	Total	Elementary[1]	Secondary[2]	Combined elementary/secondary[3]				Other[4]	Alternative[5]	Special education[5]	Charter[5]	One-teacher schools[5]
						Total	Pre-kindergarten, kindergarten, or 1st grade to grade 12	Other schools ending with grade 12	Other combined schools					
1	2	3	4	5	6	7	8	9	10	11	12	13	14	15
Ohio	3,731	3,916	3,942	2,738	1,003	176	40	60	76	25	9	61	165	0
Oklahoma	1,880	1,821	1,786	1,198	583	5	0	1	4	0	0	0	12	1
Oregon	1,199	1,273	1,238	913	274	41	30	6	5	10	58	2	24	12
Pennsylvania	3,260	3,252	3,259	2,375	802	66	20	27	19	16	13	12	102	0
Rhode Island	309	328	341	268	68	5	4	1	0	0	5	4	8	0
South Carolina	1,097	1,127	1,161	849	285	20	5	11	4	7	19	10	18	0
South Dakota	802	769	740	441	281	12	7	5	0	6	24	6	0	26
Tennessee	1,543	1,624	1,677	1,259	354	61	27	30	4	3	27	16	4	—
Texas	5,991	7,519	7,978	5,241	1,835	902	432	445	25	0	945	119	274	2
Utah	714	793	886	546	309	14	1	9	4	17	90	41	19	9
Vermont	397	393	393	276	69	48	40	8	0	0	2	61	0	3
Virginia	1,811	1,969	2,070	1,482	412	98	55	42	1	78	131	56	6	0
Washington	1,936	2,305	2,251	1,425	592	234	136	74	24	0	266	84	0	8
West Virginia	1,015	840	793	588	178	26	4	20	2	1	24	9	0	0
Wisconsin	2,018	2,182	2,222	1,552	593	77	20	45	12	0	191	10	137	0
Wyoming	415	393	380	255	108	17	8	8	1	0	27	0	1	14
Bureau of Indian Affairs	—	189	189	102	26	60	53	3	4	1	0	0	0	[6]26
Department of Defense dependents schools														
Domestic schools	—	71	69	57	7	5	1	2	2	0	0	0	0	0
Overseas schools	—	156	154	105	39	10	9	1	0	0	0	0	0	0
Other jurisdictions														
American Samoa	30	31	31	24	6	0	0	0	0	1	0	1	0	0
Guam	35	38	37	33	4	0	0	0	0	0	0	0	0	0
Northern Marianas	26	29	32	23	6	1	0	0	1	2	1	0	0	0
Puerto Rico	1,619	1,543	1,522	862	358	269	33	6	230	33	24	28	120	0
Virgin Islands	33	36	35	24	10	1	0	0	1	0	1	0	0	0

—Not available.

[1]Includes schools beginning with grade 6 or below and with no grade higher than 8.

[2]Includes schools with no grade lower than 7.

[3]Includes schools beginning with grade 6 or below and ending with grade 9 or above.

[4]Includes schools not classified by grade span.

[5]Schools are also included under elementary, secondary, combined, or other as appropriate.

[6]Data are for 1998–99.

SOURCE: U.S. Department of Education, National Center for Education Statistics, Common Core of Data (CCD), "Public Elementary/Secondary School Universe Survey," 1990–91, 2000–01, and 2003–04. (This table was prepared July 2005.)

Public elementary schools, by grade span, average school size, and state or jurisdiction: 2003–04

			Schools, by grade span						Average number of students per school[2]	
State or jurisdiction	Total, all elementary schools	Total, all regular elementary schools[1]	Pre-kindergarten, kindergarten, or 1st grade to grades 3 or 4	Pre-kindergarten, kindergarten, or 1st grade to grade 5	Pre-kindergarten, kindergarten, or 1st grade to grade 6	Pre-kindergarten, kindergarten, or 1st grade to grade 8	Grade 4, 5, or 6 to grade 6, 7, or 8	Other grade spans	All elementary schools	Regular elementary schools[1]
1	2	3	4	5	6	7	8	9	10	11
United States	65,758	64,721	5,030	23,472	13,547	5,502	12,341	5,866	476	482
Alabama	938	928	90	303	163	76	209	97	480	482
Alaska	194	192	1	21	111	23	16	22	321	322
Arizona	1,261	1,231	61	233	352	358	162	95	509	514
Arkansas	711	709	117	139	235	7	133	80	381	382
California	6,579	6,396	174	2,012	2,462	758	985	188	614	630
Colorado	1,196	1,195	30	552	261	60	227	66	411	411
Connecticut	824	809	105	294	115	59	152	99	460	467
Delaware	137	135	33	48	6	3	32	15	528	533
District of Columbia	139	138	4	21	80	11	17	6	354	356
Florida	2,350	2,330	27	1,510	142	78	486	107	737	742
Georgia	1,637	1,634	39	966	70	12	398	152	660	661
Hawaii	208	207	3	63	108	8	25	1	551	554
Idaho	417	413	37	111	155	19	64	31	366	368
Illinois	3,189	3,086	310	772	423	718	542	424	442	453
Indiana	1,420	1,413	107	597	348	26	259	83	459	459
Iowa	1,023	1,020	92	339	223	15	220	134	291	292
Kansas	977	975	87	287	252	95	185	71	299	300
Kentucky	1,007	995	50	480	141	90	199	47	437	441
Louisiana	1,037	1,013	96	335	178	79	229	120	456	461
Maine	518	517	67	96	69	109	93	84	250	250
Maryland	1,085	1,060	13	627	137	32	218	58	540	548
Massachusetts	1,464	1,458	194	515	166	100	284	205	443	444
Michigan	2,698	2,684	241	1,032	394	168	520	343	411	412
Minnesota	1,256	1,118	121	316	396	52	199	172	398	440
Mississippi	599	597	84	109	130	41	132	103	515	515
Missouri	1,560	1,549	126	510	321	112	300	191	379	380
Montana	497	495	20	63	219	118	52	25	173	173
Nebraska	885	867	0	0	546	227	80	32	198	200
Nevada	406	395	6	191	97	19	69	24	659	674
New Hampshire	375	375	53	109	52	47	74	40	363	363
New Jersey	1,911	1,898	283	534	199	270	352	273	483	484
New Mexico	575	562	26	215	138	18	123	55	357	362
New York	3,187	3,169	278	1,186	550	127	640	406	583	585
North Carolina	1,770	1,766	61	1,021	54	111	434	89	537	538
North Dakota	322	322	12	32	195	46	23	14	176	176
Ohio	2,738	2,726	378	808	596	147	526	283	405	406
Oklahoma	1,198	1,198	65	333	163	313	215	109	352	352
Oregon	913	894	55	391	177	82	182	26	383	388
Pennsylvania	2,375	2,375	284	859	497	104	443	188	466	466
Rhode Island	268	267	25	120	35	2	48	38	398	399
South Carolina	849	847	56	409	81	19	218	66	569	571
South Dakota	441	441	17	112	103	111	76	22	183	183
Tennessee	1,259	1,251	154	474	102	184	273	72	495	497
Texas	5,241	5,134	567	2,036	761	115	1,177	585	545	553
Utah	546	531	21	107	347	5	42	24	515	528
Vermont	276	242	13	25	113	66	16	43	207	228
Virginia	1,482	1,475	41	840	142	13	305	141	540	542
Washington	1,425	1,358	68	416	527	71	233	110	431	446
West Virginia	588	584	88	220	95	41	107	37	320	321
Wisconsin	1,552	1,493	124	635	219	119	307	148	355	358
Wyoming	255	254	26	48	101	18	40	22	191	191

See notes at end of table.

Public elementary schools, by grade span, average school size, and state or jurisdiction: 2003–04—Continued

State or jurisdiction	Total, all elementary schools	Total, all regular elementary schools[1]	Schools, by grade span						Average number of students per school[2]	
			Pre-kindergarten, kindergarten, or 1st grade to grades 3 or 4	Pre-kindergarten, kindergarten, or 1st grade to grade 5	Pre-kindergarten, kindergarten, or 1st grade to grade 6	Pre-kindergarten, kindergarten, or 1st grade to grade 8	Grade 4, 5, or 6 to grade 6, 7, or 8	Other grade spans	All elementary schools	Regular elementary schools[1]
1	2	3	4	5	6	7	8	9	10	11
Bureau of Indian Affairs	102	102	5	4	22	67	3	1	215	215
Department of Defense dependents schools										
Domestic schools..................	57	57	15	17	4	2	9	10	438	438
Overseas schools	105	105	7	23	47	6	18	4	470	470
Other jurisdictions										
American Samoa	24	24	1	0	0	21	1	1	491	491
Guam	33	33	0	24	0	0	7	2	683	683
Northern Marianas................	23	23	0	2	10	0	1	10	301	301
Puerto Rico.......................	862	830	51	5	762	7	24	13	297	297
Virgin Islands	24	24	0	1	22	0	1	0	408	408

[1]Excludes special education and alternative schools.
[2]Average for schools reporting enrollment data.
NOTE: Includes schools beginning with grade 6 or below and with no grade higher than 8. Excludes schools not reported by grade level, such as some special education schools for the disabled.

SOURCE: U.S. Department of Education, National Center for Education Statistics, Common Core of Data (CCD), "Public Elementary/Secondary School Universe Survey," 2003–04. (This table was prepared July 2005.)

Public secondary schools, by grade span, average school size, and state or jurisdiction: 2003–04

State or jurisdiction	Total, all secondary schools	Total, all regular secondary schools[1]	Schools, by grade span							Vocational schools[2]	Average number of students per school[3]	
			Grades 7 to 8 and 7 to 9	Grades 7 to 12	Grades 8 to 12	Grades 9 to 12	Grades 10 to 12	Other spans ending with grade 12	Other grade spans		All secondary schools	Regular secondary schools[1]
1	2	3	4	5	6	7	8	9	10	11	12	13
United States	22,782	18,810	3,251	3,175	665	13,910	685	297	799	1,100	722	816
Alabama	403	308	33	88	7	233	32	5	5	75	667	691
Alaska.........................	85	72	18	19	2	43	2	0	1	2	522	585
Arizona	560	466	86	46	13	398	5	2	10	73	665	699
Arkansas.....................	424	400	53	190	5	106	44	2	24	20	434	439
California	2,187	1,373	334	274	34	1,505	20	6	14	0	955	1,447
Colorado	401	339	60	64	4	262	4	3	4	2	612	694
Connecticut................	240	180	30	11	6	163	7	15	8	17	778	959
Delaware.....................	44	36	11	1	24	7	0	0	1	5	958	1,006
District of Columbia	43	38	11	2	1	29	0	0	0	2	462	488
Florida........................	481	456	17	35	19	385	4	5	16	26	1,482	1,558
Georgia......................	356	341	15	3	6	326	1	0	5	0	1,178	1,222
Hawaii	54	53	11	8	0	34	0	0	1	0	1,196	1,215
Idaho..........................	223	160	38	52	3	109	16	0	5	9	440	557
Illinois........................	1,005	792	158	62	24	630	12	31	88	54	698	814
Indiana.......................	448	397	71	85	2	259	1	1	29	29	812	837
Iowa	424	389	54	88	0	271	7	2	2	0	413	442
Kansas.......................	423	419	63	90	4	258	6	1	1	0	412	415
Kentucky....................	337	254	27	62	5	235	2	5	1	10	629	767
Louisiana	312	279	50	46	181	29	1	1	4	9	697	741
Maine.........................	156	129	17	10	1	126	1	0	1	27	541	541
Maryland....................	269	196	21	7	1	221	3	5	11	25	1,148	1,333
Massachusetts.............	334	285	36	34	8	252	1	1	2	40	878	915
Michigan....................	843	703	107	89	22	553	18	5	49	45	703	791
Minnesota	836	470	78	217	55	275	89	63	59	12	396	660
Mississippi	327	232	36	60	6	188	25	3	9	89	634	634
Missouri	650	576	66	192	2	343	21	11	15	61	550	554
Montana.....................	362	358	186	0	0	174	1	0	1	0	173	175
Nebraska	333	333	25	196	0	106	6	0	0	0	342	342
Nevada	127	100	19	20	4	76	1	4	3	3	968	1,125
New Hampshire	97	97	18	0	0	76	2	0	1	0	734	734
New Jersey.................	462	397	65	36	7	325	14	2	13	55	1,015	1,095
New Mexico................	205	169	34	37	6	112	6	1	9	1	556	645
New York....................	995	880	100	138	28	622	16	0	91	25	906	962
North Carolina	390	372	19	8	21	332	4	2	4	7	1,016	1,046
North Dakota	200	193	14	131	4	37	4	1	9	7	234	234
Ohio...........................	1,003	915	160	137	37	583	28	17	41	75	697	714
Oklahoma...................	583	583	100	0	0	400	62	3	18	0	346	346
Oregon.......................	274	241	37	33	5	187	7	3	2	0	686	762
Pennsylvania...............	802	713	104	160	9	412	29	9	79	81	899	909
Rhode Island	68	50	8	0	0	50	4	1	5	13	860	987
South Carolina..................	285	227	29	14	9	206	13	9	5	40	922	961
South Dakota....................	281	266	96	11	0	174	0	0	0	0	158	163
Tennessee	354	317	28	27	3	257	19	12	8	23	813	842
Texas	1,835	1,480	344	182	12	1,225	16	10	46	30	763	916
Utah	309	220	95	35	11	60	74	7	27	2	674	916
Vermont.....................	69	55	8	21	0	40	0	0	0	14	642	642
Virginia.......................	412	346	31	5	36	295	3	0	42	48	1,103	1,151
Washington.................	592	447	111	66	23	335	25	15	17	10	627	792
West Virginia...............	178	132	18	19	2	123	10	3	3	33	618	676
Wisconsin	593	482	70	57	10	402	14	31	9	1	525	628
Wyoming.....................	108	94	31	7	3	61	5	0	1	0	331	365

See notes at end of table.

Public secondary schools, by grade span, average school size, and state or jurisdiction: 2003–04—Continued

State or jurisdiction	Total, all secondary schools	Total, all regular secondary schools[1]	Schools, by grade span							Vocational schools[2]	Average number of students per school[3]	
			Grades 7 to 8 and 7 to 9	Grades 7 to 12	Grades 8 to 12	Grades 9 to 12	Grades 10 to 12	Other spans ending with grade 12	Other grade spans		All secondary schools	Regular secondary schools[1]
1	2	3	4	5	6	7	8	9	10	11	12	13
Bureau of Indian Affairs	26	26	1	8	0	17	0	0	0	0	365	365
Department of Defense dependents schools												
Domestic schools...........	7	7	2	0	0	5	0	0	0	0	504	504
Overseas schools	39	39	2	22	1	14	0	0	0	0	469	469
Other jurisdictions												
American Samoa	6	5	0	0	0	6	0	0	0	1	676	737
Guam	4	4	0	0	0	4	0	0	0	0	2,256	2,256
Northern Marianas.........	6	6	1	1	0	4	0	0	0	0	682	682
Puerto Rico.................	358	335	172	28	0	5	142	0	11	14	584	590
Virgin Islands	10	8	5	0	0	4	1	0	0	1	850	950

[1]Excludes vocational, special education, and alternative schools.
[2]Vocational schools are also included under appropriate grade span.
[3]Average for schools reporting enrollment data.
NOTE: Includes schools with no grade lower than 7. Excludes schools not reported by grade level, such as some special education schools for the disabled.

SOURCE: U.S. Department of Education, National Center for Education Statistics, Common Core of Data (CCD), "Public Elementary/Secondary School Universe Survey," 2003–04. (This table was prepared July 2005.)

States requiring testing for initial certification of teachers, by skills or knowledge assessment and state: 2004 and 2005

State	Assessment for certification, 2004					Assessment for certification, 2005				
	Basic skills exam	Subject-matter exam	General knowledge exam	Knowledge of teaching exam	Assessment of teaching performance	Basic skills exam	Subject-matter exam	General knowledge exam	Knowledge of exam teaching	Assessment of teaching performance
1	2	3	4	5	6	7	8	9	10	11
Alabama	X	(1)		(1)	X	X	X		X	X
Alaska	X									
Arizona		X		X	X		X		X	
Arkansas	X	X		X	X	X				X
California	X	(2)			X	X				X
Colorado		X								
Connecticut	X	X				X	X		X	X
Delaware	X					X	X	(3)		
District of Columbia	X	X			X	X	X			
Florida	X	X	X	X	X	X	X		X	
Georgia	X	X				X	X			
Hawaii	X	X		X			X		X	
Idaho		(3)	(4)	(4)			X		X	X
Illinois	(5)	(6)		X		X	X			X
Indiana	X	X				X	X			
Iowa	X									
Kansas		X		X			X		X	
Kentucky	(5)	X		X	X		X		X	X
Louisiana	X	X	X	X	X	X	X			
Maine	X									
Maryland	X	X		X	X	X	X		X	X
Massachusetts		(7)				X	X			X
Michigan	X	X	(8)			X	X			X
Minnesota	X		X	X		X	X		X	
Mississippi		X		X						
Missouri	(5)	X		(9)		X	X			X
Montana										
Nebraska	X									
Nevada	X	X		X						
New Hampshire	X	X				X	X			
New Jersey		X	(10)		X					
New Mexico	X	X	X	X		X	X		X	X
New York			X	X			X		X	
North Carolina	(5)	X								
North Dakota	(5)		X	X						
Ohio		X		X	X					
Oklahoma	X	X	X	X	X					
Oregon	X	X			(11)					
Pennsylvania	X	X	(12)	X		X	X		X	X
Rhode Island[14]		X							X	X
South Carolina	X	X		X	X		X		X	
South Dakota	X	X			X					
Tennessee	(13)	X		X		X	X		X	X
Texas		X		X						
Utah				(14)			X			X
Vermont	X	X				X	X			
Virginia	X	X				X	X		X	
Washington	(5)					X	X			X
West Virginia	X	X		X	X	X	X		X	X
Wisconsin	X					X	X			
Wyoming										

X State requires testing.

[1] Institution's exit exam.

[2] Subject-matter exam or completion of an approved subject-matter program.

[3] All secondary endorsements require a Praxis II content-area test.

[4] Early Childhood/Early Childhood Special Education Blended Certificate requires two Praxis II tests—Early Childhood and Early Childhood Special Education; Elementary Certificate requires two Praxis II tests—content and pedagogy; and Exceptional Child Certificate requires two Praxis II tests—basic skills for special education and specific special education area.

[5] For admission to teacher education program.

[6] Prior to student teaching.

[7] Two-part exam covers communication and literacy skills and the subject-matter knowledge for the certificate.

[8] Elementary certificate exam (subject-area exam).

[9] If no subject knowledge assessment is designated.

[10] For elementary education.

[11] For Oregon graduates.

[12] Includes mathematics.

[13] Basic skills exams in reading, math, and writing are covered in the Praxis Pre-Professional Skills Test.

[14] Level I license requirement.

SOURCE: National Association of State Directors of Teacher Education and Certification, *The NASDTEC Manual on the Preparation & Certification of Educational Personnel in the United States & Canada, 2004 and 2005.* (This table was prepared August 2005.)

Public and private elementary and secondary teachers, enrollment, and pupil/teacher ratios: Selected years, fall 1955 through fall 2014

Year	Teachers (in thousands)			Enrollment (in thousands)			Pupil/teacher ratio		
	Total	Public	Private	Total	Public	Private	Total	Public	Private
1	2	3	4	5	6	7	8	9	10
1955..............	1,286	1,141	[1] 145	35,280	30,680	[1] 4,600	27.4	26.9	[1] 31.7
1960..............	1,600	1,408	[1] 192	42,181	36,281	[1] 5,900	26.4	25.8	[1] 30.7
1965..............	1,933	1,710	223	48,473	42,173	6,300	25.1	24.7	28.3
1970..............	2,292	2,059	233	51,257	45,894	5,363	22.4	22.3	23.0
1971..............	2,293	2,063	[1] 230	51,271	46,071	[1] 5,200	22.4	22.3	[1] 22.6
1972..............	2,337	2,106	[1] 231	50,726	45,726	[1] 5,000	21.7	21.7	[1] 21.6
1973..............	2,372	2,136	[1] 236	50,446	45,446	[1] 5,000	21.3	21.3	[1] 21.2
1974..............	2,410	2,165	[1] 245	50,073	45,073	[1] 5,000	20.8	20.8	[1] 20.4
1975..............	2,453	2,198	[1] 255	49,819	44,819	[1] 5,000	20.3	20.4	[1] 19.6
1976..............	2,457	2,189	268	49,478	44,311	5,167	20.1	20.2	19.3
1977..............	2,488	2,209	279	48,717	43,577	5,140	19.6	19.7	18.4
1978..............	2,479	2,207	272	47,637	42,551	5,086	19.2	19.3	18.7
1979..............	2,461	2,185	[1] 276	46,651	41,651	[1] 5,000	19.0	19.1	[1] 18.1
1980..............	2,485	2,184	301	46,208	40,877	5,331	18.6	18.7	17.7
1981..............	2,440	2,127	[1] 313	45,544	40,044	[1] 5,500	18.7	18.8	[1] 17.6
1982..............	2,458	2,133	[1] 325	45,166	39,566	[1] 5,600	18.4	18.6	[1] 17.2
1983..............	2,476	2,139	337	44,967	39,252	5,715	18.2	18.4	17.0
1984..............	2,508	2,168	[1] 340	44,908	39,208	[1] 5,700	17.9	18.1	[1] 16.8
1985..............	2,549	2,206	343	44,979	39,422	5,557	17.6	17.9	16.2
1986..............	2,592	2,244	[1] 348	45,205	39,753	[1] 5,452	17.4	17.7	[1] 15.7
1987..............	2,631	2,279	352	45,487	40,008	5,479	17.3	17.6	15.6
1988..............	2,668	2,323	[1] 345	45,430	40,189	[1] 5,242	17.0	17.3	[1] 15.2
1989..............	2,734	2,357	377	45,741	40,543	5,198	16.7	17.2	13.8
1990..............	2,753	2,398	[1] 355	46,451	41,217	[1] 5,234	16.9	17.2	[1] 14.7
1991..............	2,787	2,432	355	47,322	42,047	5,275	17.0	17.3	14.9
1992..............	2,822	2,459	[1] 363	48,145	42,823	[1] 5,322	17.1	17.4	[1] 14.7
1993..............	2,870	2,504	366	48,813	43,465	5,348	17.0	17.4	14.6
1994..............	2,926	2,552	[1] 374	49,609	44,111	[1] 5,498	17.0	17.3	[1] 14.7
1995..............	2,978	2,598	380	50,502	44,840	5,662	17.0	17.3	14.9
1996..............	3,054	2,667	[1] 387	51,375	45,611	[1] 5,764	16.8	17.1	[1] 14.9
1997..............	3,134	2,746	388	51,968	46,127	5,841	16.6	16.8	15.1
1998..............	3,221	2,830	[1] 391	52,475	46,539	[1] 5,937	16.3	16.4	[1] 15.2
1999..............	3,306	2,911	395	52,876	46,857	6,018	16.0	16.1	15.2
2000..............	3,331	2,941	[1] 390	53,358	47,204	[1] 6,155	16.0	16.0	[1] 15.8
2001..............	3,390	3,000	390	53,992	47,672	6,320	15.9	15.9	16.2
2002..............	3,428	3,034	[1] 394	54,584	48,183	[1] 6,401	15.9	15.9	[1] 16.2
2003..............	3,447	3,049	[1] 399	54,860	48,541	[1] 6,319	15.9	15.9	[1] 15.9
2004[2]..............	3,501	3,100	401	54,593	48,270	6,323	15.6	15.6	15.8
2005[2]..............	3,526	3,122	404	54,725	48,375	6,349	15.5	15.5	15.7
2006[2]..............	3,570	3,161	409	54,993	48,574	6,419	15.4	15.4	15.7
2007[2]..............	3,601	3,188	413	55,102	48,664	6,439	15.3	15.3	15.6
2008[2]..............	3,625	3,209	416	55,154	48,696	6,458	15.2	15.2	15.5
2009[2]..............	3,650	3,230	420	55,221	48,740	6,481	15.1	15.1	15.4
2010[2]..............	3,680	3,256	424	55,352	48,842	6,510	15.0	15.0	15.3
2011[2]..............	3,718	3,288	430	55,551	49,004	6,547	14.9	14.9	15.2
2012[2]..............	3,769	3,333	436	55,839	49,248	6,591	14.8	14.8	15.1
2013[2]..............	3,825	3,382	443	56,225	49,584	6,641	14.7	14.7	15.0
2014[2]..............	3,887	3,437	451	56,688	49,993	6,695	14.6	14.5	14.9

[1]Estimated.
[2]Projected.
NOTE: Data for teachers are expressed in full-time equivalents. Data for private schools include kindergarten and a relatively small number of nursery school teachers and students. Ratios for public schools reflect totals reported by states and differ from totals reported for schools or school districts. Some data have been revised from previously published figures. Detail may not sum to totals because of rounding.

SOURCE: U.S. Department of Education, National Center for Education Statistics, *Statistics of Public Elementary and Secondary Day Schools*, 1955–56 through 1984–85; Common Core of Data (CCD), "State Nonfiscal Survey of Public Elementary/Secondary Education," 1985–86 through 2003–04; Private School Universe Survey (PSS), 1989–90 through 2001–02; and *Projections of Education Statistics to 2014*. (This table was prepared July 2005.)

Estimated average annual salary of teachers in public elementary and secondary schools: Selected years, 1959–60 through 2004–05

School year	Current dollars					Constant 2004–05 dollars[2]		
	All teachers	Elementary teachers	Secondary teachers	Wage and salary accruals per full-time-equivalent (FTE) employee[1]	Ratio of average teachers' salary to accruals per FTE employee	All teachers	Elementary teachers	Secondary teachers
1	2	3	4	5	6	7	8	9
1959–60.........	$4,995	$4,815	$5,276	$4,749	1.05	$30,958	$31,413	$34,420
1961–62.........	5,515	5,340	5,775	5,063	1.09	33,413	34,055	36,830
1963–64.........	5,995	5,805	6,266	5,478	1.09	35,398	36,080	38,945
1965–66.........	6,485	6,279	6,761	5,934	1.09	37,012	37,722	40,618
1967–68.........	7,423	7,208	7,692	6,533	1.14	39,749	40,629	43,357
1969–70.........	8,626	8,412	8,891	7,486	1.15	43,773	42,687	45,118
1970–71.........	9,268	9,021	9,568	7,998	1.16	44,723	43,531	46,170
1971–72.........	9,705	9,424	10,031	8,521	1.14	45,209	43,900	46,728
1972–73.........	10,174	9,893	10,507	9,056	1.12	45,559	44,300	47,050
1973–74.........	10,770	10,507	11,077	9,667	1.11	44,279	43,198	45,541
1974–75.........	11,641	11,334	12,000	10,411	1.12	43,086	41,949	44,414
1975–76.........	12,600	12,280	12,937	11,194	1.13	43,552	42,446	44,717
1976–77.........	13,354	12,989	13,776	11,971	1.12	43,615	42,423	44,993
1977–78.........	14,198	13,845	14,602	12,815	1.11	43,454	42,373	44,690
1978–79.........	15,032	14,681	15,450	13,825	1.09	42,066	41,084	43,236
1979–80.........	15,970	15,569	16,459	15,088	1.06	39,433	38,443	40,641
1980–81.........	17,644	17,230	18,142	16,520	1.07	39,044	38,128	40,146
1981–82.........	19,274	18,853	19,805	17,866	1.08	39,260	38,402	40,342
1982–83.........	20,695	20,227	21,291	18,950	1.09	40,418	39,504	41,582
1983–84.........	21,935	21,487	22,554	19,878	1.10	41,311	40,467	42,477
1984–85.........	23,600	23,200	24,187	20,819	1.13	42,773	42,048	43,836
1985–86.........	25,199	24,718	25,846	21,732	1.16	44,391	43,543	45,530
1986–87.........	26,569	26,057	27,244	22,650	1.17	45,787	44,905	46,951
1987–88.........	28,034	27,519	28,798	23,705	1.18	46,390	45,538	47,654
1988–89.........	29,564	29,022	30,218	24,655	1.20	46,762	45,905	47,796
1989–90.........	31,367	30,832	32,049	25,647	1.22	47,354	46,547	48,384
1990–91.........	33,084	32,490	33,896	26,794	1.23	47,357	46,507	48,520
1991–92.........	34,063	33,479	34,827	27,999	1.22	47,245	46,435	48,304
1992–93.........	35,029	34,350	35,880	29,058	1.21	47,113	46,200	48,258
1993–94.........	35,737	35,233	36,566	29,811	1.20	46,852	46,191	47,938
1994–95.........	36,675	36,088	37,523	30,606	1.20	46,742	45,993	47,822
1995–96.........	37,642	37,138	38,397	31,561	1.19	46,703	46,078	47,640
1996–97.........	38,443	38,039	39,184	32,789	1.17	46,374	45,887	47,268
1997–98.........	39,350	39,002	39,944	34,346	1.15	46,636	46,224	47,340
1998–99.........	40,544	40,165	41,203	35,978	1.13	47,234	46,792	48,002
1999–2000......	41,807	41,306	42,546	37,800	1.11	47,339	46,771	48,176
2000–01.........	43,395	42,929	44,013	39,257	1.11	47,509	46,999	48,186
2001–02.........	44,660	44,192	45,252	40,031	1.12	48,043	47,540	48,680
2002–03.........	45,776	45,480	46,095	41,004	1.12	48,185	47,874	48,521
2003–04.........	46,752	46,408	47,120	42,547	1.10	48,159	47,805	48,538
2004–05.........	47,750	47,487	48,100	—	—	47,750	47,487	48,100

—Not available.

[1]Calendar-year data from the U.S. Department of Commerce have been converted to a school-year basis by averaging the two appropriate calendar years in each case.
[2]Constant 2004–05 dollars based on the Consumer Price Index, prepared by the Bureau of Labor Statistics, U.S. Department of Labor, adjusted to a school-year basis.

NOTE: Some data have been revised from previously published figures.
SOURCE: National Education Association, *Estimates of School Statistics*, 1959–60 through 2004–05, and unpublished tabulations; U.S. Department of Commerce, Bureau of Economic Analysis, National Income and Product Accounts, 1959 through 2004. (This table was prepared January 2006.)

Estimated average annual salary of teachers in public elementary and secondary schools, by state or jurisdiction: Selected years, 1969–70 through 2004–05

State	Current dollars							Constant 2004–05 dollars[1]						Percent change, 1989–90 to 2004–05 in constant dollars
	1969–70	1979–80	1989–90	1999–2000	2002–03	2003–04	2004–05	1969–70	1979–80	1989–90	1999–2000	2002–03	2003–04	
1	2	3	4	5	6	7	8	9	10	11	12	13	14	15
United States	$8,626	$15,970	$31,367	$41,807	$45,776	$46,752	$47,750	$43,773	$39,433	$47,354	$47,339	$48,185	$48,159	0.8
Alabama	6,818	13,060	24,828	36,689	38,246	38,325	38,863	34,598	32,248	37,482	41,544	40,259	39,478	3.7
Alaska	10,560	27,210	43,153	46,462	49,685	51,736	52,424	53,587	67,187	65,147	52,610	52,300	53,293	-19.5
Arizona	8,711	15,054	29,402	36,902	40,894	41,843	42,905	44,205	37,171	44,388	41,785	43,046	43,102	-3.3
Arkansas	6,307	12,299	22,352	33,386	37,753	39,314	40,495	32,005	30,369	33,744	37,803	39,740	40,497	20.0
California	10,315	18,020	37,998	47,680	56,283	56,444	57,876	52,344	44,495	57,365	53,989	59,245	58,143	0.9
Colorado	7,761	16,205	30,758	38,163	41,275	43,319	44,161	39,384	40,014	46,435	43,213	43,447	44,623	-4.9
Connecticut	9,262	16,229	40,461	51,780	54,362	57,337	58,688	47,001	40,073	61,083	58,631	57,223	59,062	-3.9
Delaware	9,015	16,148	33,377	44,435	50,772	49,366	50,869	45,747	39,873	50,389	50,314	53,444	50,852	1.0
District of Columbia	10,285	22,190	38,402	47,076	50,763	57,009	58,456	52,192	54,792	57,975	53,305	53,435	58,725	0.8
Florida	8,412	14,149	28,803	36,722	39,465	40,604	41,081	42,687	34,937	43,483	41,581	41,542	41,826	-5.5
Georgia	7,276	13,853	28,006	41,023	45,533	45,988	46,526	36,923	34,206	42,280	46,451	47,929	47,372	10.0
Hawaii	9,453	19,920	32,047	40,578	44,464	45,479	44,273	47,970	49,187	48,381	45,947	46,804	46,848	-8.5
Idaho	6,890	13,611	23,861	35,547	40,148	41,080	42,122	34,964	33,608	36,023	40,250	42,261	42,316	16.9
Illinois	9,569	17,601	32,794	46,486	51,289	54,230	55,629	48,559	43,461	49,509	52,637	53,988	55,862	12.4
Indiana	8,833	15,599	30,902	41,850	45,097	45,791	46,851	44,824	38,517	46,652	47,387	47,470	47,169	0.4
Iowa	8,355	15,203	26,747	35,678	38,921	39,432	40,347	42,398	37,539	40,379	40,399	40,969	40,619	-0.1
Kansas	7,612	13,690	28,744	34,981	38,123	38,623	39,190	38,628	33,803	43,394	39,610	40,129	39,785	-9.7
Kentucky	6,953	14,520	26,292	36,380	38,981	40,240	41,002	35,284	35,853	39,693	41,194	41,032	41,451	3.3
Louisiana	7,028	13,760	24,300	33,109	36,878	37,918	38,880	35,664	33,976	36,685	37,490	38,819	39,059	6.0
Maine	7,572	13,071	26,881	35,561	38,121	39,864	40,940	38,425	32,275	40,582	40,266	40,127	41,064	0.9
Maryland	9,383	17,558	36,319	44,048	49,677	50,261	52,331	47,615	43,354	54,830	49,876	52,291	51,773	-4.6
Massachusetts	8,764	17,253	34,712	46,580	52,043	53,181	54,596	44,474	42,601	52,404	52,743	54,782	54,781	4.2
Michigan	9,826	19,663	37,072	49,044	54,071	54,412	55,693	49,863	48,552	55,967	55,533	56,917	56,049	-0.5
Minnesota	8,658	15,912	32,190	39,802	42,833	45,375	46,906	43,936	39,290	48,597	45,068	45,087	46,740	-3.5
Mississippi	5,798	11,850	24,292	31,857	34,555	35,684	36,590	29,422	29,260	36,673	36,072	36,373	36,758	-0.2
Missouri	7,799	13,682	27,094	35,656	38,826	38,006	38,971	39,577	33,784	40,903	40,374	40,870	39,150	-4.7
Montana	7,606	14,537	25,081	32,121	35,754	37,184	38,485	38,597	35,895	37,864	36,371	37,636	38,303	1.6
Nebraska	7,375	13,516	25,522	33,237	37,896	38,352	39,456	37,425	33,374	38,530	37,635	39,890	39,506	2.4
Nevada	9,215	16,295	30,590	39,390	41,795	42,254	43,394	46,762	40,236	46,181	44,602	43,995	43,526	-6.0
New Hampshire	7,771	13,017	28,986	37,734	40,519	42,689	43,941	39,435	32,142	43,760	42,727	42,652	43,974	0.4
New Jersey	9,130	17,161	35,676	52,015	54,166	55,592	56,600	46,331	42,374	53,859	58,897	57,017	57,265	5.1
New Mexico	7,796	14,887	24,756	32,554	36,687	38,067	39,328	39,561	36,759	37,374	36,861	38,618	39,213	5.2
New York	10,336	19,812	38,925	51,020	52,600	55,181	56,200	52,451	48,920	58,764	57,771	55,368	56,842	-4.4
North Carolina	7,494	14,117	27,883	39,404	43,076	43,211	43,313	38,029	34,858	42,094	44,618	45,343	44,511	2.9
North Dakota	6,696	13,263	23,016	29,863	33,210	35,441	36,449	33,979	32,749	34,747	33,814	34,958	36,508	4.9
Ohio	8,300	15,269	31,218	41,436	45,452	47,482	48,692	42,119	37,702	47,129	46,919	47,844	48,911	3.3
Oklahoma	6,882	13,107	23,070	31,298	34,854	35,061	37,141	34,923	32,364	34,828	35,439	36,688	36,116	6.6
Oregon	8,818	16,266	30,840	42,336	47,600	49,169	50,790	44,748	40,164	46,559	47,938	50,105	50,649	9.1
Pennsylvania	8,858	16,515	33,338	48,321	51,800	51,835	52,700	44,951	40,779	50,330	54,715	54,526	53,395	4.7
Rhode Island	8,776	18,002	36,057	47,041	51,076	52,261	53,473	44,534	44,451	54,435	53,265	53,764	53,834	-1.8
South Carolina	6,927	13,063	27,217	36,081	41,279	41,162	42,207	35,152	32,255	41,089	40,855	43,451	42,401	2.7
South Dakota	6,403	12,348	21,300	29,071	32,416	33,236	34,040	32,492	30,490	32,156	32,918	34,122	34,236	5.9
Tennessee	7,050	13,972	27,052	36,328	39,677	40,318	41,527	35,776	34,500	40,840	41,135	41,765	41,531	1.7
Texas	7,255	14,132	27,496	37,567	40,001	40,476	41,009	36,816	34,895	41,510	42,538	42,106	41,694	-1.2
Utah	7,644	14,909	23,686	34,946	38,413	38,976	39,965	38,790	36,813	35,758	39,570	40,435	40,149	11.8
Vermont	7,968	12,484	29,012	37,758	41,603	42,007	44,535	40,434	30,826	43,799	42,754	43,792	43,271	1.7
Virginia	8,070	14,060	30,938	38,744	43,152	43,655	44,763	40,952	34,717	46,707	43,870	45,423	44,969	-4.2
Washington	9,225	18,820	30,457	41,043	44,949	45,434	45,712	46,813	46,470	45,980	46,474	47,315	46,801	-0.6
West Virginia	7,650	13,710	22,842	35,009	38,508	38,461	39,139	38,820	33,853	34,484	39,641	40,535	39,618	11.2
Wisconsin	8,963	16,006	31,921	41,153	42,871	42,882	43,466	45,483	39,522	48,191	46,598	45,127	44,172	-9.8
Wyoming	8,232	16,012	28,141	34,127	37,876	39,532	40,392	41,774	39,537	42,484	38,643	39,869	40,722	-4.9

[1]Constant dollars based on the Consumer Price Index (CPI), prepared by the Bureau of Labor Statistics, U.S. Department of Labor, adjusted to a school-year basis. The CPI does not account for differences in inflation rates from state to state.

NOTE: Some data have been revised from previously published figures.
SOURCE: National Education Association, *Estimates of School Statistics*, 1969–70 through 2004–05. (This table was prepared January 2006.)

Federal on-budget funds for education and related programs, by agency: Selected fiscal years, 1970 through 2005
[In thousands of current dollars]

Agency	1970	1975	1980	1985	1990	1995	2000	2003	2004	2005[1]
1	2	3	4	5	6	7	8	9	10	11
Total	$12,526,499	$23,288,120	$34,493,502	$39,027,876	$51,624,342	$71,639,520	$85,944,203	$124,374,489	$131,720,129	$141,788,214
Department of Education	4,625,224	7,350,355	13,137,785	16,701,065	23,198,575	31,403,000	34,106,697	57,442,854	62,903,421	71,013,428
Department of Agriculture	960,910	2,219,352	4,562,467	4,782,274	6,260,843	9,092,089	11,080,031	12,423,631	13,009,615	13,808,319
Department of Commerce	13,990	38,967	135,561	55,114	53,835	88,929	114,575	166,000	176,500	155,800
Department of Defense	821,388	1,009,229	1,560,301	3,119,213	3,605,509	3,879,002	4,525,080	5,639,857	5,684,278	5,500,008
Department of Energy	551,527	764,676	1,605,558	2,247,822	2,561,950	2,692,314	3,577,004	4,053,579	4,116,387	4,145,927
Department of Health and Human Services	1,796,854	3,675,225	5,613,930	5,322,356	7,956,011	12,469,563	17,670,867	24,704,292	25,426,845	25,922,738
Department of Homeland Security	†	†	†	†	†	†	†	226,722	246,970	226,056
Department of Housing and Urban Development	114,709	-52,768	5,314	438	118	1,613	1,400	1,200	1,500	1,300
Department of the Interior	190,975	300,191	440,547	549,479	630,537	702,796	959,802	1,251,392	1,275,344	1,332,750
Department of Justice	15,728	61,542	60,721	66,802	99,775	172,350	278,927	503,089	525,270	541,916
Department of Labor	424,494	1,103,935	1,862,738	1,948,685	2,511,380	3,967,914	4,696,100	5,977,300	5,687,600	5,789,100
Department of State	59,742	89,433	25,188	23,820	51,225	54,671	388,349	494,747	490,017	620,715
Department of Transportation	27,534	52,290	54,712	82,035	76,186	135,816	117,054	130,300	129,090	124,800
Department of the Treasury	18	1,118,840	1,247,463	290,276	41,715	49,496	83,000	300	0	0
Department of Veterans Affairs	1,032,918	4,402,212	2,351,233	1,289,849	757,476	1,324,382	1,577,374	2,519,896	2,844,965	3,137,329
Other agencies and programs										
ACTION	†	7,081	2,833	1,761	8,472	†	†	†	†	†
Agency for International Development	88,034	78,896	176,770	198,807	249,786	290,580	332,500	525,400	571,000	550,100
Appalachian Regional Commission	37,838	45,786	19,032	4,745	93	10,623	7,243	13,204	8,237	8,100
Barry Goldwater Scholarship and Excellence in Education Foundation	†	†	†	†	1,033	3,000	3,000	3,000	3,000	5,000
Corporation for National and Community Service	†	†	†	†	†	214,600	386,000	498,000	493,000	569,000
Environmental Protection Agency	19,446	33,875	41,083	60,521	87,481	125,721	98,900	115,400	123,600	175,200
Estimated education share of federal aid to the District of Columbia	33,019	55,487	81,847	107,340	104,940	78,796	127,127	161,470	184,749	210,513
Federal Emergency Management Agency	290	290	1,946	1,828	215	170,400	14,894	†	†	†
General Services Administration	14,775	22,532	34,800	†	†	†	†	†	†	†
Harry S Truman Scholarship fund	†	†	-1,895	1,332	2,883	3,000	3,000	3,000	4,000	3,000
Institute of American Indian and Alaska Native Culture and Arts Development	†	†	†	†	4,305	13,000	2,000	5,000	6,000	6,000
Institute of Museum and Library Services	†	†	†	†	†	†	166,000	249,000	207,000	290,000
James Madison Memorial Fellowship Foundation	†	†	†	†	191	2,000	7,000	2,000	2,000	2,000
Japanese-United States Friendship Commission	†	†	2,294	2,236	2,299	2,000	3,000	3,000	3,000	3,000
Library of Congress	29,478	63,766	151,871	169,310	189,827	241,000	299,000	389,000	402,000	405,000
National Aeronautics and Space Administration	258,366	197,901	255,511	487,624	1,093,303	1,757,900	2,077,830	2,479,036	2,629,900	2,528,600
National Archives and Records Administration	†	†	†	52,118	77,397	105,172	121,879	243,000	244,000	260,000
National Commission on Libraries and Information Science	†	449	2,090	723	3,281	1,000	2,000	2,000	1,000	1,000
National Endowment for the Arts	340	4,754	5,220	5,536	5,577	9,421	10,048	11,583	10,531	11,139
National Endowment for the Humanities	8,459	63,955	142,586	125,671	141,048	151,727	100,014	100,934	125,071	119,325
National Science Foundation	295,628	535,294	808,392	1,147,115	1,588,891	2,086,195	2,955,244	3,954,505	4,104,589	4,224,180
Nuclear Regulatory Commission	†	7,093	32,590	30,261	42,328	22,188	12,200	13,400	11,800	8,600
Office of Economic Opportunity	1,092,410	16,619	†	†	†	†	†	†	†	†
Smithsonian Institution	2,461	5,509	5,153	7,886	5,779	9,961	25,764	40,799	41,850	49,826
United States Arms Control Agency	100	0	661	395	25	†	†	†	†	†
United States Information Agency	8,423	9,405	66,210	143,007	201,547	294,800	†	†	†	†
United States Institute of Peace	†	†	†	†	7,621	12,000	13,000	17,000	16,000	28,000
Other agencies	1,421	5,949	990	432	885	500	300	9,600	10,000	10,445

†Not applicable.
[1]Estimated except U.S. Department of Education, which are actual budget reports.
NOTE: To the extent possible, amounts reported represent outlays, rather than obligations. Some data have been revised from previously published figures. Detail may not sum to totals because of rounding. Negative amounts occur when program receipts exceed outlays.

SOURCE: U.S. Department of Education, National Center for Education Statistics, unpublished tabulations. U.S. Office of Management and Budget, *Budget of the U.S. Government, Appendix*, fiscal years 1972 through 2006. National Science Foundation, *Federal Funds for Research and Development*, fiscal years 1970 through 2005. (This table was prepared November 2005.)

Federal on-budget funds for education, by level/educational purpose, agency, and program: Selected fiscal years, 1970 through 2005

[In thousands]

Level/educational purpose, agency, and program	1970	1975	1980	1985	1990[1]	1995[2]	2000[3]	2003[4]	2004[5]	2005[6]
1	2	3	4	5	6	7	8	9	10	11
Total	$12,526,499	$23,288,120	$34,493,502	$39,027,876	$51,624,342	$71,631,845	$85,944,203	$124,374,489	$131,720,129	$141,788,214
Elementary/secondary education	5,830,442	10,617,195	16,027,686	16,901,334	21,984,361	33,616,134	43,790,783	59,274,219	62,653,231	67,959,233
Department of Education[7]	2,719,204	4,132,742	6,629,095	7,296,702	9,681,313	14,029,000	20,039,563	30,749,304	33,689,396	37,716,135
Education for the disadvantaged	1,339,014	1,874,353	3,204,664	4,206,754	4,494,111	6,808,000	8,529,111	11,253,024	12,486,303	14,638,210
Impact aid program[8]	656,372	618,711	690,170	647,402	816,366	808,000	877,101	1,097,047	1,238,536	1,329,712
School improvement programs[9]	288,304	700,470	788,918	526,401	1,189,158	1,397,000	2,549,971	6,752,890	7,459,849	8,419,049
Indian education	†	40,036	93,365	82,328	69,451	71,000	65,285	115,864	114,434	129,891
English Language Acquisition	21,250	92,693	169,540	157,539	188,919	225,000	362,662	565,126	644,956	839,578
Special education	79,090	151,244	821,777	1,017,964	1,616,623	3,177,000	4,948,977	8,490,699	9,749,398	10,226,542
Vocational and adult education	335,174	655,235	860,661	658,314	1,306,685	1,482,000	1,462,977	1,942,716	1,945,155	2,030,362
Education Reform—Goals 2000[10]	†	†	†	†	†	61,000	1,243,479	531,938	50,765	102,791
Department of Agriculture	760,477	1,884,345	4,064,497	4,134,906	5,528,950	8,201,294	10,051,278	11,215,285	11,725,259	12,643,027
Child nutrition programs[11]	299,131	1,452,267	3,377,056	3,664,561	4,977,075	7,644,789	9,554,028	10,828,285	11,206,422	12,163,890
McGovern-Dole International Food for Education and Child Nutrition Program[12]	†	†	†	†	†	†	†	†	150,000	88,000
Agricultural Marketing Service—commodities[13]	341,597	248,839	388,000	336,502	350,441	400,000	400,000	200,000	171,000	188,000
Special milk program	83,800	122,858	159,293	15,993	18,707	(11)	(11)	(11)	(11)	(11)
Estimated education share of Forest Service permanent appropriations	35,949	60,381	140,148	117,850	182,727	156,505	97,250	187,000	197,837	203,137
Department of Commerce	†	†	54,816	†	†	†	†	†	†	†
Local public works program—school facilities[14]	†	†	54,816	†	†	†	†	†	†	†
Department of Defense	143,100	264,500	370,846	831,625	1,097,876	1,295,547	1,485,611	1,684,258	1,642,139	1,698,606
Junior R.O.T.C.	12,100	12,500	32,000	55,600	39,300	155,600	210,432	252,058	292,737	307,051
Overseas dependents schools	131,000	252,000	338,846	613,437	864,958	855,772	904,829	1,056,100	959,296	995,965
Domestic schools[8]	†	†	†	162,588	193,618	284,175	370,350	376,100	390,106	395,590
Department of Energy	200	300	77,633	23,031	15,563	12,646	†	†	†	†
Energy conservation for school buildings[15]	†	†	77,240	22,731	15,213	10,746	†	†	†	†
Pre-engineering program	200	300	393	300	350	1,900	†	†	†	†
Department of Health and Human Services	167,333	683,885	1,077,000	1,531,059	2,396,793	5,116,559	6,011,036	7,570,973	7,727,454	7,785,402
Head Start[16]	†	403,900	735,000	1,075,059	1,447,758	3,534,000	5,267,000	6,666,783	6,774,420	6,843,230
Payments to states for AFDC work programs[17]	†	†	†	†	459,221	953,000	15,000	—	—	—
Social Security student benefits[18]	167,333	279,985	342,000	456,000	489,814	629,559	729,036	904,190	953,034	942,172
Department of Homeland Security	†	†	†	†	†	†	†	452	500	556
Tuition assistance for educational accreditation—Coast Guard personnel[19]	†	†	†	†	†	†	†	452	500	556
Department of the Interior	140,705	220,392	318,170	389,810	445,267	493,124	725,423	962,995	983,290	1,024,510
Mineral Leasing Act and other funds										
Payments to states—estimated education share	12,294	27,389	62,636	127,369	123,811	18,750	24,610	57,730	65,090	97,980
Payments to counties—estimated education share	16,359	29,494	48,953	59,016	102,522	37,490	53,500	81,000	85,000	128,000
Indian Education										
Bureau of Indian Affairs schools	95,850	141,056	178,112	177,265	192,841	411,524	466,905	512,562	520,611	517,647
Johnson-O'Malley assistance[20]	16,080	22,251	28,081	25,675	25,556	24,359	17,387	16,908	16,666	16,510
Education construction	†	†	†	†	†	†	161,021	293,795	294,923	263,373
Education expenses for children of employees, Yellowstone National Park	122	202	388	485	538	1,000	2,000	1,000	1,000	1,000
Department of Justice	8,237	9,822	23,890	36,117	65,997	128,850	224,800	445,400	482,500	506,100
Vocational training expenses for prisoners in federal prisons	2,720	3,039	4,966	8,292	2,066	3,000	1,000	8,000	4,000	—
Inmate programs[21]	5,517	6,783	18,924	27,825	63,931	125,850	223,800	437,400	478,500	506,100
Department of Labor	420,927	1,097,811	1,849,800	1,945,268	2,505,487	3,957,800	4,683,200	5,972,000	5,675,000	5,778,000
Job Corps	†	175,000	469,800	604,748	739,376	1,029,000	1,256,000	1,423,000	1,438,000	1,688,000
Training programs—estimated funds for education programs[22]	420,927	922,811	1,380,000	1,340,520	1,766,111	2,928,800	3,427,200	4,549,000	4,237,000	4,090,000

See notes at end of table.

Federal on-budget funds for education, by level/educational purpose, agency, and program: Selected fiscal years, 1970 through 2005—Continued

[In thousands]

Level/educational purpose, agency, and program	1970	1975	1980	1985	1990[1]	1995[2]	2000[3]	2003[4]	2004[5]	2005[6]
1	2	3	4	5	6	7	8	9	10	11
Department of Transportation	45	50	60	60	46	62	188	†	†	†
Tuition assistance for educational accreditation—Coast Guard personnel[19]	45	50	60	60	46	62	188	†	†	†
Department of the Treasury	†	847,139	935,903	273,728	†	†	†	†	†	†
Estimated education share of general revenue sharing[23]										
State[24]	†	475,224	525,019	†	†	†	†	†	†	†
Local	†	371,915	410,884	273,728	†	†	†	†	†	†
Department of Veterans Affairs	338,910	1,371,500	545,786	344,758	155,351	304,093	445,052	514,578	551,000	604,000
Noncollegiate and job training programs[25]	281,640	1,249,410	439,993	224,035	12,848	†	†	†	†	†
Vocational rehabilitation for disabled veterans[26]	41,700	73,100	87,980	107,480	136,780	298,132	438,635	514,578	551,000	604,000
Dependents' education[27]	15,570	48,990	17,813	13,243	5,723	5,961	6,417	—	—	—
Other agencies										
Appalachian Regional Commission	33,161	41,667	9,157	4,632	93	2,173	2,588	2,019	2,495	2,500
National Endowment for the Arts	†	3,686	4,989	4,399	4,641	7,117	6,002	9,035	8,951	9,469
Arts in education	†	3,686	4,989	4,399	4,641	7,117	6,002	9,035	8,951	9,469
National Endowment for the Humanities	20	149	330	321	404	997	812	203	326	325
Office of Economic Opportunity	1,072,375	16,619	†	†	†	†	†	†	†	†
Head Start[28]	325,700	†	†	†	†	†	†	†	†	†
Other elementary and secondary programs[29]	42,809	16,612	†	†	†	†	†	†	†	†
Job Corps[30]	144,000	†	†	†	†	†	†	†	†	†
Youth Corps and other training programs[31]	553,368	7	†	†	†	†	†	†	†	†
Volunteers in Service to America (VISTA)[32]	6,498	†	†	†	†	†	†	†	†	†
Other programs										
Estimated education share of federal aid to the District of Columbia	25,748	42,588	65,714	84,918	86,579	66,871	115,230	147,717	164,921	190,603
Postsecondary education	**$3,447,697**	**$7,644,037**	**$11,115,882**	**$11,174,379**	**$13,650,915**	**$17,618,137**	**$15,008,715**	**$29,499,694**	**$32,432,975**	**$36,405,123**
Department of Education[7]	1,187,962	2,089,184	5,682,242	8,202,499	11,175,978	14,234,000	10,727,315	22,706,436	25,340,999	28,769,589
Student financial assistance	†	†	3,682,789	4,162,695	5,920,328	7,047,000	9,060,317	14,092,384	14,968,595	14,667,843
Federal Direct Student Loan Program[33]	†	†	†	†	†	840,000	-2,862,240	5,115,949	3,246,326	1,333,342
Federal Family Education Loan Program[33]	2,323	111,087	1,407,977	3,534,795	4,372,446	5,190,000	2,707,473	1,216,003	4,661,638	10,210,063
Higher education	1,029,131	1,838,066	399,787	404,511	659,492	871,000	1,530,779	1,930,342	2,041,113	2,205,433
Facilities—loans and insurance[33]	114,199	16,292	-19,031	5,307	19,219	-6,000	-2,174	-5,702	-4,859	-567
College housing loans[33,34]	†	†	14,082	-164,061	-57,167	-46,000	-41,886	-31,590	31,691	-24,335
Educational activities overseas	774	1,881	3,561	1,838	82	†	†	†	†	†
Historically Black Colleges and Universities Capital Financing, Program Account	†	†	†	†	†	†	150	133	151	292
Gallaudet College and Howard University	38,559	111,971	176,829	229,938	230,327	292,000	291,060	336,261	342,593	326,085
National Technical Institute for the Deaf	2,976	9,887	16,248	27,476	31,251	46,000	43,836	52,656	53,751	51,433
Department of Agriculture	†	6,450	10,453	17,741	31,273	33,373	30,676	93,626	93,831	98,661
Agriculture Extension Service, Second Morrill Act payments to agricultural and mechanical colleges and Tuskegee Institute	†	6,450	10,453	17,741	31,273	33,373	30,676	93,626	93,831	98,661
Department of Commerce	8,277	14,973	29,971	2,163	3,312	3,487	3,800	4,200	4,000	4,000
Sea Grant Program[35]	†	1,886	3,123	2,163	3,312	3,487	3,800	4,200	4,000	4,000
Merchant Marine Academy[36]	6,160	10,152	14,809	†	†	†	†	†	†	†
State marine schools[36]	2,117	2,935	12,039	†	†	†	†	†	†	†
Department of Defense	322,100	379,800	545,000	1,041,700	635,769	729,500	1,147,759	1,673,399	1,780,339	1,907,602
Tuition assistance for military personnel	57,500	86,800	—	77,100	95,300	127,000	263,303	548,599	594,350	645,026
Service academies	78,700	86,200	106,100	196,400	120,613	163,300	212,678	268,708	286,222	292,774
Senior R.O.T.C.	108,100	116,500	—	354,000	193,056	219,400	363,461	521,221	525,239	577,500
Professional development education[37]	77,800	90,300	—	414,200	226,800	219,800	308,317	334,871	374,528	392,302

See notes at end of table.

Federal on-budget funds for education, by level/educational purpose, agency, and program: Selected fiscal years, 1970 through 2005—Continued

[In thousands]

Level/educational purpose, agency, and program	1970	1975	1980	1985	1990[1]	1995[2]	2000[3]	2003[4]	2004[5]	2005[6]
1	2	3	4	5	6	7	8	9	10	11
Department of Energy	3,000	3,000	57,701	19,475	25,502	28,027	†	†	†	†
University laboratory cooperative program	3,000	3,000	2,800	6,500	9,402	8,552	†	†	†	†
Teacher development projects	†	†	1,400	†	†	†	†	†	†	†
Energy conservation for buildings—higher education[15]	†	†	53,501	12,705	7,459	7,381	†	†	†	†
Minority honors vocational training	†	†	†	150	†	†	†	†	†	†
Honors research program	†	†	†	120	6,472	2,221	†	†	†	†
Students and teachers	†	†	†	†	2,169	9,873	†	†	†	†
Department of Health and Human Services	981,483	1,686,650	2,412,058	516,088	578,542	796,035	954,190	1,692,847	1,535,283	1,559,247
Health professions training programs[38]	353,029	599,350	460,736	212,200	230,600	298,302	340,361	882,396	698,256	700,000
Indian health manpower	†	†	7,187	5,577	9,508	27,000	16,000	31,000	29,000	30,000
National Health Service Corps scholarships	†	1,206	70,667	2,268	4,759	78,206	33,300	46,300	45,000	45,000
National Institutes of Health training grants[39]	†	154,875	176,388	217,927	241,356	380,502	550,220	711,441	740,506	762,247
National Institute of Occupational Safety and Health training grants	8,088	7,182	12,899	8,760	10,461	11,660	14,198	21,666	22,521	22,000
Alcohol, drug abuse, and mental health training programs[40]	118,366	83,727	122,103	43,617	81,353	†	†	†	†	†
Health teaching facilities[41]	†	353	3,078	739	505	365	110	44	†	†
Social Security postsecondary students' benefits[42]	502,000	839,957	1,559,000	25,000	†	†	†	†	†	†
Department of Homeland Security	†	†	†	†	†	†	†	33,900	41,100	42,500
Coast Guard Academy[19]	†	†	†	†	†	†	†	22,000	22,300	22,900
Postgraduate training for Coast Guard officers[43]	†	†	†	†	†	†	†	8,700	8,300	8,600
Tuition assistance to Coast Guard military personnel[19]	†	†	†	†	†	†	†	3,200	10,500	11,000
Department of Housing and Urban Development[34]	114,199	-55,418	†	†	†	†	†	†	†	†
College housing loans[33,34]	114,199	-55,418	†	†	†	†	†	†	†	†
Department of the Interior	31,749	50,844	80,202	125,247	135,480	159,054	187,179	234,197	246,154	269,640
Shared revenues, Mineral Leasing Act and other receipts—estimated education share	6,949	15,480	35,403	71,991	69,980	82,810	98,740	135,070	142,300	164,300
Indian programs										
Continuing education	9,380	13,311	16,909	24,338	34,911	43,907	57,576	71,356	76,212	78,619
Higher education scholarships	15,420	22,053	27,890	28,918	30,589	32,337	30,863	27,771	27,642	26,721
Department of State	30,850	50,347	†	†	2,167	3,000	319,000	387,000	399,600	528,200
Educational exchange[44]	30,850	50,347	†	†	—	†	319,000	387,000	399,600	528,200
Mutual educational and cultural exchange activities	30,454	50,300	†	†	—	†	303,000	372,000	381,600	509,200
International educational exchange activities	396	47	†	†	—	†	16,000	15,000	18,000	19,000
Russian, Eurasian, and East European Research and Training	†	†	†	†	2,167	3,000	†	†	†	†
Department of Transportation	11,197	11,885	12,530	55,569	46,025	59,257	60,300	65,000	66,000	66,000
Merchant Marine Academy[36]	†	†	†	19,898	20,926	30,850	34,000	58,000	56,000	56,000
State marine schools[36]	†	†	†	19,777	8,269	8,980	7,000	7,000	10,000	10,000
Coast Guard Academy[19]	9,342	9,780	10,000	11,857	12,074	13,500	15,500	†	†	†
Postgraduate training for Coast Guard officers[43]	1,655	1,855	2,230	3,499	4,173	5,513	2,500	†	†	†
Tuition assistance to Coast Guard military personnel[19]	200	250	300	538	582	414	1,300	†	†	†
Department of the Treasury	†	268,605	296,750	†	†	†	†	†	†	†
General revenue sharing—estimated state share to higher education[23,24]	†	268,605	296,750	†	†	†	†	†	†	†

See notes at end of table.

Federal on-budget funds for education, by level/educational purpose, agency, and program: Selected fiscal years, 1970 through 2005—Continued

[In thousands]

Level/educational purpose, agency, and program	1970	1975	1980	1985	1990[1]	1995[2]	2000[3]	2003[4]	2004[5]	2005[6]
1	2	3	4	5	6	7	8	9	10	11
Department of Veterans Affairs	693,490	3,029,600	1,803,847	944,091	599,825	1,010,114	1,132,322	2,005,318	2,293,965	2,533,329
Vietnam-era veterans	638,260	2,840,600	1,579,974	694,217	46,998	†	†	†	†	†
College student support	†	†	1,560,081	679,953	39,458	†	†	†	†	†
Work-study	†	†	19,893	14,264	7,540	†	†	†	†	†
Service persons college support	18,900	74,690	46,617	35,630	8,911	†	†	†	†	†
Post-Vietnam veterans	†	†	922	82,554	161,475	33,596	3,958	1,172	1,044	968
All-volunteer-force educational assistance	†	†	†	196	269,947	868,394	984,068	1,712,611	1,942,781	2,109,610
Veterans	†	†	†	†	183,765	760,390	876,434	1,548,421	1,768,253	1,905,181
Reservists	†	†	†	196	86,182	108,004	107,634	164,190	174,528	204,429
Veteran dependents' education	36,330	114,310	176,334	131,494	100,494	95,124	131,296	277,920	332,140	404,751
Payments to state education agencies	†	†	†	†	12,000	13,000	13,000	13,615	18,000	18,000
Other agencies										
Appalachian Regional Commission	4,105	2,545	1,751	—	—	2,741	2,286	9,045	2,500	2,600
National Endowment for the Humanities	3,349	25,320	56,451	49,098	50,938	56,481	28,395	34,058	29,824	29,000
National Science Foundation	42,000	60,283	64,583	60,069	161,884	211,800	389,000	535,000	566,000	561,000
Science and engineering education programs	37,000	60,283	64,583	60,069	161,884	211,800	389,000	535,000	566,000	561,000
Sea Grant Program[35]	5,000	†	†	†	†	†	†	†	†	†
United States Information Agency[45]	8,423	9,405	51,095	124,041	181,172	260,800	†	†	†	†
Educational and cultural affairs[44]	†	†	49,546	21,079	35,862	13,600	†	†	†	†
Educational and cultural exchange programs[46]	†	†	†	101,529	145,307	247,200	†	†	†	†
Educational exchange activities, international	†	†	1,549	1,433	3	†	†	†	†	†
Information center and library activities	8,423	9,405	†	†	†	†	†	†	†	†
Other programs										
Barry Goldwater Scholarship and Excellence in Education Foundation	†	†	†	—	1,033	3,000	3,000	3,000	3,000	5,000
Estimated education share of federal aid to the District of Columbia	5,513	10,564	13,143	15,266	14,637	9,468	11,493	12,668	18,380	17,755
Harry S Truman Scholarship fund[33]	†	†	-1,895	1,332	2,883	3,000	3,000	3,000	4,000	3,000
Institute of American Indian and Alaska Native Culture and Arts Development	†	†	†	—	4,305	13,000	2,000	5,000	6,000	6,000
James Madison Memorial Fellowship Foundation	†	†	†	†	191	2,000	7,000	2,000	2,000	2,000
Other education	**$964,719**	**$1,608,478**	**$1,548,730**	**$2,107,588**	**$3,383,031**	**$4,719,655**	**$5,484,571**	**$6,532,502**	**$6,576,820**	**$7,207,515**
Department of Education[7]	630,235	1,045,659	747,706	1,173,055	2,251,801	2,861,000	3,223,355	3,435,182	3,437,807	3,896,802
Administration	47,456	108,372	187,317	284,900	328,293	404,000	458,054	548,318	525,188	525,452
Libraries[47]	108,284	225,810	129,127	85,650	137,264	117,000	†	†	†	†
Rehabilitative services and disability research	473,091	709,483	426,886	798,298	1,780,360	2,333,000	2,755,468	2,871,797	2,893,992	3,350,748
American Printing House for the Blind	1,404	1,994	4,349	4,230	5,736	7,000	9,368	14,875	18,627	20,602
Trust funds and contributions[33]	†	†	27	-23	148	†	465	192	0	0
Department of Agriculture	135,637	220,395	271,112	336,375	352,511	422,878	444,477	473,620	462,125	467,631
Extension Service	131,734	215,523	263,584	325,986	337,907	405,371	424,174	450,520	439,125	445,631
National Agricultural Library	3,903	4,872	7,528	10,389	14,604	17,507	20,303	23,100	23,000	22,000
Department of Commerce	1,226	2,317	2,479	†	†	†	†	†	†	†
Maritime Administration Training for private sector employees[36]	1,226	2,317	2,479	†	†	†	†	†	†	†
Department of Health and Human Services	24,273	31,653	37,819	47,195	77,962	138,000	214,000	299,950	310,000	325,000
National Library of Medicine	24,273	31,653	37,819	47,195	77,962	138,000	214,000	299,950	310,000	325,000
Department of Homeland Security	†	†	†	†	†	†	†	192,370	205,370	183,000
Federal Law Enforcement Training Center[48]	†	†	†	†	†	†	†	185,000	147,000	171,000
Estimated disaster relief[49]	†	†	†	†	†	†	†	7,370	58,370	12,000
Department of Justice	5,546	42,818	27,642	25,517	26,920	36,296	34,727	19,589	25,170	25,816
Federal Bureau of Investigation National Academy	2,066	5,100	7,234	4,189	6,028	12,831	22,479	17,630	15,072	15,464
Federal Bureau of Investigation Field Police Academy	2,500	5,254	7,715	10,220	10,548	11,140	11,962	1,959	10,051	10,352
Narcotics and dangerous drug training	980	1,152	2,416	83	850	325	286	—	47	0
National Institute of Corrections	†	31,312	10,277	11,025	9,494	12,000	†	†	†	†

See notes at end of table.

Federal on-budget funds for education, by level/educational purpose, agency, and program: Selected fiscal years, 1970 through 2005—Continued

[In thousands]

Level/educational purpose, agency, and program	1970	1975	1980	1985	1990[1]	1995[2]	2000[3]	2003[4]	2004[5]	2005[6]
1	2	3	4	5	6	7	8	9	10	11
Department of State	20,672	28,113	25,000	23,791	47,539	51,648	69,349	107,747	90,417	92,515
Foreign Service Institute	15,857	20,750	25,000	23,791	47,539	51,648	69,349	107,747	90,417	92,515
Center for Cultural and Technical Interchange[44]	4,815	7,363	†	†	†	†	†	†	†	†
Department of Transportation	3,964	11,877	10,212	3,785	1,507	650	700	600	890	900
Highways training and education grants	2,418	3,250	3,412	1,500	—	—	—	—	—	—
Maritime Administration Training for private sector employees[36]	†	†	†	1,135	1,507	650	700	600	890	900
Urban mass transportation—managerial training grants[50]	1,546	2,627	500	1,150	†	†	†	†	†	†
Federal Aviation Administration[51] Air traffic controllers second career program	—	6,000	6,300	—	—	—	—	—	—	—
Department of the Treasury	18	3,096	14,584	16,160	41,488	48,000	83,000	†	†	†
Federal Law Enforcement Training Center[48]	18	3,096	14,584	16,160	41,488	48,000	83,000	†	†	†
Other agencies										
ACTION[52]	†	7,045	2,833	1,761	8,472	†	†	†	†	†
Estimated education funds	†	7,045	2,833	1,761	8,472	†	†	†	†	†
Agency for International Development	88,034	78,896	99,707	141,847	170,371	260,408	299,000	489,200	536,000	513,200
Education and human resources	61,570	58,349	80,518	115,104	142,801	248,408	299,000	489,200	536,000	513,200
American schools and hospitals abroad	26,464	20,547	19,189	26,743	27,570	12,000	†	†	†	†
Appalachian Regional Commission	572	1,574	8,124	113	†	5,709	2,369	2,140	3,242	3,000
Corporation for National and Community Service[52]	†	†	†	†	†	214,600	386,000	498,000	493,000	569,000
Estimated education funds	†	†	†	†	†	214,600	386,000	498,000	493,000	569,000
Federal Emergency Management Agency[53]	290	290	281	405	215	170,400	14,894	†	†	†
Estimated architect/engineer student development program	40	40	31	155	200	—	—	†	†	†
Estimated other training programs[54]	250	250	250	250	15	—	—	†	†	†
Estimated disaster relief[49]	—	—	—	—	—	170,400	14,894	†	†	†
General Services Administration Libraries and other archival activities[55]	14,775	22,532	34,800	†	†	†	†	†	†	†
Institute of Museum and Library Services[47]	†	†	†	†	†	†	166,000	249,000	207,000	290,000
Japanese-United States Friendship Commission	†	†	2,294	2,236	2,299	2,000	3,000	3,000	3,000	3,000
Library of Congress	29,478	63,766	151,871	169,310	189,827	241,000	299,000	389,000	402,000	405,000
Salaries and expenses	20,700	48,798	102,364	130,354	148,985	198,000	247,000	334,000	352,000	353,000
Books for the blind and the physically handicapped	6,195	11,908	31,436	32,954	37,473	39,000	46,000	48,000	49,000	52,000
Special foreign currency program	2,273	2,333	3,492	4,621	10	†	†	†	†	†
Furniture and furnishings	310	727	14,579	1,381	3,359	4,000	6,000	7,000	1,000	0
National Aeronautics and Space Administration Aerospace education services project	350	600	882	1,800	3,300	5,923	6,800	—	—	—
National Archives and Records Administration Libraries and other archival activities	†	†	†	52,118	77,397	105,172	121,879	243,000	244,000	260,000
National Commission on Libraries and Information Science	†	449	2,090	723	3,281	1,000	2,000	2,000	1,000	1,000
National Endowment for the Arts	340	1,068	231	1,137	936	2,304	4,046	2,548	1,580	1,670
National Endowment for the Humanities	5,090	38,486	85,805	76,252	89,706	94,249	70,807	66,673	94,920	90,000
Smithsonian Institution	2,461	5,509	5,153	7,886	5,779	9,961	25,764	40,799	41,850	49,826
Museum programs and related research	2,261	4,203	3,254	4,665	690	3,190	18,000	35,000	34,000	40,000
National Gallery of Art extension service	200	300	426	675	474	771	764	799	850	826
Woodrow Wilson International Center for Scholars	†	1,006	1,473	2,546	4,615	6,000	7,000	5,000	7,000	9,000
U.S. Information Agency—Center for Cultural and Technical Interchange[44]	†	†	15,115	18,966	20,375	34,000	†	†	†	†
U.S. Institute of Peace	†	†	†	—	7,621	12,000	13,000	17,000	16,000	28,000

See notes at end of table.

Federal on-budget funds for education, by level/educational purpose, agency, and program: Selected fiscal years, 1970 through 2005—Continued

[In thousands]

Level/educational purpose, agency, and program	1970	1975	1980	1985	1990[1]	1995[2]	2000[3]	2003[4]	2004[5]	2005[6]
1	2	3	4	5	6	7	8	9	10	11
Other programs										
Estimated education share of federal aid for the District of Columbia	1,758	2,335	2,990	7,156	3,724	2,457	404	1,085	1,449	2,154
Research programs at universities and related institutions[56]	**$2,283,641**	**$3,418,410**	**$5,801,204**	**$8,844,575**	**$12,606,035**	**$15,677,919**	**$21,660,134**	**$29,068,074**	**$30,057,103**	**$30,216,343**
Department of Education[57]	87,823	82,770	78,742	28,809	89,483	279,000	116,464	551,932	435,219	630,902
Department of Agriculture	64,796	108,162	216,405	293,252	348,109	434,544	553,600	641,100	728,400	599,000
Department of Commerce	4,487	21,677	48,295	52,951	50,523	85,442	110,775	161,800	172,500	151,800
Department of Defense	356,188	364,929	644,455	1,245,888	1,871,864	1,853,955	1,891,710	2,282,200	2,261,800	1,893,800
Department of Energy	548,327	761,376	1,470,224	2,205,316	2,520,885	2,651,641	3,577,004	4,053,579	4,116,387	4,145,927
Department of Health and Human Services	623,765	1,273,037	2,087,053	3,228,014	4,902,714	6,418,969	10,491,641	15,140,522	15,854,108	16,253,089
Department of Homeland Security	†	†	†	†	†	†	†	—	—	—
Department of Housing and Urban Development	510	2,650	5,314	438	118	1,613	1,400	1,200	1,500	1,300
Department of the Interior	18,521	28,955	42,175	34,422	49,790	50,618	47,200	54,200	45,900	38,600
Department of Justice	1,945	8,902	9,189	5,168	6,858	7,204	19,400	38,100	17,600	10,000
Department of Labor	3,567	6,124	12,938	3,417	5,893	10,114	12,900	5,300	12,600	11,100
Department of State	8,220	10,973	188	29	1,519	23	†	†	†	†
Department of Transportation	12,328	28,478	31,910	22,621	28,608	75,847	55,866	64,700	62,200	57,900
Department of the Treasury	†	†	226	388	227	1,496	†	300	†	†
Department of Veterans Affairs	518	1,112	1,600	1,000	2,300	2,500	†	†	†	†
ACTION	†	36	†	†	†	†	†	†	†	†
Agency for International Development	†	†	77,063	56,960	79,415	30,172	33,500	36,200	35,000	36,900
Environmental Protection Agency	19,446	33,875	41,083	60,521	87,481	125,721	98,900	115,400	123,600	175,200
Federal Emergency Management Agency	†	†	1,665	1,423	†	†	†	†	†	†
National Aeronautics and Space Administration	258,016	197,301	254,629	485,824	1,090,003	1,751,977	2,071,030	2,479,036	2,629,900	2,528,600
National Science Foundation	253,628	475,011	743,809	1,087,046	1,427,007	1,874,395	2,566,244	3,419,505	3,538,589	3,663,180
Nuclear Regulatory Commission	†	7,093	32,590	30,261	42,328	22,188	12,200	13,400	11,800	8,600
Office of Economic Opportunity	20,035	†	†	†	†	†	†	†	†	†
U.S. Arms Control and Disarmament Agency	100	†	661	395	25	†	†	†	†	†
Other agencies	1,421	5,949	990	432	885	500	300	9,600	10,000	10,445

—Not available.

†Not applicable.

[1]Excludes $4,440,000,000 for federal support for medical education benefits under Medicare in the U.S. Department of Health and Human Services. Benefits excluded from total because data before fiscal year (FY) 1990 are not available. This program has existed since Medicare began, but was not available as a separate budget item until fiscal year 1990.

[2]Excludes $7,510,000,000 for federal support for medical education benefits under Medicare. See footnote 1.

[3]Excludes $8,020,000,000 for federal support for medical education benefits under Medicare. See footnote 1.

[4]Excludes $8,000,000,000 for federal support for medical education benefits under Medicare. See footnote 1.

[5]Excludes $7,342,000,000 for federal support for medical education benefits under Medicare. See footnote 1.

[6]Estimated. Data for the U.S. Department of Education are actual numbers and those for the other agencies are estimates. Excludes $8,033,000,000 for federal support for medical education benefits under Medicare. See footnote 1.

[7]The U.S. Department of Education was created in May 1980. It formerly was the Office of Education in the U.S. Department of Health, Education, and Welfare.

[8]This program allowed the Secretary to make arrangements for the education of children who resided on federal property when no suitable local school district could or would provide for the education of these children.

[9]School Improvement programs include many programs, such as No Child Left Behind, 21st Century Community Learning Centers, Class Size Reduction, Charter Schools, and Safe and Drug-Free Schools.

[10]This program included the School-To-Work Opportunities program, which initiated a national system to be administered jointly by the U.S. Departments of Education and Labor. Programs in the Education Reform program have been transferred to the School Improvement program or discontinued in FY 2002. Amounts in this program reflect balances that are spending out from prior-year appropriations.

[11]Starting in FY 1994, the Special Milk program was included in the Child Nutrition program.

[12]The Farm Security and Rural Investment Act of 2002 (Public Law 107-171) carries out pre-school and school feeding programs in foreign countries to help reduce the incidence of hunger and malnutrition, and improve literacy and primary education.

[13]These commodities are purchased under Section 32 of the Act of August 24, 1935, for use in the child nutrition programs.

[14]This program assisted in the construction of public facilities, such as vocational schools, through grants or loans. No funds have been appropriated for this account since FY 1977, and it was completely phased out in FY 1984.

[15]This program was established in 1979. Funds were first appropriated for this program in FY 1980.

[16]The Head Start program was formerly in the Office of Economic Opportunity, and funds were appropriated to the U.S. Department of Health, Education, and Welfare, Office of Child Development, beginning in 1972.

[17]This program was created by the Family Support Act of 1988. It provides funds for the Job Opportunities and Basic Skills Training program. This activity was replaced by Temporary Assistance for Needy Families program.

[18]After age 18, benefits terminate at the end of the school term or in 3 months, whichever is less.

[19]This program was transferred from the U.S. Department of the Treasury to the U.S. Department of Transportation in 1967. This program was transferred to the U.S. Department of Homeland Security in March of 2003.

[20]This program provides funding for supplemental programs for eligible American Indian students in public schools.

[21]This program finances the cost of academic, social, and occupational education courses for inmates in federal prisons.

[22]Some of the work and training programs included in this program were in the Office of Economic Opportunity and were transferred to the U.S. Department of Labor in 1971 and 1972. Beginning in FY 1994, the School-to-Work Opportunities program is included. This program is administered jointly by the U.S. Departments of Education and Labor.

[23]This program was established in FY 1972 and closed in FY 1986.

[24]The states' share of revenue-sharing funds could not be spent on education in FYs 1981 through 1986.

[25]This program provides educational assistance allowances in order to restore lost educational opportunities to those individuals whose careers were interrupted or impeded by reason of active military service between January 31, 1955, and January 1, 1977.

[26]This program is in "Readjustment Benefits" program, Chapter 31, and covers the costs of subsistence, tuition, books, supplies, and equipment for disabled veterans requiring vocational rehabilitation.

[27]This program is in the "Readjustment Benefits" program, Chapter 35, and provides benefits to children and spouses of veterans.

[28]Head Start program funds were transferred to the U.S. Department of Health, Education, and Welfare, Office of Child Development, in 1972.

[29]Most of these programs were transferred to the U.S. Department of Health, Education, and Welfare, Office of Education, in 1972.

[30]The Job Corps programs were transferred to the U.S. Department of Labor in 1971 and 1972.

[31]These programs were transferred to the U.S. Department of Labor in 1971 and 1972.

[32]These programs were transferred to the Action Agency in 1972.

[33]Negative amounts occur when program receipts exceed outlays.

[34]This program was transferred from the U.S. Department of Housing and Urban Development to the U.S. Department of Health, Education, and Welfare, Office of Education, in FY 1979.

[35]This program was transferred from the National Science Foundation to the U.S. Department of Commerce, October 1970.

[36]This program was transferred to the U.S. Department of Transportation in FY 1981 by Public Law 97-31, from the U.S. Department of Commerce.

[37]Includes special education programs (military and civilian); legal education program; flight training; advanced degree program; college degree program (officers); and "Armed Forces Health Professions Scholarship" program.

[38]Does not include higher education assistance loans.

[39]Alcohol, drug abuse, and mental health training programs are included starting in FY 1992.

[40]Beginning in FY 1992, data were included in the National Institutes of Health training grants program.

[41]This program closed in FY 2004.

[42]Postsecondary student benefits were ended by the Omnibus Budget Reconciliation Act of 1981 (Public Law 97-35) and were completely phased out by August 1985.

[43]Includes flight training. This program was in the U.S. Department of the Treasury in 1965 and was transferred to the U.S. Department of Transportation in 1967. This program was transferred to the U.S. Department of Homeland Security in March of 2003.

[44]This program was transferred from the U.S. Department of State to the International Communication Agency (I.C.A.) in 1977. In FY 1998 pursuant to the Foreign Affairs Reform and Restructuring Act of 1998, this program was transferred to the U.S. Department of State.

[45]This program was transferred from the U.S. Department of State to the International Communication Agency (I.C.A.) in 1977.

[46]This program was in the "Educational and Cultural Affairs" program in FYs 1980 through 1983, and became an independent program in FY 1984.

[47]This program was transferred to the Institute of Museum and Library Services in FY 1997. Program was formerly in the U.S. Department of Education.

[48]This program was transferred to the U.S. Department of Homeland Security in FY 2003.

[49]The disaster relief program repairs and replaces damaged and destroyed school buildings. In FY 1994 and FY 1995, funds were for repairs due to the Northridge Earthquake in California. In FY 1994, $37.2 million was spent on school districts; $4.2 million was spent on community colleges and $43.8 million spent on universities. In FY 1995, $74.4 million was spent on school districts; $8.4 million on community colleges and $87.6 million on colleges and universities. This program was transferred from the Federal Emergency Management Agency to the U.S. Department of Homeland Security in FY 2003.

[50]This program was transferred to the U.S. Department of Transportation in FY 1968 from the U.S. Department of Housing and Urban Development.

[51]The Federal Aviation Administration, an independent agency, was transferred to the U.S. Department of Transportation in FY 1967.

[52]The National Service Trust Act of 1993 established the Corporation for National and Community Service. In 1993, ACTION became part of this agency.

[53]The Federal Emergency Management Agency was created in 1979, representing a combination of five existing agencies. The funds for the Federal Emergency Management Agency in FY 1970 to FY 1975 were in the other agencies. This agency was transferred to the U.S. Department of Homeland Security in March of 2003.

[54]These programs include the Fall-Out Shelter Analysis, Blast Protection Design through 1992. Starting in FY 1993, earthquake training and safety for teachers and administrators for grades 1 through 12 are included.

[55]This program was transferred from the General Services Administration to the National Archives and Records Administration in April 1985.

[56]Includes federal obligations for research and development centers and R & D plant administered by colleges and universities. FY 2003 and FY 2004 are estimated.

[57]Total outlays for FYs 1965 and 1970 include the "Research and Training" program. FY 1975 includes the "National Institute of Education" program. FYs 1990 through 2005 include outlays for the Office of Educational Research and Improvement and Institute for Education Sciences.

NOTE: Some data have been revised from previously published figures. To the extent possible, amounts reported represent outlays rather than obligations. Detail may not sum to totals because of rounding. Negative amounts occur when program receipts exceed outlays.

SOURCE: U.S. Department of Education, Budget Service, unpublished tabulations. U.S. Office of Management and Budget, *Budget of the U.S. Government, Appendix*, fiscal years 1972 through 2005; National Science Foundation, *Federal Funds for Research and Development*, fiscal years 1970 through 2004. (This table was prepared July 2004.)

U.S. Department of Education appropriations for major programs, by state or jurisdiction: Fiscal year 2004
[In thousands]

State or jurisdiction	Total	Grants for the disadvantaged[1]	Block grants to states for school improvement[2]	School assistance in federally affected areas[3]	Vocational and adult education[4]	Education for the handicapped[5]	Language assistance[6]	American Indian education	Degree-granting institutions[7]	Student financial assistance[8]	Rehabilitation services[9]
1	2	3	4	5	6	7	8	9	10	11	12
Total, 50 states and D.C.[10]	$53,989,179	$13,566,485	$5,892,003	$1,048,228	$1,823,341	$10,653,463	$542,302	$95,933	$1,933,684	$15,825,875	$2,607,866
Total, 50 states, D.C., other activities, and other jurisdictions	56,415,663	14,288,727	6,199,159	1,159,991	1,895,927	10,900,168	681,215	95,933	1,981,849	16,503,812	2,708,882
Alabama	971,504	216,080	97,680	2,981	32,882	172,447	1,879	1,734	71,425	318,609	55,786
Alaska	262,694	43,743	30,641	101,071	5,700	33,945	862	9,518	13,605	13,855	9,756
Arizona	1,247,016	268,007	103,904	154,088	36,763	166,854	16,454	9,956	25,742	414,762	50,486
Arkansas	574,081	139,907	62,504	654	19,891	108,076	1,872	1,085	29,628	175,529	34,937
California	6,702,294	2,105,302	738,558	65,347	224,481	1,166,585	161,549	6,460	171,207	1,802,367	260,438
Colorado	655,053	137,375	68,300	15,995	24,361	140,982	7,070	650	24,924	207,592	27,805
Connecticut	476,906	124,009	57,159	6,745	17,126	126,836	5,381	0	12,318	107,154	20,179
Delaware	150,179	36,949	30,669	84	6,923	31,394	725	0	7,234	26,432	9,769
District of Columbia	444,909	54,513	30,191	1,768	6,166	16,488	680	0	261,533	60,325	13,244
Florida	2,720,223	672,757	279,005	11,772	103,041	592,150	36,273	50	52,488	840,139	132,547
Georgia	1,527,380	436,563	172,667	19,955	56,064	292,011	11,255	4	60,884	398,891	79,087
Hawaii	243,798	49,294	30,929	44,980	8,816	38,434	2,187	0	17,684	40,108	11,366
Idaho	264,039	52,447	32,160	6,481	9,876	51,805	1,298	365	6,918	87,705	14,985
Illinois	2,201,727	583,773	245,737	19,870	72,918	483,587	25,929	102	65,787	604,610	99,415
Indiana	967,867	193,848	95,340	142	39,305	243,556	4,276	0	27,516	301,170	62,714
Iowa	497,986	74,907	48,059	449	18,780	115,509	2,193	148	21,829	187,534	28,577
Kansas	492,616	103,490	50,988	21,050	17,228	102,617	2,976	972	23,694	143,384	26,217
Kentucky	796,814	200,066	92,279	564	29,745	153,456	1,812	0	28,507	240,437	49,949
Louisiana	1,051,886	305,048	132,655	8,681	35,284	177,342	2,328	771	46,272	297,700	45,806
Maine	244,374	52,341	35,052	2,385	8,473	53,006	500	128	10,677	66,015	15,798
Maryland	769,381	182,573	85,993	6,986	28,496	191,196	5,868	176	36,590	191,196	40,306
Massachusetts	1,060,810	260,543	111,975	755	31,239	268,610	9,673	48	34,580	295,765	47,622
Michigan	1,721,750	467,795	209,962	3,851	60,890	379,978	8,220	3,126	32,871	462,829	92,226
Minnesota	765,431	120,343	75,528	13,638	27,277	181,571	6,109	3,281	28,727	266,467	42,490
Mississippi	734,896	184,211	88,065	3,642	22,675	113,772	972	363	31,789	249,028	40,379
Missouri	1,014,445	211,579	107,997	20,125	36,367	214,198	3,130	79	27,172	334,956	58,842
Montana	261,444	46,588	36,236	41,092	7,559	35,591	500	2,948	17,442	62,108	11,381
Nebraska	370,240	59,602	39,522	20,050	10,945	70,652	1,864	662	10,699	138,632	17,614
Nevada	258,739	72,791	34,938	3,591	13,044	62,989	5,707	748	4,611	46,246	14,074
New Hampshire	190,854	33,838	32,828	8	8,308	45,631	533	0	5,639	52,795	11,274
New Jersey	1,237,628	298,626	136,516	15,485	44,172	342,268	16,278	63	25,320	304,140	54,759
New Mexico	553,966	130,625	53,922	85,010	14,051	86,420	5,494	7,962	26,431	121,420	22,631
New York	4,262,351	1,374,189	490,180	11,285	108,542	730,008	47,908	2,965	71,845	1,283,073	142,355
North Carolina	1,400,050	315,387	141,347	14,447	53,705	295,267	8,884	3,518	66,149	416,413	84,934
North Dakota	199,753	34,672	31,032	27,064	5,832	25,704	500	1,567	11,196	52,520	9,665
Ohio	1,896,513	450,224	210,413	2,569	70,043	415,057	6,439	0	39,182	586,876	115,710
Oklahoma	781,499	162,251	81,276	37,641	25,175	139,221	2,916	21,995	41,276	229,885	39,863
Oregon	605,314	160,699	63,025	3,042	21,517	122,415	4,952	2,435	13,003	181,624	32,601
Pennsylvania	1,969,524	489,460	221,395	1,261	71,344	405,852	9,384	0	44,945	605,674	120,209
Rhode Island	231,194	51,457	30,858	4,076	8,759	42,459	1,768	0	6,673	74,259	10,884
South Carolina	787,697	187,751	80,758	3,244	29,386	167,496	2,443	0	39,759	230,228	46,633
South Dakota	443,482	39,789	31,431	42,130	6,343	30,689	535	3,048	8,193	271,518	9,805
Tennessee	1,011,588	227,346	104,873	2,636	38,362	220,855	3,686	0	39,374	311,653	62,804
Texas	4,521,245	1,309,715	509,263	77,710	153,289	894,651	74,350	319	128,426	1,175,386	198,136
Utah	446,421	60,677	39,420	9,179	17,739	102,053	3,397	1,044	14,013	173,860	25,041
Vermont	156,953	32,987	30,274	6	5,641	24,943	500	134	7,963	44,737	9,768
Virginia	1,495,837	221,503	107,971	38,472	42,325	265,781	7,273	10	43,584	706,974	61,942
Washington	962,235	208,448	97,266	53,018	34,131	211,817	9,607	4,406	32,330	263,774	47,436
West Virginia	405,323	105,989	50,557	22	13,363	72,712	500	0	22,354	114,290	25,535
Wisconsin	832,676	179,775	92,517	12,553	33,544	200,319	4,914	2,538	36,662	216,321	53,532
Wyoming	146,590	34,633	30,190	8,577	5,458	26,209	500	553	5,012	26,906	8,553

See notes at end of table.

507

U.S. Department of Education appropriations for major programs, by state or jurisdiction: Fiscal year 2004—Continued
[In thousands]

State or jurisdiction	Total	Grants for the disadvantaged[1]	Block grants to states for school improvement[2]	School assistance in federally affected areas[3]	Vocational and adult education[4]	Education for the handicapped[5]	Language assistance[6]	American Indian education	Degree-granting institutions[7]	Student financial assistance[8]	Rehabilitation services[9]
1	2	3	4	5	6	7	8	9	10	11	12
Other activities											
Indian Tribe (Set-Aside)	274,722	101,862	34,950	0	14,938	87,103	5,000	0	0	0	30,870
Other	412,880	79,678	50,413	109,968	21,243	22,579	127,782	0	0	0	1,217
Other jurisdictions											
American Samoa	29,305	9,845	7,712	0	409	5,935	1,162	0	540	2,692	1,010
Guam	48,543	8,648	11,292	0	876	14,636	1,200	0	1,734	8,186	1,971
Marshall Islands	1,903	0	0	0	0	0	0	0	1,903	0	0
Federated States of Micronesia	15,204	0	0	0	0	0	0	0	1,607	13,597	0
Northern Mariana Islands	20,130	4,282	4,366	0	511	4,973	912	0	1,605	2,297	1,183
Palau	1,775	0	0	0	159	0	0	0	1,615	0	0
Puerto Rico	1,581,295	505,426	188,443	1,600	33,318	102,328	2,725	0	36,716	648,134	62,605
Virgin Islands	40,725	12,501	9,980	195	1,131	9,151	132	0	2,445	3,030	2,160

[1]Title I, formerly called Chapter 1, Education Consolidation and Improvement Act of 1981, includes Grants to Local Education Agencies (Basic, Concentration, Targeted, and Education Finance Incentive Grants; Reading First State grants); Even Start; Migrant Education grants; Neglected and Delinquent Children grants; and Comprehensive School Reform Grants.

[2]Title VI, formerly called Chapter 2, Education Consolidation and Improvement Act of 1981, includes Teacher Quality State Grants; 21st Century Community Learning Centers; Educational Technology State Grants; State Grants for Innovation Programs; State Assessments, including No Child Left Behind; Education for the Homeless Children and Youth; Rural and Low-Income Schools Program; Small, Rural School Achievement Program; Fund for the Improvement of Education—Comprehensive School Reform; Safe and Drug-Free Schools and Communities State Grants; State Grants for Community Services for Expelled or Suspended Students; and Mathematics and Science Partnerships.

[3]Includes Impact Aid—Basic Support Payments; Impact Aid—Payments for Children with Disabilities; and Impact Aid—Construction.

[4]Includes Vocational Education State Grants; English Literacy and Civics Education State Grants; Tech-Prep Education; State Grants for Incarcerated Youth Offenders; and Adult Basic and Literacy Education State Grants.

[5]Includes Special Education—Grants to States; Preschool Grants; and Grants for Infants and Families with Disabilities.

[6]Includes Language Assistance State Grants.

[7]Includes Institutional Aid to Strengthen Higher Education Institutions serving significant numbers of low-income students; Other Special Programs for the Disadvantaged; Cooperative Education; Fund for the Improvement of Postsecondary Education; Fellowships and Scholarships; and annual interest subsidy grants for facilities construction.

[8]Includes Pell Grants; Leveraging Educational Assistance Partnership, formerly the State Student Incentive Grants; Federal Supplemental Educational Opportunity Grants; Federal Work-Study; Guaranteed Student Loans interest subsidies; and Federal Perkins Loans—Capital Contributions.

[9]Includes Rehabilitation Services—Vocational Rehabilitation Grants to States; Supported Employment State Grants; Client Assistance State Grants; and Independent Living State Grants; Services for Older Blind Individuals; Protection and Advocacy for Assistive Technology; and Protection and Advocacy of Individual Rights.

[10]Total excludes other activities and other jurisdictions.

NOTE: Data reflect revisions to figures in the *Budget of the United States Government, Fiscal Year 2006*. Detail may not sum to totals because of rounding.

SOURCE: U.S. Office of Management and Budget, unpublished tabulations. (This table was prepared July 2005.)

Appropriations for Title I, No Child Left Behind Act of 2001, by type of appropriation and state or jurisdiction: Fiscal years 2004 and 2005

[In thousands]

State or jurisdiction	Total, fiscal year 2004	Fiscal year 2005		State agency programs		Comprehensive School Reform	Even Start	Reading First State Grants	State Grants for Innovative Programs, fiscal year 2005	State Assessments, fiscal year 2005
		Total	Grants to local education agencies[1]	Neglected and Delinquent	Migrant					
1	2	3	4	5	6	7	8	9	10	11
Total, 50 states and D.C.[2]	$13,566,485	$13,906,260	$12,140,934	$47,649	$376,580	$187,255	$195,352	$958,489	$194,234	$389,521
Total, 50 states, D.C., other activities, and other jurisdictions	14,288,727	14,651,638	12,739,571	49,600	390,428	205,344	225,095	1,041,600	198,400	411,680
Alabama	216,081	223,002	194,434	1,202	2,704	2,988	3,051	18,623	2,873	6,599
Alaska	43,743	44,767	33,703	264	6,801	495	1,014	2,491	985	3,624
Arizona	268,007	287,362	248,135	1,744	6,410	3,667	3,899	23,507	3,839	7,809
Arkansas	139,907	145,535	124,322	303	5,142	1,881	1,927	11,961	1,758	5,202
California	2,105,301	2,115,160	1,782,922	3,240	126,526	27,680	27,810	146,982	24,373	33,527
Colorado	137,375	146,309	123,665	483	7,457	1,917	1,911	10,877	2,924	6,663
Connecticut	124,009	121,985	107,594	1,077	2,996	1,772	1,618	6,928	2,212	5,771
Delaware	36,949	38,414	33,817	294	303	495	1,014	2,491	985	3,643
District of Columbia	54,513	54,866	49,954	138	438	732	1,014	2,590	985	3,332
Florida	672,757	707,175	609,443	1,709	22,742	8,722	9,666	54,893	10,170	15,739
Georgia	436,563	455,777	401,779	1,090	8,643	6,129	6,314	31,822	5,804	10,270
Hawaii	49,294	53,414	47,518	244	739	669	1,014	3,229	985	3,942
Idaho	52,447	52,558	42,115	184	4,536	690	1,014	4,020	985	4,201
Illinois	583,772	597,357	538,448	1,971	2,333	8,371	8,402	37,833	8,309	13,407
Indiana	193,848	198,259	172,071	1,207	5,166	2,869	2,650	14,295	4,160	8,211
Iowa	74,907	73,979	63,983	518	1,669	1,132	1,014	5,663	1,814	5,272
Kansas	103,490	101,097	80,341	400	11,548	1,352	1,214	6,242	1,793	5,246
Kentucky	200,066	215,023	185,539	772	7,160	2,731	2,923	15,897	2,564	6,211
Louisiana	305,048	313,969	277,777	1,233	2,408	4,130	4,401	24,020	3,024	6,788
Maine	52,341	55,920	48,790	194	2,087	704	1,014	3,131	985	3,975
Maryland	182,573	190,256	171,796	1,140	524	2,645	2,721	11,430	3,593	7,500
Massachusetts	260,543	255,654	230,405	1,728	1,775	3,578	3,507	14,660	3,862	7,837
Michigan	467,795	485,184	434,040	592	8,546	6,560	6,717	28,730	6,703	11,396
Minnesota	120,343	123,757	108,893	176	2,357	1,729	1,654	8,948	3,271	7,097
Mississippi	184,211	190,685	167,439	764	1,358	2,496	2,590	16,038	1,952	5,445
Missouri	211,578	222,339	196,279	1,298	1,618	3,072	3,069	17,003	3,668	7,594
Montana	46,588	47,378	41,625	134	953	596	1,014	3,057	985	3,720
Nebraska	59,602	62,092	50,867	263	5,133	819	1,014	3,996	1,135	4,421
Nevada	72,791	76,563	67,770	268	224	990	1,076	6,234	1,481	4,856
New Hampshire	33,838	36,742	32,310	324	142	460	1,014	2,491	985	4,035
New Jersey	298,627	302,752	271,609	2,548	2,034	4,358	4,141	18,062	5,544	9,944
New Mexico	130,624	123,757	109,295	324	865	1,781	1,700	9,792	1,306	4,636
New York	1,374,190	1,355,345	1,232,206	3,143	9,468	18,841	19,191	72,497	11,760	17,730
North Carolina	315,388	331,745	287,345	854	6,952	4,462	4,560	27,573	5,308	9,648
North Dakota	34,672	36,395	32,136	69	221	464	1,014	2,491	985	3,488
Ohio	450,223	432,138	385,984	2,685	2,466	6,656	5,981	28,367	7,355	12,212
Oklahoma	162,251	160,319	140,047	589	2,010	2,259	2,157	13,256	2,248	5,815
Oregon	160,699	152,461	124,284	1,251	12,899	2,222	1,919	9,886	2,217	5,777
Pennsylvania	489,460	534,771	476,974	977	10,390	7,036	7,467	31,928	7,536	12,439
Rhode Island	51,457	53,522	47,986	509	69	759	1,014	3,184	985	3,810
South Carolina	187,750	201,109	178,282	1,261	536	2,668	2,819	15,542	2,646	6,314
South Dakota	39,789	41,226	36,167	244	815	495	1,014	2,491	985	3,639
Tennessee	227,346	230,018	203,229	472	531	3,234	3,220	19,332	3,587	7,492
Texas	1,309,714	1,370,937	1,173,904	2,742	57,381	17,685	18,550	100,675	15,713	22,681
Utah	60,677	65,480	55,430	677	1,736	884	1,014	5,740	1,817	5,276
Vermont	32,987	34,080	29,144	397	608	426	1,014	2,491	985	3,472
Virginia	221,503	242,750	216,198	977	793	3,377	3,409	17,996	4,635	8,805
Washington	208,448	213,876	176,327	710	15,455	2,934	2,756	15,695	3,924	7,915
West Virginia	105,989	114,096	103,025	475	84	1,492	1,615	7,405	1,027	4,286
Wisconsin	179,775	181,537	162,951	1,240	614	2,702	2,519	11,512	3,522	7,412
Wyoming	34,633	35,366	30,640	549	217	455	1,014	2,491	985	3,400

See notes at end of table.

Appropriations for Title I, No Child Left Behind Act of 2001, by type of appropriation and state or jurisdiction: Fiscal years 2004 and 2005—Continued

[In thousands]

State or jurisdiction	Total, fiscal year 2004	Fiscal year 2005							State Grants for Innovative Programs, fiscal year 2005	State Assessments, fiscal year 2005
		Total	Grants to local education agencies[1]	State agency programs		Comprehensive School Reform	Even Start	Reading First State Grants		
				Neglected and Delinquent	Migrant					
1	2	3	4	5	6	7	8	9	10	11
Other activities										
Indian Tribe Set-Aside............	101,862	102,599	91,322	0	0	1,567	4,502	5,208	0	2,000
Other nonstate allocations.....	79,678	80,221	8,436	1,240	10,000	9,103	16,631	34,810	0	11,680
Other jurisdictions										
American Samoa	9,845	10,554	8,462	0	0	132	307	1,653	263	379
Guam	8,648	9,411	7,546	0	0	117	274	1,474	566	815
Northern Marianas................	4,282	4,453	3,660	0	0	60	133	600	177	256
Puerto Rico.......................	505,426	524,699	467,838	711	3,849	6,932	7,484	37,885	2,778	6,479
Virgin Islands	12,501	13,441	11,371	0	0	177	412	1,481	382	551

[1]Includes Basic, Concentration, Targeted, and Education Finance Incentive Grants.
[2]Total excludes other activities and other jurisdictions.
NOTE: Detail may not sum to totals because of rounding. These are preliminary estimates for fiscal year 2005.

SOURCE: U.S. Department of Education, Budget Service, Elementary, Secondary, and Vocational Education Analysis Division, unpublished tabulations. (This table was prepared July 2005.)

U.S. Department of Agriculture obligations for child nutrition programs, by state or jurisdiction: Fiscal years 2003 and 2004
[In thousands of dollars]

State or jurisdiction	Total, fiscal year 2003	Fiscal year 2004							
		Total	Special milk	School lunch[1]	School breakfast	State administrative expenses	Commodities and cash in lieu of commodities[2]	Child and adult care	Summer food service
1	2	3	4	5	6	7	8	9	10
United States[3]	$11,072,230	$11,545,006	$14,371	$6,495,288	$1,732,059	$136,667	$988,881	$1,932,125	$245,614
Alabama	218,757	216,062	58	127,226	34,236	2,641	14,742	32,785	4,373
Alaska	30,965	31,145	8	18,293	3,598	516	1,511	6,876	343
Arizona	225,404	242,291	126	143,895	36,114	2,801	16,012	42,104	1,239
Arkansas	132,302	135,003	26	74,373	23,396	1,736	9,996	23,428	2,048
California	1,434,712	1,493,347	687	892,272	229,241	17,158	106,217	232,699	15,074
Colorado	105,213	109,780	136	66,229	13,490	1,443	8,076	19,602	805
Connecticut	88,247	89,000	355	54,357	11,598	1,096	10,932	9,870	791
Delaware	28,525	30,731	33	14,135	3,852	509	2,362	8,525	1,316
District of Columbia	26,330	38,099	6	14,398	3,808	417	13,968	3,121	2,382
Florida	638,052	655,189	89	376,648	103,116	7,223	51,907	99,946	16,260
Georgia	442,516	482,052	28	261,885	84,096	5,172	48,973	70,993	10,905
Hawaii	45,378	43,172	8	28,001	6,336	622	2,818	4,648	740
Idaho	46,057	48,530	201	30,546	7,019	612	3,434	4,395	2,323
Illinois	437,349	446,795	2,671	255,714	43,093	5,629	38,193	91,681	9,815
Indiana	188,472	205,058	288	118,015	26,511	2,281	25,537	28,532	3,894
Iowa	99,987	99,363	95	55,782	11,418	1,281	11,363	18,384	1,040
Kansas	102,728	110,506	136	56,285	13,438	1,469	8,816	28,900	1,461
Kentucky	186,933	200,009	103	111,633	37,571	2,262	17,429	23,675	7,336
Louisiana	276,131	290,600	46	156,763	49,631	3,431	22,438	51,246	7,045
Maine	38,547	39,258	79	19,940	5,124	626	3,231	9,457	801
Maryland	154,491	155,757	414	83,998	21,066	2,121	12,710	31,999	3,448
Massachusetts	180,479	182,209	448	91,712	22,637	2,487	18,127	42,156	4,642
Michigan	290,336	294,187	765	167,524	41,549	3,593	28,433	48,595	3,729
Minnesota	179,696	183,696	904	83,472	18,185	2,726	19,685	55,948	2,774
Mississippi	190,011	197,519	6	113,322	38,939	2,260	13,338	25,598	4,055
Missouri	211,783	219,698	425	121,694	34,239	2,535	19,049	35,296	6,460
Montana	33,446	38,599	37	15,946	3,805	584	8,716	8,645	866
Nebraska	72,924	76,049	80	35,914	7,054	1,178	8,896	22,108	819
Nevada	53,818	57,731	88	38,065	9,426	665	4,738	4,015	733
New Hampshire	23,012	24,862	195	13,544	2,691	380	4,766	2,634	653
New Jersey	223,633	229,955	781	131,050	22,298	2,775	23,340	43,021	6,691
New Mexico	122,330	124,640	14	57,136	18,708	1,739	7,809	34,094	5,141
New York	782,836	770,045	934	429,700	101,436	9,308	58,453	136,674	33,542
North Carolina	365,074	382,468	164	205,617	62,954	4,499	31,466	73,019	4,749
North Dakota	25,483	26,006	93	11,252	2,332	510	2,415	8,940	463
Ohio	328,420	349,495	724	193,723	47,164	4,026	41,058	57,444	5,357
Oklahoma	178,656	189,681	54	93,504	31,218	2,430	13,961	46,242	2,272
Oregon	115,154	120,755	148	63,794	22,782	1,585	9,085	21,721	1,640
Pennsylvania	322,719	347,428	710	198,589	44,476	3,766	37,675	49,741	12,471
Rhode Island	33,954	34,112	94	19,438	4,570	536	2,050	6,409	1,016
South Carolina	194,990	206,122	10	118,039	38,370	2,234	17,179	22,405	7,886
South Dakota	31,666	32,811	37	17,558	3,999	518	3,920	6,086	694
Tennessee	227,281	246,625	37	139,614	39,009	2,908	20,264	38,604	6,190
Texas	1,196,411	1,270,382	73	741,731	248,395	13,088	83,041	159,437	24,617
Utah	89,676	95,540	61	52,134	8,786	1,336	11,507	19,948	1,768
Vermont	17,625	18,005	113	8,849	2,745	351	1,736	3,861	349
Virginia	197,086	211,645	233	124,205	30,809	1,681	22,542	26,978	5,196
Washington	188,073	195,938	268	108,928	26,674	2,443	18,227	36,864	2,534
West Virginia	80,555	80,472	34	42,497	14,958	1,107	5,638	14,565	1,675
Wisconsin	151,369	159,232	1,223	87,785	12,170	2,025	19,422	33,660	2,948
Wyoming	16,639	17,352	23	8,566	1,930	350	1,683	4,553	247

See notes at end of table.

U.S. Department of Agriculture obligations for child nutrition programs, by state or jurisdiction: Fiscal years 2003 and 2004—Continued

[In thousands of dollars]

State or jurisdiction	Total, fiscal year 2003	Fiscal year 2004							
		Total	Special milk	School lunch[1]	School breakfast	State administrative expenses	Commodities and cash in lieu of commodities[2]	Child and adult care	Summer food service
1	2	3	4	5	6	7	8	9	10
Other activities									
Administrative costs and other costs	8,833	9,576	0	0	0	772	8,804	0	0
Department of Defense dependents schools........	6,774	5,341	0	5,328	12	0	0	0	0
Other jurisdictions...................	**198,086**	**194,531**	**1**	**119,555**	**30,181**	**2,603**	**12,867**	**19,949**	**9,376**
American Samoa	0	0	0	0	0	0	0	0	0
Guam......................................	5,015	5,945	0	4,340	1,353	213	0	39	0
Northern Marianas..............	0	0	0	0	0	0	0	0	0
Puerto Rico...........................	186,171	181,784	0	111,077	28,131	2,145	12,317	19,353	8,762
Virgin Islands	6,900	6,801	1	4,138	697	245	550	557	614
Undistributed[4]	24,348	185,323	-396	9,500	24,654	-472	36,766	103,622	11,648

[1]Includes the Special Meal Assistance program.
[2]Commodities are based on preliminary food orders for fiscal year 2004.
[3]Excludes other activities, other jurisdictions, and undistributed.
[4]Undistributed amount reflects the difference between preliminary state earnings reports and federal obligations as of September 30, 2004. Undistributed amount under school lunch includes obligations for American Samoa and the Northern Marianas Islands.

NOTE: Data are based on obligations as reported September 30, 2004. Detail may not sum to totals because of rounding.
SOURCE: U.S. Department of Agriculture, Food and Nutrition Service, Budget Division, unpublished tabulations. (This table was prepared July 2005.)

U.S. Department of Health and Human Services allocations for Head Start and enrollment in Head Start, by state or jurisdiction: Fiscal years 2001 through 2004

State or jurisdiction	2001 Allocations in thousands	Enrollment[1]	2002 Allocations in thousands	Enrollment[2]	2003 Allocations in thousands	Enrollment[3]	2004 Allocations in thousands	Enrollment[4]
1	2	3	4	5	6	7	8	9
United States[5]	$5,346,145	804,598	$5,627,581	810,472	$5,739,294	808,140	$5,828,994	797,579
Alabama	95,374	16,498	100,154	16,529	103,588	16,509	105,500	16,374
Alaska	11,656	1,586	12,104	1,839	12,126	1,817	12,353	1,634
Arizona	89,629	12,865	96,913	13,297	100,174	13,215	102,023	13,215
Arkansas	57,381	10,818	61,024	10,930	62,645	10,915	63,808	10,879
California	758,591	97,667	801,430	98,687	811,487	98,767	823,694	98,933
Colorado	61,805	9,826	65,716	9,872	66,428	9,843	67,676	9,820
Connecticut	47,931	7,207	49,985	7,224	50,604	7,129	51,401	7,148
Delaware	11,831	2,243	12,286	2,231	12,537	2,214	12,771	2,197
District of Columbia	23,203	3,343	24,091	3,403	24,408	3,403	24,865	3,403
Florida	236,056	34,657	252,370	35,610	255,501	35,350	260,307	35,574
Georgia	151,340	23,140	161,740	23,414	163,757	23,400	166,837	23,450
Hawaii	21,166	3,073	21,977	3,073	22,248	3,063	22,665	3,063
Idaho	20,158	2,890	21,663	3,347	21,820	2,939	22,411	2,957
Illinois	248,855	39,805	259,780	39,619	263,047	39,640	267,111	39,672
Indiana	85,241	14,256	88,667	14,145	93,523	14,148	95,093	14,234
Iowa	47,381	7,689	49,495	7,620	50,109	7,717	51,050	7,775
Kansas	44,951	7,897	47,909	8,013	49,503	7,924	50,433	7,949
Kentucky	99,054	16,419	103,473	16,190	104,829	16,091	106,799	16,071
Louisiana	128,484	21,969	135,048	22,136	141,892	22,108	144,497	21,982
Maine	24,770	3,958	26,661	4,002	26,991	3,970	27,344	3,979
Maryland	71,713	10,487	74,929	10,527	75,851	10,235	77,277	10,344
Massachusetts	99,675	13,004	104,182	13,040	105,476	12,981	107,299	13,011
Michigan	215,873	35,112	225,290	35,269	228,045	35,099	232,215	35,124
Minnesota	65,523	10,164	69,643	10,331	70,369	10,332	71,119	10,339
Mississippi	149,606	26,624	155,259	26,742	157,165	26,762	160,121	26,754
Missouri	108,305	17,718	113,256	17,646	115,663	17,573	117,837	17,473
Montana	18,944	2,971	20,117	2,982	20,365	2,952	20,747	2,945
Nebraska	32,142	4,982	34,580	5,252	35,008	5,203	35,709	5,080
Nevada	18,367	2,694	19,786	2,754	23,315	2,754	23,698	2,754
New Hampshire	12,388	1,632	12,861	1,632	13,018	1,632	13,257	1,632
New Jersey	120,245	15,329	125,176	15,262	126,711	15,099	127,761	15,130
New Mexico	45,919	7,618	49,185	7,749	50,852	7,651	51,790	7,451
New York	398,522	48,952	418,239	49,493	422,350	49,473	430,086	49,300
North Carolina	124,580	18,991	132,667	19,202	137,403	19,125	139,360	19,098
North Dakota	15,750	2,287	16,036	2,307	16,697	2,357	17,009	2,353
Ohio	226,942	38,072	236,999	38,081	239,770	38,017	244,102	38,029
Oklahoma	72,190	13,228	76,910	13,460	78,784	13,474	80,249	13,474
Oregon	54,785	9,129	57,105	9,199	57,704	9,052	58,893	8,716
Pennsylvania	209,346	31,104	219,115	30,986	222,603	30,908	226,002	30,868
Rhode Island	20,412	3,150	21,184	3,150	21,446	3,150	21,802	3,150
South Carolina	74,963	12,184	78,507	12,248	80,223	12,248	81,718	12,248
South Dakota	17,513	2,925	18,079	2,827	18,301	2,827	18,644	2,827
Tennessee	107,146	16,344	112,344	16,507	116,072	16,473	118,217	16,437
Texas	429,075	67,572	454,292	67,664	475,422	67,764	474,092	67,785
Utah	35,858	5,403	36,270	5,527	36,709	5,527	37,399	5,518
Vermont	12,553	1,573	13,023	1,573	13,183	1,573	13,429	1,569
Virginia	89,890	13,612	95,366	13,772	96,214	13,768	98,142	13,768
Washington	92,257	11,106	97,247	11,167	98,022	11,001	100,193	1,118
West Virginia	46,713	7,590	48,625	7,650	49,227	7,650	50,152	7,650
Wisconsin	83,337	13,478	86,941	13,489	88,082	13,515	89,784	13,532
Wyoming	10,760	1,757	11,882	1,803	12,028	1,803	12,252	1,793

See notes at end of table.

U.S. Department of Health and Human Services allocations for Head Start and enrollment in Head Start, by state or jurisdiction: Fiscal years 2001 through 2004—Continued

State or jurisdiction	2001		2002		2003		2004	
	Allocations in thousands	Enrollment[1]	Allocations in thousands	Enrollment[2]	Allocations in thousands	Enrollment[3]	Allocations in thousands	Enrollment[4]
1	2	3	4	5	6	7	8	9
Other activities								
Migrant programs	246,905	33,355	257,815	33,850	260,201	33,609	264,621	33,154
Support activities	—	†	210,255	†	†	†	†	†
American Indian/Alaska Native programs	171,289	23,632	181,794	23,837	183,412	23,802	186,704	23,737
Training and other assistance	—	†	—	†	169,688	†	174,078	†
Research, demonstration, and evaluation	—	†	—	†	20,000	†	20,000	†
Monitoring program review	—	†	—	†	26,051	†	39,746	†
Other jurisdictions	**240,376**	**43,650**	**259,125**	**44,290**	**268,137**	**44,057**	**261,973**	**41,500**
Puerto Rico	216,476	35,894	234,304	36,920	243,016	36,687	246,792	37,498
Pacific jurisdictions	14,381	6,209	14,943	6,209	15,128	6,209	7,262	3,060
Virgin Islands	9,519	1,547	9,878	1,161	9,992	1,161	7,919	942

—Not available.

†Not applicable.

[1]The distribution of enrollment by age was as follows: 4 percent were 5 years old and over; 54 percent were 4-year-olds; 35 percent were 3-year-olds; and 7 percent were under 3 years of age. Handicapped children accounted for 13 percent in Head Start programs. The racial/ethnic composition was American Indian/Alaska Native, 4 percent; Hispanic, 30 percent; Black, 34 percent; White, 30 percent; Asian, 2 percent; and Hawaiian/Pacific Islander, 1 percent.

[2]The distribution of enrollment by age was as follows: 5 percent were 5 years old and over; 52 percent were 4-year-olds; 36 percent were 3-year-olds; and 7 percent were under 3 years of age. Handicapped children accounted for 13 percent in Head Start programs. The racial/ethnic composition was American Indian/Alaska Native, 3 percent; Hispanic, 30 percent; Black, 33 percent; White, 28 percent; Asian, 2 percent; and Hawaiian/Pacific Islander, 1 percent.

[3]The distribution of enrollment by age was as follows: 5 percent were 5 years old and over; 53 percent were 4-year-olds; 34 percent were 3-year-olds; and 8 percent were under 3 years of age. Handicapped children accounted for 12.5 percent in Head Start programs. The racial/ethnic composition was American Indian/Alaska Native, 3.1 percent; Hispanic, 30.5 percent; Black, 31.5 percent; White, 27.9 percent; Asian, 1.8 percent; and Hawaiian/Pacific Islander, 1.0 percent.

[4]The distribution of enrollment by age was as follows: 5 percent were 5 years old and over; 52 percent were 4-year-olds; 34 percent were 3-year-olds; and 9 percent were under 3 years of age. Handicapped children accounted for 12.7 percent in Head Start programs. The racial/ethnic composition was American Indian/Alaska Native, 3.1 percent; Hispanic, 31.2 percent; Black, 31.1 percent; White, 26.9 percent; Asian, 1.8 percent; Hawaiian/Pacific Islander, 0.9 percent; and multiracial/other, 5.0 percent.

[5]Excludes other activities and other jurisdictions.

NOTE: Detail may not sum to totals because of rounding.

SOURCE: U.S. Department of Health and Human Services, Office of Human Development Services, unpublished tabulations. (This table was prepared July 2005.)

Average mathematics literacy, reading literacy, science literacy, and problem-solving scores of 15-year-olds, by sex and country: 2003

Country	Mathematics literacy			Reading literacy			Science literacy			Problem solving		
	Total	Male	Female	Total	Male	Female	Total	Male	Female	Total	Male	Female
1	2	3	4	5	6	7	8	9	10	11	12	13
OECD total[1]	489 (1.1)	494 (1.3)	484 (1.3)	488 (1.2)	472 (1.4)	503 (1.3)	496 (1.1)	499 (1.3)	493 (1.3)	490 (1.2)	489 (1.4)	490 (1.3)
OECD average[2]	500 (0.6)	506 (0.8)	494 (0.8)	494 (0.6)	477 (0.7)	511 (0.7)	500 (0.6)	503 (0.7)	497 (0.8)	500 (0.6)	499 (0.8)	501 (0.8)
Australia	524 (2.1)	527 (3.0)	522 (2.7)	525 (2.1)	506 (2.8)	545 (2.6)	525 (2.1)	525 (2.9)	525 (2.8)	530 (2.0)	527 (2.7)	533 (2.5)
Austria	506 (3.3)	509 (4.0)	502 (4.0)	491 (3.8)	467 (4.5)	514 (4.2)	491 (3.4)	490 (4.3)	492 (4.2)	506 (3.2)	505 (3.9)	508 (3.8)
Belgium	529 (2.3)	533 (3.4)	525 (3.2)	507 (2.6)	489 (3.8)	526 (3.3)	509 (2.5)	509 (3.6)	509 (3.5)	525 (2.2)	524 (3.1)	527 (3.2)
Canada	532 (1.8)	541 (1.9)	530 (1.9)	528 (1.7)	514 (2.0)	546 (1.8)	519 (2.0)	527 (2.3)	516 (2.2)	529 (1.7)	533 (2.0)	532 (1.8)
Czech Republic	516 (3.5)	524 (4.3)	509 (4.4)	489 (3.5)	473 (4.1)	504 (4.0)	523 (3.4)	526 (4.3)	520 (4.1)	516 (3.4)	520 (4.1)	513 (4.3)
Denmark	514 (2.7)	523 (3.4)	506 (3.0)	492 (2.8)	479 (3.3)	505 (3.0)	475 (3.0)	484 (3.6)	467 (3.2)	517 (2.5)	519 (3.1)	514 (2.9)
Finland	544 (1.9)	548 (2.5)	541 (2.1)	543 (1.6)	521 (2.2)	565 (2.0)	548 (1.9)	545 (2.6)	551 (2.2)	548 (1.9)	543 (2.5)	553 (2.2)
France	511 (2.5)	515 (3.6)	507 (2.9)	496 (2.7)	476 (3.8)	514 (3.2)	511 (3.0)	511 (4.1)	511 (3.5)	519 (2.7)	519 (3.8)	520 (2.9)
Germany	503 (3.3)	508 (3.6)	499 (3.9)	491 (3.4)	471 (4.2)	513 (3.9)	502 (3.6)	506 (4.5)	500 (4.2)	513 (3.2)	511 (3.9)	517 (3.7)
Greece	445 (3.9)	455 (4.8)	436 (3.8)	472 (4.1)	453 (5.1)	490 (4.0)	481 (3.8)	487 (4.8)	475 (3.9)	449 (4.0)	449 (4.9)	448 (4.1)
Hungary	490 (2.8)	494 (3.3)	486 (3.3)	482 (2.5)	467 (3.2)	498 (3.0)	503 (2.8)	503 (3.3)	504 (3.3)	501 (2.9)	499 (3.4)	503 (3.4)
Iceland	515 (1.4)	508 (2.3)	523 (2.2)	492 (1.6)	464 (2.3)	522 (2.2)	495 (1.5)	490 (2.4)	500 (2.4)	505 (1.4)	490 (2.2)	520 (2.5)
Ireland	503 (2.4)	510 (3.0)	495 (3.4)	515 (2.6)	501 (3.7)	530 (3.7)	505 (2.7)	506 (3.1)	504 (3.9)	498 (2.3)	499 (2.8)	498 (3.5)
Italy	466 (3.1)	475 (4.6)	457 (3.8)	476 (3.0)	455 (5.1)	495 (3.4)	486 (3.1)	490 (5.2)	484 (3.6)	470 (3.1)	467 (5.0)	471 (3.5)
Japan	534 (4.0)	539 (5.8)	530 (4.0)	498 (3.9)	487 (5.5)	509 (4.1)	548 (4.1)	550 (6.0)	546 (4.1)	547 (4.1)	546 (5.7)	548 (4.1)
Korea, Republic of	542 (3.2)	552 (4.4)	528 (5.3)	534 (3.1)	525 (3.7)	547 (4.3)	538 (3.5)	546 (4.7)	527 (5.5)	550 (3.1)	554 (4.0)	546 (4.8)
Luxembourg	493 (1.0)	502 (1.9)	485 (1.5)	479 (1.5)	463 (2.6)	496 (1.8)	483 (1.5)	489 (2.5)	477 (1.9)	494 (1.4)	495 (2.4)	492 (1.9)
Mexico	385 (3.6)	391 (4.3)	380 (4.1)	400 (4.1)	389 (4.6)	410 (4.6)	405 (3.5)	410 (3.9)	400 (3.9)	384 (4.3)	387 (5.0)	382 (4.7)
Netherlands	538 (3.1)	540 (3.1)	535 (3.5)	513 (2.9)	503 (3.7)	524 (3.2)	524 (3.1)	527 (4.2)	522 (3.6)	520 (3.0)	522 (3.6)	518 (3.6)
New Zealand	523 (2.3)	531 (2.8)	516 (3.2)	522 (2.5)	508 (3.1)	535 (3.3)	521 (2.4)	529 (3.0)	513 (3.4)	533 (2.2)	531 (2.6)	534 (3.1)
Norway	495 (2.4)	498 (2.8)	492 (2.9)	500 (2.8)	475 (3.4)	525 (3.4)	484 (2.9)	485 (3.5)	483 (3.3)	490 (2.6)	486 (3.1)	494 (3.2)
Poland	490 (2.5)	493 (3.0)	487 (2.9)	497 (2.9)	477 (3.6)	516 (3.2)	498 (2.9)	501 (3.2)	494 (3.4)	487 (2.8)	486 (3.4)	487 (3.9)
Portugal	466 (3.4)	472 (4.2)	460 (3.4)	478 (3.7)	459 (4.3)	495 (3.7)	468 (3.5)	471 (4.0)	465 (3.6)	470 (3.9)	470 (4.6)	470 (3.9)
Slovak Republic	498 (3.3)	507 (3.9)	489 (3.6)	469 (3.1)	453 (4.3)	486 (3.3)	495 (3.7)	502 (4.3)	487 (3.9)	492 (3.4)	495 (4.1)	488 (3.6)
Spain	485 (2.4)	490 (3.4)	481 (2.2)	481 (2.6)	461 (3.8)	500 (2.5)	487 (2.6)	489 (3.9)	485 (2.6)	482 (2.7)	479 (3.6)	485 (2.6)
Sweden	509 (2.6)	512 (3.0)	506 (3.1)	514 (2.4)	496 (2.8)	533 (2.9)	506 (2.7)	509 (3.1)	504 (3.5)	509 (2.4)	504 (3.0)	514 (2.8)
Switzerland	527 (3.4)	535 (4.7)	518 (3.6)	499 (3.3)	482 (4.4)	517 (3.1)	513 (3.7)	518 (5.0)	508 (3.9)	521 (3.0)	520 (4.0)	523 (3.3)
Turkey[3]	423 (6.7)	430 (7.9)	415 (6.7)	441 (5.8)	426 (6.8)	459 (6.1)	434 (5.9)	434 (6.7)	434 (6.4)	408 (6.0)	408 (7.3)	406 (5.8)
United Kingdom[3]	508 (2.4)	512 (2.9)	505 (3.9)	507 (2.5)	492 (3.1)	520 (3.6)	518 (2.5)	520 (3.1)	517 (4.0)	510 (2.4)	506 (3.0)	514 (3.5)
United States	483 (2.9)	486 (3.3)	480 (3.2)	495 (3.2)	479 (3.7)	511 (3.5)	491 (3.1)	494 (3.9)	489 (3.5)	477 (3.1)	477 (3.4)	478 (3.5)
Non-OECD countries												
Brazil	356 (4.8)	365 (6.1)	348 (4.4)	403 (4.6)	384 (5.8)	419 (4.1)	390 (4.3)	393 (5.3)	387 (4.3)	371 (4.8)	374 (6.0)	368 (4.3)
Hong Kong-China	550 (4.5)	552 (6.5)	548 (4.6)	510 (3.7)	494 (5.3)	525 (3.5)	539 (4.3)	538 (6.1)	541 (4.2)	548 (4.2)	545 (6.2)	550 (4.0)
Indonesia	360 (3.9)	362 (3.9)	358 (4.6)	382 (3.4)	369 (3.4)	394 (3.9)	395 (3.2)	396 (3.1)	394 (3.8)	361 (3.3)	358 (3.1)	365 (4.0)
Latvia	483 (3.7)	485 (4.8)	482 (3.6)	491 (3.7)	470 (4.5)	509 (3.7)	489 (3.9)	487 (5.1)	491 (3.9)	483 (3.9)	481 (5.1)	484 (4.0)
Liechtenstein	536 (4.1)	538 (7.2)	521 (6.3)	525 (3.6)	517 (7.2)	534 (6.5)	525 (4.3)	538 (7.7)	512 (7.3)	529 (3.9)	535 (6.6)	524 (5.9)
Macao-China	527 (2.9)	538 (4.8)	517 (3.3)	498 (2.2)	491 (3.6)	504 (2.8)	525 (3.0)	529 (5.0)	521 (4.0)	532 (2.5)	538 (4.3)	527 (3.2)
Russian Federation	468 (4.2)	473 (5.3)	463 (4.2)	442 (3.9)	428 (4.7)	456 (3.7)	489 (4.1)	494 (5.3)	485 (4.0)	479 (4.6)	480 (5.9)	477 (4.4)
Serbia and Montenegro	437 (3.8)	437 (4.2)	436 (4.5)	412 (3.6)	390 (3.9)	433 (3.9)	436 (3.5)	434 (3.7)	439 (4.2)	420 (3.3)	416 (3.9)	424 (3.9)
Thailand	417 (3.0)	415 (4.0)	419 (3.4)	420 (2.8)	396 (3.7)	439 (3.0)	429 (2.7)	425 (3.7)	433 (3.1)	425 (2.7)	418 (3.8)	431 (3.1)
Tunisia	359 (2.5)	365 (2.7)	353 (2.9)	375 (2.8)	362 (3.3)	387 (3.3)	385 (2.6)	380 (2.7)	390 (3.0)	345 (2.1)	346 (2.5)	343 (2.5)
Uruguay	422 (3.3)	428 (4.0)	416 (3.8)	434 (3.4)	414 (4.5)	453 (3.7)	438 (2.9)	441 (3.7)	436 (3.6)	411 (3.7)	412 (4.6)	409 (4.2)

[1] Illustrates how a country compares with the OECD area as a whole. Computed taking the OECD countries as a single entity, to which each country contributes in proportion to the number of 15-year-olds enrolled in its schools.
[2] Refers to the mean of the data values for all OECD countries, to which each country contributes equally, regardless of the absolute size of the student population of each country.
[3] Response rate is too low to ensure comparability with other countries.

NOTE: Scales were designed to have an average score of 500 points and standard deviation of 100. Possible scores range from 0 to 1000. Standard errors appear in parentheses.
SOURCE: Organization for Economic Cooperation and Development (OECD), Program for International Student Assessment (PISA), 2003, *Learning for Tomorrow's World, 2003*, and *Problem Solving for Tomorrow's World, 2003*. U.S. Department of Education, National Center for Education Statistics, PISA, 2003, *International Outcomes of Learning in Mathematics Literacy and Problem Solving, 2003*. (This table was prepared March 2005.)

Mean scores and percentage distribution of 15-year-olds scoring at each mathematics literacy proficiency level, by country: 2003

Country	Mean score		Percentage distribution at levels of proficiency													
			Below Level 1[1]		Level 1[2]		Level 2[3]		Level 3[4]		Level 4[5]		Level 5[6]		Level 6[7]	
1	2		3		4		5		6		7		8		9	
OECD total[8]	489	(1.07)	11.0	(0.32)	14.6	(0.32)	21.2	(0.28)	22.4	(0.32)	17.6	(0.25)	9.6	(0.19)	3.5	(0.19)
OECD average[9]	500	(0.63)	8.2	(0.17)	13.2	(0.16)	21.1	(0.15)	23.7	(0.18)	19.1	(0.17)	10.6	(0.13)	4.0	(0.10)
Australia	524	(2.15)	4.3	(0.45)	10.0	(0.51)	18.6	(0.62)	24.0	(0.71)	23.3	(0.64)	14.0	(0.53)	5.8	(0.45)
Austria	506	(3.27)	5.6	(0.70)	13.2	(0.84)	21.6	(0.90)	24.9	(1.14)	20.5	(0.84)	10.5	(0.85)	3.7	(0.52)
Belgium	529	(2.29)	7.2	(0.56)	9.3	(0.49)	15.9	(0.65)	20.1	(0.71)	21.0	(0.62)	17.5	(0.69)	9.0	(0.48)
Canada	532	(1.82)	2.4	(0.26)	7.7	(0.36)	18.3	(0.61)	26.2	(0.67)	25.1	(0.60)	14.8	(0.55)	5.5	(0.45)
Czech Republic	516	(3.55)	5.0	(0.69)	11.6	(0.90)	20.1	(0.96)	24.3	(0.95)	20.8	(0.87)	12.9	(0.80)	5.3	(0.53)
Denmark	514	(2.74)	4.7	(0.50)	10.7	(0.62)	20.6	(0.89)	26.2	(0.88)	21.9	(0.83)	11.8	(0.86)	4.1	(0.50)
Finland	544	(1.87)	1.5	(0.23)	5.3	(0.38)	16.0	(0.57)	27.7	(0.65)	26.1	(0.89)	16.7	(0.64)	6.7	(0.46)
France	511	(2.50)	5.6	(0.68)	11.0	(0.77)	20.2	(0.82)	25.9	(0.99)	22.1	(0.97)	11.6	(0.72)	3.5	(0.40)
Germany	503	(3.32)	9.2	(0.84)	12.4	(0.81)	19.0	(1.05)	22.6	(0.82)	20.6	(1.02)	12.2	(0.87)	4.1	(0.48)
Greece	445	(3.90)	17.8	(1.21)	21.2	(1.15)	26.3	(1.04)	20.2	(1.01)	10.6	(0.87)	3.4	(0.53)	0.6	(0.17)
Hungary	490	(2.84)	7.8	(0.80)	15.2	(0.81)	23.8	(1.05)	24.3	(0.93)	18.2	(0.90)	8.2	(0.73)	2.5	(0.42)
Iceland	515	(1.42)	4.5	(0.40)	10.5	(0.55)	20.2	(1.02)	26.1	(0.88)	23.2	(0.81)	11.7	(0.61)	3.7	(0.36)
Ireland	503	(2.45)	4.7	(0.57)	12.1	(0.84)	23.6	(0.83)	28.0	(0.82)	20.2	(1.06)	9.1	(0.76)	2.2	(0.33)
Italy	466	(3.08)	13.2	(1.19)	18.7	(0.93)	24.7	(1.03)	22.9	(0.84)	13.4	(0.73)	5.5	(0.43)	1.5	(0.19)
Japan	534	(4.02)	4.7	(0.65)	8.6	(0.72)	16.3	(0.80)	22.4	(1.02)	23.6	(1.24)	16.1	(0.96)	8.2	(1.14)
Korea, Republic of	542	(3.24)	2.5	(0.32)	7.1	(0.65)	16.6	(0.80)	24.1	(0.98)	25.0	(1.08)	16.7	(0.81)	8.1	(0.93)
Luxembourg	493	(0.97)	7.4	(0.45)	14.3	(0.65)	22.9	(0.87)	25.9	(0.79)	18.7	(0.85)	8.5	(0.59)	2.4	(0.31)
Mexico	385	(3.64)	38.1	(1.71)	27.9	(1.02)	20.8	(0.87)	10.1	(0.84)	2.7	(0.39)	0.4	(0.10)	#	(†)
Netherlands	538	(3.13)	2.6	(0.65)	8.4	(0.95)	18.0	(1.11)	23.0	(1.14)	22.6	(1.34)	18.2	(1.09)	7.3	(0.58)
New Zealand	523	(2.26)	4.9	(0.44)	10.1	(0.63)	19.2	(0.71)	23.2	(0.90)	21.9	(0.80)	14.1	(0.60)	6.6	(0.44)
Norway	495	(2.38)	6.9	(0.50)	13.9	(0.82)	23.7	(1.16)	25.2	(1.01)	18.9	(1.00)	8.7	(0.57)	2.7	(0.35)
Poland	490	(2.50)	6.8	(0.61)	15.2	(0.76)	24.8	(0.75)	25.3	(0.94)	17.7	(0.89)	7.8	(0.49)	2.3	(0.31)
Portugal	466	(3.40)	11.3	(1.11)	18.8	(0.99)	27.1	(0.99)	24.0	(1.03)	13.4	(0.94)	4.6	(0.47)	0.8	(0.16)
Slovak Republic	498	(3.35)	6.7	(0.85)	13.2	(0.86)	23.5	(0.88)	24.9	(1.08)	18.9	(0.82)	9.8	(0.68)	2.9	(0.38)
Spain	485	(2.41)	8.1	(0.66)	14.9	(0.87)	24.7	(0.78)	26.7	(1.02)	17.7	(0.65)	6.5	(0.62)	1.4	(0.25)
Sweden	509	(2.56)	5.6	(0.52)	11.7	(0.60)	21.7	(0.84)	25.5	(0.95)	19.8	(0.81)	11.6	(0.57)	4.1	(0.49)
Switzerland	527	(3.38)	4.9	(0.45)	9.6	(0.57)	17.5	(0.80)	24.3	(0.98)	22.5	(0.72)	14.2	(1.05)	7.0	(0.90)
Turkey	423	(6.74)	27.7	(2.01)	24.6	(1.33)	22.1	(1.12)	13.5	(1.27)	6.8	(1.05)	3.1	(0.82)	2.4	(1.02)
United Kingdom[10]	508	(2.43)	5.2	(0.54)	12.5	(0.67)	21.2	(1.20)	25.6	(0.88)	20.6	(0.73)	11.0	(0.73)	3.9	(0.43)
United States	483	(2.95)	10.2	(0.80)	15.5	(0.81)	23.9	(0.80)	23.8	(0.79)	16.6	(0.73)	8.0	(0.53)	2.0	(0.36)
Non-OECD countries																
Brazil	356	(4.83)	53.3	(1.94)	21.9	(1.09)	14.1	(0.86)	6.8	(0.78)	2.7	(0.47)	0.9	(0.36)	0.3	(0.16)
Hong Kong-China	550	(4.54)	3.9	(0.72)	6.5	(0.64)	13.9	(1.00)	20.0	(1.25)	25.0	(1.17)	20.2	(1.00)	10.5	(0.94)
Indonesia	360	(3.91)	50.5	(2.08)	27.6	(1.05)	14.8	(1.07)	5.5	(0.71)	1.4	(0.39)	0.2	(0.09)	#	(†)
Latvia	483	(3.69)	7.6	(0.86)	16.1	(1.08)	25.5	(1.17)	26.3	(1.15)	16.6	(1.17)	6.3	(0.70)	1.6	(0.36)
Liechtenstein	536	(4.12)	4.8	(1.33)	7.5	(1.66)	17.3	(2.78)	21.6	(2.54)	23.2	(3.09)	18.3	(3.22)	7.3	(1.73)
Macao-China	527	(2.89)	2.3	(0.60)	8.8	(1.34)	19.6	(1.40)	26.8	(1.77)	23.7	(1.71)	13.8	(1.55)	4.8	(0.96)
Russian Federation	468	(4.20)	11.4	(1.03)	18.8	(1.09)	26.4	(1.13)	23.1	(1.02)	13.2	(0.92)	5.4	(0.58)	1.6	(0.38)
Serbia and Montenegro	437	(3.75)	17.6	(1.35)	24.5	(1.08)	28.6	(1.16)	18.9	(1.11)	8.1	(0.88)	2.1	(0.41)	0.2	(0.10)
Thailand	417	(3.00)	23.8	(1.28)	30.2	(1.25)	25.4	(1.12)	13.7	(0.85)	5.3	(0.53)	1.5	(0.31)	0.2	(0.10)
Tunisia	359	(2.54)	51.1	(1.37)	26.9	(0.95)	14.7	(0.75)	5.7	(0.61)	1.4	(0.30)	0.2	(0.12)	#	(†)
Uruguay	422	(3.29)	26.3	(1.30)	21.8	(0.80)	24.2	(0.89)	16.8	(0.68)	8.2	(0.65)	2.3	(0.33)	0.5	(0.17)

†Not applicable.

#Rounds to zero.

[1]Less than or equal to 357.77 score points. Does not meet the requirements for proficiency at level 1.

[2]A score greater than 357.77 and less than or equal to 420.07. Indicates an ability to answer questions involving familiar contexts where all relevant information is present and the questions are clearly defined.

[3]A score greater than 420.07 and less than or equal to 482.38. Indicates an ability to interpret and recognize situations in contexts that require no more than direct inference, extract relevant information from a single source, and employ direct reasoning for literal interpretations of results.

[4]A score greater than 482.38 and less than or equal to 544.68. Indicates an ability to execute clearly described procedures, interpret and use representations based on different information sources, and develop short communications reporting their interpretations, results, and reasoning.

[5]A score greater than 544.68 and less than or equal to 606.99. Indicates an ability to work effectively with explicit models for complex concrete situations that may involve constraints or call for making assumptions, select and integrate different representations, reason with some insight, and construct and communicate explanations and arguments based on their interpretations and actions.

[6]A score greater than 606.99 and less than or equal to 669.3. Indicates an ability to develop and work with models for complex situations, work strategically using broad, well-developed thinking and reasoning skills, and communicate their interpretations and reasoning.

[7]A score greater than 669.3. Indicates an ability to conceptualize, generalize, and utilize information, link different information sources and representations, and formulate and precisely communicate actions and reflections regarding findings and interpretations.

[8]Illustrates how a country compares with the OECD area as a whole. Computed by taking the OECD countries as a single entity to which each country contributes in proportion to the number of 15-year-olds enrolled in its schools.

[9]Refers to the mean of the data values for all OECD countries, to which each country contributes equally, regardless of the absolute size of the student population of each country.

[10]Response rate was too low to ensure comparability with other countries.

NOTE: Mean score was designed to have an average of 500 points, and a standard deviation of 100. Standard errors appear in parentheses. Possible scores range from 0 to 1000. Detail may not sum to totals because of rounding.

SOURCE: Organization for Economic Cooperation and Development, *Program for International Student Assessment (PISA), 2003, Learning for Tomorrow's World*, 2003. U.S. Department of Education, National Center for Education Statistics, PISA, 2003, *International Outcomes of Learning in Mathematics Literacy and Problem Solving: PISA 2003 Results From the U.S. Perspective.* (This table was prepared March 2005.)

Average fourth-grade mathematics scores, by content areas, index of time students spend doing mathematics homework (TMH) in a normal school week, and country: 2003

Country	Mathematics overall	Average score by content area					Index of time students spend doing mathematics homework (TMH) in a normal school week					
		Number[1]	Patterns and relationships[2]	Measurement[3]	Geometry[4]	Data[5]	High TMH[6]		Medium TMH[7]		Low TMH[8]	
							Percent	Mean score	Percent	Mean score	Percent	Mean score
1	2	3	4	5	6	7	8	9	10	11	12	13
International average	495 (0.8)	495 (0.7)	495 (0.7)	495 (0.7)	495 (0.7)	495 (0.6)	18 (0.2)	489 (1.3)	56 (0.3)	500 (0.9)	26 (0.3)	494 (1.6)
Armenia[9]	456 (3.5)	473 (3.0)	461 (4.1)	465 (3.1)	431 (3.8)	417 (3.6)	33 (1.3)	467 (5.1)	65 (1.3)	465 (3.5)	2 (0.3)	‡ (†)
Australia[10]	499 (3.9)	479 (4.3)	495 (3.7)	514 (3.7)	524 (3.7)	525 (3.6)	7 (0.8)	486 (13.0)	43 (2.1)	500 (4.6)	50 (2.1)	505 (4.4)
Belgium (Flemish)	551 (1.8)	549 (1.9)	542 (1.9)	550 (1.4)	533 (1.8)	548 (2.2)	9 (0.7)	538 (3.9)	48 (1.7)	549 (2.7)	43 (2.0)	557 (2.0)
Chinese Taipei	564 (1.8)	568 (1.8)	555 (2.4)	557 (1.6)	553 (2.5)	564 (2.3)	11 (0.6)	546 (3.5)	62 (1.1)	569 (2.0)	27 (1.2)	561 (2.7)
Cyprus	510 (2.4)	514 (2.7)	519 (2.4)	506 (2.3)	505 (2.3)	509 (2.3)	14 (0.6)	494 (4.6)	76 (0.9)	521 (2.4)	10 (0.6)	497 (5.3)
England[10]	531 (3.7)	519 (4.1)	523 (3.9)	535 (3.3)	542 (3.7)	552 (3.4)	4 (0.6)	489 (14.3)	37 (1.8)	531 (4.8)	59 (1.9)	540 (4.2)
Hong Kong, SAR[10,11]	575 (3.2)	574 (3.3)	568 (3.5)	563 (2.7)	557 (2.9)	562 (2.3)	24 (1.0)	575 (3.8)	71 (0.9)	580 (3.2)	5 (0.5)	530 (5.6)
Hungary	529 (3.1)	524 (2.9)	545 (3.7)	532 (2.7)	514 (3.3)	513 (3.2)	17 (0.9)	515 (4.9)	78 (1.1)	538 (3.1)	5 (0.9)	535 (10.6)
Iran, Islamic Republic of	389 (4.2)	410 (3.7)	394 (3.9)	398 (3.2)	416 (3.9)	356 (4.4)	31 (2.3)	404 (5.1)	52 (1.8)	391 (5.0)	17 (2.3)	376 (8.1)
Italy	503 (3.7)	502 (3.6)	496 (4.3)	504 (3.4)	522 (3.5)	497 (3.0)	24 (1.1)	496 (5.2)	52 (1.1)	504 (4.5)	24 (1.6)	512 (3.6)
Japan	565 (1.6)	556 (2.0)	554 (1.4)	568 (1.6)	559 (1.9)	593 (1.6)	8 (0.6)	543 (4.6)	57 (1.8)	568 (2.3)	35 (2.1)	565 (2.7)
Latvia	536 (2.8)	531 (2.6)	532 (3.4)	545 (2.6)	523 (2.2)	526 (2.7)	25 (1.1)	525 (4.1)	71 (1.1)	546 (2.7)	4 (0.6)	517 (9.1)
Lithuania[12]	534 (2.8)	535 (2.9)	531 (3.0)	540 (2.7)	524 (2.2)	517 (2.5)	29 (1.2)	527 (3.8)	66 (1.3)	545 (3.1)	5 (0.6)	510 (10.7)
Moldova, Rep. of	504 (4.9)	507 (4.7)	521 (5.1)	505 (4.0)	501 (4.9)	477 (4.3)	31 (2.0)	518 (6.3)	66 (1.9)	504 (5.4)	3 (0.6)	494 (10.9)
Morocco[13]	347 (5.1)	359 (4.7)	360 (4.7)	345 (5.5)	362 (4.9)	355 (5.0)	22 (1.3)	362 (5.9)	58 (1.9)	365 (4.8)	20 (2.1)	353 (12.3)
Netherlands[10]	540 (2.1)	536 (2.2)	527 (2.4)	545 (2.2)	521 (3.2)	553 (2.4)	1 (0.2)	‡ (†)	10 (0.8)	508 (6.6)	89 (0.9)	546 (1.8)
New Zealand	493 (2.2)	475 (2.3)	495 (2.9)	503 (2.0)	517 (1.8)	522 (2.0)	7 (0.4)	489 (6.7)	41 (1.1)	491 (3.3)	52 (1.3)	504 (3.1)
Norway[14]	451 (2.3)	440 (2.2)	439 (2.7)	475 (2.2)	478 (2.2)	479 (2.3)	12 (1.0)	447 (4.7)	56 (1.8)	462 (3.2)	32 (2.1)	467 (4.0)
Philippines	358 (7.9)	380 (7.4)	382 (7.0)	330 (7.8)	335 (8.8)	384 (7.5)	17 (0.8)	349 (7.0)	52 (1.7)	362 (6.7)	31 (1.9)	372 (15.7)
Russian Federation	532 (4.7)	532 (4.6)	531 (5.0)	538 (3.8)	528 (4.8)	505 (4.1)	38 (1.3)	531 (5.3)	59 (1.2)	537 (4.7)	2 (0.4)	‡ (†)
Scotland[10]	490 (3.3)	475 (3.3)	495 (2.9)	499 (3.1)	511 (2.5)	516 (2.7)	6 (0.8)	477 (6.8)	40 (2.0)	488 (4.2)	54 (2.2)	498 (3.4)
Singapore	594 (5.6)	612 (6.0)	579 (5.4)	566 (4.6)	570 (5.5)	575 (3.9)	40 (1.5)	604 (6.0)	49 (1.3)	595 (5.8)	11 (0.6)	575 (7.2)
Slovenia	479 (2.6)	461 (2.7)	490 (2.7)	497 (2.8)	498 (2.2)	486 (2.7)	14 (0.9)	466 (6.7)	76 (1.2)	490 (2.6)	10 (0.9)	455 (8.6)
Tunisia[13]	339 (4.7)	360 (4.1)	330 (4.7)	308 (5.5)	346 (5.1)	308 (4.7)	22 (2.2)	373 (8.6)	50 (2.8)	365 (6.3)	28 (3.0)	365 (8.0)
United States[10]	518 (2.4)	516 (2.6)	524 (2.7)	500 (2.1)	518 (2.2)	549 (2.0)	12 (0.6)	504 (4.0)	63 (1.3)	524 (2.7)	25 (1.5)	520 (3.5)

†Not applicable.
‡Reporting standards not met.
[1]Topic includes whole numbers; fractions and decimals; integers; and ratio, proportion, and percent.
[2]Topic includes patterns, equations and formulas, and relationships.
[3]Topic includes attributes and units and tools, techniques, and formulas.
[4]Topic includes lines and angles, two- and three-dimensional shapes, congruence and similarity, locations and spatial relationships, and symmetry and transformations.
[5]Topic includes data collection and organization, data representation, and data interpretation.
[6]High level indicates more than 30 minutes of mathematics homework assigned 3–4 times a week.
[7]Medium level includes all possible combinations of responses not included in the high or low level categories (see below for details on the low level).
[8]Low level indicates no more than 30 minutes of mathematics homework assigned no more than twice a week.

[9]Response rate for the TMH index was at least 70 but less than 85 percent of the students, with missing data having not been explicitly accounted for in the analysis.
[10]Met international guidelines for participation rates only after replacement schools were included.
[11]SAR=Special Administrative Region.
[12]National Desired Population does not cover all of the International Desired Population.
[13]Response rate for the TMH index was at least 50 but less than 70 percent of the students, with missing data having not been explicitly accounted for in the analysis.
[14]Students had received 4 years of formal schooling, but first grade is called "First grade/preschool."
NOTE: TMH index data are provided by students. Data are for fourth-grade students or equivalent in most countries. Possible scores range from 1 to 1,000. Detail may not sum to totals because of rounding. Standard errors appear in parentheses.
SOURCE: International Association for the Evaluation of Educational Achievement (IEA), Trends in International Mathematics and Science Study (TIMSS), 2003, TIMSS 2003 International Mathematics Report, by Ina V. S. Mullis et al. (This table was prepared March 2005.)

Average eighth-grade mathematics scores, by content areas, index of time students spend doing mathematics homework in a normal school week, and country: 2003

Country	Mathematics overall	Average score by content area					Index of time students spend doing mathematics homework (TMH) in a normal school week					
		Number[1]	Algebra[2]	Measurement[3]	Geometry[4]	Data[5]	High TMH[6]		Medium TMH[7]		Low TMH[8]	
							Percent	Mean score	Percent	Mean score	Percent	Mean score
1	2	3	4	5	6	7	8	9	10	11	12	13
International average[9]	467 (0.5)	467 (0.5)	467 (0.5)	467 (0.5)	467 (0.5)	467 (0.5)	26 (0.2)	468 (0.8)	54 (0.2)	471 (0.6)	19 (0.2)	456 (1.0)
Armenia	478 (3.0)	473 (3.1)	489 (2.6)	488 (3.3)	481 (3.1)	419 (2.7)	35 (1.3)	490 (3.9)	60 (1.2)	478 (3.7)	4 (0.4)	475 (7.5)
Australia	505 (4.6)	498 (4.6)	499 (4.4)	511 (4.3)	491 (4.8)	531 (3.8)	19 (1.6)	520 (6.0)	50 (1.5)	509 (5.4)	31 (2.0)	497 (5.5)
Bahrain	401 (1.7)	380 (1.9)	411 (2.5)	388 (2.1)	438 (2.1)	414 (2.1)	18 (0.8)	387 (3.3)	69 (1.2)	409 (2.0)	13 (1.1)	398 (4.9)
Belgium (Flemish)	537 (2.8)	539 (2.7)	523 (2.8)	535 (2.5)	527 (3.1)	546 (2.9)	13 (1.1)	542 (4.5)	42 (1.4)	546 (3.2)	44 (2.0)	532 (3.7)
Botswana	366 (2.6)	382 (2.2)	377 (2.7)	377 (2.0)	335 (3.9)	375 (2.7)	25 (0.8)	385 (3.9)	53 (0.8)	368 (2.6)	22 (0.9)	355 (3.0)
Bulgaria	476 (4.3)	477 (4.1)	481 (4.0)	473 (4.6)	484 (4.5)	458 (3.9)	33 (1.8)	482 (6.4)	54 (1.5)	478 (4.6)	14 (1.5)	469 (5.4)
Chile	387 (3.3)	390 (3.1)	384 (3.1)	404 (2.9)	378 (3.3)	412 (3.4)	10 (0.7)	387 (6.9)	43 (1.0)	389 (3.8)	47 (1.4)	388 (3.7)
Chinese Taipei	585 (4.6)	585 (4.6)	585 (4.9)	574 (4.4)	588 (5.1)	568 (3.4)	18 (1.5)	611 (6.0)	45 (1.2)	594 (4.4)	37 (2.0)	563 (5.6)
Cyprus	459 (1.7)	464 (1.5)	455 (1.7)	459 (2.2)	457 (2.4)	458 (1.7)	21 (0.8)	459 (2.8)	70 (0.7)	469 (1.8)	9 (0.6)	438 (5.3)
Egypt	406 (3.5)	421 (3.0)	408 (3.9)	401 (3.3)	408 (3.6)	393 (3.2)	26 (0.8)	402 (4.3)	60 (1.0)	418 (3.6)	14 (0.7)	419 (4.7)
England[10]	‡ (†)	‡ (†)	‡ (†)	‡ (†)	‡ (†)	‡ (†)	‡ (†)	‡ (†)	‡ (†)	‡ (†)	‡ (†)	‡ (†)
Estonia	531 (3.0)	523 (3.1)	528 (2.6)	528 (3.0)	540 (2.6)	535 (2.8)	28 (1.3)	519 (4.0)	66 (1.3)	538 (3.2)	7 (1.2)	523 (10.3)
Ghana	276 (4.7)	289 (5.1)	288 (4.8)	262 (3.7)	278 (4.3)	293 (4.1)	24 (0.9)	288 (5.8)	56 (0.9)	280 (4.5)	20 (1.0)	275 (7.5)
Hong Kong, SAR[11,12]	586 (3.3)	586 (3.2)	580 (3.2)	584 (3.3)	588 (3.6)	566 (3.0)	32 (1.9)	600 (3.5)	49 (1.5)	587 (3.6)	19 (1.5)	566 (7.6)
Hungary	529 (3.2)	529 (3.6)	534 (3.1)	525 (3.1)	515 (3.1)	526 (2.9)	20 (1.2)	516 (5.8)	77 (1.2)	537 (3.1)	3 (0.5)	501 (14.1)
Indonesia[13]	411 (4.8)	421 (4.6)	418 (4.5)	394 (4.9)	413 (4.6)	418 (4.0)	37 (1.1)	435 (4.3)	48 (0.8)	406 (5.3)	15 (0.8)	391 (7.3)
Iran, Islamic Republic of	411 (2.4)	416 (2.3)	412 (3.1)	399 (2.6)	437 (3.1)	404 (2.6)	24 (1.2)	420 (3.8)	52 (0.9)	414 (2.8)	25 (1.1)	403 (3.4)
Israel[14]	496 (3.4)	504 (3.3)	498 (3.2)	480 (3.4)	488 (3.7)	492 (3.3)	33 (1.4)	498 (3.9)	55 (1.3)	505 (4.1)	12 (0.9)	479 (6.3)
Italy	484 (3.2)	480 (3.2)	477 (3.4)	500 (3.2)	469 (3.5)	490 (3.0)	54 (1.4)	484 (3.8)	40 (1.1)	487 (3.6)	7 (0.7)	471 (8.0)
Japan	570 (2.1)	557 (2.3)	568 (2.0)	559 (2.0)	587 (2.1)	573 (1.9)	6 (0.7)	565 (10.1)	36 (1.5)	566 (2.8)	58 (1.9)	576 (2.1)
Jordan	424 (4.1)	413 (4.4)	434 (4.4)	418 (4.4)	446 (4.0)	430 (3.5)	25 (0.8)	425 (4.7)	64 (1.1)	437 (4.1)	11 (0.9)	411 (4.9)
Korea, Republic of[15]	589 (2.2)	586 (2.1)	597 (2.2)	577 (2.0)	598 (2.6)	569 (2.0)	11 (1.0)	582 (4.3)	46 (1.6)	592 (2.6)	43 (2.0)	590 (2.8)
Latvia	508 (3.2)	507 (3.2)	508 (3.2)	500 (3.0)	515 (3.3)	506 (3.8)	33 (1.3)	502 (4.7)	61 (1.3)	516 (3.0)	6 (0.7)	508 (9.3)
Lebanon	433 (3.1)	430 (3.3)	448 (3.1)	430 (3.7)	459 (3.0)	394 (4.0)	42 (1.7)	436 (3.5)	52 (1.7)	437 (3.5)	5 (0.6)	412 (7.6)
Lithuania[13]	502 (2.5)	500 (2.7)	501 (2.4)	492 (3.0)	506 (2.5)	502 (2.5)	32 (1.4)	493 (3.1)	63 (1.3)	509 (3.0)	5 (0.8)	490 (8.7)
Macedonia, Republic of[14]	435 (3.5)	438 (3.5)	442 (3.6)	434 (3.6)	442 (3.7)	419 (3.6)	26 (1.1)	440 (4.5)	61 (1.3)	444 (3.9)	13 (1.3)	439 (6.0)
Malaysia	508 (4.1)	524 (4.0)	495 (3.9)	504 (4.5)	495 (4.8)	505 (3.2)	33 (1.3)	515 (4.4)	56 (1.1)	510 (4.5)	11 (0.8)	485 (5.9)
Moldova	460 (4.0)	463 (3.8)	464 (4.2)	468 (4.0)	463 (4.7)	428 (3.4)	38 (1.4)	472 (4.3)	57 (1.3)	458 (4.6)	5 (0.5)	437 (8.3)
Morocco[13,16,17]	387 (2.5)	384 (2.7)	400 (2.8)	376 (3.4)	415 (2.3)	374 (2.5)	34 (1.5)	390 (4.5)	52 (1.1)	392 (3.2)	14 (1.0)	380 (4.8)
Netherlands[11]	536 (3.8)	539 (3.6)	514 (4.0)	549 (3.7)	513 (4.1)	560 (3.1)	19 (1.3)	540 (5.2)	62 (1.4)	542 (4.4)	19 (1.7)	518 (6.5)
New Zealand	494 (5.3)	481 (6.0)	490 (5.2)	500 (4.8)	488 (4.6)	526 (5.1)	14 (1.1)	488 (5.1)	49 (1.8)	505 (6.0)	37 (2.1)	492 (7.2)
Norway	461 (2.5)	456 (2.3)	428 (2.7)	481 (2.9)	461 (2.8)	498 (2.5)	26 (1.3)	454 (4.0)	52 (1.3)	466 (2.5)	22 (1.3)	472 (3.5)
Palestinian National Authority	390 (3.1)	385 (3.6)	392 (3.5)	386 (2.8)	423 (3.1)	390 (2.8)	27 (1.1)	393 (3.5)	65 (1.1)	398 (3.5)	8 (0.6)	371 (6.6)
Philippines	378 (5.2)	393 (5.1)	400 (5.2)	372 (4.8)	344 (5.3)	390 (4.5)	24 (0.9)	390 (5.4)	54 (1.0)	382 (5.5)	22 (1.2)	361 (6.6)
Romania	475 (4.8)	474 (4.9)	480 (4.7)	485 (4.7)	476 (4.9)	445 (4.6)	68 (1.6)	492 (4.5)	28 (1.4)	451 (6.4)	3 (0.4)	437 (13.0)

See notes at end of table.

Average eighth-grade mathematics scores, by content areas, index of time students spend doing mathematics homework in a normal school week, and country: 2003—Continued

Country	Average score by content area						Index of time students spend doing mathematics homework (TMH) in a normal school week					
	Mathematics overall	Number[1]	Algebra[2]	Measurement[3]	Geometry[4]	Data[5]	High TMH[6]		Medium TMH[7]		Low TMH[8]	
							Percent	Mean score	Percent	Mean score	Percent	Mean score
1	2	3	4	5	6	7	8	9	10	11	12	13
Russian Federation	508 (3.7)	505 (4.0)	516 (3.2)	507 (3.9)	515 (4.2)	484 (3.2)	53 (1.2)	509 (4.4)	45 (1.2)	511 (3.4)	2 (0.2)	‡ (†)
Saudi Arabia	332 (4.6)	307 (5.3)	331 (4.7)	338 (3.4)	382 (4.3)	339 (3.8)	15 (1.0)	315 (8.1)	62 (1.6)	335 (4.6)	23 (1.6)	345 (5.7)
Scotland[11]	498 (3.7)	484 (4.2)	488 (3.9)	508 (3.6)	491 (3.3)	531 (3.7)	8 (0.8)	493 (5.8)	46 (2.1)	507 (4.5)	46 (2.5)	496 (4.1)
Serbia[13]	477 (2.6)	477 (2.8)	488 (2.5)	475 (2.5)	471 (3.0)	456 (2.6)	25 (1.3)	466 (4.1)	54 (1.2)	481 (3.5)	20 (1.7)	497 (3.5)
Singapore	605 (3.6)	618 (3.5)	590 (3.5)	611 (3.6)	580 (3.7)	579 (3.2)	38 (1.1)	621 (3.1)	51 (0.9)	604 (3.8)	11 (0.8)	566 (7.8)
Slovak Republic	508 (3.3)	514 (3.3)	505 (3.3)	508 (3.7)	501 (3.6)	495 (2.9)	11 (0.9)	495 (6.4)	81 (1.4)	511 (3.4)	8 (1.3)	500 (7.7)
Slovenia	493 (2.2)	498 (2.0)	487 (2.3)	496 (2.3)	483 (2.5)	494 (2.3)	25 (1.1)	482 (2.9)	71 (1.2)	500 (2.5)	4 (0.8)	463 (8.8)
South Africa	264 (5.5)	274 (5.4)	275 (5.1)	298 (4.7)	247 (5.4)	296 (5.3)	21 (0.8)	275 (8.1)	58 (0.8)	270 (6.3)	20 (1.0)	260 (5.4)
Sweden	499 (2.6)	496 (2.6)	480 (3.0)	512 (2.6)	467 (3.4)	539 (3.0)	4 (0.5)	453 (7.0)	38 (1.4)	494 (3.5)	58 (1.5)	509 (2.7)
Tunisia	410 (2.2)	419 (2.3)	405 (2.4)	407 (2.2)	427 (2.0)	387 (2.2)	39 (1.1)	410 (2.7)	50 (1.1)	414 (2.2)	11 (0.9)	414 (4.3)
United States[16]	504 (3.3)	508 (3.4)	510 (3.1)	495 (3.2)	472 (3.1)	527 (3.2)	31 (1.0)	518 (4.1)	60 (0.9)	506 (3.2)	9 (0.9)	461 (6.3)

†Not applicable.

‡Reporting standards not met.

[1]Topic includes whole numbers; fractions and decimals; integers; and ratio, proportion, and percent.

[2]Topic includes patterns, algebraic expressions, equations and formulas, and relationships.

[3]Topic includes attributes and units and tools, techniques, and formulas.

[4]Topic includes lines and angles, two- and three-dimensional shapes, congruence and similarity, locations and spatial relationships, and symmetry and transformations.

[5]Topic includes data collection and organization, data representation, data interpretation, and uncertainty and probability.

[6]High level indicates more than 30 minutes of mathematics homework assigned 3–4 times a week.

[7]Medium level includes all possible combinations of responses not included in the high or low level categories (see below for details on the low level).

[8]Low level indicates no more than 30 minutes of mathematics homework assigned no more than twice a week.

[9]The international average of 467 may sometimes appear as 466. In that case, the TIMSS 2003 average for eighth-graders published in the National Center for Education Statistics report reflects the deletion of England from the average.

[10]Did not satisfy guidelines for sample participation rates.

[11]Met guidelines for sample participation rates only after replacement schools were included.

[12]SAR=Special Administrative Region.

[13]National Desired Population does not cover all of International Desired Population.

[14]National Defined Population covers less than 90 percent of National Desired Population.

[15]Korea tested the same cohort of students as other countries, but later in 2003, at the beginning of the next school year.

[16]Nearly satisfied guidelines for sample participation rates only after replacement schools were included.

[17]Response rate for the TMH index was at least 70 but less than 85 percent of the students, with missing data having not been explicitly accounted for in the analysis.

NOTE: TMH index data are provided by students. Data are for eighth grade or equivalent in most countries. Possible scores range from 1 to 1,000. Standard errors appear in parentheses. Detail may not sum to totals because of rounding.

SOURCE: International Association for the Evaluation of Educational Achievement (IEA), Trends in International Mathematics and Science Study (TIMSS), 2003, TIMSS 2003 International Mathematics Report, by Ina V. S. Mullis et al. (This table was prepared April 2005.)

Percentage of lesson time spent on various mathematics activities, yearly mathematics instructional time, and mathematics instructional time as a percentage of total instructional time in eighth grade, by country: 2003

Country	Reviewing homework	Listening to lecture-style presentations	Working problems with teacher's guidance	Working problems on their own without teacher's guidance	Listening to teachers reteach and clarify content/procedures	Taking tests and quizzes	Participating in classroom management tasks not related to the lesson's content/purpose	Other student activities	Students' average yearly mathematics instructional time, in hours	Mathematics instructional time as a percent of total instructional time
1	2	3	4	5	6	7	8	9	10	12
International average	11 (0.1)	19 (0.1)	22 (0.2)	18 (0.2)	11 (0.1)	10 (0.1)	5 (0.1)	4 (0.1)	123 (0.4)	‡ (†)
Armenia	10 (0.5)	14 (0.8)	26 (1.1)	19 (0.9)	13 (0.6)	11 (0.6)	4 (0.3)	4 (0.3)	‡ (†)	13 (0.3)
Australia	8 (0.5)	15 (0.8)	23 (1.2)	28 (1.2)	9 (0.4)	7 (0.4)	7 (0.6)	3 (0.4)	136 (2.9)	13 (0.1)
Bahrain	13 (0.5)	24 (0.9)	17 (0.5)	12 (0.5)	12 (0.3)	13 (0.5)	6 (0.5)	6 (0.3)	142 (0.8)	16 (0.1)
Belgium (Flemish)	7 (0.4)	14 (1.0)	26 (1.0)	20 (0.9)	16 (0.8)	11 (0.4)	4 (0.3)	2 (0.2)	123 (2.2)	13 (0.3)
Botswana	13 (0.9)	16 (1.1)	19 (1.1)	21 (1.2)	11 (0.8)	10 (0.7)	6 (0.5)	5 (0.4)	‡ (†)	‡ (†)
Bulgaria	10 (0.6)	18 (1.3)	26 (1.0)	16 (0.8)	17 (0.9)	8 (0.5)	3 (0.4)	2 (0.3)	96 (1.7)	11 (0.2)
Chile	10 (0.4)	18 (0.8)	21 (0.9)	18 (0.8)	14 (0.7)	11 (0.5)	6 (0.4)	3 (0.3)	160 (4.1)	14 (0.4)
Chinese Taipei	12 (0.5)	42 (1.3)	13 (0.6)	7 (0.5)	9 (0.4)	10 (0.4)	3 (0.3)	3 (0.3)	141 (2.0)	13 (0.2)
Cyprus	22 (0.4)	16 (0.5)	20 (0.5)	14 (0.4)	12 (0.4)	10 (0.5)	5 (0.2)	2 (0.2)	75 (0.4)	8 (0.1)
Egypt	11 (0.4)	18 (1.0)	17 (0.8)	15 (0.7)	15 (0.8)	11 (0.4)	6 (0.3)	7 (0.4)	‡ (†)	‡ (†)
England[3]	‡ (†)	‡ (†)	‡ (†)	‡ (†)	‡ (†)	‡ (†)	‡ (†)	‡ (†)	‡ (†)	‡ (†)
Estonia	10 (0.4)	12 (0.6)	25 (1.0)	25 (0.8)	11 (0.5)	13 (0.6)	3 (0.3)	2 (0.3)	125 (1.2)	12 (0.2)
Ghana	11 (0.4)	16 (0.9)	20 (0.8)	18 (0.7)	12 (0.7)	12 (0.4)	17 (0.4)	6 (0.4)	‡ (†)	15 (0.5)
Hong Kong, SAR[4,5]	8 (0.4)	36 (1.5)	18 (0.7)	16 (0.8)	9 (0.7)	6 (0.3)	4 (0.5)	4 (0.4)	145 (5.2)	15 (0.5)
Hungary	12 (0.4)	13 (0.7)	25 (0.9)	25 (1.0)	10 (0.4)	10 (0.4)	3 (0.3)	3 (0.3)	112 (2.0)	11 (0.2)
Indonesia[6]	12 (0.5)	25 (1.1)	20 (0.9)	14 (0.9)	12 (0.5)	12 (0.7)	3 (0.4)	3 (0.5)	169 (4.4)	13 (0.4)
Iran, Islamic Republic of[7]	12 (0.6)	17 (0.8)	18 (0.7)	14 (0.7)	15 (0.7)	11 (0.5)	6 (0.3)	6 (0.6)	115 (3.5)	12 (0.4)
Israel[7]	14 (0.6)	15 (0.8)	22 (0.7)	21 (0.8)	11 (0.4)	10 (0.5)	5 (0.5)	3 (0.3)	‡ (†)	‡ (†)
Italy	15 (0.6)	22 (0.6)	19 (0.6)	13 (0.6)	13 (0.4)	11 (0.5)	4 (0.3)	2 (0.3)	132 (1.7)	13 (0.2)
Japan	7 (0.6)	29 (1.3)	28 (1.1)	11 (1.0)	15 (0.9)	6 (0.4)	2 (0.2)	2 (0.4)	107 (2.6)	10 (0.2)
Jordan	15 (0.7)	23 (1.0)	17 (0.8)	13 (0.8)	11 (0.5)	9 (0.4)	6 (0.4)	6 (0.5)	110 (0.9)	12 (0.2)
Korea, Republic of[8]	6 (0.3)	30 (1.2)	19 (0.6)	20 (0.7)	9 (0.4)	8 (0.4)	5 (0.3)	3 (0.3)	109 (1.2)	9 (0.1)
Latvia	8 (0.6)	12 (0.7)	25 (1.1)	22 (0.9)	11 (0.6)	15 (0.7)	2 (0.2)	4 (0.4)	122 (1.4)	13 (0.3)
Lebanon	24 (1.6)	17 (0.9)	23 (1.1)	8 (0.8)	10 (0.6)	11 (0.6)	4 (0.4)	4 (0.4)	‡ (†)	‡ (†)
Lithuania[6]	9 (0.5)	7 (0.6)	30 (1.2)	26 (0.9)	11 (0.7)	14 (0.6)	1 (0.2)	2 (0.2)	122 (0.9)	11 (0.2)
Macedonia, Republic of[7]	7 (0.3)	37 (1.1)	19 (0.7)	15 (0.7)	6 (0.4)	8 (0.4)	3 (0.3)	4 (0.3)	80 (1.2)	9 (0.2)
Malaysia	13 (0.7)	21 (1.0)	21 (0.9)	16 (0.8)	9 (0.5)	8 (0.4)	6 (0.4)	6 (0.4)	120 (1.4)	12 (0.1)
Moldova	9 (0.6)	15 (1.0)	23 (1.0)	18 (0.9)	11 (0.9)	14 (0.8)	4 (0.7)	5 (0.6)	‡ (†)	‡ (†)
Morocco[6,9]	‡ (†)	‡ (†)	‡ (†)	‡ (†)	‡ (†)	‡ (†)	‡ (†)	‡ (†)	‡ (†)	‡ (†)
Netherlands[4]	15 (1.1)	13 (0.7)	21 (2.0)	28 (2.5)	7 (0.5)	8 (0.5)	5 (0.5)	4 (0.4)	94 (1.4)	9 (0.1)
New Zealand	7 (0.4)	17 (0.8)	24 (1.1)	23 (1.3)	9 (0.4)	8 (0.4)	7 (0.5)	4 (0.5)	136 (1.7)	14 (0.2)
Norway	8 (0.4)	19 (0.6)	26 (1.2)	25 (1.5)	10 (0.4)	6 (0.3)	4 (0.3)	3 (0.4)	114 (2.3)	13 (0.3)
Palestinian National Authority	13 (0.6)	23 (1.0)	18 (0.8)	16 (0.9)	11 (0.5)	9 (0.3)	6 (0.3)	6 (0.4)	127 (2.3)	14 (0.3)
Philippines	19 (0.4)	20 (0.9)	16 (0.8)	15 (1.0)	11 (0.5)	16 (0.7)	7 (0.3)	6 (0.4)	193 (3.6)	17 (0.4)
Romania	9 (0.4)	24 (0.8)	29 (1.0)	15 (0.7)	10 (0.4)	9 (0.5)	3 (0.3)	2 (0.2)	120 (2.1)	13 (0.3)
Russian Federation	11 (0.2)	20 (0.7)	20 (0.7)	18 (0.7)	8 (0.4)	18 (0.5)	1 (0.2)	3 (0.4)	128 (2.1)	15 (0.3)
Saudi Arabia	15 (1.0)	16 (1.6)	13 (1.0)	8 (0.7)	23 (2.2)	12 (1.0)	6 (0.4)	7 (0.8)	110 (1.0)	11 (0.2)
Scotland[4]	8 (0.3)	22 (0.7)	26 (1.3)	22 (1.5)	8 (0.5)	14 (0.3)	6 (0.5)	3 (0.5)	142 (2.2)	14 (0.3)
Serbia[6]	7 (0.4)	25 (1.4)	23 (1.2)	20 (1.2)	9 (0.5)	7 (0.4)	3 (0.3)	5 (0.5)	107 (1.5)	13 (0.2)
Singapore	11 (0.4)	27 (0.7)	19 (0.6)	15 (0.5)	9 (0.3)	8 (0.3)	6 (0.4)	4 (0.4)	114 (1.6)	13 (0.2)

See notes at end of table.

Percentage of lesson time spent on various mathematics activities, yearly mathematics instructional time, and mathematics instructional time as a percentage of total instructional time in eighth grade, by country: 2003—Continued

| Country | Percentage of time in mathematics lessons students spend on various activities in a typical week | | | | | | | | Students' average yearly mathematics instructional time, in hours | Mathematics instructional time as a percent of total instructional time |
| | Reviewing homework | Listening to lecture-style presentations | Working problems with teacher's guidance | Working problems on their own without teacher's guidance | Listening to teachers reteach and clarify content/procedures | Taking tests and quizzes | Participating in classroom management tasks not related to the lesson's content/purpose | Other student activities | | |
1	2	3	4	5	6	7	8	9	10	11
Slovak Republic	8 (0.3)	17 (0.7)	27 (0.9)	17 (0.7)	13 (0.5)	12 (0.4)	3 (0.3)	3 (0.3)	[1]126 (1.9)	[1]14 (0.3)
Slovenia	11 (0.4)	21 (0.8)	24 (0.7)	22 (0.9)	10 (0.6)	6 (0.3)	2 (0.2)	4 (0.4)	116 (1.3)	11 (0.1)
South Africa	[2]15 (0.9)	[2]13 (0.7)	[2]19 (0.9)	[2]18 (0.9)	[2]11 (0.6)	[2]12 (0.6)	[2]7 (0.4)	[2]5 (0.4)	‡ (†)	‡ (†)
Sweden	4 (0.4)	11 (0.6)	37 (1.8)	28 (1.8)	9 (0.3)	6 (0.3)	3 (0.3)	3 (0.4)	[1]91 (1.6)	[1]10 (0.2)
Tunisia	[1]18 (0.9)	[1]14 (1.0)	[1]17 (0.9)	[1]18 (0.9)	[1]14 (0.8)	[1]13 (0.7)	4 (0.4)	[1]4 (0.5)	‡ (†)	‡ (†)
United States[9]	13 (0.5)	18 (0.7)	21 (0.6)	18 (0.6)	11 (0.3)	11 (0.4)	5 (0.3)	4 (0.4)	[2]135 (2.2)	13 (0.2)

†Not applicable.
#Rounds to zero.
‡Reporting standards not met.
[1]Data available for at least 70 but less than 85 percent of students, with missing data having not been explicitly accounted for in the analysis.
[2]Data available for at least 50 but less than 70 percent of students, with missing data having not been explicitly accounted for in the analysis.
[3]Did not satisfy guidelines for sample participation rates.
[4]Met guidelines for sample participation rates only after replacement schools were included.
[5]SAR=Special Administrative Region.
[6]National Desired Population does not cover all of International Desired Population.

[7]National Defined Population covers less than 90 percent of National Desired Population.
[8]Korea tested the same cohort of students as other countries, but later in 2003, at the beginning of the next school year.
[9]Nearly satisfied guidelines for sample participation rates only after replacement schools were included.
NOTE: Percentage of time in mathematics lessons students spend on various activities in a typical week provided by teachers. Mathematics instructional time provided by teachers and total instructional time provided by schools. Data are for eighth grade or equivalent in most countries. Detail may not sum to totals because of rounding. Standard errors appear in parentheses.
SOURCE: International Association for the Evaluation of Educational Achievement (IEA), Trends in International Mathematics and Science Study (TIMSS), 2003, *TIMSS 2003 International Mathematics Report*, by Ina V. S. Mullis et al. (This table was prepared April 2005.)

Average size and scores of eighth-grade mathematics classes and Index of Teachers' Emphasis on Mathematics Homework (EMH), by country: 2003

Country	Overall average class size	Percentage distribution and mean scores of mathematics classes, by average class size								Index of Teachers' Emphasis on Mathematics Homework (EMH)[1]					
		1 to 24 students		25 to 32 students		33 to 40 students		41 or more students		High EMH[2]		Medium EMH[3]		Low EMH[4]	
		Percent	Mean score	Percent	Mean score	Percent	Mean score	Percent	Mean score	Percent	Mean score	Percent	Mean score	Percent	Mean score
1	2	3	4	5	6	7	8	9	10	11	12	13	14	15	16
International average	30 (0.1)	29 (0.5)	461 (1.9)	35 (0.5)	473 (1.4)	24 (0.5)	470 (2.1)	13 (0.3)	448 (1.7)	30 (0.5)	473 (1.4)	51 (0.6)	469 (0.9)	19 (0.4)	453 (1.7)
Armenia	[5] 27 (0.9)	39 (4.4)	474 (5.6)	43 (4.3)	485 (5.0)	7 (1.8)	460 (9.9)	11 (2.8)	462 (8.4)	[6] 65 (4.6)	481 (4.2)	31 (4.7)	474 (6.6)	4 (2.1)	467 (11.5)
Australia	26 (0.5)	31 (4.2)	482 (9.4)	65 (4.7)	518 (5.9)	4 (2.2)	492 (14.2)	# (†)	‡ (†)	10 (3.0)	544 (19.7)	56 (4.1)	518 (5.9)	34 (3.8)	475 (9.5)
Bahrain	32 (0.1)	6 (0.7)	451 (5.8)	52 (2.7)	402 (2.1)	40 (2.6)	395 (3.5)	3 (0.0)	412 (3.8)	15 (2.5)	389 (6.1)	72 (3.7)	404 (2.3)	14 (3.1)	396 (8.7)
Belgium (Flemish)	20 (0.3)	90 (2.3)	538 (3.3)	10 (2.3)	553 (10.5)	# (†)	‡ (†)	# (†)	‡ (†)	9 (2.5)	555 (6.5)	30 (3.8)	555 (5.8)	60 (3.9)	529 (5.6)
Botswana	37 (0.4)	1 (0.7)	‡ (†)	14 (2.6)	392 (9.1)	60 (4.3)	360 (3.7)	25 (4.1)	362 (4.1)	44 (4.6)	364 (4.0)	49 (4.5)	368 (4.0)	7 (2.5)	379 (7.0)
Bulgaria	22 (0.5)	64 (4.2)	468 (4.9)	32 (3.9)	503 (8.0)	3 (2.4)	423 (5.0)	1 (0.0)	‡ (†)	53 (4.2)	483 (6.1)	38 (3.6)	467 (7.7)	9 (2.5)	469 (15.6)
Chile	35 (0.4)	9 (1.5)	385 (17.0)	22 (2.6)	384 (8.1)	47 (3.6)	390 (5.7)	23 (3.0)	389 (6.9)	10 (2.2)	401 (14.9)	49 (3.6)	388 (5.1)	40 (3.3)	383 (5.5)
Chinese Taipei	37 (0.4)	4 (1.5)	598 (28.9)	14 (2.8)	567 (11.5)	65 (4.0)	575 (4.7)	17 (3.2)	636 (8.7)	29 (3.9)	602 (8.6)	39 (3.9)	588 (6.3)	32 (3.9)	570 (7.6)
Cyprus	26 (0.1)	21 (1.9)	463 (3.2)	79 (1.9)	460 (2.0)	# (†)	‡ (†)	# (†)	‡ (†)	35 (3.1)	455 (3.2)	65 (3.1)	462 (2.3)	# (†)	‡ (†)
Egypt	38 (0.6)	3 (1.2)	422 (13.8)	9 (2.1)	428 (11.3)	61 (4.1)	403 (4.3)	27 (3.7)	407 (7.5)	23 (3.3)	401 (8.6)	57 (3.8)	409 (4.8)	20 (3.2)	406 (8.1)
England[7]	[8] ‡ (†)	‡ (†)	‡ (†)	‡ (†)	‡ (†)	‡ (†)	‡ (†)	‡ (†)	‡ (†)	[6] ‡ (†)	‡ (†)	‡ (†)	‡ (†)	‡ (†)	‡ (†)
Estonia	27 (0.5)	32 (3.4)	523 (5.1)	41 (4.2)	530 (4.3)	27 (3.8)	550 (5.4)	‡ (†)	‡ (†)	12 (2.3)	540 (9.9)	78 (3.2)	532 (3.3)	9 (2.5)	518 (14.1)
Ghana	[5] 37 (1.0)	16 (2.7)	232 (7.4)	18 (3.1)	249 (8.9)	29 (4.0)	292 (9.0)	37 (4.7)	289 (9.1)	48 (5.0)	271 (7.9)	37 (5.0)	275 (7.1)	15 (3.0)	284 (10.2)
Hong Kong, SAR[9,10]	39 (0.3)	3 (1.1)	504 (28.1)	6 (1.6)	513 (21.3)	49 (4.1)	575 (5.7)	43 (4.1)	612 (4.7)	26 (3.7)	598 (6.0)	50 (4.6)	593 (6.0)	24 (4.0)	566 (10.0)
Hungary	22 (0.4)	64 (3.9)	522 (4.2)	35 (4.0)	540 (6.5)	2 (0.9)	‡ (†)	# (†)	‡ (†)	8 (2.0)	532 (8.9)	90 (2.2)	530 (3.5)	2 (0.9)	‡ (†)
Indonesia[11]	40 (0.5)	23 (1.7)	413 (8.6)	10 (2.8)	366 (20.0)	38 (4.1)	413 (8.3)	48 (4.3)	421 (6.7)	45 (3.9)	421 (7.4)	45 (4.4)	402 (9.4)	10 (2.6)	412 (15.3)
Iran, Islamic Republic of	29 (0.4)	23 (2.9)	397 (5.7)	50 (4.6)	413 (4.5)	25 (3.3)	420 (6.0)	3 (1.4)	431 (13.7)	63 (4.4)	417 (3.2)	26 (4.1)	406 (7.2)	12 (2.8)	399 (9.3)
Israel[12]	[5] 34 (0.4)	9 (2.2)	512 (18.3)	23 (3.7)	500 (9.2)	64 (4.5)	490 (4.9)	4 (1.7)	531 (4.5)	50 (3.8)	501 (5.4)	44 (4.1)	500 (6.3)	4 (1.5)	438 (17.8)
Italy	22 (0.3)	78 (3.1)	483 (3.4)	22 (3.1)	488 (8.3)	# (†)	‡ (†)	# (†)	‡ (†)	71 (3.5)	482 (3.2)	25 (3.2)	489 (8.4)	4 (1.5)	480 (11.2)
Japan	35 (0.2)	3 (1.2)	561 (6.1)	18 (2.6)	557 (4.5)	78 (2.6)	571 (2.7)	1 (1.0)	‡ (†)	7 (2.2)	583 (23.4)	29 (3.8)	573 (6.9)	64 (3.9)	567 (2.5)
Jordan	35 (0.7)	14 (2.8)	430 (9.4)	26 (3.6)	424 (13.3)	32 (4.4)	417 (5.9)	28 (3.8)	428 (7.4)	30 (3.8)	422 (5.5)	55 (4.4)	430 (6.3)	14 (2.8)	410 (8.6)
Korea, Republic of[13]	[8] 37 (0.4)	1 (0.9)	‡ (†)	20 (3.0)	569 (4.6)	57 (4.6)	594 (2.9)	22 (3.5)	600 (7.0)	[14] 9 (2.1)	582 (10.8)	31 (3.6)	589 (4.7)	60 (3.5)	591 (3.5)
Latvia	24 (0.7)	52 (3.5)	497 (4.4)	42 (3.4)	519 (5.5)	3 (1.0)	527 (20.3)	3 (1.7)	506 (12.6)	17 (2.9)	523 (8.8)	75 (3.8)	505 (3.5)	6 (2.6)	500 (11.7)
Lebanon	29 (0.9)	32 (3.9)	429 (6.0)	44 (4.8)	429 (5.1)	16 (3.1)	443 (10.4)	8 (3.1)	464 (8.7)	45 (4.6)	433 (4.6)	45 (4.4)	436 (5.8)	9 (1.9)	401 (13.1)
Lithuania[12]	25 (0.3)	39 (3.2)	486 (4.2)	61 (3.2)	510 (3.0)	# (†)	‡ (†)	# (†)	‡ (†)	13 (2.7)	512 (7.7)	76 (3.6)	501 (3.4)	11 (2.6)	477 (11.3)
Macedonia, Republic of[12]	28 (0.4)	24 (3.5)	439 (9.2)	58 (4.3)	435 (5.9)	17 (3.6)	429 (13.7)	1 (1.0)	‡ (†)	22 (3.3)	450 (8.1)	66 (3.9)	428 (5.2)	12 (2.6)	432 (13.8)
Malaysia	37 (0.4)	1 (0.7)	‡ (†)	18 (3.3)	514 (11.0)	56 (4.4)	503 (5.1)	25 (3.5)	515 (8.8)	60 (4.5)	508 (5.0)	34 (4.2)	515 (8.5)	5 (1.9)	466 (10.1)
Moldova	[5] 24 (0.5)	56 (4.5)	449 (6.0)	38 (4.6)	460 (7.0)	5 (2.5)	485 (25.2)	1 (0.6)	‡ (†)	[6] 43 (4.8)	451 (6.1)	52 (5.0)	463 (7.9)	5 (1.9)	468 (10.1)
Morocco[11,15]	‡ (†)	6 (2.0)	‡ (†)	27 (3.9)	394 (8.9)	50 (3.7)	385 (8.9)	14 (3.1)	‡ (†)	[14] 54 (6.2)	391 (5.9)	37 (4.3)	391 (5.2)	11 (4.1)	389 (11.1)
Netherlands[9]	26 (0.3)	33 (3.9)	514 (9.4)	66 (4.1)	546 (5.8)	# (†)	‡ (†)	# (†)	‡ (†)	7 (2.4)	550 (15.3)	82 (3.7)	541 (4.9)	11 (2.6)	495 (14.1)
New Zealand	27 (0.4)	22 (3.0)	469 (8.9)	72 (4.1)	500 (5.7)	6 (3.2)	538 (17.8)	# (†)	‡ (†)	7 (2.1)	479 (15.6)	67 (4.1)	510 (6.6)	25 (4.2)	471 (5.3)
Norway	25 (0.3)	34 (3.8)	467 (4.3)	65 (3.6)	460 (3.5)	1 (0.7)	‡ (†)	1 (0.7)	‡ (†)	25 (3.4)	460 (6.4)	46 (4.3)	465 (3.8)	29 (4.3)	455 (5.0)
Palestinian National Authority	39 (0.6)	6 (2.0)	398 (20.0)	17 (2.8)	393 (7.4)	27 (3.9)	394 (8.9)	50 (3.7)	385 (4.2)	30 (4.0)	389 (6.4)	58 (4.3)	391 (4.6)	12 (2.5)	388 (14.9)
Philippines	54 (0.7)	1 (0.6)	‡ (†)	1 (0.7)	‡ (†)	7 (2.0)	448 (23.4)	91 (2.1)	372 (5.4)	24 (4.0)	358 (10.9)	61 (4.8)	384 (7.1)	15 (3.7)	377 (19.1)
Romania	24 (0.5)	51 (4.5)	469 (6.7)	46 (4.5)	480 (7.4)	3 (1.4)	534 (34.7)	1 (0.0)	‡ (†)	78 (3.3)	478 (5.5)	21 (3.3)	463 (10.1)	1 (0.7)	‡ (†)
Russian Federation	24 (0.6)	47 (4.2)	500 (5.1)	47 (3.6)	515 (5.0)	6 (3.4)	533 (11.0)	# (†)	‡ (†)	56 (3.5)	514 (4.3)	43 (3.5)	499 (4.7)	1 (0.5)	‡ (†)
Saudi Arabia	28 (0.5)	36 (5.3)	333 (7.5)	26 (4.4)	340 (8.1)	29 (5.8)	330 (5.6)	8 (3.0)	325 (4.1)	14 (3.0)	331 (8.9)	69 (3.0)	332 (4.6)	17 (3.0)	346 (15.0)
Scotland[9]	[5] 27 (0.5)	33 (3.9)	457 (7.2)	56 (4.4)	520 (6.2)	11 (3.4)	548 (10.1)	1 (0.7)	‡ (†)	45 (1.7)	549 (10.6)	45 (4.6)	527 (5.7)	10 (4.5)	477 (6.2)
Serbia[11]	26 (0.4)	38 (3.7)	464 (4.4)	51 (4.0)	483 (3.8)	11 (2.9)	489 (8.2)	# (†)	‡ (†)	34 (4.1)	474 (4.9)	45 (4.3)	481 (4.5)	21 (3.7)	470 (5.6)
Singapore	38 (0.2)	2 (0.6)	‡ (†)	8 (1.6)	613 (18.0)	63 (2.7)	606 (5.0)	26 (2.5)	607 (5.7)	59 (2.4)	620 (4.2)	33 (2.5)	592 (6.6)	8 (1.3)	563 (13.1)

See notes at end of table.

Average size and scores of eighth-grade mathematics classes and Index of Teachers' Emphasis on Mathematics Homework (EMH), by country: 2003—Continued

Country	Overall average class size	Percentage distribution and mean scores of mathematics classes, by average class size								Index of Teachers' Emphasis on Mathematics Homework (EMH)[1]					
		1 to 24 students		25 to 32 students		33 to 40 students		41 or more students		High EMH[2]		Medium EMH[3]		Low EMH[4]	
		Percent	Mean score	Percent	Mean score	Percent	Mean score	Percent	Mean score	Percent	Mean score	Percent	Mean score	Percent	Mean score
1	2	3	4	5	6	7	8	9	10	11	12	13	14	15	16
Slovak Republic	25 (0.4)	42 (4.6)	498 (4.7)	53 (4.7)	512 (5.4)	5 (1.8)	543 (19.7)	# (†)	‡ (†)	5 (1.5)	510 (12.4)	79 (2.9)	511 (4.0)	16 (2.7)	492 (6.3)
Slovenia	22 (0.3)	70 (4.1)	491 (3.0)	30 (4.1)	500 (4.1)	# (†)	‡ (†)	# (†)	‡ (†)	13 (2.9)	490 (9.2)	85 (3.1)	495 (2.5)	3 (1.0)	473 (9.7)
South Africa	[8]45 (1.3)	4 (1.2)	309 (35.8)	14 (3.0)	290 (23.8)	30 (3.7)	265 (11.7)	52 (4.1)	249 (8.7)	[6]26 (3.4)	266 (9.2)	54 (3.9)	267 (9.6)	20 (3.3)	250 (9.1)
Sweden	21 (0.4)	71 (3.6)	491 (3.3)	27 (3.7)	522 (5.5)	1 (1.0)	‡ (†)	# (†)	‡ (†)	17 (2.8)	503 (7.0)	25 (3.2)	506 (6.0)	59 (3.7)	494 (4.0)
Tunisia	34 (0.3)	1 (1.0)	‡ (†)	26 (3.3)	404 (3.6)	71 (3.5)	412 (3.2)	2 (1.1)	‡ (†)	12 (2.5)	423 (9.1)	84 (3.0)	407 (2.2)	4 (1.6)	442 (11.3)
United States[15]	[5]24 (0.4)	56 (2.9)	504 (3.9)	39 (2.7)	510 (5.1)	4 (1.2)	531 (16.4)	1 (0.7)	‡ (†)	27 (2.5)	531 (8.0)	62 (2.9)	504 (3.8)	11 (2.2)	471 (9.5)

†Not applicable.

#Rounds to zero.

‡Reporting standards not met.

[1]Index based on teachers' responses to two questions about how often they usually assign mathematics homework and how many minutes of mathematics homework they usually assign.

[2]High EMH indicates the assignment of more than 30 minutes of homework in about half of the lessons or more.

[3]Medium level includes all possible combinations of responses not included in the high or low level categories (see below for details on the low level).

[4]Low level indicates no assignment or the assignment of less than 30 minutes of homework in about half the lessons or less.

[5]Class size data available for at least 70 but less than 85 percent of students, with missing data having not been explicitly accounted for in the analysis.

[6]EMH data available for at least 70 but less than 85 percent of students, with missing data having not been explicitly accounted for in the analysis.

[7]Did not satisfy guidelines for sample participation rates.

[8]Class size data available for at least 50 but less than 70 percent of students, with missing data having not been explicitly accounted for in the analysis.

[9]Met guidelines for sample participation rates only after replacement schools were included.

[10]SAR=Special Administrative Region.

[11]National Desired Population does not cover all of International Desired Population.

[12]National Defined Population covers less than 90 percent of National Desired Population.

[13]Korea tested the same cohort of students as other countries, but later in 2003, at the beginning of the next school year.

[14]EMH data available for at least 50 but less than 70 percent of students, with missing data having not been explicitly accounted for in the analysis.

[15]Nearly satisfied guidelines for sample participation rates only after replacement schools were included.

NOTE: Background data provided by teachers. Data are for 8th grade or equivalent in most countries. Possible scores range from 0 to 1000. Detail may not sum to totals because of rounding. Standard errors appear in parentheses.

SOURCE: International Association for the Evaluation of Educational Achievement (IEA), Trends in International Mathematics and Science Study (TIMSS), 2003, *TIMSS 2003 International Mathematics Report*, by Ina V. S. Mullis et al. (This table was prepared April 2005.)

Eighth-grade students' perceptions about mathematics and hours spent on leisure activities, by country: 2003

Country	Index of students' self-confidence in learning mathematics (SCM)[1]						Average hours spent each day[2]							
	High SCM		Medium SCM		Low SCM		Watching TV or videos	Playing computer games	Playing or talking with friends	Doing jobs at home	Playing sports	Reading for enjoyment	Using the Internet	Working at a paid job
	Percent	Average achievement	Percent	Average achievement	Percent	Average achievement								
1	2	3	4	5	6	7	8	9	10	11	12	13	14	15
Armenia	41 (1.1)	505 (4.0)	40 (1.0)	468 (3.7)	19 (0.9)	462 (4.1)	1.8 (0.03)	‡ (†)	‡ (†)	‡ (†)	‡ (†)	‡ (†)	‡ (†)	‡ (†)
Australia	50 (1.7)	542 (4.5)	31 (1.1)	483 (3.7)	19 (1.2)	451 (6.4)	2.0 (0.03)	0.9 (0.02)	1.7 (0.04)	1.0 (0.02)	1.6 (0.03)	0.7 (0.02)	1.3 (0.03)	0.4 (0.03)
Bahrain	44 (0.9)	437 (2.0)	38 (0.9)	379 (2.4)	18 (0.6)	366 (3.2)	2.0 (0.03)	1.2 (0.02)	1.6 (0.03)	1.2 (0.02)	1.5 (0.03)	0.9 (0.02)	1.4 (0.03)	0.6 (0.02)
Belgium (Flemish)	45 (0.9)	556 (3.2)	30 (0.7)	526 (3.0)	25 (0.8)	518 (3.5)	2.1 (0.03)	1.0 (0.03)	1.9 (0.03)	0.9 (0.02)	1.6 (0.03)	0.5 (0.01)	1.3 (0.03)	0.2 (0.02)
Botswana	38 (0.9)	390 (2.8)	45 (0.8)	361 (2.5)	17 (0.8)	352 (3.4)	1.4 (0.03)	0.5 (0.02)	2.1 (0.04)	2.3 (0.03)	1.5 (0.02)	1.8 (0.03)	0.7 (0.02)	0.6 (0.03)
Bulgaria	33 (1.3)	519 (5.5)	39 (1.4)	467 (4.2)	28 (1.2)	445 (4.8)	2.5 (0.04)	1.1 (0.04)	2.6 (0.05)	1.5 (0.03)	1.2 (0.04)	0.7 (0.03)	1.0 (0.04)	0.3 (0.02)
Chile	35 (0.9)	427 (3.9)	42 (0.7)	369 (3.4)	23 (0.7)	361 (3.9)	2.2 (0.02)	0.7 (0.02)	2.3 (0.03)	1.5 (0.02)	1.8 (0.03)	0.6 (0.01)	0.7 (0.02)	0.3 (0.02)
Chinese Taipei	26 (1.0)	661 (4.1)	30 (0.7)	593 (5.1)	44 (1.1)	534 (4.0)	1.7 (0.03)	1.4 (0.04)	1.4 (0.03)	0.7 (0.01)	1.0 (0.02)	1.0 (0.02)	1.4 (0.04)	0.2 (0.01)
Cyprus	46 (0.8)	503 (2.0)	32 (0.8)	437 (2.2)	22 (0.7)	407 (3.6)	2.1 (0.03)	1.3 (0.02)	2.1 (0.03)	1.0 (0.03)	1.7 (0.03)	0.9 (0.02)	1.2 (0.02)	0.6 (0.02)
Egypt	58 (1.0)	437 (3.3)	35 (0.9)	383 (3.7)	7 (0.4)	374 (5.3)	0.8 (0.02)	0.7 (0.02)	0.8 (0.02)	1.3 (0.03)	1.1 (0.02)	1.0 (0.02)	0.6 (0.02)	0.6 (0.02)
England[3]	‡ (†)	‡ (†)	‡ (†)	‡ (†)	‡ (†)	‡ (†)	‡ (†)	‡ (†)	‡ (†)	‡ (†)	‡ (†)	‡ (†)	‡ (†)	‡ (†)
Estonia	41 (0.9)	569 (3.2)	32 (0.7)	520 (3.1)	28 (0.8)	489 (3.5)	2.3 (0.03)	1.1 (0.03)	2.8 (0.03)	1.1 (0.02)	1.4 (0.03)	0.7 (0.02)	1.5 (0.04)	0.4 (0.02)
Ghana	— (†)	— (†)	— (†)	— (†)	— (†)	— (†)	0.7 (0.02)	0.6 (0.02)	1.2 (0.03)	1.5 (0.03)	1.3 (0.02)	1.7 (0.03)	0.8 (0.03)	0.8 (0.03)
Hong Kong, SAR[4]	30 (0.9)	627 (2.9)	38 (0.7)	581 (4.1)	33 (0.9)	556 (4.0)	2.3 (0.03)	2.0 (0.04)	1.6 (0.03)	0.7 (0.01)	1.0 (0.03)	1.1 (0.02)	2.0 (0.03)	0.1 (0.01)
Hungary	44 (1.0)	574 (3.3)	32 (1.0)	507 (3.9)	24 (0.8)	479 (3.9)	2.1 (0.03)	1.1 (0.03)	2.2 (0.03)	1.1 (0.02)	1.5 (0.03)	0.8 (0.02)	0.6 (0.03)	0.2 (0.02)
Indonesia	27 (1.1)	420 (6.6)	59 (0.8)	408 (4.5)	15 (0.9)	416 (4.7)	1.5 (0.03)	0.5 (0.02)	1.3 (0.03)	2.2 (0.03)	1.1 (0.02)	1.1 (0.02)	0.3 (0.02)	0.8 (0.03)
Iran, Islamic Republic of	35 (0.9)	447 (3.5)	49 (0.8)	399 (2.6)	16 (0.7)	377 (3.4)	1.6 (0.03)	0.4 (0.02)	1.4 (0.03)	1.5 (0.03)	1.4 (0.04)	1.0 (0.02)	0.2 (0.02)	0.7 (0.05)
Israel	59 (1.2)	526 (3.5)	30 (0.9)	461 (3.8)	11 (0.7)	451 (5.7)	2.5 (0.04)	1.9 (0.02)	2.3 (0.03)	1.4 (0.03)	1.6 (0.03)	0.9 (0.02)	1.8 (0.04)	0.6 (0.02)
Italy	46 (0.9)	521 (3.3)	29 (0.9)	466 (3.6)	25 (1.0)	439 (3.4)	1.8 (0.03)	1.0 (0.02)	2.6 (0.03)	1.1 (0.03)	1.8 (0.03)	0.7 (0.02)	0.6 (0.02)	0.9 (0.02)
Japan	17 (0.6)	634 (3.1)	38 (0.7)	580 (2.7)	45 (0.8)	538 (2.3)	2.7 (0.03)	0.9 (0.02)	1.6 (0.04)	0.6 (0.01)	1.3 (0.03)	0.9 (0.02)	0.6 (0.02)	0.1 (0.01)
Jordan	49 (1.2)	463 (4.7)	38 (1.0)	400 (3.7)	13 (0.7)	390 (4.4)	1.5 (0.03)	0.9 (0.03)	1.2 (0.03)	1.3 (0.03)	1.2 (0.03)	0.9 (0.02)	0.6 (0.03)	0.6 (0.03)
Korea, Republic of[5]	30 (0.7)	650 (2.8)	36 (0.6)	592 (2.5)	34 (0.8)	534 (2.3)	1.7 (0.03)	1.5 (0.03)	1.8 (0.03)	0.7 (0.01)	0.7 (0.02)	0.6 (0.01)	1.7 (0.03)	0.1 (0.01)
Latvia	34 (1.0)	555 (3.4)	33 (0.9)	499 (3.2)	33 (1.0)	473 (3.4)	2.4 (0.03)	1.0 (0.02)	2.8 (0.03)	1.6 (0.03)	1.3 (0.03)	0.8 (0.03)	0.8 (0.03)	0.5 (0.02)
Lebanon	43 (1.4)	462 (3.6)	44 (1.1)	416 (3.1)	13 (0.7)	403 (4.4)	1.8 (0.04)	1.3 (0.03)	1.6 (0.03)	1.3 (0.03)	1.6 (0.03)	1.0 (0.03)	1.0 (0.03)	0.8 (0.03)
Lithuania	36 (1.0)	552 (3.1)	37 (0.9)	486 (2.8)	26 (0.9)	456 (2.7)	2.1 (0.03)	1.1 (0.03)	2.6 (0.04)	1.6 (0.04)	1.1 (0.03)	0.6 (0.02)	0.7 (0.03)	0.3 (0.02)
Macedonia, Republic of	33 (1.0)	482 (4.0)	37 (1.0)	418 (4.7)	31 (1.0)	424 (3.9)	2.3 (0.04)	1.3 (0.03)	2.2 (0.03)	1.6 (0.03)	1.8 (0.03)	1.0 (0.02)	0.9 (0.03)	0.6 (0.03)
Malaysia	39 (1.2)	546 (4.2)	45 (1.0)	490 (3.7)	16 (0.7)	471 (4.4)	2.1 (0.04)	0.8 (0.03)	1.5 (0.03)	1.7 (0.02)	1.1 (0.02)	1.2 (0.02)	0.6 (0.02)	0.3 (0.02)
Moldova, Republic of	30 (1.2)	494 (5.0)	50 (0.9)	451 (4.5)	20 (1.1)	441 (5.3)	1.9 (0.04)	0.7 (0.02)	2.0 (0.04)	2.2 (0.06)	1.3 (0.03)	1.1 (0.03)	0.7 (0.03)	0.5 (0.03)
Morocco	‡ (†)	‡ (†)	‡ (†)	‡ (†)	‡ (†)	‡ (†)	1.3 (0.04)	2.3 (0.06)	1.3 (0.03)	1.8 (0.03)	1.4 (0.02)	1.2 (0.02)	0.5 (0.03)	0.8 (0.04)
Netherlands	45 (1.4)	557 (4.4)	33 (1.0)	527 (4.7)	23 (1.0)	511 (4.8)	2.1 (0.05)	1.2 (0.04)	2.6 (0.05)	0.8 (0.02)	1.7 (0.04)	0.5 (0.02)	1.5 (0.04)	0.8 (0.05)
New Zealand	43 (1.4)	534 (6.4)	36 (1.1)	475 (5.4)	21 (0.9)	452 (4.1)	2.1 (0.04)	1.0 (0.04)	1.8 (0.05)	1.0 (0.02)	1.5 (0.03)	0.7 (0.03)	0.9 (0.04)	0.6 (0.03)
Norway	46 (1.1)	502 (2.0)	32 (0.8)	445 (2.9)	21 (0.8)	405 (3.4)	2.2 (0.03)	1.1 (0.03)	2.7 (0.03)	1.0 (0.03)	1.8 (0.03)	0.6 (0.02)	0.6 (0.03)	0.7 (0.02)
Palestinian National Authority	43 (1.0)	428 (3.9)	41 (0.9)	370 (2.9)	16 (0.6)	355 (3.6)	1.2 (0.02)	0.7 (0.02)	1.3 (0.02)	1.5 (0.03)	1.1 (0.03)	1.0 (0.02)	0.5 (0.02)	0.6 (0.03)
Philippines	29 (0.7)	405 (6.1)	59 (0.7)	369 (4.8)	12 (0.5)	366 (6.5)	1.6 (0.04)	0.6 (0.02)	1.7 (0.03)	1.9 (0.03)	1.4 (0.02)	1.2 (0.02)	0.5 (0.03)	0.8 (0.04)
Romania	30 (1.2)	533 (4.6)	45 (1.1)	465 (4.5)	25 (0.9)	442 (5.4)	2.0 (0.04)	0.9 (0.03)	2.1 (0.03)	1.7 (0.05)	1.3 (0.03)	1.0 (0.03)	0.8 (0.04)	0.5 (0.03)
Russian Federation	43 (1.1)	548 (3.0)	30 (0.8)	492 (4.1)	27 (0.8)	466 (4.6)	2.0 (0.03)	1.0 (0.03)	2.5 (0.04)	1.6 (0.03)	1.3 (0.02)	1.1 (0.03)	0.4 (0.02)	0.2 (0.02)
Saudi Arabia	41 (1.4)	361 (4.8)	43 (1.1)	321 (5.4)	16 (0.9)	303 (5.8)	1.6 (0.05)	1.1 (0.03)	1.3 (0.03)	1.5 (0.04)	1.2 (0.04)	0.9 (0.02)	0.8 (0.05)	0.8 (0.03)
Scotland	52 (1.5)	524 (3.9)	32 (1.0)	477 (3.8)	15 (0.9)	456 (5.0)	2.2 (0.03)	1.4 (0.04)	2.7 (0.03)	0.8 (0.02)	1.7 (0.03)	0.6 (0.02)	1.4 (0.03)	0.5 (0.03)
Serbia	44 (1.1)	530 (2.8)	26 (0.7)	458 (3.2)	30 (1.1)	422 (3.4)	2.1 (0.03)	1.4 (0.04)	2.1 (0.03)	1.3 (0.03)	1.7 (0.03)	0.8 (0.02)	0.6 (0.03)	0.3 (0.02)
Singapore	39 (0.8)	639 (3.0)	34 (0.7)	594 (3.9)	27 (0.7)	571 (4.6)	2.3 (0.02)	1.4 (0.02)	1.7 (0.03)	0.7 (0.02)	1.4 (0.02)	0.9 (0.02)	1.6 (0.02)	0.2 (0.02)

See notes at end of table.

Eighth-grade students' perceptions about mathematics and hours spent on leisure activities, by country: 2003—Continued

Country	Index of students' self-confidence in learning mathematics (SCM)[1]						Average hours spent each day[2]							
	High SCM		Medium SCM		Low SCM		Watching TV or videos	Playing computer games	Playing or talking with friends	Doing jobs at home	Playing sports	Reading for enjoyment	Using the Internet	Working at a paid job
	Percent	Average achievement	Percent	Average achievement	Percent	Average achievement								
1	2	3	4	5	6	7	8	9	10	11	12	13	14	15
Slovak Republic	40 (1.1)	556 (3.7)	35 (1.0)	487 (3.9)	25 (1.0)	462 (4.1)	2.5 (0.03)	1.1 (0.03)	2.8 (0.03)	1.5 (0.03)	1.9 (0.04)	0.9 (0.02)	0.6 (0.03)	0.4 (0.02)
Slovenia	40 (0.9)	533 (3.2)	39 (1.0)	474 (2.5)	20 (0.9)	453 (2.8)	2.2 (0.03)	1.3 (0.03)	2.0 (0.03)	1.2 (0.03)	1.7 (0.03)	0.8 (0.02)	1.1 (0.03)	0.4 (0.02)
South Africa	37 (0.9)	300 (8.3)	48 (0.9)	242 (3.9)	15 (0.8)	255 (9.9)	1.5 (0.03)	0.7 (0.02)	2.0 (0.03)	1.8 (0.03)	1.6 (0.02)	1.6 (0.03)	0.8 (0.02)	0.8 (0.02)
Sweden	49 (1.3)	534 (2.6)	36 (0.9)	477 (3.1)	16 (0.9)	446 (3.4)	2.1 (0.03)	1.1 (0.03)	2.8 (0.03)	1.0 (0.02)	1.6 (0.03)	0.6 (0.02)	1.7 (0.04)	0.4 (0.02)
Tunisia	44 (1.0)	436 (2.7)	36 (0.8)	399 (2.5)	20 (0.9)	384 (2.2)	1.4 (0.02)	0.8 (0.03)	1.5 (0.02)	1.9 (0.03)	1.5 (0.02)	1.3 (0.02)	0.7 (0.02)	0.6 (0.02)
United States	51 (0.8)	534 (3.3)	29 (0.6)	483 (3.5)	20 (0.6)	461 (3.6)	2.2 (0.03)	1.1 (0.02)	2.4 (0.03)	1.2 (0.02)	1.8 (0.02)	0.7 (0.01)	1.8 (0.03)	0.6 (0.02)

—Not available.
†Not applicable.
‡Reporting standards not met.

[1]Index based on students' responses to four statements about mathematics: 1) I usually do well in mathematics; 2) Mathematics is more difficult for me than for many of my classmates; 3) Mathematics is not one of my strengths; 4) I learn things quickly in mathematics. Average is computed across the four items based on a 4-point scale: 1. Agree a lot; 2. Agree a little; 3. Disagree a little; 4. Disagree a lot. Students showing positive attitudes a little or a lot of the time across the four statements were assigned to the high level. Students showing negative attitudes a little or a lot of the time across the four statements were assigned to the low level. Students showing mixed attitudes across the four statements were assigned to the middle level.

[2]Number of hours based on: No time = 0; Less than 1 hour = 0.5; 1–2 hours = 1.5; More than 2, but less than 4 hours = 3; 4 or more hours = 4.5. Activities are not necessarily exclusive; students may have reported engaging in more than one activity at the same time.
[3]Did not satisfy guidelines for international participation rates.
[4]SAR=Special Administrative Region.
[5]Korea tested the same cohort of students as other countries, but later in 2003, at the beginning of the next school year.
NOTE: Data are for eighth grade or equivalent in most countries. Detail may not sum to totals because of rounding. Standard errors appear in parentheses.
SOURCE: International Association for the Evaluation of Educational Achievement (IEA), Trends in International Mathematics and Science Study (TIMSS), 2003, *TIMSS 2003 International Mathematics Report*, by Ina V. S. Mullis et al. (This table was prepared April 2005.)

Average fourth-grade science scores in content areas and average time spent teaching science in school, by country: 2003

Country	Average score by content area								Average yearly science instructional time in hours		Science instructional time as a percent of total instructional time[1]	
	Science overall		Life science		Physical science		Earth science					
1	2		3		4		5		6		7	
Armenia	437	(4.3)	435	(4.4)	429	(4.3)	450	(3.6)	‡	(†)	‡	(†)
Australia	[2]521	(4.2)	[2]523	(3.8)	[2]518	(3.9)	[2]518	(4.1)	[3]45	(2.6)	5	(0.3)
Austria	—	(†)	—	(†)	—	(†)	—	(†)	—	(†)	—	(†)
Belgium (Flemish)	518	(1.8)	524	(1.7)	507	(2.3)	522	(1.7)	‡	(†)	‡	(†)
Canada	—	(†)	—	(†)	—	(†)	—	(†)	—	(†)	—	(†)
Chinese Taipei	551	(1.7)	540	(1.6)	554	(2.0)	559	(2.6)	84	(1.0)	11	(0.2)
Cyprus	480	(2.4)	482	(2.1)	479	(2.3)	487	(2.5)	[3]46	(1.4)	5	(0.2)
Czech Republic	—	(†)	—	(†)	—	(†)	—	(†)	—	(†)	—	(†)
England	[2]540	(3.6)	[2]532	(3.1)	[2]546	(3.2)	[2]535	(3.5)	‡	(†)	‡	(†)
Greece	—	(†)	—	(†)	—	(†)	—	(†)	—	(†)	—	(†)
Hong Kong, SAR[4]	[2]542	(3.1)	[2]535	(2.6)	[2]548	(2.7)	[2]536	(2.7)	[3]77	(5.4)	8	(0.5)
Hungary	530	(3.0)	536	(2.5)	526	(2.7)	526	(3.7)	[3]54	(1.0)	6	(0.1)
Iceland	—	(†)	—	(†)	—	(†)	—	(†)	—	(†)	—	(†)
Iran, Islamic Republic of	414	(4.1)	424	(4.6)	419	(4.5)	428	(3.0)	‡	(†)	‡	(†)
Ireland	—	(†)	—	(†)	—	(†)	—	(†)	—	(†)	—	(†)
Israel	—	(†)	—	(†)	—	(†)	—	(†)	—	(†)	—	(†)
Italy	516	(3.8)	521	(3.5)	512	(3.5)	519	(3.7)	[5]73	(2.3)	[5]8	(0.3)
Japan	543	(1.5)	530	(1.3)	557	(1.7)	535	(1.9)	81	(1.2)	8	(0.2)
Korea, Republic of[6]	—	(†)	—	(†)	—	(†)	—	(†)	—	(†)	—	(†)
Kuwait	—	(†)	—	(†)	—	(†)	—	(†)	—	(†)	—	(†)
Latvia	532	(2.5)	531	(2.3)	532	(2.6)	534	(2.9)	‡	(†)	‡	(†)
Lithuania	512	(2.6)	[2,7]516	(2.0)	[2,7]512	(2.5)	[2,7]503	(3.2)	53	(1.6)	6	(0.2)
Netherlands	[2]525	(2.0)	[2]547	(1.8)	[2]505	(1.9)	[2]503	(2.3)	[3]33	(1.8)	3	(0.2)
New Zealand	520	(2.5)	520	(2.3)	516	(2.3)	522	(2.3)	[3]65	(3.5)	7	(0.4)
Norway	466	(2.6)	480	(2.2)	456	(2.3)	473	(2.8)	[5]38	(1.8)	[5]4	(0.2)
Philippines	332	(9.4)	330	(9.0)	343	(9.6)	324	(9.2)	[5]176	(3.2)	[5]16	(0.4)
Portugal	—	(†)	—	(†)	—	(†)	—	(†)	—	(†)	—	(†)
Russian Federation	526	(5.2)	526	(4.7)	527	(5.2)	527	(6.0)	[3]33	(1.2)	5	(0.2)
Scotland	[2]502	(2.9)	[2]506	(3.1)	[2]503	(2.6)	[2]498	(2.6)	‡	(†)	‡	(†)
Singapore	565	(5.5)	506	(3.1)	503	(2.6)	498	(2.6)	64	(0.6)	7	(0.1)
Slovenia	490	(2.5)	489	(2.9)	497	(2.3)	490	(2.7)	[5]75	(2.2)	[5]9	(0.3)
Thailand	—	(†)	—	(†)	—	(†)	—	(†)	—	(†)	—	(†)
Tunisia	314	(5.7)	290	(5.9)	324	(5.3)	336	(4.8)	‡	(†)	‡	(†)
United States	[2]536	(2.5)	[2]537	(2.2)	[2]531	(2.3)	[2]535	(2.5)	[5]83	(3.0)	[5]8	(0.3)

—Not available.

†Not applicable.

‡Does not meet reporting standards.

[1]Computed as the ratio of science instructional time to the total instructional time averaged across students.

[2]Met guidelines for participation rates only after replacement schools were included.

[3]Data are available for at least 50 but less than 70 percent of the students.

[4]SAR=Special Administrative Region.

[5]Data are available for at least 70 but less than 85 percent of the students.

[6]Korea tested the same cohort of students as other countries, but later in 2003, at the beginning of the next school year.

[7]National Desired Population does not cover all of International Desired Population.

NOTE: Data are for fourth grade or equivalent in most countries. Detail may not sum to totals because of rounding. Standard errors appear in parentheses.

SOURCE: International Association for the Evaluation of Educational Achievement (IEA), Trends in International Mathematics and Science Study (TIMSS), 2003, *TIMSS 2003 International Science Report*, by Ina V. S. Mullis et al. (This table was prepared October 2005.)

Average eighth-grade science scores in content areas and average time spent studying out of school, by country: 2003

Country	Average score by content area						Index of time students spend doing science homework (TSH) in a normal school week[1]					
	Science overall	Life science	Chemistry	Physics	Earth science	Environmental science	High TSH Percent	High TSH Average achievement	Medium TSH Percent	Medium TSH Average achievement	Low TSH Percent	Low TSH Average achievement
1	2	3	4	5	6	7	8	9	10	11	12	13
International average	473 (0.5)	474 (0.5)	474 (0.5)	474 (0.5)	474 (0.5)	474 (0.5)	13 (0.2)	458 (1.3)	44 (0.2)	466 (0.9)	43 (0.3)	467 (0.9)
Armenia	461 (3.5)	[2]453 (3.3)	[2]466 (4.2)	479 (3.2)	[2]460 (3.7)	[2]417 (4.4)	— (†)	— (†)	— (†)	— (†)	— (†)	— (†)
Australia	527 (3.8)	[3]532 (3.8)	[3]506 (3.8)	[3]521 (3.7)	[3]531 (4.2)	[3]536 (3.4)	9 (0.8)	520 (6.4)	35 (1.6)	530 (3.3)	56 (2.0)	530 (4.4)
Bahrain	438 (1.8)	[2]445 (1.9)	[2]441 (2.6)	[2]443 (2.0)	[2]440 (2.4)	[2]439 (3.1)	13 (0.7)	426 (4.1)	56 (1.3)	441 (2.5)	31 (1.4)	445 (2.6)
Belgium (Flemish)	516 (2.5)	[3]526 (2.4)	[3]503 (2.0)	[3]514 (2.5)	[3]508 (2.5)	[3]523 (2.7)	— (†)	— (†)	— (†)	— (†)	— (†)	— (†)
Botswana	365 (2.8)	[2]370 (2.7)	[2]348 (3.1)	[2]371 (3.2)	[2]361 (3.1)	[2]381 (3.3)	14 (0.7)	378 (6.1)	45 (1.0)	368 (3.2)	40 (1.2)	366 (3.6)
Bulgaria	479 (5.2)	474 (5.2)	482 (5.7)	485 (5.0)	491 (4.9)	[2]464 (5.0)	— (†)	— (†)	— (†)	— (†)	— (†)	— (†)
Chile	413 (2.9)	[2]427 (2.7)	[2]405 (3.3)	[2]401 (3.1)	[2]435 (3.1)	[2]436 (2.9)	[4]12 (1.2)	[4]588 (4.6)	[4]37 (1.3)	[4]581 (4.0)	[4]51 (2.1)	[4]561 (3.5)
Chinese Taipei	571 (3.5)	[3]563 (3.1)	[3]584 (4.0)	[3]569 (3.3)	[3]548 (3.1)	[3]560 (3.1)	— (†)	— (†)	— (†)	— (†)	— (†)	— (†)
Cyprus	441 (2.0)	[2]437 (2.2)	[2]443 (2.6)	[2]450 (1.7)	[2]447 (2.1)	[2]441 (2.3)	—	‡	‡	‡	‡	‡
England[5]	‡ (†)	‡ (†)	‡ (†)	‡ (†)	‡ (†)	‡ (†)	‡	‡	‡	‡	‡	‡
Egypt	421 (3.9)	[2]425 (3.7)	[2]442 (3.8)	[2]414 (4.1)	[2]403 (4.4)	[2]430 (4.0)	23 (0.7)	416 (4.4)	64 (0.8)	436 (4.0)	13 (0.6)	430 (6.6)
Estonia	552 (2.5)	[3]547 (2.4)	[3]552 (2.1)	[3]544 (2.4)	[3]558 (2.9)	[3]540 (2.2)	— (†)	— (†)	— (†)	— (†)	— (†)	— (†)
Ghana	255 (5.9)	[2]256 (5.6)	[2]276 (6.6)	[2]239 (5.4)	[2]254 (5.6)	[2]267 (6.2)	25 (1.2)	267 (8.5)	54 (1.0)	262 (6.0)	22 (1.0)	258 (8.1)
Hong Kong, SAR[6,7]	556 (3.0)	[3]551 (2.9)	[3]542 (2.6)	[3]555 (2.8)	[3]549 (2.9)	[3]555 (2.6)	6 (0.5)	548 (4.6)	43 (1.4)	563 (2.9)	50 (1.4)	554 (3.9)
Hungary	543 (2.8)	[3]536 (2.7)	[3]560 (3.1)	[3]536 (2.7)	[3]537 (3.1)	[3]528 (2.9)	— (†)	— (†)	— (†)	— (†)	— (†)	— (†)
Indonesia[8]	420 (4.1)	[2]424 (3.9)	[2]391 (3.8)	[2]430 (4.0)	[2]431 (3.8)	[2]454 (3.4)	— (†)	— (†)	— (†)	— (†)	— (†)	— (†)
Iran, Islamic Republic of	453 (2.3)	[2]447 (2.6)	[2]445 (2.7)	[2]445 (3.0)	[2]468 (2.9)	[2]487 (2.1)	8 (0.7)	451 (5.6)	42 (1.4)	457 (2.9)	49 (1.7)	452 (2.7)
Israel[9]	[10]488 (3.1)	[3]491 (3.0)	[3]499 (3.4)	[3]484 (2.9)	[3]485 (3.0)	[3]486 (2.9)	13 (0.9)	480 (4.7)	43 (1.6)	485 (4.3)	44 (2.0)	505 (3.4)
Italy	491 (3.1)	[3]498 (3.2)	[3]487 (3.3)	470 (3.2)	[3]513 (3.2)	[3]497 (3.0)	14 (1.0)	489 (5.9)	41 (1.1)	487 (3.7)	45 (1.4)	496 (3.7)
Japan	552 (1.7)	[3]549 (2.0)	[3]552 (2.1)	[3]564 (1.9)	[3]530 (2.1)	[3]537 (2.0)	— (†)	— (†)	— (†)	— (†)	— (†)	— (†)
Jordan	475 (3.8)	[2]448 (4.0)	[2]467 (4.4)	[2]465 (3.8)	[2]472 (4.0)	[2]442 (3.7)	19 (0.9)	466 (4.2)	52 (1.2)	478 (3.9)	29 (1.5)	499 (5.0)
Korea, Rep. of[11]	558 (1.6)	[3]558 (1.6)	[3]529 (2.5)	[3]579 (1.6)	[3]540 (1.9)	[3]513 (3.2)	4 (0.4)	549 (6.3)	26 (1.7)	562 (2.4)	70 (2.0)	559 (1.9)
Latvia	513 (2.9)	[3]511 (2.5)	[3]514 (3.2)	[3]512 (2.4)	[3]514 (2.8)	[3]508 (3.3)	— (†)	— (†)	— (†)	— (†)	— (†)	— (†)
Lebanon	393 (4.3)	[2]360 (5.0)	[2]433 (4.9)	[2]419 (4.0)	[2]395 (4.0)	[2]374 (5.1)	— (†)	— (†)	— (†)	— (†)	— (†)	— (†)
Lithuania[8]	519 (2.1)	517 (2.4)	[3]534 (2.3)	[3]519 (2.7)	[3]512 (2.7)	[3]507 (2.0)	— (†)	— (†)	— (†)	— (†)	— (†)	— (†)
Macedonia[9]	449 (3.6)	[2]448 (3.8)	[2]467 (3.9)	[2]458 (3.1)	[2]440 (4.3)	[2]442 (3.7)	20 (1.0)	513 (4.4)	49 (0.9)	510 (3.6)	31 (1.3)	510 (4.6)
Malaysia	510 (3.7)	[3]504 (3.7)	[3]514 (3.8)	[3]519 (3.6)	[3]502 (3.8)	[3]513 (3.2)	— (†)	— (†)	— (†)	— (†)	— (†)	— (†)
Moldova	472 (3.4)	[2]466 (3.7)	[2]479 (3.9)	[2]479 (3.7)	[2]475 (4.0)	[2]454 (3.8)	[12]14 (0.7)	[12]391 (5.3)	[12]47 (1.1)	[12]396 (3.4)	[12]39 (1.3)	[12]408 (3.5)
Morocco[7,8]	[10]396 (2.5)	[2]390 (2.6)	[2]402 (2.7)	[2]410 (2.7)	[2]397 (3.4)	[2]396 (3.3)	— (†)	— (†)	— (†)	— (†)	— (†)	— (†)
Netherlands[7]	536 (3.1)	[3]536 (3.3)	[3]514 (2.6)	[3]538 (3.4)	[3]534 (3.2)	[3]539 (2.8)	— (†)	— (†)	— (†)	— (†)	— (†)	— (†)
New Zealand	520 (5.0)	[3]523 (5.1)	[3]501 (5.6)	[3]515 (4.7)	[3]525 (4.8)	[3]525 (3.9)	10 (1.3)	519 (6.2)	41 (1.6)	531 (6.9)	48 (2.0)	518 (5.1)
Norway	494 (2.2)	[3]496 (2.5)	[3]485 (3.0)	[3]488 (2.6)	[3]517 (2.7)	[3]496 (2.9)	13 (0.8)	485 (3.7)	44 (1.2)	493 (3.1)	43 (1.7)	503 (2.3)
Palestinian National Authority	435 (3.2)	[2]435 (3.6)	[2]444 (3.9)	[2]432 (3.6)	[2]439 (3.0)	[2]444 (3.7)	21 (1.1)	433 (4.4)	56 (1.3)	442 (3.4)	23 (1.3)	441 (4.8)
Philippines[13]	377 (5.8)	[2]387 (5.8)	[2]342 (6.1)	[2]380 (4.7)	[2]377 (5.7)	[2]403 (5.4)	17 (0.7)	381 (7.5)	50 (0.8)	379 (5.7)	33 (1.2)	381 (7.2)
Romania	470 (4.9)	471 (4.8)	474 (4.9)	473 (4.1)	469 (5.2)	472 (4.7)	— (†)	— (†)	— (†)	— (†)	— (†)	— (†)
Russian Federation	514 (3.7)	[3]514 (3.3)	[3]527 (4.0)	[3]511 (3.4)	[3]518 (3.3)	[3]491 (3.2)	— (†)	382 (6.0)	61 (1.5)	402 (4.6)	31 (1.7)	403 (4.6)
Saudi Arabia	398 (4.0)	[2]412 (3.9)	[2]382 (4.8)	[2]394 (3.9)	[2]394 (4.0)	[2]410 (3.8)	8 (0.7)	487 (14.2)	27 (0.4)	508 (5.0)	71 (1.5)	517 (3.4)
Scotland[7]	512 (3.4)	[3]512 (3.3)	[3]499 (3.2)	[3]515 (3.0)	[3]515 (3.8)	[3]511 (3.5)	3 (0.4)	— (†)	— (†)	— (†)	— (†)	— (†)
Serbia[8]	468 (2.5)	[2]468 (2.6)	474 (2.4)	471 (2.6)	471 (3.0)	[2]457 (2.4)	— (†)	— (†)	— (†)	— (†)	— (†)	— (†)
Singapore	578 (4.3)	[3]569 (4.0)	[3]582 (4.2)	[3]579 (3.4)	[3]549 (3.9)	[3]568 (3.8)	18 (0.7)	595 (4.1)	48 (0.7)	585 (4.4)	34 (0.9)	564 (5.5)

See notes at end of table.

Average eighth-grade science scores in content areas and average time spent studying out of school, by country: 2003—Continued

Country	Average score by content area						Index of time students spend doing science homework (TSH) in a normal school week[1]					
	Science overall	Life science	Chemistry	Physics	Earth science	Environmental science	High TSH		Medium TSH		Low TSH	
							Percent	Average achievement	Percent	Average achievement	Percent	Average achievement
1	2	3	4	5	6	7	8	9	10	11	12	13
Slovak Republic..........	517 (3.2)	[3] 514 (2.9)	[3] 519 (3.6)	[3] 519 (2.9)	[3] 523 (3.3)	[3] 509 (2.8)	— (†)	— (†)	— (†)	— (†)	— (†)	— (†)
Slovenia................	520 (1.8)	[3] 521 (2.2)	[3] 532 (2.6)	[3] 509 (1.8)	[3] 523 (2.2)	[3] 515 (2.2)	— (†)	— (†)	— (†)	— (†)	— (†)	— (†)
South Africa...........	244 (6.7)	[2] 250 (6.0)	[2] 285 (5.9)	[2] 244 (6.2)	[2] 247 (6.3)	[2] 261 (6.6)	17 (0.7)	234 (9.6)	52 (0.9)	246 (7.9)	32 (0.9)	263 (7.4)
Sweden.................	524 (2.7)	[3] 528 (2.7)	[3] 526 (2.6)	[3] 525 (2.9)	[3] 532 (3.3)	[3] 499 (2.6)	— (†)	— (†)	— (†)	— (†)	— (†)	— (†)
Tunisia................	404 (2.1)	[2] 417 (2.0)	[2] 413 (2.5)	[2] 386 (2.5)	[2] 408 (2.0)	[2] 436 (2.2)	9 (0.6)	398 (4.0)	35 (0.9)	400 (2.8)	56 (1.2)	411 (2.6)
United States[9]......	[10] 527 (3.1)	[3] 537 (3.0)	[3] 513 (3.2)	[3] 515 (2.9)	[3] 532 (2.9)	[3] 533 (2.9)	13 (0.7)	519 (4.3)	43 (1.4)	530 (3.4)	45 (1.7)	531 (3.7)

—Not available.
†Not applicable.
‡Reporting standards not met.
[1]Index based on students' reports on the frequency and amount of science homework they are given. High level indicates more than 30 minutes of science homework assigned 3–4 times a week. Low level indicates no more than 30 minutes of science homework no more than twice a week. Medium level includes all other possible combinations of responses.
[2]Country average significantly lower than international average.
[3]Country average significantly higher than international average.
[4]Students were asked about natural science; data pertain to grade 8 physics/chemistry course.
[5]Did not satisfy guidelines for sample participation rates.
[6]SAR=Special Administrative Region.
[7]Met guidelines for sample participation rates only after replacement schools were included.

[8]National Desired Population does not cover all of International Desired Population.
[9]National Defined Population covers less than 90 percent of National Desired Population.
[10]Did not meet international sampling or other guidelines.
[11]Korea tested the same cohort of students as other countries, but later in 2003, at the beginning of the next school year.
[12]Met guidelines for sample participation rates only after replacement schools were included.
[13]Students study only biology at grade 8.
NOTE: Data are for eighth grade or equivalent in most countries. Detail may not sum to totals because of rounding. Standard errors appear in parentheses.
SOURCE: International Association for the Evaluation of Educational Achievement (IEA), Trends in International Mathematics and Science Study (TIMSS), 2003, *TIMSS 2003 International Science Report,* by Ina V. S. Mullis et al. (This table was prepared October 2005.)

Pupils per teacher in public and private elementary and secondary schools, by level of education and country: Selected years, 1985 to 2003

	Elementary							Junior high school (lower secondary)							Senior high school (upper secondary)						
Country	1985	1990	1996	2000	2001	2002	2003	1985	1990	1996	2000	2001	2002	2003	1985	1990	1996	2000	2001	2002	2003
1	2	3	4	5	6	7	8	9	10	11	12	13	14	15	16	17	18	19	20	21	22
Australia	[1]13.8	—	18.1	17.3	17.0	16.9	16.6	—	—	—	—	—	12.5	[2]12.4	3.2	—	—	—	—	12.5	[2]12.4
Austria	11.3	11.6	12.7	—	14.3	14.4	14.4	9.2	7.7	9.2	—	9.8	9.8	10.0	15.2	12.4	8.5	—	9.9	10.3	10.2
Belgium	—	—	—	15.0	13.4	13.1	13.1	—	—	—	—	—	9.3	10.6	—	—	—	—	—	9.3	9.6
Canada	18.1	17.1	17.0	18.1	18.3	—	—	16.0	15.5	20.0	18.1	18.4	—	—	16.0	15.3	19.5	19.5	17.2	—	—
Denmark	12.7	11.2	11.2	10.4	10.0	10.9	10.8	10.2	9.3	10.1	11.4	11.1	10.9	10.8	14.8	13.3	12.1	14.4	13.9	14.2	13.4
France	—	—	19.5	19.8	19.5	19.4	19.4	16.9	14.6	16.0	14.7	13.5	13.7	13.7	—	21.0	13.1	10.4	11.2	10.6	10.6
Germany[3]	20.7	20.3	20.9	19.8	19.4	18.9	18.7	—	—	—	15.7	15.7	15.7	15.6	23.7	—	—	13.9	13.7	13.6	13.7
Ireland	—	—	22.6	21.5	20.3	19.5	18.7	—	—	—	15.9	15.2	14.3	13.7	7.2	8.3	—	—	—	14.3	13.7
Italy	12.8	10.7	11.2	11.0	10.8	10.6	10.9	9.6	8.5	10.8	10.4	9.9	9.9	10.3	10.8	10.7	9.8	10.2	10.4	10.3	10.8
Japan	—	[1]20.8	19.7	20.9	20.6	20.3	19.9	—	18.6	16.2	16.8	16.6	16.2	15.7	—	16.2	15.6	14.0	14.0	13.7	13.5
Netherlands	20.2	19.2	20.0	16.8	17.2	17.0	16.0	12.7	12.4	18.1	19.9	18.7	19.4	18.8	—	—	14.1	13.1	12.8	15.9	15.7
New Zealand	20.1	19.1	22.0	20.6	19.6	19.6	19.9	—	—	—	—	—	—	—	—	—	—	—	—	13.8	10.9
Norway	—	—	—	12.4	11.6	11.5	[1]11.7	—	—	—	9.9	9.3	10.3	[1]10.4	—	—	—	9.7	9.2	9.2	[1]9.2
Portugal	—	—	—	12.1	11.6	11.0	—	—	—	—	10.4	9.9	9.3	—	—	—	—	7.9	8.0	7.5	—
Spain	26.8	21.2	18.0	14.9	14.7	14.6	14.3	21.4	18.8	17.8	—	—	13.7	13.3	15.3	14.8	14.2	—	—	8.3	7.9
Sweden	11.6	10.6	12.7	12.8	12.4	12.5	12.3	10.8	10.2	12.2	12.8	12.4	12.2	12.1	13.1	11.9	15.2	15.2	16.6	14.1	14.1
Turkey	31.1	30.6	—	30.5	29.8	27.5	25.9	41.3	48.4	—	[2]17.6	[2]17.3	[2]17.6	[2]17.4	11.0	12.1	—	14.0	17.2	17.7	18.0
United Kingdom	19.7	22.0	21.3	21.2	20.5	19.9	[2]20.0	—	18.5	16.0	16.3	17.0	15.5	15.5	11.1	13.9	15.3	[2]12.5	[2]12.3	[2]12.5	[2]12.6
United States	17.0	15.6	16.9	15.8	16.3	15.5	15.5	16.5	15.9	17.5	16.3	17.0	15.5	15.5	16.2	15.8	14.7	14.1	14.8	15.6	15.6

—Not available.

[1]Public schools only.

[2]Includes only general programs in lower and upper secondary education.

[3]Data for 1985 are for the former West Germany.

NOTE: In this table, U.S. data for elementary correspond to grades 1 through 6; junior high school corresponds to grades 7 through 9; and senior high school corresponds to grades 10 through 12.
SOURCE: Organization for Economic Cooperation and Development (OECD), Education Online Database; *Annual National Accounts, Vol. 1, 1997*; and *Education at a Glance, 2002 through 2005.* (This table was prepared October 2005.)

Number of bachelor's degree recipients per 100 persons of the typical age of graduation, by sex and country: 2002 and 2003

Country	Male and female		Male		Female	
	2002	2003	2002	2003	2002	2003
1	2	3	4	5	6	7
Australia	50.7	54.8	43.0	46.7	58.8	63.4
Austria	18.0	19.0	17.9	18.7	18.1	19.4
Belgium[1]	19.2	—	18.7	—	19.7	—
Canada	—	—	—	—	—	—
Czech Republic	15.4	17.3	14.3	15.9	16.6	18.8
Denmark	34.4	38.6	23.4	25.1	45.7	52.3
Finland	51.8	55.8	37.7	40.4	66.4	72.2
France	39.0	41.5	32.9	34.9	45.3	48.4
Germany	19.2	19.5	19.3	19.3	19.1	19.7
Hungary	31.1	33.6	23.2	24.6	39.3	43.2
Iceland	40.0	44.2	27.2	29.4	53.1	59.1
Ireland	30.9	36.8	25.6	29.7	36.2	44.0
Italy	22.4	27.8	19.2	24.0	25.6	31.6
Japan	34.1	34.4	40.2	40.1	27.6	28.5
Korea, Republic of	31.5	31.7	31.6	32.1	31.3	31.2
Mexico	16.5	14.3	15.6	13.3	17.4	15.3
Netherlands	38.6	42.5	34.4	36.4	42.9	48.7
New Zealand	41.6	39.0	31.8	29.1	51.3	49.1
Norway	41.1	42.0	29.7	30.0	52.8	54.2
Portugal	—	—	—	—	—	—
Spain	33.1	32.0	26.4	25.5	40.0	38.9
Sweden	35.2	38.4	26.5	28.6	44.1	48.5
Switzerland	20.8	20.9	23.3	23.5	18.3	18.4
Turkey	—	—	—	—	—	—
United Kingdom	—	—	—	—	—	—
United States	36.1	33.4	29.7	27.6	42.9	39.4

—Not available.

[1]Data for Flemish Belgium only.

NOTE: The recipients per 100 persons ratio relates the number of people of all ages earning bachelor's degrees in a particular year to the number of people in the population at the typical age of graduation. The typical age is based on full-time attendance and normal progression through the education system (without repeating a year, taking a year off, etc.); this age varies across countries because of differences in their education systems.

SOURCE: Organization for Economic Cooperation and Development (OECD), Education Online Database. Retrieved November 1, 2005, from http://stats.oecd.org/WBOS/Default.aspx. (This table was prepared November 2005.)

Percentage of bachelor's degrees awarded in science, by field and country: Selected years, 1985 through 2003

Country	All science degrees[1]					Natural sciences[2]					Mathematics and computer science[3]					Engineering				
	1985	1990	1995	2000	2003	1985	1990	1995	2000	2003	1985	1990	1995	2000	2003	1985	1990	1995	2000	2003
1	2	3	4	5	6	7	8	9	10	11	12	13	14	15	16	17	18	19	20	21
Australia	—	—	19.3	21.1	23.7	—	—	9.9	7.6	5.5	—	—	3.8	5.1	10.2	—	—	5.6	8.5	8.0
Austria	16.8	19.6	21.1	25.7	26.5	5.0	5.3	6.0	5.0	5.3	4.1	5.2	5.3	3.4	3.4	7.7	9.0	9.9	17.3	17.8
Belgium[4]	—	—	—	—	24.6	4.6	—	—	—	7.0	1.7	—	—	—	2.8	—	—	—	—	14.9
Canada	17.1	16.4	16.7	20.0	—	4.9	6.0	6.5	8.1	—	4.5	4.2	3.8	4.3	—	7.7	6.2	6.4	7.6	—
Czech Republic	—	—	—	29.5	30.2	—	—	—	4.2	4.7	—	—	—	8.4	4.2	—	—	—	16.9	21.4
Denmark	—	—	—	10.5	11.4	6.3	4.4	2.5	6.8	3.2	—	—	—	3.1	1.1	16.2	21.7	17.0	0.6	7.1
Finland	39.3	33.5	37.2	32.2	28.8	7.7	4.1	4.0	3.9	2.6	6.3	5.9	6.9	3.3	4.5	25.3	23.4	26.3	24.9	21.8
France	—	—	—	30.1	27.1	—	—	—	12.2	9.0	—	—	—	5.5	4.7	—	—	—	12.5	13.4
Germany[5]	23.8	31.3	31.6	31.7	30.1	5.0	7.2	6.7	6.4	6.0	2.3	3.5	5.2	4.9	5.8	16.5	20.5	19.7	20.3	18.3
Hungary	—	—	—	12.6	—	—	—	—	1.1	—	—	—	—	1.2	—	—	—	—	10.4	—
Iceland	—	—	—	16.5	17.3	—	—	—	6.0	4.7	—	—	—	4.0	6.6	—	—	—	6.5	6.1
Ireland	28.8	34.1	32.3	29.3	27.0	12.8	14.1	16.9	11.5	8.4	4.0	6.3	4.7	7.2	9.6	12.0	13.7	10.7	10.6	8.9
Italy	19.5	19.7	19.5	27.5	25.6	8.1	7.6	6.8	5.9	5.1	3.1	3.9	3.8	3.2	2.9	8.3	8.3	8.9	18.4	17.6
Japan	22.7	23.5	22.8	18.9	18.2	2.4	2.4	3.4	—	0.0	—	—	—	—	0.0	20.3	21.0	19.3	18.9	18.2
Korea, Republic of	—	—	—	36.9	37.8	—	—	—	6.3	6.6	—	—	—	4.3	3.9	—	—	—	26.3	27.3
Mexico	—	—	—	23.0	28.1	—	—	—	2.2	2.5	—	—	—	6.7	8.9	—	—	—	14.1	16.8
Netherlands	21.8	21.1	—	16.2	—	8.5	7.1	—	3.2	—	1.2	1.6	1.6	1.9	—	12.1	12.4	—	11.1	—
New Zealand	20.5	19.5	—	17.8	20.4	11.7	8.2	—	11.2	5.8	5.5	5.5	—	1.9	8.7	3.3	5.8	3.2	4.7	5.8
Norway	—	12.9	16.8	11.6	16.5	2.5	2.1	3.1	0.7	0.4	1.8	0.6	0.5	3.4	6.5	—	10.2	13.2	7.5	9.7
Poland	—	—	—	16.7	17.0	—	—	—	2.7	2.6	—	—	—	2.0	3.0	—	—	—	12.0	11.4
Portugal	—	—	15.0	17.5	18.2	6.5	6.7	2.2	1.7	2.9	—	—	2.8	3.6	2.4	—	10.5	9.9	12.2	12.9
Spain	13.9	15.0	18.2	22.7	24.7	5.5	5.7	4.3	5.3	4.7	1.3	2.6	4.5	4.3	4.6	7.0	6.7	9.4	13.1	15.4
Sweden	15.4	24.0	26.4	27.7	—	2.6	4.1	3.9	3.7	—	1.6	4.7	5.5	3.7	—	11.3	15.2	17.0	20.3	—
Switzerland	20.2	23.0	22.3	25.1	23.9	10.3	11.2	10.4	6.0	5.6	2.1	3.7	3.7	1.8	3.6	7.9	8.1	8.3	17.3	14.7
Turkey	23.0	20.6	20.9	24.1	21.7	3.6	4.6	5.1	7.4	6.4	1.6	2.1	2.7	3.6	3.8	17.8	13.8	13.1	13.1	11.5
United Kingdom	—	—	—	28.5	31.2	—	—	—	12.5	13.0	—	—	—	5.8	8.5	—	—	—	10.2	9.7
United States	21.7	16.9	—	17.1	17.6	6.3	5.1	—	6.6	6.0	5.5	4.0	3.3	3.9	5.2	9.8	7.8	6.7	6.6	6.4

—Not available.

[1]Includes life sciences, physical sciences, mathematics/statistics, computer science, and engineering.

[2]Includes life sciences and physical sciences.

[3]Includes mathematics/statistics and computer science.

[4]Data for Flemish Belgium only.

[5]Data for 1985 are for the former West Germany.

NOTE: Data in this table refer to degrees classified by the Organization for Economic Cooperation and Development (OECD) as International Standard Classification of Education (ISCED), level 5A, first award. This level corresponds to the bachelor's degree in the United States.
SOURCE: Organization for Economic Cooperation and Development (OECD), Education Online Database. Retrieved October 31, 2005, from http://stats.oecd.org/WBOS/Default.aspx. (This table was prepared November 2005.)

Percentage of graduate degrees awarded in science, by field and country: Selected years, 1985 through 2003

Country	All science degrees[1]						Natural sciences[2]						Mathematics and computer science[3]						Engineering					
	1985	1990	1996	1999	2000	2003	1985	1990	1996	1999	2000	2003	1985	1990	1996	1999	2000	2003	1985	1990	1996	1999	2000	2003
1	2	3	4	5	6	7	8	9	10	11	12	13	14	15	16	17	18	19	20	21	22	23	24	25
Australia	—	—	14.0	17.9	15.2	15.5	—	—	5.4	6.3	4.0	3.6	—	—	3.8	3.8	4.9	7.2	—	—	4.7	7.7	6.3	4.7
Austria	43.3	37.7	38.8	38.4	39.2	35.4	14.2	12.3	17.5	15.0	16.7	14.9	7.3	4.6	4.7	3.6	4.7	5.3	21.7	20.8	16.6	19.8	17.7	15.1
Belgium[4]	—	—	—	17.6	—	18.8	—	—	—	7.0	—	9.5	—	—	—	2.4	—	4.9	—	—	—	8.3	—	4.4
Canada	19.7	20.0	22.3	23.0	22.4	—	7.5	7.8	7.7	7.9	7.4	3.5	2.8	3.4	3.5	3.6	4.1	—	9.4	8.8	11.2	11.5	10.9	—
Czech Republic	—	—	—	21.3	21.0	12.4	—	—	—	5.6	5.3	3.5	—	—	—	6.3	7.9	2.2	—	—	—	9.3	7.7	6.7
Denmark	16.0	22.2	12.3	—	30.2	27.8	4.1	5.8	3.1	—	9.8	8.1	2.7	4.8	1.5	—	2.5	4.1	9.2	11.6	7.8	—	15.4	15.7
Finland	47.6	30.6	28.3	31.1	28.7	28.1	24.0	14.7	11.6	8.5	11.3	10.3	6.3	5.4	4.0	3.9	2.4	3.5	17.2	10.5	12.7	18.7	14.9	14.3
France	—	—	—	21.0	26.4	34.4	—	—	—	6.4	13.5	17.1	—	—	—	1.6	5.6	8.5	—	—	—	13.0	7.3	8.9
Germany[5]	27.7	33.2	38.6	38.9	38.1	36.0	18.7	23.5	25.5	25.2	24.9	22.2	1.8	2.3	3.5	4.0	3.7	4.2	7.2	7.4	9.5	9.8	9.5	9.6
Hungary	—	—	—	13.5	9.9	7.7	—	—	—	4.8	1.7	1.7	—	—	—	1.2	0.7	1.1	—	—	—	7.6	7.5	4.9
Iceland	—	—	—	30.7	35.9	20.5	—	—	—	20.0	19.4	10.3	—	—	—	—	—	1.0	—	—	—	10.7	16.5	9.2
Ireland	31.4	34.5	23.1	24.8	28.1	21.0	18.9	19.5	10.9	4.0	6.9	5.1	2.6	5.8	3.0	16.0	15.2	10.0	9.9	9.3	9.2	4.8	6.0	6.0
Italy	—	—	—	13.1	11.7	12.8	—	—	—	1.0	0.3	2.8	—	—	—	6.5	5.8	3.9	—	—	—	5.6	5.7	6.1
Japan	50.1	54.6	—	42.4	51.7	38.5	9.5	9.5	10.2	8.8	8.5	10.2	—	—	—	—	0.0	0.0	40.5	45.1	44.4	42.4	41.9	38.5
Korea, Republic of	—	—	—	48.3	48.4	45.6	—	—	—	8.8	8.4	10.2	—	—	—	4.1	5.7	3.1	—	—	—	35.4	34.3	32.3
Mexico	—	—	—	22.7	31.4	20.0	—	—	—	14.3	18.9	6.8	—	—	—	2.0	4.1	2.5	—	—	—	6.4	8.4	10.8
Netherlands	—	28.9	18.6	17.6	—	24.2	20.6	17.7	4.4	6.8	—	3.9	—	1.5	3.7	2.0	8.7	0.7	7.5	9.7	10.6	8.8	1.2	19.7
New Zealand	45.1	22.6	16.7	24.4	20.5	16.7	24.6	13.8	12.7	13.4	11.6	6.7	5.4	4.7	1.1	1.5	1.4	6.0	15.1	4.0	3.0	9.4	7.5	4.1
Norway	40.1	33.4	38.3	21.0	22.0	22.0	17.9	8.0	8.7	15.0	14.9	11.8	3.5	2.1	1.9	4.3	4.6	5.6	18.7	23.3	27.7	—	2.5	4.7
Poland	—	—	—	3.1	3.3	4.1	—	—	—	0.6	0.7	0.8	—	—	—	0.9	0.7	0.6	—	—	—	1.7	1.9	2.7
Portugal	—	—	—	—	39.3	—	—	—	—	—	11.7	—	—	—	—	—	9.4	—	—	—	—	—	18.2	—
Spain	35.6	26.9	36.0	40.1	36.1	35.8	28.6	19.7	24.8	24.8	23.9	22.7	1.8	1.4	4.1	4.2	5.4	5.7	5.1	5.7	7.1	11.1	6.8	7.3
Sweden	48.0	48.5	32.3	41.5	40.5	32.2	21.2	19.4	9.2	14.4	14.3	11.4	6.8	9.2	5.9	4.1	4.0	3.8	20.0	19.9	17.1	23.0	22.2	17.0
Switzerland	30.7	30.2	40.1	41.5	42.7	32.6	20.3	22.0	25.8	11.4	11.7	9.8	2.8	1.7	4.1	17.0	19.5	12.6	7.6	6.5	10.1	13.1	11.6	10.2
Turkey	35.8	24.0	—	29.8	25.7	22.9	6.6	7.6	—	8.0	7.6	6.9	2.8	3.3	—	3.0	3.0	3.2	26.3	13.2	—	18.7	15.2	12.7
United Kingdom	—	14.5	—	21.8	21.7	22.1	—	4.2	—	6.0	7.4	7.5	—	3.4	—	4.7	5.0	6.2	—	6.9	—	11.0	9.2	8.4
United States	13.5	14.5	13.8	13.7	13.0	13.7	4.5	4.2	4.0	3.8	3.4	3.4	2.8	3.4	3.2	3.1	3.4	4.0	6.3	6.9	6.7	6.8	6.2	6.4

—Not available.

[1] Includes life sciences, physical sciences, mathematics/statistics, computer science, and engineering.
[2] Includes life sciences and physical sciences.
[3] Includes mathematics/statistics and computer science.
[4] Data for Flemish Belgium only.
[5] Data for 1985 are for the former West Germany.

NOTE: Data in this table refer to degrees classified by the Organization for Economic Cooperation and Development (OECD) as International Standard Classification of Education (ISCED), level 5A, second award and ISCED 6. ISCED 5A, second award, corresponds to master's and first-professional degrees in the United States, and ISCED 6 corresponds to doctor's degrees.
SOURCE: Organization for Economic Cooperation and Development (OECD), Education Online Database. Retrieved October 31, 2005, from http://stats.oecd.org/WBOS/Default.aspx; and previously unpublished tabulations. (This table was prepared November 2005.)

Foreign students enrolled in institutions of higher education in the United States and other jurisdictions, by continent, region, and selected countries of origin: Selected years, 1980-81 through 2003-04

Continent, region, and country	1980–81 Number	Percent	1985–86 Number	Percent	1990–91 Number	Percent	1995–96 Number	Percent	2000–01 Number	Percent	2001–02 Number	Percent	2002–03 Number	Percent	2003–04 Number	Percent
1	2	3	4	5	6	7	8	9	10	11	12	13	14	15	16	17
Total	311,880	100.0	343,780	100.0	407,530	100.0	453,787	100.00	547,867	100.0	582,996	100.0	586,323	100.0	572,509	100.0
Africa	38,180	12.2	34,190	9.9	23,800	5.8	20,844	4.59	34,217	6.2	37,724	6.5	40,193	6.9	38,150	6.7
Eastern Africa	6,260	2.0	6,730	2.0	7,590	1.9	7,596	1.67	13,516	2.5	15,331	2.6	15,996	2.7	14,831	2.6
Central Africa	1,130	0.4	1,540	0.4	1,650	0.4	1,346	0.30	1,859	0.3	1,972	0.3	2,371	0.4	2,331	0.4
North Africa	7,310	2.3	5,980	1.7	4,540	1.1	3,422	0.75	5,184	0.9	5,593	1.0	5,218	0.9	4,487	0.8
Southern Africa	1,480	0.5	2,360	0.7	2,840	0.7	2,657	0.59	3,304	0.6	3,443	0.6	3,017	0.5	2,679	0.5
West Africa	22,000	7.1	17,580	5.1	7,180	1.8	5,818	1.28	10,346	1.9	11,385	2.0	13,590	2.3	13,821	2.4
Nigeria	17,350	5.6	13,710	4.0	3,710	0.9	2,093	0.46	3,820	0.7	4,499	0.8	5,816	1.0	6,140	1.1
Asia	94,640	30.3	156,830	45.6	229,830	56.4	259,893	57.27	302,058	55.1	324,812	55.7	332,298	56.7	324,006	56.6
East Asia	51,650	16.6	80,720	23.5	146,020	35.8	166,717	36.74	189,371	34.6	196,813	33.8	199,666	34.1	189,874	33.2
China	2,770	0.9	13,980	4.1	39,600	9.7	39,613	8.73	59,939	10.9	63,211	10.8	64,757	11.0	61,765	10.8
Hong Kong	9,660	3.1	10,710	3.1	12,630	3.1	12,018	2.65	7,627	1.4	7,757	1.3	8,076	1.4	7,353	1.3
Japan	13,500	4.3	13,360	3.9	36,610	9.0	45,531	10.03	46,497	8.5	46,810	8.0	45,960	7.8	40,835	7.1
Korea, Republic of	6,150	2.0	18,660	5.4	23,360	5.7	36,231	7.98	45,685	8.3	49,046	8.4	51,519	8.8	52,484	9.2
Taiwan	19,460	6.2	23,770	6.9	33,530	8.2	32,702	7.21	28,566	5.2	28,930	5.0	28,017	4.8	26,178	4.6
South and Central Asia	14,540	4.7	25,800	7.5	42,370	10.4	45,401	10.00	71,765	13.1	86,131	14.8	93,767	16.0	98,138	17.1
India	9,250	3.0	16,070	4.7	28,860	7.1	31,743	7.00	54,664	10.0	66,836	11.5	74,603	12.7	79,736	13.9
Pakistan	2,990	1.0	5,440	1.6	7,730	1.9	6,427	1.42	6,948	1.3	8,644	1.5	8,123	1.4	7,325	1.3
South East Asia	28,450	9.1	50,310	14.6	41,440	10.2	47,774	10.53	40,916	7.5	41,868	7.2	38,865	6.6	35,994	6.3
Indonesia	3,250	1.0	8,210	2.4	9,520	2.3	12,820	2.83	11,625	2.1	11,614	2.0	10,432	1.8	8,880	1.6
Malaysia	6,010	1.9	23,020	6.7	13,610	3.3	14,015	3.09	7,795	1.4	7,395	1.3	6,595	1.1	6,483	1.1
Philippines	—	—	3,920	1.1	4,270	1.0	3,127	0.69	3,139	0.6	3,295	0.6	3,576	0.6	3,467	0.6
Singapore	—	—	3,930	1.1	4,500	1.1	4,098	0.90	4,166	0.8	4,141	0.7	4,189	0.7	3,955	0.7
Thailand	6,550	2.1	6,940	2.0	7,090	1.7	12,165	2.68	11,187	2.0	11,606	2.0	9,982	1.7	8,937	1.6
Europe	25,330	8.1	34,310	10.0	49,640	12.2	67,358	14.84	80,584	14.7	81,579	14.0	78,001	13.3	74,134	12.9
Eastern Europe	1,670	0.5	1,770	0.5	4,780	1.2	18,032	3.97	27,674	5.1	29,591	5.1	29,167	5.0	27,710	4.8
Western Europe	23,660	7.6	32,540	9.5	44,860	11.0	49,326	10.87	52,910	9.7	51,988	8.9	48,834	8.3	46,424	8.1
France	—	—	3,680	1.1	5,630	1.4	5,710	1.26	7,273	1.3	7,401	1.3	7,223	1.2	6,818	1.2
Germany[1]	3,310	1.1	4,730	1.4	7,000	1.7	9,017	1.99	10,128	1.8	9,613	1.6	9,302	1.6	8,745	1.5
Greece	3,750	1.2	4,440	1.3	4,360	1.1	3,365	0.74	2,768	0.5	2,599	0.4	2,341	0.4	2,126	0.4
Spain	—	—	1,740	0.5	4,300	1.1	4,809	1.06	4,156	0.8	4,048	0.7	3,633	0.6	3,631	0.6
United Kingdom	4,440	1.4	5,940	1.7	7,300	1.8	7,799	1.72	8,139	1.5	8,414	1.4	8,326	1.4	8,439	1.5
Latin America	49,810	16.0	45,480	13.2	47,580	11.7	47,253	10.41	63,634	11.6	68,358	11.7	68,950	11.8	69,658	12.2
Caribbean	10,650	3.4	11,100	3.2	12,610	3.1	10,737	2.37	14,423	2.6	13,879	2.4	14,895	2.5	15,606	2.7
Central America	12,970	4.2	12,740	3.7	15,950	3.9	14,220	3.13	16,764	3.1	18,826	3.2	18,856	3.2	19,264	3.4
Mexico	6,730	2.2	5,460	1.6	6,740	1.7	8,687	1.91	10,670	1.9	12,518	2.1	12,801	2.2	13,329	2.3
South America	26,190	8.4	21,640	6.3	19,020	4.7	22,296	4.91	32,447	5.9	35,653	6.1	35,199	6.0	34,788	6.1
Brazil	—	—	2,840	0.8	3,900	1.0	5,497	1.21	8,846	1.6	8,972	1.5	8,388	1.4	7,799	1.4
Colombia	—	—	4,010	1.2	3,180	0.8	3,462	0.76	6,765	1.2	8,068	1.4	7,771	1.3	7,533	1.3
Venezuela	11,750	3.8	7,040	2.0	2,890	0.7	4,456	0.98	5,217	1.0	5,627	1.0	5,333	0.9	5,575	1.0
Middle East	84,710	27.2	52,720	15.3	33,420	8.2	30,563	6.74	36,858	6.7	38,545	6.6	34,803	5.9	31,852	5.6
Iran	47,550	15.2	14,210	4.1	6,260	1.5	2,628	0.58	1,844	0.3	2,216	0.4	2,258	0.4	2,321	0.4
Jordan	6,140	2.0	6,590	1.9	4,320	1.1	2,222	0.49	2,187	0.4	2,417	0.4	2,173	0.4	1,853	0.3
Lebanon	6,770	2.2	7,090	2.1	3,900	1.0	1,554	0.34	2,005	0.4	2,435	0.4	2,364	0.4	2,179	0.4
Saudi Arabia	10,440	3.3	6,900	2.0	3,590	0.9	4,191	0.92	5,273	1.0	5,579	1.0	4,175	0.7	3,521	0.6
Turkey	—	—	2,460	0.7	4,080	1.0	7,678	1.69	10,983	2.0	12,091	2.1	11,601	2.0	11,398	2.0
North America[2]	14,790	4.7	16,030	4.7	18,950	4.6	23,644	5.21	25,888	4.7	27,039	4.6	27,227	4.6	27,650	4.8
Canada	14,320	4.6	15,410	4.5	18,350	4.5	23,005	5.07	25,279	4.6	26,514	4.5	26,513	4.5	27,017	4.7
Oceania	4,180	1.3	4,030	1.2	4,230	1.0	4,202	0.93	4,624	0.8	4,852	0.8	4,811	0.8	4,534	0.8
Stateless[3]	240	0.1	190	0.1	80	#	30	#	10	#	87	#	33	#	19	#

—Not available.

#Rounds to zero.

[1]Data for 1980–81 and 1985–86 are for West Germany (Federal Republic of Germany before unification).

[2]Excludes Mexico and Central America, which are included with Latin America.

[3]Home country unknown or undeclared.

NOTE: Totals and subtotals include other countries not shown separately. Data are for "nonimmigrants" (i.e., students who have not migrated to this country). Detail may not sum to totals because of rounding.

SOURCE: Institute of International Education, *Open Doors: Report on International Educational Exchange*, various years. (This table was prepared March 2005.)

Total public direct expenditures on education as a percentage of the gross domestic product, by level and country: Selected years, 1985 through 2002

Country	All institutions[1]						Primary and secondary institutions						Higher education institutions					
	1985	1990	1995	2000	2001	2002[2]	1985	1990	1995	2000	2001	2002[2]	1985	1990	1995	2000	2001	2002[2]
1	2	3	4	5	6	7	8	9	10	11	12	13	14	15	16	17	18	19
Average for year	5.3	4.9	4.9	5.2	5.1	4.9	3.7	3.5	3.5	3.5	3.6	3.6	1.1	1.0	0.9	1.2	1.1	1.0
Average for countries reporting data for all years	5.4	5.2	5.3	5.4	5.2	5.3	3.7	3.7	3.6	3.6	3.6	3.7	1.1	1.1	1.1	1.4	1.1	1.1
Australia	5.4	4.3	4.5	5.1	4.5	4.4	3.5	3.2	3.2	3.9	3.6	3.6	1.7	1.0	1.2	1.2	0.8	0.8
Austria	5.6	5.2	5.3	5.8	5.6	5.4	3.7	3.6	3.8	3.8	3.8	3.7	1.0	1.0	0.9	1.4	1.2	1.1
Belgium[3]	6.3	4.8	5.0	5.2	6.0	6.1	4.0	3.4	3.4	3.4	4.0	[4]4.1	1.0	0.8	0.9	1.3	1.2	[4]1.2
Canada	6.1	5.4	5.8	5.5	4.9	—	4.1	3.7	4.0	3.3	3.1	—	2.0	1.5	1.5	2.0	1.5	—
Czech Republic	—	—	4.8	4.4	4.2	4.2	—	—	3.4	3.0	2.8	2.8	—	—	0.7	0.8	0.8	0.8
Denmark	6.2	6.2	6.5	8.4	6.8	[5]6.8	4.7	4.4	4.2	4.8	4.2	[5,6]4.1	1.2	1.3	1.3	2.5	1.8	[5,6]1.9
Finland	5.8	6.4	6.6	6.0	5.7	5.9	—	4.3	4.2	3.6	3.7	3.8	—	1.2	1.7	2.0	1.7	1.7
France	—	5.1	5.8	5.8	5.6	5.7	—	3.7	4.1	4.1	4.0	4.0	—	0.8	1.0	1.0	1.0	1.0
Germany[7]	4.6	—	4.5	4.5	4.3	4.4	2.8	—	2.9	3.0	2.9	3.0	1.0	—	1.0	1.1	1.0	1.0
Greece	—	—	3.7	3.8	3.8	[5]3.9	—	—	2.8	2.7	2.4	[5]2.5	—	—	0.8	0.9	1.1	[5]1.2
Hungary	—	5.0	4.9	4.9	4.6	5.0	—	3.5	3.3	3.1	2.8	3.1	—	0.8	0.8	1.0	0.9	1.0
Iceland	—	4.3	4.5	6.0	6.1	6.8	—	3.3	3.4	4.7	5.0	[5,6]5.4	—	0.6	0.7	1.1	0.9	[5,6]1.0
Ireland	5.6	4.7	4.7	4.4	4.1	[5]4.1	4.0	3.3	3.3	3.0	2.9	[4]3.0	0.9	0.9	0.9	1.3	1.1	[4]1.1
Italy	4.7	5.8	4.5	4.6	4.9	4.6	3.2	4.1	3.2	3.2	3.6	3.4	0.6	1.0	0.7	0.8	0.8	0.8
Japan	—	3.6	3.6	3.6	3.5	3.5	—	2.9	2.8	2.7	2.7	[6]2.7	—	0.4	0.4	0.5	0.5	[6]0.4
Korea, Republic of	—	—	3.6	4.3	4.8	4.2	—	—	3.0	3.3	3.5	3.3	—	—	0.3	0.7	0.4	0.3
Luxembourg	—	—	4.3	—	3.6	—	—	—	4.2	—	3.6	[6]3.9	—	—	0.1	—	—	[6]—
Mexico	—	3.2	4.6	4.9	5.1	5.1	—	2.2	3.4	3.4	3.8	3.5	—	0.7	0.8	0.9	0.7	1.0
Netherlands	6.2	5.7	4.6	4.8	4.5	4.6	4.1	3.6	3.0	3.2	3.1	3.3	1.5	1.6	1.1	1.3	1.0	1.0
New Zealand	—	5.5	5.3	7.0	5.5	5.6	—	3.9	3.8	4.9	4.3	4.4	—	1.2	1.1	1.7	0.9	0.9
Norway	5.1	6.2	6.8	6.7	6.1	6.7	4.0	4.1	4.1	3.9	4.6	4.2	0.7	1.1	1.5	1.7	1.3	1.4
Poland	—	—	5.2	5.2	5.6	[5]5.5	—	—	3.3	3.8	4.0	[5]4.0	—	—	0.8	0.8	1.1	[5]1.1
Portugal	—	—	5.4	5.7	5.8	[5]5.7	—	—	4.1	4.2	4.2	[5]4.2	—	—	1.0	1.0	1.0	[5]0.9
Russian Federation	—	—	3.4	3.0	3.0	4.0	—	—	1.9	1.7	1.7	[4,5]2.7	—	—	0.7	0.5	0.5	[4,5]0.7
Spain	3.6	4.2	4.8	4.4	4.3	4.3	2.9	3.2	3.5	3.1	3.0	2.9	0.4	0.7	0.8	1.0	1.0	1.0
Sweden	—	5.3	6.6	7.4	6.3	6.7	—	4.4	4.4	4.9	4.3	[4]4.6	—	1.0	1.6	2.0	1.5	[4]1.6
Switzerland	4.9	5.0	5.5	5.4	5.4	5.7	4.0	3.7	4.1	3.9	3.9	4.0	0.9	1.0	1.1	1.2	1.3	1.4
Turkey	—	3.2	2.2	3.5	3.5	[5]3.4	—	2.3	1.4	2.4	2.5	[5]2.3	—	0.9	0.8	1.1	1.0	[5]1.0
United Kingdom	4.9	4.3	4.6	4.8	4.7	5.0	3.1	3.5	3.8	3.4	3.4	3.7	1.0	0.7	0.7	1.0	0.8	0.8
United States	4.7	5.3	5.0	5.0	5.1	5.3	3.2	3.8	3.5	3.5	3.8	3.8	1.3	1.4	1.1	1.1	0.9	1.2

—Not available.

[1]Includes preprimary and other expenditures not classified by level.

[2]Includes public subsidies to households attributable for educational institutions and includes direct expenditure on educational institutions from international sources.

[3]Data are for Flemish Belgium only.

[4]Direct expenditure on higher education institutions from international sources exceeds 1.5 percent of all public expenditure.

[5]Public subsidies to households not included in public expenditure.

[6]Postsecondary non-higher education included in both secondary and higher education.

[7]Data for 1985 are for the former West Germany.

NOTE: Direct public expenditure on educational services includes both amounts spent directly by governments to hire educational personnel and to procure other resources, and amounts provided by governments to public or private institutions, or households. Figures for 1985 also include transfers and payments to private entities, and thus are not strictly comparable with later figures. Some data have been revised from previously published figures.

SOURCE: Organization for Economic Cooperation and Development (OECD), Education Online Database; *Annual National Accounts, Vol. 1, 1997*; and *Education at a Glance*, 2002 through 2005. (This table was prepared October 2005.)

Public libraries, books and serial volumes, library visits, and reference transactions, by state: Fiscal year 2002

State	Number of public libraries, excluding branches	Number of books and serial volumes (in thousands)	Number of books and serial volumes per capita	Library visits per capita[1]	Circulation per capita	Public library reference transactions per capita[2]
1	2	3	4	5	6	7
United States	9,137	785,075	2.8	4.5	6.8	1.1
Alabama	207	8,913	2.0	3.0	3.8	0.7
Alaska	85	2,272	3.5	4.4	5.8	0.5
Arizona	35	9,109	1.7	3.7	7.0	0.9
Arkansas	47	5,357	2.1	2.9	4.3	0.6
California	179	68,291	2.0	4.1	5.3	1.0
Colorado	115	11,469	2.7	5.8	9.9	1.3
Connecticut	194	14,336	4.2	6.5	8.9	1.2
Delaware	21	1,488	1.9	3.7	6.2	0.6
District of Columbia	1	2,650	4.6	3.5	2.1	1.9
Florida	72	30,775	1.8	4.0	5.3	1.5
Georgia	58	14,869	1.9	3.3	4.8	1.0
Hawaii	1	3,052	2.5	4.6	5.8	0.9
Idaho	106	3,636	3.1	5.8	7.9	0.8
Illinois	627	42,390	3.7	5.5	7.9	1.4
Indiana	239	23,667	4.2	6.3	11.7	1.3
Iowa	538	11,494	3.9	5.3	9.1	0.7
Kansas	323	10,691	4.8	5.8	10.1	1.2
Kentucky	116	8,154	2.0	3.6	5.4	0.5
Louisiana	65	11,092	2.5	2.9	4.0	1.1
Maine	274	6,016	5.1	5.0	7.1	0.8
Maryland	24	15,389	3.0	5.2	9.4	1.4
Massachusetts	370	30,795	4.9	5.5	7.6	0.9
Michigan	383	31,695	3.2	4.1	5.8	0.8
Minnesota	142	16,115	3.2	5.2	9.7	1.0
Mississippi	49	5,712	2.1	2.8	3.3	0.5
Missouri	148	18,204	3.6	4.5	7.7	0.9
Montana	79	2,652	2.9	4.0	5.7	0.5
Nebraska	275	6,152	4.4	5.2	8.7	0.8
Nevada	22	4,137	1.9	4.1	5.5	0.7
New Hampshire	230	5,725	4.5	4.7	7.3	0.7
New Jersey	309	31,203	3.7	5.1	6.3	0.9
New Mexico	89	4,098	2.5	3.3	4.9	0.6
New York	751	79,003	4.2	5.7	6.9	1.7
North Carolina	76	16,243	2.0	3.8	5.4	0.9
North Dakota	82	2,246	4.1	4.2	7.4	0.8
Ohio	250	48,075	4.2	6.9	14.6	1.7
Oklahoma	110	6,345	2.2	4.7	5.9	0.7
Oregon	124	8,811	2.8	5.9	13.4	0.9
Pennsylvania	451	28,548	2.4	3.4	5.1	0.8
Rhode Island	48	4,109	3.9	5.7	6.8	0.9
South Carolina	41	8,379	2.1	3.5	4.6	1.1
South Dakota	125	2,837	4.7	5.9	8.4	0.9
Tennessee	184	10,376	1.8	3.1	4.0	0.7
Texas	557	36,890	1.9	3.0	4.5	1.1
Utah	72	6,063	2.7	5.0	11.7	1.4
Vermont	189	2,739	4.7	5.2	6.7	0.8
Virginia	90	19,385	2.7	4.5	8.5	1.1
Washington	64	17,133	2.9	4.8	10.1	1.5
West Virginia	97	5,010	2.8	3.4	4.2	0.8
Wisconsin	380	18,864	3.5	5.7	9.7	1.0
Wyoming	23	2,420	4.9	5.6	7.8	0.9

[1]The total number of persons entering the library for any purpose during the year.

[2]A reference transaction is an information contact which involves the knowledge, use, recommendations, interpretation, or instructions in the use of one or more information sources by a member of the library staff.

NOTE: Data include imputations for nonresponse.

SOURCE: U.S. Department of Education, National Center for Education Statistics, *Public Libraries in the United States: Fiscal Year 2002*. (This table was prepared March 2005.)

Public schools and instructional rooms with access to the Internet, by selected school characteristics: 1994 through 2003

Schools, computers, instructional rooms, and access	All public schools	Instructional level[1]		Size of school enrollment			Metropolitan status				Percent of students eligible for free or reduced-price lunch[2]			
		Elementary	Secondary	Less than 300	300 to 999	1,000 or more	City	Urban fringe	Town	Rural	Less than 35 percent	35 to 49 percent	50 to 74 percent	75 percent or more
1	2	3	4	5	6	7	8	9	10	11	12	13	14	15
Estimated total number of schools														
1995	77,853	57,705	18,083	20,673	50,044	7,136	17,906	18,464	19,539	21,944	37,450	13,627	12,808	13,166
1997	79,125	59,695	19,430	20,540	51,169	7,416	21,071	23,419	12,637	21,998	37,525	12,250	16,302	12,864
1998	78,791	59,173	19,193	20,095	50,655	8,041	20,698	26,265	11,306	20,522	38,156	12,088	13,967	14,541
1999	78,399	59,575	17,110	20,018	50,389	7,992	21,034	26,245	11,235	19,885	35,653	13,908	16,099	11,993
2000	80,127	59,782	18,414	20,067	51,887	8,173	21,115	26,584	11,879	20,550	36,563	12,414	17,030	13,912
2001	81,066	61,640	17,627	20,665	51,968	8,433	17,997	26,260	10,180	26,628	34,928	14,753	16,627	14,710
2002	82,036	62,134	17,608	21,429	51,876	8,731	18,550	26,431	10,774	26,280	34,989	13,243	19,040	14,765
2003	82,232	62,298	17,889	21,623	51,952	8,657	18,803	26,485	10,597	26,347	32,501	14,869	18,577	16,285
1998 (standard error)	(333)	(293)	(220)	(479)	(467)	(165)	(88)	(98)	(182)	(273)	(1,530)	(1,185)	(991)	(1,263)
1999 (standard error)	(665)	(722)	(521)	(1,263)	(681)	(291)	(605)	(514)	(343)	(506)	(1,211)	(977)	(1,067)	(949)
2000 (standard error)	(650)	(569)	(359)	(697)	(206)	(217)	(1,380)	(1,746)	(1,323)	(1,478)	(1,215)	(792)	(1,071)	(923)
2001 (standard error)	(492)	(527)	(414)	(589)	(274)	(139)	(1,416)	(1,002)	(746)	(1,087)	(1,191)	(1,203)	(995)	(814)
2002 (standard error)	(780)	(647)	(371)	(761)	(253)	(145)	(963)	(922)	(1,080)	(1,289)	(1,194)	(1,050)	(1,134)	(862)
2003 (standard error)	(763)	(759)	(396)	(697)	(448)	(154)	(1,160)	(1,060)	(1,098)	(1,422)	(1,381)	(1,111)	(1,095)	(999)
Percent of schools having access to the Internet														
1994	35	30	49	30	35	58	40	38	29	35	39	35	32	18
1995	50	46	65	39	52	69	47	59	47	48	60	48	41	31
1996	65	61	77	57	66	80	64	75	61	60	74	59	53	53
1997	78	75	89	75	78	89	74	78	84	79	86	81	71	62
1998	89	88	94	87	89	95	92	85	90	92	92	93	88	79
1999	95	94	98	96	94	96	93	96	94	96	95	98	96	89
2000	98	97	100[3]	96	98	96	96	98	98	99	99	98	97	94
2001	99	99	100[3]	99	99	100[3]	97	99	100[3]	100[3]	99	100[3]	99	97
2002	99	99	100[3]	99	100[3]	100[3]	99	100[3]	100[3]	100[3]	98	100[3]	100[3]	99
2003	100[3]	100[3]	100	100	100	100	00	100[3]	100	100	100	100	100	99
1998 (standard error)	(1.3)	(1.6)	(2.1)	(3.4)	(1.4)	(2)	(2)	(2.8)	(3.2)	(3.4)	(2.0)	(2.2)	(3.0)	(3.7)
1999 (standard error)	(0.8)	(1.0)	(0.8)	(1.5)	(1.0)	(2)	(2)	(1.2)	(2.5)	(1.4)	(1.1)	(0.9)	(1.7)	(3.1)
2000 (standard error)	(0.5)	(0.7)	(0.2)	(1.7)	(0.5)	(1)	(1)	(1.2)	(1.2)	(0.9)	(0.7)	(0.7)	(1.3)	(1.7)
2001 (standard error)	(0.3)	(0.4)	(0.2)	(1.0)	(0.4)	(#)	(1)	(0.5)	(#)	(0.1)	(0.6)	(#)	(0.5)	(1.1)
2002 (standard error)	(0.5)	(0.6)	(0.5)	(1.7)	(0.2)	(#)	(1)	(#)	(2.2)	(1.0)	(1.0)	(#)	(#)	(0.9)
2003 (standard error)	(0.2)	(0.2)	(#)	(#)	(0.2)	(#)	(#)	(0.5)	(#)	(#)	(#)	(#)	(#)	(0.8)
Number of computers for instructional purposes, in thousands[4]														
1995	5,621	3,453	2,021	850	3,600	1,171	1,497	1,526	1,404	1,195	2,905	806	950	882
1997	5,959	3,701	2,258	839	3,767	1,353	1,727	2,084	934	1,214	3,154	886	1,013	890
1998	7,111	4,519	2,549	952	4,414	1,744	2,148	2,606	1,047	1,311	3,630	1,105	1,127	1,235
1999	7,806	4,923	2,728	1,021	4,952	1,834	2,320	2,975	1,022	1,489	3,900	1,245	1,429	1,170
2000	8,776	5,296	3,271	1,135	5,524	2,117	2,537	3,396	1,155	1,689	4,394	1,373	1,606	1,384
2001	10,058	6,165	3,654	1,085	6,273	2,700	2,685	3,791	1,134	2,448	4,781	1,707	1,862	1,698
2002	10,711	6,775	3,705	1,347	6,533	2,831	2,662	4,043	1,320	2,686	4,982	1,673	2,265	1,792
2003	11,180	6,879	4,087	1,275	6,709	3,196	2,825	4,188	1,357	2,810	5,049	1,923	2,248	1,960
1998 (standard error)	(183)	(145)	(94)	(53)	(136)	(106)	(74)	(129)	(58)	(77)	(198)	(114)	(89)	(155)
1999 (standard error)	(147)	(114)	(103)	(76)	(127)	(101)	(113)	(121)	(50)	(75)	(152)	(115)	(116)	(98)
2000 (standard error)	(174)	(149)	(113)	(73)	(121)	(103)	(179)	(213)	(132)	(131)	(147)	(93)	(112)	(107)
2001 (standard error)	(180)	(165)	(98)	(57)	(140)	(85)	(192)	(168)	(78)	(142)	(206)	(120)	(132)	(117)
2002 (standard error)	(237)	(187)	(105)	(101)	(181)	(101)	(158)	(173)	(172)	(164)	(170)	(172)	(137)	(136)
2003 (standard error)	(265)	(234)	(115)	(77)	(179)	(118)	(163)	(177)	(139)	(220)	(252)	(165)	(139)	(110)

See notes at end of table.

Public schools and instructional rooms with access to the Internet, by selected school characteristics: 1994 through 2003—Continued

Schools, computers, instructional rooms, and access	All public schools	Instructional level[1]		Size of school enrollment			Metropolitan status				Percent of students eligible for free or reduced-price lunch[2]			
		Elementary	Secondary	Less than 300	300 to 999	1,000 or more	City	Urban fringe	Town	Rural	Less than 35 percent	35 to 49 percent	50 to 74 percent	75 percent or more
1	2	3	4	5	6	7	8	9	10	11	12	13	14	15
Average number of instructional computers per school														
1995[4]	72	60	112	41	72	164	84	83	72	54	78	59	74	67
1997	75	62	116	41	74	183	82	89	74	55	84	72	62	69
1998	90	76	133	47	87	217	104	99	93	64	95	91	81	85
1999	100	83	159	51	98	229	110	113	91	75	109	90	89	98
2000	110	89	178	57	106	259	120	128	97	82	120	111	94	99
2001	124	100	207	52	121	320	149	144	111	92	137	116	112	115
2002	131	109	210	63	126	324	144	153	123	102	142	126	119	122
2003	136	110	228	59	129	369	150	158	128	107	155	129	121	120
1998 (standard error)	(2.3)	(2.4)	(4.9)	(2.6)	(2.5)	(13.0)	(3.6)	(4.9)	(5.2)	(3.6)	(3.7)	(6.1)	(4.5)	(7.7)
1999 (standard error)	(2.2)	(2.2)	(6.4)	(2.5)	(2.3)	(10.7)	(4.7)	(4.2)	(4.2)	(3.6)	(2.8)	(6.8)	(5.6)	(5.2)
2000 (standard error)	(2.0)	(2.4)	(5.3)	(3.1)	(2.3)	(9.0)	(4.9)	(4.3)	(5.6)	(3.6)	(3.4)	(5.9)	(5.7)	(5.5)
2001 (standard error)	(2.3)	(2.7)	(6.2)	(2.5)	(2.6)	(10.1)	(6.4)	(4.7)	(6.0)	(4.0)	(4.9)	(5.8)	(6.0)	(5.0)
2002 (standard error)	(2.8)	(2.9)	(6.4)	(4.1)	(3.5)	(10.8)	(6.4)	(5.2)	(9.3)	(4.5)	(4.7)	(8.5)	(5.3)	(5.9)
2003 (standard error)	(2.6)	(3.1)	(4.9)	(2.9)	(3.2)	(11.0)	(6.1)	(5.6)	(6.7)	(4.9)	(5.9)	(7.0)	(5.6)	(5.1)
Number of instructional computers with access to the Internet, in thousands														
1995[4]	447	232	187	59	315	73	96	131	126	94	286	46	57	36
1998	3,569	2,100	1,450	407	2,276	887	1,026	1,334	481	727	2,064	608	439	458
1999	4,809	2,773	1,945	663	2,988	1,158	1,265	1,887	691	966	2,762	778	810	428
2000	6,759	3,813	2,779	882	4,191	1,686	1,782	2,688	955	1,335	3,608	1,064	1,215	858
2001	8,500	4,936	3,357	874	5,229	2,396	2,175	3,178	1,008	2,139	4,225	1,447	1,529	1,289
2002	9,658	5,912	3,525	1,214	5,827	2,618	2,329	3,677	1,222	2,431	4,586	1,474	2,049	1,549
2003	10,361	6,225	3,935	1,156	6,169	3,036	2,593	3,887	1,264	2,616	4,751	1,724	2,121	1,726
1998 (standard error)	(173)	(148)	(79)	(38)	(140)	(73)	(87)	(105)	(46)	(73)	(151)	(79)	(48)	(78)
1999 (standard error)	(145)	(111)	(89)	(60)	(132)	(68)	(94)	(93)	(50)	(70)	(140)	(59)	(79)	(55)
2000 (standard error)	(174)	(136)	(113)	(69)	(114)	(97)	(148)	(178)	(111)	(91)	(139)	(80)	(93)	(87)
2001 (standard error)	(176)	(144)	(92)	(61)	(139)	(89)	(164)	(150)	(74)	(137)	(196)	(105)	(114)	(101)
2002 (standard error)	(236)	(183)	(105)	(97)	(183)	(102)	(145)	(160)	(162)	(148)	(167)	(158)	(129)	(122)
2003 (standard error)	(270)	(237)	(117)	(71)	(186)	(122)	(160)	(168)	(128)	(217)	(244)	(158)	(134)	(107)
Percent of instructional computers with access to the Internet														
1995[4]	8	7	9	7	9	6	6	9	9	8	10	6	6	4
1998	50	46	57	43	52	51	48	51	46	55	57	55	39	37
1999	62	56	71	65	60	63	55	63	68	65	71	62	57	37
2000	77	72	85	78	76	80	70	79	83	79	82	77	76	62
2001	85	80	92	81	83	89	81	84	89	87	88	85	82	76
2002	90	87	95	90	89	92	87	91	93	90	92	88	90	86
2003	93	90	96	91	92	95	92	93	93	93	95	90	94	88
1998 (standard error)	(1.7)	(2.5)	(2.1)	(3.4)	(2.2)	(3.4)	(3.0)	(2.8)	(4.1)	(3.4)	(2.0)	(4.2)	(2.9)	(4.6)
1999 (standard error)	(1.4)	(1.6)	(2.4)	(3.0)	(1.7)	(3.6)	(2.6)	(2.4)	(3.1)	(2.7)	(2.2)	(3.6)	(2.8)	(3.6)
2000 (standard error)	(1.1)	(1.5)	(1.2)	(2.6)	(1.3)	(1.8)	(2.1)	(1.7)	(2.5)	(2.1)	(1.2)	(2.9)	(2.6)	(3.1)
2001 (standard error)	(0.8)	(1.2)	(0.8)	(2.8)	(1.2)	(1.4)	(2.1)	(1.5)	(2.1)	(1.3)	(1.2)	(2.0)	(2.5)	(2.2)
2002 (standard error)	(0.8)	(1.1)	(0.6)	(1.8)	(0.9)	(1.3)	(1.6)	(1.2)	(1.9)	(1.4)	(1.1)	(2.0)	(1.5)	(1.6)
2003 (standard error)	(0.6)	(0.8)	(0.8)	(1.9)	(0.8)	(1.0)	(1.0)	(1.1)	(1.6)	(1.3)	(0.8)	(2.3)	(1.0)	(1.5)

See notes at end of table.

Public schools and instructional rooms with access to the Internet, by selected school characteristics: 1994 through 2003—Continued

Schools, computers, instructional rooms, and access	All public schools	Instructional level[1]		Size of school enrollment			Metropolitan status				Percent of students eligible for free or reduced-price lunch[2]			
		Elementary	Secondary	Less than 300	300 to 999	1,000 or more	City	Urban fringe	Town	Rural	Less than 35 percent	35 to 49 percent	50 to 74 percent	75 percent or more
1	2	3	4	5	6	7	8	9	10	11	12	13	14	15
Number of public school students per instructional computer with access to the Internet														
1998	12.1	13.6	9.9	9.1	12.3	13.0	14.1	12.4	12.2	8.6	10.6	10.9	15.8	16.8
1999	9.1	10.6	7.0	5.7	9.4	10.0	11.4	9.1	8.2	6.6	7.6	9.0	10.0	16.8
2000	6.6	7.8	5.2	3.9	7.0	7.2	8.2	6.6	6.2	5.0	6.0	6.3	7.2	9.1
2001	5.4	6.1	4.3	4.1	5.6	5.4	5.9	5.7	5.0	4.6	4.9	5.2	5.6	6.8
2002	4.8	5.2	4.1	3.1	5.0	5.1	5.5	4.9	4.4	4.0	4.6	4.5	4.7	5.5
2003	4.4	4.9	3.8	3.2	4.7	4.3	5.0	4.6	4.1	3.8	4.2	4.4	4.4	5.1
1998 (standard error)	(0.6)	(0.9)	(0.4)	(0.7)	(0.7)	(1.0)	(1.2)	(0.9)	(1.2)	(0.8)	(0.6)	(1.2)	(1.4)	(2.5)
1999 (standard error)	(0.3)	(0.4)	(0.3)	(0.4)	(0.4)	(0.6)	(0.8)	(0.4)	(0.6)	(0.4)	(0.3)	(0.4)	(0.8)	(2.2)
2000 (standard error)	(0.1)	(0.2)	(0.2)	(0.3)	(0.2)	(0.3)	(0.4)	(0.2)	(0.3)	(0.3)	(0.2)	(0.4)	(0.4)	(0.7)
2001 (standard error)	(0.1)	(0.2)	(0.1)	(0.3)	(0.1)	(0.2)	(0.2)	(0.2)	(0.3)	(0.1)	(0.2)	(0.2)	(0.3)	(0.3)
2002 (standard error)	(0.1)	(0.2)	(0.1)	(0.2)	(0.2)	(0.2)	(0.2)	(0.2)	(0.4)	(0.2)	(0.1)	(0.3)	(0.2)	(0.3)
2003 (standard error)	(0.1)	(0.2)	(0.1)	(0.2)	(0.1)	(0.2)	(0.2)	(0.2)	(0.2)	(0.2)	(0.1)	(0.3)	(0.2)	(0.2)
Number of instructional rooms,[5] in thousands														
1997	2,625	1,720	906	335	1,725	566	830	902	388	505	1,336	375	462	447
1998	2,709	1,772	916	349	1,740	620	839	981	390	498	1,372	413	451	471
1999	2,811	1,830	926	360	1,805	645	857	1,049	375	530	1,325	477	541	437
2000	2,905	1,864	972	377	1,871	657	866	1,086	413	541	1,380	465	570	482
2001	2,851	1,854	929	332	1,829	690	726	1,068	339	718	1,299	486	551	510
2002	2,988	2,006	919	396	1,896	696	748	1,101	378	761	1,368	451	648	520
2003	3,004	1,998	952	378	1,919	707	777	1,104	375	748	1,281	524	626	512
1998 (standard error)	(41)	(29)	(25)	(15)	(34)	(21)	(22)	(24)	(14)	(17)	(60)	(39)	(29)	(42)
1999 (standard error)	(36)	(33)	(29)	(26)	(39)	(30)	(29)	(33)	(16)	(23)	(46)	(34)	(42)	(34)
2000 (standard error)	(35)	(28)	(24)	(22)	(23)	(23)	(56)	(61)	(47)	(39)	(46)	(28)	(36)	(29)
2001 (standard error)	(31)	(30)	(18)	(17)	(23)	(15)	(49)	(46)	(24)	(36)	(48)	(34)	(35)	(29)
2002 (standard error)	(37)	(30)	(19)	(25)	(20)	(16)	(36)	(39)	(40)	(48)	(45)	(38)	(38)	(33)
2003 (standard error)	(47)	(44)	(20)	(18)	(33)	(16)	(45)	(51)	(38)	(54)	(51)	(39)	(38)	(34)
Percent of instructional rooms[5] with access to the Internet														
1994	3	3	4	3	3	3	4	4	3	3	3	2	4	2
1995	8	8	8	9	8	4	6	8	8	8	9	6	6	3
1996	14	13	16	15	13	16	12	16	14	14	17	12	11	5
1997	27	24	32	27	28	25	20	29	34	30	33	33	20	14
1998	51	51	52	54	53	45	47	50	55	57	57	60	41	38
1999	64	62	67	71	64	58	52	67	72	71	73	69	61	38
2000	77	76	79	83	78	70	66	78	87	85	82	81	77	60
2001	87	86	88	87	87	86	82	87	91	89	90	89	87	79
2002	92	92	91	91	93	89	88	92	96	93	93	90	91	89
2003	93	93	94	93	93	94	90	94	97	94	95	93	94	90
1998 (standard error)	(1.8)	(2.3)	(2.1)	(3.7)	(2.2)	(3.9)	(3.2)	(2.9)	(4.0)	(3.6)	(2.4)	(5.1)	(3.9)	(4.3)
1999 (standard error)	(1.6)	(1.8)	(2.6)	(3.2)	(1.9)	(3.0)	(2.6)	(2.5)	(3.4)	(3.0)	(2.3)	(3.4)	(3.1)	(4.4)
2000 (standard error)	(1.1)	(1.5)	(1.6)	(2.8)	(1.5)	(2.2)	(2.2)	(2.0)	(2.6)	(1.7)	(1.5)	(2.9)	(2.8)	(3.3)
2001 (standard error)	(0.9)	(1.1)	(1.2)	(2.1)	(1.1)	(1.7)	(2.1)	(1.3)	(2.2)	(1.3)	(1.2)	(2.2)	(2.4)	(2.4)
2002 (standard error)	(0.6)	(0.8)	(1.0)	(1.9)	(0.7)	(1.7)	(1.6)	(0.9)	(1.1)	(1.0)	(0.8)	(2.1)	(1.4)	(1.9)
2003 (standard error)	(0.5)	(0.7)	(0.9)	(1.6)	(0.7)	(1.1)	(1.0)	(0.9)	(0.9)	(1.2)	(1.0)	(1.4)	(1.1)	(1.5)

#Rounds to zero.

[1]Excludes combined elementary/secondary schools because of small sample size.

[2]Excludes schools with missing data for free and reduced-price lunch participation.

[3]This estimate fell between 99.5 percent and 100.0 percent and therefore was rounded to 100 percent.

[4]Includes computers used for instructional or administrative purposes.

[5]Includes all classrooms, computer labs, and library/media centers.

NOTE: Data are derived from sample surveys and are subject to sampling error. Detail may not sum to totals because of rounding. Standard errors appear in parentheses.

SOURCE: U.S. Department of Education, National Center for Education Statistics, Fast Response Survey System (FRSS), *Internet Access in U.S. Public Schools and Classrooms: 1994–2003*; and unpublished tabulations. (This table was prepared April 2005.)

Average grade that the public would give the public schools in their community and in the nation at large: 1974 through 2005

Year	All adults		No children in school		Public school parents		Private school parents	
	Nation	Local community	Nation	Local community	Nation	Local community	Nation	Local community
1	2	3	4	5	6	7	8	9
1974	—	2.63	—	2.57	—	2.80	—	2.15
1975	—	2.38	—	2.31	—	2.49	—	1.81
1976	—	2.38	—	2.34	—	2.48	—	2.22
1977	—	2.33	—	2.25	—	2.59	—	2.05
1978	—	2.21	—	2.11	—	2.47	—	1.69
1979	—	2.21	—	2.15	—	2.38	—	1.88
1980	—	2.26	—	—	—	—	—	—
1981	1.94	2.20	—	2.12	2.01	2.36	2.02	2.20
1982	2.01	2.24	2.04	2.18	2.01	2.35	1.82	1.89
1983	1.91	2.12	1.92	2.10	1.92	2.31	—	—
1984	2.09	2.36	2.11	2.30	2.11	2.49	2.04	2.17
1985	2.14	2.39	2.16	2.36	2.20	2.44	1.93	2.00
1986	2.13	2.36	—	2.29	—	2.55	—	2.14
1987	2.18	2.44	2.20	2.38	2.22	2.61	2.03	2.01
1988	2.08	2.35	2.02	2.32	2.13	2.48	2.00	2.13
1989	2.01	2.35	1.99	2.27	2.06	2.56	1.93	2.12
1990	1.99	2.29	1.98	2.27	2.03	2.44	1.85	2.09
1991	2.00	2.36	—	—	—	—	—	—
1992	1.93	2.30	1.92	—	1.94	2.73	1.85	—
1993	1.95	2.41	1.97	2.40	1.97	2.48	1.80	2.11
1994	1.95	2.26	1.95	2.16	1.90	2.55	1.86	1.90
1995	1.97	2.28	1.98	2.25	1.93	2.41	1.81	1.85
1996	1.93	2.30	1.91	2.22	2.00	2.56	1.80	1.86
1997	1.97	2.35	1.99	2.27	2.01	2.56	1.99	1.87
1998	1.93	2.41	1.91	2.36	1.96	2.51	1.81	2.20
1999	2.02	2.44	2.03	2.42	1.97	2.56	—	—
2000	1.98	2.47	1.94	2.44	2.05	2.59	—	—
2001	2.01	2.47	2.00	2.42	2.04	2.66	—	—
2002	2.08	2.44	2.08	2.40	2.06	2.61	—	—
2003	2.11	2.41	2.09	2.32	2.16	2.57	—	—
2004	1.93	2.45	1.07	2.42	2.00	2.58	—	—
2005	1.99	2.45	2.07	2.43	2.11	2.60	—	—

—Not available.
NOTE: Average based on a scale where A=4, B=3, C=2, D=1, and F=0.

SOURCE: Phi Delta Kappa, *Phi Delta Kappan*, "The Annual Gallup Poll of the Public's Attitudes Toward the Public Schools," 1974 through 2005. (This table was prepared September 2005.)

Labor force status of high school dropouts, by sex and race/ethnicity: Selected years, 1980 through 2004

Year, sex, and race or ethnicity	Dropouts[2] Number (in thousands)	Percent of total	Dropouts in civilian labor force[1] Number (in thousands)	Labor force participation rate	Unemployed Number (in thousands)	Unemployment rate	Dropouts not in labor force Number (in thousands)	Percent of population
1	2	3	4	5	6	7	8	9
All dropouts[2]								
1980	739 (33.5)	100.0 (†)	471 (26.7)	63.7 (2.18)	149 (20.7)	31.6 (2.64)	268 (20.2)	36.3 (2.18)
1985	612 (30.5)	100.0 (†)	413 (25.1)	67.5 (2.34)	147 (20.6)	35.6 (2.91)	199 (17.4)	32.5 (2.34)
1990	405 (25.7)	100.0 (†)	280 (21.4)	69.0 (2.94)	90 (16.7)	32.3 (3.57)	125 (14.3)	31.0 (2.94)
1995	604 (31.4)	100.0 (†)	409 (25.8)	67.7 (2.43)	121 (19.3)	29.6 (2.88)	195 (17.8)	32.3 (2.43)
2000	515 (39.1)	100.0 (†)	350 (32.3)	68.0 (3.55)	99 (17.1)	28.1 (4.15)	165 (22.2)	32.0 (3.55)
2001	506 (28.3)	100.0 (†)	324 (22.7)	64.0 (2.69)	116 (18.7)	35.9 (3.36)	182 (17.0)	36.0 (2.69)
2002	401 (25.2)	100.0 (†)	271 (20.7)	67.7 (2.94)	81 (15.6)	29.8 (3.50)	129 (14.3)	32.3 (2.94)
2003	457 (26.9)	100.0 (†)	271 (20.7)	59.3 (2.89)	84 (15.9)	30.8 (3.53)	186 (17.2)	40.7 (2.89)
2004	496 (28.0)	100.0 (†)	267 (20.6)	53.7 (2.82)	106 (17.8)	39.9 (3.77)	229 (19.0)	46.3 (2.82)
Male								
1980	422 (32.5)	57.1 (3.82)	305 (27.7)	72.3 (3.46)	93 (15.3)	30.5 (4.18)	117 (17.1)	27.7 (3.46)
1985	321 (30.0)	52.5 (4.67)	261 (27.0)	81.3 (3.65)	98 (16.6)	37.5 (5.02)	60 (13.0)	18.7 (3.65)
1990	215 (25.4)	53.1 (5.91)	173 (22.8)	80.2 (4.72)	63 (13.8)	36.2 (6.34)	42 (11.2)	19.8 (4.72)
1995	339 (31.9)	56.1 (4.68)	251 (27.5)	74.0 (4.13)	72 (14.7)	28.7 (4.96)	88 (16.3)	26.0 (4.13)
2000	295 (28.5)	57.3 (4.79)	220 (24.6)	74.4 (4.23)	54 (12.2)	24.5 (4.82)	76 (14.5)	25.6 (4.23)
2001	298 (29.5)	58.9 (4.88)	198 (24.0)	66.5 (4.68)	68 (14.1)	34.2 (5.77)	100 (17.1)	33.5 (4.68)
2002	214 (25.0)	53.4 (5.83)	149 (20.9)	69.5 (5.38)	35 (10.1)	23.4 (5.93)	65 (13.8)	30.5 (5.38)
2003	242 (26.6)	53.0 (5.49)	159 (21.6)	65.6 (6.45)	53 (12.5)	33.2 (6.39)	83 (15.6)	34.4 (5.22)
2004	278 (28.5)	56.0 (5.09)	166 (22.0)	59.9 (6.51)	67 (14.0)	40.4 (6.51)	112 (18.1)	40.1 (5.03)
Female								
1980	317 (27.0)	42.9 (4.23)	166 (19.6)	52.4 (4.27)	56 (11.4)	33.7 (5.58)	151 (18.7)	47.6 (4.27)
1985	291 (27.4)	47.5 (4.71)	152 (19.8)	52.2 (4.71)	49 (11.3)	32.2 (6.10)	139 (18.9)	47.8 (4.71)
1990	190 (22.9)	46.9 (6.03)	107 (17.2)	56.3 (5.99)	28 (8.8)	26.1 (7.07)	83 (15.2)	43.7 (5.99)
1995	265 (27.1)	43.9 (5.08)	157 (20.8)	59.5 (5.02)	49 (11.7)	30.9 (6.14)	107 (17.2)	40.5 (5.02)
2000	220 (23.6)	42.7 (5.30)	131 (18.2)	59.4 (5.27)	45 (10.7)	34.2 (6.59)	90 (15.1)	40.6 (5.27)
2001	207 (23.6)	40.9 (5.61)	126 (18.4)	60.6 (5.57)	48 (11.4)	38.6 (7.12)	82 (14.9)	39.4 (5.57)
2002	187 (22.4)	46.6 (5.99)	122 (18.1)	65.6 (5.70)	46 (11.1)	37.6 (7.20)	64 (13.1)	34.4 (5.70)
2003	215 (24.0)	47.0 (5.59)	112 (17.4)	52.1 (5.59)	31 (9.1)	27.6 (6.93)	103 (16.6)	47.9 (5.59)
2004	218 (24.2)	44.0 (5.52)	100 (16.4)	45.9 (5.54)	39 (10.2)	38.9 (8.00)	118 (17.8)	54.1 (5.54)
White[3]								
1980	580 (29.7)	78.5 (2.11)	392 (24.4)	67.6 (2.40)	106 (17.5)	27.0 (2.77)	188 (16.9)	32.4 (2.40)
1985	458 (26.4)	74.8 (2.50)	330 (22.4)	72.1 (2.59)	116 (18.3)	35.2 (3.24)	128 (14.0)	27.9 (2.59)
1990	303 (22.2)	74.8 (3.19)	211 (18.6)	69.8 (3.37)	56 (13.2)	26.3 (3.88)	92 (12.3)	30.2 (3.37)
1995	448 (27.0)	74.2 (2.64)	312 (22.6)	69.8 (2.77)	85 (16.2)	27.2 (3.22)	135 (14.8)	30.2 (2.77)
2000	384 (33.8)	74.6 (3.84)	280 (28.9)	73.0 (3.91)	70 (14.4)	24.9 (4.46)	104 (17.6)	27.0 (3.91)
2001	401 (25.2)	79.2 (2.55)	273 (20.8)	68.1 (2.93)	89 (16.3)	32.4 (3.57)	128 (14.2)	31.9 (2.93)
2002	281 (21.1)	70.1 (3.44)	188 (17.3)	67.0 (3.53)	48 (12.0)	25.6 (4.01)	93 (12.1)	33.0 (3.53)
2003	336 (23.1)	73.5 (3.03)	215 (18.5)	64.0 (3.30)	58 (13.2)	27.1 (3.82)	121 (13.8)	36.0 (3.30)
2004	370 (24.2)	74.6 (2.85)	196 (17.6)	53.0 (3.27)	56 (13.0)	28.8 (4.07)	174 (16.6)	47.0 (3.27)
Black[3]								
1980	146 (20.3)	19.8 (5.55)	73 (14.4)	50.0 (6.97)	40 (10.6)	‡ (†)	73 (14.4)	50.0 (6.97)
1985	132 (20.4)	21.6 (6.37)	69 (14.7)	52.3 (7.73)	30 (9.7)	‡ (†)	63 (14.1)	47.7 (7.73)
1990	86 (17.0)	21.2 (8.13)	56 (13.8)	65.3 (9.46)	30 (10.1)	‡ (†)	30 (10.1)	34.7 (9.46)
1995	109 (19.2)	18.0 (6.79)	66 (14.9)	61.0 (8.61)	27 (9.6)	‡ (†)	42 (11.9)	39.0 (8.61)
2000	111 (18.6)	21.5 (6.90)	58 (13.5)	51.9 (8.40)	27 (9.2)	‡ (†)	53 (12.9)	48.1 (8.40)
2001	85 (15.8)	16.8 (6.96)	42 (11.1)	49.9 (9.31)	21 (7.9)	‡ (†)	43 (11.2)	50.1 (9.31)
2002	79 (16.1)	19.7 (8.12)	55 (13.4)	69.8 (9.38)	27 (9.4)	‡ (†)	24 (8.9)	30.2 (9.38)
2003	88 (17.0)	19.3 (7.63)	42 (11.8)	47.8 (9.67)	19 (7.9)	‡ (†)	46 (12.3)	52.2 (9.67)
2004	91 (17.3)	18.3 (7.37)	50 (12.8)	54.4 (9.48)	39 (11.3)	‡ (†)	42 (11.8)	45.6 (9.48)
Hispanic[4]								
1980	91 (18.9)	12.3 (6.85)	60 (15.4)	65.9 (9.88)	17 (8.2)	‡ (†)	31 (11.1)	34.1 (9.88)
1985	106 (18.3)	17.3 (6.54)	73 (15.2)	68.9 (8.00)	33 (10.2)	‡ (†)	33 (10.2)	31.1 (8.00)
1990	67 (15.1)	16.5 (8.36)	32 (10.4)	‡ (†)	10 (5.8)	‡ (†)	35 (10.9)	‡ (†)
1995	174 (24.2)	28.8 (6.33)	119 (20.0)	68.6 (6.48)	35 (10.9)	29.3 (7.69)	55 (13.6)	31.4 (6.48)
2000	101 (19.8)	19.6 (7.80)	62 (15.5)	61.1 (9.58)	22 (8.9)	‡ (†)	39 (12.3)	38.9 (9.58)
2001	119 (21.5)	23.5 (7.67)	84 (18.1)	70.6 (8.24)	27 (10.2)	32.6 (10.10)	35 (11.7)	29.4 (8.24)
2002	94 (17.6)	23.4 (7.93)	62 (14.3)	66.5 (8.84)	23 (8.7)	‡ (†)	31 (10.1)	33.5 (8.84)
2003	124 (20.1)	27.1 (7.25)	68 (14.9)	54.5 (8.12)	17 (7.5)	‡ (†)	57 (13.7)	45.5 (8.12)
2004	154 (22.4)	31.0 (6.77)	87 (16.9)	56.8 (7.25)	27 (9.4)	30.7 (8.98)	67 (14.8)	43.2 (7.25)

†Not applicable.

‡Reporting standards not met.

[1]The labor force includes all employed persons plus those seeking employment. The labor force participation rate is the percentage of persons either employed or seeking employment. The unemployment rate is the percent of persons in the labor force who are seeking employment.

[2]Persons 16 to 24 years old who dropped out of school in the 12-month period ending in October of years shown.

[3]Includes persons of Hispanic origin.

[4]Persons of Hispanic origin may be of any race.

NOTE: Data are based upon sample surveys of the civilian noninstitutional population. Includes dropouts from any grade, including a small number from elementary and middle schools. Even though the standard errors are large, smaller estimates are shown to permit users to combine categories in various ways. Detail for the above race and Hispanic-origin groups will not sum to totals because data for the other racial groups are not presented and Hispanics are included in both the White and Black population groups. Some data have been revised from previously published figures. Detail may not sum to totals because of rounding. Standard errors appear in parentheses.

SOURCE: U.S. Department of Labor, Bureau of Labor Statistics, *College Enrollment and Work Activity of High School Graduates*, selected years, 1980 through 2004 and unpublished tabulations. (This table was prepared October 2005.)

Unemployment rate of persons 16 years old and over, by age, sex, race/ethnicity, and educational attainment: 2002, 2003, and 2004

Sex, race/ethnicity, and educational attainment	Unemployment rate, 2002[1]				Unemployment rate, 2003[1]				Unemployment rate, 2004[1]			
	16- to 24-year-olds[2]			25 years old and over	16- to 24-year-olds[2]			25 years old and over	16- to 24-year-olds[2]			25 years old and over
	Total	16 to 19 years	20 to 24 years		Total	16 to 19 years	20 to 24 years		Total	16 to 19 years	20 to 24 years	
1	2	3	4	5	6	7	8	9	10	11	12	13
All persons												
All education levels	12.0 (0.16)	16.5 (0.31)	9.7 (0.18)	4.6 (0.04)	12.4 (0.30)	17.4 (0.52)	10.0 (0.37)	4.6 (0.06)	11.9 (0.29)	17.0 (0.51)	9.4 (0.36)	4.4 (0.08)
Less than high school completion	18.4 (0.36)	19.0 (0.44)	17.0 (0.61)	8.4 (0.18)	19.1 (0.58)	19.6 (0.65)	18.2 (1.25)	8.8 (0.29)	18.8 (0.57)	20.0 (0.66)	16.4 (1.19)	8.5 (0.29)
High school completion, no college	12.6 (0.29)	15.9 (0.58)	11.1 (0.33)	5.3 (0.08)	13.4 (0.62)	17.4 (1.23)	12.0 (0.72)	5.5 (0.16)	12.4 (0.60)	15.8 (1.16)	11.1 (0.69)	5.0 (0.15)
Some college, no degree	7.7 (0.24)	9.2 (0.60)	7.3 (0.27)	4.8 (0.11)	7.8 (0.48)	10.3 (1.15)	7.3 (0.53)	5.2 (0.22)	7.8 (0.48)	9.1 (1.07)	7.5 (0.53)	4.5 (0.20)
Associate's degree	7.2 (0.59)	‡	7.1 (0.59)	4.0 (0.13)	6.8 (1.25)	‡	6.6 (1.26)	4.0 (0.28)	6.1 (1.16)	‡	5.9 (1.17)	3.7 (0.26)
Bachelor's or higher degree	5.8 (0.39)	‡	5.8 (0.39)	2.9 (0.06)	6.1 (0.84)	‡	6.1 (0.84)	3.1 (0.13)	5.6 (0.79)	‡	5.6 (0.79)	2.7 (0.12)
Male												
All education levels	12.8 (0.23)	18.1 (0.45)	10.2 (0.25)	4.7 (0.06)	13.4 (0.43)	19.3 (0.75)	10.6 (0.53)	5.0 (0.13)	12.6 (0.43)	18.4 (0.74)	10.1 (0.52)	4.4 (0.12)
Less than high school completion	18.7 (0.47)	20.8 (0.62)	15.1 (0.72)	7.8 (0.22)	19.3 (0.78)	21.1 (0.91)	16.3 (1.57)	8.2 (0.40)	18.8 (0.79)	21.4 (0.93)	14.7 (1.51)	7.6 (0.40)
High school completion, no college	12.7 (0.39)	16.4 (0.82)	11.3 (0.44)	5.4 (0.12)	14.0 (0.86)	19.6 (1.81)	12.1 (0.97)	5.7 (0.24)	12.7 (0.83)	16.4 (1.68)	11.4 (0.95)	5.1 (0.23)
Some college, no degree	8.1 (0.37)	9.8 (0.95)	7.8 (0.39)	4.7 (0.15)	8.3 (0.72)	11.0 (1.79)	7.7 (0.78)	5.4 (0.32)	8.7 (0.73)	10.2 (1.70)	8.4 (0.81)	4.4 (0.29)
Associate's degree	8.0 (0.88)	‡	7.6 (0.87)	4.3 (0.20)	7.8 (1.99)	‡	7.6 (2.01)	4.4 (0.43)	5.7 (1.73)	‡	5.6 (1.74)	4.0 (0.41)
Bachelor's or higher degree	6.9 (0.67)	‡	7.0 (0.67)	3.0 (0.09)	6.7 (1.36)	‡	6.8 (1.37)	3.2 (0.19)	5.9 (1.26)	‡	5.9 (1.28)	2.7 (0.17)
Female												
All education levels	11.1 (0.22)	14.9 (0.43)	9.1 (0.25)	4.6 (0.06)	11.4 (0.39)	15.6 (0.67)	9.3 (0.48)	4.6 (0.11)	11.0 (0.40)	15.5 (0.70)	8.7 (0.49)	4.4 (0.11)
Less than high school completion	17.9 (0.54)	17.0 (0.62)	20.7 (1.12)	9.5 (0.31)	18.9 (0.80)	17.9 (0.87)	22.1 (1.93)	9.8 (0.41)	18.9 (0.84)	18.4 (0.93)	20.1 (1.97)	10.0 (0.44)
High school completion, no college	12.3 (0.43)	15.4 (0.83)	10.9 (0.50)	5.1 (0.12)	12.7 (0.84)	15.1 (1.55)	11.7 (1.00)	5.2 (0.20)	12.1 (0.87)	15.2 (1.61)	10.6 (1.02)	4.9 (0.21)
Some college, no degree	7.3 (0.33)	8.8 (0.77)	6.8 (0.36)	5.0 (0.15)	7.5 (0.61)	9.8 (1.42)	6.8 (0.67)	4.9 (0.28)	7.1 (0.62)	8.4 (1.37)	6.8 (0.70)	4.7 (0.28)
Associate's degree	6.7 (0.79)	‡	6.6 (0.80)	3.7 (0.17)	6.1 (1.49)	‡	5.9 (1.49)	3.7 (0.33)	6.3 (1.57)	‡	6.2 (1.58)	3.4 (0.33)
Bachelor's or higher degree	5.1 (0.48)	‡	5.0 (0.48)	2.8 (0.09)	5.5 (0.99)	‡	5.6 (0.99)	2.9 (0.17)	5.3 (1.00)	‡	5.3 (1.01)	2.7 (0.18)
White, non-Hispanic												
All education levels	9.8 (0.18)	13.5 (0.34)	7.7 (0.20)	3.9 (0.05)	10.2 (0.35)	14.4 (0.60)	8.0 (0.42)	4.0 (0.09)	9.8 (0.34)	14.1 (0.60)	7.6 (0.41)	3.6 (0.09)
Less than high school completion	15.6 (0.43)	15.4 (0.48)	16.4 (0.97)	7.5 (0.26)	16.7 (0.73)	16.4 (0.78)	18.1 (2.06)	7.6 (0.39)	16.2 (0.73)	16.3 (0.78)	15.7 (1.93)	7.7 (0.40)
High school completion, no college	10.5 (0.33)	13.2 (0.65)	9.2 (0.38)	4.5 (0.09)	10.9 (0.73)	13.8 (1.39)	9.7 (0.85)	4.6 (0.17)	10.6 (0.71)	13.5 (1.34)	9.3 (0.84)	4.3 (0.17)
Some college, no degree	6.3 (0.26)	8.0 (0.65)	5.8 (0.28)	4.2 (0.12)	6.7 (0.54)	8.9 (1.29)	6.2 (0.60)	4.3 (0.23)	6.7 (0.54)	8.2 (1.21)	6.4 (0.60)	3.7 (0.21)
Associate's degree	6.0 (0.63)	‡	5.6 (0.62)	3.5 (0.14)	5.1 (1.29)	‡	4.8 (1.29)	3.5 (0.29)	4.9 (1.26)	‡	4.8 (1.25)	3.3 (0.28)
Bachelor's or higher degree	5.3 (0.43)	‡	5.2 (0.42)	2.7 (0.07)	5.5 (0.91)	‡	5.5 (0.92)	2.8 (0.14)	5.0 (0.86)	‡	4.9 (0.86)	2.5 (0.13)
Black, non-Hispanic												
All education levels	22.7 (0.59)	30.1 (1.16)	19.3 (0.68)	7.7 (0.17)	23.8 (1.10)	33.2 (1.78)	19.9 (1.41)	8.3 (0.35)	22.4 (1.07)	32.0 (1.75)	18.6 (1.36)	8.1 (0.35)
Less than high school completion	35.0 (1.30)	34.9 (1.62)	35.2 (2.15)	13.6 (0.63)	36.8 (1.88)	35.9 (2.12)	38.2 (4.07)	13.9 (1.02)	37.1 (1.88)	38.7 (2.15)	34.9 (3.94)	15.5 (1.07)
High school completion, no college	22.6 (0.97)	28.0 (2.00)	20.7 (1.10)	8.8 (0.30)	24.7 (2.11)	34.0 (4.38)	22.0 (2.39)	9.4 (0.63)	21.9 (2.03)	28.0 (4.03)	19.9 (2.34)	8.7 (0.60)
Some college, no degree	14.6 (0.97)	15.7 (2.62)	14.4 (1.04)	6.9 (0.34)	14.6 (1.90)	21.1 (4.95)	13.5 (2.05)	8.6 (0.81)	14.2 (1.85)	16.2 (4.46)	13.9 (2.03)	8.4 (0.81)
Associate's degree	13.3 (2.42)	‡	13.6 (2.46)	6.0 (0.49)	13.6 (5.71)	‡	12.8 (5.68)	6.1 (1.09)	6.9 (4.20)	‡	7.2 (4.42)	5.9 (1.07)
Bachelor's or higher degree	4.9 (1.43)	‡	5.0 (1.46)	4.2 (0.28)	6.8 (3.46)	‡	6.8 (3.47)	4.3 (0.62)	8.8 (3.63)	‡	8.8 (3.67)	4.2 (0.60)
Hispanic origin[3]												
All education levels	12.9 (0.40)	20.0 (0.88)	9.9 (0.42)	6.1 (0.15)	12.8 (0.78)	20.0 (1.44)	10.2 (0.93)	6.4 (0.30)	12.3 (0.75)	20.4 (1.43)	9.3 (0.87)	5.7 (0.28)
Less than high school completion	16.7 (0.68)	22.9 (1.19)	12.2 (0.78)	7.7 (0.27)	16.1 (1.19)	23.0 (1.75)	11.5 (1.66)	8.2 (0.52)	16.2 (1.19)	24.0 (1.77)	10.9 (1.61)	7.5 (0.51)
High school completion, no college	11.4 (0.66)	17.3 (1.59)	9.5 (0.70)	5.9 (0.27)	12.4 (1.50)	18.3 (3.47)	10.8 (1.64)	5.9 (0.55)	11.6 (1.43)	17.2 (3.30)	10.0 (1.56)	5.2 (0.51)
Some college, no degree	8.6 (0.75)	11.9 (2.04)	7.9 (0.80)	5.7 (0.37)	7.7 (1.48)	9.7 (3.57)	7.3 (1.62)	5.8 (0.81)	8.0 (1.45)	10.6 (3.56)	7.4 (1.59)	5.1 (0.75)
Associate's degree	7.5 (1.85)	‡	6.9 (1.84)	5.0 (0.54)	10.0 (4.49)	‡	10.2 (4.58)	5.3 (1.18)	8.0 (3.69)	‡	8.1 (3.77)	4.2 (1.05)
Bachelor's or higher degree	8.4 (1.85)	‡	8.5 (1.87)	3.4 (0.30)	11.1 (4.86)	‡	11.1 (4.87)	4.1 (0.71)	5.0 (3.22)	‡	5.0 (3.22)	3.5 (0.64)

†Not applicable.
‡Reporting standards not met.
[1]The unemployment rate is the percent of individuals in the labor force who are not working and who made specific efforts to find employment sometime during the prior 4 weeks. The labor force includes both employed and unemployed persons.
[2]Excludes persons enrolled in school.
[3]Persons of Hispanic origin may be of any race.
NOTE: Some data have been revised from previously published figures. Standard errors appear in parentheses.
SOURCE: U.S. Department of Labor, Bureau of Labor Statistics, Office of Employment and Unemployment Statistics, Current Population Survey (CPS), March 2002, 2003, and 2004, unpublished tabulations. (This table was prepared May 2005.)

Labor force participation rates and employment to population ratios of persons 16 years old and over, by highest level of education, age, sex, and race/ethnicity: 2004

Age, sex, and race/ethnicity	Labor force participation rate[1]						Employment/population ratio[2]					
	Total	Less than high school completion[3]	High school completion	College			Total	Less than high school completion[3]	High school completion	College		
				Some college, no degree	Associate's degree	Bachelor's or higher degree				Some college, no degree	Associate's degree	Bachelor's or higher degree
1	2	3	4	5	6	7	8	9	10	11	12	13
16 to 19 years old[4]	43.9 (2.14)	36.0 (0.79)	64.0 (1.53)	55.6 (1.84)	‡ (†)	‡ (†)	36.4 (2.07)	28.8 (0.75)	53.9 (1.59)	50.6 (1.86)	‡ (†)	‡ (†)
Male	43.9 (0.95)	36.4 (1.10)	66.4 (2.14)	54.4 (2.79)	‡	‡	35.9 (0.92)	28.6 (1.03)	55.5 (2.25)	48.9 (2.80)	‡	‡
Female	43.8 (0.96)	35.6 (1.15)	61.7 (2.18)	56.6 (2.45)	‡	‡	37.0 (0.94)	29.0 (1.09)	52.3 (2.24)	51.9 (2.47)	‡	‡
White, non-Hispanic	49.1 (0.86)	41.4 (1.04)	67.7 (1.84)	58.6 (2.17)	‡	‡	42.2 (0.85)	34.7 (1.01)	58.6 (1.94)	53.8 (2.20)	‡	‡
Black, non-Hispanic	31.2 (1.74)	23.7 (1.88)	53.6 (4.48)	46.6 (6.04)	‡	‡	21.2 (1.54)	14.5 (1.55)	38.6 (4.38)	39.1 (5.91)	‡	‡
Hispanic	38.2 (1.73)	31.1 (1.91)	60.5 (4.27)	53.8 (5.77)	‡	‡	30.4 (1.64)	23.6 (1.76)	50.0 (4.37)	48.1 (5.78)	‡	‡
20 to 24 years old[4]	75.0 (0.38)	67.6 (1.10)	78.9 (0.66)	70.7 (0.66)	82.4 (1.37)	83.3 (0.94)	67.9 (0.41)	56.5 (1.16)	70.1 (0.74)	65.4 (0.69)	77.6 (1.50)	78.6 (1.03)
Male	79.6 (0.69)	79.9 (1.69)	85.5 (1.04)	71.5 (1.30)	84.1 (2.72)	85.1 (1.90)	71.6 (0.77)	68.2 (1.96)	75.8 (1.26)	65.5 (1.37)	79.4 (3.01)	80.0 (2.13)
Female	70.5 (0.75)	51.3 (2.33)	70.8 (1.42)	70.0 (1.21)	81.2 (2.42)	82.0 (1.64)	64.3 (0.78)	41.0 (2.29)	63.3 (1.51)	65.3 (1.25)	76.2 (2.64)	77.7 (1.78)
White, non-Hispanic	77.8 (0.47)	67.5 (1.81)	82.0 (0.80)	72.7 (0.79)	84.8 (1.54)	85.6 (1.01)	71.9 (0.51)	56.9 (1.91)	74.4 (0.91)	68.1 (0.83)	80.8 (1.68)	81.4 (1.12)
Black, non-Hispanic	68.1 (1.63)	58.2 (4.08)	72.1 (2.63)	65.8 (2.79)	73.1 (7.57)	80.5 (5.12)	55.4 (1.74)	37.9 (4.01)	57.8 (2.89)	56.7 (2.91)	67.5 (8.00)	73.4 (5.72)
Hispanic	74.5 (1.31)	72.7 (2.31)	77.0 (2.19)	72.0 (2.72)	77.4 (5.76)	81.0 (5.82)	67.6 (1.40)	64.8 (2.48)	69.3 (2.40)	66.7 (2.86)	71.3 (6.23)	77.3 (6.21)
25 and older	66.9 (0.14)	45.1 (0.38)	63.2 (0.25)	70.3 (0.32)	76.6 (0.42)	77.9 (0.23)	64.0 (0.14)	41.2 (0.37)	60.0 (0.25)	67.1 (0.33)	73.8 (0.44)	75.8 (0.24)
Male	75.3 (0.25)	58.3 (0.73)	73.5 (0.45)	77.3 (0.59)	83.5 (0.77)	82.8 (0.40)	72.0 (0.26)	53.8 (0.73)	69.8 (0.47)	73.8 (0.62)	80.1 (0.83)	80.6 (0.42)
Female	59.3 (0.26)	32.5 (0.65)	54.1 (0.46)	64.3 (0.60)	71.5 (0.78)	72.8 (0.46)	56.7 (0.26)	29.2 (0.63)	51.5 (0.46)	61.3 (0.61)	69.1 (0.80)	70.9 (0.47)
White, non-Hispanic	66.1 (0.16)	35.8 (0.52)	60.9 (0.29)	68.6 (0.38)	76.2 (0.49)	77.3 (0.26)	63.7 (0.17)	33.1 (0.51)	58.3 (0.30)	66.1 (0.39)	73.7 (0.50)	75.3 (0.27)
Black, non-Hispanic	66.9 (0.60)	38.5 (1.44)	67.5 (1.00)	73.8 (1.28)	77.5 (1.89)	83.0 (1.13)	61.5 (0.62)	32.5 (1.39)	61.6 (1.04)	67.6 (1.36)	73.0 (2.01)	79.5 (1.21)
Hispanic	71.2 (0.56)	62.3 (0.93)	74.0 (1.01)	79.1 (1.38)	79.8 (2.09)	82.1 (1.34)	67.1 (0.58)	57.6 (0.95)	70.2 (1.06)	75.1 (1.47)	76.5 (2.21)	79.2 (1.42)

†Not applicable.
‡Reporting standards not met.
[1]Percent of the civilian population who are employed or seeking employment.
[2]Number of persons employed as a percent of civilian population.
[3]Includes persons reporting no school years completed.
[4]Excludes persons enrolled in school.
NOTE: Standard errors appear in parentheses.
SOURCE: U.S. Department of Labor, Bureau of Labor Statistics, Office of Employment and Unemployment Statistics, Current Population Survey (CPS), March 2004, unpublished tabulations. (This table was prepared April 2005.)

Median annual income of year-round, full-time workers 25 years old and over, by highest level of educational attainment and sex: 1990 through 2004

Sex and year	Total	Elementary/secondary: Less than 9th grade	Elementary/secondary: Some high school, no completion[1]	Elementary/secondary: High school completion (includes equivalency)[2]	College: Some college, no degree[3]	College: Associate's degree[4]	Bachelor's or higher degree[5]: Total	Bachelor's or higher degree[5]: Bachelor's degree[6]	Bachelor's or higher degree[5]: Master's degree[4]	Bachelor's or higher degree[5]: Professional degree[4]	Bachelor's or higher degree[5]: Doctor's degree[4]
1	2	3	4	5	6	7	8	9	10	11	12
Current dollars											
Males											
1990	$30,733 (—)	$17,394 (—)	$20,902 (—)	$26,653 (—)	$31,734 (—)	— (†)	$42,671 (—)	$39,238 (—)	— (†)	— (†)	— (†)
1991	31,613 (—)	17,623 (—)	21,402 (—)	26,779 (—)	31,663 (—)	$33,817 (—)	45,138 (—)	40,906 (—)	$49,734 (—)	$73,996 (—)	$57,187 (—)
1992	32,057 (120)	17,294 (—)	21,274 (—)	27,280 (175)	32,103 (—)	33,433 (—)	45,802 (—)	41,355 (304)	49,973 (—)	76,220 (—)	57,418 (—)
1993	32,359 (124)	16,863 (—)	21,752 (—)	27,370 (204)	32,077 (—)	33,690 (—)	47,740 (—)	42,757 (536)	51,867 (—)	80,549 (—)	63,149 (—)
1994	33,440 (246)	17,532 (453)	22,048 (319)	28,037 (322)	32,279 (300)	35,794 (430)	49,228 (707)	43,663 (633)	53,500 (854)	75,009 (3,040)	61,921 (1,619)
1995	34,551 (275)	18,354 (545)	22,185 (342)	29,510 (358)	33,883 (517)	35,201 (535)	50,481 (312)	45,266 (510)	55,216 (973)	79,667 (2,582)	65,336 (2,188)
1996	35,622 (150)	17,962 (594)	22,717 (414)	30,709 (184)	34,845 (456)	37,131 (435)	51,436 (303)	45,846 (458)	60,508 (945)	85,963 (3,317)	71,227 (3,362)
1997	36,678 (149)	19,291 (629)	24,726 (466)	31,215 (171)	35,945 (293)	38,022 (774)	53,450 (755)	48,616 (851)	61,690 (771)	85,011 (4,253)	76,234 (3,611)
1998	37,906 (291)	19,380 (600)	23,958 (547)	31,477 (169)	36,934 (291)	40,274 (539)	56,524 (421)	51,405 (349)	62,244 (847)	94,737 (12,105)	75,078 (2,507)
1999	40,333 (144)	20,429 (444)	25,035 (535)	33,184 (388)	39,221 (581)	41,638 (459)	60,201 (439)	52,985 (722)	66,243 (690)	100,000 (37,836)	81,687 (3,953)
2000	41,059 (156)	20,789 (376)	25,095 (436)	34,303 (457)	40,337 (312)	41,952 (460)	61,868 (303)	56,334 (573)	68,322 (1,506)	99,411 (20,832)	80,250 (2,446)
2001	41,617 (104)	21,361 (235)	26,209 (251)	34,723 (299)	41,045 (214)	42,776 (561)	62,223 (279)	55,929 (335)	70,899 (687)	100,000 (†)	86,965 (3,013)
2002	41,152 (100)	20,919 (213)	25,903 (207)	33,206 (311)	40,851 (195)	42,856 (673)	61,700 (201)	56,077 (385)	67,281 (1,294)	100,000 (†)	83,305 (2,076)
2003	41,939 (90)	21,217 (227)	26,468 (280)	35,412 (168)	41,348 (182)	42,871 (719)	62,075 (187)	56,502 (365)	70,640 (562)	100,000 (†)	87,131 (2,528)
2004	42,085 (89)	21,659 (191)	26,277 (234)	35,725 (148)	41,895 (175)	44,404 (931)	62,797 (798)	57,220 (393)	71,530 (490)	100,000 (†)	82,401 (2,423)
Females											
1990	21,372 (—)	12,251 (—)	14,429 (—)	18,319 (—)	22,227 (—)	— (†)	30,377 (—)	28,017 (—)	— (†)	— (†)	— (†)
1991	22,043 (—)	12,066 (—)	14,455 (—)	18,836 (—)	22,143 (—)	25,000 (—)	31,310 (—)	29,079 (—)	34,949 (—)	46,742 (—)	43,303 (—)
1992	23,139 (159)	12,958 (—)	14,559 (—)	19,427 (176)	23,157 (—)	25,624 (—)	32,304 (—)	30,326 (294)	36,037 (—)	46,257 (—)	45,790 (—)
1993	23,629 (166)	12,415 (—)	15,386 (—)	19,963 (173)	23,056 (—)	25,883 (—)	34,307 (—)	31,197 (310)	38,612 (—)	50,211 (—)	47,248 (—)
1994	24,399 (165)	12,430 (427)	15,133 (328)	20,373 (158)	23,514 (327)	25,940 (295)	35,378 (280)	31,741 (314)	39,457 (606)	50,615 (2,154)	51,119 (2,888)
1995	24,875 (160)	13,577 (490)	15,825 (293)	20,463 (162)	23,997 (274)	27,311 (428)	35,259 (313)	32,051 (273)	40,263 (556)	50,000 (2,532)	48,141 (2,373)
1996	25,808 (131)	14,414 (559)	16,953 (333)	21,175 (143)	25,167 (267)	28,083 (526)	36,461 (296)	33,525 (437)	41,901 (564)	57,624 (3,635)	56,267 (3,300)
1997	26,974 (134)	14,161 (492)	16,697 (335)	22,067 (148)	26,335 (291)	28,812 (660)	38,038 (481)	35,379 (295)	44,949 (837)	61,051 (4,737)	53,038 (3,626)
1998	27,956 (199)	14,467 (429)	16,482 (322)	22,780 (254)	27,420 (271)	29,924 (513)	39,786 (408)	36,559 (305)	45,283 (760)	57,565 (1,705)	57,796 (1,881)
1999	28,844 (216)	15,098 (492)	17,015 (298)	23,061 (279)	27,757 (369)	30,919 (318)	41,747 (275)	37,993 (614)	48,097 (862)	59,904 (4,479)	60,079 (3,130)
2000	30,327 (138)	15,798 (327)	17,919 (434)	24,970 (236)	28,697 (364)	31,071 (307)	42,706 (439)	40,415 (284)	50,139 (735)	58,957 (3,552)	57,081 (2,999)
2001	31,356 (91)	16,691 (255)	19,156 (359)	25,303 (132)	30,418 (186)	32,153 (231)	44,776 (367)	40,994 (231)	50,669 (328)	61,748 (3,976)	62,123 (2,228)
2002	31,010 (83)	16,510 (297)	19,307 (360)	25,182 (121)	29,400 (299)	31,625 (211)	43,245 (568)	40,853 (173)	48,890 (595)	57,018 (2,421)	65,715 (2,268)
2003	31,565 (85)	16,907 (256)	18,938 (327)	26,074 (118)	30,142 (176)	32,253 (241)	45,116 (291)	41,327 (204)	50,163 (454)	66,491 (3,469)	67,214 (2,462)
2004	31,990 (80)	17,023 (241)	19,162 (319)	26,029 (116)	30,816 (135)	33,481 (489)	45,911 (229)	41,681 (172)	51,316 (263)	75,036 (2,436)	68,875 (2,450)
Constant 2004 dollars[7]											
Males											
1990	$44,418 (—)	$25,139 (—)	$30,210 (—)	$38,521 (—)	$45,865 (—)	— (†)	$61,672 (—)	$56,710 (—)	— (†)	— (†)	— (†)
1991	43,845 (—)	24,442 (—)	29,683 (—)	37,141 (—)	43,914 (—)	$46,902 (—)	62,603 (—)	56,734 (—)	$68,978 (—)	$102,627 (—)	$79,314 (—)
1992	43,162 (162)	23,285 (—)	28,643 (—)	36,730 (236)	43,223 (—)	45,014 (—)	61,668 (—)	55,680 (409)	67,284 (—)	102,623 (—)	77,308 (—)
1993	42,302 (162)	22,044 (—)	28,436 (—)	35,780 (267)	41,933 (—)	44,042 (—)	62,409 (—)	55,895 (701)	67,804 (—)	105,299 (—)	82,553 (—)
1994	42,624 (314)	22,347 (577)	28,103 (407)	35,737 (410)	41,144 (382)	45,624 (548)	62,747 (901)	55,654 (807)	68,193 (1,089)	95,609 (3,875)	78,926 (2,064)
1995	42,826 (341)	22,750 (676)	27,498 (424)	36,578 (444)	41,998 (641)	43,632 (663)	62,571 (387)	56,107 (632)	68,440 (1,206)	98,747 (3,200)	80,984 (2,712)
1996	42,887 (181)	21,625 (715)	27,350 (498)	36,972 (222)	41,952 (549)	44,704 (524)	61,926 (365)	55,196 (551)	72,849 (1,138)	103,495 (3,994)	85,754 (4,048)
1997	43,168 (175)	22,704 (740)	29,101 (548)	36,738 (201)	42,305 (345)	44,750 (911)	62,908 (889)	57,218 (1,002)	72,606 (907)	100,053 (5,006)	89,723 (4,250)
1998	43,929 (337)	22,459 (695)	27,765 (634)	36,479 (196)	42,803 (337)	46,673 (625)	65,505 (488)	59,573 (404)	72,134 (982)	109,790 (14,028)	87,008 (2,905)
1999	45,732 (163)	23,163 (503)	28,386 (607)	37,626 (440)	44,471 (659)	47,211 (520)	68,259 (498)	60,077 (819)	75,110 (782)	113,385 (42,900)	92,621 (4,482)
2000	45,041 (171)	22,805 (412)	27,529 (478)	37,630 (501)	44,249 (342)	46,021 (505)	67,868 (332)	61,797 (629)	74,948 (1,652)	109,052 (22,852)	88,033 (2,683)
2001	44,390 (111)	22,784 (251)	27,955 (268)	37,037 (319)	43,780 (228)	45,626 (598)	66,369 (298)	59,655 (357)	75,623 (733)	106,663 (†)	92,759 (3,214)
2002	43,211 (105)	21,966 (224)	27,199 (217)	34,867 (327)	42,895 (205)	45,000 (707)	64,787 (211)	58,882 (404)	70,647 (1,359)	105,003 (†)	87,473 (2,180)
2003	43,056 (92)	21,782 (233)	27,173 (287)	36,355 (172)	42,449 (187)	44,013 (738)	63,728 (192)	58,007 (375)	72,521 (577)	102,663 (†)	89,451 (2,595)
2004	42,085 (89)	21,659 (191)	26,277 (234)	35,725 (148)	41,895 (175)	44,404 (931)	62,797 (798)	57,220 (393)	71,530 (490)	100,000 (†)	82,401 (2,423)
Females											
1990	30,889 (—)	17,706 (—)	20,854 (—)	26,476 (—)	32,125 (—)	— (†)	43,904 (—)	40,493 (—)	— (†)	— (†)	— (†)
1991	30,572 (—)	16,735 (—)	20,048 (—)	26,124 (—)	30,711 (—)	34,673 (—)	43,425 (—)	40,331 (—)	48,472 (—)	64,828 (—)	60,058 (—)

See notes at end of table.

Median annual income of year-round, full-time workers 25 years old and over, by highest level of educational attainment and sex: 1990 through 2004—Continued

Sex and year	Total	Elementary/secondary			College		Bachelor's or higher degree[5]				
		Less than 9th grade	Some high school, no completion[1]	High school completion (includes equivalency)[2]	Some college, no degree[3]	Associate's degree[4]	Total	Bachelor's degree[6]	Master's degree[4]	Professional degree[4]	Doctor's degree[4]
1	2	3	4	5	6	7	8	9	10	11	12
1992	31,154 (214)	17,447 (—)	19,602 (—)	26,157 (237)	31,179 (—)	34,500 (—)	43,494 (—)	40,831 (396)	48,520 (—)	62,280 (—)	61,652 (—)
1993	30,889 (217)	16,230 (—)	20,114 (—)	26,097 (226)	30,140 (—)	33,836 (—)	44,848 (—)	40,783 (405)	50,476 (—)	65,639 (—)	61,766 (—)
1994	31,100 (210)	15,844 (544)	19,289 (418)	25,968 (201)	29,972 (417)	33,064 (531)	45,094 (357)	40,458 (400)	50,293 (772)	64,515 (2,746)	65,158 (3,681)
1995	30,833 (198)	16,829 (607)	19,615 (363)	25,364 (201)	29,744 (340)	33,852 (531)	43,704 (531)	39,727 (338)	49,906 (689)	61,975 (3,138)	59,671 (2,941)
1996	31,072 (158)	17,354 (673)	20,411 (401)	25,494 (172)	30,300 (321)	33,811 (633)	43,897 (356)	40,362 (526)	50,447 (679)	69,377 (4,376)	67,743 (3,973)
1997	31,747 (158)	16,667 (579)	19,651 (394)	25,972 (174)	30,995 (342)	33,910 (777)	44,769 (566)	41,639 (347)	52,903 (985)	71,854 (5,575)	62,423 (4,268)
1998	32,398 (231)	16,766 (497)	19,101 (373)	26,400 (294)	31,717 (314)	34,679 (595)	46,108 (473)	42,368 (353)	52,478 (881)	66,712 (1,976)	66,980 (2,180)
1999	32,705 (245)	17,119 (558)	19,293 (338)	26,148 (316)	31,472 (418)	35,058 (361)	47,335 (312)	43,078 (696)	54,535 (977)	67,922 (5,079)	68,121 (3,549)
2000	33,268 (151)	17,330 (359)	19,657 (476)	27,392 (259)	31,480 (399)	34,084 (337)	46,848 (482)	44,334 (312)	55,001 (806)	64,675 (3,896)	62,617 (3,290)
2001	33,445 (97)	17,803 (272)	20,432 (383)	26,989 (141)	32,445 (198)	34,295 (246)	47,759 (391)	43,725 (246)	54,045 (350)	65,862 (4,241)	66,262 (2,376)
2002	32,561 (87)	17,336 (312)	20,273 (378)	26,442 (127)	30,871 (314)	33,207 (222)	45,408 (596)	42,897 (182)	51,336 (625)	59,870 (2,542)	66,003 (2,381)
2003	32,406 (87)	17,357 (263)	19,442 (336)	26,768 (121)	30,945 (181)	33,112 (247)	46,317 (299)	42,428 (209)	51,499 (466)	68,262 (3,561)	69,004 (2,528)
2004	31,990 (80)	17,023 (241)	19,162 (319)	26,029 (116)	30,816 (135)	33,481 (489)	45,911 (229)	41,681 (172)	51,316 (263)	75,036 (2,436)	68,875 (2,450)
Number of persons with income (in thousands)											
Males											
1990	44,406 (268.6)	2,250 (73.9)	3,315 (89.3)	16,394 (188.0)	9,113 (144.6)	— (†)	13,334 (171.8)	7,569 (132.6)	— (†)	— (†)	— (†)
1991	44,199 (268.3)	1,807 (66.3)	3,083 (86.2)	15,025 (181.1)	8,034 (136.4)	2,899 (83.6)	13,350 (171.9)	8,456 (139.7)	3,073 (86.1)	1,147 (53.0)	674 (40.7)
1992	44,752 (269.1)	1,815 (66.5)	3,009 (85.2)	14,722 (179.5)	8,067 (136.6)	3,203 (87.8)	13,937 (175.2)	8,719 (145.1)	3,178 (87.5)	1,295 (56.3)	745 (42.8)
1993	45,873 (270.6)	1,790 (66.0)	3,083 (86.2)	14,604 (178.9)	8,493 (140.0)	3,557 (92.4)	14,346 (177.5)	9,178 (145.1)	3,131 (86.8)	1,231 (54.9)	808 (44.5)
1994	47,566 (272.8)	1,895 (67.9)	3,057 (85.8)	15,109 (181.5)	8,783 (142.2)	3,735 (94.6)	14,987 (180.9)	9,636 (148.4)	3,225 (88.1)	1,258 (55.4)	868 (46.1)
1995	48,500 (324.3)	1,946 (71.6)	3,335 (93.5)	15,331 (195.8)	8,908 (151.1)	3,926 (101.3)	15,054 (194.1)	9,597 (156.7)	3,395 (94.3)	1,208 (56.5)	853 (47.5)
1996	49,764 (339.9)	2,041 (76.2)	3,441 (98.7)	15,840 (206.6)	9,173 (159.3)	3,931 (105.4)	15,339 (203.5)	9,898 (165.3)	3,272 (96.3)	1,277 (60.4)	893 (50.5)
1997	50,807 (342.6)	1,914 (73.8)	3,548 (100.2)	16,225 (208.9)	9,170 (159.3)	4,086 (107.4)	15,864 (206.7)	10,349 (168.9)	3,228 (95.6)	1,321 (61.4)	966 (52.5)
1998	52,381 (346.6)	1,870 (73.0)	3,613 (101.1)	16,442 (210.2)	9,375 (161.0)	4,347 (110.7)	16,733 (212.0)	11,058 (174.3)	3,414 (98.3)	1,264 (60.1)	998 (53.4)
1999	53,062 (348.2)	1,993 (75.3)	3,295 (96.6)	16,589 (211.1)	9,684 (163.6)	4,359 (110.9)	17,142 (214.4)	11,142 (174.9)	3,725 (102.6)	1,267 (60.1)	1,008 (53.7)
2000	54,065 (350.7)	1,968 (74.9)	3,354 (97.5)	16,834 (212.6)	9,792 (164.4)	4,729 (115.4)	17,387 (215.8)	11,395 (176.8)	3,680 (102.0)	1,274 (60.3)	1,038 (54.5)
2001	54,013 (350.5)	2,207 (79.2)	3,503 (99.6)	16,314 (209.5)	9,494 (162.0)	4,714 (115.2)	17,780 (218.0)	11,479 (177.4)	3,961 (105.8)	1,298 (60.9)	1,041 (54.5)
2002	54,108 (225.0)	2,154 (50.7)	3,680 (66.1)	16,005 (134.2)	9,603 (105.5)	4,399 (72.2)	18,267 (142.7)	11,829 (116.5)	4,065 (69.4)	1,308 (39.6)	1,065 (35.8)
2003	54,253 (225.2)	2,209 (51.4)	3,369 (63.3)	16,285 (135.3)	9,340 (104.1)	4,696 (74.5)	18,354 (143.0)	11,846 (116.6)	4,124 (69.9)	1,348 (40.2)	1,037 (35.3)
2004	55,469 (227.0)	2,427 (53.8)	3,468 (64.2)	17,067 (138.3)	9,257 (103.6)	4,913 (76.2)	18,338 (142.9)	11,701 (115.9)	4,243 (70.9)	1,305 (39.6)	1,088 (36.1)
Females											
1990	28,636 (234.7)	847 (45.6)	1,861 (67.3)	11,810 (162.8)	6,462 (123.1)	— (†)	7,655 (133.3)	4,704 (105.8)	— (†)	— (†)	— (†)
1991	29,474 (237.1)	733 (42.4)	1,819 (66.5)	10,959 (157.4)	5,633 (115.3)	2,523 (78.1)	7,807 (134.6)	5,263 (111.6)	2,025 (70.1)	312 (27.7)	206 (22.5)
1992	30,346 (239.6)	734 (42.4)	1,659 (63.6)	11,039 (157.9)	5,904 (117.9)	2,655 (80.1)	8,355 (138.9)	5,604 (115.0)	2,192 (72.9)	334 (28.7)	225 (23.5)
1993	30,683 (240.5)	765 (43.3)	1,576 (62.0)	10,513 (154.4)	6,279 (121.4)	3,067 (86.0)	8,483 (139.9)	5,735 (116.3)	2,166 (72.5)	323 (28.2)	260 (25.3)
1994	31,379 (242.4)	696 (41.3)	1,675 (63.9)	10,785 (156.2)	6,256 (121.2)	3,210 (87.9)	8,756 (142.0)	5,901 (117.9)	2,174 (72.6)	398 (31.3)	283 (26.4)
1995	32,673 (275.7)	774 (45.2)	1,763 (68.2)	11,064 (167.7)	6,329 (128.0)	3,336 (93.5)	9,406 (155.1)	6,434 (129.1)	2,268 (77.2)	421 (33.4)	283 (27.4)
1996	33,549 (289.6)	750 (46.3)	1,751 (70.9)	11,363 (176.6)	6,582 (135.7)	3,468 (99.1)	9,636 (163.2)	6,689 (136.7)	2,213 (79.3)	413 (34.4)	322 (30.4)
1997	34,624 (293.5)	791 (47.6)	1,765 (70.9)	11,475 (177.4)	6,628 (136.1)	3,538 (100.1)	10,427 (169.5)	7,173 (141.5)	2,448 (83.4)	488 (37.4)	318 (30.2)
1998	35,628 (297.1)	814 (48.3)	1,878 (73.1)	11,613 (178.4)	7,070 (140.5)	3,527 (99.9)	10,725 (171.6)	7,288 (142.6)	2,639 (86.6)	468 (36.6)	329 (30.7)
1999	37,091 (302.1)	886 (50.3)	1,883 (73.2)	11,824 (180.0)	7,453 (144.1)	3,804 (103.7)	11,242 (175.7)	7,607 (145.6)	2,818 (89.4)	470 (36.7)	346 (31.5)
2000	37,762 (304.4)	930 (51.6)	1,950 (74.5)	11,789 (179.7)	7,607 (145.6)	4,118 (107.8)	11,584 (178.2)	7,899 (148.2)	2,823 (89.5)	509 (38.2)	353 (31.8)
2001	38,228 (305.9)	927 (51.5)	1,869 (73.0)	11,690 (179.0)	7,391 (143.5)	4,190 (108.8)	12,269 (183.2)	8,257 (151.5)	3,089 (93.6)	531 (39.0)	392 (33.5)
2002	38,510 (197.6)	858 (32.1)	1,841 (46.9)	11,687 (115.8)	7,283 (92.7)	4,285 (71.2)	12,484 (119.5)	8,229 (97.9)	3,281 (62.5)	572 (26.2)	402 (22.0)
2003	38,681 (197.9)	882 (32.6)	1,739 (45.6)	11,587 (115.3)	7,354 (92.7)	4,397 (72.2)	12,735 (120.6)	8,330 (98.5)	3,376 (63.4)	567 (26.1)	462 (23.6)
2004	39,072 (198.7)	917 (33.2)	1,797 (46.4)	11,392 (114.4)	7,330 (92.6)	4,505 (73.0)	13,131 (122.4)	8,664 (100.4)	3,451 (64.0)	564 (26.0)	452 (23.3)

—Not available.
†Not applicable.
[1]Includes 1 to 3 years of high school for 1990.
[2]Includes 4 years of high school for 1990.
[3]Includes 1 to 3 years of college and associate's degrees for 1990.
[4]Not reported separately for 1990.
[5]Includes 4 or more years of college for 1990.
[6]Includes 4 years of college for 1990.
[7]Constant dollars based on the Consumer Price Index, prepared by the Bureau of Labor Statistics, U.S. Department of Labor.

NOTE: Data for 1992 and later years are based on 1990 census counts; prior years are based on 1980 counts. Total standard errors for bachelor's or higher degree are not available for 1992 and 1993 from the source document. Detail may not sum to totals because of rounding. Standard errors appear in parentheses. SOURCE: U.S. Department of Commerce, Census Bureau, Current Population Reports, Series P-60, Money Income of Households, Families, and Persons in the United States, Income, Poverty, and Valuation of Noncash Benefits, selected years, 1990 through 1994; Series P-60, Money Income in the United States, selected years, 1995 through 2002; and Detailed Income Tabulations from the CPS, 2003 through 2005. Retrieved May 17, 2005, from http://www.census.gov/hhes/www/income/dinctabs.html. (This table was prepared October 2005.)

School boards revenue and expenditures

	2001	2002	2003	2004	2005
	\$ thousands				
Total revenue	**35,230,651**	**36,895,015**	**38,409,518**	**40,035,634**	**40,854,241**
Own source revenue	9,851,322	10,121,370	10,544,256	11,078,982	11,368,047
Property and related taxes	8,105,789	8,197,216	8,523,696	8,985,717	9,241,478
Other taxes	723	695	737	781	747
Sales of goods and services	1,644,381	1,822,908	1,914,441	1,981,926	2,014,297
Interest income and investment income	74,635	71,844	75,310	78,953	79,241
Other revenue from own sources	25,794	28,707	30,072	31,605	32,284
Transfers	25,379,329	26,773,645	27,865,262	28,956,652	29,486,194
Federal government	89,923	104,689	96,651	100,407	103,785
Provincial government	25,120,176	26,494,344	27,594,042	28,680,492	29,213,866
Municipal government	169,230	174,612	174,569	175,753	168,543
Total expenditures	**35,368,073**	**36,873,300**	**38,736,273**	**40,485,457**	**41,615,062**
Education	34,624,407	36,150,312	38,007,178	39,782,766	40,927,379
Debt charges	743,666	722,988	729,095	702,691	687,683
Surplus or deficit	**-137,422**	**21,715**	**-326,755**	**-449,823**	**-760,821**

Note: Year ending December 31.
Source: Statistics Canada, CANSIM
Last modified: 2007-01-31.

School boards revenue and expenditures, by province and territory
(Newfoundland and Labrador, Prince Edward Island, Nova Scotia, New Brunswick)

	2005[1]				
	Canada	N.L.	P.E.I.	N.S.	N.B.[2]
	$ thousands				
Total revenue	**40,854,241**	**660,959**	**168,979**	**915,081**	..
Own source revenue	11,368,047	6,680	810	27,271	..
Property and related taxes	9,241,478	19,778	..	..	..
Other taxes	747	..	..	..	..
Sales of goods and services	2,014,297	5,974	737	24,850	..
Investment income	79,241	181	7	965	..
Other revenue from own sources	32,284	525	66	1,456	..
Transfers	29,486,194	654,279	168,169	887,810	..
Federal government	103,785	4,296	39	5	..
Education	103,785	4,296	39	5	..
Provincial and territorial governments	29,213,866	649,983	168,130	730,222	..
Education	28,771,044	649,983	168,130	730,222	..
Debt charges (interest)	442,822	..	2	0	..
Municipal governments	168,543	..	..	157,588	..
Education	168,543	..	..	157,588	..
Total expenditures	**41,615,062**	**686,673**	**172,125**	**900,358**	..
Education	40,927,379	686,569	172,125	899,387	..
Debt charges	687,683	104	2	971	..
Surplus or deficit	**-760,821**	**-25,714**	**-3,146**	**14,723**	..

.. : not available for a specific period of time.

1. Year ending December 31.

2. Schools boards of New Brunswick are administrated by provincial general government.

Source: Statistics Canada, CANSIM

Last modified: 2007-01-31.

Average undergraduate tuition fees for full-time students, by discipline, by province
(Canada)

	1999-2000	2000-2001	2001-2002	2002-2003	2003-2004
			dollars		
Canada					
Discipline					
Agriculture	3,061	3,159	3,216	3,301	3,487
Architecture	3,376	3,510	3,583	3,524	3,586
Arts	3,310	3,411	3,474	3,617	3,810
Commerce	3,171	3,300	3,536	3,743	3,991
Dentistry	7,863	8,424	9,105	9,703	11,733
Education	2,787	2,857	2,911	3,019	3,216
Engineering	3,481	3,624	3,776	3,865	4,371
Household Sciences	3,182	3,285	3,359	3,486	3,669
Law	3,495	4,044	4,366	5,021	5,995
Medicine	5,894	6,494	7,458	8,063	9,406
Music	3,347	3,356	3,454	3,586	3,753
Science	3,334	3,420	3,547	3,728	3,954
Total undergraduate	3,328	3,447	3,577	3,749	4,025

Note: Using the most current enrolment data available, average tuition fees have been weighted by the number of students enrolled by institution and field of study. Fees at both public and private institutions are included in the weighted average calculations.

Source: Statistics Canada, Centre for Education Statistics.

Last modified: 2004-09-01.

University enrollments by program level and instructional program
(All programs)

	2000/2001	2001/2002	2002/2003	2003/2004	2004/2005
	All programs				
	number				
Total, instructional programs	**850,572**	**886,605**	**933,870**	**993,246**	**1,014,486**
Education	66,879	69,747	72,216	76,839	72,561
Visual and performing arts and communications technologies	26,922	27,900	29,862	33,984	35,514
Humanities	123,744	129,738	136,083	147,918	145,146
Social and behavioural sciences and law	136,659	140,247	151,671	164,832	178,146
Business, management and public administration	134,517	141,165	151,695	160,539	162,849
Physical and life sciences and technologies	79,140	80,553	83,616	91,719	96,441
Mathematics, computer and information sciences	43,527	46,377	45,897	44,190	40,929
Architecture, engineering and related technologies	70,023	74,817	81,087	85,776	86,451
Agriculture, natural resources and conservation	15,420	14,841	14,487	14,613	14,640
Health, parks, recreation and fitness	74,268	80,589	84,810	91,908	97,950
Personal, protective and transportation services	1,047	1,185	1,317	1,299	1,683
Other instructional programs	78,426	79,374	81,063	79,575	82,152

Note: The data is subject to revision. For Quebec institutions, the Classification of Instructional Programs (CIP) codes assigned to programs are under review. For British Columbia institutions, the conciliation of the 2003/2004 data from Simon Fraser University is not yet completed.

Source: Statistics Canada, CANSIM

Last modified: 2006-11-07.

University enrollments by registration status and sex, by province
(Both sexes)

	2000-2001	2001-2002	2002-2003	2003-2004	2004-2005
			Both sexes		
			number		
Canada	**850,572**	**886,605**	**933,870**	**993,246**	**1,014,486**
Full-time student	**606,819**	**635,016**	**675,486**	**737,976**	**756,987**
Part-time student	**243,756**	**251,589**	**258,381**	**255,270**	**257,499**
Newfoundland and Labrador	16,140	16,275	16,908	17,550	18,048
Full-time student	13,467	13,527	13,953	14,445	14,877
Part-time student	2,673	2,748	2,952	3,105	3,171
Prince Edward Island	3,366	3,354	3,561	3,855	3,972
Full-time student	2,793	2,787	2,952	3,252	3,384
Part-time student	573	570	609	606	585
Nova Scotia	38,817	40,575	41,892	44,772	43,533
Full-time student	30,894	32,454	33,903	36,240	35,562
Part-time student	7,923	8,118	7,992	8,529	7,971
New Brunswick	23,649	24,309	24,654	25,554	24,903
Full-time student	19,089	19,602	19,887	21,123	20,364
Part-time student	4,560	4,707	4,767	4,431	4,536
Quebec	233,652	240,669	250,809	260,061	263,397
Full-time student	139,659	144,189	153,330	161,775	164,874
Part-time student	93,990	96,480	97,479	98,286	98,526
Ontario	320,112	335,724	360,285	397,776	413,409
Full-time student	242,748	254,400	275,523	316,062	333,219
Part-time student	77,367	81,324	84,762	81,714	80,190
Manitoba	31,938	34,143	35,166	38,043	39,285
Full-time student	23,352	24,822	25,230	27,846	29,025
Part-time student	8,586	9,318	9,939	10,197	10,260
Saskatchewan	31,479	32,094	34,254	34,560	32,838
Full-time student	23,874	24,261	25,923	26,478	24,819
Part-time student	7,605	7,833	8,331	8,079	8,022
Alberta	76,341	79,131	83,448	86,097	88,077
Full-time student	57,996	60,168	62,889	65,004	65,718
Part-time student	18,348	18,963	20,559	21,093	22,359
British Columbia	75,087	80,331	82,893	84,981	87,024
Full-time student	52,953	58,803	61,899	65,754	65,145
Part-time student	22,131	21,528	20,994	19,230	21,879

Note: The data is subject to revision. For Quebec institutions, the Classification of Instructional Programs (CIP) codes assigned to programs are under review. For British Columbia institutions, the conciliation of the 2003-2004 data from Simon Fraser University is not yet completed.
Source: Statistics Canada, CANSIM

Universities and colleges revenue and expenditures

	2002	2003	2004	2005	2006
			$ thousands		
Total revenue	**23,262,806**	**25,359,135**	**28,048,472**	**30,390,710**	**31,850,915**
Own source revenue	10,339,207	11,244,357	12,708,921	13,944,883	14,578,584
Sales of goods and services	8,132,232	9,026,491	9,865,103	10,843,777	11,333,439
Tuition fees	4,486,787	5,085,897	5,765,824	6,366,403	6,649,086
Other sales of goods and services	3,645,445	3,940,594	4,099,279	4,477,374	4,684,353
Investment income	396,046	370,231	821,554	900,089	945,312
Other own source revenue	1,810,929	1,847,635	2,022,264	2,201,017	2,299,833
Transfers from other levels of government	12,923,599	14,114,778	15,339,551	16,445,827	17,272,331
Transfers from federal government	1,922,197	2,270,560	2,564,931	2,767,845	2,902,432
Transfers from provincial governments	10,947,140	11,817,345	12,745,152	13,645,770	14,335,434
Transfers from local governments	54,262	26,873	29,468	32,212	34,465
Total expenditures	**23,454,251**	**25,590,341**	**28,050,725**	**30,385,993**	**31,842,146**
Education	22,989,436	25,091,972	27,475,075	29,781,257	31,211,530
Postsecondary education	22,717,330	24,820,214	27,206,559	29,483,800	30,902,499
Administration	4,662,921	4,717,093	5,161,947	5,580,693	5,861,237
Education	11,372,063	12,485,313	13,749,835	14,886,311	15,600,477
Support to students	718,845	818,445	960,656	1,063,972	1,111,258
Other postsecondary education expenses	5,963,501	6,799,363	7,334,121	7,952,824	8,329,527
Debt charges	464,815	498,369	575,650	604,736	630,616
Surplus or deficit	**-191,445**	**-231,206**	**-2,253**	**4,718**	**8,769**

Note: Fiscal year ending March 31.
Source: Statistics Canada, CANSIM
Last modified: 2007-01-31.

Universities and colleges revenue and expenditures, by province and territory
(Newfoundland and Labrador, Prince Edward Island, Nova Scotia, New Brunswick)

	2006				
	Canada	**N.L.**	**P.E.I.**	**N.S.**	**N.B.**
	\$ thousands				
Total revenue	**31,850,915**	**530,121**	**132,835**	**960,293**	**432,877**
Own source revenue	14,578,584	180,513	65,216	556,121	212,167
Sales of goods and services	11,333,439	164,007	56,213	466,880	183,680
Tuition fees	6,649,086	81,736	32,948	293,144	124,599
Other sales of goods and services	4,684,353	82,271	23,265	173,736	59,081
Investments income	945,312	2,989	3,199	26,650	7,065
Other own source revenue	2,299,833	13,517	5,804	62,591	21,422
Transfers from other levels of governments	17,272,331	349,608	67,619	404,172	220,710
Federal government	2,902,432	62,793	10,674	83,624	42,369
Provincial governments	14,335,434	286,628	56,945	320,433	178,311
Local governments	34,465	187	0	115	30
Total expenditures	**31,842,146**	**544,353**	**144,258**	**971,143**	**444,302**
Education	31,211,530	543,449	143,323	957,902	442,367
Postsecondary education	30,902,499	543,449	137,928	957,902	442,367
Administration	5,861,237	112,274	47,101	194,606	86,586
Education	15,600,477	308,740	65,686	487,699	211,633
Support to students	1,111,258	17,634	2,237	35,286	10,657
Other postsecondary education expenses	8,329,527	104,801	22,904	240,311	133,491
Debt charges	630,616	904	935	13,241	1,935
Surplus or deficit	**8,769**	**-14,232**	**-11,423**	**-10,850**	**-11,425**

Note: Fiscal year ending March 31.

1. Excludes Yukon for confidentiality purposes.

Source: Statistics Canada, CANSIM

Last modified: 2007-01-31.

University degrees, diplomas and certificates granted by sex, by province
(Both sexes)

	2000	2001	2002	2003	2004
	Both sexes				
	number				
Canada	**176,556**	**178,101**	**186,153**	**198,525**	**209,076**
Newfoundland and Labrador	2,931	2,862	2,898	2,976	3,168
Prince Edward Island	534	606	555	624	672
Nova Scotia	7,638	7,680	7,878	8,766	9,579
New Brunswick	4,032	4,101	4,395	4,557	4,944
Quebec	50,847	51,153	54,009	57,786	61,212
Ontario	67,221	68,286	70,749	75,864	80,436
Manitoba	5,340	5,397	5,580	5,871	6,309
Saskatchewan	5,793	5,694	5,739	5,865	5,835
Alberta	14,052	15,087	16,344	17,199	18,012
British Columbia	18,171	17,238	18,000	19,017	18,906

Note: The data is subject to revision. For Quebec institutions, the Classification of Instructional Programs (CIP) codes assigned to programs are under review. In addition, qualifications awarded in Quebec do not include microprogrammes and attestations. For British Columbia institutions, the conciliation of the 2003 data from Simon Fraser University is not yet completed.

Source: Statistics Canada, CANSIM

Last modified: 2006-11-07.

University degrees, diplomas and certificates granted, by program level and instructional program

(All programs)

	2000	2001	2002	2003	2004
	All programs				
	number				
Total, instructional programs	176,556	178,101	186,153	198,525	209,076
Education	22,542	22,395	23,754	24,942	25,428
Visual and performing arts, and communications technologies	5,373	5,904	5,949	6,654	7,320
Humanities	20,064	19,809	20,463	22,095	22,350
Social and behavioural sciences, and law	36,315	36,096	37,398	39,120	41,757
Business, management and public administration	33,213	34,728	37,485	40,785	43,170
Physical and life sciences, and technologies	14,730	14,808	14,283	14,685	15,186
Mathematics, computer and information sciences	8,448	9,060	10,008	10,647	11,079
Architecture, engineering and related technologies	13,305	13,839	14,766	16,380	17,460
Agriculture, natural resources and conservation	4,008	3,885	3,654	3,765	3,576
Health, parks, recreation and fitness	16,518	16,215	17,220	18,129	20,136
Personal, protective and transportation services	81	228	270	270	360
Other instructional program	1,959	1,131	903	1,053	1,254

Note: The data is subject to revision. For Quebec institutions, the Classification of Instructional Programs (CIP) codes assigned to programs are under review. In addition, qualifications awarded in Quebec do not include microprogrammes and attestations. For British Columbia institutions, the conciliation of the 2003 data from Simon Fraser University is not yet completed.

Source: Statistics Canada, CANSIM

Last modified: 2006-11-07.

Canadian Education Statistics

Population 15 years and over by highest level of schooling (1981-2001 Censuses)

	1981	1986	1991	1996	2001
	number				
Total	**18,609,285**	**19,634,100**	**21,304,740**	**22,628,925**	**23,901,360**
Elementary-secondary only	11,341,020	11,226,170	11,276,595	11,106,595	10,844,795
Less than grade 5	776,855	659,740	588,350	578,110	524,145
Grades 5-8	2,954,455	2,733,975	2,371,565	2,149,100	1,826,350
Grades 9-10	2,858,695	2,811,885	2,663,635	2,601,150	2,430,300
Grades 11-13	2,329,520	2,509,345	2,506,710	2,539,645	2,696,105
Secondary (high) school graduation only	2,421,505	2,511,215	3,146,345	3,238,595	3,367,900
Trades certificate or diploma	632,730	601,500	846,890	837,160	836,250
College education only	3,666,335	4,189,285	4,756,200	5,487,505	6,047,085
Without trade or college certificate or diploma	1,112,200	1,335,720	1,393,715	1,474,925	1,537,615
With trades certificate or diploma	1,210,240	1,225,145	1,350,170	1,405,920	1,601,275
With college certificate or diploma	1,343,885	1,628,425	2,012,310	2,606,665	2,908,200
University	2,969,200	3,617,145	4,425,055	5,197,665	6,173,225
Without degree	1,479,020	1,738,665	2,005,305	2,196,885	2,485,580
Without college education	704,230	846,735	972,595	1,036,115	1,133,685
Without certificate, diploma or degree	516,325	589,710	711,270	743,070	806,920
With trades certificate or diploma	36,005	38,430	17,255	7,210	8,080
With university certificate or diploma below bachelor level	151,905	218,590	244,070	285,830	318,685
With college education	774,790	891,930	1,032,710	1,160,775	1,351,890
Without certificate, diploma or degree	164,905	218,325	225,640	224,235	245,625
With trades certificate or diploma	97,800	104,575	127,790	121,650	153,320
With college certificate or diploma	339,135	406,045	482,150	575,240	670,205
With university certificate or diploma below bachelor level	172,950	162,990	197,130	239,645	282,740
With degree	1,490,180	1,878,480	2,419,750	3,000,780	3,687,650
With bachelor or first professional degree	1,040,300	1,329,195	1,676,605	2,084,715	2,534,010
With university certificate above bachelor level	171,795	189,000	264,845	310,700	382,955
With master's degree	222,125	293,335	394,750	501,505	642,055
With earned doctorate	55,955	66,955	83,545	103,860	128,625

Source: Statistics Canada, Census of population.

Last modified: 2005-02-17.

Population 15 years and over by highest level of schooling, by province and territory (2001 Census)
(Newfoundland and Labrador, Prince Edward Island, Nova Scotia, New Brunswick)

	2001				
	Canada	N.L.	P.E.I.	N.S.	N.B.
	number				
Total	**23,901,360**	**419,015**	**106,690**	**732,370**	**589,370**
Elementary-secondary only	10,844,795	216,920	52,255	330,365	306,975
Less than grade 5	524,145	12,630	1,065	8,120	13,040
Grades 5-8	1,826,350	51,265	10,050	57,600	68,195
Grades 9-10	2,430,300	63,870	15,880	103,080	72,500
Grades 11-13	2,696,105	49,740	12,910	90,235	66,085
Secondary (high) school graduation only	3,367,900	39,415	12,350	71,335	87,150
Trades certificate or diploma	836,250	11,140	3,485	26,475	18,755
College education only	6,047,085	103,925	25,780	183,675	133,825
Without trade or college certificate or diploma	1,537,615	16,555	4,760	28,220	25,020
With trades certificate or diploma	1,601,275	52,650	8,895	68,370	43,030
With college certificate or diploma	2,908,200	34,720	12,130	87,085	65,780
University	6,173,225	87,025	25,175	191,860	129,815
Without degree	2,485,580	47,085	12,985	89,205	63,200
Without college education	1,133,685	22,245	6,490	48,590	33,010
Without certificate, diploma or degree	806,920	17,845	5,040	36,575	25,685
With trades certificate or diploma	8,080	170	15	400	170
With university certificate or diploma below bachelor level	318,685	4,230	1,435	11,615	7,160
With college education	1,351,890	24,835	6,500	40,615	30,190
Without certificate, diploma or degree	245,625	4,205	785	5,820	5,680
With trades certificate or diploma	153,320	6,560	1,040	7,965	4,695
With college certificate or diploma	670,205	10,845	3,725	20,250	15,760
With university certificate or diploma below bachelor level	282,740	3,225	950	6,575	4,055
With degree	3,687,650	39,945	12,190	102,655	66,620
With bachelor or first professional degree	2,534,010	28,795	8,995	71,470	48,415
With university certificate above bachelor level	382,955	2,585	1,095	10,065	5,855
With master's degree	642,055	7,255	1,750	17,465	10,260
With earned doctorate	128,625	1,310	350	3,655	2,090

Source: Statistics Canada, Census of Population.

Last modified: 2004-09-01.

Population 15 years and over by highest degree, certificate or diploma, by province and territory (2001 Census)

(Newfoundland and Labrador , Prince Edward Island, Nova Scotia, New Brunswick)

	2001				
	Canada	N.L.	P.E.I.	N.S.	N.B.
	number				
Total	**23,901,360**	**419,015**	**106,695**	**732,365**	**589,370**
No degree, certificate or diploma	7,935,075	185,075	42,145	272,960	229,310
High school graduation certificate	5,499,885	70,455	20,690	128,020	134,040
Trades certificate or diploma	2,598,925	70,520	13,435	103,205	66,645
College certificate or diploma	3,578,400	45,560	15,850	107,335	81,545
University certificate or diploma below bachelor level	601,425	7,455	2,385	18,190	11,215
Bachelor's degree	2,411,475	27,245	8,615	67,765	46,485
University certificate or diploma above bachelor level	382,955	2,580	1,095	10,070	5,855
Medical degree	122,535	1,545	380	3,705	1,930
Master's degree	642,055	7,255	1,750	17,460	10,260
Earned doctorate	128,625	1,315	350	3,655	2,085

Source: Statistics Canada, Census of Population.

Last modified: 2004-09-01.

Population 15 years and over by highest degree, certificate or diploma (1986-2001 Censuses)

	1986	1991	1996	2001
	number			
Total	**19,634,100**	**21,304,740**	**22,628,925**	**23,901,360**
No degree, certificate or diploma	9,384,100	8,639,900	8,331,615	7,935,075
High school graduation certificate	3,985,820	4,967,330	5,217,205	5,499,885
Trades certificate or diploma	1,969,650	2,342,105	2,372,000	2,598,925
College certificate or diploma	2,034,465	2,494,460	3,181,845	3,578,400
University certificate or diploma below bachelor level	381,585	441,200	525,565	601,425
Bachelor's degree	1,254,250	1,585,775	1,979,465	2,411,475
University certificate or diploma above bachelor level	189,000	264,845	310,820	382,955
Medical degree	74,945	90,835	105,050	122,535
Master's degree	293,335	394,750	501,505	642,055
Earned doctorate	66,950	83,545	103,855	128,625

Source: Statistics Canada, Census of Population.

Last modified: 2004-09-01.

Canadian Education Statistics

People employed, by educational attainment

	2006		
	Both sexes	**Men**	**Women**
	%		
Total	**63.0**	**67.7**	**58.3**
15 to 24 years	58.7	57.9	59.5
25 to 44 years	82.0	86.8	77.2
45 and over	50.4	56.6	44.6
Less than Grade 9	21.5	29.5	14.5
15 to 24 years	26.5	30.9	20.9
25 to 44 years	52.1	64.6	36.3
45 and over	17.3	24.1	11.9
Some secondary school	44.9	51.3	38.3
15 to 24 years	43.4	43.5	43.3
25 to 44 years	66.8	75.6	55.2
45 and over	37.1	46.3	29.0
High school graduate	65.2	72.0	59.0
15 to 24 years	69.4	69.8	68.9
25 to 44 years	79.7	85.9	72.9
45 and over	53.6	61.1	47.9
Some postsecondary	64.0	66.6	61.3
15 to 24 years	60.6	59.0	62.0
25 to 44 years	78.0	81.7	73.8
45 and over	54.6	60.2	49.1
Postsecondary certificate or diploma[1]	72.7	76.5	69.0
15 to 24 years	78.0	77.5	78.5
25 to 44 years	86.1	90.1	82.2
45 and over	59.6	63.9	55.5
Bachelor's degree	76.8	79.4	74.5
15 to 24 years	74.7	73.0	75.6
25 to 44 years	85.9	90.3	82.4
45 and over	65.1	67.7	62.2
Above bachelor's degree	77.1	78.4	75.5
15 to 24 years	65.7	62.4	67.7
25 to 44 years	86.4	90.6	81.9
45 and over	69.0	69.3	68.5

1. Includes trades certificate.

Source: Statistics Canada, CANSIM

Internet use by individuals for educational purposes

	2005	
	As a percentage of Internet users at home[1]	As a percentage of Internet users at home who reported using Internet for educational purposes
	%	
Specific educational purposes		
Distance education, self-directed learning or correspondence courses	11.0	25.8
Researching information for project assignments or for solving academic problems	28.1	66.2
Communicating with teachers and peers (includes submission of projects or assignments)	9.1	21.5
Communicating with administration, registering or obtaining marks	10.4	24.4
Other educational purposes	3.5	8.3

Note: The Canadian Internet use survey (CIUS) tables beginning with 2005 replace the Household Internet survey (HIUS) tables from 1997 to 2003. The unit surveyed is now the individual rather than the household. Only adults aged 18 years and over were surveyed.

1. Percentage of all individuals, aged 18 years and over, who responded that they had used the Internet in the previous 12 months for personal non-business purposes at home.

Source: Statistics Canada, CANSIM

Last modified: 2006-11-01.

A

B

D

J

N

O

P

Q

R

S

Alabama

Alaska

Arizona

Arkansas

California

Colorado

Connecticut

Delaware

District of Columbia

Florida

Georgia

Hawaii

Idaho

Illinois

American Academy of Pediatrics, 5
American Association of French Teachers Conference, 636
American Association of School Librarians National Conference, 639
American Association of Teachers of French, 285
American Library Association, 302
American Library Association Annual Conference, 649
Ameritech Foundation, 2407
Annual Ethics & Technology Conference, 661
Awards and Recognition Association, 26
Career Evaluation Systems, 825
Carus Corporate Contributions Program, 2408
Center for the Study of Reading, 5003
Chauncey & Marion Deering McCormick Foundation, 2409
Chicago Community Trust, 2410
Chicago Principals Association Education Conference, 3287
Clearinghouse on Early Education and Parenting (CEEP), 170
Coleman Foundation, 2411
Community Foundation for Jewish Education, 840
Council on Library Technical Assistants (COLT), 305
Curriculum Center - Office of Educational Services, 3604
DeVry University, 3606
Dellora A & Lester J Norris Foundation, 2412
Dillon Foundation, 2413
Directory of Curriculum Materials Centers, 3406
Dr. Scholl Foundation, 2414
Easter Seals Communications, 47
Eastern Illinois University School of Technology, 3609
Educational Specialties, 872
Energy Concepts, 3616
Evanston Public Library, 2415
Executive Deputy Superintendent, 2962
Farny R Wurlitzer Foundation, 2416
Finance & Support Services, 2963
Grand Canyon University College of Education, 3622
Grover Hermann Foundation, 2417
How to Raise Test Scores, 3411
Illinois Affiliation of Private Schools for Exceptional Children, 446
Illinois Assistant Principals Conference, 3294
Illinois Association of School Business Officials, 447
Illinois Business Education Association (IBEA), 448
Illinois Citizens' Education Council, 449
Illinois Department of Education, 2964
Illinois Education Association, 450
Illinois Library Association, 451
Illinois Library Association Conference, 780
Illinois Principals Professional Conference, 3295
Illinois Resource Center Conference of Teachers of Linguistically Diverse Students, 3296
Illinois School Boards Association, 3297
Illinois School Library Media Association, 452
Illinois Vocational Association Conference, 781
Improving Student Performance, 701
Independent Schools Association of the Central States, 147
Innovative Learning Group, 894
Institute of Cultural Affairs, 250
International Awards Market, 614
International Council on Education for Teaching, 3247
Janice Borla Vocal Jazz Camp, 3633
Joyce Foundation, 2418
Kodaly Teaching Certification Program, 3640
Lloyd A Fry Foundation, 2419
Lutheran Education Association, 72
Lutheran Education Association Convention, 711

Management Simulations, 925
Midwestern Regional Educational Laboratory, 5024
National Council of English Teachers Conference, 3334
National Council of Teachers of English Annual Convention, 296, 3336
National Council on Rehabilitation Education (NCRE), 100
National Council on Student Development (NCSD), 101
National Lekotek Center, 109
National Society for the Study of Education (N SSE), 115
North Central Regional Educational Laboratory, 5049
Northern Trust Company Charitable Trust, 2420
Orff-Schulwerk Teacher Certification Program, 3660
Palmer Foundation, 2421
Philip H Corboy Foundation, 2422
Planning, Research & Evaluation, 2965
Polk Brothers Foundation, 2423
Prince Charitable Trust, 2424
Programs & Accountability, 2966
Recognition & Supervision of Schools, 2967
Regenstein Foundation, 2425
Region 5: Education Department, 2968
Requirements for Certification of Teachers & Counselors, 3431
Richard H Driehaus Foundation, 2426
Robert E Nelson Associates, 977
Robert R McCormick Tribune Foundation, 2427
Rockford Systems, 3673
School Improvement & Assessment Services, 2970
Sears-Roebuck Foundation, 2428
Sigma Tau Delta, 300
Society for Research in Child Development, 767, 5065
Specialized Programs, 2972
Spencer Foundation, 2429
Student Development Services, 2973
Sulzer Family Foundation, 2430
Teaching for Intelligence Conference, 770
Top Quality School Process (TQSP), 3448
United Airlines Foundation, 2431
Valenti Charitable Foundation, 2432
Wavelength, 3585, 3695
Workforce Education and Development, 3697

Indiana

Administration & Financial Management Center, 2975
Agency for Instructional Technology, 373, 3232
Allen County Public Library, 2433
American Camping Association National Conference, 641
Art to Remember, 2818
Arvin Foundation, 2434
Association for Educational Communications & Technology Annual Convention, 377, 3278
Ball State University, 3591
Before the School Bell Rings, 3397
Beyond Tracking: Finding Success in Inclusive Schools, 3398
C/S Newsletter, 3463
Center for Professional Development & Services, 830
Center for School Assessment & Research, 2976
Clearinghouse on Reading, English & Communicat ion, 333
Clowes Fund, 2435
Community Relations & Special Populations, 2977
Dekko Foundation, 2436
ERIC Clearinghouse for Social Studies Educatio n, 367
East Central Educational Service Center, 859
Education Conference, 3290

Educational Services Company, 871
Eli Lilly & Company Corporate Contribution Program, 2437
External Affairs, 2978
Foellinger Foundation, 2438
Hoosier Science Teachers Association Annual Meeting, 779
Indiana Association of School Business Officials, 453
Indiana Business Education Association, 454
Indiana Department of Education, 2979
Indiana Library Federation, 455
Indiana School Boards Association Annual Conference, 3298
Indiana State Teachers Association, 456
Indiana University-Purdue University of Indianapolis, IUPUI, 3626
Indianapolis Foundation, 2439
International Curriculum Management Audit Center, 3629
International Listening Association Annual Convention, 619
John W Anderson Foundation, 2440
July in Rensselaer, 3635
Law of Teacher Evaluation: A Self-Assestment Handbook, 3413
Lilly Endowment, 2441
Moore Foundation, 2442
National Educational Service, 107
National Student Exchange, 116
Office of the Deputy Superintendent, 2980
Phi Delta Kappa, 275
Piano Workshop, 3666
Priority Computer Services, 963
Professional Computer Systems, 965
Professional Development Institutes, 3669
Professional Learning Communities at Work, 3428
Revolution Revisited: Effective Schools and Systemic Reform, 3435
School Improvement & Performance Center, 2982
State Board Relations & Legal Services, 2983
Teachers Association in Instruction Conference, 3378
Teachers as Leaders, 3440
Voices in the Hall: High School Principals at Work, 3584
W Brooks Fortune Foundation, 2443
Wilderness Education Association, 138

Iowa

Book of Metaphors, Volume II, 3399
Cedar Rapids Public Library, 2444
Center for Learning Connections, 3596
Community Colleges Division, 2984
Division of Library Services, 2985
Educational Services for Children & Families, 2986
Elementary & Secondary Education, 2853, 2987
Ethical Issues in Experiential Education, 3408
Financial & Information Services, 2988
Gershowitz Grant and Evaluation Services, 2802
Iowa Business Education Association, 457
Iowa Council Teachers of Math Conference, 3300
Iowa Department of Education, 2989
Iowa Library Association, 458
Iowa Public Television, 2990
Iowa Reading Association Conference, 3301
Iowa School Administrators Association Annual Convention, 3302
Iowa School Boards Association, 3303
Iowa State Education Association, 459
Janet Hart Heinicke, 907
National Association of Media and Technology Centers, 386
Noel/Levitz Centers, 951
Profiles, 967
RJ McElroy Trust, 2445
Theory of Experiential Education, 3446

UNI Overseas Recruiting Fair, 789
Vocational Rehabilitation Services, 2991

Kansas

American Council on Education in Journalism an d Mass Communication (ACEJMC), 286
Assistant Commissioner's Office, 2992
Center for Rural Education and Small Schools Annual Conference, 682
Character Education: Restoring Respect & Responsibility in our Schools, 3537
Classroom Teacher's Guide for Working with Paraeducators Video Set, 3539
Closing the Achievement Gap, 3402
Conferencing with Students & Parents Video Series, 3541
Creating Schools of Character Video Series, 3545
Critical Thinking Video Set, 3547
Depco, 3608
Discipline Techniques you can Master in a Minute Video Series, 3550
Education Data, 863
Educational Resources, 870
Eleven Principals of Effective Character Educa tion, 3552
Finishing Strong: Your Personal Mentoring & Planning Guide for the Last 60 Days of Teaching, 3409
Fiscal Services & Quality Control, 2993
Four State Regional Technology Conference, 3620
Great Classroom Management Series DVD, 3555
Great Classroom Management Video Series VHS, 3556
Handling Chronically Disruptive Students at Risk Video Series, 3557
Hearlihy & Company, 3558
Inclusion: The Next Step DVD, 3412
Inclusion: The Next Step the Video Series, 3561
Institute for Research in Learning Disabilitie s, 5017
Integrating Technology into the Curriculum Video Series, 3562
Journalism Education Association, 294, 709, 3478, 3478
Kansas Association of School Librarians, 460
Kansas Business Education Association, 461
Kansas Department of Education, 2994
Kansas Division of Special Education, 2995
Kansas Education Association, 462
Kansas Library Association, 463
Kansas School Boards Association Conference, 3304
Kansas United School Administrators Conference, 3305
Lesson Plans and Modifications for Inclusion a nd Collaborative Classrooms, 3564
Lesson Plans for the Substitue Teacher: Elementary Edition, 3415
Mary Jo Williams Charitable Trust, 2446
Mentoring Teachers to Mastery Video Series, 3566
Motivating Students in the Classroom Video Ser ies, 3567
National Teachers Hall of Fame, 3264
On The Go! for the Educational Office Professional, 3481
On-The-Go For Educational Office Professionals, 3482
Paraeducator's Guide to Instructional & Curricular Modifications, 3483
Personal Planner and Training Guide for the Paraprofessional, 3425
Pittsburg State University, 3667
Retaining Great Teachers, 3489
School-Wide Stratigies for Retaining Great Tea chers Video Series, 3573
Sprint Foundation, 2447
Students-at-Risk Video Series, 3577
Teaching for Results, 3444

Technology Integration for Teachers, 3501
The Board, 3502
The Master Teacher, 3582
The Professor In The Classroom, 3503
Training Video Series for the Substitute Teacher, 3583
Understanding and Relating To Parents Professionally, 3450
Welcome to Teaching and our Schools, 3451
Wichita Public Library, 2448
You Can Handle Them All, 3453
You Can Handle Them All Discipline Video Series, 3586
Your Personal Mentoring & Planning Guide for the First 60 Days of Teaching, 3454

Kentucky

Ashland Incorporated Foundation, 2449
Bluegrass Regional Recycling Corporation, 822
Chief of Staff Bureau, 2996
Curriculum, Assessment & Accountability Services, 2998
EPPA Consulting, 857
Education Technology Office, 2999
Gheens Foundation, 2450
James Graham Brown Foundation, 2451
Kentucky Association of School Administrators, 913
Kentucky Department of Education, 3000
Kentucky Library Association, 464
Kentucky School Boards Association Conference, 3306
Kentucky School Media Association, 465
Kentucky School Superintendents Association Meeting, 3307
Kentucky State University, 3639
Learning Results Services Bureau, 3001
Louisville Free Public Library, 2452
Margaret Hall Foundation, 2453
Morehead State University, 3652
Office of Learning Programs Development, 3002
Performance Learning Systems, 3665
Regional Services Centers, 3003
Southeast Regional Center for Drug-Free Schools & Communities, 5066
Special Instructional Services, 3004
Support Services Bureau on Learning, 3005
VV Cooke Foundation Corporation, 2454

Louisiana

Academic Programs Office, 3007
Advance Program for Young Scholars, 3
Basics Plus, 819
Baton Rouge Area Foundation, 2455
Booth-Bricker Fund, 2456
East Baton Rouge Parish Library, 2457
Educational Support Programs, 3008
Fred B & Ruth B Zigler Foundation, 2458
Louisiana Association of Business Educators, 467
Louisiana Association of Educators, 468
Louisiana Association of School Business Offic ials (LASBO), 469
Louisiana Children's Research Center for Development & Learning, 920
Louisiana Department of Education, 3009
Louisiana Library Association, 470
Louisiana School Boards Association Conference, 3310
Management & Finance Office, 3010
Mid-South Educational Research Association Annual Meeting, 3317
National Association of Substance Abuse Trainers & Educators, 201
New Orleans Public Library, 2459

Office of Vocational Education, 3011
Research & Development Office, 3012
Shreve Memorial Library, 2460
Special Education Services, 2896, 3013

Maine

Applied Technology & Adult Learning, 3014
CIEE Annual Conference, 606
Clarence E Mulford Trust, 2461
Council on International Educational Exchange (CIEE), 245
Division of Compensatory Education, 3015
Harold Alfond Trust, 2462
Information Exchange, 5016
Institute for Global Ethics, 899
Maine Association of School Libraries, 472
Maine Department of Education, 3016
Maine Education Association, 473
Maine Library Association, 474
Maine Principals Association Conference, 3311

Maryland

Abell Foundation, 2463
Aegon USA, 2464
Aid for Education, 2816
American Association of Physics Teachers National Meeting, 637
American Dance Therapy Association, 314
American Speech-Language-Hearing Association, 288, 655, 3238, 3238
Association for Childhood Education International Annual Conference, 604
Association for International Practical Training, 214
Association for Persons with Severe Handicaps Annual Conference, 668
BBX Teacher Clearinghouse, 179
Beverly Celotta, 821
CHADD: Children & Adults with Attention Deficit/Hyperactivity Disorder, 28, 678
Career Technology & Adult Learning, 3017
Center for Research on the Education of Students Placed at Risk, 5000
Center for Social Organization of Schools, 5001
Certification & Accreditation, 3018
Childhood Education Association International, 608
Childrens Youth Funding Report, 2819
Clarence Manger & Audrey Cordero Plitt Trust, 2465
Clark-Winchcole Foundation, 2466
Commonwealth Foundation, 2467
Compensatory Education & Support Services, 3019
Division of Business Services, 3020
Dr. Anthony A Cacossa, 855
Dresher Foundation, 2468
ERIC Clearinghouse on Assessment & Evaluation, 45
Educational Systems for the Future, 873
Edward E Ford Foundation, 2469
Enoch Pratt Free Library, 2470
France-Merrick Foundation, 2471
Grayce B Kerr Fund, 2472
Henry & Ruth Blaustein Rosenberg Foundation, 2473
Hummel Sweets, 2825
Instruction Division, 3021
International Association for the Exchange of Students for Technical Experience, 254
International Clearinghouse for the Advancement of Science Teaching, 3563
International Dyslexia Association, 292
International Dyslexia Association (IDA), 293

International Dyslexia Association Annual Conference, 617
International Performance Improvement Conference Expo, 707
International Society for Performance Improvement, 66
James M Johnston Trust for Charitable and Educational Purposes, 2474
John W Kluge Foundation, 2475
Learner-Centered, 624
Learning Independence Through Computers, 384
Library Development & Services, 3022
Longview Foundation for Education in World Affairs/International Understanding, 2777
Marion I & Henry J Knott Foundation, 2476
Maryland Center for Career and Technology Education, 3648
Maryland Department of Education, 3023
Maryland Educational Media Organization, 475
Maryland Educational Opportunity Center, 927
Maryland Elco Incorporated Educational Funding Company, 928
Maryland Library Association, 476
Maryland State Teachers Association, 477
NCSS Summer Workshops, 3655
National Association of School Psychologists Annual Convention, 199, 732
National Clearinghouse for Alcohol & Drug Information, 5038
National Council for Social Studies Annual Conference, 3333
National Council for the Social Studies, 368
National Data Bank for Disabled Student Servic es, 157
National Institute of Child Health and Human Development, 2863
National School Public Relations Association, 113
National School Supply & Equipment Association, 756
National Women's Studies Association, 120, 3254
Performance Improvement Journal, 3485
Planning, Results & Information Management, 3024
Robert G & Anne M Merrick Foundation, 2477
School Equipment Show, 765
Success for All Foundation, 990
T-Shirt People/Wearhouse, 2833
Teacher Magazine, 3495
University Research, 997

Massachusetts

ART New England Summer Workshops, 3588
Annual New England Kindergarten Conference, 3276
Associated Grantmakers of Massachusetts, 2478
Beacon Education Management, 820
Boston Foundation, 2479
Boston Globe Foundation II, 2480
Boston Public Library, 2481
Carney Sandoe & Associates, 827
Center on Families, Schools, Communities & Children's Learning, 5005
Civic Practices Network, 34
Corporate Design Foundation, 845
Critical Issues in Urban Special Education: The Implications of Whole-School Change, 3602
Critical and Creative Thinking in the Classroom, 3603
Dean Foundation for Little Children, 2482
E-S Sports Screenprint Specialists, 2821
EF Educational Tours, 43
Education Development Center, 49, 864
Educational Placement Sources-US, 3466
Educational Register, 53
Educational Technology Center, 382
Effective Strategies for School Reform, 3612
Efficacy Institute, 879
Excellence in Teaching Cabinet Grant, 3260

Facing History & Ourselves, 55
George I Alden Trust, 2801
Harvard Institute for School Leadership, 3623
Harvard Seminar for Superintendents, 3624
Hyams Foundation, 2483
International Physicians for the Prevention of Nuclear War, 260
Irene E & George A Davis Foundation, 2484
James G Martin Memorial Trust, 2485
Jessie B Cox Charitable Trust, 2486
KidsCare Childcare Management Software, 3510
LG Balfour Foundation, 2487
Leadership and the New Technologies, 3642
Learning & The Enneagram, 3643
Linkage, 917
List of Regional, Professional & Specialized Accrediting Association, 3418
Little Family Foundation, 2488
Massachusetts Business Educators Association, 478
Massachusetts Department of Education, 3027
Massachusetts Department of Educational Improvement, 3028
Massachusetts Elementary School Principals Association Conference, 3312
Massachusetts Library Association, 479
Massachusetts School Boards Association Meeting, 3313
Massachusetts Teachers Association, 480
Media and American Democracy, 3649
Meeting the Tide of Rising Expectations, 713
Merrimack Education Center, 934, 5021
NASDTEC Knowledge Base, 3422
National Association of State Directors of Teacher Education & Certification, 153, 3248
National Coalition of Advocates for Students, 91
National Commission for Cooperative Education, 94
National Evaluation Systems, 947
New England History Teachers Association, 369
New England Kindergarten Conference, 3344
New England League of Middle Schools, 3345
New England Library Association, 481
Pennsylvania School Librarians Association, 543
Polaroid Education Program, 3668
Principals' Center Spring Institute Conference, 3369
Project Zero Classroom, 3671
Recruiting New Teachers, 3255
Region 1: Education Department, 3029
Regional Laboratory for Educational Improvement of the Northeast, 5058
Rogers Family Foundation, 2489
Standards and Accountability: Their Impact on Teaching and Assessment, 3680
State Street Foundation, 2490
Sudbury Foundation, 2491
TERC, 5072
TUV Product Service, 3686
Technical Education Research Centers, 994
Time to Teach, Time to Learn: Changing the Pace of School, 3447
Timothy Anderson Dovetail Consulting, 996
Trustees of the Ayer Home, 2492
Uplinc, 999
Weld Foundation, 2493
Western Massachusetts Funding Resource Center, 2494
William E Schrafft & Bertha E Schrafft Charita ble Trust, 2495
Women's Educational & Industrial Union, 139
Woodstock Corporation, 2496
Worcester Public Library, 2497

Michigan

AVKO Educational Research Foundation, 4995
Accuracy Temporary Services Incorporated, 809
Adult Extended Learning Office, 3031

Alex & Marie Manoogian Foundation, 2498
Association for Asian Studies, 211
Association for Behavior Analysis Annual Convention, 666
Association for Gender Equity Leadership in Education, 19
Association for the Study of Higher Education Annual Meeting, 674
Charles Stewart Mott Foundation, 2499
Childs Consulting Associates, 834
Chrysler Corporate Giving Program, 2500
Clonlara School Annual Conference Home Educato rs, 777
Community Foundation for Southeastern Michigan, 2501
Community Foundation of Greater Flint, 2502
Cronin Foundation, 2503
Detroit Edison Foundation, 2504
Effective Schools Products, 877
Extensions - Newsletter of the High/Scope Curriculum, 3468
Ford Motor Company Fund, 2505
Frey Foundation, 2506
General Motors Foundation, 2507
Grand Rapids Foundation, 2508
Harry A & Margaret D Towsley Foundation, 2509
Henry Ford Centennial Library, 2510
Herbert H & Grace A Dow Foundation, 2511
Herrick Foundation, 2512
Higher Education Management Office, 3033
Innovator, 3471
Instructional Programs, 3034
Kresge Foundation, 2513
Leona Group, 916
Malpass Foundation, 2514
McGregor Fund, 2515
Michigan Association for Media in Education, 482
Michigan Association of Elementary and Middle School Principals Conference, 3314
Michigan Association of School Administrators, 483
Michigan Department of Education, 3035
Michigan Education Association, 484
Michigan Education Council, 935
Michigan Elementary & Middle School Principals Association, 485
Michigan Library Association, 486
Michigan School Boards Association Fall Leadership Conference and Exhibit Show, 3315
Michigan Science Teachers Association Annual Conference, 3316
Michigan State University Libraries, 2516
NCRTL Special Report, 3479
National Center for Community Education, 3249
National Center for Research on Teacher Learning, 5032
National Heritage Academies, 948
National Student Assistance Conference, 758
North American Students of Cooperation, 124
Office of School Management, 3036
Office of the Superintendent, 3037
Postsecondary Services, 3038
Professional Development Workshops, 3670
Rebus, 971
Richard & Helen DeVos Foundation, 2517
Rollin M Gerstacker Foundation, 2518
SAP Today, 3572
School Program Quality, 3039
Steelcase Foundation, 2519
Student Financial Assistance, 3041
Teacher & Administrative Preparation, 3042
University of Michigan-Dearborn Center for Corporate & Professional Development, 3694
Wayne State University, 2520
Whirlpool Foundation, 2521

Minnesota

Andersen Foundation, 2522

Educational Publishing Summit: Creating Managing & Selling Content, 693
Educational Summit, 3611
Educational Testing Service, 875, 5012
Foundation for Student Communication, 57
Fund for New Jersey, 2567
Fundraising USA, 2822
Gifted Child Society, 59
Gifted Child Society Conference, 697
Global Learning, 249
Hoechst Celanese Foundation, 2568
Honeywell Foundation, 2569
Hyde & Watson Foundation, 2570
International Schools Services, 262
Lab Volt Systems, 3641
M&M Mars Fundraising, 2826
Mary Owen Borden Memorial Foundation, 2571
Mason Associates, 929
Merck Company Foundation, 2572
Middle States Council for the Social Studies Annual Regional Conference, 3318
National Coalition for Sex Equity in Education, 738
New Jersey Department of Education, 3083
New Jersey Department of Education: Finance, 3084
New Jersey Division of Special Education, 3085
New Jersey Education Association (NJEA), 514
New Jersey Library Association, 515
New Jersey School Boards Association Annual Meeting, 783
New Jersey State Department of Education Resource Center, 516
New Jersey State Library, 3086
Odyssey of the Mind, 126
Pro Libra, 308
Professional Development & Licensing, 3087
Prudential Foundation, 2573
Relearning by Design, 975
Sensa of New Jersey, 982
Strategies for Educational Change, 989
Teach Overseas, 279
Teacher's Guide to Classroom Management, 3496
Telemetrics, 391
Training Research Journal: The Science and Practice of Training, 3505
Troll Book Fairs, 2834
Turrell Fund, 2574
Urban & Field Services, 3088
Victoria Foundation, 2575
Warner-Lambert Charitable Foundation, 2576
Wilf Family Foundation, 2577

New Mexico

Agency Support, 3089
American Indian Science & Engineering Society Annual Conference, 648
Dale J Bellamah Foundation, 2578
Learning Services, 3090
National Association for Legal Support of Alternative Schools (NALSAS), 79
National Coalition of Alternative Community Schools, 92, 739
National Education Association of New Mexico, 518
National Information Center for Educational Media, 5043
New Mexico Department of Education, 3091
New Mexico Department of School-Transportation & Support Services, 3092
New Mexico Library Association (NMLA), 519
New Mexico School Boards Association Conference Annual Meeting, 3346
New Mexico State Library, 2579
RD & Joan Dale Hubbard Foundation, 2580
School Management Accountability, 3093
Southwest Comprehensive Regional Assistance Center-Region IX, 5068

Western History Association, 372
Western History Association Annual Meeting, 808

New York

Achelis Foundation, 2581
Adrian & Jessie Archbold Charitable Trust, 2582
African-American Institute, 363
Alfred P Sloan Foundation, 2583
Alliance for Parental Involvement in Education, 4
Altman Foundation, 2584
Ambrose Monell Foundation, 2585
American Association for Chinese Studies, 364
American Council for Drug Education, 7
American Educational Research Journal, 3458
American Express Foundation, 2586
American Montessori Society, 12
American Montessori Society Conference, 651
American-Scandinavian Foundation, 2838
Andrew W Mellon Foundation, 2587
Annual Convention, 3275
Arnold Bernhard Foundation, 2588
Arts Management in Community Institutions: Summer Training, 3460
Arts Scholarships, 2839
Association for Advancement of Behavior Therapy Annual Convention, 665
Association for Business Communication (ABC), 15
Atran Foundation, 2589
Beatrice P Delany Charitable Trust, 2590
Better Chance, 27
Bodman Foundation, 2591
Bristol-Myers Squibb Foundation, 2592
Bryant and Stratton College, 3592
Buffalo & Erie County Public Library, 2593
Business Teachers Association of New York State, 520
CDS International, 227
CUNY Teacher Incentive Program, 2840
Caleb C & Julia W Dula Educational & Charitable Foundation, 2594
Capital Cities-ABC Corporate Giving Program, 2595
Carl & Lily Pforzheimer Foundation, 2596
Carnegie Corporation of New York, 2597
Catholic Medical Mission Board, 233
Center for Education Studies, 365
Center for Educational Innovation, 829
Center for Technology in Education, 5002
Center on Human Policy, 33
Chase Manhattan Corporation Philanthropy Department, 2598
Christian A Johnson Endeavor Foundation, 2599
Classroom, 835
Cleveland H Dodge Foundation, 2600
College Board, 342, 2841
College Entrance Examination Board, 838
Competency-Based Framework for Professional Development of Certified Health Specialists, 3404
Cordell Hull Foundation for International Education, 239
Council for Aid to Education, 847
Council on Foreign Relations, 243
Cowles Charitable Trust, 2601
Cultural Education, 3095
Daisy Marquis Jones Foundation, 2602
DeWitt Wallace-Reader's Digest Fund, 2603
Delmar Thomson Learning, 3607
Dissertation Fellowships in the Humanities, 2842
EPIE Institute Educational Products Information Exchange Institut, 856
Edison Schools, 861
Edna McConnell Clark Foundation, 2604
Education Index, 3508
Educational Equity Concepts, 52
Edward John Noble Foundation, 2605
Edward W Hazen Foundation, 2606

Edwin Gould Foundation for Children, 2607
Elaine E & Frank T Powers Jr Foundation, 2608
Elementary, Middle & Secondary Education, 3096
Elmer & Mamdouha Bobst Foundation, 2609
Equitable Foundation, 2610
Eye on Education, 3554
Festo Corporation, 3618
Ford Foundation, 2611
Foundation Center, 2799
Frances & Benjamin Benenson Foundation, 2612
George Dehne & Associates, 887
George F Baker Trust, 2613
George Link Jr Foundation, 2614
Girls Incorporated, 60
Gladys & Roland Harriman Foundation, 2615
Gladys Brooks Foundation, 2616
Green Fund, 2617
Guild Notes Bi-Monthly Newswletter, 3469
Hagedorn Fund, 2618
Hasbro Children's Foundation, 2619
Henry Luce Foundation, 2620
Herman Goldman Foundation, 2621
Hess Foundation, 2622
Higher & Professional Education, 3097
Hitting the High Notes of Literacy, 699
Horace W Goldsmith Foundation, 2623
Human-i-Tees, 2824
IBM Corporate Support Program, 2624
Information Center on Education, 5015
Institute of International Education, 251
International Association of Students in Economics & Business Management (AIESC), 255
International Baccalaureate North America, 256
International Center for Leadership in Education, 901
Island Drafting & Technical Institute, 3632
J&Kalb Associates, 903
JI Foundation, 2625
JP Associates Incorporated, 906
JP Morgan Charitable Trust, 2626
Jewish Education Service of North America, 68
Jewish Educators Assembly, 69
Jewish Foundation for Education of Women, 2845
Joukowsky Family Foundation, 2627
Julia R & Estelle L Foundation, 2628
Leon Lowenstein Foundation, 2629
Levittown Public Library, 2630
Life Skills Training, 3417
Literacy Volunteers of America National Conference, 710
Louis & Anne Abrons Foundation, 2631
MacMillan Guide to Correspondence Study, 3419
Magi Educational Services Incorporated, 923
Margaret L Wendt Foundation, 2632
McGraw-Hill Foundation, 2633
Modern Language Association Annual Conference, 714
Mosaica Education, 944
NCSIE Inservice, 3480
National Academy Foundation Annual Institute for Staff Development, 720
National Center for Learning Disabilities, 89
National Center for the Study of Privatization in Education, 5034
National Center on Education & the Economy, 946, 5035
National Child Labor Committee, 5037
National Clearinghouse for Information on Business Involvement in Education, 5040
National Guild of Community Schools of the Arts Conference, 324, 747
National Reading Styles Institute, 949
National Reading Styles Institute Conference, 751
National Research Center on English Learning and Achievement, 299
New York Department of Education, 3098
New York Foundation, 2634
New York Library Association (NYLA), 522
New York School Superintendents Association Annual Meeting, 3347
New York Science Teachers Association Annual Meeting, 3348

New York State Council of Student Superintendents Forum, 784
New York State United Teachers (NYSUT), 523
New York State United Teachers Conference, 3349
New York Teachers Math Association Conference, 3350
Northeast Regional Center for Drug-Free Schools & Communities, 5050
Operation Crossroads Africa, 271
Orators & Philosophers: A History of the Idea of Liberal Education, 3423
Palisades Educational Foundation, 2635
Phoenix Learning Resources Conference, 803
Princeton Review, 962
ProLiteracy Worldwide, 337
Professional Responsibility Office, 3099
Public Relations Student Society of America, 131
Quality Education Development, 969
Quality School Teacher, 3430
Quantum Performance Group, 970
Region 2: Education Department, 3100
Regional Learning Service of Central New York, 973
Robert Sterling Clark Foundation, 2636
Rochester Public Library, 2637
Ronald S Lauder Foundation, 2638
Rookey Associates, 978
SH & Helen R Scheuer Family Foundation, 2639
SUNY College at Oswego, 3674
Samuel & May Rudin Foundation, 2640
Scholarships in the Health Professions, 2848
Seth Sprague Educational and Charitable Foundation, 2641
Sexuality Information & Education Council of the US, 135
Sidney Kreppel, 984
Starr Foundation, 2642
Stewart Howe Alumni Service of New York, 988
Superintendents Work Conference, 3377
Teachers & Writers Collaborative, 301
Teachers College: Columbia University, 3688
Tiger Foundation, 2643
Tisch Foundation, 2644
Travelers Group, 2645
Tribeca Learning Center-PS 150, 173
United Nations Development Program, 281
United States-Japan Foundation, 2811
Vocational & Educational Services for Disabled, 3101
White Plains Public Library, 2646
William Randolph Hearst Foundation, 2647
William T Grant Foundation, 2648

North Carolina

AE Finley Foundation, 2649
Auxiliary Services, 3102
Cannon Foundation, 2650
Cisco Educational Archives, 3538
Dickson Foundation, 2651
Duke Endowment, 2652
Financial & Personnel Services, 3103
First Union University, 2653
Foundation for the Carolinas, 2654
Kathleen Price and Joseph M Bryan Family Foundation, 2655
Mary Reynolds Babcock Foundation, 2656
Master Woodcraft Inc., 712
Measurement, 932
Musikgarten, 3653
National Early Childhood Technical Assistance System, 166, 5042
National Network for Early Language Learning (NELL), 298
National Society for Experiential Education Conference, 114, 757
Non-Profit Resource Center/Pack Memorial Library, 2657

North Carolina Association for Career and Technical Education Conference, 3352
North Carolina Association for Career and Technical Education, 524
North Carolina Association of Educators (NCAE), 525
North Carolina Business Education Association (NCBEA), 526
North Carolina Department of Education, 3104
North Carolina Department of Instructional Services, 3105
North Carolina Department of Public Instructio n (DPI), 527
North Carolina Library Association (NCLA), 528
North Carolina School Administrators Conference, 3353
Paideia Group, 3662
Poetry Alive!, 959
SERVE, 5060
SERVE Conference, 764
Staff Development & Technical Assistance, 3106
State Library of North Carolina, 2658
William R Kenan Jr Charitable Trust, 2659
Winston-Salem Foundation, 2660
Z Smith Reynolds Foundation, 2661

North Dakota

ATEA Journal, 3456
American Technical Education Association Annual Conference, 656
Myra Foundation, 2662
North Dakota Department of Education, 3107
North Dakota Department of Public Instruction Division, 3108
North Dakota Education Association (NDEA), 529
North Dakota Library Association, 530
North Dakota State Board for Vocational & Technical Education, 3109
North Dakota Vocational Educational Planning Conference, 793
Study & State Film Library, 3110
Tom & Frances Leach Foundation, 2663

Ohio

Akron Community Foundation, 2664
American Association for Employment in Education Annual Conference, 631
American Educational Studies Association, 647, 3235
American Foundation Corporation, 2665
American School Health Association, 14
American School Health Association's National School Conference, 654
Analog & Digital Peripherals, 3506
Association for Disabled Students, 17
Association for Integrative Studies, 20
Balance Sheet, 3461
Blind School, 3111
Brief Legal Guide for the Independent Teacher, 3400
Burton D Morgan Foundation, 2666
Creative Learning Consultants, 849
Curriculum, Instruction & Professional Development, 3112
Dayton Foundation, 2667
Direct Instructional Support Systems, 854
E-Z Grader Software, 3507
Early Childhood Education, 3113
Edison Welding Institute, 3610
Education Concepts, 862
Educational REALMS-Resources for Engaging Acti ve Learners in Mathematics and Science, 351
Educational Theatre Association Conference, 694

Eisenhower National Clearinghouse for Mathemat ics and Science Education, 310, 352
Emco Maier Corporation, 3615
Eva L & Joseph M Bruening Foundation, 2668
Fastech, 3617
Federal Assistance, 3114
GAR Foundation, 2669
George Gund Foundation, 2670
Gold Medal Products, 2823
Hobart Institute of Welding Technology, 3625
Hoover Foundation, 2671
Industrial Training Institute, 3627
Institute for Development of Educational Activities, 898
International Thespian Society, 318
Journal on Excellence in College Teaching, 3477
Kent State University, 3638
Kettering Fund, 2672
Kulas Foundation, 2673
Lilly Conference on College Teaching, 3308
Louise H & David S Ingalls Foundation, 2674
Louise Taft Semple Foundation, 2675
Marketing Education Resource Center, 926
Martha Holden Jennings Foundation, 2676
Mead Corporation Foundation, 2677
Music Teachers Association National Conference, 716
Music Teachers National Association, 320, 5026
National Association for Developmental Educati on (NADE), 78
National Career Development Association Conference, 3328
National Center for Science Teaching & Learning, 5033
National Council for History Education Conference, 3332
National Middle School Association, 110, 344, 3252, 3252
National Middle School Association's Annual Conference and Exhibition, 3340
National School Safety and Security Services, 950
National Staff Development Council, 3253
Nord Family Foundation, 2678
North American Montessori Teachers' Association, 761
Ohio Association of School Business Officials, 531
Ohio Association of Secondary School Administrators, 532
Ohio Bell Telephone Contribution Program, 2679
Ohio Business Teachers Association, 3360
Ohio Department of Education, 3115
Ohio Library Council, 533
Ohio Library Council Trade Show, 786
Ohio Public School Employees Association Convention, 3361
Ohio School Boards Association Capital Conference & Trade Show, 787
Ohio Secondary School Administrators Association Fall Conference, 3362
Ohio State Library Foundation Center, 2680
Ohio Technology Education Association (OTEA), 534
Ome Resa, 952
Owens Community College, 3661
Owens-Corning Foundation, 2681
Personnel Services, 2958, 3116
Procter & Gamble Fund, 2682
Public Library of Cincinnati, 2683
Reading Recovery Council of North America, 338
Root Learning, 979
School Finance, 2969, 3117
School Food Service, 3118
School for the Deaf, 3119
SchoolMatch by Public Priority Systems, 981
Student Development, 3121
Summit Vision, 137
Teacher Education & Certification, 2974, 3006, 3122, 3122
Thomas J Emery Memorial, 2684
Timken Foundation of Canton, 2685
Today's Catholic Teacher, 3504
Tooling University, 3690

Vocational & Career Education, 3123
Wolfe Associates, 2686

Oklahoma

Accreditation & Standards Division, 3124
At-Risk Students: Identification and Assistance Strategies, 3535
Center for the Study of Small/Rural Schools, 5004
Conflict Resolution Strategies in Schools, 3542
Cooperative Learning Strategies, 3544
Crisis Management in Schools, 3546
Curriculum Alignment: Improving Student Learning, 3548
Education Extension, 50
Federal/Special/Collaboration Services, 3125
Grace & Franklin Bernsen Foundation, 2687
Improving Parent/Educator Relationships, 3559
Improving Student Thinking in the Content Area, 3560
Managing Students Without Coercion, 3565
Mervin Bovaird Foundation, 2688
Multicultural Education: Teaching to Diversity, 3568
National Association of Trade & Industrial Instructors, 86
National Rural Education Association Annual Convention, 753
Oklahoma City University, 2689
Oklahoma Department of Career and Technology Education, 3126
Oklahoma Department of Education, 3127
Oklahoma Department of Education; Financial Services, 3128
Oklahoma Education Association (OEA), 535
Oklahoma Library Association (OLA), 536
Oklahoma School Boards Association & School Administrators Conference, 3363
Outcome-Based Education: Making it Work, 3569
Overview of Prevention: A Social Change Model, 3570
Professional Services, 2894, 3129
Public Service Company of Oklahoma Corporate Giving Program, 2690
Quality School, 3571
Retention in Education Today for All Indigenous Nations, 763
Samuel Roberts Noble Foundation, 2691
School Improvement, 3130
Site-Based Management, 3574
Southwestern Oklahoma State University, 3677
Strategic Planning for Outcome-Based Education, 3575
Strengthening the Family: An Overview of a Holistic Family Wellness Model, 3576
Superintendent/School Board Relationships, 3578
TQM: Implementing Quality Management in Your School, 3579
Teacher Link: An Interactive National Teleconference, 768
Teachers as Heros, 3580
Teaching for Intelligent Behavior, 3581
www.positivepins.com, 2836

Oregon

AFT-Oregon (American Federation of Teachers-Oregon), 537
Aprovecho Research Center, 209
Assessment & Evaluation, 3131
Collins Foundation, 2692
Community College Services, 3132
Compensatory Education Office, 3133
Deputy Superintendent Office, 3134
ERIC Clearinghouse on Educational Management, 145

Early Childhood Council, 3135
Educational Productions Inc, 3551
Ford Family Foundation, 2693
Future Music Oregon, 317
Government Relations, 3047, 3136
Interface Network, 900
International Society for Technology in Education, 383
MPulse Maintenance Software, 3646
Management Services, 2860, 3137
Measurement Learning Consultants, 933
Meyer Memorial Trust, 2694
Multnomah County Library, 2695
National Parent-Teacher Association Annual Convention & Exhibition, 750
North American Association of Educational Negotiators, 123
Northwest Regional Educational Laboratory, 3359, 5052
Office of Field, Curriculum & Instruction Services, 3138
Oregon Association of Student Councils (OASC), 538
Oregon Community Foundation, 2696
Oregon Department of Education, 3139
Oregon Education Association (OEA), 539
Oregon Educational Media Association, 540
Oregon Library Association (OLA), 541
Oregon School Boards Association Annual Convention, 3364
Pacific Northwest Council on Languages Annual Conference, 3365
Prevention Researcher, 3487
Professional Technical Education, 3140
Student Services Office, 3142
TACS/WRRC, 5071
Tektronix Foundation, 2697
Twenty First Century Schools Council, 3143

Pennsylvania

Add Vantage Learning Incorporated, 810
Alcoa Foundation, 2698
American Driver and Traffic Safety Education Association (ADTSEA), 10
American Foundation for Negro Affairs, 3236
American Friends Service Committee, 205
American Musicological Society, 315
Annenberg Foundation, 2699
Arcadia Foundation, 2700
Aspira of Penna, 815
Attention Deficit Disorder Association, 25
Audrey Hillman Fisher Foundation, 2701
Auerbach Central Agency for Jewish Education Incorporated, 818
Bayer Corporation, 2702
Bayer/NSF Award for Community Innovation, 3259
Buhl Foundation, 2703
Center for Learning, 4998
Chief of Staff Office, 3145
Connelly Foundation, 2704
Continuous Learning Group Limited Liability Company, 844
Dutch Mill Bulbs, 2820
Eden Hall Foundation, 2705
Education & Treatment of Children, 3465
Elementary Education Professional Development School, 3614
Erie County Library System, 2706
Foundation Center-Carnegie Library of Pittsburgh, 2707
Friends Council on Education, 58
Graphic Arts Technical Foundation, 182
HJ Heinz Company Foundation, 2708
Higher Education/Postsecondary Office, 3146
International Association of School Librarians hip, 306
John McShain Charities, 2709

K'nex Education Division, 3636
Lawrence A Heller Associates, 915
Learning Disabilities Association of America International Conference, 71, 625
Learning Research and Development Center, 5019
Mary Hillman Jennings Foundation, 2710
McCune Foundation, 2711
Mid-Atlantic Regional Educational Laboratory, 5022
Millersville University, 3651
Montgomery Intermediate Unit 23, 942
National Association of Catholic School Teache rs, 81
National Center on Education in the Inner Cities, 5036
Northeast Conference on the Teaching of Foreign Languages, 3356
Northeast Regional Christian Schools Internati onal Association, 785
Office of Elementary and Secondary Education, 3147
Office of the Comptroller, 3148
Opportunities Industrialization Centers Intern ational (OIC), 272
Parsifal Systems, 955
Pennsylvania Council for the Social Studies Conference, 3366
Pennsylvania Department of Education, 3149
Pennsylvania Education, 3484
Pennsylvania Library Association (PaLA), 542
Pennsylvania School Boards Association Annual Meeting, 3367
Pennsylvania Science Teachers Association, 3368
Pennsylvania State Education Association (PSEA), 544
Pennsylvania State University-Workforce Educat ion & Development Program, 3664
Pew Charitable Trusts, 2712
Prevention Service, 961
Region 3: Education Department, 3150
Research for Better Schools Publications, 3432
Richard King Mellon Foundation, 2713
Rockwell International Corporation Trust, 2714
SIGI PLUS, 5061
Samuel S Fels Fund, 2715
Sarah Scaife Foundation, 2716
Satellites and Education Conference, 788
Search Associates, 3256
Shore Fund, 2717
Stackpole-Hall Foundation, 2718
Total Quality Schools Workshop, 3691
Training & Development Programs, 2882
United States Steel Foundation, 2719
Westinghouse Foundation, 2812
William Penn Foundation, 2720
Women's International League for Peace & Freed om, 191

Rhode Island

American Mathematical Society, 650
Career & Technical Education, 3032, 3151
Champlin Foundations, 2721
East Bay Educational Collaborative, 858
Equity & Access Office, 3152
Human Resource Development, 3153
Instruction Office, 3154
National Education Association Rhode Island (N EARI), 545
Northeast and Islands Regional Educational Laboratory, 5051
Office of Finance, 3155
Outcomes & Assessment Office, 3156
Providence Public Library, 2722
Resource Development, 3157
Rhode Island Association of School Business Officials, 546
Rhode Island Department of Education, 3158
Rhode Island Educational Media Association, 547

Virginia

Washington

West Virginia

Wisconsin

Wyoming

Canada

Arts

A&F Video's Art Catalog, 6131
ART New England Summer Workshops, 3588
Alarion Press, 4658
All Art Supplies, 6132
American Academy of Arts & Sciences Bulletin, 4499
American Art Clay Company, 6133
American Art Therapy Association, 313
American Dance Therapy Association, 314
American Musicological Society, 315
Annual Conductor's Institute of South Carolina, 3589
Annual Summer Institute for Secondary Teachers, 3590
Arnold Grummer, 6134
Arrowmont School of Arts & Crafts, 6135
Art & Creative Materials Institute, 6136
Art Education, 4500
Art Image Publications, 4674
Art Instruction Schools, 6137
Art Visuals, 4675
Art to Remember, 6138
ArtSketchbook.com, 6139
Arts & Activities, 4501
Arts Education Policy Review, 4502
Arts Institutes International, 6140
Choral Journal, 4504
Choristers Guild's National Festival & Directors' Conference, 684
Clavier, 4505
College Guide for Visual Arts Majors, 3995
Coloring Concepts, 4717
Community Outreach and Education for the Arts Handbook, 3996
Creative Teaching Press, 4726
Crizmac Art & Cultural Education Materials Inc, 5205
Dover Publications, 4740
Dramatics, 4506
ERIC Clearinghouse for Social Studies Education, 367
Educational Theatre Association Conference, 694
Flute Talk, 4507
Future Music Oregon, 317
Graphic Arts Education & Research Foundation, 181
Graphix, 5236
Harmonic Vision, 6047
Instrumentalist, 4508
International Conference, 615
International Thespian Society, 318
International Trombone Festival, 623
International Workshops, 3631
Italic Letters, 3997
Janice Borla Vocal Jazz Camp, 3633
Journal of Experiential Education, 4509
July in Rensselaer, 3635
Kennedy Center Alliance for Arts Education, 319
Kodaly Teaching Certification Program, 3640
Mel Bay Publications, 4851
Midnight Play, 6048
Mondo Publishing, 4857
Money for Visual Artists, 3947
Museum Stamps, 6141
Music Ace 2, 6142
Music Educators Journal, 4510
Music Educators Journal and Teaching Music, 4511
Music Educators National Conference, 715
Music Teacher Find, 6049
Music Teachers Association National Conference, 716
Music Teachers Guide to Music Instructional Software, 4000
Music Teachers National Association, 320
Music and Guitar, 6050
Musikgarten, 3653
NAEA News, 4512

National Art Education Association, 321
National Art Education Association Annual Convention, 722
National Association for Music Education, 322
National Association of Schools of Music (NASM), 323
National Council of State Supervisors of Music, 2907
National Guild of Community Schools of the Arts, 324
National Guild of Community Schools of theArts Conference, 747
National Institute of Art and Disabilities, 325
National Standards for Dance Education News, 4531
Oranatics Journal, 4514
Orff-Schulwerk Teacher Certification Program, 3660
Phelps Publishing, 4893
Piano Workshop, 3666
Pure Gold Teaching Tools, 6051
Resource Booklet for Independent Music Teachers, 4001
Rhythms Productions, 4912
School Arts, 4002
SchoolArtsDavis Publications, 4515
SchoolArts Magazine, 4516
Studies in Art Education, 4517
Teaching Journal, 4518
Teaching Music, 4519
Ultimate Early Childhood Music Resource, 4520
http://library.thinkquest.org, 6052
http://members.truepath.com/headoftheclass, 6053
www.sanford-artedventures.com, 6055
www.songs4teachers.com, 6056

Civics & Government

AppleSeeds, 4592
Boletin, 4593
Center for Civic Education, 30
Children's Book Council, 4708
Choices Education Project, 4713
Cobblestone, 4597
Colloquoy on Teaching World Affairs, 4598
Congressional Quarterly, 4722
Directory of Central America Classroom Resources, 4031
ERIC Clearinghouse for Social Studies Education, 367
Educators Guide to FREE Social Studies Materials, 4032
Facts on File, 4768
Focus, 4600
Footsteps, 4601
Frog Publications, 4776
Goethe House New York, 4779
Greenhaven Press, 4781
Hands-On Prints, 4786
High Touch Learning, 4792
Horn Book Guide, 4796
Houghton Mifflin Books for Children, 4797
Houghton Mifflin Company: School Division, 4798
Hyperion Books for Children, 4799
Jacaranda Designs, 4808
Keep America Beautiful, 4816
Knowledge Unlimited, 4819
Lynne Rienner Publishing, 4837
Media and American Democracy, 3649
Middle States Council for the Social Studies Annual Regional Conference, 3318
NASDTEC Knowledge Base, 3422
NCSS Summer Workshops, 3655
National Council for Social Studies Annual Conference, 3333
National Council for the Social Studies, 368
National Council for the Social Studies, 4867
National Women's History Project, 4874

National Women's History Project Annual Conference, 759
New Press, 4877
NewsBank, 4878
Organization of American Historians, 4882
Pennsylvania Council for the Social Studies Conference, 3366
Perspectives on History Series, 4891
Phi Delta Kappa Educational Foundation, 4202
Population Connection, 4897
Rand McNally, 4906
Roots & Wings Educational Catalog-Australia for Kids, 4915
Routledge/Europa Library Reference, 4917
Sharpe Reference, 4928
Social Issues Resources Series, 4932
Social Science Education Consortium, 4933
Social Studies School Service, 4934
USA Today, 4962
VIDYA Books, 4965
West Educational Publishing, 4974
Western History Association Annual Meeting, 808
Winston Derek Publishers, 4978
World & I, 4981
World Bank, 4983
World Book Educational Products, 4984
World Eagle, 4985
World Resources Institute, 4986
World of Difference Institute, 4988
Worth Publishers, 4989
www.ushistory.com, 6057

Economics

American Educational Studies Association, 647
Bluestocking Press Catalog, 4689
Capitalism for Kids, 4596
Chicago Board of Trade, 4707
Junior Achievement, 4813
National Council on Economic Education, 4869

English

ABDO Publishing Company, 4648
AGS, 4649
Accelerated Reader, 5700
American Educational Studies Association, 647
Amsco School Publications, 4671
Australian Press-Down Under Books, 4681
Ballantine/Del Rey/Fawcett/Ivy, 4683
Barron's Educational Series, 4684
Beech Tree Books, 4686
Black Butterfly Children's Books, 4687
Bluestocking Press Catalog, 4689
BridgeWater Books, 4691
Brown & Benchmark Publishers, 4693
Capstone Press, 4700
Carolrhoda Books, 4702
Center for Critical Thinking and Moral Critique Annual International, 607
Center for Education Studies, 365
Center for Learning, 4998
Charles Scribner & Sons, 4706
Children's Book Council, 4708
Children's Literature Festival, 801
Children's Press, 4709
Chime Time, 4712
Clearinghouse on Reading, English & Communication, 333
Cottonwood Press, 4724
Creative Teaching Press, 4726
Cricket Magazine Group, 4727
Dial Books for Young Readers, 4733
Disney Press, 4737
Dover Publications, 4740
Dutton Children's Books, 4741

Foreign Language

Geography

History

Mathematics

Reading & Language Arts

Special Education

Technology

Sedgwick Press
Education Directories

The Comparative Guide to American Elementary & Secondary Schools, 2007

The only guide of its kind, this award winning compilation offers a snapshot profile of every public school district in the United States serving 1,500 or more students – more than 5,900 districts are covered. Organized alphabetically by district within state, each chapter begins with a Statistical Overview of the state. Each district listing includes contact information (name, address, phone number and web site) plus Grades Served, the Numbers of Students and Teachers and the Number of Regular, Special Education, Alternative and Vocational Schools in the district along with statistics on Student/Classroom Teacher Ratios, Drop Out Rates, Ethnicity, the Numbers of Librarians and Guidance Counselors and District Expenditures per student. As an added bonus, *The Comparative Guide to American Elementary and Secondary Schools* provides important ranking tables, both by state and nationally, for each data element. For easy navigation through this wealth of information, this handbook contains a useful City Index that lists all districts that operate schools within a city. These important comparative statistics are necessary for anyone considering relocation or doing comparative research on their own district and would be a perfect acquisition for any public library or school district library.

"This straightforward guide is an easy way to find general information. Valuable for academic and large public library collections." –ARBA

2,400 pages; Softcover ISBN 1-59237-223-6, $125.00

The Complete Learning Disabilities Directory, 2007

The Complete Learning Disabilities Directory is the most comprehensive database of Programs, Services, Curriculum Materials, Professional Meetings & Resources, Camps, Newsletters and Support Groups for teachers, students and families concerned with learning disabilities. This information-packed directory includes information about Associations & Organizations, Schools, Colleges & Testing Materials, Government Agencies, Legal Resources and much more. For quick, easy access to information, this directory contains four indexes: Entry Name Index, Subject Index and Geographic Index. With every passing year, the field of learning disabilities attracts more attention and the network of caring, committed and knowledgeable professionals grows every day. This directory is an invaluable research tool for these parents, students and professionals.

"Due to its wealth and depth of coverage, parents, teachers and others... should find this an invaluable resource." -Booklist

900 pages; Softcover ISBN 1-59237-122-1, $145.00 ◆ Online Database $195.00 ◆ Online Database & Directory Combo $280.00

Sedgwick Press
Health Directories

The Complete Directory for People with Disabilities, 2007

A wealth of information, now in one comprehensive sourcebook. Completely updated, this edition contains more information than ever before, including thousands of new entries and enhancements to existing entries and thousands of additional web sites and e-mail addresses. This up-to-date directory is the most comprehensive resource available for people with disabilities, detailing Independent Living Centers, Rehabilitation Facilities, State & Federal Agencies, Associations, Support Groups, Periodicals & Books, Assistive Devices, Employment & Education Programs, Camps and Travel Groups. Each year, more libraries, schools, colleges, hospitals, rehabilitation centers and individuals add *The Complete Directory for People with Disabilities* to their collections, making sure that this information is readily available to the families, individuals and professionals who can benefit most from the amazing wealth of resources cataloged here.

"No other reference tool exists to meet the special needs of the disabled in one convenient resource for information." –Library Journal

1,200 pages; Softcover ISBN 1-59237-147-7, $165.00 ◆ Online Database $215.00 ◆ Online Database & Directory Combo $300.00

To preview any of our Directories Risk-Free for 30 days, call (800) 562-2139 or fax to (518) 789-0556

The Complete Directory for People with Chronic Illness, 2007/08

Thousands of hours of research have gone into this completely updated 2005/06 edition – several new chapters have been added along with thousands of new entries and enhancements to existing entries. Plus, each chronic illness chapter has been reviewed by an medical expert in the field. This widely-hailed directory is structured around the 90 most prevalent chronic illnesses – from Asthma to Cancer to Wilson's Disease – and provides a comprehensive overview of the support services and information resources available for people diagnosed with a chronic illness. Each chronic illness has its own chapter and contains a brief description in layman's language, followed by important resources for National & Local Organizations, State Agencies, Newsletters, Books & Periodicals, Libraries & Research Centers, Support Groups & Hotlines, Web Sites and much more. This directory is an important resource for health care professionals, the collections of hospital and health care libraries, as well as an invaluable tool for people with a chronic illness and their support network.

"A must purchase for all hospital and health care libraries and is strongly recommended for all public library reference departments." –ARBA

1,200 pages; Softcover ISBN 1-59237-183-3, $165.00 ◆ Online Database $215.00 ◆ Online Database & Directory Combo $300.00

The Complete Mental Health Directory, 2006/07

This is the most comprehensive resource covering the field of behavioral health, with critical information for both the layman and the mental health professional. For the layman, this directory offers understandable descriptions of 25 Mental Health Disorders as well as detailed information on Associations, Media, Support Groups and Mental Health Facilities. For the professional, *The Complete Mental Health Directory* offers critical and comprehensive information on Managed Care Organizations, Information Systems, Government Agencies and Provider Organizations. This comprehensive volume of needed information will be widely used in any reference collection.

"… the strength of this directory is that it consolidates widely dispersed information into a single volume." –Booklist

800 pages; Softcover ISBN 1-59237-124-8, $165.00 ◆ Online Database $215.00 ◆ Online & Directory Combo $300.00

Older Americans Information Directory, 2006/07

Completely updated for 2006/07, this sixth edition has been completely revised and now contains 1,000 new listings, over 8,000 updates to existing listings and over 3,000 brand new e-mail addresses and web sites. You'll find important resources for Older Americans including National, Regional, State & Local Organizations, Government Agencies, Research Centers, Libraries & Information Centers, Legal Resources, Discount Travel Information, Continuing Education Programs, Disability Aids & Assistive Devices, Health, Print Media and Electronic Media. Three indexes: Entry Index, Subject Index and Geographic Index make it easy to find just the right source of information. This comprehensive guide to resources for Older Americans will be a welcome addition to any reference collection.

"Highly recommended for academic, public, health science and consumer libraries…" –Choice

1,200 pages; Softcover ISBN 1-59237-136-1, $165.00 ◆ Online Database $215.00 ◆ Online Database & Directory Combo $300.00

The Complete Directory for Pediatric Disorders, 2007

This important directory provides parents and caregivers with information about Pediatric Conditions, Disorders, Diseases and Disabilities, including Blood Disorders, Bone & Spinal Disorders, Brain Defects & Abnormalities, Chromosomal Disorders, Congenital Heart Defects, Movement Disorders, Neuromuscular Disorders and Pediatric Tumors & Cancers. This carefully written directory offers: understandable Descriptions of 15 major bodily systems; Descriptions of more than 200 Disorders and a Resources Section, detailing National Agencies & Associations, State Associations, Online Services, Libraries & Resource Centers, Research Centers, Support Groups & Hotlines, Camps, Books and Periodicals. This resource will provide immediate access to information crucial to families and caregivers when coping with children's illnesses.

"Recommended for public and consumer health libraries." –Library Journal

1,200 pages; Softcover ISBN 1-59237-150-7 $165.00 ◆ Online Database $215.00 ◆ Online Database & Directory Combo $300.00

To preview any of our Directories Risk-Free for 30 days, call (800) 562-2139 or fax to (518) 789-0556

Grey House Publishing
General Reference Titles

The Value of a Dollar 1600-1859, The Colonial Era to The Civil War

Following the format of the widely acclaimed, *The Value of a Dollar, 1860-2004*, *The Value of a Dollar 1600-1859, The Colonial Era to The Civil War* records the actual prices of thousands of items that consumers purchased from the Colonial Era to the Civil War. Our editorial department had been flooded with requests from users of our Value of a Dollar for the same type of information, just from an earlier time period. This new volume is just the answer – with pricing data from 1600 to 1859. Arranged into five-year chapters, each 5-year chapter includes a Historical Snapshot, Consumer Expenditures, Investments, Selected Income, Income/Standard Jobs, Food Basket, Standard Prices and Miscellany. There is also a section on Trends. This informative section charts the change in price over time and provides added detail on the reasons prices changed within the time period, including industry developments, changes in consumer attitudes and important historical facts. This fascinating survey will serve a wide range of research needs and will be useful in all high school, public and academic library reference collections.

600 pages; Hardcover ISBN 1-59237-094-2, $135.00

The Value of a Dollar 1860-2004, Third Edition

A guide to practical economy, *The Value of a Dollar* records the actual prices of thousands of items that consumers purchased from the Civil War to the present, along with facts about investment options and income opportunities. This brand new Third Edition boasts a brand new addition to each five-year chapter, a section on Trends. This informative section charts the change in price over time and provides added detail on the reasons prices changed within the time period, including industry developments, changes in consumer attitudes and important historical facts. Plus, a brand new chapter for 2000-2004 has been added. Each 5-year chapter includes a Historical Snapshot, Consumer Expenditures, Investments, Selected Income, Income/Standard Jobs, Food Basket, Standard Prices and Miscellany. This interesting and useful publication will be widely used in any reference collection.

"Recommended for high school, college and public libraries." –ARBA

600 pages; Hardcover ISBN 1-59237-074-8, $135.00

Working Americans 1880-1999
Volume I: The Working Class, Volume II: The Middle Class, Volume III: The Upper Class

Each of the volumes in the *Working Americans 1880-1999* series focuses on a particular class of Americans, The Working Class, The Middle Class and The Upper Class over the last 120 years. Chapters in each volume focus on one decade and profile three to five families. Family Profiles include real data on Income & Job Descriptions, Selected Prices of the Times, Annual Income, Annual Budgets, Family Finances, Life at Work, Life at Home, Life in the Community, Working Conditions, Cost of Living, Amusements and much more. Each chapter also contains an Economic Profile with Average Wages of other Professions, a selection of Typical Pricing, Key Events & Inventions, News Profiles, Articles from Local Media and Illustrations. The *Working Americans* series captures the lifestyles of each of the classes from the last twelve decades, covers a vast array of occupations and ethnic backgrounds and travels the entire nation. These interesting and useful compilations of portraits of the American Working, Middle and Upper Classes during the last 120 years will be an important addition to any high school, public or academic library reference collection.

"These interesting, unique compilations of economic and social facts, figures and graphs will support multiple research needs. They will engage and enlighten patrons in high school, public and academic library collections." –Booklist

Volume I: The Working Class ◆ 558 pages; Hardcover ISBN 1-891482-81-5, $145.00 ◆ Volume II: The Middle Class ◆ 591 pages; Hardcover ISBN 1-891482-72-6; $145.00 ◆ Volume III: The Upper Class ◆ 567 pages; Hardcover ISBN 1-930956-38-X, $145.00

Working Americans 1880-1999 Volume IV: Their Children

This Fourth Volume in the highly successful *Working Americans 1880-1999* series focuses on American children, decade by decade from 1880 to 1999. This interesting and useful volume introduces the reader to three children in each decade, one from each of the Working, Middle and Upper classes. Like the first three volumes in the series, the individual profiles are created from interviews, diaries, statistical studies, biographies and news reports. Profiles cover a broad range of ethnic backgrounds, geographic area and lifestyles – everything from an orphan in Memphis in 1882, following the Yellow Fever epidemic of 1878 to an eleven-year-old nephew of a beer baron and owner of the New York Yankees in New York City in 1921. Chapters also contain important supplementary materials including News Features as well as information on everything from Schools to Parks, Infectious Diseases to Childhood Fears along with Entertainment, Family Life and much more to provide an informative overview of the lifestyles of children from each decade. This interesting account of what life was like for Children in the Working, Middle and Upper Classes will be a welcome addition to the reference collection of any high school, public or academic library.

600 pages; Hardcover ISBN 1-930956-35-5, $145.00

To preview any of our Directories Risk-Free for 30 days, call (800) 562-2139 or fax to (518) 789-0556

Working Americans 1880-2003 Volume V: Americans At War

Working Americans 1880-2003 Volume V: Americans At War is divided into 11 chapters, each covering a decade from 1880-2003 and examines the lives of Americans during the time of war, including declared conflicts, one-time military actions, protests, and preparations for war. Each decade includes several personal profiles, whether on the battlefield or on the homefront, that tell the stories of civilians, soldiers, and officers during the decade. The profiles examine: Life at Home; Life at Work; and Life in the Community. Each decade also includes an Economic Profile with statistical comparisons, a Historical Snapshot, News Profiles, local News Articles, and Illustrations that provide a solid historical background to the decade being examined. Profiles range widely not only geographically, but also emotionally, from that of a girl whose leg was torn off in a blast during WWI, to the boredom of being stationed in the Dakotas as the Indian Wars were drawing to a close. As in previous volumes of the *Working Americans* series, information is presented in narrative form, but hard facts and real-life situations back up each story. The basis of the profiles come from diaries, private print books, personal interviews, family histories, estate documents and magazine articles. For easy reference, *Working Americans 1880-2003 Volume V: Americans At War* includes an in-depth Subject Index. The *Working Americans* series has become an important reference for public libraries, academic libraries and high school libraries. This fifth volume will be a welcome addition to all of these types of reference collections.

600 pages; Hardcover ISBN 1-59237-024-1; $145.00
Five Volume Set (Volumes I-V), Hardcover ISBN 1-59237-034-9, $675.00

Working Americans 1880-2005 Volume VI: Women at Work

Unlike any other volume in the *Working Americans* series, this Sixth Volume, is the first to focus on a particular gender of Americans. *Volume VI: Women at Work*, traces what life was like for working women from the 1860's to the present time. Beginning with the life of a maid in 1890 and a store clerk in 1900 and ending with the life and times of the modern working women, this text captures the struggle, strengths and changing perception of the American woman at work. Each chapter focuses on one decade and profiles three to five women with real data on Income & Job Descriptions, Selected Prices of the Times, Annual Income, Annual Budgets, Family Finances, Life at Work, Life at Home, Life in the Community, Working Conditions, Cost of Living, Amusements and much more. For even broader access to the events, economics and attitude towards women throughout the past 130 years, each chapter is supplemented with News Profiles, Articles from Local Media, Illustrations, Economic Profiles, Typical Pricing, Key Events, Inventions and more. This important volume illustrates what life was like for working women over time and allows the reader to develop an understanding of the changing role of women at work. These interesting and useful compilations of portraits of women at work will be an important addition to any high school, public or academic library reference collection.

600 pages; Hardcover ISBN 1-59237-063-2; $145.00

Working Americans 1880-2005 Volume VII: Social Movements

The newest addition to the widely-successful *Working Americans* series, *Volume VII: Social Movements* explores how Americans sought and fought for change from the 1880s to the present time. Following the format of previous volumes in the Working Americans series, the text examines the lives of 34 individuals who have worked — often behind the scenes — to bring about change. Issues include topics as diverse as the Anti-smoking movement of 1901 to efforts by Native Americans to reassert their long lost rights. Along the way, the book will profile individuals brave enough to demand suffrage for Kansas women in 1912 or demand an end to lynching during a March on Washington in 1923. Each profile is enriched with real data on Income & Job Descriptions, Selected Prices of the Times, Annual Incomes & Budgets, Life at Work, Life at Home, Life in the Community, along with News Features, Key Events, and Illustrations. The depth of information contained in each profile allow the user to explore the private, financial and public lives of these subjects, deepening our understanding of how calls for change took place in our society. A must-purchase for the reference collections of high school libraries, public libraries and academic libraries.

600 pages; Hardcover ISBN 1-59237-101-9; $145.00
Seven Volume Set (Volumes I-VII), Hardcover ISBN 1-59237-133-7, $945.00

The Encyclopedia of Warrior Peoples & Fighting Groups

Many military groups throughout the world have excelled in their craft either by fortuitous circumstances, outstanding leadership, or intense training. This new second edition of The Encyclopedia of Warrior Peoples and Fighting Groups explores the origins and leadership of these outstanding combat forces, chronicles their conquests and accomplishments, examines the circumstances surrounding their decline or disbanding, and assesses their influence on the groups and methods of warfare that followed. This edition has been completely updated with information through 2005 and contains over 20 new entries. Readers will encounter ferocious tribes, charismatic leaders, and daring militias, from ancient times to the present, including Amazons, Buffalo Soldiers, Green Berets, Iron Brigade, Kamikazes, Peoples of the Sea, Polish Winged Hussars, Sacred Band of Thebes, Teutonic Knights, and Texas Rangers. With over 100 alphabetical entries, numerous cross-references and illustrations, a comprehensive bibliography, and index, the Encyclopedia of Warrior Peoples and Fighting Groups is a valuable resource for readers seeking insight into the bold history of distinguished fighting forces.

"This work is especially useful for high school students, undergraduates, and general readers with an interest in military history." –Library Journal

Pub. Date: May 2006; Hardcover ISBN 1-59237-116-7; $135.00

To preview any of our Directories Risk-Free for 30 days, call (800) 562-2139 or fax to (518) 789-0556

The Encyclopedia of Invasions & Conquests, From the Ancient Times to the Present

Throughout history, invasions and conquests have played a remarkable role in shaping our world and defining our boundaries, both physically and culturally. This second edition of the popular Encyclopedia of Invasions & Conquests, a comprehensive guide to over 150 invasions, conquests, battles and occupations from ancient times to the present, takes readers on a journey that includes the Roman conquest of Britain, the Portuguese colonization of Brazil, and the Iraqi invasion of Kuwait, to name a few. New articles will explore the late 20th and 21st centuries, with a specific focus on recent conflicts in Afghanistan, Kuwait, Iraq, Yugoslavia, Grenada and Chechnya. Categories of entries include countries, invasions and conquests, and individuals. In addition to covering the military aspects of invasions and conquests, entries cover some of the political, economic, and cultural aspects, for example, the effects of a conquest on the invade country's political and monetary system and in its language and religion. The entries on leaders – among them Sargon, Alexander the Great, William the Conqueror, and Adolf Hitler – deal with the people who sought to gain control, expand power, or exert religious or political influence over others through military means. Revised and updated for this second edition, entries are arranged alphabetically within historical periods. Each chapter provides a map to help readers locate key areas and geographical features, and bibliographical references appear at the end of each entry. Other useful features include cross-references, a cumulative bibliography and a comprehensive subject index. This authoritative, well-organized, lucidly written volume will prove invaluable for a variety of readers, including high school students, military historians, members of the armed forces, history buffs and hobbyists.

"Engaging writing, sensible organization, nice illustrations, interesting and obscure facts, and useful maps make this book a pleasure to read." –ARBA

Pub. Date: March 2006; Hardcover ISBN 1-59237-114-0; $135.00

Encyclopedia of Prisoners of War & Internment

This authoritative second edition provides a valuable overview of the history of prisoners of war and interned civilians, from earliest times to the present. Written by an international team of experts in the field of POW studies, this fascinating and thought-provoking volume includes entries on a wide range of subjects including the Crusades, Plains Indian Warfare, concentration camps, the two world wars, and famous POWs throughout history, as well as atrocities, escapes, and much more. Written in a clear and easily understandable style, this informative reference details over 350 entries, 30% larger than the first edition, that survey the history of prisoners of war and interned civilians from the earliest times to the present, with emphasis on the 19th and 20th centuries. Medical conditions, international law, exchanges of prisoners, organizations working on behalf of POWs, and trials associated with the treatment of captives are just some of the themes explored. Entries range from the Ardeatine Caves Massacre to Kurt Vonnegut. Entries are arranged alphabetically, plus illustrations and maps are provided for easy reference. The text also includes an introduction, bibliography, appendix of selected documents, and end-of-entry reading suggestions. This one-of-a-kind reference will be a helpful addition to the reference collections of all public libraries, high schools, and university libraries and will prove invaluable to historians and military enthusiasts.

"Thorough and detailed yet accessible to the lay reader. Of special interest to subject specialists and historians; recommended for public and academic libraries." - Library Journal

Pub. Date: March 2006; Hardcover ISBN 1-59237-120-5; $135.00

The Religious Right, A Reference Handbook

Timely and unbiased, this third edition updates and expands its examination of the religious right and its influence on our government, citizens, society, and politics. From the fight to outlaw the teaching of Darwin's theory of evolution to the struggle to outlaw abortion, the religious right is continually exerting an influence on public policy. This text explores the influence of religion on legislation and society, while examining the alignment of the religious right with the political right. A historical survey of the movement highlights the shift to "hands-on" approach to politics and the struggle to present a unified front. The coverage offers a critical historical survey of the religious right movement, focusing on its increased involvement in the political arena, attempts to forge coalitions, and notable successes and failures. The text offers complete coverage of biographies of the men and women who have advanced the cause and an up to date chronology illuminate the movement's goals, including their accomplishments and failures. This edition offers an extensive update to all sections along with several brand new entries. Two new sections complement this third edition, a chapter on legal issues and court decisions and a chapter on demographic statistics and electoral patterns. To aid in further research, The Religious Right, offers an entire section of annotated listings of print and non-print resources, as well as of organizations affiliated with the religious right, and those opposing it. Comprehensive in its scope, this work offers easy-to-read, pertinent information for those seeking to understand the religious right and its evolving role in American society. A must for libraries of all sizes, university religion departments, activists, high schools and for those interested in the evolving role of the religious right.

" Recommended for all public and academic libraries." - Library Journal

Pub. Date: November 2006; Hardcover ISBN 1-59237-113-2; $135.00

To preview any of our Directories Risk-Free for 30 days, call (800) 562-2139 or fax to (518) 789-0556

From Suffrage to the Senate, America's Political Women

From Suffrage to the Senate is a comprehensive and valuable compendium of biographies of leading women in U.S. politics, past and present, and an examination of the wide range of women's movements. Up to date through 2006, this dynamically illustrated reference work explores American women's path to political power and social equality from the struggle for the right to vote and the abolition of slavery to the first African American woman in the U.S. Senate and beyond. This new edition includes over 150 new entries and a brand new section on trends and demographics of women in politics. The in-depth coverage also traces the political heritage of the abolition, labor, suffrage, temperance, and reproductive rights movements. The alphabetically arranged entries include biographies of every woman from across the political spectrum who has served in the U.S. House and Senate, along with women in the Judiciary and the U.S. Cabinet and, new to this edition, biographies of activists and political consultants. Bibliographical references follow each entry. For easy reference, a handy chronology is provided detailing 150 years of women's history. This up-to-date reference will be a must-purchase for women's studies departments, high schools and public libraries and will be a handy resource for those researching the key players in women's politics, past and present.

"An engaging tool that would be useful in high school, public, and academic libraries looking for an overview of the political history of women in the US." –Booklist

Pub. Date: October 2006; Two Volume Set; Hardcover ISBN 1-59237-117-5; $195.00

An African Biographical Dictionary

This landmark second edition is the only biographical dictionary to bring together, in one volume, cultural, social and political leaders – both historical and contemporary – of the sub-Saharan region. Over 800 biographical sketches of prominent Africans, as well as foreigners who have affected the continent's history, are featured, 150 more than the previous edition. The wide spectrum of leaders includes religious figures, writers, politicians, scientists, entertainers, sports personalities and more. Access to these fascinating individuals is provided in a user-friendly format. The biographies are arranged alphabetically, cross-referenced and indexed. Entries include the country or countries in which the person was significant and the commonly accepted dates of birth and death. Each biographical sketch is chronologically written; entries for cultural personalities add an evaluation of their work. This information is followed by a selection of references often found in university and public libraries, including autobiographies and principal biographical works. Appendixes list each individual by country and by field of accomplishment – rulers, musicians, explorers, missionaries, businessmen, physicists – nearly thirty categories in all. Another convenient appendix lists heads of state since independence by country. Up-to-date and representative of African societies as a whole, An African Biographical Dictionary provides a wealth of vital information for students of African culture and is an indispensable reference guide for anyone interested in African affairs.

"An unquestionable convenience to have these concise, informative biographies gathered into one source, indexed, and analyzed by appendixes listing entrants by nation and occupational field." –Wilson Library Bulletin

Pub. Date: July 2006; Hardcover ISBN 1-59237-112-4; $125.00

American Environmental Leaders, From Colonial Times to the Present

A comprehensive and diverse award winning collection of biographies of the most important figures in American environmentalism. Few subjects arouse the passions the way the environment does. How will we feed an ever-increasing population and how can that food be made safe for consumption? Who decides how land is developed? How can environmental policies be made fair for everyone, including multiethnic groups, women, children, and the poor? American Environmental Leaders presents more than 350 biographies of men and women who have devoted their lives to studying, debating, and organizing these and other controversial issues over the last 200 years. In addition to the scientists who have analyzed how human actions affect nature, we are introduced to poets, landscape architects, presidents, painters, activists, even sanitation engineers, and others who have forever altered how we think about the environment. The easy to use A–Z format provides instant access to these fascinating individuals, and frequent cross references indicate others with whom individuals worked (and sometimes clashed). End of entry references provide users with a starting point for further research.

"Highly recommended for high school, academic, and public libraries needing environmental biographical information." –Library Journal/Starred Review

Two Volume Set; Hardcover ISBN 1-57607-385-8 $175.00

World Cultural Leaders of the Twentieth Century

An expansive two volume set that covers 450 worldwide cultural icons, World Cultural Leaders of the Twentieth Century includes each person's works, achievements, and professional careers in a thorough essay. Who was the originator of the term "documentary"? Which poet married the daughter of the famed novelist Thomas Mann in order to help her escape Nazi Germany? Which British writer served as an agent in Russia against the Bolsheviks before the 1917 revolution? These and many more questions are answered in this illuminating text. A handy two volume set that makes it easy to look up 450 worldwide cultural icons: novelists, poets, playwrights, painters, sculptors, architects, dancers, choreographers, actors, directors, filmmakers, singers, composers, and musicians. World Cultural Leaders of the Twentieth Century provides entries (many of them illustrated) covering the person's works, achievements, and professional career in a thorough essay and offers interesting facts and statistics. Entries are fully cross-referenced so that readers can learn how various individuals influenced others. A thorough general index completes the coverage.

"Fills a need for handy, concise information on a wide array of international cultural figures."–ARBA

Two Volume Set; Hardcover ISBN 1-57607-038-7 $175.00

To preview any of our Directories Risk-Free for 30 days, call (800) 562-2139 or fax to (518) 789-0556

Universal Reference Publications
Statistical & Demographic Reference Books

America's Top-Rated Cities, 2007

America's Top-Rated Cities provides current, comprehensive statistical information and other essential data in one easy-to-use source on the 100 "top" cities that have been cited as the best for business and living in the U.S. This handbook allows readers to see, at a glance, a concise social, business, economic, demographic and environmental profile of each city, including brief evaluative comments. In addition to detailed data on Cost of Living, Finances, Real Estate, Education, Major Employers, Media, Crime and Climate, city reports now include Housing Vacancies, Tax Audits, Bankruptcy, Presidential Election Results and more. This outstanding source of information will be widely used in any reference collection.

"The only source of its kind that brings together all of this information into one easy-to-use source. It will be beneficial to many business and public libraries." –ARBA

2,500 pages, 4 Volume Set; Softcover ISBN 1-59237-184-1, $195.00

America's Top-Rated Smaller Cities, 2006/07

A perfect companion to *America's Top-Rated Cities*, *America's Top-Rated Smaller Cities* provides current, comprehensive business and living profiles of smaller cities (population 25,000-99,999) that have been cited as the best for business and living in the United States. Sixty cities make up this 2004 edition of *America's Top-Rated Smaller Cities*, all are top-ranked by Population Growth, Median Income, Unemployment Rate and Crime Rate. City reports reflect the most current data available on a wide-range of statistics, including Employment & Earnings, Household Income, Unemployment Rate, Population Characteristics, Taxes, Cost of Living, Education, Health Care, Public Safety, Recreation, Media, Air & Water Quality and much more. Plus, each city report contains a Background of the City, and an Overview of the State Finances. *America's Top-Rated Smaller Cities* offers a reliable, one-stop source for statistical data that, before now, could only be found scattered in hundreds of sources. This volume is designed for a wide range of readers: individuals considering relocating a residence or business; professionals considering expanding their business or changing careers; general and market researchers; real estate consultants; human resource personnel; urban planners and investors.

"Provides current, comprehensive statistical information in one easy-to-use source…
Recommended for public and academic libraries and specialized collections." –Library Journal

1,100 pages; Softcover ISBN 1-59237-135-3, $160.00

Profiles of America: Facts, Figures & Statistics for Every Populated Place in the United States

Profiles of America is the only source that pulls together, in one place, statistical, historical and descriptive information about every place in the United States in an easy-to-use format. This award winning reference set, now in its second edition, compiles statistics and data from over 20 different sources – the latest census information has been included along with more than nine brand new statistical topics. This Four-Volume Set details over 40,000 places, from the biggest metropolis to the smallest unincorporated hamlet, and provides statistical details and information on over 50 different topics including Geography, Climate, Population, Vital Statistics, Economy, Income, Taxes, Education, Housing, Health & Environment, Public Safety, Newspapers, Transportation, Presidential Election Results and Information Contacts or Chambers of Commerce. Profiles are arranged, for ease-of-use, by state and then by county. Each county begins with a County-Wide Overview and is followed by information for each Community in that particular county. The Community Profiles within the county are arranged alphabetically. *Profiles of America* is a virtual snapshot of America at your fingertips and a unique compilation of information that will be widely used in any reference collection.

A Library Journal Best Reference Book *"An outstanding compilation."* –Library Journal

10,000 pages; Four Volume Set; Softcover ISBN 1-891482-80-7, $595.00

The Comparative Guide to American Suburbs, 2007

The Comparative Guide to American Suburbs is a one-stop source for Statistics on the 2,000+ suburban communities surrounding the 50 largest metropolitan areas – their population characteristics, income levels, economy, school system and important data on how they compare to one another. Organized into 50 Metropolitan Area chapters, each chapter contains an overview of the Metropolitan Area, a detailed Map followed by a comprehensive Statistical Profile of each Suburban Community, including Contact Information, Physical Characteristics, Population Characteristics, Income, Economy, Unemployment Rate, Cost of Living, Education, Chambers of Commerce and more. Next, statistical data is sorted into Ranking Tables that rank the suburbs by twenty different criteria, including Population, Per Capita Income, Unemployment Rate, Crime Rate, Cost of Living and more. *The Comparative Guide to American Suburbs* is the best source for locating data on suburbs. Those looking to relocate, as well as those doing preliminary market research, will find this an invaluable timesaving resource.

"Public and academic libraries will find this compilation useful…The work draws together figures from many sources and will be especially helpful for job relocation decisions." – Booklist

1,700 pages; Softcover ISBN 1-59237-180-9, $130.00

To preview any of our Directories Risk-Free for 30 days, call (800) 562-2139 or fax to (518) 789-0556

Crime in America's Top-Rated Cities

This volume includes over 20 years of crime statistics in all major crime categories: violent crimes, property crimes and total crime. *Crime in America's Top-Rated Cities* is conveniently arranged by city and covers 76 top-rated cities. *Crime in America's Top-Rated Cities* offers details that compare the number of crimes and crime rates for the city, suburbs and metro area along with national crime trends for violent, property and total crimes. Also, this handbook contains important information and statistics on Anti-Crime Programs, Crime Risk, Hate Crimes, Illegal Drugs, Law Enforcement, Correctional Facilities, Death Penalty Laws and much more. A much-needed resource for people who are relocating, business professionals, general researchers, the press, law enforcement officials and students of criminal justice.

"Data is easy to access and will save hours of searching." –Global Enforcement Review

832 pages; Softcover ISBN 1-891482-84-X, $155.00

The Asian Databook: Statistics for all US Counties & Cities with Over 10,000 Population

This is the first-ever resource that compiles statistics and rankings on the US Asian population. *The Asian Databook* presents over 20 statistical data points for each city and county, arranged alphabetically by state, then alphabetically by place name. Data reported for each place includes Population, Languages Spoken at Home, Foreign-Born, Educational Attainment, Income Figures, Poverty Status, Homeownership, Home Values & Rent, and more. Next, in the Rankings Section, the top 75 places are listed for each data element. These easy-to-access ranking tables allow the user to quickly determine trends and population characteristics. This kind of comparative data can not be found elsewhere, in print or on the web, in a format that's as easy-to-use or more concise. A useful resource for those searching for demographics data, career search and relocation information and also for market research. With data ranging from Ancestry to Education, *The Asian Databook* presents a useful compilation of information that will be a much-needed resource in the reference collection of any public or academic library along with the marketing collection of any company whose primary focus in on the Asian population.

1,000 pages; Softcover ISBN 1-59237-044-6 $150.00

The Hispanic Databook: Statistics for all US Counties & Cities with Over 10,000 Population

Previously published by Toucan Valley Publications, this second edition has been completely updated with figures from the latest census and has been broadly expanded to include dozens of new data elements and a brand new Rankings section. The Hispanic population in the United States has increased over 42% in the last 10 years and accounts for 12.5% of the total US population. For ease-of-use, *The Hispanic Databook* presents over 20 statistical data points for each city and county, arranged alphabetically by state, then alphabetically by place name. Data reported for each place includes Population, Languages Spoken at Home, Foreign-Born, Educational Attainment, Income Figures, Poverty Status, Homeownership, Home Values & Rent, and more. Next, in the Rankings Section, the top 75 places are listed for each data element. These easy-to-access ranking tables allow the user to quickly determine trends and population characteristics. This kind of comparative data can not be found elsewhere, in print or on the web, in a format that's as easy-to-use or more concise. A useful resource for those searching for demographics data, career search and relocation information and also for market research. With data ranging from Ancestry to Education, *The Hispanic Databook* presents a useful compilation of information that will be a much-needed resource in the reference collection of any public or academic library along with the marketing collection of any company whose primary focus in on the Hispanic population.

"This accurate, clearly presented volume of selected Hispanic demographics is recommended for large public libraries and research collections."-Library Journal

1,000 pages; Softcover ISBN 1-59237-008-X, $150.00

The American Tally: Statistics & Comparative Rankings for U.S. Cities with Populations over 10,000

This important statistical handbook compiles, all in one place, comparative statistics on all U.S. cities and towns with a 10,000+ population. *The American Tally* provides statistical details on over 4,000 cities and towns and profiles how they compare with one another in Population Characteristics, Education, Language & Immigration, Income & Employment and Housing. Each section begins with an alphabetical listing of cities by state, allowing for quick access to both the statistics and relative rankings of any city. Next, the highest and lowest cities are listed in each statistic. These important, informative lists provide quick reference to which cities are at both extremes of the spectrum for each statistic. Unlike any other reference, *The American Tally* provides quick, easy access to comparative statistics – a must-have for any reference collection.

"A solid library reference." -Bookwatch

500 pages; Softcover ISBN 1-930956-29-0, $125.00

To preview any of our Directories Risk-Free for 30 days, call (800) 562-2139 or fax to (518) 789-0556

Ancestry in America: A Comparative Guide to Over 200 Ethnic Backgrounds

This brand new reference work pulls together thousands of comparative statistics on the Ethnic Backgrounds of all populated places in the United States with populations over 10,000. Never before has this kind of information been reported in a single volume. Section One, Statistics by Place, is made up of a list of over 200 ancestry and race categories arranged alphabetically by each of the 5,000 different places with populations over 10,000. The population number of the ancestry group in that city or town is provided along with the percent that group represents of the total population. This informative city-by-city section allows the user to quickly and easily explore the ethnic makeup of all major population bases in the United States. Section Two, Comparative Rankings, contains three tables for each ethnicity and race. In the first table, the top 150 populated places are ranked by population number for that particular ancestry group, regardless of population. In the second table, the top 150 populated places are ranked by the percent of the total population for that ancestry group. In the third table, those top 150 populated places with 10,000 population are ranked by population number for each ancestry group. These easy-to-navigate tables allow users to see ancestry population patterns and make city-by-city comparisons as well. Plus, as an added bonus with the purchase of *Ancestry in America*, a free companion CD-ROM is available that lists statistics and rankings for all of the 35,000 populated places in the United States. This brand new, information-packed resource will serve a wide-range or research requests for demographics, population characteristics, relocation information and much more. *Ancestry in America: A Comparative Guide to Over 200 Ethnic Backgrounds* will be an important acquisition to all reference collections.

> *"This compilation will serve a wide range of research requests for population characteristics … it offers much more detail than other sources." –Booklist*

1,500 pages; Softcover ISBN 1-59237-029-2, $225.00

The Environmental Resource Handbook, 2007/08

The Environmental Resource Handbook is the most up-to-date and comprehensive source for Environmental Resources and Statistics. Section I: Resources provides detailed contact information for thousands of information sources, including Associations & Organizations, Awards & Honors, Conferences, Foundations & Grants, Environmental Health, Government Agencies, National Parks & Wildlife Refuges, Publications, Research Centers, Educational Programs, Green Product Catalogs, Consultants and much more. Section II: Statistics, provides statistics and rankings on hundreds of important topics, including Children's Environmental Index, Municipal Finances, Toxic Chemicals, Recycling, Climate, Air & Water Quality and more. This kind of up-to-date environmental data, all in one place, is not available anywhere else on the market place today. This vast compilation of resources and statistics is a must-have for all public and academic libraries as well as any organization with a primary focus on the environment.

> *"…the intrinsic value of the information make it worth consideration by libraries with environmental collections and environmentally concerned users." –Booklist*

1,000 pages; Softcover ISBN 1-59237-195-7, $155.00 ☐ Online Database $300.00

Weather America, A Thirty-Year Summary of Statistical Weather Data and Rankings

This valuable resource provides extensive climatological data for over 4,000 National and Cooperative Weather Stations throughout the United States. *Weather America* begins with a new Major Storms section that details major storm events of the nation and a National Rankings section that details rankings for several data elements, such as Maximum Temperature and Precipitation. The main body of *Weather America* is organized into 50 state sections. Each section provides a Data Table on each Weather Station, organized alphabetically, that provides statistics on Maximum and Minimum Temperatures, Precipitation, Snowfall, Extreme Temperatures, Foggy Days, Humidity and more. State sections contain two brand new features in this edition – a City Index and a narrative Description of the climatic conditions of the state. Each section also includes a revised Map of the State that includes not only weather stations, but cities and towns.

> *"Best Reference Book of the Year." –Library Journal*

2,013 pages; Softcover ISBN 1-891482-29-7, $175.00

To preview any of our Directories Risk-Free for 30 days, call (800) 562-2139 or fax to (518) 789-0556

Grey House Publishing
Business Directories

The Directory of Business Information Resources, 2007

With 100% verification, over 1,000 new listings and more than 12,000 updates, this 2007 edition of *The Directory of Business Information Resources* is the most up-to-date source for contacts in over 98 business areas – from advertising and agriculture to utilities and wholesalers. This carefully researched volume details: the Associations representing each industry; the Newsletters that keep members current; the Magazines and Journals - with their "Special Issues" - that are important to the trade, the Conventions that are "must attends," Databases, Directories and Industry Web Sites that provide access to must-have marketing resources. Includes contact names, phone & fax numbers, web sites and e-mail addresses. This one-volume resource is a gold mine of information and would be a welcome addition to any reference collection.

"This is a most useful and easy-to-use addition to any researcher's library." –The Information Professionals Institute

2,500 pages; Softcover ISBN 1-59237-146-9, $195.00 ▯ Online Database $495.00

Nations of the World, 2007 A Political, Economic and Business Handbook

This completely revised edition covers all the nations of the world in an easy-to-use, single volume. Each nation is profiled in a single chapter that includes Key Facts, Political & Economic Issues, a Country Profile and Business Information. In this fast-changing world, it is extremely important to make sure that the most up-to-date information is included in your reference collection. This edition is just the answer. Each of the 200+ country chapters have been carefully reviewed by a political expert to make sure that the text reflects the most current information on Politics, Travel Advisories, Economics and more. You'll find such vital information as a Country Map, Population Characteristics, Inflation, Agricultural Production, Foreign Debt, Political History, Foreign Policy, Regional Insecurity, Economics, Trade & Tourism, Historical Profile, Political Systems, Ethnicity, Languages, Media, Climate, Hotels, Chambers of Commerce, Banking, Travel Information and more. Five Regional Chapters follow the main text and include a Regional Map, an Introductory Article, Key Indicators and Currencies for the Region. As an added bonus, an all-inclusive CD-ROM is available as a companion to the printed text. Noted for its sophisticated, up-to-date and reliable compilation of political, economic and business information, this brand new edition will be an important acquisition to any public, academic or special library reference collection.

"A useful addition to both general reference collections and business collections." –RUSQ

1,700 pages; Print Version Only Softcover ISBN 1-59237-177-9, $155.00

The Directory of Venture Capital & Private Equity Firms, 2007

This edition has been extensively updated and broadly expanded to offer direct access to over 2,800 Domestic and International Venture Capital Firms, including address, phone & fax numbers, e-mail addresses and web sites for both primary and branch locations. Entries include details on the firm's Mission Statement, Industry Group Preferences, Geographic Preferences, Average and Minimum Investments and Investment Criteria. You'll also find details that are available nowhere else, including the Firm's Portfolio Companies and extensive information on each of the firm's Managing Partners, such as Education, Professional Background and Directorships held, along with the Partner's E-mail Address. *The Directory of Venture Capital & Private Equity Firms* offers five important indexes: Geographic Index, Executive Name Index, Portfolio Company Index, Industry Preference Index and College & University Index. With its comprehensive coverage and detailed, extensive information on each company, *The Directory of Venture Capital & Private Equity Firms* is an important addition to any finance collection.

"The sheer number of listings, the descriptive information provided and the outstanding indexing make this directory a better value than its principal competitor, Pratt's Guide to Venture Capital Sources. Recommended for business collections in large public, academic and business libraries." –Choice

1,300 pages; Softcover ISBN 1-59237-176-0, $565.00/$450.00 Library ▯ Online Database (includes a free copy of the directory) $889.00

To preview any of our Directories Risk-Free for 30 days, call (800) 562-2139 or fax to (518) 789-0556

The Directory of Mail Order Catalogs, 2007

Published since 1981, the *Directory of Mail Order Catalogs* is the premier source of information on the mail order catalog industry. It is the source that business professionals and librarians have come to rely on for the thousands of catalog companies in the US. New for 2007, The Directory of Mail Order Catalogs has been combined with its companion volume, *The Directory of Business to Business Catalogs*, to offer all 13,000 catalog companies in one easy-to-use volume. Section I: Consumer Catalogs, covers over 9,000 consumer catalog companies in 44 different product chapters from Animals to Toys & Games. Section II: Business to Business Catalogs, details 5,000 business catalogs, everything from computers to laboratory supplies, building construction and much more. Listings contain detailed contact information including mailing address, phone & fax numbers, web sites, e-mail addresses and key contacts along with important business details such as product descriptions, employee size, years in business, sales volume, catalog size, number of catalogs mailed and more. Three indexes are included for easy access to information: Catalog & Company Name Index, Geographic Index and Product Index. *The Directory of Mail Order Catalogs*, now with its expanded business to business catalogs, is the largest and most comprehensive resource covering this billion-dollar industry. It is the standard in its field. This important resource is a useful tool for entrepreneurs searching for catalogs to pick up their product, vendors looking to expand their customer base in the catalog industry, market researchers, small businesses investigating new supply vendors, along with the library patron who is exploring the available catalogs in their areas of interest.

"This is a godsend for those looking for information." –Reference Book Review

1,700 pages; Softcover ISBN 1-59237-156-6 $350.00/$250.00 Library ☐ Online Database (includes a free copy of the directory) $495.00

Sports Market Place Directory, 2007

For over 20 years, this comprehensive, up-to-date directory has offered direct access to the Who, What, When & Where of the Sports Industry. With over 20,000 updates and enhancements, the *Sports Market Place Directory* is the most detailed, comprehensive and current sports business reference source available. In 1,800 information-packed pages, *Sports Market Place Directory* profiles contact information and key executives for: Single Sport Organizations, Professional Leagues, Multi-Sport Organizations, Disabled Sports, High School & Youth Sports, Military Sports, Olympic Organizations, Media, Sponsors, Sponsorship & Marketing Event Agencies, Event & Meeting Calendars, Professional Services, College Sports, Manufacturers & Retailers, Facilities and much more. *The Sports Market Place Directory* provides organization's contact information with detailed descriptions including: Key Contacts, physical, mailing, email and web addresses plus phone and fax numbers. Plus, nine important indexes make sure that you can find the information you're looking for quickly and easily: Entry Index, Single Sport Index, Media Index, Sponsor Index, Agency Index, Manufacturers Index, Brand Name Index, Facilities Index and Executive/Geographic Index. For over twenty years, *The Sports Market Place Directory* has assisted thousands of individuals in their pursuit of a career in the sports industry. Why not use "THE SOURCE" that top recruiters, headhunters and career placement centers use to find information on or about sports organizations and key hiring contacts.

1,800 pages; Softcover ISBN 1-59237-189-2, $225.00 ☐ Online Database $479.00

Food and Beverage Market Place, 2007

Food and Beverage Market Place is bigger and better than ever with thousands of new companies, thousands of updates to existing companies and two revised and enhanced product category indexes. This comprehensive directory profiles over 18,000 Food & Beverage Manufacturers, 12,000 Equipment & Supply Companies, 2,200 Transportation & Warehouse Companies, 2,000 Brokers & Wholesalers, 8,000 Importers & Exporters, 900 Industry Resources and hundreds of Mail Order Catalogs. Listings include detailed Contact Information, Sales Volumes, Key Contacts, Brand & Product Information, Packaging Details and much more. *Thomas Food and Beverage Market Place* is available as a three-volume printed set, a subscription-based Online Database via the Internet, on CD-ROM, as well as mailing lists and a licensable database.

"An essential purchase for those in the food industry but will also be useful in public libraries where needed. Much of the information will be difficult and time consuming to locate without this handy three-volume ready-reference source." –ARBA

8,500 pages, 3 Volume Set; Softcover ISBN 1-59237-152-3, $595.00 ☐ Online Database $795.00 ☐ Online Database & 3 Volume Set Combo, $995.00

To preview any of our Directories Risk-Free for 30 days, call (800) 562-2139 or fax to (518) 789-0556

The Grey House Homeland Security Directory, 2007

This updated edition features the latest contact information for government and private organizations involved with Homeland Security along with the latest product information and provides detailed profiles of nearly 1,000 Federal & State Organizations & Agencies and over 3,000 Officials and Key Executives involved with Homeland Security. These listings are incredibly detailed and include Mailing Address, Phone & Fax Numbers, Email Addresses & Web Sites, a complete Description of the Agency and a complete list of the Officials and Key Executives associated with the Agency. Next, *The Grey House Homeland Security Directory* provides the go-to source for Homeland Security Products & Services. This section features over 2,000 Companies that provide Consulting, Products or Services. With this Buyer's Guide at their fingertips, users can locate suppliers of everything from Training Materials to Access Controls, from Perimeter Security to BioTerrorism Countermeasures and everything in between – complete with contact information and product descriptions. A handy Product Locator Index is provided to quickly and easily locate suppliers of a particular product. Lastly, an Information Resources Section provides immediate access to contact information for hundreds of Associations, Newsletters, Magazines, Trade Shows, Databases and Directories that focus on Homeland Security. This comprehensive, information-packed resource will be a welcome tool for any company or agency that is in need of Homeland Security information and will be a necessary acquisition for the reference collection of all public libraries and large school districts.

"Compiles this information in one place and is discerning in content. A useful purchase for public and academic libraries." –Booklist

800 pages; Softcover ISBN 1-59237-151-5, $195.00 ☐ Online Database (includes a free copy of the directory) $385.00

The Grey House Transportation Security Directory & Handbook

This brand new title is the only reference of its kind that brings together current data on Transportation Security. With information on everything from Regulatory Authorities to Security Equipment, this top-flight database brings together the relevant information necessary for creating and maintaining a security plan for a wide range of transportation facilities. With this current, comprehensive directory at the ready you'll have immediate access to: Regulatory Authorities & Legislation; Information Resources; Sample Security Plans & Checklists; Contact Data for Major Airports, Seaports, Railroads, Trucking Companies and Oil Pipelines; Security Service Providers; Recommended Equipment & Product Information and more. Using the *Grey House Transportation Security Directory & Handbook*, managers will be able to quickly and easily assess their current security plans; develop contacts to create and maintain new security procedures; and source the products and services necessary to adequately maintain a secure environment. This valuable resource is a must for all Security Managers at Airports, Seaports, Railroads, Trucking Companies and Oil Pipelines.

800 pages; Softcover ISBN 1-59237-075-6, $195

The Grey House Safety & Security Directory, 2007

The Grey House Safety & Security Directory is the most comprehensive reference tool and buyer's guide for the safety and security industry. Arranged by safety topic, each chapter begins with OSHA regulations for the topic, followed by Training Articles written by top professionals in the field and Self-Inspection Checklists. Next, each topic contains Buyer's Guide sections that feature related products and services. Topics include Administration, Insurance, Loss Control & Consulting, Protective Equipment & Apparel, Noise & Vibration, Facilities Monitoring & Maintenance, Employee Health Maintenance & Ergonomics, Retail Food Services, Machine Guards, Process Guidelines & Tool Handling, Ordinary Materials Handling, Hazardous Materials Handling, Workplace Preparation & Maintenance, Electrical Lighting & Safety, Fire & Rescue and Security. The Buyer's Guide sections are carefully indexed within each topic area to ensure that you can find the supplies needed to meet OSHA's regulations. Six important indexes make finding information and product manufacturers quick and easy: Geographical Index of Manufacturers and Distributors, Company Profile Index, Brand Name Index, Product Index, Index of Web Sites and Index of Advertisers. This comprehensive, up-to-date reference will provide every tool necessary to make sure a business is in compliance with OSHA regulations and locate the products and services needed to meet those regulations.

"Presents industrial safety information for engineers, plant managers, risk managers, and construction site supervisors..." –Choice

1,500 pages, 2 Volume Set; Softcover ISBN 1-59237-160-4, $225.00

To preview any of our Directories Risk-Free for 30 days, call (800) 562-2139 or fax to (518) 789-0556

The Grey House Biometric Information Directory

The Biometric Information Directory is the only comprehensive source for current biometric industry information. This 2006 edition is the first published by Grey House. With 100% updated information, this latest edition offers a complete, current look, in both print and online form, of biometric companies and products – one of the fastest growing industries in today's economy. Detailed profiles of manufacturers of the latest biometric technology, including Finger, Voice, Face, Hand, Signature, Iris, Vein and Palm Identification systems. Data on the companies include key executives, company size and a detailed, indexed description of their product line. Plus, the Directory also includes valuable business resources, and current editorial make this edition the easiest way for the business community and consumers alike to access the largest, most current compilation of biometric industry information available on the market today. The new edition boasts increased numbers of companies, contact names and company data, with over 700 manufacturers and service providers. Information in the directory includes: Editorial on Advancements in Biometrics; Profiles of 700+ companies listed with contact information; Organizations, Trade & Educational Associations, Publications, Conferences, Trade Shows and Expositions Worldwide; Web Site Index; Biometric & Vendors Services Index by Types of Biometrics; and a Glossary of Biometric Terms. This resource will be an important source for anyone who is considering the use of a biometric product, investing in the development of biometric technology, support existing marketing and sales efforts and will be an important acquisition for the business reference collection for large public and business libraries.

800 pages; Softcover ISBN 1-59237-121-3, $225

The Grey House Performing Arts Directory, 2007

The Grey House Performing Arts Directory is the most comprehensive resource covering the Performing Arts. This important directory provides current information on over 8,500 Dance Companies, Instrumental Music Programs, Opera Companies, Choral Groups, Theater Companies, Performing Arts Series and Performing Arts Facilities. Plus, this edition now contains a brand new section on Artist Management Groups. In addition to mailing address, phone & fax numbers, e-mail addresses and web sites, dozens of other fields of available information include mission statement, key contacts, facilities, seating capacity, season, attendance and more. This directory also provides an important Information Resources section that covers hundreds of Performing Arts Associations, Magazines, Newsletters, Trade Shows, Directories, Databases and Industry Web Sites. Five indexes provide immediate access to this wealth of information: Entry Name, Executive Name, Performance Facilities, Geographic and Information Resources. *The Grey House Performing Arts Directory* pulls together thousands of Performing Arts Organizations, Facilities and Information Resources into an easy-to-use source – this kind of comprehensiveness and extensive detail is not available in any resource on the market place today.

"Immensely useful and user-friendly ... recommended for public, academic and certain special library reference collections." –Booklist

1,500 pages; Softcover ISBN 1-59237-138-8, $185.00 ☐ Online Database $335.00

The Rauch Guide to the US Adhesives & Sealants, Cosmetics & Toiletries, Ink, Paint, Plastics, Pulp & Paper and Rubber Industries

The Rauch Guides are known worldwide for their comprehensive marketing information. Acquired by Grey House Publishing in 2005, new updated and revised editions will be published throughout 2005 and 2006. Each Guide provides market facts and figures in a highly organized format, ideal for today's busy personnel, serving as ready-references for top executives as well as the industry newcomer. *The Rauch Guides* save time and money by organizing widely scattered information and providing estimates for important business decisions, some of which are available nowhere else. Each Guide is organized into several information-packed chapters. After a brief introduction, the ECONOMICS section provides data on industry shipments; long-term growth and forecasts; prices; company performance; employment, expenditures, and productivity; transportation and geographical patterns; packaging; foreign trade; and government regulations. Next, TECHNOLOGY & RAW MATERIALS provide market, technical, and raw material information for chemicals, equipment and related materials, including market size and leading suppliers, prices, end uses, and trends. PRODUCTS & MARKETS provide information for each major industry product, including market size and historical trends, leading suppliers, five-year forecasts, industry structure, and major end uses. For easy access, each *Guide* contains a chapter on INDUSTRY ACTIVITIES, ORGANIZATIONS & SOURCES OF INFORMATION with detailed information on meetings, exhibits, and trade shows, sources of statistical information, trade associations, technical and professional societies, and trade and technical periodicals. Next, the COMPANY DIRECTORY profiles major industry companies, both public and private. Generally several hundred companies are analyzed. Information includes complete contact information, web address, estimated total and domestic sales, product description, and recent mergers and acquisitions. Each Guide also contains several APPENDICES that provide a cross-reference of suppliers, subsidiaries and divisions. The Rauch Guides will prove to be an invaluable source of market information, company data, trends and forecasts that anyone in these fast-paced industries.

The Rauch Guide to the U.S. Paint Industry Softcover ISBN 1-59237-127-2 $595 ♦ The Rauch Guide to the U.S. Plastics Industry Softcover ISBN 1-59237-128-0 $595 ♦ The Rauch Guide to the U.S. Adhesives and Sealants Industry Softcover ISBN 1-59237-129-9 $595 ♦ The Rauch Guide to the U.S. Ink Industry Softcover ISBN 1-59237-126-4 $595 ♦ The Rauch Guide to the U.S. Rubber Industry Softcover ISBN 1-59237-130-2 $595 ♦ The Rauch Guide to the U.S. Pulp and Paper Industry Softcover ISBN 1-59237-131-0 $595 ♦ The Rauch Guide to the U.S. Cosmetic and Toiletries Industry Softcover ISBN 1-59237-132-9 $895

To preview any of our Directories Risk-Free for 30 days, call (800) 562-2139 or fax to (518) 789-0556

New York State Directory, 2006/07

The New York State Directory, published annually since 1983, is a comprehensive and easy-to-use guide to accessing public officials and private sector organizations and individuals who influence public policy in the state of New York. *The New York State Directory* includes important information on all New York state legislators and congressional representatives, including biographies and key committee assignments. It also includes staff rosters for all branches of New York state government and for federal agencies and departments that impact the state policy process. Following the state government section are 25 chapters covering policy areas from agriculture through veterans' affairs. Each chapter identifies the state, local and federal agencies and officials that formulate or implement policy. In addition, each chapter contains a roster of private sector experts and advocates who influence the policy process. The directory also offers appendices that include statewide party officials; chambers of commerce; lobbying organizations; public and private universities and colleges; television, radio and print media; and local government agencies and officials.

New York State Directory - 800 pages; Softcover ISBN 1-59237-145-0; $145.00
New York State Directory with Profiles of New York – 2 volumes; 1,600 pages; Softcover ISBN 1-59237-162-0; $225

Profiles of New York □ Profiles of Florida □ Profiles of Texas □ Profiles of Illinois □ Profiles of Michigan □ Profiles of Ohio □ Profiles of New Jersey □ Profiles of Massachusetts □ Profiles of Pennsylvania □ Profiles of Wisconsin □ Profiles of Connecticut □ Profiles of Indiana □ Profiles of North Carolina □ Profiles of Virginia

Packed with over 50 pieces of data that make up a complete, user-friendly profile of each state, these directories go even further by then pulling selected data and providing it in ranking list form for even easier comparisons between the 100 largest towns and cities! The careful layout gives the user an easy-to-read snapshot of every single place and county in the state, from the biggest metropolis to the smallest unincorporated hamlet. The richness of each place or county profile is astounding in its depth, from history to weather, all packed in an easy-to-navigate, compact format. No need for piles of multiple sources with this volume on your desk. Here is a look at just a few of the data sets you'll find in each profile: History, Geography, Climate, Population, Vital Statistics, Economy, Income, Taxes, Education, Housing, Health & Environment, Public Safety, Newspapers, Transportation, Presidential Election Results, Information Contacts and Chambers of Commerce. As an added bonus, there is a section on Selected Statistics, where data from the 100 largest towns and cities is arranged into easy-to-use charts. Each of 22 different data points has its own two-page spread with the cities listed in alpha order so researchers can easily compare and rank cities. A remarkable compilation that offers overviews and insights into each corner of the state, *Profiles of New York*, *Profiles of Florida* and *Profiles of Texas* go beyond Census statistics, beyond metro area coverage, beyond the 100 best places to live. Drawn from official census information, other government statistics and original research, you will have at your fingertips data that's available nowhere else in one single source. Data will be published on additional states in 2006 and 2007.

Each Profiles of... title ranges from 400-800 pages, priced at $149.00 each

Research Services Directory: Commercial & Corporate Research Centers

This Ninth Edition provides access to well over 8,000 independent Commercial Research Firms, Corporate Research Centers and Laboratories offering contract services for hands-on, basic or applied research. *Research Services Directory* covers the thousands of types of research companies, including Biotechnology & Pharmaceutical Developers, Consumer Product Research, Defense Contractors, Electronics & Software Engineers, Think Tanks, Forensic Investigators, Independent Commercial Laboratories, Information Brokers, Market & Survey Research Companies, Medical Diagnostic Facilities, Product Research & Development Firms and more. Each entry provides the company's name, mailing address, phone & fax numbers, key contacts, web site, e-mail address, as well as a company description and research and technical fields served. Four indexes provide immediate access to this wealth of information: Research Firms Index, Geographic Index, Personnel Name Index and Subject Index.

"An important source for organizations in need of information about laboratories, individuals and other facilities." –ARBA

1,400 pages; Softcover ISBN 1-59237-003-9, $395.00 □ Online Database (includes a free copy of the directory) $850.00

International Business and Trade Directories

Completely updated, the Third Edition of *International Business and Trade Directories* now contains more than 10,000 entries, over 2,000 more than the last edition, making this directory the most comprehensive resource of the worlds business and trade directories. Entries include content descriptions, price, publisher's name and address, web site and e-mail addresses, phone and fax numbers and editorial staff. Organized by industry group, and then by region, this resource puts over 10,000 industry-specific business and trade directories at the reader's fingertips. Three indexes are included for quick access to information: Geographic Index, Publisher Index and Title Index. Public, college and corporate libraries, as well as individuals and corporations seeking critical market information will want to add this directory to their marketing collection.

"Reasonably priced for a work of this type, this directory should appeal to larger academic, public and corporate libraries with an international focus." –Library Journal

1,800 pages; Softcover ISBN 1-930956-63-0, $225.00 □ Online Database (includes a free copy of the directory) $450.00

To preview any of our Directories Risk-Free for 30 days, call (800) 562-2139 or fax to (518) 789-0556

Sedgwick Press
Hospital & Health Plan Directories

The Comparative Guide to American Hospitals, 2007

This is the first ever resource to compare all of the nation's hospitals by 17 measures of quality in the treatment of heart attack, heart failure and pneumonia. This data is based on the Hospital Compare study, produced by Medicare, and is available in print and in a unique and user-friendly format from Grey House Publishing, along with extra contact information from Grey House's *Directory of Hospital Personnel*. *The Comparative Guide to American Hospitals* provides a snapshot profile of each of the nations 6,000 hospitals. These informative profiles illustrate how the hospital rates in 17 important areas: Heart Attack Care (% who receive Aspirin at Arrival, Aspirin at Discharge, ACE Inhibitor for LVSD, Beta Blocker at Arrival, Beta Blocker at Discharge, Thrombolytic Agent Received, PTCA Received and Adult Smoking Cessation Advice); Heart Failure (% who receive LVF Assessment, ACE Inhibitor for LVSD, Discharge Instructions, Adult Smoking Cessation Advice); and Pneumonia (% who receive Initial Antibiotic Timing, Pneumococcal Vaccination, Oxygenation Assessment, Blood Culture Performed and Adult Smoking Cessation Advice). Each profile includes the raw percentage for that hospital, the state average, the US average and data on the top hospital. For easy access to contact information, each profile includes the hospitals address, phone and fax numbers, email and web addresses, type and accreditation along with 5 top key administrations. These profiles will allow the user to quickly identify the quality of the hospital and have the necessary information at their fingertips to make contact with that hospital. Most importantly, *The Comparative Guide to American Hospitals* provides an easy-to-use Ranking Table for each of the data elements to allow the user to quickly locate the hospitals with the best level of service. This brand new title will be a must for the reference collection at all public, medical and academic libraries.

2,500 pages; Softcover ISBN 1-59237-182-5; $225.00

The Directory of Hospital Personnel, 2007

The Directory of Hospital Personnel is the best resource you can have at your fingertips when researching or marketing a product or service to the hospital market. A "Who's Who" of the hospital universe, this directory puts you in touch with over 150,000 key decision-makers. With 100% verification of data you can rest assured that you will reach the right person with just one call. Every hospital in the U.S. is profiled, listed alphabetically by city within state. Plus, three easy-to-use, cross-referenced indexes put the facts at your fingertips faster and more easily than any other directory: Hospital Name Index, Bed Size Index and Personnel Index. *The Directory of Hospital Personnel* is the only complete source for key hospital decision-makers by name. Whether you want to define or restructure sales territories... locate hospitals with the purchasing power to accept your proposals... keep track of important contacts or colleagues... or find information on which insurance plans are accepted, *The Directory of Hospital Personnel* gives you the information you need – easily, efficiently, effectively and accurately.

"Recommended for college, university and medical libraries." -ARBA

2,500 pages; Softcover ISBN 1-59237-178-7 $325.00 ☐ Online Database $545.00 ☐ Online Database & Directory Combo, $650.00

The Directory of Health Care Group Purchasing Organizations, 2006

This comprehensive directory provides the important data you need to get in touch with over 800 Group Purchasing Organizations. By providing in-depth information on this growing market and its members, *The Directory of Health Care Group Purchasing Organizations* fills a major need for the most accurate and comprehensive information on over 800 GPOs – Mailing Address, Phone & Fax Numbers, E-mail Addresses, Key Contacts, Purchasing Agents, Group Descriptions, Membership Categorization, Standard Vendor Proposal Requirements, Membership Fees & Terms, Expanded Services, Total Member Beds & Outpatient Visits represented and more. Five Indexes provide a number of ways to locate the right GPO: Alphabetical Index, Expanded Services Index, Organization Type Index, Geographic Index and Member Institution Index. With its comprehensive and detailed information on each purchasing organization, *The Directory of Health Care Group Purchasing Organizations* is the go-to source for anyone looking to target this market.

"The information is clearly arranged and easy to access...recommended for those needing this very specialized information." –ARBA

1,000 pages; Softcover ISBN 1-59237-0091-8, $325.00 ☐ Online Database, $650.00 ☐ Online Database & Directory Combo, $750.00

To preview any of our Directories Risk-Free for 30 days, call (800) 562-2139 or fax to (518) 789-0556

The HMO/PPO Directory, 2007

The HMO/PPO Directory is a comprehensive source that provides detailed information about Health Maintenance Organizations and Preferred Provider Organizations nationwide. This comprehensive directory details more information about more managed health care organizations than ever before. Over 1,100 HMOs, PPOs, Medicare Advantage Plans and affiliated companies are listed, arranged alphabetically by state. Detailed listings include Key Contact Information, Prescription Drug Benefits, Enrollment, Geographical Areas served, Affiliated Physicians & Hospitals, Federal Qualifications, Status, Year Founded, Managed Care Partners, Employer References, Fees & Payment Information and more. Plus, five years of historical information is included related to Revenues, Net Income, Medical Loss Ratios, Membership Enrollment and Number of Patient Complaints. Five easy-to-use, cross-referenced indexes will put this vast array of information at your fingertips immediately: HMO Index, PPO Index, Other Providers Index, Personnel Index and Enrollment Index. *The HMO/PPO Directory* provides the most comprehensive data on the most companies available on the market place today.

"Helpful to individuals requesting certain HMO/PPO issues such as co-payment costs, subscription costs and patient complaints. Individuals concerned (or those with questions) about their insurance may find this text to be of use to them." -ARBA

600 pages; Softcover ISBN 1-59237-158-2, $325.00 ☐ Online Database, $495.00 ☐ Online Database & Directory Combo, $600.00

Medical Device Register, 2007

The only one-stop resource of every medical supplier licensed to sell products in the US. This award-winning directory offers immediate access to over 13,000 companies - and more than 65,000 products – in two information-packed volumes. This comprehensive resource saves hours of time and trouble when searching for medical equipment and supplies and the manufacturers who provide them. Volume I: The Product Directory, provides essential information for purchasing or specifying medical supplies for every medical device, supply, and diagnostic available in the US. Listings provide FDA codes & Federal Procurement Eligibility, Contact information for every manufacturer of the product along with Prices and Product Specifications. Volume 2 - Supplier Profiles, offers the most complete and important data about Suppliers, Manufacturers and Distributors. Company Profiles detail the number of employees, ownership, method of distribution, sales volume, net income, key executives detailed contact information medical products the company supplies, plus the medical specialties they cover. Four indexes provide immediate access to this wealth of information: Keyword Index, Trade Name Index, Supplier Geographical Index and OEM (Original Equipment Manufacturer) Index. Medical Device Register, 2007 is the only one-stop source for locating suppliers and products; looking for new manufacturers or hard-to-find medical devices; comparing products and companies; know who's selling what and who to buy from cost effectively. This directory has become the standard in its field and will be a welcome addition to the reference collection of any medical library, large public library, university library along with the collections that serve the medical community.

"A wealth of information on medical devices, medical device companies... and key personnel in the industry is provide in this comprehensive reference work... A valuable reference work, one of the best hardcopy compilations available." -Doody Publishing

3,000 pages Two Volumes; Hardcover ISBN 1-59237-181-7; $325.00

The Directory of Independent Ambulatory Care Centers

This first edition of *The Directory of Independent Ambulatory Care Centers* provides access to detailed information that, before now, could only be found scattered in hundreds of different sources. This comprehensive and up-to-date directory pulls together a vast array of contact information for over 7,200 Ambulatory Surgery Centers, Ambulatory General and Urgent Care Clinics, and Diagnostic Imaging Centers that are not affiliated with a hospital or major medical center. Detailed listings include Mailing Address, Phone & Fax Numbers, E-mail and Web Site addresses, Contact Name and Phone Numbers of the Medical Director and other Key Executives and Purchasing Agents, Specialties & Services Offered, Year Founded, Numbers of Employees and Surgeons, Number of Operating Rooms, Number of Cases seen per year, Overnight Options, Contracted Services and much more. Listings are arranged by State, by Center Category and then alphabetically by Organization Name. Two indexes provide quick and easy access to this wealth of information: Entry Name Index and Specialty/Service Index. *The Directory of Independent Ambulatory Care Centers* is a must-have resource for anyone marketing a product or service to this important industry and will be an invaluable tool for those searching for a local care center that will meet their specific needs.

"Among the numerous hospital directories, no other provides information on independent ambulatory centers. A handy, well-organized resource that would be useful in medical center libraries and public libraries." -Choice

986 pages; Softcover ISBN 1-930956-90-8, $185.00 ☐ Online Database, $365.00 ☐ Online Database & Directory Combo, $450.00

To preview any of our Directories Risk-Free for 30 days, call (800) 562-2139 or fax to (518) 789-0556

Grey House Publishing Canada
Canadian Information Resources

Canadian Almanac & Directory, 2007

The Canadian Almanac & Directory contains ten directories in one – giving you all the facts and figures you will ever need about Canada. No other single source provides users with the quality and depth of up-to-date information for all types of research. This national directory and guide gives you access to statistics, images and over 45,000 names and addresses for everything from Airlines to Zoos - updated every year. It's Ten Directories in One! Each section is a directory in itself, providing robust information on business and finance, communications, government, associations, arts and culture (museums, zoos, libraries, etc.), health, transportation, law, education, and more. Government information includes federal, provincial and territorial - and includes an easy-to-use quick index to find key information. A separate municipal government section includes every municipality in Canada, with full profiles of Canada's largest urban centers. A complete legal directory lists judges and judicial officials, court locations and law firms across the country. A wealth of general information, the Canadian Almanac & Directory also includes national statistics on population, employment, imports and exports, and more. National awards and honors are presented, along with forms of address, Commonwealth information and full color photos of Canadian symbols. Postal information, weights, measures, distances and other useful charts are also incorporated. Complete almanac information includes perpetual calendars, five-year holiday planners and astronomical information. Published continuously for 160 years, The Canadian Almanac & Directory is the best single reference source for business executives, managers and assistants; government and public affairs executives; lawyers; marketing, sales and advertising executives; researchers, editors and journalists.

Hardcover ISBN 978-1-89502-149-3; 1,600 pages; $315.00

Associations Canada, 2007

The Most Powerful Fact-Finder to Business, Trade, Professional and Consumer Organizations
Associations Canada covers Canadian organizations and international groups including industry, commercial and professional associations, registered charities, special interest and common interest organizations. This annually revised compendium provides detailed listings and abstracts for nearly 20,000 regional, national and international organizations. This popular volume provides the most comprehensive picture of Canada's non-profit sector. Detailed listings enable users to identify an organization's budget, founding date, scope of activity, licensing body, sources of funding, executive information, full address and complete contact information, just to name a few. Powerful indexes help researchers find information quickly and easily. The following indexes are included: subject, acronym, geographic, budget, executive name, conferences & conventions, mailing list, defunct and unreachable associations and registered charitable organizations. In addition to annual spending of over $1 billion on transportation and conventions alone, Canadian associations account for many millions more in pursuit of membership interests. Associations Canada provides complete access to this highly lucrative market. Associations Canada is a strong source of prospects for sales and marketing executives, tourism and convention officials, researchers, government officials - anyone who wants to locate non-profit interest groups and trade associations.

Hardcover ISBN 978-1-59237-219-5; 1,600 pages; $315.00

Financial Services Canada, 2006/07

Financial Services Canada is the only master file of current contacts and information that serves the needs of the entire financial services industry in Canada. With over 18,000 organizations and hard-to-find business information, Financial Services Canada is the most up-to-date source for names and contact numbers of industry professionals, senior executives, portfolio managers, financial advisors, agency bureaucrats and elected representatives. Financial Services Canada incorporates the latest changes in the industry to provide you with the most current details on each company, including: name, title, organization, telephone and fax numbers, e-mail and web addresses. Financial Services Canada also includes private company listings never before compiled, government agencies, association and consultant services - to ensure that you'll never miss a client or a contact. Current listings include: banks and branches, non-depository institutions, stock exchanges and brokers, investment management firms, insurance companies, major accounting and law firms, government agencies and financial associations. Powerful indexes assist researchers with locating the vital financial information they need. The following indexes are included: alphabetic, geographic, executive name, corporate web site/e-mail, government quick reference and subject. Financial Services Canada is a valuable resource for financial executives, bankers, financial planners, sales and marketing professionals, lawyers and chartered accountants, government officials, investment dealers, journalists, librarians and reference specialists.

900 pages; Hardcover ISBN 978-1-89502-145-5 $315.00

To preview any of our Directories Risk-Free for 30 days, call (800) 562-2139 or fax to (518) 789-0556

Directory of Libraries in Canada, 2007/08

The Directory of Libraries in Canada brings together almost 7,000 listings including libraries and their branches, information resource centers, archives and library associations and learning centers. The directory offers complete and comprehensive information on Canadian libraries, resource centers, business information centers, professional associations, regional library systems, archives, library schools and library technical programs. The Directory of Libraries in Canada includes important features of each library and service, including library information; personnel details, including contact names and e-mail addresses; collection information; services available to users; acquisitions budgets; and computers and automated systems. Useful information on each library's electronic access is also included, such as Internet browser, connectivity and public Internet/CD-ROM/subscription database access. The directory also provides powerful indexes for subject, location, personal name and Web site/e-mail to assist researchers with locating the crucial information they need. The Directory of Libraries in Canada is a vital reference tool for publishers, advocacy groups, students, research institutions, computer hardware suppliers, and other diverse groups that provide products and services to this unique market.

850 pages; Hardcover ISBN 978-1-59237-222-5; $315.00

Canadian Environmental Directory, 2007/08

The Canadian Environmental Directory is Canada's most complete and only national listing of environmental associations and organizations, government regulators and purchasing groups, product and service companies, special libraries, and more! The extensive Products and Services section provides detailed listings enabling users to identify the company name, address, phone, fax, e-mail, Web address, firm type, contact names (and titles), product and service information, affiliations, trade information, branch and affiliate data. The Government section gives you all the contact information you need at every government level – federal, provincial and municipal. We also include descriptions of current environmental initiatives, programs and agreements, names of environment-related acts administered by each ministry or department PLUS information and tips on who to contact and how to sell to governments in Canada. The Associations section provides complete contact information and a brief description of activities. Included are Canadian environmental organizations and international groups including industry, commercial and professional associations, registered charities, special interest and common interest organizations. All the Information you need about the Canadian environmental industry: directory of products and services, special libraries and resource, conferences, seminars and tradeshows, chronology of environmental events, law firms and major Canadian companies, The Canadian Environmental Directory is ideal for business, government, engineers and anyone conducting research on the environment.

Hardcover ISBN 978-1-59237-218-8; 900 pages; $315.00

To preview any of our Directories Risk-Free for 30 days, call (800) 562-2139 or fax to (518) 789-0556